CONFERENCE PROCEEDINGS

CHI 2012

it's the experience!

The 30th ACM Conference on Human Factors in Computing Systems (CHI)

AUSTIN • TEXAS • USA

MAY 5-10, 2012

Association for Computing Machinery

chi2012.acm.org

SIGCHI
special interest group computer human interaction

Association for
Computing Machinery

Advancing Computing as a Science & Profession

The Association for Computing Machinery
2 Penn Plaza, Suite 701
New York, New York 10121-0701

Notice to Past Authors of ACM-Published Articles
ACM intends to create a complete electronic archive of all articles and/or other material previously published by ACM. If you have written a work that has been previously published by ACM in any journal or conference proceedings prior to 1978, or any SIG Newsletter at any time, and you do NOT want this work to appear in the ACM Digital Library, please inform permissions@acm.org, stating the title of the work, the author(s), and where and when published.

ISBN: 978-1-4503-1015-4 (Digital)

ISBN: 978-1-4503-1938-6 (Print Vol 1)

Additional copies may be ordered prepaid from:

ACM Order Department
PO Box 30777
New York, NY 10087-0777, USA

Phone: 1-800-342-6626 (USA and Canada)
+1-212-626-0500 (Global)
Fax: +1-212-944-1318
E-mail: acmhelp@acm.org
Hours of Operation: 8:30 am – 4:30 pm ET

ACM Order Number: 609121

Printed in the USA

Welcome to CHI 2012!

After nearly two years of preparation, we are thrilled to welcome you to CHI 2012 in Austin, Texas. Austin is justifiably proud of being the Live Music Capital of the World (R), and it is home to a world-class university, innovative technology and design firms, superb restaurants, exciting culture and nightlife, and genuinely friendly people--what a perfect fit for our CHI conference. We encourage you to get out and explore the city.

But we also are working hard to lure you back indoors with a phenomenal technical program. At the core of the program are over a hundred technical sessions with research papers and notes, case studies, and other exciting presentations that bring you the best new work on human-computer interaction.

We give thanks to our hundreds of review committee members and our more than one thousand reviewers--they invested thousands of hours to help make sure that we've picked the best content. All of the technical content can be found in the ACM Digital Library.

At the same time, we hope to lure you into our useful courses, engaging panels, and thoughtful invited talks. We're very excited to have Margaret Gould Stewart and Hugh Herr as our keynote speakers. In spanning from Margaret's talk on connecting the world through video to Hugh's talk on designing intelligent orthotics and prosthetics we span the scope of this conference--from social interaction with each other through computing to the very personal and intimate interaction of a human with computerized limbs or other assistive devices. We're also excited to have two special invited talks: Stu Card, SIGCHI's 2000 Lifetime Achievement Award winner, will talk about what interaction science means in today's environment; and Richard Shusterman will bridge HCI and the humanities as he introduces us to Somaesthetics and how it can improve our understanding and experience. We are also honored to have Dan Olsen, Joy Mountford, and Batya Friedman--SIGCHI's Lifetime Research, Lifetime Practice, and Social Impact awardees--each giving talks at CHI 2012. Each of the three of them has made an indelible impact on our field.

The theme of this year's CHI conference is "It's the Experience!" and from the beginning it has been our goal to ensure that CHI 2012 attendees don't only hear about HCI, but experience it with all of their senses. We are therefore delighted to have more than 60 interactivity demonstrations and installations--opportunities for you to see, feel, hear, and interact with exciting new technologies and also to reflect on technologies of the past, thanks to Roger Ibars' HWD collection--a hands-on installation of historic hard-wired input devices. We'll be featuring the full set of interactivity on Tuesday afternoon and Wednesday lunchtime; selected installations will be available at other times--check the Interactivity tab for more details. Our video program will provide another way to experience innovative forms of HCI.

CHI 2012 has new depth in Computer Games (including a new student games competition), digital arts, and the humanities. We have an unusually rich collection of Digital Arts installations--we invite you to take some time to interact with the artists and learn about how art--like science, engineering, and design--has its own ways of posing and exploring challenging questions.

And there's so much more. We will also have over 250 posters representing exciting works-in-progress and much more. Student venues at CHI 2012 include our doctoral consortium--an intimate opportunity for extensive mentoring and peer support; student research and design competitions, and the games competition. Come see the competition finalists! And let's not forget CHI Madness--a frenetic but highly efficient whirlwind tour through each days technical papers.

Even before we "formally" open the conference Monday morning, we will have had an intensive weekend of workshops where CHI attendees gather to address emerging fields, tackle challenging questions, and simply support each other in areas of common interest. The mutual support continues both in formal SIG gatherings and in informal gatherings in the convention center halls and at tables in our exhibit hall. We particularly invite you to gather together in affinity groups built around our nine communities--these communities not only shape our program, they also can help enrich your experience as an attendee.

In the end, though, it is been quite an Experience! for us. We are grateful to all the dedicated volunteers and staff that have made this conference possible. We appreciate the support of our sponsors and participation of our exhibitors. And most of all, we thank you for joining us here at the conference. We hope you find things some things that are useful, some things that are inspiring, and some things that are just plain fun. We hope you have an incredible CHI 2012 Experience!

Joseph A. Konstan
University of Minnesota
CHI 2012
General Conference Chair

Ed H. Chi
Google
CHI 2012
Technical Program Chairs

Kristina Höök
Mobile Life at KTH
CHI 2012
Technical Program Chairs

From ACM SIGCHI's President and Vice President for Conferences

SIGCHI is proud to sponsor the premier annual conference in the field of human-computer interaction. We are extremely grateful to the CHI 2012 Conference Chair Joseph Konstan, to Technical Program Chairs Ed Chi and Kristina Höök, and to their wonderful crew, who succeeded to build an impressive program and experience.

CHI 2012 marks the 30th anniversary of our society. The first conference, on Human Factors in Computer Systems, took place in Gaithersburg, MD, on March 15-17, 1982.

The second and third conferences were a year and a half apart, and from then on CHI, as the conference has been called since 1983, has been an annual event with the official name: "ACM Conference on Human Factors in Computing Systems".

The first conference drew over 900 attendees, and since then CHI has continued to grow and broaden its range of topics and contributing disciplines: the founding psychologists and software engineers began to meet new visions from ethnography, sociology, communication sciences and arts, among others. Relevant industries, as well as research institutes and academia, showed an increasing-and often long-lasting-interest and involvement (through volunteers and through sponsorship for conference expenses).

CHI is an ideal forum for people to meet formally as well as informally, to exchange knowledge and views, to share experiences, and to learn. The CHI conference brings together professionals from research and practice; people from industry, academia, and from government; long-term veterans of HCI, young professionals and students; all in an environment designed to encourage interaction. We invite you to actively participate in that interaction: introduce yourself to people, interact with presenters and speakers, renew old friendships and make new ones.

CHI is organized on behalf of ACM's Special Interest Group on Computer-Human Interaction (SIGCHI), an international community of professionals who share an interest in the many diverse facets of HCI. SIGCHI is committed both to advancing the field of HCI, to facilitate exchange of information within the SIGCHI community, and to support students to enter the domain.

The CHI conference is arguably the single most visible activity of SIGCHI, but we also sponsor and support a wide range of specialized conferences in areas ranging from interactive systems design to user interface technology to computer-supported cooperative work to "intelligent" user interfaces. Visit the SIGCHI website at http://www.sigchi.org to find our conference schedule, listing upcoming as well as past conferences.

SIGCHI and ACM produce some of the most respected publications in the field. All members receive interactions, a highly-acclaimed magazine covering the broad field of HCI and user interface design. ACM Transactions on Computer-Human Interactions (ToCHI), now in its 18th year, is our flagship journal - a quarterly publication with the top-quality archival research aimed at researchers and those translating research into practice.

SIGCHI is truly an international organization, with over 30 local chapters and 3 student chapters in 19 countries on 5 continents. We encourage all SIGCHI members to join their local chapter - or if there isn't one in your area, we would love to help you create one. And don't forget virtual communities! SIGCHI hosts dozens of electronic mailing lists on topics ranging from HCI and the Web, to HCI educations, to public policy and beyond. Those lists range from dozens of subscribers to thousands, and are an excellent way to keep up with the field and with friends and colleagues.

Finally, on behalf of ACM SGICHI, we again want to thank the conference committee and all of the hundreds of volunteers who make this conference possible. Their work makes this a rewarding experience for all of us.

Gerrit C. van der Veer
SIGCHI President

John "Scooter" Morris
SIGCHI Vice-President for Conferences

ABOUT SIGCHI

CHI 2012 is sponsored by ACM's Special Interest Group on Computer-Human Interaction (ACM SIGCHI). ACM, the Association for Computing Machinery, is an educational and scientific society uniting the world's computing educators, researchers, and professionals to inspire dialogue, share resources, and address the field's challenges. ACM strengthens the profession's collective voice through strong leadership, promotion of the highest standards, and recognition of technical excellence. ACM supports the professional growth of its members by providing opportunities for life-long learning, career development, and professional networking. ACM offers its more than 100,000 worldwide members cutting edge technical information through world class journals and magazines, dynamic special interest groups, and globally recognized conferences.

Visit www.acm.org for more information about the ACM.

SIGCHI is the premier international society for professionals, academics, and students who are interested in human-computer interaction (HCI). We provide a forum for the discussion of all aspects of HCI through our conferences, including our flagship CHI conference, publications, web sites, email discussion groups, and other services. We advance education in HCI through courses, workshops, and outreach, and we promote informal access to a wide range of individuals and organizations involved in HCI. Members can be involved in HCI-related activities with others in their region through local SIGCHI chapters. Come to the SIGCHI Town Hall meeting on Wednesday at 12:50 in Meeting Room 16AB, 4th Floor or visit www.sigchi.org to learn more about SIGCHI.

ACM, the Association for Computing Machinery http://www.acm.org/, is an educational and scientific society uniting the world's computing educators, researchers and professionals to inspire dialogue, share resources and address the field's challenges. ACM strengthens the profession's collective voice through strong leadership, promotion of the highest standards, and recognition of technical excellence.ACM supports the professional growth of its members by providing opportunities for life-long learning, career development, and professional networking. ACM offers its 87,000 global members cutting-edge technical information through world class journals and magazines, dynamic specia linterest groups and globally recognized conferences.

Table of Contents

Getting Around: Menus, Scrolling, & Advanced Navigation

Session Chair: Emmanuel Pietriga *(INRIA)*

Spectators

Session Chair: Barry Brown *(University of California, San Diego)*

Immateriality as a Design Feature

Session Chair: Joonhwan Lee *(Seoul National University)*

Privacy + Self Disclosure

Session Chair: Manfred Tscheligi *(University of Salzburg)*

Empathy & Technology: Focus on the End User

Session Chair: Jettie Hoonhout *(Philips Research Europe)*

Workplace

Session Chair: Volkmar Pipek *(University of Siegen)*

Uses of Media & Creation of Web Experiences

Session Chair: Jan Gulliksen *(Uppsala University)*

Tools for Video + Images

Session Chair: Michael Rohs *(University of Munich)*

Intimacy & Connection

Session Chair: Mary Czerwinski *(Microsoft Research)*

HCI4D: Business

Session Chair: Batya Friedman *(University of Washington)*

Pen + Touch

Session Chair: Carman Neustaedter *(Simon Fraser University)*

Affective Presence

Session Chair: Albrecht Schmidt *(University of Stuttgart)*

Literacy on the Margin

Session Chair: Juan Pablo Hourcade *(University of Iowa)*

Participatory Design with Older People

Session Chair: Steven Dow *(Carnegie Mellon University)*

Personas & Design

Session Chair: Shaowen Bardzell *(Indiana University)*

Kick it! Interfaces for Feet & Walking

Session Chair: Yang Li *(USTB)*

Music Across CHI

Session Chair: Rebecca Fiebrink *(Princeton University)*

Space: The Interaction Frontier

The Tools of the Trade

Publics & Civic Virtues

Promoting Educational Opportunity

Interfaces for Health & Well Being

Session Chair: Ian Li *(Carnegie Mellon University)*

Needle in the Haystack

Session Chair: Mark Dunlop *(University of Strathclyde)*

Understanding Online Communication

Session Chair: Sharoda Paul *(GE Global Research)*

Performative Emergency Simulation

Session Chair: Olav W. Bertelsen *(Aarhus University)*

Search Interfaces

Session Chair: Remco Chang *(Tufts University)*

Music

Session Chair: Karyn Moffatt *(McGill University)*

ICT4D

Session Chair: Brygg Ullmer *(Louisiana State University)*

Movement-Based Gameplay

Session Chair: Shaun Kane *(University of Maryland, Baltimore County)*

Beyond Paper

Session Chair: Mikael B. Skov *(Aalborg University)*

Culture, Playfulness, & Creativity

Session Chair: Lucian Leahu *(Cornell University)*

I Did That! Being in Control

Session Chair: Mary Beth Rosson *(The Pennsylvania State Universtiy)*

Teaching with Games

Session Chair: Andreas Butz *(University of Munich)*

Health + Design

Session Chair: Jodi Forlizzi *(Carnegie Mellon University)*

Dimensions of Sensory Interaction

Session Chair: Shwetak Patel *(University of Washington)*

Phone Fun: Extending Mobile Interaction

Session Chair: Ken Hinckley *(Microsoft Research)*

Learning with Children

Session Chair: Carl DiSalvo *(Georgia Institute of Technology)*

Morphing & Tracking & Stacking: 3D Interaction

Session Chair: Celine Latulipe *(University of North Carolina at Charlotte)*

Social Computing: Business & Beyond

Session Chair: Henriette Cramer *(Mobile Life @ SICS)*

Programming, Performance, & Sense Making

Session Chair: John Thomas *(IBM Research)*

Programming & Debugging

Session Chair: Niklas Elmqvist *(Purdue University)*

Organizing the Recovery

Session Chair: Ron Wakkary *(Simon Fraser University)*

Tweet, Tweet, Tweet!

Session Chair: Sadat Shami *(IBM Research)*

Me & My Mobile

Session Chair: Lynne Baillie *(Glasgow Caledonian University)*

Understanding Gamers

Session Chair: Peter Tolmie *(University of Nottingham)*

Better Together

Session Chair: Gary Hsieh *(Michigan State University)*

Bigger is Better: Large & Multiple Display Environments

Session Chair: David Dearman *(Nokia Research Center)*

What a Lovely Gesture

Session Chair: Hrvoje Benko *(Microsoft Research)*

Crowdsourcing & Peer Production II

Session Chair: Erika Poole *(Penn State)*

Usability & User Research

Session Chair: Anna Cox *(University College London)*

Do You See What Eye See

Session Chair: Andrew Duchowski *(Clemson University)*

Home & Family

Session Chair: Andrea Grimes Parker *(Georgia Institute of Technology)*

Designing for Learners' Complex Needs

Session Chair: Hilary Hutchinson *(Google)*

Groups @ Work

Session Chair: Eric Gilbert *(Georgia Institute of Technology)*

Use the Force

Session Chair: Mike Horn *(Northwestern University)*

Human Performance Gives Us Fitts'

Session Chair: Olivier Chapuis *(Univ Paris-Sud)*

With a Little Help from My Friends

Session Chair: Amy Hurst *(Carnegie Mellon University)*

CHI 2012 ORGANIZING COMMITTEE

Conference Chair
Joseph A. Konstan, *University of Minnesota*

TECHNICAL PROGRAM

Chairs
Ed H. Chi, *Google Research*
Kristina Höök, *Mobile Life @ KTH*

Papers
Susanne Bødker, *Aarhus University*
Dan R. Olsen Jr., *Brigham Young University*

alt.chi
Amanda Williams, *Wyld Collective Ltd.*
Erica Robles, *New York University*

Case Studies
Daniela Busse, *Samsung Research*
Elizabeth Buie, *Luminanze Consulting LLC*

Courses
Nancy Frishberg, *MSB Associates*
Gregorio Convertino, *Palo Alto Research Center (PARC)*

Doctoral Consortium
Steve Brewster, *University of Glasgow*
Erik Stolterman, *Indiana University Bloomington*

Interactivity
Patrick Baudisch, *Hasso Plattner Institut*
Florian 'Floyd' Mueller, *Exertion Games Lab*
Eva Hornecker, *University of Strathclyde*
Danielle Wilde, *daniellewilde.com*

Panels
Allison Druin, *University of Maryland*
Joseph 'Jofish' Kaye, *Nokia Research Center*

Special Interest Groups (SIGS)
Daphne Raban, *University of Haifa*
Kaisa Väänänen-Vainio-Mattila, *Tampere University of Technology*

Student Design Competition
Gilbert Cockton, *Northumbria University*
Thecla Schiphorst, *Simon Fraser University*

Student Research Competition
Anne Aula, *Google*
Shaowen Bardzell, *Indiana University Bloomington*

Student Game Competition
Seth Cooper, *University of Washington*
Winslow Burleson, *Arizona State University*

Video
Michael Bernstein, *MIT CSAIL*
Jeffrey Bardzell, *Indiana University, Bloomington*

Work-in-Progress (WIPs)
Lichan Hong, *Google*
Henriette Cramer, *Mobile Life @ SICS*

Workshops
Helena Mentis, *Microsoft Research Cambridge*
Ido Guy, *IBM Research Haifa*

CHI 2012 COMMUNITIES

Chairs
Arnie Lund, *Microsoft*
Bo Begole, *Samsung's User Experience Center*

Core Communities

Design
Ellen Yi-Luen Do, *Georgia Tech*
Patrick Olivier, *Newcastle University*

User Experience
Jhilmil Jain, *Microsoft*
Kath Straub, *Usability.org*

Engineering
Ruven Brooks, *Independent Consultant*
Fabio Paternò, *CNR-ISTI*

Management
Janice Rohn, *Experian*
Dennis Wixon, *Microsoft*

Featured Communities

Child Computer Interaction
Janet C Read, *University of Central Lancashire*
Panos Markopoulos, *Eindhoven University of Technology*
Allison Druin, *University of Maryland*

Digital Arts
David England, *Liverpool John Moores University*
Jill Fantauzzacoffin, *Georgia Tech*

Games and Entertainment
Regina Bernhaupt, *IRIT*
Katherine Isbister, *NYU-Poly*

Health
Karen Cheng, *University of California, Irvine*
Julie Kientz, *University of Washington*

Sustainability
Eli Blevis, *Indiana University at Bloomington*
Samuel Mann, *Otago Polytechnic*

PARTICIPATION AND VOLUNTEERING

Student Volunteer Coordinators
Vicky McArthur, *York University*
Bobby Beaton, *Virginia Tech*

Madness
Paul André, *University of Southampton*
Petra Sundström, *Salzburg University*

Social Media
Cliff Lampe, *Michigan State University*
Sean McNee, *FTI Consulting*

Publicity
Rosemary Stevens, *Ace Public Relations*
Eelco Herder, *L3S Research Center*

Local Experience
Annette Priest, *Revel Insight*

MAKING THINGS HAPPEN

Design Directors
Apala Lahiri Chavan, *Human Factors International*
Srikanth Vellore, *Human Factors International*

Webmaster
William Hudson, *Syntagm Ltd. and Hult International Business School*

Posters
Oleg Komogortsev, *Texas State University-San Marcos*

Proceedings
Max Van Kleek, *University of Southampton*
Nirmal Patel, *Georgia Tech*
Alireza Sahami Shirazi, *University of Stuttgart*
Michael Ekstrand, *University of Minnesota*

Mobile Apps
Stephen Oney, *Carnegie Mellon University*
Jason Wiese, *Carnegie Mellon University*
Eiji Hayashi, *Carnegie Mellon University*

Communications Director
Garett Dworman, Tec-Ed Inc

Program Production
Joan Johnson, *Joan Johnson Design*
Max Van Kleek, *University of Southampton*

Mailing Lists
Adam Sporka, *Czech Technical University*

ACM Staff Liaison
Ashley Cozzi, *ACM*

Sponsors and Exhibits
Carol Klyver, *Foundations of Excellence*

Conference Logistics
Janeé Pelletier, *CLC*
Allison Perrelli, *CLC*

Technology Liaison
Scooter Morris, *University of California, San Francisco*
Sara Drenner, *BI Worldwide*

CMC Liaison
Scooter Morris, *University of California, San Francisco*

Registration
Yvonne Lopez, *Executive Events*

Special thanks for the financial support provided by the following sponsors:

CHI Champion Sponsors

Autodesk®

Bloomberg

Google

ebay® | PayPal™

Microsoft®

NSF

SAP®

CHI Contributing Sponsors

facebook

NOKIA

Friends of CHI

Adobe Systems, Inc. **Disney Research** **University of Michigan School of Information**

Printed on Rolland Enviro 100
100% post-consumer fiber
Certified EcoLogo
Processed chlorine free
Manufactured using biogas energy
Printed using soy-based inks

Tell Me More? The Effects of Mental Model Soundness on Personalizing an Intelligent Agent

Todd Kulesza[1], Simone Stumpf[2], Margaret Burnett[1], Irwin Kwan[1]

[1]Oregon State University
School of EECS
Corvallis, Oregon 97333
{kuleszto, burnett, kwan}@eecs.oregonstate.edu

[2]City University London
Centre for HCI Design, School of Informatics
London EC1V 0HB, United Kingdom
Simone.Stumpf.1@city.ac.uk

ABSTRACT

What does a user need to know to productively work with an intelligent agent? Intelligent agents and recommender systems are gaining widespread use, potentially creating a need for end users to understand how these systems operate in order to fix their agent's personalized behavior. This paper explores the effects of mental model soundness on such personalization by providing structural knowledge of a music recommender system in an empirical study. Our findings show that participants were able to quickly build sound mental models of the recommender system's reasoning, and that participants who most improved their mental models during the study were significantly more likely to make the recommender operate to their satisfaction. These results suggest that by helping end users understand a system's reasoning, intelligent agents may elicit more and better feedback, thus more closely aligning their output with each user's intentions.

Author Keywords

Recommenders; mental models; debugging; music; personalization; intelligent agents;

ACM Classification Keywords

H.5.m [Information interfaces and presentation]: Miscellaneous;

INTRODUCTION

Intelligent agents have moved beyond mundane tasks like filtering junk email. Search engines now exploit pattern recognition to detect image content (e.g., clipart, photography, and faces); Facebook and image editors take this a step further, making educated guesses as to who is in a particular photo. Netflix and Amazon use collaborative filtering to recommend items of interest to their customers, while Pandora and Last.fm use similar techniques to create radio stations crafted to an individual's idiosyncratic tastes. Simple rule-based systems have evolved into agents employing complex algorithms. These *intelligent agents* are computer programs whose behavior only becomes fully specified *after* they learn from an end user's training data.

Because of this period of in-the-field learning, when an intelligent agent's reasoning causes it to perform incorrectly or unexpectedly, only the end user is in a position to better personalize—or more accurately, to debug—the agent's flawed reasoning. Debugging, in this context, refers to *mindfully and purposely* adjusting the agent's reasoning (after its initial training) so that it more closely matches the user's expectations. Recent research has made inroads into supporting this type of functionality [1,11,14,16]. Debugging, however, can be difficult for even trained software developers—helping end users do so, when they lack knowledge of either software engineering or machine learning, is no trivial task.

In this paper, we consider how much ordinary end users may need to know about these agents in order to debug them. Prior work has focused on how an intelligent agent can explain itself to end users [9,13,15,22,27,28], and how end users might act upon such explanations to debug their intelligent agents [1,11,14,16,24]. This paper, in contrast, considers whether users actually need a sound mental model, and how that mental model impacts their attempts to debug an intelligent agent. Toward this end, we investigated four research questions:

(RQ1): Feasibility: Can end users quickly build and recall a sound mental model of an intelligent agent's operation?

(RQ2): Accuracy: Do end users' mental models have a positive effect on their debugging of an intelligent agent?

(RQ3): Confidence: Does building a sound mental model of an intelligent agent improve end users' computer self-efficacy and reduce computer anxiety?

(RQ4): User Experience: Do end users with sound mental models of an intelligent agent experience interactions with it differently than users with unsound models?

To answer these research questions, we conducted an empirical study that investigates the effects of explaining the reasoning of a music recommender system to end users. We developed a prototype, *AuPair*, which allowed participants to set up radio stations and make adjustments to the songs that it chose for them. Half of the participants received detailed explanations of the recommender's reasoning, while the other half did not. Our paper's contribution is a better understanding of how users' mental models of their intelligent agents' behavior impacts their ability to debug their personalized agents.

BACKGROUND AND RELATED WORK

Functional and Structural Mental Models

Mental models are internal representations that people build based on their experiences in the real world. These models allow people to understand, explain and predict phenomena, and then act accordingly [10]. The contents of mental models can be concepts, relationships between concepts or events (e.g., causal, spatial, or temporal relationships), and associated procedures. For example, one mental model of how a computer works could be that it simply displays everything typed on the keyboard and "remembers" these things somewhere inside the computer's casing. Mental models can vary in their richness—an IT professional, for instance, has (ideally) a much richer mental model of how a computer works.

There are two main kinds of mental models: *Functional* (shallow) models imply that the end user knows how to use the computer but not how it works in detail, whereas *structural* (deep) models provide a detailed understanding of how and why it works. Mental models must be sound (i.e., accurate) enough to support effective interactions; many instances of unsound mental models guiding erroneous behavior have been observed [18].

Mental model completeness can matter too, especially when things go wrong, and structural models are more complete than functional models. While a structural model can help someone deal with unexpected behavior and fix the problem, a purely functional model does not provide the abstract concepts that may be required [10]. Knowing how to *use* a computer, for example, does not mean you can *fix* one that fails to power on.

To build new mental models, it has been argued that users should be exposed to transparent systems and appropriate instructions [21]. *Scaffolded instruction* is one method that has been shown to contribute positively to learning to use a new system [20]. One challenge, however, is that mental models, once built, can be surprisingly hard to shift, even when people are aware of contradictory evidence [28].

Mental Models of an Intelligent Agent's Reasoning

There has been recent interest in supporting the debugging of intelligent agents' reasoning [1,11,13,14,16,25], but the mental models users build while attempting this task have received little attention. An exception is a study that considered the correctness of users' mental models when interacting with a sensor-based intelligent agent that predicted an office worker's availability (e.g., "Is now a good time to interrupt so-and-so?") [28], but this study did not allow users to debug these availability predictions.

Making an agents' reasoning more transparent is one way to influence mental models. Examples of explanations by the agent for specific decisions include *why...* and *why not...* descriptions of the agent's reasoning [13,15], visual depictions of the assistant's known correct predictions versus its known failures [26], and electronic "door tags" displaying predictions of worker interruptibility with the reasons underlying each prediction (e.g., "talking detected") [28]. Recent work by Lim and Dey has resulted in a toolkit for applications to generate explanations for popular machine learning systems [16]. Previous work has found that users may change their mental models of an intelligent agent when the agent makes its reasoning transparent [14]; however, some explanations by agents may lead to only shallow mental models [24]. Agent reasoning can also be made transparent via explicit instruction regarding new features of an intelligent agent, and this can help with the construction of mental models of how it operates [17]. None of these studies, however, investigated how mental model construction may impact the ways in which end users debug intelligent agents.

Making an intelligent agent's reasoning transparent can improve perceptions of satisfaction and reliability toward music recommendations [22], as well as other types of recommender systems [9,27]. However, experienced users' satisfaction may actually decrease as a result of more transparency [17]. As with research on the construction of mental models, these studies have not investigated the link between end users' mental models and their satisfaction with the intelligent agent's behavior.

EMPIRICAL STUDY

To explore the effects of mental model soundness on end-user debugging of intelligent agents, we needed a domain that participants would be motivated to both use and debug. Music recommendations, in the form of an adaptable Internet radio station, meet these requirements, so we created an Internet radio platform (named *AuPair*) that users could personalize to play music fitting their particular tastes.

To match real-world situations in which intelligent agents are used, we extended the length of our empirical study beyond a brief laboratory experiment by combining a controlled tutorial session with an uncontrolled period of field use. The study lasted five days, consisting of a tutorial session and pre-study questionnaires on Day 1, then three days during which participants could use the AuPair prototype as they wished, and an exit session on Day 5.

AuPair Radio

AuPair allows the user to create custom "stations" and personalize them to play a desired type of music. Users start a new station by seeding it with a single artist name (e.g., "Play music by artists similar to *Patti Smith*"). Users can debug the agent by giving feedback about individual songs, or by adding general guidelines to the station. Feedback about an individual song can be provided using the 5-point

Figure 1. Users could debug by saying *why* the current song was a good or bad choice.

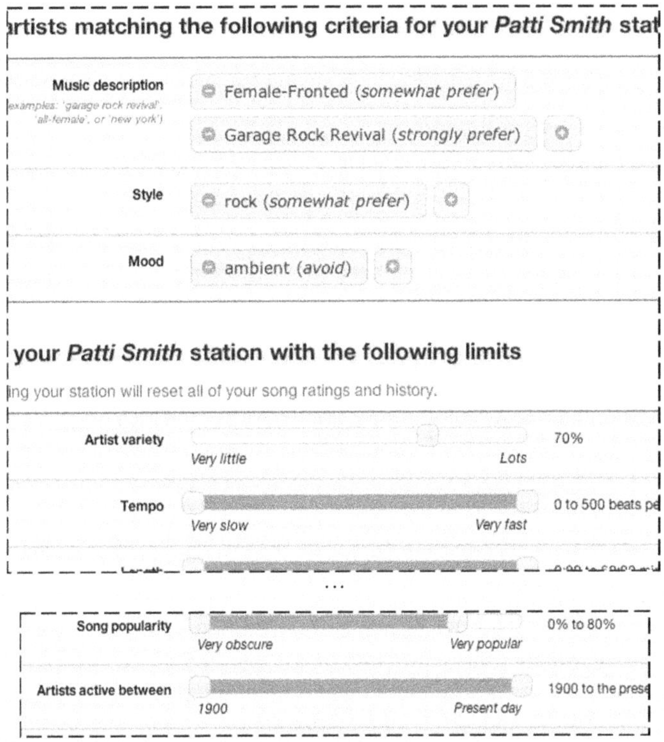

Figure 2. Participants could debug by adding guidelines on the type of music the station should or should not play, via a wide range of criteria.

rating scale common to many media recommenders, as well as by talking about the song's attributes (e.g., "This song is too mellow, play something more energetic", Figure 1). To add general guidelines about the station, the user can tell it to "prefer" or "avoid" descriptive words or phrases (e.g., "Strongly prefer garage rock artists", Figure 2, top). Users can also limit the station's search space (e.g., "Never play songs from the 1980's", Figure 2, bottom).

AuPair was implemented as an interactive web application, using jQuery and AJAX techniques for real-time feedback in response to user interactions and control over audio playback. We supported recent releases of all major web browsers. A remote web server provided recommendations based on the user's feedback and unobtrusively logged each user interaction via an AJAX call.

AuPair's recommendations were based on The Echo Nest [6], allowing access to a database of cultural characteristics (e.g., genre, mood, etc.) and acoustic characteristics (e.g., tempo, loudness, energy, etc.) of the music files in our library. We built our music library by combining the research team's personal music collections, resulting in a database of more than 36,000 songs from over 5,300 different artists.

The Echo Nest developer API includes a dynamic playlist feature, which we used as the core of our recommendation engine. Dynamic playlists are put together using machine learning approaches and are "steerable" by end users. This is achieved via an adaptive search algorithm that builds a path (i.e., a playlist) through a collection of similar artists. Artist similarity in AuPair was based on cultural characteristics, such as the terms used to describe the artist's music. The algorithm uses a clustering approach based on a distance metric to group similar artists, and then retrieves appropriate songs. The user can adjust the distance metric (and hence the clustering algorithm) by changing weights on specific terms, causing the search to prefer artists matching these terms. The opposite is also possible—the algorithm can be told to completely avoid undesirable terms. Users can impose a set of limits to exclude particular songs or artists from the search space. Each song or artist can be queried to reveal the computer's understanding of its acoustic and cultural characteristics, such as its tempo or "danceability".

Participants

Our study was completed by 62 participants, (29 females and 33 males), ranging in age from 18 to 35. Only one of the 62 reported prior familiarity with computer science. These participants were recruited from Oregon State University and the local community via e-mail to university students and staff, and fliers posted in public spaces around the city (coffee shops, bulletin boards, etc.). Participants were paid $40 for their time. Potential participants applied via a website that automatically checked for an HTML5-compliant web browser (applicants using older browsers were shown instructions for upgrading to a more recent browser) to reduce the chance of recruiting participants who lacked reliable Internet access or whose preferred web browser would not be compatible with our prototype.

Experiment Design & Procedure

We randomly assigned participants to one of two groups—a *With-scaffolding* treatment group, in which participants received special training about AuPair's recommendation engine, and a *Without-scaffolding* control group. Upon arrival, participants answered a widely used, validated self-efficacy questionnaire [5] to measure their confidence in problem solving with a hypothetical (and unfamiliar) software application.

Both groups then received training about AuPair, which differed only in the depth of explanations of how AuPair worked. The Without-scaffolding group was given a 15-minute tutorial about the functionality of AuPair, such as how to create a station, how to stop and restart playback, and other basic usage information. The same researcher provided the tutorial to every participant, reading from a script for consistency. To account for differences in participant learning styles, the researcher presented the tutorial interactively, via a digital slideshow interleaved with demonstrations and hands-on participation.

The With-scaffolding group received a 30-minute tutorial about AuPair (15 minutes of which was identical to the Without-scaffolding group's training) that was designed to induce not only a functional mental model (as with the Without-scaffolding group), but also a *structural* mental model of the recommendation engine. This "behind the scenes" training included illustrated examples of how AuPair determines artist similarity, the types of acoustic features the recommender "knows" about, and how it extracts this information from audio files. Researchers systematically selected content for the scaffolding training by examining each possible user interaction with AuPair and then describing how the recommender responds. For instance, every participant was told that the computer will attempt to "play music by similar artists", but the With-scaffolding participants were then taught how *tf-idf* (term frequency-inverse document frequency, a common measure of word importance in information retrieval) was used to find "similar" artists. In another instance, every participant was shown a control for using descriptive words or phrases to steer the agent, but only With-scaffolding participants were told *where* these descriptions came from (traditional sources, like music charts, as well as Internet sources, such as Facebook pages).

After this introduction, each participant answered a set of six multiple-choice comprehension questions in order to establish the soundness of their mental models. Each question presented a scenario (e.g., "Suppose you want your station to play more music by artists similar to *The Beatles*"), and then asked which action, from a choice of four, would best align the station's recommendations with the stated goal. Because mental models are inherently "messy, sloppy... and indistinct" [18], we needed to determine if participants were guessing, or if their mental models were sound enough to eliminate some of the incorrect responses. Thus, as a measure of confidence, each question also asked how many of the choices could be eliminated before deciding on a final answer. A seventh question asked participants to rate their *overall* confidence in understanding the recommender on a 7-point scale.

The entire introductory session (including questionnaires) lasted 30 minutes for Without-scaffolding participants, and 45 minutes for With-scaffolding participants. Both groups received the same amount of hands-on interaction with the recommender.

Over the next five days, participants were free to access the web-based system as they pleased. We asked them to use AuPair for at least two hours during this period, and to create at least three different stations. Whenever a participant listened to music via AuPair, it logged usage statistics such as the amount of time they spent debugging the system, which debugging controls they used, and how frequently these controls were employed.

After five days, participants returned to answer a second set of questions. These included the same self-efficacy and comprehension questionnaires as on Day 1 (participants were not told whether their comprehension responses were correct), plus the NASA-TLX survey to measure perceived task load [8]. We also asked three Likert-scale questions about user's satisfaction with AuPair's recommendations, using a 21-point scale for consistency with the NASA-TLX survey, and the standard Microsoft Desirability Toolkit [3] to measure user attitudes toward AuPair.

Data Analysis

We used participants' answers to the comprehension questions described earlier to measure mental model soundness. Each question measured the depth of understanding for a specific type of end user debugging interaction, and their combination serves as a reasonable proxy for participants' understanding of the entire system. We calculated the soundness of participant's mental models using the formula $\sum_i(correctness_i \times confidence_i)$, where *correctness* is either 1 for a correct response, or -1 for an incorrect response and *confidence* is a value between 1 and 4 (representing the number of answers the participant was able to eliminate). These values were summed for each question i to create a participant's comprehension score, ranging from -24 (indicating a participant who was completely confident about each response, but always wrong) to +24 (indicating someone who was completely confident about each response and always correct).

Mental models evolve as people integrate new observations into their reasoning [18], and previous studies have suggested that participants may adjust their mental models while working with an intelligent agent that is transparent about its decision-making process [14]. Furthermore, constructivist learning theory [12] places emphasis on knowledge *transformation* rather than the overall *state* of knowledge. Hence, we also calculated *mental model transformation* by taking the difference of participants' two comprehension scores (*day_5_score – day_1_score*). This measures how much each participant's knowledge shifted during the study, with a positive value indicating increasing soundness, and a negative value suggesting the replacement of sound models with unsound models.

Table 1 lists all of our metrics and their definitions.

RESULTS

Feasibility (RQ1)

Effectiveness of Scaffolding

Understanding how intelligent agents work is not trivial—even designers and builders of intelligent systems may have considerable difficulty [11]. Our first research question (RQ1) considers the feasibility of inducing a sound mental model of an algorithm's reasoning process in end users—if participants fail to learn how the recommender works given a human tutor in a focused environment, it seems unreasonable to expect them to learn it on their own.

We tested for a difference in mental model soundness (measured by comprehension scores weighted by confidence) between the With-scaffolding group and the Without-scaffolding group. The With-scaffolding group had significantly higher scores than the Without-scaffolding group, both before and after the experiment task (Day 1: Welch's t-test, p=.004, t=-3.03, df=53.64) (Day 5: Welch's t-test, p<.001, t=-3.77, df=59.87). To ensure these differences were not primarily the result of differing levels of confidence, we performed the same test without weighting the comprehension scores by confidence, finding nearly identical results (Day 1: Welch's t-test, p=.003, t=-3.09, df=55.11) (Day 5: Welch's t-test, p<.001, t=-3.55, df=59.36). Neither group's mean comprehension score changed significantly during the 5-day study (Figure 3).

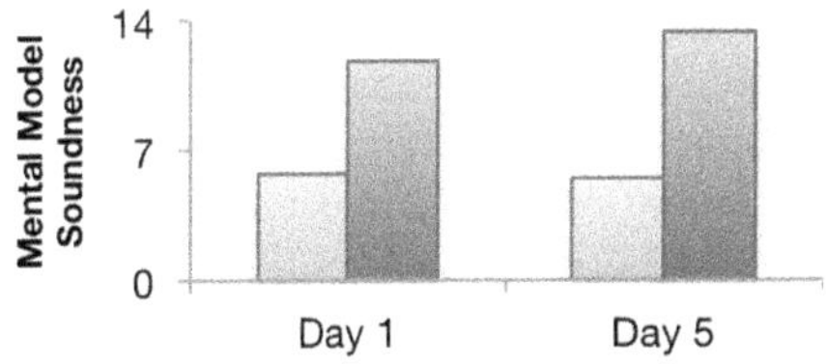

Figure 3. With-scaffolding participants (dark) held sounder mental models than without-scaffolding participants (light), both immediately following the tutorial, and five days later.

Participants also showed differences in their *perceived* mental model soundness, at least at first. On Day 1, the Without-scaffolding group was significantly less certain that they accurately understood how the system selected songs and responded to feedback (mean score of 4.5 out of 7) than the With-scaffolding group (mean score of 5.6 out of 7) (Welch's t-test, p=.015, t=-2.51, df=58.00). By Day 5, however, the Without-scaffolding group's responses had risen to a mean of 5.25, with no evidence of statistical difference against the With-scaffolding group (with a mean of 5.3).

Discussion

These results provide insights into four aspects of the practicality of end users comprehending and debugging the reasoning of an intelligent agent.

First, even a short 15-minute scaffolding tutorial effectively taught participants how the recommender "reasoned". With-scaffolding participants were significantly more likely to correctly and confidently answer the comprehension questions. This in turn suggests that the With-scaffolding participants should be better equipped to debug the recommender's reasoning than the Without-scaffolding participants, a point we investigate in RQ2.

Second, mental model soundness did not significantly improve during the five days participants interacted with AuPair on their own—simply using the system did not significantly help participants develop sounder mental

Metric	Definition
Mental model soundness	Responses to comprehension questions (sum of correct responses, weighted by confidence).
Perceived mental model soundness	Response to Likert question "Are you confident all of your statements are accurate?" after participants were asked to enumerate how they think the recommender made decisions.
Mental model transformation	Post-task mental model soundness minus pre-task mental model soundness.
Debugging interactions	Number of actions a participant used to debug the playlist (e.g., providing feedback, getting the next recommendation, or viewing a song's features), from the automated log files.
Interaction time	Length of time a participant spent on the task, i.e. listening to and interacting with *AuPair*.
Cost/benefit	Response to Likert question "Do you feel the effort you put into adjusting the computer was worth the result?"
Satisfaction	Response to Likert question "How satisfied are you with the computer's playlists?"

Table 1: Definitions for each metric used in our data analysis.

models about its reasoning. This is in contrast to recent work in interactive machine learning, which has found that for some systems (e.g., gesture recognition frameworks), repeated use taught people the most salient aspects of how the system worked [7].

Third, the soundness of participants' mental models largely persisted for the duration of the study. This appeared to be the case for both the Without-scaffolding and With-scaffolding groups, with neither groups' comprehension scores significantly changing between Day 1 and Day 5. This bodes well for end users retaining and recalling sound models initially learned about an intelligent agent.

Fourth, however, is the issue of initially building unsound models: once incorrect models were built, they were hard to shift. Even though the Without-scaffolding group formed less sound mental models, their confidence in their mental models increased, suggesting that they had convinced themselves they were, in fact, correct. Making *in situ* explanations available on an ongoing basis, such as in [9,14,26], may be a way to address this issue.

Together, these findings provide evidence that furnishing end users with a brief explanation on the structure of an intelligent agents' reasoning, such as the attributes used, how such attributes are collected, and the decision-making procedure employed, can significantly improve their mental model's soundness.

Accuracy (RQ2)

A recommender's effectiveness is in the eye of the beholder. Personalized recommendations cannot have a "gold standard" to measure accuracy—only the end users themselves can judge how well an agent's recommendations match their personal tastes. Hence, for our second research question (RQ2), we turned to a pair of more appropriate measures to explore the effects of mental model soundness on "accuracy"—cost/benefit and participant satisfaction.

Cost/Benefit

In theory, a sound mental model enables a person to reason effectively about their best course of action in a given situation [10]. Thus, we expected participants with sounder mental models (the With-scaffolding participants, according to the RQ1 results) to debug more effectively than those with less sound models. For example, knowing that the recommender could be steered more effectively by using unique, highly specific words (e.g., "Merseybeat") rather than broad, common descriptors (e.g., "oldies") should have helped such participants debug the agent's reasoning more effectively than participants who did not understand this.

Surprisingly, when using participants' perceptions of cost/benefit as a surrogate for effectiveness, the soundness of participants' mental models showed little impact on this measure of debugging effectiveness. However, mental model *transformation* was tied with cost/benefit: participants who most improved the soundness of their mental models reported that the effort of debugging was significantly more worthwhile than participants whose mental models improved less, or not at all (Table 2, row 1 & Figure 4A).

Participants' opinions of effectiveness were confirmed by their debugging interactions to adjust or assess AuPair's recommendations (e.g., providing feedback, getting the next recommendation, or viewing a song's features). The count of these debugging interactions was significantly correlated with the improvement in mental model soundness for With-scaffolding participants, while no such correlation existed among Without-scaffolding participants (Table 2, rows 2 and 3 & Figure 4B). *Sounder changes* to the mental model, then, may have had a positive effect on debugging, whereas changes in an initially unsound model did not serve the Without-scaffolding participants as well.

Further, participants who most improved the soundness of their mental models spent significantly less *time* on their interactions than others (Table 2, row 4 & Figure 4C). In light of the increases in perceived cost/benefit and debugging interactions, this suggests positive mental model transformations were linked to more efficient debugging.

An alternative explanation of the above results is that debugging interactions were responsible for participants' mental model transformations, rather than the other way around. Recall, however, that the Without-scaffolding group showed no correlation between debugging interactions and mental models (Table 2, row 3). Thus, the evidence suggests that it was the *in situ enhancement* of relatively *sound* models that was linked to improved attitudes toward debugging.

Satisfaction

Our second measure of debugging effectiveness and the accuracy of the result was participants' satisfaction with AuPair's resulting recommendations. To measure this, we asked participants (using a Likert scale) "How satisfied are you with the computer's playlists?" at the end of the study.

As with the cost/benefit results, neither treatment nor mental model soundness was predictive of participant satisfaction (Table 2, rows 5 and 6). However, here again, transformation of mental models appeared to matter—mental model transformation was marginally predictive of how satisfied participants felt with AuPair's playlists (Table 2, row 7). For example, the participant whose mental model's soundness decreased the most expressed dissatisfaction and a feeling of being unable to control the computer:

"The idea is great to be able to 'set my preferences', but if the computer continues to play what I would call BAD musical choices—I'd prefer the predictability of using Pandora."

	Metric	Statistical Test	Result	Figure
1	Mental model transformation vs. cost/benefit	Linear regression	*p*=.041, R^2=.07, F(1,60)=4.37	Figure 4A
2	Mental model transformation (With-scaffolding) vs. debugging interactions	Pearson correlation	*p*=.031, *r*=.39, t=2.27, df=28	Figure 4B
3	Mental model transformation (Without-scaffolding) vs. debugging interactions	Pearson correlation	*p*=.952, *r*=.01, t=0.06, df=30	
4	Mental model transformation vs. interaction time	Pearson correlation	*p*=.032, *r*=-.27, t=-2.19, df=60	Figure 4C
5	Satisfaction between With-scaffolding/Without-scaffolding groups	Welch's t-test	*p*=.129, t=1.53, df=59.9	
6	Satisfaction vs. mental model soundness	Linear regression	*p*=.272, R^2=.02, F(1,60)=1.23	
7	Satisfaction vs. mental model transformation	Linear regression	*p*=.053, R^2=.06, F(1,60)=3.89	
8	Satisfaction vs. cost/benefit	Pearson correlation	*p*<.001, *r*=.73, t=8.25, df=60	Figure 4D
9	Satisfaction vs. debugging interactions	Pearson correlation	*p*=.293, *r*=-.13, t=-1.06, df=60	

Table 2. Positive mental model transformations were consistently associated with better benefits, lower costs, and improved satisfaction (significant results shaded). Definitions for each metric are listed in Table 1.

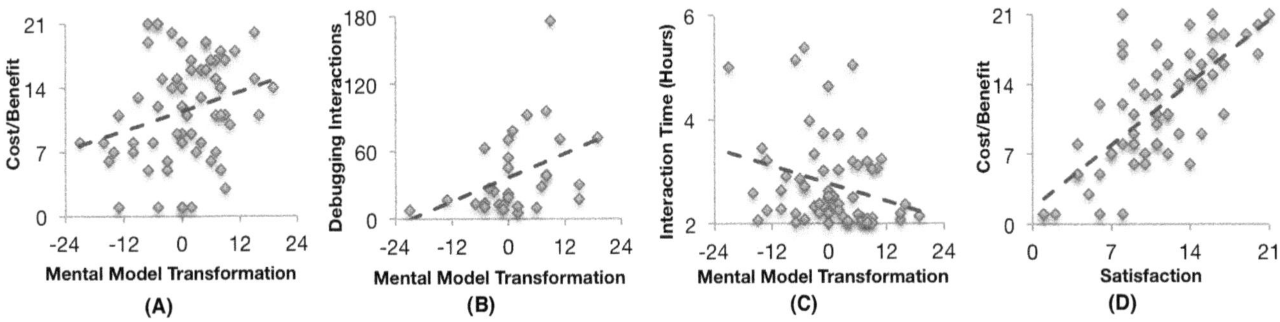

Figure 4: Scatterplots of raw data for each significant result from Table 2. Definitions for axis measurements are listed in Table 1.

Conversely, one of the participants whose mental model most increased in soundness expressed a feeling of being more in control:

"I like the idea of having more control to shape the station. Controls made sense and were easy to use. The user has a lot of options to tune the station."

Perceived cost/benefit from debugging the recommender was also significantly correlated with participant satisfaction (Table 2, row 8 & Figure 4D)—further evidence that satisfaction was indicative of an increased ability to debug the agent's reasoning. To ensure that participant satisfaction was not simply a result of time and effort invested, we tested for a relationship between reported satisfaction and the number of debugging interactions each participant performed, but found no evidence of a correlation (Table 2, row 9).

Discussion

It should be noted that one additional factor may have affected participant satisfaction. Our music database held songs by just over 5,300 artists—pandora.com, by comparison, has over 80,000 different artists [19]. Participant satisfaction may have been confounded by the fact that some participants hoped their stations would play music that was unavailable to AuPair. As one participant commented:

"The songs played weren't what I was looking for, the selection was poor. The system itself was excellent, but I need more music."

Despite this potential factor, the confluence of several metrics (cost/benefit, debugging interactions, interaction time, and satisfaction) suggests that transformations in mental model soundness translated to an improved ability to debug the recommender's reasoning, resulting in more satisfaction with AuPair's recommendations. Because our evidence suggests mental model transformations (which occurred *during* the study) helped participants debug more efficiently and effectively, continuing to provide explanations of an intelligent agent's reasoning while end users interact with the agent may help to increase their ultimate satisfaction with the agent's decisions. Such on-line explanations, however, were not investigated by the current study; we focused our exploration on the impact of explanations prior to (rather than during) user interaction with an intelligent agent.

One potential explanation of why we found no evidence that end-of-study mental model soundness was predictive of debugging ability could be that the information presented to the With-scaffolding tutorial participants was not helpful for debugging the recommender's reasoning. Instead, the most effective participants may have learned to debug by *using* the system. However, this alternative explanation is weakened by the fact that the prototype was not transparent about how it made its decisions; the only time when participants were presented with explanations of AuPair's reasoning occurred during the With-scaffolding tutorial.

Confidence (RQ3)

Presenting a complex system to unsuspecting users could overwhelm them. We are particularly concerned with peoples' willingness to debug intelligent agents—some people (especially those with low computer self-efficacy) may perceive a risk that their debugging is more likely to harm the agent's reasoning than to improve it. Similarly, computer anxiety (a "degree of fear and apprehension felt by individuals when they consider the utilisation, or actual use, of computer technology" [4]) is known to negatively impact how (and how well) people use technology, and is negatively correlated with computer self-efficacy [29].

As Table 3 shows, almost three-quarters of the With-scaffolding participants experienced an increase in their computer self-efficacy between Day 1 and Day 5. Without-scaffolding participants, conversely, were as likely to see their computer self-efficacy decrease as to increase. A X^2 comparison showed that With-scaffolding participants were significantly more likely than a uniform distribution (in which only half would increase their self-efficacy) to increase their computer self-efficacy (X^2=6.5333, df=1, p=.011). This suggests that exposure to the internal workings of intelligent agents may have helped to allay, rather than to increase, participants' perceived risk of making their personalized agents worse.

As further evidence that it was *understanding* how the system worked (rather than simply a byproduct of using it) that influenced participants' computer self-efficacy, participants' perceived mental model soundness was significantly correlated with their computer self-efficacy at the end of the study (Pearson correlation, p<.001, r=.44, t=3.81, df=60). Additionally, there was no evidence of a correlation between the number of debugging interactions participants made and their self-efficacy at the end of the study (Pearson correlation, p=.286, r=.13, t=1.07, df=60); participants did not appear to grow more confident by simply interacting with the system. Thus, participants who at least *thought* they understood the nuances of AuPair's reasoning scored higher on the computer self-efficacy questionnaire than those who expressed little confidence in their knowledge of the recommender's logic.

	Self-Efficacy		
	Did Improve	Did Not Improve	Average Change
Without-scaffolding	16	16	3.29%
With-scaffolding	22	8	5.90%

Table 3. Participants in the With-scaffolding group were likely to end the experiment with higher computer self-efficacy than when they began.

Discussion

We hope further research will shed additional light on this preliminary link between learning how an intelligent computer program reasons, and increasing levels of computer self-efficacy (and, by association, decreasing levels of computer anxiety). Challenging tasks, when successfully accomplished, have been found to have a significantly larger impact on self-efficacy than overcoming small obstacles [2]. Personalizing intelligent agents seems exactly the sort of difficult computer task that, successfully carried out, may make people say, "If I could do *that*, surely I can do *this*…", thereby reducing the obstacles of risk and anxiety toward future computer interactions.

User Experience (RQ4)

For our final research question, we looked at the potential effects of mental model soundness on perceptions of experience, such as cognitive demands and emotional responses.

Cognitive Demands

Prior work has found that explaining concrete decisions of an intelligent agent's reasoning to end users *in situ* created an increase in participants' frustration with, and mental demand of, debugging the agent (measured via the NASA-TLX questionnaire) [14]. We suspected that end users might experience similar effects when presented with prior structural knowledge. However, the With-scaffolding participants showed no significant difference to Without-scaffolding participants' TLX scores. While acquiring a sound mental model undoubtedly requires mental effort on the part of end users, we encouragingly found no evidence that this was any greater than the mental effort required to interact with an intelligent agent without a clear understanding of its underpinnings. This suggests that end users' experience with intelligent agents does not necessarily suffer when they are exposed to more knowledge of how the agent works.

Emotional Responses

We used the Microsoft Desirability Toolkit [3] to investigate participants' user experience with the AuPair music recommender. Participants were given a list of 118 adjectives and asked to underline each one they felt was applicable to their interactions with AuPair.

The Internet General Inquirer (a tool which associates participants' words with either positive or negative connotations, based on the content analysis framework proposed in [23]) revealed that With-scaffolding participants employed slightly more positive descriptions of

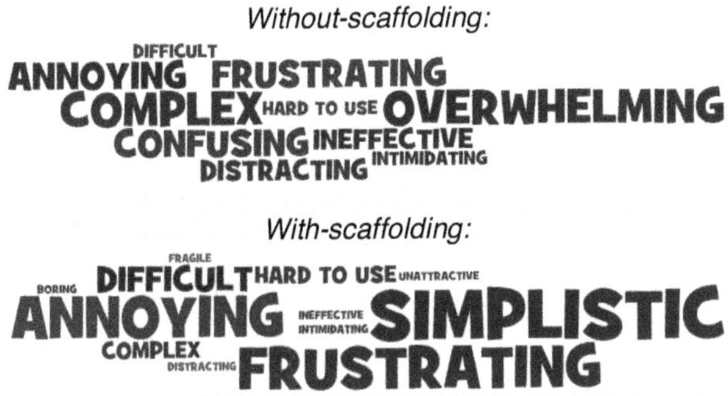

Figure 5. Tag cloud of negative descriptive terms for AuPair. Without-scaffolding participants found the system "overwhelming" and "complex" (top), whereas the With-scaffolding group (bottom) viewed it as "simplistic".

AuPair than the Without-scaffolding group (54.9% vs. 49.6%) and fewer negative descriptions (9.9% vs. 12.0%). While not statistically significant between groups, these numbers suggest that the With-scaffolding participants (with their sounder mental models) may have viewed the overall experience of interacting with AuPair in a more positive light than Without-scaffolding participants.

Participants' descriptions revealed a subtler picture of the difficulties they faced. Word clouds—in which a word's frequency is indicated by its size—of the negative descriptions show that the With-scaffolding group's complaints may have stemmed more from difficulties *using* the system than difficulties *understanding* it; these participants were apt to complain the system was "simplistic", "annoying", and "frustrating" (Figure 5, bottom), while the Without-scaffolding group appeared to have trouble even understanding the impact of their debugging interactions, citing the system as "confusing", "complex", "overwhelming", and "ineffective" (Figure 5, top).

Participants' choices of positive descriptions provide further evidence the With-scaffolding participants' mental models contributed positively to interacting with the agent (Figure 6). The phrase "easy to use" dominated their responses, alongside "innovative" and "accessible". In contrast, the Without-scaffolding participants focused on the visual appearance of the agent, with words like "clean" and "appealing". Participants with a deeper understanding of the system may have placed more emphasis on the interaction experience than aesthetics.

Discussion

Numerous benefits are associated with sound mental models, and in the case of this intelligent agent, it appears possible to gain these without impairing the user experience. This is encouraging for the feasibility of end-user debugging of recommendation systems (and possibly other types of intelligent agents), especially when the user associates a benefit with debugging the agent's reasoning.

Figure 6. Tag cloud of positive descriptive terms for AuPair. Without-scaffolding participants (top) focused on visual appearance more than With-scaffolding participants (bottom).

CONCLUSION

This paper provides the first empirical exploration of how mental models impact end users' attempts to debug an intelligent agent. By scaffolding structural models for half of our study's participants, we learned that:

- Despite the complexity inherent to intelligent agents, With-scaffolding participants quickly built sound mental models of how one such agent (a music recommender) operates "behind the scenes"—something the Without-scaffolding participants failed to accomplish over five days.
- The participants' mental model transformations—from unsound to sound—was predictive of their ultimate satisfaction with the intelligent agent's output. Participants with the largest transformations were able to efficiently adjust their recommenders' reasoning, aligning it with their own reasoning better (and faster) than other participants. These same participants were also likely to perceive a greater benefit from their debugging efforts.
- Participants presented with structural knowledge of the agent's reasoning were significantly more likely to increase their computer self-efficacy, which is known to correlate with reduced computer anxiety and increased persistence when tackling complex computer tasks.
- Participants who were presented with structural knowledge showed no evidence of feeling overwhelmed by this additional information and viewed interacting with the intelligent agent in a positive light, while participants holding only functional mental models more frequently described their debugging experience in negative terms, such as "confusing" and "complex".

This work demonstrates the value and practicality of providing end users with structural knowledge of their intelligent agents' reasoning. Our results suggest that such an approach could better support end-user personalization of intelligent agents—telling an end user more about how it *does* work may help him or her tell the agent more about how it *should* work.

ACKNOWLEDGMENTS

We thank the study participants for their help and Weng-Keen Wong for comments on this paper. This work was supported by NSF 0803487.

REFERENCES

1. Amershi, S., Fogarty, J., Kapoor, A., and Tan, D. Examining multiple potential models in end-user interactive concept learning. In *Proc. CHI*, ACM (2010), 1357-1360.
2. Bandura, A. Self-efficacy: Toward a unifying theory of behavioral change. *Psychological Review 8*, 2 (1977).
3. Benedek, J. and Miner, T. Measuring desirability: New methods for evaluating desirability in a usability lab setting. In *Proc. Usability Professionals' Association International Conference* (2002).
4. Bozionelos, N. The relationship of instrumental and expressive traits with computer anxiety. *Personality and Individual Differences 31* (2001), 955-974.
5. Compeau, D. and Higgins, C. Application of social cognitive theory to training for computer skills. *Information Systems Research, 6,2* (1995), 118-143.
6. Echo Nest, The. http://the.echonest.com (July, 2011).
7. Fiebrink, R., Cook, P., and Trueman, D. Human model evaluation in interactive supervised learning. In *Proc. CHI*, ACM (2011), 147-156.
8. Hart, S. and Staveland, L. Development of a NASA-TLX (Task load index): Results of empirical and theoretical research, Hancock, P. and Meshkati, N. (Eds.), *Human Mental Workload* (1988), 139-183.
9. Herlocker, J., Konstan, J., Riedl, J. Explaining collaborative filtering recommendations. In *Proc. CSCW*, ACM (2000), 241-250.
10. Johnson-Laird, P.N. *Mental Models: Towards a Cognitive Science of Language, Inference, and Consciousness.* Cambridge University Press (1983).
11. Kapoor, A., Lee, B., Tan, D., and Horvitz, E. Interactive optimization for steering machine classification. In *Proc. CHI*, ACM (2010), 1343-1352.
12. Kolb, D. A. *Experiential Learning*. Prentice-Hall Englewood Cliffs, NJ (1984).
13. Kulesza, T., Wong, W.-K., Stumpf, S., Perona, S., White, R., Burnett, M., Oberst, I., and Ko, A. J. Fixing the program my computer learned: barriers for end users, barriers for the machine. In *Proc. IUI*, ACM (2009), 187-196.
14. Kulesza, T., Stumpf, S., Burnett, M., Wong, W., Riche, Y., Moore, T., Oberst, I., Shinsel, A., McIntosh, K. Explanatory debugging: Supporting end-user debugging of machine-learned programs. In *Proc. VL/HCC*, IEEE (2010), 41-48.
15. Lim, B. Y., Dey, A. K., and Avrahami, D. Why and why not explanations improve the intelligibility of context-aware intelligent systems. In *Proc. CHI,* ACM (2009), 2119- 2128.
16. Lim, B. Y. and Dey, A. K. Toolkit to support intelligibility in context-aware applications. In *Proc. UbiComp*, ACM (2010), 13-22.
17. McNee, S. M., Lam, S. K., Guetzlaff, C., Konstan, J. A., and Riedl, J. Confidence displays and training in recommender systems. In *Proc. INTERACT*, IFIP (2003), 176-183.
18. Norman, D. Some observations on mental models, Gentner, D. and Stevens, A. (Eds.), *Mental Models* (1983), 7-14.
19. Pandora Media, Inc. Initial Public Offering Form S-1 (2011).
20. Rosson, M. B., Carroll, J. M., and Bellamy, R. K. E. Smalltalk scaffolding: a case study of minimalist instruction. In *Proc. CHI*, ACM (1990), 423-430.
21. Sharp, H., Rogers, Y., and Preece, J. *Interaction Design: Beyond Human-Computer Interaction* (3rd edition), John Wiley (2011).
22. Sinha, R. R. and Swearingen, K. The role of transparency in recommender systems. In *Proc. CHI Extended Abstracts*, ACM (2002), 830-831.
23. Stone, P., Dunphy, D., Smith, M., Ogilvie, D., and associates. *The General Inquirer: A Computer Approach to Content Analysis*. The MIT Press (1966).
24. Stumpf, S., Rajaram, V., Li, L., Burnett, M., Dietterich, T., Sullivan, E., Drummond, R., and Herlocker, J. Toward harnessing user feedback for machine learning. In *Proc. IUI*, ACM (2007), 82-91.
25. Stumpf, S., Rajaram, V., Li, L., Burnett, M., Wong, W.-K., Dietterich, T., Sullivan, E., Drummond, R., and Herlocker, J. Interacting meaningfully with machine learning systems: Three experiments. *International Journal of Human-Computer Studies 67*, 8 (2009).
26. Talbot, J., Lee, B., Tan, D., and Kapoor, A. EnsembleMatrix: Interactive visualization to support machine learning with multiple classifiers. In *Proc. CHI*, ACM (2009), 1283-1292.
27. Tintarev, N., and Masthoff, J. Effective explanations of recommendations: User-centered design. In *Proc. Recommender Systems* (2007), 153-156.
28. Tullio, J., Dey, A.K., Chalecki, J., and Fogarty, J. How it works: A field study of non-technical users interacting with an intelligent system. In *Proc. CHI*, ACM (2007).
29. Wilfong, J. Computer anxiety and anger: The impact of computer use, computer experience, and self-efficacy beliefs. *Computers in Human Behavior 22* (2006).

Pay Attention! Designing Adaptive Agents that Monitor and Improve User Engagement

Dan Szafir, Bilge Mutlu
Department of Computer Sciences, University of Wisconsin–Madison
1210 West Dayton Street, Madison, WI 53706, USA
{dszafir,bilge}@cs.wisc.edu

ABSTRACT
Embodied agents hold great promise as educational assistants, exercise coaches, and team members in collaborative work. These roles require agents to closely monitor the behavioral, emotional, and mental states of their users and provide appropriate, effective responses. Educational agents, for example, will have to monitor student attention and seek to improve it when student engagement decreases. In this paper, we draw on techniques from brain-computer interfaces (BCI) and knowledge from educational psychology to design *adaptive agents* that monitor student attention in real time using measurements from electroencephalography (EEG) and recapture diminishing attention levels using verbal and nonverbal cues. An experimental evaluation of our approach showed that an adaptive robotic agent employing behavioral techniques to regain attention during drops in engagement improved student recall abilities 43% over the baseline regardless of student gender and significantly improved female motivation and rapport. Our findings offer guidelines for developing effective adaptive agents, particularly for educational settings.

Author Keywords
Educational agents; adaptive agents; human-robot interaction; immediacy; passive brain-computer interfaces (BCI); electroencephalography (EEG)

ACM Classification Keywords
H.5.2 Information Interfaces and Presentation: User Interfaces – *input devices and strategies, evaluation/methodology, user-centered design*; H.1.2 Models and Principles: User/Machine Systems – *human factors, software psychology*

INTRODUCTION
Physically and virtually embodied agents offer great potential due to their capacity to afford interaction using the full range of human communicative behavior. To know when to best utilize these behaviors, these agents must be able to perceive subtle shifts in users' emotional and mental states. For instance, one factor behind the success of the best classroom teachers and one-on-one tutors is that they improve student learning by closely following student engagement and employing strategies that seek to increase attention, motivation, and involvement in the instruction. These behaviors involve a number of *verbal* acts such as directing questions, using humor, and addressing students with their first names and *nonverbal* cues such as expressions, gestures, eye-contact, smiling, posture, and proxemity [19, 20, 39]. Researchers have shown that students with teachers who effectively employ these strategies show more interest in the subject matter and display better cognitive performance [10].

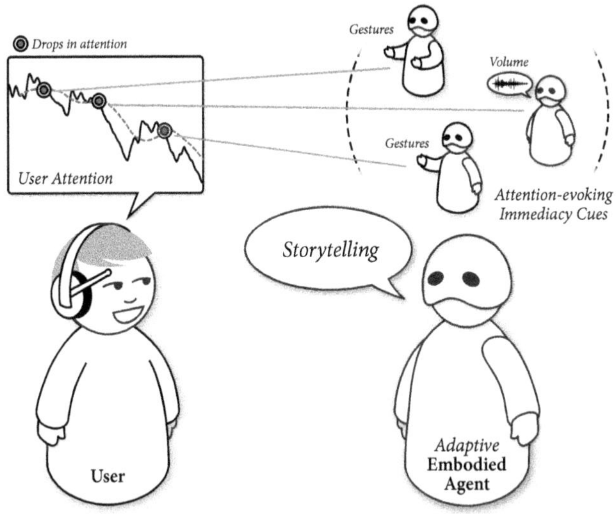

Figure 1. In our study, participants interacted with an embodied agent that monitored their attention using EEG signals in realtime and adapted its behavior to improve the discourse.

As a whole, these behaviors can be grouped under the blanket term *immediacy cues*—actions taken by speakers to decrease the psychological distance between themselves and their listeners [30]. The following excerpt from the educational literature [46] provides a vivid example of the role that these behaviors play:

Professor:	*How do you know when your teacher really means what she says?*
Third Grader:	*Well, her eyes get big and round and she* ***looks right at us****. She doesn't move and her* ***voice is a little louder****, but she talks kinda slowly. Sometimes she stands over us and looks down at us.*
Professor:	*What happens then?*
Third Grader:	*The class does what she wants!*

As in the dialogue above, human teachers change aspects of their verbal and nonverbal language to communicate to their students that they should be attending the teacher. This observation leads us to the question of how can a computer-based system monitor student engagement in a similar manner as real classroom teachers? Even if we could successfully monitor student attention, how could we then exploit that information to design agents that adapt to students and engage them in learning without disrupting the learning process? This study aims to engage these types of questions that surround the area of designing and building adaptive agents by creating a novel system in the educational domain that interacts with users and adapts in real-time to *unconscious* changes in their attentional states (Figure 1).

Educational software, from simple games such as Reading Rabbit and MathBlasters to complex and expensive language suites like Rosetta Stone, has become increasingly popular. Computer-based eduction (CBE) holds significant promise for instructional scenarios and has even shown improvement over traditional classroom education both in terms of academic achievement [1] and student motivation [44]. Further, CBE can reduce the amount of time needed for instruction as well as increase student attitudes towards learning [25]. However, there is much room for improvement as these tools "are not yet as effective as the best human tutors" [1] and "should supplement traditional instruction, not replace it" [27].

Although certain metacognitive strategies such as self-explanation can work well with CBE [1], most CBE tools lack the social and emotional aspects inherent in the traditional classroom setting. One proposed solution to this challenge is the use of virtual characters or agents, which can increase student motivation and create a more natural interaction through the use of social behaviors such as gaze, body language, and facial expressions [22]. However, modern computer systems are limited in comparison with actual teachers who can use a vast array of knowledge including their past experiences and their observations of students to inform their decisions of when and what behavior to employ.

This study seeks to answer the following question: How can we design computer-based educational tools that monitor student attention[1] and employ attention-inducing strategies to improve learning in the way human teachers do? We propose a novel approach that combines techniques and knowledge from behavioral neuroscience and educational psychology. The approach translates previous work into the physical world by utilizing a social robot that monitors real-time student attention using neural signals captured from an off-the-shelf, wireless EEG headset and models real-life educator behavior to deliver instruction. We investigate how an agent, by employing adaptive behavioral techniques to induce involvement with the instruction when significant drops in engagement are detected, might affect student achievement, motivation, and perceptions of the instructor.

[1]The terms "engagement" and "attention" are used interchangeably in this paper.

Behavioral cues	Cue affordances
Bodily cues	***Body***
Sits behind desk when teaching. (Reversed)	*Proximity*
Moves around the classroom when teaching.	*Proximity*
Sits on a desk or in a chair when teaching. (Reversed)	*Proximity*
Stands behind podium or desk when talking to the class. (Reversed)	*Proximity*
Gestures when talking to the class.	*Gestures*
Looks at the class when talking.	*Gaze*
Looks at board or notes when talking to the class. (Reversed)	*Gaze*
Has a very tense body position when talking to the class. (Reversed)	*Posture*
Has a very relaxed body position when talking to the class.	*Posture*
Smiles at individual students in the class.	*Facial Expressions*
Smiles at the class as a whole, not just individual students.	*Facial Expressions*
Touches students in the class.	*Touching*
Vocal cues	***Voice***
Uses monotone/dull voice when talking to the class. (Reversed)	*Vocal Tone*
Uses a variety of vocal expressions when talking to the class.	*Vocal Expressions*

Table 1. Verbal and nonverbal cues identified in educational settings to evaluate the effectiveness of teacher immediacy

RELATED WORK

Immediacy, Education, and Embodied Agents

Educational agents require both a means of monitoring student engagement as well as a suite of corrective actions to take when they realize that a student is no longer paying attention. Research in educational psychology has extensively investigated the various ways in which human teachers utilize vocal and nonverbal cues to achieve desired shifts in students' emotional and mental states. This literature argues that teachers display varying degrees of immediacy—the degree of perceived physical or psychological closeness between people—and that immediacy is strongly associated with the effectiveness of their teaching [23, 38].

Verbal immediacy comprises spoken content, stylistic determinations, and paralinguistic manipulations such as tone and volume, which may affect the listener positively as well as negatively [5, 21]. In general, increased immediacy can be achieved using communication content that demonstrates openness, friendliness, and empathy and an inclusive and mutual style [19].

Nonverbal immediacy includes the speaker's bodily cues and shape the listener's impressions of the speaker. In educational settings, teachers who are more expressive and use more gestures create greater immediacy and attain higher ratings by students [11]. Increasing immediacy through both verbal and nonverbal channels facilitates communication and allows people to share thoughts and feelings more easily. Furthermore, immediacy is a cyclic process whereby an increase in immediacy increases liking and brings people closer together, which, in turn, creates even greater immediacy [5]. Table 1 (adapted from [39]) lists several pivotal verbal and nonverbal behaviors that education researchers have identified in teachers who display high immediacy.

In cognitive tasks, both verbal and nonverbal immediacy have been shown to effect four major learning outcomes: student apprehension [10], motivation [11], understanding and recall of course material [23], and attitudes towards subject matter and instructors [38]. These effects have been shown to be cross-cultural [29, 28] and cross-gender [8] and can be divided into affective (student beliefs and disposition) and cognitive (recall and self-reported learning) aspects. There are two major theories as to how immediacy can be used by an instructor to positively impact student cognitive and affective learning. First, *arousal-attention theory* argues that the use of immediacy increases student arousal thus increasing student attention and engagement leading to a greater recall ability [40]. Second, *motivational theory* suggests that immediacy can increase student ambition by sparking curiosity and driving them to increased inquiry and involvement [11, 21, 40].

Education research offers strong evidence that immediacy plays a critical role in teacher-student interaction, which motivates research into how best to incorporate immediacy, presence, and proxemics in the design of educational agents. However, due to the complex nature of immediacy and the still emerging picture of how to best utilize it within the context of computer-based education, most traditional CBE systems still do not employ any form of immediacy cues. Moreover, early research into CBE has suggested that CBE systems "work better if they present themselves to students as non-human tools to assist learning rather than as emulations of human tutors" [3]. However, research in HCI provides evidence that humanlike representations improve educational outcomes such as student motivation and point to a rich design space for creating humanlike behavior such as verbal feedback that might further enhance these outcomes [33]. We argue that modern agents modeling actual human educators can surpass traditional CBE tools by utilizing arousal-attention and motivational theory.

EEG and Attention

Current computer-based tools focus on the student's comprehension of the instructional material [3] and do not consider attention and engagement, mainly due to the difficulty in inferring these cognitive states. Teachers in classroom and one-on-one tutoring situations monitor these states in real-time by reading students' behavioral cues such as direction of attention, posture, facial expressions, and responsiveness to instructional activity, and researchers have devised various self-reporting scales to measure student motivation after the fact [11, 41]. Current computational methods, however, cannot reliably capture these cues in CBE settings due to vast variability in user characteristics and environmental conditions. However, recent experiments in neuroergonomics have used electroencephalography (EEG) signals to identify subtle shifts in alertness, attention, and workload in laboratory, simulation, and real-world contexts on a second-by-second timeframe [6]. Commercially-available, low-cost wireless EEG headsets have made this approach even more feasible for brain-computer interfaces (BCIs)[34].

BCIs are a rapidly growing technology that draws on brain signals as user input. There are several forms of BCI technology currently available, which can be classified as either invasive devices that require special surgery such as electrocorticography or non-invasive methods such as EEG. Although invasive interfaces allow for better signal fidelity, non-invasive interfaces can be used by the general public, offer no risk to the user, and do not require specialized knowledge or training in their use. EEG is a particularly well-studied non-invasive method which measures event related potentials (ERPs)—positive and

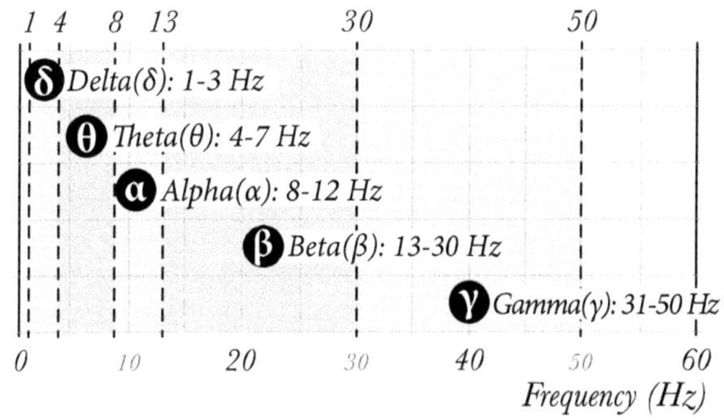

Figure 2. EEG bands and their respective frequencies.

negative charges created by inhibitory and excitatory potentials in the cerebral cortex that are created following the change in membrane conductance as neurotransmitters are released. EEG data is collected via electrodes sensitive to these changes arrayed across the scalp and is generally sequenced into signals classified by frequency (see Figure 2) that have been shown to be affected by cognitive loads in predictable ways [16]. EEG frequencies have been extensively studied and can provide insight into user mood and emotions such as anxiety, surprise, pleasure, and frustration [12, 32, 15]. Additionally, EEG measures are sensitive to cognitive states including task engagement/attention, working modality, and perception of user/machine errors [12, 13, 48].

EEG has the advantage of high temporal resolution, which offers the ability to correlate EEG data with stimuli in the external world, but has the disadvantage of low spatial resolution, which makes it difficult to determine where in the brain the signals originated from. Further, because EEG data represents a vast generalization of actual brain activity, it can be difficult to perceive small changes in user states. Finally, due to the non-invasive nature of EEG, electrode signals are highly susceptible to noise as well as influence by extraneous signals such as electromyography (EMG)—electrical signals that originate from muscles in the scalp and face as opposed to electrical signals in the brain. However, these barriers can be overcome by filtering the EEG signal and EEG has been used make accurate classifications of various cognitive tasks [26, 45]. Specifically, research has offered the following formula for calculating a signal E based on α, β, and θ waves that is highly correlated with participant task engagement [37]:

$$E = \frac{\beta}{(\alpha + \theta)} .$$

Although promising research is currently ongoing into how to best utilize EEG as input into controlling interfaces and robots, BCI design is impeded by the variability of user EEG waves. Traditional BCI systems utilize machine learning algorithms, which must be presented with large amounts of data in order to learn individual EEG patterns to create statistical models of user behavior [35]. These *active* systems where a user deliberately tries to control their brain activity and the system attempts to interpret and respond to the user's brain signals grew out of the goal of having systems for disabled users who could not interact with computers through standard input methods. Although research in this area has succeeded in various ways such as allowing disabled users to control a mouse cursor, these systems often require extensive tuning and training on both the part of the system and the user and are rarely generalizable across multiple users [36, 4].

Current research has shown a paradigm shift towards *passive* systems, which implicitly monitor user conscious and unconscious brain activity [47]. This implicit information is then used in conjunction with other active input by the user (e.g., vocal commands or gestures) to provide further context to the user's intended commands and state. Although research into passive BCI systems is still in its infancy, systems have already been built that can aid in the detection of user and machine errors and detect and adapt to user cognitive load [48, 18, 15]. Our research will build on these promising first steps into non-invasive, passive BCI systems as a means of improving user experience and user-system performance by creating a system that *reacts to* rather than is controlled by user EEG data. This process does not need to be trained by the user as it is based on the user's *unconscious* engagement levels. In effect, we have attempted to create an agent that passively monitors student engagement levels and reacts to them in real time in the manner that a human instructor would.

DESIGN

Our system leverages previous BCI research to create a novel system that monitors student attention in real time. When it detects significant drops in user engagement, it attempts to regain student attention through the use of immediacy cues informed by educational theory.

Detecting Drops in User Engagement

Agents who truly model human behavior must have a system that actively monitors users' attention levels to know the best time to use the verbal and nonverbal cues at their disposal. Our conjecture is that significant drops in user engagement measured from EEG might serve as close approximations of these times and that less engaging tasks should evoke more significant drops. Figure 3 shows sample engagement values from our preliminary experiments of a participant involved in tasks with varying levels of engagement. In this research,

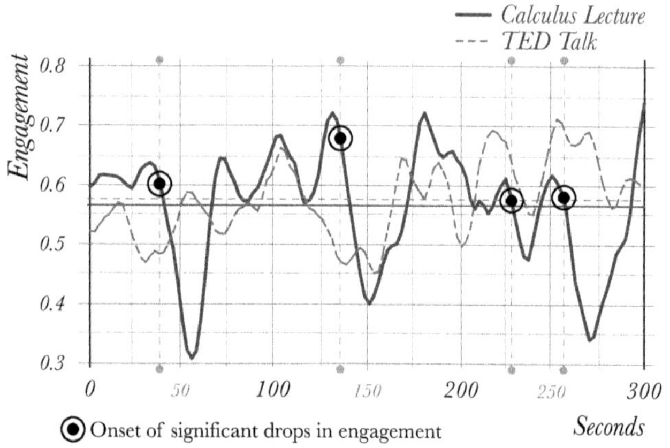

Figure 3. Engagement levels from preliminary experiments using a proprietary index of engagement as a participant watches a video of a Ted Talk (dotted line) and the same user watching a video of a calculus lecture over a six-minute period. More significant drops are seen in the calculus lecture and the onset of these drops are highlighted.

the low-cost[2] Neurosky Mindset EEG device was used as a means of testing the possibilities of off-the-shelf, low-fidelity hardware that could feasibly be used in real-world scenarios. The wireless headset gathers data using only four electrodes, which can remain dry and can quickly and easily be put on and taken off, as opposed to other EEG devices which often have many more electrodes and require special conductive liquids. The headset does not require any special training and is comfortable and usable enough for students to use in an actual classroom scenario.

The Mindset gathers EEG measurements from the FP1 region of the cortex which is known to manage learning, mental states, and concentration [17, 14, 18]. The hardware uses A1-T3 regions for grounding and filtering the signal via common mode rejection and additionally utilizes notch filters, analog and digital low- and high-pass filters, as well as proprietary algorithms to remove EMG artifacts and other noise. This filtering was verified through a pretest that assessed the presence of common artifacts such as eye-blinks. The device samples at a rate of 512Hz and is sensitive to frequencies in the range of 3-100Hz, which are broken into alpha, beta, theta, and gamma waves using Fast Fourier Transforms.

Using this device as input, we constructed a two-tiered system that analyzed EEG engagement levels and identified significant drops in attention in real-time. First, EEG levels for alpha, beta, and theta frequencies were read in from the headset. These values were smoothed using an exponentially-weighted moving average (EWMA):

$$S(t) = \begin{cases} Y(t) & : t = 1 \\ a * Y(t-1) + (1-a) * S(t-1) & : t > 1 \end{cases}$$

where S corresponds to the smoothed value produced using an EWMA, t is time, Y is the raw signal from the headset, and a is a regularization constant that is inversely proportional to the relative weighting of less recent events (a value of .015 was used in this study based on pre-test results).

Even with smoothing, the engagement signal shows high variability. To establish a consistent means of locating drops in attention levels across participants, two thresholds were created from user EEG data in real time and polled for possible losses of engagement in 15 second intervals (chosen after pretesting to identify minimum timeframe that grants sufficient data to accurately make predictions).

The first threshold compares the average slope of recent data with the average slope seen so far:

$$DT(E) = \begin{cases} 1 & : \frac{d\bar{E}(x)}{dt} < \frac{d\bar{E}(y)}{dt}, \frac{d\bar{E}(x)}{dt} < 0 \\ 0 & : otherwise \end{cases}$$

where x corresponds to a 15-second timeframe, y represents full signal seen so far, E is the smoothed engagement signal, and DT represents the derivative threshold function that outputs 1 if an immediacy cue should be displayed.

[2]At the time of this study the Neurosky Mindset was available for consumer purchase at a cost of $199.

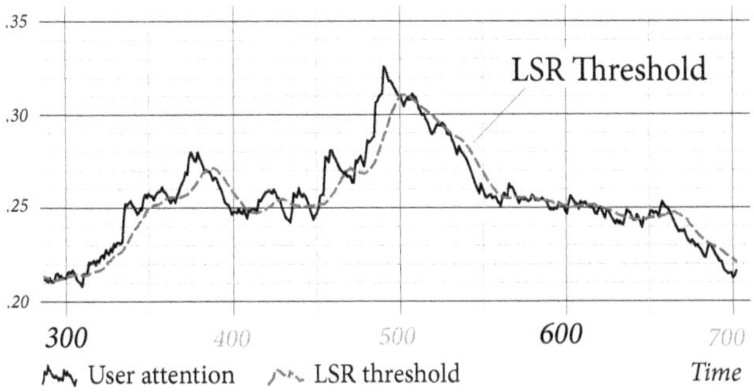

Figure 4. The LSR threshold is created by finding two lines of best fit using LSR regression. The first line is formed using all data seen so far, while the second line is based on data seen in the last time window. These values are then weighted and combined to form a rolling "average" value for user attention.

The second threshold level is based on Least-Squares Regression (LSR), which minimizes a function F, where:

$$F = \sum_{i=1}^{n} (y_i - (ax_i + b))^2 ,$$

$$\frac{\partial F}{\partial a} = 0 \text{ and } \frac{\partial F}{\partial b} = 0 .$$

Here, F corresponds to the minimized function, which generates slope a and intercept b around the data represented by x and y from the start to time n. To generate the second threshold, two LSR functions are generated, one based on the past 15-second interval and one based on all the data seen so far. These values are then averaged and weighted:

$$T = .05 * F(\bar{y}) + .95 * F(\bar{x})$$

where T is the generated threshold, $F(y)$ is the function generated by LSR around all data seen so far, and $F(x)$ is the LSR function based on the data in the latest 15-second interval (see Figure 4). This creates a constantly updating "average" level for each individual user's engagement.

Our system then suggests displaying an immediacy cue by polling both the derivative threshold and the LSR threshold as long as no cue had been performed in the 15 second window immediately prior to the data window used in the calculations. This last step was put into place due to the fact that it can take time for engagement levels to rise following the instructor's use of immediacy cues. This check was enacted in response to pre-test results to avoid situations in which participants felt that the instructor gave too many cues immediately following each other.

Agent Behavior

The design of the agent's behaviors was informed by research into educator immediacy. Immediacy cues are comprised of both verbal and nonverbal behaviors that can signal accessibility or unapproachability and indicate the level of psychological distance between participants. The behaviors used by the agent in this study included modulating spoken volume and using gaze, head nodding, and gestures.

Vocal cues including tempo, pitch, tone, and volume are used by speakers to emphasize words or phrases, add emotion, and increase listener arousal [7, 43]. In our study, we increased volume when an immediacy cue was triggered due to a loss of participant attention to re-engage the student and increase instructor clarity [10]. Increased eye contact has been reported to indicate a higher level of dominance as well as affiliation and immediacy [8]. Head nodding by an instructor has also been shown to positively affect student reactions towards educators [23]. To more accurately model real-world educational scenarios, head nodding and gaze immediacy was used across all conditions to provide for a baseline interaction between the participant and the robot.

Research on gestures suggests that people use four major categories of gestures in human-human interaction: (1) iconic, (2) metaphoric, (3) deictic, (4) and beat gestures [9]. Iconic gestures are closely related to the content of speech and represent concrete events and objects, for example raising one's hands to indicate "higher." Metaphoric gestures allow the speaker to represent ethereal concepts, such as moving one's hands in a circle to show the idea of a cycle. Deictic gestures direct attention towards things directly around the speaker or to the speaker themselves, such as pointing at one's self to highlight a self-experience. Beat gestures allow the speaker to emphasize certain words and phrases and may also be linked with internal processes in speech formulation [2].

Instructor use of gestures has been shown to have a positive effect on immediacy [23] and the use of humanlike gestures by robots has been shown to facilitate interaction between humans and robots [24]. In our study, the robotic instructor utilized metaphoric, deictic, and beat gestures, to indicate that it was conveying an abstract idea, to point toward the participant and toward itself, and to add rhythmic emphasis to its speech, respectively (see Figure 5). The robot's behaviors did not include iconic gestures due to the lack of a priori knowledge of when gestures, which are triggered by a loss in participant attention, would be used during the task.

HYPOTHESES

Two hypotheses were developed for our system based on findings in BCI literature and its potential for use with adaptive educational agents:

Hypothesis 1. Instructor immediacy cues triggered by drops in EEG-monitored engagement levels will increase student attention, thereby increasing learning performance.

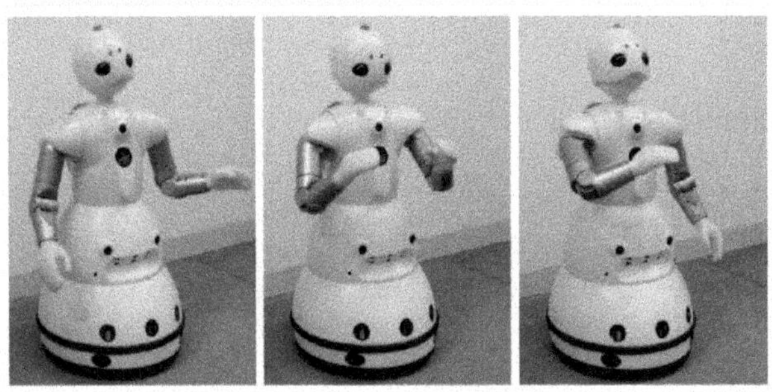

Figure 5. Examples of nonverbal immediacy gestures used by the instructor: (a) *deictic* gestures referring to the participant, (b) *metaphoric* gestures using both hands to form a gesture space containing an idea, and (c) *beat* gestures created by moving its arm rhythmically up and down.

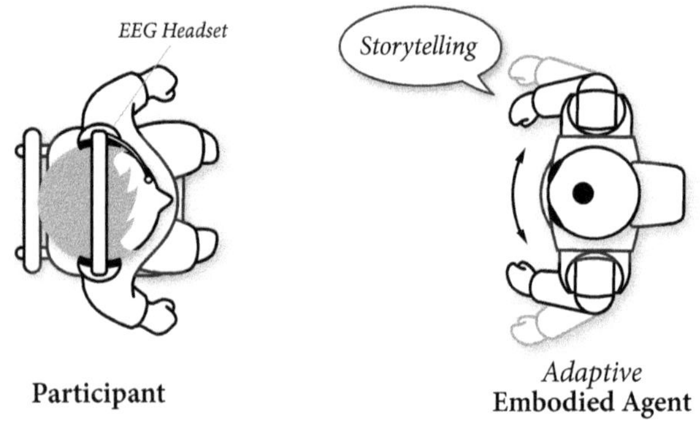

Figure 6. The spatial configuration of our experiment. In the adaptive condition, the robot used immediacy cues to regain participant attention.

Hypothesis 2. The instructor's use of immediacy cues triggered by drops in engagement will positively affect participants' motivation and evaluations of the instructor in measures of rapport.

EVALUATION

To investigate the effects of EEG-triggered adaptive immediacy cues in educational outcomes, we designed and conducted a laboratory experiment in which participants interaction with and received instruction from a humanlike robot. Below we describe the design of our experiment, our procedure and measurements, and our population.

Experimental Design

To test our hypotheses, we conducted a 3×1 between-participants study in which we manipulated the immediacy cues displayed by a Wakamaru humanlike robot, as it told participants two narrative stories. The independent variable was the introduction of the immediacy cues and included three levels: (1) low immediacy, (2) immediacy cues at random intervals, and (3) "adaptive" cues triggered by drops in their EEG-measured engagement levels. The dependent variables included participants' recall of the details of the stories, their perceptions of the robot, and self-reported learning.

Experimental Procedure

In the study, each participant was presented with a memory task that assessed the participant's recall of the details of a story narrated by the robotic teacher. After signing a consent form and being given a brief description of the experiment, participants were brought into a controlled room. Here the researcher aided the participant in putting on the wireless EEG headset and ensured good connectivity. Once the headset connection was established, the researcher left the room and the participant started interacting with the robotic instructor.

The human-robot interaction scenario consisted of five main phases: (1) introduction, (2) calibration, (3) learning, (4) distractor, and (5) evaluation, during which the robot spoke using a pre-recorded female voice modulated to a gender-neutral tone. First, the robot introduced itself and asked if the participant had any prior knowledge of the story behind the 12 signs of the Chinese Zodiac. The robot then told a pre-scripted three-minute long story about the determination of animals in the Chinese Zodiac, which was used to get baseline EEG readings that were used to build the derivative and LSR thresholds. During this calibration phase, the robot used gaze matching and head movements to make the conversation appear more natural, but did not employ other immediacy cues regardless of experimental condition. In the learning phase, the robot narrated a longer ten-minute story based on the popular Japanese folk tale "My Lord Bag of Rice." Both stories were chosen for their unfamiliarity to our participant population in order to ensure that participants had no prior task knowledge.

During the second story, instructor-participant immediacy was manipulated according to experimental condition. In the adaptive condition, the agent displayed adaptive immediacy cues by increasing its volume and employing arm gestures when a drop in engagement was identified by monitoring the participants' real-time EEG engagement data. In the random immediacy cue condition, the robot raised the volume of its voice and produced arm gestures at random intervals, the number of which was determined by the number of cues made by the instructor in the last experimental trial in the adaptive condition. In the low immediacy category, the educator told the second story in the same way it told the first story, ignoring any lapses in participant attention, although still using gaze and natural head movements that were controlled autonomously to ensure consistency between participants. While displaying an immediacy cue, the robot suspended its head movement and looked toward the participant.

After the learning phase, the instructor asked the participant four questions about the Chinese Zodiac story as a distractor task which ensured that there was a break between the learning and evaluation phases for the second story. In the last phase, the robot presented the participant with fourteen questions about the longer story to evaluate the participants' recall ability. During this question-answer period, the time between questions was controlled by the researcher behind the scenes to account for varying answer times.

Following these questions, the experimenter re-entered the room and had the participant remove the headset and fill out a post-experiment questionnaire to obtain a subjective evaluation of participant experience. Finally, participants were debriefed by the researcher and were compensated $5 for their time. The entire procedure took on average 25 minutes.

Figure 7. A participant in our study interacts with the embodied agent.

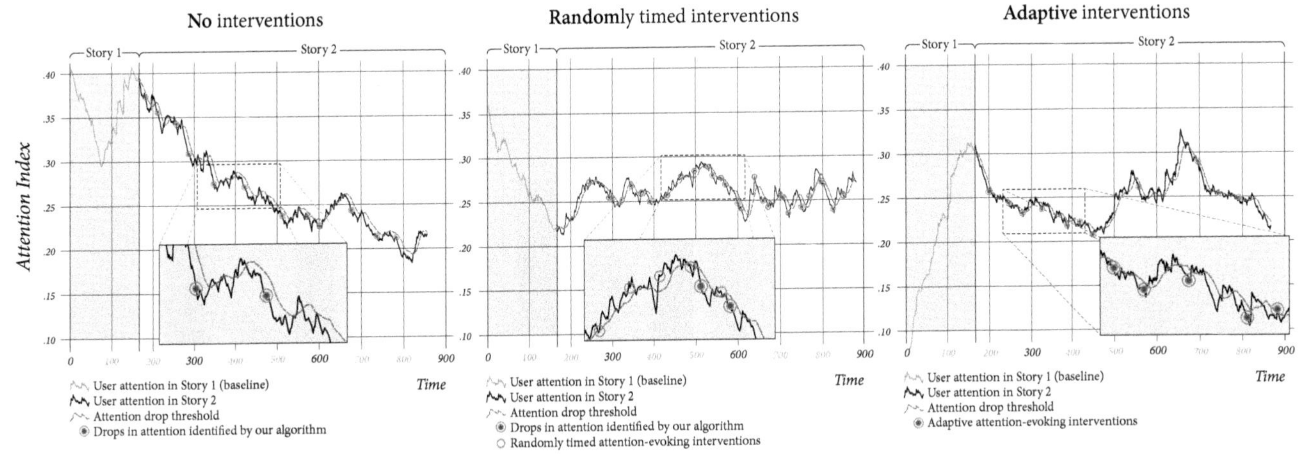

Figure 8. EEG data for three different participants in the three conditions studied. Our analysis indicates that our algorithm correctly identified real-time drops in user engagement and that instructor immediacy behavior halted downward trends in attention levels.

Participants

A total of 30 participants (15 males and 15 females) took part in this experiment. Each of the three conditions had an equal number of participants (five males and five females). All participants were native English speakers and recruited from the University of Wisconsin–Madison campus. The average age was 22.3 ($SD = 6.88$) with a range of 18-57. Prior familiarity with robots was low ($M = 3.23, SD = 1.55$) as was their familiarity with the story in the task ($M = 1.37, SD = 1.07$) in a scale of one to seven. Figure 7 shows a participant interacting with the agent.

Measurement

Objective measurements included fourteen questions that measured the participants' ability to recall the details of the "My Lord Bag of Rice" story and the participants' EEG data. Additionally, subjective measures were taken by means of a seven-point rating scale used to measure participants' responses on a post-experiment questionnaire. This questionnaire included checks on the success of our immediacy manipulations based on Richmond's Nonverbal Immediacy Scale [41] and questions regarding the participants' perception of the instructor and whether they would like to work with the robot again in the future. We utilized a modified version of Christophel's Trait Motivation Scale [11] to determine effects of the robot's behavior on student motivation.

We utilized three different checks to verify our manipulations. First, we confirmed that our algorithm successfully identified drops in attention by examining the EEG data of participants in the low immediacy condition. Second, we analyzed the EEG data of participants in the random and adaptive immediacy conditions to ensure that the agent's behaviors had a positive effect on student engagement. Finally, we constructed a five-item scale from participant responses to the post-experiment questionnaire to assess whether or not our manipulations of the robot's immediacy behavior were successful. The items asked participants how much the robot emphasized parts of story, tried to get their attention, varied the volume of its speech, used gestures, and tried to get their attention when they grew bored (Cronbach's $\alpha = .756$).

RESULTS

We utilized analysis of variance (ANOVA) to analyze our data from manipulation checks and objective and subjective measurements.

Manipulation Checks – To verify that our system was working correctly, we processed the EEG data for participants in the low immediacy condition using our algorithm to identify times when the instructor would have used immediacy cues had those participants been in the adaptive condition. We then analyzed engagement levels in the 30 second timeframes before and after each possible cue using a two-way repeated measures ANOVA using participant ID as a random effect and condition, time frame, and the interaction of the two as fixed effects. Our analysis found that average engagement levels 30 seconds prior to when our algorithm would have directed the robot to re-engage the participant were significantly higher than the average engagement levels 30 seconds after this time, $F(1, 658.5) = 7.54$, $p = .006$, suggesting that our algorithm was correctly identifying losses of engagement.

Further EEG analysis yielded no significant differences in the 30-second windows before and after the robot employed behavioral strategies to regain attention in the random, $F(1, 658.5) = 0.116$, $p = .734$, and adaptive, $F(1, 658.5) = 241$ $p = .121$, conditions, showing that agent immediacy cues successfully halted downward engagement levels. Figure 8 provides a visual summary of the EEG data collected across conditions and the points of attention loss identified by our algorithm.

Our manipulation on checks on whether the participants perceived the robot to show immediacy cues showed that the manipulation was successful and that participants were able to notice when the robot used immediacy between conditions, $F(2, 27) = 6.41$, $p = .005$, $\eta_p^2 = .322$.

Objective Results – Our first hypothesis predicted that participants who received targeted immediacy cues triggered by a drop in EEG-monitored engagement levels would have better recall of the story than other participants. Our analysis confirmed this hypothesis; the number of correct answers out of fourteen questions were on average 6.30 ($SD = 3.40$), 7.44 (SD

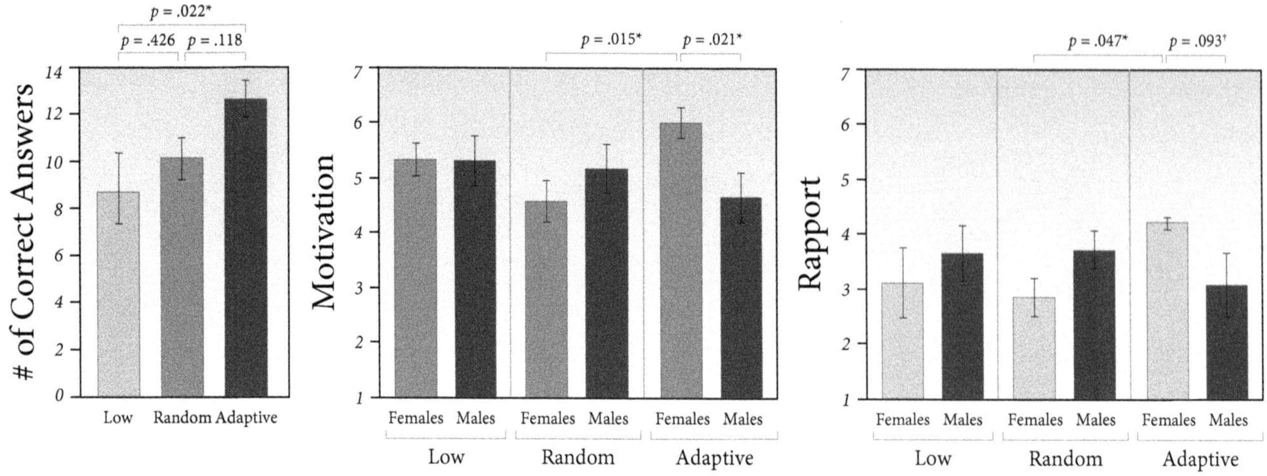

Figure 9. An analysis of our objective data supports our hypothesis that recall is positively effected by using an adaptive immediate agent.

= 1.94), and 9.00 (SD = 1.76) in the low immediacy, random immediacy, and adaptive immediacy conditions, respectively. These results showed that participants with an adaptive instructor outperformed the random condition by 23% and the low immediacy baseline by 43% with a significant difference between the low and adaptive immediacy levels, $F(1, 27) = 5.87$, $p = .022$, $\eta_p^2 = .177$, regardless of gender. No significant difference was found between the low and random conditions, $F(1, 27) = .652$, $p = .426$, $\eta_p^2 = .024$, or between random and adaptive conditions, $F(1, 27) = 2.60$, $p = .118$, $\eta_p^2 = .088$. A pairwise comparison, which contrasted the adaptive condition with the random and low immediacy conditions, revealed significantly improved recall accuracy in students with an adaptive instructor, $F(1, 27) = 5.43$, $p = .028$, $\eta_p^2 = .164$. Much of the variance in our model came from gender as well as users' prior familiarity with robots. When we controlled for these factors, our analysis showed even a greater difference between information recall scores in the adaptive immediacy condition and the combined scores in the low and random immediacy conditions, $F(1, 21) = 7.89$, $p = .003$, $\eta_p^2 = .291$.

Subjective Results – Our second hypothesis predicted that participants would more positively rate an adaptive agent than a random or non-adaptive one. This prediction was supported by the results from our female participants. Females felt significantly more rapport with the adaptive instructor than the random immediacy instructor, $F(1, 24) = 4.40$, $p = .047$, $\eta_p^2 = .155$, and reported that the adaptive agent motivated them significantly more $F(1, 24) = 6.83$, $p = .015$, $\eta_p^2 = .222$. Females also recognized that the adaptive instructor aided them and rated their own learning significantly higher in the adaptive case, $F(1, 24) = 7.98$, $p = .0094$, $\eta_p^2 = .244$.

Despite these promising results for females, we found no significant differences in males for rapport, motivation, or perceived learning across condition. This result could partially be explained by the fact that females reported marginally more general motivation about education and schoolwork than males did, $F(1, 24) = 3.33$, $p = .081$, $\eta_p^2 = .115$. We found no significant effects on the perceived humanlikeness of the agent or the perceived competency of the instructor in either gender. Figure 9 highlights the major results of our study.

DISCUSSION

Our first hypothesis predicted that the use of adaptive agents would significantly improve recall performance in a narrative task. Our results support this hypothesis; participants with an adaptive instructor had objectively better recall of story information. Our second hypothesis predicted that participants would react more favorably to an adaptive agent and evaluate it more positively in subjective measures. Our results partially supported this hypothesis; females felt more rapport with and motivation from an educator that adaptively displayed human-like immediacy behaviors, while males rated all instructors equally. These results highlight the capability of utilizing EEG signals to monitor real-time user states and the benefits of designing agents that can adapt to these states.

Participants who interacted with an adaptive educational robot that displayed high immediacy had similar responses to those who interact with adaptive human educators that demonstrate high immediacy. Our results are consistent with the predictions of the arousal-attention and motivational theories; students who are taught by an instructed with high immediacy show improved recall performance, regardless of whether the instructor is human or an agent/robot. In addition, females rated the instructor with high immediacy more favorably, consistent with previous findings on gender-based differences in social perception, which indicate that females in general are better able to decode and more sensitive to nonverbal cues [42]. These results lend credence to the idea that immediacy can improve perceived learning, which can be a positive factor in student enthusiasm for classroom as well as future performance [23, 31].

Limitations & Future Work

Despite these positive results, our data showed that the instructor's use of immediacy had no significant effect on male motivation and rapport across conditions. The particular context of this study might account for this discrepancy. First, the design of the robot may have made it more difficult for males than females to connect with a "cute" robot of a small stature that used a child-like voice while instructing them. Another possibility is that a narrative task or the specific stories used in this study might affected male and female participants and their resultant experience differently. Finally, while the immediacy cues we considered in this study were limited to metaphoric, deictic, and beat gestures and volume modulation, immediacy offers a rich design space, including cues such as prosody, proximity, and facial expressions. The limited scope of our exploration prevents us from generalizing our results to situations in which the wider range of immediacy cues are used.

Regardless of their own perceptions, both males and females had an improved recall ability, which highlights the usefulness of using our immediacy cues. Moreover, the differences in educational and experiential outcomes between students who received instruction from the robotic instruction in the adaptive versus the random conditions suggest that simply displaying immediacy cues is not sufficient—immediacy cues must be strategically utilized in response to the participants' current attentional state. Although the results of this study are limited to the narrative educational setting, we feel that future work will build on our results and demonstrate the importance of adaptive agents who respond to both conscious and unconscious input from users.

While our system achieved its intended goal of improving student learning by monitoring user attention in real-time and introducing immediacy behaviors at points at which there was a significant drop in attention, open questions remain regarding our method for identifying these points. As with any measurement of neural activity, our engagement index is prone to be affected by other signals such as muscle artifacts due to the limitations of the EEG technology. Although our system employed filters to remove such artifacts, more investigation is necessary to validate that our engagement index indeed represents underlying cognitive activity free from extraneous signals. Future work should also assess the reliability of this measure across contexts, as neural signals might be affected by aspects of the social interaction and the task at hand. Additionally, we believe that the accuracy of our algorithm might be increased by exploring other means of creating tighter thresholds.

Finally, open questions remain about the interaction between agents, gender, and adaptive immediacy. Why did females show a stronger reaction to an adaptive agent? Why did males not give evaluate more positively an instructor from whom they learned objectively more? How can our system be improved to integrate EEG monitoring with other measures such as participant gaze or body posture to improve the adaptability of agents? Our future work will seek to answer these questions towards gaining a fuller understanding of how individual differences affect responses to adaptive agents and further improving our technology.

CONCLUSION

For agents to be successfully integrated into general human-computer interaction, they must be able to accurately measure and respond to conscious and unconscious user states. In this study, we created a system in which a robotic agent informed of real-time measurements of student attention obtained from EEG data employed immediacy cues that human instructors use to recapture student attention when student neural signals indicated a decline in engagement. We found significant improvements in participant recall ability when taught by an agent that adaptively employed immediacy cues compared with agents that employed these cues at random times or that showed low immediacy. Furthermore, female participants reported more motivation, rapport, and learning with the adaptive instructor. These results demonstrate that user states can be reliably evaluated using low-cost, off-the-shelf hardware and argue that the design of truly intelligent agents must incorporate the ability to react to these states in a humanlike way. We hope that this research serves as a springboard for further investigation into the field of how adaptive behavior can aid the design of effective agents to create more fluid interactions with humans.

ACKNOWLEDGMENTS

Mitsubishi Heavy Industries, Ltd., Google Inc., and the University of Wisconsin–Madison Graduate School provided support for this research. We would like to thank Jonathan Mumm, Kohei Yoshikawa, and Erin Spannan for their help in the development of our system.

REFERENCES

1. Aleven, V., and Koedinger, K. R. An effective metacognitive strategy: learning by doing and explaining with a computer-based cognitive tutor. *Cognitive Science 26*, 2 (2002), 147–179.
2. Alibali, M. W., Heath, D. C., and Myers, H. J. Effects of visibility between speaker and listener on gesture production: Some gestures are meant to be seen. *Journal of Memory and Language 44*, 2 (2001), 169–188.
3. Anderson, J. R., Corbett, A. T., Koedinger, K. R., and Pelletier, R. Cognitive tutors: Lessons learned. *The Journal of the Learning Sciences 4*, 2 (1995), 167–207.
4. Ayaz, H., Shewokis, P., Bunce, S., Schultheis, M., and Onaral, B. Assessment of cognitive neural correlates for a functional near infrared-based brain computer interface system. In *Augmented Cognition, HCII 2009*, D. Schmorrow, I. Estabrooke, and M. Grootjen, Eds., vol. 5638 of *Lecture Notes in Computer Science*. Springer Berlin / Heidelberg, 2009, 699–708.
5. Barenger, D. K., and McCroskey, J. Immediacy in the classroom: Student immediacy. *Communication Education 49* (2000), 178–186.
6. Berka, C., Levendowski, D. J., Lumicao, M. N., Yau, A., Davis, G., Zivkovic, V. T., Olmstead, R. E., Tremoulet, P. D., and Craven, P. L. EEG correlates of task engagement and mental workload in vigilance, learning, and memory tasks. *Aviation, Space, and Environmental Medicine 78*, Supplement 1 (May), B231–B244.
7. Buller, D. B., and Aune, R. K. The effects of vocalics and nonverbal sensitivity on compliance a speech accommodation theory explanation. *Human Communication Research*, 14 (1988), 301–332.
8. Burgoon, J. K., and Dillman, L. Gender, immediacy, and nonverbal communication. In *Gender, power, and communication in human relationships*, P. J. Kalbfleisch and M. J. Cody, Eds. Psychology Press, 1995.
9. Cassell, J., Steedman, M., Badler, N., Pelachaud, C., Stone, M., Douville, B., Prevost, S., and Achorn, B. Modeling the interaction between speech and gesture. In *Proc CogSci '94* (1994), 153–158.
10. Chesebro, J. L., and McCroskey, J. C. The relationship of teacher clarity and immediacy with student state receiver apprehension, affect, and cognitive learning. *Communication Education 50*, 1 (January 2001), 59–68.

11. Christophel, D. M. The relationships among teacher immediacy behaviors, student motivation, and learning. *Communication Education 39*, 4 (1990), 323–340.
12. Cutrell, E. Tan, D. BCI for passive input in HCI. In *Proc CHI '07* (2007).
13. Ferrez, P. W., and Millan. You are wrong! automatic detection of interaction errors from brain waves. In *Proc IJCAI '05* (2005).
14. Gentili, R. J., Hadavi, C., Ayaz, H., Shewokis, P. A., and Contreras-Vidal, J. L. Hemodynamic correlates of visuomotor motor adaptation by functional near infrared spectroscopy. In *Proc IEEE '10* (2010).
15. George, L., and Lecuyer, A. An overview of research on 'passive' brain-computer interfaces for implicit human-computer interaction. In *Proc ICABB '10 Workshop: "Brain-Computer Interfacing and Virtual Reality"* (2010).
16. Gevins, A., and Smith, M. E. Neurophysiological measures of cognitive workload during human-computer interaction. *Theoretical Issues in Ergonomics Science 4*, 1 (2003), 113–131.
17. Gevins, A., Smith, M. E., Leong, H., McEvoy, L., Whitfield, S., Du, R., and Rush, G. Monitoring working memory load during computer-based tasks with EEG pattern recognition methods. *Human Factors 40* (1998), 79–91.
18. Girouard, A., Solovey, E. T., and Jacob, R. J. K. Designing a passive brain computer interface using real time classification of functional near-infrared spectroscopy. *International Journal of Autonomous and Adaptive Communications Systems* (2010).
19. Gorham, J. The relationship between verbal teacher immediacy behaviors and student learning. *Communication Education 37* (1988), 40–53.
20. Gorham, J., and Christophel, D. M. The relationship of teachers' use of humor in the classroom to immediacy and student learning. *Communication Education 39* (1990), 46–62.
21. Gorham, J., and Christophel, D. M. Students' perceptions of teacher behaviors as motivating and demotivating factors in college classes. *Communication Quarterly 40*, 3 (1992), 239–252.
22. Gulz, A. Benefits of virtual characters in computer based learning environments: Claims and evidence. *Int. J. Artif. Intell. Ed. 14* (December 2004), 313–334.
23. Harris, M., and Rosenthal, R. No more teachers' dirty looks: Effects of teacher nonverbal behavior on student outcomes. applications of nonverbal communication. In *Applications of nonverbal communication*, R. E. Riggio and R. S. Feldman, Eds. Lawrence Erlbaum, 2005, 157–192.
24. Kanda, T., Ishiguro, H., Ono, T., Imai, M., and Nakatsu, R. Development and evaluation of an interactive humanoid robot "robovie". In *Proc ICRA '02*, vol. 2 (2002), 1848 –1855.
25. Kulik, C.-L. C., and Kulik, J. A. Effectiveness of computer-based instruction: An updated analysis. *Computers in Human Behavior 7*, 1-2 (1991), 75 – 94.
26. Lee, J. C., and Tan, D. S. Using a low-cost electroencephalograph for task classification in HCI research. In *Proc UIST '06* (2006), 81–90.
27. Lowe, J. Computer-based education: Is it a panacea? *Journal of Research on Technology in Education 34*, 2 (2002), 163–71.
28. McCroskey, J. C., Richmond, V. P., Sallinen, A., Fayer, J. M., and Barraclough, R. Nonverbal immediacy and cognitive learning: A cross-cultural investigation. *Communication Education 45*, 3 (July 1996), 200–211.
29. McCroskey, J. C., Richmond, V. P., Sallinen, A., Fayer, J. M., and Barraclough, R. A. A cross-cultural and multi-behavioral analysis of the relationship between nonverbal immediacy and teacher evaluation. *Communication Education 44*, 4 (October 1995), 281–291.
30. Mehrabian, A. Immediacy: An indicator of attitudes in linguistic communication. *Journal of Personality 34*, 1 (1966), 26–34.
31. Menzel, K. E., and Carrell, L. J. The impact of gender and immediacy on willingness to talk and perceived learning. *Communication Education 48*, 1 (1999), 31–40.
32. Molina, G., Tsoneva, T., and Nijholt, A. Emotional brain-computer interfaces. In *Proc ACII '09*, IEEE (2009), 1–9.
33. Mumm, J., and Mutlu, B. Human-robot proxemics: physical and psychological distancing in human-robot interaction. In *Proc HRI '11* (2011), 331–338.
34. Nijholt, A., Bos, D. P.-O., and Reuderink, B. Turning shortcomings into challenges: Brain-computer interfaces for games. *Entertainment Computing 1*, 2 (2009), 85–94.
35. Nijholt, A., and Tan, D. Brain-computer interfacing for intelligent systems. *IEEE Intelligent Systems 23*, 3 (May-June 2008), 72–79.
36. Pfurtscheller, G., Neuper, C., Guger, C., Harkam, W., Ramoser, H., Schlogl, A., Obermaier, B., and Pregenzer, M. Current trends in Graz Brain-Computer Interface (BCI) research. *IEEE Transactions on Rehabilitation Engineering 8*, 2 (2000), 216–219.
37. Pope, A. T., Bogart, E. H., and Bartolome, D. S. Biocybernetic system evaluates indices of operator engagement in automated task. *Biological Psychology 40*, 1-2 (1995), 187–195.
38. Richmond, V. P. Teacher nonverbal immediacy use and outcomes. In *Communication for Teachers*, J. Chesebro and J. McCroskey, Eds. Allyn & Bacon., 2001, 65–82.
39. Richmond, V. P., Gorham, J. S., and McCroskey, J. C. The relationship between selected immediacy behaviors and cognitive learning. *Communication Yearbook*, 10 (1987), 574–590.
40. Richmond, V. P., and McCroskey, J. C. Influencing teacher influence through immediacy. In *Power in the classroom: communication, control, and concern*, V. P. Richmond and J. C. McCroskey, Eds. Psychology Press, 1992, 101–119.
41. Richmond, V. P., McCroskey, J. C., and Johnson, A. D. Development of nonverbal immediacy scale (nis): Measures of self-and other-perceived nonverbal immediacy. *Communication Quarterly 51*, 4 (2003), 504–517.
42. Rosip, J. C., and Hall, J. A. Knowledge of nonverbal cues, gender, and nonverbal decoding accuracy. *Journal of Nonverbal Behavior 28* (2004), 267–286.
43. Scherer, K., Ladd, D., and Silverman, K. Vocal cues to speaker affect: Testing two models. *Journal of the Acoustical Society of America 76*, 5 (1984), 1346–1356.
44. Schofield, J. W. *Computers and Classroom Culture*. Cambridge University Press, 1995.
45. Tan, D. Brain-computer interfaces: applying our minds to human-computer interaction. In *Proc CHI Workshop: "What is the Next Generation of Human-Computer Interaction?"* (2006).
46. Woolfolk, A. E., and Brooks, D. The influence of teachers' nonverbal behaviors on students' perceptions and performance. *The Elementary School Journal 85* (1985), 513–528.
47. Zander, T., and Kothe, C. Towards passive brain-computer interfaces: applying brain-computer interface technology to human-machine systems in general. *Journal of Neural Engineering 8*, 2 (2011), 025005.
48. Zander, T. O., Kothe, C., Jatzev, S., and Gaertner, M. Enhancing human-computer interaction with input from active and passive brain-computer interfaces. In *Brain-Computer Interfaces*, D. S. Tan and A. Nijholt, Eds., Human-Computer Interaction Series. Springer London, 2010, 181–199.

ReGroup: Interactive Machine Learning for On-Demand Group Creation in Social Networks

Saleema Amershi, James Fogarty, Daniel S. Weld
Computer Science & Engineering
DUB Group
University of Washington
{samershi, jfogarty, weld} @ cs.washington.edu

ABSTRACT
We present ReGroup, a novel end-user interactive machine learning system for helping people create custom, on-demand groups in online social networks. As a person adds members to a group, ReGroup iteratively learns a probabilistic model of group membership specific to that group. ReGroup then uses its currently learned model to suggest additional members and group characteristics for filtering. Our evaluation shows that ReGroup is effective for helping people create large and varied groups, whereas traditional methods (searching by name or selecting from an alphabetical list) are better suited for small groups whose members can be easily recalled by name. By facilitating on-demand group creation, ReGroup can enable in-context sharing and potentially encourage better online privacy practices. In addition, applying interactive machine learning to social network group creation introduces several challenges for designing effective end-user interaction with machine learning. We identify these challenges and discuss how we address them in ReGroup.

Author Keywords
Interactive machine learning; social network access control; example and feature-based interaction.

ACM Classification Keywords
H.5.2 [Information interfaces and presentation (e.g., HCI)]: User Interfaces.

General Terms
Algorithms, Design, Human Factors.

INTRODUCTION
Social networking sites present a conflict between our desire to share our personal lives online and our concerns about personal privacy [13, 33,37]. Well-known examples of privacy blunders include oversharing embarrassing photos with potential employers [19], accidently posting intimate conversations [30], and being fired for publicly criticizing a boss [4]. Major sites have therefore begun advocating customizable friend groups as the latest tool for helping us control with whom we share [27,31].

The currently-advocated approach to custom group creation is to pre-categorize friends in advance of sharing decisions. For example, Google+ requires friends be manually organized into "Circles" before content can be shared with them [31]. Katango [17] and Facebook's "Smart Lists" [27] attempt to aid group curation by automatically generating potential groups based on a person's social graph or common features (e.g., inferred closeness, current city). These automatically generated groups can then be manually edited for correctness or to capture other preferences.

Pre-defined groups may suffice for filtering update streams and news feeds, but usable security recommendations argue that privacy controls for sharing content should operate in context of that content [20,29,40,43]. This is because prior research has shown that willingness to share varies widely based on both content recipients and the content itself [26]. For example, a person's definition of a "close friend" may change when sharing a personal photograph versus inviting people to a party. Furthermore, Jones and O'Neill [16] recently showed that groups created for generic purposes only partially overlap with in-context sharing decisions. Ill-conceived groupings can therefore lead to information leakage, over-restriction, or additional work to revise pre-defined groups in-context.

We present ReGroup (<u>R</u>apid and <u>E</u>xplicit <u>Group</u>ing), a novel system that uses end-user interactive machine learning to help people create custom, on-demand groups in Facebook. As ReGroup (Figure 1) observes a person's normal interaction of adding members to a group, it learns a probabilistic model of group membership in order to suggest both additional members and group characteristics for filtering a friend list. ReGroup differs from prior group member suggestion systems (e.g., Gmail's "Don't forget Bob!" [11] and FeedMe [3]) in its ability to continually update its membership model based on interactive user feedback. As a result, ReGroup can tailor its suggestions to the group a person is currently trying to create (instead of being limited to making suggestions based on a predefined and static notion of similarity or interest). Facilitating on-demand creation of contextualized groups may help encourage better privacy practices in social networks.

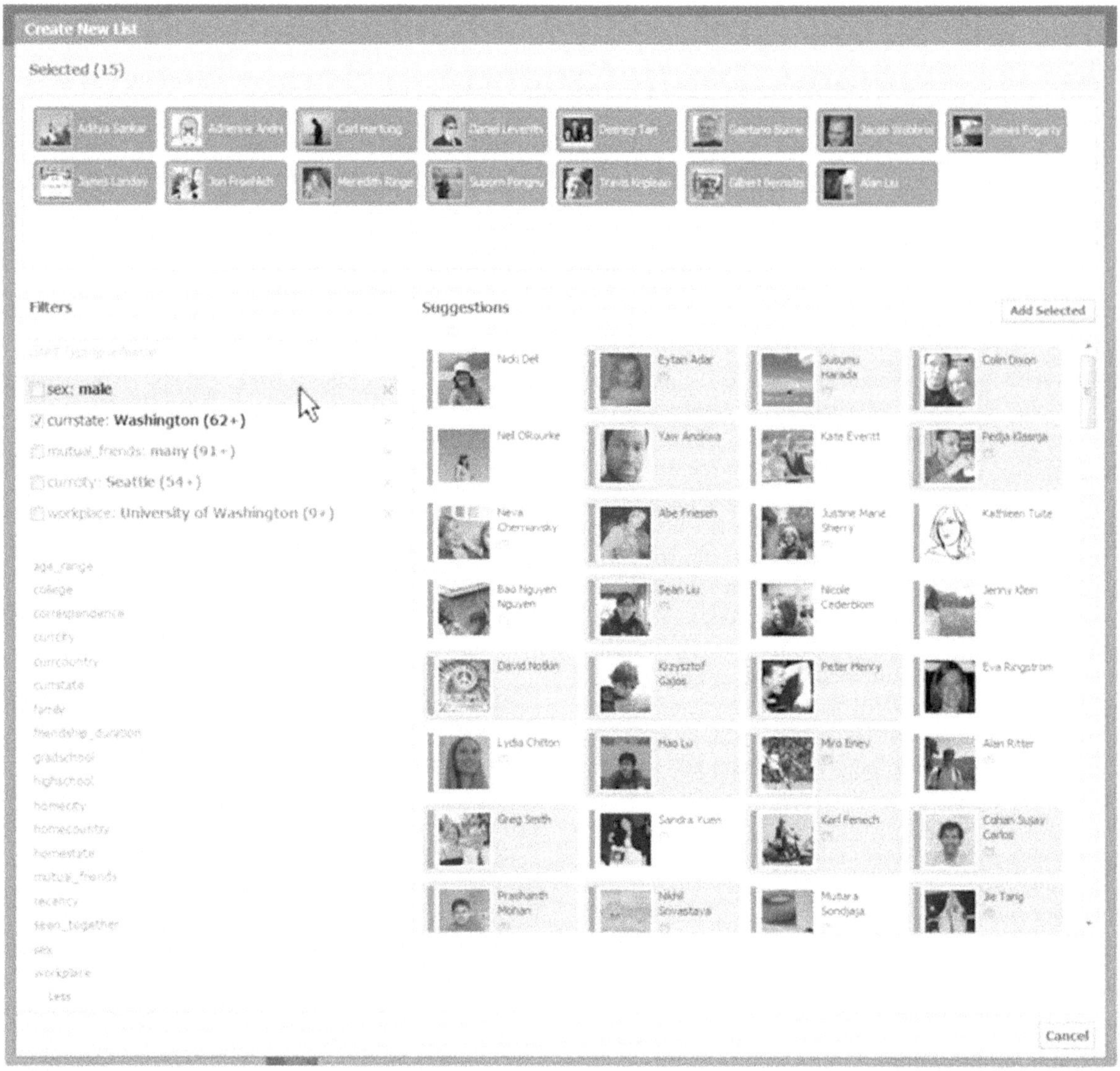

Figure 1. ReGroup uses end-user interactive machine learning to help people create custom, on-demand groups. As a person selects group members (in the *Selected* display), ReGroup suggests additional members (in the *Suggestions* display) and suggests group characteristics as filters for narrowing down a friend list (see five suggested filters at the top of the *Filters* display).

This paper makes the following contributions:

- A new approach to social access control – using end-user interactive machine learning to help people create custom groups on-demand in the context of sharing decisions.
- A discussion of several new challenges for the design of effective end-user interaction with machine learning systems, as exposed in our application to social networks.
- Novel example and feature-based interaction techniques for addressing the above design challenges in ReGroup.
- An evaluation of ReGroup compared to traditional methods of on-demand group creation. Our quantitative and qualitative analyses indicate that different techniques are effective for different types of groups and therefore integrating all techniques in online social networks can support a wider range of desired groups.

REGROUP

ReGroup uses end-user interactive machine learning to help people create custom groups on-demand. In this section, we first use an example to illustrate how a person can create a group with ReGroup. We then discuss the challenges inherent to interactive machine learning for group creation and how we address them in our design of ReGroup.

Example Usage Scenario

Ada wants to advertise a confidential research talk to relevant friends at the University of Washington, so she decides to use ReGroup to create a private group for the ad. To start, she thinks of a friend she knows will be interested in the talk, searches for them by name (via a search box, left in Figure 1) and adds them to her group (*Selected* display, top in Figure 1). ReGroup learns from this example and then tries to help Ada find other friends to include. It re-organizes her friend list to sort relevant friends to the top of the *Suggestions* display (right in Figure 1). Ada now sees several additional friends she wants to include. She adds them to her group all at once by drag-selecting and then clicking the *Add Selected* button (right in Figure 1). With these additional examples, ReGroup learns more about the group being created and again re-organizes Ada's friends to help her find more group members.

As ReGroup learns about the group Ada is creating, it also presents relevant group characteristics she can use as filters. For example, given the currently selected friends, ReGroup believes Ada might want to include other people that live in Washington, that have several mutual friends with her, or that work at the University of Washington (top of *Filters* display in Figure 1). Although not everybody Ada wants to include works at the University of Washington (e.g., some are students), she agrees that they all likely live in Washington. She clicks the "Washington" filter, causing ReGroup to remove friends who do not live in Washington. This helps Ada by reducing the number of people she must consider when finding friends to include in her group.

Ada continues interacting with ReGroup this way, explicitly adding group members and filtering when necessary, until she has included everyone to whom she wants to advertise.

Identifying Features

ReGroup's ability to suggest group members is powered by its interactive machine learning component. Machine learning works by discovering patterns in examples. A system is therefore strongly influenced by the quality of information contained in the representations of those examples (i.e., the features). We based our features on related work on social networks (e.g., [11]). We also conducted an online survey of Facebook and Google+ users to identify common groups we could support. We distributed the survey to our own Facebook and Google+ contacts, obtaining 69 responses (21 Facebook and 48 Google+) describing 244 customized groups (32 Facebook and 212 Google+). Facebook and Google+ advocate creating groups in advance, so the groups identified in our survey may not correspond to groups people would create on-demand (i.e., the composition of permanent groups may differ from groups created in context). Nevertheless, these gave a starting point from which to distill potential features.

Table 1 presents the 18 features currently used by ReGroup, each with an example group the feature might help support. In this research, we endeavored to support common groups as part of demonstrating the potential for interactive machine learning in social access control. Our features are therefore not intended to be exhaustive.

Suggesting People while Preserving End-User Control

ReGroup's group member suggestions are realized by a Naïve Bayes classifier [5]. Each friend is represented by a set of n feature-value pairs (Table 1). The probability of each friend being a member of the group g is then computed via the following Bayesian formulation:

Feature	Description/Examples
Gender, Age Range	"Sorority friends", "People my age"
Family Member	"People I'm related to"
Home City, State and Country	"Friends from my hometown"
Current City, State, Country	"Anyone I know who lives nearby"
High School, College, Graduate School	"Anyone from my department at school"
Workplace	"CoWorkers"
Amount of Correspondence	Number of Inbox, Outbox and Wall messages sent and received. "People I socialize with regularly"
Recency of Correspondence	Time since latest correspondence. "Friends I currently interact with"
Friendship Duration	Time since first correspondence [11]. "Friends I've known over 10 years"
Number of Mutual Friends	"My group of closest friends"
Amount Seen Together	Number of photos/events a person and friend are both tagged in. "People I see on a regular bases"

Table 1. The 18 features currently used by ReGroup's interactive machine learning component.

$$P(g|x_1, x_2, \ldots, x_n) = \frac{P(x_1, x_2, \ldots, x_n|g)P(g)}{\sum_{g'=g,\bar{g}} P(x_1, x_2, \ldots, x_n|g')P(g')}$$

where $P(x_1, x_2, \ldots, x_n|g)$ is the likelihood of a friend with feature values $x_1, x_2, \ldots, x_n$ being a member of g, $P(g)$ is the prior probability of any friend belonging to g, and the denominator is the probability of seeing the set of feature values in the data and serves as a normalizing constant.

The Naïve Bayes assumption considers each feature to be conditionally independent given the class, reducing the likelihood computation to:

$$P(x_1, x_2, \ldots, x_n|g) = \prod_{i=1}^{n} P(x_i|g)$$

where the probability of a group member having a particular feature value, $P(x_i|g)$, can be estimated by a frequency count of the number of current group members having that feature value over the total number of current group members. We also use Laplace smoothing to improve performance in the presence of limited training data. Although the independence assumption is often violated in real-world data, Naïve Bayes has been shown to work well in many practical applications [5]. Naïve Bayes also gracefully handles missing data and allows for a straightforward interpretation of features, both important aspects of ReGroup as will be discussed below.

ReGroup's classifier is re-trained every time a person adds friends to a group. ReGroup then reorders a person's remaining friends according to who is most likely to also belong to the group as computed by the updated classifier.

To preserve end-user control during interaction with the classifier, we made the design decision that people must *explicitly* approve every group member, as opposed to having ReGroup automatically add suggested friends.

Indirectly Training an Effective Classifier

Effective training of machine learning systems requires both positive and negative examples. Therefore, a system focused on *training an effective classifier* will be designed to solicit explicit positive and negative examples (e.g., [1]). In our case, however, a person's primary goal is to *create a group*. That is, the classifier is a disposable side effect and a person is not concerned about its generalization.

To mitigate the effects of people primarily providing positive examples, we designed ReGroup to obtain implicit negative examples during interaction. When a person selects a group member from an ordered list of friends, ReGroup increases the probability that the skipped friends (i.e., friends preceding the selection in the ordered list) are *not* intended for the group. This is achieved by assigning the preceding friends implicit negative labels in ReGroup's group membership computations. However, as this heuristic is not always correct (e.g., a person's gaze may be drawn to a friend further down in the list without having viewed or decided upon the preceding friends), an implicit negative example contributes only a partial frequency count, α, in ReGroup's computation of $P(x|g)$. ReGroup also still includes implicitly labeled friends in its list of suggestions. We found that setting $\alpha=0.2*n$, where n is the number of times a friend is skipped, worked well in practice.

Unlearnable Groups

While experimenting with early versions of ReGroup, we observed that skipped friends would sometimes continue bubbling back up in the ordered list during group creation. Further examination revealed that this occurred when (1) a friend had all the characteristics of the group, as modeled by the classifier, but (2) was skipped for some reason not captured by the system (e.g., a person planning a surprise party would obviously not invite the guest of honor). Implicit negative examples are not powerful enough to prevent repeated suggestion of such friends because of their high similarity to the many positive examples. This problem occurs in all machine learning systems when the hypothesis language is insufficiently expressive to model the true concept. However, it can be particularly frustrating in an interactive system like ReGroup, as a person can quickly grow tired of repeatedly skipping the same friend. We addressed this with an explicit penalty term, v, in our group membership estimation as follows:

$$P(g|x) = P(g|x) * v^n$$

where n is the number of times a friend was skipped. Our preliminary experiments showed that setting v=0.9 achieved the desired effect (i.e., it reduced the likelihood of a skipped friend continuing to be highly ranked when ReGroup could not learn the true concept).

Integrating Knowledge about Group Members via Decision-Theoretic Filter Suggestions

Most end-user interactive machine learning systems focus only on interaction with examples (e.g., [8, 10]). However, people often have knowledge about the shared properties of groups. We hypothesized that enabling interaction with those features might accelerate the group creation process. We chose to realize end-user interaction with features in ReGroup using faceted search [15], a popular method for helping people find items in collections (e.g., [46]). With faceted search, people find items by filtering a collection based on feature values. ReGroup provides two ways for people to filter friends by feature values:

- Via a suggested list of five top feature value filters (top of *Filters* display, left in Figure 1).
- Via a static, hierarchical list of all feature value filters (bottom of *Filters* display, left in Figure 1).

Previous methods for ordering filters have used metrics like hit count [15] or query keyword similarity [46]. However, none of these are appropriate for our domain. We therefore formulate the problem decision-theoretically. Intuitively, we want ReGroup to suggest filters that will reduce effort required during group creation. A suggested filter must therefore represent the intended group well (i.e., $P(x_i| g)$ must be high). However, this alone does not guarantee that a filter will prune unwanted friends. We therefore combine this with the expected utility of a filter as follows:

$$U(x_i) = P(x_i| g) * InformationGain(X_i)$$

Here, we use information gain to approximate the potential time savings of activating a filter [25]. We use this formulation in choosing the top five filters to suggest, as well as in ordering feature values within the static list.

Missing Data

Missing data, which can lead to unpredictable behavior in machine learning systems, is rampant in the domain of online social networks. People choose not to supply information, have strict privacy settings, or are inconsistent with their online activity. The Naïve Bayes classifier gracefully handles missing data by ignoring features with missing values when computing group membership probabilities. However, missing data can still adversely impact the usefulness of filters by leading to incorrectly filtered friends (e.g., when filtering on "Seattle", a friend who lives in Seattle might be filtered because they have not supplied this to Facebook) or incorrectly preserved friends (e.g., when filtering on "Seattle", retaining a friend who lives in Austin but has not supplied this to Facebook).

ReGroup attempts to estimate missing values by creating additional feature classifiers for predicting missing values conditioned on all other available features. Then, when applying a filter, ReGroup only eliminates friends who are *guaranteed* to be ineligible (i.e., have provided some value other than the filter value). For friends with missing data, ReGroup indicates its uncertainty by displaying a question mark under their name (see Figure 1). If a person hovers over a question mark, ReGroup displays a tooltip showing its guess for that friend's corresponding feature value. ReGroup thus avoids incorrectly eliminating friends while reducing irritation by explicitly displaying its guesses.

Implementation Details

ReGroup is implemented using Facebook's Application Platform [7] and a Firefox Greasemonkey script [12]. ReGroup uses Facebook's Application Platform to access a person's relevant information (see Table 1), while the Greasmonkey script allows ReGroup to run within a person's own Facebook account. ReGroup is not publicly available (i.e., only our study participants could access the Facebook Application and use the Greasemonkey script installed on the study computer). ReGroup accessed a participant's Facebook information only after they provided explicit and informed consent and only for enabling its interface, staying within Facebook's Terms of Service.

EVALUATION

We conducted an evaluation to explore the tradeoffs between end-user interactive machine learning for on-demand custom group creation and Facebook's current approach of allowing manual selection from an alphabetical list or searching by name [39]. We also wanted to compare a design including our feature-based interaction with a more typical design using only example-based interaction.

Interface Conditions

We evaluated the following interfaces:

- *Alphabet*. A person can search by name or scroll through an alphabetical list to find friends. This is equivalent to Facebook's current on-demand group creation process.
- *Example-Only*. Each time a person adds a friend to the group, the list of friends is reordered based on ReGroup's current estimation of group membership probability. People can also still search for friends by name.
- *Example-Attribute*. The full ReGroup design, enhancing the *Example-Only* with our decision-theoretic technique for feature-based interaction.

Design and Procedure

We ran a within-subjects study, counterbalancing order of interface conditions using a Latin square design. At the beginning of the study, we told participants they would be testing new tools for helping people create custom groups in Facebook. We also explained the tools would work in their own Facebook accounts and that they would be testing the tools by creating groups of their own friends. Participants were then informed about what data would be accessed and how it would be used. We continued only after they provided written consent and granted our Facebook Application permissions to access their data.

Next, prior to seeing any interface, participants were asked to think of six groups they could create during the study. We chose this approach to ensure groups were meaningful, as assigned groups may not correspond to distinctions a person would make among their friends. When thinking of groups, participants were instructed to imagine they were about to post a new comment or share a new photo and only wanted to share it with a select group of friends. We also provided them with a list of ten example groups based on frequent responses to our online survey (e.g., "home town friends", "close friends") to help them decide. Resulting groups ranged from typical (e.g., "Family", "CoWorkers") to more unique and nuanced (e.g., "Older Faculty Members", "People I Care About"). We also asked participants to estimate group size ("small", "medium" or "large"). The experimenter then sorted groups by estimated size and assigned them to conditions in order (thus roughly balancing groups across conditions by size).

The experimenter then demonstrated ReGroup (using the full *Example-Attribute* interface) with the experimenter's own Facebook account. Participants were told they would use three variations of the ReGroup interface. Before each condition, the participant practiced with the corresponding interface by creating a simple gender-based group. After the practice, participants used the interface condition to create two of their groups (they were not told which groups they would create until they were about to create them). To avoid exhausting participants, we limited each group to a maximum of 4 minutes (we did not inform participants of this limit, but simply asked them to stop if they reached it).

All interface actions were time-stamped and logged. All participant information and logged data was stored anonymously, using unique identifiers, on a secure server accessible only by the researchers. After each group, participants completed a short questionnaire containing 5-point Likert scales (1=strongly disagree, 5=strongly agree) about the group they just created (e.g., "I was happy with the group I just created"). At the end of the study, participants filled out a final questionnaire to comment on their overall experience and compare the interfaces (e.g., "Rank the versions to indicate which was your favorite"). The study lasted 1 hour and participants were given a $20 Amazon gift certificate for their participation.

Participants and Data

Twelve people (four female, ranging in age from 18-34) were recruited via a call for participation sent to several university mailing lists. As a result, all of our participants were technically savvy, but ranged from undergraduates to staff members from a variety of disciplines (e.g., Computer Science, Psychology, Design). We required participants to have an active Facebook account in use for at least one year and to have at least 100 friends. This was to help ensure enough activity was available to enable ReGroup's suggestions. As expected, participants varied in their composition and number of friends (mean=385.4, min=136, max=781) and their Facebook activity (ranging from every day to a few times per month). On average, our participants also had 36.3% missing data with respect to ReGroup's features.

RESULTS

We performed all of our log and Likert scale data analyses using a nonparametric repeated measures analysis of variance, after aligning the data according to the *aligned rank transform* [44] to preserve interaction effects due to having participants create two groups per condition. We also performed post-hoc pairwise comparisons when a significant effect was observed. To analyze our final ranking questions, we used a randomization test of goodness-of-fit [23] which is more robust against smaller sample sizes than a standard Chi-Square test. For each test, we ran 10,000 Monte Carlo simulations. Tables 2 and 3 show the per-condition means and standard deviations for all metrics used in our log and Likert scale data analyses, respectively. Table 3 also shows the number of participants choosing each condition for each of our ranking questions. We discuss all of our quantitative analyses in the context of our qualitative observations and feedback from participants.

We analyze our study data in terms of the overall time taken and final group sizes, the speed and effort of selecting group members, and interface element usage. Note that we cannot evaluate group accuracy because no adequate ground truth is available or obtainable. Asking participants to re-create Facebook or Google+ groups could bias their notion of those groups. Alternatively, asking participants to verify group completeness would require exhaustive labeling (recognized as error-prone [38] and analogous to list scrolling in the *Alphabet* condition).

Final Times and Group Sizes

Overall, participants created 72 groups with a total of 2077 friends. Examining the *Final Time* taken to create groups, our analysis shows a significant effect of interface condition ($F_{2,55}$=6.95, $p\approx.002$). Post-hoc pairwise analyses reveal that participants using the *Alphabet* interface took significantly less time to create groups than when using both the *Example-Only* ($F_{1,55}$=5.93, $p\approx.018$) and *Example-Attribute* ($F_{1,55}$=13.4, $p\approx.0006$) interfaces. There was no difference in *Final Time* between *Example-Only* and *Example-Attribute* conditions. One explanation for participants taking less time in the *Alphabet* condition is that both the reordering conditions (*Example-Only* and *Example-Attribute*) required additional time to update the display when reordering or filtering. Another contributing factor could be that participants in the *Alphabet* condition often attempted to recall friends by name to avoid scrolling through their entire list of friends (e.g., *"I was surprised how useless alphabetical ordering is, but keyword search was very useful"*). This may have resulted in people forgetting to include some friends and stopping early. Interestingly, participants who resorted to scrolling through the full list often felt like they missed people (e.g., *"umm, I guess that's it"*, *"there's probably more, but oh well"*). One participant also explicitly commented *"It's too easy to forget about people when it's ordered alphabetically."*

	Alphabet	*Example-Only*	*Example-Attribute*
*Final Time**	163.0/63.4s	196.9/56.8s	216.0/35.8s
Final Group Size	25.3/24.8	34.0/40.6	27.2/22.1
Mean Select Time	8.6/3.9s	13.9/16.3s	15.9/16.5s
*SD Select Time**	9.4/6.5s	13.5/8.5s	19.7/15.1s
*Mean Position**	171.8/87.2	58.1/78.9	38.5/48.8
*SD Position**	101.7/56.1	41.1/33.3	40.5/41.1
Single Selections	18.0/27.0	8.5/6.2	7.9/5.1
*Multi-Selections**	0.4/0.8	2.8/2.9	2.8/3.0
Search-Selections	4.3/4.7	2.1/2.7	2.0/2.1

Table 2. Mean/SDs of all metrics used in our log data analyses. *'s indicate a significant effect was observed.

	Alphabet	*Example-Only*	*Example-Attribute*
Happiness	3.9/0.9	3.9/1.1	4.0/0.7
*Easiness**	2.6/1.0	3.2/1.2	3.3/0.8
*Quickness**	2.3/1.0	3.0/1.2	3.4/1.0
*Favorite**	1	0	11
*Best Helped**	3	1	8

Table 3. Likert mean/SDs (1=strongly disagree, 5=strongly agree) and ranking (number of participants) responses. Metrics with *'s indicate a significant effect was observed.

Difficulty recalling friends in the *Alphabet* interface could have resulted in the shorter *Final Times* in that condition. However, one would then also expect to see larger *Final Group Sizes* in the reordering conditions because of their ability to surface relevant people, favoring recognition over recall (e.g., *"Reordering makes it much faster than alphabetical because it reminds you of people without having to do an exhaustive search"* and *"Reordering helps me quickly pick friends in the first rows. Filters keep me from frequent scrolling"*). However, our analysis showed no significant difference in *Final Group Size* across conditions. Further analysis showed the presence of a ceiling effect in all conditions, suggesting that participants were often cut short of the time they needed to complete their groups, which could account for the lack of difference in *Final Group Size*. This effect was also more pronounced in the reordering conditions (16.7%, 33.3% and 45.8% of interactions were cut short in the *Alphabet*, *Example-Only*, and *Example-Attribute* conditions, respectively).

Speed and Effort in Selecting Group Members

To compare the time between group member selections, we had to account for the fact that participants could add friends individually or in bulk (i.e., a multi-select action). In the case of a multi-select, we assigned the time between the action and the previous group member selection to the first friend in the multi-selection and assigned a time of zero to the rest of the friends. We did not see an effect of interface condition on *Mean Select Time*. We did however see a difference in *SD Select Time* ($F_{2,55}$=7.78, $p\approx.001$), with post-hoc pairwise comparisons showing significant or marginal differences in all cases: *Alphabet* was less than *Example-Only* ($F_{1,55}$=2.83, $p\approx.09$) and *Example-Attribute*

($F_{1,55}$=15.5, $p \approx .0002$), and *Example-Only* was less than *Example-Attribute* ($F_{1,55}$=5.07, $p \approx .03$).

Although we did not see an effect of condition on *Mean Select Time*, the average *Mean Select Time* was smallest in *Alphabet* (see Table 2). This is partially an artifact of the time needed to update the display in the reordering conditions. In *Example-Attribute*, a display update can also occur as a result of a filtering action. As this confounds our analysis of *Select Time*, we decided to measure the position in the display of each group member immediately before selection as a proxy for effort level. That is, if position is low, a friend was closer to the top of the display and therefore required less effort to locate. We saw a significant effect of condition on *Mean Position* ($F_{2,55}$=39.1, $p \approx .0001$), with post-hoc pairwise comparisons showing that the *Mean Position* in *Alphabet* was significantly greater than in both *Example-Only* ($F_{1,55}$=47.8, $p \approx .0001$) and *Example-Attribute* ($F_{1,55}$=67.7, $p \approx .0001$). We also saw a significant difference in consistency of position as measured by *SD Position* ($F_{2,55}$=19.6, $p \approx .0001$), again with *SD Position* being significantly greater in *Alphabet* compared to both *Example-Only* ($F_{1,55}$=2.81, $p \approx .0001$) and *Example-Attribute* ($F_{1,55}$=31.8, $p \approx .0001$). Lower positions indicate that people had to scroll less to search for friends in the reordering conditions because these conditions sorted potential group members closer to the top of the display for easy recognition and access. As expected, the *Mean Position* of selected friends in the *Alphabet* condition was roughly half, 44.6%, of the average number of Facebook friends of our participants and their *SD Position* was highly varied because group members were often evenly distributed throughout the entire alphabetical list.

Our questionnaire results provide additional evidence of reduced effort in the reordering conditions. Analyses of our Likert scale questions show an effect of condition on perceived levels of *Easiness* ($F_{2,55}$=4.33, $p \approx .018$), with the both the *Example-Only* and *Example-Attribute* interfaces being perceived as easier to use than the *Alphabet* interface ($F_{1,55}$=5.74, $p \approx .02$ and $F_{1,55}$=7.18, $p \approx .01$, respectively). Similarly, we found a significant effect of condition on perceived *Quickness* ($F_{2,55}$=6.63, $p \approx .003$) in creating groups, again with *Example-Only* and *Example-Attribute* interfaces being perceived as quicker than *Alphabet* ($F_{1,55}$=5.80, $p \approx .02$ and $F_{1,55}$=12.74, $p \approx .0008$, respectively). We saw no difference in terms of perceived *Easiness* or *Quickness* between *Example-Only* and *Example-Attribute*. Perceived *Easiness* and *Quickness* in the reordering conditions is likely due to these interfaces automatically surfacing relevant friends (e.g., "*Sometimes it really looked as if the system was reading my mind!*").

Behavioral Differences and Feature Usage

In all interfaces, participants could select friends to include one at a time (*Single Selections*), several at a time (*Multi-Selections*), or by searching for them by name (*Search-Selections*). Our participants used all of these features in each condition, however they searched for friends by name and added friends one by one less often in the reordering conditions compared to the *Alphabet* condition. In addition, we found a significant effect of condition on the number of *Multi-Selections* ($F_{2,55}$=10.9, $p \approx .0001$) with the *Example-Only* and *Example-Attribute* conditions both showing increased *Multi-Selections* compared to the *Alphabet* condition ($F_{1,55}$=17.4, $p \approx .0001$ and $F_{1,55}$=15.4, $p \approx .0002$, respectively). Increased *Multi-Selections* and fewer *Single* and *Search-Selections* in the reordering conditions is likely due to these interfaces making friends easier to add as a group by sorting relevant friends to the top of the display and filtering out irrelevant friends (in *Example-Attribute*).

Our logged data also showed that participants used the suggested and static filters when they were available (in *Example-Attribute*). Participants selected *Suggested Filters* 1.9 times on average (*SD*=1.3), selected *Static Filters* 0.9 times on average (*SD*=1.3), and *Unselected Filters* that they had previously selected 2.3 times on average (*SD*=2.8). Our observations showed that participants sometimes used the filters in clever and unexpected ways, such as selecting them temporarily to find a certain set of friends and then unselecting them to find others. One participant commented that the "*Filters helped me guide the tool*". Other comments indicate that the suggested filters served as an explanation of how the system was working (e.g., "*The filters helped me understand what patterns the tool was discovering, and thus helped understand the tool's behavior*").

Discussion

Overall, our evaluation showed that different interfaces worked well for different kinds of groups (e.g., "*[My favorite version] depended on the group I was creating*"). We observed, and participants reported, that the *Alphabet* condition appeared to work well for small groups whose members could be easily recalled by name (e.g., family members with the same name, co-authors of a paper, and members of a cross-country team). In contrast, the reordering conditions worked better for larger and more varied groups (e.g., childhood friends, local friends or friends from particular regions of the world, college friends, former and current colleagues, people in a particular field of work, and friends with a professional relationship). One participant noted that for "*most of the small groups that I wanted to create, I already knew the list in my head [so] alphabetical was easiest. However, for larger groups, reordering was most efficient.*" A likely result of this is that we found no significant difference in terms of overall participant *Happiness* with their final groups created in each condition.

Although a significant majority of our participants rated the full ReGroup interface (i.e., *Example-Attribute*) as their overall *Favorite* (χ^2=18.5, $p \approx .0001$) and felt that it *Best Helped* them create groups (χ^2=6.5, $p \approx .04$), participants did become frustrated when ReGroup was unable to model the group well, as this essentially resulted in having to search through an unordered list for group members (e.g., *"Ordering is useful for some lists, annoying for others"* and *"though I liked the filters, I think they didn't work in some cases"*). As with all machine learning based systems, the ability to model a concept is highly dependent upon the quality of the underlying data (e.g., the expressiveness of the features and the availability of data). Interestingly, some participants could tell why ReGroup was not working well in some cases (e.g., *"Groups that all have something in common that is tracked by Facebook (i.e., college) were easier to create than a group of people who are seemingly unrelated based on Facebook information."*).

RELATED WORK

Privacy continues to be a concern in online social networks [13,33,37]. Traditional mechanisms for specifying social access control lists have been too inexpressive (e.g., pre-defining lists of "Friends" or "Everyone" in Facebook) or tedious and error-prone (e.g., manual selection from an alphabetical list of friends [28,38]). This has motivated research on alternative methods. For example, Toomim *et al.* examine guard questions testing for shared knowledge [41] and McCallum *et al.* examine automatically inferring access control roles from email communication [24].

Recent interest has developed in automatic detection of communities within social networks (e.g., [16,17,22,27]). The assumption in such work is that detected communities will overlap with a person's eventual sharing needs. SocialFlows [22] automatically creates hierarchical and potentially overlapping groups based on email communication. These groups can then be edited via direct manipulation and exported to Facebook and Gmail. Katango [27] and Facebook's "Smart Lists" [17] feature also follow this model by providing a set of automatically generated friend groups which can then be manually edited for correctness. Jones and O'Neill [16] recently evaluated the feasibility of this approach by comparing manually defined groups with automatically detected network clusters. They found their automatically-detected clusters only overlapped with manually-defined groups by 66.9% on average, suggesting a need for considerable manual refinement. After following up with their participants, they further discovered that predefined groups only partially correspond to in-context sharing decisions (77.8-90.8% overlap with manually defined groups and only 33.8-76.1% overlap with automatically generated groups). In contrast, our focus on custom, on-demand group specification via end-user interactive machine learning is better aligned with usable security recommendations [20,29,40,43].

Prior work facilitating on-demand sharing or access control in social networks includes Gilbert and Karahalios's research on modeling relationship or tie strength between individuals based on network structure, communication, and shared profile data [11]. Predicted tie strength could potentially inform privacy levels for protected content. In contrast to modeling relationships, Bernstein *et al.*'s FeedMe system [3] models user interest using term-vector profiles in order to recommend people with which to share particular pieces of content. Our work differs from these in that ReGroup iteratively learns a model based on end-user provided examples and feedback. By iteratively updating the underlying model, ReGroup can tailor its group member recommendations to the specific group a person is currently trying to create. More similar to our approach of defining groups by example is Gmail's "Don't forget Bob!" feature, which recommends additional email recipients based on a few seed contacts and a social graph constructed from previous email [34]. However, ReGroup provides more control over its suggestions by continuing to iteratively update its underlying model based on further examples.

Our work also contributes to recent research on designing end-user interactive machine learning systems (e.g., [8,10]). Most similar to our work is Fang and LeFevre's interactive machine learning-based privacy wizard for online social networks [9]. Their wizard employs active learning to construct a privacy classifier that maps item-friend pairs to allow or deny actions. ReGroup differs in that we use end-user interactive machine learning as a tool for helping people select members of a group rather than for creating a robust classifier. As a result, ReGroup's design aims to balance end-user flexibility and control with speed, as opposed to an active learning approach that prioritizes speed at the potential expense of user experience [2]. Furthermore, ReGroup preserves end-user desired control of group membership [14] by requiring explicit approval of group members instead of delegating control to a classifier.

Defining groups via member examples and interaction with group characteristics is related to work on example and feature-based feedback in interactive machine learning systems [6,32,45]. Each of these explored the utility of feature or example-and-feature-based feedback for creating document classifiers. Wong *et al.* [45] allowed end-users to explicitly define relevant features by highlighting words used to update a classifier model. Other work [6,32] has taken an active learning approach to soliciting end-user labels of features and examples. Our approach differs in that we do not solicit feature-level feedback for the purpose of training a classifier. Rather, we enable feature interaction for the purpose of helping people search for relevant examples. Our approach uses a novel technique of integrating human knowledge of features into the interactive machine learning process through filtering on group characteristics. This makes our work more similar to work on faceted search and interaction [15].

Secord *et al.* [35] explored example and facet-based interaction for creating collections of music (i.e., playlists). In their system, end-users could both view songs related to given examples or enter textual queries (e.g., "lots of rock") that were then mapped to facet values (e.g., genre=rock) and used as constraints on song recommendations. Their rationale for free form, text-based facet interaction was that songs have potentially hundreds of facets and traditional static presentations of facets would be too cumbersome for interaction. The social network domain can also have an overabundance of facets, however our approach is to highlight and rank facets highly relevant to the intended group. This approach favors recognition of relevant facets instead of relying upon recall, which can be particularly useful when facets are vague or difficult to define.

Previous approaches to facet ranking for search result exploration have based ranking on hit count [15], query keywords [46], query logs and click through data [42], or user models defined by explicit ratings of documents [18]. We base ranking on statistical regularities of the currently selected group members. Most similar to our approach is Li *et al.*'s Facetedpedia [21], which extracts and ranks facets based on the top results of a keyword search. However, their ranking is based on the navigation cost of reaching the top results and therefore serves more as a sense-making tool rather than a tool to search for additional items.

CONCLUSION AND FUTURE WORK

This paper presented ReGroup, a novel system that employs end-user interactive machine learning to help people create custom groups on-demand in online social networks. Our evaluation showed that different group creation techniques helped in creating different kinds of groups. For example, the traditional search-by-name approach is efficient for small, well-defined groups where members are easy to recall by name. ReGroup's support for recognition over recall, embodied by both its group member and filter suggestions, helps for larger and more varied groups. Therefore, we advocate integrating ReGroup's novel techniques with traditional methods used in online social networks to support a wider range of potential groups.

This paper also discussed the design challenges associated with interactive machine learning in social access control and detailed how we addressed these challenges in ReGroup. One challenge was in addressing unlearnable groups, typically the result of missing information. Although we attempted to address this issue with our technique for group member prediction, it still caused some frustrations during our evaluation. Additional features should improve ReGroup's performance, but missing data is inherent to social networks. Future work might therefore aim to detect such cases and degrade gracefully. Another design decision was to focus end-user attention on creating groups, rather than on training a robust classifier. However, creating a classifier as a by-product of group creation could enable automatic group maintenance as relationships change over time. In the future we hope to evaluate ReGroup's classifiers for group maintenance and to design additional interaction techniques to support this task.

ACKNOWLEDGMENTS

We thank Michael Toomim for his thoughtful insights and Jacob O. Wobbrock and Leah Findlater for their guidance on our analyses. This work was supported in part by the National Science Foundation under awards IIS-0812590, IIS-1016713, and OAI-1028195, by Office of Naval Research award N00014-06-1-0147, by the WRF / TJ Cable Professorship, and by a Google Faculty Research Award.

REFERENCES

1. Amershi, S., Fogarty, J., Kapoor, A. and Tan, D. Overview-Based Example Selection in Mixed-Initiative Interactive Concept Learning. In *Proc. UIST 2009*, ACM Press (2009), 247-256.
2. Baum, E.B. and Lang, K. Query Learning can work Poorly when a Human Oracle is Used. In *Proc. IJCNN 1992*, IEEE Computer Society (1992), 609-614.
3. Bernstein, M., Marcus, A., Karger, D.R. and Miller, R. C. Enhancing Directed Content Sharing on the Web. In *Proc. CHI 2010*, ACM Press (2010), 971-980.
4. Chen, S. Can Facebook get you Fired? Playing it Safe in the Social Media World. Nov. 10, 2010. http://articles.cnn.com/2010-11-10/living/facebook.fired.social.media.etiquette_1_social-media-worker-posts-workplace-complaints.
5. Domingos, P. and Pazzani, M. On the Optimality of the Simple Bayesian Classifier under Zero-One Loss. *Machine Learning 29*, (1997), 103-130.
6. Druck, G., Settles, B. and McCallum, A. Active learning by labeling features. In *Proc. EMNLP 2009*, 81-90.
7. Facebook Application Platform. http://developers.facebook.com/
8. Fails, J.A. and Olsen, Jr., D.R. Interactive Machine Learning. In *Proc. IUI 2003*, ACM Press (2003), 39-45.
9. Fang, L. and LeFevre, K.. Privacy Wizards for Social Networking Sites. In *Proc. WWW 2010*, ACM Press (2010), 351-360.
10. Fogarty, J., Tan, D., Kapoor, A., and Winder, S. CueFlik: Interactive Concept Learning in Image Search. In *Proc. CHI 2008*, ACM Press (2008), 29-38.
11. Gilbert, E. and Karahalios, K. Predicting Tie Strength with Social Media. In *Proc. CHI 2009*, ACM Press (2009), 211–220.
12. Greasemonkey. http://www.greasespot.net/
13. Gross, R. and Acquisti, A. Information Revelation and Privacy in Online Social Networks. In *Proc. WPES 2005*, ACM Press (2005), 71-80.
14. Halliday, J. Facebook Changes See the Social Network Trying to be More Social. Sept. 21, 2011. http://www.guardian.co.uk/technology/pda/2011/sep/21/facebook-changes-social-network.
15. Hearst, M. Design Recommendations for Hierarchical Faceted Search Interfaces. *SIGIR Workshop on Faceted Search 2006*, ACM Press (2010).

16. Jones, S. and O'Neill, E. Feasibility of Structural Network Clustering for Group-Based Privacy Control in Social Networks. In *Proc. SOUPS 2010,* ACM Press (2010).

17. Kincaid, J. Kleiner-Backed Katango Organizes Your Facebook Friends into Groups for You. July 11, 2011. http://techcrunch.com/2011/07/11/kleiner-backed-katango-automatically-organizes-your-facebook-friends-into-groups-for-you.

18. Koren, J., Zhang, Y. and Liu, X. Personalized Interactive Faceted Search. In *Proc. WWW 2008*, ACM Press (2008), 477-486.

19. Korkki, P. Is Your Online Identity Spoiling Your Chances? Oct. 9, 2010. http://www.nytimes.com/2010/10/10/jobs/10search.html

20. Lederer, S., Hong, J.I., Dey, A.K., and Landay, J.A. Personal Privacy through Understanding and Action: Five Pitfalls for Designers. *Personal Ubiquitous Computing 8*, 6 (2004), 440-454.

21. Li, C., Yan, N., Roy, S.B., Lisham, L. and Das, G. Facetedpedia: Dynamic Generation of Query-Dependent Faceted Interfaces for Wikipedia. In *Proc. WWW 2010,* ACM Press (2010), 651-660.

22. MacLean, D., Hangal, S., Teh, S.K., Lam, M.S. and Heer, J. Groups Without Tears: Mining Social Topologies from Email. In *Proc. IUI 2011*, ACM Press (2011), 83-92.

23. Manly, B.F.J.*Randomization, Bootstrap and Monte Carlo Methods in Biology, 2nd ed.* Chapman & Hall, NY, 1997.

24. McCallum, A., Wang, X. and Corrada-Emmanuel, A. Topic and Role Discovery in Social Networks with Experiments on Enron and Academic Email. *Journal of Artificial Intelligence Research 30*, 1 (2007), 249–272.

25. Mitchell, T. *Machine Learning*. McGraw Hill, 1997.

26. Olson, J.S., Grudin, J. and Horvitz, E. A Study of Preferences for Sharing and Privacy. *Ext. Abstracts CHI 2005*, ACM Press (2005), 1985-1988.

27. Ortutay, B. Facebook to Organize Friends in 'Smart Lists'. Sept. 13, 2011. http://www.usatoday.com/tech/news/story/2011-09-13/facebook-smart-lists/50389154/1.

28. Pachal, P. Google Circles: The Dumbest Thing About Google+. June 29, 2011. http://www.pcmag.com/article2/0,2817,2387808,00.asp.

29. Palen, L. and Dourish, P. Unpacking "Privacy" for a Networked World. In *Proc. CHI 2003*, ACM Press (2003), 129-136.

30. Parker, A. Congressman, Sharp Voice on Twitter, Finds It Can Cut 2 Ways. May, 30. 2011. http://www.nytimes.com/2011/05/31/nyregion/for-rep-anthony-weiner-twitter-has-double-edge.html.

31. Pogue, D. Google+ Improves on Facebook. July 13, 2011. http://www.nytimes.com/2011/07/14/technology/personaltech/google-gets-a-leg-up-on-facebook.html.

32. Raghavan, H. and Allan, J. An Interactive Algorithm for Asking and Incorporating Feature Feedback into Support Vector Machines. In *Proc. SIGIR 2007*, ACM Press (2007), 79-86.

33. Rosenblum, D. What Anyone can Know: The Privacy Risks of Social Networking Sites. *IEEE Security & Privacy 5,* 3 (2007), 40-49.

34. Roth, M. Ben-David, A., Deutscher, D., Flysher, G., Horn, I., Leichtberg, A., Leiser, N., Matias, Y. and Merom, R. Suggesting Friends using the Implicit Social Graph. In *Proc. KDD 2010*, ACM Press (2010), 233-242.

35. Secord, A., Winnemoeller, H., Li, W. and Dontcheva, M. Creating Collections with Automatic Suggestions and Example-Based Refinement. In *Proc. UIST 2010*, ACM Press (2010), 249-258.

36. Settles, B. Closing the Loop: Fast, Interactive Semi-Supervised Annotation with Queries on Features and Instances. In *Proc. EMNLP 2011*, (2011), 1467-1478.

37. Sheehan, K. Towards a Typology of Internet Users and Online Privacy Concerns. *The Information Society 18*, (2002), 21-23.

38. Siegler, M. Zuckerberg: "Guess What? Nobody Wants to Make Lists." Aug. 26, 2010. http://techcrunch.com/2010/08/26/facebook-friend-lists/.

39. Slee, M. Friend Lists. Dec. 19, 2007. http://www.facebook.com/blog.php?post=7831767130.

40. Smetters, D.K. and Good, N. How Users Use Access Control. In *Proc. SOUPS 2009*, ACM Press (2009).

41. Toomim, M., Zhang, X., Fogarty, J. and Landay, J. Access Control by Testing for Shared Knowledge. In *Proc. CHI 2008*, ACM Press (2008), 193-196.

42. van Zwol, R., Sigurbjörnsson, B., Adapala, R., Pueyo, L.G., Katiyar, A., Kurapati, K., Muralidharan, M., Muthu, S., Murdock, V., Ng, P., Ramani, A., Sahai, A., Sathish, S.T., Vasudev, H. and Vuyyuru. U. Faceted Exploration of Image Search Results. In *Proc. WWW 2010*, ACM Press (2010), 961-970.

43. Whalen, T., Smetters, D., and Churchill, E.F. User Experiences with Sharing and Access Control. *Ext Abstracts CHI 2006*, ACM Press (2006).

44. Wobbrock, J.O., Findlater, L., Gergle, D. and Higgins, J.J. The Aligned Rank Transform for Nonparametric Factorial Analyses using only ANOVA Procedures. In *Proc. CHI 2011*, ACM Press (2011), 143-146.

45. Wong, W. Oberst,I., Das,S., Moore, T., Stumpf, S. McIntosh, K. and Burnett, M. End-User Feature Labeling: A Locally-Weighted Regression Approach. In *Proc. IUI 2011*, ACM Press (2011), 115-124.

46. Yelp.com. http://www.yelp.com

*Monsieur, azonnal kövessen engem bitte!**
An Automatically Generated Interlanguage Tailored to Speakers of Minority but Culturally Influenced Languages

Luis A. Leiva and Vicent Alabau
ITI/DSIC, Universitat Politècnica de València
{luileito,valabau}@{iti,dsic}.upv.es

ABSTRACT
Automatic localization of cultural resources and UIs is crucial for the survival of minority languages, for which there are insufficient parallel corpora (or no corpus at all) to build machine translation systems. This paper proposes a new way to compensate for such resource-scarce languages, based on the fact that most languages share a common vocabulary. Concretely, our approach leverages a family of languages closely related to the speaker's native language to construct translations in a *coherent mix* of these languages. Experimental results indicate that these translations can be easily understood, being also a useful aid for users who are not proficient in foreign languages. Therefore this work significantly contributes to HCI in two ways: it establishes a language that can improve how applications communicate to their users, and it reports insights on the user acceptance towards the method.

Author Keywords
Localization, Machine Translation, Interlingua, Cityspeak

ACM Classification Keywords
H.1.2 User/Machine Systems: Human information processing; H.5.2 User Interfaces: Natural language; I.2.7 Natural Language Processing: Machine translation

INTRODUCTION
Language is one of the most notable (and, at the same time, vulnerable) treats of our cultural heritage. With an estimated number of roughly 7,000 languages spoken worldwide [7], it follows that the vast majority of languages are minority languages in every country in which they are spoken. As such, there exists a considerable amount of native speakers that may have trouble operating UIs, because of a non-familiar vocabulary, and accessing to cultural resources that are otherwise available in other (popular) languages. Moreover, it is commonly held that the diversity of languages should not be an obstacle to mutual understanding. This is where Machine Translation (MT) becomes a clear asset for humans (and computers) to communicate.

*Blade Runner's CitySpeak: *Sir, follow me immediately please!* [8]

CHI'12, May 5–10, 2012, Austin, Texas, USA.

The traditional approach to MT is statistical, or data-driven, due to the scale at which it operates and the generalization capabilities it can provide. Under this paradigm, an MT system learns statistical parameters from a series of source-target language pairs. Therefore, a fundamental problem arises when no proper training data are available, as it often occurs with minority languages, as the MT system becomes useless. What is more, the number of potential bilingual translators of uncommon languages is hard to find, and so this is both expensive and not scalable. Fortunately, the expansive movements of migratory populations, combined with the historical dominance of some cultures, have resulted in a large common vocabulary among some linguistic areas, leading to what is known as *Sprachbunds* [4] — groups of languages that have become similar in some way because of geographical proximity and/or language contact. For instance, some examples of Sprachbund include the following:

Uralic: Estonian, Finnish, Hungarian, *Mordvinian*, *Kanthy*.
Nguni: Xhosa, Zulu, Ndebele, *Hlubi*, *Phuthi*.

In both cases, the first 3 languages are supported by some online translation systems. However, the other 2 are not. Overall, according to [7], it is estimated that more than a 10% of the world population could not be assisted by any MT system.

In this paper we exploit the Sprachbund concept to allow MT systems to handle minority languages. Our approach is entitled Culturally Influenced Interlanguage (CI^2), since we employ a family of languages closely related to the speaker's native language ($L1$) to construct translations in a *coherent mix* of these languages, i.e., preserving some features of $L1$. Note that it is assumed that the MT system has training pairs in those related languages, but the user is not proficient in any of them.

BACKGROUND AND RELATED WORK
The given context of our method is inspired by "Cityspeak", a polyglot street jargon devised in the film *Blade Runner* that incorporated words from many different languages (Spanish, French, Chinese, German, Hungarian, and Japanese) [8]. Needless to say this solution is not practical, as the users would need to learn a complex mix of highly unrelated languages. Historically, however, a large amount of effort has been invested in the development of new languages that would standardize a vocabulary common to the widest possible range of languages. Amongst these constructed languages, the most popular example is Interlingua, in which words may be taken from any language as long as they are present in a series of control languages. Interlingua tends

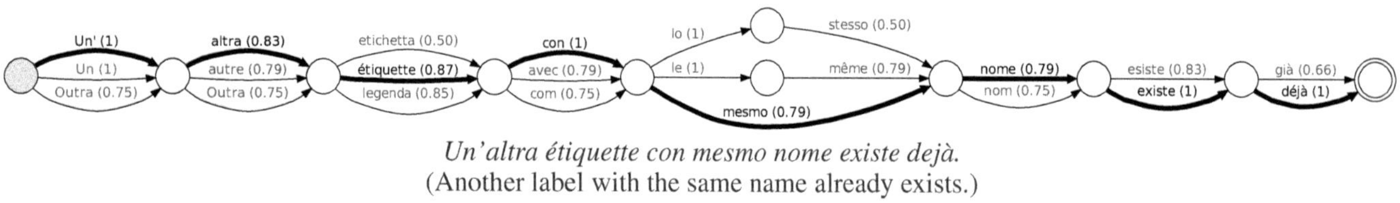

Figure 1: CI^2 can construct a sentence tailored to the Spanish language by using three related languages: Italian (top branches), French (central branches), and Portuguese (bottom branches). Each node in the graph is transited according to the maximum probability of belonging to the Spanish vocabulary (depicted in parentheses). As observed in the last 3 transitions, branches are collapsed either when a word is common to two (or more) of the base languages, or when no compatible alignments between such a base languages are found. Since this method is performed statistically, it can be completely extrapolated to other language families.

to be the lowest common denominator among such control languages (mostly Indo-European), providing also a simple grammar and regular word formation, but still it must be learned. Instead, a sentence could be formed in a way that it will be close to the vocabulary of $L1$. In these circumstances, it seems reasonable that people could easily understand multilingual translations, since such translations would be similar to their native language (Figure 1). In the same way as adaptive user interfaces try to fit the needs of a specific user (or group of users), CI^2 aims to construct a pseudo-language for the users so as to better communicate with them (Figure 2).

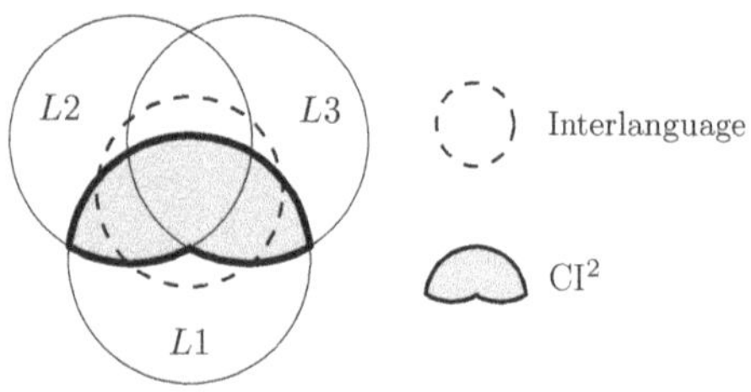

Figure 2: Artificially constructed interlanguages follow the Interlingua approach, i.e., they tend to the lowest common denominator among a series of control languages. CI^2, however, would employ only a subset of those control languages that intersect with the user's native language ($L1$).

To the best of our knowledge, there is little research that relates to our work; i.e., using multilingual information from different languages to better communicate the meaning of a message. For instance, Dagan et al. [2], to resolve lexical ambiguities in non-restricted text, concluded that "two languages are more informative than one". In Information Retrieval, Gollins and Sanderson [3] combined translations from two different languages to disambiguate search queries. The drawback of their approach is that it was limited to lemmatized dictionary entries, as presumably a common term would be present in the auxiliary languages involved. On the other hand, in HCI, the 'collaborative translation' concept has been explored. It is a fairly new approach to support monolingual translation (i.e., translation by people who speak only the source or target language, but not both) that unfortunately can be extremely slow (e.g., Hu et al. [5] reported an average speed of 40 sentences translated per day).

CI^2 SYSTEM OVERVIEW

Let us consider the following scenario: users whose native language is $L1$ want to understand a message in the source language S. Suppose that $L1$ is an under-resourced language, meaning that an automatic translation system cannot be built for it. At most, there is a vocabulary V available for $L1$, obtained e.g. from a regular dictionary. However, $L1$ belongs to a family of languages $L2, L3, \ldots, LN$ with a reasonable set of resources. Specifically, paired corpora are available to build a Statistical Machine Translation (SMT) system [6].

A first approach to overcome the problem is to build such an SMT system and hope that the user would be able to guess the meaning for any of the auxiliary languages. However, these translations may have vocabulary not understandable by the user. Our proposal is aimed to offer multilingual sentences in such a way that the communication channel maximizes the probability of understanding. CI^2 is defined as *a mix of languages tailored to the native language of the user.* This way, CI^2 tries to converge to a common ground by leveraging the resemblances that exist between the base languages that are used.

Formally, given a source string $\boldsymbol{s}$ and a vocabulary V for $L1$, the CI^2 system searches for the sentence $\boldsymbol{i} \in CI^2$ with highest posterior probability, $\hat{\boldsymbol{i}} = \arg\max_{\boldsymbol{i}} \Pr(\boldsymbol{i}|\boldsymbol{s}, V)$. After some mathematical transformations we obtain the expression

$$\hat{\boldsymbol{i}} \approx \arg\max_{\boldsymbol{i}} \left[\Pr(\boldsymbol{i}|V, \hat{\boldsymbol{t}}_2, \ldots, \hat{\boldsymbol{t}}_N) \max_{\boldsymbol{t}_2,\ldots,\boldsymbol{t}_n} \prod_{n=2}^{N} \Pr(\boldsymbol{t}_n|\boldsymbol{s}) \right] \quad (1)$$

where $\Pr(\boldsymbol{t}_n|\boldsymbol{s})$ are SMT systems built with Moses [6] for each auxiliary language. The first term is a graph that combines the best translations $\hat{\boldsymbol{t}}_2, \ldots, \hat{\boldsymbol{t}}_N$ and assigns to each word the probability of belonging to V. It is measured as the edit distance with respect to the closest word in the vocabulary, normalized by word length. Figure 1 illustrates this model.

EVALUATION

Due to the exploratory nature of this research, we carried out the experimentation in our department, which is located in Spain. Only for evaluation purposes, we assumed that Spanish was a minority language influenced by its neighboring countries: Portugal, Italy, and France. This way, we would have the necessary resources to perform the study: *1)* Spanish belongs to a known Sprachbund (Romance languages); *2)* there exists publicly available parallel corpora for this language family; and *3)* we can easily recruit a representative user sample of native speakers. The experiments consisted in translating Swedish (*Sv*) sentences to CI^2, which would be formed by a mix of Portuguese (*Pt*), French (*Fr*), and Italian

(*It*). We chose *Sv* as the source language so that participants would not understand the original sentences. The following hypotheses were evaluated:

- **H1**: CI² translations should look familiar to the user.
- **H2**: CI² translations should be easier to read and understand with respect to the base languages.

Participants
Seventeen volunteers (5 females) were recruited via email and word-of-mouth communication. The average age was 31.7 (SD=7.4). They were told to rank their level of language proficiency in a 1-5 Likert scale (1: not proficient, 5: almost native) for *Pt* [1.68 (0.8)], *Fr* [2.25 (1.0)], and *It* [1.87 (0.6)].

Design
To evaluate **H1**, we tested in Study 1 (S1) if there were differences regarding the number of unknown words among CI² translations and its 3 base languages. We carried out a one-way (continuous factor) analysis of variance (ANOVA), since we verified that both normality and homocedasticity did hold between groups. Interaction effects were considered at the $p < .05$ level for each of the tested conditions. On the other hand, **H2** was evaluated on the basis of the following criteria:

1. *Fluency*: Is the translation readable?
2. *Comprehension*: Is the translation understandable?
3. *Adequacy*: Regarding the reference sentence (in Spanish), is meaning really preserved?

In this second study (S2) we carried out two different experiments. In the first part we analyzed CI² translations in terms of the above mentioned criteria. In the second part we verified if any of the base languages would work better than CI².

Apparatus
We used the KDE4 corpus, which comprises the localization files of the popular software libraries, and is publicly available at the OPUS project [9]. This corpus has 92 paired languages and 8.89M sentence fragments. We trained an MT system with 167K sentences of each base languages (2.2M of running words), and reserved 100 *Sv* sentences for testing. Once the 100 test sentences were automatically translated to the base languages, we assembled the CI² translations according to Eq. (1). Next we selected two partitions for human evaluation. The first partition included 5 sentences, and the second one was formed by 10 sentences. All of them were randomly selected. We analyzed such translations and observed that the proportion of each language assigned by Eq. (1) was 25.2% *It*, 25.3% *Pt*, 12.6% *Fr*, and 36.9% common (including punctuation characters). Finally we developed two applications and a final survey to collect users' data.

Procedure
In S1, the sentences in the first partition were shuffled with their corresponding translations in *It*, *Fr*, and *Pt* (5 translations each). Overall, in this experiment users had to assess 20 sentences,which were presented in random order, by clicking on those words that were completely unknown to them. Table 1 summarizes the number of words for each language in both test partitions. ANOVA revealed that there were no statistically significant differences on word count $[F(3,16) = 2.12, p = .137, \eta^2 = 0.33]$.

Study	# Sentences	Pt	Fr	It	CI²
S1	5	16 (2.7)	18 (4.6)	16.6 (2.3)	12.8 (1.1)
S2	10	13.4 (2.2)	13.7 (2.6)	13.0 (3.1)	11.8 (2.7)

Table 1: Mean (and SD) number of words per sentence (per language) in both experiments.

Regarding S2, users were sequentially presented with a set of 10 *Sv* and CI² sentences. Each translation would be assessed in a 1-5 Likert scale based on the three criteria mentioned in Design section, followed by a ranking that would compare CI² and its base languages. To assess the adequacy criterion, users were given groundtruth Spanish translations of the source sentences. Eventually we acquired $17 \times 5 \times 4 = 340$ samples for S1, and $17 \times 10 \times 3 = 510$ samples for S2.

Finally, participants filled out a survey which was adapted from the System Usability Scale (SUS) questionnaire [1]. The goal was to measure the (subjective) user's appreciation towards the quality of CI² translations. Users could also complement the survey with freeform comments and ideas.

RESULTS
In S1, regarding the number of unknown words in each sentence, there were statistically significant differences between languages $[F(3,327) = 18.25, p < .001, \eta^2 = 0.33]$. Post hoc comparisons using the Tukey HSD test indicated that the mean number of unknown words in CI² (Table 2) was significantly lower in comparison to *Fr* and *It* ($p < .001$ and $d > 0.45$ in both cases). However, for *Pt* there was no statistical significance regarding CI² ($p = .23, d = -0.36$). This result indicated that participants were confident while reading sentences both in CI² and *Pt*. Considering that no participant was proficient in that language, this can be explained because of the fact that Spanish and Portuguese have strong mutual influences.

Pt	Fr	It	CI²
0.95 (0.9)	1.96 (1.5)	2.26 (1.2)	1.32 (1.0)

Table 2: S1 results. Mean (and SD) number of unknown words.

In the first part of S2, besides of the obtained high scores (Table 3), we did not find strong correlations between fluency, comprehension, and adequacy (in all cases, $0.1 < \rho < 0.3$). Nonetheless, in the second part of S2 it was interesting to observe that CI² translations were chosen in first place 64% of the time over the other languages for these cases (Figure 3a).

Fluency	Comprehension	Adequacy
4.14 (0.7)	4.26 (0.6)	4.26 (0.9)

Table 3: S2 results, part 1. Mean (and SD) criteria scores. Values were comprised between 1 (worse) and 5 (better).

Regarding the adapted SUS questionnaire, the average score was 67.65 (SD=12.16) — SUS scores are ranged between 0 and 100. This suggested that users were satisfied with CI^2 translations. We inspected each SUS question individually, and observed that, overall, they were scored as expected. For instance, *"I think that I could understand CI^2 frequently"* and *"I found CI^2 very interesting"* were notably ranked as positive; and, conversely, *"I found the sentences unnecessarily complex"* or *'I found CI^2 very cumbersome to understand"* were ranked as negative.

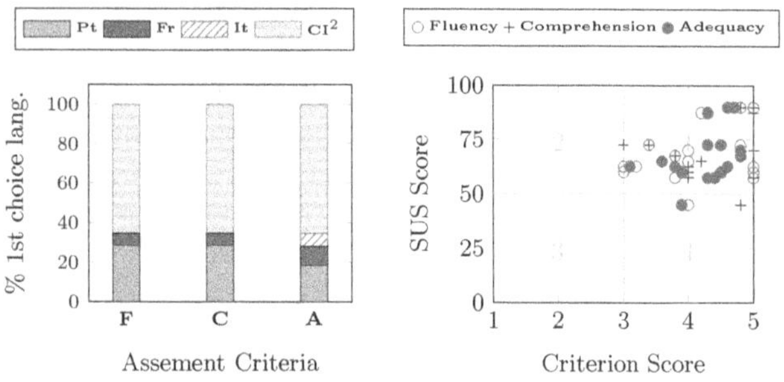

(a) (b)

Figure 3: S2 results, part 2. [3a] Percentage of times a language was chosen in first position in terms of fluency (F), comprehension (C), and adequacy (A). [3b] SUS against these (averaged) assessment criteria. Quad. #1: Users that liked CI^2 and indeed it worked for them. Quad. #3: Users that did not like CI^2 and it did not work for them.

The viewpoint that users agreed most was that *"CI^2 is interesting and useful"*. One skeptical user reported that *"It surprised me! Translations were really helpful"*. Interestingly, some users remarked that *"CI^2 translations were really easy to deal with, sometimes ever better than the reference sentences"*. That is because the KDE4 corpus was automatically generated by an MT system following partial post-edition; therefore some sentences may not be completely error-free. Finally, although a few people did not find CI^2 very appealing (SUS < 50), Figure 3b shows that it worked quite successfully for them (score ≥ 4).

DISCUSSION

In light of the results, we envision a wealth of scenarios where CI^2 could be used. For instance, in some geographical areas several languages and dialects often do meet; however a few of them are official, and therefore governmental support is limited for the rest. In these cases, CI^2 would be an economic alternative to convey meaning, foster dialog between ethnic groups, and favor social integration. In this regard, we also believe that CI^2 may encourage people to improve their language skills, by making connections with the proposed vocabulary. Although it seems clear that users would not learn new grammatical structures with CI^2, we do hypothesize that it can be useful to learn new languages, or at least to be accustomed to them. For instance, the user could infer the meaning of new words by using the context of the sentences.

Importance to HCI and Limitations

Beyond the utility that our method provides from a general point of view, it can be a valuable asset for localizing software programs, as we have shown. Additionally, further applications in HCI exploring this potential include:

- Providing access to digital resources (e.g., web pages or electronic books) that cannot be translated by current systems to the minority languages.
- Bridging the gap between the linguistic competence of the user and the UI of the underlying computer system (e.g., selecting the appropriate vocabulary in command menus).
- Promoting the acceptance of UIs into developing countries that are still gaining access to technologies.
- Since CI^2 sentences are closer to the user's native language and hence are better understood, CI^2 can speed up the monolingual translation workflow in UIs like [5].

Finally, a strong limitation of CI^2 is that it would not work with related languages with unrelated alphabet glyphs (e.g., Romance languages have inherited many terms from Greek, however Greek uses a completely different alphabet set).

CONCLUSION

We have introduced CI^2, an automatically generated interlanguage that is tailored to the user (or groups of users thereof). It has been shown that CI^2 can serve as a communication channel across language barriers. Our research has been backed up with empirical evidence for Spanish speakers with little knowledge of foreign languages. CI^2 may also work with other language families, due to their mutual intelligibility. Future work includes replicating the same evaluation with other Sprachbunds, so that we can consolidate the foundations of our method. We hope that CI^2 will allow more people to share their knowledge with others worldwide, no matter which language do users or applications speak.

ACKNOWLEDGMENTS

This work is partially supported by MIPRCV (CSD2007-00018), erudito.com (TSI-020110-2009-439) and iTrans2 (TIN2009-14511) projects, and by GV/2010/067 and UPV/2009/2851 grants.

REFERENCES

1. Brooke, J. SUS: A "quick and dirty" usability scale. In *Usability Evaluation in Industry*. Taylor and Francis, 1996.
2. Dagan, I., Itai, A., and Schwall, U. Two languages are more informative than one. In *Proc. ACL* (1991), 130–137.
3. Gollins, T., and Sanderson, M. Improving cross language retrieval with triangulated translation. In *Proc. SIGIR* (2001).
4. Hickey, R., Ed. *The Handbook of Language Contact*. Wiley-Blackwell, 2010.
5. Hu, C., Bederson, B. B., Resnik, P., and Kronrod, Y. Monotrans2: a new human computation system to support monolingual translation. In *Proc. CHI* (2011), 1133–1136.
6. Koehn, P., Hoang, H., Birch, A., Callison-Burch, C., Federico, M., Bertoldi, N., Cowan, B., Shen, W., Moran, C., Zens, R., Dyer, C., Bojar, O., Constantin, A., and Herbst, E. Moses: open source toolkit for statistical machine translation. In *Proc. ACL* (2007), 177–180.
7. Lewis, M. P., Ed. *Ethnologue: Languages of the World*, 16th ed. SIL International, 2009.
8. Sammon, P. *Future Noir: The Making of Blade Runner*. Orion Books, 1997.
9. Tiedemann, J. News from OPUS - A collection of multilingual parallel corpora with tools and interfaces. In *Proc. RANLP* (2009), 237–248.

"Then Click *OK!*" Extracting References to Interface Elements in Online Documentation

Adam Fourney afourney@cs.uwaterloo.ca
Ben Lafreniere bjlafren@cs.uwaterloo.ca
Richard Mann mannr@uwaterloo.ca
Michael Terry mterry@cs.uwaterloo.ca

Cheriton School of Computer Science
University of Waterloo

ABSTRACT
This paper presents a recognizer for identifying references to user interface components in online documentation. The recognizer first extracts phrases matching a list of known components, then employs a classifier to reject coincidental matches. We describe why this seemingly straightforward problem is challenging, then show how informal conventions in documentation writing can be leveraged to perform classification. Using the features identified in this paper, our approach achieves an average F1 score of 0.81, and can correctly distinguish between actual command references and coincidental matches in 93.7% of test cases.

Author Keywords
Named Entity Recognition; Online Documentation

ACM Classification Keywords
H.5.2 Information Interfaces and Presentation: Miscellaneous

INTRODUCTION
The Internet contains a wealth of reference material, tutorials, and other documentation related to the use of interactive systems. Written for the benefit of users, this documentation is expressed in natural language. However, from the perspective of a software system, this documentation is opaque and unactionable.

Recently, the CHI community has demonstrated interest in the problem of automatic identification of references to user interface components within online documentation. For example, work by Ekstrand *et al.* demonstrates how a custom search engine can extract commands mentioned in software tutorials, so that those commands can be listed in the snippets presented as part of enhanced search result pages [1]. Similarly, query-feature graphs, by Fourney *et al.* , pair high-level search query terms with the corresponding user interface elements mentioned in collections of technical documentation [3]. Also closely related is work by Lau *et al.* [4], which has demonstrated the possibility of extracting *action-target-value* triples from how-to instructions, with the goal of advancing machine-guided help systems. In their work, *targets* correspond to interface widgets.

The problem of identifying user interface elements mentioned within documentation is a domain-specific instance of *named entity recognition*. In the context of technical documentation, we are interested in the problem of extracting named entities that refer to interface components, such as commands, menu items, dialogs, settings, and tools within the interface.

In this paper, we introduce a named-entity recognizer for detecting user interface elements mentioned within HTML documents. We call this specific problem *named widget recognition*. In the following sections, we enumerate the specific challenges for this problem, then discuss how certain informal conventions in tutorial writing can be leveraged to better detect named entities in this context. From these conventions, we derive a set of features and a general classification strategy that leads to accurate recognition of user interface elements referenced within text.

CHALLENGES AND RECOGNITION STRATEGIES
Web-based tutorials and documentation use natural language to describe how to perform specific tasks with interactive applications. To be clear and unambiguous, authors typically refer to user interface elements by their given, visible names (i.e., captions or labels) [4, 3]. For example, an author may write that the user should invoke the "Undo" command from the "Edit" menu.

Given this practice, an obvious strategy to named widget recognition is to simply search the documentation for strings matching known widget labels. This tact requires a complete list of widget captions, but numerous, reliable approaches exist for automatically enumerating and extracting the captions of widgets in both web [5] and desktop [3, 6] applications. We refer to this overall strategy as the *baseline* approach to named widget recognition. This baseline approach has been employed in the past by the query-feature graphs work by Fourney *et al.* in [3], and by the enhanced search results work by Ekstrand *et al.* in [1].

While simple and straightforward, the baseline strategy is prone to error. Consider, for example, a tutorial describing various options for converting a colour image to black and white with the GIMP raster graphs software[1]. In the full tutorial, approximately 170 distinct phrases match the labels or captions of components found in the GIMP user interface.

[1] http://www.gimp.org/tutorials/Color2BW/

CHI'12, May 5–10, 2012, Austin, Texas, USA.

"Here is what I get if I use desaturate instead. Duplicate the original image (Ctrl+D) and right-click on the copy. Select <Image> Image -> Colors -> Desaturate. Unlike the grayscale mode change above, the channels are not remixed in different percentages, so we should expect different results."

Figure 1. An excerpt from a tutorial describing how to convert a colour image to black and white using GIMP [1]. Substrings matching the names of GIMP commands are outlined in rectangles. False positive matches are crossed out.

However, upon inspection of the tutorial, only approximately 50 phrases are actual references to GIMP operations, making the false positive rate of this approach greater than 70%. An excerpt from this tutorial is listed in Figure 1, with all matches outlined with rectangles and false positives crossed out.

Online documentation also often includes its own set of menus, menu items, and controls for navigating and interacting with the website. These documentation widgets can also generate false matches when employing the baseline approach.

In the following sections, we identify a number of sources of information that can be employed to improve upon this baseline accuracy.

Leveraging Prior Beliefs

In the previous example, the term "desaturate" can be found in the first sentence (Figure 1). This term is highly technical, and rarely occurs in more general writing. Without additional evidence, we would expect that the use of this term refers to GIMP's "Desaturate" command. Conversely, in the second sentence, we encounter the term "image". This term is very generic, and occurs in many contexts beyond GIMP tutorials. Without additional evidence, we assume that it represents a false detection. Thus, by estimating how often a phrase refers to a widget in a given corpus, it is possible to correctly label many named widget references without any further consideration of the context in which the matches occur.

Leveraging Informal Conventions

In sentence 3 of Figure 1, the term "Image" twice refers to actual, named widgets. In such situations, further evidence is needed to overcome the prior expectation that generic phrases do not represent commands. This additional evidence is provided by informal conventions that are often employed in tutorial writing. For example, command names are often capitalized, and are occasionally styled to appear differently than the surrounding text (in this case, with a bold weighting). Special punctuation is also often employed to specify menu hierarchies (e.g., "->" in "File->Open"). The use (or lack of use) of these conventions can also factor into the classification of terms.

Leveraging Page Context

Page context can provide additional evidence to help correctly identify named widgets in cases where the online documentation contains links and website navigation with names matching those of the software it is documenting (e.g., "Help", "About", etc.). Specifically, matches that occur in regions of the page that resemble site navigation reduce the confidence that the matching term directly references a user interface widget.

Given this foundation, we now describe a feature set and a general classification framework that enables accurate recognition of named widgets.

CLASSIFICATION FRAMEWORK

Identifying UI components referenced in web documentation is a three step process. First, the document is examined for substrings matching the names of known interface components or commands (the baseline approach described above) to yield a set of *candidate matches*. In the second step of the process, a set of features is extracted from the context of every candidate match (where the features are derived from the cues and informal conventions discussed above). In the final step, a classifier determines which substring matches are indeed references to widgets.

Feature Extraction

To more correctly classify candidate named widgets, we employ the following set of features.

Capitalization

Recognizing the tendency for authors to capitalize references to commands, our classifier employs two related capitalization features: 1) Whether a candidate match's first token is capitalized, and 2) the total number of capitalized tokens within the match sequence. For example, "Save Selection to File" has three of its four tokens capitalized, including the first.

Next and Previous Tokens

The *next and previous tokens* features record the tokens immediately preceding and following the candidate named widget. These features are designed to model common phrases in which named widgets appear (e.g., "the File menu"). They also model conventions for describing menu hierarchies, such as the use of ">" or "->".

Next and Previous Candidates

Given a candidate match, the *next candidate* and *previous candidate* features record the candidate matches found before and after the current match. All tokens occurring between candidate matches are ignored. These features are designed to recognize and leverage common command sequences (e.g., "Copy and Paste") as well as parent-child relationships expressed in menus (e.g., "Edit > Paste As > New Layer").

Element Occupancy Ratio and Element Type

In web-based tutorials, references to interface elements are often expressed with some styling that makes the text visually distinct from the surrounding text. The *element occupancy ratio* feature models these markup differences as follows. First, we identify the HTML element directly enclosing the candidate match. We then compute the ratio between the number of tokens making up the candidate and the total number of tokens enclosed by the HTML element. For example, the word "pencil" exhibits a $1:4$ ratio in the phrase

"`<p>Select the pencil tool</p>`", but a 1: 1 ratio in the phrase "`Select the <b>pencil</b> tool`". In addition to the element occupancy ratio, we extract a feature recording the *type* of the enclosing element.

Text-to-Tag Ratio and Location (wrt. the Start of the Page)
Tutorial content, and hence named widgets, often make up the "main content" of the enclosing HTML document (as opposed to secondary content such as navigation, headers, and advertisements). In the information extraction literature, the *text-to-tag ratio* has been found to be a good feature for discriminating between main and secondary content [8]. Specifically, main content is typified by regions of the HTML document containing many text tokens, but few HTML tags. These regions are said to have a high text-to-tag ratio. Similarly, main article content is often found in the central region of an HTML file, somewhere between header content and footer content. Thus, we use the *location* of the match within the HTML document to help rule out candidates that are likely part of a tutorial's site navigation.

Notably absent from this list of 10 features is any representation of our prior beliefs regarding the likelihood that a candidate match represents a named entity. Prior beliefs are those held before considering evidence (i.e., features), and are modelled by the classifier directly. We describe the classifier next.

A Naive Bayes Classifier with Witten-Bell Smoothing
The features outlined above are compatible with many modern text classification and information extraction techniques. In this work, we elected to construct a recognizer that employs naive Bayes classification. While potentially less effective than more complex techniques (e.g., [2]), naive Bayes classifiers have nonetheless proven to be effective general purpose classifiers, and are certainly sufficient for demonstrating the feasibility of named-widget recognition. Moreover, naive Bayes classifiers confer a number of unique advantages. First, the number of parameters in a naive Bayes model scales linearly with the number of features and classes [7]. As a result, comparatively less training data is required to produce an effective classifier. Additionally, the "naive" independence assumption affords the ability to independently learn the feature distributions, thus enabling efficient training in the types of distributed systems typical of existing web indexing platforms.

In order to classify commands, we employ a separate binary naive Bayes classifier for each UI component we would like to recognize. When classifying a candidate match, we invoke only the classifier corresponding to that named component. For example, substrings matching the text "File" invoke the classifier corresponding to the system's *File* menu.

By treating commands separately rather than collectively via a single class or classifier, we ensure that the framework is able to directly model the subtle differences in context in which named entities are expected to occur (e.g., enabling the classifier to learn menu structures). Unfortunately, the strategy aggravates the problem of sparse data, and the training data may not include mentions of every available widget. To overcome the sparse data problem, we use Witten-Bell smoothing [9]. Witten-Bell smoothing uses the training data to estimate the likelihood of novel events. It then uses this estimate, together with a more general "backoff" model, to redistribute probability mass, thus filling in missing information. In our case, the backoff model is constructed by pooling the training data for all named entities into a single "generic widget" class. As a concrete example, suppose that the training data does not include any examples of the "Cut" command. With Witten-Bell smoothing, we can use what we know about commands in general to predict how references to the "Cut" command might appear in text.

EVALUATION
To evaluate the accuracy of the classification framework, we trained classifiers for each of the software applications listed in Table 1. In the following sections, we describe how the necessary training data was collected, how the classifiers were evaluated, and report the results of the evaluation.

Generating Training Data
In the course of conducting previous research with query-feature graphs [3], we had previously amassed a corpus of thousands of web documents pertaining to each of the software applications listed in Table 1. These corpora were collected using standard web crawling procedures. To generate training data for a particular application, we randomly sampled 35 documents from the associated document collection. We then identified candidate matches within each document, and manually labeled each as either referring to a command or not. Since terminology varies in generality from application to application (e.g., the names of commands in GIMP tend to be technical), and because we sampled an equal number of pages for each application, the number of labeled examples in each training set differ.

Evaluation and Results
In order to measure the accuracy of the classifiers, we employed leave-one-out validation on a per-page basis: in each round, the classifier is trained with items found in all but one of the web documents, and is evaluated using the withheld document. We report the results of this experiment in Table 1. To provide a point of comparison, the table also presents the accuracy achieved when using only the baseline approach.

The results suggest that the classification framework performs well. The tested classifiers are able to accurately label an average of 93.7% of all candidate named entities, surpassing the baseline accuracy by a wide margin. Viewed as a retrieval problem, the classifier returns an average of 75% of all actual named widgets (i.e., recall), with an average true-positive rate of 87% (i.e., precision). This yields an overall F1 score of 0.81.

To verify the classifiers were modelling the phenomena as expected, we manually inspected the conditional probability tables making up the various naive Bayes classifiers. Through this inspection, we found that the classifiers were indeed modelling various structural aspects of the target interface. For example, our approach automatically learns that the most likely token to follow a reference to GIMP's "Fuzzy Select" command is the word "tool", which is expected since "Fuzzy

	GIMP	Inkscape	Thunderbird	Total
Classifier:				
True +	598	405	445	1448
False +	53	91	71	215
True -	2040	2668	4215	8923
False -	133	181	164	478
Precision	0.92	0.82	0.86	0.87
Recall	0.82	0.69	0.73	0.75
F1 score	0.87	0.75	0.79	0.81
Accuracy	93.4%	91.9%	95.2%	93.7%
Baseline:				
F1 score	0.41	0.30	0.22	0.30
Accuracy	25.9%	17.5%	12.4%	17.4%

Table 1. Evaluation results characterizing the performance of the proposed classification framework. For comparison, the final two rows of the table present performance characteristics of the baseline method.

Feature Set	F1 score
Next and Previous Candidate Matches	0.78
Next and Previous Tokens	0.63
Capitalization	0.63
Text-to-Tag Ratio / Location	0.59
Element Occupancy Ratio / Element Type	0.50
No features (i.e., using the prior distribution directly)	0.50

Table 2. Classification performance when using only the features named in the leftmost column.

Select" is a tool that appears in GIMP's toolbox. Similarly, the words "window" or "dialog" are the most likely tokens to follow references to GIMP's "Channels" window.

Finally, to determine the relative importance of the various features employed by the classifier, we re-ran the experiment with classifiers employing various subsets of the available features. For example, we found that classifiers employing *only* the "Next and Previous Candidates" features achieve an overall F1 score of 0.78 across the three applications. Similarly, the classifiers utilizing only the "Capitalization" features achieve an overall F1 score of 0.63. The difference between these scores reflects the relative importance of the associated features. Of all features, "Element Occupancy Ratio" and "Element Type" were the least effective (F1 score of 0.50), providing less inferential leverage than we would have liked. A summary of the F1 scores for the various feature sets is listed in Table 2.

DISCUSSION AND FUTURE WORK

In this paper, we have demonstrated a system that draws upon informal practices in tutorial writing to detect references to named widgets in online documentation. The resulting named widget recognizer provides the foundation for a number of new interaction possibilities, including: (1) new means of indexing and searching tutorials, (2) the ability for users to invoke commands directly from within tutorial text, (3) the creation of summaries that highlight important steps in long tutorials (i.e., generating "Quick Start" guides), and (4) the automatic generation of macros or macro templates.

As with any complex system, there are a number of limitations of our recognizer worthy of further discussion.

First, our recognizer compares online documentation against a list of known widgets, and disambiguates between meaningful references and spurious/coincidental string matches. Our recognizer is both trained and evaluated using automatically generated lists of all strings in a user interface (e.g., captions, labels, tooltips, etc.). A limitation of this approach is that it does not consider cases where online documentation refers to a widget using alternative text (e.g. "click the 'No' button" when the button is actually labeled "Cancel"). Consideration of such novel synonyms can be expected to lower the recall scores as compared to the results reported in Table 1. This situation can be partially ameliorated by adding common synonyms to the list of widget names, but a more general solution for detecting novel synonyms remains a topic of future work.

Additionally, our system cannot disambiguate between distinct widgets that share a common name. For instance, in the GIMP 2.6 interface, both a menu and a panel share the caption "Layers". Fortunately, this does not significantly impact the applicability of the proposed technique to applications such as improved tutorial indexing or tutorial summarization. Moreover, we can often rely on the user to differentiate between multiple possible interpretations. In the future, we hope to leverage additional context to automatically disambiguate between identically named widgets.

Despite the aforementioned considerations, the proposed recognizer can be immediately applied to existing research, including query-feature graphs [3], the work of Lau *et al.* [4], and the work of Ekstrand *et al.* [1].

REFERENCES

1. M. Ekstrand, W. Li, T. Grossman, J. Matejka, and G. Fitzmaurice. Searching for software learning resources using application context. In *Proc. UIST'11*, pages 195–204, New York, NY, USA, 2011. ACM.
2. J. R. Finkel, T. Grenager, and C. Manning. Incorporating non-local information into information extraction systems by gibbs sampling. In *Proc. ACL'05*, pages 363–370, Stroudsburg, PA, USA, 2005. Association for Computational Linguistics.
3. A. Fourney, R. Mann, and M. Terry. Query-feature graphs: bridging user vocabulary and system functionality. In *Proc. UIST'11*, pages 207–216, New York, NY, USA, 2011. ACM.
4. T. Lau, C. Drews, and J. Nichols. Interpreting written how-to instructions. In *Proc. IJCAI '09*, pages 1433–1438, 2009.
5. G. Little and R. C. Miller. Translating keyword commands into executable code. In *Proc. UIST '06*, pages 135–144, New York, NY, USA, 2006. ACM.
6. V. Ramesh, C. Hsu, M. Agrawala, and B. Hartmann. Showmehow: translating user interface instructions between applications. In *Proc. UIST'11*, pages 127–134, New York, NY, USA, 2011. ACM.
7. S. Russell and P. Norvig. *Artificial Intelligence A Modern Approach*, chapter 20, page 718. Prentice Hall, 2nd edition, 2003.
8. T. Weninger and W. H. Hsu. Text extraction from the web via text-to-tag ratio. *Database and Expert Systems Applications, International Workshop on*, 0:23–28, 2008.
9. I. Witten and T. Bell. The zero-frequency problem: estimating the probabilities of novel events in adaptive text compression. *Information Theory, IEEE Transactions on*, 37(4):1085 – 1094, July 1991.

"Oh, dear Stacy!" Social Interaction, Elaboration, and Learning with Teachable Agents

Amy Ogan[*], Samantha Finkelstein[*], Elijah Mayfield[*], Claudia D'Adamo[†], Noboru Matsuda[*], Justine Cassell[*]

[*]Carnegie Mellon University
5000 Forbes Avenue
Pittsburgh, PA 15213
{aeo, slfink, emayfiel, mazda, justine}@cs.cmu.edu

[†]Wheaton College
26 E. Main Street
Norton, MA 02766
claudiadadamo@gmail.com

ABSTRACT

Understanding how children perceive and interact with teachable agents (systems where children learn through teaching a synthetic character embedded in an intelligent tutoring system) can provide insight into the effects of social interaction on learning with intelligent tutoring systems. We describe results from a think-aloud study where children were instructed to narrate their experience teaching Stacy, an agent who can learn to solve linear equations with the student's help. We found treating her as a partner, primarily through aligning oneself with Stacy using pronouns like *you* or *we* rather than *she* or *it* significantly correlates with student learning, as do playful face-threatening comments such as teasing, while elaborate explanations of Stacy's behavior in the third-person and formal tutoring statements reduce learning gains. Additionally, we found that the agent's mistakes were a significant predictor for students shifting away from alignment with the agent.

Author Keywords

Teachable agents; peer tutoring; impoliteness; rapport; ECA

ACM Classification Keywords

H.5.2 [Information interfaces & presentation]: User Interfaces - Graphical user interfaces; K.3.1 [Computers & Education]: Computer Uses in Education

INTRODUCTION

Teachable agents are a specific type of tutoring system that provides a platform for children to learn through teaching [3]. Such systems give students the opportunity to engage in peer tutoring exercises that may increase self-efficacy and motivation, and even contribute to learning [9, 18].

The success of teachable agents has been referred to as the tutor learning effect [3]. A number of theories have been proposed to explain this effect, including increased motivation to learn the material [23], increased reflection on already learned material [19], and increased effort turning knowledge into coherent, communicable ideas [10,11,29].

Among real children, while both tutors and tutees achieve significant learning gains from peer tutoring sessions, peer tutors learn more when their tutees struggle with the material [28]. This increase in learning gains is hypothesized to relate to increased reflection, self-explanation, and necessary reworkings of the problem from multiple perspectives. This may even lead to the tutor learning additional domain material not explicitly covered in the session [23].

Unfortunately, Walker et al. [28] found that tutee errors, while helpful for tutor learning gains, generally lead to less learning for the tutee. Research into the development of successful teachable agents can address this issue, as agents may play the role of a struggling tutee without evoking concern about detrimental consequences for a child. Teachable agents also allow researchers to examine how specific tutee behaviors affect how different children tutor, and thus learn, in identical educational environments.

However, one of the notable challenges with using teachable agents is that there are many components of human peer tutoring that are still not completely understood. For example, researchers have proposed that there are substantial social aspects of peer tutoring that are responsible for evoking tutor learning effects, such as a strong feeling of accountability for ensuring the tutee is learning the proper information [24], as well as a desire to avoid the face-threat of not being able to fully respond to tutee questions [28]. While prior research has shown that children do treat virtual characters similarly to peers in both language use and nonverbal behavior [5], one of the open questions in teachable agent research is whether child tutors are capable of the social motivations described here with a virtual tutee, and whether these social behaviors effect the same tutor learning benefits that can be seen with human peer tutoring.

While *cognitive* process data is relatively easy to collect in a technologically-enhanced learning system in which students work through problems [27], *social* process data that elucidates children's relationship with the agent is not. To our knowledge, analyses connecting the social processes that occur in either human-agent or human-human peer tutoring to learning gains have not been carried out, making it difficult to understand how social perceptions affect and change the course of these educational sessions. In this work, we therefore examine how children interact with Stacy, a teachable agent designed to learn linear equations with the help of a child tutor.

Using a think-aloud technique, we assess how children talk to and about Stacy throughout two tutoring sessions, and how their dialogue changes based on Stacy's success, perceived competence, and the length of time the students spend working with the agent. We examine the varying levels to which students choose to suspend disbelief and talk to Stacy as a peer – applauding her successes and reassuring her after failures – and when they instead choose to align themselves with the human experimenter in the room and refer to Stacy as *it* or *she*. We explore these linguistic nuances as they relate to the participants' social behaviors, and examine how these factors, among others, affect learning. We present results that indicate that it is in fact primarily social behaviors that correlate with increased learning gains, and that an *outside-system* perspective, where perceptions of Stacy's partner status are abandoned for viewing Stacy as a *she* or an *it,* predict fewer learning gains.

By examining how children interact with teachable agents, we begin to understand the social processes of human peer tutoring. This also allows us to delve into the more general area of human-agent interaction, addressing foundational questions about how children perceive the agency and competency of virtual characters, with implications for designing better teachable agents as learning interventions, and better agents in general.

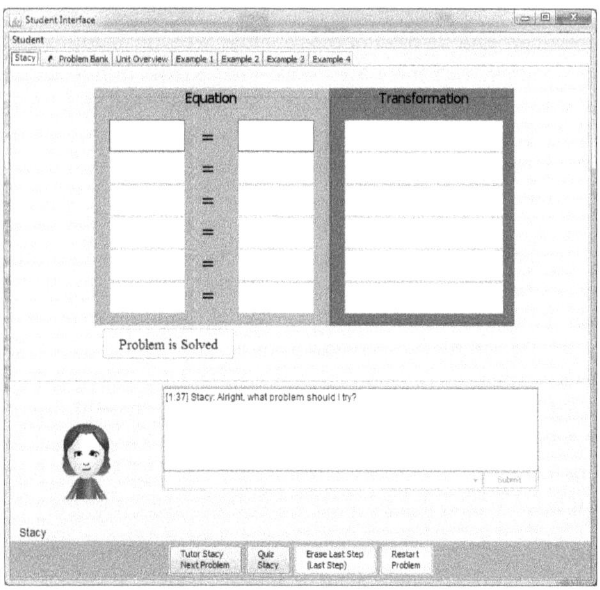

Figure 1. The SimStudent interface, with Stacy in the lower right corner.

RELATED WORK

The efficacy of teachable agents has received support in the literature, with several systems demonstrating the success of this intervention for user learning gains (e.g., [3, 17]). Although many more teachable agent systems have been developed than have been evaluated, it has been shown that children can achieve learning gains by tutoring a teachable agent. In fact, this learning result can be stronger than when the child is being taught by a virtual tutor, as demonstrated in an evaluation of the Betty's Brain system [3].

Investigators are also trying to understand the impact of social moves with teachable agents. Some propose that bringing off-task social conversation into educational dialogues may allow for cognitive rest, increase engagement, provide memory cues, and promote trust and rapport-building with the agent [12]. Gulz et al. [12] developed an interface where an embodied agent learns through either simply *observing* what the child is doing or requiring the child to explicitly explain the rules using a multiple choice dialogue interface. The system also allows users to engage in open-ended chat with the agent as both a motivational tool and a way to evaluate if this type of behavior might affect self-efficacy and generally improve feelings about math. They found a trend indicating that students allowed to engage in off-task chat had a more positive game experience and that their teachable agents had learned more of the material, but the evaluation did not take social process data about the type of social interaction nor how it changed over the course of the interaction into account.

A substantial amount of research also indicates that one's perceptions of the motivations for learning and of the learning partner affect how people speak and even the resulting learning gains. For example, Bargh and Schul [2] found that people primed to believe they were studying for a quiz to teach others about the material performed much better on the assessment than people who were preparing for the exam for themselves. This result is mirrored in virtual agent studies, where children achieve smaller learning gains when they believe they are teaching a virtual agent that represents themselves than when they are teaching a virtual agent that is presented as a different (virtual) student [7]. Chase et al. refer to this as the protégé effect. When interacting with the agent representing an other, students spend more time on learning activities, attribute mental states and responsibility to their agents, and are more likely to acknowledge errors by displaying negative affect and justifying and explaining why their agent has failed. However, the social mechanisms behind this effect have not been explored.

There is also research indicating that these varied learning effects change depending on the user's *belief* about whether they are interacting with a human or a computer agent. Even when agent responses are identical, students do not spontaneously offer the kinds of self-explanations to an agent that they produce when they believe they are interacting with a human. Instead they tend to answer questions with short keywords, providing no explanation [20, 21].

Okita et al. also explored whether the mere belief that a student was interacting with another real person makes a difference in learning gains [15]. Participants were given a script to use to teach a virtual character who responded identically to everyone, controlling for potential differences in dialogue. Regardless, participants who believed they were talking to a virtual character that was an avatar of a human in another room learned more from the tutoring session than participants who believed they were talking to an autonomous agent.

There are a number of potential explanations for this phenomenon. Students have reported that the social motivations of teaching, such as feeling accountability for helping another person prepare for an exam, forced them to gain deeper understanding of the materials [3]. Chase et al. [7], based on attribution statements for success and failure, hypothesize another social explanation for the learning by teaching effect. By having a second party who shares in the interaction and can take the blame for mistakes, rather than only (a representation of) oneself, the social implications could be that the student's ego is protected from the psychological ramifications of failure, which might in turn facilitate learning.

Conversely, other students interviewed by Biswas et al. [3] proposed a more cognitive explanation of the effectiveness of the tutor learning effect - that it is the need for the clear, conceptual organization of materials required by teaching that produces learning gains. Additionally, the explicit self-explanation that must occur in order to teach someone else has also been hypothesized as the main factor responsible for tutor learning [23]. While a cognitive explanation would hold regardless of who (or what) tutors believe they are interacting with, the mere belief results described above require the tutor to attribute some form of agency or social motivation to the teachable agent. Those results, then, suggest that there is some social aspect affecting the learning process, though details have not been explored until the current study.

HYPOTHESES

Cognitive hypotheses of learning by teaching suggest that tutors will engage in more mental organization of the material and perform more self-explanation as they tutor, leading to learning gains [10,11,16,20,25]. Therefore, we expected analysis of think-aloud protocols to demonstrate that (1) thinking about the state of the agent's knowledge, (2) reflecting on the agent's performance, and (3) providing extended explanations of domain material would result in improved learning gains for the participant.

On the other hand, previous literature has also hypothesized that it is social factors that motivate the tutor effect [3, 7, 11, 15]. Given conflicting prior work on whether social relationships can be formed with virtual agents [5,16,17,18] we chose to look at the type of language students used when referring to the agent as a clue to their social stance. We expected that speaking directly to the agent using pronouns such as you (e.g. "you got it right, Stacy"), which we call inside-system language, would be correlated with learning. Conversely, we expected that outside-system language, i.e. referring to the agent as she or it, would be less associated with learning gains because it demonstrates a reduced social relationship with the virtual peer. Similarly, we expected that increased use of explicit social dialogue moves in the think-aloud would promote learning gains.

In summary, we are interested in three primary questions: how do (1) increased cognitive (or meta-cognitive) reflection moves (2) inside-system vs. outside-system language and (3) increased social moves correlate with learning? We expected that both cognitive and social moves would improve learning gains, while outside-system language would hurt learning gains. Additionally, to support the creation of future teachable agent systems that can re-engage the child with the agent right as they began to slip away, we investigate what factors may affect shifts in alignment throughout the dialogue. We predicted that Stacy's competency would predict alignment-shifting, with students tending to use inside-system language when Stacy performs well, and outside-system language when Stacy begins to make mistakes.

SIMSTUDENT DESCRIPTION

Our study was carried out using the SimStudent platform [13]. SimStudent is a Learning by Teaching environment in which students interact with a virtual tutee named Stacy which inductively learns procedural rules in various domains. SimStudent starts off the interaction with a knowledge base of production rules that relate to a specific domain. In our work, the domain is linear equations, and the tutee's knowledge base includes the four basic math operations. SimStudent modifies and adds production rules to this knowledge base as students demonstrate problems.

As shown in Figure 1, the SimStudent interface consists of a set of domain overview materials, a set of worked-out example problems, a problem bank sorted by problem difficulty, and an interface for completing problems. While working, students create a linear equation and enter it into the interface for Stacy to try. Stacy completes steps based on her current production rules. After each step, Stacy asks the tutor if the rule she just applied was a good move. The response reinforces her learning algorithm, and allows the tutor to recognize and correct errors.

At times, Stacy may not have an appropriate rule to apply, and then will ask the tutor for help entering the next step. When a student demonstrates a step for Stacy, she creates a generalized rule by checking which operators can result in the input the student provides. If the example is divide by 3 for 3x=6, she might generalize to "divide by the first number." If the student tells Stacy that a step is incorrect, she uses inductive logic to determine constraints to only use the rule in appropriate situations - e.g., if a new negative example says that it is incorrect to divide by 2 for 2x+3=5, she might add the constraint "when the left hand side does not have a constant term".

Throughout the interaction Stacy also asks the tutor other questions, such as, "Why should I do this problem?", or "I did [x] before, why can't I do that here?" These questions are intended to provoke reflection and self-explanation in the tutor. Students can select an answer from a drop-down box or can type in their own explanation.

At any point in time, tutors can have Stacy take a quiz on the material. Tutors can use this quiz both to test that she has acquired the knowledge they have taught, as well as to understand where her misconceptions lie. As she passes sections of the quiz, new problem types appear that give tutors an indication of the domain rules they should be working on next with Stacy.

While Stacy is embodied, her image is not articulated and has a cartoon-like appearance. She is modeled using an agent creation system that mimics characters on the Nintendo Wii system, and has three poses: a standard pose, a questioning pose in which she appears to be thinking, and a happy pose that is seen when the tutor marks a step correct.

STUDY

Participants

12 students (2 girls and 10 boys), ranging from entering 7th grade to entering 10th grade, were recruited from an e-mail list of parents who had previously indicated interest in research participation. All students reported experience with algebra. Students came for two 90-minute sessions, and were compensated $40 at the completion of both sessions.

Equipment

Students sat at a desktop computer, with the SimStudent interface pre-loaded. A chart showing twelve classrooms labeled with different school grades was taped to the wall on their left. A digital video camera recorded participants on their right side, and captured their position in the chair, the grade chart behind them, and part of the screen. They were provided scratch paper and were invited to use it, though only some did.

Procedure

In the first session, students first took a pre-test which consisted of algebra problems. Once completed, students were asked to look at an image of Stacy, and place a post-it on the grade chart beside them to indicate what grade they thought she was in. They were told they could move the post-it to update their choice at any time. Next, students watched an 8-minute video describing Stacy, and were given instructions on how to think-out-loud during a study. Once finished, students began working with Stacy, and were reminded to speak out loud whenever they became quiet. Students were told that their goal was to help Stacy learn how to solve equations with variables on both sides to help her pass four sections of a quiz.

In the second session, students immediately began working with Stacy in the think-aloud protocol. They worked until either Stacy passed all four quiz sections, or 45 minutes had passed. They then completed the post-test, which took anywhere from 10-35 minutes. They were asked some final interview questions, and were compensated for their time.

LEARNING GAINS

Before we investigated students' behaviors in the tutoring sessions, we calculated pretest and posttest scores to assess their learning gains over the course of the intervention, which were significant ($t = 2.84$, $p < .02$, effect size 0.56σ). Significance was calculated using a student's paired t-test across each student's pretest and posttest scores. We also collected the following demographic data for each participant: school grade, gender, and previous tutoring experience; however, none of these variables were significantly correlated with learning gains.

We then computed normalized learning gains using the standard formulation to account for differences in children's prior knowledge:

$$normalized\ gain = \frac{posttest - pretest}{1 - pretest}$$

Normalized gain is used in our subsequent results sections to explore relations to learning.

OBSERVATIONS FROM THE VERBAL PROTOCOL

Observationally, students made comments during the think-aloud in three primary categories: social moves, tutoring strategies, and (meta)cognitive evaluations of Stacy's knowledge. In this section, we discuss notable examples of social and tutoring utterances.

Social Moves

Students made social comments to Stacy with varying frequency, with one student never saying anything social at all, and some making a social move every ten utterances. Positive social moves were common, particularly on day one, including compliments:

Stacy: Would this be a good move?
P12: Yes! You're a smart person.

Congratulatory praise: *P12: You got it, Stacy. Congratulations! Let's try the quiz again.*

Reassurance: *P10: You're almost there Stacy! Oh, Stacy. You were so close.*

Empathy: *P10: Negative 8? Oh dear. You didn't like that one, did you?*

Not all social moves were so clearly positive, however. We observed many comments that could be characterized as *face-threatening*, by which is meant dialogue moves that threaten the other person's identity management, or positive sense of him or herself [4]. Examples were students playfully insulting and teasing Stacy throughout the conversation, particularly during the second session. This included students minimizing her successes:

P7: You got lucky Stacy.
P8: Problem is solved, no thanks to you.
P7: Yes Stacy listened for once.

Being overtly face-threatening:
P7: Oh God. You fail Stacy. Oh God.
P8: That's terribly not right.

Using sarcasm:
Stacy: I think the problem is solved.
P10: Really? Well I don't.

Stacy: I'm stuck and I don't know what to do next. Can you show me what to do?
P10: Hmm, really? Yeah, I've heard that one before.

Expressing frustration:
P12: Argh, you annoy me so much.
P2: Stacy, what are you doing?!

These utterances were typically said with a playful tone, and it's important to note that, qualitatively, the students did not seem to be harboring actual frustration, annoyance, anger, or any strong negative emotion. Instead, they seemed to engage in the teasing one would observe among friends.

Tutoring
Most students, for at least part of their session, took their role as tutor seriously. All students made comments at some point about what they should do to make sure Stacy was learning, with various degrees of serious analysis about her knowledge. Participant 4 made many of these formal tutoring moves, though very few social moves:

P4: All right, so Stacy got the first problem right, and didn't have a clue how to do the next problem.
P4: I don't think she knows how to deal with parentheses.
P4: All right, so I'm just going to use their example problem now.
Stacy: Why should I do this problem?
P4: You should do this problem because you got this problem wrong, and I want to see what you did not understand about it.

This utterance also depicts a common phenomenon in our data, which we call face-saving alignment. Students who made many formal tutoring moves and few social moves often used outside-aligned speech to discuss what Stacy did and did not know, which we hypothesize is because it would be face-threatening to discuss her incompetencies with her in detail, along the lines described by Reeves and Nass [16]. When Stacy prompts the participant back into inside-aligned speech with a question, the child does provide an answer, though it has less specific elaborations about what exactly they thought Stacy was doing wrong. The students who made fewer social moves such as teasing may not have felt the same sense of rapport that the social students felt, and might not have been comfortable being face-threatening with Stacy the way the social students did.

DATA ANNOTATIONS
In order to adduce evidence for the hypotheses we lay out above, we analyzed the linguistic behaviors of the children in our corpus, based on annotation of the think-aloud protocols in the way described below.

Coding Scheme
Each think-aloud session in our data set was divided into utterances by a human annotator, based on pauses in speech and thought completeness. Our data consists of 3,433 utterances from 12 participants over 20 sessions (four participants finished the tutoring task in their first session, returning only for the posttest on day two).

These utterances were then coded in five categories developed to evaluate our hypotheses. The coding was carried out by two independent coders who first evaluated interrater reliability by independently coding a random child's full dialogue. Reliability is given for each coding category below in a Cohen's K [8]. Every utterance was given a code from every category, with *none* always as an option in the case that the utterance contained no features for that category. Our five coding categories and their sub-categories are described below.

1. A *social* utterance, either *positive* that represents feelings including hope, encouragement, or excitement (e.g. "yay, dear Stacy, you can do it!") or *negative* expressing face-threat or frustration (e.g. "got this one right, no thanks to you.") (interrater reliability Cohen's K = .773)
2. A *tutoring* move that included conceptualizations of Stacy's knowledge and informed decisions about how to proceed (e.g. "now I'll give you an example fractions problem because you got that one wrong last time"), and elaborations about domain material (e.g. "now you need to divide to make sure the variable is alone on that side of the equation.") (Cohen's K = .686)
3. An *alignment* based on pronoun use, including inside-system alignments such as *you* and *inclusive-we* (e.g. "you got this one wrong, Stacy, we should do a new one now"), and outside-system alignments such as *she, Stacy*, and *exclusive-we* (e.g. "Stacy doesn't know fractions, we'll see if she can do this one now.") (Cohen's K=.823)
4. A *cognitive* or metacognitive assessment about Stacy's knowledge that was either *simple* (e.g. "She gets this one") or *elaborated* (e.g. "Okay, Stacy doesn't understand the distributive part."). These elaborations are a hypothesized mechanism for learning, as described earlier in the paper. (Cohen's K=.823)

5. A *correctness* evaluation of Stacy's knowledge as being either *correct* or *incorrect*. (Cohen's K = .707)

Analysis Methods

Our quantitative experiments are framed around exploring the effects and interactions of coded language behaviors in the five categories described above. In the upcoming sections, we report our results from several quantitative experiments that explore:

1. Correlations between language behaviors, learning gains, and participant attributes to examine how participant features and behaviors are associated with agent interaction and learning.
2. Shifts in behavior between sessions 1 and 2 to better understand how increased exposure to the system affects language behaviors.
3. How specific linguistic behaviors in the child affect upcoming child alignment on a turn-by-turn level using a novel machine learning approach.

DIALOGUE BEHAVIORS AND LEARNING GAINS

We first investigated children's learning gains as they related to the relative frequencies of their dialogue moves.

For each child *c* in the set of children *C*, we calculate probabilities that an utterance will have a label *l* for label category *L* (where the labels represent the language behaviors we coded). This results in a value $P(L = l \mid C = c)$ for each possible pairing of category label and child. For each category, these probabilities sum to 1 for each student. For each variable individually, we perform a linear regression to fit normalized learning gain and evaluate significance of the regression using a one-way ANOVA test. Labels with a statistically significant relationship to learning gain are summarized in Table 1.

We found a significant positive correlation between negative social moves, such as face-threatening or teasing comments, and student learning gains.

We also found significant negative correlations between learning gains and three specific student behaviors: (1) aligning outside of the system by talking *about* Stacy rather than *to* Stacy, (2) describing very formal tutoring moves such as stating what they planned to do, why they were doing it, and what they hoped it would achieve, and (3)

Annotation Label	Gain r^2	Sig.
Alignment: Outside	-.510	**
Tutoring	-.314	*
Cognitive-elaborated	-.316	*
Social-negative	.646	***

Table 1. Behaviors which explain significant variance in normalized learning gain. Significance marked as * (p < .05), ** (p < .01), * (p < .001)**

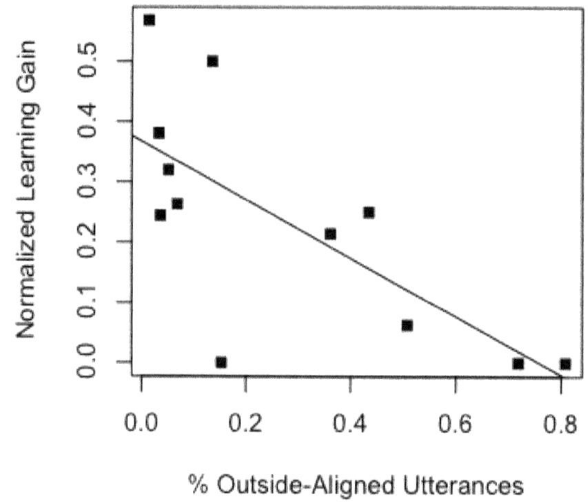

Figure 2. Correlation of relative percentage of outside-aligned utterances to normalized learning gains

giving elaborate cognitive assessments about Stacy's understanding of the material, such as explaining what exactly it is, in detail, that Stacy knows or doesn't know.

None of the other dialogue behaviors were significantly correlated to learning, nor did they demonstrate any significant correlation to any of the demographics collected.

Cognitive elaboration and outside alignment

Because previous human-human peer tutoring research reports that increased elaboration is associated with learning gains [23], we conducted further analysis to understand why elaborations were negatively correlated with learning in our study. We found that there was a significant correlation between cognitive elaboration and outside-system alignment, and that it is the outside-system alignment that's driving the significance (see the following section.) When we controlled for alignment, the effects of cognitive elaboration on learning gains were not significant, though they still trended negatively, $p<.4$. Closer examination found that 39% of utterances that involved elaborations were preceded by inside-aligned student moves, indicating that students were breaking away from alignment with Stacy to explain her cognitive state in the third person.

ALIGNMENT SHIFT PREDICTION

Overall, we found that shifting away from direct communication with the agent and instead talking *about* Stacy in the third person was more negatively correlated with learning than any other annotated student behavior.

In the next experiment, we attempt to *predict shifts* in child alignment within a single session based on our coding of the think-aloud utterances. This gives us insight into what behaviors are most likely to indicate a child's upcoming break in rapport (shifting to outside-alignment) so we know how to address this issue in the design of future learning interventions.

We treat this as a three-way classification task. Machine learning was performed using the SIDE text mining toolkit [14]. We built a Naïve Bayes model and evaluated accuracy through leave-one-child-out cross validation, where eleven students are used to train each model, and that model is tested against the sessions from the held-out child. This is done twelve times and the accuracy is averaged.

In a given model, we choose a window size of *n* utterances Then we define two features for each category label: a numeric feature marking how many times this feature occured in the previous *n* utterances, and a boolean feature marking whether the label was observed at all in the window. We then add one additional feature marking whether Stacy made an incorrect move since the most recent utterance.

Through cross-validation, we find window size *n*=6 to be the most predictive. This model has 70.9% accuracy in predicting upcoming alignment overall (predicting outside alignment with precision = .611, recall = .745, κ=.554).

We observe several interesting characteristics of the model. Relatively little adjustment is made based on observing a behavior once in the window. Observing a behavior two or more times, however, has a more drastic effect. For instance, one negative social move in the recent window drops the probability only slightly, while two or more drop the probability near zero. On the other hand, elaborated cognitive moves have a similar pattern in the opposite direction, with a slight increase in likelihood when only one is observed, but virtual certainty of outside alignment if two or more elaborated moves have been observed in the last six utterances. What this suggests is that individual moves in any category are possible across a broad range of interactional styles. However, repeating the same style of moves (such as elaborated cognitive moves, or negative social moves) more than once in quick succession gives the model the evidence it needs that recent moves fit into an outside-aligned or inside-aligned pattern.

Qualitatively, it appears that students' alignment often reflects their perceptions of Stacy's ability. At one point in the interaction, participant P4 is inside-aligned, talking to Stacy and telling her what to do:

P4: Ok so 10c+3, and your 10c... So you have to div.. If 10c=3 you have to divide by 10.

When he then evaluates her subsequent performance as poor, he switches alignment to outside the system, talking to the experimenter (and demoting her in grade level):

P4: And I'm going to move her back to about 7th grade cause she can't solve this.

Although we did not make a distinction between calling Stacy 'she' and 'it' in our coding scheme due to the infrequent occurrences of 'it', we believe that a shift between the use of one of these pronouns to the other might, in a larger data set, have just as much significance as a shift from inside to outside alignment. Where the shifts from

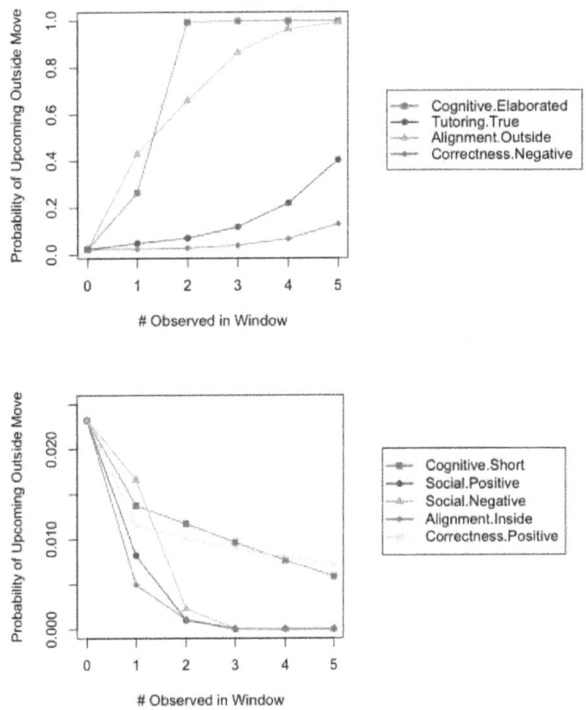

Figure 3. Impact of each feature individually on prediction of upcoming outside-aligned moves (holding all other features constant at 0)

"she" to "it" occur, they seem to follow a similar pattern to switches between inside ("you") and outside alignment ("she"). For example, participant P2 at one point in the interaction is aligned outside the system, talking about Stacy:

P2: She didn't do problem number 8.

This is followed by two steps which were correct, but the participant wrongly evaluated as incorrect:

P2: No that's not right...No.

Stacy then takes five correct steps followed by two incorrect steps, at which point the participant dehumanizes her in his speech:

*P2: Uh.... Um... I don't think **it** knows how to distribute things.*

In addition to predicting shifts in alignment, we were also interested in discovering what behaviors were most predictive of upcoming social moves, given that these moves were such a strong predictive feature for alignment, and were also associated with learning gains. We attempted to replicate this experiment to predict upcoming social moves; however, accuracy above chance was much weaker (K < .2). This suggests that the factors that are responsible for influencing children's use of social moves are likely outside of our coding scheme, and further research is necessary to determine what these features are and how they play a role.

BEHAVIOR SHIFTS ACROSS SESSIONS

As tutoring interventions ideally happen over an extended period of time, and we know that language changes among human interlocutors as they become more familiar with one another, we examined differences in the children's linguistic behavior between sessions 1 and 2. In our study eight participants returned to engage with the tutoring intervention on a second day. Investigating only these participants, we had 8 sessions comprised of 1,164 utterances that represent the first interaction a participant has with the agent, and eight sessions comprised of 1,387 utterances representing the second session on a later day. Quantitative measures of shifts in each annotation are given in Table 2. Significance is calculated using unpaired student's t-tests between utterance distributions in each day.

On day 2 of the intervention, we saw that while positive social moves decreased, negative social moves significantly increased. Additionally, simple cognitive evaluations increased, as did both negative and positive statements about Stacy's correctness on the task.

Annotation	Day 1	Day 2	Shift %	Sig.
- Social	.024	.050	108.3	***
+ Social	.056	.037	-34.5	**
- Correctness	.109	.173	58.9	***
+ Correctness	.226	.291	28.7	***
Cog Simple	.305	.439	43.9	***
Cog Elab	.024	.025	4.2	NS
Inside Align	.092	.112	21.7	NS
Outside Align	.215	.241	+12.3%	NS
Tutoring	.137	.119	-13.4	NS

Table 2. Distributions of behavior in separate days, and normalized shift in those behaviors. Significance marked as * ($p < .05$), ** ($p < .01$), * ($p < .001$), or Not Significant.**

DISCUSSION

A number of authors have posited that human peer tutoring is successful because of the increased elaboration of material that is necessitated by interaction between tutor and tutee [22, 23]. However our results demonstrated the opposite effect – that increased elaboration and reflection resulted in fewer learning gains. Further exploration found that the driving force behind this effect is that elaborations were strongly correlated with outside-aligned speech, which in turn was strongly associated with negative learning gains. We also saw that 39% of the time, students switched from inside to outside-aligned speech for the purpose of this elaboration, taking themselves out of a role as Stacy's partner and assuming the role of Stacy's observer.

We hypothesize that this switch to outside-aligned speech occurs because students who don't feel comfortable with Stacy – those with fewer social behaviors – don't want to offend Stacy by directing their detailed assessment of her incompetencies to her. We believe these students are doing face-saving alignment – an unconscious switch from inside to outside-aligned speech when they want to elaborate about Stacy's abilities. We also hypothesize that this switch away from partnership and alignment with Stacy removes some of the social motivations of peer tutoring, and that making the kind of useful tutoring moves that consist of elaborating information about domain material, but without the scaffolded support of the system, make it difficult for the child to maintain an effective peer relationship with the agent.

Because previous research has shown that elaboration and self-explanation is so beneficial to learning, we propose that learning by teaching interventions should have provisions to allow students to elaborate on knowledge as part of a joint activity with the agent, to discourage them from disaligning with the system. Stacy has very limited social moves, and is only able to ask a handful of open-ended questions designed to prompt the student to elaborate. However, Stacy could not respond to these elaborations, nor could she encourage the child to elaborate while remaining *inside* the system. It's possible that children picked up on Stacy's inability to respond, which is what lead them to disalign. It is also possible that if Stacy were able to scaffold how one could reflect and elaborate while continuing to co-construct knowledge with the child, the participants would have been able to follow suit. Future work will examine different ways of encouraging inside-aligned speech during reflection and elaboration.

In addition, we found that tutoring moves were negatively correlated with learning. Based on qualitative observation of students' verbalizations, these moves were also highly formal speech like their elaborations, and may also indicate that in these turns, students were playing the role of tutor and not socially engaging with the tutee.

These findings highlight the importance of role in tutoring, with students who speak to Stacy as a peer rather than a socially-distant tutee achieving the highest learning gains. We found that negative social moves, such as teasing and face-threat, were the most predictive of learning gains. These moves are also indicative of rapport between interlocutors, and are thought to mostly take place between intimates [25]. In fact, the literature on social moves among middle-schoolers makes it clear that alliance building is not confined to supportive behaviors. Episodes of playful confrontation, name-calling, and insulting sequences are prominent in middle-school communication [1]. It is notable that students who produce many of these utterances achieve the highest learning gains, indicating that in human-agent peer tutoring, the social role of the child is vital, and that a strict tutor-role division may not be the most beneficial. We suggest that systems should support rapport-building dialogue – including what may appear at first to be agent abuse.

We found that the frequency of these intimate teasing comments increased on students' second session, indicating that students may naturally gain more rapport with the agent over time. In fact, according to the theory of rapport proposed by [26], as applied by [6], positive statements in a relationship decrease over time, which may indicate that students felt more comfortable with the agent and thus had less need for positive statements. Upon resuming the second day, several students made explicit social opening statements:

P12: Ok. Let's try it again, Stacy.
P7: Stacy, come back for you!

However, our investigation found that it was not possible to predict when these social moves would occur from the features in our coding scheme. In future work we will examine how we can support critical rapport-building in this context by looking at what behaviors lead children to tease and in other ways ally themselves with a teachable agent or real human tutee.

We also saw that agent mistakes are an important factor in the likelihood that children will shift into outside-aligned speech. Making errors is realistic, and there is evidence that in human-human peer tutoring, these are the places where tutors do the most learning [28]. Instead of trying to create perfectly competent agents, we propose designing agents that are able to acknowledge their errors socially, in particular after committing several contiguous errors. Additionally, we found that the child's assessment of the agent's correctness was a greater predictor of alignment-shift than actual correctness. We propose that agents should keep the participant immersed in the experience by making teasing or joking face-threatening moves of their own following an incorrect assessment of their ability. In future work we will observe human-human pairs and their strategies for defusing these situations, and extract social moves following errors that lead to more learning.

We hypothesize that systems designed with agents that can interact socially with the child could prevent children from facing the identity crises we saw children experience during the course of our study. Stacy's limited social interactions but realistic learning patterns may have confused students, with some indicating they weren't sure about how to interact with Stacy – as an agent, a machine, a peer, a tutee. One participant's utterance sums up this conflict precisely:

P13: I'm mad at the computer because it's not – I'm mad at Stacy because she's not understanding what I'm saying. [pause] But I'm holding it in 'cause it's not nice to be mean to your students… even though this isn't really a student.

Finally, we do see that significant learning gains were achieved with our program, which adds to the evidence that a learning-by-teaching paradigm is successful with agents.

Of course, it's important to note that our data were derived from the kind of think-aloud protocol that would likely not occur outside of a lab study. In a paradigm where students typed directly to the agent rather than speaking aloud, such alignment shifts may not have occurred. While we believe our results are insightful, we acknowledge they may be different from how students would speak to an agent during full dialogues via chat. Think-alouds also encourage the child to verbalize what they might have otherwise kept to themselves, perhaps artificially encouraging less social children to resort to face-saving alignment that wouldn't have been necessary with a different methodology.

Additionally, we emphasize that these results are not causal. It may be the case that feeling self-efficacious about learning leads to gaining more rapport with the agent, rather than the increased rapport driving learning. It also may be the case that it is not the switch to outside-aligned speech that is causing negative learning gains, but a third factor such as frustration that is causing the students to dis-align as well as learn less. It is also important to note that this work only describes interactions with the agent in a procedural domain. Students may use different behaviors in other creativity-based or declarative learning domains. Our future work aims to address these limitations.

CONCLUSION

This work presents the most thorough analysis to date of social interaction with teachable agents. This is the first work that looks at the association between learning gains, social moves, and tutoring/elaboration moves with an embodied virtual peer, and it is thus notable that the human-human results are not mirrored in this work.

Children who acted as though the teachable agent was in the room, who spoke directly to her and engaged her in conversation (even though she rarely replied!) were more successful in the learning task. This was particularly true for students who produced the most teasing and face-threatening utterances.

Based on this research, we recommend designing systems that are able to provide better social support for (1) scaffolding inside-aligned elaboration, (2) modeling appropriate elaborations within a peer-tutoring context, and (3) encouraging inside-alignment in response to agent errors through increased social dialogue.

ACKNOWLEDGEMENTS

The research reported here was supported by National Science Foundation Award Nos. DRL-0910176 and IIS-0968485 and the Institute of Education Sciences, U.S. Department of Education, through Grant R305A090519 to Carnegie Mellon University. This work is also supported in part by the Pittsburgh Science of Learning Center, which is funded by the National Science Foundation Award No. SBE-0836012. The opinions expressed are those of the authors and do not represent views of the funders.

REFERENCES

1. Ardington, A. Playfully negotiated activity in girls' talk, *J. of Pragmatics*, 38(1) (2006), 73-95.
2. Bargh, H., Schul, Y. On the cognitive benefits of teaching. *J. of Educ. Psych*, 72(5) (1980), 593-604.
3. Biswas, G., Leelawong, K., Schwartz, D., Vye, N., and TAG-V. Learning By Teaching: A New Agent Paradigm for Educational Software. *Applied Artificial Intelligence*, 19, (2005), 363-392.
4. Brown, P., and Levinson, S. *Politeness: Some Universals in Language Usage*. New York: Cambridge University Press, 1987.
5. Cassell, J. Towards a Model of Technology and Literacy Development: Story Listening Systems. *J. of Applied Developmental Psych*, 25(1) (2004), 75-105.
6. Cassell, J., Gill, A. and Tepper, P. Coordination in Conversation and Rapport. In *Proc. EmbodiedNLP 2007*. 41-50.
7. Chase, C., Chin, D., Oppezzo, M., Schwartz, D. Teachable Agents and the Protégé Effect: Increasing the Effort Towards Learning. *J. Sci. Educ. Tech.,* 18 (2009), 334-352.
8. Cohen, J. A coefficient of agreement for nominal scales. *Educ. and Psych Measurement*, 20(1) (1960). 37-46.
9. Cohen, P., Kulik, J., Kulik, C. Educational Outcomes of Tutoring: A Meta-analysis of Findings. *J. of Educational Research.* 19(2) (1982), 237-248.
10. Coleman, E., Brown, A., Rivkin, A. The effect of instructional explanations on learning from science texts. *J. of the Learning Science*, 6(4) (1997), pp. 347-365.
11. Fantuzzo, J. W., King, J., Heller, L.R. Effects of reciprocal peer tutoring on mathematics and school adjustment: A component analysis. *J. of Educ. Psych*, 84(3) (1992), 331-339.
12. Gulz, A., Haake, M. and Silvervarg, A. Extending a Teachable Agent with a Social Conversation Module - Effects on Student Experiences and Learning. In *Proc. AIED 2011*. 106-114.
13. Matsuda, N., Yarzebinski, E., Keiser, V., Raizada, R., Stylianides, G., Cohen, W. W. Learning by Teaching SimStudent – An Initial Classroom Baseline Study comparing with Cognitive Tutor. *In Proc AIED 2011*, Springer, 213-221.
14. Mayfield, E. and Rosé, C.P. An interactive tool for supporting error analysis for text mining. In *Demo Session NAACL 2010*.
15. Okita, S., Bailenson, J., and Schwartz, D.L. Mere belief in social action improves complex learning. *In Proc. ICLS 2008*. 132-139.
16. Reeves, B., and Nass, C. The Media Equation: how people treat computers, televisions and new media like real people and places. Cambridge: Cambridge University Press, 1996.
17. Reif, F. and Scott, L.A. Teaching scientific thinking skills: Students and computers coaching each other. *Amer. J. Physics.* 67(9), 1999, 819-831.
18. Rohrbeck, C. A., Ginsburg-Block, M. D., Fantuzzo, J. W., and Miller, T. R. Peer-assisted learning interventions with elementary school students: A meta-analytic review. *J. of Educ. Society.* 95(2), (2003), 240-257.
19. Roscoe, R.D., and Chi, M. Understanding Tutor Learning: Knowledge-Building and Knowledge-Telling in Peer Tutors' Explanations and Questions. *Review of Educ. Research.* 77(4), (2007), 534-574.
20. Rosé, C.P., Bhembe, D., Siler, S., Srivastava, R., and VanLehn, K. The Role of Why Questions in Effective Human Tutoring. In *Proc. AIED 2003*, IOS Press. 55-62.
21. Rosé, C.P., Jordan, P., Ringenberg, M., Siler, S., VanLehn, K., and Weinstein, A. Interactive conceptual tutoring in Atlas-Andes. In *Proc AIED 2001*. IOS Press, 256-266.
22. Rosé, C. P., and Torrey, C. Interactivity versus Expectation: Eliciting Learning Oriented Behavior with Tutorial Dialogue Systems, In *Proc. Interact 2005.* 323-336.
23. Sharpley, A., Irvine, J., and Sharpley, C. An Examination of the Effectiveness of a Cross-age Tutoring Program in Mathematics for Elementary School Children. *Amer. Educ. Research J.* 20(1), (1983), 103-111.
24. Slavin, R. E. Research on cooperative learning and achievement: What we know, what we need to know. *Contemporary Educ. Psych,* 21, (1996), 43-69.
25. Straehle, C. A. '"Samuel?" "Yes dear?" Teasing and conversational rapport', *Framing in Discourse*. New York: Open University Press. (1993). 210-229.
26. Tickle-Degnen, L., and Rosenthal, R. The nature of rapport and its nonverbal correlates. *Psych. Inquiry*, 1, (1990), 285-293.
27. VanLehn, K. The behavior of tutoring systems. *Internatl. J. of Artificial Intelligence in Educ.* 16(3), (2006), 227-265.
28. Walker, E., Rummel, N., and Koedinger, K. R. Integrating collaboration and intelligent tutoring data in the evaluation of a reciprocal peer tutoring environment. *Research and Practice in Tech. Enhanced Learning*, 4(3), (2009), 221-251.
29. Webb, N. M. Peer interaction and learning in small groups. *J. of Educ. Psych.* 13(1), (1989), 21-39.

From Participatory to Contributory Simulations: Changing the Game in the Classroom

Stefan Kreitmayer[1,3], Yvonne Rogers[3], Robin Laney[1], Stephen Peake[2]

1. Department of Computing
The Open University
Milton Keynes, UK
{s.kreitmayer, r.c.laney}@open.ac.uk

2. Department of Design
The Open University
Milton Keynes, UK
s.r.peake@open.ac.uk

3. UCLIC
University College London
London, UK
y.rogers@ucl.ac.uk

ABSTRACT

There is much potential for supporting collaborative learning with interactive computer simulations in formal education and professional training. A number of simulations have been developed for single user and remote interaction. In contrast, our research is concerned with how such learning activities can be designed to fit into co-located large group settings, such as whole classrooms. This paper reports on the iterative design process and two in-the-wild evaluations of the 4Decades game, which was developed for a whole classroom of students to engage with a climate simulation. The system allows students to play and change the rules of the simulation, thereby enabling them to be actively engaged at different levels. The notion of Contributory Simulations is proposed as an instructional model that empowers groups to make informed, critical changes to the underlying scientific model. We discuss how large-group collaboration was supported through constraining an ecology of shared devices and public displays.

Author Keywords

Contributory Simulations; participatory simulations; ubiquitous computing; ambient displays; serious games; collaborative learning; tablets

ACM Classification Keywords

H.5.2 [Information Interfaces and Presentation]: User Interfaces - Interaction styles;

General Terms

Design, Human Factors

INTRODUCTION

Simulations and role-play activities are often used in classroom-based teaching in addition to lectures and discussion. They allow groups of students to think for themselves about a topic by engaging in active problem solving. While younger audiences are often given well-structured problems with pre-defined solutions, higher-level education and professional training courses recognize the need to involve mature students more deeply in the framing of real-world problems and in the critical analysis of these framings.

Examples of real-world problems include complex, global challenges such as climate change. Policy makers in corporations, NGOs and governments need to be trained in thinking about how to solve these by using, on the one hand, scientific and economical models that are based on mathematics and, on the other hand, working out how to deal with uncertainty in numerous ways. Developing practical fluency in using a combination of precision and possibility is critical to this kind of thinking and is key to the success of training courses at this level.

Our research is concerned with how interactive simulations can be designed to be more effective as learning tools for this kind of professional training. In particular, we are interested in how ubiquitous technologies can be used to support simulation-based learning activities that take place during high-profile, multi-day executive training workshops. Initially, we designed 4Decades - an interactive learning tool – in the form of a Participatory Simulation that encourages teams to collaboratively explore a given model alongside discussing and reflecting upon uncertainties. When played by two teams in a real-world training context it was found to promote high levels of collaboration and problem-solving. However, it was identified that it could be improved if the simulation could also enable critical changes to be made to the underlying mathematical model as well as interacting with the visible dimensions at the user interface. A second iteration of the simulation was developed, which we called a contributory simulation, distinguishing it from participatory simulations. The main difference is that our simulation enables teams to explore a hypothetical world and revise it. Decisions were made based on outcomes and interventions, through changing the rules of the simulation. The extent to which having this level of functionality aids thinking collaboratively about complex global problems is discussed. Our findings establish the feasibility of designing contributory simulations using shareable devices and ambient displays and suggest potential for future design and research in this area.

BACKGROUND

Figure 1 shows the different approaches to learning with simulations, that are positioned in relation to one another in terms of the extent to which they include observation versus role-playing and are malleable versus rigid. The majority of early computer simulations that were designed to teach complex topics in science, economics, and so on, were at the fixed and observational end of the continuums. They also ran mainly on single-user desktop applications. These include microworlds that were developed in the 1980s [4] and Scientific Discovery Learning, based on predesigned computational models, in the 1990s [3]. More recently, software tools that allow students to design and test their own systems models, such as NetLogo or StarLogo TNG [9] have been developed. These can be defined as more malleable. Other developments include Massively Multi-player Online Role-Playing Games (MMORPGs) and Serious Games – again largely played on single user desktop machines.

While desktop machines offer the benefits of sophisticated graphical interfaces and powerful computational resources, their affordances for face-to-face interaction in large groups are limited. In many learning contexts where human-human interaction is at the heart of a topic's complexity, for example, in management and political science, educators have instead relied on using paper-based interaction and board games. A limitation of such media is that they can consume large amounts of valuable class time and preparation/evaluation and has meant that many educators have refrained from using simulations in their courses [6].

An alternative approach that has recently been promoted is to provide interlinked technologies in co-located settings that support face-to-face collaborative learning. Roschelle et al. [13], for example, envision new forms of collaborative interaction taking place in the classroom that goes beyond the limitations of paper and desktops. Potential benefits of this form of real-time collaboration include rapid information sharing within the whole class of students and the teacher's ability to monitor and mediate interaction. To enable this, one idea is to provide students with a network of tablet computers. AlAgha [1], for example, recently proposed an extensive architecture for classroom collaboration based on multiple networked interactive tabletops. Another benefit of having a heterogeneous mix of devices is that they can provide Multiple Linked Representations (MLR) that can support peer collaboration as well as individual agency [11]. Moher [12] used tablet devices combined with low-tech ambient displays. His approach - Embedded Phenomena - supported long-term installations for scientific discovery learning in middle-school classrooms. A set of devices were shared by the students in a classroom and used as observation points to collaboratively collect data about simulated processes. The Embedded Phenomena approach aims to help groups of students become a community of authentic scientific practitioners.

Another approach that emphasizes role-playing as a key component is Participatory Simulations [2,16]. These allow learners to explore a model from the perspective of virtual elements within the simulation. Ubiquitous technologies have been used to immerse large, co-located groups of learners in shared, interactive computer simulations. While such embodied learning experiences with complex systems can be engaging and motivating, it has been suggested that Participatory Simulations may be best suited for illustrating the basic idea of a topic, rather than a detailed account [2]. Depending on the case, this may be enough to satisfy a particular goal, e.g. to trigger a discussion about a specific perspective on the topic, which may then feed into other forms of classroom instruction [14].

Scientific Discovery Learning [3] is the instructional paradigm which Embedded Phenomena inherit from Participatory Simulations. Learners are presented with predesigned models and predesigned ways of interacting with them or observing their autonomous progression over time. In the context of entertainment oriented simulations of urban planning and biology, Turkle [15] warns that certain ways of interacting with predefined simulations can result in superficial understanding or factually wrong conclusions about the topic, particularly when the underlying models are not revealed to learners. This call for transparency is in-line with Jonassen's [8] distinction between the black box approach typically taken in microworlds (which Participatory Simulations are a form of [2]) and the glass box approach where the underlying models are explicated and can potentially be modified by learners. Wilensky and Reisman [17] describe such a glass box approach to teaching biological phenomena through scientific modeling. Their approach allows individual students to reflect on emergent properties of complex systems (e.g. the dynamics of predator-prey populations) by manipulating models of local elements (e.g., the behavior of individual animals).

The goal of our research is to extend this approach by combining large-group role-play and malleable models, to enable groups to change and reflect upon aspects of the underlying model in relation to a shared experience of playing the simulation.

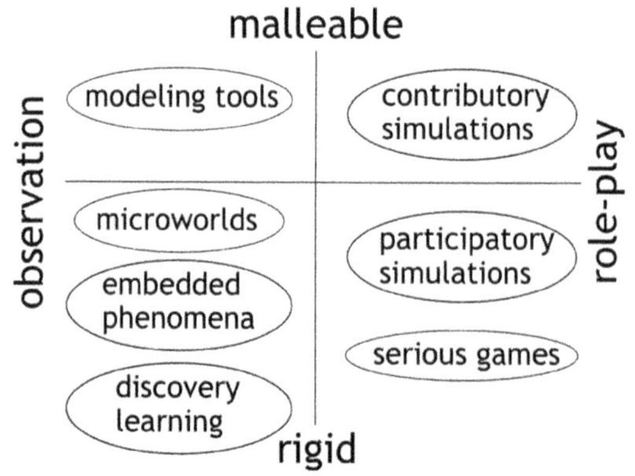

Figure 1: Related approaches to learning with simulations

METHOD

The aim of our research is to explore how interactive simulations, using ubiquitous technologies, can be designed to support collaborative learning in large-group professional training workshops. In particular, we are interested in enabling large groups of students who are immersed in professional training to put into practice what they are learning about a complex topic in lectures over an intensive period of 2–3 days. The objective is to enable them to think creatively and reflectively and to explicitly discuss with each other the rationale for making decisions to solve given problems in a domain.

Towards this goal, 4Decades was designed and evaluated in a series of management courses on sustainable business leadership. To begin, we developed a participatory simulation that would encourage role-playing. We describe the real-world setting before elaborating on the initial design. A second iteration extended the simulation to enable the students to interact and change the underlying model, itself. The idea behind this form of contributory simulation was to enable deeper exploration of the domain by allowing the participants to change the rules and dimensions underlying the model, which in turn, can have an impact on the consequences of their subsequent decisions. Participants can thus experience the domain from the perspective of decision-makers as well as from the perspective of scientists and modeling experts who influence decision-making directly or indirectly through their interpretations of the world.

Fitting in the real world

Professional training workshops often rely on a combination of formal lectures and active learning components, such as case studies or simulations. Because the topics are often complex and controversial in nature, group discussions are considered an integral means for participants to share their perspectives, reflect on their experiences and in so doing support collaborative learning. Discussions also allow the workshop facilitators to interact with the whole group in order to monitor learning and to moderate potential tensions and misunderstandings in the group. When simulations and games are integrated into training workshops, discussions are likely to arise within the context of collaborative playing. They can also be extended to take place outside of the simulation in debriefing sessions [5]. The benefit of having multiple levels of discussion throughout the training sessions is that it provides more opportunities for the students to step in and out and reflect on possible solutions, trade-offs and issues. Figure 2 illustrates how we proposed the simulation game being integrated with lectures and discussions and how the different stages contributed to each other. It is cyclical in nature, showing how subsequent cycles of the game and discussions can be augmented with ad-hoc lectures.

The setting

The 4Decades simulation was designed for deployment in a series of international executive training workshops on sustainable business leadership run by the University of Cambridge. The aim of these workshops is to bring together large groups (typically 25-30) of mid to high-level managers from different professional and cultural backgrounds in order to increase their practical understanding of sustainability leadership. The overarching goal is to enable participants to help their organizations achieve better ways of addressing global problems. Lectures, case studies and simulations have been designed to provide applicable knowledge and foster collaborative leadership skills. Much emphasis is placed on illustrating the interrelation between local policy making and complex global problems, such as climate change.

Climate politics are of direct relevance to the agendas of the participants on the course. As a result of the instructional design being constantly evaluated and refined, the workshop organizers have learned to value the integration of active learning experiences that allow participants to put into practice some of the theoretical knowledge learned in class. Previous deployments of off-the-shelf paper-based simulations and board games had not been satisfactory for these workshops, due to lack of scientific accuracy and/or excessive time cost. The workshop organizers value computer simulations in principle for their power to let participants rapidly explore scientific models that are relevant to their courses. However, they hesitated to deploy off-the-shelf desktop packages, arguing that the single-user orientation and lack of the affordances for face-to-face communication conflicted with the goal of their workshop – which is to provide socially rich, co-located activities for collaborative learning. They asked us to develop a custom-built experience that could support co-located groups of participants learning together and solving problems that were more related to their course material. To this end, we decided to develop a simulation that could run on inter-connected tablets that pairs or small groups could interact with together and use to spark multiple discussions.

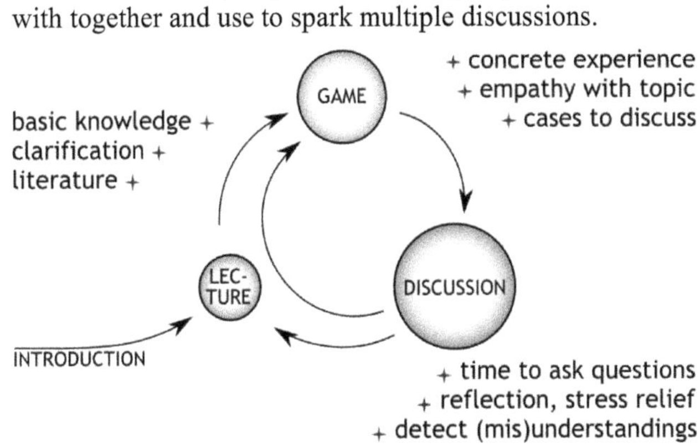

Figure 2: Our proposed pedagogical approach where lectures provide the fundamental knowledge required to play the game

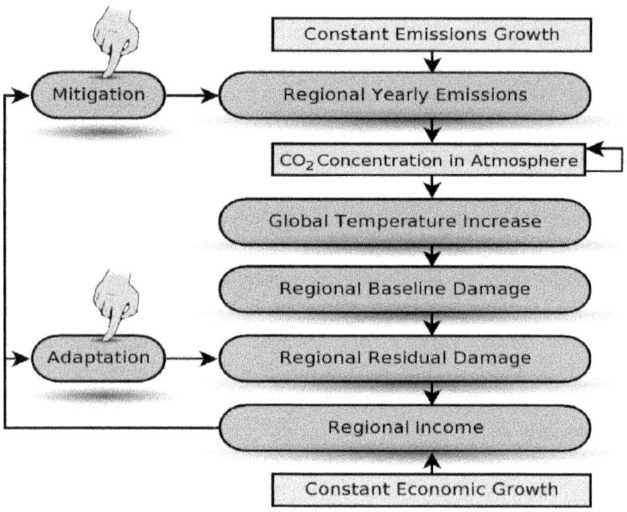

Figure 3: Flow diagram of the economic model. The rounded boxes are variables that users can see.

Figure 4: Room layout in version 1 (left) and version 2 (right). Each team shares 4 tablets on a large table and an ambient display. In version 2 there is an additional ambient display.

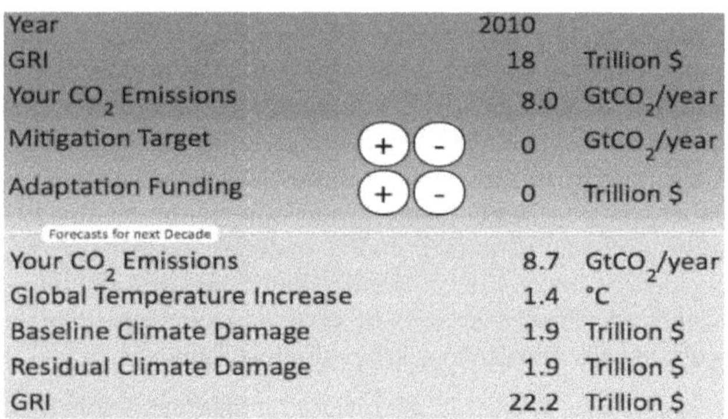

Figure 5: User interface on each tablet. Information is clearly structured in rows and columns. The lower half shows a forecast to the next round. Four large buttons in the center.

Mitigation				Adaptation				Emissions				°C	Baseline Damage			
3	4	4	2	1	1	1	1	6.2	5.2	5.2	7.2	1.1	1.4	1.1	1.1	1.5
3	3	4	3	2	1	1	2	4.5	3.5	2.5	5.5	1.8	2.9	2.3	1.9	3.2
1	2	3	2	3	2	2	3	4.7	2.7	0.7	4.7	2.4	5.0	4.0	2.9	5.4
1	0	1	1	3	1	2	3	5.0	4.0	1.0	5.0	3.0	8.0	6.4	4.7	8.7

Mitigation				Adaptation				Emissions				°C	Baseline Damage			
5	5	5	5	0	0	0	0	4.2	4.2	4.2	4.2	0.9	0.5	0.5	0.5	0.5
4	4	4	4	0	0	0	0	1.5	1.5	1.5	1.5	1.3	0.5	0.5	0.5	0.5
3	3	3	3	0	0	0	0	-0.2	-0.2	-0.2	-0.2	1.4	0.6	0.6	0.6	0.6
4	4	4	4	0	0	0	0	-3.0	-3.0	-3.0	-3.0	1.1	0.2	0.2	0.2	0.2

Figure 6: Section of a team's ambient display after 2 matches. Each row represents a round. The full image would show two more columns for residual damage and income to the right.

The scientific model

A number of meetings with the organizers were carried out to understand fully the topic of climate change and the problem-solving activities planned for the participants. Our aim, in agreement with the organizers, was to create a socially engaging activity that would enable the participants to play with a scientific or economic model. The activity was expected to address a number of learning goals: to give participants concrete experience with concepts and numbers that are central to the workshop curriculum; to highlight some of the challenges surrounding decision-making under complexity and uncertainty and to provoke a critical discussion about the simulated topic. It was agreed that the simulation should challenge participants to address the question: *What will be the cost of anthropogenic climate change and how should policy makers balance investments between greenhouse gas mitigation, adaptation to climate change and residual repairs within the next 40 years?* The topic was chosen because of its key relevance to both the workshop curriculum as well as participants' professional situations as policy makers in international organizations. A simple economic model (see Figure 3) was designed, intended to enable participants, in the role of governments, to control spendings in terms of CO_2 mitigation and adaptation to global climate change effects. On the one hand, both mitigation and adaptation cost money. On the other hand, both have the potential to save (more) money indirectly by reducing climate-related damage in different ways. Balancing investments over repeated cycles (decades) becomes a challenge when the goal is to maximize income. By providing participants with multiple copies of this model – which were termed *regions*, in order to avoid comparison with real countries – and linking the regions with a shared global temperature, the climate-economic situation of several governments on one planet is approximated. The model was set so that mitigation spending benefits the whole planet, whereas adaptation spending only benefits a single region that spends the money. This set of rules gives rise to a socially complex 'tragedy of the commons' situation that it was hoped would encourage collaboration within teams.

In order to ensure equitable playing conditions within teams, all regions were defined as being equal in size. The facts and numbers used in the model were based on a collation of recent economic and scientific literature, complemented with approximations where necessary. A more in-depth description of the design rationale can be found in [10].

In order to structure the task of exploring the model, it was decided that two teams would play, each controlling a separate planet (or alternative realities of the same planet). A game was devised of four rounds in which each region decides on their mitigation and adaptation spending. Each team tries to achieve the highest income for their planet after four rounds of the game, proceeding in decades from 2010.

The collaborative simulation interface

It was decided that the interface should be simple and immediately accessible by all participants. This was in part, because there was little time to train the students to learn a new system as the workshops were run on a tight schedule. To begin, we considered using multi-touch tabletops to support interaction with the simulation. However, a limitation of tabletops is they can only support small group sizes (5–6). This would have required several such surfaces to be placed in a room in order to involve the whole group of 30 participants. The cost and logistics of this possible design was a major obstacle. Moreover, multiple tabletops would have fragmented the class into small groups working with little awareness of the others, whereas our goal was to have two large teams competing with one another, being aware of how each other was faring.

Our solution was to use a network of eight shareable tablet devices that supported the same simulation in real time, four for each team. Figure 4 shows the eight tablet devices distributed on two large square tables, with each table representing one of two competing planets and the four tablets per table representing the *regions* on the planets. To show the record of each team's previous decisions and outcomes, a large shared ambient display was assigned to each team. The results of each round were updated after each round. The data displayed was designed to enable the two teams to reflect on their decision-making; to infer how the model worked and to draw conclusions about improving their collaboration and performance in the game while seeing what the other team had chosen to do.

Constraining interfaces to encourage collaboration

A number of constraints on awareness, control and the availability of information [18] were used with the goal of increasing collaboration. These decisions mainly concerned the user interfaces on the individual tablets and the way the network of tablets was controlled. As Figure 5 shows, the user interface on each tablet was designed to be simple. Only few variables are displayed. Moreover, only two variables can be controlled directly. Four large buttons allow participants to increase and decrease values for mitigation and adaptation spending in coarse steps (only whole numbers). In response to a participant pressing a button, the lower half of the screen shows a forecast of what the region's state would be in the next game round if the chosen values were kept.

The forecast was placed below the four manipulation buttons, so that participants could see the values change directly. The rationale was that this would incentivize them to remove their hands immediately after touching it, thus freeing the screen for other collaborators to use. A deliberate delay of one second was imposed on the responsiveness of the buttons, in order to slow down the exploration process, such that other participants could follow the changes more easily. While the forecast allows participants to quickly try out possible investment decisions and evaluate predicted outcomes, its scope was deliberately limited to one local region (as opposed to the whole team/planet) and only one round of the game. Acting strategically on a global and/or long-term level, therefore, requires participants to collaborate on a larger scale. For example, it was expected that participants would be encouraged to coordinate their strategic ideas with other team members across the table or to use the team's shared ambient display.

Additional constraints on interaction were imposed through external control of the networked tablets. In particular, the facilitator controlled the timing of the game rounds. Between game rounds, the tablets turned into a non-interactive state, to make it easier for the facilitator to draw attention to salient aspects or to moderate discussions.

STUDY 1: PARTICIPATORY SIMULATION

A series of lab tests were run with small groups of participants to ensure the simulation was robust, understandable, challenging and engaging. Feedback was received on the usability of the technological set-up and the game mechanics. The first deployment of 4Decades was during a four-day workshop at a conference center. In order to provide an opportunity for participants to put into practice the theoretical knowledge from the first two days, a hands-on session was scheduled at the end of day two after a series of lectures on climate science and economics. A session was scheduled to last for 90 minutes, comprising a brief introduction to the simulation, four matches of playing the game and a final debriefing discussion.

In order to allow enough time for setting up the technology on site, the session took place in a separate meeting room which was not used for other activities. Participants were initially handed badges indicating the team they belonged to. As they entered the room, the facilitator showed each team their table, asking half the participants to sit in pairs at the tablets and the other half to gather around the table. It was explained that the roles within the team would be swapped after each of the four matches. The facilitator further explained what the tables and tablets represented, the objective of the game and the numbers and buttons on the interface. Five minutes later the group was ready to play a brief practice match during which the facilitator explained how the elements on a team's ambient displays showed their decisions on the left, the outcomes of the decisions further right, and how after every round of decision making one row of data was added to the display as a record. The facilitator also encouraged participants to help themselves to the prepared pens and blank paper sheets and some printed tables of mitigation cost and adaptation efficiency. Since all the technical terms used in the simulation had been covered in prior lectures, participants were ready to play without any further introduction to the topic. The game lasted for 55 minutes and the subsequent debriefing discussion was concluded after 10 minutes when nobody had any further comments.

Figure 7: Sharing tablets in pairs. Partners tended to keep their hands close to the devices, always ready to point and press buttons.

The aim of the first trial was to investigate how participants used the tablets and ambient displays, and how engaging and useful they found the activity. We were also interested in whether the game would trigger a critical discussion based on an understanding of the model and reflection on what was taught in the prior lectures.

Evaluation

Since this was the first deployment of the prototype in the wild, an exploratory approach to evaluation was taken with the aim of collecting a wide range of potentially relevant data while also keeping the observation as unobtrusive as possible. A questionnaire was provided by the workshop organizers at the end of the session. An additional web survey was sent to participants after a delay of several months to elicit long lasting impressions.

Field notes were also taken by two researchers in the room, video was captured from all 4 corners of the room and a small microphone on each table was used to capture audio. Screen shots of the ambient displays were used to analyze team strategies.

Use of devices and displays

Our observations of the teams revealed that as soon as the facilitator initiated the first round, all eyes were on the tablet devices. Seated pairs were immediately engrossed in pressing the buttons and watching the numbers change, thinking aloud together while exploring the interface. Standing participants watched the tablets over their team-mates' shoulders. It appeared that the tablet interfaces were immediately accessible and understood by participants. Sharing the tablets worked seamlessly as tablets were kept centered between pairs and participants naturally drew their hands back after pressing buttons, thus effectively releasing control and freeing the screen for others to peek in (Figure 7). Standing participants seemed to benefit from this affordance as they often used their mobility to peek into several tablets to assist collaboration from more of a bird's eye view. Standing participants were also engaged in dialogue with pairs. They contributed mostly in verbal form, e.g. suggesting theories and strategies, directing attention to other regions or data on the ambient displays, but rarely touching the tablets directly. No difficulties regarding the usability of the tablets and ambient displays were observed or mentioned in the debriefing discussion. Swapping roles between sitting and standing participants after each match allowed every participant to use the tablet interface.

After each round, the decisions of each region and the respective outcomes were added to the shared record on each team's ambient display as an additional row (see Figure 6) and thereafter, many participants were eager to see their team's results following each round, appearing on the screen. Comparing a team's results immediately with the other team's results was the main use of the ambient displays in the early matches. As new data was added to the tables on the ambient displays, the participants became quicker at knowing what to look for, helping them to reflect more readily on the aggregate data and theorize about their implications. Increasing numbers of participants spent time focused on their own team's or the other team's scores, discussing ideas in small sub-groups or pairs. Some of these discussions happened as independent threads outside the main action at the tables. The ambient displays were further used in the debriefing discussion to recall significant moments and support arguments with concrete data. For example, figure 6 shows that the team found consensus on a strategy for match 2, whereas in match 1 different regions had entered different values.

Over the course of the four matches, the extent of collaboration could be seen to gradually increase from controlling the simulation via tablets in pairs, to sub-team tactics, to team strategies and whole-classroom exchange of information. In the first matches, most of the talking occurred between pairs sitting by the tablets, changing the values on the screen, while the others were either watching intently or talking to their closest neighbors. Decisions in the game were made on a local basis without consulting the whole team. Later matches were characterized by efforts to establish a shared awareness of the whole team's situation and a team-wide strategy, as groups realized that local decisions affected the state of the simulation for the whole team. Increasingly, seated participants made eye contact and verbal contact with other seated participants across the table and standing participants started walking between regions, comparing values between devices, making suggestions and engaging in clarifications and arguments.

Minor clarifications were handled in a lightweight fashion among peers, thus allowing the facilitator to stay in the background, casually observing the whole-room interaction and the data on the ambient displays. At the end of each round, when the tablets switched to a non-interactive state and the data was updated on both teams' ambient displays, the overall attention of the teams shifted noticeably from the tables to the whole room. Sometimes the facilitator would use these breaks between the rounds as opportunities to get the attention of the whole class, e.g. to provide additional information, without interrupting the flow of the game.

Participant satisfaction

Participants were engrossed in the activity from the beginning of the game and stayed engaged throughout the 90 minutes session. The whole session was rated on a Likert scale, from 1 to 5, with an average score of 4.1, which is close to the whole course's average rating of 4.23. Out of 20 responses nobody gave the lowest score of 1. Another indication of its success, was receiving several invitations from delegates to deploy 4Decades in their organizations and the workshop organizers asking us to deploy the simulation again in their next workshop.

Supporting reflection and critical discussion

When reflecting on their strategies during the debriefing discussion, participants related their game experience to the roles of real-world policy makers, emphasizing the value of whole-team communication. Two participants from different teams summarized their team's collaboration:

"There was a lot of really good collaborative policy making going on, probably on both teams. Especially after the first [match] everybody started to kind of communicate across the table. And that fairly rapidly got us towards [winning]"

"You think you've made an agreement and then [...] a region changes their opinion [...] you put that to the global level, and you see exactly how that, that same psychology plays out but far worse, with far bigger stakes."

A surprising observation was that, despite the fact that the winning condition was explicitly as 'the planet with the highest global income by 2050', there was an internal dispute in both teams regarding whether income or stabilizing global temperature should be prioritized:

"The money was a driver, but... I think we didn't... erm... we certainly could have made a lot of our decisions based on trying to keep the temperature down."

In the debriefing discussion many nodded in agreement with a participant contrasting the amount of feedback from the simulation with expectations based on prior lectures:

"We were slightly surprised that a bit more spending on mitigation in the early decades didn't deliver a better result [than an adaptation-focused strategy], which is what you'd have thought from what we were hearing and discussing today."

Despite critical discussions about the discrepancy between expected and produced output values, participants' efforts to attribute this discrepancy to specific aspects of the model were rare and imprecise. Instead, it appeared more likely that they perceived the game as a *black box* that delivered certain outputs based on certain inputs and unknown transfer characteristics which were not intended to be known or criticized. This conjecture can be seen as supported by participants' frequent use of words such as 'reward', 'punishment' or 'penalty' when referring to feedback from the game.

In order to address the critical comments made by the participants about the limitations of the underlying model we decided to refine the model and make it possible for the participants to be able to change the underlying rules. These were the mitigation cost function, the function for adaptation efficiency and the winning condition. Our overall aim was to find effective ways of enabling the teams to engage in meaningful design decisions. Given that the interface, the configuration of networked tablets and ambient displays was found to be very usable and highly engaging we chose not to change these.

DESIGN ITERATION

In order to make the model and its underlying assumptions more transparent to participants, it was decided to give groups the ability to be more involved in the design of the simulation. In particular, we looked for ways to enable the groups to create variations of the original simulation that they could immediately evaluate through play.

Our starting point was a thematic analysis of the participants' discussions and comments, which resulted in two aspects that were found most controversial: first, the question of what it means to 'win' the challenge of climate change; and, second, the payoffs of mitigation and adaptation investments. These two aspects were found to also be controversial in the domain literature, as they touch on many scientific unknowns, speculations about future technology and socio-political disputes [7]. Our approach was to offer a range of choices (in addition to the assumptions that we had provided in the first version) to account for more optimistic as well as more pessimistic views represented in the mainstream climate literature.

To address the needs of different winning conditions, we decided to let participants choose between any of the five existing variables in the model that were considered potentially meaningful: income, emissions, baseline damage and residual damage. Further options were whether to play for high or low values and whether winning should be per planet or per region.

The payoffs in our model depend mainly on two functions: the cost of mitigation and the efficiency of adaptation. We therefore decided to let participants change these functions.

Figure 8: One team temporarily gathers around a single tablet to choose the model parameters and winning condition for the next match, while the other team is engaged in discussion.

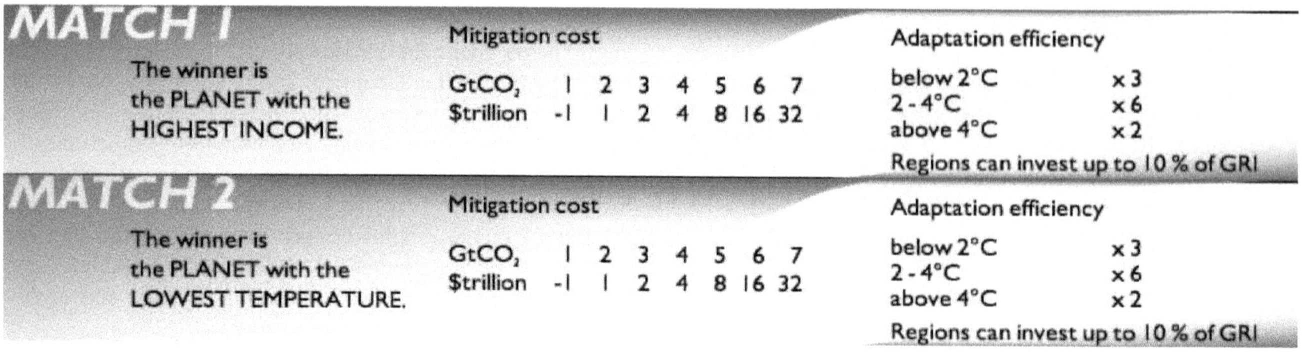

Figure 9: Screenshot of the ambient display for the game settings. This view represents what players saw at the end of match 2.

Since the game was structured in short matches, several of which could be played in one session, there was scope for groups to create and test about 4 different variations to the game. We chose to enforce turn-taking between teams for creating variations before each match, such that one team sets the rules for matches 1 and 3 and the other team for matches 2 and 4. The chosen solution involved a series of multiple-choice menus on one single tablet per team (see figure 10).

Since participants could not be expected to memorize all the game settings of all the current and previous matches, a third ambient display was added (figure 9). This enabled a record of their changes to be referenced by the teams. The room layout was changed to a symmetrical arrangement of displays to make space for the third display while ensuring equal conditions for both teams (right half of figure 4).

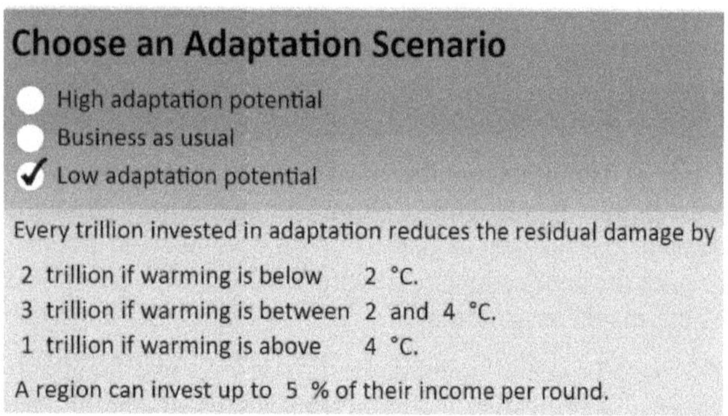

Figure 10: The group can choose between 3 different scenarios reflecting different beliefs about adaptation. Similar multiple-choice menus exist for mitigation and the winning condition.

STUDY 2: CONTRIBUTORY SIMULATION

Version 2 of the simulation was deployed in another workshop, similar to the workshop in which version 1 of 4Decades had been deployed. However, the conditions differed in a number of ways. First, participants did not have prior lectures on the topic. Intrigued by the buzz and social atmosphere witnessed in the first workshop using 4Decades, the organizers insisted on scheduling the game as an ice-breaker right at the beginning of the 7-day workshop. To compensate for the lack of prior lectures, the facilitator explained the basic concepts of the topic in a condensed 20-minute micro-lecture prior to introducing the game. To accommodate the lecture and the newly added features, a longer time slot of two hours was scheduled and chairs were provided for all 26 participants. A 15 minute debriefing discussion was also included.

Evaluation

The same data collection methods were used as in study 1, except that the web-based survey was replaced by a paper-based questionnaire for participants to complete in stages after each match, in order to account for their individual, immediate reactions to aspects of the activity. Likert scales and open questions were designed to give insight into usability and learner satisfaction, with an emphasis on the newly added features.

Use of devices and displays

Similar to study 1, the group was immediately engrossed in sharing the tablets and the use of the ambient displays. Talk across the table increased in the later matches. Again, no usability problems were observed or reported regarding the new ambient display or the tablets. Figure 8 shows a team gathered around one single tablet for the purpose of editing the game settings, while the other team were using the break for a discussion. The figure also shows how teams had turned their devices towards the corners of the table, in order to share the devices in a circular layout, with chairs around the table. This orientation was found in both teams. No explicit pairing of participants around the tablets was suggested by the facilitator. Nevertheless, tablets were shared equitably in a seamless way. It appeared that the groups paid more attention to the content on the screens, rather than the physical devices. Small changes to the seating occurred occasionally, as some participants walked around the table for over-the-shoulder interaction with other regions.

Figure 9 shows different winning conditions and mitigation/adaptation scenarios chosen by the participants for the first 2 matches. When deciding about the winning condition for match 3, the team asked the facilitator's permission to create a winning condition that was more complex than the options provided by the multiple-choice menu. In particular, the team wished to play for 'highest income per planet' with the addition that a team loses immediately if their global temperature rises above 3 degrees. The suggestion was accepted and so the group continued to play with multiple winning conditions.

While teams decided on game settings for the next match, they were often hunched over a single tablet (figure 8), discussing as a whole team. During these discussions participants pondered and clarified concepts, reflecting on earlier settings and strategies and compared the settings with regard to their implications for game strategies. The following excerpt (before match 4) illustrates this:

A: In this [optimistic mitigation] setting we'll break even at the second gigatonne.
B: So that means we can afford a lot more mitigation.
Several: Yeah / That's right / Exactly / Yes we can.
C: Let's go for that one.

Supporting reflection and critical discussion

Similar to study 1, there was much discussion about the relation between inputs and outputs of the simulation. These observations were discussed in the context of specific assumptions that went into the various user-created versions of the simulation. The discussion about winning conditions was concluded with the argument that real-world governments were currently playing a 'one condition game', while they should be playing a 'two condition game'. Several participants suggested that future versions of the simulation should allow the definition of multiple winning conditions as a standard feature.

Several participants indicated that they perceived the session as too rushed and would have preferred fewer matches in exchange for more time to discuss during and between rounds. It was argued that conversations in the team provided important opportunities for peer teaching. Analysis of conversations during game-play showed that much time was spent clarifying domain knowledge which the audience of study 1 had already brought into the game.

Participant satisfaction

Nearly all the participants thought the simulation was very worthwhile. The organizers' wish that the game serve as an icebreaker to help people get to know each other was supported by the ratings. Only 1 out of 26 participants agreed with the questionnaire statement "I would have preferred a 90 minute lecture on the topic instead of the game". 2 somewhat agreed, 2 answered neutral, 9 somewhat disagreed and 12 disagreed. Participants further found that the game provoked a useful discussion about the topic. In the debriefing discussion, it was made explicit that many players would have liked more time for reflection and discussion between the matches. The group almost unanimously agreed that changing the winning condition added an interesting perspective to the game. Further deployments of 4Decades were requested by the organizers.

DISCUSSION

Our findings show how both participatory and contributory simulations can engage large co-located groups in collaborative interactions resulting in much discussion about complex global challenges. In particular, the use of Multiple Linked Representations, presented via ambient displays, can support large group collaboration at multiple levels, enabling teams to have a shared reference of theirs and each other's solutions and ideas. The constrained combination of being able to easily manipulate rules and vary core dimensions of the simulation was found to support a high level of distributed team working. Groups were able to understand the complex system from both a local and global perspective, through having multiple conversations, observations and interactions that took place at and between the tables, tablets and ambient displays.

Adding the functionality of changing the rules in the contributory simulation between rounds also enabled the teams to gain a better understanding of the underlying mathematical model and to see how they connected with the visible dimensions at the user interface. In particular, it enabled them to hypothesize together and contest what-if scenarios of future decades, in terms of climate policies and also in terms of how the planet responds to those policies.

Perhaps, the most striking finding is that collaboration increased over the course of several matches, from operating the tablets in pairs, via sub-team tactics, to team strategies and whole-classroom exchange of information. This development was observed in both sessions and indicates that the ecology of devices supported collaboration at multiple levels.

The provision of very simple constrained interfaces on the tablets meant it was easy for the groups to swap roles from being the drivers of the game, changing the variables for a given planet, to taking a more global role, observing what other members of their and the other teams were doing. Those standing at the tables were also able to relay to each other what the current thinking was and to suggest agreed strategies for subsequent rounds. The fact that no one mentioned problems with the interface or how to use the system suggested that it was for the large part transparent, enabling them to focus on their interactions with each other.

Future iterations of 4Decades could increase the scope of how participants are able to interact with the simulation, for example, entering arbitrary numbers, float numbers, text or visual programming. This would allow the exploration of more sophisticated modeling tasks but the potential downside is that the participants may focus more on the simulation and less on discussing their strategies, trade-offs and solutions, with each other.

In sum, key design features that contributed to the success of using the contributory simulation include:

• the transparent interface and distributed system of displays not requiring prior learning or knowledge.

• the constraints of the tablet interface (only giving local, short-term information and control), so participants needed to collaborate beyond the tablets in order to effect strategies on a global and long-term level.

• the gradual increase of real-time data on the team-shared ambient displays (availability of information).

• no absolute winning condition, but criteria that require teams to compare, interpret and discuss each other's results.

This suggests that this type of interactive simulation could be generalized to other learning settings for complex challenges and global problems, such as pandemics, waste, water and energy.

CONCLUSIONS AND FUTURE WORK

This paper introduced the notion of Contributory Simulations based on the iterative design and in-the-wild evaluation of 4Decades. Our findings show that Contributory Simulations using a distributed ecology of devices and displays can be a powerful way of putting the material learnt in lectures into the hands of the participants, enabling much excited and engaged discussion to ensue. Importantly, using tight constraints on awareness, control and availability of information was seen to engender beneficial aspects of collaboration. In particular, collaboration increased over time from the local to the global. To investigate the generalizability of our observations, we are planning to conduct a series of follow-up studies with Contributory Simulations for a range of audiences, covering a variety of topics. These studies will further explore different designs for allowing large co-located groups to make quantitative and structural changes to computational models.

ACKNOWLEDGMENTS

This research was funded by The Open University, UK. We would like to thank Vaiva Kalnikaitė for taking field notes and Jörn Ketelsen for help with some of the programming.

REFERENCES

1. AlAgha, I., Hatch, A., Ma, L., and Burd, L. Towards a teacher-centric approach for multi-touch surfaces in classrooms. *Proc of ITS Tabletop*, ACM (2010).

2. Colella, V. Participatory simulations: Building collaborative understanding through immersive dynamic modeling. *The Journal of the Learning Sciences* 9, 4 (2000), pp. 471–500.

3. De Jong, T., and Van Joolingen, W. Scientific discovery learning with computer simulations of conceptual domains. *Review of educational research* 68, 2 (1998).

4. DiSessa, A. *On "Learnable" Representations of Knowledge: A Meaning for the Computational Metaphor.* Massachusetts Institute of Technology, A. I. Laboratory, 1977.

5. Fanning, R., and Gaba, D. The role of debriefing in simulation-based learning. *Simulation in Healthcare* 2, 2 (2007), 115.

6. Faria, A., and Wellington, W. A survey of simulation game users, former-users, and never-users. *Simulation & Gaming* 35, 2 (2004), 178.

7. Hulme, M. *Why we disagree about climate change : understanding controversy, inaction and opportunity.* Cambridge University Press, Cambridge, 2009.

8. Jonassen, D., and Strobel, J. Modeling for meaningful learning. *Engaged learning with emerging technologies* (2006), 1–27.

9. Klopfer, E., Roque, R., Huang, W., Wendel, D., and Scheintaub, H. The simulation cycle: Combining games, simulations, engineering and science using StarLogo TNG. *E-Learning and Digital Media, E-Learning and Digital Media*, Vol.6, No. 1, pp. 71–96

10. Kreitmayer, S., Peake, S., Laney, R., and Rogers, Y. Designing a large multi-player simulation game to encourage reflection and critical debate. *Proc. of ECGBL '10* (2011).

11. Lyons, L., Lee, J., Quintana, C., and Soloway, E. Preliminary evaluation of a synchronous co-located educational simulation framework. *Proc. of CHI '06*, ACM (2006).

12. Moher, T. Embedded phenomena: supporting science learning with classroom-sized distributed simulations. *Proc. of CHI '06*, ACM (2006), 691–700.

13. Roschelle, J., Tatar, D., Chaudbury, S., Dimitriadis, Y., Patton, C., and DiGiano, C. Ink, improvisation, and interactive engagement: Learning with tablets. *Computer* 40, 9 (2007), 42–48.

14. Stroup, W., Ares, N., Hurford, A., and Lesh, R. Diversity-by-design: The what, why, and how of generativity in next-generation classroom networks. *Foundations for the future in mathematics education* 367 (2007).

15. Turkle, S. From powerful ideas to powerpoint. Convergence: *The International Journal of Research into New Media Technologies* 9, 2 (2003).

16. Wilensky, U., and Stroup, W. Learning through participatory simulations: network-based design for systems learning in classrooms. *Proc. CSCL '99,* ISLS (1999).

17. Wilensky, U. and Reisman, K. Thinking like a wolf, a sheep, or a firefly: Learning biology through onstructing and testing computational theories - an embodied modeling approach. *Cognition and Instruction*, 2006

18. Yuill, N., and Rogers, Y. Mechanisms for collaboration: A design and evaluation framework for multi-user interfaces. To appear in *TOCHI*, ACM (2012).

The Impact of Tutorials on Games of Varying Complexity

Erik Andersen, Eleanor O'Rourke, Yun-En Liu, Richard Snider, Jeff Lowdermilk, David Truong, Seth Cooper, and Zoran Popović
Center for Game Science
Department of Computer Science & Engineering, University of Washington
{eland,eorourke,yunliu,mrsoviet,jeff,djtruong,scooper,zoran}@cs.washington.edu

ABSTRACT
One of the key challenges of video game design is teaching new players how to play. Although game developers frequently use tutorials to teach game mechanics, little is known about how tutorials affect game learnability and player engagement. Seeking to estimate this value, we implemented eight tutorial designs in three video games of varying complexity and evaluated their effects on player engagement and retention. The results of our multivariate study of over 45,000 players show that the usefulness of tutorials depends greatly on game complexity. Although tutorials increased play time by as much as 29% in the most complex game, they did not significantly improve player engagement in the two simpler games. Our results suggest that investment in tutorials may not be justified for games with mechanics that can be discovered through experimentation.

Author Keywords
games; analytics; tutorials; multivariate testing

ACM Classification Keywords
H.5.0 Information interfaces and presentation: General

INTRODUCTION
Teaching new players how to play a game is challenging but crucial for engaging and retaining players. As a result, game designers frequently utilize tutorials to aid the learning process. Since tutorials are typically the first part of a game that new players encounter, effective tutorial design is important for retaining new players. Although modern games employ a wide varety of tutorial styles, including hints, help buttons, manuals, and interactive training challenges, the relative effectiveness of these styles is not well understood. As a result, designers must rely on intuition, personal experience, existing examples, and extensive user testing when designing tutorials. A deeper understanding of how tutorial design decisions impact player engagement and retention would help game developers create more learnable interfaces and spend valuable resources more wisely.

CHI'12, May 5–10, 2012, Austin, Texas, USA.

Learnability is widely accepted as a central component of usability, and it has been studied in the field of Human Computer Interaction for decades [11, 20, 23]. In this paper, we draw tutorial ideas from the HCI literature and present a large-scale comparative study of their effectiveness in video game tutorials. Although many factors influence tutorial design, we chose to focus on four specific tutorial characteristics: the presence of tutorials, the context-sensitivity of tutorial instructions, the freedom given to users during the tutorial, and the availability of additional help on demand. We examined the importance of these characteristics by conducting a multivariate experiment across three games that we developed: Refraction, Hello Worlds, and Foldit. These games belong to different genres and vary in complexity.

We present results gathered from over 45,000 players showing that the value of tutorials depends greatly on the complexity of the game. In Foldit, the most complex and least conventional game we studied, tutorials increased play time by as much as 29% and player progress by as much as 75%. However, we found that tutorials had a surprisingly negligible effect on player engagement in Hello Worlds and Refraction, which are less complex and more similar to other games in their respective genres. Giving tutorial instructions as closely as possible to when they were needed, rather than out of context in an up-front manual, increased play time by 16% and progress by 40% in Foldit but had no effect in the other two games. We found no evidence to support the claim that restricting player freedom in order to focus the player's attention on a target concept improves learnability. Providing help on-demand improved player engagement in Foldit, but had no effect in Hello Worlds and even negative effects in Refraction. Our results suggest that investment in tutorials may not be justified for games that can be learned through experimentation, and that the players of these games, at least, seem to learn more from experimentation than from reading text.

Tutorial presence
The first feature we considered was tutorial *presence*: whether the game provides a tutorial to its players or not. Although some successful games provide no instructions to players, such as Tetris (Pajitnov 1984), Pac-Man (Namco 1980), and Super Mario Brothers (Nintendo 1985), the use of tutorials has become very common. Therefore, we wanted to examine the impact of tutorial presence.

Hypothesis 1: *Games with tutorials will exhibit better player engagement and retention than games without tutorials.*

We examined this hypothesis by comparing versions of each game with and without tutorials.

Context-sensitivity

Another feature we considered was the *context-sensitivity* of tutorials. Existing tutorials can be divided into two categories: those that provide contextually relevant suggestions from within the application interface and those that provide documentation outside of the application context. HCI researchers have studied both types of tutorials extensively; however, the effect of context-sensitivity on tutorial success is unclear, and the existing literature does not show a clear preference for either type of information.

Historically, tutorials have been provided through primarily textual documentation that is accessed outside the application context. While paper manuals and online documentation require minimal resources to generate, they present a number of challenges for users, who struggle to keep track of instructions when switching between the tutorial and the application [1, 15, 17]. As a result, many researchers have worked on improving external software documentation by incorporating screenshots, graphics, animations, and annotations into textual content [9, 12, 13, 21].

Despite these improvements, many researchers argue that contextually relevant tutorials have greater potential for improving application learnability [4, 14, 10]. This idea is supported by situated learning, a popular learning model in education based around teaching concepts in the same context in which they will be applied [18]. Game expert James Gee also highlights the importance of teaching new mechanics just before the player needs to use them, rather than presenting them out of context [7]. Tooltips, which provide brief textual help when the user hovers over an interface component, are one of the most successful forms of contextual help [6]. On the other hand, context-sensitive help can be more frustrating than helpful, as shown by Microsoft's Office Assistant [24].

Commercial video games have used both context-sensitive and context-insensitive tutorials successfully. Up-front manuals, which present game mechanics out-of-context at the very beginning of a game, can be seen in the popular online Flash games Cursed Treasure[1] and Epic Battle Fantasy 3[2]. Other games present instructions in-context, just as the player needs to use them. This strategy can be seen in the highly-rated Flash game In the Company of Myself[3] and the popular console game Portal (Valve Corporation). To learn more about the value of context-sensitivity in game tutorials, we included both styles of presentation.

Hypothesis 2: *Tutorials that present instructions in context will be more effective than tutorials that present information out of context.*

In this study, we compare tutorials that present information out of context in an up-front manual and tutorials that present information in context just before the player needs to use a particular concept.

Freedom

We also considered tutorial *freedom*, or the degree to which tutorials force users to perform the mechanics being described. While requiring users to practice specific game mechanics could improve tutorial effectiveness, it could also frustrate players. As a result, it is not clear if and when reducing player freedom improves engagement.

Game designers have often cited the importance of allowing users to experiment while learning new concepts [7, 22]. James Gee argues that such experimentation is most effective when it occurs in a safe environment where functionality is reduced and mistakes are not punished [7]. Software learnability researchers Kelleher and Pausch argue that restricting user freedom improves tutorial performance. They found that an interactive tutorial for the Alice computer programming environment that restricts user freedom, called Stencils, helped users finish the tutorial sequence more quickly and with fewer errors than a paper-based tutorial with the same content [14]. How different types of interfaces are affected by reduced player freedom, however, is currently unknown.

Many video games provide players with complete freedom during the tutorial. Braid (Number None 2008), for instance, provides the player with background suggestions for keys to press during gameplay, but does not force the player to perform the suggested action. At the same time, the use of more restrictive stenciling strategies is also popular, and can be found in PopCap's tower defense game Plants vs. Zombies (PopCap 2009), the simulation game SimCity 4 (Maxis 2003), and Facebook game Cityville (Zynga 2010). We included tutorials of both types in order to determine the value of restricting player freedom.

Hypothesis 3: *Tutorials that restrict player freedom improve engagement and retention.*

In this study, we compare tutorials that restrict player freedom using the stenciling technique proposed by Kelleher and Pausch [14] and those that give players complete freedom to ignore the tutorial content.

Availability of help

Finally, we considered the *availability of help*. Many applications provide access to documentation on-demand through help buttons, but it is unclear whether this type of information has a strong effect on interface learnability. Although it seems likely that providing access to on-demand help would positively impact learnability, it is not known how much users take advantage of on-demand information when it is available.

James Gee argues that manuals are most effective when they are accessed on-demand, after the user has become familiar with the basic interface elements and has developed specific questions [7]. Commercial software applications rely heavily on the availability of on-demand documentation, and help

[1] `http://www.kongregate.com/games/IriySoft/cursed-treasure-dont-touch-my-gems`
[2] `http://www.kongregate.com/games/kupo707/epic-battle-fantasy-3`
[3] `http://www.kongregate.com/games/2DArray/the-company-of-myself`

buttons can be found in many ubiquitous products such as Microsoft Word (Microsoft Inc. 2010) and iTunes (Apple Inc. 2001). On-demand tutorials are also common in games. For example, help buttons are available in the Flash game Epic Battle Fantasy 3 and the real time strategy game Starcraft 2 (Blizzard 2010). To determine the impact of on-demand help in games, we included tutorials with and without this feature.

Hypothesis 4: *Having on-demand access to help improves player retention.*

In this study, we compare games that provide access to tutorial manuals on-demand through a help button with games that do not, both with and without other types of tutorial instructions.

STUDY METHODOLOGY

Over the past decade, researchers have begun to use the Internet to collect large quantities of data on player behavior. This has given rise to a data-driven evaluation methodology that has been widely used by companies like Amazon, Microsoft, and Google to support interface design decisions [16][19][8]. Such evaluation models frequently use simple A/B testing, in which a baseline sample is compared to a variety of single-variable test samples. This methodology has been used to evaluate games as well; Andersen et al. used A/B testing to show that gameplay affects average play time more than animations and audio [2], and that secondary game objectives are most effective when they support the primary objectives [3].

In this study, however, we wanted to compare a large variety of tutorial designs defined by multiple variables. We also had a limited understanding of which combinations of tutorial characteristics would be most effective. As a result, we chose to perform a multivariate experiment considering four independent variables and a total of eight conditions, rather than using a simple A/B test.

Our games

We performed tutorial experiments on three games developed by our research group: Refraction, Hello Worlds, and Foldit. All three games contain puzzle elements, but otherwise differ greatly in their format, complexity, and player bases. We consider two of the games, Refraction and Hello Worlds, to be "casual" games. We define "casual" games as those that rely on familiar game mechanics, take only a few hours to complete, and do not require a download.

Refraction, which involves solving spacial puzzles by splitting lasers into fractional amounts, was originally designed as a math-learning game. Each level is played on a grid that contains laser sources, target spaceships, and asteroids, as shown in Figure 1. Each target spaceship requires a fractional amount of laser power, indicated by a yellow number on the ship. The player can satisfy the targets by placing pieces that change the laser direction and pieces that split the laser into two or three equal parts. All targets must be correctly satisfied at the same time to win.

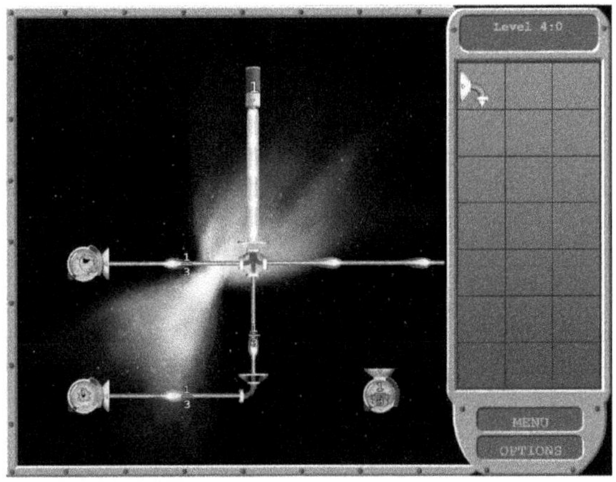

Figure 1. A level of Refraction. The goal is to use the pieces on the right to split lasers into fractional pieces and redirect them to satisfy the target spaceships. The user can pick up and put down pieces by clicking on them. The pieces are designed to be as intuitive as possible. The grid interface, pipe-flow game mechanics, and spatial reasoning puzzles are similar to many other puzzle games.

Although Refraction was originally designed to teach math concepts, the game has found success with an adult audience on the popular Flash website Kongregate, where it has been played over 480,000 times since its release in September 2010. The use of fractions as a game mechanic is relatively uncommon, but similar spacial reasoning puzzles and pipe flow mechanics appear in many other games on Kongregate and elsewhere. The artwork for the laser sources, target spaceships, asteroids, and laser manipulators was designed to utilize affordances to make the functionality of each piece as clear as possible. Refraction is freely available and can be played by anyone with a web browser.

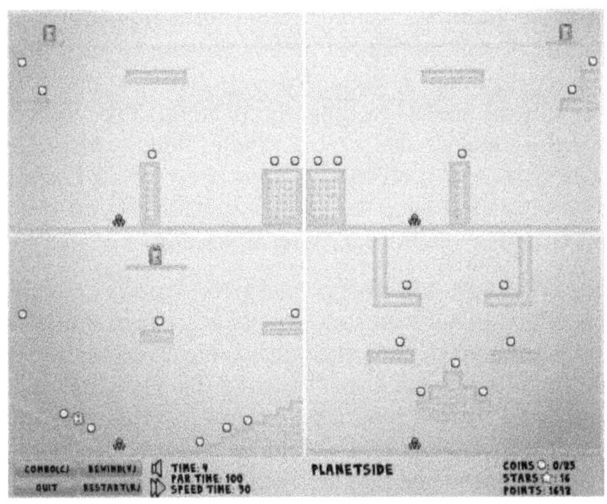

Figure 2. A level of Hello Worlds, a puzzle-platformer game. The game interface is similar to thousands of other games in the platformer genre, except that the player exists in multiple worlds at the same time. As a result, the basic game mechanics for navigating using keyboard input may be familiar to players. The player advances through each level by opening and closing doors, a common goal mechanic.

Hello Worlds is a puzzle game that offers a simple twist on the standard platformer genre. Platformers typically involve navigating a character through a two-dimensional world by running, jumping, and avoiding obstacles. In Hello Worlds, the character exists in multiple worlds at the same time, and interacts with the obstacles in each world simultaneously, as shown in Figure 2. The player must find a path through the worlds to reach various doors that open and close worlds or complete the level. While the puzzle element of Hello Worlds is uncommon, the basic game mechanics for navigating using keyboard input are used in many existing platformers. Hello Worlds is available for free on the Flash game website Kongregate, and has been played over 1,300,000 times since its release in May 2010.

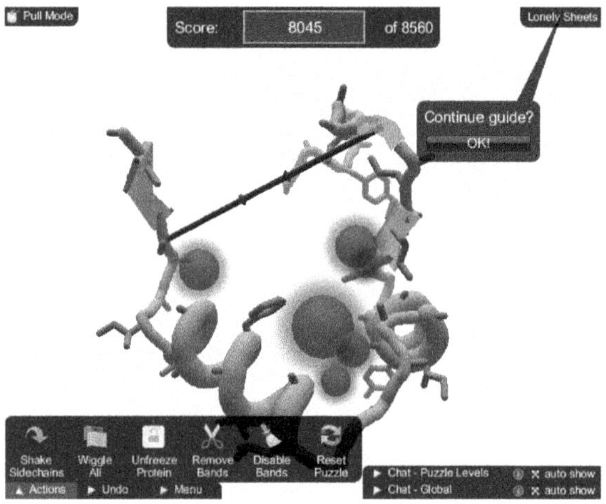

Figure 3. A puzzle in Foldit, a game in which players manipulate protein models and try to pack the shape as tightly as possible. The game is complex, has an interface with many tools and buttons, and offers a gameplay experience that is very different from other games. Therefore, players cannot rely on prior knowledge of other games very much when trying to learn how to play Foldit.

Foldit is a multiplayer, online game in which players compete and collaborate to fold protein structures efficiently [5]. Players can manipulate 3D protein structures, shown in Figure 3, by pulling on them, freezing pieces to prevent them from moving, and launching optimizations that will computationally improve the protein. Each folded protein is given a score which is used to rank solutions. Foldit has a set of offline tutorial puzzles designed to prepare players for online competitions, which we used for this study.

Foldit differs from Refraction and Hello Worlds in several key ways. First, players must download and install Foldit from a website in order to play, and must create an account to participate in online competitions. Second, the gameplay mechanics required to fold proteins are unique to this game, and as a result it is unlikely that players can benefit from past gaming experience when playing Foldit. Finally, it is much more complex than the two "casual" games and requires an understanding of some unconventional mechanics, such as placing rubber bands to hold the protein together, or running a wide variety of optimizations. Since Foldit players are working to solve complex, open scientific problems through gameplay, we do not consider this a "casual" game.

Metrics

Collecting data on player behavior through large-scale anonymous experiments has strengths and weaknesses. One key advantage is that, in contrast to laboratory user studies, our experiments are conducted "in the wild" where players do not know that they are being observed. As a result, participants are playing under their own motivation, and our findings reflect their natural behavior. However, one important limitation is that we have no interaction with our participants, and we cannot know what they are thinking or feeling. Therefore, we must infer the effects of tutorials on player engagement by measuring their behavior.

We measure player engagement in three ways. First we count the number of unique levels each player completes. Second, we calculate the total length of time that they played the game. Since players occasionally idle for long periods, we aggregated moves the player made in 30-second intervals, removing periods of two or more consecutive idle intervals from the total play time. Finally, we measured the return rate, defined as the number of times players loaded the game page in Refraction and Hello Worlds, and as the number of times the game was restarted in Foldit. While these metrics are not precisely the same as "engagement" or "learnability," we argue that they are closely related, given that players are free to leave at any time and cannot advance in a game without learning its associated rules and strategies. If the purpose of tutorials is to teach game mechanics to the player, the ability to complete levels should be the ultimate test of whether the player has learned those mechanics.

We modified each of the games to randomly assign new players to one of the eight experimental conditions. We focused solely on new players for this experiment; veteran players who were already familiar with the games were not included in our analysis. In Refraction and Hello Worlds, we tracked players using the approach described in [2], storing progress and experimental condition through the Flash cache. One drawback of this method is that if players changed computers or deleted their Flash cache, they were treated as new players. However, since the Flash cache is inconvenient to clear and this action deletes all progress in the game, we considered this risk to be small. For Foldit, we tracked players using their Foldit account and stored the condition number locally on their machine. Players who logged in on multiple machines were tracked by their account and discarded to prevent the inclusion of players who played multiple tutorial versions.

STUDY DESIGN

We performed a multivariate experiment with four variables: *presence*, *context-sensitivity*, *freedom*, and *availability of on-demand help*. We picked these variables to capture the most salient differences in tutorial implementations seen in successful games. We included a total of eight experimental conditions, shown in Table 2, each representing a combination of values for the four variables. Table 1 shows a breakdown of the concepts that each game introduces and the order in which they are introduced. The following sections explain how the four variables are implemented in each game.

Tutorial presence

We wanted to examine how the addition of tutorials affected player behavior. Therefore, the first variable in our experi-

Hello Worlds			Refraction			Foldit		
Concept	Level	Page	Concept	Level	Page	Concept	Level	Page
Character Movement (S)	1	1	Powering Ships	1	1	Clashes	1	1
Collecting Coins	1	2	Benders (S)	1	1	Pulling Sidechains	1	1
Using Doors (S)	1	1	Multiple Benders	3	-	Rotating the Camera	2	2
Red Doors	1	3	Ship Input Direction	3	4	Score	2	2
Overworld Doors	O	5	Asteroids	4	1	Shake (S)	3	3
Star Types	O	6	Coins	5	3	Pulling the Backbone (S)	4	4,5
Multiple Worlds	2	1	Splitters (S)	6	5	Undo	4	8
Combo View (S)	2	4	Fractional Ships (S)	6	4	Voids	5	6
Rewind (S)	3	4	Magnifying Glass (S)	7	6	Reset	5	8
Green Doors	6	3	Combiners (S)	33	7	Wiggle (S)	6	7
Blue Doors	10	3	Expanders (S)	37	8	Hydrogen Bonds	7	9
			Multiple Input Ships (S)	43	9	Wiggle Again (S)	7	7
			Multiple Denominators	44	9	Rubber Bands (S)	8	10
						Translating the Camera	9	2
						Rubber Bands Again (S)	9	10
						Freeze (S)	10	11
						Backbone Color	11	12
						Rebuild (S)	11	12
						Hydrophobics	12	13
						Exposeds	12	-
						Tweak Rotate (S)	13	14
						Tweak Shift (S)	14	15
						Tweak Rotate Again (S)	15	14
						Secondary Structure Mode (S)	16	16

Table 1. A breakdown of concepts taught in each game. The concepts are listed by the order in which they were taught in the context-sensitive condition. Concepts were either taught in a specific level as part of a context-sensitive tutorial or in the manual used by the context-insensitive tutorial and the on-demand help. Concepts marked with an "(S)" were stenciled during the blocking conditions. Foldit is more complex than the other two games and required many more tutorials.

Condition	Presence	Context	Freedom	Help
Insensitive+Help	Present	Insensitive	Nonblocking	On-demand
Insensitive	Present	Insensitive	Nonblocking	None
Sensitive+Help	Present	Sensitive	Nonblocking	On-demand
Sensitive	Present	Sensitive	Nonblocking	None
Blocking+Help	Present	Sensitive	Blocking	On-demand
Blocking	Present	Sensitive	Blocking	None
Help Only	None	N/A	N/A	On-demand
No Tutorials	None	N/A	N/A	None

Table 2. The eight tutorial conditions that we implemented for our multivariate experiment, based on four independent variables: presence, context-sensitivity, freedom, and availability of help. These conditions were designed to represent a wide range of existing tutorial designs and evaluate multiple hypotheses simultaneously.

ment was *presence*, resulting in two conditions: *tutorials* and *no tutorials*. For conditions in which there were *no tutorials*, the game explained nothing on its own and players were forced to either experiment or seek help outside the game. The conditions with *tutorials* are further broken into more categories in the following sections.

Context-sensitivity

To evaluate the effect of tutorial context-sensitivity on engagement and player retention, we introduced an additional variable, *context-sensitivity*. For conditions in which tutorials were present, we organized the tutorials from each game into two versions: *context-sensitive* and *context-insensitive*.

For the *context-sensitive* version, we tried to introduce each concept as closely as possible to when the player needed to use it. Therefore, for each of the concepts in Table 1, we added a short message explaining that concept to the first level in the game requiring knowledge of it. Some tutorials also contained contextual images to reinforce the text. Each message was controlled for size so that it could be easily ignored. Additionally, the player could dismiss any tutorial message.

In Refraction, as shown in Figure 4(a), the instructions appeared in a notification bar at the top of the main grid. Refraction also contained "just-in-time" messages that would activate when the player tried to do something that was not allowed. For example, when a player powered a target spaceship with less than the required amount, a message saying "too little power" appeared over the spaceship. Each of these messages appeared every time the spaceship was underpowered, but player could click "don't show again," which would cause that particular message to stop appearing.

Foldit tutorial messages appeared in pop-up boxes as shown in Figure 4(b). In Refraction and Foldit, longer context-sensitive messages were sometimes displayed across multiple pages, which the user could advance by clicking on the "next" or "Tell me more..." button.

In Hello Worlds, shown in Figure 4(c), help icons were scattered throughout the game to give the player information when appropriate. These help icons were activated whenever the player stood over them, as shown in 4(c). When activated, the text relating to that help icon would appear in the space above the icon, allowing the user to easily read or ignore it. If the player's avatar then moved off of the help icon, the text would immediately disappear. If the player moved their avatar back over the help icon, the text would reappear.

For the *context-insensitive* version, we grouped the concepts of each game into multi-page manuals by topic and order of introduction. Since each game requires a different number of concepts, the length of the context-insensitive manuals varied across the games: 9 pages for Refraction, 16 for Foldit, and 6 for Hello Worlds. The manuals for Refraction, Foldit, and Hello Worlds are shown in Figures 5(a), 5(b), and 5(c), respectively. The manual consisted of a brief textual description of each of the game's concepts accompanied by

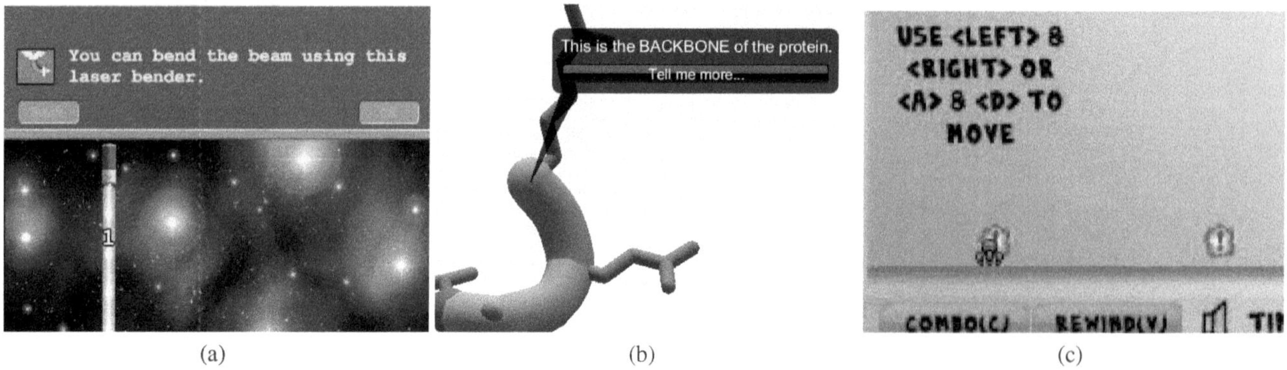

Figure 4. Screenshots of the context-sensitive tutorials. For Refraction, shown in Figure 4(a), a window appeared at the top of the screen containing text, pictures, an OK button to continue, and a back button to return to a previous message. Foldit's tutorial, shown in Figure 4(b), included a small box containing tutorial text, which related to the protein at hand, and a "Tell me more..." button to go onto the next message. For Hello Worlds, shown in Figure 4(c), blue help icons could be found throughout the game. Tutorial text appeared above an icon whenever the player's avatar overlapped with it.

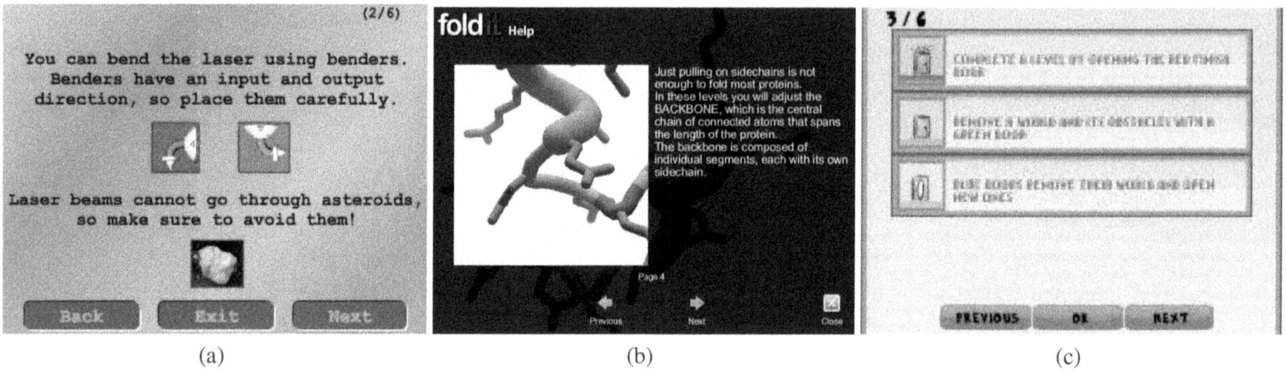

Figure 5. Screenshots of the context-insensitive tutorials. All three games featured a large window containing text, pictures, page numbers, "Next" and "Previous" buttons, and a "Close" button to help the player navigate and understand the concepts of the game. The layout of this window varied from game to game. Figure 5(a) shows the layout for Refraction, Figure 5(b) shows the layout for Foldit, and Figure 5(c) shows the layout for Hello Worlds.

relevant pictures associated with that concept. These manuals appeared before the player could interact with any levels, forcing them to interact with the manual in some way before playing the game. The player could navigate between pages with the "next" and "back" buttons and gauge their progress using page numbers present on each page. The player could also close the manual at any time by clicking the "close" button.

Due to their length, we broke the Refraction and Foldit tutorials into logical "chapters." As the player advanced, new chapters became available. At each new stage, the *context-insensitive* tutorial reappeared showing the first page in the new chapter, and the player could navigate to previous chapters if desired. Refraction had three chapters, displayed at the beginnings of worlds one, five and six respectively. Foldit had four chapters, displayed every four levels.

Freedom

To evaluate the effect of tutorial freedom, we divided the context-sensitive condition described above into two conditions: *blocking* and *nonblocking*. To create the *blocking* condition, we identified several concepts from each game that involved using a new tool, a new interface object, or a new keyboard key. We then added a "stencil" for each of these concepts that forced the player to use the new tool, blocking forward progress in the game until the player performed the desired action. After completing the stencil, freedom to interact with the full user interface was restored. We implemented stencils slightly differently in each game due to their different interaction styles.

In Refraction, when the player encountered a stencil, the game drew the player's attention to the target interface object by making the entire window gray except for that object, displaying the instructions on a notification bar at the top of the screen, adding an animated yellow arrow that pointed to the object, and ignoring all user input directed at anything other than the object. This implementation is shown in Figure 6(a). If a level had both context-sensitive tutorial messages and a stencil, then the game forced the player to click somewhere on the screen to advance each tutorial message before forcing the player to complete the stencil instructions.

In Foldit, the game displayed a message telling the player what to do, as shown in Figure 6(b). The screen was not grayed out, and the user could still manipulate the camera and interact with game's user interface controls. However, the game prevented the player from manipulating the protein in any other way until they performed the desired action. In

(a) (b) (c)

Figure 6. Screenshots of the blocking tutorials. A blocking tutorial prevented the player from continuing until they completed a specified action. For Refraction, shown in Figure 6(a), the tutorial grayed out the interface except for a window containing tutorial text, an object for the player to interact with, and an arrow pointing at that object. Foldit, shown in Figure 6(b), used a small text box to tell the player what action they needed to perform. Hello Worlds, shown in Figure 6(c), grayed out the screen except for character, the tutorial text, and the interface buttons whenever the blocking tutorial was active.

some levels the player needed to advance through preceding context-sensitive tutorial messages to reach the stencil.

In Hello Worlds, as in Refraction, a gray window was drawn over the entire game except for the player's avatar, the message text, and the user interface buttons. Since the user primarily interacts with Hello Worlds through the keyboard, the displayed message associated with each stencil told the user what key(s) to press to continue, as shown in Figure 6(c). All other keys were ignored until the user pressed one of the valid keys. The user was allowed to interact with the interface buttons, such as "quit," but could not make any progress on the level until completing the instructions in the stenciled message.

Availability of help

To evaluate whether players would look for help when they needed it, and to measure the effect of tutorial availability on player engagement, we added another variable, *availability of help*, with two possibilities: *on-demand help*, and *no help*. We created a version of the game with on-demand help for each of the previously described conditions.

There are many ways to give tutorial information on-demand. For this experiment, we added a help button to the main toolbar of each game. Since Foldit's main toolbar can be closed, another floating help button was added near the score display. Clicking on this help button opened the same manual used in the context-insensitive tutorial condition described previously. The manual included only the concepts which the player could have encountered up to that point. If later levels introduced new concepts, the help manual did not include those concepts until the user reached that level. In order to make the help provided as context-sensitive as possible, the manual automatically opened to the page that most closely related to the level the user is currently playing. If desired, the player could view all of the pages of the help screen with the "next" and "back" buttons. The player could close the help screen and return to the current level by clicking on a "close" button. When activated, the help screen covered the main interaction area for each game and restricted gameplay until the player closed the tutorial.

DATA ANALYSIS AND RESULTS

We collected data from Refraction and Foldit for approximately two weeks, accumulating 13,158 Refraction players and 9,743 Foldit players. During this period, Kongregate added a new badge to Refraction, pushing the game to the top of the "new badges list" and attracting many new players. Kongregate also featured Hello Worlds on the front page of its website as a "badge of the day," allowing us to collect data from 22,417 Hello Worlds players over a two-day period.

Table 3 shows the results of our experiment. Our measurements of levels completed and time played were not normally distributed, so we used on a non-parametric test, the Wilcoxon/Kruskal-Wallis 2-sample test, to analyze levels completed and time played for large-scale effects. The Z-value reported for this test is a standard normal random variable, a scaled version of the distribution of relative rankings of the lower-ranked condition. For return rate, we used Pearson χ^2 analyses to compare the percentages. The variance in our measures was very high, so a great deal of data was necessary to show statistical significance at the $p = 0.05$ level.

Tutorials were only justified in the most complex game

To evaluate whether tutorials improved player engagement, we compared the version of the game with no tutorials to the versions with context-sensitive tutorials and context-insensitive tutorials. The "presence" section of Table 3 shows the results for these comparisons.

We expected to find that including tutorials, either in-context or out-of-context, would lead to higher engagement than providing no instruction at all. In Foldit, this was the case. Foldit players with context-sensitive tutorials played 75% more levels and 29% longer than those with no tutorials. Players with context-insensitive tutorials played 25% more levels and 12% longer than with no tutorials. We found no significant effects for return rate.

However, tutorials were not as effective in the other two games. We found no significant effects for either comparison in Refraction. In Hello Worlds, we found no significant

Experimental variable	Game	Condition	Player Count	Time Played		Levels Completed		Return Rate	
Presence	Foldit	Context sensitive	1242	*660s*	$p < 0.001$	*7*	$p < 0.001$	19.16%	$p = 0.408$
		No Tutorials	1210	*510s*	$Z = -5.070$	*4*	$Z = -10.982$	20.50%	$\chi^2 = 0.686$
		Context insensitive	1147	*570s*	$p = 0.010$	*5*	$p < 0.001$	19.62%	$p = 0.594$
		No Tutorials	1210	*510s*	$Z = -2.592$	*4*	$Z = 4.353$	20.50%	$\chi^2 = 0.284$
	Refraction	Context sensitive	1634	990s	$p = 0.437$	15	$p = 0.294$	28.46%	$p = 0.925$
		No Tutorials	1678	1050s	$Z = -0.778$	16	$Z = -1.049$	28.61%	$\chi^2 = 0.009$
		Context insensitive	1687	1020s	$p = 0.483$	15	$p = 0.272$	28.45%	$p = 0.922$
		No Tutorials	1678	1050s	$Z = 0.702$	16	$Z = 1.099$	28.61%	$\chi^2 = 0.010$
	Hello Worlds	Context sensitive	2817	750s	$p = 0.697$	10	$p = 0.537$	*17.96%*	$p < 0.001$
		No Tutorials	2815	720s	$Z = -0.389$	10	$Z = -0.618$	*21.60%*	$\chi^2 = 11.733$
		Context insensitive	2754	690s	$p = 0.572$	10	$p = 0.770$	20.59%	$p = 0.356$
		No Tutorials	2815	720s	$Z = -0.565$	10	$Z = 0.292$	21.60%	$\chi^2 = 0.854$
Context sensitivity	Foldit	Context sensitive	1242	*660s*	$p = 0.014$	*7*	$p < 0.001$	19.16%	$p = 0.779$
		Context insensitive	1147	*570s*	$Z = -2.470$	*5*	$Z = -7.727$	19.62%	$\chi^2 = 0.079$
	Refraction	Context sensitive	1634	990s	$p = 0.901$	15	$p = 0.994$	28.46%	$p = 0.998$
		Context insensitive	1687	1020s	$Z = -0.124$	15	$Z = 0.008$	28.45%	$\chi^2 = 0.000$
	Hello Worlds	Context sensitive	2817	750s	$p = 0.348$	10	$p = 0.736$	*17.96%*	$p = 0.013$
		Context insensitive	2754	690s	$Z = -0.938$	10	$Z = -0.337$	*20.59%*	$\chi^2 = 6.175$
Freedom	Foldit	Blocking	1210	630s	$p = 0.454$	*7*	$p = 0.007$	18.93%	$p = 0.881$
		Non-blocking	1242	660s	$Z = -0.749$	*7*	$Z = 2.697$	19.16%	$\chi^2 = 0.022$
	Refraction	Blocking	1634	930s	$p = 0.142$	14	$p = 0.139$	26.37%	$p = 0.187$
		Non-blocking	1551	990s	$Z = -1.467$	15	$Z = -1.477$	28.46%	$\chi^2 = 1.743$
	Hello Worlds	Blocking	2729	723s	$p = 0.740$	9	$p = 0.376$	18.94%	$p = 0.346$
		Non-blocking	2817	750s	$Z = -0.332$	10	$Z = -0.886$	17.96%	$\chi^2 = 0.889$
Availability of help	Foldit	Help (aggreg.)	4939	600s	$p = 0.536$	5	$p = 0.208$	18.34%	$p = 0.130$
		No help (aggreg.)	4809	600s	$Z = -0.619$	5	$Z = -1.258$	19.55%	$\chi^2 = 2.297$
		Help Only	1238	*570s*	$p = 0.036$	*4*	$p = 0.001$	18.98%	$p = 0.347$
		No Tutorials	1210	*510s*	$Z = -2.101$	*4*	$Z = -3.197$	20.50%	$\chi^2 = 0.885$
	Refraction	Help (aggreg.)	6608	960s	$p = 0.806$	15	$p = 0.515$	28.50%	$p = 0.528$
		No help (aggreg.)	6550	990s	$Z = 0.245$	15	$Z = 0.651$	28.00%	$\chi^2 = 0.399$
		Help Only	1678	*900s*	$p = 0.031$	*14*	$p = 0.013$	27.43%	$p = 0.451$
		No Tutorials	1655	*1050s*	$Z = -2.161$	*16*	$Z = -2.496$	28.61%	$\chi^2 = 0.569$
	Hello Worlds	Help (aggreg.)	11302	720s	$p = 0.626$	10	$p = 0.972$	*18.56%*	$p = 0.021$
		No help (aggreg.)	11115	720s	$Z = 0.487$	10	$Z = 0.035$	*19.78%*	$\chi^2 = 5.314$
		Help Only	2864	754s	$p = 0.434$	11	$p = 0.190$	*18.44%*	$p = 0.003$
		No Tutorials	2815	720s	$Z = -0.782$	10	$Z = -1.310$	*21.60%*	$\chi^2 = 8.875$

Table 3. Summary of data gathered during the experiment, organized around our four experimental variables of *presence*, *context-sensitivity*, *freedom*, and *availability of help on-demand*. Statistically significant results are shown in blue italics. Our results show that tutorials only had positive effects on player behavior in Foldit, that context-sensitive tutorials outperformed context-insensitive tutorials in Foldit, that restricting player freedom did not improve engagement in any game, and that providing access to help on-demand was beneficial in Foldit, ineffective in Hello Worlds, and actually harmful in Refraction.

effects for levels completed and time played, and we found that 3.5% *fewer* players returned with context-sensitive tutorials than with no tutorials.

In contrast to our expectations, our results show that tutorials are only useful for improving player engagement in some games. It may be the case that tutorial value depends on game complexity. Refraction and Hello Worlds are typical of their genres and have intuitive interfaces. Foldit, on the other hand, is unconventional, complex, and requires deep strategy and spatial insight. Another possible explanation is that Foldit players are more patient. Since the barrier to play a downloadable game like Foldit is higher than for online casual games like Refraction and Hello Worlds, players who are willing to overcome this barrier may be willing to devote more time reading the tutorials. Further work is necessary to know the exact reasons for this effect. Regardless, our results show that tutorials may only be worthwhile for complex games, such as Foldit, and may not be worth the investment of time and resources in games with mechanics that are more easily discovered through experimentation, such as Refraction and Hello Worlds.

Context-sensitivity can improve engagement

We next evaluated the importance of presenting tutorial information in context. We expected that presenting information as closely as possible to when the player needed it would be better than presenting information out of context. The results for the comparison of context-sensitive and context-insensitive tutorials are shown in the "context-sensitivity" section of Table 3.

Context-sensitivity improved player engagement in Foldit. Foldit players played 40% more levels and 16% longer with context-sensitive tutorials than context-insensitive tutorials. However, we did not find positive effects for context-sensitivity in the other two games. We found no significant effects for Refraction. In Hello Worlds, we found that the return rate was about 2% less with context-sensitive tutorials than with context-insensitive tutorials.

Therefore, the importance of context-sensitivity in a particular game depends on whether tutorials positively impact player engagement in that game. For complex games where tutorials are beneficial, such as Foldit, presenting the information in context seems beneficial. However, for games in which tutorial presence does not have an impact, it does not matter whether or not the information is presented in context.

Tutorial freedom did not affect player behavior

To evaluate whether restricting player freedom would improve tutorial effectiveness, we compared the versions with context-sensitive blocking tutorials to those with context-sensitive nonblocking tutorials. The results of this comparison are shown in the "freedom" section of Table 3.

We expected that blocking tutorials would focus player attention and improve learning. In Foldit, we found a significant effect for levels completed, but the median number of levels completed remained constant at 7 levels. We found no significant effects for Refraction and Hello Worlds.

Therefore, we found no evidence supporting the practice of restricting player freedom in order to focus player attention on target interface objects. This result may further reinforce our conclusion that players learn how to use the interface primarily through experimentation, and that forcing the player to perform a series of actions may not be effective. It may also be the case that players do not like having their freedom restricted and that this cancels out any positive effects on learning. Further examination is necessary to understand whether restricting player freedom improves player engagement and learning in some cases.

On-demand help harmed and helped player retention

We next evaluated whether player engagement would be improved by providing additional help that players could access when needed. We expected that providing additional help in this way would be beneficial. The results for the following comparisons are shown in the "availability of help" section of Table 3.

To look for large-scale effects of providing on-demand help in general, we first aggregated the four conditions with a help button and the four conditions without a help button and compared them against each other. We found only one significant effect across all three games, which was a 1.2% increase in return rate for Hello Worlds.

We then assumed that the effect of providing help on-demand would be strongest when no other instructions were given. Therefore, we compared the version with a help button and no other tutorials with the version with no help button and no tutorials. In Foldit, providing a help button in this case increased engagement. Players played about 12% longer with a help button than without. We found a significant effect on the number of levels completed but this effect did not change the median. However, we found negative effects in the other two games. In Hello Worlds, players returned about 3% less frequently with on-demand help than without. In Refraction, we found that players with on-demand help completed 12% *fewer* levels than those without access to help, and played for 15% *less* time.

The negative impact of the help button, particularly in Refraction, is difficult to explain. Only 31% of players that had access to the help button in Refraction ever used it. One possible explanation is that the knowledge that there is help available discourages players from putting as much effort into the game. It is also possible that players will only click "help" if they are already frustrated, and will quit even sooner if they are unable to find the help they need. We can only speculate at this point, however, since multivariate testing does not tell us what players are thinking. Future studies are needed to reproduce and understand this effect. Nevertheless, it is clear that players can respond unpredictably to tutorial implementations, and that tutorials can harm player retention unexpectedly. This points to the importance of testing tutorial implementations to avoid unexpected negative effects.

CONCLUSION

Our examination of tutorials in three games of varying complexity showed that tutorial effectiveness depends on the complexity of the game. Tutorials had the greatest value in the most unconventional and complex game, Foldit, increasing play time by as much as 29%. However, tutorials had *surprisingly little* impact on player behavior in Refraction and Hello Worlds, which are less complex, more similar to other games, and easier to learn through experimentation. Our results suggest that tutorials may not be effective for such games, and that designers should consider the complexity and discoverability of game mechanics when deciding whether to invest resources in tutorials. It is unlikely that a single approach will work for tutorial design in all games.

Since players seem to learn more from exploring than from reading text, we believe that it is important to design early levels in a way that maximizes a player's ability to experiment and discover game mechanics. A key question that arises is how to facilitate this experimentation while ensuring that the player learns how to play and does not become frustrated. We found little evidence to suggest that restricting player freedom to focus attention on a particular interface object or game mechanic is beneficial. Although it may be tempting to provide help on-demand, we found that adding a help button was only effective in Foldit, and actually *reduced* player progress by 12% and play time by 15% in Refraction. Future work is needed to understand how to break down a complex game into smaller "chunks" that can be learned through exploration, how to detect when a player is confused or frustrated, and how to intervene, if necessary, in a way that causes learning without negatively impacting engagement.

One of the drawbacks of our methodology is that we do not know demographic information about our players. It is likely that each game attracted different kinds of players and that self-selection contributed to the differences in player behavior that we observed. However, we believe that it is most useful to tailor tutorials for the players who do self-select to play each game because they are the players who are likely to play the most.

Since we only tested tutorials in Refraction, Hello Worlds, and Foldit, we cannot know for sure how these results generalize to other games and genres. In particular, our games are not representative of commercial games, and as a result we can draw no conclusions about the effectiveness of tutorials in games that players must purchase. Further research with a wider variety of games is required to determine whether our results will apply to commercial games and games of different genres.

Furthermore, future work is necessary to understand how tutorial *presentation* affects player behavior. There are many ways to design tutorials, and we only experimented with basic designs. Although video game tutorials frequently include audio, animations, and videos, we only examined tutorials containing pictures and text. Another question is whether designers should integrate tutorials into the main game progression or provide them in a separate "tutorial mode" that can be avoided entirely, as suggested by [1] and utilized in highly successful games such as Deus Ex (Ion Storm Inc. 2000). Future experiments with a greater variety of tutorial styles will improve our understanding of how to design effective tutorials.

Our results point to the importance of analytics and large-scale analysis of player behavior because these effects would be difficult to discover without large amounts of data. We believe that this methodology will continue to provide valuable insights that improve our understanding of good game design. Such experiments are important because player behavior is often counterintuitive; each of our four hypotheses turned out to be either incorrect or incomplete. Furthermore, we believe that the ability of games to attract large numbers of participants, allowing researchers to perform tests with many experimental variables, will make them an important mechanism for future HCI research.

ACKNOWLEDGMENTS

We would like to acknowledge the members of the Refraction, Hello Worlds, and Foldit teams for developing the games and making this work possible. We also thank Anthony Pecorella and August Brown of Kongregate for promoting our games and helping us gather data. This work was supported by the University of Washington Center for Game Science, DARPA grant FA8750-11-2-0102, the Bill and Melinda Gates Foundation, NSF grant IIS0811902, two NSF Graduate Fellowships, Adobe, and Intel.

REFERENCES

1. E. Adams. The designer's notebook: Eight ways to make a bad tutorial. *Gamasutra*, 2011.
2. E. Andersen, Y.-E. Liu, R. Snider, R. Szeto, S. Cooper, and Z. Popović. On the harmfulness of secondary game objectives. In *FDG '11: Proceedings of the Sixth International Conference on the Foundations of Digital Games*, New York, NY, USA, 2011. ACM.
3. E. Andersen, Y.-E. Liu, R. Snider, R. Szeto, and Z. Popović. Placing a value on aesthetics in online casual games. In *CHI '11: Proceedings of the SIGCHI conference on Human factors in computing systems*, New York, NY, USA, 2011. ACM.
4. L. Bergman, V. Castelli, T. Lau, and D. Oblinger. Docwizards: A system for authoring follow-me documentation wizards. In *UIST '05 Proceedings of the 18th annual ACM symposium on User interface software and technology*, New York, NY, USA, 2005. ACM.
5. S. Cooper, F. Khatib, A. Treuille, J. Barbero, J. Lee, M. Beenen, A. Leaver-Fay, D. Baker, Z. Popović, and F. Players. Predicting protein structures with a multiplayer online game. *Nature*, 466(7307):756–760, August 2010.
6. D. K. Farkas. The role of balloon help. *ACM SIGDOC Asterisk Journal of Computer Documentation*, 17, 1993.
7. J. P. Gee. Learning by design: Games as learning machines. *Interactive Educational Multimedia*, 8:15–23, 2004.
8. Google Website Optimizer. http://www.google.com/websiteoptimizer/.
9. F. Grabler, M. Agrawala, W. Li, M. Dontcheva, and T. Igarashi. Generating photo manipulation tutorials by demonstration. In *ACM SIGGRAPH 2009*, New York, NY, USA, 2009. ACM.
10. T. Grossman and G. Fitzmaurice. Toolclips: An investigation of contextual video assistance for functionality understanding. In *CHI '10 Proceedings of the 28th international conference on Human factors in computing systems*, New York, NY, USA, 2010. ACM.
11. T. Grossman, G. Fitzmaurice, and R. Attar. A survey of software learnability: Metrics, methodologies and guidelines. In *CHI '09: Proceedings of the 27th international conference on Human factors in computing systems*, New York, NY, USA, 2009. ACM.
12. S. M. Harrison. A comparison of still, animated, or nonillustrated on-line help with written or spoken instructions in a graphical user interface. In *CHI '95 Proceedings of the SIGCHI conference on Human factors in computing systems*, New York, NY, USA, 1995. ACM.
13. J. Huang and M. B. Twidale. Graphstract: Minimal graphical help for computers. In *UIST '07 Proceedings of the 20th annual ACM symposium on User interface software and technology*, New York, NY, USA, 2007. ACM.
14. C. Kelleher and R. Pausch. Stencils-based tutorials: Design and evaluation. In *CHI '05 Proceedings of the SIGCHI conference on Human factors in computing systems*, New York, NY, USA, 2005. ACM.
15. K. Knabe. Apple guide: A case study in user-aided design of online help. In *CHI '95 Conference companion on Human factors in computing systems*, New York, NY, USA, 1995. ACM.
16. R. Kohavi, R. M. Henne, and D. Sommerfield. Practical guide to controlled experiments on the web: listen to your customers not to the hippo. In *KDD '07: Proceedings of the 13th ACM SIGKDD international conference on Knowledge discovery and data mining*, pages 959–967, New York, NY, USA, 2007. ACM.
17. T. Lau, L. Bergman, V. Castelli, and D. Oblinger. Sheepdog: Learning procedures for technical support. In *IUI '04 Proceedings of the 9th international conference on Intelligent user interfaces*, New York, NY, USA, 2004. ACM.
18. J. Lave and E. Wenger. *Situated learning: Legitimate peripheral participation*. Cambridge University Press, Cambridge, England, 1991.
19. G. Linden. Early Amazon: Shopping cart recommendations, 2006. http://glinden.blogspot.com/2006/04/early-amazon-shopping-cart.html.
20. J. Nielsen. *Usability Engineering*. Morgan Kaufmann, San Francisco, CA, USA, 1993.
21. S. Palmiter and J. Elkerton. An evaluations of demonstrations for learning computer-based tasks. In *CHI '91 Proceedings of the SIGCHI conference on Human factors in computing systems: Reaching through technology*, New York, NY, USA, 1991. ACM.
22. S. G. Ray. Tutorials: Learning to play. *Gamasutra*, 2010.
23. B. Shneiderman. *Designing the User Interface: Strategies for Effective Human-Computer Interaction*. Addison-Wesley Longman Publishing Co., Inc., Boston, MA, USA, 1986.
24. J. Xiao, R. Catrambone, and J. Stasko. Be quiet? evaluating proactive and reactive user interface assistants. Technical report, Georgia Institute of Technology, Atlanta, GA, USA, 2003.

Tales from the Front Lines of a Large-Scale Serious Game Project

Rilla Khaled
Center for Computer Games Research
IT University of Copenhagen
rikh@itu.dk

Gordon Ingram
Interactions Lab, School of Management
University of Bath
g.ingram@bath.ac.uk

ABSTRACT
Serious games have received much positive attention; correspondingly, many researchers have taken up the challenge of establishing how to best design them. However, the current literature often focuses on best practice design strategies and frameworks. Fine-grained details, contextual descriptions, and organisational factors that are invaluable in helping us to learn from and reflect on project experiences are often overlooked. In this paper, we present five distinct and sometimes competing perspectives that are critical in understanding factors that influence serious game projects: *project organisation, technology, domain knowledge, user research*, and *game design*. We explain these perspectives by providing insights from the design and development process of an EU-funded serious game about conflict resolution developed by an interdisciplinary consortium of researchers and industry-based developers. We also point out a set of underlying forces that become evident from viewing the process from different perspectives, to underscore that problems exist in serious game projects and that we should open the conversation about them.

Author Keywords
Serious games; learning games; game design; reflective design; interdisciplinary research

ACM Classification Keywords
H.5.m [Information Interfaces and Presentation (e.g. HCI)]: Miscellaneous;

INTRODUCTION
The notion that games could have agendas in addition to entertainment holds appeal for many audiences - educators, parents, and activists, to name but a few. Efforts to create games of this nature have been taking place for some time, under the umbrella of serious games [1, 39]. Whereas games have been attacked for being too influential in terms of promoting violence while also being too frivolous, serious games have managed to benefit from the intersection of these qualities, namely, the possibility to educate, inform, train, and persuade in an entertaining and compelling manner. But hype aside, effective serious games are complicated design undertakings. No one would dispute that designing a great game takes talent, just as no one would dispute that designing an effective learning tool requires skill. Serious games are expected to serve both purposes well; they are faced with a double burden. A number of researchers have suggested design strategies, mechanics, and patterns that support current best practice based on existing serious games, and previous design experience, e.g. [18, 22]. Other researchers have adopted more holistic approaches to serious game design, and have suggested design methodologies and frameworks, e.g. [1, 12, 39]. This work is helpful in guiding us at a theoretical and abstract level.

What the present literature gives us less insight into is the complex process of the evolution of a serious game. It rarely conveys a sense of the tensions, dynamics, and subtle contextual factors that act on large-scale, ongoing game development projects. Tales about these experiences are being told, but often they are transmitted only in oral form, as candid coffee break confessions from one colleague to another. These stories disappear from the final cut of serious games literature, leaving no recorded trace, which in academia is akin to never having existed. For researchers and practitioners from novice to veteran alike, this can lead to hidden and undiscussed tensions needing to be discovered anew, despite their prevalence across serious games efforts.

In this paper, we illuminate some of these tensions, dynamics, and factors. We share insights from the design and development process of an EU-funded serious game project being undertaken by an interdisciplinary consortium. The goal of this project is to develop a game that facilitates children in learning about conflict resolution. We show how the serious game creation process can be understood in deeper, more nuanced ways that facilitate reflection on practice if it is understood as an interweaving of different, occasionally competing agendas and perspectives. We critically examine our experiences from five perspectives: *project organisation, technology, domain knowledge, user research*, and *game design*. In doing so, we illustrate the inherently messy nature of serious game design as a practice. We also present a set of underlying forces at work in projects of this nature that emerge from viewing our process through these perspectives, as these forces play profoundly important roles in shaping the trajectory of game creation. Our game is still a work in progress, but we find it important to point out these tensions as they emerge. In reflecting on our process so far, our intention is to bring to light those parts of serious game projects that often remain backgrounded and hidden.

A REFLECTIVE CRITICAL STANCE ON PROCESS

The reflective critical stance we adopt in this paper has a provenance within the design literature. In 1983, Schön proposed the *reflective practitioner perspective* [30], which has since been widely embraced by the design community. More recently, Sengers et al. proposed *reflective design* as an approach in which reflection is foregrounded as a dominant organising quality of design [31]. They suggested that reflection could be used for a number of purposes, including as a lens during the design process, as a way of uncovering limitations and challenging dominant assumptions, as a means for supporting users in reflecting on their lives, and for inviting dialogue between designer and user. Reflection as a tool for understanding design consequences contextualised in the world is also a commonplace practice, as evidenced by the growing number of retrospective accounts in the interaction design (IxD) literature, e.g. [14]. Within more industry-oriented writing, we see similar accounts in the way of game postmortems. *Game Developer* [38], a well-known industry-focused magazine, regularly publishes postmortems contributed by game designers and developers. Typically these document the development of a game after it has been released, detailing and dissecting positive and negative aspects. Recently, one designer wrote a meta postmortem based on two years worth of previous postmortems to identify whether there were patterns in game development pitfalls [32]. He noted that 56% of the problems volunteered by postmortem authors focused on process issues. Within the industry-based game community, then, process problems are already noted as ubiquitous.

Several of the aforementioned works, particularly those presenting retrospective reports, focus on reflections on practice after the fact. In contrast, we wish to examine project tensions and forces as they emerge, as this would circumvent the "resolved" qualities many retrospective reports acquire. We also choose to report on these experiences now because of their fleeting nature. Once projects finish and time passes, experiences that spur process insights or changes to practice can lose their potency. But this does not render the experiences or insights any less important. Unlike the IxD literature, such reflections are still rare within the serious games literature. Perhaps due to its youth, it currently focuses on successes and best practice as gleaned from previous projects or the literature of other disciplines. To move the field towards maturation, researchers and practitioners should be able to share their war stories. This is the stance we adopt in this paper, which we see as a complement to the existing literature.

THE SIREN PROJECT

The game we discuss in this paper is the core focus of a European Commission 7th Framework Programme (FP7) funded three year project, which began in September of 2010. Our ongoing goal is to develop a serious game to support children in learning about conflict resolution, that can be played in the classroom, and that will allow players to explore a variety of conflict handling behaviours. The game will be playable in both single player and multiplayer modes, it will feature content that will adapt based on player behaviour, and will partially rely on emotion detection and recognition.

The project is being undertaken by an interdisciplinary consortium made up of six small teams, five of which hail from academic research backgrounds, and one of which is a serious game development studio. Each research team belongs to a distinct community, with separate traditions, epistemologies, and work practices. All six teams have been tasked with leading work packages related to their own areas of expertise, on the understanding that the work packages will eventually dovetail together to produce the final game, as well as encompass design and evaluation tasks.

Due to the dovetailing of the project work packages, limiting focus to one's own work package has not been possible. All of the partners have needed to at least partly understand each others' contributions, both for reasons related to task balancing, but also to make sense of their own responsibilities. Three teams have been researching sociology and psychology literature on conflict with a special focus on children, including best practice for conflict management and resolution. A different grouping of three teams have been conducting user research with children and teachers who represent potential future users. All of the partners have been involved in developing functional and nonfunctional requirements. Two teams not involved in user studies have commenced work on early technology demonstrators. Three teams are developing the underlying technologies that were promised in the final version of the game, namely, procedural content generation (PCG), interactive story-telling, and natural user interfaces (NUI), and a fourth team has also committed to developing intelligent agents for the game. Finally, the industry partner has been tasked with developing assets, GUIs, and final versions of the game software.

FIVE PROJECT PERSPECTIVES

When reading the literature on serious games, it often seems that diverse project concerns will naturally weave together. Further, the retrospective nature of many reports presents a view of process where there was never ambiguity or contradiction in terms of needs or design perspectives. Within our project, and indeed serious game projects in general, we propose that there are at least five active perspectives: *project organisation*, *technology*, *domain knowledge*, *user research*, and *game design*. All of them are operational in shaping the final game. When viewed individually, however, the perspectives are radically different from one another. To gain a nuanced understanding of how serious game projects are fueled and shaped, exploration of each perspective is critical.

Project organisation

In 2009, the European Commission launched a call for applications for its FP7 ICT funding scheme. These application calls are often quite specific in terms of expected characteristics of funded projects. The call that our consortium responded to was ICT-2009.4.2: Technology-enhanced learning. In particular, our application was targeted for Outcome (c): "Innovative adaptive and intuitive systems for learning featuring affective and emotional approaches, including related new forms of assessing learning outcomes as well as feedback/guidance mechanisms (innovative diagnostic techniques) to the learner and the teacher" [11]. The funding call went on to state: "Work may relate to serious games and immersive environments and include advances in the combination of simulation, story telling, and collaborative learning" [11]. Thus, from the beginning of the funding process, various project constraints and evaluation criteria had been set.

In response to the call, our consortium was formed, with each member pledging to contribute relevant specialised expertise. We then assembled an application for a three-year project. For projects of this type, applicants are required to describe work plans in terms of work packages, which are blocks of research or development led by one project partner that culminate in one or more project deliverables that must be delivered by particular dates. In writing the application, we thus committed to a specific organisational structure and set of project deliverables prior to any real experience of the project itself.

Some months after submitting our application, we learned that we had been successful. Our project officially commenced in September of 2010 at a kick-off meeting in Athens, when many of the consortium members met each other for the first time. The Athens meeting also served as the first time we encountered the large disciplinary gaps that exist in our consortium, which contains experts on PCG in the context of games, NUI and emotional detection, intelligent agents and robotics, interactive story telling, culturally-relevant game design, character-centric IxD, and childhood from an anthropological perspective. At times, we literally did not understand what other members within our consortium were talking about. While the participatory design literature emphasises the importance of establishing shared vocabularies between designers and users [24], we found such a lingua franca was necessary just within the consortium itself, to better understand each others' perspectives, experiences, and needs.

Within the organisation science, software engineering, and serious games literature, project organisation has been noted as having a strong influence on project performance [7, 17, 37]. With so many types of expertise represented in our consortium, any decision making has involved coordinating diverse philosophies and expectations with regards to the user research, the theory on conflict management and resolution, the game design, and the use of certain technologies, all while satisfying individual partner responsibilities and overall project responsibilities. In an ethnographic study of a serious games company, Tran and Biddle suggest that factors that contribute most positively to team collaboration are *role respect* – understanding one's own contribution to the game as well as the efforts, contributions, and working habits of others, *iterative development* – requiring frequent meetings, constant evaluation, and high levels of team member involvement, and *shared vision* – having a common understanding about what the game product should be [37]. The heterogeneous and distributed nature of our team, coupled with the research bent of the project have made all of these factors difficult to control. In terms of Constantine's organisational paradigms for software projects, we found ourselves adopting an *open* paradigm of organisation. The open paradigm is noted to be excellent for complex problem solving, information sharing, and practical adaptation, but can in the worst case be inefficient, complicated, and lead to endless processing [7].

To reach our project goals, we sought guidance from several methodologies. For the software development aspects of the project, we looked to agile methodologies, which have arisen in response to "high risk" projects with changing requirements that must be delivered on tight schedules [6]. Many industry-based game developers have also used and adapted agile methods to suit their needs, leveraging the concept of iteration to develop playtestable prototypes [4]. As noted earlier, researchers from the serious games community have proposed patterns and frameworks for the development of serious games [1, 18, 22, 39]. For user participation aspects, we looked to participatory and user centered design methods [24, 28]. Noting that none of the traditions exactly fit the needs of our project and different disciplinary practices, we assembled a set of modified methods from software engineering, IxD, and game design. Serious games as a general practice will always struggle with suggesting "best practice" processes at the project level, because serious games are an umbrella genre of diverse games. Every serious game is associated with a specific domain and development context, and involves different groupings of stakeholders with particular disciplinary traditions. All of these factors must be taken into account in devising a process that supports the needs of the project and the perspectives of the stakeholders.

Requirements, disciplinary traditions, and project organisation are a hidden input into serious games. It is tempting to envisage game development as a smooth procession from an idea to design to implementation. But numerous other organisation factors, from proposal requirements, to team communication, to methodological decisions have a very real impact on the final product. To some extent, a large part of the organisation for our project was set in place even before the project began. One year in, we have worked hard to develop open channels of communication within the consortium and to move towards a joint vision for the project, but much remains to be done.

Technology

During the design phase of any interactive system, technology creates constraints. Often, these constraints arise for historical reasons. For example, if the new system is intended to replace a legacy system, then characteristics and affordances of the legacy system may partially constrain what can be done with the new technology. Other times, these constraints are based on surrounding infrastructures, and underlying platform capacities. Our project also features a third kind of constraint: technologies that must be featured in the solution. As mentioned earlier, from the beginning of our project, we were aware that we essentially had a contractual obligation to make use of particular technologies in our system, that is, adaptive computing in the form of PCG and AI-based player modelling, intuitive systems in the form of NUI, and interactive storytelling.

The technologies involved in our project are domain agnostic, in the sense that they could be used in any number of domain contexts (ranging, for example, from conflict resolution to assisting the visually impaired). As a consequence, whereas project teams tasked with responsibilities related to user research and game design could not fully begin making decisions prior to research phases, the technology-focused teams were able to begin development work as soon as the project commenced. These teams have already produced functional early prototypes of the various necessary technology solutions. They have begun collaborating and sharing in-house software with one another to establish how to usefully connect these technologies. So even before some of the important macro-level game design decisions were reached, underlying architectural choices were quietly taking shape.

Whereas a naive perspective might suggest that technology decisions should be shaped by game design decisions, the game studies literature provides counterexamples showing that this is often not the case. Montfort and Bogost, for example, pointed out how many of the design tropes we associate with games arose in response to hardware constraints imposed by the Atari VCS, an early mainstream gaming console [23]. This trend has been continued by serious games, as one of their typical value propositions is the technological progress they deliver [1, 21, 40]. Our game design concepts have constantly been coupled to considerations for how to maximise the individual and collaborative potential of the requisite underlying technologies. For example, the team concerned with contributing NUI technology developed a component that infers players' attention levels according to gaze detection on the screen. Part of the design challenge has become to determine how the game should respond in accordance to differing levels of player attention. The conflict resolution literature highlights the importance of emotions in conflict management and resolution, but the emotions discussed in the literature typically concern frustration, anger, and sadness, as opposed to level of attention, which falls within the broader domain of affect. Players' attention levels certainly do impact on the play and learning experience, and could be leveraged very usefully to adapt game contents. But they address an aspect of affective design that is different from that examined in the domain literature.

While some of the technologies have not readily formed an affinity with the problem domain, others have seemed more immediately applicable. For example, the conflict resolution literature proposes narrative structures as a metaphor for understanding conflict, which fits well with the narrative focus of interactive storytelling. Our progress in the interactive storytelling domain has been slower than some of the other technology components, however, partially because it has been contingent on the user research and literature findings.

In step with our ambitions for developing ground-breaking technology, we have been tethered by the limitations of existing computing platforms available to our users. This presents a paradox for the value proposition of technological progress presented by serious games advocates. Scholars have noted that one of the biggest challenges for serious games is integration within existing infrastructures, whether these be ideological, pedagogical, or technological [9, 16]. Egenfeldt-Nielsen, for example, conducted an empirical study to explore the practical challenges of introducing serious games to the classroom. Over a seven week period, he encountered numerous technological challenges, including a shortage of computers, a lack of technical support, and vandalism by the students [10]. We committed to implementing player modeling within the game, which translated to the constraint that only one player would be able to play per computer as it is currently infeasible to conduct (individual) player modeling on computers being used by two or more players. But early explorations of the technology set-ups in the schools participating in our project revealed that not all of them had computer labs. In some schools there was only one computer per classroom. While we have not yet settled on a solution, a potential workaround we are considering is inviting these schools to play the games in the computer labs of the nearest participating partner. This, of course, will end up impacting on how evaluation can be conducted down the line, and more long term, whether our games can indeed be integrated into the infrastructures of schools. We find ourselves needing to balance our project commitments and personal desires to innovate against the realities of classroom technology facilities.

Domain knowledge

The "serious" in *serious games* is largely explained by the intended relation to the real world inherent in the mechanics, content, objective, or outcome of a game [3]. As such, a fundamental aspect of a serious game is that it has real world relevance. To this end, an invaluable resource is existing research within the relevant subject domain. But the transition from literature to game design is not always obvious. Moving from literature to game design requires significant creativity. At a more subtle level, it requires scope reduction.

As no one in our consortium is already a conflict resolution expert, three partners have taken on the task of exploring the sociology and psychology literature on conflict. This process has helped us to develop a better understanding of how conflict management has been, could be, and should be addressed. Simultaneously, it has helped us to articulate what we are not doing in our project.

There is no shortage of research on conflict resolution, and part of the task of those involved in literature reviews has been to establish which of the research to draw from. Our choices regarding literature have undeniably been shaped by an awareness that we will need to proceduralise and computationalise these concepts, transforming them into game components, mechanics, and scenarios. For example, one popular definition of conflict proposed by Deutsch that we have adopted presents conflict in a way that strongly resonates with game-based challenge: "a conflict of interests occurs when the actions of one person attempting to reach his or her goals prevent, block or interfere with the actions of another person attempting to reach his or her goals" [8]. Another definition proposed by Thomas that we have also taken into consideration positions conflict as a process, which again seems well-suited to procedural representation: "the process which begins when one party perceives that another has frustrated, or is about to frustrate, some concern of his".

Beyond definitions alone, in step with learning more about conflict, we have essentially been developing literature-informed views of conflict that support game-based stories and technology-based representations of conflict. We now see conflict as follows: it is a dyadic event – while it may involve many participants, it is an interaction between two opposing sides. It is also an episode of social interaction – even if not always a constructive one – with a recognizable temporal duration. As such, it has much in common with narrative. Indeed, Laursen and Hafen explicitly compared the typical plot of conflict to that of a play or novel, and we see potential in translating these concepts to game design: "There is a protagonist and an antagonist (conflict participants), a theme (conflict topic), a complication (initial opposition), rising action (conflict behaviors), climax or crisis (conflict resolution), and denouement (conflict outcome)" [19].

Understanding the constituent components of conflict is one thing; educating young people on how to resolve it is another; and communicating how to do so using games as a medium is yet another. Bodine and Crawford noted that the way conflict resolution is typically approached in schools includes third party settlement of disputes, reactive responses after conflict has reached a critical point, and breaking of school rules as key focal points [2]. To facilitate young people in dealing with their conflicts more proactively and effectively, Bodine and Crawford developed a six-phase problem-solving process. In order, these phases include: *setting the stage*, *gathering perspectives*, *identifying interests*, *creating options*, *evaluating options*, and *generating agreement*. The process-based perspective was appealing to us because it echoed with major rhetorical strengths of computer games, namely, the ability to represent processes and for players to enact those processes themselves [3]. We also found resonance for this model in Gee's principles for learning in games, namely the *Probing Principle* and the *Multiple Routes Principle* [15]. Bodine and Crawford's process also echos classic HCI models, namely GOMS [5], and Norman's human action cycle [25].

The flip side to relying on certain views and perspectives means that others have not been incorporated. Conflict perspectives which are less well-suited for representation through games and technology have correspondingly received less attention from us. Games and technology have become a literature filter for this project. Even though we set out to enrich our game experience, context, and content with relevant research, as a side-effect of the nature of our project, we inevitably introduced a skew into our interpretation of the existing literature.

User Research

As the last three decades of HCI have shown, user research greatly improves the relevance and longevity of technology. A key goal of our project has been to develop games about conflict resolution that can fit into learning contexts and regular classrooms. Developing such games requires asking a series of questions that the domain literature cannot answer. Questions we have found ourselves asking in order to progress with design include: what conflicts do children from our target group actually experience in a school setting? What do children between the ages of 9 – 11 deem as acceptable methods of conflict resolution? What are the conflict resolution philosophies of the schools involved in the project? Do the students receive specialised instruction on conflict resolution? Which class subject should the game be played in? How game-literate are these students, and what does this suggest about what kind of game we should design?

To establish how to meet the needs of our end users, and their understandings of, and responses to conflict, three partners have been conducting user research with students and teachers in schools in the UK, Portugal, and Greece. The project member who has been tasked with much of the user research efforts, who is also an author of this paper, has a background in anthropology.

Children can be challenging user research participants, due to reasons including shyness, attention span, difficulties in articulating abstract concepts, and awkwardness surrounding power issues between interviewer and interviewee. To further complicate issues, conflict tends to be a sensitive topic for people in general. To mitigate these concerns, the partners in our project are employing a number of methods. These include ethnographies conducted at school, interviews with students and teachers, cultural probes, and data collection using the comics tool *Pixton* [26]. Here we reflect on the ethnography and interview process.

The anthropologist commenced his user research by conducting ethnographies at two schools in the UK, where he spent two weeks sitting in on classes and observing playground events. Next, he embarked on the interview phase, during which he interviewed 47 students from the aforementioned schools. His objectives were to find out about conflict situations they had either been involved in personally or had recently witnessed, what conflict resolution strategies they had adopted, and their emotional responses following these incidents. In addition, he conducted interviews with two teachers from these schools to gain insight into how teachers approached conflict resolution in their classrooms.

On transcribing and coding the data gathered, a number of recurrent themes were observed. These included conflicts related to jokes going wrong or being misunderstood, conflicts related to cultural and religious identity and norms, and conflicts related to breaking promises and deception. In terms of resolution strategies, the most common responses were: physical aggression, verbal aggression, and withdrawal. With regards to teachers, their strategies for mediating conflicts tended towards trying to keep students apart until their emotional responses had calmed in terms of intensity. Afterwards, they encouraged conflicting parties to talk to each other to obtain both perspectives.

In interpreting the data, the anthropologist made an effort to relate his findings to the theoretical constructs introduced in the previous section, but noted that drawing strict connections between the theory and the observed data was often difficult. For example, while much of the literature we have relied on to date discusses conflict from an overall perspective, the students were only able to recount experiences from individual perspectives, that are partial at best. Furthermore, much of the literature conceptualises conflict from adult perspectives, which does not necessarily translate to children.

The early user research data was met with interest from other project partners, but also triggered additional questions often related to specific, technology-related responsibilities. For example, the partners involved in PCG and NUI were both keen to find out about what emotions students were feeling *while* conflicts were taking place, because they were interested in using it as game input to drive adaptation. Not being familiar with the ins and outs of the technology implementation plans, however, emotions experienced during conflicts had not been a core focal point for the anthropologist during the initial user research phase. In addition, from early on in the project, for practical and ethical reasons, analysing emotions generated during interpersonal conflicts in situ was ruled out. But to doubly complicate matters, the participants involved in the user research were not always adept at articulating conflict-related concerns. Even when the anthropologist had asked the participants about their emotions, it was rarely the case that they were able to fully elaborate on them.

Our user researchers have in many ways needed to be the most knowledgeable about everyone else's needs, as they have been the single point of contact with the users. They have also had to become experts at conducting research with the specific user group, which in this case is children. This highlights an interesting tension: as technology and technology projects become increasingly complex, we expect more and more from user researchers. We expect them to be in possession of social science and design research skills, meanwhile, we also expect them to understand (to some degree) the complicated internal workings of technology. In our project, as one of our core objectives is to develop ground-breaking technology, this effect has been exacerbated.

Within the field of IxD, there are widely understood paths for moving from user research towards design ideation stages. The same cannot be said for serious game design, which rests, in large part, on design practices borrowed from mainstream game design. Current game design processes privilege the perspective of game designers. Typically, a designer comes up with a concept, which initially relies very little on player opinions and input. Fullerton and others have advocated for playtesting of game concepts with real players from early on [13, 29]. Even so, future players rarely shape the game design from the beginning – their involvement generally begins once a playtestable game exists. Whether or not this is problematic for game design, a lack of early player involvement is problematic for serious game design. In a related vein, while it is unusual to think of user requirements in relation to mainstream games, such requirements are needed for serious games, sometimes with different requirements needed by different stakeholders. With the exception of a handful of works e.g. [27, 33, 34], little research to date discusses how to incorporate the perspectives of end users and future players into design. Further emblematic of the problem, user research processes do not straightforwardly map to game design processes. So not only is there little precedent for right ways to incorporate such data, there are also few obvious ways. Having user research injected into our project has been both eye-opening and baffling, as we continue to attempt to bridge the gap between the players and the game.

Game design

Conflict resolution can be taught in a number of ways. It can range from indirect methods - including day-to-day skills gleaned from normal social interactions - to the explicit - including role play exercises, workshops, classroom-based instruction, and cognitive behavioural therapy exercises. From the inception of this project, we were contractually obliged to develop a serious game. So part of our research has been establishing what affordances games as a medium offer for teaching and learning about conflict resolution. Simultaneously, we have been attempting to progress the game design in a manner that suits the needs and expectations of the diverse members of the project consortium.

Within the serious game design literature, there is widespread acknowledgement of the complex interrelations involved in designing a serious game. The insights provided often centre on how to design effective, entertaining, and pedagogically meaningful game mechanics. Several sets of such best practice design guidelines for serious games exist, ranging from mechanics that have been observed in existing serious games [1, 18], mechanics that have been observed in popular games [15, 35], and design suggestions that are derived from broader theoretical perspectives, such as behaviourist psychology [20], and situated learning [9]. The literature also describes potential design processes to adopt [12] and frameworks of operation [1, 39].

While partners were tasked with user research and conflict scenario design efforts, no particular partner was tasked with game design, which is not interchangeable with the aforementioned tasks. Allocating the design decision making to one partner alone would have created a bottleneck in terms of management, decision making, and effort. As such, the game design responsibility dynamic that has emerged in the consortium is that both no one and everyone is responsible for the game design. In moving towards a game design that satisfies all of our criteria, we have simultaneously progressed along two channels: exploration of the literature and of qualities of existing games and serious games that could be beneficial in our project, and design ideation strictly related to conflict resolution. Whereas the former has progressed smoothly, the latter has proved to be a delicate undertaking.

The design ideation has involved trying to marry technology needs and perspectives, theory demands and constraints, and user requirements and ethnographic insights, for the purpose of producing game design concepts. Each of these perspectives on their own, in fact, could inspire separate and distinct game designs. At some points, this process has felt almost deadlocked, as it has been nigh impossible to move forward with any design decisions before getting clearance from other partners. They have understandably not felt comfortable locking decisions in place without first fully understanding their own domains of concern, as decisions made at this point could have unforeseen ramifications and limiting consequences down the track. Our task has been to try to incrementally weave together these distinctive threads into a cohesive artifact and experience, in step with the insights that keep progressively emerging as different partners continue their particular project tasks. As well as remaining cognisant of interweaving on a design concept level, though, we have also had to deal with the human aspect of collaboration. This has included establishing how to promote preferred concepts while not stepping on the toes of, or creating friction with other consortium members, negotiating when necessary, and knowing when to choose our battles.

For example, one design concept proposed by the team tasked with PCG technology was inspired both by Thomas's scheme of five conflict management modes [36], and the need to create PCG content. The game consisted of a multiplayer resource management game lasting for a number of rounds, in which players oversee different sets of workers, and must barter, compete, and cooperate with each other to survive. The bartering and socialising mechanics of the game could be mapped to different modes of conflict handling strategies, thus the design supported the tracking of strategic tendencies amongst certain players. Furthermore, the game scenarios were to be adapted procedurally in response to players' strategies. The PCG team were optimistic about this concept, but were careful to not commit to it too deeply as they felt that the concept could easily be rejected by the other partners.

Following the PCG team's proposal of the resource management concept to the consortium, the team developing intelligent agents presented a different design concept. This concept was based around a theater director metaphor that enabled players to act as conflict mediators, and also maximised the potential to explore interesting behaviour for intelligent agents. Naturally, the different technology-focused partners suggested and gravitated towards design solutions that optimally leveraged their own technologies. As our project does encompass a number of distinct agendas, the consortium decided that the most sustainable, efficient, and manageable path of progress would be to come up with separate minigame designs, and to present the collection of these minigames as the complete Siren game. The divide-and-conquer approach to game design seemed like one that would ease project complications by giving all partners a degree of autonomy.

But this approach of presenting a collection of minigames did not feel sufficiently cohesive to an author of this paper. She proposed an overall game frame story to house the minigames. In the frame story, the player is dreaming, and encounters a number of recurring dreams that each correspond to minigames developed by the different partners. The recurring dreams are eating over the space of the player's dreamscape, so the player's objective is to resolve the conflicts to dissipate the dreams. The dream metaphor as an organising system dynamic seemed to have a number of advantages. It was a meta-level solution for narrative inconsistency caused by multiple minigames. It facilitated independent team work on separate minigames highlighting different technologies. Furthermore, it provided a plausible context for consideration of conflict, as dreams often echo real life events whilst incorporating fantasy; not unlike practice runs of life.

On hearing about this concept, however, the other author of this paper was not completely happy. He raised concerns about whether the dream metaphor was too scary for the age group. He also queried whether there was a need for a game frame story, and whether the coherence was more for the sake of developing a cohesive game in keeping with our existing expectations of games, or whether it would be genuinely advantageous for students learning about conflict resolution. His question in fact highlighted one the classic tensions involved in developing serious games – what to prioritise: game experience or serious application? In addition, he voiced concerns that if our game felt too "game-like" and was too far removed from the reality of the classroom then teachers would not embrace it. The conservative perspective he presented seemed at odds with the future-oriented research encouraged by the European Commission, but emphasised the importance of serious games needing to fit into their surroundings to stand a chance of success and adoption. Amongst our consortium, opinions are still split. Creating watered-down compromises of everyone's visions is not an appealing option, as good design is rarely a matter of finding averages.

UNDERLYING FORCES: INVISIBLE, UNINVITED TEAM MEMBERS

As the above discussion highlights, the dynamics of design and development for larger-scale serious game projects are complex. Work flows are messy, often difficult to explain, and collaboration requires a lot of time and translation effort. What has gradually become evident is that there are many different, sometimes hidden forces involved in large projects. More conventional software engineering methodologies, which favour positivist and modernist perspectives, often cast stories about technology as grand narratives of progress. But these have the effect of backgrounding more minor narratives and underlying forces. Here we examine some of the forces that have been acting on our project. Identifying them facilitates us in turning a critical eye towards our work, it helps us to develop a better awareness of interactions involved in projects, and informs us in terms of where to usefully invest effort. We do not present general solutions for how to address these forces, but do briefly describe how we have been responding to their effects on our specific project.

Technology adds rigidity to the solution space

Before our project had even begun, certain factors had already been set in stone, especially with regards to technology solutions. In terms of our grant agreement, successful development and integration of the technologies discussed above plays as important a role in the evaluation as does successful addressing of the problem domain. Some of the technologies naturally map to the problem domain, while others do not. As the maxim goes, there is freedom within constraints. In our case, it has sometimes seemed that technology has added constraints to the solution of a *different* problem: we have found ourselves trying to build bridges between these problems, transforming one into the other. Or from another perspective, technology has brought rigidity to the solution.

We understand rigidity as somewhat different in nature from a constraint – whereas constraints bound a design solution space, rigidity is within the solution space. That is, certain aspects, features, or forms already exist within the solution space, and part of the design challenge is to make the rest of the design solution connect with rigid aspects. Technology has brought rigidity to our project in more indirect ways as well. It has heavily informed how we have come to understand conflict resolution research – such as our focus on emotions, our understandings of conflict-as-episodic and conflict-as-narrative, and procedural interpretations of conflict events. The technology lens acting on our readings of the conflict resolution research has already impacted on how conflict resolution will ultimately be represented and experienced by our players. As technology is central to our project, we cannot avoid this rigidity. We have, however, begun more openly acknowledging it, which has freed up partners to suggest solutions, interpretations, and philosophies that do not readily support technocentric understandings. This has broadened our understanding of the problem space, encouraged debate amongst consortium members, and made us more thoughtful about usefully leveraging technology.

IxD is IxD and game design is game design

As our discussion of the literature review activities and user research highlights, there is no straightforward way to interface between either research-informed understandings of phenomena or user research-informed perspectives of phenomena to game design. This is an issue faced by design in general and serious games in particular, expressly because of the contradictory qualities of "serious games". Breaking these contradictory qualities down into some of their constituent parts, two bodies of literature that surround the serious games literature broadly include game design literature and the IxD literature. Unfortunately, neither literature provides us with clear answers. The game design literature provides much insight into how to design games, but has little guidance for how to conduct early stage design research with end users (players), or how to fold these insights back into the design process. The IxD literature, on the other hand, features well-developed and well-tested methods for incorporating user perspectives, but unsurprisingly sheds little light on how to move from user insights to game mechanics and game concepts. The serious games design literature itself often focuses closely on insights from the learning sciences, or psychological principles supporting post-game consequences, but rarely provides in depth treatments of how to incorporate players. To address this under-explored area, one of our objectives has become to document and reflect on our ongoing experiences with user research-informed serious game design. Our user researchers and game designers have been working together in this regard, and are currently looking into repurposing Scaife et al.'s informant design framework [28] for use in a game design context.

Deep down we are not all the same

Our project team is made up of individuals with diverse knowledge bases, epistemologies, agendas, and assumptions about how to conduct research. This diversity of background was required for us to fulfill our project objectives. But the more diverse the members of project consortia are, the more a burden is placed on all project members in terms of needing to understand each other's specialised domains. We touched on this issue above with regards to the anthropologist needing to be knowledgeable about a topic far outside of his background, and the burden placed on user researchers as technology becomes progressively more complex. In fact, this is a concern faced by most of the partners involved in our project. For example, some technology-focused partners have found it equally difficult to make sense of user research methods and some of the more intangible design processes. The learning curve for everyone has been increased by the dovetailing of project responsibilities and the open paradigm of organisation we adopted, with its relatively flat management structure and decision-making processes of negotiation and consensus. For interdisciplinary projects taken on in the future involving new disciplines or foci, this situation cannot be avoided. But measures can be taken to acknowledge the diversity and to create bottom-up contexts of crossover interests. Recently we conducted a workshop featuring some of the consortium partners to address some of the semantic and conceptual impasses that we kept encountering. The workshop served as a review session of collective project vision and as a forum for in-depth examination of the responsibilities of different partners. It culminated in the shared authoring of a revised version of a game design document, and resulted in greater feelings of project cohesion.

Encapsulation hinders design process collaboration

In software engineering, encapsulation is understood as a way of hiding away details of object data, components, and the inner workings of procedures. In order to acquire some autonomy, as well as facilitate progress in an overall process that has sometimes felt logically deadlocked, we have often encapsulated our responsibilities and conducted work individually in our separate teams. While this has the short term appearance of economising on time, the long term consequence has often not followed suit. When regrouping at meetings featuring members from across the consortium, or during task handover from one partner to another, issues have arisen ranging from a lack of understanding, to lack of agreement and endorsement, through to lack of ability to integrate. The obvious alternative is deeper collaboration at all points along the process. As discussed above, this is a surprisingly costly undertaking, both in terms of time, work effort, and at the human level. In fact, our process has been characterised by alternations between faster, autonomous work sprints followed by slower, collaborative work, on occasion associated with a degree of backtracking. So, while in the context of software engineering encapsulation supports collaboration, in the case of our design process it has sometimes hindered it. Within the consortium, we have now opted to pursue tighter collaboration and less encapsulation, as it has generally led to more rewarding experiences. One way we are doing this by having certain individuals participate in tasks that are interdependent, as these individuals will be able to relay understandings to others. Another way is by creating more joint tasks, which necessitates greater coordination and collaboration.

CONCLUSIONS

Large-scale serious game projects need to satisfy many different constraints. They involve numerous stakeholders, including researchers from different traditions, practitioners, funding bodies, and users. They also draw together distinct and sometimes competing perspectives – project organisation, technology, domain knowledge, user research, and game design. All of these perspectives have an effect on one another. They cannot be cleanly separated. The trajectory of tasks conducted from each perspective is intertwined with that of other perspectives. As tasks motivated from one perspective are advanced, tensions can be created on tasks from others.

In this paper we presented a reflective examination of our process so far of working in an interdisciplinary team to design a serious game to facilitate young people in learning about conflict resolution. In focusing on five different perspectives, we brought to light some factors that are often overlooked once projects draw to a close, including methodological discrepancies, funding and evaluation criteria, selection processes for literature, burdens placed on user researchers, mismatches between research agendas and contexts of use, and disagreements amongst project members. We demonstrated how project concerns are complex, interwoven, and inseparable, resulting in what occasionally feels like deadlock. We also described a number of underlying forces that emerged from examinations of the perspectives: the rigidity of technology, the lack of a well-trodden path between IxD and game design, communication gaps between project members caused by complexity and expertise, and autonomous project work being at odds with collaborative project work.

Throughout, we have attempted to avoid presenting a grand narrative perspective of our progress. A grand narrative would have underplayed the idiosyncratic details of the smaller constituent stories that characterise the nature of our project. If we do not acknowledge the existence of these little stories, we lose the ability to be reflective about and accountable for decisions made and courses of action sought, because the grand narrative of large projects gradually over-write and come to stand in for what actually happened. Because of rosy retrospection and the research-oriented drive to provide value, it is tempting to paint increasingly more positive pictures of research endeavours. While positive post-hoc overall narratives do provide us with optimism, they are less helpful from a methodological perspective for people currently mired in project processes. We provide these real-time observations from the front lines of a large-scale serious game project.

ACKNOWLEDGEMENTS

We thank the entire SIREN team, who are the ever-patient protagonists of these stories. This work has been supported in part by the EU FP7 ICT project SIREN (project number: 258453).

REFERENCES

1. Annetta, L. The “i's” have it: A framework for serious educational game design. *Review of General Psychology 14*, 2 (2010), 105–112.
2. Bodine, R., and Crawford, D. *The Handbook of Conflict Resolution Education: A Guide to Building Quality Programs in Schools*. Jossey-Bass Inc. Publishers, 1998.
3. Bogost, I. *Persuasive Games: The Expressive Power of Videogames*. The MIT Press, 2007.
4. Bornemann, K. The elusive 'quick iteration' - tips for indie devs. `http://altdevblogaday.com/2011/08/05/the-elusive-quick-iteration-tips-for-indie-devs/`, August 2011.
5. Card, S. K., Newell, A., and Moran, T. P. *The Psychology of Human-Computer Interaction*. L. Erlbaum Associates Inc., Hillsdale, NJ, USA, 1983.
6. Cockburn, A. *Agile Software Development*. Addison-Wesley Professional, 2001.
7. Constantine, L. L. Work organization: paradigms for project management and organization. *Commun. ACM 36* (October 1993), 35–43.
8. Deutsch, M. *The resolution of conflict: Constructive and destructive processes*. Yale University Press, New Haven, Connecticut, 1973.
9. Egenfeldt-Nielsen, S. Third generation educational use of computer games. *Journal of Educational Multimedia and Hypermedia 16*, 3 (2007), 263–281.
10. Egenfeldt-Nielsen, S. Beyond fun. ETC Press, Pittsburgh, PA, USA, 2008, ch. Practical barriers in using educational computer games, 20–26.
11. European Commission. FP7 Cooperation Work Programme: Information and Communication Technologies. Published on European Commission CORDIS FP7 ICT website, July 2009.
12. Flanagan, M., and Nissenbaum, H. A game design methodology to incorporate social activist themes. In *Proceedings of the SIGCHI conference on Human factors in computing systems*, CHI '07, ACM (New York, NY, USA, 2007), 181–190.
13. Fullerton, T. *Game Design Workshop, Second Edition: A Playcentric Approach to Creating Innovative Games (Gama Network Series)*, 2 ed. Morgan Kaufmann, February 2008.
14. Gaver, W., Bowers, J., Kerridge, T., Boucher, A., and Jarvis, N. Anatomy of a failure: how we knew when our design went wrong, and what we learned from it. In *Proceedings of the 27th international conference on Human factors in computing systems*, CHI '09, ACM (New York, NY, USA, 2009), 2213–2222.
15. Gee, J. P. *What Video Games Have to Teach Us About Learning and Literacy*. Palgrave Macmillan, 2003.
16. Gros, B. Digital games in education: The design of games-based learning environments. *Journal of Research on Technology in Education 40*, 1 (2007), 23–38.

17. Hoegl, M., Weinkauf, K., and Gemuenden, H. G. Interteam coordination, project commitment, and teamwork in multiteam r&d projects: A longitudinal study. *Organization Science 15* (January 2004), 38–55.

18. Isbister, K., Flanagan, M., and Hash, C. Designing games for learning: insights from conversations with designers. In *Proceedings of the 28th international conference on Human factors in computing systems*, CHI '10, ACM (New York, NY, USA, 2010), 2041–2044.

19. Laursen, B., and Hafen, C. A. Future directions in the study of close relationships: Conflict is bad (except when it's not). *Social Development 19* (2010), 858–872.

20. Linehan, C., Kirman, B., Lawson, S., and Chan, G. Practical, appropriate, empirically-validated guidelines for designing educational games. In *Proceedings of the 2011 annual conference on Human factors in computing systems*, CHI '11, ACM (New York, NY, USA, 2011), 1979–1988.

21. Losh, E. Making things public: democracy and government-funded videogames and virtual reality simulations. In *Proceedings of the 2006 ACM SIGGRAPH symposium on Videogames*, Sandbox '06, ACM (New York, NY, USA, 2006), 123–132.

22. Malone, T. W. What makes things fun to learn? heuristics for designing instructional computer games. In *Proceedings of the 3rd ACM SIGSMALL symposium and the first SIGPC symposium on Small systems*, SIGSMALL '80, ACM (New York, NY, USA, 1980), 162–169.

23. Montfort, N., and Bogost, I. *Racing the Beam: The Atari Video Computer System*. The MIT Press, 2009.

24. Muller, M. J. The human-computer interaction handbook. L. Erlbaum Associates Inc., Hillsdale, NJ, USA, 2003, ch. Participatory design: the third space in HCI, 1051–1068.

25. Norman, D. A. *The Psychology of Everyday Things*. Basic Books, New York, 1990.

26. Pixton. Pixton. `http://www.pixton.com`, September 2011.

27. Rankin, Y. A., McNeal, M., Shute, M. W., and Gooch, B. User centered game design: evaluating massive multiplayer online role playing games for second language acquisition. In *Proceedings of the 2008 ACM SIGGRAPH symposium on Video games*, Sandbox '08, ACM (New York, NY, USA, 2008), 43–49.

28. Scaife, M., Rogers, Y., Aldrich, F., and Davies, M. Designing for or designing with? informant design for interactive learning environments. In *Proceedings of the SIGCHI conference on Human factors in computing systems*, CHI '97, ACM (New York, NY, USA, 1997), 343–350.

29. Schell, J. *The Art of Game Design: A book of lenses*, 1 ed. Morgan Kaufmann, Aug. 2008.

30. Schön, D. A. *The Reflective Practitioner: How Professionals Think in Action*. Basic Books, 1983.

31. Sengers, P., Boehner, K., David, S., and 'jofish Kaye, J. Reflective design. In *Proceedings of Critical Computing*, ACM Press (2005), 49–58.

32. Shirinian, A. Dissecting the postmortem: Lessons learned from two years of game development self-reportage. *Game Developer Magazine* (February 2011).

33. Sotamaa, O. Perceptions of player in game design literature. In *Situated Play: Proceedings of the 2007 Digital Games Research Association Conference*, B. Akira, Ed., The University of Tokyo (Tokyo, September 2007), 456–465.

34. Sotamaa, O., Ermi, L., Jäppinen, A., Laukkanen, T., Mäyrä, F., and Nummela, J. The Role of Players in Game Design: A Methodological Perspective. In *Proceedings of the 6th DAC Conference* (Copenhagen, 2005), 34 – 42.

35. Squire, K. From content to context: videogames as designed experience. *Educational Researcher 35*, 8 (2006), 19 – 29.

36. Thomas, K. W. Conflict and conflict management: Reflections and update. *Journal of Organizational Behavior 13*, 3 (1992), 265–274.

37. Tran, M. Q., and Biddle, R. Collaboration in serious game development: a case study. In *Proceedings of the 2008 Conference on Future Play: Research, Play, Share*, Future Play '08, ACM (New York, NY, USA, 2008), 49–56.

38. UBM TechWeb. Game developer magazine. `http://www.gdmag.com/homepage.htm`, September 2011.

39. Winn, B. The design, play, and experience framework. In *Handbook of Research on Effective Electronic Gaming in Education*. IGI Global Publication, Hershey, Philadelphia, July 2008, 1010 – 1024.

40. Zyda, M. From visual simulation to virtual reality to games. *Computer 38* (September 2005), 25–32.

Not Doing But Thinking: The Role of Challenge in the Gaming Experience

Anna L Cox
UCL Interaction Centre
University College London
anna.cox@ucl.ac.uk

Paul Cairns
Dept of Computer Science
University of York
paul.cairns@york.ac.uk

Pari Shah
Psychology & Language Sciences
University College London
zcjtbb4@ucl.ac.uk

Michael Carroll
Dept of Computer Science
University of York
mjpc@cs.york.ac.uk

ABSTRACT
Previous research into the experience of videogames has shown the importance of the role of challenge in producing a good experience. However, defining exactly which challenges are important and which aspects of gaming experience are affected is largely under-explored. In this paper, we investigate if altering the level of challenge in a videogame influences people's experience of immersion. Our first study demonstrates that simply increasing the physical demands of the game by requiring gamers to interact more with the game does not result in increased immersion. In a further two studies, we use time pressure to make games more physically *and* cognitively challenging. We find that the addition of time pressure increases immersion as predicted. We argue that the level of challenge experienced is an interaction between the level of expertise of the gamer and the cognitive challenge encompassed within the game.

Author Keywords
Games; immersion; challenge.

ACM Classification Keywords
K.8.0 Personal Computing: General - Games

General Terms
Experimentation

INTRODUCTION
Videogames are possibly the most successful application of computing by almost any measure. For instance, the games industry now exceeds cinema in terms of sales [5] and eight out of ten homes in the UK own a next-generation videogame console [29]. What underlies this success is undoubtedly the experiences that people have with games, but what exactly those experiences are and how they influence people is only just beginning to be understood.

There are currently several approaches to defining and measuring gaming experience (GX) and whilst these differ in emphasis and detail, there are general overlaps in how gaming experience is understood. At the most basic level, GX arises from engagement with games and it is useful to both quantify that engagement [1] and to understand the components of a game that lead to engagement [4]. There are also concerns for specific aspects of gaming experience such as immersion, the sense of being cognitively involved in the game to the exclusion of the world around you [12, 15], and presence, the sense of being actually present in the world of the game as if it were real [26]. Both of these concepts are included in more general approaches to GX that attempt to cover all the major components of experiences that may arise from playing videogames not just immersion and presence but also enjoyment, flow, emotions and so on [20]. These more general descriptions of GX even extend to include wider, more complex aspects of gaming such as narrative and social relationships [21, 9].

These descriptions of GX provide frameworks in which to understand how different aspects of games lead to specific experiences. Research in this area covers diverse features from the controllers used to play [26] and the scenarios used to motivate the game [22] to the Quality of Service provided in networked games [30] and even the reviews games receive [18].

Underpinning the study of GX is the need for effective metrics. Those descriptions of GX mentioned above are operationalised as questionnaires that allow for the quantification of GX. Other richer, more complex measures are also possible such as the use of patterns to classify behaviour of players [10] or the use of log or telemetry data [13].

Whilst much is being done, there are still many fundamental questions that remain. The aim of this paper is to address one such question by considering the role of challenge in GX.

Immersion

In the work reported here, we are specifically concerned with the concept of immersion. This is the sense of being absorbed in a game to the exclusion of all else outside of the game. The experience of immersion in videogames is commonly reported by players, reviewers and designers of games [3] and, in various guises, is common to many of the theories of GX. Typical consequences of immersion are a sense of dissociation from the real world, a loss of the sense of time and a high degree of cognitive and emotional involvement in the gameplay and its outcome [15].

Whilst immersion is recognized as important in GX, the field of positive psychology is dominated by the theory of Flow [8]. Flow is an extreme experience combining elements of skill, progress, challenge and focus to produce an optimal experience. It is best characterized as the sporting experience of being "in the zone" but can also be experienced in factory work and playing chess. Within videogames, flow is considered to be an important component of GX [6, 7]. Others have tailored this theory specifically for gaming with the concept of GameFlow [27] but whereas flow is the experience had by players, GameFlow is the features of a game that are proposed to generally lead to flow experiences. As such, flow and GameFlow both relate to optimal experiences. However, when flow is formulated in the context of GX and particularly measuring GX, flow is actually operationalised to be a graded experience where people can grade their level of flow e.g. [20]. This makes little sense – an athlete cannot be "a bit in the zone" and gamers cannot be a bit in flow.

In contrast, immersion is acknowledged as a graded experience ranging from engagement, through engrossment to total immersion [3]. It is only total immersion that can be viewed as being analogous to flow [25]. When playing a videogame, many people are having much more prosaic experiences than those conceived by the notion of flow. When in flow, by definition, one is not monitoring other activities in the environment. But when immersed in a videogame, other things can be going on that the player is attending to. For instance, in mobile games, the player might also be waiting for a bus and thus actively monitoring the environment for the arrival of a bus, checking to see if it has the required route number as well as applying focused attention and engagement in playing a game on their phone. The player is somewhat immersed but definitely not in flow.

Challenge

Across the several different GX theories, there are concepts that consistently occur as important constituents of GX. One such concept is challenge. Indeed, without a challenge that is perceived as worthy, games are simply not enjoyed as much [16]. However, challenge, as used in this context, is that reported by the gamer on reflection of their experience. How this relates to the actual challenge presented by games has only begun to be examined [22] and even then the definition of challenge is purely in terms of players' perception of difficulty. It is possible that respondents to a questionnaire incorporating challenge elements are merely asserting the challenge experienced as some sort of halo response to a generally positive (or negative) GX. And even if this were not the case, none of the approaches are precise about what specifically the challenges are that lead to a particularly good (or bad) GX.

Designers of games necessarily consider how to make a game challenging to the gamer [23]. There are two main ways to achieve this: push the gamer's physical limits; or push the gamer's cognitive limits [14, 19]. The gamer's physicality limits the speed with which interactions with the game can be conducted, and the accuracy with which actions can be performed. The gamer's cognitive abilities have a limiting effect on speed and accuracy of the problem solving activities required by the game.

Immersion is believed to specifically arise from the level of challenge experienced by gamers. As such, challenge, as perceived by the player, is a component that goes into the make-up of immersion [15] and can be isolated as its own factor of immersion. However, as with other aspects of GX, what is undefined is what sort of challenge is required in order to increase the immersive experience. In this paper we explore how both the cognitive and physical abilities of a gamer can be challenged, and investigate which has the greater effect on the level of immersion experienced. In our first experiment we manipulate the number of interactions required to make progress in the game and thus the speed with which the gamer must interact with the game. Our second and third experiments manipulate the level of time pressure under which the participants play the game. In contrast to experiment one which simply manipulates the number of actions the participants have to make, the addition of time pressure in experiments two and three means that participants have to also think faster. We hypothesise that it is the cognitive challenge that will have the greater effect on immersion.

Expertise

Csikszentmihalyi [8] suggests that flow is achieved as a result of an appropriate balance between the perceived level of challenge and the person's skills. Given the relationship between immersion and flow, we are interested in whether immersion is also sensitive to the balance between skill and challenge.

Therefore, in addition to manipulating time pressure and number of interactions, we also explore the role of expertise in immersion. We hypothesize that, if the gamer finds the game too challenging, where this level of challenge is too high in proportion to their skills, they are more likely to experience anxiety and may 'give-up' playing the game. However if the inverse is true, whereby the gamers skills are too high and the game is not challenging enough, then the gamer will be in a state of boredom. When a gamer is in either of these states (anxiety or boredom), they are less likely to be immersed in the game. In two of the studies reported here, we therefore also explore the role of expertise in combination with challenge to see how the two together influence immersion.

Overview of the experiments

To experimentally investigate the role of challenge on immersion, it is necessary to manipulate games within the strictures of experimental control to provide the different sorts of challenge. The ideal is two versions of the same game that differ only in the physical or cognitive challenge that they present.

For the first experiment, manipulating physical challenge could have been done by simply requiring more actions to achieve the same effects, eg two mouse clicks to select an object rather than one. However, unless this is plausibly motivated by the game, players will perceive such naïve manipulations as unnecessarily awkward and immersion could be reduced simply because of frustration at poor game design. The aim for the game in the first experiment was therefore to provide essentially the same playing experience with the same level of difficulty but that simply required more actions to keep playing. As will be seen this manipulation does seem to have been successfully achieved.

For the second and third experiments that intend to manipulate the cognitive challenge, it is not enough to provide more difficult puzzles or tasks for players as such increases in cognitive challenge may leave the players unable to make any progress in the game and decreases could leave the game too easy to be interesting. Instead, we chose to manipulate the time pressure on the player. This would mean that players would be required to achieve the same cognitive tasks but at different rates. This contrasts with the physical challenge of the first experiment in that if players failed to meet the cognitive challenge in the second two experiments then the game would end very quickly whereas in the first experiment, failure to keep up with the physical challenge would not mean immediate game over and the players would have the opportunity to subsequently act quickly to make up for lost time.

Of course it must be acknowledged that in manipulating challenge whilst maintaining comparability between experimental conditions, it is difficult to completely disentangle physical and cognitive challenge. Nonetheless, in the first experiment the emphasis of the manipulation is on physical challenge whereas on the latter two it is on cognitive challenge.

It should also be noted that the first experiment was devised in parallel with the second and third experiments due to the circumstances of the researchers involved. Thus, the design of the second and third experiments did not directly build on that of the first even though they did conceptually. Naturally, all three experiments drew on the same background research.

EXPERIMENT 1: INVESTIGATING THE EFFECT OF SPEED OF INTERACTION ON IMMERSION

The first experiment investigated how altering the level of physical effort required from players influenced their sense of immersion within the developed game. This was altered by changing the relative game 'intensity', represented by the level of activity required to play the game.

A number of possible effects could have been observed. Compelling players to be more active may have caused them to focus more intently upon the game, increasing their attention and potentially immersion. Conversely, 'frantic' gameplay could overstress players, preventing them from appreciating other aspects of the game, decreasing the cohesiveness of their experience and thus reducing their overall immersion level.

In addition, we explore the effect of expertise by categorizing players according to their prior experience with the game genre, in this case, Tower Defence Games.

Method

Design

This was a between subjects design with two conditions. The independent variable was the relative amount of effort required by the game: low effort (LEff) and high effort (HEff). The dependent variable was the participant's sense of immersion within the game, as calculated through participant responses to the Immersive Experience Questionnaire (IEQ) [15].

Participants

41 students from the University of York took part in the study; however, one participant's results were removed due to inattention and lack of effort during the study. As a result, there were 40 participants for analysis (29 male). Ages ranged from 18 to 24 (mean = 20.9).

Game experience and attitudes varied between the participants, ranging from those who played games less than once per month, to game programmers and even the chair of the York University LAN (Local Area Network) gaming society.

Materials

The game used in this study was a Tower Defense (TD) game purpose built for research in GX in general and this study in particular. The basic idea is common to all TD games where enemies (creeps) move from one side of the screen to the other along a set path. The player must place towers along the path to damage, hinder and ideally destroy all creeps before they reach the other side. Creeps have various characteristics such as speed, tolerance to damage and so on. Towers also vary in how they affect creeps, how fast they fire and they can further be upgraded to improve their characteristics. Towers and upgrades cost money which is generated by killing creeps. Players start with 20 lives and one is lost each time a creep manages to cross the screen. Play stops if all lives are lost or after eight minutes when the creeps stop attacking.. Because the pattern of creeps is the same each time, a simple measure of performance is how long a player survives before 20 creeps make it across the screen.

The advantage of using a specially developed game is that we could exercise experimental control over the gameplay to achieve a manipulation of physical challenge whilst maintaining the level of cognitive challenge. To do this, we used the notion of the game being "balanced." That is, the game is balanced if the amount of damage per second that players can buy matches the amount of damage that is needed to kill creeps at the required rate. To achieve this, the towers and creeps were specified so that despite the apparent range of differences between firepower of towers and the strength and speed of the creeps, provided the player placed the towers reasonably well and continually spent all income earned from killing creeps there would always be enough firepower to destroy the creeps. The only cognitive challenge would be where to place the towers and to a large extent that would not matter too much.

The initial game setup was determined through testing to create an appropriate rate of play. This was then reduced by approximately one third to create the low effort condition (LEff), and increased by approximately one third to form the high effort condition (HEff). In the LEff condition, players earned small amounts of money sufficient to buy powerful towers whereas in the HEff condition, players earned more money to by more but weaker towers than in the LEff condition. In both conditions, the game was balanced.

It may be argued that the HEff condition required more cognitive effort because of the task of having to frequently buy or upgrade towers, that is, the apparent time pressure. However, this is not the case because to a large extent it did not matter how players spent their money, simply that they spent it. Also, there was no specific time pressure to act at any particular moment. Falling behind in spending could be compensated for by a rapid burst of spending at a later point.

The game was loaded in a resolution of 1440x900 (full-screen) on a 15.5" laptop with a 2.2GHz Intel Core2 Duo processor, 4GB DDR2 RAM and an NVidia GeForce 8600M GT graphics card. A basic, ambidextrous mouse was provided for input, and on-ear headphones were supplied to allow sound effects and music to be heard.

Immersion was measured using the IEQ [15] which consists of 31 questions. An additional 3 questions were added to the questionnaire to explore to game playing habits and how players rated their own ability. These questions were used in order to estimate player expertise.

Procedure

The game included an in-game tutorial, page one of which was loaded prior to participant arrival. Players were required to read, or at least navigate through the pages of, this tutorial before access to the actual game was provided.

Participants then played the game for either eight minutes or until the player had run out of lives. Upon reaching a game-over condition, players were asked to immediately inform the investigator that they had finished playing. Participants were then provided with the IEQ and again left alone to answer this privately. When they had completed the IEQ, participants were asked if they had any further questions or comments, before being orally debriefed.

Participants received a £5 Amazon voucher for taking part.

Results

The purposes of the different experimental conditions were to impose significantly different levels of physical effort whilst keeping difficulty constant. Table 1 shows the number of actions and performance (seconds survived) of participants in each condition. There was a significant difference between the number of actions performed in each condition ($F(1, 38) = 13.17$, $p < 0.001$). Participants in the HEff condition performed, on average, over 60% more actions than those in the LEff condition. There was no difference in performance between the conditions ($F(1, 38) = 0.032$ $p = 0.86$). These results demonstrate the success of the setup of each experimental condition in achieving the intended effects.

	Low Effort	High Effort
Actions	48.7 (19.8)	78.2 (30.5)
Performance (s)	391.1 (99.5)	397.1 (112.2)
Immersion	112.2 (15.6)	113.5 (12.7)

Table 1: Mean number of Actions, Performance and Immersion (and standard deviations) in the experimental conditions

Table 1 also shows the immersion levels of participants in each condition. The results obtained demonstrate no significant effect of physical effort upon immersion ($F(1, 38) = 0.09$, $p = 0.766$).

Expertise

Data analysis using Pearson's r (two-tailed) indicated a significant positive correlation between expertise and performance ($r(38) = 0.62$, $p < .001$), confirming the adopted measure of expertise was appropriate for this study. Participants were divided into three expertise groups using a three-way split. The lower group (N = 13) was termed 'insufficient expertise' (IX), the middle group (N = 16) 'low expertise' (LX) and the upper group (N = 11) 'high expertise '(HX).

Table 2 shows the performance of the different expertise groups in each condition. Players in the IX group performed significantly differently ($F(2, 37) = 12.78$, $p < 0.001$). Additionally, IX players performed a significantly different number of 'upgrade' actions relative to the number of total actions performed ($F(2, 37) = 13.19$, $p < .001$), with many performing no upgrades at all (38% against 0% in the other two groups) (see Table 3). As such, players from this group were missing out on important gameplay elements, indicating that they had not fully read or understood the provided tutorial and the basic mechanics of the game. For these reasons, it was decided to exclude IX players' results from further analysis as these were not representative of the gaming experience of typical game players.

	Level of Expertise		
	Insufficient (IX)	**Low (LX)**	**High (HX)**
Overall	299.6 (118.9)	431.3 (60.7)	451.7 (52.8)
LEff	328.1 (123.7)	415.9 (70.8)	439.6 (64.5)
HEff	266.3 (114.5)	446.6 (48.4)	461.8 (44.5)

Table 2. Mean (standard deviation) of performance in the different expertise groups

	Level of Expertise		
	Insufficient (IX)	**Low (LX)**	**High (HX)**
Actions	51.1 (32.1)	88.9 (22.2)	94.8 (16.5)
Upgrades	23.4 (28.1)	57.3 (19.4)	65.3 (18.9)

Table 3: Mean (standard deviation) of the number of actions and upgrades in the different expertise groups

The immersion levels of players in the LX and HX groups are shown in Figure 1. Immersion levels are consistent across both groups in the LEff condition (LX = 115.5 (s.d.=14.5), HX = 115.0 (s.d.=12.7)). However in the HEff condition, immersion levels increase for the LX group (123.0 (s.d.=8.7)), but decrease for the HX group (104.2 (s.d.=9.6)). These results show a statistically significant main effect of expertise ($F(1, 23) = 4.48$, $p = .045$) and an interaction between expertise and physical challenge at a level approaching significance ($F(1, 23) = 4.03$, $p = .057$).

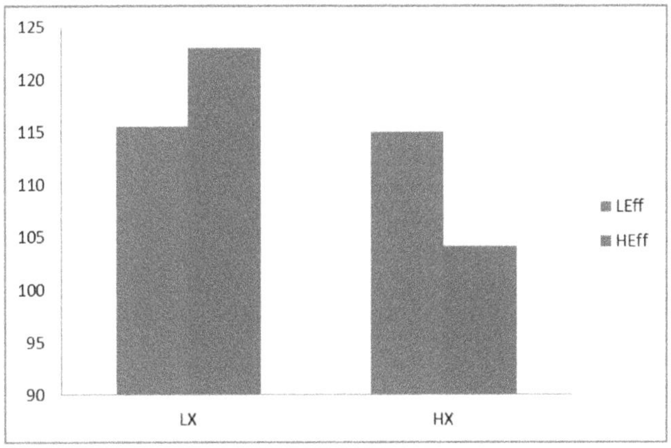

Figure 1: Mean immersion scores in the low and high expertise groups

	Low (LX)	**High (HX)**
LEff	14.1 (3.44)	13.2 (2.16)
HEff	14.9 (2.75)	11.0 (2.83)

Table 4. Mean (standard deviation) of challenge in the different expertise groups

Analysing just the challenge factor of immersion, the means and sd for challenge are given in Table 4. The pattern of results is similar to that for overall immersion but there is a main effect of expertise ($F(1,23) = 4.42$, $p=0.047$) but no interaction effect between expertise and physical challenge ($F(1,23)=1.67$, $p=0.209$).

Discussion

The experimental setup had the desired effects. The number of actions performed increased dramatically and, most importantly, significantly in the high effort condition, indicating an increased level of physical effort being placed upon the participants in this condition. The consistent performance of players' shows that this difference is not as a result of the amount of time spent playing in either condition, demonstrating conditions were equal in difficulty and supporting the requirement that the increase in the level of physical effort required does not impact performance.

Despite this success in manipulating the number of actions required to play the game, but not the game difficulty, the observed levels of immersion were consistent between conditions, demonstrating that physical effort alone does not impact significantly on the level of immersion experienced.

Where players are actually able to fully engage in the game, that is discounting 'insufficient expertise' players, it is clear that those with low expertise view the two experimental conditions equally. However, those with more experience are less immersed in the HEff condition than the LEff despite performing at a similar level. The Low expertise players have a fine time in the Leff condition, and a slightly better time when pushed to go faster. However, for those with more experience and skill (HX), the requirement to play faster is frustrating as the speed with which they must complete actions in the game negatively impacts on their abilities to apply their strategies. Indeed, some of these players commented in debriefing that they did not have time to work out which towers were best to deploy.

The same picture is seen when considering only the challenge factor with high expertise group in the HEff condition rating the challenge lowest. This may seem contradictory: the HEff condition should produce higher challenge. It does however support the view that the questionnaire, measures the player's perception of challenge in the context of the overall gaming experience, and that, when evaluating the GX, the gamer values cognitive challenge rather than physical challenge (at least in this game genre).The low scores on the challenge factor suggest that the High expertise players found the HEff condition not to be challenging perhaps because it was an unfair or unreasonable challenge. When a player is an expert, the challenge of this game is cognitive (identifying which towers are best from a strategic perspective) not physical.

EXPERIMENT 2: INVESTIGATING THE EFFECT OF TIME PRESSURE ON IMMERSION

For experiment 2, the aim was to investigate the effect of time pressure on gaming. In contrast to the manipulation used in experiment one, we hypothesized that the addition of time pressure would manipulate the level of cognitive challenge within the game. This is because the player is not only required to complete more actions per time unit in order to play the game, but that they also have to think more quickly in to stay in the game and maintain immersion. It was therefore predicted that participants who play the experimental game under time pressure will have significantly higher overall immersion scores and 'challenge' scores than those who play the game under no time pressure. As the focus in this study was on the explicit link between challenge and immersion, expertise was not considered in relation to challenge. Instead of taking statistical account of it, it was experimentally controlled by balancing the levels of expertise between the experimental conditions.

METHOD

Design

The study was a between subjects design. The independent variable was the level of challenge in the experimental game, i.e. whether the game had time pressure or no time pressure. The dependent variable was the participant's questionnaire scores on the IEQ.

Participants

There were 22 participants (12 male) from University College London with an age range of 18-22 years old and an average age of 20.1 years.

Materials

The PC game Bejeweled [2], was used in both conditions. The game can be played in either "simple" or "timed" mode. The aim of the game is to swap adjacent gems to align sets of 3 or more gems of the same colour. Scores are dependent on gems being aligned and sets being created.

The timed mode used for the time pressure condition has a Gem Meter which displays the amount of time the player has left to play shown by the length of the green line on the meter. To prevent time running out, the player must keep finding as many sets of the same gem colour as possible. The more sets found, the more power the Gem meter obtains and this in turn enables bonuses as well. If, however, the player has long intervals between finding sets, the length of the gem meter would gradually decrease so long as no sets are being made. As the game progressed, the participant would find it more difficult to make sets of gems and the Gem meter would decrease more quickly. If the participant failed to make any sets, then their time would eventually run out and the game would be over.

The simple game, used for the no time pressure condition, also has a Gem Meter, however the meter increases in power if sets are made but does *not* decrease in power if the player is unable to make sets of gems. Participants are therefore not playing against time. The game is completed when there were "no more moves left" i.e., when sets could no longer be made.

The IEQ [15] was used to measure the levels of immersion experienced.

Procedure

Participants first filled out a questionnaire that asked questions about their general gaming experience and particularly their experience with the experimental game Bejeweled. This enabled us to further divide the participants in each condition so that half of the participants would have played the experimental game and half would not have. The participants were then given a set of standardized instructions, which were specific to the experimental condition.

Participants were required to play the game Bejeweled. Those in the time pressure condition played the 'timed' version of the game and those in the no time pressure condition played the 'simple' version of the game.

The participants were asked to play the game for approximately 15 minutes in each condition unless the game ended before this. Participants then completed the IEQ.

Results

There was no significant difference in the scores achieved by participants in the two groups (time pressure mean score = 5603 (s.d.=6212), no time pressure mean score = 3501 (s.d. = 3187) $t(20)=0.998$, $p>0.05$).

The descriptive statistics presented in Table 5 clearly show that those in the time pressure condition have a much higher immersion score than those in the no time pressure condition. This was confirmed by paired samples t-tests: overall immersion scores $t(10)=6.36$, $p<0.05$); challenge $t(10)=9.59$, $p<0.05$.

Questionnaire Scores	Time Pressure	No Time Pressure
Total immersion*	113.5 (11)	81.3 (8.60)
Challenge*	15.6 (1.12)	8.82 (1.78)

Table 5. Mean (standard deviation) of the overall immersion score and the challenge factor score.

Discussion

There was no difference in the scores in the two conditions, thus any differences found in levels of immersion cannot be attributed to one group being better than another.

The results and analysis for experiment 2 clearly show a significant difference between the conditions on both the overall immersion questionnaire scores and the scores for the challenge factor. This confirms our hypothesis that it is the addition of cognitive challenge that impacts on the GX.

In experiment 1 we argued that those with insufficient experience were not representative of the gaming experience of typical game players. The participants in experiment 2 fell in to two broad categories, those who had played Bejewelled before, and those who were complete novices. We therefore have not analysed differences between participants with different levels of experience, but simply ensured they were equally distributed between the experimental groups. In study 3 we therefore explore the role of expertise in the context of time pressure.

EXPERIMENT 3: INVESTIGATING THE INTERACTION BETWEEN TIME PRESSURE AND EXPERTISE ON IMMERSION

The aim of this study was to test the hypothesis that expertise interacts with the level of cognitive challenge imposed by the game and thereby mediates the level of immersion experienced. We manipulated this by selecting participants who were either expert or novice at a particular game (Tetris), and tested how immersed they were whilst playing the game, that was either high in challenge or low in challenge. In this study, the challenge of the game was determined by the level at which the participant was playing the game, so the higher the level, the more challenging the game. The difference in levels is in the speed at which the game progresses, thus making this manipulation analogous to that in study 2.

It was thus hypothesised that 'experts' will be more immersed when playing the experimental game at a higher level, but will be in a state of boredom when playing the game at a lower level. It was also predicted that 'novices' will be more immersed when playing the experimental game at a lower level, but will be in a state of anxiety when playing the game at a higher level.

Method

Design

The study was a mixed design, which was carried out in a laboratory setting. The within subjects independent variable was the level of the experimental game (Tetris) that was being played (which was either low- level 1 or high- level 6). This would indicate the level of challenge within the game. The between subjects variable was the level of expertise (expert or novice). The dependent variable was the participant's questionnaire scores on the immersion questionnaire (IEQ).

Participants

There were 20 participants (10 male) from University College London. Their age range was 18-26 years old and the average age was 19.3.

Materials

The PC puzzle game Tetris [28] was used in both conditions. The aim of Tetris is to make as many lines as possible by stacking up the pieces that fall one by one from above. The pieces are stacked accordingly, by either rotating their positions (to ensure a correct fit) or by moving the piece towards the left or the right of the screen (depending on where the player wants to place the piece). In order for the player to make the lines, the pieces must be packed tightly so that there are no 'gaps'. As they progress through each level, the speed at which the pieces fall from above will increase, making it more difficult and more challenging for the gamer to decide how and where to place the piece in the stack.

Additionally, participants were given a questionnaire that asked about their gaming experience. This was a similar questionnaire to that used in study 2, which provided information as to whether the participant plays and how often they play computer games, the kind(s) of computer games they enjoy playing and kind(s) they find challenging. It also asked the participants whether they had played the experimental game Tetris before. If they answered 'yes' to this question, they were asked how often they play the game and were also asked to give an honest rating of how 'good' they think they are at it on a scale of 1-10 (where 1= novice and 10= expert). This gave us an indication of their abilities and skills regarding the game and therefore enabled us to assign the participants to each condition so there would be 10 participants who rated themselves closer to being 'expert' at playing Tetris and 10 participants who rated themselves closer to being 'novice'.

Immersion was measured using the IEQ as in the previous studies. An additional questionnaire asked participants to rate their levels of boredom and anxiety.

Procedure
Participants first completed the gaming questionnaire. They then played each condition (at level 1 or at level 6) for approximately 15 minutes. Order of play level was counterbalanced between participants.

When in the level 1 (the low challenge) condition, they were allowed to complete levels 1 and 2 but once they had reached the third level, they were asked to restart the game. They were asked to do this for the entire duration of the gaming portion of the study (restarting the game whenever they reached level 3).

The participants in the level 6 (the high challenge) condition were allowed to play the game until the game ended, i.e. when the stack had reached the top and no more lines could be made. Once their game was over, they were asked to restart the game at level 6. They too were asked to do this for the entire duration of the gaming portion (restarting the game at level 6 whenever the game ended).

Once participants had completed each condition of the game, they were asked to complete the IEQ. Participants were also asked to rate how bored or anxious they were (on a scale of 1 to 10) after playing in each condition.

Results
When playing Tetris at a high level experts were more immersed (mean = 110.4, sd = 12.68) than when playing at a low level (mean = 81.9, sd = 12.34). The novices on the other hand, were more immersed when playing Tetris at a low level (mean= 106.2, sd = 9.93) than when playing at a high level (mean = 83.2, sd = 17.04).

There was a highly significant interaction, ($F(1,18)=53.37$, $p<0.001$). As the level of challenge increases, experts become more immersed in the game and novices become less immersed in the game. The repeated measures ANOVA however, also showed that there was not a significant main effect of level of expertise ($F(1,18)=0.93$, $p>0.05$) or of level of challenge ($F(1,18)=0.61$, $p>0.05$), suggesting that the level of expertise in the game (expert or novice) and the level of challenge (low or high) do not vary significantly when expertise is unaccounted for.

	Low	High
Expert	7.8 (2.44)	13.9 (1.28)
Novice	14.7 (2.41)	14 (2.21)

Table 6: Descriptive statistics of the challenge factor scores of the low level and high level conditions.

Table 6 clearly shows that the experts mean challenge score for the high level condition was almost double that of the low level condition, suggesting that the experts found the high level condition to be far more challenging than the low level condition.

The novices however, had a slightly higher mean challenge score in the low level condition than in the high level condition. The mean challenge scores for both conditions are extremely high (given that the maximum possible challenge score is 20) with a difference of just 0.7 between the low level conditions.

Discussion
Whilst the effect of challenge shows no influence on immersion when there is no consideration of expertise, when expertise is factored in, there is a significant interaction showing that expertise and challenge interact in an important way in leading to immersion. This result mirrors the well-known effect in flow whereby it is only through balancing skill and challenge that flow is achieved. Immersion however is a much more general experience than flow and moreover is graded so that people can assess themselves to be more or less immersed. Nonetheless, the same pattern is seen where those who are less experienced are more immersed at lower levels of challenge and conversely those with more experience are more immersed at higher levels of challenge.

GENERAL DISCUSSION AND CONCLUSIONS
The final experiment might give the impression that immersion behaves like flow with a balance of challenge and expertise leading to better gaming experiences but this needs closer scrutiny. The classic view of flow is that achieving the balance of challenge and expertise leads to the optimal experience, flow, and regardless of how expert you are, the balance gives the same top end flow experience. Here though all players achieve some degree of immersion in all of the games. Immersion is higher though when the balance of challenge and expertise is better. This then supports the idea that as players become more immersed they move towards total immersion or flow [25].

Additionally, this picture of increasing immersion is in contrast to the situation in the first experiment. The game of Tetris offers little subtlety: blocks fall and the only challenge is posed by how fast they fall. Thus experts at Tetris see the game, know the game and their expertise is challenged at higher levels. By contrast, tower defense games offer a variety of challenges where success requires strategic thinking and games vary substantially in which strategies are successful. High expertise players know this and require time to assess the relative strengths and weaknesses of the towers in order to deploy them optimally. However, the tower defense game in the first study did not require this level of strategic thinking.

These results suggest that whilst the balance of skill and challenge is important, it is also important that players perceive themselves as having the suitable skills. With Tetris, this was possible and so the higher challenge was more immersive. With the tower defense game of the first study, this was not so straightforward and the higher skill players recognized their inability to assess the challenge and therefore their skills in relation to the challenge. These players were less immersed being less able to deploy their higher skills against the higher challenge. Lower expertise players however, unaware of the challenges they faced were much more able to just get on and play the game and so were able to be equally immersed regardless of the physical challenge they faced.

High expertise is not only a matter of high skill levels but also the ability to use expertise to reflect on the matters at hand [24]. The effects seen here present something of a converse of the Dunning-Kruger effect [17]. For the Dunning-Kruger effect, those with low expertise were unable to properly understand feedback and therefore failed to re-evaluate themselves appropriately in light of feedback. Those with high expertise better understand feedback and so re-evaluate themselves more accurately in response to feedback. Here by contrast, those with low expertise just got on with playing and enjoying the game whilst those with those with high expertise mis-perceived the challenge presented due to the shallow nature of the game and therefore enjoyed themselves less.

The first and second study together also show that whilst it is important that players have activities to engage them, it is not simply a matter of having stuff to do. Immersion does not arise from physical challenge but from the cognitive challenge of solving problems quickly not simply acting quickly.

Our findings are novel in the context of GX. Whilst the many approaches to GX acknowledge the role of challenge in leading to positive gaming experiences, there has been little attempt to qualify what form these challenges must make and how they relate to players expertise. The studies here present a first attempt to provide construct validity to the notions of GX through explicitly manipulating the concepts believed to underpin GX from an objective perspective of what constitutes challenge.

Of course, this work only begins to scratch the surface of the types of challenge that games offer and the myriad of GX that can therefore arise. Further work should not only explore challenges arising at the basic level such as time pressure but also things that lead to higher scores or collecting more bonus points. In addition, this research suggests that challenges at higher levels such as the level of strategy and possibly even narrative are important for immersion. There is always concern for the limitation of lab studies such as these and what challenges players expect over a longer term engagement with games are currently unspecified.

Throughout all of this, it is also clear that challenge cannot be considered in isolation but must always be analysed in relation to the expertise of players. Even this is not simple in that challenge is distinct from the perceived challenge as indicated in the first study so that when attempting to achieve immersion through a balance of challenge and skill, players must first be able to perceive that such a balance is possible.

ACKNOWLEDGMENTS

We thank the EPSRC for supporting the first experiment on grant TS/G002843/1. And we would like to thank all our participants for giving their time to play games for us, and the reviewers for their insightful comments that improved this paper.

REFERENCES

1. Brockmyer, J., Fox, C., Curtiss, K., McBroom, E, Burkhart, K., Pidruzny, J. (2010) The development of the Game Engagement Questionnaire: A measure of engagement in video game-playing. *J. of Exp. Social Psychology*, 45(4), 624-634.
2. Bejeweled: http://www.1001onlinegames.com/games/puzzle/bejeweled.html
3. Brown, E. & Cairns, P.A,, (2004). A grounded investigation of game immersion. *CHI 04*, 31-32.
4. Calvillo-Gamez, E., Cairns, P., Cox, A.L. (2010) Assessing the core elements of the gaming experience. In Bernhaupt, R. (ed) *Evaluating user experience in games*, Springer, 47-71
5. Chatfield, T. (2009) Videogames now outperform Hollywood movies. *The Observer, Sunday 27th Sept 2009*
6. Chen, J. (2007) Flow in games (and everything else). *Comm. ACM,* 50(4), 31-34.
7. Cowley, B., Charles, D., Black, M., Hickey, R. (2008) Toward an understanding of flow in video games. *ACM Computers in Entertainment,* 6(2), 20:1-20:27
8. Csikszentmihalyi, M. (1990). *Flow: The Psychology of Optimal Experience.* New York: Harper and Row.
9. de Kort, Y. A. W., IJsselsteijn, W. A., Poels, K. (2007). Digital Games as Social Presence Technology: Development of the Social Presence in Gaming Questionnaire (SPGQ). *Presence 2007.*

10. El-Nasr, M.S., Aghabeigi, B., Milam, D., Erfani, M., Lameman, B., Maygoli, H., & Mah, S. (2010) Understanding and evaluating cooperative games. *CHI '10. ACM, New York, NY, USA*, 253-262

11. Epps, A. (2007) *Immersion in video-games: How is immersion related to attention?* Unpublished MSc Thesis, UCL

12. Ermi, L., Mayra, F. (2005) Fundamental Components of the Gameplay Experience: Analysing Immersion. *Proc. of DIGRA 2005*

13. Gagne, A., El-Nasr, M.S., & Shaw, C. A Deeper Look at the use of Telemetry for Analysis of Player Behavior in RTS Games. *International Conference on Entertainment Computing (ICEC 2011), 2011*

14. Hsu, S.H., Wen, M.H., Wu, M.C. (2007) Exploring design features for enhancing players challenge in strategy games. *Cyberpsychology & Behaviour* 10 (3), 393-397

15. Jennett, C., Cox, A. L., Cairns, P., Dhoparee, S., Epps, A., Tijs, T., & Walton, A. (2008). Measuring and defining the experience of immersion in games. *International Journal of Human-Computer Studies*, 66(9), 641-661.

16. Juul, J. (2009) Fear of failing? The many meanings of difficulty in video games. In Wolf, M and Perron, B. (eds) *The Video Game Theory Reader 2.* New York: Routledge, 237-252.

17. Kruger, J., Dunning, D, (1999) Unskilled and unaware of it: How difficulties in recognizing one's own incompetence lead to inflated self-assessments. *Journal of Personality and Social Psychology*, Vol 77(6), 1121-1134

18. Livingston, I., Nacke, L., Mandryk, R. (2011) Influencing Experience: The Effects of Reading Game Reviews on Player Experience. *International Conference on Entertainment Computing (ICEC 2011), 2011*

19. Orvis, K.A., Horn, D.B., Belanich, J., (2008) The roles of task difficulty and prior videogame experience on performance and motivation in instructional videogames. *Computers in Human Behaviour* 24 (5), 2415-2433

20. Poels, K, deKort, Y, IJsselsteijn, W. (2007) "It is always a lot of fun!" - exploring dimensions of digital game experience using focus group methodology. *FuturePlay 2007,* 83-89

21. Qin, H., Rau, P.L.P., Salvendy, G., (2009) Measuring player immersion in the computer narrative. *International Journal of Human-Computer Interaction* 25 (2), 107-133

22. Qin, H., Rau, P.L.P., Salvendy, G., (2010) Effects of different scenarios of game difficulty on player immersion. *Interacting with Computers* 22, 230-239

23. Schell, J. (2008) *The Art of Game Design.* Burlington MA: Morgan Kaufmann.

24. Schon, D (1983) *The Reflective Practitioner.* London: Basic Books

25. Seah, M., Cairns, P. (2008) From Immersion to addiction in videogames. In England, D. and Beale, R. *Proc. of HCI 2008*, vol 1 BCS, 55-63

26. Skalski, P., Tamborini, R, Shelton, A., Buncher, M, Lindmark, P. (2011) Mapping the road to fun: Natural video game controllers, presence, and game enjoyment. *New Media & Society,*

27. Sweetser and Wyeth. 2005. GameFlow: a model for evaluating player enjoyment in games. *Comput. Entertain.* 3, 3 (July 2005), 3-3.

28. Tetris: http://www.capehostpro.com/play-tetris.htm

29. Wallop, H. (2009) Eight out of ten homes own a next-gen console. *The Daily Telegraph, 15th Jan 2009*

30. Wijnants, M., Agten, S, Quax, P., Lamotte, W. (2009) Investigating the relationship between QoS and QoE in a mixed desktop/handheld gaming setting. *CoNEXT Student Workshop '09,* 29-30

Understanding User Experience in Stereoscopic 3D Games

Jonas Schild
Entertainment Computing Group
University of Duisburg-Essen
Forsthausweg 2,
47057 Duisburg, Germany
jonas.schild@uni-due.de

Joseph J. LaViola Jr.
University of Central Florida
Department of EECS
4000 Central Florida Blvd.
Orlando, FL 32816 USA
jjl@eecs.ucf.edu

Maic Masuch
Entertainment Computing Group
University of Duisburg-Essen
Forsthausweg 2,
47057 Duisburg, Germany
maic.masuch@uni-due.de

ABSTRACT
Recent advances in digital game technology are making stereoscopic games more popular. Stereoscopic 3D graphics promise a better gaming experience but this potential has not yet been proven empirically. In this paper, we present a comprehensive study that evaluates player experience of three stereoscopic games in comparison with their monoscopic counterparts. We examined 60 participants, each playing one of the three games, using three self-reporting questionnaires and one psychophysiological instrument. Our main results are (1) stereoscopy in games increased experienced immersion, spatial presence, and simulator sickness; (2) the effects strongly differed across the three games and for both genders, indicating more affect on male users and with games involving depth animations; (3) results related to attention and cognitive involvement indicate more direct and less thoughtful interactions with stereoscopic games, pointing towards a more natural experience through stereoscopy.

Author Keywords
Games; stereoscopy; player experience; game experience; S3D; play; genre; presence; immersion; simulator sickness.

ACM Classification Keywords
H.5.m [Information Interfaces and Presentation (e.g., HCI)]: Miscellaneous; K.8.0 [Personal Computing]: General - Games.

General Terms
Experimentation; Human Factors.

INTRODUCTION
Since the success of James Cameron's Avatar, many new digital media productions have promoted stereoscopic 3D vision as a strong benefit, be it movies, 3DTV, or games. The Sony Playstation 3 and the Nintendo 3DS offer stereoscopic 3D (S3D) gaming on consoles while driver-based solutions such as Nvidia 3D Vision or TriDef let the user play in S3D on the PC. In both cases, existing games and well known game concepts are extended with S3D vision as a toggle option. Nevertheless, to have such an option, players are required to purchase new display systems, glasses, or consoles. It remains unclear whether S3D actually offers a substantial additional value to players. Industry representatives announce S3D gaming as "the most exciting and engaging way to deliver an immersive game experience"[1]. While recent studies actually indicate an increased engagement and improved experience, the reason for such an effect is not understood (e.g., game performance is not necessarily improved by S3D vision [16,24]). In addition, negative impacts on user experience through S3D are known as well: visual discomfort is expected to occur, especially at intensive depth levels involving large parallax settings or drastic changes in depth [9].

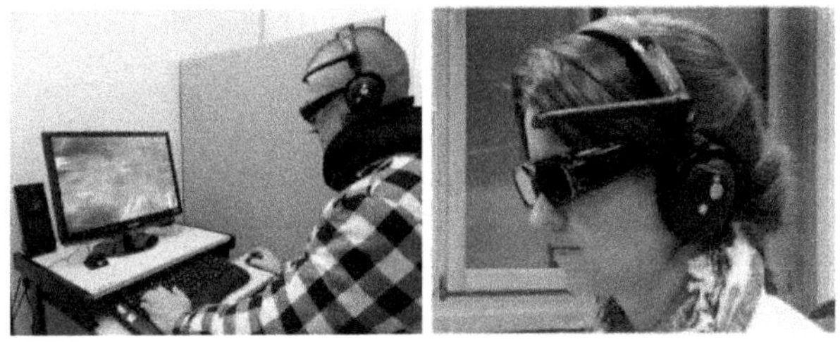

Figure 1: Setup (left) and equipment (right) consisting of Nvidia 3D Vision glasses, MindSet NeuroSky, and ear plugs beneath the headset.

We expect subjective player experience in S3D gaming to differ both positively and negatively from monoscopic gameplay. In this paper, we focus on understanding the quality of the actual impact and why users feel the way they do when playing games in 3D stereo over a 2D display. How do different game concepts and target groups affect the experience? Can we automatically improve every experience with S3D, as often promised by industry and expected by users? By answering these questions, game designers can begin to take this knowledge and use it to assist in developing more compelling 3D stereo games.

[1] see http://www.thegamecreators.com/pages/newsletters/newsletter_issue_86.html#10

We conducted a study among 60 participants to compare subjective player experience of three different games played in S3D and in monoscopic vision. The study applies four empirical tools: questionnaires on game experience, spatial presence and simulator sickness, and the NeuroSky MindSet.

RELATED WORK

Benefits and Disadvantages of Stereoscopic Vision

The impact on experience of playing games using S3D compared to regular monoscopic displays is unknown. Such a subjective experience while playing a game is often referred to as user experience [1], player experience [20], or game experience. Positive and negative effects of stereoscopic vision on user experience have been intensively studied in the domain of image perception, 3DTV, and with virtual reality applications. According to Tam et al., S3D image sequences are generally preferred over non-stereoscopic versions, perceived depth is rated greater for S3D sequences than for non-stereoscopic ones, and perceived sharpness of stereoscopic sequences is rated the same or lower compared to non-stereoscopic sequences [30]. In addition, animations in depth are perceived faster in S3D [23]. S3D also has a powerful impact on providing information about spatial location, size, shape, or orientation of 3D objects [10]. Virtual scenes [13] and video clips [11] experienced in S3D induce an increased perceived presence. The latter study also reports more attention towards details requiring more time to explore a S3D scene. S3D images are generally perceived more naturally and induce a better viewing experience [27].

In contrast to these benefits, current stereoscopic displays with a fixed screen plane cause several human visual cues to conflict with each other; the most prominent ones being accommodation and convergence. This conflict is known to result in a negative experience due to visual discomfort [17] associated with symptoms of visual fatigue (e.g., sore eyes, eye strain, headache, blurred vision) [7]. A common solution is to reduce parallax settings to a comfortable viewing range [28], effectively limiting stereoscopic effects. Additional distortions occurring from exaggerated disparity may include cross-talk, binocular rivalry, blur, compression artifacts, noise [34], or geometric distortions [33]. For objective assessment of image quality, 2D image quality metrics are not appropriate and 3D quality metrics are not available yet [34]. In addition, the perceived quality of stereoscopic presentations depends on the 3D display (driver, electronics), varying with individual user physiology [8]. Even watching good quality 3DTV induced symptoms of simulator sickness in a pre-/post-comparison [22]. Such symptoms are already noticeable after less than five minutes of exposure [14].

Stereoscopy in Digital Games

There has been little academic research on player experience with stereoscopic gaming. Zachara and Zagal reviewed the failure of Nintendo's Virtual Boy. They describe a lack of focused design and emphasize a need for stereoscopic game mechanics [35]. Rajae-Joordens evaluated gameplay of Quake III: Arena on an autostereoscopic, lenticular display for 2D vs. S3D display modes [24]. S3D caused an increase in emotional arousal while the heart rate remained unaffected. A questionnaire showed significantly higher presence and engagement results for S3D. Additionally, no visual symptoms or simulator sickness was found. The gaming performance (score) initially was higher in S3D but equal to 2D after prolonged use. Most of the participants (85%) preferred S3D over 2D. LaViola and Litwiller also investigated user performance benefits of S3D with 40 participants playing five current digital games. Their results indicate that although participants preferred playing in S3D for the tested games, it did not provide any significant advantage in overall user performance and learning. Still, the users reported an improved experience and increased engagement while playing in S3D. Interestingly, the variety of the evaluated games showed no influence to these results [16].

In a recent study, Takatalo et al. evaluated user experience of Need for Speed Underground (a racing game published in 2003) played at a resolution of 800 x 600 pixels in S3D with two different parallax settings and monoscopic vision using a multifactorial between-subjects design [29]. Compared to monoscopic vision, they found a higher presence experienced with medium parallax settings only, not with high settings, probably due to visual discomfort. With their slightly lower resolution setting, they did not find any effect in emotional factors such as the experienced flow, fun or enjoyment. However, in another study, novel display technology (e.g., higher resolution) was found to amplify impact from S3D on user experience [32].

Overall, previous work proposes that S3D in some games is generally preferred. However, it remains unclear exactly how player experience actually benefits from stereoscopic presentation. How does it relate to known advantages of stereoscopy in general? What is the impact of varying game design, modern stereoscopic display technology and rendering quality on novel stereoscopic gaming experience?

USER STUDY

The aim of our study was to examine how player experience differs between playing a game being presented in stereoscopic vision (SV) and playing it in monoscopic vision (MV). We hypothesize that:

1. Stereoscopy results in a different game experience compared to a monoscopic display.
2. Playing stereoscopic games confirms benefits and flaws of experiencing other stereoscopic visuals (e.g., movies, 3DTV), resulting in increased presence and increased simulator sickness.
3. These results are independent of the game.

The participants were tasked with playing through pre-selected sections of one of three different games.

Selecting the Games

Before the study, more than 20 S3D-enabled games were tested based on several suitability criteria. None of the games were primarily designed with stereoscopy in mind but provided stereoscopic vision as an option, provided through the 3D vision driver. Other 3D related aspects (ghosting, double vision) were tested subjectively on the test system (glasses, display, computer, display driver) as recommended before. Besides stereoscopic properties, we focused on game playability. The games needed to provide easy entry to keep the whole test setting within a reasonable time-frame and suitable to untrained players who might have never held a gamepad before. Game controls thus had to be similar between the games and should avoid a possible impact from active body movements on psycho-physiological measures (i.e., on a steering wheel compared to body passiveness when a game only requires single keystrokes). Hence, all selected games had to be playable using cursor keys and a few additional keys on the keyboard. The games needed to appeal to a broad audience but also needed to differ significantly in genre and visual setup. The latter aspect refers to the strong depth effect of stereoscopy on the user. For each game, two parts were selected, one for each experimental session. The parts were selected to offer similar game mechanics and tasks within each game while allowing gameplay for both casual and experienced players. The S3D settings for each game were set to provide a comfortable viewing on the used display.

James Cameron's Avatar: The Game, UbiSoft, 2009 (AV)

AV is a 3D action game played in third person view. The player controls the player character through a 3D game world and has *full control over the camera view* in a certain range around the player model. The task is to explore the 3D world, to collect items, to interact with non-player characters, and to shoot enemy creatures. The first session consisted of the first level of the game, the second session started with the middle part of the second level.

Blur, ActivisionBlizzard, 2010 (BL)

BL is a racing game where the player controls a car from a third-person view while the camera *moves into depth*. This effect is exaggerated when the player switches into a boost mode, drastically increasing the speed. Six races at medium difficulty were selected, three from the first and three from the second level.

Trine, Nobilis/Frozenbyte, 2009 (TR)

TR is an action-adventure game where the player controls one of three different fantasy characters through a side-scrolling world with primarily *lateral camera animations*. The world is constructed from 3D models and spans across several depth planes, thus leaving a spatial impression. For the playing sessions we selected the start of the game and the first part of the second level.

Participants

We recruited 60 participants (26 male, 34 female) from our university, all students. The study was advertised via bulletin and online forums. The age of the chosen sample varied between 19 and 33 years, with a median of 21 years. For both AV and BL half of the participants were male, while TR was played by 14 females and six males. The median age for AV was 22 years and 21 years for the other two games. A similar age is important as stereoscopic vision abilities are strongly affected of aging [4]. All of the participants successfully passed a prior S3D vision test. The participants were offered free fruits, candy and beverages during the test sessions. They received "study points" they need to earn in order to conduct experiments in their courses. The evaluation was approved by our ethics board.

Equipment

The testing room was designed with a constantly low light source that did not interfere with the shutter glasses. The games were run on a quad-core desktop PC running Windows 7, with a GeForce GTX 275 graphics card and a Samsung 22" display at 120 Hz with 1680 x 1050 pixel resolution. Nvidia 3D Vision Driver version 6.14.12.5896 was used to generate 3D stereo. To later sort out any participants possibly faking play activities, the gaming sessions were recorded using Fraps (Version 3.0) by Beepa Pty Ltd. For the recordings, we used decreased resolutions and frame rate to ensure interactive frame rates>25 fps. A MindSet headset was connected via bluetooth. We recorded the data using open source software Puzzlebox Synapse by Brainstorms. Due to stability problems, the software had to be controlled using an external PC. Thus, sound could not be provided using the Mindset and so participants had to wear additional in-ear headphones beneath the MindSet device. Since there was an impact on the subjective feel and comfort by wearing the full gear (glasses, headset, and earplugs, see Figure 1), the participants had to wear the 3D Vision glasses during both sessions (MV and SV). In monoscopic display, both shutters of the glasses are open, providing an image slightly darker than without glasses but brighter than the stereoscopic version and similar in color tone (altered towards yellow).

Design and Procedure

All participants had to play a game in both vision modes (SV, MV) in a within-subject design. The sequence of the vision modes was randomized to alleviate possible learning effects and a potential impact from small differences between first and second levels. The population was randomly broken into three groups of twenty users, where each group played one of the three games (AV, BL, TR) in both vision modes. The purpose of this decision was to enforce a comparison between vision modes, not between games. It further allowed us to reduce duration times of the testing sessions and to minimize impact from personal preference. The order of vision modes was randomized in a mixed design, where half of the participants started with SV and the other half with MV, equally distributed across games and gender. To minimize impact from personal preference for a certain game or genre, the games were randomly selected and equally distributed across gender.

Metrics

Our choice of metrics was based on Affective Ludology [21], an approach which propagates a mixture of subjective self-reporting tools and objective psycho-physiological metrics to assess both cognitive and emotional sides of gameplay experience. In addition to demographic data, we asked participants about prior experience with gaming as well as with stereoscopic entertainment (games, TV, cinema). At the end of each trial, each participant was asked for their personal preference of vision modus and problems experienced during the sessions.

To assess user experience of game play, several tools have been proposed, mostly questionnaires (e.g. [2]) and/or psycho-physiological data [5]. We used the Game Experience Questionnaire's (GEQ)[2] core questionnaire module. It contains seven dimensions: Immersion (Imm), Flow (Flo), Competence (Com), Tension (Ten), Challenge (Cha), Positive Affect (PoA), and Negative Affect (NeA). These are each measured using five to six items per dimension (36 in total), each on 1-to-5 disagree-agree response Likert-scales. We used the German version provided by Nacke [21]. The GEQ further includes a social presence module and a post-game module which were discarded in this study to shorten the overall test duration.

Presence was measured by the MEC Spatial Presence Questionnaire (MEC-SPQ) [31]. It includes four process factors: Attention Allocation (AA), Spatial Situation Model (SSM), Spatial Presence:Self Location (SP:SL) and Spatial Presence:Possible Actions (SP:PA). Two additional variables relating to states and actions (Higher Cognitive Involvement (HCI) and Suspension of Disbelief (SoD)) are also part of the MEC-SPQ. We used the short version offering four items for each scale.

Possible dizziness or other subjective disorders were measured using the Simulator Sickness Questionnaire (SSQ) [15]. It contains three dimensions, Nausea (Nau), Oculomotor (Ocu), and Disorientation (Diso), measured through 16 items on a 4-level Likert scale (ranging from "no symptoms" to "severe symptoms"). The three dimensions are then combined to create a Total SSQ metric (Tot). In our study, we used the German translation previously applied by Mehlitz [18].

Psychophysiological data was acquired using the NeuroSky MindSet. The headset measures electroencephalogram (EEG) data using contact dots. Three of these dots are included in the left ear cushion while the forth dot rests on the subject's forehead. The data consists of custom interpretations in so-called eSense meters: Attention (Att) and Meditation (Med). Although little data on the validity of these scales is available, previous work indicates positive correlations of Att and Med with self-reported attention [25] and stress levels [3] .

[2] GEQ, developed by K. Poels, W. A. IJsselsteijn, and Y. A. W de Kort at the Game Experience Lab Eindhoven (NL), (http://www.gamexplab.nl) in the European project FUGA.

Procedure

All participants were informed about the aim and procedure of the study and had to sign an agreement including a list of possibly occurring symptoms such as epilepsy, vision disorders or dizziness. All participants were tested for stereoscopic vision through the medical test image provided by the Nvidia driver settings. This introduction took about seven minutes on average. The experiment began with a five-minute introduction to the experiment and the signature of the participation agreement. In the following ten minutes, the participants completed a questionnaire at another PC that focused on demographic data and personal prior experience with games and stereoscopic vision. The participants were then seated in front of the gaming PC. They were introduced to the gear (3D vision glasses, MindSet and earbuds) and were asked to remain seated in a constant position. Before the tests started, the game was presented and could be tested for about ten minutes, until the participant understood the core game mechanics and was able to control and play for her- or himself.

Each of the two following gaming sessions, one per vision mode, lasted about fifteen minutes. During play, the participants were left alone by the experimenters, who could not see the current display content. Each gaming session was followed by a questionnaire session of about fifteen minutes. The whole experiment took about 1.5 hours per participant.

RESULTS AND ANALYSIS

Demographic information

We collected data of frequency of play for all participants. Ten participants never played computer games (16.7%), 32 played 1-5 hours per week (53.3%), 11 played 6-10 hours per week (18.3%), and seven played 11-20 hours per week (11.7%). None of our participants played more than 20-30 or more than 30 hours per week. The typical weekly playing duration was 4.9 hours across all participants. Male subjects (7.3 hours per week) played noticeably more frequently than females (3 hours per week).

The participants had the most genre-related experience with Jump'n'Run (38%), Strategy (37%), RPG (33%), and Puzzles (32%). More than a fifth listed Action RPG (23%), Ego-Shooter (23%), and Adventures (20%), followed by Sports (18%), Simulations (17%), Racing (13%), Fighting (11%), and Education games (2%). Again, experience with genre differed between both genders: females are better used to Puzzle games (38%), Jump'n'Run (32%), and Strategy/RPG games (21% each). Males had generally higher experience levels, maximizing in Strategy (58%), Ego-Shooter/RPG (50% each), and Jump'n'Run/Action-Shooter (46% each). Considering BL, Racing was better known among males (27%) than among females (3%).

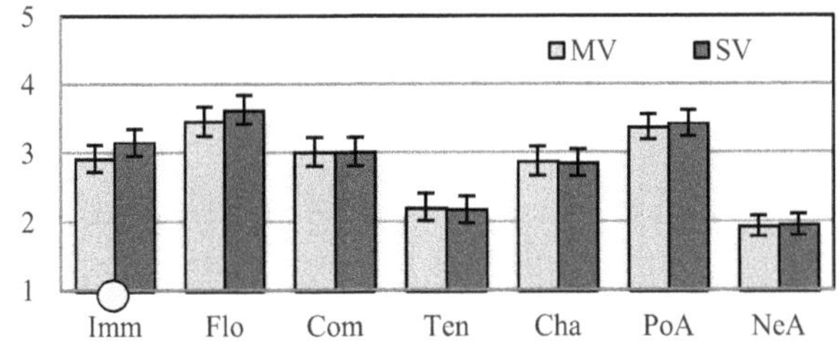

Figure 2. GEQ data across all groups– a significant difference between mono and stereo vision was only found in Immersion. (Error bars show 95% CI, ○=p<.05; ◉=p<.01; ●=p<.001)

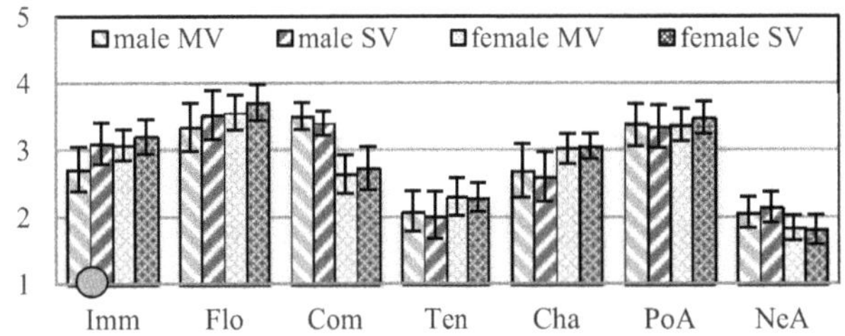

Figure 3. GEQ Data – gender vs. vision mode. No effects on female subjects. Males experienced higher immersion.

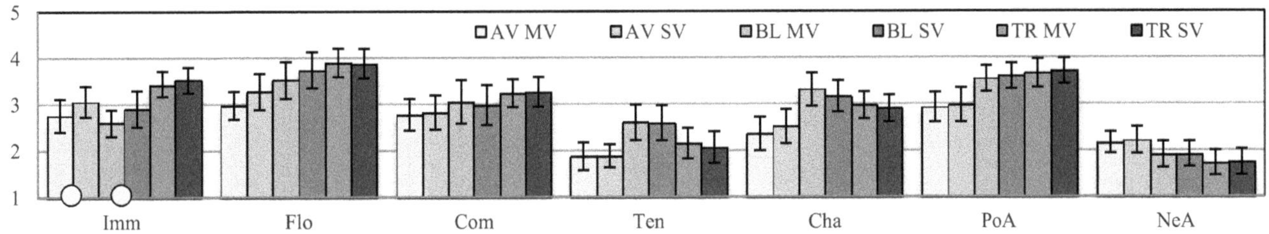

Figure 4. GEQ data – game vs. vision mode: Immersion in Avatar and Blur shows significant differences between vision modes.

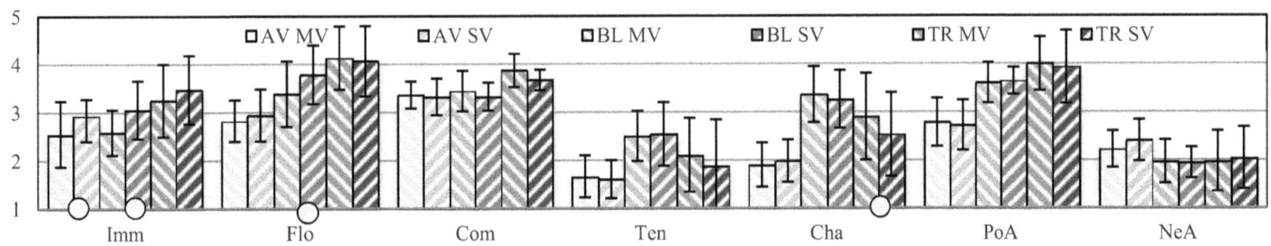

Figure 5. GEQ data – male subjects only – game vs. vision mode: stereoscopy impacts male subjects' Immersion in Avatar, Immersion and Flow in Blur, and Challenge in Trine.

Only a few of the participants had played the games we tested. Seven reported to have previously played AV one to ten times (11.7%), one had played BL one to ten times (1.7%) and two had played it for more than 25 times (3.3%, they were in the AV group). One player had previously played TR one to ten times (1.7%).

Prior experience with S3D was collected for cinema, TV and digital games. Of the 60 participants, four had never seen a 3D cinema movie, 34 one to three times and 22 four to nine times. Fifteen had previously watched 3DTV one to three times, one had watched four to nine times, the others never. Only six participants had previously played S3D games (10%). These results were similar for both genders.

GEQ

Comparing SV with MV, the GEQ data revealed higher mean values of Immersion, Flow, Positive Affect, and Negative Affect and lower mean values in Tension and Challenge in the stereo condition (see Figure 2). A dependent two-sample T-Test revealed significant differences only for Immersion (t_{59}=-3.293, p<.01).

Looking at these results for each gender (see Figure 3), a dependent two-sample T-Test confirmed the significant difference only among male participants (t_{25}=-3.676, p<.01) showing a higher immersion in SV than in MV. Female participants showed no significant difference.

We found differences for the three particular games (see Figure 4), as only AV and BL revealed a significantly higher Immersion (AV: t_{19}=-2.348, p<.05; BL: t_{19}=-2.291, p<.05). More effects became visible for the male group only (see Figure 5). Again, Immersion in SV was higher than in MV for AV (t_9=-2.318, p<.05) and BL (t_9=-2.318, p<.05). For males playing BL, a Wilcoxon-Signed-Rank test showed a significantly higher Flow value in SV than in MV (Z=2.214, p<.05). In TR, male subjects experienced Challenge significantly lower under SV than under MV condition (t_5=3.841, p<.05). No effects were found in the female group.

MEC-SPQ

All presence dimensions of the MEC-SPQ with one exception had higher mean values in SV than in MV (see Figure 6). Significant differences were found in AA (Z=2.522, p<.05), SP:SL (Z=5.071, p<.001), and SP:PA (t_{59}=-4.707, p<.001). The differences in SSM and SoD were not significant. In contrast, the mean values of HCI in stereo were significantly below those in the mono condition (Z=-4.568, p<.001).

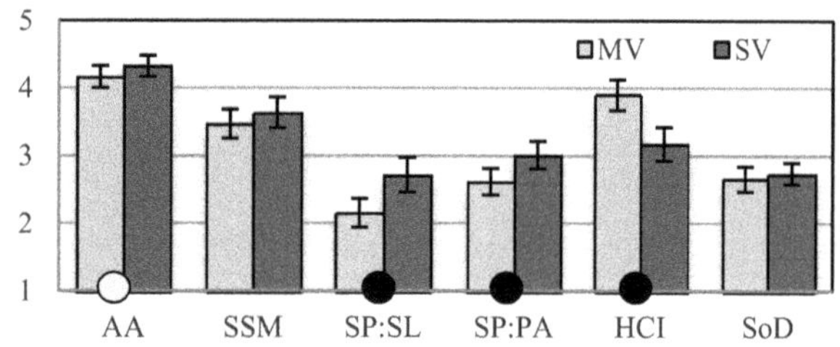

Figure 6. MEC-SPQ with Attention Allocation (AA), Spatial Situation Model (SSM), Spatial Presence:Self Location (SP:SL), Spatial Presence:Possible Actions(SP:PA), Higher Cognitive Involvement (HCI), Suspension of Disbelief (SoD).

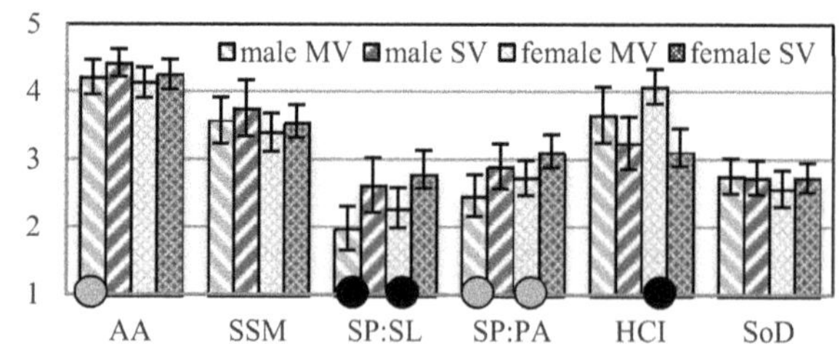

Figure 7. MEC-SPQ vision mode x gender. Different characteristics in presence for male and female subjects. (Error bars show 95% CI, ○=p<.05; ●=p<.01; ●=p<.001)

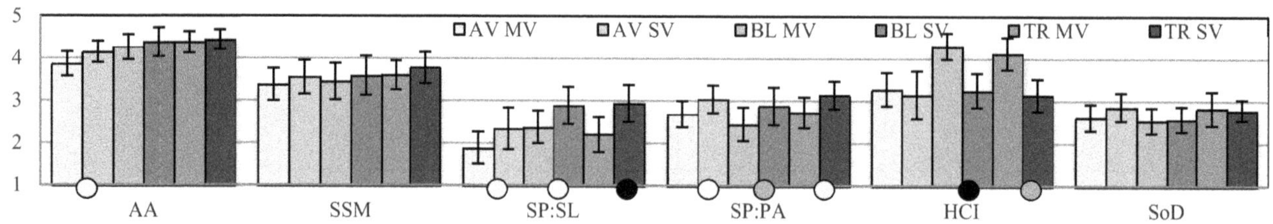

Figure 8. MEC-SPQ games x vision mode. All games provide enhanced presence in SV with some differences in AA and HCI.

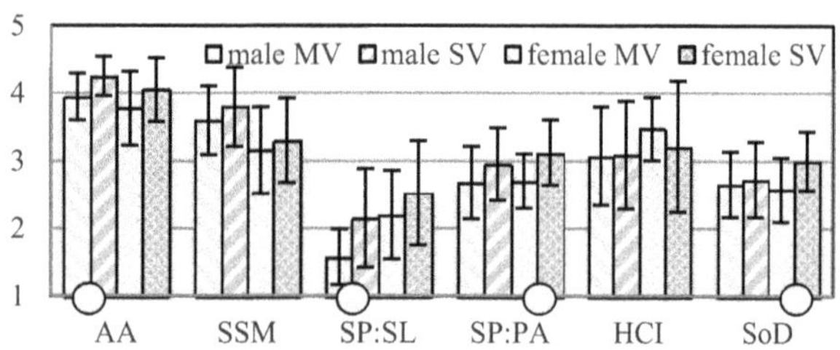

Figure 9. MEC-SPQ Avatar gender vs. vision mode. Both gender groups were affected by SV.

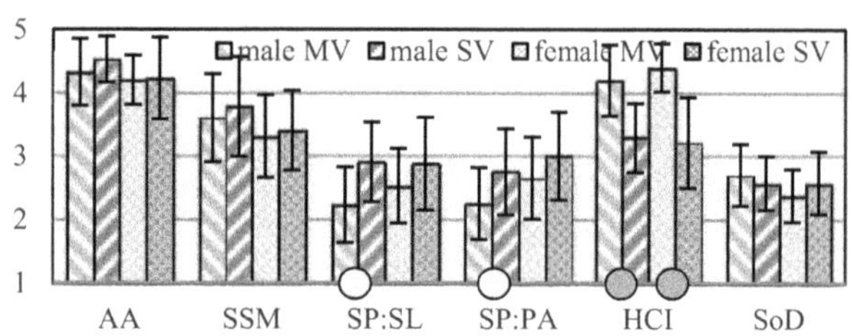

Figure 10. MEC-SPQ Blur gender vs. vision mode. More effects could be found in the male group.

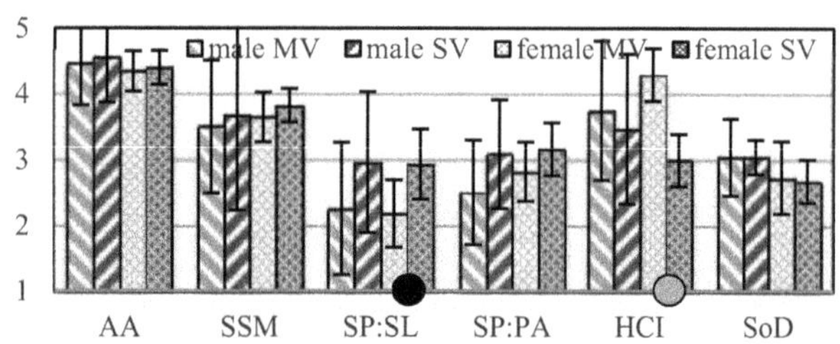

Figure 11. MEC-SPQ Trine gender vs. vision mode. Only female users report differences between MV and SV.

As with the GEQ, we extracted gender specific differences (see Figure 7): Female subjects had significantly higher values in SV than in MV for SP:SL (t_{33}=-4.361, p<.001) and SP:PA (t_{33}=-3.428, p<.01). They had significantly lower values of HCI in stereo than in mono (Z=-4.095, p<.001). Male subjects had significantly higher values in stereo for AA (Z=2.742, p<.01), SP:SL (Z=3.654, p<.001), and SP:PA (t_{25}=-3.175, p<.01).

Looking at the particular games (see Figure 8), SV increased presence in all three games: We found significantly higher values of Spatial Presence:Self Location (AV: Z=2.459, p<.05, BL: t_{19}=-2.848, p<.05, TR: t_{19}=-5.902, p<.001) and Spatial Presence:Possible Action (AV: t_{19}=-2.483, p<.05, BL: t_{19}=-3.023, p<0.01, TR: t_{19}=-2.554, p<.05) in stereo than in mono. Again, the games evoked different characteristics as well. Only AV induced significantly higher values of Attention Allocation in SV than in MV (t_{19}=-2.596, p<.05). Only BL and TR showed significantly lower values of Higher Cognitive Involvement in SV than in MV (BL: Z=-3.733, p<.001, TR: Z=-3.136, p<.01). Again, means of SSM and SoD were not significantly different within any of the game groups.

Interestingly, these effects showed different characteristics when analyzed for each gender. AV (see Figure 9) affected both genders, but in different aspects: stereo significantly pushed SP:PA (t_9=-2.547, p<.05) and SoD (Z=2.214, p<.05) for female users, while it increased AA (t_9=-2.714, p<.05) and SP:SL (Z=1.973, p<.05) for male users. In BL (see Figure 10), stereo had more effect for the male group, where SP:SL (t_9=-2.976, p<.05) and SP:PA (t_9=-2.535, p<.05) were significantly higher in SV than in MV. HCI was significantly lower for both male (t_9=3.636, p<.01) and female subjects (t_9=3.952, p<.01). In contrast to the TR group (see Figure 11), stereo only affected female subjects whose SP:SL (t_9=-6.101, p<.001) was significantly higher and HCI (Z=-3.171, p<.01) was lower compared to MV.

SSQ

Stereoscopic vision also had an impact on the amount of experienced symptoms of simulator sickness (see Figure 12): The mean value of Total SSQ was significantly higher (Z=2.353, p<.05) in SV than in MV. All three subscales (Nausea, Oculomotor and Disorientation) also showed higher SV mean values, but only the difference in Ocu was significant (Z=2.853, p<.01). Surprisingly, this increase in symptoms was only reported by the male subjects. They showed significantly higher values in SV for all subscales and the total value (Nau: Z=2.138, p<.05; Ocu: Z=3.154, p<.01; Diso: Z=2.205, p<.05; Tot: Z=3.241, p<.01). The female subjects reported lower mean values in SV than in MV, but these differences were not significant.

Within the game conditions over all participants, no significant differences between SV and MV were found. Only when focusing on the male group, we found SV causing significantly more symptoms in total for AV (Z=2.325, p=.05) and BL (t_9=-3.503, p<.01). For male subjects playing AV, Ocu (Z=2.111, p<.05) and Diso (Z=2.032, p<.05) were higher in SV than in MV. For males playing BL, Nau (Z=2.121, p<.05), Ocu (t9=-2.954, p<.05), and Diso (Z=2.271, p<.05) were significantly higher in SV. No effects were found for Trine, nor for the female group playing any game.

MindSet

We had to exclude eight of the subjects due to erroneous data in at least one condition. Of the remaining sample, 29 were female and 23 were male. We interpreted the data using arithmetic mean values for Attention and Meditation of each session. Attention showed a significantly lower value in SV than in MV (t_{51}=4.338, p<.01). This effect (see Figure 13) can be found in both gender groups (female: t_{28}=3.450, p<.01; male: t_{22}=2.646, p<.05). Regarding the games (see Figure 14), Attention was significantly lower while playing AV (Z=-2.166, p<.05) and BL (t_{18}=4.307, p<.001) in SV than playing in MV. TR did not evoke any significant differences.

S3D Preference and Other Findings

Comparable to previous findings, 51 participants (85%) had more fun with the SV mode. Of the nine others, five had played BL, three had played AV and one TR (6 male, 3 female). We also asked for any problems during play. Our subjects reported more problems with game controls (36.7%) and the gear (33.3%) than with the display (16.7%). For some participants (11.7%), the game difficulty was too low. We further collected both positive and negative comments (see Table 1). The positive ones state a new and fun experience with a more spatial connotation; the negative remarks were related to comfort and reported unsuitable game interaction for stereoscopic vision (quick camera movements, distracting HUD display).

Positive comments	Negative comments
• more fun	• more eye strain
• more intensive game feel	• uncomfortable glasses
• better spatial visualization	• 3D effects distract from game play
• more spatial feeling	• 3D display is unsuitable for quick camera movements, only great when you stand still
• more plasticity of the environment	• looking at HUD information is easier in Mono 3D
• more immersive impression	
• new quality of play experience	
• much more realistic	

Table 1. Positive and negative comments on S3D gaming.

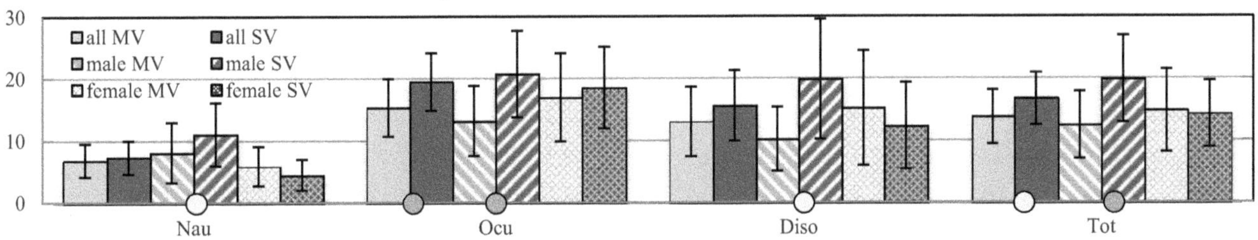

Figure 12. SSQ – all groups and gender vs. vision mode. SV had effect on all participants, but more significantly on male subjects. (Error bars show 95% CI, ○=p<.05; ◐=p<.01; ●=p<.001)

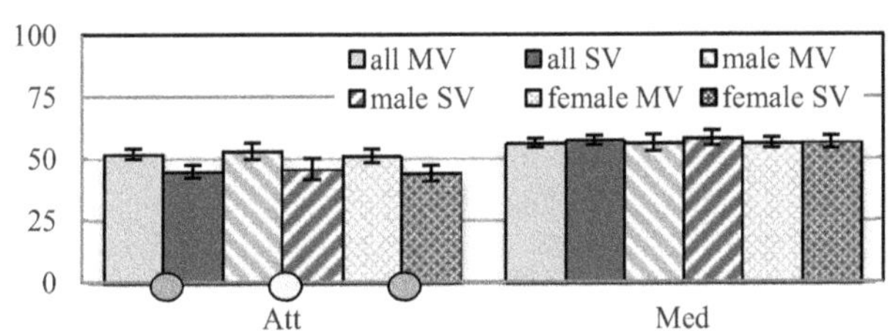

Figure 13. MindSet - gender vs. vision mode. Attention significantly decreases among all participants in SV.

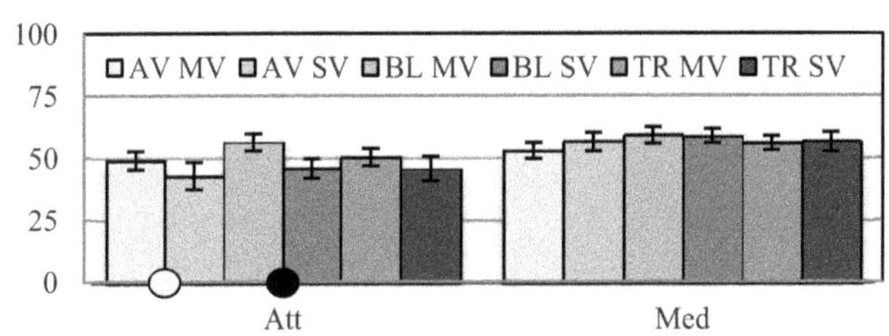

Figure 14. MindSet - games vs. vision mode. The effects for Attention through SV were only confirmed in AV and BL.

	Total		Avatar		Blur		Trine	
	male	female	male	female	male	female	male	female
GEQ	Imm+		Imm+		Imm+			
	Imm+		Imm+		Imm+, Flo+		Cha–	
MEC–SPQ	AA+, SP:SL+, SP:PA+, HCI–		AA+, SP:SL+, SP:PA+		SP:SL+, SP:PA+, HCI–		SP:SL+, SP:PA+, HCI–	
	AA+, SP:SL+, SP:PA+	SP:SL+, SP:PA+, HCI–	AA+, SP:SL+	SP:PA+, SoD+	SP:SL+, SP:PA+, HCI–	HCI–		SP:SL+, HCI–
SSQ	Tot+, Ocu+							
	Nau+, Ocu+, Diso+, Tot+		Ocu+, Diso+, Tot+		Nau+, Ocu+, Diso+, Tot+			
MindSet	Att–		Att–		Att–			
	Att–	Att–						

Table 2: The impact of stereoscopic vision on player experience for all metrics across the particular groups (games and gender) (+ means a significant increase, – indicates a significant decrease compared to monoscopic presentation).

DISCUSSION AND FUTURE WORK

According to the GEQ data alone, stereoscopy resulted in increased Immersion and thus enhanced game experience, confirming our first hypothesis. Most of the other results in MEC-SPQ and SSQ correspond to previous findings on stereoscopic applications (i.e., stereoscopic games) seem to induce an increased spatial presence, but cause a higher level of simulator sickness than monoscopic games. This also confirms our second hypothesis. Interestingly, and other than what we had expected based on previous findings [16,24], all of these effects are strongly altered by the choice of games which clearly rejects our third hypothesis. In addition we found a strong impact from the gender of the players, which we did not expect to happen.

The Impact of Game and Gender

Stereoscopic vision affects particular users differently for varying games (as summarized in Table 2). GEQ only showed differences for male users: BL caused males to report higher Flow; in TR they experienced less Challenge when playing in S3D. SV seems to have more impact on Immersion in those games which offer a lot of depth animation (AV, BL) than in a side-scrolling game (TR). For the former two games, males were more strongly affected in game experience and simulator sickness than females.

Similarly, the MEC-SPQ had different impact for the games and gender. SV in BL increased presence primarily in males; SV in AV had an effect on presence in both gender groups. SV in TR had more impact in presence on females.

Effects of simulator sickness were found to be increased in SV for the whole sample, but again differently for the separate games and gender (i.e., males mainly playing AV and BL were affected). The TR group did not report any such impairment, nor did the female subjects which partly contradicts previous findings [12]. This effect could relate to the used display technology, as a previous study using a lenticular display did not find an impact on SSQ [24].

We consider the strong impact of SV across all metrics on males to be affected for two reasons. First, our male users stated a greater prior experience with game genres and report more frequent use of digital games than female subjects. Thus, the effect of SV could be also related to experience than just gender. A second aspect is a possible higher affinity of males for 3D animations and spatially complex environments and the known gender difference in spatial abilities (i.e., males can solve spatial problems faster and more accurately than females [6]).

At the same time however, SV was strongly preferred for any choice of game in both gender groups. Hence, it will require further research to allow forecasting preference and quality assessment from analyzing user experience characteristics. Our data does not indicate whether the distinctive preferences found may result from a possible novelty factor of stereoscopic games and may vanish with longer playing times.

Attention in S3D Gaming

An increased spatial presence was generally experienced while playing stereoscopic games. Players felt more directly located within the stereoscopic game and increasingly urged to actively participate. More attention was also allocated by the game. At the same time, higher cognitive involvement was reduced under SV, so players seem to less actively reflect their playing on a meta-level. As with game experience, these effects differed for the three games. While BL had more impact on male users, TR only affected female users in their spatial presence. In AV, we found similar effects for both male and female users.

The MindSet data showed a lower mean Attention during SV game play. It is questionable how this decrease might be related with the MEC-SPQ values of increased AA and decreased Higher Cognitive Involvement in SV. We did not find any correlation of Attention with any other metric. However, as the MindSet is primarily designed as an input device in order to allow players active control of a computer using brain activities, we would rather expect this value to reflect self-induced or conscious attention. As such, it does not contradict the increase of AA found in the stereo MEC-SPQ which reports how a game allocates or draws attention of a player. Hence, we argue that stereoscopic presentation draws more attention but leads to less thoughtfulness and attentiveness, possibly contributing to a more intuitive and natural interaction with a game. A possible reason could be the generally more natural visual experience with stereoscopic images, also reported in [27].

The Difference of S3D in Current Games and Movies

Besides the Immersion effect, SV had only little overall impact on game experience as no other differences were found across all participants. In general, the GEQ is able to show such differences, visible when analyzing the variances between the three games: All but one GEQ-dimension were significantly different between the three games in MV, correctly reflecting their differences. In SV however, only four of seven dimensions were different for the three games, they were effectively more similar to each other in SV than in MV in terms of game experience. We have to note that none of the evaluated games were primarily designed for stereoscopic vision. As previously stated, all current games have SV as an option and must remain playable without it [26].

In comparison, stereoscopic movies are thoroughly produced for S3D presentation, taking into account actual movie theater configurations and display settings [19]. They differ in parts (e.g., cutting, scene transitions) from their monoscopic versions. Movie makers can build on a long history of stereoscopic cinematography that directs visual attention towards certain depths of interest within a scene. These solutions are hardly applicable in games, where the camera and scene depths often change dynamically and interactively. Many current games further suffer from certain S3D rendering problems and interface artifacts.

Goals and Actionable Steps for the Future

Our goal in subsequent work will be to develop a game design which is experienced differently when presented in stereoscopic vision. The effects found here give a first direction, indicating an impact of depth animation, showing that SV can contribute to a particular game experience, when taking into account how the design affects the core target group. Future assessment should also examine if the given results for these games are valid for similar games, allowing for systematically estimating a benefit of stereoscopy for a certain type of game or genre.

CONCLUSIONS

This paper provides a comprehensive study on the impact of stereoscopy on gaming experience. We analyzed three different games by comparing two vision modes using GEQ, MEC-SPQ, SSQ and EEG-related metrics. Our results contain three major contributions. First, we confirm previous findings that playing games in S3D is clearly preferred over mono. It increases experiences of presence and immersion while causing more symptoms of simulator sickness. Second, we show for the first time that these effects depend strongly on the game and the gender of the user. For a racing game with compelling 3D camera movement, we found more impact on male users, while a side-scrolling-game with less spatial animations had more effect on female users. Avatar, offering dynamic 3D scenes with side- and depth-relative camera movements, affected both genders. Third, a higher Attention Allocation in S3D was accompanied by a reduced Higher Cognitive Involvement, indicating a more direct and unconscious interaction with stereoscopic games, effectively offering a more natural player experience. Future research needs to confirm these results for other games, helping to understand which particular design characteristics actually contribute to a more compelling experience through stereoscopic vision.

ACKNOWLEDGEMENTS

Many thanks go to our students, who helped with the experiments, especially Liane Bölicke, Christian Hierhammer and Sebastian Kirch, and to the participants.

REFERENCES

1. Bernhaupt, R. User Experience Evaluation in Entertainment. In R. Bernhaupt, ed., *Evaluating User Experience in Games Concepts and Methods*. Springer London, 2010, 3-7.
2. Brockmyer, J.H., Fox, C.M., Curtiss, K.A., McBroom, E., Burkhart, K.M., and Pidruzny, J.N. The development of the Game Engagement Questionnaire: A measure of engagement in video game-playing. *Journal of Experimental Social Psychology*, 45 (2009), 624-634.
3. Crowley, K., Sliney, A., Pitt, I., and Murphy, D. Evaluating a Brain-Computer Interface to Categorise Human Emotional Response. *2010 10th IEEE International Conference on Advanced Learning Technologies*, (2010), 276-278.
4. Dodgson, N. Variation and extrema of human interpupillary distance. *Stereoscopic Displays and Virtual Reality Systems XI 5291*, (2004), 36–46.
5. Drachen, A., Nacke, L.E., Yannakakis, G., and Pedersen, A.L. Correlation between Heart Rate, Electrodermal Activity, and Player Experience in First-Person Shooter games. *Proceedings of the 5th ACM SIGGRAPH Symposium on Video Games*, ACM New York, NY, USA (2010), 49-54.
6. Gaulin, S.J.C. and McBurney, D.H. *Evolutionary Psychology*. Prentice Hall, 2003.
7. Hoffman, D., Girshick, A., Akeley, K., and Banks, M.S. Vergence–accommodation conflicts hinder visual performance and cause visual fatigue. *Journal of Vision 8*, 3 (2008), 1-30.
8. Holliman, N., Froner, B., and Liversedge, S. An application driven comparison of depth perception on desktop 3D displays. *Proceedings of SPIE*, January (2007), 64900H-64900H-12.
9. Howarth, P. Potential hazards of viewing 3-D stereoscopic television, cinema and computer games: a review. *Ophthalmic & physiological optics : the journal of the British College of Ophthalmic Opticians (Optometrists) 31*, 2 (2011), 111-22.
10. Hubona, G.S., Wheeler, P.N., Shirah, G.W., and Brandt, M. The relative contributions of stereo, lighting, and background scenes in promoting 3D depth visualization.

ACM Transactions on Computer-Human Interaction 6, 3 (1999), 214-242.

11. Häkkinen, J., Kawai, T., Takatalo, J., Leisti, T., Radun, J., and Hirsaho, A. Measuring Stereoscopic Image Quality Experience with Interpretation Based Quality Methodology. *System 6808*, January (2008), 27-31.

12. Häkkinen, J., Pölönen, M., Takatalo, J., and Nyman, G. Simulator sickness in virtual display gaming. *Proceedings of the 8th conference on Human-computer interaction with mobile devices and services - MobileHCI '06*, ACM Press (2006), 227-230.

13. IJsselsteijn, W., Ridder, H. de, Freeman, J., Avons, S.E.E., and Bouwhuis, D. Effects of Stereoscopic Presentation, Image Motion, and Screen Size on Subjective and Objective Corroborative Measures of Presence. *Presence: Teleoperators & Virtual Environments 10*, 3 (2001), 298–311.

14. Jumisko-Pyykko, S., Utriainen, T., Strohmeier, D., Boev, A., and Kunze, K. Simulator sickness — Five experiments using autostereoscopic mid-sized or small mobile screens. *2010 3DTV-Conference: The True Vision - Capture, Transmission and Display of 3D Video*, IEEE (2010), 1-4.

15. Kennedy, R., Lane, N., and Berbaum, K. Simulator Sickness Questionnaire: An enhanced method for quantifying simulator sickness. *The International Journal of Aviation Psychology 3*, 3 (1993), 203-220.

16. LaViola Jr, J.J. and Litwiller, T. Evaluating the benefits of 3d stereo in modern video games. *Proceedings of the 2011 annual conference on Human factors in computing systems*, ACM (2011), 2345–2354.

17. Lambooij, M.T.M., IJsselsteijn, W. a., and Heynderickx, I. Visual Discomfort in Stereoscopic Displays : A Review. *Proceedings of SPIE 6490*, May 2010 (2007), 64900I-64900I-13.

18. Mehlitz, M.A. Aufbau eines medizinischen Virtual-Reality-Labors und Entwicklung eines VR-gestützten neuropsychologischen Testsystems mit einer präklinischen und klinischen Evaluationsstudie. 2004. http://webdoc.sub.gwdg.de/diss/2004/mehlitz/mehlitz.pdf.

19. Mendiburu, B. *3D movie making: stereoscopic digital cinema from script to screen*. Elsevier, 2009.

20. Nacke, L.E. and Drachen, A. Towards a Framework of Player Experience Research. *Proceedings of EPEX'11 at FDG 2011, Bordeux, France*, (2011).

21. Nacke, L.E. Affective Ludology. *Technology*, (2010).

22. Obrist, M., Wurhofer, D., Förster, F., et al. Perceived 3DTV Viewing in the Public : Insights from a Three-Day Field Evaluation Study. *Human Factors*, (2011), 167-176.

23. Palmisano, S. Consistent stereoscopic information increases the perceived speed of vection in depth. *Perception 31*, 4 (2002), 463-80.

24. Rajae-Joordens, R.J.E. Measuring experiences in gaming and TV applications. *Probing Experience*, (2008), 77–90.

25. Rebolledo-Mendez, G., Dunwell, I., Martinez-Mirón, E., et al. Assessing NeuroSky's Usability to Detect Attention Levels in an Assessment Exercise. *Lecture Notes in Computer Science 5610*, Human-Computer Interaction. New Trends (2009), 149–158.

26. Schild, J. and Masuch, M. Fundamentals of Stereoscopic 3D Game Design. *Proceedings of ICEC 2011*, Ifip (2011), 155-160.

27. Seuntiens, P.J., Heynderickx, I., IJsselsteijn, W.A., et al. Viewing experience and naturalness of 3D images. *Proceedings of SPIE 6016*, 0 (2005), 601605-601605-7.

28. Shibata, T., Kim, J., Hoffman, D.M., and Banks, M.S. The zone of comfort: Predicting visual discomfort with stereo displays. *Journal of vision 11*, 8 (2011), 1-29.

29. Takatalo, J., Kawai, T., Kaistinen, J., Nyman, G., and Häkkinen, J. User Experience in 3D Stereoscopic Games. *Media Psychology 14*, 4 (2011), 387-414.

30. Tam, W.J., Stelmach, L.B., and Corriveau, P.J. Psychovisual aspects of viewing stereoscopic video sequences. *Proceedings of SPIE 3295*, SPIE (1998), 226-235.

31. Vorderer, P., Wirth, W., Gouveia, F.R., et al. MEC spatial presence questionnaire (MEC-SPQ): Short documentation and instructions for application. *Report to the European Community, Project Presence: MEC (IST-2001-37661)*, (2004).

32. Ware, C. and Mitchell, P. Reevaluating stereo and motion cues for visualizing graphs in three dimensions. *Proceedings of the 2nd symposium on Applied perception in graphics and visualization - APGV '05*, ACM Press (2005), 51.

33. Woods, A., Docherty, T., and Koch, R. Image distortions in stereoscopic video systems. *Stereoscopic displays and applications IV 1915*, February 1993 (1993), 36–48.

34. You, J., Jiang, G., Xing, L., and Perkis, A. Quality of Visual Experience for 3D Presentation – Stereoscopic Image. In M. Mrak, M. Grgic and M. Kunt, eds., *High-Quality Visual Experience*. Springer Berlin Heidelberg, Berlin, Heidelberg, 2010, 51-77.

35. Zachara, M. and Zagal, J.P. Challenges for Success in Stereo Gaming : A Virtual Boy Case Study. *Proceedings of the International Conference on Advances in Computer Entertainment Technology*, ACM (2009), 99–106.

Health Promotion as Activism: Building Community Capacity to Effect Social Change

Andrea G. Parker[1], Vasudhara Kantroo[2], Hee Rin Lee[3], Miguel Osornio[1], Mansi Sharma[1] & Rebecca E. Grinter[1]
[1]College of Computing, Georgia Institute of Technology, [2]Nokia R&D,
[3]School of Informatics & Computing, Indiana University
agrimes@cc.gatech.edu, vasudhara@gmail.com, hl34@indiana.edu, mosornio3@gatech.edu, mansi388@gmail.com, beki@cc.gatech.edu

ABSTRACT
As HCI researchers have designed tools to promote wellness, disease has often been approached as a general problem. In contrast, public health research argues for an activist approach focused on how certain groups disproportionately experience disease and eliminating these disparities. Taking this activist stance, we examine how technology can reduce health inequalities by disrupting power relationships and helping communities pursue social change. We discuss our tool, Community Mosaic (CM), which allows individuals to share their healthy eating ideas with one another as a means of advocating behavior change. Our results characterize how CM helped facilitate activism (*i.e.*, collective efforts to counter local challenges to healthy living) and shift users' attitudes regarding their role as advocates for health. We contribute to the field of HCI by using our findings to present a set of recommendations for future research focused on designing and evaluating health promotion tools using an activist lens.

Author Keywords
Activism; collective action; community; health; low-income; nutrition; social change; wellness.

ACM Classification Keywords
H.5.3 [Information Interfaces and Presentation]: Group and Organization Interfaces - Collaborative computing;

INTRODUCTION
Researchers argue that Information and Communication Technologies (ICTs) such as social media and mobile phones have made it easier for lay people to address issues of societal importance [14,18,27]. For example, within HCI, designers have created tools to help citizens use natural resources more judiciously and become lobbyists for environmentally conscious behavior change [6,27]. The diverse body of work using ICTs to encourage social change (*i.e.*, the transformation of societies) is characterized by its activist focus, whereby the status quo is challenged through an explicit examination of marginalized groups, societal problems, and the power relationships that perpetuate inequality [2,5,6,14,27].

In this paper we examine how an activist perspective might help HCI researchers design and evaluate tools that address health inequities and the ecological influences on behaviors and attitudes. We focused on a specific inequity: the disproportionate amount of diet-related health problems in low-income neighborhoods and amongst ethnic minority groups such as African Americans [1,35]. Researchers argue that to eliminate these inequities it is critical to examine the ecology of health management, including the cultural, economic, and political influences on health practices [1,33,35,36]. Yet, while HCI researchers have investigated a number of health concerns (*e.g.*, physical fitness and chronic illness [4,10]), there has been less work specifically focused on health inequalities. Furthermore, while designers have created tools that address the psychological, physiological and behavioral barriers to health [4,10,23], less research has explored how ICTs can address ecological barriers (though important research in this area is beginning to emerge, *e.g.*, see [12,13,22]).

To begin exploring the design space of activist health promotion tools, we developed Community Mosaic (CM). CM helps users advocate healthy living by sharing their ideas (via photo and text messages) for how to eat nutritiously within the local community. These ideas are then visualized on an interactive public display. In a three-month field study, we examined how CM impacted participants' ability to advocate social change (*i.e.*, healthier eating amongst residents). In this paper, we discuss how using CM affected users' confidence in their ability to improve the world around them, how important they believe it is to help others, and their perception of the value of their efforts. Further, we demonstrate how a community-anchored device can encourage social change by acting as a counterpoint to existing local health challenges.

Our work makes two contributions to HCI research. First, through our evaluation of CM, we demonstrate the positive impact that approaching health promotion as a form of activism can have, as well as challenges that arise. Second, we present three recommendations for future research on health activism in HCI: 1) complement the prevalent psychological and behavioral views of health management with an ecological perspective, 2) encourage wellness through collective action, and 3) carefully negotiate competing values and perspectives on how to best address health inequity.

RELATED WORK

Health activism involves challenging the "existing order and power relationships that are perceived to influence some aspects of health negatively or impede health promotion" [36]. From grassroots approaches to institutionally backed top-down efforts, health activists have fought for a range of issues, such as the elimination of racial discrimination in healthcare and the establishment of public health warnings about the dangers of tobacco use [36]. Researchers have used community-based participatory research to help communities identify local health issues, brainstorm ways to overcome them and take action to change social norms [33].

Our focus is on the inequity that exists between high and low-income communities and between ethnic majority and minority groups in the United States (U.S.). Low-income households have poorer health outcomes than more affluent ones and African Americans, Hispanics and other ethnic minorities fare worse on health and wellness than Caucasian Americans [1]. The World Health Organization (WHO) attributes these differences to the *social determinants of health*, that is, "the conditions in which people are born, grow, live, work and age that can contribute to or detract from the health of individuals and communities" [1]. The WHO adds that these conditions are caused by the unequal distribution of income, goods, services and power [35]. In our work, we explore to what extent considering such conditions can lead to the design of health applications that address these inequalities.

Digitally-Enabled Activism

We view activism as a set of interrelated concerns that commonly characterize societal change efforts (computer-mediated and otherwise). Though these features do not exhaustively define activism, they provide a useful starting point for articulating a health activism research agenda within HCI. First, inherent in activist efforts is an explicit or implicit confrontation with morality, as attempts for social change are driven by an articulation of what is "right", "best", and "fair" and how the current social order does not live up to that standard [6,7,27,36]. In HCI, previous work on environmental sustainability has yielded persuasive tools that help users change their behaviors in an ethically responsible way [6]. Such tools have helped users see the impact of their behaviors (*e.g.*, energy consumption patterns) on the earth's health [7].

In pursuing social change, activists often address issues of inequality by advocating on behalf of marginalized or underserved groups. Such advocacy involves explicitly acknowledging that quality of life, opportunities to thrive, and access to goods and services are unevenly distributed across society [36]. For example, Bardzell [2] has argued that feminist theory can help interaction designers avoid marginalizing people by accounting for their perspectives in design. Focusing on inequality raises issues of politics and the organization and distribution of power relationships within and between groups [5,15]. For example, in Zimbabwe, Dialup Radio (an information distribution system for mobile phones) empowered local NGOs and rural citizens to challenge the government's tight control of broadcast media outlets [14].

Issues of conflict, particularly the structural forces working for and against groups, are also surfaced [11,36]. This reflects a concern not only with the manifested issue but also the underlying causes of the problem. For example, when Maitland *et al.* [22] studied the challenge of healthy eating in low-income communities they recommended shifting the focus of ICT design away from persuading individuals to change because their participants needed help with socio-economic barriers. We build on this work by describing the evaluation of a tool designed to address such barriers and presenting implications for future work of this type. Sociologists have argued that a structural approach to studying health is deterministic, discounting the existence of individual agency [34]. Accordingly, in our work we do not conceive of structural forces as insurmountable, but as part of the ecology of health management in which people both are affected by, and react to social forces.

Finally, activism involves examining forms of resistance [15,20]. Such resistance may be realized through collective mobilization, whereby the existing social order is challenged [36]. The "social order" refers to a society's system of social structures (*e.g.*, socioeconomic stratification), institutions (*e.g.*, the government and healthcare industry), and norms. ICTs can facilitate collective resistance of this order by making collaboration, coordination and information dissemination easier, more efficient, and more engaging [18]. For example, networked devices have enabled new political alliances through the coordination of lay people from diverse interests groups [15].

The exploration of how technology can mobilize collectives to effect social change (and address associated issues of power, inequity, and conflict) is a burgeoning pursuit within HCI. Questions remain, including whether, and if so how, existing applications and infrastructure have helped citizens address societal issues [25]. Our field has a unique opportunity to study the impact of new tools and their ability to help people address serious societal issues. In this paper, we seek to provoke dialogue on this topic by focusing attention on activist health technology.

Health Promotion in HCI

Medical researchers and government agencies have called for social action to end ethnic health disparities in the U.S. [1]. A growing number of HCI researchers have begun to explore how technology can help in this effort [12,13,22]. Yet, overall, few projects have used activism as a lens for designing and evaluating wellness tools. Leveraging the characteristics of activism presented in the previous section, we overview three aspects of previous HCI health research and discuss open questions.

First, previous work has often examined how ICTs can address behavioral and psychological barriers to health. For example, researchers concerned with obesity prevention have focused on lack of exercise and high caloric intake [4,19]. Work has also focused on the role that online communities can play in addressing personal motivation to change [26]. Far less research has focused on the design of health applications that explicitly address the impact of structural forces on people's ability to manage their health (*e.g.*, poverty's effect on health decision making).

Second, much research has approached disease as a general problem. For example, researchers have studied diabetes as an issue in the overall U.S. population, examining how health applications can affect the way that people understand their disease [10,23]. To compliment this work, there exists opportunity to focus on health inequalities, exploring the design of tools that address disease amongst groups who disproportionately experience it. In the growing body of HCI research on developing countries, researchers have increasingly focused on both the structural forces on health (such as politics, educational opportunities, and economics) and health inequalities (*e.g.*, [30]). A similar focus is needed in the developed world as well, given the health disparities in that context [35]. Recent fieldwork and systems exploring health in low-income U.S. neighborhoods represent steps in this direction [12,22].

Finally, while research has focused on health management in close-tie social networks (*e.g.*, friends and family [4,16]), less work has looked at mobilizing larger collectives to resist societal inequities by empowering them to be agents for social change. To explore this space, in our previous work, we designed and evaluated EatWell [12], a system that helps community members share audio stories about how they have tried to eat nutritiously in their local neighborhoods. In our current research, we extend that work by developing Community Mosaic (CM). In contrast to EatWell, CM supports information sharing by allowing community members to submit healthy eating ideas visually and receive feedback on how viewers react to their contributions. Furthermore, we specifically examined the extent to which CM helped develop users' capacity to be health advocates.

COMMUNITY MOSAIC

Focusing on activist concerns creates opportunities for new types of health promotion systems. To begin unpacking the implications of such an approach, we created Community Mosaic (CM). CM helps lay people encourage others in their neighborhood to eat healthfully by sharing how they have been able to make healthy eating decisions themselves—information that is, hopefully, locally and culturally relevant to other community members. CM aims to address the disproportionate amount of diet-related health problems in low-income African American neighborhoods by mobilizing people to speak out about the feasibility of eating nutritious foods. Additionally, we gave community members the sole authority to contribute to the system, rather than facilitate the dissemination of nutrition advice from medical experts. While information from the latter is certainly valuable, our goal was to place power in the hands of the community and examine the effect of health advocacy by lay people. (As we will discuss later, this decision yielded benefits and challenges.)

Our design approach was motivated by research showing that within low-income, predominantly African American neighborhoods, collectivist (emphasizing communal responsibility) approaches to health promotion are particularly effective [13]. For example, in the lay health advisor model, community members (not medical experts) are given resources and support to be advocates for healthy behaviors within their social networks [28]. In our evaluation of CM we examined the usefulness of providing a technological resource for such health advocacy.

CM has two interface points, the first being a user's cell phone. We chose cell phones because they are widely owned by lower-income individuals [12]. The second interface point is the CM Visualization software. This software runs on a touch-screen monitor that we installed in a public space within an Atlanta, GA YMCA branch. (The YMCA is a non-profit organization that provides resources to local communities such as exercise facilities and childcare.)

We used an iterative design process to create CM, beginning with formative focus groups at the same YMCA branch discussed above. Thirty-one YMCA members and staff attended these sessions, brainstorming how technology could best support health advocacy in their community. Their recommendations led us to develop CM; for example, 1) emphasize how the community is succeeding at eating healthfully (instead of focusing on the challenges), and 2) help residents take steps to eat well in spite of the local barriers to doing so. To prepare CM for our field study, we created a series of increasingly high-fidelity prototypes that were evaluated for robustness and basic usability with HCI experts. In the remainder of this section we detail the functionality of the resulting prototype.

Experience Sharing: In the CM Visualization (see Figure 1), users are greeted with the following prompt: *"How are we eating healthfully today? Share your experiences. Send pictures, text or both. Inspire others in the community."* Users send picture (MMS) and text (SMS) messages from

Figure 1. The CM Visualization runs on a touch-screen monitor (top). Larger screenshots of the CM Visualization are also shown, including the Main Screen (middle) and Detail Screen for one message (bottom).

their cell phones to the CM phone number to document their healthy eating experiences. The messages that users send can include anything that they feel relates to healthy eating (*e.g.*, specific foods, establishments, and people). Messages are displayed in the CM Visualization software that runs on a 42" touch-screen monitor (see Figure 1).

CM Visualization Main Screen: The CM Visualization works as follows. The Main Screen shows a set of buildings that are evocative of the Atlanta skyline. Each building window represents one message that someone has shared. As messages are sent to CM, the building windows illuminate, either showing a small version of the picture shared, or if the user has only shared a text message, the CM logo. For aesthetic purposes, windows are populated based upon a pre-defined pattern that spreads messages evenly across the buildings. Windows with messages that have been sent "today" are overlaid with a blue flickering light, helping users locate new content.

CM Visualization Detail Screen: Users can press any of the illuminated building windows. Once a window is pressed, the Detail Screen for the message pops up (see Figure 1), showing the photo (if any), the text (if any), the date and time it was sent and how many times the message has been viewed. All messages are shown anonymously (the sender's name and telephone number are not displayed) in an attempt to help users feel comfortable sharing their meals and ideas. At the bottom of the Detail Screen, viewers can scroll through thumbnails representing other messages that the same user has sent. They can then press any thumbnail to view that message's Detail Screen.

On the right side of the Detail Screen is the Community Response Panel; here users can quickly share their reactions to the message's healthy eating strategy by pressing buttons that say: 1) I'm inspired to try this, 2) I want to learn more about this, and 3) I hope others in the community will try this. A tally appears next to each button showing the number of times it has been pressed. The bottom of the CM Visualization Main Screen displays the total number of times users have been inspired to try ideas shared in CM.

Update Messages: Once a week, each user receives a personalized SMS telling them 1) how many CM messages were shared in the past week and 2) how often people were inspired to try messages that they have personally shared (based on the number of times that viewers pressed the "I'm inspired to try this" button for that user's messages).

Our SMS/MMS Gateway software (developed in Java) processes messages sent to the CM phone number. The gateway runs on a Google Android G1 phone that parses and sends message data to a server hosted at our University, where the data is then stored in a MySQL database. The CM Visualization software was written in Adobe Flex and PHP and is shown in a full-screen mode web browser on a 42" Samsung TSN-2 touch-screen monitor.

METHOD

We conducted a 12-week field study with 43 participants in three phases: pre-CM deployment data collection (3 weeks), the CM deployment (6 weeks), and post-deployment data collection (3 weeks).

Study Site

The CM Display was installed in a public location of a local YMCA branch. This particular branch is located in a predominantly African American neighborhood (95%) in Atlanta where the median income is 34% below the state average (according the most recent U.S. census data at factfinder.census.gov). We chose this community because it is a setting partially characterized by low access to healthy foods and a disproportionate experience with health challenges. We were also motivated by previous work showing that such settings can also be characterized by experiential knowledge about local resources for healthy eating [12]. Our goal was to see whether CM tapped into these strengths and addressed the inequities. While the

YMCA provides exercise facilities and health programs, they also provide services unrelated to physical fitness. And, since anyone could use CM (even if not enrolled in our study) our participants had the opportunity to reach individuals with a variety of interests.

Participant Overview

We recruited participants by placing flyers in the YMCA, making announcements in exercise classes and asking participants to encourage others to sign up. Before we installed CM, we used a survey based upon the Transtheoretical Model (TTM) of behavior change to understand how healthfully participants were already eating [17]. The TTM measures the stages through which individuals progress as they attempt health behavior change—from *Pre-contemplation* to *Maintenance*. Thirty-nine participants fully completed the survey. Most had recently tried to eat less fat or intended to in the near future (the *Preparation* stage, n=22). Many had been eating a low-fat diet for the past 1-5 months (*Action*, n=10) or for more than six months (*Maintenance*, n=5). One participant was not thinking about changing her eating habits (*Pre-contemplation*, n=1) and one was just beginning to (*Contemplation*, n=1). As such, the majority of our participants were interested in eating nutritiously, making them excellent individuals to study as we examined how CM might empower people to advocate healthy eating.

Thirty-four females and seven males participated in the CM field study. While we attempted to achieve a gender balance, we had a much greater enrollment response from females. Most participants were aged 18-47 (n=28), with the rest aged 48-57 (n=9) and 58-67 (n=3). Twelve were married and 24 had children. Thirty-one were employed, eight were not, and two were retired. Thirty-nine participants reported their income. Roughly half had an annual household income between $13k and $45k/year (n=19) and the remainder had incomes from $45,501 to over $100k/year (n=20). Forty participants identified as Black, two as White and one as Black/White/Indian. While the membership of the YMCA branch that we worked with is primarily African American, there is some cultural diversity and as such we felt it important to include the few non-Black participants who signed up for the study.

Data Collection & Analysis

Pre-CM Deployment: Participants attended an introductory session at the YMCA where we described the study, how to send messages to CM, and how to use the CM Display. They also completed a pre-intervention survey that asked demographic questions and questions about their nutrition-related habits and attitudes (*e.g.*, how important it is to advise others to eat well, and if they felt that they know enough about healthy eating to advise others). Participants were also asked to send 1-2 messages per month (or more, if they liked), for the duration of the study.

CM Deployment: The CM Display was installed at the YMCA for six weeks and was functioning for 25 days during this period, due to system glitches, thefts and disturbances of system components. Anyone at the YMCA could use the display, even if not formally enrolled in our study. During the deployment period, we conducted semi-structured interviews (15-20 minutes each) with 29 of our participants (20 participants completed two interviews, nine completed one). Interview topics included participants' experience sending messages and using the CM Display, their motivation for sending messages, and to what extent their use of CM affected their nutrition-related attitudes and their perception of their ability to help the community.

Post-CM Deployment: After the 6-week CM deployment, participants filled out a post-intervention survey that repeated the nutrition-related questions from the pre-intervention survey. Twenty-seven participants also came to one of five focus group sessions (about 20 minutes each). Focus groups were open-ended, and the discussion was guided by two broad topics: how useful (or not) CM is for helping to improve the community's eating habits and how CM could be improved. All participants who completed the interviews and focus group received a $60 gift card (the rest received a $30 gift card).

We completed an inductive analysis [32] of the interview and focus group transcripts, examining each transcript line by line to derive a set of codes describing the emergent phenomena in the data. Codes were then iteratively clustered to arrive at higher-level categories and the themes that we present in this paper. We computed descriptive statistics for our survey data and used the Wilcoxon signed-rank test to analyze the changes in pre- and post-CM deployment responses to the Likert scale survey questions.

RESULTS

Our system logs showed that CM users shared 278 messages (average=6, min=0, max=32) and viewed messages a total of 1585 times (an average of 63 messages each day that the display was up and running). As anyone at the YMCA could interact with the CM Display, this total includes messages viewed by study participants and YMCA patrons who were not formally enrolled in our study.

In our evaluation we examined a number of topics, such as the relative value of visual imagery and text, and the impact of CM on participants' eating behaviors. However, in this paper we focus our discussion on how participants used CM to advocate healthy behaviors to other community members. We also discuss how using CM affected participants' attitudes regarding their ability to advocate healthy eating and the importance of doing so. Through our findings, we show how a community-anchored digital tool can facilitate health activism (*i.e.*, collective efforts to counter local and cultural challenges to healthy living) and help shift users' attitudes regarding their role as advocates for health behavior change.

Health Advocacy in Community Mosaic

CM helped participants counter cultural and environmental barriers to nutritious eating by reflecting on and challenging the status quo. In particular, they tried to inspire others to adopt healthy habits and expose them to new, yet practical, ideas for doing so.

Counteracting Local Barriers to Healthy Eating

In our interviews, 16 (55%) participants described challenges to healthy eating within the African American culture or their local environment. For example, participants expressed concern over the prevalence of diet-related health problems such as diabetes and high blood pressure within the African American population. As we discussed earlier, the disproportionate existence of these problems amongst African Americans is well documented [1]. Others spoke about the abundance of fast food and the challenge of finding healthy foods in their community. P6 described how CM made her more aware of this challenge:

> When I look around in the community, the healthy choices for you know like... restaurants and places to eat are just not there and by having something like [CM] visible, it just, it makes me think I don't want to eat at a lot of the places that I see in this community; I may wanna, maybe cook my own food.

P8 also described the challenge to nutritious eating she faces because of the racial makeup of her neighborhood:

> This week I was trying to find something quick without having anything greasy and [I realized] that there is nothing available... Eating in my community has always been hard because of the demographics, because of the race of people that lives in my community... the options, again, are limited.

P8's presumption is supported by studies showing that predominantly African American neighborhoods have fewer grocery stores than predominantly Caucasian ones, even when controlling for income [24]. Furthermore, the grocery stores that are in African American neighborhoods tend to have a smaller supply of healthy foods such as low-fat starches and meats [31]. CM reminded our participants of how this inequity is reflected in their own neighborhood.

However, 10 participants further described how CM is a useful way of addressing the local barriers to healthy eating. They explained that CM's presence in the YMCA reminds them of the importance of, and ideas for, nutritious eating. This reminder was particularly critical in the face of the prevalent information about, and access to, unhealthy options in the community. For example, P9 discussed how the community needs the information in CM because:

> We can get a really good deal on... fast food or [fried chicken] wings... That's what people are inundated with. If you drive down some of the main streets in the community there's not... information encouraging you to improve your health or making those resources available to you.

Zoller [36] states that health activism involves challenging the existing power relationships that inhibit healthy living. In our study, one relevant issue of power was the inequity in healthy food access that our participants felt was unique to their community compared to other areas of Atlanta. As such, their comments suggest that CM served as a vehicle for engaging in activism by reflecting on the problems in the existing social order. In the next section we further describe the steps they took to challenge these problems.

Activism Through Inspiration and Exposure

In line with the design goal of CM, participants wanted to pique others' interest in wellness and inspire them to engage in healthy behaviors. Thirteen participants (45%) specifically discussed sending messages to incite behavior change. They did not only use CM to gain ideas for themselves or discuss nutrition generally; they desired to motivate community members to eat more nutritious foods. For example, P6 hoped to influence even one person to stop eating fried foods. Others tried to show CM viewers that it is not as difficult as one might think to eat healthfully.

Participants further described how CM helped them share information in a new way, moving beyond word-of-mouth as a means of healthy advocacy. The system's fixed presence at the YMCA meant that users could repeatedly show others the feasibility of eating well. As P31 said:

> The more we saturate [one another] with facts [about healthy eating]... the more it affects you, the more you think about it, the more it becomes, you know, part of your being.

Other participants described the value of CM in terms of how it supports the sharing of realistic and practical ways for people to change their habits. P7 explained how CM helped the community "spark change" one person at a time:

> As oppose to going to Wendy's and getting that $0.99 burger... we have something constantly giving us ideas [so we can] say, 'Well, you know what, let me just go to... Subway and get a sandwich with lots of vegetables.'

The constant presence of CM, and more importantly, the content therein, helped participants take action against the draw of unhealthy foods within the community. As such, CM helped participants begin to challenge the status quo within the community—the abundance of unhealthy food access and the limited availability and promotion of healthy food. Our findings show that CM functioned as more than just an information gateway. It was also a platform for small-scale social change whereby the existing power relationships within the community were challenged. This happened as community members resisted the foods that vendors made readily available by suggesting other viable options. Examining participants' reactions to CM with an activist lens provides unique insight by highlighting the political nature of the tool within the community.

Innovation

CM was not only useful for sharing basic information about healthy eating (*e.g.,* saying that it is important to eat vegetables). Many (n=9, 31%) participants described how they chose to share more innovative and creative foods that people may not have previously known about. They shared establishments, snacks and meals that may have been outside of message viewers' normal routine. For example, P9 shared foods that she felt people might not think of, like an organic protein shake that she sweetens with Stevia (a natural sweetener). In addition to highlighting new ideas for what to eat, some people shared creative ideas for *how* to eat. For example, P4 introduced viewers to her vegetarian lifestyle. P28 shared how she handles the large portion sizes provided at a Jamaican restaurant she frequents:

> I normally just take the meal and divide it into three servings and then just add veggies or a salad with each serving...A lot of times when we eat out the portions are so large and we feel like we have to just consume all of it. So I was just hoping that [my idea] might inspire someone.

These findings suggest that many participants did not simply share any meal that they felt was healthy, but purposefully and selectively chose those experiences that might best expand viewers' understanding of how to eat healthfully. In summary, these participants tried to encourage behavior change by giving message viewers a fresh perspective on eating nutritiously. While some activists attempt societal change through social critique or public demonstrations [15], another important way of responding to social issues is the articulation, by those affected, of pragmatic ways in which change can occur. And this sharing of practical, yet innovative ideas is precisely what we saw happen in our evaluation of CM.

Becoming an Advocate: 3 Key Attitudinal Shifts

We now move our discussion to the three attitudinal shifts that characterize how participants began to see themselves as health advocates. After using CM, they described feeling an increased sense of 1) competence in terms of their healthy eating knowledge, 2) the importance of their personal involvement in health advocacy, and 3) the potential impact of their ideas.

Competence & Views on the Importance of Advocacy

Our survey results showed that at the end of the study, participants felt more strongly that they know enough about healthy eating to give advice to the local community (Z=-2.06, p<.05). Our interview data provide insight into the reasons behind this increased confidence. Most participants (n=22, 76%) felt that their messages were useful because they were detailed, the foods they discussed were both healthy and tasty, or the idea they shared was based on previous nutritional knowledge that they had obtained. These results suggest that the process of sharing messages in CM helped users realize that they, based on their practical experience with trying to eat nutritiously, had important ideas that might benefit others. At the end of the study, participants also felt more strongly that it is *important* for them to give healthy eating advice to others (Z=-2.93, p<.01). In summary, our findings suggest that participants began developing the mindset of a health activist (*i.e.*, someone interested in encouraging social change) by engaging in two attitudinal shifts: they became more confident in their ability to advocate health and saw more value in helping others to eat healthfully.

Table 1: Participant Visits to the CM Display

# Visits	0	1-3	4-7	8+
% Participants	29%	34.2%	18.4%	18.4%

Potential for Impact

During our interviews, many participants (n=10, 34%) also said that they valued seeing viewers' reactions to their messages (in the SMS updates and at the CM Display) because it showed them, in a small way, how many times they inspired others towards change. Our survey data helps substantiate these findings: most participants said that they help to improve the community's health by sharing messages in CM (n=30, 81%). Interestingly, we saw these positive results though participants had relatively limited information about how viewers reacted to their messages. The CM update messages, while seen as useful, only provided each user with basic information summarizing the number of times the "I'm inspired to try this" button was pressed for his or her messages. Furthermore, as Table 1 shows, participants had a modest amount of interaction with the CM Display: most visited it less than eight times over the 6-week deployment and 29% did not visit it at all.

Our results suggest that even small amounts of feedback can help contributors see the impact they have on their community. At the same time, one direction for future work would be to provide more detailed feedback to CM users regarding *how* the information they have shared is helping to transform the community's behaviors. Indeed, while many participants felt their messages were valued, some were unsure of how much they actually motivated viewers to change their habits. Ultimately, these participants felt that their ability to impact social change relies not only on their contributions but what the community does with that information. Future research on health advocacy systems should explore engaging ways of giving users more detailed feedback on the influence they are having.

STUDY LIMITATIONS

Our study was conducted over a relatively short time period. An important direction for future work will be to examine the impact of longer-term interactions with health advocacy tools such as CM. Another limitation of this work is that while participants felt confident in the ideas they shared, there was little external validation of the healthiness of these ideas. We did moderate CM messages based upon a set of YMCA guidelines; for example, we were required to filter out messages that encouraged dangerously low caloric intake. Still, while CM users shared many ideas that on the surface appear to be healthy (*e.g.*, smoothies, kale salad, and baked sweet potatoes), a nutrition expert did not carefully evaluate them. In addition, as users frequently shared only a photo of a meal, determining and assessing the specific ingredients in the dish was often impossible for viewers. Finally, as messages were shared anonymously, viewers did not have a straightforward method of assessing content contributors' credibility. In summary, these limitations suggest two directions for future work on systems that support health advocacy: 1) examine previous research on online communities to identify potential mechanisms for conveying contributor expertise, and 2) explore how the involvement of nutrition experts affects user engagement, and encourages or inhibits the development of lay content contributors into effective health advocates.

DISCUSSION

Zoller [36] offers a theoretical perspective on how the field of health communication can be moved productively forward by using an activist lens that focuses on issues of power, inequality and the structural influences on health. A focus on similar issues is a valuable way for HCI to not only understand the broader context in which health and wellness is facilitated and inhibited; such a focus can also help us conceive of new ways that technology can help people live healthier lives. In the remainder of this paper, we propose an agenda for HCI research on health activism that involves a shift in how we examine the context of health management, promoting health through collective action, and carefully negotiating competing values.

Re-Thinking the Context of Health Management in HCI

Previous HCI research has often conceived of health and wellness as ideal states challenged mainly by an individual's lack of motivation, interest, knowledge, or access to social support [4,10,23,26]. Of course, these are important challenges that present great opportunities for technological innovation. However, broader structural challenges to health have been less explicitly confronted—challenges such as the imbalance of power between food vendors and the residents of predominantly African American communities. In our evaluation of CM, we examined how the content in CM pushed back on the unhealthy food advertisements and resources available within the community. Doing so helped us to understand CM as not simply an information appliance but as a political actor, giving the community an opportunity to broadcast their own health messaging and not just receive messaging from local food corporations. Public health researchers and policy makers regularly examine the ecology of health management [1]. HCI researchers should similarly study users' broader context of health decision-making to better appreciate how health and wellness tools might sit within users' lives, and ultimately facilitate social change (*e.g.*, as in [12,21,22,30]). Doing so necessitates approaching the pursuit of health not only as a matter of individual behavioral change but also explicitly confronting the community, cultural, and society-level forces that shape the conditions in which people live.

An examination of such contextual factors raises a complementary set of questions to those that HCI researchers have typically explored in the past. For example, previous research has examined how physicians' use of computers in the exam room impacts their interaction with patients [3]. A consideration of the broader ecology of health and a critical focus on social justice would suggest stepping back to question, for example, how feasible it is for different populations to even access healthcare. For example, ethnic minority groups in the U.S. are significantly less likely than others to have health insurance, and those who do seek treatment consistently report receiving lower-quality healthcare [1]. Considering these issues could affect how HCI researchers design health applications. For example, research might focus on supporting communication between individuals and healthcare providers other than physicians, such as community health workers (*e.g.*, [30]). Another idea would be to examine the particular reasons for which ethnic minority groups report lower quality care and brainstorm tools that might help patients and providers identify ways to repair their relationship. In future HCI research on health, thoroughly examining "change" as a matter of social transformation (and not only individual modification) will necessitate a study of the forces that have led the collective to be what they are and those forces that hinder or help the collective in pursuing change.

Health Promotion Through Collective Action

In addition to understanding the ecological context of health management, one significant opportunity for future HCI health research is further examining how collectives can be organized to pursue social change. In writing about environmental sustainability, Dourish [7] suggests not only focusing on systems that persuade individuals to modify their behaviors but also "persuade people of the effectiveness of collective action and of their own positions within that collective". Doing so, he argues not only develops individuals who care about the earth's health, but also has the potential to shape larger-scale movements. Through our field evaluation of CM, we identified ways in which our participants were persuaded of the importance and value of advocating healthy eating to their friends, family and broader community. As they cared for others by sharing ideas and as they received feedback on these ideas, participants' attitudes changed regarding the value of health advocacy more broadly.

Based upon the positive results of our work, we encourage future research to study the design of applications that not only help users address social issues through the tool, but also help them become advocates of change apart from the tool. Such a design orientation is particularly important, as HCI projects are often short-term, yielding prototypes that are eventually removed from users. To better understand the potential of new ICTs to facilitate real social change, it will be critical to examine not only how the tool itself can enable social change but also to what extent users are more prepared to change the world around them (*e.g.*, due to their increased desire to effect change).

We also suggest that future work explore new ways in which technology can enable the collective pursuit of change in the context of health. Researchers have evaluated systems that facilitate the pursuit of wellness goals by leveraging small social networks of friends and larger networks of strangers in online communities [4,26]. Previously, such computer-mediated groups have provided informational, emotional and instrumental support to one another. But, how else might technology facilitate collective action? We can understand the range of possibilities by conceiving of collective action along two dimensions: the locus of change (a continuum from individual betterment to societal transformation) and the amount of change pursued (a continuum from partial to radical change) [36]. While tools might help collectives encourage people to modify their behaviors (as was the case with CM), other systems might help groups address social structures themselves. For example, applications could help citizens rally together to challenge government agencies to supplement existing legislation (partial change) or an overhaul of the healthcare system (radical change). Recent work by Maitland [21] and the growing body of HCI research on collective action outside of the health domain provide useful starting points for future research in this area (*e.g.*, see [14,18,27]).

Negotiating Values

Within HCI and related fields, numerous researchers have advocated a careful focus on how stakeholder values are embedded into the design of ICTs [8]. Furthermore, recent work critiquing persuasive technology (tools with the explicit goal of shifting behaviors and attitudes) has encouraged designers to consider the line between persuasion and coercion and whose viewpoints are incorporated into systems encouraging behavior change [29]. Activist research on societal health issues must also carefully consider how values are designed into future applications. For example, stakeholders will undoubtedly have varied perspectives on topics such as the underlying causes of health inequity and how these problems are best addressed (*e.g.*, through environmental transformation or improved access to healthcare).

An example of this value tension arose in our work between the YMCA and CM contributors. Recall that the YMCA requested we filter CM messages based upon a list of guidelines; for example, messages could not advocate caloric intake below a certain level or mention commercial weight loss programs such as Weight Watchers. These guidelines helped protect the welfare of YMCA members, but also the interests of the YMCA (*e.g.,* ensuring it is not seen as endorsing a particular weight loss program). As we filtered messages, the YMCA's values became intertwined CM users': what the YMCA felt was appropriate to share ultimately superseded users' opinions. Based upon our experience, we see the value of future research on activist health systems transparently informing stakeholders of each party's interests and how they are harmonious or conflicting. Such transparency could help resolve conflicts or unite stakeholders based upon shared values.

When developing tools that address health injustices, researchers may also be forced to make value assessments, taking a stand for what they feel is "right" and "wrong". As researchers approach the design of health promotion technologies from an activist perspective, they should carefully evaluate their place within the project and the values they are upholding and reinforcing. Focusing on these concerns more closely aligns health technology research with the existing and emerging agendas within HCI that have a focus on values at their core (*e.g.*, [2,9]).

CONCLUSION

Previous HCI research has often focused on behavioral, psychological and physiological challenges to wellness. In our design and evaluation of CM, we used an ecological perspective, attempting to address cultural and economic disparities in health, and examining how the system nudged political relationships and affected community members' capacity to be change agents. Based on our results and the precedent of activist research in public health, we presented recommendations for future work in HCI that approaches health promotion as a form of activism. We hope that our findings and recommendations will catalyze future inquiry into how ICTs can address serious health disparities.

ACKNOWLEDGMENTS

We thank the YMCA, Blanche Payne, our participants, and our colleagues who provided feedback on this paper. This work was funded by Humana and graduate fellowships from the Ford Foundation and Microsoft Research.

REFERENCES

1. *HHS Action Plan to Reduce Racial and Ethnic Health Disparities*. Department of Health and Human Services.
2. Bardzell, S., "Feminist HCI: taking stock and outlining an agenda for design," *CHI'2010* (2010), 1301-1310.
3. Chen, Y., Ngo, V., Harrison, S. and Duong, V., "Unpacking exam-room computing: negotiating computer-use in patient-physician interactions," *CHI'11* (2011), 3343-3352.
4. Consolvo, S., Everitt, K., Landay, J.A., "Design Requirements for Technologies that Encourage Physical Activity," *CHI'06*, ACM (2006), 457-466.
5. DiSalvo, C., Light, A., Hirsch, T., Le Dantec, C.A., Goodman, E. and Hill, K., "HCI, communities and politics," *CHI'10*, ACM (2010), 3151-3154.
6. DiSalvo, C., Sengers, P. and Brynjarsdóttir, H., "Mapping the landscape of sustainable HCI," *CHI'10*, ACM (2010), 1975-1984.
7. Dourish, P., "HCI and environmental sustainability: the politics of design and the design of politics," *DIS'2010*, ACM (2010), 1-10.
8. Friedman, B. and Freier, N.G., "Value Sensitive Design," in Fisher, K.E., Erdelez, S. and McKechnie,

E.F. (eds.), *Theories of information behavior: A researcher's guide*, Information Today, Medford, NJ, 2005, 368-372.

9. Friedman, B., Kahn, P.H. and Borning, A., "Value Sensitive Design and Information Systems," in *The Handbook of Information and Computer Ethics*, John Wiley & Sons, Inc., 2009, 69-101.
10. Frost, J. and Smith, B.K., "Visualizing health: imagery in diabetes education," *DUX'03*, ACM (2003), 1-14.
11. Garrett, R.K., "Protest in an Information Society: a review of literature on social movements and new ICTs," *Information, Communication & Society 9*, 2 (2006), 202-224.
12. Grimes, A., Bednar, M., Bolter, J.D. and Grinter, R.E., "EatWell: Sharing nutrition-related memories in a low-income community," *CSCW'08*, ACM (2008), 87-96.
13. Grimes, A. and Grinter, R., "Designing Persuasion: Health Technology for Low-Income African American Communities," *Persuasive'07*, Springer-Verlag (2007), 24-35.
14. Hirsch, T., "Communities real and imagined: designing a communication system for zimbabwean activists," *C&T'09*, ACM (2009), 71-76.
15. Kahn, R. and Kellner, D., "New Media and Internet Activism: From the 'Battle of Seattle' to Blogging," *New Media & Society 6*, 1 (2004), 87-95.
16. Kimani, S., Berkovsky, S., Smith, G., Freyne, J., Baghaei, N. and Bhandari, D., "Activity awareness in family-based healthy living online social networks," *IUI'2010*, ACM (2010), 337-340.
17. Kristal, A.R., Glanz, K., Curry, S.J. and Patterson, R.E., "How Can Stages of Change be Best Used in Dietary Interventions?," *Journal of the American Dietetic Association 99*, 6 (1999), 679-684.
18. Kuznetsov, S., Odom, W., Moulder, V., DiSalvo, C., Hirsch, T., Wakkary, R. and Paulos, E., "HCI, politics and the city: engaging with urban grassroots movements for reflection and action," *CHI'11 Extended Abstracts*, ACM (2011), 2409-2412.
19. Lester, J., Hartung, C., Pina, L., Libby, R., Borriello, G. and Duncan, G., "Validated caloric expenditure estimation using a single body-worn sensor," *Ubicomp'09*, ACM (2009), 225-234.
20. Lievrouw, L.A., "Oppositional and activist new media: remediation, reconfiguration, participation," *PDC'06*, ACM (2006), 115-124.
21. Maitland, J., "Towards negotiation as a framework for health promoting technology," *SIGHIT Rec. 1*, 1 (2011), 10-19.
22. Maitland, J., Chalmers, M. and Siek, K., "Persuasion not Required: Improving our Understanding of the Sociotechnical Context of Dietary Behavioural Change," *Pervasive Health'09*, IEEE (2009), 1-8.
23. Mamykina, L., Mynatt, E., Davidson, P. and Greenblatt, D., "MAHI: investigation of social scaffolding for reflective thinking in diabetes management," *CHI'08*, ACM (2008), 477-486.
24. Morland, K., Wing, S., Diez Roux, A. and Poole, C., "Neighborhood characteristics associated with the location of food stores and food service places," *American Journal of Preventive Medicine 22*, 1 (2002), 23-29.
25. Morozov, E., *The Net Delusion: The Dark Side of Internet Freedom*. PublicAffairs, New York, NY, 2011.
26. Newman, M.W., Lauterbach, D., Munson, S.A., Resnick, P. and Morris, M.E., "It's not that i don't have problems, i'm just not putting them on facebook: challenges and opportunities in using online social networks for health," *CSCW'11*, ACM (2011), 341-350.
27. Paulos, E., Honicky, R. and Hooker, B., "Citizen Science: Enabling Participatory Urbanism," in Foth, M. (ed.) *Handbook of Research on Urban Informatics: The Practice and Promise of the Real-Time City*, Information Science Reference, Hershey, PA, 2009.
28. Plescia, M., Groblewski, M. and Chavis, L., "A Lay Health Advisor Program to Promote Community Capacity and Change Among Change Agents," *Health Promotion Practice 9*, 4 (2008), 434-439.
29. Purpura, S., Schwanda, V., Williams, K., Stubler, W. and Sengers, P., "Fit4life: the design of a persuasive technology promoting healthy behavior and ideal weight," *CHI'11*, ACM (2011), 423-432.
30. Ramachandran, D., Canny, J., Das, P.D. and Cutrell, E., "Mobile-izing health workers in rural India," *CHI'2010*, ACM (2010), 1889-1898.
31. Sloane, D.C., Diamant, A.L., Lewis, L.B., Yancey, A.K., Flynn, G., Nascimento, L.M., Mc Carthy, W.J., Guinyard, J.J. and Cousineau, M.R., "Improving the Nutritional Resource Environment for Healthy Living Through Community-based Participatory Research," *Journal of General Internal Medicine 18*, 7 (2003), 568-575.
32. Thomas, D.R., "A general inductive approach for qualitative data analysis," *American Journal of Evaluation 27*, 2 (2006), 237-246.
33. Wallerstein, N.B. and Duran, B., "Using Community-Based Participatory Research to Address Health Disparities," *Health Promotion Practice 7*, 3 (2006), 312-323.
34. Williams, G.H., "The determinants of health: structure, context and agency," *Sociology of Health & Illness 25*, 3 (2003), 131-154.
35. World Health Organization, *Closing the gap in a generation: Health equity through action on the social determinants of health*, 2008.
36. Zoller, H.M., "Health Activism: Communication Theory and Action for Social Change," *Communication Theory 15*, 4 (2005), 341-364.

Augmented Perception of Satiety: Controlling Food Consumption by Changing Apparent Size of Food with Augmented Reality

Takuji Narumi, Yuki Ban, Takashi Kajinami, Tomohiro Tanikawa and Michitaka Hirose
Graduate School of Information Science and Technology,
The University of Tokyo
7-3-1 Hongo, Bunkyo-ku Tokyo, Japan
{narumi, ban, kaji, tani, hirose}@cyber.t.u-tokyo.ac.jp
81-3-5841-6367

ABSTRACT
The main contribution of this paper is to realize a method for modifying perception of satiety and controlling nutritional intake by changing the apparent size of food with augmented reality. As a possible method for decreasing rates of obesity, we focused on controlling food intake implicitly without any effort.

We hypothesized that ambiguous perception of satiety can be applied to control our food intake. Recent psychological studies have revealed that the amount of food consumed is influenced by both its actual volume and external factors during eating. Based on this knowledge, we sought to control perception of satiety gained from the same amount of food by changing its apparent size. We also proposed a method for food-volume augmentation using real-time shape deformation. Our results suggest that this augmentation can control the perception of satiety and food intake.

Author Keywords
Perception of Satiety; Human Food Interaction; Cross-modal Interaction; Augmented Reality

ACM Classification Keywords
H.5.1 [Information Interfaces and Presentation (I.7)]: Multimedia Information Systems - Artificial, augmented, and virtual realities;

INTRODUCTION
Obesity has become a serious public health concern all over the world [1]. Obesity is defined as a medical condition in which excess body fat has accumulated to the extent it may result in adverse health effects. Obesity has become particularly prevalent in the United States, affecting one out of three Americans. Moreover, while obesity used to be a problem only in developed countries, developing countries are recently seeing their overweight population increase. Obesity increases the risk of many medical conditions, both physical and mental. It is associated with increased risk of cardiovascular disease, diabetes mellitus, certain types of cancer, obstructive sleep apnea, and osteoarthritis. Furthermore, obesity has been shown to decrease life expectancy [2]. A combination of excessive food intake and lack of physical activity has been defined as major cause of obesity [3]. Obesity risk can be decreased through limiting food intake and exercising. Thus, obesity is one of the leading preventable causes of death worldwide [4].

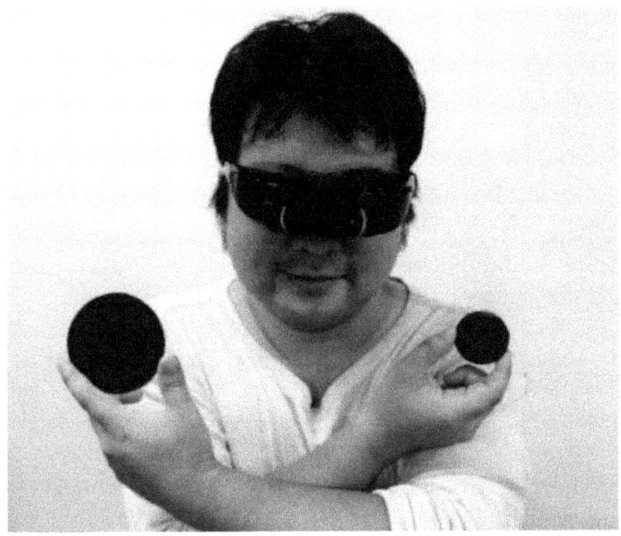

Figure 1. An augmented reality system to control our food consumption by changing visual size of food.

To decrease rates of obesity, many researchers have developed systems to promote physical activity using human-computer interaction techniques [5, 6]. Conversely, there are few studies on how such techniques can be used to modify food intake. However, computer-mediated human-food interactions are attracting recent research attention in the HCI community [7]. Wellness in particular is a growing research interest. For example, Mankoff et al. developed a system for analyzing individuals' food purchases at grocery stores and suggested a method for how users might make healthier selections from logs of receipts [8]. Noronha et al. has developed a crowdsourcing nutritional analysis system that estimates users' food intake (and the types of food eaten) in order to change their eating habits [9].

One limitation of these methods is that they are based on conscious education. This requires continuous effort on the part of the consumer in order to change their eating habits. Sustaining highly conscious effort when performing an intended behavior can be difficult. However, if aspects of eating behavior are controlled subconsciously, we may be able to modify food intake with minimal effort. Thus, our present research focuses upon controlling food intake implicitly by using human-computer interaction techniques.

Humans cannot accurately assess the volume or nutrition value of the food they consume. Therefore, humans estimate the volume of food eaten by using indirect cues: distension in the stomach and bowels, elevated blood-glucose levels, and apparent size of food. This estimation is inaccurate because some kinds of cues are evaluated relative to an individual's surroundings.

Recent studies in psychology and economics have revealed that the amount of food consumed at a given time is influenced by both characteristics of the food itself and environmental factors during eating. Theses can include plate size, package size, type of food, lighting, and socializing [13-32]. For example, if a person decides to eat a certain amount of soup, the size of the bowl acts as a contextual cue. This subsequently influences how much s/he serves and eats. Using these contextual cues can make it difficult to estimate the proper amount of food to eat.

We hypothesize that this ambiguity in perception of satiety can be applied to a method for controlling our food intake. Eating is a perceptual experience that involves the integration of various sensations including vision, audition, olfaction, and the trigeminal sensations. Our senses are highly interconnected. Perception through one sensory system is changed by stimuli that are simultaneously received through other senses. This phenomenon is referred to as "cross-modality" [10]. As a result, retaining the impression from an eating experience can be modified significantly by changing stimuli through only one modality.

Augmented reality has recently undergone significant growth in several fields of study. Augmented reality has great potential for enhancing and modifying our perception of real life experiences. This is accomplished by presenting computer-generated virtual sensations in a semantic context with real environmental elements. We suggest that the experience of eating can be modified using an augmented reality system, and that this can aid our ability to control food intake.

Recent research has conducted virtual eating experiments using the cross-modal effect and augmented reality technology. For instance, we have developed a "Pseudo-gustatory" display that changed the perceived taste of food and presented desired flavors through a cross-modal (visual and olfactory) augmented reality [11].

Another example is Hashimoto's "straw-like user interface" (SUI). This interface allows the user to virtually experience the sensations of drinking by representing data collected on the actual pressures, vibrations and sounds produced when drinking through an ordinary straw [12]. Their results suggest users can experience the sensation of drinking even though they are not consuming any liquid.

The goal of the current study is to control the perception of satiety obtained from the same amount of food by changing contextual cues through augmented reality. We first discuss results from previous conventional studies on the influence of contextual cues on the perception of satiety and food consumption. Next, we propose a method for food-volume augmentation using real-time shape deformation. Finally, we report the results of our food-volume augmentation system for controlling food consumption (Figure 1).

FACTORS THAT AFFECT THE PERCEPTION OF SATIETY AND FOOD CONSUMPTION

As previously mentioned, the perception of satiety and the volume of consumed food are influenced by several external cues such as apparent volume, portion size, plate size, package size, variety of foods, lighting, and socializing. These cues are organized into the eating environment and the food environment.

The eating environment refers to the ambient factors during eating that are independent of the food itself. This can include the atmosphere during the meal and social interactions. The atmosphere during the meal includes ambient characteristics such as temperature, lighting and sound. For example, people tend to eat more under cold conditions than under hot conditions [13]. This is because our bodies need energy to regulate body temperature. Thus, we need more energy to maintain warmth in a colder atmosphere.

Lighting can also influence food consumption. Dimmed or soft lighting has been shown to increase eating duration. Conversely, bright illumination decreases the duration people will stay in a restaurant. However, warm lighting (e.g., via candlelight) influences people to stay longer and consume more food [14, 15].

In addition to lighting, soft music generally influences longer meal times and greater food consumption [16]. On the other hand, people tend to spend less time in a dining area when ambient music or noise is too loud and discomforting [17].

These environmental factors are assumed to decrease our perceived perception of satiety and increase our food consumption because people are made to feel more comfortable. This allows them to enjoy and spend more time with their meal.

Social interactions can also influence eating behaviors. For instance, the presence of others can influence food consumption because eating duration tends to be longer when we eat with others. One study has shown that eating with friends can increase both food consumption and the duration of a meal [18].

Furthermore, observing someone else's eating behavior can affect how much food we eat; this observation can provide cues to estimate a "normal" consumption volume. This effect occurs even when observing a stranger's eating behavior. De Castro has shown that food consumed with one person increased by 33% as compared to when eating alone [19]. Additionally, increasing the number of people present at the meal increases the amount of food consumed. These results suggest that external social cues can help us estimate a "normal" consumption volume; this can have a great impact on our perception of satiety.

Other factors contributing to the food environment include the way that food is provided (e.g., salience, variety, package/portion size and apparent volume).

"Saliency of food" refers to how well food surfaces to the conscious mind. People will be aware of their hunger and tempted to eat unplanned food when they see or smell it. Thus, appearance and smell of food influences our eating activities and the amount of food consumed. For example, Wansink et al. have reported that candies placed in clear jars were consumed 46% more quickly than those placed in opaque jars [20]. A recent physiological study suggests that the visibility of a tempting food can enhance hunger by increasing the emission of dopamine, a neurotransmitter related to pleasure and reward [21].

Increasing the variety of food presented simultaneously relieves the perception of satiety and increases the total amount of food consumed. Rolls et al. have shown that people consume an average of 23% more yogurt when they are offered an assortment of three different flavors than when offered only one flavor [22]. Moreover, Kahn et al. have shown that increasing the variety of colors of M&M candies increases consumption, even though the taste of the candies in each color is the same [23]. It is considered that the reason for these effects variety gives us a chance to enjoy the food and relieves the perception of satiety.

The third external factor related to food is package or portion size. Recent studies have revealed that package and portion size have a great impact on food consumption. Rolls et al. showed that a larger portion size of an amorphous food (e.g., macaroni and cheese) significantly leads to greater food consumption [24]. They have also shown that intake of a packaged snack is directly influenced by the size of the package, even if the total amount of the snack in the package is not visible. Furthermore, increased food consumption from bigger packages is not compensated for at the next meal [25].

Child development research has shown that portion size begins to influence children's eating behavior between the ages of three and five years [26]. Therefore, the relationship between estimated perception of satiety and portion size might be acquired early on in life. It is conceivable that we learn the relationship between package and portion size and develop a psychological constraint influencing the appropriate amount of food we should consume.

The apparent volume of food can also influence eating behavior. Given that estimating portion size is often a relative judgment [27], apparent food volume is assessed according to the size of neighboring objects such as other food, dishes, cups, cutlery and a person's hand. This relates to the Ebbinghaus illusion, whereby humans cannot help but compare food as smaller/larger when viewed in contrast with smaller/larger neighboring objects.

Even if these perceptual cues are inaccurate, they offer cognitive shortcuts that allow us to decide how to engage in eating behaviors with minimal cognitive effort. For instance, Wansink et al. showed that a larger serving bowl [28] and serving spoon size [29] increases food consumption. On the other hand, Mishra et al. showed that a larger fork size increases food consumption only in a restaurant, but not in the laboratory [30]. This might suggest that the size of cutlery may only work as an external cue in familiar settings.

Vertical-horizontal illusions can also influence how we estimate the volume of a drink in a glass. The Vertical-horizontal illusion is an optical illusion where people tend to focus on the vertical dimension at the expense of the horizontal dimension of a cylindrical object [31]. Wansink et al. have shown that this basic visual bias can influence teenagers to pour and drink 88% more juice or soda into short, wide glasses than into tall, narrow glasses that held the same volume. They believed that they poured the same volume, but this bias was still prevalent. Similar results were found with regular people and veteran bartenders [32].

As we have described in this section, the perception of satiety is influenced by several factors. Controlling these contextual cues by evoking an illusionary effect with human-computer interaction techniques may allow us to control (enhance or weaken) our perception of satiety. This can be accomplished without changing the real volume of food. Thus, the current study will control food intake by using augmented reality technology.

By mediating the control of contextual cues by digital technology, we can (1) reduce total food intake as a means to lose weight and (2) control the valence of nutritional value. In other words, this technology could support decreased food intake and influence the consumption (more consumption or less consumption) of a specific type of food (greens, certain macronutrients, etc.). This could help control eating behavior adequately according to the meal and its contents.

Unfortunately, we are not aware of any studies comparing the impact of external factors on satiety perception directly. Thus, it is necessary to identify the most suitable factor(s) from the external cues we have reviewed to this point. First, we chose not to use the size of dishes or cutlery for affecting perception of satiety. While the size of utensils has the advantage of being useful with various kinds of food, including liquids, utensils don't always work as satiety modifiers under familiar settings [30]. People know that the size of the dish is constant, and this can disturb attempts to change perceived satiety.

Given that the size of food is inconsistent in many cases, we consider it unlikely that we would induce a learning effect with our paradigm. Therefore, our research focuses on changing the apparent size of food. We consider that combining the effect of physical utensils and the imaginary apparent size of a food item is more effective in modifying our perception. However, we can utilize this effect by changing utensils physically, not computationally. Meanwhile, it is difficult to change the size of food without the aid of a computer program. This is another major reason for choosing to assess apparent food size as a suitable satiety modifier.

The apparent size of a food item can be modified easily by using augmented reality technology. Since food is placed in the foreground of our sight, it is easy to recognize the food by a camera put around our eyes and deform it. Conversely, given that dishes are in the background of food, it is difficult to recognize these items with a camera. Thus it is difficult to deform these items in order to keep them consistent with surroundings.

We propose a method for food-volume augmentation using real-time shape deformation for controlling the perception of satiety. This is accomplished by using the same amount of food, but we change contextual cues affecting food consumption with augmented reality technology.

AUGMENTED PERCEPTION OF SATIETY SYSTEM TO CONTROL OUR FOOD CONSUMPTION

As described in the previous chapter, the comparison of an objects' size is a relative judgment, and this relativity can evoke a change in perceived food-volume. We cannot evoke this change effectively when we scale the whole of our sight, because it does not change relative to the size of other objects. Therefore, we have to construct an augmented reality where we scale food consistently with its surroundings.

The current study focuses on finger-food eating because comparing a food object with our own body is the most basic element of size recognition. We decided to construct an augmented reality technology where we scale a food item while making sure the user perceives the food as if they were actually holding it. This "real" hold of the food enables us to compare the size of a food item and the user's hand. This may be effective for manifesting the illusion of the perception of satiety.

System Overview

Here we present an augmented reality paradigm where we change only the size of food in the visual field through head-mounted display (HMD). We also deform the shape of the user's hand as if s/he really were handling the virtually scaled food. This gives the users the impression that there is a difference in food size although they are holding the food in a certain size.

Figure 2 shows the setup of our system. The system consists of a laptop PC, a video see-through HMD (HMD + WEB camera), and food. In this system, users wear only a video see-through HMD (Figure 3).

Figure 2. The setup of the augmented satiety system: Laptop PC, HMD+WEB Camera and Food (Cookie).

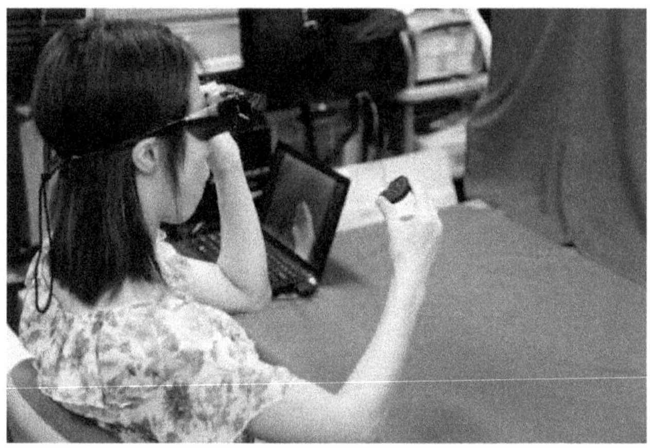

Figure 3. The user wears video see-through HMD and sees the deformed cookie and her hand.

Real-time Scaling of Food Appearance

Figure 4 shows the flow of image processing for changing the scale of food. Each step is discussed in more detail in the following sections.

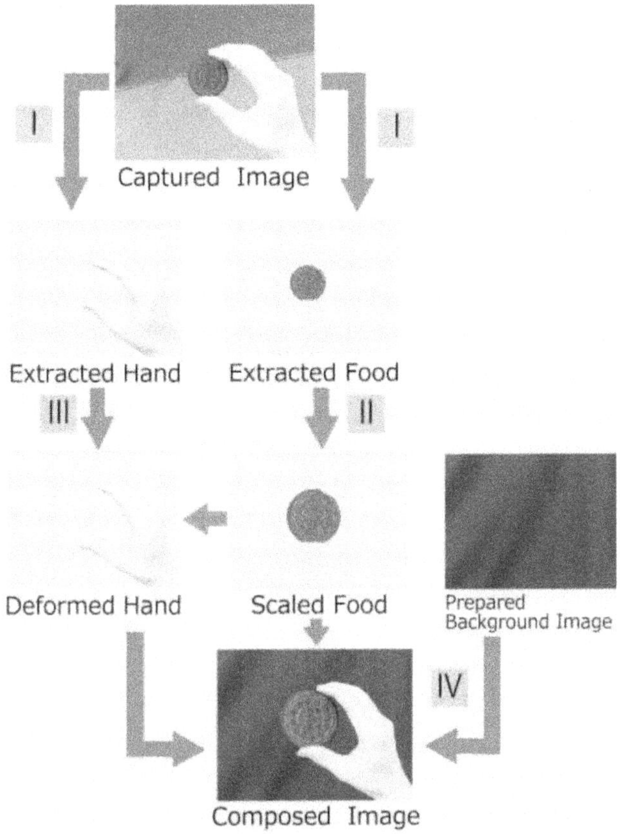

Figure 4. Image processing method for scaling the appearance of food.

I. Extraction of the Food and User's Hand in the Captured Image

First, we extracted the area of the food item and the user's hand from captured image based on the color. We made up a blue background with Chroma key, which eases color extraction. We made up a blue-back environment using a blue tablecloth as shown in Figure 3, which is not an unusual situation for a dining table, and here we consider it acceptable for an initial user study to test the effectiveness of the proposed system.

II. Food Scaling

We scaled the appearance of the food (up/down) while maintaining the centroid of its area. Here we defined the scale factor as R. In addition, we calculated the change of the food's outline.

III. Hand Deformation

We used a deformation algorithm based on the position of control points on the hand [33]. Using this algorithm, we deformed the shape of the hand easily and naturally using three control points. We defined the points where the user's fingers contacted the food as "contact points." The two contact points between the food and hand, and the centroid of the user's hand, are referred to as the control points. Below we describe the algorithm generated to naturally deform the shape of the hand for this particular hold.

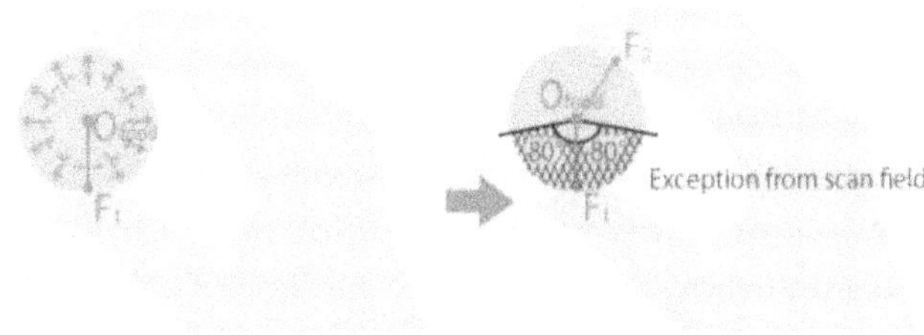

Figure 5. Detection of contact points between food and fingers. O_{food} is the centroid on the area detected as food. F_1 and F_2 are contact points between hand and food.

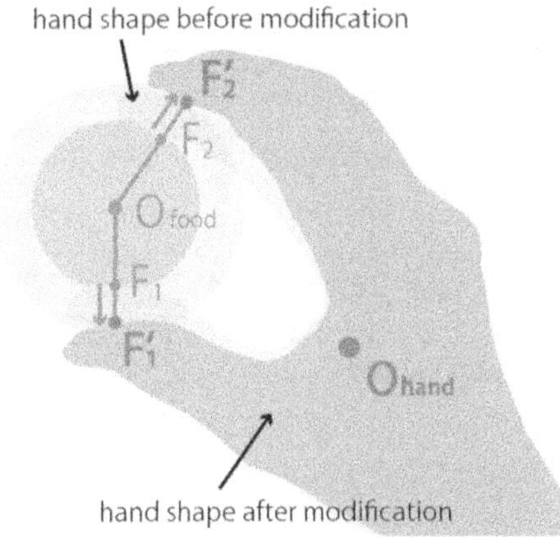

Figure 6. Scaling of food and deformation of hand.

We mainly focus on the situation where the user holds the food with the index finger and thumb; this can be seen in the upper image of Figure 4. The system uses the two contact points between the food and hand (one is on the thumb and the other is on the index finger) and the centroid of the user's hand as the control points. Before we calculated the hand deformation, we detected the user's two fingers with which s/he held the food and the position where his/her fingers contacted the food.

The first contact point is detected as the point in the portion of user's hand nearest to the centroid of the detected food area (O_{food}); this contact point is defined as F_1.

The second contact point is the point nearest to O_{food} in the area excluding the vicinity of F_1; this is defined as F_2. We defined the sector area, the center, which is line F_1O_{food}, and the central angle, which is ± 80 degree; this is shown as the meshed area on the right in Figure 5. These detected contact points (F_1, F_2), and the centroid of the user's hand (O_{hand}), are used as the control points before deformation.

Figure 6 shows how we deformed the shape of the user's hand. During the deformation process, we replaced F_1 and F_2 with F'_1 and F'_2 where the user's fingers contacted the virtually scaled food according to the change in the outline of food calculated in section II. In other words, we enlarged/shrunk F_1O_{food} and F_2O_{food} to R times as described in the following expression for determining the coordinates of F'_1 and F'_2.

$$F_1 O_{food} : F'_1 O_{food} = F_2 O_{food} : F'_2 O_{food} = 1 : R$$

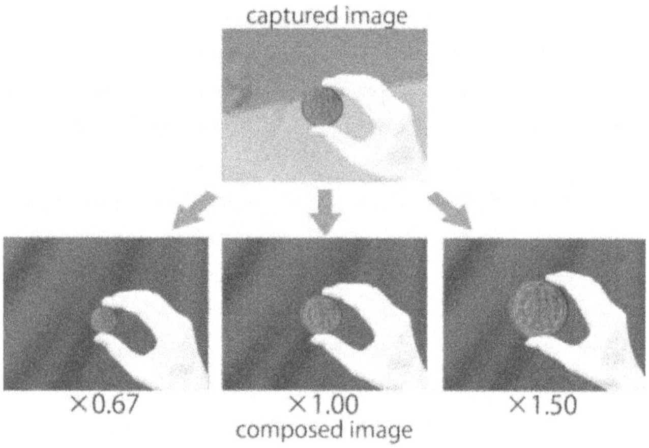

Figure 7. The result of scaling of food appearance

We next used these two replacement control points of F'_1, F'_2 and the centroid of the user's hand (O_{hand}) as the updated control point coordinates. We deformed hand shape to move from F_1, F_2, and O_{hand} to F_1', F'_2, and O_{hand} based on the algorithm described in [33].

While previous figures show the situation when a user's thumb is detected first, this algorithm works well even if a user's index finger is detected first. Furthermore, this method tolerates other grip types. Figure 7 and 8 show examples of food scaling and hand deformation.

IV. Image Composition

Finally, we overlaid the scaled food and deformed hand images over the background image which we prepared in advance. This is used for visual feedback. Figure 7 shows the result of image processing for scaling a cookie held with a hand. Figure 8 (a), (b) and (c) shows another example of the composition with a bagel. Figure 8 (d), (e) and (f) shows another pattern of food deformation. In these figures, a hamburger is enlarged/shrunk. These figures seem natural except for minor image artifacts (e.g., blue points around the thumb in Figure 8c).

USER STUDY

We conducted a user study to investigate how the food consumption would change by changing the scale factor of the food's size with our method. In the current study, we examined whether our system would change consumption volume even though users are not consciously paying attention to a change in volume. Participants were not made aware of the true purpose of the experiment.

Subjects

The study consisted of 12 subjects (8 male and 4 female). The subjects' ages ranged from 22 to 36 and the average age was 25.6 years-old. The subjects were screened to determine that they were in good health, had no food allergies/restrictions, were not currently dieting for weight-loss or trying to gain weight, were not depressed, were not using medication known to affect appetite, and were not pregnant or lactating. The subjects were not informed of the actual purpose of the study.

Design

The experiment used a within-subjects design. On 3 separate days, subjects came to our laboratory to eat cookies. We used NABISCO's OREO cookies because of their availability and familiarity. Its original size was 32 [mm] in diameter. Its energy density was 5.3 [kcal/g].

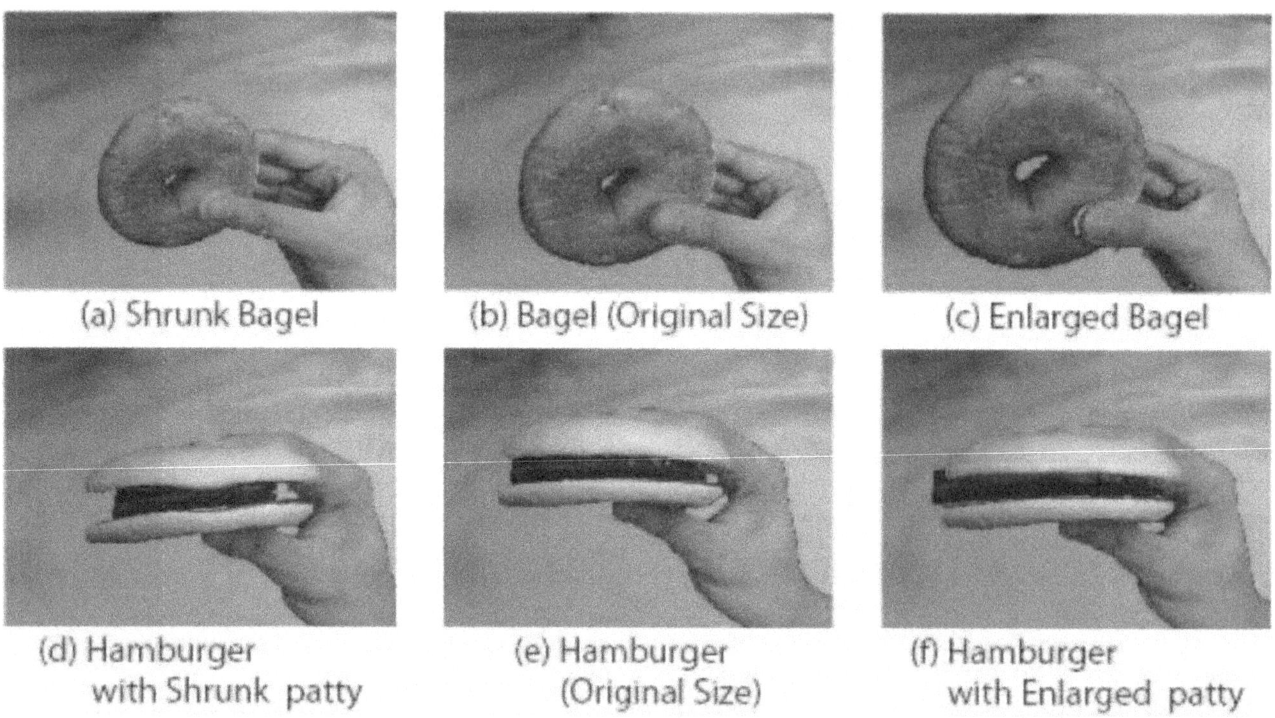

Figure 8. Examples of scaled food

During each testing session, subjects were presented with one of three apparent size changes by our augmented reality system: shrunk condition (× 0.67), normal condition (× 1.0) and enlarged condition (× 1.5). The appearance of the cookie in each condition is shown in Figure 7. To eliminate any effect of presentation order of apparent size, the presentation order was randomly assigned and balanced across subjects. The test days were separated by at least 2 days in order to prevent any satiation effects.

Procedures

Subjects were asked to keep their activity level as similar as possible on the day before each testing session. They were also asked to eat a similar meal as their last meal prior to the experimental session. During the day of each testing session, subjects were instructed not to consume any food for 2 hours prior to the experiment. Subjects kept a brief record of their activity patterns and food intake on the day prior to, and each day of, the testing session. Prior to each testing session, subjects recorded their life cycle and we made sure that subjects had followed the prescribed protocol prior to each session: at least two hours had passed since their last meal, there was no significant change in diet since the previous testing session and that their activity level had been similar as previous days prior to the testing session (e.g., no all-night work or hard exercise). If activity patterns and menu differed from that of the day prior to the previous testing session, we postponed the testing session for at least one day.

The first portion of the experiment required subjects to perform a calculation task. This task was used to ensure that subjects did not know the true nature of the experiment. Subjects were next asked questions regarding their hunger conditions. We describe these questions below.

Subjects were next set up with the HMD and were instructed to eat as many cookies and drink as much water as they desired. Subjects were told that they did not have to eat the entire cookie, and we allowed them to have leftovers. We passed a cookie out of the viewing area of HMD, and had the subject hold the cookie as shown in the upper image of Figure 6. We asked subjects to look at the cookie carefully before they ate it; they were also asked to take a look at the cookie each time they took a bite. This is done because the apparent size will not influence changes in the perception of satiety if subjects don't actually see the food. During a preliminary experiment, we found that some subjects ate cookies without even looking because of a narrow viewing angle of the HMD. Therefore, we included the instruction to view the cookie prior to each bite in this experiment. We allowed subjects to only drink water; when they drank we turned off the HMD to ensure that the user did not see anything.

After the subject stopped eating, we had them perform another calculation task and asked questions identical to those asked prior to the experiment.

Visual analogue scale ratings

Subjects completed ratings of hunger and satiety immediately before and after the experiment. Subjects rated their hunger, thirst, nausea, fullness, and how much food they thought they could eat when completing the analogue scales. All questions are shown in Table 1.

For example, subjects answered the question "How hungry are you now?" by rating hunger on a 100 mm line anchored by "not hungry at all" on the left and "extremely hungry" on the right. Other anchors in other questions consisted of the phrases "not at all" and "extremely" combined with the adjectives "thirsty," "nauseated," and "full." The anchors for the rating of prospective consumption were "nothing at all" and "large amount." If a rating during the current testing session had changed more than 30[mm] compared with the rating from his/her prior testing session, we postponed his/her testing session. This method for clarifying the control of hunger states has been commonly used in previous research [26].

The subjects were asked to rate the palatability of the cookie on a 100 mm visual analogue scale prior to the experiment. We originally planned that subjects whose palatability rating was less than 40 mm would be excluded from this experiment in order to avoid inflicting them. However, all subjects found the cookie highly palatable; thus, no subjects were excluded based on this criteria.

Results

Average cookie consumption volume and standard error of the mean in each experimental condition are as follows: shrunk condition (× 0.67): 91.9 ± 11.0 g; normal condition (× 1.0): 81.1 ± 8.0 g; enlarged condition (× 1.5): 75.0 ± 8.5 g. Figure 9 illustrates the normalized results based on the consumption volume under normal conditions by subject. Figure 10 shows the ratings of hunger and satiety before and after the testing session by experimental condition. We used a repeated measures ANOVA and Wilcoxon signed-rank tests with Bonferroni-Holm correction. This test revealed a significant main effect of size, $F(2, 33)=4.17$, with Bonferroni-Holm correction showed a significant difference between the volumes of cookie consumed in the enlarged versus the shrunk condition ($p = 0.014$).

These results indicated that subjects consumed significantly greater amounts of the cookie when they ate a visually smaller cookie relative to a visually larger cookie. There was also a trend where subjects consumed more when viewing the smaller cookie relative to when they ate the normal cookie ($p = 0.097$). However, there was no significant difference in consumption between the visually larger cookie and the normal cookie ($p = 0.293$). Water intake during each testing session did not differ by apparent size of the cookie.

Only one subject stopped eating before the entire cookie was eaten. All other subjects stopped eating when they finished eating the entire body of one cookie.

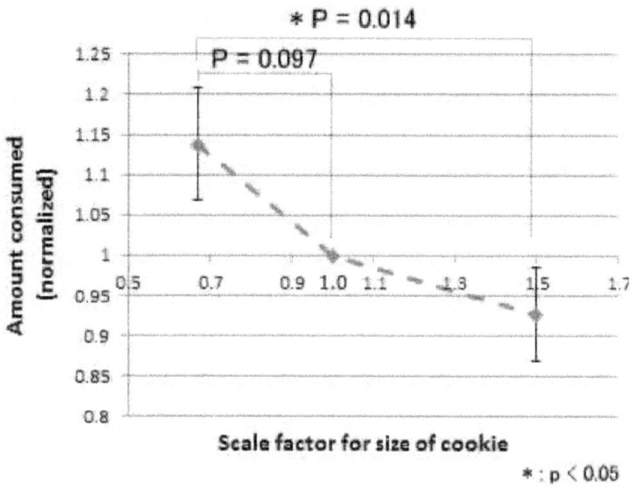

Figure 9. Amount of cookies consumed (± standard error of the mean) during the experiment by size (Scale factor for visual size of the cookies normalized by original size).

Discussion

Across all conditions of the cookie's apparent size, no significant differences were found prior to the testing session on ratings of hunger, thirst, nausea, fullness and prospective consumption. There were also no significant differences on these ratings after each testing session. These results point to the validity of our experimental design. These results also showed that our system maintains perceived fullness even after subjects ate the food. This is particularly compelling given that consumption is only influenced by visual augmentation of the food. Our results suggest that increasing the apparent size of a food item affects food intake and the perception of satiety; this is accomplished from the same amount of food during a single meal.

Contextual cues beyond the comparison between the apparent size of the cookie and the subject's hand were not provided because we used a blue-backed booth in this study. One subject did comment that she noticed the apparent size of the cookie was different from day to day. She thought that this was caused by a lack of constancy in the zoom factor of the camera. This suggests that the size comparison between the cookie and the subject's hand did not work fully as a cue to estimate the satiety in all of our subjects. If other types of contextual cues, such as a comparison between the apparent size of the cookie and other surrounding objects, were used we may have seen a more robust effect.

No subject mentioned experiencing an abnormality in proprioception even though s/he saw a virtually scaled cookie in her/his deformed hand. We have previously shown visuo-haptic interaction affects when subjects identify the shape of a grasped object [34]. We suggest that the subjects did not experience this abnormality of proprioception given that this effect was produced by our augmented satiety system.

LIMITATION

The current study has some limitations. First, the system may not have changed perception of satiety drastically. The results of our study, and previous research, suggests that the more the apparent size of a food changes, the more our consumption volume changes. However, drastically modifying the apparent size of a food, and our proprioception, may interfere with the ability to eat. For example, we may feel that we cannot put a food that is drastically scaled up in our mouth. This abnormality may limit the range of alternations in satiety perception.

Second, our algorithm is only useful for food eaten with the fingers. This was done to focus on a comparison between

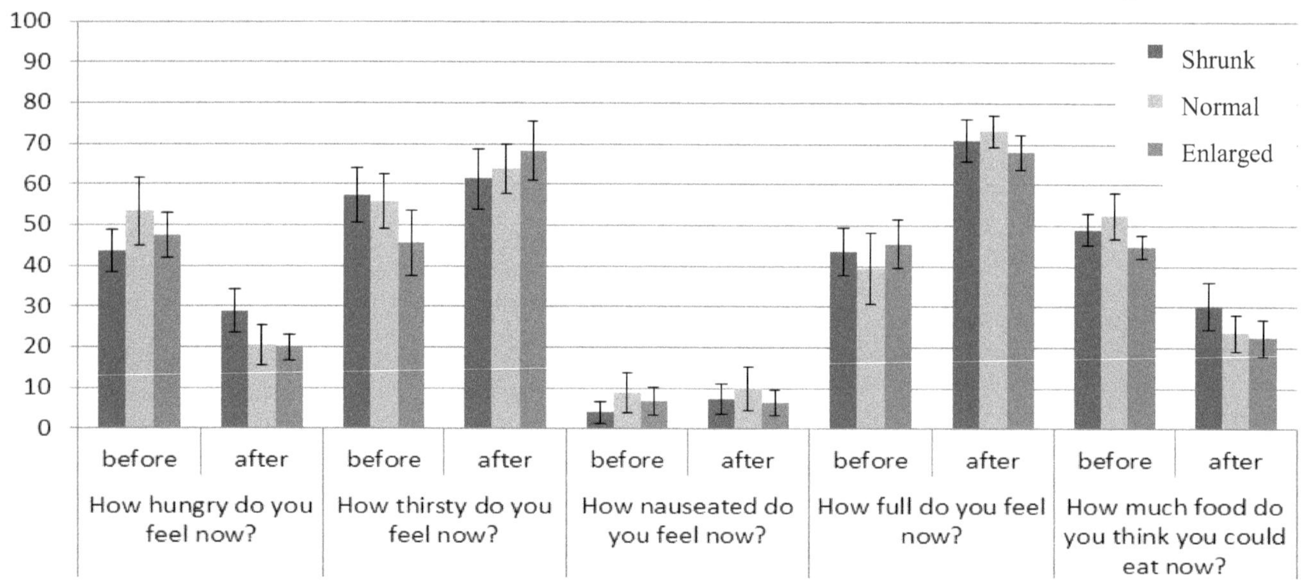

Figure 10. Ratings of hunger and satiety before and after the testing session in experimental condition.

(Average ± standard error of the mean)

an object and our body as a basic element of size recognition. Meanwhile, our method can be used with cutlery by expanding our method to define rigid parts of cutlery and deforming the food by keeping the rigid part unchanged. We may also use this expanded method to change the size of a glass in our hands for liquid food. Thus, a modified method would only need contact points between food/glass and body/cutlery for deformation.

Finally, our current method cannot be used with arbitrary backgrounds. However, we believe this method can be expanded with arbitrary backgrounds by employing a different food-recognition paradigm (e.g., natural feature-point based recognition used in [11]) and a content-aware filling algorithm [35]. One limitation of a content-aware filling algorithm is that it may produce visual artifacts around the food. These artifacts likely would have been observed in our shrunk condition. Thus, we did not use this algorithm for the current study. However, one advantage of the content-filling algorithm is that it will reduce other artifacts (such as blue dots around a thumb found in Figure 8c). Future research should examine the utility of this content-filling algorithm to determine whether it improves the quality of our current method.

CONCLUSION

The purpose of the current study was to control the perception of satiety and food intake implicitly by changing a contextual cue affecting food consumption. This was accomplished by using an augmented reality paradigm. We proposed a method for food-volume augmentation using shape deformation processing in real-time. This is based on previous research in the field of psychology. With this method, we can scale food while ensuring that a subject perceives that they were really holding the food. This "real" feeling of holding the food enables a comparison of the size of a food item and the subject's hand; this is effective for creating the illusion of apparent food size and the perception of satiety.

We developed a prototype system for implementing the proposed method. We conducted the current study to evaluate the effectiveness of this system. Our results showed that our system could change the consumption volume of a food item (cookie) by changing only its apparent size with augmented reality. This suggested that we could control the perception of satiety and nutritional intake. The ability to control our consumption with minimal effort is a conspicuous merit of our system. Previous research [8, 9] has shown that conscious education can change user behavior in certain settings. Thus, our system might be even more useful if individuals use it with a sense of purpose.

Future research should seek to quantify and assess the effect of apparent size. For example, we will attempt to reveal the relationship between apparent food size in augmented reality and the rate of change in food consumption volume. Technological improvement is needed such that additional object recognition methods can be utilized with our augmented reality paradigm.

The present study examined the effect of augmented reality during a single meal. It is important to determine whether our effects can be sustained over a longer period. Through these assessments, we aim to realize a more effective system. While the current study is the first step, and has its limitations, we believe that the proposed system can help individuals more effortlessly control their food consumption. This should have significant effects on promoting nutritional health. Additionally, these HCI techniques may be helpful for setting up treatment regimens to diminish obesity's negative impact on public health.

ACKNOWLEDGMENTS

This research was partially supported by the Ministry of Education, Science, Sports and Culture, Grant-in-Aid for Research Activity Start-up, 23800013, 2011.

REFERENCES

1. World Health Organization, Obesity: preventing and managing the global epidemic. Geneva: World Health Organization, 1998.
2. Haslam DW and James WP: Obesity, Lancet 366 (9492): 1197-1209, 2005.
3. Lau DC, Douketis JD, Morrison KM, Hramiak IM, Sharma AM, and Ur E: 2006 Canadian clinical practice guidelines on the management and prevention of obesity in adults and children. CMAJ 176 (8): S1-13, 2007.
4. Mokdad AH, Marks JS, Stroup DF and Gerberding JL: Actual causes of death in the United States, 2000, JAMA 291 (10): 1238-45, 2004.
5. Maitland J and Chalmers M: Designing for peer involvement in weight management. In Proceedings of the 2011 annual conference on Human factors in computing systems (CHI '11), pp.315-324, 2011.
6. Consolvo S, Everitt K, Smith I and Landay JA: Design requirements for technologies that encourage physical activity. In Proceedings of the SIGCHI conference on Human Factors in computing systems (CHI '06), pp. 457-466, 2006.
7. Grimes A and Harper R.: Celebratory technology: new directions for food research in HCI. In Proceedings of the twenty-sixth annual SIGCHI conference on Human factors in computing systems (CHI '08), pp. 467-476, 2008.
8. Mankoff J, Hsieh G, Hung HC, Lee S and Nitao E: Using Low-Cost Sensing to Support Nutritional Awareness. In Proceedings of Ubicomp 2002, pp. 371-378, 2002.
9. Noronha J, Hysen E, Zhang H and Gajos KZ: Platemate: crowdsourcing nutritional analysis from food photographs. In Proceedings of the 24th annual ACM

symposium on User interface software and technology (UIST '11), pp. 1-12, 2011.

10. Shimojo S and Shams L: Sensory modalities are not separate modalities: plasticity and interactions, Current Opinion in Neurobiology 2001 Aug;11(4):505-9, 2001.

11. Narumi T, Nishizaka S, Kajinami T, Tanikawa T and Hirose M: Augmented Reality Flavors: Gustatory Display Based on Edible Marker and Cross-Modal Interaction, In Proceedings of the 2011 annual conference on Human factors in computing systems (CHI '11), pp.93-102, 2011.

12. Hashimoto Y, Inami M and Kajimoto H: Straw-like User Interface (II): a new method of presenting auditory sensations for a more natural experience, Euro Haptics 2008, pp.484-493, 2008.

13. Brobeck JR: Food intake as a mechanism of temperature regulation, Yale Journal of Biology and Medicine, 20:545-552, 1948.

14. Sommer R: Personal Space. Behavioral Basis of Design. Englewood Cliff, NJ: Prentice-Hall, 1969.

15. Lyman B: A Psychology of Food. More Than a Matter of Taste. Van Nostrand-Reinhold, 1989.

16. Caldwell C and Hibbert SA: The influence of music tempo and musical preference on restaurant patrons' behavior. Psychology and Marketing, 19:895-917, 2002.

17. North AC and Hargreaves DJ: The effects of music on responses to a dining area. Journal of Environmental Psychology, 24:55-64, 1996.

18. Bell R and Pliner PL: Time to eat: the relationship between the number of people eating and meal duration in three lunch settings. Appetite 41:215-218, 2003.

19. de Castro JM: Family and friends produce greater social facilitation of food intake than other companions. Physiology and Behavior, 56:445-455, 1994.

20. Wansink B, Painter JE and Lee YK: The office candy dish: proximity's influence on estimated and actual consumption. International Journal of Obesity, 30(5):871-875, 2006.

21. Volkow ND, Wang GJ, Fowler JS, Logan J, Jayne M, Franceschi D, Wong C, Gatley SJ, Gifford AN, Ding YS and Pappas N: "Nonhedonic" food motivation in humans involves dopamine in the dorsal striatum and methylphenidate amplifies this effect, Synapse, 44:175-180, 2002.

22. Rolls BJ, Rowe EA, Rolls ET, Kingston B, Megson A and Gunary R: Variety in a meal enhances food intake in men. Physiol. Behav. 26:215-221, 1981.

23. Kahn BE and Wansink B: The influence of assortment structure on perceived variety and consumption quantities. Journal of Consumer Research, 30:519-533, 2004.

24. Rolls JB, Morris EL and Roe LS: Portion size of food affects energy intake in normal-weight and overweight men and women, American Journal of Clinical Nutrition, Vol. 76, No. 6, pp.1207-1213, December 2002

25. Rolls BJ, Roe LS, Kral TVE, Meengs JS and Wall DE: Increasing the portion size of a packaged snack increases energy intake in men and women, Appetite, Vol. 42 Issue 1, pp. 63-69, 2004.

26. Rolls BJ, Engell D and Birch LL: Serving portion size influences 5-year-old but not 3-year-old children's food intakes. Journal of the American Dietetic Association, 100(2): 232-234, 2000.

27. Coren S: A size-contrast illusion without physical size differences, The American Journal of Psychology, Vol. 84(4), pp.565-566, 1971.

28. Wansink B and Cheney MM: Super Bowls: serving bowl size and food consumption. The Journal of the American Medical Association. 13;293(14):1727- 1728, 2005.

29. Wansink B, Van Ittersum K and Painter JE: Ice cream illusions bowls, spoons, and self-served portion sizes. American Journal of Preventive Medicine, 31(3):240-243, 2006.

30. Mishra A, Mishra H and Masters TM: The Influence of Bite Size on Quantity of Food Consumed: A Field Study, Journal of Consumer Research, 2012. (published online June 2011)

31. Piaget J: The Mechanisms of Perception, Routledge & Kegan Paul Pliner, London, 1969.

32. Wansink B and Van Ittersum K: Bottoms up! The influence of elongation on pouring and consumption, Journal of Consumer Research, 30:455-463, 2003.

33. Schaefer S, McPhail T and Warren J: Image deformation using moving least squares. ACM Transactions on Graphics 25, 3, pp. 533-540, 2006.

34. Ban Y., Kajinami T., Narumi T., Tanikawa T. and Hirose M.: Modifying an Identified Curved Surface Shape Using Pseudo-Haptic Effect, The 2012 IEEE Haptics Symposium (HAPTICS2012), 2012.

35. Herling J and Broll W: Advanced self-contained object removal for realizing real-time Diminished Reality in unconstrained environments, In Proc. of 9th IEEE International Symposium on Mixed and Augmented Reality (ISMAR2010), pp.207-212, 2010.

Laying the Table for HCI: Uncovering Ecologies of Domestic Food Consumption

Annika Hupfeld
School of Computer Science
University of Nottingham
Nottingham NG8 1BB
psxah4@nottingham.ac.uk

Tom Rodden
School of Computer Science
University of Nottingham
Nottingham NG8 1BB
tar@cs.nott.ac.uk

ABSTRACT
Food contributes fundamentally to our well-being: physically, mentally, and socially. Unsurprisingly then, the importance of food to our lives has long been recognized in the social sciences, and more recently, in Human-Computer Interaction. Yet, despite ongoing trends towards the digital augmentation of domestic environments, little consideration has been given to the impact of the material aspects of food consumption in the home. This paper takes an ecological approach to uncovering the role spaces, tabletops, and artefacts play in the social organization of domestic eating practices. Based on our findings of interviews with seven households in England, we discuss implications for those seeking to digitally augment domestic dining.

Author Keywords
Food; eating; tableware; tabletop; augmentation; domestic technology; ubiquitous computing.

ACM Classification Keywords
H.5.m [Information Interfaces and Presentation]: Miscellaneous;

General Terms
Human Factors; Design.

INTRODUCTION
Food and dining are fundamental to our lives. At the most basic level, they contribute to our physical and mental well-being. Socially, it is an important part of life events, such as birthdays, weddings, and funerals, as well as to everyday gatherings with friends and family. Much of our individual, cultural, and national identities are associated with food. In view of the centrality of food and eating to human experience, then, its relevance to human-computer interaction scholars and practitioners becomes apparent.

Food has already been the subject of both technical and empirical investigation in HCI. Everyday kitchens [4], dining tables [13], and coffee mugs [14] have been digitally augmented with sensors and displays to become smart, context-aware, and trackable. On the empirical side, a range of studies have explored the role of digital technologies in food provision and preparation [15].

In this paper, we are interested in what happens when food gets onto the table. In moving beyond stages of domestic food choice and preparation towards consumption, we shift focus onto the dining table. We present a study of people's dining practices with practical emphasis on the tabletop interactions, the spaces where dining occurs, and the artefacts and activities involved. We suggest that it is the everyday processes, practices and meanings surrounding food consumption in the home that interaction designers seeking to digitally augment the space must engage with in order to successfully weave technologies into the fabric of everyday life. In doing so, we make the following contributions:

- We provide an introduction to the approaches taken to domestic eating in the social sciences and HCI
- We offer an account of domestic food consumption highlighting the distinctive role of the space, table and artefacts involved
- We reflect on the implications of our findings for those seeking to augment domestic eating experiences

Our studies focus on the evocative nature of the artefacts around the dining table and the emotional attachments people have with them. They also stress a number of key differences in the nature of food consumption. These would include differences between everyday and celebratory dining, between the various roles within a family, and between the different levels of conviviality involved.

The remainder of this paper is organized as follows. We start by giving an introduction to current approaches to studying and designing for domestic eating practices and experiences in the social sciences and human-computer interaction. From there we draw some implications for our own research approach. We then explicate and reflect on our study findings in the context of tangible, tabletop and ubiquitous computing. We conclude by outlining potential avenues for further research into the space.

BACKGROUND

Food and eating have received broad interest across a range of social sciences. Each discipline has brought its own approaches and perspectives to the topic, casting light on the physical, mental, social, cultural, and symbolic dimensions of domestic food consumption.

Social Sciences Perspectives

Anthropology has tended to take a holistic approach to studying food. Working in the structuralist tradition, to Mary Douglas '*food is [] the medium through which a system of relationships within the family is expressed*' (as cited in [39]). Ethnographies in the domain have uncovered the role of food in the personal, social and cultural construction of memory [34] and in the establishment of social bonds and rivalries through food exchange [26]. Material culture studies, specifically, has emphasized our shaping of domestic artefacts and their shaping us [29]. Miller, for instance, studied how council estate tenants applied a range of home-making strategies to their kitchens in order to create a sense of ownership [28].

Psychology's concern has chiefly been with the sensory, emotional, and cognitive dimensions of eating, nutritional socialization, and eating disorders. Macht et al [25], for instance, highlight food, the physical environment, and social factors as significant in contributing to positive eating experiences. The focus here tends to be on the individual rather than social or cultural groups. Working from a social psychological standpoint, Csikszentmihalyi and Rochberg-Halton [7] present the range of meanings people associate with their domestic artefacts, such as memories, values, and social relationships, some of which were related to food.

Sociology's focus has been on the social practices surrounding food. Gender studies, in particular, have much contributed to an understanding of food consumption in the home. Kemmer et al. [22] found eating patterns became more formalized and shared meals took on symbolic importance to young couples setting up home together. Often it is women who hold the main responsibility for (but not always control over) doing the 'feeding work'. Women's role has been characterized as the expression and reflection of both care and affection towards the family [31] and their subordination to men [8]. Kaufmann presents an in-depth study of cooking and eating [21]. It shows the way they actively produce family and are central to its continuity, breakdown, and reconstitution, a point also made by [1]. Kaufmann exploits the table as a particular lens for his discussion of the changing social life around eating. However, the dominant emphasis has been placed on social practice and neglected the role of spaces and artefacts involved in domestic food consumption.

HCI and food

Moving on to HCI, a range of work in ubiquitous computing, tabletop interaction, and tangible user interfaces has related to the enhancement of our domestic spaces, tabletops, and artefacts with sensing and computing capabilities.

In the area of ubiquitous computing researchers have thought about ways of digitally augmenting the kitchen space to help people shop for food [30], find recipes [1, 33], master cooking activities [4, 16, 20, 27], maintain a healthy diet [5], and even communicate through food [2]. A recent overview of food-related work in HCI by Grimes and Harper [15] notes the field's tendency to frame our interactions with food as imbued with problems in need of a (technological) solution. As an alternative, they call for promoting the celebratory aspects of human-food interaction [15]. An example in this space is the Living Cookbook [36], which allows users to share stories and experiences around the preparation of food with others.

The table as a domestic surface lends itself for digital augmentation. Indeed, an entire subfield within HCI is dedicated to the task of studying and designing tools and experiences for interactive tabletops. Yet, this work heavily weighs towards the office domain and centres around the use of media on tables. Two works considering tabletops in the dining context are the diet-aware dining table [24] that monitors the diner's food intake, and Tea Place [23], an ambient multimodal display responding to the colour of tea placed on the table. A focus for this work has been on the table where consumption occurs, with little emphasis on how the objects got to and from the table. Gaver et al.'s History Tablecloth [4], by contrast, was designed as a digital layer that sits on top of a dining table. It traces the food prints of objects placed on it, thereby subtly revealing various social patterns within the home.

Since Tangible User Interfaces (TUIs) emerged two decades ago, there has been a shift from the *physical* augmentation of the graphical user interface [9] to the *digital* augmentation of everyday artefacts [19]. An early example of a 'smart' object is the MediaCup [14] which collects, infers and communicates use information to remote participants. Similarly, the Lover's Cups [6] light up when used by remote users to promote intimacy.

In summary, there exists a rich body of work around the digital augmentation of domestic food spaces and the artefacts within them. A particular emphasis has been on food provision and preparation. In contrast, spaces and artefacts associated with food consumption, like the dining room, dining table, and tableware, have received little attention. Our interest then is in understanding the social practices surrounding food consumption and the role of the spaces and artefacts implicated in these practices.

METHODOLOGY

An ecological approach

As we have seen, there is a range of possible approaches to studying and designing for social interactions around food.

In our study we took an ecological approach to understanding domestic eating, paying particular attention to the artefacts, spaces, people, and their mutual relations. These relations have been found to be significant to the expression and reconfiguration of our values and identity [7], as a resource for thinking [18], and as glue for social relationships [26]. Given the premise in HCI that technology can augment social experiences we are interested in examining existing relationships and experiences with artefacts to gain insight into how digital augmentation might change these experiences.

Participants

Participants were recruited via university mailing lists. Among our respondents we were interested in professionals living in a shared family household[1]. Choosing middle-class professionals increased the likelihood of domestic work being shared among family members [38].

Gender	Women		Men	
	P1, P3, P4, P7, P8		P2, P5, P6	
Age	30s	40s	50s	60s
	P1, P3, P8	P2, P6, P7	-	P4, P5
Lifecycle stage	Without children	With school children	With teenage children	With adult children
	P3	P1, P6, P8	P2	P4, P5

Table 1. Participants' gender, age, and stage in the life course.

Eight participants from seven households were selected (two participants, a married couple, lived together). Five of the participants were women (P1, P3, P4, P7, P8) and three were men (P2, P5, P6), ranging in age from their 30s to 60s. Except for one (a retiree) all our participants were in full-time employment at the time of interview. Professions included three students, one lecturer, one associate professor, one research consultant, one operations manager, and one retiree. Participants also reflected a range of stages across the life course. Seven participants were married, one co-habiting with their partner. Children were part of all but two of the households, one of which had children living away from their parents (P4 and P5) and one was without children (P3). The households with children had two to three children aged between 5 and 17 years. One household had an exchange student staying with them (P7).

[1] The term 'household' and 'family' is used interchangeably in this paper. Yet, it is understood that not every household makes a family and vice versa. Many contemporary households have moved beyond the traditional model of the nuclear family [1] and include single-person, single-parent, re-married or co-habiting partners or families extending across multiple households, for instance.

Method

Our study was based around a semi-structured interview with participants. Before the interview, participants were asked to take photographs of their dining table at the beginning and end of a meal for three meals or more. Participants were encouraged to capture a variety of occasions and types of meals. Participants were asked to send their photos to the researcher before the interview (examples are shown in Fig. 1). Printouts of the photographs were then used as conversational prompts during the interview. Two participants were unable to send their pictures before the interview, but showed digital copies on their smart phones instead.

Figure 1. Sample of photographs taken by participants.

All participants were interviewed individually within a week after the photographs were taken. Interviews took place in meeting rooms and offices at the participant's workplace or at their home wherever possible. Interviews typically lasted between 30 to 40 minutes and loosely covered the following topics. First, interviewees were asked to describe to the researcher the pictures they had taken of their dining spaces with the aim of eliciting *contextual information*, such as setting, situation, people present, etc. Interviewees were then asked in detail about their *tableware*, such as its use, origin, history, meanings and the practices surrounding it, followed by questions about the *table setting*, *tables* and *spaces* in which family meals took place. Throughout the interview, participants were encouraged to raise and follow topics and questions of their own concern.

Analysis

Interviews were audio recorded and transcribed verbatim. Additionally, video data was captured of the interviewee's interactions with the photographs during the interview to preserve any references to the pictures (e.g. pointing out objects). Pictures were used to complement verbal accounts, but not formally analyzed. This was because the quality of the pictures varied between participants, and as a consequence, the degree to which tableware and settings were visible. As pictures were only snapshots of one particular stage of an entire meal, they also varied in what they showed. Some pictures, for instance, had been taken before the table was fully set. Verbal data was qualitatively analyzed for emergent themes which were then grouped into categories and repeatedly cross-checked with the data.

FINDINGS

Presenting our data with the dining table as our anchor, we start by explicating where dining tables are located in the home and how people make decisions on how to use them. Next, we turn our attention to the tables themselves and examine how they are prepared for eating, how serving takes place, how the seating order is managed, and the meal orchestrated. Finally, we focus in on some of the artefacts we find on dining tables, and investigate questions of meaning and ownership.

Spaces

We found that the space and location of the table framed and marked the degree of formality of a meal. In those households with an extra space for dining (P1, P2, P4, P5, P6, P8), one tended to be constructed for formal occasions while the other was associated with everyday informal meals (Fig. 2).

Figure 2. Formal and informal spaces: the conservatory (top) will only be used on weekends and with guests, while the breakfast bar in the kitchen (bottom) is used on an everyday basis.

Configuring the Space: Formal and Informal

The formality of a meal was constructed out of a number of factors, such as occasion, social context, and type of food. Formal occasions included non-everyday situations, such as weekend meals, and special occasions, such as birthdays, involving guests and/or special foods: *"And if we have friends round and we cooked a proper meal we'd almost always eat in the dining room."* (P8). P6 frames formal occasions as follows: *"I guess what characterizes a formal meal is that somehow we have marked it out as a formal meal, just sort of by saying in some sense we have a Sunday lunch today or we've invited someone to Sunday lunch, that's turned it into a meal, a formal meal, because you've got some guests say or it might be something like a birthday meal you know for one of the children."*. Formality is not a hard and fast rule, but rather something that is defined and redefined by the household. P2 points to the extra time and effort involved in staging a meal as formal: *"That's in the conservatory which we eat at from time to time. I think that was a Sunday kind of dinner and we're more likely to eat in there. I don't know, it's almost as if we couldn't be bothered to sometimes but it's nice to. [] And of course, if anyone else, if any other friends are around or whatever then we'd eat in there."*.

Informal spaces, typically the kitchen, would be used on weekdays mostly for meals involving only the core members of the household. Where using the kitchen table was not used out of necessity, it was done out of the convenience of not having to carry food and tableware to a separate room and back. The transition between food preparation and consumption could thus be handled much more efficiently, but was deemed inappropriate for visitors other than child friends.

Tabletop

Just as spaces were configured for informal and formal use, so too were tables.

Preparing the Table: Mixed and Dedicated Use

Whether a table was used for dining only or used for other purposes, such as work and play, again, depended on how many tables were available and where they were located.

In households with one dining table only, typically located in the kitchen, multi-purpose use was very common. While in one household mixed use seemed to be a necessity due to space constraints (P3), in another multi-purpose use was welcome and deliberate, and a lot of the family activity revolved around the kitchen table (P7). As the social center of the house, the kitchen table was regularly used for family members to work: *"If everyone's really really hungry and we've all been working and the table is a mess it will just be a case of pushing everything to the far end of the table. So quite often, even if it's five of us ((laughs)), half the table will be taken up with stuff and we'll be cramped at this end []. To be honest, I mean generally it's very rare that that table is completely clear and is dedicated for eating. [] I think it's just reflective of the fact that we're a busy family"*, P7. The shared use of the table for family life and work is indicative of the family's mixed lifestyle where home and work have no clear boundaries and become intermingled. Fig. 3 shows the spatial arrangement of home and work on P7's the kitchen table.

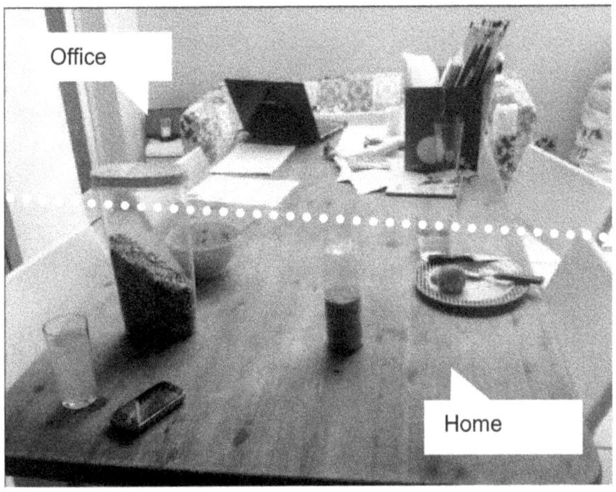

Figure 3. Mixed used of table: eating in the foreground with laptop and paper work in the background. The plastic plate (right) and mobile phone (left) indicate the participant's daughter and husband having had breakfast there.

In households with two tables, one in the kitchen and one in the dining room, the one in the dining room tended to be subject to multi-purpose use, while the kitchen table tended to be reserved for eating purposes only. Dedicated use of a table typically involved it being completely cleared before the table was prepared for eating. For efficiency, on some of these tables, items that were regularly used, such as table mats and salt and pepper mills would remain on the table, marking its function as a table dedicated to eating.

Seating order around the table: Inscribed and Ad-Hoc

Whether seating arrangements around the table are fixed or produced ad-hoc depended on the social context of a meal.

Inscribed seating arrangements involve a strict hierarchy of places for core members of the household. Rarely these arrangements have been explicitly negotiated but instead have evolved over time. Typically they are linked with the family member's role in enabling shared family meals. It was common for the person who does most of the cooking to sit closest to where food was prepared or tableware stored. P4 affirms: "*No, no, no. I will always sit here 'cause I'm near the kitchen and I do most of the running around.*" Physical requirements can lead members to claim a place for them, such as sufficient leg space or space for special chairs: *"I kept bumping into things so I made [spouse] sit there ((laughs)). I think it's because I have to get up to go to the kitchen more often so I used to get quite annoyed sitting there. So we tried lots of places and this seems to be the place where we're all happiest."* P8. Finally, there are social requirement that determine the seating arrangement, such as the need to supervise young children as P8's comment illustrates: *"I have to sit next to my son because he's quite naughty so I have to keep an eye on him and make sure that he doesn't, well, make sure that he eats his food, because he usually just procrastinates and he used to get down from the table and things like this."* We see here how P8's role in supplying food and tableware leads her to re-negotiate the seating arrangement. Conversely, a re-negotiation of the seating arrangement enables family members to claim a certain role within the family. P4's example draws on family meals with her grown-up children at which her daughter refuses to adopt the role currently held by her mother: *"My daughter sits there when she comes because she made an announcement that she didn't want to do any running around and if she sat there she was further from the door than if she sat there [], and if there's five with the two boys here as well then there's a bit more shuffling around although she still jokes and maintains here place at that side of the table."*, P4.

Ad Hoc arrangements often existed alongside inscribed ones to accommodate non-core members, such as visitors. Usual seating arrangements would be temporarily modified or abandoned for the sake of letting visitors choose their own seats or to consider relationships between people at the table. In P2's household the daughter's boyfriend regularly joins the family for dinners and prefers to be seated next to the daughter. Hence, the usual arrangement has to adapt.

Serving: Continuous and Upfront

Further, differences in the way the serving of food was done had an impact on the creation and perception of formality and conviviality.

Continuous serving of food involved all food being brought to the table, where eaters could then typically serve themselves. Continuous serving was more common for elaborate meals either on weekends or when visitors were around. Bringing all food to the table was considered to be more social as P7 posits: *"We bring food to the table and I think that's probably because we're quite kind of social eaters we all like kind of chat around food and also it means people can just take what they need really."*.

Serving upfront, on the other hand, involved placing food directly onto plates in the kitchen before bringing it to the table. Serving upfront was mainly done for efficiency: it allowed families to use fewer pieces of tableware, and thus to minimize the time for setting the table. Unsurprisingly, serving upfront was most typical for weekday family meals. P7 talks about 'feeding' her daughter and friends: *"[] we do tend to have quite a few kids you know as extra guests in the house and that really would be a case of just find the nearest clean plate, put food on, stick it on the table and then move it away as quickly as possible when they're finished ((laughs))."* Similarly to the structure of a meal, the way food is served both indicates and shapes the level of conviviality.

Orchestrating the Meal: Structured and Unstructured

Different degrees of structure characterized the domestic table settings at different meal times. While dinners and weekend lunches tended to be highly structured, breakfasts were much less so. In the United Kingdom, children attending school tend to have lunch at school while parents have lunch at work, and so weekday lunches would normally not be taken at home.

Structured meals tended to be marked by a clear beginning and end. The table would be completely set and everyone was required to sit down at the table before meals would start. Disruptions to the meal were highly unwelcome and to be avoided as were distractions. Commensality and experiencing the meal as a family or group is what makes structure important to a meal. Managing structure during meals can be challenging, however, particularly when young children are involved. P8, a mother of two children aged 5 and 7 speaks of the difficulty of achieving synchronism during meal times. Talking about her son, she says: *"[] sometimes we get cross because he's not eating and then eventually he will but it can take like twenty, twenty-five minutes to persuade him. Usually [daughter] gets really impatient so she goes off and gets her pudding. We try and make her wait but sometimes she doesn't and then we have our pudding as well."*. Her son's pace of eating is out of tune with the rest of the family. While he slows meals down, her daughter tries to speed them up, each of them taking control of the structure of the meal. A degree of structure would still be visible when individual household members were away or running late: *"My husband was going to be late, so actually although we set it for four there were only three of us eating, [] and that's just a setting for [spouse] for when he comes in later and we've got some food here, I just leave the food out and he comes helps himself"*, P7. The place setting would mark the missing member's presence during shared meals. Literature on domestic cultures has found similar roles for family photographs marking the presence of physically absent family members [17].

Unstructured meals are characterized by no clear start and end. Breakfast would commonly be unstructured: different schedules meant that there was some, little or no crossing-over, so that household members would arrive at and leave the table at different times, sometimes seeing each other at breakfast only fleetingly or not at all. As a result, household members would organize their own breakfast and the table was either incompletely set or not at all. In one family, household members organized their breakfast around access to the bathroom. So, while structure enables family members to achieve sociality, the lack of it helps individual members get eating done under the constraints of living in a shared household.

Tableware

When we think of tableware, we think of it as a set of pieces matching in shape, material and pattern. While one or more sets obtained as a unit did exist in most households, the histories and origins of tableware collections could be complex, sometimes including pieces obtained from various people or places over long periods of time. Attached to them were different notions of ownership.

Using the Tableware: Sets and Assortments

Assortments of tableware were considered to be pieces of tableware that did not match in material, color, pattern or size. It was common for non-matching pieces of tableware to pre-date both partners' life as a couple. The assortment had come together as a result of combining two households in the process of moving in together. Sometimes, additional pieces of tableware had then been acquired cheaply or were given to partners from other family members or friends. P6's statement describing their assortment of is summative of many other instances: *"I think I probably had one set of four before I was married, very very old, you know, [] they're an assortment, [] I think they're mainly things that we've been sort of given or picked up from other people, from other members of family or something but they're really, just really utility things, [] as I say there's two and four and three and two of different types and sizes of plates."*, P6. Assortments are 'utility things', inexpensive, disposable, and replaceable, that serve their purpose in everyday contexts. On special occasions, however, assortments can conflict with how the family sees itself and would like to be seen by others. P1 explains what triggered their decision to replace their assortment with a set: *"We had some friends to stay, I think ((laughs)) we just kind of thought, o god this is a bit embarrassing, but, you know, we're still eating off these (scrubby) plates now that we live in a proper house and have proper jobs and all the rest of it, so ((laughs))."* [P1]. The assortment as a manifestation of the couple's life as students is at odds with their life as a family. The visit from friends brings this conflict to the surface and triggers the purchase of a set of tableware that is in accordance with what they understand as proper.

Strikingly, it is common for couples to be given sets of tableware as a wedding present, carefully chosen by the partners themselves before the event. The set then marks the transition to a new period in the partners' lives and establishes their identity as a couple. Where partners come together without a wedding and a wedding gift as a tangible manifestation of their bond, the set fails to contribute to a shared identity, not least due to differences in taste. P2 co-habits with his partner who had brought two sets of tableware into the relationship: *"Personally, I'm not big into patterns or those sort of things. I mean I don't mind them, they're quite nice, but I'm not sure if, if it was solely down to me to go out and buy it, a set, I don't think I would go and buy those but I don't dislike them."*. While the set of tableware can act as a symbol and anchor of a family's self-image and life style, the matching of pieces also plays a role in establishing a feeling of conviviality during shared meals among extended family and friends. Unlike assortments sets also have a sense of completeness attached to them when there are matching numbers of pieces. Completeness became significant when planning to pass on tableware to the children. An important consideration when buying sets of tableware was thus whether broken pieces could be easily replaced to keep the set complete: *"I think it's very much, very much more the sense of, you know, this is something that's, that is sort of in the family and ideally you would want to pass it on as a set and, and if you don't replace breakages as, you know, as they occur then the replacement might be increasingly difficult as time goes on."*, P5. The importance of completeness is still evident on the receiving end. Breakages of individual items would be highly upsetting and so some pieces would only be used in a safe environment, on special occasions, in an almost ritualised manner: "*My mom was a big collector of crystal it's probably a Polish thing and so there are glasses that I (used) again only when we have people around but then a few of them have broken over time I tend to only take them out for me if I'm sitting down and having a glass of wine and that's not always with a meal. Sometimes I'm sitting down just having a snack and I just use that glass and it's nice to be recollected in that way."* (P3). Yet, the attachment is not without ambiguity. While these items are highly cherished for their ability to re-enact family rituals, invoke shared memories and a sense of belonging among family members, the tableware itself does not meet P3's taste: *"When my mom passed away she left oh, she was a big fan of, it's really revolting actually but it looks like a lettuce leaves bowl like salad and some spoons shaped like lobsters. I don't know why lobsters but it's for tomato which is very strange and it's quite horrible but it comes out at Christmas occasionally if my brother's family is there I bring them out because of the family association."*

Ownership: Appropriated and Assigned

While the entire household typically shares ownership of tableware, there are pieces that individual household members have some sense of ownership of, either through subtle appropriation over time, assignment of use, or through way of having received the piece by someone else.

Appropriated items are pieces or classes of tableware that participants have a personal preference for or relation to. Typically, these were cups and bowls, but can include other items as well. A preference for the form (P2, P6) or colour (P7) of a particular piece or class of tableware could motivate its appropriation. Again, personal attachment could make the loss or breakage of a favourite item highly upsetting, as P6 reports: *"I used to have a very specific odd bowl which was just my bowl which I used for breakfast but that recently got broken. I was very upset about that, so I no longer have my personal bowl"*. Family members tended to be aware of each other's preferences and avoided using other's favourite items for themselves. P7 describes how she and her husband make their respective favourite mugs available for each other: *"I always try to use one of two cups for [spouse] to make tea and I probably go out of my way to-, if it's not clean I will go and clean that cup to make sure he actually has his tea in that cup and he does the same for me I think."* The awareness of and extra effort involved in making items available can be understood as a display of care and affection towards other family members.

Yet, preferred pieces of tableware would normally not be used in a communal context. Favourite cups, for instance, tended to be more common between meals and during breakfast. It might be that the role of matching tableware is to both establish and reflect group membership during the meal that the use of personal pieces would break. Indicative of the tenuousness of managing individual preferences in a shared family context is P2's account of his step-daughter's habit of secretly exchanging cutlery before a meal: *"[] if I lay her small ones out for hers, if she thinks there's no one's looking then she'll swap them from someone else's plate to the bigger, bigger set. So I know that she prefers using them."* While the girl cares enough about her preferred cutlery to exchange it, doing so secretly shows that she doesn't feel the right to claim it for herself.

Figure 4. Assigned tableware: the two children have their own personal tableware made of plastic (back) with prints on them while the parents use pieces of the family's set (front).

Alternatively, pieces of tableware could be assigned to family members due to special requirements or temporarily to visitors. P8 habitually allocates each visitor a unique cup they can recognize and hold on to throughout their visit to avoid running out of tableware later in the day: *"We do it deliberately actually so you know whose is whose, because if they're all the same you can't tell whose is whose so and when particularly when [spouse]'s family come round they be two, three, six, seven adults drinking tea, and we drink a lot of tea so everyone has to come in and I allocate them a cup. They have to have that cup for the rest of the day."*

The need to avoid breakages could lead parents to give their children plastic tableware (Fig. 4). Designing tableware for children is a fairly recent phenomenon and linked to current ideas of what childhood means [10]. The distinctness of the tableware marks out children's special status within the family, which can become problematic in the children's transition into adulthood. A mother reports how she continues to assign her eleven year daughter plastic plates, recognizing the inadequacy of it: *"[] apart from this tableware here, this is out of a hamper, it's plastic and that's because [youngest daughter], I tend to put things on plastic plates for her. I think it's just because she's young and I'm probably still treating her like a baby."*, P7. Again, the plastic plates are only given to the daughter however when she eats alone or with friends, but never when eating with other family members. This is because: *"I'm not sure that she would say anything but I think that I that I just wouldn't want [] to mark her out as being any different really and not serving her a proper plate."*, P7. This mother has difficulty letting her daughter move into adulthood, but it can also be the children who hold on to their childhood, to the discontent of their parents. P2 comments on his step-daughters' use of plastic beakers: *I find them a bit, you know, I find that I think they kind of seem like they're a bit like they're safety cups for five year olds almost rather than using glass, glasses."*.

Technology and Media at the Table

Technologies and media, such as mobile phones, laptops, eReaders, and newspapers were generally unwelcome during meals. As they would divert attention away from the meal they tended to be sanctioned at the table, a rule which wasn't always adhered to:*"It's a time to chat really more than anything it's just a way of getting together and catching up but yeah the girls try to and sometimes I'm, I do this, they try to use the phone and text at the table which really really bugs me and sometimes I do."*, P7. This mother's account illustrates how individuals' engagement with technology can counteract the establishment of conviviality.

When eating alone, on the other hand, technology and media are a common and largely accepted accompaniment to meals (Fig. 5). P7's eleven year old daughter would typically have her breakfast in front of the television, as would do a mother for lunch once a month when working from home (P8). Laptops for doing work or browsing, and reading eReaders, books and newspapers were equally attractive past-times during solitary meals. Equally acceptable are technology and media when they are shared or shareable. In many families, for instance, meals were accompanied by listening to the radio – the choice of channel had to be negotiated as a family to meet both the parents' and children's interests – or solving cross word puzzles in the weekend newspaper as P8 reports: *"We have a no-iPhones-at-the-table rule but sometimes we break that, it's very important, because we both work, one of the things we've always done is, we've all ate together and we do spend ten or fifteen minutes with all of us there eating at the weekend on a Saturday we get the newspaper and we also do the quiz in the [newspaper]"*. Here the pastime of solving crossword puzzles has been incorporated as a family ritual enriching their limited shared time together.

Figure 5. The accompaniment of media such as books and laptops was common when eating alone.

DISCUSSION AND DESIGN IMPLICATIONS

So far we have seen some of the ways in which artefacts and spaces shape and are sensitive to the social contexts in which they appear. What might this mean for HCI researchers and technology developers? With any study of this nature, there is a tension between the need for distilled advice and the risk of presenting simplistic potentially reductionist "truths". In the following, we propose a set of concepts to sensitize interaction designers and technologists to some of the challenges and opportunities involved in designing around domestic eating.

Again, focusing on the spaces and artefacts involved, the concepts mark four dimensions, each of which points towards the social relationships they reflect and change, enable and disrupt between the individual, the household, and society.

Mundanity and Celebration

The dimension of the celebratory and the mundane emphasizes the tension between routine and special dining occasions. While having distinct characteristics these both often take place in the same space using similar artefacts.

Interaction designers may want to think about the degree to which their designs foreground and background the nature of an occasion. For example, we can imagine a digital tabletop that supports people in orchestrating the particular character of an occasion or in making someone feel special while subtly enabling or reflecting the more mundane social interactions around the table in an everyday context (such as Gaver's History Tablecloth).

The blending and overlap between the special and the everyday also means that technologists need to be aware of the ways in which artefacts are foregrounded by people in different ways during formal and informal dining and that the technology needs to recognize this in terms of set up and availability. For example, we might invest considerable time in setting up table technology for a birthday party but resist its use for breakfasts.

Independence and Socialization

Family life is an on-going negotiation of roles and boundaries between individual members and the family as a whole signalled through a range of gestures and rituals.

Interaction designers might wish to think about how their designs might draw upon the boundaries between independence and socialization and the gestures that signal them. Might these be used playfully within families or even between different settings?

Beyond the challenge of recognizing gestures technologists may wish to understand how best to signal boundary definition and exploit the boundary. How might these boundaries be used? For example, should these boundaries by used to constrain interaction with other communication technologies or highlight their use to others at the table?

Isolation and Conviviality

The artefacts of dining have a role in shaping the group at a table. The use of some artefacts invited family members in while some exclude others.

Interaction designers seeking to augment dining may want to think about the affordances of their designs to promote either sharing within the context or isolation and removal from it. While a digitally augmented table surface could provide a resource for conversation and social interaction at family dinners [15], when eating alone its content may focus on only one member or connect to people remote from the setting.

We would draw technologists' attention to the ways in which context imbues digital artefacts with particular values. When eating with others digital devices may be agents of separation drawing people's attention "away from the table". Yet at another time of the day (e.g. breakfast) they may be thought of as tools of organization.

Reminiscence and Identity

Over a lifetime of use dining artefacts are invested in cognitively and emotionally, change ownership and meanings. (e.g. when tableware becomes a family heirloom).

Interaction designers may want to extend their design considerations beyond the immediate context to which their design will be deployed and consider the potential trajectories a dining artefact might take over its lifetime of use. The digital augmentation with narratives is one example of how artefacts have been made to become more evocative of the past, but also tends to fix its meaning. What others are possible and how might they be used?

Technologists may wish to think of how the artefacts of dining may build their own record of use. How might they build a contextual footprint that can be exploited by others to relive previous experiences or highlight past uses. Equally, designers of technology may simply wish to recognize dining as point of reminiscing and sharing of stories and think how different media may be delivered to support this.

CONCLUSION

The digital augmentation of our domestic spaces is well underway. While our homes, including our kitchens, are generally accepting of new technologies, the table, and spaces of food consumption more generally, seem to continue to resist augmentation. In fact, food consumption as a core domestic activity has had little attention as an area of empirical investigation in HCI. In this paper, we have taken a closer look at the dining table and the artefacts and spaces associated with it. In doing so, we have uncovered their role in shaping and being shaped by a complex of social interactions surrounding eating at home. Our findings can point towards some of the challenges we face in bringing digital technologies to the table, but also inspire opportunities for digital innovation.

While appropriate to the exploratory nature of our work, clearly, there are limitations to our choice of sample and setting. Naturally, domestic ecologies of eating vary between household arrangements, as well as across socio-economic and cultural contexts. [39]. Also, in talking to only one or two members of a household, there is a risk in biasing views towards individual eaters. As prior research has shown, for instance, children play a key role in shaping and structuring family life [37]. We encourage researchers to explore dining beyond the voices and perspectives presented in this paper. It is only by gaining a rich picture of the everyday nature of food and eating in HCI that we can start to make more informed choices about their digital augmentation.

ACKNOWLEDGMENTS

This work is supported by the Horizon Doctoral Training Centre at the University of Nottingham (RCUK Grant No. EP/G037574/1) and by the RCUK's Horizon Digital Economy Research Institute (RCUK Grant No. EP/G065802/1).

REFERENCES

1. Aberg, J. An Evaluation of a Meal Planning System: Ease of Use and Perceived Usefulness. *Proc. BCS-HCI 2009,* ACM Press (2009), 278-287.
2. Abeyrathne, D., Peiris, R., Ranashinghe, N., Fernando, O., Cheok, A. Food Internet Communication. *Proc. ACE 2010*, ACM Press, (2010), 49-52.
3. Beardsworth, A. and Keil, T. *Sociology on the Menu.* Routledge, New York (1997).
4. Bonanni, L., Lee, C.H., Selker, Counter Intelligence: Augmented Reality Kitchen. *Proc. CHI 2005*, ACM Press (2005).
5. Chi, P., Chen, J., Chu, H., Chen, B. Enabling Nutrition-Aware Cooking in a Smart Kitchen. *Proc. CHI 2007 Extended Abstracts*, ACM Press (2007), 2333-2338.

6. Chung, H., Lee, C.H., Selker, T. Lover's Cups: Drinking Interfaces as New Communication Channels. *Proc. CHI EA 2006,* ACM Press (2006), 375-380.

7. Csikszentmihalyi, M. and Rochberg-Halton, E. *The Meaning of Things: Domestic Symbols and the Self.* Cambridge University Press (1981).

8. Devault, M. 'Conflict and Deference'. In Counihan, C. and van Esterik, P. (eds.) *Food and Culture: A Reader*, Routledge (1997).

9. Fitzmaurice, G., Ishii, H., and Buxton, W. Bricks: Laying the Foundations for Graspable User Interfaces, in *Proc. Of CHI 1995*, ACM Press (1995), 442-449.

10. Forty, A. *Objects of Desire*. Thames & Hudson (1986).

11. Gaver, W. (2001) "Designing for ludic aspects of everyday life", *ERCIM News*, No.47. www.ercim.org/publication/Ercim_News/enw47/gaver.html

12. Gaver, W., Beaver, J., Benford, S. Ambiguity as a Resource for Design. *Proc. CHI 2003*, ACM Press (2003), 233-240.

13. Gaver, W., Bowers, J., Boucher, A., Law, A., Pennington, S., Villar, N. The History Tablecloth: Illuminating Domestic Activity. In *Proc. DIS 2006,* ACM Press (2006), 199-208.

14. Gellersen, H., Beigl, M., Krull, H. The MediaCup: Awareness Technology Embedded in an Everyday Object. In *HUC 1999*, 27-29, (1999), 308-310.

15. Grimes, A. and Harper, R. Celebratory Technologies: New Directions for Food Research in HCI. In *Proc. CHI 2008*, ACM Press (2008), 467-476.

16. Hamada, R., Okabe, J., Ide, I., Satoh, S., Sakai, S., Tanaka, H., Cooking navi: assistant for daily cooking in kitchen. *Proc. International Multimedia Conference* (2005), 371-374.

17. Hollows, J. *Domestic Cultures*. Open University Press, (2008).

18. Hutchins, E. *Cognition in the Wild*. MIT Press (1996).

19. Ishii, H., Ullmer, B. Tangible Bits: Towards Seamless Interfaces between People, Bits and Atoms. In *Proc. CHI 1997*, ACM Press (1997), 234-241.

20. Ju, W., Hurwitz, R., Judd, T. and Lee, B., CounterActive: an interactive cookbook for the kitchen counter. *Proc. CHI 2001*, ACM Press (2001), 269-270.

21. Kaufmann, J.-C. *The Meaning of Cooking*. Polity Press (2010).

22. Kemmer, D, Anderson, A., Marshal, D. Living together and eating together: changes in food choice and eating habits during the transition from single to married/cohabiting. In *Sociological Review*, 1998.

23. Lee, K., Cho, H., Park, K., Hahn, M. Ambient Lamp Display in the Active Home Ubiquitous Computing Environment for Relaxing and Mediation. *FGCN 2007,* 6-8, IEEE (2007), 81-86.

24. Liu, S., Chu, H., Hsu, J., Chen, C., Lin, T., Chen, C., Huang, P. The Diet-Aware Dining Table: Observing Dietary Behaviors over a Tabletop Surface. *Pervasive Computing*, Springer (2006), 366-382.

25. Macht, M., Meininger, J., Roth, J. The pleasures of eating: a qualitative analysis. *Journal of Happiness Studies*, 6, Springer (2005), 137–160.

26. Mauss, M. *The Gift*. Routledge (2001).

27. Mennicken, S., Karrer, T., Russell, P., Borchers, J. First-Person Cooking: A Dual-Perspective Interactive Kitchen Counter. *Proc. CHI 2010*, ACM Press (2010), 3403-3408.

28. Miller, D. Appropriating the state on the council estate. In *Man*, 23, (1988), 353-372.

29. Miller, D. *Home Possessions: Material Culture Behind Closed Doors*. Berg (2001).

30. Mulrooney, B., McDermott, M., Earley, N. NutraStick: portable diet assistant. *Proc. CHI 2006*, ACM Press (2006), 1855-1860.

31. Murcott, A. "It's a pleasure to cook for him": food, mealtimes, and gender in some South Wales households. In Gamarnikow, E., Morgan, E., Purvis, J., Taylorson, D. (eds) *The Public and the Private*. Heinemann (1983).

32. Ochs, E., Shohet, M. The Cultural Structuring of Mealtime Socialization. *New Directions for Child and Adolescent Development, No. 111,* Wiley (2006).

33. Palay, J., Newman, M. SuChef: An In-Kitchen Display to Assist with "Everyday" Cooking. *Proc. CHI 2009*, ACM Press (2009), 3973-3978.

34. Sutton, D. *Remembrance of Repasts*. Berg (2001).

35. Tales of Things, www.talesofthings.com.

36. Terrenghi, L., Hilliges, O., Butz, A. Kitchen Stories: sharing recipes with the Living Cookbook. *Personal Ubiquitous Computing*, 11, Springer (2007), 409-414.

37. Valentine, G. Eating In: Home, Consumption and Identity. *The Sociological Review*, 47, (1999), 491-524.

38. Warde, A. and Hetherington, K. English households and routine food practices: a research note. In *The Sociological Review* 42, 4, Wiley (1994), 758-78.

39. Wood, R. *The Sociology of the Meal*. Edinburgh University Press (1995).

panavi: Recipe Medium with a Sensors-Embedded Pan for Domestic Users to Master Professional Culinary Arts

Daisuke Uriu, Mizuki Namai, Satoru Tokuhisa, Ryo Kashiwagi, Masahiko Inami, Naohito Okude
Graduate School of Media Design, Keio University (KMD)* & Keio-NUS CUTE Center†
* 4-1-1, Hiyoshi, Kohoku-ku, Yokohama-city, Kanagawa, Japan 223-8526
† I-Cube Building, 21 Heng Mui Keng Terrace, #02-01-01, Singapore 119613
{uriu, mizukichen, tokuhisa, kashiwagi, inami, okude}@kmd.keio.ac.jp

ABSTRACT
"*panavi*," a recipe medium, supports cooking experience for domestic users to master professional culinary arts in their kitchens by managing temperature and pan movement properly. Utilizing a sensors-embedded frying pan—providing projected images, LED indications, and vibration—wirelessly connected with a computer system that shows text messages with sounds, the panavi system analyzes sensors' data, recognizes users' conditions, and provides the users with situated instructions. Describing our vision, design process, implementation, and user study that outlines experience of challenging professional cooking, this paper introduces a design framework model of this recipe medium for domestic usage. Throughout revealing the design process—from ideation to the finished research artifact as a whole cooking support system—this research suggests how to design interactive systems responding to human situated actions, for use as daily commodities enriching domestic user experience.

Author Keywords
Cooking; Kitchen; Interaction Design; Situated Actions; Ubiquitous Computing; Research through Design

ACM Classification Keywords
H.5.2 User Interfaces: Interaction styles

General Terms
Design

INTRODUCTION
A famous American chef named Julia Child debuted on the TV program "The French Chef" in 1963, what can now be considered the pioneering cooking show. In contrast to her high level of French cooking skills that she had accumulated over years of practice, the humorous show consisted of general cooking instructions. Throughout the show, she discussed and commented contextually regarding what she was doing. When making an omelet, for example, she stirred the eggs, put them in the pan, and roughly shook the pan while heating it. Her cooking show, translating traditional print or verbal recipe sharing to the medium of video or TV, was a great hit with domestic audiences in the US.

Cooking medium has entered a transitional period with regards to HCI. Cooking instruction systems based on new digital platforms such as iPhone or Nintendo DS have already become commonplace [1, 17]. Vita Craft released an automatic temperature control cooking pan that works with a special IH cooking heater in Japan [19]. ThinkGeek also released a temperature sensor embedded frying pan [3]. Highly-smart kitchens provide new experiences such as remote communication through cooking [20], prevention of memory loss [24], or making invisible information visible using augmented reality [5, 6]. Although computerized kitchens and utensils have provided us with convenience, domestic users still have limited means to utilize professional culinary arts, such as proper temperature management or proper handling of the pan, especially when following a recipe that is not easy to understand. To cook quickly, smartly, and beautifully like professionals, one has to apprentice for years which may be as difficult as training to become champion athletes.

This paper introduces "*panavi*" (Figure 1), a recipe medium for domestic users to master professional cooking culinary arts, normally inherited through life-long training experience under apprenticeship of other chefs. 'panavi,' its name deriving from the combination of frying-'pan' and 'navi'gation, guides users to control the fire, move the pan properly, and cook sequentially with the instructions via sound, light, vibration, projection of the pan, and also the monitor display. Users inspect current temperature and follow the instructions projected on the pan as shown in Figure 4-a, b. The system analyzes the embedded motion-sensor's degree of tilt, recognizes the users' cooking condition, and provides text instructions on the display with audible alerts. The panavi system, a package of these technical functions, is designed as a recipe medium suitable for usage in domestic kitchens enabling users to master professional method, approach, and technique for cooking.

Our initial prototype of panavi described in this paper is a "*Research Artifact*" [26] produced to conduct interaction design research in domestic environments, especially kitchens. Activities in kitchens cannot be planned as a static model, be-

Figure 1. Cooking the Recipe of Carbonara Mediated by "panavi"

cause it seldom causes uncertain troubles due to users' activities basically based on situated actions [21]. Therefore this research attempts to obtain ways of designing computer mediated artifacts that support uncertain domestic environments.

This paper follows Zimmerman's principles for "*Research through Design*" that evaluates how a Research Artifact could contribute to the HCI community; *Process, Invention, Relevance*, and *Extensibility* [26]. Firstly, this paper contextualizes this work in previous researches and also defines contributions to the HCI community (*Relevance, Invention*). Secondly, it describes our design process: what our initial motivation and hypotheses is, how we developed the panavi system in several iteration processes through hardware sketching with "trial and error" cooking, a preliminary user study to find deficiencies of design, and the design of our first prototype (*Process*). Thirdly, it presents the design and architecture of panavi with instructions of how to use this system (*Invention*). Fourthly, revealing user experience of this new recipe medium, we describe a user study of three groups including four persons actually challenging to cook the recipe for spaghetti *Carbonara* as instructed by the panavi system (*Invention* and defining *Extensibility*). Finally, this paper defines two ways the HCI research community can leverage on this research (*Extensibility*); 1) A consideration about how to make an interactive system supporting users' situated actions [21], especially how it supports the difference in skill between users, 2) A model of interactive artifact design supporting domestic everyday affairs, consisting of basic technological framework and a design methodology for interaction designers: how to design a smart device with communication functionality for the real home environment.

RELATED STUDIES

In the latter of 1980's, Winograd [25] suggested to design computer systems as tools for human lives rather than the "perfect" Artificial Intelligence (AI) as if another human being. At the same period, Suchman [21] criticized applying AI for designing HCI systems by ethnographically surveying the usability of the Xerox copy machine. In Suchman's description, examinees cannot easily utilize the machine, since the programmed instructions do not support their situated actions: the errors and problems they actually face are not expected by the system. Traditional media formats for recipes basically describe steps toward a perfect completion of cooking in text, which is usually difficult for non-professional users to reproduce the taste of meals.

Cooking support systems corresponding to users' situated actions have been considered in HCI context since nobody is able to cook by going ahead with planned actions. Bradbury et al [7] designed an interactive cookbook supporting situated actions using eye-tracking and speech recognition technologies. Olivier et al [18] realized a situated coaching system by integrating projection systems, RFID, accelerometers, and under-floor pressure sensing technologies. Hamada et al [13] designed a cooking assistant system enabling users to cook several menus at the same time, recognizing the procedure and managing/keeping the time. While, Chi et al [9] designed a kitchen providing real-time feedback, tracking the number of calories in food ingredients.

Providing situated suggestions by real-time sensing and giving feedback, our system embeds the sensors in the physical pan wirelessly connected with the computer system. The combination of the pan and the interactive recipe application does not mean just a technical innovation, but provides a new user experience enabling users to enjoy daily cooking with trials and errors rather than skill-improving or automation-cooking. Mennicken et al [16] designed a very creative kitchen experience as if users can cook with a professional chef. Our work also suggests a new user experience to challenge a difficult recipe with situated assistances by following the video of chef's cooking.

Furthermore, the panavi system integrates various technological aspects the previous works have used; using image, video, and sound instead of traditional text based recipes [11, 20], designing situated navigations by monitoring and recording conditions in videos and image [4, 24], or replacing everything related with cooking with a cooking agent robot [22]. Augmented Reality visualization using the projector compensates user's senses by showing invisible things [5, 6] or provides efficient information for cooking such [14]. The sensor embedded knife [15] distinguishes what ingredients the user slices. The sensor embedded pan [3] monitors the current temperature on the LCD display in its handle. A consumer product [19] enables automated cooking by integrating a sensors embedded pan with a special IH cooking machine.

This research contributes to the HCI community firstly to provide a medium for recipes as a whole cooking support system, and secondly to suggest how to design an interactive system responding to human situated actions, for use as daily commodity to enrich the user experience in domestic life. This paper's contribution is neither technical innovations nor scientific theory, as the technical element of the current prototype already has been used in both the research and the consumer product field. Main contribution of this prototype is integrating each technical element as a medium, analyzing the sensors data from the pan and suggesting to users what to do, depending on each condition. This combination of analysis and feedback demonstrates a solution to human situated actions. The cooking process in the kitchen is generally tricky to deal with as it involves high temperature, water, cooking ingredients, kitchen utensils, and the unique experience of each user; meaning that there is no way to perfectly calculate the plan of the dishes ahead of time, and that the user must handle situated actions. Our design process case study from ideation to finished research artifact gives the CHI design community knowledge to develop smart daily commodities supporting domestic life.

DESIGN PROCESS

panavi system was designed through an iterative process that consists of hardware sketching, software sketching, and small tests that the authors actually use for an 'imperfect' prototype. Before arriving to our first prototype described in this paper, we went through three phases; 1) the iterative sketching cycle—making three hardware prototypes with software sketching and conducting experiments four or five times by the authors using the prototypes, 2) a preliminary user study of the basic prototype with two persons, 3) implementation by designing a robust hardware prototype and re-configuring the software.

Vision

Firstly, we focused on temperature control or maintaining the fire. Although temperature control is one of the most important skills for cooking, descriptions about it written in the cooking book are very ambiguous; low heat, medium heat, or high heat. It is said that some professional chefs can sense the temperature of pan, ingredients, or oil by physical sensation. Some touch the pan and feel the heated oil to sense the temperature, while others listen to the sound of water in the heated pan to gage temperature as well. However, it is very challenging for domestic amateurs to practice these physical sensation, therefore we decided to develop a system providing real-time temperature sensing and feedback.

Model Recipe

Prior to the sketching, we chose a recipe of Italian pasta Roman-styled *Carbonara* as an initial menu, because this recipe requires some cooking ways including sensitive temperature control, which is difficult to master. We quoted a recipe of Tsutomu Ochiai [2] a famous Japanese chef of Italian cuisines who sometimes appears in TV. After a trial and error process as described below, we formed an original cooking sequence for this system by arranging his recipe, referring to his texts and video tutorials.

Iterative Hardware Sketching Process

Lower-fidelity iterative sketching process such as paper prototyping, drawing scenarios, or making videos has been required before designing the actual hardware when designers create an interactive artifact [8]. However, the kitchen is complex environment where accidents frequently occur. There are constraints to ensure the design through the lower-fidelity sketching for developing the tools used in the kitchen. Therefore we adopted an iterative hardware sketching cycle from the beginning of our prototyping.

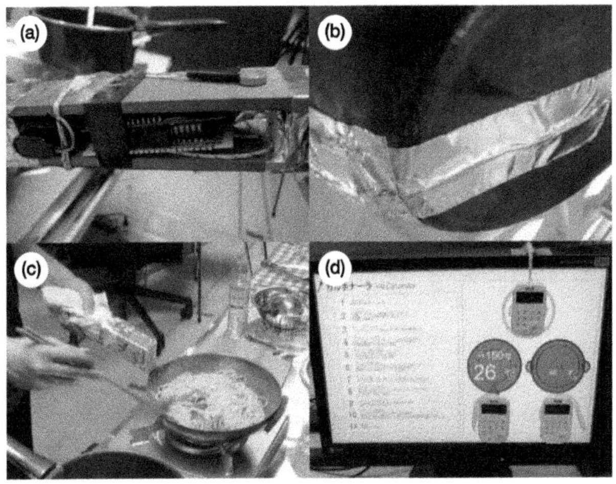

Figure 2. Initial Hardware Sketching; (a) Circuit, (b) Thermocouple Probe, (c) Experimental Cooking Using the Pan, (d) Display

Our iterative hardware sketching process consists of 1) making a trial hardware and software sketch, 2) test cooking using the sketch; the authors actually attempted to make *Carbonara* using the trial hardware and software, 3) finding problems and considering an improved plan, and 4) making a new prototype. At the initial stage, an iron-made pan with the thermocouple probe attached with aluminum tape, whose handle embedded a "MOXA" prototyping circuit with wireless communication function [23] and a full color LED, was crafted. The members of our developing team attempted experimental cooking several times, referring to the paper recipe and using this prototype (See, Figure 2). Through these trials, we found problems; the LED cannot be seen under concentration, the temperature sensor cannot measure correct temperature, and the assumed temperature settings were not suitable for actual use. Hence, we adopted a new idea projecting temperature value on the pan's surface, changed the position of the temperature sensor, and also configured temperature settings at each point on the recipe.

Preliminary User Study

After a basic prototype shown in Figure 3 was designed through the iterative sketching process, we conducted a preliminary user study with two amateur users, attempting to cook using the prototype in the domestic kitchen. In this study, users cooked *Carbonara* using the pan integrated with projection of temperature value, LED indications corresponding to proper temperature settings, and the embedded temperature sensor. During cooking, the users were required to coordinate the fire to keep the proper temperature which the system indicated, referring to the text recipe sequence displayed on the monitor and viewing current temperature's degree shown on the monitor or the projection.

Reflection toward the Final Prototype

From this user study, we observed that users had difficulty making a satisfying dish. Even if the users can keep the proper temperature control, the *Carbonara* sauce may be baked without physical actions such as stirring ingredients and shaking the pan. Hence, we added onscreen navigations

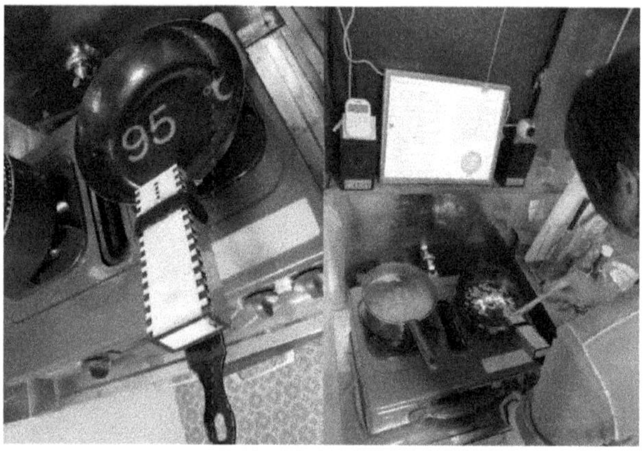

Figure 3. Left: The Prototype Used in the Preliminary User Study, Right: Setting of the Preliminary Study

in the form of stirring, shaking and moving by embedding an accelerometer in the handle of the pan that senses the pan's moves. In addition, we decided to provide video instructions to support text recipes on the navigation display. After this trial and error process, the current design of the system described in the following section was finalized.

DESIGN: FUNCTIONS AND INSTRUCTIONS

Special Frying-Pan

The special frying-pan (Figure 4-a) that can be used to cook ingredients over the heated stove, provides some instructions via LED lamps, vibration, and projection images. Five color LED lamps indicate temperature conditions and a vibration motor moves when the users' temperature control is good, which are embedded within the handle of the pan. The instructional graphics by the projection can also be checked on the display monitor to support the recognition of the projection when the pan is removed from the stove or when the projection cannot be recognized since there is much ingredient on the pan. If part of the system fails, other parts could still help the user (i.e. if the projector fails, the display and the LED indication work). See, Table 1. The temperature color changes from white to blue, green, yellow, and red, depending on the value, which also synchronizes with the LEDs. White is the default color or indicates when the condition temperature is too low, blue indicates 5-10 degrees lower than the proper temperature setting, green indicates when it is at the proper temperature within 5 degrees, yellow indicates 5-10 degrees higher, and red indicates over 15

TEMP (°C)	A	- 149	150 - 159	160 - 169	170 - 179	180 -
	B	- 0	54 - 64	65 - 74	75 - 84	85 -
	C	- 69	70 - 79	80 - 89	90 - 99	100 -
Color		White	Blue	Green	Yellow	Red
Sound		–	the second hand of a clock	the second hand of a clock	the second hand of a clock	warning tone
Vibration		–	–	ON	ON	ON

Table 1. Parameters to Cook the Carvonara Programed in the System.

degrees to high. When the pan is being heated, the system makes a sound like the second hand of a clock at 1-sec intervals. When the color is red, it makes a warning tone. The user is required to stay within the green zone by controlling the stove by turning it off or cooling the pan. In addition, the instructions about actions such as shaking or stirring appear. When the pan should be shaken, an animation of an arrow will be displayed on the surface as shown in Figure 4-b. At the same time, the user is required to observe the specific instruction by referring to the texts on the display.

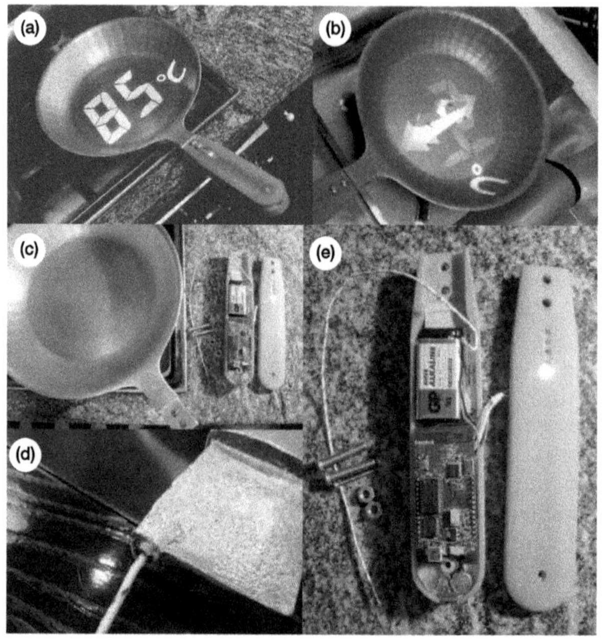

Figure 4. Special Fry-ing Pan; (a) Current Temperature is Projected, (b) Temperature and Action are Indicated, (c) Separated the Body and the Handle, (d) Stainless Made Small Pipe, (e) Inner Circuit of the Handle

Display

There are three modes displayed on the main panel (Figure 5-b-1) that are loadable by touching a particular tab, which are 'Summary,' 'Detail,' and 'Condition' at anytime. The Summary mode (Figure 5-a) displays an overview of the text recipes and current progress. Detail mode (Figure 5-b) displays a detailed culinary art of the text recipe with video instructions, Condition (Figure 5-c) displays the boiling time, current temperature and the pan's movement like the dashboard of a car.

The current Step Panel and Checkbox (Figure 5-b-2) displays the title of each step (Table 2) and the check box that manages the procedure. The user touches the box when the current step's tasks are completed and the system recognizes it and loads the new navigation setting as the next step. Comment Panel (Figure 5-b-3) indicates the instruction massages including advice, caution, or alert texts depending on the current condition, which the user should notice continuously during the cooking process. Temperature Panel (Figure 5-b-4) is an auxiliary tab used when the user wants to check the temperature not referring Condition mode. Timer Panel (Figure 5-b-5), displays the target time to finish cooking, the

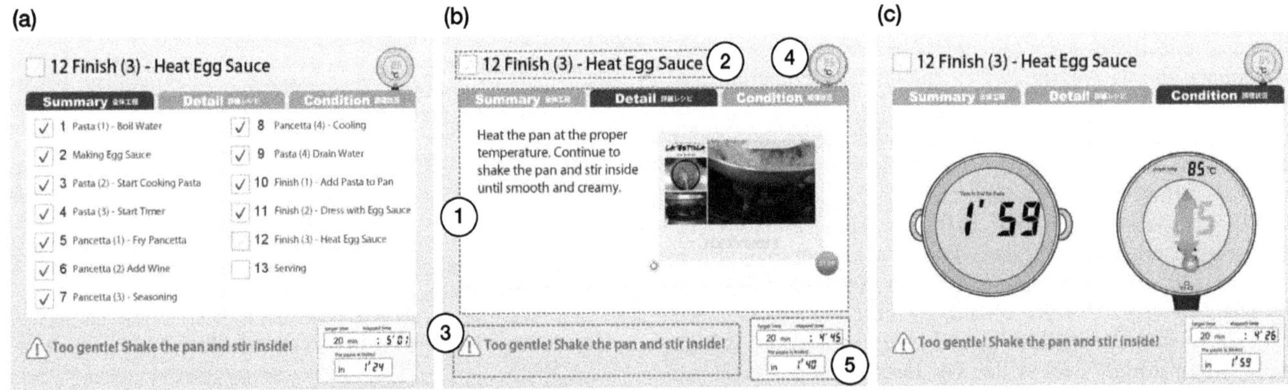

Figure 5. Three Kinds of Setting Displayed in the Monitor; (a) Summary, (b) Detail, (c) Condition / Name of each Area [See, (b)]; (b-1) Main Panel, (b-2) Current Step Panel and Checkbox, (b-3) Comment Panel, (b-4) Temperature Panel, (b-5) Timer Panel

elapsed time, and the timer of boiling the pasta, which is also a supplemental function to Condition mode.

IMPLEMENTATION & ARCHITECTURE

panavi system mainly consists of three parts; the special kitchen utensil (frying-pan) with embedded sensors and actuators, the display system connecting the computer with the touch monitor and the projection system, and the software system showing cooking sequence information (Figure 6).

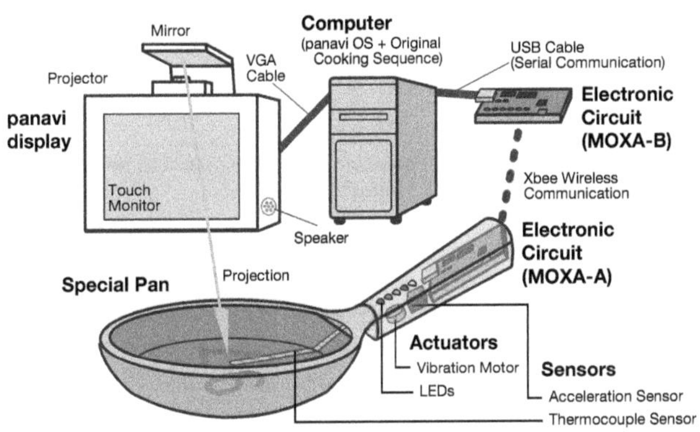

Figure 6. System Architecture

Special Pan

The main body of the pan is formed of cast aluminum, with a handle made of Bakelite that can be clamped to the body (Figure 4-c, e). The pan is embedded with two sensors. One is the J-type thermocouple sensor measuring the current temperature with a fast response speed that can sense the temperature shift continuously. A small, stainless steel pipe is implanted in the pan from one end of the handle to the center of the pan in order to embed the sensor. Another is the acceleration sensor also embedded in the handle sensing the movement of the pan. A MOXA [23] (MOXA-A in Figure 6) is embedded in the pan's handle, which wirelessly communicates with the computer system by sending the sensors' value to another MOXA (MOXA-B in Figure 6) connected with the computer as a server client. On the surface of the pan, the proper temperature and the instructions regarding movements are displayed from the projector. Actuators, LEDs and vibration motors are embedded in the handle, controlled by the signals from the computer system via MOXA-B.

Display and Computer

The computer is connected with 'panavi display' packaging touch panel monitor and projector, and 'panavi OS' with the 'Original Cooking Sequence' works as an Adobe Flash application on the computer (as shown in Figure 6). The panavi OS displays the instructions by analyzing the sensors' degrees against parameters programed in the system.

Original Cooking Sequence

The original cooking sequence models the recipe of *Carbonara*, consisting of videos and photos in addition to the general text recipes. For the panavi OS, this cooking sequence was reconstructed by the development team and its procedure is divided into 13 steps (as shown in Table 2). Each step is programmed with settings; temperature, sounds, and vibrations settings etc. (as shown in Table 1).

Preparing Pasta (Table 2, Step 1-4) When the checkbox of the Step 1 is touched, the elapse time counter from the beginning (See, Figure 5-5) starts. The normal cooking time is set to 20 minutes. When Step 4 is checked, the pasta timer shown in the Detail mode starts. The user should complete cooking the pancetta by the end of the time limit. The boiling time for the pasta is set to 6 minutes.

Frying Pancetta (Table 2, Step 5-7) At the Step 5, the temperature setting A (Figure 1-A, 165°C) is applied. In the Comment Panel (Figure 5-3) the instruction message is displayed; "*Stop Heating*" if the current temperature is too high, "*A little hotter*" if slightly higher, "*Keep at this temperature*" if it is on the proper setting, or "*Heat up a little more*" if it is slightly lower. The user is required to follow the instructions and keep the proper temperature.

Cooling Down (Table 2, Step 8-9) From the Steps 8 to 11, the temperature setting B (Figure 1-B, 70°C) is applied, because this setting is optimized to cool the pan. The instruction messages are displayed as follows; "*Cool the pan on the wet washcloth*" if the current temperature is higher than the proper temperature or "*Go to the next step*" if lower.

Finishing (Table 2, Step 10-12) On the Step 10 and 11, the instruction messages are displayed as follows; "*Cool the pan on the wet washcloth*" if the current temperature is much higher than the proper temperature, "*Wait a moment till the temperature drops*" if slightly higher than the proper temperature, or "*Put the egg sauce*" if lower. The users are urged to follow the instructions because the sauce will burn if the temperature is too high. After the Step 12 begins, the temperature setting C (Figure 1-B, 85 °C) is applied, which is optimized to heat the egg sauce with the pasta. This step models "*Stirring the sauce constantly until it comes to a boil and has thickened with shaking and swinging the pan*," which is required for high level skills. The instruction messages are displayed as follows; "*Remove the pan from fire and shake*" if the temperature is higher than the proper degree or "*Heat up a little more*" if lower. In addition, the messages also have instructions about movements fed from the acceleration sensor; "*Shake the pan and stir inside*" when the pan is not shaken. The user must keep the temperature to 85 °C stirring the sauce very quickly.

USER STUDY

This section describes the user experience of cooking using the panavi system. In order to earn detailed user experiences, we observed how the system effects the users' behavior while cooking, verified the usability of the current prototype, and found its problems. The user study was conducted in an environment specially constructed in our research laboratory similar to the kitchen, as shown in Figure 7 and Figure 8-A. Total of four beginner or intermediate level persons in three groups without experience of making *Carbonara* were selected, because experts or professional chefs are able to cook without the system.

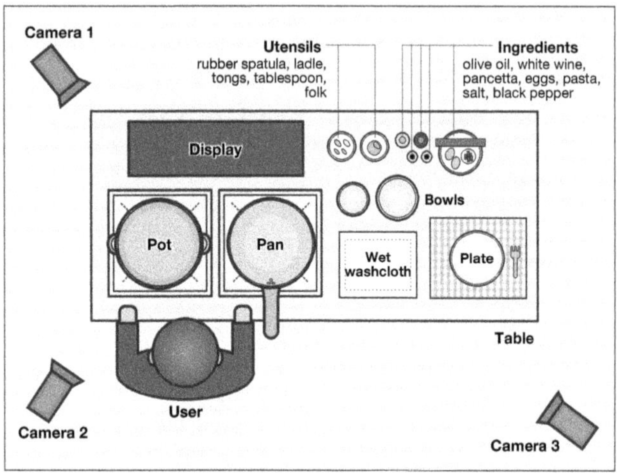

Figure 7. Layout of the User Study

In this study, we consider not only general or common findings but also each user's originality; their respective backgrounds, and experiences about cooking. Not only does it improve the users' skills but it provides fruitful experiences such as challenging to difficult recipes, enjoying cooking actions, and tasting delicious dishes even at home. Design researchers should not only evaluate the effectiveness of the system itself, but they must verify real experience of users with systems [12]. Because our work is not a scientific experiment system, we considered that quantitatively measuring user experience and effectiveness is not suitable, therefore focused on how each user's experience has changed from their everyday cooking lives. This report describes the detailed experience including the user's own context and differences among individuals; each user's characters, previous experiences, and creative impressions through the user studies.

Step 1. Pasta (1) - Boil Water
Boil 8 cups of water in the pot.

Step 2. Making Egg Sauce
Beat a whole egg with an extra egg-yolk in a bowl. Then add 15 grams of grated cheese and small amount of freshly-ground black pepper, and beat them well again.

Step 3. Pasta (2) - Start Cooking Pasta
Put one and a third of tablespoons of salt and 70 grams of pasta into the pot.

Step 4. Pasta (3) - Start Timer
Start the timer for boiling pasta. (Keep boiling for 6 minutes.)

Step 5. Pancetta (1) - Fry Pancetta
Heat a teaspoon of olive oil in a pan. Add 30 grams of diced pancetta and fry over high heat to the proper temperature. Keep cooking until crispy and brown.

Step 6. Pancetta (2) Add Wine
Turn off the stove temporarily and add 10ml of white wine. Heat it again at the proper temperature until almost no liquid remains in the pan.

Step 7. Pancetta (3) - Seasoning
Turn off the stove and move the pan onto a wet washcloth. Add 50ml of boiled water from pasta pot to the pan along with a table spoon of fresh water. Shake the pan until oil and water are mixed well.

Step 8. Pancetta (4) - Cooling
Keep the pan under the proper temperature.

Step 9. Pasta (4) - Drain Water
After the pasta timer rung, drain the water from pasta well.

Step 10. Finish (1) - Add Pasta to Pan
Add pasta and mix it to be dressed with the pancetta.

Step 11. Finish (2) - Dress with Egg Sauce
Add the egg sauce into the pan. Stir with a spatula about 15 seconds until the yellow and the white of the egg uniformly combined.

Step 12. Finish (3) - Heat Egg Sauce
Heat the pan at the proper temperature. Continue to shake the pan and stir inside until smooth and creamy.

Step 13. Serve
Serve immediately to avoid after heat.

Table 2. Original Cooking Sequence's Texts Displayed in the Main Panel (Figure 5-b-1) of the Detail Mode (Figure 5-b).

Method

The user study was conducted in the following sequence. At first, the authors interviewed each user about his/her cooking experience, home environment, and other related things about cooking and diet in 5 - 10 minutes as a prior interview. Before starting the cooking, we introduced how to use this system in about 5 minutes and then gave the user about 5 minutes to learn the functions of panavi, actually heating the pan and showing the changes of the temperature's degree, and touching the display to operate the system. In addition, we explained what the end goal of the process is by showing the photo of completed *Carbonara*, Figure 8-a. During the cooking, we did not help the user in all tasks except when troubles such as system errors occurred. After the cooking, we interviewed the user in about 60 minutes as the posterior interview. The users were required to specifically explain intentions and impressions about each action, activity, and process of cooking, watching a video of his/her cooking.

This study was video-recorded in 90 minutes per group, total about 270 minutes. The scene when the user did the cooking was recorded by three video cameras each set at different locations as shown in Figure 7; Camera 1 is to capture the user's actions, Camera 2 is to capture the display, and Camera 3 is to capture the pan and actions on the kitchen table. During the prior interview, we recorded the user's face and voices using one camera. The posterior interview was recorded by one camera when the user talks, watching the monitor showing the video taken during the cooking activity.

Our user study method is constructed by arranging "video-cued recall method" Costello et al. [10] adopted to verify their media art works. The method is a way to interview the user watching the video of when he/she experienced the work in order to reveal the detailed user experience of the artwork. Moreover, it prevents ambiguous answers based on the user's objective interpretation comparing to the way to depend on the user's recollections. This method intends to restress the user, because the user can experience the work in a natural situation. In the case of our study, we did not interrupt nor ask the user about intentions or impression during the cooking sequence. To understand detailed feedback at each point during cooking and make thick descriptions about user experience, this method is highly efficient.

Users

For this user study, we asked four persons in their twenties to use this system because we assumed they would be potential users if this future work becomes commercialized. Recipe books, cooking schools, and digital recipe contents are frequently engaged with young persons in their twenties in Japan. Therefore we considered to earn the user experience as our first user study.

User A, an attendee of Study 1, is a 23 years old male with little experience in cooking. He has an experience of living on his own for a brief time, but lives with his parents now. Although he has tried to do basic cooking such as fried rice or miso soup, he could not make them well. As a result, he does not do any cooking recently.

User B, an attendee of Study 2, is a 24 years old female undergoing simple cooking once or twice a week. She lives with her parents and gives some help to the parents' cooking ever since she was young. Her parents have interests in food and cooking, and hold their own home garden. Raised in such a family environment, she has basic knowledge of cooking, but has not had a chance to challenge authentic menus.

Study 3 was designed to see two persons co-cooking in the domestic kitchen, so two attendees were selected; User C, a 24 years old male, and User D, a 22 years old female. They are colleagues at the same graduate school. User C lives with his parents and brothers, having a wide experience as a Boy Scout member when he was young and in part-time jobs at a restaurant when he was an undergraduate student. He has basic cooking knowledge and does cooking 3 or 4 times a week. User D lives on her own for 5 years and has a habit of cooking. After starting to be the single life, she mastered the recipe book for beginners her mother gave her, and utilizes web sites in order to expand her cooking repertoire.

Results

Study 1, User A

Since User A did not have much knowledge about cooking, he could not understand instructions and as a result, spent a lot of time cooking. Despite this, he followed each step carefully and completed his *Carbonara*; although the pasta was too soft. We describe highlighted scenes from the sequence (Table 2) in the following paragraphs.

While the Step 5, he started to cook after reading the recipe texts. In the posterior interview, he explained that he could not understand the detailed instructions for example "*Cold the pan put on the wet washcloth*"; he had no idea such as stopping the heating or using the washcloth after heating.

During the Step 7, even though the alert bell was ringing to announce the boiled time has passed, he did not seem like he was in a rush. After the cooking, he said "*I could not understand how the pasta will be affected by not carrying out the procedures quickly.*"

On the Step 11, he was about to turn on the stove even though the system says "*Keep the fire off.*" Then, he checked the monitor again, noticed his misunderstanding, and stopped to turn on the fire without minding the time. After the cooking, he said "*I was so anxious to re-read the Main Panel of the Detail mode many times.*"

Finally, on the Step 12, he finished heating the egg sauce with pasta very well in 2 minutes, by checking the video and the projection images on the pan and preventing 'red' or 'yellow' temperature indication (Figure 8-B). However, he could not stop heating the pan even after the sauce was thick and creamy. As a result, his *Carbonara* sauce was slightly baked compared to the perfect example (Figure 8-b). After the cooking, he said "*I could not image the completion, because I had never eaten this menu.*" Eventually, all of his cooking was finished in 32 minutes, which is over 10 minutes later than the normal cooking time.

In the posterior interview, he discussed some aspects of the design. For example, he said "*I could not judge between the important steps and the omissible ones throughout the all steps, because it was too much information for me to understand and follow. If I cook while talking to my mother on the phone, I can do it well as she comments directly. In case of using this system, it is challenging for me to think about all things.*" He also commented "*I would not like to use this system when my girlfriend comes to my home, because it does not look smart to depend on the machine like this. I like to use this system as a practice in private.*"

Study 2, User B

User B, having a habit of cooking, had conducted most steps without difficulty. Rather, she seemed to enjoy the process

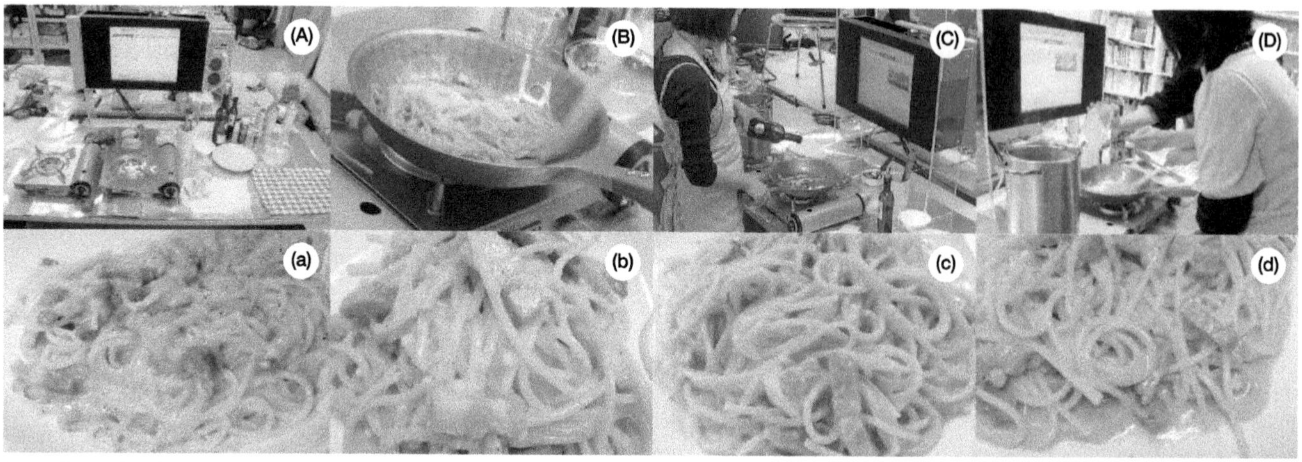

Figure 8. (A) Setting of the User Study (a), Carbonara the Author Cooked, (B) User A Heated the Egg Sauce Very Well., (b) Carbonara Sauce was Slightly Baked., (C) User B Poured the Wine in the Pan with Imitating the Chef's Action., (c) Carbonara User B Cooked., (D) User C Put the Egg Sauce into the Pan while User D Grasped the Pan and Stirred the Ingredient Using a Rubber Spatula., (d) Their Carbonara was Slightly Sloppy.

of cooking like playing a game, and completed a delicious *Carbonara* except it was slightly scorched at the end.

She easily finished the steps following the instructions until the Step 4. She was amazed to the visualized temperature degree at the navigation on the Step 5. When the temperature reached to the proper setting, she sensed the vibration from the handle of the pan and lowered the heat. Furthermore, when the system indicated the "yellow" temperature, she kept the pan away from on the stove and waited until it returned back to "green." She speedily finished this step in 210 seconds from the beginning, when the ingredients have been baked slightly.

While the Step 6, she poured the wine in the pan imitating the chef's action shown in the video after checking the video two or three times, (Figure 8-C). After that, she turned on the fire and heated the pan until water evaporated. In the posterior interview, she said "*At first, I could not understand the meaning of the task on this step. It was difficult so I tried carefully, different from the previous steps.*"

During the Step 7, the alert bell for the pasta rang. After the cooking, she said "*At this time, I thought to improve my cooking's speed, being aware of time.*"

On the Step 12, she started the tasks after checking how to cook by reading the recipe texts aloud. The chef Ochiai [2] in the video said "*Don't turn the heat on high,*" she also repeated this sentence. When the arrowed line was displayed on the surface of the pan, she immediately responded to the signal and stirred the ingredients. She had completed the entire cooking sequence in 18 minutes, which is 2 minutes shorter than the normal cooking time.

She was engaged in the process with swinging tempo, sometimes reading the texts aloud and speaking to herself. In the posterior interview, she said "*I am very satisfied to make a delicious menu (Figure 8-c). I have felt the process was easier than I had imagined. But I might fail something to do without using the panavi.*" She has really enjoyed the cooking with the panavi.

Study 3, User C & D

User C and D conducted the steps by dividing the tasks flexibly. Firstly, in the early steps, they enjoyed talking with one another, but in the latter part of the process they talked less and seemed to be concentrating on the work. Although they completed the dish perfectly before Step 12, their *Carbonara* was undercooked on the last step and were disappointed with the result.

On the Step 2, while User D made the egg sauce, User C provided the instructions to her by referring to the video. After that, they divided the tasks in several scenes, which had not been decided before the cooking. This division was conducted flexibly on a case-by-case basis, according to the posterior interview.

While the Step 5, User D took the pan and turned on the fire, and then User C measured oil using a spoon and poured it in the pan. After that, they continued to cook at low heat for a while, but the pan's temperature was not close to the proper degree (165 °C). Then, User C turned the fire up after viewing the monitor of the Condition mode and checking how far the current temperature was from the proper degree.

As a result of their collaboration, they completed the cooking with time to spare until the Step 7. When starting the Step 8, User C saw the Condition and checked the proper temperature for this step (70 °C). When the pan's temperature had been lowered to the proper degree, the alert bell for the pasta rang.

At first on the Step 11, User C put the egg sauce in the pan while User D grasped the pan and stirred the ingredients using a rubber spatula (Figure 8-D). However on the Step 12, she exchanged places with him and began to adjust the fire standing on his side, because User D was not able to shake the pan well. After a short time, User C removed the pan from the fire and put it on the wet washcloth, because the temperature had been too high. From the posterior interview, User C said "*I checked if it is suitable for the finish, but I judged it needs to be more time heated and put it on the stove again.*" After a while, he checked it again and arranged the pasta on a plate. They have completed the cooking in about 15 minutes and 30 seconds, which was the fastest time among 3 groups. However, in the interview, we noticed User C worried about what the dish would be like if it was heated a little longer. As a result, their *Carbonara* was slightly sloppy (Figure 8-d).

Throughout the cooking, User C frequently checked the proper temperature referring to the Main Panel of the Condition mode, while User D read the recipe texts many times. The videos were rarely used and they cooked relying on their experiences. But from the interview, User C said "*We'd forgotten about watching the video*." Since they had not seen the videos, as a result, they could finish the cooking very quickly. Both User C and D said "*I want to cook it again using the system*," because they were disappointed in quality of the pasta sauce.

Reflections

This study revealed the difference between the understandings of instructions for each group, because the users had distinctive prior knowledge and skills about cooking. User A, the beginner, repeated the same video at least twice or three times on each step, and also tried to faithfully follow the all of instructions. As a result, he ran over the normal time substantially. In contrast, User B finished the cooking quickly without watching the videos and depended on her own experience, except when she was dealing with the steps she thought was difficult. User C and D also used their own ways and completed the steps sometimes without checking the navigation.

We perceived the main feature of this system (the combination of sensing, analyzing, and navigation supporting users' situated actions) took care each user's differences, even for beginner users. Although User A had little knowledge about cooking and stumbled throughout many steps, he eventually succeeded on the Step 12, which requires a high skill level. The other two groups also controlled the temperature and moved the pan well at this point.

On the other hand, however, the system sometimes could not respond to the users' situated actions because the instructions by texts and video tutorials are fixed and not changeable. For example, User C and D skipped to check the video tutorials since they understood basic ways to cook only when referring to the text tutorials, but they regretted not to see the videos at Step 12. If the system could suggest the users to inspect this navigation, they may not fail this process.

The current system is able to support cooking conditions such as the temperature or movements but does not support any other contexts. This is because the system cannot recognize if the user understands the tutorials, forgets to check, or is worrying about what to do. Regarding these aspects, HCI systems, especially cooking support media, should not only sense users' conditions but also understand what the users need under some contexts and provide proper directions considering the individual experience and skills.

Furthermore, as a technical issue, the current system cannot navigate the timing of judging when the heating should be stopped especially on the Step 5 and 12. It would not judge when the heating should be stopped, because the system cannot recognize some changes; how the pancetta is fried on the Step 5, how the moisture of the egg sauce is evaporated, and how long the sauce is heated to be creamy and not baked on the Step 12. The possibility of adding other functions to the system (e.g. measuring water amount, multiple-sensing temperatures, etc.) to solve this issue should be discussed.

CONCLUSION

Designing Smart Daily Commodities

This paper described panavi, a new recipe medium format utilizing a special pan that analyzes sensors data, recognizes users' conditions, and provides the users suitable navigation messages based on each situations. It consisted of an iterative sketching and prototyping process, an implementation for the initial menu *Carbonara* that requires specific temperature and movement control, and a user study of three groups.

Throughout the design process and the user study, we developed the system in the temporal kitchen set in our research place, and obtained a model for designing daily commodities (e.g. kitchen utensils) as smart objects enriching our everyday life experiences. This model consists of a technical framework and a methodology. The technical framework is the integration of sensor-embedded tool(s), wireless communication modules, and operating system; sensing and analyzing users' state, and generating feedback suitable for each user's situations. But this framework itself is not an innovative aspect. Rather, the methodology is important; the integrated technical elements should be designed as a whole system through the prototyping process in real domestic environments. In our case, panavi has been designed in in the mock kitchen environment, not in a scientific research lab. This process is a way of designing user experience instead of 'usability evaluation oriented researches' Greenberg [12] strongly criticized. It is also an example of how to design artifacts supporting Suchman's situated actions [21]. If (HCI) designers challenge to develop a new system for domestic users, they will be able to apply this basic model in a certain domestic context.

The basic design model of the panavi system—the sensor embedded daily commodities communicating wirelessly with computer system—enables the users to concentrate in cooking without noticing if it is a computing device. The appearance and usability of the pan seems the same as normal consumer products. Furthermore, the wireless communicative sensor-embedded tools are needless of any massive equipment to construct the system. Integrated systems based on HCI technologies, focusing on cooking support (e.g. [6, 7, 9, 16, 18, 20]), require complex or ambitious architecture, however, this design model is simple but sufficient and easy to set in current domestic kitchens.

Future Visions

This recipe medium may be applied to other menus. For example, French chefs skillfully move the pan with a high temperature in a minute when making an omelet, Japanese chefs season ingredients into tasty soup by sensitively controlling its temperature and osmotic pressure, or Chinese chefs dynamically move the pan to cook fried rice. As future works, we would like to measure and model chefs' cooking ways such as temperature and movement controls, and apply these data to navigation, and produce various kinds of recipe working on future prototype.

The design model of the sensor-embedded frying pan may also be applied to other kitchen utensils such as small and large pods, bowls, knives and chopping blocks [15], and etc. If multiple "smart" utensils may be integrated in a navigation application, this system will support various scenes; for more challenging and sophisticated menus, and multiple food preparations at the same time [13].

Developing the panavi system challenged us to design computer artifacts to be used in an extreme environment, the kitchen that is always associated with water and fire. Moving towards Ubiquitous Computing environments, HCI design is required to adapt with usages in uncertain but exciting everyday life. We will proceed to develop and improve this system to be more suitable for real domestic contexts and encourage people's daily cooking to become more enjoyable.

ACKNOWLEDGMENTS

This research is granted by CREST., JST until March 2010. After that, it is carried out under Keio-NUS CUTE Center. Lastly, we thank Jeffrey Tzu Kwan Valino Koh, Yan Yan Cao, and Chihiro Sato on supporting to revise this paper.

REFERENCES

1. Kraft foods inc., ifood assistant. http://www.kraftrecipes.com/media/ifood.aspx.
2. Web la bettola. http://www.la–bettola.co.jp/.
3. Digital thermometer pan. *Ubergizmo.com* (2008), http://www.ubergizmo.com/2008/11/digital–thermometer–pan/.
4. Aoyama, H., Ozeki, M., and Nakamura, Y. Smart cooking support system based on interaction reproducing model. *Proc. CEA '09* (2009), 39–46.
5. Arroyo, E., Bonanni, L., and Selker, T. Waterbot: exploring feedback and persuasive techniques at the sink. *Proc. CHI '05* (2005), 631–639.
6. Bonanni, L., Lee, C.-H., and Selker, T. Attention-based design of augmented reality interfaces. *Proc. CHI EA '05* (2005), 1228–1231.
7. Bradbury, J. S., Shell, J. S., and Knowles, C. B. Hands on cooking: towards an attentive kitchen. *Proc. CHI EA '03* (2003), 996–997.
8. Buxton, B. *Sketching User Experiences: Getting the Design Right and the Right Design (Interactive Technologies)*. Morgan Kaufmann, 2007.
9. Chi, P.-Y. P., Chen, J.-H., Chu, H.-H., and Lo, J.-L. Enabling calorie-aware cooking in a smart kitchen. *Proc. PERSUASIVE '08* (2008), 116–127.
10. Costello, B., Muller, L., Amitani, S., and Edmonds, E. Understanding the experience of interactive art: Iamascope in beta_space. *Proc. IE 2005* (2005), 49–56.
11. Fukuda, T., Nakauchi, Y., Noguchi, K., and Matsubara, T. Human behavior recognition for cooking support robot. *ROMAN2004* (2004), 359–364.
12. Greenberg, S., and Buxton, B. Usability evaluation considered harmful (some of the time). *Proc. CHI '08* (2008), 111–120.
13. Hamada, R., Okabe, J., Ide, I., Satoh, S., Sakai, S., and Tanaka, H. Cooking navi: assistant for daily cooking in kitchen. *Proc. MULTIMEDIA '05* (2005), 371–374.
14. Ju, W., Hurwitz, R., Judd, T., and Lee, B. Counteractive: an interactive cookbook for the kitchen counter. *Proc. CHI EA '01* (2001), 269–270.
15. Kranz, M., Schmidt, A., Maldonado, A., Rusu, R. B., Beetz, M., Hörnler, B., and Rigoll, G. Context-aware kitchen utilities. *Proc. TEI '07* (2007), 213–214.
16. Mennicken, S., Karrer, T., Russell, P., and Borchers, J. First-person cooking: a dual-perspective interactive kitchen counter. *Proc. CHI EA '10* (2010), 3403–3408.
17. Nintendo. Personal trainer: Cooking. http://personaltrainercooking.com/.
18. Olivier, P., Xu, G., Monk, A., and Hoey, J. Ambient kitchen: designing situated services using a high fidelity prototyping environment. *Proc. PETRA '09* (2009), 47:1–47:7.
19. Perton, M. Vita craft rfiq cookware uses rfid to control temps. *Engadget* (2006), http://www.engadget.com/2006/01/13/vita–craft–rfiq–cookware–uses–rfid–to–control–temps/.
20. Siio, I., Mima, N., Frank, I., Ono, T., and Weintraub, H. Making recipes in the kitchen of the future. *Proc. CHI EA '04* (2004), 1554–1554.
21. Suchman, L. A. *Plans and Situated Actions: The Problem of Human-Machine Communication (Learning in Doing: Social, Cognitive and Computational Perspectives)*. Cambridge University Press, 1987.
22. Sugiura, Y., Sakamoto, D., Withana, A., Inami, M., and Igarashi, T. Cooking with robots: designing a household system working in open environments. *Proc. CHI '10* (2010), 2427–2430.
23. Tokuhisa, S., Ishizawa, T., Niwa, Y., Kasuya, K., Ueki, A., Hashimoto, S., Koriyama, K., and Inakage, M. xtel: a development environment to support rapid prototyping of "ubiquitous content". *Proc. TEI '09* (2009), 323–330.
24. Tran, Q. T., Calcaterra, G., and Mynatt, E. D. Cookfs collage: Déjà vu display for a home kitchen. *Proc. HOIT 2005* (2005), 15–32.
25. Winograd, T., and Flores, F. *Understanding Computers and Cognition: A New Foundation for Design*. Addison-Wesley Professional, 1987.
26. Zimmerman, J., Forlizzi, J., and Evenson, S. Research through design as a method for interaction design research in hci. *Proc. CHI '07* (2007), 493–502.

Keep in Touch: Channel, Expectation and Experience

Rongrong Wang
Virginia Tech
Blacksburg, VA 24060
wangr06@vt.edu

Francis Quek
Virginia Tech
Blacksburg, VA 24060
quek@vt.edu

Deborah Tatar
Virginia Tech
Blacksburg, VA 24060
dtatar@vt.edu

James Keng Soon Teh
IDMI, National University of Singapore
james.tks@gmail.com

Adrian David Cheok
Graduate School of Media Design, Keio University
adriancheok@kmd.keio.ac.jp

ABSTRACT
This paper investigates whether and how digitally mediated social touch (remote touch) may influence the sense of connectedness toward a speaker and the emotional experience of what is being communicated. We employ an 'augmented' storytelling methodology where we manipulate the modality of an 'emotive' channel that accompanies the speech, and the contextual expectation of the listener. Comparing a remote upper-arm touch against a similarly timed flashing light, we explore the importance of the touch modality in affect conveyance. Our second manipulation involves two cover stories where the listener is told that the touch or flashing light is triggered either by the storyteller expressively squeezing a touch input device while speaking, or by measured 'high points' in the mental state of the storyteller. Our results show that the story accompanied by communicative touch resulted in a significant increase in the sense of connectedness with the storyteller over the speech-only condition, and a trend toward greater affective conveyance.

Author Keywords
Remote Touch; Connectedness; Empathy; Affect; Emotional Experience; Multimodality; Haptics; Computer Mediated Communication

ACM Classification Keywords
H.5.2 Information Interfaces and Presentation: Miscellaneous—*Optional sub-category*

General Terms
Experimentation, Human Factors

INTRODUCTION
Human communication is not just about conveying information streams. Facial expression, gesture, 'body language', physical touch and voice prosody all function with speech to convey aspects of communication that strings of symbols alone cannot carry. In our current political season, for example, a politician's speech is often judged by how well he or she has 'connected' with the electorate. The voters want to sense that somehow the speaker empathizes with their situation, and the speaker wants to induce in the listener a sense of empathy with his or her viewpoint. This paper investigates how remote touch in conjunction with speech may influence this sense of connectedness or empathy toward the speaker and the emotional experience of what is being communicated.

Digital communication has expanded to incorporate a number of non-verbal channels such as video to convey gestures and facial expressions, high fidelity sound to capture prosody, and accompanying textual interaction. Touch, however, has not received equivalent attention, and hence is less studied. This is problematic since touch plays a significant role in natural human interaction to convey affect, intimacy, and to increase connectedness and empathy.

Most of previous pioneering work in remote touch have focused on the design and prototype of remote touch systems. However there has been little exploration of whether and how remote touch can influence the affective components in human communication. Notable exceptions include: Haans [12, 11] and [24]. Wang [24] prototyped an armband using shape memory alloy which can produce a squeeze sensation on the user's upper arm. The in-between study recruited two groups of participants to listen to a sad story that had a happy ending with or without remote touch channel. The result shows that participants with the augmented remote touch channel experience a significant reduction in sadness and a trend toward increased joviality. This study suggests that remote touch channel can influence people's emotional experience.

This raises two research questions that we hope to answer in this paper. First, is the specific *modality* important to the conveyance of affect? Perhaps the results of altered affect comes from altering the listener's attention, causing her to focus on the affective components of the story conveyed in speech? Can the same effect be achieved by any channel other than touch? In other words, is there anything special about the remote touch channel other than as a signaling mechanism? Second, how does the context of the communication affect one's perception of connectedness or affect? We manipulated the expectation of communicative intent in our study to address this question. Does it matter if the recipient think that the touch and speech were co-generated by the speaker in the process of speaking or if she believes that the touch is the result of some unintended measurement of the speaker's affective state?

We present a similar upper-arm touch device that is paired with a pressure-sensitive casing for a cellular phone. The idea is to enable experience of touch communication in conjunction with speech. We designed a study to investigate the importance of the touch *modality* and the impact of the context or expectation of the recipient of the dual-channel communication. In the subsequent sections, we shall outline the relevant related work (covering both the role of touch in human communication and the design and testing of remote touch systems); describe our interactive speech/touch system; discuss the design and results of our study; and present our discussion and conclusions.

RELATED WORK

Touch as Emotion Communication

Despite the importance of touch in different domains of social life, its role in emotion communication has received little attention compared to facial and vocal displays of emotion [23]. Based on existing research on touch and emotion communication, generally there are four claims:

First, touch is capable of communicating and eliciting the valenced emotions (i.e. either positive or negative). Wolff [28] studied the development of smiling in the early life of the infant and reported that the widely known game of 'pat-a-cake' becomes an effective generator of positive emotions in infants as indicated by their intense and broad smiles. Wolff inferred that tactile stimulation, and not other stimulation, resulted in infant smiling because the infants played the game without being able to see or hear the interactive adult. Touch seems to be an extraordinary powerful sensory system for communicating hedonically valenced emotions. The skin contains receptors that directly generated hedonic values, either because there are portions of the skin that are erogenous or because there are nerve endings that are nociceptive. Studies have also indicated that touch is capable of eliciting negative emotion. Brossard and Decarie [3] explored a number of stimuli varying in complexity that reinforced infants most effectively, laying a hand on the infants' abdomens for 30s with little pressure (i.e. static touch) took the most amount of time to reinforce infant smiling. Furthermore, infants displayed the most amount of tension when they were touched statically.

Second, touch amplifies the intensity of emotional displays from the face and voice [18]. Third, Hertenstein et al [15] indicate that touch can communicate distinct emotions in a robust fashion. 248 subjects (124 unacquainted dyads) participated in their study. The randomly designated encoder entered the lab to find the blindfolded decoder. The encoder was presented emotion words on sheets of paper and asked to communicate the specific emotion by making contact with the decoder's body using any form of touch he/she deems appropriate. The results show that all emotions including anger, fear, happiness, sadness, disgust, love, gratitude and sympathy were decoded at greater than chance levels without significant level of confusion. Its accurate rates for emotions are comparable to the accuracy rates observed in facial and vocal studies of emotions.

Fourth, the meaning of touch is largely shaped by context. Jones and Yarbrough [16] found that there is no one-to-one correspondence between meaning and touch. Their context-based analysis study on meanings of touch shows that that similar touches may have different meanings while similar meanings can lead to different touches. Context plays a critical role in shaping the meaning of touch. With context, touch can convey meanings including closeness, support, appreciation, comfort, reassurance, anger, hate etc.

These literatures in emotion communication not only show that touch can communicate different emotions but also suggests that touch conveying affect in an immediate non-symbolic manner. By "non-symbolic", we mean no predefined meaning or code is needed for affect conveyance using touch. The sender of touch does not try to make a statement when touching others and the recipient just receive the touch without trying to decode the meaning of the touch. We also note that this does not cover certain aspects socially codified physical interaction such as a handshake that obviously has a symbolic component in its meaning [16]. This characteristics of touch is important. If the way that touch conveys affect is the same as message passing, it can be easily replaced by a speech/textual communication channel and thus the significant of research on digitally mediated touch will be very limited.

Digitally Mediated Touch to Increase Sense of Connectedness

Prior research in digitally mediated touch has focused on increasing connectedness between individuals. However, most of these work have been focused on the design of remote touch system. Very few studies are available that report on the empirical system validations beyond the level of anecdotal descriptions of user experiences [10]. On the other hand, in contrast from the results suggested from psychology and communications literature, most of the remote 'social touch' technology is used for message passing (an extensive review of the literature that comes to this conclusion can be found in [24]). Either by design or by user decision, users of the technology typically performed conscious encoding of symbolic messages and used the devices as signaling channels, in essence, using the remote touch device as some kind of tactile Morse Code. Following, we shall present several instances of prior research relating to remote touch devices that increase connectedness between individuals.

Brave and Dahley describe an inTouch [2] system that used a pair of linked devices with rollers that mirror each other's movements. Users placed their hands on the rollers, and as they moved the rollers, the paired device would mirror the roll in displacement and force. Users reported that the device supported 'playful' interaction. Chang et al presented the ComTouch system designed to enable symbolic communicative function through a tactile interface [4] that is attached to cellphone and utilizes encoded haptic patterns in communication. They reported preliminary studies in which benefits were found with the tactile channel for 1. Redundancy between voice and haptics for emphasis, 2. Mimicry of haptic patterns to indicate attention and camaraderie, and 3. Turn taking signals. Apart from mimicry, the haptic interaction was used to transmit symbolically coded messages. Mueller et al [19] and DiSalvo et al [7] describe a 'hug' devices that support remote hugging. An inflatable koala bear serves as the input device. When it is squeezed, a paired inflatable vest inflates to simulate a hug. After 4 seconds, the hug ends, and a 'kissing sound' is sent back to the koala to express 'appreciation'. The target use was to support intimacy between people in close relationships. A user test was not reported (the system was presented to a design workshop). The consensus was that the pumps for the vest inflation was too noisy and slow, and that the participants did not think that the system was useful in daily life.

In another device called LumiTouch [5], two picture frames on the desks of a pair of users serve as interfaces. The photograph of each user adorns the frame of the other user. When the sender squeezes the picture frame on her desk, her partner's picture frame would glow. In a test with a random user pairs, the subjects developed interpersonal symbolic signals (the authors called this an 'interpersonal language') that were sent over the devices. "Users created different combinations of light intensities, colors, and pulses and agreed with each other upon private meanings to their interaction. One user used a pulsing green and blue series to communicate "Good luck" and a flashing red "Good bye, I am busy now." Rovers and van Essen designed two related devices HIM [21] and FootIO [22]. Both devices are used within instant messaging to convey hapticons (similar as emoticons), where encoded tactile patterns represent the emotion that people in chatting deliberately send out. We note that emoticons are not immediate expressions of emotion, but are part of a symbol system to communicate para-linguistic information through a channel of symbols [20, 13], and have to be interpreted for correlation with real emotions.

Several observations from these work reviewed above include: 1. Some of the systems were designed with symbolic communication as integral components in the meaning of touch; 2. Even when symbolic communication was not specifically prescribed, users tend to use the systems to transmit deliberately encoded messages, turning a rich human touch system into a low-bit-rate signaling tool; 3. The most commonly cited 'non-verbal' communication resulting from these devices was 'playful interaction' – the promise of broader affect conveyance was not in evidence, and 4. Few user studies were reported on the affective use of the systems, making it hard to derive design principles for enabling immediate affective interaction through remote touch. We believe the lack of understanding of whether and how remote touch may facilitate the affect conveyance in tele-communication contributes to the usage of touch as a symbolic channel. In this paper we will explore whether and how remote touch may affect people's attitude to the speaker and their emotional experience differently when it is used as a communicative or information signal channel.

Pressure as One Dimension of Touch

From childhood, we are exposed to many types of touch (e.g., patting, stroking, kissing, hugging, squeezing, pinching, poking, and jabbing). All these forms can be conceptualized into a number of dimensions. A few researchers have proposed analytic frameworks to describe touch. For example, Geldard [8] categorized properties of touch into mechanical (i.e. locus, intensity, duration, and frequency) and non-mechanical (i.e. thermal, chemical and electrical). Weiss [27] proposed a conceptual framework in which she considers four dimensions of touch: duration, location, action and intensity. Hertenstein [14] build a physical touch space upon Weiss's framework including parameters (location, frequency, duration, and extent of surface area) and qualities of touch (action, intensity, velocity, abruptness and temperature). With such a huge and complex design space, itself is a big challenge to choose a reasonable starting point.

Clynes explores the pressure dimension of touch as an output modality of seven basic emotions in his book "Sentics: the touch of emotion"[6]. In that study, the subject sits in a chair with a straight back and no armrests. His/her middle finger rests on a finger rest one inch high so that other fingers are relaxed in a natural position without touching anything. The finger remains in touch with the finger rest throughout and not lifted off at any time. Researchers request each subject to produce an action for a particular emotion thirty to fifty times at varying intervals a few seconds apart. Clynes measured the force and the direction of the finger tip action. They found surprisingly that over 400 participants produced very similar dynamic forms for each of seven basic emotions (love, joy, anger, hate, grief, sex, and reverence). When they replayed the recorded dynamic profile of finger tip pressure action to another group of participants, participants can recognize these emotions clearly. Bailenson and his colleagues did a similar study in virtual environment, in which they request 1st group of participants to produce a handshake using a commercial available handshake device for a particular emotion and 2nd group of participants to recognize emotions from recorded dynamic profiles of handshake. They also find the similar results in digitally mediated touch condition [1].

Clynes and Bailenson's work informs that pressure may be a good place to start the investigation of remote touch because pressure can provide rich emotion range for us to explore and relatively easy to implement. We will take remote pressure transmission as our start point for the similar reason.

REMOTE TOUCH DEVICE

Our previous prototype with Shape Memory Alloy (SMA) is lightweight, very quite in operation, and was able to activate quickly (able to produce a squeeze in 300 milliseconds). However, because SMA typically only contracts 3$\sim$5% in length, the pulling force is quite limited. Users comment that the force provided by armband is much softer compared to a normal human squeeze. This low force level also makes user's sensation of squeeze sensitive to rise-time of the SMA.

Users can only feel the squeeze when the SMA is activated quickly. We achieved this speed by over-driving the SMA in our first prototype for our study reported in [24]. This reduced the life of the SMA considerably.

For the current study, we designed a new remote touch device prototype [25] shown in Figure 1. This prototype is composed of two main parts: the output armband , and a squeeze input device.

Figure 1(a) and 1(b) show our output armband design. It employs a servo motor as the mechanical actuator that retracts a fabric layer in the armband worn by the touch recipient. The armband is designed to wrap around the upper arm of the user and has a width of about 7cm approximating the width of an adult's palm, and can provide maximum pulling force off around 120N in 0.2s.

Figure 1(c) and 1(d) show the touch input part of our prototype. It comprises force sensors embedded in an acrylic case designed to house a Google Nexus One smart phone, and the control electronics. The case is made of acrylic pieces and is precisely cut into the required shape using a 2D laser cutter. Two Flexi-Force sensors are mounted along one side of the case (see Figure 1(c)). The control circuit (Figure 1(c))includes a Bluetooth module and a micro-controller PIC-16F76. After initial calibration, this input part can detect soft/medium/hard levels of squeeze force on the phone. It is also able to distinguish such squeezes from the normal force by which one would hold the phone. Once a squeeze is detected, the control circuit will send a signal to the phone via Bluetooth.

When a paired phone case is paired with an output armband, the armband will deliver a squeeze with a force that corresponds to the pressure detected in the phone case. Our perception study with 22 subjects shows that 100% of users agree or strongly agree that they can easily feel the squeezes they are assigned to experience. 86.4% of users report that the squeeze is similar to human touch, although they can feel a difference [25].

EXPERIMENT

Since we are interested to explore how the touch modality and context modulate people's emotional experience, we decide to use stories as emotion elicitation. We use the same story and a similar study protocol as was used in Wang and Quek [24]. We invite participants to listen to the emotive story recording told by a professional actress. We are interested to examine the closeness they feel to the storyteller, the emotion they experience in hearing the story

Recall that our previous study in [24] found a significant decrease in sadness and a trend towards increased joviality when one listens to the story with remote touch as opposed to without. Our current study design is discern if the second channel effect is unique to touch or if some other arbitrary similarly synchronized channel would suffice. We also want to know if the contextual expectation that the touch received is expressively generated by the speaker is a significant factor in the experience.

Cover Story For Communicative Condition: "A female storyteller is going to tell you a story. In additional to audio, she is allowed to use a soft object in her hand to express her mental state. Every time she squeezed the soft object, the remote pressure transmission device will be in action and you will feel a squeeze on your arm (or, you will see a flashing light on your monitor). Now enjoy the story."

Cover Story For Measurement Condition: "A female storyteller is going to tell you a story. Her mental state is monitored in real time by a device. Every time her mental state reaches a high point, the remote pressure transmission device will be in action and you will feel a squeeze on your arm (or, you will see a flashing light on your monitor). Now enjoy the story."

Table 1. Cover stories for the *Communicative* and *Measurement* conditions

Figure 2 illustrates our study design. At the highest level, our study compares the *Speech+Additional Channel* (where *Additional Channel* may be touch or a flashing light) against the base *Speech Only* condition. For *Additional Channel* conditions, we manipulate two factors: Type of channel (*Remote Touch* vs *Flashing Light*) and Expectation of the participants (*Communicative* vs *Measurement*). The *Remote Touch* vs *Flashing Light* manipulation is designed to ferret out the importance of modality. In both conditions the signal is 'on/off', of the same duration (1 second in this study), and synchronizes with some emotionally laden portion of the verbal story stream. Hence, any difference in effect between these conditions must be related to modality. The *Communicative* vs *Measurement* manipulation is designed to determine the influence of context on affective and connectedness experience. The two conditions differ only in the cover story communicated to the participant. In the *Communicative* condition, the participant understands that the touch or flash they receive is triggered by the expressive intent of the storyteller as she squeezes an object for expressive effect as she tells the story. In the *Measurement* condition, the participant is told that the touch or flash they receive is the outcome of an 'emotion measurement device' that monitors emotional high points in the storyteller. Table 1 contains the respective cover stories. We denote these different conditions CT and CL for communicative touch and light, and MT and ML for measurement touch and light respectively.

Emotional High Points and Story Narration

A suitable story used in this experiment should be: 1) emotive so it has the power to influence the listener's emotional state; 2) not widely known. If some subjects have heard about the story before it might reduce the reliability of our experimental results; 3) be attractive to a wide range of people with different backgrounds. We decide to avoid stories dealing with sensitive topics such as religion and politics. We chose and edited a story named Story of Stevie. This story is emotion-laden and has a happy ending.

The story is about a boy with Down's Syndrome who found purpose bussing tables in a truck stop cafe. He is diagnosed with a heart problem that forced him to stop working. The story continues that this boy's absence was noticed by truck drivers who then spread the word. Every time a truck driver stopped at the cafe, he would leave money and mark a napkin

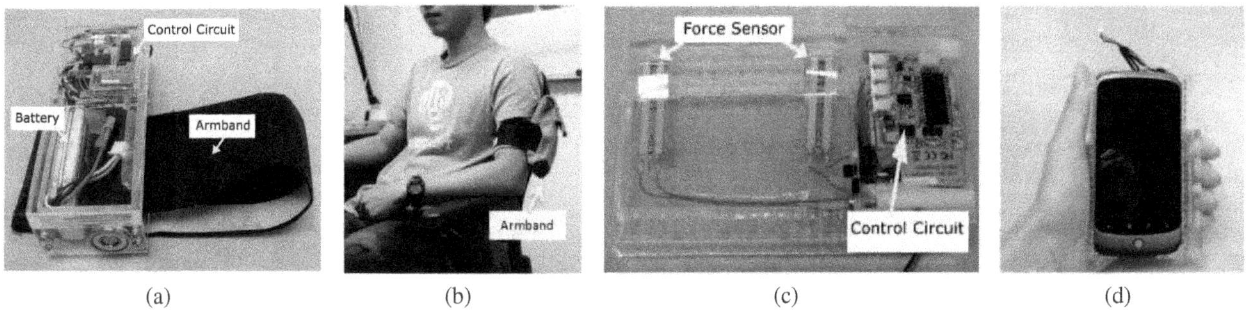

Figure 1. Remote Touch System: (a) Armband, (b) Armband Attachment, (c) Force Sensor, (d) Squeezable Case and Phone

	Speech + Additional Channel		Speech Only
Expectation \ Channel	Remote Touch	Flashing Light	Base Condition
Communicative	CT	CL	
Measurement	MT	ML	

Figure 2. Experiment Design

'for Stevie'. The story ends happily with enough money collected for Stevie's operation that returns him to health and his favorite activity, bussing tables at the cafe.

We employed the same 'emotional high points' used by [24] to determine where the touch or flashing light would be administered in the story audio stream. These high points were obtained by proposing 29 possible touch points in the story to 6 participants who evaluated these points in response to the question "Is this an emotional high point in this story?" in 1-5 scale. Fourteen touch signals are chosen which got highest scores.

We provided the story and 'touch' points to a professional actress. She was asked to narrate the story in a conversational style. She was also asked to hold a soft object in hand to help her keep her vocal narration congruent with touch activities. The recording of her narration serves as the audio stimulus in this study.

Participants

Twenty female and twenty male participants are recruited from on-campus listservs and a participant recruiting system maintained by Psychology Department at Virginia Tech. The participants include undergraduate/graduate students and university staff members. Participants from Psychology Department are compensated with 1 course credit for participation and participants from other sources are compensated with 5 dollars for their participation. Their age range is from 18 to 44 with an average of 23.13.

Procedure

Participants are gender balanced and randomly assigned into one of five experiment conditions. At the start of the study, participants are asked to fill a background information form. At this point, the participants are told their respective cover stories from Table 1. For familiarization with the study setup (room, audio equipment, and their assigned study condition), the participants were given a story practice session in which they will listen to a story about a distinguish alumnus of their institution. This familiarization story is accompanied with touches or light flashes in the same fashion as our stimulus story (the touch or flash points were identified in the same way as for our stimulus story). For participants in with-additional-channel condition, the experimenter ensured that participants can feel touch sensation clearly or see the flashing light on the monitor clearly, and are comfortable with the signal.

We use pre- and post-Positive Affective Negative Affective Schedules (pre- and post-PANAS) to measure the changes in subjects' current feelings and emotions. This form is adopted from Positive Affective Negative Affective Schedules Expanded form (PANAS-X) [26]. After the practice session, the participants are asked to fill a pre-PANAS form, after which the study stimulus ('Story of Stevie' with respective touch or flash signals) is administered. After the storytelling session, participants are asked to fill a post-PANAS form and a 10-question quiz about the content of the story. A semi-structured interview follows, which include questions:

1. How close do you feel to the storyteller? Please use the liker scale 1 (not at all) to 7 (extremely) to indicate
2. Why do you feel connected this way?
3. What is in your mind when you get squeezed or see the flashing light?
4. (Only for Touch Condition) How do you rate the sound level accompanying the remote pressure transmission device when it is in function?

The entire study takes about one hour.

Data Collection and Analysis

The pre- and post-PANAS test we use to measure emotion involves the participants responding 60 words relating to emotions on a scale of 1 (not at all) to 7 (extremely). This yields a scale that measures the instantaneous affective state of the respondent [26]. The internal consistency reliabilities (Cronbach's coefficient alpha) are high, generally ranging from .85 to .90 for positive affect, and .85 to .90 for negative affect. Additionally, the correlation between positive affect and negative affect is generally low, ranging from -.05 to -.35, giving quasi-independence between positive affect and negative affect [26].

We also use a semi-structured interview to evaluate the sense of connectedness the participants feel toward the storyteller and why, and their understanding of the additional channel and their strategy in understanding it. The interview is audio-recorded and transcribed. This yielded 90 pages of transcriptions that were analyzed using an open coding methodology.

We developed a questionnaire consisting of 10 multiple-choice questions based on facts in the story. This is to check whether the participant is involved in the experiment and to validate their data. Data from participants who scored less than 7 out of 10 in this questionnaire were removed from the study.

Results

Closeness Rating. We did one-way ANOVA to compare the closeness rating of CT, MT, CL, ML with that of the base condition. Figure 3 shows that participants in the with-additional-channel conditions all showed a trend of a higher degree of closeness to the storyteller. In particular, participants in CT reported highest closeness to the storyteller among all conditions which is significantly higher than that in the base condition ($p < 0.05$). For each bar in the graph, the central red mark is the median, the edges of the box are the 25th and 75th percentiles, the whiskers extend to the most extreme data points not considered outliers, and outliers are plotted by red cross individually.

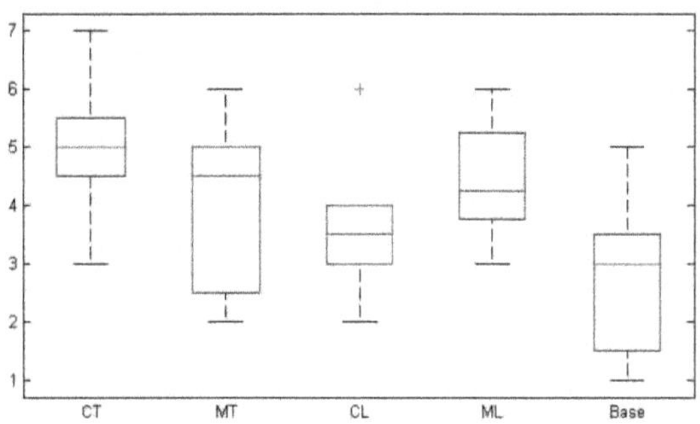

Figure 3. Closeness Rating Across Conditions

We divide all participants in each condition into a *close group* when their closeness rating is between 5 and 7 and the rest (1-4) into a *not-close group.* Figure 4 shows the number of participants falling in *close* and *not-close group* across all conditions. Applying a Fisher Exact Test, we found that the CT condition had significantly ($p < 0.05$) more participants in the *close* group than the *base* group. The same test on the other conditions (MT, ML) showed a trend toward closeness though not crossing the threshold for significance. The trend was not seen for the CL condition.

To take a closer look at how channels and expectations affect peoples's feeling of connectedness, we did a two-way ANOVA using channel and expectation as two variables and participants' closeness rating as dependent variable. The results suggest a possible main effect of Channel ($p < 0.3$)

Condition / Group	CT	MT	CL	ML	Base
Close	6	4	1	4	1
Not-close	2	4	7	4	7

Figure 4. Close Group and Not-Close Group Across Conditions

and a statistically significant interaction effect ($p < 0.05$). Figure 5 shows the interaction plot of channels and expectations. The X-axis shows two manipulations of expectation (*Communicative* vs *Measure*), and the Y-axis shows the rating of sense of closeness toward the storyteller. The red marked points are the means in the *Remote Touch* condition, and the blue marked points are the means in the *Flashing Light* condition.

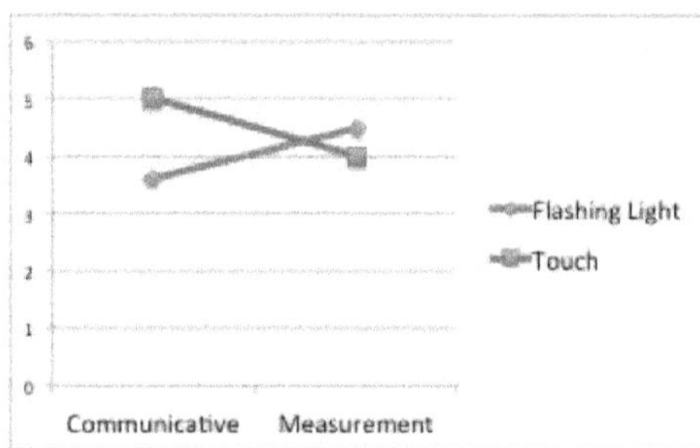

Figure 5. Interaction Plot of Channel and Expectation

Why do you feel close this way? We coded participants' answers to "Why do you feel close to the storyteller at this level" into five categories:

1. "The story is nice."
2. "The way she told story." and "The way she carries her emotion in her voice."
3. "Own personal experience makes me feel close."
4. "The squeeze feels like a personal physical contact and helps me visualize the activity." (Only in CT and MT)
5. "The flashing light makes me feel more about her feelings." (Only in CL and ML)
6. "Not much in common", and "I don't like her story."

Figure 6 shows how many participants's comments falls into each category across conditions. Note: participants may mention multiple categories in their comments.

We counted positive comments (Category 1 to 5) made by each participant and compared the number across conditions. Overall participants with additional channel made more the positive comments about the their feelings to the story and storyteller than participants in base conditions. And the number of positive comments in CT is significantly higher than the base condition ($p < 0.05$). Then we did two-way ANOVA by using channel and expectation as two variables and the

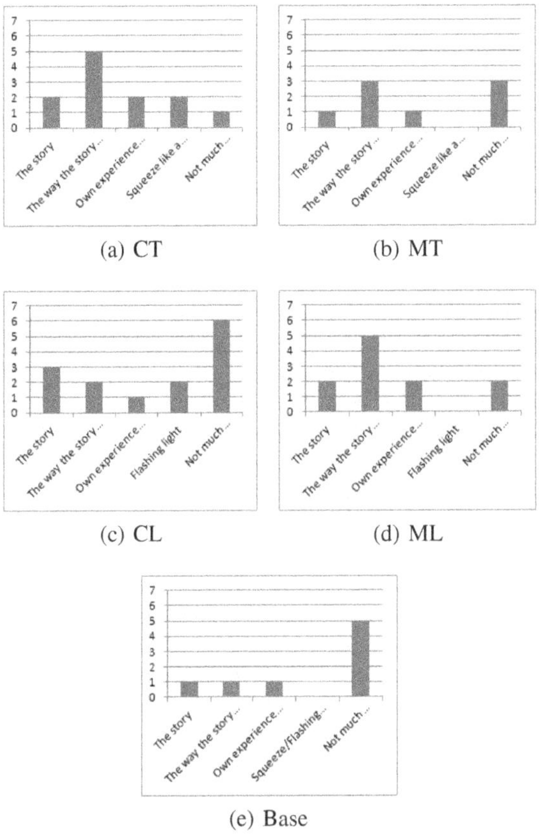

Figure 6. Comments on Closeness across conditions

number of positive comments made by each participant as dependent variable. We again found the significant interaction effect ($p < 0.05$).

We did the same analysis for negative comments (Category 6). The number of negative comments in different conditions shows the similar trend: $CT < ML < MT < CL$. Two-way ANOVA also shows the significant interaction effect ($p < 0.05$).

These analysis results based on participants' comments agree with what we find in their closeness ratings. It suggests strongly that communicative remote touch makes people feel more connected to the storyteller than the base condition. It also suggests that remote touch and flashing light have different characteristics in modulating people's sense of connectedness toward others: remote touch seems work better as a communicative channel while flashing light is more congruent as a measurement/signal channel.

Emotion Experience. We compared participants' emotion states before and after the story session using pre-PANAS and post-PANAS. Figure 7 shows the mood changes in negative emotions, positive emotions, sadness and joviality in different conditions. The negative emotion of participants in CT, MT and CL all showed a trend of reduction while there are not much changes in ML and Base conditions. There shows an increase of positive emotion in with-Touch conditions while there shows a trend of reduction of in ML and base conditions. There is not much change in positive emotion in CL condition. For sadness emotion, there are not much change across all conditions. There shows an increase in joviality in CT, MT, CL and Base condition while there is not much difference in ML.

We take the emotion brought out by the story in the base condition as a baseline. The results suggest that CT, MT and CL are sharing and enhancing similar emotion experience in negative emotions and joviality, that is the story about Stevie with a happy ending reduces the participants' negative emotions and increases their joviality.

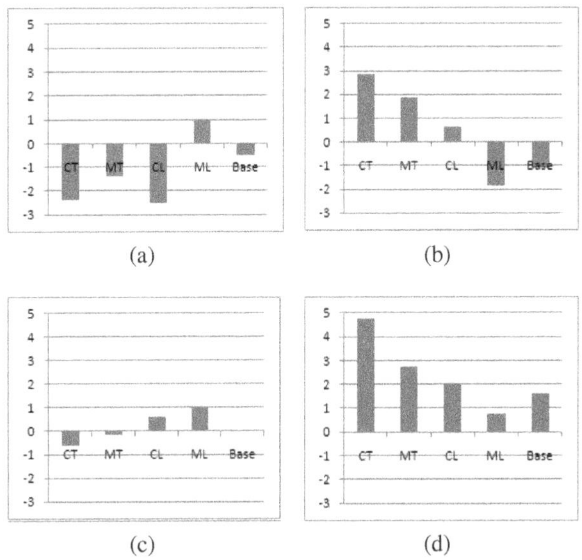

Figure 7. Emotion Experience Changes Across Conditions: (a) Changes in Negative Emotions, (b) Changes in Positive Emotions, (c) Changes in Sadness, (d) Changes in Joviality

Effects of Additional Channels. In the semi-structured interviews, we asked participants explicitly about the effects of remote pressure transmission or flashing light in their process of listening to the story. Our open-coding process yielded seven categories from our participant responses that may be summarized by the following seven statements.

1. "It coincides with my own feelings."
2. "I can understand why the pressure is applied or the light flashes happened most of the time."
3. "It feels like a physical contact." (Only for CT and MT.)
4. "It makes me more attentive."
5. "Not much effects." (Only showed in MT and ML)
6. "Not sure what it means/Trying to figure out", and "I don't understand." (Only showed in CT and CL)
7. "It is a distraction to me."

Figure 8 shows the number of participants from the different conditions that fall into each category. Note that because of the free-form nature of the comments, some participant responses can fall into multiple categories. There appeared to

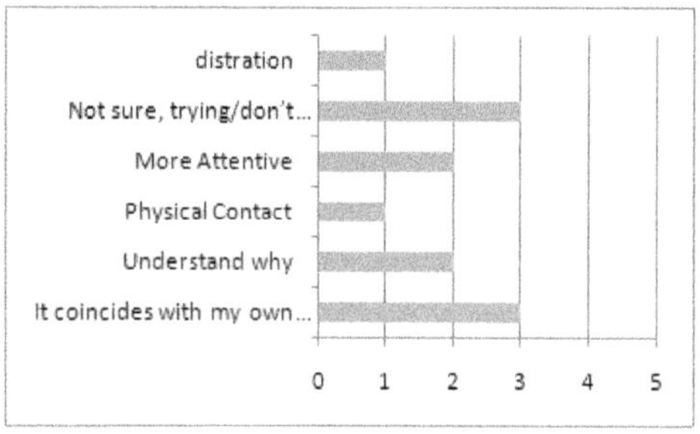

(a) CT

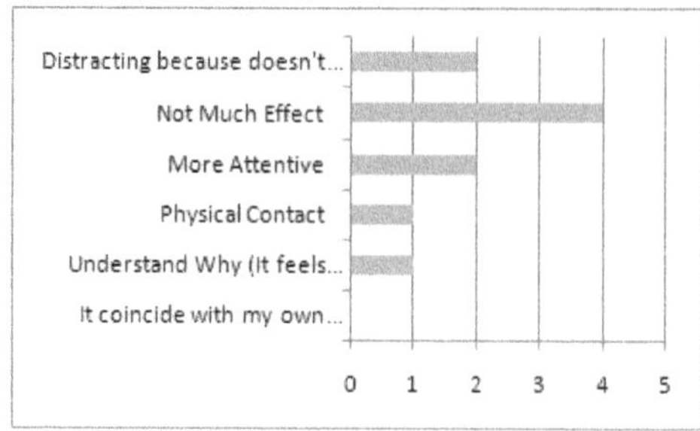

(b) MT

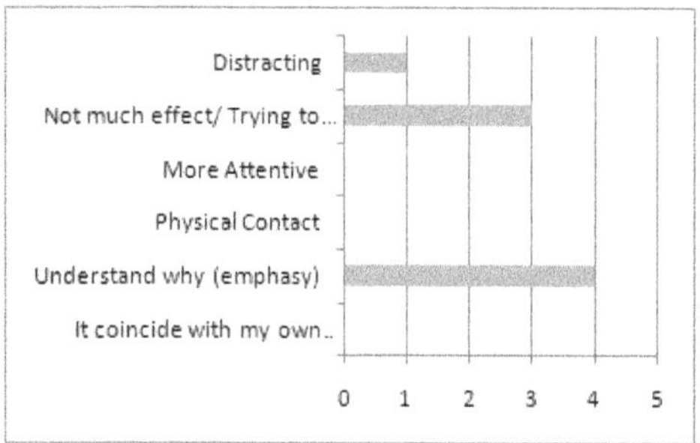

(c) CL

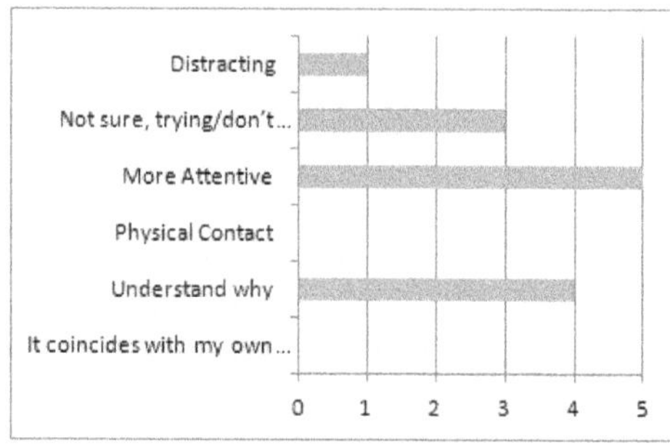

(d) ML

Figure 8. Effects of Additional Channel

be a subtle difference in viewpoint between participants in the *measurement* (MT and ML) conditions and the *communicative* (CT and CL) conditions. In the former, the comments appeared to take an 'observer's' perspective (e.g., "(Additional channel) does not have much effects on me,"), while participants in the latter conditions seemed to treat the additional channels as part of the 'communicative package' (e.g., "I am not sure what it (additional channel) means). I am trying to figure out."). This suggests that the participants accepted the cover story concerning the context of the additional channel – a measurement to interpret separately from the speech as opposed to a part of the communication to be understood.

DISCUSSION

Comparison Across Modalities

We first examine the difference between channels (remote touch vs flashing light).

***CT* vs *CL*.** As is shown in Figure 8(a) and Figure 8(c), participants seem more emotionally involved in CT than in CL. In CT, three out of eight participants in CT reported that the touch coincides with their own feeling or intensifies their feeling, while none in CL reported so. For example one participant in CT reported: "It makes me feel ... jump a little bit, kind of. Cause I already feel that. The squeeze intensified it. Kind of." And another participant stated: "I notice that it almost always squeeze when I got goose bumps. Almost always when I get goose bumps, I will get a squeeze. Or when I get a squeeze, and I get goose bumps. They are very close to each other. " Further, two participants in CT report that remote touch channel made them more attentive. One participant said that touch helped him to visualize the storyteller and her activity as a physical contact sitting across a coffee table. He stated: "The squeeze on my arm makes me feel like she sits very close to me... She is like sitting at the coffee table, squeezing my hand."

In contrast, no such comments were made by participants in the CL condition. Some participants in the CL condition, however, reported that they had a better understanding of the storyteller's feelings. Four participants report that although they did not feel similarly, they could understand why the storyteller may have squeezed the touch device at the particular junctures in the story.

This observation is supported by our *A Fisher Exact Test* results that show that CT participants felt a sense of closeness to the storyteller. CT participants also experienced a stronger trend toward reduction in negative emotions and an increase in joviality. This suggests that the CT condition invoked greater empathy toward the storyteller's perspective. In the CL condition, the participants may have an understanding of why the storyteller may have been emotionally moved by a story although the listener did not empathize with the feeling as much.

***MT* vs *ML*.** In this comparison, the expectation that the signal depicts a measurement is held constant, and the difference is only in modality (touch vs flashing light). Interestingly, more participants in the flashing light condition reported that they were more attentive than those in the touch condition (5 out of 8 in ML and 2 out of 8 in MT). We note that this is a slight reversal from the *communicative* context comparison. Also, more participants in the ML condition reported understanding the emotions of the storyteller than in the MT condition (4 out of 8 in ML and 1 out of 8 in MT) – See Figure 8(b) and 8(d) for these count.

We conjecture that this effect toward greater comprehension of emotional state and attention in the flashing light condition derives from the cultural experience of the participants in associating measured values with light indicators as opposed to touch. They were thus more facile in evaluating the measured signal as a light flash than as a touch.

Comparison Across Expectations (Context)

We proceed to examine the difference across expectations contrasting the effects of communicative intent with passive measurement.

***CT* vs *MT*.** As we described in previous session, participants in CT and MT listened to the same story recording and were touched in the exactly same point in the story. The only difference between CT and MT is their expectation of communicative intent. In the CT case, they expect the touch to be part of the communication produced by the storyteller, while in MT they believe that the touch is a signal measurement indicator. This seems to make a big difference in the reported effects of touch.

First, in CT 5 out of 8 participants report their feeling coincides with the storyteller or they can understand her feelings while no such experience of empathy found in the responses provided by participants in the CT condition. In only one case did a participant in the MT condition say that the correspondence between the touch and speech were intuitively correspondent ("it feels intuitive when the voice and touch matches"), and even in this case, the participant did not report empathy with the storyteller – only that she could understand the match.

Second, the majority of MT participants (6 out of 8) report that their feelings toward the story were not influenced by the touch, and some even said that the touch was distracting from the story. The majority of MT participants reported the touch confused or distracted them because the touch episodes did not correlate with their own emotion states or expectation. On the other hand only 3 out of 8 participants in CT reported they were trying to figure out the reason for the touches and one of them found "the touch is a little bit distracting" because of that.

One possible interpretation for the difference is in the way the multi-modal communication is experienced in a communicative context. In the CT condition, the participant believes that both speech and touch find their origin in the communicative intent of the storyteller. Hence, they interpret these as a single multimodal compound, in essence creating a single meaning from both channels. That is, they derive the meaning of the communication from both speech and touch simultaneously (i.e. $Speech + Touch = Meaning$). Hence, this single emotion-laden meaning has greater potency in inducing empathy in the recipient, and did not seem confusing, conflicting, or distracting.

In the MT condition, only the speech channel is part of the communicative package intended by the storyteller. The touch is a signal indicator that is to be reconciled to the meaning the participant experiences from the communicative stream. Using the same notation from our CT discussion, in this case $Speech = Meaning$, leaving the need to understand the measured mental state of the storyteller. Hence, the participants did not report empathy with the storyteller, and furthermore, the need to perform the added reconciliation step caused the participants to experience greater distraction and confusion.

This interpretation seems likely given our understanding of how speech and non-speech channels (like gesture, eye-gaze, and body posture) are fused in communication [9], and how the only difference between CT and MT is in the expectation of how touch is produced.

***CL* vs *ML*.** In this axis of comparison, we see a trend where ML resulted in a stronger sense of connectedness than CL. This is surprising since in the CL condition, the participant expects that the light signal is in response to the storyteller's communicative intent. Furthermore, participants in the ML condition reported that the light made them more attentive (5 out of 8), while none of the CL participants reported this effect.

We draw again on the notion that culturally, we are familiar with the associating of light indicators to measured signals to possibly explain this effect. Hence, the ML signal is easier to interpret than the CL situation, where the participant had to associate the flash with communicative intent.

We note, however, that all conditions with additional channels (CT, CL, MT, ML) resulted in a trend towards a greater sense of closeness to the storyteller than the *base* speech-only condition, although only the CT effect was significant. This may suggest that any additional signal indicating the emotional state of the speaker may influence the sense of closeness.

This result and interpretation are consistent with Chang et al's work in [5] and Kaye's work in [17], both of which used flashing light as an interface to increase the sense of connectedness between users.

As we found, the combination of *Speech + Communicative Touch* enhances the sense of connectedness significantly and also suggests a trend of greater emotional experience. More importantly, this is achieved when users experienced the communicative touch in an immediate "non-symbolic" way without pre-defined message coding-decoding process. We believe *Speech*, provided as a contextualizing channel for touch, plays a key role in retaining the capacity of touch in conveying sense of connectedness and affect in an immediate fashion. Without a contextualizing channel, users will tend to use the device to send messages with some kind of 'tactile Morse code' in order to 'give meaning' to the touch interaction [5]. This may severely compromise the immediacy of touch for affect conveyance.

CONCLUSION

In this paper we investigate how remote touch and contextual expectation in conjunction with speech influence people's empathy to the speaker. The results show that participants in *Speech + Communicative Touch* condition experienced the sense of connectedness toward the storyteller significantly higher than that in *Speech Only* condition though participants in all *with-additional-channel* conditions experienced the similar trend in varying degrees. Participants using *Communicative Touch* also showed a stronger trend of an increase in joviality and reduction in negative emotions.

ACKNOWLEDGE

This project has been partially supported by NSF grant CNS-0551610 "Interfaces for the Embodied Mind", Center for Human Computer Interaction at Virginia Tech, and the Singapore NSF International Research Centre at Singapore Funding Initiative. We thank Steve Harrison for his insightful discussions and our subjects for their participation.

REFERENCES

1. Bailenson, J. N., Yee, N., Brave, S., Merget, D., and Koslow, D. Virtual interpersonal touch: Expressing and recognizing emotions through haptic devices. *Human Computer Interaction 22*, 3 (2007), 325–353.
2. Brave, S., and Dahley, A. intouch: a medium for haptic interpersonal communication. In *CHI97*, 363–364.
3. Brossard, L., and Decarie, T. Comparative reinforcing effects of eight stimulations on the smiling responses of infants. *J. Child Psych. & Psychiatry 9* (1968), 51–60.
4. Chang, A., O'Modhrain, S., Jacob, R., Gunther, E., and Ishii, H. Comtouch: Design of a vibrotactile communication device. In *DIS'2002*.
5. Chang, A., Resner, B., Koerner, B., Wang, X., and Ishii, H. Lumitouch: an emotional communication device. In *CHI'2001*.
6. Clynes, M. *Sentics: The Touch of Emotions*, 1st edition ed. Anckor Press/DoubleDay, Garden City, New York, 1977.
7. DiSalvo, C., Gemperle, F., Forlizzi, J., and Montgomery, E. The hug: an exploration of robotic form for intimate communication. In *IEEE Wksp on Robot & Hum. Int. Comm.* (2003).
8. Geldard, F. Some neglected possibilities of communication. *Science 131* (1960), 1583–1588.
9. Goldin-Meadow, S. *Hearing Gesture: How our hands help us think.* Belknap Press, 2003.
10. Haans, A., and Ijsselsteijn, W. Mediated social touch: A review of current research and future directions. *Virtual Reality 9* (2006), 149–159.
11. Haans, A., IJsselsteijn, W. A., Graus, M. P., and Salminen, J. A. The virtual midas touch: helping behavior after a mediated social touch. In *CHI '08 extended abstracts*, 3507–3512.
12. Haans, A., Nood, C. d., and IJsselsteijn, W. A. Investigating response similarities between real and mediated social touch: a first test. In *CHI '07 extended abstracts*.
13. Harris, R. B., and Paradice, D. An investigation of the computer-mediated communication of emotions. *J. Applied Sciences Res. 3*, 12 (2007), 2081–2090.
14. Hertenstein, M. J. Touch: Its communicative functions in infancy. *HUMAN DEVELOPMENT 45* (2002), 70–94.
15. Hertenstein, M. J., Holmes, R., McCullough, M., and Keltner, D. The communication of emotion via touch. *Emotion 9*, 4 (2009), 566–573.
16. Jones, S. E., and Yarbrough, A. E. A naturalistic study of the meanings of touch. *Communication monographs 52* (1985).
17. Kaye, J. J. I just clicked to say i love you: rich evaluations of minimal communication. In *CHI '06 extended abstracts*.
18. Knapp, M. L. Hall, J. A. *Nonverbal communication in human interaction*. Fort Worth, TX: Harcourt Brace College Publishers, 1997.
19. Mueller, F., Vetere, F., Gibbs, M., Kjedskov, J., Pedell, S., and Howard, S. Hug over a distance. In *CHI' 05 Extended Abstracts*.
20. Riva, G. The sociocognitive psychology of computer-mediated communication: The present and future of technology-based interactions. *Cyberpsychology & Behavior 5*, 6 (2002), 581–598.
21. Rovers, A. F., and van Essen, H. Him: A framework for haptic instant messaging. In *CHI '2004*.
22. Rovers, A. F., and van Essen, H. A. a. Guidelines for haptic interpersonal communication applications: an exploration of foot interaction styles. *Virtual Reality 9*, 2 (2006), 177–191.
23. Stack, D. M., Bremner, G., and Fogel, A. The salience of touch and physical contact during infancy: Unraveling some of the mysteries of the somesthetic sense. In *Blackwell handbook of infant development.* Blackwell Publishing, Malden, MA US, 2001, 351–378.
24. Wang, R., and Quek, F. Touch & talk: contextualizing remote touch for affective interaction. In *Pro. 4th Int'l Conf. on Tangible, Embedded, & Embodied Interaction*, TEI '10, ACM, 13–20.
25. Wang, R., Quek, F., Teh, J. K. S., Cheok, A. D., and Lai, S. R. Design and evaluation of a wearable remote social touch device. In *Int'l Conf. on Multimodal Int. & the Wksp on Machine Learning for Multimodal Int.*, ICMI-MLMI '10, ACM, 45:1–45:4.
26. Watson, D., and Clark, L. A. The panas-x: Positive and negative affect schedule-expanded form, 1994.
27. Weiss, S. J. Measurement of the sensory qualities in tactile interaction. *Nursing Res. 41*, 2 (1992), 82–86.
28. Wolff, P. *Observations on the early development of smiling*. London: Methuen & Co, 1963, ch. Determinant of infant behavior II, 113 – 138.

TAP & PLAY: An End-User Toolkit for Authoring Interactive Pen and Paper Language Activities

Anne Marie Piper, Nadir Weibel, James D. Hollan
Distributed Cognition and Human-Computer Interaction Lab
Department of Cognitive Science, University of California, San Diego
9500 Gilman Dr., La Jolla, CA 92093-0515
{apiper, weibel, hollan}@ucsd.edu

ABSTRACT
Hybrid paper-digital interfaces are a promising approach for supporting language activities. The familiarity of pen and paper makes it a particularly attractive media for many user groups, including young children. Digital pens enhance interaction with traditional paper content by playing and recording audio and recognizing handwriting and gestures. Currently, generating custom interactive paper documents involves some programming, limiting its use by many user groups (e.g., educators and families) who might especially benefit from application of hybrid paper-digital interfaces in their practices. To address this need, we developed an end-user Toolkit for Authoring Pen and Paper Language Activities (TAP & PLAY). This paper describes the iterative development of the toolkit, its accessibility for novice non-technical users, and use in three different contexts for early language learning. We demonstrate and document the system's usability, generality, and utility for people who want to create and tailor their own custom interactive paper-based language activities.

Author Keywords
Children; Digital Pen; End-User Authoring Toolkit; Language Activities; Learning

ACM Classification Keywords
H.5.2 User Interfaces: Input Devices and Strategies

General Terms
Design; Human Factors

INTRODUCTION
Even after all the advances in computer interface design, modern computers can be difficult to use or inappropriate for some tasks. Pen with paper, in contrast, is a familiar, flexible, and pervasive interface. Hybrid paper-digital interfaces enabled by digital pens (e.g., Anoto[1]) bridge the simplicity of pen and paper interaction with the processing, memory, and multimodal input/output capabilities of a computer. Digital pen technology has been introduced into a variety of contexts (e.g., [10, 25, 20]) and as commercial products (Livescribe[2], LeapFrog Tag[3]). However, creating interactive paper-based content requires programming expertise and access to complex software development toolkits. This paper introduces TAP & PLAY, a pen-based interface for authoring interactive paper materials. It enables non-technical end-users to independently create custom paper materials that work with a Livescribe digital pen. TAP & PLAY could support many applications, but here we document its use for authoring language learning activities.

Many language learning activities are paper-based and may benefit from the capabilities of digital pens. Language development for young children often involves parents and teachers reading picture books with them. Early childhood education classrooms have words written on paper posted around the instructional space. Walls are filled with printed posters, children's artwork, and early writing samples. These materials could be augmented with sounds or audio content. The audio recording and playback facilities of digital pens could also capture audio descriptions by children who are unable to write. When children do learn to write, pencil on paper is often the first interface they use. Digital pens could provide guidance and foster independence in writing. Similarly, digital pen technology promises to benefit foreign language learning goals such as improving auditory comprehension and pronunciation. Moreover, the ability to dynamically record, replay, and archive audio content as well as the history of interaction that reflects a student's progress provides a new data collection facility for language instruction.

While there are many language-based computer programs for children (i.e., for phones, tablets, and desktop computers), there is a need to explore early learning experiences that might be best supported by paper materials. This paper presents the development and refinement of an end-user toolkit for authoring interactive paper materials. In addition to rapid iterative testing with 10 users, we deployed this toolkit in three contexts with over 70 users from age three to 61. Our data indicate that the toolkit is both easy to use and useful for a variety of language and communication activities.

[1] http://www.anoto.com
[2] http://www.livescribe.com
[3] http://www.leapfrog.com

RELATED WORK

Paper is a flexible medium with many affordances not supported by current digital systems [18, 8, 9, 11]. The idea of linking paper documents with a digital system has been investigated in numerous research projects, including Wellner's Digital Desk [24], MacKay's A-Book [10], and the Audio Notebook [21]. More recently, digital pen and paper technology has been explored for scenarios such as document editing [3], linking handwritten and audio notes [2], text processing [23], PowerPoint presentations [19], field and laboratory scientific notebooks [25, 22], and collaborative annotations [20]. Oviatt et al. [15, 13] describe the challenges and opportunities for multimodal digital pen and paper systems.

Commercial versions of digital pen technology enable mainstream use of pen-based systems for education. The Livescribe[2] pen supports linking handwritten notes with audio content and is marketed as a study aid. LeapFrog developed several versions of a digital pen for language and literacy development, including the Tag (ages 4-8), Tag Junior (age 2-4), and FLY Pentop Computer (age 10-13)[3]. Several researchers have examined digital pen technology for math learning [14, 5], but relatively little research explores the potential of digital pen technology for a broader class of language development and communication activities.

One challenge is that educational content provided by commercial digital pens (e.g., LeapFrog) is static and not customizable. Several toolkits have been developed to support hybrid paper-digital interaction and to help developers build custom pen and paper applications [26, 4, 12]. Commercial digital pen products by Anoto and Livescribe also have software development toolkits. However, using these toolkits requires programming experience and therefore development of custom applications remains inaccessible to many user groups who may know how to best exploit digital pens.

This paper introduces a general end-user toolkit for authoring interactive paper materials. As with other prototyping toolkits (e.g., [6, 7]), TAP & PLAY enables rapid creation of custom user interfaces. The software allows dynamic linking and reassigning of various regions of paper with a variety of audio resources. TAP & PLAY is also a physical toolkit in that the system allows facile coupling of digital interactions with a variety of paper and physical materials. TAP & PLAY extends the earlier work of Piper et. al. [17] on a toolkit specifically tailored for therapists working with older adults with aphasia. The motivation for an end-user authoring toolkit arose during a year-long field study of speech-language therapy involving older adults with aphasia [16]. We extend this prior work in three ways: (1) we describe the iterative development of a general end-user authoring toolkit, (2) we evaluate and improve the usability of the toolkit through rapid iterative user testing, and (3) we examine the toolkit's generality and flexibility by deploying it in three real-world contexts.

SYSTEM DESIGN

TAP & PLAY is an application that runs on Livescribe digital pens. These pens integrate a processor, memory, and an infrared camera into what appears to be a normal pen. They exploit Anoto's digital pen technology to interpret a unique dot-pattern printed on standard paper. By decoding the printed pattern, the device can track its exact position on paper in real-time. Unique to the Livescribe pen is a built-in speaker, microphone, and OLED display. TAP & PLAY allows users to create interactive regions on dot-patterned paper and program them with a combination of the three basic interactions supported by Livescribe digital pens: (1) audio recording, (2) audio playback, and (3) handwriting recognition. By exploiting this functionality, TAP & PLAY supports creation of custom multimodal applications for specific user populations. TAP & PLAY is designed for two categories of users: *content authors* who use the digital pen to create a pen and paper application, and *content users* who use the developed materials for their specific needs. Authoring multimodal content with TAP & PLAY is completely paper-based and does not require access to traditional software development environments or a separate computer. Instead, content authors "program" the pen and paper materials using a special paper-based authoring interface we have developed.

Programming Multimodal Interactions

The authoring interface consists of paper-based control panels that enable the creation of multimodal interactive paper regions. Authors can use any kind of Livescribe dot-patterned paper and assign particular interactions to specific regions of a page. Interacting with a paper region with the digital pen can initiate the playback of audio that has been previously recorded or that is stored in the pen's sound library (e.g. animal sounds, traffic noises), can start the recording of the user's speech, or can enable the recognition of their handwriting. Figure 1 shows the TAP & PLAY control panels. Figure 2 illustrates the process of creating an interactive region

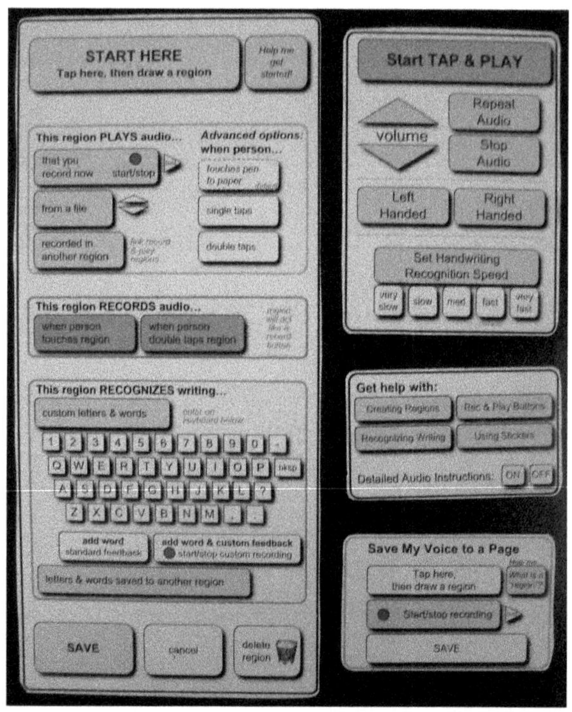

Figure 1. ***Clockwise from top left:*** **main control panel for authoring, general interface controls, help buttons, and quick custom audio widget.**

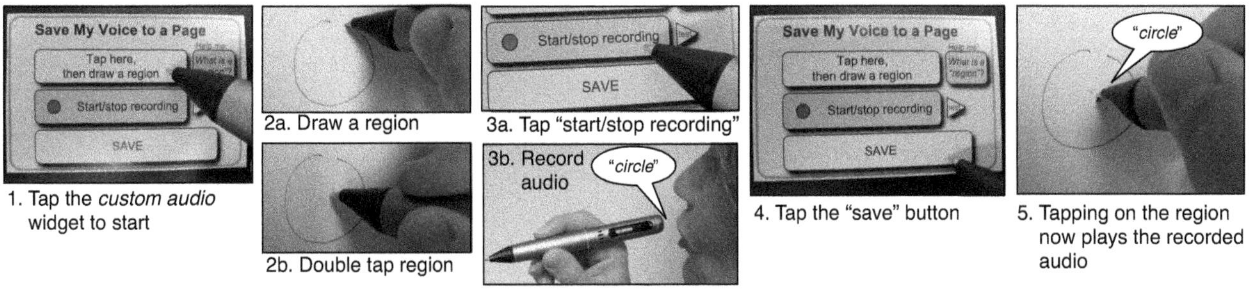

Figure 2. The quick custom audio widget allows users to quickly and easily record speech and save it to any paper with the Livescribe dot pattern.

with the *quick custom audio* widget. Additionally, a panel of help buttons (Fig. 1, right-middle) provide supplementary audio instructions for novice authors, and a general interface controls pen settings such as volume, left- vs. right-handed usage, and handwriting recognition speed (Fig. 1, right-top).

Content authors use the pen to tap on the control panels and TAP & PLAY guides them through the authoring process (experienced authors can disable detailed audio prompts). The largest control panel (Fig. 1, left) is the full-featured interface for authoring materials. This control panel allows authors to create playback regions, record regions, and handwriting recognition regions. After defining a new region by drawing it on paper, the main control panel can be used to add the specific interactions and content.

Interactive regions can be layered on top of each other, with the upper regions redefining a specific subregion with different interactions. Also, layering can be achieved by pen-based interactions. Authors can decide to activate specific interactions on *pen-down* (when the pen touches the paper interface), on *single tap* (when the pen taps the paper and then is lifted) or on *double tap*. Observations of an early toolkit [17] indicate that recording audio and saving it to a page was the most frequently used facility. Based on this, we created the *quick custom audio* widget (Fig. 1, right-bottom; Fig. 2) to enable rapid definition of regions that play back recorded speech.

Paper Materials

One distinctive advantage of paper is that it can be manipulated and shaped in many ways. Thus, since user interfaces developed with TAP & PLAY use traditional paper, they can be cut up and glued or taped together or to other objects. Since we wanted to emphasize this unique affordance, we made available a range of paper-based materials with the Livescribe dot pattern. TAP & PLAY works on standard Livescribe notebooks, printed pages, cardboard, stickers (varying sizes and transparency), magnetic paper, post-it notes, and more (as shown in Fig. 3). Authors can use these materials to create hand-drawn paper-digital applications or can print on top of them as they would do with any other paper material.

RAPID ITERATIVE PROTOTYPE REVIEW

A central design goal for TAP & PLAY is to help novice users, particularly people who do not know how to program, quickly figure out how to use the pen-based interface and begin authoring their own multimodal documents. Because we are designing the system to broaden access to pen and paper technology, it must therefore be quick and easy to use by people with diverse backgrounds and without requiring technical programming expertise. The questions we addressed during the initial phase of research include:

- Do users without digital pen experience understand the idea of a pen-and-paper-based interface?
- Can users quickly determine how to get started authoring their own paper documents?
- Is the basic functionality of the system (creating play, record, and handwriting recognition regions) easy to use?
- Do the audio and text prompts provide clear and sufficient support for navigating the system?

We conducted iterative prototype testing with 10 users (age 20-61, mean=37.5, stdev=15.4) to address these questions. Each participant used TAP & PLAY individually. We video recorded each evaluation session, noted points of confusion and areas for improvement, and logged all interactions on the pen. None of the users had experience with digital pen technology prior to this study. Participants held diverse occupations, including a lawyer, social worker, therapist, elementary school teacher, medical equipment salesperson, non-profit fundraiser, and university students. Only one of the ten participants had any programming experience.

As part of the rapid iterative prototype review we dynamically made adjustments to the user interface layout, workflow for authoring, and cueing presented via the pen's audio speaker and OLED display. Our goal was to iteratively refine the prototype based on user data to quickly achieve a usable design before beginning evaluation in specific application domains. The flexibility of a paper-based control panel and the software we have developed allowed us to rapidly update the system to

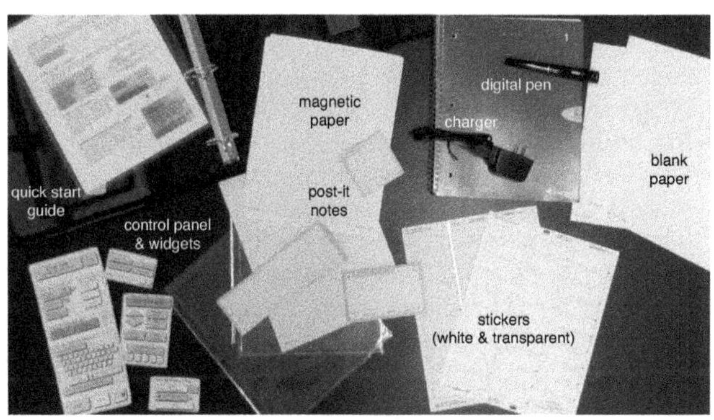

Figure 3. TAP & PLAY material set.

Context of Deployment	Content Designed For	Content Authors	Content Users	Deployment Length
Early childhood education	Young children in classes of 25 (age 3-5)	Teachers & assistant teachers (19)	37 (age 3-5)	11 weeks
Home language activities	Individual children at home (age 3-5)	Parents & grandparents (4)	2 (age 3-4)	6 weeks
Language tutoring	Foreign language students (age 3-65)	Adult instructor (1)	8 (age 3-9)	8 weeks
Total		*24*	*47*	

Table 1. Participants involved in field deployment of TAP & PLAY. Content authors created content with TAP & PLAY. Content Users are the groups who used the custom materials created by the authors.

reflect feedback from users. In some testing sessions, updates were made on-the-spot in collaboration with the user. Participants cut up the paper control panel and reconfigured it to reflect their expectations of the workflow. Similarly, researchers and participants collaboratively crossed out and relabeled buttons and prompts to evolve designs.

Findings and Design Iteration

Getting started was the most salient challenge for users. Some participants (P1-P5) took approximately 20-25 minutes to learn basic functionality of authoring their own interactive paper documents. These users spent at least five minutes trying to understand the idea of authoring interactive paper and how to get started with the toolkit. One initial challenge is that users must first understand interaction with a digital pen, including how the pen detects its position on paper printed with the dot pattern, how to attend to cues provided by the pen's speaker and OLED display, and how to tap the pen on paper-based buttons and widgets. A second challenge is to understand how to program the pen with the paper-based user interface to generate their own interactive documents. Programming with TAP & PLAY is a multistep process with several decision points. Moreover, the idea of "programming" pen and paper to perform specific interactions is an unfamiliar concept. Several users were intimidated by the idea of programming the pen with TAP & PLAY. One participant said, "I can use a regular computer, but this I'm not so good at." Even before starting, at least six participants mentioned that they were not good at this sort of activity.

Partway through the evaluation (after P5), we realized that the key to getting users started quickly and easily is to have them focus first on the *quick custom audio* widget. This presents the idea of authoring interactive paper in a clear and concise way. For participants 6-10, we first showed them the *quick custom audio* widget. These participants rapidly acquired the concept of authoring interactive paper documents and were able to program the pen to perform basic functions within 10 minutes. This finding informs how we introduce the system in the contextual evaluations described below.

We also addressed the challenge of getting started by adding a large "start here" button to direct users' attention to the starting point as well as a "help me get started" audio help button. In addition, we created supplementary paper materials (e.g., a tips and hints page) to support initial learning. One user said, "I'd want a user manual to give me instructions." Another person commented, "It's easy to navigate but you still need something to read like a manual." Throughout the user testing we noted the places where users needed additional audio cueing and iterated our design to provide needed support. The system now provides a setting for detailed versus minimal audio instructions depending on user needs.

We made several design modifications to streamline the authoring process. In an early toolkit version, users were required to enter an "edit mode" to start authoring content. We removed the need for modes and now with four steps (achievable through both the full control panel and the custom audio widget) a user can program the pen to play custom audio when a specific region is tapped. We improved the color-coding and layout of the control panel to enhance readability. Iterative prototype testing allowed us to improve the navigation, layout, workflow, and help facilities provided by TAP & PLAY. The resulting usability of the system is documented below, based on use by more than 70 people in field deployments.

CONTEXTUAL EVALUATIONS

Following the rapid iterative prototype review, we wanted to understand how well the system supports a variety of language activities. We conducted field deployments to address the following questions:

- Are users within different educational contexts (schools, homes) able to integrate the system into their practices?
- Do they use the system in meaningful ways?
- Does the system address important language and communication needs for each user group?

We deployed the TAP & PLAY system with: four groups of early childhood education teachers, two families for home use, and one foreign language instructor. We focused on educational scenarios that involve young children. This complements prior work on digital pens for older adult language rehabilitation [16, 17]. Table 1 summarizes participants. Each group received their own Livescribe pen loaded with TAP & PLAY and a binder with various paper materials printed with the dot pattern (see Fig. 3).

The research team introduced the toolkit to participants and video recorded them learning to use the system. Based on what we learned in our early prototype testing, we introduced the idea of authoring interactive documents by using the *quick custom audio* widget. Our evaluation of the field deployments is primarily qualitative, including field notes detailing system use and the environment, video data of teachers and children using the system, still images capturing the applications end-users created, and interviews describing challenges and opportunities for the system by all people involved. We transcribed interviews and categorized observational data, photos, and video recordings to identify high-level themes. Raw data is presented in quotes whereas our observations and interpretations are reported directly in the text.

Context 1: Early Childhood Education Classrooms

We deployed TAP & PLAY with teachers and teaching assistants (n=19) in four early childhood education classrooms.

Figure 4. Three children (age 4-5) reading interactive books with TAP & PLAY.[5]

Two classes have three to four year old children and the other two classes have four to five year old children. Our research team introduced TAP & PLAY to the four lead teachers in a group setting. The lead teachers then introduced the toolkit to their larger group of assistant teachers.

Adding audio content to books

A basic activity that most teachers created involved programming interactive stickers to read or play sounds associated with parts of a book. Some of the teachers recorded part of the story read aloud or questions about the story and attached the stickers to the corresponding pages of the book. Children independently used the pen to listen to the story (see Fig 4).

Commenting on this activity, one teacher said, "They pick it up so fast, it is incredible. It was really, really easy for them, from the beginning." She also commented on how the children were fascinated by the pen when it started to interact with them, "The book, you know, asks them questions, and they were responding to the pen. First they looked at me when it started talking, they said, 'It's magic!'" She also compared this to her observations of how her students typically read a book, get bored quickly, and want to switch to another activity. She explained, "They wanted to read the same book over and over again, which is really rare. They kept asking, 'Can I do it again, can I try it again?' Usually they don't read the book, they just flip through the pages and whoop it's over."

Teachers were pleased by the autonomy that students demonstrated with this activity. This same teacher said, "I really like it. You don't need an adult to always be there. All I had to say was, 'so this pen... if you tap on a rectangle, it will talk to you.' And then I opened a page and asked them, 'do you see another one?' And they just right away knew exactly what to do." She also commented, "I think [this activity] was really successful because they can be by themselves and still learn without someone standing over them the whole time and reading everything." Another teacher used this approach as an independent reading activity for non-native English speakers. She said, "I have a couple children who don't speak English fluently. They can just pick up this book, tap on it, and try to follow along with the words, which is another way for them to learn English."

Linking a child's speech with books and art

Several teachers mentioned the challenge of capturing and documenting a child's comments. One teacher said, "It's hard to write as fast as they are speaking, so sometimes we get close enough but it's not their exact words." To solve this problem, teachers in one classroom setup an activity that had children add audio comments to various books and pieces of art. One teacher (see Fig. 5) asked two students (age 3-4) about a book. As they described the contents of a page and answered his questions, he recorded their voices and linked it to the book using interactive stickers. The students were able to independently tap on stickers within the book and listen to their answers.

[5]All participants (parents on behalf of children) consented to the use of photos for publication.

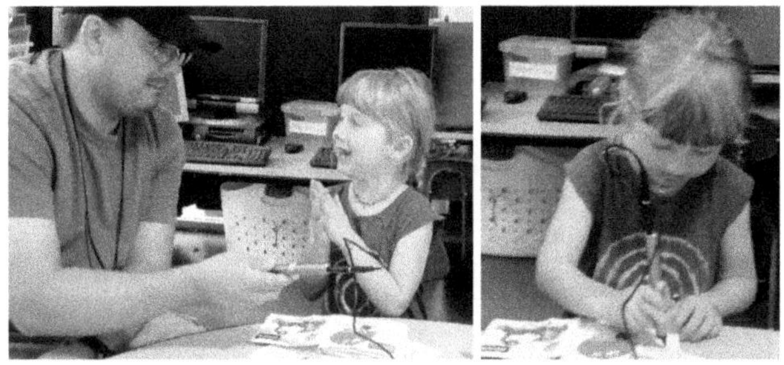

Figure 5. Teacher asks a child (age 4) questions about a book. He records her answers using an interactive sticker. The student listens to her answers by tapping the stickers in the book.

This teacher said, "You could use just like a regular recorder but you have nothing to attach it to. So this is nice to be able to attach it to the picture directly." He continued, "The parents like to hear their children talk about the pictures versus us talk to them about their pictures. So it's nice to be able to hear their children speak about [the pictures]." Several days later another teacher in this classroom also implemented this idea. She had students describe their artwork and recorded their descriptions using TAP & PLAY. She added an interactive sticker to each drawing and observed as the children listened to their narrations (Fig. 6).

Figure 6. Students (age 3) record and replay descriptions of artwork.

Sign language learning

One of the teachers was interested in how TAP & PLAY might support sign language learning. Initially she was skeptical about how well her students (age 4-5) would be able to learn sign language, but knowing about the success of TAP & PLAY in other settings, she decided to give it a try. She used a pre-existing poster showing different letters of the alphabet and the associated signs. She then attached stickers to each letter and recorded the name of the letter, it's phonetic sound, and an example of a word starting with this letter. By using TAP & PLAY and the interactive sign language poster (Fig. 7) she created, children were able to independently practice the signs for letters of the alphabet.

Figure 7. A student (age 4) practices sign language letters with the help of TAP & PLAY .

The teacher explained that the pen helped in a different way than other tools she has used in the past, such as an alphabet song and a person showing signs for the letters. She said, "They can do it on their own, they can go back, you know. With the song it just keeps going." She continued, "There are books, but the meaning of the sign is written and they still can't read." Finally, she mentioned ideas for expanding this activity, "You don't have to do just the alphabet, you can do it also with actual signs and kind of teach them little sentences." A similar activity was created by another teacher. She printed words and signs on dot pattern paper and then recorded the spoken meaning. Children could use these word cards as reference when writing or rearrange them to create interactive sentences.

English-Spanish dictionary

In several of the classes, Spanish is taught on a regular basis. One of the Spanish teachers decided to use TAP & PLAY as part of her daily Spanish activity. Most of the children using TAP & PLAY (age 3-4) already had Spanish in the past as part of the school curriculum, and they have been exposed to basic vocabulary (e.g., animals, vehicles, colors, and clothes). The teacher wanted to consolidate the words she was teaching them to create a stronger connection between the English and Spanish words. She used blank letter-sized Livescribe pages and cut-outs from old books to create an interactive and multimodal English-Spanish dictionary for the children (Fig. 8). Each page contained images of objects beginning with a certain letter in English. The teacher wrote the English and Spanish name next to each image. Tapping on the words written in English or Spanish plays that word aloud.

Children primarily interacted with the application in small groups of two or three, sometimes with the supervision of the teacher, sometimes by themselves. They used the pen naturally, continuously switching between English and Spanish, and often repeating words aloud after listening to the pen's recording. When asked about the Spanish translation of a particular word, they instantly tapped the pen on the correct translation. One child who was not participating in the session grabbed a *normal* pen from the table and started to tap on objects and on the patterned pages expecting it to work as the TAP & PLAY pen. The children used the digital pen and materials in a playful, game-like manner. The activity appeared fun for the children, as many smiled and laughed as they used the interactive dictionary.

Figure 8. Spanish-English class with TAP & PLAY. Children are interacting with the pen supervised by a teacher (left) or by themselves (center). *Right:* an example of one page of the English-Spanish dictionary.

The Spanish teacher was pleased by how the children took to this activity. She commented on one student, "She was so into the pen. She was repeating every single word. This is rare." In general, children liked the pen because "it is fun" and "it makes sound." One of them said, "It's cool. When it is stops for a long time, I'll make it go again." TAP & PLAY was also able to keep the children focused on the Spanish activity for longer than usual. The teacher commented, "You can see the attention span... Some of the children really have a hard time staying focused, and this helps." She continued, "Usually we just tell them a story, spelling one word first in English and then in Spanish, so they can relate. TAP & PLAY allowed us to continue working in the same way, having them relate the Spanish with the English directly."

Context 2: Home Language Activities

With two of the children from the Early Child Education Center, we followed up on the usage of TAP & PLAY in a home setting with their parents and grandparents. Both children speak multiple languages; English and Spanish at school and one or more other languages at home. After observing the use of TAP & PLAY for foreign language learning in school, we decided to explore how the toolkit might support language activities at home.

Audio Memory

One of the two children (age 4) is bilingual (English and Italian) and sometimes has difficulties spelling words in the two languages due to different vowel pronunciation. For example, the letter 'a' is often pronounced *æ* in English and *a* in Italian, while the letter 'e' is pronounced *i* in English and *ε* in Italian[6], causing some confusion.

In order to introduce new words and work on their pronunciation in Italian, the grandmother (age 61) created an audio version of a well-known memory game (see Fig. 9). She prepared a set of interactive cards using cardboard paper imprinted with the Livescribe pattern on one side and a sticker on the other side. The grandmother recorded pairs of cards as follows: one card plays an animal sound (from the library of pre-recorded sounds that came with TAP & PLAY), while the other card plays a question such as "I am a dog. What sound do I make?" The child tapped the pen on different cards to find pairs. After finding a match, the child turned over the cards and listened to the pronunciation of the word. The grandmother asked her to repeat the word and find two other words that started with the same letter from the set of picture cards that she prepared (Fig. 9, right).

[6]Using the standard International Phonetic Alphabet (IPA).

Figure 9. ***Left*****: four-year-old child playing "Audio Memory" with her grandmother.** ***Right*****: interactive cards used as part of the game.**

The activity was challenging at first. An audio-only memory game that does not have pictorial cues resulted in a much more difficult activity that the grandmother anticipated. "Since they are plain paper cards, I could separate the questions on the right and the animal sounds on the left, and easily change the rules of the game, since it was too difficult for her," she commented, "but she did great and she could easily use the pen to listen multiple times to the recorded content." The grandmother explained her ideas for evolving this activity: "Instead of having me listening to her pronunciation and checking if she found the right words directly with her, in the future I could add a *record button* and have her record this by herself, without needing my presence during the game, but only afterwards to check the answers."

Interactive home games

The second family was a multi-ethnic family living in the United States but with roots in Italy, France, and Portugal. Their daughter has contact with family members all over the world and is therefore exposed to many different languages (two at school plus three at home). The parents created a set of games exploring different aspects of language and geography. They created three distinct games, by exploiting existing materials and attaching stickers, or by using the provided Livescribe notebook in combination with paper materials that they cut from a book. Figure 10 shows the materials they created and the child playing two of the games with her mother.

Figure 10. Interactive home games. ***Top*****: the child (age 3) playing the** ***spell by listening*** **game (left) and the** ***family map*** **game (right) with her mother.** ***Bottom*****: a collection of games created with TAP & PLAY.**

The parents first augmented an existing game that involved dice with letters on each face paired with a set of cards showing objects and their spelling in English (see Fig. 10, top-left). With only the object on the card visible, children had to arrange the dice to spell the word on the card. On the sides of the dice, the parents attached a sticker and recorded the sound of each letter. The daughter used the pen to explore letter sounds and arrange the dice into words. When she wanted to check her spelling, she could tap on a sticker on the card and listen to the word read and spelled aloud.

The second activity (Fig. 10, top-right) involved finding the location of different friends and family members on a world map. The parents prepared interactive arrows by cutting up livescribe sticky paper and attaching it to different locations on the map. For each arrow, the parents recorded the names of people living in that place. The daughter tapped on the arrows and listened to the recording to find out who lived where.

The family also used the Livescribe notebook to create a picture-audio trivia game, in which they could ask a question such as, "I am warm and bright, I come in the morning and go at night. Who am I?" The daughter listened to the prompt and then selected one of four images. She was able to check her answer by tapping the sticker that was attached to the image (Fig. 10, bottom).

The parents commented on their daughter's interest in the games. The father said, "She was much more engaged. She saw that she had a voice and there was an opportunity for her to actually give the answer. She felt like she was on her own in front of the game." He also mentioned, "Normally, if we are there she wants us to help. Instead here was the pen that was helping, so that allowed her to be more independent." While the child responded well to all of the games, the father commented on the map game in particular: "This was an absolute success for her, and we really enjoyed it... She liked the fact that the map was big. She could locate where the people were very easily." In terms of learning, her father said, "It was amazing how excited she was to discover friends and family in different places by listening to their names. She really made the connection between the location and the people living there, and this is because of the link between the image and the audio."

Finally, the father stressed the range of activities that TAP & PLAY supports: "Possibilities are countless, there is no limit apart of your own imagination. With other educational toys like the LeapFrog ones... you can't change the games." He said, "With TAP & PLAY you spend time planning and you think about how the child is going to react. You also tailor it to the specific likes of the child. It is really good for both the child and the parent, for establishing the link between the two. In the end you spend more time together."

Context 3: Supporting Foreign Language Learning

To further understand the potential of TAP & PLAY to aid foreign language learning, we deployed the toolkit with an Italian language teacher who works with students (age 3-65) learning the language to communicate with distant family members or to be able to read and speak while traveling. Teaching activities are typically structured as individual tutoring sessions or as interactive group sessions in which students participate in a specific activity together, sometimes taking turns, or in group conversations. The instructor explored the use of TAP & PLAY in these different contexts.

Learning language through songs
The instructor uses song as a vehicle for foreign language instruction. As part of a summer language camp for children (age 3-7), she created a set of eight posters, each representing a verse of a well-know Italian song. Using TAP & PLAY, she recorded each verse of the song, programmed clear stickers to play the verses, and attached the stickers to the paper posters (see Fig. 11). The instructor also created stickers for keywords and attached them to specific locations that were purposely left blank. On each poster, interacting with the main sticker plays the verse associated with it, while tapping the sticker on top of a blank space plays the missing word.

We observed the Italian instructor using these interactive posters during her summer language camp. She demonstrated how to use the pen and the children immediately asked to try it on their own. For this group activity, the instructor asked the students to say the vocabulary word that was missing in each sentence. The student who answered correctly got to use the pen to tap on the poster and check their answer. The novelty of the digital pen and chance to use it in front of their peers was motivating for the students. The instructor explained, "I was surprised myself how TAP & PLAY can be easily used and how it fascinated the kids. They really wanted to use the pen. I was not prepared for this. Usually I have to ask them to do something or to answer my questions, but with this, they wanted to make the paper talk by themselves."

Group word learning
After observing the kids' excited use of the pen with posters, the instructor spontaneously created another group activity. Working on the floor with children around her, she drew a tree and different fruit on a piece of paper. Students took turns recording the names of various fruits in Italian. Surprisingly, one of the students (age 7) was able to independently use the

Figure 11. Italian instructor created interactive posters that play parts of a song and key vocabulary words.

quick custom audio widget to add her voice to a drawing on paper. Reflecting on how the student could easily use the pen, the instructor commented, "It is a wonderful tool for the children to explore and invent something new by themselves. They can start from a point that I created and end in something different that we created together."

TAP & PLAY worked well for the Italian instructor's needs. "This pen facilitates my work a lot. I can apply it directly to something I already create on paper," she said. The ability to make existing materials interactive by using dot pattern stickers was particularly useful. She explained, "Instead of using an external recorder that I have to start and stop, moving off the focus of the class... I am able to work easily by just touching some areas. The connection is much stronger." Finally, she emphasized the importance of the pen's portability, "You can take it out of the classroom too... You can be anywhere and just use this very simple, but powerful tool."

Targeting Language Development Outcomes
At the end of the study, we surveyed eight educators involved in this project about how well TAP & PLAY supports developmental goals for young children. Since most activities were designed for children under age five, we evaluated how well TAP & PLAY supports the goals described within the California Preschool Learning Foundations [1] (also used by the classes in our study). Participants rated 48 areas of development (covering self, reading, writing, speaking, and mathematics). Table 2 lists the top 12 areas of development that are best supported by TAP & PLAY.

Developmental Goal	Mean	Stdev
Vocabulary in listening	4.88	0.35
Vocabulary in speech	4.88	0.35
Use language to create oral narratives about personal experiences	4.88	0.35
Sound differences in the home language and English	4.88	0.35
Phonological awareness when reading	4.75	0.46
Alphabetics and word/print recognition	4.75	0.46
Participate in read-aloud activity	4.75	0.46
Demonstrate awareness that print carries meaning	4.75	0.46
Writing strategies (grasping and using different drawing/writing tools)	4.71	0.49
Understand story structure	4.71	0.49
Show an increasing understanding of book reading experience	4.64	0.48
Positive group participation	4.63	0.52

Table 2. Participant ratings for top 12 areas of development supported by TAP & PLAY. Scores are from a five-point Likert scale, 1="does not support at all" and 5="supports extremely well".

DISCUSSION
Early childhood education teachers, language instructors, parents, and grandparents quickly implemented new interactive paper activities. During these field deployments we observed the development of a variety of digital pen applications: adding audio content to books, linking audio narrations directly to children's artwork, learning sign language, a multimodal English-Spanish dictionary, multi-lingual games for home use, and "singing posters" for children in a summer language camp. In this section, we summarize key findings from the present study and plans for future work.

Linking Audio with Paper
TAP & PLAY demonstrates an effective approach for linking audio content with a variety of paper materials. The toolkit allows facile coupling of rich audio information with many forms of paper-based content. We reported on novel applications of multimodal paper-digital interfaces in three contexts, but the approach has the potential to support many activities related to language development, speech rehabilitation, audio archiving, and supporting recall or reminiscence.

Integration with Physical Objects
Often the limitation of digital pen and paper publishing architectures is that they require specialized software and a printer to print the unique dot pattern. TAP & PLAY not only enables easy linking of audio with paper materials but also allows integration with physical objects through stickers printed with the dot pattern. This simple extension yields a powerful approach that was (1) the most frequently used part of the material set and (2) the key component of enabling a new class of multimodal language activities. Interactive stickers allowed users to naturally integrate multimodal content with physical objects, including dice, maps, books, and posters.

Supporting Existing Work Practices
The user groups we studied have highly specialized practices involving paper-based content. Classrooms are filled with paper labels, posters, instruction sheets, and more. Additionally, children have established practices that involve specialized paper interfaces such as reading from hardback books, writing on lined paper, and creating art projects with construction paper and glue. Our toolkit, along with the introduction of interactive stickers, allowed content authors to build on their current practices and supplement existing materials by adding audio content. The unique ability of TAP & PLAY to support these practices and the use of pre-existing paper content is a central reason for its success.

Learning Pen and Paper Authoring
At the outset of this study, it was unknown how well end-users would understand and carry out their own "programming" of paper-digital materials. We found through early usability testing that teaching pen-and-paper programming through the custom audio widget is a useful didactic approach. This widget simplifies the complex concept of dynamically creating references between dot pattern space and audio content. An important property of our toolkit is its paper-based authoring interface; the interface may be cut up (or even ripped), menu items can be relabeled or amended, and the entire UI can be reconfigured to fit the needs of each individual user. This stands in sharp contrast to purely digital authoring tools.

A Natural Interface for Children
During the course of the study, we observed how digital pens and TAP & PLAY materials moved from the hands of content authors (teachers, parents, and grandparents) to the hands of children. The vast majority of adults authoring materials showed some initial reluctance in having children use the pen, and several asked what would happen if a child broke the pen. It also seemed that many adults initially thought that the digital pen was a complex tool that would be too difficult for children to manage. On the contrary, children used TAP & PLAY without fail, easily holding the pen and tapping on interactive materials. Even though a pen is usually a writing device, it is a natural device for tapping and selecting interactive regions on paper. When asked what he normally uses a pen for, one student (age 3) answered, "for tapping." Another (age 5) commented while using the pen, "You just tap here and it plays." We observed the ease with which children recorded their voice with the pen. One child (age 7) even created her own interactive region with the control panel.

Independent and Collaborative Use
Participants commented on the potential of TAP & PLAY to support independent work. Several teachers reported that TAP & PLAY kept the children focused on the activity much longer than other approaches. One teacher stated, "I was surprised by how interactive they were. They were asking and responding, and they wanted to do it like five times for the same book." She also said, "They didn't even need us there... As soon as they heard the question, which means that they're really listening, they would respond with the correct answer." In each setting we also observed collaborative use of the system, and in many cases collaborative authoring of content. This was particularly evident in the Italian language summer camp. As another example, a teacher worked with three students to create a story. He drew with the digital pen and the children collaboratively narrated the story.

Limitations and Future Work
Participants wanted to share materials with others and to be able to transfer information between digital pens. Currently sharing between pens is not possible, although we are building a solution that allows sharing of custom materials. In addition, for this study, we printed all materials and distributed them to participants. We envision a web interface that would enable participants to print their own paper materials with the dot pattern on a centralized printer. Each group who participated in the contextual deployment only received one pen (i.e., one pen per classroom). This limited the types of activities that were possible. Exploring the use of multiple pens and providing facilities to share information between pens are important next steps in this research. We described how users in different contexts began to integrate this system into their practices and how the content they created was used by children. While the results of these initial deployments are very promising, we plan more formal evaluations in the future.

This paper primarily describes language learning activities for children, but we are also exploring use of the TAP & PLAY system for other populations. For example, digital pens are an appropriate pointing device for older adults with limited dexterity [16]. Another area of interest involves children with special needs. Since the inception of TAP & PLAY, several parents and relatives of children with autism have requested access to the system. We see potential for this type of flexible, paper-based system to support language development and therapy activities involving a wide range of populations. We plan to further develop and explore TAP & PLAY in a wide range of domains to assess its generality for authoring multimodal materials.

CONCLUSION

This paper presents the development of an end-user toolkit for authoring custom paper-digital materials. We examine the usability and utility of this toolkit for novice, non-technical users. An important contribution of this work is a long-term field deployment of the TAP & PLAY authoring system involving over 70 adults and children in language learning contexts. This allowed us to study how educators and parents incorporate digital pen technology into their daily activities, and in turn, we identified ways in which TAP & PLAY might be improved to support literacy development and language instruction. By empowering end-users as content authors, we observed novel and innovative uses of digital pen technology for language-related activities.

ACKNOWLEDGMENTS

We thank our study participants for making this work possible and Livescribe for donating digital pens. Support for this research was provided in part by NSF grant #0729013.

REFERENCES

1. California Department of Education. Preschool Learning Foundations, Volume 1. `http://www.cde.ca.gov/re/pn/fd/documents/preschoollf.pdf`, 2008.
2. Chiu, P., and Wilcox, L. A dynamic grouping technique for ink and audio notes. In *Proc. UIST* (1998), 195–202.
3. Conroy, K., Levin, D., and Guimbretière, F. ProofRite: A Paper-Augmented Word Processor. Tech. Rep. CS-TR-4652, University of Maryland, USA, May 2004.
4. Guimbretière, F. Paper Augmented Digital Documents. In *Proc. UIST '03* (2003), 51–60.
5. Jeong, Y., Gunawardena, A., and Koedinger, K. R. Designing a pen-based flashcard application to support classroom learning environment. In *Proc. CHI '10* (2010), 4695–4698.
6. Landay, J. A., and Myers, B. A. Interactive sketching for the early stages of user interface design. 43–50.
7. Lee, J. C., Avrahami, D., Hudson, S. E., Forlizzi, J., Dietz, P. H., and Leigh, D. The calder toolkit: wired and wireless components for rapidly prototyping interactive devices. In *Proc. DIS '04* (2004), 167–175.
8. Luff, P., Heath, C., and Greatbatch, D. Tasks-in-interaction: paper and screen based documentation in collaborative activity. In *Proc. CSCW '92* (1992), 163–170.
9. MacKay, W. Is paper safer? The role of paper flight strips in air traffic control. *ACM TOCHI 6*, 4 (1999).
10. Mackay, W. E., Pothier, G., Letondal, C., Bøegh, K., and Sørensen, H. E. The Missing Link: Augmenting Biology Laboratory Notebooks. In *Proc. UIST '02* (2002), 41–50.
11. Nomura, S., Hutchins, E., and Holder, B. The uses of paper in commercial airline flight operations. In *Proc. CSCW '06* (2006), 249–258.
12. Norrie, M. C., Signer, B., and Weibel, N. General Framework for the Rapid Development of Interactive Paper Applications. In *Proc. CoPADD '06* (2006), 9–12.
13. Oviatt, S. Multimodal interfaces. *The human-computer interaction handbook: Fundamentals, evolving technologies and emerging applications* (2003), 286–304.
14. Oviatt, S., Arthur, A., Brock, Y., and Cohen, J. Expressive pen-based interfaces for math education. In *Proc. CSCL* (2007), 573–582.
15. Oviatt, S., Cohen, P., Wu, L., Vergo, J., Duncan, L., Suhm, B., Bers, J., Holzman, T., Winograd, T., Landay, J., Larson, J., and Ferro, D. Designing the user interface for multimodal speech and pen-based gesture applications: state-of-the-art systems and future research directions. *Hum.-Comput. Interact. 15*, 4 (2000).
16. Piper, A. M., Weibel, N., and Hollan, J. Introducing multimodal paper-digital interfaces for speech-language therapy. In *Proc. ASSETS '10* (2010), 203–210.
17. Piper, A. M., Weibel, N., and Hollan, J. Write-N-Speak: Authoring Multimodal Digital-Paper Materials for Speech-Language Therapy. *Transactions on Accessible Computing (TACCESS)* (2011).
18. Sellen, A. J., and Harper, R. *The Myth of the Paperless Office*. MIT Press, November 2001.
19. Signer, B., and Norrie, M. C. Paperpoint: a paper-based presentation and interactive paper prototyping tool. In *Proc. TEI '07* (2007), 57–64.
20. Steimle, J., Brdiczka, O., and Mühlhäuser, M. CoScribe: Integrating Paper and Digital Documents for Collaborative Knowledge Work. *IEEE Transactions on Learning Technologies 2*, 3 (2009), 174–188.
21. Stifelman, L., Arons, B., and Schmandt, C. The Audio Notebook: Paper and Pen Interaction with Structured Speech. In *Proc. CHI '01* (2001), 182–189.
22. Tabard, A., Mackay, W. E., and Eastmond, E. From individual to collaborative: the evolution of prism, a hybrid laboratory notebook. In *Proc. CSCW '08* (2008), 569–578.
23. Weibel, N., Ispas, A., Signer, B., and Norrie, M. C. Paperproof: a paper-digital proof-editing system. In *Proc. CHI '08* (2008), 2349–2354.
24. Wellner, P. Interacting with paper on the digitaldesk. *Communications of the ACM 36*, 7 (1993), 87 – 96.
25. Yeh, R., Liao, C., Klemmer, S., Guimbretière, F., Lee, B., Kakaradov, B., Stamberger, J., and Paepcke, A. Butterflynet: a mobile capture and access system for field biology research. In *Proc. CHI '06* (2006), 571–580.
26. Yeh, R. B., Klemmer, S. R., Paepcke, A., Bastéa-Forte, M., Brandt, J., and Boli, J. Iterative Design of a Paper + Digital Toolkit: Supporting Designing, Developing, and Debugging. Tech. Rep. CSTR 2007-10, Stanford University, CS Department, March 2007.

At Home with Surface Computing?

David S. Kirk[2], Shahram Izadi[1], Otmar Hilliges[1], Stuart Taylor[1], Abigail Sellen[1], Richard Banks[1]

[1]Microsoft Research Cambridge
7 JJ Thomson Ave., Cambridge, UK, CB3 0FB
{shahrami; otmarh, asellen; stuart; rbanks}@microsoft.com

[2]Computing Sciences
Newcastle University,
Newcastle, NE1 7RU, UK
david.kirk@newcastle.ac.uk

ABSTRACT
This paper describes a field study of an interactive surface deployed in three family homes. The tabletop technology provides a central place where digital content, such as photos, can be easily archived, managed and viewed. The tabletop affords multi-touch input, allowing digital content to be sorted, triaged and interacted with using one or two-handed interactions. A physics-based simulation adds dynamics to digital content, providing users with rich ways of interacting that borrows from the real-world. The field study is one of the first of a surface computer within a domestic environment. Our goal is to uncover people's interactions, appropriations, perceptions and experiences with such technologies, exploring the potential barriers to use. Given these devices provide such a shift in interaction, will people be able to engage with them in everyday life in the ways we intend? In answering this question, we hope to deepen our understanding of the design of such systems for home and consumer domains.

ACM Classification: H5.2 Information interfaces and presentation: Graphical user interfaces.

General terms: Design, Human Factors

Keywords: Interactive surfaces and tabletops; multi-touch; physics-simulation; field-study; home

INTRODUCTION
Although interactive surfaces and multi-touch are an established area of HCI research – dating back over two decades [3] – it is only recently that these technologies have become the focus of much media attention. The internet is abuzz with talk of new products, and research in this area is growing apace, reflecting this enthusiasm. In many ways this is understandable, given that these technologies change the ways we can interact with computers. The "natural" style of interaction afforded by the direct multi-touch displays, the form-factor, and their collaborative nature, are the often-cited appeals of such technologies.

It is therefore unsurprising that many companies are now beginning to market interactive surfaces, particularly in tablet and phone form-factors. Larger interactive tabletops are becoming commercially available. However, their costs currently are fairly prohibitive for the everyday consumer market. This is likely to change in years to come, as the cost of the hardware falls.

As interactive tabletops become more available, we can easily posit a world where people will want to procure such novel technologies for their homes. But how will real users respond to and learn to interact with such technologies, when they are placed in their homes? In this paper we present one of the first deployments of a multi-touch tabletop device in a domestic setting. Our overall goal is to investigate the potential for surface computing in the home. Specifically, in this paper we seek to observe what people's interactions, perceptions and experiences are of such novel computing technologies and interfaces, as a means to further inform the design space. Given that these devices provide such a revolutionary shift in form of interaction, will people be able to interact with them in the ways we intend?

Figure 1: Our interactive surface, a bespoke tabletop, with an embedded multi-touch display and overhead camera for imaging physical objects on the surface (left), with a custom physics-enabled photo application (right).

To explore this question, we have built and evaluated an interactive tabletop, in-the-field with three families, for a month at a time. The vision-based tabletop system, shown in Figure 1, was built from the ground up, in-house. We have developed a media management application for these devices, which provides a central place for users to manage and archive their digital photos (see also Figure 1). Although by no means feature-rich, this application has instead been designed to be rich in the interactions it affords, to allow us to more closely observe how real families interact with interactive tabletops. The application therefore supports multi-touch input, allowing digital content to be sorted, triaged and interacted with using one or two-handed interactions. A physics-based simulation adds dynamics to digital content, providing users with rich ways of interacting that borrows from the real-world.

Previous work [9] on this system reported on the more sociological aspects of the deployment, describing how the technology integrated, and at many times disrupted, social and organisational practices in the home. In this prior work the technology was very much used as a probe to enrich our understandings of the home, ideas around family and practices around digital media management.

In this paper we describe our findings that pertain more towards the *interactions* that our surface computer offered, in particular around the multi-touch and physics-enabled techniques to manipulate the virtual. We were particularly interested in understanding whether this interaction paradigm shift, away from the desktop, would work outside of the lab. Specifically, with our deployment we wanted to investigate the following questions in detail:

- Can households naturally learn to use multi-touch gestures, and do bimanual or multitouch patterns of use evolve over time?
- How does a physics-based, hands-on interactional model affect the ways such a technology was used? And does such a model actually allow users to develop their own interaction strategies?
- Can we design a system that successfully blends the virtual and physical? In particular how do we maintain the benefits of the virtual when designing an interface that closely resembles the ways in which we manipulate objects in the real world?

While the answers to these questions are specific to the device we have constructed, we believe that exploring these issues will have generalizable implications for informing the design and development of future surface and tabletop systems for home environments. As we conclude, these questions and our observations during the field deployment open up an interesting discussion around the notion of *intuitive* or *natural user interfaces* in general.

RELATED WORK

Lab studies have uncovered many affordances of tabletop systems. Much of this work considers tabletop use in the context of co-located collaboration [14, 16, 17]. These have led to guidelines for the development of tabletops [15, 18].

Although studies and interaction techniques are common in the tabletop literature, real world applications have been less forthcoming. Photo manipulation and organisation has become one popular application area [2, 17]. Given that the field is fairly new, it is understandable that studies of tabletops have mainly been within the confines of laboratories – to evaluate some of the basic affordances of these systems in more controlled settings. However, real-world deployments are now beginning to emerge, including knowledge workers' use of large tablet displays [12], use of tabletops within museums [6], and other public and shared spaces [20], including schools [14] and universities [22]. Wigdor et al. [21] presents a longitudinal study of a multi-touch tabletop deployed within an office. Hancock et al. [6] describe the use of physics-enabled tabletops for sandtray therapy for children. Although not a tabletop, CityWall [13] studies the use of a single multi-touch wall within a public space for a week, revealing many findings with regard to the social phenomena surrounding such novel technologies.

We wish to extend this literature by considering the use of tabletops and surface computing in the home. Mazalek et al. have begun to explore this space with their TViews system [10], a tangible tabletop which allowed multiple users to interact through wireless pucks on a large horizontal display. Rather than considering tangible tabletops, we wish to more closely understand the adoption of direct multi-touch tabletops within the domestic domain, and further also evaluate the more advanced techniques emerging from the tabletop literature, such as physics-based interactions [23]. In doing so, we wish to ground our work in the field, focusing on in-situ rather than lab-based studies. Ultimately if we wish to have such technologies widely adopted in the real world, we need to better understand how people will interact with them as part of their everyday lives.

AN INTERACTIVE TABLETOP FOR THE HOME

For this deployment we purposefully kept the features of the system basic, using the field study itself as a means for eliciting more advanced user requirements for future iterations of our tabletop media management system. Given our study's dual purpose of also learning more about surface computing in general, we decided to design a system that was *interaction-rich*, even if not *feature-rich*. Therefore we aimed to provide users with hands-on and intuitive multi-touch manipulation of virtual objects, supporting a variety of direct one and two-handed interactions.

We chose to add physical behaviors to virtual objects and use physical gestures wherever possible for interaction. Our aim was to imitate the openness and ease with which we manipulate photos in the real world. Much work has been done recently in the area of physics on tabletops (see [23] for a review), and we felt this was critical to include in the design and study of the system, as it is clearly a relevant technology for surface computing. We were keen to understand whether users would see such features as a novelty, which wore off, or whether they would find them integral to system use.

Physical Design and Underlying Technology

From prior experience of the home deployments of technologies and understanding that the technology would live in peoples' homes, we decided to design a device that looked more like a bespoke piece of furniture than a piece of technology. We also initially investigated the possibility of procuring existing off-the-shelf hardware, but given costs of devices and availability, and our aesthetic goals for the device, we settled for developing a solution in-house from the ground-up.

We chose a common Frustrated Total Internal Reflection (FTIR) based technique for multi-touch sensing [5]. The display screen was constructed using an acrylic sheet, covered with a thin sheet of silicon rubber and a layer of drafting film, and finally edge-lit with Infrared (IR) LEDs for touch sensing. A projector was mounted inside the unit in order to back project onto the surface. A camera was similarly positioned inside to image the display surface. These images were processed on an internally stored PC, using custom GPU-based computer vision techniques. This allowed us to process multiple touch contacts at 60Hz, with little latency, giving an acceptable rate of interaction. The projection gave a display size of 47cm x 35.5cm (18½" x 14"), which a single person or two people could comfortably interact around. Due to the anticipated usages and placement of the device, the display was set at waist-level allowing people to stand rather than sit to interact. We were careful to set the height of the surface to support ease of use, without undue strain, when standing.

To fit with the goal of making a device for the home, we were careful in the physical design to try and hide much of the technology from the user. The cameras, projector and connected PC were all encased. A wooden top with an extended space to the side and shelves allowed devices, ornaments and other objects to be kept by the device. A digital camera and dock was placed on one of these shelves to allow people to take and upload photos.

Interacting with the Tabletop Archive

The application running on our multi-touch tabletop is built using a 3D graphics engine (currently Direct3D). We leverage the metaphor of peering inside the tabletop to reveal a 3D virtual world confined by four virtual walls, which correspond to the bounds of the tabletop display. The virtual camera is set so that you are looking at the 3D scene from a birds-eye view (see Figure 1, 2 and 3).

Objects such as photos are controlled using a gaming physics engine (NVIDIA's PhysX). We model multi-touch input in this world using a technique described in [23], which approximates each finger touching the surface to a series of virtual objects that can interact with others in the 3D scene.

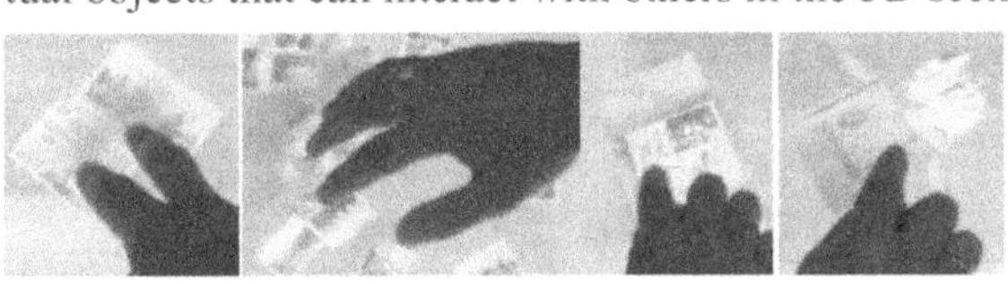

Figure 2: Flicking two photos (left) and gathering multiple objects using multiple touching fingers (middle). Blue shading provides feedback of touch points. Tipping boxes (right).

For users, this means virtual objects begin to move more fluidly and behave more tangibly. Photos and scanned objects have inertia and acceleration, can be flicked from one side of the surface to the other (see Figure 2 left), can collide with one another and bounce off walls, or be spun and rotated by applying torque. As we model multi-touch input, the user is free to use multiple fingers, and one or two hands to gather multiple objects simultaneously, pile them, separate two piles out using a sweeping gesture and so forth (see Figure 2 middle). This behaviour is unscripted, in the sense that users are free to define their own ways of interacting within the bounds of the physics simulation.

This approach of leveraging physics is clearly inspired by prior work such as Bumptop [1] – although the original Bumptop system only supported interaction with one point of contact. This is one of the core novel aspects of the technology that we wanted to evaluate with households. Of course a literal translation of the physical world sometimes limits the qualities of the digital. Therefore in certain instances we supported scripted gestures, such as a multi-fingered gesture for scaling virtual objects.

Getting Content onto the Tabletop

Content could be automatically uploaded to the table using either a digital camera docking station or other USB memory storage device. The system tracks files that it currently contains in order to prevent multiple downloads of the same picture. Once uploaded, content is automatically arranged in piles within the 3D world, and can be spread out to access individual objects by a flick of the hand.

Inspired by fieldwork around real photos in the home [9] we use the metaphor of *virtual shoeboxes* for containment. This is an easily identifiable real-world analogy, and provides a loose way to partition the media on the tabletop. Boxes can be moved and rotated using similar interactions used for photos. Box lids can be opened and closed using a pinch gesture. Once opened, applying multiple contacts off center, as shown in Figure 2 right, spills box contents. To make the process of getting objects into boxes as straightforward as possible, an open box carries a magnetic force, which essentially attracts any colliding objects into the box.

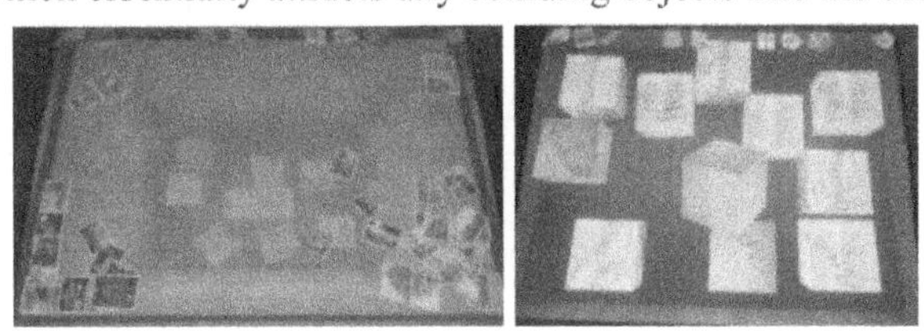

Figure 3: The photo floor (left) and box basement (right).

Clutter was a concern in early UI versions. As boxes were created less virtual floor space was available for working with digital photos and scans. After iterative testing we decided to separate storage and interaction spaces into two virtual 'floors'. The analogy we use is to have boxes stored in the basement – or at the bottom of the tabletop – from where they can be brought to the top level, to be spilled out, loosely arranged, displayed and subsequently tidied up and stored back in the basement (see Figure 3). To give the user a sense of this two-level arrangement and the ability to overview the boxes stored in the archive, the "photo floor" is slightly transparent (as shown in Figure 3 left).

So far we have illustrated how users interact with objects that are already in the system. Interactions such as manipulating photos or boxes can be modeled quite nicely using physics-enabled multi-touch. However, other core features for our application did not easily map to such a literal gesture manipulation paradigm. In order to expose these features to our users we reverted to a collection of virtual buttons along the top edge of the screen. Functionality included the creation of new, empty boxes and also their deletion once no longer needed. Further icons are provided for users to move between the two floors, retrieving boxes from the lower storage level (or vice versa) by touching a particular box and the icon to move between floors. The system also provides an easy means for labeling boxes (and objects) with ink – by switching to annotation mode using a virtual button. In this mode users use their fingers to scribble on boxes and draw onto photographs.

We also decided to introduce a set of shortcuts allowing users to rapidly arrange objects an ordered grid in order to get a quick overview over many photos at once. A "slideshow" mode then allows users to rapidly view and cycle through these photos up-close, by repositioning the virtual camera.

FIELD TRIAL

It is a common strategy for evaluations of user interfaces to take place in the lab and to have a formal experimental structure. Our research goals were instead concerned with understanding the practicalities of everyday interaction with multi-touch and physics-enabled surfaces in-the-wild. As such, an observational, in situ analysis of user interaction in the home was more suitable for our purposes.

Accordingly, we conducted an in-depth field study of our tabletop prototype in three different family homes, each deployment lasting for about a month. Given time constraints, we built and deployed three tabletop units in parallel, one for each family. This coupled with the technical complexity of the system – comprising of custom hardware, GPU processing, and a 3D physics-based UI – made for an extremely demanding deployment. Similar systems deployed in the field have only supported a single system deployment [10, 13], but we felt this was important to help generalise our results.

We officially visited each family once per week for several hours at a time, but also took opportunities to capture field data during times when we were called out to fix technical problems. Data consisted of a written diary left with each family and video and audio recordings both of the participants directly interacting with the UI and whilst being interviewed about their use and experiences of the system. This usually involved capturing footage for extended periods, where multiple family members closely interacted with the device to show us the media they had stored.

In terms of spending time in the field with families, we wanted to get a balance between capturing enough data and ensuring the families had time on their own with the system (being careful to ensure that we were not coaching them in how they should be using it). During the field trial all families had at least some members go on short breaks, frequently returning with new content for the tabletop. At the end of the deployment we also collected system logs of device use and copies of all content uploaded and conducted an exit interview.

Participants

Our families were recruited by word of mouth and email advertisement and all came from the local area. We recruited families with the requirement that they did not have children under the age of 6 (as the back of the device was exposed and therefore possibly hazardous to small children), and that they had previous exposure to using digital photography. Participants were rewarded for participation by being able to keep the digital camera and docking station that was provided with the tabletop. Some users had prior experience of using multi-touch technology, such as iPhone use.

Household A: consisted of a recently married couple in their early 30's, he was a biostatistician and she was an economist at a local university. Both travelled frequently. Both had a post-graduate level of education.

Household B: consisted of a married couple (in their mid-30s), with a six year old son. The father worked in medical research and the mother in biotech. Both had a post-graduate level of education. During the trial for 2 weeks the family had their maternal grandmother staying to look after the little boy during his summer holidays from school.

Household C: consisted of a married couple (late 30s-early 40s) with two teenage daughters (aged 15 and 18). The father worked in software development and the Mother was a housewife. The father had a graduate degree, the mother high school level education. This family had maternal grandparents staying for much of the trial.

Data Analysis

Logged data of system use was collated and summarized after the field trial had ended. The video data of interviews and usage data of the system were then closely analyzed by the research team. Transcriptions of interesting moments of interaction and reflection were transcribed and from this, deeper themes were explored.

FINDINGS

General Patterns of Use

All three households chose to have their device situated in their living room. Households B and C kept their systems running continuously, while Household A turned it on only when they intended to use it for uploading materials or displaying photos to friends, family and other guests. This was due mainly to concerns about the possible energy consumption of the unit. Due to the time taken to install and configure the device, participants were given little training from us regarding the device (~30 minutes overview each).

Inevitably, as with most prototype systems, there were occasional technical problems. Due to the fact that the system was vision-based, adverse lighting conditions affected the touch sensing. However, because we rendered feedback in the UI when touch-points were sensed (see Figure 2), households became very adept at detecting when rogue touch points were appearing on the surface, and would devise workarounds. For example, Household B moved the orientation of light sources in the house, and Household C drew curtains at times when the surface was being used under direct sunlight. By exposing the users to some of this technical maintenance we found they were able to devise fairly sophisticated means to work around these limitations on their own.

Despite these problems, we observed substantial use of the tabletop during deployment, as summarized in **Table1**.

	Nr. days deployed	Nr. days used	Nr. photos kept	Nr. boxes kept
Household A	27	13 (48%)	312	21
Household B	30	21 (70%)	765	30
Household C	32	18 (56%)	429	25

Table1: General usage statistics per household. (Note days deployed includes days travelling/vacationing).

In the remainder of this paper we focus on investigating the users' perceptions of the UI, their uses of multi-touch, physics and 3D, and in general, how they interacted with this novel surface computing technology. We avoid findings pertaining to the media management features of the system (this is instead the focus of [9]).

Ways of the Hands

We were extremely pleased with the speed in which users picked up the gestural vocabulary for interacting, even when training had been kept to a minimum. Manipulation of photos and boxes in particular were rapidly discovered. On the first session most users were able to move, scale, rotate, flick and pile photos. Flicking was particularly evident and users formed strategies for flicking multiple objects into boxes rapidly. Basic interaction with boxes was also straightforward for users, such as moving, opening, closing, rotating and hovering up content.

Throughout the study we observed many one-handed multi-touch interactions, and much bimanual interaction. Users switched effortlessly between using one and two hands. The great degree of bimanual contrasts with some lab studies of photo work on multi-touch tabletops [19].

Users also developed markedly different hand gestures to achieve the same UI actions. This is perhaps best illustrated by Household A. In Figure 4, we show just some of the hand gestures utilised by both husband and wife during a 20 minute period of sustained interaction (observed during the middle of the trial). Here the users switched from using a single finger to move a single small object (a) to grabbing and moving a larger object with multiple fingers of one hand (b) and then finally moving multiple objects one-at-a-time by using the index fingers of both hands (c). This illustrates how diverse and fairly complex chains of hand gestures could be devised for simply moving virtual objects. We observed how the wife distinguished and switched fluidly between precise selection of a single small target using her index finger, and more coarse selection and movement using multiple fingers of a single hand.

Likewise in the same session, the husband goes on to open a box using one hands' index and middle finger (f) and then close it using the index fingers of both hands (g), and rotate a photo bimanually (h), whilst the wife rotated a photo using a single finger placed in the corner (i) and finally both rotated using a more typical thumb and forefinger pinch (j). Although this open-ended set of hand gestures may feel complex to master, these were in fact lightweight for users to achieve, and we began to observe these throughout the trial. Users felt at ease experimenting with new techniques, and also switching between techniques gracefully.

We often observed sequential interaction with objects as shown in [19], where users interacted with objects one at a time. However, even with these single object interactions, we observed large use of the second hand, which was often used alongside the first to divide the labor between hands [4]. This again contrasts with [19]. That being said we also observed many instances of interaction with multiple objects (although perhaps not as plentiful as sequential use). These were often for more coarse movement of objects, such as gathering up, piling or rummaging through photos.

Here we noted about half the participants would not directly touch on photos, but instead would use more of a collision model, bringing their fingers in on the sides of objects to either push them away or more commonly bring them towards themselves. Although not conclusive, this is interesting as the model does not directly translate to drag-and-drop metaphors where movement is achieved by direct selection, but instead suggests a model that derives more from physical interaction. Returning to Household A, we see later in the session the wife sweeping multiple photos to one side using multiple fingers of one hand, while she searches for a specific photo to show us Figure 4 (d), she then introduces her second hand to speed this process up and again divide up the labor (e).

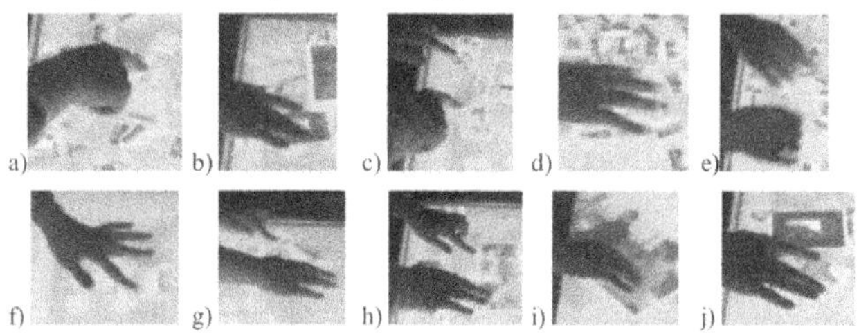

Figure 4: Different hand postures. Users switch fluidly between multiple uni- and bi-manual interactions.

The use of multi-touch and bimanual use is also highlighted in **Table 2**. Here we highlight the total minutes the families interacted with the tabletop on a daily basis (not including days they were away for travel). We also logged whether during each minute, the user(s) were interacting predominately with one, two or more fingers (this is shown as a percentage). This gives a *rough* sense of how many fingers were typically used during interactions with the tabletop. Note that we did not count contacts appearing and disappearing rapidly, which did not move, or did not lead to any UI actions, as these may have been falsely triggered by adverse lighting. We also did a simple distance measure between contacts to again *roughly* predict when contacts could not physically belong to same hand, suggesting bimanual use.

	Total use (min)	Mins/ day	1 finger	2 finger	> 2 finger	Bi-manual
Household A	1351	104	37%	44%	19%	31%
Household B	2396	114	42%	47%	11%	22%
Household C	2657	148	29%	38%	33%	45%

Table 2: More detailed usage statistics. Column two shows total interaction time per family, recorded when 1 or more finger was active. Fourth, fifth and sixth estimates the percentage of this time that 1, 2 or more than 2 contacts were sensed. The last column estimates percentage of overall bimanual use.

Overall our logs, video data and interviews demonstrate multi-touch gestures and bimanual use was plentiful. This was interesting given that the size of the display is a little smaller than other tabletops and we had felt occlusion caused by two hands could be an issue. Already through the field deployment we were seeing results that contrast with lab-based studies of tabletop photo work [19].

Curse of Single Touch

The data also highlights single finger use. This in some ways is to be expected, particularly when moving a single object or clicking buttons. However, when we began to unpack other moments *when* and *why* users switched to a single finger, we found a subtle, but yet critical difference between how users interacted with objects in the virtual and the physical. In the real-world, we often use two hands to provide finer motor control (for example imagine trying to control a ball rolling across a table with one finger as opposed to entirety of your hand). In the digital however, more hands or fingers does not necessarily equate to more control. Indeed users often have the opposite way of perceiving fine control, we often observed users reverting to single touch to carry out fine-grained interactions, for example to position an object precisely.

This reverting to a single finger was also the case when physics-based interactions led to unpredictable results in the UI. For example, when boxes filled up they would become more unstable suggesting they may accidently tip over. Under these conditions using multiple fingers leads to more force to hold the box in place, so in terms of control more fingers are better than one. However, we observed that if the box did show signs of tipping, the users would in fact do the opposite – removing all fingers from the box and using a single finger to carefully move it. This actually made the box less stable, and led to tipping and user frustration.

One consideration here is that when users are touching the virtual box, they are not directly interacting with it. Even if the tabletop gives the impression of directness, there is an intermediary – the computer – so reverting back to the simplest form of interaction, a single finger, allows users to make better sense of the actions of the computer in response to their input.

Beyond the Desktop

In general people appreciated the hands-on nature of the system and the physics-based interactions. It gave a sense of familiarity when interacting digitally, and at the same time distinguished it from standard computing interfaces. Users had a sense that they were interacting with something new and different.

Excerpt 1 – [Household A]
Interviewer 1: have you looked at it like it's a computer?
Anne: No, because we rarely see the first screen (meaning the windows desktop)

This is perhaps best illustrated again through example – the elderly grandfather in Household C walking us through his photo collection on the tabletop. This participant stated he had little if no computer expertise. At first during his interactions he struggled and needed instruction from his daughter to recover his box from the virtual basement. He continually asked *"What button do I press?"* referring to the icons on the top of the screen. However, once the box was on the photo-level, he managed with little instruction to open the box with a pinch gesture, get the contents out of the box, scale and show each photo to us, and rescale them back using bimanual input, before finally flicking each photo back in the box and closing the lid, as highlighted in Figure 5. Whilst interacting, he was fully engaged with us, describing the story behind each photo. It is interesting that the only time he stalled was interacting with the icons at the top of the screen.

When interviewed (with his daughter present), he alluded to what qualities of this interface he found beneficial:

Excerpt 2 - [Household C]
Karen: He (the granddad) doesn't really like computers but as soon as he was here, he was up here [pointing to tabletop]
Karen: I was saying wasn't I mum, that if he'd seen that there was a computer based thing behind it then the block would have come up and he wouldn't have done it
Granddad: Yeah because it's touch init, it's like er fun.
Interviewer 1: do you like the fact that you can do that?
Granddad: Yeah I'm a hands-on kind of person, I've always worked with my hands, everything I do is with me hands, up here [points to head] is a little bit slower than me hands.

The granddad clearly sees a computer as requiring a technical mind, something that requires expertise and a mindset he will never have, but instead this device allows him to engage and express himself with his *hands*. It is interesting that as the daughter points out – there is a PC hidden in the tabletop – but because of the tangible quality of the direct touch and the physics, the granddad feels qualitatively differently about this device. He was confident enough to interact, and manipulate objects based on the hands-on skills he has acquired from the real-world.

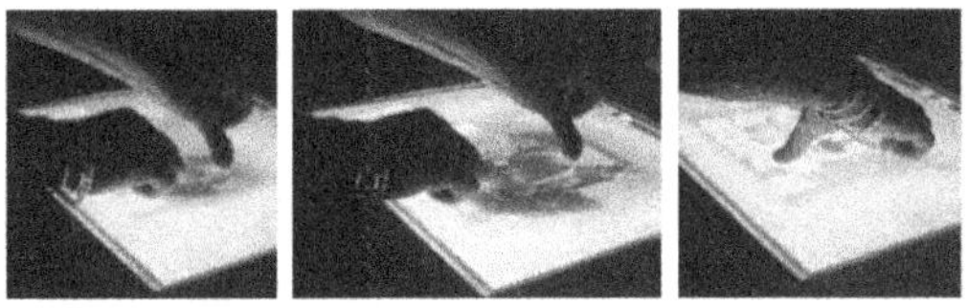

Figure 5: The granddad in household C takes his box from the basement and shows us photos using bimanual input to scale the photos and a pinch gesture to close and open boxes.

The physics also added an organic feeling to the UI that people greatly appreciated. As illustrated in the following:

Excerpt 3 - [Household B]
Carol: And the whole physics-I like! It's just that interaction that you don't get. I guess you could put it in a normal computer but it's just a bit more funky, more real.

Excerpt 4 - [Household A]
Victor: The physics of this stuff is really cool. I mean it feels really like it's a real object. A feature that I, now that I'm playing with it, would like to have, is a full hand. Does it do this? (Manages to gather up many objects using his entire hand)

Again the physics gives the interaction a "real" or tangible quality. In excerpt 4, the participant is enticed to play and experiment with the system, and quickly discovers new unanticipated interactions are feasible. In excerpt 3, the participant hints at how the physics adds further distance between this device and a regular PC. She goes on to say:

Excerpt 5 – [Household B]
Carol: The things have a space have a feeling, you are not dealing with files you're dealing with things, I think that has the edge, it is very different it does transform the way you think about these things because you have to think twice to realise that it is a file.

...

Mike: Once you get into it's just a room basically, in the beginning yes you think about it more analytically, but once you get used to it, it just becomes a room, and it becomes a room with real boxes

This further alludes to how the physics and the real-world metaphors, coupled with the tabletop hardware allowed the families to further shift from the idea that they were interacting with a normal computer and desktop metaphors. This seemed critical for all the families, but why? Again Household B provides some answers:

Excerpt 6 – [Household B]
Carol: I think I have watched my pictures more with this thing.
Mike: because you have it always there and available
Interviewer 2: Is that a good thing or a bad thing?
Carol: I think it is good, and if I have to go to the computer to look at pictures I will probably end up doing something related to work.

...

Carol: I do not want a computer in my living room!
Interviewer 1: Why?
Carol: Because the keyboard and cables ... it's ugly.

Here the participants clearly identify the PC with work and the workplace, whereas this device has a more playful or appliance-like quality that seems more suited for the home.

As we have seen, the perception of this device as "not a PC" seems due to a combination of factors: its hands-on interaction, the illusion of physics, and its aesthetic qualities. However, as we will go on to discuss, all of this can also create a tension when considering what the device is for, in particular, the tension between work and play.

All Play and No Work?

When interviewed families reported a lot on "playing with the device". They liked the randomness that the physics gave the process of displaying pictures.

Excerpt 7 - [Household A]
Anne: What I liked about the slide show is that it's not as stiff as the digital photo frame.
Anne: Here you can make it very random and stuff which I like.

Figure 6: Physics used to randomly arrange photos before a slideshow.

Here the non-deterministic nature of the physics added a touch of unpredictability or spontaneity to the interaction. Indeed, we saw users play on this spontaneity further by arranging the photos into an aligned grid (using the relevant UI button), and then proceed to shuffle the photos around slightly before starting a slideshow, as shown in Figure 6.

The physics by its very nature added non-determinism to the interaction, which was suitable for playful interactions. However, there were times that the interactions were too literal and almost too real. For example, participants would get frustrated by moments when carefully arranged and sorted boxes would accidently spill due to adverse collisions. Another example is that participants complained about the need to tidy away photos after displaying them or tidy up the basement when it became cluttered. One couple went to extreme cases, when they wanted to ignore the ensuing clutter in the digital by turning off the display.

Excerpt 8 – [Household B]
Carol: Whenever it was messy yes it was like oh my god not only have I got to clean up my house on a Saturday but now I have to clean up the flippin desktop.

Excerpt 9 – [Household C]
Karen: I'm normally tidying it up after people have used it, but then I have a problem with symmetry.

Other frustrations were caused by the "effort" required by the physics interfaces to do such simple things as tipping over the boxes. Many users struggled to do this gesture efficiently, instead opting to use the "arrange in a grid" button to pull the photos automatically out of the box. Here some of the problem was down to the lack of 3D input on the surface. In the real-world, tipping over a box is a simple endeavour because we can pick the box up and have all degrees-of-freedom (DOF) available for manipulation. However, with the interactive surface the input is bound to a 2D plane, which must somehow be mapped onto the 3D world – inevitably the DOFs in interacting are lost. The analogy is like trying to interact with small physical boxes on a desk but only being able to push or nudge them with fingertips, instinctively we wish to pick the boxes up and interact with them using all 6DOFs.

This clearly highlights an important design trade-off as to when to create an interaction that borrows from the real-world, and when to instead *offload* to the virtual. Being too literal in the translation of the digital tabletop can lead us to missing some of the benefits and efficiency of the virtual (as also highlighted by [1]). In this case we saw that, while aspects of physics helped create playful interactions, the physical work and unpredictability this entailed added to users' perceptions that this was mainly a device for play rather than one for productivity and efficiency.

It's a Small World!

These issues surrounding the literalness of the UI also play out in the finite space that users had in the virtual 3D world. This coupled with the fact that the space was shared by all family members, children and adult alike meant there was a real "battle" for space. This is perhaps best illustrated in the following vignette:

Excerpt 10 - [Household B]
Mike: It's like he [referring to their 6 year old son] *would have his own area with permission only to open boxes to yeah mess about but he cannot change for example where the pictures go in this box or in that box.*
Interviewer 1: Would he be able to open your boxes?
Mike: Yeah I guess so but with permission, he cannot modify anything he cannot write on certain pictures for example or certain boxes things like that.
Carol: As long as he has his own space I don't think he'll go and try to mess up ours.
[Pause]
Luke (the son): I will.

Excerpt 11 – [Household B]
Luke: what I found fun was playing around with all of the pictures and letting mum and dad tidy them up.

This vignette demonstrates the contention in the household over the shared space. Because the system was democratic, the son had equal rights to explore the space, open boxes and so forth. He used this space more as a play area. He would upload photos of his toys, make a mess (which was almost encouraged with the physics) and not even need to tidy up. In some ways, this was the only space in the home that he had such freedoms so he made the most of this.

'Hands-off' Computing

The democratic nature of surface computing is often seen as a real benefit of these systems, in particular supporting co-located collaboration more effectively [15, 17, 18]. However, although on the first deployment visit we saw evidence of co-located collaboration, by the end of the trial it had all but disappeared. Instead, participants got into the practice of interacting on their own to, for example, interacting to arrange photos before calling others over to view the show, rather than directly touch the surface.

This contention in collaboration has begun to be uncovered in the tabletop literature [11, 16, 24], but it really was paramount in the homes we studied. Participants were indeed almost hesitant to use the system at the same time:

Excerpt 12 - [Household B]
Interviewer 2: So when you have used it have you used it together or on your own?
Carol: We mostly use it on our own or otherwise we would start.
Mike: You would start fighting.
Carol: Yeah unless you're in presentation mode.
Mike: In presentation mode it's fine

Part of this could be where the tabletop was placed, or perhaps the form-factor, in particular the limits of the screen size. However, it is interesting that participants comfortably interacted side-by-side during our deployment visit, and were happy to interact bimanually on their own at the tabletop. Instead it seemed that many of the social norms of the real-world were simply ignored in the digital domain. People would be happy taking objects out of each other's hands, competing for screen real-estate, and fighting over objects such as photos and boxes. This clearly was done in a playful way, but participants did mediate access to the device to avoid even these playful conflicts.

DISCUSSION

So to return to the question raised in the title of our paper, were people at home with surface computing? And more specifically did they engage with this novel form of interaction in the ways we intended? When it comes to interacting with such devices, we had assumed that the open nature of interaction supported by a combination of multi-touch and physics would make the system intuitive to use. And indeed this was partly borne out: Both young and old were clearly engaged with the system, and in certain cases with little existing computing expertise.

We found that a number of factors contributed to this. One set of factors had to do with the interaction model, and the use of virtual physics, which led to more open interactions allowing users to more readily experiment and develop their own strategies for interaction. These became extremely elaborate and sophisticated as the trial progressed, allowing users to switch between many different strategies for interaction. We also saw clear evidence of the ways in which households fluidly adopted multi-finger and two-handed methods of interaction, as the situation demanded. Accordingly, we would suggest it is important for designers not to overly prescribe a single interaction model. Bimanual interaction of the kind we observed has not previously been observed in shorter-term studies e.g. [19] and only emerged in our work due to prolonged interaction with the system (> 1 week). Importantly, this *ad hoc* and fluid use of bimanual gesture contrasts with prior work such as [19].

Although our system was designed to be *interaction-rich* rather than *feature-rich* we still had to design a user interface that occasionally had to go beyond the literal to enable certain features. Whenever possible we opted for gestures that at least borrowed from the real world such as two fingers to resize images. However, metaphorical gestures such as the pinch to zoom are not always a feasible choice, especially when exposing functionalities that are *not* possible in the physical such as copy and paste. These functionalities are often abstract concepts therefore we usually revert to non-literal metaphors to expose them to the user (typically menu-entries). If we strive to inform the design of real-world applications based on physics-enabled interactions we need to derive ways to enable all three types of interactions: the literal, the metaphorical and the abstract.

A "Natural" User Interface?

Through our study we have also begun to look more critically at a (somewhat overloaded) term that has become synonymous with surface computing – *natural* – suggesting an interface akin to real-world interaction (also see [8]). However, from our study, we have begun to question what this really means from the perspective of everyday users. One example comes in tipping the box, where the most natural interaction – to simply pick the box up and spill out the contents – was unavailable due to lack of 3D input. This made what at first appears a natural gesture, tipping a box by direct touch, a wholly unnatural one, which was a poor imitation of the real-world. Users opted instead to perform a simple button press to perform this action.

Another example is when users fell back to interacting with a single finger, particularly when the physics-simulation meant virtual objects were behaving unexpectedly. Here even though we tried to provide an illusion of interacting directly with a real object, users clearly saw that their interactions were being mediated and processed – by the computer. To make better sense of the computers actions, they would interact cautiously and limit their interactions to a single finger, and observe how the system reacted. Although almost an implicit action, users were simply limiting input to the computer to better make sense of the output.

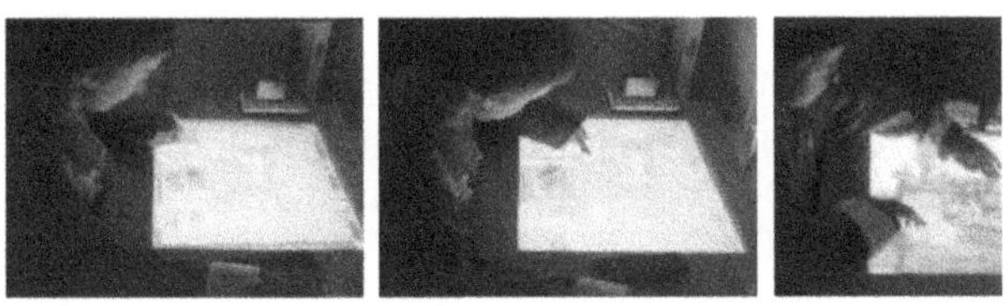

Figure 7: Interacting with digital objects. Switching from interacting with a mouse (left), to hybrid bimanual interaction using touch and mouse (middle), to bimanual touch input.

We want to use one final rare and yet remarkable example, which we include here in our discussion, rather than our findings section, to inspire us to think more about how the lines between desktop and real-world metaphors can be blurred. During the last few days of deploying the tabletop, Luke discovered the presence of a mouse plugged into the back of the device. When observing him we saw he was using both touch and mouse, and had become quite adept at distinguishing what interactions in the UI were optimised for which input. For example, Figure 7 (left) shows how Luke uses the mouse to move around the virtual, something he quotes as being *"hard work"* with touch. He also uses the mouse to interact with the buttons on top of the screen as this aided his reach and accuracy. However, for zooming he understands he needs two touches, and proceeds to touch a single finger down, and use the mouse cursor creating the necessary second touch point Figure 7 (middle). He then almost exclusively switches to manipulating objects – the boxes and photos – by touch Figure 7 (right).

Our field-study uncovered interesting tensions arising from the interplay between real-world and desktop-based metaphors. Despite problems caused by mixing these concepts it is *both* that makes surface computing a compelling experience. Our deployment has highlighted the need to develop a sophisticated understanding of *how* to design user interfaces that that seamlessly blend digital and physical interaction metaphors, optimising interplay between both worlds.

Design Guidelines

We conclude by drawing out our main findings and highlighting their impact on the design of tabletop interfaces in the home.

1) *Flexibility of hand configurations and rapid transitions.* We observed regular single finger, multiple fingers and bimanual hand configurations during the study. Users implicitly transitioned between different hand and finger-based configurations, and we feel that it is important for designers not to overly prescribe a single model. Bimanual interactions of this kind were not observed in shorter term studies e.g. [19] and only emerged due to prolonged interaction with the system (> 1 week). This is a crucial finding that goes against prior work such as [19].

2) *Causes of hand configurations and transitions.* Many different factors impacted user hand configurations. For example, when users perceived that a virtual physics object needed to be stabilized or controlled, they switched to using a single finger (which interestingly is not the way we typically bring a physical object under control). The fidelity of the task also resulted in different hand poses. Users switched from single and multi-finger for fine control over a single object, to using two hands for coarse multi-object interactions. Another under explored factor was that of the *confidence* the user has in the system. For example, if the system failed to respond in a predictable way, the user typically reduced the number of fingers interacting.

3) *Perceptions of tabletop device and physics-based interactions.* Hand-based interactions and physics allowed users to learn the system in ways they would not have been able to with a regular computer. They saw it as a hybrid virtual/digital world. Beyond a regular PC, but had some reservations due to the fact that it was still 'technology'.

4) *Battling between virtual and real analogies.* We observed how on many occasions the mental model of the user was battling between real world analogies and their experiences of WIMP. This can lead to confusion and interesting findings. e.g. users assumed less fingers would

give more control for physics-enabled virtual objects (less like the real world), but also trying to open boxes using double click instead of using real world metaphor.

5) *Literal translation of the real world is not always good for tabletop design.* Some of the physics interactions made for hard work for the user, and the virtual space was limited due to the 3D physics. This shows that simply replicating the real in the virtual is not without its downsides, and ultimately these metaphors should be used liberally, but carefully thought through, and not too literally.

6) *Tabletops are not always beneficial for collaboration.* There is a huge body of work on tabletop systems for collaboration. However, in practice we saw little examples of collaboration. People genuinely avoided parallel use and would often become agitated when interacting side by side.

7) *Challenge the term natural user interaction (NUI).* We often think that NUI means touch based input. For children in our study natural meant the mouse and double click. Evidence from the study really demonstrates that 'natural' is an overloaded and often confused term.

CONCLUSIONS

We have evaluated a novel multi-touch and physics enabled interactive tabletop in three real family homes, providing a grounded understanding of tabletop UI design in domestic spaces. In doing this we have explored how such devices can be used in everyday homes and with regular users. By capturing a rich data set regarding peoples' interactions and perceptions of such devices the study has assessed the value of multi-touch, physics and surface computing, thinking deeply about the design of such devices. It has allowed us to see where the emulation of physics fits well, and equally where it may hinder the kinds of things that families want to accomplish. This raises a design challenge of building an interface for a system which supports both work and play, and which at once can incorporate affordances of both the physical and digital world in ways that optimize both.

REFERENCES

1. Agarawala, A. and Balakrishnan, R. 2006. Keepin' it real: pushing the desktop metaphor with physics, piles and the pen. In *Proc. CHI* '06 (April 22 - 27, 2006).
2. Apted, T., Kay, J., and Quigley, A. 2006. Tabletop sharing of digital photographs for the elderly. In *Proceedings CHI* '06).
3. Buxton, B., Multi-touch systems that I know and love, http://www.billbuxton.com/multitouchOverview.html
4. Guiard. Y., Asymmetric division of labor in human skilled bimanual action: The kinetic chain as a model. The Journal of Motor Behavior, 19(4):486–517, 1987.
5. Han, J. Y. 2005. Low-cost multi-touch sensing through frustrated total internal reflection. In *Proceedings of* UIST '05).
6. Hancock, M., et al. 2010. Supporting sandtray therapy on an interactive tabletop. In *Proc. CHI '10.*
7. Hornecker, E., "I don't understand it either, but it is cool" – Visitor Interactions with a Multi-Touch Table in a Museum. *Proc. of IEEE Tabletop 2008.*
8. Jacob, R.J. et al. Reality-based interaction: a framework for post-WIMP interfaces. In CHI '08. ACM, New York, NY, 201-210.
9. Kirk, D. et al. 2010. Opening up the family archive. In *Proc. Of CSCW '10.* ACM, New York, NY, 261-270.
10. Mazalek, A., et al. The TViews Table in the Home, *In Proc. IEEE TABLETOP'07.*
11. Marshall, P, et al (2009) Fighting for control: children's embodied interactions when using physical and digital representations. In *Proc. CHI '09*, 2149-2152
12. Morris, M.R., Brush, A.J., Meyers, B., A Field Study of Knowledge Workers' Use of Interactive Horizontal Displays. In *Proc. IEEE Tabletop 2008.*
13. Peltonen, P. et al. It's Mine, Don't Touch!: interactions at a large multi-touch display in a city centre. In *CHI* '08 (Florence, Italy, April 05 - 10, 2008).
14. Piper, AM & Hollan, J. D. (2009) Tabletop displays for small group study: affordances of paper and digital materials. In *Proc. of CHI '09.* ACM, 1227-1236
15. Scott, S. D., Grant, K. D., and Mandryk, R. L. 2003. System guidelines for co-located, collaborative work on a tabletop display. In *Proceedings ECSCW* '03).
16. Scott, S. D., et al. Territoriality in collaborative tabletop workspaces. In *Proc. of ACM* CSCW '04.
17. Shen, C., Lesh, N., and Vernier, F. 2003. Personal digital historian: story sharing around the table. *Interactions* 10, 2 (Mar. 2003), 15-22.
18. Shen, C., et al. 2006. Informing the Design of Direct-Touch Tabletops. *IEEE Comput. Graph. Appl.* 26, 5 (Sep. 2006)
19. Terrenghi, L., et al. Affordances for manipulation of physical versus digital media on interactive surfaces. In Proceedings of CHI '07. ACM, New York, NY, 1157-1166.
20. Van de Mortel, D., Ju, H., Apartgame: a multi-user tabletop game platform for intensive public use. In IUI '07: pages 49–52, NewYork, NY, USA, 2007.
21. Wigdor, D. et al., Living with a Tabletop: Analysis and Observations of Long Term Office Use of a Multi-Touch Table. In Proc. *IEEE Tabletop*. 2007.
22. Wigdor, D. et al (2009) WeSpace: the design development and deployment of a walk-up and share multi-surface visual collaboration system. In *Proc. CHI '09*, 1237-1246
23. Wilson, A.D. et al (2008) Bringing Physics to the Surface. In *Proc. of UIST '09.* ACM, 67-76
24. Zhang, X. and Takatsuka, M. Put That There NOW: Group Dynamics of Tabletop Interaction under Time Pressure. *In TABLETOP 2007*. pp. 37—43.

StoryCrate: Tabletop Storyboarding for Live Film Production

Tom Bartindale[1], Alia Sheikh[2], Nick Taylor[1], Peter Wright[1], Patrick Olivier[1]

[1] Culture Lab
School of Computing Science
Newcastle University, UK
{t.l.bartindale,nick.taylor,p.c.wright,
p.l.olivier}@ncl.ac.uk

[2] BBC Research & Development
Centre House,
56 Wood Lane,
London, UK
alia.sheikh@bbc.co.uk

ABSTRACT
Creating film content for broadcast is a high pressure and complex activity involving multiple experts and highly specialized equipment. Production teams are under continuous pressure to produce ever more creative and groundbreaking content while reducing the budgets and human resources required. While technologies are being developed for digitizing and streamlining sections of the production workflow, a gap remains between creative decisions made on location, and those made during digital editing and post-production. We describe a prototype tangible, tabletop interface to be deployed on a film shoot, which uses a storyboard as a shared data representation to drive team creativity. We define creativity in terms of team production, discuss our implementation and describe a deployment in which the prototype was used by a professional production team during a film shoot. Finally we describe a number of interesting interactions that were observed and consider the implications of our design decisions on the creative process of film making and the benefits of tangible, tabletop collaborative interactive displays in live film production.

AUTHOR KEYWORDS
Broadcast; tangible interface; collaborative work; inter-disciplinary; prototype, storyboarding; editing.

ACM Classification Keywords
H.5.3 [Information interfaces and presentation (e.g., HCI)]: Group and Organization Interfaces - Collaborative computing.

INTRODUCTION
Producing media content for broadcast is a time consuming and expensive process involving a large number of skilled and experienced staff. BBC (British Broadcasting Corporation) has for many years been at the cutting edge of broadcast technology research, developing innovative technologies relating to teletext, video on demand services and digital television standards to enhance users' viewing experience. Recently BBC has developed a set of digital workflow tools to improve efficiency in the production process. This paper describes a collaboration between interaction design researchers and BBC Research and Development which aimed to integrate the media production process and its multiple technological components, bridging in-house digital production workflow products and new interaction techniques and technologies to drive existing production staff to produce better content. To enable our understanding of this domain we developed a technology prototype designed to facilitate collaborative production in a broadcast scenario, which we deployed and evaluated during a professional film shoot. We present our design rationale, the prototype implementation, and report on our initial findings regarding the use of interactive technologies to support the complex processes involved in these types of broadcast production. Our contribution is twofold: The design and deployment of a system to drive awareness and ownership in live production, towards understanding how collaborative design elements benefit

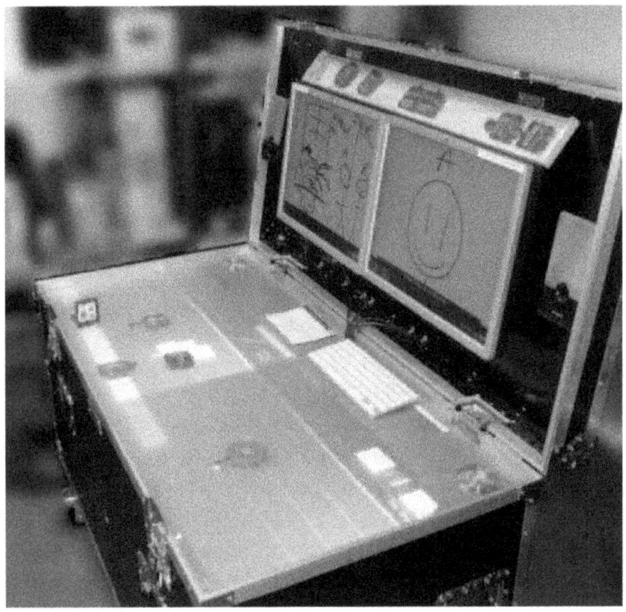

Figure 1. StoryCrate Prototype.

highly creative yet specialized environments; Demonstrating that technology in a live context can be designed to facilitate creativity by using atomic functionality and graphical state representation. Rather than assume that design paradigms from other domains translate directly to this domain, we present specific elements that drive creative practice in an existing live production workflow.

MAKING TELEVISION

Making broadcast television involves multiple skilled personnel each with an expertise in a different aspect of the production process. Many of these roles are highly reliant on digital and other technologies and developments in camera optics, HD recording and cloud media storage are having a significant impact on production practice. Although production processes vary tremendously, ranging from blockbuster movie sets with hundreds of crew to wildlife documentaries with three multi-skilled team members, they typically share a common workflow pattern.

This workflow consists of a number of stages in which separate groups of people contribute to the final product. A typical workflow, shown in Figure 2, follows a linear order: (i) a concept is developed through a group creative process; (ii) this is written as a script; (iii) the director designs camera angles through the script; (iv) this is translated into a shoot order, the actual order in which shots will be filmed on set; (v) the shoot order is followed by the crew on set, and annotated with metadata by hand e.g. "boom in shot" or "incorrect dialogue"; and (vi) the raw footage, metadata and script are passed to an editor, who works with the director to produce a final edit for broadcast.

Figure 2. The broadcast production workflow.

Systems such as INGEX [7] for tape-less recording, and Redux [26] (the technology behind BBC iPlayer) for distribution, archiving and playlist creation, are innovations that digitize this workflow, but are primarily used for either a specific digitization task, or disseminating media to the public. Although these systems facilitate capture, transport and storage of content, footage still needs to be interpreted by the director and editor, this requires a re-reading of paper annotations made on location by other members of the team.Many of these new production technologies aim to integrate media and metadata throughout the workflow, from shooting to broadcast, to streamline data transmission, storage and access. Instead of facilitating data transfer forwards through the workflow, our proposal is to move creative decisions that would traditionally be performed in the editing and post-production phase back up the workflow into the shoot phase, thereby making use of the creative team already in place. Rather than reduce the number of production staff with more "creative" briefs (typically the editor and director in the editing phase), by moving creative decision-making earlier in the workflow we can make better use of the context in which the production team operate and its proximity to the shoot, and use technology to transfer information about these decisions into post-shoot phases. Better support for creative decision-making earlier in the process, and better capture and communication of these decisions should reduce the time currently spent searching and interpreting notes for clips during the editing phase.

Because the director's vision drives content creation, they set the agenda for the shoot and make the principal creative decisions during the filming process. They lead a team of specialist production staff, including lighting and sound engineers, camera operators and a script supervisor, who must all be given enough information to perform their function effectively. Such teams are usually organized within a hierarchical team structure, where the further away in the hierarchy team members are from the director, the less awareness they will have of the current progress, the creative rationale and the end result. In addition to this, many decisions that are made during the shoot are not acted upon immediately, but are decisions that the director and editor will act upon later, during editing.

This workflow is implemented throughout the television production industry, and generally performs well in cases where the production team has a rigid and well defined production process and a fixed script. However, it is less appropriate for smaller, multi-skilled teams where there is an expectation of quicker throughput from scripting to broadcast. Our goal was to develop digital tools to support creative decision-making and the production process of such smaller production teams. Our hypothesis is that by creating a shared, visible representation of the shoot phase of production we can push the point at which a number of creative decisions are made earlier in the workflow. By having earlier decision-making, more members of the team can be involved and the number of decisions that have to be made at edit time (using interpreted data) by director and editor will be reduced. By allowing crew members to have more awareness of the effect of their role on content creation we aim to: (i) facilitate more flexibility and opportunities for trying new ideas; (ii) allow the transfer of production notes transparently between processes; and (iii) facilitate creative contribution by all members of the production team.

WHY STORYBOARD?

A script, written for production, represents the creative vision of the writer. A director interprets the script by turning it into a sequence of camera angles or 'shots',

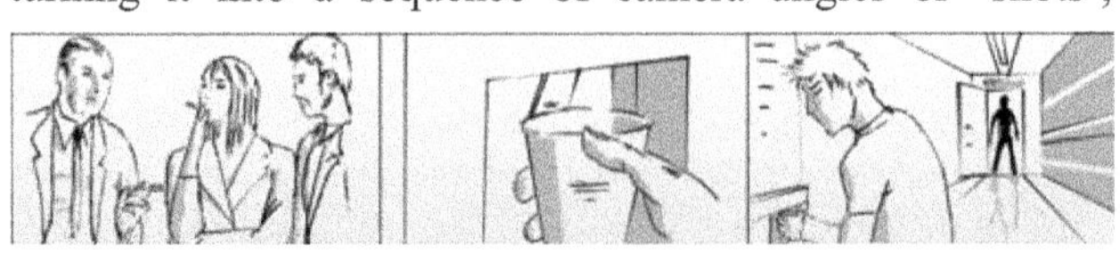

Figure 3. Three example storyboard frames.

designating close-ups, cutaways of objects and locations, used to guide the shooting timetable, actors call sheets and equipment usage. This is then visualized using a still image of each shot (see Figure 3), laid out alongside the script. Most often this is a sequence of stylized drawings, representing characters, props camera angles and perspective [21].

Big budget productions such as Hollywood blockbusters use storyboards to plan high-risk sequences and special effects to reduce re-shoot costs and manage risk. Before the advent of digital filmmaking, storyboards were also used extensively for smaller productions and documentaries. The process of planning and creating storyboards was a time-intensive, but valuable and money-saving, part of the workflow in which a cross section of the crew would pre-plan all required shots to reduce lengthy camera setups and tape slicing [10]. In modern television production, practices have changed and these lists of shots are produced by, and distributed to, a much smaller subset of the production team (often just the director) or not produced at all. One unintentional side effect of this change in workflow practice is the loss of an external representation of the film shoot (i.e. a representation that is visible and shared between the members of the production team).

While other functionally equivalent representations exist (e.g. timetables, shooting orders) a storyboard is a familiar, simple to use, and well understood means of representing the creative output of a production. We therefore chose to reproduce and revise the storyboard in digital form, as a dynamic shared representation for collaborative use by members of the production team during film shoots. As an external representation it aims to allow any team member to have access to shoot progress and to understand their own role in relation to it.

DRIVING CREATIVITY

Rather than facilitate a specific team function, our goal was to facilitate individuals existing roles, supporting creativity in the context of their skill area within the team.. Our prototype design therefore needed to take account of the different forms of creativity and creative input in film production. Baer *et al.* postulate that creativity is domain specific, and thus creativity is best understood in terms of specific describable user events [1]. A review of the literature on creativity, including Shneiderman *et al.*'s extensive work on the fundamentals of actionable creativity led us to a list of key high-level issues that we needed to address when designing film production and a creative practice [20]. Using a grounded approach to inform our prototype design, we have drawn on aspects of actionable creativity within the literature and have categorized collaborative creative practice within broadcast media according to the following six themes.

Exploring Alternatives

Existing content can trigger our imagination with respect to other creative possibilities. Users explore creative alternatives, either spontaneously or triggered by existing content, and add these new ideas to the collection of creative alternatives. A number of design elements can facilitate this process, for example, Santanen *et al.* argue that "the likelihood of new association formation is an inverse function of cognitive load" [18], which suggests that designing to reduced cognitive load will facilitate creative use of a new technology.

Changing Roles

As multi-faceted individuals we are used to re-applying skills to new scenarios. When users change roles (either explicitly or by intervening with others), we share our experience and skills implicitly across role boundaries. Users change roles depending on the situation, sharing experience and skill dynamically throughout the production process without explicit intention to multi-skill. In the 'Handbook of Creativity', Yamamoto supports this by describing how role flexibility within a scenario leads to a higher creative output within a group [25].

Linking to the Unexpected

In addition to the exploration of alternatives, we can consider team members' levels of spontaneous use of unexpected or unplanned processes to accomplish tasks as a measure of group creativity. Interestingly, Goldenberg. suggests that rather than allowing users to explore a large possibility space, defining a structure in a domain leads to a more creative team, as team members are not overwhelmed by possible actions [9]. These *unexpected* outputs may be new ideas that don't relate exactly to the task in hand, but that drive the creative process further by linking unrelated ideas together.

Externalization of Actions

As individuals we manipulate an internal representation of the problem space in order to drive creativity. If members within a team each have access to other members' representations, they are less limited by their own and can use these external inputs as triggers for creative thought. A study by Warr *et al.* shows that although externally triggered new ideas were generated by interpersonal verbal communication users found an external representation added context and a new level of situational understanding enabling more creative group work [23]. A study on Visual DJs reveals building displays to support externalization encourages creativity within subtle creative expression [12].

Group Communication

It is well understood that during collaboration group members communicate on a variety of levels. By facilitating a wide range of interaction types and styles, interpersonal conversations should be richer, and lead to a quicker understanding of each other's ideas. This communication can be explicit, e.g. where users engage in verbal exchanges, but also occurs as a result of non-verbal 'back channel' behavior, where users observe non-verbal cues from one-another. Firestien *et al.* describe "a synergistic relationship between the field of creative problem solving and communication", suggesting that creative practice, team communication and creativity itself are inherently linked [6].

Random Access

In computer science, random access is the ability to access data out of sequence at any time. In media production, the ability to playback and reference media that was recorded at other times is an important capability that is likely to support creativity. If users are not limited to a linear production workflow, they are able to construct conceptual and other (e.g. stylistic) links between a wider range of content. Hocevar *et al.* describe this abstract relational process as "divergent thinking", and talk about the need to design for "fluency, flexibility, originality, redefinition and elaboration" when facilitating creativity [11].

Although the measurement of creativity is still an open question, defining discrete aspects of collaboratively driven content creation informs the interaction design process, allowing us to gauge success and inform study design.

DESIGN RESPONSE

Our design response was developed through a process of: (i) mapping our thematic categorization of the creative process onto the roles, skills, processes and practical constraints of television production; and (ii) selecting and configuring interaction technologies and techniques to support these mappings while respecting the practical constraint of television production.

Scott *et al.*'s extensively cited guide for collaborative tabletop design identifies a number of affordances of tabletop interfaces: natural interpersonal interaction; transitions between personal and group work; transitions between tabletop collaboration and external work; flexible user arrangements; and simultaneous user interactions [19]. Waldner *et al.* describe in detail how tangible interaction facilitates collaborative interaction [23], and Buxton identified the cognitive benefits of bi-manual control and inputs using physical tools [3]. Although modern displays offer multi-touch interaction (for multiple users), using physical tools or objects has the potential to offer a more natural externalization of a user's actions, of which co-located users are more likely to be peripherally aware. Production crew already carry a number of physical objects, such as radios, clipboards and recording equipment, so providing a space to place these while they interact with any system is an important design factor to consider.

Hornecker *et al.* argue that graspable interfaces resolve ambiguities, embody actions visibly for communication partners and maintain a performative meaning during manipulation, enhancing understanding and shared experience [14]. Using these physical representations we can drive group communication, facilitating role changing by providing expressive yet natural interaction for non-expert interface users.

Russell *et al.* suggest that large, multi-user displays can support a user's understanding and manipulation of concepts within a social context [17]. Elrod supported this argument, and described how electronic whiteboards in presentation scenarios encouraged a wider audience to participate in discussion [5]. With current technology we can now combine high-resolution large form factor displays and tabletop interfaces to create large collaborative interfaces for complex information (e.g. many HD videos).

Stewart *et al.*'s work on single display groupware highlights the benefits of a single interaction focal point, providing a shared feedback space and facilitating "coupled navigation" where users change task mode seamlessly in union [21]. Conversely, he warns of a potential design problem: that users may actually collaborate less. That is, since users can act on their own, there may be no imperative to communicate with others in order to complete a task.

Peripheral awareness interfaces are a category of information display that provide situated contextual information in a user's environment. Slideshow is a typical example of such an interface and allows users to ingest an array of information relevant to a task at hand both directly and indirectly [4]. While peripheral awareness underpins or supplements a number of the creative practices identified (e.g. externalisation of actions), it is important to also be sensitive to the distinct roles of the users and the varying demands placed on them spatially (where they need to be on the set), temporally (when something is happening) and cognitively. Placing the point of interaction with the system within reach of all members of the team reduces physical barriers, and encourages spontaneous use and the exploration of ideas without the risk of having leaving the relative safety of their *natural location* within the shoot. Current infrastructure demands that video equipment be physically connected on set to operate reliably. Since film shoots can be in any location, the envisaged prototype must also be easy to transport, configure and operate outside of a controlled environment as discussed when designing MediaCrate [2]. Furthermore, crews are naturally reticent about use new or untested equipment, and it is therefore desirable that any prototype has a 'look and feel' that is consistent with traditional equipment and requires as little specialist knowledge to operate as is possible.

Our understanding of the creative practices we wished to support, the realities of television production, and the limitations and affordances of interaction technologies led us to select a tabletop interface for our prototype implementation. Tabletops not only afford collocated collaboration and peripheral awareness, but readily support tangible interaction, and can be cast in a physical form that is both appropriate to a production environment and familiar to crew members. By using aspects of an agile development process we can develop a prototype that realises independent atomic elements of functionality that

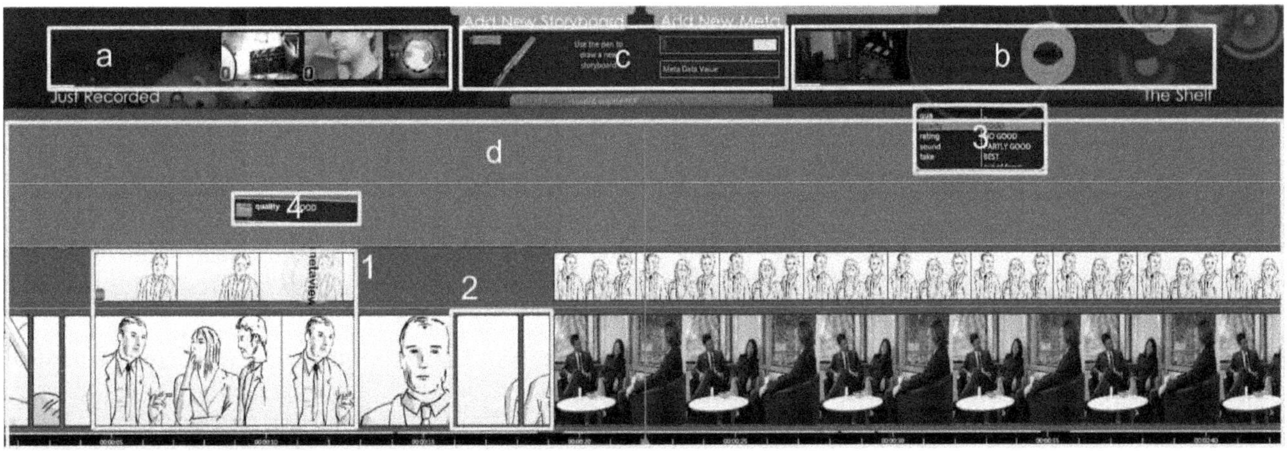

Figure 4. StoryCrate interface.

the users themselves can appropriate to realise a workflow. This encourages random access to features, as each one would operate independently from another, providing a 'buffet' of tools which different crew members can both use, and learn to use from the observation of each other's use.

WHAT IS STORYCRATE

StoryCrate is an interactive table consisting of a computer with two rear-projected displays behind a horizontal surface creating a 60" x 25" high-resolution display, with two LCD monitors mounted vertically behind it. Shaped plastic tiles used to control the system are optically tracked by two PlayStation 3 Eye Cameras in infrared through the horizontal surface using fiducial markers and the reacTIVision [14] tracking engine. The entire device and all associated hardware is housed in a 1.5m long flight case on castors, with power and Ethernet inputs on the exterior, and was built to be robust and easily transportable to shoot locations. StoryCrate is written in Microsoft .NET 4, utilizing animation and media playback features built into Windows Presentation Foundation.

StoryCrate is built to take on location, and connects via Ethernet to the digital recording system used by BBC. StoryCrate uses Secure Shell to connect to the Linux based recording system, and monitors the recording directory, downloading new clips and XML metadata as they are created. StoryCrate keeps track of all media recorded during the shoot so that content can be used at any point, regardless of when it was filmed, providing random access to content for users. Before shooting, StoryCrate is pre-loaded with a storyboard (created in Final Cut Pro) that includes the script, shot descriptions and storyboard images edited into expected timings. On StoryCrate, this is represented as a linear timeline, where each media item is represented as a thumbnail of the media on the display. Almost the entire display is filled with this shared representation of filming state, providing users with a single focal point for keeping track of group progress. During the shoot, a take or clip appears on the device shortly after it is filmed, and can be manipulated and previewed on StoryCrate as a thumbnail. The interface is based on a multi-track video editor, where all footage is presented on the display together, allowing users to see and make links between all available clips. Time is represented horizontally, and a selection of multiple takes (limited to five, as prior experience shows that single shots would be filmed to completion, rather than spliced) of a shot vertically (elements (1) and (2) in Figure 4).

StoryCrate provides discrete functional elements for the following tasks, where each task is independent of another, allowing for complete flexibility and role sharing in how users choose to operate it:

- Adding textual metadata to clips;
- Playback of both the timeline and individual clips;
- Selecting in- and out-points on clips;
- Moving, deleting, inserting and editing clips on the timeline;
- Adding new hand-drawn storyboard content.

The interface is divided into four key areas (see (a), (b), (c) and (d) in Figure 4) within which Media Tiles can placed. Clips from the recording system arrive in area (a) within ten seconds of a take being filmed, and can be moved from here to either the timeline (d) or the shelf (b) for later use. This flexibility in workflow allows users to delay decisions about incoming media, and the ability to quickly move clips around provides an easy method of trying out sequencing and edit ideas, as well as exploring alternatives.

Actions are performed by physically moving acrylic *control* objects which when placed on the surface interact contextually with elements of the interface, providing a critical externalization of digital actions. Clips are moved around the display by placing one end of the *move control* on the clip to be moved, and the other end at the destination point. The control consists of two tangible objects joined by a sprung cord. Lifting the destination end control moves the clip, and lifting the source end control cancels the operation. This control seamlessly performs inserts or

Figure 5. Tangible controls for StoryCrate.

moves depending on the destination location. By using both tangible and bi-manual controls, users' actions are externalized and other members of the team are more readily aware of changes. Clips are animated between positions both to avoid losing context while performing actions, and to support others' understanding the context when viewed from a distance.

Clips located on the timeline (d) are played back sequentially using the *play head control*, which when placed on the timeline represents the current playback position, with the timeline scrolling horizontally underneath it. When rotated, it can also be used to scroll or scrub through the timeline. The full resolution output is displayed on the right hand vertical monitor (see Figure 1), which is visible from a distance to all team members. Clips can also be looped on the left-hand monitor by placing the *preview control* on a clip. By placing the *preview control* to the right of the *play head control* spatially, previews of future clips are automatic. Clips can be removed from the interface at any point by placing the *delete control* down. After a two second timeout, the clip is removed when the control is lifted. This prevents accidental deletions and allows other users to intervene in critical actions.

Depending on the director, footage may arrive in large sections with multiple takes within a single block of video. To segment these and cut out useful shots, the *clipping control* is used (Figure 5). This controls the left-hand monitor and is physically attached, and oriented perpendicular to the *preview control* so that they cannot be placed down simultaneously, thereby enforcing an important functional constraint within the tangible control. When placed on a clip it takes over the entire timeline display, and controls for the in-point and the out-point are used to place accurate markers within the clip. This forces all users to collaborate on one specific task, while also allowing a high-resolution positioning. When the operation is complete, the *clipping control* is removed and the clip is updated. Multiple takes of the same shot can be stacked on top of each other, as shown in (1) in Figure 4, by using the *take selector control* to select the clip to playback within the main sequence.

Metadata takes the form of text key-value pairs and can be added by placing the *add meta control* onto a clip (see (3) in Figure 4). A list is displayed next to the control and extra buttons located on the control allow the user to navigate the list and select the required metadata tag. This fine-grained list control is implemented using physical contextual buttons as more than one parameter (provided by rotation) is required to navigate the list. Metadata presence is displayed as an icon on a clip, and in more detail by placing the *meta-view control* on the Media Tile (see (4) in Figure 4).

An important feature of StoryCrate is its facility to allow the addition of new storyboard content *during* a shoot, allowing users to explore different creative avenues. This is accomplished using a digital Anoto pen (see (c) in Figure 4) and drawing a new still frame on the pad provided. When docked, this image appears immediately as a clip on the shelf (see (b) in Figure 4) like other media. New metadata pairs can be added by typing directly on the keyboard (see (c) in Figure 4), and these are directly available to the *add meta control*. These text and freehand drawing capabilities are the only uses for the keyboard and Anoto pen, which prevents ambiguity regarding their functionality, promotes the visibility of these actions, and facilitates faster and more spontaneous input.

Potential conflicts during use, such as two users simultaneously wanting to add metadata are negotiated by providing only one physical control for each action. This requires users to negotiate for functionality, forcing externalization of their intentions.

When a tangible control is manipulated by a user it displays a subtle expanding circle animation emanating from the center of the object. Similarly, when the software moves thumbnails beneath an object on the surface a smaller visual indication is made around all tangible objects placed on the display. These promote users' direct and peripheral awareness that the interface is responding to their input and that of others. When the shoot is complete, StoryCrate exports the timeline as an Apple XML Interchange [27] file, which can be directly imported into a video editing system, retaining all metadata, editing and take information. An editor can use this file directly at a later date, using it as a starting point for the editing process.

THE DEEP END

A film shoot is a time-constrained, multi-disciplinary creative process which is dependent on a multitude of changing factors e.g. crew dynamics, team experience, location, weather and finances. Production teams have learnt to thrive in these un-predictable environments, and members perform skilled roles and maintain relationships of trust and mutual understanding that minimize the need for complex and detailed communication between team members.

It is impossible to replicate all of the factors that characterize television production environments in a laboratory experiment. Rogers "Why it's worth the hassle", comments that Ubiquitous computing is difficult to evaluate due to context of use, and that traditional lab studies fail to capture the complexities and richness of a domain [16]. Consequently, beyond obvious usability issues, lab-based studies are unlikely to be able to predict how a real production team will use, and adapt to, the new technology when it is deployed 'in the wild'. Consequently, we chose to deploy StoryCrate on a live film shoot to evaluate how a real crew would use specific aspects of its functionality, and see the impact StoryCrate had on their workflow.

Deploying a prototype for real world use involves creating a robust system, both in terms of the software and its mechanical properties. Although high fidelity prototyping has been shown to be an effective approach it is not as widely deployed in interaction design as, say, agile programming for systems design. One notable hurdle to prototype deployments in a highly skilled environment, such as television production, is the trust that crew have in their equipment. Crew members come to rely on specific functionality and become used to idiosyncrasies of their own equipment, knowing possible pitfalls and fault points. They are also acutely aware of the long lead-in times of learning to use new equipment effectively, and the inevitable process of discovering pitfalls and idiosyncrasies in new equipment. This is especially the case when there is an awareness that the equipment has not been extensively tested in a live environment. When designing for such critical systems we cannot naively assume that errors will not occur, and consequently our approach was to implement extensive backup and restore functionality, in addition to the clear visual feedback associating all user actions.

THE ANTICIPATED WORKFLOW

StoryCrate's discrete elements of functionality were based on activities performed as part of a traditional workflow. However, three use cases reflect our expectations about how StoryCrate could potentially improve creativity during a shoot, and in our study we paid particular attention to observing whether aspects of these emerged.

Clip Review

This is where StoryCrate is used for clip reviewing. The director maintains control over it and uses it during breaks to explain current progress and show the rest of the crew what they produced and how content is progressing. Clips are batch processed into the storyboard at intervals by the production team and only shown to actors when director is happy with a complete section of the storyboard.

Context Explanation

This is where StoryCrate is updated whilst filming. The director explains shot context and ideas using StoryCrate to get the crew up to speed. Specific shot characteristics can be demonstrated and continuity aspects discussed. The storyboard is incrementally created and can be viewed by anyone at any time.

Logging

This is where StoryCrate is used by production assistants and crew to log shots and add metadata useful for editing. The director does not have direct interaction with the system, but allows its use as a logging tool for monitoring shoot progress and logging by the rest of the crew.

In all these cases, we expect shots to be inserted into the storyboard during the shoot. This creates a rough edit by the end of the active shoot that can be reviewed immediately or at a later stage.

THE STUDY

To effectively observe a crew in their natural environment we reproduced a standard configuration for a TV short production. We commissioned a three-minute script, specifying two to four characters (due to budget limitations) and four distinct scenes. We used each of these scenes as a different phase of the test. The director then worked with a visual artist to develop a pictorial storyboard representing his vision for camera angles and shots. These frames were combined with the script into a Final Cut Pro project, and imported into StoryCrate before the shoot.

During the shoot, we used aspects of Millens's 'rapid ethnography' approach for field tests [15]. Three ethnographers were paired with filmographers, who were tasked with observing different areas of the team; crew at StoryCrate, crew around StoryCrate, and crew physically distant from StoryCrate. The ethnographers were briefed with suggested thematic codes to use while observing, and notes were to be time stamped throughout. In the outer observation space, two further observers filmed and documented the study process as a whole. Figure 6 summarizes the full set of participants and the members of the film crew and the actors.

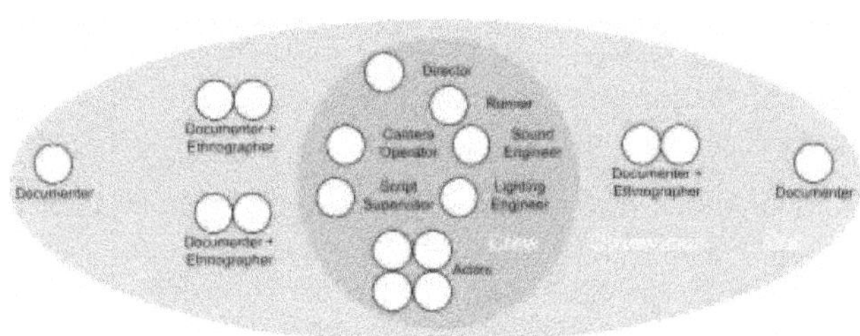

Figure 6. Observation Strategy

We hired a crew of seven who work full time in the industry to fulfill their normal roles (director, camera operator, sound recordist, script supervisor/assistant director, runner, makeup and lighting) and four actors, exactly as in a traditional shoot. Some had experience working together, and some had not. We ran a half day training session to introduce the crew to basic operation of the device. A short video and scripted tutorial were used to describe each functional element of the device, although we were careful to avoid leading the crew members as regards our anticipated scenarios of use. The crew was asked to create short thirty-second clips about themselves, each time rotating roles. Each member was encouraged to try a variety of tools in StoryCrate.

The main film shoot was split into four sessions (one for each scene) each lasting half a day. At the start of each session, we gave a briefing to the crew about the technology they had at their disposal, and the scene they were to shoot. From that point onwards, all organizational responsibility was handed off to the production team themselves. At the end of each session, short interviews were performed with each member of the crew.

Figure 7. The film shoot, Inset: Daniel - ***designated operator***

The goal of the study was to understand the impact of StoryCrate on the practices of this particular production team. Furthermore, because storyboards are not in common use (even in paper form), it was important to distinguish between team interaction based around the existence of a storyboard, and interactions facilitated by StoryCrate. We therefore only allowed the crew to use StoryCrate for the first and last session, used a printed paper storyboard for the second session, and no storyboard at all for the third session.

Although the film shoot was managed in a traditional manner, with the director taking operational control, we explicitly encouraged the use of StoryCrate. The director was briefed to use the system in a way that facilitated the shoot, but also to be open to changes in team working practices. Importantly, our briefing emphasized the importance of concentrating on quality of product.

STORIES

Here we report the result of our initial analysis, for which we selected five significant facets of interaction that were observed during the deployment. Demonstrated with specific examples, we have selected quotes from crew interviews to discuss how our design choices influenced the shoot and explore avenues of investigation for later analysis.

Designated Operator

After the initial training session, we were informed by the director that they would be appointing Daniel, the runner, to be the designated operator of StoryCrate (Figure 7). Violet, the script supervisor reported: *"I found it helpful having one person that was permanently there moving clips down because I felt like I wouldn't have had time to do that myself."* This suggests that although our design facilitates non-hierarchical operation of the device, a designated operator was needed to maintain data in order to for the rest of the crew to spontaneously interact. Violet explained: *"it's too slow to keep anything up so you can't really build up a full storyboard on what you are doing."* Daniel's primary role as operator was to enter logging information that was called out by Violet, marking clips as they were shot. Here we can clearly see our expectation of a logging system coming into play, although we had expected crew to use it for their own data individually and independently.

It appeared that the trust relationships within the team were quickly established, and that the runner was given the operator role because it was perceived that he was the most competent. Daniel supports this: *"I spent quite a long time with story crate yesterday getting used to it so maybe they thought 'Dave can do it'"*. But even within this designated role he was subject to hierarchical overruling: *"when the Crate needed to be used and the director wanted to use the Crate then actually he displaced me from the Crate and took over himself."*

Artistic Collaboration

At the beginning of the fourth shoot the director decided that he was going to shoot the scene completely differently to the way it was storyboarded. While waiting for actors to finish makeup, he gathered the crew around StoryCrate and spent 20 minutes drawing out each new storyboard tile as Daniel inserted them into a new timeline. The script supervisor commented: *"in gathering round and discussing round the storyboard, I felt like that was a good moment to make your creative input and it facilitated that."* This clearly supports our expected use case of facilitating creative input within the team, allowing users to contribute to a discussion, and be aware of resulting changes.

The cameraman mentioned that displaying this new content in a timeline context was helpful: *"it was a useful opportunity to just have a glance at what he was planning to do. The way he was explaining it wasn't particularly clear. But because most of the storyboard was already there, being able to see the thing at a glance helped."* This also suggests that although StoryCrate was too time-consuming for operation during the shoot, the ability to have a shared public representation of the new plan was helpful.

The facility for hand-drawn input to the system motivated the lighting engineer to contribute. He had initially declined to engage with the StoryCrate as he felt it was outside of his professional role. In training, when he was asked to explain how he would light a particularly difficult shot, he used the pen and pad to draw a simple representation of his idea, treating it solely as a paper copy. Although this was not subsequently inserted explicitly into StoryCrate, a digital copy would be transferred to the editor.

These initial observations demonstrate that the ability to create new content during the shoot was a useful functionality of the interface, and that the director's use of the shared display to scaffold explanation and discussion of plans within the group drove creativity and ownership of ideas, even without passing this data through the workflow to the editor.

Media Playback

During the second session, where the crew was without StoryCrate, an 'over the shoulder' camera angle became difficult as no one could recall the previous shot angles, and where actors were stood (to maintain continuity). Using the digital recording system, playback is limited to single files from a list, and vital sections have to be memorized to recall them. Enraged at the inability to play back previous clips to match against, the director shouted "*this is where we really need the [expletive] Crate*".

It was decided by the crew that to start session four, various shots from the first day would be re-taken. For the crew, this involved re-dressing the set, re-setting the lighting and matching the camera angles. The director commented: "*Then we used it [StoryCrate] to check the sequence of storyboards and whether we had got the shots we needed. It became a much more general reference point as the two days had gone on because we had done so much that we could – needed to go back and check we weren't missing stuff.*" At this point StoryCrate was used primarily for reviewing clips from the previous day to match up the current environment with the pre-recorded version, using it is a master reference to what had been shot and what was good quality. This functionality was a key aspect of our expectations, the use of playback for clip review to assess continuity. The sound operator summarized this functionality: *"you see and hear playback, which otherwise on a film set may not be quite so easy. I mean, there's like a central place that you can go to."* Without the independent units of functionality that StoryCrate provides this would not have been possible, as this practice was outside the traditional workflow of a production team. With this analysis we hope to ascertain how this playback functionality drove efficiency within the team, for example, by allowing them to re-shoot parts they would not have had time to otherwise. Interestingly the large vertical display was used by most of the team from a distance while performing their roles in situ, so this physical aspect of its configuration alone was a useful component.

Equipment Integration

We integrated StoryCrate into the recording infrastructure so no additional effort was required on the part of the user. However, this caused ambiguity in the perceived purpose of StoryCrate. Daniel commented: "*I do wonder if I've just been sat there dragging clips to a viewable area where [the recording system] is doing that at the same time.*" Due to this seamless integration, it was confusing for the crew to separate which piece of equipment was of interest to the study, and which was well tested equipment, as both were new to them. As we observed, this led to StoryCrate primarily being used as a large screen playback device, visible to the whole crew. Interestingly this differs from our expectation of playback at the end of a shoot, as it was used primarily to guide new shots, rather than review an entire scene.

Due to the design of the study, the crew were unaware how the resulting data from StoryCrate was going to be used by an editor later in the production process. Because of this, they felt obliged to contribute towards the central repository of metadata, but lacked an understanding of how their input was beneficial to others (e.g. the editor). Daniel stated: *"It's difficult to know without seeing a finished product and seeing how well it helps the editors but just from being able to show someone who has just taken shots 'oh what does this look like?' and come over and say 'oh it's like this' is very useful.*"

This highlights an interesting aspect of prototyping in the wild: although we have expectations as to how users may interact with a prototype, we cannot design for transient factors produced by external equipment which affect the process as a whole.

Tangible Controls

During implementation, the issue of how robust a prototype needed to be to effectively elicit information about key design features rather than be overshadowed by 'in the wild' operational problems relating to deployment. As it turned out, hardware tracking issues were raised during the study, and these were partly overcome by the designated operator learning other ways to accomplish a task. Violet commented: *"I found it frustrating trying to drag stuff down and it wouldn't, and that just becomes more time-consuming than it's worth when it's not obeying.*" Whereas Daniel said: *"having all the lumpy bits you put on, I found I needed another couple of [objects] and couldn't quite put my hands on them, but that's just a storage thing if you get into the habit of putting everything in the right place, then you know where they are.*" This suggests that although at first the implementation was problematic, tangible controls became usable by spatially arranging them in known locations. The issue of durability and robustness come into play here, and it is worth noting that although the interface became hard to use for particular tasks, these were non-dependent tasks and thus the system was flexible and could function even through technical problems.

As in Daniel's earlier quote, tangible objects facilitated the transfer and holding of power over the interface, primarily during points where users gathered around it. This reinforces our expectation that the director would still have ultimate control over the device and would initiate playback sessions. While one person held control over the move and play head tangible, most other actions were irrelevant as they interfered with the primary user's task.

CONCLUSION

We have presented a prototype collaborative system for augmenting traditional film production during a shoot.. The interface uses a storyboard to present a single point of reference for the entire crew, enabling a greater awareness of current progress, facilitating creativity and ownership of content within the team and driving decisions made on site directly into the current digital workflow. Rather than design for a particular workflow, we define aspects of creative practice relevant to film production, using this to inform our implementation. We then use a prototype to elicit responses from the domain by placing it on a real film shoot, observing user communication, creativity in practice and team awareness, towards understanding collaborative design in this context.

We articulate five interaction scenarios from our observation, discussing how tabletop and tangible design decisions influenced team interaction with the device, and how this may drive the creative workflow within the team. We will be using these initial scenarios to guide further in-depth investigation into our data, at all times referring back to the creative aspects which we defined and the affordances of co-located surface computing for media production. Wider concepts can also be investigated from this study, such as the benefit of the storyboard in modern film practice and the value of a single reference point in unpredictable environments. We describe the context and environment in which shared tangible interactive displays can be used to encourage practice, and hope to encourage other researchers to use exploratory prototyping as a method of driving forward existing processes in complex social domains.

REFERENCES

1. Baer, J. The case for domain specificity of creativity. *Creativity Research Journal 11*, 2 (1998), 173–177.
2. Bartindale, T., Hook, J., Olivier, P. Media Crate: tangible live media production interface. In *Proc. TEI* ACM Press (2009), 255-262
3. Buxton, B. Two-Handed Input in Human-Computer Interaction. In *Haptic Input*. 2008, 11.1.
4. Cadiz, J.J., Venolia, G., Jancke, G., and Gupta, A. Designing and deploying an information awareness interface. In *Proc. CSCW*, ACM Press (2002), 314.
5. Elrod, S., Bruce, R., Gold, R., et al. Liveboard: a large interactive display supporting group meetings, presentations, and remote collaboration. In *Proc. CHI*, ACM Press (1992).
6. Firestien, R. and McCowan, R. Creative problem solving and communication behavior in small groups. *Creativity Research Journal 1*, 1 (1988), 106-114.
7. Fletcher, J., Kirby, D.G., and Cunningham, S. Tapeless and paperless: automating the workflow in tv studio production. *BBC Research White Paper 141*, September (2006).
8. Goodwin, N.C. Functionality and usability. *CACM 30*, 3 (1987), 229-233.
9. Goldenberg, J. Essays on Science and Society: Creative Sparks. *Science 285*, 5433 (1999), 1495-1496.
10. Hart, J. *The art of the storyboard: storyboarding for film, TV, and animation*. Focal Press, 1999.
11. Hocevar, D. Measurement of creativity: Review and critique. *Journal of Personality Assessment 45*, (1981), 450-464.
12. Hook, J., Green, D., McCarthy, J., Taylor, S., Wright, P., Olivier, P. A VJ centered exploration of expressive interaction. In *Proc CHI.* (2011), 1265-1274.
13. Hornecker, E. Understanding the benefits of graspable interfaces for cooperative use. *Cooperative Systems Design*, 71 (2002).
14. Kaltenbrunner, M. and Bencina, R. reacTIVision: a computer-vision framework for table-based tangible interaction. In *Proc. TEI*, (2007), 69 - 74.
15. Millen, D.R. Rapid ethnography. In *Proc. DIS*, ACM Press (2000), 280-286.
16. Rogers, Y., Connelly, K., Tedesco, L., et al. Why it's worth the hassle: the value of in-situ studies when designing. In *Proc. Ubicomp*. (2007), 336-353.
17. Russell, D., Drews, C., and Sue, A. Social Aspects of Using Large Public Interactive Displays for Collaboration. *Lecture Notes in Computer Science 2498*, (2002), 663-670.
18. Santanen, E.L., Briggs, R.O., and Vreede, G.-J. de. The Impact of Stimulus Diversity on Creative Solution Generation: An Evaluation of the Cognitive Network Model of Creativity. In *Proc. HICSS*, IEEE Computing (2003).
19. Scott, S.D., Grant, K.D., and Mandryk, R.L. System guidelines for co-located, collaborative work on a tabletop display. In *Proc. ECSCW*, ACM Press (2003), 159-178.
20. Shneiderman, B. Creativity support tools. *CACM 45*, 10 (2002), 116-120.
21. Stewart, J., Bederson, B., and Druin, A. Single display groupware: a model for co-present collaboration. In *Proc. CHI*, ACM Press (1999), 286–293.
22. Tumminello, W. *Exploring storyboarding*. Cengage Learning, 2005.
23. Waldner, M., Hauber, J., Zauner, J., Haller, M., and Billinghurst, M. Tangible tiles: design and evaluation of a tangible user interface in a collaborative tabletop setup. In *Proc. CHI*, ACM Press (2006), 151–158.
24. Warr, A. and O'Neill, E. Tool support for creativity using externalizations. In *Proc. Creativity & Cognition*, ACM Press (2007), 127.
25. Yamamoto, K. Relationships between creative thinking abilities of teachers and achievement and adjustment of pupils. *The Journal of Experimental Education 32*, 1 (1963), 3–25.
26. History of the 'BBC Redux' project. *BBC Internet Blog*, 2008. http://www.bbc.co.uk/blogs/bbcinternet/2008/10/history_of_the_bbc_redux_proje.html.
27. Final Cut Pro Opens up with XML Interchange Format. http://developer.apple.com/appleapplications/fcpxml.htm

LightGuide: Projected Visualizations for Hand Movement Guidance

Rajinder Sodhi[1,2] **Hrvoje Benko[1]** **Andrew D. Wilson[1]**

[1]Microsoft Research
One Microsoft Way
Redmond, WA 98052
{benko, awilson}@microsoft.com

[2]Department of Computer Science
University of Illinois
201 North Goodwin Avenue, Urbana, IL 61801
rsodhi2@illinois.edu

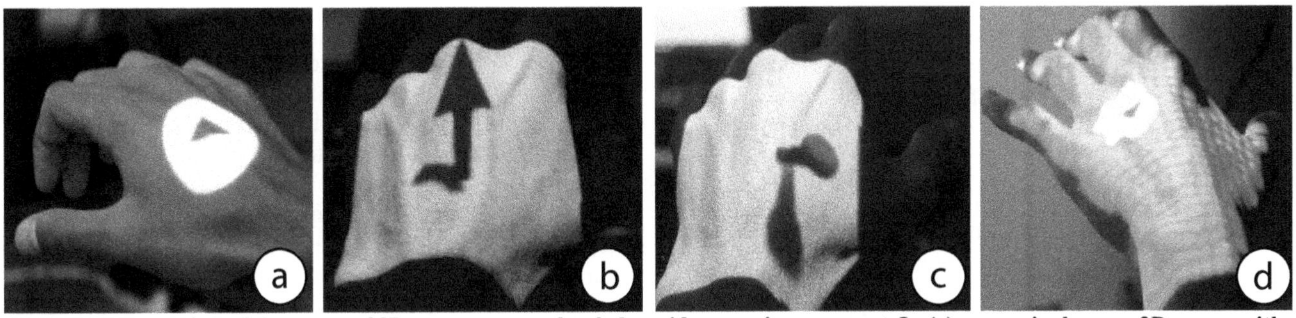

Figure 1. An overview of the range of 3D cues we created to help guide a user's movement. In (a), a user is shown a 2D arrow with a circle that moves in the horizontal plane, (b) shows a 3D arrow, (c) a 3D path where blue indicates the movement trajectory and (d) uses positive and negative spatial coloring with an arrow on the user's hand to indicate depth.

ABSTRACT

LightGuide is a system that explores a new approach to gesture guidance where we project guidance hints directly on a user's body. These projected hints guide the user in completing the desired motion with their body part which is particularly useful for performing movements that require accuracy and proper technique, such as during exercise or physical therapy. Our proof-of-concept implementation consists of a single low-cost depth camera and projector and we present four novel interaction techniques that are focused on guiding a user's hand in mid-air. Our visualizations are designed to incorporate both feedback and feedforward cues to help guide users through a range of movements. We quantify the performance of *LightGuide* in a user study comparing each of our on-body visualizations to hand animation videos on a computer display in both time and accuracy. Exceeding our expectations, participants performed movements with an average error of 21.6mm, nearly 85% more accurately than when guided by video.

Author Keywords

On-demand interfaces; on-body computing; appropriated surfaces; tracking; spatial augmented reality;

ACM Classification Keywords

H.5.2 [Information interfaces and presentation]: User Interfaces - Input devices & strategies;

INTRODUCTION

When performing gestures that are intricate or that require a great deal of technique, physical feedback from an instructor can often be useful for performing a movement. For example, when someone wants to perform the proper technique for a weight training exercise, an instructor often gives instantaneous feedback by gradually correcting the position of the user's body through physical touch.

While this exchange seems crucial, the availability of such a resource disappears when a user is no longer in the presence of an instructor. Instead, directing human movement is usually accomplished through video recordings, diagrams, animations, or textual descriptions. We rely on a bevy of online resources that include detailed graphical imagery or do-it-yourself videos (see Figure 2). However, without incremental and real-time feedback, interpreting and following a set of movements can still be a challenge.

In this paper, we explore an alternative approach to movement guidance where body movement can be directed using projected visual hints. Our system, *LightGuide*, provides users with real-time incremental feedback for movement guidance that is projected directly on their hand (see Figure 1). *LightGuide* provides a unique benefit to existing gesture guidance methods: users can focus their attention directly on the body-part rather than divide their attention between a video screen and the movement. Users can move their body-parts freely in space, releasing the user from always being orientated towards a video screen. All our system requires is a projector and depth-sensing camera. While our system does not require a user to be physically instrumented with a device, these hints can also be used in a body-worn [12,13] or on limited-screen space handheld devices, such as smartphones.

Thus, our work provides three primary contributions: First, we introduce a series of unique visualizations for movement guidance that incorporate feedback and feedforward cues. Second, we contribute a prototype system, *LightGuide*, which is comprised of a single overhead projector and depth-sensing camera to sense the user and their movements. Our proof-of-concept system facilitates the display of our visual hints on a user's body and allows us to replay pre-recorded or system-generated 3D paths at a user-driven pace or dynamically controllable speeds. Finally, we show results of our quantitative comparative evaluation, qualitative user feedback and discuss the pros and cons of our approach.

MOTIVATION

We can envision a number of practical applications that leverage on-body projected hints for guidance. For example, imagine an amateur athlete working on punching exercises during martial arts training. With projected hints, the system can direct the user towards the optimal reach of the arm to ensure that the shoulder is not overextended to cause injury. In another example, physical therapy patients recovering from an injury can be guided through practicing exercises at home. Novice musicians learning to play an instrument can by directed to the correct posture when their form begins to drift. We believe that all of these movements can be guided with correct spatially registered projections on a user's body.

RELATED WORK

Our on-body projection approach draws from a variety of fields, including computer-aided instruction, augmented reality, and projection-based guidance. Here we focus on the relevant related work from these areas to position and understand the contributions of the present work.

Computer-Aided Task Guidance

Receiving task guidance through computer-aided instruction has been a research focus for decades. Demonstration through animated-videos have shown that computer-based instruction can improve task performance, particularly in assembly based tasks [31]. Palmiter and Elkerton showed that well placed textual hints with animated videos can also give immediate benefits for task performance [23]. Others have explored adding graphical visual hints to video in post to help users explore a range of dance movements [29]. While these hints are statically placed in video, previous literature has also looked at using co-located real-time feedback and feedforword mechanisms to provide on-demand assistance to guide users through gestural tasks [3,11]. Such systems lead users in-situ, while a user is in the process of performing the gesture. Our work draws upon this prior research where we explore how co-located projection-based on-body hints can help show similar improvements for movement tasks.

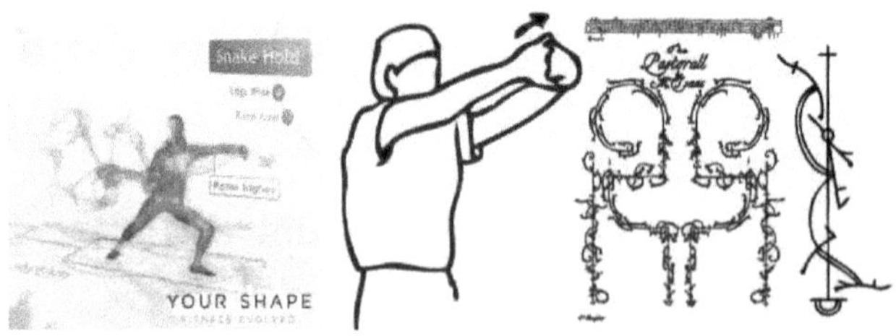

Figure 2. Examples of how people currently follow instruction for movement (e.g. Kinect virtual avatar, stretching, rhythmic dance notation [4]**).**

Task Guidance in Augmented Reality

The field of Augmented Reality (AR) has shown a number of methods to provide guidance by using head-mounted displays or mobile devices to convey instructions that are superimposed on virtual or real world video feeds [1,8]. Feiner et al. explored using AR to guide users through repairing laser printers. More recently [21,22], AR has been demonstrated for a variety of tasks, such as playing the guitar or manufacturing. In tangible AR, White et al. explored using a variety of graphical representations through 'ghosting' to enable the discovery and completion of gestures [32]. While these approaches are promising, head-mounted displays can be cumbersome for users to wear and diminutive screens can constrain the user experience.

Augmenting Environments with Projectors

Recent advancements in projection technology have made it possible to imbue user's environments with projection capabilities [24,26,27,33]. For example, Wilson and Benko explored using a series of depth-sensing cameras and projectors to transform a room-sized environment to enable un-instrumented surfaces (e.g., a desk) to emulate interactive displays.

In addition, the emergence of miniaturized projection technology has opened up the possibility of appropriating the user's body as a display surface where even a user's hand alone contains more surface area than a typical smart phone [12,13]. In addition to body-worn projection systems, handheld [5,6] and head-mounted projectors [15] also allow users to be mobile, without requiring their environments to be permanently instrumented with projectors and cameras [18,20,25]. All of these projection-based approaches are similar to our approach using a depth-sensing camera for tracking and a projector to turn an arbitrary surface into an interactive display.

Projection-Based Guidance

The use of projection-based augmented reality AR for guiding users through tasks has been a research vision in recent years [10]. Kirk et al. looked at using projection in remote collaborative scenarios (e.g., remote Lego building) with real-time projection guidance co-located next to the user's hand on a static desk [19]. Similarly, Rosenthal et al.

found that combining static text and pictorial instructions on a screen with micro-projection based guidance on physical objects improved overall task performance [28]. In contrast to prior literature, we explore projecting visual-hints with real-time feedback directly on the user's hand that is tracked in mid-air for movement guidance.

DESIGN CONSIDERATIONS FOR GUIDING MOVEMENT

To provide in-situ guidance for the user's movement, visual hints need to *convey* a sense of where to move next. We are motivated by the idea that one can co-locate the instruction for the movement with the body part that needs to be moved along a desired path. To inform the design of such hints and the validity of the overall approach, we focused this work on projected hints on the user's hand as it moves freely in space. We believe that our approach allows the user to focus their attention on body part and the movement itself. Through our initial exploration as well as leveraging prior literature, we highlight six critical aspects that need to be considered when designing on-body guidance hints: (1) feedback, (2) feedforward, (3) scale, (4) dimension, (5) perspective and (6) timing.

Feedback

Feedback components provide information about the current state of the user during the execution of the movement. This feedback can come in the form of a user's current position, the path the they took (e.g., [3]), or their error or deviation from the path, to name a few. For example, with position, the feedback can either be relayed to the user in a relative sense (e.g. a user's projected "progress" along a movement path) or in an absolute sense (e.g. a user's absolute deviation from a movement path).

Feedforward

Feedforward components provide information to the user about the movement's shape *prior* to executing the movement. As described in [3,11], the feedforward can come in the form of showing the user where to go next, a segment of the movement path ahead, or simply show the user the entire movement path. One possible downside for showing the whole movement is for sufficiently complex paths, path self-occlusions may obstruct a user's view of where to move next.

Scale

To gain insight into how to convey scale, we consider Steven's Power Law which describes a relationship between magnitude of a stimulus (e.g., visual length, visual area, visual color) and its perceived intensity or strength (projected line, projected circle, projected intensity) [2]. That is, the relationship allows us to understand how users perceive visual cues, e.g., the area of a circle, color, or the length of a line, and describes how well they convey the scale of a movement (e.g., what is the distance I should move my hand to get from point A to point B when a projected line denotes distance versus using area or color to denote distance?).

Dimension

As found in [17] the way in which the user perceives the structure of the task greatly affects their performance for high-dimensional input. As such, how we convey where to move in three-dimensions depends on how intuitive the user finds the visual hint. For certain users, the most intuitive way to get from point A to point B may be in the form of a visual hint that is broken down into two distinct components, e.g. where to move horizontally and vertically. In contrast, for others, a single metaphor hint may be the most perceptually intuitive, e.g. go from point A to B all in one simultaneous task.

Perspective

One aspect of conveying an on-body visual hint is to explore egocentric and exocentric viewpoints [30] (e.g. a first person and third person perspective, respectively) With an egocentric viewpoint, we want users to get a greater sense of presence where the hints become a *natural extension* of their bodies, reinforcing guidance by "tugging" the user's hand along the movement path. In contrast, with an exocentric viewpoint, rather than seeing guided hints embodied in the user, they are seen at an overview (e.g., a video).

Timing

In our design of an on-body visual hint, we feel that there are two main approaches that may effectively communicate timing in motion: *system imposed timing* and *self-guidance.* For system imposed timing, users follow a visual hint that is displayed at a system specified speed. A visual hint can convey a range of dynamics, such as in keeping the speed constant or changing it dynamically throughout the movement. For self-guidance, the user can see a visual hint and choose the pace at which they react to the hint.

LIGHTGUIDE PROJECTED HINTS

We describe a set of visual hints that follow important aspects of the design space we have highlighted. Our visual hints can be used to help guide a user's movement in all three translational dimensions. To our knowledge, this is the first implementation of on-body projected hints for real-time movement guidance. While this is a rather large design space with many possible solutions, our iterative design process included an analysis of 1D, 2D and 3D visual hints and offers a set of compelling solutions that can inform future designs. We focus our descriptions on the final hint design which resulted from our iterative process, but encourage the reader to see the accompanying video for a more complete reference of alternatives.

In this initial exploration we have chosen to focus and verify our ideas by tackling hand translation first (i.e., movements in the x, y and z dimensions), without any rotations of the hand. As such, we leave a visual vocabulary for 3D rotations to future work.

Follow Spot

The Follow Spot can be seen in Figure 3(a)-(b). Through our initial pilots, we found the most intuitive metaphor for

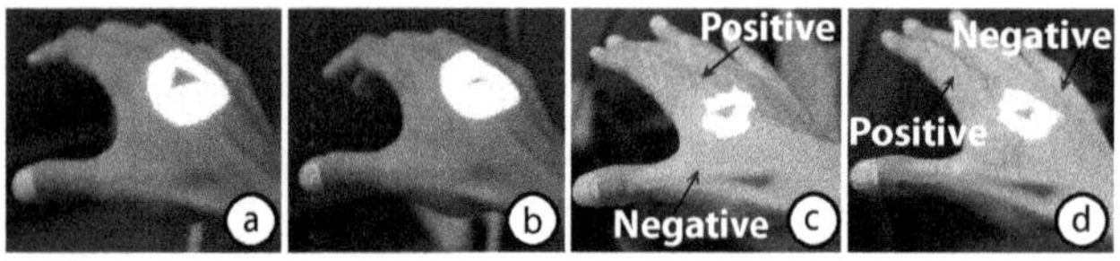

Figure 3. In (a)-(b) the *Follow Spot* shows a user a white circle and a black arrow reduces in size when user moves their hand up, (c)-(d) the *Hue Cue* shows positive coloring (blue) which represents the direction a user should follow horizontally while moving away from the negative coloring (red).

users was to use 1D visual length (e.g. distance), which is reflected in the mapping specified by Steven's Law [2]. To specify feedback in depth, the 1D arrow points away from the user to signal moving up and points the arrow towards the user to signal moving down. The size of the arrow dictates the distance to the target depth position communicating the scale of the movement. That is, as the user moves up in the z-direction to hit a target depth as specified by a large black arrow pointing away from the user, the tip of the arrow decreases in size until it becomes a black horizontal line. The visual hint otherwise contains no feedforward mechanism.

Hue Cue

We create a visual hint that utilizes negative and positive spatial coloring to indicate direction and the space a user should occupy, shown in Figure 3(c)-(d). The cue uses a combination of spatial coloring in x and y and depth feedback in z to guide a user's movement in three dimensions. The feedforward component is conveyed in the positive coloring, shown in blue and the negative coloring for feedback in red. To perform the whole movement, a user can continuously move toward the blue and away from the red. In order for a user to see if they are moving at the correct depth, a *Follow Spot* hint is projected in the middle of the hand.

3D Arrow

We create a more direct mapping to visualize direction by conveying a simple 3D Arrow to the user, shown in Figure 4(a)-(b). The benefit of using a *3D Arrow* is that direction for all three dimensions, *x, y and z* can be conveyed in a single metaphor. Additionally, to engage the user's egocentric viewpoint, we render the *3D Arrow* from the user's perspective and add shading to emphasize its 3D shape.

3D Pathlet

We create a *3D Pathlet* metaphor where users are shown a small segment of the path ahead in the movement. This visual hint allows users to see a segment of the path, denoted in blue in Figure 4(c)-(d) as a form of feedforwad. The red dot provides users with their relative position, projected on the movement path. The benefit of the *3D Pathlet* is that users can see changes in direction of curved motions along the path well before they execute the movement. Figure 4(c)-(d) shows a user completing a movement shaped in the form of the alphabet letter 'N'

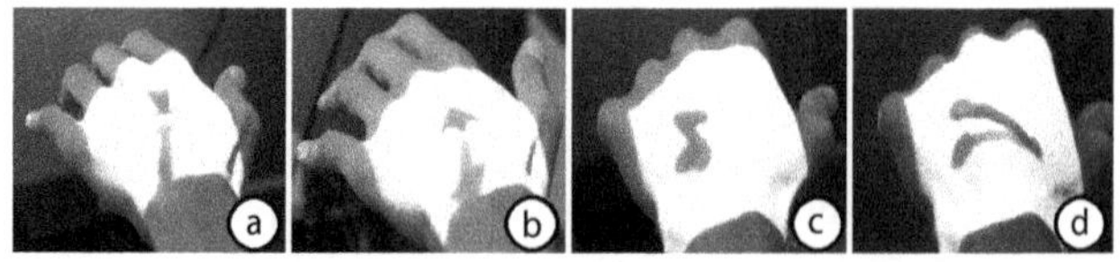

Figure 4. In (a)-(b), the *3D Arrow* is shown pointing down and up, (c)-(d) the *3D Pathlet*, shows the user (red dot) a small segment of what is ahead in the path (denoted in blue).

displayed at a 45-degree angle. Additionally, for perspective, a similar shadow is used to emphasize the *3D Pathlet*'s shape. As shown in Figure 5, when the user distorts their hand significantly, the 3D illusion is diminished.

Movement Guidance Algorithm

LightGuide can replay any pre-recorded movement (e.g., recorded with a depth sensor) or ideal generated path (e.g., parametric wave). For a path, we summarize our algorithm (Figure 6) as follows: The path is first pre-processed into segments, where a segment is composed of two points in the order with which we wish to guide the user. The path is then translated to the user's current hand position where the visual hint is rendered. As the user follows a visual hint, any deviation from the path can result in an absolute, relaxed-absolute or relative projection (Figure 6(a)-(c)). The user continues through the path using one of these three approaches until the path is complete.

The absolute projection results in a visual hint that immediately guides the user back to the movement path once deviated, the relaxed-absolute movement slowly guides the user back to the movement path and the relative projection simply shows the user the next direction of the movement without requiring the user to be directly on the path. Each projection type is task dependent. For example, a dancing movement may be less stringent about following the exact path and could thus use a relative projection. In contrast, an exercise movement where a user can potentially strain a muscle if done incorrectly may use an absolute or relaxed-absolute projection. Based on our initial pilots, we chose to have the *Follow Spot* use an absolute mapping, the *Hue Cue* to have a relative mapping in *x and y* and an absolute mapping in *z,* while the *3D Arrow* and *3D Pathlet* use a relative mapping.

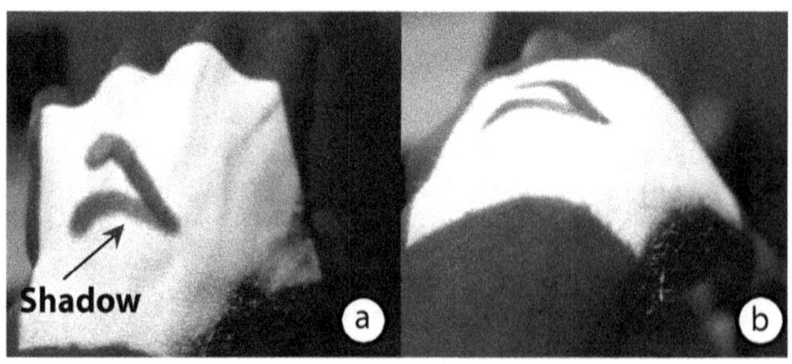

Figure 5. In (a), the *3D Pathlet* creates an illusion of the path extending beyond your body where the shadow emphasizes the 3D nature of the hint. In (b), the illusion is diminished when the user's hand is orientated at an extreme angle.

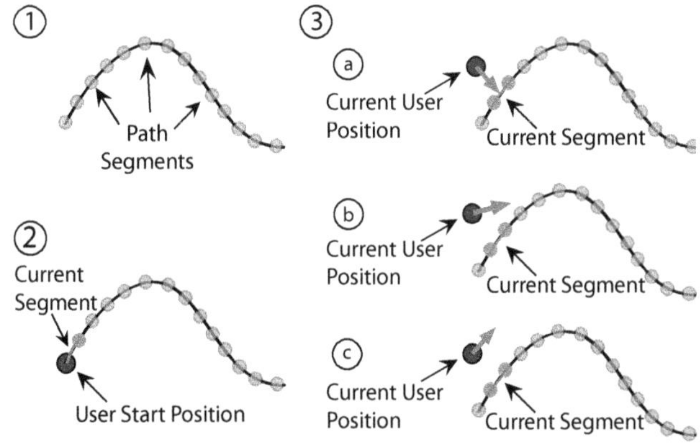

Figure 6. Our algorithm first breaks down the path into smaller segments. The path is translated to the user's current hand position and the visual hint is rendered to begin guiding the user. When the user deviates from the desired path, the visual hint can, (a) direct the user back to the closest point on the path, (b) incrementally bring the user back to the path, or (c) guide the user through a relative movement.

Dynamics

For *system imposed timing*, LightGuide can replay the visual hint so that it follows the movement path automatically in space at any speed. To ensure that the visual hints do not move off of the user's hand, we followed the same procedure as [12] in which we compute a derivative map of the depth image to check for large changes in the boundaries at the contours of the hand. That is, if the visual hint reaches the contour of the hand, it stops moving until a user has adequately caught up to the path. For the *self-guidance* approach, the system relies on the user to direct themselves through the movement. A visual hint describes the motion trajectory through feedback and feedfoward cues and a user can choose their own pace.

LIGHTGUIDE IMPLEMENTATION

Our proof-of-concept LightGuide system, seen in Figures 7, consists of two primary components. First is a commercially available Microsoft Kinect Depth Camera, which provides 640x480 pixel depth images at 30Hz. The second component is a standard off the shelf InFocus IN1503 wide-angle projector (1280x1024 pixels) [16]. The depth camera and projector are both rigidly mounted to a metal stand positioned above the user. This ensures that we could adequately see the user's hand motions as well as to ensure that our projected visual hints would fully cover the user's hands.

The visual hints are rendered from a fixed perspective that assumes a user is looking down a 45-degree angle towards their hand. While occlusion (particularly self-occlusion) is a fundamental problem with all projector-camera systems, we do not feel that this played a significant role in users' interactions. In the future, multiple projectors and cameras can be used to help reduce the effects of occlusions on more complex unconstrained movements.

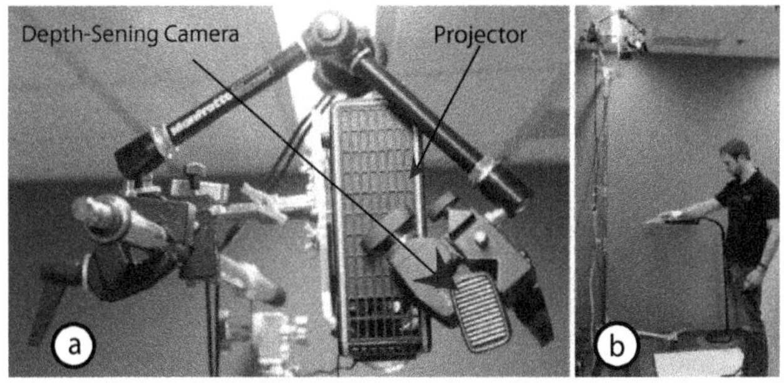

Figure 7. (a) LightGuide uses a single projector and depth sensing camera, (b) the projector and depth camera are fixed over the user's body.

Projector Camera Calibration

For the visual hints to be correctly projected on a user's hand, we must first unify the projector and camera into the same coordinate space. We calibrate our projector to the depth camera as the camera already reports real world coordinates (mm). The intrinsic parameters of the projector can be modeled using the diagonal field of view and the center of projection. To compute the extrinsic parameters, we require four non-coplanar correspondences between points that can be seen in the depth camera and projector. Once we establish correspondences between the 2D points of the projector and the 3D points of the camera, we use the POSIT algorithm [7] to find the position and orientation of the projector.

Hand Tracking

The prototype system first transforms every pixel in the input image into world coordinates and then crops pixels outside of a volume of 1 cubic meter. This removes the floor, walls and other objects in the scene (e.g. a desk). The prototype then identifies the user's arms by determining continuous regions along the depth image. The system then finds the farthest point along the entire arm by tracing through the continuous region eventually reaching the most distant point along the hand. To extract the user's hand, we assume a constant hand length [14] which worked well in our tests. A distance transform [9] is then used on the resulting image and the maxima is assumed to be the center position of the hand.

USER STUDY

The purpose of this study was to demonstrate the feasibility of our approach and to determine if our prototype is capable of guiding a user's hand in mid-air. Specifically, we wanted to know how accurately users follow on-body projected visualizations. We also wanted to investigate how the accuracy and behavior of a user changes for paths at varying depth levels. In addition to following, we also explored the accuracy and speed of self-guided movements where users dictate their own pace of a movement.

To place LightGuide's performance in context, we compared our method to video as we felt it was representative of a resource that users currently utilize. The *video condition*, shown in Figure 8, is comprised of a 3D

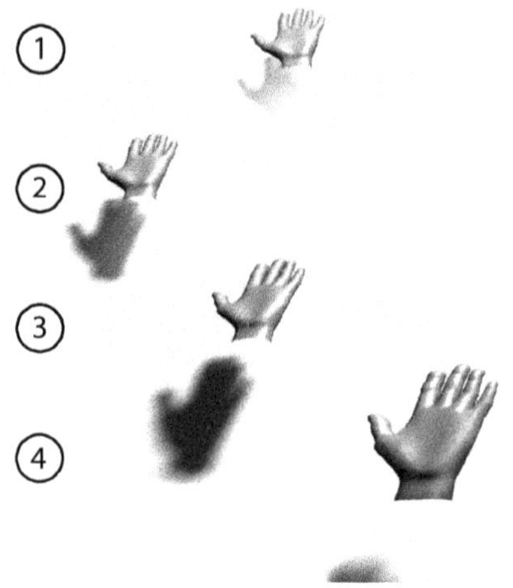

Figure 8. A rendering of the 3D hand that is used in our video condition. The motion is an arc that moves towards the user and gradually increases in depth.

model of hand that follows an ideal, system-generated path. Although our animated video does not provide nearly as much visual context to participants as a real life video, a system controllable video allowed us to remove the effects of any human or tracking error that could affect the movement paths. More importantly, the animated video allowed us to control the perspective of the video (e.g. rendered from the user's perspective) as well as precisely control the speed and timing of replayed movements. While we feel that the best performance with our system can be attained by using both video and on-body hints, our comparison independently measures the effect of our visual hints and video for movement guidance.

Participants

We recruited 10 right-handed participants from our local metropolitan area (2 female) ranging in age from 18 to 40. All participants were screened prior to the study to ensure their range of motion was adequate to perform our tasks. The study took approximately 90 minutes and participants received a gratuity for their time.

Test Movements

Our goal was to support interactions on a variety of movements. For our user study, we included five different paths: a line which must be traced back and forth, a square, a circle, an 'N', and a line plus a curve (Figure 9). These paths share similar characteristics to the types of movements patients are asked to perform in physical therapy sessions (see Motivation). The paths, seen in Figure 9, range in length from 300 to 630mm (mean = 438.1 mm, SD = 130.6mm). To ensure that we adequately tested a variety of depth levels, we vary the paths at three different angles: 0°, 45° and 90° with respect to the horizontal plane in the participant's frame of reference.

Procedure

During the experiment, participants were instructed to stand at a comfortable position underneath the overhead projector and depth-sensing camera. Prior to starting, we verified that

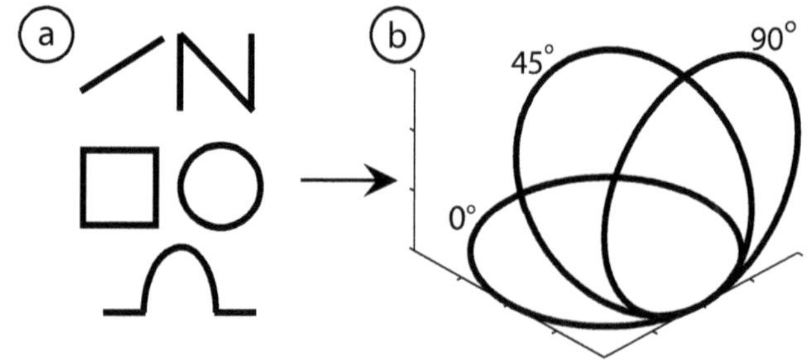

Figure 9. In (a) the test paths used in our study, (b) each path is oriented at 0°, 45° and 90° (only a circle path is shown).

each participant had enough room to move their hand while being adequately tracked by the system.

The primary task consisted of a participant moving their hand in space following specific hand guidance visual hints. By 'following', we mean that a visual hint would begin moving in space at a speed of 30 mm/sec. and participants would follow the hint and respond to its cues. Our choice of 30mm/sec for visualization speed was chosen through informal pilot studies that had users try out a variety of speeds. 30 mm/sec was chosen to be the most comfortable constant speed while still producing reasonable hand motions. To quantify how users perform a movement at their own pace, a secondary task was included where the same *3D Arrow* was used without any system imposed timing. That is, the *3D Arrow* would only change position if the user responded to the direction indicated by the *3D Arrow*. We refer to this as *self-guided.*

We performed a within subjects experiment and in total, we tested 6 visual hints: *Follow Spot, 3D Follow-Arrow, 3D Self-Guided Arrow, 3D Pathlet, Video on Hand,* and *Video on Screen.* Here on, we refer to our two *3D Arrow* conditions as *3D F-Arrow* and *3D SG-Arrow.* All except the *Video on Screen* condition were projected on the participant's hand. Our baseline *Video on Screen* condition was shown to a participant on a computer monitor situated directly in front of the user. Importantly, participants were told to keep their hands flat (facing down) during the entire experiment to ensure that the visual hints would consistently appear on their hands between trials as well as to ensure consistent hand tracking performance by our system.

To provide consistent start location for each movement, we marked the desired starting hand location with markers on the floor in front of the participant and asked them to return to the marker before beginning each new trial. In each trial, participants were instructed to hold out their hand and follow the guidance cues completing a single path as accurately as possible. We asked the participant to keep the visual hint at the center of their hand. Once the path was completed, the system would sound a 'chime' and a red circle would appear on the participant's hand signaling the user to return to the start position. In total, participants were asked to follow a single visualization over our 15 test paths;

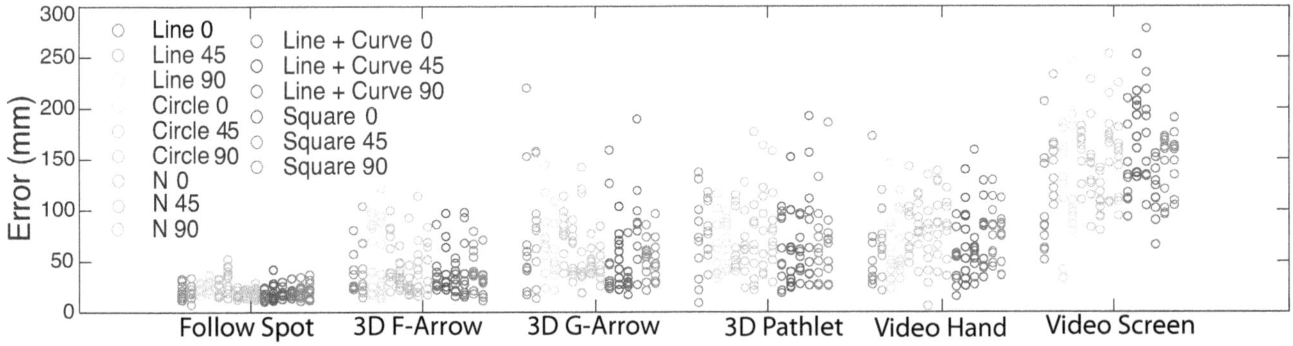

Figure 10. Overall distribution of unscaled deviations from a path. The circles denote users while colors show the 15 unique paths.

presentation order was randomized. The procedure was repeated for each of our conditions.

Before each measurement phase, participants were allowed to practice using the visual hints to move through a path. Each condition lasted approximately 10 minutes, of which 5 minutes was used for practice and 5 minutes for measurement. Between conditions, we allocated 5 minutes for participants to rest in order to reduce the effects of hand fatigue.

Each session produced 90 trials (6 conditions x 5 paths x 3 angles) per participant. To counter-balance the conditions, the presentation of each condition was randomized to remove the effects of ordering. Users were interviewed after each session followed by a short post-study interview. We recorded video of the participants and measured their position, hand-orientation and time.

RESULTS

We separate our analysis into two components: *Movement Accuracy and Movement Times.*

Our 10 participants produced a total of 900 movement trials on 15 unique paths. During the study, we experienced only a single type of outlier relating to the tracking of a user's hand. The tracking results would change depending on if the user would self-occlude their hand (e.g., rotate towards the principal axis of the camera). Additionally, we experienced 21 trails (2%) where users would lean their bodies into the capture volume, leading to momentary erroneous hand measurements that would only appear in the outer extents of the capture volume. The erroneous measurements in the outer extents were filtered in post-data analysis allowing us to use all trial measurements in our final analysis.

Movement Accuracy

We take a two-fold approach on measuring the accuracy of movements: deviation from the path and fit (e.g., see [14]). In both cases, to determine accuracy, we use the absolute Euclidian distance from the closest point as an error metric.

As in prior literature [12], we highlight two sources of systematic error: 1) non-linearity and improper calibration of the projector and camera (e.g., the location of the projected visualization differs from where the camera expects it to be) and 2) inaccuracy in the hand tracking, especially when the user's hand begins to leave the capture volume. Overall, we found a small global systematic offset between the camera and projector where the average X-offset across users was 9.02mm to the left of a path and a Y-offset of 1.05mm below a path, which is in agreement to findings in previous literature [12,14].We did not apply these global X/Y offsets, as participants would compensate for the system inaccuracy in the 'following' conditions by moving their hand until the visualization appeared at the center of their hand. In the self-guided condition, the location of the *3D G-Arrow* was sufficiently well placed in all our trials so that participants could see the visual hint.

Movement Deviations

We analyzed the average deviations of users across all paths and visualizations using their raw, unscaled, distances to the closest point on the path, (see full distribution in Figure 10 and a single user's performance in Figure 11). Using a standard ANOVA, we found that there was a significant difference between our visual hints ($F_{[5,\ 894]}$ = 276.5, $p < .001$) . A post-hoc Bonfferoni-corrected t-test on the *Follow spot* and *3D F-Arrow* performed significantly better than both video conditions with average deviations of 24.6mm (SD = 9.0mm) and 49.9mm (SD = 29.17mm) respectively (t_{16} = 25.6, $p < .001$, t_{26} = 122.5, $p < .001$).

Additionally, the distribution highlights the difficulties users had in perceiving scale for our animated videos. Surprisingly, a Bonfferoni-corrected t-test comparing the accuracy of our video conditions show that significantly smaller deviations can be achieved by showing an identically rendered video, on the user's hand (t_{56} = 93.0, $p < .001$).

Movement Shape

Although the unscaled distribution in Figure 10 shows that our users were not able to achieve the desired scaling on a path with the *video screen* condition, the results do not explain how well users do at performing the shape of the movement. To help analyze shape, we use the Iterative Closest Point (ICP) algorithm to register the user's movements to our model paths [34]. With ICP, we have the flexibility of rotating, translating and scaling an object in all three axes to find the best match. For our purposes, we

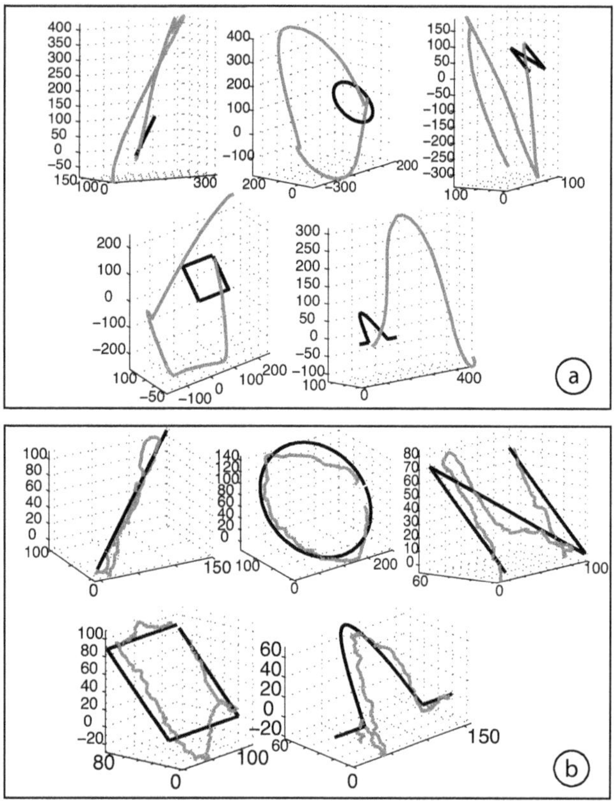

Figure 11. A single user's performance on paths oriented at 45° using the *Video Screen* (top) and *Follow Spot* (bottom row) visual hint. The ground truth is denoted in black and the user's movement is shown in red. Axis units are in mm.

exclude rotation from our ICP transformation as our path's unique characteristics are defined by their angle of rotation. That is, we wanted to see how well users perceived angles in video and excluding rotation allowed us to analyze deviations from angled motions.

Figure 12 shows results on the change in deviation when a user's path is scaled and translated with ICP. On average, participants using the *video screen* condition deviated from the desired path by 25.1mm (mean SD = 7.3mm), while the *video hand* condition faired comparably. Participants using the *Follow Spot* condition showed significantly less deviation at 13.7mm (mean SD = 6.6mm) ($t_{16} = 11.4$, $p < .001$).

Additionally, our results indicate that there was a significant performance difference in orientation of the paths in the *video screen* condition ($F_{[2, 147]} = 24.6$, $p < .001$). On average, participants performed angled movements with an average deviation of 43.2mm (SD = 9.3mm), approximately 40% less accurately than flat or vertical movements.

Movement Times

We break down movement measurements into two components: self-guided times for the *3D SG-Arrow* compared to the video conditions and distances ahead or behind a path for each of our visual hints.

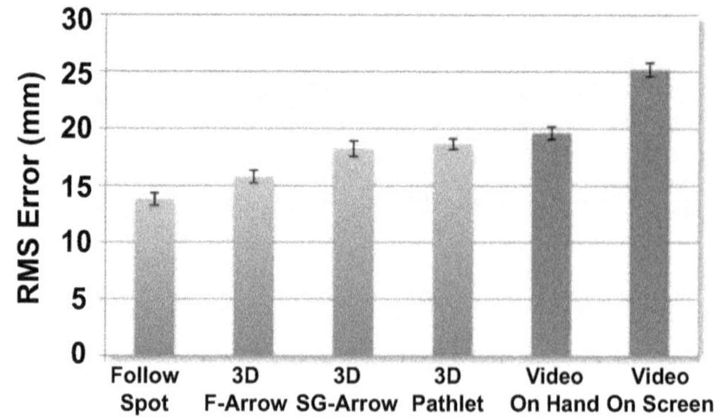

Figure 12. The Iterative Closest Point Algorithm is used to analyze the performance of a user's shape. A user's movement is translated and scaled iteratively until their motion converges to the ideal path. Error bars encode standard error of the mean.

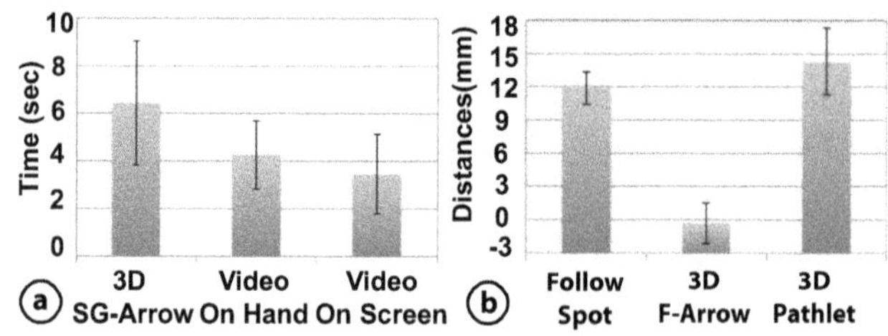

Figure 13. (a) Participants movement times were analyzed in the 3D SG-Arrow condition and compared to video on hand and video on screen and (b) shows participant's average distance behind each projected visualization.

Self-Guided Times

The average movement times across all users and paths for the *3D G-Arrow, video screen,* and *video hand* are visualized in Figure 13(a). With the *3D SG-Arrow*, although participants were able to perform the movements with more accuracy over both video conditions, movement times for video were significantly faster ($F_{[2, 447]} = 54.9$, $p < .001$).

On average, participants performed *video screen* movements with a mean of 3.45s (SD = 1.67s), nearly twice as fast as the *3D SG-Arrow*. These results reflect our observation that participant's tendencies were to first see the whole path conveyed on video, where users acquire the gist of the entire movement. In contrast, users with the *3D SG-Arrow* would perform movements in situ, figuring out direction as they moved along the path.

Distance Ahead/Behind Paths

Figure 13(b) displays the average distance (mm) participants were in front, or behind each of the visualizations in the 'following' conditions. To illustrate how participants follow a *3D F-Arrow*, Figure 14 displays a single participant's movement on a circle that is oriented at 45 degrees with the respect to a canonical horizontal X-Y plane.

User Feedback

In the video condition, users were able to quickly perform movements, but often expressed frustration with the lack of

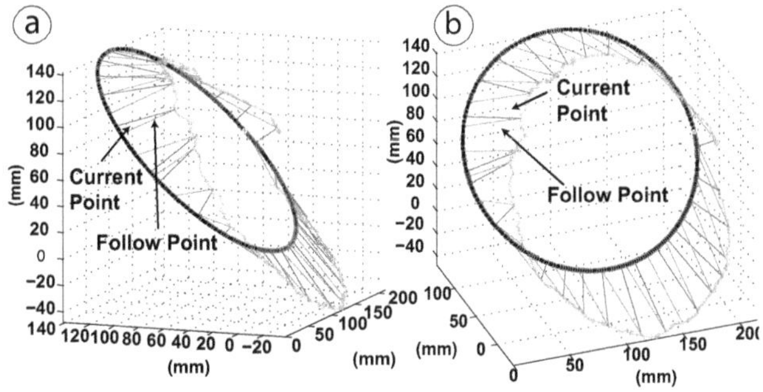

Figure 14. The plots show the same movement from two perspectives of how far in-front or behind a user's hand is compared to the projected visual hint. Green denotes a participant's path, the red line shows the actual position of the hint and the blue line shows the projected point on the path.

feedback. As one participant described for video, "It was harder to reproduce subtle movements, then to follow. It was also harder to judge elevation based on the size of the hand." Importantly with video, users also described the lack of feedforward hints. As one participant said, "With video, you have global features. You just never know what's coming next."

With the *Follow spot* visualization, users commented on the general ease of understanding of the visualization. For example, as a participant explained, "The circle one was simplest, it was only telling you up or down. Less displayed info made it easier." Similarly, another participant noted, "For me, the best visualization was probably the circle with the arrow, as once I was used to the mechanics of it, it became somewhat second nature." With the *3D Pathlet*, users commented on the benefits of knowing what was coming up ahead in the movement. As a participant described, "The feedback was great and I liked seeing where I was going." Although occlusions were not prevalent in all paths, users occasionally commented on a "disappearing red ball." As a result, participants would tend to overshoot a path, as they were unable to see how much of the path they had consumed.

Following and Leading

A majority of our users in our interviews (8/10) said they preferred the 3D *SG-Arrow* over all other visualizations. The ability for users to shape their own tempo was important to their overall satisfaction with the visualization. As a participant noted, "Creating my own tempo made it easier to concentrate on where I was moving." Another participant described, "If I go faster, I feel like I can do it better. Moving at my own speed lets me concentrate on what the system wants me to do. Because it's reacting to me, I can focus on the shape of the path. I didn't have to follow a slower system when I could do better."

DISCUSSION

The results of our study support our approach of guiding users' movements with on-body projections in that users were able to perform more accurately with our system over video. Our reasoning for using an animated video was to adequately control for perspective, tracking error and speed. However, we hypothesize that the reason for the large difference in scale was that we only provided users with a single shadow on a white horizontal plane for visual context. Thus, a more representative measure of accuracy with our hints can be seen in our analysis with ICP, where the *Follow Spot* visual hint did significantly better than all other conditions. In general, users' qualitative feedback also reflected our empirical findings where general comments positively reflected the ease of understanding the hint.

However, this accuracy comes at a cost. With our *3D SG-Arrow*, users were able to accurately guide themselves through a path, but were unable to do so at the same speed as video. One reason for this behavior may be attributed to users being able to see the movement before completing the path, getting the gist of the motion. Although we have highlighted scenarios where users are no longer in the position to look at a video screen (e.g., when they are using body-worn projection systems), a more beneficial scenario for on-body projections may be attained when combined with video. One strategy users can take is to view the gist of the motion and see the visual context in video, and then use our on-body hints to perfect the motions.

Our findings also showed that when the exact same video was moved from the screen to the hand, there was a significant performance difference in scale. While this may be attributed to the lack of visual context, or a change in scale (e.g., the video on the hand was smaller), another possibility could be that users were able to more accurately calibrate for the desired movement of their hand when the video was rendered in the same location as the physical body-part we were attempting to guide.

Surprisingly, at times users would become so immersed in the visual hints that it became unclear to them whether they were moving their hand or if it was the visualization that was moving in space. This reaction reflects similar findings in previous literature [27] where projected light was used to 'trick' viewers into thinking a static car was moving along a road.

Among the visual hints, the *3D F-Arrow* showed the most promising behavior with regard to user's consistently keeping pace with system imposed timing. That is, by simply conveying a sense of the next point along the path through direction alone, users were able to more accurately predict where to move next. Our user opinions suggest that when the task is not rhythmic in nature or requires a fixed speed/accuracy, the most benefit may be obtained by allowing the user to dictate their own pace. This allows users to have the flexibility to decide how they want to interpret and react to the visual hints.

CONCLUSION AND FUTURE WORK

In this paper, we described and evaluated four on-body projected visual hints to help guide a user's movement in mid-air. In addition, we introduced LightGuide, a proof-of concept system that uses an overhead projector and camera to display our visual hints which can replay movements at a user guided or system imposed speed. Our results suggest that users can follow our on-body hints accurately for movement of a single body part in space and can do so at a system controlled speed.

While our chief goal with the present work was to demonstrate that on-body projected hints could be used for movement guidance, we have only tested these visual hints on a user's hand. For example, these visual hints could just as easily be shown on the rest of your arms, torso and legs assuming the rest of the user's body is tracked (e.g. with the Kinect skeletal tracker). Furthermore, we have yet to explore guidance of two or more body parts (e.g. two hands) simultaneously. Another important question moving forward is how to adapt or add rotational visual hints to allow guiding a user's full range of motion.

Finally, there are many fascinating cognitive questions we would like to investigate. For example, does projecting the same visual hint on a screen allow the user to perform the movement just as accurately as projecting the hint on your body? Can on-body visual hints be used to distort the user's sense of their space, allowing us to control their range of motion? While we have helped to define what the design space of projected hints might look like to explore guidance first, we have yet to answer the question of how well users *learn* a particular movement. In addition, we have yet to explore how well users perform the dynamics of a movement, particularly when users are guided through alternating speeds. Our work has allowed us to answer the fundamental question of whether or not on-body projected hints are possible, but many interesting questions lie ahead.

ACKNOWLEDGMENTS

We thank the Microsoft Research VIBE and ASI groups, as well as the 2011 Microsoft Research interns, for helping us improve LightGuide.

REFERENCES

1. Baird, K.M. and Barfield, W. Evaluating the effectiveness of augmented reality displays for a manual assembly task. *Virtual Reality 4*, 4, 1999, 250-259.
2. Banaji, M.R. Stevens, Stanley Smith (1906–73). *Journal of Personality and Social Psychology*, 1994.
3. Bau, O. and Mackay, W.E. OctoPocus: a dynamic guide for learning gesture-based command sets. *Proc. UIST*, 2008, 37–46.
4. Britannica. http://britannica.com/EBchecked/topic/150794/dance-notation.
5. Cao, X. and Balakrishnan, R. Interacting with dynamically defined information spaces using a handheld projector and a pen. *Proc. UIST*, 2006, 225-234.
6. Cao, X., Forlines, C., and Balakrishnan, R. Multi-user interaction using handheld projectors. *Proc. UIST*, 2007, 43-52.
7. Daniel Dementhon, L.D. Model-Based object pose in 25 lines of code. *Proc. of IJCV 15*, 1 (1995), 123-141.
8. Feiner, Steve, Blaire Macintyre, D.S. Knowledge-Based augmented reality. *Commun. ACM 36*, 7, 1993, 53-62.
9. Felzenszwalb, P.F. and Huttenlocher, D.P. *Distance transforms of sampled functions*. 2004.
10. Flagg, M. and Rehg, J.M. Projector guided painting. *Proc. UIST*, 2006, 235-244.
11. Freeman, D., Benko, H., Morris, M.R., and Wigdor, D. ShadowGuides: Visualizations for In-Situ Learning of Multi-Touch and Whole-Hand Gestures. *Proc. ITS*, 2009, 165-172.
12. Harrison, C., Benko, H., Wilson, A.D., and Way, O.M. OmniTouch: Wearable multitouch interaction everywhere. *Proc. UIST*, 2011, 441-450.
13. Harrison, C., Tan, D., and Morris, D. Skinput: Appropriating the body as an input surface. *Proc. CHI*, 2010, 453-462.
14. Holz, C. and Wilson, A. Data miming: inferring spatial object descriptions from human gesture. *Proc. CHI*, 2011, 811–820.
15. Hua, H., Brown, L.D., and Gao, C. Scape: Supporting Stereoscopic Collaboration in Projective Environments. *Proc. CG*, 2004, 66-75.
16. InFocus. http://www.infocus.com.
17. Jacob, R. The perceptual structure of multidimensional input device selection. *Proc. CHI*, 1992, 211-218.
18. Kane, S.K., Avrahami, D., Wobbrock, J.O., and Harrison, B. Bonfire: A Nomadic system for hybrid laptop-tabletop interaction. *Proc. UIST*, 2009, 129-138.
19. Kirk, D. and Stanton Fraser, D. Comparing remote gesture technologies for supporting collaborative physical tasks. *Proc. CHI*, 2006, 1191-1200.
20. Mistry, P. and Maes, P. WUW-wear Ur world: a wearable gestural interface. *Proc. CHI*, 2009, 4111-4116.
21. Motokawa, Y. and Saito, H. Support system for guitar playing using augmented reality display. *Proc. ISMAR*, 2006, 243-244.
22. Neumann, U. and Majoros, A. Cognitive, performance, and systems issues for augmented reality applications in manufacturing and maintenance. *Proc. of VR*, 1998, 4-11.
23. Palmiter, S. and Elkerton, J. An evaluation of animated demonstrations of learning computer-based tasks. *Proc. CHI*, 1991, 257-263.
24. Pinhanez, C. The Everywhere Displays Projector: A Device to create ubiquitous graphical interfaces. *Proc. UbiComp*, 2001, 315-331.
25. Raskar, R., Beardsley, P., Van Baar, J., et al. RFIG Lamps: interacting with a self-describing world via photosensing wireless tags and projectors. *Proc. of SIGGRAPH*, 2004, 406–415.
26. Raskar, R., Welch, G., Cutts, M., Lake, A., Stesin, L., and Fuchs, H. The office of the future: A unified approach to image-based modeling and spatially immersive displays. *Proc. SIGGRAPH*, 1998, 179-188.
27. Raskar, R., Welch, G., Low, K.L., and Bandyopadhyay, D. Shader lamps: Animating real objects with image-based illumination. *Proc. Eurographics*, 2001, 89-102.
28. Rosenthal, S., Kane, S.K., Wobbrock, J.O., and Avrahami, D. Augmenting On-Screen Instructions with Micro-Projected Guides: When it works, and when it fails. *Proc. UbiComp*, 2010, 203-212.
29. SynchronousObjects. http://synchronousobjects.osu.edu.
30. Tan, D.S., Pausch, R., and Hodgins, J. Exploiting the cognitive and social benefits of physically large displays. 2004.
31. Watson, G., Curran, R., Butterfield, J., and Craig, C. The effect of using animated work instructions over text and static graphics when performing a small scale engineering assembly. *Proc. CE*, 2008, 541–550.
32. White, S., Lister, L., and Feiner, S. Visual Hints for tangible gestures in augmented reality. *Proc. ISMAR*, 2007, 1-4.
33. Wilson, A.D. and Benko, H. Combining multiple depth cameras and projectors for interactions on, above and between surfaces. *Proc. UIST*, 2010, 273–282.
34. Zhang, Z. Iterative point matching for registration of free-form curves and surfaces. *JCV 13*, 2 1994, 119-152.

Understanding Flicking on Curved Surfaces

Simon Voelker Christine Sutter Lei Wang Jan Borchers

RWTH Aachen University
52056 Aachen, Germany
{voelker, borchers}@cs.rwth-aachen.de
{christine.sutter, lei.wang}@psych.rwth-aachen.de

ABSTRACT
Flicking is a common interaction technique to move objects across large interactive surfaces, but little is known about its suitability for use on non-planar, curved surfaces. Flicking consists of two stages: First, visually determining the direction in which to flick the object, then planning and executing the corresponding gesture. Errors in both stages could influence flicking accuracy. We investigated flicking interactions on curved interactive surface to evaluate which type of error influences accuracy. Therefore, we carried out three user studies to analyze how each stage of flicking on a curved surface is influenced. Our main findings are: 1) Flicking gestures are more accurate if horizontal and vertical surface are joined by a continuous curve than if they are separated by an edge or gap. 2) Flicking gestures on curved surfaces are mostly influenced by the motor execution stage of the gesture rather than the visual perception stage. 3) Flicking accuracy decreases as the starting point of the gesture is moved closer to the curve. 4) We conclude with a first mathematical model to estimate the error users will make when flicking across a curve.

Author Keywords
Curved surface; touch-input; flicking

ACM Classification Keywords
H.5.2 Information Interfaces and Presentation: *User Interfaces - Ergonomics, Theory and methods*

General Terms
Design, Human Factors, Measurements

INTRODUCTION
Moving objects around is a common action on large interactive tabletops and surfaces. For this, users have to touch the object and drag it to its destination. For long distances, this operation can become slow and awkward as the target position moves beyond the user's reach.

To improve the efficiency of these movements, several approaches have been proposed. One of the simplest solutions

CHI'12, May 05–10, 2012, Austin, TX, USA.

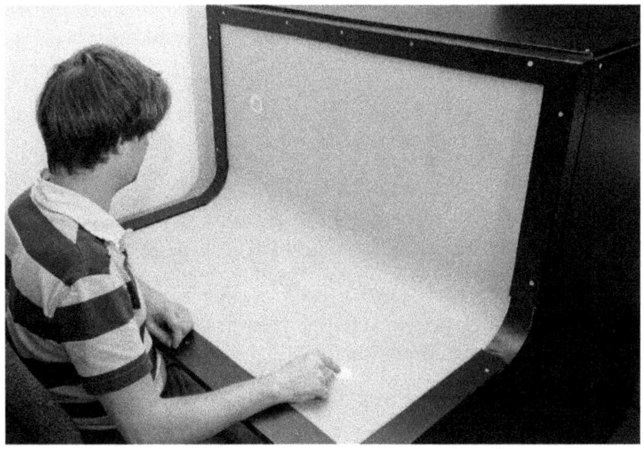

Figure 1. A user performing a flicking gestures on on the *BendDesk*, our prototype of a curved interactive surface.

is to flick the object to its target position. This simulates the real-world throwing action that people use to move objects, e.g., a book, over a large distance on a table. To flick a digital object on an interactive surface, the user performs a sliding gesture into the direction of the target, then lets go, and the object continues to move into the direction thus indicated. In this paper, we are not interested in questions of velocity or how far the object travels, focusing instead on better understanding the direction of flicking gestures.

To conduct this gesture, a user has to first visually identify the spatial relation between source object intended target position, then create and execute a motor plan such that her sliding gesture points in the direction of the target. This implies that flicking accuracy depends on how accurately the user can (1) identify the correct direction with her visual system and (2) create and execute the motor plan using her motor system.

Identifying the correct direction on a planar surface is not very complex, because the three-dimensional line between the source object and the target position lies directly on the surface on which the digital object will move. Furthermore, the user can use the usually rectangular frame around the surface as a basic reference system. This leads to the assumption that the accuracy of flicking gestures on planar surfaces depends mostly on the motoric ability to derive and execute the motor plan of the sliding gesture.

Prior research has proposed systems with multiple but discrete interactive horizontal and vertical surfaces, such as the DigiTable [2] or the WeSpace [22]. More recently, research systems like BendDesk [20] or Curve [25] have begun to merge these horizontal and vertical surfaces using a curved section into a single large curved interactive surface (1). According to Weiss et al. [20], this new form factor has several benefits over planar horizontal surfaces, but increases the complexity of flicking gestures. On a curved surface, in contrast to a normal planar tabletop, the shortest line between an object and its target position will span the 3D space between the surfaces unless object and target happen to be on the same planar display section. The user has to map this direct 3D line onto the curved surface to identify the correct direction from the source object to the target position for flicking.

In this paper, we investigate how accurately users can conduct flicking gestures on curved surfaces, and how the visual perception and motor systems influence this accuracy.

Furthermore, we examine if there are any regularities that can be used to derive a model of this gesture, to define guidelines for implementing more accurate flicking gestures on curved surfaces.

In the following, we present three studies that investigate flicking accuracy in different setups.

The first study compares a system with horizontal and vertical displays connected via a continuous curve, to a system with vertical and horizontal surfaces separated by a gap (like a multitouch table with a nearby monitor), and to a system with both surfaces adjacent to each other but with a straight edge ("fold") between them. The goal of this study is to analyze if the continuous curved connection has any effect on visual perception on the accuracy of the visual planning stage of a flicking gesture, even though the curve is only on the intended trajectory without being involved directly in the interaction.

The second study compares the accuracy of flicking gestures from different areas, and in different directions, on a curved surface. Its goal is to derive a mathematical model to help estimate and thus correct systematic errors users may make when flicking across a curve.

The third and final study analyzes the impact of where the curve lies along the flicking trajectory (closer to the beginning or closer to the target location), to derive recommendations for when and where to use flicking gestures on curved surfaces.

APPLICABILITY OF CURVED SURFACES

Combining vertical and horizontal surfaces is not new. In fact, a desktop computer workspace consists of a combination of both surfaces: an interactive vertical display and a horizontal table. Morris et al. [11] showed that each of these surfaces have different advantages for different tasks, and that an interactive system that is used to replace this workspace has to offer a vertical and a horizontal surface to address the user's needs. Nevertheless, providing both surfaces in a disconnected manner causes users to quickly lose awareness of surface not in focus [12].

Wigdor et al. found that it is possible to replace desktop systems with horizontal interactive surface [23]. Nevertheless, having to look downwards onto such a surface and having to stand while using it, is too uncomfortable for productive work.

In 1994, Sun's seminal *Starfire* video prototype [19] already proposed a single, curved horizontal and vertical interactive display surface for use in the office. More recent research has followed through on this idea, merging those two orthogonal surfaces with a curved area [20, 25]. Three benefits arose from these such curved surfaces: (1) Users are able to sit while interacting, allowing long-term usage. (2) The concave curve area enables continous inter-screen touch interaction, e.g., dragging from one surface to another. (3) The continuous display supports the impression that both areas belong to one large workspace.

These findings, combined with recent developments in bendable organic light-emitting diodes (OLEDs) and touch sensing technology suggest that curved surfaces could replace the traditional desktop computer workspace as envisioned by Tognazzini's Starfire [19]. Air traffic controller workstations, with their frequent combination of horizontal and vertical interactive screens, are another example of a likely candidate for adopting curved displays. Interaction with nonplanar surfaces has, consequently, recently become a topic of interest in HCI. This makes studying the basic interaction techniques for curved surfaces, and the mental models that users develop when using them, relevant to the CHI community.

RELATED WORK

The DigitalDesk [21] introduced one of the first interactive tabletop workspaces. The Sun Starfire vision video [19] envisioned a much larger desk consisting of horizontal and vertical areas merged into one curved interactive surface. In contrast to a purely horizontal surface, Starfire's curved surface mimicked a typical office workplace with its horizontal table and vertical computer display. This provided users with the ability to choose which surface they wanted to use for which task, and Starfire included the suggestion of a flicking gesture to move objects. In recent years, this concept of a curved surface as a desk workspace was picked up by Weiss et al. [20] and Wimmer et al. [25]. On all of these systems, moving digital objects around is one of the most frequent interaction techniques. Over the last years several techniques have been proposed as alternatives to dragging. They divide into two groups of movement control mechanisms, closed-loop and open-loop.

Closed-loop control techniques, such as dragging, provide the user with continuous real-time feedback, allowing them to correct their movement as they approach the target. Through this real-time correction, these types of movement control mechanisms are very accurate. However, they also force the user to pay attention to movement action until the action is completed. Dragging in particular can become cumbersome or physically impossible if it extends beyond the user's natural reach. This may require the user to reposition herself, potentially dropping and re-grabbing the object in the process, paying attention to avoid triggering unintended effects at the intermediate drop location. An example of these techniques is the Pick-and-Drop technique by Rekimoto [16], which allows the user to pick up an object by tapping it with a pen, and drop it in a different location.

Open-loop control techniques, such as Drag-and-Throw [3] or Shuffle [6], let the user define the direction in which the object should move at the beginning of the action. Once the automatic part of the movement was initiated, they do not provide the user with opportunities for interaction, so they cannot be corrected anymore. This leads to the problem that open-loop techniques are less accurate than closed-loop techniques. However, the user does not have to focus on the moving object during its automatic movement, until it arrives at the target position. Most open-loop techniques also allow the user to move objects to positions beyond their reach.

Flicking is one of the most common open-loop techniques. It is fairly natural, like moving a physical object across a large surface by pushing or flicking it in the designated direction. On interactive surfaces, flicking is usually executed with one finger or the entire hand [24, 26, 1]. Hinrichs and Carpendale [9] showed that even users that had never used an interactive tabletop readily used this gesture to move digital objects. To simulate the flicking of a physical object more realistically, Sato et al. [18] compared a vision-based approach in which users conducted a flicking gesture above the table to users flicking a real marble.

However, none of the above approaches investigated flicking gestures in more detail, or evaluated its accuracy. This was only studied for flicking gestures using a pen or mouse. Reetz et al. [15] showed that, in contrast to closed-loop techniques, flicking is faster but, especially for small targets, very inaccurate. They proposed a new gesture called Superflick that allows users to control the direction while the object is moving. Adding this online correction to flicking gestures significantly improved their accuracy. Another study by Moyle and Cockburn [13] compared linear mouse and pen flicking gestures, and found mouse flicking to be more accurate. They also showed that downwards flicking gestures where conducted more slowly than those pointing upwards.

HARDWARE SETUP

For our experiments, we used an interactive curved-surface tabletop with the same specifications as the BendDesk system by Weiss et al. [20]. However, we used four instead of three identical infrared cameras to improve finger tracking robustness. All cameras operated at the same resolution of 640×480 px and framerate of 60 fps.

For the first user study comparing the effect of the curve on perception, we had to adapt this setup. For the *Gap* condition with separated surfaces, we covered the curved area of the table with a wooden frame (fig. 3(b)). This provided users with the impression that the horizontal and vertical surfaces were two separated displays. Furthermore, we disabled the projection in the curved surface such that the top line of pixels on the horizontal surface beneath the gap was vertically directly connected to the bottom line of the vertical surface above the gap. This reduced the resolution of the system from 1024×1024 px to 1024×860 px.

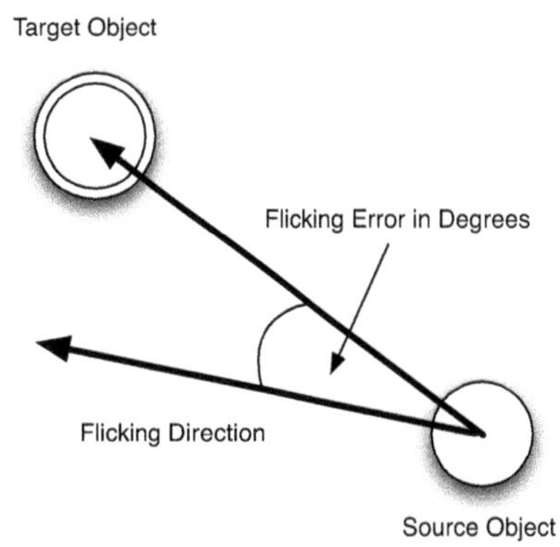

Figure 2. Error measurement for flicking gestures. Errors were measured in degrees difference from the target direction to make them independent of distance.

For the *Edge* condition with adjacent planar surfaces, we replaced the entire curved acrylic surface segment with a horizontal and a vertical stripe that were placed directly orthogonal to each other (fig. 3(c)). The vertical surface was placed at the same distance to the user as in the other conditions. In this setup, the depth of the horizontal surface was 50 cm, and the height of the vertical surface was 55 cm. As in the separated display condition, the top pixel line of the horizontal surface was directly connected to the bottom pixel line of the vertical surface. The resolution of this setup was 1024×1075 px.

GENERAL PROCEDURE

Participants were seated in front of the table, in a dimly lit room for best infrared tracking results. They worked throughout three different flicking studies. Each study was introduced by a standardized instruction and a practice trial to familiarize participants with the task. The study order was randomized for each user so that no study could benefit from learning effects.

The goal of each study was to flick a digital source object onto a digital target using the index finger of the dominant hand. To conduct the flicking gesture, participants had to put their index finger onto the digital source object, and slide their finger along the surface in the direction in which they wanted to flick the object. After executing the flick gesture, the source object moved in the computed direction at constant speed until it hit the surface boundaries. Then the interactive start area went blank, and a new trial appeared. Participants were instructed to solve each task as fast and accurately as possible.

To measure the direction, we recorded all touch points of the user's sliding movement, and computed a direction vector with a first-degree Least Squares regression. This method to determine the direction was also used by Reetz et al. [15] for gestures with a pen on a tabletop. They analyzed several approaches to computing the direction, and found that first-degree Least Squares regression was closest to users' expectations. To estimate gesture accuracy, we used the flicking error as a dependent variable. It was defined as the angle in degrees between the direct line along the surface from the

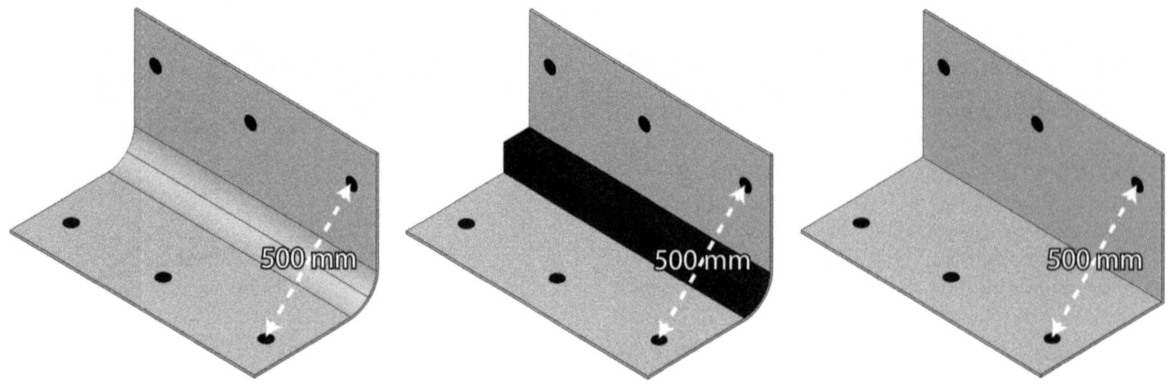

(a) Curve condition (b) Gap condition (c) Edge condition

Figure 3. Table setup conditions with object and target positions.

source object to the target, and the direction vector defined by the user's actual input (Fig. 2).

USER STUDY 1: FLICKING ACROSS THE CURVE

This first study investigated if the continuity of a curved surface has any effect on flicking accuracy, even if neither the source object nor the target lie inside the curve segment. We compared flicking accuracy between three different table conditions: Curve (fig. 3(a)), Gap (fig. 3(b)) which simulated the combination of a table and a vertical screen, and Edge (fig. 3(c)).

Participants

24 participants (21 males) age 20–39 (mean 27) volunteered for the study. Of these, 15 were computer scientists, 2 business administration managers, 4 school teachers, 2 medical scientists, and 1 mechanical engineer. All participants had normal or corrected-to-normal vision. 21 out of 24 participants were right-handed.

Task design and procedure

The experimental task and the conditions are depicted in figure 4. The system displayed the source object as a blue dot (diameter 50 px) and the target as a red circle (diameter 60 px). We defined the distance between source and target as the Euclidean distance between these two points in real-world 3D space (fig. 3). This distance resulted from the current position of the source and target as illustrated in figure 4. Therefore, the distance on the surface between source and target was different for each table condition, being smallest in the Gap condition and largest in the Edge condition.

Source and target appeared in 3 different positions on the surface. For upward flicking movements (away from the user), the source appeared within the horizontal area either 10 cm from the left edge, in the center, or 10 cm from the right edge, while the target appeared within the vertical area, again 10 cm from the left edge, centered, or 10 cm from the right edge. Downward movements were tested analogously. This resulted in 9 different tasks presented, with 3 repetitions for each movement direction. The order of start positions was randomized, and for each start position the order of trials was randomized as well.

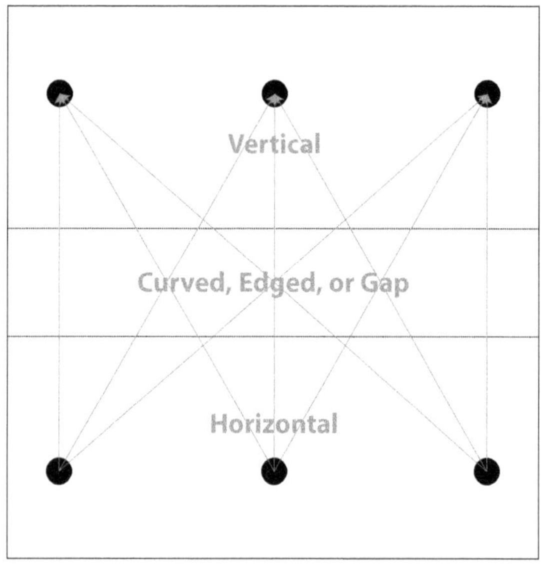

Figure 4. User study 1: Flicking tasks for the upwards direction. In the downwards direction the source object and the target exchanged positions.

Participants were randomly assigned to one of the table types (8 participants per table type). They worked through a trial block with upward movements (27 trials) and through another block with downward movements (27 trials). The experiment lasted about 5 minutes.

The experimental design was a 3 (table types) $\times$ 2 (flicking direction) mixed design with repeated measurements. We hypothesized the following outcomes:

H1: Interacting on a continuous surface (Curve or Edge conditions) will be more accurate than on a disrupted interface

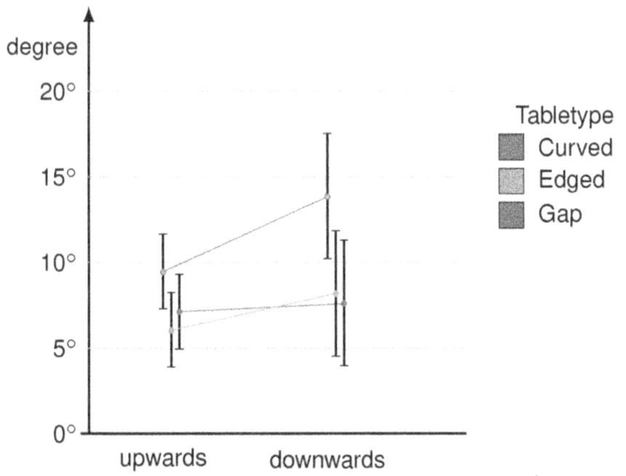

Figure 5. Diagram of the mean flicking errors dependent on flicking direction and table type. Whiskers denote 95% confidence intervals.

(table with gap through covered curve). Additionally, we wanted to explore if the smoothly curved surface would be of further benefit for flicking compared to the Edge condition with orthogonal planes.

H2a: If users take the active arm as a reference line (ones own body as frame of reference), then flicking downwards should be more accurate than flicking upwards.

H2b: If users visually represent the task by a virtual line (external coordinates as frame of reference), then flicking downwards should be less accurate than flicking upwards. This was assumed because for downward movements, the effector will block a part of the interface from view.

Results and discussion

A 3 (table type) × 2 (flicking direction) mixed ANOVA with repeated measurements revealed significant main effects for the factors table type ($F(2, 21) = 3.62; p = 0.001$) and flicking direction ($F(1, 21) = 13.68; p = 0.044$). The interaction showed a trend ($F(2, 21) = 3.21; p = 0.061$). Flicking errors were most present for the Gap condition (13.68°) and decreased for the Curve and Edge conditions (7.3° and 7.1°, respectively). Furthermore, upward flicking was more accurate than downward flicking (7.5° vs. 9.9°).

In summary, when comparing table types with a continuous versus separated surface (H1), the results clearly showed more accurate flicking actions for the continuous surfaces than for the separated one. This is in accordance with H1. This clearly shows that flicking accuracy depends on the user's visual perception and on the ability to visually identify the spatial relations between the source and the target. If flicking accuracy would only depend on the user's motor system, there would be no difference between the continuous table conditions and the separated table condition. It also shows that a continuous surface improves the user's ability to identify the correct flicking direction to hit the target. This could be explained by the fact that in contrast to the continuous surfaces, in the separated table condition, users have to develop a mental model of how both surfaces are connected, which is difficult for surfaces with different orientations as in our setup.

We also looked for differences between the two continuous surface conditions Curve and Edge. We did not find any further facilitation of operations for the Curve condition. However, 7 of 8 users in the Edge conditions stated that they needed more time to plan their flicking gesture, because they tried to identify a point on the edge between the horizontal and vertical surfaces as a reference point to determine the direction to the target. Probably, the disadvantage of edge surface was compensated through a more extensive movement planning. It could be presumed that poorer accuracy in edge surfaces would be observed, if the planning time would have been kept equal across different surfaces. Time required for movement planning, which indicates the demand on the cognitive system, will be taken into account in future works. Considering the direction, we assumed that users plan the action either with reference to internal coordinates (e.g., posture of the effective limb) or with reference to distal coordinates (e.g., anticipated visual source trajectory). We found that flicking upwards was more accurate than downwards. This is in line with the alternative hypothesis (H2b). It seems beneficial to have a full view of the surface when planning and executing the flicking action, especially when interacting with a disrupted surface.

USER STUDY 2: FLICKING IN DIFFERENT AREAS

In the second study, we compared flicking on the horizontal, vertical, and curved area to investigate if there are differences in flicking accuracy on these different areas of a curved surface.

Participants

A total of 16 participants (13 males), age 20–39 (mean=27) volunteered for the study. The group consisted of 12 computer scientists, 2 business administration managers and 2 medical scientists. 14 out of 16 participants were right-handed. All participants had normal or corrected-to-normal vision.

Task design and procedure

Figure 6 depicts the experimental task and conditions. The system again displayed the source as a blue colored dot (diameter 50 px) and the target as a red colored circle (diameter 60 px). In contrast to the first study, the distance between source and target was measured as the distance on the surface between these two points, and was 29 cm (300px) for all conditions. Trials appeared in 3 different areas (horizontal area, curve, vertical area), 2 different source positions (left side or right side) and 7 different flicking angles (with 3 repetitions each): (1) 90°, (2) 75°, (3) 60°, (4) 45°, (5) 30°, (6) 15° and (7) 0°. Participants worked through a block of trials with upward movements and through another block with downward movements. This resulted in 252 trials total. The order of trials per source position was randomized. We used a 3 (area) × 2 (flicking direction) × 7 (flicking angle) design with repeated measurements. The experiment lasted about 15 minutes. We assumed that a larger flicking angle would yield a lower flicking performance, especially within the curve:

H3: The flicking error is smaller for flicking within the horizontal area than within the vertical area or the curve.

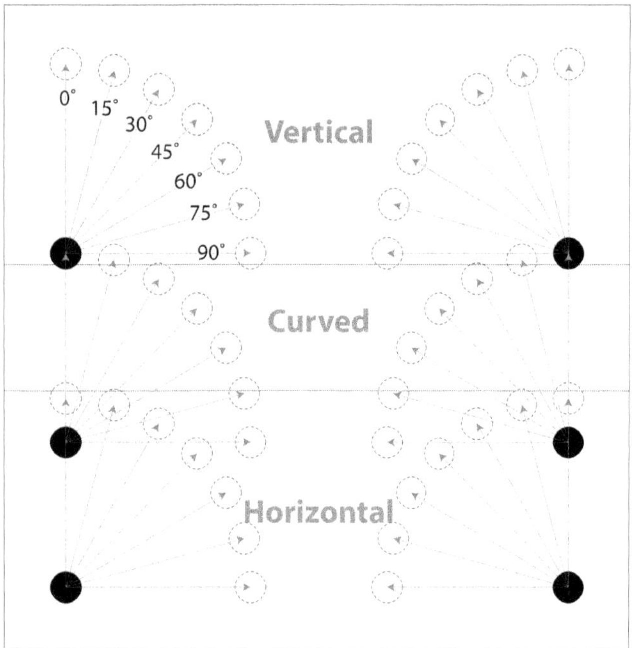

Figure 6. Flicking task in the second user study in the upwards direction.

H4: The flicking error increases with larger flicking angle. Especially flicking within the curve will be affected by the flicking angle.

H5: Flicking downwards is less accurate than flicking upwards.

Results and discussion

A 3 (area) × 2 (flicking direction) × 7 (flicking angle) ANOVA with repeated measurements showed significant main effects for the factors flicking direction ($F(1, 15) = 18.78; p = 0.001$) and flicking angle ($F(6, 90) = 12.81; p < 0.0001$), and a trend for the factor area ($F(2, 30) = 3.05; p = 0.062$). The interaction area × direction × angle was also significant ($F(12, 180) = 2.48; p = 0.005$). The main effect of flicking angle showed a severe inaccuracy for flicking at 0° (error at 10.9°), for all other angles the flicking error ranged from 6.7° to 7.5°. Furthermore, flicking upwards was more accurate than flicking downwards (6.9° vs. 8.3°). There was a trend that flicking within the horizontal area was more accurate than flicking in the curve or within the vertical area (7.0° vs. 8.0° and 7.8°). The three-way interaction revealed nearly similar accuracy for flicking at angles between 15° and 90°. When flicking downwards, actions were most inaccurate at 0°, irrespective of the interaction area. For upward flicking, this inaccuracy was only observed for interactions within the curve, but not for actions within the horizontal or vertical area.

There are two main findings from this study: First, we successfully replicated the impact of flicking direction that was observed in study 1: flicking upwards was more accurate than flicking downwards (H5). The impact of the interaction area was only partially confirmed. There was a trend for more accurate flicking within the horizontal area, especially for downward flicking at an angle between 15° and 90° (H3). Second, and completely contrary to our hypothesis, we did not find an increase of flicking errors with increasing flicking angle (H4). Accuracy was comparable for flicking angles between 15° and 90°, and interactions were more accurate than for flicking at 0°. This result is quite surprising and in contrast to findings from dragging actions. However, in our general discussion we will discuss the potential responsibility of motor constraints for this outcome.

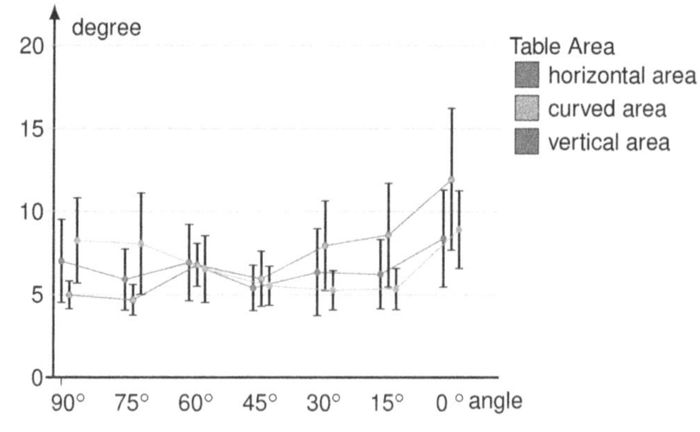

(a) Upwards direction

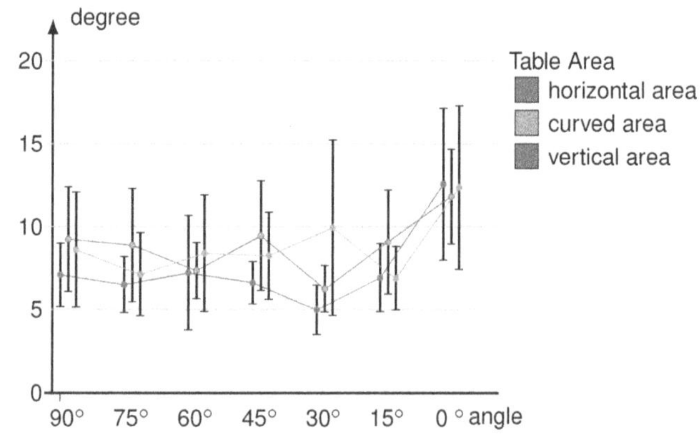

(b) Downwards direction

Figure 7. Mean flicking errors dependent on the different areas and angles. Whiskers denote 95% confidence intervals.

USER STUDY 3: FLICKING THROUGH THE CURVE

In this study we investigated if the relative position of the curved area between the source object and the target position has any influence on flicking accuracy. Additonally, we investigated if the lateral position of the source object has an effect on accuracy.

Participants

A total of 14 participants (11 males) aged 20–39 (mean=26) volunteered for the study. The group consisted of 10 computer scientists, 2 business administration managers and 2 medical scientists. All participants were right-handed and had normal or corrected-to-normal vision.

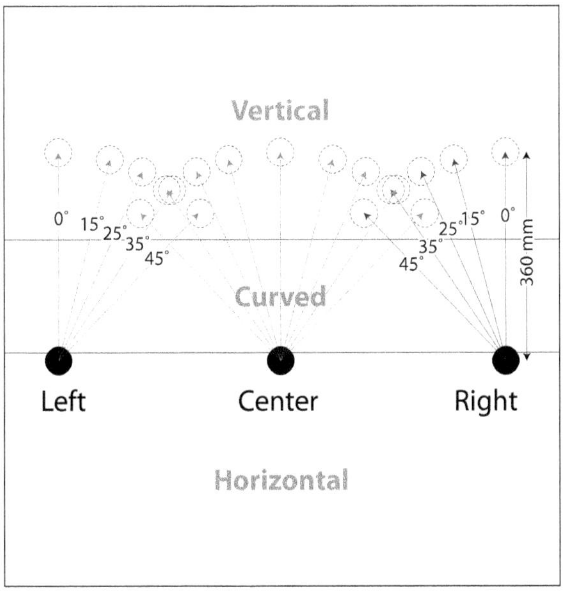

Figure 8. Flicking task in the third user study in the condition close to the curve.

Task design and procedure

Figure 8 depicts the experimental task and conditions. The system again displayed the source as a blue colored dot (diameter 50 px) and the target as a red colored circle (diameter 60 px). The distance between source and target was 368 px (35 cm).

Trials appeared at 2 different distances from the curve (start position closer to (10 cm) or farther away from (20 cm) the curve center), with 4 different combinations of source position and movement direction (flicking from left to right, from the center to the right, from the center to the left, and from right to left) and 5 different flicking angles, with 3 repetitions each: (1) 45°, (2) 35°, (3) 25°, (4) 15°, (5) 0°. Participants worked through a block of trials with the start position near the curve, then through another block with the start position farther away from the curve. This resulted in 120 trials total. Order of trials per source position and order of source positions were randomized. The study is based on a 2 (distance between source and curve center) × 4 (start position × sideward direction) × 5 (flicking angles) design with repeated measurements. The study lasted about 10 minutes.

We hypothesized the following outcomes:

H6: The flicking error increases if the source position is closer to the curve.

H7: The flicking error is higher at 0° than when flicking sideways (replication of findings from study 2).

Results and discussion

A 2 (distance between source and curve center) × 4 (start position × sideward direction) × 5 (flicking angles) ANOVA with repeated measurements revealed significant main effects of the factors "distance from curve" ($F(1,13) = 7.14; p = 0.019$), "start position and sideways direction" ($F(3,39) = 10.63; p = 0.000$) and "flicking angle" ($F(4,52) = 9.21; p = 0.000$). Flicking was more accurate when the source was positioned farther away from the curve center than when it was directly at the curve (7.8° vs. 9.7°). Flicking accuracy was almost similar for flicking angles between 15° and 45° (error: 7.6° - 8.4°), and remarkably decreased at 0° (error: 11.8°). The impact of flicking angle was more pronounced for start positions near the curve than farther away, yielding a significant interaction ($F(4,52) = 4.11; p = 0.006$). The factor "start position and sideways direction" further showed flicking operations were most accurate when the source was positioned to the right side, with flicking to the left (error: 7.0°), and least accurate when the source was centered, with flicking to the right (error: 10.9°). The three-way interaction ($F(12,156) = 3.04; p = 0.001$) showed an impact of flicking angle for all start positions and sideways directions, except when the source was on the right side. This was the most accurate condition, and the impact of angle nearly diminished.

Finally, we found a significant performance decrease for flicking actions that originated near the curved area (H6). This finding supports our assumption that the curved surface induces a perceptional bias. It seems that its impact decreases the farther away the action takes place. Furthermore, we successfully replicated the impact of flicking angle observed in study 2 (H7). For all source positions we found very inaccurate flicking actions at 0°, except for the source positions on the right side. Here, flicking was most accurate, and flicking angle had almost no effect on performance. Please note, that in our study all participants were right-handed. Thus, when the source was in the right position flicking performance was most accurate compared to the center or left position of the source. We conclude that for right-handed users a spatial alignment between dominant hand and source facilitates motor control, while all other source positions required somewhat awkward postures of the moving limb and therefore restricted motor control. Consequently, left-handed users should feel most comfortable and be most effective when the source is in the left position. This will be addressed in future studies.

GENERAL DISCUSSION

As described previously, a flicking gesture consists of two different stages: a visual planing stage, in which the user has to determine the spatial relation between the source and the target, and a motoric execution stage in which she executes a sliding gesture in the previously determined direction towards the target. Errors that influence flicking accuracy can appear in both of these stages. To improve flicking on curved surfaces, we first have to understand how, where and which errors can appear, and how they affect the flicking gesture.

The visual planing stage can be biased through contextual factors so that perception errors occur. Previous psychological research has demonstrated various perceptual illusions that impact visual planning performance. Classic phenomena referring to such perception biases are the Mueller-Lyer illusion of length [17], the Ponzo illusion of distance and object size [5], and the Poggendorff illusion of vertical offsets

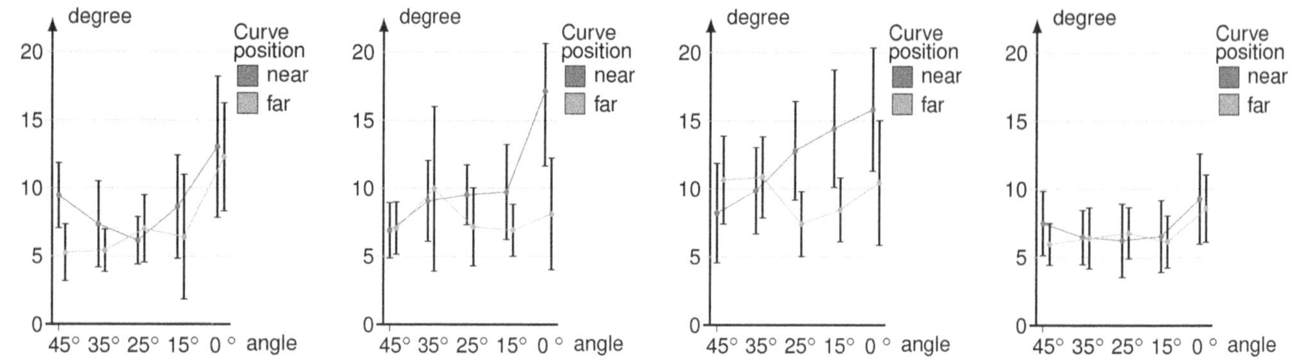

(a) From left to right (b) From center to the left (c) From center to the right (d) From right to left

Figure 9. Mean flicking errors dependent on the different start positions and directions, and on the distance between source object and the center of the curve. Whiskers denote 95% confidence intervals.

[7]. These examples indicate that the shape of an interactive tabletop could be such a contextual factor leading to an error that influences the visual planning phase. We assume that this error is extremely strong in the separated "Gap" table condition of the first user study, leading to the larger flicking error that we observed compared to the continuous conditions.

Another of these contextual factors could be the curved area. This would explain the different flicking error rates in the third user study, in which only the distance between the source object and the center of the curved area changed.

In contrast to the visual planning state, the inaccuracy of the motoric execution stage is less context-specific, and manifests itself primarily in movement execution. The major source of motor inaccuracy is the motor noise originating from noise in the nervous system, which is responsible for controlling the movement apparatus [4]. The magnitude of motor noise has been proven to be a function of the number of involved joints in an action and the resolution of the involved joints per se. Previous studies have demonstrated differences in performance between the muscle groups controlling the various upper limb joints. For instance, the hand was proven to be superior to the forearm [8], and evidence was found that the fingers may possess a higher resolution than the wrist or forearm [14]. Langolf et al. [10] investigated the relationship between Fitts' Index of Difficulty (ID) and movement time for different upper limbs (finger, wrist, and whole arm) over a wide range of movement distances. As predicted by Fitts' Law, the movement time turned out to be a function of increasing ID. However, the slope of the function differed remarkably between finger, wrist, and whole arm. If the reciprocal of the slope was supposed to infer the information-processing capacity of the motor system, then the fingers showed a much higher information-processing rate (38 bits/sec) than the hand (23 bit/sec) and the arm (10 bit/sec).

The results of the second user study showed a tendential main effect of the area. Movements within the horizontal area turned out to be more precise than movements executed in the curve, while the most difficult movements were those in the vertical area. This finding matches the results of Langolf et al. [10]. The working areas were at different distances to the user's body. When the working area was within the horizontal area, the arm was bent and relaxed in front of the chest, and flicking could be carried out by simply moving the index finger. In contrast, if the working area was in the vertical area, the arm was stretched out straight. In order to accomplish the same action, movement of the whole arm, including all upper limb joints (wrist, elbow, and shoulder) had to be coordinated. Therefore, we assume that the effect of different flicking accuracies on different areas of the curved surface is an error in the motor execution phase.

Additionally, we observed a similar error in the third user study that follows the same pattern described in [10]. Note, that in this study all users were right-handed. The results showed that the most accurate flicking gestures were made from the right position, which is the closest position to the right arm. In this condition, users could leave their arm in a very comfortable position, and could use only finger movement to conduct the flicking gesture. In contrast to that, in the other conditions of the test, users had to conduct a more complex movement that involved the entire hand. Consequently, we assume an opposite pattern of results for left-handed users. This has to be proved in future studies.

Another effect that we observed was that, independent of the source position, flicking gestures directly upwards or downwards (0°) showed the largest error. This is in direct contrast to the findings that were made by Weiss et. al [20] in which users shot at different targets by defining a line with a two-finger tap. They showed that hitting objects that are placed directly above or below was highly accurate, in contrast to other target positions. These differences can only be explained by a motor error of the flicking gesture, because according to their study, users can identify the correct direction to these targets very well. That most users had significant problems with this flicking direction can be explained by the way they executed this gesture. We observed basically two different hand postures in this task: In the first posture, users placed their hand directly above the source object, and used their entire arm to conduct the gesture (fig. 10(a)), which ac-

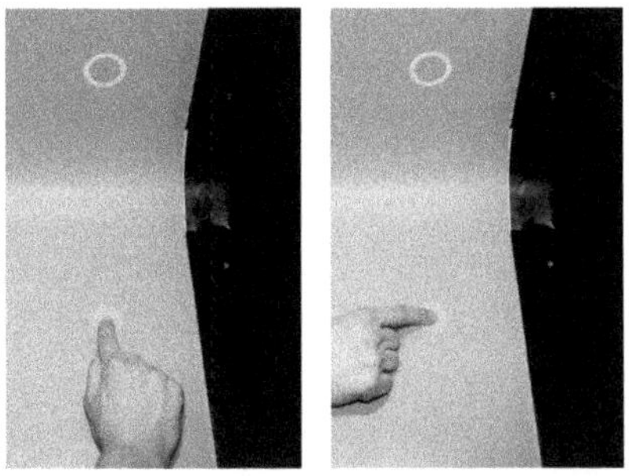

(a) hand below (b) hand on the side

Figure 10. Hand postures for flicking directly upwards.

cording to [10] leads to inaccurate execution of the gesture. In the second posture, users placed their hand lateral to the source object, and moved only their finger. However, since fingers can only be moved radially in this posture, a sliding gesture pointing directly upwards or downwards is not possible this way (fig. 10(b)). These issues do not occur when simply tapping with two fingers to define a direction, explaining the different results from [20] mentioned above.

PRELIMINARY MATHEMATICAL MODEL OF FLICKING ERROR

To explain the relationship between the flicking angle and the flicking error, we developed a first rough mathematical model from the data acquired at the center position of the third user study. In this model, we redefined the flicking error as a signed angle. The negative values means error to the right. Therefore, we have nine angles (-45° to -15° to the left of the target, 15° to 45° to the right of the target, and 0° directly above the target). The angular error are shown in Figure 11.

We approximated these results with the following sinusoidal function: $a + b \times sinus(c * Angle)$. From our data, the best-fit parameters are: $a = 1.162$, $b = -8.656$, and $c = 3.444$. Although this function is only a very rough approximation of the results and can only be used to give a hint about the flicking error by flicking angle, it shows that flicking can be described by a mathematical function.

CONCLUSION

This paper investigated flicking gestures on curved surfaces. Flicking is a common and simple gesture that lets users move digital objects across large interactive surfaces. Its accuracy can be influenced by two types of errors: an error in the visual identification of the spatial relation between the source object and the target object, and an motor error in the planning and execution of the gesture. We presented three studies analyzing flicking accuracy on curved interactive surfaces, and for each condition identified which error types influenced accuracy. Table 1 summarizes our results and suggests from what factors the effects appear to originate. This is a first attempt to systematically explore empirical findings for this technique, to make the results more digestible for practical purposes,

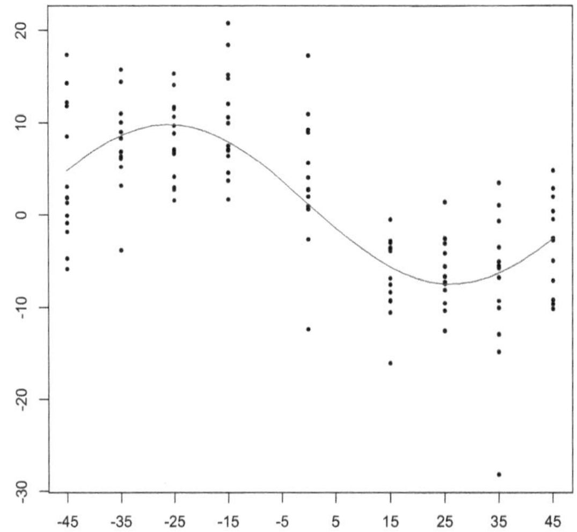

Figure 11. Visualization of the first mathematical model to predict the flicking error and the flicking angle for flicking gestures across the curved area. Each dot is a data point, and the blue line is the fitted model.

User study	Factors for flicking errors	Perceptual error	Motor error	Shown in figure
1	Table configuration	x	x	5
	Flicking direction		x	5
2	Area condition		x	7
	Flicking direction		x	7
	Flicking angle	x	x	7
3	Distance to curve	x		9
	Sideways position		x	9
	Flicking angle	x	x	9

Table 1. Suspected origins of errors in our flicking user studies.

e.g., to derive guidelines for curved surface interaction design. Clearly, the validity of our suggested classification will need to be confirmed through additional experiments.

FUTURE WORK

We are only beginning to understand how users interact with curved surfaces as a new class of devices. Even studying a basic gesture such as flicking in depth has shown that our methodical understanding of this interaction is still in its infancy. Our initial mathematical model for angle-specific systematic errors is a first approximation; such a model would enable us to correct these systematic errors and improve flicking accuracy, but the observed data exhibits higher-frequency patterns that warrant further study, to improve the predictive power of our initial model and its usefulness as a design tool.

The errors that occur in the motor stage also require further analysis, by focusing on hand movement during gesture execution. Furthermore, cognitive load caused by movement planing could also be used as relevant criterion beside accuracy in order to characterize flicking movements. Finally, we intend to create mathematical model of how flicking works on the various areas of curved surfaces.

ACKNOWLEDGMENTS

This work was funded in part by the German B-IT Foundation. We thank Thorsten Karrer, Jan-Peter Kraemer, and Chat Wacharamanotham for there helpful comments on this paper.

REFERENCES

1. Cao, X., Wilson, A., Balakrishnan, R., Hinckley, K., and Hudson, S. Shapetouch: Leveraging contact shape on interactive surfaces. In *3rd IEEE International Workshop on Horizontal Interactive Human Computer Systems '08*. (2008), 129 –136.
2. Coldefy, F., and Louis-dit Picard, S. Digitable: an interactive multiuser table for collocated and remote collaboration enabling remote gesture visualization. In *Proc. Computer Vision and Pattern Recognition '07*, IEEE (2007), 1 –8.
3. Collomb, M., Hascoët, M., Baudisch, P., and Lee, B. Improving drag-and-drop on wall-size displays. In *Proc. Graphics Interface 2005*, Canadian Human-Computer Communications Society (2005), 25–32.
4. Faisal, A. A., Selen, L. P. J., and Wolpert, D. M. Noise in the nervous system. *Nature Review Neuroscience 9* (2008), 292–303.
5. Fineman, M. *The Nature of Visual Illusion*. New York: Dover, 1996.
6. Geissler, J. Shuffle, throw or take it! working efficiently with an interactive wall. In *Proc. CHI '98*, ACM (1998), 265–266.
7. Green, R. T., and Hoyle, E. M. The poggendorff illusion as a constancy phenomeno. *Nature 200* (1963), 611–612.
8. Hammerton, M., and Tickner, A. H. An investigation into the comparative suitability of forearm, hand and thumb controls in acquisition tasks. *Ergonomics 9* (1966), 125–130.
9. Hinrichs, U., and Carpendale, S. Gestures in the wild: studying multi-touch gesture sequences on interactive tabletop exhibits. In *Proc. CHI '11*, ACM (2011), 3023–3032.
10. Langolf, G. D., Chaffin, D. B., and Foulke, J. A. An investigation of fitts' law using a wide range of movement amplitudes. *Journal of Motor Behaviour 8* (1976), 113–128.
11. Morris, M., Brush, A., and Meyers, B. Reading revisited: Evaluating the usability of digital display surfaces for active reading tasks. In *Proc. TABLETOP '07* (2007), 79 – 86.
12. Morris, M., Brush, A., and Meyers, B. A field study of knowledge workers' use of interactive horizontal displays. In *Proc. TABLETOP '08* (2008), 105 – 112.
13. Moyle, M., and Cockburn, A. Analysing mouse and pen flick gestures. In *Proc. SIGCHI-NZ Symposium On Computer-Human Interaction '02* (2002), 266–267.
14. Penfield, W., and Rasmussen, T. *The cerebral cortex of man*. New York: Macmillan, 1950.
15. Reetz, A., Gutwin, C., Stach, T., Nacenta, M., and Subramanian, S. Superflick: a natural and efficient technique for long-distance object placement on digital tables. In *Proc. Graphics Interface '06*, Canadian Information Processing Society (2006), 163–170.
16. Rekimoto, J. Pick-and-drop: a direct manipulation technique for multiple computer environments. In *Proc. Symposium on User Interface Software and Technology '97*, ACM (1997), 31–39.
17. Restle, F., and Decker, J. Size of the mueller-lyer illusion as a function of ist dimensions: Theory and data. *Theory and data. Perception and Psychophysics 21* (1977), 489–503.
18. Sato, T., Fukuchi, K., and Koike, H. Implementation and evaluations of vision-based finger flicking gesture recognition for tabletops. In *3rd IEEE International Workshop on Horizontal Interactive Human Computer Systems '08*. (2008), 137 –144.
19. Tognazzini, B. The starfire video prototype project: a case history. In *Proc. CHI '94*, ACM (1994), 99–105.
20. Weiss, M., Voelker, S., Sutter, C., and Borchers, J. Benddesk: dragging across the curve. In *Proc. Interactive Tabletops and Surfaces*, ACM (2010), 1–10.
21. Wellner, P. The digitaldesk calculator: tangible manipulation on a desk top display. In *Proc. Symposium on User Interface Software and Technology '91*, ACM (1991), 27–33.
22. Wigdor, D., Jiang, H., Forlines, C., Borkin, M., and Shen, C. Wespace: the design development and deployment of a walk-up and share multi-surface visual collaboration system. In *Proc. CHI '09*, ACM (2009), 1237–1246.
23. Wigdor, D., Perm, G., R., K., Esenther, A., and Shen, C. Living with a tabletop: Analysis and observations of long term office use of a multi-touch table. In *Proc. TABLETOP '07* (2007), 60 – 67.
24. Wilson, A. D., Izadi, S., Hilliges, O., Garcia-Mendoza, A., and Kirk, D. Bringing physics to the surface. In *Proc. Symposium on User Interface Software and Technology '08*, ACM (2008), 67–76.
25. Wimmer, R., Hennecke, F., Schulz, F., Boring, S., Butz, A., and Hussmann, H. Curve: revisiting the digital desk. In *Proc. Nordic Conference on Human-Computer Interaction '10*, ACM (2010), 561–570.
26. Wu, M., and Balakrishnan, R. Multi-finger and whole hand gestural interaction techniques for multi-user tabletop displays. In *Proc. Symposium on User Interface Software and Technology '03*, ACM (2003), 193–202.

MirageTable: Freehand Interaction on a Projected Augmented Reality Tabletop

Hrvoje Benko[1] Ricardo Jota[1,2] Andrew D. Wilson[1]

[1]Microsoft Research
One Microsoft Way,
Redmond, WA 98052
{benko | awilson}@microsoft.com

[2]VIMMI / Inesc-ID
IST / Technical University of Lisbon
1000-029 Lisbon, Portugal
jotacosta@ist.utl.pt

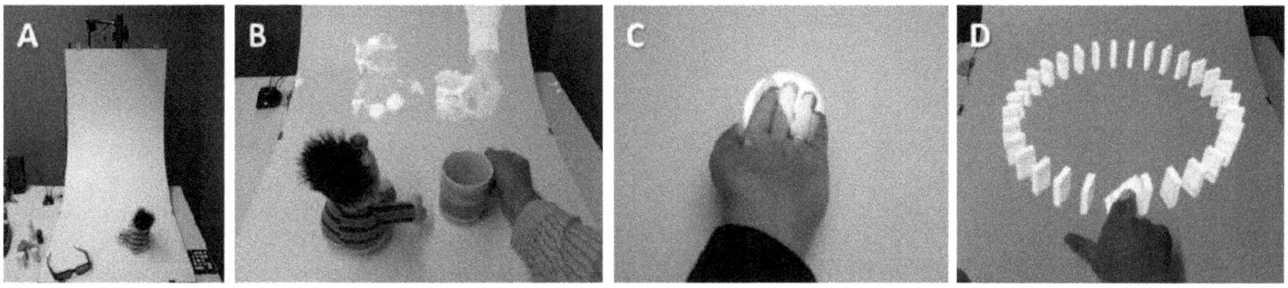

Figure 1. MirageTable is a curved projection-based augmented reality system (A), which digitizes any object on the surface (B), presenting correct perspective views accounting for real objects (C) and supporting freehand physics-based interactions (D).

ABSTRACT

Instrumented with a single depth camera, a stereoscopic projector, and a curved screen, *MirageTable* is an interactive system designed to merge real and virtual worlds into a single spatially registered experience on top of a table. Our depth camera tracks the user's eyes and performs a real-time capture of both the shape and the appearance of any object placed in front of the camera (including user's body and hands). This real-time capture enables perspective stereoscopic 3D visualizations to a single user that account for deformations caused by physical objects on the table. In addition, the user can interact with virtual objects through physically-realistic freehand actions without any gloves, trackers, or instruments. We illustrate these unique capabilities through three application examples: virtual 3D model creation, interactive gaming with real and virtual objects, and a 3D teleconferencing experience that not only presents a 3D view of a remote person, but also a seamless 3D shared task space. We also evaluated the user's perception of projected 3D objects in our system, which confirmed that users can correctly perceive such objects even when they are projected over different background colors and geometries (e.g., gaps, drops).

Author Keywords

3D interaction; spatial augmented reality; projector-camera system; projective textures; depth camera; 3D digitization; 3D teleconferencing; shared task space;

ACM Classification Keywords

H.5.2 [Information Interfaces and Presentation]: User Interfaces - Graphical user interfaces;

INTRODUCTION

Overlaying computer generated graphics on top of the real world to create a seamless spatially-registered environment is a core idea of Augmented Reality (AR) technology. AR solutions have thus far mostly focused on *output* technologies such as head-worn and handheld displays, or spatially projected visualizations [3, 4].

While improving the output solutions is critical to wider adoption of AR, we believe that most AR solutions suffer from fundamentally impoverished *input* from the real world. For example, in order to interact with virtual content, users are often encumbered with on-body trackers, head-worn displays, or required to interact "through the screen" in handheld AR scenarios. Second, such systems have a limited understanding of the real-time changes of the environment. Lastly, while interacting with the virtual content users often lack the ability to employ any of the fine-grained motor skills that humans rely on in our interactions with the physical world. In comparison with reality, interaction with the virtual world is greatly impoverished.

Depth cameras capture the "range image" (i.e., the per-pixel distance from the camera to the nearest surface) and have the potential to drastically increase the input bandwidth between the human and the computer. Such cameras (e.g., Kinect[1], PrimeSense[2], Canesta[3]) enable inexpensive real-time 3D modeling of surface geometry, making some traditionally difficult computer vision problems easier. For example, with a depth camera it is trivial to composite a false background in a video conferencing application.

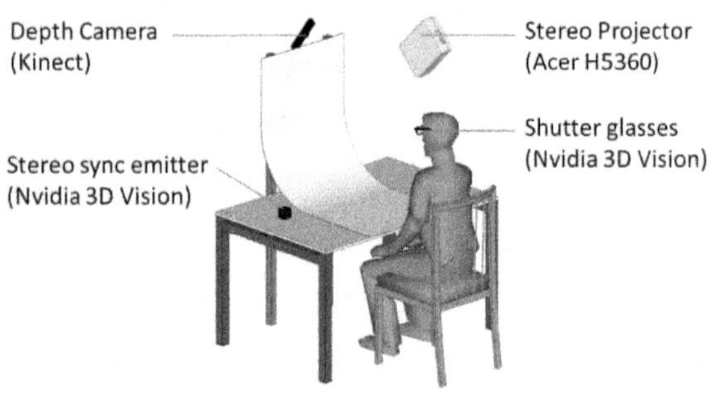

Figure 2. MirageTable setup with the stereoscopic projector mounted on the ceiling above the curved screen.

In this paper, we demonstrate using a depth camera's high-bandwidth input stream to create richer spatial AR experiences with minimal instrumentation of the user. In particular, we present an interactive system, *MirageTable*, which combines a depth camera, a curved screen and a stereoscopic projector (Figure 2). This system can present correct perspective 3D visualizations to a single user. These appear spatially registered to the real world and enable freehand interactions with virtual content.

Motivation and Contributions

We are motivated by a simple idea: can we enable the user to interact with 3D digital objects alongside real objects in the same physically realistic way and without wearing any additional trackers, gloves, or gear.

To illustrate the power of this concept, we provide an example from our system. Imagine that you walk up to the MirageTable with a single bowling pin and place it on the table (Figure 3a). You can instruct the system to make an instant 3D copy of it and you copy it multiple times to create a set of virtual pins to play with. The system tracks your head and you can see these captured pins in correct 3D perspective stereoscopic views on the table. From your perspective, they all look just like your original physical pin (Figure 3b). Then you scoop up a virtual 3D bowling ball in your hand, and throw it at the bowling pins. The virtual ball leaves your hand, rolls down the surface of the table, and knocks down the pins (Figure 4c). A strike! In this simple game example, we blurred the line between the physical and the virtual world in a variety of ways, and made both physical and virtual objects appear collocated in space and behave in the same physical way.

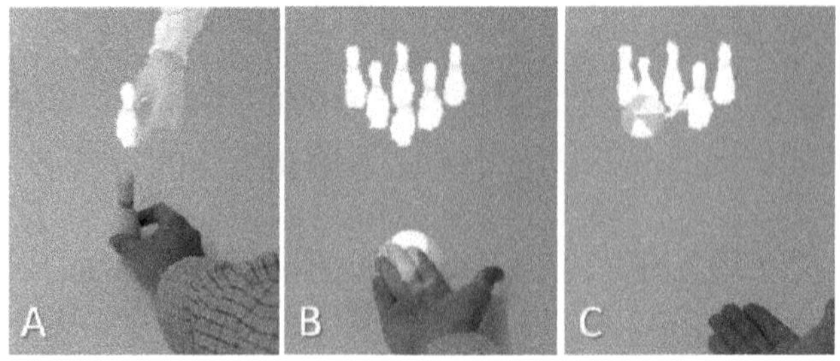

Figure 3. "Bowling" on MirageTable: A) a single bowling pin gets digitized six times, B) virtual ball held by the user's hand, C) thrown ball knocks down previously scanned pins.

MirageTable demonstrates that many interactive aspects needed for a convincing spatial AR experience can be facilitated by the exclusive use of the depth camera input stream. In particular, in this paper we show how the real-time depth information enables:

1) Instant 3D capture of physical objects and the user,
2) Rendering those captures and other 3D content in correct stereographic perspective manner,
3) Perspective projections on non-flat and changing real surfaces,
4) Robust tracking of the user's head without the need of worn trackers or instruments,
5) Freehand interactions with virtual objects in much the same way users manipulate real world objects: through physically realistic behaviors and without gloves, trackers, or instruments.

While these capabilities have been demonstrated independently before [16,17,20,27], MirageTable demonstrates how integrating them together enables a compelling spatial AR experience. Our contributions are trifold: (1) system design and implementation, (2) three prototype applications (including our 3D teleconferencing that not only presents a 3D view of a remote person, but also a seamless 3D shared task space), and (3) a user study on 3D perception and image quality in our system.

Our experiments confirmed that users of our system can correctly perceive projected 3D objects (i.e., fuse a stereo image), even when such objects are projected on top of a background which varies in color or topology (e.g., gaps, drops, or other physical discontinuities). These results are important to the future designers of similar experiences, as they highlight both the limitations of our approach and the areas of technology where improvements will greatly enhance the overall user experience in the future.

RELATED WORK

Our review focuses on two closely related areas: projection based augmented reality solutions, and the use of depth sensing cameras for user input. For a comprehensive review

[1] http://www.xbox.com/kinect
[2] http://www.primesense.com
[3] http://www.canesta.com

of all AR solutions for superimposing computer generated imagery on the real world, we refer the reader to [3].

Projection Based Augmented Reality Solutions

Numerous research projects have highlighted the benefits of projectors to simulate novel interfaces on top of the real world (e.g., [14,16,23,27]). Projectors have been used to transform existing 2D surfaces into interactive surfaces [13, 18,29], to simulate texturing and reflectance properties [4, 17], shadowing and day lighting [23], and animate user-manipulated terrain [14].

We were primarily inspired by the Office of the Future (OOTF) [16] and LightSpace [29] projects. OOTF independently demonstrates a working projective texturing prototype and structured light depth capture prototype at 3Hz [16]. However, the authors only envisioned the entire working real-time system. We present a fully functioning integrated system, and extend the OOTF idea, by eliminating user-worn tracking equipment for tracking the user's gaze, body or hands, and by facilitating physically-realistic high-fidelity interactions with virtual objects.

LightSpace demonstrates how multiple depth cameras and multiple projectors can be combined to augment the surfaces of the entire room [29]. While LightSpace enables interactions in hand and between surfaces, it did not provide correct perspective views, or allow for 3D virtual objects which we explore here.

Interactions Facilitated by Depth Cameras

Many techniques exist to capture 3D information of the scene (e.g., stereo, structured light, shape from silhouette, time of flight). The major advance of the current generation of depth-sensing cameras is their ability to do so in real-time, without high computational cost, and at low cost per device. For example, Microsoft Kinect showcases the application of depth-sensing cameras for controller-free motion-controlled gaming. We are interested in supporting high fidelity interactions that make a direct analog to the real world. Such interactions are previously demonstrated by Wilson [27], as well as freehand interactions above the table or around the room [29]. HoloDesk [9] showcases similar depth-camera interactions, using a configuration based on a beam splitter to visualize the interactions.

While not using a depth sensing camera, Starner et al. [20] demonstrate a workbench which automatically digitizes any physical object on its surface using a shape-from-silhouette approach. We extend this work with real-time capture which provides the capture of the user as well as physical objects placed on the table, and a high level of freehand interactivity with the captured content. Other projects explored digitization of 3D objects albeit with more focus on capture quality, rather than real-time interactivity [2,10].

Lastly, curved displays and projections over several available surfaces are often employed to extend the viewing area to provide a seamless interface and increase the level of immersion [6,15]. Several proposed curved tabletop displays combine the horizontal and vertical surfaces into one seamless experience [22,26]. In contrast to our system, the existing curved tabletop solutions have primarily focused on more traditional 2D interactive surface applications.

MIRAGETABLE IMPLEMENTATION

MirageTable is a projected tabletop configuration that is designed to explore the feasibility of using 3D projections directly on the physical scene. One of the major benefits of this approach for creating AR experiences is that projector-based augmentations do not obstruct the user's view with additional equipment (e.g., no head-worn displays or half-silvered mirrors [4,5]). In MirageTable, the virtual augmentation is performed by directly projecting virtual content on the surfaces in front of the user, e.g., the tabletop itself, the physical objects and the user's hands and arms above the tabletop.

Furthermore, MirageTable can instantly digitize physical objects, re-project them alongside their real counterparts, and enable the manipulation of such virtual objects that is similar to that of real physical objects. The end result is a 3D scene imaged by the user that seamlessly mixes real and virtual objects (Figure 4).

MirageTable consists of a 120Hz DLP projector (Acer H5360, 1280x720 pixels), a Kinect depth camera, a pair of shutter glasses (Nvidia 3D Vision), a curved screen, and the computer that powers the experience. All components are configured above the tabletop as shown in Figure 2.

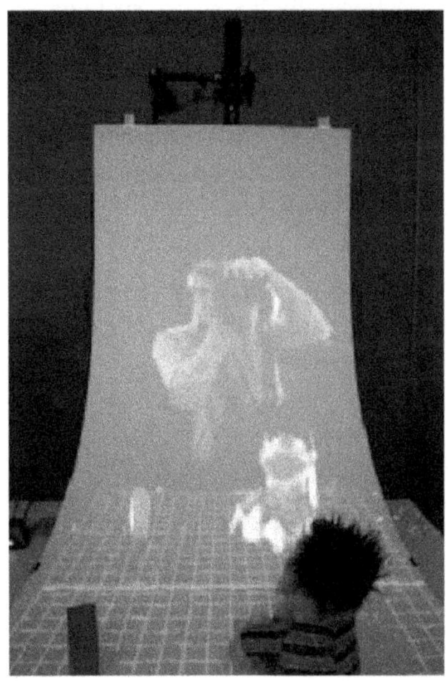

Figure 4. Mirror view of real-time captured data of the user and the objects on the tabletop (stereo projection is disabled in this picture for clarity). Note that, even though the screen curves, the 3D captured data as well as the grid which represents the tabletop surface appears correct from the user's perspective.

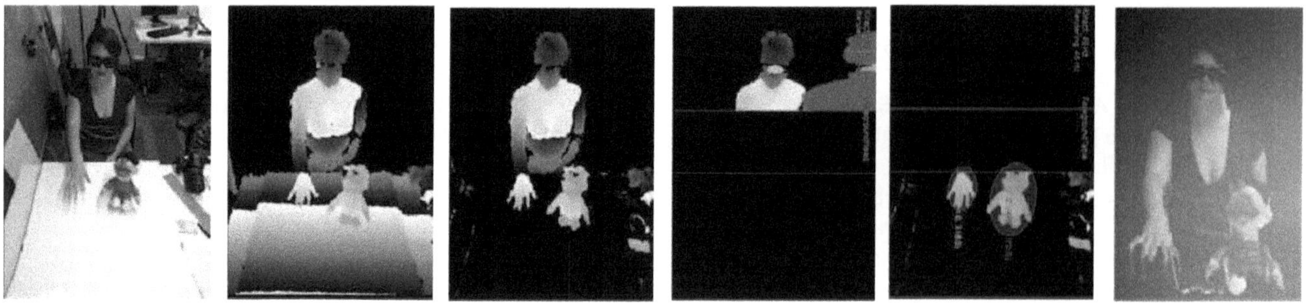

Figure 5. MirageTable image capture and processing pipeline: Color and Depth image are acquired every frame. Foreground is computed by subtracting the previously acquired background image. Head Tracking finds the user's glasses in the depth image. Proxy Particles are assigned to the tracked objects on top of the tabletop to facilitate physically realistic behaviors. Real-Time Mesh is constructed from Foreground image and textured by Color image. Note that the captured mesh can be viewed from many viewpoints.

The curved screen is constructed of a single sheet of off-white low-density polyethylene (LDPE) plastic. LDPE is a tough, flexible and impact resistant material with a matte surface suitable for projection. The screen is 90cm deep, 60cm wide, and 80cm tall, with a curvature radius of 50cm.

We use a curved surface primarily as a seamless projection surface. The curvature itself is not necessary, but it helps by not having visible seams in the experience. In fact, the system would work well in the corner of the room or if the desk was placed next to the wall. What is important is that there are surfaces available to project on and we can capture its configuration in the calibration stage.

The Kinect camera is mounted above the screen (Figure 2) and is oriented to capture the top of the table as well as the user's upper body. The 120Hz stereoscopic projector is suspended from the ceiling, displaying content on the curved screen and on objects above and on it. Lastly, shutter glasses provide the stereo viewing capability to the user. The glasses are the only piece of instrumentation that the user needs to wear, and only if stereo viewing is desired.

Our system is calibrated so that the position and orientation of both the camera and projector are known in the real-world coordinate system (i.e., calibrated with respect to the real-world screen). We follow the camera and projector calibration methods as outlined in the LightSpace project by Wilson and Benko [29]. As part of the initial calibration step, we capture the geometry of the curved screen so that our projection system can account for distortion that would otherwise be caused by the shape of the screen surface. We capture the screen geometry by placing the depth camera in front of the setup, calibrating the camera from that perspective and then capturing the empty scene. This empty scene depth map can also be used as a background baseline to easily segment all new objects or user body parts in the scene (e.g., Foreground image in Figure 5).

We now describe three core capabilities that together facilitate MirageTable: a) provision of the correct 3D perspective view, 2) real-time capture and replay of acquired mesh data, and 3) high-fidelity physical interactions with virtual objects based on the real geometry of the scene.

Correct 3D Perspective Views

To provide correct 3D perspective view of the virtual scene, MirageTable must track the user's head location and gaze as well as project imagery onto the scene in such a way that it appears correct from the user's viewpoint [25].

Head Tracking

In MirageTable, the user's eyes are occluded by the shutter glasses. Thus, rather than track the eyes, we track the location of the glasses in the depth image and use that information to compute the user's viewpoint.

To localize the glasses in the depth image of the head, we exploit the fact that their reflectivity disturbs the depth values reported by Kinect, i.e., the depth image of the head appears as if it has "holes" at the glasses (see Foreground and Head Tracking images in Figure 5). We track the aggregate location of those holes with respect to the head. This gives a good estimate of the mid-point between the eyes. While it is also possible to extract the 3D orientation of the glasses by averaging the available depth values around the glasses, this measurement is fairly noisy with the current camera and not needed for obtaining the correct perspective in projective texturing (see below). For stereoscopic views, we apply a fixed offset from the midpoint to arrive at an estimate of the location of each eye.

Projective Texturing

To provide correct perspective visualizations, we synthesize the projector images through the use of a projective texture approach [19] that requires two rendering passes. The scene is first rendered from the perspective of each eye, taking into account both the virtual content and real-time digitized objects (e.g., user's hand) in order to correctly handle occlusions.

We then use those renderings as textured light sources and project them onto the captured real-world geometry. The second pass renders those re-projected views from the perspective of the projector (again, one per eye). The result of this pipeline is the virtual image which looks correct only from the eye point of the user since it correctly takes into account the shape of the physical projection surface [15,16] (Figure 6). For example, the virtual ball appears correctly in the hand of the user in Figure 7a, but that same ball is actually projected over multiple surfaces in Figure 7b.

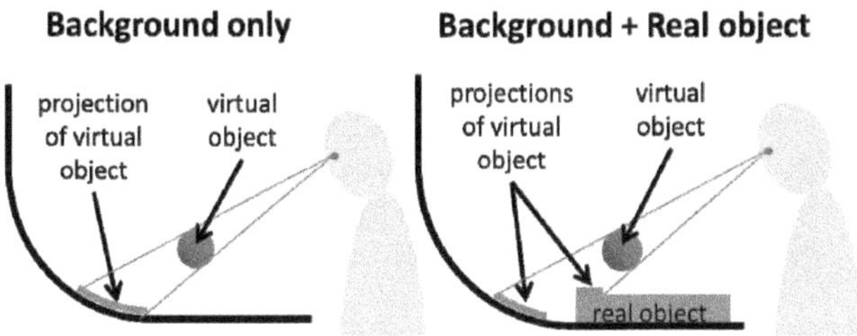

Figure 6. Projective texturing requires that the system takes into account the geometry of real objects on the tabletop at every frame in order to correctly present perspective 3D virtual information to the user's eye.

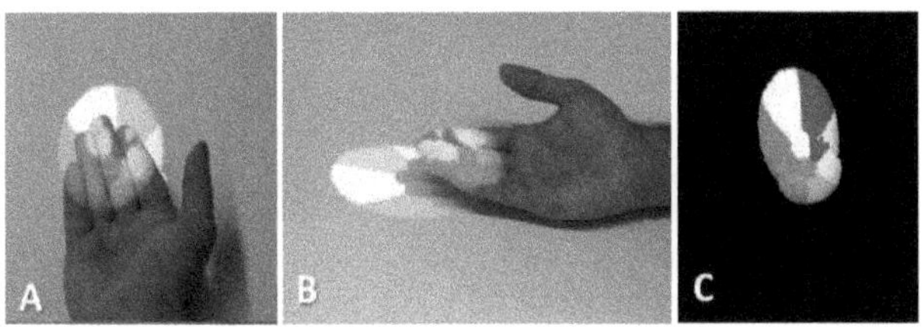

Figure 7. Projective texturing of the ball in the user's hand: A) correct user's perspective, B) side view (off-axis), C) the projected image used to create this effect. Note that part of the ball is correctly projected on top of the user's hand and the rest is on the background. The projection appears distorted from any perspective other than viewpoint in A.

While it can be disturbing to focus on a plane that is far behind the actual location of the virtual 3D object, this is typically not a problem in MirageTable. Due to the simulation of physical gravity, the projected virtual objects tend to be near to the surface on which they are projected, and so appear at about the correct focusing distance.

3D Capture and Replay of the Real World

MirageTable exploits the depth camera as a continuous 3D digitizer. This is similar to [20]; however, today's depth cameras make this computationally feasible in real-time and at low computational cost. In order to ensure maximum performance, we implemented a custom vertex shader to render dense captured geometry in real-time on a GPU (Nvidia GeForce GTX 580).

The objects are digitized by capturing their real-time 3D geometry and texture. We do not restrict capture to specific objects or body parts, but rather include anything that occupies physical space and can be imaged by our camera (e.g., cups, wooden blocks, and body parts such as user's hands). For example, both the user as well as the objects on the table are captured and projected mirrored in Figure 4.

Mirroring the captured geometry when displaying can be particularly advantageous with MirageTable. Our system suffers from visibility constraints typical of any single camera system, i.e., only the visible side is captured without requiring the user to move the object or the camera to capture all visible sides (e.g., [10]). By mirroring the object, the system can show the captured side to the user, resulting in a better illusion of the 3D object. If a simple rotation in place was applied, the system would need to infer the correct centroid for each object which is difficult from a front surface alone. Mirroring the entire scene does not suffer from this problem. Additionally, mirroring the capture scene has a benefit of not overlaying the captured object directly on top of the real object.

We use captured geometry in many different scenarios: it can be used (or stored) as a digital copy of the real object, it can be played back (e.g., as a 3D mirror), it can be transferred to a remote location for 3D remote teleconferencing, or it can be used to account for real world geometry when projecting virtual objects as shown in the previous section. These scenarios are further discussed later in the paper.

Freehand Physically Realistic Interactions

The last main feature of MirageTable is the simulation of physically realistic interactions with virtual 3D content. MirageTable aims to minimize the differences between physical and virtual objects, making them appear correctly side by side and furthermore to enable the user to interact with them in similar ways. In our system, the user can hold a virtual object, move it, or knock it down, since all virtual and real objects participate in a real-world physics simulation. Grasping a virtual object is currently not supported due to complexities of inferring grasping forces from depth camera images. Our physics simulation runs using a commercial Nvidia PhysX game engine.

Ideally this simulation would directly accommodate the real-time deformable geometry of the captured objects; however, current physics engines lack support for such complex simulations. Instead, we approximate the captured geometry with proxy particles (tiny tightly-packed spheres) as seen in Figure 8. Using proxy particles to facilitate

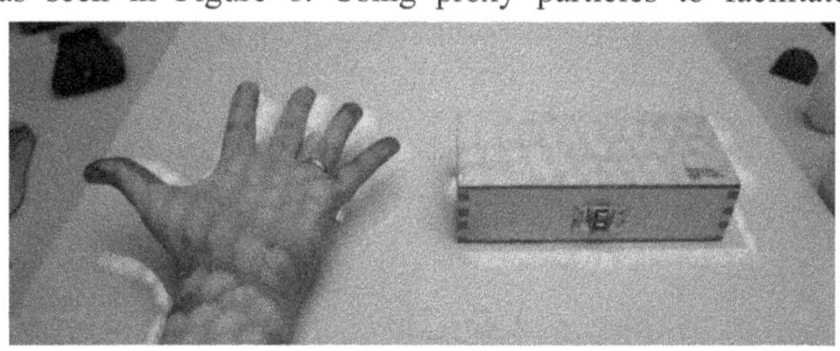

Figure 8. Proxy particles shown re-projected on top of the geometry they are representing in the physics simulation.

freehand interactions was demonstrated previously on 2D interactive screens to better simulate touch and gestural interactions [8,30], but we extended it to three dimensions.

To generate correct proxy particles, we first segment the available depth data from the table image into discrete objects, i.e., each real object becomes a separate tracked component (see Proxy Particle image in Figure 5). Next we subsample this geometry and assign a sphere proxy particle (1cm radius) for each 2cm patch of captured geometry. These sphere proxy particles are placed in the 3D scene at the precise location of the corresponding patch of geometry (Figure 8). From then on, they participate in a physics simulation together with all other virtual objects, except that they are set to not collide with one another. This process is repeated every frame.

In addition to placing proxy particles frame-to-frame, we impart a force vector to each that corresponds to the overall movement vector of the tracked object (e.g., the hand). This allows for the correct collision response when colliding with objects, and enables lateral movement of virtual objects (i.e., when holding the virtual ball in one's hand, one expects it to follow the hand's movement).

MirageTable Interactive Scenarios

MirageTable makes it possible to quickly compose complex virtual 3D scenes by successive capture and replication of physical objects. For example, it is possible to build an entire virtual castle using only a single physical brick piece (Figure 9a) or, as previously described, to build a set of bowling pins by repeatedly scanning a single pin (Figure 3). In order to ensure that the user's hands are not captured in the scene as well, the controls for initiating capture, undoing the last capture and manipulating the entire captured virtual scene are currently mapped onto a few buttons on keypad to the side of the projection surface (Figure 9a inset). We tested our 3D modeling capabilities with architects on early implementation of this system and found that complex models can be constructed using very limited set of physical objects [11].

The shared participation of captured and virtual content in a physics simulation enables a variety of game-like experiences (e.g., [27]). We have prototyped a simple dominos game (Figure 9b) and a previously described bowling experience (Figure 3). To enable these game experiences, the captured objects must have volumes that approximate their real counterparts. This is challenging in our system, since we only capture surfaces that face the camera. However, for each captured object we perform a simple 3D shape approximation that provides acceptable results in our physics simulation: starting with the captured side of the object that faces the camera we fill in the bottom of the object by projecting additional vertices down to the plane of the table and then mirror the object. Filling the bottom is important in order that the object stands up in our interactive physics simulation, while mirroring the object

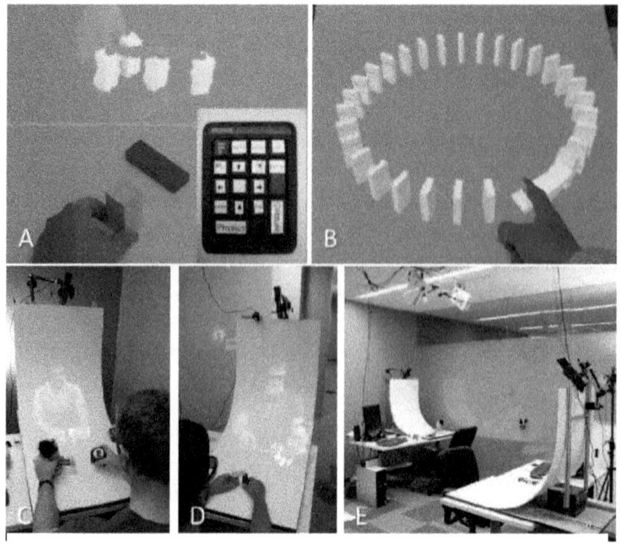

Figure 9. MirageTable interactive scenarios: A) virtual model construction (inset shows the control keypad), B) virtual dominos game, C-D) two users collaborating with our 3D shared task space teleconferencing prototype E) two MirageTable setups used for teleconferencing.

presents the best captured side of the object to the user. This approach works best for symmetrical objects. A more elaborate solution using multiple cameras [20] or modeling the object while it is being rotated [10] are possible, and we hope to integrate them into our experience in the future.

Real-time captured geometry may also be shared with a remote participant to facilitate 3D remote collaborations. We assembled two MirageTable setups and streamed the depth information over a network connection (Figure 9e). The unique benefit of this setup is that two users share not only the 3D image of each other, but also the tabletop task space in front of them (in contrast to sharing task space videos [28]). The curvature of the screen makes a seamless connection between the view of the user, their gestures, and their objects on the tabletop. The MirageTable remote collaboration experience is akin to sitting at the same desk opposite of one another (Figure 9c-d).

EVALUATIONS OF PROJECTIVE TEXTURING QUALITY

MirageTable is a projection-based augmented reality system, which enables the user to reach into the scene to hold and manipulate 3D virtual objects. This core ability depends on whether the system can provide the correct perspective view regardless of the distortions caused by the real objects in the scene (e.g., user's hands).

We explored this core question in two experiments, in which we evaluated *image quality degradation* and *user's depth perception* when viewing 3D virtual objects over various geometries and colored backgrounds. These evaluations offer some early proof that the user can perceive the object's 3D shape and position even when projected on highly distorted, non-uniform and backgrounds of varying color, such as the user's hand.

Effect of Projection Surface on Image Quality

We wanted to assess how the projected image of the 3D object is impacted by a variety of irregular projection surfaces. To do so, we placed a camera at a fixed location looking at the virtual 3D beach ball projected on the tabletop. The ball was positioned 10 cm above the tabletop surface. We disabled head-tracking and fixed the camera location to a known (measured) point, ensuring a good projective texture view of the ball. Stereo viewing was disabled for this experiment. The test setup can be seen in Figure 10a.

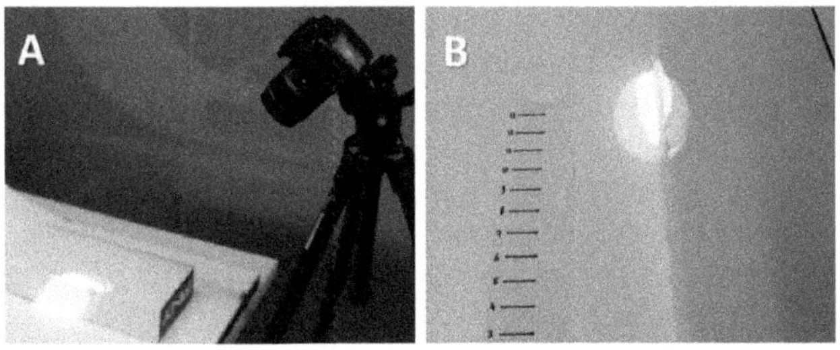

Figure 10. The experiment setup showing *drop* condition: A) the side view showing the camera, the 6cm high box on the surface, and the distorted projection of the virtual ball, B) the perspective image taken by the camera in figure A where the ball appears correct. Note the fixed tick marks used in our depth perception experiment.

To quantify the image degradation, we computed the root mean square (RMS) difference between the image of the ball on the white background (*base*) to the image of the ball when projected over 8 different combinations of color and geometry backgrounds (Figure 11). Since each image is taken from the same location, with the same lighting and camera parameters, the only degradation is due to the change in projection surface. Our system attempts to compensate for this through projective texturing. While our system performs no active color compensation, we included different color backgrounds in this evaluation as such conditions would be common in many applications. Colors chosen (white, red-white, red, and black) represent a sensible range of different color intensities. Active color compensation would further minimize these differences [3,15,17]; however, such setups are most effective when the projector is the only illumination source in the room.

Results

When examining RMS values associated with the recorded images, it appears that the geometric distortions lead to roughly similar and relatively small RMS differences. This is encouraging, as it indicates that our projective texturing technique succeeded in accounting for a variety of geometric distortions as well as for conditions when the projection is split over surfaces substantially varying in depth (*drop* and both *hand* conditions).

When comparing color vs. geometry distorted backgrounds, color conditions (including *bare hand*) yielded substantially greater RMS differences. This is not surprising, as RMS

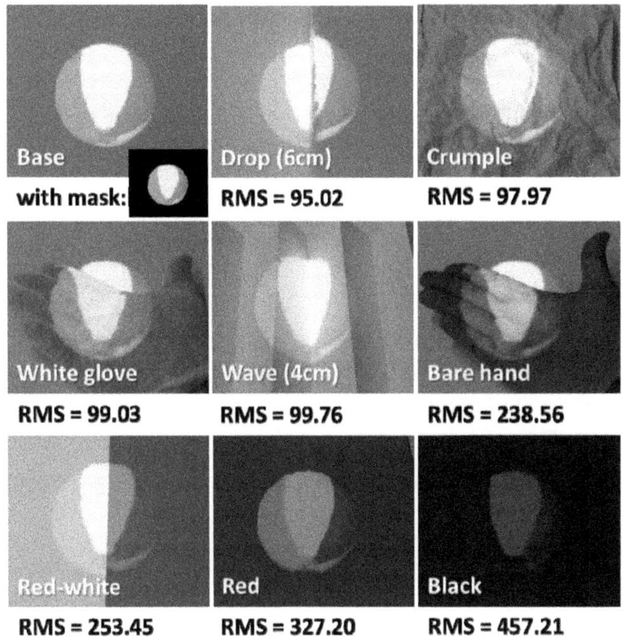

Figure 11. Nine captured images of the 3D virtual ball when presented over backgrounds differing in geometry (*drop*, *crumple*, *wave*), color (*base*, *red-white*, *red*, *black*), and in front of user's hand (*bare hand*, *white glove*). Images shown in order of increasing RMS difference from *base*. RMS difference was computed only for the portion of the image (see *mask*) where there were lit pixels in the base image, all other pixels were ignored. *Drop* was caused by a white box (6 cm high) which split the image in half (see Figure 10), *crumple* was a randomly crumpled sheet of white paper, while *wave* was a repeatedly folded piece of white paper (each ridge was 4cm long). Two hand conditions show user's hand 5 cm above the surface.

error measures absolute pixel differences; however, visual inspection of the images does not yield the same perceived ordering for most humans. The human eye readily compensates for color differences [12], and therefore, we postulate that *while the images coming from geometry backgrounds yielded closer images to the base, the geometry distortions will have a greater impact on the user's 3D perception than the color background.* We tested this hypothesis in our second experiment.

Effect of Projection Surface on Depth Perception

To evaluate the effect various irregular projection surfaces have on user's perception of 3D volume and depth, we conducted a second study. In this experiment the users rated the depth of a sphere (the same ball from the previous experiment) floating above the table in a 3D graphical scene. This task is similar to that used previously to evaluate the effectiveness of volumetric displays [7] as well as effects of shadows on depth perception [24]. We recruited 10 participants (ages 25–52, 3 female) from our organization. The participants were screened for stereopsis and were compensated with a small gratuity.

Each participant sat in front of MirageTable, and observed the ball floating above various projection surfaces (as shown in Figure 10b). Their head location was tracked and they wore shutter glasses giving them stereoscopic perspective views of the 3D object. The participants were not allowed to reach into the scene or interact with it in any way, forcing them to base their depth estimates purely on visual cues.

Head tracking was limited to a small volume in order to prevent users from taking viewpoints which would trivialize the depth perception task, but in order to allow them to use motion parallax cues in their depth estimates. The participant's viewpoint was always centered on the ball to ensure optimal viewing from any head location. These constraints were explained to the participant prior to the experiment.

To test the effects of different backgrounds and projective texturing on depth perception, we chose the following 6 surface material conditions from the first experiment: *base, drop, crumple, wave, red-white,* and *red.* These were chosen to adequately cover the space of representative distortions, while limiting the overall number of conditions. We opted not to test the hand conditions, since it is difficult to control for their size, shape and color between participants; however, we note that hand conditions are essentially a combination of the color and geometry deformations well represented by the set of conditions.

The participant's task was to determine the depth of the ball by indicating a tick mark at the same depth. The uniformly distributed tick marks (labeled 1–12, 2cm apart) were permanently fixed to the surface as seen in Figure 10b. Our test presented the spheres at 4 different depths (each 6cm apart aligning with tick marks 2, 5, 8, and 11, with 2 being closest to the participant) all aligned with the central axis of the table in order to maintain the same horizontal location throughout all surface material conditions (e.g., for *drop* or *red-white conditions* the ball always appeared directly on the "edge"). We randomly varied ball height (10–15cm) and size (6–10cm diameter) for each trial to prevent the participants from judging the depth purely based on ball size or projection location difference. All tested depths were within arm's length of the participant (<80cm).

Overall, we tested 6 Conditions x 4 Depths with 4 repetitions for a total of 96 ratings per participant. The order of conditions was counterbalanced to reduce the effects of ordering and the participants had 4 practice trials before each condition to familiarize themselves with the task. Participants took about 30 min to complete the study.

The procedure for each trial was as follows. The experimenter hit a key on the keyboard to begin a trial. The ball was projected at some depth on the table and a "chime" was sounded to indicate the beginning of the trial. The participant had exactly 3 seconds to observe the ball after which it disappeared. The participant then spoke their depth estimate which was recorded by the experimenter.

Results

Our experimental setup did not account for differing inter-ocular distance for each participant. Thus our participants' depth estimates will include a bias due to the resulting slight error in the stereo presentation. To account for such participant bias, we first needed to normalize their responses. We performed a linear regression analysis on the data from the *base* condition for each participant and used this linear model to correct the data across all other conditions for that participant.

Even without accounting for participant bias, participants were reasonably accurate in their estimates, with an average depth estimate error of 1.2 tick marks (~2.4cm). Applying the per-participant correction resulted in a smaller overall average error (~1.3cm). This result confirms that even with difficult geometric and color distortions, our projective texturing method compensates well enough for users to fuse the stereo images and accurately discern the depth of a given 3D object.

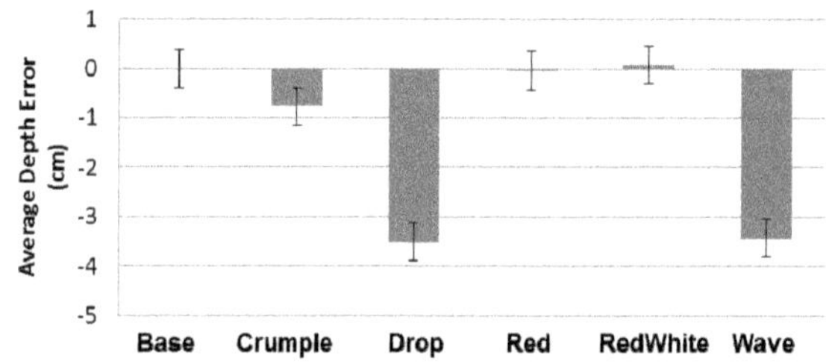

Figure 12. Average depth error (cm) after correcting for participant bias (error bars show 95% conf. intervals).

Using repeated measures ANOVA we found significant main effects on Condition ($F_{5,936}$= 78.992, p<<0.001), where the conditions with the highest amounts of geometric distortions (*drop* and *wave*) caused the highest participant judgment error (Figure 12). This confirmed our hypothesis from the first experiment. Note that the negative sign of error means that the participant believed that the object was closer than it really was.

The interaction between Condition and Depth was also significant ($F_{15,936}$=3.282 p<<0.001). The closest depth (tick 2) showed the most converged estimates across conditions, while other depth values showed a difference between *drop* and *wave* and the other conditions (Figure 13).

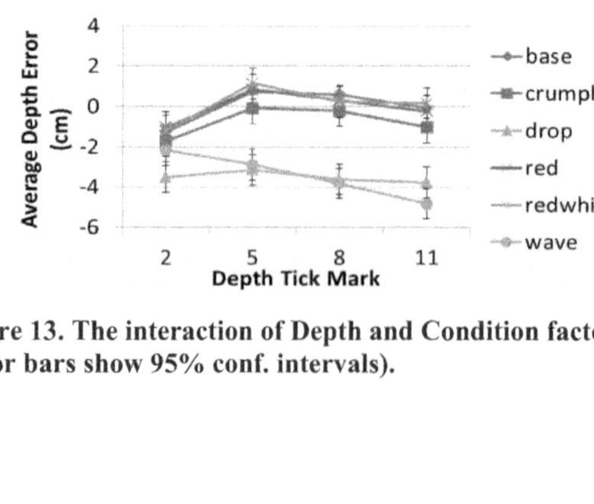

Figure 13. The interaction of Depth and Condition factors (error bars show 95% conf. intervals).

Lastly, when asked to subjectively rank different projection surfaces in order of preference for "perceiving the 3D object above the table with the least distortion", the participants showed clear preference for non-geometrically distorted surfaces. The ranking summary is shown in Figure 14.

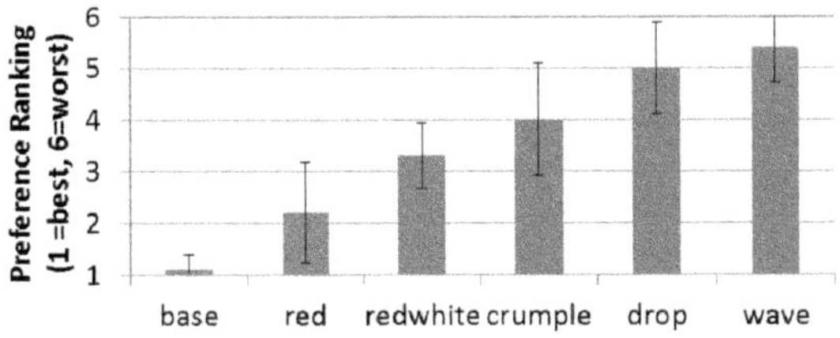

Figure 14. Subjective preferences of conditions in depth ranking experiment (error bars show standard deviation).

Summary of Findings

The study results show impressive performance of users in our system. For example, even under significant geometric distortions in the wave condition, participants performed with a relatively low average error of 3.7cm when estimating depth. On average their error was much smaller (~1.3cm). This error is much lower than the size of the object that they observed. These results indicate that even when the object is presented on a distorted background, the users are still able to fuse the stereoscopic image and perceive the image as a 3D object over the table. This provides evidence that even when reaching into a projected scene, the user can perceive 3D shape and color of the object while manipulating it using their bare hands. Simply stated, our system is capable of "fooling" the eye and presenting the correct 3D views on all backgrounds tested.

However, another important observation from our experiments is that while the users *can* perceive 3D shape over distorted geometry backgrounds, they *do not prefer* such visualizations. Indeed, they prefer backgrounds that vary in color to the ones that vary in geometry and are significantly worse in making their depth estimates with the latter. The reader can make their own assessment from images in Figure 11. We conclude that, while projective texturing lessens the impact of such distorted geometry backgrounds, they should be avoided when possible, or when convincing 3D visualizations are desired. An interesting extension of our work would be to automatically place 3D objects in the scene such that they tend to be projected on the flattest, most uniform backgrounds. This is possible in our system, because the system knows the geometry and location of all real objects on the tabletop.

DISCUSSION AND FUTURE WORK

MirageTable takes a step towards the idea that we can interact with virtual content in the same physically-realistic, high fidelity way that we expect from the real world. However, that vision is far from complete. While MirageTable tackled the problems of correct real-time perspective projections and real-world geometry-driven interactions, many areas of improvement remain. For example, the fidelity of our capture and interactions would improve with higher resolution, less noisy depth cameras. The need to provide correct perspective stereo views currently restricts MirageTable to a single user. Supporting two or three simultaneous users is technically feasible [1] and would enable interesting applications.

Also, we currently only capture the front faces of objects on the tabletop, leaving many gaps and incomplete geometries. This impacts the quality of projective texturing. We would like to capture the entire geometry of the object, this could be accomplished either with multiple cameras [20] or with object rotation [2, 10]. We hope to build on the approach of Izadi et al. [10] where a moving object is reconstructed from multiple captured frames. In addition, we are experimenting with mounting multiple cameras above the tabletop to provide multiple simultaneous views for more complete 3D models. Another approach would be to recognize the object and then render a clean CAD model [2]. This would work well for designed rigid objects, e.g., *Lego* blocks.

Another limitation is that MirageTable currently requires the user to scoop or catch the object from below in order to hold it in their hand. Simulating realistic grasping behaviors given depth camera input remains an open research problem. While some solutions have been proposed (e.g., pinch detection [8], or depth-aware optical flow [9]), several important issues, such as self-occlusions, inferring forces from images, as well as reliable finger tracking still need to be solved for convincing grasping interactions.

In this paper, we have focused on describing and evaluating the core technical aspects of our system. However, we currently offer no proof that our proposed application scenarios are convincing or useful. While such in-depth evaluations are beyond the scope of this paper, they are important in order to understand the usefulness of this technology. As we continue to refine our applications, we hope to report on their usage and the benefits they offer (e.g., we are currently investigating how our shared task space 3D teleconferencing interface changes the dynamics of remote collaborations).

Finally, it is encouraging to notice (from our current anecdotal evidence) that our users responded most positively to the interactive scenarios which required that all components of the system come together: when the 3D shared projections are combined with the ability to interact with the scene with their bare hands and when virtual objects behaved in physically realistic ways (e.g., the bowling ball example in Figure 3).

CONCLUSION

We present MirageTable, a spatial AR interactive system that allows the user to visualize and interact with virtual 3D objects spatially co-located with real objects on the tabletop. Our work contributes a novel implementation which combines simple and instantaneous 3D capture and replay, correct 3D perspective views and freehand physics-based interactions for a compelling spatial AR experience. In addition to our system and several interactive application scenarios, we contribute two experiments that confirmed the validity of our projection approach.

While we are still very far from an implementation of a working version of Sutherland's "Ultimate Display" [21] or Star Trek's *Holodeck*, MirageTable shows the potential of the projector/depth camera system to simulate such scenarios and move the interactions from computer screens to the space around us.

REFERENCES

1. Agrawala, M., Beers, A.C., McDowall, I., Fröhlich, B., Bolas, M., and Hanrahan. P. 1997. The two-user Responsive Workbench: support for collaboration through individual views of a shared space. In *Proc. of ACM SIGGRAPH '97.* 327-332.
2. Anderson, D., Frankel, J., Marks, J., Agarwala, A., Beardsley, P., Hodgins, J., Leigh, D., Ryall, K., Sullivan, E., and Yedidia, J. S. 2000. Tangible interaction + graphical interpretation: a new approach to 3D modeling. In *Proc. of ACM SIGGRAPH '00.* 393-402.
3. Bimber, O. and Raskar, R. 2005. Spatial Augmented Reality: Merging Real and Virtual Worlds. A. K. Peters, Ltd., Natick, MA, USA.
4. Bimber, O., Fröhlich, B., Schmalstieg, D., and Encarnacao, L. M. 2002. The virtual showcase. *IEEE Comput. Graph. Appl.* 21, 6 (November 2001). 48-55.
5. Bimber, O., Encarnacao, L.M., and Branco, P. 2001. The Extended Virtual Table: An Optical Extension for Table-Like Projection Systems. *Presence: Teleoper. Virtual Environ.* 10, 6. 613-631.
6. Cruz-Neira, C., Sandin, D.J., and DeFanti, T.A. 1993. Surround-screen projection-based virtual reality: The design and implementation of the CAVE. In *Proc. of ACM SIGGRAPH '93.* 135–142.
7. Grossman, T. and Balakrishnan, R. 2006. An evaluation of depth perception on volumetric displays. In *Proc. of ACM Advanced Visual Interfaces (AVI '06).* 193-200.
8. Hilliges, O., Izadi, S., Wilson, A., Hodges, S., Garcia-Mendoza, A., and Butz, A. 2009. Interactions in the Air: Adding Further Depth to Interactive Tabletops. In *Proc. of ACM UIST '09.* 139-148.
9. Hilliges, O., Kim, D., Izadi, S., Weiss, M. and Wilson, A.D. 2012. Holodesk: Direct 3D Interactions with a Situated See-Through Display. In *Proc. of ACM SIGCHI '12.*
10. Izadi, S., Kim, D., Hilliges, O., Molyneaux, D., Newcombe, R., Kohli, P., Shotton, J., Hodges, S., Freeman, D., Davison, A., and Fitzgibbon, A. 2011. KinectFusion: Real-time 3D Reconstruction and Interaction Using a Moving Depth Camera. In *Proc. of ACM UIST '11.* 559-568.
11. Jota, R., and Benko, H. 2011. Constructing Virtual 3D Models with Physical Building Blocks. In *CHI 2011 Extended Abstracts.* 2173-2178.
12. McCann, J.J. 1992. Rules for colour constancy. *Ophthal. Physiol. Opt.,* Vol. 12. 175-177.
13. Pinhanez, C. S. 2001. The Everywhere Displays Projector: A Device to Create Ubiquitous Graphical Interfaces. In *Proc. of UBICOMP '01.* 315–331.
14. Piper B, Ratti C, Ishii H. 2002. Illuminating clay: a 3-D tangible interface for landscape analysis. *In Proc. of ACM SIGCHI '02.* 355-362.
15. Raskar, R., Brown, M.S., Yang, R. Chen, W.-C., Welch, G., Towles, H., Seales, B., and Fuchs. H. 1999. Multi-projector displays using camera-based registration. In *Proc. of Visualization (VIS '99).* 161-168.
16. Raskar, R., Welch, G., Cutts, M., Lake, A., Stesin, L. and Fuchs, H. 1998. The office of the future: a unified approach to image-based modeling and spatially immersive displays. In *Proc. of ACM SIGGRAPH '98.* 179-188.
17. Raskar, R., Welch, G., Low, K.-L., and Bandyopadhyay, D. 2001. Shader Lamps: Animating Real Objects With Image-Based Illumination. In *Proc. of the Eurographics Workshop on Rendering Techniques.* 89-102.
18. Rekimoto, J. and Saitoh, M. 1999. Augmented Surfaces: A Spatially Continuous Work Space for Hybrid Computing Environments. In *Proc. of ACM SIGCHI '99.* 378–385.
19. Segal, M., Korobkin, C., van Widenfelt, R., Foran, J., and Haeberli, P. 1992. Fast shadows and lighting effects using texture mapping. In *Proc. of ACM SIGGRAPH '92.* 249-252.
20. Starner, T., Leibe, B., Minner, D., Westyn, T., Hurst, A., and Weeks, J. 2003. The Perceptive Workbench: Computer-vision-based gesture tracking, object tracking, and 3D reconstruction for augmented desks. In *Journal of Machine Vision and Applications*, vol. 14. 59-71.
21. Sutherland, I.E. 1965. The Ultimate Display. In *Proc. of the IFIP Congress.* 506-508.
22. Tognazzini, B. 1994. The "Starfire" video prototype project: a case history. In Proc. of ACM SIGCHI '94. 99-105.
23. Underkoffler, J., Ullmer, B., and Ishii, H. 1999. Emancipated pixels: Real-world graphics in the luminous room. *In Proc. of ACM SIGGRAPH '99.* 385–392.
24. Wanger, L. 1992. The effect of shadow quality on the perception of spatial relationships in computer generated imagery. In *Proc. of ACM Interactive 3D Graphics '92.* 39-42.
25. Ware, C., Arthur, K. and Booth, K. 1993. Fish tank virtual reality. In *Proc. of ACM SIGCHI '93.* 37-42.
26. Weiss, M., Voelker, S., Sutter,C., and Borchers, J. 2010. BendDesk: dragging across the curve. In *Proc. of ACM International Conference on Interactive Tabletops and Surfaces (ITS '10).* 1-10.
27. Wilson, A. 2007. Depth-Sensing Video Cameras for 3D Tangible Tabletop Interaction. In *Proc. of IEEE International Workshop on Horizontal Interactive Human-Computer Systems (TABLETOP '07).* 201–204.
28. Wilson, A. and Robbins, D. C. PlayTogether: Playing Games across Multiple Interactive Tabletops, *IUI 2007 Workshop on Tangible Play: Research and Design for Tangible and Tabletop Games.*
29. Wilson A. and Benko H. 2010. Combining multiple depth cameras and projectors for interactions on, above and between surfaces. In *Proc. of ACM UIST'10.* 273-282.
30. Wilson, A. D., Izadi, S., Hilliges, O., Garcia-Mendoza, A., and Kirk, D. 2008. Bringing physics to the surface. In *Proc. of ACM UIST '08.* 67-76.

How Screen Transitions Influence Touch and Pointer Interaction Across Angled Display Arrangements

Fabian Hennecke, Wolfgang Matzke, Andreas Butz
Media Informatics Group, University of Munich
Amalienstraße 17, 80333 Munich, Germany
{fabian.hennecke, andreas.butz}@ifi.lmu.de, wolfgang.matzke@gmx.net

ABSTRACT

Digital office environments often integrate multiple displays in a variety of arrangements. We investigated the combination of a horizontal and a directly connected vertical display, which together form a digital workspace. In particular, we were interested in the effect of the physical transition (bezel, edge or curve) on dragging. In a study participants performed dragging tasks across both display planes with direct touch as well as a pointing device. Contrary to our expectations, we found no significant effect on task completion time. Only regarding accuracy the curved transition performed better than edge and bezel. Interestingly, the subjective judgment did generally not match the objective results. These findings suggest that we need to rethink our understanding of display continuities in terms of usability as well as user satisfaction.

Author Keywords

Display connection; interactive surfaces; transition; dragging; tabletops.

ACM Classification Keywords

H.5.2 [Information Interfaces and Presentation]: User Interfaces - Input Devices and Strategies;

General Terms

Design, Human Factors.

INTRODUCTION

In today's computerized offices, a variety of display arrangements can be found. While the most common combination of two or more displays is a horizontal row, other display combinations are possible. An assembly of conventional displays will mostly involve crossing (a) a screen bezel [15] or (b) a hard edge [4] connecting the displays. Recently also (c) a curved segment was proposed as a display connection [14, 16, 17]. Current research mainly focuses on the effects of screen bezels in horizontal display arrays [13]. Apparently, users tend to organize their data according to display borders, since these prevent the usage of combined displays as one large screen [2, 7].

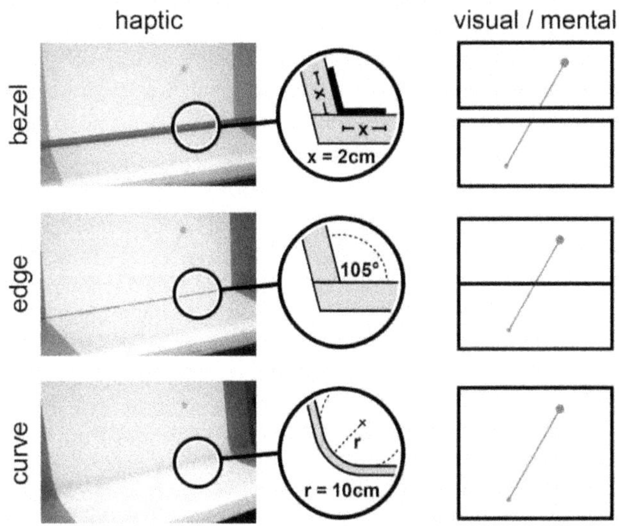

Figure 1: Three different connection types with different levels of haptic, visual and mental continuity: bezel, edge and curve.

Bezels affect both pointer and direct touch input. Pointer interaction is influenced by bezels as the pointer might jump from one display to the other in an unexpected way [3]. For touch interaction, the haptic continuity of the display arrangement is essential. Screen bezels of systems such as the Acer Iconia [1] present a clear obstacle for direct input while displays without such barriers offer a more continuous input [4]. Curved display combinations aim to maximize the degree of haptic continuity using a curved connection area [14, 16, 17].

We present a study in which we investigated the effects of these different connection types between two angled displays on touch and pointer interaction. We built three otherwise similar display setups with different connection types: a bezel, an edge and a curve (see Figure 1). Participants had to complete different dragging tasks across the connections. Against our expectations we did not find strong objective differences between the three setups. However, we identified several effects on the users' subjective perception of touch and pointer interaction across displays, which did not generally match the objective results. As a conclusion we propose to rethink the understanding of display connections and their influence on touch and pointer interaction.

RELATED WORK

As our work uses dragging tasks to judge direct and indirect input mechanisms on a large display, it largely draws on prior evaluations based on such tasks. Foley et al. proposed a taxonomy of general task types for graphical user interfaces [5]. Pathing tasks were fundamental in their description as they continuously involve time in contrast to simple positioning or orienting tasks. Forlines et al. used a dragging task to evaluate the difference between pointer and touch interaction on interactive surfaces [6]. Weiss et al. evaluated the effects of the curved connection on their BendDesk on touch input in different dragging directions [16]. Due to the underlying large interactive surface in our study we also considered the entire human arm as a chain of actuators as described by Guiard [8].

EVALUATION

We conducted a user study to examine the effect of the three different connection types (bezel, edge, curve) on dragging tasks across display borders. The following research questions were investigated: (RQ1) To what extent does the type of display connection affect the input accuracy? (RQ2) To what extent does the type of display connection affect the task completion time? (RQ3) To what extent does the type of display connection affect the subjective assessment of the display and the input?

Participants and Design

In order to keep all parameters other than the connection type fixed (overall: width: 120cm, internal angle: 105°; horizontal display: height 72cm, depth 35cm; vertical display: height 38cm), we used a reconfigurable display setup based on rear-projection and FTIR touch sensing. As the reconfiguration of the interactive surface took too long for a within-subject design we conducted a between-group study with *connection type* as the between-group factor. Each connection type was tested with 16 participants. Consequently, 48 people participated in the study (21 females and 27 males, aged between 22 and 35, 46 right- and 2 left-handed). We used touch as well as pointer interaction with two different task conditions (constrained, unconstrained). This combination of within-subject factors (*input*, *task*) was counterbalanced using a 4x4 Latin Square.

Task and Procedure

Each participant was initially seated centered in front of the display. They had an extensive training phase prior to the study, which included two runs of each *input* x *task* combination. Only the third run was used for statistical analysis. In the end, each participant completed a questionnaire based on ISO 9241-9:2000 [10].

Connection Type

To emulate the most common connection – two monitors placed with bezels next to each other – our (1) *bezel* setup consisted of two acrylic plates. We used a wooden strip (height 4cm, thickness 3mm) within the connection area to separate both display planes. By removing the strip, we created a direct connection between both displays with an (2) *edge*. For the third type of transition we exchanged the acrylic plates. The new plate had a continuous (3) *curve* with a radius of 10cm connecting both planar display segments (see Figure 1).

Input

We tested direct (1) *touch* interaction with FTIR sensing and indirect (2) *pointer* interaction with an optical mouse. To allow dragging a virtual object between the display planes even without a direct connection, we combined two interaction techniques for both inputs: Flick [12] and Stitching [9]. The dragged object could be flicked across the connection and picked up again afterwards. In addition users could beam the object to the other surface in a small area next to the connection similar to the pen-based Stitching described by Hinckley et al. [9]. The bezel in the respective setup consisted of a wooden strip mounted in front of the edge connection. Consequently the pointer had to bypass the occluded display area behind the bezel to simulate a real bezel. As we did not want the resulting pointer movement to suffer from a warping effect, but rather be fluid and understandable, we derived the last-known pointer movement direction near the bezel and beamed the pointer to the other display in that direction similar to the Mouse ether technique [3]. This enabled dragging the object fluently across the bezel connection.

Dragging Tasks

We varied the task conditions for each input modality (see Figure 2). In the first task the user had to drag an object from a starting point on the horizontal plane to a target area on the vertical plane and vice versa (1) without any constraints. In the second task the users were (2) constrained as they were asked to follow the shortest virtual path shown between both points as fast and accurately as possible. No further constraining mechanisms (e.g. a constraining force) were used. To obtain meaningful data we used a two-way path design based on ISO 9241-9:2000 [10]. In the bezel condition the length was extended by the height of the bezel to assure that distances of equal length had to be covered on the display itself.

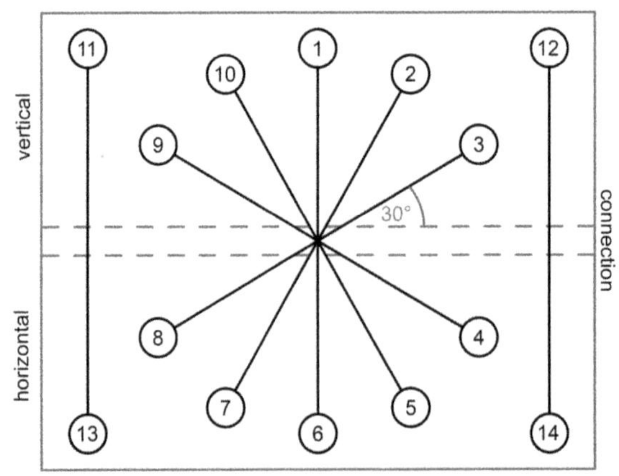

Figure 2: Arrangement of the dragging paths across the display: participants dragged from each point to its counterpart - with and without a constraining path shown.

Measures

There were two sources of objective data. In order to assess the accuracy, the path deviation (PD) was calculated. It is defined (as in MacKenzie et al. [11]) as the mean distance between the user input and the shortest virtual path along a line perpendicular to that path, and it is measured in pixels. Second, the task completion time (TCT) was measured. It is defined as the time between starting the dragging motion and releasing the object in the target area.

In addition, post-questionnaires were used to assess the participants' opinion regarding display configuration and in particular the connection types. We used 5-point Likert scales ranging from '1' being the best to '5' being the worst rating for all questions.

Statistical tests and analysis

All objective data (PD, TCT) were analyzed with a 3x2x2 analysis of variances (mixed ANOVA) with the between-groups factor *connection type* and the within-subject factors *task* and *input*. Subjective ratings were combined into three categories: 'acceptable' ('1', '2'), 'neutral' ('3') and 'not acceptable' ('4', '5') for further analyses. To give a general overview we only report the subjective ratings with the help of the 'acceptable' category.

RESULTS

We combine and compare objective data as well as subjective ratings and observations in four categories: *accuracy*, *speed*, *convenience* and *further findings*.

Accuracy

For the accuracy in terms of PD we found a significant effect of the connection type, $F(2, 45) = 4.509$, $p<.05$. Post-hoc tests (Bonferroni) revealed a significant difference between edge (M=36.5px) and curve (M=27.9px) with $p<.05$. No other significant differences between the connection types (bezel: M=30.3px) were found for these conditions. Further investigations using a 3x2 mixed ANOVA only for the constrained task show significant differences of PD between curve and edge, $F(2, 45) = 201.883$, $p<.05$, for both inputs. There were also significant effects ($p<.05$) of task ($F(1,45) = 176.526$) and input x task ($F(1,45) = 15.320$) on user's accuracy. No further significant effects (e.g. connection type x input) were found.

The percentage of participants who rated the touch accuracy as "acceptable" on the entire display (bezel 62,5%, curve 56,3%, edge 37,5%) and within the connection area (bezel 31,3%, curve 31,3%, edge 12,5%) is in line with our measurements. Interestingly the ratings for mouse input are reversed: edge receives a lot of good ratings for the entire display and the connection area (81,3%/68,8%) while bezel (43,8%/37,5%) and curve (37,5%/43,8%) are rated worse.

Additionally we created plot diagrams from participants' input data. They show various effects of the connection and perspective: (1) We found deviations for touch input from the shortest virtual path for all connections in the unconstrained task just as Weiss et al. [16]. Beside this we also noticed that the dragging paths are much more scattered across the transition in the edge setup compared to curve and bezel. (2) With pointer input in the constrained task participants tend to drag along an inwards bulged trajectory in the upward direction (13-11 and 14-12, see Figure 2) on the horizontal display. Interestingly the trajectory is bulged outwards for the downward direction between the same points. (3) There is a general tendency towards curved trajectories in both task conditions and all task axes with pointer input despite the centered vertical axes (1-6, 6-1, see Figure 2). We assume that this tendency, which is stronger for the unconstrained task as expected is caused by two factors. First, perspective distortion on the large display seems to be mainly responsible as all except the centered task axis are affected. Second, a problem with users' mental model of indirect pointer movement seems to have an influence on the trajectories. Obviously pointer interaction on the horizontal display plane is much more affected than on a vertical display to which users are accustomed. Further pointer movement was in line with common knowledge (e.g. target overshoots).

Speed

Although the mean TCT for each connection type tended to decrease from bezel via edge to curve, we didn't find a significant effect of connection, $F(2, 45) = 2.415$, $p>.05$. But as expected there was a significant effect of task ($F(1,45) = 41.057$, $p<.05$). Participants completed the unconstrained task (M=9869.4ms) faster than the constrained one (M=11705.1ms). Additionally we found a significant effect of input ($F(1,45) = 222.001$, $p<.05$). Pointer input (M=8134.3ms) was faster than touch input (M=13440.2ms) which might be caused by the relatively small movement of the mouse compared to direct touch.

Despite the lack of a significant difference, the perceived interaction speed was rated differently. Mouse input was generally rated acceptable concerning the entire display (curve 93,8%, edge 93,8%, bezel 81,3%) and the connection area (edge 93,8%, bezel 81,3%, curve 81,3%). However, more participants were satisfied with a curve regarding the speed of touch input on the entire surface (curve 75%, edge 50%, bezel 37,5%) as well as the connection area (curve 37,5%, edge 18,8%, bezel 12,5%).

Convenience

Curve is rated best (75,0%) followed by edge (56,3%) and bezel (31,3%) regarding the oddness of transition for pointer and touch input (curve: 62,5%, bezel: 43,8%, edge: 6.5%). Asked about the haptic convenience within the connection area they preferred the curve to bezel and edge (curve 50,0%, bezel 37,5%, edge 25,0%). Bezel's bad ratings for the connection area might be caused by rather unnatural arm poses described in the next section.

Further Observations

In the edge setup users tend to keep contact with the interactive surface for the entire touch-based dragging task, even across the connection, although transition techniques

(Flick and Stitching) were introduced to them. It seems to encourage the users to interact as close to the edge as possible due to its visual output until the edge. This led to extreme finger and wrist poses during the dragging tasks in the connection area. In addition to a bent wrist, users had to rotate their arms to continue dragging through the transition. This rotation was obviously also done to avoid occlusion of the surface by the user's arm. Although there was no mention of increased arm or wrist fatigue these postures looked rather unnatural.

CONCLUSION AND FUTURE WORK

Our results reveal actual as well as perceived effects of the different connection types on cross-display interaction. We showed how the connection influences the user's perception of touch and pointer interaction and the way users interact across a connection. Based on the results of our study we argue for using a curved connection in angled display combinations for touch input. It received good subjective ratings, allows the highest dragging accuracy and avoids any hard visual breaks. In contrast to this there is no clear preference for pointer input as users rated all connections similarly using a mouse. Maybe the effect of the large planar display areas, which are quite similar to traditional displays normally used with pointer input outweigh the effect of the rather small connection area. Our study also revealed that the objective results regarding time and error rate are not necessarily in line with the subjective user ratings for the connections. Therefore we propose to not only rely on objective criteria such as accuracy or task completion time but also on the users' assessment of the display connection while developing new display setups.

Although a curved connection seems to be preferable compared to a bezel or an edge another display angle might influence the results. As the haptic break of an edge connection becomes smaller with an increased angle this could lead to different subjective results and even different accuracy measures. Consequently future studies definitely need to investigate this matter. It will also be interesting to investigate other aspects of such display combinations such as their size, curve radius and different transition techniques revealing their effects on usability and user satisfaction. In addition, we suggest investigating the influence of different haptic and visual continuities of display connections on user satisfaction with touch input. Connections with a low haptic continuity (e.g. an edge) but a comparatively high visual continuity might trouble the user. In contrast to this a bezel provides two separate display planes that are visually and haptically separated and therefore gets better ratings. As pointer input is not influenced by haptic continuity it is obviously not affected by this difference. Future studies with a rounded edge could provide further insights on this.

ACKNOWLEDGMENTS

We'd like to thank our patient study subjects for their time and the CHI reviewers for a fruitful rebuttal phase.

REFERENCES

[1] Acer: *http://us.acer.com/ac/en/US/content/iconia.* Accessed: 2012-12-28.

[2] Ball, R. and North, C. 2005. An Analysis of User Behavior on High-Resolution Tiled Displays. *INTERACT 2005* (2005), 350--363.

[3] Baudisch, P. et al. 2004. Mouse ether: accelerating the acquisition of targets across multi-monitor displays. *CHI 2004* (2004), 1379--1382.

[4] Microsoft: 2007. *http://www.microsoft.com/presspass/exec/jeff/10-23convergence.mspx*. Accessed: 2011-12-28.

[5] Foley, J.D. et al. 1984. The human factors of computer graphics interaction techniques. *IEEE Computer Graphics and Applications*. 4, 11 (1984), 10--48.

[6] Forlines, C. et al. 2007. Direct-touch vs. mouse input for tabletop displays. *CHI 2007* (2007), 647--656.

[7] Grudin, J. 2001. Partitioning digital worlds: focal and peripheral awareness in multiple monitor use. *CHI 2001* (2001), 458--465.

[8] Guiard, Y. 1987. Asymmetric Division of Labor in Human Skilled Bimanual Action: The Kinematic Chain as a Model. *Journal of Motor Behavior*. 19, 4 (1987), 486--517.

[9] Hinckley, K. et al. 2004. Stitching: pen gestures that span multiple displays. *AVI 2004* (2004), 23--31.

[10] ISO 9241-9 Ergonomic Requirements for Work with Visual Display Terminals, Non-keyboard Input Device Requirements. (2000).

[11] MacKenzie, I.S. et al. 2001. Accuracy measures for evaluating computer pointing devices. *CHI 2001* (2001), 9--16.

[12] Reetz, A. et al. Superflick: a Natural and Efficient Technique for Long-Distance Object Placement on Digital Tables. *GI 2006* 163--170.

[13] Robertson, G. et al. 2005. The large-display user experience. *IEEE computer graphics and applications*. 25, 4 (2005), 44--51.

[14] Tognazzini, B. 1994. The "Starfire" Video Prototype A Case History. *CHI 1994* (1994), 99--105.

[15] Uray, P. et al. 2005. MRI - A Mixed Reality Interface for the Masses. *SIGGRAPH 2006* (2005), 3-3.

[16] Weiss, M. et al. 2010. BendDesk: Dragging Across the Curve. *ITS 2010* (2010), 1--10.

[17] Wimmer, R. et al. 2010. Curve: Revisiting the Digital Desk. *NordiCHI 2010* (2010), 561--570.

How Small Can You Go? Analyzing the Effect of Visual Angle in Pointing Tasks

Juan Pablo Hourcade and Natasha E. Bullock-Rest
University of Iowa, Department of Computer Science
14 MacLean Hall, Iowa City, IA 52242 USA
juanpablo-hourcade@uiowa.edu, natasha.bullock.rest@gmail.com

ABSTRACT
People are increasingly using wireless mice from across rooms as they use computers as entertainment centers. As a consequence, they often have to point at targets occupying small visual angles. In this note we present the results of a study on pointing performance for targets occupying small visual angles. Our results suggest there is a steep degradation of pointing performance in both accuracy and speed for targets occupying a visual angle below 3 minutes of arc.

Author Keywords
Pointing; accuracy; efficiency; visual angle.

ACM Classification Keywords
H.5 [Information interfaces and presentation (e.g., HCI)]: Miscellaneous.

INTRODUCTION
An increasing number of people who are using computers to hold and manage all their digital media (e.g., music, movies, photos) are often operating them from a distance. For instance, many new homes in the United States have one large room (no walls) that includes kitchen, living and dining spaces. Many people have their media centers in these large rooms, often controlled by a computer. Due to the distance between, for example, the kitchen and the place where the computer is, many people operate their computers using wireless mice so they do not have to walk over to the computer every time they want to switch media. This results in pointing tasks with targets occupying small visual angles.

Programmers size visual targets in software using pixels. The size at which they appear on the screen depends on the size of the display, its resolution, and zoom settings. We will refer to this size as *display size*. The *visual angle* occupied by a target may be different for the same display size depending on the distance between the user and the display. In addition, if using a mouse to point, the size of targets in terms of *motor space* (i.e. how far a user would physically have to move the mouse to go from one end of a target to the opposite end) will vary depending on operating system settings for mouse cursor speed and acceleration. See Figure 1 for a diagram showing motor space, visual angle and display size.

Motor space plays a role in pointing performance as demonstrated, for example, by Blanch et al.'s study on semantic pointing [2]. There is some evidence that larger visual angles can affect performance [3][8]. In addition, there is evidence that large displays appear to benefit users' performance in spatial tasks in virtual environments when compared with smaller displays that occupy the same field of view [1][10]. This is coupled with studies of pointing performance with large displays from oblique angles [6] and long distances [7].

Our concern in this note is learning about the impact of small visual angles on pointing tasks. We present the results of a study suggesting a steep decrease in pointing performance in both accuracy and speed for targets occupying a visual angle below 3 minutes of arc. The results can be used to develop target-sizing guidelines for expected ranges of cursor speeds, display sizes, resolutions and distances to displays.

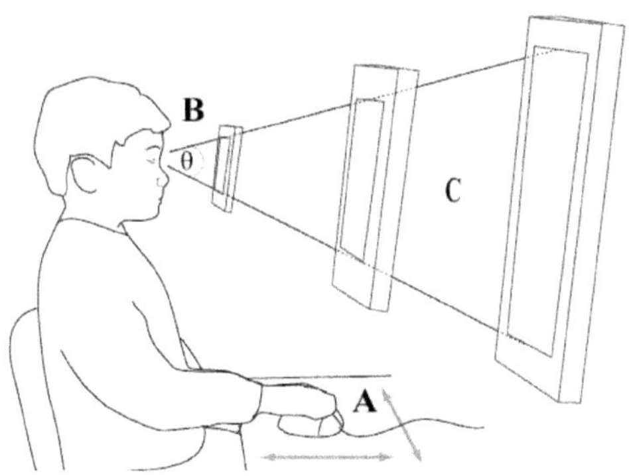

Figure 1. Motor space (A), visual angle θ (B), and three display sizes (C).

RESEARCH OBJECTIVE
Our research objective was to learn about the relationship between pointing performance and visual angle for small

visual angles. A secondary objective was to learn if PointAssist [5], a free, open source tool designed to help with pointing tasks would improve the pointing performance of users attempting to click on targets occupying small visual angles. To assist in pointing, PointAssist detects the type of motion that occurs when users have difficulty pointing at a target (e.g., an icon), and slows the speed of the mouse cursor to provide extra precision in those cases.

STUDY SETUP

Participants

The participants were twelve adults (age min=25, q1=27.5, median=31.5, q3=37.75, max=69). Ten were male and two were female. Eleven used their right hand to hold the mouse, and one used the left hand. They used a computer a mean of 46 hours a week (min=16, q1=29, median=40, q3=53, max=100) and a mouse for a mean of 32 hours per week (min=0, q1=16, median=30, q3=43, max=80). All had at least 20/20 vision based on asking them to read letters from a Snellen eye chart. They were recruited through posters and word of mouth at our University. All participants were compensated.

Materials

We used a Dell XPS laptop running Windows Vista. We used a Dell optical mouse (6.6cm wide, 12.1cm long, 3.6cm high) as an input device and a 21" widescreen LCD display using a 1440 by 900 pixel resolution. The display's width was 43cm. The cursor speed was set to 8 (corresponds to the fifth tick from the left in Windows Vista). The "enhance pointer precision" option was turned on.

We used a modified version of software used in a previous study [5], providing feedback when the cursor is inside the target by changing its shape (see Figure 2). It presents participants with pointing tasks that involve moving the mouse cursor from the middle of a green square toward a light blue target circle, and clicking on the light blue target circle. The light blue target circles always appear to the right of the green square. We presented targets in only one direction because we were not interested in researching the effect of angles on pointing tasks. Tasks ended as soon as participants clicked, regardless of whether the click was inside or outside the target. More details on how tasks are presented in the study software can be found in [5].

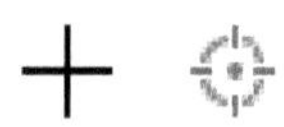

Figure 2. On the left, the default cursor. On the right, the cursor when inside a target. Both were 19 by 19 pixels.

Procedure

We conducted the study in an office at our University's Department of Computer Science. After providing demographic information, participants conducted nine practice tasks with PointAssist turned off to ensure that they could understand what to do. A researcher instructed them to complete tasks as quickly and accurately as possible.

The study software presented target circles of three different diameters: 4, 6 and 8 pixels. See Table 1 for equivalent sizes in millimeters for size on the screen. The center of the target circles appeared at one of three distances from the starting position: 128, 256 and 512 pixels. The combination of three target sizes and three distances yielded a total of nine distinct tasks.

Screen (pixels)	Screen (mm)
4	1.2
6	1.8
8	2.4

Table 1. Size of targets on the screen in pixels and millimeters.

Participants completed a total of four blocks of tasks after practicing. Each block was completed at a different physical distance from the screen. The distances were 115.5, 231, 287, and 355.5cm. These distances were calculated so the smallest 4 pixel target would occupy the following angles in the participants' field of view (in arc minutes): 4, 2, 1.6, and 1.4. Note that 20/20 vision is defined as the visual acuity needed to discriminate two points separated by 1 arc minute (or 1/60th of a degree) [4]. The order in which participants experienced the four distances was balanced using a fully balanced Latin Square.

At each distance, participants completed two sub-blocks, one completed with PointAssist turned on and the other with PointAssist turned off. Participants were randomly assigned to starting each block with PointAssist turned on or off (half started with PointAssist on and half with PointAssist off). The study software switched PointAssist on and off automatically and the participants were not told that they would be testing two modes of pointing. Each sub-block in the study consisted of the nine distinct tasks for a total of 72 tasks in the study. The study software presented the nine tasks in random order.

After participants completed all tasks, we asked them to complete a simple questionnaire asking them how easy or difficult tasks were at each distance from the display using a five-point scale (1-"very hard", 5 -"very easy").

Design

The independent variables were: target size, amplitude (i.e., distance to target from initial cursor position), physical distance from the display, block number, and PointAssist status (all within-subjects). The dependent variables were: accuracy, movement time, target reentry, and number of sub-movements. Accuracy for each task was 100 if the participant pressed and released the mouse button while inside the target, 0 otherwise. Movement time was measured starting when participants moved the mouse cursor from the middle of the green square and ending when they released the mouse button as part of a click. Target reentry refers to the number of times participants entered the target (not counting the first time). The number of sub-movements was based on PointAssist's parsing of sub-movements [5].

RESULTS

The study software logged every mouse event into a Microsoft Access database. For the statistical analysis, we exported data to SPSS 17.0. We used repeated measures ANOVAs for normally distributed data and Friedman's test for the remaining data. We concentrate our analysis on the impact of physical distance from the display.

Accuracy

Physical distance from the display had a statistically significant effect on accuracy (chi-square=12.982, df =3, sig=.005). Figure 3 shows a clear decline in accuracy rates for the smallest visual angles. There were also statistically significant differences for 4 pixel targets between those occupying 1.6 and 1.4 arc minutes, and differences worth noting (p=.059) for 6 pixel targets between those occupying 3 and 2.1 arc minutes.

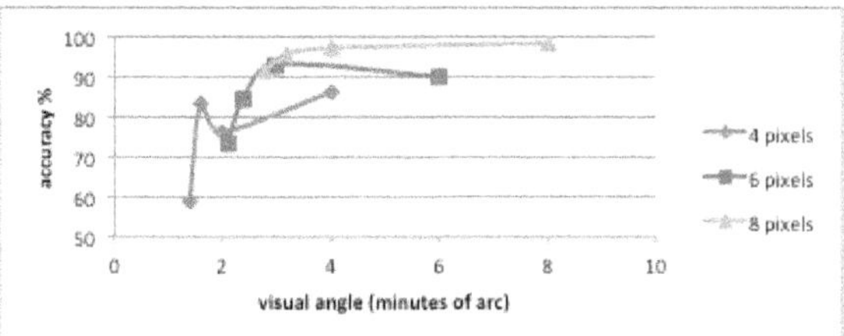

Figure 3. Accuracy by visual angle and target size.

Movement Time

Physical distance from the display also had a statistically significant effect on movement time (F(3, 33)=21.225, p<.001, power=1.0). Figure 4 shows a similar pattern to the one with accuracy rates. There were also statistically significant differences within specific target sizes. For example, for 4 pixel targets, between those occupying 4 and <=2 arc minutes, for 6 pixel targets between those occupying 6 and <=3 arc minutes, and for 8 pixel targets between those occupying 3.2 and 2.8 arc minutes.

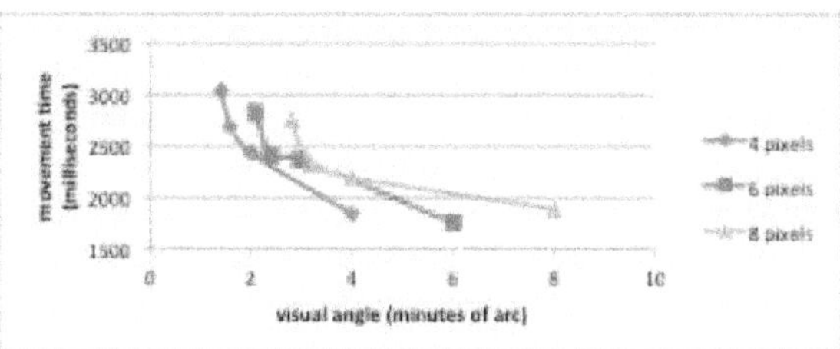

Figure 4. Movement time by visual angle and target size.

Target Reentry and Sub-Movements

Physical distance from the display did not have a statistically significant effect on target reentry (p=.087, power=.545). It did have a statistically significant effect on the number of sub-movements (F(3, 33)=18.9, p<.001, power=1.0). Participants had more sub-movements with smaller visual angles.

PointAssist

PointAssist did not have a statistically significant effect on accuracy or movement time.

Fitts' Law Measures

We conducted a linear regression using both Fitts' index of difficulty and the effective index of difficulty for each physical distance at which participants conducted tasks [9]. We obtained higher correlation coefficients when using Fitts' index of difficulty, consistent with previous studies where participants face tasks so difficult that spending extra time on them does not result in higher accuracy (e.g., [5]). Figure 5 shows Fitts' index of performance by target diameter and visual angle. Again, we see the same pattern, with differences by target diameter and a clear dip in performance for visual angles beginning at about 3 minutes of arc.

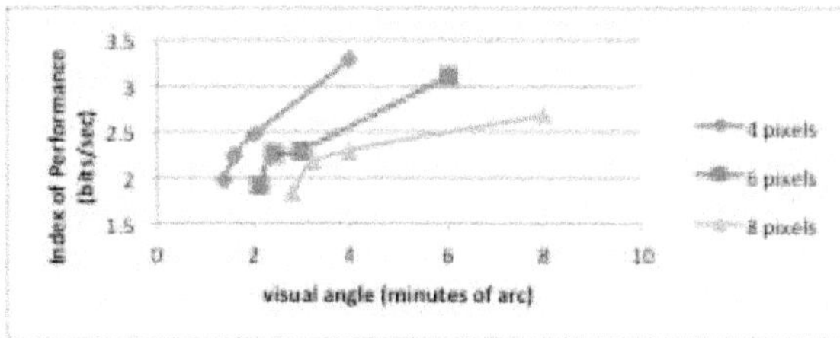

Figure 5. Fitts' index of performance by visual angle and target size.

Adjusting Model to Include Visual Angle

In the standard form of Fitts' law, shown in the equation below, MT is movement time, a and b are empirically determined constants, A is amplitude, and W is the diameter of the target.

$$MT = a + b \log_2 (A/W + 1)$$

We conducted a linear regression for the equation above using data from all four distances from the display (36 data points from nine unique combinations of amplitude and target diameter times four distances to the display). The resulting R^2 coefficient was only 0.19, suggesting a need to modify the model to take into account visual angle.

Given the clear impact of visual angle on movement time and accuracy, we explored how visual angle could be included as an extension to Fitts' law to better predict movement time. We studied taking into account visual angle by itself in a third term:

$$MT = a + b \log_2 (A/W + 1) + c \log_2 (1/V + 1)$$

The third term includes a third empirically determined constant c, and V, the visual angle. Conducting regression yielded a relatively low R^2 coefficient of 0.66 (a=954, b=116, c=1772), which was still a great improvement over using Fitts' law by itself. Note that most Fitts' law studies average values for all tasks with the same target sizes and amplitudes when fitting the model (this typically results in 9 to 12 points). This means we are fitting 3-4 times the points most Fitts' law studies try to fit, which by itself should reduce the fit to the model. While we do not expect this to be a definitive model, it provides a sense for the mathematical relationship between visual angle and pointing performance.

Participant Reported Ease/Difficulty

Not surprisingly the distance from the display at which tasks were conducted had a statistically significant effect on perceived ease and difficulty ($p<.001$). For the closest distance, ten out of twelve participants selected the highest ease score, while for the farthest distance, nine out of twelve selected the lowest two ease scores.

DISCUSSION

The analysis of results consistently shows that the decline in pointing performance for smaller visual angles, both in terms of accuracy and movement time is not linear. Instead, the plots of visual angle against dependent variables suggest that performance steeply deteriorates for targets occupying visual angles below 3 arc minutes. This is supported by pairwise comparisons between visual angles for specific target sizes.

These findings could be taken into account, for example, in the design of user interfaces for entertainment applications such as media players that may often be operated at a distance. Common sense target size guidelines could be developed based on the distribution of display sizes, screen resolutions, cursor speeds, and room sizes for the target market. The following equation provides an example of how target sizes could be calculated.

$$TiP = D \tan(AM/60)\ (WSiP/WS)$$

TiP is the target size in pixels, D is the distance from the user to the screen, AM is the desired size of the target in arc minutes, $WSiP$ is the width of the screen in pixels and WS is the width of the screen (measured in the same unit as D). For example, for the screen width and resolution used in this study, with D=7.5m, a target size 3 minutes of arc wide would have to be 22 pixels wide.

The main limitation of our study is that we used very small targets due to limits in the size of our facilities, which limits the environmental validity of the study. However, participants had reasonable performance with these target sizes at the closest distance to the display. Other factors could have also influenced the results. For example, since participants had little experience conducting pointing tasks away from the display, they may have taken a bit of extra time and care when farther away from the display, increasing movement times across all target sizes. This may explain the differences by target size in the charts showing visual angle plotted against movement time and index of performance.

CONCLUSION

We have presented the results of a study investigating the relationship between targets with small visual angles and pointing performance. The results suggest there is a steep decline in pointing performance for targets with visual angles below 3 minutes of arc.

ACKNOWLEDGEMENTS

We would like to thank Alicia Trillo for her valuable feedback on the study software.

REFERENCES

1. Bakdash, J. Z., Augustyn, J. S., and Proffitt, D. R. (2006). Large displays enhance spatial knowledge of a virtual environment. *Proceedings of APGV '06*. ACM Press: pp. 59-62.
2. Blanch, R., Guiard, Y. & Beaudouin-Lafon, M. (2004). Semantic Pointing: Improving Target Acquisition with Control-Display Ratio Adaptation. *Proceedings of CHI 2004*. ACM Press: pp. 519-526.
3. Cockburn, A. and Brock, P. (2006). Human On-Line Response to Visual and Motor Target Expansion. *Proceedings of Graphics Interface 2006*, 81-87.
4. Holladay, J.T. (1997). Proper Method for Calculating Average Visual Acuity. *Journal of Refractive Surgery, 13*, 388-391.
5. Hourcade, J.P., Nguyen, C.M., Perry, K.B. and Denburg, N.L. (2010). PointAssist for Older Adults: Analyzing Sub-Movement Characteristics to Aid in Pointing Tasks. *Proceedings of CHI 2010*. ACM Press: pp. 1115-1124.
6. Jota, R., Nacenta, M.A., Jorge, J.A., Carpendale, S. and Greenberg, S. (2010). A comparison of ray pointing techniques for very large displays. In *Proceedings of Graphics Interface 2010* (GI '10), 269-276.
7. Kopper, R., Silva, M.G., McMahan, R.P. and Bowman, D.A. (2008). *Increasing the Precision of Distant Pointing for Large High-Resolution Displays*. TR-08-17, Computer Science, Virginia Tech.
8. Kovacs, A.J., Buchanan, J.J. and Shea, C.H. (2008). Perceptual influences on Fitts' law. *Exp. Brain Research, 190*, 99-103.
9. Soukoreff, R.W. and MacKenzie, I.S. (2004). Towards a standard for pointing device evaluation, perspectives on 27 years of Fitts' law research in HCI. *International Journal of Human-Computer Studies, 61*(6), 751-789.
10. Tan, D. S., Gergle, D., Scupelli, P., and Pausch, R. 2006. Physically large displays improve performance on spatial tasks. *ACM Trans. Comput.-Hum. Interact. 13*, 1, 71-99.

Human Computation Tasks with Global Constraints

Haoqi Zhang[1], Edith Law[2], Robert C. Miller[3], Krzysztof Z. Gajos[1], David C. Parkes[1], Eric Horvitz[4]
[1]Harvard SEAS, Cambridge, MA, {hq, kgajos, parkes}@eecs.harvard.edu
[2]Carnegie Mellon University, Pittsburgh, PA, edith@cmu.edu
[3]MIT CSAIL, Cambridge, MA, rcm@mit.edu
[4]Microsoft Research, Redmond, WA, horvitz@microsoft.edu

ABSTRACT
An important class of tasks that are underexplored in current human computation systems are complex tasks with global constraints. One example of such a task is itinerary planning, where solutions consist of a sequence of activities that meet requirements specified by the requester. In this paper, we focus on the crowdsourcing of such plans as a case study of constraint-based human computation tasks and introduce a collaborative planning system called Mobi that illustrates a novel *crowdware* paradigm. Mobi presents a single interface that enables crowd participants to view the current solution context and make appropriate contributions based on current needs. We conduct experiments that explain how Mobi enables a crowd to effectively and collaboratively resolve global constraints, and discuss how the design principles behind Mobi can more generally facilitate a crowd to tackle problems involving global constraints.

Author Keywords
Human Computation; Crowdware; Mixed-Initiative Interaction; Groupware; Collaborative Planning

ACM Classification Keywords
H.5.3 [Information Interfaces and Presentation]: Group and Organization Interfaces

General Terms
Design, Human Factors

INTRODUCTION
Human computation [16, 9] is an evolving paradigm with numerous studies and applications over the last decade. Most human computation tasks explored to date are simple and easy to parallelize. However, several recent studies (e.g., Soylent [1], CrowdForge [7], PlateMate [13]) have tackled more complex tasks by using workflows that link together independent modules that harness different types of human effort. These workflows serve as algorithms that coordinate among the inputs and outputs of different task modules, allowing complex tasks to be decomposed into manageable subtasks that the crowd can contribute to independently without having to reason about other modules or the task at large.

*The first two authors have equal contribution in this work.

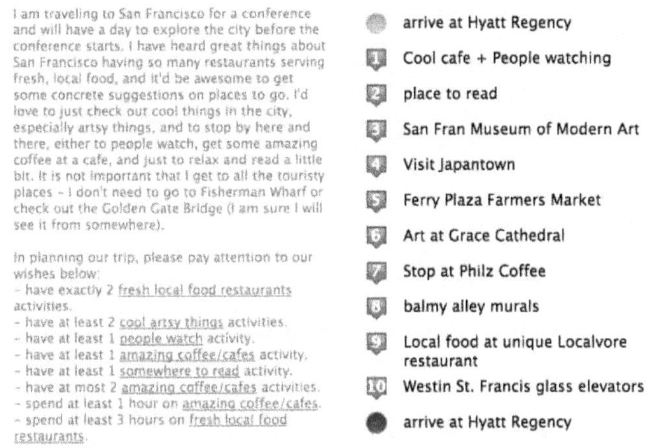

Figure 1. Planning mission (left) and itinerary (right)

Within studies of human computation, an important class of underexplored tasks are those in which the solution must satisfy a set of global requirements. For example, in leveraging the crowd to write an essay, a requester may want to specify requirements on the desired tone, tense, length, structure of arguments, and style of exposition that must hold consistently throughout a piece of writing. Some requirements, e.g., presenting a balanced perspective on a situation, touch upon different components of the essay and depend on its composition. Similar considerations arise in creative tasks such as graphic design, and more mundane tasks such as meeting scheduling. As good solutions rely on the composition as a whole and are marked by interdependence among solution components, such tasks are not amenable to the divide and conquer approach used in most crowdsourcing systems.

As a focal example, consider the problem of crowdsourcing itinerary planning. Planning events such as vacations, outings, and dates often involve an *itinerary* (Figure 1), which contains an ordered list of activities that are meant to be executed in sequence over the course of an event. People going on a trip have preferences and constraints over the types of activities of interest (e.g., "I want a coffee break right after lunch"), how long to spend on different activities (e.g., "I want to spend at least 2 hours in parks"), the composition of activities (e.g., "I want to focus on art galleries and museums for the day"), the budget, and the time available, which define a set of global requirements that an itinerary should satisfy.

Decisions on any particular activity in the itinerary may naturally influence other decisions. As simple examples, spending time on one activity leaves less time for another, and moving to one location introduces distances to other locations.

To handle tasks with global requirements, we introduce a novel *crowdware* paradigm that provides a single workspace in which a crowd of individuals contribute opportunistically based on their knowledge and expertise and the current solution context, and in which the system (indirectly) coordinates the crowd problem solving effort to resolve global constraints. Crowdware takes inspiration from *groupware* [3], which suggest principles and ideas on communication and collaboration within a shared context, that help a group to accomplish a joint task. We consider how to apply such principles and ideas to crowd workers, who differ from groups in that individuals are only briefly involved, are less willing to spend time grasping the solution context or take meta-level actions, and may not consider the desires of other crowd workers when making decisions.

We focus on itinerary planning as a case study of coordinating a crowd to tackle tasks with global constraints. We introduce a collaborative itinerary planning system called Mobi, which takes as input a planning mission containing a set of qualitative and quantitative constraints as articulated by the user and produces as output an itinerary that satisfies the mission. The crowd participates via a single interface—displaying the current itinerary and a stream of ideas generated thus far—that allows individuals to contribute opportunistically given the current context and to see their contributions incorporated into the solution in real-time. Mobi focuses the crowd's attention on aspects of the evolving plan that needs work by prominently displaying a list of automatically generated *todo* items, which point out violated constraints, provide suggestions on how to address them, and promote activities directed at the refinement of the itinerary.

Mobi allows users to specify their desires and needs in *natural language*, thereby enabling complex constraints and preferences to be expressed and used in the planning process. We present two studies, which show that Mobi's design promotes a collaborative planning environment in which the crowd can effectively produce custom-tailored itineraries that satisfy the stated global constraints in user missions. In the first study, we test the effect of displaying the automatically generated todo items on the rate at which quantitative constraints are resolved by the crowd, and measure the contribution patterns of the crowd workers. We find that the use of todo items promotes satisfaction of constraints at a significantly faster rate than when the items are not displayed, and that the crowd's editing patterns show evidence of both collaboration and opportunistic planning.

The second study seeks to understand whether the end users believe that crowd-generated itineraries satisfy their stated requirements. We find that users feel that the itineraries contain many activities of interest, mostly or fully satisfy their mission requirements, and are useful for their actual trips. After presenting these results, we revisit and summarize the design principles behind Mobi and discuss how they can in general facilitate a crowd to tackle problems involving global constraints.

RELATED WORK

Planning can be viewed as an *iterative task* in which workers make successive edits to improve the solution. There has been some attention on iterative tasks in human computation [11], and an interesting recent example is work by Kittur [6] that recruits workers to collaborate in Etherpad to translate a poem. Workers were able to see their edits reflected in real time (as in Mobi), and could communicate to explain their edits via chat. One difference in Mobi is that the system uses its sense of the progress made so far, e.g., how full the itinerary is, which constraints are violated, etc., to prompt users on what needs work so as to guide the problem-solving process. Other recent systems recruit a crowd to plan (e.g., Turkomatic [8] and CrowdPlan [10]); our work differs in that we consider planning tasks with global requirements.

Wikipedia can be viewed as an example of a system in which (mostly expert and highly dedicated) contributors write and edit articles to resolve a set of global constraints as defined by Wikipedia's standards. Much like the way todo items are used in Mobi to drive progress, template messages and cleanup tags are used in Wikipedia [17] to alert editors of changes that need to be made to improve an article. Such messages are typically managed by human contributors, whereas in Mobi todo items are managed in an automated manner whenever possible.

Several models have been proposed to describe how people generate plans to achieve goals. The *successive refinement* model advocates a top-down approach, where a high-level goal is decomposed into subgoals iteratively, down to a sequence of elementary actions [14]. In contrast, the planning of many everyday activities (e.g., errands) is often *opportunistic*—i.e., planning decisions happen whenever opportunities arise [4, 5], so that a decision or observation in one part of the plan may suggest new ideas or illuminate problems in a different part of the plan, causing the planner to refocus his attention. Opportunistic planning may involve both top-down and bottom-up processing. For example, in an errand planning experiment [4], it was found that subjects would start making detailed plans (e.g., sequencing individual errands), and then switch to planning on a more abstract level (e.g., by discovering clusters of errands), and back and forth as they refined the plan. Mobi is designed with the opportunistic planning model in mind, where individuals in the crowd are allowed to contribute freely as they see fit based on their observations of what needs work given the current solution context.

Real-life planning is a difficult problem for computers; despite advances in automated planning [12], a major challenge is in making sense of people's goals, preferences and other 'soft' considerations [2]. Currently, the automated planner in Mobi supports workers by automatically checking constraints and computing trip times and routes. In the future, automation may play a more active role in the planning process by learning about different requirements, suggesting activities and their composition in the itinerary, or even detecting and adding important constraints that may have been missed by the requester.

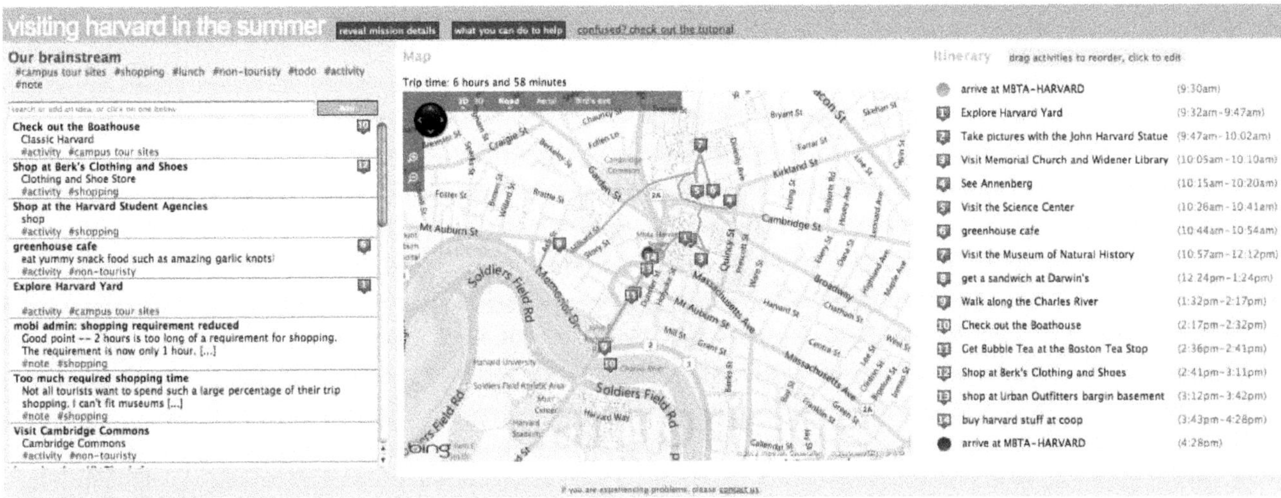

Figure 2. The Mobi planning interface consists of the information panel (top), the brainstream (left), and the itinerary viewer (right).

There are several existing commercial systems that either allow groups to plan trips for themselves or to ask friends and other members for suggestions. Examples include Gogobot, triporama, Kukunu, and FriendTripper. Mobi differs from these systems in that it seeks to produce not only suggestions for activities but an itinerary satisfying a set of global requirements, and can focus the crowd on making contributions where they are most needed.

MOBI: A SYSTEM FOR CROWD ITINERARY PLANNING

Mobi takes as input a planning mission consisting of preferences and constraints, and generates an itinerary by having a crowd plan asynchronously using a shared interface. Workers invited to contribute can view the current plan and all ideas proposed thus far, and make contributions as they see fit. Edits can be made at any time and without restrictions, and the itinerary is automatically saved after each change. We now describe Mobi's interfaces for specifying the planning mission and for assembling the itinerary, and discuss how these two interfaces support the process of generating itineraries and resolving constraints. Mobi's planning interface is shown in Figure 2.

Specifying the Planning Mission

Our target users, also referred to as *requesters*, are people who are interested in planning a trip. To start planning, the requester enters a planning mission using a simple web interface, which specifies the title and description of the trip, start/end locations and times, and whether they will use public transit or drive between locations in addition to walking.

Requesters can express two kinds of constraints: *qualitative* and *quantitative*. Figure 1 shows an example of a planning mission that includes both types of constraints. Qualitative constraints are specified in natural language (e.g., in a paragraph), and describe the nature of the trip, what the user hopes to accomplish, who they are traveling with, etc. Quantitative constraints are specified by creating *categories* using arbitrary natural language phrases (e.g., "cool artsy things," "by the ocean"), and assigning preferences and limitations over those categories. One can specify constraints on the number of activities in each category (e.g., "I want to have up to two *museum visits*"), as well as on the amount of time to spend on activities in each category (e.g., "I want to spend at least two hours on *cool artsy things*"). Such constraints can also be used to express the preferred combination of activities in the plan (e.g., "I want to spend half of my time on activities *by the ocean*, and the other half on activities *in the city*"). In our prototype, the domain-specific language for quantitative constraints allows for constraints encoded in the form of "*I want* $\{$*at most, at least, exactly*$\}$ *[number]* $\{$*activities, hours*$\}$ *of* $\{cat_1, cat_2, \ldots, cat_n\}$," where cat_i refers to the i-th category.

Both qualitative and quantitative constraints contain natural language, and can express 'soft' considerations that the computer cannot tackle alone. In addition to these constraints, the system maintains a pair of time constraints, which state that the cumulative duration of the activities in the itinerary should not be significantly less than, or greater than, the duration of the trip specified by the user.

Assembling the Itinerary

Once a requester specifies a planning mission, workers can use Mobi's planning interface to view the mission by clicking on the *reveal mission details* button in the *information panel* (see Figure 2, on top). The planning interface consists of two key components – the brainstream and the itinerary viewer.

Brainstream

The *brainstream* (see Figure 2, on left) is a collection of everyone's ideas. An idea can be an activity ("something to do or see") or a note ("a thought about the plan").

To view ideas in the brainstream, one can either scroll down the list, click on a hashtag to display ideas belonging to a particular category, or use the auto-completing search box. Clicking on an idea reveals additional details via a dialog box, and presents the option to edit the idea, or in the case of an activity, an option to add it to or remove it from the current

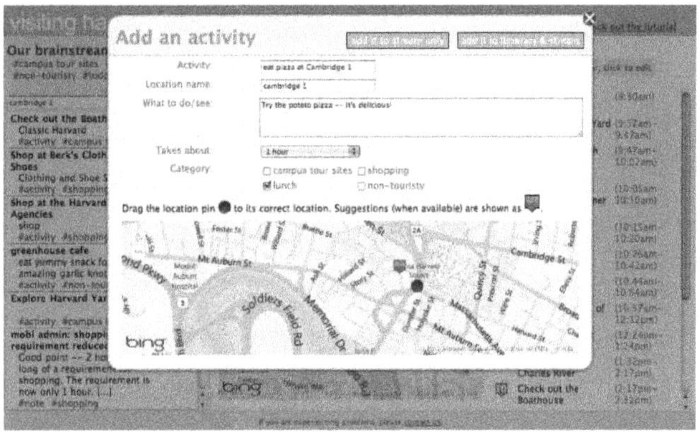

Figure 3. Adding a new activity to the brainstream via a dialog box

Figure 4. The brainstream displays system-generated todo items, alerting workers about what needs work.

itinerary. A blue badge next to an activity indicates that it is already in the current itinerary.

To add a new idea (an activity or a note), one can type a title into the search box and click 'add'. If similar ideas already exist, a drop down list will appear, which helps to prevent duplicates and promote editing. For notes, workers can fill in a description if desired. For activities, the activity editor (see Figure 3) asks workers to provide the name of the location, what to do or see, the activity's duration, and the (requester-defined) categories that the activity belongs in. In the same editor, workers can view a map, which allows them to mark the location of the point of interest. Workers can decide to add the activity to both the itinerary and the brainstream, or only to the brainstream for the time being.

The brainstream allows people to brainstorm together and build upon each other's ideas. It keeps around all alternative activities, and allows workers to quickly access them through the hashtags and the search box. By adding notes, workers can identify areas that need work or raise questions about the plan's feasibility, that other workers or the requester can help to address or provide further comments on. The brainstream's design draws inspirations from social technologies such as Twitter and Piazza, which aggregate information into a feed or stream that one can then easily process.

If the current itinerary does not satisfy a stated quantitative constraint or is over time or under time, the violated constraints are automatically turned into *todo items* that are displayed at the top of the brainstream in a different color, alerting workers to what needs work (e.g., see Figure 4). The todo items suggest specific actions, e.g., "Add more lunch activities," or, "The itinerary is over time. Try reordering itinerary items. You can also edit or remove items." Todo items also provide natural language explanations of how the current itinerary violates particular constraints, e.g., "You need exactly one lunch activity but there is currently none in the itinerary," or "The itinerary is over time because the trip must end by 9pm."

We note that the system is able to check arbitrary quantitative constraints and generate todo items without understanding the meaning of the natural language categories; this is because workers associate activities with the categories they belong in when they are suggested. As we will show in the next section, todo items are an important design element that helps to accelerate the speed with which quantitative constraints are resolved.

Itinerary Viewer

The *itinerary viewer* (see Figure 2, on right) consists of an itinerary and a map. The itinerary displays the activities in order, alongside the times during which they are scheduled to take place, with travel times between locations automatically computed and accounted for. It is accompanied by a map showing the activities' locations and routes between locations. The map and itinerary allow crowd workers to see at a glance whether the plan is coherent, that is, if any activities are out of place (e.g., lunch happening too early, activities whose order can be swapped to avoid unnecessary back-and-forth travel), or if too much or too little time is spent on an activity. The itinerary doubles as an editor—workers can drag and drop activities to rearrange their order, and click an activity to see its details, edit it, or remove it from the itinerary. On any itinerary change (i.e. via adding, removing, editing, or reordering of activities), the itinerary, activity times, map display, trip time, and todo items automatically update, which provides direct feedback to the workers as they refine the itinerary.

Mobi promotes collaboration by making the plan always visible and editable by everyone. This follows the WYSIWIS ('What You See Is What I See') principle [15], which ensures that all participants have equal access to shared information. Mobi also supports *opportunistic planning*, by providing support for both top-down and bottom-up planning, and a fluid way to move back and forth between the two. For example, as workers plan at a detailed level (e.g., suggesting activities in the brainstream), they may become aware of shortcomings of the current itinerary, which in turn prompts them to start considering the itinerary as a whole; likewise, when workers

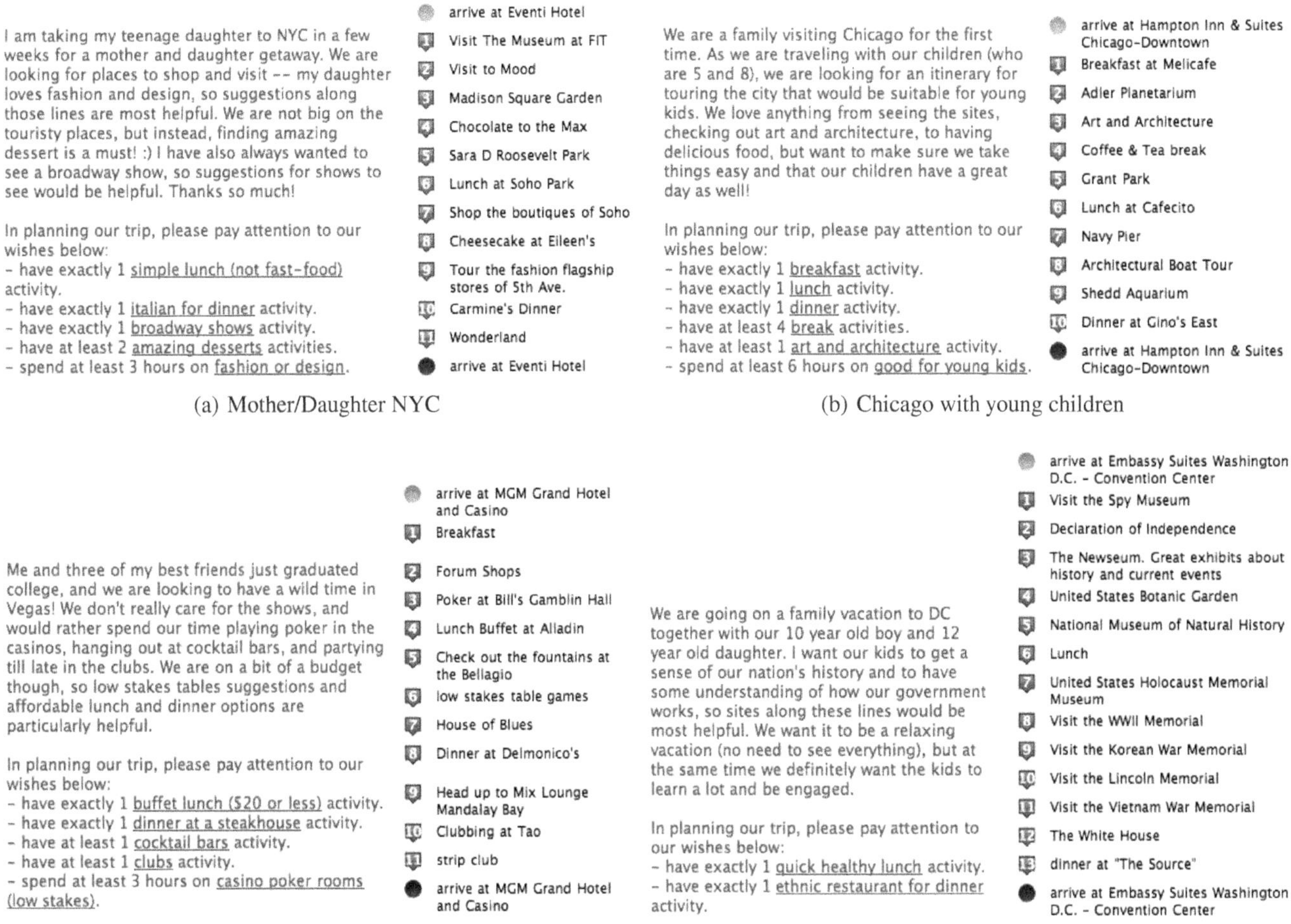

Figure 5. Experiment: planning missions and the corresponding itineraries generated by the crowd in the todo items condition

refine the itinerary, they may think of new activities to add to the brainstream, or ways to elaborate on the details of a particular activity in the current itinerary.

EXPERIMENT: TODO OR NOT TODO

We hypothesize that elements of Mobi's design, namely todo items and having a shared interface in which the crowd can work off the current solution context and existing ideas, promotes the crowd to effectively and collaboratively resolve the users' stated constraints so as to produce itineraries that satisfy planning missions. Focusing first on quantitative constraints, we conducted an experiment using two versions of Mobi—one that displays todo items and one that does not—to evaluate the effect of todo items on how quickly the crowd can reach feasible solutions that satisfy the stated constraints.

Method

We created custom day-trip planning missions for each of eight major U.S. cities: New York, Chicago, DC, Las Vegas, Los Angeles, San Francisco, Seattle, and San Diego. We recruited Mechanical Turk workers in the U.S. who have a 95% or higher approval rating to contribute to the planning missions, by working on human intelligence tasks (HITs) in which the Mobi interface was fully embedded. The interface is nearly identical to that shown in Figure 2, with the addition of a submit button on the bottom, a 'HIT instructions' button replacing the 'what you can do to help' button in the information panel, and the addition of a 'continue to improve the itinerary' todo item that displays only when there are no other todo items (i.e. all quantitative constraints are satisfied). Turkers were asked to make 'micro-contributions' as they plan the trip with other Turkers, and were told that they can submit a HIT as soon as they have made *any* contribution. Turkers were paid 15 cents per HIT, and no verification was used other than requiring Turkers to have made some edit (however small) to the brainstream or itinerary before submitting the task. For half of the cities, the version with todo items was posted prior to that with no todo items, and the order of posting was reversed for the other cities. Missions were posted for up to four days. Other than the display of todo items, the interface, job description, and instructions are identical in the two conditions.

Results I: The Generated Itineraries

Figure 5 shows a sample of the planning missions and the corresponding itineraries generated by Turkers in the todo condition. All eight itineraries satisfy the stated quantitative con-

	NYC	Chicago	Las Vegas	DC
# unique workers	17	15	16	21
# workers with winning ideas	6	5	7	8
# activities in brainstream	35	16	18	28
# activities in itinerary	11	10	11	13
# edits in brainstream	50	54	43	57
# edits in itinerary	193	140	75	154
# notes in brainstream	1	0	9	1
# of HITs	64	31	47	50
Total cost	$9.60	$4.65	$7.05	$7.50

Table 1. Summary statistics about the final itineraries of the examples shown in Figure 5, including contributions by and payments to Turkers. Winning ideas are activity suggestions that are in the final itinerary.

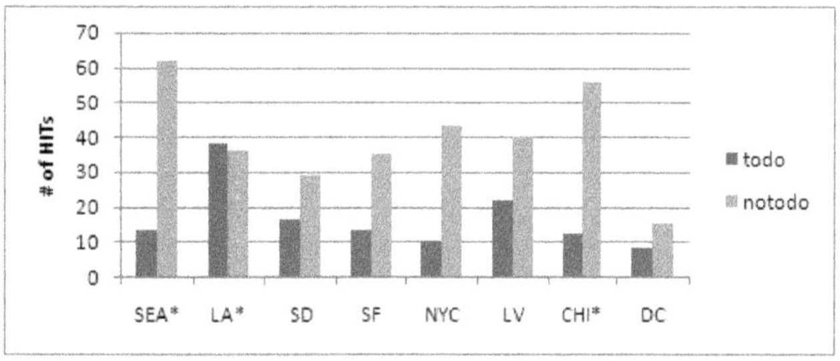

Figure 6. Number of HITs required to satisfy all quantitative and system generated time constraints for each city in the todo and no todo conditions. For cities marked by an asterisk, itineraries in the no todo condition still have violated constraints; in such cases we reported the number of HITs thus far.

straints. From the final itineraries, it appears that Turkers not only pay attention to the quantitative constraints, but also the mission description, e.g., by filling the itinerary with government/history related activities in DC, and by offering low-cost options in Vegas.

Table 1 summarizes, for each of the examples shown in Figure 5, statistics about the final itineraries, different types of edits Turkers made, and the amount of money paid to workers. We see that the final itineraries contain original ideas from multiple workers. Specifically, Turkers generated just over twice as many ideas for activities as are in the final itineraries, and generally used notes sparingly. When notes were added, they provided commentary on alternative suggestions ("They are a better place then Pasty's by far, and have better service, plus that perfect dessert."), noted errors in activities ("Barbary Coast isn't called 'Barbary Coast' anymore"), presented general advice ("You can buy a MealTicket which will allow you to eat free at many places."), or pointed out problems with the plan ("why are we eating so much dinner?").

Results II: Influence of Todo Items

Results show that when prompting users with todo items, quantitative constraints are satisfied significantly more quickly than when todo items are not displayed. We measure the speed of the process in number of HITs performed. One spammer in the no-todo condition submitted multiple HITs for a single piece of work (e.g. adding an activity, filling in its details, and placing it into the itinerary) as three separate HITs. For this worker, only the itinerary-changing HITs were counted, but for all other workers, all HITs were counted.

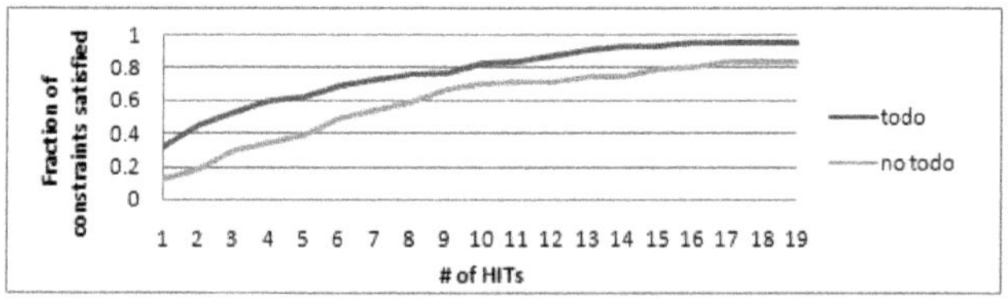

Figure 7. Cumulative distribution of the violation duration of constraints in the todo versus no todo conditions, showing the fraction of constraints satisfied after at most k HITs since the time it was last violated.

We make three observations. First, we found a significant difference ($t(7) = 3.65, p = 0.0082$) in the number of HITs it took to satisfy (for the first time) all of the stated quantitative constraints between the todo condition ($\mu = 16.5, \sigma = 9.65$) and the no todo condition ($\mu = 39.5, \sigma = 14.8$);[1] see Figure 6 for a city-by-city breakdown.

Second, there is also a significant difference ($t(7) = 4.247$, $p = 0.0038$) in the number of HITs it took to satisfy *all* constraints for the first time (this includes system generated time constraints) between the todo condition ($\mu = 22.5, \sigma = 8.5$) and the no todo condition ($\mu = 45.38, \sigma = 13.9$).

Finally, as constraints can be violated and satisfied repeatedly throughout the planning process, we sought to understand how quickly constraints are satisfied on average. We introduce the notion of the *violation duration* of a constraint, which is the number of HITs it takes for a constraint to be satisfied by the itinerary since it was last violated (which could be when it is first introduced). The average violation duration of quantitative constraints is shorter for the todo condition ($\mu = 5.64, \sigma = 6.34$) compared to the no todo condition ($\mu = 10.5, \sigma = 10.97$); the result is statistically significant ($t(134) = 3.206, p = 0.0017$).

Figure 7 shows the cumulative distribution of the violation durations of constraints in the todo versus no todo conditions. We observe that for any violation duration (in number of HITs), a larger fraction of the constraints are satisfied within that duration in the todo condition than the no todo condition. We also see that more than half of all violated constraints become satisfied after three or fewer HITs in the todo condition.

Figure 8 shows, for the todo versus no todo conditions, the rate at which *each* constraint gets satisfied as workers contribute to the planning effort for the Seattle and Chicago planning missions. We observe that constraints are satisfied much more quickly in the todo condition. The Chicago case is particularly interesting; whereas in the todo condition a worker violated a previously satisfied constraint while editing and proceeded to make successive edits that led to satisfying all of the constraints, in the no todo condition a satisfied constraint was violated and then left unaddressed for a significant amount of time. This example illustrates the power of immediate feedback—when an edit to the itinerary violates

[1] In some cases for the no todo condition, no itinerary satisfied all the stated requirements in the course of the experiment. In such cases the number of HITs completed thus far was used as a lower bound for comparison.

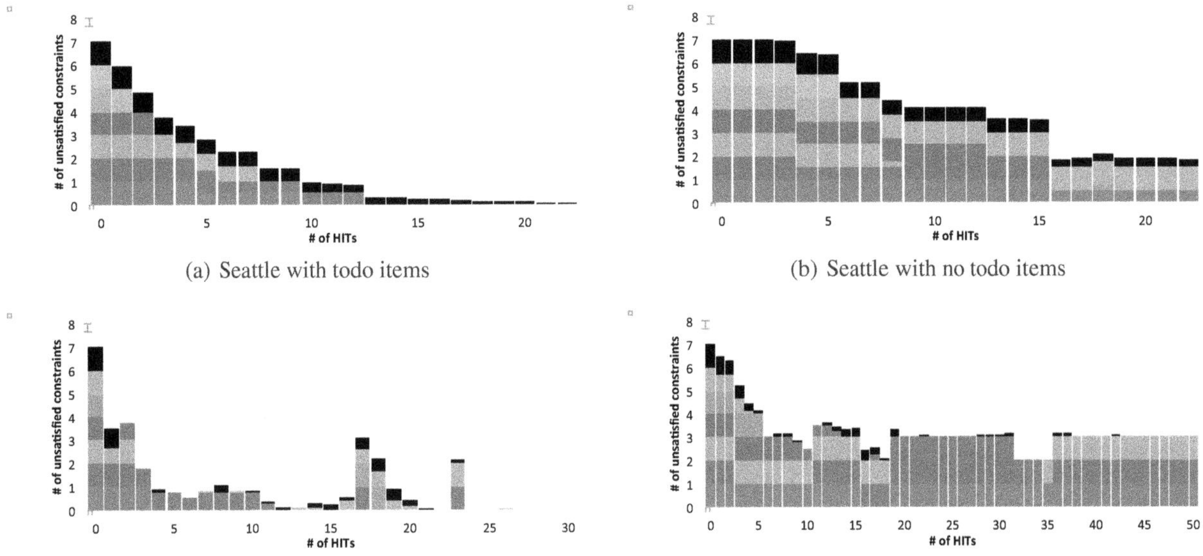

(a) Seattle with todo items

(b) Seattle with no todo items

(c) Chicago with todo items

(d) Chicago with no todo items

Figure 8. The unsatisfied constraints during the planning process for the Seattle and Chicago missions. The height of each bar indicates the number of constraints unsatisfied after k HITs. Each colored segment represents a particular quantitative constraint, and its height indicates the extent to which it is violated. The black segment represents the percent by which the itinerary is over time or under time (when it is greater or less than 5%).

some constraints, the automatically generated todo items are able to not only alert workers as to what needs fixing, but also make them aware that their edits have direct effects on the constraints associated with the planning mission.

Results III: Editing Patterns

Having shown that todo items play an important role in focusing the crowd's effort towards satisfying the quantitative constraints, we turn to investigate the crowd's work process while using Mobi in the todo condition. In particular, we look for evidence of collaborative behavior from the crowd, and at the way that they plan using the current context of the plan.

We focus first on the process of generating ideas for activities. We observe that roughly half the edits to the brainstream contain new suggestions (52%) while the other half (48%) are edits of existing ideas in the itinerary. Of the edits, 72% are edits on ideas that originated from someone else (i.e., other than the person editing), which suggests that workers are working off others' contributions as they refine ideas and the itinerary. When editing an activity, we see that edits are predominantly on an activity's duration (80%), but there are also edits to change title/descriptions (7%) and to correct an item's location coordinates (12%). Although duration edits are often in the context of resolving some constraints, edits to the title, description, and location are particularly encouraging to see as they suggest that the interface is providing (via the brainstream, map, and itinerary) means for users to discover and improve on existing ideas.

Turning to the patterns of itinerary edits, we observe that most of the contributions come from adding (31%) and reordering activities (32%), but that workers also edit existing ideas (22%) and remove activities (14%). This is encouraging to see because workers are using the different actions available to them to plan as they see fit as they improve the itinerary. When tasks are left to run after the quantitative constraints are all satisfied, we observe that itineraries continue to evolve; workers replace activities in the itinerary with other activities, reorder the itinerary, edit existing items, and so on. While constraints may be violated during such edits, workers were reminded of such violations by the todo items and violated constraints were quickly satisfied again (e.g., see Figure 8(c)). This suggests that new ideas can continue to be generated and incorporated into the itinerary; in fact, workers are encouraged to do both because they are paid for such contributions and because we display a todo item that asks workers to continue to improve the itinerary whenever all quantitative constraints are met.

Throughout the experiment, we saw very few Turkers who blatantly tried to game the system. The kinds of gaming behavior we did observe generally fell into two categories. In one, a Turker under-specifies an activity, either by creating an activity without filling in its description and location, or by adding a note containing a suggestion for an activity instead of just adding the suggested activity. In the other, a Turker would fully specify an activity, but use two or even three HITs to do so, by spending a HIT on creating the activity, another to edit its details, and another to add it to the itinerary – when all this can be accomplished with a single 'add activity' action.

While it is certainly useful to consider refinements that would curb such behaviors (e.g., by requiring activities to contain descriptions, by not allowing workers to submit HITs in which they have only edited their own ideas, etc.), we note that such gaming behaviors from a small set of Turkers did not seem to have a negative influence on the planning processes nor the resulting solutions. In particular, we saw that

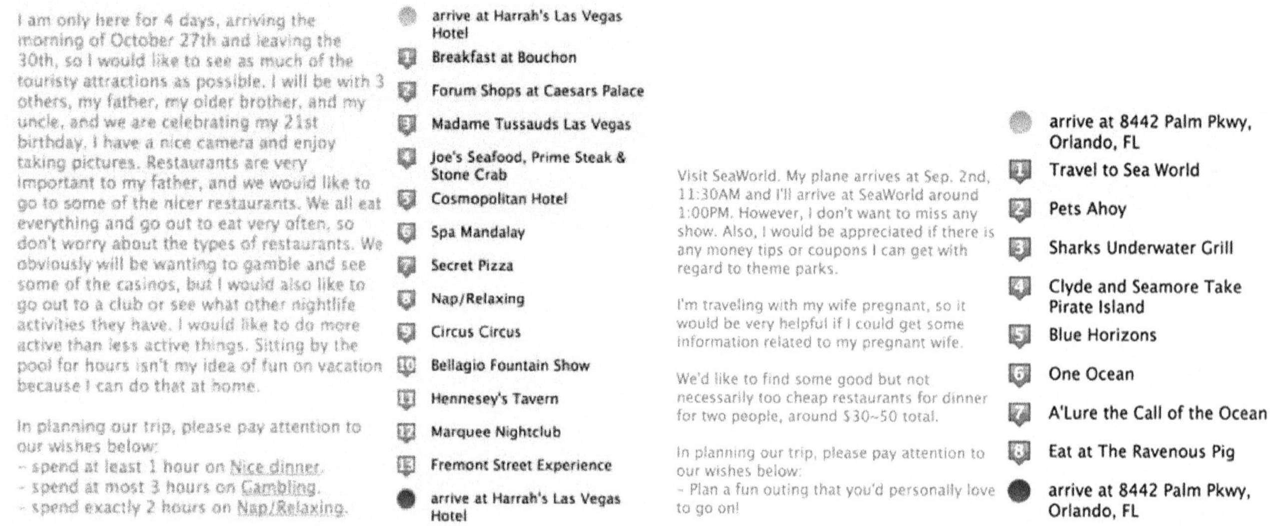

(a) Subject 1: Las Vegas (b) Subject 2: Orlando

Figure 9. User study: planning missions and corresponding itineraries generated by the crowd

poorly formed ideas were simply ignored, removed from the itinerary, or edited by another worker who discovered them via the auto-complete search box in the brainstream, which occurred as a natural part of the iterative process through which workers improved the itinerary.

END-TO-END USER STUDY

Having seen that workers can resolve quantitative constraints effectively using Mobi, we conducted a user study through which we seek to evaluate how well the generated itineraries satisfy not only *quantitative* constraints, but also the stated *qualitative* constraints, from the perspective of requesters.

Method

We recruited 11 subjects to participate in the study via the use of several university mailing lists. We specified requirements that participants be actually planning a forthcoming trip to a major U.S. city. Recruited subjects are a mix of undergrads, graduate students, and research scientists. We report on the responses of 10 of the users, as one of the users specified a trip destination that is not a major U.S. city. Subjects were instructed to describe their planning mission, which includes qualitative and quantitative preferences and constraints. Participants were given unlimited access to Mobi for over a week, during which they were free to modify their planning mission or to participate in the planning process. Missions were crowdsourced on Mechanical Turk as was done in the todo versus no todo experiment. At the end of the study, subjects were given a questionnaire, which asked them to evaluate the final itinerary and to describe their experiences using Mobi. Subjects were each paid $30 for their participation.

The trip destinations specified by the users include Boston, New York City, San Francisco, Las Vegas, Orlando, and Washington DC. The planning missions vary in length and specificity. Figure 9 provides two examples of user missions and the generated itineraries.

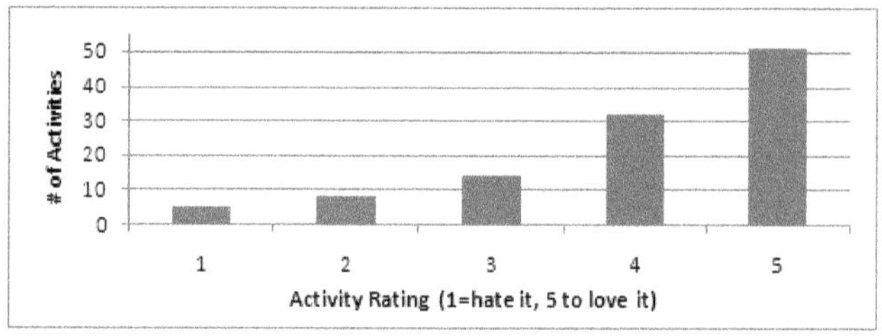

Figure 10. Histogram of activity ratings

Results

To see how well the generated itineraries satisfy the end users' requirements, we consider three measures of the *quality* of an itinerary, namely the extent to which it (1) contains activities that the requester likes, (2) satisfies the qualitative and quantitative constraints specified in the planning mission, and (3) serves its purpose as a plan that is feasible, useful, and executable in real life.

1. Do itineraries contain activities that the requesters like?

Users were shown each of the itinerary activities (title, description, start time, end time, duration) and asked to rate how much they think they would enjoy each activity on a 5-point scale (1="hate it", 5="love it").

Figure 10 shows a histogram of the activity ratings across all 10 participants. The mean rating was 4.03 ($\sigma = 0.44$). Users also mentioned that the activities are diverse, interesting, and often unknown to them prior to using Mobi.

2. Do itineraries satisfy the qualitative and quantitative constraints specified in the planning mission?

All of the users answered that their itinerary fulfilled most or all of the requirements they had specified. Some users noted specific activities that they do not like (e.g., "I just happen to be afraid of bungee jumping because it seems so unsafe, but a similar activity would be fun," "I am under age so the wine thing would not be great for me but everything else sounds great.") or complained about too many activities (e.g., "There was far far far too much packed into a single day, but the ideas were all totally interesting.") or visiting too many parts of a city in one day (e.g., "For the most part, it was a good mix of things to do. I was not expecting to travel so much uptown/downtown in one day though.") These problems can be partially explained by the fact that many constraints (e.g., the notion that an itinerary shouldn't be too packed) are assumed or missed and therefore not explicitly stated by the users. One potential solution is to have the requesters evaluate the itineraries as they are being created and add the missing constraints to the planning mission. In fact, as a preliminary test, we took two of the users' feedback and entered them as todo items (i.e., "Let's just stay midtown and remove downtown activities," "The harbor island suggestions are great but one island would be enough. Please adjust time durations accordingly so the day is not so packed."). After resuming the task, we observe that after just a few HITs workers have already addressed the issue by removing offending activities, reordering activities (so that meals occur at reasonably hours), and adding additional activities (replacing a concert downtown with a Broadway show in midtown).

3. Are the itineraries feasible, useful, and executable in real-life settings?

We asked users if they *would* or *did* use the itinerary in real-life. All users expressed that they would use the itinerary as is, some version of the itinerary, or selective ideas in the itinerary. When asked *"If Mobi were made available for general use, how likely would you want to use such a tool again for recruiting the crowd to help you plan a trip?"*, 7 out of 10 users answered *likely* or *very likely*, 2 answered *neutral* and only 1 answered *unlikely*, showing the usefulness of Mobi in practice.

Three users actually followed the itinerary or used the ideas in the itinerary in their real-life trips. One subject reported that "having other people involved in the idea-creation process was extremely helpful. It sparked all sorts of ideas that I kept in the back of my head throughout the weekend." Another subject remarked that his "trip was mostly in the plan, but all restaurant plans changed due to necessity during the trip."

We found a dichotomy of users: those who are interested in obtaining a *fully-specified itinerary* and those who are interested in a *loose itinerary* that contains an unordered set of suggested activities that leave room for exploration. An interesting solution is to allow requesters to choose between a fully specified or loose itinerary, which in turn translate into constraints that specify the maximum number of activities in the itinerary, the amount of buffer time between activities, and whether activities need to be ordered.

One of the most frequently mentioned benefits of Mobi is that both the *idea generation* and the *planning* are fully automated, thereby "integrating all the factors one would consider in planning an itinerary," yet making "the time spent creating the plan minimal." Most users (7 out of 10) said that they are comfortable with an anonymous crowd planning their trip. Furthermore, results show that requesters mostly left the planning up to the crowd. In particular, 3 out of 10 users said that they never or rarely checked on the progress of the itinerary, 5 did so occasionally, and only 2 frequently. Likewise, 7 out of 10 users said that they never went back to modify the mission details or add notes. As one user puts this succinctly: "the process seemed to work smoothly without my intervention."

DISCUSSION

Having demonstrated the effectiveness of Mobi for helping the crowd to resolve qualitative and quantitative constraints in the itinerary planning setting, we now revisit the elements of Mobi's design and discuss how these elements may in general inform the design of systems that facilitate a crowd to tackle problems involving global constraints.

Keeping the crowd, the solution, and the context together

Compared to the design of most other crowdsourcing systems for tackling complex tasks, Mobi is distinguished in its use of a single structured interface through which the crowd is exposed to the current solution and the global problem-solving context. This unified view provides a shared context that allows contributors to coordinate and communicate more effectively with one another than approaches where participants are forced to work on different subtasks in separate contexts.

Interactions are less controlled, but still structured

Mobi allows workers to choose how they want to contribute to the task. In our studies, we found that workers generate a diverse set of ideas, and make various types of contributions while problem solving. This freedom is particularly important for resolving global constraints as we do not know *a priori* the specific contributions that are needed. Rather, contributions are context dependent. While interactions are less controlled this way, note that the interaction is still highly structured; the crowd selects from a well-specified set of actions, todo items guide the crowd towards useful actions, and real-time feedback is provided on the effects of actions (e.g., via map, trip times, and todo items).

A language for human-computer communication

In the background, Mobi's automation computes routes and times, checks for violated constraints, and generates todo items. Mobi understands, for example, when all of the quantitative constraints are satisfied; this ability enables Mobi to take such actions as prompting the crowd for future revisions and asking the crowd or requester to check for potential problems. Mobi can do these things without knowing what the constraints mean, because the inputs that it seeks from the crowd include the categories of suggested activities. This information is sufficient for the system to check for violated constraints, and therefore assist in the planning process.

A fluid way to refine goals

With complex problems, requirements can change over time as ideas and partial solutions stream in. In Mobi, a requester can add or revise requirements, write notes, or even directly alter the plan throughout the planning process. The crowd can react to such changes just as they react to the current solution at any other point in the planning process. The iterative nature of the task and the ease with which workers can grasp the current solution and access alternative suggestions make it easy for the crowd to see and respond to such refinements.

CONCLUSION

To date, many human computation systems have relied on the assumption that problems can be solved in an algorithmic manner, using explicit procedures that outline the operations that need to be done and how they are ordered. We argue for an alternative *crowdware* paradigm, where workers contribute to solving complex tasks in a less controlled environment, allowing them to view and build upon each other's ideas and to contribute as they wish, while being steered towards a solution by system-generated advice and alerts.

Using itinerary planning as a case study, we introduce a prototype named Mobi, which draws on groupware ideas and uses explicit processes (e.g., automatic generation of todo items) to generate itineraries that satisfy complex, interdependent constraints. Our results show that constraints are resolved efficiently using this design, and that end users find that the generated itineraries satisfy their stated quantitative and qualitative constraints. The design principles explored in research on Mobi bring into focus several research opportunities, including the formulation of novel combinations of crowdware and workflow approaches to enhance the ability of participants to effectively contribute to solving complex problems that are hard to decompose.

On potential extensions of Mobi, we are interested in studying ways to handle the implied constraints that are assumed or missed, such as the common sense knowledge that people may desire a bathroom break every few hours. The challenge is to make implied constraints visible so they can be tackled like other constraints; possible approaches include having the crowd identify them, using automated procedures to detect and learn about such constraints, and asking requesters to provide feedback. A related direction is to encapsulate *qualitative* constraints in todo items, which would allow workers to see everything that needs work in one place.

While we are using Mechanical Turk as an experimentation platform, we are interested in exploring Mobi as a social system, with friends and community members coming to help. This introduces opportunities for identifying individuals who can best contribute to (particular aspects of) a mission and routing tasks appropriately. Finally, we envision rich opportunities to integrate different types of automation into Mobi—to detect failures, handle uncertainties, incorporate richer forms of user preferences, and combine automated and human planners in a synergistic way.

ACKNOWLEDGMENTS

Mobi was initially formulated and prototyped at Microsoft Research during summer internships there by Haoqi Zhang and Edith Law, who thank Anne Loomis Thompson and Paul Koch for technical assistance on an earlier prototype. Haoqi Zhang and Edith Law are generously funded by a NSF Graduate Research Fellowship and a Microsoft Graduate Research Fellowship respectively.

REFERENCES

1. Bernstein, M. S., Little, G., Miller, R. C., Hartmann, B., Ackerman, M. S., Karger, D. R., Crowell, D., and Panovich, K. Soylent: a word processor with a crowd inside. In *UIST* (2010), 313–322.
2. Chen, L., and Pu, P. Survey of preference elicitation methods. Tech. rep., Swiss Federal Institute Of Technology In Lausanne (EPFL), 2004.
3. Ellis, C. A., Gibbs, S. J., and Rein, G. Groupware: some issues and experiences. *Communications of the ACM 34*, 1 (1991), 38–58.
4. Hayes-Roth, B., and Hayes-Roth, F. A cognitive model of planning. *Cognitive Science 3* (1979), 275–310.
5. Kamar, E., Horvitz, E., and Meek, C. Mobile opportunistic commerce: Mechanisms, architecture, and application. In *AAMAS* (2008).
6. Kittur, A. Crowdsourcing, collaboration and creativity. *XRDS 17* (December 2010), 22–26.
7. Kittur, A., Smus, B., Kraut, R., and Khamkar, S. Crowdforge: Crowdsourcing complex work. In *UIST* (2011).
8. Kulkarni, A. P., Can, M., and Hartmann, B. Turkomatic: automatic recursive task and workflow design for mechanical turk. In *CSCW* (2011).
9. Law, E., and von Ahn, L. *Human Computation*. Synthesis Lectures on Artificial Intelligence and Machine Learning. Morgan and Claypool, June 2011.
10. Law, E., and Zhang, H. Towards large-scale collaborative planning: Answering high-level search queries using human computation. In *AAAI* (2011).
11. Little, G., Chilton, L. B., Goldman, M., and Miller, R. C. Turkit: human computation algorithms on mechanical turk. In *UIST* (2010), 57–66.
12. Nau, D., Ghallab, M., and Traverso, P. *Automated Planning: Theory & Practice*. Morgan Kaufmann Publishers Inc., San Francisco, CA, USA, 2004.
13. Noronha, J., Hysen, E., Zhang, H., and Gajos, K. Z. Platemate: Crowdsourcing nutrition analysis from food photographs. In *UIST* (2011).
14. Sacerdoti, E. D. *A structure for plans and behavior*. Elsevier North-Holland, 1977.
15. Stefik, M., Bobrow, D. G., Foster, G., Lanning, S., and Tatar, D. Wysiwis revised: early experiences with multiuser interfaces. *ACM Trans. Inf. Syst. 5* (April 1987), 147–167.
16. von Ahn, L. *Human Computation*. PhD thesis, Carnegie Mellon University, 2005.
17. Wikipedia:template messages/cleanup, 2011. Available at `http://en.wikipedia.org/wiki/Wikipedia:Template_messages/Cleanup`. Accessed September 22, 2011.

Strategies for Crowdsourcing Social Data Analysis

Wesley Willett*, Jeffrey Heer†, Maneesh Agrawala*
*Computer Science Division, University of California, Berkeley
{willettw, maneesh}@cs.berkeley.edu
†Computer Science Department, Stanford University
jheer@cs.stanford.edu

ABSTRACT
Web-based social data analysis tools that rely on public discussion to produce hypotheses or explanations of patterns and trends in data rarely yield high-quality results in practice. Crowdsourcing offers an alternative approach in which an analyst pays workers to generate such explanations. Yet, asking workers with varying skills, backgrounds and motivations to simply "Explain why a chart is interesting" can result in irrelevant, unclear or speculative explanations of variable quality. To address these problems, we contribute seven strategies for improving the quality and diversity of worker-generated explanations. Our experiments show that using *(S1) feature-oriented prompts*, providing *(S2) good examples*, and including *(S3) reference gathering*, *(S4) chart reading*, and *(S5) annotation* subtasks increases the quality of responses by 28% for US workers and 196% for non-US workers. Feature-oriented prompts improve explanation quality by 69% to 236% depending on the prompt. We also show that *(S6) pre-annotating charts* can focus workers' attention on relevant details, and demonstrate that *(S7) generating explanations iteratively* increases explanation diversity without increasing worker attrition. We used our techniques to generate 910 explanations for 16 datasets, and found that 63% were of high quality. These results demonstrate that paid crowd workers can reliably generate diverse, high-quality explanations that support the analysis of specific datasets.

Author Keywords
Information Visualization; Social Data Analysis; Crowdsourcing

ACM Classification Keywords
H.5.3 Group & Organization Interfaces: Collaborative computing.

INTRODUCTION
Making sense of large datasets is fundamentally a human process. While automated data mining tools can find recurring patterns, outliers and other anomalies in data, only people can currently provide the explanations, hypotheses, and insights necessary to make sense of the data [22, 24]. Social data analysis tools such as Sense.us [8], Pathfinder [18] and Many Eyes [30] address this problem by allowing groups of web-based volunteers to collaboratively explore visualizations, propose hypotheses, and seek out new insights. Controlled experiments have shown that groups can use these tools to discover new, unexpected findings [8, 29]. However, eliciting high-quality explanations of the data requires seeding the discussion with prompts, examples,and other starting points to encourage contributions [8, 32].

Outside the lab, in real-world web-based deployments, the vast majority of the visualizations in these social data analysis tools yield very little discussion. Even fewer visualizations elicit high-quality analytical explanations that are clear, plausible, and relevant to a particular analysis question.

We recently surveyed the Many Eyes website and found that from 2006 to 2010, users published 162,282 datasets but generated only 77,984 visualizations and left just 15,464 comments. We then randomly sampled 100 of the visualizations containing comments and found that just 11% of the comments included a plausible hypothesis or explanation for the data in the chart. The low level of commenting may represent a shortage of viewers or may be due to *lurking* – a common web phenomenon in which visitors explore and read discussions, but do not contribute to them [31, 20]. When comments do appear, they are often superficial or descriptive rather than explanatory (Figures 2a, 2b). Higher-quality analyses sometimes take place off-site [5] but tend to occur around limited (often single-image) views of the data curated by a single author. Ultimately, marshaling the analytic potential of crowds calls for a more systematic approach to social data analysis; one that explicitly encourages users to generate good hypotheses and explanations.

In this paper we show how paid crowd workers can be used to perform the key sensemaking task of generating explanations of data. We develop an analysis workflow (Figure 1) in which an analyst first *selects charts*, then uses crowd workers to carry out *analysis microtasks* and *rating microtasks* to generate and rate possible explanations of outliers, trends and other features in the data. Our approach makes it possible to quickly generate large numbers of good candidate explanations like the one in Figure 2c, in which a worker gives several specific policy changes as possible explanations for changes in Iran's oil output. Such analytical explanations are extremely rare in existing social data analysis systems.

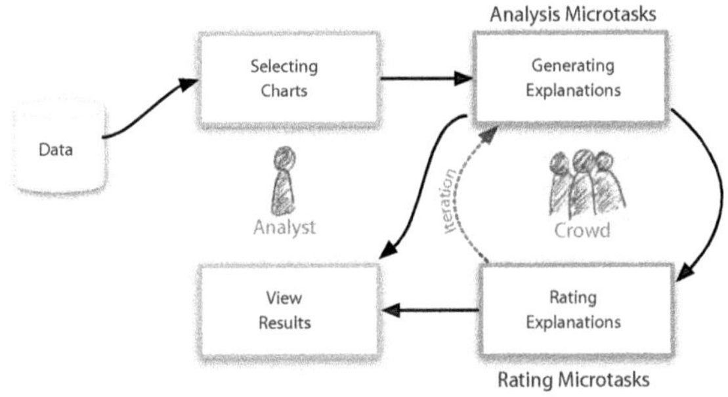

Figure 1. Our workflow for crowdsourcing data analysis.

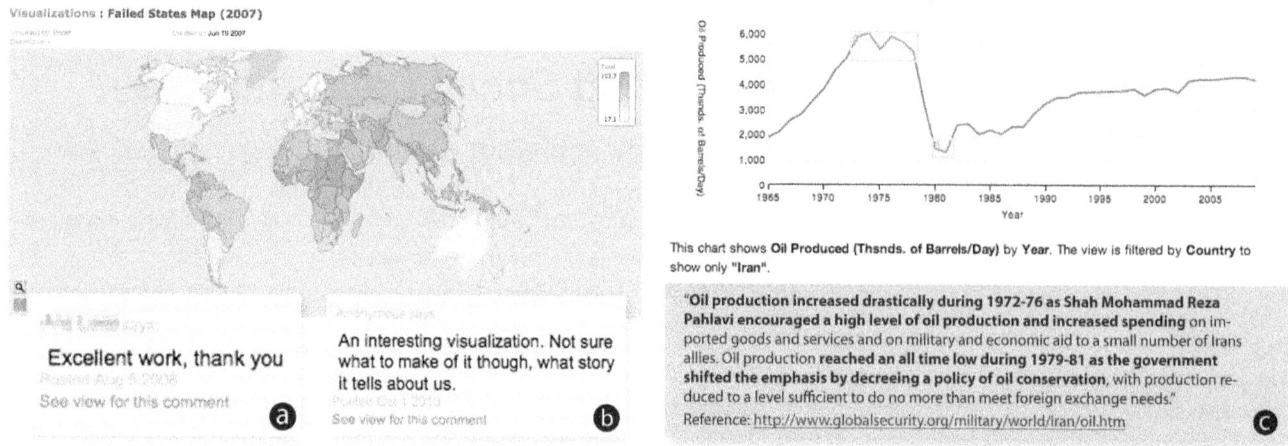

Figure 2. Comments on social data analysis on sites like Many Eyes (a,b) often add little value for analysts. We show that crowd workers can reliably produce high-quality explanations (c) that analysts can build upon as part of their broader analyses. (Emphasis added.)

Yet, simply asking workers with varying skills, backgrounds, and motivations to "Explain why a chart is interesting" can result in irrelevant, unclear, or speculative explanations of variable quality. We present a set of seven strategies that address these problems and improve the quality of worker-generated explanations of data. Our seven strategies are to: *(S1) use feature-oriented prompts, (S2) provide good examples, (S3) include reference gathering subtasks, (S4) include chart reading subtasks, (S5) include annotation subtasks, (S6) use pre-annotated charts*, and *(S7) elicit explanations iteratively*. While some of these strategies have precedents in other crowdsourcing systems [17, 21], the main contribution of this work is to demonstrate their impact in the context of collaborative data analysis.

We have applied these strategies to generate 910 explanations from 16 datasets, and found that 63% were of high quality. We also conducted six experiments to test the strategies in depth. We find that together our first five strategies (S1-S5) increase the quality ratings (a combined measure of clarity, plausibility, and relevance) of responses by 28% for US workers and 196% for non-US workers. Feature-oriented prompts (S1) are particularly effective, increasing the number of workers who explain specific chart features by 60%-250% and improving quality by 69%-236% depending on the prompt. Including chart annotation subtasks (S5) or pre-annotating charts (S6) also improves workers' attention to features. Additionally, iterative rounds of explanation generation (S7) can produce 71% new explanations without increasing worker attrition. Finally we show how workers can help analysts identify the best unique explanations – providing quality ratings that correlate strongly with our own and identifying redundant explanations with 72% accuracy. Our results show that by recruiting paid crowd workers we can reliably generate high-quality hypotheses and explanations, enabling detailed human analyses of large data sets.

RELATED WORK

We build on two main areas of related work; asynchronous social data analysis and applications of paid crowdsourcing.

Asynchronous Social Data Analysis

Social data analysis systems such as Sense.us [8], Pathfinder [18], Many Eyes [30], and Swivel [27] were built under the assumption that people can parallelize the work required to analyze and make sense of data. Motivated users can visualize, share, and discuss datasets but, as we've noted, few of the visualizations exhibit high-quality analytical discussion. In fact, many of the commercial websites no longer exist.

Heer and Agrawala [6] discuss a variety of issues in designing asynchronous social data analysis systems to improve sensemaking. They suggest that these systems should facilitate division, allocation and integration of analysis work, support communication between workers and provide intrinsic and extrinsic incentives. Building on these suggestions, Willett et al.'s CommentSpace [32] demonstrates that dividing social data analysis into concrete subtasks can improve the quality of analysts' contributions. In this work, we further break the task of generating explanations into smaller *microtasks* in which paid workers explain features of the data and other workers rate those explanations.

Applications of Paid Crowdsourcing

With the rise of online labor marketplaces such as Amazon's Mechanical Turk (`www.mturk.com`), researchers have focused on the use of paid crowdsourcing to supplement purely computational approaches to problem solving and user testing [12, 23]. In the context of visualization, recent work has used crowdsourced workers to perform graphical perception experiments on the effectiveness of charts and graphs [7, 14]. We also pay crowd workers to make judgments about charts and graphs and to provide graphical annotations, but we focus on analytical sensemaking tasks.

Other work has examined how to incorporate human computation into larger workflows. Soylent [2] uses paid workers to perform document editing tasks within a word processor, using a Find-Fix-Verify pattern to break editing tasks into smaller subtasks. Similarly, our workflow helps an analyst break down complex data analysis operations into *analysis microtasks* that many workers can perform in parallel and *rating microtasks* that help the analyst consolidate the results of the parallel analyses. We also take inspiration from CrowdForge [13], Jabberwocky [1], TurKit [17], and Turkomatic [15] which provide general-purpose programming models for leveraging crowds to perform complex tasks.

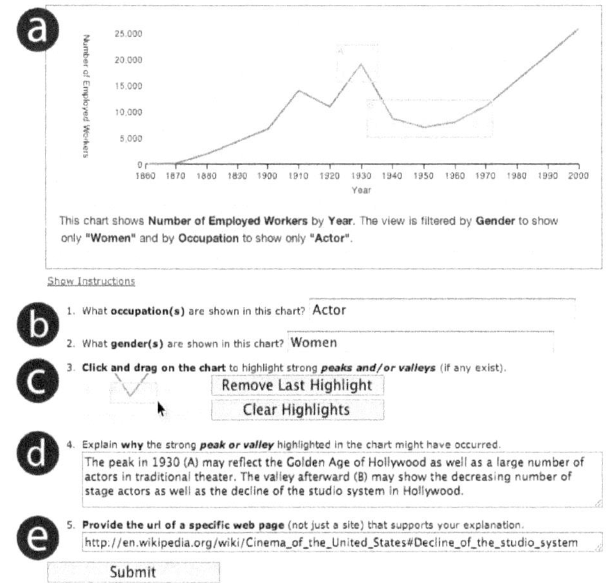

Figure 3. An example analysis microtask shows a single chart (a) along with chart-reading subtasks (b) an annotation subtask (c) and a feature-oriented explanation prompt designed to encourage workers to focus on the chart (d). A request for outside URLs (e), encourages workers to check their facts and consider outside information.

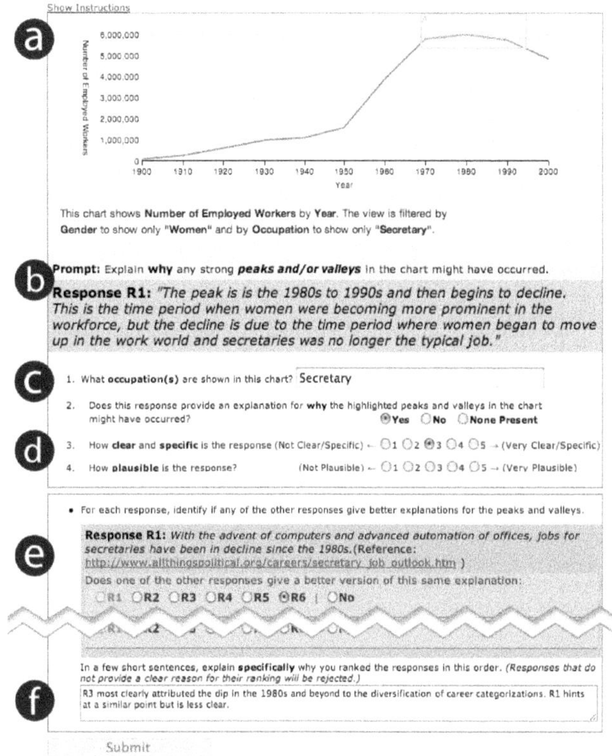

Figure 4. An example rating microtask showing a single chart (a) along with explanations (b) from several workers. The task contains a chart-reading subtask (c) to help focus workers' attention on the charts and deter scammers, along with controls for rating individual responses (d), indicating redundant responses (e), and summarizing responses (f).

A WORKFLOW FOR CROWDSOURCING DATA ANALYSIS

Hypothesis (or explanation) generation is a key step of Pirolli and Card's [22] sensemaking model and it requires human judgment. Developing good hypotheses often involves generating a diverse set of candidate explanations based on understanding many different views of the data. Our techniques allow an analyst to parallelize the sensemaking loop by dividing the work of generating and assessing hypotheses into smaller *microtasks* and efficiently distributing these microtasks across a large pool of workers.

We propose a four-stage workflow (Figure 1) for crowdsourcing data analysis. An analyst first *selects charts* relevant to a specific question they have about the data. Crowd workers then examine and explain these charts in *analysis microtasks*. Optionally, an analyst can ask other workers to review these explanations in *rating microtasks*. Finally, the analyst can *view the results* of the process, sorting and filtering the explanations based on workers' ratings. The analyst may also choose to iterate the process and add additional rounds of analysis and rating to improve the quality and diversity of explanations.

Selecting Charts

Given a dataset, an analyst must initially select a set of charts for analysis. The analyst may interactively peruse the data using a visual tool like Tableau [28] to find charts that raise questions or warrant further explanation. Alternatively, the analyst may apply data mining techniques (e.g., [10, 16, 33]) to automatically identify subsets of the data that require further explanation. In general, our workflow can work with any set of charts and is agnostic to their source.

In our experience, analysts often know *a priori* that they are interested in understanding specific features of the data such as outliers, strong peaks and valleys, or steep slopes. Therefore, our implementation includes R scripts that apply basic data mining techniques to a set of time-series charts in order to identify and rank the series containing the largest outliers, the strongest peaks and valleys and the steepest slopes. The analyst can then review these charts or post them directly to crowd workers to begin eliciting explanations. We leave it to future work to build more sophisticated data mining algorithms for chart selection.

Generating Explanations

For each selected chart, our system creates an analysis microtask asking for a paid crowd worker to explain the visual features within it. Each microtask contains a single chart and a series of prompts asking the worker to explain and/or annotate aspects of the chart (Figure 3). The analyst can present each microtask to more than one worker to increase the diversity of responses.

Rating Explanations

If a large number of workers contribute explanations, the analyst may not have the time to read all of them and may instead wish to focus on just the clearest, most plausible or most unique explanations. In the rating stage the analyst enlists crowd workers to aid in this sorting and filtering process. Each *rating microtask* (Figure 4) includes a single chart along with a set of explanations authored by other workers. Workers rate explanations by assigning each a binary (0-1) *relevance* score based on whether it explains the desired feature of the chart. Workers also rate the clarity (how easy it is to interpret) and plausibility (how likely it is to be true) of each response on a numerical (1-5) scale. We combine these ratings into a numerical *quality* score (0-5) that mea-

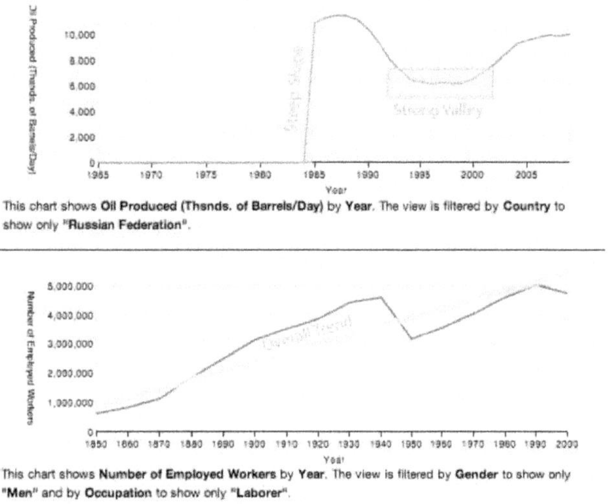

Figure 5. Sample charts from the oil production and US census datasets used in our examples and experiments. Depending on their interests analysts may with to focus workers' attention on a variety of different features of a chart, including *slopes*, *valleys*, and *overall trends*.

sures how well a worker's response explains the feature they were asked to focus on, using the formula:

$$quality = (clarity + plausibility)/2 \times (relevance).$$

Analysts can use these scores to quickly assess the quality of responses and quantitatively identify the best explanations. Workers also mark each redundant response by indicating any other response in the set that provides a better version of the same explanation.

View Results

Once workers have generated explanations, the analyst can view the responses and incorporate them into their own analyses. If the explanations have been rated, the analyst can sort and filter them using the ratings and can hide redundant responses. For example the analyst may examine only the most plausible, unique explanations. Optionally, the analyst can examine and organize the results further using a collaborative visualization environment such as CommentSpace [32]. An analyst may also choose to have workers iterate on a task, generating additional unique explanations or explanations that improve on the best responses from a prior round.

STRATEGIES FOR ELICITING GOOD EXPLANATIONS

Simply asking workers to look at a chart and explain why it is interesting may not produce good results. We consider five types of problems that can reduce the quality of these explanations and discuss strategies (S1-S7) designed to mitigate these problems.

Example datasets. For illustration we focus our discussion of the strategies on two time series datasets (Figure 5); historical data on world oil production by nation from 1965-2010, and US census counts of workers by profession from 1850-2000. We consider other datasets later in the paper.

Problem 1: Irrelevant Explanations

A chart may be interesting for many reasons, but analysts are often interested in understanding specific visual features such as outliers or overall trends. Without sufficiently detailed instructions, workers may explain features irrelevant to the analyst. For example, workers may comment on the visual design of the chart rather than the features of the data.

S1. Use feature-oriented explanation prompts. Refining the prompt to focus on the specific features the analyst is interested in increases the likelihood that workers will provide relevant explanations. Consider the line charts in Figure 5. An analyst may be interested in *peaks and valleys* or *steep slopes and flat regions* in the oil production chart because such features indicate significant events in the oil market. Alternatively, the analyst may be interested in longer-term tendencies of the labor market as indicated by the *overall trend* of the census chart. For other charts, analysts may be interested in more complex features such as clusters, repeating patterns, and correlations between dimensions.

A feature-oriented prompt might ask workers to *"explain the peaks and/or valleys in the chart (if any exist)"*. A specific prompt like this can increase the chance that workers will refer to peaks and valleys in their explanations, and also makes it easier for workers to note the absence of these features. Such negative explanations can be just as informative as explanations of the features themselves.

Problem 2: Unclear Expectations

Workers may not know what typical and atypical charts look like or what kinds of explanations they are expected to produce. Similarly, they may not know how to identify specific features like peaks or slopes.

S2. Provide good examples. To introduce workers to a dataset or feature type, analysis microtasks can include example charts showing several representative views. Similarly, including example responses may help to establish expectations and calibrate workers to the style and level of detail expected in their response [3]. In our implementation, analysts can generate examples by selecting a small set of charts (typically 2-3) and performing the analysis microtask themselves. We then package the example charts with the analyst's responses and present them to workers before they begin their first microtask. To reduce the amount of work an analyst needs to do before launching a new dataset, the examples may come from different datasets analyzed earlier. However, the data, chart type, and desired features should be similar to the new dataset.

Problem 3: Speculative Explanations

Explanations of data invariably depend on outside information not present in the data itself. Often interpretations are speculative or based on assumptions from prior experience.

S3. Include reference gathering subtasks. To encourage validation, an analysis microtask can require workers to provide references or links to corroborating information on the web (Figure 3e). Requiring such links may encourage workers to fact-check more speculative answers and may also uncover useful resources that the analyst can use later in the analysis process. However, asking workers to gather outside references may increase the time and effort associated with a microtask, and may increase worker attrition.

Problem 4: Inattention to Chart Detail

In an effort to increase their payment, workers may proceed quickly through the microtask without thoughtfully considering the prompt. They may also attempt to scam the task by entering junk responses. Even well-intentioned workers may not attend to the chart features specified in the instructions.

S4. Include chart reading subtasks. Chart reading questions (Figure 3b) can focus workers by requiring them to inspect axes, legends or series (*"What country is shown in this chart?"*), to extract a value from the chart (*"In what year did the number of workers peak?"*), or perform a computation based on the chart (*"How many more workers were there in 2000 than in 1900?"*). Such questions force workers to familiarize themselves with the data and can draw attention to important aspects of a particular chart like missing data or a non-zero axis. Additionally, because "gold standard" answers to such chart reading questions are known a priori, we can automatically check workers' answers and eliminate responses from spammers or workers who do not understand the instructions. Including such gold standard questions is a well known technique for improving result quality in crowdsourcing tasks [21, 26]. In our case these questions also help direct workers' attention to chart details.

S5. Include annotation subtasks. Requiring workers to visually search for and mark features in the chart can further focus their attention on those details. For example, the microtask may ask workers to first annotate relevant features of a chart and then explain those features (Figure 3c). Such annotations encourage attention to details and support deixis [9], allowing workers to ground their explanations by pointing directly to the features they are explaining. In our implementation each annotation is labeled with a unique letter ("A","B","C",...) so workers can refer to them in their text explanations. The worker-drawn annotations are also amenable to further computation. For example, when summarizing responses, a system could aggregate marks from multiple workers to highlight hot spots on a particular chart, or to calculate a collective "best guess" for the overall trend of a time series [6].

S6. Use pre-annotated charts. Alternatively, the analyst can pre-annotate visual features in the chart (Figure 5) so that workers pay attention to those details. Such annotations help focus workers on specific chart details and also reduce irrelevant explanations (Problem 1). Although pre-annotating charts greatly reduces the possibility that workers will attempt to explain the wrong feature, creating such annotations may require the analyst to perform additional data mining or manual annotation on the dataset.

Problem 5: Lack of Diversity

Multiple workers may generate similar explanations while leaving the larger space of possible explanations unexplored.

S7. Elicit explanations iteratively. As with other human computation tasks [17], analysis microtasks can be run in multiple, sequential stages, in which workers see a chart along with the best explanations generated in prior iterations. The analyst may elicit more diverse responses by asking workers to generate explanations that are different from the earlier ones. Alternatively, the analyst can increase explanation quality by asking workers to expand and improve upon the earlier explanations.

DEPLOYMENT

We have deployed our crowdsourced data analysis workflow on Amazon's Mechanical Turk and used workers to generate 910 explanations for 64 different charts drawn from 16 different datasets.

Our deployment included the census and oil datasets described earlier, as well as data on world development (UN food price indices, life expectancy data by nation), economics (US foreign debt, employment and housing indices for major US cities, return on investment data for US universities), and sports (team winning percentages from the NBA and MLB, historical batting averages of professional baseball players, olympic medal counts by nation, and Tour de France standings). As a proof-of-concept, we generated a set of 2 to 5 charts for each dataset that exhibited a particular characteristic, such as sharp peaks, valleys or steep slopes. In some cases we selected charts by hand, while in others we used our data-mining scripts to automatically select the charts.

We (the authors) examined and rated all 910 responses generated by workers and scored them using the quality metric described earlier in the Workflow section. We assigned $quality >= 3.5$ to 276 of the 435 responses (63.4%) that used our strategies but were not part of our experiments, indicating that most explanations were very good. Throughout the deployment, we found that workers consistently generated high-quality explanations for all datasets and provided numerous explanations that we had not previously been aware of. For example, one worker who examined the US debt dataset suggested that a large spike in British purchases of US debt might be due to Chinese purchases through British brokers. In another case, five different workers examining a chart of baseball player John Mabry's batting average (Figure 6c) independently attributed a prominent valley to a mid-season trade that reduced his at-bats. Other novel insights are shown in Figures 2, 4, and 6.

EXPERIMENTS

A full factorial experiment to evaluate all seven strategies would be prohibitively large. Instead we evaluated the strategies as we developed them. We first tested five initial strategies (S1-S5) together to gauge their overall impact. We then examined the effects of S1, S2, and S5 in a factorial experiment. Based on these results, we added three additional experiments to compare reference gathering (S3), annotation strategies (S5 and S6), and iteration (S7). Finally, we examined the results of our rating microtasks.

Experiment 1: Strategies S1-S5 in Two Worker Pools

To evaluate the cumulative impact of the first five strategies (S1-S5) we had one pool of workers complete analysis microtasks that included all of them (*strategies* condition) while a second pool completed the same microtasks but without the strategies (*no-strategies* condition).

Non-US workers represent a large portion of the workers on Mechanical Turk [11] and can often provide results more

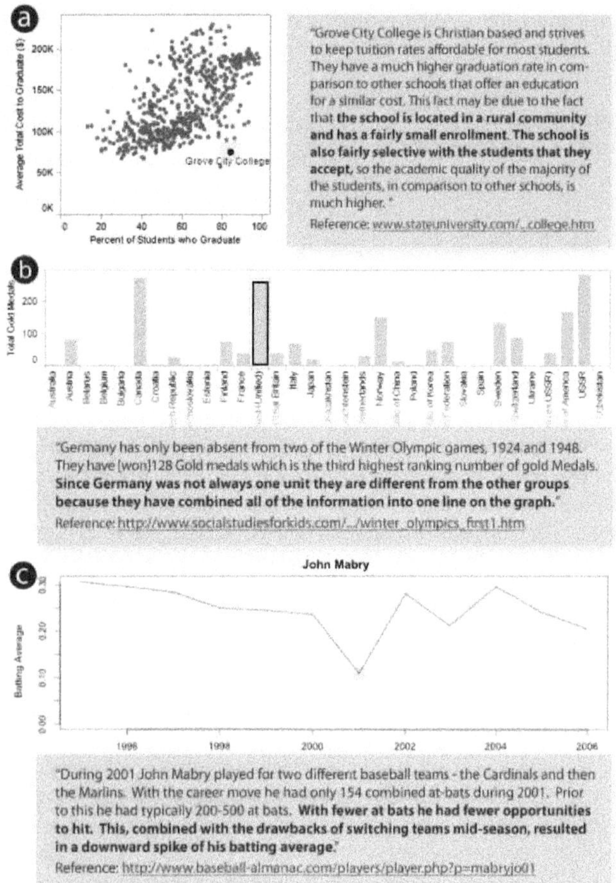

Figure 6. Sample explanations generated for charts showing university tuition and graduation rates (a), olympic medal counts by country (b), and historical batting averages (c). In each case we asked workers to explain a single outlier on a pre-annotated chart. (Emphasis added.)

quickly and cheaply than US-based workers. However, studies of Mechanical Turk have shown that workers from outside the United States exhibit poorer performance on content analysis [25] and labeling tasks [4]. We designed the experiment to determine if a similar performance gap exists for data analysis tasks and whether our strategies could improve results from these workers.

We hypothesized that: (1) Results from *US workers* would be of higher quality than results from *non-US workers*, but (2) employing strategies S1-S5 would increase the quality of explanations produced by workers in both groups.

Methods

Over the course of the experiment, we ran 200 analysis microtasks using Mechanical Turk. We divided these microtasks into 8 experimental conditions:

$$2\,strategy\ variants \times 2\,worker\ pools \times 2\,datasets = 8$$

The microtask in the *no-strategies* condition asked workers to "explain why any interesting sections of chart might have occurred". In the *strategies* condition, the microtask (Figure 3) included a **feature-oriented prompt (S1)** asking workers to "explain why any strong peaks and/or valleys in the chart might have occurred" and an **annotation subtask (S5)** that instructed workers to highlight those peaks and valleys. The microtask was preceded by instructions that included three **example charts (S2)** with annotations and explanations. The *strategies* condition also included a **reference-gathering subtask (S3)** that required workers to provide the URL of a website that corroborated their explanation. To help safeguard against scammers, we included **chart-reading (S4)** subtasks in both conditions. We also asked workers to fill out a demographic questionnaire.

We used both the oil production and US census datasets and selected five charts from each dataset with the largest variance. All of the resulting charts exhibited a range of features including peaks, valleys, slopes, and large-scale trends.

We collected five explanations for each of the charts. We also restricted each worker to a single condition (either *strategies* or *no-strategies*) and allowed workers to explain each chart only once, for a maximum of 10 responses per worker. We paid workers $0.05 per microtask during some early trials, but later increased the pay rate to $0.20 per microtask to reduce completion time. We based these rates on prior studies [7, 19] which have shown that while pay rate impacts completion time, it has little impact on response quality.

Results

Over the course of the experiment, 104 different workers produced responses for the 200 microtasks. To assess how well workers understood the tasks, we (the authors) calculated quality scores for each response (as described in the Workflow section). We also analyzed the content of the responses, labeling each one as either an *"explanation"* if it explained the chart features or a *"description"* if it simply described the features. We also examined whether or not each response referred to *"peaks or valleys"*, *"steep slopes or flat regions"*, or an *"overall trend"*.

We observed no significant difference in response quality, completion time, or length between the census and oil productions datasets in either worker population, indicating that producing explanations was of similar difficulty across both datasets. Thus, we combine the results from both datasets in all subsequent analyses.

Worker Pools. We found that worker pool had a significant main effect on quality ($F_{1,198} = 12.2, p < 0.01$). Response quality was higher for US workers ($\mu = 2.23, \sigma = 1.79$) than for non-US workers ($\mu = 1.37, \sigma = 1.87$) (Figure 7) in part because 83% of responses from US workers contained relevant explanations, while only 42% of responses from non-US workers did so. Instead, 34% of non-US workers described the chart rather than explaining it, and 24% produced responses that were so poorly written we could not classify them. The poor performance of non-US workers may reflect their lack of familiarity with the datasets as well as a language barrier. In our demographic questionnaire, only 35% of non-US workers in the census conditions could accurately describe the US census, versus 100% of US workers. Less than 20% of non-US workers reported English as their native language, versus 95% of US workers.

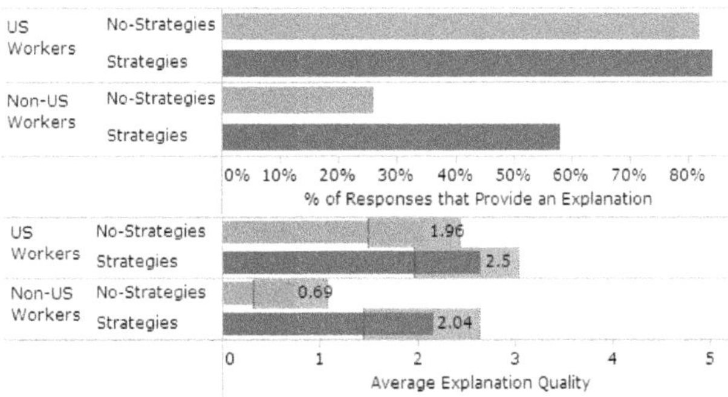

Figure 7. Percent of responses containing an explanation(top) and average explanation quality(bottom), by worker group (*US / non-US* workers) and strategy condition (*strategies / no-strategies*) in Experiment 1. Error bars give 95% confidence intervals.

We also found that across US and non-US groups, workers in the *strategies* condition produced higher quality responses ($\mu = 2.27, \sigma = 2.00$) than those in the *no-strategies* condition ($\mu = 1.33, \sigma = 1.62$) ($F_{1,198} = 14.5, p < 0.01$). However, the improvement in average quality of responses for non-US workers (196%) was much larger than for US workers (28%). These results suggest that using strategies S1-S5 makes a bigger difference when workers are culturally unfamiliar with the task and/or dataset.

Prompts. The introduction of strategies S1-S5 greatly increased workers' attention to peaks and valleys in the data. Workers in the *strategies* condition, which included a feature-oriented "*peaks and valleys*" prompt (S1) along with examples (S2) and annotation subtasks (S5) that reinforced the prompt, referred to peaks and valleys very consistently (90% of *US* and 68% of *non-US* responses). Workers in the *no-strategies* condition, however, referenced very few of these features (16% of *US* and 6% of *non-US responses*). The *no-strategies* workers often referred to overall trends or slopes in the data or failed to provide an explanation at all.

Completion Times and Attrition. Across both pools, workers took significantly longer to complete each microtask in the *strategies* condition (Median=4 minutes 11 seconds) than they did in the *no-strategies* condition (Median=2 minutes 48 seconds) ($t = -3.668, p < 0.01$). We computed attrition as the percentage of participants who began a microtask but quit without completing it and found an attrition rate of 67% for workers in the *strategies* condition. Attrition was 23% in the *no-strategies* condition. These results suggest that workers are less willing to complete analysis microtasks that include additional subtasks like chart reading and reference gathering.

Because *non-US* workers generated such low quality explanations, we used only US workers in our subsequent experiments. Also, because we saw similar results in Experiment 1 across both the oil production and US census datasets, we used only the census dataset in Experiments 2-5.

Experiment 2: Exploring Individual Strategies

Our experience in Experiment 1 led us to believe that three strategies, **feature-oriented prompts (S1)**, **examples (S2)**, and **annotation subtasks (S5)**, had the greatest impact on response quality. To better understand the effects of these

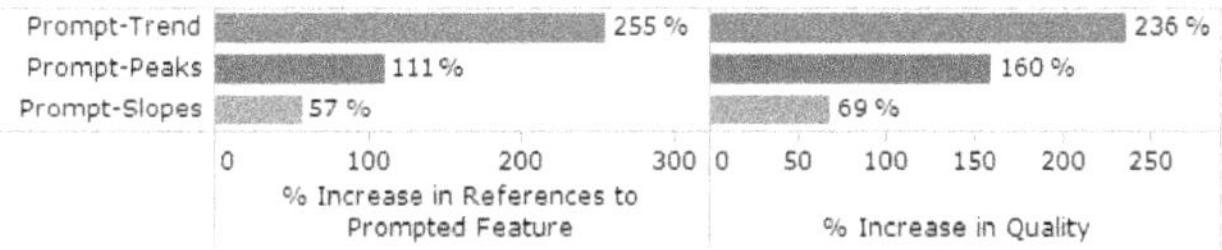

Figure 8. Percent increase in references to prompted feature (left) and quality (right) for each feature-oriented prompt (S1) in Experiment 2.

strategies, we conducted a factorial experiment that varied each one independently. We hypothesized that: (1) Feature-oriented prompts (S1) would improve quality by increasing the proportion of responses that explained the specified feature; (2) Examples (S2) would improve quality, especially when paired with a feature-oriented prompt, by familiarizing workers with the prompt and chart type as well as the expected length, style, and content of good responses; (3) Annotation subtasks (S5) would encourage workers to mark the prompted feature and thereby improve quality by increasing the number of relevant responses.

Methods

In Experiment 2, we ran 160 explanation microtasks divided into 16 conditions:

$$(4 \ \ prompts\ ) \times (2 \ \ \begin{matrix} examples \\ variants \end{matrix}\ ) \times (2 \ \ \begin{matrix} annotation \\ variants \end{matrix}\ ) = 16$$

Our 4 prompts included three feature-oriented prompts (S1) *prompt-slopes*, *prompt-trend*, and *prompt-peaks*, and one control prompt, *prompt-control*. In the *prompt-slopes* conditions, we asked workers to "explain why any sharp slopes and/or flat regions in the chart might have occurred", while in the *prompt-trend* conditions we asked workers to "explain why the overall trend in the chart might have occurred". The *prompt-peaks* and *prompt-control* conditions used the same prompts as the *strategies* and *no-strategies* conditions from Experiment 1, respectively.

To test the examples strategy (S2), we included an *examples* condition that showed workers three examples of high-quality explanations and a *no-examples* conditions that provided only short text instructions. To test annotation subtasks (S5), we included a *worker-annotation* condition that required workers to mark features in the charts and a *no-annotation* condition that did not. For consistency with Experiment 1, we included reference-gathering subtasks (S3) and chart-reading subtasks (S4) in all conditions.

Results

Prompts. Including a feature-oriented prompt (S1) increased the percentage of responses that referred to that feature by between 60% and 250% compared to the control condition, depending on the feature (Figure 8). Workers in the *prompt-peaks* ($\chi^2 = 8.455$), *prompt-slopes* ($\chi^2 = 5.952$), and *prompt-trend* ($\chi^2 = 37.746$) were all significantly more likely (all $p < 0.02$) to explain their prompted feature than workers in *prompt-control*. Similarly, including prompts increased response quality by between 69% and 236% compared to *prompt-control*. This increase was significant for workers in *prompt-trend* ($U = 372.0, p < 0.001$) and *prompt-peaks* ($U = 564.5, p = 0.008$). The increase for *prompt-slopes* ($U = 624.5, p = .064$) was not quite significant, probably because *prompt-control* workers were already more likely to explain slopes (35% of responses) than peaks or trends (both 23% of responses).

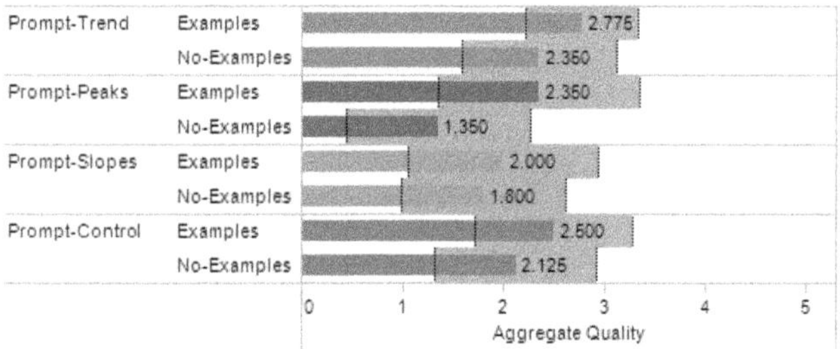

Figure 9. Average response quality by prompts (*prompt-trend, prompt-peaks, prompt-slopes,* or *prompt-control*) and examples (*examples, no-examples*). Error bars show 95% confidence intervals.

Providing Examples. Workers in the *examples* conditions produced higher quality responses ($\mu = 2.41, \sigma = 1.78$) than workers in the *no-examples* conditions ($\mu = 1.91, \sigma = 1.77$) (Figure 9), but the difference in quality was not significant ($U = 2717.5, p = 0.09$). Examples also improved the quality and consistency of annotations. Workers in the *worker-annotation* condition who saw examples of high-quality responses with annotated features, emulated the examples (Figures 2c and 4). Workers who did not see such examples created annotations that were more difficult to interpret and often annotated more features than they explained.

Annotation. In the *worker-annotation* condition, workers annotated chart features that were relevant to the prompt in 60 of the 80 trials. Workers who received a feature-oriented prompt as well as an annotation subtask referred to the feature specified in their prompt more frequently (S1 and S3: 85%) than workers who received a feature-oriented prompt without an annotation subtask (S1 only: 72%), but the difference was not quite significant ($\chi^2 = 3.142, p = 0.076$). Many *worker-annotation* workers also referred to their annotations by letter in their responses, providing clear deictic references to features. Neither the average time to complete the explanation microtask nor the attrition rate were significantly different between the *worker-annotation* and *no-annotation* conditions.

Reference-Gathering. In Experiment 2, we asked workers in all 16 conditions to gather references from the web to support their responses. Out of the 160 responses, 151 included valid URLs, of which 137 were unique. We assigned each reference a quality score from 1-5 based on how well it supported the explanation. Workers in the *examples* condition generated higher quality URLs ($\mu = 2.73, \sigma = 0.96$) than those in the *no-examples* case ($\mu = 2.4, \sigma = 1.0$) but these differences were not significant ($U = 3018, p = 0.08$).

Experiment 3: Reference Gathering

Based on results from Experiments 1 and 2, we hypothesized (1) that **reference gathering (S3)** increased response quality, but (2) the effort required to gather references contributed to high attrition. To test this hypothesis, we ran an experiment with 50 trials split between two conditions; the *gathering* condition was identical to the *strategies* condition in Experiment 1, while the *no-gathering* condition omitted the reference gathering subtask but was otherwise identical.

Results

The 25 responses in the *gathering* condition produced 20 unique URLs and URL quality was similar to Experiment 2 ($\mu = 2.67, \sigma = 1.02$). Surprisingly, however, the *no-gathering* condition produced significantly higher-quality explanations ($\mu = 3.38, \sigma = 1.55$) than the *gathering* condition ($\mu = 2.22, \sigma = 1.94$) ($U = 211.5, p = 0.046$). Additionally, the median completion time for *no-gathering* microtasks was only 2 minutes 36 seconds, significantly faster than the 3 minutes 45 second median for *gathering* tasks ($U = 175.5, p = 0.008$), suggesting that while reference gathering produces useful references, it does so at the cost of speed and quality. Given the low number of trials and high variance, further study is necessary to fully understand this relationship.

Experiment 4: Annotation Strategies

In our first two experiments, we found that **annotation subtasks (S5)** helped workers focus on chart features and facilitated deixis. In some cases, however, the analyst may wish to **pre-annotate charts (S6)** to focus workers' attention on specific features. To compare the trade-offs between these two strategies, we conducted another study with 50 trials split between two conditions – *worker-annotation*, in which we asked workers to mark the prompted feature before they explained it, and *pre-annotation*, in which the feature was pre-marked. We hypothesized that workers in the *pre-annotation* condition would generate more responses that explained the prompted feature than those in the *worker-annotation* condition.

Results

We found no significant differences between the two conditions. However the number of response that explained the prompted feature ("peaks and valleys") was high in both the *pre-annotation* (88%) and *worker-annotation* (96%) cases. In 84% of the trials in the *worker-annotation* condition, workers marked the exact same peak or valley that we had highlighted in the *pre-annotation* condition, suggesting we shared a common notion of which peaks or valleys were important.

Experiment 5: Iteration

In our fifth experiment, we tested whether **eliciting explanations iteratively (S7)** could improve the diversity of workers' explanations. First, we asked one group of workers (the *initial* condition) to generate explanations for a dataset. After a second group rated these explanations, we asked a third group of workers (the *iteration* condition) to generate additional explanations that were different from the first set. We hypothesized that (1) the *iteration* condition would produce mostly new explanations, but (2) would have a higher rate of attrition, since later workers might feel unable to author a response that differed from the initial explanations.

We conducted 25 trials in the *initial* round, producing five explanations each for the five US census charts. In the *iteration* round, we conducted 25 more trials, in which we showed new workers the same five charts, along with the initial explanations. We instructed *iteration* workers to generate new explanations that were "different from the explanations already shown". Both conditions included pre-marked charts (S6), but were otherwise identical to the *strategies* condition in Experiment 1.

Results

The 25 trials in the *initial* condition produced 36 distinct explanations, while the 25 trials in the *iteration* condition produced 35 explanations. Of the *iteration* explanations, 71% had not been proposed in the first round. The attrition rate for the *iteration* condition (75.3%) was also slightly lower than the attrition rate in the *initial* round (80.2%), indicating that iteration can increase the diversity of explanations without increasing attrition.

Experiment 6: Rating

In order for rating microtasks to provide an effective means of sorting explanations and identifying duplicates, workers must be able to generate consistent ratings. To test this, we conducted a final experiment in which we asked workers to rate a subset of the explanations generated during our broader deployment. We hypothesized that (1) quality ratings assigned by workers would be similar to our own quality ratings and that (2) workers would consistently detect and label redundant explanations.

Methods

We asked 243 Mechanical Turk workers to rate 192 different explanations across 37 charts. Using the interface shown in Figure 4, workers rated each response according to the criteria (relevance, clarity, and plausibility) described in the Workflow section. We compared these ratings against our own quality ratings for the same results.

Workers also indicated redundancy as follows: for each explanation, workers could mark at most *one* other response as providing a better version of the same explanation. For each worker, we then formed a redundancy graph with the explanations as the nodes. We linked two explanations with an undirected edge if the worker marked them as redundant. To identify groups of redundant explanations we computed the transitive closure of this graph. Each connected component then represented a unique explanation and all explanations within a component were redundant.

To reduce scamming in the rating microtask we also included one "gold standard" explanation on five of the charts. We purposely based the content of each "gold standard" explanation on one of the worker-generated explanations, but modified the language to ensure that workers could not identify it as an exact duplicate. We used these "gold standard" explanation with known redundancy to test whether or not workers could successfully detect redundant explanations.

Results

In total, the workers produced 1,334 individual ratings for the 192 different explanations. We compared these to our own quality ratings for the same responses.

Rating Consistency. A Pearson's chi-square test showed very strong agreement ($\chi^2 = 78.81, p < 0.01$) between workers' *relevance* scores and our own, indicating that workers were good at identifying responses that did not explain the requested feature. A Spearman's rank correlation coefficient

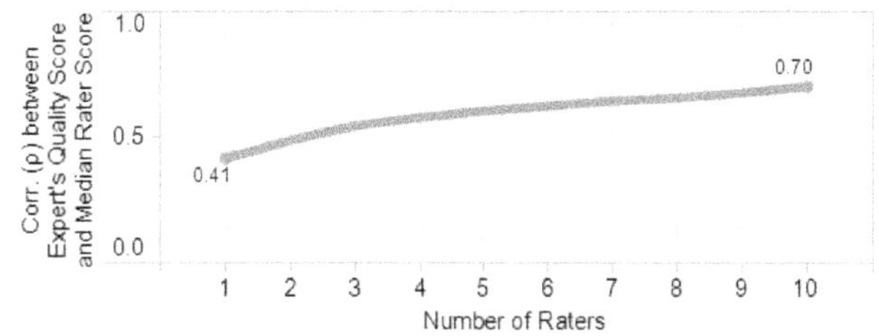

Figure 10. Correlation between our quality scores and the median workers' scores. For each number of raters, we randomly sample from a set of 10 ratings for 25 different explanations. The chart shows average correlations after 10,000 sampling iterations.

showed that workers' overall *quality* scores and our scores were moderately correlated ($\rho = 0.42$).

Because not all workers' ratings are reliable, an analyst may wish to combine ratings from multiple workers to obtain a more accurate result. To estimate the effect of using multiple raters, we took the set of responses that had been rated by at least ten raters and repeatedly sampled a subset of the ratings for each response.

For example, to estimate the effectiveness of using three raters, we randomly selected three worker's ratings for each response and used the median of them as the response's quality score. We then computed the correlation between the median scores and our own quality scores for all responses. To control for sampling error we randomly sampled and recomputed the correlation 10,000 times for each number of raters (Figure 10). Using the median score from multiple workers produced results that correlated more strongly with our own - increasing steadily from a moderate correlation ($\rho = 0.41$ when using one rater) to a strong one ($\rho = 0.70$ with ten raters).

Redundancy. We tested workers' ability to detect redundant responses by examining the results from the 25 rating microtasks in which we seeded the set of responses with a known redundant explanation. Across these 25 microtasks, workers connected the known redundant explanation to the explanation on which it was based 72% of the time. Workers agreed strongly on 35% of the pairs, with *all* five raters indicating the same redundancy relationship.

DISCUSSION

We have demonstrated that paid crowd workers can reliably produce high quality explanations and novel insights. In fact, in our deployment we found that 63% of the responses we sampled contained good explanations – far more than in tools like Many Eyes. Moreover, we found that using several basic strategies (S1-S5) can greatly improve explanation quality, particularly when users are unfamiliar with the data. Because paid crowd workers are readily available and can provide good explanations, these results suggest that we may be able to conduct targeted social data analysis at a much larger scale than was possible in previous systems.

In practice, strategies may only be appropriate in certain circumstances. For example, reference gathering (S3) is useful if an analyst requires citations or references for their analyses. However, in our experience, reference gathering causes workers to take longer and can reduce the diversity of explanations, since workers cannot pose hypotheses for which they have no references. Instead, it may be better to make references optional or provide bonuses for good references.

Similarly, while both annotation strategies we tested (S5,S6) improved workers' attention to prompted details, they are useful in different situations. Annotation subtasks (S5) are more useful when the specific features of interest are not yet known, while pre-annotated charts (S6) are useful for directing workers' attention to more subtle features that are relevant to the analyst, but not obvious to workers.

Finally, our analysis of workers' performance on rating microtasks demonstrates that crowd workers can provide high-quality ratings that correlate strongly with our own. However, using multiple workers produces more accurate ratings. Redundancy checking subtasks provide a reliable approach for identifying unique explanations, however, quality-control mechanisms such as "gold standard" questions with known responses may be necessary to make certain that workers understand the task.

While crowd workers generated good explanations for the wide range of public-interest datasets we tested, they may fare less well with domain-specific data. In future work, we plan to apply similar strategies to elicit targeted analysis help from expert communities, volunteers, and enthusiasts.

CONCLUSION

Our work demonstrates how the key sensemaking task of generating explanations can be broken down and performed systematically by paid workers. Relying on paid crowd workers rather than ad-hoc volunteers allows us to marshal the analytic power of hundreds of workers in a systematic way. By packaging simple charts within analysis microtasks and dispatching them en-masse to the crowd, we can solicit large numbers of high-quality explanations much more predictably than we could using existing social data analysis platforms. Moreover, we demonstrate that using a straightforward set of strategies, we can mitigate common problems such as irrelevant explanations, unclear and speculative worker expectations, and inattention to chart detail.

ACKNOWLEDGEMENTS

We would like to thank Björn Hartmann for his helpful input. This work was partially supported by NSF grants CCF-0963922 & CCF-0964173 and a gift from Greenplum/EMC.

REFERENCES

1. Ahmad, S., Battle, A., Malkani, Z., and Kamvar, S. The jabberwocky programming environment for structured social computing. In *Proc. UIST* (2011).
2. Bernstein, M. S., Little, G., Miller, R. C., Hartmann, B., Ackerman, M. S., Karger, D. R., Crowell, D., and Panovich, K. Soylent: a word processor with a crowd inside. In *Proc. UIST* (2010), 313–322.
3. Boud, D. *Enhancing learning through self assessment*. Routledge, 1995.
4. Chandler, D., and Kapelner, A. Breaking monotony with meaning: Motivation in crowdsourcing markets. *U. of Chicago mimeo* (2010).
5. Danis, C. M., Viegas, F. B., Wattenberg, M., and Kriss, J. Your place or mine?: Visualization as a community component. In *Proc. CHI* (2008), 275–284.
6. Heer, J., and Agrawala, M. Design considerations for collaborative visual analytics. *Information Visualization 7*, 1 (2008), 49–62.
7. Heer, J., and Bostock, M. Crowdsourcing graphical perception: Using mechanical turk to assess visualization design. In *Proc. CHI* (2010), 203–212.
8. Heer, J., Viégas, F., and Wattenberg, M. Voyagers and voyeurs: Supporting asynchronous collaborative visualization. *Comm. of the ACM 52*, 1 (2009), 87–97.
9. Hill, W. C., and Hollan, J. D. Deixis and the future of visualization excellence. In *Proc. of IEEE Visualization* (1991), 314–320, 431.
10. Hurley, C. B., and Oldford, R. W. Pairwise Display of High–Dimensional Information via Eulerian Tours and Hamiltonian Decompositions. *JCGS 19*, 4 (2010), 861–886.
11. Ipeirotis, P. Demographics of mechanical turk. *New York University, Tech. Rep* (2010).
12. Kittur, A., Chi, E. H., and Suh, B. Crowdsourcing user studies with mechanical turk. In *Proc. CHI* (2008), 453–456.
13. Kittur, A., Smus, B., and Kraut, R. Crowdforge: crowdsourcing complex work. In *CHI Extended Abstracts*, ACM (2011), 1801–1806.
14. Kong, N., Heer, J., and Agrawala, M. Perceptual guidelines for creating rectangular treemaps. *IEEE TVCG 16* (2010), 990–998.
15. Kulkarni, A., Can, M., and Hartman, B. Collaboratively Crowdsourcing Workflows with Turkomatic. In *Proc. CSCW* (2012).
16. Lee, E.-K., Cook, D., Klinke, S., and Lumley, T. Projection pursuit for exploratory supervised classification. *JCGS 14*, 4 (2005), 831–846.
17. Little, G., Chilton, L., Goldman, M., and Miller, R. Turkit: tools for iterative tasks on mechanical turk. In *Proc. SIGKDD*, ACM (2009).
18. Luther, K., Counts, S., Stecher, K., Hoff, A., and Johns, P. Pathfinder: an online collaboration environment for citizen scientists. In *Proc. CHI* (2009), 239–248.
19. Mason, W., and Watts, D. J. Financial incentives and the "performance of crowds". *SIGKDD Explor. Newsl. 11* (May 2010), 100–108.
20. Nielsen, J. Participation inequality: Encouraging more users to contribute. *Jakob Nielsen's Alertbox* (2006). http://www.useit.com/alertbox/participation_inequality.html.
21. Oleson, D., Sorokin, A., Laughlin, G., Hester, V., Le, J., and Biewald, L. Programmatic gold: Targeted and scalable quality assurance in crowdsourcing. In *Proc. HComp* (2011).
22. Pirolli, P., and Card, S. The sensemaking process and leverage points for analyst technology as identified through cognitive task analysis. *The Analyst 2005*, 1–6.
23. Quinn, A. J., and Bederson, B. B. Human Computation: A Survey and Taxonomy of a Growing Field. In *Proc. CHI* (2011).
24. Russell, D. M., Stefik, M. J., Pirolli, P., and Card, S. K. The cost structure of sensemaking. In *Proc. CHI* (1993), 269–276.
25. Shaw, A. D., Horton, J. J., and Chen, D. L. Designing incentives for inexpert human raters. In *Proc. CSCW* (2011), 275–284.
26. Sorokin, A., and Forsyth, D. Utility data annotation with amazon mechanical turk. In *Computer Vision and Pattern Recognition Workshops* (2008), 1 –8.
27. Swivel. http://www.swivel.com.
28. Tableau. http://www.tableausoftware.com.
29. Viégas, F., Wattenberg, M., McKeon, M., Van Ham, F., and Kriss, J. Harry potter and the meat-filled freezer: A case study of spontaneous usage of visualization tools. In *Proc. HICSS*, Citeseer (2008).
30. Viégas, F., Wattenberg, M., Van Ham, F., Kriss, J., and McKeon, M. Manyeyes: a site for visualization at internet scale. *IEEE TVCG 13*, 6 (2007), 1121–1128.
31. Whittaker, S., Terveen, L., Hill, W., and Cherny, L. The dynamics of mass interaction. In *Proc. CSCW* (1998), 257–264.
32. Willett, W., Heer, J., Agrawala, M., and Hellerstein, J. CommentSpace: Structured Support for Collaborative Visual Analysis. In *Proc. CHI* (2011).
33. Wills, G., and Wilkinson, L. Autovis: automatic visualization. *Information Visualization 9* (March 2010), 47–69.

Direct Answers for Search Queries in the Long Tail

Michael S. Bernstein[1], Jaime Teevan[2], Susan Dumais[2], Dan Liebling[2], Eric Horvitz[2]
[1] MIT CSAIL
32 Vassar St., Cambridge MA
msbernst@mit.edu
[2] Microsoft Research
One Microsoft Way, Redmond WA 98052
{teevan, sdumais, danl, horvitz}@microsoft.com

ABSTRACT
Web search engines now offer more than ranked results. Queries on topics like weather, definitions, and movies may return inline results called *answers* that can resolve a searcher's information need without any additional interaction. Despite the usefulness of answers, they are limited to popular needs because each answer type is manually authored. To extend the reach of answers to thousands of new information needs, we introduce *Tail Answers*: a large collection of direct answers that are unpopular individually, but together address a large proportion of search traffic. These answers cover long-tail needs such as the average body temperature for a dog, substitutes for molasses, and the keyboard shortcut for a right-click. We introduce a combination of search log mining and paid crowdsourcing techniques to create Tail Answers. A user study with 361 participants suggests that Tail Answers significantly improved users' subjective ratings of search quality and their ability to solve needs without clicking through to a result. Our findings suggest that search engines can be extended to directly respond to a large new class of queries.

Author Keywords
Search user interfaces; query log analysis; crowdsourcing

ACM Classification Keywords
H5.2 [Information interfaces and presentation]: User Interfaces – Graphical user interfaces.

General Terms
Design; Human Factors.

INTRODUCTION

While search engines have long connected people to *documents*, they are now beginning to also connect people directly to *information*. The results page is no longer just a plain list of page titles and snippets. For popular topics such as weather, movies, and definitions, search engines may add custom interfaces with direct results (e.g., "77°F, partly cloudy"). These direct results, known as *answers* [7], allow searchers to satisfy their information need without clicking through to a web page. Answers have a measurable impact on user behavior in search result pages, and many users seek answer types repeatedly once they realize that they exist [7]. For common needs, answers demonstrate the value of customizing the interface to deliver information rather than documents.

Unfortunately, answers are only available for a small percentage of common needs [7,13]. Few manually curated answers exist, and those that do focus on popular query types like weather. In contrast, most searchers' information needs are unpopular: half of all queries are unique [20], and users rarely see most answers [7]. It has not been feasible for search engines to create answers to cover the long tail of less popular information needs: search engines must author the content, test which queries to trigger on, find a data source to feed the answer, and keep the answer up-to-date as the web changes [1]. As a result, searchers only receive relevant direct answers when they have extremely common information needs.

We extend search engine answers to a broad new class of queries in the long tail. By doing so, we show that *search engines can aggregate user knowledge to improve not just result rankings, but the entire search user experience.* We introduce *Tail Answers*, automatically generated search engine answers that support a large set of less common information needs. These information needs include the normal body temperature for a dog (Figure 1), substitutes for molasses, the currency in Ireland, and many more (Figure 2). Each of these needs may occur thousands of times per year, but are too far in the tail of query traffic to be worth assigning programmers, designers, testers, and product management staff to create and maintain answers.

To push answer content down into the long tail (without an exponentially-sized editorial staff), our insight is to aggregate the knowledge of thousands of everyday web users. We turn to web users in each of the three major steps of creating Tail Answers: 1) We identify answer candidates

Figure 1. Tail Answers are inline direct responses for search results. This Tail Answer addresses body temperature for dogs.

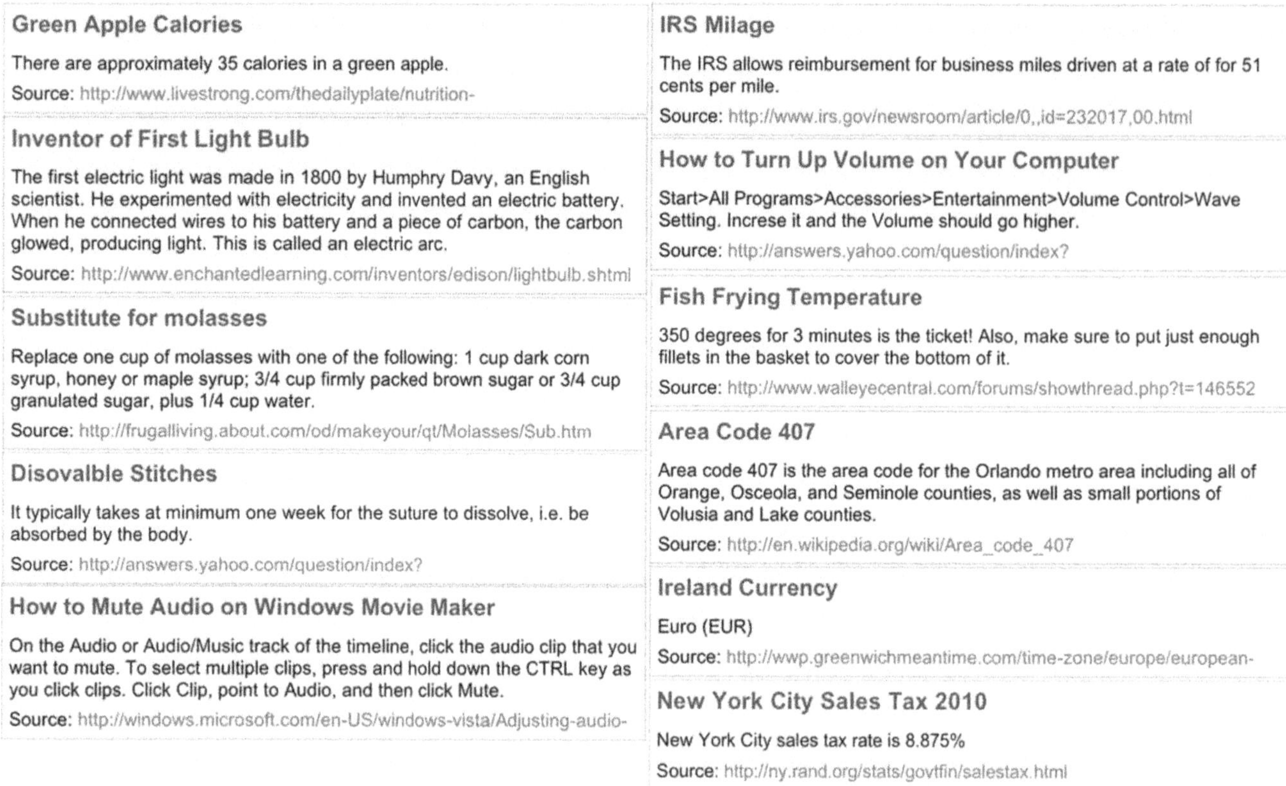

Figure 2. Tail Answers address less common information needs. These examples (including errors) were produced by the data mining and crowdsourcing processes described in the paper. They trigger on related queries, e.g., *apple calories*.

using aggregate search and browsing patterns; 2) We filter those answer candidates to ones which represent directly answerable needs, using search logs and paid crowdsourcing; 3) We extract the answer content from the web, using paid crowds to copy and paste content from the page, then author and edit the final answer text. The entire process can be effectively automated.

Following a survey of related work, we describe how we use log analysis and crowdsourcing to generate Tail Answers for information needs that search engines would not normally be able to address directly. We then present the results of an evaluation of Tail Answers that shows they significantly improved the subjective search experience, compensating for poor results and reducing perceived effort. We conclude by detailing extensions of these techniques for authoring smart snippets, integrating automatic question-answering systems, and creating new classes of answers. Our work suggests that search engines can use aggregate search patterns and crowdsourcing to improve the search experience far beyond simply better result ranking.

RELATED WORK

Search engine answers and result snippets can have a powerful influence on the web search user experience. Nearly half of the abandoned queries in a Google sample displayed a snippet that might have made any additional clicks unnecessary [13]. One quarter of all queries may already be addressed directly in the result page, especially for needs like spell checking, query monitoring, and learning about a term [17]. Successful answers will thus *cannibalize* clicks from the rest of the search results, and searchers will repeat queries to trigger an answer once they learn of it [7]. Even when no answer exists, searchers often use queries for repeated navigation, for example searching for *chi 2012* whenever they want to find the CHI papers deadline [19]. Search result snippets can also sometimes address information needs directly [8]; the snippet for a page, for example, may contain the answer in the text.

Some long-tail information needs can be addressed with automatic information extraction. Many question-answering systems are designed to address information needs with short phrases such as using search result *n*-grams to identify answers [2,5,14]. A second approach is open-domain information extraction, for example TextRunner [3]. These approaches work best when facts are repeated across multiple web pages. Finally, systems can employ curated knowledge bases such as YAGO [18] and match on them to answer some queries. However, automated approaches can make mistakes that are obvious to humans.

Question-answering systems have also recruited crowds to deliver results: for example, Aardvark [9] and Quora (www.quora.com) use members to answer questions. Rather than find domain experts, Tail Answers recruits crowd members with only basic knowledge of web search and the search context. This enables Tail Answers to cover broad content, but it raises challenges when workers do not

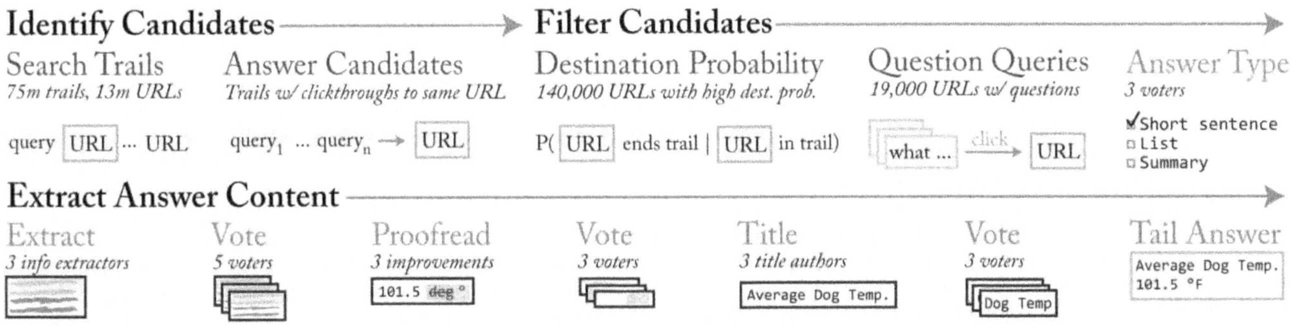

Figure 3. An overview of the three phase Tail Answers creation process, which involves 1) identifying answer candidates, 2) filtering the candidates to ones that address "answerable" needs, and 3) extracting the Tail Answer content. Steps that are implemented via data mining are indicated in blue, and those implemented via crowdsourcing are indicated in orange.

have necessary expertise. ChaCha (www.chacha.com) also uses paid, on-demand staff or crowds for question answering, but they do not vet or edit the results and do not create reusable information artifacts.

Our crowdsourcing algorithm depends on several quality control techniques from the literature. We build on the idea of gold standard tasks [12]: questions that the requester has labeled with ground truth. To cheaply and robustly control for quality, we create ground truth tasks for which the worker's answer must include at least one phrase from an inclusion list and none from an exclusion list. This inclusion/exclusion technique extends gold standard questions beyond exact matching (e.g., multiple choice) to open-ended writing or extraction tasks. Then, once the raw text is extracted, we use crowdsourcing approaches inspired by iterative text refinement [15] and proofreading [4] to improve the answer quality. Crowd planning algorithms could later be used to create high-level summaries for complex topics [11]. Search engines have also used crowds for relevance judgments; our work is the first to use crowd work to expand the search user experience.

Tail Answers improves on related work by creating the first set of direct responses for a broad set of uncommon queries. We contribute new query log mining and crowdsourcing quality control techniques to create Tail Answers in an automated fashion. We provide the first controlled, empirical evidence that these answers improve the user experience, often as much as search result quality.

TAIL ANSWERS

In this section, we describe how we create Tail Answers to extend search engine answers to tens of thousands of new information needs. Tail Answers are special results inserted inline in the search interface, as shown in Figure 1. The Tail Answer contains edited text from a webpage where other searchers found the solution to the same information need. Above the answer text is a concise title to aid skimming, and below it is a link to the source web page for attribution and further exploration. Each Tail Answer is targeted at one particular information need, although it may trigger for many different queries. When a user issues a query that matches a triggering query for a Tail Answer, that answer appears at the top of the search results.

Although answers for popular queries are currently manually authored, Tail Answers have an automated process to identify information needs that are appropriate for an answer and to author a direct result that addresses the need. In this work, we represent an information need as a set of queries with a similar intent. For example, the queries *dog temperature*, *dog fever*, and *average temp dog thermometer* represent the information need in Figure 1. In addition, we assume that Tail Answers can be associated with a web page that contains the answer (e.g., the page www.natural-dog-health-remedies.com/dog-temperature.html).

To create a Tail Answer, then, our system needs to:

1. **Identify** pages that are answer candidates,
2. **Filter** candidates that answers cannot address, and
3. **Extract** the Tail Answer content.

To accomplish these goals, we extract knowledge about answers from the activities of thousands of web users. To identify information needs, we use large-scale log analysis of web browsing patterns. To filter the needs, we augment log analysis with paid crowdsourcing. To extract answer content, we use paid crowdsourcing. Figure 3 represents this process visually. We now describe each step in detail, highlighting the technical challenges we solved to improve answer quality.

Identifying Answer Candidates

We begin by identifying information needs, which we call *answer candidates*. An answer candidate is a set of queries associated with a URL from a search result page (Table 1). A key idea is to identify browsing patterns that suggest searchers are finding a compact solution to an information need. We use query log analysis to populate our set of answer candidates. To do so, for each search session in our browser logs, we extract a *search trail* [20]: a browsing path beginning with a search query and terminating with a session timeout of thirty minutes. We then group all search trails on the first clicked URL from the result page. For each URL in our dataset, we now have a set of queries that led to the URL and a set of trails that describe what users did after clicking through to the URL.

Filtering Answer Candidates

From these answer candidates, we must identify those that are intended for fact-finding [10] and will produce good answers. Some answer candidates have information needs that are too complex to answer; others have underspecified queries where the information need may not be clear. We developed three filters to find promising answer candidates. These filters look for particular types of 1) navigation behavior, 2) query behavior, and 3) information needs.

Filtering by Navigation Behavior: Destination Probability

Our first filter uses the search trails to identify web pages where people quickly end their search sessions. We assume that after a query, people typically end up at web pages containing information that addresses their need. If users stop browsing after they reach a page, that page likely solves the need. If users continue browsing or searching, on the other hand, the page may not succinctly satisfy their need. For example, queries such as *new york times* are often navigational [6]: searchers click on www.nytimes.com in the results, then often keep browsing and click on a link to read an article. Other information needs, like buying a new car, are complex and persist across multiple sessions [9], so searchers will typically keep browsing and returning to the search page. But, for web pages like the CHI call for papers, searchers will issue a query (e.g., *chi 2012 deadline*), click through to the page, find what they are looking for, and end their search session.

We formalize the idea of trail-ending web pages with a measurement we call *destination probability*. The destination probability for a web page is the observed probability that a searcher will end their session at that web page after clicking through to the page from the search results. In our search trails, the step immediately after a query is a click on a result web page. If a high percentage of trails end after that click (i.e., if their trail length is two), the destination probability will be high. If most trails instead include actions that return to the result page or browse to other URLs, the destination probability will be low. In other words, the destination probability for a URL is the observed probability that a click to the URL from the search result page is the last action in the search trail.

Page Title and URL	Sample Queries	Type
How to Force Quit on Mac ehow.com/how_5178032_force-quit-mac.html	*force quit mac* *force quit on macs* *how to force quit mac*	Short
Area Code 410 areacodehelp.com/where/area_code_410.shtml	*what area code is 410* *410 area code* *area code 410 location*	Short
How to bake a potato howtobakeapotato.com	*baked ptato* *how long do you cook potatoes in the oven* *best way to bake a potato*	List
Rummy 500 rules rummy.com/rummy500.html	*rules of gin rummy 500* *rummy 500* *how to play rummy 500*	Summary
Pandora Radio pandora.com	*radio* *pandora* *pandora radio log in*	—

Table 1. Pages with high destination probability, queries to them, and their crowd-voted answer category. All but the bottom row had a question query: the lack of a question signals that Pandora would not be appropriate for an answer.

Web pages with high destination probability are strong candidates for Tail Answers. We filter out any answer candidates that have destination probability of less than 0.3 or fewer than three search trails in our dataset. The 30% cutoff was tuned empirically to balance the number of possible answers (false negatives) with the number of pages with unanswerable content (false positives). Table 1 lists five web pages with high destination probabilities. For example, one contains instructions for how to bake a potato.

Filtering by Query Behavior: Question Words

Destination probability identifies pages where searchers appear to be finding immediate answers for their information needs. However, it can be very hard to infer the fact-finding intent from queries that are only two or three words long. For example, an answer for the query *dissolvable stitches* would be valuable if the searcher wanted to learn how long the stitches take to dissolve, but would not if they want to learn the stitches' history.

To avoid this problem, we make use of the minority of searchers who write queries using question words. Question-word queries are useful because they tend to be expressed in natural language, are longer than typical queries, and are more explicit (e.g., *how long do dissolvable stitches last*). These properties make the information need relatively easy to understand. Use of question words also tends to indicate fact-finding intent. We assume that question-word queries often overlap significantly with the unspecified information needs from the other queries, for example that *where is 732 area code* and *732 area code* have similar needs. When this is not the case, we rely on paid crowd members later to disambiguate the most common information need from the set of all queries.

We filter the answer candidates to remove any that had fewer than 1% of their clicks from question queries. The question words we currently look for are: *how*, *what*, *when* and *who*. The bottom row of Table 1 demonstrates the kind of error that can occur without a question word filter.

Filtering by Information Need: Answer Type

While question words are useful for identifying answer candidates, neither they nor other types of behavioral log data can help the system understand whether a concise answer could address the information need. Knowing the expected length of the answer is important because crowd workers often extract too much text in order to guarantee that they captured the correct information and thus will be paid. However, overly verbose answers are not useful to searchers. Knowing what kind of answer to expect, for example a short phrase, can help the system perform automatic quality control using length.

To solve these problems, we use paid crowdsourcing via Crowdflower to categorize answer candidates into types. Crowdflower is built on top of Amazon Mechanical Turk and uses hidden quality-control questions known as *gold standard* questions to filter out poor-quality workers. By prototyping many answers, we developed the following three categories as useful for workers to identify:

- **Short** answers with very little text. For example: "The optimal fish frying temperature is 350°F."
- **List** answers, which typically contain a small set of directions. For example: "To change your password over Remote Desktop: 1) Click on Start > Windows Security. 2) Click the Change Password button. […]".
- **Summary or long list** answers, which synthesize large amounts of content. For example, pages requiring deep reading such as "Impact of Budget Cuts on Teachers" and "Centralized vs. Decentralized Organizations".

Workers were asked to read all of the queries that led to the web page, as well as the page itself, and then vote on the best matching category. The third column in Table 1 labels each example with its voted answer type.

Although short answers and list answers can be extracted from the web page and edited into an answer, summary answers require more synthesis. For this reason, we leave the generation of summary answers to future work. We use the data about whether an answer is a short answer or a list answer to give workers more specific instructions as they extract answer content and to enforce a maximum number of characters workers can extract from a page.

Extracting the Tail Answer

At this point, we have a set of answer candidates that can be addressed succinctly and factually by the search engine, but each candidate is only represented by a web page and a set of queries. To create an actual answer, we need to extract the information from the web page related to the unifying need, edit it for readability, and write a short answer title. Because automatic extraction algorithms are not yet reliable, we use paid crowdsourcing via Crowdflower.

The algorithm we developed to guide the crowd to create Tail Answers is as follows. Workers: 1) *extract* (i.e., copy and paste) as little text as possible from the web page using the associated queries as a guide, 2) *proofread* and edit the extracted information into an answer, and 3) *title* the answer descriptively. This information is compiled into a visually distinct search result and presented to searchers who issue the queries associated with the intent, or similar queries. Figure 3 contains a graphical representation of these steps.

Worker quality control is a major challenge for the generation of the Tail Answer title and text. Lazy Turkers

Spooning is a type of cuddling. When you spoon, you lay on your side with your back to your partner's chest and the partner behind wraps his or her arms around you and fits around you like a puzzle. The name likely came because of the way two spoons rest on each other, filling all the nooks. The "little spoon" is considered the person in front, the "big spoon" is considered the person in back. Another explanation I have read for the origin of the expression: In days of old, when a proper young man visited a proper young lady, he was supposed to do something to keep his hands occupied and away from her body. An acceptible activity was sit and carve a wooden spoon while conversing. Of a similar vintage, when the couple threw another log in the fireplace late in the evening, the neighbors would see a burst of sparks from the chimney, and know that someone was "sparking."

Figure 4. In this example workers extracted all of the text when an inclusion/exclusion lists was not used. Orange text is the same answer with inclusion/exclusion lists.

[4] will copy/paste introductory text from each page instead of the answer, and even well-intentioned, pre-qualified workers will extract entire paragraphs or large sections of the page to be sure that it contains the right answer. As a result, early prototype versions of Tail Answers were much too long and of poor quality (Figure 4).

One popular quality control technique is to generate a set of potential responses and ask workers to vote on which is the best. For example, we asked three different workers to copy and paste text from the web page and then had five other workers vote to select the best extraction. However, if there are no short extractions, the answer will be long; worse, workers tend to vote for long extractions.

So, it is necessary to add another layer of quality control to help guarantee that the extractions are short and targeted. We adapt the gold standard technique, which requires workers to demonstrate competence by agreeing with the answers to pre-authored example questions for each job [12]. Crowdflower uses gold standard testing by silently inserting gold standard questions into the worker's stream, and only keeps work from people who answer at least 70% of the gold standard questions correctly. Most gold standard tasks involve workers exactly matching the requester's input. For example, for voting we can enforce that workers agree with the authors' selection of which option is the best.

Unfortunately, requiring exact agreement fails for open-ended tasks like extraction. There are often several valid extractions for a page, and it can be just as important to specify which text workers should *not* include. To address this issue, we introduce *inclusion/exclusion lists* for gold standard testing for text generation. To use an inclusion/exclusion list for page extraction, the requester identifies sections of the page that *must* be in the extraction, as well as sections of the page that *must not* be in the extraction, in order for the work to be accepted. By doing so, we are able to tightly scope the areas of the page that are off-limits, as well as information that must be included in the answer for it to be correct. Figure 4 is a representative example of how training workers using inclusion/exclusion gold leads to shorter, more targeted answers.

We implement this technique using negative look-ahead in regular expressions. We also use inclusion/exclusion gold in the title generation step, making sure that workers submit relevant phrases or words and that they do not copy and paste queries verbatim. Inclusion/exclusion gold standards could be useful for other open-ended crowdsourcing tasks like proofreading, replacing expensive approaches such as Find-Fix-Verify [4] as well as qualifier tasks, which cut down on the worker pool significantly.

Implementation

To generate a set of Tail Answers, we began with a one-week sample of browsing behavior from opt-in users of a widely-distributed browser toolbar starting March 22, 2011. We filtered the sample to users in the US who use English when searching. The resulting search trails represent over 2 billion browse events from over 75 million search trails for over 15 million users. We filter pages with too little data by removing ones that have been clicked fewer than three times. Filtering via destination probability and question words resulted in 19,167 answer candidates, including those in the top four rows of Table 1.

The query and web page occurrences that make up the answer candidates are distributed similar to power laws, so there are a few pages with many queries and a large number of pages with our minimum of three queries. Answer candidates had a median of three queries (μ=5.2, σ=7.4), 37% of the unique queries contained question words, and the median query had only been issued once in the dataset (μ=7.37, σ=35.0). If each answer candidate were to receive the same number of queries every week for a year as it did during our sample week, the median answer would trigger 364 times per year (μ=1992, σ=6318).

We sampled 350 answer candidates from this set for which to create Tail Answers. We combined several different sampling methods in order to get broad coverage: 100 needs were chosen randomly from the dataset in order to represent the tail more heavily, and 250 were chosen by weighted query popularity to represent query volume.

The number of workers in each stage is a tradeoff between cost and quality. Based on previous work (e.g., [4,15]), we recruited three to five workers for extraction and voting. Three workers voted on whether each of the 350 information needs should be addressed by a short answer, a list answer, or a summary answer, for 4.2¢ per need. Of the 350 needs, one hundred forty six (42%) were short phrase answers, one hundred twenty seven (36%) were short list answers, and seventy seven (22%) were summary answers. We focus here just on the short phrase answers, although the process is identical for short list answers and the results are similar. Three workers created extractions for each need (7¢), and five workers voted on the best extraction (10¢). Ten of the 146 answers were voted out by workers for having no good extractions. Of the remainder, three workers proofread the extraction (9¢), and three workers voted on the best alternative (6¢). Three workers authored potential titles (4.2¢), and three workers voted on the best title and filtered the answer if none were appropriate (4.2¢).

At the end of the process, 120 of the 146 short answer candidates became finalized Tail Answers. A number of examples are shown in Figure 2. The cost per answer was 44.6¢ plus a small extra fee for Crowdflower and the expense of the partial results for answers that got voted out. If we were to build Tail Answers for each of the roughly 20,000 candidates in our dataset, it would cost roughly $9,000. This cost can be lowered by combining extraction and title authoring into one task.

EVALUATION

In this section, we aim to better understand Tail Answers. Using manual judgments, we show they are high quality and relevant. We then present a controlled user study that shows that Tail Answers significantly improved users' ratings of search result quality and their ability to solve needs without clicking. To remove a source of variation in these evaluations, we focus on the short answers only.

Answer Quality

We first ask whether Tail Answers are high quality. This question has several dimensions: correctness, writing quality, query accuracy, and whether major search engines already have an answer to address the need. We hand-labeled each of the answers with whether the title or the content had writing errors, whether the answer was correct, whether a major search engine already had such an answer, and whether the answer addressed each query in its training set. Two authors labeled each answer; any disagreements were settled by a third rater.

We found that most Tail Answers had high-quality writing in their title and their content (Table 2). Of the titles with writing errors, workers had suggested a correct version 50% of the time, but it had been voted down. Likewise, 30% of the contents with an error had a correct version available, but the workers did not vote for it.

Correctness was more variable: some common errors are displayed in Table 3. Over two thirds of the Tail Answers were judged fully correct (Table 2). A common minor error (18.3%) occurred when the title did not match the answer: workers who wrote the answer title sometimes paid attention to the original queries rather than the content of the answer. This could be addressed through improved interfaces for the workers and more rigorous quality control in voting. (About 45% of the incorrect answers had a correct version extracted that was not the winner of the popular vote.) Other problems occurred for dead links (i.e., the data could not be extracted) and for dynamic pages (e.g., a "What's My IP?" application and YouTube videos), where workers were unable to signal that the page had no useful information. Two changes would help Tail Answers' accuracy: 1) identifying when dynamic content would make an answer impossible to build, and 2) better quality control to make sure titles are on-topic in the voting stage, since they are written after the answer content.

	High Quality	Minor Error	Major Error
Title Writing	83.3%	14.2%	2.5%
Content Writing	82.5%	14.2%	3.3%
Correctness	68.3%	18.3%	13.3%

Table 2. Hand-labeled writing and correctness ratings.

Low-Quality Tail Answer	Problem
Resume Writing A Curriculum Vitae, commonly referred to as CV, is a longer (two or more pages), more detailed synopsis. It includes a summary of your educational and academic backgrounds as well as teaching and research experience, publications, presentations, awards, honors, affiliations and other details.	Title does not match the answer
Cary Grant Cary Grant was born on January 18, 1904.	Title does not match the answer
What Reallyhappens.com Most recent WRH radio show from Rense Radio.	Dynamic page has no useful text to extract
Double Irish Tax The Double Irish method is very common at the moment, particularly with companies with intellectual property.	Extracted text is too general

Table 3. Examples of common errors in Tail Answers.

Fourteen percent of the Tail Answers we generated already had answers available on Bing, a major search engine. Unit conversions (e.g., mL in a tablespoon) were the most common, followed by weather, definitions, and dates. These answers could be filtered in a deployed system, or could be used to replace manually generated answers, which are expensive and time consuming to maintain.

We investigated how closely the answers matched the apparent intent of the queries that represented the intent. (Many queries, like *chi 2012*, may not express the searcher's full intent.) In 58% of the unique queries, it was clear that the Tail Answers addressed the query's intent. About 7% of queries were more general than the answer (e.g., the query was *az municipal court* and the answer gave the phone number to the court), so it is difficult to know whether the answer would have satisfied the information need. Likewise, 23% of queries were generally related to the answer, and the judgment would depend on the exact intent (e.g., a query for *B.C.E.* was associated with an answer for *C.E.*, the Common Era). About 12% of the unique queries were not good matches: about 9% of the queries expressed a more specific need than the answer had (e.g., the query was *fredericksburg VRE* [Virginia Railway Express] but the answer focused on the entire VRE), and about 3% of queries were unrelated to the answer. Often, pages like *C.E.* covered multiple information needs, but workers had to choose just one need for the answer. Clustering these queries into overlapping keyword sets and building separate answers for each would help.

User Evaluation

We also wanted to understand whether Tail Answers positively or negatively impact users' impressions of the search engine result page. In particular, we wanted to know whether Tail Answers improved users' subjective impressions of search results, and whether Tail Answers could compensate for poorer search rankings.

Method

We recruited 361 people (99 female, 262 male) at Microsoft to participate in our study. Most were in their 30s (30%) or 40s (42%), and used search engines hourly (58%) or daily (41%). About 30% held nontechnical jobs. Participants could complete the study from their own computers, and we raffled off $25 gift certificates in return. Participants did not know the purpose of the experiment.

We created a custom version of the Bing search engine that inserted Tail Answers at the top of the search results whenever the user issued a matching query. We gathered a sample of thirty Tail Answers from the 120 we created. Participants were shown five queries, each taken from a randomly chosen Tail Answer, and chose one they found interesting. Participants were required to invent reasons they would issue each query, which is less realistic than showing the Tail Answer when someone has the real information need. However, by giving participants a choice of queries, we hoped they would focus on more personally meaningful tasks. After choosing a query, participants were shown the result page and asked for their level of agreement on a seven point Likert scale with two statements about the search results: 1) "This is a very useful response for the query," and 2) "This page contains everything I need to know to answer the query without clicking on a link."

Our experiment used a two-by-two research design. Each query was randomly assigned either to the *Answer* condition, which displayed a Tail Answer, or to a *No Answer* condition, with no answer. It was also randomly assigned either to the *Good Ranking* condition, where the search engine displayed results ranked 1 through 10, or a *Bad Ranking* condition, which displayed results ranked 101 through 110. In the Bad Ranking condition, the search results were typically much poorer. All conditions appeared to return top-ten results, and we hid ads and other answers. Participants would see each of the conditions randomly as they rated new queries, and were required to rate at least ten queries to be entered in the lottery. At the conclusion of the study, participants filled out a final survey.

We hypothesized that Tail Answers would improve the user experience of the search engine. However, we were also interested in how users would react when Tail Answers fired on inappropriate queries or had incorrect results.

Results

Participants rated 3963 result pages. Mean ratings are reported in Table 4 and Table 5. To analyze the results, we used a linear mixed effects model, which is a generalization of ANOVA. We modeled participant, and query (nested in answer), as random effects. Ranking and answer were fixed effects. We also included an interaction term for ranking*answer. This model allowed us to control for

	Tail Answer	No Tail Answer
Good Ranking	5.81	5.54
Bad Ranking	5.12	3.73

Table 4. Mean Likert scale responses to: "This is a very useful response for the query."

	Tail Answer	No Tail Answer
Good Ranking	5.06	4.10
Bad Ranking	4.54	2.66

Table 5. Mean Likert scale responses to: "This page contains everything I need to know to answer the query without clicking on a link."

variation by answer, query, and user in our analysis. Finally, because participants were more likely to choose certain queries in our dataset, we weighted the observations so that each answer was represented equally in the data. Weighting observations is a common technique when the sample distribution does not match the population; removing the weighting produces very similar results, but we felt that weighting would be the most accurate way to represent all answers equally. We ran the model twice, once for the first Likert scale (1) overall subjective opinion of the result page, and once with the second Likert scale (2) ability to solve the information need without clicking a link.

Tail Answers and result ranking both had significant effects on overall rated result usefulness (Table 4). In the statistics to come, we note that weighting the sample leads to non-integer degrees of freedom. Tail Answer appearance, $F(1, 4307.8) = 292.0$, $p < .001$, had an estimated effect of 0.34 points on result usefulness. Good ranking, $F(1, 4306.0) = 570.6$, $p < .001$, had an estimated effect of 0.68 points on result usefulness. Result ranking, which is central to search engines, had an effect size just twice the effect size of Tail Answers: 0.34 vs. 0.68. The interaction was significant, $F(1, 4309.95) = 106.5$, with an estimated effect size of 1.03 points. The large interaction effect indicates that answers are particularly helpful when search results are poor.

Tail Answers were also useful at solving information needs without needing to click through to a result (Table 5). The addition of Tail Answers to the search results, $F(1, 4293.0) = 631.4$, $p < 0.001$, had an estimated positive effect of 1.01 points on users' rating. Good ranking, $F(1, 4291.4) = 270.3$, $p < 0.001$, had a smaller effect of 0.50 points on users' ratings, and the interaction term remained large: $F(1, 4295.8) = 60.49$, $p < 0.001$, effect size of 0.91 points. The study design removed other answers from the search results in order to control for variation. It is possible that our effect sizes would be smaller if other answers were included.

Overall, the inclusion of Tail Answers had a positive effect on users' search experience as reflected in their ratings. The impact of Tail Answers was nearly half as much as result ranking, where search engines focus much of their effort. That positive effect was more than doubled when participants were asked whether they needed to click through to a URL. Answers were able to fully compensate for poorer search results, suggesting that a single answer can be as important as good search engine ranking.

Survey Feedback

Participants filled out the survey at the completion of the experiment and provided feedback on the writing, correctness, and usefulness of Tail Answers. Participants found Tail Answers useful (μ=5.8 / 7, σ=1.4), especially for directed, fact-oriented queries. For many of these queries, Tail Answers addressed the information need directly in the search results. A common theme in the responses was, "it told me exactly the right answer to my question." Participants were enthusiastic that a search engine could answer such unstructured queries. Most participants did not suspect that the Tail Answers were being human-edited.

While participants generally thought the answers were accurate (μ=5.3, σ=1.4) and well-written (μ=5.4, σ=1.4), relevance was a challenge. The crowd tended to create Tail Answers based on the most visible or understandable need in the query logs. When there were multiple information needs on a single URL, the answer would not cover all queries. For example, the only query with clear intent about the Phoenix Municipal Court asked about the court's phone number, so the answer was built around the phone number. However, that answer did not completely address more general queries like *phoenix municipal court*. In other cases, participants pointed out that the Tail Answer covered the high-level concept but did not have enough detail to fully satisfy their information need. In the future, we believe that it will be important to better target queries either by using the crowd to filter the set of trigger queries, or by A/B testing and measuring click cannibalization [7].

Some participants trusted Tail Answers implicitly, and others wanted more information about sources. Because Tail Answers look like they are endorsed by the search engine, we are particularly sensitive to accuracy and trust.

Generally, participants felt that Tail Answers were concise and well-written. We view this as a success, because extractions in earlier iterations on Tail Answers were much too long. The crowd-authored text had direct readability benefits: one participant remarked that Tail Answers avoided the ellipses and sentence fragments common in search result snippets. Participants occasionally requested richer structure, such as tables and images.

DISCUSSION

We have shown that search engines can cheaply and easily answer many of searchers' fact-finding queries directly. We presented evidence that Tail Answers can improve the user experience, often roughly as significantly as search result quality. Although search engines have used large-scale log data and paid judges to improve search result ranking, our findings suggest that there are new ways human effort can be applied to re-envision the search user experience.

Question Query	Algorithmic Result	
	Accepted	Rejected
What is a substitute for molasses?	brown sugar, honey	baking, recipes
What is the cost of mailing letters in the US?	44¢ to 39¢	12, 37¢, mail
Where is area code 559?	State of California	Selma CA, Clovis
How much nicotine is in a light cigarette?	Low density, 6mg	milligrams, 14mg

Table 5. Here, an automated question-answering system proposed Tail Answers and crowds filtered them.

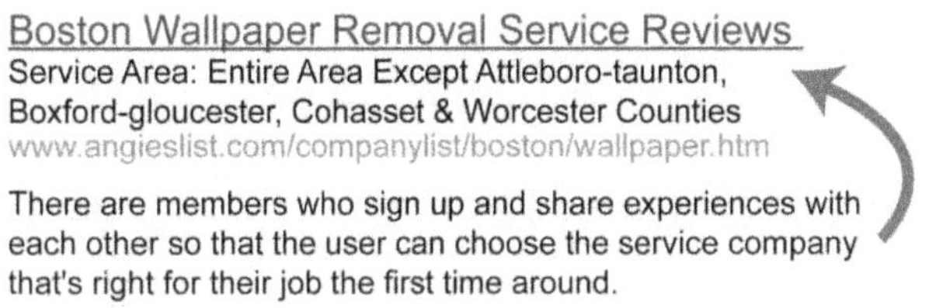

Figure 5. The Tail Answers crowd extraction algorithm (bottom) can suggest replacements for result snippets (top).

Challenges

Because Tail Answers are presented in a way that appears authoritative, they can potentially spread incorrect or misleading information without oversight. Even simple errors like triggering a Tail Answer on the wrong query can undermine people's trust in the search engine; our evaluation suggested that trimming the query trigger list is an important step for making Tail Answers deployable.

Tail Answers may be particularly tempting targets for search engine spam because of the authority they carry. With Tail Answers, a few members of the crowd would have significant direct control over search results by including advertisements or misinformation. However, a small group of trusted individuals could check for these problems and send answers back if there are problems.

Like result snippets, Tail Answers extract information from web pages and present that content to searchers. Unlike snippets, however, the intent behind the extraction is to fully address the searcher's information need, rather than to direct the searcher to the page. In this way, Tail Answers cannibalize page views. But without the underlying web content, the answers would not exist. To incentivize content providers, one option may be for the search engine to redirect a portion of the query's advertising revenue to pages that provide valuable content. Search engines will continue walking the line between attributing sources and highlighting the most useful information from that source.

Extensions: A.I., Snippets, and More Answer Types

Despite the challenges, we believe that the insight gained through Tail Answers can deeply extend the vocabulary of search interfaces. We have prototyped several extensions and share some early results in this section.

Artificial Intelligence-Driven Information Extraction

To extract content from web pages and turn that content into an answer, we used paid crowdsourcing. As

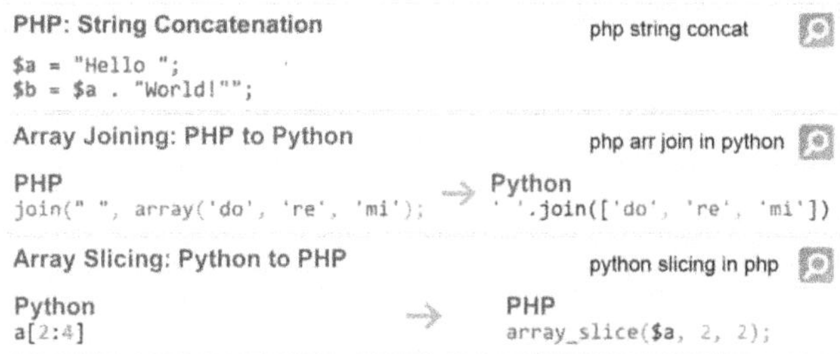

Figure 6. Code tutorial answers. Within a domain, Tail Answers like these can specialize their user interface.

technologies advance, this balance may shift: automatic systems may assume more or all of the responsibility. Our experiments with automatic systems such as AskMSR [5] and TextRunner [3] suggest that they produce too many poor guesses to be useful. However, a hybrid approach that uses the crowd to vet the answers provided by machine intelligence could be cheap and accurate. To explore this, we connected the AskMSR question-answering system to our dataset of Tail Answer queries, and asked it to generate candidate answers for the question queries. We then used the crowd to vote whether each answer was correct. Table 5 demonstrates early results, for example returning "brown sugar" as a substitute for molasses while filtering out highly-rated false positives like "baking". This vote was much cheaper than paying for extraction and proofreading.

Smart Snippets for Popular Queries

In addition to standalone answers, the crowd can help with snippets, the short page summaries that appear underneath the page title in search results. Instead of tail needs, popular queries are a good match for snippet improvement because they are seen by a large number of searchers. In particular, we focus on popular queries that have high click entropy (i.e., people click on many different results for the query). Queries like *wallpaper* have high click entropy because they have multiple meanings (e.g., computer desktop art versus home wall decoration), and searchers may not have enough information scent [16] in the snippets to make good choices. We can use the extraction routine from Tail Answers to find snippets for these sites. Figure 5 demonstrates the resulting improvements to a high-visibility search snippet for the query *wallpaper*.

New Classes of Answers

We have thus far explored short and list-style answers, but there are many more possible answer types that could be developed with our approach. For example, answers could be created to help users achieve high-level goals like creating a website or planning a vacation to Yosemite [11]. They could also summarize web content, automatically create answers for spiking queries or news stories, or even connect searchers with other users who might be able to help solve their information need [9]. To create more sophisticated answers, we expect to transition from generic crowd workers in Mechanical Turk to more expert workers like those found on oDesk. We could also give other searchers the ability to edit the answer, much like

Wikipedia. The amount of effort and cost could be applied differentially, based on potential gain, with more invested in more popular or high impact information needs.

Because Tail Answers are general-purpose, it is impossible to provide custom user interfaces. However, if we focus on a particular set of information needs, we can build special user interfaces and data extraction requirements. Figure 6 shows example answers we have built for translating commands between programming languages, for example understanding how to translate PHP's array join syntax into Python. We began with a list of programming primitives in Python, then asked workers to volunteer the mapping into PHP. With this mapping, the Tail Answers can return results for functions in either language, as well as translate between the languages, with a specially designed interface.

Destination probability can also help identify new kinds of answers. For example, pages with telephone area codes tended to have high destination probability. Armed with this information, search engines might start building answers specifically for area code queries.

CONCLUSION

Search engines increasingly aim to return information rather than links. Search companies devote significant resources to build a small number of inline answers for topics like weather and movies. Unfortunately, most information needs are unlikely to ever trigger answers. In response, we have introduced Tail Answers: succinct inline search results for less frequent and extremely varied information needs. To build Tail Answers, we draw on the aggregate knowledge of thousands of web users. We mine large-scale query logs for pages that tend to end search sessions, select candidates where searchers have used information key terms like question words, and use paid crowds to remove candidates that cannot be answered succinctly. Finally, crowds extract the information from the web page, edit it, and title it. Our evaluation of Tail Answers demonstrates that they can significantly improve the search user experience and searchers' ability to find the information they are looking for without navigating to an external web page. We demonstrate the generalizability of these techniques by prototyping ways they could be used to improve other aspects of the search engine interface.

REFERENCES

1. Adar, E., Teevan, J., Dumais, S.T., and Elsas, J.L. The web changes everything. *Proc. WSDM '09*, (2009).
2. Agichtein, E., Lawrence, S., and Gravano, L. Learning to find answers to questions on the Web. *ACM TOIS 4*, 2 (2004), 129-162.
3. Banko, M., Cafarella, M.J., Soderland, S., Broadhead, M., and Etzioni, O. Open information extraction for the web. *IJCAI '072*, University of Washington (2007).
4. Bernstein, M.S., Little, G., Miller, R.C., et al. Soylent: A Word Processor with a Crowd Inside. *Proc. UIST '10*, (2010).
5. Brill, E., Dumais, S., and Banko, M. An analysis of the AskMSR question-answering system. *Proc. EMNLP '02*, (2002).
6. Broder, A. A taxonomy of web search. *ACM SIGIR Forum 36*, 2 (2002), 3.
7. Chilton, L.B. and Teevan, J. Addressing people's information needs directly in a web search result page. *Proc. WWW '11*, (2011).
8. Cutrell, E. and Guan, Z. What are you looking for?: an eye-tracking study of information usage in web search. *Proc. CHI '07*, (2007).
9. Horowitz, D. and Kamvar, S.D. The anatomy of a large-scale social search engine. *Proc. WWW '10*, (2010).
10. Kellar, M., Watters, C., and Shepherd, M. A field study characterizing Web-based information-seeking tasks. *JASIST 58*, 7 (2007), 999-1018.
11. Law, E. and Zhang, H. Towards Large-Scale Collaborative Planning: Answering High-Level Search Queries Using Human Computation. *Proc. AAAI '11*, (2011).
12. Le, J., Edmonds, A., Hester, V., and Biewald, L. Ensuring quality in crowdsourced search relevance evaluation. *Proc. SIGIR '10 Workshop on Crowdsourcing for Search Evaluation*, (2010).
13. Li, J., Huffman, S., and Tokuda, A. Good abandonment in mobile and PC internet search. *Proc. SIGIR '09*, (2009).
14. Lin, J. An exploration of the principles underlying redundancy-based factoid question answering. *ACM TOIS 25*, 2 (2007).
15. Little, G., Chilton, L., Goldman, M., and Miller, R.C. Exploring iterative and parallel human computation processes. *Proc. HCOMP '10*, (2010).
16. Pirolli, P. *Information foraging theory: adaptive interaction with information.* Oxford Press, 2007.
17. Stamou, S. and Efthimiadis, E.N. Queries without clicks: Successful or failed searches. *Proc. SIGIR '09 Wkshp on the Future of IR Evaluation*, (2009).
18. Suchanek, F.M., Kasneci, G., and Weikum, G. YAGO : A Core of Semantic Knowledge Unifying Wikipedia and WordNet. *WWW '07*, (2007).
19. Teevan, J., Liebling, D.J., and Ravichandran Geetha, G. Understanding and predicting personal navigation. *Proc. WSDM '11*, (2011).
20. White, R.W., Bilenko, M., and Cucerzan, S. Studying the use of popular destinations to enhance web search interaction. *Proc. SIGIR '07*, (2007).

Distributed Sensemaking: Improving Sensemaking by Leveraging the Efforts of Previous Users

Kristie Fisher[1,2], Scott Counts[1], Aniket Kittur[3]

[1]Microsoft, [2]Microsoft Research
1 Microsoft Way
Redmond, WA 98052 USA
{kfisher, counts}@microsoft.com

[3]Carnegie Mellon University
5000 Forbes Ave
Pittsburgh, PA 15213
nkittur@cs.cmu.edu

ABSTRACT
We examine the possibility of *distributed* sensemaking: improving a user's sensemaking by leveraging previous users' work without those users directly collaborating or even knowing one another. We asked users to engage in sensemaking by organizing and annotating web search results into "knowledge maps," either with or without previous users' maps to work from. We also recorded gaze patterns as users examined others' knowledge maps. Our findings show the conditions under which distributed sensemaking can improve sensemaking quality; that a user's sensemaking process is readily apparent to a subsequent user via a knowledge map; and that the organization of content was more useful to subsequent users than the content itself, especially when those users had differing goals. We discuss the role distributed sensemaking can play in schema induction by helping users make a mental model of an information space and make recommendations for new tool and system development.

Author Keywords
Sensemaking, search, collaboration, knowledge mapping.

ACM Classification Keywords
H.5.m [Information interfaces and presentation (e.g., HCI)]: Miscellaneous;

INTRODUCTION
A large majority of people engage in information seeking behaviors online: 81% of online adults research products; 68% make travel reservations; 89% use search engines; 75% get health information; 71% buy something online[1]. Beyond simply seeking information, people engage in *sensemaking:* constructing a mental representation of interrelated pieces of information relevant to accomplishing a goal, such as planning a vacation, planting a garden, or understanding a current news event [26, 30].

In most cases, after each sensemaking episode in which an individual develops a useful mental representation of an information space for herself, her work is essentially lost, benefiting no one else[2]. Furthermore, if asked today, she may have forgotten much of what she spent so much time learning in the first place. With users spending at least a third of their time online finding and gathering information [15], usefully capturing such efforts represents a significant opportunity. In this paper we explore this possibility by examining the viability of *distributed* sensemaking in the context of web search. We use the term distributed sensemaking here to refer to an iterative process in which users save and organize their own sensemaking efforts, which are then available to subsequent users with whom they are neither collaborating nor communicating, and may not even know.

At its best, distributed sensemaking could help convey the information, evidence, judgments, relations and perspectives that individuals process during sensemaking, increasing the depth and/or speed for each subsequent information seeker. On the other hand, the costs of integrating information from others may be prohibitive, or may lead to biases or gaps otherwise avoided, especially if the goals or expertise of the initial and subsequent users differ. The focus of this paper is on addressing the questions of whether, and in what ways, this type of sensemaking actually helps users.

Potential Advantages
Potential benefits of distributed sensemaking include: 1) saving the user time and/or effort during sensemaking, 2) higher quality sensemaking within a given amount of time, and 3) compensating for a user's lack of knowledge on a given sensemaking topic.

These benefits could be accomplished in two ways. First, having access to the output of other users' sensemaking efforts could lead to more content and/or more relevant content. Second, the user could leverage the way another

[2] Reviews do incorporate some of this, but only for the things people actually buy, and also is highly biased towards those with either very positive or negative experiences [12].

user has *organized* content for a particular topic. That is, even if the content itself is not ideally tailored to the user, perhaps the content categories or the notes the previous user included could help the user to abstract a "schema" or mental model of the information space she is trying to make sense of. Studies from cognitive psychology suggest that people form such models through the induction of relational schemas which explicate the relationships between items [8, 13]. These theories suggest an important distinction between the structure of the content and the content itself, with structure being especially important for learning and generalization. For example, novice problem solvers are likely to focus on surface similarities between problems, while experts focus on deep structural similarities [4].

Thus helping users gain expertise in an area may require not only providing them with appropriate content, but also supporting their development of an organizational schema or mental model. This schema could facilitate the user's search for content that is relevant by helping prioritize and focus information gathering. In the context of distributed sensemaking, users would leverage schemas created, iterated, and passed on by previous users, generating a "virtuous cycle" of increasing ease and quality of sensemaking.

Potential Disadvantages

Distributed sensemaking might fail to facilitate, or even hinder, sensemaking. First, for a given sensemaking topic two users are likely to have different preferences, different levels of expertise, unique needs, and so on. This could render the content and its organization irrelevant or confusing to subsequent users. Starting from the output of someone else's sensemaking would make the task *more* effortful and more time-consuming for the user, because she would first have to make sense of the previous person's efforts before engaging in her own sensemaking. This raises a number of questions regarding the cost of distributed sensemaking. How quickly and accurately can a user parse the output of someone else's sensemaking? How does the overhead of figuring out that user's sensemaking process balance again the benefit of leveraging their effort? As subsequent users continue to iterate a sensemaking task, how is this cost-benefit ratio changed?

RELATED WORK

Understanding and improving sensemaking has become a prominent topic of HCI research. Computational models have been developed that characterize how people seek out and determine the relevance of information they find on the web (i.e., SNIF-ACT & ACT-IF; see [23] for a review). As described below, several prototype systems have also been developed to assist individual users with sensemaking by providing an organizational space for them to save and annotate information and by incorporating machine learning algorithms to help with information classification.

Tools for Sensemaking

An early example of such a tool was SenseMaker [2], which emphasized the need for interfaces that could support the organization and exploration of diverse sources of information at different "levels of granularity." More recently, SSIGS [25] allowed a user to create a visual representation of online information in the form of a "knowledge tree" in a web browser side-bar. ScratchPad [11] allowed users to take and arrange "snapshots" of web content akin to visual bookmarks. Entity Workspace [3] was created to support sensemaking in the medical profession by integrating search engine capabilities with document reading and note taking.

Collaborative Search & Sensemaking

Research and tool development in *collaborative* sensemaking aims to support groups of two or more people explicitly working together on web-based sensemaking tasks. Tools such as SearchTogether help users better accomplish goals such as shopping and travel planning [18]. Social interactions and collaboration can also shape an individual's internet search behaviors even when the users are not engaging in synchronous, joint web searching [6].

This collaborative or social component of search and sensemaking is likely to become even more relevant in the future with the explosion in popularity of online social networking, and the availability of the web on a growing number of hand-held devices. Accordingly, several efforts have been made to develop tools and systems to support collaborative search and sensemaking, both when people are working together in time and space [1, 19, 21], and when they are collaborating remotely [14].

Distributed and Iterated Information Organization

The previous work on collaborative search and sensemaking typically has supported groups of users explicitly collaborating towards a common goal, at least at some level [6, 14, 22]. The group of internet users at large is a vastly bigger set of people to draw on for sensemaking assistance. Can individuals benefit from the sensemaking of previous users, even those they don't know? Or, conversely, would exposure to someone else's efforts induce more cost than benefit? Systems like Wikipedia and delicious provide proofs of concept that distributed effort can generate high quality content [9] and useful information organizations [10]. These systems often involve coordination among contributors, as in Wikipedia, or are less task-focused, in the case of social bookmarking. Research on Mechanical Turk [17] shows that iterated effort by a group of people unknown to one another can solve fairly difficult tasks such as decoding text in a blurred image. Together, the systems and research around Wikipedia, social bookmarking, and crowd sourcing suggest that users engaged in sensemaking tasks on the web may benefit from the sensemaking efforts of other users previously engaged in a similar sensemaking task.

RESEARCH STUDY

To study the iterative process of distributed sensemaking, we needed a common artifact that participants could jointly author. For this we turned to digital knowledge maps. Digital knowledge maps are one way to create an "external representation" of sensemaking, and having such a representation has been recommended by several other researchers [14, 28, 29]. We will use the term "knowledge map" to refer to a visual representation of the output of a sensemaking task. That is, knowledge maps consist of information items and a representation of how those items are related.

We observed the process and outcome of sensemaking when users created knowledge maps with and without previous users' knowledge maps to build from. We also asked users to complete detailed surveys about their experience, and analyzed looking patterns as users examined knowledge maps created by other users. Together these measures bear on the "value proposition" of distributed sensemaking: that the process and outcome of sensemaking for any given user is improved by leveraging the efforts of previous users.

Knowledge Map Pilot

We first conducted a pilot study to test the viability and usefulness of this approach using a low-fidelity prototype. A low-fidelity approach helps to ensure that the results would not be constrained by existing technological factors, such as how specific tools influence the ease of annotation or organization of information. It also minimizes training and more closely captures participants' thought processes, though it has drawbacks such as making it difficult to quantify and compare participants' work and to scale up to a larger sample. As such our goal with this pilot was to determine the kind of functionality a tool would need to support for a larger study on distributed sensemaking, and to ascertain early on the likely viability of such a study.

In the pilot study, participants were asked to engage in the sensemaking task of selecting an appropriate venue for a party from a variety of local venues. To generate the source materials, we collected and printed out approximately 200 pieces of evidence from the web, including reviews, menus, maps, photos, and general information, which were pasted onto card stock. We then provided participants with a large whiteboard placed horizontally on a table, annotation tools such as post-it notes and markers, and a folder with all of the evidence. Additional participants, who were unknown to the initial users, were brought in for each initial map, and completed the same task but starting with the end state of the first participant's workspace. During the experiment we employed a think-aloud protocol (shown to provide information about participants' working memory contents without affecting them; [5, 20]), and also captured images of their workspace every few minutes. Results of the pilot were promising, as subsequent participants reported finding the maps and annotations of the first participants useful. One example of the iterative construction process between participants is shown in Figure 1. All participants used structured spatial layouts, often constructing grids with competitors on one axis and features to compare them on another axis. Participants also added annotations, using sticky notes on specific evidence or writing comments on the whiteboard relating to dimensions or competitors. Some interesting emergent themes are discussed below:

Provenance. We were initially concerned that users would either find the organization and annotations of others useless and simply start over, or would base their decisions on the results of the previous participant without examining the evidence for themselves, but neither turned out to be true. Although most participants used others' organizational schemas, all also explored provenance data: *why* someone made an annotation, such as adding stickies indicating items as particularly helpful or organizing items in certain ways. This highlights the importance of enabling users to make informed risk/reward decisions about using the work of others (for example by enabling users to directly view underlying evidence). Showing such provenance information has been shown to have significant impact on trust in other user-generated content systems [7, 16, 24, 27].

Collaborative dimension discovery. Participants learned not only about the features of venues that others found important but also about the dimensions that others found useful for evaluating those features. For example, one participant created a column for the dimension "type of music" which was later found to be useful and adopted by future participants who had not initially thought of it.

Externalization of prior knowledge. We also found evidence that capturing participants' prior knowledge could be extremely helpful. For example, one participant who was native to the area annotated maps with sticky notes that indicated whether or not the venue was on the more desirable side of a river in town. This information was important because while the farther side of the river was much less desirable than the closer side, it appeared essentially equivalent in terms of distance on the map.

Overall, the results of the pilot study were promising in suggesting that spatial landscapes of information developed by one person could be useful for others and that simple tools supporting spatial layouts could be used to further investigate distributed sensemaking. We also found evidence that people not only found the content of others' maps useful, but potentially more useful were the organization and relations between competitors and dimensions. This suggests that "knowledge maps" could provide an important function in promoting the development of rich mental schemas. We further examine these issues through a larger study using digital knowledge maps.

User Study

Building from the results of the pilot study, a more in-depth user study was conducted in order to better quantify the

	This participant (P2) started with the organization and annotations of the previous participant (P1). P1 had organized the information with the rows corresponding to the top four venues, with summaries (orange text) such as "good food" or "good snacks, good service, decent music", but with idiosyncratic columns.
	P2 in the process of reorganizing the information landscape according to his own mental model. The landscape resulted in clearly structured columns, differentiating benefits for each venue listed on the left, and annotations on post-it notes for some of the evidence.
	After P2 was finished, P3 was brought in to do the same task. This figure shows the final results of P3's landscape, which has changed very little from P2's landscape, suggesting the utility of P2's landscape (and confirmed by post-experiment questioning).

Figure 1. Pictures from the pilot experiment. Participants iteratively constructed a "knowledge map" for the sensemaking task of selecting a venue for a party.

effects of distributed sensemaking. The user study consisted of two phases. The primary purpose of the first phase was to assemble a collection of knowledge maps that would be used by people in the second phase. In the second phase, we analyzed users' sensemaking output under different conditions of distributed sensemaking and we tracked their eye movements while they examined other users' knowledge maps.

Phase 1: Knowledge Map Creation & Iteration

To create knowledge maps in this phase of the study, participants were first asked to use a search engine to find resources on the web that were related to one of the following six sensemaking topics:

1. Planning a multi-day trip to a local national park.
2. Exploring options for starting a vegetable garden at your home.
3. Planning a small gala with food and entertainment for your work team (approx. 30 people).
4. Entertaining friends from out-of-town for the weekend with tourist activities, etc.
5. Exploring options for attending a local professional sporting event.
6. Finding resources for do-it-yourself kitchen remodeling.

After finding useful web content, participants used a screen capture tool to capture images of relevant search results, including image, video and any other type of search result. Thus the items making up our sensemaking knowledge maps were snips of web search results. Participants pasted the screen capture images onto a PowerPoint slide and organized them in whatever way most the "made sense" to them.

This method enabled us to build on our pilot by incorporating a greater variety of tasks, as well as by using a digital environment that supported flexibility for organizing and annotating content. Starting with a blank PowerPoint slide meant that participants were able to organize information in a way that was largely free of system constraints. PowerPoint allowed participants to spatially position items in any 2-dimenstional layout, size items, connect them with lines and arrows, add labels and notes, color-code, and so on. Thus this approach provided a low-effort way for participants to externalize their mental model of how relevant pieces of information were related to one another and to the sensemaking goal. As subsequent participants iterated on these knowledge maps, they were able to modify them with relative ease.

Twelve participants from our company (2 female), with an average age of 35.58 (*SD* = 8.16) were each asked to create knowledge maps using the method described above. Participants were recruited via internal e-mail solicitation, and they participated in the study by performing the task at their own workstation and then e-mailing us their resulting knowledge maps.

Three participants each created two knowledge maps, with the result being a set of six knowledge maps, one for each of the six sensemaking topics. Participants were asked to keep track of how much time they spent creating each map, taking no more than 20 minutes. They also completed a survey about the knowledge map they created and their experience in the task. These maps were then distributed to three subsequent users who were told specifically to start with the provided map and add, delete, change, or move as much or as little of the content from the previous user as they desired.

This process was then repeated for a second iteration group and then a final iteration group, resulting in a knowledge map for each topic that had been created with the input of four users. The knowledge maps participants created in each round of iteration were evaluated and compared to the initial maps they were given in order to track what had and had not changed during each round.

One notable limitation is that the search results snips used to build knowledge maps were not live, which severely impairs the ability of a subsequent user to evaluate and use them. To reduce this problem, we told users to only include search result snips and not snips of pieces of a web page, so that subsequent participants could see both a preview of the content of the website visited by the other user, as well as the web address in case they wanted to visit the site themselves.

Phase 2: Distributed Sensemaking & Eye-tracking

The next phase of the study was the primary investigation. 21 participants (5 female), all members of our company and with an average age of 37.19 (*SD* = 10.06) were recruited via internal e-mail.

Value of Iteration for Sensemaking Participants first created knowledge maps for three different topics, one in each of three conditions: 1) Starting from a "blank slate" with no access to another user's map (Solo Condition), 2) Building from one of the maps created in Phase 1 by a single other user (Other Condition), and 3) Building from one of the maps that had been iterated in Phase 1 by four other users (Iterated Condition). This allowed us to test for benefits of previous sensemaking: how did the input of a single user or of multiple previous users impact sensemaking in comparison to sensemaking "from scratch"?

The order in which they completed the three tasks was counter-balanced across participants. When completing the task in the Other and Iterated conditions the participants were told simply that the knowledge maps had been "created by one other user," and "had been created with the input of several users over time," respectively. In each case, they were told to work from the knowledge map they had been given, changing as little or as much as they would like in order to create their own knowledge map for the given topic. Participants were given a time limit of 20 minutes to complete each task, but most did not choose to use all of the allotted time. Participants completed a detailed survey to evaluate their experience in each of the three conditions, and the knowledge maps they created were evaluated and compared to the knowledge maps that they had been given.

Parsing the Sensemaking of Others Participants were then shown two additional knowledge maps, each on a different topic. They were not told which sensemaking topic had been given to the user who created the map, and they were not told that one map had only been created by one user and that the other map had been iterated on by several users. Participants' task was to examine the map and try to figure out what it was about in order to answer some questions about it. They were told to look at the map for as much or as little time as necessary. While participants examined each map, we recorded their eye movements. To do this we used a Tobii X50 eye tracker and the accompanying Tobii Studio software. The Tobii system records eye position at 40ms intervals and defines a fixation as he maintaining of eye position for 100ms. For our analyses, total fixation time was summed for pre-defined regions of the screen containing different types of content. This process allowed us to examine how much total time participants needed to accurately assess what the knowledge map was about and to determine what aspects of the knowledge map participants paid the most attention to when trying to understand it. Recall that the effort required to make sense of another person's map represents a potential downside of distributed sensemaking. Comparing this process across maps made by a single other person versus those that were iterated provided a more nuanced picture, with the possibility that iteration mitigates the risk of the organization of any single other user being difficult to understand.

Knowledge maps and sensemaking topics were counter-balanced across participants. At the end of the study, we conducted informal interviews with each participant, and they were permitted to give additional open-ended feedback about the viability of a distributed sensemaking system and their ideas and preferences for specific tools and features.

RESULTS

Properties of Created & Iterated Knowledge Maps

The knowledge maps created by participants in the first phase of the study had some interesting consistencies, most notably in how they were organized. The most popular way of organizing content was to create small groupings of content and give a text label to each group (83% of all maps created across all four rounds of creation and iteration), as shown in Figure 2. Furthermore, the way a map was organized tended to be quite stable over the rounds of iteration. For the first round of iteration, four out of the six topic maps maintained their original organizational structure. The only two maps whose organizational structure was changed started out as being a disorganized "collage" or a hybrid structure (groups and networks) and ended up being transformed into a group and label structure. In the second and third rounds of iteration, five out of the six maps maintained their group structure. We find this result surprising given that participants were free to choose any 2-dimensional organizational structure. Also, in sensemaking tools developed by previous researchers [11, 26], a network or hierarchy was the only type of organizational structure available to users, but neither of those was spontaneously used by our participants.

The typical look and content of the knowledge maps were as follows. The maps on average, across creation and iterations, contained about 13 search result snips (M = 12.67, SD = 5.00) with a range from six to 25 items. When these items were organized into groups, there tended to be between four and five on average (M = 4.67, SD = 2.73). When iterating on others' knowledge maps, participants added about six new items on average (M = 6.04, SD = 5.62), with a range of zero to 24 items. Similarly, participants deleted about six items on average (M = 5.88, SD = 5.62), with a range of zero to 17. Participants also tended to add and delete organizational groups of items with an equivalent rate (add: M = 2.17 groups, SD = 2.22; delete: M = 1.88 groups, SD = 2.33).

Potential Advantages & Disadvantages

Descriptive statistics for all of the analyses described below are in Table 1 (survey data) and Table 2 (eye tracking data). Unless stated otherwise, for all comparisons described below, ANOVAs with planned comparisons (with Bonferroni correction) were used to compare means when

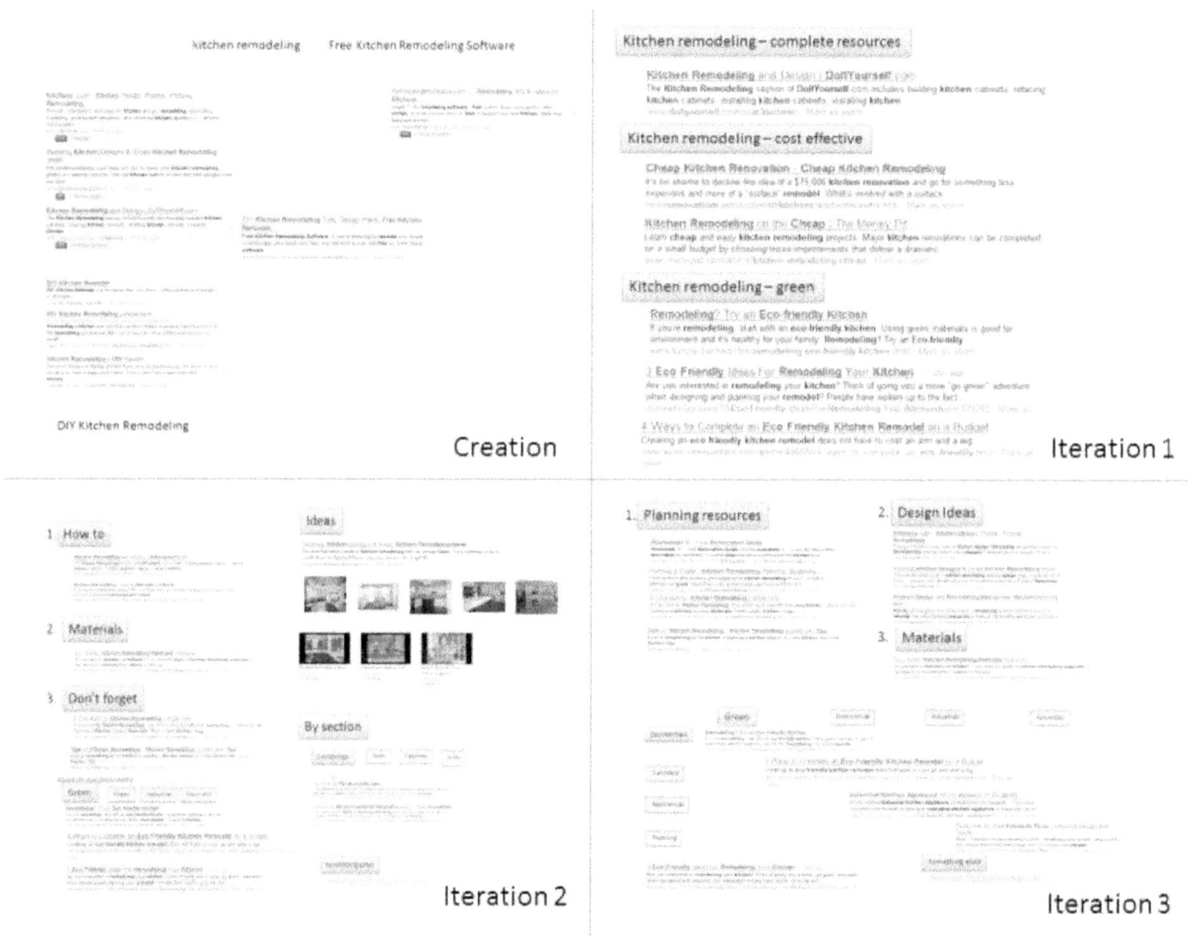

Figure 2. Example of a "knowledge map" that was created and then iterated on over time by three subsequent users. The topic of the map was *Exploring options for "do it yourself" kitchen remodeling.* The first user found some relevant resources and made an attempt to start organizing them into groups, but the second user was able to greatly improve on the organization. The third user expanded on the organizational groupings, adding a numbered step-by-step process for how to sort through the resources. The final user changed little of the organizational structure, and tried to synthesize it. The fourth person also started building an arrangement of rows and columns based on labels from the third user in order to provide a resource for many different combinations of options reflecting different needs (e.g., "cost effective," "industrial"). Note: for space reasons, we use this example to highlight schema emergence through iteration, with smaller text not meant to be readable.

Map Creation Task (Distributed Sensemaking)						
	Solo		Other		Iterated	
	M	*SD*	*M*	*SD*	*M*	*SD*
Time to Create Map (minutes)	15.52	3.49	14.33	3.95	13.67	4.52
Rating of Cognitive Effort for Creation	4.14	1.42	3.71	1.45	3.24	1.37
Self-rated Map Quality	4.90	1.26	4.29	1.19	5.48	1.12
Helpfulness of Other Users' Maps	-	-	3.57	1.86	4.86	1.85
Self-rated Helpfulness to Others	4.90	1.26	4.74	0.86	5.62	0.97
Map Examination (Eye-tracking)						
	Other		Iterated			
	M	*SD*	*M*	*SD*		
Map Clarity	4.19	2.09	6.24	0.89		
Understanding Author Intent	4.67	1.46	5.95	0.67		
Likelihood of Creating a Similar Map Organization	2.95	1.75	5.19	1.17		
Likelihood of Creating a Map with Same Content	4.76	1.00	5.67	1.02		

Table 1. Descriptive statistics for survey and creation time data for the two tasks in Phase 2 of the study. For all survey items, participants used 1-7 rating scales, with 1 representing the negative valence (e.g., "High effort," "Very unclear") and 7 representing the positive valence (e.g., "Low Effort," "Very clear").

there were three conditions of interest for a measure, and dependent t-tests were used when there were two conditions. Note that the results do not change when data are analyzed with non-parametric tests.

Time and Effort

Turning to results of the second phase of the study, people spent the most time creating a knowledge map in the Solo Condition and the least time creating a knowledge map in the Iterated Condition. However, the difference among these three conditions was not statistically significant, $F(2, 40) = 2.10$, $p = .14$. A similar pattern was observed for users' ratings of the "cognitive effort" that creating a knowledge map required in each condition. On a scale of 1 (very low effort) to 7 (lots of effort), the average rating for the Solo Condition suggests it was neither very easy nor very difficult. Effort in the Other and Iterated conditions were rated as being somewhat less effortful, but the ratings in these three conditions were not statistically different from each other, $F(2, 40) = 2.20$, $p = .12$. A direct comparison between the Solo and Iterated conditions was borderline significant, $t(20) = 2.38$, $p = .054$. Thus, while the effects are in the direction of distributed sensemaking being beneficial, we cannot draw conclusions about time and effort savings, with the exception of a trend-level reduction in effort when compared to starting from scratch. We note that particularly for time spent, the variance was high and therefore these effects may only be teased out with considerably greater numbers of subjects.

Quality and Helpfulness

Though time spent was similar across conditions, what users were able to accomplish within that period of time appears to be of higher quality and greater use when working with the iterated knowledge maps. Using a scale of 1 (low quality) to 7 (high quality), participants rated the quality of the maps they created the highest in the Iterated Condition, followed by the Solo Condition, and lastly the Other Condition. These quality ratings were significantly different from one another, $F(2, 40) = 5.68$, $p = .007$, and paired contrasts with a Bonferroni correction revealed a significant difference between Other and Iterated, $p = .005$. Participants felt *their own* sensemaking superior when starting with content organized and iterated on by multiple previous participants.

Participants also rated the knowledge maps of others in the Iterated Condition as being significantly more helpful than those in the Other Condition, $t(20) = 2.38$, $p = .027$. Furthermore, participants were asked to rate how helpful they thought the knowledge map would be to another user if that user was asked to work from the knowledge map in a sensemaking task for the same topic. Again, participants thought their map would be most helpful to others when they had constructed it in the Iterated Condition, followed by the Solo Condition, and lastly the Other Condition.

Value of Organization

We asked participants to describe *why* they rated the knowledge maps given to them in the Other and Iterated conditions as helpful or not helpful. In the Other condition, four of the participants who rated the map helpful (i.e., greater than 4 on the rating scale) mentioned the quality of the organization as the primary reason for their rating, while only one person mentioned the content. For the Iterated Condition, nine people who rated the map as helpful cited organization of the map versus three due to content. Most of the reasons cited when the map was rated un-helpful were due to the content the map contained (5 people) rather than the organization of the map (1 person). Some quotes from this free-form section of the survey that highlight the importance of well-organized content over the content itself are listed below:

- *Although I deleted 50% of what was on the other knowledge map, it gave me some ideas right away on where to look and which factors or questions I should consider during my search.*
- *Helpful only because there were groupings of ideas that I used to form my ideas for what would be useful.*
- *I liked the structure - it was helpful things to see the thought process laid out.*

Understanding the Sensemaking of Others

To further probe the idea that structure was most helpful to subsequent users, we turn to results of the eye-tracking portion of the study. Recall that we tracked eye movements of participants as they read knowledge maps created by previous participants (see Figure 3). The purpose of this task was to understand how, and how well, participants could make sense of other people's sensemaking activities. We focus on the comparison between working with knowledge maps generated by a single other person versus those iterated by four people.

Participants looked for a roughly equal amount of time at both the Other knowledge map and the Iterated knowledge map; the difference was not significantly different, $t(20) = 1.03$, $p = .32$. They were also highly accurate in both conditions at discerning the topic of the knowledge map, though slightly more so in the Iterated condition (Other: 81% correct, 5% close, 14% incorrect; Iterated: 86% correct, 14% close); the difference in performance proportions was in the expected direction, but not significant, as revealed by a chi-square homogeneity of proportions test, $X^2(2, N = 21) = 0.82$, $p = .66$.

Diving in deeper, we examined looking time across different aspects of the knowledge maps. Specifically we compared time spent looking at content (the *links* in the search results, and content *boxes* containing clusters of results, such as groups of images) versus organizational elements like *labels*. Looking times for links, labels ($M = 6.52$, $SD = 6.33$), and boxes ($M = 6.80$, $SD = 5.57$) are not significantly different from one another for Iterated maps, $F(2, 36) = .44$, $p = .65$. However, there is a significant difference among looking times for links, labels, and boxes for the knowledge maps in the Other condition, with links looked at considerably longer than organizational elements, $F(2, 26) = 6.38$, $p = .006$. From this we infer that iteration allows a schema to emerge, reducing visual focus on content elements (links).

After viewing each knowledge map, participants completed a survey. Participants were asked whether it was clear how the items in the map were related to one another (rated from 1 – not clear, to 7 – very clear), and they rated the Iterated maps as being significantly more clear than the Other maps, $t(20) = 4.22$, $p < .001$. Participants also said that they could more easily understand what the author was thinking in the Iterated maps compared to the Other maps, $t(20) = 3.29$, $p = .004$.

Participants were also asked to rate how likely they would be to create a similar map if they were given the same topic (1 – not at all likely to 7 – very likely). Participants said that they would be much more likely to *organize* content in the same way that the Iterated maps were organized relative to the Other maps, $t(20) = 4.03$, $p = .001$. They also said that they would be more likely to include the same content as the Iterated map compared to the Other map, $t(20) = 3.10$, $p = .006$, though this difference was a bit smaller than that for organization.

DISCUSSION

We examined the process of distributed sensemaking in which participants iteratively engaged in a sensemaking task using the results of others' work. Overall we found statistically significant increases in self-rated quality and helpfulness, and a modest reduction in effort, when using iterated maps with no corresponding increases in time spent. Our eye tracking data, rating data, and other qualitative feedback suggest that these gains were due to the accumulation of an organizational framework, or schema, across users and over the rounds of iteration. While the usefulness of the content often changed from person to person, the structure of that content remained consistent and useful. For example, two people looking to start a garden may live in different cities, or one in the country and the other in the city, so specific content such as which seeds to plant will change, but they both benefit from the content dimensions of "design ideas", "how to", and so on. That this structure did not start to emerge until a map had been iterated once (see Figure 2) speaks to the value of building on others' work: this organizational structure is not necessarily something a person is going to think of in an initial 15 minutes of sensemaking.

Our survey results also indicated that many users would simply prefer to start from scratch rather than with the initial content collection of a single other user. A fruitful area for future research may be exploring how systems for distributed sensemaking can encourage users to get over the hump of the initial round of iteration. However, despite this "first iteration hump", it did not appear difficult for users to parse the meaning of another person's knowledge map, even when the content and/or organization of this knowledge map were less than ideal. Specifically, we found in the case of knowledge maps created by just a single user,

	Other		Iterated	
	M	*SD*	*M*	*SD*
Total	30.26	17.10	27.02	12.56
Links	15.07	12.27	8.36	6.55
Labels	5.95	3.18	6.52	6.33
Boxes	5.95	5.91	6.80	5.57

Table 2. Descriptive statistics for looking time data (in secs) from the Map Examination (eye-tracking) task.

participants could make an accurate assessment of that user's information goal in a short amount of time.

Importantly, these findings provide evidence that people do not have to collaborate directly in order to help one another make sense of information, nor even know each other. If one user can pass along the "structure" or "schema" of their thought process with respect to a topic—even by simply providing some meaningful sub-topics helpful in organizing relevant information—it can facilitate the sensemaking process of a subsequent user. Our eye tracking results also showed that with further iteration on knowledge maps, users shift to using a greater balance of structural dimensions versus content dimensions. As such they provide an interesting relation to the Chi et al. [4] findings discussed earlier in which the transition from novice to expert was accompanied by a shift in focus from surface to structural features. In the case of distributed sensemaking, the expertise can be thought of as embodied in the artifact itself, which develops deeper and more useful structural organization with further iteration.

The impact and generalizability of our results should be considered in light of the limitations inherent in our study design. First, the knowledge map creation procedure constrained behavior to some extent (e.g., that people had to use a single power point slide). Second, our participant sample could arguably be considered "experts" in sensemaking with digital information, as they were employees at a technology company (though again we point to the diversity in job descriptions). Finally, and perhaps most importantly, we were only able to put knowledge maps through a few stages of iteration. The effects of distributed sensemaking over tens to hundreds of iterations are left to future research.

In summary, we find both promise and challenge in the distributed sensemaking approach. Iteration on distributed knowledge maps can lead to greater improvements in quality and usefulness in a given amount of time than when starting from scratch, even when individuals are working for themselves and not for others. These benefits occurred with only four rounds of iteration and a simple interface not optimized for knowledge maps; exploring new interfaces for constructing knowledge maps and greater iterations are important future work. Furthermore, benefits due to greater structure and organization of the maps transferred across individuals even when the content of the maps did not, demonstrating the value of the approach across differences in contexts, goals, and expertise.

However, we also found challenges in first iteration adoption of knowledge maps, with many users preferring to start from scratch than to start with a map that has not been iterated on. Importantly, the system must encourage users to iterate beyond the initial creation, as significant improvements in quality and helpfulness were seen in the fully iterated knowledge maps. Approaches to doing so include both machine methods, such as automatic alignment of first-round knowledge maps to produce maps that look more like iterated maps; as well as human methods, such as leveraging paid crowds to bootstrap the system or enforcing constraints such as requiring users to integrate some first-round maps in order to benefit from iterated ones.

CONCLUSION

In this paper we examined the idea of distributed sensemaking, in which users who are unknown to one another iteratively engage in a web search-based sensemaking task. This form of sensemaking could harness effort that today is lost when users work in isolation. We

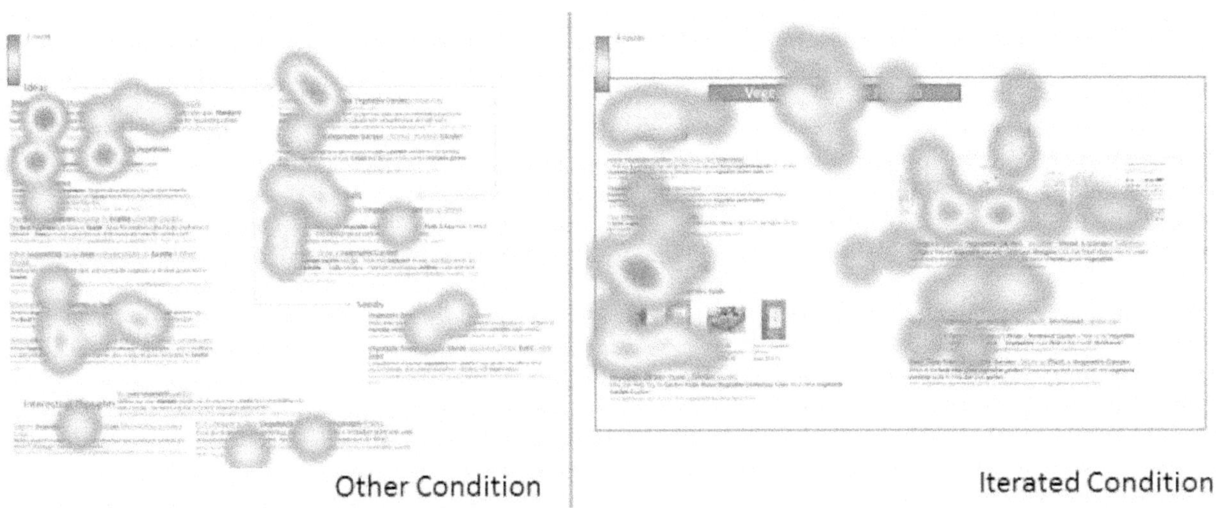

Figure 3. Example eye-tracking results for the topic, *Exploring options for starting a vegetable garden at your home*. Across all topics, in the Other condition (map created by one other user), participants spent more time looking at the search result content relative to the organizational labels. Here the labels "Ideas" and "Interesting Thoughts" receive little to no visual attention. In the Iterated condition (map created by one user and iterated on by three subsequent users), participants looked for equal amounts of time at the different types of content in the knowledge map. Here the labels given to groups of content items receive heavy visual attention.

showed that iterating knowledge maps over only four users allowed a collectively-generated schema to emerge, leading to significant improvements in sensemaking quality and helpfulness. We also identify a key startup obstacle in the distributed sensemaking process; users preferring to use maps that have been iterated on multiple times versus starting over, but prefer to start from scratch when given a map iterated on only once. Overcoming this startup cost will be a key factor in realizing the potential of distributed sensemaking.

ACKNOWLEDGMENTS

We thank our participant volunteers. This work was supported by NSH grants OCI-0943148, IIS-0968484, IIS-1111124, and the Center for the Future of Work.

REFERENCES

1. Amershi, S., & Morris, M.R. CoSearch: A system for co-located collaborative Web search. In *Proc. CHI, 2008*, 1647-1656.
2. Baldonado, M.Q.W., & Winograd, T. SenseMaker: An information-exploration interface supporting the contextual evolution of a user's interests. *Proc. CHI, 1997*, 11-18.
3. Billman, D., & Bier, E. Medical sensemaking with entity workspace. In *Proc. CHI, 2007*, 229-232.
4. Chi, M.T.H., Feltovich, P.J., and Glaser, R. Categorization and representation of physics problems by experts and novices. *Cognitive science 5*, 2 (1981), 121–152.
5. Davey, B. (1983). Think aloud: Modeling the cognitive processes of reading comprehension. *J. of Reading, 27*(1), 44-47.
6. Evans, B.M., & Chi, E.H. Towards a model of understanding social search. *Proc. CSCW, 2008*, 485-494.
7. Erickson, T., Smith, D., Kellogg, W., Laff, M., Richards, J., & Bradner, E. (1999). Social translucent systems: social proxies, persistent conversation, and the design of "babble". In *Proc. CHI 1999.*
8. Gentner, D. Structure-mapping: A theoretical framework for analogy. *Cognitive science 7*, 2 (1983), 155–170.
9. Giles, G. Internet encyclopaedias go head to head. *Nature, 438* (2005), 900-901.
10. Golder, S. & Huberman, B. (2006). Usage Patterns of Collaborative Tagging Systems. *Journal of Information Science*. 32(2).
11. Gotz, D. The ScratchPad: Sensemaking support for the web. In *Proc. WWW, 2007*, 1329-1330.
12. Hu, N., Pavlou, P., & Zhang, J. (2006). Can Online Reviews Reveal a Product's True Quality? Empirical Findings and Analytical Modeling of Online Word-of-Mouth Communication. In *Proc. EC, 2006.*
13. Hummel, J.E. and Holyoak, K.J. A symbolic-connectionist theory of relational inference and generalization. *Psychological Review 110*, 2 (2003), 220.
14. Keel, P.E. EWall: A visual analytics environment for collaborative sense-making. *Information Visualization, 6* (2007), 48-63.
15. Kellar, M., Watters, C., & Shepherd, M. (2007). A Field Study Characterizing Web-Based Information-Seeking Tasks. *J. of American Society for Information Science, 58*(7), 999-1018.
16. Kittur, A., Chi, E., & Suh, B. (2008). Can You Even Trust a Wiki? Impacting Perceived Trustworthiness in Wikipedia. In *Proc. CSCW 2008.*
17. Little, G., Lydia, B., Chilton, M., & Miller, R. (2010). Exploring Iterative and Parallel Human Computation Processes. In *Proc. HCOMP, 2010.*
18. Morris, M.R. A survey of collaborative Web search practices, In *Proc. CHI 2008*, 1657-1660.
19. Morris, M.R., & Horvitz, E. SearchTogether: An interface for collaborative Web search. In *Proc. UIST 2008*, 3-12.
20. Nielsen, J., Clemmensen, T., & Yssing, C. (2002). Getting access to what goes on in people's head: reflections on the think-aloud technique. In *Proc. CHI 2002.*
21. Paul, S.A., & Morris, M.R. CoSense: Enhancing sensemaking for collaborative web search. In *Proc. CHI, 2009*, 1771-1780.
22. Paul, S.A., & Reddy, M. (2010). Understanding Together: Sensemking in Collaborative Information Seeking. In *Proc. CSCW 2010.*
23. Pirolli, P. Rational analyses of information foraging on the web. *Cognitive Science, 29* (2005), 343-373.
24. Pirolli, P., Wollny, E., & Suh, B. (2009). So you know you're getting the best possible information: A tool that increases Wikipedia credibility. In *Proc. CHI 2009.*
25. Qu, Y. (2003). A sensemaking-supporting information gathering system. In *CHI EA 2003.*
26. Russell, D.M., Stefik, M.J., Pirolli, P., Card, S.K. The cost structure of sensemaking. In *Proc. CHI, 1993*, 269-276.
27. Shneiderman, B. (2000). Designing trust into online experiences. *Communications of the ACM, 43*(12), 57-59.
28. Suthers, D.D. Collaborative knowledge construction through shared representations. In *Proc. HICSS-38, 2005.*
29. Umapathy, K. Requirements to support collaborative sensemaking. In *CSCW CIS Workshop, 2010.*
30. Whitaker, S. Making sense of sensemaking, in *HCI remixed: Reflections on the works that have influenced the HCI community*, MIT Press, Boston, MA, USA, 2008.

Improving Command Selection with CommandMaps

Joey Scarr[†], Andy Cockburn[†], Carl Gutwin[‡], Andrea Bunt[*]

[†]Computer Science
University of Canterbury
Christchurch, New Zealand
{joey,andy}@cosc.canterbury.ac.nz

[‡]Computer Science
University of Saskatchewan
Saskatoon, Canada
gutwin@cs.usask.ca

[*]Computer Science
University of Manitoba
Winnipeg, Canada
bunt@cs.umanitoba.ca

ABSTRACT
Designers of GUI applications typically arrange commands in hierarchical structures, such as menus, due to screen space limitations. However, hierarchical organisations are known to slow down expert users. This paper proposes the use of spatial memory in combination with hierarchy flattening as a means of improving GUI performance. We demonstrate these concepts through the design of a command selection interface, called CommandMaps, and analyse its theoretical performance characteristics. We then describe two studies evaluating CommandMaps against menus and Microsoft's Ribbon interface for both novice and experienced users. Results show that for novice users, there is no significant performance difference between CommandMaps and traditional interfaces – but for experienced users, CommandMaps are significantly faster than both menus and the Ribbon.

Author Keywords
Expertise; spatial memory; commands; hierarchies.

ACM Classification Keywords
H.5.2 [User Interfaces]: Interaction Styles.

INTRODUCTION
Most GUI applications provide access to commands using visual components such as menus, toolbars, or the Ribbon interface seen in Microsoft Office. When an application has a large number of commands, designers often use a hierarchical navigation structure to partition the components (e.g., with menus or Ribbons) – partly to save screen space, but also to provide semantic groupings of commands (e.g., "File," "Insert," or "View") that simplifies search for novice users. However, hierarchical structures have been shown to be less efficient for expert users (e.g., [7]) – experts already know which commands they want and where those commands are, but a hierarchical selection widget requires additional navigation actions that take more time and increase the chance of navigation errors.

This problem has been recognized by researchers, and alternative command-selection techniques have been studied

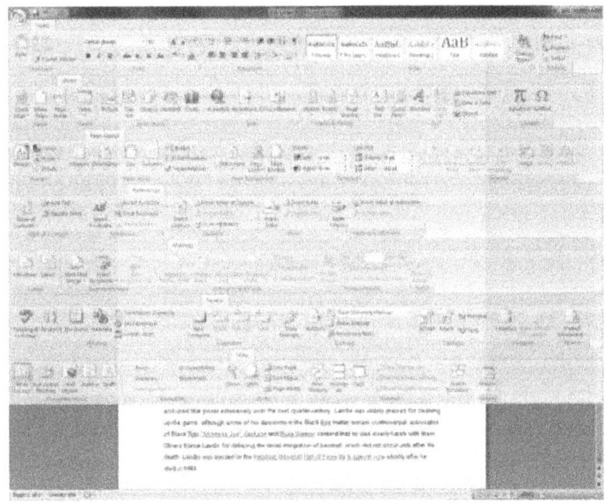

Figure 1. An example CommandMap for Microsoft Word.

that allow better performance for experts. For example, command languages, marking menus, and shortcut keys have all been shown to perform better than standard controls (e.g., [27, 30]). These alternative approaches gain their performance advantage through the use of flat (rather than hierarchical) organizations of commands, and rapid memory-based selection mechanisms. For example, when people become experienced with marking menus or shortcut keys, they begin to retrieve the correct command using muscle memory rather than visual search; similarly, experts with command languages use retrieval of the correct command from memory.

Although these techniques have been shown to be effective, they have characteristics that may not fit well with existing GUI styles. Most WIMP (Windows, Icons, Menus and Pointer) based systems use a strongly visual presentation style because of its advantages for novices, and are heavily invested in existing widget types (like standard menus and Ribbons); this means that it may be difficult to ask users to switch to a radically different interaction paradigm such as a command language; in addition, these systems are most often used with a mouse, which can make gesturing (as used with marking menus) more difficult.

What other kind of fast retrieval could be used to improve expert performance in traditional GUI applications? In this paper, we explore the use of spatial memory as a fast retrieval mechanism that could replace hierarchical selection techniques, and that can fit the general appearance and presentation style of GUI systems. Previous research has shown that spatial memory is a powerful and persistent mechanism for fast retrieval (e.g., [17, 32]), but this idea has not been studied in detail for command interfaces, other than in a few small experiments.

One inspiration that spatial memory can be used in this way comes from anecdotes about expert use of complex applications such as AutoDesk's Maya. Experienced users of these systems often arrange several visual toolbars in a stable spatial arrangement, and then hide and show the tools when needed. Following from these examples, and as a way to evaluate the effectiveness of spatial memory as a command-selection mechanism, we developed a technique called *CommandMaps (CMs)*. CMs have two main properties: they show all (or at least a substantial fraction) of an application's commands at once, and they do so in a spatially-stable fashion, allowing users to build up spatial memory of frequently-used commands (Figure 1).

We carried out studies to compare the performance of CMs to standard GUI command-selection techniques (menus and Ribbons) both for experts and novices. We found that for novices, there were no overall differences between CMs and the standard GUI techniques, showing that a spatial memory approach does not impose an extra burden when users are just starting out with an interface.

When users had more experience with the interface, there were much larger differences in favour of CMs. Selections with CMs needed significantly less time than both menus (34% faster) and Ribbons (25% faster); furthermore, the error rate with CMs was one-tenth of the other interfaces. CMs were also strongly preferred by participants.

These results show that spatial memory can be successfully used as a command-selection mechanism in GUI interfaces, and that the CommandMaps instantiation of this idea should be considered by UI designers as a way to dramatically improve performance ceilings for expert users.

RELATED WORK

Interfaces for Improved Performance with WIMP

User performance in WIMP interfaces is dominated by two operations. The first is the need to locate a desired command among those available, and the second is the time to select it using the mouse (or other similar device). Pointing time is commonly modelled using Fitts' Law [15], a logarithmic function of target width and distance from the cursor. The time to locate a target, on the other hand, has been shown to depend on the users' expertise or familiarity with the interface [9]. Novice users must rely on visual search (typically a linear function of target count), while experts can decide about their location (a log function [19, 20]).

Improvements to traditional WIMP interfaces have sought to make accessing commands more efficient by reducing either pointing time or search time. One such line of work involves alternative command organizations. For example, *pie menus* [5] aim to reduce pointing time by having menu items centred around the cursor when the menu is invoked. *Marking menus* extend pie menus by allowing experts to leverage their spatial knowledge using gestural selections that pre-empt menu display [22]. While keyboard methods, such as shortcut keys, can also reduce pointing time [27], few users make the transition from mouse to keyboard [30].

Work on adaptive interfaces has examined using past user behaviour to either spatially promote likely commands [13, 16, 25] or to visually highlight them [14, 16]. Theoretically, spatial relocation has potential benefits in reducing pointing time and visual search time (if users perform a top-down linear search; see [4] for an analysis of visual search paths). However, empirical evaluations demonstrate that spatial relocation can harm performance [16, 25], and performance models attribute this to the increased reliance on visual search rather than rapid decision [9]. Adaptive visual highlighting aims to leverage visual pop-out effects to decrease visual search time by focussing the search space. For example, Findlater *et al.* [14] empirically demonstrate that 'ephemeral adaptation' improves menu selection performance. However, the benefits of the technique are likely to diminish as users gain expertise in target location.

Spatial Memory

Considerable research on human memory of object locations has been carried out, both in psychology (e.g., [2, 3, 28]) and in HCI (e.g., [10-12]). Much psychology work has been done on memory for navigation: for example, Thorndyke [33] divides spatial knowledge into three types: landmark knowledge, procedural or route knowledge, and survey knowledge (a global overview of the space). Survey knowledge is related to object location memory (the type of memory at issue in this research), and studies have shown that expert human retrieval of object locations is governed by the Hick-Hyman Law [19, 20] (which states that retrieval time is proportional to the log of the number of items in the set), and that spatial learning is governed by a power law of practice [26] (which states that performance improves quickly at first, and levels off with experience).

Several researchers in HCI have explored the use of spatial memory in computer interfaces, and studies have shown that although abilities can vary widely [31], people are capable of using spatial memory to remember large numbers of items, and retrieve them quickly. For example, retrieval of 100 web pages using the memory-based Data Mountain technique [29] was significantly faster than with a standard bookmarking system, and the spatial memory also persisted over several months [10]. Other research, however, suggests that the form of presentation is critical, and that when location is used as the only retrieval cue, spatial memory fares less well [21].

There are relatively few studies that investigate spatial memory as a command-selection mechanism for interfaces. One of these is the *ListMaps* interface [17], which showed that a 15x15 grid of buttons was faster for experts than a linear list of 225 alphabetical items, but considerably slower for novices. This work indicates that the potential value of spatial memory as a fast retrieval technique must be balanced against the time it takes to learn item locations. Another study tested a spatially-stable arrangement of page thumbnails as a document-navigation interface, and showed that spatial memory outperformed scrolling (and that the difference increased dramatically with revisitation) [8].

Hierarchical Navigation

Three decades of research since Miller's [24] analysis of performance with different menu structures has produced extensive and apparently conflicting empirical evidence of the relative merits of 'broad and shallow' versus 'narrow and deep' hierarchical structures. Recent work, however, demonstrates that the apparent conflict between study results can be explained by differences in the experimental conditions [7] – specifically, performance improves with breadth (shallow hierarchies) when item selection performance is a logarithmic function of number of candidate items; but performance follows a 'U' shape with breadth when selection performance is a linear function of the number of items. Logarithmic performance is possible when users can both anticipate a target's location (e.g., by drawing on spatial memory or their knowledge of ordered data) and rapidly control the interface mechanics to acquire the item (e.g., by pointing). Linear performance results when the user either has to visually search for the item (e.g., an unknown target location, or a random data order) or when the interface mechanics constrain selection performance (e.g., stepping through a list one item at a time using an arrow key).

Combining prior findings on spatial memory and hierarchical navigation therefore suggests that expert performance can be enhanced by supporting spatially stable items in the shallowest possible hierarchy.

STUDY 1: USERS' SPATIAL KNOWLEDGE OF GUIS

Our overall hypothesis is that spatial memory can be the basis for command-selection interfaces. To test the basic premise of this hypothesis, we carried out a study to see whether experienced users of a real-world application (Microsoft Word 2010) have built up spatial knowledge of familiar commands in the Ribbon interface.

Method

Twelve participants were recruited from a local university; all considered themselves to be experienced Word 2010 users (7 male, 5 female, mean age 25.1). A study system (Figure 2) running on a Windows 7 PC with a 1600x1200 monitor prompted participants through three tasks.

Task 1: determine familiar commands. Participants were asked to inspect the study system's mock-up of the Word 2010 interface and to indicate which Ribbon-based commands they were familiar with (this was a subjective decision with no strict categories of use). These commands were then used in the remaining tasks.

Task 2: specify locations with Ribbon hidden. For each command determined in Task 1, the participant was shown the name and icon of the command, and asked to click on the location of the command with the Ribbon interface hidden. The participant then clicked on a blank space where they thought the Ribbon item would be (see Figure 2). The study system recorded these locations to determine the error in people's spatial memory of the command's location.

Task 3: select commands using the Ribbon. After specifying a location in Task 2, the participant was asked to find that command with the Ribbon interface. Participants clicked on a Ribbon tab to show that tab, and then on the command to complete the task. The system recorded the number of tab switches and clicks used to correctly complete the task.

Participants completed Task 1, then interleaved Tasks 2 and 3 for each of their selected commands. Commands were presented in a random order, and each command was shown twice overall.

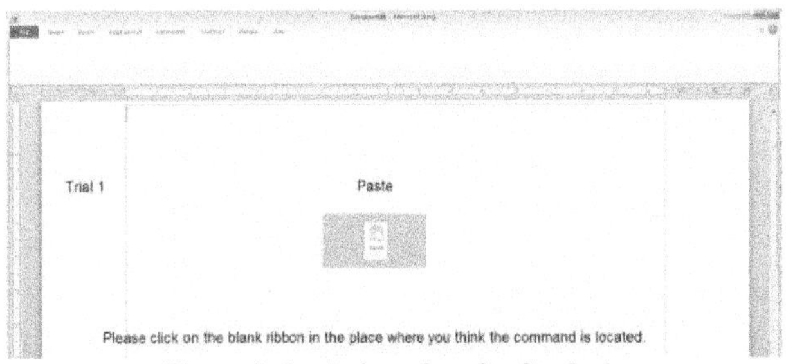

Figure 2. Study interface for Study 1.

Results

Number of familiar commands. Overall, participants chose a mean of 59.6 commands as "familiar" (median 62, standard error 6.72). Many participants appeared to select all of the commands that they had previously used in the interface, rather than just those they used frequently, so we expected a range of actual familiarity with the commands.

Error distance with blank Ribbon. Participants' clicks on the blank Ribbon were on average 147 pixels from the centre of the correct command. There were several outliers, however (see Figure 3), suggesting that some commands were not as well-known as the participant believed. The median error value (less sensitive to outliers) was 92 pixels, which represents approximately 2.5cm on the study monitor. Figure 3 shows the distribution of error distances.

Number of tab selections. When selecting commands with the (visible) Ribbon, participants most often found the command with a single tab selection (one selection was the minimum since the Ribbon was closed at the start of each trial). However, more than one tab selection was needed in 28% of trials; the overall average was 1.95 selections to find the correct command.

These results provide us with two main findings. First, for many commands, people do have a good spatial memory of the commands' locations in the GUI: 50% of commands (i.e., about 30 commands) were known to within 100 pixels. Second, people know the tab location of most of their familiar commands, but for a sizeable subset (28%), they needed more than one selection to find the command.

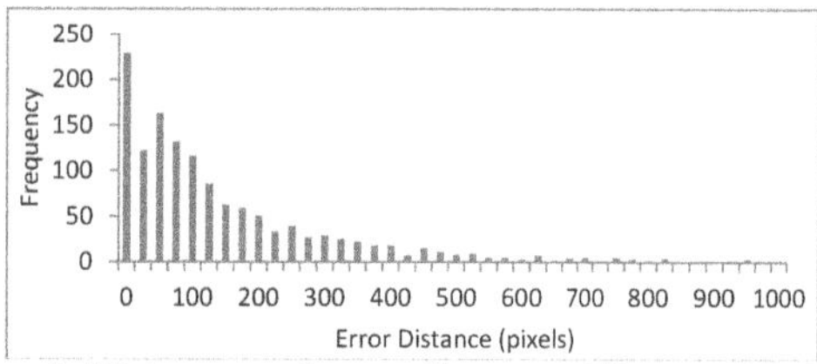

Figure 3. Histogram of error distances. Bins are 25 pixels.

COMMANDMAP DESIGN AND PERFORMANCE MODEL

CommandMap Overview

CommandMap interfaces (e.g., Figure 1) are intended to replace traditional command interfaces such as menus, Ribbons and toolbars. They provide multiple stacked Ribbons that are concurrently displayed when the user presses a dedicated mouse button or command key (e.g. CTRL). Command selections are then made by clicking on the appropriate icon in the CommandMap.

When activated, CommandMaps rapidly fade in to a configurable opacity level (allowing the underlying workspace to be viewed). They remain displayed until their activation key is released, allowing multiple commands to be issued in sequence without reposting.

CommandMap Objectives

Compatible with traditional interaction

Traditional WIMP interfaces have dominated desktop interaction for thirty years. Although faster command invocation mechanisms (such as shortcuts) are available for experts, it is known that these facilities are lightly used [6, 23] and that most users are content to 'make do' with mouse driven selections. CommandMaps therefore maintain the familiar 'point and click' style of interaction.

Improve performance for knowledgeable users

The primary objective for CommandMaps is to improve performance for knowledgeable users. Many office workers use the same computing tools for years or decades, and they are therefore likely to be knowledgeable much longer than they are novice. CommandMaps use two methods to improve knowledgeable user performance: *spatial stability* and *hierarchy flattening.*

Spatial stability. As discussed in Related Work there is extensive empirical evidence showing that consistent spatial placement facilitates location learning and improves selection performance by supporting rapid spatial decisions.

Hierarchy flattening. Traditional interfaces display only a small subset of commands at a time, so command hierarchies are used to partition command subgroups. The result is that even when users know the ultimate location of their targets (as shown by Study 1), they need to mechanically navigate the command hierarchy to satisfy interface requirements. Furthermore, each hierarchical level constitutes an interaction mode, introducing the risk of mode errors – e.g., "Zoom" is not displayed at its known location if the "Home" tab is selected. Scarr *et al.* [30] observed that interface expertise is best supported when interfaces provide a flat command structure. CommandMaps provide a graphical means for hierarchy flattening, maximising the proportion of commands immediately available and reducing the risk of mode errors.

Maintain performance by novice users

While CommandMaps are primarily intended to improve performance by knowledgeable users, it is important that they do not harm novice performance.

Maximise workspace display

When using a desktop application, the user's attention is likely to be on the workspace, such as their document or spreadsheet. Commands must be available on demand, but for much of the time they produce visual clutter and consume space that might be better reserved for the workspace. CommandMaps maximise the workspace by using a modal separation of workspace and commands.

Performance Models: CommandMaps, Menus, Ribbons

To formalise our analysis of the relative merits of CommandMaps, Ribbons, and menus we used the Search, Decision, and Pointing (SDP) model [1, 9] to make theoretical performance predictions. SDP was specifically designed to model performance with menu systems across hierarchical structures and levels of expertise. Our use of SDP also accounts for the proportion of selections requiring the previously selected parent item to be changed.

The SDP model [1, 9] calculates the time to select an item as the sum of time taken at each hierarchical level. The key component of the model is the time taken at each level, which is calculated as the "search/decision time" plus the pointing time (from Fitts' Law). Search/decision time depends on whether the user can decide about an item's location or must visually search for it, with experts being able to make spatial decisions, while novices must rely on visual search. Decision time uses the Hick-Hyman Law of choice reaction time [19, 20], which is a logarithmic function of the number of equally probable choices. Visual search time is a linear function of the number of candidates. The transition from novice visual search to expert decision is modelled using a power law of practice [26]. The reader should refer to Ahlström et al. [1] for a more detailed explanation of the SDP modelling process.

Model assumptions and theoretical performance issues

Using the model to compare CommandMaps, menus, and Ribbons exposes several important theoretical issues about their use. In particular the modelling process demonstrates that knowledgeable use of CommandMaps involves a single decision and pointing activity, while menu use involves two (one for selecting the right menu, and another for selecting the item). Ribbon use is more involved, depending on whether the Ribbon is minimized or not and on whether the target item is within the current tab (details below).

To simplify modelling we make a series of assumptions. We model 210 commands that are evenly divided across seven groupings (approximately reflective of Microsoft Word), with all commands being equally probable. We assume that command selections begin with the cursor located at the centre of the workspace, that tab/menu targets are 20 pixels wide, and that Ribbon items are 40 pixels wide. We also assume error-free performance. Predictions are calculated in a simple spreadsheet using previously published calibration parameters [9]. The spreadsheet is accessible at *removed for anonymity*.

CommandMap. We model novice selections as requiring a two level search process: first searching for the appropriate tab marker in the CommandMap, then searching for the desired command within that group. While two levels of searching are required, only a single pointing activity is necessary in the flat display. Experts are modelled using a single-level decision between all commands, followed by a single pointing activity. The mean pointing amplitude with CommandMaps is assumed to be 250 pixels.

Figure 4 shows expert performance predictions with the three interfaces as the proportion of selections involving a switch between parent items increases. CommandMaps are predicted to have constant fast performance of approximately 1.5s. Their speed is due to the single decision/pointing activity regardless of the need to switch from the previously selected parent.

Menu. All selections, regardless of expertise, involve a two level acquisition process. Users first search for (novice) or decide about (expert) the menu and point to it. They then search/decide and point to the item in the menu. We assume mean amplitude of 500 pixels from the screen centre to the top level menu, and amplitude of 300 pixels for second level selections (half way through a 30 item menu).

Figure 4 shows a constant expert menu prediction of approximately 3s. This slow performance is due to the two decisions and pointing actions for every selection.

Ribbon. The Ribbon can be minimised, causing it to disappear after each selection, which requires a tab to be clicked before it reappears. In this case Ribbon interaction (and model) is nearly identical to menus, involving a two-level search/decision and pointing process.

Modelling performance with the non-minimised Ribbon is theoretically interesting because it is *sometimes* necessary to switch the parent tab and sometimes unnecessary. For novices we use a two level searching process (as for CommandMaps and menus); however, time for first level pointing is only included when a tab-switch is necessary.

For experts, it is unclear whether acquisitions involve a single decision for a 'global' target (e.g., the user thinks "Bold" and recalls its spatial location) or two decisions (e.g., the user thinks "Home tab", "Bold"). If two decisions are involved, then selections within the currently selected tab involve a superfluous decision, wasting a small amount of time. However, if only a single decision is made then users are likely to encounter mode errors when tab changes are required – for example, the user thinks "Bold", recalls its location from memory, and encounters a mode error when the target is not where expected because the 'View' tab is selected. Anecdotal reports suggest that Ribbon users do make frequent mode errors, lending support to the one-level decision model.

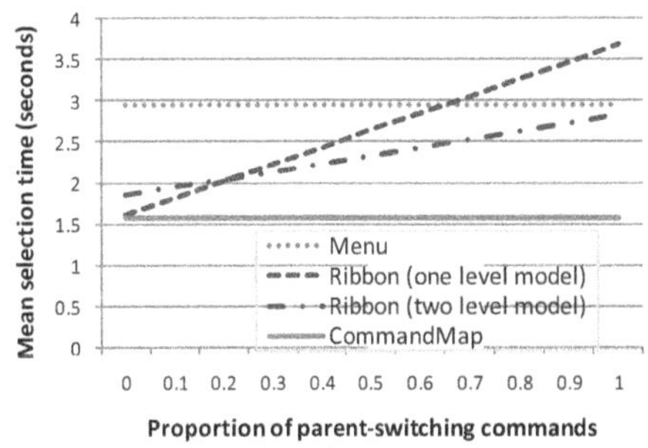

Figure 4. Predicted expert performance across proportion of commands requiring a tab change.

Figure 4 shows expert predictions for both one- and two-level Ribbon models (using the same pointing distances as menus). Ribbons are predicted to match CommandMaps only when no selections involve switching parents, and to gradually deteriorate as the proportion of parent switching increases. Note that the one-level model predicts that Ribbons will be worse than menus when most selections involve a tab switch.

STUDY 2: KNOWLEDGEABLE USE OF COMMANDMAPS

Studies 2 and 3 compare user performance with CommandMaps, Ribbons, and menus when knowledgeable and when novice. Study 4 then compares performance with two variant CommandMap designs for allowing window geometry manipulation. All participants completed Studies 2-4 in a single one hour session.

The primary aim of CommandMaps is to improve performance by knowledgeable users who have developed spatial awareness of command locations. Study 2 therefore tests the following hypotheses:

H1: Knowledgeable users can select commands faster using CommandMaps than when using Ribbons and menus.

H2: There is no performance difference between CommandMaps and Ribbons when selecting commands contained in the most recently used tab, but CommandMaps are faster than the Ribbon for tasks requiring switching between different parent tabs.

H3: Subjectively, users will prefer CommandMaps.

Hypotheses 1 and 3 are important but straightforward performance and preference comparisons. Hypothesis 2 is more nuanced, examining the theoretical performance model's assumptions. As the one-level model of Figure 4 shows, we predict no difference between CommandMaps and Ribbons for *non-switching* tasks. However, the model also predicts that CommandMaps will perform much better than Ribbons and menus when switching is required.

Procedure

To achieve the interface familiarity necessary to examine knowledgeable user performance, we based the experiment on a widely used desktop application: Microsoft Word 2007. All participants completed tasks using three interfaces: a Ribbon replicating the actual Word Ribbon, a menu, and a CommandMap. The menu design used seven top-level menus matching the Ribbon's tabs, with underlying menus containing all of the items in each tab, and similar group separation. The CommandMap, shown in Figure 1, presented all of the Ribbon tabs laid out from top to bottom within the window. None of the interfaces implemented third level pop-up/drop-down items – for example, clicking on the colour swatch drop-down arrow A· did not post the associated dialog.

As participants may not have encountered the Word commands used in the experiment, and because no participant could have had prior experience with our tailor-made menu or CommandMap interfaces, they were required to complete two blocks of tasks with each interface: *familiarisation* and *performance*. The *familiarisation* block was used to assure familiarity with the location of commands in each interface condition, while the *performance* block was used for experimental analysis.

Tasks were initiated by clicking a 'Next' button in the centre of the window, which displayed a sidebar prompt containing the name and icon for a target. Task timing began when the prompt was displayed and ran until the correct item was selected. Incorrect selections produced an audible beep. Participants were instructed to complete tasks "as quickly and accurately as possible".

Three sets of command targets were generated, with each set consisting of a total of six commands located in three different tabs: three in the Home tab, two in the Insert tab, and one in the View tab. Each participant used the same command set for *familiarisation* and *performance* with one interface, and then different command sets for subsequent interfaces. The order of command set and interface was counterbalanced using a Latin square.

The *familiarisation* block comprised 30 trials, with 5 selections for each of the six targets. The *performance* block contained 90 trials, with 15 selections for each of the same six targets. The order of target selection within each condition was established with a one-off random process, where the selection sequence was repeatedly regenerated until it met our constraint that 50% of selections would involve a tab switch when using the Ribbon.

Participants completed NASA-TLX [18] worksheets after each interface, and at the end of the experiment they ranked the three interfaces for preference.

Participants and Apparatus (for studies 2-4)

18 participants were recruited from a local university (16 male, 2 female). The experiment was performed on a Windows 7 desktop with a 2.66 GHz Intel Core 2 Quad and 8GB of RAM. A 22″ screen was used, running at a resolution of 1680×1050.

Design

The experiment is designed as a 3×2 analysis of variance for within-subjects factors *interface {ribbon, menu, commandmap}* and *parent {same, different}*. The factor *parent* allows analysis of the impact of moving between different interface structures – tasks are *same* when the current selection occurs in the same menu or Ribbon tab as the last one; otherwise they are *different*. The dependent measures are task time and error rate.

Results

We analysed task time data with and without trials containing incorrect selections, with both analyses producing the same statistical outcomes.

Mean acquisition times (errors removed) were fastest with *commandmap* (1.57 s, s.d. 0.4), followed by *ribbon* (2.11 s, s.d. 0.8) and *menu* (2.40 s, s.d. 0.4), giving a significant main effect of *interface*: $F_{2, 34} = 114.0, p < .001$. Bonferroni corrected pairwise comparisons (total $\alpha = .05$) confirm that *commandmaps* were faster than *ribbon* (by 25%) and *menu* (by 34%). We therefore find support for **H1**.

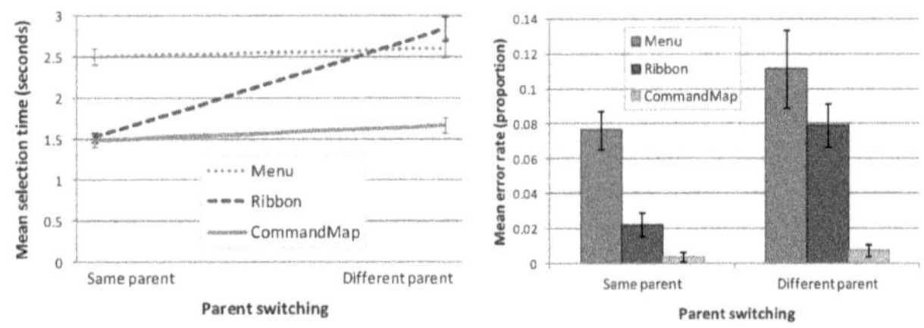

(a) Task time (b) Errors

Figure 5. Results for Study 2, with (a) shown as a line chart for consistency with Figure 4. Error bars show standard error.

As expected, there was a significant effect of *parent* ($F_{1, 17} = 155.5, p < .001$), with *same* selections faster than *different*. Importantly, though, there was a strong *interface* × *parent* interaction ($F_{2, 34} = 187.4, p < .001$). This is shown in Figure 5a: *commandmaps* and *ribbon* performed similarly for *same* tasks, but *commandmap* was relatively faster in *different* tasks (the lines in the figure show linear interpolation between data for *same* and *different* tasks with each interface). We therefore find support for **H2**. The model predictions shown in Figure 4 are confirmed by Figure 5a, including the crossover effect of *ribbon* performance becoming worse than menus in *different* tasks.

The proportion of trials containing an error was much lower with *commandmaps* (0.6%) than either *ribbon* (5%) or *menu* (9%): $F_{2, 34} = 21.6, p < .001$. A significant *interface* × *parent* interaction ($F_{2, 34} = 5.26, p < .05$), evident in Figure 5b, is caused by *commandmap* error rates being relatively unaffected by *parent*, while *ribbon* and *menu* have much higher errors in *different* parent tasks (suggestive of the hypothesised mode errors).

The combination of time and error data is important, as it shows that *commandmaps* do not increase errors to achieve their improved temporal performance – they are both faster and more accurate than menus and Ribbons.

User response to CommandMaps was positive, with 14 participants ranking it as their first preferred interface, two rating *ribbons* first, and two *menus*: $\chi^2=16.0,\ p < .001$. CommandMaps were also rated as having the lowest workload on all significant NASA-TLX measures (Table 1). We therefore find support for **H3**.

	Menu		Ribbon		CM		χ_r^2	Sig
Mental demand	3.1	(1.1)	3.4	(0.9)	2.5	(1.2)	11.9	< .005
Physical demand	3.7	(1.1)	3.5	(0.9)	2.4	(1.0)	11.6	< .005
Temporal demand	2.9	(1.1)	3.2	(0.9)	2.4	(1.2)	9.3	< .01
Hard work	3.1	(0.9)	3.1	(1.0)	2.0	(1.1)	10.5	< .01
Frustration	3.3	(1.0)	2.9	(1.0)	1.9	(1.1)	13.4	< .005

Table 1. Mean (st. dev.) NASA-TLX values (1= low, 5=high).

STUDY 3: NOVICE USE OF COMMANDMAPS

CommandMaps are primarily intended to enhance knowledgeable users' performance, but novice performance is also important. Study 3 therefore compares novice performance with CommandMaps, Ribbons, and menus. Since CommandMaps display all commands at once, there is a risk that visual search performance will be impaired by the need to visually scan many concurrent candidates.

Procedure

The experiment involved acquiring randomly located targets in logical groupings using CommandMap, menu, and Ribbon interfaces. Five groups of 24 items each were created to populate the interfaces (*animals*, *cartoon characters*, *food*, *office items*, and *sports*). Only items from *animals*, *food*, and *sports* were used as targets. The groups were intentionally unconnected with computing to avoid transfer effects from traditional interface experience.

Tasks were presented to participants using an identical prompting interface to Study 2. Participants completed twenty-four tasks with each interface before proceeding to the next interface (interface order counterbalanced using a Latin square). The tasks with each interface comprised selecting eight unique targets in each of three different groups (e.g., eight different animals). The order of task presentation was manipulated such that half of the tasks involved switching parent group and half did not (to test the impact of searching within and across tabs). To reduce learning effects across tasks (and hence emulate novice visual search) no target item was reused throughout the experiment, and the location of all items (parents and items within groups) was randomised for every trial. Participants provided comments and rated the ease of finding targets at the conclusion of each interface condition, and at the end of the experiment they ranked the three interfaces for perceived performance and preference.

Participants, apparatus, and design are identical to Study 2.

Results

Mean acquisition times were similar with *commandmap* (4.45 s, s.d. 1.73) and *ribbon* (4.38, s.d. 1.4), but slower with *menu* (5.74, s.d. 1.6), giving a significant main effect of *interface* ($F_{2,34} = 110.9,\ p < .001$). In pairwise posthoc comparisons (Bonferroni adjusted T-Tests), menus were slower than both *ribbon* and *commandmap,* but there was no difference between *commandmap* and *ribbon* ($T_{17}<1$).

There was a significant *interface*×*parent* interaction ($F_{2,34} = 12.3,\ p < .001$; Figure 6), with *ribbon* slightly faster than *commandmap* for *same* tasks, but *commandmap* slightly faster than *ribbon* for *different* tasks. Pairwise comparisons between *commandmap* and *ribbon* in each of these conditions (*same* and *different*) show no significant difference ($p > .05$).

Error analysis showed a 2.8% error rate with *commandmap,* 5.1% with *ribbon,* and 16% with *menu*: $F_{2,34} = 35.2,\ p < .001$. There were marginally more errors with *different* parent (9.2%) than with *same* (6.6%): $F_{1,17} = 4.1,\ p = .06$. There was no *interface*×*parent* interaction ($F_{1,17} < 1$).

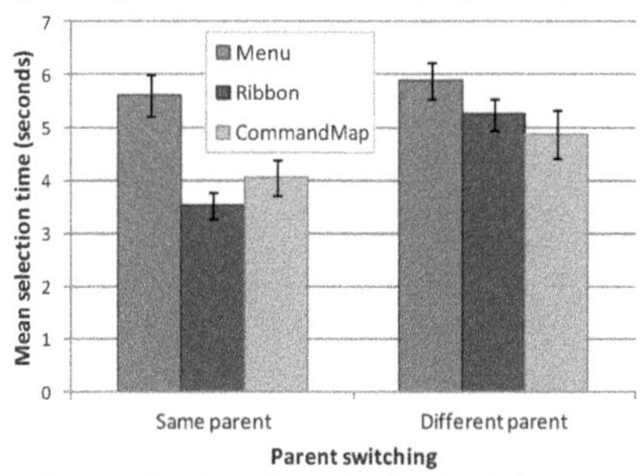

Figure 6. Mean selection times in Study 3. Error bars show standard error.

Subjective responses to the question "It was easy to find targets" (1 disagree, 5 agree) indicated greatest ease with *commandmap* (mean 3.5, s.d., 1.0), followed by *ribbon* (3.2, 1.0) and *menu* (2.4, 0.9): Friedman $\chi^2=10.0,\ p < .005$. Eleven participants ranked *commandmap* as their preferred interface for the task, four preferred the *ribbon*, and two preferred *menus*: $\chi^2=7.9,\ p < .05$. Comments on the *commandmap* presentation were mixed, with one participant stating *"Too much to see at once"*, and another saying *"I like how you can see all the buttons at once."*

The key finding is that novice performance is similar when using CommandMap and Ribbon designs; both are substantially better than menus.

STUDY 4: COMMANDMAPS AND WINDOW GEOMETRY

Studies 2 and 3 used large, static windows, but any practical deployment will need to accommodate variable window sizes and positions. This raises questions of how CommandMaps should respond to window geometry manipulation, and how this affects their performance. The following sections describe and test two CommandMap designs for responding to window geometry manipulation – one based on scaling within the window boundary, and another using a pop-up window.

Scaling and Pointing Lens CommandMap

Scaling CommandMaps are dynamically resized in response to window size manipulations so that items maintain relative spatial location. To avoid distortion when windows are resized on only one dimension, they maintain a 1:1 aspect ratio using the smaller window dimension. They are anchored to the top-left corner of the window. To assure that targets remain discernable at small scales a pointing lens is used to magnify the area under the cursor.

Pop-up CommandMaps

Pop-up CommandMaps are displayed in a pop-up window of constant (full) size. Like menus, the location of the CommandMap is anchored in the top-left window corner by default, but it is repositioned outside the window boundary when necessary for the entire CommandMap to appear within the display. Therefore, when the window is small, or when the window intersects a screen edge, the CommandMap extends outside the window boundary.

Evaluating the Designs

We compared knowledgeable user performance with *scaling* and *pop-up* CommandMaps at three different window *sizes*: full size (1280×1024), 50% (640×512), and 25% (320×256). The 50% size represents a realistic lower bound for window size with a standard desktop application. The 25% size represents an extreme limit of interaction.

Procedure

Experimental tasks involved selecting the same six targets used for the *commandmap* condition in Study 2. Participants initially performed a block of 'refresher' trials, selecting each of the six targets twice (data discarded). They then made 36 selections with *scaling* and 36 with *pop-up* interface (order counterbalanced). The 36 selections comprised 12 at each *size* (full, 50% and 25%), consisting of two repetitions of each of the six targets. The targets were ordered such that each selection used a different window size to the preceding one (e.g., a participant might select target 1 at full size, then target 2 at 25%, then target 3 at 50%, and so on) in order to maximise abrupt transitions between window sizes. Tasks were presented to users using the same prompting interface as Studies 2 and 3.

Participants, Apparatus, and Design

Participants and apparatus are identical to Studies 2 and 3. The design is a 2×3 RM-ANOVA for within-subjects factors *interface {scaling, popup}* and *size {full, 50, 25}*. The main dependent measure is task time.

Results

The error rate was low (a total of 10 across 1296 trials), so error analysis was not conducted. *Popup* (mean 1.54, s.d. 0.33) was much faster than *scaling* (2.65, 1.1), giving a significant effect of *interface* ($F_{1,17} = 82.1, p < .001$). There was also a significant main effect of *size* ($F_{2,34} = 81.5, p < .001$), but this was due to *scaling* performance deteriorating as *size* decreased, while *popup*'s performance remained stable, leading to a significant *interface* × *size* interaction ($F_{2,34} = 77.7, p < .001$). *Popup* outperformed *scaling* even at *full* size, where the two conditions were identical. This suggests that the abrupt transitions between sizes were a significant detriment to performance with *scaling* – one participant commented *"I found I lost my sense of where things were as the scale changed."* All participants preferred the popup interface.

Popup's performance stability across window size is important. In Study 2, the *commandmap* mean of 1.57 s was 25% faster than *ribbon*, and *popup*'s mean in Study 4 was nearly identical at 1.54s. We did not include *ribbon* in Study 4, but it would clearly have performed worse than it did in Study 2 due to its progressive elision of items into additional hierarchical levels (see Figure 7). The results of Study 4 therefore suggest that the advantage for popup CommandMaps over the Ribbon will exceed 25% with small windows.

Figure 7. The Word Ribbon at 320 px width, necessitating additional hierarchical traversal to reach targets.

DISCUSSION

To summarise the results, Study 1 confirmed that users have a good memory for the spatial location of commands, but that their memory for the parent item containing commands is relatively weak. Studies 2 to 4 then tested CommandMaps. Study 2 demonstrated that CommandMaps provide substantial performance benefits for knowledgeable users – they were 34% faster than menus and 25% faster than the Ribbon. The results confirmed the predictive performance model, including a cross-over effect with Ribbon performance being worse than menus for selections involving a parent switch. CommandMaps were also much less error prone, with 0.6% errors compared to 5% and 9% with Ribbons and menus respectively. Study 3 showed that novice visual search for randomly located items in CommandMaps is faster than menus, but not significantly different to Ribbons. The study also showed that the relative performance of CommandMaps and Ribbons depends on whether selections involve switching from the previous parent item. Study 4 demonstrated that popup CommandMaps remain efficient regardless of window size.

Why did CommandMaps succeed?

The empirical results closely matched the theoretical predictions generated by the performance model (Figures 4 and 5a). Furthermore, the preferred 'one-level model' of Ribbon use anticipated frequent mode errors when parent switches are required, as observed with the Ribbon's 5% error rate (as compared to 0.6% with CommandMaps).

The theoretical model mechanically implements predictions using previously reported parameters [9] (eliminating any chance of calibration 'bias'), and the model's formulae for expert performance attend only to the number of interface levels, the timing associated with location decisions at each level, and pointing requirements. Therefore, we attribute CommandMaps' success to their two defining properties – stability of item location (allowing spatial decisions), and maximally flattened hierarchy (allowing acquisition with a single decision and pointing action).

CommandMaps in the real world

The experiment focused on command selection performance, with tasks involving repeated selection of a small set of serially presented targets. While real work sometimes involves executing a series of commands (e.g., changing the zoom level, inserting a symbol, and formatting it) it normally interleaves activities on the workspace with command selections. This raises concerns about whether the experimental findings will generalise to real use, discussed below.

Impact of the small target set on spatial memory. Study 3 involved repeated selections of six target items. The small set was used to assure participants had a good spatial knowledge of target location (emulating expertise), but it is possible that the method induced spatial location memory that is artificially refined. We are confident that the results will generalise to larger active command sets for two reasons. First, Study 1 shows that participants have a good spatial knowledge of approximately 30 items (50% of a mean 59.6 "familiar items"). Second, prior studies have demonstrated that users can efficiently draw on spatial memory for large item sets (e.g. [29]).

Activating control. Our experimental interface used the CTRL key to activate the CommandMap, but this requires bimanual operation with one hand on the key and another on the mouse. Our experimental participants issued an intense series of command selections, so it was natural for them to keep one hand on or near the control key. However, during real work the non-dominant hand might be otherwise occupied, demanding a homing action to the activating key. Two solutions to this concern are first, the CommandMap could be posted by clicking in a designated area (e.g., window title); similar to how the current Ribbon can be posted once 'minimized'; second, a dedicated mouse button could be used to activate the CommandMap mode, allowing unimanual selection. Similarly, on a touchscreen device, the CommandMap could be activated with a specific gesture (e.g., four finger touch).

Workspace overlay. To display the full set of commands simultaneously, the CommandMap covers the user's work or content area with a configurable transparent overlay. While this overlay allows the underlying area to remain visible, it is possible users may respond less favourably to having their content somewhat obscured when invoking commands that allow previews prior to final selection (e.g., font size). We hope, however, that the substantial performance benefits of the CommandMap design outweigh this potential downside, which would be present for only a subset of commands.

Initial user reaction. Study 2 shows that novice visual search performance is similar between Ribbons and CommandMaps. However, there are two concerns on initial user reaction. First, three participants indicated that the number of controls was 'overwhelming' when first viewing the CommandMap, but this impression quickly dissipated on use. Second, there is an absence of control affordance due to the omission of obvious controls at their familiar location. Both of these concerns are short-term effects that might be eased with a help display after installation.

Limit of number of commands. While CommandMaps utilise screen real estate to a much higher degree than conventional techniques, there is still a limit to the number of commands that can be displayed at once. In situations where the available command set is too large, a hierarchical structure must still be employed. However, we still anticipate a performance increase over contemporary interfaces if the hierarchy is as shallow as possible. Furthermore, CommandMaps in their current form are unable to support certain features of the Ribbon, such as contextual tabs, due to a lack of screen space. Anyone designing a practical implementation of CommandMaps will therefore have to keep screen size limitations in mind when choosing control arrangements.

CONCLUSIONS

In modern user interfaces, hierarchical command organisations are common. However, we showed that users can remember the spatial locations of controls without the need for hierarchy, implying that hierarchy traversal is inefficient for experienced users.

We presented the notion of combining spatial memory and flat hierarchies to support efficient command access and instantiated these ideas within CommandMaps. We generated performance models supporting our design and empirically validated them through two studies: one demonstrating a speed increase for expert users of 34% over menus and 25% over Microsoft's Ribbon, and the other showing no significant performance difference for novices. Subjective responses indicated that CommandMaps was preferred across both experiments. Finally, we evaluated two alternative designs allowing CommandMaps to remain effective at smaller window geometries, with a "pop-up" design performing significantly better than one that scaled widgets according to the window dimensions.

There are a number of directions for future work. Our experiments used menus and Ribbons as baseline comparators due to their dominance in contemporary interfaces. However, comparisons with other command invocation techniques are needed, particularly with those that have been shown to support expert use, such as marking menus [22]. A second area of future work involves exploring ways to combine CommandMaps with other performance optimizations, particularly for systems that have a predictive capacity. For example, ephemeral adaptation [14] or a related scheme could be used to emphasize likely commands.

Alternatively, a subset of frequently used commands could remain visible in workspace mode (similar to Gajos' Split Interface [16]). Finally, studies with more complex tasks would provide insight into the strengths and limitations of the CommandMap design when command invocation is intermixed with content manipulation.

ACKNOWLEDGEMENTS

We would like to thank our study participants for the use of their valuable time. This work was partially funded by Royal Society of New Zealand Marsden Grant 10-UOC-020.

REFERENCES

1. Ahlström, D., Cockburn, A., Gutwin, C. and Irani, P. Why it's Quick to be Square. in *Proc. CHI'10*, (2010).
2. Andrade, J. and Meudell, P. Short report: Is spatial information encoded automatically? *Quarterly Journal of Experimental Psychology 46A* (1993), 365-375.
3. Baddeley, A.D. *Human Memory*. Erlbaum, (1990).
4. Byrne, M., Anderson, J., Douglass, S. and Matessa, M. Eye Tracking the Visual Search of Click-Down Menus. in *Proc. CHI'99*, ACM, (1999), 402-409.
5. Callahan, J., Hopkins, D., Weiser, M. and Shneiderman, B. An Empirical comparison of Pie Versus Linear Menus. in *Proc. CHI*, (1988), 95-100.
6. Carroll, J. and Rossen, M. Paradox of the active user. in Carroll, J. ed. *Interfacing Thought: Cognitive Aspects of HCI*, MIT Press, 1987, 80-111.
7. Cockburn, A. and Gutwin, C. A Predictive Model of Human Performance with Scrolling and Hierarchical Lists. *HCI 24*, 3 (2009), 273-314.
8. Cockburn, A., Gutwin, C. and Alexander, J. Faster Document Navigation with Space-Filling Thumbnails. in *Proc. CHI'06*, ACM Press, (2006), 1-10.
9. Cockburn, A., Gutwin, C. and Greenberg, S. A Predictive Model of Menu Performance. in *Proc. CHI'07*, ACM Press, (2007), 627-636.
10. Czerwinski, M., van Dantzich, M., Robertson, G. and Hoffman, H. The Contribution of Thumbnail Image, Mouse-Over Text and Spatial Location Memory to Web Page Retrieval. in *Proc. INTERACT*, (1999), 163-170.
11. Darken, R.P. and Sibert, J.L. Wayfinding strategies and behaviors in large virtual worlds. in *Proc. CHI '96*, ACM, (1996), 142-149.
12. Ehret, B. Learning Where to Look: Location Learning in Graphical User Interfaces. in *Proc. CHI'02*, 211-218.
13. Findlater, L. and McGrenere, J. A comparison of static, adaptive, and adaptable menus. in *Proc. CHI'04*, ACM, (2004), 89-96.
14. Findlater, L., Moffatt, K., McGrenere, J. and Dawson, J. Ephemeral adaptation. in *Proc. CHI'09*, ACM Press, (2009), 1655-1664.
15. Fitts, P.M. The Information Capacity of the Human Motor System in Controlling the Amplitude of Movement. *J. Experimental Psych. 47* (1954), 381-391.
16. Gajos, K., Czerwinski, M., Tan, D. and Weld, D. Exploring the Design Space for Adaptive Graphical User Interfaces. in *Proc. AVI'06*, (2006), 201-208.
17. Gutwin, C. and Cockburn, A. Improving List Revistation with ListMaps. in *Proc. AVI'06*, 396-403.
18. Hart, S. and Staveland, L. Development of NASA-TLX. in *Human Mental Workload*, 1988, 139-183.
19. Hick, W.E. On the rate of gain of information. *Quarterly Journal of Experimental Psychology 4* (1952), 11-26.
20. Hyman, R. Stimulus information as a determinant of reaction time. *Experimental Psych. 45* (1953), 188-196.
21. Jones, W. and Dumais, S. The Spatial Metaphor for User Interfaces: Experimental Tests of Reference by Location versus Name. *ACM TOIS 4*, 1 (1986), 42-63.
22. Kurtenbach, G. and Buxton, W. User Learning and Performance with Marking Menus. in *Proc. CHI'94*, (1994), 258-264.
23. Lane, D.M., Napier, H.A., Peres, S.C. and Sandor, A. Hidden costs of graphical user interfaces. *I.J. HCI 18*, 2 (2005), 133-144.
24. Miller, D. The depth/breadth tradeoff in hierarchical computer menus. in *Proc. HFES*, (1981), 296-300.
25. Mitchell, J. and Shneiderman, B. Dynamic versus Static Menus. *ACM SIGCHI Bulletin 20*, 4 (1989), 33--36.
26. Newell, A. and Rosenbloom, P.S. Mechanisms of Skill Acquisition and the Law of Practice. in Anderson, J. ed. *Cog. Skills & Acquisition*, Erlbaum, 1981, 1-55.
27. Odell, D., L. , Davis, R., C., Smith, A. and Wright, P., K. Toolglasses, marking menus, and hotkeys: a comparison of one and two-handed command selection techniques. in *Proc. Graphics Interface*, (2004), 17-24.
28. Postma, A. and De Haan, E. What Was Where? Memory for Object Locations. *Quarterly Journal of Experimental Psychology 49A*, 1 (1996), 178-199.
29. Robertson, G., Czerwinski, M., Larson, K., Robbins, D., Thiel, D. and van Dantzich, M. Data Mountain. in *Proc. UIST'98*, (1998), 153-162.
30. Scarr, J., Cockburn, A., Gutwin, C. and Quinn, P. Dips and Ceilings: Understanding and Supporting Transitions to Expertise in User Interfaces. in *Proc. CHI'11*, ACM, (2011), 2741-2750.
31. Silverman, I. and Eals, M. Sex differences in spatial abilities: Evolutionary theory and data. in *The Adapted Mind*, Oxford University Press, (1992).
32. Tak, S., Cockburn, A., Humm, K., Ahlstroem, D., Gutwin, C. and Scarr, J. Improving Window Switching Interfaces. in *Proc. INTERACT'09*, (2009), 187-200.
33. Thorndyke, P.W. and Goldin, S.E. Spatial learning and reasoning skill. *Spatial orientation: Theory, research, and application* (1983), 195-217.

Improving Scrolling Devices with Document-Length-Dependent Gain

Andy Cockburn[†], **Philip Quinn**[†], **Carl Gutwin**[‡], **Stephen Fitchett**[†]
[†]Computer Science, University of Canterbury, Christchurch, New Zealand
andy@cosc.canterbury.ac.nz, philip.quinn@canterbury.ac.nz, stephen.fitchett@pg.canterbury.ac.nz
[‡]Computer Science, University of Saskatchewan, Saskatoon, Canada, gutwin@cs.usask.ca

ABSTRACT

We describe a method for applying gain to events reported by scrolling input devices such as scroll wheels. By treating document length as an input to our gain functions, the method allows rapid document traversal regardless of document length; it also allows slow and precise scroll control at shorter distances. An initial experiment characterises four diverse scrolling input devices – a standard 'notched' scrollwheel, a high performance 'inertial' wheel, an isometric scrolling joystick, and a trackpad – and the results are used to calibrate several gain function parameters. A second experiment validates the method, showing that it allows faster scrolling in long and short documents than current scrolling-device gain methods, and that subjective preferences favour it.

Author Keywords

Scrolling; control-display gain; empirical studies.

ACM Classification Keywords

H.5.2 [User Interfaces]: *Input devices and strategies*;

INTRODUCTION

Scrolling provides a simple means for working with documents that are too large to be conveniently displayed within a single view. Commensurate with its importance, scrolling interactions have been extensively researched, producing innovative devices, techniques, and behaviours. Surprisingly, though, there has been little public research into one of the most basic and universal scrolling problems – that of supporting appropriate gain functions to allow both precise repositioning actions as well as rapid movement across large distances. Although most pointing devices include scroll controls (e.g., scrollwheels) there has been little research into optimising their performance.

Scrolling and mouse-based targeting are similar in that both have a wide range of control requirements – from small precise pixel actions to long range movement. Yet gain functions for scrolling are relatively unstudied (with Hinckley [11] being a notable exception, reviewed later). For pointing, however, gain studies are common, and they are known to improve performance [6, 7].

Two main problems complicate the design of effective scroll gain functions. First, many scrolling input devices allow only coarse levels of control. For example, the range of physical movement enabled by most mouse scroll-wheels is approximately 10mm linearly without 'clutching' (the process of temporarily disengaging from the wheel in order to reposition the finger). Furthermore, this limited movement is often discretised into 5 or 6 coarse 'notches'. By contrast, clutch-free mouse pointing extends over approximately ten times this linear distance, on two dimensions, with hundreds of registered points per cm. The second problem complicating the design of scroll gain functions is that the linear range of control requirements for scrolling is much larger than that of cursor pointing. Pointing requires at most a few thousand pixels be addressable on the x or y dimensions. Documents, however, can be thousands of pages long, with each page containing roughly a thousand linear pixels, any of which might be considered a target for positioning the scrolled display.

The conflict between the low fidelity of scrolling input controls and the wide range of possible scrolling targets means that clutching with scrolling input devices is often pronounced, causing users to frenetically repeat scrolling actions, exhibited as 'clawing' a scrollwheel or 'scratching' a touchscreen. Consequently, many scroll devices, such as standard notched scrollwheels, are best used only for short range movement, and when longer movements are required users should switch to an alternative control, such as dragging the scroll thumb (as part of a scrollbar). However, expecting users to make a distance-based choice between scrolling methods is inefficient: decisions take time, they can be made incorrectly, and they require that the user switch their attention from the task to the interface. As a result, users may avoid the decision and try to use a single technique regardless of its comparative inefficiency for a particular range of distances (e.g., people may often use the scroll wheel for long distances, even when this takes far longer than using the thumb). Given that devices such as scrollwheels are already in common use, it is reasonable to expect that these controls should be usable for all scrolling needs – no one would consider using two mice for pointing (one for near targets and another for far ones), yet curiously, this is the equivalent expectation for scrolling.

Two observations – that documents vary greatly in length, and that scrolling mechanisms are inefficient at long distances – lead us to the idea of making gain functions that are dependent on document length. Document-length-dependent (DLD) gain is a simple method that can substantially improve the performance of scrolling input devices. Our method of evaluation involves a rapid calibration process to understand device characteristics, which could be performed by the device manufacturer or by individuals seeking tailored performance. The gain function allows pixel-precise movement as well as rapid document traversal, regardless of length. Experiments validate the technique's effectiveness across a diverse range of devices.

The specific contributions of this paper are as follows:

- An empirical characterization of human performance with different scrolling devices: a notched scrollwheel, an isometric 'ScrollPoint' joystick, an inertial scrollwheel, and two-finger trackpad scrolling.
- Details of our document-length-dependent gain function.
- Empirical results demonstrating that performance and preferences are improved by our gain function.

SCROLLING FRAMEWORK & RELATED WORK

Abowd and Beale's interaction framework [1] subdivides interaction into translations from the user's motor actions to input events, from input events to system state, from state to output, and from output to perception. We use this framework to clarify scrolling activities and to classify prior research.

User → Input: Motor action

Several previous studies have examined input device capabilities, including Buxton's analysis of position, motion, and pressure input for controlling multiple input dimensions [4], Card, Mackinlay and Robertson's morphological analysis of input [5], and Jacob *et al.*'s mapping between input device and user task [15]. These analyses focus on pointing requirements, and none share our specific focus on document scrolling.

Most scrolling devices are isotonic, using either linear or rotary movement to control absolute position, relative position, or rate of movement. Absolute position control assigns specific meaning to fixed locations: for example, touching the bottom of a trackpad slider might map directly to the bottom of a document. Relative position control normally involves manipulating instant-to-instant displacement (e.g., pointing with a mouse), but it is can also be used to control displacement between a 'marked' location and a tracked one, as is the case when using middle-button autoscroll to control scroll speed (e.g., [9]). With *rate of movement* control the velocity of interaction is the primary input parameter, with examples including the speed of gestural flicks on a touchscreen (e.g., [2]) and the speed of rotary movement (e.g., [16, 17]). While most devices are isotonic, Zhai's IBM 'ScrollPoint' mouse uses an isometric knob for high performance scrolling [11, 19], making scroll speed proportional to the force applied to the knob. One benefit of rotary and isometric input methods is that they can be continually operated without clutching.

Input → System: Device/driver events

Input devices translate motor actions into electronic events which are interpreted and modified by low level driver software before being forwarded to applications. Quantization and driver gain critically affect this process.

Quantization problems occur when input discretisation impedes performance. This arises in many aspects of scrolling, such as mapping from a constrained range of scrollbar positions to a large range of potential views, or the coarse scroll increments supported by notched scroll wheels. The impact of quantization has been examined in several pointing studies (e.g., [7]), but we are unaware of similar analysis for scrolling.

Scrolling devices report raw events corresponding to the degree of a user's manipulation, which is translated into a magnitude of movement m (measured in number of lines or pixels) by software device drivers. The drivers can also attend to the reported m value and the time since the last event (Δt) and use these to apply transformations to the device events, typically using gain functions to improve performance. While there have been many studies of pointing gain (e.g., [6, 7]), there has been little public research on scroll gain, with Hinckley *et al.* [11] being a notable exception.

Hinckley *et al.* [11] describe a scrollwheel gain function (Equation 1) and a methodology for evaluating scrolling performance. Their experiments demonstrate that their gain function improves scrollwheel performance.

$$\Delta y = k_1(1 + k_2\Delta t)^{\alpha} \qquad \text{Equation 1.}$$

In this equation, Δy is the resultant gain, k_1, k_2, and α are constants, and Δt is the time between scroll events. The Δy gain value is used to multiply event magnitude m. For negative values of α, this function caps gain to a maximum value of k_1. Recognising the limitation of capped gain for long distance scrolling, Hinckley *et al.* [12] patented 'distance-based accelerated scrolling', in which rapid repeated scrollwheel clutches have an additive effect on gain, while pauses or direction reversals cancel it. This requires calibration of timeout values and threshold levels to distinguish small pauses from clutched reacquisition of the scrollwheel. We are unaware of any evaluation of the method, and we include it in Experiment 2.

System→Output→User: Display update and perception

Applications are responsible for updating the display in response to events reported from the driver. The default behaviour is to adjust the viewport by the magnitude requested, but applications can apply other effects based on particular needs. For example, 'speed dependent automatic zooming' [13] reduces motion blur by automatically zooming away from documents at high scroll speeds, and 'content aware scrolling' [14] allows documents to stipulate particular scroll paths based on document content. Techniques such as these change the basic scrolling behaviour, adding side effects to scroll-based movement, such as zooming or path alteration. In contrast, our goal with DLD-gain is to improve performance of basic scrolling using ubiquitous devices such as scroll wheels.

DOCUMENT-LENGTH-DEPENDENT GAIN

In Human-Computer Interaction, gain functions are used to amplify the raw signals from a device to assist the user in achieving their tasks. The level of gain calculated by the function(s) depends on some input parameter. For example, 'pointer acceleration' [7] is a gain function whereby pointer movement is amplified dependent on mouse velocity – when the mouse moves quickly, the user is assumed to want to move far, so higher gain assists them in doing so.

The specific goals of our document-length-dependent scrolling gain functions are as follows:

Pixel-level control. Recent scrolling devices and drivers allow smooth document movement by reporting high resolution (sub-line) scroll increments. Our gain functions enable smooth sub-line scroll increments even when the minimal scroll increment reported by the device/driver is an integral number of lines – the functions smooth out rough devices.

Constant time for full document traversal. Regardless of document length, the gain function should allow the entire document to be traversed (from start to end) in a near-constant time. Without this property device efficiency is likely to decrease as document length increases.

Efficient regardless of range. The gain function must remain efficient across all movement ranges – lines, paragraphs, pages, chapters, and entire books.

Subjectively appealing. Users must find the gain-modified device satisfying and comfortable for all movement ranges.

Details of the gain method

Our gain method uses three functions to map from device velocity to a resultant gain level: a slow movement function (SMF), a fast proportional function (FPF), and a slow-to-fast transition function (SFTF), described below.

As mentioned in related work, two parameters can be derived from each scrolling event – the magnitude of the movement (m) and the time since the last event (Δt). From these values we calculate a device velocity for each event ($v=m/\Delta t$), which is input to our functions to determine a gain level (g). The gain level is then used as a multiplier to the initial event magnitude to calculate a resultant scrolling distance ($d=g\times m$). This approach differs to Hinckley *et al.* [11] in that our functions calculate gain based on device velocity rather than Δt alone. Doing so allows the functions to receive a wider range of input values, particularly at high scroll-speeds (demonstrated by the calibration experiment). The three component functions are described below.

Slow movement function. SMF controls gain (g_s) during precise scrolling actions – it maps from the device velocity (v) to gain level using Equation 2. Figure 1 shows that this gives a rapid increase through fractional gain levels up to a capped constant level k_s (set to 1 by default). Fractional gain allows devices that report line-based scroll increments to support pixel-level smooth scrolling. The parameter α determines the rate of gain increase, which could be set through a user preferences dialog. Note that Equation 2 is independent of document length, meaning that slow document movement is consistently controlled across all documents.

$$g_s = k_s - k_s\alpha^{-v} \qquad \text{Equation 2.}$$

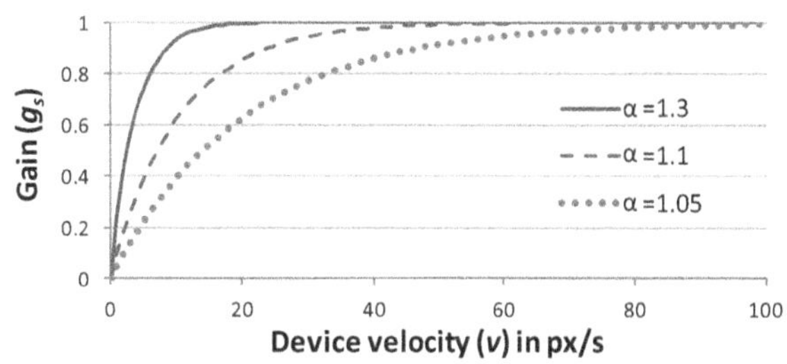

Figure 1. The slow movement function allows line-based devices to offer pixel scroll control through fractional gain.

Fast proportional function. The FPF function calculates gain (g_f) based on the *proportion* of the document that is visible in the viewport (see Equation 3). High gain levels are therefore possible for long documents or for documents that are viewed when closely zoomed. This is analogous to the behaviour of the scroll thumb – the number of document lines traversed when dragging the thumb depends on the ratio of document length to viewport size. The constant k_f allows adjustment of the maximum scrolling gain, and can be used to account for differences in device report granularity and for user preferences.

$$g_f = k_f \times \frac{document\ length}{viewport\ size} \qquad \text{Equation 3.}$$

$$p_s = 1 - p_f \qquad \text{Equation 4.}$$

$$p_f = \begin{cases} 0, & if\ v/v_{max} < initial \\ \frac{v/v_{max} - initial}{final - initial}, & if\ initial \le \frac{v}{v_{max}} \le final \\ 1, & if\ v/v_{max} > final \end{cases} \qquad \text{Equation 5.}$$

$$g = (p_s \times g_s) + (p_f \times g_f) \qquad \text{Equation 6.}$$

Slow-to-fast transition. The SFTF function controls the transition between slow-movement and fast-proportional functions. It does so by linearly transitioning between the proportional contribution of the SMF and FPF gain functions (p_s, p_f), based on the proportion of maximum device velocity (v/v_{max}). This transition is shown in Figure 2, Equation 4 and the piecewise Equation 5. The transition to using FMF begins when the device velocity exceeds an *initial* threshold, and it is complete at a *final* threshold. The gain calculation is shown in Equation 6.

The overall effect of these functions is similar to an exponential mapping from v to g, but the gain onset is postponed until high velocities to assist users with document control when moving short distances.

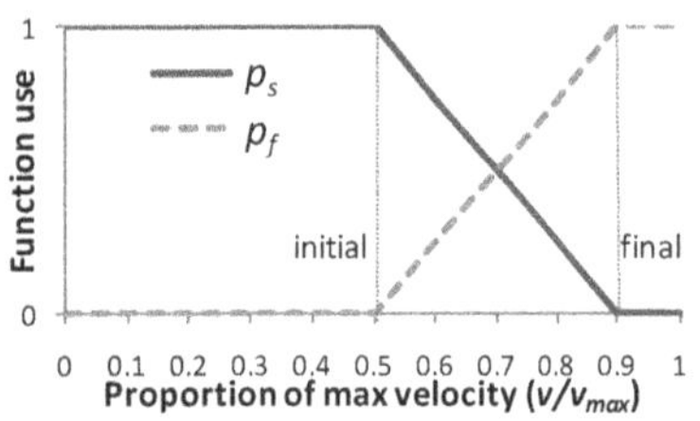

Figure 2. Slow-to-fast transition function, which controls the proportional contribution of slow and fast functions.

The potential drawback of the technique is that the fast proportional function (Equation 3) will produce high gain levels in long documents, which may cause control problems (exhibited as overshooting) when the *initial* threshold is accidentally attained. This effect will be more severe in long documents, since the interpolation gradient between the slow and fast functions will be steeper.

To investigate and evaluate the idea of document-length-dependent gain, we carried out two experiments. The objective of Experiment 1 was to understand important aspects of human control with four substantially different scrolling input devices, to characterise their event streams, and to use this data to calibrate the DLD-gain parameters identified in the previous section. Experiment 2 then validated DLD-gain by analysing human performance when using it; this study also examines the trade-off between fast long-distance movement and a steep interpolation function.

EXPERIMENT 1: CALIBRATING SCROLLING DEVICES

Calibrating DLD-gain would be straightforward if all users had exactly the same physical capabilities, if these capabilities were identically expressed in upward and downward scroll directions, if device event streams were smooth, and if all devices produced exactly the same range of values in their event reports. None of these are likely to be true. Experiment 1 therefore answers several questions that are used to calibrate DLD-gain parameters, as follows:

Q1: Is it necessary to separately calibrate v_{max} for different participants, directions, and devices? Equation 5 shows that v_{max} is a critical value controlling the transition between slow precise movement and fast proportional movement. If there is little variation between participants, directions, and devices then a single value would be sufficient for all, but if variation is substantial then individual calibration is necessary for participants, directions and devices.

Q2: Is smoothing necessary to reduce noise in event streams? If the m and Δt values reported by a device driver are substantially unstable while the user attempts to control the device at a constant velocity, then the resultant scrolling behaviour will be jerky, particularly at high gain levels. By understanding the characteristics of the event stream, simple procedures may adequately smooth event reports.

Q3: Is it necessary to diminish events for over-sensitive devices? The slow movement function (Equation 2) is capable of generating fractional gain levels (<1). These low gain levels allow pixel scrolling with devices that report integral line scroll increments, but importantly, they should also improve control of 'twitchy' devices that report unexpectedly fast scroll speeds for small motor effects.

The experiment answers these questions using four scrolling devices that use very different control mechanisms: a low-end traditional '*notched*' scrollwheel (Microsoft Wheel Mouse Optical), an '*inertia*' free-wheeling scrollwheel (Logitech M905), two-finger scrolling on a *trackpad* (Apple Magic Trackpad), and a mouse-mounted *isometric* scroll knob (IBM ScrollPoint).

Participants and apparatus

Thirteen university students (3 female; mean age 23.5, s.d. 1.9) took part in the experiment, all of whom used computers for at least 7 hours per week. Their participation lasted approximately 40 minutes.

The experiment ran on an Apple iMac with a 21.5″ display at 1920×1080 native resolution. The software was written in JavaScript and ran in Firefox 5. The drivers for each device were configured to use their lowest gain settings; we confirmed that these settings produced constant gain (no acceleration) by tracing function calls in the driver code[1].

Procedure

All participants used the four scrolling devices in both scrolling directions (up and down), completing all trials with one device before proceeding to the next (order counter-balanced). Participants completed NASA-TLX [10] worksheets after each device. With each device the procedure consisted of two repetitions (one for scrolling downward, one for upward) of the following activities: *familiarisation*, *v_{max} calibration*, and *slow scrolling*.

Familiarisation with each device/direction combination consisted of four repetitions of operating the device to match the left-to-right velocity of a series of orange vertical lines shown inside a progress bar. Each vertical line traversed the progress bar in three seconds. The participant's control of scroll velocity was indicated by progressively shading the progress bar grey, with a green leading edge. An abstract representation of scroll velocity was used (rather than scrolling text) to reduce transfer effects from prior scrolling experience.

[1] Available at: `http://opensource.apple.com/source/IOHIDFamily/IOHIDFamily-315.7.16/IOHIDSystem/IOHIPointing.cpp`

V_{max} calibration. To calibrate maximum velocity with the device/direction combination, participants were prompted to scroll 'As fast as comfortably possible'. They clicked a 'Start' button then began operating the device as fast as possible. A progress bar automatically filled at a rate of ¼ per second. This process was repeated four times in each direction, with the first trial discarded as familiarisation.

Slow scrolling. The final condition prompted users to scroll "smoothly and slowly to match the shown rate", with a document displaying pixel-scrolling at 2.5 lines per second (40 px/s). They repeated the four second task four times.

Results

Q1: Is separate v_{max} calibration needed?

We analyse v_{max} variation between directions and devices using a 4×2 repeated-measures analysis of variance for factors *input device* and *direction*. The dependent variable is the average speed during each trial (px/s). We applied the Aligned Rank Transform for nonparametric factorial analysis [18] to accommodate a non-normal distribution.

The isometric device reported dramatically higher maximum scroll speeds (mean 12358 px/s) than the other three devices at 1769, 568 and 431 px/s with *inertia, notch,* and *trackpad* respectively ($F_{3,36} = 48.3$, $p < .001$). *Direction* showed a significant main effect, with mean *down* speed (4045 px/s) faster than *up* (3518 px/s): $F_{1,12} = 52.2$, $p < .001$. A *device* × *direction* interaction ($F_{3,36} = 8.85$, $p < .001$), was caused by *inertia* having a larger difference between *up* and *down* directions than other devices.

These results demonstrate that device- and direction-dependent v_{max} calibration is necessary.

There was also substantial cross-participant variation in v_{max}, particularly with *inertia* and *isometric* devices. Figure 3 shows the range, median, mean, and interquartile range of v_{max} values across participants with the devices, suggesting that individual v_{max} calibration is important.

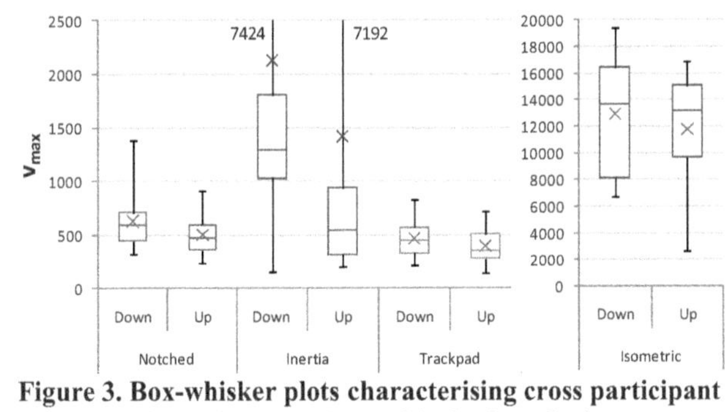

Figure 3. Box-whisker plots characterising cross participant variation in v_{max} values with the four devices.

Q2: Is smoothing necessary?

Figure 4 shows typical event streams with each of the four devices during v_{max} trials. It illustrates that clutching is prevalent with *notched* and *trackpad* (the velocity frequently decreases to zero while the fingers are repositioned on the device), and that users were better able to maintain a constant velocity with *inertia* and *isometric.*

The *trackpad* and *isometric* event streams frequently included paired 'corrective' events of small magnitude with extremely small Δt values (typically ~1ms), resulting in extremely high peak velocities. We account for these by summing Δt and m across events within a 10msec window.

Two further steps were taken to smooth DLD-gain's performance in response to noisy event streams. First, our implementation sets v_{max} to the 70th percentile of velocity attained during maximum velocity calibration trials. Doing so means that v_{max} is an attainable velocity, rather than one that can only be accidentally hit when the device reports a 'spike'. Second, to reduce the tendency for high variance in event stream velocities to produce jerky post-gain velocities, we average DLD-gain (g) over a window of w event reports (w=7 in our implementation). The event window is reset if no events are received for w_t seconds (0.5s) and when the scroll direction reverses.

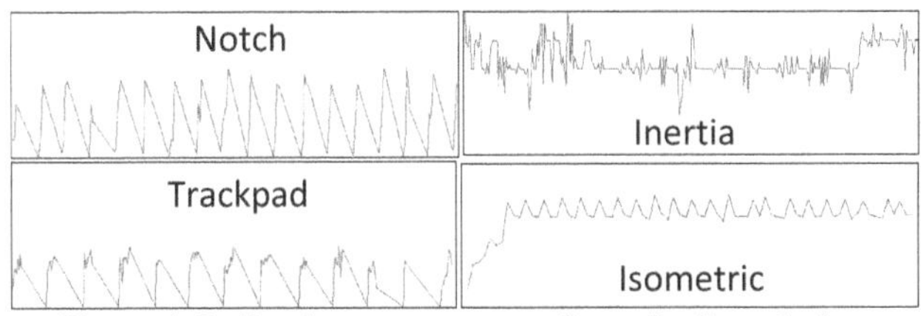

Figure 4. Indicative event streams from the four devices (magnitude *m* on y-axis, time on x-axis).

Q3: Is it necessary to diminish events for sensitive devices?

Slow trials involved operating the devices to match the velocity of a document shown scrolling at 40 px/s. Event stream analysis showed that participants operated three of the devices at roughly twice the intended speed: 82, 69 and 82 px/s with *notch, inertia,* and *trackpad. Isometric* was extremely fast at 4835 px/s, which suggests that users will have difficulty with slow and precise movement unless its event reports are diminished – confirmed by Experiment 2.

Subjective responses

NASA-TLX worksheet responses [10] on a five point scale from low (1) to high (5) showed significant differences (Friedman χ^2 test, $p < .05$) between devices for physical effort (means of 3.8, 2.8, 3.4, and 2.1 with *notch, inertia, trackpad* and *isometric* respectively), temporal demand (means of 3.3, 3.4, 3.1, and 2.2), and hard work (3.5, 3.5, 3.5, 2.1). The absence of clutching with *isometric* best explains its low perceived workload. However, participant comments also stated that *isometric* was *"too sensitive to control, need to highly concentrate on it"*, and *"I never feel like I have good control even if I can match a target rate".*

Resultant calibration

Table 1 shows the DLD-gain parameters used in Experiment 2 for the three devices. These values were attained by first finding k_s and α values that allowed precise control for line and paragraph movement, then finding k_f, *initial* and *final* values that allowed rapid long range movement. Experiment 2 compares DLD-gain performance with '*hinckley*' gain (the best scroll gain function we are aware of). We used Hinckley *et al.*'s function [11], supplemented with their "additive" technique [12], which accumulates gain across rapidly repeated clutching actions. '*Hinckley*' parameters for Equation 1 are also shown in Table 1, established through a similar process.

	Hinckley			*DLD*				
	k_1	k_2	α	k_s	α	k_f	*initial*	*final*
notched	4	8	-2.5	5	1.005	1	0.9	1.0
inertia	8	16	-3	2	1.005	0.2	0.5	1.0
isometric	10	15	-3	0.1	1.003	0.016	0.8	0.9

Table 1. Gain parameters for *hinckley* and *DLD* conditions.

EXPERIMENT 2: VALIDATING DLD-GAIN

We validate DLD-gain in a three-part experiment. The first part compares performance with three devices using DLD-gain against that of the same devices using Hinckley's gain functions. It uses an extremely long document (20,000 lines; 333 pages at 60 lines per page) that will cause DLD-gain to produce very high gain levels when the user exceeds the *initial* speed threshold – DLD-gain is therefore likely to be 'twitchy' at medium speeds. Part 1's hypothesis is:

> **H1:** DLD-gain improves performance compared to Hinckley's gain functions in an extremely long document.

Hinckley's gain functions are used as the comparator because they represent the state-of-the-art – they are known to improve performance with notched scrollwheels [11], and our pilot testing demonstrated that they radically improved performance with inertia and isometric devices, particularly for long distances.

Part 2 of the experiment analyses user performance with DLD-gain when scrolling in shorter documents, testing the following hypothesis.

> **H2:** scrolling performance with DLD-gain improves as document length decreases.

Finally, when switching between documents of different lengths user performance and preferences may be adversely affected by 'unpredictable' gain. This is tested in Part 3:

> **H3:** user performance with DLD-gain is not adversely affected when switching between document lengths.

These hypotheses are tested using Hinckley *et al.*'s method for analysing mechanical aspects of scrolling performance [11], which involves bidirectional tapping between target lines at controlled scroll distances. The target line is indicated by showing a mark at its location in the scroll trough and by highlighting the target line green (Figure 5). A target is acquired by pressing the space bar when the target line rests within a marked central region of the viewport (six lines wide). Pressing the space bar when the target is outside the target region constitutes an error, and the trial continues until successfully acquired. Completing one trial automatically begins the next, alternating between downward and upward scrolling. We used a wide range of distances representing movement across lines, paragraphs, pages, chapters, and books.

Part 1: Hinckley gain versus DLD-gain

Experiment 2 Part 1 compares performance with three devices when using DLD-gain and when using Hinckley's gain functions. The devices were *notch, inertia,* and *isometric*, with *trackpad* discarded for expediency due to its calibration similarity to *notch* in Experiment 1. As our research objective is to improve performance of scrolling devices, other methods for scrolling (such as the dragging the scroll-thumb) were disabled.

The experiment analyses performance across scrolling distance and direction. Pilot testing demonstrated that long distance scrolling with Hinckley's function can be prohibitively time-consuming, so to avoid prolonged and frenetic use of the device, trials were capped at 15 seconds.

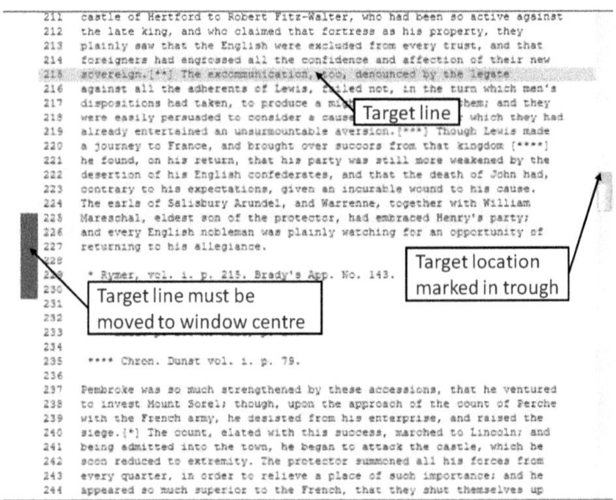

Figure 5. Experimental interface. Tasks involve moving the green target line into the central window region (left).

Design and Procedure

The primary dependent measure is acquisition time, with a secondary dependent measure for number of target overshoots and undershoots (necessitating a change in scrolling direction).

Data are analysed using a 2×3×5×2 ANOVA for within subjects factors *input device, gain, distance,* and *direction*:

Gain $\in$ *{hinckley, DLD}* ×
Input device $\in$ *{notch, inertia, isometric}* ×
Distance $\in$ *{7, 49, 343, 2401, 16807}* ×
Direction $\in$ *{up, down}* ×*3 repetitions*

With each device, participants completed nine device familiarisation trials with no gain. They then completed a v_{max} calibration for the *up* and *down* directions using the same procedure as Experiment One. The main experimental trials consisted of six selections at each of five levels of distance, with shorter distances preceding longer ones. The six trials consisted of three bi-directional repetitions (downward then upward thrice), with the first discarded as target familiarisation.

All trials with each *input device* were completed before moving on to the next *input device*, within which, all trials with each *gain* level were completed before moving on to the next gain. Six orders of *input device* and *gain* were balanced using a Latin square.

Participants and apparatus

Sixteen university students (6 female; mean age 25.5, sd. 4.5) took part in the experiment, with participation lasting approximately 40 minutes.

The experiment ran on a Microsoft Window 7 PC with a 22″ display at 1680×1050 native resolution. The experimental software was written in JavaScript and ran in Firefox 6. Device drivers were configured to produce constant gain (no scroll acceleration). The document used for the study was 20,000 lines of raw text from David Hume's *A History of England.*

Part 1: Results

At the longest scrolling distance (16807 lines) most trials were automatically terminated before the 15 second time cap with *hinckley* (90%, 62%, and 100% with *notch, inertia,* and *isometric* respectively), but comparatively few were automatically terminated with *DLD* (6%, 17%, and 9% respectively). In the following analysis the time cap value of 15 seconds is inserted for all time capped trials (consequently, substantially underestimating times with *hinckley* for distance 16807). *Direction* was found to have no significant effects or interactions, so we collapsed the analysis across *direction* and report results of a 2×3×5 ANOVA for *gain, device,* and *distance.*

Mean trial times with *DLD* (5.82s) were significantly faster than *Hinckley* (6.8s), leading us to accept **H1**: $F_{1,15} = 86.5, p < .001$. There was also significant main effect of *device* ($F_{2,30} = 15.8, p < .001$), with *inertia* fastest (6.0s), followed by *notch* (6.1) and *isometric* (6.8). As expected, *distance* showed a significant main effect: $F_{4,60} = 815.6, p < .001$.

Importantly, all interactions were also significant. Figure 6(a-c) separately show the *gain* × *distance* interactions for each device ($F_{4,60} = 117.0, p < .001$). The figures show that *hinckley* gain was slightly faster than DLD-gain for most short scrolling distances. For longer distances, however, DLD-gain was much faster, especially when considering that nearly all long distance *hinckley* trials were prematurely terminated by the 15 second cap.

To produce an estimate of how long it would have taken participants to complete the 16807 distance trials using *hinckley,* we used the distance completed during the 15 seconds of scrolling to calculate an average speed, and extrapolated for the remaining distance. This produces a mean estimate of 33 seconds for *notch*, 21 seconds with *inertia*, and 85 second with *isometric*, suggesting that long distance scrolling is impractical using *hinckley* gain. Regardless of *DLD*'s faster overall performance, its slightly worse performance at the 343 line distance is notable (*index of difficulty*=5.6 in Figure 6). We attribute this to participants accidentally hitting the *initial* threshold and consequently experiencing high gain levels due to the extreme document length strongly influencing Equation 3. This explanation is supported by scrolling path analysis, which shows significantly higher target overshooting with *DLD* (passing over the target and changing direction to return). The mean number of overshoots per trial was 0.67 with *hinckley* and 1.14 with *DLD* ($F_{1,15} = 41.0, p < .001$). Note that the number of overshoots characterises interaction but does not necessarily imply a performance problem – for example, a rapid ballistic phase of movement will promote overshooting, while gradual slow target approach will not.

As the *isometric* device was shown to be particularly sensitive in Experiment 1, we conducted a planned comparison between *DLD* and *hinckley* for it at the shortest distance, revealing means of 1.57s with *DLD* and 2.1s with *hinckley* ($F_{1,15} = 7.4, p < .05$). Although further analysis is required, this suggests that *DLD*'s slow movement function can be effective in aiding slow precise control.

Subjective responses for workload (using the NASA Task Load Index [10]) favoured *DLD.* Table 2 summarises these values, showing that where significant differences were detected, they all favoured *DLD.* The table suggests that participants found *DLD* most beneficial with the *notch* device for which physical and temporal workloads were particularly high with *hinckley*. Participants showed higher mean values for success when using *DLD* with all devices, and they rated it significantly higher for comfort. Despite

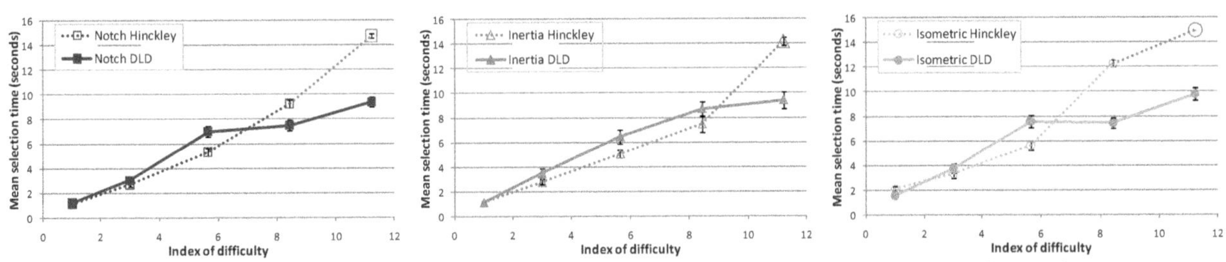

(a) Notch (b) Inertia (c) Isometric

Figure 6. Mean selection time with the three devices with Hinckley and DLD Gain. The enlarged red final data point with Hinckley gain indicates that most trials exceeded the automatic 15 second time cap. Index of difficulty = *log₂(distance/width+1)*.

these positive results, participants were near evenly split in their preferences for control.

Participants' comments reinforced these findings. One participant stated that when using *hinckley* with the *notch* device there was "*strain on finger, particularly index*" and "*very slow scrolling far away*". Another stated that *hinckley* with the *isometric* device was "*Hard to manipulate*". However, several participants commented on overshooting problems with *DLD*: "*kept over scrolling, hyper sensitive*" and "*didn't like how it jumped when I was close to target.*"

	Notch		Inertia		Isometric	
	DLD	Hinckley	DLD	Hinckley	DLD	Hinckley
Mental load	2.8(1.4)	2.2(1.1)	2.3(1.1)	2.1(1.1)	2.3(1.1)	2.0(1.1)
Physical load	***2.5(1.0)***	***4.3(1.0)***	2.2(1.0)	2.8(1.3)	2.4(1.1)	2.6(1.4)
Temporal load	***2.4(0.7)***	***4.1(0.9)***	2.6(0.9)	3.0(1.0)	2.8(0.9)	3.2(1.0)
Success	***3.6(0.9)***	***2.6(0.9)***	4.0(0.8)	3.4(0.8)	***3.5(1.1)***	***2.4(0.8)***
Hard work	***2.9(0.8)***	***4.1(0.9)***	2.4(0.8)	2.9(1.0)	3.1(0.9)	3.0(1.1)
Frustration	2.9(1.1)	3.2(1.2)	2.2(1.0)	2.4(0.9)	3.2(0.9)	2.9(1.0)
Comfort Pref.	***16***	***0***	***13***	***4***	***12***	***3***
Control Pref.	10	7	8	9	9	8

Table 2. Mean (st. dev.) NASA-TLX values (1= low, 5=high). Significant results are bold-italic, using Friedman tests for all but comfort and control preferences (which used χ^2 tests).

DLD's slight performance disadvantage for short distances and its substantial advantage for long distances (in this extremely long document) are indicative of a performance trade-off. When navigating long documents such as manuals, users are likely to need to move large distances (e.g., cross referencing the index), and these results show that for movements exceeding 10 pages (*notch* or *inertia*), *DLD* substantially outperforms *hinckley*. Part 2 examines *DLD's* performance in shorter documents.

Part 2: DLD-gain performance across document length

Hypothesis 2 examines DLD-gain's performance in shorter documents (10 and 100 pages). For expediency, experiment parts 2 and 3 were conducted using only the *inertia* device (which happened to have the smallest performance difference between *hinckley* and *DLD* in Part 1).

Participants completed trials at a subset of Part 1 distances (7, 49, and 343 lines) in a 600 line document and in a 6000 line document (recall that Part 1 used a 20000 line document). Trials were otherwise administered exactly as for Part 1, with the same progression through increasing movement distances and repetition of the two directions.

Part 2: Results

Acquisition time and overshoot data are analysed using a 3×3 RM-ANOVA for factors *distance* (7, 49, and 343) and *document length* (600, 6000, and 20000 lines).

Figure 7(a) summarises the acquisition time results, with *hinckley* data from Part 1 also shown for comparison. There was a significant main effect of *document length* ($F_{2,30} = 20.3, p < .001$), with means of 2.4, 2.8, and 3.7 for lengths 600, 6000 and 20000 respectively. Means for *distance* were also significant ($F_{2,30} = 37.9, p < .001$). Importantly, though, there was a significant *length* × *distance* interaction ($F_{4,60} = 14.3, p < .001$), caused by acquisition times increasing less steeply across distance in shorter documents. ANOVA of overshoots (summarised in Figure 7(b)) shows the same statistical effects, with overshooting much more prevalent in the 20,000 line document. We therefore accept **H2**.

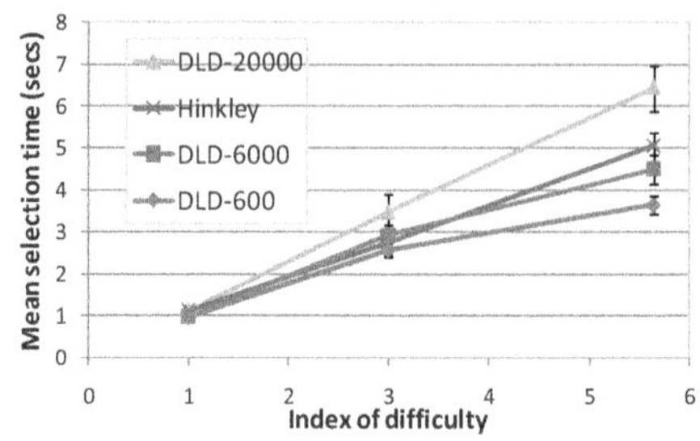

(a) Time

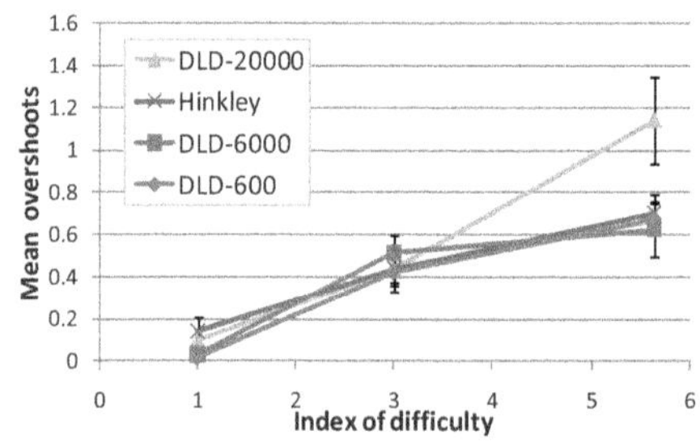

(b) Overshoots

Figure 7. Part 2 results, including *hinckley* data from Part 1.

We conducted planned comparisons between *hinckley inertia* data from Part 1 with *DLD* 600 and *DLD 6000* data from Part 2, using separate 2×3 RM-ANOVA for *gain* and *distance*. As suggested by Figure 7(a), in the 600 line document *DLD* (mean 2.4s) was significantly faster than *hinckley-inertia* (mean 3.0s): ($F_{1,15} = 20.5, p < .001$). There was also a significant *gain*×*distance* interaction ($F_{2,30} = 21.9, p < .001$) due to performance with *hinckley-inertia* deteriorating more rapidly across distance than *DLD*. Comparison of *DLD* performance in the 6000 line document with *hinckley-inertia* shows no main effect of *gain*, but a significant *gain*×*distance* interaction ($F_{2,30} = 4.3, p < .001$). Analysis of overshoots showed no significant effects involving *gain*.

These results suggest that DLD-gain outperforms Hinckley gain with the inertia wheel in a ten page document. This supports the explanation that DLD's slightly worse performance than Hinckley gain in middle-distance scrolling in Experiment 2 Part 1 was due to the performance trade-off in allowing rapid extremely long distance scrolling at the cost of 'twitchy' performance in middle distance scrolling. Experimental concerns with this assessment are presented in the Discussion.

Part 3: DLD-gain performance with document switching

Hypothesis 3 is motivated by the risk that performance may be adversely affected when rapidly switching between documents of different lengths (which will cause different gain behaviours with DLD). The change in gain behaviour is analogous to switching between different mouse gain settings, which temporarily disrupts pointing performance.

Participants completed two repetitions of bidirectional acquisitions with the following distance and document length tuples, in the following order: *(49, 20000), (343, 600), (16807, 20000), (7, 600)*. This order was used to maximise abrupt transitions between document lengths, and therefore maximise changes in DLD-gain behaviour. To allow a comparison between scrolling times when working within one document and when switching between document lengths, we compare data from Part 3 (which we termed '*switching*' trials) with data from the same distance and document length combinations in Experiment Parts 1 and 2 ('*non-switching*' trials).

Part 3: Results

Acquisition time data are analysed using a 2×4 RM-ANOVA for factors *task-type* and *distance-length*. The levels of *task-type* are *non-switching* and *switching*, with *non-switching* data extracted from the equivalent conditions in Parts 1 and 2 (where participants used the *inertia* device for the same distance and length conditions is a constant document length). The levels of *distance-length* were (7,600), (49, 20000), (343, 600) and (16807, 20000).

Figure 8 summarises the results. There were no significant negative effects of switching between different document lengths. The mean acquisition time for *non-switching* trials (4.4s) was similar to that for *switching* trials (4.1s): $F_{1,15} = 2.48$, $p = .14$. There was a marginal *task-type*×*distance-length* interaction ($F_{3,45} = 2.49$, $p = .07$), but as Figure 8 shows, this is due to *switching* being faster than *non-switching* trials at the longest distance-document combination, which (although not significant) is likely due to participants becoming more familiar with the inertia device later in the experiment. We therefore accept **H3.**

DISCUSSION

The results of Experiment 2 show that DLD-gain allows faster scrolling in extremely long documents than existing state-of-the-art gain functions, that its performance is faster still in more typical document lengths, and that performance is not harmed by switching between documents of different lengths. Subjective preferences were also favourable. These are good results, which suggest that the utility of scrolling devices such as scroll-wheels can extend far beyond their commonplace restriction to short-distance movement. The following paragraphs describe challenges to general use of DLD-gain, and areas for further work.

Experimental limitations for further work

These current results provide a strong foundation for further empirical analysis of DLD-gain's performance. We will pursue three main areas in further work.

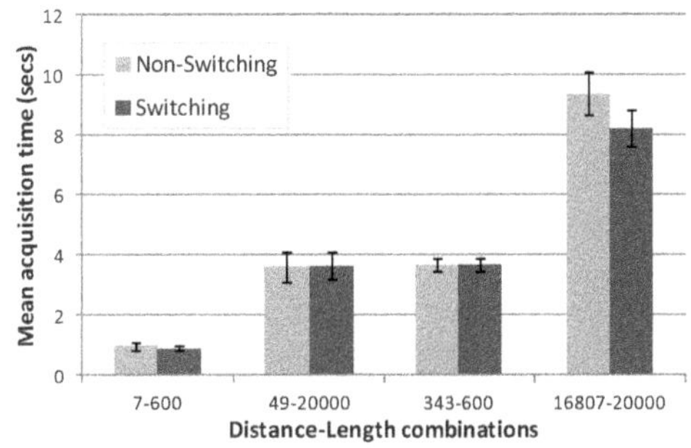

Figure 8. Part 3 results: effects of switching between different document lengths (Non-Switching data is from Parts 1 and 2).

First, we will compare DLD-gain with previous gain functions in typical document lengths. Experiment 2 Part 2 demonstrated that performance with DLD-gain improves in shorter documents, but we also compared DLD results from Part 2 with Hinckley gain results from Experiment Part 1. This comparison is reasonable because Hinckley's gain functions are not affected by document length, but there are risks of learning effects and of task prompting effects (the scroll trough mark is smaller in a long document). We are confident that direct comparisons with short documents will confirm the results. Our second main area for further work is to conduct these comparisons with multiple devices.

Third, an important part of the motivation for DLD-gain was to enable scrolling devices to support the full range of scrolling activities, regardless of distance. We think DLD-gain achieves this objective, but in future work we will seek empirical evidence demonstrating the use of DLD-gain enhanced devices in favour of dragging the scroll thumb.

Application gain, rather than device

DLD-gain requires information about document length and viewport size that is unavailable to device driver software. It is most likely that DLD-gain would be implemented by particular applications or interface toolkits. This raises three concerns: first, how could application designers calibrate their software to work with many different devices; second, how would users adapt to inconsistent scrolling across applications; and third, how does DLD-gain interact with different device gain settings? For calibration parameters, without changes to driver protocols, the application would need to support a table lookup dependent on automatic device detection or user-specification of their main device. The second issue of inconsistent scrolling behaviour seems relatively minor as many applications already support scrolling enhancements that result in varied performance. Experiment 2 Part 3 also provided preliminary evidence that users are robust to sudden large changes in scrolling gain behaviour. The third issue of interaction between device driver gain and DLD-gain is interesting and we intend to conduct further studies using the method of Casiez and Roussel [6] to examine and manipulate device gain.

Comparison with other techniques

Finally, many research systems are known to improve scrolling performance, with several using some form of zooming output effect (e.g., OrthoZoom [3], SDAZ [11], and SFT [8]) or oscillatory input gestures (e.g., Cyclopan [16] and the virtual scroll ring [17]). DLD-gain is different in that it maintains traditional mechanisms for scrolling input and output. However, empirical comparison with these and other techniques remains interesting.

CONCLUSIONS

Specific devices for scrolling, such as scrollwheels, are provided on most pointing devices, but there has been surprisingly little publicly accessible research into improving their performance. Consequently, these devices have limited applicability, and in particular, they become inefficient for long distance scrolling. We presented three gain functions, collectively called document-length-dependent gain, that improve performance with scrolling devices. They do so by making the maximum attainable gain level a function of document length, which allows long documents to be traversed quickly. Experimental results demonstrated that the technique improves performance and preferences over existing gain methods in a variety of document lengths and navigation distances.

ACKNOWLEDGEMENTS

Thanks to the experimental participants and the paper reviewers. This work was supported by a Royal Society of New Zealand Marsden Grant 10-UOC-020.

REFERENCES

1. Abowd, G. and Beale, R. Users, systems and interfaces: A Unifying Framework for Interaction. in *People and computers VI. Proc. British HCI '91. 20*, 1991, 73-87.
2. Aliakseyeu, D., Irani, P., Lucero, A. and Subramanian, S. Multi-flick: An evaluation of flick-based scrolling techniques for pen interfaces. in *Proc. CHI'08*, ACM Press, (2008), 1689-1698.
3. Appert, C. and Fekete, J. OrthoZoom Scroller: 1D Mutli-scale navigation. in *Proc. CHI'06*, ACM Press, (2006), 21-30.
4. Buxton, W. Lexical and pragmatic considerations of input structures. *SIGGRAPH Computer Graphics 17*, 1 (1983), 31-37.
5. Card, S., Mackinlay, J.D. and Robertson, G. A morphological analysis of the design space of input devices. *ACM Transactions on Information Systems 9*, 2 (1991), 99-122.
6. Casiez, G. and Roussel, N. No more Bricolage! Methods and Tools to Characterize, Replicate and Compare Pointing Transfer Functions. in *Proc. UIST '11*, ACM Press, (2011).
7. Casiez, G., Vogel, D., Balakrishnan, R. and Cockburn, A. The Impact of Control-Display Gain on User Performance in Pointing Tasks. *Human-Computer Interaction 23*, 3 (2008), 215-250.
8. Cockburn, A., Gutwin, C. and Alexander, J. Faster Document Navigation with Space-Filling Thumbnails. in *Proc CHI '06*, ACM Press, (2006), 1-10.
9. Cockburn, A., Savage, J. and Wallace, A. Tuning and Testing Scrolling Interfaces that Automatically Zoom. in *Proc. CHI '05*, ACM Press, (2005), 71-80.
10. Hart, S. and Staveland, L. Development of NASA-TLX (Task Load Index): Results of Empirical and Theoretical Research. in Hancock, P. and Meshkati, N. eds. *Human Mental Workload*, 1988, 139-183.
11. Hinckley, K., Cutrell, E., Bathiche, S. and Muss, T. Quantitative Analysis of Scrolling Techniques. in *Proc. CHI '02*, ACM Press, (2002), 65-72.
12. Hinckley, K. and Cuttrell, E. Distance-based accelerated scrolling. US Patent: 7,173,637 B1, 2007.
13. Igarashi, T. and Hinckley, K. Speed-dependent Automatic Zooming for Browsing Large Documents. in *Proc. UIST '00*, ACM Press, (2000), 139-148.
14. Ishak, E. and Feiner, S. Content-aware scrolling. in *Proc. UIST '06*, ACM Press, (2006), 155-158.
15. Jacob, R., Sibert, L., McFarlane, D. and Mullen, M. Integrality and separability of input devices. *ACM Transactions on Human-Comptuer Interaction. 1*, 1 (1994), 3-26.
16. Malacria, S., Lecolinet, E. and Guiard, Y. Clutch-free panning and integrated pan-zoom control on touch-sensitive surfaces: the cyclostar approach. in *Proc. CHI '10*, ACM Press, (2010), 2615-2624.
17. Moscovich, T. and Hughes, J. Navigating documents with the virtual scroll ring. in *Proc. UIST '04*, ACM Press, (2004), 57-60.
18. Wobbrock, J., Findlater, L., Gergle, D. and Higgins, J. The Aligned Rank Transform for Nonparametric Factorial Analyses Using Only ANOVA Procedures. in *Proc. CHI '11*, ACM Press, (2011), 143-146.
19. Zhai, S., Smith, B. and Selker, T. Improving Browsing Performance: A Study of Four Input Devices for Scrolling and Pointing Tasks. in *Proc. INTERACT'97*, (1997), 286-292.

Aural Browsing On-The-Go: Listening-based Back Navigation in Large Web Architectures

Tao Yang, Mexhid Ferati, Yikun Liu, Romisa Rohani Ghahari, Davide Bolchini
Indiana University, School of Informatics at IUPUI
535 W. Michigan Street, Indianapolis, IN 46202, U.S.A.
{taoyang, mferati, yikliu, rrohanig, dbolchin}@iupui.edu

ABSTRACT
Mobile web navigation requires highly-focused visual attention, which poses problems when it is inconvenient or distracting to continuously look at the screen (e.g., while walking). Aural interfaces support more eyes-free experiences, as users can primarily *listen to* the content and occasionally look at the device. Yet, designing aural information architectures remains a challenge. Specifically, back navigation is inefficient in the aural setting, as it forces users to listen to each previous page to retrieve the desired content. This paper introduces *topic-* and *list-based back*: two navigation strategies to enhance aural browsing. Both are manifest in Green-Savers Mobile (GSM), an aural mobile site. A study (N=29) compared both solutions to traditional back mechanisms. Our findings indicate that topic- and list-based back enable faster access to previous pages, improve the navigation experience and reduce perceived cognitive load. The proposed designs apply to a wide range of content-intensive, ubiquitous web systems.

Author Keywords
Aural web; mobile web; info architecture; back navigation.

ACM Classification Keywords
H.5 [Information Interfaces and Presentation];

INTRODUCTION
A student walks to school while listening to music; a mom jogs in the park while listening to her favorite podcast; a scientist walks to lunch while listening to the latest news.

These situations share a common thread: listening to digital content in a mobile setting. Whereas existing audio content follows an elementary, linear structure (e.g., playlists, podcasts or audio books), it is much less obvious to design *aural* interactions for highly-structured, hypertextual content, such as a large website. This would call for investigating the interplay among listening to content, being on-the-go, interacting (occasionally) with a mobile device, and navigating a large information architecture (Figure 1).

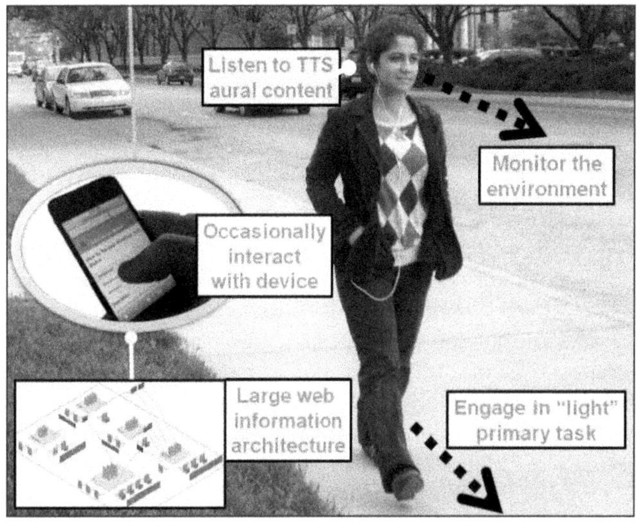

Figure 1. A mobile scenario for browsing aural websites.

Aural interfaces have shown to have potential to support eyes-free experiences [24, 25], as users can mainly *listen* to content (e.g., in Text-To-Speech form) and occasionally *look* at the mobile device. A recent study on driving scenarios indicates that *audio-based* interfaces – though slower to interact with – can be less distracting from the primary task (e.g., monitoring the environment) compared to visual interfaces [8]. Yet, one of the most perplexing challenges of designing effective aural interfaces is to understand the navigation issues in large information architectures [5, 6]. The aural perceptual channel, in fact, is much narrower than our visual bandwidth; this makes the aural navigation of complex hierarchical and hypertextual structures a very difficult and frustrating task [1, 5, 26].

Aurally browsing non-trivial web architectures is especially cumbersome in those frequent situations in which users need to go *back* to previously visited pages. In visual navigation, users can easily master the flow of pages through at-a-glance page scanning. Aural back navigation, however, becomes quickly unmanageable when many pages need to be backtracked: each non-useful back click is a detrimental waste of time and cognitive effort, as the user is forced to *listen to* some part of the page to recognize it [12]. The structural linearity of audio, combined with the rigid linearity of existing web history strategies, easily leads to ineffective aural experiences [3]. How can the experience of back navigation be improved in aurally browsing a

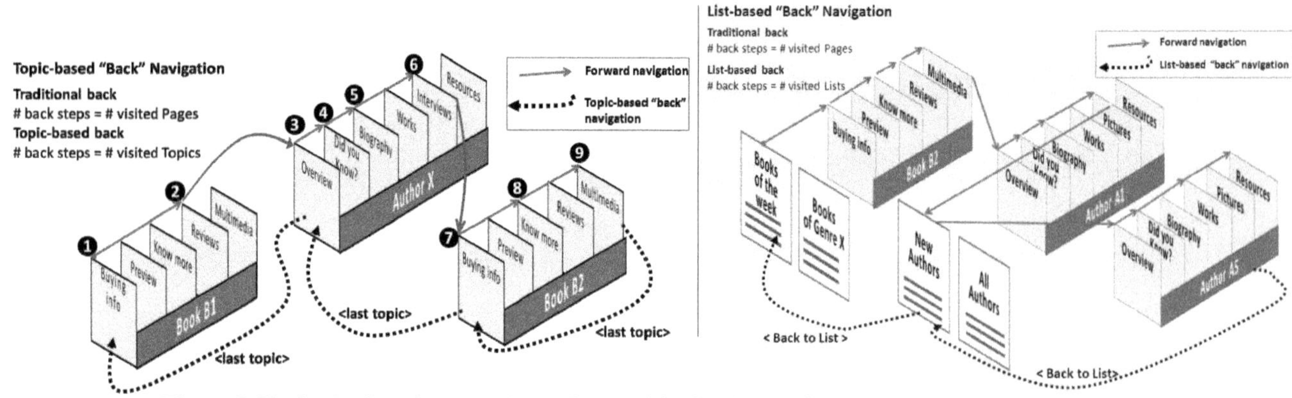

Figure 2. Topics (rather than pages) are the cognitive landmarks in topic-based back navigation (left); list-based back enables users to directly navigate to previously visited list pages (right).

mobile web application? How can people interact with the aural backtracking history while on the go?

To address these questions, this paper introduces and evaluates *topic-* and *list-based back*, two conceptual design strategies to support effective "back" navigation in complex aural information architectures, especially for mobile contexts. Both aural navigation strategies are manifest in Green-savers Mobile (GSM in short), an aural mobile website. GSM was used to set up a controlled evaluation study (N=29) in which participants browsed aural content in a simulated walking environment using either the advanced navigation strategies or a traditional "back" mechanism for aural browsing tasks of equivalent complexity. To control the navigation, we combined the design strategies with two "commodity" input modalities commonly available on smart phones (clicking on an explicit link, or using custom touch gestures). We measured task efficiency, navigation experience and perceived cognitive load for each condition. In short, our findings suggest that the advanced navigation solutions, when each compared to traditional back mechanisms, enable faster access to previous pages, improve the navigation experience, and reduce cognitive load. Whereas these strategies might make little difference for the visual web, our work shows that they are enhancing navigation performance and experience in auditory browsing, especially when audio is experienced in the pervasive mobile context (with sporadic interaction with the device and dual-task situations). In the following sections we illustrate the aural browsing strategies, the study design, and the results. We then discuss the implications and limits of our research to advance the design of the aural web.

BACK BROWSING STRATEGIES FOR THE AURAL WEB

Topic-based Back Navigation

In very large web applications, the change of navigational context (e.g., reaching a new type of content or a new section) is not taken into consideration by current history or backtracking strategies (e.g., the back button of the browser), that simply model every navigation unit as a "page." Collections of pages, however, are commonly "held" together and conceptually designed to represent a coherent information entity, or "topic". For example, in Amazon.com, a main topic is a "book." A book topic generally consists of a number of pages, such as buying information, customer reviews, and a book preview. Users traverse pages, and in traversing pages, they navigate topics. Aural users can benefit by navigating *back through topics* instead of through pages, as topics represent clear landmarks for new content and navigation contexts.

Imagine a scenario in which users are moving from the "buying info" page ❶ of book B1 (see Figure 2 left) to the book reviews ❷. From there, they navigate to the book's author ❸, listen to trivia ❹ and biographical information about the author ❺, listen to an interview ❻, and directly navigate to another book written by the same author by following a suggested navigation path (e.g., "see other books of this author"). As users need to go "back" to the first visited book by using existing back mechanisms, they would need to backtrack *page by page* through this path, with the known detrimental consequences of "listening" to every previous page. Instead, by using a *topic-based navigation strategy* (Figure 2 left), users can directly access the last *visited topics* (not pages), and thus visit (in sequence) the current book, the visited author and the first book. Topics are defined at conceptual design time during the planning of large web information architectures [3].

In the example of Figure 2 (left), a traditional back strategy (the back of common browsers) would require eight back clicks to get back to the desired page (Buying info of Book B1). Topic-based back would only require three clicks, gaining a potential 62% in backtracking efficiency, without considering the decreased demand on cognitive effort (i.e. removing the need to listen and pay attention to every visited page). Given the constrained linearity of the aural medium, this "shortcut" back navigation can be extremely beneficial in aural, mobile situations.

List-based Back Navigation

Let us now consider a complementary perspective. Users not only traverse content (topics), but also *list pages,* which are the fundamental mechanism to access content. For example (Figure 2 right), users can visit the page "Books of

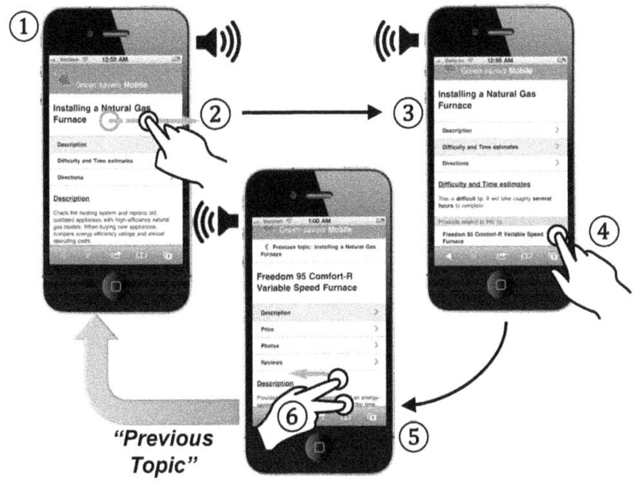

Figure 3. Topic-based back with custom gesture: ❶ Green Tip 1, Description; ❷ Move to ❸ Tip 1, Time estimates; ❹ Go to a related product; ❺ Product 1, Description; ❻ Two-finger swipe left to go back to Tip 1. Icons from [14].

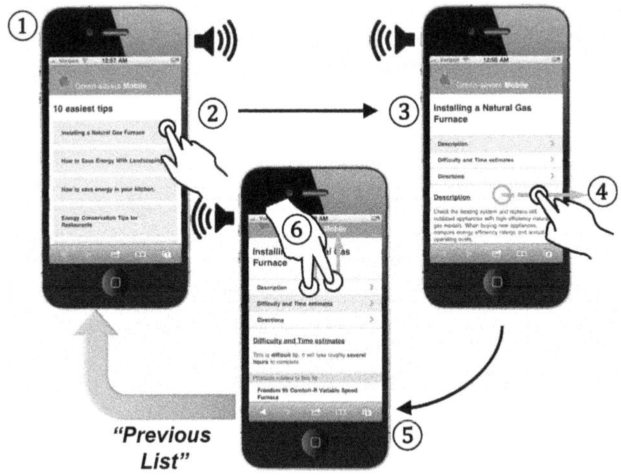

Figure 4. List-based back with custom gesture: ❶ List of tips ❷ Choose the first tip; ❸ Tip 1, Description; ❹ Go to the next section of the tip; ❺ Tip 1, Time estimates; ❻ Two-finger swipe up to go back to the previous list (list of tips).

the Week", pick a book, browse its details, navigate to the author, discover from here a list of emerging authors, choose another author, and browse her biography. If users want to go back to the "Books of the Week" list to pick another book, 11 steps are needed in our example. This means that 11 pages would have to be listened to (at least to recognize the content) in an auditory interface. An efficient aural back does not have to work this way. Navigation strategies conceptually based on the *access structures* (list pages) would allow users to aurally go "up" *directly* to the list pages previously visited, thus skipping unnecessary navigation steps through content (topic) pages. With a *list-based back*, users can simply backtrack to the list of "Books of the Week" with 2 steps, gaining a potential 81% in backtracking efficiency, without considering the reduction in cognitive effort. As such, list-based back would be especially beneficial in contexts in which users often go back to previously visited lists to regain orientation and restart a navigation path. Both conceptual patterns (topic- and list-based back) are applicable to a variety of aural interaction scenarios, such as the use of screen readers [1, 3, 6, 20], as well as for aurally navigating a large website on-the-go using a mobile device.

REIFYING DESIGNS

To investigate and evaluate the implications of these navigation strategies on the interplay between aural mobile browsing and interacting with complex architectures, we have reified topic-based back (Figure 3) and list-based back (Figure 4) in GSM, an aural web-based mobile application prototype on energy saving tips and green products for the home (http://discern.uits.iu.edu:8670/NSF_MOBILE/). This mobile site was developed to demonstrate aural mobile navigation in a non-trivial, web information architecture. The information architecture of GSM includes 4 types of topics (tip, product, tax credit, and rebate), overall 65 topic instances, 43 list page instances, and 6 types (64 instances) of hypertextual associations (e.g., products related to a tip, tips related to a product, rebates available for a product).

GSM is optimized for touch-screen mobile devices, specifically Apple's iPhone or iPod Touch, with iOS 4.1. To auralize content, GSM features dynamic, real-time text-to-speech (TTS) of page content and links. The custom TTS script, which is based on the API of the iSpeech service (www.ispeech.org), converts the text visible on the screen to audio, which is played back to the user in the same order in which it appears on screen. The back navigation strategies dynamically populate the user's backtracking history based on the current browsing session. Navigation functions have also been parameterized to alternatively exhibit topic- or list-based behavior. In terms of input to control navigation, GSM supports explicit link labels (e.g., Go back to <List Page Name>), and, alternatively, custom touch gestures (see Figure 3 and 4) to alleviate the demand of focused visual attention to the device.

EVALUATION HYPOTHESES

Based on the principles of topic- and list-based back navigation as applied to an aural mobile scenario, we hypothesize that:

H1: With respect to traditional back, *topic-based back* enables faster navigation to previously visited content pages, yields a better navigation experience and reduces perceived cognitive load.

H2: With respect to traditional back, *list-based back* enables faster navigation to previously visited list pages, yields a better navigation experience and reduces perceived cognitive load.

H3: The proposed custom gestures support topic-based navigation better than label clicking.

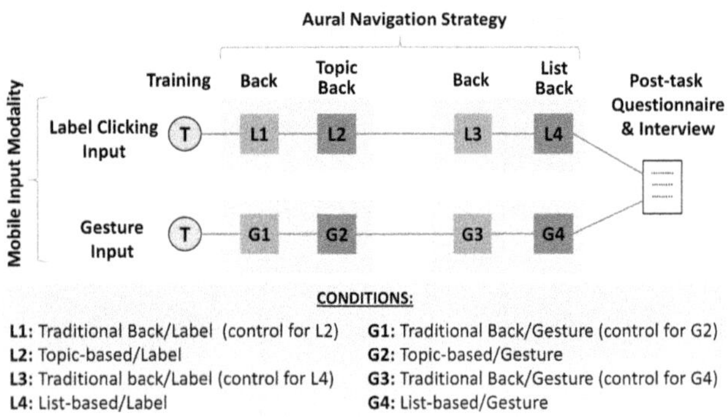

Figure 5. Synopsis of the study design.

H4: The proposed custom gestures support list-based navigation better than label clicking.

STUDY DESIGN

Physical Set Up

The evaluation study was conducted in a controlled environment, where we set up an 89-foot long path that users had to walk on while executing aural browsing tasks. The path included 10 sharp turns and 5 stop signs (on the ground) to simulate a real-world scenario in which people are required to avoid other people or objects in their way (Figure 6 left). We recorded the interaction with GSM (through a mounted video camera) and the walking behavior along the path (through a distant observer with video camera). Participants were encouraged to walk on the path as naturally as possible, and listen to the TTS content and links provided by the application. They were asked to only look to the device when necessary to activate a link.

Study Variables

The independent variables were the aural navigation strategy (traditional back, topic-based back, or list-based back) and input modality (custom gesture input or label clicking). Dependent variables were task efficiency (time-on-task, number of pages viewed), effectiveness (task success rate), degree of distraction from walking path (missed stop signs and steps out of the path), self-reported navigation experience and perceived cognitive load.

Participants

We recruited 29 participants (14 males and 15 females), all undergraduate students from a large Midwestern university; all of them spoke English fluently, and had no hearing or walking impairment. Participants were all daily users of Apple iPhone or iPod Touch. For approximately 60 minutes of participation, each participant received a $15 gift card.

Procedure

Participants were randomly assigned to either gesture-input group (G) or label clicking group (L). Participants in either group individually attended a 10-minute basic training (T) session in which they were briefed about the general content of GSM and the navigation features available. Participants were then introduced to both topic- and list-based back for 3-4 minutes and were given approximately 15 minutes to practice the two navigation strategies and input modalities on their own.

Figure 6. Simulated path that users walked while doing tasks (left); capturing participant's navigation behavior (right).

The gesture group (G) was instructed to use the custom finger gestures to activate topic- and list-based back. For the control group (traditional back), users were instructed to go back to previously visited pages using one finger swipe right. The label group (L) was instructed to click on an explicit link labels when available (i.e., anchor: Back to <*topic name*>) to perform the same back operations. Both groups went through four stages of tests – two tasks per stage – totaling eight tasks per participant (see Figure 5). The first stage included traditional back/label (L1) and traditional back/gesture (G1), both as control conditions for topic-based navigation. The second stage included topic-based/label (L2) and topic-based/gesture (G2), both as experimental groups for topic-based navigation. Stage three and four covered traditional back/label (L3) and traditional back/gesture (G3) as control for list-based navigation. List-based/label (L4) and list-based/gesture (G4) were the experimental groups for the list-based navigation strategy.

Fourteen participants went through stages in an order of 1, 2, 3, and 4, while 15 participants follow the order of 3, 4, 1, and 2. Navigation tasks were designed to cover multiple instances of all types of navigation structures relevant for topic- and list-based back. The designed tasks fall under the "fact finding" category of Kellar et al. [17]. Appendix A reports two examples of the tasks used, one for topic-based navigation and one for list-based navigation. The structure of the tasks (i.e., expected page types in the architecture) is the same across stages. The only difference is the set of *instances* of topics and list pages that were covered.

During each task, participants were asked to use the application while walking on the predefined path marked with tape. Deviations from the line or missed stop signs (breaks on the course) during the task were recorded as distractions. Three types of distraction indicators were captured: 1. *number of stop signs missed*: the number of stop signs that a user walked across without stopping; 2. *number of step-outs*: the number of times that a user stepped out of the predefined path; and 3. *unnecessary stop-time*: the amount of time users spent standing still when they were not supposed to. After each stage, participants rated their navigation experience using the navigation-related module of the DEEP usability index [34]; they also

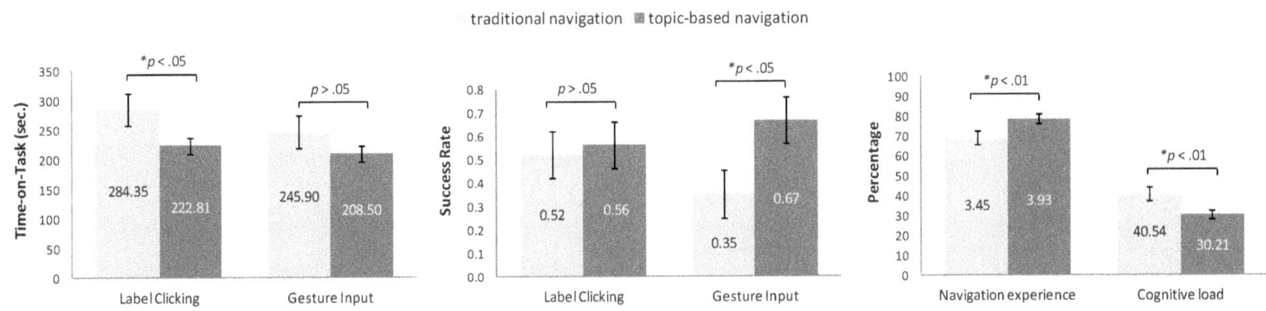

Figure 7. Topic-based back significantly reduces time-on-task when label clicking input is used (left); significantly increases success rate when gesture input is used (middle); and yields better ratings for navigation experience and cognitive load (right).

rated their perceived cognitive load on the NASA TLX scale [15].

In a post-test interview, participants were asked three main questions about their navigation experience: (1) *Which of the three navigation strategies – if any – did you find most helpful in completing your tasks? (2) Please explain in your own words what each strategy does; (3) What difficulties – if any – did you encounter in using the back navigation?*

ANALYSIS

For the quantitative data, 2 × 2 mixed-model ANOVAs were used to analyze the efficiency and effectiveness of the two novel back navigation strategies, and the effect of the input type. We used the navigation strategy (traditional back vs. topic-based/list-based back) as the within subject factor and the input type (label clicking vs. gesture input) as the between subject factor. Six outcome variables were compared: time-on-task, success rate, distractions, pages viewed, navigation experience, and cognitive load. The scales used for measuring navigation experience (DEEP) and perceived cognitive load (NASA TLX) were reliable in all the experimental conditions (Cronbach's Alpha > .82). This indicates that they were good instruments for capturing the factors of the user experience we set out to measure. For the qualitative analysis of the interviews, we extracted recurrent themes and grouped comments by type. The emerging issues highlight user preferences for the navigation strategies, and difficulties faced while using back navigation in combination with the input modalities.

RESULTS

Topic-Based Back vs. Traditional Navigation

Topic-based Back Reduces Time-on-Task

As indicator of navigation efficiency, we operationalized time-on-task as the amount of time it took users to either accomplish or give up on a task. Average time-on-task differs significantly between topic-based and traditional back ($F_{(1, 26)} = 6.75$, $p < .05$, $\eta^2 = .206$). Users spent significantly less time to accomplish the tasks using topic-based back (M = 215.65 sec., SE = 9.48) than using traditional back navigation (M = 265.12 sec., SE = 18.73).

No significant interaction was found between navigation strategy and input type. A special pattern, however, was detected: topic-based back only significantly reduced time-on-task in the label clicking condition, but not in the gesture input condition (see Figure 7 left).

Topic-based Back with Gesture Increases Success Rate

As indicator of navigation effectiveness, we measured users' task performance by either pass (full completion of the task) or fail (partial completion, completion with assistance, give up, or missing target). The success rate was calculated by averaging the scores of the related tasks. Success rate did not differ significantly between topic-based and traditional back ($F_{(1, 26)} = 4.16$, $p > .05$, $\eta^2 = .138$). Nevertheless, the success rate using topic-based back (M = .58, SE = .07) was still much higher than using traditional back (M = .42, SE = .07). Although no significant interaction was found, we noticed that topic-based back significantly increased the success rate in the gesture input condition, but not in the label clicking condition (see Figure 7 middle). Moreover, the combination of topic-based back and gesture input yielded the best success rate (67% on average) across conditions.

Distraction from Walking Task

Unnecessary stop-time was significantly reduced using topic-based back ($F_{(1, 26)} = 6.8$, $p < .05$, $\eta^2 = .207$) (Figure 8). Topic-based back reduced (although not significantly) both the number of stop signs missed ($F_{(1, 26)} = .23$, $p > .05$, $\eta^2 = .009$) and the number of step-outs ($F_{(1, 26)} = .14$, $p > .05$, $\eta^2 = .005$). No significant interaction between navigation strategy and input type was found for each of the three distraction indicators (number of stop-signs missed, number of step-outs, and unnecessary stop-time).

Number of Pages Viewed

Number of pages viewed did not differ significantly between topic-based back and traditional back ($F_{(1, 26)} = .05$, $p > .05$, $\eta^2 = .002$). On average, the number of pages viewed using topic-based back (M = 17.50, SE = 1.14) was only slightly less than the number viewed using traditional back (M = 17.13, SE = .88). There was also no significant interaction between navigation strategy and input type.

Better Navigation Experience and Reduced Cognitive Load

Users' navigation experience and perceived cognitive load in the two navigation conditions are compared in Figure 7

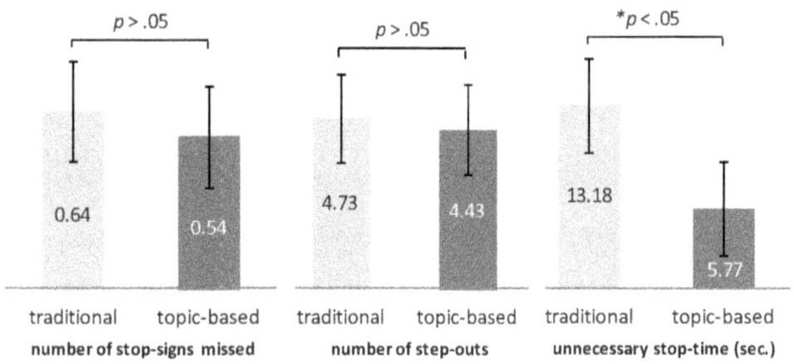

Figure 8. Topic-based back partially reduces distraction, especially the number of unnecessary stops (when users stop to focus on the device).

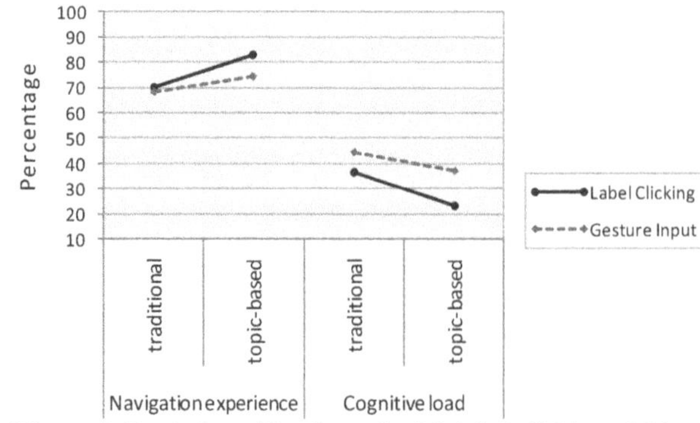

Figure 9. Topic-based back used with label clicking yields better ratings for navigation experience and cognitive load.

(right). Regardless of the input type used, users had significantly better navigation experience using topic-based back (M = 3.93, SE = .12) than traditional back (M = 3.45, SE = .18) ($F_{(1, 27)} = 9.22$, $p < .01$, $\eta^2 = .255$). Moreover, users' cognitive load was significantly higher in the traditional back (M = 40.54, SE = 4.35) than in the topic-based back condition (M = 30.21, SE = 3.17) ($F_{(1, 26)} = 10.47$, $p < .01$, $\eta^2 = .287$). These results indicate that topic-based back navigation has the potential to improve the experience of navigating an aural website and reduce the cognitive load in accomplishing aural browsing tasks.

No significant interaction between navigation strategy and input type was found for either navigation experience or cognitive load. It is worth noting, however, that gesture input significantly worsened the perceived cognitive load in topic-based back (M = 37.72, SE = 5.36; t = 2.47, $p < .05$) with respect to label clicking (M = 22.98, SE = 2.66). In addition, when label clicking input was used, topic-based back enhanced navigation experience and reduced cognitive load to a higher degree than when gesture input was used. This is clearly indicated by the different slopes between the solid and the dotted lines in Figure 9. In sum, the above evidence suggests that gesture input might not work as well as label clicking for the topic-based back navigation.

List-Based Back Navigation vs. Traditional Navigation

List-based Back Reduces Time-on-Task

Time-on-task differed significantly between list-based back and traditional back ($F_{(1, 26)} = 16.94$, $p < .05$, $\eta^2 = .394$). It took users significantly less time to accomplish the tasks using list-based back (M = 130.00 sec., SE = 9.09) than using traditional back (M = 173.38 sec., SE = 9.75). No significant interaction was found between navigation strategy and input type.

List-based Back and Success Rate

Success rate did not differ significantly between the two navigation strategies ($F_{(1, 26)} = 2.97$, $p > .05$, $\eta^2 = .102$). Nevertheless, the success rate using list-based back (M = .57, SE = .08) was still much higher than using traditional back (M = .39, SE = .08). Significant interaction was found between navigation strategy and input type ($F_{(1, 26)} = 4.27$, $p < .05$, $\eta^2 = .141$). List-based back significantly increased success rate with label clicking, but not with gesture input (see Figure 10 left). The combination of list-based back and label clicking input yielded the best success rate (71% on average) across all conditions.

Distraction

Although not significant, list-based back reduced the number of stop-signs missed ($F_{(1, 25)} = .49$, $p > .05$, $\eta^2 = .019$), the number of step-outs ($F_{(1, 25)} = 2.81$, $p > .05$, $\eta^2 = .101$) and the unnecessary stop-time ($F_{(1, 25)} = 3.87$, $p > .05$, $\eta^2 = .134$) (Figure 10 middle). No significant interaction between navigation strategy and input type was found for each of the three indicators.

Number of Pages Viewed

The number of visited pages did not differ significantly between the two navigation strategies ($F_{(1, 26)} = 2.27$, $p > .05$, $\eta^2 = .080$). Nevertheless, on average, users still browsed less pages using list-based back (M = 12.46, SE = .80) than using traditional back navigation (M = 13.98, SE = .83). No significant interaction was found by taking into consideration the input type used.

Better Navigation Experience and Reduced Cognitive Load

Regardless of input type, users had significantly better navigation experience using list-based back (M = 4.19, SE = .11) than traditional back (M = 3.54, SE = .15) ($F_{(1, 27)} = 18.67$, $p < .01$, $\eta^2 = .409$). Additionally, users' cognitive load was significantly higher in the traditional back condition (M = 38.94, SE = 3.55) than in the list-based back condition (M = 23.62, SE = 2.85) ($F_{(1, 24)} = 14.07$, $p < .01$, $\eta^2 = .370$). These results indicate that, list-based back navigation has the potential to improve the experience of navigating a website and reduce the cognitive load in aural browsing tasks.

Findings from post-test interviews

Emerging but Not Translucent Mental Model

The navigation strategies were not fully understood by all participants. Three of 29 participants (10%) correctly explained the topic-based back, while 16% (5 out of 29) correctly explained the list-based back strategy. For both advanced navigation strategies, 30% (9 out 29) of participants gave partially complete answers, while the remaining 44% (13 out of 29) gave confusing answers, showing difficulty in articulating an accurate mental model of the navigation mechanisms that they used.

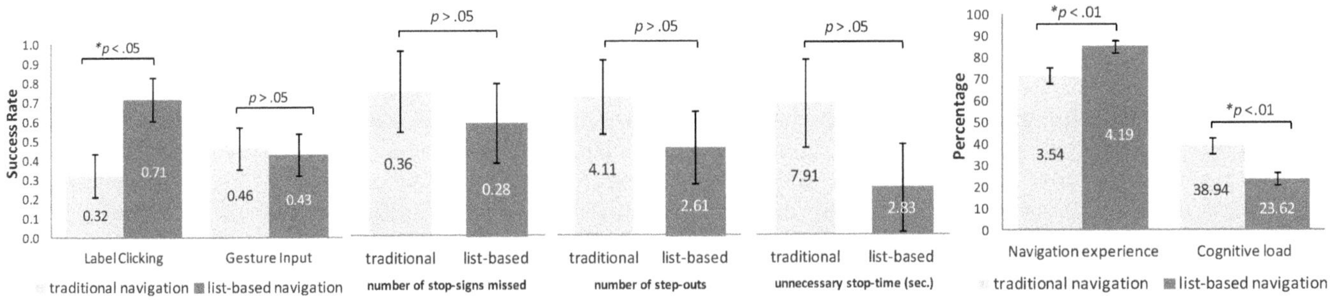

Figure 10. List-based back significantly increases success rate when label clicking input is used (left); reduces distractions (middle); and yields better ratings for navigation experience and perceived cognitive load (right).

The most common explanation of topic-based back revolved around the general notion of "last" page (21%, or 6 out of 29), or "main" page (10%, or 3 out 29). P3: *"[List-based back] is a more detailed version of the back button".* P8: *[Topic-based back] sends you back to the main page".* Other comments (accounting for 25% of participants) gave more accurate explanations. P22: *"[List-based back] with a single click takes you to a previous list".* P17: *"[Topic-based back] navigates through topics you visited".* Overall, although list-based back was better understood than topic-based navigation, it is clear that users did not immediately conceptualize the new strategies in their key mechanisms.

List-based Back Preferred over the Other Strategies

Overall, 55% (16 out of 29) preferred the list-based back more than traditional and topic-based back navigation. Topic-based back was preferred by 25% (7 out of 29), while 10% (3 out of 29) preferred both advanced navigation strategies equally. The remaining 10% (3 out of 29) preferred the traditional back. Some users' comments reveal that they prefer and understand list-based back better than topic-based back navigation. Some of the comments included: P12: *"[List-based back] is easy to navigate, straight to the point"*; P18: *"topic-back was a bit hard to find".*

Overall Difficulties Encountered by Users

In terms of navigation problems, 24% (7 out of 29) of participants had no difficulties whatsoever. The remaining participants had difficulties of different sources, such as: non-responsive touch for gesture and label clicking alike (24%, 7 out of 29), hard-to-hit small buttons (14%, 4 out of 29), confusing website layout (14%, 4 out of 29) and occasional application freezing (10%, 3 out of 29). Finally, two participants suggested including also a *forward* topic- and list-based navigation. This would facilitate back *and forth* movements across the trail of topics and lists.

DISCUSSION

Topic-based and List-based Back Increase Efficiency

Our study confirms hypotheses H1 and H2, as it shows that both topic-based back and list-based back are important time-savers in aural mobile browsing. On average, compared to traditional back, topic-based back saved about 49.47 seconds, while list-based back saved about 43.38 seconds. Since each task was supposed to be completed within approximately 4-5 minutes, a 40 to 50 seconds reduction is a 17% gain in navigation efficiency. This is an important gain, but it is much lower than what we anticipated based on the conceptual navigation modeling (Figure 2), which did not consider the mobile setting, input type, the prototype limitations, and human error.

Gesture Semiotics in Aural Mobile Contexts

As we consider the input type used, an interesting finding emerges: topic-based back significantly increased success rate only when gesture input was used, whereas list-based back was effective only with label clicking. This finding can be interpreted by considering the semiotic of our custom gestures [2], i.e., whether the gesture used transparently conveys the intended functional meaning.

On the one hand, our data suggest that "two-finger swipe left" gesture successfully conveys the meaning of "moving back to a previously visited *topic*". Participants remembered to use it and used it accurately. On the other hand, the "two-finger swipe *up*" gesture used to convey "last-list" was probably a poor design decision. The original rationale for this gesture was to resemble the "move up" paradigm used in hierarchical directories. The semiotics of this custom gesture, however, was not transparent enough to immediately convey its functional meaning, and this caused difficulties for the users during the test. As a consequence, *label clicking* for list-based navigation offered users a more transparent semiotics or information scent [28], as it provided an explicit name indicating the target destination (i.e., the actual title of the last list page).

For the topic-based back navigation, users were more successful in completing the tasks using gesture, though it required relatively high cognitive load. This shows that users can perform better using gesture in topic-based back, but they need more time to get adjusted to use the gesture. These findings resonate with those of "Slide Rule" [16], in which participants were faster but made more errors using a touch screen than using physical buttons. Collectively, our results partially confirm hypothesis H3; list-based back, however, is more effective when label clicking is used. Therefore, hypothesis H4 is not supported by our findings.

More than Expected Page Visits

Unexpectedly, neither of the two advanced navigation strategies significantly reduced the number of pages visited to accomplish the tasks. The reason behind this may be two-fold. First, the implementation of the custom gesture on the prototype pages had some bugs that occasionally caused the unresponsiveness of gesture interaction. Thus, as users clicked incorrect links or used a gesture unintentionally, the number of pages visited increased. Second, some users failed to notice the correct cue on the page and started browsing around to find the link. This may have been due to the position, styling and labeling of the links. Overall, these factors do not undermine the potential of topic- and list-based strategies, but indicate important details about the experimental instruments and page design that might have skewed the actual navigation behavior.

Topic-based and List-based Back Reduce Distraction

Results of our observation of users' physical behavior suggest that both the topic- and list-based back navigations help to reduce distraction from a simple walking task. Our findings suggest that these two navigation strategies better support eyes-free aural experiences. They involve less user attention compared with traditional back navigation, which requires users to continuously interact with a page and click on the back button to traverse back to each and every page.

Enhancement in Navigation Experience

For both advanced navigation strategies, the ratings of navigation experience were significantly higher than the control group, particularly on two questionnaire items: "the website provided enough guidance for me to navigate through the content" and "it was easy for me to return to previous pages." The former item implies that users considered both navigation strategies as *guidance* to the content. The latter confirms that topic- and list-based back can make back navigation much easier than traditional back. This finding puts in better perspective the lack of transparent mental model as previously discussed. The fact that most users were not able to fully articulate the basic mechanisms governing the navigation strategies, did not prevent them from consistently acknowledging their ultimate utility for navigating complex architectures.

Reducing Perceived Cognitive Load

Our findings show that both advanced navigation strategies reduced cognitive load especially on two fronts: "physical demand" and "temporal demand." This evidence indicates that participants felt less rushed and needed less physical operation in accomplishing the browsing tasks. Moreover, list-based back resulted in significantly lower rates in user's frustration. Collectively, this evidence suggests that the second half of H1 (topic-based back yields a better navigation experience and reduces perceived cognitive load) and, similarly, H2, are also confirmed.

Validity and Limitations of the Study

Internal Validity

We used several strategies to maximize internal validity. First, we adopted a within-subject design in which both performance data *and* self-reported, subjective experiences were collected. Second, we captured not only the standard task performance and experience indicators, but also a number of contextual measures (stop signs missed, step-outs, and unnecessary stops) that are representative of critical factors in mobile scenarios. Third, to mitigate the learning effect within subjects, we carried out a consistent training session with each participant before the experiment, so that the participants' knowledge about the website could reach a common threshold of familiarity with the site. Finally, the order of the advanced navigation conditions was also counterbalanced across participants.

Even though traditional back was always presented before the advanced navigation, we argue that this potential learning effect is minimal. In fact, there was no double exposure to the same parts of the application because the actual tasks assigned were equivalent only in terms of types of navigation path, but differed in terms of traversed pages. Consequently, the only thing participants were familiar with before entering the advanced condition was the site structure. A limit of our experimental design is the fact that the walking path was exactly the same across conditions. The habituation to the path, however, is partially mitigated by the counterbalancing of the advanced strategies and the differences in the tasks. Also, the initial training and the simplicity of the path left little to learn after the first walk.

External Validity

The purpose of topic- and list-based navigation strategies is not to replace the existing back links of a given web application, but to enable aural users to perform navigation at a higher, conceptual level (which is at the same time more natural and efficient) on top of existing navigation structures. As such, topic- and list-based readily complement existing research on strategies for aural page structuring [21], by operating at the level of the information architecture of a site. Designers who work on large-scale, engineered web architectures (e.g., thousands of pages) will easily recognize a mapping between the information architecture of their websites and the proposed navigation semantics. In fact, most of the proposed design concepts (topics, parts of a topic, list pages) are constantly underlying the rapidly changing patterns of most complex, content-intensive web applications [29]. These aural navigation commands can be applied to all known types of information architectures, with one exception. Websites with simply structured content units (e.g., a one page description of a product) would not benefit from topic-based back, which would assume the availability of multiple pages for a topic. Similarly, sites with few list pages would not benefit much by the "shortcuts" of list-based back. As we did with GSM, topics and lists can be conceptually identified at design time (or reverse-engineered from existing sites) and marked on the information architecture. The user's history session can then be tracked on the server; on the client side, topic- and list-back links (or gesture listeners) are dynamically generated based on the simple navigation rules of the two patterns, and included in the page templates.

RELATED WORK

Research on supporting eyes-free, aural experiences is gaining momentum in combination with the pervasive presence of advanced mobile devices. As a most recent example, the Apple iPhone 4S SIRI personal assistant promotes a highly semi-aural paradigm, where aural output is the primary modality, complementary to the visual display.

Brewster et al. [7] argue that when users focus their visual attention on visually-demanding interfaces, they face difficulty navigating their environments. Borden [4] also emphasizes that visual interfaces often need most of the cognitive resources of the user in order to complete simple tasks, such as clicking a button. Hence, visual interfaces may be highly distracting when used in parallel to other visual activities (such as walking, jogging or driving) since both draw from the same pool of limited cognitive resources [33].

From this perspective, there has been extensive work that explored ways to use audio to replace visual feedback in mobile scenarios [30, 13] and in content-rich web applications in general [18, 32]. For instance, BlindSight [19] enables users to access their contact lists or digital calendars using audio cues, thus without being forced to look at the mobile device at all times. In this context, topic-based back, for example, can support re-finding of appropriate "conceptual" entities (rather than actions or steps) in the array of personal information. One could easily find the "next event" scheduled, or the "last meeting" attended. In a similar vein, Ec(h)o [31] is an example of advanced "audio guide" that enables museum visitors to focus their attention to the exhibited objects, while listening to complementary explanations. In these scenarios, topic- and list-based back can facilitate the aural navigation in the collection by jumping directly to the previously visited work of art or area (set of works) of the collection.

Past works on web structures have demonstrated the importance of back navigation [9, 10]. For example, by analyzing log files, Catledge and Pitkow found that back navigation accounts for 41% of all the web interaction activities [9]. They also found that a user's navigation history usually shows "a spoke and hub structure" [9], which is analog to accessing topics via a list. Capitalizing on the characteristics of web navigation history, Milic-Frayling et al. tried to substantially enhance back navigation experience by visualizing the types and the structure of a user's navigation trail [22, 23]. They introduce a browser feature called "SmartBack" [23], which can automatically detect the dynamic "hubs" of in-depth web browsing. In a complementary perspective, Cui et al. specifically propose that "navigation history" should be designed by prioritizing the key content that a user has visited and skip "less meaningful pages" [11]. Topic-based back embraces this general notion and formalizes it into a reusable and systematic design approach for the aural web.

CONCLUSIONS AND FUTURE WORK

The novel contribution of this research is to introduce and evaluate two back navigation patterns that can significantly improve the aural browsing of large websites in mobile scenarios. Our work is a fundamental step in addressing the structural, conceptual transformations that are much needed when moving from the visual to the aural web. Whereas current sites do offer mechanisms to navigate across sets of pages (e.g., menus, tabs, breadcrumbs), these common visual patterns need to be rethought for auditory navigation. To address this problem, we introduced two higher-level, conceptual back shortcuts suitable for aural browsing. Topic-based back leverages the notion of topic to quickly shortcut back across several collections (and therefore skipping tabs, breadcrumbs and menus). List-based back leverages list pages to directly navigate up to lists across several navigation trails. We demonstrated and empirically evaluated the potential of topic- and list-based back to enhance aural back browsing while on-the-go. Our findings suggest that the principles guiding those strategies result in significant improvements in navigation effectiveness and efficiency. In a parallel research effort, we are evaluating topic- and list-based back to support aural browsing for blind users of screen readers, in close collaboration with the Indiana School for the Blind. Our rationale is that the same aural interaction strategies used to navigate mobile websites might *also* enhance traditional web browsing when looking at the screen is not an option.

ACKNOWLEDGMENTS

We thank all study participants, as well as J. Luebke, J. Carey and T. Tiede for their work on prototyping and evaluation. We also thank J. George-Palilonis for feedback on earlier versions of the paper. This research is based upon work supported by the NSF under grant IIS-1018054.

APPENDIX A: Aural Navigation Tasks*

Task A: Navigating Back to a Visited Topic

[Access a topic instance and browse its details] Small changes in your energy consumption at home can make a great difference on your electric bill over time. Find a list with all the energy saving tips that you can complete in 10 minutes or less. From this list, find out how to save energy with your computer and listen to the specific directions on how to do so.

[Navigate to a related topic] While thinking to renew your computer equipment, look for a ViewSonic monitor and find out how much it costs. Check to see if there are any rebates for the monitor, and if so, determine how much money you would get back.

[Back to visited topic] Go back to keep on listening to further instructions on how to save energy with your computer.

Task B: Navigating Back to a Visited List

[Access a topic instance and browse its details] The Winter season is coming and you want to take proper precautions on how to save on your gas bill. Find a list with all the saving tips related to all areas of the house. From this list, find out more about re-sealing windows and doors and then read all the directions on how to do so.

[Navigate to a related topic] While thinking about doors and windows, look for a door draft stopper kit. First, check the reviews of this item, then see if there is a rebate for it, and how you can get it.

[Back to visited list] Choose another green tip related to Spring.

**** Tasks with equivalent structure were assigned in Stages 1-4.***

REFERENCES

1. Asakawa, C., and Itoh, T. User Interface of a Home Page Reader. *Proc. ASSETS* (1998), 149-156.
2. Billinghurst, M. Gesture-based Interaction. In Buxton, W. (Eds.), *Human Input to Computer Systems: Theories, Techniques and Technology* (2011).
3. Bolchini, D., Colazzo, S., Paolini, P., and Vitali, D. Designing Aural Information Architectures. *Proc. SIGDOC* (2006), 51-58.
4. Borden IV, G. R. An Aural User Interface for Ubiquitous Computing. *Proc. ISWC* (2002), 143.
5. Borodin, Y., Bigham, J. P., Stent, A., and Ramakrishnan, I. V. Towards One World Web with HearSay3. *Proc. W4A* (2008), 130-131.
6. Borodin, Y., Mahmud, J., Ramakrishnan, I.V. Context Browsing with Mobiles-When Less is More. *Proc. Int. MobiSys Conferences* (2007), 3-15.
7. Brewster, S., Lumsden, J., Bell, M., Hall, M., and Tasker, S. Multimodal 'eyes-free' interaction techniques for wearable devices. *Proc. CHI* (2003), 473-480.
8. Brumby, D. P., Davies, S. C. E., Janssen, C. P., and Grace, J. J. Fast or safe? How Performance Objectives Determine Modality Output Choices while Interacting on the Move. *Proc. CHI* (2011), 473-482.
9. Catledge, L., and Pitkow, J. Characterizing browsing strategies in the World Wide Web. *Computer Networks and ISDN Systems* 27, 6 (1995), 1065-1073.
10. Cockburn, A., McKenzie, B., and Jasonsmith, M. Pushing Back: Evaluating a New Behaviour for the Back and Forward Buttons in Web Browsers. *IJHCS*, 57, 5 (2002), 397-414.
11. Cui, Y., Oulasvirta, A., and Ma, L. Event Perception in Mobile Interaction: Toward Better Navigation History Design on Mobile Devices. *IJHCI*, 27, 5 (2011), 413-435.
12. Di Blas, N., and Paolini, P. There and Back Again: What Happens to Phoric Elements in a Web Dialogue. *Document Design*, 4, 3 (2003), 194-206.
13. Dicke, C., Wolf, K., & Tal, Y. Foogue: eyes-free interaction for smartphones. *Proc. Mobile HCI* (2010), 455-458.
14. Gestureworks. http://gestureworks.com/
15. Hart, S. G., and Staveland, L. E. Development of NASA-TLX: Results of Empirical and Theoretical Research. *Adv. in Psychology*, 52 (1988), 139-183.
16. Kane, S. K., Bigham, J. P., and Wobbrock, J. O. Slide Rule: Making Mobile Touch Screens Accessible to Blind People Using Multi-touch Interaction Techniques. *Proc. ASSETS* (2008), 73-80.
17. Kellar, M., Watters C., and Shepherd M. A Goal-based Classification of Web Information Tasks. *Proc. SIGCOMM 2006*, 101-112.
18. Kolias, C., Kolias, V., Anagnostopoulos, I., Kambourakis, G., Kayafas, E. Design and implementation of a VoiceXML-driven wiki application for assistive environments on the web. *Personal and Ubiquitous Computing*, 14(6), 2010, 527-539.
19. Li, K. A., Baudisch, P. and Hinckley, K. Blindsight: Eyes-free Access to Mobile Phones. *Proc. CHI* (2008), 1389-1398.
20. Mahmud, J., Borodin, Y., Ramakrishnan, I.V. CSurf: A Context-driven Non-visual Web Browser. *Proc. WWW* (2007), 31-40.
21. Michailidou, E., Harper, S., and Bechhofer, S. Investigating Sighted Users' Browsing Behavior to Assist Web Accessibility. *Proc. ASSETS* (2008), 121-128.
22. Milic-Frayling, N., and Rodden, K. WebScout: Support for Revisitation of Web Pages within the Navigation Session. *Proc. IEEE WI* (2003), 689-693.
23. Milic-Frayling, N., Jones, R., Rodden, K., Smyth, G., Blackwell, A., and Sommerer, R. Smartback: supporting users in back navigation. *Proc. WWW* (2004), 63-71.
24. Oakley, I., & Park, J.-S. Designing eyes-free interaction. In *Proc. HAID Conf.* (2007), 121-132.
25. Raman, T. V., & Chen, C. L. Eyes-Free User Interfaces. *Computer* (2008), 41(10), 100-101.
26. Ramakrishnan, I.V., Stent, A., and Yang, G. Hearsay: Enabling Audio Browsing in Hypertext Content. *Proc. WWW* (2004), 80-89.
27. Sato, D., Zhu, S., Kobayashi, M., Takagi, H., and Asakawa, C. Sasayaki: Voice Augmented Web Browsing Experience. *Proc. CHI* (2011), 2769-2778.
28. Spool, J. M., Perfetti, C., and Brittan, D. Designing for the Scent of Information, UIE.com (2004).
29. Van Duyne, D. K., Landay, J. A., Hong, J. The Design of Sites *(2n Ed.), Prentice Hall* (2007).
30. Vazquez-Alvarez, Y., and Brewster, S. A. Eyes-Free Multitasking: The Effect of Cognitive Load on Mobile Spatial Audio Interfaces. *Proc. CHI* (2011), 2173-2176.
31. Wakkary, R., & Hatala, M. Situated play in a tangible interface and adaptive audio museum guide. *Personal and Ubiquitous Computing*, 11, 3 (2007), 171-191.
32. Wang, L., Roe, P., Pham, B., and Tjondronegoro, D. An audio wiki supporting mobile collaboration. *Proc. SAC* (2008), 1889-1896.
33. Wickens, C. D. Multiple resources and performance prediction. *Th. Issues in Erg. Sc.* (2002), *3*(2), 159-177.
34. Yang, T., Linder, J., and Bolchini, D. DEEP: Design-oriented Evaluation of Perceived usability. *IJHCI* 2011.

PolyZoom: Multiscale and Multifocus Exploration in 2D Visual Spaces

Waqas Javed, Sohaib Ghani, and Niklas Elmqvist
Purdue University
West Lafayette, USA
{wjaved, sghani, elm}@purdue.edu

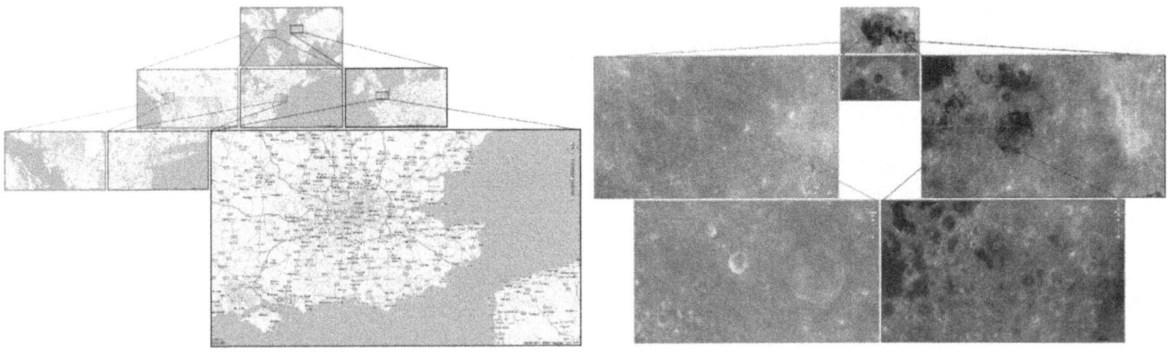

Figure 1. PolyZoom focus hierarchies where the color-coded selections and the connecting lines make the parent-child relationships explicit.

ABSTRACT

The most common techniques for navigating in multiscale visual spaces are pan, zoom, and bird's eye views. However, these techniques are often tedious and cumbersome to use, especially when objects of interest are located far apart. We present the PolyZoom technique where users progressively build hierarchies of focus regions, stacked on each other such that each subsequent level shows a higher magnification. Correlation graphics show the relation between parent and child viewports in the hierarchy. To validate the new technique, we compare it to standard navigation techniques in two user studies, one on multiscale visual search and the other on multifocus interaction. Results show that PolyZoom performs better than current standard techniques.

Author Keywords

Multifocus interaction; comparative visualization; maps; navigation; visual exploration; visual analytics; interaction.

ACM Classification Keywords

H.5.2 Information Interfaces and Presentation: User Interfaces—*Interaction styles*; I.3.6 Computer Graphics: Methodology and Techniques—*Interaction techniques*

INTRODUCTION

A *multiscale visual space* has different visual representation depending on the zoom level used to view the space [14]. Navigation in such multiscale visual spaces is becoming increasingly important for many everyday tasks. For example, Google Maps is essentially a large, two-dimensional, and multiscale geospatial dataset. The same could be said about many visualizations, such as zoomable treemaps, large adjacency matrices, or high-resolution scatterplots. However, multiscale navigation has been shown to be a difficult problem because of the phenomenon known as *desert fog* [11], where the immediate environment in the viewport is devoid of navigational cues due to its multiscale nature. For example, in Google Maps, seeing continents on the world map will not help the user in finding a specific park in a city. Zooming into the map to search for the target will automatically cause a loss of overview. However, maintaining an awareness of the full space is necessary for effectively exploring the space, otherwise the navigation process can easily become tedious [4].

We present PolyZoom, a navigation technique for two-dimensional multiscale visual spaces that allows users to iteratively build a hierarchy of focus regions, thereby maintaining their awareness of multiple scales of the visual space at the same time (Figure 1). Using PolyZoom, users can progressively narrow down the search space by creating regions of increasing magnification into areas of interest on the visual space. This allows the user to be aware of the space at different scales, so they can easily backtrack if they make a mistake during the visual exploration. In addition to this, PolyZoom also supports multifocus interaction [2] where several regions of interest can be compared side by side while preserving their spatial relation and context.

We have implemented PolyZoom using Adobe Flash. The application lets the user to smoothly navigate in a large and multiscale visual space using the PolyZoom technique, as well as using standard pan and zoom. Our implementation currently supports four different visual spaces: the Google Maps world map, the NASA Universe dataset, a Lunar dataset, and a Martian dataset.

The extra spatial awareness provided by PolyZoom comes at the cost of smaller map viewports and suboptimal use of screen space. To study the impact of this on visual exploration, we performed two user studies comparing the new technique to standard pan and zoom. In the first study, participants were asked to perform a multiscale navigation task that required them to search for a particular target using navigational cues at different levels of scale. In the second study, we studied the multifocus capabilities of the technique by asking users to compare potential targets to a specific source object. Despite the extra space required for the PolyZoom technique, results from both studies indicate a performance improvement for the new technique.

BACKGROUND

Here we review general techniques for navigating in 2D spaces, highlighting issues that make navigation difficult.

Common Navigation Techniques

Scrolling is one of the standard techniques for navigating large workspaces, but it can be cumbersome when the space to explore is large. Igarashi and Hinckley [8] proposed a method of speed-dependent automatic zooming (SDAZ) to automatically vary the zoom level depending on the zoom rate. Ishak and Feiner presented content-aware scrolling [9] to vary the direction, speed, and zoom during scrolling based on content properties. Despite these improvements:

Scrolling has little multiscale capability and requires considerable effort when exploring large 2D workspaces.

Panning allows users to directly manipulate the position of the viewport on the visual space, while *zooming* changes the viewport's magnification level (i.e., viewport space size). Since the original infinitely zoomable canvas proposed in Pad [14], there has been a large amount of work in this area. Furnas and Bederson present the space-scale diagram [4] as a method for understanding zoom and pan actions as paths through space-scale. Multiple studies show that combining zooming and panning is more efficient than only panning [4, 20]. However, panning and zooming alone is insufficient:

Pan and zoom for a large visual space means giving up either overview or detail, and can be ineffective [3, 4].

Overview+detail techniques use multiple windows to present both magnified and bird's eye views of the space. The overview window shows the entire workspace while the detail window shows the current focus. Hornbæk and Frøkjær [7] found that overview and detail techniques are easy to use and can outperform pan+zoom and fisheye views for some tasks. Of particular interest to our work is DragMag [21]—discussed in more detail below—which is an overview+detail technique where the user directly drags a focus region on the visual space to control an associated magnification window. In general, overview and detail techniques have been shown to be effective in navigating large spaces [6, 12]. However, overview+detail has problems:

Overview+detail divides user attention between viewports, and scales poorly to high magnification ratios.

Focus+context techniques combine a focus region shown in great detail integrated with the surrounding context, typically using distortion. Magnifying lenses [1] and fisheye views [3] are commonly used focus+context techniques. Rubber sheet stretching [18] is another model of distorting 2D space. Elmqvist et al. [2] propose a space-folding technique called Mélange that combines different parts of the workspace. Despite the benefits achieved through focus+context techniques:

Focus+context is unstable [5], scales poorly to large spaces [7], and the focus transition is nonintuitive [15].

Multiscale Navigation

Multiscale navigation is defined as spatial navigation in a multiscale visual space, i.e. a space that has different visual representation depending on the magnification used to view the space. Multiscale representations are important in many domains such as cartography (where small-scale maps are generated through the abstraction of large-scale datasets), visualization (examples such as zoomable adjacency matrices, treemaps, and data cubes are all multiscale spaces), and even common documents (which exhibit both macro- and micro-level structure). The original Pad [14] provided an infinitely zoomable multiscale space, and introduced the concept of semantic zooming for navigating such structures. However:

Multiscale navigation is difficult due to missing navigational cues at different levels of scale ("desert fog" [11]).

Multifocus Interaction

Multifocus interaction [2] provides a way to simultaneously view and compare multiple regions of interest while exploring large visual spaces such as geographical maps. Below we review prior work in this domain.

Split-screen techniques divide the screen into multiple viewports that each show a portion of the full workspace, and has been adopted for multifocus interaction in the past. Plaisant et al. [17] used a split-screen for exploring large time series data. Shoemaker and Gutwin [19] combine the split-screen approach with dynamic focus creation that automatically define focus regions as the interaction points move further apart. However, these and other techniques have the following characteristic in common:

Split-screen techniques support multifocus awareness, but provide little spatial relations between viewports and generally do not allow for creating cascading viewports.

Many of the focus+context techniques can also be used for multifocus interaction. Techniques like fisheye views [3, 19], rubber sheet [18], and space folding [2] support multiple focus regions. However, there are issues with such methods:

Multifocus+context techniques do not permit creating focus hierarchies, which is needed for multiscale awareness.

Javed and Elmqvist [10] propose a multifocus overview+detail technique called *stack zooming* that lets the user build a cascaded hierarchy of focus regions. The technique supports most requirements, however, it has a limitation:

Stack zooming is designed for one-dimensional visual spaces (e.g., time series), and its adaptation to two-dimensional visual spaces (e.g., maps) is non-trivial.

POLYZOOM: TECHNIQUE

The PolyZoom technique was designed for exploring multiscale 2D spaces. We summarize our design goals as follows:

- **Multiscale awareness:** Most overview+detail techniques are not effective when navigating large multiscale spaces, since large differences in magnification between overview and detail make navigation impractical. We aim to provide awareness of the visual space at multiple scale levels.
- **Multifocus awareness:** Many tasks require viewing several regions simultaneously, e.g., for side-by-side comparison [2]. We thus want to support multiple foci.
- **No distortion:** Spatial distortion can be confusing because it introduces non-linear elements into the display, elements that are typically not visually stable under translation [5]. We thus want to avoid spatial distortion.
- **No overlap:** We want the technique to avoid overlapping viewports and instead efficiently fill the available space.

The PolyZoom technique lets users build focus hierarchies by selecting regions of interest in a viewport, thereby spawning a child viewport at higher magnification. This gives the user awareness of multiple levels of scale simultaneously. As shown in Figure 2, three focus regions (A, B, and C) have been created on the visual canvas. Each new viewport forms a parent-child relation where the new viewport becomes the child of the parent viewport in which the selection was made. The new viewport can further act as a parent for multiple new viewports by performing the same selection operation. For example, in Figure 2, the viewports A and B, children of the main viewport, are the parents of viewports D and E, respectively. This parent-child viewport relation provides not only overview at multiple scale levels, but also facilitates backtracking while navigating in a multiscale visual space.

Our approach of letting users create focus regions that spawn magnification viewports is reminiscent of the DragMag technique [21], where a magnifying glass metaphor is used to control a zoom window on top of a base window. However, PolyZoom takes the basic DragMag concept further by allowing the user to create hierarchies of zoom windows (i.e., focus regions within zoom windows), thereby producing a multiscale navigation technique. Furthermore, because PolyZoom also supports creating multiple children for each viewport, it inherently supports *multifocus interaction* [2, 19], the capability of comparing multiple focus regions side-by-side. Unlike previous multifocus techniques, such as space folding [2] and multiple fisheye views [19], it does so without using distortion in the display.

The three main design aspects of PolyZoom are (1) the layout algorithm, which dictates the positioning of different viewports on the screen; (2) the viewport size management algorithm, which manages the size of different viewports; and (3) correlation graphics, which provide explicit linking between parent and child viewports. In the following subsections we will discuss each of these in detail.

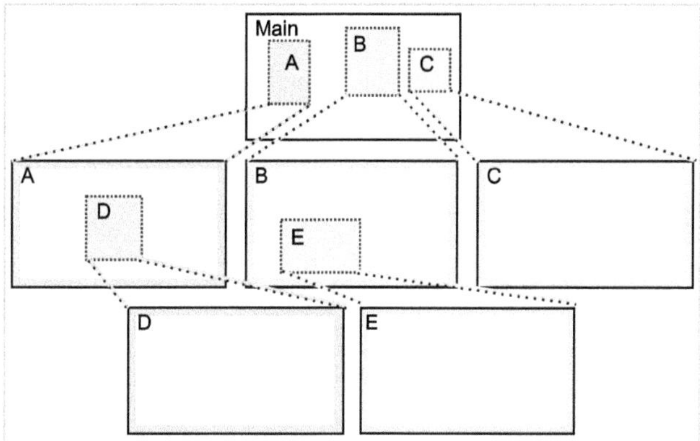

Figure 2. General layout mechanism for PolyZoom. Color-coded zoom areas and corresponding colored frames show parent-child relationships, and visual lines make the relations explicit.

Layout

For the PolyZoom technique, we aimed for a layout that is easy to understand, allows effective side-by-side comparisons at a given level of the focus hierarchy, and is logical and predictable based on the underlying tree structure. Based on these requirements, we use a stack-based algorithm to lay out a focus hierarchy as multiple viewports on the screen. This is done by splitting the vertical space so that each consecutive level in the focus hierarchy is allocated a vertical segment, starting with the focus root at the top of the space. Next the horizontal space in each segment is divided and allocated as viewports to the focus regions on that level in the hierarchy. This layout generates a visual tree structure that makes it easy to relate parent and child viewports, thereby allowing the user to keep track of the context of any focus region all the way to the root of the focus hierarchy. Figure 2 shows an example layout where viewports A, B, and C are children of the main viewport, and viewports D and E are the children of viewports A and B, respectively.

The layout algorithm restricts the vertical positioning of viewports based on the parent-child relation, but makes no assumption on their horizontal positioning. This means that focus regions for a level in the hierarchy can be reordered in a vertical segment, e.g., for side-by-side comparison.

The layout also makes each viewport the same size. For most visual spaces, such as for maps and images, the aspect ratio between width and height is fixed. This means that no dimension in a focus region should be stretched or squashed. For these situations, because PolyZoom allows the user to freely select 2D focus regions, the viewports may need to show some additional area of the visual space outside the selection in order to preserve the aspect ratio. This is done by fitting a rectangle of the correct aspect ratio to the selection (which most likely does not have the correct aspect ratio). This is only necessary if the underlying visual space is sensitive to varying aspect ratio. Another approach is to restrict the aspect ratio of the focus area during selection.

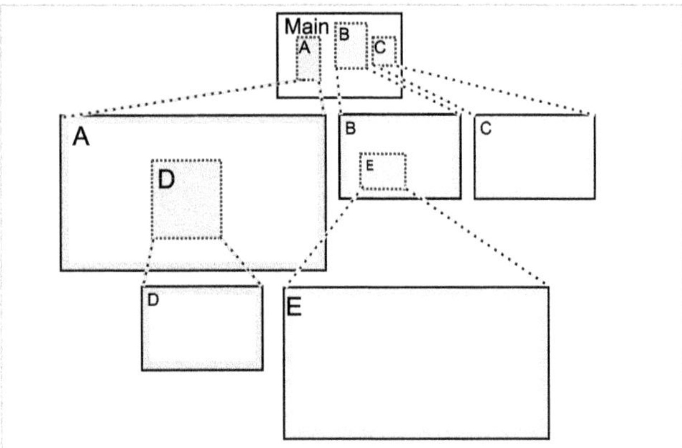

Figure 3. Viewport size management mechanism for PolyZoom. Two windows A and E are selected as active viewports, causing them to be allocated a larger part of the available view space.

Viewport Size Management

So far we have kept viewport size constant when performing the layout of the focus hierarchy in the visual space. However, viewport size plays an important role for the effectiveness of PolyZoom: if viewports become too small as the focus hierarchy grows, it will be difficult to see details in each individual viewport. On the other hand, not all viewports are important all the time, and this will change as the user navigates in the visual space. Hence, dividing the view space equally among all the viewports is not always optimal.

As an alternative, we provide an interest-based viewport size management algorithm that dynamically changes the sizes of individual viewports while keeping their aspect ratio constant. The algorithm allows users to dynamically flag the viewports that are currently of interest as being *active* (or even to let the active viewport be determined by the mouse pointer). Active viewports are assigned a magnification factor M that captures how much larger an active viewport will be compared to a passive one (if $M = 1$, this algorithm reverts to the equal-sized viewport layout algorithm above).

The algorithm proceeds by finding which of the vertical or horizontal dimensions of the focus hierarchy requires the most amount of space. For the vertical axis, this amounts to summing up each level of the hierarchy, where a level has value M if there is at least one active viewport in the level, and 1 if there is none. For the horizontal axis, we select the level with the maximum sum, where the sum of a level is computed by counting each active viewport as M, and each passive one as 1. Finally, we compare the horizontal and vertical sums and select the maximum as the deciding factor (the intuition is that the axis with the maximum sum will require the most display space). This factor is then used to determine both width and height of passive and active viewports based on the magnification factor M.

Figure 3 shows an example of applying this algorithm. Viewports A and E are active. Based on the magnification ratio $M = 2$, the passive viewports are given considerably less space. In this example, the vertical sum is $2M + 1$ (dominant) and the horizontal is $M + 2$ (for level 2 in the hierarchy).

Correlation Graphics

For maintaining the full context of viewports in the focus hierarchy, we want to make the relationship between parent and child viewports explicit. Prior work [10] in this field uses correlation graphics to achieve this. We adopted this idea for PolyZoom as follows:

- **Color-coded selection areas:** The selection areas in a viewport are rendered as color-coded and semi-transparent rectangles in the viewport the selection was made. This makes it easy to identify the extent of selected space that corresponds to a particular viewport in its parent window. For example, in Figure 2, three regions A, B, and C have been selected in the main viewport. The selection regions are highlighted using three different colors.
- **Color-coded viewport frames:** We use the same color-coding for the frames around child viewports to indicate the relation to the selection region in the parent (Figure 2).
- **Correlation links:** We use explicit correlation links as color-coded lines that connect the selection region in the parent to the child viewport (Figure 2). These are helpful in the presence of a large number of viewports, but may cause visual clutter. For this reason, we only link the base of a focus region to the top of each child viewport.

POLYZOOM: SYSTEM

We built a web-based prototype implementation of PolyZoom for multiscale and multifocus navigation in 2D multiscale visual spaces. Our implementation supports the Google Maps dataset, NASA Universe, a Lunar dataset, and a Martian dataset. Even though our prototype is tailored to these datasets, there is nothing in the technique that prevents it from being implemented for other datasets, such as Bing Maps, DeepZoom[1], or general 2D visual spaces.

Our implementation (Figure 1) starts with a single main viewport that displays the complete visual space (i.e., for Google Maps, the whole world). Users can pan and zoom normally in this viewport just like in a normal Google Maps implementation, i.e., using dragging and the mouse wheel or the Google Maps navigation widget. In addition to this standard functionality, we also allow users to specify focus regions by left-clicking on the map to start a rubber band rectangular selection, and left-clicking again to finish the selection. This creates a new focus region that becomes a child of the main viewport. The selected area in the main viewport is drawn as a color-coded and semi-transparent rectangle. This new child viewport has the exact same functionality as its parent; specifically, it can have its own children if the user

[1] `http://www.microsoft.com/silverlight/deep-zoom/`

performs a focus region selection inside its borders. Furthermore, each viewport can naturally have more than one child. The system also supports all three correlation graphics described above to maximize the user's spatial awareness.

The interaction design of navigating parents and children has different alternatives depending on the application. In our implementation, navigating in a child viewport will update the size and position of its corresponding selection region in the parent; analogously, moving the selection area of a child in a parent viewport is the same as panning the child itself. A child viewport is specified in relative coordinates to its parent, so panning or zooming a parent will automatically pan or zoom the child a corresponding amount. Finally, parents are immutable from the viewpoint of a child, so children viewports are restricted to the bounds of the parent, thereby preventing interaction in one child to affect other siblings.

EVALUATION

PolyZoom provides spatial awareness simultaneously at multiple different levels of scale. However, this comes at the cost of reduced viewport size for each individual focus region. In addition, as can be seen in some of the figures in this paper, laying out a hierarchy of focus regions with a fixed aspect ratio means that the entire screen cannot be fully utilized. In other words, PolyZoom has both potential advantages and disadvantages over the standard pan and zoom operations that are common when navigating in spatial datasets such as Google Maps.

To better understand these tradeoffs, we performed two user studies comparing PolyZoom to standard pan and zoom interaction. Our study designs were influenced by the multiscale search operationalization proposed by Pietriga et al. [16]. Thus, the first study focused on multiscale search, and required participants to navigate in a hierarchy of visual cues on different levels of scale. The second study was aimed at the multifocus aspects, and required participants to compare foci in different locations on the visual space.

Both studies were performed back to back and with the same participants. However, the order of performing a study was balanced between participants. In this section, we discuss common aspects of both studies, whereas in subsequent ones, we describe their unique details.

Participants

We recruited 12 participants (11 male, 1 female) from the student population at our university (average age 22.2, median age 23). Participants were all self-selected volunteers, had normal or corrected-to-normal vision, were not color blind (self-reported), and were paid $10 upon completing a full experimental session. No particular skills were required other than basic knowledge of operating a computer.

Apparatus

The experiment was conducted on a standard 3 GHz dual-core desktop computer with 4 GB RAM and running Microsoft Windows XP. The computer was equipped with a standard two-button mouse (with mouse wheel), a keyboard, and a 19" LCD monitor set to 1280×1024 resolution. Participants only used the mouse to interact during the trials. The experimental application was maximized on the screen.

Navigation Technique (T)

We used Navigation Technique T as a factor for both studies:

- *Standard Pan and Zoom (S):* Navigation in map windows with all of the basic navigation techniques supported by Google Maps. Participants were able to create multiple map windows, and had access to the standard Google Maps overview for each window.
- *PolyZoom (P):* Navigation using the PolyZoom navigation technique; no standard overview viewport.

In the context of Pietriga et al.'s operationalization of multiscale search [16], the *Standard Pan and Zoom* technique (*S*) that serves as our baseline and comparison is equivalent to the "Pan-Zoom + Overview" technique that is most efficient in their experiment, with the difference that we use the standard overview window provided by the Google Maps API. On the other hand, Nekrasovski et al. [13] found that the presence of an overview had no impact on multiscale search, so we think this small discrepancy will have minimal impact.

Software and Dataset

We used our PolyZoom implementation in Adobe Flash/Flex (described above) as the experimental software using the Google Maps standard dataset. This allowed us to use both standard pan and zoom, as provided by the Google Maps API, as well as the PolyZoom technique as discussed above. Depending on the Technique factor, we restricted the use of PolyZoom—participants could still pan and zoom using the normal Google Maps user interface in both conditions.

In Study 2, we asked participants to compare two different regions on the map. In a real setting, a user may solve this task using two or more Google Map windows viewed side-by-side. To support this strategy, we implemented our map windows for the standard pan and zoom option as internal frames in a multiple document interface (MDI). We chose a MDI design (as opposed to creating separate browser windows) so that we were able to instrument the windows for the purpose of control and measurements for the user study.

For the standard pan and zoom condition, tasks started with a single map window, but participants were able to create additional windows simply by clicking a button. Each window supported basic operations such as resizing (by dragging on the lower-right corner of the window), bringing to top (by clicking anywhere on the window), and closing (by clicking on an X in the title bar). Beyond clicking on windows directly, users could switch between windows by clicking on their titles in a taskbar implemented inside our MDI interface. Pressing Shift-Tab also cycled between windows.

For both navigation techniques, viewports could be navigated using all of the basic navigation techniques supported by Google Maps: pan (left-drag), zoom (mouse-wheel), navigation widget, etc. In the PolyZoom condition, participants could also use the PolyZoom technique as described above, but were not allowed to create multiple windows.

Procedure

Upon starting an experimental session, participants were first allocated to a study order (i.e., Study 1 or 2 first). For each study, the experiment administrator described the overall task. The participant was then assigned to an order of techniques for the study, which we blocked on.

At the start of each technique block, participants were asked to complete a set of training trials. During this training session, the administrator demonstrated how to operate the technique and how to use it to solve the task. Participants were then asked to solve training trials on their own. They were allowed to ask questions during the training trials (not during real trials). Training continued until the participants indicated that they were ready to proceed to the timed trials.

A trial started when the participant clicked on a button in a dialog box that interleaved each trial. This dialog box served as an intermission between trials. Clicking on the button started the timer. Participants were instructed to complete the task as quickly as possible. The means of ending a trial (stopping the timer) was different for the two studies:

- For **Study 1**, the trial ended when the user had found and clicked on the red balloon that served as the target.
- For **Study 2**, the trial ended when the user had entered a target name they thought was correct and clicked "OK".

At the end of each study, participants were asked to provide comments and to give 5-point Likert scale ratings on how efficient, how easy, and how rewarding the different techniques were to use.

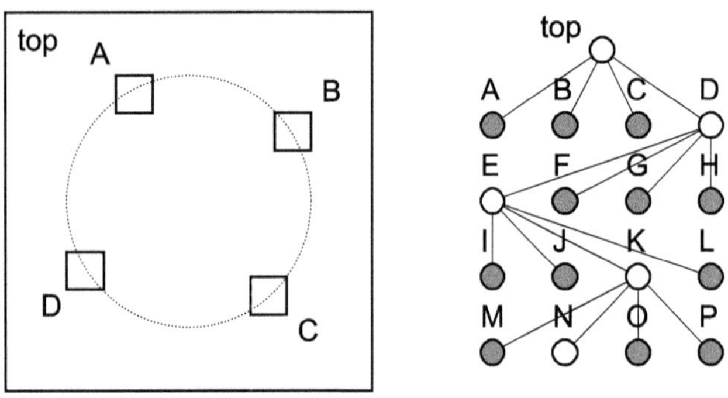

Figure 4. Top level view of the cue hierarchy (left) and complete sample visual cue (right). Red nodes represent dead ends, white nodes are correct choices that give rise to new options. The bottom white node (N) represents the target. The correct path is D, E, K, and N.

STUDY 1: MULTISCALE VISUAL SEARCH

Our first user study was designed to test the basic multiscale navigation functionality of PolyZoom in comparison with the standard pan and zoom provided in Google Maps (the winning technique in the experiment by Pietriga et al. [16]).

Task

The intuition behind our scenario in this study was that multiscale search consists of knowledge at several different levels of scale. To mimic this multiscale knowledge, we asked participants to navigate a hierarchy of visual cues, in the form of identical squares. This would emulate situations where a user knows a little about the target at different zoom levels, e.g., "it is a city near a coast", but several alternatives may have to be pursued to determine which one is correct.

Starting from the top view (shown at the start of a trial), and at each subsequent level in this hierarchy, four visual cues were shown as squares on the visual space. The visual cues form a hierarchy, where three of the four visual cues are dead ends, and only one is the correct and contains four new visual cues in turn. This parent-child relationship between correct visual cues continues for a given number of levels (depending on an experimental factor, see below).

Inside a visual cue, the squares representing the new visual cues were equally spaced, with a random starting offset, on the periphery of an invisible circle centered in the middle of the space. The radius of this circle was equal to one third of the parent cue's width, and the width of a square representing a visual cue is one tenth of the width of the parent. Figure 4 gives an overview, and Figure 5 gives an example.

The cues at different levels of the hierarchy were made visible only when a user is at a zoom level greater than or equal to the zoom level associated with that cue hierarchy level. When zooming into a visual cue representing a dead end, the contents of the square would turn a transparent red (Figure 5(b)) to indicate this fact. When zooming into a visual cue at the bottom of the hierarchy, the final target—a red balloon—would appear (Figure 5(d)). The trial ended (stopping the timer) when the participant clicked the balloon.

To simulate the effect of noticeable change in a multiscale visual space with a change in scale, there was a difference of three zoom levels between two adjacent levels of the cue hierarchy. This difference was also sufficient to ensure that at a time, only one of the visual cue at the previous levels of cue hierarchy is visible (Figure 5(b) and (c)).

Nevertheless, it should be noted that the visual cue hierarchy is *not* a complete tree, where dead ends are only unveiled at the bottom level. We chose to "short-circuit" incorrect search branches immediately by indicating that they are dead ends as soon as the participant zoomed into the visual cue. If we had used a complete tree, PolyZoom would likely benefit because it would offload the participant from having to remember each zoom decision at each node in the tree. The choice not to do this was made to keep the comparison fair. Because this design was in effect (thus minimizing the amount of backtracking arising from errors), we also chose *not* to control for random chance (which we do in Study 2).

Study Design

We used a full-factorial within-participants design:

	12	participants
×	2	**Navigation Technique** *T* (S, P)
×	3	**Hierarchy Level** *L* (3, 4, 5)
×	4	repetitions
	288	Total trials (24 per participant)

The *L* factor modeled the number of levels in the visual cue hierarchy, and we included it to study the effect of naviga-

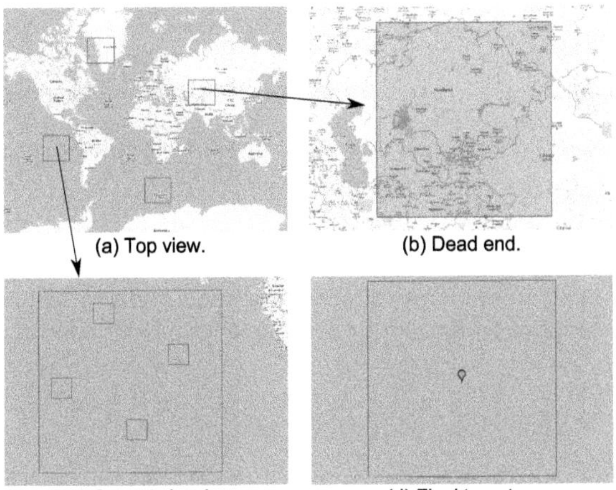

(a) Top view. (b) Dead end. (c) Correct visual cue. (d) Final target.

Figure 5. Scenario for Study 1. (a) View at the start of a trial; (b) Visual cues that represent dead ends are colored red when zoomed in; (c) The correct visual cue yields the next level in the hierarchy when zoomed in; (d) Zoom-in on the last level of the correct visual cue, where the target becomes a red balloon that needs to be clicked to finish the experiment.

tional depth on multiscale navigation. The deeper the hierarchy, the more stress will be placed on the navigation techniques: more zoom stacks in PolyZoom, and more backtracking for standard zoom and pan.

We organized the trials in blocks based on technique. Block order and the order of visual cue hierarchy levels within each block were randomized across participants to counteract learning effects. During the experiment we collected the time it took the participants to complete a task. Completion times were averaged for the four repetitions.

Hypotheses

H1 *P will be faster than S.* We believe that PolyZoom's increased multiscale awareness will favor the technique.

Results

We followed common statistical practice to improve the robustness of our completion time data by removing outliers (trials outside two standard deviations of the average) and averaged between the four repetitions per participants. The omitted trials were all above the average, and likely resulted from interface mistakes. We then analyzed the completion time measurements using a repeated-measures analysis of variance (RM-ANOVA, normality and equality of variances assumptions valid). We found a significant main effect of Technique T on completion time ($F(1,11) = 7.33, p < .0071$). Figure 6(a) shows completion times per technique and hierarchy level; the average times were 27.47 (s.d. 5.80) seconds for PolyZoom (P), and 29.39 (s.d. 6.13) seconds for standard pan and zoom (S). This constitutes an approximate 6.5% speedup for PolyZoom over standard pan and zoom, which is a small but non-negligible value.

Not surprisingly, there was also a significant main effect of Hierarchy Level L on completion time ($F(2,22) = 51.76, p < .0001$). Completion time was roughly linear with the number of levels in the visual cue hierarchy. Pairwise comparison of levels using a Tukey HSD showed that levels were significantly different ($p < .05$) with completion times ordered $3 < 4 < 5$. However, we found no significant interaction between T and L. This signifies that there is no difference in how the techniques manage increasing scale.

Participants were able to create multiple windows in the standard pan and zoom condition, but few did so: only in 10 out of the 144 trials for the S condition did participants create additional windows, and even in those situations, the maximum number of windows ever created was 2. Creating a second window is not an advantageous strategy for this task, but the low number of instances this happened means there should be only a very small impact on our results.

Subjective Feedback

Subjective ratings are shown in Figure 7 (left); differences were significant (Friedman test, $p < .05$) except for reward. In their comments also, participants found PolyZoom useful for the given task. One of them stated "[PolyZoom] is cool," and another wrote "PolyZoom was very useful."

Discussion

Our results confirmed hypothesis H1: participants performed the multiscale search task 6.5% faster using PolyZoom than using standard pan and zoom. While the speedup is fairly small, this is nevertheless a significant result given the optimality of pan and zoom as indicated by related work—for example, Pietriga et al. [16] found that pan and zoom performed better than two advanced lens-based techniques, and Hornbæk and Frøkjær [7] showed that overview+detail was superior to panning and fisheye views.

The experimental application was maximized on the screen at all times, which meant that both techniques had access to the same, constant amount of display space. The explanation for these results is likely that PolyZoom provides more awareness of the visual space than pan and zoom with a single overview. Our findings indicate that the impact of viewports becoming successively smaller, as well as suboptimal use of display space, did not decrease performance for PolyZoom, at least not in situations covered in our experiment.

The solution strategy that users adopted with PolyZoom was interesting and worth describing: for each level in the visual cue hierarchy, the user would create *one* focus region centered on one of the four visual cues. This new viewport would immediately allow the user to determine whether this was a dead end or not, and if it was, the user would simply move the selection area in the parent to the next visual cue. In other words, participants only ever had a single viewport open at each zoom level. For pan and zoom, on the other hand, the participants were forced to continually pan and zoom the single viewport to focus on each visual cue.

The question is whether and how these results generalize, and we think there are both qualitative and quantitative answers to this question. On a qualitative level, we believe that it is easy to see the usefulness of PolyZoom for general multiscale navigation, and we can foresee the technique being used for even larger and more complex visual spaces than those tested in our experiment. On a quantitative level, we found no significant interaction between technique and hierarchy level, which seems to indicate that PolyZoom's performance did not degrade as the number of levels in the visual cue hierarchy increased. On the other hand, since PolyZoom keeps every step of the navigation process visible, it is clear that there *does* exist a limit to how far it will scale (although it is always possible to restart PolyZoom on a new position in the space, foregoing the existing focus hierarchy). However, it should be noted that in our evaluation, the condition $L = 5$ used the full 23 zoom levels of the Google Maps dataset, which clearly is a large and realistic multiscale visual space.

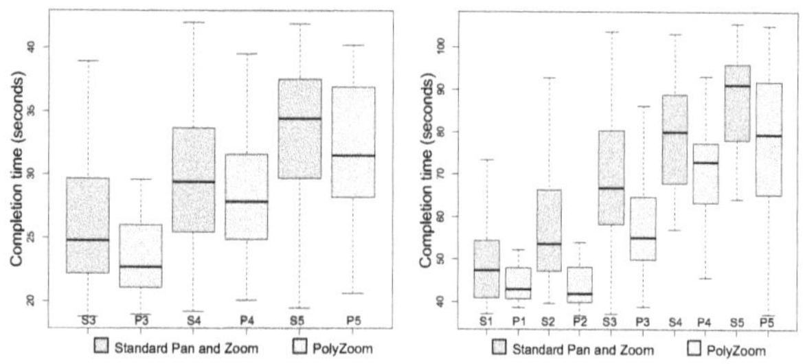

(a) Completion times (S1). (b) Completion times (S2).

Figure 6. Performance metrics for both Study 1 and Study 2 as a function of the level *L* and discovery order *D*, respectively.

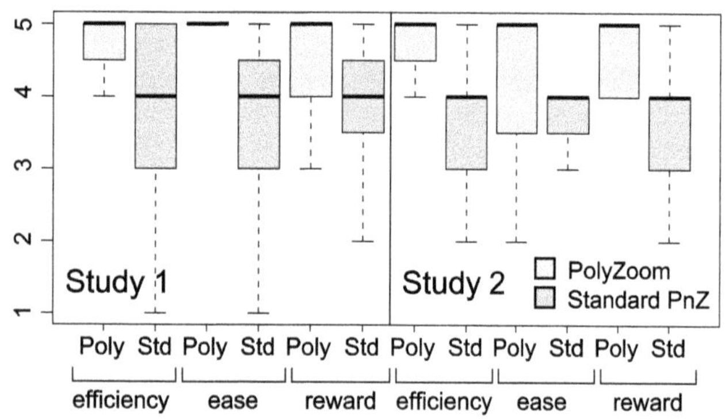

Figure 7. Subjective ratings for both studies (Likert 1-5 scale).

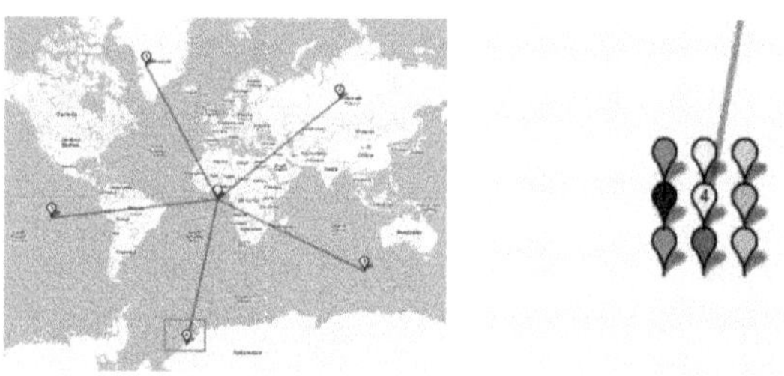

(a) Overall view. (b) Detail view.

Figure 8. Scenario for Study 2. (a) Overall trial view. The target in the center is the source, and the targets at the spokes of the circle are destinations. (b) Detail view of target 4 (indicated in the overview with a red rectangle) showing the 3 × 3 grid of colored balloons (only visible at maximum zoom) used to represent a target.

STUDY 2: MULTIFOCUS COMPARISON

Our second study was intended to explore the multifocus capabilities of PolyZoom. The novel technique provides a way to manage a hierarchy of viewports, whereas the de facto standard for looking at multiple regions in the same visual space is to open two or more windows and compare them side by side. We wanted to see whether the ever-shrinking viewports of PolyZoom would actually result in better performance than the multiple window approach.

Task

The motivation for the task in our second study was to capture situations when a user is trying to compare a particular region in a visual space with a set of candidate regions to find the one that matches. For this reason, we designed this task as a multifocus comparison task.

A trial setup consisted of a *source target* placed at the center of the visual space, and five potential *destination targets* arranged with equal spacing on the periphery of a virtual circle centered at the source. The source was connected to all destinations by a straight line. The task consisted of determining which of the five destination target exactly matches the appearance of the source. Figure 8(a) gives an example.

Actually determining the appearance of a target—source or destination alike—required navigating to the maximum zoom level in the visual space for the target to be unveiled. A target is a 3×3 grid of colored balloons where the center balloon is always yellow (Figure 8(b)). The colors used were red, green, blue, black, yellow, purple, cyan, and grey. The source target has a unique configuration of colors, and one of the destination targets—the *actual target*—has the exact same configuration. All other destination targets have the same color configuration but with two randomly swapped colors. This was done to ensure that all destination targets would be similar to the source, precluding matching on just a part of the source's color configuration.

Completing the trial consisted of finding the actual target and inputing its number (shown in both overview and detail views, see Figure 8) into a text field and clicking a button.

Study Design

We used a full-factorial within-participants design:

	12	participants
×	2	**Navigation Technique** T (S, P)
×	5	**Discovery Order** D (1, 2, 3, 4, 5)
×	2	repetitions
	240	Total trials (20 per participant)

We wanted to counterbalance the impact of random chance in the navigation, so we introduced a factor D for which order the participant would discover the actual target. In other words, while we told the participants that the program randomly selected one destination target to be the actual target prior to the participant starting the trial, this was not actually the case. Instead, the application counted the number of destination targets as they were unveiled (i.e., viewed at the maximum zoom level), and made the n:th destination target the actual target. With D taking on all values $\{1,2,3,4,5\}$, and with two repetitions, it is easy to see that all participants twice encountered all orderings of when they found the actual target. This design mimics the counterbalancing done by Pietriga et al. [16] and controls the impact of participants being "lucky" and choosing the right target every time.

We again organized the trials in blocks by technique. Technique order was balanced and discovery orders were randomized to counteract learning effects. During the experiment we measured time and correctness. To detect guessing, if a participant answered without ever having unveiled the actual target, we counted that as a wrong answer. This was also true for the last target, so participants were not able use elimination (we informed participants of this fact).

Hypotheses

H2 *P will be faster than S.* We think that PolyZoom's explicit multifocus support will outperform pan and zoom with access to multiple windows; no predictions on correctness.

Results

As in Study 1, we removed outliers and calculated the average across all repetitions of a trial. We then analyzed the completion times using a repeated-measures analysis of variance (as before, all assumptions were valid). We found a significant main effect of technique T on completion time ($F(1,11) = 28.10, p = .0001$). Figure 6(b) shows the completion times per technique and order; the average times were 60.7 (s.d. 17.6) seconds for PolyZoom, and 68.31 (s.d. 19.1) seconds for standard pan and zoom, an 11% speedup.

Not surprisingly, the discovery order D had a significant main effect on completion time ($F(4,44) = 46.08, p < .0001$). The effect was roughly linear, as expected, and the pairwise differences in completion time between orders were significant (Tukey HSD, $p < .05$). We found no interaction effects between the two factors T and D, however.

We analyzed the correctness using logistic regression, but found no significant main or interaction effects of T or D on this metric. In general, correctness for Study 2 was high, with more than 90% of all trials being answered correctly.

For the number of windows, all participants created at least two windows when solving the task (there was no single trial with less than two windows). This tells us that participants were using an appropriate strategy, i.e., putting one window on the source target and then creating at least one window for comparing destination targets. Two was also the most common number, used in 32% of trials. These findings are also consistent with our informal observations from the study.

Subjective Feedback

Differences in subjective ratings (see Figure 7 (right)) were significant (Friedman test, $p < .05$) except for ease of use. Like for Study 1, comments given by the participants were in favor of PolyZoom; for example, "PolyZoom [was] better," and "[the standard pan and zoom] technique did not help."

Discussion

Our results again confirm our hypothesis H2: participants were 11% faster when using PolyZoom than when they were using standard panning and zooming with two or more map windows. This is significant given that spawning multiple windows, each supporting pan and zoom, is the current baseline for existing tools such as Google Maps. In fact, our experimental platform made creating new map windows trivial by providing an explicit button for this, whereas in a real window environment you would need to duplicate your browser window to achieve this. In other words, we suspect a lightweight technique such as PolyZoom that incorporates multiple viewports may compare even better.

The reason for PolyZoom performing better than standard pan and zoom is fairly straightforward: PolyZoom not only makes creating multiple viewports easy, but it also provides an explicit correlation between viewports. We did not evaluate this latter characteristic in Study 2, but we think it is easy to see that giving the user an awareness of the spatial relation of viewports may be highly useful in many situations.

It is worth noting that we did *not* compare PolyZoom against existing multifocus interaction techniques such as space-folding [2], multiple fisheyes [19], or rubber sheet interaction [18]. However, none of these techniques support multi-level awareness, and they all rely on visual distortion which is visually unstable and can cause hunting effects [5]. While it would be interesting to compare PolyZoom directly to these techniques, we leave this for future work.

Finally, in terms of generalizing these results, we again give both qualitative and quantitative arguments. For a qualitative argument, we believe that PolyZoom will also generalize to other, and potentially more complex, multifocus tasks than the ones studied here. For example, our task only involved comparing two regions, but it is easy to see that PolyZoom could be used to compare three, four, or more regions. As for the quantitative argument, we again saw no significant interaction between technique and discovery order. In other words, participants were not degrading in performance as a function of how late the actual target came in the order of visitation. While this will again clearly not scale indefinitely, we still think that it indicates that our results will generalize outside the context of our experimental setup.

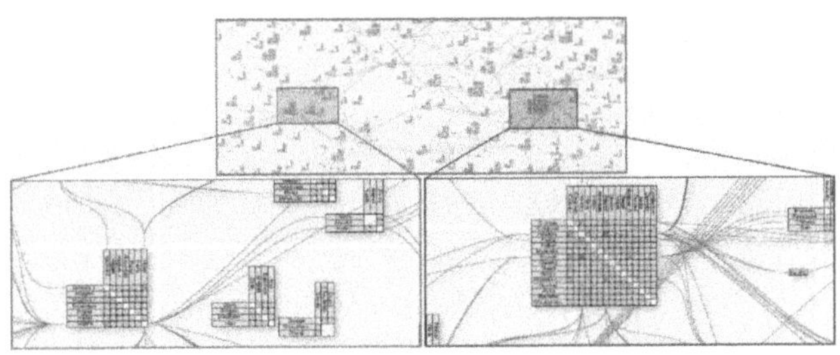

Figure 9. PolyZooming in the 20 years of UIST diagram.

POLYZOOM: BEYOND MAPS

While both of our studies used the multiscale geographical world maps through Google Maps, none of the actual tasks actually made use of the geographical data itself. We used the Google Maps example because it is familiar to our participants, and it also represents the actual state of the art of what people use today when interacting with maps.

However, as we have already established, PolyZoom can be used for any 2D visual space, not just geographical maps.

Figure 1 shows a visual exploration session in a Lunar dataset where the user is comparing the different craters on the lunar surface. Similarly, we envision applying PolyZoom to a variety of multiscale spaces defined by visualization techniques, including large adjacency matrices, multiscale hierarchies, and multiresolution high-dimensional data. Figure 9 shows an example of zooming in the large UIST co-authorship graph created by Henry, Dragicevic, and Fekete (`http://www.aviz.fr/gallery/uist20years_v2.jpg`). Our findings in this paper easily confirm the general utility of PolyZoom for multiscale spaces and we foresee much advances for other datasets.

CONCLUSIONS AND FUTURE WORK

We have presented PolyZoom, a multiscale and multifocus navigation technique in which users progressively build hierarchies of focus regions that are rendered on the screen simultaneously. We have implemented PolyZoom for Google Maps, NASA Universe, and other multiscale datasets, and we use this implementation to compare the technique to pan and zoom in two controlled experiments involving human subjects. Our findings show that PolyZoom is superior for both multiscale search as well as multifocus comparison. In the future we plan to continue to improve these tasks through interest-based, topology-aware, and semantic methods.

REFERENCES

1. C. Appert, O. Chapuis, and E. Pietriga. High-precision magnification lenses. In *Proceedings of the ACM Conference on Human Factors in Computing Systems*, 273–282, 2010.
2. N. Elmqvist, N. Henry, Y. Riche, and J.-D. Fekete. Mélange: Space folding for multi-focus interaction. In *Proceedings of the ACM Conference on Human Factors in Computing Systems*, 1333–1342, 2008.
3. G. W. Furnas. Generalized fisheye views. In *Proceedings of the ACM Conference on Human Factors in Computer Systems*, 16–23, 1986.
4. G. W. Furnas and B. B. Bederson. Space-scale diagrams: Understanding multiscale interfaces. In *Proceedings of the ACM Conference on Human Factors in Computing Systems*, 234–241, 1995.
5. C. Gutwin. Improving focus targeting in interactive fisheye views. In *Proceedings of the ACM Conference on Human Factors in Computing Systems*, 267–274, 2002.
6. K. Hornbæk, B. B. Bederson, and C. Plaisant. Navigation patterns and usability of zoomable user interfaces with and without an overview. *ACM Transactions on Computer-Human Interaction*, 9(4):362–389, 2002.
7. K. Hornbæk and E. Frøkjær. Reading of electronic documents: The usability of linear, fisheye, and overview+detail interfaces. In *Proceedings of the ACM Conference on Human Factors in Computing Systems*, 293–300, 2001.
8. T. Igarashi and K. Hinckley. Speed-dependent automatic zooming for browsing large documents. In *Proceedings of the ACM Symposium on User Interface Software and Technology*, 139–148, 2000.
9. E. W. Ishak and S. Feiner. Content-aware scrolling. In *Proceedings of the ACM Symposium on User Interface Software and Technology*, 155–158, 2006.
10. W. Javed and N. Elmqvist. Stack zooming for multi-focus interaction in time-series data visualization. In *Proceedings of the IEEE Pacific Visualization Symposium*, 33–40, 2010.
11. S. Jul and G. W. Furnas. Critical zones in desert fog: Aids to multiscale navigation. In *Proceedings of the ACM Symposium on User Interface Software and Technology*, 97–106, 1998.
12. V. Kaptelinin. A comparison of four navigation techniques in a 2D browsing task. In *Proceedings of the ACM Conference on Human Factors in Computing Systems*, 282–283, 1995.
13. D. Nekrasovski, A. Bodnar, J. McGrenere, F. Guimbretière, and T. Munzner. An evaluation of pan & zoom and rubber sheet navigation with and without an overview. In *Proceedings of the ACM Conference on Human Factors in Computing Systems*, 11–20, 2006.
14. K. Perlin and D. Fox. Pad: An alternative approach to the computer interface. In *Computer Graphics (ACM SIGGRAPH '93 Proceedings)*, 57–64, 1993.
15. E. Pietriga and C. Appert. Sigma Lenses: Focus-context transitions combining space, time and translucence. In *Proceedings of the ACM Conference on Human Factors in Computing Systems*, 1343–1352, 2008.
16. E. Pietriga, C. Appert, and M. Beaudouin-Lafon. Pointing and beyond: an operationalization and preliminary evaluation of multi-scale searching. In *Proceedings of the ACM Conference on Human Factors in Computing Systems*, 1215–1224, 2007.
17. C. Plaisant, B. Milash, A. Rose, S. Widoff, and B. Shneiderman. LifeLines: Visualizing personal histories. In *Proceedings of the ACM Conference on Human Factors in Computing Systems*, 221–227, 1996.
18. M. Sarkar, S. S. Snibbe, O. J. Tversky, and S. P. Reiss. Stretching the rubber sheet: A metaphor for visualizing large layouts on small screens. In *Proceedings of the ACM Symposium on User Interface Software and Technology*, 81–91, 1993.
19. G. Shoemaker and C. Gutwin. Supporting multi-point interaction in visual workspaces. In *Proceedings of the ACM Conference on Human Factors in Computing Systems*, 999–1008, 2007.
20. J. J. van Wijk and W. A. A. Nuij. Smooth and efficient zooming and panning. In *Proceedings of the IEEE Symposium on Information Visualization*, 15–22, 2003.
21. C. Ware and M. Lewis. The DragMag image magnifier. In *Extended Abstracts of the ACM Conference on Human Factors in Computing Systems*, 407–408, 1995.

Looking Glass: A Field Study on Noticing Interactivity of a Shop Window

Jörg Müller †, Robert Walter †, Gilles Bailly †, Michael Nischt †, Florian Alt ‡
†Quality and Usability Lab, Telekom Innovation Laboratories, TU Berlin
Ernst-Reuter-Platz 7, 10587 Berlin
firstname.lastname@tu-berlin.de
‡University of Stuttgart
Pfaffenwaldring 5a, 70569 Stuttgart
florian.alt@vis.uni-stuttgart.de

ABSTRACT
In this paper we present our findings from a lab and a field study investigating how passers-by notice the interactivity of public displays. We designed an interactive installation that uses visual feedback to the incidental movements of passers-by to communicate its interactivity. The lab study reveals: (1) Mirrored user silhouettes and images are more effective than avatar-like representations. (2) It takes time to notice the interactivity (approximately 1.2s). In the field study, three displays were installed during three weeks in shop windows, and data about 502 interaction sessions were collected. Our observations show: (1) Significantly more passers-by interact when immediately showing the mirrored user image (+90%) or silhouette (+47%) compared to a traditional attract sequence with call-to-action. (2) Passers-by often notice interactivity late and have to walk back to interact (the *landing effect*). (3) If somebody is already interacting, others begin interaction behind the ones already interacting, forming multiple rows (the *honeypot effect*). Our findings can be used to design public display applications and shop windows that more effectively communicate interactivity to passers-by.

Author Keywords
Interactivity, Noticing Interactivity, Public Displays, User Representation

ACM Classification Keywords
H.5.1 Multimedia Information Systems: Evaluation/Methodology.

INTRODUCTION
A major challenge when creating engaging public displays is that people passing by are usually not aware of any interactive capabilities. Unlike privately owned devices, such as mobile phones or PCs, people simply do not know or expect that they are interactive - an effect that has been amplified by displays having been used for static ads from their very advent. If public displays cannot communicate their interactivity, they will be hardly used and not fulfill their purpose. We believe that this issues will become even more apparent in the future as current LCD technology for public displays are likely to be replaced by technologies that more closely resemble traditional paper (e.g., e-paper [5]). As a consequence, passers-by might not even be able to notice that a surface is digital, unless the content is constantly moving.

Figure 1. Two groups of users (lined up in multiple rows) having a social experience with the looking glass. Users are represented by their silhouette on the display.

To put this problem in context, passers-by of public displays need to (1) notice the display, (2) understand that it is interactive, and (3) be motivated to interact with it (not necessarily in this order). Müller *et al.* [19] discuss the role of attention and motivation. However, relatively little is known about understanding interactivity (2), which is at the focus of this paper. Previous solutions involve calls-to-action and attract loops [14]. A *call-to-action*, like a "Touch to start" label, can be effective. However, text or symbols are language and culture dependent and complex to understand subconsciously. *Attract loops*, such as a video of a person interacting, can create an atmosphere of an arcade game and be complex to understand in a similar manner.

In this paper we investigate how feedback to the passer-by's incidental movements (e.g., a mirror image) can be used to communicate the interactivity of a display (see Figure 1). As humans are very efficient at recognizing human motion [2] as well as their own mirror image [18], this technique benefits from these perceptual mechanisms.

After discussing psychological foundations, we report and discuss the results of a lab and a field study. In the initial lab study we were able to show that a real-time video image or silhouette of the user are equally effective for recognizing interactivity. Avatar-like and more abstract representations are less effective. We measured an average time of 1.2s people required to recognize interactivity for the mirrored video. In the subsequent field study we deployed and tested three displays in a shop over the course of three weeks. Our observations show: (1) Significantly more passers-by interact when immediately showing the mirrored user image (90% more) or silhouette (47% more) compared to a traditional attract sequence with call-to-action. (2) Passers-by often recognize interactivity after they already passed. Hence they have to walk back - we call this the *landing effect*. (3) Often passers-by notice interactivity because of somebody already interacting. They position themselves in a way that allows them to see both the user and the display, allowing them to understand the interactivity. If they start interacting themselves, they do so behind the person interacting hence forming multiple rows.

Our observations can be useful for designers of public displays who need to communicate interactivity to passers-by, and more generally, for any designer of devices where users do not know in advance that the device is interactive.

RELATED WORK

Attracting *attention* with public displays and kiosks is not easy [8][11][19], and has been described as the 'first click problem' [11]. Huang *et al.* observed the passer-by's attention towards (non-interactive) public displays and show that most displays receive little attention [8]. One solution is to use stimuli for attracting attention [8][19]. However, this is challenging as in public space, many other objects strive for the user's attention [8]. Another solution suggests using physical objects. For instance Ju *et al.* [11] show that a physical attract loop (animatronic hand) is twice as effective as a virtual attract loop (virtual hand). While physical objects seem to attract more attention than digital content, they are less flexible and more difficult to update with new content.

We conducted a literature review and identified 6 techniques used for *communicating interactivity* of both public displays and tabletops: (1) A *call-to-action* [14], often a simple text label such as "touch screen to begin" was used in [11], [14] and [16]. (2) An *attract sequence* which is originally described as a slideshow [14]. Some multitouch installations used constantly moving objects [22][7]. Arcade machines also use a video that either explains the interaction or shows a user performing the interaction. (3) Nearby *analog signage*, either with a simple call-to-action or a more complex manual, has been used in many deployments, e.g., [14][16][22]. (4) The *honeypot effect* [1] describes the effect of people being attracted by persons already interacting with a device. Brignull *et al.* observed this effect and divided the people around the display into the phases peripheral attention, focused attention, and interacting. Further observations of the honeypot effect are reported in [16][22][17]. (5) *Persons inviting passers-by to interact* can be either users who have already noticed the interactivity of the display and now motivate their friends [16][22], or researchers standing next to the device inviting users and explaining the interaction [9]. (6) *Prior knowledge* that a device is interactive can either be used if users pass by the same device multiple times, or if they know the device (e.g., the Microsoft Surface, as in [16]).

After people noticed interactivity, *immediate usability* is important. The term has been introduced in the context of Shneiderman's CHI photo kiosk [14]. Users should be able to use the interface after observing others or using it themselves for a brief period of time (15-60s). Marshall *et al.* [16] observed that even a delay of a few seconds after touching an interactive tabletop is problematic. Users are likely to give up and think that the device is not interactive or broken.

Perceived affordances [20] are derived from Gibson's concept of affordances, which are properties of an organism's environment that have a certain relation to the body and skills of the organism. These properties make certain actions possible (afford them). While affordances exist independent of their perception, it is important how they can be perceived by users. More recently, Norman proposed the more general concept of signifiers [21]. Signifiers may be any information in the environment that indicate that a certain action is possible or appropriate. This is especially interesting in the context of public displays, as, for example, smears on a screen may indicate that it is a touch screen.

Several researchers have proposed to use a *shadow or mirror image* of users of large displays to indicate and support interaction. They have been used in the context of artistic installations [13], pointing tasks on large displays [26], and interaction above a tabletop [6]. In the context of public displays, Michelis [17] deployed public displays showing a camera image of what was happening in front of the screen and augmented it with digital effects guided by motion, like clouds of numbers or growing flowers. The focus of this study was on the motivation to interact rather than noticing interactivity. Thus, no different user representations were compared and no baseline, like call-to-action, was tested. While these works explored various aspects of shadow and mirror metaphors, their application and properties to communicate interactivity of displays has not yet been explored.

Attract sequence and call-to-action are practical solutions to communicate interactivity. In the following we explore the representations through mirror images as an alternative.

PSYCHOLOGICAL CUES & INTERACTIVITY

When it comes to noticing interactivity, several concepts from psychology provide useful hints as to how such an interactive system should be designed. Table 1 shows that for a certain interaction it is possible to compare whether the manipulation has been intentional (or not) and whether the effect has been noticed by the user (or not). Dix *et al.* [3] discuss a continuum of intentionality between explicit and incidental interaction. Explicit interaction refers to the case where users intentionally manipulate an interactive system. Incidental interaction refers to situations where the interaction is neither intended nor the effect noticed after the fact, such as when a user enters a room and the temperature is adjusted automati-

	Noticed Effect	Unnoticed Effect
Intentional Manipulation	Explicit Interaction [3]	–
Unintentional Manipulation	**Inadvertent Interaction**	Incidental [3] / Implicit [24] Interaction

Table 1. While incidental / implicit interaction assumes that the user does not notice the effect, we can distinguish the case where the user inadvertently interacts and then sees the effect.

cally, without the user noticing. A similar concept is implicit interaction [24], which describes situations where the user interacts without being aware of interacting. As users become aware of the fact that they are interacting, implicit and incidental interaction turn into explicit interaction. To describe the situation where users manipulate a device incidentally, but become aware of the effect and thus the fact that the device is interactive, we use the term *inadvertent interaction*. When users perceive that a device reacts to their incidental movements, this reaction can be perceived in three ways. It can be perceived as (1) a *representation* of the user, (2) an effect being *caused* by the user, or (3) an *animate* object reacting to the user. For all of these perceptions, powerful perceptual mechanisms exist. While the focus of this paper is on the *representation* of the user, we will also shortly review psychological foundations for perceptions of causality and animacy.

Representation: Recognizing Oneself

There are two ways how one could potentially recognize oneself in a mirror: appearance matching and kinesthetic-visual matching [18]. Appearance matching is based on a comparison of the image seen in a mirror with the knowledge of how oneself looks like. Kinesthetic-visual matching is based on the correlation between the own motion and the visual feedback in the mirror. The question whether some organism can recognize itself in a mirror has been a topic of investigation since the early work of Gallup [4]. They learned that only humans, chimpanzees, and orang-utans show this behavior. Humans can recognize themselves already in the first months of life [18]. For recognizing somebody else's reflection in a mirror, visual-visual matching can be used instead of kinesthetic-visual matching (if we can see both the person and the reflection). This is presumably easier than kinesthetic-visual matching (it is learned early in childhood).

When users control a representation of themselves on a display (e.g., mouse pointer or mirror image), they need to understand that they are in control. This is similar to the questions of psychology how humans perceive which part of the world is one's own body (ownership) and controlled by oneself (agency) [10]. From psychology we learn: (1) Visual feedback can override proprioceptive feedback, such that people feel agency for parts of the world which are not actually their own body. People might forget about their real surroundings when immersed in the virtual representation. (2) People assume more often that they control something that they do not actually control than vice versa (overattribution). (3) People can experience a continuum between more and less agency, depending on the correlation (amount of noise and delay) [10]. It is important to minimize noise and delay to improve the perception of agency.

Abstraction, Biological Motion, and Body Schema

Humans can not only use appearance matching, but also kinesthetic-visual matching, to recognize their mirror image. So it is possible to abstract the user representation and still have users recognize themselves. This gives the designer of a device much more artistic freedom in designing the user representation. Fortunately, humans have direct perception of the motion of humans and animals from minimal information. It was shown that a video of a dynamic array of point lights (at skeletal joints) is sufficient to see the presence of a walker [2]. For recognizing gender, the upper body joints are more relevant, and adding more points besides shoulders, elbows, wrists, and hips (70% accuracy) does not improve accuracy [12]. From static images of point lights without motion however, not even the presence of a human can be seen. For this paper it is especially interesting that we can recognize ourselves and friends, and that we are more effective in recognizing ourselves (43% accuracy) than our friends (36%, 16.7% chance), despite the fact that we see our friends walking more often [2]. This is explained by the fact that both executed and perceived motion are represented in isomorphic representations (the body schema) and can easily be translated into each other.

Concluding, a system could use minimal representations similar to point light displays to represent users, but it is very important that the representation is dynamic. Upper body parts like wrists and torso might be most effective. In order to use the body schema for representation, however, the feedback needs to directly match to the movements of specific body parts (e.g., head or hand). More abstract feedback that cannot directly be matched to body parts (e.g., averages of the movements of multiple body parts) often needs more time to be recognized [27].

Perceptual Causality and Animacy

Besides for recognizing themselves, humans also have perceptual mechanisms for causality and animacy. This is impressively demonstrated by 2D movies of simple moving geometric shapes [25]. If an object 'hits' another, and this second object is 'pushed' away, humans have a strong impression that the first object caused the motion of the second. If there is more than a 50-100 ms delay between the two events, this perception starts to disappear. Similarly, objects that start from rest, change direction to avoid collision, or have directed movement towards a goal can appear to be 'alive' [25]. Perceptual causality and animacy can be used to communicate interactivity, and in these cases, known cues causing these perceptions should be used (e.g., collision). In particular, causality can be combined with mirror representations. As interacting with mirror representations alone is not very motivating, physics simulations provide motivating interaction and increase the perception of interactivity.

Relevance for this Paper

In this paper we focus on the representation of the user as a cue to interactivity, because such a user representation is a very general tool to support multiple interaction techniques.

From these psychological foundations, we learn the following: (1) There are efficient perceptual mechanisms that support this self-recognition (2) It is unclear how recognition of oneself degrades when the representation is abstracted. (3) It seems crucial that the correlation between the user's movement and feedback is high (low noise and delay). (4) The feedback should be directly matchable to a certain body part, in order to use the efficient body-schema representation. (5) User representations can be combined with perceptual causality (or animacy) to strengthen the perception of interactivity and provide a more interesting application.

STUDIES

To explore how inadvertent interaction and representations of the user can be used to communicate the interactivity of public displays, we conducted a series of three user studies. We developed a series of prototypes that were successively refined based on the results of these studies. During these studies the focus was on noticing interactivity rather than attention or motivation. We simply relied on the motion of the user representation to capture attention and on a very simple game (playing with balls) to motivate users. More elaborate attention grabbing or motivating techniques would probably increase the total number and duration of interactions.

Hardware and Implementation

The system was deployed on large portrait-oriented LCD screens of different sizes ranging from 40" to 65". To detect passers-by and users the Microsoft Kinect sensor was employed. The code runs on a recent linux workstation machine.

We use the 3d rendering capabilities of *OpenGL* to display the user's mirrored image or silhouette and other virtual objects. For detecting users we rely on the *OpenNI* framework, which provides unique IDs and pixel masks to separate them from the background. The mirrored user representations are directly embedded into the scene to the lower half of the screen (see Table 2) and interacts with other virtual objects (balls). We use the *Bullet* physics library to simulate the behavior of these objects constrained to 2d plane. Since the simulation is optimized for rigid bodies, we approximate the users' shape with small objects along their contour which are continuously tracked between frames. We record the depth image stream and user activities for later analysis.

Study Design

In the following we present a pre-study and two consecutive studies on noticing interactivity. We began with a *pre-study* to see if and how passers-by are interacting with a public display. This was followed by a controlled *lab study* removing the attraction and motivation criteria. Hence, we could measure the time required to recognize if the test application was in an interactive or non-interactive (video playback) mode. The study further included the influence of the user representations for which we evaluated multiple levels of abstractions. Finally, in an "in the wild" *field study* we compared immediate, inadvertent interaction against an attract sequence combined with a call-to-action. We also again compare different user representations. The focus of this study however is on exploring the noticing of interactivity "in the wild".

PRE-STUDY

Our prototype showed the silhouette of the passer-by on a 46" portrait LCD monitor. Passers-by could interact with a virtual ball using simulated physics. The display was installed for three days around lunchtime in front of a university cafeteria. Users were observed from a hidden position and interviewed on opportunity basis. Interrater reliability was satisfactory (Cohen's Kappa=0.61) [15]. We observed 832 passers-by, of which 456 (54.8%) looked at the display, 171 (20.6%) interacted with the display, and 141 (16.9%) stopped walking to interact. People played for 2 to 182 seconds ($\mu = 26s$), and stated to mostly have left for time pressure. Interestingly, most persons interacted in groups – most single passers-by rather hurried past the display.

There are two important conclusions from this study. First, a large percentage of all passers-by interacted (in a university setting), so the design is very promising for our purpose. Second, almost no passer-by interacted alone. As our design supported only single-use, this posed problems as mostly groups of 2-5 users tried to interact simultaneously. Also, almost all passers-by stopped before interacting, while we expected more people interacting while passing by.

LAB STUDY

The objective of this study was to determine the impact of the abstraction of the representation of the user on how quickly users can notice that a display is interactive. We compared the user representations *mirror, silhouette, avatar,* and *abstract*. In this study, we only focused on noticing interactivity. We asked participants to pay attention to the display and decide whether the display reacted to their movements or not. No additional virtual objects, that would potentially have biased the motivation of the participants, were shown on the screen. This lab study setup provided a baseline of how quickly users can decide whether a display is interactive under optimal conditions using the different representations. The lab design provided a high degree of control, while at the same time providing a lower degree of ecological validity. To counterbalance, the study was followed by a field study, which offers high ecological validity but less control.

Conditions

The conditions were (a) Mirror image: an interactive colored image of the user (on a black background), (b) Silhouette: a white filled silhouette of the user, (c) Avatar: a 2d avatar including head, torso, and hands, and (d) Abstract: just the head of the user, with abstract eyes and mouth.

All of these conditions can be directly matched to body parts by the user (see section Psychological Cues & Interactivity). For the expected interaction distance at the shop windows the camera could not capture both feet and head of the user. Based on the studies of point-light displays that show that upper body parts are most relevant, we decided to position the camera so that these parts were visible. Based on the same studies, we expect the gain in speed and accuracy from adding feet to the avatar to be low. Related work on stimulus-response compatibility [27] indicates that stimuli that can be directly matched to body parts are more effective than those which cannot. Therefore, we decided for the abstract condition to directly represent the head of the user (instead of, e.g., an average of multiple body parts). All four of these interactive conditions were also presented as non-interactive conditions. In this case, a video of another user interacting with the display was started as soon as the user stepped in front of the display. These non-interactive conditions should simulate situations where either just a random video was shown on a display, or a different user (e.g,. standing behind the participant) would interact with the display.

Task and Stimulus

Users were asked to walk past the display back and forth following a line on the ground placed at a constant 2m distance. On the display, one of the 4x2 different conditions was shown. Users carried a device (Logitech Presenter) and were asked to click on the left button when they believed the display to react to their movements, and the right button when they believed the display not to react to their movements. Users were asked to be as fast and accurate as possible. Time was measured from the moment when they entered the FOV of the camera (and thus appeared on the screen in the interactive conditions) until they pressed a button.

Apparatus and Design

A 82" portrait LCD display was used to present the content. The representation of the user was created using a Microsoft Kinect camera and software using OpenNI, NITE, and Processing. A within subjects design was used with n=16 participants recruited from a pool of non-computer scientists. Variables measured were time and accuracy.These 4x2 conditions were repeated in 10 blocks. The order was counterbalanced using a latin square within the participants, and randomized between the participants.

Results

The *selection time* was measured as the time from when the stimulus appeared (as the user entered the camera's field of view) to the time when the user made a choice. An ANOVA revealed a significant effect for *representation* on selection time ($F_{3,45} = 80.76, p < .0001$). It also revealed a representation * interactivity interaction effect on selection time ($F_{3,45} = 6.75, p < .0001$). A post-hoc Tukey test showed that Mirror (1.2s) and Silhouette (1.6s) are significantly faster than Avatar (2.8s) and Abstract (2.8s) in the interactive condition. In the non-interactive condition, Mirror (1.2s) is significantly faster than Silhouette (1.7s) and Avatar (2.1s) which are significantly faster than Abstract (2.8s).

An ANOVA also revealed a significant effect for representation on *accuracy* ($F_{3,45} = 43.09, p < .0001$). It also revealed a representation * interactivity interaction effect on accuracy ($F_{3,45} = 5.84, p < .0001$). A post-hoc Tukey test shows that Mirror (100%) and Silhouette (97.5%) are significantly more accurate than Abstract (84.3%) and Avatar (81.2%) in the interactive condition. In the non-interactive condition, Mirror (98.8%) and Silhouette (97.5%) are significantly more accurate than Avatar (86.3%) which is significantly more accurate than Abstract (73.1%). Finally, the ANOVA revealed a significant effect for *block id* on accuracy ($F_{9,135} = 5.84, p < .0001$). A post-hoc Tukey test shows that users are less accurate in the first block (74.2%) than in the other blocks (mean:91.6%).

Figure 2. Study location: Displays were finally installed in three shop windows (B, E, F)

Discussion

From this experiment we learn that (1) the Mirror and Silhouette representation are similarly efficient, but both more efficient than the Avatar and Abstract representation, and (2) it takes considerable time to distinguish the interactive and the non-interactive conditions even in an optimal environment (1.2s vs. 1.6s). The fact that the Silhouette is efficient is good, because it provides much more artistic freedom for the designer of a display. While the lab study provided control, ecological validity was low. Therefore, we decided to compare the two most promising representations, Mirror and Silhouette, to a combination of two common traditional techniques, call to action and attract loop, and a purely causal technique in a field study.

FIELD STUDY

The objective of this study was to explore how users would notice interactivity and interact with public displays using different user representations "in the wild". We compared the two most effective user representations, (Mirror) Image and Silhouette, to the most common strategy in industry, call-to-action combined with an attract loop, and a merely causal condition without user representation. This comparison was regarding their ability to attract users to interact with the display as well as their general effect on the social situation in an urban place. A field study was chosen in order to maximize ecological validity, sacrificing the control of the lab.

Deployment

Three displays were deployed for three weeks in shop windows of a store in the city center of Berlin (see Figure 2). Windows on one side of the store (D, E, F) were close to a well-frequented sidewalk, windows on the other side (A, B) were near a subway entrance. To decide in which windows to install the displays we observed 200 passers-by of the street-facing side of the store (C, D, E, F) during afternoon until night. The observations showed that there are large differences in how many passers-by look into each shop window. The percentages are: Main door C (6%), small window D (12%), small window (13%), small bright window (19%), large window E (29%), small window (16%), large window (29%), second door F (large and bright, 33%). For people walking from right to left, for whom the second door was the first window they saw, even 66% looked into the window. It seems that the large and bright windows attract more attention, especially if surrounding windows differ. Also for people walking from right to left, we noticed a large percentage (17%) looking straight away from the last window. Apparently, they looked down a road at the crossing. For the deployment we used three LCD monitors in portrait format (65", 46", 46"). Cameras (Microsoft Kinect) were installed below the monitors. For the first week of deployment we moved the displays between the windows A, B, C, D, E, F (see Figure 2). While window B had the advantage that people could play relatively undisturbed from passers-by, windows E and F had a larger number of passers-by and attracted most views. Therefore we decided to install the 65" display in window B, and two 46" displays in windows E and F. For the background image we initially tried different artistic contents, but could not observe a large influence of our contents on behavior. The final content was an advertisement for the store and was created by a professional advertising agency.

Conditions

In our study we tested two variables: user representation (Image vs. Silhouette vs. No Representation) and interactivity cue (inadvertent interaction vs. attract sequence with call-to-action). Regarding the application, we opted for a very simple ball game. Ten balls were displayed on the screen, and users could play with them (kick them) using the contour of their representation. The whole game took place in the 2d plane of the user representation. In the Image condition, the user's image from the color camera was extracted from the background and shown on the display. In the Silhouette condition, the silhouette of the user was shown on the display, and in the No Rrepresentation condition, just the balls were rendered, but no user representation was shown (but interaction was as in the other conditions). In the inadvertent interaction condition, when nobody was in front of the screen, just the background image and balls were shown. The interaction started as soon as users entered the FOV of the camera. In the attract sequence with call-to-action condition, a video of a person demonstrating the interaction was shown together with a label "Step Close to Play" (see Table 2). The video showed a person in the corresponding visualization (Image, Silhouette, and No Representation) stepping close to the camera and then playing with the balls. When the user entered the FOV of the camera with a closer distance (1m), the screen was switched to interaction, the user was represented in the corresponding visualization and could play with the balls. Conditions were counterbalanced and automatically switched every 30 minutes. This was done to minimize the influence of time of day on the results.

Data Analysis

We collected both qualitative and quantitative data. Qualitative data was gathered from observations, semi-structured interviews, and manual video recording. As quantitative data, complete interaction logs (from NITE person tracking) and videos from the depth camera were kept from each display over three weeks. For anonymity reasons we did not record the camera image, but only the (anonymous) depth image.

Qualitative data collection was conducted daily during three weeks. As displays worked best and most interaction occurred in the late afternoon and evening, at least two researchers were present during these times. Additional observations were conducted as needed. Observations were conducted from inconspicuous positions like the other side of the street or near the subway entrance, where it was common to see waiting people. During the observations, video was recorded using video cameras that looked similarly to mobile phones (FLIP HD). Furthermore, field notes were kept. Every day interesting findings were presented and discussed in a meeting of the entire research team. Eventually, the team agreed on a specific focus for following observations.

From the depth videos we recorded roughly 1500 hours of videos. We selected 11 consecutive days for manual coding. We implemented an analysis software that automatically searched the log files for scenes, in which a user was detected for more than 4 seconds. In accordance to [16] and [22], interactions which followed each other within less than 20s were merged to single sessions. All sessions were then manually reviewed and annotated. We observed 502 interactions. Inter-rater reliability was substantial (Cohen's Kappa=.75) [15]. During the analysis, we grouped our findings in four categories: *image, silhouette, and call-to-action, the landing effect, dynamics between groups*, and *dynamics within groups*.

Attract Loop with Call-to-Action

No Representation Silhouette Image

Table 2. Representations. We tested three user representations: No Representation, Silhouette, and Image. All three representations were tested in an "attract loop with call-to-action" as well as in a "inadvertent interaction" version. In this figure, the corresponding attract loops (a video of somebody stepping close to the display and starting to interact) are shown. In the inadvertent interaction condition, the person in front of the display was shown in the same representation, just without the call to action ("Step Close to Play").

	No-representation	Silhouette	Image
Call-to-action	67	59	79
Inadvertent interaction	60	87	150

Table 3. Total number of interactions in the different conditions during 11 days of field study. Inadvertent interaction attracts significantly more interactions than call-to-action. Further, Image works significantly better than Silhouette and No-representation.

Findings

Image, Silhouette, and Call-to-action

The total number of interactions during the 11 coded days is shown in Table 3. We compared the number of interactions per day. ANOVA reveals a significant effect for interactivity cue (call-to-action vs. inadvertent interaction) ($F_{1,11} = 12.6 p < .001$). A post-hoc Tukey test shows that passers-by interact more with the inadvertent interaction condition than

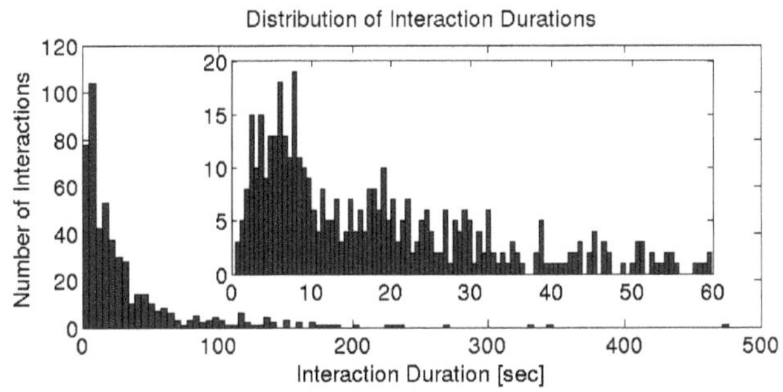

Figure 3. Interaction Durations: In order to investigate how well the different conditions communicate interactivity, we needed a large number of situations where nobody was currently interacting with the screen. Hence we intentionally designed the interaction not to be especially motivating for extended play. The mean duration of interactions was 31s, but many interactions only lasted for a few seconds. Surprisingly, some users seemed to be motivated to play for many minutes.

Figure 4. In the call-to-action condition people sometimes spent considerable time in front of the display (1) before stepping closer (2). In this case, the two women are surprised by seeing themselves and walk away (3). On the next window, they encounter inadvertent interaction in the Silhouette condition and start playing (4).

with the call-for-action. ANOVA also reveals a significant effect for user representation ($F_{2,22} = 13.1$). A post-hoc tukey test shows that Image is more efficient than Silhouette and No representation. Finally, ANOVA also reveals a user representation*interactivity cue interaction ($F_{2,22} = 6.8, p < 0.005$). As expected, there are no significant differences between user representation for call-to-action. User representations differ only in the inadvertent interaction condition. Many interactions with the display only lasted for seconds (Figure 3).

The interviews revealed different preferences for the user representations. The shop owner preferred the Silhouette as people were covered in company colors. For users there was no clear preference, and many said that they liked the representation they discovered first. Users who preferred the Image representation described it as more "authentic", more "fun", and they liked to see themselves and their friends. Users who preferred the Silhouette representation described it as more "anonymous" and said that they liked it when bystanders could not see their image. Some also said that they did not like to see themselves, so they preferred the Silhouette representation. In the Image representation, also some users mentioned that they do not like to be observed by a camera, which they did not say for the Silhouette representation. From our observations we found, that in the call-to-action conditions, people spent several seconds in front of the display before following the instructions ("Step Close to Play") (compare Figure 4). In this vignette, two girls observe the display for some time, before one steps close and activates the interaction in the Image condition. They are surprised by seeing themselves and walk away. A few meters further, they notice a second display running the inadvertent interaction Silhouette condition, where they start to play. When interviewed how they noticed interactivity, most people said that they saw themselves on the display. Some also said that they saw themselves and a friend / partner at the same time. Only very few stated to have seen the representation of another person walking in front of them.

When a crowd had already gathered around the display, it was sometimes very difficult to distinguish which effect was caused by whom. This was especially true for the Silhouette and obviously the No Representation conditions. In these cases we observed people copying the movements of other users and seemingly interacting with the screen, although they were not represented on the screen. Sometimes they were not even standing in the field of view of the camera. This can be an example of *overattribution* (compare section on psychological cues), where people assume they are causing some effects although they are not.

Over time, knowledge about the presence and interactivity had built up among people who pass the location regularly. In the third week of deployment, a number of people who interacted said that they had seen somebody else interacting, e.g., "a few weeks ago" or "earlier that day", but had not tried interaction themselves. There were also a few regular players. For example, we noticed from the logs that between 7-8am, there was considerable activity in front of the displays. Observations revealed that a number of children played regularly with the displays on their way to school. We observed them waiting expectantly at the traffic light, then crossing the street directly to the display to play with it. Such interaction is obviously different from situations where people encounter the displays for the first time.

Design Recommendations: Inadvertent interaction outperforms the attract loop with call-to-action in attracting interactions. The Image representation also outperforms the Silhouette and interaction without user representation. In contrast to the lab study, the Image representation works significantly better than the Silhouette. From this we learn that Image representations are a powerful cue to communicate interactivity, although Silhouettes may have some benefits like more artistic freedom in designing the content and provide more anonymity. As most people recognize themselves on the display rather than someone else, displays should be positioned so that people can see themselves well when passing by. Over time, as knowledge about the interactivite device builds up, these interactivity cues become less important.

The Landing Effect

One striking observation regarding the moment when people start to interact was that often, people stop late and have to walk back (see Figure 6 for this effect with a couple, and Figure 5 for this effect in a group). In Figure 5, a group of young men is passing the display. The seventh person in the group looks at the display but keeps on walking with the group. Some meters further the person suddenly turns around and walks back, followed by a second person. They then start to interact, and are soon joined by other group members. In this paper we refer to these cases as the *landing effect*.

Figure 5. Landing effect for a group: A group of people passes the display (1). Only at the next shop windows person A stops (2), turns around, and walks back to the display (3). As he starts interacting (4) more and more people from the group join. (5)

Figure 6. Landing effect for a couple: As the couple passes by, the woman notices the screen and stops. As her partner walkes on, she drags him back to the screen. Both start interacting. (The scene is from the depth video logs that were annotated)

Regarding the number of landing effects, interestingly ANOVA reveals a significant effect for interactivity cue ($F_{1,11} = 23.1, p < 0.0001$). A post-hoc Tukey test shows that more landing effects are observed in inadvertent interaction (18.5% of all interactions) than in call-to-action (8%). There was no significant effect for visualization. We observed this behavior only for people passing by the displays (not waiting), when nobody was yet interacting with the displays, and who apparently did not know before that the displays were interactive (e.g., because they already interacted with them).

The landing effect often led to conflicts when one person in a group noticed the interactivity. If the first persons in a group suddenly stopped and turned around, the following people would sometimes bump into them. More often, the whole group stopped rather than walking on. When a following person in a group however noticed interactivity, the first would usually walk on for some time before they noticed that somebody stopped and stop themselves. This situation created a tension in groups as to whether people who already continued walked back or whether the person interacting would abandon the display and join the group. In some cases the group simply walked on after some waiting, causing the interacting person to continue playing only for a short moment and then hurry (sometimes even run) to re-join the group.

Our interviews revealed more details about this behavior. One man who had walked back (Image condition) stated that he had seen from the corner of his eye two persons on the screen walking into the same direction. He was curious and walked back, accompanied by his wife. When he saw himself on the display, he understood that it was interactive and explained it to his wife. They both started to play with it. For another couple, the man stated that he saw something moving from the corner of the eye and walked back. His wife stopped, but did not follow him. He noticed that the display was interactive upon seeing himself, but only played very shortly before again joining his wife. It is quite possible that users did not interact, because they only noticed interactivity after they had already passed the displays and did not want to walk back to further explore.

Because we installed multiple displays along the same trajectory, passers-by had the option to notice interactivity on one screen, but then interact with another one. When they noticed the second screen, they already expected that it was also interactive and stopped earlier. One man for example said to have noticed the balls jumping away on the first screen, but then did not walk back. When he noticed the second screen, he decided to stop his friend. They saw their representations and played for a short moment. Often, after playing with one screen, people also searched the other windows of the shop for further screens. If they saw further screens, they often also played with those (see Figure 4).

Design Recommendations: The landing effect is in line with our observation from the lab, that people need approximately 1.2s (Image) and 1.6s (Silhouette) to recognize interactivity. They also need to notice the display first and be motivated to interact. With an average walking speed of 1.4 m/s, by the time passers-by have decided to interact, they have already passed the display. This effect is so strong that it should be designed for in any public display installation. Displays should be placed so that, when people decide to interact, they are still in front of the display and do not have to walk back. Optimally, when users stop friends walking in front of them, also the friends should still be able to interact with the display without walking back. This could be achieved by designing very wide displays (several meters), or more practically, a series of displays along the same trajectory. Another solution would be to place displays in a way so that users walk directly towards them, but this is possible only for very few shop windows.

Dynamics Between Groups

We observed many situations in which different groups started to interact. The first group (or person) usually causes what has been previously termed the "honeypot effect". We found that people passing by firstly observed somebody making unconventional movements while looking into a shop window (the manipulation [23]). They subsequently positioned themselves in a way that allowed them to see and understand the reason for these movements – usually in a location that allowed both the persons interacting as well as the display to be seen (see Figure 7). In this figure, a man interacting with the display with expressive gestures attracts con-

Figure 7. The Honeypot Effect: As people notice a person making uncommon gestures, they position themselves in a way allowing both the screen as well as the interacting person to be seen. They also often position themselves so that they are not represented on the screen.

Figure 8. Multiple Rows: The girl from group A noticed interactivity first. Woman B positioned herself behind them to see what happens and also started interacting. Later, a couple C stopped behind them and started interacting in a third row.

siderable attention. The crowd stopping and staring at him and the display partially blocks the way for other passers-by. Newcomers seem to be first attracted by the crowd, then follow their gaze, then see the man interacting, follow his gaze, repositioning themselves so they can see both the man and the display. They also seem to prefer to stand a little bit to the side, so that they are not represented on the screen. The audience is mostly positioned behind the user. We observed this pattern regularly. When people in the audience decided to join the interaction, they accordingly did so *behind* the ones already interacting, not next to them (see Figure 8). In this figure, the little girl in the front noticed the interactivity first, followed by her mother, who then stopped to explore the display together with the daughter (the father did not walk back and is standing behind the camera). The young woman behind them was attracted by their interaction and eventually also started interacting behind them. This again attracted the couple behind them, of which the girl finally also started interacting in a third row. In some cases, such multiple rows where then again observed by people in the subway entrance. In the few cases where other people started to interact in the same row as people already interacting, we were able to observe social interaction between the users, which we did not observe for different groups interacting behind each other.

People interacting with the screens were usually standing in the way of others. The resulting conflicts were solved in different ways. For the screen installed near the subway entrance, passers-by usually tried to pass behind the ones already interacting, not disturbing them. When multiple rows of people interacted, this was not possible however, and they passed in front of them (Figure 8). When a large group passed by, we sometimes observed that the person interacting abandoned the display. This again sometimes let someone from the coming group take the place and start to play. We also saw some occasions, where users deliberately moved between the display and the person interacting and interacted for a very short moment.

Design Recommendations: The honeypot effect is a very powerful cue to attract attention and communicate interactivity. Displays which manage to attract many people interacting will be able to attract more and more people. The honeypot effect even works after multiple days, as people who have seen somebody interacting previously may also try the interaction in the future (see subsection on Image, Silhouette and, Call-to-Action). To achieve this, displays should be designed to have someone visibly interacting with them as often as possible. This can be achieved by improving motivation and persuading people to play longer. Because the audience repositions themselves such that they can see both the user and the display, the environment needs to be designed to support this. In our case, both the subway entrance and the narrow sidewalk limited the possible size of the audience. In order to support more audience, displays should be visible from a wide angle, or considerable space should be available directly in front of the displays. This is also necessary as different groups start to interact behind each other. This interaction behind each other should also be supported, e.g., by increasing the maximum interaction distance beyond the distance from where single groups normally interact.

Dynamics Within Groups

We discovered that the vast majority of interactions were performed by people being in a group. The only cases of single people interacting we observed personally were children before or after school, men after waiting for a considerable amount of time near the subway entrance, a man in rags, and a man filming himself while playing. One man for example waited for many minutes directly in front of one screen, while incidentally interacting with it through his movements. After some time, he was approached by an apparent stranger, who showed him the display and the fact that he was interacting. The man seemed surprised, and continued to play a little bit with the display. While a considerable number of single people passes by the store, they usually walk faster and look more straight ahead and downwards. When we interviewed some of them, only very few had noticed the screens at all, and nobody had noticed that the screens were interactive.

Between 1 and 5 people interacted simultaneously ($\mu = 1.5$). Often the first person in a group noticed the display first, while this was not always the case.

We discovered that people strongly engaged with the game and apparently identified more with their representation on the screen than the possible influence of their movements on people around them (see section on Psychological Cues). This sometimes led to situations where people were not aware anymore of their neighbors (people belonging to one group usually line up next to each other), even though they were able to see their representation on the screen. This focus on the virtual space led in some situations to that people accidentally hit or bumped into each other. Another observation was that people usually started interaction with very subtle movements and continously increased the expressiveness of their movements. This process sometimes took just a few seconds and sometimes extended over many minutes. The subtle movements at the beginning were sometimes just slight movements of the head or the food. Later, people proceeded to extensive gesturing with both arms, jumping, and even acrobatic movements like high kicks with the legs.

Design Recommendations: The most important observation from this section is that very few persons who are alone interact. This observation is supported by the results of the prestudy. Therefore it is important to understand how groups notice interactivity, and public displays should always be designed to support groups. Even if just one person is interacting, the display must provide some value for the other group members. When users strongly engage with their representation on the screen, they may forget about their real surroundings. According to our observations, more slowly moving objects make users conduct also slower movements, which increases safety.

CONCLUSION

From this paper we learn that: (1) Using the mirror image of users such that passers by inadvertently interact with public displays is an effective way of communicating interactivity. Mirror images are more effective than silhouettes and avatars, and more effective than a traditional attract loop with a call-to-action. (2) Noticing interactivity needs some time, which leads to the *landing effect*. When passers-by decide to interact with public displays, they have often already passed them, so they have to walk back. This can be mediated e.g., by installing multiple displays in a row. (3) Users from a different group often start to interact *behind* the ones already interacting, forming multiple rows. Because also, the vast majority of interacting persons are in groups, public displays should support multiple users, in particular when interacting behind each other. We hope that mirror representations for inadvertent interaction will also be applied to other devices beyond public displays, e.g., tables or floors. Finally, we believe that public displays that effectively communicate their interactivity have the potential to make urban spaces all over the world more fun and engaging to be in.

ACKNOWLEDGEMENTS

We thank Albrecht Schmidt and Daniel Michelis for their valuable feedback. Furthermore, we thank the staff of the Telekom Shop *4010* in Berlin for their support during the study. This work was supported by the European Institute of Innovation and Technology, the Alexander von Humboldt Foundation and the European Union 7th framework programme under grant agreements no. 215893 and 244011.

REFERENCES

1. Brignull, H., and Rogers, Y. Enticing people to interact with large public displays in public spaces. In *Proc. of INTERACT '03* (2003), 17–24.
2. Cutting, J. E., and Kozlowski, L. T. Recognizing friends by their walk: Gait perception without familiarity cues. *Bulletin of the Psychonomic Society 9*, 5 (1977), 353–356.
3. Dix, A., Finlay, J. E., Abowd, G. D., and Beale, R. *Human-Computer Interaction (3rd Edition)*. Prentice-Hall, Inc., 2003.
4. Gallup JR, G. G. Chimpanzees: Self-recognition. *Science 167*, 3914 (1970), 86–87.
5. Heikenfeld, J., Drzaic, P., Yeo, J.-S., and Koch, T. A critical review of the present and future prospects for electronic paper. *Journal of the Society for Information Display 19*, 2 (2011), 129–156.
6. Hilliges, O., Izadi, S., Wilson, A. D., Hodges, S., Garcia-Mendoza, A., and Butz, A. Interactions in the air: adding further depth to interactive tabletops. In *Proc. of UIST '09*, A. D. Wilson and F. Guimbretière, Eds., ACM (2009), 139–148.
7. Hinrichs, U., and Carpendale, S. Gestures in the wild: studying multi-touch gesture sequences on interactive tabletop exhibits. In *Proc. of CHI '11*, ACM (New York, NY, USA, 2011), 3023–3032.
8. Huang, E., Koster, A., and Borchers, J. Overcoming assumptions and uncovering practices: When does the public really look at public displays? In *Proc. of Pervasive '08*. Springer, 2008, 228–243.
9. Jacucci, G., Morrison, A., Richard, G. T., Kleimola, J., Peltonen, P., Parisi, L., and Laitinen, T. Worlds of information: designing for engagement at a public multi-touch display. In *Proc. of CHI '10*, ACM (New York, NY, USA, 2010), 2267–2276.
10. Jeannerod, M. The mechanism of self-recognition in humans. *Behavioural Brain Research 142*, 1-2 (2003), 1–15.
11. Ju, W., and Sirkin, D. Animate objects: How physical motion encourages public interaction. In *PERSUASIVE'10* (2010), 40–51.
12. Kozlowski, L. T., and Cutting, J. E. Recognizing the sex of a walker from a dynamic point-light display. *Perception Psychophysics 21*, 6 (1977), 575–580.
13. Krueger, M. W. *Artificial reality II*. Addison-Wesley, 1991.
14. Kules, B., Kang, H., Plaisant, C., Rose, A., and Shneiderman, B. Immediate usability: a case study of public access design for a community photo library. *Interacting with Computers 16*, 6 (2004), 1171 – 1193.
15. Landis, J. R., and Koch, G. G. The measurement of observer agreement for categorical data. *Biometrics 33*, 1 (1977), 159–174.
16. Marshall, P., Morris, R., Rogers, Y., Kreitmayer, S., and Davies, M. Rethinking 'multi-user': an in-the-wild study of how groups approach a walk-up-and-use tabletop interface. In *Proc. of CHI '11* (2011), 3033–3042.
17. Michelis, D., and Mueller, J. The audience funnel. *International Journal of Human-Computer Interaction* (2010).
18. Mitchell, R. W. Mental models of mirror-self-recognition: Two theories. *New Ideas in Psychology 11*, 3 (1993), 295–325.
19. Müller, J., Alt, F., Michelis, D., and Schmidt, A. Requirements and design space for interactive public displays. In *Proc. of ACM Multimedia '10*, ACM (New York, NY, USA, 2010), 1285–1294.
20. Norman, D. A. Affordance, conventions, and design. *interactions 6* (May 1999), 38–43.
21. Norman, D. A. The way i see it: Signifiers, not affordances. *interactions 15* (November 2008), 18–19.
22. Peltonen, P., Kurvinen, E., Salovaara, A., Jacucci, G., Ilmonen, T., Evans, J., Oulasvirta, A., and Saarikko, P. It's mine, don't touch!: interactions at a large multi-touch display in a city centre. In *Proc. of CHI '08*, ACM (New York, NY, USA, 2008), 1285–1294.
23. Reeves, S., Benford, S., O'Malley, C., and Fraser, M. Designing the spectator experience. In *Proc. of CHI '05*, ACM (New York, NY, USA, 2005), 741–750.
24. Schmidt, A. Implicit human computer interaction through context. *Personal and Ubiquitous Computing 4*, 2/3 (2000), 191–199.
25. Scholl, B. J., and Tremoulet, P. D. Perceptual causality and animacy. *Trends in Cognitive Sciences 4*, 8 (2000), 299 – 309.
26. Shoemaker, G., Tang, A., and Booth, K. S. Shadow reaching: a new perspective on interaction for large displays. In *Proc. of UIST '07*, ACM (New York, NY, USA, 2007), 53–56.
27. Wilson, M. Perceiving imitatible stimuli: Consequences of isomorphism between input and output. *Psychological Bulletin 127*, 4 (2001), 543–553.

Urban HCI: Spatial Aspects in the Design of Shared Encounters for Media Façades

Patrick Tobias Fischer, Eva Hornecker
Department of CIS, University of Strathclyde, Glasgow G1 1XH, UK
Fischer@cis.strath.ac.uk, Eva.Hornecker@cis.strath.ac.uk

ABSTRACT

Designing interactive applications for Media Façades is a challenging task. Architectural sized large-scale screens can result in unbalanced installations, and meaningful interaction is easily overshadowed by the drastic size of the display. In this paper we reflect on urban technology interventions by analyzing their spatial configuration in relation to the structuring of interaction. We outline basic categories and offer a new terminology to describe these interactive situations designed for the built environment.

Author Keywords

Media Façade; Urban Screens; Media Intervention; Shared Encounter; Architecture; Social Technology; Urban HCI.

ACM Classification Keywords

H.5. Information Interfaces and Presentation

General Terms

Human Factors, Design

INTRODUCTION

In the book "Production of Space", Henri Lefebvre argues that urban space is a complex social product and that space is produced by spatial practices [21]. So how can novel technologies integrate gracefully into this context? We employ the term *Urban HCI* to emphasize the situation that is composed of the built environment, the interface and any associated computer system, and the social context. Urban HCI focuses on situations outside the lab and inside the city where context is activity and not just a location point. Even though its focus is not on screen-based interaction, a prominent medium has found increased use over the past few years. Media Façades and Urban Screens have become experimental platforms for artists and creative coders exploring new forms of communication and adding cultural value to architecture. Real-time systems transform these displays from a passive medium into an interactive visual medium. Nevertheless, most of these screens are installed solely for (passive) advertising purposes. While advertisers focus mainly on visibility and pedestrian flow to create as much exposure as possible, we focus on aspects beyond recall efficiency. We build on the concept of *Shared Encounters* which bridges existing research in architecture, urbanism, social sciences, anthropology and computer science. Adapted from Goffman's "Behaviour in Public Places" [14], a Shared Encounter is defined as "an ephemeral form of communication and interaction augmented by technology" [29] and "[...] the interaction between two people or within a group where a sense of performative co-presence is experienced by mutual recognition of spatial or social proximity" [39]. We consider them as short intermezzos in our habitually predetermined everyday urbane life, or as dérive creating works that are integrated in the built environment, without demands of permanence in time. They are a symbolic intervention, with the ambition to understand urban space, not as data source but as experience itself.

The emerging interest in Media Façades within HCI research can be recognized in a slowly increasing number of published case studies [2, 5, 36] and design processes [6, 13]. The slow pace of progress results from the difficulties of the medium itself that often demands compromises. Usually, various stakeholders are involved in the (production) process and only rarely is extended airtime (longer than 8 minutes, see e.g. [1]) provided for interactive pieces. This poses a problem for the development of appropriate evaluation methods. Moreover, there is the lack of language for describing spatial phenomena and relations. With this paper we want to further the discourse about the role of spatial aspects in Urban HCI and propose a terminology for spatial relations and phenomena in technological media interventions in urban space.

In the following, we first introduce the domain of Media Façades and briefly outline existing models from the HCI literature on public screen interaction, discussing to what degree these are applicable to Media Façades. We then describe two interventions we have created for this medium. By comparing the setup and interaction patterns at different exhibition venues, as well as those of other Media Façade installations at the same venue, we illustrate important aspects of spatial design. Our contribution in this paper is to demonstrate that Shared Encounters should focus on the interaction design *in front of the screen* and think about the overall space, rather than just the interaction *on* the screen. We propose a terminology for describing the structure of this space. We believe that this may inform the design process and the integration of installations into new locations by providing a better conceptual understanding of the interrelation of an installation with the space.

BACKGROUND

Harrison and Dourish [18], and others [16, 28, 33] have pointed out that locations are not just containers of geometric spaces (settings), but become a place when space becomes meaningful; place is created through cultural interactions and context. Media Façades allow content producers to change the meaning of a location for a short time, changing the situation, and ideally provide the public with the opportunity to engage creatively and communicatively with the urban environment.

Media Façades

The sorts of Media Façades we focus on are projections or LED-based displays of much larger scale than public displays [25] or urban screens. The façade sizes we have experience with range from $40m^2$ to $273m^2$ with a resolution of 0.34 – 3.63pixel per inch (ppi). This is at the lower end of the scale, since bigger façades may cover an entire building of up to $900m^2$ (e.g. Kunsthaus, Graz), with only 0.03ppi, where content mostly has aesthetic and ornamental function. At this upper end of the scale a Media Façade enters the domain of architectural sized elements, and adopts sculptural functionalities. It is obvious that the potential forms of interaction at this scale go beyond touch screens. This has the positive effect that potentially more people can engage with the installation simultaneously, creating social engagement and co-presence in front of the façade.

Making large displays interactive is a challenge, because people do not usually assume them to be interactive. Most host passive advertising or news channels; some are reactive, for example [4, 9], or visualize sensor data as ambient or generative information [8]. A few allow pedestrians to interact, enrich or participate (with the community) by adding content [26]. The latter is a concern for the façade owner. User-generated content needs monitoring for content considered inappropriate. But this prevents rich real-time interaction. However, with our own installations we observed that this is less of a problem if the spatial setup imposes social norms (e.g. if authorship is visible) and makes people refrain from posting inappropriate content. We therefore believe that the design of urban installations can exploit such effects to produce *social space*.

Models of Public Screen Interaction

The emergence of large screens and embedded UbiComp displays has turned 'space' into a relevant category for HCI. Various models for understanding public screen interaction have been proposed. [32, 35] describe the interaction process with public displays and present an onion-layer model of how people approach the display (from seeing a display from afar, observing it, to interacting peripherally and directly). But these models are often system-centric and primarily describe the information available to the system. Other models (e.g. [3, 12, 27, 31]) focus on performative interaction in public space, distinguishing different roles. They describe the relations between performers and spectators, and transitions between roles, distinguishing between active performers (Actors), participants who co-engage with the performer, passive observers and bystanders. Sheridan [31] and Reeves [27] in particular, provide useful terminology and basic interaction models for the design and evaluation process. However, large distances, architectural influences, and relations between displays of architectural scale and human scale are rarely discussed. Most models for interaction with public displays presume displays that rely on direct manipulation interaction (touch) or react to proximity. They describe the interaction with displays that are relatively small in comparison to the Media Façades we focus on. Issues of scale and spatial organisation, of context and environment are rarely considered in these frameworks.

So how can Urban HCI describe people's interaction with digital systems in relation to the structure of public space? The work of anthropologist Adam Kendon [20] offers a spatial analysis of human interaction which has been used successfully in HCI by Marshall et al [23]. Furthermore, the typology of Edward T. Hall, who coined the term proxemics [17], or urbanists' views on the city such as William H. Whyte [37] might help to understand urban space.

More quantitative approaches come from mobility research, particularly for estimating the value of advertising billboards. With parameters such as viewing angle, distance to street, competing nearby visual stimuli, numbers of passers-by, a so-called G-Value is calculated that estimates how many people per hour will remember an advertisement. While these parameters might be useful, the G-value does not tell us much about the actual experience or people's behaviour. Related to these parametric approaches that measure and describe the built environment, is Space Syntax [19]. Concepts such as integration / segregation, visual stability, mazelikeness, drift and isovists provide mathematical measures that can be used in scientific modelling and simulation. These approaches have already been used for the analysis of public interventions by Fatah gen. Schieck [30]. These research attempts also attract neuroscientists like Wiener who aim to correlate affective effects, experience and behaviour in the built environment using Space Syntax [38]. Even if we are not aiming for a parametric approach; the terminology of Space Syntax might be useful to describe advanced spatial concepts and properties.

OUR URBAN INTERVENTIONS

We now describe two successive versions of our installation, the Spread.gun and the SMSlingshot. Our analysis will focus largely on the SMSlingshot that we have exhibited in a variety of places, but we will also refer to the first instantiation Spread.gun. We prefer to call these exhibitions 'interventions' since they intervene in public spaces, changing their nature and use ephemerally. These are not permanent as the term installation might suggest.

Motivation and Design of Spread.gun and SMSlingshot

The Spread.gun was the result of a call for participation in the Media Façade Festival 2008. Our initial idea was to create an ancient Greek agora like situation, where the communication channel employed by advertisers is opened up

Figure 1. The Spread.gun setup and its process of spatial use

to the public, creating a digital speaker's corner. At that time we had no experience of what it means to design for Media Façades and experienced similar challenges as identified later by Daalsgard [5].

For example, our initial concept did not fit with the given physical properties of the Media Façade (Daalsgard's challenge No. 2: Integration into physical structures and surroundings). Furthermore, we were required to use digital street furniture owned by the sponsors (Daalsgard's challenge No. 5: Aligning stakeholders and balancing interests). Further challenges are described in [13]. However, our main vision survived. The Spread.gun resembled an ancient cannon that could be loaded with digital messages from a city terminal's touch screen (Figure 1). After the cannon was loaded, the message could be shot onto the façade using a pinball trigger. The intervention ran on 3 different day's during the festival. A limitation of the Spread.gun apart from lack of robustness (Daalsgard's challenge No. 3) and high system complexity was how it dealt with the social space in front of the interfaces. The emerging situation was rather similar to that at a supermarket or ATM. People lined up in front of the touch screen, with their back to other people's faces, and would then move on to the cannon. There was little discussion and sociality. Even though we recognized the problem, our spatial design thinking was not as elaborate as today. The main impetus that drove the design of the subsequent SMSlingshot was to enhance embodied interaction. An expressive gesture should clearly define the performer. Our design principle was to draw the action into the space in front of the screen. People should be able to pose and use the space like actors use a stage.

The interface itself has the shape of a wooden slingshot (see figure 2). It embeds a 2.1 inch display and 12 wooden keys arranged like a mobile phone keypad. A high frequency modem transmits typed text to the rendering PC when a message is 'shot'. A use sequence during an intervention is to hand the SMSlingshot to an observer, who then starts to key a statement into the device (thereby turning into a performer). The performer can then choose a colour

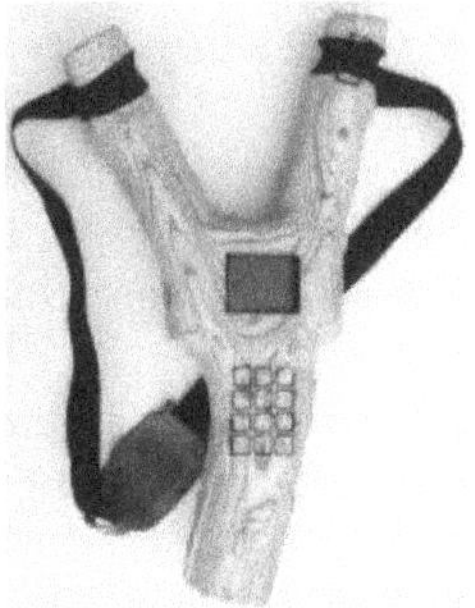

Figure 2. SMSlingshot

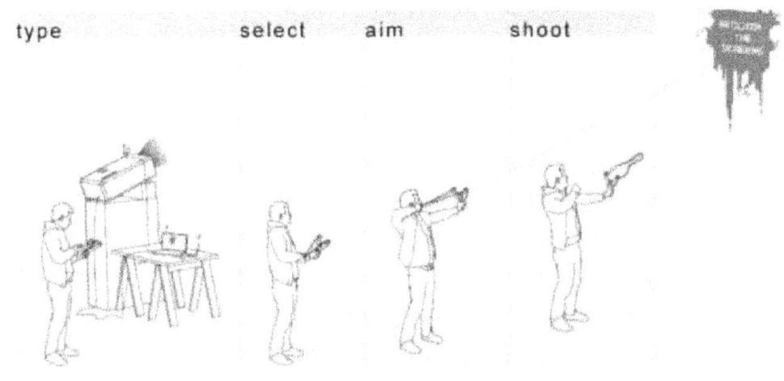

Figure 3. Interaction with the SMSlingshot

for the text background. Next, they aim at a spot on the Media Façade by holding up the device while pulling the rubber band. A laser beam lights up if the rubber band is pulled to show the aim. Once the band is let loose, the virtual message "is shot" on the façade, rendered as a coloured splat carrying the message. Then, the SMSlingshot is often handed to another person who wants to have a go.

In the course of our exhibitions it became apparent that SMSlingshot transports and creates many values (cf. values of third wave HCI [11]) we were not initially aware of. In particular, the ability to cover a very large potential interaction space in front of the Media Façade helped to not only generate interaction between user and system, but also to create a social interaction space.

ANALYSING SITUATIONS BY SPACE AND DISPLAY TYPES

Exhibiting in a variety of places helped us to realize the role of spatial setup and differences in scale, and their effects on the success of an intervention. Our systems have been exhibited at several venues over the past three years, each constituting a different architectural setting and context. The SMSlingshot was shown outdoors at an art festival (White Night, Riga 2009), in an indoor exhibition (Technical Museum, Berlin 2010), a conference and demo context (TEI, Boston 2010), Contemporary Museum of Art, Mallorca 2010), during a theatre award ceremony (São Paulo, FILE 2010), at a pedestrian walkway (São Paulo 2010, Eindhoven 2010), on a plaza (Media Façade Festival, Madrid, Liverpool and Berlin 2010), and within a branded space Museumsquartier Vienna 2010 for Amnesty International). Not only did the context of venues change, but the spatial setting was unique to each place, often requiring adaptation of the technical setup. All interventions began after dusk, as projections are not visible in daylight, with the positive side effect that passersby are not in a rush.

William H. Whyte [37] conducted pioneering field studies on informal, spontaneous interaction in the streets of Manhattan through observation of common spatial patterns; e.g. he found that street conversations occur typically on corners and in front of entrances and stairways. In a similar manner, we analyzed the use of our interventions with regard to performer, participant and observer roles. To investigate the role of spatial relation and interaction, we analyzed the various situations we exhibited in, distinguishing between

Figure 4. Top to bottom: Plaza, hybrid, walkway, and open plan setting

different types of spaces and displays. Most of our interventions were recorded to identify interaction patterns and spatial effects. Collected data includes photos and videos recorded 'on the ground', as well as maps, aerial photos and videos from an elevated position, as well as field notes and interviews with users. Analysis and comparison of this material informed the development of our model (Fig. 5). This was derived via a systematic iterative analysis of the data, focusing on the implications of spatial configurations, from which the categories in our model successively emerged.

In the following we characterise types of spaces and displays to describe the different venues and compare configurations of urban installations. Comparing these with other systems installed at the same location, we highlight core differences in configuration and propose a terminology that offers a framework for describing spatial setups for Shared Encounters.

Basic Categories

Our main distinction of situations in the built environment is between a plaza and walkway. Most of our outdoor settings can be categorized by one main type, even if some have a hybrid character. The hybrid feel becomes prevalent if streets rather than buildings border a plaza. The setting then becomes open plan instead of feeling intimate and enclosed. This also changes the ratio between **Display Space** and **Interaction Space,** which will be discussed later-on.

Another relevant distinction concerns the vertical position of the display, which is either on ground level or in an elevated position. While advertising tends to prefer elevated positions to maximize display space and visibility, ground level displays promote more interactivity, being in reach-of-grasp. For example, we observed people running towards ground level projections in order to 'perform' in collaboration with the primary performer holding the SMSlingshot. Their idea was to have their silhouette stencilled out on the wall by the coloured splash being shot. Other possible façade positions and orientations are explored by creative installations like Bus-Tops [7] or Canopy [34] which use displays in horizontal positions above ground and dramatically change the relation between pedestrian and display. The resulting display and interaction space for these setups is rather different to what we are examining here. Because of their orientation these displays probably defy the definition of a façade.

Figure 4 shows the spectrum from enclosed plaza to open plan situations, where streets cut through the setting and situation and environmental complexity increase. Streets usually reduce the interaction space**.** They often create an imbalance with the space from where the façade can be seen from (Display Space), making it difficult to understand the interaction unless explicit cues are given. For example, the graphics of the SMSlingshot application emulate the flight and squash of a paint bomb, illustrating that someone 'threw' a message from somewhere in front of the façade.

An Overview of Types of Spaces and Displays

Figure 5 summarizes and illustrates the different types of spaces we have identified, using a plaza situation as example. In the following, we present and discuss these and their interrelations. Depending on installation type, context, and environment, these spaces can differ in size and position. They can also change in size throughout the intervention time and often overlap (discussed under 'dynamics').

Figure 5. Types of spaces

Identified relevant spaces are:

- **Display Spaces** are the areas from which a display can be seen.
- **Interaction Space** is the space used to carry out a form of communication with the installation. It belongs to a single person, but can overlap with other person's interaction space.
- **Potential Interaction Spaces (PIS)** are spaces where the interaction between system and performer can potentially occur.
- **Gap Spaces** are spaces that create distance, either between human and system or among humans.

- **Social Interaction Spaces (SIS)** are those areas where people congregate, being attracted by the system, and have a Shared Encounter.
- **Comfort Spaces** provide a sense of physical and psychological ease. Protective features like walls, pillars, trees, etc. draw people subconsciously towards them.
- **Activation Spaces** are spaces where some displays can be seen from, often triggering curiosity, but interaction is not possible.

Display Space
Display Spaces are areas from which a display can be seen. This refers to the Media Façade, but also to other elements considered as 'displays' forming part of the installation. We will discuss this under 'people as displays'.

Interaction Space
The Potential Interaction Space (PIS) encompasses all areas where interaction could occur, whereas the (actual) Interaction Space is the space used at a specific moment in time. Several things can constrain this space. For example, a performer usually cannot stay long enough on a street to finish their action without risk to life. Of course this may cease to apply when there are few cars (e.g. at night) or the road is closed. Other restrictions might be an obstructed view of the façade, and any restrictions via system design. The PIS is an intermediate space that creates flexibility in the formation of observers, participants and performers. It allows diversity of action, and eases movement between the roles of observer, participant and performer. A setup such as that provided by the SMSlingshot does not convey that actions need to be carried out at a specific location - the PIS is theoretically everywhere.

Maximizing the Interaction Space
Urban interventions can create different sizes of Interaction Spaces. There is a continuum that the designer can choose the right degree from, even if it is hard to get it right. At this point we want to illustrate various sizes of Interaction Spaces by reviewing two more installations; Lummoblocks [15] and Rafael Lozano-Hemmers Body Movies [22].

Figure 6 shows an overlay of interaction spaces (green) on photos of the situations. For the Spread.gun (a) there were two rather small spaces for interacting with the Media Façade, one at the touch screen terminal, where people could type in messages and load the Spread.gun, and one behind the cannon to aim and shoot. This split of the interaction space meant that people often approached the cannon first, making it difficult for them to understand how the system works. Also, social interaction was minimal due to the small size of this space, and it was rarely occupied by multiple people (apart from parents with children). Even couples did not approach the interaction space together, but one would wait and observe instead of participating.

Lummoblocks (b) also has two Interaction Spaces, but of larger size. It was shown at the same venue as the SMSlingshot. The installation is a two player public game based on Tetris [15]. One player moves a falling block right and left, the other rotates it. Both players have an individual areal in which to move in order to move or rotate the block. Both see a birds-eye view of themselves on the screen, so they can determine where they are within the interactive space. The interaction space for each performer is approximately 6m wide. Observers usually position themselves behind this space and this configuration generates an arena situation. Observers quickly start to judge performer's competence to play and shout what to do.

Figure 6. Different sizes of Interaction Spaces. (figure 6.d from [22] licensed under Creative Commons)

The SMSlingshot (c) intervention enlarges the interaction space by creating *several* interaction spaces around the device. First, there is the keypad and the embedded LCD that allows asynchronous interaction from the façade. Since people in urban spaces often walk in groups of two or more, the interface is also seen by nearby people, who peek at the screen, interfere by pressing buttons or suggest messages. This creates a **Social Interaction Space** (Figure 6 c/B) around the device, where messages are reviewed or other topics around the intervention are discussed. This is related to the 'honeypot effect' described by Brignull [3] and to F-formations [20, 23], but we here distinguish between participants in the situation and pure observers. In addition, the Potential Interaction Space allows the performer to interact with other things while handling the slingshot. Adding more slingshots creates multiple Interaction Spaces, transforming the Potential Interaction Space (PIS, Figure 6 c/A) into actual Interaction Space. However, despite of the large size of the SMSlingshot's PIS nobody ever tested how far it extends.

The biggest installation in terms of the size of interaction space determined by system design we know to date is Rafael Lozano-Hemmers installation Body Movies (6d).

His installations explore relational architecture at the intersection between new technologies, public space and performance art. They comprise façades of $400m^2$ to $1800m^2$ and up to double this space in front of the façade. Lozano-Hemmer uses façades at ground level. This is crucial for this installation, creating a strong connection between façade and interaction space. Strong floodlights are positioned at the opposite side of the plaza directed towards the façade [23]. These allow people to cast shadows of 2 to 30 meters in size. On the same façade, multiple projectors display people in various positions that can be revealed and mimicked with one's shadow silhouette. If all positions have been mimicked the projection changes. This technique creates an interaction field where passers-by automatically become part of the installation as they enter the plaza, willing or not.

We have illustrated several techniques of urban interaction that create different sizes of interaction space and will now outline further spaces to think about in façade designs.

Gap Space

Gap spaces create distance to the system or between humans. They may have multiple causes, some induced by the built environment, from social or cultural conventions (cf.[17]) or by system design. Street entertainers are very aware of this and often arrange the audience in the beginning of their show, asking them to come closer, sit in the first row or to leave a gap to avoid congestion. Explicit arrangements are rarely the case in media installations since there is usually no facilitator. Gaps between people occur naturally and 'closing' them can be difficult. However, from studying interaction principles in plaza or walkway situations, we can estimate gap spaces for future designs. With Media Façades the most common Gap Space is generated through the screen position. With the Spread.gun, for example, interface affordances and associations affected spatial arrangements. Observers did not position themselves in front of the cannon. A triangular space between cannon and Media Façade remained empty and was occasionally perceived as 'dangerous'. It was interpreted as belonging to the interface, extending the Interaction Space of the person operating the cannon. People crossing it tended to apologize for doing so, just as people do when they cross into the line of view when people take photos. Here, the interface metaphor (ballistic device) generates an extended Interaction Space that can bridge Gap Spaces.

Figure 7. Gap Spaces

Figure 7 shows two different types of Gap Spaces. One is in front of the façade and the second between a Comfort Space and a Social Interaction Space. The gap in front of the façade is created through the elevation of the Media Façade. As stated earlier, interaction is more encouraged if a projection is at ground level as in the Body Movies installation. The second Gap Space is located between the spaces used by different roles. People in the Comfort Space position themselves as observers, away from participants and performers. This gap has been observed in a plaza situation. Performers and participants mix in a crowd, forming the Social Interaction Space. Observers keep apart from it via this gap, remaining at Hall's public distance [17].

For the Lummoblocks installation, three gap spaces were common: One is created (by system design) between the two players' Interaction Spaces. The second results from the elevated Media Façade. The third emerged between the players, and the observer and participant crowd. Like the space between street entertainers and their viewers, this gap emerges automatically but unlike an entertainer, a system cannot minimize the gap by asking viewers to come closer.

For Body Movies, gap spaces are evenly distributed between little groups of 2-3 people. The installation does not attempt to remove Gap Spaces in the physical world, but does so through the shadows cast in the 'virtual' world. Partial anonymisation closes a social gap on the screen. People can act in real-time on the façade, detached from their normal role in public space. They start to play with other people's shadows and do things they would not do in real life. Touching people's shadow without breaking personal space makes the piece so playful among unacquainted people.

'Detaching' performers from the physical world can bring them together in the 'virtual' world. In Lummoblocks the players are brought together in the virtual world, but at the same time a gap between the player and the audience is created. The players are positioned in front of the façade, and their visual field is completely occupied by it. Gap Spaces are harder to close the greater the space is. In plaza situations there are usually few, especially if the projection goes to the ground. In walkway situations the space is usually open plan and streets, signs, street furniture, trees, etc. create more and greater gaps.

Social Interaction Spaces

Social Interaction Spaces (SIS) are spaces that emerge as soon as more than two people come together and the chance of a social encounter is given. The Social Interaction Spaces we are especially interested in emerge through the situation that an interactive installation or intervention creates. For Shared Encounters it is essential to create SIS areas.

Spread.gun is a good example of how the setup of an installation can prevent a Social Interaction Space from emerging around the interface. The configuration of people is not social in any way. People face others' backs when waiting for their turn. This changed for the SMSlingshot intervention. People gathered around the interface, and easily started to talk or discuss e.g. the political implications of the work. Lozano-Hemmer's work establishes no Social Interaction Space on the plaza itself in front of the façade, but primarily creates a sense of co-awareness on the screen.

Social Interaction Spaces can also host different roles. Whereas with the SMSlingshot, the performer and participants could mingle, with Lummoblocks observers and participants mingled, while the performers were left outside of the SIS. Dynamic aspects can also contribute to the emergence of SIS. For example, the process of typing a message (this takes about 45-60 sec.) on the SMSlingshot creates an opportunity for social interaction within a group. This can result in longer interactions, because the message is discussed while typing or after passing the slingshot around. Often social activities integrate along the interaction with the slingshot. Observed activities range from suggesting new messages, reviewing messages, holding items initially carried by the performer so that s/he can use both hands to shoot, snatching the device from each other, and so on.

The most extreme reach of SIS was when people from nearby office buildings approached the artists/researchers. They had a deeper relationship with the space 'occupied' by the projection, and pointed out where they work, talked about their job, and were very interested in the project. Not only did they tend to stay very long, but they also pulled acquainted people into the place due to their presence. They proudly explained to them what was going on and explained the interaction. This shows a really extreme case of how an intervention becomes a Shared Encounter.

Comfort Spaces

Comfort spaces are spaces near architectural elements that provide physical or psychological comfort. They are created by the built environment. The setup of the Media Façade influences which comfort spaces are suitable for observing, providing line of sight and giving observers the feeling of being 'out of the way'. Protecting one's back is an instinctive behaviour. In the diagram (Figure 5) this is illustrated by a man leaning with his back to the wall. It also shows a comfort space at the edge of the plaza beneath a tree. Here, not only the tree provides protection, but also an extended view into the streets seems to please human needs and thus attract observers. These spaces are not always positive for a Shared Encounter and may interfere with designers' intentions of achieving a certain situation in a given setting.

Activation / Noise Space

Activation Spaces are regions near the fringe of the Display Space where ongoing interaction with a Media Façade is not necessarily seen from. Here, a full understanding of the situation cannot be established, unless the work is already known, and misunderstandings are likely. From an artist's perspective this could also be seen as space that does not pay tribute to the interactive artwork or even compromises its aesthetic expression. It is an area of heavy noise which is uncontrolled, especially when façades are elevated high above ground casting a large Display Space.

Again, if we look at the Body Movies installation we find that these difficult zones are handled quite well. The unity of the piece is not compromised by distance and is well bordered. People in the Activation Spaces can still understand the situation because the interaction technique of casting a shadow is well known. With SMSlingshot we had a different experience. Especially in open plan settings where scene complexity is high, people did not always understand that the projection is interactive. Some observers reported that they realized that the projections might be interactive because of the metaphor of throwing a colour bag on a façade. While this interaction technique is common in street art culture and natural for the urban environment, it is less well understood than the one in Body Movies and thus seems to perform less well within Activation Spaces.

EXAMPLE ANALYSIS

In this section we illustrate how spatial design thinking could have been useful for an intervention at the Museumsquartier in Vienna for Amnesty International if we had been aware of the described spaces at this point. Figure 8 (see also 4b) illustrates the hybrid plaza walkway situation and different spaces. The context provided restricted choice of which façade to project onto, and where to place temporary structures like a pavilion/tent, a podium, desk and the projector.

Figure 8. Space types in Vienna's Museumsquartier

The projection had to be elevated due to the façade geometry, and a natural gap space emerged. This was further intensified by an entrance for an underground parking space accessed from the main street. Options for softening this gap were limited. We covered the illumination of the parking driveway to reduce its visual salience, which interfered with the façade. Figure 8 also shows how the relation between display space and PIS changes in rather open plan scenarios. The display space is much bigger than the Potential Interaction Space (PIS). We eventually chose PIS 1, a rather obvious straightforward decision. But putting up temporary structures (tent, desk, etc), transformed PIS 1 from an open plan setting into a more central position. In retrospect this was a mistake. It would have been best to position the SMSlingshots in a pedestrian flow, where people walk nearby performers and participants, increasing the probability to engage with them. One of the main pedestrian ways went parallel to the building through the gap space under the projection, neither a good place for performers' action, nor convenient for reading the messages on the screen. But nevertheless a lot of passers-by stopped here and watched the performers from the front. It is unclear if it would have been better to block this gap space and force pedestrian flow through the PIS.

A lot of pedestrians also came from the park through the Activation Space, crossed the street over a zebra crossing and proceeded to walk to an entrance through PIS 2. Even though PIS 2 was a stopping point for observers, they rarely crossed the gap space to PIS 1, our actual interaction space. It remains an open question what would have happened if we had chosen PIS 2 or used a spot in the Activation Space.

PEOPLE AS DISPLAYS

So far, we have mainly discussed different types of spaces and less their visible components. Depending on the setting, a façade can create a display space that is multitudes bigger than the actual interaction space. Interactivity might then not be discovered by some people. However, urban space is inherently a social space we share with other people and their activities. People observe and react to other people's actions. Hence interaction spaces can be spotted by seeing other people watching people (cf. [3], [37]). Users' and observers' actions also effectively function 'as a display'. We now discuss how role-based activity can serve as display which is effectively part of the intervention.

Observer Display

People begin to act as an observer display when they glance repeatedly in a certain direction. This makes other people eventually do the same. We do not know how big the impact of an observer display is and from how far it can be seen. Some individuals observe the situation for a long time, some first check out the situation from different angles, and then position themselves in a Comfort Space and don't move anymore for a long time.

The Participants' Display

Participants' displays are of a more active nature. During the SMSlingshot interventions we saw participants helping the performer (Social Space) by taking stuff off their hands so they could type and shoot, suggesting messages, showing where the delete or colour button is, teaching others how to pull the rubber band, etc. Other forms of display generated consisted of photographing the performer, photographing the shot message and distributing the slingshot to various groups.

The participant's activity of helping is a friendly, social display that is beneficial for the intervention. However, in some cases we observed a negative display, which kept other interested people outside (like a wall), blocking attempts to engage. During an intervention in Liverpool a fairly large crowd formed a single Social Interaction Space around the performer, rendering most of his action and hence display of action invisible for observers. Furthermore, people crossing the plaza mainly saw the backs of people with little space between them and thus did not feel invited in (cf. [20]). When approaching the crowd from the front, one could see the performer, but doing this would be unusual without an invitation. This might also explain why things work better on the street, where participants usually do not form such a strong 'shield'. On the street, people are more loosely organized, making it easier for others to join.

The Performer Display

When we consider people's activity as a display, the performers' interaction with a system is the most direct form of display. This requires a revealed or amplified interaction (as defined by Reeves [27]), since with hidden manipulation (e.g. tapping on a mobile phone) there is no visible performer display. We can not only define roles through the interaction design, but also estimate the size of the performer display. Figure 9 shows different actions and their resulting display size.

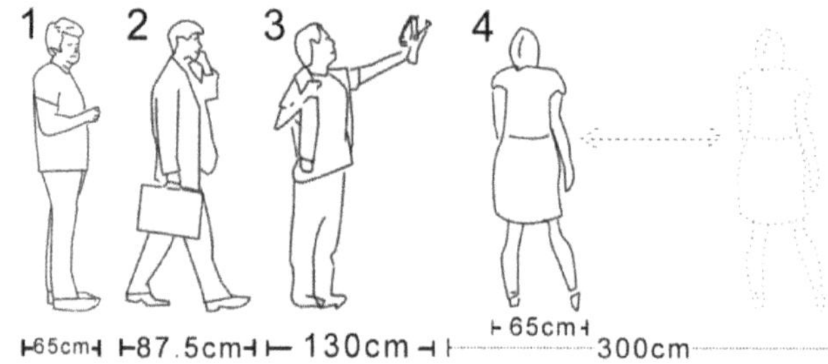

Figure 9. Different sized performer displays

One of the design intentions with SMSlingshot was to draw the interaction from the façade into the space in front of it. The idea was to provide opportunity to pose with large gestures and position oneself in space after typing the message and aiming. However, it turned out that performers do not roam around much, possibly because they are 'glued' to their group, which they don't want to leave or do not want to appear as if they might 'steal' the device.

Over time, we increased the performer display by offering multiple slingshots. While this does not change the size much, we observed an action that might do so. At an intervention in Vienna where three SMSlingshots were operating at a point, people decided to shoot simultaneously. This created a much bigger attention effect for observers. The synchronisation of performer displays (a common flash mob tactic) seems to be somehow conspicuous for viewers; indicating an increase of size of this type of display.

DYNAMICS OF SITUATIONS

The arrangement of situations becomes more complicated to design for if we switch from a static to a dynamic view of a situation, as people change their roles over the course of an intervention. Spaces are created when people walk up, they grow when the pedestrian flow brings new people in, and they shrink or vanish if people leave. Reviewing the dynamic aspects of Shared Encounters is beyond the scope of this paper, but two short observations are noted here.

In Liverpool a spatial practice emerged that defined a new role within the intervention. Some people began to distribute the slingshot to different groups within the crowd without being explicitly asked to do so. The slingshot interface was thus able to 'invade' a group. This was different from 'passing the torch', as is usually done by handing the device over to another person after using it. This decreased effort, since groups did not have to decide to go towards the interface; the interface itself joins and leaves. However, most dynamics are difficult to handle, especially large ones. At some sites, situations ranged from emptiness to overcrowding. For the Spread.gun this was a problem, since only one person could be active. The design of SMSlingshot opened up participation to several people at once.

DISCUSSION

Our analysis of the different settings for urban interventions has enabled us to develop a terminology and conceptual framework, which takes account of aspects not considered so far in the literature, in particular the relation of situated digital interfaces to the built environment. Our approach of Urban HCI takes a different view (compared to Ubiquitous Computing) by taking situated architectural effects (instead of the anytime, anywhere paradigm) into account (cf. [10, 24]) and focuses on how to integrate technology into urban everyday life and architectural space. The examples we have given here demonstrate that a digital system is not simply set in a given setting, but a situation is created. This situation comprises the intervention itself, its spatial setup, the given architectural and urban design structures or layouts (which influence pedestrians action), all of which interplay in how the installation will be used. We hope to contribute to a better understanding of spatial setup factors that influence the success of such an installation, and to provide a model that helps to conceptualize relevant spatial relations. We adopt a role-based view similar to Sheridan, Reeves, and Finke [3, 12, 27, 31] and extend it by describing the spaces used by performers, participants and observers. This contributes to Dalsgaard's [5] second and sixth challenge, the integration of new installations into existing physical environments, and the diversity of situations. We propose a terminology that enables us to describe and compare Shared Encounters at Media Façades.

We believe that our model and terminology are not only useful for describing existing situations, but may also be used productively when planning 'new situations'. On a pragmatic level, the terminology proposed here might also be helpful when explaining to stakeholders and sponsors why a certain setup is important (e.g. having to move a fixture to make space for a social congregation space). Disciplined thinking about the different spaces and display types can inform the design strategy for the creation of new installations and may provide guidance when installing an existing installation at a new location.

For example, if gap spaces are needed to provide a passageway (preventing congestion), then an elevated display might be a better choice than one at ground level. Vice-versa, if the installation is to attract people towards the façade and a sense of spatial continuity is to be created, then a ground level display is preferable. Virtual, social, role-based or physical blocks and barriers between the different spaces should be avoided, so that the Interaction Space can attract social interaction around it. If gaps are purposely created, the designer needs to employ interface metaphors that bridge across Gap Spaces (we have found that 'shooting' works well) or to create a clear, visual connection.

Furthermore, it is advisable to maximize the Potential Interaction Space, increasing the potential for social interaction (observers and participants kept away from performers at Lummoblocks, and Spread.gun barely generated any social interaction). Multiple instances of a (mobile) interface can increase the PIS and may foster co-awareness between performers. We have found split-up interaction spaces to be problematic - at the Spread.gun this resulted in confusion. Factors such as good visibility of the interaction, flexibility in how and where the interface is used, and being able to hand over the device allow for the interaction spaces to move around quickly, turning participants into performers. Our observations furthermore highlighted the role of comfort zones, which allow people to observe while feeling at ease. Whenever we set up a table or projector tripod, even a ladder, people tended to gravitate towards these. Conscious use of existing comfort spaces or the creation of temporary ones can thus support an installation.

We have discussed how the form and size of interfaces along with performer, participant, and observer displays increase and extend the façade's Display Space. However, imbalanced or oversized Display Spaces can dominate a situation. Thus, the ratio between Display and Interaction Spaces should be carefully considered. We chose the term display, because it can be applied to objects as well as subjects. This abstraction enables the designer to think about what effect to achieve, while leaving it open what kind of display to employ (human, architectural or system-generated).

We do not attempt to provide a comprehensive framework, as there may be further kinds of spaces. In further research we will continue to apply our model to different situations and to extend it, focusing on user experience issues – i.e. we have made the informal observation that shooting over a larger distance to the façade makes for a stronger user experience, being more fun and potentially creating a feeling of 'empowerment'. We also found that the SMSlingshot had less affective impact when used indoors (with a relatively small screen) then at large outdoors façades.

CONCLUSION

As we approach third wave HCI [11], concepts like Shared Encounters have obvious problems in how to measure success. We cannot answer the question of why one encounter is better than another, but we have proposed a terminology for describing and analysing the spatial setup of interactive Media Façade interventions, which takes account of the social use of space and of the existing structure of the built environment. This terminology highlights the interrelation of an installation with the surrounding space as well as core aspects that can inform the design process and help designers to more explicitly reason about how to install and structure an installation within a new location. This can support intentional temporary place/making, helping the designer anticipate how the system will be used. In short, before we can properly design Shared Encounters that use digital interfaces as a link between urban environments and humans, we must first learn how to accurately describe - a future aim of Urban HCI research.

ACKNOWLEDGMENTS. We thank Susa Pop and Miriam Struppek as representatives for all the fantastic curators that supported us, SICSA for PhD funding, Paul Marshall and Kenton O'Hara for useful feedback and of course the incredible VR/Urban collective that makes this research happen.

REFERENCES

1. BBC. *Bigscreen Content Guidelines. http://www.bbc.co.uk/bigscreens/media/130111_contentguidelines.pdf. 02.08.2011.*
2. Boring, S., et al. Multi-user interaction on media facades through live video on mobile devices. *Proc. of CHI*, ACM, (2011), 2712 - 2724.
3. Brignull, H., Rogers, Y. Enticing people to interact with large public displays in public spaces. *Proc. of INTERACT, IOS Press,* (2003), 17 - 24.
4. Bruges, J. *Platform 5. http://www.jasonbruges.com /projects/uk-projects/platform-5. 02.08.2011.*
5. Dalsgaard, P.,Halskov, K. Designing urban media facades: cases and challenges. *Proc. of CHI*, ACM, (2010), 2277 - 2286.
6. Dalsgaard, P., et al. Towards a Design Space Explorer for Media Facades. *Proc. of OzCHI*, ACM, (2008).
7. Dieu, P. L., Dennen, A. *Bus-Tops. http://bus-Tops.com. 21.07.2011.*
8. doubleNegatives. *Corpora. http://doublenegatives.jp /installations/Corpora/index.htm. 02.08.2011.*
9. Eyl, F. *Aperture. http://www.fredericeyl.de/aperture/. 02.08.2011.*
10. Fallman, D. Mobility as involvement: on the role of involvement in the design of mobile support systems for industrial applications. *AI & Soc.*, 25, 1, (2010), 43-52.
11. Fallman, D. The New Good: Exploring the Potential of Philosophy of Technology to Contribute to Human-Computer Interaction. *Proc. of CHI*, ACM, (2011), 1051 - 1069.
12. Finke, M., et al. Lessons learned: game design for large public displays. *Proc. of DIMEA 2008*, ACM, (2008).
13. Fischer, P. T., et al. VR/Urban: Spread.gun - Design Process and Challenges in Developing a Shared Encounter for Media Façades. *Proc. of British HCI*, (2010).
14. Goffman, E. *Behaviour in Public Places.* The Free Press, New York, 1966.
15. Guitiérrez, C., et al. *Lummoblocks. http://www.lummo.eu/lummotetris.html. 21.07.2011.*
16. Gustafson, P. Meanings of Place: Everyday Experience and Theoretical Conceptualizations. *Journal of Environmental Psychology*, 21, 1, (2002), 5 - 16.
17. Hall, E. T. *The Hidden Dimension.* Anchor, 1966.
18. Harrison, S., Dourish, P. Re-Place-ing Space: The Roles of Place and Space in Collaborative Systems. *Proc. of CSCW*, ACM, (1996).
19. Hillier, B. *Space is the Machine: A Configurational Theory of Architecture.* Cambridge Univ. Press, 1998.
20. Kendon, A. Spacing and Orientation in Co-present Interaction. *Proc. of COST 2102 Training School*, Springer Heidelberg, (2009), 1 - 15.
21. Lefebvre, H. *The production of space.* Blackwell Publishing Ltd., 1991.
22. Lozano-Hemmer, R. *Body Movies. Relational Architecture 6. http://www.lozano-hemmer.com/body_movies.php. (seen 21.07.2011).*
23. Marshall, P., et al. Using F-formations to Analyse Spatial Patterns of Interaction in Physical Environments. *Proc. of CSCW*, ACM, (2011), 445 - 454.
24. McCullough, M. *Digital Ground.* MIT Press, 2005.
25. Peltonen, P., et al. "It's Mine, Don't Touch!": Interactions at a Large Multi-Touch Display in a City Centre. *Proc. of CHI*, ACM, (2008), 1285 - 1294.
26. Peltonen, P., et al. Extending Large-Scale Event Participation with User-Created Mobile Media on a Public Display. *Proc. of MUM*, ACM, (2007), 131 - 138.
27. Reeves, S., et al. Designing the spectator experience. *Proc. of CHI*, ACM, (2005), 741 - 750.
28. Relph, E. C. *Place and Placelessness.* Pion, 1984.
29. Schieck, A. F. g., et al. Exploring Digital Encounters in the Public Arena. In K. S. Willis, et al. (eds). *Shared Encounters,* Springer, London, 2010, 179-195.
30. Schieck, A. F. g., O'Neill, E. The Urban Screen as a platform for communication. *Proc. of CHI*, ACM, (2009)
31. Sheridan, J. G., et al. Understanding Interaction in Ubiquitous Guerilla Performances in Playful Arenas. *Proc. of HCI,* Springer, (2004), 3-18.
32. Streitz, N., et al. Ambient Displays and Mobile Devices for the Creation of Social Architectural Spaces. In K. O'Hara (eds). *Public and Situated Displays,* Kluwer Academic Publisher, 2003.
33. Tuan, Y.-F. *Space and Place.* University of Minnesota Press, Minneapolis, 1977.
34. UnitedVisualArtists. *Canopy. http://www.uva.co.uk/work/canopy.*
35. Vogel, D., Balakrishnan, R. Interactive Public Ambient Displays: Transitioning from Implicit to Explicit, Public to Personal, Interaction with Multiple Users. *Proc. of UIST*, ACM, (2004), 137 - 146.
36. Wally, B., Ferscha, A. Ambient Façades. *Proc. of UbiComp*, ACM, (2008).
37. Whyte, W. H. *City: Rediscovering the Center.* Anchor, 1990.
38. Wiener, J. M., Franz, G. Isovists as a means to predict spatial experiences and behaviour. *Proc. of Spatial Cognition IV*, Springer, (2004), 42 - 57.
39. Willis, K. S., et al. Shared Encounters. In K. S. Willis, et al. (eds). *Shared Encounters,* Springer, 2010, 1-15.

Chained Displays: Configurations of Public Displays Can Be Used to Influence Actor-, Audience-, and Passer-By Behavior

Maurice ten Koppel **Gilles Bailly** **Jörg Müller** **Robert Walter**

Quality and Usability Lab, Telekom Innovation Laboratories, TU Berlin, Germany
Firstname.Lastname@tu-berlin.de

ABSTRACT
Most interactive public displays currently rely on flat screens. This form factor impacts how users (1) notice the public display (2) develop motivation and (3) (socially) interact with the public display. In this paper, we present *Chained Displays*, a combination of several screens to create different form factors for interactive public displays. We also present a design space based on two complementary concepts, *Focus* and *Nimbus*, to describe and compare chained display configurations. Finally, we performed a field study comparing three chained displays: *Flat*, *Concave,* and *Hexagonal*. Results show that *Flat* triggers the strongest honeypot effect, *Hexagonal* causes low social learning, and *Concave* triggers the smallest amount of simultaneously interacting users among other findings.

Author Keywords
Public displays; Form factor; Chained displays; Field study.

ACM Classification Keywords
H.5.m [Information Interfaces And Presentation]: Miscellaneous.

INTRODUCTION
Interactive public displays are increasingly becoming prevalent within public spaces such as airports, fares, public transit stations, and shopping areas. For instance, users can use them to get information, watch multimedia content, or to play games. However, several studies reported three widespread problems: (1) noticing the public displays, (2) developing motivation to interact and (3) designing for parallel or collaborative interaction. While most public displays rely on one single *flat* screen, we argue that different form factors impact user behavior and can alleviate the previous limitations.

We propose *Chained Displays* (Figure 1) as alternative to the widespread flat public displays. Chained displays consist of a combination of several screens to create a large non-flat continuous display surface. Thereby they provide designers the opportunity to create novel display configurations by changing the quantity of and the angularity between the displays.

In order to analyze the large variety of chained displays configurations, we propose a design space based on two complementary concepts: *Nimbus and Focus* [2]. *Nimbus* refers to a sub-space within which a person projects their presence. *Focus* is its counterpart and represents a sub-space within which a person focuses their attention. We use these two concepts to describe and compare two promising chained displays configurations: *Concave* and *Hexagonal.* We also compare them to the traditional *Flat* configuration (see Figure 1). We discuss these different configurations in regard to actor- (people interacting with the displays), audience- (by-standers observing actors), and passer-by (people passing by the installation) behavior as well as five commonly observed effects on public displays.

We conducted a field study to compare the three chained display configurations within the entrance hall of a university canteen. In particular, we examined how the angularity between the displays impacted actor-, audience- and passer-by behavior. As motivation for people to interact with the chained displays, we designed an engaging but simple gestural version of the classical *space invaders* game. Our findings, based on observation, questionnaires and interviews, reveal how the three chained displays were unique in terms of social learning, group approach, the strength of the honeypot effect, the amount of simultaneous interaction, and where individuals position themselves in front of the displays.

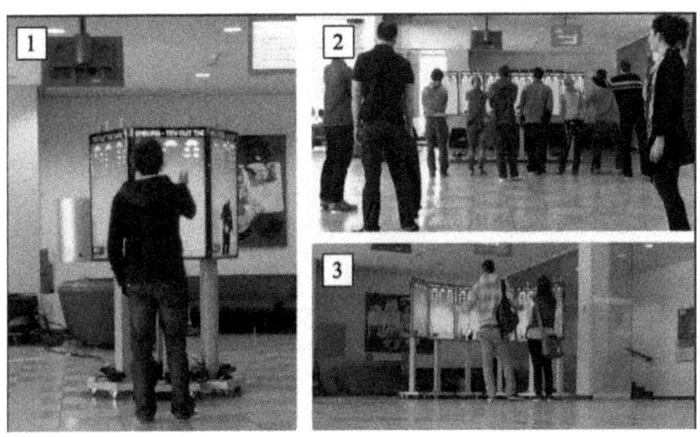

Figure 1: *Chained Displays*: (1)*Hexagonal*: actors can limitedly see other screens resulting in low social learning (2) *Flat* attracts more people (Honeypot) because actions and their effects can be observed (3) *Concave*: actors have a limited interaction space resulting in few simultaneously interacting users.

The primary contributions of the paper are:

- A novel class of generic non-flat public displays.
- A design space based on two complementary concepts: Nimbus and Focus.
- A field study comparing 3 public display configurations.

RELATED WORK

Non-flat public displays

Non-flat displays have been proposed within the context of augmented reality [17], immersive environments [12] and handheld devices [32]. In the context of public displays, most displays are based on horizontal [21] or vertical [18] *flat* screens. The orientation of public displays can impact users' behavior [31]: Rogers et al. showed that people collaborate more effectively when situated around the tabletop than in front of a wall display [31]. We argue that non-flat displays can also impact the behavior of users.

Few spherical displays have been proposed [3, 8, 20], but their medium size (16"-24") limits their practical application for public displays. Beyer et al. investigated cylindrical displays in [4]. A lab study involving single users indicated that the cylindrical shaped displays invited users to actively move around the display. This study demonstrates that non-flat public displays can impact the behavior of users, however fails to capture the social complexities that are inherent to public spaces such as performative interaction [10]. For this reason, we conducted a field study comparing three display configurations.

Field studies on public displays

Several field studies [6,7,9,21,25,26] have been conducted to capture "natural" user practices with public displays. For instance, Peltonen *et al.* installed a wide multi-touch display in Helsinki [26]. They observed and highlighted several social effects such as social learning, performative interaction and issues related to the intrusion of virtual spaces. Cao *et al.* [7] deployed a collaborative multiplayer game and reported on the playing, spectating and social experience of the game. These studies shed light on social phenomena emerging around public displays. What remains unknown is how the form factor of the public display contributed to the observed effects.

We now review five main effects related to public displays that are used to guide our analysis on the impact of the form factors on user behavior. Moreover, we will explicitly report on these effects based on our own observations during the field study.

Stages of interaction

Several models have been proposed to describe the different stages of interacting with a public display [13, 24, 33, 36]. For instance, the *audience funnel* [24] describes 6 stages of interaction. First, people are unaware of the public display (*passing-by*). Then, after *viewing and reacting* to the public display, users test the interactivity of the screen with *subtle interaction* (e.g. they might wave their hand). They come closer to the screen to perform *direct interaction* with the device. In the context of multiple displays, users might start interacting with other screens (*multiple interaction*). Finally, they can perform *follow-up actions* such as taking a photo of the device. This model is especially relevant for our setup as it focuses on both multiple displays and gestural interaction.

Performative interaction

Users of public displays are simultaneously in three different relationships [29]: (1) the interaction with the public display; (2) the perception of oneself within the situation and (3) acting out a role for others to observe [10]. The experience people have with public displays is determined by the interaction between these roles. This can for instance result in social embarrassment [27], but it can also lead to users showing off [29].

Reeves *et al.* differentiated two ways in which users can be observed [29]: *manipulations* and *effects*. *Manipulations* refer to the performer's gestures while *effects* refer to the visible result of the interaction on the display. Installations making manipulations highly visible might trigger hesitance to interact but can favor social learning and foster the social experience around the display [27]. We argue that the form factor of public displays contributes strongly to the visibility of manipulations and effects, yet its impact is poorly understood.

Personal space

Personal space is the "invisible bubble" around the self used as mechanism to control the desired state of privacy [1]. The proxemics between people depends on many factors such as the social relationship [1]. In the context of public displays, we differentiate between the intrusion of *personal* and *virtual* space. Both intrusions lead to social discomfort and could result in people leaving the display [21,26]. Modifying the form factor of a public display changes the size of the interaction space. This can impact the number of simultaneous users or the level of social comfort.

F-Formations

F-formations is a tool to analyze how the organization of space supports or blocks social interactions [22]. It refers to the specific spatial arrangement people persist during social interaction in which people maintain a shared attention area referred to as the *shared transactional segment* [19]. While social interaction typically structures these spatial arrangements, spatial structures can in return also influence the f-formation and thereby the resulting social interaction [19]. The form factor of a public display is an example of such a spatial structure and thus plays a crucial role in influencing the user experience. However, this effect has only been investigated within lab studies (e.g. [31, 34]).

Honeypot effect

The *honeypot effect* [6] is the social effect of people being attracted to the public display by other people standing in close vicinity to it. It creates a social atmosphere around the public display in which people do not only signal their interest towards the display but also express that they are open for social interaction. Several field studies on public displays [24, 26] reveal that the honeypot effect is powerful in attracting users: once there is an initial crowd, people will be attracted by it and thereby again attract others [16]. Except for the location of the public display [6], it is not clear how this effect can be catered for and whether the form factor of the public display can influence this effect.

In summary, only few studies proposed different form factors for public displays and never compared them in a field study. While several effects have been observed during field studies, it is unsure how the form factor contributed. For these reasons, we conducted a field study contrasting form factors and report on the five described effects (*stages of interaction*, *performative interaction*, *personal space*, *f-formations* and *honeypot effect*).

CHAINED DISPLAYS

Chained displays consist of a combination of several screens to create large non-flat display surfaces (Figure 2). Each screen is linked to its neighbor screens in order to maintain a "global continuity". By changing the angularity between displays, we can easily modify the form factor of the display surface. Our chained displays also include a depth sensor (e.g. Microsoft Kinect) to allow users to perform mid-air gestures in front of the displays.

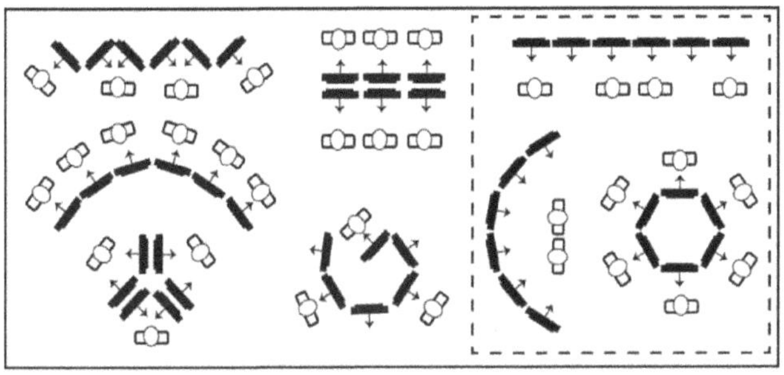

Figure 2: An overview of possible 6-chained display configurations. In dashed lines: the chained displays we tested

We used 40" LCD displays to build our chained displays. They were chosen for their wide viewing angles and thin bezel. We also built specific stands designed for this setup in order to (1) guarantee a high level of stability, (2) easily transport the displays and (3) have the screens close to each other whatever the angularity. While the minimal chained display configuration relies on 2 screens, our setup is based on 6 screens. This is a good compromise between (1) the number of users it can support (2) the number of possible configurations and (3) practicalities to run the experiment.

DESIGN SPACE

We propose a design space to describe and compare chained display configurations. This is followed by an analysis of the three tested chained displays according to our design space. Finally, we discuss how the design space helps in understanding how the configurations impact the five aforementioned effects.

Scope and Definition

To precisely understand the interaction between users and the system as well as interaction between users many factors need to be considered such as location of the display, the architecture of the hall/room, the flow of people, the type of population around, the form factor of the displays, etc. Some tools such as proxemic interactions [15] can help to reason about social interaction around public displays. In this article, we use the concepts of *Nimbus* and *Focus* [2, 30] to analyze how chained displays configurations influence *actors*, *audience* and *passers-by*.

The *Nimbus and Focus* concepts [2] have been applied in other contexts such as virtual reality [2], privacy [5, 23] or multimedia streams [14]. *Nimbus* is defined as a sub-space within which a person projects their presence. *Focus* is its counterpart and represents a sub-space within which a person focuses their attention. While Nimbus is related to the question "*Where can I be perceived?*". Focus is more related to the question "*What can I observe?*", We argue that these two concepts can help to reason about the behavior of individuals around public displays. Although they are insufficient to precisely describe the complex environment of public displays, they form a basis on which more complex concepts can be described.

Due to the huge size of possible chained displays configurations, we decided to mainly focus on "curved" configurations: configurations where the angularity between each pair of screens is similar. In particular, we distinguish *Concave* and *Hexagonal* (the latter as an example of a Convex configuration) as well as *Flat* (as baseline) to systematically illustrate our analysis. These three configurations (Figure 2) are both simple and sufficiently different to highlight the differences between chained display configurations in regard to our two concepts.

To understand the experience people will have with chained displays, we apply the Nimbus and Focus concepts to the four main components of the public display: The *public display* itself, its *actors*, its *audience* and its *passers-by*.

Public display

The concepts of Nimbus and Focus are originally defined for persons. We argue that the same terms can be used to describe from where a display can be perceived and what it can 'perceive', i.e. what its interaction area is.

Nimbus: Inspired by the concept of Isovist [11, 35], the nimbus of a public display refers to a sub-space from which the content of the system's displays can be perceived. Figure 3 illustrates strong differences in terms of Nimbus of the system. Whereas the content presented on *Flat* can only be perceived from one side, *Hexagonal* can be perceived from all around it. Finally, *Concave* has the lowest nimbus.

Focus: Inspired by the concept of aura [2], the Focus of a public displays includes the sub-part within space for which the interaction is enabled. Figure 4 shows that the interaction space decreases when the curvature increases.

Actors

Nimbus: The nimbus of actors can be described in relation to their physical body (manipulations) or their representation on the screen (effects). Because the public display itself blocks visibility, increasing the curvature increases the physical nimbus of the actor (Figure 5). In addition, *Hexagonal* favors the nimbus of manipulations rather than effects. Indeed, certain audience members (D2) and actors (A2) can see the face of actors (dotted line) and the subtle interaction performed in front of them but cannot see their screens (*effects*). Notice that the distance of the actor from the screen in *Hexagonal* (to a lesser extent in *Concave*) impacts the nimbus area of the actor. For instance, direct touch interaction reduces the nimbus of the actor.

Focus: Only *Hexagonal* limits the number of screens (1-3) that actors can see simultaneously. However, it offers the opportunity for actors to see other actors (A2) and audience members (D2) in their peripheral vision during interaction (Figure 6). Once again, the distance of the actor from the screen modifies the observable area.

Audience members and passers-by

As passers-by and audience members share a lot of similarities in regard to their nimbus and focus, they are discussed together.

Nimbus: Whatever the configuration (Figure 7), an audience member can be seen by other audience members (or passers-by) from the back (D4) or the side (D2). Moreover, in *Hexagonal*, an audience member can be perceived from the front (D2) but only by some actors (A2).

Focus: In *Flat* and *Concave*, audience members can simultaneously see *manipulations* and *effects* performed by all actors. This in contrast to *Hexagonal*, where only the *manipulations* of up to 4 actors and the *effects* of up to 2 actors can be observed. They can in return see other audience members from the front (D1).

Discussion

The concepts of Nimbus and Focus provide a tool to analyze the differences between chained displays in a systematic way. We also derived five main effects of public displays from literature: *Stages of interaction*, *Performative interaction*, *Personal space*, *f-formations* and *Honeypot effect*. Equipped with these concepts, we can now revise our original research question: How does the shape of chained displays influence actor, bystander and passer-by behavior? A more specific version would be: How do different focus and nimbus of chained displays influence stages of interaction, performative interaction, personal space, f-formation and the honeypot effect? In order to address this research question we conducted a field study.

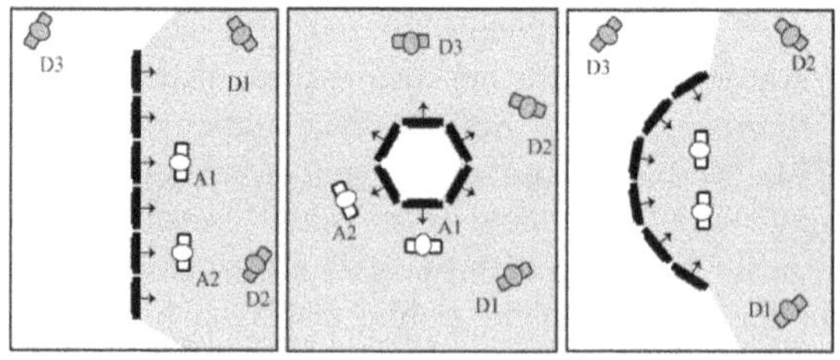

Figure 3: Public display Nimbus for each configuration: Flat, Hexagonal and Concave (in white actor, in gray audience member).

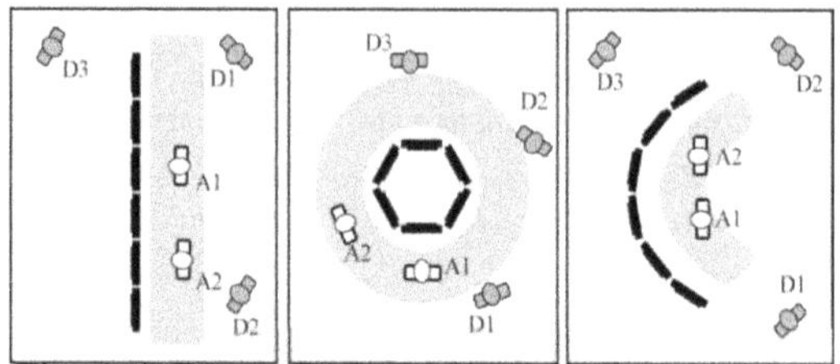

Figure 4: Focus of three chained displays configurations: Flat, Hexagonal, Concave.

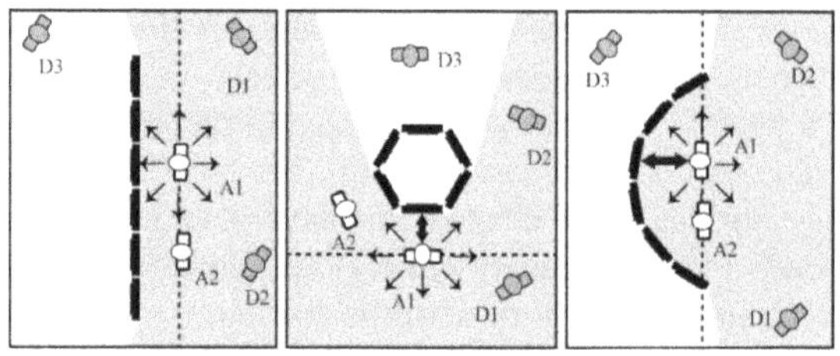

Figure 5: Actor nimbus depending on the configuration.

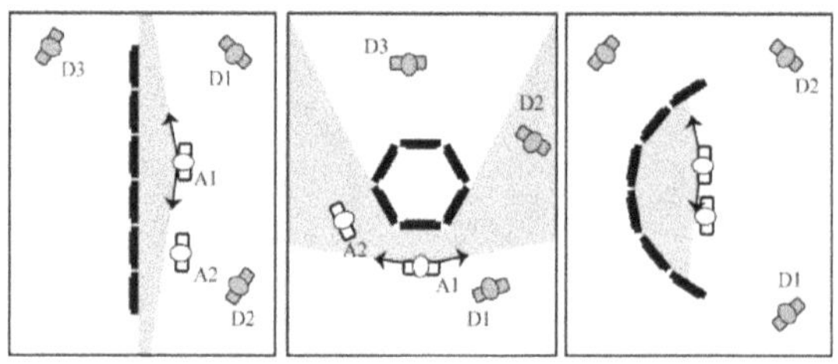

Figure 6: Actor focus for each configuration.

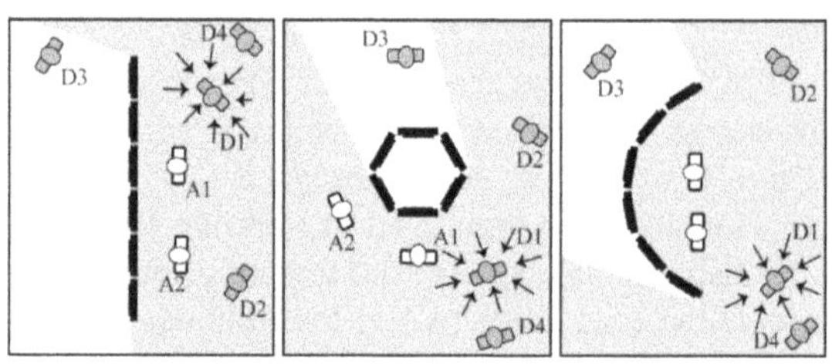

Figure 7: Audience nimbus for each configuration.

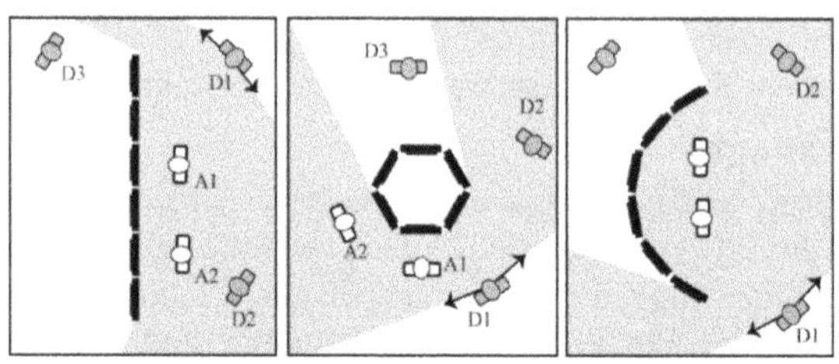

Figure 8: Audience focus for each configuration.

FIELD STUDY: COMPARING CHAINED DISPLAYS

The goal of the field study was 1) to qualitatively compare three chained displays configurations (*Flat*, *Hexagonal* and *Concave)*, 2) to investigate the impact of form factor on actor-, audience- and passer-by behavior 3) to understand the influence of Nimbus and Focus on stages of interaction, performative interaction, personal space, f-formations and the Honeypot effect.

Game content as motivation

To motivate people to interact with the chained displays we designed a simple gestural version of the classical *space invaders* game (Figure 9). It was implemented in Flash and used the OpenNI framework to capture depth images and the OpenCV library for processing depth images. The design of the game was guided by 5 principles:

Immediate usability. Users interacted as soon as they entered in the interaction space: Their body contour appeared on the screen and they started to shoot projectiles immediately. So, novice users only required a minimum amount of knowledge to start playing the game.

Ad-hoc gaming. The game was designed to let people join and leave when they want to (no need to wait for the next round or to achieve a specific goal after which the round is ended). Users could engage in short interactions but could also play for a long time as aliens were regenerated.

Gestural interaction. The game is based on body gesture interaction to reward demonstrative interaction. For instance, users need to move their hands in order to define the direction of projectiles. Moreover, users have to move their body to avoid aliens' projectiles.

Advanced control and difficulty. We created advanced controls to invite intermediate users to actively explore the possibilities and to keep expert users motivated. Spreading the arms increases the shooting frequency while moving the arms up increases the shooting power. Finally, the difficulty increases over time by aliens shooting faster.

Deployment

The three chained display configurations were deployed for three days in the entrance hall of a university canteen in Berlin. Figure 10 provides an overview of the space: People mainly come from two entries (A & B) and move towards the canteen (C). After lunch, they leave the canteen (points D & E) by exiting through the entrance hall. This hall has several advantages: it is big, has a strong flow of people and is indoors. However, the population is not heterogeneous: It is mainly composed of students (and personnel of the University) and a high proportion of large groups (>5). The displays were positioned in the area F, directly besides the main walking path for users. People walked parallel to the flat or concave displays, while passing on one side of the hexagonal display (people could still circulate around the configuration). One alternative placement would have been to position the hexagonal display directly on the main walking path, so that people would circulate to both sides.

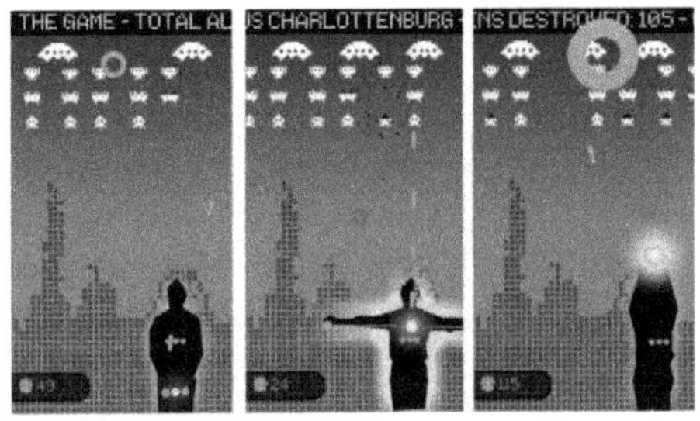

Figure 9: Left: users standing in front of the displays immediately started interacting. Middle: By spreading the arms the shooting frequency is increased. Right: By moving the arms up the shooting power is increased.

The side position was chosen because (1) the position was the same for all three displays, eliminating confounding effects of position (2) positioning on the side of the walking path is more realistic. Indeed, positioning of public displays is strongly regulated. For example, the OSHA standard [28] explicitly mentions "Exit routes must be free and unobstructed". Thus, the majority of all advertising columns are placed to the side of the main walking path.

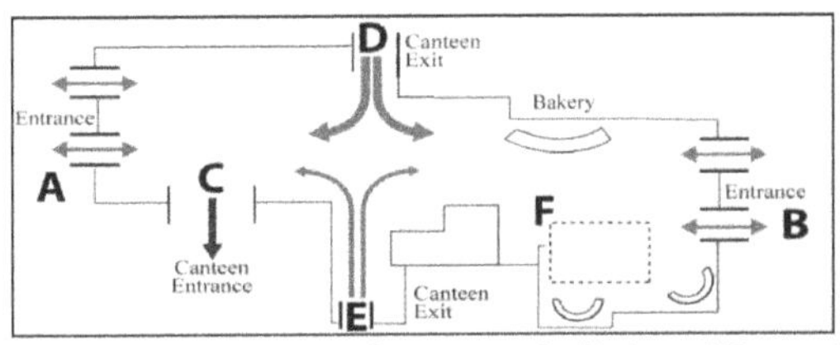

Figure 10: Overview of entrance hall. A and B are the entrances of the space. The chained displays were installed in area F

Data collection and Analysis

We used two methods to collect data:

Direct observations and videos. Our primary data collection method was direct observation. Three researchers observed the displays and kept field notes. We also deployed several cameras capturing how users approached and interacted with the chained displays. Videos were used to review situations from the field notes in more detail.

Interviews. We approached those who played for at least 10 seconds to fill in the survey right after they stopped playing. The survey had 24 questions (inspired by [18]) and covered items related to the user and social experience, personal space and f-formations. We also conducted semi-structured interviews with actors and audience members.

The data was analyzed qualitatively by two researchers. As a guide for analysis, the concepts of stages of interaction, performative interaction, personal space, f-formations and the Honeypot effect were used. Qualitative and explorative analysis was chosen because of the early stage of research regarding interactive public displays, which does not yet provide accepted theories that lend themselves to hypothesis formulation. Because of the social nature of the research question, we emphasize ecological validity over a controlled setting.

Design

Each configuration was tested for a single day (3 days in total) during lunch time (from 11:00 am to 2:00 pm). The first day we tested *Flat*, followed by *Hexagonal* and finally *Concave*. To understand to what extent a novelty factor was present, we included an item in the survey asking whether actors had just seen the installation for the first time (day 1: 93.8%, day 2: 73.1%, day 3: 59.1%). The results indicate that a global awareness of the presence of the game was developed over the test days. While it is a limitation of our study, it was impossible to test the 3 configurations at the same time. Moreover, the questionnaire showed that still a large number of users playing the game on the third day were still new users (72.7%).

FINDINGS

Over the three days, on the order of 250 people interacted with the game ranging from relatively short interactions (a couple of seconds) to long interactions of around 5 minutes.

Findings from the survey

We compared the responses of the 66 collected surveys about configurations but our analysis returned no significant differences. In general, people responded they had a positive experience with the game. People who played the game reported that they only had few worries of social embarrassment. Moreover, none to few issues of personal space were experienced. In terms of the social experience created by the game, few people felt they created new contacts but judged the social experience more towards natural as unnatural. Players responded that they did not change their behavior towards others. In response to whether they observed other players using the screens, and whether they observed the actions, respondents were neutral: not declining but also not fully agreeing.

Observation and video analysis

In this section we report on our observations. Our observations are organized according to the process how an individual approaches the display. After the approach, we describe how individuals and groups position themselves in front of each configuration and the impact on the number of simultaneously interacting users. We also report on social embarrassment and social learning. Finally, we mention the size of the audience.

Individual approaching

We observed two distinct ways in how people approached the displays:

(1) Many people started out as part of the audience and after brief observation of the game, directly approached the displays having a sense of what actions to perform. This process looked similarly for the three tested configurations.

(2) Passers-by passed through the interaction space, noticed the interactivity and were intrigued to interact. In *Flat*, passers-by only made a small detour when they noticed the display as the chained display was positioned in parallel and not far from the natural walking path (Figure 11-top). In *Concave*, they performed the same detour, however, many showed a hesitance to enter the shape and thereby did not notice the interactive component (Figure 11-bottom). We argue this is due to the shape of the chained display that affords a clear entry point.

Finally, *Hexagonal* triggers different passing-by behavior. Here passers-by only have the front screen to get a reaction of the system as the other screens were too far from the natural walking path. As a consequence, many noticed the interactivity of the setup too late and did not stop. For those passers-by who did notice it in time, we observed that they followed the curved path around the displays, almost as if the displays had a gravitational pull (Figure11-middle).

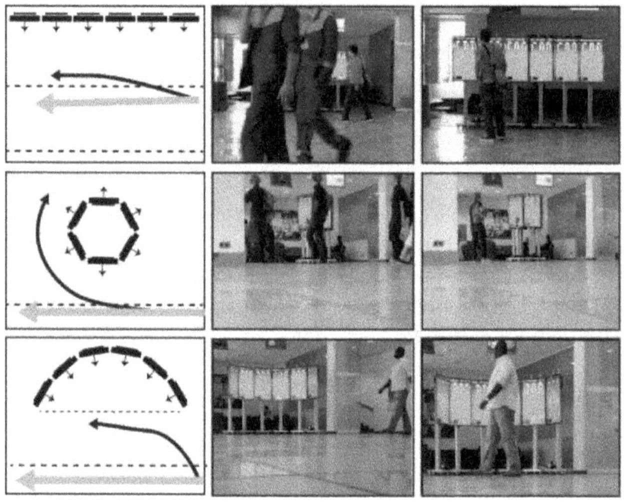

Figure 11: Top: A user noticing interactivity while passing by *Flat*. Middle: A user orbiting around the Hexagonal (several instances of the *same* user are displayed to describe the path. Bottom: a user avoiding the inner space of the Concave.

Individual positioning

We observed that the configurations influence where individuals position themselves in front of chained displays (Figure 12) especially in the case of few actors being present (up to 2 persons).

In *Flat*, we observed that individuals frequently approached one extremity of the public display even if no other actors were present. Individuals seemed to maintain a rule to maximize the amount of personal space with others, anticipating where joining strangers could position themselves (Figure 12-top). This is in contrast to *Hexagonal*, where individuals generally annexed the neighboring screen of an actor (Figure 12-middle). Probably, the physical distance between them was large enough for people to feel comfortable. Finally, in *Concave*, the first user generally positioned himself/herself in the middle of the setup. When a second individual approached, s/he frequently waited for the actor to leave or positioned himself/herself at one extremity (at the limit of the interaction space) as shown in figure 12-bottom.

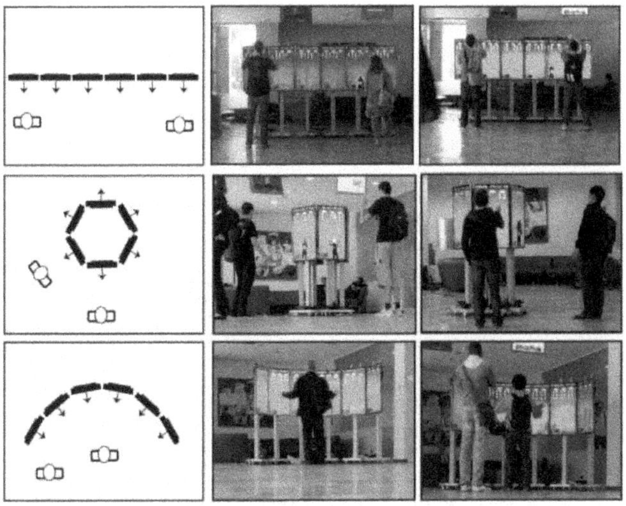

Figure 12: Top: people maintained a *safe* distance in *Flat.* Middle: strangers occupying neighbor screens in Hexagonal. Bottom: *Concave* afforded 1 to 2 players simultaneously

Our findings contrast with [4] who found that actors are generally positioned in the middle of a flat display. This might be explained by the fact that the user study tested single user interaction where users did not have to anticipate other users.

Group approaching

We observed that within all conditions, groups generally followed one "brave" member who initiated the interaction. The group quickly followed, but the members positioned themselves differently within the conditions.

Flat: Once a brave member had initiated the interaction, the rest of the group approached the display and divided up in front of the display in order to have one screen per group member as shown Figure 13-top.

Hexagonal: After a member initiated the interaction, the rest of the group usually formed an audience around the player (figure 13-middle). At many occasions, we observed that a member of the group tried to play at a neighboring screen, but returned quite quickly to re-join the audience of the other player. It seemed the relatively large distance from the group signaled detachment of the group and as a result he/she returned to the group.

Concave: The group also formed an audience around the first player but at a larger distance. Moreover, we sometimes observed that the brave individual returned to the group and someone else would take his place (Figure 13-bottom).

Simultaneous interaction

We observed that the form factor impacts the number of simultaneous actors (Figure 14). While we frequently observed 5 simultaneous actors in *Flat*, it was generally limited to 2 or 3 in *Hexagonal* and 1 or 2 in *Concave*.

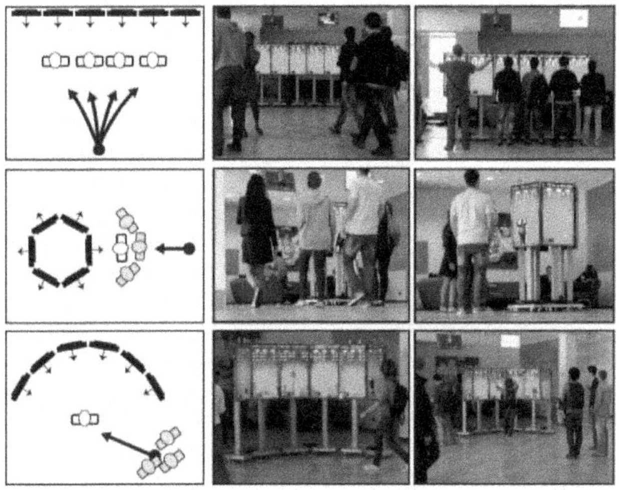

Figure 13: Top: a group approaching and dividing in front of the screens. Middle: A group approaching and centering around one screen. Bottom: A group member detaching to play.

Surprisingly, in the case of *Hexagonal*, people did not interact with the screens that were not oriented in the direction of the pathway: people seem to interact with screens only if it does not force them to diverge from their initial pathway. We expect that moving *Hexagonal* to a location directly in the pathway (i.e. towards the center of the large hall) would increase the number of simultaneous actors. Finally, as mentioned above, *Concave* affords interaction for only 1 or 2 actors due to the lack of personal space.

Figure 14: Left: multiple people playing simultaneously. Middle: Only the 2 front displays are occupied. Right: *Concave* afforded 1 to 2 users.

Social learning

Our game supports novice users (intuitive gestures) and lets more experienced users discover advanced gestures. We observed that many people discovered these advanced gestures and often learned them by mimicking successful other users. We frequently observed in *Flat* and *Concave* that actors copy (Figure 15) each other's gestures even if these gestures were not correct. Surprisingly, mimicking happened to a lesser extent in *Hexagonal* although actors could easily observe manipulations of other actors. This may be explained by the fact that for social learning to occur, it is important that actors can see both *manipulations* and the *effects* of other (successful) actors as opposed to seeing only the *manipulations*.

Figure 15: Example of social learning for *Flat.* The user with the black shirt stayed a long time without performing advanced gestures. He starts performing them by mimicking the two students.

Social embarrassment

Most actors had no worries of social embarrassment (most of passers-by were students) whatever the configuration. They frequently performed very expressive gestures as soon as they discovered them. Some of them even took the opportunity to make a small spectacle for their groups or other audience members (Figure 16-middle and -right). However, we also observed some audience members anxiously standing in the proximity of the display (Figure 16-left). It seems that social embarrassment is more likely to manifest itself in a hesitance to interact as opposed to non-expressive behavior.

Figure 16: Left: Hesitance to interact. Middle and right: Example of performative interaction

Size of the audience

We observed that *Flat* triggered more audience than the two other configurations. At occasions, different rows of people were formed to observe what was happening. *Hexagonal* triggered less audience than expected.

DISCUSSION

We now revisit the five effects derived from the literature according to the findings of the field study and the concepts of Nimbus and Focus.

Stages of interaction

Configurations with a large system nimbus get noticed better. Given our deployment location, the flat configuration was noticed by most people, followed by the cylindrical and the concave display. This can be explained by the fact that flat configuration had the largest system nimbus given the deployment location, followed by the cylindrical and the concave configuration. Note that the nimbus not only depends on the configuration itself but also on the environment. Had the cylindrical configuration been installed directly in the walking path, it would probably have had a larger nimbus and been noticed by more people.

Configurations with a large system focus (interaction space) better communicate interactivity. We observed that the most important factor for passers-by noticing interactivity is the intersection between the interaction space and the walking path. We argue that the directions of the natural walking paths are an important factor for creating interaction. This directionality is not directly reflected in the design space, but needs to be considered in particular regarding Nimbus.

Performative interaction

Configurations making actors' effects and manipulations highly visible favor social learning. Flat favors social learning because actors can easily observe other actor's *effects* (*System Nimbus*) and *manipulations (Actor Nimbus).* This allows actors to mimic other successful actors and thereby learn the system. In the *Hexagonal,* people can better see other actors' *manipulations* but have limited (or no) view on their *effects.* Thereby, social learning is limited.

Configurations do not seem to impact the hesitance to interact or the expressivity of behavior. Social embarrassment is more likely to manifest itself in a hesitance to interact as opposed to non-expressive behavior. Although no clear behavioral difference between the configurations emerged, *Concave* and *Flat* seemed to attract more performative behavior. They had a smaller nimbus considering the person itself, but the overlapping of the nimbus of the actor and the representation of the actor was larger. For these configurations, the space directly in front of the chained display signals a highly observable stage for an actor to perform his actions.

Personal space

Configurations with a large interaction space have the highest amount of simultaneous users. Configurations with a high system Focus seem to afford more simultaneous users. However, for the hexagonal display, this was only true for the interaction areas that intersected with the walking path of users. Therefore, the size of the intersection between the interaction space and the walking path better explains our observations than only considering the size of the interaction space.

Configurations with a small interaction space do not create more social discomfort nor make people leave. We did not observe occasions where people invaded the personal space of another person playing and thereby making the other person leave. It seems that when a display is occupied, people rather observe the actor and wait for their turn. This is particularly true for displays with a rather small interaction space, e.g. the concave display.

F-formations

The maintenance of the shared transactional space is essential for the cohesion of the group. While *Hexagonal* areas allow groups of actors to position themselves in a slight angle towards each other, we observed that isolated group members quickly returned to the screen where the rest of the group focused on. Audience members and actors have the opportunity to monitor the *manipulations* of multiple players but they lose the shared focus because the *effects* can no longer be observed. In contrast, although *Flat* changed the f-formation to a shoulder-to-shoulder interaction it still allowed groups to observe (virtually) what the other group members were doing (effects) and thereby maintained their "shared transactional space" [19]. In conclusion, the maintenance of the *shared transactional space* is of more importance for the cohesion of the group than the increase of monitoring each other's actions.

Concave configurations favor turn-taking. As this configuration only affords space for a single or two users, a group of people split up in an observing and an interacting group. As the observing group tended to observe from a distance, the social communication between the groups necessarily decreased.

Honeypot effect

Judged by the size of the audience, *Flat* triggered the strongest honeypot effect. We argue that *Flat* catalyzed the Honeypot effect more because (1) its position triggered the highest number of simultaneous actors and (2) all passers-by can observe many *manipulations* and *effects* due to the orientation and the location of the setup (parallel to the walking path). Although we observed something different than we anticipated (*Hexagonal* would trigger the strongest honeypot effect), the configuration with high system, actor and audience nimbus (in our test situation *Flat*) triggered the strongest honeypot effect.

CONCLUSION

We proposed chained displays as alternative to the flat form-factor commonly used within the context of public displays. We then proposed a design space based on two static concepts: *Nimbus and Focus*. It serves to describe and compare chained displays as well as to reason about the 5 commonly described effects found within the literature. We performed a field study and qualitatively compared three chained displays (*Flat*, *Hexagonal* and *Concave*) in an "in the wild" situation. Observations show that each configuration (and more generally form factor) impacts actor-, audience- and passer-by behavior.

From the field study, we learned that *Flat* created the highest honeypot effect, triggered individuals to position themselves at the extremities of the display, triggered groups to divide and occupy multiple screens, and fostered social learning. *Hexagonal* allowed strangers to comfortably play on adjacent screens. *Concave* created the lowest amount of simultaneously interacting people, and caused groups to split into actors and audience. These results can help designers to consider different form factors for public displays as they trigger different user behavior.

Importantly, contrary to our first assumption, the concept of Nimbus and Focus must be extended from the persons themselves to their representations on the screen. Social learning, for example, only occurred if users could see the effects of other people actions on the screen and was strongest when they could see both the manipulations and the effect. Similarly, the honeypot effect was strong for the flat display where audiences could see both manipulations and effects of actions, and weak for the cylindrical display, where the manipulations could be seen from a large area, but not the effects.

The field study also highlighted some limitations of our design space, which provides a simplified model based on two *static* concepts (Nimbus and Focus) to describe user behavior around a public display. Our observations from the field suggest that the natural walking path is an important *dynamic* factor that strongly influences the noticing of interactivity and thus impacts user behavior. In future work, we plan to include this dynamic factor in our design space and to perform a field study comparing different locations for our configurations.

ACKNOWLEDGEMENT

This work was supported by the Alexander von Humboldt Foundation and the European Institute of Innovation and Technology. We also wish to thank Sarah Kleideiter and Hossein Maktoufi for their help during the field study.

REFERENCES

1. Altman, I. 1975. The environment and social behavior: Privacy, personal space, territory, crowding. Monterey, Calif.: Brooks/Cole Pub. Co.
2. Benford, S., Bullock, A., Cook, N., Harvey, P., Ingram, R., Lee, O. 1993. From Rooms to Cyberspace: Models of Interaction in Large Virtual Computer Spaces. *Interacting with Computers*. 217-237.
3. Benko, H., Wilson, A. D., and Balakrishnan, R. 2008. Sphere: multi-touch interactions on a spherical display. *ACM UIST '08*, 77-86.
4. Beyer, G., Alt, F., Müller, J., Schmidt, A., Haulsen, I., Klose, S., Isakovic, K., Schiewe, M.: Audience Behavior around Large Interactive Cylindrical Screens. *ACM CHI '11*, 1021-1030.
5. Boyle, M., Greenberg, S. 2005. The Language of Privacy: Learning from Video Media Space Analysis and Design. *ACM ToCHI*, Vol. 12, No 2. P328-370.
6. Brignull, H. and Rogers, Y. 2003. Enticing people to interact with large public displays in public spaces. *IFIP INTERACT 2003*, p. 17–24.
7. Cao, X., Massimi, M., & Balakrishnan, R. 2008. Flashlight jigsaw: an exploratory study of an ad-hoc multi-player game on public displays, *ACM CSCW '08*, 77-86
8. Companje, R., van Dijk, N., Hogenbirk, H. and Mast, D. 2007. Globe4D, Time-Traveling with an Interactive Four- Dimensional Globe. *ACM MULTIMEDIA '06*, 959–960.
9. Coutrix, C., Kuikkaniemi, K., Kurvinen, E., Jacucci, G., Avdouevski, I., Mäkelä, R. 2011. FizzyVis:

Designing for Playful Information Browsing on a Multitouch Public Display. *ACM DPPI'11.*

10. Dalsgaard, P., & Hansen, L. K. 2008. Performing perception - staging aesthetics of interaction. *ACM TOCHI*, 15(3), 1-33.
11. Dalton, S. N., Marshall, P., & Dalton, R. C. 2010. Measuring environments for public displays: A space syntax approach. *ACM CHI EA'10, 3841-3846*
12. Elumen's Vision Dome. www.virtuale3d.com/elumens.html
13. Finke, M., Tang, A., Leung, R., & Blackstock, M. 2008. Lessons learned: Game design for large public displays. *DIMEA '08*, 23-33.
14. Fernado, O., Adach, K., Cohen, M. 2004. Phantom Sources for Separation of Listening and Viewing Positions of Multipresent Avatars in Narrowcasting Collaborative Virtual Environments. IDCSW'04. 170-175.
15. Greenberg, S., Marquardt, N., Ballendat, T., Diaz-Marino, R. and Wang, M. 2011. Proxemic Interactions: The New Ubicomp?. Interactions 18, 1 (2011), 42-50.
16. Hornecker, E., Marshall, P., & Rogers, Y. 2007. From entry to access: How shareability comes about. *ACM DPPI'07,* 328-342
17. Hua, H., Brown, L. D., Gao, C., and Ahuja, N. 2003. A New Collaborative Infrastructure: SCAPE. *IEEE VR'03*, 171–179.
18. Jacucci, G., Morrison, A., Richard, G., Kleimola, J., Peltonen, P., Parisi, L., & Laitinen, T. 2010. Worlds of information: Designing for engagement at a public multi-touch display. ACM *CHI'10*, 2267-2276
19. Kendon, A. 2010. Spacing and orientation in co-present interaction. Development of Multimodal Interfaces: Active Listening and Synchrony, 1-15.
20. Kettner, S., Madden, C. and Ziegler, R. 2004. Direct Rotational Interaction with a Spherical Projection. *Creat. & Cog. Symp. on Int.: Syst., Pract. and Theory.*
21. Marshall, P., Morris, R., Rogers, Y., Kreitmayer, S., & Davies, M. 2011. Rethinking multi-user: An in-the-wild study of how groups approach a walk-up-and-use tabletop interface. *ACM CHI '11*, 3033-3042.
22. Marshall, P., Rogers, Y., & Pantidi, N. 2011. Using f-formations to analyse spatial patterns of interaction in physical environments. *ACM CSCW '11*, 445-454.
23. Mataxas, G. Markopoulos, P. 2008. "Aware of What?" A Formal model of Awarness Systems that Extends the Focus-Nimbus. *Enginnering Interactive Systems*. 429-446.
24. Michelis, D., & Müller, J. 2011. The audience funnel: Observations of gesture based interaction with multiple large displays in a city center. In *International Journal of Human-Computer Interaction*, (1), 1-1.
25. Müller, J. Walter, R., Bailly, G., Nischt, M., Alt, F. 2012. Looking Glass: A Field Study on Noticing Interactivity of a Shop Window. *ACM CHI'12.*
26. Peltonen, P., Kurvinen, E., Salovaara, A., Jacucci, G., Ilmonen, T., Evans, J., Oulasvirta, A., Saarikko, P. 2008. It's mine, don't touch!: Interactions at a large multi-touch display in a city centre. *ACM CHI '08*, 1285-1294
27. Perry, M., Beckett, S., O'Hara, K., & Subramanian, S. 2010. Wavewindow: Public, performative gestural interaction. *ACM ITS '10,* 109-112
28. OSHA. United states Departement of Labor, section regulations, paragraph 1910.37(a) 3. www.dol.gov.
29. Reeves, S., Benford, S., O'Malley, C., & Fraser, M. 2005. Designing the spectator experience. *ACM CHI'05,* 741-750.
30. Rodden, T. 1996. Populating the Application: A Model of Awareness for Cooperative Applications. *ACM CSCW'96*. 87-96
31. Rogers, Y., & Lindley, S. 2004. Collaborating around large interactive displays: Which way is best to meet. *Interacting with Computers*, 16(6), 1133-1152.
32. Roudaut, A., Pohl, H., Baudisch, P. 2011. Touch input on curved surfaces. *ACM CHI'11*, 1011-1020.
33. Russell, D., Drews, C., & Sue, A. 2002. Social aspects of using large public interactive displays for collaboration. *ACM Ubicomp'02*, 663-670.
34. Ryall, K., Forlines, C., Shen, C., & Morris, M. R. 2004. Exploring the effects of group size and table size on interactions with tabletop shared-display groupware. *ACM CSCW '04,* 284-293.
35. Scupelli, P. G., Kiesler, S., & Fussell, S. R. 2007. Using isovist views to study placement of large displays in natural settings. *ACM CHI EA '07*, 2645-2650.
36. Vogel, D. and Balakrishnan, R. Interactive public ambient displays: Transitioning from implicit to explicit, public to personal, interaction with multiple users. *ACM UIST'04*, 137-146.

Investigating the Presence, Form and Behavior of Virtual Possessions in the Context of a Teen Bedroom

William Odom, John Zimmerman, Jodi Forlizzi, Hajin Choi, Stephanie Meier, Angela Park
Human-Computer Interaction Institute
Carnegie Mellon University
{wodom, johnz, forlizzi}@cs.cmu.edu , {hajin.choi, smeier, anglea.park}@andrew.cmu.edu

ABSTRACT
Over the past several years, people have acquired more and more *virtual possessions*. While virtual possessions have become ubiquitous, little work exists to inform designers on how these growing collections should be displayed and how they should behave. We generated four design concepts that changed the form and behavior of these digital things, making them more present within a teen bedroom. We then conducted speed dating sessions [9] to investigate how these new forms and behaviors influence perceptions of value. Sessions revealed how new technologies might better support self-exploration and reflection, as well as how they could complicate identity construction processes. Findings are interpreted to detail opportunities and tensions that can guide future research and practice in this emerging space.

Author Keywords
Teenagers; Virtual Possessions; User Enactments; Speed Dating; Design Methods; Bedroom; Home

ACM Classification Keywords
H.5.m. Information interfaces and presentation (e.g., HCI): Miscellaneous.

INTRODUCTION
Most teens feel the greatest sense of place attachment to their bedroom [6]. Here they live with their things, make sense of their lives, and work to understand the complex changes and challenges of growing up [25]. The bedroom provides moments for solitude and reflection, a social space to engage parents and peers, and a canvas to experiment with an evolving sense of self [17]. Teens display and curate their precious material possessions in their bedrooms in order to explore their changing values and aspirations, and project them to different audiences. Through this process, they construct value with their things; mentally reassigning an individualized sense of worth as they possess and repeatedly use their things over time [3]. The bedroom provides teens with their first opportunity to author a space, to create their own aesthetic and sense of style in negotiation with their parents [25].

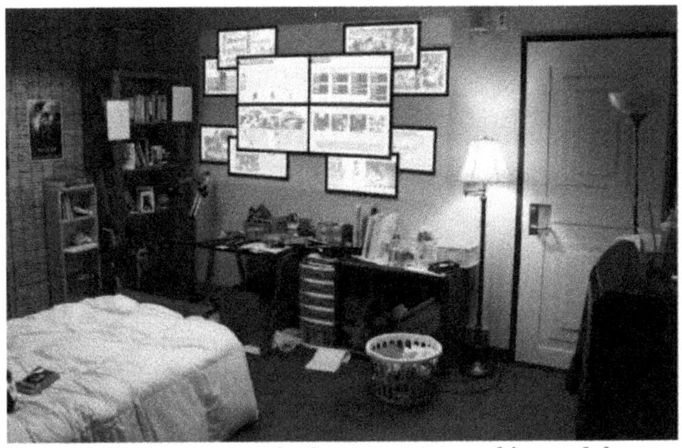

Figure 1. The messy teen bedroom prototyped in our lab.

Digital devices and services have become an increasingly large part of teen life [18] and teens commonly alternate their attention and interactions between their material and *virtual possessions*. Virtual possessions include things that are increasingly immaterial (e.g., books, music, and photos) and things that never had a lasting material form (e.g., game avatars, electronic message archives, social networking profiles, and metadata traces logged during interactions with various systems). Our previous fieldwork with teens investigating value construction with material and virtual possessions in their rooms, and how these materials shaped teens' identity construction processes revealed that they work to make virtual things more present, and that they draw on them as critical resources for self-reflection and self-presentation to different social groups [22].

The study reported here focuses new forms and behaviors of virtual possessions that support curation and presentation of self to different audiences. Specifically, we wanted to understand how on how making virtual possessions more present in the bedroom and giving them new forms and behaviors influence teens' perceived value of these things. To do this, we generated four design concepts: an auto-redecorating bedroom, postcards sent from a teen's past, electronic gift giving, and a system for curation of multiple selves. We then constructed a bedroom in our lab and conducted speed dating sessions [9] with 14 teens. This provided a prism for investigating aspects of several potential futures that teens may or may not desire.

Speed dating sessions revealed that teens desire (i) to have their virtual possessions more present as long as they can control this presence, (ii) to curate multiple presentations of self while retaining a sense of authenticity, and (iii) new forms and behaviors that better support reflection on past self and on the relationship they have with another. These findings suggest significant opportunities for the HCI community to create new forms and behaviors for virtual things in order to modify people's perceived value of them, particularly in terms of *ability to investigate one-on-one relationships* and *supporting reflection on the past*. They also reveal an opportunity to develop richer forms of metadata, and the infrastructure required for its capture, storage, retrieval, and sensitive treatment.

Our research makes two contributions. First, it advances the HCI community's understanding of how teenagers construct value with their virtual things, alluding to future product and service forms. Second, it provides a case demonstrating how speed dating with user enactments can work to investigate potential futures.

BACKGROUND AND RELATED WORK

Technology use in and around the home

The ways in which technology affects the social and moral order of the home, and how it might be better designed to improve domestic life continue to be major areas of concern in HCI. Edwards and Grinter [11] discuss how even relatively simple technologies can disrupt domestic routines and practices. Subsequent work has emphasized developing technologies that make people feel more in control of their lives, rather than focusing on control of devices and services [8]. Building on the issue of control, Woodruff et al. [29] illustrated how ceding control to a smart home can help families focus on building social relationships. More generally, Vetere et al. [28] describe the complex ways technologies mediate intimate relationships and the need to make new designs more rich, nuanced and expressive.

Teenagers and their domestic places have received less attention in HCI. March and Fleuriot [21] explored how technology mediates teens' need for private space within their parents' home. Durrant et al. [10] proposed ways that teenagers' curation of digital photos opens up opportunities for intergenerational interaction and identity construction. Hodkinson and Lincoln [17] suggest teens increasingly use social media technologies to extend boundaries beyond the bedroom. Additional work has investigated how teens work to maintain offline relationships through interactive technology [e.g.,26]. More generally, teens are seen as defining new social mores through their use and appropriation of social computing technologies [e.g., 4].

Our work picks up these threads, advancing HCI's understanding of how teens control and might better control their bedroom. Our user enactments investigate digital photos and social networks, and how digital possessions and social computing services might change the way teens desire to express themselves and construct value with their possessions, both digitally and materially.

Privacy and self-disclosure

As everyday technologies have become networked, a wealth of literature has emerged concerning privacy and unwanted disclosure. Palen and Dourish [23] unpack the multi-dimensional nature of privacy practices, drawing attention to how they are not limited to tensions between people, but also involve a person's internal conflicts over how disclosure shapes their self-concept. Many important works too numerous to mention here have since built on this seminal article, working to reduce unwanted disclosure across mobile platforms and networked services (see [1] for an in depth review). Outside of HCI, Goffman's [15] sociological work reveals a range of performative practices people engage in to manage self impression and disclosure to different social audiences. Giddens [14] later argues that the act of managing presentations of self across different settings can lead to an integrated, holistic life narrative.

Additionally, there is growing interest in how to support designers in considering user values (such as privacy) throughout the design process [e.g., 12]. Much of this work helps illustrate how designing technologies reflective of users' values can productively open the space for people to construct a deeper sense of value or 'worth' with these things [see 7]. Our user enactments investigate both the context and forms for new technology for both self-reflection and self-presentation. Our designs are intended to probe, in order to better reveal the issues and tensions around privacy, disclosure, self-presentation, and self concept.

Digital content, archives and collections

Recently, researchers have begun to explore the implications surrounding the virtualization of material artifacts, such as photos [27] and familial possessions [20]. Approaches to designing digital objects characterized by immaterial qualities are continuing to emerge in parallel [16]. New research also describes how people develop attachment to digital artifacts. Kirk and others [20] present a values-oriented approach to designing tools to support archiving of cherished digital artifacts. Kaye et al. [19] describe how digital archives can function as rich resources for identity construction and presentation. Van House [27] details how digital photos presented online can support curation of identity to different groups. Our research draws on these themes to inspire our designs for the bedroom.

OUR PRIOR RESEARCH

Previously we conducted ethnographic interviews with 21 teens in their bedrooms to investigate their perceived value of virtual and material possessions, and how these materials shaped teens' identity construction practices [22]. Our findings detailed design opportunities for value construction activities with immaterial things. These include:

Value in presence—Teens worked to make their virtual possessions more present. This included: constantly changing backgrounds on personal devices; printing status updates and comments from friends to display in their rooms; and maintaining a persistent, online connection in order to monitor the virtual world.

Value in self-reflection—Teens used their virtual possessions to reflect on their past. This included investigating how many times they listened to a song;

storing printed status updates; and reflecting on popular culture and other images featured on their computer previously. They used both system logs and human constructed metadata to understand who they have been.

Value in curation of multiple selves—Teens used virtual possessions to 'curate' different selves to different audiences. Actions included applying interface 'skins' on gaming consoles; encoding photos of a shared experience into the metadata of songs in playlists given as gifts; and tagging/untagging of photos as well as restricting/granting access to photos and other social media content.

TEEN BEDROOM SPEED DATING STUDY

The goal of this study was to advance our understanding of how the design of virtual possessions that were intended support identity construction activities might influence perception of value and meaning. We chose to conduct speed dating sessions with "user enactments" (UE) [9] to help better understand our target audience as well as potential opportunities and risks in the design space. In real-life speed dating, people have dating props such as a wine glass, café table and candle. They go on many very short dates in a single evening, and at the end, they know very little about any of the people they met. However, they have developed a much better and more realistic vision of what they want in a partner. Speed dating with user enactments follows the same approach. Design teams create rich scenes of possible futures. They then bring in representative participants who find themselves in a familiar scene and then experience a "sip" of what the future might be like. Prior to each enactment, participants are asked to reflect on their current practices and desires for the future. At the conclusion, they are asked to reflect on how the enactment may have complicated or supported these desires, or led to unexpected experiences. By combining wide exploration across multiple structured engagements, user enactments provide a broad perspective to find new design opportunities and to reveal potential underlying social tensions around new technology.

Our process followed three steps. First, we synthesized the strands of related research and findings from our field study through repeated discussion and affinity diagramming. Second, we operationalized our insights in the form of applications for engaging with virtual possessions. Third, we conducted speed dating sessions with teens to reveal design opportunities and implications.

We began with in-depth review sessions of our field data, related research and design opportunity areas. During these sessions we made affinity diagrams and free form diagrams to gain a perspective on the situation. We then held several concept generation sessions, resulting in 94 concepts. We clustered these thematically to understand the overall design space and to more clearly articulate visions of preferred and undesirable futures. We iteratively filtered these clusters based on their fit to: design opportunities, the importance of the issue probed by the concept, and the feasibility of realizing the concept through a user enactment. We then more fully realized twelve remaining concepts by making detailed scenarios and through body storming [5]. Again, we filtered these concepts resulting in the final set we developed into user enactments.

Our enactments required a teenager's bedroom, which we constructed in our lab (Figure 1). Our design process for this began with printing photos of teen rooms we collected in our previous study and placing them on the wall. Using them as a resource, we then constructed a bedroom space, continually tweaking and augmenting it until it "felt" like the rooms we had visited. A major addition to the room included twelve overlapping displays that fill the wall above the teen's desk. These were made from black and white foam-core, and we used a high definition projector to create the illusion that they functioned as independent screens. We intentionally created a set of displays that could be easily integrated into the bedroom, while at the same time might be perceived as overwhelming. We hoped this tension might provoke teens to critically reflect on the amplified presence of technology in their personal space.

Similar to Schön's notion of design as a reflective conversation with materials [24], we engaged in a reflective dialogue with the narrative and the problem framing each design raised. Through repeated meetings to critique scenarios, we iteratively refined the user enactments, often increasing the fidelity by using props and acting out scenes in order to developed a consistent narrative flow. We then repeatedly piloted the enactments. Piloting helped refine our design of the physical bedroom. It also revealed unanticipated narrative problems, which we addressed by developing a specific order for enactments. Finally, piloting helped to find the harmony between giving participants too much freedom and making the scenario mostly exposition.

We crafted the scenarios around a fixed set of digital content provided by two teenagers (male and female, respectively). We chose to do this for two reasons. First, participants have different sets of virtual possessions (e.g., some have large music collections, while some listen to music online; some archive text messages, while others are less meticulous; etc.). Reliance on participants' personal collections would have removed an important control: making sure participants reactions were based on the same stimuli. Additionally, it would make the enactments only as rich as the collections teens keep *now*. Second, acquiring teens' personal collections and building personalized versions of the room would have significantly increased our efforts. One of the key challenges with designing new technology is to reduce the risk of development for things people do not ultimately desire. Our intention was to ground our intuitions and avoid making an over commitment to a specific design direction. We needed to do UE to help reduce the risk associated with taking a conceptual leap to an emerging design space that has few existing conventions to draw on.

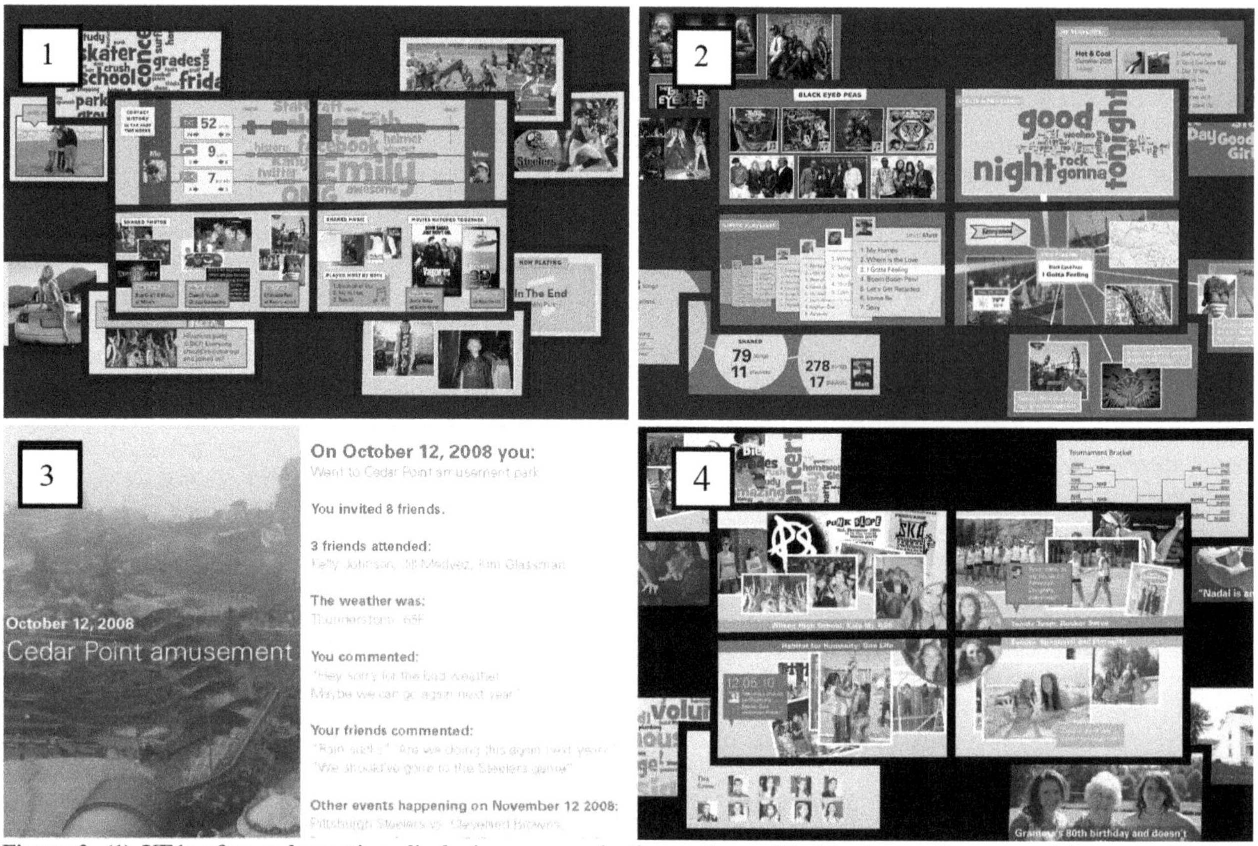

Figure 2. (1) UE1: after redecoration, displaying communication pattern with friend as well as shared interests. (2) UE2: displaying gifted playlists and personally inscribed data. (3) UE3: Postcard from the past composed of metadata scraped from social networking pages. (4) UE4: four views of self: (clockwise from top-left) School, Sports team, Family, Church.

User Enactments for Speed Dating

UE 1: Redecorating Bedroom—The participant enters the bedroom after dinner in order to read an Act from Romeo & Juliet to prepare for an upcoming exam. 12-displays show various collections, including: a visualization of messages exchanged with friends over the last two weeks, favorite music, photos of a wild party with comments, provocative pop-culture images, and personal photos related to sports and family. A confederate (of the same gender) plays the participant's friend. They show up and enter the room, triggering five of the screens to automatically re-decorate; presenting new information of shared activities and interests between the two friends. The screens highlight events both attended, images from parties, a visualization of communication patterns, and images of the two friends in Halloween costumes from a time before they knew each other (see figure 2.1). The confederate alludes to the meaning and function of the displays through a semi-structured conversation. After a few minutes of discussion, another confederate in the role of a parent knocks. The participant presses a remote to change the displays to "parent approved," masking the provocative image and party photos. The participant then allows the parent to enter and drop off folded laundry.

This enactment explored issues surrounding the control of virtual possession displays against the backdrop of different social audiences entering and exiting the room. It investigated questions including: Do teens value a system that automatically presents digital content relevant to particular people in the room? Will virtual possessions from a teen's past (i.e. Halloween photos) conflict with their current perception of self?

UE 2: Gift Giving—The participant is sitting in the room listening to music, while waiting for a friend. The song she/he is listening to is from a playlist given as a gift to them by their girl/boyfriend. 12-displays present machine and human-produced metadata for the current song as well as a collection of annotated photographs assembled by the girl/boyfriend from visit to an amusement park together. Metadata for the photos lists the time, day, and weather information as well as a topographical map. Other screens display a set of gifted playlists, information about listening habits between girl/boyfriend and participant, and wordclouds of lyrics (see figure 2.2). After spending a few minutes in the room, a confederate friend arrives, notices the screens, and engages the participant in a semi-structured conversation alluding to the meaning and function of the displayed information.

This enactment aimed to investigate questions including: Is a digital gift perceived to be more valuable if it reveals more of the effort someone put into making it? To what extent could social or machine-logged metadata help support the work of crafting a digital thing expressive of a social relationship between two people?

UE 3: Postcards from past—The participant sits in the bedroom when a parent confederate arrives with two postcards mailed to her/him. The postcards present information and metadata scraped from a teen's social networking account from two years ago. One summarizes personal stats, including the number of: friends on Facebook, people they most frequently tagged in photos, untaggings of self in photos, etc. The other (see figure 2.3) shows an amusement park trip shared with friends, including both social information (e.g. friends that attended, comments about the event) as well as other metadata (e.g. weather and temperature, other events happening that day, celebrities visiting the park that year). After a few minutes, the parent confederate returns to say dinner is ready.

The enactment explored questions including: Would receiving a physical postcard constructed from old metadata be perceived to support or conflict with self-reflection? How far is 'too far' for teens to look into their past? Does revealing that the system keeps digital traces of activity make teens feel uneasy?

UE 4: Curating Multiple Selves—Sitting in their bedroom after school, the participant views four different versions of their social networking profile targeted at four different audiences: family, school friends, sports team, and church (see figure 2.4). These are linked to incoming and outgoing digital communication. They enable the teen to post status updates, comments and other content to each group individually. After a few moments she/he receives a text message from a member of the sports team, and this quadrant highlights. She/he reads the text message (on a phone provided to them). A few moments later a different quadrant indicates another text message has arrived from a school friend. The corresponding quadrant highlights and she/he reads that message. The enactment concludes when a parent confederate knocks and asks her/him to get ready for sports practice.

This enactment investigated questions including: Will teens perceive the ability to explicitly manage different presentations of self to different groups valuable? Are teens disturbed by the explicit fragmentations of their social groups, and the presence of this information in their room?

Participants and Data Analysis

We recruited 14 teenagers ranging in age from 14-17; eight female and six male. Teens were recruited through flyers posted in several different areas of Pittsburgh and through word of mouth. Throughout the paper we refer to each participant with a sex specific pseudonym followed by her or his age (e.g., Sally-15). The design of screens for Enactments 1, 2 and 4, which emphasize personal content, were adapted to feature sex specific names for both the participant's character and their friends.

Before beginning the enactments, researchers gave participants a bedroom tour, introducing "their" digital and physical belongings. Researchers primed participants for each enactment by offering brief explanations of interfaces and then describing an activity to start with. Participants were also asked to reflect on their own everyday behaviors and experiences. This provided researchers with additional insights, and primed participants for drawing connections between their own lives and the possible future presented in each enactment.

During the enactments we played popular contemporary music popular in the background to deemphasize that this was taking place in a lab. Following each enactment we conducted semi-structured interviews, asking participants to reflect on their experience. We began by asking about their everyday practices, and then transitioned to talking about the specific enactment. This technique appeared to help participants fluidly make connections between the daily experience and the potential futures. Sessions lasted between 75 and 90 minutes.

We video recorded the speed dating sessions, which resulted in nearly 18.5 hours of video. We also took notes during sessions. The research team then met weekly over the course of four months to repeatedly review the video and notes in order to draw out underlying themes. Textual documents were coded using these themes. We also created conceptual models and affinity diagrams to reveal connections across participants and across enactments.

FINDINGS

During pre-enactment interviews, teens commonly described themselves as technology users and reported using computers and mobile phones everyday. All teens had personal bedrooms. Upon first entering our bedroom, many noted similarities between it and their own room in terms of objects and messiness. In the following sections, we present several examples taken from speed dating sessions that capture four primary emerging themes: the desire for presence and imperative of control; desire for curation of multiple selves and tensions surrounding authenticity; desire for self reflection by looking back; and desire to investigate relationships through evidence of action.

Presence and control

Almost every participant had a strong, positive reaction to how the 12-displays made their virtual possessions much more present within the bedroom. They valued that the displays could both support representing their self to others and investigating who they are right now. In terms of the increased presence, teens stressed the importance of controlling the display, both in terms of turning it on and off, and in terms of managing the content. Sara-15: "*...I like that it's bigger in the room. ...more available to me. I can lie around on my bed ...look at it, think about how to connect with people, but then it needs to go away. If I can't ...it's going to make me paranoid or obsessed.*" Similar to Sara, several teens described how the constant presence of their virtual things might lead to obsessive behaviors.

Participants related the practice of displaying objects in their rooms to the 12-displays. Anna-15: "*It's all the things that are out* [on display] *that make up a big part of who I am. ...This* [motions to the 12-displays], *you can see those connections between your different things. ...Those connections can kind of show who you are in a way. ...It's not really different from physical things, but there's no way to do that today.*" Anna's statement captures what many teens said, how seeing relationships and connections among their things could make them more valuable.

Several teens described how elements of UE1-Redecoration and UE4-Multi-self could help support self-development and discovery. They seemed very much aware of the work they were doing in their bedrooms to understand themselves. Derek-16: "*I'm figuring out who I am and coming into my self as a person. This could be really useful for thinking about who I am and who I might be comfortable being.*"

The enactments showed that the desire for control involved both turning displays on and off as well as curation of what was displayed. Sara-16: "*there are photos on Facebook of me and my friends that I want to have up in my room but I can't.* [parents will not allow] *...They are an important part of me and my life ...that* [my parents] *aren't part of. ...I'd want to have* [photos of friends] *up, like posters on the wall, ...Like live with them. ...But a big part of living with them is also living my life outside of them. ... I have to have some real space away from them.*"

The display of specific content from electronic messages also emerged as highly contentious and in some cases inappropriate. Sam-16: "*having the actual messages of like texts or Facebook displayed up there, I think I would panic. Even if I could control it, what if someone walked in the room?* ...[They're] *way too personal, who knows what someone's going to send you and who'd see it.*"

Interestingly, UE1-Redecoration's screens presented wordclouds of text message archives (either the cumulative sent by self or those exchanged with friend). This provoked some teens to speculate on potential workarounds offered by this alternative form: "*I write so many texts to so many people I lose track of what I've said. ...Those* [wordclouds] *feel like they'd give me time to pause and think about the meaning of what's sent. ...It feels like a special thing that I'd have with someone else. ...Other people could see it, but we'd be the one's that'd know what it means.*" (Mary-16).

Authenticity and Multiple Selves

UE1-Redecoration and UE4-Multi-self explored how teens would react when confronted with technologies that explicitly displayed presentations of self to different social groups. During our iterative piloting of UE-4, we used university students as stand-ins for teens. These college students often reacted negatively to the idea of displaying different representations of self to different social groups. Our teen participants, however, had an entirely different reaction: "*I need them to be separate because I can't express everything I want to if everyone is listening. ...I don't want to seem fake, I mean I'm real to everyone, but in ways that make sense in each situation. This* [application] *would be really helpful*" (Mary-16). Mary's reflection captures how teens were typically comfortable with having multiple digital presentations of self clearly segmented and manageable.

The automatic and manually-triggered redecorations of the room to present content tailored to a person or social group in UE1-Redecoration did raise concerns. Redecorating was perceived to evoke contrived, inauthentic presentations. Mary-16: "*...the screens show a lot about my relationship with a friend in a different kind of way than the physical things leftover from* [shared] *experiences with them. But I would rather look at it on my own to think about what we've done together. ...Having* [the screens] *change when she comes in feels strange. ...It seems like I'm stalking her. ...If she's coming* [over] *...I want to focus on being there with my friend.*" Several other teens described how the redecorating screens could cause peers or parents to perceive they are hiding aspects of their lives from them, potentially leading to awkward and undesirable situations.

Self reflection by looking back

Several enactments triggered reflections on how records of their interactions with digital materials could surface as resources for looking back on who they were at different times in their life. In what follows, we detail how teens drew on the applications to envision how they could be used for reflecting on the past. We then highlight how teens unexpectedly linked the perceived value of these things with less frequent interactions with them over time.

The enactments provoked teens to consider how technical systems keep traces of their interactions as metadata and how access to this data could shape their perceptions of virtual possessions. We suspected the personal-behavior postcard (in UE3), which presented machine-captured metadata summarizing a teen's behavior from two years ago, would cause conflicts by prying 'too far back' into the past to their 'pre-teen' days. Surprisingly, this was often not the case and most teens desired to, as Mary-16 stated, "*go back more into the past ...to when I can't even remember*". Some participants described how the postcards could stimulate co-exploration of the past with friends or family: "*I don't know what was happening when I was younger and I like the idea of the [postcards] going back a few years each time I get them until they were back to when I was a baby. ...I've wondered about what was happening then, but I don't bring it up with my parents much.* ...[postcards] *would provide a little bit of information to start a conversation*" (Eric-16).

Teens also described how mundane records of their online activities might support a new way of recalling past experiences: "*Who I'm tagging* [in photos] *now, shows who I'm around.* [My] *friends are a big part of who I am. ...Knowing that information when I'm older feels like it would make me think a lot about what I was doing then and who I was*" (Tim-16). In some cases, teens envisioned the postcards would accrue value over longer periods of time: "*...how many times I untagged myself from a photo or who* *was tagging me and when and where. ....In five years, ten years, twenty years, that could be a really special way of thinking about what was happening in my life then*" (Stephanie-17). However, several teens expressed that a lack of transparency in when and how this data was captured over time, and where it was stored, as well as the potential to be reminded of fights with parents and friends could complicate the perceived value of these things.

During interviews following UE1-Redecoration, several teens described how materials taken from bedroom walls were rarely captured. In some cases, they expressed a desire to 'save' the state of their virtual possession displays to revisit them. Anna-15 uses a bedroom wallpaper metaphor: "*Everything in my room and on my walls is a reflection of me. ...I put new things up and take other things down ...here* [in this application] *there are pictures of friends, bands everyone liked, different pictures of you and what you're into. ...They could keep layering on top of each other like wallpaper. ...You could peel back the layers and see what's underneath. ...it would be making a saved record* [of my life] *from what I do over time.*"

Other teens described how revisiting the spatial layout of virtual possessions decorating the room could stimulate a different experiences of remembering: "*...when I'm older it would be cool to bring up all of my digital things and how they were arranged in my room during different years. ...it feels different than thinking about an experience that's in a photo. ...It's not about remembering an experience I had, more like what it felt like to be in my room when looking up at how I arranged everything*" (Marisa-17). When probed further on how frequently she would use this kind of application, Marisa stated: "*I'd probably come back to it every four or five years. Like after I finish college or I've gotten married. ...what I'd treasure is going back* [to it] *when my life is changing and immersing myself in who I was and think about where I'm going.*"

Marisa's comment captures how several teens speculated the value of these things as resources may in part be tied to the rate at which they are encountered. Interestingly, the potential value of infrequency became one of the largest unexpected themes, emerging across several participants and enactments. This theme emerged in some cases in relation to the multiple selves application (in enactment 4). Eric-16 describes saving different 'states' of his different social groups to revisit in the future: "*...the meaning won't come from seeing them everyday. ...It's like the photo albums of me when I was a child. I look at them every other year. ...This* [application] *would be like that. You could save what you're doing ...and have it as a special way of thinking about who you were by who was around you.*"

Understanding relationships through evidence of action

The majority of digital content represented across all UEs usually centered on some form of evidence of action. This included forms constructed to explicitly reinforce a social relationship, such as the gifted playlist in UE2. It also included many implicit forms symbolic of shared practices or exchanges, such as the graphical breakdowns illustrating the number of times tagged in a photo with a friend (UE3); or the times a song has been listened to collectively among friends (UE2). In what follows, we describe how teens drew on these forms to envision how they could support reflection on valued social relationships.

In UE1-Redecoration, the communication summary screen becoming present as the friend enters provides an implicit evidence of action; it illustrates the frequency of SMS messages, emails and phone calls exchanged between two friends. This screen in particular provoked several discussions. Katie-17 describes how these records could construct a social portrait only readable to friends in the relationship: "*It makes me think of a landmark to remember people by. I can look at it and see when we were interacting and think about what we were doing. ...It's something that only her eyes would understand.*" Marisa-17 envisions how the low resolution of this implicit form might stimulate more active recollections of relationships compared to photos: "*...in a photo album there are lots of memories and in this there are lots of memories too. ...The way I think I would use them to remember is different. Like with a photo album, I look at it, I see each photo and, like that, I remember what was happening then because I'm seeing it. ...With the* [communication visualization] *only I know what went on when all those messages were sent and so I have to think back, and put it all together myself...*"

Many teens described holding onto the physical cases and discs from mix-CDs given to them by friends even though they accessed the music on digital music players. Some teens reflected on the less expressive qualities of other digital gifts: "*...for me, one of the most important things about getting a card that someone made is having it around during that momentary time that's special in my life. ...* [and] *think about what went into it. ...With e-cards there's nothing personal about them, nothing real went into it so they don't feel like they represent much*" (Eric-16).

However, reactions to the gifted song playing in UE2-Gift tended to contrast Eric's sentiment. Tim-16 describes the explicit evidence of work conveyed by the application: "*It's using the digital medium in ways that are hard to do with the physical. ...What I mean is a person can put together these photos and tag them with comments and put other information ...the point is all of this comes together to make an experience that's different than listening to music someone gave you sometime. ...I see it like a handwritten letter. ...when I read it, it's like that person is coming through the paper because they went through the trouble to write and had an intention. ...*[the digital gift] *feels like the* [girlfriend] *put some effort into making it say something.*" Tim's statement captures what several teens remarked on, how different kinds of metadata could be used to explicitly convey the work that went into crafting a unique digital thing symbolic of a valued relationship.

DISCUSSION AND IMPLICATIONS

Our findings produced a range of insights on how the presence, form and behavior of virtual possessions shape teens' sense of identity and how they might help them better curate different aspects of self. In what follows, we first discuss how speed dating sessions challenged findings from our prior study and produced some unexpected results, specifically in terms of: increasing presence, balancing authenticity and multiple selves, and looking back on the past and exploring personal relationships.

Increasing Presence

We previously observed teens working to display virtual possessions in their bedrooms and to breakdown boundaries between the material and virtual world. However, from this fieldwork, it was unclear if teens desired systems that significantly amplify the presence of their digital collections. We expected teens to find the 12-screen display to be invasive, overwhelming, or even inhibiting. However, nearly all had positive reactions, valuing how it could provide a better understanding of their things and support their work to understand themselves and their relationships. These perceptions were clearly contingent on teens having control over the presence (and absence) of their virtual things but not the presences of the displays.

There is an opportunity to rethink the bedroom in terms of digital displays as well as how new interaction methods might lead to better situated control over screens' contents. In addition, there is an opportunity to better leverage screens currently found in bedrooms (mobile phone, computer, television), helping them to work together as a more integrated and artful display system. Further, virtual things can be made present in many ways, and screens are only one option. There is also an opportunity for creating physical forms (e.g., the postcards in UE3), light based forms or even auditory forms, which could support familiar ways of manipulating the presence and absence of things.

Authenticity and multiple selves

Our prior fieldwork described how teens drew on their virtual possessions to curate different presentations of self to others. Our user enactments made this "fragmentation" of a teen's self more explicit through UE1's auto-redecoration and UE4's curation of four different selves. We wanted to investigate if future technologies should acknowledge or even reinforce the fragmentation, or if they should work to make teens feel more whole.

Redecoration particularly seemed like a good idea, as it is less explicit than UE4's four selves and it builds on the inherent strength of virtual possessions to instantaneously appear and disappear; something physical possessions cannot do. However, teens perceived the socially reactive display in UE1 as potentially inauthentic and attention seeking. Teens instead desired to be with friends or family when in their presence, and then to use virtual possessions to reflect on these relationships later when alone.

The multiple selves screen in UE4 raised issues over unwanted self-disclosure. Teens appeared quite comfortable when faced with seeing their self as multiple, curated selves. They felt the fragmentation could somehow make their lives seem more manageable. In some cases, they envisioned how saved records of these fragmentations could provide resources for reflecting on personal growth across life transitions and stages.

One explanation of this could be that teens have more segmented lives than other people. They move between their home and bedroom, partially controlled by their parents, and their high school, controlled by both peers and school rules. As they work to construct a self identity, they have the experience of being at least two people much more than young adults who create a separate life when they leave their parents' home and begin to control their own space. In keeping with Giddens [14], this surface-level fragmentation can be crucial to teens' work to construct a unified life narrative and, in essence, develop a concrete sense of self. Nonetheless, these issues are indicative of how the teen world is different from other populations, and what is expressed here must be viewed carefully before being applied to other groups of people. It does however raise some interesting general issues for investigating how people living together, such as couples, form and learn to share space, and share physical and virtual possessions that are representative of the couple or collective group.

Exploring the past and personal relationships

Our prior fieldwork revealed that teens used virtual possessions to reflect on their near past self. They often did not possess many virtual things that dated more than a few years into their past. UE1's presentation of Halloween photos depicting the teen at a young age as well as discussions following UE3's postcards both aimed to provoke teens to confront their earlier in their lives. We anticipated teens would find they complicated their current self-image; however, this often was not the case. Many teens desired to go deeper into their past, and they perceived collections of metadata operationalized by the postcards to be valuable for looking back on their practices. At the same time, their reflections indicated the value associated with the cards may come from occasional interaction, rather than constant presence.

Several UEs used forms that summarized personal relationships by revealing evidence of action. We displayed visualizations of communications sent and received (UE1), wordclouds of text messages indicating the frequency of word usage (UE1), favorite shared media (UE1), interfaces for making digital gifts more present (UE2), and experiences like trips shared together (UE3). While most social networking visualization tools currently offer a view of a person's complete network, these unintentionally provided windows into individual relationships. Teens reacted positively to these concepts, often describing how they could become aesthetically integrated into bedroom practices and provide mechanisms for actively expressing the social bond shared with another person. They clearly desired ways to see the evidence of the actions taken by themselves and others as a way of understanding who they are with that person and possibly where they want to go with that person.

Design Opportunities and Considerations

Collectively, these findings suggest many opportunities for the design of new technologies that increase the perceived value of teens' ever growing collections of digital things. Our findings highlight the importance of both human and machine-produced metadata. Systems that elicit human produced metadata and devices and systems that generate their own metadata have not been designed to support reflection on past self or reflection on the relationship with another. Going further, this indicates an opportunity for richer forms of metadata that can better support these desires. The opportunities include infrastructure for capture, storage, and retrieval; devices that keep and share metadata; and interactive tools that support display and reflection. Here, we detail two opportunity areas to advance the form and behavior of virtual possessions and open up new ways for teens to draw on them as resources in the bedroom.

Ability to investigate one-on-one relationships—A common factor shaping teens' perceived value of virtual possessions centered on how they could provide resources for investigating a one-on-one relationship with a friend. These findings generally match prior research on teens' ritual exchanges of text messages to express and affirm close relationships [26]. However, the digital materials used in these social processes are becoming more diverse, and questions surrounding how they could enrich social relationships are complex. Socially reactive virtual possessions becoming present when friends and family entered the room was clearly disruptive. Teens wanted to develop relationships with specific people when they were around, and to use technologies to explore, reflect on and "live with" these relationships when alone.

There is an opportunity to develop systems that capture metadata related to shared activities. In particular, teens described how being "tagged" together with friends on social networking sites enabled them to explore experiences with particular people over time. This kind of data could summarize how shared actions between two people have evolved over time. This opportunity highlights how everyday interactions with digital technology create layers of metadata, which could provide unique resources for viewing, exploring and expressing social relationships.

There is also an opportunity to use virtual possessions to represent actions between two people. The visualizations of SMS and email exchanges between friends in UE1 provoked several reflections from teens on how they could provide a new kind of "landmark to remember people." These low-resolution exchanges triggered speculations on how this communication could support active recollection of shared experiences. This also led to the visualizations being perceived as publicly presentable within the room, while remaining privately 'readable' only to those in the relationship. In a sense, systems can capture actions that are evidence of friendship, which help build and sustain a specific relationship. These materials can help create aesthetic forms of digitally mediated social exchanges open to being actively drawn on, or simply persist in the background. This direction could build on the history of work in HCI at the intersection of ambiguity in design [13] and slow technology [16] to explore how as these visual and interactive forms could be integrated into and slowly emerge as facets of bedroom culture and space over time.

Supporting reflection on the past through new materials—Teens' reflections across enactments showed how virtual possessions could provide resources for reflecting on their past. Several teens desired to 'save' versions of displays. Anna drew on the metaphor of wallpaper to describe how she would use saved states of her bedroom to "peel back the layers" and experience a sense of place from the past. There seems to be an opportunity to create applications that record the history of people's virtual possessions and enable them to view how they changed in the future. For example, an application could save versions of desktop images on past computers. As virtual possessions grow in number, more opportunities to create a history of their arrangement will also grow.

Teens also strongly perceived value in aggregations of metadata that capture information about their actions from the past (e.g., the postcards in UE3). It is currently unclear how to extract both human and machine-produced metadata from third party services. New systems can be developed to begin archiving digital records to create new resources for reflection. An example of this could be a background display that visually communicates thematic shifts in one's status updates, or simply the occurrence of momentous and mundane events over many years across life transitions.

Several teens also wanted to visit their virtual possessions several years into the future. This suggests opportunities for systems that anticipate making virtual possessions re-emerge in people's lives over longer periods of time. An example of this could be a system that actively archives summaries of events attended or photos posted online, and delivers them to their owners years into the future.

Practical and ethical issues for designers and developers—There are many ways to advance the form, presence and behavior of virtual possessions to investigate significant social relationships and reflection on one's sense of self. However, these opportunities also raise possible negative outcomes. When exploring these emerging design spaces it is important to consider how complications could emerge around metadata and evidence of action, as well as new risks of persistent digital records.

While metadata could enrich close friendships, it could also emphasize counting actions as opposed to the value of individual actions. Metadata captured by systems could become the currency by which relationships become defined; this may not always be the most relevant way to support social relationships. Additionally, as virtual possessions are increasingly created through and archived by third party services, they are given a lasting permanence different than material possessions. This makes virtual things increasingly vulnerable to surfacing in unintended contexts, highlighting how complex being able to 'forget' them will be. Future systems should support this need and, indeed the act of forgetting can itself be considered an opportunity [2]. These issues are crucial when critically considering the role of future technology in positively supporting the forming and sustaining of social relationships, moving toward a concrete concept of self, and reflecting back on the past. These should be considered as the HCI community moves forward in developing systems that support value construction activities with virtual things.

CONCLUSION

We conducted user enactments with teenagers to investigate the role of future technologies in the bedroom could play in supporting (or complicating) identity construction processes. With this paper, we hope to develop insights about how new systems could be created to help people construct more value with their virtual things. Speed dating UE provided a way of moving beyond studies of teens' current practices. It allowed us to engage teens in confronting possible benefits and tensions as they drew on their own experiences to make sense of possible futures. Findings highlighted several new opportunities for increasing the presence and advancing the form and behavior of virtual possessions, and key tensions related to their development. We are currently developing technology probes based on these findings.

ACKNOWLEDGMENTS

This work is partly supported by NSF grant IIS-1017429 and by Google. We thank the teens (and their parents) that took part in the study and the reviewers for their comments.

REFERENCES

1. Ackerman, M., Mainwaring, S. 2005. Privacy issues and human-computer interaction. Garfinkel, S., Cranor, L. (eds.) *Security and Usability*, 381-400, O'Reilly.
2. Bannon, L. 2006. Forgetting as a feature, not a bug: the duality of memory and implications for ubiquitous computing. *CoDesign,* Vol. 2, 1, 3-15.
3. Belk, R. 1988. Possessions and the Extended Self. *Journal of Consumer Research*, 15, 2, 139-168.
4. boyd, danah. 2007. Why Youth (Heart) Social Network Sites: The Role of Networked Publics in Teenage Social Life. *Youth, Identity, and Digital Media Volume*, 1-26.
5. Buchenau, M. and Suri, J. F. Experience Prototyping. In *Proc. of of of DIS*, (2000) ACM Press, 424-433.
6. Chawla, L. 1992. Childhood Place Attachments. In Altman, I. (ed.). *Place Attachment*. Plenum, 63-86.
7. Cockton, G. 2006. Designing worth is worth designing. *Proc. of NordiCHI '06*, 165-174.
8. Davidoff, S., Lee, M., Yui, C., Zimmerman, J., Dey, A. 2006. Principles of smart home control. *Proc of UbiComp '06*, 19-34.
9. Davidoff, S., Lee, M., Dey, A., Zimmerman, J. 2007. Rapidly exploring application design through speed dating. *UbiComp '07*, 429-446.
10. Durrant, A., Frohlich, D., Sellen, A., Lyons, E. 2009. Home curation versus teenage photography: photo displays in the family home. *Int. J. Hum.-Comput. Stud.* 67(12): 1005-1023.
11. Edwards, K., Grinter, R. 2001. At Home with Ubiquitous Computing: Seven Challenges. *Ubicomp '01*, 256-272.
12. Friedman, B. 2006. Value sensitive design. *Interactions, 3*, 6, 16-23. ACM Press.
13. Gaver, W. Beaver, J., Benford, S. 2003. Ambiguity as a resource in design. *Proc. of CHI '03*, 233-240.
14. Giddens, A. 1991. *Modernity and Self-Identity: Self and Society in the Late Modern Age*, Stanford University Press, 187-201.
15. Goffman, E. 1959. *The Presentation of Self in Everyday Llife*. New York: Double Day.
16. Hallnas, L., Redstrom, J. 2001. Slow Technology: Designing for Reflection. *Personal Ubiquit. Comput. 5*, 3, 201-212.
17. Hodkinson, P., Lincoln, S. 2008. Online Journals as Virtual Bedrooms? Young People, Identity, and Personal Space. *YOUNG 16,* 1, 27-46.
18. Ito, M. et al. 2010. *Hanging Out: Kids Living and Learning with New Media.* MIT Press.
19. Kaye, J. et al. 2006. To have and to hold: exploring the personal archive. *Proc. of CHI '06*, 275-284.
20. Kirk, D., Izadi, S., Sellen, A., et al. 2010. Opening up the family archive. *Proc. of CSCW '10*, 261-270.
21. March, W., Fleuriot, C. 2006. Girls, technology and privacy: "is my mother listening?" *Proc. of CHI '06.*
22. Odom, W. Zimmerman, J., Forlizzi, J. 2011. Teenagers and Their Virtual Possessions: Design Opportunities and Issues. *Proc. of CHI '11*, 1491-1500.
23. Palen, L., Dourish, P. 2003. Unpacking "Privacy" for a Networked World. *Proc. of CHI' 03*, 129-136.
24. Schön, D., Bennet, J. 1996. Reflective Conversation with Materials. *Bringing Design to Software*, 171-189.
25. Steele, J., Brown, J. 1995. Adolescent room culture: Studying media in the context of everyday life. *Journal of Youth and Adolescence*, *24,* 5, 551-576.
26. Taylor, A., Harper, R. 2002. Age-old practices in the 'new world': a study of gift-giving between teenage mobile phone users. *Proc. of CHI '02*, 439-446.
27. Van House, N. 2009. Collocated photo sharing, storytelling, and the performance of self. *Int. J. Hum.-Comput. Stud. 67*, 12, 1073-1086.
28. Vetere, F. et al. 2005. Mediating intimacy: designing technologies to support strong-tie relationships. *Proc. of CHI '05*, 471-480.
29. Woodruff, A, Augustin, S., Foucault, B. 2007. Sabbath day home automation: "it's like mixing technology and religion". *Proc. of CHI '07*, 527-536.

Technology Heirlooms? Considerations for Passing Down and Inheriting Digital Materials

William Odom[1], Richard Banks[2], Richard Harper[2], David Kirk[3], Siân Lindley[2], Abigail Sellen[2]

Carnegie Mellon University[1]
Human-Computer Interaction Institute
PA 15213 Pittsburgh, USA
wodom@cs.cmu.edu

Microsoft Research Cambridge[2]
Cambridge CB3 0FB, UK
{rbanks r.harper, sianl, asellen}@microsoft.com

Newcastle University[3]
Culture Lab
Newcastle, UK, NE1 7RU
david.kirk@ncl.ac.uk

ABSTRACT

Material artifacts are passed down as a way of sustaining relationships and family history. However, new issues are emerging as families are increasingly left with the digital remains of their loved ones. We designed three devices to investigate how digital materials might be passed down, lived with and inherited in the future. We conducted in-home interviews with 8 families using the devices to provoke discussion about how technology might support (or complicate) their existing practices. Sessions revealed families desired to treat their archives in ways not fully supported by technology as well as potential tensions that could emerge. Findings are interpreted to detail design considerations for future work in this emerging space.

Author Keywords

Technology Heirlooms; Memories; Digital Inheritance; Design-oriented HCI; Technology Probes; Design

ACM Classification Keywords

H5.m. Information interfaces and presentation (e.g., HCI): Miscellaneous.

INTRODUCTION

Material artifacts are passed down across generations of family members as a way of sustaining social relationships and bolstering ideas of shared heritage, history and values. These heirloom objects often offer connections to the past that extend before and potentially beyond the current owner's life. As we live more of our lives "online", it is interesting to ask how digital content will find its place among these physical collections of things that connect us to the past. After all, digital technology makes it possible for people to accumulate vast and diverse digital archives. In the future will children look back over their grandmother's digital photos or Facebook content to explore what her life was like? Will these digital things be passed down the same way as physical things are?

Figure 1. The three 'technology heirloom' devices: the Timecard (left), BackupBox (center), and the Digital Slide Viewer (right).

Research in the HCI community has illustrated a diverse range of ways people are drawing on digital objects to reflect on and reminisce about the past [e.g., 14]. Very recent work has described new complications that are emerging as loved ones pass away and leave complex assortments of digital remains for the living to come to terms with [e.g., 16, 19]. Many of these issues point to the fact that we are seeing a proliferation of personally meaningful digital artifacts. However, little work to date has progressed beyond explorations of current practice to explore how these sensitive materials might persist over time, across owners and across generations in the future.

With this in mind, we designed three devices (see Figure 1) as a way of encouraging people to think more concretely about how digital materials might be inherited in the future. The aim was to use these design artifacts to explore how the processes of passing down digital materials among family members might be better supported as well as to reveal potential unintended consequences that could emerge. They are: the *Digital Slide Viewer,* which packages treasured family photo albums in the form factor of a traditional slide viewer; *Timecard,* a device that enables people to assemble, present and hide away digital content of multiple family members along a chronological timeline; and *Backup Box,* which locally stores a person's Twitter archive on a daily basis in a form that can be handed down. We conducted in-home interviews with 8 families, using the devices to provoke discussions about how technology might fit within (or complicate) their practices of inheriting and passing down digital collections in the future. These sessions opened up discussions that provided insights into how families desired to treat their archives in ways not fully supported by technology. They also revealed emergent tensions as members critically considered futures embodied by (and beyond) the devices and reflected on consequences that could emerge.

With these findings in mind, this paper concludes with a discussion of four design considerations aimed at sensitizing the design space toward better supporting the work of inheriting, living with and passing down significant digital materials: designing technologies to be put away; supporting the moral work of safeguarding; enabling multiple roles; and enabling multiple representations in the archive.

BACKGROUND AND RELATED WORK

Artifacts play important roles as triggers for personal and shared memories. Over time these things signify our relationships with each other and can mediate how people remember their loved ones. The roles material artifacts play in supporting personal and familial memory [2] as well as ideas of family history and heritage [10] have been central concerns across several disciplines in the social sciences and humanities. Currently, there is a growing literature exploring the process of *passing down* objects as not merely reflecting our relationships with loved ones, but in essence *constituting* them over time [6]. A special emphasis has been given to how objects signify human relationships with the living as well as stand in as proxy for the departed [17].

With the increasing presence of digital artifacts and systems in everyday life, the nature of human interactions is shifting—people now commonly mediate between material things and digital technologies. It is not surprising then that research related to the effects of digital artifacts being left behind by departed loved ones is starting to emerge in quite a vital way. Based on an empirical study of bereaved families, Massimi and Baecker [16] speculate on future challenges related to digital inheritance, including: the claiming problem—digital materials lack clear affordances for inheriting, and the afterlifelog problem—reimagining the role of digital materials representing the lives of departed family members could provide opportunities for family members to remember loved ones. In a related study, Odom et al. [19] describe how relationships with the departed loved one continues to evolve, often mediated by inherited objects. It suggests concerns such as supporting the endurance of a cohesive archive and developing richer tools for contextualizing inherited digital content.

More generally, there exists a history of research in the HCI community exploring the recording and archiving personal or family memories. Kaye et al. [13] describe how digital archives could better support the work of self-reflection and understanding. Kirk & Sellen [14] present a values-oriented approach to support the archiving of families' cherished digital materials. Importantly, they highlight how the movement and storage of artifacts around the home plays central roles in preserving them for future generations.

Additionally, several projects [e.g., 8, 24] have designed and studied devices in laboratory environments that, in varying ways, enable families to attribute audio annotations to physical objects and digital photos. These studies speculated that shifting interaction away from the PC and toward dedicated devices may be more appropriate for supporting social practices of storytelling. Outside of the lab environment, Petrelli et al. [21] present a rare example of how reminiscence could be triggered by encasing audio recordings of family events in the form of a vintage FM radio.

Collectively, these strands of research have made important contributions to understanding how interactive technologies could better support digitally capturing family memories and revisiting them. They also reveal how new problems are emerging as members attempt to make sense out of inherited digital content, and consider how they themselves will pass down their digital legacy. Our work attempts to bring these strands of research together. We want to investigate how digital technology might fit within (or complicate) families' existing practices, and how the design space could be critically developed through and sensitized by these understandings. Beyond work that has gone before, we do this by grounding discussion around a set of working prototype devices that aim to make concrete new ideas for dealing with families' growing legacies of data.

METHODOLOGY

We designed three working devices to critically explore potential future interactions, experiences and practices surrounding the inheritance of digital content. Although these objects offer some diversity in design we synthesized a methodological approach that united them. Specifically, we used them to provoke reflection on the materials themselves and encourage a dialogue about (and beyond) the stances and potential futures they embody. Our methodology drew from a number of approaches, including speculative design [9], critical design [3], reflective design [23], technology probes [12], and design-oriented HCI [5].

The process leading to the development of these devices consisted of the following. We conducted review sessions of theoretical literature and empirical studies (many are noted previously). We then ideated many design concepts and progressively refined and clustered several conceptually related sets to construct an understanding of the overall design space. Comparable to Schön's notion of design as a reflective conversation with materials [22], we engaged in a reflective dialogue with theoretical and empirical materials, and iterative development and critique of the design concepts themselves, to arrive at our final devices.

We intended the form and presentation of each respective device to be resolved to the extent that, at first glance, they might appear relatively familiar in comparison to other domestic artifacts. We wanted the devices' material aesthetics to, on the surface, evoke a sense of the warm qualities associated with antique or heirloom objects (e.g., veneered oak composing an old chest compared to plastics encasing many contemporary appliances). The three devices are designed as a visual family, each encased in a European Oak veneer with a single surface of color. Further, the digital technology of each artifact is integrated into a form characterized by affordances that enable them to be fluidly opened up and put away. These design choices were influenced in part by prior work illustrating how the qualities of certain materials, such as wood, can inspire a perceived sense of durability [20]; and how the invocation, experience and putting away of inherited objects—digital and physical—appears central in supporting meaningful, self-determined interactions with them [19].

Nonetheless, it is important to point out that the notion of 'designing an heirloom' can seem contradictory. The ways in which an object achieves heirloom status is highly idiosyncratic and heterogeneous; what one family may regard as an heirloom will likely not retain the same meaning for another. Additionally, heirlooms often directly owe to the people that possessed them previously and the material histories inscribed through their use over time.

Thus, it must be stressed quite crucially that we did not aim to evaluate our design concepts *per se*. Indeed, a more traditional 'evaluation' would require a deployment for many years—if not decades—to understand how the devices shaped people's practices and experiences as they accumulated digital content and were (or were not) passed down to another generation. Rather, we used the devices to provoke discussion around—and beyond—the potential futures they might embody and inspire; and to explore issues and insights that emerge through these discussions. Additionally, we populated the devices with digital content from a research team member's personal collection, as opposed to each family's specific content. This team member's digital content captured years of personal and family experiences, as well as materials left behind after the loss of a close elder family member. Nonetheless, this clearly has limitations. The digital materials left behind by, for example, a teenager or middle-aged person would be different. However, this approach did appear effective in providing families with enough context to understand and relate the devices to their own lives, while remaining open enough to encourage them to envision new ideas or uses. In what immediately follows, we describe each of the concepts in turn, and then provide details on our participants and study.

The Digital Slide Viewer is a device for the local archiving of different collections of a family's digital photographs (see Figure 2). The device is an augmented vintage analog slide viewer popular in the United Kingdom in the 1970s. Physical slide tokens, laser cut from acrylic, symbolically correspond to photo albums previously stored online or locally by a family. The slides and viewer are stored and organized in an oak case. Each slide has a unique strip of color on its back, which is recognized by a color sensor to determine which album should be made viewable from internal memory. When a slide is inserted, the photos in the corresponding album become viewable, which may be sequentially explored by tilting the device left, to move backward, or right, to move forward, in the set. The digital slide viewer is driven by a Gadgeteer [18] microprocessor board, which several sensors and devices are plugged into, including: a 100x100 pixel display; an SD card (in an internal SD reader) for image storage; an RGB reader for detecting a unique color present on each slide token (to invoke different photo collections); and a breakout board with two tilt sensors for supporting navigation. A mini USB connector powers the device. Content for the photo albums was supplied by a research team member and models their exact organization. These 20 albums cover a diverse range of events over several years, including family trips and moments in a young child's life as well as mundane experiences (e.g., a family informally creating artwork together).

Figure 2. From left to right: The viewer in case with the slides; View of a photo; Families often desired to store the slide viewer in spaces where other significant artifacts were kept.

Issues framing the rationale for this concept included: How would the form and presentation of this device be perceived to support or complicate participants' existing practices of viewing family photos, against the backdrop of their own physical and digital albums? How would integrating digital photo albums into an artifact that may already be familiar to some members shape perceptions of these digital materials?

Timecard enables family members to construct and present a timeline representing the life of a loved one, which is stored and displayed on a dedicated device (see Figure 3). Timelines can be created for a departed family member as a form of memorial, or simply to map the lives of several family members as a matter of preserving family history. Family members can add digital content (e.g. text, images) to the system via a web interface and backend online service, which is used to transfer content locally to the device. During the upload phase, people are able to attribute specific dates to the content, which dictate where items appear on the timeline. The Timecard case includes doors that enable it to easily be opened up or put away; the touch screen sits behind the doors. It is stand-alone and can sit of a shelf or on display elsewhere in the home. A fanless mini-PC runs the Timecard application displayed on the screen.

Figure 3. From left to right: Children from F4 interact with historical metadata; The timeline UI view; Several families placed Timecard (closed up) on display with other things in the home.

Photos can randomly cycle in full screen mode. Touching a photo brings up a timeline view of all the images of a person chronologically; the timeline (and collated content) can then be explored via the touchscreen. In addition to personal annotations, family members can attribute metadata of historical events (scraped from Wikipedia) to the timeline to help better contextualize the life and times of an ancestor. We speculated this design choice might make the life stages of different ancestors more meaningful for future generations. A research team member that had recently experienced the loss of an elder close family member provided the content Timecard presented in this study. This included physical objects and photos that he had been bequeathed (which were later scanned), as well as photos over the years that depicted the member in different life stages.

Issues framing the rationale for this concept included: How might technologies fit within, extend or complicate families' practices of remembering and commemorating the lives of loved ones? How could these narratives be passed down and how could chronology affect these practices? We were also interested in where families perceived they would keep an artifact like this in their home and how it would be treated considering its potentially sensitive nature. For example, would enabling content to be made public shape perceptions of its placement in storytelling practices?

BackupBox is a digital store of a lifetime of Tweets posted to the micro-blogging website Twitter.com (see figure 4). Through a WIFI connection, it copies messages from the internet to a self-contained hard drive. There they are preserved for a future time when they might be drawn on as a resource to revisit the mundane and extraordinary moments of a family member's life captured by their Twitter account. We selected Twitter in contrast to other social media accounts (e.g., Facebook) as we speculated the 140 character limit for each entry would produce more concise and easily accessible entries. However, during the study participants speculated on how their own digital materials (e.g., Facebook content) might relate to—and extend beyond—the BackupBox concept, which we will discuss in detail later.

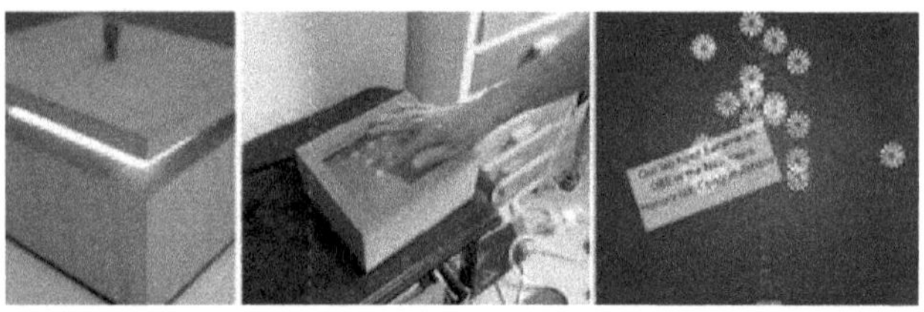

Figure 4. From left to right: The removable lid; Mom2 presses a icon to open a Tweet; UI design for an opened Tweet.

The physical form consists of a box with a removable lid, intended to conceal the growing archive of digital materials so as to not attract attention, while still inviting exploration if a family member chooses to open it up. The user interface presents Tweets in chronological order along the X axis; the Y axis indicates the time of day each Tweet was posted. The interface is navigated via a touch screen and each Tweet item in the timeline is symbolically represented as a non-descript flower; touching a specific element will present the contents of the message. A fanless mini-PC runs the BackupBox application displayed on the screen. Considering the potentially sensitive nature of some messages, we speculated this design choice could provide an additional layer of comfort by requiring people to physically invoke the content beyond just removing the lid. The Twitter content on BackupBox at the time of the study was archived from nine months of the device routinely backing up one of our research team members' Twitter account.

Issues framing the rationale for this concept included: Would the BackupBox surface tensions around the processes of passing down personal digital content that is created and stored online? Would family members perceive a physical instantiation of a digital service to be valuable? Would family members perceive social media content, such as Twitter data, to be similar or different to existing perceptions of materials to be passed down in a family archive?

Participants and Data Analysis

We recruited 8 families (F1-F8) from the southeastern region of the United Kingdom to participate in our study. This approach clearly has limitations; for example, it makes the results hard to generalize to another population of users. However, we wanted to focus on a specific group to gain a richer descriptive understanding of the space as a whole to inform what might be salient issues for future research. Two parents from each family participated (with the exception of (F5); only the mother participated). All families had at least 1 child; F2, F4, F5, F6 and F8 all had young or teenage children, all of whom participated in the study. F1, F3 and F7 had children in their early to mid-twenties which all lived outside of the parents' home; 4 out of 5 of these young adults participated. Three families (F1, F6, F7) had members representing two generations that participated (i.e. children and parents); the remainder had members representing three generations that took part in the study (i.e. children, parents and grandparents). 5 of the 8 families had experienced the loss of at least one grandparent in the past 5 years; all inherited objects from these experiences. In total 36 people participated in the study—15 children (ages ranging from 9-25), 15 parents (mid 30s-early 50s), and 6 grandparents (late 60s-late 70s). The occupations of parents ranged from schoolteacher to IT consultant to plumber; occupations of non-student children included sales attendant, law clerk, and barista; all grandparents were retired. We recruited this participant pool as they could offer a range of experiences with physical and digital objects.

All interviews were conducted at the parents' home, where family members collectively convened prior to the interview. The choice of the parents' home appeared most appropriate as they typically housed an assortment of artifacts ranging from heirlooms that had been passed down over at least one generation, to objects that were anticipated to be passed down to their children. One home visit was conducted per family and lasted between 2 to 3 hours. Visits began with parents (at times together with grandparents and/or children) giving us a tour of their home, with emphasis on where they kept heirlooms or objects that might become heirlooms. They were asked to describe stories associated with these artifacts, how they were received, who is responsible for them, and reasons for keeping them in particular spaces. We also explored if members possessed digital collections they desired to hold onto (and potentially pass down), and where they were kept. We then asked members to gather a selection of artifacts emerging in the tour and to arrange them in a central room in the home. This was to provide a rich backdrop of participants' possessions that could serve as a basis for comparison when exploring the devices.

All participating members then reconvened in the central room (often living room or kitchen). We conducted a brief discussion to clarify experiences surrounding the artifacts arranged in the room. We then began sessions using the devices. We were careful to make clear that all the devices are concepts to be used as starting points for discussion about and beyond them; family members were encouraged to envision what they would (or would not) want them to be. One device was introduced at a time, and each had a specific semi-structured session conducted with it. However, members were free to go between devices if desired. For each device, researchers offered a short narrative providing background context, illustrating how it could be interacted with in the process. These introductions were kept brief. Emphasis was placed on family members exploring the device and coming to their own interpretations of it; they were encouraged to imagine what kind of future each device projects and consider what that would be like.

At appropriate moments during sessions of exploration and discussion, we posed open-ended questions. Questions were designed to critically elicit reflections on topics including: how narratives persist with personal artifacts as they are passed down; how and when cherished objects are used; what kind of family 'image' they construct; how physical and digital archives are maintained and how the social roles of members surrounding their care may change; and where they will go when they are passed down. Members were asked to contrast their descriptions with how the device might or might not fit within their practices. We altered the order devices were introduced to families across the study. After all devices had been discussed, we asked members to take us on another tour of their home, this time considering where they would keep them in their home and why.

All interviews were audio recorded, which resulted in nearly 20 hours of recordings; photographs were additionally taken to document objects and spaces discussed during the interview. We listened to recordings and transcribed segments relevant to heirlooms and interview questions (as opposed to general chat), which were organized into themes. Meetings were held with the research team to discuss and corroborate emergent themes; we coded the textual documents using these themes. In addition, we created affinity diagrams using sticky notes to order findings across families and reveal unexpected connections.

FINDINGS

In what follows, we present several examples taken from field observations with families, which we feel capture the core themes emerging across our interviews. We refer to participants by their role — GF (Grandfather), GM (Grandmother) Mom, Dad, S (Son), D (Daughter) — followed by a number indicating the family. In the case of children, the reference includes a second number indicating the child's age. For example D4-13 would stand for a 13-years-old daughter from family 4.

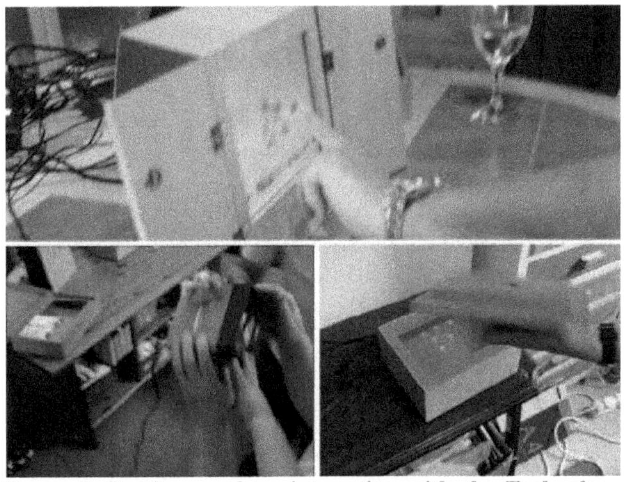

Figure 5. Family members interacting with the Technology Heirlooms during in home interview sessions.

The storage and safekeeping of family heirlooms

Interviews in families' homes revealed a diverse range of material and digital artifacts members kept and desired to pass down. In what follows, we first describe families' perceptions of their material heirlooms and their digital collections. We then detail how families drew on the devices to envision alternatives to better support their practices.

Despite representing some of their most valued possessions, families commonly described 'using' their heirlooms infrequently, at times several years lapsing in between these instances. It was also common for families to clearly differentiate heirlooms from other domestic objects: "*We don't use them like you'd use a* [television] *remote. ...Their purpose is something bigger.*" (Mom3). Instead, practices surrounding heirlooms were bound up with having them present and ensuring their safekeeping. Dad1 describes an album containing photos and memorabilia of his family's ancestors: "*we rarely go back to them. ...it's having that peace of mind that they're there* [motioning to bookshelf] *and we'll see to it that they're there until it's time for my kids to take them.*"

Safekeeping was understood as occurring across generations and was bound up with the passing on of items. In some cases, older members preemptively passed down heirlooms to ensure their transfer to the next generation:

"*...making sure* [they] *make it through time, that feels as important as the things themselves. ...telling my daughter what they mean, the people they represent, while she has them, that's going to help them last*" (GM5). Similar to their material heirlooms, families sought to safeguard treasured digital collections for future generations. These included things such as: digital photos, videos, documents, and to some extent, artworks and music.

Various tensions were bound up with the notion of safeguarding digital collections, however, especially relating to practices surrounding their backing up. For example, it was a common strategy for families to use external hard drives to back up their digital collections. However, in some cases the extra task (and hassle) of updating a secondary storage location led to the external hard drive being routinely neglected. In others, families described a general distrust over the longevity of their personal computers, which led them to create extensive backups on physical media (e.g., CDs or DVDs). Tensions also emerged with this approach, namely due to doubts over how long these media would last and the physical space their storage required. Other concerns included the potential to lose the physical media: "*the problem with CDs is if we lose one ... we'd lose a whole a chapter of the kids growing up*" (Dad8); as well as concerns that the aesthetics of physical media failed to convey the preciousness of the content. As Mom7 put it: "*they deserve better than that.*"

The use of online services to store digital family collections is an alternative to creating local backups, and members from all families reported using photo sharing services (e.g. Facebook, Flickr) or email to share select family photos with specific people to varying extents. However, these services were viewed as supporting *sharing* rather than the *safekeeping* of sentimental content: "*We put things online to share them, not to preserve them. ...all our intimate* [digital] *memories, we want to know where they are, keep them in order. ...the thought of them being where someone could get at them. That makes us uneasy*" (Dad6). Parents in two families (F4, F7) maintained accounts through the cloud storage service dropbox.com, and similar concerns also emerged: "*I'll put things for my work or my music in dropbox, but I wouldn't put anything too valuable to us there. What if our account was hacked or deleted? ...it feels too risky*" (Dad7). When possible, we probed teenagers' perceptions of storing content online. They typically reported fewer immediate reservations about hosting personal content online, but tended to react strongly against integrating their own digital content into family collections.

Unexpectedly, some families drew on the physical forms of Timecard and, especially, BackupBox to propose alternatives that might help alleviate some of tensions mentioned above. While these ideas varied, they were united insofar as they proposed that a storage system distributed among people was an appropriate way to preserve familial content. Consider Dad4's reflection: "*my brother, my wife's brother. ...they would be the guardian of our kids if we passed away. We'd do the same for them. ...it makes sense that they could guard our* [digital] *things and we could do the same. ...So if one of our homes burned down or our thing* [i.e. device] *died, there'd still be one or two copies out there, like at my brother's or at Mum's place. Same would go for them.*"

Dad4's reflection captures how some families drew on the devices to propose potential uses of technology that might better support their desires to safely preserve precious digital archives over time.

Embodied digital forms: settling in and setting the tone

The embodiment of digital content in physical forms conveyed through our devices provoked discussions across home visits. Below we detail how families saw ways in which physical properties might enable them to treat, relate to and live with sentimental digital content.

A primary theme across interviews centered on how capturing digital family archives in forms distinct from the computer might both project and engender a deeper sense of care for these materials: "*Putting our family photos and videos and all in a different folder* [on our computer] *doesn't do them justice. There is so much on* [our computer] *that we won't give a toss about in a year. ...our photos, videos, that's the bit that matters.* ......[The devices] *get away from all the clutter. ...they show you care and makes you want to care for them, tend to them*" (Mom3). GM5 similarly noted, "*there's something about being able to say 'what's important, it's all in here' and pick it up, give it to someone or keep it in a special place that suits it.*" Other families speculated on potential benefits of storing digital content in domestic spaces populated by their treasured material things. For example, when considering where the Digital Slide Viewer would be stored in their home, F1 selected a small living room cupboard that housed several sentimental items: "*...having it packed up next to the Chinese boards and albums and medals. ... seeing it age with them, the things we'll always have. It feels right. ...we want to hold onto our* [digital] *family photos like those things I suppose. Putting it there makes it feel like it's findings its place. ..with our things, in our home*" (Mom1).

Four of the eight families (F3, F5, F6, F8) we interviewed possessed only a single computer, all of which were desktops set up in home office or kitchen locations. These families in particular reflected on how moving their sentimental digital archives to other domestic places could better prime interactions with them: "*we have this chest. ...It has little trinkets and bits and bobs that we've saved over the years, some old stuff from me Mum. ...this is where it* [Digital Slide Viewer] *should go. Opening* [the chest], *seeing those things and bringing out the* [digital] *slide box, that'd be a more natural way of coming to them* [photos] *than booting up the computer*" (Dad6). Mom6 then continued: "*We've got this habit about the chest. When we get into it, it sets a tone. It's time to take a moment and look through them. ...having it* [Digital Slide Viewer] *in the chest, it'd blend right in. ...with what we're already doing and the things that've always been there.*" Mom8 contrasts Timecard's location in her living room with the home office-based computer: "*I don't walk by our computer in the office and think of the memories that're on it. ...This feels somewhere in between. ...it'd remind me of the memories in there, but if it's closed up, we could walk past it and leave it at that. ...That makes it feel like a more complete part of our life.*"

Additionally, the vintage form factor of the Digital Slide Viewer itself appeared to help set the tone for reminiscing about the past. Members of several families recognized its form, which led to discussions about their lives when they last used one. After one such discussion with her son and granddaughter, GM2 noted: "*seeing something familiar from the past, it triggers all these memories and associations I haven't thought about in a while. ...it feels like a real way of starting to get back to the past and remember it, with the photos and all.*" Often younger members were actively included in these discussions as the device was passed around; in some cases, they initiated discussions themselves: "D4-13: *Mummy you had one of these. Is this what you used to look at pictures?* M4: *Yes I did. It was* [grandmother's], *she can tell you where she got it from.*"

Collectively, this sample of reflections helps illustrate how giving digital collections physical properties might better support the dynamics of living with them over time, from intentional engagement to simply letting them persist among other significant domestic possessions and spaces.

Curating, Integrating and Changing Roles

Families adopted several practices to construct a meaningful whole out of collections of heterogeneous artifacts they desired to pass down. In what follows, we provide an overview of these practices, before detailing how Timecard in particular provoked discussions about potential benefits and complications technology might present in this context.

A common practice we observed across families was the use of notes and other materials to explicitly detail the history of family artifacts to preserve their meanings. These instances ranged from Dad2's collection of his great grandfather's medals and other artifacts from World War One, to Mom6's scrapbook owing to her own life as well as to several departed ancestors. Across these examples, family members included short notes and, at times, materials detailing local and historical events occurring when specific artifacts were in use to help communicate their significance to future generations.

It was also common for families to consciously prune collections of important physical materials to avoid creating an archive of undesirable size and scale, and to underpin a sense of coherence. We found both parents and grandparents engaged in this practice and while at times difficult, it was considered an essential part of ensuring cherished familial artifacts made it to the next generation.

However, the constraints families imposed on their material archives did not always translate to their digital collections. Mom5 contrasts her family's physical photo albums with their digital collections: "*With the* [physical] *albums we have to decide what to put in there and what's not quite worth it. ...On our computer they pile up. We have so many photos on there now and we keep taking more. ...It starts to feel endless, really.*" In two cases (F5, F6), families elected to print out physical copies of digital photos and integrate them into physical albums, to make them easier to manage and pass down. However, when posed with the question of how (or if) families would wish to cull their digital collections for the future, most members were ambivalent.

While archives of material things supported heterogeneity in a way that digital archives did not, they were typically associated with one branch of a family. Discussions of Timecard highlighted that having a place to collate content from multiple sources would also be desirable: "*...thinking about when my Dad passed away. I have some digital photos of him and my sister does, and we both have some of his things. ...If we were able to put some of them* [digital things] *together, when we're feeling up to it, that would be meaningful. ...We could have something celebrating his life, and us with him*" (Dad7). Mom1 speculated on the potential benefits of distributed curation of sensitive digital materials over time: "*having a place where my brother could add an event in one of our parent's lives and I could leave it for a while, and then add something. ...let things come out slowly over time, that would be valuable. ...it would create a new record of our family.*"

Digital archives were also noted for supporting collaboration within nuclear families. However, this also raised concerns. Some families perceived that this could complicate meaning: "*If everyone is putting in things like moments in history or notes about a person, it's going to make things confusing. There has to be some kind of quality control*" (Dad1). Timecard triggered other families to consider how social roles of members would be supported: "*We* [parents] *take most of the responsibility for preserving things about our parents' lives and our lives with the kids. ...I like how we could all see it and add to it. That is useful for everyone. But we* [parents] *need to be able to make sure it doesn't become a mess*" (Mom6).

In some cases Timecard triggered intergenerational discussions among living family members in the room about past experiences and family history. For example, after interacting with a metadata tag relating to the date of India's independence (15 August 1947), D4-13 felt prompted to ask her Grandmother about her life during this time period. After describing what her life was like as a young girl then, GM4 reflected on what she remembered of her father immediately following World War II. At the conclusion of GM4's story, Dad4 remarked: "*well, that's a bit of our family history I haven't heard. I wish we could've recorded* [it] *in this box* [Timecard], *right then and there.*" Dad4 highlights the potential value of capturing emergent conversations about family members' own lives; this opens a space to consider how such records could make interactions with the device richer in the future.

However, some discussion emerged about how perceptions of past experiences can shift over time and how technology could pose challenges: "*Even if we remember things from the past the same, the way we feel about them can change. ...like if a photo or summit later reminds us of a falling out we had with a relative. We chuck it in the bin to be done with it. ...So if I put something in there* [motioning to Timecard], *I should also be able to take it out*" (S3-25). His remarks represent discussions that emerged with the Timecard and the Digital Slide Viewer: the need to take things out of digital archives as fluidly as they are put in.

Tensions over new digital materials in the family archive

Our aim with Backup Box was to provoke family members to consider the potential role of social networking data, such as Twitter updates, within family archives. Backup Box was highly contentious across families. Several related kinds of criticism emerged, as we describe.

Several families possessed diaries written by ancestors now considered important parts of the family archive. These diaries tended to contain mundane information (e.g., a list of household chores completed on any given day) with a sprinkling of extraordinary events (e.g., marriage of family member, birth of child). When asked to speculate on similarities and differences among the diaries and Backup Box, family members drew strong distinctions. Dad7's perception of the difference between his father's diaries and social media content is exemplary of members of several families' sentiments: "*when I open one of his diaries and see what he wrote, I know he sat down and thought for a moment, and that feels significant. ...with stuff like Twitter, people rattle things off, sometimes without thinking ...the intention is different and I suppose that makes a huge difference.*"

Backup Box also raised issues over the potentially vast amounts of social networking content other family members would have to reconcile with. D3-22 prospectively considered what it would be like to receive her brother's social networking archive: "*He posts stuff to Twitter and Facebook literally all of the time. I can't imagine how many updates there would be for one or two years, let alone a decade. How would we deal with that?*" Other participants speculated on how years worth of Twitter data could trap a small amount of meaningful insights from a person's life within a sea of trivial entries, potentially making it difficult to explore or let go of: "*If I got, say, Mum's Twitter. I'm sure there'd be some stuff I'd enjoy seeing, but I'd have no idea how to find it. ...I'd probably keep it, but not know what to do*" (D1-21).

When D3-22 concluded reflecting on her brother's social media content (mentioned above), she noted: "*And it's so much about him, but not all that much about us. ...or our family.*" This statement captures deeper concerns echoed by members of several families: that social media content is often targeted at different audiences, which could make its place in the family archive controversial. Mom2 describes how this quality could lead to undesirable experiences: "*online it's easy to act* [in] *very different ways to different people. Even I confess to that, and I wouldn't exactly want other people to know about this. ...it feels a little scary that we could learn something about someone that maybe we weren't supposed to know, or didn't want to.*" Teenagers in the families we interviewed typically were frequent users of social networking services, and also reacted against the inclusion of their content in the family archive. D6-17 reflects on her personal social media content: "*I could see looking back on it myself, but it would be weird if other people in my family used it to think about me. I'd rather make myself something that would go in it. ...something that'd show my family something special about me.*"

Related concerns also emerged around how a device like BackupBox could cause family members to self-censor the social networking content they posted, or paralyze these practices completely. Some families proposed ways to work around these tensions, such as using a special hash tag or a specific application to send updates only to Backup Box.

DISCUSSION AND DESIGN CONSIDERATIONS

It is clear physical and digital objects hold significant places in families' lives, and that these are envisaged as retaining this significance over time and across generations. A key contribution of our study is to surface insights on how technology might open up new opportunities for passing down and inheriting digital materials, as well as new complications that they could introduce. Our findings reveal a range of ways families desired to treat and live with their significant digital materials. Several of these cases were characterized by their desires to treat these archives differently, integrate them into more appropriate places in the home, and tend to their care and safety. Other instances suggested how technology might better support social practices of creating more cohesive sets of materials to be passed down, creating archives from multiple branches of the family, and documenting conversations that emerge around them. The devices also raise a range of potential consequences that could emerge if careful consideration is not given to new technological interventions. In what follows we present several research and design considerations for the HCI community that emerged from the study.

Designing technologies to be put away— Similar to material heirlooms, participants perceived value in supporting the dynamics of living with treasured digital collections, from knowing their location, to tending to their well being, to actively interacting with them. That the physical forms, material qualities and affordances of our devices enabled them to be packaged away, discretely displayed, or actively explored seemed to resonate with families and some of their existing rituals, practices and values. Reforming digital materials in this way allows them to fit into the wider ecology of archived materials in the home and situates them within a familiar context of artifact-mediated reflecting, remembering and learning about the past. Beyond designing explicitly for 'use', this consideration emphasizes the aesthetics of integrating treasured digital materials into environments as a whole over time, a notion parallel to 'slow technology' [11]. Collectively, these findings suggest that to support more sensitive and nuanced engagement with cherished *digital* familial content requires the artful design of technologies that can be put away, drawn on alongside others, and which evoke rich experiences when interacted with. This is more complex than it sounds; comments about the fractious intrusions of waiting for machines to 'boot up' are indicative of this.

Supporting the moral work of safeguarding—Notions of the value of 'deep storage' [14], redolent in our interviews, highlight clear unresolved tensions between digital and physical materials. For example, the encasing of our devices may last 100 years (or longer), while their technological components may last for only 5 years. This highlights the need to design new storage systems that are extremely robust and can handle sporadic use. There are opportunities to explore combined advances in solid-state storage and low power consumption. Although even with hardware innovation it is hard to imagine end users not having to engage with some degree of archive maintenance, as such advances will not resolve significant issues of evolving file format standards and ensuing compatibility issues. We suggest the ritual work of preservation may accommodate issues of safeguarding. Several instances from our findings suggest that tending to material heirlooms is itself a significant act: rituals of care could therefore be appropriated as opportunities for the physical maintenance and updating of these technologies.

While the Cloud offers a technical solution to problems of storage, our findings reveal that knowing *where* one's sensitive digital materials are located is bound to the sense that one is keeping them safe. 'Storing' these kinds of sensitive materials in online places raised concerns, especially in terms of ceding the higher-level social and moral work of safekeeping to a third party service. An approach to safeguarding raised by participants themselves, which lends particularly well to digital technologies (as opposed to physical possessions), is the distribution of storage devices and the (redundant) copying of familial archives across multiple homes and branched families. This would leverage the value of existing social-familial networks and could help alleviate immediate concerns over the loss of cherished content, while supporting the higher-level work of safekeeping content in morally and socially appropriate ways.

Enabling multiple roles in the archive—The solution pointed to above would need to be nuanced, however. One of the largest issues our devices provoked families to consider was the various roles members play in maintaining family archives, and how they would be supported in these roles by future technologies. From contributing new materials, to curating collections (organizing and editing etc.), family members play important roles in sustaining the family archive [15]. So while technologies might open up opportunities for mirroring archives across homes, richer combinations would need to be carefully considered.

Families suggested Timecard's indirect, distributed nature could create an opportunity for mapping family history "slowly over time". In other cases it seemed to open the opportunity to support storytelling and the recording of family history. Both of these opportunities potentially illustrate how a digital artifact from the past might accrue value through repeated interaction, and resonate with prior research [8, 24] suggesting the prospect of integrating multiple family perspectives as beneficial.

However, it was clear that family members' approaches to archiving were expected to differ, and this raised concerns over how 'quality control' could be upheld. These issues raise significant questions for future research. How does the architecture of new technology reinforce the moral accountability of access to the content? Who has the right to delete or edit entries? How is this accountability represented in the system? What is the communicative structure that envelops the archive and provision of material within it, and how is this negotiated through technology? Better understanding these concerns seems a crucial part of designing new systems to support the persistence of a family's digital legacy across generations. Research proposing implications for 'forgetting' as a feature in system design [e.g., 1] could be leveraged in future explorations, as could emerging research on multi-lifespan design [7].

Enabling multiple representations in the archive—While previous research suggested people desired to pass down their social networking content to other family members [19], families across our study reacted strongly against having a technology like the BackupBox. In particular, these instances highlighted tensions around integrating social networking content from members within the collective family archive. Participants made key distinctions between the thoughtful recording of one's life believed to be reflected in their ancestors' diaries, and their own practices of posting less mindful social networking content targeted at multiple audiences, often outside of the family. These reactions surfaced clear boundaries members had for how they wanted to author their presentation of self within the family archive. Prior work has explored how technology could productively support members in presenting different representations of their selves to each other through novel tools for curating family photo collections [4]. While there are clear differences between curated photos and social networking data, this work could be leveraged to further explore how different aspects of unique social bonds between family members could be preserved, while also leaving space for authorship of one's self image in the family archive as a whole.

CONCLUSION

We designed three devices aimed at provoking families to consider how technology might fit within their practices of inheriting, living with and passing down digital collections in the future. Families' reactions revealed several ways digital materials fall short of supporting the values and practices they associated with physical heirlooms, and highlighted new opportunities for design. While researching in this space is inherently challenging, our methodology provided a way to engage family members in confronting potential benefits and tensions projected by our devices and draw on their own experiences to make sense of possible futures—and envision ideas beyond them. These reactions provided salient points to consider as people increasingly acquire cherished digital collections that they may desire to pass down alongside material heirlooms. Based on these findings we proposed *designing technologies to be put away, supporting the moral work of safeguarding, enabling multiple roles*, and *enabling multiple representations in the archive* as considerations for future HCI research and practice. Importantly, our devices did not explicitly explore how to address the challenges that the sheer size and scale of meaningful digital content pose as families increasingly amass larger archives. Designing new forms and ways of interacting with massive archives of sentimental materials marks a clear area for future research. Ultimately, we hope this study will inspire future research into how technologies can better support the range of experiences that come with inheriting, living with and passing down treasured digital possessions over time and across generations.

ACKNOWLEDGMENTS

We thank Alex Taylor and Mike Massimi for their thoughts on this paper, as well as Phil Gosset, Tim Regan, and Mark Selby for their help on this project.

REFERENCES

1. Bannon, L. 2006. Forgetting as a feature, not a bug: the duality of memory and implications for ubiquitous computing. *CoDesign*, Vol. 2, 1, 3-15.
2. Belk, R. 1990. The Role of Possessions in Constructing and Maintaining a Sense of Past. *Advances in Consumer Research*, 17, 669-676.
3. Dunne, T., Raby, F. 2001. *Design Noir: The Secret Life of Electronic Objects*. Birkhauser.
4. Durrant, A., Taylor, A., Frohlich, D., Sellen, A., Uzzell, D. 2009. Photo Displays and Intergenerational Relationships in the Family Home. *Proc. of BCS HCI '09*, 10-19.
5. Fallman, D. 2003. Design-oriented human-computer interaction. In *Proc. Of CHI '03*, 225-232.
6. Finch, J., Mason, J. 2000. *Passing On: Kinship & Inheritance in England.* Routledge.
7. Friedman, B., Nathan, L. 2010. Multi-lifespan Information System Design: A Research Initiative for the HCI Community. *Proc. of CHI '10*, 2243-2246
8. Frohlich, D., Murphy, R. 2000. The Memory Box. *Personal Ubiquitous Comput.* 4, 4, 238-240.
9. Gaver, B., Martin, H. Alternatives: Exploring Information Appliances through Conceptual Design Proposals. In *Proc.of CHI '00*, 2000, 209-216.
10. Hallam, E., Hockey, J. 2001. *Death, Memory and Material Culture.* Oxford: Berg.
11. Hallnas, L., Redstrom, J. 2001. Slow Technology: Designing for Reflection. *Personal Ubiquit. Comput. 5,* 201-212.
12. Hutchinson, H. et al. 2003. Technology probes: inspiring design for and with families. *Proc. of CHI '03*, 17-24.
13. Kaye, J. et al. 2006. To have and to hold: exploring the personal archive. *Proc. of CHI '06*, 275-284.
14. Kirk, D., Sellen, A. 2010. On human remains: Value and practice in the home archiving of cherished objects. In *ACM Trans. Comput. –Hum. Interact.* 17, 3, 10.
15. Kirk, D. Izadi, S., Sellen, A., et al. 2010. Opening up the family archive. *Proc. of CSCW '10*, 261-270.
16. Massimi, M., Baecker, R. 2010. A Death in the Family: Opportunities for Designing Technologies for the Bereaved. *Proc. of CHI '10*, 1821-1830.
17. Miller, D., Parrot, F. 2009. Loss and Material Culture in South London. *J. of R. Anthro. Inst.*, Vol. 15, 3, 502-519.
18. .Net Gadgeteer. http://research.microsoft.com/en-us/projects/gadgeteer/
19. Odom, W., Harper, R., Sellen, A., Kirk, D., Banks, R. 2010. Passing on and putting to rest: Understanding bereavement in the context of interactive technologies. *Proc. of CHI '10*, 1831-1840.
20. Odom, W., Pierce, J., Stolterman, E., Blevis, E. 2009. Understanding why we preserve some things and discard others in the context of interaction design. *Proc. of CHI '09*, 1053-1062.
21. Petrelli, D., Villar, N., Kalnikaite, V., Dib, L., Whittaker, S. 2010. FM radio: family interplay with sonic mementos. *Proc. Of CHI '10*, 2371-2380.
22. Schön, D., Bennet, J. 1996. Reflective Conversation with Materials. *Bringing Design to Software*, 171-189.
23. Sengers, P., Boehner, K., David, S., Kaye, J. 2005. Reflective design. *Proc. of CC '05*, 49-58.
24. Stevens, M, Abowd, G., Truong, K., Vollmer, F. 2003. Getting into the Living Memory Box: Family archives and holistic design. *Personal Ubiquitous Comput*, 7, 210-216.

Digitality and Materiality of New Media: Online TV Watching in China

Qi Wang, Xianghua Ding, Tun Lu and Ning Gu
School of Computer Science
Fudan University
Shanghai 201203, China
{qi_wang, dingx, lutun, ninggu}@fudan.edu.cn

ABSTRACT
This paper examines issues of digitality and materiality of new media, grounded in a study of online TV watching in China. Particularly, by looking at how people make choices and decisions regarding TV watching in everyday life, we highlight material and digital properties of new media TV, and how they support and condition actions and interactions around them. The study illustrates that materiality and digitality are complementary, instead of one substituting the other, and are highly intertwined in the hybrid media environment around which meaningful experiences are conditioned and produced. It also suggests that an analytic distinction between materiality and digitality is fruitful in unpacking the complex relations between media technologies and social experiences.

Author Keywords
TV; materiality; digitality; new media; new media TV; online TV.

ACM Classification Keywords
H5.m. Information interfaces and presentation (e.g., HCI): Miscellaneous.

General Terms
Design; Human Factors.

INTRODUCTION
Today, television (TV) and computing are co-evolving. On the one hand, TV is increasingly computerized [3], as manifested in new TV products enhanced by computing capabilities (e.g. recording, archiving, rewinding, pausing and fast forwarding), such as Tivo and Sky+. On the other hand, computers and the Internet have also become a new platform for TV watching. Not only can people now download movies or TV shows from the Internet, but they can also watch them on the fly through Internet TV services such as Hulu and Google TV and other general video sharing websites such as YouTube. As such, TV broadcasting is made possible not just through TV networks, but also through computer networks; not just through traditional TV sets, but also through new computing devices, including laptops, iPads, and cell phones. For convenience, we refer to the former as computerized TV and the latter as new media TV, as a way to distinguish them from old or traditional TV.

This paper focuses on issues of new media TV in use. So far, much of the work on TV in HCI has been focused on computerized TV [3, 14, 22], but little attention has been paid to new media TV. Although computerized TV and new media TV share similar characteristics such as increased flexibility in terms of when and how to watch, they are different mainly in their material properties such as infrastructure, screen size, mobility, and image and sound effects. For the former, although it has been enhanced by computing capabilities, its physical form still remains the same and it is still largely placed within the home environment. As for the latter, TV has been moved to more universal computing platforms, ranging from cell phones to desktops with a variety of physical shapes, sizes, and mobility. It also comes with new computing and communicating capabilities such as searching, sharing, commenting, etc.

How does the new platform of computer and the Internet shape practices and meanings of TV watching? To answer this question, we conducted an empirical study of new media TV watching in China. China provides an interesting site for this investigation. In China, while the development and adoption of computerized TV is still in its infancy (mainly in the form of IPTV. TV recording technologies such as PVR and DVR have made little presence in China's TV market), new media TV has been on a rapid rise in recent years. According to CNNIC's (China Internet Network Information Center) report, about 62.1% of Chinese netizens (totally 301 million) watch TV online (data collected prior to July 2011). It is the 7th most popular network service after search engine (79.6%), instant messaging (79.4%), online music (78.7%), online news (74.7%), blogging (65.5%) and online gaming (64.2%) [6]. Overall, there are two kinds of new media TV in China, one being online video streaming platforms such as PPTV, PPS, and Xunlei[1] and the other video sharing websites focusing on short and original video clips such as Youku and Tudou[2].

A close look at new media TV in use in China, particularly through the choices and decisions people make, highlights the material and digital properties of old and new media, and their roles in shaping TV watching experiences. Here, we use digitality to refer to capabilities and effects brought by digitalization or when things are turned into bits and bytes. For example, with digitalization, now we can compress huge amount of data including text, video and audio to a high degree, access it easily, transfer it remotely, and communicate with others instantly. Materiality is, then, used to refer to capabilities and effects resulted from the more tactile physical and material properties, such as portability, density, and scarcity. When turning to an "information society", digitality is often framed as substituting or replacing materiality, as implicated in phrases such as "substitution of bits for atoms" or "atoms to bits" (e.g. [12]). However, digitality, no matter how powerful it is, always relies and is conditioned upon some physical materials, as argued by Dourish and Mazmanian, "*even in this information-rich environment, the physical world persistently makes itself felt*" [11]. We found similar themes of materiality in shaping old and new media experiences in our study, and will discuss how digitality and materiality work together in shaping TV watching experiences.

Our work draws on and extends previous discussions on hybridity between digital and physical in support of actions and interactions (e.g. [8, 9, 19]). Lindtner et al., for example, use hybrid cultural ecology to highlight the ways in which physical and digital spaces, as well as socio-economical environments, are combined to form an environment in which collaborations around gaming occur [19]. Jenkins's notion of media convergence concerns the flow of content and the migratory behavior of audiences across multiple media platforms [15]. On the design front, Crabtree and Rodden and others have explored how to incorporate physical and digital elements to create new interactive experiences [4, 8, 17]. We take their work further by focusing on digitality and materiality as two aspects of the same thing, rather than two different environments or artifacts. By analytically distinguishing between them, we hope to unpack the complex relationships between media technologies and social experiences.

In what follows, we first present a brief literature review of TV studies and describe the research site and methods used for the study. We then describe digital and material characteristics of new media TV, and illustrate how they condition various practices around it. After that, we discuss the change of old TV in use in relation to the new media TV, and how social media is employed in TV watching experiences, both old and new. We conclude by showing how conceptualizations of materiality and digitality help to unpack the complex relationships between digital characteristics, material properties and social practices.

[1] PPTV (www.pptv.com), PPS (www.pps.tv) and Xunlei Kankan (www.xunlei.com)

[2] Youku (www.youku.com) and Tudou (www.tudou.com)

LITERATURE REVIEW

TV has arguably played a crucial role in contemporary socio-cultural life. While some portray TV watching as a negative social force [20, 21], others highlight the more positive aspects of TV [1, 13, 23, 27]. Particularly, TV has long been found to be central in providing resources for collective self-expressions and the production of social and cultural identities [1, 23, 27]. Silverstone, for example, suggested, "*And equally it is clear how in the forms of television, in the structures of its schedules, in the patterns of the media calendar and in the array of channel choice, the medium provides yet another route into consumer culture, offering itself as an object of choice to a more or less active/passive spectator.*" [23]. Studies of old TV also find that TV can radically structure our daily schedules. Gauntlett and Hill, for example, show how TV works for coordination of family routines and helps to bind and create social order [13]. This way, old TV, relevant TV networks, and timetables have all become part of everyday infrastructures and media, through which our everyday lives are organized, and cultural identities are expressed.

TV started to attract attention from the field of HCI when it became increasingly computerized (e.g. [3, 14, 22]). These studies highlight the new freedom provided by computing technologies. Irani et al. use "plasticity" to describe the flexibility and openness within the patterns of television viewing brought about by digital technologies such as set-top boxes, digital video recorders, and on demand services [14]. Barkhuus and Brown also emphasize that the use of new recording technologies such as PVR increases the choices and flexibility of TV watching, which in turn has changed TV watching from a passive to a more active activity [3]. While these studies have revealed increased choices and flexibility with computerized TV, the physical form and location of TV sets still largely remain the same. As often installed and placed in the home environment, TV is usually examined in relation to domesticity [3, 14, 22].

On the new media front, the work that most closely resembles our own is the research on online video sites and the role of commenting and chatting. Barkhuus studied web-based video watching (either downloaded or streaming), and found the number of viewers among US college students who use traditional TV sets is decreasing, and they are more likely to choose online media to watch when available [2]. By researching youth involvement on YouTube, Lange discovered the practice of sharing and commenting helps to create, maintain and develop social networks [18]. He describes how the way users manipulate media indicates different types of social relationships.

Weisz et al. emphasize that online watching becomes more active, social and engaging when combining chatting and watching together, and found chatting can lead to a positive influence on relationships, despite possible distraction from dedicated watching [26].

RESEARCH SITES AND METHODS

This study was primarily based on PPTV, the top online TV platform in China. However, we also covered the use of other popular online TV platforms including PPS, Youku and Tudou. PPTV, with over 200 million subscribers, is the first platform worldwide that has more than 8 million audience members online simultaneously. Users can either download its client, or use its website to watch TV. It provides both movies and TV shows, covers shows from China as well as from abroad, and supports both recorded videos and live TV broadcasts. These different video resources are organized based on genres and types, as well as locations of their productions (e.g. American dramas, Korean entertainment shows, Japanese animation movies, etc.). On its front page, it recommends and presents the most recent and popular shows, but users can also search to find particular shows to watch. They can also comment and rate shows on PPTV.

We obtained and analyzed part of PPTV log data (Jul/26/2011-Aug/1/2011). Each record of the log contains information of user ID, IP address, show name, genre, as well as time consumption. We statistically analyzed the data to understand the overall distribution of PPTV users, especially its geographical distribution.

We also conducted in-depth interviews with a total of 17 PPTV users (11 male and 6 female). PPTV provided a list of 20 people who had called the PPTV customer service and left their contact information, and 7 were willing to be interviewed. We then used snowball-sampling method to recruit 10 other informants starting with our own social circles who had watched PPTV. Our informants were of diverse backgrounds such as students, blue-collar workers, storeowners, foreign IT company employees, and government employees. They also came from different parts of the country including Beijing, Shanghai, Shandong, Guangdong, Guangxi, Hubei, etc. Their age varied between 20 and 35, representing the age range of the main new media TV users in China. Our interviews were semi-structured, covering details of their recent TV watching experiences with both old and new media TV (e.g. what, where, how, and with whom TV was watched), as well as their socialization and commenting practices around TV watching. All interviews were conducted in Chinese over the phone, recorded under their permission, and later transcribed. Besides interviews, we also collected data from Sina Weibo[3] on the subject of online TV watching. The Weibo data (also in Chinese) was mostly collected by searching the keywords "PPTV" and names of some of the most popular shows broadcasted on PPTV (e.g. "Super Girl").

We then applied a grounded theoretical approach for the analysis of the data [24]. We started analysis while the data was being collected. Through open and axis coding of the interview and Weibo transcripts, themes started to emerge. We then iteratively posed more questions around these themes in later interviews. When emerged themes started to repeat themselves, we stopped the data collection process. In this paper, we will use representative individual quotes to illustrate our points. All of the names used are pseudonyms, and relevant quotes were later translated for this paper.

CHARACTERISTICS OF NEW MEDIA TV

More freedom with digitalization

Similar to previous findings of computerized TV [3, 13], we also found people had obtained a lot more freedom from new media TV, especially in terms of time. One direct consequence is that TV schedules are no longer effective in structuring people's daily activities anymore as audiences can now tailor watching based on their own schedules. One of our informants Zheng described a typical situation, "*When I missed something, I would take a look at PPTV (to see whether they have it online).*" Actually, the fixed schedule was seen as the main obstacle for people to watch live broadcasts, especially for those who had very unpredictable schedules. Shilie, a celebrity event planner, described, "*The time is too rigid. I think it is because of my work. Won't you feel bad that you watch two episodes today, and then you have to work and won't have time to follow it up the next day? So I just don't do it.*" Almost all our informants reported that they would not be constrained by TV schedules anymore. So watching has also become decoupled from show broadcasting with new media TV, as with TV recording technologies such as PVR and VCR [3, 13].

We further identified several digital characteristics of the new media, around which more freedom in terms of choices and control were resulted. The first is the richness of content. Not only can they find almost all shows of old TV now on new media TV, but also they can even find content that was not previously available there. Yaya commented, "*I feel TV is too limited now, compared to the Internet. It is too limited in terms what you can watch.*" Particularly, new media TV provides shows that are unavailable through China's current TV network. Several of them reported that they used the new media TV just to watch shows from Hong Kong, Korea, Japan, and U.S.. The second characteristic of new media TV is the freedom in terms of when, how and where to watch. With new media TV, they now can watch TV based on their own daily schedules, can easily skip scenes, rewind, pause, and fast forward, and can take it to other places beyond home such as offices, labs,

[3] Sina Weibo (www.weibo.com) is the biggest microblogging website in China.

and coffee houses. Finally, the main advantage of new media TV is its capability to easily integrate with other resources and connect one with other people through computing and communication functions such as searching, IM, social network sites and microblogging. For example, Shilie commented, *"If you watch it online, you can chat at the same time while watching... for example, especially for those live and competitive kinds of shows, you can discuss them with your friends"*. So it is through these characteristics of the new media, including richness of content, more freedom, more control, as well as the new computing and communication enhancement that have made new media TV a preferred alternative for these young audiences.

...but conditioned upon infrastructural and other materiality

While new media TV provides more freedom for TV watching, as similarly shown in studies of computerized TV (e.g.[3]), what make them different are their material aspects, including the underlying infrastructures upon which they are based. Computerized TV is still largely based on a dedicated TV broadcasting infrastructure, either cable or satellite; whereas new media TV is based on a more general infrastructure - the Internet. Figure 1 shows the geographical distribution of PPTV users in China based on the log analysis. The deep grey areas are provinces with the Internet population above 34.3% [7], and they align well with the black circles indicating PPTV population above 4‰. It suggests that Internet penetration or the Internet infrastructure is probably the most important factor in shaping PPTV adoption. It also means, access and availability of new media TV deeply relies upon the Internet infrastructure, which, according to the figure, is very unevenly distributed.

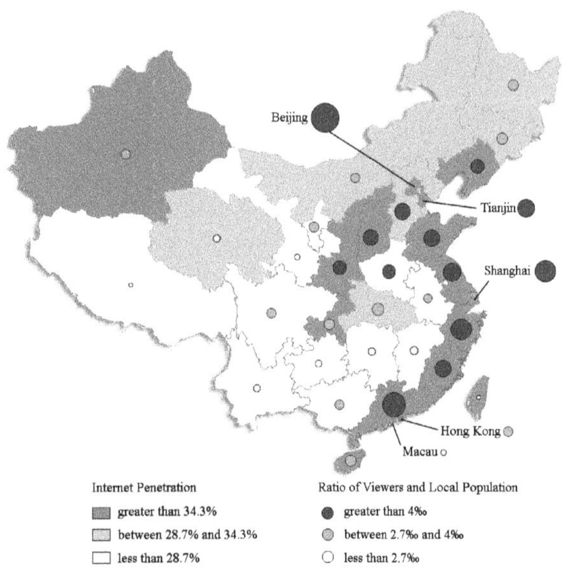

Figure 1. PPTV Viewer Distribution Map in China

Besides accessibility, new media TV watching experience is also conditioned on infrastructural resources available such as bandwidth. Like other high demand Internet applications [25], we found infrastructural properties were constantly made visible through new media TV. Zhan was a storeowner, and explained that he could only watch TV when there was not much Internet traffic, *"um...the net speed is bad because it is shared by several households. We have (only) 2 mega byte bandwidth. So it is always 'ka' (卡, not smooth) when you watch movies online. Usually I will pick the time when there are not so many people using the net to watch movies online, and it will be much better."* Yaya described she would only watch online TV at home, not school, because *"um...the net speed in school is not good enough. It is 'ka' sometimes, not as good as that at home."* Zhaogan similarly mentioned his watching behavior was conditioned on Internet connections, *"usually, I don't use it (PPTV) much when I am in school. Basically, if I do use it, it will be with the cable in the Guanghua building because the wireless is sort of (slow)."* Wan described how he chose what to watch based on network conditions, *"The wireless installation is not so good here, and the connection is sort of slow, so I won't watch long videos when I am outside. Because it takes long time to buffer and I can't stand, I only watch short ones"*. Through these ways, infrastructures have shaped when, where, and what new media TV is watched. It suggests that while new media TV provides more freedom, it doesn't mean people can now watch TV "anytime and anywhere". As with other new media applications such as online gaming, online TV watching is also necessarily linked to an infrastructure.

Besides infrastructure, the use of new media TV is also conditioned on other aspects of materiality, such as portability, screen size, computer power and memory, image quality, and others. We found, in some occasions, these material conditions also shaped how, when, where and what to watch, and also whether they would choose old or new media TV to watch, an issue we will elaborate more in the subsequent sections.

NEW MEDIA TV IN USE

Now, we will illustrate how various TV watching practices are supported and constrained by digital and material properties of the new media, including new expressions made possible by digitalization, deep watching encouraged by the Internet, background TV supported and constrained by computer resources, and cross-generation gate-keeping practices around computers.

New expressions by digitalization

The expressive capability of TV has long been acknowledged in TV literatures. Silverstone, for example, stated that TV watching *"inevitably revealed the tension in contemporary society between the increasingly international cultural-industrial complex, and the possibilities released for those powers for self-expression, through denial, transcendence or transformation*" [23]. Now the expressive capacity of TV is further enhanced by the great increase of possibilities, resources and means for watching. The choice is not just between watching or not watching, or which channels to watch, but also between whether it is through old or new media TV, where to watch, and specific details of how to watch, all made possible by digitalization. As such, new media TV provides new means to reflect and express moods, preferences and attitudes.

Particularly, we uncovered the numerous ways in which new media TV was employed for self-expressions. First, with timeshifting brought by new media TV, we argue that watching *live* broadcasts obtains new expressive capabilities. As mentioned above, watching live broadcasts is relatively rare for our informants, mainly due to its time constraints. While it was rare, however, when they did it, it became an indication of something really significant to them as it usually requires extra effort such as scheduling their lives, or staying up all night waiting. For example, Shilie described how the attraction of the show determined whether she would watch live broadcasts or not, "*For example, the Super Boy shows...I like Super Boy, and I would surely stay there and wait for the live broadcast.*" Indeed, now live broadcasts overall have been used only for special shows that personally matter to them. Liuqi reported she would only watch live broadcasts for important ceremonies, "*I do have watched live broadcasts. I watched the Taiwan Golden Melody Award ceremony through the live broadcast...um, I would be anxious (to know the result) such as Golden Melody, Golden Bell, and Golden Horse, hehe.*" This resonates with what John Dewey pointed out that "*The only way it can become aware of its nature and its goal is by obstacles surmounted and means employed.*"[10]. Live broadcasts, compared to recorded videos, pose a kind of obstacle to watch and become a means through which people express what matters and what is important to them.

Secondly, the specific control made available by new media TV also provides means for people to express their care for shows. For example, whether they would take pains to download the gigabyte size movies to ensure high resolution and smoothness is associated with their enthusiasm for the show, as Jiad described, "*That depends, if it is the movie that I've been looking forward to watching, I will surely choose the high resolution one, and download it. Like the Transformers 3, I would download 2 or 3 gigabytes of it. That will be spectacular!* " Other specific setups and details of how the show is watched is also telling about their attitudes toward the show, such as whether it was full screen or not, whether they would skip scenes or follow it from the beginning to the end, or whether they watched it with full or divided attention. For example, Liuqi reported, "*if it is the show that I like, then I will watch it from the beginning to the end, and if it is not, then I will drag through it.*" Jiad told us he would use full screen as a way to avoid QQ distractions for those "big" movies, which he felt serious about. Xiaoshu reported that she would allocate attention differently based on her seriousness about the show. As such, the choices in terms how to watch new media TV, including material properties of a show such as the bulkiness of a downloaded movie, have all become ways to reflect users' attitudes and care for the show.

Furthermore, the rich choices of content also make it easy to express one's emotional states and to address one's moods. People would commonly choose what to watch based on their mood. Lan reported, "*There might be some quarrels in my work, and I feel upset, so I would choose Korean entertainment shows, those funny shows from Korea, to adjust my mood at home.*" We found many similar comments from Sina Weibo, such as this one, "*The frustration, when thinking of the Super Girl show tonight, will be all gone.*" While the Super Girl show is often associated with being naïve or immature by adults, interestingly we found it played effective roles in mood adjustment for young people. Some also reported that they would share inspiring movies to encourage others when they are depressed. So in a way, watching TV has become a means to deal with emotional disturbance.

Deep watching encouraged by the Internet

We found different video clips and other resources were often explored to support deeper exploration of shows, a practice we call *deep watching.* Often this includes digging into older video materials. For example, when a new version of a very popular TV show comes out a decade after its original one, it becomes a common practice that people dig out the old ones to compare and recollect their memory. A typical example is revealed in discussions of the new Princess Pearl (还珠格格, a very popular comedy TV series in China) on Weibo, "*When I watched the new Princess Pearl, I reviewed the old version right away, and found its ranking on PPS went up rapidly. Haha, I guess there were just so many people like me...*" Jiangbing reported how the release of her idol's movie triggered her to find his old movies to watch, "*I've saved all his movies. If he has new movies to come out, I would review his previous ones. But usually I wouldn't remember to do it (reviewing them)*". More commonly, when they watched an episode of show that was of particular interest to them, they would go back to catch up with the old ones. It was also very common that people would transition from old to new media TV to finish up shows that were suspended or interrupted from old TV broadcasting. As such different media sources are combined, through which the integrity of the show is ensured. In addition, while previous research finds that many times people just collect and archive shows but rarely revisit them [3], our study suggests that triggers such as new releases, new versions, and some events are important for people to revisit their collections.

Although similar practices also exist for other storage media such as DVDs, deep watching has become much more easily practiced with the improved accessibility and availability made possible by the Internet. It was common that when people realized something of interest was coming out, they would directly search for relevant information on the Internet, as a way to learn more about a topic, or to locate quality resources. Jiad described such a case, "*If there are hot events coming out, for example, the maiden flight of China's 5th generation of J-20 fighter jet...when I watched the relevant news, on XinWenLianBo (新闻联播 Network News Broadcast) or 30 Minute News, I will go to search relevant in-depth interview programs to learn more about it.*" This way, he gained more perspectives and details to deepen his understanding of the development and meaning of the event. Liuqi took that as a way to locate quality shows, "*I really like Tao Jingying's hosting style, and I will watch any shows that are hosted by her. At first, I watched her 'DaXueShengLeMei (大学生了没 College Students or Not)', and then all of sudden, she mentioned 'XingGuangDaDao (星光大道 Avenues of Star)' in the show, so I searched for information about XingGuangDaDao, and found that singing contest was really good.*" Similar uses were also reported in Sina Weibo. So it was evident that, with a web search a click away, media content combination and navigation were very much encouraged.

Background TV conditioned on computer materiality

Many times, users do not directly interact with TV, but rather, they arrange TV as part of a desirable environment for other activities. We call this practice *background TV*, concerning how people use their idle or peripheral attention to watch while engaging in other activities. Although background TV is also practiced with old TV as shown in other studies [3, 14], it is generally limited to the home environment. Now with the availability of new media TV, background TV has been taken into new settings.

First, widespread computers, portable devices and the Internet have brought TV into others places including offices, labs, stores, libraries, study rooms and others. Zhaogan's example was the most telling one. He reported that he often used new media TV to watch his favorite shows while he was studying in the study room, "*That is something... basically it is when I am writing something there, I will raise my head to glance it (PPTV). Basically it is when I am tired I will raise my head to glance it. That is, I am not staring at the screen.*" Since he only chose movies that he had watched before, he didn't need to follow the plot closely, making it suitable for background watching. At the same time, he also used both mute and headsets to ensure it won't interfere with others. Residing in a study room, and with the muted movie at the background, he obtained a balance between study and leisure, "*This way, I can relax and at the same can still get things done.*" In both work and entertainment, TV watching has been commonly used to occupy idle and peripheral attention. Jiangbing, a graduate student at school, reported she would watch online TV when waiting in between experiments in her lab. So here, the richness of choices, the widespread use of computers and the mobility of devices have allowed online TV watching to be integrated with other activities, and incorporated into more settings.

At the same time, background TV is also subject to new digital and material conditions, including the rich choices of content, as well as the screen size, memory, and CPU power of computers. Zhan used new media TV to accompany online gaming and described how the screen size of his computer made it possible, "*I always watch it while I am playing games. Mine (screen) is 19 inches, 19 inch wide screen. You know, for this game, Menghuanxiyou (梦幻西游, a popular MMORPG in China), it does not affect watching (TV)...I can be online, for 20 to 30 minutes, and I only need to do something once in a while. So I always watch it this way...I don't need to use the full screen to play the game. It only takes one third of the screen space, so it won't affect (watching). Because for the PP(TV), you can use a small window.*" Zheng reported similar experiences, and further commented that some entertainment shows were especially suitable for this purpose, "*Because it (the show) is just for fun, which means you only need to know it, and you don't need to watch it closely. Because, for example, if I watch movies, I won't watch it this way, right? It is just Kangxilaile (康熙来了, an entertainment show from Taiwan). Kangxilaile, you only need to listen to it, right? And the size of the screen...sometimes, I only need to glance it, so I don't care about the image quality, so it doesn't matter if it (the window) is small.*" What is interesting is that, both of them mentioned the screen size, suggesting that it is an important factor in supporting the simultaneous use of new media TV together with other tasks on computers. Lan's case further revealed how this practice was conditioned on computer materiality, as his computer was not powerful enough to do this, "*The game is a high demand one (on the computer， and my computer is not powerful enough, hehe, so when I play the game, I will always close other programs, and will watch it when the game is over.*" These interviews suggest that, computer materiality including processor power, storage capacity, and screen size, has conditioned how background TV can play out.

Cross-generation gate-keeping around computers

The computer, compared to the TV set, is generally considered to be more complex to use and less accessible to novice users, especially the elderly. So the employment of computers as the new platform for TV watching has also created troubles and called for gate-keeping practices in the home. Almost all our informants reported cases when they helped their parents to use new media TV to watch. Shilie said, "*If I don't initiatively show it to them, they will never watch it. But, if, for example, if it is my mom, and if she is following a show, and if she really wants to watch it, she will use it to watch, and I will set it up for her, and she will watch it one episode after another. But she doesn't have such initiatives, for example if I am not home, for her to use it to watch herself.*" Zhaogan tried to make it easier for her mom to use new media TV by saving links in "favorites" on the web, "*It seems she (his mom) is not so familiar with it, so usually she doesn't like it. Generally, I will add the link to the 'favorite' for her, so she only needs to click it and watch.* " Yang described how he would recommend movies for his father, "*For example, he likes moves from Hong Kong TVB, and I will tell him what good movies are there, and he will go there to search.*" The cross-generation gate-keeping practice was not just for parents, but also for younger kids. Our informants reported they once lent their iPads or laptops to their nieces or younger sisters, and set up kids' movies for them to watch. So the complexity and the learning curve associated with the new media platform have posed challenges for less technically literate people, which then lead to gate-keeping practices around them.

OLD TV: DECREASED USE BUT HEIGHTENED MEANING

Now let's turn to old TV, emphasizing the new meanings it obtained with the availability of new media TV. As reported in related studies [3], youths had rarely watched old TV anymore, as it seemed too rigid and inflexible compared to new media TV. For the 17 people we interviewed, except for one informant who just formed a family and watched old TV everyday with his wife during dinner, all the rest reported that it was rare for them to watch old TV. This shift influenced their material choices around TV in a variety of ways. For those who lived together with their parents, new media TV was commonly used as a way to resolve TV conflicts with other family members. Others who lived independently from their families either didn't bother to set up the cable or didn't buy a TV set at all. Still others had been reluctant to upgrade their TV sets. Zhan, who was a big game fan and had three computers at home, said, "*I don't bother to upgrade it, because I barely watch TV anymore and always watch it on my computer. If I have to choose (between TV and the computer) to upgrade the screen, I will choose the computer for sure*". Almost all of them reported that they now only watched old TV for special live broadcasts, which was rare and only on yearly basis.

However, rare use does not necessarily mean less significance, but rather, we found it had a special place in people's TV watching experiences. Indeed, the occasional use of old TV could indicate something really meaningful and significant to them. Zhan reported that only some special sport events would make him stay up late for watching it on old TV, "*except for finals of World Cup or of NBA that I will watch on TV, for all the rest, I generally just watch them on my computer.*" Lan shared a similar story, "*You can get any videos or movies online, so except for something like the national day (we just celebrated our 60th anniversary in China), the big parade of the national day which I watched on TV, I have no interest (to watch them on TV) for others.*" So for these spectacular live shows, the material conditions of old TV including the big screen, the good image quality, and the smoothness of the show (without issues of "ka" caused by network latency as in new media TV) made it a preferred choice. Jiangbing's comment was representative, "*The good thing about it is, since the TV screen is bigger, that is, um...it feels more immersive and attractive than smaller ones.*" It suggests that although new media TV provides much richer content and more flexibility, old TV still plays certain roles in daily TV watching experiences, due to its screen size, image quality, and show smoothness.

Old TV watching was also practiced and valued for family time. Several of our informants used "accompany" to describe their old TV watching experiences. Yaya made it clear, "*Oh, for the TV set in the living room? I barely watch it, except for accompanying my mom.*" Watching old TV to accompany parents was the most prominent for people who were away most of the time and got home just for summer or other vacations. Shilie described that she would watch TV with her parents when she was home, "*If I am home, I will usually accompany and watch TV together with my parents at night*" "Accompany" was also commonly mentioned among the two newly married couples. Lixing, who was just married, reported that they would save some shows to be watched on old TV during their dinner time, "*We will still wait and watch it on TV (even though they have become available online already), because usually when we are having dinner, there is no good show (on TV).*" At the same time, we found it had been rare for new media TV to be employed for family purposes. As pointed by our informants, new media TV was limited in its material conditions for this use. For example, Zheng pointed out that PPTV was only for personal use. "*If I watch it online, it is rare for me to co-watch it with others. The screen is so small, and also (there are issues with) headsets and bad sound effects...*"This suggests that the different material properties of old and new media TV have led them to be distinguished and appropriated for personal or family uses.

Interestingly, we also found old TV had obtained some nostalgic value. Qiansu described, "*It has been rare for me to watch TV anymore since I went to college... So that kind feeling, like watching TV in a stealthy way as what we did when we were kids, is gone. When I got home and watched TV in my fresh and sophomore years, I felt so good about it even when just watching ads. It was very satisfying, so TV watching has become a sweet childhood memory.*" We found many similar comments from Weibo such as this one, "*tonight, we three siblings are watching the Super Girl show. We've been watching and chatting and appraising...watching and laughing...and we also need to keep quiet because our mom is sleeping [shh]. Feel so good and so happy···It has been long for watching TV together with my young sister and brother. The old feeling has come back...chatting and laughing... so happy [yay!][yay!]*". So although rarely watched anymore, old TV has special values for people, as it represents their childhood memories.

Relatedly, old TV had also been leveraged to get rid of "esthetic fatigue" resulted from the heavy use of new media, Jiangbing reported how she got tired from using the Internet and sitting in front of the computer all the time in school, and watched old TV to take a break from it, "*I've got enough (of the Internet) from the school. I will watch TV for sure (when home)...*" It was also confirmed by other anecdotes that they would occasionally watch some "very bad" shows on TV just to take a break from the Internet, or other more popular shows. This reminds us of the dialectic relationship between old and new media TV. That is, meanings of one kind media can only be examined and understood in its relation to other media.

SOCIAL MEDIA IN TV WATCHING

Previous research has uncovered the importance of TV as a topic for socialization. TV is so popular that it is commonly talked about at work - the so-called "water cooler TV" (Barkhuus cited [16]). It is even documented people trying to be synchronized with their colleagues in terms of TV watching so they can talk about it the next day [3]. We similarly found that TV was a common topic among colleagues and friends in our study; they would also share good TV shows or movies within their own social circles through social media. What's more, we found social media have been commonly integrated into TV watching processes whether it comes as a component of online TV platform such as the commenting feature on PPTV, or an independent general social media platform, such as Sina Weibo. Actually, sometimes, it was hard to tell whether the use of social media was associated with online or offline TV watching merely based on the blogging content. So when discussing the role of social media, we do not distinguish between online and offline TV.

While TV provides an important topic for socialization, however, TV watching itself is often considered to be an isolated or asocial activity, especially when compared with the physical movie theater. Our informants were all very conscious about the integral public and social element of movie theaters. Qiansu described, "*Anyway, if you go to the movie theater, everyone will see the same thing, and we will respond together simultaneously, so I won't feel lonely. It is definitely much better than watching movies on PPS alone at home.*" Xiaoshu also commented, discussion is an integral part of theater going, "*If it is in the movie theater, it will surely make things different. We would surely talk about it afterwards. Or even during the movie, when there something super funny, or sometimes it might not be that funny, but if a few laughed badly, we will all get influenced.*" Compared to watching movies in the theater, it seems TV watching is associated with a lack of corresponding social atmosphere.

Yet, the arrival of social media can potentially improve the sociality of TV watching, both online and offline. We found people did make use of social media for this purpose. It was evident in some microblogging messages, e.g. "*10:30pm every Friday, Super Girl! Although we've passed the start chasing age, and although it is purely for fun, when a lot of friends, or classmates who are distributed in different cities all watch the same show at the same time, it is just so fun.*" This way, social media provided opportunities to expand social interactions beyond the collocated people, including others remotely. It is important to note that remote co-watching sociality was especially valuable when it was hard to find others in their physical world to share and discuss TV. That was a recurring problem for those watching TV alone or at home, as family members often have different watching preferences and conflicts are common regarding which TV channel to watch, especially between different generations or genders. Qiansu said, "*They (Roommates) don't like to watch it. Usually it is just me who watch it, and then I will find people with similar interests on Weibo.*" So social media provided opportunities for our informants to socialize with peers who might not be in the same location, but who share the same interests.

However, despite the potential of social media to support distributed co-watching, its enhancement was still very limited, especially for new media TV. Mainly because when people watched TV based on their own schedules, it was hard to find out who was watching the same show anymore. Qiansu's comment was revealing, "*We will discuss more if it is a live broadcast. For others, there is nothing to discuss, because you two are not watching the same show, and probably not the same episode.*" Indeed the most heated discussion on social media is usually associated with live broadcasts. So although technically, it is possible for new media TV to be co-watched remotely, practically it is often limited due to awareness and synchronization issues.

Although limited for direct social interactions, social media has been commonly leveraged to address emotional responses to TV. Indeed, watching TV can be very emotional, especially for some special shows, such as funny comedies, sport events (e.g. World Cup finals or NBA finals), and other competitive shows (e.g. the Super Girl show). In this respect, social media provided a good way to discuss and express their emotional responses and attitudes through commenting and communications. Many informants reported that they only commented when they watched something especially good or bad. One extreme example is when reading some opposite opinions. Almost all our informants mentioned these were the moments that they felt most compelled to comment. Wan provided a typical example, "*um...sometimes, because I personally like Naruto (a famous Japanese animation about ninja) and some people don't behave quite well... probably they are fans of other animation movies...so they say bad things using some dirty words, and I would reply and say I like it...*" So the use of social media, or the commenting and discussing, is highly associated with one's emotional responses to the show and to others' opinions.

An interesting finding is that it seems breaks were important times for interactions through social media. All informants reported that they would use a gap or a break to interact with others. For example, Yang made use of half-times of some sports shows, and Xiaoshu took advantage of commercial breaks to discuss with others. Interestingly, buffering also provided opportunities for that, as reported by Xiaoshu, "*When it was buffering, I quickly glanced the comments at the bottom.*" It was noted from previous research that social chatting could make watching more engaging, even sometimes distracting [26]. Our study further suggested that whether it was distracting or not was also a result of people's active work, in that they were consciously and skillfully utilizing breaks and managing interactions to minimize their distractibility.

DISCUSSIONS

Through the preceding discussions, we hope to have illustrated the importance of digitality and materiality in shaping TV watching experiences. Especially, we argue that an analytic distinction between them helps explicate relevant media phenomena. It is not enough to say that old and new media are converged [15], or that physical and digital artifacts are combined to support interactions and actions [19]. Although we can clearly see these at work in our data, e.g. people transitioned from old TV to new media TV to finish shows, and new social media were integrated into TV watching experiences. However, our work complicates this argument by showing how materiality, as an inherent aspect of new media, plays important roles in enabling and constraining new media experiences. For example, although the new Internet infrastructure and the portable devices have allowed background TV to be practiced into new settings, the accessibility and availability of computing and infrastructural resources also pose constraints on where and how it can be practiced. So, in understanding new media TV experiences, we must include materiality in our discussions on digitality. Moreover, focusing on both digitality and materiality also helps us to understand the differences and relationships between different media platforms. With the freedom brought by digitalization, both new media TV and computerized TV (e.g. enhanced with PVR and DVR technologies) support time shifting practices and provide similar expressive capabilities. However, as they are incorporated into different physical forms, they are subject to different material constraints and taken into different fabrics of life. For instance, it is easy to imagine that new media TV is better supporting deep watching and widespread background TV, whereas computerized TV makes a better platform for shared watching and family time.

What is more interesting is that, not only do different kinds of media support different practices and embody different meanings, but also their meanings are dependent on each other. For example, the arrival and popularity of new media TV has transformed the value and meaning of old TV, as old TV has been saved and leveraged for special purposes, such as family time, special occasions, nostalgic values, and getting rid of esthetic fatigue from new media TV. So from our study, we can see that old and new media TV are not just made into different uses, or converge to support interactions, they are also involved in a dialectic relationship where the meanings of old and new are dependent on each other.

This finding certainly differs from previous views in which digitality is seen to be replacing materiality, or bits "substitute" atoms, a view that is often advocated in the context of information society. As computing technologies continue to enter into more spheres of our everyday lives, we will continue to see more digitalized versions of previous physical artifacts and practices, such as digital calendars, e-books, digital photography, online shopping, online conferencing, etc. However, as we have seen here, no matter how they are developed, some special meanings resulting from the material properties can never be reproduced digitally. As shown in our study, materiality can afford and support special meanings. Similar to Bourdieu's view of consumption as class discrimination [5], we argue TV watching is also an expression, and the addition of new media provides new dimensions for discrimination and expression of one's attitudes, priorities and life styles, instead of simulation or substitution.

CONCLUSIONS

Built on previous work on hybrid media [19], and inspired by Dourish and Mazmanian's materiality of information [11], we further conceptualize, tease apart and distinguish between digitality and materiality involved in media technologies. Through this kind of investigation, we hope we are able to talk about and unpack the complex interactions between digital characteristics, material properties, and social practices. We draw a number of related conclusions from this work.

First, while digitalization is often associated with more freedom and more flexibility, they are in the end conditioned upon material properties. And the conditioning is not just in its production [11], but also in the consumption of digital goods. For example, computing resources and the underlying technological infrastructures often shape people's new media TV watching behavior.

Second, materiality shapes social affordances and meanings around digital products. For example, the screen size, the image quality and the sound effect all have impact on whether it will be used for social or personal purposes. Also, the complexity involved in using computers have also led to gate keeping practices cross generations. Further, old TV sets, with their fixed location in the household, and their historical roles in the family, carry special meanings with regard to family time and childhood memories.

Third, the relationship between digitality and materiality is complementary, not replacing. This is not just manifested in their working together to support new experiences around new media TV, but also in people's selective use of old and new media based on their particular materiality and digitality. More interestingly, traditional TV is used in relation to new media TV, in that it is used to get rid of esthetic fatigues from the Internet.

Finally, TV has long been considered as a medium for cultural and individual expressions [1, 23, 27], and when it is more digitalized, it becomes even more so. Because digitalization provides more nuanced controls in terms of how TV is watched (e.g. full screen or not, high or low resolution, and live broadcasts or recorded videos), through which one's attitudes, priorities, and seriousness can be expressed. Just as Appadurai stated, "*Because of the sheer multiplicity of the forms in which they appear (cinema, television computers, and telephones) and because of the rapid way in which they move through daily life routines, electronic media provide resources for self-imagining as an everyday social project.*" [1] We believe, with the continual digitalization of media, there is an increase in the multiplicity of forms for expressions that the hybrid media environment can support.

ACKNOWLEDGMENTS

Thanks to Charlotte P. Lee, Silvia Lindtner, Julie Starr and our reviewers for their valuable feedback. The work is supported by the Shanghai Science & Technology Committee Key Fundamental Research Project under Grant No. 11JC1400800.

REFERENCES

1. Appadurai, A. *Modernity at large: Cultural dimensions of globalization.* University Of Minnesota Press, 1996.
2. Barkhuus, L. Television on the Internet: New practices, new viewers. *In Proc. CHI'09 Extended Abstracts*, ACM Press (2009), 2479-2488.
3. Barkhuus, L. and Brown, B. Unpacking the television: User practices around a changing technology. *Transactions on Computer-Human Interaction (TOCHI) 16*, 3 (2009), 1-22.
4. Benford, S., Greenhalgh, C., Reynard, G., Brown, C. and Koleva, B. Understanding and constructing shared spaces with mixed-reality boundaries. *Transactions on Computer-Human Interaction (TOCHI) 5*, 3 (1998), 185-223.
5. Bourdieu, P. *Distinction: A social critique of the judgement of taste.* Harvard University Press, 1984.
6. CNNIC. The 28th China Internet Network Development Statistical Report.
7. CNNIC. The 27th China Internet Network Development Statistical Report.
8. Crabtree, A. and Rodden, T. Hybrid ecologies: Understanding cooperative interaction in emerging physical-digital environments. *Personal Ubiquitous Computing 12*, 7 (2008), 481-493.
9. De Souza E Silva, A.S. From cyber to hybrid: Mobile technologies as interfaces of hybrid spaces. *Space and culture 9*, 3 (2006), 261-278.
10. Dewey, J. *Art as experience.* Perigee, 2005.
11. Dourish, P. and Mazmanian, M. Media as material: Information representations as material foundations for organizational practice, *Third International Symposium on Process Organization Studies*, 2011.
12. Doyle, P. Value-based marketing. *Journal of Strategic Marketing 8*, 4 (2000), 299-311.
13. Gauntlett, D. and Hill, A. *TV living: Television, culture, and everyday life.* Routledge, London, 1999.
14. Irani, L., Jeffries, R. and Knight, A. Rhythms and plasticity: Television temporality at home. *Personal and Ubiquitous Computing 14*, 7 (2010), 621-632.
15. Jenkins, H. *Convergence culture: Where old and new media collide.* NYU press, 2006.
16. Johnson, S. Watching TV makes you smarter. *The New York Times 24* (2005).
17. Koleva, B., Schn A Delbach, H., Benford, S. and Greenhalgh, C. Traversable interfaces between real and virtual worlds. *In Proc. CHI'00*, ACM Press (2000), 233-240.
18. Lange, P.G. Publicly private and privately public: Social networking on YouTube. *Journal of Computer-Mediated Communication 13*, 1 (2008), 361-380.
19. Lindtner, S., Nardi, B., Wang, Y., Mainwaring, S., Jing, H. and Liang, W. A hybrid cultural ecology: World of Warcraft in China. *In Proc. CSCW'08*, ACM Press (2008), 371-382.
20. Milavsky, J.R. *Television and aggression: A panel study.* Academic Press, 1982.
21. Putnam, R.D. *Bowling alone: The collapse and revival of American community.* Simon and Schuster, New York, 2001.
22. Rode, J.A., Toye, E.F. and Blackwell, A.F. The domestic economy: A broader unit of analysis for end user programming. *In Proc. CHI'05 Extended Abstracts*, ACM Press (2005), 1757-1760.
23. Silverstone, R. *Television and everyday life.* Routledge, London, 1994.
24. Strauss, A.L. and Corbin, J. *Basics of qualitative research.* Sage Newbury Park, CA, 1990.
25. Wang, Q., Ding, X., Lu, T., Xia, H. and Gu, N. Infrastructural experiences: An empirical study of an online arcade game platform in China. *In Proc. CSCW'2012*, ACM Press (2012).
26. Weisz, J.D., Kiesler, S., Zhang, H., Ren, Y., Kraut, R.E. and Konstan, J.A. Watching together: Integrating text chat with video. *In Proc. CHI'07*, ACM Press (2007), 877-886.
27. Williams, R. *Television: Technology and cultural form.* Fontana, London, 1974.

Writing the Experience of Information Retrieval: Digital Collection Design as a Form of Dialogue

Melanie Feinberg
School of Information, University of Texas at Austin, Austin, TX 78701
feinberg@ischool.utexas.edu

ABSTRACT
In the context of digital libraries and other online resource collections, the substance of interaction is generated to a large degree through the selection, description, organization, and arrangement of the aggregated items. Within information studies, researchers [such as 32, 6] have shown how individual events of selection and description inevitably form judgments about the collected materials. This paper describes a process in which designers purposefully use the elements of selection, description, organization, and arrangement to "write" a resource collection as a form of rhetorical expression. The design process was implemented in two classroom settings. In the more successful second implementation, the role of the audience in structuring a rhetorical interaction was emphasized, and collection design was conceptualized as designing a dialogue between author and audience. The formalized critique of existing collection designs was a key element in enabling this dialogic orientation.

Author Keywords
Experience design; digital collections; rhetoric; criticism

ACM Classification Keywords
H.5.2 Information Interfaces and Presentation: Misc

General Terms
Design

INTRODUCTION
Within information studies and computer science, we tend to conceptualize information seeking as a simple, well-defined task [16]. In this mode, one approaches a resource collection, such as the recipe Web site Epicurious, with a specific need in mind, such as finding a casserole recipe for the office potluck. Accordingly, there is an equal, longstanding tendency to characterize the ideal information supplied to address that need as objectively isolated, neutrally described fact [35]. If I seek potluck casserole recipes, then lo, that is what I should receive.

However, just as philosophers of science, such as Bryant and Ereshevsky, have complicated the notion of scientific fact and its accompanying taxonomy [11, 19], emphasizing the pragmatic and interpretive elements involved in providing accounts of scientific data, scholars of classification have repeatedly shown how, within resource collections such as libraries and databases, events of item selection, attribute definition, and category assignment inevitably form interpretive judgments about the collected materials [see, for example, 32, 6; this orientation is pervasive in current classification research]. An objective neutrality, in other words, is an untenable design principle for resource collections, be they composed of physical materials or digital ones.

To continue the office potluck example, if the casserole recipes that I receive all contain meat products, then Epicurious is communicating a rhetorical position to me, that main dishes should include meat. Similarly, if the recipes feature inexpensive ingredients, then Epicurious is telling me that potlucks are informal, not elegant. In fact, whatever the search results might be, Epicurious will be expressing its own idea of what a "potluck casserole" means; this interpretive activity cannot be avoided. As judgments accumulate throughout the Web site, they form a larger perspective on food, on preparing and eating it, and even its cultural significance. As a user of Epicurious, I receive more than instructions for making turkey tetrazzini, or whatever "potluck casserole" I choose; I receive a whole approach to cooking, as expressed through the selection, description, and organization of recipes.

This notion, that resource collections communicate a specific interpretation of their contents, has been widely accepted in classification research and other related areas, such as archival science and museum studies [see, for example, 17, 27]. However, implications for the collection designer's task have yet to be widely explored. For example, practice guides and standards for controlled vocabularies continue to portray the designer of these systems as a compiler of data, who documents a subject domain by objectively identifying categories to describe it [10]. In contrast, a design process that directly acknowledges the difficulties with a neutral perspective would portray the collection designer more like an author, who forms positions and determines how to express them creatively and persuasively through the selection, organization, and arrangement of resources in a collection. Users would interact with resulting collection in a manner similar to the "information flaneur," in which users encounter materials for various reasons of engagement, and not just query resolution [16]. In this perspective, an information system's usefulness and interest is located partly in its ability to enact an interpretive frame that differs from a user's current way of thinking and that challenges existing ideas and expectations regarding the collection's subject matter, in the same way that the flaneur prowls a city to experience its eclectic mix of people, places, and things. If my encounter with Epicurious expands my notion of "casserole" by including dishes like Asian hotpots and Mexican tingas, in addition to standard American fare, then I have found some new ideas, in addition to recipes.

This paper describes a continuing project to enact a design process for resource collections that views this design space as a rhetorical situation, rather than a scientific problem. The motivating research question asks what it means to "write" a digital resource collection, and what it means to be the author of one. The language of classification theorists, such as Beghtol and Kwasnik, often refers to information systems as "making arguments" or "forming theories," which clearly suggests the domain of rhetoric [6, 29]. However, both the materials of expression and the means by which the user audience engages with this expression are less certain in the resource collection context than with common forms of rhetorical communication, such as linear text. We know how to use sentences and paragraphs to write an essay, and we can expect that our audience will read it from beginning to end, and that our audience will be reading the essay primarily to engage with our ideas, even if they don't end up agreeing with them. In contrast, it's less clear how we deploy the mechanisms of resource selection, organization, and metadata description to create sustained, persuasive arguments, especially when our user audience shapes their own path through the system, and when that audience may have their own information-related goals that do not entirely align with our authorial vision. This study suggests that the form of rhetoric articulated through digital resource collections is most effectively described as designing a dialogic experience between author and audience, as opposed to making the audience agree with what the author proposes. This conceptualization aligns with Kenneth Burke's idea of rhetoric as a process of *identification* [12]. For Burke, rhetoric becomes a means of bridging differences in beliefs, values, and goals; successful rhetorical expression illuminates a path to joint action or understanding, framed by shared interests. In the context of resource collections, the act of persuasion requires active audience engagement to structure the interactive experience; the author acknowledges and works with, instead of against, that audience power. Such notions of audience engagement enacted through the structure provided by an author are closely related to the reader-response school of literary theory as exemplified by Wolfgang Iser [28]. (While the influence of Bakhtin [2] is noted whenever the concept of dialogue is linked to expression, his work is less central to the orientation used here.)

The concept of persuasion at the heart of this research project is based in the tradition of rhetoric, in which the goal is to advance a position and potentially achieve agreement regarding that position. Bogost has articulated the rhetorical stance in the context of video games and noted the differences between this approach and that of persuasive technologies, as seen in the work of Fogg and others [8, 22]. Persuasive technologies encourage users to act in accordance with existing plans; for example, in Consolvo's UbiFit project, an ambient display motivates users to achieve exercise goals they have already set [14]. In contrast, rhetorical approaches attempt to persuade people to adopt new goals or accept new ideas.

BACKGROUND

Previous work has described the initial creation of a design process focused on the development of rhetorically focused resource collections and an implementation of that process in a classroom environment [20, 21]. To provide context for the subsequent implementation reported here, I present a brief overview of the process as deployed in the first implementation.

The design process for rhetorical collections includes these activities:

- Learning.
- Envisioning.
- Strategizing.
- Sketching.
- Revisiting, reflecting, and refining.
- Analysis and critique.

The following sections describe each activity. It should be noted that, while many of these activities are not uncommon in design-oriented fields, they are all unusual in the context of resource collection development, as seen in library and information studies. This is because, in the traditional mode of information seeking, the emphasis is on finding the correct, objective way to describe information, and not on the user experience. While, as described in the introduction, the ideal of neutrality as a design principle has been convincingly refuted, this conceptual shift has yet to translate to the collection design space.

Learning

The designer acquires more information about:

- The subject area of the collection being designed.
- The structure, content, and format of potential documents to include in the collection.
- The user audience being targeted.

The designer performs this research following standard practices for each information type, such as domain analysis for the subject area, interviews and focus groups for user research, and content and genre analysis of potential documents.

Envisioning: persona and scenario development

Personas encapsulate characteristics of a selected target audience [34] and synthesize user research in a way that forms believable characters and not merely data composites [33]. Next, the designer imagines a diverse set of experiences that show how these personas might interact with a potential document collection [13]. By reflecting on these scenarios, the designer can begin to perceive the extent of the design problem.

Strategizing: a plan to achieve the nascent vision

The designer uses ideas generated from initial scenario development to postulate a tentative strategy for how the still-amorphously-defined information collection might communicate its position to the identified audience. This strategy is presented through a systematic design document, called the *brief,* which includes the following sections:

- Authorial goals, or the position being articulated on the collection's subject matter.
- Audience characteristics, including beliefs, values, and information needs.
- Design rationale, or the strategies of resource selection and description that convey the position to the audience through the document collection.

Sketching

The designer synthesizes the ideas generated from the Envisioning, Learning, and Strategizing activities by sketching how different collection elements—selected resources, descriptive information, and access mechanisms—come together as a coordinated work of expression.

Revisiting, refining, and reflecting

Synergistic development of scenarios, brief, and sketches continues until a viable design emerges through the intersection of the three documents, which together represent the potential audience experience of the collection (through personas and scenarios), the communicative goals and strategies of the designer/author (through the design strategy brief), and the union of resource selection, description, and access mechanisms that support the audience experience and communicative goals (through the sketches). Together, these documents represent a considered negotiation between an author's desire for expression, an audience's information needs and associated tasks, and the shape of the subject domain.

Analysis and critique

The candidate design is systematically examined and revamped before proceeding to implementation, in accordance with practice in many design fields [36, 39].

Design outcomes

The outcome of this process comprises the three related design documents developed during the coordinated activities: user scenarios, strategy brief, and sketches. Together, these documents present a unified design vision for a collection of information resources that is organized and arranged to communicate a unique perspective on the subject matter that it makes accessible.

Embarassed by my own persona: reservations about authorship

In the first classroom implementation, conducted in the spring semester, 2010, 15 master's students in an information studies program used the design process to create digital video libraries that each presented a unique perspective within the same subject area of "sustainability." The students selected their collection resources from a common pool of videos, and they all worked in an easy-to-use digital video library environment, the Open Video Digital Library Toolkit [25], for "sketching." These constraints focused the students on the primary expressive mechanisms of description (via abstracts, titles, cross-references, and other video metadata), organization (via the creation and assignment of browsing categories), and arrangement (via the establishment and description of thematic subcollections), as opposed to visual design or interface elements, which the toolkit standardizes.

Students successfully created resource collections that presented rhetorical positions on the subject matter, as expressed through the mechanisms of resource selection, description, organization, and arrangement [21]. However, student reflective essays showed lingering discomfort with the idea of authorship. The findings suggested that students could not clearly envision the role that an audience would have in shaping their own interactions with the collections; accordingly, this made the student authors feel like they shouldn't assert their own ideas too strongly. For example, one student worried that her authorial persona "catered" to her audience instead of "challenging" them, and she felt "embarrassed" at this "manipulation." The students had instinctively formulated their rhetorical strategies to work *against* audience power, by saying what they thought an audience would want to hear, instead of *with* audience power, by imagining their designs as a conversation between equals.

To address these issues, I planned a second classroom implementation of the design process, which reoriented the idea of authorship as one of two actors in a dialogic process, with the audience taking a role that demands equal presence. In this view, a compelling interaction requires that both participants, author and audience, take an active role in the retrieval process; both are, in effect, writing not just the resource collection, but writing the experience of retrieval. I hoped that by adapting the idea of writing to encompass the structuring of a dynamic process, as opposed to a static product, the student designers would be more likely to both acknowledge the equal agency of the audience and to embrace their own agency more fully. Such notions of engaged audiences have precedent in rhetoric as well as in the reader-response school of literary theory.

METHOD AND RESEARCH QUESTIONS

To encourage these changes, I made the following adaptations for the second classroom implementation:

- Throughout class sessions, I referred to the design product as "writing the collection experience as a type of performative document" as opposed to writing a collection, and I described the author's role as negotiating a balance between authorial and audience goals, "in other words, as designing a dialogue."
- I expanded the Learning activity to include a written, directed critique of an existing resource collection, with required consideration of author, audience, and critical perspectives.
- I elongated the Analysis and Critique activity to incorporate three critiques over separate weeks, one each from the perspective of author, audience, and critics.

My corresponding research questions were:

- How did designers' conceptualizations of their process, their product, and their role change from the first implementation to the second?
- How did collection designs change from the first implementation to the second?

These research questions limit the scope of the project to the ways that notions of dialogue and audience power affect the designers, and accordingly any changes in the implemented designs. This project is not concerned with actual audience reactions. Such an approach is not unusual in rhetorical and literary criticism, in which an "implied audience" is read, by a critic, through its instantiation by an author in a text [7].

I initiated the practice of formalized criticism as a precursor to design, in addition to the practice of critique from within the design process, to help bridge a perceived gap in both the critical skills and the confidence of the student designers. The "crit" session as a means of generating new knowledge by reflecting on in-progress ideas is an established activity in design fields, including architecture and HCI [36, 38, 23]. However, in most traditions of design practice, the design judgment employed by experts in the context of a crit session is seen as the result of long experience as a designer, with accompanying standards of rigor generated through the conventions of the design community, to which a student is exposed over a long period of what Lave and Wenger would describe as legitimate peripheral participation, or gradual accumulation of expertise, responsibility, and standing [30]. In the first implementation of the design process, the student designers did not feel sufficiently confident to apply critical judgments to their own work and that of their peers; they confided their misgivings about their practice as authors only in final essays.

A more formal employment of criticism, as finds expression in art, literature, and culture, in addition to design fields, has been advocated for interaction design [31, 3, 5]. In this kind of interpretive analysis, the critic attempts to uncover a deeper significance for a text or artifact, often by combining the technique of close reading, or detailed, sustained interpretation of the text, with a particular theoretical orientation (such as a reading of Shakespeare's *The Tempest* from the perspective of post-colonialism). Incorporating a more structured episode of such critical inquiry into the collection design process seemed an especially appropriate means to developing a keener sense of design judgment in this case, because of the analogy with writing. In composition courses, textual analysis is often taught in conjunction with writing skills, and budding authors are often told by experienced practitioners to read others' work, as well as to write themselves. Moreover, because case studies that incorporate systematic criticism into design process have not previously been reported in HCI literature, this project provides an opportunity to demonstrate the value of formal critique in actual practice.

To develop critical skills in preparation for the critique assignment, I structured three class sessions to address each of the three perspectives I had designated for their analysis: that of the audience, of the author, and of the critic. In the audience session, we discussed how an audience generates meaning or "performs" a text through reading it; in the author session, we discussed how authors create a text that their audience will enact, in some sense how authors "construct" through their choices an audience persona for the actual audience to take on; and in the critic session, we discussed how the critic might take an overall look at how this audience/author relationship is negotiated in the text. For each session, we prepared by reading articles from literary studies, rhetoric, and interaction design, and, importantly, we put these notions into practice by applying them to example resource collections that had been created in the previous classroom implementation.

We did not begin developing any of the design products—personas and scenarios, briefs, sketches—until after the critique project was completed. Then, after initial drafting of the three products, the three-fold structure of author, audience, and critic returned in the Analysis and Critique phase of the process. The author-focused critique of in-progress designs was a peer critique, conducted in a structured format; for the audience-focused critique, four students from the first classroom implementation returned to take on the role of audience members; and for the critic-focused critique, four faculty experts attended.

FINDINGS

Five students enrolled in the second class implementation. While the sample size was small, the richness of the collected data, as accumulated through a 15-week semester, greatly lessens the impact of this limitation. To avoid borrowings from the first class to the second, the second class designed collections in the subject area of "alternative medicine and wellness" instead of sustainability.

Students described their roles as authors, their relationship with the audience, and their process as designers in markedly different terms than students in the first implementation. The collection designs were also qualitatively different, in consistent ways, from the first implementation. The following two sections provide details for each of these assertions.

Participant notions of roles and goals

The students in the second implementation used strikingly different language to describe their roles as authors. This altered conceptualization of authorship also led to a different way of framing their design situations and accompanying work process.

In the first class, students tended to adapt their own messages to what they imagined the audience would like to hear, more in the way that one would appease an opponent, instead of in the way that one would cooperate with a partner. For example, 11 of 15 projects emphasized how simple personal actions, such as recycling household waste, could contribute to sustainability. In providing rationale for this choice, one student explained that her collection "strives to present the videos and accompanying text in a casual, low-commitment manner...The audience needs simple ways to impliment [sic] the conceptual ideas into their day-to-day lives."

None of the students actually thought that using vinegar and water to clean one's kitchen counters would result in a sustainable society; they all believed that such problems required long-term infrastructure solutions in addition to individual minor actions. But they took these positions in their collections because they thought that, in the words of one student, being "positive and encouraging" would be more persuasive to a broader audience. In the end, though, some of them felt like pandering manipulators, fooling people into believing that if they went to the farmer's market and bought local produce, they would save the planet. Because they didn't see the audience as active agents to really engage with, they shrank from their own potential power as authors.

In contrast, students in the second class assigned equal importance to their ideas and the goals of the audience. Instead of thinking, as the first group did, "I believe X, but I think the audience will respond to Y, so I will design my collection to speak Y," participants in the second implementation understood their problem space as "If I believe X, and the audience thinks Y, how can I get from Y to X?" They framed their challenge as, in the words of one participant, "Dave," "facilitating understanding for the audience," by first acknowledging their differences and

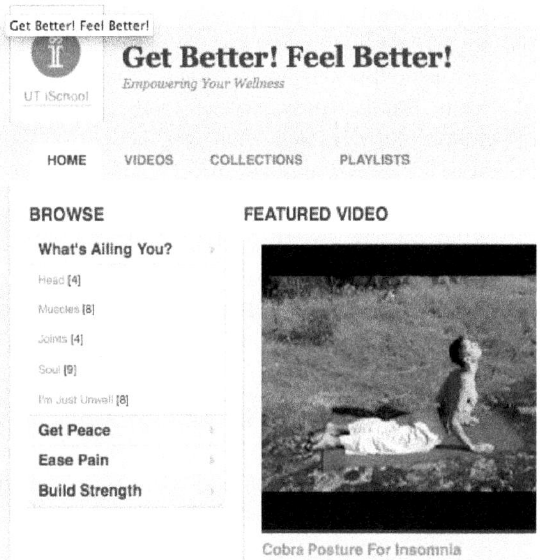

Figure 1: Browsing categories informed by using personas to model potential author/audience relationship

showing how those differences could be bridged, as opposed to ignoring the differences and pretending that they didn't exist. Another participant, "Isabella," elaborated that she had attempted to "construct a critical audience, willing and able to evaluate conflicting arguments," as a means of structuring a conversation between author and user. A third student, "Edie," contended that "ultimately, the negotiating of these [author and audience] spaces in an exercise in relationship building," further commenting that "if the author recognizes and respects the partnership and cooperation necessary to create a persuasive and interactive experience, neither author nor audience will feel compromised."

One way in which these different conceptions of author/audience roles played out in design work was in different attitudes toward personas and scenarios for the two implementations. In the first class, students were skeptical of personas as a design tool. As one participant complained, "I am troubled in placing too much stock into fictitious people, regardless of the level of believability of their actions and who they represent. I also do not know if real people are necessarily better..." Students in the second class, however, embraced personas as a vital element of their authorial process. Another participant, "Jessica," described her authorial goals as showing the holistic benefits—mind, body, and spirit—of wellness practices. Her personas, however, were a waitress and a food truck owner who were both short of money and on their feet all day; they wanted relief from chronic pain without the requirement of health insurance, which they didn't have. Jessica then puzzled over how to provide quick access to material related to physical conditions while not ignoring mental and spiritual connections to bodily systems. As depicted in Figure 1, one way that Jessica managed this problem was to include a browsing category for "ailments" but to include within it not just areas of the physical body but also "soul," and, provocatively, "I'm just unwell," a category that brought together a diverse assortment of material, from South American spiritual cleansing to clearing out nasal passages with a neti pot.

While participants in the second class did characterize their roles as authors consistently, they did not always find it easy to negotiate the author/audience balance they described. Indeed, Edie noted how at one point, she felt like she and her audience (as exemplified by her personas) were in a dysfunctional relationship, not one of equal partners:

I found myself time and time again too willing to compromise, too willing to lose my own voice in order to give the people what they want. I was the kind of partner who apologizes for things she shouldn't be sorry for and standing down when she should be holding her ground.

In contrast to students from the first class, however, Edie reasoned that being too conciliatory towards audience needs was, in the end, a disservice to both herself and to the audience. Audience values must be taken into account by the author, but the goal is to facilitate understanding, not to let the audience take over the discourse entirely. As Dave put it, "if a designer prioritizes audience needs to the point that the message is lost...what's the point?"

Participant design innovations

The collection designs themselves showed qualitative differences from one implementation to the next. In comparison with the first class, the collections from the second implementation were more thematically cohesive and more creatively provocative.

To provide evidence for these claims, I present one case study from each class. The case study from the first class, Sustainability Is Easy, was selected by all the students in the second class as the object of their written critiques, so I can include their interpretations of it.

Through its selection, description, and arrangement of videos, the Sustainability Is Easy collection, shown in Figure 2, asserts that simple individual activities can nonetheless increase overall sustainability. Its featured video, for example, depicts a trip to the farmer's market to buy locally grown food. Its top browsing category groups material by the type of household project described in a video (with no categories for larger-scale projects undertaken by communities, governments, or corporations), and its second browsing category categorizes videos based on the degree of easiness for each project. The collection's relentlessly upbeat tone ("Drip irrigation is a great, simple way to save water in your garden") emphasizes the hope that a little bit of individual effort can solve a big problem.

However, while the general position advocated by Sustainability Is Easy is direct and clear, its expression is muddled by trying to directly address a scattershot set of potential audience information needs: for example,

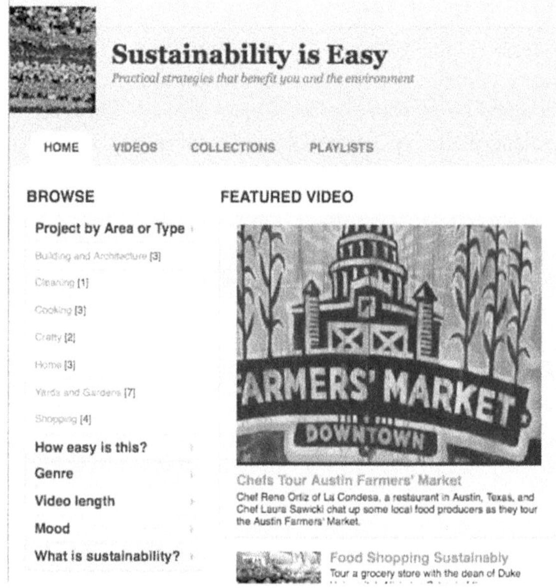

Figure 2: Sustainability Is Easy collection

browsing menus for mood, genre, video length, and general sustainability definitions have no connection to the overall rhetorical goals. Students from the second class criticized these diverse access mechanisms as contributing to conceptual incoherence and a resulting dilution of rhetorical power. Isabella suggested that this fragmentation emphasized the shallowness of the primary message, lessening the impact of the experience:

...the navigation elements do not present a coherent path to understanding how sustainability is easy. Because of this, we cannot participate in a transformative narrative...

In other words, without providing some evidence for the assertion that the videos in the collection will really enable the audience to contribute to sustainability, the audience has no real motivation for either understanding or action. Dave concurred, writing that "people need a reason beyond the fact that something is easy to make a switch to sustainable living practices."

Edie elaborated that the collection design, while perhaps meant to be encouraging, inscribes the audience as incapable of understanding the broader context of sustainability and contributing to larger-scale action, suggesting that "the social space the design constructs is one where consumers needn't take much responsibility." Edie's comments imply a lack of trust and respect on the part of the Sustainability Is Easy author toward the audience. Overall, the students' critiques of Sustainability Is Easy showed how, despite its clearly conveyed message, the collection strains to work *against* perceived limitations—as opposed to *with* those constraints.

The collection designs from the second implementation, in contrast, emphasized thematic consistency over access diversity, as a mechanism to facilitate understanding of the author's position by an audience with different goals,

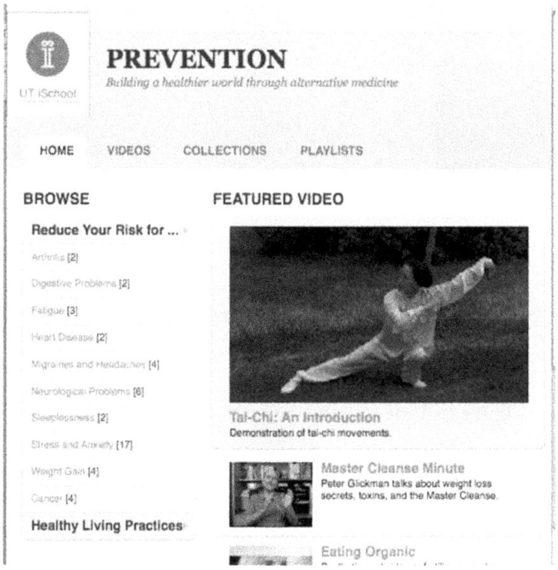

Figure 3: Prevention collection

Figure 4: Categories under Healthy Living Practices challenge audience preconceptions of medical knowledge

beliefs, and values. Dave's collection, our primary case study, focused on the relationship between alternative medicine practices and maintaining overall wellness. Dave used the theme of prevention to concentrate this idea, as shown in Figure 3.

In contrast to the diverse set of browsing categories employed by Sustainability Is Easy, Prevention includes just two thematically related categories: Reduce Your Risk For...which includes potential health problems, and Healthy Living Practices, which includes alternative systems that may address those problems (in addition to other problems). Dave refined these categories over many weeks, remarking that this process "was probably one of the most difficult parts of authoring this collection, and one place where the tension between author and audience was most evident." Dave struggled to structure and label these categories in a way that hinted at common ground between author and audience. Dave's personas were coming to the collection with specific fears of, or perhaps experience with, particular symptoms or conditions, whereas Dave wanted to emphasize the broad benefits of holistic practices for preventing many connected problems, not just isolated ones. If Dave called the category something like "Symptoms and Problems," though, then the idea of prevention was lost.

In addition to encouraging the audience to think about the goals of health-related practices in a different way, from a focus on alleviating symptoms to an awareness of larger networks and their overall maintenance, Dave wanted the audience to consider a wide set of knowledge systems as having bearing on these issues. Accordingly, the categories presented under healthy living practices encompass a variety of traditions, as Figure 4 illustrates.

The audience is challenged to consider the relationships between "angels," "acupuncture," and "shamanism" and the conditions under which such connections might hold. Even enthusiasts of herbal remedies and Chinese medicine might be initially taken aback at seeing these practices grouped with "angels," but this placement does underscore the holistic—physical, mental, spiritual—emphasis of many alternative medicine traditions. All the student designers in the second class felt empowered to pursue such creative and evocative pathways; they felt confident that by creating a thematically consistent collection that considered, but was not limited to, initial audience goals and beliefs, the audience would be able to find its bearings and productively engage more challenging aspects of the rhetorical artifact they had created. This consistency enabled a sort of trust that provided groundwork for a more equal author/audience relationship. As Isabella explained, "the designer should establish a relationship by giving small fulfillments on the emotional promise, and making further promises." In other words, a consistent structure has the potential to enable a larger meaning to emerge when the user interacts with it. However, although the author enables this meaning, the author does not determine it; the ultimate expression relies on audience action.

In Isabella's collection, the browsing categories offer a narrative progression that hopes to demonstrate how "alternative medical systems, no matter how strange, have internal logics and may be understood by examining them as systems of knowledge." Figure 5 shows how the logical progression of browsing categories, from Ailment to Cause of Ailment, then Healing Acts, Explanations (systems in which the healing acts make sense) and finally Perspectives (different ways to react to and assess these knowledge pathways) provides context for the initially quite strange items within any particular category.

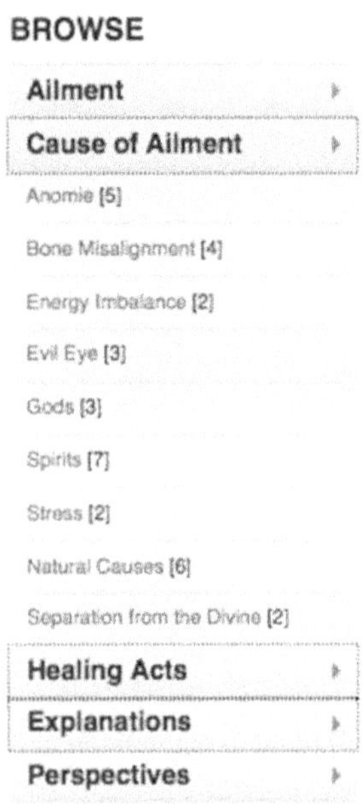

Figure 5: Browsing categories in Causes and Cures collection illuminate the logical structure of alternate knowledge systems

Individual video records show potential narrative flows to link these concepts, as Figure 6 depicts: the ailment, lovesickness, is caused by the evil eye, and healed by witchcraft; this progression makes sense in the knowledge system of brujeria, and this video approaches the system from a "mondo" perspective. (What does "mondo" mean? The audience can pursue this path by looking through the items placed in this category.)

DISCUSSION

On a basic level, these findings provide additional support for preliminary conclusions that the design process used in this study does facilitate the creation of digital resource collections that embrace their identity as rhetorical artifacts, where the selection, description, organization, and arrangement of included materials (here, digital videos) produces a coherent position on the collection's subject matter [20, 21]. These findings also demonstrate that the changes made to the second implementation of the design process—the characterization of the project as "writing the collection experience" as a "form of dialogue between author and audience," the use of a structured critique of an existing rhetorical collection to explore these ideas before beginning design, and an elongated, varied phase of critique for the in-progress designs—resulted in clearly identifiable changes to the ways that designers perceive their roles and their process, and increased the thematic consistency and creativity of the designs themselves. Additionally, these findings enable reflection upon the notion of authorship as a productive way to approach the design of resource collections, and upon the role of criticism in understanding, developing, and researching information artifacts.

Figure 6: Video metadata forms a narrative

Collection designers as authors of dialogic experience

All information systems enact an interpretive frame upon their contents, shaping users' perceptions of the included resources. As classification research has conclusively shown, it is impossible for information objects in a collection to "speak for themselves" in a neutral, objective way, without some level of judgment applied by the collection designer [32, 6]. While it may seem tempting to "aim for" a neutral collection, such an approach fails to grasp the inevitable human decision making that permeates all information collections. Moreover, this willful blindness can be seen as an abdication of moral responsibility; pretending to an impossible objectivity is a deceptive act.

It may seem equally tempting to design a collection based on what one thinks the audience expects or wants. Paradoxically, perhaps, this approach can also be seen as a type of ethical failure, because it refuses to acknowledge the ultimate power of the audience as critical agents able to agree or to disagree. This approach can also be limiting rhetorically; the audience will never reach a new understanding if an opportunity to explore and assess the author's perspective is not offered.

In contrast, the dialogic approach advocated in this study emphasizes the value of active engagement between an author's ideas and audience beliefs, goals, and values. While it is more common to imagine that "rhetoric" entails any means necessary, including manipulation and deceit, to coerce an audience, this is not the case, although as Aristotle observed, rhetoric comprises a set of tools that can be used for good or ill [1]. I would suggest that the rhetorical process foregrounds audience action as stemming from deliberate choice informed by the flow of ideas. Inspired by feminist epistemology, Foss and Griffin characterize such a rhetoric as "invitational" [24]. The student designers found this notion of invitational rhetoric to resonate strongly with their goal to structure a dialogue between themselves as authors and their user audience.

Such ideas align well with several transformative critical practices that have found currency within interaction design. There is a clear connection with the goals articulated in Scandinavian participatory design, for example, and Ehn and Kyng's well-known manifesto to design with users, not for or by them [18]. There is also a close link with feminist notions of situatedness and located accountability [26, 37]. Both these approaches acknowledge that designers—authors—have their own perspectives, expertise, and goals, and that a designer's motivations are problematic when they are hidden or denied, not because they exist. A designer (author) who truly respects an audience will be inspired by differences in perspective, and thus will be able to use conflicts in beliefs, values, and goals productively, in the manner of equal partners in a conversation, where the outcome is uncertain and is therefore potentially exciting, revelatory. The resource collections created in the context of this study, with their provocative category structures and other thematically compelling features, provide evidence for this assertion. As the student designers came to understand, in such an environment of equality, the audience cannot be patronized. The author must work to understand the audience's convictions but not reproduce them; instead, the author uses these as a foundation for new understanding on everyone's part, the author included.

The idea of a rhetorical dialogue, and the roles of author and audience, instead of user and designer, can be of value in various forms of interaction design. "Audience-centered" design may help to rehabilitate the concept of the user as an active, vital agent whose beliefs and values are to be understood and respected, in order that the story be heard and dialogue ensue. Too often, in system design, the "user" is decomposed into a faceless set of tasks and needs, whose success at getting things done is prioritized over thoughts and feelings [16]. As this study suggests, however, an audience must be understood at a much deeper level if the author is to succeed at initiating a true conversation.

Criticism in design education and practice

This dialogic rhetorical approach to collection design was partly enabled through the student designers' experiences with the structured, formalized critique of an existing collection. Students were required to produce a written critical analysis that considered the example collection from the perspective of the author, from the perspective of the audience, and from the perspective of an information critic surveying the negotiated relationship between the two. Moreover, they were required to present their ideas through a standard essay format, with a clear unifying thesis, and to bolster their observations with reference to course readings from rhetoric, literary studies, design, and information criticism [15, 23, 31, 4].

The work performed in the critique markedly reinforced the notions of dialogic design that the project was attempting to instill in the participants and directly informed the resulting collection designs. One form of inspiration involved the recognition of relatively deep thematic problems in the example, Sustainability Is Easy, and an accompanying resolve to avoid such issues in their own designs. But another form of inspiration was generated from sustained engagement with the work of scholars and critics of design, rhetoric, and so on, and from the application of these ideas to the example collection. Isabella, for example, employed Lowgren and Stolterman's notion of "use qualities," and in particular their characterizations of seductivity and control/autonomy, to provide depth and structure to her critique, and then also used those concepts to propel her own project.

The results of this study provide clear empirical evidence that critical inquiry of the form endorsed by Bardzell, Bolter, and Lowgren can be an important and productive component of interaction design education [5]. The student designers read scholarly work that took a critical perspective; they used their understanding of this work to create their own critical accounts of a design example; and they were then able to extend that thinking to produce their own innovative collection designs, even though they had never engaged in this sort of design activity before. It may be argued that experienced designers do not need to articulate formal criticism in this way, that they can express sophisticated design judgments through activities such as sketches and "crit" sessions without employing a structured analysis of the sort described here. I do not think, however, that the utility of those activities is denied by exploring the complementary potential of criticism in a practice, as well as an educational, setting. Assuming a critical gaze forces one to look at a design differently, to develop a new vocabulary for describing how things work and what effects are produced. The form of attention produced through critical engagement with existing artifacts can, this study suggests, can be a direct engine of creativity and innovation.

ACKNOWLEDGMENTS

My sincere thanks to Gary Geisler and the students in INF 385U, Digital Media Collections, spring 2010 and 2011, for making this work possible. I also thank Pedja Klasnja and Chris LeDantec for their helpful notes on earlier drafts.

REFERENCES

1. Aristotle. *On rhetoric*. George Kennedy, trans. New York: Oxford Press, 1991.
2. M. Bakhtin. *The dialogic imagination*. Caryl Emerson and Michael Holquist, trans. Austin, TX: University of Texas Press, 1982.
3. J. Bardzell. Interaction criticism and aesthetics. *Proceedings of ACM CHI 2009,* pp. 2357–2366, 2009.
4. J Bardzell and S. Bardzell. Interaction criticism: A proposal and framework for a new discipline of HCI. *Proceedings of ACM CHI 2008,* pp. 2463–2472, 2008.
5. J. Bardzell, J. Bolter, and J. Lowgren. Interaction criticism: three readings of an interaction design, and what they get us. *Interactions,* 32–37, 2010.

6. C. Beghtol. Relationships in classificatory structure and meaning. In C. Bean and R. Green, editors. *Relationships in the organization of knowledge*. Boston: Kluwer Academic Publishers, 2001.
7. E. Black. The second persona. *Quarterly Journal of Speech,* 56(2), 109–119, 1970.
8. I. Bogost. *Persuasive games: the expressive power of video games*. Cambridge, MA: MIT Press, 2007.
9. G. Bowker and S. L. Star. *Sorting things out*. Cambridge, MA: MIT Press, 1999.
10. V. Broughton. *Essential thesaurus construction*. London: Facet Publishing, 2006.
11. R. Bryant. *Discovery and decision: exploring the metaphysics and epistemology of scientific classification*. Cranbury, NJ: Associated University Presses, 2000.
12. K. Burke. *A rhetoric of motives*. Berkeley, CA: University of California Press, 1969.
13. J. Carroll and M. B. Rosson. Getting around the task-artifact cycle: how to make claims and design by scenario. *ACM Transactions on Information Systems,* 10(2), 181–212, 1992.
14. S. Consolvo, et al. Activity sensing in the wild: a field trial of UbiFit Garden. *Proceedings ACM CHI 2008,* 1797–1806.
15. C. DiSalvo. Design and the construction of publics. *Design Issues* 25(1): 48–63, 2009.
16. M. Dörk, S. Carpendale, and C. Williamson. The information flaneur: a fresh look at information seeking. *Proceedings of ACM CHI,* pp. 1215–1224, 2011.
17. W. Duff and V. Harris. Stories and names: archival description as narrating records and constructing meanings. *Archival Science,* 2, 263–285, 2002.
18. P. Ehn and M. Kyng. The collective resource approach to systems design. In G. Bjerknes, P. Ehn, and M. Kyng, eds. *Computers and democracy: a Scandinavian challenge*. Aldershot, UK: Avebury, 19–57, 1987.
19. M. Ereshevsky. *The poverty of the Linnaean hierarchy*. Cambridge, UK: Cambridge University Press, 2007.
20. M. Feinberg. An integrative approach to the design of knowledge organization schemes. *Proceedings of the ISKO Conference,* 2010.
21. M. Feinberg. Compiler to author: a process for designing rhetorically aware document collections. *Journal of the American Society for Information Science and Technology,* 62(9), 1784–1796, 2011.
22. B. J. Fogg. *Persuasive technology: using computers to change what we think and do*. San Francisco: Morgan Kauffman, 2007.
23. J. Forlizzi and C. Lebbon. From formalism to social significance in communication design. *Design Issues* 18(4): 3-13, 2002.
24. S. Foss and C. Griffin. Invitational rhetoric. *Communication Monographs* 62, 2–18, 1995.
25. G. Geisler. Open Video Digital Library Toolkit software. Documented at http://www.open-video-toolkit.org/
26. D. Haraway. Situated knowledges: the science question in feminism and the privilege of partial perspective. *Feminist Studies* 14(3), 575–599, 1988.
27. E. Hooper-Greenhill. *Museums and the interpretation of visual culture*. London: Routledge, 2000.
28. W. Iser. *The act of reading: a theory of aesthetic response*. Baltimore, MA: Johns Hopkins University Press, 1980.
29. B. Kwasnik. The role of classification structures in reflecting and building theory. In R. Fidel, B. Kwasnik, and P. Smith, eds. *Advances in Classification Research,* vol. 3. Medford, NJ: Learned Information, 1992.
30. J. Lave and E. Wenger. *Situated learning: legitimate peripheral participation*. Cambridge, UK: Cambridge University Press, 1991.
31. J. Lowgren and E. Stolterman. *Thoughtful interaction design: A design perspective on information technology*. Cambridge, MA: MIT Press, 2004.
32. J-E. Mai. Classification in context: relativity, reality, and representation. *Knowledge Organization,* 31 (1), 39–48, 2004.
33. L. Nielsen. From user to character: an investigation into user-descriptions in scenarios. *Proceedings of DIS,* pp. 99–104, 2002.
34. J. Pruitt and J. Grudin. Personas: practice and theory. *Proceedings of DUX,* pp.1-5, 2003.
35. B. Rayward. Visions of Xanadu: Paul Otlet and hypertext. *Journal of the American Society for Information Science,* 45(4): 235–250, 1994.
36. A. Snodgrass and R. Coyne. *Interpretation in architecture: design as a way of thinking*. London: Routledge, 2006.
37. L. Suchman. Working relations of technology production and use. *Computer Supported Cooperative Work* 2, 21–39, 1994.
38. T. Vetting Wolf, J. Rode, J. Sussman, and W. Kellogg. Dispelling design as the "black art" of CHI. *Proceedings of ACM CHI,* pp.521–530, 2006.
39. J. Zimmerman, J. Forlizzi, and S. Evenson. Research through design as a method for interaction design research in HCI. *Proceedings of ACM CHI 2007,* pp. 493–502, 2

The Mismeasurement of Privacy: Using Contextual Integrity to Reconsider Privacy in HCI

Louise Barkhuus
Mobile Life @ Stockholm University
164 40 Kista, Sweden
barkhuus@mobilelifecentre.org

ABSTRACT

Privacy is a widely studied concept in relation to social computing and sensor-based technologies; scores of research papers have investigated people's 'privacy preferences' and apparent reluctance to share personal data. In this paper we explore how Ubicomp and HCI studies have approached the notion of privacy, often as a quantifiable concept. Leaning on several theoretical frameworks, but in particular Nissenbaum's notion of contextual integrity, we question the viability of obtaining universal answers in terms of people's 'general' privacy practices and apply elements of Nissenbaum's theory to our own data in order to illustrate its relevance. We then suggest restructuring inquiries into information sharing in studies of state-of-the-art technologies and analyze contextually grounded issues using a different, more specific vocabulary. Finally, we provide the first building blocks to such vocabulary.

Author Keywords

Privacy; user studies; location-based services; ubiquitous computing; online social networks

ACM Classification Keywords

H.1.2 [User/Machine Systems]: Human factors;

INTRODUCTION

With sensor-based and networked technologies built into the fabric of our everyday lives, from mobile personal devices to work places and public areas, personal information is now more accessible and sharable than ever before. This leads to a natural level of concern as to who has access to one's personal information and how it is shared. Research is therefore increasingly addressing issues of personal privacy. As opposed to data privacy (also referred to by Iachello and Hong as 'data protection' [21]), where laws and even constitutions prescribe what can and cannot legally be shared, personal privacy addresses the more fluid notion of privacy around a person, such as one's right to control personal information flow.

Issues of personal privacy in particular emerge in relation to the use of mobile devices that can take advantage of context information such as identity and location of a user, because mobile applications share information that was previously unsharable. Just as the digitization of music not only made it possible to edit music after recording but also enabled effortless (sometimes illegal) sharing, digitization of other information presents equally mixed advantages.

Many studies have investigated users' information management within interactive, mobile systems as well as individual's concern for information sharing when using mobile and sensor-based applications, studies that are relevant for CHI in terms of future design and development of technologies. However, despite research addressing overall concerns relating to personal privacy in these systems, there is a shortage of empirical studies focusing on the underlying contextually grounded reasons for people's privacy concern or lack thereof. Desiring to uncover simple rules and guidelines for design of sensor-based technology, many researchers have instead investigated narrow issues of information sharing such as *with whom* people would like to share particular information, and *when*, but few such studies have applied more theoretical notions of privacy to their data analysis or developed theoretical frameworks (with some notable exceptions [1, 12, 30]). With the limited analytical treatment of privacy, empirical findings are often locked into the context of the study. In this paper we argue that privacy is not an easily measurable unit and that we as HCI researchers and practitioners need to approach the notion through more contextually grounded measures. We hope to provide researchers with better insights into the concept of privacy and better tools to study this often slippery notion. We base our argument on Nissenbaum's theory of 'Contextual Integrity' [29], which views privacy as the appropriate flow of information rather than a static act of sharing. Illustrating key issues from the theory with our own empirical data, we provide evidence for the shortcomings of previous scenario-based studies of sensor-based services; we then provide recommendations for

CHI'12, May 5–10, 2012, Austin, Texas, USA.

research approaches to privacy and suggest the first important distinctions within a new privacy vocabulary.

TECHNOLOGY AND INDIVIDUALS' PRIVACY SENSITIVITIES

Researchers have already expressed concerns about digital technologies' ability to easily distribute even simple personal data such as birthplace and date; it has been argued that because electronic data can be shared more easily than paper-based directories, new standards for protecting personal information were needed [28]. In the mid-nineties, new telephone systems capable of displaying the caller's number (caller ID) were challenged as privacy invading, as they left the caller unable to remain anonymous until he/she chose to reveal him/herself [26]. More recently, sensor-based personal technologies such as location tracking applications and public surveillance have presented new challenges to the individual's sense of personal privacy. A number of studies have explored individual preferences for sharing information (such as location) through survey instruments, usually involving descriptions of likely scenarios of use [5, 25]. In Tang et al.'s study user-created data was used to generate scenarios about which participants answered questions regarding location-sharing preferences [35]. Using interview methods, other studies have explored issues such as attitude toward the sharing of online media [20], or WiFi snooping of content from personal laptops [24]. These studies set the scene for understanding initial reactions to information management, and provide a valuable foundation for later research. Yet, a basic challenge in this work is the inherent ambiguity in the definition of privacy itself, as well as questions over the generalizability of specific results.

Where most of these studies look at particular aspects of privacy concern, others have attempted to take a broader, more theoretical stance. Palen and Dourish, for example, provide a thorough analysis of privacy issues within socio-technical systems. Leaning on Altman's theory that describes privacy as dialectic and dynamic control processes for privacy boundaries, the authors analyze several relevant prototype and implemented systems. They point to the disparity that privacy regulation is not static or rule-based, yet technology, by definition, relies on both rules and stable functionality. The authors emphasize that the importance is not the specific privacy settings within the technology itself, but rather how the technology fits into cultural practices of privacy management [30]. Dourish and Anderson similarly argues that privacy cannot be viewed only as economic rationality, where personal information is provided in exchange for the benefit of a service or social value [16]. An interesting proposition following this argument is to view privacy as based on accountabilities of presence [37]. Our approach to privacy builds partly on this work in that we agree with the importance of fitting technology into already existing cultural practices. While these discussions focus on the issues governing interpersonal privacy management as a way to inform researchers and developers more broadly in terms of technology design, we propose a more contextually grounded approach to actual empirical research and a more dynamic use of the concept of privacy within HCI.

Another relevant theoretical approach is that of Boyle and Greenberg [13]; the researchers provide a taxonomy for different technical types of support for privacy in the use of video media awareness systems and describe a vocabulary for individual's modalities of privacy control. This vocabulary provides a useful and clear description of *how* individuals control their privacy in relation to media awareness. In this paper, however, we address the basic issue of *why* privacy is so important to use of sensor-based systems in order to continue answering how people negotiate privacy in everyday situations.

Location-Based Technologies

These issues of privacy are particularly relevant to location sharing. Location-based systems have entered many people's lives in the form of friend finders (such as foursquare, Gowalla and Facebook), map based searches (as provided with for example Google maps) and way-finding systems (GPS navigators). Such applications introduce a new set of privacy issues related not only to surveillance but also to simple factors such as control of impression management and interpersonal privacy [30]. It is therefore no surprise that many studies of people's privacy concerns and preferences for data sharing have focused particularly on location. Where some studies have based their findings on scenario testing [5], others have deployed systems with real-time sharing of location [36] or focused on commercial systems [20, 27]. These efforts to pinpoint aspects of people's concerns regarding location sharing are of particular interest in this paper. Where, from a naïve perspective, a person's location is not sensitive information (in that a person is generally physically visible to others), the recording and sharing of this information with people outside the physical vicinity make this information potentially sensitive. Researchers have, since early prototype systems, attempted to determine and predict specific location sharing practices [14, 25] and attributed results to the concept of 'privacy preferences'. However, most technology-focused studies of personal privacy preferences/perceptions have yet to provide a clear description of how these findings fit into a broader understanding of personal privacy.

The Understanding of Privacy

Nissenbaum's theory of *contextual integrity* [29] emphasizes that there is no aspect of human life that is "not governed by [context-specific] norms of information flow" [29, p. 119], those being cultural, ethical or moral norms. We are able to fluently transform our behavior according to these norms just as we appropriate our actions with people we have different relationships with. She argues that there are no such thing as universal privacy norms but that these are distinct to each situation, and assist in maintaining contextual integrity. *Contextual integrity* describes a desirable state that people strive towards by keeping perceived-private information private according to the context. For example, people expect to share medical information with doctors but not with employers. Where it in some cultures yearly salary is perceived as private, within others it is normal to share this information. Contextual integrity thereby explains how privacy is grounded in each context, governed by pre-existing norms and values. To explain her theory of contextual integrity, she highlights three principles that dominate the public discussion of privacy policy: (1) protecting the privacy of individuals against government intrusion, (2) restricting access to sensitive personal information and (3) protecting personal space. It is argued that because many new socio-technical and sensing technologies (for example public surveillance) fall into grey areas or even outside these principles, there is no pre-defined understanding of privacy in these situations. The argument relates to Boyle and Greenberg's explanation of "inadvertent privacy violations" where the media space design aligns poorly with social and human factors [13]. It thus appears rather narrow to attempt to generate generalized, rule-based principles about personal privacy preferences. Understanding personal privacy concern requires a contextually grounded awareness of the situation and culture, not merely a known set of characteristics of the context.

The current popular attempt to provide general guidelines about privacy preferences is flawed exactly because of the user studies' lack of situational foundation. We suggest that other, more theoretical, measures are included in the broader discussion of privacy in relation to technology studies. In the following section we expand on Nissenbaum in relation to our own empirical data to support our argument.

THE CASE FOR CONTEXTUAL INTEGRITY

To support our proposition that privacy should be approached as a much more flexible notion and to explain the theory of contextual integrity, we lean on empirical data focusing on mobile personal information management. The data is from a project studying university students' use of a mobile social network (Facebook); this group is of particular interest since they illustrate common use of a network that is highly integrated into their daily lives. We do not claim that these students represent the broader population but rather that this sub-population represents a particular set of values in an extreme, highly social, highly mobile setting. Their practices illuminate aspects of privacy that so far have been ignored. The project itself focuses on broader issues; here we focus on their information-sharing and privacy perceptions (see [12] and [6] for further details on the project). The data consist of qualitative semi-structured interviews with 60 students as well as data collection from their online profiles. All participants accessed their online social network mostly from their mobile device (iPhone, Blackberry), resulting in very integrated use where other types of text communication such as text messaging were placed side by side in terms of importance.

In this section we examine three parts from Nissenbaum's theory in an aim to provide real-life examples of how privacy is perceived, negotiated and articulated: social appropriateness, distribution and change of norms. We apply our own data selectively, acknowledging (and emphasizing) that one particular online social network does not contain generalizable behavior,. We aim to exemplify particular characteristics of Nissenbaum's theory to build our argument.

Social appropriateness

Part of Nissenbaum's reasoning refers to how norms of appropriateness determine what personal information is fitting to reveal in a particular context. Each social setting prescribes what kind of information is expected to be shared; it is appropriate to share medical data with doctors but not with distant acquaintances and it is normal to share romantic details with friends but not with colleagues. These norms are primary to behavior and inform the contexts wherein actions are performed. Among our participants it was clear that such concept of social appropriateness was in place regarding their use of the online social network. Just as face-to-face contexts are governed by norms, so were the online communication situations that the participants reported. This communally understood behavior, or as Mancini et al. refer to as 'unspoken code of conduct' [27], contributes to a general understanding of social context, and participants had few problems with others overstepping their bounds of privacy. In the few cases where such overstepping had occurred, swift action by the participants had been taken, such as unfriending a friend who repeatedly sent unwanted messages. This general understanding of limits and bounds was in place partly because the network had been part of the participants' lives for 3+ years but more importantly because they had the ability to weigh situations and act accordingly.

Nissenbaum also stresses how an important part of norms of appropriateness is the distinction between different relationships, different social roles. How a person behaves is dependent on the other people present in the context. For our participants it was clear that their personal information sharing was grounded in their own perception of their social relations present on Facebook. Their content sharing was meant for their full set of friends with few exceptions. As in other research [20], none of the participants had divided their friends into sub-groups, providing reasons that this is a time-consuming task or due to unawareness of this feature. Instead they were reasonably aware who was on their friend list and shared information accordingly. The 'mom test' was not uncommon, illustrated by this male participant: "I am friends with my mom on Facebook so I guess I am okay with my mom seeing it." Participants' content was self-censored to fit the 'greatest common divisor'.

Another method of tailoring the content to the socially appropriate situation was to publish content that was specifically understood by a subgroup but not by the rest of the group. While the study took place the university held an 'end of semester' extended weekend and although it was known internally by students that a lot of drinking took place, the status messages were cryptic enough to leave outsiders with some ambiguity as to what was going on. Participants wrote content such as: "[name of special weekend]...Worlds greatest college weekend...love you" and another participant wrote: "thinks [name of special weekend] is going great =]". The plausible deniability that vague messages provided was enough for the participants to find them acceptable, even though the vast majority stated that alcohol in pictures or status message was improper, especially because two thirds were under 21, the legal drinking age in the US. It was necessary for the participants to manage their content tightly due to their broad set of friends, conforming to the notion of social appropriateness.

Challenges to Research

Nissenbaum points out that although norms of appropriateness are part of everyday life, these norms are not explicitly addressed in research that informs privacy policies. We also find that much research relating to privacy issues and technology has, if not simply ignored context, then attempted to generalize to other contexts on the basis of characteristics. It is not uncommon for studies to inquire to their participants' preferences for information sharing on the basis of scenarios or personas rather than within an actual sharing situation. Before commercial sharing applications were available this seemed acceptable, but even with experience sampling made possible in networked mobile devices, the 'experience' tracked is still too complex to generate general rules from. Our concern here is not simply the quality of research methods but the approach to privacy that many studies take, attempting to gather information that can inform design in the form of 'people's general preferences for privacy'. By studying behavior as predictable and generalizable, personal privacy research is missing out on opportunities to understand people's underlying motivations for sharing and not sharing in the first place. This brings us to a discussion of the distribution of information, or information flow.

Information Flow

Another set of norms that Nissenbaum uses to explain privacy in terms of contextual integrity is the concept of information flow. Like the norms of social appropriateness, existing norms of information flow are engrained into everyday life, again in particular related to different relationships. Relationships are in essence defined by what type of information we share with one another. People share more intimate information with close friends and more general information with acquaintances. What we tell people about ourselves is in a sense as important as what we hold back in terms of forming relationships, a factor that should inform our understanding of privacy. These norms of information flow help explain the sudden concern over sharing personal information such as present location or preferences for particular material commodities. Yet, most people also have an exhibitionist desire to share at least some personal information with different sets of people, described as "self-exposure".

Reasons to share personal information

Before the advent of online social services such as Flickr, Twitter and Facebook, many people found it difficult to imagine the value of sharing with superficial relations trivial, personal information as is done now through status messages and photos of small everyday events (and for many it still is). But interest in others' personal lives have always been part of human nature, and with the introduction of reality shows in the late '90s more and more people have been getting their '15 minutes of fame', to the joy and entertainment of others. What appealed to our participants were some of the same factors that are at play in reality television where apparently normal people (as opposed to people with particular abilities leading to their fame such as singing, acting, writing or sports) have their personal lives exposed. It is the dual pleasure of both being able to expose ones' self and being able to 'snoop' on others' private lives that is at play here. A female participant for example expressed why she found Facebook so intriguing: "It's for the same reason that, you know, people find celebrities entertaining and so many gossip, you know, it's like reading about other people's life, especially when you know them, is just really entertaining". Exposing personal information in essence makes the person 'feel famous', especially when others comment on content (in public or semi-public), which is re-affirmed as the person is able to see others' personal information and comment on it. The network, in this sense, fulfilled a need for self-exposure but at the same time users were able to manage their personal information. The dual desires to expose private personal information to seek attention and to 'snoop' on others' personal lives work well in an online social network where relationships are dominated by weak ties [17].

Reasons not to share personal information

Obviously there is also personal information that people are not interested in sharing with (selected) others and this is the area of which most research has addressed. Many studies, particularly of ubicomp technologies, focus on what information people do not wish to share. However, what many of these studies ignore and misunderstand is the distinction between different intents behind not wanting to share a piece of personal information. A participant who responds that they would not share a particular piece of information with a particular other is not necessarily *worried* about the other person obtaining this information or expressing privacy concern. There are multiple contextual factors at play. Here we propose a simplified explanation where there are two reasons for not sharing information, one a genuine concern about others knowing something (a *secret*) and the other simple *modesty* or politeness, not wanting to 'burden' others with seemingly insignificant information. Where *modesty* governs particularly weak ties (e.g. we do not have genuine *concern* about the person next to us in the coffee shop knowing our name and position, yet we would not walk over and volunteer that info); *secrets*[1] govern to a higher degree close ties (e.g. we would not expect our close friend to tell our spouse what we have bought them as a Christmas present). The closer a relationship gets, the more information is often exchanged between the partners and the more potential 'secret' or 'relationship specific' information exist. In an odd way new social media technology supports the *modesty*-motivated desire not to share, by making it available for easy access rather than having to specifically provide the information. While people are not sharing information specifically with each other, they are making personal information available to interested others; it is not a motivation to hide information but a motivation to adhere to common practices of what information to (explicitly) share with specific people in specific situations (information flow based on relationships). It was clear from our study that the participants were able to negotiate their shared content to fit with both motivations of modesty (by not 'forcing' information on anyone) and secrets (by not revealing inappropriate information to people on their friend list).

Negotiating information sharing on the ground

As we have argued, supported by Nissenbaum, information flow defines individual social relationships, but digital technologies are not very good at managing groups of relationships, except laboriously. Facebook does have an option to separate friends into groups and publishing content to specific groups only; however, despite its apparent usefulness, none of our participants had taken advantage of this feature, either because they were not aware of it or because they did not want to spend the time on customization. Perhaps, one of the problems with this tool is that a friend list is still static when it has been created. Following the principles of contextual integrity, each status message and each picture should be published to a new unique list of friends. Another obvious flaw, based in the user interface, is that receivers of the messages cannot see who the message had been shared with, which subset of friends or the sender's whole network; this prevents the message from being socially translucent [18]. Instead of using friend subsets, the participant showed us how they negotiated the sharing by going by 'greatest common devisor. When asked if they worried about their privacy, a male participant said that he did not but "I am conscious of what I put up there", indicating that he would rather censor the content than fiddle with detailed privacy settings. This highlights the point that controlling information flow is negotiated on the ground, locally, instead of through a complex set of settings behind several pages, which was not transparent to view at each posting[2].

The area where most self-presentation management took place for the participants was in relation to pictures posted on Facebook. One female participant for example said: "People that take pictures of me are people who are allowed to take pictures of me I guess, like friends..." and another participant said "If there is a picture where I don't look my best I don't want to be tagged and I will untag it." The same participant expressed how she was able to check out her boyfriend and how she would look through his profile on occasion: "...there have been a few incidents were, like he will be tagged in a picture with another girl and I will ask 'what was that?' and it is nothing that has been too problematic..." Identity management was conducted as an ongoing activity where the personal information sharing was constantly held up against the social norms of information flow, norms tailored to the participants' relationships.

Research often points to the discrepancy between expressed privacy concern and apparent oversharing, or inflated self-reports of concern that do not fit with actual information protection behavior [1]. We found part of a potential explanation in that several participants were not sure exactly who they where sharing their content with. One participant, for example, replied to our question of which friends he shared content with: "I think... I don't even really know... I think it is just private, I mean only people from [the university] can search me or my other networks..." It was not uncommon to be unsure of their actual settings, which in return questions, if not the validity, at least the usefulness of studies viewing 'friends-only' sharing as a 'privacy enhancing behavior' [34]. Instead, we note how information-sharing practices were negotiated on the ground, within single experiences; if our participants experienced something negative, they changed behaviors.

This data should clearly illustrate our earlier emphasis that studying privacy preferences is complex and should be rooted in context. No matter how detailed a scenario is given within a study and no matter how many characteristics of participants' real life is based on real information, each situation is unique for the individual, and each decision to share or not is decided within that context.

Change of Norms

As a final characteristic from Nissenbaum's theory, we turn our attention to the changing of norms over time. What was appropriate to know about other people at one time is not the same today. Where in the 1990s it was inappropriate or at least questionable to be aware of the caller's identity

---

[1] By secrets we do not mean juicy tales of cheating spouses but simple daily relationship negotiations, such as not wanting a spouse to hear a heart-to-heart talk with a friend.

[2] Facebook has recently changed the way users chose who to share content with and selecting people and lists appears to be slightly more transparent.

before picking up the phone, it is today inconceivable not to have the caller ID function on cell phones. Especially with technological development, norms change rapidly, some more subtly than others.

Several of our participants made reference to changes of this sort. They had encountered something undesired, such as an unwanted post on their profile, and had de-friended the offender; their friend-accepting behavior consequently became more conservative, and most participants claimed that they knew virtually all of their friends personally and had met them in real life. We propose that even within an online social network norms change, and participants illustrated a change in social norms in their transition from high school to university. Where it was appropriate to accept (and possibly interact) with all friend requests in high school, now more moderate norms reigned.

One problem with inquiries into privacy preferences and concern in relation to prototype technologies is these technologies' lack of establishment among the people testing them. Much of the research within ubicomp and HCI uses prototypes, which can be a useful tool for receiving early feedback to new technologies, but which can be more complicated for studies predicting behavior manifested within repeated and socially established use. Looking at early preferences for potential sharing of certain data does not generate invalid findings but because their lack of grounding within actual lived situations they merely provide a tiny slice of potential human behavior in potential situations. It is therefore not only difficult to describe generic preferences among people but it is questionable how useful such prescriptions are long-term. At best they represent a snapshot in time, describing how current norms influence behavior.

We now step outside Nissenbaum's theory and continue by looking at a well-studied type of personal data in terms of concern for sharing: location. Ubicomp research, in particular, has maintained location as a focus of research, partly due to recent technological developments and partly due to its wide appeal in social applications. By illustrating the use of location within our own data, this discussion adds to the argument that preferences for personal privacy are grounded in contextual integrity.

LOCATION SHARING AND PRIVACY

Location has recently become a type of personal information that is possible to record and share, in real time, through our pervasive mobile devices. This intriguing type of personal information can have useful and productive applications (such as locating emergency calls from cell phones, locating nearest point of interest and locating friends of interest), but can also aid misuse (locating victims by criminals and stalkers, targeted but unwanted advertisements, and locating by unwanted friends/family). More importantly, the very essence of personal privacy includes the permission to 'hide', that is, placing oneself in seclusion, away from self-selected people. The prospect of being located is therefore also distressing for people if not in full control of this information. Referring back to Nissenbaum's concept of contextual integrity, it should be clear how general societal norms, in terms of the appropriateness of real-time location sharing, have yet to develop; so far we adhere to common sense. It is therefore no surprise that research has been particularly curious about people's concern for location sharing.

Many studies of privacy concern relating to location have been scenario based; participants were provided with descriptions of situations (often based on person-relevant data) and then asked if they were comfortable sharing particular location information with particular people [5, 10, 11, 25, 35]. Others have employed actual sharing technologies and in-situ studies [4, 22, 23, 31, 36, 38]. Each study focuses on particular elements of behavior or perception, for example how *much* concern individuals express [5], how their level of concern influences their privacy settings [36, 38] or people's willingness to share location information with others depending on location and recipients [2, 14, 25]. Most of this work attempts to pin down people's perceptions and preferences of sharing personal data with a wide, but specified, set of people.

Different Types of Location

In these studies the concept of location is addressed as *a single type* of information. Papers conclude and generalize about 'location privacy' based on the location type that they are looking at, despite other studies and other applications using and studying different granularities of location as well as different types of location information. Where some applications rely on exact geo-referenced locations using latitude and longitude, others use user-entered place names. Yet others (for example commercial 'check-in' services such as Gowalla, foursquare and Facebook's check in) use community-named locations. The level of accuracy also differs, but with most commercial systems now using GPS, with WiFi fingerprinting as backup, the imprecision of early systems has decreased. Unfortunately, treating such diverse information as a single entity waters down analysis and generalizability between studies. Systems and findings are compared inappropriately to other systems and research, leading to analogies and conclusions that may not be justified. 'Location' is, like the notion of privacy, a vague concept, interpreted variously according to context.

One way this problem manifests is that reviews of literature on location sharing services often do not actually mention what type of location data was shared. The difference between sharing a named location (such as 'Home', 'Peet's Coffee', 'University and 9th Av') and exact geo-referenced location is significant for social appropriateness; where providing a self-defined location is better in upholding accountability and contextual integrity, a geographical reference is more likely to reveal locations with no social translucence [18]. Similarly, the difference between 'checking in' and constant background updating also poses a significant shift in accountability; a manual check-in is controlled by the user, but a location provided by background updating can be misunderstood by even the closest friends. This is particularly relevant when adhering to the view that privacy is based on accountabilities of presence [33, 37].

Some studies do address the issue of disclosing location at different levels of granularity; Consolvo et al., [14] for example, directly asked people about which level of location information they would reveal and Hecht et al., looked at manually entered location [19]. There is a major difference of the user's perception between sharing location with different granularity and of different type, and little research so far has addressed this issue. Comparing or contrasting people's preferences for sharing geo-referenced location with sharing self-defined, text-based locations makes little sense, owing to social norms around providing this information [32]. In fact, the increased social translucence of self-defined location not only adds contextual information, it can also contribute to maintaining personal relationships [4] and is therefore likely more rewarding to use.

Motivations for Sharing Location

Although some studies have looked into motivations for sharing location digitally with friends or sharing with third parties [6, 14, 15], few studies have been able to ground their studies in real situations. In the studies that have investigated why and how their participants wanted to share location information in particular situations, the situations were mainly provided as scenarios, or location was given only as a geo-referenced type [5, 11, 25, 36].

Our own data confirmed that individuals occasionally use Facebook to post their location. Yet, their understanding of social appropriateness prevented them from just showing up at a friend's location unless explicitly invited. "That would be creepy," participants explained. The norms in our (Western) society (at least since the telephone was widely adopted) dictate that people do not 'just show up' but make prior social engagements. This transferred to Facebook even though the knowledge of people's whereabouts was now often more detailed. Interestingly, this use is in contrast to social networks that were specifically developed for meet-ups such as Dodgeball[3]. We have earlier pointed out how specifically inviting status messages can lead to real-life meet-ups, but that these were almost always mediated by other communication [6].

This common rule in turn made location a fairly uninteresting status to post for our participants unless it was in the context of something more 'status-worthy' and we found less than 5% of their status messages contained reference to present location. The surprising finding that none of the participants 'checked in' (through Facebook's own feature) or pushed Gowalla or foursquare locations to their Facebook profile was very likely a feature of our student sample. They lived in a small college town with few core social spots and possibly felt the need to convey their identity [15] through other expressions.

Inquires into people's 'privacy preferences' and 'privacy practices' are often based on the belief that privacy is of clear concern to all. But while people of course do have such concerns, these are rarely well articulated or generalizable, even within individuals. Studies often inquire what types of information the participants are willing to share, and in what situations, but the analyses often neglect to inquire the deeper reasons why people are not willing to share particular information. Studies that have asked this question often find different reasons than those of privacy. Consolvo et al., for example, in their initial study of location-sharing preferences, highlights issues of privacy between hierarchical relations; employees are more cautious about sharing location information with their managers, which would then indicate a generic predictor with whom people want to share information with [14]. However, in the authors' later technology implementation of Reno, they point out that participants mainly turned off automated sharing in order not to 'spam' the people they shared location with [22]. Bales et al. also found that the 'off setting' in their location-sharing system CoupleVibe was used merely out of courtesy for the sharing partner, for example due to a known time difference, instead of a clear preference for privacy [3]. And in our own study of Connecto, groups of co-workers, including a manager, shared location throughout the study without expressing any significant concern [4]. This ties back to the discussion of modesty versus secrecy in terms of motivations. Even these few examples show how modesty is also too simple a concept to explain motivations; so where people might seem reluctant to share location data by answering negatively in a study or survey, the reasons for this are contextually defined. Unfortunately the data from the many studies that look at sharing preferences skews our knowledge of real users' motives and more broad considerations for their privacy.

We now turn to a discussion of possible implications for research that this rather rigid notion of privacy in HCI research is contributing to.

IMPLICATIONS FOR RESEARCH

As described in this paper, the actual data that are often shared, or imagined shared, are in no case homogenous across studies; where some share a community-defined location, others share an exact geo-referenced location, etc. This is in itself not problematic because different systems make use of different types of data, but when researchers compare findings across studies, the fallacy is to think that these can inform one another and together build a

[3] Dodgeball was a text-message based social network existing from 2000 to 2009. It enabled people to see which of their friends were nearby, focusing on social gathering.

generalized notion regarding 'privacy behavior'. It is for example impossible to ask if people have any concerns about sharing their 'location' and get a useful answer, since location is not a discrete piece of data; it is an interpretive type of information that can be perceived differently by different people depending on a range of details; it is always contextually dependent. A major gap in the discussion is therefore one of data type. People's answer to 'where are you' depends on the situation, as witnessed by the location-sharing studies that were based on self-input locations (such as [4] and [22]). Sometimes the importance is a specific restaurant, other times it is simply the city. The choice depends on numerous factors, all grounded in the specific context of the information provider and his/her receivers. Unfortunately, geo-referenced systems are not flexible enough to support different granularity, apart from simple obfuscation. Geo-referenced systems therefore do not provide well for individual accountability; in a world where the pub is next door to the library, the goal to uphold contextual integrity can easily fail. We therefore suggest that location-sharing studies emphasize granularity and data type of location before trying to generalize uses and sharing preferences; by examining location sharing in context one can better understand the diverse set of privacy issues.

Our second implication can be found in our finding that many studies are not grounded in actual user situations. Although many studies use real user data, it is rare to see studies that implemented real systems with real data sharing or which used in-situ survey data. Instead users are asked to evaluate potential situations on the basis of their own data. Although these studies might introduce us to basic issues of personal information management and hint at early reactions to sharing potentially sensitive data, they should not be mistaken for rule-generating or theory-informing research. When, as Nissenbaum suggests, all decisions and potential privacy violations are based in the real-life context informed by social norms, it is not possible to generalize further than the studies' own context. We therefore call for more contextually-grounded research that explores privacy issues in the wild.

Third and finally, the issues we as researchers should address regarding privacy are more complex than just *concern*. Privacy is also a way for us to maintain distance to weak-tie acquaintances and it is something we maintain by not 'bothering' others, as illustrated above. There are many reasons for hesitancy to share personal information, from courtesy and modesty to uncertainty about the audience. Few studies within HCI and ubicomp today have been able to pinpoint exactly *why* their participants reacted the way they did, only answering *how* they reacted and *what* their practices were. If we view privacy in a broader light, it transforms (as Palen and Dourish has also pointed out [30]) into the everyday negotiations done to manage not only the availability of one's personal information, but also the information that one receives about others. This important characteristic of privacy leads us to emphasize that it is the *appropriation of behavior* in the situation that informs new research and not a behavioristic belief that people's actions are based on a structured set of privacy concerns. Instead of focusing on the *how* and *what* in terms of people's preferences for personal data sharing, we need a foundation of research that looks at *why*.

CONCLUSION

In this paper we have attempted to frame and discuss the notion of privacy as it is studied and presented in relation to HCI and ubicomp technologies. It is no doubt a slippery notion that tends to be used for any kind of concern about personal information recording and sharing. With location detection being of particular interest, many studies have examined concern for the sharing of personal location data, real-time as well as recorded. We believe that a great portion of this research is not grounded in real-world situations and is therefore unable to provide more than coarse generalizations, which in many cases are easily predicted by applying already-present theoretical frameworks such as Nissenbaum's contextual integrity [29], Altman's theoretical privacy framework (as used by Palen and Dourish [30]) and Agre's discussion of 'the new landscape' [1].

With illustrations from our own study of practices among highly mobile users of an online social network, we emphasized how articulated privacy concerns were less visible among our participants but that they instead adjusted their practices according to social norms. They changed behavior (e.g. being more conservative in their friend acceptances) mainly after having experienced something negative, something that made them question their private integrity. Although we do not claim that our data set, collected from a very homogeneous and non-representative set of people, provides generalizable findings about broader aspects of privacy, we found it useful to illustrate some of the points of our argument.

From our analysis of literature and our own empirical data it is clear that privacy concerns are not easily measurable. People want accountability for their actions, they want control over their own personal data, and they want plausible deniability for their recorded and shared personal data. When data is already semi-public, for example when a person is out in public or self-posts information online, sharing does not violate any sense of privacy, except if this sharing goes beyond what is commonly conceivable in accordance with contextual integrity. It is therefore reasonable to state that people prefer manual systems where they keep control over their data and in which they can define the shared data themselves, from situation to situation (such as for example self-defined labels). At the same time it is important not to underestimate the social consideration people have for one another, particularly in close relationships (strong ties); they are simply not interested in providing more information than necessary in scenarios of personal information sharing due to modesty but also because this can also lead to complex scenarios of sense of reciprocity (see Bales et al., for a discussion [3]).

Our major aim with this paper is to call for a more nuanced treatment of the notion of privacy within HCI. In fact we will go as far as to suggest minimizing the use of this loaded and commonly-misunderstood word. Often, research is in fact addressing issues of information sharing practices and concern for revealing personal data. Using the word *privacy*, particularly to elicit data from participants, not only introduces the complexity of multiple interpretations of the word but also automatically stamps the data as sensitive. Location information, for example, is in many public situations the most available data about a person, free for all to see; yet many current studies present a general concern for sharing such information widely.

We therefore suggest that future studies use a different, more specific vocabulary for empirical research. Such vocabulary should explicitly distinguish between carefully determined reasons *why* individuals want to share or not share information before looking at how and what. Our initial analysis here uncovered the notions of secrecy and modesty, concepts that provide a first step for such distinction. We suggest that the next steps are taken in the direction of uncovering the established sense of social appropriateness and its influence on people's information sharing practices. Yet such investigation should distinguish between social norms and personal appropriateness due to their distinct characteristics and influence of behavior. Viewing social norms and personal appropriateness as fluid notions will prevent overarching generalizations based on situational characteristics and instead provide a better understanding of why, rather than how, individuals want to share personal information. Only by utilizing such detailed vocabulary can we begin to gain a better insight into personal information sharing practices.

ACKNOWLEDGMENTS

The author would like to thank Nis Bornoe for help with the fieldwork. Also thanks to Leysia Palen and Paul Dourish for thoughtful comments on the paper. Finally, thanks to Valerie Polichar for editorial assistance.

REFERENCES

1. Agre, P. Introduction. In Agre, P. and Rotenberg, M. *Technology and privacy: the new landscape.* MIT Press. 1998.
2. Anthony, D. Henderson, T. and Kotz, D. 2007. Privacy in Location-Aware Computing Environments. IEEE Pervasive Computing 6, 4 (October 2007), 64-72.
3. Bales, E., Li, K. A. and Griswold. W. 2011. CoupleVIBE: mobile implicit communication to improve awar eness for (long-distance) couples. In Proc. of CSCW '11. ACM, New York, NY, USA, 65-74.
4. Barkhuus, L., Brown, B., Bell, M., Sherwood, S., Hall, M. and Chalmers, M. 2008. From awareness to repartee: sharing location within social groups. In Proc. CHI '08. ACM, New York, NY, USA, 497-506.
5. Barkhuus, L. and Dey, A.K. Location-Based Services for Mobile Telephony: a study of users' privacy concerns. In Proceedings of Interact 2003, pp. 207-212.
6. Barkhuus, L. and Tashiro, J. 2010. Student socialization in the age of facebook. In Proc. of CHI '10. ACM, New York, NY, USA, 133-142.
7. Bell, G. and Dourish, P. 2007. Yesterday's Tomorrows: Notes on ubiquitous computing's dominant vision. *Personal Ubiquitous Computing.* 11, 2, 133-143.
8. Bell, M., Reeves, S., Brown, B., Sherwood, S., MacMillan, D., Ferguson, J. and Chalmers, M. 2009. EyeSpy: supporting navigation through play. In Proc. of CHI '09. ACM, New York, NY, USA, 123-132.
9. Bell, M., Chalmers, M., Barkhuus, L., Hall, M., Sherwood, S., Tennent, P., Brown, B., Rowland, D., Benford, S., Capra, M. and Hampshire, A. 2006. Interweaving mobile games with everyday life. In Proc. of CHI '06. ACM, New York, NY, USA, 417-426.
10. Benisch, M., Kelley, P.G. Sadeh, N. and Cranor, L. F. Capturing location-privacy preferences: quantifying accuracy and user-burden tradeoffs. In *Personal and Ubiquitous Computing*, December 6., 2010, 1-16.
11. Bernheim Brush, A.J., Krumm, J. and Scott. J. 2010. Exploring end user preferences for location obfuscation, location-based services, and the value of location. In Proc. of Ubicomp '10. ACM, 95-104.
12. Bornoe, N. and Barkhuus, L. 2011. Online Social Networks On-The-Go: An Exploration of Facebook on the Mobile Phone. Horizon paper in Proc. of CSCW EA 2011.
13. Boyle, M. and Greenberg, S. 2005. The language of privacy: Learning from video media space analysis and design. *ACM Transactions of Computer-Human Interaction.* 12, 2 (June 2005), 328-370.
14. Consolvo, S., Smith, I. E. Matthews, T., LaMarca, A., Tabert, J. and Powledge, P. 2005. Location disclosure to social relations: why, when, & what people want to share. In Proc. of CHI '05. ACM, 81-90.
15. Cramer, H., Rost, M. and Holmkvist, L.E. 2011. Performing a check-in: emerging practices, norms and 'conflicts' in location-sharing using foursquare. In Proc. of MobileHCI '11. ACM, 57-66.
16. Dourish, P. and Anderson, K. 2006. Collective Information Practice: Exploring privacy and security as social and cultural phenomena. Human-Computer Interaction. 21, 3 (September 2006), 319-342.
17. Ellison, N. B., Steinfield, C. and Lampe, C. 2007. The Benefits of Facebook ''Friends:'' Social Capital and College Students' Use of Online Social Network Sites. Journal of Computer-Mediated Communication 12 (2007), pp. 1143-1168.

18. Erickson, T., Smith, D. N., Kellogg, W. A., Laff, M., Richards, J.T. and Bradner, E. 1999. Socially translucent systems: social proxies, persistent conversation, and the design of "babble". In Proceedings of the SIGCHI conference on Human factors in computing systems: the CHI is the limit (CHI '99).
19. Hecht, B. Hong, L., Suh, B., Chi, E.H. Tweets from Justin Bieber's Heart: The Dynamics of the "Location" Field in User Profiles. In Proc. of CHI '11. ACM, New York, NY, USA.
20. Hull, G., Lipford, H. R. and Latulipe, C. Contextual gaps: Privacy Issues on Facebook. In Ethics of Information Technology, 2010, Springer.
21. Iachello, G. and Hong, J. End-user privacy in human-computer interaction. Foundational trends of human-computer interaction, 1, 1 (jan, 2007), pp. 1-137.
22. Iachello, G., Smith, I., Consolvo, S., Abowd, G. D., Hughes, J., Howard, J., Potter, F., Scott, J., Sohn, T. and Hightower, J. et al. Control, Deception, and Communication: Evaluating the Deployment of a Location-Enhanced Messaging Service. In Proc. of UbiComp '05, Springer, 213-231.
23. Jedrzejczyk, L. Price, B. A., Bandara, A.K. and Nuseibeh, B. 2010. On the impact of real-time feedback on users' behaviour in mobile location-sharing applications. In Proc. of SOUPS '10. ACM, New York, NY, USA, Article 14.
24. Klasnja, P., Consolvo, S., Jung, J., Greenstein, B.M., LeGrand, L., Powledge, P. and Wetherall, D. 2009. "When I am on Wi-Fi, I am fearless": privacy concerns and practices in everyday Wi-Fi use. In Proc. of CHI '09. ACM, New York, NY, USA, 1993-2002.
25. Lederer, S., Mankoff, J. and Dey, A.K. 2003. Who wants to know what when? privacy preference determinants in ubiquitous computing. In Proc. of CHI EA '03. ACM, New York, NY, USA, 724-725.
26. Lyon, D and Zureik, E. Surveillance, Privacy, and the New Technology. In Lyon, D. and Zureik, E. *Computers, Surveillance, & Privacy* (eds). University of Minnesota Press. 1996.
27. Mancini, C. Thomas, K., Rogers, Y., Price, B.A., Jedrzejczyk, L., Bandara, A. K., Joinson, A. N. and Nuseibeh, B. 2009. From spaces to places: emerging contexts in mobile privacy. In Proc. of Ubicomp '09. ACM, New York, NY, USA, 1-10.
28. Mayer-Schönberger, V. Generational Development of Data Protection in Europe. In Agre, P. and Rotenberg, M. *Technology and privacy: the new landscape*, pp. 219-243. MIT Press. 1998.
29. Nissenbaum, H. Privacy as Contextual Integrity. Washington Law Review 79 (30), 2004.
30. Palen, L. and Dourish, P. 2003. Unpacking "privacy" for a networked world. In Proc. CHI '03. ACM, 129-136.
31. Sadeh, N. Hong, J., Cranor, L., Fette, I., Kelley, P., Prabaker, M. and Rao, J. 2009. Understanding and capturing people's privacy policies in a mobile social networking application. Personal and Ubiquitous Computing, 13, 6 (August 2009), 401-412.
32. Schegloff, E.A. 1972. Notes on a Conversational Practice: Formulating Place, in D. N. Sudnow (ed.), Studies in Social Interaction (New York: MacMillan, The Free Press, 1972), 75-119.
33. Shklovski, I., Vertesi, J., Troshynski, E., Dourish, P. 2009. The Commodification of Location: Dynamics of Power in Location-Based Systems. In Proc. of Ubicomp '09, 11-20.
34. Stutzman, F. and Kramer-Duffield, J. Friends Only: Examining a Privacy Enhancing Behavior in Facebook. In *Proceedings of CHI '10*. ACM Press, 1553-1562.
35. Tang, K. P., Lin, J., Hong, J.I., Siewiorek, D.P. and Sadeh, N. 2010. Rethinking location sharing: exploring the implications of social-driven vs. purpose-driven location sharing. In Proc. of Ubicomp '10. ACM, New York, NY, USA, 85-94.
36. Toch, E., Cranshaw, J., Drielsma, P.H., Tsai, J.Y., Kelley, P.G., Springfield, J., Cranor, L., Hong, J. I. and Sadeh, N. 2010. Empirical models of privacy in location sharing. In Proc. of Ubicomp '10. ACM, 129-138.
37. Troshynski, E., Lee, C. and Dourish, P. 2008. Accountabilities of presence: Reframing location-based systems. In Proc. of CHI '08, ACM, New York, 2008.
38. Tsai, J. Y., Kelley, P., Drielsma, P., Cranor, L. F., Hong, J.I. and Sadeh, N. 2009. Who's viewed you?: the impact of feedback in a mobile location-sharing application. In Proc. of CHI '09. ACM, 2003-2012.

Tag, You Can See It! Using Tags for Access Control in Photo Sharing

Peter F. Klemperer*, Yuan Liang*, Michelle L. Mazurek*, Manya Sleeper*, Blase Ur* Lujo Bauer*, Lorrie Faith Cranor*, Nitin Gupta*, Michael K. Reiter†

*Carnegie Mellon University
Pittsburgh, PA
{klemperer, yliang, mmazurek, msleeper}@cmu.edu
{bur, lbauer, lorrie, nitingupta}@cmu.edu

†University of North Carolina
Chapel Hill, NC
reiter@cs.unc.edu

ABSTRACT

Users often have rich and complex photo-sharing preferences, but properly configuring access control can be difficult and time-consuming. In an 18-participant laboratory study, we explore whether the keywords and captions with which users tag their photos can be used to help users more intuitively create and maintain access-control policies. We find that (a) tags created for organizational purposes can be repurposed to create efficient and reasonably accurate access-control rules; (b) users tagging with access control in mind develop coherent strategies that lead to significantly more accurate rules than those associated with organizational tags alone; and (c) participants can understand and actively engage with the concept of tag-based access control.

Author Keywords

Access control; human factors; tagging; privacy

ACM Classification Keywords

H.1.1. User/Machine Systems: Human Factors; D.4.6 Security and Protection: Access controls

INTRODUCTION

Users often have rich and complex sharing preferences for digital content, including online photo sharing [1, 4]. For example, a user may wish to share photos of a work picnic only with co-workers who participated in the event, while blocking those same co-workers from seeing photos taken at a family party. However, non-experts have difficulty using currently available mechanisms to create and maintain access-control policies that capture their sharing preferences [8, 24].

Tags, including descriptive keywords and captions users add to their photos, could potentially help users create and maintain fine-grained access-control policies more intuitively. Currently, users tag photos for purposes including organization, search, communication, and description (hereafter collectively termed *organizational tags*) [5]. Improvements in automated and assisted tagging — including location tagging via GPS-enabled smartphones and facial-recognition tools found in services like Picasa and Facebook — are making tags increasingly available while decreasing user burden. More broadly, "users have learned to find data by describing what they want ... instead of where it lives" [20], and data management using tag-like organization is emerging in systems such as music management in iTunes, note-taking programs like Evernote or Springpad, and file-tagging mechanisms built into Windows and MacOS.

Systems that use such tags to define access-control policies have been prototyped [3] [6]. However, the usability of tag-based access control has not been investigated using users' own content, tags, and access-control policies. In this paper, we employ an 18-participant laboratory study using participants' own photos to explore the feasibility of tag-based access-control rules for photo sharing. Although tag-based access control could potentially apply to broader categories of digital content, we draw on photo sharing as an initial case study both because users have varied access-control preferences for photos and because systems that allow users to tag photos are already in use.

To explore the efficacy of tag-based access-control rules, we consider the following research questions:

- ***Q1: Can organizational tags be repurposed as-is to create effective access-control rules?***: Users already create tags for purposes including organization, search, description, and communication. To allow tag-based access control to function with minimal overhead, can rules based on these currently available tags capture user preferences?
- ***Q2: Does tagging with access control in mind improve the performance of tag-based access control?***: For tag-based access control to be practical, users must intuit how adding and removing tags affects their access-control policies. When tagging with access control in mind, do users' tags more accurately capture their preferences?

- ***Q3: How do users engage with the concept of tag-based access control?***: Tag-based rule creation should be intuitive and understandable for users. What strategies do users employ when simultaneously tagging photos for both their current, organizational purposes and access control? What do users understand and like about tag-based access control, and what impediments does tag-based access control present? Can users understand and suggest tag-based access-control rules that support their preferences?

We found that organizational tags could be repurposed to create efficient and reasonably accurate access-control rules. When participants tagged photos with access control in mind, they were typically able to develop coherent strategies and create tags that supported significantly more accurate rules than those created from organizational tags alone. We also observed that participants understood the concept of tag-based rules and were able to actively engage in rule suggestion.

We first discuss related work and then detail our methodology. We next present some basic data about our participants' demographics, access-control policies, and tags. We proceed to our main results and analysis and then discuss some study limitations. We conclude by highlighting implications for the design of tag-based access-control systems.

RELATED WORK

This work focuses on photos as a case study to explore how tags could be used for access control. Prior work has examined tag-based access control from both system-building and machine learning standpoints, but only in a limited way concerning usability. The broader literature includes research on both access-control preferences and user-created tags.

Tag-based access control and management

Tag-based access-control systems have been prototyped. Au Yeung et al. implemented a system with access-control policies specified in terms of photos' tags; usability was outside their scope [3]. Hart et al. designed a tag-based access-control system for blogs that performed better than typical privacy tools on a generic blog [6], but they did not examine users' actual preferences for their own content, as we do.

Other work has investigated using tags to predict or recommend access-control policies. Vyas et al. used tags to automatically recommend privacy policies for content, while Squicciarini et al. used a combination of automated image-content analysis and tags to predict privacy policies [25, 23]. In contrast, we allowed users to explicitly define tags for access control.

Prior work also investigated semantic tagging for file and document management [20]. Several distributed file systems have been constructed on this principle [15, 18, 19]. Future systems could include tag-based access control.

Access-control policies and preferences

Studies have demonstrated that users have varied and complex photo-sharing preferences. Miller and Edwards classify digital photographers into two groups: those who share primarily with real-life friends, and those who focus on sharing broadly with online communities [11]. Besmer and Lipford report that concerns about photo privacy are driven by "identity and impression management" rather than by fears about physical safety [4]. Ahern et al. found that sharing decisions were often affected by the location where photos were taken and photo content. They note that sharing decisions are influenced by how easily users can create nuanced policies, demonstrating a need for usable policy management [1].

Beyond photo sharing, research indicates that, while information-sharing preferences can often be categorized into broad classes, exceptions are frequent and important [9, 14]. Other studies report that sharing preferences are frequently dynamic, depending on content lifecycles, the context of sharing requests, and expectations about how shared data will be used [10, 16]. Other work suggests sharing decisions may be governed by the difficulty of setting and updating policies, reinforcing the idea that users must be able to easily set up access-control policies [22, 24].

Tagging

We investigate creating access-control policies from photo-management tags. A number of researchers have examined tagging behavior. Ames and Naaman categorized photo tags as organizational or communicative and intended for oneself or others [2]. Kirk et al. found users often group photos by event [7]. Nov et al. found that users' tagging motivations influence the number of unique tags they create [13].

More broadly, Zubiaga et al. suggest that taggers who categorize rather than describe content provide better inputs to automated classifiers [26]. Gupta et al. provide a survey of tagging motivations, content, and recommendations [5].

METHODOLOGY

We designed an exploratory laboratory study during which participants performed three separate tagging tasks. The first task focused exclusively on *organizational tagging* to help a user organize and search her photos, while the second and third tasks focused on organizational tagging in combination with tagging for access control. These tasks provided insight into participants' tagging behaviors and strategies (Q3). Tags from these tasks were also used to create machine-generated access-control rules that roughly approximated users' policies. Some of these rules were shown to the participants to demonstrate the tag-based access-control concept and stimulate discussion (Q3). We also used the tags and machine-generated rules during post-processing to evaluate the efficacy of organizational tags for access control (Q1) and to compare the performance of organizational-only tags to combined organizational and access-control tags (Q2).

Recruitment

We used advertisements on Craigslist, in the university's newspaper, on a university research participant website, and on posters around Pittsburgh to recruit English-speaking participants who take at least 100 photos per year. Because we were interested in the usefulness of existing organizational tagging strategies for access control, we required that participants add keyword tags or captions to photos "often" or "always." We eliminated participants who only tagged photos on Flickr or Facebook since Flickr tags tend to be created for sharing [11], and Facebook tags are limited to people's names. We felt that including such users would skew the results, although excluding them may limit generalizability.

Qualified participants were asked to upload 40 photos they had previously tagged. To prompt potential participants to provide photos for which they might have varied access preferences, we provided them with a list of 17 suggested photo categories, including "up to 15 photos that you haven't posted publicly and wouldn't want to share with the general public," "3 photos with trees in them," and "3 photos with your relatives in them." We also asked them whether they would be willing to share the photos with "some," "none," or "all" of several groups of people. Potential participants who answered "none" or "all" to all categories were eliminated. As we discuss in detail in the Limitations section, we believe these measures were successful.

We sent our screening survey to 152 people, 63 of whom completed the survey. Of those 63, we rejected 39 people who only tagged photos on Facebook or Flickr, 5 who did not tag frequently enough, and 1 who lacked English proficiency. The remaining 18 people made up our participants.

Procedures

Qualified participants were invited to our lab for the main part of the study, which lasted between 1.5 and 2.5 hours. During this portion of the study, we observed their organizational tagging behaviors and their strategies for incorporating access control into their tagging schemes. We also presented participants with machine-generated, tag-based access-control rules, both to demonstrate tag-based rules and to gauge their reactions. For this portion of the study, we used the Picasa desktop photo software and custom web interfaces.

Warmup task

We gave each participant a brief tutorial on tagging photos in Picasa. As a warmup task, we asked her to add at least one tag to each of five sample photos unrelated to her own photos.

T1: Organizational tagging

T1 was designed to evaluate how effective organizational tags can be for expressing access-control policies.

Prior to the lab session, we stripped all existing tags from the participant's photos, saving these *original tags* for later reference. In the lab, we asked the participant to re-tag her stripped photos with the objective of finding the photos more easily in the future, adding as many tags as she would like. We asked participants to re-tag their photos so we could observe each participant's tagging behavior using a think-aloud procedure.

Collecting access-control preferences

Next, we collected a set of the participant's access-control preferences for her study photos. These preferences served as ground truth for creating and evaluating access-control rules.

We collected a list of people with whom the participant might want to share photos. We first prompted for three people with whom she had a close relationship, including household members, friends, and significant others. We then prompted for four to seven people with whom she had less close relationships, such as supervisors, friends of friends, neighbors, and colleagues. From here forward, we will refer to this entire set of people as the participant's *friends*.

We then presented the participant with an *access grid* mapping her photos to her friends. We added a "Public" friend column to represent posting a photo publicly, in connection with the participant's real name. For each combination of friend and photo, we asked the participant to select a preference from the following options:

- **Strong allow**: Allow access; would be upset if the friend were not able to view the photo.
- **Weak allow**: Allow access; would not be very upset if the friend were not able to view the photo.
- **Strong deny**: Deny access; would be upset if the friend were able to view the photo.
- **Weak deny**: Deny access; would not be very upset if the friend were able to view the photo.
- **Neutral**: Absolutely no preference between allowing and denying the friend access to the photo.

To confirm understanding, we asked the participant to point out and explain one example for each type of preference (or to explain why that preference would not be needed).

Example rules

At this point, we introduced the participant to the concept of tag-based access-control rules. To aid this introduction, we created a set of machine-generated best-fit access-control rules for each of the participant's friends. Rule generation is described in more detail below. Each friend was assigned zero or more rules of the form "If *tagged / not tagged* with *tag*, then *allow / deny*," combined with *and* and *or* as appropriate. Each friend was also assigned a *default rule* of allow or deny, which applied to any photos not covered by the other rules. Some friends were assigned only default rules — for example, the participant's spouse might be assigned the simple rule of "always allow" access to all photos. The participant's boss, by contrast, might be assigned a more complicated ruleset with three rules: "If tagged with *landscape*, then *allow*"; "if tagged with *work*, then *allow*"; and the default rule "otherwise deny."

We applied the machine-generated rulesets to the participant's photos, resulting in a set of allowed and denied photos for each friend. In the interest of time, we selected two example rulesets to present, including at least one example with at least one non-default rule. If no non-default rulesets were created, we showed the participant a default-only ruleset, as well as a generic non-default example prepared in advance.

Our goal with these examples was to familiarize the participant with the idea of tag-based access-control rules and get preliminary reactions, rather than to evaluate the success of these rules in detail. We designed a simple rule-display interface, shown in Figure 1, intended only to demonstrate the

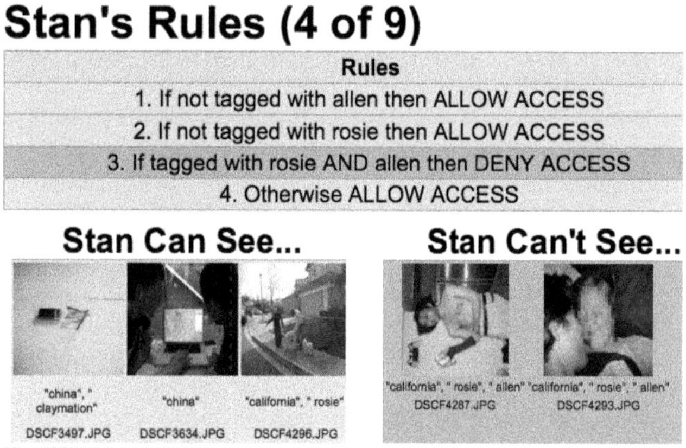

Figure 1. The interface we used to demonstrate machine-generated rules and their effective access policy. (Names changed and faces blurred.)

machine-generated rules and stimulate discussion. The interface displayed the text rules for a given friend at the top of the screen and a thumbnail photo display at the bottom. The photo display distinguished the photos the friend was and was not allowed to see under the rules. Each photo was displayed with its tags to help the participant understand how the rules were applied. This interface was not intended to simulate any real system for managing tag-based access control.

T2: Tagging for access control

After using the sample machine-generated rules to introduce the concept of tag-based access control, we returned to Picasa for T2. We invited the participant to add to and/or delete from the tags she had added in T1, with the joint objectives of finding photos more easily and creating tag-based access-control rules. As before, we observed the participant's tagging behavior and strategies using a think-aloud mechanism.

Detailed review of machine-generated rules

Next, we explored how successful the participant's T2 strategy had been and gathered detailed feedback on the tag-based access-control concept. We used the tags from T2 and the participant's access-control preferences to create a new set of machine-generated access-control rules for each friend. We showed the participant all the resulting rulesets, using the same interface, one friend at a time. For each friend, we asked detailed questions about how accurately the rules reflected the participant's preferences, including for other photos she had taken in the past or might take in the future.

We also used our interface's *"show conflicts" view* to highlight any photos that were misclassified. We asked how upset the participant was about the misclassifications and how they affected her view of the ruleset's overall success. We also asked how she might change the tags or the ruleset to more accurately reflect her preferences.

T3: Refinement and wrap-up

To examine what the participant had learned, we invited her to add to and/or delete tags from T2, this time keeping in mind what she had learned during the detailed rule review. Once again, the goal of the tagging was to make both finding photos and developing access-control rules easier. As before, a think-aloud mechanism helped us observe the participant's behavior and strategy. Although we created rules from these tags for post-processing and analysis, in the interest of time we did not show these rules to the participant. Finally, we asked each participant a series of general questions about her photo-tagging and sharing habits.

Machine-generated rules and analysis

We used machine-generated rules both to demonstrate tag-based access-control rules to our participants and to conduct post-interview analysis. For demonstration, we were mainly interested in creating rules that were somewhat human-readable and would provoke discussion (Q3). In post-interview analysis, we used the machine-generated rules to investigate Q1 and Q2: Could we construct reasonably well-fitting access-control rules from organizational tags, and would tags modified with access control in mind produce better rules? For this purpose, a rough approximation seemed sufficient, so we did not attempt to find an optimal rule-generating algorithm or construct the best possible rules for each participant.

To achieve both goals, we created rules using an open-source implementation of the c4.5 decision-tree algorithm [12].[1] We trained the algorithm for each friend, lumping together weak and strong preferences into *allow* and *deny* categories and using default sensitivity settings. Photos with neutral preferences were ignored during training.

We displayed the results of the training to the participants and used them in our later analyses. We did not use separate training and test sets, because we wanted to establish a baseline scenario for how tags aligned with access-control policies. Future work might separately consider finding the optimal algorithm for generating rules, as well as how well rules generated from one set of photos could predict access-control policies for other photos.

We report the results of generating rules from the participants' original tags, as well as their tags from tasks T1, T2 and T3, in the Results and Analysis section.

DEMOGRAPHICS, POLICIES, AND TAGS

Table 1 lists demographic information for our 18 participants. Half were men, and half were women. The subjects trended young (between 18-32) and technologically focused: 10 of the 18 self-identified as science, technology, engineering and math (STEM) professionals or students. This bias toward youth and STEM professions may limit the generalizability of this study. Other work related to tagging and access control has also focused on similarly young populations [23, 25].

Our 18 participants provided between 40 and 48 photos each and listed 7 to 10 friends, plus Public. Overall, they expressed 6847 access preferences, each for one combination of a photo and a friend. 15.7% of preferences were strong allow, 40.8%

[1] http://www2.cs.uregina.ca/~dbd/cs831/notes/ml/dtrees/c4.5/tutorial.html

Code	*Age*	*Gender*	*Occupation*	*Photos/year*	*Tag software*
P01	23	F	STEM professional	1001-5000	Picasa
P02	20	F	engineering student	101-500	iPhoto
P03	27	F	service industry	501-1000	Picasa, Facebook, Tumblr
P04	32	F	STEM professional	1001-5000	Skydrive
P05	24	F	student	1001-5000	iPhoto
P06	23	M	engineering student	501-1000	Picasa
P07	22	M	engineering student	101-500	Picasa
P08	24	M	student	101-500	Picasa
P09	18	M	engineering student	5001+	Picasa
P10	24	M	STEM professional	5001+	Photoshop Album
P11	26	M	STEM professional	1001-5000	Flickr
P12	28	F	art, writing	5001+	Lightroom
P13	23	M	clothing designer	51-100	Twitter, Yfrog, Photobucket
P14	20	M	engineering student	1001-5000	Picasa
P15	19	F	music student	501-1000	Picasa
P16	29	F	anthropology student	1001-5000	iPhoto
P17	25	M	STEM professional	501-1000	Picasa
P18	18	F	art student	1001-5000	iPhoto

Table 1. Participant demographics.

were weak allow, 11.0% were strong deny, 14.9% were weak deny, and the remaining 17.5% were neutral. The distribution of preferences, however, varied widely across participants. P11 was most permissive, allowing 87.8% of access combinations; P04 was most restrictive, denying 80.0% of access combinations.

In T1, participants used on average 2.6 total tags per photo; P07 used the most, with 5.0, while P08 used the fewest, with 1.0. It is also possible to count the number of unique tags (e.g., counting the tag "family" once whether it was used once or many times). We will refer to this count as "unique" tags. Considering only each participant's unique tags, the average was 1.2 per photo, with a minimum of 4 tags for 48 photos (P13) and a maximum of 130 tags for 40 photos (P03).

RESULTS AND ANALYSIS

Our results show that tags created for organization can often be used to create reasonably effective access-control rules (Q1). Asking users to update their tagging schemes with access control in mind produced even more accurate rules, in many cases with only limited modifications to the tags (Q2). We also observed that most participants quickly understood tagging for access control and were able to develop and apply a modified tagging strategy (Q3).

In the first two subsections, we describe results related to Q1 and Q2, respectively. Taken together, qualitative results from both subsections also address Q3.

Organizational tags can express many access policies

Overall, organizational tags performed well as the basis for access-control policies. Rules generated automatically from the participants' T1 tags were highly accurate, resulting in few false allow or false deny conflicts and indicating that the tags were expressive enough to be useful for such policies. Overall, the rules generated conflicts for only 7.8% of non-neutral photo-friend combinations in T1, with a conflict rate under 5% for one-third of participants. The best case for organizational tags was no conflicts for P11, who had a very simple allow-most policy. The worst observed case was user P08, with 19% conflicts, due in part to his use of long, complex tags that were not repeated across photos. Figure 2 shows the rate of conflicts in each of the three tasks.

As a control, we compared our results to a simple default policy of either allow all or deny all, choosing the more accurate option for each participant-friend combination. In case of ties, we chose deny all to preserve privacy. This default policy, illustrated in Figure 2, produced more than twice as many conflicts as T1 (15.8% to 7.8%, significant, paired Wilcoxon, $\alpha = 0.05$).

Considering T1 conflicts in more detail, we found that for most conflicts (83.5%), the suggested rules disagreed with the less-serious weak preferences, bolstering the case that it is possible to make effective rules from organizational tags. To some extent, this reflects the fact that most non-neutral preferences were weak; however, we find that across participants, the proportion of conflicts with weak preferences was greater than the proportion of all preferences that were expressed as weak preferences (χ^2 per participant, aggregated using Fisher's combined test, $p < 0.05$).

In access control, false allows (erroneously granting access) are often of greater concern than false denies (erroneously denying access). In T1, 57% of conflicts were false allows. We might expect this to mirror the proportion of preferences that were deny preferences (since conflicts with those would be false allows); however, only 31% of preferences were deny preferences, a proportion significantly lower than that of the false allows (χ^2 and Fisher's combined test, as above, $p < 0.05$). More positively, most of those false allows conflicted only with weak preferences: just 13% of conflicts (less than 1% of decisions) were false allows that conflicted with a strong preference. We hypothesize that a classification algorithm tuned against false allows would ameliorate this further.

For most participants, a small number of photos were responsible for most conflicts. In T1, only 27% of all photos were misclassified by the machine-generated rules at least once, for any friend. The worst case was P04, for whom 60% of photos were misclassified at least once; for more than two-thirds of participants, fewer than one-third of all photos were ever misclassified. This suggests that minor improvements in tagging or rule generation might reduce conflict rates considerably.

Simple rules from organizational tags

Another way to evaluate the performance of tag-based access-control policies is to consider their complexity; policies with too many rules or rules with too many clauses could prove incomprehensible to users. We measure rule complexity in two ways: by counting the number of non-default rules generated for each friend, and then by counting the number of unique tags used in those rules.

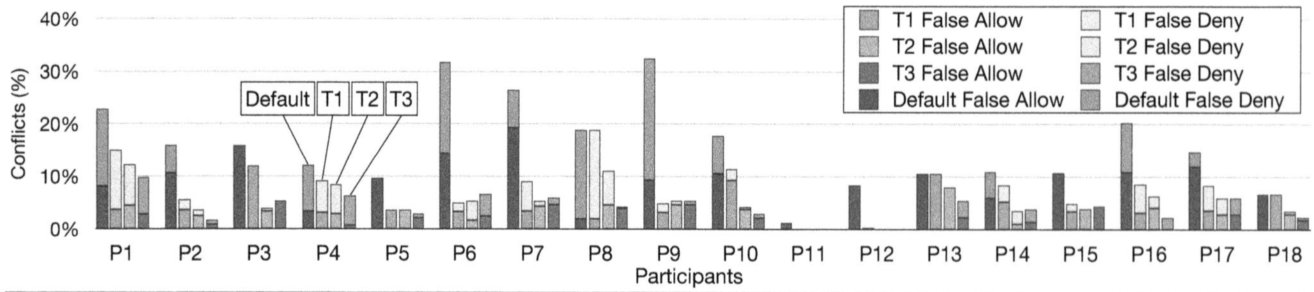

Figure 2. Conflict rate across tasks, for all participants, distinguishing false allows and false denies. For each participant, we show four vertical bars, one each for the default policy, T1, T2, and T3. The default policy is the more accurate of allow all and deny all for each friend. For most participants, the conflict rate was highest for the default and decreased in consecutive tasks. P11 had no conflicts, and P12 had only 0.02% false deny conflicts in T2.

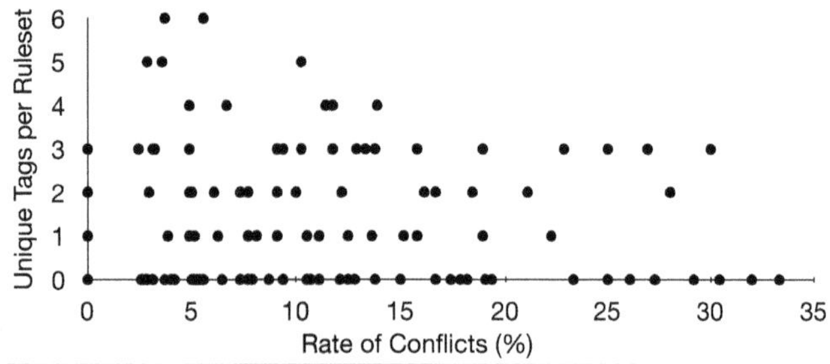

Figure 3. Rule complexity (measured in unique tags per ruleset) versus accuracy (measured in conflict rate), for 168 participant-friend combinations. A value of zero unique tags denotes a default-only ruleset (deny all or allow all). In general, many rules are both simple and accurate, and few rules are both complex and inaccurate.

By both of these measures, the rules we generated were fairly simple. In T1, more than half of the 168 participant-friend combinations resulted in default-only rules. Among the 75 non-default cases, an average of 2.8 non-default rules were made for each friend. Even the worst case was relatively straightforward: the largest four rulesets contained only 4 non-default rules each. Examining the unique tags used in each ruleset yields similar results. On average, non-default rulesets for T1 contained only 2.4 unique tags. The worst case, rulesets containing six unique tags, occurred only twice among the 75 non-default rulesets.

It is also interesting to consider the relationship between accuracy and rule complexity. Prior to the study, we hypothesized that more-accurate rulesets would also be more complex, necessitating a tradeoff between expressiveness and ease of use. To examine this, we plot rule complexity (measured by unique tag count) against accuracy (measured by conflict rate), for all 168 participant-friend combinations, in Figure 3. The results show many instances of rulesets that are both simple and accurate: examples include allowing a spouse to see all photos, forbidding the public to see any photos, or allowing a boss to see only photos tagged with "work." We also see many rulesets in the top-left and bottom-right, indicating at least some tradeoff between accuracy and complexity, with few instances of rules that are both complex and inaccurate.

Reactions to sample rules

After creating machine-generated rules from the T1 tags, we showed each participant two rules and asked for general reactions. Many participants liked these rules and found them intuitive. For example, P05 said the rules for a former teacher, which denied access to photos from a friend's wedding and a graffiti-covered landmark, made sense because the rules "conceptualized what [she] was thinking." P17 said rules created for a friend with a child his son's age matched "the intuitive rule that [he] made" while setting up his preferences: the friend could see only photos containing P17's son.

However, the rules created from the organizational tags were not always fully successful. In some cases, the tags included in the rules were too general or too specific. For example, P09 said a rule denying his roommate access to photos tagged with "gf" was too general, as he wouldn't need to restrict all photos containing his girlfriend. Other participants were generally satisfied with the rules but flagged some exceptions. P14 said a rule for a former teacher "seem[ed] roughly accurate," but he was upset that the teacher could see one embarrassing, slightly lewd picture. In other cases, the machine-generated rules appeared coincidental, fitting the participant's preferences but using tags with little or no relation to the participant's policy decision-making.

Reactions to tag-based access control

After reviewing the sample rules, we asked participants for their overall impressions of tag-based access control, and found that the concept typically made sense. On a five-point Likert scale, 13 participants said the concept made complete sense or some sense (scores of 5 or 4), two were neutral (score of 3), and one said the concept did not make sense (score of 2). Two others said it depended on circumstances (no score).

Among those who said the concept made complete sense, several said making policy using tags would save time or be "more efficient" (P03). Tag-based rules worked particularly well for P11, who had a subtle preference for preventing his family from seeing certain combinations of people: "If they can avoid seeing me and my girlfriend together, I'd probably use it for that."

P06, the only participant to say tag-based rules did not make sense, explained that he would need "a large number of tags to make it easier to make rules." P09, who chose neutral, expressed related concerns about scalability: "The results are great, but if you added more photos these rules would break down."

Ad-hoc access control with organizational tags

As another indicator that organizational tags may be appropriate for access-control policies, we found that several participants already used photo tagging to help implement their intended policies in various ad-hoc ways. P17 tagged his photos based mainly on the events at which they were taken; he used these tags to help him sort out which photos should be shared with whom on PicasaWeb. In the organization task, P01 tagged photos of herself with her boyfriend to keep track of things she didn't want her family to see.

Similarities between organizational and original tags

As described in Methodology, we also requested participants' original tags — that is, tags they added to the photos prior to the study — to confirm that the tags created in T1 were not highly different from tags the participants normally create. We were able to collect original tags for half our participants.

Our results indicate the two sets of organizational tags were reasonably similar. The overall rate of conflicts for rules generated from the original tags is 10.6%, compared to 8.5% for rules from T1 tags for the same 9 participants (not significant, paired Wilcoxon test, $p > 0.2$). This includes an outlier in P06, whose original photos included captions that were markedly different from the keyword tags he used in T1, resulting in a conflict rate of 25.9% for his original tags compared to 4.9% for his T1 tags. Original-tag conflict rates for the other 8 participants for whom this data was available were within 3 percentage points of the T1 rates. This provides a rough indication that T1 aligns with natural tagging behaviors for the majority of participants.

Tagging for access control provides improvement

Although access-control policies generated from organizational tags performed reasonably well, we found that policies generated from dual organization/access-control tags performed even better. The overall conflict rate improved significantly[2] from 7.8% in T1 to 5.2% in T2, and the worst-case rate improved from 18.9% (P08) to 12.2% (P01). Across participants, the average improvement was 2.7 percentage points.

We observed a smaller but still significant improvement between T2 and T3, as participants fine-tuned their tags after viewing rules. The overall conflict rate improved to 4.2%, and the worst case improved to 9.8% (P01). Individual participants' conflict rates dropped 1.1 percentage points on average.

The ratios of weak to strong conflicts and of false allows to false denies did not change significantly among T1, T2 and T3. Unsurprisingly, participants were more concerned with false allows than false denies. During the detailed rule review, we asked participants to report how upset they were about each conflict on a five-point Likert scale. Comparing median upsetness per participant, we find that false allows cause significantly more upset (paired Wilcoxon test, $p < 0.01$).

[2]Unless otherwise noted, significance tests in this section use a Friedman repeated-measures test to establish differences among the tasks, then paired Wilcoxon tests (chosen a priori) to separately compare T1 to T2 and T2 to T3. $\alpha = 0.05$.

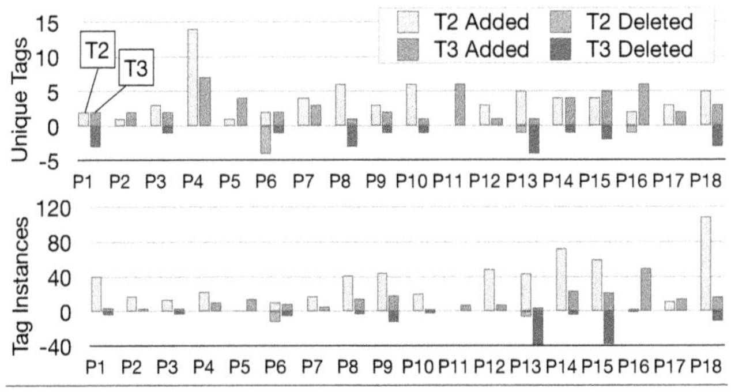

Figure 4. The unique tags and total tag instances added and deleted in T2 and T3, per participant.

Limited modifications for access-control tagging

Overall, participants made few modifications to their T1 tags in T2, averaging 33 modifications each, or less than one modification per photo. On average, participants only added or deleted 4 unique tags. Most of these changes (97%) were additions; only three participants deleted any tags in T2. P18 made the most modifications (108 additions, 5 unique); P11, by contrast, made no modifications.

Participants made even fewer refinements in T3, averaging 19 additions or deletions each (less than 0.5 per photo). P15 made the most (59, 7 unique), and P02 made the fewest (3, 2 unique). The refinement step was more balanced between addition and deletion; 65% of modifications were additions, and 10 participants deleted at least one tag. Figure 4 shows each participant's overall and unique modifications in both tasks.

Rule complexity across tasks

The overall pattern of avoiding complex, inaccurate rules was maintained across T2 and T3. The distribution of the complexity-accuracy tradeoff appeared to shift slightly, with more complex-but-accurate rules and fewer simple-but-inaccurate rules. This is attributable in part to a drop in default-only rulesets, from 93 in T1 to 66 in T2 and 59 in T3, as policies become more precise. However, this change was not signficant.

Strategies for access-control tagging

Participants appeared to follow one of three tagging strategies in T2: leveraging content-based tags for access control, using tags specifically designed to indicate access-control policy, or using a hybrid of content- and policy-based tags. Most participants articulated a clear strategy and applied it consistently, demonstrating that they had quickly grasped the concept of tag-based access control.

Five of 18 participants used the content-based strategy. At the extreme, P11 made no modifications because he felt his organizational tags were sufficient to specify his policy. P05 added "kiddos" to photos containing children, because their parents might not want those photos to be shared. P16 added "Belize" to one photo and changed "outside Sleeping Bear Lake" to just "Sleeping Bear Lake" on another; in both cases her modifications placed the photo in question into a group with other photos for which she had similar policy preferences. Participants using this strategy added, on average, 14 new tags and 4 new unique tags in T2.

Five other participants used an entirely policy-based strategy, creating tags indicating sharing policies like "private," "public," and "for friends." P09, who adopted this strategy, said he "would separate the two ideas [content and policy tags] completely." On average, participants using this strategy in T2 added 51 new tags and 4 new unique tags each.

The remaining eight participants used a hybrid strategy that combined policy- and content-based tags. Some of these participants used tags that conveyed both content and policy information, such as a "family" tag indicating family members could access photos containing family members. P07 used tags like these for family, close friends, and general friends. Others used both content and policy tags to form a combined policy: P10 wanted to restrict photos with the "private" tag from most people, as well as photos with "strange" or "weird" content from some of his less-close friends. Participants using the hybrid strategy added, on average, 31 new tags and 4 new unique tags in T2.

During the detailed rule review after T2, we asked participants to suggest ways to improve the machine-generated rules. Many were able to articulate simple rules that matched their tagging strategies more closely than the automated rules. For example, P02 noted the machine-generated rules did not pick up on her strategy to restrict photos tagged "goofy" from less close friends.

Refinement strategies in T3

As previously noted, participants refining their tags after the detailed rule review made few additional modifications. The modifications they did make generally demonstrated a strong grasp of tag-based access control and a consistent approach to making tags that would facilitate better rules.

Most participants used T3 to adjust the granularity of their access-control-tagging scheme. For example, P03 originally tagged photos she didn't want made public with "drunk"; in T3, she added a "very drunk" tag to distinguish permissions for different levels of drunkenness. P18 changed policy tags on some photos to distinguish between "friends" and "close friends." Others used T3 to make rules more generalizable: P16 added "landscape" tags on top of "Sleeping Bear Lake" to make a broader category, "because if it's restricted to lake pictures," her friends were "not going to be seeing much."

Other participants added tags that were not necessary for creating policies for the photos and friends in the study, but could be useful for broader policies. For example, P17 added a "Pittsburgh" tag to photos taken in Pittsburgh; these photos were already classified correctly for the friends in the study, but he wanted to make a rule to share the photos explicitly with friends from Pittsburgh. T3 was also frequently used to make corrections or fix inconsistencies in tags. P10 consolidated "weird" and "strange" into one "weird" tag after noticing both were used in rules.

Only one participant overhauled her entire tagging scheme in T3: after viewing her rules, P15 switched from a policy-based strategy in which she assigned tags based on who *should* see the photos to an inverse strategy of tagging based on who *should not* see the photos.

LIMITATIONS

There are several important limitations to our study design. First, our results are limited by the participants we recruited and the photos they provided. As discussed in Demographics, our subject pool skewed young and technical; it also included only people willing to upload their photos to our recruitment website. The generalizability of the photos provided was also limited by our request that participants upload previously tagged photos. We requested tagged photos so we could examine the ecological validity of tags created in our lab (as discussed in Results and Analysis). During recruitment, we attempted to encourage participants to upload a range of photos with different access preferences. We believe we succeeded, in part because participants expressed deny preferences for 25% of photo-friend combinations, including photos with sensitive content like alcohol, unprofessional behavior, and skinny dipping. We also asked participants about their current photo sharing preferences: 14 participants said they had published 80% or less of their study photos online. Most used various access-control mechanisms to protect photos they did publish, including setting privacy preferences on websites like Facebook and Picasa Web Albums. Participants distinguished clearly between these protected photos and photos published "publicly" on Tumblr, Twitter, personal websites and blogs. However, we acknowledge participants were unlikely to share their most private photos with us.

A second set of limitations concerns our use of machine-generated access-control rules. The algorithm has no access to the context and meaning of tags and no insight into the policy the participant intended when tagging for access control. As a result, some rules appeared strange or arbitrary to the participants, potentially driving them toward explicit policy-based tags like "private" and "public." We chose to use machine-generated rules to establish a standardized baseline for comparison accross tasks and provoke discussion with the participants. We also did not attempt to optimize our rule-generation mechanism or produce the best possible machine-generated rules. A better algorithm might result in fewer conflicts or strike a better balance among strong and weak conflicts and false allows and false denies.

Other limitations concern scale and generalizability. Our quantitative results measure only how well the rules fit the photos provided by the participants for the study; we talked to participants about how well the rules would generalize to other photos and friends, but cannot draw firm conclusions. Similarly, we cannot comment on whether the rules would remain tractable when dealing with thousands of photos and hundreds of friends, family members, and acquaintances.

DISCUSSION

Our results indicate that tag-based access-control seems promising. In this section, we discuss potential design implications that arose from our findings and observations.

Automated rule generation

Participants were generally supportive of automated rule generation, and several explicitly said that they would like a system that suggested access-control rules for their photos. As P12 put it, "That's kinda handy." Participants also did not seem to mind suggesting tweaks to automatically generated rules that did not completely capture their preferences. Although asking users to fill in an access-control grid for all their photo and preference combinations, as we did in the study, would be unrealistic in an actual system, such a system could potentially leverage users' willingness to tweak slightly incorrect rules by asking for a small set of ground-truth preferences over time and using these preferences to offer suggestions for baseline rules. Such a feature might be especially useful for people just starting to use a tag-based access-control system: results from our pilot testing indicate that users may better understand a tag-based rule system when it is demonstrated with their own tags and photos, rather than with generic examples.

Additionally, we did not try to optimize the machine-learning algorithm to reduce policy conflicts. Current work in privacy policy prediction promises to reduce conflicts further than observed in this work [23, 25].

Varied approaches to exception handling

Participants showed varying levels of preference flexibility when presented with tag-based rules. We categorize a user as *flexible* if, when presented with conflicts during the detailed rule review, she generally indicated this new access-control setting was also acceptable. In contrast, a *strict* user would attempt to modify her tags and propose new rules to resolve the majority of conflicts.

The 18 participants were evenly split between flexible and strict. P03 was representative of flexible users, saying, "If a couple more things got cut off than I intended, then it wouldn't matter to me so much." P10 felt similarly, explaining, "There's no reason for her to see relative photos, but I don't care too much." In contrast, P08 was representative of the strict users. When he encountered conflicts, he decided to create a number of additional tags and suggest associated rules to resolve those conflicts, saying, "One tag doesn't suffice for these three groups; [even] three tags are not enough."

A system design should account for people with both flexible and strict preferences. Stricter users could potentially be satisfied by providing an option for exception handling; however, providing such an option would need to be balanced with encouraging users to create generalizable rules to promote usability. P18 provides an example of this dynamic. She said that she had a large number of Facebook friends, and, while most of the time she would want to set permissions for groups, she would need some individual exceptions but not so many that the exceptions would became hard to manage.

Interface-supported rule management

Our results indicate that it is possible to repurpose organizational tags to create rules that capture the majority of a participant's preferences. However, a practical system must also help users create and manage rules and understand the impact of tag and rule changes.

Although our rule-display interface was not intended to represent a real system, we asked participants for their impressions of it to gain some insight into potentially useful design features. As expected, most participants used the text rules to understand the future impact of the policy, and the photos to understand the immediate impact. P03 found both the rules and photos useful, saying he was worried about "not remembering how you tagged very specific photos ... I think seeing them is a more visceral response." A few participants mentioned that the photo display might be hard to use for larger sets of photos.

A tag-based access-control system could help users set policy by appropriately displaying relevant photos and rules, as well as demonstrating what would happen if the user changed tags or rules. The Expandable Grid [17], for example, could be used to demonstrate the impact of rule adjustments.

System support for manual tagging

Our users were able to actively and successfully engage in tagging for access control immediately after being exposed to tag-based access control (Q2). A practical system could further encourage tagging for access control in a variety of ways. One possibility is checking tags for consistency: for example, asking whether a user missed one tag in a group of photos she otherwise tagged similarly, noting slight changes in spelling, or highlighting use of close synonyms like P10's "strange" and "weird."

Additionally, a practical system could detect the types of tags frequently used in rules and remind the user to add these tags. We found that users tended to add descriptive, people, or permission tags when tagging for access control in T2. Displaying frequently used tags in such categories might nudge the user to create tags that are more useful for access-control rules. In addition, we investigated only user-provided keyword tags. However, person- and location-based tags were among the most common to appear in the access-control rules. Such tags are well supported by existing automation tools, including Picasa's face-detection feature (turned off during our study). Automated support for tagging is an emerging tool that could reduce user burden and help users add more, and more accurate, tags [21].

CONCLUSION

Overall, we found that tag-based rules are promising for use in an access-control system. Organizational tags can be repurposed to create reasonable access-control policies, and when participants actively create tags for access control, policies based on these tags are yet more accurate. Participants are able to suggest and engage actively with tag-based rules.

These results suggest that it would be possible to create a usable access-control system with tag-based rules and minimal tagging overhead. It may be possible to additionally aid users with appropriate support for automated rule generation, exception handling, intuitive policy management, and automated tag generation and correction.

ACKNOWLEDGMENTS

This research was supported by the National Science Foundation via grants CNS-0831407 and DGE-0903659, by CyLab at Carnegie Mellon under grants DAAD19-02-1-0389 and W911NF-09-1-0273 from the Army Research Office, and by the ARCS Foundation. We thank Greg Ganger, Saranga Komanduri, and Raja Sambasivan for their help and advice.

REFERENCES

1. Ahern, S., Eckles, D., Good, N. S., King, S., Naaman, M., and Nair, R. Over-exposed?: privacy patterns and considerations in online and mobile photo sharing. In *Proc. CHI*, 2007 (2007), 357–366.
2. Ames, M., and Naaman, M. Why we tag: motivations for annotation in mobile and online media. In *Proc. CHI* (2007), 971–980.
3. Au Yeung, C., Kagal, L., Gibbins, N., and Shadbolt, N. Providing access control to online photo albums based on tags and linked data. In *Social Semantic Web* (2009).
4. Besmer, A., and Richter Lipford, H. Moving beyond untagging: photo privacy in a tagged world. In *Proc. CHI* (2010), 1563–1572.
5. Gupta, M., Li, R., Yin, Z., and Han, J. Survey on social tagging techniques. *SIGKDD Explor. Newsl. 12* (November 2010), 58–72.
6. Hart, M., Castille, C., Johnson, R., and Stent, A. Usable privacy controls for blogs. In *Proc. ICCSE* (2009), 401–408.
7. Kirk, D., Sellen, A., Rother, C., and Wood, K. Understanding photowork. In *Proc. CHI* (2006), 761–770.
8. Maxion, R. A., and Reeder, R. W. Improving user-interface dependability through mitigation of human error. *Int. J. Hum.-Comput. Stud. 63* (July 2005), 25–50.
9. Mazurek, M. L., Arsenault, J. P., Bresee, J., Gupta, N., Ion, I., Johns, C., Lee, D., Liang, Y., Olsen, J., Salmon, B., Shay, R., Vaniea, K., Bauer, L., Cranor, L. F., Ganger, G. R., and Reiter, M. K. Access control for home data sharing: Attitudes, needs and practices. In *Proc. CHI*, 2010 (2010), 645–654.
10. Mazurek, M. L., Klemperer, P. F., Shay, R., Takabi, H., Bauer, L., and Cranor, L. F. Exploring reactive access control. In *Proc. CHI* (2011), 2085–2094.
11. Miller, A. D., and Edwards, W. K. Give and take: a study of consumer photo-sharing culture and practice. In *Proc. CHI* (2007), 347–356.
12. Mitchell, T. *Machine Learning*. McGraw-Hill, 1997.
13. Nov, O., Naaman, M., and Ye, C. What drives content tagging: the case of photos on Flickr. In *Proc. CHI* (2008), 1097–1100.
14. Olson, J. S., Grudin, J., and Horvitz, E. A study of preferences for sharing and privacy. CHI EA (2005), 1985–1988.
15. Ramasubramanian, V., Rodeheffer, T. L., Terry, D. B., Walraed-Sullivan, M., Wobber, T., Marshall, C. C., and Vahdat, A. Cimbiosys: a platform for content-based partial replication. In *Proc. NSDI* (2009), 261–276.
16. Razavi, M. N., and Iverson, L. A grounded theory of information sharing behavior in a personal learning space. In *Proc. CSCW* (2006), 459–468.
17. Reeder, R., Bauer, L., Cranor, L., Reiter, M., Bacon, K., How, K., and Strong, H. Expandable grids for visualizing and authoring computer security policies. In *Proc. CHI* (2008), 1473–1482.
18. Riva, O., Yin, Q., Juric, D., Ucan, E., and Roscoe, T. Policy expressivity in the anzere personal cloud. In *Proc. SOCC* (2011), 14:1–14:14.
19. Salmon, B., Schlosser, S. W., Cranor, L. F., and Ganger, G. R. Perspective: semantic data management for the home. In *Proc. FAST* (2009), 167–182.
20. Seltzer, M., and Murphy, N. Hierarchical file systems are dead. In *Proc. HotOS* (2009), 1–1.
21. Sigurbjörnsson, B., and van Zwol, R. Flickr tag recommendation based on collective knowledge. In *Proc. WWW* (2008), 327–336.
22. Smetters, D. K., and Good, N. How users use access control. In *Proc. SOUPS* (2009), 15:1–15:12.
23. Squicciarini, A. C., Sundareswaran, S., Lin, D., and Wede, J. A3p: adaptive policy prediction for shared images over popular content sharing sites. In *Proc. Hypertext and Hypermedia* (2011), 261–270.
24. Voida, S., Edwards, W. K., Newman, M. W., Grinter, R. E., and Ducheneaut, N. Share and share alike: exploring the user interface affordances of file sharing. In *Proc. CHI* (2006), 221–230.
25. Vyas, N., Squicciarini, A. C., Chang, C.-C., and Yao, D. Towards automatic privacy management in Web 2.0 with semantic analysis on annotations. In *Proc. CollaboateCom* (2009), 1–10.
26. Zubiaga, A., Körner, C., and Strohmaier, M. Tags vs shelves: from social tagging to social classification. In *Proc. Hypertext and Hypermedia* (2011), 93–102.

Curation, Provocation, and Digital Identity: Risks and Motivations for Sharing Provocative Images Online

Rebecca Gulotta, Haakon Faste & Jennifer Mankoff
HCII – Carnegie Mellon
{rgulotta, hfaste, jmankoff}@andrew.cmu.edu

ABSTRACT

Among the billions of photos that have been contributed to online photo-sharing sites, there are many that are provocative, controversial, and deeply personal. Previous research has examined motivations for sharing images online and has identified several key motivations for doing so: expression, curation of identity, maintaining social connections, and recording experiences. However, few studies have focused on the perceived risks of posting photos online and even fewer have examined the risks associated with provocative, controversial, or deeply personal images. In our work, we used photo-elicitation interviews to explore the motivations for posting these types of images and the perceived risks of doing so. In this paper, we describe our findings from those interviews.

Author Keywords
Flickr; photos; digital rights; privacy; identity; sharing

ACM Classification Keywords
H.5.m. Information interfaces and presentation (e.g., HCI): Miscellaneous.

General Terms
Design; Experimentation

INTRODUCTION

Online photo-sharing sites have become invaluable social, creative, and educational resources as visual repositories for a wide range of pictures that depict the human experience. Amongst their vast archives, there are a startling number of deeply personal pictures that reveal facets of life not ordinarily shared online. Examples include brutal acts of violence, women in labor, and innumerable other topics. These photos provide value for contributors who want to preserve them and share them with others. Viewers benefit from images that allow them to explore unknown places, learn about other's experiences, and find new inspiration.

Though the nature of what makes a photo provocative, revealing, or controversial is influenced by the subjective values held by both the sharer and the viewer, our definition is adapted from the concerns of social network users. As discussed by boyd and Ellison [2], such content would involve the disclosure personal information, damage to one's reputation, or the risk of physical or emotional harm. The sharing of this photographic content online is important because of its value for understanding how we manage personal aspects of our identity, but there are a number of open questions that surround this phenomenon. What are users' motivations for sharing provocative images? What are the perceived risks of sharing these images, and how do they influence how we curate and express our identities online?

In this paper we discuss the phenomena of posting personal, revealing, and controversial images online, and how the curation of digital identity and expectations about risks and audience influence the contribution of those photos. We performed a qualitative study of contributors of provocative online photos to learn about issues of sensitivity and risk. Our findings, drawn from interviews and surveys, explore how users conceptualize their digital rights, motivations for putting these photos online, and expectations and perceived risks in doing so. We conclude with opportunities drawn from these findings.

PHOTO SHARING ONLINE

The rise of cheap, portable cameras has led to an increase in social uses of photographs [4]. While they were once reserved for special occasions, cameras are now used to document our everyday lives. As a result, the expectations and culture surrounding the use, value, and appropriateness of photography have shifted.

In a research study centered on the popular online photo-sharing site Flickr (*www.Flickr.com*) and photo-sharing in general [5], Van House *et al.* wrote that people contribute photos to define and record their identity, maintain relationships, curate and cultivate a self-representation, and express themselves by sharing their work. Work by Cox *et al.* [3] supports these findings, adding that digital photo-sharing provides greater opportunities for self-expression than traditional hobby groups or photo-clubs, because of the freedom associated with Flickr's weak social ties.

Content and risk are at the center of ongoing discussions about what is acceptable to share online. Increasingly, news stories describe the repercussions people face when sharing sensitive photographs and other information. Despite this, little has been done to explore how users perceive these risks and how this perception is influenced by use of social photo-sharing sites. Ahern *et al.* conducted interviews with Flickr users that assessed the extent to which their privacy concerns

CHI'12, May 5–10, 2012, Austin, Texas, USA.

were related to the ideas of security, social disclosure, identity, and convenience [1]. The study revealed two related findings: that participants' concerns about privacy vary based on factors like who appeared in the photos (*i.e.,* family, children, friends), and that participant's pre-study predictions about their privacy preferences differed greatly from the choices they made when posting photographs [1]. However, this work did not address the nuances of these risks in depth, nor the motives for the contribution of provocative images.

Though provocative and revealing images are a subset of the larger collection of photos shared online, the growing prevalence of photo-sharing tools makes exploration of these issues increasingly important. Not everyone posts pictures from weekend parties or protest rallies, but millions of people share photos online that reveal facets of their own identity, or the identity of others. Individuals cannot control all aspects of their digital identity because photos shared by others are often beyond their control.

Our study examines the ways in which people establish and curate their identities online. In a study of Facebook users, Zhoa et al. [6] found that users intentionally create profiles that represent an idealized version of themselves. They suggest that this behavior is tied to Facebook users' use of real names and the high percentage of relationships on the site that are "anchored," or tied directly to offline relationships. They contrast this finding with research on digital anonymity, which they suggest has shown that people use anonymity to act out their underlying impulses.

The Digital Landscape of Photo-Sharing Sites

Our work contributes information about provocative or risky images and identifies divergences between previous observations of general image sharing behaviors and those of our participants. We chose to focus our study on Flickr and its users. We recruited from Flickr (rather than competitors such as Facebook or Picasa) because of the open nature of the majority of the photos shared on the site. However, we also collected data about other sites where our participants shared photos for comparison. In this way, our contribution is relevant to topics far broader than just Flickr and addresses the general phenomena of sharing provocative photos online.

STUDY DESIGN

We recruited participants using advertisements that called for people who had used Flickr, generally, to post personal photographs publicly online. These advertisements were posted to online research boards (*e.g.,* Craigslist), social networking sites (*e.g.,* Twitter and Facebook), and around our university campus. We also directly contacted Flickr members either through local area group discussion boards or by sending messages to individual users. All of the people who responded to the advertisements were screened to ensure that they had posted photos to Flickr that were relevant to our work. More specifically, we were interested in people who had posted photos containing nudity or sexual situations, that expressed strong political or religious beliefs, that depicted physical ailments and harm, that documented criminal acts and, more generally, that revealed unconventional or "risky" aspects of their identity.

Participants

There were 10 participants in our study. Participants had a wide variety of backgrounds and occupations, although all of them had attended at least some college. The average age was 39 (S.D. = 14). Three participants identified as female, six identified as male, and one identified as gender queer. The participants shared a wide range of photos, including naked photos, sexually explicit art, photos depicting them engaging in criminal acts, and photos depicting political viewpoints such as support for gay rights.

We met with each participant for a single 1-2 hour session focused on exploring their experiences with photo-sharing sites and their feelings about sharing provocative material. Participants began by completing a short survey to tell us about their Flickr use (frequency, number of contacts, and so on) and any other photo-sharing sites they used. Next, we conducted a semi-structured interview. We used photo elicitation as a central part of our interview process. Photo elicitation incorporates photos into interviews as a way of stimulating conversation and focusing discussions. During the interviews, the participant and the interviewer both shared a computer screen and discussed the photos that were publicly viewable on the participant's stream. The photos served as a starting point for conversations about image sharing and as memory aids for participants. Interviews were conducted in person (9 participants), and over Skype with screen sharing (1 participant).

FINDINGS

After the interviews were completed, they were transcribed and coded. We used affinity diagramming to identify connections and draw findings from that data. Coded pieces of the transcripts were physically arranged into clusters based on themes present in the data. This allowed us to explore relationships between participants.

Support for Previous Work

Broadly speaking, though no two participations shared the same combinations of motivations, our participants were motivated to share photos for the same reasons that have been observed by previous researchers. For our participants, the provocative or personal photos they posted online were largely a reflection of their offline identity. As such, they had the same general goals for posting these photos as they would for any photo. Indeed, most of the people we spoke with did not feel that their content was "provocative" *per se*, but rather that it was a reflection of themselves, their interests, and their values in life. This reinforced the broad applicability of the frameworks described in the previous literature.

Even though participants posted photos that others might find inappropriate online, all of the participants demonstrated an awareness of social norms associated with the websites they used. Off-line networks, like family and friends, were reflected in the facets of identity they displayed in different online contexts. Several of our participants described intentionally filtering their photos in response to contextual norms based on both the content of the images and the interests of the audience.

We did observe a degree of reticence about posting images and information online because of the potential ways in which they could be used by others. The Internet was generally viewed as a public domain, and most people recognize that posted information is not "safe" from theft or misuse. Participants also had a general distrust of the public—not because they mistrust people at large, but because of the vast nature of the Internet.

While our findings partially confirmed existing theories about online photo sharing, they also extend previous research by providing insight into the particular concerns of people who post provocative and personal photos online.

All of the users we spoke to expressed clear personal motivations for posting provocative photos online, but were also highly aware and respectful of the rights of others. We observed conflicting motivations among everyone we interviewed: between their desires to explore and expand their sense of personal identity and/or that of their group, *versus* their desire to protect their identity (or that of others) from possible harm. Specifically, our analysis identified three unexpected trends with regard to provocative content: (1) people advocate for the right to be themselves, (2) they advocate for the rights of others, and (3) they seek to protect others. These findings, outlined in Figure 1, are described in detail in the following sections.

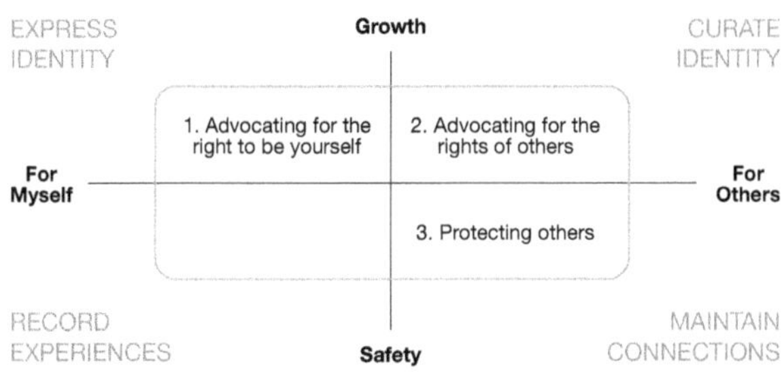

Figure 1. Motivations for sharing images online identified in previous research [5] (blue text) can be divided across two principal axes relevant to sharing provocative content: the desire to improve myself while considering others (horizontal), and the mutual desire for growth and safety of expression/identity (vertical). Our three main findings reflect the mechanisms that people use to accomplish these goals (green box). Specifically, people are motivated to advocate for the rights and protection of others because they perceive the direct personal benefits of being pro-socially active. Note: the focus of our study (i.e., people who post provocative photos) largely excluded the lower left quadrant.

1. Advocating for the Right To Be Yourself

The first novel trend we observed was the importance of a concept we call self-advocacy, wherein people advocate for the "right" to be themselves online. Despite an acute awareness of social norms, six participants expressed strong feelings of entitlement to be themselves online, which superseded concerns about the implications of their actions. In several of the interviews, participants expressed feeling indignant or upset by the need to censor themselves to conform to social norms. Here P4 describes her thought process: *"[my family members] already know I'm [a] weird artist person anyway, and my mom doesn't really approve of me photographing burlesque dancers, but she already knows that about me, is that I'm like that."* She balanced her initial misgivings about publicly posting these pictures against her wish to promote her experiences and beliefs.

Similarly, in response to unwanted attention received after posting a picture of her navel tattoo, P10 noted *"the fact that these people were infringing upon me and being rude to me I felt was their mistake and I shouldn't have to change my behavior for their being an asshole. I'm very indignant about that."* While she was uncomfortable with viewers' comments, she later explained that she kept the photo online because of its value to her as a representation of something she loves and wants to share with her friends.

These examples illustrate the tension between the differing values and actions of our participants. Those same participants who expressed concerns about judgment from their social circles were nonetheless willing to post images that could elicit disparaging responses. This discrepancy is similar to that identified by Ahern *et al.* [1]: when it comes to privacy online, people often incorrectly predict the choices they will make when sharing photos. The key difference is that our participants were clearly aware of their seemingly contradictory motivations—expressing their true identity and protecting themselves—and were actively choosing to accept the risks involved.

2. Advocating for the Rights of Others

A complementary thread in our interviews was the motivation to advocate for the rights of others. Three of our participants viewed their photos as a means for expressing their allegiance to the identity of differing groups. P6 spoke about feeling a sense of responsibility to use his educational status to support the gay community in Taiwan, his home country. He said *"I'm ... higher educated than most the people in Taiwan, and some of my friends they ... just graduate from high school. But I want to, by posting the picture to Flickr and show the link of my Flickr pictures on Facebook... to show to my friends and try to influence them, and just that being gay is not really a terrible thing."*

In another example, a participant who has posted nude images of herself online discussed her advocacy for peoples' rights to represent themselves honestly. P1 said, *"I find it very important for me to be that way in terms of educating people or teaching people to be who they are, and to be honest, and to be real. Be real, and whether that's on a personal basis with my family or like on Flickr, with the world at large."* She described how she has received messages from people who viewed her photos and who have thanked her for being honest and encouraging them to be more comfortable with expressing themselves in a similar way. People are motivated to advocate for what they value, and the growth of others is important to their curation of self. Indeed, advocating for the rights of others to express their identities not only ensures people's right to express their own identity, it acknowledges that ultimately identity is socially constructed. People advocate for others' rights because they know that their identities are shaped by processes beyond individual control.

3. Protecting Others

Despite participants' willingness to violate numerous social norms, we found a universal cautiousness about putting others at risk. Although the degree to which they shared compromising pictures of others varied, all ten participants in our study expressed the desire to protect others through their actions. Sharing potentially risky content online was viewed as a personal choice, and participants did not want to infringe on others' rights to make that choice.

For example, P5 discussed his experience posting pictures of a friend who had expressed concern with revealing damaging details of his personal life to his students and colleagues. P5 mentioned that his friend *"is very concerned about his privacy. And also just of sort of generally about the Internet, he is also just very concerned about that. So I have to be very cautious and I've had to remove photographs of him."* Although the participant was using his photos as a venue to express his beliefs, he did not want to put anyone else as risk to do so.

Only one participant in our study explicitly declared that her goal for posting photos was to provoke others. Even given this extreme ambition, she was careful to protect the identities of the other people, like friends and strangers, who appeared in her photos. Though she did post sensitive pictures of her friends, she described how she deliberately left out any information that could be used to identify them. Thus people are motivated not only to advocate for others' rights to express their identity, they actively work to protect those same rights.

RECOMMENDATIONS AND DISCUSSION

Ultimately, the value of digital photographs as identity-building resources makes it important that we (1) encourage the growth and development of photo sharing sites, (2) provide users with tools to make informed decisions about what to share online, and (3) develop systems that are sensitive to users' concerns. Our findings suggest several ways to support these goals.

First, there is an opportunity to motivate people to be confidently different by encouraging them to express who they already are. Online image sharing environments are promising forums for this kind of self-actualizing behavior. Although it is impossible for people to objectively know how much information to reveal online or how inhibited to be when expressing themselves, and despite the potential risks of alienation from identity-supporting online groups, we nevertheless feel that photo-sharing can be an effective means of personal growth and that posting "boundary-pushing" content should gently be encouraged by interactive systems.

Second, while people are afraid to damage their reputation among anchored relationships, they are nonetheless motivated to advocate for what they value in others. As a consequence, systems should be designed that strengthen users' ability to celebrate and personalize community norms through the curation of photographic social media. This highlights the need for systems that are sensitive to people's decision-making processes and to their desires to both express opinions, protect themselves, and protect the subjects of their photos.

Finally, while it is risky to trust others online because their motivations are opaque, people nonetheless demonstrated universal respect for the rights of friends and strangers to choose how to express their identity for themselves. There is therefore an opportunity to support online behaviors and etiquette that sets clear expectations around the importance of protecting these basic "online identity rights." We recommend that future researchers interested in studying the propagation of identity online in contemporary life—where the lines between real and virtual are increasingly blurred—pursue efforts that further elaborate the ethical and practical implications of these rights as they pertain to the expression and curation of identity.

ACKNOWLEDGMENTS

We thank our participants and Ian Li, Tawanna Dillahunt, Queenie Kravitz for their support and contributions to this work. This work was funded by Google, NSF IIS-0916459 and an NSF Graduate Fellowship – NSF 0750271.

REFERENCES

1. Ahern, S., Eckles, D., Good, N., King, S., Naaman, M., & Nair. R. (2007). Over-exposed? Privacy pattern and considerations in online and mobile photo-sharing. *CHI 2007,* 357-366.
2. Boyd, D.M., & Ellison, N.B. (2007). Social Network Sites: Definition, History, and Scholarship. *Journal of Computer-Mediated Communication* **13**(1): 210-230.
3. Cox, A.M., Clough, P.D., & Marlow, J. (2008). Flickr: A first look at user-behavior in the context of photography as serious behavior. *Information Research* **13**(1).
4. Van Dijck, J. (2008). Digital photography: Communication, identity, memory. *Visual Communications* **7**(1):57-76.
5. Van House, N., Davis, M., Takhteyev, Y., Good, N., Wilhelm, A., Finn, M., & Hall, S. (2004). From "What?" to "Why": The social uses of personal photos. *Current* **10.**
6. Zhoa, S., Grasmuck, S., & Martin, J. (2008). Identity construction on Facebook: Digital empowerment in anchored relationships. *Computers in Human Behavior* **24**:1816-1836.

The Implications of Offering More Disclosure Choices for Social Location Sharing

Karen P. Tang
Donald Bren School of Information & Computer Sciences
University of California, Irvine
kptang@ics.uci.edu

Jason I. Hong, Daniel P. Siewiorek
Human-Computer Interaction Institute
Carnegie Mellon University
{jasonh, dps}@cs.cmu.edu

ABSTRACT
We compared two privacy configuration styles for specifying rules for social sharing one's past locations. Our findings suggest that location-sharing applications (LSAs) which support varying levels of location granularities are associated with sharing rules that are less convoluted, are less likely to be negatively phrased, and can lead to more open sharing; users are also more comfortable with these rules. These findings can help inform LSA privacy designs.

Author Keywords
Privacy; rules; configuration; location sharing.

ACM Classification Keywords
H.3.5. Online Information Services: Data Sharing.

INTRODUCTION
Advances in location sensing and mobile technology have made it easy for people to share their location with others. Many location-sharing applications (LSAs) frame these disclosures using social motivations, stating that awareness of others' current location can encourage more social serendipity and better social grounding [8]. However, location sharing also exposes end-users to potential privacy risks. Consider Foursquare and Facebook Places, which lets users browse historical feeds of their friends' locations. With these LSAs, more location information is being shared within one's network, as these feeds have implicitly turned what was once *current* location sharing into a much more persistent and continuous sharing of *past* locations.

Sharing historical data, however, is a double-edged sword. On one hand, sharing more data provides better awareness of a person's whereabouts and activities, which can be helpful for increasing social capital between weak ties [7]. On the other hand, sharing data streams can make it easier to aggregate information. For example, by sharing past locations, one could infer favorite activities (e.g., which restaurants someone frequents) or travel routines (e.g., when someone arrives home, what routes they take when going home). In light of these privacy risks, it is important to design privacy controls for sharing *past* locations.

One repeated finding in the privacy literature is that LSAs should support varying levels of granularity [6, 8, 9, 11, 12, 15]. Providing both precise and vague descriptions of location allows for plausible deniability [9], a necessary social phenomenon that provides better impression management [15]. Other work has revealed that there are additional factors which can be helpful in configuring sharing preferences, including mood [6], time [13], and geographic references [13]. Nearly all of these studies have been conducted on scenarios for sharing *current* locations.

In our work, we investigate whether these same factors are useful for sharing *past* locations. More importantly, we also investigate the implications of designing privacy configurations that support large sets of privacy filters. Based on thirty interviews, our results suggest that configurations that support varying location granularities can lead to sharing rules that are less complex, more open, and are selections that users are more comfortable with. These results have important implications for future LSAs that are weighing the benefits of having flexible privacy controls for specifying sharing preferences.

RELATED WORK
For LSAs, it is common to find privacy controls where users must specify with whom to share their locations. Many systems use a buddy list, where locations are only shared with people on that list [3, 14]. Other systems use group-based controls [8, 12], incorporate different location granularities [8, 9, 12], or allow users to specify when disclosures should occur [12, 13]. Some LSAs have used mood-based privacy preferences as well [6]. Each of these privacy filters has been used in the context of sharing *current* locations. In our work, we examine whether these filters are also useful for sharing *past* locations.

To do this, we examine two different privacy configuration styles (Table 1). The baseline configuration style uses an all-or-nothing approach that is commonly seen in current LSAs, where users either share no location information or a specific geographic description (i.e., an address or street intersection). The experimental configuration style allows users to share varying granularities of location information that are less descriptive than an address or street intersection. In both configurations, users can use privacy filters to restrict the conditions in which their location is shared with others. These filters are based on past work and include limiting sharing by mood, time, and receiver type.

Our work provides an initial look at the implications for designing privacy controls that support *multiple* privacy filters. Past work in economics have shown that providing a large choice set can have both positive and negative effects. On one hand, having more choices offers a better match between one's preferences and allows for more flexibility in one's decision making [10]. However, deciding amongst several choices can also lead to an increased cognitive load for users, a greater sense of confusion, and a less satisfying decision [5]. In our work, we look at how additional disclosure options influences location privacy preferences.

In summary, our study compares two configuration styles for specifying privacy preferences for location sharing. We focus on two research questions. First, we explore how different configuration styles affect users' sharing preferences. Second, we assess users' perceived comfort levels with their specified set of sharing preferences. We then discuss how our results differ from past work and its impact on the design of future privacy UIs for LSAs.

STUDY DESIGN

We recruited 30 participants, ages 20-54 years ($\bar{x}$=28.1, sd=7.3), from a local university; 18 participants were male. 10 participants were undergraduates, 11 were graduate students, and nine were administrative staff. Of the 21 students, thirteen had non-technical backgrounds.

Recruitment for the study was advertised as a usability evaluation of a university-wide experimental LSA for mobile phones called Social Beacon. These evaluations were conducted as hour-long interviews. Each interview began with an online tutorial explaining Social Beacon's location-sharing features and was based on seven scenarios describing why one might choose to share his location with others. These scenarios revolved around three themes: 1) to increase awareness about others (e.g., find out where friends went last night), 2) to meet new friends (e.g., find others who frequent the same places), and 3) to get place recommendations (e.g., others may suggest a new restaurant based on one's past visits). The tutorial also explained that, by default, Social Beacon would continuously update participants' locations and automatically share this data with others within the university. In particular, whenever location information was shared, Social Beacon would disclose one week's worth of *past* locations, in addition to the user's *current* location. To change this behavior, users could configure their privacy settings to limit their sharing.

We presented two kinds of privacy configurations for specifying sharing preferences and counter-balanced them for ordering effects. In each configuration, participants defined a sharing rule using the privacy filters and disclosure granularities available for that particular configuration. To ensure that participants openly expressed their rules in as flexible a manner as possible, the rule specifications were done as pen-and-paper exercises. Participants were instructed that the researchers would later

	Baseline	Experimental
Location Granularity	*Nothing* or *Specific geographic* (address)	*Nothing*, *Specific geographic* (address), *General geographic* (city or neighborhood), *Specific semantic* (business names, like Starbucks or personal labels, like home), or *General semantic* (type of place, like coffee shop)
Privacy Filters	*Time of Day* (5-8pm, evenings), *Day of Week* (weekends), *Frequency of Visits* (after 2 visits), *Current Transportation* (driving, walking), *Current Mood* (positive/neutral/negative)	

Table 1. The privacy configurations differed in the location granularities offered, but offered the same privacy filters. Examples of granularities & filters provided in parentheses.

add their written rules into the system after installing the application. In reality, Social Beacon was a hypothetical LSA used to ground considerations of privacy concerns for location sharing. To maintain the system's realism, we only recruited participants who owned smartphones, as this LSA would have been deployed on such a platform. At the end of the study, we disclosed our experimental manipulation.

Privacy Configuration Exercises

In each privacy configuration, participants defined rules for how Social Beacon should share their locations. Each rule was required to have three parts: 1) who they want to share their location with, 2) how the location should be described (i.e., what level of location granularity should be shared), and 3) under what conditions should the location be shared. When specifying the "who" portion of the rule, each participant referenced the same set of 8 relationship types: strangers, classmates/coworkers, acquaintances, casual friends, close friends, spouse/significant other, bosses/ professors, and family members. These relationship types were based on past work involving location sharing [2, 6].

The two privacy configurations differ only in the types of location descriptions that can be shared with others. The baseline configuration is modeled after the all-or-nothing approach that many existing LSAs use for location sharing. In this configuration, users choose between sharing no geographical information or a precise geographical description (as depicted by a pin on a map, like an address). In the experimental configuration, users can share nothing or choose from four location abstractions, borrowed from past work [11, 15]. These abstractions can be semantic or geographic references that are general or specific (Table 1).

In both conditions, participants can add privacy filters to specify the conditions in which they would like to share their locations. Participants add these filters by using subordinate conjunctions (e.g., "except", "only if") and can reference 5 variables (Table 1): time of day, day of week, frequency of visits, their current transportation mode, and their current mood (positive, negative, or neutral).

Limitations of Study Design

Our study uses paper-based privacy configuration exercises and a hypothetical LSA. We used several techniques to ensure that Social Beacon's status was not apparent to participants. In fact, all of our participants were surprised to learn that no software would actually be installed. It is possible that the privacy configurations measured people's *perceived* preferences rather than their actual preferences, similar to past ecommerce studies [1]. To alleviate this concern, we followed a think-aloud protocol to encourage participants to reflect and consider their privacy concerns, similar to what was done in [6]. Interview responses seemed to confirm that participants were thoughtful when expressing their sharing preference for location sharing.

KEY FINDINGS

Our participants created 121 and 148 privacy rules in the baseline and experimental configurations, respectively.

Q1a: Expressions of Sharing Rules: Who, What, When

Table 2 (top) shows how many participants shared their locations for each relationship type in both conditions. As expected, in the baseline configuration, participants were more willing to share with spouses and family, and least willing to share with bosses and strangers. This finding echoes past results that say people are more comfortable sharing with their close ties than with their weak ties [15].

Since Social Beacon was advertised as a university-wide LSA, there is an implicit social network for location sharing. The link between LSAs and SNSs is important. Past work has shown that SNSs typically have more weak ties (casual friends) than strong ties (close friends) [7]. This property has important implications for location sharing. Rows D-G in Table 2 make up the types of weak-tie relationships that are typically found in SNSs (while row F is also a weak tie, few users include a significant number of strangers in their SNSs). The baseline condition shows very few participants chose to share past locations for these groups ($\bar{x}$=1.0/30). In the experimental configuration, many more shared some level of their past location information with these groups ($\bar{x}$=17.25/30). These results suggest that additional location granularities can lead to significantly different sharing outcomes (McNemar's $\chi^2(1)=8.40$, $p<0.003$) and may encourage participants to share past locations when they would not have done so otherwise. When considering all relationship types, participants were more likely to hide past locations in the baseline condition. This result is similar to prior work [11], but show that they extend to sharing of past (and not just current) locations.

Table 2 (bottom) shows how often each privacy filter appeared in participants' sharing rules. For example, the most popular filters referenced time and day variables. 41 rules in the baseline configuration referenced a time or day (33.9%). In the experimental configuration, 26 rules contained time- or day-related privacy filters (17.6%). As these make up a non-trivial percentage of all the user-defined sharing rules, this suggests that LSAs should consider including temporal filters in their privacy controls.

An important finding we observed is that the experimental configuration resulted in less complex sharing rules (wich we define as having fewer conditions). We found that the experimental rules contained fewer subjective conjunctions (McNemar's $\chi^2(1)=5.38$, $p<0.02$) and referenced fewer privacy variables (McNemar's $\chi^2(1)=75.2$, $p<0.0001$). Thus, participants were more likely to share rules like "always share my general geographic location" (no subjective conjunction or privacy filters) vs. "only share my location if I'm in a good mood and it's a weekend" (multiple privacy filters, expressed with the subjective conjunction "only if"). Having less complex rules is an important outcome, as simpler rules tend to require less cognitive load for when users need to re-examine their privacy preferences. Moreover, as computer-mediated communication becomes more context-aware, other types of data, beyond location, will also be shared. Thus, having simpler sharing rules for one type will be a more scalable privacy solution for when context-aware apps support other kinds of sharing. Though, by adding location granularities, we are also adding a level of complexity to the design of an LSA's privacy UI. Thus, while the resulting rule set is structurally simpler, further work is needed to address how to incorporate the privacy filters and location granularities into a UI so that it does not visually overwhelm users.

		Baseline Configuration		Experimental Configuration				
		No Location	Specific Geographic	No Location	General Semantic	Specific Semantic	General Geographic	Specific Geographic
A	Spouse/Sig. Other	1	29	0	19	3	3	16
B	Family	10	20	5	6	0	20	5
C	Close Friends	20	10	1	4	16	9	9
D	Casual Friends	29	1	12	5	0	16	0
E	Acquaintances	29	1	16	2	0	13	0
F	Classmates/Coworkers	28	2	9	4	0	21	0
G	Boss/Professors	30	0	0	0	0	16	0
H	Strangers	30	0	0	0	0	11	0

	Time	Day	Frequency of Visits	Transportation	Mood	Time+Day	Time+Day+Mood	No Filters
Baseline	5	11	0	5	9	8	17	66
Experimental	8	11	2	5	8	4	3	107

Table 2. (top) # of participants (out of 30) that preferred a certain location granularity for each relationship. Numbers may be >30 in the experimental condition since participants can share ≥1 location granularities. (bottom) # of rules containing the specified filters to limit location sharing ("only share if..."). A rule can contain multiple filters or no filters.

Q1b: Negative vs. Positive Phrasing of Sharing Rules

23.6% of the baseline rules had negative sharing language (e.g., "do *not* share my location if I'm in a bad mood" vs. "do share my location if I'm in a good or neutral mood"). In contrast, this occurred in significantly fewer experimental rules (10.8%; McNemar's $\chi^2(1)$`52.1, $p<0.0001$). In past work, negative rules were only examined in terms of blacklists, where users specified who should not receive their data. To our knowledge, this is the first study to examine how negative (i.e., exclusionary) language is used in the context of other privacy variables. In particular, our findings suggest that LSAs should build privacy UIs to support negative phrasing, as it may be a better match to how participants naturally express their privacy concerns. Most existing LSAs rely almost exclusively on positive phrasing (e.g., "only share my location in X condition").

Q2: Perceived Comfort of User-Defined Rule Sets

Using a 5-point Likert scale, participants reported higher comfort scores ($\bar{x}_e=3.9$, $sd_e=0.68$; $\bar{x}_b=3.2$, $sd_b=0.71$) in the experimental configuration (Mann-Whitney=240, $p<0.001$). On one hand, this result is promising because, as previously indicated, the experimental configuration led users to share their location information in more situations and to more relationship types. Thus, it is encouraging to see that more sharing did not decrease users' perceived comfort level.

DISCUSSION

In our work, we present a comparative study using location granularity as an independent variable to determine its impact on end-user privacy preferences for location sharing. Our study investigates this issues in the context of a group-based approach that supports multiple privacy filters. This experimental design is distinct from prior work in that past studies have examined privacy rules along one, but not all, of these dimensions. For example, IMBuddy [7] looked at privacy rules that supported different location granularities, but without the use of privacy filters. Work by Benisch et al. considered some privacy filters but did not vary location granularity and they used optimization-based equations to calculate users' sharing preferences [4]. This is distinct from our user-centric approach that references a user's natural expression of their sharing preferences through two privacy configuration exercises.

Despite these differences, several past studies have reported perceived comfort scores, though this is all done in the context of sharing only *current* locations. For example, past work has found that user were more comfortable sharing current locations with varying location granularity [6, 9] and when using time-related privacy filters (vs. no filters) [4]. Our work extends these results in two ways. First, we show that these user preferences persist when sharing *past* locations. Second, we show that, even when presented with several types of privacy filters, users still prefer having additional location granularities. In other words, users did not seem to mind the additional complexity of adding more disclosure options for sharing past locations.

CONCLUSION AND FUTURE WORK

In conclusion, our results show that privacy configurations that support varying location granularities can significantly change how privacy rules are defined and under which conditions locations are shared. In particular, we provide empirical evidence that including more abstract location descriptions can lead to more open location sharing, less complex rules, and fewer negatively phrased rules. Users were also more comfortable with privacy configurations that offered varying granularities. In future work, we will implement our privacy configurations in an actual LSA; this will allow us to evaluate whether additional location granularities enables LSAs to better match users' perceived preferences, as well as their real-world privacy preferences.

REFERENCES

1. Ackerman, M.S., Cranor, L.F. and Reagle, J. (1999). Privacy in e-commerce: examining user scenarios and privacy preferences. In E-Commerce '99, 1-8.
2. Anthony, D., Kotz, D. and Henderson, T. (2007). Privacy in Location-Aware Computing Environments. *IEEE Perv Comp*, 6 (4), 64-72.
3. Barkhuus, L., Brown, B., Bell, M., et al. (2008). From awareness to repartee: sharing location within social groups. In CHI '08, 497-506.
4. Benisch, M., Kelley, P.G., Sadeh, N., et al. (2011). Capturing Location Privacy Preferences: Quantifying Accuracy and User Burden Tradeoffs. *PUC*, to appear.
5. Chernev, A. (2003). When More Is Less and Less Is More: The Role of Ideal Point Availability and Assortment in Consumer Choice. *J Consumer Research*, 30 (2), 170-183.
6. Consolvo, S., Smith, I., Matthews, T., et al. (2005). Location Disclosure to Social Relations: Why, When, & What People Want to Share. In CHI '05, 82-90.
7. Ellison, N.B., Steinfield, C. Lampe, C. (2007). The benefits of Facebook "friends:" social capital and college students' use of online social network sites. *JCMC*, 12 (4), article 1.
8. Hsieh, G., Tang, K.P., Low, W.Y., and Hong, J.I. (2007). Field Deployment of IMBuddy: A Study of Privacy Control and Feedback Mechanisms for Contextual IM. In Ubicomp '07, 91-108.
9. Iachello, G., Smith, I., Consolvo, S., et al. (2005). Control, Deception, and Communication: Evaluating the Deployment of a Location-Enhanced Messaging Service. In Ubicomp '05, 213-231.
10. Lancaster, K. (1990). The Economics of Product Variety: A Survey. *Marketing Science*, 9 (3), 189-206.
11. Lin, J., Xiang, G., Hong, J.I., et al. (2010). Modeling People's Place Naming Preferences in Location Sharing. In Ubicomp '10, 75-84.
12. Patil, S. and Lai, J. (2005). Who Gets to Know What When: Configuring Privacy Preferences in an Awareness Application. In CHI '05, 101-110.
13. Sadeh, N., Hong, J.I., Cranor, L., et al. (2008). Understanding and Capturing People's Privacy Policies in a Mobile Social Networking Application. *PUC*, 13 (6), 401-412.
14. Tang, J.C., Yankelovich, N., Begole, J., et al. (2001). ConNexus to Awarenex: Extending Awareness to Mobile Users. In CHI '01, 221-228.
15. Tang, K.P., Lin, J., Hong, J.I., et al. (2010). Rethinking Location Sharing: Exploring the Implications of Social-Driven vs. Purpose-Driven Location Sharing. In Ubicomp '10, 85-94.

Interactivity as Self-Expression: A Field Experiment with Customization and Blogging

S. Shyam Sundar*+, Jeeyun Oh*, Saraswathi Bellur*, Haiyan Jia*, Hyang-Sook Kim*
*Media Effects Research Laboratory
The Pennsylvania State University
University Park, PA 16802, USA
+Department of Interaction Science
Sungkyunkwan University
Seoul, Korea
{sss12, jzo120, sxb979, huj116, hxk256}@psu.edu

ABSTRACT
A paradigmatic quality of interactive interfaces is that they allow users to express themselves, thereby converting message receivers into communication sources. We define this quality as Source Interactivity [26, 29], and test its effects on user experience with a field experiment (N=141) of a portal site featuring cosmetic customization, functional customization and blogging (active versus filter). In demonstrating the psychological influence of source-based interactivity on such outcomes as user engagement, sense of agency, sense of community, intrinsic motivation and attitudes toward the interface, we discuss how designers can use them for creating interactive tools for self-expression.

Author Keywords
Interactivity; Customization; Blogging; User Engagement.

ACM Classification Keywords
H.5.m. Information interfaces and presentation (e.g., HCI): Miscellaneous.

INTRODUCTION
In acknowledging that interactivity in media interfaces has fundamentally reshaped human-computer interaction [29], researchers and designers have sought to distinguish between different kinds of interactive tools as they address a fundamental empirical question: What kinds of interactivity work in which ways under what circumstances? Among the myriad conceptualizations of interactivity, the one that dramatically changes the nature of communication is its ability to allow the user to go beyond being a mere receiver of messages and actually serve as a source. Modern interactive media offer plenty of opportunities for users to act as gatekeepers, recommenders and even creators of messages. For example, Google News allows readers to customize their choice of news categories to display and also set individualized preferences for news sources. Thus, users are able to actively dictate not only the genres of news content that they encounter but also how and from whom they receive it. From simple display and ringtone settings on one's mobile phone to more complex sharing and privacy options on a social networking site, designers are bestowing users with more choice and control. While such customization features allow the users to gatekeep information for themselves, interactive tools of social media enable them to go a step further and serve as a source for others, by bookmarking, forwarding, tagging, commenting, tweeting and blogging information. The phenomenal growth of blogging services is a testimony to the powerful psychological appeal of users themselves serving as communication sources [24, 25].

Conceptually, customization and content creation mirror the functions of journalistic sources in traditional media (namely, gatekeeping and story-telling), and can therefore be seen as imbuing "sourceness" to users. They represent two different forms of "source interactivity," defined as the extent to which users are enabled by the interface to serve as primary sources (and/or gatekeepers) of information [26, 29]. Greater source interactivity allows users to actively dictate the source, nature, form and content of interaction, with higher agency and control [25]. In this way, source interactivity serves as a tool for self-expression, be it in the form of indicating preferences or generating messages.

Operationally defining interactivity in this way could be potentially useful not only for researchers interested in the user experience of interactivity but also for designers seeking user-centered design goals. Making the user the source of communication and affording greater self-expression can be meaningful objectives for designers of interactive tools. Source interactivity could perhaps occupy a distinct position in UI design, quite apart from the plethora of tools that simply offer manipulation of the interface without an emphasis on self-expression. However, this would require empirical verification of source interactivity as a psychologically salient dimension of UX. Will users recognize the different forms of source interactivity as tools of self-expression? Are some tools more desirable than others? Is there a source-interactivity threshold beyond which user experience is affected adversely? The larger question is: What are the individual and cumulative effects of different forms of source interactivity on user experience?

An answer to this question requires us to examine different tools of self-expression within the same interface rather than separately, as has been done in previous research. With this in mind, we conduct a user study of an interface that offers two forms of customization (functional and cosmetic) and also gives users the opportunity to express themselves by either generating self-created content (active blogging) or sharing other-created content (filter blogging). We situate these different forms of source interactivity along a continuum of self-expression (discussed in the next section). This source-interactivity continuum serves as a basis for addressing the practical implications of our study: How do different forms of source interactivity, and the subsequent scope for self-expression that they offer, inform the psychology of HCI? What can we learn about interfaces of portals (e.g., iGoogle, Netvibes) and other systems that allow users to actively customize and express themselves? How do we build affordances that can foster a sense of "sourceness" and its allied outcomes?

SOURCE INTERACTIVITY CONTINUUM

Source interactivity is the degree to which the user is able to actively serve as a source of communication, rather than passively consume prepackaged information as a receiver. Websites that offer no opportunities for the user to customize information rank low on source interactivity whereas those that allow users to express themselves would score high [26]. Therefore, we think of source interactivity as a continuum of self-expression that is made possible by specific affordances of interactive interfaces such as customization. By customizing, users are actively browsing, selecting, organizing and making the interaction their "own" unique experience. This can be achieved in two ways: Functional and Cosmetic. Functional customization involves tailoring features mainly to fulfill task-based goals, whereas cosmetic customization is presentation-driven, such as changing hair color of an avatar, setting cell phone screen savers, desktop background, and so on [18]. At the higher end of the source interactivity continuum, users are not only managing and organizing content, but also actively disseminating and creating content of their own. It could be in the form of uploading YouTube videos, writing blogs, collaborating on Wikipedia, reviewing products and services, and many other Web 2.0 affordances that imbue users with a sense of "sourceness." Here again, a distinction could be made between sharing existing content with others and creating new content, with the latter scoring higher on "sourceness." Operationally then, customization (be it cosmetic, functional, or both) signals higher source interactivity than a non-customizable interface, while sharing content would rank higher and creating original content even more so, on a continuum of the degree of self-expression afforded by the interface.

An open empirical question is the degree to which these different forms of source interactivity contribute to users' sense of agency (or perceived ability to assert themselves). Studies using the *agency model of customization* [24, 25, 28] have identified two key psychological mechanisms—sense of control and sense of identity—that enable users to feel agentic [19]. By applying this to the source interactivity continuum, we can expect greater levels of identity and control when users engage in blogging compared to customizing content. However, a practical question facing the interface designer is whether to include both customization and content-generation features (such as blogging) on the same interface. Is it desirable to include all possible forms of source interactivity on a given interface in order to boost its overall affordance of self-expression? Do some forms of source interactivity evoke a higher sense of control, while others evoke a higher sense of identity? Are they cumulative, or alternatively, is it possible that one type of source interactivity may counteract another?

To answer these and other questions, we conducted a field experiment that examined three forms of source interactivity on a personalized portal site that was especially created for this study (cf. Method section)--Functional customization (operationalized as the extent to which users can choose and edit task-based widgets); Cosmetic customization (operationalized as the affordance for users to modify the look of the interface); and Blogging (operationalized as the extent to which users can recommend existing content or create new content).

While previous research has examined the effects of blogging and customization separately [e.g., 8, 24, 26, 28], we study them together on the same interface. This enables us to test both their unique and interaction effects, allowing us to advance existing knowledge of source interactivity and offer practical guidelines pertaining to ideal combinations of customization and content-generation features on an interface. In the sections below, we review prior studies that allowed us to derive testable hypotheses for constructive replication.

PSYCHOLOGICAL EFFECTS OF CUSTOMIZATION

Our notion of self, and related psychological factors such as self-esteem, self-representation, and self-identity, have a profound influence on the ways in which we think, feel and behave [9]. Several studies in the fields of psychology and communication show how linking messages to one's values and beliefs can increase one's identity and sense of personal relevance [22]. Interactive technologies can do the same by letting users customize the interface. Indeed, studies have shown that customization holds strong emotional and cognitive appeal to users. For instance, when users were told to modify the characteristics of a conversational agent, they perceived the customized agent as more likable, trustworthy and useful, even though the customizability was only an illusion [34]. Another study showed that customization increases task efficiency in data management and reduces mental demand of users [23], even considering the extra time needed to customize the interface. Users of a personalized My Yahoo! page showed better attitudes towards the website than their counterparts who used a non-customized version of the same site [16]. Enjoyment of online gaming was also found to be elevated among users who were allowed to customize their avatars [3]. Customization in e-learning websites has been shown to enhance perceived group support and foster interactions with peers [35].

So what is it that makes customization so appealing to users? Recent studies have identified some of the key psychological factors [19, 28], including sense of control, sense of identity, and sense of agency. Sense of control is the extent to which the user feels in charge of the interaction with an interface. Sense of identity refers to the degree to which users perceive that the end product of their customization efforts is a reflection of themselves (values, ideas, beliefs etc). Sense of agency is a measure of "sourceness", i.e., the extent to which the user feels they are being an active agent, initiating actions [28, 29]. In fact, a study comparing websites with personalized features to those with customizable features [28] showed that sense of agency imbued by user-initiated customization, rather than system-initiated tailoring, is key to inducing better attitudes toward customizable websites. Taken together, these studies show why customizing their own portal is likely to influence users' sense of identity and sense of agency, thereby inducing more positive attitudes toward the portal site. Thus, we propose the following hypotheses:

H1: Higher degree of functional customization will result in higher sense of identity (H1a), higher sense of agency (H1b), and more positive attitudes towards the site (H1c).

H2: Higher degree of cosmetic customization will result in higher sense of identity (H2a), higher sense of agency (H2b), and more positive attitudes towards the site (H2c).

PSYCHOLOGICAL EFFECTS OF BLOGGING

Since their advent in 1991 [33], blogs have played a significant role in the domain of user-generated content [14]. In its role either as a form of personal journaling or one of filtering external events [32], blogging enables users to create and/or share content. In general, blogging is associated with positive outcomes. Researchers have found that various forms of blogging, such as video blogs, personal journals, political and collaborative blogs, increased users' likelihood of interacting with other users within online communities (e.g., following blog rolls), which in turn resulted in a greater number of other social interactions, such as participation in community forums [14]. Similarly, active bloggers who create and share their own stories demonstrated a greater level of attachment to the community, as compared to non-bloggers [4].

Akin to the roles played by sense of identity, control and agency in driving the effects of customization, psychological empowerment via sense of community and sense of agency has characterized the perceived effects of blogging [8, 24]. A collaborative blog website of a university yielded a greater sense of community among students who participated in the blogging program [8]. Another study showed that the type of blogging–originally creating content and sharing it (active blogging) or sifting content from other sources and sharing it (filter blogging)–makes a difference in users' psychological experiences. Specifically, active blogging led to an increased sense of community, which in turn influenced one's feelings of being autonomous, whereas filter blogging increased one's sense of agency and subsequently made them feel a sense of influence over others in the community [24]. Based on this, we proposed the following hypotheses for study:

H3a: Active blogging will result in higher sense of community than filter blogging

H3b: Both active and filter blogging will result in a similar level of sense of agency.

H3c: Both active and filter blogging will result in a similar level of positive attitudes towards the portal site.

While previous research has studied blogging in isolation, we investigate how it interacts with other affordances of self-expression on the interface, such as functional and cosmetic customization. Theoretically, this also highlights a key distinction between users acting as a source for self (i.e., customization) versus others (i.e., blogging).

RQ: How do the different types of source interactivity vary in usability (RQ1), perceived competency (RQ2), intrinsic motivation to use the site (RQ3), and behavioral intention to use the site (RQ4)?

SOURCE INTERACTIVITY AND USER ENGAGEMENT

In recent years, scholars have emphasized the importance of moving beyond usability concerns toward understanding user experience, and design interfaces to make them engaging to users [11]. User engagement has been defined as a psychological state of being involved, absorbed, immersed, or being in a flow-like state [5, 7, 12, 21]. Higher levels of source interactivity, such as customization. have been shown to foster interactions among students [35], presence among game players [3], and perceived involvement in website users [16]. These psychological outcomes are likely to contribute to a heightened level of *absorption*, defined as a state of deep involvement with an interface that includes temporal dissociation, focused immersion, heightened enjoyment, and control [1].

Apart from such self-reported indicators, recent work on engagement has included behavioral metrics that can objectively reflect the degree to which users are engaged in the task at hand. For instance, Businessweek.com calculated user engagement based on the number of comments per posting on their website [30]. Other scholars have devised a user engagement metric in social networking sites that is calculated on the basis of the weighted sum of activities ranging from simple log-ins to writing forum messages [2]. Considering that deeply engaged users would be more willing to exert effort and manage their online activity, creating their own content (via blogging) would be the highest form of engagement that such users show in personal dashboard sites. Beyond the individual level, responding to other users' questions and blogposts will also contribute in sparking further discussion and contributions from others users as well [6]. In keeping with this, we operationalize the behavioral dimension of user engagement as the number of comments and replies generated by study participants during the course of our study.

RQ: How do the different types of source interactivity features vary in the degree of absorption (RQ5), and the number of comments (RQ6)?

METHOD

To address our research questions and hypotheses, we conducted a 3 (Functional customization: no vs. low vs. high) × 2 (Cosmetic customization: absent vs. present) × 2 (Blogging: active vs. filter) fully factorial field experiment wherein human subjects used the test site for two weeks.

Participants

Study participants were recruited by posting an ad in the local newspaper. All participants went through the informed consent procedure prior to their participation. After successful completion of the study, they were offered a monetary compensation of $35 in the form of gift cards. In all, 141 participants (108 females) took part in this study, with mean *age* of 45.13 years, over three periods of data collection in Spring, 2011.

Procedure

All participants were first asked to fill out a pretest questionnaire that asked about their general technology usage and previous experience with portal sites. Using a randomization script, we assigned participants to one of the 12 experimental conditions. One day before the study started, they received an instructional email with the link to one of our stimulus websites, login information, introduction of the website functions, and an activity table listing all possible activities to perform on the website. With the information from the instructional email, participants were expected to start browsing and interacting with the website for two weeks. During the two weeks, participants were requested to log into the website for at least 20 minutes every day. To make the experience realistic and to create a sense of readership, a number of confederates interacted with the participants as if they were Portal users as well, but in fact no interaction among participants was possible or allowed.

To ensure interaction between participants and the websites, we assigned various tasks to participants on a daily basis. In Week 1, participants received emails with specific tasks every day, whereas in Week 2, they were allowed to interact with the site freely. (In the second round of data collection, the order was reversed to counter-balance the effect of emailing). The email suggested that participants try out one of the features on the website, e.g., "Did you know that you could check the weather on your portal via the Tools Gadget? The Weather tool lets you view the weather for State College. It gets real-time weather information from weather.com and updates automatically every minute. It also provides three-day forecast. If you have not tried it yet, feel free to explore this gadget today!"

Repeated post-test questionnaires were sent to the participants at the end of the first week and second week. Participants with 0 logins were excluded from the study after Week 1; those who were inactive or who did not respond to the questionnaire were reminded through email.

Stimuli

Twelve stimulus websites were created using the WordPress platform to test the effects of functional customization, cosmetic customization and blogging. On every website, there were four tabs: Homepage, blogs, Q&A, and Portal feeds. Several features were listed on the navigation bar, including Portal home, my blog, change theme (only available in Cosmetic Customization), change avatar, and play music. See Figure 1 for an example.

Figure 1. Sample Portal homepage

On the homepage, there were three columns: gadgets, blog, and RSS feeds. A total of six default gadgets were present on the homepage, including Email (Gmail/Hotmail/Yahoo!), Date and Time, Google News, YouTube, Wikipedia and Weather. These were chosen from the most-used list in the iGoogle gadgets directory. Users were also given a list of default RSS feeds covering seven major categories such as technology, business, and politics. We chose the top-ranked blog for each of the categories from technorati.com. Other default functions included rearranging the three columns (gadgets, blog, and RSS feeds) or rearranging gadgets or feeds within the column, changing avatar, listening to Pandora, and posting on a Q&A board.

On the main menu bar, the Blogs tab allowed participants to see the latest blog posts. The Q&A tab showed the discussion board where participants could post questions or answers; however, they did not see posts from other participants. They could only see posts from the confederates, thus keeping content constant..

Other than these default features and functions, the websites had different settings, so participants in different conditions were allowed to perform certain types of activities with regard to adding/editing gadgets and RSS feeds, changing website themes, and engaging in active or filter blogging (see next section on "Independent Variables").

Nine video tutorials and text instructions were accessible under the "Help" tab, covering all site features, so participants could refer to them as needed.

Independent Variables

The three independent variables—functional customization, cosmetic customization, and blogging—were manipulated to vary the level of source interactivity on the stimulus websites. Baseline level of "source-ness" was achieved by default features, including the setting of display name, uploading an avatar, and choosing the type of music to play on the Portal website.

Functional customization was operationalized as the affordance of changing—choosing, adding or removing—the functional features, such as gadgets and RSS feeds, on the website. In this study, it had three levels: no vs. low vs. high. In control condition, or "no" condition, no functional customization options, but only the preset of default gadgets and RSS feeds were provided. In the low condition, participants were allowed to pick one of three widgets from each of the nine categories (News, Tools, Communication, Lifestyle, etc.). Similarly, users were given links to the Top-3 RSS feeds, as rated by technorati.com and were asked to select one RSS feed from each one of five categories (technology, business, politics, entertainment, etc.). In the high condition, participants were directly linked from their Portal homepage to Google Gadgets Directory (http://www.google.com/ig/directory), where they could search and choose from more than 220,000 gadgets. For RSS feeds, they were allowed to use a RSS search engine (www.rsssearchhub.com) to look for any topic or any source to subscribe. The total number of gadgets and RSS feeds present on the homepage were the same in all conditions. (Apart from adding equivalence across conditions, this also helped in ensuring that the Portal's appearance would not get cluttered with several widgets and feeds, inadvertently leading to negative usability issues).

Cosmetic customization was operationalized as the affordance of tailoring the look of the website. The experimental (present) condition allowed participants to choose from six WordPress blog themes (see Figure 1 for example), whereas in the control (absent) condition, participants were unable to change from the default blue theme. A number of themes were pretested, and the six chosen ones were rated about medium in attractiveness.

User-generated content, operationalized as *Blogging* in this study, had two forms: filter blogging and active blogging. Filter blogs allowed participants to choose a news source and a message to re-disseminate with their comments or additional information. A "blog it" button appeared whenever participants moused-over an RSS feed. Clicking the button would directly add the link and the first few sentences from that feed to their blog post. They could then add their own preface before publishing the post. Active blogs, on the other hand, did not necessarily have outbound linking, but allowed participants to write about any topic of their choice. The two types of blogs differed in the extent to which participants were able to choose a topic to write about freely, and thus the degree of "source-ness" that they perceived during the practice of blogging.

Dependent Variables

In the post-test questionnaires, we measured the following variables using 9-point Likert-type scales.

Website Assessments

Participants were asked to make quick evaluations of the websites in terms of *perceived interactivity*, *perceived customization*, and *usability*.

Attitudinal and Behavioral Responses

We measured participants' *attitudes* towards each of the features on the websites as well as towards the Portal website. Attitudinal measures towards the website included questions asking participants' agreement with the following eleven descriptors: appealing, useful, positive, good, favorable, attractive, exciting, pleasant, likable, high quality, and interesting [27].

To measure *behavioral intention* towards portal, 10 questions asked about the likelihood that participants would perform the following behaviors in the future: "bookmark the website for future use", "recommend it to others", "visit it again in the future" and so on [13].

Psychological Mechanisms

Absorption was measured by self-reported level of temporal dissociation: "Time appeared to go by very quickly", "I lost track of time", and "I spent more time than I had intended" [1]. *Sense of agency* was measured using three items describing feeling of an assertive voice: "I feel that I have control over my own voice", "I feel that I am able to assert myself", and "I feel I have a distinct voice" [24]. *Sense of identity* was measured using six items such as "I feel the website reflects my personal identity", "the website is now a true representation of who I am", and "the website fits my image" [24]. *Sense of community* was measured using seven items including "this website has made me feel that I am part of a community", "this website has induced a feeling of belonging in me", and "I experience a sense of kinship when going through this site" [16]. Participants were asked to self-report *perceived competency* of managing the website as well. There were six questions which included "I think I was pretty good with handling the website", and "I am satisfied with my performance." We also asked if participants were *intrinsically motivated* to engage with the websites via 14 questions such as "I am doing it for my own good", "I am supposed to do it" (reverse-coded), and "I believe that this activity is important for me" [10].

Interaction Measures

Log data were collected automatically to record participants' login times, browsing duration, number of gadgets added/deleted, etc. One of the behavioral measures that could reflect their engagement with the websites and other "users" was the *number of comments*, which was a sum of the *number of comments* that they posted on others' blog entries and the *number of answers* that they posted on the Q&A discussion board. The number of blogposts created by each user could not be included in our user- engagement metric since our study instruction required the participants to create at least one blogpost each day. It is important to note here that the "other users" in the study were not other participants in the sample. Instead, a team of researchers posed as other users of the Portal. They followed a predetermined experimental protocol to manage the blogging tasks and instructions to sustain the blogging manipulation in the study.

Control Variables

Power usage was measured by participants' perceived capability in managing technologies in general. Twelve questions were asked, including "I think most of the technological gadgets are complicated to use", and "I have to have the latest available upgrades of the technological devices that I use" [20]. *Previous experience* with Portal-like websites and blog sites were measured. 23% of our participants had used iGoogle services before the study, and 17% had blog accounts with services like Blogspot or WordPress. We also measured how *agentic* people felt that they normally were in their everyday conduct. The following three items were used: "I get to make my own decisions in my life", "I feel in control when I work", and "I am competent in my own field."

RESULTS

A 3 (Functional customization: no vs. low vs. high) x 2 (Cosmetic customization: absent vs. present) x 2 (Blogging: active vs. filter) repeated measures analysis of covariance (ANCOVA) was conducted, with power usage, individualism, sense of agency in life, previous usage of iGoogle and blogs, age and gender of the participants entered as covariates, and the time of questionnaire administration (Week 1 or Week 2) as the repeated factor.

Effects on Perceived Customization and Interactivity

For perceived customization and perceived interactivity, the score was averaged across the two weeks.

Perceived customization: Both low functional customization (M = 5.79) and high functional customization (M = 5.66) were rated higher than the control condition (M = 4.76), F (2, 136) = 3.44, $p < .05$, $\eta^2 = .16$. Cosmetic customization elicited higher ratings of perceived customization (M = 5.72) than the control condition (M = 5.09) at a marginally significant level, F (1, 136) = 3.42, $p = .06$, $\eta^2 = .16$.

Perceived interactivity: Participants in the high functional customization condition scored higher on perceived interactivity (M = 6.61) than those in control condition (M = 5.41), with participants in the low level of functional customization condition scoring in the middle (M = 6.30), F (2, 136) = 5.16, $p < .01$, $\eta^2 = .21$. Participants in the active blogging condition (M = 6.49) scored higher on perceived interactivity than their counterparts in the filter blogging condition (M = 5.72), F (1, 136) = 6.10, $p = .05$, $\eta^2 = .21$.

Effects on Sense of Identity, Agency, and Community

H1a and H2a (Sense of identity): Participants reported higher sense of identity under low functional customization (M = 3.47, SE = .56) than high functional customization (M = 3.30, SE = .50) or control conditions (M = 2.46, SE = .56) across two weeks, F (2, 120) = 3.62, $p < .05$, $\eta^2 = .24$. Tukey's HSD post hoc test showed that the difference between low and control conditions was significant at $p < .05$. Neither the cosmetic customization feature nor the blogging type showed any effects on identity.

H3a (Sense of community): As predicted by H3a, the participants who were involved in active blogging reported greater sense of community (M = 2.72, SE = .50) than those involved in filter blogging (M = 2.05, SE = .53) across two weeks, F (1, 120) = 4.53, $p < .05$, $\eta^2 = .25$. Interestingly, functional customization also influenced the sense of community such that low level of functional customization imbued greater sense of community in users (M = 2.90, SE = .56) compared to the high level of the feature (M = 2.45, SE = .50) and the control condition (M = 1.79, SE = .56). Low and control conditions were significantly different.

H1b, H2b, and H3b (Sense of Agency): As shown in Figure 2, there was a significant three-way interaction between all three types of source interactivity. Low level of functional customization elicited higher sense of agency than other conditions when it was combined with both cosmetic customization and active blogging features (M = 7.95, SE = .63) (right side), but created less sense of agency than others when there was only active blogging but no cosmetic customization available (M = 6.93, SE = .63) (left side), F (2, 120) = 3.28, $p < .05$, $\eta^2 = .25$.

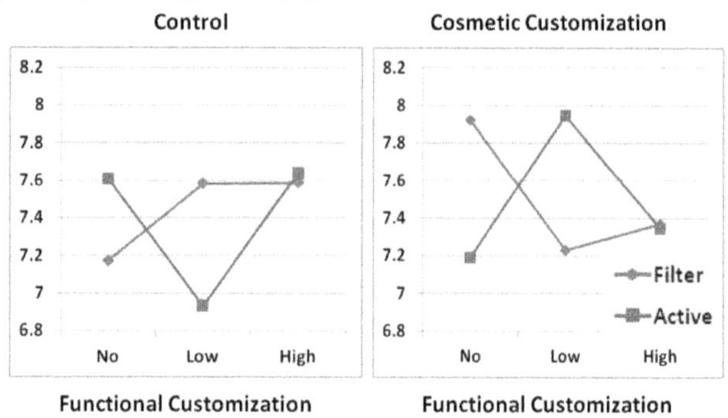

Figure 2. Three-way interaction effect on sense of agency

H1c, H2c, and H3c (Attitude towards the portal): Participants who used cosmetic customization reported more positive attitudes towards the site (M = 4.77, SE = .50) than those in the control condition (M = 3.98, SE = .48) across the two weeks, F (1, 120) = 6.74, $p < .05$, $\eta^2 = .24$. Likewise, participants who did active blogging showed more positive attitudes (M = 4.67, SE = .47) than those who did filter blogging (M = 4.08, SE = .50), F (1, 120) = 4.09, $p < .05$. Functional customization did not significantly influence participants' attitudes towards the portal.

RQ1 (Usability): Active blogging (M = 5.89, SE = .39) was found to be more usable than filter blogging (M = 5.34, SE

= .41) across two weeks, F (1, 120) = 5.14, $p < .05$, $\eta^2 = .20$. No effects were found for either type of customization.

RQ2 (Perceived competency): Participants who did active blogging reported feeling more competent to use the portal website (M = 6.46, SE = .44) than those who did filter blogging (M = 5.77, SE = .46), F (1, 120) = 6.32, $p < .05$, η^2 = .22. Other source interactivity features did not significantly influence the level of perceived competency.

RQ3 (Intrinsic motivation to use the portal): Participants in the active blogging condition were more intrinsically motivated to use the portal website (M = 5.31, SE = .47) than those in the filter blogging condition (M = 4.65, SE = .50), F (1, 120) = 4.87, $p < .05$, $\eta^2 = .19$. In addition, a significant time-by-condition effect, F (1, 120) = 4.31, p < .05, showed that participants without cosmetic customization were less intrinsically motivated to use the portal site in Week 2 (M = 4.36) than in Week 1 (M = 5.10), with no difference for those given cosmetic customization.

RQ4 (Behavioral intention to use the portal): A significant two-way interaction between functional customization and the type of blogging activity was found, F (2, 120) = 6.46, p < .01, η^2 = .26 (Figure 3). When participants did active blogging, the higher the level of functional customization, the higher their behavioral intention to use the portal site. In contrast, there was a curvilinear effect of functional customization for filter blogging.

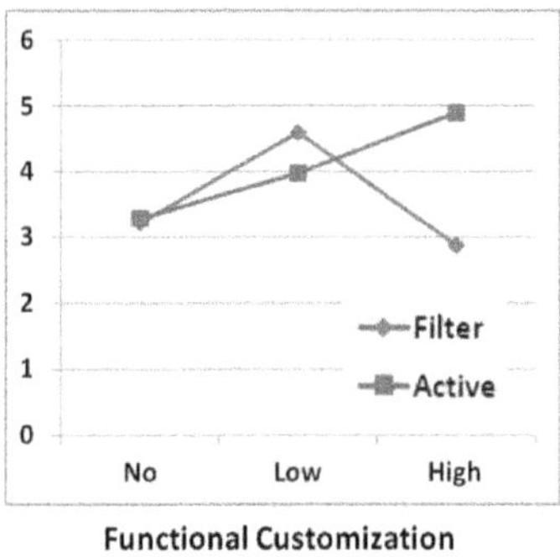

Figure 3. Two-way interaction effect on behavioral intention

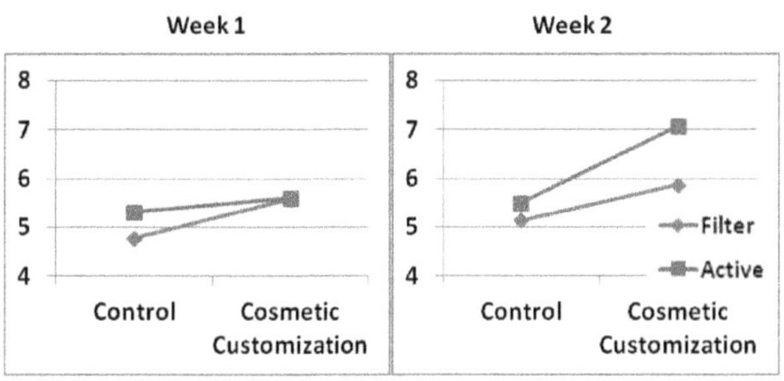

Figure 4. Time-by-cosmetic-by-blogging interaction effect on absorption

RQ5 (Absorption): Two significant three-way interactions emerged: time-by-cosmetic-by-blogging (Figure 4), and time-by-functional-by-blogging (Figure 5). As shown in Figure 4, participants reported being more absorbed in Week 2 (M = 7.08, SE = .60) than Week 1 (M = 5.61, SE = .65) when they had both cosmetic customization and active blogging, with other conditions remaining almost the same over two weeks, F (1, 120) = 4.77, $p < .05$, $\eta^2 = .21$. Also, they reported being less absorbed when they had the highest level of functional customization but only had filter blogging in their portal sites in Week 1, compared to other conditions (left side of Figure 5). In Week 2, active blogging increased the level of absorption for those who had the medium level of functional customization (right side of Figure 5), F (2, 120) = 3.86, $p < .05$.

RQ6 (Number of comments): A significant two-way interaction between cosmetic customization and blogging, F (1, 120) = 4.69, $p < .05$, η^2 = .14, revealed that while participants in the cosmetic customization condition commented more when they were asked to do filter blogging whereas their counterparts in the non-cosmetic control condition commented more when they were asked to do active blogging (Figure 6).

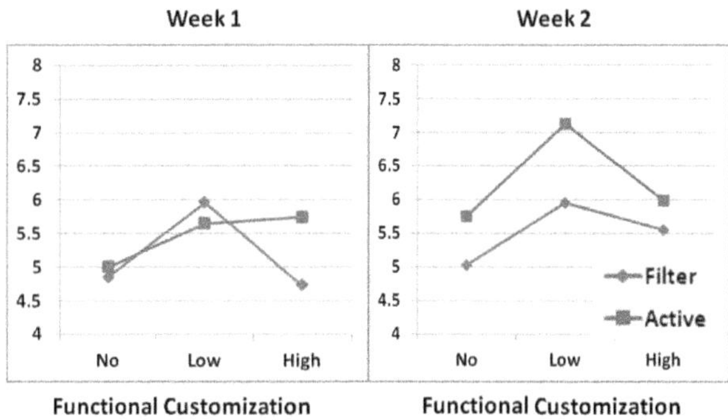

Figure 5. Time-by-functional-by-blogging interaction effect on absorption

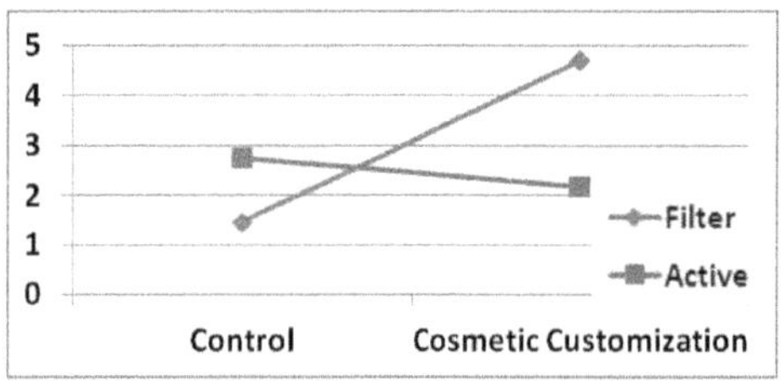

Figure 6. Two-way interaction effect on the number of comments

SUMMARY & DISCUSSION

The primary objective of the study is to understand the individual and cumulative effects of different forms of source interactivity on user engagement and experience. Our results show that self-expression in the form of making cosmetic changes to the interface and engaging in active, rather than filter, blogging resulted in several favorable outcomes. Functional customization, however, was preferred in moderation. These findings are qualified by several interaction effects between the three source-interactivity affordances, some over time.

Active blogging and cosmetic customization sustain user-engagement

At the end of two weeks, active blogging was more likely to

sustain users' level of absorption than filter blogging, especially when it was combined with cosmetic customization or a modicum of functional customization. Therefore, one way to engage users over time is to provide options for creating personal content along with options for customization, but with a moderate number of choices. When users made use of colored themes and patterns to customize their Portal cosmetically, their intrinsic motivation sustained over the entire duration of the study. In contrast, the intrinsic motivation of those without the Change Theme option decreased over time. Although the study site offered only six options of customizable themes to choose from, even this small pool was effective in keeping the users motivated and engaged. The "sleeper effect" [17] for cosmetic customization suggests that allowing users to express their aesthetic taste can sustain their interest even after the novelty wears off. The implication for interface designers is obvious—include cosmetic customization options whenever possible. In addition, our study showed that the combination of active blogging and cosmetic customization was most powerful in sustaining user absorption over two weeks (Fig. 4), with a larger effect size. Therefore, designers may want to combine active blogging with customizable options.

Effortful customization could result in decision fatigue that could be combated with active self-expression

The relative difficulty of filter blogging was found to be detrimental when combined with unlimited choices of gadgets and feeds, i.e., high functional customization. This reduced usability of filter blogging manifested itself in the form of lower behavioral intentions (Fig. 3). On the positive side, active blogging appears to enhance the appetite for performing effortful functional customization. Allowing free self-expression appears to energize users to engage in effortful customization activities related to task. Filter blogging, on the other hand, peaked at low level of functional customization, thereby suggesting that interface features that call for selection and filtering have a threshold, crossing which may mean losing repeat visitors to the site. Theoretically, this implies greater need for decision-making—and hence "decision fatigue" [31]—during the course of filter blogging, and should therefore be avoided on interfaces that call for other forms of effortful decision-making, particularly given the effect size of this interaction.

Cosmetic customization could stimulate user participation, in lieu of active self-expression

The higher number of comments (in the form of replies to others' blog posts) generated by users in the filter blogging condition shows that users' need for self-expression is so strong that it drives them to produce more comments when they are deprived of one type of source interactivity (i.e., no scope for active blogging) while given the other (cosmetic customization)—a decent-sized effect considering all the noise factors of a field experiment. Hence, designing community-oriented websites is not always a matter of adding countless options for communicating with others; rather, the key is to ensure that users do not expend all their self-expression by active blogging and instead reserve some of it for more social forms of self-expression as well, such as commenting. As our findings suggest, offering some customization options in the interface, without providing blog-like features for content generation, can stimulate other types of participation in community forums on the site, such as commenting and replying to other users. This role of cosmetic customization as a stimulant of user participation can be effectively leveraged by designers of online communities.

Customizing from a convenient choice-set encourages sense of community

Our study revealed an interesting behavioral pattern with respect to functional customization and users' choice-set behaviors. We found that a pre-selected, shorter set of choices is likely to be better for users than an exhaustive list that displays a vast array of choices. This echoes other findings in studies of human choice behavior [15]. In our study, users in the high functional customization condition, who were given an unlimited choice-set for adding gadgets and feeds, did not appreciate the opportunity, even though they rated it as highly interactive. In terms of overall user experience, the optimal level of functional customization was the low level, which fostered greater sense of community than both high and control conditions. Thus, another way to build sites that evoke a sense of community (apart from active blogging) is by providing cues that give users an impression of selecting and choosing from a shared, predetermined list of gadgets and content, ideally with ratings and other cues about quality. In practice, several sites and services employ such cues, in the form of Most Emailed News Stories, Critics' Top Movie Picks, and so on.

Non-linear combinations of source-interactivity features are needed to build a sense of agency

Participants' sense of agency was at its highest when optimal levels of all three forms of source interactivity were present together: low, rather than high, level of functional customization (i.e. limited number of choices), presence, rather than absence, of cosmetic customization, and active, rather than filter, blogging. Removing cosmetic customization from this combination of source-interactivity features was particularly detrimental to users' sense of agency. In general, users can be made to feel like active agents of action by offering different forms of source interactivity features that complement each other and contribute to their self-expression needs. In fact, the 3-way interaction with sense of agency reveals that different combinations of the three forms of source interactivity can affect user experience in different ways. For example, active blogging leads to higher sense of agency when accompanied by both cosmetic customization and (some amount of) functional customization or neither, compared to the presence of one or the other. In addition, a high level of functional customization does serve to make the user feel more agentic, but only in the absence of cosmetic customization. These findings suggest carryover as well as threshold effects among the different forms of source interactivity, which provide ready guidelines to designers who will now have to worry about how certain combinations of source-interactivity features may be more empowering than others. It means that they will need to think about self-expression tools on the interface in terms of toggle effects rather than as a cumulative affordance leading linearly to positive outcomes.

Power of active blogging substantiates the source interactivity continuum

Active blogging was rated as more interactive than filter, verifying our continuum of source interactivity—when the user is able to actually generate new content, they perceive a higher level of interactivity in the interface than when they are simply filtering, bookmarking or forwarding existing content. What's more, they found the relatively simpler affordance (often just a text field with a Publish button) more empowering. Even though the task of coming up with one's own topic to write about and actually composing something to say may seem onerous, our participants rated active blogging as higher in usability compared to the convenience of simply pressing the Blog It button that often appears next to already published articles. These users also had a higher sense of community, were more intrinsically motivated to use the site and had more positive attitudes towards it. The active-blogging feature alone was quite powerful enough in creating a sense of community ($\eta^2 = .25$), whereas evoking a sense of agency of similar effect size required all three source-interactivity features to operate in tandem. An obvious design implication is that simple text-field options, whereby users can write and publish online, can go a long way in enhancing the quality of UX, particularly for building community, as evidenced by the dramatic popularity of Twitter and the Status Update function in Facebook. From a psychological point of view, the height of customization appears to be when users can generate their own content, thus extending the scope of the agency model [25]. Under the model, if making active choices and decisions via functional customization contributes to a sense of control, cosmetic customization and active blogging provide a heightened sense of identity. Thus, self-expression achieved either via asserting one's identity or via more active control of functional choices allows for a creation of sense of agency that is key in explaining source-interactivity outcomes. For designers of customizable interfaces, this means an emphasis on letting the user be the source of new content rather than simply a selector of preset options.

CONCLUSION

Even though our two-week long user study provided perceptual verification of the source-interactivity continuum, the effects of each of the three components were anything but straightforward when considered together in one interface. While the affordance of active blogging appears to gratify the need for self expression, and cosmetic customization serves to maintain user interest in the interface, filter blogging provides lesser self-expression by comparison, and like functional customization, seems to require greater decision-making, resulting in a reduction of perceived agency. Therefore, more is not necessarily better for these affordances, and designers will need to find an optimal level. The challenge is to provide sufficient opportunities for expression without undermining user control. In conclusion, conceptualizing interactivity in terms of making users the source of communication offers designers an opportunity to devise interface tools specifically geared toward self expression, and thereby influence a number of psychological outcomes that are novel in UX studies, such as perceptions of agency, identity, community and engagement, with important implications for their attitudes toward the interface, intrinsic motivation to use it and intention to reuse it.

ACKNOWLEDGEMENTS

This research is supported by the U. S. National Science Foundation (NSF) via Standard Grant No. IIS-0916944 and by the Korea Science and Engineering Foundation under the WCU (World Class University) program funded through the Ministry of Education, Science and Technology, S. Korea (Grant No. R31-2008-000-10062-0). We thank NSF REU awardees, Ann Sciandra and Ashley Gabel, for their assistance.

REFERENCES

1. Agarwal, R. and Karahanna, E. Time flies when you're having fun: Cognitive absorption and beliefs about information technology usage. *MIS Quarterly 24*, 4 (2000), 665-694.
2. Baghaei, N., Kimani, S., Freyne, J., Brindal, E., Berkovsky, S. and Smith, G. Engaging families in lifestyle changes through social networking. *International Journal of Human-Computer Interaction 27*, 10 (2011), 971-990.
3. Bailey, R.W., and Bolls, P. How avatar customizability affects children's arousal and subjective presence during junk food-sponsored online video games. *CyberPsychology & Behavior 12*, 3 (2009), 277-283.
4. Baker, J.R. and Moore, S.M. Blogging as a social tool: A psychosocial examination of the effects of blogging. *CyberPsychology & Behavior 11,* 6 (2008), 747-749.
5. Busselle, R. and Bilandzic, H. Fictionality and perceived realism in experiencing stories: A model of narrative comprehension and engagement. *Communication Theory 18*, 2 (2008), 255-280.
6. Cheng, R., and Vassileva, J. User motivation and persuasion strategy for peer-to-peer communities. In *Proc. HICSS'38* (2005), Hawaii, USA, 193-202.
7. Csikszentmihalyi, M. *Flow: The psychology of optimal experience*. New York: Harper and Row, 1990.
8. Firpo, D., Kasemvilas, S., Ractham, P. and Zhang, X. Generating a sense of community in a graduate educational setting through persuasive technology. In *Proc. Persuasive Technology*, ACM Press (2009), Article 41.

9. Flemming, M.A. and Petty, R.E. Identity and persuasion: An elaboration likelihood approach. In M. A. Hogg & D. J. Terry (Eds.), *Attitude, behavior, and social context: The role of norms and group membership*. Mahawah, NJ: Erlbaum, 2000.

10. Guay, F., Vallerand, R.J., and Blanchard, C. On the assessment of situational intrinsic and extrinsic motivation: The situational motivation scale. *Motivation and emotion 24,* 3 (2000), 175-213.

11. Hassenzahl, M. and Tractinsky, N. User experience: A research agenda. *Behavior and Information Technology 25*, 2 (2006), 91-97.

12. Higgins, E.T. Value from hedonic experience and engagement. *Psychological Review 113,* 3 (2006), 439–460.

13. Hu, Y. and Sundar, S.S. Effects of online health sources on credibility and behavioral intentions. *Communication Research 37*, 1 (2010), 105-132.

14. Huang, C., Shen, Y-Z., Lin, H-X. and Chang, S-S. Bloggers' motivations and behaviors: A model. *Journal of Advertising Research 47*, 4 (2007), 472-484.

15. Iyengar, S. and Lepper, M. When choice is demotivating: Can one desire too much of a good thing? *Journal of Personality and Social Psychology 79* (2000), 995–1006.

16. Kalyanaraman, S. and Sundar, S.S. The psychological appeal of personalized content in Web portals: Does customization affect attitudes and behavior? *Journal of Communication 56* (2006), 110–132.

17. Kumkale, G.T. and Albarracin, D. The sleeper effect in persuasion: A meta-analytic review. *Psychological Bulletin 130* (2004), 143-172.

18. Marathe, S.S. and Sundar, S.S. The 'me' revolution in mediated communication: Investigating the psychology of cosmetic and functional customization. In *Proc. International Communication Association*, 2011.

19. Marathe, S.S. and Sundar, S.S. What drives customization? Control or identity? In *Proc. CHI 2011*, ACM Press (2011), 781-790.

20. Marathe, S.S., Sundar, S.S., Bijvank, M.N., et al. Who are these power users anyway? Building a psychological profile. In *Proc. International Communication Association*, 2007.

21. O'Brien, H.L., Toms, E.G., Kelloway, E.K. and Kelley, E. Developing and evaluating a reliable measure of user engagement. In *Proc. American Society for Information Science and Technology*, 2008.

22. Petty, R.E. and Cacioppo, J.T. Involvement and persuasion: Tradition versus integration. *Psychological Bulletin 107* (1990), 367-374.

23. Rivera, D. The effect of content customization on learnability and perceived workload. In *Proc. CHI '05 extended abstracts on Human factors in computing systems*, ACM Press (2005), 1749–1752.

24. Stavrositu, C., and Sundar, S.S. (2008). Can blogs empower women? Designing agency-enhancing and community-building interfaces. In *Proc. Ext. Abstracts CHI 2008*, ACM Press (2008), 2781-2786.

25. Sundar, S.S. Self as source: Agency and customization in interactive media. In E. Konijn, S. Utz, M. Tanis, and S. Barnes (Eds.), *Mediated interpersonal communication* (pp. 58-74). New York: Routledge, 2008.

26. Sundar, S.S. Social psychology of interactivity in human-website interaction. In A. N. Joinson, K.Y.A. McKenna, T. Postmes, and U-D. Reips (Eds.). *The Oxford handbook of Internet psychology*, (pp. 89-104). Oxford University Press Oxford, UK, 2007.

27. Sundar, S.S., Kalyanaraman, S. and Brown, J. Explicating website interactivity: Impression-formation effects in political campaign sties. *Communication Research 30* (2003), 30-59.

28. Sundar, S.S., and Marathe, S.S. Personalization versus customization: The importance of agency, privacy, and power usage. *Human Communication Research 36* (2010), 298–322.

29. Sundar, S.S., Xu, Q., and Bellur, S. Designing interactivity in media interfaces: A communications perspective. In *Proc. CHI 2010,* ACM Press (2010), 2247-2256.

30. Ulken, E. Measuring user engagement: Lessons from BusinessWeek. *Online Journalism Review.* http://www.ojr.org/ojr/people/eulken/200904/1696/.

31. Vohs, K.D., Baumeister, R.F., Schemeichel, B.J., Twenge, J.M., Nelson, N.M. and Tice, D.M. Making choices impairs subsequent self-control: A limited-resource account of decision making, self-regulation, and active initiative. *Journal of Personality and Social Psychology 94* (2008), 883-989.

32. Wei, L. Filter blogs vs. personal journals: Understanding the knowledge production gap on the Internet. *Journal of Computer-Mediated Communication 14* (2009), 532–558.

33. Winer, D. *The history of weblogs*. 2002. http://oldweblogscomblog.scripting.com/historyOfWeblogs.

34. Xiao, J., Stasko, J., and Catrambone, R. The role of choice and customization on users′ interaction with embodied conversational agents: Effects on perception and performance. In *Proc. CHI 2007*, ACM Press (2007), 1293-1302.

35. Yu, F.-Y. Scaffolding student-generated questions: Design and development of a customizable online learning system, *Computers in Human Behavior* 25, 5 (2009), 1129-1138.

CrossingGuard: Exploring Information Content in Navigation Aids for Visually Impaired Pedestrians

Richard T. Guy & Khai N. Truong
Department of Computer Science
University of Toronto
Toronto, ON, Canada, M5S 3E4
{guy, khai}@cs.toronto.edu

ABSTRACT

Visually impaired pedestrians experience unique challenges when navigating an urban environment because many cues about orientation and traffic patterns are difficult to ascertain without the use of vision. Technological aids such as customized GPS navigation tools offer the chance to augment visually impaired pedestrians' sensory information with a richer depiction of an environment, but care must be taken to balance the need for more information with other demands on the senses. In this paper, we focus on the information needs of visually impaired pedestrians at intersections, which present a specific cause of stress when navigating in unfamiliar locations. We present a navigation application prototype called CrossingGuard that provides rich information to a user such as details about intersection geometry that are not available to visually impaired pedestrians today. A user study comparing content-rich information to a baseline condition shows that content-rich information raises the level of comfort that visually impaired pedestrians feel at unfamiliar intersections. In addition, we discuss the categories of information that are most useful. Finally, we introduce a micro-task approach to gather intersection data via Street View annotations that achieves 85.5% accuracy over the 9 categories of information used by CrossingGuard.

Author Keywords

Visually Impaired Pedestrians; Wayfinding; Navigation Aids; Geographic Data.

ACM Classification Keywords

H.5.2. User Interfaces: User Centered Design

General Terms

Human Factors, Design, Experimentation

INTRODUCTION

Navigating unfamiliar locations on foot often requires that one learn new traffic and location clues from the environment. For visually impaired individuals, this presents special challenges because many of the cues one uses to determine when and where to walk in an urban environment are visual [10]. Streets names are presented on signs that are often not accessible to people with little or no vision, and choosing a direction to cross is difficult without being able to see a target on the other side of the street. Moreover, many city maps and GPS navigation aids, even accessible aids, focus on streets rather than on pedestrian paths, making the assumption that those streets that are good for cars will have sidewalks that are good for pedestrians.

In this paper, we address the problem of orientation and mobility for visually impaired pedestrians by examining their specific navigation needs. Through a series of formative interviews with visually impaired pedestrians and Orientation and Mobility (O&M) specialists, we found that intersections present a point of stress, particularly when navigating in a new area. For instance, one participant from our formative study told us:

"Just arriving at an unfamiliar corner, you have no way of knowing what you are dealing with. You may be able to tell from traffic what it is, if you stay there long enough. But it's either familiarity with an area or what someone has told you. Otherwise, there is no way to tell just by arriving at a street corner." (F1— formative study participant 1)

The quote above represents a common refrain in our formative study. Pedestrians expressed that it is hard to gather information about an unfamiliar intersection even if car noise is present. They rely on prior knowledge or on guides, which limits their ability to travel independently. Their feedback about what kind of information would help them to navigate with confidence motivated us to develop CrossingGuard, a new navigation aid for visually impaired pedestrians that provides "sidewalk to sidewalk" directions along with detailed information about the geometry (shape and width) of intersections and about traffic control systems.

To explore the effect of more detailed information on the comfort level of visually impaired pedestrians, we performed a study comparing the CrossingGuard information and instructions against a baseline set of instructions based on commercially available navigation aids. Results demonstrate that possessing detailed information about intersections raises the comfort level of visually impaired pedestrians, which can in turn help them travel more independently. We also investigate which information is most helpful in an effort to streamline the presentation of information. Results show that participants use a wide array of information, but they consider information about traffic signaling, intersection shape, and road width to be the most important information.

Although the information we present in CrossingGuard likely exists in some mapping systems, it is not accessible to users or developers in a standard format. Thus, we explored the use of Amazon's Mechanical Turk as a plausible means for extracting such relevant information about intersections from still images taken from Google Street View. We demonstrate that Turk users are able to collect the 9 categories of information used by the CrossingGuard application with 85.5% accuracy.

RELATED WORK

Visually impaired pedestrians rely on accessible infrastructure, technological aids, and specialized training when they approach and cross an intersection. Technological aids can complement both accessible infrastructure and the techniques taught by Orientation and Mobility (O&M) specialists.

Intersection Design and O&M Training

The O&M manual, written primarily for O&M practitioners, explains an eight-step strategy employed by most visually impaired people [28]. They include (1) detecting the intersection, (2) locating the crosswalk and crossing, (3) determining traffic signaling, (4) locating an APS if available, (5) aligning to cross, (6) determining when to cross, (7) starting to cross, and (8) maintaining correct alignment. Intersections can be designed with accessibility in mind, for instance by including an Accessible Pedestrian Signal (APS) or tactile markers in sidewalks. However, budget constraints often limit the availability of these solutions. Conflicting requirements make it difficult to design intersections that meet the needs of all users. For instance, the sloped curves that wheelchair users require sometimes make it more difficult for visually impaired pedestrians to square off to the street they are crossing. For an overview of accessible engineering practices including a discussion of what kinds of options are available and appropriate, see [5, 6].

Technological mobility aids

Previous work on accessibility applications for visually impaired pedestrians focuses on challenges in orientation. Properly orienting one's self involves both current location and desired heading.

Orientation applications deploy location-sensing technology coupled with a map to locate and guide users through their environment. Strategies for location detection include augmenting the environment through, for instance, infrared markers [7,17] and using a signal-based location sensor such as GPS. In the rest of this section, we focus on signal-based location sensing because it does not require infrastructural change, though our results on the type of information that visually impaired pedestrians require can be of use for infrastructure based accessibility applications.

Loomis *et al.* [16] and Golledge *et al.* [9] present early work in orientation. Loomis *et al.*'s system uses highly accurate differential GPS, an electronic compass, GIS, and spatial audio to name streets and other landmarks in their proper location in space. Dhristi [11] focuses on responding to dynamic information about the environment rather than the static information typical of GIS. For instance, the system allows users to dynamically reroute themselves in response to road closures and other unexpected changes. Another influential system is the MOBIC dialogue system, which introduces multi-tiered directions that provide progressively more detailed information about a scene [23]. MOBIC addresses the key question of what *kinds* of information a system should present in the context of visually impaired users. Our own work presents a partial answer to this question by providing participant feedback about the perceived helpfulness of an array of potential information.

More recent work has found that visually impaired individuals using navigation devices travel to new areas faster [19] and with less errors and halts [13] than using physical maps or direct experience. Several commercially available GPS navigation aids are marketed directly to visually impaired people. Trekker Breeze [24] is a leading stand-alone device that supports orientation using a commercial GPS receiver. Sendero [21] is a commercial product that uses the wireless and location-sensing capabilities of smart phones. However, these systems are agnostic to sidewalks, and some of the information they share is taken straight from GIS databases, including postal codes or the name of the city. This raises the question of what kind of information about a location should be included in a mobile GPS.

Visually impaired pedestrians often have specific information needs. Völkel *et al.* [26] note that the preferred route for a visually impaired pedestrian may not be the most direct route. Their RouteCheckr application allows a user to include specific criteria that can alter routes to be more suitable for the specific travel needs of the person. Bradley and Dunlop [4] compared the directions that sighted people and blind people give, and found that visually impaired users are best able to follow instructions that focus on sensory, motion and social contact information rather than on structural or street-area information. Their work motivates the need for further understanding about the types of information that visually impaired users need to feel safe while traversing a new environment.

Nonverbal audio and haptic feedback are two novel information presentation strategies that have been studied in the context of visually impaired pedestrians. The SWAN system [27, 29] presents several kinds of audio information with nonverbal, spatialized sound. Sound beacons, which are nonverbal audio signals, lead a user towards the next waypoint in a predefined route. Features of the environment like park benches or bus stops are also represented by audio icons or though highly compressed speech called earcons or speercons. Haptic route information was investigated in [2, 3, 12, 25] among others. Their work demonstrates that physical feedback can be used to lead a visually impaired individual along a path as well as alert them to obstacles.

Several aspects of this work will build upon features of the systems that have been described in the literature. In particular, greater knowledge about the effect of navigation aids on visually impaired pedestrians as well as the information they should include will explored as a way of enhancing the efficacy of such systems. Furthermore, our investigation of a crowd-sourced mechanism to construct accessible maps presents an opportunity to expand such systems beyond the boundaries of an area that was mapped for research purposes.

FORMATIVE STUDY

To develop an understanding of visually impaired pedestrians' travel practices and requirements, we performed a pair of formative, structured interviews with 4 visually impaired individuals and two O&M specialists. The first interview focused on the strategies visually impaired pedestrians use to identify, navigate, and cross both familiar and unfamiliar intersections. We used these results to develop a prototype navigation system to elicit more detailed feedback about the information needs of the participants. All but one of the participants (F3) returned for a second interview, which was focused on design criteria for a mobile navigation application. Across both interviews, we were interested not just in what an application should provide to the user but on how to optimize the amount of attention we asked of the user.

Information gathered from the interviews corroborated literature describing that pedestrians are taught to approach street crossings with a multi-phase plan [28]. First, they identify the intersection using the downward curve, changes in sound volume, wind, and, for some individuals, light intensity. Once they are at an intersection, they assess the traffic patterns to solve the primary challenges of crossing *direction* and *timing*. Knowing the crossing direction requires insight about the shape of the intersection. Crossing timing requires that the pedestrians understand when traffic will let them cross, when they have the right of way, how long they have to cross, and how long the crossing will take. Intersection shape and width and the presence of traffic signals (lights or stop signs) are also important information when assessing crossing timing.

Participants described feeling uncomfortable with new intersections in particular, which is a hindrance for traveling to new areas independently even for advanced travelers:

"Any new [intersections], I am not able to do them unless I learn how first, unless I get [his O&M instructor] first. I'm not going to try some new one that I don't know." (F4)

Weather and other conditions can affect how well participants understand traffic patterns. For example, wet roads create more noise and significantly more echoes, which makes it harder to assess the shape of the intersection. Also, time of day affects the traffic level at an intersection, making it difficult to understand when to cross and how much time the pedestrian has.

All participants reported trouble identifying alleys and driveways, which may be missed altogether or mistaken for roads. Several participants noted that current GPS systems for pedestrians give routes that follow streets, but that they do not account for the presence of sidewalks:

"I once crossed the street and there was no sidewalk on the other side. [..] I went down for about 200 feet just to see if there was going to be a sidewalk and there wasn't and I had to go back and cross and find it on the other side.." (F2)

Our formative study uncovered several design criteria for a GPS based mobile accessibility application. The device should include information about the shape of the intersection including the directions of available crossings, the width of streets, and the presence of islands and other features of the roadway that affect crossing time. It should also relay information about the traffic signaling system in place. The system should give directions that follow sidewalks rather than focusing on roads. A final design criterion is the tradeoff between providing the user with detailed information and occupying their attention when they should be listening to traffic cues in their environment. In order to satisfy this criterion, we designed a study to investigate what categories of information are most helpful.

THE CROSSINGGUARD SYSTEM

Based on findings from our formative study, we developed the CrossingGuard system to provide "sidewalk to sidewalk" directions for visually impaired pedestrians; that is, the route follows known sidewalks and explicitly directs the user when to cross intersections. In addition, we designed the system to help users understand intersection geometry by including information about the size and shape of the streets that meet in the intersection as well as details about traffic signaling. Finally, we designed the system to complement the user's assessment of the environment by organizing the detailed information about the intersections into groups, which one can easily access when appropriate.

User Interaction

Prior to navigation, users must input their desired destination into the system. The user can specify the street addresses with existing input techniques such the keyboard or the phone's built in voice recognizer. Because the purpose of this project investigates what detailed navigation information to provide to visually impaired pedestrians and its effect on their comfort when they travel unfamiliar environments, we did not explore novel support for inputting the destination; however, it is an important aspect of the system that needs attention in a final product.

Users can interact with the application through a set of simple gestures with the mobile phone. To identify *"What is here?"* users perform a single tap. The device shares information about the nearest intersection if they are within 40m of an intersection or about the road they are following if they are on the sidewalk between intersections. At an intersection, users can ask the system *"Where could I go?"* by performing a double tap. The device shares what streets meet at the intersection and what direction they lead. To hear *"What should I do from here to get to my destination?"* the user swipes left or right across the screen. If the user should cross an intersection, the device says what street to cross and presents information about the crossing. If the user should follow a sidewalk, the device says what sidewalk to follow and alerts the user to any alleys that are between her and the next intersection. See Figure 1 for an example of each question at a sample intersection.

Back End: Supporting Information

The back end for CrossingGuard must identify relevant geographic information for the user's location, translate it to answers for the three questions supported by the CrossingGuard application, and provide route-planning support when a user enters a new destination. A critical need is information about the locations of sidewalks rather than just streets in the area of interest. Sidewalk information can compliment other geometric information such as the location of streets and the angle at which one or more streets intersect, which is available in many geographic databases. However, to be of use, CrossingGuard must interpret the information for use by visually impaired pedestrians.

We based our prototype system on the data available through the OpenStreetMap (OSM) project [18]. OSM is a collaborative, open source mapping initiative. Contributors utilize GPS traces, government data, and an online interface to annotate a world map with details including both locations and meta-data about roads and footpaths. We chose to use OSM because it has exhaustive information in the downtown area of our city.

OSM defines a labeled graph with geometry: *nodes* represent locations in space while *ways* represent connections between *nodes*. *Ways* can correspond to either closed-form loops like the footprint of a building or to traversable paths including streets, sidewalks, walking paths, and railways. Both *nodes* and *ways* contain meta-data including street names and other data, the presence of lights or other traffic control implements, and, for *nodes*, latitude and longitude.

CrossingGuard includes an online service that interprets the OSM graph in terms of intersections and constructs a route between a user-supplied start and stop. This entails three steps. First, we parse the map graph and interpret metadata. Second, we utilize the graph topology to group the map into human-traversable paths and intersections that represent instances where a human traversable path crosses a street. Next, using the geographic metadata, we construct a natural language explanation of the layout of each intersection.

Interaction	Crossing Guard Response	Baseline Response
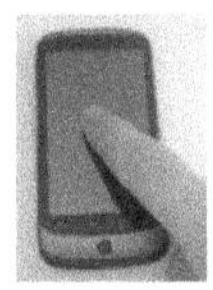 To ask the system *"What is here?"* the user performs a single tap.	*"Lighted, slanted plus intersection. You are west of the center of the intersection."*	*"Plus intersection"*
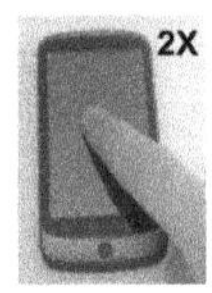 To ask the system *"Where could I go?"* the user performs a double tap.	*"Jones St. leads east and west. Main St. leads north. King St. leads south."*	
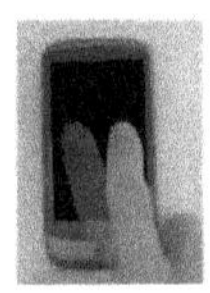 To ask the system *"What should I do from here to get to my destination"* the user performs a left or right scroll.	*Cross Jones St. This is in the same line of travel from your current bearing. This crossing has 4 lanes. The road is a heavy traffic road. Tram rails in crossing".*	*"Cross Jones St."*

Figure 1: Gestures to prompt mobile phone for information about the local area. The system responses on the right are an example of the base line instructions and information we included in our user study.

Intersections are described as either "T", "plus", or "multi-way" depending on whether 3, 4, or 5+ streets meet at the intersection. If streets meet at a non-right angle (non-equal angles for multi-way streets), the description alerts users that the shape is skewed. Finally, we construct a route between the start and stop locations that utilizes only human-traversable paths. A key feature of the routes constructed by our algorithm is that they are "sidewalk to sidewalk" routes rather than repurposed vehicle-oriented routes as utilized by commercial GPS systems, even systems designed for pedestrian use.

EVALUATION

We designed a user study to test whether having the more detailed information that CrossingGuard provides can raise the comfort level of users as they prepare to cross an unfamiliar intersection compared to base line information that is available on some commercially available GPS navigation systems. Our formative study suggested that a key metric to judge our sidewalk-based routing information is whether it reduces the stress associated with traveling in a new area. Stress associated with safe and efficient navigation is one of the key challenges to independent travel for visually impaired people [10]. Participants were recruited to walk a short route downtown and were presented with either the information and instructions available in CrossingGuard or a baseline set of instructions based on commercially available GPS navigation devices. We used their self-reported comfort level to test whether having detailed information raises the level of comfort that participants felt before crossing unfamiliar intersections.

Participants

We recruited 10 visually impaired participants to test our device on a route in the downtown area. Participants were between the ages of 29 and 60 and were required to use a white cane for everyday travel. Their degree of visual impairment ranged from totally blind (2 participants) to light sensitivity (6 participants) to some vision (less than 3% total vision: 2 participants). Two participants reported familiarity with commercially available GPS devices. No participants had previously walked in the study area, and no participants reported other physical or cognitive impairments.

Study Design

Participants followed a route that included 10 intersections. The device was pre-programmed with the information that would be returned by the CrossingGuard system as well as baseline information simulating what is available in commercially available applications. At each intersection, a participant could hear only one of the two types of information. The type of information that a participant heard alternated through the course of the study, with the initial information type counterbalanced within each visual impairment group described above.

The baseline information was designed to be consistent with commercially available GPS applications and what is available in a Trekker Breeze [24]. The information provided by such systems does include the shape of an intersection and the names and directions of streets, but none of the other information that is provided by CrossingGuard. Furthermore, the shape information was limited to the number of streets that met at an intersection ("T", "plus", or "multi-way") and information about irregularities in the intersection shape was omitted. For a full list of the categories of information that the CrossingGuard condition could share, see Table 2.

At each intersection, the participant was asked to describe the intersection before them as best they could without using a device. Next, they listened to all three interactions, and we asked them to rate how comfortable they were crossing the indicated street using a 7-point Likert scale where 1 corresponded to "I would not cross without assistance" and 7 corresponded to "I feel totally comfortable crossing." After giving their rating, participants were asked to cross without any assistance from the researcher. After crossing, they were asked about information in the instruction that they found helpful or unhelpful and about any information about the intersection that they would like to know.

Study participants were asked to traverse the route without the assistance of the researcher. However, a spotter walked within 3 meters of the participant at all times to ensure that they remained safe. Also, we asked the participant to declare when they began crossing any street so we could prevent them from walking into oncoming traffic.

Completing the route took between 54 and 75 minutes depending on the walking speed of the participant. Afterward, we administered a brief follow up interview to ask about general comfort while traversing the route and what information they found helpful.

Apparatus

Participants were provided an HTC Nexus One phone loaded with the modified CrossingGuard application described above. A script was created to specify to the application which of the two information types should be provided to the user at the different intersections. The responses were presented via bone conducting headphones, which avoid muffling ambient noise by relaying sound through the cheekbone rather than the ear canal. A hardware amplifier was used to ensure that the participants could comfortably hear the audio outdoors.

RESULTS

Access to richer information raised the comfort level of participants at unfamiliar intersections. In addition, we report on *what* information was most helpful as well as on general suggestions to improve the function of navigation applications.

Comfort Level when Crossing the Intersections

Participants' rankings to the question, *"Given the information you have heard about this intersection, how comfortable do you feel crossing the street here?"* demonstrate a significant effect of amount of information on comfort level using a within-subjects ANOVA ($F_{1,9}$=14.641; $p<0.005$). Possessing more detailed information about an intersection raised the median perceived comfort level before crossing the street by 1.0 points on the 7-point Likert scale (see Figure 2). This shows that *having more detailed information does increase comfort levels for visually impaired pedestrian.*

Participants crossed intersections of varying size, and we anticipated that the size of the intersection would affect comfort ratings. We divided the route into primary intersections (4 lanes of traffic, traffic light) versus secondary intersections (2 lanes of traffic, stop sign) and tested for an effect of intersection size (primary vs. secondary) on participant comfort. Although size does affect comfort ($p<0.0001$), there was not a significant interaction between crossing size and comfort ($p=0.84$). This suggests that primary intersections create more discomfort for visually impaired pedestrians but that having more detailed information about the crossing reduces discomfort at both primary and secondary intersections.

Mental model of the intersections

At each intersection, we asked participants to describe the intersection as best they could prior to hearing anything from the device. All participants reported using hearing as their primary sensory tool. Of interest are the kinds of information participants were able to report and the accuracy of their descriptions. Using open coding [17], we identified 8 types of information that participants used to describe intersections: Traffic Level, Stop Sign/Light, One-way Street, Intersection Shape, Presence of Bikes, Street Car, Width, and presence of an APS. Table 1 shows that all 10 participants used traffic level as a descriptor at least once, but that traffic level and the presence of a stop sign or light were both the most common types of description.

We noted several errors in participant descriptions. Seven of 10 participants committed a total of 14 errors while describing intersections along the route; 5 of these involved misclassifying a light as a stop sign or vice versa. Participants said that this type of error could lead to delays in travel or more serious consequences:

"If there is no light then it is hard to decide when to cross.

Description Type	Average number of times (of 10) that participants used this descriptor to describe an intersection	Number of people (of 10) that used this descriptor to describe at least one intersection.
Traffic Level	6.5	10
Stop sign/ Light	6.75	8
Intersection Shape	3.667	6
Street Car	1.167	6
Width	2.167	6
APS	1.333	6
One-way Street	1.2	5
Bike Traffic	1.5	4

Table 1: The left column shows the categories of information about an intersection that participants used to describe unfamiliar intersections. The center and right column show that traffic level and the presence of traffic control were the most salient features of unfamiliar intersections.

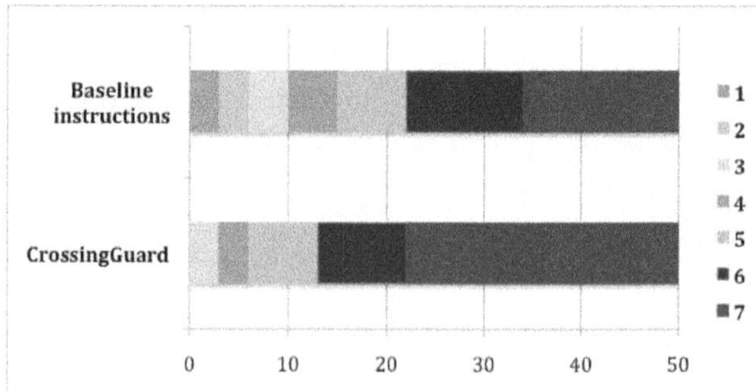

Figure 2. Access to detailed instructions increased the number of participants reporting higher comfort when crossing an unfamiliar intersection.

We can't make eye contact with the driver. If it's a controlled light it might be waiting for me to press a button." (P8)

Other errors included incorrectly identifying the shape of the intersection or the width of the street and mistakenly thinking that an intersection had an APS. Although not counted as an error in our analysis, many participants showed hesitancy when describing intersections. For instance, one participant stated confidently that there was a light at an intersection that had a stop sign. As she listened longer, she grew less confident. She decided there must be a stop sign, and then a light again, and finally decided it was a stop sign but that she was unsure.

Both the information that participants used and the errors they made provide evidence that the *shape, traffic level, and traffic control device (light or stop) are the most salient features of intersections*. Eight types of information were mentioned by at least 5 out of 10 participants, suggesting that a GPS navigation application should include richer information about the intersection. Access to richer information allows pedestrians to travel with greater confidence:

"If I know it is a light I can pace myself to be at the corner as it changes. Sighted people do that as they walk. It would save time and let us walk faster, like sighted people." (P3)

Perceived Value of Application Data

Particularly Helpful Information

At each intersection, we asked participants to list information from the device that they found helpful, and later we used open coding to classify the responses. Then we computed the percentage of time that each listed piece of information was rated as helpful. For instance, tram rails are only mentioned if the street that the participant was crossing had tram rails (4 crossings) and the participant heard the CrossingGuard instructions at that location (5 participants.) This meant that there were $5 \times 4 = 20$ times that a participant heard "tram rails in crossing" while there were $5 \times 10 = 50$ times that a participant heard how wide the road was. During the follow-up interview, we also asked participants specifically to rate the helpfulness of each piece of information on a 7-point

Likert scale where 1 meant "I would never use this" and 7 meant "I would always find this helpful."

Table 2 highlights that the presence of a traffic signal was the most important piece of information reported both during and after the study. An anomaly exists between the reported helpfulness of shape when we asked about helpful information during the walk versus when we asked to rate information in a follow up interview. Shape was presented in both CrossingGuard and control instructions (though shape information was more detailed in the CrossingGuard condition – see the Study Design section, above), so it was not as salient to users when it was presented as part of more information. Nevertheless, it as an important piece of information based on both the Likert scale response and on user comments:

"[Shape] influences the line I take crossing and it helps me interpret the traffic if it seems like it's doing something I don't understand." (P5)

As a participant follows a sidewalk to the next intersection, the CrossingGuard system alerts the user to the presence of alleys along the route. Alleys were defined as any roads marked "alley" or "service" in the OSM data. All but one participant commented that they liked knowing the alleys were there. Two reasons were given for wanting to know about alleys: there were sometimes mistaken for streets and they represent a place where vehicles might enter the roadway:

"[I slowed down because] I wasn't sure what that truck was doing. Knowing there was an alley told me it could cross my line of travel." (P5)

The one exception said he found alleys to be something he would not use and therefore did not want to listen to.

Self-reported Influences on Navigation Comfort

Participants cited a wide array of influences on their comfort level while traveling. We noted two ways in which access to more detailed information seemed to make participants more comfortable while traveling an unfamiliar route. First was the confidence that they understood the intersection where they were standing:

"Getting info about intersections such as whether they were plus intersections or there was a light or stop sign does take a layer of anxiety out of travel because it gives me information I wouldn't be certain of on my own." (P5)

Information	Percent of time mentioned as helpful	Helpfulness rating (7 point Likert scale)
Traffic Signaling	42	6.81
Tram Rails	35	4.77
Road Width	30	6.05
One-way Street	30	5.64
Intersection Shape	22	6.73
Traffic Level	22	5.05

Table 2: Helpfulness rating for the information presented in the CrossingGuard condition. We present both the percent of time that participants self-reported a category as helpful and the mean helpfulness rating on a 7-point Likert scale.

"I had enough information. Where to go and what the street was like, especially the traffic. Is it busy or not? It's my first time to know this stuff." (P7)

Although we took measures to minimize the variance of pedestrian and vehicle traffic during the study by running sessions at times of relatively similar traffic and using a within-subjects design, we did notice variability in outside factors influencing comfort. For example, one participant was able to use the clicking of a woman's heels as a cue for when and where to cross the street. Several noted confusion about cars that were turning right and appeared to be waiting for the pedestrian to cross. A common complaint was that intersections with very little traffic parallel to the participant's direction of travel were difficult to time:

"This will be hard. There's no traffic on Jones. A car can't pull up beside me and go through." (P11)

This variance serves to underscore the different criteria that influence each stage of an intersection crossing.

Participants also noted that the knowledge they gained from CrossingGuard helped to prepare them for what to expect from vehicle traffic:

"I sometimes wait even through traffic is going where I want to go. But if I know there is no light and a car is going in my direction, I can just go." (P5)

DISCUSSION

Potential Use Cases for CrossingGuard

The most common use case participants listed for a navigation aide was traveling to new areas. Other participants noted that it would be useful when there are changes to one's normal routine, including visits to the doctor or adjusting to new daily patterns:

"Recently, my office moved, and it is still new for me. I don't know where anything is and where I can go for lunch. This device would be very helpful if you are going to new places." (P8)

Increasing comfort in new areas is important because participants described feeling less comfortable traveling to new areas or unfamiliar settings. Many had experienced dangerous or uncomfortable moments due to changing conditions or unexpected obstacles:

"One night at 2 in the morning, I simply went for a walk, crossed what I thought was ok but it was one of those [intersections] with the turning lanes and platforms so when I thought I was heading back home I was heading in the opposite direction because you have to cross one platform to get to the other." (P1)

Having a rich set of information made participants feel more confident that they could navigate in a new area:

"It was really neat with the GPS. I love the independence it can give a person who is visually challenged." (P1)

Particularly salient for some participants was that having more information made them feel more included in a sighted community:

"Knowing what street I'm on. Just knowing! I think I'm more included if I have that because everybody else knows it." (P9)

Furthermore, participants liked the more detailed mental map that they were able to create using the information in the device.

"I like to know things because I'm nosey. Also, if you know the street, you can put 2 and 2 together and figure out other streets that might intersect." (P3)

User Feedback on Application Design

Participants generally found the application easy to use:

"It's a very easy and friendly user interface. Not complicated.... I tried GPS a few years ago but this is the best. It gives lots of information, more accessible, easy to use." (P8)

Three participants had to perform gestures multiple times in order to get the phone to respond. Participants were able to repeat gestures as many times as they needed. Touch screens have differing levels of sensitivity, so gestures need to be designed with the specific capabilities of both the device and the user in mind [15]. Participants had trouble understanding some words in the eSpeak TTS engine, though they commented that it may be a matter of getting used to the engine.

The parameters of our study, which required that people be able to meet us in a part of the city with which they were unfamiliar, created a situation where the participants considered themselves to be advanced travelers. However, they offered suggestions for people that are not as advanced. In particular, they suggested that the device take care to repeat details like street names as often as possible. Rather than saying "This crossing has 2 lanes," the device should say, "Jones St. has 2 lanes" so that users are able to hear the street name twice. As one participant explained:

"A lot of us have learning disabilities or hearing disabilities. Everyone processes things just a bit differently." (P9)

One participant found it difficult to remember all of the specific details in the crossing instruction, and suggested that we change that interaction to a multi-step process. The first swipe would relay the crossing instruction. Further swipes would cycle through more information about the crossing in decreasing order of importance so that the user can choose both what to listen to and how fast to cycle through the information.

Since they already carry a cane, several participants commented that they liked to use the device on a mobile phone, which keeps them from having to carry one more device [14].

Finally, participants suggested that we extend CrossingGuard to include the location of public transit stops and the location of points of interest along the route. Both of these pieces of information are available in open formats. Future versions of CrossingGuard will include information about attractions from Foursquare and Yelp as well as transit information, which is available through OSM.

Wayfinding in other locations

One point of confusion for participants was our decision to use cardinal directions. Toronto, where we ran our study, is at an "angle" compared to true north so the direction locals call "north" is actually northeast and "east/west" streets actually run northeast/southwest. An improved design would incorporate local knowledge into the descriptive vocabulary. We designed CrossingGuard to operate in other locales by modularizing intersection logic and intersection description. Local terminology (for instance, uptown-downtown) can be inserted in a customized description module to account for local custom. In the same way, new logic to handle novel intersection types like roundabouts can be included in the intersection logic module.

CROWDSOURCING CAPTURE OF REQUIRED DATA

CrossingGuard uses OpenStreetMap to calculate intersection geometry and capture meta-data that raises the comfort level of visually impaired pedestrians. However, OSM's accuracy and completeness varies depending on location. For rural and suburban areas in particular, the sidewalk information on which we base our work is not available. To facilitate the collection of the information that our participants identified as most useful, we developed a prototype crowd sourced Web application (Figure 3) that displays a Google Street View image beside an overhead map and asks users to identify features of the intersection in view.

Collecting Data

Mechanical Turk [1] is a web service offered by Amazon that lets users complete a simple task in exchange for a small payment. We designed a task to allow users to quickly annotate screenshots from Street View with information discovered to be important in our user study. A single task for a Turk user consists of a series of views of the center of an intersection, one taken from each street that meets at the intersection (A). Each image covers a 90-degree horizontal field of view and is taken as close to 30m from the intersection center as possible. An overhead shot (B) gives the user a bird's eye perspective of the center of the intersection (red marker) and the position of the Street View image (blue marker). Finally, each image corresponds to an HTML form (C) with a series of yes or no questions about the intersection that pertain to the point of view of the image. A mouseover image (D) corresponding to each question provides guidance about what type of annotation the question pertains to. If the intersection is a T shape

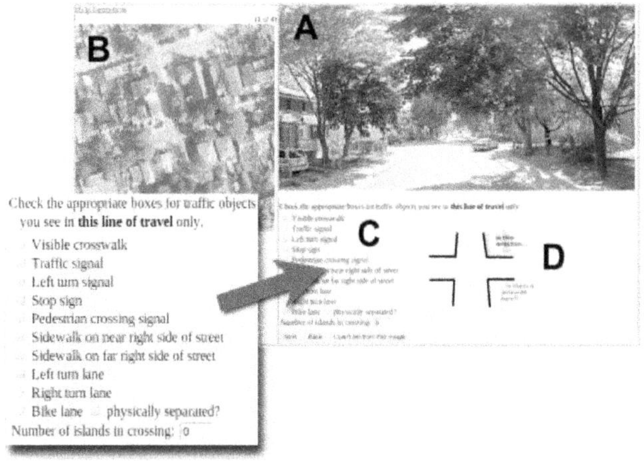

Figure 3: The Mechanical Turk interface showing an overhead view and a Google Street View picture of the intersection. The mouseover image corresponding to "Sidewalk on the far right side of the street" is visible.

(degree of center node = 3) we change the questions to account for the fact that one road does not exist.

We asked raters to consider 11 annotations for each street at an intersection. See Table 3 for a full list of the available annotations. The annotations represent information that was requested by users as well as other information that is not available in current, open databases.

Deployment and Results

We deployed the Mechanical Turk interface on all 125 intersections in a 2 square mile section of our city. Three unique Turk users scored each intersection for a reward of $0.05 each. A final rating for each answer was chosen by majority vote. Turk users completed 378 tasks in under 40 hours of wall time. In addition to Turk users, two researchers traversed each intersection to gather the same information in person. Discrepancies between the ratings of the two researchers were resolved by consensus.

Table 3 shows that accuracy across all questions was 85.5% compared to local raters, but that there is a split between annotations that Turk users were able to identify with accuracy greater than or equal to 87% and annotations that Turk users were unable to identify with 80% accuracy.

Type of Information	MTurk Accuracy (%)
Left Turn Lane	94
Left Turn Signal	94
Stop Sign	94
Right Turn Lane	93
Bike Lane	90
Traffic Signal	87
Sidewalk	78
Pedestrian Signal	73
Visible Crosswalk	67

Table 3: Accuracy of Mechanical Turk users' ability to accurately identify features of intersections through Google Street View still images as compared to local raters.

Elements in the roadway are most accurately captured while elements on the periphery or on the other side of the street (particularly pedestrian signals) represent a challenge for the current Turk interface, which only gives users a static view of the intersection.

We also noted a significantly low accuracy score for marking a visible crosswalk, which is attributed to ambiguity about the definition of a visible crosswalk. Turk users were looking for visible indicators of a legal crossing, which meant a painted signal in the intersection that a crossing was safe. However, the local coders marked intersections with legal crossings even if the only evidence that the crossing was legal was depressed sidewalk curbs and traffic control rather than pavement markings. This uncovers an important point of confusion at many intersections: visible road markings are not a reliable signal that a road is safe to cross. Some intersections contain clues such as pedestrian signals that may not be visible to all users. Other low traffic streets may have no markings at all. It is important to alert visually impaired pedestrians when the crossing is ambiguous because they may present unanticipated challenges.

Our preliminary results show that the data that we present in CrossingGuard can be cheaply and accurately produced across a wide geographic area by breaking the intersections into small annotation tasks. Future work will focus on an annotation procedure for Mechanical Turk that allows users to explore an intersection in the Street View interface to better examine the sides of the street and the opposite side of a crossing.

CONCLUSION

Navigation in new areas is a source of stress for visually impaired people because they feel that they lack the information to travel safely and confidently. We investigate the effect of richer information about intersections along a route by showing that more detailed information does increase comfort when crossing an unfamiliar intersection and by exploring what information is most helpful. We also prototype a method to gather and deliver the information that raises comfort.

Using insights from a set of formative interviews, we designed CrossingGuard to provide a route along pedestrian routes and to provide detailed information about street crossings. We also created a Mechanical Turk mechanism to gather the detailed information required to assist a visually impaired pedestrian when navigating in new areas. Turkers were able to annotate 9 categories of information using Street View images with 85.5% accuracy.

From a user study designed to examine the effect of additional information on comfort level, we found that having greater information about intersections raised the comfort level of participants, which is one of the key requirements for a system that will help visually impaired pedestrians travel independently. In particular, knowing the intersection shape, road widths, and traffic signaling type were listed as the most helpful information in CrossingGuard.

ACKNOWLEDGEMENTS

The authors wish to thank Natasha Woodcock and Martin Courcelles with the Canadian National Institute for the Blind for valuable feedback about prototype design. In addition, we thank Nikola Banovich and Koji Yatani for the feedback throughout the study process.

REFERENCES

1. Amazon's Mechanical Turk. www.mturk.com.
2. Amemiya, T. and Sugiyama, H. 2009. Haptic handheld wayfinder with pseudo-attraction force for pedestrians with visual impairments. In *Proc. ASSETS '09*. ACM, NY, 107-114.
3. Amemiya, T. and Sugiyama, H. 2010. Orienting Kinesthetically: A Haptic Handheld Wayfinder for People with Visual Impairments. ACM Trans. Access. Comput. 3, 2, Article 6 (November 2010), 23 pages.
4. Bradley, N.A. and Dunlop, M.D. 2005. An Experimental Investigation into Wayfinding Directions for Visually Impaired People. Personal Ubiquitous Comput. 9, 6 (November 2005), 395-403.
5. Bentzen, B.L., J.M. Barlow and L. Franck. 2000. Addressing Barriers to Blind Pedestrians at Signalized Intersections. In *ITE Journal*, Vol. 70, No. 9. pp 32–35
6. Carter, D., Barlow, J. Accessible Pedestrian Signals: A Guide to Best Practice. Produced by the National Cooperative Highway Research Program Project. 2007.
7. Crandall, W., Brabyn, J., Bentzen, B.L., Myers, L., 1999. "Remote infrared signage evaluation for transit stations and intersections." In *The Journal of Rehabilitation Research & Development*. Vol 36, No. 4. 359-368.
8. eSpeak Text to Speech. http://espeak.sourceforge.net/.
9. Golledge, R.G., Loomis, J.L., Klatsky, R.L., Flury, A., Yang, X.L., "Designing a personal guidance system to aid navigation without sight: progress on the GIS components." International journal of geographical information systems. Vol. 5, No. 4, 2007.
10. Guidice N.A., and Legge G.E. (2008). "Blind Navigation and the Role of Technology" in *The Engineering Handbook of Smart Technology for Aging, Disability, and Independence.* Helal, A., Mokhtari, M., and Abdulrazak, B., Eds. Jon Wiley & Sons, Inc., pp 479-500.
11. Helal, S Moore, S.E., and Ramachandran, B. 2001. Drishti: An Integrated Navigation System for Visually Impaired and Disabled. In *Proc. ISWC* '01. IEEE Computer Society, Washington, DC, USA, 149-.
12. Heuten, W., Henze, N., Boll, S., and Pielot, M. 2008. Tactile wayfinder: a non-visual support system for wayfinding. In Proceedings of the 5th Nordic conference on Human-computer interaction: building bridges (NordiCHI '08). ACM, NY, 172-181
13. Ishikawa, T., Fujiwara, H., Imal, O., and Okabe, A. 2007. Wayfinding with a GPS-based mobile navigation system: A comparison with maps and direct experience. In *Journal of Environmental Psychology.* Vol 28.1. pp 74-82.
14. Kane, S.K., Jayant, C., Wobbrock, J.O.,, and Ladner, R.E. 2009. Freedom to roam: a study of mobile device adoption and accessibility for people with visual and motor disabilities. In *Proc.* ASSETS. ACM, NY, 115-122.
15. Kane, S.K., Wobbrock, J.O., and Ladner, R.E. 2011. Usable Gestures for Blind People: Understanding Preference and Performance. In *Proc. CHI* '11. ACM, NY, 413-422.
16. Loomis, J.M., Golledge, R.G., Klatzky, R.L., Speigle, J.M., and Tietz, J. 1994. Personal guidance system for the visually impaired. In *Proc ASSETS '94*, ACM NY, 85-91
17. Marston, J.R. 2001. "Empirical Measurement Of Barriers To Public Transit For The Vision-Impaired And The Use Of Remote Infrared Auditory Signage For Mitigation." In *Proc. CSUN 16th Technology & Persons with Disabilities Conference.* LA, CA.
18. The OpenStreetMap Project. www.openstreetmap.org
19. Ponchillia, P.E., Rak, E.C., Freeland, A.L., and LaGrow, S.J. 2007. "Accessible GPS: Reorientation and Target Location Among Users with Visual Impairments" in *Journal of Visual Impairment & Blindness.* Vol 101, No. 7. pp 1-19.
20. Ross, D.A., Blasch, B.B. 2000. Wearable interfaces for orientation and wayfinding. In *Proc. ASSETS.* ACM, New York, NY, USA
21. Sendero GPS for the Blind, www.senderogroup.com.
22. Strauss, A., and Corbin, J. 1990. *Basics of Qualitative Research: Grounded Theory, Procedures, and Techniques*. Sage, NY, NY.
23. Strothotte, T. Fritz, S., Michel, R., Raab, A., Petrie, H., Johnson, V., Reichert, L., and Schalt, A. 1996. Development of dialogue systems for a mobility aid for blind people: initial design and usability testing. In *Proc ASSETS* '96. ACM, NY, 139-144
24. Trekker Breeze. Available at www.humanware.com.
25. Van Erp, J.B.F., Van Veen, H.A., Jansen, C., and Dobbins, T. 2005. Waypoint navigation with a vibrotactile waist belt. ACM Trans. Appl. Percept. 106-117.
26. Völkel, T and Weber, G. 2008. RouteCheckr: personalized multicriteria routing for mobility impaired pedestrians. In *Proc. 10th SIGACCESS.* ACM, New York, NY, 185-192.
27. Walker, B.N. and Lindsay, J. 2006. Navigation Performance with a Virtual Auditory Display: Effects of Beacon Sound, Capture Radius, and Practice. In *Human Factors*, 48, 2. 265-27
28. Wiener, W.R., Welsh, R.L., and Blasch, B.B., *Foundations of Orientation and Mobility Volume II.* American Foundation for the Blind Press, NY. Ch. 12.
29. Wilson, J., Walker, B.N., Lindsay, J., Cambias, C., and Dellaert, F. 2007. SWAN: System for wearable audio navigation. In Proceedings of the 11th International Syposium on Wearable Computers (ISWC 2007)

SpaceSense: Representing Geographical Information to Visually Impaired People Using Spatial Tactile Feedback

Koji Yatani[1,2], Nikola Banovic[1], Khai N. Truong[1]
[1]University of Toronto
Department of Computer Science
{koji, nikola, khai}@dgp.toronto.edu
[2]Microsoft Research Asia
HCI group
koji@microsoft.com

ABSTRACT
Learning an environment can be challenging for people with visual impairments. Braille maps allow their users to understand the spatial relationship between a set of places. However, physical Braille maps are often costly, may not always cover an area of interest with sufficient detail, and might not present up-to-date information. We built a handheld system for representing geographical information called SpaceSense, which includes custom spatial tactile feedback hardware—multiple vibration motors attached to different locations on a mobile touch-screen device. It offers high-level information about the distance and direction towards a destination and bookmarked places through vibrotactile feedback to help the user maintain the spatial relationships between these points. SpaceSense also adapts a summarization technique for online user reviews of public and commercial venues. Our user study shows that participants could build and maintain the spatial relationships between places on a map more accurately with SpaceSense compared to a system without spatial tactile feedback. They pointed specifically to having spatial tactile feedback as the contributing factor in successfully building and maintaining their mental map.

Author Keywords
Vibrotactile feedback; handheld devices; touch screens; geographical information representation; users with visual impairments; assistive technology.

ACM Classification Keywords
H.5.2 [Information Interfaces and presentation]: User Interfaces – *Haptic I/O, Voice I/O.*

General Terms
Human Factors

INTRODUCTION
Acquiring knowledge about an environment can be challenging for people with visual impairments. They often need support by sighted people to understand what is in the environment, where venues are positioned, and their spatial relationship with each other. They sometimes also need to physically navigate an environment multiple times before they can develop a familiarity with the environment. Although such activities can help visually impaired people increase their independence and confidence in their navigation, burdens associated with these activities often discourage them to explore and learn an environment [33].

Braille maps (*a.k.a.* tactile maps) are an effective way for visually impaired people to develop an understanding of the spatial relationships between a set of places in addition to identifying directions between them [3, 7]. Prior work has shown that Braille maps can help visually impaired people prepare for their future trips to an area [3, 12]. But, they use physical materials that are often costly to produce, may not always cover an area of interest with sufficient detail, and might not present updated information [26].

We explore a way of representing geographical information to visually impaired users on a handheld device. We chose this form factor because mobile devices have been interwoven into their daily life (*e.g.*, calling someone for help, and sending an email) [12]. Thus, a map application on mobile devices can provide users with easy access to geographical information and encourage their spatial learning about the area of interest. Our investigation includes the use of two feedback channels—auditory (speech) feedback and tactile feedback—to present places of interest, provide detailed information about those locations, and present routes to those points.

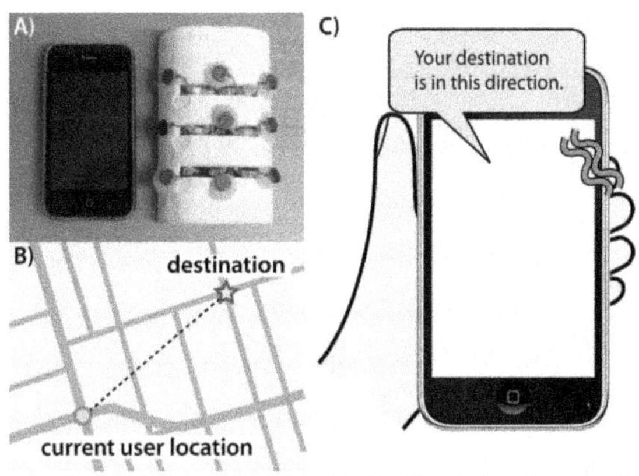

Figure 1. A) The spatial tactile feedback hardware. Nine vibration motors are embedded in the sleeve that fits to an iPhone; B) An example geographical information being browsed by the user (with the destination north-east from the user's location); C) Spatial tactile feedback conveys the general direction towards the destination.

The main contribution of this work is the design and evaluation of a system that helps people learn directions to a location and its spatial relationships with other locations on a map through use of spatial tactile feedback to represent geographical information. Our map system, SpaceSense, is a mobile application for touch-screen devices enhanced with custom spatial tactile feedback hardware. This hardware embeds nine vibration motors aligned in a 3 × 3 grid (Figure 1A), and can be used to generate vibrotactile feedback in different positions of the user's palm and fingers holding the device. Through this spatial tactile feedback, SpaceSense offers high-level information about the direction towards the destination when the user browses route information (Figure 1B and 1C). Furthermore, SpaceSense provides directional information towards other locations that the user may know or like through vibrotactile feedback. In this manner, SpaceSpace can help visually impaired users maintain high-level spatial relationships between multiple locations. SpaceSense also adapts the Review Spotlight system [35] for summarizing online user reviews about nearby locations. It reads out the most frequently-used adjective-noun word pairs extracted from online reviews to offer an overview of what people often mention about a specific place. Thus, the user can obtain information about a location before deciding whether she wants to further learn routes to it and its spatial relationships to other locations.

Through a user study with twelve visually impaired users, we learned that participants were able to build and maintain the spatial relationship between four places more accurately with SpaceSense than a system without spatial tactile feedback. Participants also explicitly mentioned benefits with having spatial tactile feedback in building and maintaining their mental map. Additionally, the Review Spotlight presentation through the auditory channel was received positively by the participants because of its succinct presentation about a location.

RELATED WORK

Braille maps have been recognized as an effective means of learning spatial relationships between multiple objects for people with visual impairments [3]. Herman *et al.* [8] found that visually impaired people can indicate the locations of objects in a space fairly accurately after they were exposed to a miniaturized version of the space layout. However, these maps are physical, and their production cost is often considerable. These maps may sometimes not have sufficient detail or updated information of the space. Digital maps can address these issues; in this section, we review computer systems to support learning spatial relationships between multiple objects for visually impaired people.

Interfaces for Map Exploration

Auditory feedback is often used to make map information accessible to people with visually impairments [9, 27, 37, 39]. To allow them to explore and learn geographical information, touch-based interaction can be integrated with such audible map systems. For example, the NOMAD system [23] uses a touchpad placed under a paper Braille map to detect which part of the map the user is contacting. When the user touches an area on the map that contains information, the system generates speech feedback to describe the user's contact point. Jacobson [11] developed a similar system which replaces the use of static Braille maps with dynamically generated maps. It provides auditory feedback (either sound or speech) to describe what the user is touching and its surrounding content. Jacobson validated that visually impaired users could reconstruct map information after they used such a system. Parente and Bishop [22] showed that vibrotactile feedback when combined with speech and non-speech audio feedback helps visually impaired users discover the boundaries of mapped elements (*e.g.*, boundaries of states in the United States map). Lahav and Mioduser [16] showed that a virtual environment system, which combines speech audio and force feedback through a joystick, enabled visually impaired users to build a cognitive map of an indoor location, and successfully navigate the corresponding physical space based on this cognitive map.

Some map systems describe path information (*e.g.*, the length or shape of a street). Google's Intersection Explorer is a hand-held application which allows the user to drag her finger on the screen to explore walkable paths that a person can take from any intersection [10]. With non-speech sound cues, Timbremap [30] helps users trace routes on a mobile device and learn geometrical patterns of walkable path segments. Its evaluation showed that visually impaired users could learn non-trivial geometries using only touch and simple audio cues. Similarly, Crossan and Brewster demonstrated that the combination of force feedback and sound feedback can also facilitate the learning of trajectories [6].

The main focus of SpaceSense is to provide visually impaired users with a high-level understanding of the spatial relationships between multiple locations instead of the exact shape of a street or a building. Thus, our system can complement these existing systems by facilitating the acquisition of route information and high-level spatial information for multiple locations. Kane *et al.* [13] developed three techniques which allow visually impaired users to identify the target locations displayed on a touch-sensitive tabletop. Their techniques can be used for learning spatial relationships between multiple locations, but may not be appropriate for devices with a small form factor. Our exploration also examines the effect of vibrotactile feedback in learning spatial relationships.

Interfaces for Navigation and Wayfinding

Another opportunity for people with visual impairments to explore and learn about places is *in situ* during navigation. There are a number of commercially available systems [28, 31, 32, 33] and open-source systems [17] that provide speech navigation instructions and information about points of interest. Azenkot *et al.*'s system [2], ChattyEnvironment [5] and Talking Points [29] are examples of location-aware navigation systems which help the user learn nearby places.

Past research also has explored ways to provide visually impaired users with trajectory information for wayfinding. Marston *et al.* [18] showed that visually impaired users can navigate an environment faster using a continuously-generated beeping 3D sound which encodes the direction to the next waypoint than Talking Signs [31] (using sound feedback when the user pointed the device towards the next waypoint). Wilson *et al.* [38] showed that the user can successfully learn information about her environment (*e.g.*, obstacles in the way) encoded as different dimensions of the sound (*e.g.*, a sound type, pitch, and rhythm) or time-compressed speech.

Tactile feedback has also been used to aid visually impaired people in wayfinding. Ross and Blasch [25] compared speech audio, non-speech audio, and tapping haptic feedback to indicate the direction in which a user should walk. They found that visually impaired users overall performed navigation tasks fastest and with fewest errors using the haptic interface, with non-speech audio coming in close second. Zelek *et al.* [39] showed that a haptic glove, which conveys the locations of obstacles in an environment through vibrations on different fingers, could help users identify where they can walk. Amemiya and Sugiyama [1] developed a mobile device using force feedback to provide the user with a sensation of being pulled towards the destination by the device, allowing her to navigate at her normal walking speed.

These projects aim to help visually impaired users learn their environment *in situ* and reinforce their cognitive map of the geographic area. SpaceSense attempts to provide an additional means which helps the user prepare for future trips (*i.e.*, prior to physically visiting a space) by supporting the learning of map information and spatial relationships of objects using tactile feedback which differentiates it from prior work.

THE SPACESENSE SYSTEM

SpaceSense is a map application that runs on a handheld touch-screen device (an iPhone in our current prototype) enhanced by our custom spatial tactile feedback system. Our motivation for choosing a mobile touch-screen device is that it allows for taps and flick gestures—interactions that are easy for visually impaired users to perform [14, 19]. In the remainder of this section, we describe our hardware for producing spatial tactile feedback, and the interactions supported by SpaceSense: identifying locations, learning place details, and learning directions.

Spatial Tactile Feedback Hardware

Figure 1A shows the hardware for our spatial tactile feedback system. Similar to SemFeel [36], we built a special case that embeds vibration motors on the backside of the mobile device. However, our prototype uses nine vibration motors aligned in a 3×3 grid. Any two of the motors are separated with a gap of at least 2 cm, and each motor vibrates at 200 Hz when activated. The placement of the motors is partly based on psychological understanding that it is difficult to distinguish two vibration sources located closer than 1 cm [21], but is adopted primarily so that the system can have greater spatial granularity than the SemFeel prototype [36]. SpaceSense uses all the vibration motors except the one located in the center.

For audio feedback, SpaceSense uses the FliteTTS[1] package to read out information through a synthesized voice. We use this package instead of the VoiceOver functionality already built in some of the iPhone devices because we wanted the ability to precisely tune the timing of the speech feedback.

Interactions

Identifying Locations

SpaceSense allows the user to select places of interest from a pre-defined list of categories ("restaurant," "café", "bar," "hotel," "attraction," and "bank" in the current prototype system). The system retrieves up to 20 locations (using Yelp API[2]) sorted by distance within a 2 km radius centered on the user's current simulated location. After the user selects a category, SpaceSense begins to present information about each location, starting with the closest.

SpaceSense offers spatial information in an exo-centric manner similar to when a person views at a map. It reads the name and street address of each place, and uses spatial tactile feedback to indicate the place's distance and cardinal direction. For instance, if the place is to the west of a referenced location (*e.g.,* the hotel where the user may be staying on an upcoming trip), the left side of the device vibrates (north is always set to the top of the device). We designed the current prototype to provide vibration at four different strength levels (100%, 80%, 60%, and 30% strength output of a vibration motor) to represent the distance (below 200 m, below 500 m, below 1 km, or farther than 1 km, respectively).

The user can perform an upward or downward flick gesture to navigate the category list and subsequent location list. The user can also repeat the current item by double-tapping the screen. We use a double tap gesture because the user is less likely to perform a double tap accidentally than a single tap. The user can select a category by rightward flick gestures. These gestures are also used for navigation and selection consistently throughout the system.

Learning Place Details

After the user selects a location, SpaceSense presents her with general information about the location, including the name, address, and phone number. The user can navigate this information using upward or downward flick gestures.

---

[1] https://bitbucket.org/sfoster/iphone-tts
[2] http://www.yelp.com/developers/documentation/v2/overview

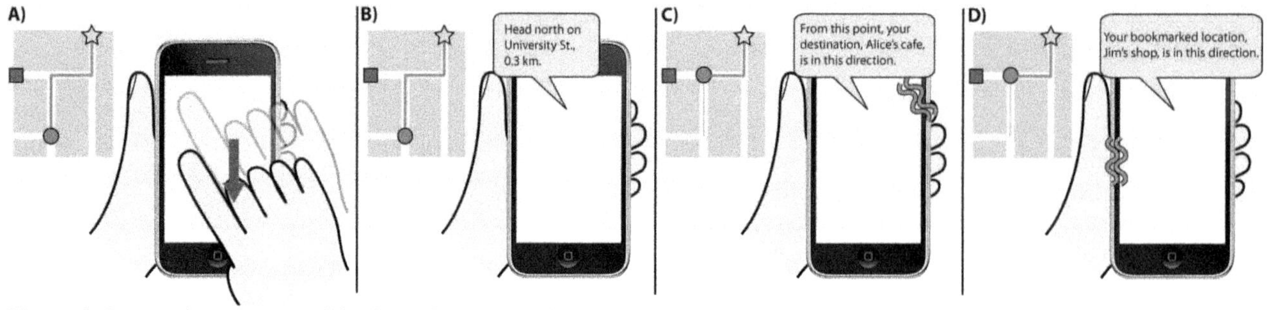

Figure 2. Interactions supported by SpaceSense. The circle, star and square in the map represent the user's simulated location, destination, and bookmarked location, respectively: A) The user performs a downward flick gesture to get the next instruction; B) SpaceSense reads out the street name and orientation; C) Spatial tactile feedback conveys the high-level direction towards the destination. In this example, the user feels vibration from the top-right side of the device because the destination is located to north-east from the user's simulated location; D) Spatial tactile feedback is also provided for the bookmarked location.

Item	Example
Name	Moonbean Coffee Shop
Address	30 St. Andrew St.
Phone	416 595 0327
Distance	0.6 km
Review words	Soy latte, friendly staff, back patio, good coffee, front patio, great coffee, little café, great person, great place, reasonable price.

Table 1. An example of place details provided by SpaceSense.

SpaceSense also offers an overview of what people mention about a specific public or commercial location on online review Websites (such as Yelp.com). It uses the adjective-noun word pairs extracted from the original review text that Review Spotlight [35] normally presents in a visual interface. Instead of visually displaying, SpaceSense reads out the ten most frequently mentioned adjective-noun word pairs through the speech feedback instead of the original review text ("review words" in Table 1).

The user can add the location to their bookmark list by using a two-finger rightward flick gesture on the touch screen. This bookmark functionality allows the user to save and quickly access places that she likes.

Learning Directions

Finally, SpaceSense gives the user directions to a location. The user can perform a rightward flick gesture to select a location while she is browsing the details of that location (as described in the previous section). The system then begins to provide step-by-step walking instructions (using speech feedback) obtained through the Google Directions API[3]. The system presents each step of the instructions in the cardinal directions along with its walking distance (*e.g.*, "head north on University Ave., 0.3 km") one at a time (Figure 2B). SpaceSense also offers audio descriptions about the intersection at which a simulated performance of the previous step would put the user (*e.g.*, "You are now at University Ave. and College St.").

The system conveys the distance and direction to the destination through spatial tactile feedback. For example, if the destination is located to the north-east from the current intersection, the top-right side of the device will vibrate (Figure 2C). Spatial tactile feedback is provided every time the system presents an intersection. In this manner, SpaceSense shows the user how the relationships of the destination and other locations change through the simulated movements of the referenced location similar to when reading a map.

The interactions in this mode are consistent to other modes in SpaceSense. The user can perform upward or downward flick gestures to navigate the route instructions (upward for moving to the previous instruction and downward for moving to the next instruction). The user can also double-tap on the screen to repeat the current instruction.

SpaceSense also provides spatial tactile feedback about nearby bookmarked locations. It will vibrate in the direction of a bookmarked location near the simulated route while the speech feedback indicates the location's name. For example, in Figure 2D, the system will vibrate on the left side of the device to indicate the bookmarked location. We designed this feature to help the user build and maintain spatial relationships between multiple places of interest.

EVALUATION

The target usage scenario of SpaceSense is when the user searches for locations that support a particular activity before she travels outside. Thus, a laboratory study reflects this scenario better than a study in which participants are walking on the street. Our laboratory study consisted of two parts to independently evaluate how well SpaceSense can support this scenario in a holistic manner: 1) user feedback on the overall system; and 2) an evaluation of the system's effect on the learning of routes and the spatial relationships between multiple locations. All conversations between the investigator and participants were audiotaped and transcribed for the analysis.

Participants

We recruited twelve visually impaired users (4 male and 8 female; P1–P12). The level of their visual impairments

[3] https://code.google.com/apis/maps/documentation/directions/

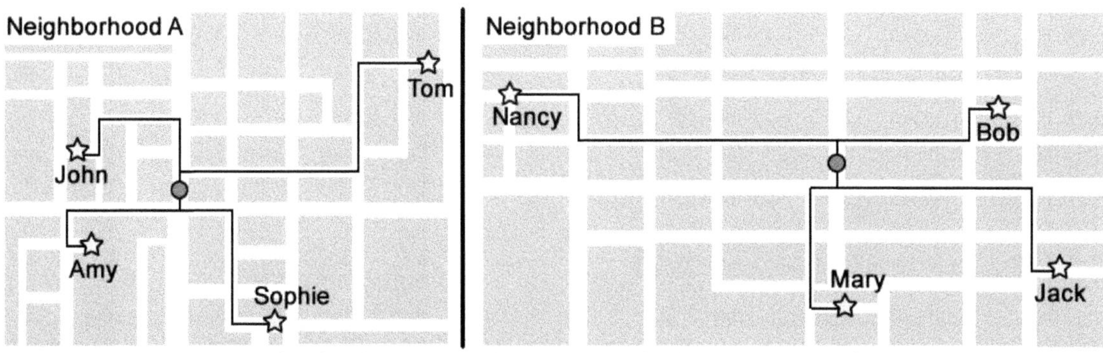

Figure 3. The two neighborhoods with four hypothetical locations used in the user study, and routes to those locations from a given starting point.

varied: 10 of them were blind, and 2 had low vision. Before the experiment, we asked them to describe familiar areas in the city, and none of them expressed a significant familiarity of the areas used in this experiment. Additionally, we asked participants about their familiarity with the locations used in the second part of the study; none was familiar with either location as well. The entire study took on average 80 minutes in total for participants to complete. Participants were compensated with $50 for their participation after the study.

Part A: User Feedback on the Overall System Design

We demonstrated the full system to participants and allowed them to interact with the system. We then interviewed participants to examine SpaceSense from a usability perspective. We encourage them to provide feedback on any aspect of the system by asking them to comment on the design of the gestures, the different features of the system, and potential use scenarios.

We also examined whether an audio adaptation of Review Spotlight [35] could be useful in providing visually impaired users with descriptive information about a public or commercial place. We prepared two places (a restaurant and a café) for this task. For each location, we prepared two presentations for reviews: *ReviewSpotlight* (reading out adjective-noun word pairs most frequently mentioned in Yelp.com) and *ReviewHighlights* (reading out sentences with approximately 50 words extracted from the review text, provided in Google Map). Participants were asked to express their opinions about both presentations.

Part B: Learning Routes and Spatial Relationships

To examine whether spatial tactile feedback can help visually impaired people learn routes and develop a high-level understanding of the spatial relationships between multiple locations, we asked participants to learn the directions to four locations from the same neighborhood, one at a time (Figure 3). For each destination, another location from the same neighborhood was set in the bookmark list beforehand; thus, each instruction provided to participants would always include directional information towards the destination and one other place as explained in the Learning Directions section. The combination of the destinations and bookmarked places

Neighborhood A		Neighborhood B	
Destination	Bookmark	Destination	Bookmark
Amy	John	Bob	Mary
John	Tom	Mary	Nancy
Tom	Sophie	Nancy	Jack
Sophie	Amy	Jack	Bob

Table 2. The combinations of the destinations and bookmarked places used in the study.

used in the study was determined as shown in Table 2. This setup allowed us to examine how well our system design could help participants learn spatial relationship between multiple locations.

We selected two neighborhoods in a North American city with an area of approximately 4 km^2. For each neighborhood, we set the starting point near the center, and selected four locations which were on average 770 m from the starting point, and required three turns to reach. We labeled these locations as the stores of four hypothetical persons (Figure 3).

Participants were allowed to navigate the route instructions freely by using flick gestures or double-taps (explained in the Learning Directions section) until they felt comfortable with the route. The experimenter helped the participants when the system did not register gestures or taps accurately, but did not provide any information about the route information. The participants held the mobile device with their non-dominant hand, and used the dominant hand to interact with the device.

After the participants went through the directions to one location, they were asked to reproduce the route with acrylic pieces and indicate the locations of the destination and the bookmarked place (Figure 4). This route reconstruction is a common task used to probe the visually impaired user's understanding of spatial knowledge [15], and was used to evaluate the effects of the two feedback types on the participant's understanding of the route information. We prepared thin rectangular pieces with four different lengths for streets (3 cm, 6 cm, 9 cm, and 12 cm long for loosely representing from very short to very long street segments), L-shape pieces for corners, and circles for the destination and the bookmarked place. The participants were allowed to use any piece to compose a route. But we instructed that they could compose all routes without using

Figure 4. A participant creating a route with acrylic pieces after she has learned route instructions from the system.

multiple rectangular pieces to make a longer street. The experimenter did not correct the participant's route composition at any point.

After participants were exposed to the directions to all the locations and composed routes, the experimenter asked them to draw locations of all the places—indicating their perception of the positions of the four locations—on a blank sheet of paper with a blue marker (Figure 5). This drawing was used to examine the effects of the two feedback types on learning the spatial relationships between the four locations. The experimenter made annotations for later analysis, but did not make any correction even if the spatial relationships among the four locations indicated by participants were incorrect. We simplified the drawing requirements; thus, it is unlikely that individual drawing skills affected the results.

For this part of the experiment, we set up two conditions to compare: *Tactile* (the interface design explained in the previous sections) and *Audio* (an interface which provided all information including the direction and distance for each location through only speech feedback). In the *Audio* condition, the system read out the direction and distance towards the destination and bookmarked location (*e.g.*,"Your destination, Amy's café, is to north-east, 0.5 km"). We tuned the speed of the speech feedback at a slower rate than the iPhone VoiceOver so that participants could follow the information provided by the system more easily. The presentation order of the two interface conditions and the maps were counter-balanced across the participants. We fixed the combinations of destinations and bookmarked locations (Table 2), but we randomized their presentation order for each participant. At the beginning of the task, we provided all participants with training and practice using each interface until they were comfortable with the procedure.

PART A RESULTS

All participants could navigate the route instructions and understand the information presented through the spatial tactile feedback hardware after receiving the explanation from the investigator. None of them experienced difficulty performing the flick or double-tap gesture.

Participants commented that they would use SpaceSense before they need to visit an unfamiliar area. For example, P9 explained that she could develop independence and

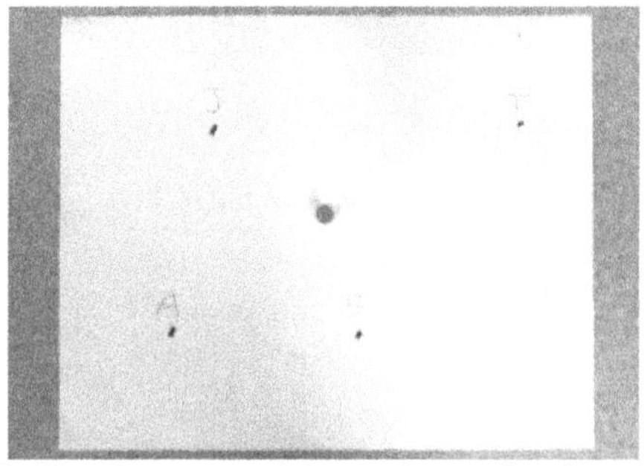

Figure 5. The dots a participant drew after learning four places in Neighborhood A with our SpaceSense system's tactile interface. The red pin at the center of the paper indicates the starting point.

confidence with navigation enabled by SpaceSense's support for pre-trip map exploration.

> *I don't really go outside by myself, but I think [SpaceSense] could give a little bit more independence. You can ask people when you are on the street, but it would be neat to do it by yourself [ahead of time]. I don't walk very far at this point, but it would give me more confidence.* [P9]

We found that all of the participants preferred *ReviewSpotlight* over *ReviewHighlight* for presenting information about public and commercial locations. They liked its succinct presentation. They also liked that the *ReviewSpotlight* presentation summarized all reviews instead of presenting one particular review. Some explicitly commented that the *ReviewSpotlight* presentation was easier to follow than *ReviewHighlights*.

> *The first one (ReviewSpotlight) is obviously a better one, much much better. It's clear in a sense, because of its form. The other one (ReviewHighlight) is more jumpy... Your brain has to sort out... It stops randomly too much, and is missing data. It (ReviewHighlight) would be something you have to replay.* [P3]

PART B RESULTS

We next analyzed data on participants' learning of routes and spatial relationships between four places in a map and acquisition of information about places. We report task completion time, accuracy, and comments from participants.

Task Completion Time

Participants used the system on average for 201 seconds to learn the route instructions (*InstructionTime*) and 95 seconds to reproduce a route with acrylic pieces (*CompositionTime*). Table 3 shows *InstructionTime* and *CompositionTime* across the conditions and neighborhoods. Participants were exposed to both conditions but with different neighborhoods. Thus, we ran a two-way mixed ANOVA on both time measures for the conditions and neighborhoods. It did not reveal a significant difference on either *IntructionTime* (Condition: $F_{(1,10)}$=0.04, Neighborhood: $F_{(1,10)}$=0.29, Condition × Neighborhood: $F_{(1,10)}$=0.26, p>.05 for all) or *CompositionTime* (Condition:

Neighborhood	*InstructionTime* A	*InstructionTime* B	*CompositionTime* A	*CompositionTime* B
Tactile	*203* (64)	*195* (136)	*86* (16)	*97* (32)
Audio	*188* (99)	*220* (83)	*103* (45)	*95* (28)
				Mean (SD)

Table 3. The time participants spent in learning the route instructions (*InstructionTime*) and reproducing a route with acrylic pieces (*CompositionTime*).

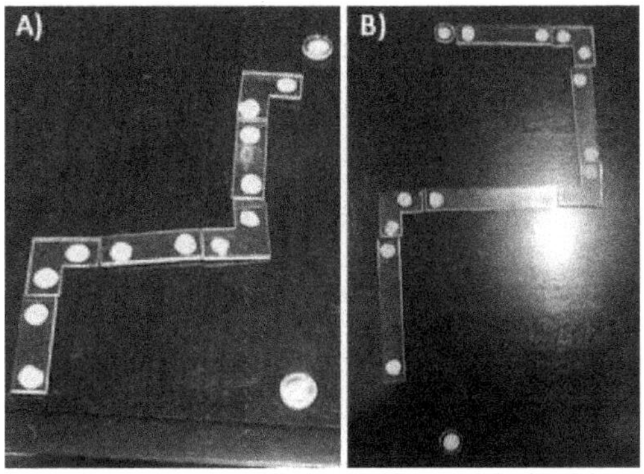

Figure 6. Route compositions to Tom with Sophie as the bookmarked place in Neighborhood A made by two different participants: A) A composition close to the correct route; B) An incorrect composition.

$F_{(1,10)}$=1.18, Neighborhood: $F_{(1,10)}$=0.06, Condition × Neighborhood: $F_{(1,10)}$=0.51, p>.05 for all).

Route Accuracy

Figure 6 shows examples of the routes created by participants. We adapted an evaluation approach used by Passini *et al.* [24] to analyze the route compositions. We used the following metrics:

- *NumberElementsError*: The number of unnecessary acrylic pieces that participants used to recreate a route. The correct number of pieces was always seven because there were four different streets and three corners/turns in each route.
- *FormElementsError*: The Levenshtein distance (the minimum number of operations required to transform one sequence into the other) between the participant's route composition and the correct route composition.
- *PositionError*: The number of incorrect orientations of the L-shape pieces.
- *PlacementError*: The number of street blocks used with the incorrect length.

We added three metrics to measure the accuracy of the positions of the destination and bookmarked place:

- *DestinationDistanceError*: The absolute difference of the straight line distance between the starting point and destination from the one in the correct route composition.
- *BookmarkDistanceError*: The absolute difference of the straight line distance between the starting point and bookmarked place from the one in the correct route composition.

Condition	Error Number	Form	Position	Placement
Tactile	*0.80* (1.27)	*0.83* (1.28)	*0.77* (1.18)	*2.75* (1.16)
Audio	*0.83* (1.18)	*0.88* (1.18)	*0.54* (0.93)	*2.79* (1.13)
t value	$t_{93.4}$=0.16	$t_{93.4}$=0.16	$t_{89.4}$=1.05	$t_{93.9}$=0.18
Condition	**DestDist**	**BookDist**	**PlaceAngle**	
Tactile	*2.11* (1.47)	*2.67* (1.90)	*53.0* (35.8)	
Audio	*2.25* (1.82)	*2.55* (1.73)	*46.7* (33.8)	
t value	$t_{89.3}$=0.39	$t_{93.2}$=0.33	$t_{84.4}$=1.48	*Mean* (SD)

Table 4. The seven error metrics measured on the route composition. Welch's t-tests did not show a significant difference in any of the metrics at the 95% confidence level.

- *PlaceAngleError*: The absolute difference of the angle between the edge connecting the starting point and destination and the one connecting the starting point and the bookmarked place from the one in the correct route composition.

Two of the researchers independently estimated the values for these three metrics for each route composition. We then used the average value for the analysis.

Table 4 illustrates the error metrics for the route composition. Because each participant was exposed to a different map for each condition, we used unpaired Welch's t-tests for our statistical analysis. Our analysis did not show any significant difference between the *Tactile* and *Audio* conditions at the 95% confidence level.

Route instructions were given through the speech feedback in both conditions. Therefore, it is sensible that we did not observe large differences in the accuracy of the route compositions. A difference between the two conditions could appear in their understanding of spatial relationships between the four places in a map. We, thus, analyzed the drawings of the four places provided by the participants.

Drawn Places Accuracy

For the place drawings (Figure 5), we used different neighborhoods for the two feedback conditions. Therefore, comparing and determining the accuracy of the two drawings by each participant was not straightforward. We decided to use subjective ratings to evaluate the spatial relationship between any two of the places from the starting point with three levels of correctness ratings:

2: Very close to the correct placement of the two places,

1: Neither completely correct nor incorrect, and

0: Not correct.

For the example shown in Figure 5, the rating between S and T (Sophie and Tom) was 2. The rating between A and S (Amy and Sophie) was 1 because the orientation between the two places is not correct but their relative positions from the starting point are close to the correct answer.

With several randomly chosen drawings, we confirmed that this rating scheme could represent the accuracy of the drawings. Two of the researchers then independently rated all the drawings. They only knew which neighborhood each drawing was for. To measure the inter-rater reliability of

Neighborhood	Places	*Tactile*	*Audio*
A	Amy-John	*0.91* (0.73)	*0.50* (0.76)
	Amy-Sophie	*1.00* (0.58)	*0.67* (0.47)
	Amy-Tom	*1.08* (0.18)	*1.00* (0.81)
	John-Sophie	*0.83* (0.68)	*0.83* (0.89)
	John-Tom	*0.75* (0.38)	*1.00* (0.82)
	Sophie-Tom	*1.50* (0.50)	*0.75* (0.69)
	Average	***1.01* (0.59)**	***0.79* (0.78)**
B	Bob-Jack	*0.16* (0.37)	*0.58* (0.83)
	Bob-Mary	*0.50* (0.76)	*0.33* (0.55)
	Bob-Nancy	*0.58* (0.73)	*0.41* (0.60)
	Jack-Mary	*0.33* (0.47)	*0.33* (0.55)
	Jack-Nancy	*0.50* (0.76)	*0.17* (0.37)
	Mary-Nancy	*1.33* (0.74)	*0.25* (0.38)
	Average	***0.57* (0.75)**	***0.35* (0.59)**

Mean (SD)

Table 5. The ratings for all the combinations of two places in each map across the two conditions.

this ordinal scale, we calculated the Cohen's κ with the squared weighting [4]. In this calculation, the disagreements of the ratings were weighted according to their squared distance from perfect agreement. As a result, the weighted Cohen's κ was .92 (95% CI: [.87, .96]), showing a strong agreement. The average rating was used to determine the accuracy of each drawing.

Table 5 shows the ratings for the correctness of the spatial relationship of all possible pairs of places in each map across the two conditions. A Mann-Whitney test found a significant difference in the correctness ratings between the *Tactile* and *Audio* conditions (Z=1.96, p<.05, the effect size r=0.23). The drawings created by participants after they used SpaceSense were more accurate than those which provided map information using the speech feedback solely. The main difference was in what direction participants perceived the locations to be from one location to another.

Results also indicate that Neighborhood B was seemingly harder than Neighborhood A for participants to learn. But regardless of the neighborhoods, participants understood the spatial relationships between locations better with the SpaceSense system than the *Audio* condition.

User Feedback

Overall, as one participant mentioned, the system provided information in a way that was very similar to what she experienced when orientation and mobility specialists taught her routes.

> *I like that the coordinate is actually on my hand... When I first started to learn how to do routes, my instructor would draw maps on my hand and use the exact same points as coordinates like the vibration system uses (for the directional information).* [P5]

Participants expressed that SpaceSense allowed them to develop a rich cognitive map of an area in a way that is similar to and possibly even better than with Braille maps.

> *[The vibration] was helpful because it gave me a very visual sense of where things should be... Instead of having to have someone label and make the map tactile, [the system] did that for me. And instead of having to take out a piece of paper with streets and stuff labeled and then have to look and see "ok this is south-west," for example, the vibration gave me that visual sense.* [P5]

Most of the participants noted that the strength of the SpaceSense system lies in its use of both the auditory and tactile channels. Particularly, they liked having directional information provided through the tactile channel.

> *It gave me information about the direction more quickly. Because it takes more time to say "north-east" or "south-west." But feeling the vibration in your hand gets the information to my brain more quickly.* [P2]

Participants felt that they were able to develop a mental map of the locations more quickly with SpaceSense than the system using only speech feedback. The tactile feedback provided in each step of the directions helped to confirm their mental map.

> *I could anticipate the next direction based on the vibration of the locations. It took longer [to do the same thing] with audio... I sort of knew which direction was next because the vibration was pointing me to a particular direction. So I could anticipate the audio instruction. I could anticipate that because of the vibration.* [P3]

In comparison, when only given audio interface, the participants described needing to work harder to construct a cognitive map.

> *I had to abstractly think where we are going, and put the information provided by the system together. It is a little easier to put together in the map with the tactile stimulation with the combination of the sound as supposed to [the audio condition].* [P4]

DISCUSSIONS

Information Overload through the Audio Channel

We found that the place drawings by the participants were more accurate in the *Tactile* than the *Audio* condition. The major reason participants found benefits with having a separate feedback channel for directional information was that spatial tactile feedback enhanced their memory of the spatial relationships between locations. They explicitly mentioned that the information was overwhelming in the *Audio* condition. P4 pointed out that it was difficult for her to maintain all the information in her mind.

> *(In the Audio condition), I had to listen to the audio over and over just to get the direction, right or left. And I had to keep track of Mary's store, Bob's store, the two names of the people. And then I had to keep track of the directions to get there.* [P4]

But participants explained that receiving directional information over the tactile channel lessened the need to concentrate heavily on the speech feedback. P4 explained this as follows.

With the tactile stimuli, you get the directions in your hand. So you don't have to worry (about the directions) because you can feel it. So you take it away from your memory. And now you just focus on how to get there. [P4]

Their subjective impressions were corroborated by the difference in their drawing of spatial relationships between four locations across the two conditions. Thus, we conclude that spatial tactile feedback can help participants understand spatial relationships between multiple locations.

Errors and Limitations with Learned Routes and Spatial Relationships

The accuracy of the route and spatial relationships between places was not high. One reason might be that participants still often had to process information provided through the speech feedback even while the spatial tactile feedback provided the directional information. Further research is necessary to understand what an effective presentation of geographical information would be to support visually impaired people to gain accurate route information and cognitive map of multiple locations.

The current SpaceSense system only provides high-level spatial relationships between locations and covers straight streets. When visually impaired users actually navigate space later, they may also need other information, such as the shape of a street or intersection. We believe that integration with a system like Timbremap [30] would enable users to gain such information. Future work includes extending SpaceSense to support the user's acquisition of both high-level and low-level geographical information.

Succinct Presentations about Places

The audio adaptation of Review Spotlight was received positively by the participants mainly because of its succinct presentation of reviews. This is in line with the findings reported in [35], but our study confirms that the Review Spotlight presentation can benefit visually impaired users as well. However, as participants indicated, they may want to access to portions of the original review text to gain more detailed information. This was discussed in the original Review Spotlight work, which incorporates a hyperlink on the adjective-noun word pair to the sentences from which the clicked word pair was extracted [35]. A faithful adaptation of the Review Spotlight system is out of the scope of this work; however, future work should investigate how an audio-based system can effectively support both a quick overview and exploration of details in online user reviews through the speech feedback.

STUDY LIMITATIONS

There are several limitations to mention in this study. Our user study included only four places in one neighborhood. During the presentation of route instructions, only two places were presented through the spatial tactile feedback (the destination and bookmarked place). Future work needs to investigate how the number of places in the space and the number of places presented in the route instructions can affect people's learning of spatial relationships.

There are several aspects of the system which were not covered in this paper. For example, due to the large difference in the number of congenitally and after-birth blind participants, we did not examine the effect of this difference in learning spatial relationships. Our current implementation of SpaceSense uses the exo-centric presentation of directions. But the ego-centric presentation can benefit users better in some cases (*e.g.*, while the user is navigating the space physically). Our study shows that participants were able to learn routes and the spatial relationship between places through an exo-centric presentation of the map information similar to when a person reads a map before visiting a location; further research is necessary to investigate how to best present the spatial relationship of locations through a system like SpaceSense while the user is navigating *in situ*.

CONCLUSION

We developed SpaceSense, a handheld system using spatial tactile feedback to help visually impaired people acquire details about places, learn the directions to a place, and understand high-level spatial relationships between multiple locations. Our user study showed that participants could maintain spatial relationships between four places on a map more accurately when directional information was also presented using spatial tactile feedback than only speech feedback. We also found that the Review Spotlight presentation through the auditory channel was received positively by the participants.

REFERENCES

1. Amemiya, T., Sugiyama, H. Haptic handheld wayfinder with pseudo-attraction force for pedestrians with visual impairments. *ASSETS 2009*, ACM (2009), 107-114.
2. Azenkot, S., Prasain, S., Borning, A., Fortuna, E., Ladner, R. E., Wobbrock, J. O. Enhancing independence and safety for blind and deaf-blind public transit riders. *CHI 2011*, ACM (2011), 3247-3256.
3. Blasch, B., Wiener, W., Welsh, R. *Foundations of orientation and mobility, 2nd Ed.* American Foundation for the Blind, New York, NY, USA, 1997.
4. Cohen, J. Weighted kappa: Nominal scale agreement with provision for scaled disagreement or partial credit. *Psychological Bulletin 70*, 4 (1986), 213-220.
5. Coroama, V. Experiences from the design of a ubiquitous computing system for the blind. *Ext. Abstracts CHI 2006*, ACM (2006), 664-669.
6. Crossan, A. Brewster, S. Multimodal trajectory playback for teaching shape information and trajectories to visually impaired computer users. *ACM Trans. Access. Comput. 1*, 2 (2008), Article 12, 34 pages.
7. Helal, A., Moore, S. E., Ramachandran, B. Drishti: An integrated navigation system for visually impaired and disabled. *ISWC 2001*, IEEE (2001), 149-157.
8. Herman, J. F., Herman, T. G., Chatman, S. P. Constructing cognitive maps from partial information: a demonstration

study with congenitally blind subjects. *Journal of Visual Impairment & Blindness 77*, 5 (1983), 195-198.

9. Heuten, W., Wichmann, D., Boll, S. Interactive 3D sonification for the exploration of city maps. *NordiCHI 2006*, ACM (2006), 155-164.
10. Intersection Explorer. https://market.android.com/details?id=com.google.android.marvin.intersectionexplorer
11. Jacobson, R.D. Navigating maps with little or no sight: A novel audio-tactile approach. *CVIR 1998*, 95-102.
12. Kane, S.K., Jayant, C., Wobbrock, J. O., Ladner, R. E. Freedom to roam: a study of mobile device adoption and accessibility for people with visual and motor disabilities. *ASSETS 2009*, ACM Press (2009), 115-122.
13. Kane, S.K., Morris, M.R., Perkins, A.Z., Wigdor, D., Ladner, R.E., Wobbrock, J.O. Access overlays: improving non-visual access to large touch screens for blind users. *Proc. UIST 2011*, ACM (2011), 273-282.
14. Kane, S. K., Wobbrock, J. O., Ladner R. E. Usable gestures for blind people: understanding preference and performance. *CHI 2011*, ACM (2011), 413-422.
15. Kitchin, R. M., Jacobson, R. D. Techniques to collect and analyze the cognitive map knowledge of persons with visual impairment or blindness: issues of validity. *Journal of Visual Impairment & Blindness* (1997), 360-376.
16. Loadstone Project. http://www.loadstone-gps.com
17. Loomis, J. M., Golledge, R. G., Klatzky, R. L., Speigle, J. M., Tietz, J. Personal guidance system for the visually impaired. *ASSETS 1994*. ACM Press (1994), 85-91.
18. Marston, J. R., Loomis, J. M., Klatzky, R. L., Golledge, R. G., Smith E. L. Evaluation of spatial displays for navigation without sight. *ACM Trans. Appl. Percept. 3*, 2 (2006), 110-124.
19. McGookin, D, Brewster, S., Jiang, W-W. Investigating touchscreen accessibility for people with visual impairments. *NordiCHI 2008*, ACM (2008), 298-307.
20. Paladugu, D. A., Wang, Z., Li, B. On presenting audio-tactile maps to visually impaired users for getting directions. *Ext. Abstracts CHI 2010*, ACM (2010), 3955-3960.
21. Palmer, C. I., Gardner, E. P. Simulation of motion of the skin IV responses of pacinian corpuscle afferents innervating the primate hand to stripe patterns on the optacon. *J. Neurophysiol. 64*, 1 (1990), 236-247.
22. Parente, P., Bishop, G. Bats: the blind audio tactile mapping system. *ACMSE '03*. (2003)
23. Parkes D. Nomad: an audio-tactile tool for the acquisition, use and management of spatially distributed information by partially sighted and blind persons. *Proc. Maps and Graphics for Visually Handicapped People*, (1988), 24-29.
24. Passini, R., Proulx, G., Rainville, C. The spatio-cognitive abilities of the visually impaired population. *Environment and Behavior 22* (1990), 91-118.
25. Ross, D. A., Blasch, B. B. Wearable interfaces for orientation and wayfinding. *ASSETS 2000*, ACM (2000), 193-200.
26. Rowell, J., Ungar, S. Feeling our way: tactile map user requirements—a survey. *ICC 2005*, International Cartographic Association (2005).
27. Sánchez, J., Sáenz, M., Pascual-Leone, A., Merabet, L. Navigation for the blind through audio-based virtual environments. *Ext. Abstracts CHI 2010*. ACM (2010), 3409-3414.
28. Sendero GPS. http://www.senderogroup.com/products/shopgps.htm
29. Stewart, J., Bauman, S., Escobar, M., Hilden, J., Bihani, K., Newman M. W. Accessible contextual information for urban orientation. *UbiComp 2008*, ACM (2008), 332-335.
30. Su, J., Rosenzweig, A., Goel, A., de Lara, E., Truong, K. N. Timbremap: enabling the visually-impaired to use maps on touch-enabled devices. *MobileHCI 2010*, ACM (2010), 17-26.
31. Talking Signs. http://www.talkingsigns.com/
32. Trekker. http://www.humanware.com/en-canada/products/blindness/talking_gps/trekker/_details/id_88 /trekker.html
33. Trekker Breeze. http://www.humanware.com/en-canada/products/blindness/talking_gps/trekker_breeze/_detai ls/id_101/trekker_breeze.html
34. Yang, R., Park, S., Mishra, S. R., Hong, Z., Newsom, C., Joo, H., Hofer, E., Newman, M. W. Supporting spatial awareness and independent wayfinding for pedestrians with visual impairments. *Proc. ASSETS 2011*, ACM Press (2011), 27-34.
35. Yatani, K., Novati, M., Trusty, A., Truong, K. N. Review spotlight: a user interface for summarizing user-generated reviews using adjective-noun word pairs. *CHI 2011*, ACM (2011), 1541-1550.
36. Yatani, K., Truong, K. N. SemFeel: a user interface with semantic tactile feedback for mobile touch-screen devices. *UIST 2009*, ACM (2009), 111-120.
37. Walker, B. N., Lindsay, J. Navigation performance with a virtual auditory display: Effects of beacon sound, capture radius, and practice. *Human Factors 48*, 2 (2006), 265-278.
38. Wilson, J., Walker, B. N. Lindsay, J., Cambias, C., Dellaert, F. SWAN: system for wearable audio navigation. *ISWC 2007*, IEEE (2007), 1-8.
39. Zelek, J. S., Bromley, S., Asmar, D., Thompson, D. A haptic glove as a tactile-vision sensory substitution for wayfinding. *Journal of Visual Impairment & Blindness 97*, 10 (2003), 1-24.
40. Zhao, H., Plaisant, C., Shneiderman, B., Lazar, J. Data sonification for users with visual impairment: a case study with georeferenced data. *ACM Trans. Comput.-Hum. Interact. 15*, 1 (2008), Article 4, 28 pages.

The User as a Sensor: Navigating Users with Visual Impairments in Indoor Spaces using Tactile Landmarks

Navid Fallah, Ilias Apostolopoulos, Kostas Bekris, Eelke Folmer
Department of Computer Science and Engineering
University of Nevada, Reno
Reno, NV 89557-0208
{navid,ilapost,bekris,efolmer}@cse.unr.edu

ABSTRACT
Indoor navigation systems for users who are visually impaired typically rely upon expensive physical augmentation of the environment or expensive sensing equipment; consequently few systems have been implemented. We present an indoor navigation system called Navatar that allows for localization and navigation by exploiting the physical characteristics of indoor environments, taking advantage of the unique sensing abilities of users with visual impairments, and minimalistic sensing achievable with low cost accelerometers available in smartphones. Particle filters are used to estimate the user's location based on the accelerometer data as well as the user confirming the presence of anticipated tactile landmarks along the provided path. Navatar has a high possibility of large-scale deployment, as it only requires an annotated virtual representation of an indoor environment. A user study with six blind users determines the accuracy of the approach, collects qualitative experiences and identifies areas for improvement.

Author Keywords
Mobility; Visual Impairment; Indoor Navigation.

ACM Classification Keywords
H.5.2 [User interfaces]: Voice I/O

General Terms
Design, Measurement

INTRODUCTION
Navigation relies on a combination of mobility and orientation skills [9]. People typically employ *path integration*, where they orient themselves relative to a starting position using proprioceptive data, or *landmark-based* navigation, where they rely upon perceptual cues together with an external or cognitive map [27]. Path integration allows for exploring unfamiliar environments in which users may build a cognitive map by observing landmarks [28]. Whereas sighted people primarily use vision to identify landmarks, individuals with visual impairments employ their compensatory senses, such as touch, hearing and even smell [35]. Studies show small differences in path integration ability between sighted and individuals with visual impairments [27], but cognitive mapping is significantly slower for people with visual impairments [25, 35] often leading to reduced mobility [12].

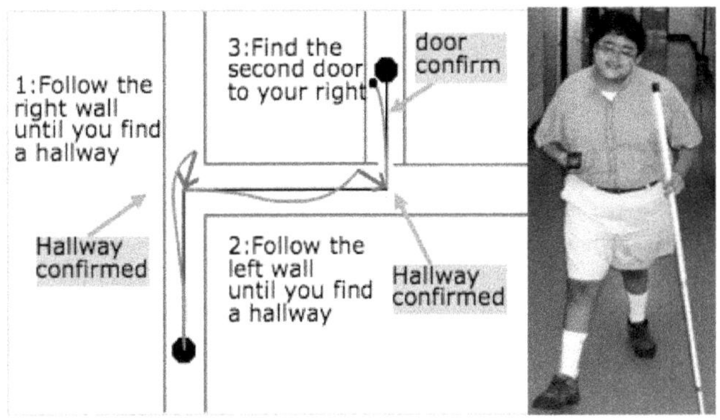

Figure 1. Sample path directions provided by Navatar and user confirmations of tactile landmarks.

Various indoor and outdoor navigation systems for users with visual impairments have been developed. Whereas outdoor navigation systems rely on GPS for locating the user, indoor navigation systems use different techniques, described in the following section, as GPS signals cannot be received inside buildings. Indoor systems have not been implemented at a large scale as they often require expensive physical augmentation of the environment or they require the user to carry expensive sensing and computing equipment, which may further impede their mobility.

This work presents an inexpensive navigation system called Navatar that does not augment physical infrastructure and that depends only on lightweight sensors available in popular devices such as smartphones. Navatar exploits the unique tactile sensing capabilities of users with visual impairments [8] by having its users confirm the presence of anticipated landmarks, such as doors and hallway intersections along the provided path that are extracted from a virtual representation of the environment (see Figure 1). This type of interaction seamlessly integrates with how users with visual impairments navigate familiar spaces as this includes the identification of known tactile landmarks [19]. In prior research a feasibility study with blindfolded users was performed [4]. This paper evaluates Navatar with blind users.

RELATED WORK

Certain navigation devices have been developed that provide local obstacle-avoidance capabilities to users with visual impairments [36, 40]. Most navigation systems, however, are able to locate the user and provide directions to a specified destination. Outdoor navigation systems [26, 34] mainly use GPS for localization purposes, but indoor systems cannot use GPS signals, as buildings block them. To surpass this issue, alternative localization techniques have been developed that can be distinguished into three different categories.

Dead-Reckoning techniques estimate the user's current location based on a previously estimated or known location. While the user is moving, dead reckoning estimates the user's location by interpreting readings from one or more sensors that the user carries such as accelerometers, magnetometers, and gyroscopes [21, 15, 31, 29]. The initial location is typically determined using GPS [15], RFID tags [21], or cellular phone positioning [31]. The main drawback of this technique is the error accumulates over time as dead reckoning is a recursive process and each sensor has some inaccuracy. One significant benefit of this approach is the low installation cost, as it does not require physical infrastructure.

Beacon-based approaches augment the physical space with identifiers. Such beacons can be retro-reflective digital signs detected by a camera [39], infrared [34, 37] or ultrasound identifiers [30]. Beacons can be integrated with dead-reckoning to correct the accumulated error through environmental knowledge [15], RFID tags [21], ultrasound beacons [20], and map-matching [21, 29]. Especially, Radio Frequency Identifier (RFID) tags have attracted a lot of attention in this direction [22, 7, 3]. Nevertheless, locating identifiers may be hard, as beacons may require line of sight or close proximity to the human. Other beacon based techniques use triangulation to locate the user. For example, wireless network positioning systems [32, 24, 23] may triangulate the location of base stations using the provided signal strength or could be building signal strength maps. Wireless nodes often suffer from multi-path effects or interference. Another drawback is the significant time and cost spent installing and calibrating beacons. Though RFID tags are cheap, a large amount of them is required to cover a whole building. Installing them in non-carpeted environments, such as concrete floors or tiles is often prohibitively expensive.

Sensor-based solutions employ sensors, such as cameras that can detect pre-existing features of indoor spaces, such as walls or doors. For instance, a camera system matches physical objects with objects in a virtual representation of the space [17] to locate the user. However, cameras require good lighting conditions, and may impose a computational cost prohibitive for portable devices. An alternative makes use of a 2D laser scanner [14, 13]. This method achieves 3D pose estimation by integrating data from inertial sensors, the laser scanner, and knowledge of the 3D structure of the space. While this method achieves accurate localization, it relies upon expensive and heavy sensors, which may further impede the mobility of users with visual impairments as they already carry devices such as a cane or a Braille display.

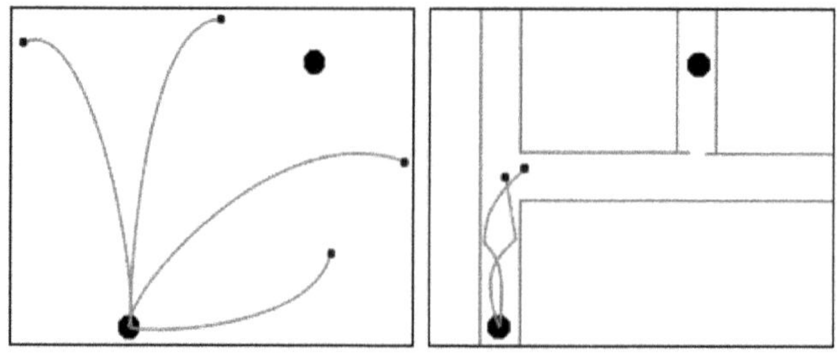

Figure 2. Veering is likelier to occur in outdoor environments (left) than in indoor environments (right) as navigation is often constrained by physical infrastructure such as walls.

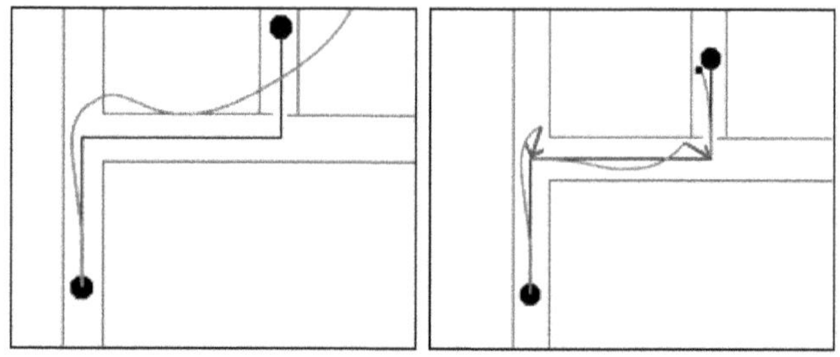

Figure 3. Error in location estimation using dead reckoning quickly grows unbounded (left) but using periodic synchronization with a beacon with a known location (right) errors can be mitigated.

DESIGN OF NAVATAR

Localization is required in any navigation system to be able to detect veering, e.g., when the user is deviating from the intended path. Precise localization in indoor environments comes at a significant cost; for example, large scale augmentation of indoor environments with RFID tags is often prohibitively expensive. Veering is likelier to occur in outdoor environments than in indoor environments as navigation is typically constrained by physical infrastructure, such as walls (see Figure 2).

To facilitate large-scale deployment of an indoor navigation system, we argue that less precise but less expensive localization solutions may need to be explored. Of the three techniques discussed in the related work section, dead reckoning does not require expensive sensing or augmentation of the environment. Dead reckoning can be achieved with commodity portable devices such as a smartphone, which have integrated accelerometers and magnetometers. To achieve a better level of localization accuracy, the proposed approach integrates inexpensive sources of dead-reckoning data with sensing information that comes from a human user. Dead reckoning is relatively accurate for short distances where error can be mitigated by periodic sensing of beacons with a known location [21, 20] (see Figure 3). The novelty in this approach is the utilization of a human as a sensor rather than just an actuator.

The cognitive mapping of indoor spaces by people with visual impairments has been extensively studied [19, 38, 11]. Tactile landmarks that are easily sensed through touch, such as doors, hallway intersections and floor transitions, play an important role in the cognitive mapping of indoor spaces by users with visual impairments [19, 6]. Sounds or even smells may also be used as landmarks [6]. Users who are blind have better tactile sensing capabilities than sighted people [8].

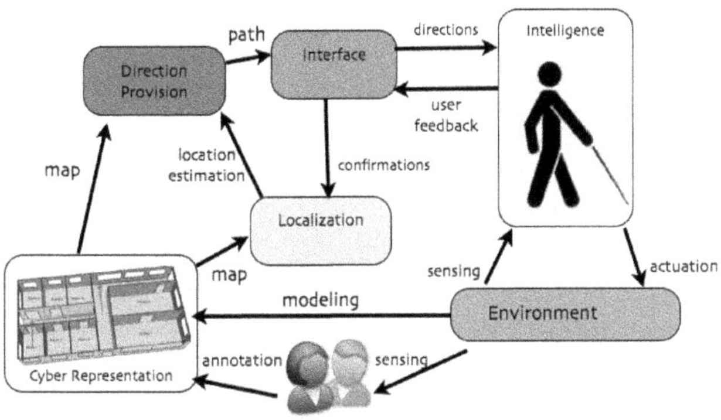

Figure 4. Navatar system overview showing the communication between the different components.

System Overview

Because the identification of tactile landmarks already plays a significant role in how users with visual impairments navigate familiar spaces, our navigation system combines dead reckoning with sensor based localization by incorporating a role for the user as an "intelligent sensor" that confirms the presence of a landmark. Landmarks along the provided path are embedded in directions (*"..until you reach a hallway intersection"*). The successful execution of the direction (and hence the presence of the anticipated landmark) is confirmed by the user.

Navatar aims to augment navigation capabilities of users with visual impairments, but it is not a local obstacle avoidance system, as this requires being able to track movable objects, such as trashcans, chairs and tables. The location of such objects may change and it is difficult to keep track of them. Instead the focus is on immutable landmarks, such as, hallway intersections, staircases and doors.

Figure 4 lists a high-level overview of the four different components of Navatar, which are: (1) a virtual representation component that stores annotated models of indoor environments; (2) the localization component that provides a location estimate of the user; (3) the direction provision component that provides directions to a user specified location; and (4) the interface component that interacts with the user.

Virtual Representation

Instead of 2D maps, 3D models are used to more accurately represent indoor environments with multiple levels and features like low ceilings, ramps, uneven floors and rails, which are often impediments to navigation for users with visual impairments. In order to exploit crowd sourcing it may be easier for sighted users to annotate 3D models with tactile landmarks. The use of virtual worlds is further motivated by the observation that thousands of 3D models of the exteriors of public buildings have been successfully created through crowd-sourcing efforts. They can be found on virtual globe applications, such as Google Earth. Google recently announced the availability of indoor maps for several airports and malls in the US [2]. Furthermore, 3D models of indoor spaces are becoming available [1] and can be created with little effort using tools such as Google Sketchup.

Localization

To localize the user, this work followed a Bayesian filtering approach called particle filters [10]. Each particle contains (a) an estimation of where the user might be located and (b) a weight of how probable this estimate is. As the user moves in the environment each particle location is updated based on a distribution of error in steps detected (pedometer and compass). The weight of the particle is updated based on the user's confirmations of anticipated landmarks. Weights are also affected by map information. For instance, when a particle is inside a wall, its weight is zero. The particles that have low weight, such as particles inside a room, while the user has not confirmed a door, are replaced with new particles to achieve more accurate localization.

In some cases the user might fail to confirm the presence of a landmark, which can be problematic for localization. To solve this problem particles are monitored. If all the particles have progressed beyond the landmark, which the system expects to be recognized, the failure is detected. Navatar will be able to self-correct by providing new directions. Specific implementation details of the particle filters process can be found in related work [4, 5] as their discussion is outside the scope of this paper.

Direction Provision & Interaction

Given a map, Navatar computes the shortest path using the A* algorithm [33] and identifies landmarks along the path upon which directions are generated. Directions are provided using synthetic speech and are of the following form:

- Moving to a landmark, i.e., *"Follow the wall to your left until you reach a hallway intersection"*.
- A turn direction, i.e., *"Turn Left"*.
- An action on a landmark, i.e., *"Open the door and take the stairs down"*.

For moving to a landmark, Navatar uses directions that include wall following and door counting rather than metric information based on the results of preliminary studies (see following). Users confirm the successful execution of each direction (and the presence of landmarks) by tapping the screen.

Preliminary Studies

The number of landmarks that need to be confirmed and the number of directions provided can significantly affect accuracy and performance. A feasibility study with 10 blindfolded users [4] focused on determining the effectiveness of different types of directions. Two versions of providing directions were tested: (1) metric-based directions (i.e., *"walk 20 steps until there is a hallway on your right"*); and (2) landmark-based directions (i.e., *"walk until you have passed three doors on your left"*). For each type of direction the distance to be navigated varied, as well as the number of landmarks to be confirmed. The user had to confirm the successful execution of a direction before receiving the next one. The highest rate of success was achieved for landmark-based directions involving few reliable landmarks, such as hallway intersections. Especially when landmarks, such as doors, are close to each other, they become harder to distinguish.

A second study with eight blindfolded users focused on integrating localization and path planning [5]. It investigated whether localization was accurate enough to allow directions to be computed on at run-time on the phone. Experiments show that the path can be adjusted when users fail to correctly follow directions by depending upon localization estimates. This work also explores the use of multiple particle filters, where each filter uses a different assumption for the user's average step length, which helps to adaptively estimate the value of this parameter on the fly. For localization, multiple particle filters are executed in parallel. Each one of them is employing a different set of assumptions regarding the capabilities of the user depending on pedometer and compass data from the smartphone and landmark confirmations by the user. For a small but sufficient number of particles per filter (50-100), as well as number of filters (7), each iteration of the algorithm required on average less than 200ms, sufficient for real-time tracking. Ground truth was collected by a vision-based system carried by the user, which is described in the following section.

USER STUDY

Though preliminary user studies were conducted with blindfolded participants, this study specifically focused on users who are visually impaired.

Instrumentation

Navatar has been implemented in Java for the Android mobile platform. A 3D model of the Engineering building of the University of Nevada, Reno was created using Google Sketchup using the Keyhole Markup Language (KML). Sketchup allows for creating named components and adding such a component to a location in the model. This allows for augmenting this model with addressing information and landmarks such as doors, hallway intersections, ramps and staircases. Though it is possible to plan paths in 3D models, this was anticipated to be too computationally intensive to be performed on the phone and hence a parser was created that extracts intermediate 2D maps that are more suitable for path planning, since the user is grounded anyway. Figures 6 and 7 show representations of extracted maps for the first and the second floor. For the estimation of the user's location 10 particle filters were used in parallel, with each filter having between 50-100 particles. Preliminary studies found the phone's compass to occasionally interfere with metal studs in the wall leading to highly noisy data. To avoid this, consecutive compass readings were averaged over a time period and then the measured value was discretized into one of eight possible directions.

A commercial beacon based localization system called Hagisonic StarGazer was used to capture the ground truth. Passive landmarks with unique identifiers were installed on the ceiling with a resolution of one identifier per three feet. An infrared camera worn by the user provides ID, distance and angle to the closest landmark. An open source library is used to access the camera, which allows the creation of a map of landmarks. To use the system for human localization, the camera and a battery are installed on a belt that the user wears. The camera is worn on the back to avoid occlusion. The user

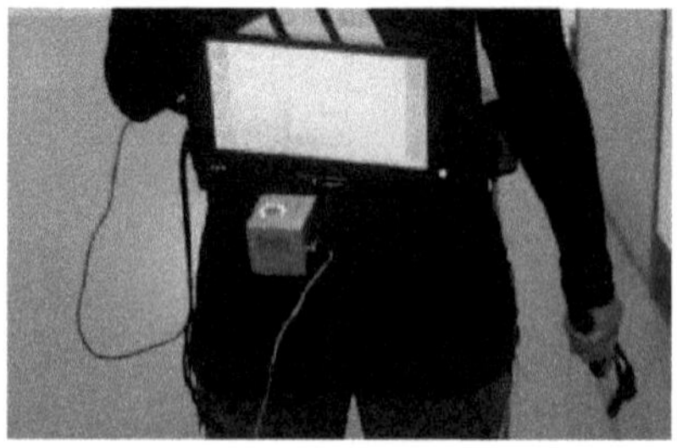

Figure 5. User carrying the StarGazer camera and tablet for measuring the ground truth.

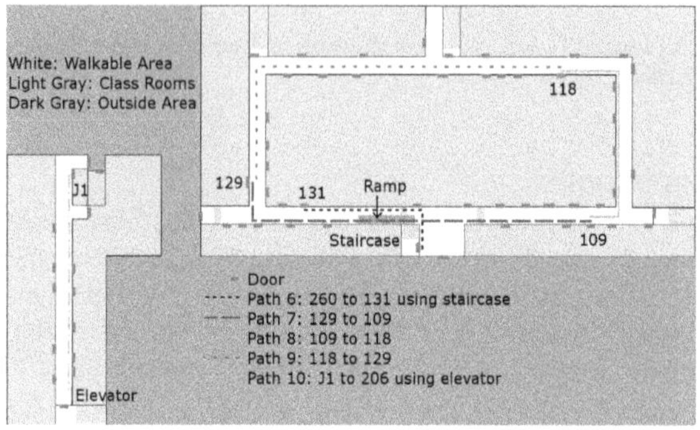

Figure 6. The map of the first floor

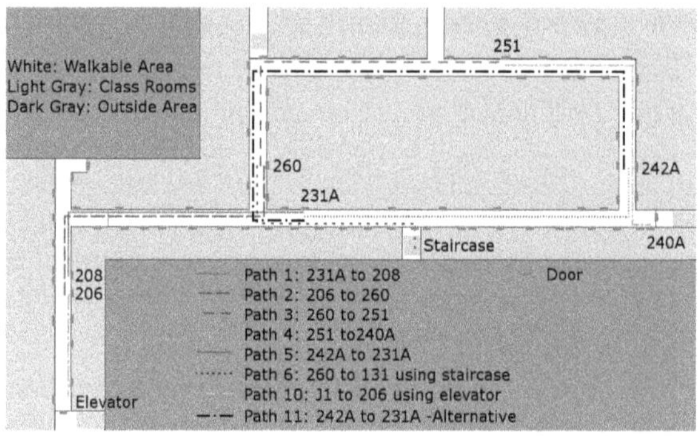

Figure 7. The map of the second floor

carries a tablet in a backpack that records the landmark information received from the camera and calculates the user's location from the map based on the relative landmark location (see Figure 5). The accuracy of the camera is 2 cm when installed on a flat surface; but the camera is sensitive to tilt and might result in incorrect readings when installed on a belt. To reduce the noise the ground truth is smoothed using an outlier detection algorithm.

Participants

Six users were recruited (3 female, average age 51.83, SD=18.21) to participate in a user study. Participants were recruited through the local National Federation of the Blind chapter. All participants were visually impaired, e.g., three were totally blind (TB), two legally Blind (LB) and one had low vision (LV)). All participants used a cane for navigation. None had any self-reported impairments in mobility or hearing. One user did not own a phone, four owned a cell phone and one owned a smartphone. None of the participants had been in the Engineering building prior to the user studies.

Path	231A-208	206-260	260-251	251-240A	242A-231A	260-131	129-109	109-118	118-129	J1-206	*242A-231A*	Avg	stdev
Path Length (m)	43.89	49.38	51.21	45.72	57.61	57.61	58.52	36.58	64.01	50.29	95.10	55.45	15.26
# of Directions	5	7	6	7	5	11	10	7	5	7	9	7.18	2.04
# of Words	33	47	45	47	33	84	76	47	33	51	61	50.64	16.94
Landmarks	2	4	4	4	7	12	7	3	1	6	5	5.0	3.0
- Hallway Inters.	1	2	2	2	1	2	2	2	1	1	3	1.73	0.65
- Doors	1	2	2	2	6	8	3	1	1	4	2	2.91	2.26
- Stairs	0	0	0	0	0	1	1	0	0	0	0	0.18	0.40
- Ramp	0	0	0	0	0	0	1	0	0	0	0	0.09	0.30
- Floor transition	-	-	-	-	-	Stairs	-	-	-	Elev.	-	-	-
Success Rate	1.00	1.00	0.83	1.00	0.50	0.50	0.83	0.83	1.00	1.00	0.83	0.61	0.24
Average time(s)	72.29	115.31	107.34	79.73	100.81	227.39	135.20	80.21	95.10	136.97	162.93	119.39	45.32
Time stdev	12.28	44.42	14.12	16.88	31.47	69.82	35.29	33.10	26.59	34.21	33.12	-	-
Average # steps	81	107	93	82	111	148	132	77	117	107	164	111	31
Steps stdev	15	34	35	14	24	57	36	17	21	27	63	28	16

Table 1. Profiling data for each path

User id	1	2	3	4	5	6	Avg	stdev
Age	62	44	54	31	37	79	51.83	18.21
Gender	F	F	M	M	F	M	-	-
Type of VI	TB	TB	LB	LB	TB	LV	-	-
Path 231A-208	1.36	0.58	0.48	0.38	0.83	0.99	0.77	0.37
Path 206-260	1.94	1.09	0.71	0.31	0.72	0.51	0.88	0.58
Path 260-251	1.85	1.04	1.68	0.23	0.33	10.11 **F**	2.54	3.77
Path 251-240A	0.76	0.55	0.54	0.55	0.24	0.33	0.50	0.19
Path 242A-231A	14.77 **F**	1.32	15.15 **F**	1.22	2.81 **F**	1.83	6.18	6.82
Path 260-131	4.00 **F**	0.46	4.97 **F**	0.96	2.78 **F**	1.48	2.44	1.78
Path 129-109	1.22	1.60	0.76	0.83	2.14 **F**	1.68	1.37	0.53
Path 109-118	0.90	0.69	0.83	0.86	4.89 **F**	1.55	1.62	1.63
Path 118-129	1.11	1.73	0.99	1.59	1.28	1.89	1.43	0.36
Path J1-206	1.25	1.84	0.67	1.21	0.77	1.30	1.17	0.42
Path 242A-231A(Alt)	2.07 **F**	0.98	0.99	0.87	1.14	2.73 **F**	1.46	0.76
Avg Step length (m)	0.40	0.73	0.63	0.51	0.40	0.68	0.56	0.14
Success rate	0.73	1.00	0.82	1.00	0.64	0.82	0.84	0.14

Table 2. Distance between the desired destination and the user's position upon completion (m). F indicates a failed path.

Procedure

For the user study, 11 paths were tested; and these paths were created so as to have approximate equal lengths with the smallest amount of overlap between paths. Two paths involve transitions between floors. Specific characteristics of each path such as its length and number of landmarks present can be found in Table 1. Initially 10 paths were created but in a previous study [5] one path (242A-231A) was found to lead to large errors in location estimation as it involves traveling a relatively large distance with only doors as landmarks (see Figure 7). To evaluate the effectiveness of planning longer but more accurate paths that lead along more distinguishable landmarks an alternative version of this path was created (*242A-231A*) that includes 3 hallway intersections.

The application provides directions through text to speech using the smartphone's speaker and the user confirms executing each direction by tapping the screen. Because touch screens are notoriously inaccessible to users with visual impairments a successful tap was indicated using a vibrotactile cue. All users were right handed and navigated with the cane in their right hand. Users were asked to hold the phone in their left hand but hold it relatively still as to achieve higher accuracy in step detection. Participants were equipped with the StarGazer camera and backpack containing the tablet. None of the participants felt the belt and backpack impeded their mobility in any way.

User studies were conducted over a weekend with few students present in the building to avoid interference. Hallways were cleared of any obstacles and all doors to offices were closed. Prior to the user study the user followed one path to have them become familiar with the phone and the direction provision and to initialize the pedometer (though the pedometer continues to calibrate itself). For each path participants were led to the start location upon which the observer would select the right path and activate the direction provision. Navatar can recover from users missing landmarks or confirming them too early or too late. If the user could not complete a provided direction, the observer would intervene and cancel the current path, mark it as a failure and guide the user to the next start location. After the user study, participants were interviewed using a questionnaire to collect qualitative experiences.

Results

Table 1 shows the success rate of each path, the average time and standard deviation it took to execute each one and the average number of steps and the standard deviation for each path. 85% (SD=20%) of the paths were completed successfully. Though the use of multiple particles in a previous study with blindfolded users [5] was able to mitigate individual differences between step lengths, for some users with visual impairments this turned out to be difficult to achieve. Table 2 lists the distance between the target destination and the user's position upon completion of the path. There was no observation of users unable to confirm a landmark, but system failures occur when the system thinks the user has arrived at their destination when they actually have not arrived yet. Paths were considered a success when the user was able to navigate within 2.0 meter of the target location. A length of 2.0 meter was chosen, as this is approximately the range that can be sensed using a cane held in the hand and to correct for the actual user location as the user was wearing the camera on their back. Failures are indicated using an **F** in table 2. For all paths and users an average error of 1.85 meter (SD=2.74) was found.

Paths that involved counting many doors, (e.g., 242A-231A and 260-131) had the lowest success rates and users were often observed to scuttle from door to door, which made it harder for the system to pick up steps. Similar to an early study with blindfolded users [5] path (242A-231A) has a low success rate (50%). The alternative path for (242A-231A) on average took longer to complete (163 seconds) than the original path (101 seconds) but has a higher success rate (83%) and a lower average error (6.18 versus 1.46 meter). This may indicate that planning longer paths that include more distinguishable landmarks may increase accuracy. The completion rate for all paths improves from 85% to 88%, and the average error reduces to 1.42 (SD=1.50) if results for the original path are excluded.

Qualitative Results

Non-directed interviews with open-ended question were used to collect qualitative experiences. None of the participants had used a navigation system before but all users had previously experienced getting lost in outdoor as well as indoor environments. Depending on the space all users engage in cognitive mapping when this space is unfamiliar to them. Primarily tactile landmarks, such as doors or windows are used in cognitive mapping, but one user noted using sounds as well, such as the sound of a water cooler or an air conditioning unit. Cognitive mapping was typically limited to smaller spaces such as rooms. None of the participants had freely explored large indoor environments out of fear of getting lost. Participants typically used a sighted guide when navigating in unfamiliar environments, which would help with working out a route. Three users preferred routes with many landmarks but would avoid ones with too many turns as that was found to be confusing.

A 5-point Likert scale was used to measure the usability of the system. All users found that the directions were easy to follow (M=4.66, SD=0.58) and that Navatar navigated them efficiently (M=4.66, SD=0.58). They also agreed this system could minimize the chance that they would get lost in unfamiliar environments (M=4.66, SD=0.58). Overall they liked using the system (M=4.66, SD=0.58). Despite Navatar failing to guide user 5 to the target destination for four paths, this user remained positive about the system. Upon further inquiry this user stated: "I have never used such a system before and I think it could be really helpful, despite its current shortcomings". Suggestions for improvement included: (1) improving the accuracy; (2) being able to repeat directions; (3) offer Braille output; (4) not holding the phone in the hand but in a pocket and (5) for directions involving stairs indicating whether you need to go up or down the stairs. This last suggestion was caused by the system providing directions dynamically so depending on the estimate of the user location the system would direct *"go down the stairs"* but if the system's estimate were beyond or on the stairs this direction would be omitted. One user preferred to not hold the phone in the hand as this user prefers to use this hand to protect their face while navigating. Repeating directions was already implemented as directions are calculated dynamically based on the system's current estimate of the location of the user. This functionality was not made available to the participants to keep the study simple and avoid any false confirmations.

DISCUSSION AND FUTURE WORK

Overall the system was able to successfully guide users to their destination in 85% of the paths. The experiences and results collected were encouraging. The following issues need to be addressed in order to improve the accuracy of Navatar. The sensors used are inexpensive but also erroneous and to improve step detection, rather than holding the phone in the hand better results may be achieved by placing at a different part of the body such as the legs.

Detecting steps was more difficult as some users would scuttle when counting doors and alternative direction provision strategies may need to be employed. When following walls users typically have a firmer stride, so wall following in direction provision may be preferred over door counting. Scuttling may not be avoided completely as users with visual impairments often have inefficient gait due to predominantly sedentary behaviors during the developmental years [16]. Alternatively, a pressure sensor could be embedded in the user's shoes to detect steps, which may be more precise than detecting steps using an accelerometer, but this may add to the cost of the system.

Future user studies will include a larger number of users who are visually impaired and will also involve navigating in more complex environments, such as open spaces, and involving a larger variety of landmarks, or sounds and smells. The intention is also to explore planning safer paths that lead along a larger number of landmarks or include landmarks that are more distinguishable. In the current system the next direction is provided manually based on the user's confirmation of successfully executing the direction. The studies demonstrate that sufficiently accurate localization is achievable, which may allow for automatic direction provision similar to how car navigation systems provide directions. This could make navigation more efficient and reduce cognitive load, as the user does not have to engage in tasks such as identifying doors. Confirmations of landmarks will still be incorporated periodically as to mitigate the error of dead reckoning localization.

A significant benefit of Navatar is that it can be installed at a much lower cost than alternative indoor localization systems. The StarGazer system used for measuring ground truth cost over $2,000 and three days to install for two floors of the building where the user study was conducted. It also requires the user to carry a heavy, awkward sensor. For comparison creating the 3D model and annotating it with landmarks only took 3 hours using Google Sketchup, with the use of an existing 2D floor plan, which is available for most buildings. Future research will study how to automatically extract landmarks, such as doors or staircases, from the geometry of a 3D model rather than annotating them manually. This would allow for using models that are created using robotic mapping [18]. As some annotations such as room numbers need to be annotated by sighted humans, to facilitate crowd-sourcing efforts, the intention is to explore how models can be most easily annotated and how annotations can be verified.

To improve obstacle avoidance and successful landmark recognition, it is desirable to leave users' hands free. Users could wear a wireless headset with a microphone worn on one ear leaving the other ear free to listen to any sounds in the immediate environment. Speech recognition could be used that allows users to verbally provide a destination, e.g., *"lead me to room 334"*. Further down the road, Navatar could facilitate answering spatial queries such as *"where is the nearest fire escape?"*.

CONCLUSION

This paper presents an indoor navigation system called Navatar that allows for navigating a user with visual impairments by exploiting the physical characteristics of indoor environments, taking advantage of the unique sensing abilities of users with visual impairments, and minimalistic sensing achievable with a smartphone. A user study with six visually impaired users evaluated the accuracy of Navatar and found that users could successfully complete 85% of the paths. To improve its accuracy more sophisticated techniques need to be developed that allow for detecting the unique steps of users with visual impairments using low cost sensing. Once its accuracy is further improved, Navatar is anticipated to have a high probability of large-scale deployment due to its low installation cost and its potential to leverage crowd-sourcing efforts for the annotation of virtual indoor models

REFERENCES

1. National university of singapore library, `http://nuslibrary.appspot.com/`, last accessed: 12/29/2011.
2. A new frontier for google maps: mapping the indoors, `http://googleblog.blogspot.com/2011/11/new-frontier-for-google-maps-mapping.html`, last accessed: 12/28/2011.
3. Amemiya, T., Yamashita, J., Hirota, K., and Hirose, M. Virtual leading blocks for the deaf-blind: A real-time way-finder by verbal-nonverbal hybrid interface and high-density rfid tag space. In *Proc. of the IEEE Virtual Reality* (Washington, DC, USA, 2004).
4. Apostolopoulos, E., Fallah, N., Folmer, E., and Bekris, K. E. Feasibility of interactive localization and navigation of people with visual impairments. In *11th IEEE Intelligent Autonomous Systems (IAS-10)* (Ottawa, CA, August 2010).
5. Apostolopoulos, E., Fallah, N., Folmer, E., and Bekris, K. E. Integrated localization and navigation of people with visual impairments. In *IEEE Int. Conf. on Robotics and Automation (ICRA'12)* (Minnesota, May 2012).
6. B Tsuji, G Lindgaard, A. P. Landmarks for navigators who are visually impaired. In *Proceedings International Cartography Conference* (2005).
7. Bessho, M., Kobayashi, S., Koshizuka, N., and Sakamura, K. Assisting mobility of the disabled using space-identifying ubiquitous infrastructure. In *Proc. of the 10th Int. ACM SIGACCESS Conf. on Computers and Accessibility (ASSETS)*, ACM (Halifax, Nova Scotia, Canada, 2008), 283–284.
8. Bhattacharjee, A., Ye, A., Lisak, J., Vargas, M., and Goldreich, D. Vibrotactile masking experiments reveal accelerated somatosensory processing in congenitally blind braille readers. *J Neurosci 30*, 43 (Oct 2010), 14288–14298.
9. Foulke, E. Spatial abilities: Development and physiological foundations, New York, 1982, ch. Perception, cognition, and mobility of blind pedestrians., 55–76.
10. Fox, D., Burgard, W., and Thrun, S. Markov localization for mobile robots in dynamic environments. *Journal of Artificial Intelligence Research (JAIR) 11* (1999), 391–427.
11. Giudice, N. A., Bakdash, J. Z., and Legge, G. E. Wayfinding with words: spatial learning and navigation using dynamically updated verbal descriptions. *Psychol Res 71*, 3 (May 2007), 347–358.
12. Golledge, R. Geography and the disabled: A survey with special reference to vision impaired and blind populations. *Transations of the Intstitute of British Geographers 18* (1993), 63–85.
13. Hesch, J. A., Mirzaei, F. M., Mariottini, G. L., and Roumeliotis, S. I. A 3d pose estimator for the visually impaired. In *Proc. of the IEEE/RSJ Intern. Conference on Intelligent Robots and Systems (IROS)* (Oct. 11-15 2009), 2716–2723.
14. Hesch, J. A., and Roumeliotis, S. I. An indoor localization aid for the visually impaired. In *Proc. of the IEEE International Conference on Robotics and Automation (ICRA)* (Roma, Italy, April 10-14 2007), 3545–3551.

15. Hollerer, T., Hallaway, D., Tinna, N., and Feiner, S. Steps toward accommodating variable position tracking accuracy in a mobile augmented reality system (2001). 31–37.

16. Horvat, M., Ray, C., Ramsey, V., Miszko, T., Keeney, R., and Blasch, B. Compensatory analysis and strategies for balance in individuals with visual impairments. *Journal of Visual Impairment and Blindness 97*, 1 (2003), 695–703.

17. Hub, A., Diepstraten, J., and Ertl, T. Design and development of an indoor navigation and object identification system for the blind. In *Proc. of the 6th Int. ACM SIGACCESS Conf. on Computers and Accessibility (ASSETS)*, ACM (Atlanta, GA, USA, 2004), 147–152.

18. Jensen, B., Weingarten, J., Kolski, S., and Siegwart, R. Laser Range Imaging using Mobile Robots: From Pose Estimation to 3d-Models. In *Proc. 1st Range Imaging Research Day* (2005), 129–144.

19. Kalia, A. A., Legge, G. E., and Giudice, N. A. Learning building layouts with non-geometric visual information: the effects of visual impairment and age. *Perception 37*, 11 (2008), 1677–1699.

20. Kleeman, L. Optimal estimation of position and heading for mobile robots using ultrasonic beacons and dead-reckoning. In *IEEE Int'l Conference on Robotics and Automation* (1992), 2582–2587.

21. Koide, S., and Kato, M. 3-d human navigation system considering various transition preferences. In *Systems, Man and Cybernetics, 2005 IEEE International Conference on*, vol. 1 (2005), 859–864.

22. Kulyukin, V., Gharpure, C., Nicholson, J., and Pavithran, S. Rfid in robot-assisted indoor navigation for the visually impaired. In *Proc. of the IEEE/RSJ Int. Conf. on Intelligent Robots and Systems* (Sendai, Japan, Sept. 28-Oct.2 2004), 1979–1984.

23. Ladd, A. M., Bekris, K. E., Rudys, A., Kavraki, L. E., and Wallach, D. S. On the feasibility of using wireless ethernet for indoor localization. *IEEE Transactions on Robotics and Automation 20*, 3 (June 2004.), 555–559.

24. Ladd, A. M., Bekris, K. E., Rudys, A., Marceau, G., Kavraki, L. E., and Wallach, D. S. Robotics-based location sensing using wireless ethernet. In *Eight ACM International Conference on Mobile Computing and Networking (MOBICOM 2002)*, ACM Press (Atlanta, GA, September 2002), 227–238.

25. Lahav, O., and Mioduser, D. Multisensory virtual environment for supporting blind persons' acquisition of spatial cognitive mapping – a case study. In *Proceedings of World Conference on Educational Multimedia, Hypermedia and Telecommunications 2001*, C. Montgomerie and J. Viteli, Eds., AACE (Norfolk, VA, 2001), 1046–1051.

26. Loomis, J. M., Golledge, R. G., and Klatzky, R. L. Navigation system for the blind: Auditory display modes and guidance. *Presence: Teleoper. Virtual Environ. 7*, 2 (1998), 193–203.

27. Loomis, J. M., Klatzky, R. L., and Golledge, R. G. Navigating without vision: basic and applied research. *Optometry and Vision Science 78*, 5 (May 2001), 282–289.

28. Lynch, K. *The Image of the city*. MIT Press., Cambridge, Ma.,, 1960.

29. Nakamura, K., Aono, Y., and Tadokoro, Y. A walking navigation system for the blind. *Systems and computers in Japan 28*, 13 (1997), 1610–1618.

30. Ran, L., Helal, S., and Moore, S. Drishti: An integrated indoor/outdoor blind navigation system and service. *IEEE International Conference on Pervasive Computing and Communications* (March 2004), 23–30.

31. Retscher, G. Pedestrian navigation systems and location-based services. In *3G Mobile Communication Technologies, 2004. 3G 2004. Fifth IEE International Conference on* (2004), 359–363.

32. Riehle, T. H., Lichter, P., and Giudice, N. A. An indoor navigation system to support the visually impaired. In *30th Annual International Conference of the IEEE Conference on Engineering in Medicine and Biology Society (EMBS)* (Aug. 2008), 4435–4438.

33. Rina, D., and Pearl, J. Generalized best-first search strategies and the optimality of a*. *Journal of the ACM 32*, 3 (1985), 505–536.

34. Ross, D. A., and Blasch, B. B. Development of a wearable computer orientation system. *Personal Ubiquitous Comput. 6*, 1 (2002), 49–63.

35. Semwal, S. K. Wayfinding and navigation in haptic virtual environments. *IEEE International Conference on Multimedia and Expo* (Aug 2001), 559 – 562.

36. Shoval, S., Borenstein, J., and Koren, Y. Auditory guidance with the navbelt - a computerized travel aid for the blind. *IEEE Transactions on Systems, Man and Cybernetics 28*, 3 (August 1998), 459–467.

37. Sonnenblick, Y. An indoor navigation system for blind individuals. In *Proceedings of the 13th annual Conference on Technology and Persons with Disabilities (CSUN)* (Northridge, Los Angeles, March 1998).

38. Stankiewicz, B. J., and Kalia, A. A. Acquisition of structural versus object landmark knowledge. *J Exp Psychol Hum Percept Perform 33*, 2 (Apr 2007), 378–90.

39. Tjan, B., Beckmann, P., Giudice, N., and Legge, G. Digital sign system for indoor wayfinding for the visually impaired. In *Proc. of the IEEE Conf. on Computer Vision and Pattern Recognition - Workshop on Computer Vision Applications for the Visually Impaired* (San Diego, CA, June 2005).

40. Yuan, D., and Manduchi, R. Dynamic environment exploration using a virtual white cane. In *Proc. of the IEEE Conf. on Computer Vision and Pattern Recognition* (San Diego, CA, June 20-25 2005), 243–249.

Guidelines are Only Half of the Story: Accessibility Problems Encountered by Blind Users on the Web

Christopher Power, André Pimenta Freire, Helen Petrie, David Swallow
Department of Computer Science, University of York
Deramore Lane, York, YO10 5GH, UK
{cpower, apfreire, helen.petrie, dswallow}@cs.york.ac.uk

ABSTRACT
This paper describes an empirical study of the problems encountered by 32 blind users on the Web. Task-based user evaluations were undertaken on 16 websites, yielding 1383 instances of user problems. The results showed that only 50.4% of the problems encountered by users were covered by Success Criteria in the Web Content Accessibility Guidelines 2.0 (WCAG 2.0). For user problems that were covered by WCAG 2.0, 16.7% of websites implemented techniques recommended in WCAG 2.0 but the techniques did not solve the problems. These results show that few developers are implementing the current version of WCAG, and even when the guidelines are implemented on websites there is little indication that people with disabilities will encounter fewer problems. The paper closes by discussing the implications of this study for future research and practice. In particular, it discusses the need to move away from a problem-based approach towards a design principle approach for web accessibility.

Author Keywords
Web accessibility; web accessibility guidelines; user evaluation; blind users.

ACM Classification Keywords
H.5.2 [User interfaces]: Evaluation/methodology;
H.5.4 [Hypertext/Hypermedia]: User issues;

INTRODUCTION
In the information society, the Web provides people with the ability to tap into news, commerce and social information at any time. Indeed, one could say that users are drowning in information. However, not all people can use this vast resource of information equally. The persistence of websites that are not accessible, meaning that people with disabilities cannot use them [15], results in these users are living in an information desert in comparison to their mainstream peers [22]. Even worse, recent studies show that the Web is becoming less accessible to people with disabilities over time [16].

In 1999 the Web Accessibility Initiative (WAI) of the World Wide Web Consortium (W3C) defined the first version of the Web Content Accessibility Guidelines (WCAG 1.0). WCAG 1.0 was published to promote web accessibility and to provide a comprehensive set of guidelines on how to prepare web content so that people with disabilities could use the web regardless of their needs and preferences [32]. WCAG 1.0 comprised 14 guidelines, and, within these guidelines, 65 checkpoints (CPs) that described how developers could adapt their web content in order to make it accessible. Each checkpoint was assigned a priority level, Priority 1 through Priority 3, which indicated the importance of the CP in terms of its impact on accessibility of content to different groups of disabled users [31]. If a web page satisfied all Priority 1 CPs it was said to be conformant at Level A. Likewise, if a website satisfied all Priority 1 and 2 CPs, the website was conformant at Level AA. Finally, if a website satisfied all CPs, it was conformant to Level AAA.

For almost a decade WCAG 1.0 served as the *de facto* standard for web accessibility. It can be argued that WAI's original goal of raising awareness accessibility was achieved [17], with WCAG 1.0 becoming the basis for legislation in a number of countries [2], and it is heavily referenced in web accessibility practice [28, 31].

However, the impact of WCAG 1.0 on improving the accessibility of the Web remained quite low throughout the period of its use. Evaluations using automated tools covering a small subset of the guidelines [13, 14, 33], expert evaluations using a combination of automated testing tools and human judgment [19, 30], and user evaluations with disabled participants [4, 10, 24] all found the level of accessibility of web pages to be extremely low in both the public and private sectors.

This low level of accessibility is likely to be the result of several different factors. For instance, despite awareness of accessibility increasing over the last decade at the level of government and legislation, the level of knowledge in the community of web commissioners and web masters remains quite low. In 2005, Petrie et al. [24] reported that 30% of websites claiming conformance to some level of WCAG 1.0 overstated their level of conformance. The authors hypothesized that this may be that web commissioners do not understand the differences between automated and manual testing, and therefore attribute more importance to the former when making conformance claims. This hypothesis is supported by the work by Lazar et al. [18], who found that the role of accessibility tools and related guidelines remained unclear to many of the site owners they surveyed. The most alarming aspect of the Lazar et al. study was the fact that 22% of site owners had no knowledge at all about accessibility guidelines.

In addition to this, there have been several criticisms leveled at the provision of support to developers for testing websites for accessibility based on WCAG 1.0. WCAG 1.0 was evaluated with 12 experienced web developers who were novices to accessibility [7]. This evaluation demonstrated that developers struggled with both the navigation through WCAG documents as well as the language used in them. Other work has also pointed to ambiguities in the language, as well as the required level of technical knowledge of accessibility in order to read and interpret the guidelines, as being barriers to their uptake in accessibility practice [11].

However, the most obvious and important concern about WCAG 1.0 was the lack of empirical evidence that a website which is Level AAA conformant was more usable by people with disabilities than a Level A website. There are two examples of empirical data being collected regarding WCAG 1.0. Rømen and Svanæs [29] collected data with 7 users on 2 websites and found that only 27% of problems identified by users were covered by the guidelines. Secondly, the Disability Rights Commission (DRC) [10] conducted a Formal Investigation into access and inclusion on the Web. The result of this investigation is still the largest known accessibility evaluation to date with 1000 websites being evaluated with automated testing and 100 websites being evaluated by experts and disabled users. For the user evaluations, 913 tasks were undertaken over the 100 websites chosen, with participants being selected from a wide variety of people with disabilities. Only 19% of websites met even Level A conformance to WCAG 1.0. In the user evaluations, it found that of the problems reported by users 45% of them were not covered by WCAG 1.0 CPs. As a consequence of these results, the equating of accessibility to conformance to WCAG 1.0 is highly suspect, and the accessibility community has indicated that this is an important issue to be addressed [17].

In 2008 the WAI released a new version of WCAG. WCAG 2.0 attempted to address many of the criticisms that had been leveled at WCAG 1.0. These new guidelines [6] are organized in a more hierarchical manner. Within WCAG 2.0 there are four Principles about web content accessibility: content should be Perceivable, Operable, Understandable and Robust. These principles group guidelines in a more structured hierarchy than was present in WCAG 1.0. Further, Guidelines under each of these Principles have been rephrased to be solutions to specific user requirements, such as the provision of text alternatives for non-text content (Guideline 1.1). Then, for each Guideline there are Success Criteria (SC). SCs are testable statements that a developer can use to determine if web content is accessible. It is against these SC that a website is measured for conformance, with each SC having a priority level, Level A, AA or AAA, relating to conformance levels that are similar to WCAG 1.0.

In order to future-proof WCAG 2.0 against the fast evolution of technology, the WAI removed the technical aspects of accessibility from the Guidelines and SCs. Technical information regarding how to implement web content with existing web technologies is now provided in separate documents [8]. These documents describe techniques that have been determined by the WCAG Working Group to be *sufficient* to meet the SC. It is also possible to meet an SC without using these sufficient techniques. For example, developers can provide implementations and evaluate them with users to show they pass the SC. However, it is reasonable to expect that the majority of web developers will implement the sufficient techniques in their own websites. In addition to these organizational changes, the WAI has provided multiple documents for understanding accessibility, WCAG and other related concepts (e.g. user agents, authoring tools) [9].

However, despite all of these changes, studies have demonstrated that many of the problems from WCAG 1.0 persist in WCAG 2.0. Petrie et al. [26] conducted interviews with 14 web accessibility evaluators, and found that they were very unclear on the differences between automated testing and manual testing of accessibility, in particular on what can be tested through automated tools. Brajnik et al. [5] had 22 expert and 27 non-expert evaluators perform accessibility evaluations using WCAG 2.0 and found that for 50% of SCs evaluators were unable to come to an 80% level of agreement about whether a problem was present in a page. Further, when using WCAG 2.0 20% of the problems reported by expert evaluators were false positives and they also missed 32% of true accessibility problems. For non-experts, the results were even worse, with higher levels of both false positives and false negatives. Alonso et al. [3] also found that a group of 25 beginner evaluators struggled to consistently rate problems according to WCAG 2.0. One cause of this lack of success in identifying accessibility problems was in the interpretation of the Guidelines and SCs. All of these results demonstrate that there are understandability and interpretation problems with WCAG 2.0.

Of greater concern is that in the three years following the release of WCAG 2.0, there appears to have been little improvement in the level of web accessibility. Lopes et al. [22] crawled 30 million web pages, performing automated accessibility tests. Under 4% of elements on these web pages met all relevant SCs that could be tested automatically. This is not a very good result given that automated testing covers only a small proportion of WCAG 2.0.

Beyond all of these issues, there is still the looming problem of a lack of empirical evidence that demonstrates that conformance to WCAG 2.0 leads to more accessible websites for disabled users. This is in contrast to web usability guidelines such as the widely used guidelines from the U.S. Department of Health and Human Sciences that cite empirical research to establish the strength of evidence supporting their application [1], and to accessibility guidelines that have been defined and validated for specific user groups [20, 21]. Indeed, there are very few examples of empirical studies of WCAG 2.0. To date, only one known paper, that of the current authors, provides (remote) user evaluations of one of the WCAG 2.0 SCs and related techniques [27].

This paper presents a study that addresses these issues and answers the following empirical questions on the relationship between WCAG conformance and accessibility as actually experienced by disabled users:

- For the web accessibility problems encountered by people with visual disabilities, what percentage of those problems would be addressed by correctly implementing existing SCs in WCAG 2.0?
- Do blind users encounter accessibility problems on web pages when they have conformed to WCAG 2.0 SCs?

METHOD

Design

The study involved a task-based user evaluation with blind users on selected websites and collecting information about the problems they encounter. Participants undertook a concurrent think aloud protocol, where they spoke about what they were thinking and doing as they were carrying out their tasks. Participants were asked to rate the severity of each problem they encountered using a four point scale (Cosmetic, Minor, Major, Catastrophic), adapted from the severity rating scale defined by Nielsen for usability problems [23]. A total of 10 different users, assigned from the participant group in no particular order, evaluated each of 16 websites.

Participants

Thirty-two blind participants took part, of whom 22 were male and 10 were female. Their ages ranged from 18 to 65 years (median = 39 years). 17 participants had no residual vision, 12 had only light/dark perception and three had a very little central vision. Most participants (20 out of 32) had been blind since birth, and the remainder of the participants had been blind for a period between three years and 47 years.

All participants used screenreaders as their primary assistive technology to access computers, 30 out of 32 used JAWS and 2 used WindowEyes. The WindowEyes users used version 7.11. JAWS versions varied from as early as JAWS 5.0 to JAWS 11.0 (the most up-to-date version available when the study was conducted). 12 users rated themselves experts with their screenreader, 6 as advanced users, 12 as intermediate and 2 as having only a basic command of their screenreader.

The participants rated their experience with computers on a scale from 1 (not at all) to 7 (extensive). Their ratings of computer experience ranged from 4 to 7, with 87% of the participants rating their experience as 5 or above. Most of the participants (29 out of 32) had been using the Internet for seven years or more. Internet Explorer was the most popular browser used by participants, being mentioned as primary navigator by all but one participant, who used Firefox.

Each participant was reimbursed with £15 per hour for his/her participation in the study.

Equipment and software

The evaluations were performed using a personal computer running Windows XP Operating System (Service Pack 3), equipped with speakers, keyboard and 2-button mouse with scrollwheel. Users had the choice of either version 10.0 of the JAWS screenreader or version 7.11 of the WindowEyes screenreader. Participants also could choose one of two web browsers: Internet Explorer 8.0 or Firefox 3.5. Morae 3.1 was used to record the participants with their concurrent verbal protocol, their facial expressions and the computer desktop.

Websites and tasks

Seventy-two websites from the DRC study [10] that still existed were chosen as the initial pool of websites to be used in this study. The home page of each website was manually audited to establish its conformance to WCAG 1.0 and WCAG 2.0. Only the home page was audited as the DRC study found that the conformance of the home page correlates highly with other pages on a website. However, very few of these websites met WCAG 1.0 or 2.0 conformance on initial testing, so further websites that claimed good conformance to WCAG 1.0 or 2.0 were sought from many sources.

A set of 16 websites was selected for inclusion in the study using the conformance results. This set of websites included websites from the private and public sectors, local and central government, public services, non-profit organizations and commercial websites. Unfortunately, in spite of seeking widely for websites with conformance to WCAG 1.0 Level AAA, WCAG 2.0 Level AA and Level AAA, very few such sites could be found. Table 1 shows the list of websites and information about their level of conformance to WCAG 1.0 and WCAG 2.0. For each website, the level of conformance (column *Conf.* with values A, AA, AAA and Fail for failure) is shown, along with the number of CPs/SCs violated and the number of *instances* of violations (column *Inst.*)

The *instances* of violations of CPs/SCs (*Inst.*) is the number of times each CPs/SCs is violated. For example, a website has two different CPs/SCs violated: there are 10 images without alternative text (CP 1.1/SC 1.1.1) and 22 missing headings (CP 5.1/SC 2.4.6). The *instances* of violations is 32.

Table 1 shows that only 1 website with WCAG 2.0 Level AAA and 1 website with WCAG 2.0 Level AA could be found. In addition, a number of sites, which conformed to WCAG 1.0 at A or AA, failed WCAG 2.0 conformance. When examining the ways in which websites failed to conform, it was noted that 3 of the websites (Digizen, JISC and Royal Mail) failed one SC a single time, specifically SC 3.3.1 ("error identification"), and otherwise conformed to Level A of WCAG 2.0. Therefore, in some analyses, which will be noted, these websites are classified as Level A conformant websites.

For each website, two or three typical tasks of varying levels of difficulty were created. Tasks involved simple operations such as finding information about council tax, booking tickets for a concert and finding an exhibit on display in a large museum. Tasks required between two and 8 steps to be completed, with an average of four steps per task.

Procedure

Evaluations took place in the Interaction Laboratory in the Department of Computer Science at the University of York. Participants were briefed about the study and asked to sign an informed consent form. Participants, with assistance from the researcher when needed, adjusted the browser and screenreader to the participant's preferred settings. Each website was introduced to the participants and they undertook tasks on the website while providing a concurrent verbal protocol. When participants were quiet for an extended period of time, they were prompted for their thoughts by the researcher. When participants encountered a problem, the researcher asked them to pause briefly and rate the problem for severity using the four point scale. This procedure was repeated for each website. At the end of the session, participants were debriefed, and were invited to ask questions about the study. All web pages visited by users were archived for further analysis.

Data analysis

Three coders independently identified and categorized accessibility problems on a subset of videos from the evaluation sessions.

	WCAG 1.0			WCAG 2.0			User Problems				
Website	Conf.	CPs violated	Inst.	Conf.	SCs violated	Inst.	Cos.	Min.	Maj.	Cat.	Total
www.lflegal.com	AA	2	5	AAA	0	0	6	27	12	6	51
www.green-beast.com	AA	3	23	AA	3	9	11	24	11	2	49
www.york.gov.uk	AA	4	16	Fail	5	7	5	29	25	11	70
www.nhsnss.org	AA	6	30	Fail	9	31	10	29	32	21	92
www.copac.ac.uk	A	8	21	A	2	6	9	25	17	6	57
www.theaa.com	A	9	68	Fail	9	58	7	22	20	5	54
www.dh.gov.uk	A	9	91	A	6	31	6	44	30	14	94
www.digizen.org.uk	A	9	80	Fail	12	46	2	6	15	31	54
www.jisc.ac.uk	A	12	58	Fail	13	216	5	12	19	15	51
www.royalmail.com	A	15	50	Fail	7	103	5	23	19	7	54
www.pret.co.uk	A	16	184	Fail	21	141	13	24	14	3	54
www.tuc.org.uk	A	23	146	Fail	17	97	17	36	34	13	100
ww.britishmuseum.org	Fail	8	130	Fail	8	86	16	73	44	23	156
www.nhsdirect.nhs.uk	Fail	10	30	Fail	20	163	14	36	21	9	80
www.ford.co.uk	Fail	27	124	Fail	33	244	19	44	57	49	169
www.ticketmaster.co.uk	Fail	29	757	Fail	35	1118	12	96	62	28	198

Table 1. List of websites evaluated in the study, with conformance levels to WCAG 1.0 and WCAG 2.0, number of different CPs/SCs violated and instances of violations, and instances of user problems grouped by severity levels

The three coders compared their initial set of user problems and their categorizations in order to develop a unified list of user problems and user problem categories. Several iterations of coding and discussion were needed before a final set of categories was agreed. Then, using this set of categories, the main coding of all the user sessions was performed.

For each user problem, an analysis was conducted as to whether it had one or more *relevant* WCAG 1.0 CPs and/or WCAG 2.0 SCs (CPs/SCs). A set of guidelines *covered* a user problem if one or more CPs/SCs was identified to be *directly relevant* to the user problem, meaning it was clear that it addressed the problem encountered by the user. In the analysis, some user problems were identified as having *marginally relevant* CPs/SCs, meaning that the CPs/SCs could be interpreted as addressing the user problem from a certain point of view, but it was not totally clear that it was relevant. For each user problem, the web page on which it was encountered was evaluated to see if it passed the *directly relevant* and *marginally relevant* CPs/SCs.

RESULTS

Table 1 shows the number of user problems for each website, identified at each severity level: cosmetic (*Cos.*), minor (*Min.*), major (*Maj.*) and catastrophe (*Cat.*). The participants encountered 1383 instances of accessibility problems across the 16 websites. The mean number of problems per website was 86.4.

User problems and WCAG conformance

Analyses were performed on how the number of problems encountered by users relate to the conformance of the websites to both WCAG 1.0 and WCAG 2.0.

For WCAG 1.0, Figure 1 presents the mean number of problems on websites that were non-conformant, Level A or Level AA conformant (there being no Level AAA conformant websites for WCAG 1.0). There was a significant difference between the mean number of problems found on websites with the different conformance levels ($F = 12.35$, $df = 2, 13$, $p < 0.001$). A set of Tukey HSD post-hoc tests showed that the difference between non-conformant and Level A conformant websites was significant ($p < 0.001$) and that the difference between non-conformant and Level AA websites was also significant ($p < 0.005$).

For WCAG 2.0, Figure 2 shows the mean number of problems on websites that were non-conformant, conformant to Level A and conformant at any level. An interesting observation is that three of the non-conformant websites that failed Level A by only violating SC 3.3.1 had some of the fewest user problems (see Table 1 entries Digizen - www.digizen.org.uk, JISC - www.jisc.ac.uk and Royal Mail - www.royalmail.com).

It was not possible to make a comparison between the individual levels of conformance as there were so few websites that conformed to Level AA or Level AAA (see section Websites and tasks).

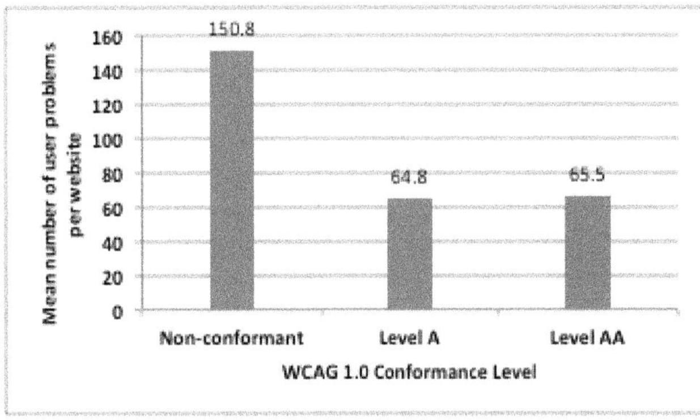

Figure 1. Mean number of instances of user problems per website grouped by WCAG 1.0 conformance levels.

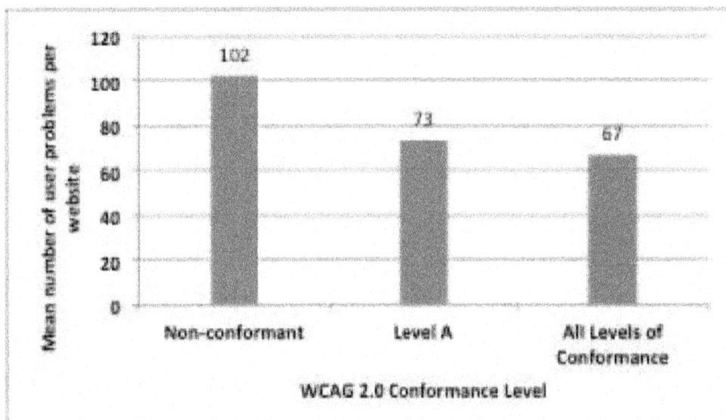

Figure 2. Mean number of instances of user problems per website grouped by WCAG 2.0 conformance levels.

A one-way ANOVA between non-conformant websites and Level A conformant websites showed no significant difference in the mean number of problems ($F = 1.107$ $df = 1,12$, n.s.). One would expect a decrease in the number of user problems between non-conformant and Level A websites. A one-way ANOVA between non-conformant websites and websites that conformed at any level of WCAG 2.0 also failed to show a significant difference ($F = 2.351$ $df = 1,14$, n.s.). Again, one would expect a decrease in the number of problems between non-conformant websites and conformant websites. In these analyses the three websites which failed SC 3.3.1 on one occasion only were classified as Level A (see section Websites and tasks).

User problems and WCAG CPs/SCs violated

Analyses were performed on how the number of user problems relate to the number of CPs/SCs violated and the number of instances of CPs/SCs violated. For the following analyses, the TicketMaster website was omitted as the number of problems per user was more than 2 standard deviations above the mean for all the websites making it an outlier.

For WCAG 1.0, there was a significant correlation between the number of CPs violated and the mean number of problems per website per user ($r = 0.53$, $df = 14$, $p < 0.05$).

For WCAG 2.0, there was also a significant correlation between the number of SCs violated and the mean number of problems per website per user ($r = 0.54$, $df = 14$, $p < 0.05$).

For the instances of violations of CPs/SCs, there was no significant correlation between the instances of violations of WCAG 1.0 CPs or WCAG 2.0 SCs and the mean number of problems per website per user.

User problems and coverage by WCAG CPs/SCs

Analyses were performed on the extent to which user problems are covered by WCAG 1.0 CPs and WCAG 2.0 SCs.

For WCAG 1.0, Figure 3 shows the breakdown of user problems into categories of relevance of CPs and whether those CPs have been implemented on the website where the problem was encountered. The total percentage of user problems that were *covered* by CPs was 43.3% (the sum of bars 2 and 3 in Figure 3) and only a small percentage of those were implemented by developers (5.7% of all user problems, bar 3 in Figure 3, or 13.3% of all user problems *covered* by WCAG 1.0). This means that of the problems encountered by users on websites, well over half (57.1%) were not covered by WCAG 1.0.

For WCAG 2.0, Figure 4 shows a similar breakdown of user problems into categories of relevance and implementation of SCs. The total percentage of user problems that were covered by SCs was 50.4% (the sum of bars 2 and 3 in Figure 4) and a similarly small percentage of these were implemented by developers (8.4% of all user problems, bar 3 in Figure 4, or 16.7% of all user problems with relevant SCs). This means that for WCAG 2.0, the current set of guidelines for web accessibility, almost half of the problems encountered by users on websites are not covered.

A Related Samples Wilcoxon Signed Rank Test showed there was no significant difference in the coverage of user problems between WCAG 1.0 and WCAG 2.0 across the five relevance and implementation categories ($W_+ = 1.5$, $df = 1$, $p = 1.0$).

User Problems not covered by WCAG 2.0 SCs

Analyses were performed to determine what categories of user problems WCAG 2.0 SCs do not cover well. As there was no difference in the *coverage* of user problems between WCAG 1.0 and WCAG 2.0, the analysis for WCAG 1.0 is not presented here but is broadly similar in results.

Table 2 presents user problem categories where WCAG 2.0 SCs did not cover at least 10 problems.

Of the six categories not *covered* by WCAG 2.0 SCs, there were two categories that accounted for 13.5% of all user problems. *Content not found in pages where expected by users* describes problems where users confidently followed a link to a page, but a piece of information that they expected to find there was missing. For example, on a museum website, users followed a link to an object in the museum collection but did not find any information about the room in which that object is displayed, which they expected.

The category *Content found in pages where not expected by users* describes the inverse situation. For this category of problems, users eventually found the information they were looking for, but not where they expected it and not by a logical process of following the navigation provided by the website. For example, on the Automobile Association website (theAA.ccom), users were looking for driving tips. They did find this information under the link "Learn to Drive", but they were surprised that they were on such a page which did not match their mental model of the information architecture of such a site.

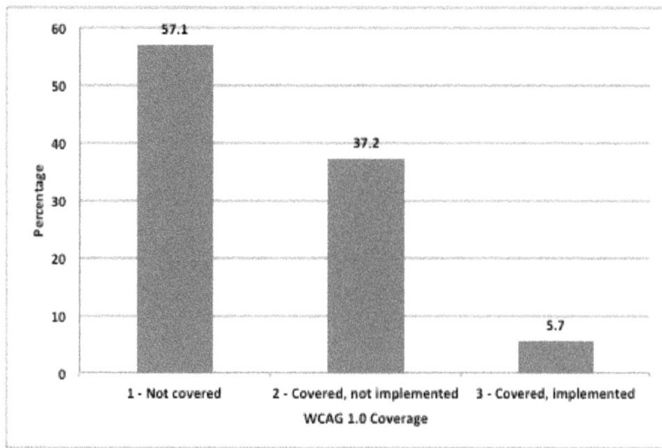

Figure 3: Categories of user problems divided by relevance of WCAG 1.0 CPs and implementation.

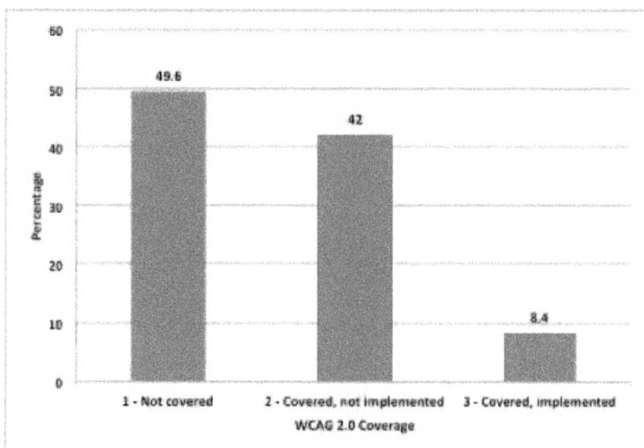

Figure 4: Categories of user problems divided by relevance of WCAG 2.0 SCs and implementation

Other categories had only a small percentage of their problems covered by WCAG 2.0. In the category *Irrelevant content before task content*, users often encountered problems with large blocks of content irrelevant to their task occurring before the relevant content.

Category	Total User Problems	% (No.) Covered by WCAG 2.0
Content found in pages where not expected by users	99	0
Content not found in pages where expected by users	88	0
Pages too slow to load	27	0
No alternative to document format (e.g. PDF)	17	0
Information architecture too complex (e.g. too many steps to find pages)	15	0
Broken links	10	0
Functionality does not work (as expected)	50	26.0 (13)
Expected functionality not present	29	34.5 (10)
Organisation of content is inconsistent with web conventions/common sense	39	35.9 (14)
Irrelevant content before task content	86	45.3 (39)
Users cannot make sense of content	65	67.6 (44)
No/insufficient feedback to inform that actions has had an effect	72	68.1 (49)

Table 2. Categories of user problems with total number of problems and percentage (number) of user problems covered by WCAG 2.0 SCs.

For example, when users were seeking information about insurance plans, the relevant page had lengthy descriptions of why it was important to buy insurance before a summary of insurance plans, the relevant content on the page. While there is an SC (2.4.1) that addresses skipping blocks of content repeated on multiple pages (e.g. main menu bars), there is nothing in this SC, or any other SC, describing the types of problems associated with irrelevant content that is unique to a single page.

User problems covered by WCAG 2.0 SCs

In order to understand why WCAG 2.0 SCs do not solve some problems encountered by users, analyses were performed on problems encountered on webpages where relevant SCs were implemented and yet users still had problems. Table 3 presents the categories of problems where more than 20% of the user problems in the category met these criteria of SC implementation and users having problems.

The largest number of user problems in Table 3 are in the category *Link destination not clear*, which accounted for 8.5% of all problems encountered by users. In 35.0% of problems in this category, the website had properly implemented SC 2.4.4 regarding the description of link purpose, and yet users still had problems determining where the links lead. This indicates that the sufficient techniques for this SC, which are primarily aimed at addressing the problems of blind, screenreader users, are in fact not sufficient.

Category description	Total User problems	% (No.) Covered by WCAG 2.0 and implemented
Language too complicated for perceived target audience	9	33.3 (3)
Link destination not clear	117	35.0 (41)
Difficult to scan pages for specific items	8	37.5 (3)
No enhancements to multimedia content	31	51.6 (16)
Meaning in content is lost or modified due to transformations	6	83.3 (5)
No alternative to information presented in tables	12	100.0 (12)
Heading structure violated	9	100.0 (9)

Table 3. Categories of user problems with their total number of problems and percentage (number) of user problems covered by WCAG 2.0 SCs and implemented.

The category with the second largest number of user problems in Table 3 concerns enhancing multimedia with audio description. Audio description is an enhancement for multimedia where an additional audio track that describes what is happening in the video is played along with the original audio tracks to provide blind viewers with descriptions of vital visual information [12]. For a page containing pre-recorded videos, it passes SC 1.2.3 (Level A), if it provides an audio description or another alternative for all these videos. The only other alternative mentioned by WCAG is a text description of the videos with a text transcript of the audio tracks, all indexed by time. However, in a somewhat complex relationship between SC 1.2.3 and SC 1.2.5, if audio description (as opposed to the text description) is provided for all pre-recorded videos, the page also passes SC 1.2.5 (Level AA). As shown in Table 3, there were 31 problems in the category *No enhancements to multimedia content: audio description*. Of those problems, 51.6% of the web pages passed SC 1.2.3 at Level A by providing an appropriate text description. These problems were covered by WCAG 2.0 and were implemented correctly, but users rejected that implementation because they wanted an audio description. The remaining problems in the category were covered by

WCAG 2.0, but not implemented properly because there was no audio description or any other alternative provided.

DISCUSSION AND CONCLUSIONS

This evaluation of 16 websites by 32 users has revealed a complex relationship between problems encountered by blind, screenreader users and WCAG 2.0.

Firstly, for WCAG 1.0, there was a significant decrease in the mean number of user problems between non-conformant websites and Level A conformant websites. The same was true when non-conformant websites were compared to Level AA websites.

However, for WCAG 2.0, there was no significant decrease in the mean number of user problems when comparing non-conformant websites and Level A conformant websites. There were so few websites that conformed to Level AA and Level AAA, similar tests could not be performed for those conformance levels. However, the same was true when non-conformant websites were compared to websites of all conformance levels.

These findings are quite unexpected. It seems that the upgrade to WCAG 2.0 has not had the expected effect. For WCAG 2.0, one would expect there to be a larger decrease in the number of user problems from non-conformant websites to Level A conformant websites than there was for WCAG 1.0. However, the results show conformance of a website to WCAG 2.0 Level A does not mean that users will encounter fewer problems on it and as a result it does not necessarily mean that following WCAG 2.0 will "make content accessible to a wider range of people with disabilities"[6].

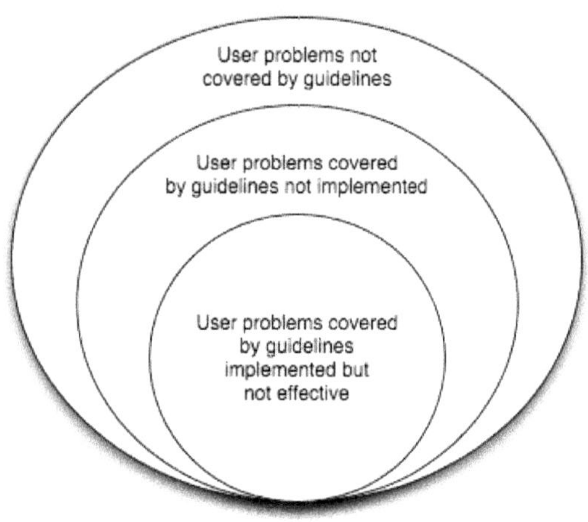

Figure 5: The overall set of user problems divided into three types: problems not covered by guidelines, those covered by guidelines but the guidelines are not implemented and those covered by guidelines with guideline implementations.

However, for WCAG 2.0 there was a correlation between the number of problems encountered by users and the number of SCs violated. These results indicate that the current WCAG 2.0 priority levels are too crude of an accessibility measure.

The results showed three different types of problems encountered by users. These types of problems are presented in Figure 5.

When user problems were compared to WCAG 1.0, 57.1% did not have a CP that could be clearly identified as being *directly relevant*. For WCAG 2.0, only 49.6% of problems were addressed by *directly relevant* SCs. This means only half of the problems encountered by users were *covered*, thus the title of this paper. The move from WCAG 1.0 to WCAG 2.0 has not increased the coverage of user problems, as one would have expected. For those problems covered by WCAG 2.0, only 16.7% of the directly relevant SCs are being implemented on websites. This is a serious problem for three reasons. First, it indicates that web developers still struggle with creating accessible websites, possibly because their understanding of the guidelines is low or because of a lack of tool support. Second, for those SCs not implemented, it is not possible at this time to determine whether the user problems would be addressed by implementing the directly relevant SCs. Finally, for those SCs that were implemented, the implementations failed to solve the user problems. This shows that proposed implementations for solving accessibility problems *must* be evaluated with disabled users.

The results showed that blind users reported problems when they encountered unexpected content or when they could not find content on a website. WCAG 2.0 does not cover these problems. Some may assert that these are not accessibility problems, but instead are usability problems and do not need to be addressed in WCAG 2.0. The authors disagree with this assertion for the following reasons. First, web accessibility is about ensuring that people with disabilities can use the Web. In order for this to be achieved, we must address *all* of the problems that disabled users encounter on web pages.

Second, previous research has shown many problems are shared by blind users and mainstream users [25]. In that research, blind users reported significantly higher severity ratings than their mainstream peers for shared problems. That result makes it critical that these shared problems are solved. The information architecture problems described above would likely impact both disabled users and mainstream users.

Finally, WCAG 2.0 already contains a number of Guidelines and SCs that relate to usability problems, such as providing proper feedback and helping users identify errors. All of these points support the inclusion of a broader range of problems in WCAG 2.0.

The results of this study indicate that it is time to move away from the problem-based paradigm for web accessibility, where our primary goal is to eliminate problems encountered by users. Taking a lesson from usability research, web accessibility research must define a much broader set of design principles, based on user data, that focuses on the use of the web by people with disabilities – not just on the problems they encounter. Once those design principles are clearly understood, only then can we look at proposing rules and heuristics that web developers can apply to evaluate their success in creating websites that people with disabilities can use well. This new paradigm will help us to discover the second half of the accessibility story.

ACKNOWLEDGMENTS

We would like to thank all the participants who took part in this study for their time and valuable input. Author André P. Freire was supported by CNPq – Brazilian Ministry of Science, grant 200859/2008-0.

REFERENCES

1. *Research Based Web Design & Usability Guidelines*. U.S. General Services Administration, 2004.
2. *Equality Act 2010*. Government Equalities Office, 2010.
3. Alonso, F., Fuertes, J. L., González, Á. L. and Martíez, L. On the testability of WCAG 2.0 for beginners. In *Proc. of W4A'10*, ACM (2010).
4. Babu, R. and Singh, R. (2009) Evaluation of Web Accessibility and Usability from Blind User's Perspective: The Context of Online Assessment, in *(AISeL), A. E. L., ed. Americas Conference on Information Systems (AMCIS) 2009*, San Francisco, Paper 623, 2009.
5. Brajnik, G., Yesilada, Y. and Harper, S. Testability and validity of WCAG 2.0: the expertise effect. In *Proc. of ASSETS 2010*, ACM (2010), 43-50.
6. Caldwell, B., Cooper, M., Guarino Reid, L. and Vanderheiden, G. *Web Content Accessibility Guidelines (WCAG) 2.0*. Web Accessibility Initiative (WAI), World Wide Web Consoritum (W3C), 2008. Retrieved from http://www.w3.org/TR/WCAG20/ on Jan. 15, 2012.
7. Colwell, C. and Petrie, H. Evaluation of guidelines for designing accessible Web content. *SIGCAPH Comput. Phys. Handicap.*, 70 (2001), 11-13.
8. Cooper, M., Guarino Reid, L., Vanderheiden, G. and Caldwell, B. *Understanding WCAG 2.0: A guide to understanding and implementing Web Content Accessibility Guidelines 2.0*. Web Accessibility Initiative (WAI), World Wide Web Consortium (W3C), 2010. Retrieved from http://www.w3.org/TR/UNDERSTANDING-WCAG20/ on Jan. 15, 2012.
9. Cooper, M., Guarino Reid, L., Vanderheiden, G. and Caldwell, B. *Techniques for WCAG 2.0: Techniques and Failures for Web Content Accessibility Guidelines 2.0*. Web Accessibility Initiative (WAI), World Wide Web Consortium (W3C), 2010. Retrieved from http://www.w3.org/TR/WCAG20-TECHS/ on Jan. 15, 2012.
10. Disability Rights Commission. *The Web: access and inclusion for disabled people - A formal Investigation conducted by the Disability Rights Commission*. Disability Rights Commission, 2004,
11. Donnelly, A. and Magennis, M. Making Accessibility Guidelines Usable. In *Proc. Universal Access: Theoretical Perspectives, Practice and Experience*, Springer (2003), 56-57.
12. Freed, F. and Rothberg, M. Accessible Digital Media Guidelines, National Centre for Accessible Media Website, (2006). Retrieved from http://ncam.wgbh.org/invent_build/web_multimedia/accessible-digital-media-guide on Jan. 15, 2012.
13. Goette, T., Collier, C. and Daniels White, J. An exploratory study of the accessibility of state government Web sites. *Universal Access in the Information Society*, *5*, 1 (2006), 41-50.
14. Hackett, S. and Parmanto, B. A longitudinal evaluation of accessibility: higher education web sites. *Internet Research*, *15*, 3 (2005), 281-294.
15. Henry, S. L. *Introduction to Web Accessibility*. Web Accessibility Initiative (WAI), World Wide Web Consortium (W3C), 2005. Retrieved from: http://www.w3.org/WAI/intro/accessibility.php on Jan. 15, 2012.
16. Kane, S. K., Shulman, J. A., Shockley, T. J. and Ladner, R. E. A web accessibility report card for top international university web sites. In *Proc. of W4A'07*, ACM (2007), 148-156.
17. Kelly, B., Sloan, D., Phipps, L., Petrie, H. and Hamilton, F. Forcing standardization or accommodating diversity?: a framework for applying the WCAG in the real world. In *Proc. of W4A'05*, ACM (2005), 46-54.
18. Lazar, J., Dudley-Sponaugle, A. and Greenidge, K.-D. Improving web accessibility: a study of webmaster perceptions. *Computers in Human Behavior*, *20*, 2 (2004), 269-288.
19. Lazar, J. and Greenridge, K.-D. One year older, but not necessarily wiser: an evaluation of homepage accessibility problems over time. *Universal Access in the Information Society*, *4*, 4 (2006), 285-291.
20. Leporini, B. and Paternò, F. Applying Web Usability Criteria for Vision-Impaired Users: Does It Really Improve Task Performance? *International Journal of Human-Computer Interaction*, *24*, 1 (2008), 17-47.
21. Leuthold, S., Bargas-Avila, J. A. and Opwis, K. Beyond web content accessibility guidelines: Design of enhanced text user interfaces for blind internet users. *International Journal of Human-Computer Studies*, *66*, 4 (2008), 257-270.
22. Lopes, R., Gomes, D. and Carriço, L. Web Not For All: A Large Scale Study of Web Accessibility. In *Proc. of W4A'10*, ACM (2010), 10.
23. Nielsen, J. *Usability Engineering*. Morgan Kaufmann, Boston, MA, 1993.
24. Petrie, H., Badani, A. and Bhalla, A. Sex, lies and web accessibility: the use of accessibility logos and

statements on e-commerce and financial websites. In *Proc. of ADDW 2005*, University of Dundee (2005).
25. Petrie, H. and Kheir, O. The relationship between accessibility and usability of websites. In *Proc. of CHI'07*, ACM (2007), 397-406.
26. Petrie, H., Power, C., Swallow, D., Velasco, C. A., Gallagher, B., Magennis, M., Murphy, E., Collin, S. and Down, K. The value chain of web accessibility: challenges and opportunities. In *Proc. of ADDW 2011*, Sun SITE Central Europe (2011).
27. Power, C., Petrie, H., Freire, A. and Swallow, D. Remote Evaluation of WCAG 2.0 Techniques by Web Users with Visual Disabilities. In *Proc. of UAHCI: Design for All and eInclusion, 6765*, (2011), 285-294.
28. Regan, B. Accessibility and design: a failure of the imagination. In *Proc. of W4A'04*, ACM (2004), 29-37.
29. Rømen, D. and Svanæs, D. Evaluating web site accessibility: validating the WAI guidelines through usability testing with disabled users. In *Proc. of the 5th NordiCHI 2008*, ACM (2008), 535-538.
30. Sloan, D., Gregor, P., Booth, P. and Gibson, L. Auditing accessibility of UK Higher Education web sites. *Interacting with Computers, 14*, 4 (2002), 313-325.
31. Thatcher, J., Burkes, M. R., Heilmann, C., Henry, S. L., Kirkpatrick, A., Lauke, P. H., Lawson, B., Regan, B., Rutter, R., Urban, M. and Waddel, C. D. *Web accessibility: web standards and regulatory compliance.* Friends of ED, 2006.
32. Vanderheiden, G., Chisholm, W. and Jacobs, I. *Web Content Accessibility Guildeines 1.0.* Web Accessibility Initiative (WAI), World Wide Web Consortium (W3C), 1999. Retrieved from: http://www.w3.org/TR/WAI-WEBCONTENT/ on Jan. 15, 2012.
33. Williams, R. and Rattray, R. An assessment of Web accessibility of UK accountancy firms. *Managerial Auditing Journal, 18*, 9 (2003), 710-716.

Interpretation and Trust: Designing Model-Driven Visualizations for Text Analysis

Jason Chuang, Daniel Ramage, Christopher D. Manning, Jeffrey Heer
Computer Science Department
Stanford University
{jcchuang, dramage, manning, jheer}@cs.stanford.edu

ABSTRACT

Statistical topic models can help analysts discover patterns in large text corpora by identifying recurring sets of words and enabling exploration by topical concepts. However, understanding and validating the output of these models can itself be a challenging analysis task. In this paper, we offer two design considerations — *interpretation* and *trust* — for designing visualizations based on data-driven models. Interpretation refers to the facility with which an analyst makes inferences about the data through the lens of a model abstraction. Trust refers to the actual and perceived accuracy of an analyst's inferences. These considerations derive from our experiences developing the Stanford Dissertation Browser, a tool for exploring over 9,000 Ph.D. theses by topical similarity, and a subsequent review of existing literature. We contribute a novel similarity measure for text collections based on a notion of "word-borrowing" that arose from an iterative design process. Based on our experiences and a literature review, we distill a set of design recommendations and describe how they promote interpretable and trustworthy visual analysis tools.

Author Keywords

Visual analysis, text, statistical models, design guidelines

ACM Classification Keywords

H.5.2 Information Interfaces: User Interfaces

INTRODUCTION

To make sense of complex data, analysts often employ *models*: abstractions (often statistical) that represent data in terms of entities and relationships relevant to a domain of inquiry. Subsequent visual representations may depict a model, source data, or both. A central goal of visual analytics research is to augment human cognition by devising new methods of coupling data modeling and interactive visualization [47].

By suppressing noise and revealing structure, model-driven visualizations can greatly increase the scale of an analysis. However, unsuitable or unfamiliar abstractions may impede interpretation. Ideally, model abstractions should correspond to analysts' mental models of a domain to aid reasoning. Reliable discoveries arise from analysts' ability to scrutinize both data and model, and to verify that a visualization shows real phenomena rooted in appropriate model assumptions.

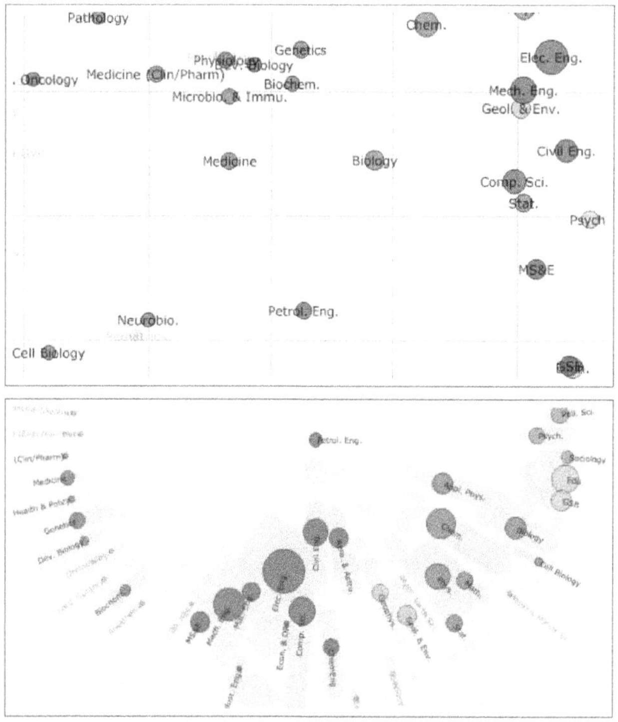

Figure 1. The curious case of Petroleum Engineering. The top visualization shows a 2D projection of pairwise topical distances between academic departments. In 2005, Petroleum Engineering appears similar to Neurobiology, Medicine, and Biology. Was there a collaboration among those departments? The bottom visualization shows the undistorted distances from Petroleum Engineering to other departments by radial distance. The connection to biology disappears: it was an artifact of dimensionality reduction. The visual encoding of spatial distance in the first view is *interpretable*, but on its own is not *trustworthy*.

Consider the visualizations in Figure 1, which depict "topical similarity" between university departments in terms of their published Ph.D. theses. We fit a statistical topic model (latent Dirichlet allocation [4]) to the text and compute similarity using the angle (cosine) between departments' topic vectors. In the top view, we project departments to 2D via principal component analysis of the similarity matrix. Using this visualization we note an unexpected trend: over the years Petroleum Engineering pulls away from other engineering departments, and in 2005 it is situated between Neurobiology, Medicine, and Biology. This observation comes easily, as the visualization is readily *interpretable*: pixel distance on the screen ostensibly represents topical similarity. However, the display is the result of a chain of transformations: topic modeling, similarity measures, and dimensionality reduction. Can an analyst *trust* the observed pattern?

The bottom view instead shows undistorted distances from Petroleum Engineering to the other departments. The relationship with Biology evaporates: it is an artifact of dimensionality reduction. Stripping a layer of modeling (projection) enables validation and disconfirms the initial insight.

In this paper we introduce interpretation and trust, two design considerations for model-driven visual analytics. We define **interpretation** as the *facility with which an analyst makes inferences about the underlying data* and **trust** as the *actual and perceived accuracy of an analyst's inferences*. Designs lacking in either restrict an analyst's ability to generate and validate insights derived from a visualization.

Our understanding of these issues is shaped by our experiences designing the Stanford Dissertation Browser and refined via a survey of text analysis and visualization research. The Dissertation Browser is a visual analysis tool for investigating shared ideas and interdisciplinary collaboration between academic departments. We initially envisioned an interface using existing statistical models. However, we quickly arrived at a working visualization that revealed unexpected shortcomings in the underlying model. Our design work instead involved close collaboration among HCI and NLP researchers to develop and evaluate models that better supported our analysis goals. In a subsequent literature review, we observed that many tools lack consideration of how model abstractions align with analysis tasks; iterative design often focuses on the visual interface alone, not modeling choices.

In this paper, we first present selected examples from prior work, drawing attention to issues of interpretation and trust as well as highlighting successful design decisions. We then describe our experience of building the Dissertation Browser. In the process, we contribute a novel similarity measure for text collections based on the notion of "word-borrowing" and show how it arose from our iterative design process. Finally we contribute a series of design process recommendations for constructing interpretable and trustworthy visual analysis systems. While we focus on the domain of exploratory text analysis, we believe our recommendations can help inform the design of a wide range of model-driven visualizations.

RELATED WORK AND CASE STUDIES

A rich and growing literature considers the use of modeling methods to drive text visualizations. Many, such as tag clouds [50], analyze documents by their constituent words to support impression formation [56], augment search [43], reveal language structure [49, 52], or aid document comparison [16, 17]. Other analyses infer latent topics [22, 23, 24, 25, 34, 46, 53], sentiment [5, 36, 51], or word relationships (e.g., overlap [44], clustering [26, 28], or latent semantics [18, 29]) from text. For large corpora, a common approach is to model document similarities, and visually convey patterns in the corpus via dimensionality reduction [9, 10, 13, 30, 38, 54, 55]. A related literature concerns "science mapping" [6, 7, 8, 32, 40, 42], often via 2D projection of academic citation networks.

Here, we review in greater detail a subset of this prior work. We choose three classes of visual analysis tools due to their widespread use and significant research attention: summaries via word clouds, document visualization using latent topic models, and investigative analysis of entity-relationship networks. We pay particular attention to visual designs and model abstractions, and discuss how they relate to analysis tasks.

Text Summarization with Word Clouds

Word clouds are a popular visualization method used to summarize unstructured text. A typical word cloud shows a 2D spatial arrangement of individual words with font size proportional to term frequency. Despite documented perceptual issues [39], word clouds are regularly found both in analysis tools and across the web [50]. Though simple, a word cloud rests on a number of modeling assumptions. Input text is typically treated as a "bag of words": analyses focus on individual words ignoring structures (e.g., word position, ordering) and semantic relationships (e.g., synonym, hypernym). Most implementations assume raw term counts are a sufficient statistic for indicating the importance of terms in a text.

The ostensible goal of most word clouds is to provide a high-level summary of a text. Is the visualization well suited for the task? A strength of word clouds is that they are highly *interpretable* and directly display the *units of analysis*, words and word-level statistics. Users can readily assess word distributions and identify key recurring terms. Studies found summary information provided by a word cloud can help form meaningful impressions [14] and answer broad queries [43].

To enable more specialized tasks, however, changes are required to the underlying language model. For decades, researchers have anecdotally noted that the most descriptive terms are often not the most frequent terms [31]. Significant absence of a word can be a distinguishing indicator of a document's content relative to a corpus. To better support document comparison, Parallel Tag Clouds [17] apply G^2 statistics to surface both over- and under-represented terms. Others note that single words account for only a small fraction of descriptive phrases used by people [48]. To better capture sentiment in restaurant reviews, Review Spotlight [56] extends the bag-of-words model to consider adjective-noun pairs ("great service" vs. "poor service", instead of just "service"). By modifying the unit of analysis, the tool improves impression formation while retaining a familiar visual design.

In-depth analyses may require more than inspection of individual words. Analysts may want additional context in order to *verify* observed patterns and *trust* that their interpretation is accurate. For example, does the presence of the word "matrix" indicate an emphasis on linear algebra, the use of matrices to represent network data, or a scatterplot matrix for statistical analysis? Interactive techniques can provide *progressive disclosure* across modeling abstractions, e.g., selecting a word in a cloud can trigger highlighting of term occurrences in a view of the source text. In other tools, changes in visual design are accompanied by corresponding changes in the model. WordTree [52] discloses all sentences in which a term occurs using a tree layout. Taking into account the frequency of adjacent terms, WordTree expands branches in the tree to surface recurring phrase patterns. DocuBurst [16] applies radial layout to show word hierarchy; the tool infers word relationships by traversing the WordNet hypernym graph.

Document Visualization using Latent Topic Models

A growing body of visual analytics research attempts to support document understanding using topic modeling. Latent Dirichlet allocation (LDA) [4] is a popular method of discovering latent topics in a text corpus by automatically learning distributions of words that tend to co-occur in the same documents. Given as input a desired number of topics K and a set of documents containing words from a vocabulary V, LDA derives K topics β_k, each a multinomial distribution over words V. For example, a "physics" topic may contain with high probability words such as "optical," "quantum," "frequency," "laser," etc. Simultaneously, LDA recovers the per-document mixture of topics θ_d that best describes each document. For example, a document about using lasers to measure biological activity might be modeled as a mixture of words from a "physics" topic and a "biology" topic.

Latent topics are often presented to analysts as a list of probable terms [12], which imposes on the analysts the potentially arduous task of inferring meaningful concepts from the list and verifying that these topics are responsive to their goals. In this case, modeling abstraction increases the gulf of evaluation [27] required to interpret the visualization.

Evaluations of existing visualizations indicate that an analysis of "topical concepts" can provide an overview of a collection [19], but that the value of the model decreases when the analysis tasks become more specific [28]. Beyond "high-level understanding," many existing systems (e.g., [23, 53]) stop short of identifying specific analysis tasks or contexts of use. This omission makes it difficult to assess their utility.

Notable issues of *trust* arise in the application of topic models to specific domains. Talley et al. [46] examined the relationships between NIH-supported research and NIH funding agencies. To characterize research output, the authors applied LDA to uncover 700 latent topics in 110,000 grants over a four-year period. To *verify* that the topics accurately capture significant research fields, the authors manually rated individual topics and noted the presence of a large number of "junk" or nonsensical topics. The authors *modified* the model by removing 1,200 non-informative words from the analysis and inserting 4,200 additional phrases. The authors then performed extensive parameter search and removed poor topics from the final model before incorporating model output into their analysis. Hall et al. [25] studied the history of Computational Linguistics over forty years. The authors applied LDA on 14,000 papers published at multiple conferences to analyze research trends over time, and recruited experts to verify the quality of every topic. The experts retained only 36 out of 100 automatically discovered topics, and manually inserted 10 additional topics not produced by the model. In many real-world analyses, extensive research effort is spent on validating the latent topics that support the analysis results.

Investigative Analysis of Entity-Relation Networks

One particularly successful class of visual analysis tools uses entity-relation models to aid investigative analysis. In the context of intelligence analysis, "entities" may include people, locations, dates, and phone numbers; "relationships" are modeled as connections between them. Example systems include FacetAtlas [11], Jigsaw [45] (a VAST'07 challenge winner), and Palantir [35] (a VAST'08 challenge winner).

In contrast to other text visualization systems, these tools exhibit clearly-defined units of analysis and provide strong support for model verification, model modification, and progressive disclosure of model abstractions. First, the units of analysis (people, places, events) are *well-aligned to the analysis tasks*. The entity-relationship model provides an interpretable analytical abstraction that can be populated by statistical methods (e.g., using automated entity extraction [21]) and modified by manual annotations (e.g., selecting terms in source text) or other override mechanisms (e.g., regular expressions). Jigsaw uses a simple heuristic to determine relations among entities: co-occurrence within a document. This model assumption is readily interpretable and verifiable, but might be revisited to infer more meaningful links. To foster trust, Palantir provides an auditable history for inspecting the provenance of an observed entity or relation.

Progressive disclosure, particularly in the form of linked highlighting, is used extensively by both Jigsaw and Palantir to enable scalable investigation and verification. According to Jigsaw's creators, the "workhorses" of the tool are the list view (which groups entities by type and reveals connections between them) and the document view (which displays extracted entities within the context of annotated source text). In contrast, Jigsaw's cluster view receives less use, perhaps due to the interpretation and trust issues inherent in assessing an arbitrary number of automatically-generated groupings.

Summary

Across these examples, we note that successful model-driven visualizations exhibit relevant *units of analysis* responsive to delineated *analysis tasks*. However, we also find that many text visualizations fail to align model abstractions with real-world tasks; iterative design often considers interface elements, but not modeling choices. These observations emphasize a recurring lack of attention to model design and a need for principled approaches. In the remainder of this paper, we share both a case study exploring these issues and a set of process-oriented design guidelines for model-driven systems.

THE DESIGN OF A DISSERTATION BROWSER

Our interest in model-driven visualization stems from our experiences working on an interdisciplinary team involving social scientists, NLP and HCI researchers. We were tasked with investigating the impact of interdisciplinary collaboration at Stanford University. Our approach adopted the idea that we could identify influences and convergent lines of research across disciplines by detecting shared language use within university-wide publications. Manually reading the document collection is infeasible due to both the size of the corpus and the expertise required to discern topical overlap between papers. The project also receives the attention of university administrators who wish to evaluate the effectiveness of various research institutes on campus. Do multi-million dollar collaborative centers return suitable intellectual dividends? Our collaboration has resulted in the Stanford Dissertation Browser, a visual analysis tool for exploring 16 years of Ph.D. theses from 75 departments.

Identifying the Units of Analysis

The social scientists hypothesized that interdisciplinary collaborations foster high-impact research, and wanted to identify ideas that might bridge disciplines. For example, they posited that statistical methods are topically situated at the center of the sciences and engineering. What data, models and representations would enable rapid assessment of such hypotheses? We began by collecting 16 years of dissertation abstracts, for which text and metadata were readily available.

Early conversations with our collaborators emphasized the need to examine large scale patterns in the university's output. A first step toward that goal is to survey the research at a "disciplinary" level. Such a survey might suggest areas of horizontal knowledge transfer — such as application of theory, methodology, or techniques across domains — that could be verified as interdisciplinary collaborations. Because each department approximately acts as its own discipline, the university's 75 *academic departments* were suggested as a sensible baseline unit of analysis. Each department's school (such as Engineering or Medicine) provides further organizational context that is meaningful to our collaborators and target audience within the university. A visualization that demonstrates which departments share content would allow our collaborators to discover unexpected areas of inter-disciplinary collaboration and verify known ones.

Our collaborators also emphasized the need to assess the impact of interdisciplinary initiatives, which requires tracking the topical composition of involved groups over time. Our collaborators want to correlate change in research output to the formation of academic ties that cross disciplinary boundaries, such as the creation of research institutes, joint grant proposals, and co-authorship. *Time*, in this case the year of filing, is therefore necessary for the analysis tasks.

Textual similarity provides one means of identifying which disciplines are sharing information. Because each dissertation is associated with one or more departments, the content of these dissertations was seen as a reasonable basis for inferring whether two departments are working on the same content as seen through the words in their published dissertations. We thus explored various text-derived similarity measures as the basis of these similarity scores.

Data and Initial Models

Our dataset contains abstracts from 9,068 Ph.D. dissertations from Stanford University published from 1993 to 2008. These dissertations represent over 97% of all Ph.D. degrees conferred by Stanford during that time period. The text of the abstract could not be recovered for the remaining 263 dissertations. The advisor and department of each dissertation are included as metadata as well as the year of each publication. The abstracts average 181 words in length after tokenization, case-folding, and removal of common stop words and very rare terms (occurring in fewer than five dissertations). The total vocabulary contains 20,961 word types.

These words serve as the input to our models, from which we derive scores of departmental similarity based on the text of each department's dissertations. We initially constructed two models, each representing a common approach to textual similarity in the literature. The first metric is based on **word similarity**, measuring the overlap of words. The second is **topic similarity**, in which we measure similarity in a lower dimensional space of inferred topics.

TF-IDF Word Similarity

We can compute the **word similarity** of departments as the cosine similarity of TF-IDF vectors representing each department, a standard approach used in information retrieval [41]. Each component i of the vector for a department v_D is computed by multiplying the number of times term i occurs in the dissertations from that department (TF) by the inverse document frequency (IDF), computed as $\log(N/df_i)$ where N is the number of dissertations in the dataset and df_i is the number of dissertations that contain the term i. We define the word similarity of two departments D_1 and D_2 as the cosine of the angle between their corresponding TF-IDF vectors v:

$$\cos(v_{D_1}, v_{D_2}) = \frac{v_{D_1} \cdot v_{D_2}}{\|v_{D_1}\| \|v_{D_2}\|}$$

LDA Topic Similarity

While TF-IDF is effective for scoring similarity for documents that use exactly identical words, it cannot assign a high score to the shared use of related terms (e.g., "heat" and "thermodynamics") because each term is represented as its own dimension in the vector space. To address term sparsity issues, we apply latent Dirichlet allocation (LDA) [4] to infer latent topics in the corpus, and represent documents as a lower-dimensional distribution over the topics.

We compute the **topic similarity** of two departments D_1 and D_2 as the cosine similarity of their expected distribution over the topics θ_d learned by LDA. This expectation is the average distribution over latent topics for dissertations in that department, and is computed simply as $\mathbb{E}[\theta_D] = \frac{1}{|D|} \sum_{d \in D} \theta_d$.

Accounting for Time

In both of the models above, we quantify the similarity of departments over time by computing a time-aware signature vector. To compute the vector for a department D within a year y, we sum across all dissertations in D either in the year y or in the preceding two years $y-1$ and $y-2$, weighting the current year by $\frac{1}{2}$, the preceding year by $\frac{1}{3}$ and the remaining year by $\frac{1}{6}$. The extra years are included in the signature to reduce sparsity and account for the influence of a student's work prior to completing a dissertation.

Visualizations: Landscape, Department & Thesis Views

The first visualization we created is the *Landscape View* (Figures 1 & 2). The intention of the view was to reveal global patterns of change in department's topical compositions. We encode academic departments as circles, with areas proportional to the number of dissertations filed in a given year. Distance between circles encodes one of the similarity measures, subject to PCA projection. We ensured visual stability by limiting the amount of movement between adjacent years under the projection. Time is controlled by a slider bar that enables analysts to view an animation of temporal changes or immediately access a specific year.

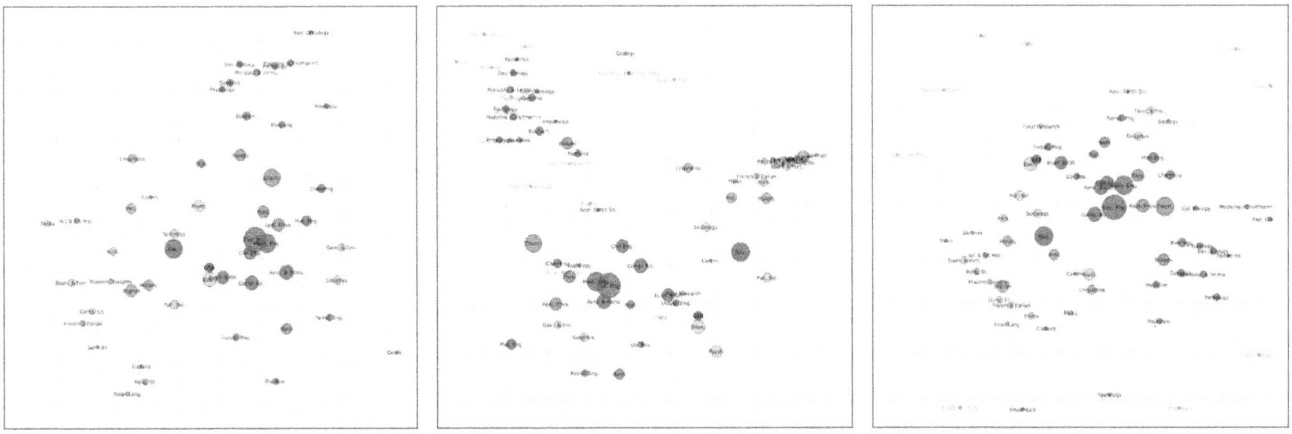

Figure 2. Departmental relationships seen in Landscape View. From left to right: (a) TF.IDF similarity, (b) LDA topic similarity, and (c) Department mixture proportions. These overviews seem plausible, but each makes different predictions and offers little guidance in choosing a model.

Consider the landscapes in Figure 2. Word similarity suggests a relatively uniform landscape, while topic similarity predicts tight overlap of research topics in Medicine (purple) and Humanities (orange) with a relative diverse set of topics in Engineering (blue) and Sciences (green). Which measure best characterizes the university's research output? Without an interactive validation mechanism or an external ground truth, we were left with no way to choose between the similarity measures, nor to trust that the projection faithfully represents the similarity scores derived from each model. The social scientists were unable to confirm whether the observations (in any of the views) correspond to interdisciplinary work, nor to gain insight about the nature of potential collaborations.

In response to these issues of trust, we designed the *Department View* to focus on a single department at a time. This view explicitly shows the distance from a focused department to every other department (i.e., a single row in the similarity matrix). Similarities are encoded as radial distances from the focused department at the center of the display. The remaining departments are arranged around the circle, first grouped by school, then alphabetically within school. A circular representation was chosen to avoid a false impression of rank-ordering among departments and to fit in a single display without scrolling. By restricting the data visible at a single time, the department view avoids projection artifacts.

This view enabled our collaborators to observe expected patterns (e.g., connections between economics and business) and discover surprises. For example, contrary to their expectations, they found that statistics and computer science were not becoming consistently more similar: indeed, they were most similar in 1999. This surprise suggests the need for an even deeper level of verification: to examine the dissertations that contribute to the high (or low) similarity scores of two departments in a given year.

The department view also reveals peculiarities in the underlying models. Figure 3 centers on English, and corresponds to the landscape view in Figure 2(b). This figure immediately suggests a fundamental issue in the topic similarity score derived from latent topic models: how to appropriately select

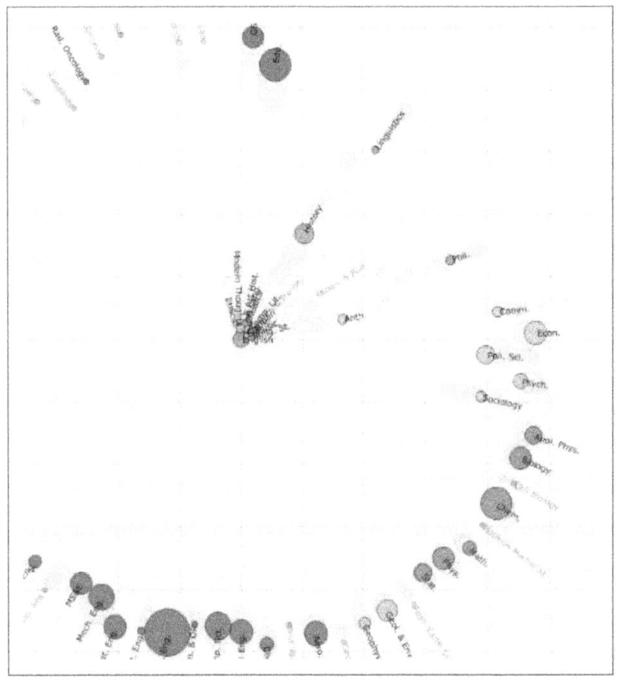

Figure 3. Department View using LDA topic similarity, focused on the English department. While the overview (Fig. 2(b)) seems plausible, we now see that the humanities have been clustered far too aggressively.

the number of topics K used to model the corpus. For the model in Figure 3, we chose the topic count that maximizes the perplexity of held-out data—the technique most commonly used to select the number of topics. However, the visualization demonstrates that the model clearly has too few topics to adequately describe variation within the humanities. A larger number of topics may mitigate this effect, but we lack data-driven metrics for making a principled selection.

As a result, we added the *Thesis View* (Figure 4) to support validation and exploration of observed similarity scores. The thesis view is presented in response to a click on the centered department in the department view. Every thesis from

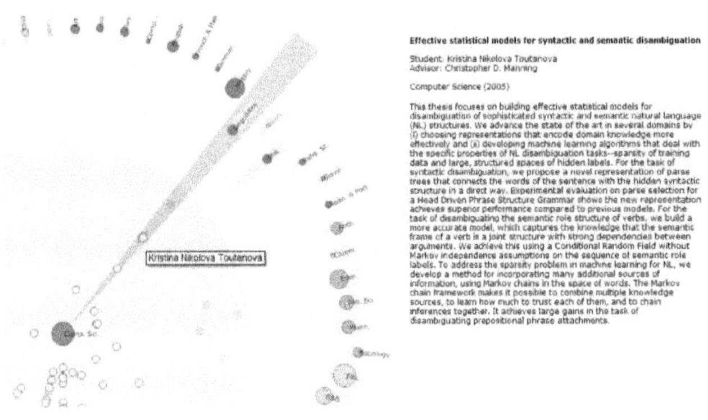

Figure 4. The Thesis View shows individual dissertations as small circles placed between the focus department and the next most similar department. Reading the original text of the dissertation enables experts to evaluate observed dept-dept similarities, and confirm the placement of three computational linguistics Ph.D.s that graduated in 2005.

the focused department, as well as the most similar theses from other departments, are added to the visualization within a concentric circle between the focus and the other departments. The angular position of a thesis aligns with the most similar department, excluding the focus; the radial position is a function of the ratio of the dissertation's similarity to those two departments. This encoding provides a simple means to note theses that might connect two departments.

Upon mouse-over, the text of the thesis abstract is shown, enabling analysts to read the source text and judge whether the two departments are sensible anchors for the dissertation. This view enables users to explore the relationships between departments at a fine-grained level, providing texture and context to the observed department-level similarities.

Evaluating the Models

To assess our modeling options, we conducted an expert review. We invited academic domain experts (professors and graduate students) to use the interface and recorded their responses. We found that the visualizations benefit from being *model agnostic*: they display departmental similarity, but otherwise are not constrained by other modeling assumptions. Thus, we can use the visualizations to compare the results of different modeling approaches.

Using the landscape view, participants could not fully justify their observations. Many potentially interesting patterns turned out to be projection artifacts, ultimately leading us to remove this view from the tool. Using the department view, participants were adept at noting similarities that violated their assumptions. Both word and topic similarity led to many such instances. Rather than identify a preferred model, we became increasingly skeptical of both approaches.

The successes and mistakes of each similarity model were revealed by the thesis view through the (mis)placement of individual dissertations with respect to the other departments. Participants were able to discover systematic errors made by topic similarity. For instance, several biology dissertations were spuriously linked to computer science and vice versa because of the existence of a computational biology topic that connected the dissertations, even though many dissertations made use of only the biology or computer science words in the computational biology topic. The TF-IDF measure used for word similarity, on the other hand, often assigned documents very high similarity to departments that happened to heavily use a common rare word.

We also used our own domain knowledge to examine the relationships between dissertations and departments. The placement of three computational linguistics Ph.D.s that graduated in 2005 provides an illustrative example (Figure 4). We expected these dissertations to fall on the line between computer science and linguistics. In the latent topic model's similarity function, two of them did, but several unrelated dissertations were deemed substantially more similar to linguistics than the computational linguistics dissertations. We discovered this was due to a shared latent topic that covered both linguistics and information retrieval. While the TF-IDF model succeeds in placing these three dissertations between computer science and linguistics, it failed to accurately describe the relationship between the two departments: a year with only one dissertation (2000) is the year of maximum similarity even though the dissertation is not computational in nature.

Revising the Model: Department Mixture Proportions

The high frequency of "mismatch" between experts' mental models and our similarity scores led us to revisit our modeling assumptions. First, we wished to avoid arbitrary parameters such as the number of latent topics (K) and realized that we might better exploit the available metadata. Second, we had implicitly assumed that our similarity measure should be symmetric, as required by the mathematical definition of a metric. However, this need not be true of analysts' views of departmental similarity. In response, we formulated a novel similarity score that we call the **department mixture proportion**. This measure uses a supervised machine learning approach to directly represent the contents of each department, our primary unit of analysis. We estimate the similarity of two departments by measuring how often dissertations from one department "borrow" words from another.

To compute the department mixture proportion, we use the machinery of Labeled LDA[1] [37], which models each document as a latent mixture of known labels. In a two-step process, we first learn latent topics using the departments associated with each dissertation as labels. In a second inference step where labels are subsequently ignored, we infer department mixtures for each thesis.

We train a Labeled LDA model using the departmental affiliations of dissertation committee members as labels. Thus the departments themselves are the "topics". Each dissertation may have one or more labels. During training, we learn both the per-topic term distributions (β_k) and initial label-based topic mixtures (θ'_d). In Labeled LDA, topical term distributions are allowed to take on any word, as in normal LDA training. However, per-document topic mixtures are restricted to only labels associated with the document. For example, the

[1]Our Labeled LDA implementation is available online at `http://nlp.stanford.edu/software/tmt/`

topic mixture for a thesis labeled "Biology" and "Chemistry" is zero for all topics except the two labeled departments.

Using the learned topical term distributions (β_k), we next ignore all labels and perform standard LDA inference on each dissertation (as if we were seeing it for the first time). This results in a new topic mixture (θ_d) in which the dissertation can "borrow" words from *any* department, not just the ones it was initially labeled with. We average the distributions for all dissertations in a given department to construct the department mixture proportion. The values of this averaged distribution are the desired similarity scores.

In short, we first determine the term distributions of each department, and then use these distributions to answer a simple hypothetical: if we let each dissertation borrow words from *any* department, what mixture of departments would it use? The resulting mixture proportion tells us the fraction of words in each dissertation that can be best attributed to each department. The similarity of a department D_1 to D_2 is now simply the value at index D_2 in θ_{D_1}. Unlike the previous measures, this score need not be symmetric. For instance, Music may borrow more words from Computer Science than Computer Science does from Music, which indeed we find in several years where computational music Ph.D. dissertations are filed. We find that this new similarity score ameliorates many of the "mismatches" identified by our earlier expert review.

System Deployment & Use

We first deployed the Dissertation Browser[2] outside of our research team in March 2010, as part of a presentation to the University President's Office. For convenience, we launched the tool on the web, where it remained available after the presentation. Our collaborators found the primary value of the tool to be in validation and communication. They noted the start of a large-scale Biophysics project connecting Biology and Physics in 2006. Several finer stories were discovered that exhibit interdisciplinary collaboration and knowledge transfer. In one case, the visualization demonstrated a strong connection between two departments driven by a small number of individuals centered around the Magnetic Resonance Systems Research Lab. This lab graduated a series of Electrical Engineering Ph.D. students in the 1990's who worked on EE-aspects of various MRI techniques. Around the same time, a hire in Radiology held a courtesy appointment in Electrical Engineering. For the next decade, the influence of these groups strongly connected the two departments until both eventually moved onto other research areas.

As we made no effort to publicize our tool, we were taken by surprise when the system gained public attention from users on the web (e.g., in hundreds of Twitter comments) beginning in December 2010. The majority of tweets expressed interest or enjoyment in the use of the tool (*"geeky and cool"*, *"i could spend hours on this site"*). Several pointed to specific patterns (*"In 2003 Edu was closer to PoliSci than English"*, *"Watch Psychology and Education PhD theses doing the hokey-pokey over time"*). Later, over a dozen science and tech blogs (including Hacker News, Discover Magazine and Flowing Data) posted articles about the tool. We observed commenters interpreting specific patterns of interest: *"I was not surprised to see the link between Computer Science and Philosophy. Heartened by a slight connection between dissertations in Computer Science and Genetics."* and *"Aha, so there are terms that are common between civil engineering and biology but not between civil engineering and religion or art history."* We also observed issues of trust: *"[browser] thinks neurobiology is closer to electrical engineering than to biology. It is easy to see why that might be so based on key vocabulary terms (voltage, potential, conductance, ion), but ..."*. From these and similar comments, we note that the ability to transition between levels of model abstractions enabled users to interrogate the model and assess unexpected correlations.

[2]The Stanford Dissertation Browser is available online at `http://vis.stanford.edu/dissertations/`

DESIGN GUIDELINES

To facilitate interpretation and trust in model-driven visualizations, we distilled a set of guidelines from both our experiences and literature review. Along with illustrative examples, we now present process-oriented recommendations for model and visualization design:

- **Align** the analysis tasks, visual encodings, and modeling decisions along appropriate *units of analysis*.
- **Verify** the modeling decisions: ensure that model output accurately conveys concepts relevant to analysis.
- Provide interactions to **modify** a model during analysis.
- **Progressively disclose** data to support reasoning at multiple levels of model abstraction.

Model Alignment

We use the term *alignment* to describe the correspondences among modeling decisions, visual encoding decisions, and an analyst's tasks, expectations, and background knowledge. We consider a visual analysis system to be well-aligned when the details surfaced in the visualization are responsive to analyst's tasks, while minimizing extraneous information that might confuse or hamper interpretation. Alignment does not result from interface design alone; both the visualization and model may require iterative design.

Identify Units of Analysis

Alignment requires a sufficient understanding of users, their tasks, and the context of use. Such *domain characterization* [33] relies on methods familiar to HCI researchers (e.g., interviews, contextual inquiry, participant-observation). However, these techniques may be foreign to model designers in fields such as statistics or machine learning. To facilitate communication among stakeholders with varying backgrounds, we found it useful to frame insights in terms of *units of analysis*: entities, relationships, and concepts about which the analysts reason. These units serve as a resource for evaluating models and their fitness to the analysis task.

With the Dissertation Browser, we engaged in participatory design meetings with our collaborators to determine the units of analysis. This process led us to realize that changes in inter-department similarity could provide answers to the social scientists' research questions. In turn, we were led to depict similarity data in the visualization and avoid the potentially confusing route of trying to convey topical composition. In later iterations we further aligned our model with this unit of analysis: we reduced the number of abstractions by computing similarity directly as the department mixture proportion. This eliminated the need to set model parameters such as the number of topics and freed analysts from unnecessarily assessing and classifying latent topics.

Assess Reliability vs. Relevance Tradeoffs

Selecting the appropriate units of analysis often involves a balance between how reliably a concept can be identified, and how relevant the concept is to the analysis task. The final units of analysis reflected in a visual analysis tool may result from a compromise: the units should correspond to the analysts' questions but must also be practical to model.

In the Dissertation Browser, we quantify "units of research" as academic departments. While our social science collaborators would ideally like to assess research at a finer granularity (e.g., trends in microbiology or evolutionary systems), we lacked reliable means to quantify such units of research. LDA models have the potential to discover unnamed research activities, but in our case collapsed all of the humanities into a single topic. Similarly, while investigating historical trends using LDA models, Hall et al. [25] found that only 36 out of 100 automatically inferred "topics" were judged relevant by experts in the field. Named organizations such as departments can be identified reliably, and correspond to concepts that the analysts can comprehend and verify during analysis. More generally, we recommend leveraging available metadata to provide reliable and relevant units of analysis.

Enumerate Model Assumptions

To assess alignment, it is valuable to explicitly enumerate the assumptions implicit in a modeling approach. Common assumptions in quantitative statistics are that data values are independently and identically distributed according to a known probability distribution (e.g., Gaussian, Poisson, etc.). Within text processing, many models are predicated on a bag-of-words assumption that ignores word ordering and relations. Understanding such assumptions is important for determining if a model is appropriate for the given units of analysis. Enumerating assumptions also provides a resource for design, suggesting potential starting points for alternative models.

While designing the Dissertation Browser, we assumed that similarity must be based on a proper metric, and hence symmetric. Once we identified this assumption, it freed us to consider the possibility of asymmetric similarity scores, ultimately leading to a "word borrowing" model based on the department mixture proportion. In Review Spotlight [56], the mismatch between the bag-of-words model and sentiment perception was resolved by making adjective-noun pairs the units of analysis, yielding improved performance.

Model Verification

Once candidate models have been identified, we need to assess how well they fit an analyst's goals. An analytical abstraction based on identified units of analysis can often be realized by different modeling approaches. Verification may require collaboration among designers and domain experts to assess model quality and validate model output.

Assess Model Fit

In domains with objective accuracies, one can take a quantitative approach to verification: common evaluation measures include precision (e.g., comparing model output to known ground truth data) or internal goodness-of-fit statistics (e.g., information criteria such as AIC and BIC). However, one should ensure that such metrics correlate with analysis goals. Domains such as text interpretation may be subjective in nature and so difficult to quantify. For LDA topic models, quality is typically measured in perplexity, which describes the "distinctiveness" of the learned topics. While perplexity is a sensible measure of encoding quality in an information-theoretic sense, in our case it did not correspond to our task: identifying concepts representing coherent "research topics."

Conduct End-User Evaluations

HCI evaluation methods can enable verification. For example, task-based user studies or real-world deployments may be used to assess how well a system aids analysis tasks. Walkthroughs with representative users can help designers gauge analysts' familiarity with a presented analytical abstraction. A potential trade-off is that if analysts don't fully understand the model (e.g., higher gulf of evaluation) but gain more useful and verifiable insights, a less familiar model may be preferred. In our case, we found that expert review was a relatively lightweight means to assess model quality by cataloging instances in which users believed the model to be in error. These "mismatches" became points of comparison across modeling options. An interesting challenge for future work is to better correlate the results of user-centered evaluation with less costly model quality metrics: Can we identify or invent better metrics that reliably accelerate verification?

Enable Comparison via Model-Agnostic Views

Another method for verification is triangulation: comparing the output of multiple models or parameter settings and gauging agreement. To enable cross-model comparison in a model-driven visualization, the visualized units of analysis should be stable across modeling choices. We use the term *model-agnostic views* to describe visualizations that use a single analytical abstraction to compare the output of various underlying modeling options. To be clear, such views rely on a stable abstraction; what they are "agnostic" to is the inferential machinery of the models. For example, the Dissertation Browser uses inter-department similarity as the shared unit of analysis, enabling comparisons with any model that can generate suitable similarity scores. Interactive comparison of parameter settings and modeling options can be invaluable to model designers when assessing choices. Providing similar facilities to end users is also helpful, but might best be treated as a "last resort" when an accurate, well-aligned model can't be found.

Model Modification

Even with careful attention to alignment and verification, a model's output may be incorrect or incomplete. Whether due to limited training data or inaccurate yet pragmatic modeling assumptions, analysts often require mechanisms to modify a model abstraction over time. The approaches listed below constitute ways to interactively improve model alignment.

Modify Model Parameters

A simple form of model modification is to adjust free parameters. Examples include setting the number of topics in an LDA model or adjusting threshold values for data inclusion (e.g., weights on edges in a social network). We have found that this ability is critical for early stage model exploration. While ideally this would not be necessary in a final analysis tool, in practice one rarely finds a "perfect" model. Consequently it is important for analysts to be able to assess various parameterizations. One challenge is to support real-time interactivity, as changes of model parameters may require expensive re-fitting or other operations. For such cases, visual analysis tools might provide facilities for scheduling offline, batch computation across a range of parameter values.

Add (Labeled) Training Data

Another approach to model modification is to introduce additional training data. For example, an analyst might add new text documents labeled as positive or negative examples of a category. In the context of the Dissertation Browser, new inference procedures might incorporate expert annotations into the model fitting process. To avoid costly re-fitting, designers might leverage techniques for online, interactive machine learning [1, 20]. An important research challenge is to design reflective systems that elicit the most useful training data from users, perhaps using active learning methods [15].

Adjust The Model Structure

Analysts familiar with a modeling method may wish to directly edit the model structure. An analyst might add new latent variables or conditional dependencies within a Bayesian network, or add a new factor to a generalized linear model. In this case, the model itself becomes a unit of analysis, requiring that users possess sufficient modeling expertise.

Allow Manual Override

An alternative approach is to bypass the modeling machinery entirely to override model output. For example, to correct modeling mistakes or impose relations outside the scope of the model or source data. Analysts may wish to delete or modify inferred LDA topics. Hall et al. [25] removed 64 topics and inserted 10 hand-crafted topics in order to complete their investigation; Talley et al. [46] removed poor topics and flagged questionable topics in their visualization. Similar to model agnostic views, manual override benefits from an analytical abstraction decoupled from any inferential machinery. However, overrides may prove problematic with dynamic data: should overrides persist when modeling incoming data?

Progressive Disclosure

By abstracting source data, models can improve scalability, surface higher-order patterns and suppress noise. However, they might also discard relevant information. To compensate, model-driven visualizations can enable analysts to shift among levels of abstraction on-demand. *Progressive disclosure* is the strategy of drilling down from high-level overview, to intermediate abstractions, and eventually to the underlying data itself. Progressive disclosure balances the benefit of large-scale discovery using models with the need for verification to gain trust. A tool can support reasoning and improve interpretation by displaying the right level of detail when it is needed. The critical concerns are that detailed data (1) is revealed on an as-needed basis to avoid clutter and (2) highlights the connections between levels of abstraction to aid verification. We identify two primary interaction techniques for achieving progressive disclosure: semantic zooming [3] and linked highlighting (a.k.a. "brushing and linking") [2].

Disclosure via Semantic Zooming

Semantic zooming changes the visible properties of an information space based on the current "zoom" level, exposing additional detail within an existing view. Using semantic zooming for progressive disclosure entails incorporating elements across different levels of modeling abstraction. The Dissertation Browser uses semantic zooming to move from department view to thesis view: individual dissertations are visualized in relation to the higher-level departmental structure. We hypothesize that semantic zooming is particularly effective for facilitating interpretation if it can show the next level of abstraction within the context of an established abstraction. Semantic zooming relies on a hierarchical organization of relevant model abstractions or metadata.

Disclosure via Linked Highlighting

Another option is to present different levels of analytical abstraction in distinct visualizations. Linked selection and highlighting between views can then enable investigation: given distinct visualizations at different levels of abstraction (e.g., a network of extracted entities and a document viewer) highlight the cross-abstraction connections (e.g., the occurrences of the entity in the document). Perhaps the simplest case is showing details-on-demand. The Dissertation Browser shows the source text of a dissertation abstract in a separate panel when a thesis is selected. Linked highlighting is desirable if the different levels of abstraction are more effectively presented using disjoint visual encodings — that is, when combining levels via semantic zooming is either impossible or inadvisable. When faced with non-hierarchical relations or simultaneous inspection of three or more levels of abstraction, linked views are likely to be preferable to semantic zooming.

Choosing Levels of Analytical Abstraction

A primary design challenge for progressive disclosure is to select the proper levels of abstraction. We consider this an instance of (vertical) model alignment that depends on the identified units of analysis. Another outstanding question is how "deep" progressive disclosure should go. For example, comments from Dissertation Browser users suggest that our design would be further improved by incorporating word-level details to aid verification of thesis-level similarities (e.g., what words does Civil Engineering "borrow" from Biology?). In most instances, we find that progressive disclosure should terminate in the original source data, enabling analysts to connect model abstractions to the raw input.

CONCLUSION

Text visualization research has traditionally focused on improving the effectiveness of a visualization without considering how the underlying model itself affects or can be adapted towards an analysis goal. This oversight constitutes a limitation in the face of big data applications and the growing need for models. Moreover, machine learning research has normally been content with formal measures of model quality, with less emphasis on user- and task-centric evaluations, even though the limited effectiveness of formal measures has become increasingly evident. In this paper, we proposed *interpretation* and *trust* as criteria to guide the design of model-driven visualizations. We described the design of the Stanford Dissertation Browser, and demonstrated how a novel "word-borrowing" similarity measure arose through an iterative design process that considered task analysis, visualization design, and modeling choices in a unified fashion. We contributed strategies (*align*, *verify*, *modify*, *progressive disclosure*) as practical aids for designers to achieve interpretability and trustworthiness in visual analysis tools. With these strategies, HCI methods can play an important role in the formulation of new interfaces, algorithms, evaluations, and models to enable productive analytic reasoning with massive data sets.

ACKNOWLEDGMENTS

This research was part of the Mimir Project, and was supported by the President's Office at Stanford, the Boeing Company and National Science Foundation Grant No. 0835614.

REFERENCES

1. Amershi, S., Lee, B., Kapoor, A., Mahajan, R., and Christian, B. CueT: human-guided fast and accurate network alarm triage. In *CHI* (2011), 157–166.
2. Becker, R. A., and Cleveland, W. S. Brushing scatterplots. *Technometrics 29* (1987), 127–142.
3. Bederson, B. B., and Hollan, J. D. Pad++: a zooming graphical interface for exploring alternate interface physics. In *UIST* (1994), 17–26.
4. Blei, D. M., Ng, A. Y., and Jordan, M. I. Latent Dirichlet allocation. *J Machine Learning Research 3* (2003), 993–1022.
5. Bollen, J., Pepe, A., and Mao, H. Modeling public mood and emotion: Twitter sentiment and socio-economic phenomena. In *ICWSM* (2011).
6. Börner, K., Maru, J. T., and Goldstone, R. L. The simultaneous evolution of author and paper networks. *PNAS 101* (2004), 5266–5273.
7. Boyack, K. W., Börner, K., and Klavans, R. Mapping the structure and evolution of chemistry research. In *ISSI* (2007), 112–123.
8. Boyack, K. W., Mane, K., and Börner, K. Mapping Medline papers, genes, and proteins related to melanoma research. In *InfoVis* (2004), 965–971.
9. Boyack, K. W., Newman, D., Duhon, R. J., Klavans, R., Patek, M., Biberstine, J. R., Schijvenaars, B., Skupin, A., Ma, N., and Börner, K. Clustering more than two million biomedical publications: Comparing the accuracies of nine text-based similarity approaches. *PLoS ONE 6*, 3 (2011), e18029.
10. Boyack, K. W., Wylie, B. N., and Davidson, G. S. Domain visualization using VxInsight for science and technology management. *JIS&T 53* (2002), 764–774.
11. Cao, N., Sun, J., Lin, Y.-R., Gotz, D., Liu, S., and Qu, H. FacetAtlas: Multifaceted visualization for rich text corpora. In *InfoVis* (2010), 1172–1181.
12. Chang, J., Boyd-Graber, J., Wang, C., Gerrish, S., and Blei, D. M. Reading tea leaves: How humans interpret topic models. In *NIPS* (2009), 288–296.
13. Chen, C. CiteSpace II: Detecting and visualizing emerging trends and transient patterns in scientific literature. *JIS&T 57* (2006), 359–377.
14. Clough, P. D., and Sen, B. A. Evaluating tagclouds for health-related information research. In *Health Info Management Research* (2008).
15. Cohn, D. A., Ghahramani, Z., and Jordan, M. I. Active learning with statistical models. *J Artificial Intelligence Research 4* (1996), 129–145.
16. Collins, C., Carpendale, S., and Penn, G. DocuBurst: Visualizing document content using language structure. *Computer Graphics Forum 28*, 3 (2009).
17. Collins, C., Viégas, F. B., and Wattenberg, M. Parallel tag clouds to explore and analyze faceted text corpora. In *VAST* (2009), 91–98.
18. Crossno, P., Dunlavy, D., and Shead, T. LSAView: A tool for visual exploration of latent semantic modeling. In *VAST* (2009), 83–90.
19. Cutting, D. R., Karger, D. R., and Pedersen, J. O. Constant interaction-time scatter/gather browsing of very large document collections. In *SIGIR* (1993).
20. Fails, J. A., and Olsen, Jr., D. R. Interactive machine learning. In *IUI* (2003).
21. Finkel, J. R., Grenager, T., and Manning, C. D. Incorporating non-local information into information extraction systems by Gibbs sampling. In *ACL* (2005), 363–370.
22. Gardner, M. J., Lutes, J., Lund, J., Hansen, J., Walker, D., Ringger, E., and Seppi, K. The Topic Browser: An interactive tool for browsing topic models. In *NIPS (Workshop on Challenges of Data Vis)* (2010).
23. Gretarsson, B., O'Donovan, J., Bostandjiev, S., Llerer, T. H., Asuncion, A., Newman, D., and Smyth, P. TopicNets: Visual analysis of large text corpora with topic modeling. *Trans on Intelligent System and Technology 3*, 2 (2011).
24. Griffiths, T. L., and Steyvers, M. Finding scientific topics. *PNAS 101* (2004).
25. Hall, D., Jurafsky, D., and Manning, C. D. Studying the history of ideas using topic models. In *EMNLP* (2008), 363–371.
26. Hearst, M. A., and Pedersen, J. O. Reexamining the cluster hypothesis: Scatter/Gather on retrieval results. In *SIGIR* (1996), 76–84.
27. Hutchins, E. L., Hollan, J. D., and Norman, D. A. Direct manipulation interfaces. *Human-Computer Interaction 1* (1985), 311–338.
28. Ke, W., Sugimoto, C. R., and Mostafa, J. Dynamicity vs. effectiveness: studying online clustering for scatter/gather. In *SIGIR* (2009), 19–26.
29. Landauer, T. K., Laham, D., and Derr, M. From paragraph to graph: Latent semantic analysis for information visualization. *PNAS 101* (2004), 5214–5219.
30. Lin, X. Visualization for the document space. In *Vis* (1992), 274–281.
31. Luhn, H. P. The automatic creation of literature abstracts. *IBM J of Research and Development 2*, 2 (1958), 159–165.
32. Moya-Anegón, F. d., Vargas-Quesada, B., Chinchilla-Rodríguez, Z., Corera-Álvarez, E., Munoz-Fernández, F. J., and Herrero-Solana, V. Visualizing the marrow of science. *JIS&T 58*, 14 (2007), 2167–2179.
33. Munzner, T. A nested process model for visualization design and validation. In *InfoVis* (2009), 921–928.
34. Newman, D., Asuncion, A., Chemudugunta, C., Kumar, V., Smyth, P., and Steyvers, M. Exploring large document collections using statistical topic models. In *KDD (Demo)* (2006).
35. Palantir technologies. `http://www.palantirtech.com`, 2011.
36. Procter, R., Vis, F., Voss, A., Cantijoch, M., Manykhina, Y., Thelwall, M., Gibson, R., Hudson-Smith, A., and Gray, S. Riot rumours: how misinformation spread on Twitter during a time of crisis. `http://www.guardian.co.uk/news/datablog/2011/dec/08/twitter-riots-interactive`, 2011.
37. Ramage, D., Hall, D., Nallapati, R., and Manning, C. D. Labeled LDA: A supervised topic model for credit attribution in multi-label corpora. In *EMNLP* (2009), 248–256.
38. Risch, J. S., Rex, D. B., Dowson, S. T., Walters, T. B., May, R. A., and Moon, B. D. The STARLIGHT information visualization system. In *InfoVis* (1997).
39. Rivadeneira, A. W., Gruen, D. M., Muller, M. J., and Millen, D. R. Getting our head in the clouds: toward evaluation studies of tagclouds. In *CHI* (2007).
40. Rosvall, M., and Bergstrom, C. T. Maps of random walks on complex networks reveal community structure. *PNAS 105* (2008), 1118–1123.
41. Salton, G., Wong, A., and Yang, C. A vector space model for automatic indexing. *Communications of the ACM 18*, 11 (1975), 613–620.
42. Sandstrom, P. Scholarly communication as a socioecological system. *Scientometrics 51*, 3 (2002), 573–605.
43. Sinclair, J., and Cardew-Hall, M. The folksonomy tag cloud: when is it useful? *J of Information Science 34* (2008), 15–29.
44. Smalheiser, N. R., Torvik, V. I., and Zhou, W. Arrowsmith two-node search interface: a tutorial on finding meaningful links between two disparate sets of articles in MEDLINE. *Computer M&P in Biomedicine 94*, 2 (2009), 190–197.
45. Stasko, J., Görg, C., Liu, Z., and Singhal, K. Jigsaw: Supporting investigative analysis through interactive visualization. In *VAST* (2007), 131–138.
46. Talley, E. M., Newman, D., Mimno, D., Herr, B. W., Wallach, H. M., Burns, G. A. P. C., Leenders, A. G. M., and McCallum, A. Database of NIH grants using machine-learned categories and graphical clustering. *Nature Methods 8*, 6 (2011).
47. Thomas, J., and Cook, K., Eds. *Illuminating the Path: The Research and Development Agenda for Visual Analytics*. IEEE Press, 2005.
48. Turney, P. D. Learning algorithms for keyphrase extraction. *Info Retr 2*, 4 (2000).
49. van Ham, F., Wattenberg, M., and Viegas, F. B. Mapping text with phrase nets. In *InfoVis* (2009), 1169–1176.
50. Viégas, F. B., and Wattenberg, M. TIMELINES: Tag clouds and the case for vernacular visualization. *Interactions 15* (2008), 49–52.
51. Wanner, F., Rohrdantz, C., Mansmann, F., Oelke, D., and Keim, D. A. Visual sentiment analysis of RSS news feeds featuring the US presidential election in 2008. In *VISSW* (2009).
52. Wattenberg, M., and Viégas, F. B. The Word Tree, an interactive visual concordance. In *InfoVis* (2008), 1221–1228.
53. Wei, F., Liu, S., Song, Y., Pan, S., Zhou, M. X., Qian, W., Shi, L., Tan, L., and Zhang, Q. TIARA: a visual exploratory text analytic system. In *KDD* (2010).
54. Wise, J., Thomas, J., Pennock, K., Lantrip, D., Pottier, M., Schur, A., and Crow, V. Visualizing the non-visual: spatial analysis and interaction with information from text documents. In *InfoVis* (1995), 51–58.
55. Wong, P. C., Hetzler, B., Posse, C., Whiting, M., Havre, S., Cramer, N., Shah, A., Singhal, M., Turner, A., and Thomas, J. IN-SPIRE contest entry. In *InfoVis* (2004).
56. Yatani, K., Novati, M., Trusty, A., and Truong, K. N. Review Spotlight: a user interface for summarizing user-generated reviews using adjective-noun word pairs. In *CHI* (2011), 1541–1550.

V-Model: A New Innovative Model to Chronologically Visualize Narrative Clinical Texts

Heekyong Park
Dept. Biomedical Engineering
College of Medicine
Seoul National University
Seoul, 110-799 KOREA
care01@snu.ac.kr

Jinwook Choi, M.D., Ph.D.
Dept. Biomedical Engineering
College of Medicine
Seoul National University
Seoul, 110-799 KOREA
jinchoi@snu.ac.kr

ABSTRACT
Visualizing narrative medical events into a timeline can have positive effects on clinical environments. However, the characteristics of natural language and medical environments make this representation more difficult. This paper explains the obstacles and suggests a solution called the V-Model. The V-Model is a new innovative time model that was developed to represent chronological narrative events in a medical domain. Forty medical students participated in evaluating this model. The experimental results show the new model successfully solved the modeling requirements and had better usability compared to conventional timeline models. All the participants assessed the new timeline as very useful in effectively understanding a patient's history.

Author Keywords
Timeline; visualization; patient history; natural language; clinical reports.

ACM Classification Keywords
H.5.2 [Information interfaces and presentation]: User Interfaces – Natural language.

INTRODUCTION
A chronological view of a patient's history is very important. In Gill et al. [1], healthcare professionals have (strongly) agreed that the use of a timeline would make clinical audits easier, enhance time efficiency, reduce clinical errors, improve patients' safety and quality of care, and provide other benefits.

A lot of important information is not stored as a database record and can be found only in clinical documents. It would be useful if the information from multiple clinical reports could be integrated on a timeline view. However, this is not a simple task due to the characteristics of natural language. Li and Hripcsack pointed out that diversity, implicitness, granularity, fuzziness and uncertainty, incomplete-interval, and other problems are obstacles in processing the temporal information of narrative clinical documents[2]. The same problems arise when dealing with a narrative patient history on a timeline.

There have been efforts to visualize patient clinical history using timelines. Various types of clinical information (i.e., raw clinical data, abstracted data, and natural language text) have been utilized in previous works. Cousins and Kahn [3] first introduced the concept of a timeline in a medical domain. They developed time line browser, an interactive environment for displaying and manipulating sets of timelines. Plaisant et al. [4, 5] developed LifeLines that reorganize and visualize patient history to enhance navigation and analysis. Personal histories, medical records, and other types of biological data were displayed. Bui et al. [6, 7] introduced the TimeLine system with the goal to provide a generalized methodology that could be applied to tailor UIs for different medical problems. These studies dealt with the visualization of raw clinical time-oriented data. The Knave-II system offered timeline visualization on both raw data and multiple levels of concepts abstracted from the data. By using knowledge based reasoning, abstracted data were derived from selected time-oriented data [8-10]. Little work has been done on displaying narrative text in a timeline. Bashyam et al.[11] designed and implemented a problem-oriented medical record (POMR) view of information extracted from clinical documents. However, problem centric visualization may exclude some useful information contained in clinical documents (e.g., narrative descriptions about situations that caused problematic symptoms). Jung et al.[12] made a generic approach to construct timelines of narrative clinical records but focused on explicit temporal expressions and present tense sentences only.

Difficulties in representing temporal information and its context are the main obstacles in developing a successful timeline system for narrative clinical documents. Solutions for these issues of representation have been suggested. In regards to granularity issues, LifeLines suggested a zooming function [4, 5] and KNAVE-II proposed a content-based zoom method [10]. Implicit problems were solved by graphical variations of point/interval notation. TVQL modeled ambiguous temporal relationships with sliders, boxes, and line segments[13]. Combi et al.[14] defined

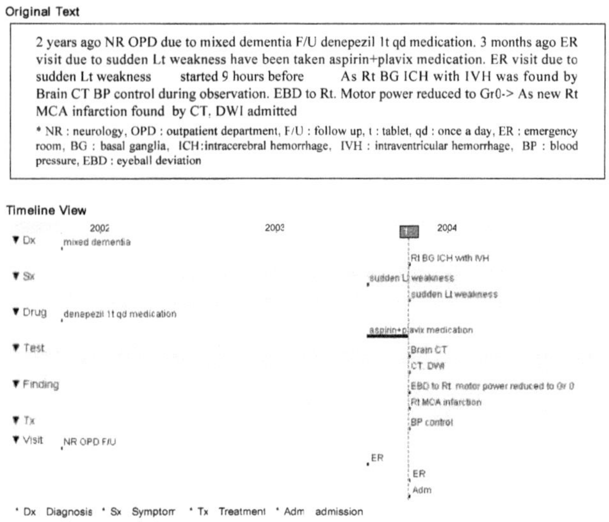

Figure 1. Difficulties in visualizing clinical documents on conventional timeline (for explanation purpose, we represented all unclear events as a point).

graphical symbols that represented starting instant, ending instant, minimum duration, and maximum duration so that undefined durations could be represented. Causality relation is one of the key features to understanding clinical context in its original description. Hallet [15] proposed causality relation to be selectively displayed in visual navigator, using color-coded arrows.

Previous works have suggested various solutions to chronologically represent patient histories. Their ideas were based on representing point/interval events as a point and time span proportion as time length in timeline space. In this paper, we call this type of approach the conventional method, and propose a new chronological visualization frame.

In the following sections, we define four problems in representing a narrative patient history in a timeline, and propose the V-Model as a chronological context representation model for narrative clinical documents.

METHODS

DERIVATION OF VISUALIZATION PROBLEMS FROM CLINICAL TEXTS

Fifty discharge summaries from Seoul National University Hospital were randomly selected and analyzed. We reviewed the documents to derive difficulties in mapping narrative clinical events into a conventional timeline. The problems can be summarized as causality, non-explicitness, granularity, and reasoning issues. For comparison purposes, we used the view from LifeLines in the following figures, to show examples of conventional timelines.

Causality

Causality is an important feature that helps in understanding clinical situations. However, it is hard to catch causal relationships from a timeline, which simply shows the time span of occurrences. With a timeline, physicians should extrapolate the context using medical knowledge. Sometimes this gets very hard even for physicians. For example, in Figure 1, a CT test was done twice on date T1. The original text describes why each CT test was done. However the conventional timeline represents only temporal occurrences without causal links. From this view, the physician cannot determine which event had caused the patient to receive another CT.

Non-explicitness

Since clinical texts record patients' chief complaints and situations, informal temporal expressions can be found frequently, e.g., "Since this *Korean Thanksgiving Day*, the weakness has gotten worse." The *Korean Thanksgiving Day* is calculated based on the lunar calendar. Therefore, the exact date varies each year. It would be difficult to interpret such kinds of expressions into a Gregorian calendar date. Moreover, especially for Korean women, the expression is not merely temporal information. It also implies the meaning of *after hard working*, which describes the situation that caused the symptom. If this temporal expression is directly converted into a calendar date, one meaningful context would be missed. In this paper, we use *non-explicitness* to refer all conventional temporal expression problems: implicitness, fuzziness and uncertainty, incomplete-interval problem, and omission of temporal expression cases.

Implicit temporal expressions are expressions that are difficult to extrapolate the temporal quantity they originally implied. For instance, "had a drug medication until *recently*" may refer a week ago or a month ago.

Fuzziness and uncertainty are imprecise expressions, such as "one month ago", "2 or 3 days". For example, to represent "seizure restarted *in mid-March*", "mid-March" is converted into a possible time range, e.g., "March 10 to March twenty". Moreover, the range may be different among systems since the possible occurrence range is interpreted based on one's experience. This will increase the confusion in representing such events.

Incomplete-interval events frequently appear in clinical documents. A considerable number of events are written referencing only one of the start, middle, or end time points. For example, only the start time of Glivec medication is reported in "8/7 Glivec 400mg qd restart -> planned short term F/U 8/12 discharge". Representing the Glivec usage interval is difficult since the information on the end point is not available.

Clinical documents tend to be very compact and frequently *omit temporal expressions.* Representing events without temporal expressions is very difficult problem. Only the sequence can be extrapolated, and there is no information on which position and how much space should be skipped to represent them.

Previous suggestions to the above problems were mainly variations of the point/interval notation. However, a timeline view full of such notations would make a patient history view more complex and worse than the original narrative text. Additionally, deciding the possible range requires a wide range of medical knowledge, which is unrealistic. Furthermore, not all events' interval ranges can be solved by domain knowledge.

Medical reports often contain non-temporal terms, which imply *temporal hints*. For example, "post-op (post-operation)" gives a hint that the event happened close to a previous "operation" event. A chief complaint that is followed by hospital visit information can inform that the two events are temporally close events. Although these are not time expressions, it would be useful if these hints can be merged into the timeline, like time information

Granularity

Clinical documents contain temporal expressions written in diverse granularity levels. For instance, "the patient has increased seizure … *since three days ago. One day ago*, increased respiration rate, chest wall retraction, … *Since two hours before*, respiration rate increased, moaning and groaning, so that visited pediatric emergency room (PER)". Current timeline methods represent temporal events in a fixed granularity level. This view causes several problems. Coarser information cannot be represented in a finer granularity view, and finer information can be accessed after doing some more actions like zooming. When there is a long healthy periods among one's medical history (e.g., *94* GB empyema with distal CBD stone-> cholecystectomy with choledocholithotomy done *02`5* HCV related LC dx *02`8* acute cholangitis), the timeline will contain a long blank space, which can cause confusion and unnecessary scrolling.

Reasoning

It is important to capture temporal relationships between clinical events. For example, sensing "duration of fever before admission" is useful in making medical decisions. The sequences of an event are also useful in tracing medical histories. For example, visual disturbance in Figure 2 becomes a chief complaint if it has occurred before the hospital visit. If the visual disturbance occurred during a local NS visit, it is not a chief complaint and may imply the severity of the patient's condition or the fact that it was an emergency situation. Therefore, a timeline should provide sufficient information for temporal reasoning, i.e., quantitative temporal relation (e.g., 3 days before, for 2 weeks, etc) and qualitative temporal relation (e.g., during, before).

However, the temporal relation is often hard to infer in conventional timelines. As shown in Figure 2, the internal sequence can be interpreted ambiguously. The temporal relationship from a non-explicit time event is also a difficult problem. From the sentence "03.9.13. *persistent fever*,

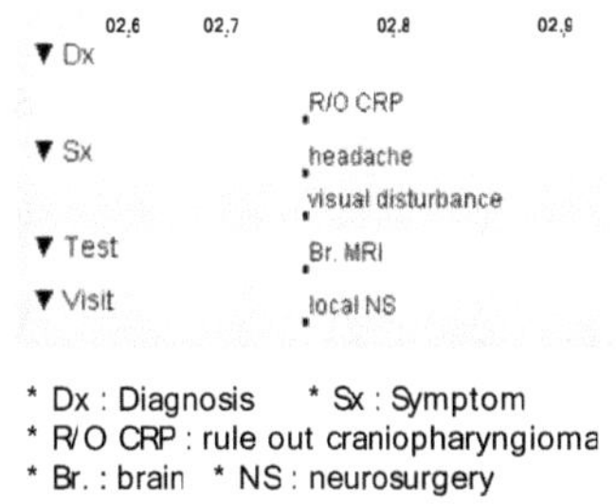

Figure 2. An example of ambiguous temporal sequence

Blood Cx (1 of 3) enterococcus found added vancomycin … 03.9.21. *fever*, hypotension developed", extrapolating the temporal distance between the two fever occurrences is impossible or to complex.

Purpose

The goal of this study was to propose a time model that is appropriate for chronologically visualizing a patient's history described in clinical narrative texts.

Design goals

We set requirements that took into consideration the representation of narrative clinical events and its utilization (reasoning and visualization aspects).

Representation: The model should be able to represent any kind of medical event preserving the integrity of the original context. Especially, the model should be able to solve causality, non-explicit temporal information, and uneven granularity problems.

Reasoning: The model should provide sufficient information for quantitative and qualitative temporal reasoning.

Visualization: The model should provide an intuitive and easy *view* that helps to understand a patient's clinical history.

V-Model

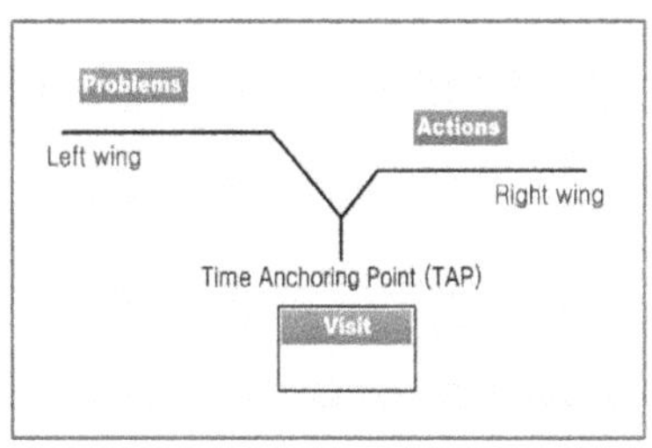

Figure 3. V-Model structure

Figure 3 shows the structure of our V-Model. The V-Model has an alphabet '*v*' like graphical structure, which has two wings. The set of wings models causal-result relationships expressed in a sentence. The left wing states *problems* and the right wing states *actions*. *Problems* are events that caused a patient to visit or be admitted to a hospital (i.e.,

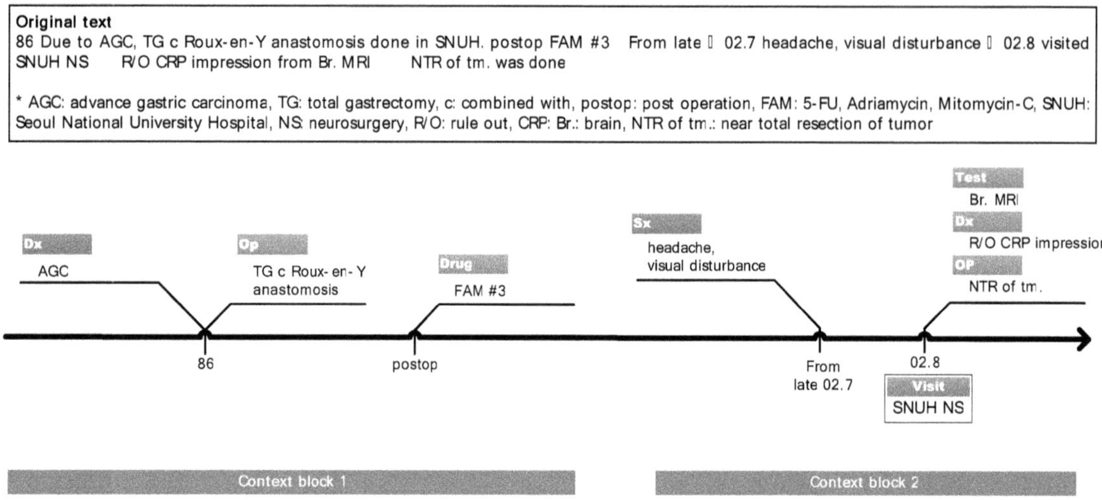

Figure 4. V-Model example (Note that the gray context block rectangles are not part of V-Model visualization. Added to help understanding).

chief complaints, purpose), or events that caused medical actions listed in the following *Actions* (i.e., symptoms, diagnoses, findings, etc) to be carried out. *Actions* are all medical events that happened in a hospital with the purpose of caring for a patient. *Actions* may include medical tests, prescription/administration of medications, treatments, operations, findings, diagnoses, plans, etc. The causality in the V-Model explains the cause of the visit or the cause of the medical actions. For example, a problem-action link describes why the patient received an operation, what medical tests were done due to the problematic symptoms, what was the diagnosis when the patient visited with the complaints, etc. To facilitate the (future) automatic mapping process, all symptoms and purposes are identified as *problems*. Additionally, some findings or diagnoses are restrictively allowed to be *problems* when the events are explicitly stated as a causal event in a sentence. For instance, from the sentence *"in 1986, TG (total gastrectomy) c (combined with) Roux-en-Y anastomosis was done due to AGC (advanced gastric cancer)"*, the AGC is identified as a *problem* since it was textually represented as a causal event (stated with the *"due to"* phrase).

It was not our intention to link causal relations which explain medical mechanisms (e.g., relations between medications and disease responses). In many cases, the causal mechanism may be ambiguous even among physicians and hard to identify automatically. Our strategy was to convey the original context on a timeline and let caregivers properly interpret the information for their use.

The bottom middle point of the v-structure is the *Time Anchoring Point (TAP)*. The *TAP* represents temporal information when problems and actions took place. Below the *TAP*, we represent *visit* information. The reason for separating visit information is that the information is one of the key references when physicians review one's clinical history and it also provides insight to temporal relations like other time expressions.

All the events in the V-Model accompany a semantic type box. Since one wing may contain a bunch of events, this provides a quick overview of the flow of events on a semantic level. To enhance readability, we colored the box in red when an event was a problem and in blue when it was an action, respectively. This color code draws attention to a new problem, which can help one to quickly access a new problem-action set.

Figure 4 shows an example of a representation by the V-Model. Our model represents the data as the original context, why the patient visited the hospital, and which actions were done to treat the problems. This is a different view from conventional timelines, which represent just the occupation time of events.

CHARACTERISTICS OF THE V-MODEL

The V-Model excels in representing narrative clinical events chronologically. With its special v-like structure and modeling strategies, the V-Model is able to resolve natural language representation problems, supports information for reasoning, and visually helps to understand a patient's history quickly (Table 1).

Representation aspects

The V-Model can represent causality relations, non-explicit temporal information, and uneven granularity expressions.

First, the V-Model provides a frame to connect causality relations (P1). In the V-Model, the multiple causality problem mentioned in Figure 1 is modeled as two v-structures (Figure 5). With the timeline, we can infer that

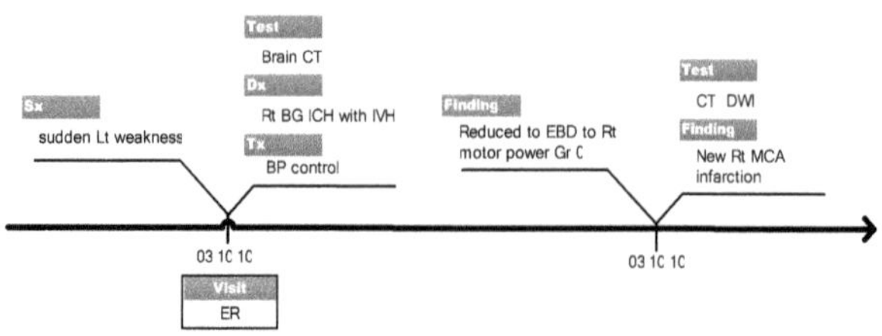

Figure 5. multiple causality in V-Model

	Id	Distinctive Features	Related Issue
Representation	P1	connection of Problem-Action relationship (P-A connection)	causality
	P2	non-explicit temporal expression (non-explicitness)	granularity
	P3	temporal proximity implied in medical terms (proximity hint)	non-explicitness
	P4	uneven granularity (uneven granularity)	non-explicitness
	P5	implicit internal sequence	non-explicitness
Reasoning	R1	Problem starts before Action (P precedes A)	reasoning
	R2	qualitative temporal relation (qualitative relation)	reasoning
	R3	temporal distance from non-explicit event (implicit distance)	reasoning
Visualization	V1	intuitive view in discovering Problem-Action relationship (intuitive P-A relation)	visual enhancement
	V2	blocking effect of Problem-Action relationship among successive events (blocking effect)	visual enhancement
	V3	overview of events' flow	visual enhancement
	V4	dynamic scaled timeline (dynamic scale)	visual enhancement
	V5	highly readable history view in tracing long period events (long history)	visual enhancement

Table 1. Distinctive features of V-Model

the second CT test was done due to 'EBD to Rt motor power decrease'. The opposite directed pair of wings also enables linking a problem to a temporally apart action event. For example, in Figure 4, the chief complaint of headache and visual disturbance, which started from late July 2002, is connected to the related actions done at SNUH NS, which occurred several days or weeks later.

Second, the V-Model solves non-explicitness issues by its unique modeling strategy. The V-Model allows *TAP* to contain diverse temporal expressions unless exactly matched to a calendar date. This is possible by following two features. First, the V-Model uses a dynamic scaled timeline. Second, events in a patient's clinical documents mostly appear in chronological order.

The original text in Figure 6 contains temporal expressions that are (a) the fuzzy and semi-interval case, (b) the omitted case, and (c) the conventional case. Contrary to conventional timeline methods, there is no problem in representing and understanding such cases (P2).

Implicitness on a finer granularity level is also solved by simple wrapping in the wing structure (P5). For instance, in Figure 4, 'Br. MRI, r/o CRP diagnosis', and 'NTR of tm.' share the same temporal expression "02.8". However, it seems clear that the events are sequential events that occurred on a different day or at a different time. The V-Model does not require an internal order or temporal gap to model such cases.

Some medical domain terms are utilized to guess the temporal distance proximity (P3) (expressions are utilized like time expressions (P3).). For example, in Figure 4, we allow the *postop* expression to appear in TAP. From this timeline, we can approximate that the FAM treatment was done temporally close to the previous operation.

Third, the V-Model represents uneven granularity expressions in one timeline view (P4). Displaying the coarser past histories together with the recent finer ones in one timeline is more natural and informative. Furthermore, the V-Model view can convey emergent situations described on a level of hours or minutes, which is generally ignored in conventional timelines.

(a) from early 2002, Lt. leg weakness developed 02.6 Op.(Operation) on back-waist in Wooridul hospital after the operation Lt. U/E weakness, hypesthesia developed -> (b) had been received treatments in herbal medicine clinic (c) after this Korean Thanksgiving Day, weakness worsened, Lt. facial hypesthesia developed

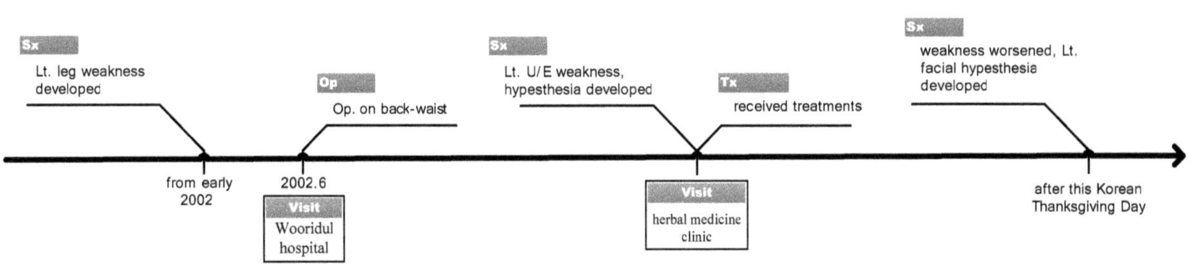

Figure 6. Non-explicit time events represented in V-Model timeline

Reasoning aspects

V-Model provides information for qualitative and quantitative reasoning.

First, the V-Model shows the relationship that problems start before actions (R1). Since the V-Model separately structures causal problems from related actions, we can extrapolate that *Problems* occurred before *Actions* although they have the same time expression. The internal sequence ambiguity problem mentioned in Figure 2 is solved by the V-Model.

Second, reasoning the other qualitative relationships is also possible (R2). This inference is done by calculating the *TAP* information manually whereas conventional timelines show the relationship intuitively (Figure 7). This weakness of performing manual calculations is deemed acceptable when considering the other powerful advantages that the *TAP* expression presents.

Third, the V-Model suggests TAP as a reference time point in temporal reasoning between non-explicit events (R3). The patient in Figure 4 had an operation with the near total resection of tumor in August 2002. Let us suppose one asks for information on "how long did it take to have an operation after the visual disturbance?" Although we only know the intermediate time of the visual disturbance, we can simply infer that "it took about two months", by using the TAP expression.

Visualization aspects

The visual display of the V-Model is highly effective in making the readability and understanding of a patient's history easier. The two wings help to discover problem-action relations intuitively (V1). Moreover, successive events in causal relations can be blocked visually (V2) (e.g., the two context blocks in Figure 4). In addition, the semantic information tag helps to quickly grasp event flows (V3). One can quickly determine the situation without reading in detail. For example, in Figure 8, we can determine the clinical situation that due to a problem occurring on Dec. 19th, the patient visited the emergency room on Dec. 20th, and a medical test, findings, treatment, and diagnosis were done.

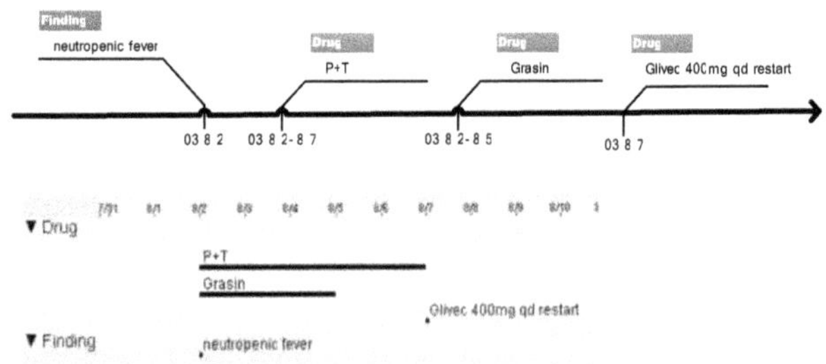

Figure 7. Interval representation of V-Model and LifeLines.

Our model's compact representation also improves the readability. The use of a dynamic scaled timeline (V4) is effective when there are long periods of blank history. The effectiveness is maximized when displaying a long history. (V5). Many of the previous clinical timeline systems have tried to organize events in semantic categories. A space is allocated for each category to collect events of that type. However, this manner of space allocation is a terrible distraction when reviewing a patient's history. One has to scroll the page up and down multiple times to trace the sequences of an event. Since our model visualizes events in a both vertically and horizontally compact space (by dynamic scale and semantic tag position), it prevents mistakenly missing sparse data, reduces scrolling behaviors, and enables a physician to determine a patient's history faster.

EVALUATION

Experimental design

Experiments were designed to evaluate the suitability of the V-Model dealing with narrative medical documents. First step, we evaluated whether our solutions (Table 1) properly solved the design requirements. Second step, we assessed the usability of our timeline. Finally, third step, we interviewed the participants to gather qualitative comments on the users' experience after using the visualization examples. The three experiments were carried out for two groups, the V-Model group and the conventional timeline model group. Forty medical students participated in these experiments. Twenty students were assigned to the V-Model group and the other twenty students to the

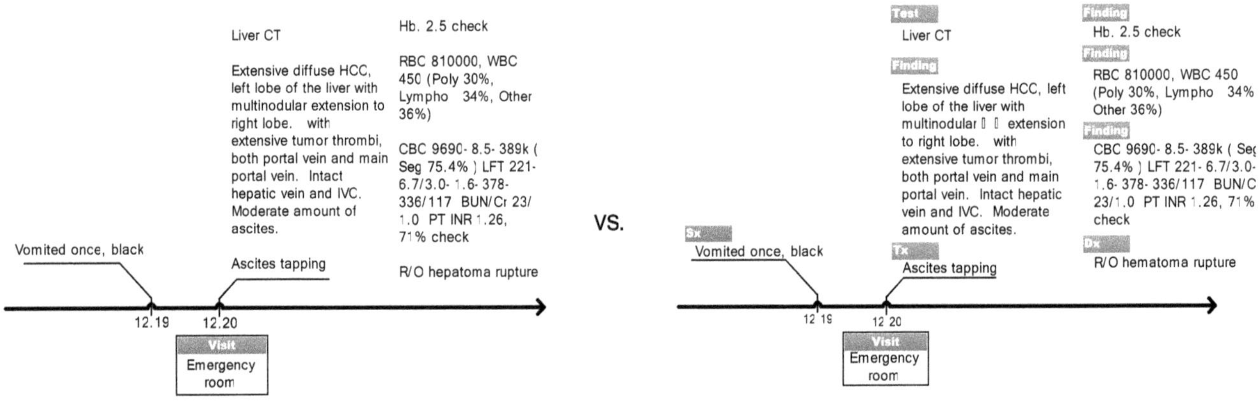

Figure 8. semantic overview

conventional timeline model group. Half of each group had experienced clinical rotations.

LifeLines

For this experiment, we used LifeLines [4, 5] as a representative of conventional timelines. There were two reasons for selecting the view of LifeLines as the control. First, LifeLines has been evaluated as one of the best known visualization environments that deals with history browsing tasks in a medical domain [16]. Second, it provides an open source program that produces the LifeLines view.

We excluded the zooming function in this experiment, which is one of the powerful features of LifeLines. There were two reasons for this. First, since the V-Model was designed on a conceptual level, we were not concerned with the physical level zooming function. Second, the time spent in zooming would increase the response time, which was one of the main evaluation measures. Therefore, the zooming function could have been a negative bias for LifeLines.

To compare texts containing non-explicit temporal events, we made some rules to show them in the LifeLines view. Since LifeLines receives input data represented as explicit start date and end date pairs, we represented the month-level temporal expressions as if they occurred on the 15th day of the month, and year-level expressions as if they occurred on January 1st. For incomplete intervals, we modeled them as if they occurred at the described time point if the data needed to be represented on the timeline. For example, "02.7 headache, visual disturbance" was modeled as starting on July 15, 2002 and ending on July 15, 2002.

In LifeLines, one point or interval represents one event. However, we represented a timespan using the V-Model's representation method, which could involve more than one event. For example, "*02.7 headache, visual disturbance*" was originally displayed as one timespan for *headache* and another timespan for *visual disturbance*; however, we modeled them as a single point, representing both the headache and the visual disturbance events.

Step 1: Q-A experiment

In this step, we justified our solutions in Table 1 by dividing them into representation, reasoning, and visualization categories, to assess the expression power, informative power in temporal reasoning, and easy-to-catch features, respectively. For this experiment, we created information seeking problems that mainly asked about the clinical situation of a given timeline. With the questions for the representation category, we measured how well the representation conveys its intentional meaning, for given a situation that contains an unresolved natural language case. For the reasoning category, we measured if one could successfully reason qualitative or quantitative temporal relations using a given timeline. Additionally, we measured how fast this could be done. For the visualization aspect, we measured how much faster one can determine a clinical situation with our visual aids.

We carefully designed the questions to show a difference between the V-Model and conventional timelines. For example, to evaluate the "P-A connection (P1)", we designed a query that asked about the causality relation from an ambiguous case like the cause of the CT test in Figure 1 (e.g., "Why the patient had to take the CT test again on Oct. 10th, 2003?"). However, to test the "intuitive P-A relation (V1)", we created the same type of questions but asked about a simpler case, in which both model users could infer the causality clearly. The questions were designed to be as easy as possible so that any participant even without medical knowledge could solve the question. The questions for "proximity words (P3)" and "temporal omission (P2)" were tested in the V-Model group only since the two cases are impossible to represent in conventional models; therefore, we could not do a comparative test for P3 and P2.

For the evaluation of "uneven granularity (P4)" and "dynamic scale (V4)", we showed both of the two types of timelines to both groups, and asked them to choose one model. For P4, we asked them to choose a model that represents uneven granularity in one timeline view (e.g., "Which timeline shows that the respiration rate increase had started since *two hours* before visiting the pediatric emergency room?"). And for V4, we suggested a patient history which had a blank period of several decades and asked which type of representation (dynamic vs. static view) was more useful in reviewing the patient's history. Although it seems clear that the V-Model supports "implicit sequential events (P5)" and "overview of events' flow (V3)", it was very hard to evaluate the features objectively with simple questions. Therefore, we excluded the evaluation of these two features.

Step 1 of the evaluation was intended to be completed within twenty minutes. One to five questions were developed for each evaluation item. We made the test on web pages that showed the timeline example set on the left frame and a question and answer choices set on the right frame. All the examples used in this evaluation were ones selected from fifty real discharge summaries. We recorded the answer(s) and response time for each question.

Step 2: Usability questionnaire

To compare the usability of the two visualization models, we adapted System Usability Scale (SUS) questions [17]. SUS is one of the popular and simple, ten-item attitude Likert scale providing a global view of subjective assessments on usability. We modified the ten general questions for the evaluation of the V-Model.

The odd numbers are positive questions and even numbers are negative questions. After experiencing the timeline model in step 1, the subjects were asked to choose their answers from the Likert scale (1-5) to the above ten questions. A sample of the original text and representation of the converted timeline was also provided on the questionnaire test page. The answers were collected as numbers ranging from 1 to 5 (from strongly disagree (1) to strongly agree (5)).

Step 3: Qualitative comments

In this evaluation, we interviewed the participants. The participants were asked three common questions.

1. What was your impression of the model?
2. Do you think this timeline view would be helpful in a clinical environment? If so, what are some examples?
3. What are the advantages and disadvantages of model and things that can be improved?

In addition, other issues were also interactively discussed. We recorded the comments by voice recorder.

RESULTS

Step 1: Evaluating requirements

The experimental results of step 1 are shown in Table 2. The differences between the two groups were analyzed by chi-square test (or Fisher's exact test) and t-test at a 0.05 confidence level.

Representation aspects

Accuracy is used as a measurement to evaluate representation power. For the *P-A connection (P1)*, the V-Model had three times higher accuracy. The V-Model participants could answer the causality seeking questions since the V-Model explicitly connects the Problem and Action, which the LifeLines does not. Eighty-seven and half percent of the V-Model participants could determine *temporal proximity (P3)* from non-temporal TAP expressions. Additionally, 85% of subjects in the V-Model group correctly answered for *non-explicitness (P2)*. This indicates that the non-explicit temporal expression case was successfully modeled in the timeline. All of the participants in the V-Model group and 95% of the participants in the LifeLines group agreed that the V-Model represented *uneven granularity* in one view (*P4*).

Reasoning aspects

To evaluate whether the timeline sufficiently provide information for temporal reasoning, we analyzed accuracy. Moreover, to compare the performance, we analyzed the response time. Both groups achieved considerably high accuracy without any statistical difference in R1 (P precedes A) and R3 (qualitative relation). The V-Model was more effective in reasoning R1. However, unlike our expectations, there was no significant difference in the time spent for R2. Reasoning implicit distance (R2), which is impossible in LifeLines view, was also successful in the V-Model (100% accuracy)

Evaluation item	num. of questions	n	LifeLines (N=20) n_c (accuracy)	LifeLines (N=20) RT (sec.) mean (sd)	V-Model (N=20) n_c (accuracy)	V-Model (N=20) RT (sec.) mean (sd)	Statistical analysis chi-squred test (p-value)	Statistical analysis t-test (p-value)
Representation								
[P1] P-A connection	2	40	12 (30 %)	63.11 (36.51)	36 (90 %)	52.77 (32)	<0.000	0.182
[P2] non-explicitness	1	20	-	-	17 (85 %)	40.39 (13.78)	-	-
[P3] proximity	2	40	-	-	35 (87.5 %)	35.52 (20.83)	-	-
Reasoning								
[R1] P precedes A	1	20	17 (85 %)	39.97 (18.75)	20 (100 %)	15.74 (3.8)	0.231	<0.000
[R2] qualitative relation	2	40	37 (92.5 %)	10.41 (8.09)	32 (80 %)	13.2 (7.6)	0.105	0.116
[R3] implicit distance	1	20	-	-	20 (100 %)	18.77 (6.26)	-	-
Visualization								
[V1] intuitive P-A relation	2	40	34 (85 %)	43.37 (20.34)	36 (90 %)	29.7 (13.91)	0.499	<0.000
[V2] blocking effect	1	20	17 (85 %)	79.95 (34.22)	15 (75 %)	55.33 (20.45)	0.695	0.009
[V5] long history	1	20	12 (60 %)	122.98 (46.9)	18 (90 %)	41.35 (13.77)	0.028	<0.000

* N : number of participants, n : number of data, n_c : number of correct answer

Evaluation item	Group	n	LifeLines	V-Model
[P4] uneven granularity (selection) (2 questions)	V-Model participants (N=20)	40	0 (0%)	40 (100%)
	LifeLines participants (N=20)	40	2 (5%)	38 (95%)
	mean	80	5%	97.50%
[V4] dynamic scale (preference) (1 question)	V-Model participants (N=20)	20	1 (5%)	19 (95%)
	LifeLines participants (N=20)	20	6 (30%)	14 (70%)
	mean	40	17.50%	82.50%

* N : number of participants, n : number of data

Table 2. Q-A experimental results

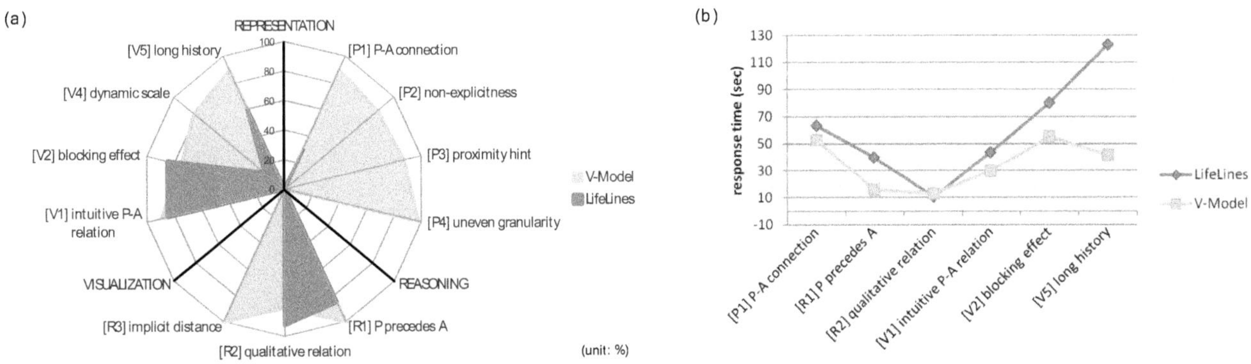

Figure 9. Overall accuracies and response times

Visualization aspects

We compared response times to determine how effectively our model helped in understanding a patient's medical history. Response times were statistically significantly faster in the V-Model group for all the evaluation items (V1, V2, V5). In regards to the dynamic scale preference problem (V4), a prominent number of participants from both groups selected the dynamic timeline of the V-Model as more appropriate for patient history. Although LifeLines users were unfamiliar with the V-Model, 70% of the LifeLines users chose this unfamiliar timeline description as better.

Total assessment

Figure 9 shows (a) the accuracy and average percentage for the selected model (P4, V4) and (b) the response time for all the evaluated items. Figure 9 (a) shows that the V-Model achieved considerably good performance for all the requirements and had advantageous characteristics. However, the conventional approach could not handle the natural language problems mentioned in this study. And in Figure 9 (b), the V-Model apparently took less time to answer all the questions except for the weak point of the model, qualitative relation reasoning (R2). To summarize, the V-Model was evaluated as an excellent model to deal with patient history in natural language.

Step 2: Usability questionnaire

Figure 10 shows the answer distribution of the usability questionnaire, grouping the results related to positive questions and negative ones. The V-Model was assessed as superior to the LifeLines in terms of usability. A prominent number of participants agreed or strongly agreed to questions asking about the advantageous aspects of the V-Model. None of them answered negatively (scores of 1 or 2). In regards to the negative questions, except for question number 10, at least seventy percent of the participants disagreed or strongly disagreed with the questions. Contrary to the assessments for the V-Model, LifeLines' results did not exhibit any striking pattern.

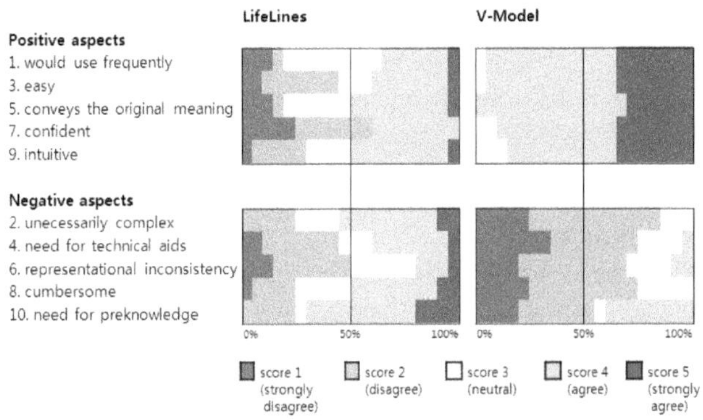

Figure 10. Usability questionnaire results

Step 3: Qualitative Comments

All of the participants in the V-Model group remarked that the V-Model was very efficient in determining a patient's history and the view was easy to read. Many of them strongly expressed their desire that this kind of view be serviced in the near future. Some of them commented our model was very innovative. They stated that this model is valuable since it removed duplicated events, represented causality relations, and reduced the number of clicks to review distributed clinical reports. They also stated that this timeline would be very helpful, especially in presenting a patient's history. From their clinical rotation experience, the V-Model automatically visualized the preliminary tasks they had to do manually for preparing patient presentations.

The weakness of the V-Model was also pointed out. Some were confused with the right wing as if the wing stood for continuity of an event. There were opinions that the time information was not notable. Although they could understand the V-Model in a short amount of time by themselves, they stated that some explanation or time was needed to understand this foreign timeline. Some mentioned that multiple problem-action links occurring at the same time seemed strange. However, after explaining this, they agreed that this separation is necessary and better than representing it as a single v-structure.

There were ideas for improvements in the V-Model. Improvements in durational notation and emphasizing temporal granularity units were suggested. Challenges for interface issues were also discussed. Linking the timeline with related materials, editing functions, providing a more summarized view, and a problem-oriented timeline were suggested to make the timeline adaptation more useful. Some also mentioned about including a zooming function but others disliked that idea.

The participants in the conventional model group expressed mostly negative opinions. Some indicated that the LifeLines view would be helpful when tracing one categorical event or when finding an occurrence date to search for a related document. However, most of the students said that the conventional view would not be helpful in a clinical environment. They expressed that the timeline is impractical in tracing chronological situations. Several common severe problems were pointed out. Consecutively moving up and down to trace a patient's history is annoying. Moreover, the temporal order was hard to determine. Due to the absence of representing causality, understanding the entire situation was difficult.

DISCUSSION

With a new graphical concept time frame, the V-Model was able to successfully and innovatively resolve visualization issues of narrative clinical text events into a timeframe. By using the V-Model, we will be able to simply automate the process of extracting and modeling the causality relations to broad medical events without the help of deep domain knowledge, and to preserve the context of the original text. The simplicity and favorable response from medical students are very promising.

However, for practical use in a clinical environment, interface issues need to be resolved. Since a patient history timeline deals with integrating lifelong healthcare data, improvements in showing abnormalities, categorical overviews, providing aggregation functions, and better interval representation are needed.

CONCLUSION

In this paper, we analyzed the problems in chronologically representing narrative patient histories. As a solution, we suggested a new innovative time model, the V-Model. Forty medical students participated in evaluating the V-Model. In conclusion, the V-Model was shown to excel in representing narrative medical events in a timeline.

ACKNOWLEDGMENTS

This work was supported by the National Research Foundation of Korea (NRF) grant funded by the Korea government (MEST) (No. 2010-0028079, 2011-0018259)

REFERENCES

1. Gill, J., et al., Presenting patient data in the electronic care record: the role of timelines. JRSM Short Rep, 2010. 1(4): p. 29.
2. Zhou, L. and G. Hripcsak, Temporal reasoning with medical data--A review with emphasis on medical natural language processing. Journal of Biomedical Informatics, 2007. 40(2): p. 183-202.
3. Cousins, S.B. and M.G. Kahn, The visual display of temporal information. Artificial Intelligence in Medicine, 1991. 3(6): p. 341-357.
4. Plaisant, C., et al., LifeLines: visualizing personal histories. Proceeding of the SIGCHI conference on Human factors in computing systems: common ground. 1996, ACM: Vancouver, British Columbia, Canada. p. 221-227.
5. Plaisant, C., et al., LifeLines: using visualization to enhance navigation and analysis of patient records. Proc AMIA Symp, 1998: p. 76-80.
6. Bui, A.A.T., D.R. Aberle, and K. Hooshang, TimeLine: Visualizing Integrated Patient Records. Information Technology in Biomedicine, IEEE Transactions on, 2007. 11(4): p. 462-473.
7. Bui, A.A., et al., Automated medical problem list generation: towards a patient timeline. Stud Health Technol Inform, 2004. 107(Pt 1): p. 587-91.
8. Martins, S.B., et al., Evaluation of an architecture for intelligent query and exploration of time-oriented clinical data. Artif. Intell. Med., 2008. 43(1): p. 17-34.
9. Martins, S.B., et al., Evaluation of KNAVE-II: a tool for intelligent query and exploration of patient data. Stud Health Technol Inform, 2004. 107(Pt 1): p. 648-52.
10. Goren-Bar, D., et al., KNAVE II: the definition and implementation of an intelligent tool for visualization and exploration of time-oriented clinical data, in Proceedings of the working conference on Advanced visual interfaces. 2004, ACM: Gallipoli, Italy. p. 171-174.
11. Bashyam, V., et al., Problem-centric organization and visualization of patient imaging and clinical data. Radiographics, 2009. 29(2): p. 331-43.
12. Jung, H., et al., Building timelines from narrative clinical records: initial results based-on deep natural language understanding, in Proceedings of BioNLP 2011 Workshop. 2011, Association for Computational Linguistics: Portland, Oregon. p. 146-154.
13. Hibino, S. and E.A. Rundensteiner, User interface evaluation of a direct manipulation temporal visual query language, in Proceedings of the fifth ACM international conference on Multimedia. 1997, ACM: Seattle, Washington, United States. p. 99-107.
14. Combi, C., L. Portoni, and F. Pinciroli, Visualizing Temporal Clinical Data on the WWW. Artificial Intelligence in Medicine, W. Horn, et al., Editors. 1999, Springer Berlin / Heidelberg. p. 301-311.
15. Hallett, C., Multi-modal presentation of medical histories, in Proceedings of the 13th international conference on intelligent user interfaces. 2008, ACM: Gran Canaria, Spain. p. 80-89.
16. Combi, C., Keravnou-Papailiou, Elpida, Shahar, Yuval, Temporal Information Systems in Medicine, ed. s. Edition. 2010: Springer.
17. Brooke J. SUS: A 'quick and dirty' usability scale. In: Jordan PW, Thomas B, McClelland l, editors. Usability evaluation in industry. London: Talylor & Francis; 1996. P. 189-94.

JigsawMap: Connecting the Past to the Future by Mapping Historical Textual Cadasters

Hyungmin Lee[1], Sooyun Lee[1], Namwook Kim[2], Jinwook Seo[1]

[1]Department of Computer Science and Engineering
Seoul National University
1 Gwanak-ro, Gwanak-gu, Seoul 151-744, Korea
{hmlee, hisyun, jseo}@hcil.snu.ac.kr

[2]Samsung Techwin
Republic of Korea
namw.kim@samsung.com

ABSTRACT
In this paper, we present an interactive visualization tool, JigsawMap, for visualizing and mapping historical textual cadasters. A cadaster is an official register that records land properties (e.g., location, ownership, value and size) for land valuation and taxation. Such mapping of old and new cadasters can help historians understand the social/economic background of changes in land uses or ownership. With JigsawMap, historians can continue mapping older or newer cadasters. In this way, JigsawMap can connect the past land survey results to today and to the future. We conducted usability studies and long term case studies to evaluate JigsawMap, and received positive responses. As well as summarizing the evaluation results, we also present design guidelines for participatory design projects with historians.

Author Keywords
JigsawMap; interactive visualization; graph layout; case study; cadaster; history

ACM Classification Keywords
H.5.m [Information interfaces and presentation (e.g., HCI)]: Miscellaneous

General Terms
Design, Human Factors

INTRODUCTION
Historians refer to prior written records to learn about the social and economic aspects of past events. They often have to analyze a large amount of historical data for several years before reaching a sound conclusion. When the sheer volume of such records overwhelms the historians' analytical capability, only a fraction of the data is reviewed at once or the tasks are distributed among other experts for collaborative analysis. The former approach may be simpler and lead to a more rapid conclusion. However, it is difficult to generalize this conclusion. The latter approach may take a longer time before any meaningful conclusion can be drawn, but it usually generates more generalizable results in the end.

The Kyujanggak Institute for Korean Studies (KIKS) preserves many invaluable historical records of pre-modern Korean history in its archives, among which are many pre-modern cadasters (from the 17th to 19th century). A cadaster contains information about each land piece surveyed, such as its owners, shape, address, etc. The pre-modern cadasters kept in the KIKS cover most cities and urban areas in the Joseon Dynasty (the most recent and last dynasty in Korean history). Thus, they provide a valuable resource for historical analyses of the temporal and spatial changes of the land's ownership, development status, and residential areas [9].

However, there are major hurdles in analyzing these pre-modern cadasters. There are no cadastral maps accompanying the textual cadasters, i.e., there are no records of the terrestrial coordinates of each land piece. Instead, only the information on the approximate land survey directions and neighboring land pieces was recorded during the survey. Fortunately, there exist modern cadastral maps to which historians can refer to figure out the geographical locations of the land pieces represented only by texts. To make things worse, the volume of the pre-

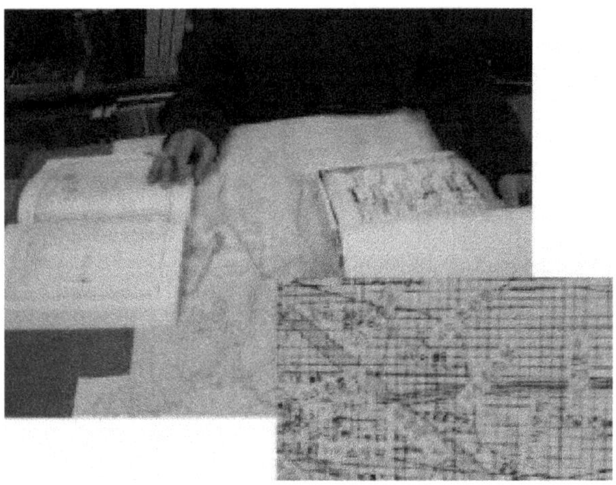

Figure 1. A historian mapping a pre-modern textual cadaster (books on the table) onto a modern cadastral map (map on the table) using sticky notes and highlighters.

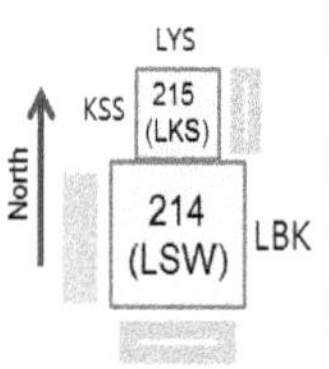

Global Index	Survey Direction	4-Neighbor Information East	West	North	South	Area	Owner
212	West	JRW	LBK	Road	Mountain	783	KMB
213	West	KMB	LSW	Road	LKS	1445	LBK
214	West	LBK	Creek	LKS	Road	4080	LSW
215	North	Road	KSS	LYS	LSW	1924	LKS
216	South	LKS	Creek	LSW	LYS	2940	KSS

Textual Land-book Format (names are abbreviated)

Figure 2. Original format of a textual cadaster (right), and a concept diagram of how the record is visualized (left).

modern cadasters is gargantuan, because it covers the records for most of the Korean peninsula across two centuries.

In the past, historians manually matched the pre-modern cadasters and modern cadastral maps using sticky notes and highlighters (Figure 1). This task was like placing an endless pile of jigsaw pieces on to a map. They chose a small rural village to evaluate the feasibility of an attempt to solve this large jigsaw puzzle [11]. It was labor intensive, time consuming and, thus, not scalable. They estimated that it might take several decades for a historian to manually match all of the pre-modern cadasters in the possession of the KIKS. This matching of cadasters is not only a challenging problem in Korea, but also in other Asian or European countries where historical cadasters exist. At the same time, because of the ambiguity or uncertainty involved in the matching process, designing an interactive visualization tool for this process is also closely related to research on uncertainty visualization.

We teamed up with historians to design and develop an interactive visualization tool called JigsawMap to help them match the pre-modern cadasters with modern cadastral maps. We used a participatory design method where the historians provided constant feedback during the design process. Once the tool was built, we conducted long-term case studies with historians, in which we obtained positive feedback about JigsawMap.

The organization of this paper is as follows. First, we describe the datasets and tasks in detail. Next, we present the design rationale and explain the interface design. We then introduce studies related to our work. A summary of our evaluation is presented in the next section. Finally, we discuss our conclusion and directions for future works.

DATASETS AND TASKS

The historians who we worked with have a goal of mapping all pre-modern textual cadasters onto the modern cadastral maps. By connecting the two, they can figure out the actual geospatial layout of the cadasters. If a complete mapping were established for every textual cadaster in the possession of the KIKS, historians would be able to use them for analyzing the temporal and spatial changes in the land ownership, land development status, and residential areas of pre-modern Korea.

In this section, we explain the two datasets and the historians' task in detail. Then, we introduce the task flow using JigsawMap and explain how the interactive tool helps each step of the historians' task thoroughly.

Pre-modern Textual Cadasters

Until the early 20th century, the Korean government kept the land survey data in a textual document format without using any geographical maps. The survey result was recorded in the simple format depicted in Figure 2. A land surveyor starts from an arbitral land piece in a village. She/he records the size and shape, the fertility rating used for taxation purposes, the four-neighbor (NWSE) information, and the direction in which the surveyor moved from the previous land piece during his/her survey (i.e., survey direction). Then, once the information on a given land piece was collected, she/he moves on to the next land piece. This process is repeated until she/he has the complete records of all land pieces in the village. The surveyor did not record explicit locations in the cadaster. Instead, only the estimated direction of his/her physical movement during the survey was recorded along with the four-neighbor information, resulting in a giant singly-linked list of the land pieces (Figure 3).

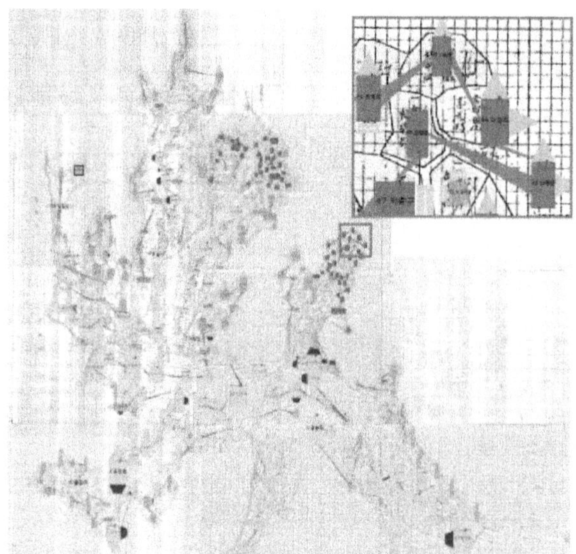

Figure 3. Result of a mapping task (overlapped mode). A node link diagram on a cadastral map is a visual representation of a textual cadaster. The enlarged region above is a magnified view of some land pieces.

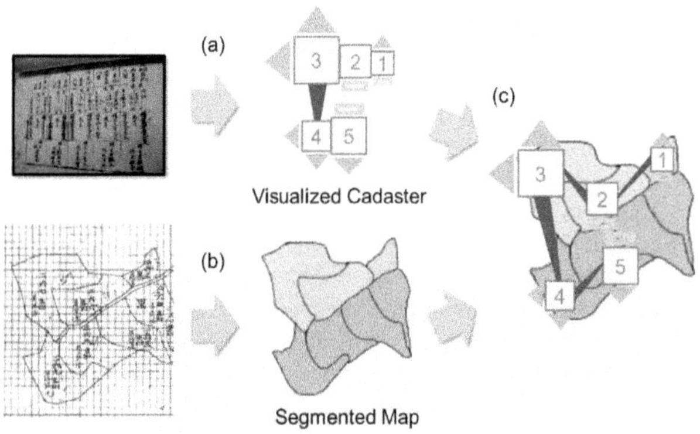

Figure 4. Task flow diagram. (a) Cadaster visualization (b) Cadastral map segmentation (c) Matching process

The KIKS preserves about 1300 volumes of textual survey books covering two centuries (from the late 18th to early 20th). They are the only copies left in existence. The Korean government is funding research projects for the purpose of computerizing the textual land survey data to encourage scalable historical research.

Modern Cadastral Maps

Modern cadastral maps have the location information and registered owner of each land piece. The cadastral maps used in this project were made in 1914. There is an approximately ten-year gap between the latest pre-modern textual cadasters and these cadastral maps. Historians assumed that there was no significant change during this ten year period, such as the ownership, land configuration, and land type. Thus, they chose to use these maps to connect the land pieces from the pre-modern cadasters.

Paper-based Mapping Process and Obstacles

The historians' mapping task begins by choosing a starting position or a land piece on a map as the first land piece in the textual cadaster. They have to guess the first land piece based only on textual information such as the neighbor information, size of land pieces, terrain description, etc. Then they traverse down the linked-list of land pieces in the textual cadaster to find more mappings to the map. However, after mapping a few more land pieces, they may notice that something is wrong, judging by the owners, land size, etc., in which case they have to try other land pieces as a starting point. This first step largely depends on the historians' intuition and they have to repeat this process until the mapping result of a starting location makes sense. Therefore, this step may take an arbitrarily long time.

Even after a mapping of the first land piece is successfully found, there are several obstacles throughout the mapping process. First, some actions are difficult to undo, since the task is done manually with sticky notes and highlighters to mark on a physical paper. Second, the mapping between land pieces in a pre-modern cadaster and land pieces in a cadastral map is not always one-to-one. Multiple land pieces in the textual cadaster can be mapped to one land piece in the cadastral map. Third, for some land pieces, historians cannot find appropriate matching pieces, because of the land pieces being split into smaller pieces or the appearance of new land pieces as a result of cultivation. Fourth, some land pieces may be included in a different town in the modern cadastral map, because of changes in the town boundary. Lastly, the ambiguity of the directional information in the textual cadaster provides another set of major challenges ("north" in the record could actually mean NNE or NNW).

Due to these difficulties, it takes about one to two months for an experienced historian to build a complete mapping of a small rural village. So it may take a few historians decades to finish all of the pre-modern textual cadasters preserved in the Korean history museum.

Task Flow in JigsawMap

JigsawMap is designed to tackle the obstacles encountered in the mapping process using highlighters and sticky notes by extending and improving upon historians' paper-based task flow (Figure 4). The task is divided into three stages: textual cadaster visualization (Figure 4a), cadastral map segmentation (Figure 4b), and an interactive matching process (Figure 4c).

Cadaster visualization and cadastral map segmentation serve as preprocessing steps before starting the matching task. In the cadaster visualization step, a graph layout is generated from the land survey data, in order to recover the original geospatial layout of the land pieces. Each node in the graph layout contains survey information, including the owner's name, land size and its four neighbors, which is presented directly to the user to provide crucial visual cues in the matching process. Cadastral map segmentation is a process used to extract the individual land pieces from the cadastral map. Each land piece is labeled with the land owner's name, land type, and a unique identifier.

The matching task is used to associate the land pieces (nodes of the graph layout) in the textual cadaster with the land pieces (segmented regions) on the cadastral map. Now, with JigsawMap, the task can be performed more accurately and efficiently, because the graph layout of the cadaster and the segmented cadastral map reveal information that was previously invisible. The details of each stage are described in the next three sections.

Visualization of Textual Cadaster

We chose the node-link diagram to visualize the textual cadaster, because the land survey information is recorded in sequential order from one land piece to another following the survey direction. The nodes resemble the sticky notes that were heavily used in the historians' manual paper-based matching task.

We developed a graph layout algorithm that generates a node-link diagram from the textual cadaster. Each node corresponds to a land piece. The size of a node is

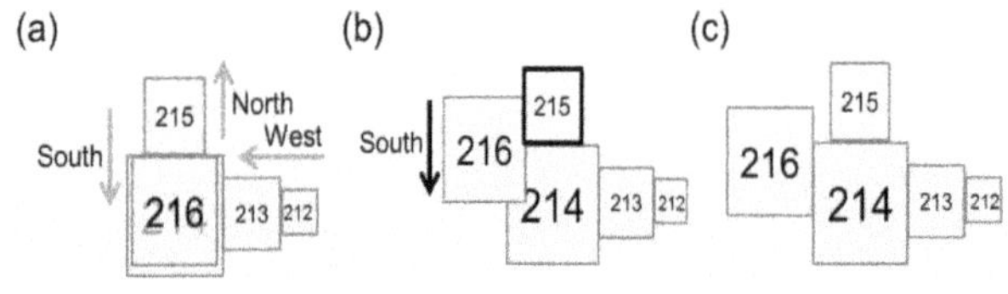

Figure 5. Example of node placement for the cadaster in Figure 2. (a) Nodes are placed according to the survey direction. 214 and 216 are overlapped. (b) Since 215 is the east neighbor of 216, 216 is shifted slightly to the NW to satisfy both the neighborhood condition and the survey direction. (c) Resolve minor node overlaps by shifting in a less-crowded direction.

proportional to the land size of the corresponding land piece. Neighboring nodes on the survey path are connected with directional edges. We used tapered edges which are the most readable visualization according to [6,7].

Nodes Overlap Removal

If the nodes are sequentially placed by following the land survey direction, some nodes will always overlap when the land survey direction reverts back to where the previous node was. This is due to the low granularity of the survey directions recorded by the surveyor. For example, an overlap occurs when it is recorded that the land surveyor moved to the north and then travelled back to the south for the next land piece (Figure 5a).

These overlapped nodes have to be detected and moved to appropriate locations (Figure 5b). First, we search through the nodes nearby and choose candidates that should be moved considering their four neighbors, land owner's name and distance. Then, a node is chosen as one of the candidates if the land owner's name of the node matches one of the neighbor's names of the overlapped node. Among these candidates, the node that is closest to the overlapped node is selected. If no candidates are detected, an alternative heuristic is used: since the overlap should be resolved without changing the topological direction of the land survey direction, one of the closest diagonal directions has to be selected. For example, if it did not have any candidates, node 216 would have been located southwest of node 215, since the land survey direction is south. Finally, minor node overlaps are resolved by shifting the overlapped node slightly in a less-crowded direction (Figure 5c). Sometimes overlaps cannot be resolved, because the surrounding nodes are too crowded. In this case, we intentionally allow an edge crossing to resolve the problem.

Visualization of land survey direction and four neighbors

The land survey direction and four neighbors of each land piece are crucial information for the matching process. Figure 6 shows how we visualize the information in the node-link diagram.

The four neighbors are either terrains or other land pieces. The terrain information is visualized as symbols and shown all the time.

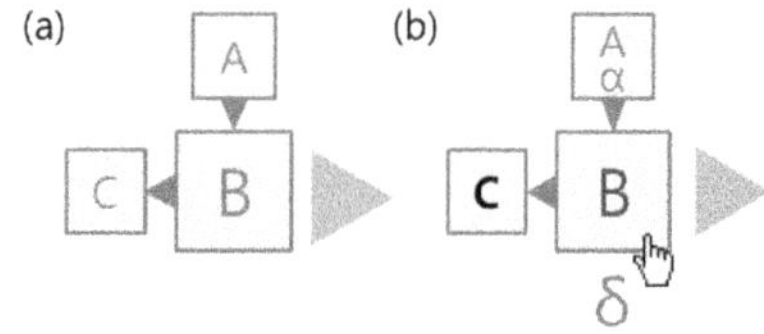

Figure 6. Survey direction and four neighbors. (a) Three nodes are shown as an example of visualization of a textual cadaster. (b) Names of its neighbors (C, α, δ) are shown when the mouse cursor is hovered over B. Since the west neighbor C is identical to the actual node in the west, it is highlighted in bold face. Unmatched neighbors (α and δ) are shown in normal face.

When the mouse cursor is hovered over a node, its neighboring land owner's names are shown (Figure 6b). When the owner's name of a neighboring node in the graph layout is identical to the actual neighbor's name in the direction, the label of the matched land is shown in bold face. All non-matching labels are shown in regular face.

Cadastral Map Segmentation

While mapping from the textual cadaster to the cadastral map, historians had to mentally parse the corresponding geographic information on poor quality hand-drawn maps that were drawn about a century ago, in which the land boundaries and gridlines overlap with each other, and both are irregular and discontinuous and consist of broken pixels (Figure 7a). To facilitate the mapping process, it is desirable to develop a tool that extracts and labels the regions on the map. The segmented regions are color-coded based on the land types. Once labeled, researchers can easily look up the land owner.

We provide both semi-automatic and sketch-based methods to segment the map image into pixel regions. Since the former method does not always produce desirable results, due to the poor quality of the map image, a sketch-based segmentation tool is provided as an alternative.

This semi-automatic segmentation process is conducted in four-stages. First, it removes the grid lines by scanning horizontally and vertically and classifying the scan lines

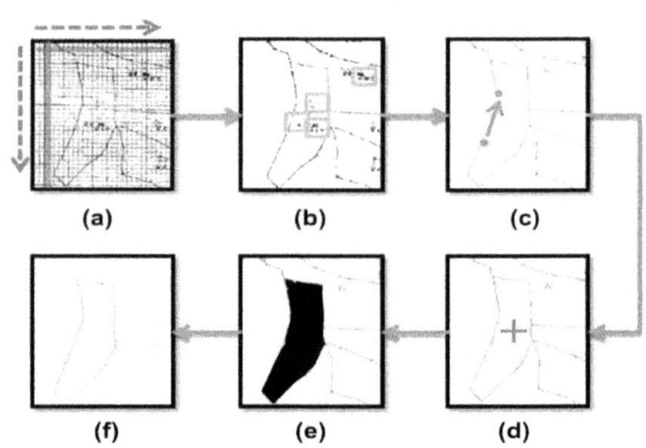

Figure 7. Map segmentation algorithm. (a) Remove grid lines. (b) Remove letters. (c) Close holes. (d) Select a region. (e) Run region growing. (f) Construct a polygon boundary.

based on the pixel intensities; if a scan line contains a pixel intensity above a certain threshold, it is considered to be a grid line (Figure 7a). Second, it removes characters by constructing connected components and examining each of them to find resemblance to a character; squareness and the number of branch points are used as character features (Figure 7b). Third, holes are closed by tracing a ray from end point to end point (Figure 7c). In the final stage, the user selects a region to extract (Figure 7d). A region growing method is then applied to construct a pixel region (Figure 7e). In addition, if desirable, a minimum-perimeter polygon algorithm is used to construct a polygon from the pixel region (Figure 7f).

The sketch-based segmentation tool is used when a land piece is not extracted perfectly with the semi-automatic segmentation tool. The user can directly segment the land pieces in the following steps. First, the user sketches a land piece by dragging the mouse pointer along its boundary. Then, a child window is shown and the user needs to input the unique identifier. The child window captures the magnified view of the land piece. This view is helpful for the user to read the unique identifier on the map. After this step, the region segmented by the user is filled with color according to the land type.

Matching Process

The user performs the matching task by comparing the node-link diagram with the segmented cadastral map (Figure 8a, b). First, the user selects the best starting point and starts linking land pieces (Figure 8c) and matching nearby land pieces (Figure 8d) until the matching process is no longer able to proceed. The user now has to find another starting point and repeat the above steps. The user may utilize clues such as the four neighbors, terrain, etc., during the process. The detailed user interactions for this process in JigsawMap are explained in a later section.

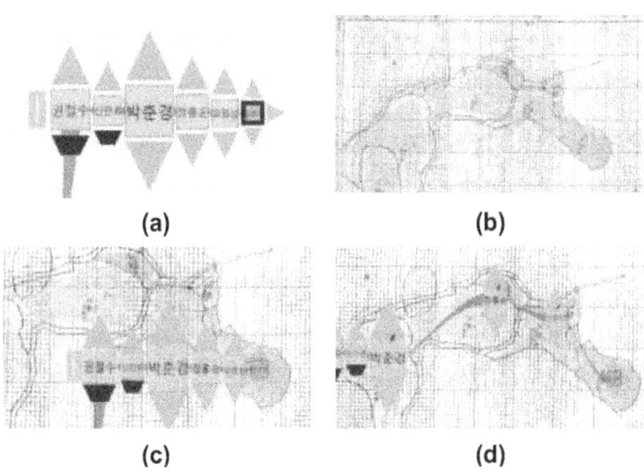

Figure 8. Matching process. (a) Visualized textual cadaster and (b) Segmented cadaster map. The land pieces in both (a) & (b) are surrounded by mountains. (c) The starting point is matched. (d) A few more following land pieces are sequentially matched.

DESIGN RATIONALE

In this section, we explain the rationale behind our design decisions and implementation of JigsawMap with domain experts.

Design based on task observations

The historians formulated the task flow as they performed the task. There is a certain goal in every step of the task. We should understand these goals to design an appropriate interface or interaction. We should also find out what makes the task uncomfortable and tedious through observations.

Give the feeling of direct engagement

The historians used highlighters and sticky notes to record their matched results on the map. To ease the learning curve of using JigsawMap, we have to support the direct manipulation of the layout through intuitive and familiar interactions with the right affordances. We decided to model the interactions based on the historians' accustomed actions with highlighters and sticky notes.

Enable search by name

The owner names are very important hints for finding the candidate nodes for matching. Especially, at the beginning of the matching process, the historians check the owner names to find out if there are similar names in the cadaster and map. For this reason, the owner names should be searchable to provide clues for the matching process.

Visualize the invisible

Making an automatic algorithm that finds perfectly matched results is very difficult, if not impossible. Thus, we visualize the important characteristics of the data which were inconspicuous in the original textual cadasters. With important features embossed in the overview, the user will be able to match places where the features were not visible before.

Control the amount of information to visualize

The cadaster contains various information on the land. Visualizing such information helps understand the data, but showing too much information at once could hinder the matching process. In the design process, we had to decide the information necessary for each task. There may be information that is important to historians, but seems irrelevant to non-historians. Thus, we closely collaborated with the historians to decide which information needs to be shown for each task.

JIGSAWMAP INTERFACE DESIGN

Our working prototype (Figure 9) is implemented using Microsoft Silverlight 4.0. JigsawMap has two view modes: separate mode and overlapped mode.

In separate mode, the user can compare the cadastral map and the visualized cadaster separately. By comparing these two views side by side, the user can skim and mark the start

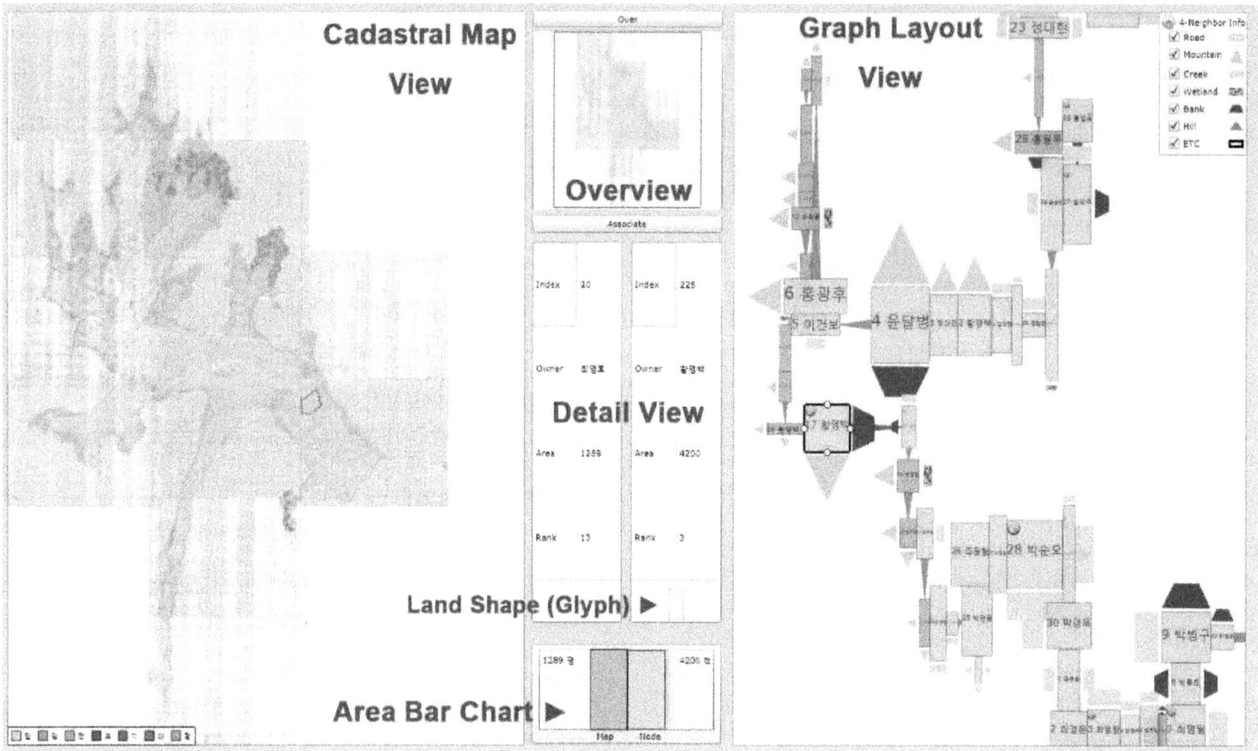

Figure 9. Overview of JigsawMap in the separate mode (Note that some widgets around the edge are cropped to show the main views better). The user can segment each land piece in the cadastral map view and adjust the layout of the land pieces in the graph layout view. He or she selects the matching land pieces in the two views and associates them by clicking on the "Associate" button.

location candidates. The cadastral map view is in the left window and the graph layout view is on the right. Each window supports zooming and panning.

The overlapped mode merges the left and right views, overlaying the visualized cadaster on the cadastral map (Figure 3). In this mode, the user can directly manipulate the nodes that are on top of the map. It is like putting sticky notes on top of the map. The user can switch the mode back and forth by clicking on the "Over" button.

An overview of the cadastral map and detailed views are placed in the center part of the interface. In the detailed view, the land information of the textual cadaster and cadastral map is shown. The land shape information in the cadaster is visualized with glyphs. In the cadaster, most of the land pieces are rectangular, but some of them have irregular shapes (e.g., an arc shape). The bar chart in the center shows the size of the selected land pieces in the cadastral map and cadaster. The user can check if they are of similar size using the bar chart.

Matching Process Interaction

The user interaction in the matching process using JigsawMap is as follows. At first, the user selects some land pieces (segmented regions in the cadastral map and nodes from the visualized cadaster) that she/he thinks are matched. The user can select them by clicking on the left mouse button. In overlapped mode, clicking on a node will automatically select the segmented regions behind it. After selection, the user can check the size of the selected land pieces with the area bar chart. If they are convinced of their selections, the user can connect them by clicking on the "Associate" button or using the context menu that appears when the right mouse button is clicked. After the association, red pin icons appear on the matched nodes, meaning that these nodes cannot be moved unless the user dissociates them first. The user can undo/redo any action whenever she/he feels that there is a mistake. There is also a re-layout function that can be applied from a user-selected land piece. This function can be used during the task to automatically re-layout all of the nodes in the graph layout starting from the selected node.

RELATED WORK

This project is based upon previous research in many different fields such as user interface design, information visualization, and image processing. First, we review studies on dealing with multiple maps. Then, we show works on changing the layout of the existing map data, followed by graph layout algorithms preserving the relative node positions. Finally, we summarize the existing techniques related to JigsawMap's segmentation method.

User Interfaces for Browsing Overlaid Multiple Maps

There are previous works on designing mapping systems for overlaid multiple maps. MapSynthesizer [2] is a prototype map browser based on MapCruncher [3], with which users can search and compare overlaid multiple maps. MapSynthesizer is designed based on expert interviews about how people correlate maps. JigsawMap differs from MapSynthesizer in that it links a textual cadaster to a geographical map. Hypercities [8] is a web-based map browser or an open platform developed for research and education. Hypercities is also used for history research and for many courses in UCLA. Geo-temporal information including historical maps are shared and explored on this platform. MapSynthesizer and Hypercities are similar to our project, since they are also platforms for merging geo-spatial information.

Generating Layout using Geo-spatial Data

Morphing a real map into a meaningful spatial layout like a Treemap [15] is one of the important research issues in geo-spatial visualization. HiVE (Hierarchical Visualization Expression) [16] has expressions for describing space-filling rectangular layouts. Among them, there is 'spatially-ordered' layout [18] that preserves the relative positions of the geographical elements in a space-filling layout. This layout can produce a Treemap from geographical map data. In JigsawMap, we have to map the spatial layout generated from an ambiguous textual geographical data onto a real map, which is a uniquely challenging task that, to the best of our knowledge, has not been addressed in the past.

Graph Layout Algorithms

In JigsawMap, the visualization of the textual cadasters is one of the key components. Since the textual cadasters encode the geographical relationships between the land pieces, it seems natural to visualize them using graph visualization methods. There are extensive works on generating overlap-free graph layouts [1]. Gansner *et al.* presented a study on graph layout algorithms that reduce the number of edge overlaps while preserving their hierarchy [4]. Our graph layout should preserve both the horizontal and vertical relative positional relationships, since it is composed of geospatial data. There was an attempt made to place nodes in a fixed grid first and then route edges to minimize the edge crossing, bending, length and density [13]. In our visualization, the edges cannot be freely rerouted, because they not only link the nodes sequentially, but also enable the direction information to be visualized. X-Y ordering [10] is a post-processing algorithm that resolves node overlaps while preserving their relative positional relationships. Since we can only partially infer the relative positional relationships among the land pieces from the cadasters, directly applying this algorithm does not guarantee a better layout.

Image Segmentation

Wikimapia [17] is a collaborative mapping platform where the user can segment the world map into geographical regions in a wiki fashion. It provides a simple interface with which the user sets the boundary points to define a region. There are also similar services such as Google Map Maker [5] and OpenStreetMap [12] that collect geospatial information by segmenting the map into geometric primitives; points, lines and polygons. JigsawMap, although targeting a different domain, takes a similar approach by providing a simple sketch-based segmentation and goes one step further to automate the segmentation process.

EVALUATION

Pilot Study

We did a pilot study with a Computer Science graduate student who does not have background in this kind of task. This study was done with an early prototype of JigsawMap to find usability problems or errors. We explained about the data and the purpose of our tool and showed a 3-minute demo. We allowed the participant to ask questions about the interactions of JigsawMap and the description of the data during the test.

The test took about 40 minutes. The participant matched about 70 land pieces, which is about 15% of the town. The results of the test were mostly similar to those of the Korea historians.

However, some of the matched results were not identical to those of the historians. This was mainly due to the N:1 matching cases where the participant sometimes matched too many or too few nodes to a land piece of the cadastral map (or vice versa). A meticulous examination of the land area information can resolve this problem. Unfortunately, there was no visualization that allowed differences in the land area data to be shown in the early prototype. Due to this problem, the participant commented that comparing the area information was not very intuitive, due to the irregular shaped land pieces in the cadastral map. Based on this feedback, we included the area bar chart to help the user compare the area data.

Longitudinal Evaluation

We conducted long-term case studies following the principles of MILC (Multi-dimensional In-depth Long-term Case Studies) [14], which is a participatory design method, with two historians. We had a meeting with each participant every two weeks for five months. Each meeting took about an hour. We preceded the meeting with the following protocols. First, we got the overall feedback from the historians about their two weeks experience using JigsawMap. Next, we exchanged questions. We mainly asked questions about the historical background of the data to understand the task and data better. The historians usually inquired about the functionality of JigsawMap in detail and the feasibility of their ideas on improving it. Then, we introduced and installed a new version of JigsawMap which was improved based on the feedback from the previous meeting. Finally, we observed the historians using the new version and received their initial feedback on it.

The next two sub-sections describe case studies with the two historians: a graduate student (P1) and undergraduate student (P2) from a Korean history department.

Case 1

This user was a graduate student (P1) who has professional experience in cadaster studies. P1 was used to the manual paper-based matching task. During the evaluation, we asked P1 to use JigsawMap to match land pieces of Gayang-ri, a town surrounded by mountains.

P1 commented that the visualization of the textual cadasters is one of the most satisfactory features compared to the paper-based matching task. The clues mainly used by P1 to find a starting land piece for the matching process were: the terrain in the four neighbors (e.g., Figure 6), the similarity of the land owner names, and the irregular shaped (e.g., arc) land pieces in the cadaster. P1 stated that the area chart was very useful for checking the size of the land pieces.

P1 noted that some of the land information is not necessary in the matching task. According to this statement, information such as the price and fertility were excluded from the tooltip popup. In contrast, the terrain information was considered very useful and important for the matching task. Therefore, we modified the interaction to show the terrain visualization of the four neighbors in a land piece all the time. P1 also mentioned that he wanted to have keyboard shortcuts and that he is familiar with word processors and spreadsheets, so we added keyboard shortcuts based on these programs (e.g., shift/ctrl click, ctrl+c/v).

Case 2

P2 is an undergraduate student in a Korean history department. P2 had no experience in the matching task before and had no background information on the cadaster to be examined. A brief background explanation and tutorial of JigsawMap was given to P2 before the evaluation. P2 worked with Yogok-ri, a town located in the valleys. The feedback from P2 about the strengths of JigsawMap was similar to that of P1.

P2 noted that she used a different approach when she was unable to carry on with the task. At first, she tried to find other candidate locations that could be far away from the current place. However, she often had problems in merging different groups. If dangling nodes remain, it means that there is something wrong and discerning the correct matching will be time consuming. Thus, she decided to follow the survey direction, finding other candidates nearby when she came to a dead-end. P2 said that working this way improved the overall performance. After hearing this anecdote, P1 affirmed that it is a reasonable approach to stay on track in the survey direction.

P2 finished the matching task in about two weeks. The total time was about 20 hours, working for 2~4 hours per day. The working time included a brief seminar on the background of the cadaster and cadastral map, as well as a tutorial of JigsawMap. Considering this, P2 finished the task in a significantly shortened time compared to that taken by experts to complete the manual paper-based task.

Post Usability Test with a Domain Expert

We additionally interviewed and tested our tool with a Korean history graduate student (P3). P3 understood the purpose of our research because he had been working on linking cadaster and cadastral maps manually. The whole process took about 90 minutes. First of all, we interviewed P3 for about 30 minutes about how he had worked manually. We asked P3 how he found starting points, the hints he used to find them, the progress of the research, and difficulties of the task. After the interview, we gave him a 10 minute tutorial with a demo. We asked P3 to use JigsawMap with the town he is working on as a warm-up and received initial feedback about it for 30 minutes. Lastly, P3 tested JigsawMap with a town he was not aware of and this step took about 15 minutes.

In the interview, P3 mentioned that he had been working on a town which is located in a plain with the paper-based method. P3 processed about 70 percent of the town in about 2 months. P3 worked for 2~3 hours on a usual day and 5 hours on weekends. The names of the owners were a very good hint in P3's case, in that almost 15 percent of his matched results were due to the land owner's name. Furthermore, their family names were also reliable clues for matching. P3 stated that the natural terrains visualized as the four neighbors of the land pieces were also helpful for finding candidates. For example, a land piece surrounded by a mountain could be easily matched to the map.

DISCUSSION

Summary of Historical Findings

Historians have found significant facts by linking cadasters to cadastral maps. Using JigsawMap, they reconfirmed their findings. In addition, they commented that our visualization will be useful for making further discoveries. We introduce some interesting findings made during the evaluation.

Disagreement of land owner names

There is only about a ten year gap between the cadastral map and cadasters in our research. For this reason, the historians hypothesized that the land owner names in these two cases would be almost the same or similar. However, when they tried to find matching land pieces by using the owner names, the result was not good. The historians concluded that the representation of the land piece was recorded by the different standards adopted at that time.

Representation of Four Canonical Directions

As explained previously, the land survey direction and four neighbors of the Korean pre-modern cadasters were recorded using four canonical directions (NSEW). When fulfilling the task, there were some cases where the direction information did not make sense compared with the trace of the nearby neighbors. The historians formulated a hypothesis that there may be exceptional cases of direction representation. For example, the direction where the king lived may have been expressed as north. The historians are studying the social aspects of that time to find historical evidences for this hypothesis.

Newly Constructed Roads

There are some long, straight roads located in the modern cadastral map. The land pieces divided by these roads share the same land owner name and are usually matched to a single land piece in the textual cadaster. The historians found that these roads were newly constructed in the 20th century.

Hidden Implications of Land Survey Direction

There are some survey directions that are unique. For example, the land surveyor walked a long way across a big mountain, rather than finishing recording the land pieces around it first. The historians are researching these survey directions to find hidden patterns and understand any social background behind the unique survey directions.

Further Interdisciplinary Work

The visualized cadasters are a rich source of information. Collaboration with researchers in other related fields will be necessary for analyzing the different aspects of them. For example, geologists can use this information to study the irrigation system at that time, because rivers and banks are recorded on the cadasters. Anthropologists may be interested in the record of agricultural land use. Further interdisciplinary work will activate relevant research in various related fields.

Design Guidelines When Working with Historians

We worked with the historians for about half a year and learned some rules of thumb that were useful in the design process. We generalize and suggest them as guidelines. We think that these will be useful when collaborating with historians.

Be Aware of Time Scale

There are many different kinds of temporal data. Most data used for visualization are evenly-spaced over time and relatively short in length. However, the data used in the history field are mostly irregular in time. The time range can vary by hundreds of years. Therefore, when designing temporal or time-line visualizations for historical studies, these characteristics should be noted.

Be Concerned about Background of the Record

During the project, we found that more than one name may represent a single person. At first we thought that the historians made some typographical errors when computerizing the materials. However, it was due to an historical issue. The historians explained that some of the letters used at that time have more than one pronunciation. In this case, there might be some background knowledge that is trivial for historians, but not for computer scientists. These unknown data properties can cause misconceptions. Thus, it is important to fully understand the background of the data to design a credible tool.

Bridge the experienced and novice users

Expertise in the domain can have both positive and negative effects on the task performance with JigsawMap. In our study, the experienced user (P1) was inspired by the feedback from the novice user (P2) who tried to use JigsawMap in a novel way. P1 mentioned that he was so used to working manually with papers and highlighters that he tended to do the task in the same way, even when using our tool. On the other hand, novice users may receive useful tips from experienced users. Thus, if we can bridge them in the design process, we can design a system that can actually improve the performance of both groups.

Field Studies

In order to verify the records of historical data, historians may go on field studies. Asking the purpose of the field study and sharing the log of the result can be a valuable process. The collected data can be proactively used in the design process.

Additional Anecdote

P2 told us about one episode when she was using the tool. She was doing a part time job in an engineering laboratory. The students in the lab were reluctant to ask about the history books P2 was studying in her free time. They were confused about the Chinese letters in the book P2 was reading. Later on, during the evaluation session with us, P2 installed the tool in her workplace and used it during her break time. When the students saw P2 doing the task with our program, they were very curious about the collaboration work we did. They were impressed about the collaboration between historians and computer scientists. They asked many questions about us and other HCI field studies as well.

Generalizability of Our Approach

Mapping historical textual cadasters is not an isolated problem in Korea. Similar problems also exist in other countries such as Japan and China. In China, land information was recorded in a "fish-scale register" in the 17th century, where the land pieces were drawn like fish scales. This system also lacks the exact coordinates, so our approach is also applicable in a similar way. There are some European countries such as Ireland that have historical cadasters to analyze in conjunction with modern cadastral maps.

Mapping historical textual cadasters requires dealing with uncertainty because of the ambiguity involved in the mapping process. JigsawMap helps historians match the historical artifacts by interactively resolving the ambiguity. Since it deals with uncertainty, the interaction design in

JigsawMap is closely related to the visualization of uncertain data or uncertainty visualization. Especially, we think that our approach and design can be generalized to such a research domain as the visualization of geospatial data with uncertainty.

CONCLUSION AND FUTURE WORK

We designed a novel interactive visualization tool, JigsawMap, for connecting pre-modern textual cadasters to more recent cadastral maps through close collaboration with historians. Professional historians are currently working on digitalizing textual cadasters in a larger scale, and will be using JigsawMap for mapping them. A visual representation of textual cadasters based on node-link diagram visualization helped the historians to easily identify the land pieces to start the matching process with. Longitudinal case studies and short usability studies were conducted to evaluate JigsawMap. We came up with design guidelines by carefully analyzing the feedback and comments from the participants. These guidelines will be useful when collaboratively designing an interactive tool with historians.

There are several aspects of JigsawMap that could be improved in future works. Our graph layout algorithm does not generate a feasible layout when the town is located in a flatland, where there are few mountains and rivers. While JigsawMap significantly reduces the time required to map a cadaster, it is not scalable enough to deal with all of the villages in a nation over a period of several decades. Crowdsourcing the matching task might be a feasible approach to scale up the process. We will also focus on making the task more playful in the next step of our research. Since our task resembles a puzzle game, we will work on interfaces that will make this task fun and competitive. Finally, we are planning to support the comparison of multiple cadasters. This research will help historians see the temporal and spatial changes at a glance.

ACKNOWLEDGMENTS

We wish to thank Prof. Kuen-tae Kim (Department of Korean History, Seoul National University) for his help with the cadasters and cadastral maps. This work was supported by grants from Microsoft Research and the National Research Foundation of Korea (NRF) funded by the Korea government (MEST) (No. 2011-0030813 & 2011-0005526). The ICT at Seoul National University provided the research facilities for this study.

REFERENCES

1. Di Battista, G., Eades, P., Tamassia, R. and Tollis, I G., Algorithms for drawing graphs: an annotated bibliography. *Computational Geometry: Theory and Applications 1994*, 4, 5, (1994), 235-282.
2. Elias, M., Elson, J., Fisher, D. and Howell. J, Do I live in a flood basin?: synthesizing ten thousand maps. In *Proc. SIGCHI 2008*, ACM (2008), 255-264.
3. Elson, J., Howell, J., and Douceur, J. R., MapCruncher: integrating the world's geographic information. *SIGOPS Operating System Review 2007*, 41, 2 ACM (2007), 50-59.
4. Gansner, E. R., Koutsofios, E., North, S. C. and Vo, K.-P., A Technique for Drawing Directed Graphs. *Trans. on Software Engineering 1993*, 19, 3 IEEE (1993), 214-230.
5. Google Map Maker, Sep 2011. http://www.google.com/mapmaker.
6. Holten, D. and van Wijk, J. J., A user study on visualizing directed edges in graphs. In *Proc. SIGCHI 2011*, ACM (2009), 2299-2308.
7. Holten, D., Isenberg, P., van Wijk, J.J. and Fekete, J., An extended evaluation of the readability of tapered, animated, and textured directed-edge representations in node-link graphs. In *Proc. PacificVis 2009*, IEEE (2009), 195-202.
8. Hypercities. http://hypercities.com/.
9. Kim, K., The Grasp on the Chinchôn and the Landholder through the Land Register and the Cadastral Survey, *KYUJANGGAK 2010*, 37 KIKS (Kyujanggak Institute for Korean Studies), (2010), 1-30.
10. Lyons, K., A., Cluster busting in anchored graph drawing, In *Proc. CASCON 1992*, 1, (1992), 7-17.
11. Miyajima, H., Comparative analysis of Kwangmu yang'an and Cadastral, *Research on the Cadastral Survey in Chosôn dynasty*, Minumsa(1997), 199-248.
12. OpenStreetMap, Sep 2011. http://openstreetmap.org.
13. Rohrschneider, M., Heine, C., Reichenbach, A. Kerren, A. and Scheuermann, G., A Novel Grid-Based Visualization Approach for Metabolic Networks with Advanced Focus&Context View, *In Proc. 17th International Symposium on Graph Drawing 2009*, Lect. Notes Comp. Sci.. Edited by Emden Gansner DE, Springer (2009), 268-279.
14. Shneiderman, B. and Plaisant, C., Strategies for evaluating information visualization tools: multi-dimensional in-depth long-term case studies. In *Proc. AVI BELIV 2006*, ACM (2006), 1-7.
15. Shneiderman, B. Tree visualization with tree-maps: 2D space-filling approach. *Trans. on Graphics 1992*, 11, 1 ACM (1992), 92-99.
16. Slingsby, A., Dykes, J. and Wood, J., Configuring Hierarchical Layouts to Address Research Questions. *Trans. on Visualization and Computer Graphics 2009*, 15, 6 IEEE (2009), 977-984.
17. Wikimapia, Sep 2011. http://wikimapia.org.
18. Wood, J. and Dykes J., Spatially ordered treemaps. *Trans. on Visualization and Computer Graphics 2008*, 14, 6 IEEE (2008), 1348-1355.

Semantic Interaction for Visual Text Analytics

Alex Endert
Virginia Tech
Blacksburg, VA USA
aendert@vt.edu

Patrick Fiaux
Virginia Tech
Blacksburg, VA USA
pfiaux@vt.edu

Chris North
Virginia Tech
Blacksburg, VA USA
north@vt.edu

ABSTRACT
Visual analytics emphasizes sensemaking of large, complex datasets through interactively exploring visualizations generated by statistical models. For example, dimensionality reduction methods use various similarity metrics to visualize textual document collections in a spatial metaphor, where similarities between documents are approximately represented through their relative spatial distances to each other in a 2D layout. This metaphor is designed to mimic analysts' mental models of the document collection and support their analytic processes, such as clustering similar documents together. However, in current methods, users must interact with such visualizations using controls external to the visual metaphor, such as sliders, menus, or text fields, to directly control underlying model parameters that they do not understand and that do not relate to their analytic process occurring within the visual metaphor. In this paper, we present the opportunity for a new design space for visual analytic interaction, *called semantic interaction,* which seeks to enable analysts to spatially interact with such models directly within the visual metaphor using interactions that derive from their analytic process, such as searching, highlighting, annotating, and repositioning documents. Further, we demonstrate how semantic interactions can be implemented using machine learning techniques in a visual analytic tool, called *ForceSPIRE*, for interactive analysis of textual data within a spatial visualization. Analysts can express their expert domain knowledge about the documents by simply moving them, which guides the underlying model to improve the overall layout, taking the user's feedback into account.

Author Keywords
Visualization; visual analytics; interaction

ACM Classification Keywords
H5.m. Information interfaces and presentation (e.g., HCI): Miscellaneous.

General Terms
Design; Human Factors; Theory

INTRODUCTION
Visual analytics bases its success on combining the abilities of statistical models, visualization, and human intuition for users to gain insight into large, complex datasets [23]. This success often hinges on the ability for users to interact with the information, manipulating the visualization based on their domain expertise, interactively exploring possible connections, and investigating hypotheses. It is through this interactive exploration that users are able to make sense of complex datasets, a process referred to as sensemaking [19].

The two primary parts of sensemaking are *foraging* and *synthesis*. Foraging refers to the stages of the process where users filter and gather collections of interesting or relevant information. Then, using that information, users advance through the synthesis stages of the process, where they construct and test hypotheses about how the foraged information may relate to the larger plot. Tools exist that support users for either foraging or synthesis – but not both.

In this paper we present *semantic interaction*, combining the foraging abilities of statistical models with the spatial synthesis abilities of analysts. Semantic interaction is based on the following principles:

1. Visual "near=similar" metaphor **supports** analysts' spatial cognition, and is generated by statistical models and similarity metrics. [22]
2. **Use** semantic interactions within the visual metaphor, based on common interactions occurring in spatial analytic processes [4] such as searching, highlighting, annotating, and repositioning documents.
3. **Interpret** and map the semantic interactions to the underlying parameters of the model, by updating weights and adding information.
4. **Shield** the users from the complexity of the underlying mathematical models and parameters.
5. Models **learn** incrementally by taking into account interaction during the entire analytic process, supporting analysts' process of incremental formalism [10].
6. **Provide** visual feedback of the updated model and learned parameters within the visual metaphor.
7. **Reuse** learned model parameters in future or streaming data within the visual metaphor.

To demonstrate the concept of semantic interaction, we present a prototype visual analytics tool, ForceSPIRE, for spatial analysis of textual information. In ForceSPIRE, the user interaction takes on a deeper, more integrated role in the exploratory spatial analytic process. This is done through *capturing* the semantic interaction, *interpreting* the analytical reasoning associated with the interaction, and *updating* the statistical model, and ultimately updating the spatialization. Hence, users are able to leverage semantic interaction to explore and analyze the data interactively, while the system is responsible for properly updating the underlying statistical model.

RELATED WORK

Foraging Tools

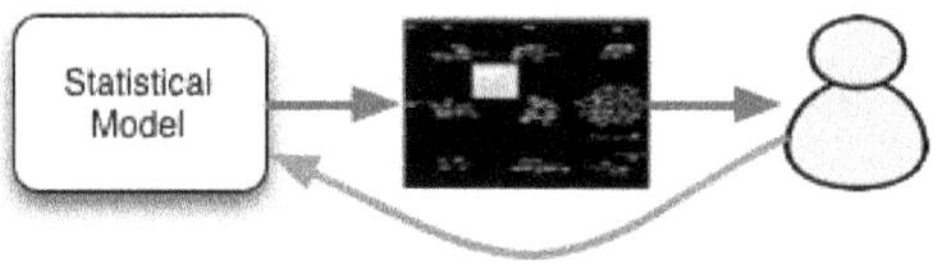

Figure 1. A model of interaction with foraging tools. Users interact directly with the statistical model (red), then gain insight through observing the change in the visualization (blue).

We categorize foraging tools by their ability to pass data through complex statistical models and visualize the computed structure of the dataset for the user to gain insight (Figure 1). Thus, users interact with these tools primarily through directly manipulating the parameters of the model used for computing the structure. As such, users are required to translate their domain expertise and semantics about the information to determine which (and by how much) to adjust these parameters. The following examples further describe this category of tools.

Visualizations such as IN-SPIRE's "Galaxy View" (shown in Figure 3) present users with a spatial layout of textual information where similar documents are proximally close to one another [25]. An algorithm creates the layout by mapping the high-dimensional collection of text documents down to a two-dimensional view. In these spatializations, the spatial metaphor is one from which users can infer meaning of the documents based on their location. The notion of distance between documents represents how similar the two documents are (i.e., more similar documents are placed closer together). For instance, a cluster of documents represents a group of similar documents, and documents placed between two clusters implies those documents are connected to both clusters. These views are beneficial as they allow users to visually gain a quick overview of the information, such as what key themes or groups exist within the dataset. The complex statistical models that compute similarity between documents are based on the structure within the data, such as term or entity frequency. In order to interactively change the view, users are required to directly adjust keyword weights, add or remove documents/keywords, or provide more information on how to parse the documents for keywords/entities upon import.

Similarly, an interactive visualization tool called iPCA uses Principal Component Analysis (PCA) to reduce high-dimensional data down to a two-dimensional plot, providing users with sliders and other visual controls for directly adjusting numerous parameters of the algorithm, such as individual eigenvalues, eigenvectors, and other components of PCA [15]. Through adjusting the parameters, the user can observe how the visualization changes. This allows users to gain insight into a dataset, given they have a thorough understanding of PCA, necessary to understand the implications behind the changes they are making to the model parameters.

Alsakran et al. presented a visualization system, STREAMIT, capable of spatially arranging text streams based on keyword similarity [3]. Again, users can interactively explore and adjust the spatial layout through directly changing the weight of keywords that they find important. In addition, STREAMIT allows for users to conduct a temporal investigation of how clusters change over time.

Synthesis Tools

Figure 2. A model of interaction with synthesis tools. Users manually create a spatial layout of the information to maintain and organize their insights about the data.

Synthesis tools focus on allowing users to organize and maintain their hypotheses and insight regarding the data in a spatial medium. In large part, this is done through presenting users with a flexible spatial workspace in which they can organize information through creating spatial structures, such as clusters, timelines, stories, etc. (Figure 2). In doing so, users externalize their thought processes (as well as their insights) into a spatial layout of the information.

For example, Analyst's Notebook [2] provides users with a spatial workspace where information can be organized, and connections between specific pieces of information (e.g., entities, documents, events, etc.) can be created. Similarly, The Sandbox [26] enables users to create a series of cases (collections of information) which can be organized spatially within the workspace.

From previous studies, we found cognitive advantages associated with the manual creation of a spatial layout of the information [4]. By providing users a workspace in which to manually create spatial representations of the information, users were able to externalize their semantics of the information into the workspace. That is, they created spatial structures (e.g., clusters, timelines, etc.), and both the structures as well as the locations relative to remaining layout carried meaning to the users with regards to their sensemaking process. Marshall et al. have pointed out that

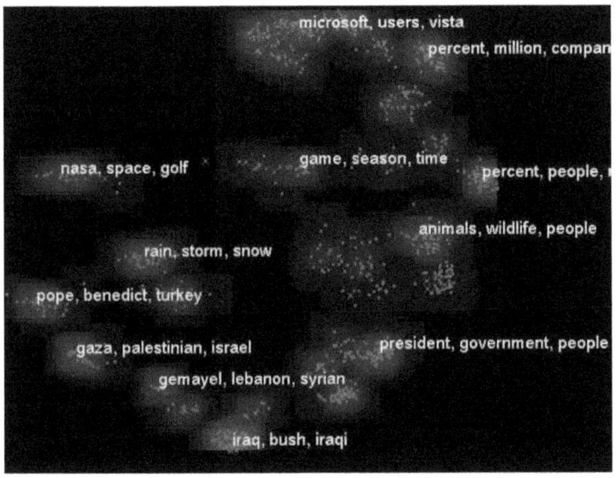

Figure 3. The IN-SPIRE Galaxy View showing a spatializtiation of documents represented as dots. Each cluster of dots represents a group of similar documents.

allowing users to create such informal relationships within information is beneficial, as it does not require users to formalize these relationships [17].

From this related work, we believe a trend is emerging in how interaction is currently handled in many visual analytic systems where complex statistical models are used – users are required to *go outside of the metaphor*. That is, while the visual representation given to users is spatial, the methods of interaction require users to step outside of that metaphor and interact directly with the parameters of the statistical model using visual controls, toolbars, etc.

There has been some work in providing more easy to use interactions for updating statistical models. For example, relevance feedback has been used for content-based image retrieval, where users are able to move images towards or away from a single image in order to portray pair-wise similarity or dissimilarity [24]. From there, an image retrieval algorithm determines the features and dimensions shared between the images that the user has determined as being similar. We view this as one example where the interaction stays in the spatial metaphor of the visualization.

Also, spatializations of document sets exist that allow users to place "points of interest" into the spatial layout. In VIBE, users are allowed to define multiple points of interest in the spatial layout that correspond to a series of keywords describing a subject matter of interest to the user [18]. Similarly, Dust & Magnet [27] allows users to place a series of "magnets" representing keywords into the space and observe how documents are attracted or repelled from the locations of these magnets. Through both of these systems, users can interact in the spatial metaphor through these placements of "nodes" representing keywords. However, the focus of semantic interaction is on interacting with data (i.e., documents), an important distinction discussed in the following section.

From the sensemaking loop presented by Pirolli and Card [19], we learn that in intelligence analysis, that analytic process consists not only of the information that is explicitly within the dataset being analyzed, but also the domain knowledge of the analyst performing the analysis. It is through this domain knowledge that analysts interact and explore the dataset to "make sense" of the information. Thus, we believe this interaction (and the domain knowledge associated with it) is equally important as the raw data, and must be incorporated into the visualization by tightly coupling the model with the interaction.

From this body of work, we most notably come away with an understanding that 1) analysts fundamentally understand the spatial metaphor used in many spatial visualizations, 2) many of these systems are constructed using complex mathematical algorithms to transform high-dimensional data to two dimensions, and 3) in most cases these algorithms can be controlled by analysts largely through visual controls (e.g., sliders, knobs, etc.) to directly adjust parameters of the algorithms, updating the spatial layout.

SEMANTIC INTERACTION

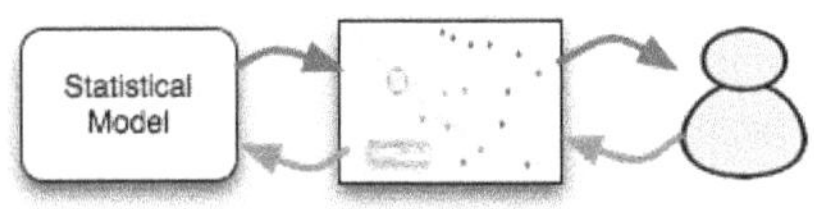

Figure 4. A model of semantic interaction. Users are able to interact directly in the spatial metaphor. The system updates the corresponding parameters of the statistical model based on the analytic reasoning of the users. Finally, the model updates the visualization based on the changes, thus unifying the synthesis and foraging stages of the sensemaking loop.

In the purest sense, semantic interaction refers to interaction occurring *within* a spatial visualization, with the added benefit that it is tightly coupled to the model calculating the spatial layout (Figure 4). Given the previous work of what interaction in visual analytic tools *is*, semantic interaction occupies a new design space for interaction. It merges the ability to change the statistical model while maintaining the flexibility and familiar methods for interacting within the metaphor of spatial visualizations. Users can benefit from semantic interactions in that they can interact within a metaphor which they are familiar with, performing interactions which are part of the spatial analytic process [4], without having to focus on formal updates to the model.

Semantic interaction leverages the cognitive connection formed between the user and the spatial layout. The following intelligence analysis scenario is representative of the strategies and interactions of analysts when performing an intelligence analysis task of textual documents in a spatial visualization, as previously found by Andrews et al. [4], and further motivates and explains the concept of semantic interaction:

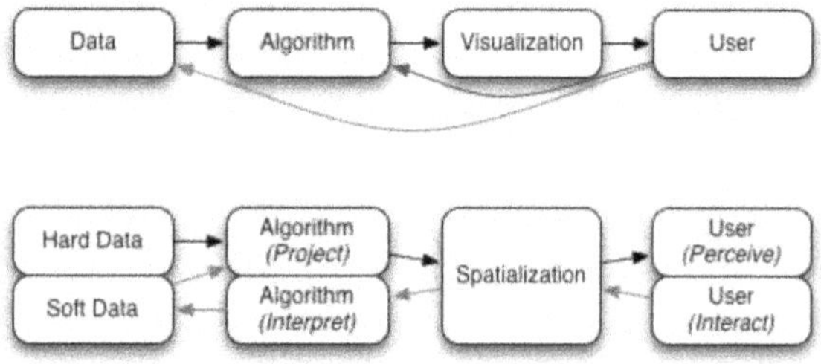

Figure 5. (top) The basic version of the "visualization pipeline". Interaction can be performed on directly the Algorithm (blue arrow) or the data (red arrow). (bottom) Our modified version of the pipeline for semantic interaction, where the user interacts within the spatial metaphor (purple arrow).

> *During her analysis, an intelligence analyst finds a suspicious and interesting phrase within a document. While reading through the document, she highlights the phrase "suspicious individuals were spotted at the airport", in order to more easily recall this information later. After she finishes reading the document, she moves the document into the bottom right corner of her workspace, in the proximity of other documents related to an event at an airport. To remind herself of her hypothesis, she annotates the document with "might be related to Revolution Now terrorist group". Now, with the goal of further examining the events at the "airport", she searches for the term, continuing her investigation.*

In addition to the three forms of semantic interaction in the scenario, Table 1 provides a list of various forms of semantic interaction, including how each can be used within the analytic process of investigating textual information spatially. We do not claim that this list is complete, but instead point out that each of these interactions can relate to a user's reasoning within the analytic process.

Designing for Semantic Interaction

In order for analysts to interact with information in a spatial metaphor, it must first be created. Following the model of the visualization pipeline [13], this creation calls for a series of mathematical transformations, turning raw data into a spatial layout – much the way many of the visualizations mentioned previously are constructed. However, these visualizations *fit* this model, as their user interactions are primarily focused on directly modifying the statistical model (as well as other attributes of the visualization or data transformation). Designing for semantic interaction requires a fundamentally different model for how tools integrate user interaction – one that can *capture the interaction*, *interpret the associated analytical reasoning*, and *update the appropriate mathematical parameters*.

Figure 5 illustrates this model, where the spatialization is treated a medium through which the user can perceive

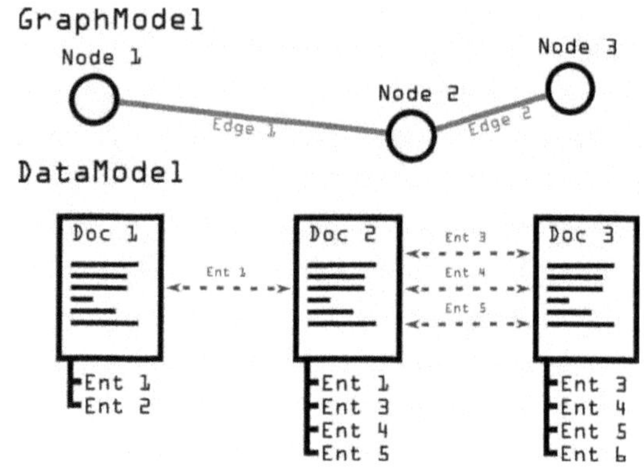

Figure 6. Overview of how nodes and edges in ForceSPIRE's force-directed layout are created from documents (Doc) and entities (Ent), respectively.

information and gain insight, as well as interact and perform his analysis. Through expanding the pipeline to accommodate for semantic interaction, it is a more appropriate match to the user's sensemaking process.

Capturing the Semantic Interaction

A non-trivial first step in the model is capturing the user interaction. Much research has been done in this area, primarily for the purpose of maintaining process history (e.g., [5], [21], [12], etc.). When considering how to capture interaction, one decision to be made is at what "level" to capture it. For example, GlassBox [6] captures interaction at a rudimentary level (i.e. mouse clicks and key strokes), while Graphical History [14] keeps track of a series of previous visualizations as a user changes the visualization during the exploration of the data.

Semantic interaction is captured at a *data level*, as the interactions occur on the data, and within the spatial metaphor. Using the earlier analytic scenario, the interaction being captured would be:

- The highlighted **phrase**
- When the highlighting occurs (**timestamp**)
- The **color** chosen for the highlight
- The **document** in which the highlight occurs
- The new document **location**
- The text of the **annotation**

By capturing (and storing) the interaction history, we can interpret the analytical reasoning of the user. Thus, we not only capture the interaction, but also *use it.*

Interpreting the Associated Analytical Reasoning

In interpreting the interaction, the goal is for the system to determine the analytical reasoning associated with the interactions and update the model accordingly. From previous findings [4], we can associate analytical reasoning with forms of semantic interaction (see Table 1). It is essentially the model's task to determine *why*, in terms of the data, the interaction occurred. To answer this question, we do not propose that this model can accurately gauge user intent. Instead, the goal is to calculate, based on the data,

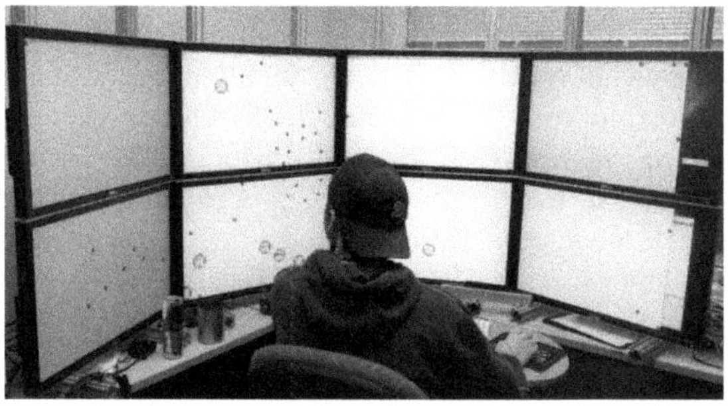

Figure 7. Using ForceSPIRE on a 32 megapixel large, high-resolution display.

what information is consistent with the captured interaction. For instance, we associate text highlighting with adding importance to the text being highlighted. We do not claim that we can associate the interaction of highlighting to the intuition that spurred the analyst to highlight the text, which is far more challenging, and arguably impossible.

We refer to the captured and interpreted interactions as *soft data*, in comparison to the *hard data* that is extracted from the raw textual information (e.g., term or entity frequency, titles, document length, etc.). We define soft data as the stored result of user interaction as interpreted by the system. In representing interaction as soft data, the algorithm can calculate and reconfigure the spatial layout accordingly. Figure 5 illustrates how our approach differs from the traditional visualization pipeline.

There has been previous work in capturing and interpreting reasoning from user interaction. For instance, Dou et al. [7] performed a study where financial analysts were asked analyze a dataset using WireVis, an interactive financial transaction visualization. The tool developers then analyzed the captured interaction, and assumptions were made about the reasoning of the analysts at specific points in the investigation. These results were compared to the analysts' self-recorded reasoning, and found to be accurate up to 82%. While our work has similar goals (i.e., interpreting the analytical reasoning associated with the analysts through an evaluation of the interaction) our model does so through tightly integrating the interaction with the underlying mathematical model. In doing so, the interpretation can be done algorithmically.

Updating the Underlying Model

Through metric learning of distance weights, the layout uses the soft data to update the underlying model. Depending on the algorithm used to compute the spatial layout, the precise parameters being updated will vary. In general, this will refer to weighting of a combination of dimensions that will help guide the model as to which dimensions the user finds important.

FORCESPIRE: SYSTEM OVERVIEW

ForceSPIRE is a visual analytics prototype designed for specific forms of semantic interaction (document movement, text highlighting, search, and annotation) for

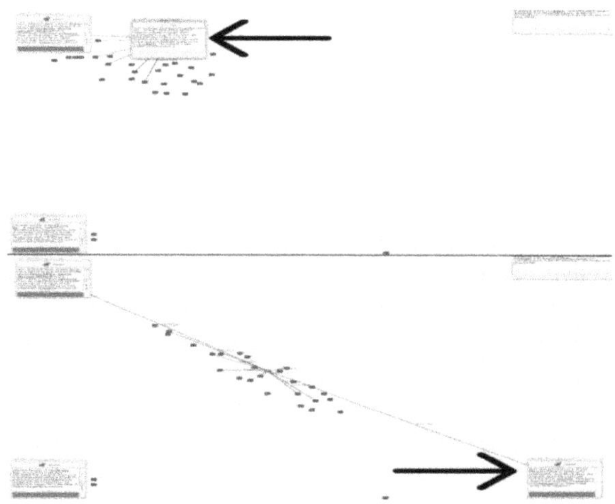

Figure 8. Moving the document shown by the arrow, ForceSPIRE adapts the layout accordingly. Documents sharing entities with the document being moved follow.

interactively exploring textual data. The system has a single spatial view (shown in Figure 12), where a collection of documents is represented spatially based on similarity (i.e., documents closer together are more similar).

ForceSPIRE is designed for large, high-resolution displays (such as the one shown in Figure 7). As semantic interaction emphasizes the importance of context in which the interaction takes place (e.g., highlighting text in the context of the document), having the full detail text available in the context of the spatial layout is beneficial over having a single document viewer. Further, the physical

Table 1. Forms of semantic interaction. Each interaction corresponds to reasoning of users within the analytic process.

Form of Semantic Interaction	*Associated Analytic Reasoning*
Document Movement	• Similarity/Dissimilarity • Create spatial construct (.e.g timeline, list, story, etc) • Test hypothesis, see how document "fits" in region
Text Highlighting	• Mark importance of phrase (collection of entities) • Augment visual appearance of document for reference
Pinning Document to Location	• Give semantic meaning to space/layout
Annotation, "Sticky Note"	• Put semantic information in workspace, within context
Document Coloring	• Create visual group/cluster • Mark group membership
Level of Visual Detail	• Change ease of visually referencing information (e.g. full detail = more important = easy to reference)
Query Terms	• Expressive search for entity

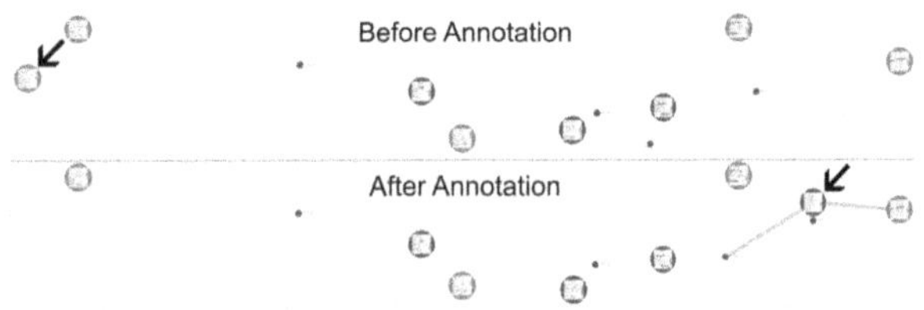

Figure 9. The Effect of adding an annotation ("these individuals may be related to Revolution Now") to the document shown with an arrow. As a result, the document becomes linked with other documents mentioning the terrorist organization "Revolution Now".

presence of these displays creates an environment in which the virtual information (in this case the documents) can occupy persistent physical space. As a result, users are further immersed into the spatial metaphor, as they can point and quickly refer to information based on the physical locations.

Constructing the Spatial Metaphor

The spatial layout of the text documents is determined by a modified version a force-directed graph model [11]. This model functions on the principle of nodes with a mass connected by springs with varying strengths. Thus, each node has attributes of attraction and repulsion: nodes repel other nodes, and two nodes attract each other only when connected by a spring (edge). The optimal layout is then computed by iteratively calculating these forces until the lowest energy state of all the nodes is reached. A complete description of this algorithm can be found in [11].

We apply this model to textual information by treating ***documents*** as ***nodes*** (an overview is shown in Figure 6). The entire textual content of each document is parsed into a collection of entities (i.e., keywords). The number of entities corresponds to the ***mass*** of each document (heavier nodes do not move as fast as lighter nodes). A ***spring*** (or edge) represents one or more matching ***entities*** between two nodes. Therefore, the initial distance metric is a based on co-occurrence of terms between documents. For example, two documents containing the term "airport" will be connected by a spring. The strength of a spring (i.e. how close together it tries to place two nodes) is based on two factors: the number of entities two documents have in common, and the ***importance value*** associated with each shared entity (initially, importance values are created using a standard tfidf method [16]). The sum of all importance values add up to 1.

The resulting spatial layout is one where similarity between documents is represented by distance relative to other documents. ***Similarity*** in this system is defined by the strength of the spring between two documents. A stronger spring (and therefore a larger amount of shared entities) will pull two documents closer together, and thus represent two similar documents.

Semantic Interaction in ForceSPIRE

The semantic interactions in ForceSPIRE are: placing information at specific locations, highlighting, searching, and annotating in order to incrementally change the spatial layout to match their mental model. The primary parameters of the force-directed model that are being updated through this learning model are the importance values of the entities.

Document Movement. The predominant interaction in a spatial workspace is positioning (and repositioning) documents. In previous work, we have demonstrated how users can perform both *exploratory* and *expressive* forms of this type of interaction [9]. In ForceSPIRE, we allow for the following exploratory interaction (i.e., interaction that allows users to explore the structure of the current model, but does not change it). Users are able to interactively explore the information by ***dragging*** a document within the workspace, ***pinning*** a document to a particular location (see Figure 8), as well as ***linking*** two documents. When dragging a document, the force-directed system responds by finding the lowest energy state of the remaining documents given the current location of the dragged document. Mathematically, this adds a constraint to the stress function being optimized (in this case the force-directed model). This allows users to explore the relationship of that document in comparison to the remaining documents.

In addition to the exploratory dragging of a document, users have the ability to ***pin*** a document. By pinning a document, users are able to incrementally add semantic meaning to locations in their workspace. By specifying key documents to user-defined locations, the layout of the remaining documents will adapt to these constraints. Thus, users can explore how documents are positioned based on their similarity (or dissimilarity) to the pinned documents. For instance, if the layout places a document between two pinned documents, it may imply that the particular document holds a link between the two pinned documents, sharing entities that occur in both.

Finally, users can perform an expressive form of this interaction by ***linking*** two documents, performed by dragging one document onto another pinned document. In doing so, ForceSPIRE calculates the similarity between the documents, and increases the importance value of the entities shared between both documents. As a result, the layout will place more emphasis on the characteristics that make those two documents similar.

Highlighting. When ***highlighting a term***, ForceSPIRE creates an entity from the term (if not already one), and the importance value of that term is increased. Similarly, ***highlighting a phrase*** results in the phrase being first parsed for entities, then increasing the importance value of each of those entities. For example, Figure 11 shows the effect of highlighting the terms "Colorado" and "missiles" in the document pointed to with the arrow. As a result, the

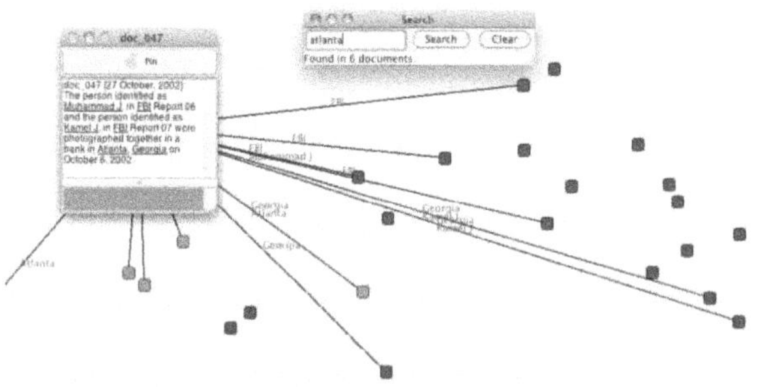

Figure 10. Searching for the term "Atlanta", documents containing the term highlight green within the context of the spatial layout. Additionally, the importance value of entity "Atlanta" is increased.

other documents containing that term are clustered more tightly.

Searching. When coming across a term of particular interest, analysts usually search on that term in order to find other occurrences. In a spatial workspace, this is of particular importance, because the answer to "where the term is also found" is not only given in terms of what documents, but also where in the layout those documents occur. The positions of documents containing the term are shown in context of the entire dataset, from which users can infer the importance of that term (as shown in Figure 10).

ForceSPIRE first creates an entity from the search term (unless it is already one), then increases the importance value of the search term. Figure 10 gives an example of how a search result appears in ForceSPIRE. Searching for the term "Atlanta", documents that contain the term are highlighted green, and links are drawn to show where the resulting documents are in relation to the current document.

Annotation. Annotations (i.e., "sticky notes") are also viewed as a form of semantic interaction, occurring within the analytic process, from which analytic reasoning can be inferred. When a user creates a note regarding a document, that semantic information should be added to the document. For example, if Document A refers to "Revolution Now" (a suspicious terrorist group), and Document B refers to "a group of suspicious individuals", and the user has reason to believe these individuals are related to Revolution Now, adding a note to Document B stating "these individuals may be related to Revolution Now" is one way for the user to add semantic meaning to the document.

ForceSPIRE handles the addition of the note (shown in Figure 9) by 1) parsing the note for any currently existing entities, then 2) increasing the importance value of each, and 3) creating any new springs between other documents sharing these entities. In the example in Figure 9, edges are created between Document B and Document A (as well as any other documents that mention "Revolution Now"). Additionally, if the note contains any new entities not currently in the model, they are created, with the intent that any future entities that may match to that note can be linked at that time. ForceSPIRE also handles cases where notes are edited, with text added or removed from the note, by updating the entities associated with the document, and adjusting the importance values of these entities accordingly.

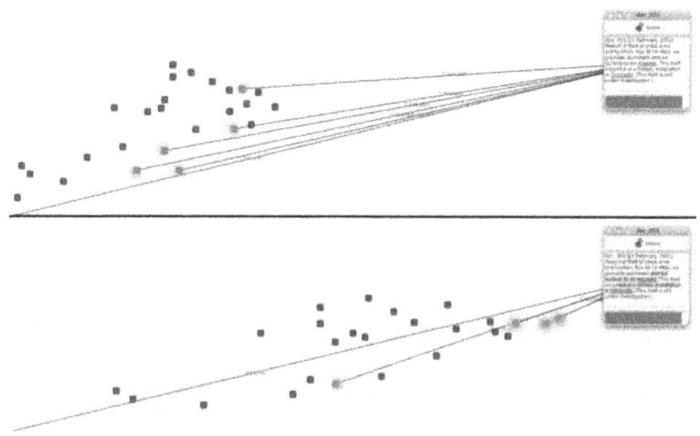

Figure 11. The effect of highlighting a phrase containing the entites "Colorado" and "missiles". Documents containing these entities move closer, as the increase in importance value increases the edge strength.

Model Updates

Each of the semantic interactions in ForceSPIRE impacts the model by updating the importance values of entities, and the mass of each document. The calculation for updating the importance value of an entity is the same for each interaction. If an entity was "hit" (i.e., it was included in a highlight, it was searched, it was in a note, etc.), ForceSPIRE increases its importance value by 10%. As the sum of all importance values of entities adds up to 1, ForceSPIRE subtracts an equal amount from all other entities' importance values. As a result, importance values decay over time, and entities that are rarely used during the analysis have less impact on the layout. The mass of a document uses a similar calculation, in that each time a document is "hit" (i.e., text was highlighted, it was the result of a search hit, etc.), it increases by 10%.

When *undoing* an interaction using the standard "Control+Z" keyboard shortcut, a linear history of the interactions will be reversed, and the importance values of affected entities will be returned to their prior values (as well as document masses). As for the locations of the documents, the reverted importance values and document masses will be responsible for updating the layout. However, this does not guarantee that the layout will return to the exact previous view, and the user may find it necessary to perform small adjustments.

The model updates used in ForceSPIRE serve as an initial approach at how to couple semantic interactions with model updates. Other, more complex methods may exist, and we encourage further research in this area. Sensemaking is a complex exploratory process. As such, semantic interaction

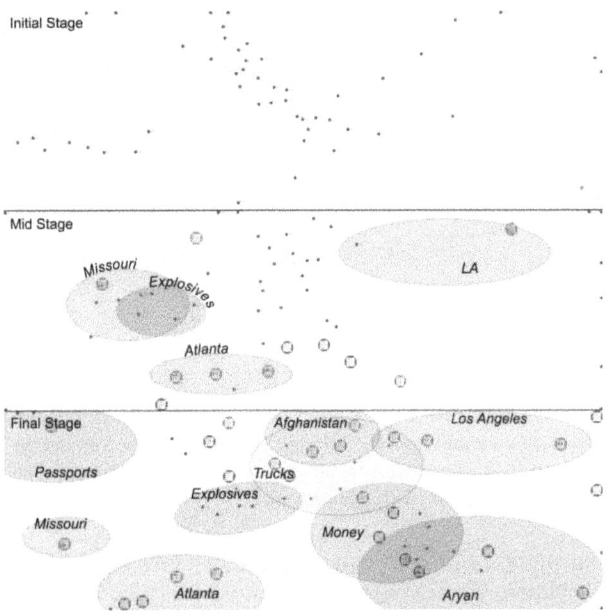

Figure 12. The incremental change of the spatial layout (main view of ForceSPIRE) from the initial to the final state. Through semantic interaction, the layout incrementally changed based on the semantic input of the user. We labeled the regions based on what the user told us the regions meant to him at each stage.

can enable analysts to explore their hypothesis in-situ, while the provenance of their insights is captured and stored. An open area of research is what analyzing the soft data might reveal about the analytic process. For instance, if the importance values of entities converge on a small number of entities, specific biases might be revealed. Similarly, instances during the analysis when new hypotheses are being explored may be indicated by diverging importance values.

Use Case

We demonstrate the functionality of ForceSPIRE through the following use case. In this scenario, we simulate an intelligence analysis scenario where the task is to find a hidden terrorist plot in a pre-constructed, ficticious textual dataset. The dataset consists of 50 text documents, containing a complex terrorist plot (explosives are being transported to various cities in the U.S. using trucks). The combination of the task of finding the hidden terrorist plot and the textual dataset is representative of daily work performed by professional intelligence analysts [8]. The analysis described below lasted 70 minutes, and was performed by an individual computer science graduate student.

The user began the investigation by loading the collection of documents into ForceSPIRE. The documents were automatically parsed for entities using the LingPipe keyword extraction library [1]. From these entities, an initial layout was generated, shown in Figure 12(top). From this layout, he began investigation by reading through the more central documents. While reading through the documents, he ***highlighted*** phrases of interest. For example, he highlighted the phrase "Nizar A. is now known to have spent six months in Afghanistan". In doing so, ForceSPIRE increased the importance value of the entities within the phrase, particularly "Afghanistan" and "Nizar A". As a result, the layout forms more tightly around those entities. Each change incrementally changes the layout.

Continuing with his investigation, he began ***searching*** for words of interest (e.g., "weapons", "Colorado", "Atlanta", etc.). ForceSPIRE provided him with quick visual feedback on where in the dataset each terms showed up (the search result for "Atlanta" is shown in Figure 10). In addition to gaining an overview of the distribution of the term within the dataset (by highlighting each document containing the term green), ForceSPIRE treats performing a search as either creating a new entity from the search term, or increasing the importance value if an entity corresponding to the search term already exists. As a result of the multiple search terms and highlights corresponding to locations (e.g., "Atlanta", "Los Angeles", "Missouri", etc.), ForceSPIRE adapts the spatialization by creating a more geographic-oriented layout (shown in the "Mid Stage" layout in Figure 12).

During further investigation, he began opening more documents and ***adding annotations*** to documents where he found information missing that he knew. For example, Figure 9 shows how he opened one document where "suspicious individuals" were mentioned. Earlier, he read a document containing information about a terrorist organization named "Revolution Now". While reading about the suspicious individuals, the other information in the document triggered him to make a connection between these individuals and Revolution Now. He made added a note to the document about the suspicious individuals stating "these individuals may be related to Revolution Now". As a result, ForceSPIRE parsed the note for entities, added them to the document, and pulled the document closer to other documents containing the entity "Revolution Now".

After continuing his investigation in this manner, he ultimately made the connections within the dataset to uncover the terrorist plot. The progression of the spatial layout, shown in Figure 12, shows the final layout, where he was able to pinpoint regions of the layout as being important in his finding. Some of the spatial locations of clusters are a result of him ***pinning*** documents to that region (e.g., "Atlanta", "Los Angeles", etc.). These pinned documents are shown in red. Perhaps more interestingly is not the regions that were created as a result of him pinning documents to that location, but rather how the remaining documents respond in the layout. For example, in the final state shown in Figure 12, a group of documents began to emerge in the middle of all the pinned locations. Upon examining these documents, he discovered that these

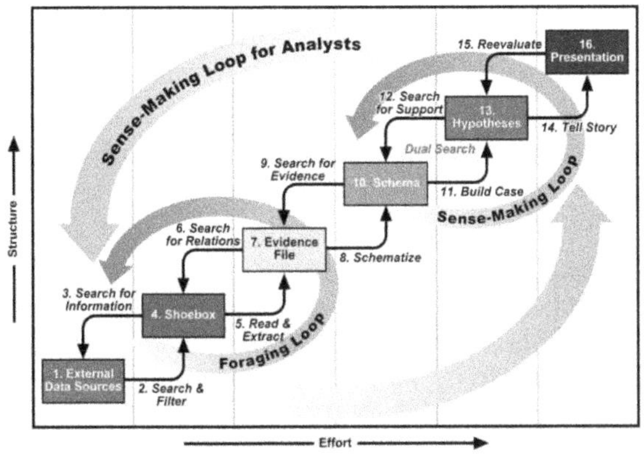

Figure 13. The sensemaking loop, illustrating the complex sequence of steps used by intelligence analysts in order to gain insight into data.

documents are about the terrorist organization using "U-Haul" or "Ryder" trucks for transportation between these locations. ForceSPIRE placing these documents in between these cities in the layout was helpful, as these documents contain information "connecting" the events in these locations. Immediately after noticing this event, he also made use of the expressive form of interaction, performed by dragging two of these documents together to determine what made them similar. After seeing that it was indeed terms such as "Ryder" and "U-Haul", the layout formed more tightly around these terms.

ForceSPIRE interpreted the analytical reasoning of the user through the creation of new entities that were not found by the initial keyword extraction, as well as the increase of importance values of existing entities. This is evidenced by the creation of 39 new entities during the course of the analysis. LingPipe extracted 89 initial entities from this dataset, and at the time of completing our investigation ForceSPIRE included 128. Examples of newly created entities are "big event", "grenades", "Fisher Island", "weapons", and others. The ability for new entities to be created via semantic interaction did not interfere with the fluid sensemaking process of the user. Instead, it aided the process by creating new entities, which in turn created semantically relevant connections within the dataset.

In addition to creating new entities, existing entities dynamically changed their importance value based on the interpreted analytical reasoning of the semantic interactions. Examples of entities that changed their importance values are "Atlanta", "Revolution Now", "Colorado", "L.A.", and others. As a result, the ForceSPIRE incrementally adapted the layout based on the user input. This shows that adjusting importance values, creating entities, and changing locations of key documents helped the user discover the structure of the dataset, and ultimately make out the hidden terrorist plot.

DISCUSSION

Unifying the Sensemaking Loop

With the fundamentally different role occupied by semantic interaction, we explore a new design space for interaction in visual analytic tools. With the addition of soft data, and a model capable of interpreting the user's analytical reasoning, we leverage interactions that are already occurring in the spatial analytic process to further aid users in their sensemaking process.

With semantic interaction, the amount of formalization between foraging and sensemaking (Figure 13) on the part of the user is reduced. For instance, in moving a document, users can formulate a hypothesis based on that document, expecting similar documents to follow. ForceSPIRE attempts to update the layout based on the interaction, and gives the user feedback. Thus, the foraging stage occurs as a result of the hypothesis being formed through semantic interaction. By not forcing users to over-formalize their analytic reasoning too early in order to forage for the relevant information, semantic interaction creates a more seamless transition between foraging and synthesis, unifying the sensemaking loop.

Future Work

Semantic interaction, as a concept, opens up many possibilities for further research, such as: what interactions to capture and store, which parameters of the model to update, how to store the soft data, and which models present a metaphor that can be extended upon.

In order to make more concrete claims regarding the usability and effectiveness of ForceSPIRE (and thus, of semantic interaction), a formal user study is needed. Our plan is to introduce ForceSPIRE to professional intelligence analysts and have them solve scenarios that model their daily task, such as one of the VAST datasets [2020]. The observations and feedback from these users will provide ecological validity for semantic interaction.

CONCLUSION

In this paper we have discussed how the concept of semantic interaction leads to a new design space for interaction in spatializations of textual information. Semantic interactions occur directly within the spatial metaphor, support spatial cognition, and exploit spatial analytic interactions. We describe semantic interaction, discussing the three components required – capturing the interaction, interpreting the analytical reasoning, and updating the mathematical model. Further, we present ForceSPIRE, designed for semantic interaction with textual information, discussing its functionality and demonstrating how it can be used through a use case. Lastly, we discuss how semantic interaction has the opportunity to unify the sensemaking loop, creating a more seamless analytic process. In allowing users to interact within the spatial metaphor, they can remain more focused on their analysis of the data, without having to become experts in the underlying mathematical models of the system.

ACKNOWLEDGEMENTS
This research was funded by the NSF grant CCF-0937071 and the DHS center of excellence.

REFERENCES
1. *Alias-i. 2008. LingPipe 4.0.1.* City, 2008.
2. *i2 Analyst's Notebook.* City.
3. Alsakran, J., Chen, Y., Zhao, Y., Yang, J. and Luo, D. STREAMIT: Dynamic visualization and interactive exploration of text streams. In *Proceedings of the IEEE Pacific Visualization Symposium*, 2011.
4. Andrews, C., Endert, A. and North, C. Space to Think: Large, High-Resolution Displays for Sensemaking. In *Proceedings of the CHI '10,* 2010.
5. Callahan, S. P., Freire, J., Santos, E., Scheidegger, C. E., C, Silva, u. T. and Vo, H. T. VisTrails: visualization meets data management. In *Proceedings of the SIGMOD international conference on Management of data* (Chicago, IL, USA, 2006). ACM.
6. Cowley, P., Haack, J., Littlefield, R. and Hampson, E. Glass box: capturing, archiving, and retrieving workstation activities. In *Proceedings of the workshop on Continuous archival and retrival of personal experences* (Santa Barbara, California, USA, 2006). ACM.
7. Dou, W., Jeong, D. H., Stukes, F., Ribarsky, W., Lipford, H. R. and Chang, R. *Recovering Reasoning Processes from User Interactions*. IEEE Computer Graphics and Applications, 2009.
8. Endert, A., Andrews, C., Fink, G. A. and North, C. Professional Analysts using a Large, High-Resolution Display. In *Proceedings of the IEEE VAST Extended Abstract* (2009).
9. Endert, A., Han, C., Maiti, D., House, L., Leman, S. C. and North, C. *Observation-level Interaction with Statistical Models for Visual Analytics*. IEEE VAST, 2011.
10. Frank M. Shipman, I. and Marshall, C. C. Formality Considered Harmful: Experiences, Emerging Themes, and Directions on the Use of Formal Representations inInteractive Systems. *ACM CSCW*, 8, 4, 1999, 333-352.
11. Fruchterman, T. M. J. and Reingold, E. M. Graph drawing by force-directed placement. *Software: Practice and Experience*, 21, 11 1991, 1129-1164.
12. Gotz, D. *Interactive Visual Synthesis of Analytic Knowledge*. IEEE VAST, 2006.
13. Heer, J. *prefuse manual*, 2006.
14. Heer, J., Mackinlay, J., Stolte, C. and Agrawala, M. Graphical Histories for Visualization: Supporting Analysis, Communication, and Evaluation. *IEEE Transactions on Visualization and Computer Graphics*, 14, 6 , 2008, 1189-1196.
15. Jeong, D. H., Ziemkiewicz, C., Fisher, B., Ribarsky, W. and Chang, R. iPCA: An Interactive System for PCA-based Visual Analytics. *Computer Graphics Forum*, 28, 2009, 767-774.
16. Karen A Statistical Interpretation of Term Specificity and its Application in Retrieval. *Journal of Documentation*, 28, 1972, 11-21.
17. Marshall, C. C., Frank M. Shipman, I. and Coombs, J. H. VIKI: spatial hypertext supporting emergent structure. In *Proceedings of the European conference on Hypermedia technology* (Edinburgh, Scotland, 1994). ACM.
18. Olsen, K. A., Korfhage, R. R., Sochats, K. M., Spring, M. B. and Williams, J. G. Visualization of a document collection: the vibe system. *Information Process Management*, 29, 1 1993, 69-81.
19. Pirolli, P. and Card, S. Sensemaking Processes of Intelligence Analysts and Possible Leverage Points as Identified Though Cognitive Task Analysis *Proceedings of the International Conference on Intelligence Analysis,*2005, 6.
20. Plaisant, C., Grinstein, G., Scholtz, J., Whiting, M., O'Connell, T., Laskowski, S., Chien, L., Tat, A., Wright, W., Gorg, C., Zhicheng, L., Parekh, N., Singhal, K. and Stasko, J. Evaluating Visual Analytics at the 2007 VAST Symposium Contest. *Computer Graphics and Applications, IEEE*, 28, 2 2008, 12-21.
21. Shrinivasan, Y. B. and Wijk, J. J. v. Supporting the analytical reasoning process in information visualization. In *Proceedings of the CHI '08* (Florence, Italy, 2008). ACM.
22. Skupin, A. *A Cartographic Approach to Visualizing Conference Abstracts*. IEEE Computer Graphics and Applications, pp. 50-58, January/February, 2002.
23. Thomas, J. J., Cook, K. A., National, V. and Analytics, C. *Illuminating the path*. IEEE Computer Society, 2005.
24. Torres, R. S., Silva, C. G., Medeiros, C. B. and Rocha, H. V. Visual structures for image browsing. In *Proceedings of the conference on Information and knowledge management* (New Orleans, LA, USA, 2003). ACM.
25. Wise, J. A., Thomas, J. J., Pennock, K., Lantrip, D., Pottier, M., Schur, A. and Crow, V. *Visualizing the non-visual: spatial analysis and interaction with information for text documents*. Morgan Kaufmann Publishers, 1999.
26. Wright, W., Schroh, D., Proulx, P., Skaburskis, A. and Cort, B. The Sandbox for analysis: concepts and methods. In *Proceedings of the CHI '06* (New York, NY, 2006). ACM.
27. Yi, J. S., Melton, R., Stasko, J. and Jacko, J. A. Dust & magnet: multivariate information visualization using a magnet metaphor. *Information Visualization*, 4, 4, 2005, 239-256.

Touché: Enhancing Touch Interaction on Humans, Screens, Liquids, and Everyday Objects

Munehiko Sato[1,2*], Ivan Poupyrev[1], Chris Harrison[1,3]

[1] Disney Research Pittsburgh, 4720 Forbes Avenue, Pittsburgh, PA 15213 USA {munehiko.sato, ivan.poupyrev} @disneyresearch.com

[2] Graduate School of Engineering, The University of Tokyo, Hongo 7-3-1, Tokyo 113-8656 Japan

[3] HCI Institute, Carnegie Mellon University, 5000 Forbes Avenue, Pittsburgh, PA 15213 USA chris.harrison@cs.cmu.edu

ABSTRACT

Touché proposes a novel *Swept Frequency Capacitive Sensing* technique that can not only detect a touch event, but also recognize complex configurations of the human hands and body. Such contextual information significantly enhances touch interaction in a broad range of applications, from conventional touchscreens to unique contexts and materials. For example, in our explorations we add touch and gesture sensitivity to the human body and liquids. We demonstrate the rich capabilities of *Touché* with five example setups from different application domains and conduct experimental studies that show gesture classification accuracies of 99% are achievable with our technology.

Author Keywords: Touch; gestures; ubiquitous interfaces; sensors; on-body computing; mobile devices.

ACM Classification Keywords

H.5.2 [Information interfaces and presentation]: User Interfaces - Graphical user interfaces; Input devices & strategies.

INTRODUCTION

Touché is a novel capacitive touch sensing technology that provides rich touch and gesture sensitivity to a variety of analogue and digital objects. The technology is *scalable*, i.e., the same sensor is equally effective for a pencil, a doorknob, a mobile phone or a table. Gesture recognition also scales with objects: a *Touché* enhanced doorknob can capture the configuration of fingers touching it, while a table can track the posture of the entire user (Figures 1b, 6 and 7).

Sensing with *Touché* is not limited to inanimate objects – the user's body can also be made touch and gesture sensitive (Figures 1a and 9). In general, *Touché* makes it very easy to add touch and gesture interactivity to unusual, non-solid objects and materials, such as a body of water. Using *Touché* we can recognize when users touch the water's surface or dip their fingers into it (Figures 1c and 10).

* *This work was conducted over the course of a one-year research internship at Disney Research, Pittsburgh.*

CHI'12, May 5–10, 2012, Austin, Texas, USA.

Notably, instrumenting objects, humans and liquids with *Touché* is trivial: *a single electrode* embedded into an object and attached to our sensor controller is sufficient to computationally enhance an object with rich touch and gesture interactivity. Furthermore, in the case of conductive objects, e.g., doorknobs or a body of water, the object itself acts as an intrinsic electrode – no additional instrumentation is necessary. Finally, *Touché* is inexpensive, safe, low power and compact; it can be easily embedded or temporarily attached anywhere touch and gesture sensitivity is desired.

Touché proposes a novel form of capacitive touch sensing that we call *Swept Frequency Capacitive Sensing* (SFCS). In a typical capacitive touch sensor, a conductive object is excited by an electrical signal at a fixed frequency. The sensing circuit monitors the return signal and determines touch events by identifying changes in this signal caused by the electrical properties of the human hand touching the object [46]. In SFCS, on the other hand, we monitor the response to capacitive human touch over a *range of frequencies*. Objects excited by an electrical signal respond differently at different frequencies, therefore, the changes in

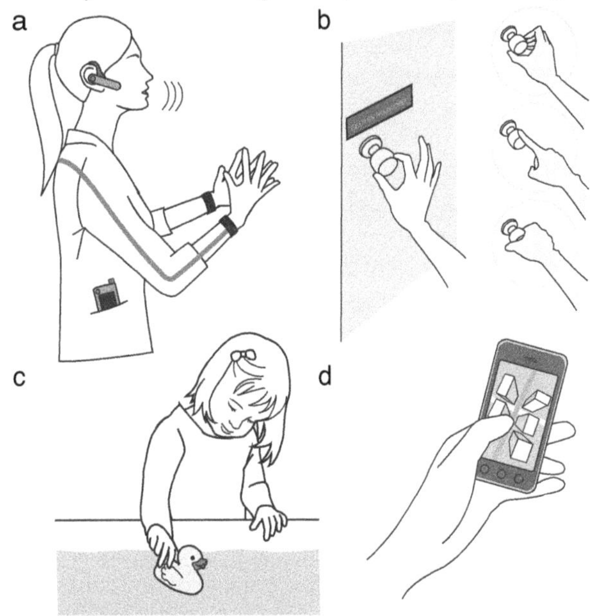

Figure 1: Touché applications: (a) on-body gesture sensing; (b) a smart doorknob with a "gesture password"; (c) interacting with water; (d) hand postures in touch screen interaction.

the return signal will also be frequency dependent. Thus, instead of measuring a *single* data point for each touch event, we measure a *multitude* of data points at different frequencies. We then use machine learning and classification techniques to demonstrate that we can reliably extract rich interaction context, such as hand or body postures, from this data. Not only can we determine that a touch event occurred, we can also determine *how* it occurred. Importantly, this contextual touch information is captured through a *single electrode*, which could be simply the object itself.

Although electromagnetic signal frequency sweeps have been used for decades in wireless communication and industrial proximity sensors [35], we are not aware of any previous attempt to explore this technique for *touch interaction*. Our contributions, therefore, are multifold:

1) We propose and develop a novel capacitive touch sensing technology, called Swept Frequency Capacitive Sensing. It allows for minimally instrumented objects to capture a wealth of information about the context of touch interaction. It also permits novel mediums for capacitive touch and gesture sensing, such as water and the human body.

2) We report a number of innovative applications that demonstrate the utility of our technology including a) smart touch interaction on everyday objects, b) tracking human body postures with a table, c) enhancing touchscreen interaction, d) making the human body touch sensitive, and e) recognizing hand gestures in liquids.

3) We conduct controlled experimental evaluations for each of the above applications. Results demonstrate recognition rates approaching 100%. This suggests *Touché* is immediately feasible in a variety of real-world applications.

RELATED WORK AND APPROACHES

The importance of touch and gestures has been long appreciated in the research and practice of human-computer interaction (HCI). There is a tremendous body of previous work related to touch, including the development of touch sensors and tactile displays, hand gesture tracking and recognition, designing interaction techniques and applications for touch, building multitouch, tangible and flexible devices. See [2, 6, 21, 24, 25, 27, 44] for a subset of previous work on touch.

The foundation for all touch interaction is touch sensing, i.e., technologies that capture human touch and gestures. This includes sensing touch using cameras or arrays of optical elements [15, 22], laser rangefinders [4], resistance and pressure sensors [31] and acoustics [16, 17] – to name a few. The most relevant technology is *capacitive touch sensing,* a family of sensing techniques based on same physical phenomenon – *capacitive coupling.*

The basic principles of operation in most common capacitive sensing techniques are quite similar: A periodic electrical signal is injected into an electrode forming an oscillating electrical field. As the user's hand approaches the electrode, a weak capacitive link is formed between the electrode and conductive physiological fluids inside the human hand, altering the signal supplied by the electrode. This happens because the user body introduces an additional path for flow of charges, acting as a charge "sink" [46]. By measuring the degree of this signal change, touch events can be detected.

There is a wide variety of capacitive touch sensing techniques. One important design variable is the choice of signal property that is used to detect touch events, e.g., changes in *signal phase* [19] or *signal amplitude* [1, 25, 30] can be used for touch detection. The signal excitation technique is another important design variable. For example, the earliest capacitive proximity sensors in the 1970s were oscillating at resonant frequency and measured signal dumping as additional capacitance that would affect the resonant frequency of the sensing circuit [35]. The choice of topology of electrode layouts, the materials used for electrodes and substrates and the specifics of signal measurement resulted in a multitude of capacitive techniques, including charge transfer, surface and projective capacitive, among others [1, 25].

Capacitive sensing is a malleable and inexpensive technology – all it requires is a simple conductive element that is easy to manufacture and integrate into devices or environments. Consequently, today we find capacitive touch in millions of consumer device controls and touch screens. It has, however, a number of limitations. One important limitation is that capacitive sensing is not particularly expressive – it can only detect when a finger is touching the device and sometimes infer finger proximity. To increase the expressiveness, matrices of electrodes are scanned to create a 2D capacitive image [6, 21, 30, 37]. Such space multiplexing allows the device to capture spatial gestures, hand profiles [30] or even rough 3D shapes [36]. However, this comes at the cost of increased engineering complexity, limiting its applications and precluding ad hoc instrumentation of our living and working spaces. Current capacitive sensors are also limited in materials they can be used with. Typically they cannot be used on the human body or liquids.

In this paper, we advocate a different approach to enhancing the expressivity of capacitive sensing – by using *frequency multiplexing.* Instead of using a single, pre-determined frequency, we sense touch by sweeping through a range of frequencies. We refer to the resulting curve as a *capacitive profile* and demonstrate its ability to expand the vocabulary of interactive touch without increasing the number of electrodes or the complexity of the sensor itself.

Importantly, our technology is not limited to a single electrode. Sensor matrices can be easily constructed and would bring many of the unique sensing dimensions described in this paper. However, in the current work, we focus on a single electrode solution, as that is the simplest – and yet allows for surprisingly rich interactions. At the same time, it is compact, inexpensive and can be easily integrated into a variety of everyday objects and real world applications.

SWEPT FREQUENCY CAPACITIVE SENSING

The human body is conductive, e.g., the average internal resistance of a human trunk is ~100 Ω [42]. Skin, on the

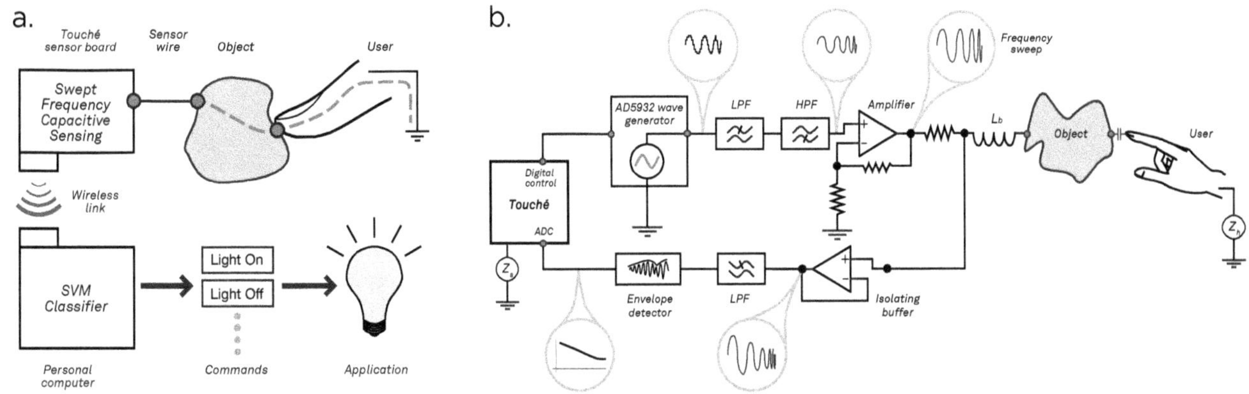

Figure 2: (a) Touché architecture (b) Swept Frequency Capacitive Sensing with Touché.

other hand, is highly resistive, ~1M Ω for dry undamaged skin [42]. This would block any weak constant electrical (DC) signal applied to the body. Alternating current (AC) signal, however, passes through the skin, which forms a capacitive interface between the electrode and ionic physiologic fluids inside the body [10]. The body forms a charge "sink" with the signal flowing though tissues and bones to ground, which is also connected to the body through a capacitive link [25, 46].

The resistive and capacitive properties of the human body oppose the applied AC signal. This opposition, or electrical *impedance*[1], changes the *phase* and *amplitude* of the AC signal. Thus, by measuring changes in the applied AC signal we can 1) detect the presence of a human body and also 2) learn about the internal composition of the body itself. This phenomenon, in its many variations, has been used since the 1960s in medical practice to measure the fluid composition of the human body [10], in electro-impedance tomography imaging [5] and even to detect the ripeness of nectarine fruits [13]. More recently, it has been used in a broad variety of capacitive touch buttons, sliders and touchscreens in human-computer interaction [6, 19, 30, 46].

The amount of signal change depends on a variety of factors. It is affected by *how a person touches the electrode*, e.g., the surface area of skin touching the electrode. It is affected by the *body's connection to ground*, e.g., wearing or not wearing shoes or having one or both feet on the ground. Finally, it strongly depends on *signal frequency*. This is because at different frequencies, the AC signal will flow through *different paths* inside of the body [10]. Indeed, just as DC signal flows through the path of least resistance, the AC signal will always flow through the path of least *impedance*. The human body is anatomically complex and different tissues, e.g., muscle, fat and bones, have different resistive and capacitive properties. As the frequency of the AC signal changes, some of the tissues become more opposed to the flow of charges, while others less, thus changing the path of the signal flow (see [10] for an overview of the bioelectrical aspects of human body impedance).

Therefore, by sweeping through a range of frequencies in capacitive sensing applications, we obtain a wealth of information about 1) how the user is touching the object, 2) how the user is connected to the ground and 3) the current configuration of the human body and individual body properties. The challenge here is to reliably capture the data and then find across-user commonalities – static and temporal patterns that allow an interactive system to infer user interaction with the object, the environment, as well as the context of interaction itself.

SFCS presents an exciting opportunity to significantly expand the richness of capacitive sensing. We are not aware of previous attempts to design SFCS touch and gesture interfaces, investigate their interactive properties, identify possible application domains, or rigorously evaluate their feasibility for supporting interactive applications[2]. All relevant capacitive touch sensing techniques use a *single frequency*.

One of the reasons why SFCS techniques have not been investigated before could be due to computational expense: instead of sampling a single data point at a single frequency, SFCS requires a frequency sweep and analysis of hundreds of data points. Only recently, with the advance of fast and inexpensive microprocessors, has it become feasible to use SFCS in touch interfaces. Another challenge in using SFCS is that it requires high-frequency signals, e.g., ~3 Mhz. Designing conditioning circuitry for high-frequency signals is a complex problem. We will discuss these challenges and solutions in detail in the next section of this paper.

TOUCHÉ IMPLEMENTATION

The overall architecture of *Touché* is presented on Figure 2a. The user interacts with an object that is attached to a *Touché* sensor board via a single wire. If the object itself is conductive, the wire can be attached directly to it. Otherwise, a single electrode has to be embedded into the object and the wire attached to this electrode.

[1] Impedance is defined as a total opposition of circuit or material to AC signal at a *certain frequency*. Impedance consists of resistance and reactance, which, in case of human body, is purely capacitive [10].

[2] We reported preliminary explorations of SFCS technology in [29].

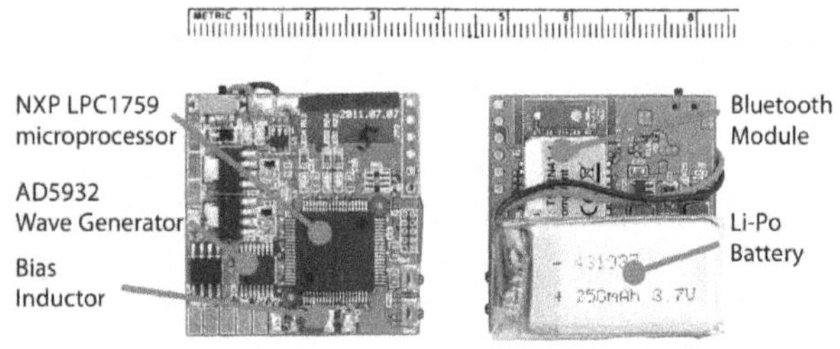

Figure 3: Touché sensing board: 36x36x5.5 mm, 13.8 grams.

Touché implements SFCS on a compact custom-built board powered by an ARM Cortex-M3 microprocessor (Figure 3). The on-board signal generator excites an electrode with sinusoid sweeps and measures returned signal at each frequency. The resulting sampled signal is a *capacitive profile* of the touch interaction. We stress that in the current version of *Touché* we do not measure phase changes of the signal in response to user interaction. We leave this for future work.

Finally, the capacitive profile is sent to a conventional computer over Bluetooth for classification. Recognized gestures can then be used to trigger different interactive functions. While it is possible to implement classification directly on the sensor board, a conventional computer provided more flexibility in fine-tuning and allowed for rapid prototyping.

Sensor board design

An ARM microprocessor, NXP LPC1759 running at 120 MHz, controls an AD5932 programmable wave generator to synthesize variable frequency sinusoidal signal sweeps from 1 KHz to 3.5 MHz in 17.5 KHz steps (i.e., 200 steps in each sweep, see Figure 2b). The signal is filtered to remove environmental noise and undesirable high frequency components and is also amplified to 6.6 Vpp (Figure 4a), which is then used to excite the attached conductive object. In the current design we tune *Touché* to sense very small variations of capacitance at lower excitation frequencies by adding a large bias inductor L_b (~100 mH), a technique used in impedance measurement. By replacing it with a bias capacitor, we can make *Touché* sensitive to very small inductive variations, e.g., copper coil stretching.

The return signal from the object is measured by adding a small sensing resistor, which converts alternating current into an alternating voltage signal (Figure 4b). This signal is then fed into a buffer to isolate sensing and excitation sections; an envelope detector then converts the AC signal into a time-varying DC signal (Figure 4c). The microprocessor samples the signal at a maximum of 200 KHz using a 12-bit analog-digital converter (ADC). A single sweep takes ~33 ms, translating to a 33 Hz update rate.

Currently, the sampling rate of ADC is a main limiting factor for speed: a dedicated ADC with a higher sampling rate would significantly increase the speed of *Touché*. Sampling is much slower at low frequencies, as it takes longer for the analogue circuitry to respond to a slowly varying signal. In applications where an object does not respond to low frequencies, we swept only in the high frequency range, tripling the sensor update rate to ~100 Hz.

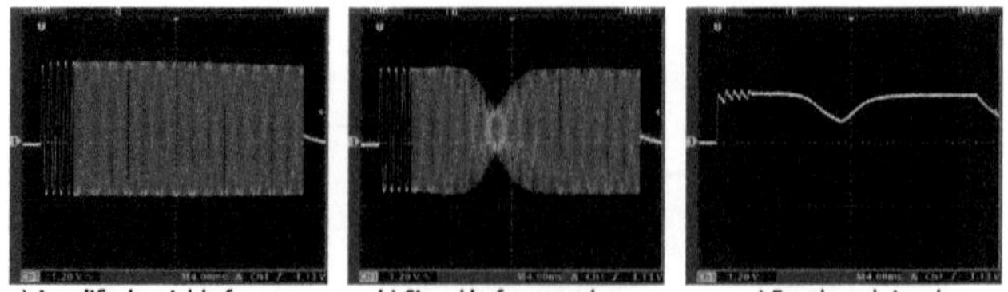

a) Amplified variable frequency sinusoidal signal b) Signal before envelope c) Enveloped signal

Figure 4: Variable frequencies sweep and return signal.

Touché Sensing Configurations

There are two basic sensor configurations. First, the *user is simply touching on object or an electrode* (Figures 5a and 5c). This is the classic capacitive sensor configuration that assumes that both the sensor and the user are sharing common ground, even through different impedances. For example, if the sensor were powered from an electrical outlet, it would be connected to the ground line of a building. The user would be naturally coupled to the same ground via a capacitive link to the floor or building structure. Although this link may be weak, it is sufficient for *Touché*.

In the second case, the sensor is *touching two different locations of the user body* with its ground and signal electrodes (Figures 5b and 5d). In this configuration *Touché* measures the impedance between two body locations [10].

Communication and Recognition

For classification, we use a Support Vector Machine (SVM) implementation provided by the Weka Toolkit [12] (SMO, C=2.0, polynomial kernel, e=1.0) that runs on the aforementioned conventional computer. Each transmission from the sensor contains a 200-point capacitive profile, from which we extract a series of features for classification.

The raw impedance values from the frequency sweep have a natural high-order quality. As can be seen in Figure 6-10, the impendence profiles are highly continuous, distinctive and temporally stable. Therefore, we use all 200 values as features without any additional processing. Additionally, we compute the derivative of the impedance profile at three different levels of aliasing, by down-sampling profiles into arrays of 10, 20, 40 and using [-1, 1] kernel, yielding another 70 features. This helps to capture shape features of the

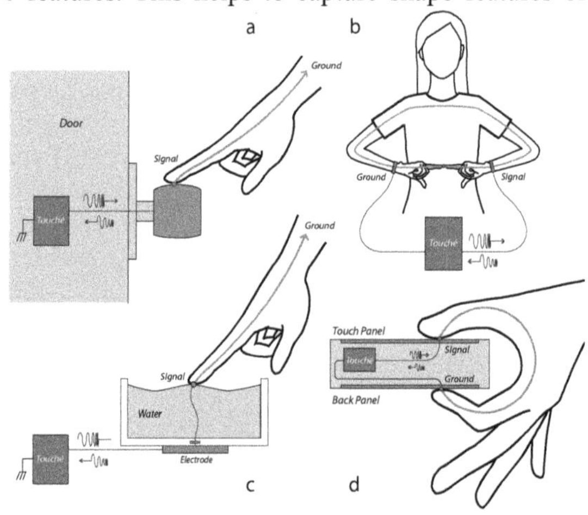

Figure 5: Configurations of *Touché* applications.

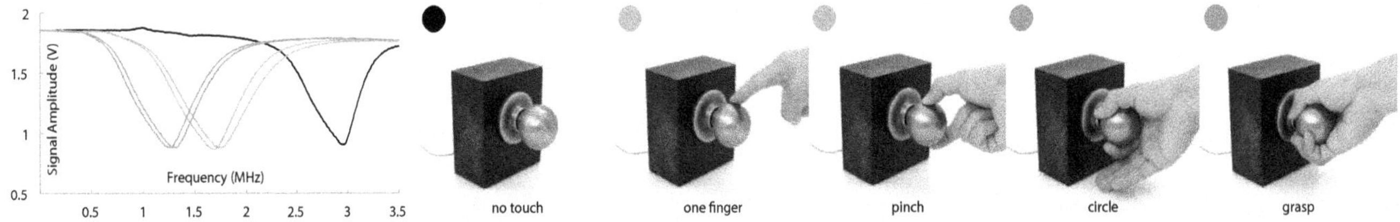

Figure 6: Capacitive profiles for making objects touch and grasp sensitive (doorknob example).

profile, independent of amplitude, e.g., it is easy to see the peaks minima in Figures 6-10 – more difficult is to see the visually subtle, but highly discriminative peak slopes. Moreover, using the derivative increases robustness to global variations in impendence, e.g., an offset of signal amplitude across all frequencies due to temperature variations. As a final feature, we include the capacitive profile minima, which was found to be highly characteristic in pilot studies (see Figures 6-10). Once the SVM has been trained, classification can proceed in a real-time fashion.

EXAMPLE TOUCHÉ APPLICATIONS

The application space of *Touché* is broad, therefore at least some categorization is pertinent to guide the development of the interfaces based on this technology. We identified five application areas where we felt that *Touché* could have the largest impact – either as a useful enhancement to an established application or a novel application, uniquely enabled by our approach:

- making *everyday objects* touch gesture sensitive
- sensing *human* bimanual hand gestures
- sensing *human* body configuration (e.g., pose)
- enhancing *traditional touch interfaces*
- sensing interaction with *unusual materials* (e.g., liquids)

In the rest of this section we propose a single exemplary application for each category, highlighting the utility and scope of our sensing approach. We then evaluate these applications experimentally in the next section of the paper.

Making objects touch and grasp sensitive

If analogue or digital objects can be made aware of how they are being touched, held or manipulated, they could configure themselves in meaningful and productive ways [14, 28, 34, 37, 38]. The canonical example is a mobile phone which, when held like a phone, operates as a phone. However, when held like a camera, the mode could switch to picture-taking automatically.

Touché offers a lightweight, non-invasive sensing approach that makes it very easy to add touch and gesture sensitivity to everyday objects. Doorknobs provide an illustrative example: they lie in our usual paths and already require touch to operate. Yet, in general, doorknobs have not been infused with computational abilities. A smart doorknob that can sense how a user is touching it could have many useful features. For example, closing a door with a tight grasp could lock it, while closing it with a pinch might set a user's away message, e.g., "back in five minutes". A sequence of grasps could constitute a "grasp password" that would allow an authorized user to unlock the door (Figure 1b).

Objects such as doorknobs can be easily instrumented with *Touché* (Figures 5a). More importantly, existing conductive structures can be used as sensing electrodes, for example, the brass surface of a doorknob. Our *Touché* sensor could be connected to these elements with a single wire, requiring no further instrumentation (Figure 6). Contrast this to previous techniques that generally require a matrix of sensors [20, 30, 37, 38]. We present detailed experimental evaluations of *Touché* in this context later in this paper.

Body Configuration Sensing

Touché can be used to sense the configuration of the entire human body. For example, a door could sense if a person is simply standing next to it, if they have raised their arm to knock on it, are pushing the door, or are leaning against it. Alternatively, a chair or a table could sense the posture of a seated person – reclined or leaning forward, arms on the armrests or not, one or two arms operating on the surface, as well as their configuration (Figure 7). More importantly, this can occur *without instrumenting* the user. Similar to everyday objects, conductive tables can be used as is, just by connecting a *Touché* sensor. Non-conductive tables would require a single flat electrode added to their surface or could simply be painted with conductive paint.

Sensing the pose of the human body without instrumenting the user has numerous compelling applications. Posture-sensing technologies are an active area of research, with applications in gaming, adaptive environments, smart offices, in-vehicle interaction, rehabilitation and many others [9]. We view *Touché* as one such enabling technology, with many exciting applications. To this end, we report an evaluation of body posture sensing with a *Touché*-enhanced table in the following Touché Evaluation section.

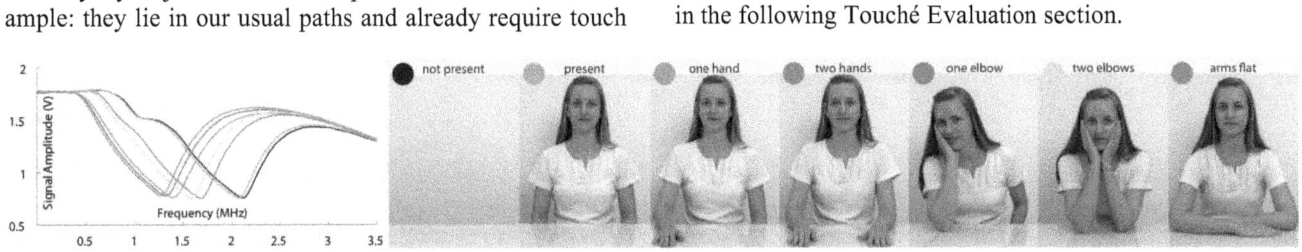

Figure 7: Capacitive profiles for sensing body postures (table examples).

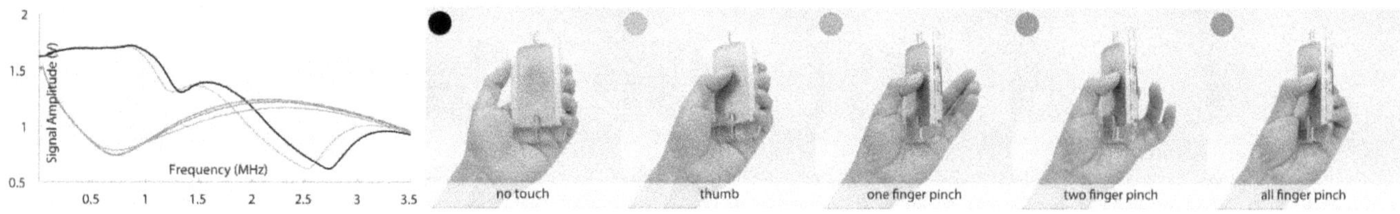

Figure 8: Capacitive profiles for enhancing touchscreen interaction with a hand posture sensing.

Enhancing Touchscreen Interaction

Touché brings new and rich interaction dimensions to conventional touch surfaces by enhancing touch with sensed *hand posture* (Figure 1d) For example, *Touché* could sense the configuration of fingers holding a device, e.g., if they are closed into a fist or held open, whether a single finger is touching, all five fingers, or the entire palm (Figures 8). The part of the hand touching could be also possibly be inferred, e.g., fingertips or knuckles, a valuable extra dimension of natural touch input [16].

These rich input dimensions are generally invisible to traditional capacitive sensing. Diffuse infrared (IR) illumination can capture touch dimensions such as finger orientation [39] and hand shape [22]. However, sensing above the surface is challenging as image quality and sensing distance is severely degraded by traditional diffuse projection surfaces ([18] offers an expensive alternative). An external tracking infrastructure can also be used. This, however, prohibits the use of mobile devices and introduces additional cost and complexity [20, 40].

Touché provides a lightweight, yet powerful, solution to bring hand posture sensing into touchscreen interaction. There are many possible implementations – one is presented in Figures 5d and 8. At the very minimum, this would enable a touch gesture similar to a mouse "right click". Right click is a standard and useful feature in desktop GUI interfaces. However, it has proved to be elusive in contemporary touch interfaces, where it is typically implemented as a tap-and-hold [16]. Additionally, combining hand pose and touch could lead to many more sophisticated interactions, such as gesture-based 3D manipulation and navigation (Figure 1d), advanced 3D sculpting and drawing, music composition and performance, among others.

In general, *Touché* could prove particularly useful for mobile touchscreen interaction, where input is constrained due to small device size. In this context, a few extra bits of input bandwidth would be a welcomed improvement. Detailed controlled experiments evaluating gesture sensing on a simulated mobile device are reported subsequently.

On-Body Gesture Sensing

Unlike inanimate physical objects, the human body is highly variable and uncontrolled, making it a particularly challenging "input device". Compounding this problem is that users are highly sensitive to instrumentation and augmentation of their bodies. For a sensing technique to be successful, it has to be minimally invasive. Research has attempted to overcome these challenges by exploring remote sensing approaches, including bio-acoustics [17], EMG [33] and computer vision [15], each of which has its own distinct set of advantages and drawbacks. *Touché* is able to sidestep much of this complexity by taking advantage of the conductive properties of the body and appropriate the skin as a touch sensitive surface while being minimally invasive.

Because humans are inherently mobile, it is advantageous to define an *on-body* signal source and charge sink for Touché. As our hands serve as our primarily means of manipulating the world, they are the most logical location to augment with *Touché*. In this case, the source or sink is placed near the hands, for example, worn like a wristwatch. The other electrode can be placed in many possible locations, including the opposite wrist (Figure 5b and 9), the waist, collar area, or lower back [11]. As a user touches different parts of their body the impedance between the electrodes varies as the signal flows through slightly different paths on and in the user's body. The resulting capacitive profile is different for each gesture, which allows us to detect a range of hand-to-hand gestures and touch locations (Figure 9).

It is worth noting the remarkable kinesthetic awareness of a human being [3], which has important implications in the design of on-body interfaces [17]. As the colloquialism "like the back of your hand" suggests, we are intimately familiar with our bodies. This can be readily demonstrated by closing one's eyes and touching our noses or clapping our hands together. In addition to our powerful kinesthetic senses, we have finely-tuned on-body touch sensations and hand-eye coordination, all of which can be leveraged for digital tasks.

A wide array of applications can be built on top of the body. One example is controlling a mobile phone using a set of

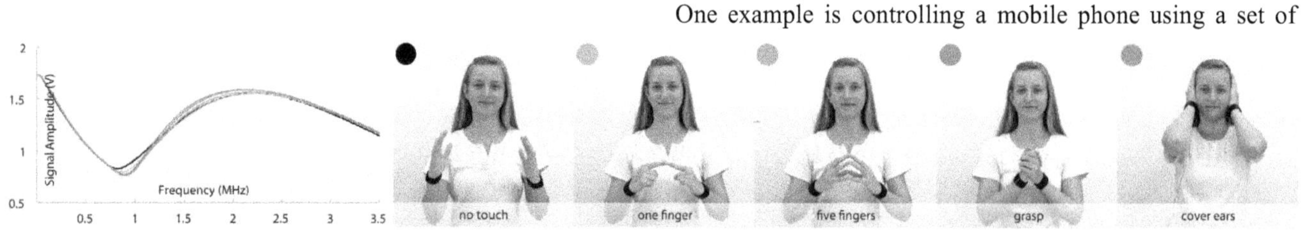

Figure 9: Capacitive profiles for on-body Sensing with wrists-mounted *Touché* sensors.

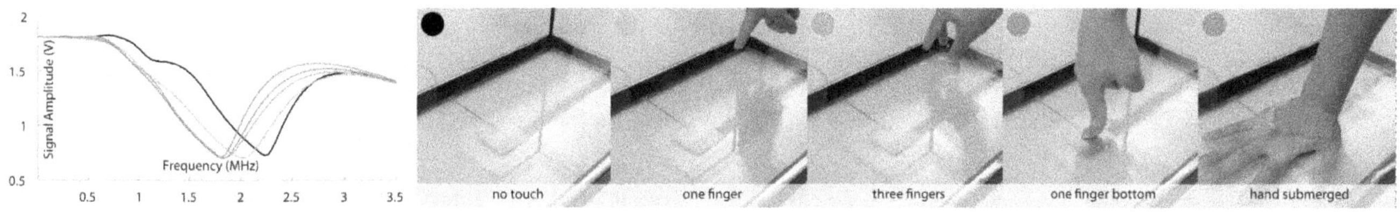

Figure 10: Capacitive profiles for interacting with water.

on-body gestures (Figure 1a). For example, making a "*shh*" gesture with index finger touching to the lips, could put the phone into silent mode. Putting the hands together, forming a book-like gesture, could replay voicemails. We evaluate feasibility of using a simple gesture set in the next section.

Sensing Gestures in Liquids

The real world does not consist only of hard and flat surfaces that can be easily enhanced with touch sensitivity. Liquid, viscous, soft and stretchable materials are important elements of everyday life. Enhancing these materials with touch sensitivity, however, is challenging. Although there is a growing body of research sensing touch for textile, paper and silicon materials [8, 32, 44], enhancing a body of liquid with rich touch sensing has mostly remained out of reach, and is a good example of *Touché*'s application range.

By interacting with water, we do not mean using touch screens under water, but *touching the water itself*. In particular, our approach can distinguish between a user *touching* the water's surface and *dipping* their finger into it (Figure 10), which is difficult to accomplish with current capacitive touch sensing techniques [7]. Resistive e.g., [31] touchpads *would* work under water, but require users to physically press on the surface, which is not truly interaction with the liquid, but rather with a submerged touchpad. Mechanical [41] or optical [26] techniques introduce large external sensing apparatus, prohibiting ad-hoc and mobile interactions. Furthermore, optical sensing generally requires controlled lighting and clear liquids. Water-activated electrical switches [45] can be used to detect the presence of water, but not the *user* playing with water. These are just a few of the challenges of user-liquid interaction.

Touché can easily add touch sensitivity to various amounts of liquid held in any container (Figures 5c). Simply by placing the electrode on the bottom of the water vessel, we can detect a user touching the surface, dipping their fingers in the water, and so on (Figures 10). The container can be made of any material, and the electrode can be affixed to the outside – although putting it inside increases sensitivity.

Applications of water sensing are mostly experiential, such as games, art and theme park installations and interactive aquariums. We can also track indirect interactions, i.e., when users are touching water via a conductive object. In this way children's water toys and eating utensils could be easily enhanced with sounds and lights (Figure 1c).

TOUCHÉ EVALUATION

In the previous section we described five example application domains where *Touché* could enhance touch interaction. For our evaluation, we selected an exemplary configuration and gesture set from each of these five domains designed specifically to tax our system's accuracy. Not only does this minimize the potential for accuracy ceiling effects, but also enables us to estimate the "sweet spot" in gesture set size and composition through several post-hoc analyses that are discussed subsequently.

These studies serve several purposes: 1) to demonstrate the wide variety of applications and interactions enabled by *Touché*, 2) to underscore the immediate feasibility of *Touché*, 3) to explore the potential richness of gesture vocabularies our system could support, and 4) to establish the baseline performance of the recognition engine.

Participants

We used two groups of 12 participants. The first group completed the first four studies (9 males, 3 females, mean age 27.6). A second group of 12 completed the final liquid study created at a later date (10 males, 2 females, mean age 28.6). Each study was run independently allowing us to distribute data collection over approximately a seven-day period. This permitted us to capture natural, real-world variations in e.g., humidity, temperature, user hydration and varying skin resistance. Although we do not specifically control for these factors, we show that our system is robust despite their potential presence. In fact, our "walk-up" general classifiers were specifically designed to model these temporal and inter-participant variances.

Procedure

The five studies followed the same basic structure described below. Each study was run independently; the entire experiment took approximately 60 minutes to complete.

Training

Participants were shown pictographically a small set of gestures and asked to perform each sequentially. While performing gestures, the participants were told to adjust their gestures slightly, e.g., tighten their grip. This helped to capture additional variety that would be acquired naturally with extended use, but impossible in a 60-minute experiment.

While the participants performed each gesture, the experimenter recorded 10 gesture instances by hitting the spacebar and then advanced the participant to the next gesture until all gestures were performed. This procedure was repeated three times providing 30 instances per gesture per user. In addition to providing three periods of training data useful in post-hoc analysis, this procedure allowed us to capture variability in participant gesture performance, obtaining more gesture variety and improving classification.

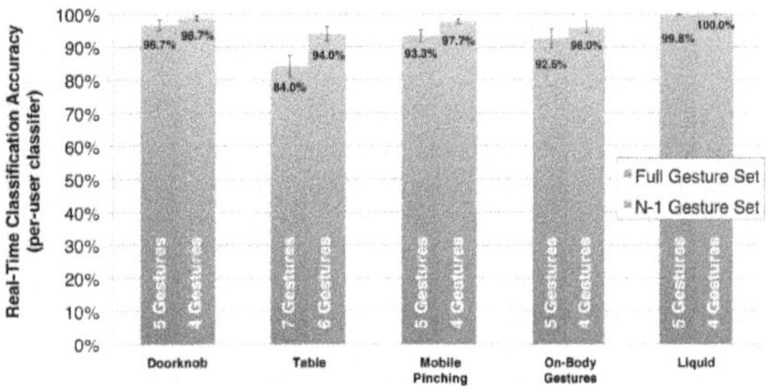

Figure 11. Real-time, per-user classification accuracy for five example applications.

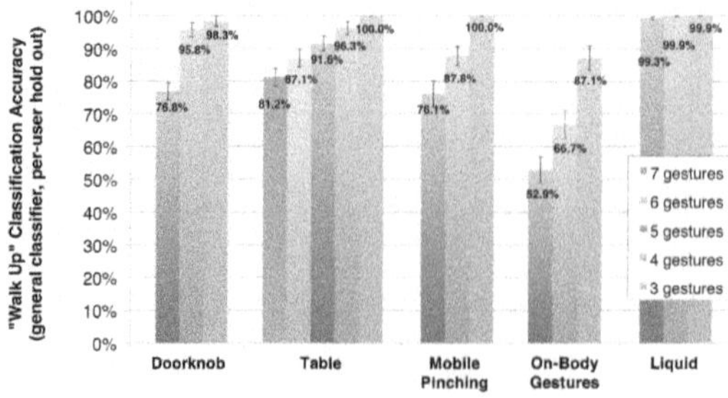

Figure 12. "Walk Up" classification accuracy for five example applications.

Testing

Following the training phase, collected data were used to initialize the system for a real-time classification evaluation. Participants were requested to perform one of the gestures from the training set randomly selected and presented on a display monitor. The system – invisible to both the experimenter and participants – made a classification when participants performed each gesture. A true positive result was obtained when the requested gesture matched the classifier's guess. The experimenter used the spacebar to advance to the next trial, with five trials for each gesture.

Accuracy Measures

Our procedure follows a per-user classifier paradigm where each participant had a custom classifier trained using only his or her training data. This produces robust classification since it captures the peculiarities of the user. Per-user classifiers are often ideal for personal objects used by a single user, as would be the case with, e.g., a mobile phone, desktop computer, or car steering wheel.

To assess performance dimensions that were not available in a real-time accuracy assessment, we ran two additional experiments post-hoc. Our first post-hoc analysis simulated the live classification experiment with *one fewer* gestures per set. The removed gesture was the one found to have the lowest accuracy in the full gesture set. For example, in the case of the grasp-sensing doorknob study, the *circle* gesture was removed, leaving *no touch*, *one finger*, *pinch* and *grasp* (Figure 6) Accuracy typically improves as the gesture set contracts. In general, we sought to identify gesture sets that exceeded the 95% accuracy threshold.

Our second post-hoc analysis estimated performance with "walk up" users – that is, classification without any training data from that user, a *general classifier*. To assess this, we trained our classifier using data from eleven participants, and tested using data from a twelfth participant (all combinations, i.e., 12-fold cross validation). This was the most challenging evaluation because of the natural variability of how people perform gestures, anatomical differences, as well as variability in clothes and shoes worn by the participants. However, this accuracy measure provides the best insight into potential real-world performance when per-user training is not feasible, e.g., a museum exhibit or theme park attraction. Moreover, it serves as an ideal contrast to our per-user classifier experimental results.

EVALUATION RESULTS

Figures 6 though 10 illustrate the physical setup and accompanying touch gesture sets for each of the five application domains we tested. Real-time accuracy results for all five studies are summarized in Figure 11. "Walk -up" accuracies with different-sized gesture sets are shown in Figure 12.

Study 1: Making Objects Touch and Grasp Sensitive

A doorknob was an obvious and interesting choice for our touch and grasp sensing study setup (Figure 6). We used a brass fixture that came with a high-gloss coating, providing a beneficial layer of insulation. A single wire was soldered to the interior metallic part of the knob, and connected to our sensor. As doors are fixed infrastructure, we grounded our sensor in this configuration. This is a minimally invasive configuration that allows for existing doors to be easily retrofitted with additional touch sensitivity.

A set of five gestures was evaluated as seen in Figure 6: *no touch*, *one finger*, *pinch*, *circle*, and *grasp*. This setup performed well in the real-time per–user classifier experiment, at 96.7% accuracy (SD=5.6%). Dropping the *circle* gesture increased accuracy to 98.6% (SD=2.5%).

Walk-up accuracy was significantly worse for five gestures – 76.8% (SD=9.2%), where the *circle* gesture was responsible for 95.0% of the errors. Once the *circle* gesture was removed, walk-up accuracy improves to 95.8% (SD=7.4%).

Study 2: Body Configuration Sensing

To evaluate performance of *Touché* in body posture recognition scenarios, we constructed a sensing table. This consisted of a conventional table with a thin copper plate on top of it, covered with a 1.6 mm glass fiber and resin composite board (CEM-1) (Figure 7). A single wire connected copper plate to the *Touché* sensor board. The static nature of a table meant that we could ground the sensor to the environment in this configuration.

A set of seven gestures was evaluated: *not present*, *present*, *one hand*, *two hands*, *one elbow*, *two elbows*, *arms* (Figure 7). Average real-time classification performance with seven gestures was 92.6% (SD=9.4%). Eliminating the *two elbows* gesture boosted accuracy to 96.0% (SD=6.1%).

Walk-up accuracy at seven gestures stands at 81.2%. As seen in Figure 12, accuracy surpasses 90% with five gestures (*not present*, *present*, *one hand*, *two hands*, *two elbow;* 91.6%, SD=7.8%). With only three gestures (*presence*, *two hands*, *two elbow*), accuracy is 100% for every participant.

Study 3: Enhancing Touchscreen Interaction

The application possibilities of *Touché* to touchscreen interaction are significant and diverse. For both experimental and prototyping purposes we chose mobile device form factor (Figure 8). Mobility implies the inability to ground the sensor, making this setup particularly difficult.

As a proof of concept, we created a pinch-centric gesture set which could be used for, e.g., a "right click", zoom in/out, copy/paste, or similar function [23]. Our mobile device mockup has two electrodes: the front touch surface, simulating a touch panel, and the backside of the device. A *Touché* sensor is configured to measure the impedance between these two surfaces through the participant's hand connecting them (Figure 5d).

Figure 9 depicts a set of five gestures that were evaluated: *no touch*, *thumb*, *one finger pinch*, *two finger pinch* and *all finger pinch*. Per-user classifier accuracy with all gestures is 93.3% (SD=6.2%). Removing the *two finger pinch* brings accuracy up to 97.7% (SD=2.6%). Walk-up accuracy at five gestures is 76.1% (SD=13.8%), too low for practical use. However, by reducing the gesture set to *no touch*, *thumb* and *one finger pinch*, accuracy is 100% for all participants, showing the immediate feasibility for mobile applications.

Study 4: On-Body Gesture Sensing

Unlike the previous three studies, human-gesture sensing has a predefined device – the human body. This leaves us with two design variables: sensor placement and gestures. For this study, we chose to place an electrode on each wrist, worn like a watch. The *Touché* sensor measured impedance between wrist electrodes through the body of participants. Due to the highly variable and uncontrolled nature of the human body, this experimental condition was the most challenging of our five studies.

Our gesture set consisted of five gestures: *no touch*, *one finger*, *five fingers*, *grasp*, and *cover ears* (Figure 9). Real-time, per-user classification accuracy was 84.0% (SD = 11.4%) with five gestures. Removing a single gesture – *one finger* – improved accuracy to a useable 94.0% (SD=7.4%). In contrast, walk- up accuracy with a general classifier does significantly worse, with all five gestures yielding 52.9% accuracy (SD=13.8%). Reducing the gesture set to three (*no touch*, *five fingers*, *grasp*) only draws accuracy up to 87.1% (SD=12.5%) – stronger, but still too low for robust use.

This divergence in accuracy performance between per-user and general classifiers is important. The results suggest that for on-body gestures where the user is both the "device" and input, per-user training is most appropriate. This should not be particularly surprising – unlike doorknobs, the individual differences between participants are very significant, not only in gesture performance, but also in their bodies' composition. A per-user classifier captures and accounts for these per-user differences, making it robust.

Study 5: Touching Liquids

We attached a single electrode under a 250 mm-wide and 500 mm-long fish tank, and filled it to a depth of 35 mm of water. The electrode was separated from the liquid by a pane of 3 mm-thick glass and attached to the *Touché* sensor board via a single wire (Figures 5c).

Our test liquid gesture set consisted of *no touch*, *one finger tip*, *three finger tips*, *one finger bottom*, and *hand submerged* (Figure 10). This experimental condition performed the best of the five. Real-time, per-user classification accuracy with the full gesture set was 99.8% (SD=0.8%). "Walk-up" classification performance was equally strong with all five gestures: 99.3% (SD=1.4%). Removing *three finger tips* improves accuracy up to 99.9% (Figure 12).

Anatomical Factors

Touché is sensitive to variations in users' anatomy. To test if anatomical variations have a systematic effect on classification accuracy, we ran several post hoc tests. We found no correlation between accuracy and height (1.6 ~ 1.9m), weight (52 ~ 111kg), BMI (19.6 ~ 32.3), or gender. This suggests the sensing is robust across a range of users.

DISCUSSIONS AND CONCLUSION

Touché has demonstrated that multi-frequency capacitive sensing is valuable and opens new and exciting opportunities in HCI. Would it be possible to achieve the same results with fewer sampling points? What are the optimal sweeping ranges and resolutions needed to achieve maximum performance and utility of such a sensing technique?

Optimizing and fine-tuning SFCS for specific configurations and uses is a subject of future work and, therefore, beyond the scope of the current paper. In general, however, designing any SFCS solutions can be considered as a sampling problem, i.e., how many samples and what frequency bands would allow us to accurately identify the state of the system? In the current implementation of *Touché* we used 200 samples between 1 KHz and 3.5 MHz. Empirically, we found it to be a good trade-off between speed and accuracy of the recognition. More importantly, it allowed us to capture details of shapes of capacitive profiles, which was important in some of the *Touché* applications, e.g., in hand-to-hand gestures. Therefore, decreasing the sweep resolution would improve performance, but also reduces the robustness of gesture recognition in some of applications.

We found that it was difficult, if not impossible, to determine a-priori which frequency bands are most characteristic for specific interactions, applications, users, materials and contexts. Indeed, around 1 MHz looks useful on Figure 9, but not at all on Figure 10. Therefore, we designed the most general sensing solution by sampling over a broad range of frequencies. Consequently, *Touché* – without any modification – enables a rich swath of interactions from humans, to doorknobs, to water. This would be impossible if we limited the range of frequencies. However, in practical applications the sensing can be limited to a range of frequencies that are most appropriate for a particular product, reducing cost and improving robustness.

Our work on *Touché* was broadly motivated by the vision of disappearing computers postulated by Mark Weiser [43]. He argued that computer must disappear in everyday objects and "*... the most profound technologies are those that disappear*". As powerful and inspiring as this vision is, it imposes a significant problem: how we will interact with computers that are invisible? From the end-user perspective, the interface will appear as a computer as long as there are buttons to press and mice to move, and thus will never truly disappear. Completely new interaction technologies are required, and we hope that this work contributes to the emergence of future ubiquitous computing environments.

AKNOWLEDGEMENT

We are thankful to Zhiquan Yeo, Josh Griffin and Scott Hudson for their significant contributions in developing early prototypes of *Touché* and helping to understand the principles of its operation [29]. We thank Jonas Loh for his efforts on exploring initial applications of *Touché*. We are thankful to Disney Research and The Walt Disney Corporation for continued support of this research effort. Finally, we thank anonymous reviewers for their insightful comments as well as subjects who participated in the experiments.

REFERENCES

1. Barrett, G. and Omote, R. Projected-Capacitive Touch Technology. *Information Display*. (26) 3, 2010. 16-21.
2. Bau, O., Poupyrev, I., Israr, A., Harrison, C., Teslatouch: electrovibration for touch surfaces. in *UIST'10*, 283-292.
3. Buxton, W. and Myers, B., A Study in Two-Handed Input. in *CHI'86*, 321-326.
4. Cassinelli, Á., Perrin, S., Ishikawa, M., Smart laser-scanner for 3D human-machine interface. in *CHI EA'05*, 1138-1139.
5. Cheney, M., Isaacson, D., Newell, J.C. Electrical impedance tomography. *SIAM Review*, *41*, 1, 1999. 85-101.
6. Dietz, P. and Leigh, D., DiamondTouch: A Multi-User Touch Technology. in *UIST '01*, 219-226.
7. Dietz, P.H., Han, J.Y., Westhues, J., Barnwell, J., Yerazunis, W., Submerging technologies. in *SIGGRAPH'06 ETech*, 30.
8. Follmer, S., Johnson, M., Adelson, E., Ishii, H., deForm: an interactive malleable surface for capturing 2.5 D arbitrary objects, tools and touch. in *UIST '11*, 527-536.
9. Forlizzi, J., Disalvo, C., Zimmerman, J., Hurst, A., The SenseChair : The lounge chair as an intelligent assistive device for elders. in *DUX '05*, 1-13.
10. Foster, K.R. and Lukaski, H.C. Whole-body impedance - what does it measure? *The American journal of clinical nutrition*, *64* (3). 1996. 388S-396S.
11. Gemperle, F., Kasabach, C., Stivoric, J., Bauer, M. , Martin, R. Design for wearability. in *IEEE ISWC'98,* 116-122.
12. Hall, M., Frank, E., Holmes, G., Pfahringer, B., Reutemann, P., Witten, I.H. The WEKA data mining software: an update. *SIGKDD Explorations*, *11*, 1, 2009. 10-18.
13. Harker, F.R. and Maindonald, J.H. Ripening of Nectarine Fruit. *Plant physiology*, *106*, 1994. 165-171.
14. Harrison, B.L., Fishkin, K.P., Gujar, A., Mochon, C., Want, R., Squeeze me, hold me, tilt me! An exploration of manipulative user interfaces. in *CHI '98*, 17-24.
15. Harrison, C., Benko, H., Wilson, A., OmniTouch: wearable multitouch interaction everywhere. in *UIST'11*, 441-450.
16. Harrison, C., Schwarz, J., Hudson, S., TapSense: enhancing finger interaction on touch surfaces. in *UIST'11*, 627-636.
17. Harrison, C., Tan, D. , Morris, D., Skinput: Appropriating the Body as an Input Surface. in *CHI '10*, 453-462.
18. Hilliges, O., Izadi, S., Wilson, A.D., Hodges, S., Garcia-Mendoza, A., Butz, A., Interactions in the air: adding further depth to interactive tabletops. in *UIST '09*, 139-148.
19. Hinkley, K. and Sinclair, M., Touch-sensing input devices. in *CHI '99*, 223-230.
20. Kry, P.G. and Pai, D.K. Grasp Recognition and Manipulation with the Tango. *in ISER'06*. 551-559.
21. Lee, S.K., Buxton, W., Smith, K.C., A multi-touch three dimensional touch-sensitive tablet. in *CHI '85*, 21-25.
22. Matsushita, N. and Rekimoto, J., HoloWall: designing a finger, hand, body and object sensitive wall. *UIST'97*, 209-210.
23. Miyaki, T., Rekimoto, J. GraspZoom: zooming and scrolling control model for single-handed mobile interaction. in *MobileHCI '09*, 81-84.
24. Paradiso, J. and Hsiao, K., Swept-frequency, magnetically-coupled resonant tags for realtime, continuous, multiparameter control. in *CHI EA '99*, 212-213.
25. Philipp, H. Charge transfer sensing. *Sens. Review*, *19*. 96-105.
26. Pier, M.D. and Goldberg, I.R., Using water as interface media in VR applications. in *CLIHC '05*, ACM, 162-169.
27. Poupyrev, I. and Maruyama, S., Tactile interfaces for small touch screens. in *UIST '03*, 217-220.
28. Poupyrev, I., Oba, H., Ikeda, T., Iwabuchi, E., Designing embodied interfaces for casual sound recording devices. in *CHI EA'08*, 2129-2134.
29. Poupyrev, I., Yeo, Z., Griffin, J.D., Hudson, S., Sensing human activities with resonant tuning. in *CHI EA '10*, 4135-4140.
30. Rekimoto, J., SmartSkin: An Infrastructure for Freehand Manipulation onInteractive Surfaces. in *CHI '02*, 113-120.
31. Rosenberg, I. and Perlin, K. The UnMousePad: an interpolating multi-touch force-sensing input pad. in *SIGGRAPH'09*, Article 65. *65:1-65:9.*
32. Russo, A., Ahn, B.Y., Adams, J.J., Duoss, E.B., Bernhard, J.T., Lewis, J.A. Pen-on-Paper Flexible Electronics. *Advanced materials*, (*23*) 30. 2011. 3426-3430.
33. Saponas, T.S., Tan, D.S., Morris, D., Balakrishnan, R., Turner, J., Landay, J.A., Enabling always-available input with muscle-computer interfaces. in *UIST '09*, 167-176
34. Sato, M. Particle display system: a real world display with physically distributable pixels. in *CHI EA '08,* 3771-3776.
35. Skulpone, S., Dittman, K. Adjustable proximity sensor. *US Patent 3,743,853*, 1973.
36. Smith, J.R. Field mice: Extracting hand geometry from electric field measurements. *IBM Systems Journal*, *35*. 587-608.
37. Song, H., Benko, H., Izadi, S., Cao, X., Hinckley, K., Grips and Gestures on a Multi-Touch Pen. in *CHI '11*, 1323-1332.
38. Taylor, B. and Bove, V., Graspables: Grasp-recognition as a user interface. in *CHI '09*, 917-926.
39. Wang, F. and Ren, X., Empirical evaluation for finger input properties in multi-touch interaction. in *CHI '09*, 1063-1072.
40. Wang, R.Y. and Popovic, J. Real-time hand-tracking with a color glove. *in SIGGRAPH '09*, Article 63, 63:1-63:8
41. Watanabe, J., VortexBath: Study of Tangible Interaction with Water in Bathroom for Accessing and Playing Media Files. in *HCI '07*, 1240-1248.
42. Webster, J.G. Ed, *Medical instrumentation: application and design*. Wiley, 2010.
43. Weiser, M. The computer for the 21st century. *Scientific American* (9). 94-104.
44. Wimmer, R. and Baudisch, P., Modular and Deformable Touch-Sensitive Surfaces Based on Time Domain Reflectometry. in *UIST '11*, 517-526.
45. Yonezawa, T. and Mase, K., Tangible Sound: Musical instrument using fluid media. in *ICMC2000*.
46. Zimmerman, T.G., Smith, J.R., Paradiso, J.A., Allport, D., Gershenfeld, N., Applying electric field sensing to human-computer interfaces. in *CHI '95*, 280-287.

Detecting Error-Related Negativity for Interaction Design

Chi Thanh Vi
Department of Computer Science
University of Bristol
vi@cs.bris.ac.uk

Sriram Subramanian
Department of Computer Science
University of Bristol
sriram@cs.bris.ac.uk

ABSTRACT
This paper examines the ability to detect a characteristic brain potential called the Error-Related Negativity (ERN) using off-the-shelf headsets and explores its applicability to HCI. ERN is triggered when a user either makes a mistake or the application behaves differently from their expectation. We first show that ERN can be seen on signals captured by EEG headsets like Emotiv™ when doing a typical multiple choice reaction time (RT) task – Flanker task. We then present a single-trial online ERN algorithm that works by pre-computing the coefficient matrix of a logistic regression classifier using some data from a multiple choice reaction time task and uses it to classify incoming signals of that task on a single trial of data. We apply it to an interactive selection task that involved users selecting an object under time pressure. Furthermore the study was conducted in a typical office environment with ambient noise. Our results show that online single trial ERN detection is possible using off-the-shelf headsets during tasks that are typical of interactive applications. We then design a Superflick experiment with an integrated module mimicking an ERN detector to evaluate the accuracy of detecting ERN in the context of assisting users in interactive tasks. Based on these results we discuss and present several HCI scenarios for use of ERN.

Author Keywords
Electroencephalography; EEG; Brain Computer Interface; Error Related Negativity; Flick; User interface

ACM Classification Keywords
H.5.2 [Information interfaces and presentation]: User Interfaces - Graphical user interfaces;

INTRODUCTION
The availability of off-the-shelf EEG headsets like Neurosky™ and Emotiv™ has opened possibility of exploring a whole range of BCI applications for everyday use. These low-cost (typically ranging from $100 to $300) and portable devices are being used in a wide range of application including task classification [16], gaming [13], and recognizing user's intended selection [1]. To date, most of these applications have been based on using P300 (a peak elicited at about 300ms after an event onset) which can be considered as a composite index of both attention and memory [16]. Another form of signal that could be used but is often ignored in interactive applications is the Error-related negativity (ERN).

An ERN is a form of an Event Related Potential (ERP) that can be triggered in the brain when a user either makes a mistake or the application behaves differently from her expectation. This pattern is produced in a person's brain when she is aware of the obvious error(s) that s/he has made; either through system feedback or individual realization [8]. For example, ERN would be produced when pressing the LEFT key while intending to press the RIGHT key in a multiple choice RT task. It also appears, but with lower amplitude when a person is confused about the decision that s/he has made [3]. Usually these ERN signals appear and peak within 150ms of the committed action [9].

If ERN signals can be detected during an interactive task they can be used in detecting and correcting errors or in augmenting users' experiences in those activities. An ERN detection module provides another medium for HCI designers to access users' intentions, which is intuitive and directly from the users' brain. This has great potential in many types of interactive application such as in gaming, spatial navigation tasks and aiding object selection. For example, when ERN is detected the system can prompt the user to check if the selection is the intended target.

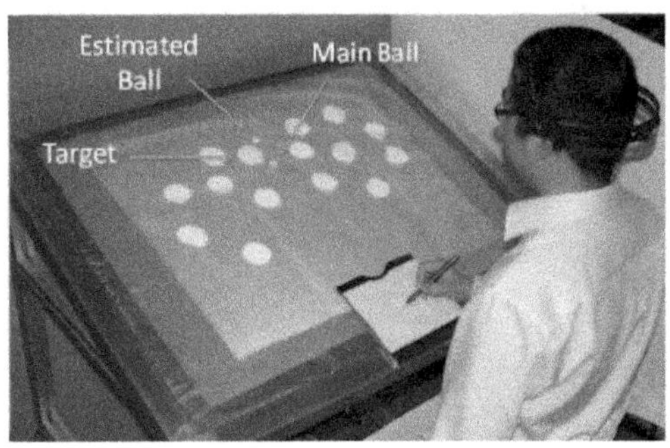

Figure 1. A user performing a Superflick [19] while wearing an off-the shelf EEG headset to see if ERN detection can aide in an object selection task.

However it is difficult to detect a clear ERN pattern due to noisy EEG signals and lack of effective real-time algorithms. Most research in detecting ERN is focused on being able to detect it over an average of multiple trials relying on offline methods (see [3, 17] for examples). As ERN is known to appear when using multiple-choice RT tasks, most research is done on Flanker task [6]. Flanker task is a visual experiment where the participant has to respond to a central and directed symbol that is surrounded by distracting symbols. There are very few ERN detection algorithms that work in real-time as well as on multiple-choice RT tasks that are not Flanker tasks.

Additionally, most ERN experiments are performed using expensive, non-portable sensing devices such as NeuroScan systems from NeuroScan™, g.BCIsys from g.tec™ or ActiveTwo from Biosemi™. These devices have the benefits of not only more sensing channels (up to 256 electrodes therefore can cover all channels in the 10-20 international system), but also higher and user selectable sampling frequencies of up to 16 kHz. These systems also introduce less noise in the signals because of better sensing electrodes and integrated amplifier/ converter module.

In comparison off-the-shelf EEG headsets have at best 14 channels, a sampling frequency of about 1 kHz and introduce more noise due to wireless transfer of EEG signals. Due to these limitations it is not clear if these devices can capture ERN patterns. However, due to their price and portability their use is being increasingly explored within HCI. In this paper we investigate the appropriateness of these off-the-shelf EEG headsets in detecting ERNs and also the effectiveness of real-time algorithms in doing so on a single trial and in real-time.

We first describe an online single trial ERN detection technique that is verified using data acquired from the frontal-central cortex of the human brain. We then show that we can detect ERN online on a single trial in an object selection task. This demonstrates the abilities of harnessing ERN in interactive applications in office conditions. Both our experiments show that we can detect ERNs using the Emotiv Headset with an accuracy of up to 70%.

These rates are indicative of the type of accuracy one can expect from off-the-shelf EEG sets. Improvements in learning techniques can improve this accuracy but it is unlikely that detection accuracy will reach 100%. It is therefore expected that with high detection accuracy users might become over-resilient on a system detecting ERNs which can increase the cost of recovery from the error. In order to examine this issue we conducted a final study where we compare users' error-rates when performing Superflick [19], a modified pointing task, with different potential ERN success rates. The results of the experiment show that ERN detection rates of 65 to 80% are acceptable to interactive applications. We finally discuss the implications of our results to interactive applications.

The contributions of this paper are: (a) we demonstrate that off-the-shelf EEG devices such as the Emotiv headset can measure ERN from channels in the front-central part of the brain; (b) we demonstrate that it is possible to detect these ERN signals online (as opposed to offline) from a single trial in a task that is closer to the types of tasks encountered in HCI; (c) through a final experiment we show that detection accuracies in the region of 65 to 80% are sufficient to use these techniques in real-time interactive applications.

RELATED WORK

Brain Computer Interface and sensing techniques

There are many methods to detect neural data that can be used in a BCI system. Some notable ones are functional Magnetic Resonance Imaging (fMRI), functional Near-Infrared Spectroscopy (fNIRS) and Electroencephalography (EEG).

fMRI measures the change in blood flow which is related to brain activity by sensing the magnetic field around the scalp. fMRI is an effective technique for brain function imaging in medical science. It can quantify neural activities with high spatial resolution but fMRI machines are big, expensive and produce loud noises [12]. Moreover, this technique is vulnerable to the existence of metal objects and head movements [21], both of which are common when using a computer. For these reasons, it is not favoured by HCI researchers.

fNIRS measures the concentration of blood oxygen using infrared light [24]. This method has been used mostly to measure the user's mental workload [12, 21]. It is comparable to EEG due to its low cost and portability. However, it has lower temporal resolution compared to EEG making it difficult to detect fast responses after an event occurs [12].

EEG records electrical fields produced by neuronal activity [5]. It is a popular non-invasive brain imaging method because of its lower cost (compared to fMRI), portability and high temporal resolution [12]. There are two approaches to measuring EEG signals: invasive (implanting an array of electrodes in the cortex layer of brain) and non-invasive (attaching a number of electrodes to the scalp). Non-invasive approaches have more opportunities for use in everyday use.

Measuring and Processing EEG Signals

Raw EEG signals can be mapped to application control using one of two learning methods: *Operant Conditioning* and *Pattern Recognition*. In *Operant Conditioning*, the users need to be trained to control their own brain activity while they are provided with real time feedback. For example, users train the system such that when they think about right hand movement or a foot movement the application navigates through a virtual street [5]. Alternatively, *Pattern Recognition* uses signal processing and machine learning techniques to reveal the mental states or activities of *untrained* users [5]. The second method has the benefit of making it easier for users and can make a BCI application universal for general people, rather than a specific individual.

Pattern Recognition method has been widely used in neuroscience to discover the neural activity inside a human's brain. For example, a P300 speller uses pattern recognition to detect the P300 pattern to help spelling/ typing letters [7] as well as selecting the intended object [1]. This speller works by flashing rows and columns in a random order of a grid of alphabets. The user concentrates and counts the number of flashes over his/her intended letter. A P300 pattern then appears after the flash over the intended letter and will be clear enough from noise to be detected after a few flashes.

Error Related Negativity (ERN)

ERN is a pattern observed when a user makes an error in a reaction time task. Its shape is a negative deflection which appears in the ongoing EEG right after the time the decision was made. The ERN also appears when users have feedback about their response accuracy [14]. Its amplitude is large when the user is clearly aware of his/her error and is small when user is confused (where errors are caused by data limitation) [3]. However, despite the change in amplitude, ERN latency seems to be consistent (about 100ms after the event). Interestingly, the amplitude of ERN does not depend on the behaviour accuracy itself but the user's perception about it [3, 25].

To date most of experiments involving ERN detection are done offline by averaging over multiple trials. Participants are asked to perform a multiple-choice task in which trials with incorrect responses were used to archive a clear ERN pattern. For example, Gehring et.al [10] used this methods to determine the effect of a speed/ accuracy trade off on different representations of ERN. Scheffers and Coles [3] use this method to conclude that ERN is a manifestation of the ongoing monitoring system in the brain which compares the expected response and the actual response.

However, in an interactive application, ERN will be most useful when it can be detected immediately after it happens. This requires the online detection of the ERN pattern (as opposed to offline) from EEG signals. One way to achieve this is by caching and averaging a small number of patterns in a limited time in order to refine a reasonably clear ERN [20]. This method requires a waiting time to collect sufficient signals and therefore delays the progress of error correction as it goes through multiple trials.

Various attempts have also been made to detect ERN from a single trial. One example is from Ferrez and Millan [8] where they train a Gaussian classifier to recognize error and correct trials on a single trial basis but after the experiment was completed (so considered an offline single-trial approach). Another example is from Dal Seno et.al. [4] who used a Linear Discriminant Analysis (LDA) classifier to cross check with every spelled letter using a P300 speller. The reported performance of the online version varies from 58% to 69%. This result is just better than chance but still encouraging, as this is one of the few attempts at detecting ERN online and from a single trial.

All the above experiments have been carried out on EEG headsets with up to 256 electrodes and with sampling frequency up to 16 kHz. Most importantly these approaches rely on having access to Fz, Cz, Pz and Oz channels. We are not aware of any attempt to detect ERN from a low-cost portable headset where the number of channels and sampling frequency are limited. Hence, we investigate if a low cost, features limited EEG headset can detect ERN and benefit to HCI.

ONLINE ERN DETECTION

The online, single trial ERN detection algorithm we present below is an adapted version of the logistic regression algorithm from Christoforos et.al [2].

If the user makes a decision (i.e by pressing a button) in a Flanker Task at time t we can create an epoch $x(t)$ for a channel around that decision moment. The total length of $x(t)$ is l samples (which is the number of samples in that epoch). We need to design a supervised classifier so that its output:

$$y(t) = \beta^T * x(t)$$

is expected to be maximally discriminated between two cases: either there is ERN or no ERN in that time window. This output $y(t)$ is a real number.

β: coefficient matrix [l x 1] that is unique for each channel.

We tested this algorithm with different signal pre-processing methods. For example, we tested with $x(t)$ as EEG signals from all channels at a time moment t following the method from [18]. This type of input does not give us a good classification. We also tried to design a coefficient matrix for all channels but did not receive a good result.

In our approach $x(t)$ is signal samples of a time windows (combination of two windows: before and after pressing button). Figure 2 presents the procedure of classifying an EEG epoch which is one of two types: ERN and no ERN.

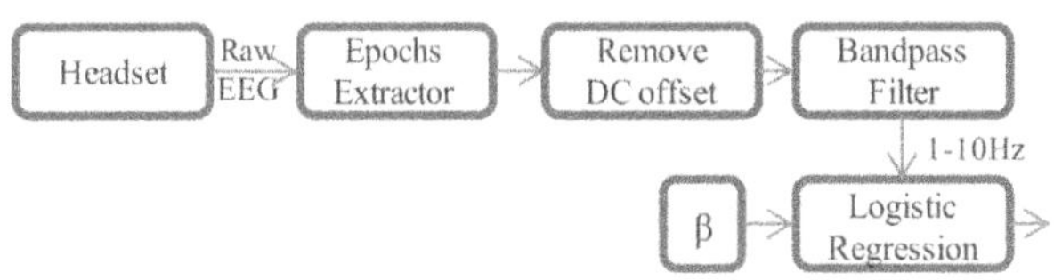

Figure 2. Online Single Trial ERN Detection Procedure

The next step is to find the coefficient matrix to satisfy the expectation of $y(t)$.

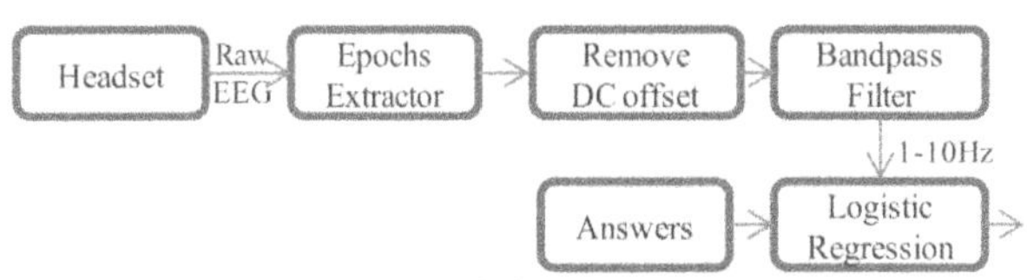

Figure 3. Coefficient matrix extractor

Figure 3 explains the procedure of finding the coefficient matrix β using a supervised logistic regression machine learning technique which is briefly explained in [2]. Once the coefficient matrix is found, it can be used to classify an EEG epoch into one of two: there is ERN or there is no ERN.

EXPERIMENT 1: FLANKER TASK

To validate the above algorithm on a low cost, portable EEG device, we designed a Flanker Task that is similar to [18]. Twelve local students (7 males) were recruited to participate in this study. Each completed this experiment individually.

To mimic the experimental conditions in [3, 25] for a typical Flanker task experiment and reduce noise in data collection, the participant was seated in front of a screen in a dimly lit room. Participants were told to sit comfortably and minimize eye movement and blink as infrequently as possible while performing the task.

Participants were asked to perform a version of Flanker Task where they had to press one of two keys to specify the direction of a central arrow that was bounded by flanker arrows. There were two types of arrows, each type had two stimuli: congruent stimuli (<<<<< and >>>>>) and the incongruent stimuli (<<><< and >><>>). All 4 stimuli were used in our trials in a random order.

For each trial there was a fixation cross in the centre of the screen for 500ms. It was replaced with one of four stimuli. The stimulus was presented for 100ms before the screen was cleared. Participants were asked to response by pressing one of two buttons corresponding to the direction of the central arrow. At this time a string "-" appeared to mark each interval of 1000ms waiting. After the participant's response, the screen remains clear for 500ms. All stimuli were presented in white font on a black background. At a viewing distance of around 100 cm, the visual angle of the arrow stimuli was 0.4° vertically and 0.6° horizontally, and between them was 0.3° space. This procedure is similar to the task carried out in [3] and [6]

Participants wore an Emotiv Epoc Neuroheadset that has the ability to capture raw EEG in 14 channels (of the 10-20 international system) from different locations around the human head. At first, participants were given one practice block of 40 trials. After that, they performed 4 blocks of 40 trials in which EEG signals were collected. Participants had 2 minutes to rest after each block. We collected a total of 1920 trials from all participants of the experiment.

SIGNAL PROCESSING

The EEG signals, captured from the Emotiv headset, were divided into 2-second length epochs 1 second before and 1 second after the key press moment). With the sampling frequency at 128Hz (after downgrading from 1024Hz), the length of each epoch is 256 samples. The first 200ms of each epoch were used to remove DC offset following which all epochs were filtered in 1-10Hz to remove components that are not in the ERN frequency bands of that particular epoch. Figure 4 shows examples of single trial ERN in the two cases when the trial was incorrect (Fig 4a) and correct (Fig 4b). These examples were picked to demonstrate the difference in the ERN pattern from a single trial.

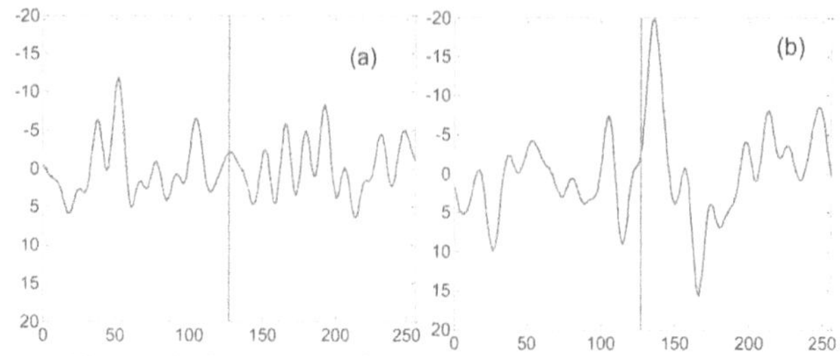

Figure 4. Examples of single trial ERN for two cases: incorrect (a) and correct (b). The x axis is number of samples (1 sec = 128 samples). The y axis is amplitude (uV). The red line is the key press moment (sample number 127).

RESULTS

For each channel, half of the trials (= 80 trials) were used for training via a logistic regression technique and other half were used for testing. We performed a t-test on $y(t)$ (calculated by multiplying $x(t)$ with the coefficient matrix) for each channel per user to check if there was a significant difference between two types of output (ERN and no ERN epochs). Based on the results of the t-test we found that on average F3, F4, F8, FC5, FC6, AF4 were the channels that yielded significant differences in $y(t)$ implying they are best suited to detect an ERN pattern from a signal $x(t)$.

From the test trials we found that using data from F4 channel can discriminate the two types of responses best: 69.7% of correct trials were classified as correct and about 70.3% of erroneous trials were classified as incorrect.

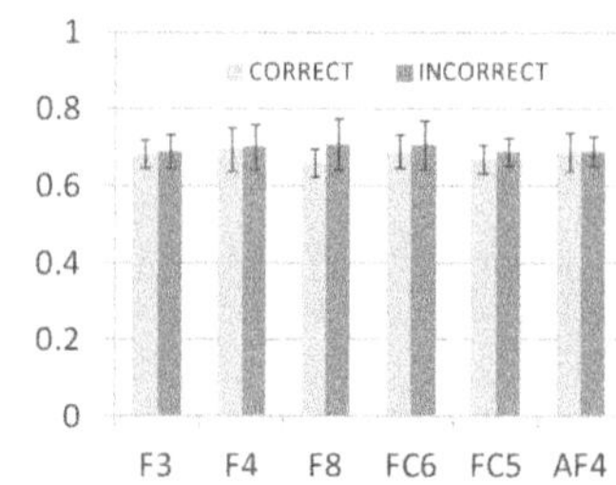

Figure 5. Classifier accuracy on a single trial basis

Figure 5 shows the average accuracy of different sensing channels on which the algorithm works most effectively. It was observed that those channels, which correspond to the frontal lobe, produce better classifications than other channels. This matched the literature about the origin of ERN, which is from the Anterior Cingulate Cortex (ACC) [26]. This also satisfies the fact that ERN has the frontal-central distribution of the human brain.

Figure 6 illustrates the average EEG signals over all epochs belonging to two cases: correct and incorrect.

To investigate the efficiency of the classifier further, we used the Receiver Operating Characteristic (ROC) Analysis [23]. It has two distinct inputs: hit rate (or true positive rate) and false alarm rate (or false positive rate) as two separate performance measures. ROC analysis has been used in machine learning recently to justify how good a classifier is by evaluating its discriminating power [15]. Figure 7 shows four ROC curves of 4 frontal-central channels. The further the curve is from the diagonal line, the more effective that classifier is. The area under the curve (AUC) gives an indication of how well the classifier is performing. The AUC of 1 indicates a perfect classifier and 0.5 indicates a random chance of classification. Our classifier achieves an average of 0.77 across all channels. The AUC for the best six channels (F3, F4, F8, FC5, FC6, and AF4) are shown in Figure 8.

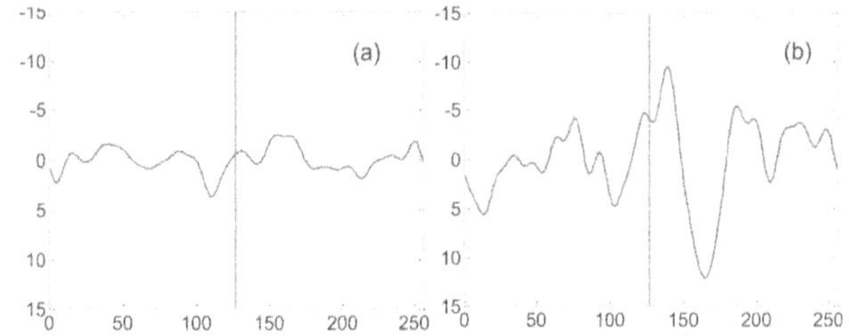

Figure 6. EEG signals at channel AF4 with number of samples in the x-axis (1 sec = 128 samples) and uV in the y-axis. (a) Correct Epochs and (b) Incorrect Epochs. The vertical red line is the moment when key was pressed.

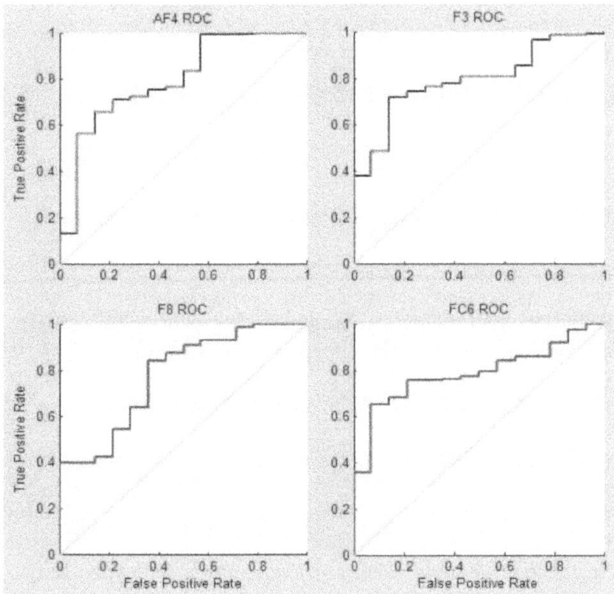

Figure 7. ROC curve for 4 channels: AF4, F3, F8, and FC6

Discussion

The result of the above Flanker Task demonstrate that Emotiv™ device is capable of capturing EEG signals with sufficient quality for a classifier to be able to detect ERN with an accuracy of about 70%. This initial result suggests that we can achieve ERN detection rates that can benefit interactive applications where these can be further improved through manipulating the feedback mechanism such that any likely error (or mistake) is noticed earlier by the user. This can provoke higher amplitude of ERN, further increasing the probability of accurately detecting it. As a result it will enhance the advantage of using ERN as the system can "sense" that the user made a mistake and interrupt or undo the last action.

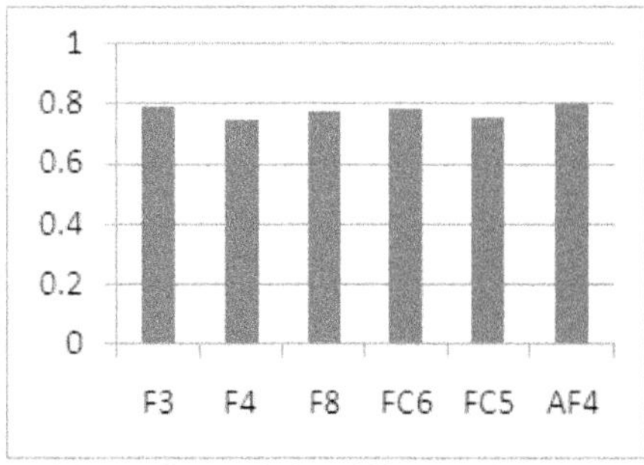

Figure 8. AUC for different channels

EXPERIMENT 2: BUTTONS SELECTION

Compared to Flanker tasks, a visually rich environment, like the one a user might encounter in an interactive application requires more users' mental workload. This will trigger neuronal activities from different parts of the brain; all of which can interfere with ERN signals. Mouse inputs in interactive tasks require free hand movements over longer distance which can cause bioelectrical signals from hand muscle activity. These activities will bring artifacts to EEG signals [22]. For these reasons it is not clear whether ERNs can be detected in a visually rich environment.

The main goal of this experiment is two-fold: first to confirm that an interactive task other than Flanker Task will produce an ERN pattern that can be measured using our portable EEG set and secondly to check whether the pattern can be classified using our online detection algorithm.

We designed a task that retains the main elements of a multiple-choice RT task while at the same time offering a visually rich environment that goes beyond the Flanker task and be closer to what might be expected of an interactive application.

Task: Button selection

In this task the user had to select an object with the size of a 160 x 55 pixel button. In each trial, the user was asked to select a button in a limited time. There are 7 buttons with text from 'Link 01' to 'Link 07' which were arranged in an ascending order from top to bottom. The trial began when user clicked on the START button. A message at the top of the screen showed which button needed to be clicked (Figure 9a). The user then moved the mouse cursor toward the required button. A timer was placed at the top right of the screen to show elapsed time since the trial started. The timer was to put pressure on user to complete the trial as quickly as possible. The user must finish the trial in a limited time (1.4s) otherwise a TIME OUT message would appear and the trial restarted. We chose 1.4s because 1.3s was the average time for an experienced user to complete the task.When the mouse cursor was moving toward the desired button and there was 30 pixels distance remaining to reach, the order of the buttons may change (Figure 9b). The probability for the buttons' order to change was 50%.

Because the position of the desired button was changed when the cursor was very near, user may not have enough time to change their decision to click on the intended button but still aware of the result of their action. The intention was to provoke an ERN in this case. When user clicked on a button, a message notified user if they had clicked on the correct one. There was a 3 second waiting time before a new trial started.

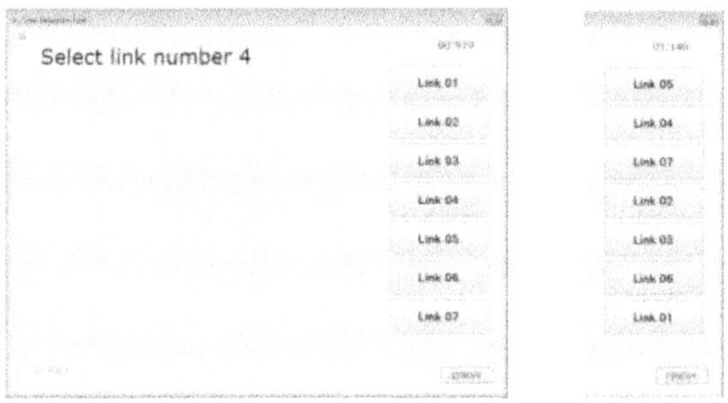

(a) (b)

Figure 9. User interface of the task at the moment of (a) start trial and (b) cursor is near the desired button.

Design and procedure

Nine students (6 males) recruited from the local university took part in this experiment. All of them knew about the Emotiv device but had never tried it before. Each of them was given the consent form and information sheet informing them about the task details. They were asked to sit comfortably but alerted to the task. They were also instructed to blink less during the experiment, especially around the deciding moment (mouse click). The experiment took place in an office environment with ambient noise.

Participants were given some practice trials to become familiar with the task until they confirmed they were ready to start the experiment in which data was collected. Each participant performed 4 blocks of 40 trials each and there was 2 minute break between each block.

Data Collection and Analysis

Signals were collected using the Emotiv neuroheadset. They were then divided into 1.5 second epochs around mouse click moments, 0.5 seconds before and 1 second after. The moments that a participant saw the result of their action were also captured as it is assumed that was when s/he realized that s/he has made a correct or incorrect choice. The epochs were then divided into two groups where the first group was used to compute the coefficient matrix (β). The second group was formed with the remaining data.

This coefficient matrix was then used to classify epochs of the second half. There were two cases to classify: participants clicked on the desired button successfully or they performed it unsuccessfully. The classifier performed the classifying task on a single trial basis. Epochs were divided based on the probabilities of having ERN and not having ERN. The result then was compared with the ground truth of participants' confirmation.

We do the classification and analysis offline but using the online detection algorithm. The primary goal here is to verify the effectiveness of the algorithm not to provide users with real-time feedback in an interactive task.

Result

We visually inspected the EEG signals around the moments when a participant clicked a mouse button to see if ERN patterns can be observed or not. ERN pattern was clearly visible in epochs where participants made an incorrect decision (clicked on a wrong button). As the trial result was displayed immediately after user clicked, the epochs of displaying moments were the same as the epochs around mouse click moments.

Figure 10 shows the mean of EEG signals around the moments when a participant click (select an object).

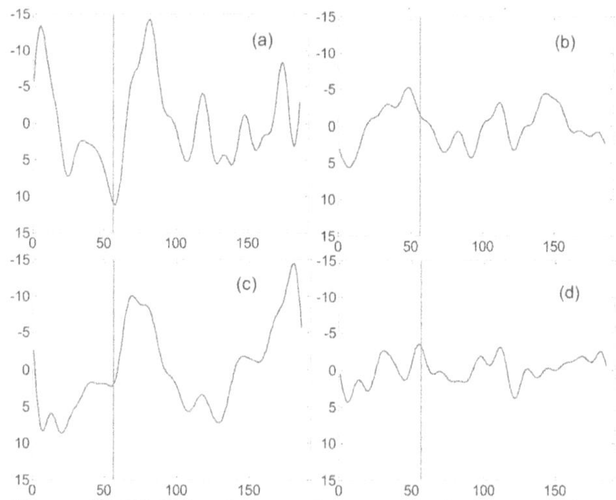

Figure 10. EEG signals around moments where a participant made an incorrect decision (a, c) and correct decision (b, d) at channel F3 (top) and FC5 (bottom). The red lines mark the moment that the mouse button was clicked.

In addition, the Logistic Regression algorithm can classify epochs belonging to those two cases: correct and incorrect responses. The coefficient matrices (β) of the same participant from the first half of data were multiplied with the extracted epochs $x(t)$ to produce output $y(t)$. We perform a t-test on $y(t)$ for each channel per user to check if there is a significant difference between two types of output: correct (user clicked on a correct button) and incorrect (user clicked on an incorrect button). We investigated further based on the t-test result and found that the accuracy of the classifier on incorrect decision moments and correct decision moments were 64% and 67% at channel F3 and 63% and 69% at channel FC5. The results from this experiment are similar in accuracy to the result of the Flanker Task. It is notable that those two channels that have the best classifying accuracy are in frontal-central part of human brain which is consistent with the result obtained from Flanker Task.

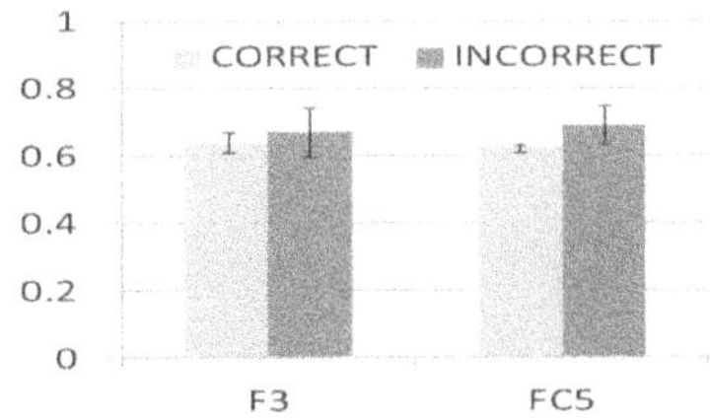

Figure 11. Single trial classification accuracies

Discussion

The result obtained from this experiment confirms the existence of an ERN pattern in a non-Flanker task. Those patterns can be seen clearly in epochs when participants commit an incorrect decision. Moreover, this result confirms that ERN patterns appeared in a normal application in a working condition as long as the ERN triggering condition is designed properly.

The method investigated in this experiment demonstrates the ability to detect an ERN pattern using a off the shelf EEG headset. It also demonstrates the ERN detection on a single trial basis. This is promising for HCI designers as the ultimate purpose is not to develop an effective and robust classifier but to harness this type of ERP into HCI.

While one might argue that we processed EEG data offline, it is worth noting that we used a detection algorithm that is essentially an online detection algorithm that works on a single trial basis. This algorithm can be used as a light weight module and can be run in the background of the system. Thus, it can be easily brought to an online version with the same design and signal processing methods.

The questions that remains is how useful this classification level is when ERN is applied to interactive applications and is 65% to 70% accuracy enough in effectively assisting users. The answer varies depending on the types and purposes of each task. Therefore, we designed the next experiment in order to demonstrate at least one set of applications that benefit from this level of ERN classification accuracy.

EXPERIMENT 3

The goal of the experiment was to determine whether the accuracies of the ERN classifier can benefit interactive applications and improve users' performance. It is unlikely that ERN classifying rate can reach 100% at all time. Therefore we design this experiment to justify the trade-off between ERN accuracies and benefits toward users.

The chosen application for this experiment was similar to Superflick [19]. Superflick is a pointing technique which is based on Flick (sliding/ throwing the object across the table) but adds a correction step. Flick is an open-loop technique, providing fast movement but requires practice to achieve accuracy. Superflick offers a "remote drag-and-drop" correction phase if the object is off the target. In our experiment we integrate a "simulated ERN detection" module into Superflick to test if there are any performance differences between different types of detection accuracies.

There are several reasons why we pick this specific pointing technique to explore performance. The main motivation is that it is easy to establish ground truth to compare the different techniques. Secondly, Flick is a popular interaction technique that has been studied extensively in the HCI literature for both handheld and tabletop environments. Thirdly, the authors have experience with the Flick technique and understand how the Superflick design can be improved through the introduction of an ERN detection module. This allows us to examine the effect of various ERN detection rates on users' performance.

The simulated ERN detection module consists of a random function used to mimic the ERN classifier. There are 4 types of accuracy: 50%, 65%, 80% and 100% to simulate the probabilities that the classifier will detect ERN patterns. The random function was controlled so that accuracies were as precise as required. During the experiment, participants were not aware that the ERN module was simulated.

Task and Technique

Participants had to move an object onto a target. The task started with the animated ball to move (the main ball – the lower yellow circle in Figure 1) located at the middle bottom of the screen. The target was a green circle and was assigned randomly among 15 targets.

The participant used a stylus to flick the object onto the target. As soon as the flick action was completed (by lifting the stylus of the touch surface) a circle appeared at the estimated final position of the main ball (the estimated ball – the higher yellow circle in Figure 1) which was calculated based on the distance and duration of the flick gesture. This instant visual feedback allowed the user to know whether or not the ball would actually hit the target. This was done to help with potentially triggering an ERN (although we do not capture these signals but rely on our controlled random function). At this point the mimicked ERN detection module will be triggered causing either the red (mimicking ERN detected) or the green (mimicking ERN not detected) light to be visible. The main ball then moved from the start point toward the estimated ball with the speed of 1200 pixels per second. When the main ball was moving, the user had a chance to remotely drag-and-drop the estimated ball to the target (as in SuperFlick). During the drag process, the main ball automatically moves toward the estimated ball. The trial finished when the main and the estimated balls met each other for over 200ms. This threshold was set to prevent accidental overlaps of the two balls. If they met inside the target, the trial was marked as successful and unsuccessful otherwise. A new trial started after 3s waiting and the user interface was reset to the original condition (with a new target).

The simulated ERN detection worked as follow: 250ms after the main ball left the start position, the ERN detection light, which was placed at the bottom right corner of the screen, started showing red if ERN pattern was detected (estimated ball was not inside the target) and green if not. In case of the light indicating red, the main ball's speed decreased dramatically to 15% of the original speed (180 pixels per second). The user then had more time to remotely correct the position.

The task was built in C# for the experiment, and was installed in a bottom-projected tabletop system. The table was 105x88x106cm (w x d x h) with display size of 72.5x60cm and projector resolution of 1280x1024 pixels. Participants used a Wacom CTE 430 tablet (dimensions: 210 x 208, active area: 127.6 x 92.8mm) for input.

Design and Procedure

Nine local students (5 females) with age from 21 to 41 participated in this experiment. All of them heard about the Emotiv headset but never had used it before. They were given a consent form and information sheet explaining about the purpose of the experiment. Participants were not aware that we were simulating ERN detection. They wore the EEG headset, stood comfortably but alerted to the task in front of the tabletop, and were led to believe that their EEG signals were used to assist them in their task. But instead of detecting ERN based on the measured EEG signals, we created a detection module which is a controlled random function. The accuracy of this detection module was controlled to simulate the accuracy rates.

Participants were given 1 block of 50 trials or more to practice until they were familiar with the task and ready to start. After that, they performed 4 blocks (with minimum 50 trials) with ERN accuracies of 50%, 65%, 80% and 100%. A block was finished when number of trials was more than the minimum number of trials and ERN detection accuracy reached the required number.

Result

Figure 12 illustrates the percentage of successful trials (the main ball ended inside the target). We applied one-way ANOVA test with Bonferroni post hoc multiple comparisons on the data and found that there was significant difference between groups ($F = 17.517$, $p < 0.001$). However, there were no significant difference between groups of 65%, 80% and 100% ($p > 0.5$).

We also analyzed the number of unsuccessful trials when there were red and green lights separately. The intention was to check if users made mistakes naturally when the main ball moved slowly (red light); and if there were more unsuccessful trials when the main ball moved with full speed (green light).

Their mean values are shown Table 1. We ran one-way ANOVA test with Bonferroni post hoc multiple comparisons on those data and found no significant difference between groups in case of Red light ($p > 0.5$). It was noteworthy that even there was significant difference between groups in case of Green light ($F = 11.741$, $p < 0.01$), there was no significant difference between groups (50%, 65%), (65%, 80%), and (80%, 100%) ($p > 0.5$).

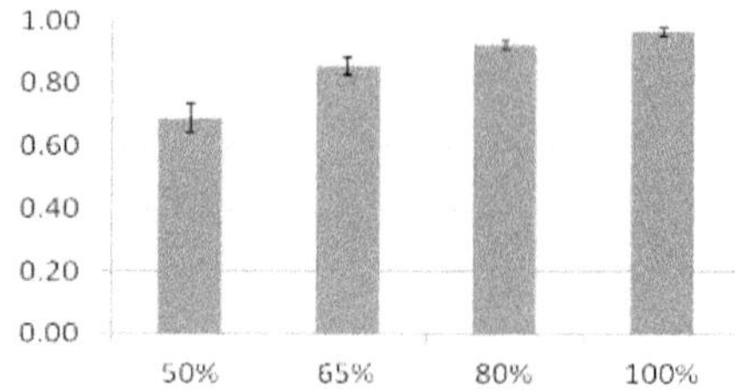

Figure 12. Accuracies of Superflick with different ERN detection accuracies

	50	65	80	100
Red	0.12	0.03	0.06	0.03
Green	0.47	0.35	0.22	0.00

Table 1. Mean % of unsuccessful trials with the two indication light

Discussion

The results obtained from participants show that when integrate ERN detection module with 65% accuracy was as good as 80% accuracy. This was proved as no significant differences were found between two groups in term of overall accuracy and when ERN was not detected (incorrectly). Our results also show that integrating an ERN detection module might not prove beneficial if the detection accuracies are lower than 65%.

The classifier with 65% accuracy may provide higher error rate compared to 80% and 100% accuracies but still benefits interactive tasks. If a system has very high accuracy (less error rate), it can promote hasty commitment to selections [11]. This is because users overly rely on the system and know that there is little cost for making mistakes. In the real world, the cost of an error may be much higher. Therefore, a system with lower classification accuracy may require more attention but has lower cost of recovery hence still offers benefits to the users.

These results confirm that ERN classification accuracy with Emotiv can benefit interactive tasks as good as other expensive devices, yet offer the advantages of portability, low-cost and instantaneous classification.

This experiment also shows an opportunity to assist users in pointing and table top applications using ERN. In these tasks, objects are usually out of range for users to select therefore they need to use several techniques such as drag-and-drop, radar, etc. ERN integration does not replace these techniques but provides better performance and more precise selections for users.

DISCUSSION

ERN has the potential to enrich interactive applications. The results from the studies in this paper can provide guidance on how best to begin harnessing ERN for such interactive experiences.

Employ ERN to Assist Interactive Tasks

The studies in this paper have shown that it is possible to detect ERN patterns using an off-the-shelf EEG headset on an online single-trial basis. If integrated into interactive tasks, an ERN detection module provides another medium for HCI designers to access users' intentions, which is intuitive and directly from the users' brain. This module can be designed as a lightweight background feature.

An ERN pattern will appear in any multiple-choice RT task, of which the button selection task used in this work is just one example. The ERN pattern can be detected within 150ms of the event onset. This means within this time window the user becomes aware that they have made a mistake; the interactive application can know this and respond. In most cases this type of information is not available without access to the user's EEG signals. Even if knowledge of user error is available in some other way (such as text auto correction, prediction techniques) it may not offer as fast response as ERN detection.

The nature and scope of usage of the ERN signal will depend on the usage context, the creativity of the designer and on the ability of the user to ignore recommendations that are incorrect or inappropriate.

Dealing with incorrect classification

Detecting ERN correctly is a challenge. We can be reasonably sure that even the best classifier will never achieve 100% accuracy in an online single trial system. Consequently, an interruption management system is needed to be integrated into the system. This can reduce the disturbance to users when the system makes suggestions based on incorrectly detected ERNs. For example, if a user chooses to ignore a suggestion that pops up based on a confirmed ERN, the pop up must not prevent the user interacting with the user interface. Designers wishing to use ERN in their applications must be careful to ensure that such ERN-based suggestions do not stop the user from working with the system.

Potential Applications of ERN

As ERN is elicited in any multiple choice RT time task when the user is confused or aware of their accidental action this has great potential in many type of interactive applications. We suggest some of them as follow:

Gaming conditions: ERN can be used to provide users with a new form of experience in gaming. For example, in time critical missions (like shooting a character in World-of-war craft) sometimes network delays and other external factors may affect the overall outcome of the mission or battle. In these cases if an ERN is detected this can be used in systems decision making process either by giving the player another chance or changing the time-stamp of user triggered events to make the outcome seem as the user intended.

Aiding Object Selection: Selecting a static target among a selection of objects is a multiple choice reaction time task. The user starts with deciding on the target then makes an initial open-loop movement followed by a final correction phase where they move the pointer or finger on the target to select it. In this correction phase if the user usually receive visual feedback on whether or not their selection was successful. This feedback combined with the initiation of the correction-phase movement can trigger ERNs if the movements are fast enough. Thus it should be possible for an ERN detection module to detect errors in users' intention and attempt to correct it. In many instances the cost of recovering from a wrong button press or a pointer selection can be quite high – the application might be launched and the user would have to close it before re-launching the right application. In these circumstances when ERN is detected the system can prompt the user if the target was selected correctly potentially helping the user.

ERN detection can be combined with P300 to reduce the user's mental load and frustration (error-recovery is time consuming and difficult) that is associated with working with P300 data. For example, in a object selection using P300 on a multi-touch table [27], ERN can be used as final confirmation that the object is the user's intended selected object. This will be very useful because it is difficult to confirm using only P300 that the selected object on the table is the one that the user wanted. Moreover, ERN usage can eliminate the trial of hitting the BACK button to de-select an object in P300 spelling which is time consuming and requires high concentration. This can also be applied into object selections on a tabletop for people in working condition so that the time spent in correcting wrong selection will be reduced and efficiency improved.

Mobile Spatial Navigation: Sometimes, a user still needs help in using and navigating using electronic maps on the fly (i.e. Google maps). HCI designers may integrate ERN into the system so that it can detect the confusion and error awareness moments in order to provide appropriate suggestion based on the location. One obstacle is EEG is known to be sensitive to movements such as walking and moving your body. This can make the EEG signal very noisy reducing the accuracy of the ERN detector. Before being fed into the classifier, EEG signals may need to be carefully pre-processed.

Multiple users' applications: ERN use can be extended to multiple users scenarios where a person's ERN is made visible to the entire team so team-support is available when the user is confused. For example if a gamer is confused in navigation or shooting activity, his/her teammates can assist him, or in collaborative table top applications, other people may give help and suggestion to a person whose avatar is being shown as confused or aware that they have made a wrong selection encouraging collaborative peer-learning.

CONCLUSION

The experiments described in this paper offer some valuable guidelines for HCI designers. We show that ERN patterns can be detected using an off the shelf EEG headset on an online single trial basis. Moreover, we apply this model to an interactive task to illustrate that it can work with normal interactive applications in a working environment with ambient noise. We finally show that accuracies in the region of 65 to 80% are sufficient for ERN to be effectively integrated into HCI applications. In our discussions we suggested novel ways in which HCI applications could benefit from ERN.

ACKNOWLEDGEMENT

We thank Dr. Nick Yeung (Oxford Neuroscience, University of Oxford) for providing access to shared data and useful discussions in the initial stages of the project.

REFERENCES

1. Campbell, A., Choudhury, T., Hu, S., Lu, H., Mukerjee, M.K., Rabbi, M., and Raizada, R.D.S. NeuroPhone: brain-mobile phone interface using a wireless EEG headset, in ACM SIGCOMM. (2010), 3-8.
2. Christoforos, A., Dimitris, T., Niall, A., and David, H. Temporally adaptive estimation of logistic classifiers on data streams. ADAC. 3, 3: (2009), 243-261.
3. Scheffers, MK, and Coles, MG. Performance Monitoring in a Confusing World: Error-Related Brain Activity, Judgments of Response Accuracy, and Types of Errors. Proc. of JEPHPP. 26, 1: (2000), 141-151.
4. Dal Seno, B., Matteucci, M., and Mainardi, L. Online detection of P300 and error potentials in a BCI speller. Computational Intelligence and Neuroscience (2010).
5. Dornhege, G., R.Millan, J.d., Hinterberger, T., J.McFarland, D., and Muller, K.-R. Toward Brain-Computer Interfacing. MIT Press. (2007), 393-408.
6. Eriksen, C. and Schultz, D. Information processing in visual search: A continuous flow conception and experimental results. Attention, Perceptionn & Psychophysics. 25, 4: (1979), 249-263.
7. Farwell, L.A. and Donchin, E. Talking off the top of your head: toward a mental prosthesis utilizing event-related brain potentials. Electroencephalography and clinical neurophysiology. 70, 6: (1988), 510-523.
8. Ferrez, P.W. and Millán, J.D.R. You are wrong!: automatic detection of interaction errors from brain waves, in Proc. of IJCAI. (2005), 1413-1418.
9. Ganushchak, L.Y. and Schiller, N.O. Brain errormonitoring activity is affected by semantic relatedness: An event-related brain potentials study. J. Cognitive Neuroscience. 20, 5: (2008), 927-940.
10. Gehring, W.J., Goss, B., Coles, M.G.H., Meyer, D.E., and Donchin, E. A Neural System for Error Detection and Compensation. Psychological Science: (1993).
11. Gutwin, C. and Cockburn, A. Improving list revisitation with ListMaps, in AVI, ACM. (2006).
12. Hirshfield, L.M., Solovey, E.T., Girouard, A., Kebinger, J., Jacob, R.J.K., Sassaroli, A., and Fantini, S. Brain measurement for usability testing and adaptive interfaces: an example of uncovering syntactic workload with functional near infrared spectroscopy, in CHI. (2009), 2185-2194.
13. Hjelm, S.I. and Browall, C. Brainball - using brain activity for cool competition. NordiCHI: (2000).
14. Holroyd, C. and Coles, M. The neural basis of human error processing: reinforcement learning, dopamine, and the error-related negativity. Psych review, 4: (2002).
15. Honghu Liu, G.L. Testing Statistical Significance of the Area under a Receiving Operating Characteristics Curve for Repeated Measures Design with Bootstrapping. J. Data Science. 3: (2005), 257-278.
16. Lee, J.C. and Tan, D.S. Using a low-cost electroencephalograph for task classification in HCI research, in UIST. (2006), 81-90.
17. Miltner, W.H.R., Braun, C.H., and Coles, M.G.H. Event-related brain potentials following incorrect feedback in a time-estimation task: Evidence for a neural system for error detection. J. Cognitive Neuroscience: (1997), 788-798.
18. Parra, L., Alvino, C., Tang, A., Pearlmutter, B., Yeung, N., Osman, A., and Sajda, P. Linear Spatial Integration for Single-Trial Detection in Encephalography. NeuroImage. 17, 1: (2002), 223-230.
19. Reetz, A., Gutwin, C., Stach, T., Nacenta, M., and Subramanian, S. Superflick: a natural and efficient technique for long-distance object placement on digital tables, in Proc. of GI. (2006), 163-170.
20. Shenoy, P. and Tan, D.S. Human-aided computing: utilizing implicit human processing to classify images, in CHI, ACM. (2008), 845-854.
21. Solovey, E.T., Girouard, A., Chauncey, K., Hirshfield, L.M., Sassaroli, A., Zheng, F., Fantini, S., and Jacob, R.J.K. Using fNIRS brain sensing in realistic HCI settings: experiments and guidelines, in UIST. (2009).
22. Sörnmo, L. and Laguna, P. Bioelectrical Signal Processing in Cardiac and Neurological Applications. Elseiver. (2005).
23. Van Erkel, A.R. and Pattynama, P.M.T. Receiver operating characteristic (ROC) analysis: Basic principles and applications in radiology. European J. Radiology. 27, 2: (1998), 88-94.
24. Villringer, A. and Chance, B. Non-invasive optical spectroscopy and imaging of human brain function. Trends in Neurosciences. 20, 10: (1997), 435-442.
25. Yeung, N., Botvinick, M.M., and Cohen, J.D. The Neural Basis of Error Detection: Conflict Monitoring and the Error-Related Negativity. Psych review: (2004).
26. Yeung, N. and Cohen, J.D. The Impact of Cognitive Deficits on Conflict Monitoring: Predictable Dissociations Between the Error-Related Negativity and N2. Psych Science. 17: (2006), 164-171.
27. Yuksel, B.F., Donnerer, M., Tompkin, J., and Steed, A. A novel brain-computer interface using a multi-touch surface, in CHI. (2010), 855-858.

Implanted User Interfaces

Christian Holz[1,2]
christian.holz@hpi.uni-potsdam.de
[1]Autodesk Research
Toronto, Ontario, Canada

Tovi Grossman[1], **George Fitzmaurice**[1]
{firstname.lastname}@autodesk.com
[2]Hasso Plattner Institute
Potsdam, Germany

Anne Agur[3]
anne.agur@utoronto.ca
[3]Department of Anatomy
University of Toronto

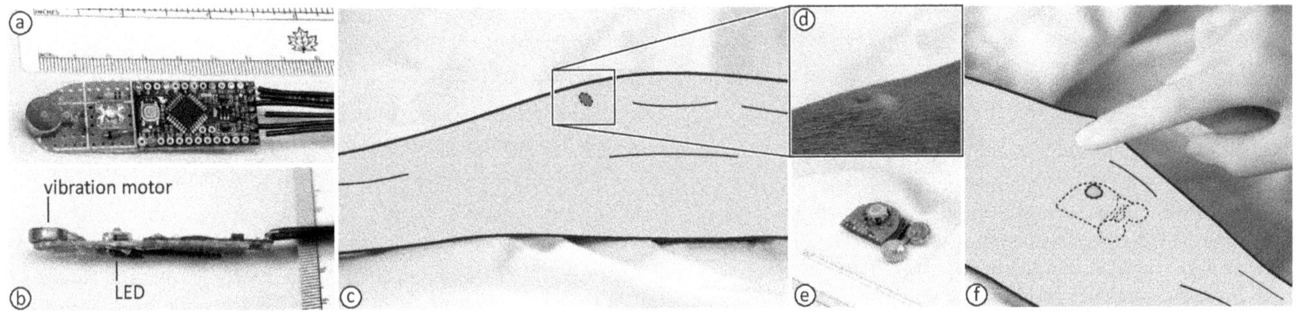

Figure 1: ***Implanted user interfaces*** **allow users to interact with small devices through human skin. (a-b) This output device is implanted (c) underneath the skin of a specimen arm. (d) Actual photograph of the LED output through the skin. (e) This standalone prototype senses input from an *exposed* trackball (f) and illuminates it in response.** ***Note: Throughout this paper, illustrations have been used in place of actual photographs of the specimen, to ensure ethical and professional standards are maintained.***

ABSTRACT

We investigate *implanted user interfaces* that small devices provide when implanted underneath human skin. Such devices *always* stay with the user, making their implanted user interfaces *available at all times*. We discuss four core challenges of implanted user interfaces: how to sense input through the skin, how to produce output, how to communicate amongst one another and with external infrastructure, and how to remain powered. We investigate these four challenges in a technical evaluation where we surgically implant study devices into a specimen arm. We find that traditional interfaces do work through skin. We then demonstrate how to deploy a prototype device on participants, using artificial skin to simulate implantation. We close with a discussion of medical considerations of implanted user interfaces, risks and limitations, and project into the future.

Author Keywords

Implanted devices; implanted interfaces; implantables; mobile devices; augmented humans; wearable computing; disappearing mobile devices; wireless power.

ACM Classification Keywords

H.5.2 [Information interfaces and presentation]: User Interfaces. Input devices & strategies.

INTRODUCTION

In 1991, Mark Weiser wrote that "the most profound technologies are those that disappear. They weave themselves into the fabric of everyday life until they are indistinguishable from it" [47]. Weiser's seminal vision is close to becoming today's reality. We now use mobile devices to place calls and send emails on the go, maintain our calendars and setup reminders, and quickly access information. While these devices have not yet disappeared, they have become an integral part of our lives, to the point where we have arguably become dependent on them [14]. For example, in a recent survey of 200 Stanford students that owned iPhones, nearly a quarter of those surveyed reported that the iPhone felt like an extension of their brain or body [28].

In this paper, we propose manifesting these dependencies on external devices by implanting them underneath human skin, allowing users to interact with them through *implanted user interfaces*. While implanted devices have existed for a long time in the medical domain, such as hearing aids or pacemakers, they support only limited interaction, and cannot support personal tasks. Unlike other types of mobile devices, such as wearables [40] or interactive clothing [33], implanted devices are with the user *at all times*. Implanting thus truly allows always-available interaction [37].

Before implanted user interfaces can become a reality, numerous questions must be considered. In this paper, we explore four core challenges: How can users produce input? How can the devices provide output? How can the devices communicate and transfer information? How can the devices remain powered?

After discussing these challenges, we perform a technical evaluation, where we surgically implant seven devices into a specimen arm. We evaluate and quantify the extent to which traditional interface components, such as LEDs, speakers, and input controls work through skin (Figure 1b&c). Our main finding is that traditional interface components do work when implanted underneath human skin, which provides an initial validation of the feasibility of implanted user interfaces.

Motivated by these results, we conduct a small qualitative evaluation using a prototype device (Figure 2a), for the purpose of collecting user feedback. As a substitute for actually implanting this device, we place it under a layer of artificial skin made from silicon, which affixes on the user's skin (Figure 2b). We conclude our exploration of implanted user interfaces with a comprehensive discussion of medical assessment, limitations, and potential for future work.

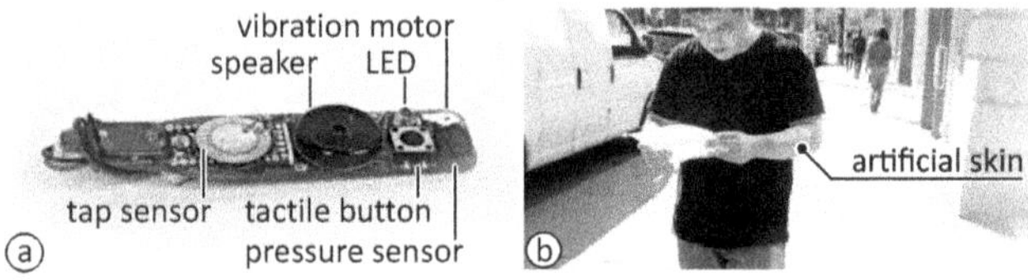

Figure 2: We covered a prototype device (a) with a layer of artificial skin (b) to collect qualitative feedback from use in an outdoor scenario. Participants received output triggers *through* the artificial skin and responded with input.

RELATED WORK

The work in this paper is related to input and output on and through the body, wearable devices, and human implants.

Input and Output on the Body

Recent on-body systems have allowed users to provide touch input on their bodies using a depth camera [13, 16] or by capturing acoustic sensations [17]. To produce output, systems often feature wearable projectors [16, 17], which, however, may complicate outdoor use and impede mobility. Implanted user interfaces, in contrast, are fully contained and mobile.

Input and Output *with* the Body

Sensing body activity directly presents an alternative to using the body as a spatial input canvas, such as sensing muscle tension [37], tongue motions using prototypes worn inside the mouth [21, 36] and micro-devices integrated into worn contact lenses [19].

Direct *output* through the body has been shown with electrodes that stimulate the user's muscles [44] or the user's ear to influence the sense of balance [9]. Uses of such output systems include learning gestures or receiving real-time feedback in gaming environments.

Results in these research areas are impressive and encouraging. However, our focus is on implanted devices as standalone units with no coupling to the user's biological system.

Wearable Devices

While users typically carry mobile devices inside pockets, retrieving them to start interacting imposes a significant overhead on usage time [2]. As mobile devices shrink to very small sizes, users can instead attach them directly to their bodies [40, 41]. *Disappearing mobile devices* prototype smallest-possible visual sensors and researchers have speculated on the possibility of implanting them [31].

Instead of attaching devices to the body, clothing has been made interactive by using conductive thread to sense pinches [24] and touch on clothing, such as on keypads made of fabric [33] or entire touchpads [35].

Wearable devices typically need to be explicitly put on or removed, either on a daily basis, or for specific activities. We see implanted user interfaces as a complement to wearable devices, which could potentially provide a more permanent solution.

Human Implants

Active medical implants typically maintain life-crucial functionality (e.g., pacemakers), improve body functionality to restore normal living (e.g., hearing aids), or monitor the user's health [8]. Passive implants are also commonly used for medical purposes, such as for artificial joints.

While swallowed and not implanted, physicians have also used small pill-sized autonomous microcomputers to record data from inside the body and transmit it to a receiver for external visualization (e.g., capsule endoscopy [12]).

For interactive purposes, electrodes have been implanted in the context of brain-computer interfaces [49] and speech production [4]. Moore and Kennedy powered such an implanted electrode using induction through the scalp [30].

Humans have experimented with adding new abilities to their bodies, such as implanting a small magnet to their finger [48] or an RFID chip into their body. Masters and Michael discuss issues surrounding human-centric applications of RFID implants, such as automatically opening doors and turning on lights [29]. Warwick's Project Cyborg investigates user interaction through an implanted RFID chip with devices in the proximity, as well as the interaction of implants with user's nervous system [46]. Ullah et al. discuss in- and on-body wireless communication [45] in the context of *body area networks* [22]. Relevant work can also be found in the art community. For example, Stelarc attached an ear-replica to his arm, which used a miniature microphone to transmit recorded sounds wirelessly [43].

These medical and non-medical examples demonstrate the feasibility of implanting devices. However, such devices are typically passive, and do not provide any mechanisms for direct interaction with the actual implant. In the next section, we introduce *implanted user interfaces*, which could support such interaction.

IMPLANTED USER INTERFACES

We consider *implanted devices* as devices that are surgically and permanently inserted under the human's skin. Implanting devices that possess user interfaces would allow users to *directly* interact with them, allowing them to support a wide range of applications and tasks, beyond the medical usages prevalent today.

Implanted devices have several advantages over mobile and wearable devices. First, implanted devices do not need to be manually attached to the user's body. They stay out of the way of everyday or recreational activities (e.g. swimming or showering). Second, implanted devices have the potential to be completely *invisible*. This would avoid any social stigmas of having such devices. Third, implanted devices, along with the information they store and provide, always travel with the user; the user can never lose or forget to take them. The devices and applications become *part* of the user.

Despite these potential benefits, there has been little or no investigation of implanted user interfaces from an HCI perspective. Given the continuous miniaturization of technology [31], we believe implanted user interfaces could become a reality in the future. Below, we outline some of the core design considerations, with the hope of bringing these issues to the attention of the HCI community.

Design Considerations

We see four core challenges associated with implanted user interfaces and their use through human skin: 1) providing input to and sensing input on implanted devices, 2) perceiving output from and producing output from implanted devices, 3) communication among implanted devices and with external devices, and 4) power supply to implanted devices.

1) Input through implanted interfaces

Since implanted devices sit under the skin, they are not directly accessible through their interfaces. This makes providing input to them an interesting challenge.

One option is to use contact-based input through the skin, such as a button, which would additionally offer tactile and audible feedback to the user. Tap and pressure sensors allow devices to sense how strongly touches protrude the skin, while brightness and capacitive sensors detect a limited range of hover. Strategic placement of touch-based sensors could form an input surface on the skin that allows for tapping and dragging. Audio is an alternative implanted user interface. A microphone could capture speech input for voice activation.

Fully implanted and thus fully concealed controls require users to learn their locations, either by feeling them through skin or by indicating their location through small marks. Natural features such as moles could serve as such marks. Partial exposure, in contrast, would restore visual discoverability and allow for direct input. Exposing a small camera, for example, would allow for spatial swiping input above the sensor (e.g., optical flow of the fingerprint [20, 31]). All such input components, whether implanted or exposed, are subject to accidental activation, much like all wearable input components. Systems have addressed this, for example, by using a global on/off switch or requiring a certain device posture [18].

2) Output through implanted interfaces

Device output typically depends on the senses of sight (i.e., visual signals), hearing (i.e., audio signals) and touch (e.g., vibration and moving parts). Stimulation of other senses, such as taste and smell, is still only experimental (e.g., taste interfaces [38]).

The size constraints of small devices require sacrificing spatial resolution and leave room for only individual visual signals, such as LEDs. Furthermore, visual output may go unnoticed if the user is not looking directly at the source. While audio output is not subject to such size constraints, its bandwidth is similar to the visual output of a single signal: varying intensities, pitches, and sound patterns [31]. Tactile output of single elements is limited to the bandwidth of pressure to the body and intensity patterns (e.g., vibration [50]). Tactile feedback may be particularly suited towards implanted user interfaces, since it could provide output noticeable only to the host user and no one else.

3) Communication and Synchronization

To access and exchange data amongst each other or with external devices, implanted devices need to communicate.

If devices are fully implanted under the skin, communication will need to be wireless. Bluetooth is already being used to replace wired short-range point-to-point communication, such as for health applications (e.g., in body area networks [22]). Wi-Fi, as an alternative, transmits across longer distances at higher speeds, but comes at the cost of increased power usage and processing efforts.

Equipping implanted devices with an *exposed port* would enable tethered communication. Medical ports are already used to permit frequent injections to the circulatory system [25]. Ports and tethered connections are suitable for communication with external devices, but not amongst two devices implanted at different locations in a user's body. Such devices would still require wireless communication.

4) Power supply through implanted interfaces

A substantial challenge for implanted devices is how they source energy. As power is at a premium, implanted devices should employ sleep states and become fully active only after triggering them.

A simple way to power an active implanted device is to use a replaceable battery. This is common with pacemakers, which typically need surgical battery replacement every 6-10 years. Rechargeable batteries would avoid the need for surgery and recharging could be wireless, through technology known as inductive charging [34]. If the implanted device is close to the skin surface, inductive charging may work through the skin [30]. Alternatively, an exposed port could provide tethered recharging to an implanted device. Finally, an implanted device could harvest energy from using the device [3] or from body functions (e.g., heartbeats [27] or body heat [39]). We direct the reader to Starner's overview for more information [39].

Summary

We have described some of the key challenges, and discussed possible components that could support the interface between the human and the implantable. However, there is little understanding of how well these basic interface components actually function underneath human skin.

EVALUATING BASIC IMPLANTED USER INTERFACES

The purpose of this evaluation was to examine to what extent input, output, communication, and charging components remain useful when implanted underneath human skin. In addition, we provide a proof of concept that these devices can in fact be implanted, both fully under the skin and with exposed parts.

We performed this evaluation in collaboration with the Department of Surgery in the Division of Anatomy at the University of Toronto, Canada. The procedure of the study underwent full ethics review prior to the evaluation and received approval from the Research Ethics Board.

Devices

We evaluated seven devices featuring twelve controls in total, which were traditional input and output components as well as components for synchronization and powering common in conventional mobile devices. As shown in Figure 3, we tested four basic sensors for direct touch input: button, pressure sensor, tap sensor. In addition, we tested two devices that could potentially detect hover above the skin: capacitive and brightness sensor. We also tested a microphone for auditory input. For output, we tested an LED (visual), vibration motor (tactile), and speaker (audio). For charging, we evaluated an inductive charging mat, and for communication, we tested Bluetooth data transfer. These devices do not exhaust all possible implanted interface components, but we chose them as some of the more likely components that could be used.

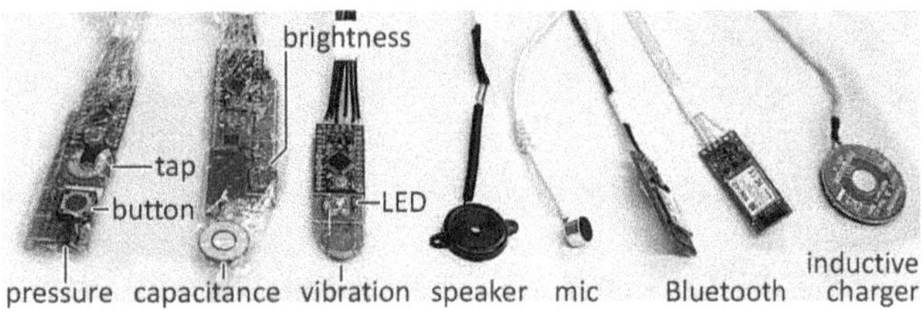

Figure 3: These devices were implanted during the study. Plastic bags around devices prevent contact with tissue fluid.

Cables connected each of the devices to a laptop computer to ensure reliable connectivity and communication with the devices throughout the study (Figure 4). The laptop logged all signals sent from the input components on the devices, including device ID, sensor ID, sensed intensity and timestamp. The laptop also logged time-stamped output triggers, including output component ID, intensity and frequency.

All active devices used an ATmega328 microcontroller with a 10-bit precision AD converter. The chip forwarded all measurements to the laptop and also computed length of impact as well as average and maximum intensities. We also recorded all background intensities separately.

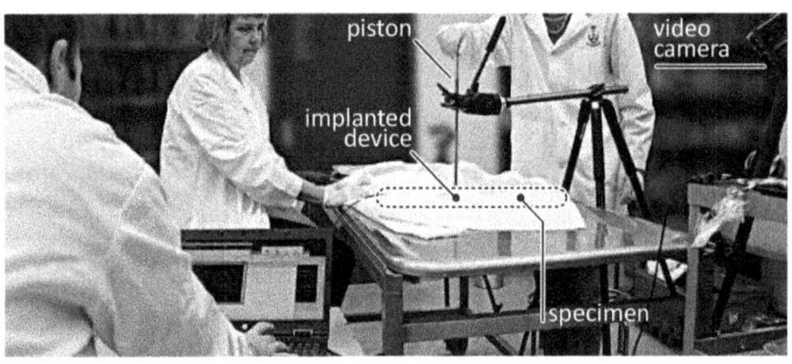

Figure 4: Study setup with input apparatus set up. A piston repeatedly dropped from controlled heights onto the sensors.

Experimenters

The study was administered by an experimenter and an experimenter assistant, both with HCI backgrounds, and an anatomy professor, who carried out all of the surgical procedures (Figure 4). Because the focus of this study was on the technical capabilities of the devices themselves, external participants were not necessary.

Procedure

We conducted the evaluation in two sessions. In the *baseline session*, the devices lay on the table shown in Figure 4. In the *implant session*, each of the seven devices was implanted into a cadaveric specimen, one at a time. An external video camera documented the entire implant session, and parts of the baseline session. The experimenter configured and initialized the devices through the laptop and monitored the incoming data, while the assistant performed the necessary interactions with the devices.

Medical Procedure

One lightly embalmed cadaveric upper limb specimen (dark-skinned male, 89 years old) was used for this study. With light embalming, the tissues remained pliable and soft, similar to fresh and unembalmed tissue [1]. The skin and subcutaneous tissues remained mobile.

Each of the seven devices was enclosed by two thin transparent plastic bags to prevent malfunction due to penetration by tissue fluid (as shown by the left-most two devices in Figure 3). To insert devices, the skin was incised and separated along the tissue plane between the skin and underlying subcutaneous tissue at the cut end of the limb, about 7.5cm proximal to the elbow joint, which was 20cm from the insertion point. Once the plane was established, a long metal probe was used to open the plane as far distally as the proximal forearm, creating a pocket for the devices. Each of the devices was inserted, one at a time, into the tissue plane and the wires attached to the devices were used to guide the device into the pocket between the skin and subcutaneous tissue of the proximal forearm (Figure 5). Distal to the insertion site of the device, the skin remained intact. All devices were fully encompassed by skin, with no space between device and skin or tissue, or any opening.

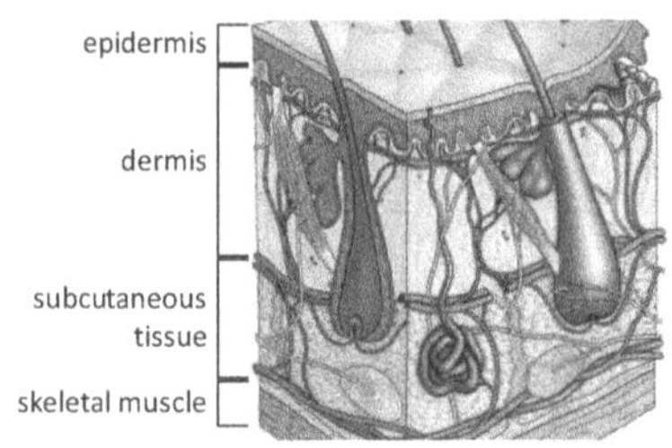

Figure 5: Illustration of skin layers. All devices were implanted between the skin and the subcutaneous fatty tissue.

Study Procedure and Results

We now report the study procedure along with results separately for each of the seven devices.

1) Touch Input Device (pressure sensor, tap sensor, button)

To produce input at controlled intensities, we built a stress test device as shown in Figure 4. The assistant dropped a piston from controlled heights onto each input sensor to produce predictable input events.

For the pressure and tap sensors, the piston was dropped from six controlled heights (2cm to 10cm in steps of 2cm), repeated five times each, and the intensities from the sensors were measured. For the button, the piston was dropped from seven heights (3mm, 7mm, 1cm, 2cm-10cm in 2cm steps), also repeated five times each, and we recorded if the button was activated. Subjectively, the piston dropping from 10cm roughly compared to the impact of a hard tap on a tabletop system. Dropping from 1cm produces a noticeable but very light tap.

Apparatus details

The pressure sensor used a voltage divider with a circular 0.2" Interlink Electronics force sense resistor (100g-10Kg) and a 10KΩ resistor. The button was a 12mm (H4.3mm) round PTS125 hardware button. The touch sensor was a Murata 20mm piezoelectric disc. The microcontroller captured events at 30kHz. The piston was a 60g metal rod.

Results

Force sensor: Skin softened the peak pressure of the dropping piston, whereas the softening effect shrunk with increasing impact force (Figure 6). We analyzed the measured voltages and, by relating them back to the force-resistance mapping in the datasheet, obtained an average of 3N in differences of sensing impact between conditions.

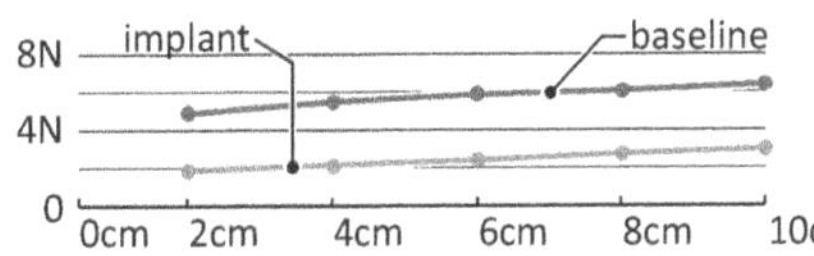

Figure 6: On average, skin accounts for 3N overhead for impact forces on pressure and touch sensors.

Button: Figure 7 illustrates the effect of skin dampening on the impact of the dropping piston. In the baseline condition, the piston always activated the button, whereas only dropping from a height of 1cm and higher achieved enough force to activate the button through the skin at all times.

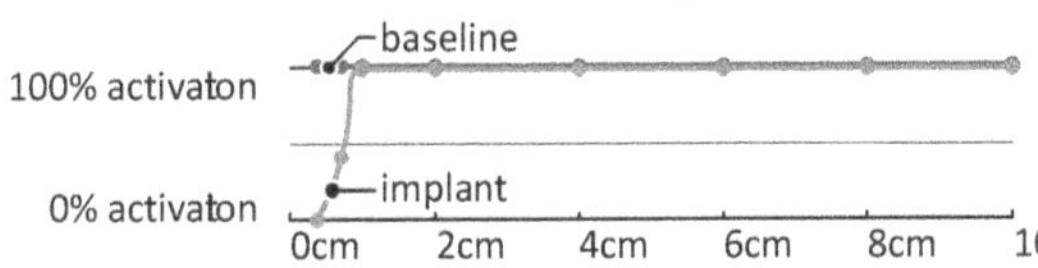

Figure 7: The piston activated the button from all tested heights in the baseline condition, but activated the button reliably only from a height of 1cm and up when implanted.

Tap sensor: In both conditions, the piezo tap sensor produced the maximum voltage our device could measure in response to the impact of the piston from all tested heights. The piston therefore activated the tap sensor reliably with all forces shown in Figure 6.

2) Hover Input Device (capacitive and brightness sensor)

To produce hover input, the assistant used his index finger and slowly approached the sensor from above over the course of 3s, rested his finger on it for 3s, and then slowly moved his finger away. The assistant repeated this procedure five times for each of the two sensors.

Apparatus details

The capacitive sensor was a 24-bit, 2-channel capacitance to digital converter (AD7746). The brightness sensor used a voltage divider with a 12mm cadmium sulfide 10MΩ photoresistor and a 10KΩ resistor. Both sensors captured hover intensities at 250Hz. Three rows of fluorescent overhead lighting illuminated the study room.

Results

For both sensors, we averaged the five curves of measured signal intensities to account for noisy measurements.

Brightness sensor: Without the finger present, skin diffused incoming light, resulted in reduced brightness (Figure 8 left). The environmental light explains the differences in slopes between baseline and implant condition; as the finger approaches the sensor, light reflected from surfaces can still fall in at extreme angles in the baseline condition. Skin in contrast diffuses light and thus objects approaching the sensor result in a less pronounced response.

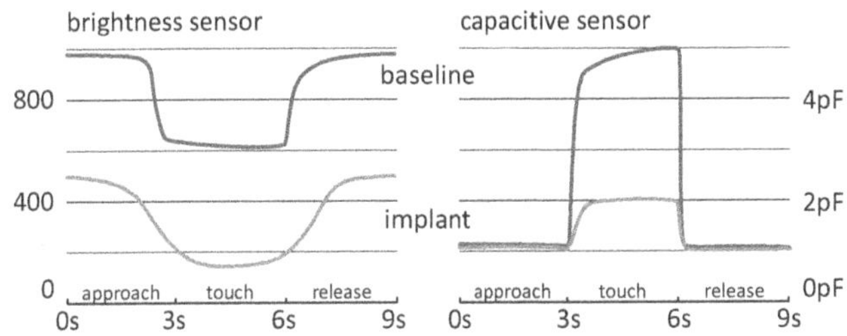

Figure 8: (left) Impact on sensed brightness and on sensed capacitance (right). Curves average the values of all five trials.

Capacitive sensor: Similar to the brightness sensor, the capacitive levels were offset when sensing through the skin (Figure 8 right). The signal of a touching finger was comparably strong in the baseline condition, but caused only a milder difference in sensed capacitance through the skin.

3) Output Device (red LED, vibration motor)

To evaluate the LED and motor, we used a descending staircase design to determine minimum perceivable intensities [5,26]. For each trial, the experimenter triggered components to emit output at a controlled intensity level for a duration of five seconds. The assistant, a 32 year old male, served as the participant for the staircase study to determine absolute perception thresholds. The method started with full output intensity, which the participant could clearly perceive. The experimenter then decreased the intensity in discrete steps, and the participant reported if he could perceive it. If he did not, the experimenter increased output intensities in smaller steps until the participant could perceive it. We continued this procedure until direction had reversed eight times [23, 26]. The last four reversal values then determined the absolute perception threshold [23].

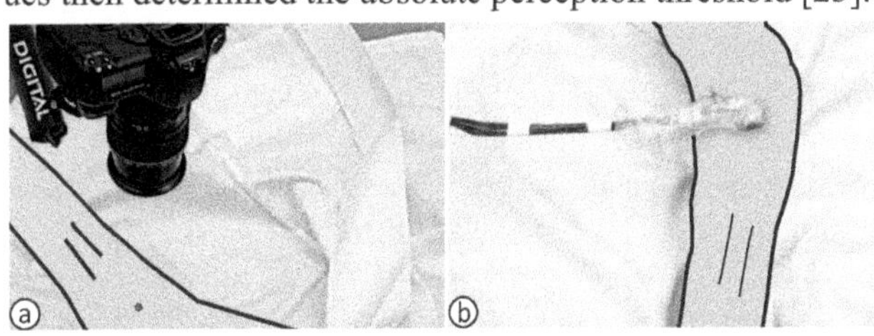

Figure 9: (a) A camera captured the intensity of produced light and (b) an accelerometer measured vibration intensities.

At each step, we also measured the actual output intensities. We captured the LED output with a camera focusing onto the LED at a fixed distance, aperture and exposure time (Figure 9a). An accelerometer placed directly above the vibration motor captured output intensities (Figure 9b).

Apparatus details

The LED was a red 3000mcd square light. The vibration motor was a 10mm (H3.4mm) Precision Microdrives shaftless 310-101 vibration motor. The external camera was a Canon DSLR EOS5D and captured 16bit RAW images.

Results

LED: The staircase methodology yielded the absolute threshold for perceiving LED output at 8.1% intensity required in the baseline condition and 48.9% intensity required through the skin. Figure 10 (left) shows the actually produced intensities determined by the external camera.

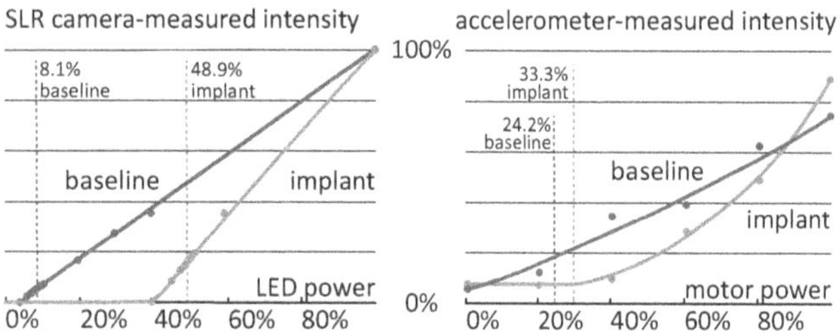

Figure 10: (left) Minimum perceivable LED intensity. (right) The accelerometer did not pick up a signal through skin at motor intensities of 40% and lower. Dotted lines indicate the participant's absolute perception thresholds.

Vibration motor: The accelerometer captured a signal through the skin only when the motor was powered at 40% intensity and higher; lower intensities were indistinguishable from background noise (Figure 10 right). The baseline condition with the accelerometer resting on the motor directly shows an expected linear decay. The shown values represent the mean standard deviation of the three values read by the accelerometer. The difference in personal perception of the vibration was small (24.2% vs. 33.3%).

4) Audio Device (speaker and microphone)

To evaluate the speaker, we again used a descending staircase design to determine minimum perceivable audio levels. We conducted the evaluation from two distances: 25cm (*close*) and 60cm (*far*). These distances simulated holding the arm to one's ear to listen to a signal (*close*) and hearing the signal from a resting state with the arms beside one's body (*far*). The stimulus was a 1kHz sine wave signal [11]. During each step, an external desktop microphone measured actual output signals from 5cm away in the *close* condition, and 60 cm away in the *far* condition.

To evaluate the implanted microphone, we produced audio as input from two distances (25cm, 60cm). Two desktop speakers pointed at the microphone and played five prerecorded sounds at ten volume levels (100%, 80%, 60%, 40%, 20%, 10%, 8%, 4%, 2%, 1%). Three of the sound playbacks were voice ("one", "two", "three", "user"), one was a chime sound.

Apparatus details

The implanted microphone was a regular electret condenser microphone. The external microphone was an audio-technica AT2020 USB. The speaker was a Murata Piezo 25mm piezoelectric buzzer. The laptop recorded from both microphones at 44.1kHz with the microphone gain set to 1.

Results

Speaker: We first applied a bandpass filter of 100Hz to the recorded signal around the stimuli frequency to discard background noise. The assistant could perceive the stimuli sound at a level of 5.2dB at only 0.3% output intensity in the *baseline* session, and at 7% in the *implant* session (Figure 11). The perceivable decibel levels compare to other results [11]. Figure 11 illustrates the additional output intensity needed to achieve comparable sound pressures.

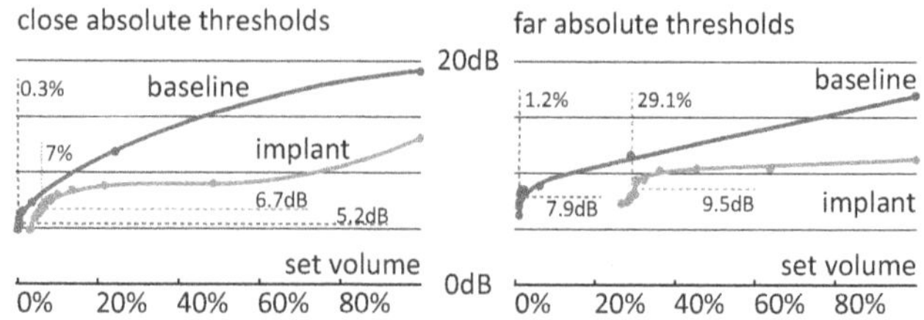

Figure 11: Sound perception through skin is possible, but skin substantially takes away from the output intensity (left). This effect grows with the distance between listener and speaker (right). Dotted lines indicate absolute perception thresholds.

Microphone: The skin accounted for a difference in recorded sound intensities of 6.5dB (±3dB) for the close-speaker condition and 6.24dB (±2.5dB) in the far-speaker condition. At full output volume, skin dampened the volume of the incoming sound by less than 2% when close by 25cm away, but almost 10% with speakers 60cm away.

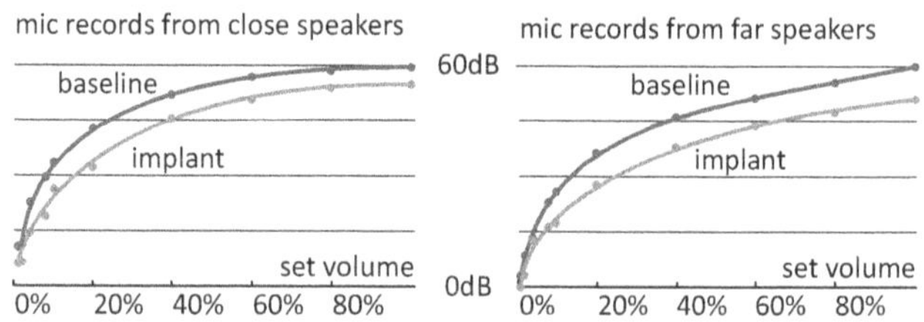

Figure 12: The differences in perceived sound intensities were nearly constant between the implant and the baseline session.

5) Powering Device (Powermat wireless charger)

To evaluate the powering device, we docked the receiver to the powering mat (Figure 13). In the *baseline* session, the two devices docked directly. In the *implant* session, the receiver was implanted, and the powering mat was placed on the surface of the skin directly above the implant.

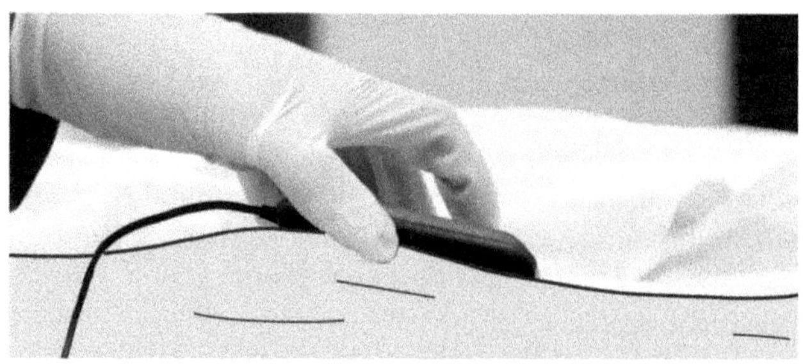

Figure 13: The wireless charging mat docks to the receiver, which is implanted inside the specimen.

Once docked, we separately measured the voltages and currents the receiver supplied with a voltmeter and an ampere-meter. We took five probes for each measurement, each time capturing values for five seconds for the meters to stabilize. We measured the provided voltages and the drawn current with four resistors: 2KΩ, 1KΩ, 100Ω, 56Ω.

Apparatus details

The powering device was a PMR-PPC2 Universal Powercube Receiver with a PMM-1PA Powermat 1X. The voltmeter and ampere-metre was a VC830L digital multimeter.

Results

The Powermat receiver output a nominal voltage of 5.12V in the baseline condition. Through skin, the provided voltage was unsubstantially smaller (5.11V).

As shown in Figure 14, skin did not impact the current drawn by the device for low resistances. For the 56Ω resistor, the difference was 7mA, still providing 80mA, which should easily power an Arduino microcontroller.

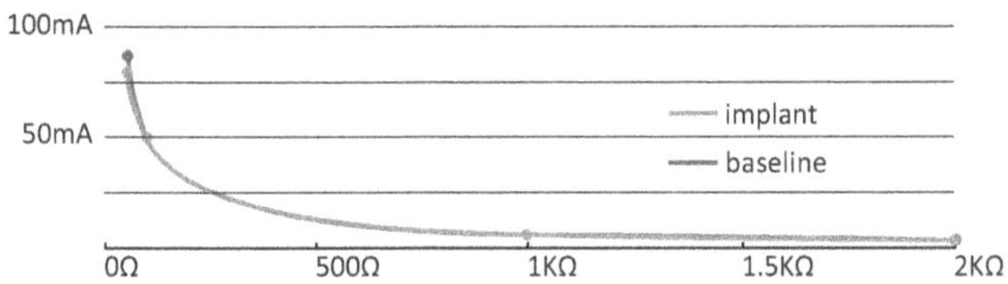

Figure 14: Skin affected the current provided through the wireless connection only at higher current values.

6) Wireless Communication Device (Bluetooth chip)

To test the performance of the wireless connection between two chips, one was external and one implanted with no space between chip and encompassing skin in the *implant* session. The *baseline* session tested both devices placed outside. We evaluated the connection at two speed levels (slow: 9600bps, fast: 115200bps), sending arrays of data in bursts between the devices (16KB, 32KB, 128KB) and calculating checksums for the sent packages. The receiving device output time-stamped logs of number of received packages and its calculated checksum. The test was fully bidirectional, repeated five times and then averaged.

Apparatus details

The Bluetooth modules were Roving Networks RN-42 (3.3V/26μA sleep, 3mA connected, 30mA transmitting) connected to an ATmega328 controller. The RN-42 featured an on-board chip antenna with no external antenna.

Results

For the slow transmission speed, no packet loss occurred in either condition. The effective speed rate was 874B/s in both conditions (Figure 15 left).

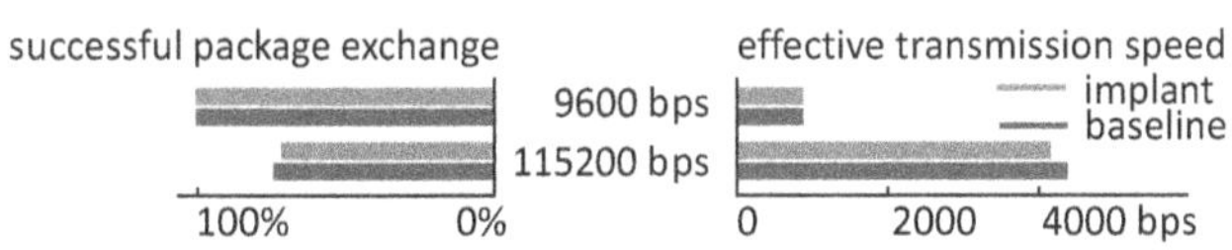

Figure 15: (left) Bluetooth exchanges data reliably when running slow, but comes with data loss when running fast. (right) Implanting affected fast transmission rates negatively.

For the fast transmission speed, the devices received 74% of the sent packages on average in the baseline and 71% when sent through skin (Figure 15 right). The effective speed differed by 200B/s (4.4KB baseline vs. 4.2KB skin). We found no differences in direction.

Discussion

Overall, all traditional user interface components that were implanted worked under the skin, sensing input through the skin, emitting output that could be perceived through the skin, and charging and communicating wirelessly.

Regarding input, skin expectedly required user input to increase in intensity to activate sensor controls. Despite this required intensity overhead, all tested input sensors did perceive input through the skin, even at the lower levels of intensity we tested. This leaves enough dynamic range for the sensors' additional degrees of freedom, such as detecting varying pressure. As for hover detection, skin incurs an offset of brightness and diminishes capacitive signals, but both sensors responded to the approaching finger.

While output appears diminished through the skin, detection is possible at low-enough intensity levels, such that output components, too, can leverage a range of intensities for producing output.

Powering the device through the skin yielded enough voltage to have powered any of the implanted devices. It is also enough to power our *3in3out* prototype device, which we will describe in the next section. More measurements with lower resistances remain necessary to determine the maximum throughput of the tested inductive power supply beyond the 100mA levels.

While skin affected the throughput of the fast wireless communication and accounted for a 3% higher loss of packages and a 0.2KB/s drop in speed, it did not affect the slow condition. The flawless wireless communication in 9600bps enables reliable data exchange. Results found in the related area of body-area networks differ, as transmission goes through the body or arm, not just skin [19].

Exploring Exposed Components

In addition to quantitatively evaluating input components, we wanted to prototype an exposed implanted interface component. To do so, we mounted a Blackberry trackball control on the back of an Arduino Pro Mini 8MHz board and soldered batteries to it. The trackball was a fully autonomous standalone device. We programmed the trackball to emit a different light color when the user swiped the ball horizontally or vertically.

To expose the roller ball, the skin and plastic cover over the roller ball were carefully incised using a scalpel. The incision was about 3mm in length, so only the roller ball was exposed. Once implanted into the specimen, the experimenters took turns interacting with the device, which worked as expected. Figure 1f illustrates the exposed trackball. Note that this exploration took place *after* the quantitative evaluation had fully finished. The incision made for this exploration had no effect on our earlier evaluation.

QUALITATIVE EVALUATION

To explore initial user feedback on implanted user interfaces, we built and deployed a prototype device covered with a layer of artificial skin on users. Our goal was to gain initial insights on how users may feel about walking around with an interactive implanted device and to demonstrate how such devices can be prototyped and tested outside controlled lab conditions.

Study Device: We built the *3in3out* device specifically for the qualitative evaluation (Figure 2a). It features three input controls (button, tap sensor, pressure sensor) and three output components (LED, vibration motor, piezo buzzer). A Li-Po battery powers the standalone *3in3out* device.

The device implemented a game as an abstract task that involved receiving output and responding with input. At 30-90 second intervals, a randomly chosen output component triggered the user, who had to respond using the correct input: pressure sensor for the LED, tap sensor for the motor, and button for the speaker. While the LED kept blinking, the speaker and vibration motor repeated their output trigger every 10s. Without a response, the trigger timed out after one minute. Participants received points based on the speed and accuracy of their responses.

Simulating Implants: Artificial Skin

We created artificial skin to cover our prototype and simulate actual implantation with the aid of a professional prosthetics shop, which had years of experience modeling body parts. The artificial skin is diffuse and diffused light, dampened sound and vibration in roughly the same manner to the real skin in our evaluation. Participants in the study confirmed that the artificial skin qualitatively felt like real skin. As the focus of this study was on obtaining qualitative feedback, we did not calibrate the characteristics of the artificial skin to match the absolute quantitative properties of skin we measured in our evaluation. We did not need the artificial skin to match the Bluetooth properties of skin either, because our qualitative study did not include communication devices.

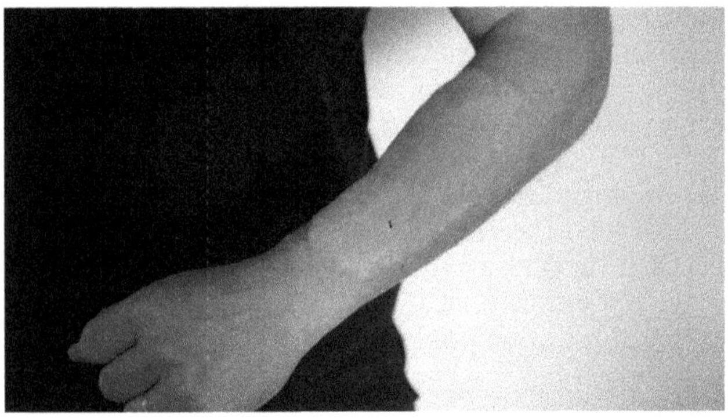

Figure 16. Artificial skin, created from silicon, covered the *3in3out* device to simulate implantation and allow for testing.

To create the artificial skin, we mixed Polytek Platsil-Gel 10 with Polytek Smith's Theatrical Prosthetic Deadener, which is known to produce silicone with skin-like feel and consistency. We added skin-color liquid foundation and enhanced the skin look with red, blue and beige flocking. We then poured the silicone mixture into a mold customized to fit a human arm, added the device wrapped in Seran foil, and positioned a clay arm, so that the silicone assumed the correct shape. We then affixed the artificial skin to users' arms using ADM Tronics Pros-Aide medical grade adhesive. The final layer of artificial skin measured 4.5" × 2" (Figure 16) and was 1-2mm thick above the device (i.e., similar to anterior surface skin [10], which we studied).

Task and Procedure

We designed a set of six primary tasks to distract from wearing the prototype device, which interrupted participants while carrying out those tasks: 1) ask a person for the time, 2) board public transport and exit after two stops, 3) ask a person for directions to the post office, 4) pick-up a free newspaper, 5) buy a coffee, and, finally, 6) sit in a park, finish the coffee and read the newspaper. Participants' secondary task was to respond to the triggers that the *3in3out* device emitted, and try to achieve a high score. The device recorded response times, errors and point totals. The study took place in downtown Toronto, Canada on a summer day, which represented a realistic worst-case scenario; both, direct sunlight and noise levels were very intense.

Participants first received a demonstration of the device and practiced its use. The participant then left the building to perform all primary tasks, and returned after approximately 60 minutes. Participants filled out a questionnaire after the study, sharing their impression when using the device in public environments and any the reactions they received.

Participants

We recruited 4 participants (1 female) from our institution. Participants were between 28 and 36 years old and wore the prototype device on their left arm. We reimbursed participants for using public transport and buying coffee.

Results

Overall, participants found the device easy to use. All liked the tap sensor ("easy to use") and button ("easy to find", "haptic feedback"), but none enjoyed the pressure sensor. For output components, all ranked the LED lowest for perception relative to the other output components, the speaker medium, and the vibration motor best ("really easy to notice"). While these results suggest that the device might work better in environments quieter and/or darker than the noisy city setting in direct sunlight, participants were able to see the LED blinking when looking at it.

While participants mentioned receiving curious looks from others when interacting with their arm, no external person approached a participant, even though they spent time in casual settings (e.g., coffee place and public transport).

Most importantly, the results of our study demonstrate that implanted user interfaces can be used to support interactive tasks. This evaluation also provides a methodology to pave the way for future evaluations and mockups of more elaborate devices and applications of implanted user interfaces.

MEDICAL CONSIDERATIONS

While the goal of this paper is to consider implanted user interfaces from an HCI perspective, it is also important to discuss some of the medical considerations. Below we discuss some of the issues surrounding the feasibility of implanted user interfaces.

Location

In our study, the devices were implanted under the skin on the front of the forearm, just distal to the elbow joint. This location was chosen as the devices could be easily activated by an individual with their other hand and would not be in an area where damage by impact is likely. For the most part, these devices could be implanted deep into the skin in the subcutaneous tissue anywhere in the body where the devices are accessible and can transmit signals. This includes the upper and lower limbs, the chest wall, abdomen, etc. Areas covered by thick skin, such as the palms and soles of the feet, would not be suitable for implantables, as the skin is too thick and tough to interact. The thickness of human skin ranges between 0.5mm on the eyelids to 4+mm on the palms and soles of the feet [10].

The superficial placement of the devices, directly under the skin, facilitates device activation and signal transmission. The devices can be inserted between the skin and subcutaneous tissue, providing a minimally invasive approach. The deep underlying tissues, e.g., muscle, would not be disrupted. Similarly, pacemakers are placed under the skin in the chest or abdominal regions and the wires that are extending from the heart are connected to the pacemaker. Only a small skin incision that is later closed with sutures is needed to insert the pacemaker. The device remains stationary in its implanted location due to the fibrous nature of subcutaneous tissue.

The tracking ball was the only device we implanted that required surface exposure. The device worked very well under the experimental conditions, but much work needs to be done to assess the medical implications of a long-term insertion of an exposed device.

Device parameters

Tissue fluid will penetrate a device that is not encased in a protective hull, and affect its function. The hull's material must be carefully chosen to be pharmacologically inert and nontoxic to body tissues. For examples, pacemakers are typically made from titanium or titanium alloys, and the leads from polyether polyurethanes. *In vivo* testing would need to be carried out to determine what materials are most suitable.

The device should be as small as possible, so it is easily implantable and cosmetically acceptable to the recipient. Functionality and minimal disruption of the contour of the skin are important considerations.

Risks

The main medical risk of implanting devices is infection. Infection can be caused by the procedure of implanting the devices. There are also possible risks to muscles if the device is implanted any deeper than the subcutaneous tissue. The material used for the casing could also possibly cause infections, so it will be important that the material being used passes through proper testing. It is very difficult to hypothesize about other types of risks without performing testing. The wear of skin depends on the pressure applied to it; while paraplegics get sore skin from body weight resting on single spots through bones, skin is unlikely to wear from manual pressure. The proposed input with implanted devices is short and low in force and intensity, making skin unlikely to wear. One risk that is relatively low is that of the skin actually tearing. Skin is very strong and it is unlikely the small devices would cause any damage. However, determining the long-term effects of interactions with implanted devices on skin requires further studies.

Implications and Future Studies

All of the input and output devices were functional under the experimental conditions of this study. Further cadaveric study is needed to determine if gender, skin color and site of implantation affect device function. In the next phase, testing would also be carried out on unembalmed tissue, although the skin of lightly embalmed and unembalmed specimens is similar, loose and pliable in both cases. Finally, the medical implications of long-term insertion of devices of this nature require detailed study.

DISCUSSION AND LIMITATIONS

The results of our study shows that traditional user interfaces for input, output, wireless communication and powering function when embedded in the subcutaneous tissue of the forearm. Having obtained an evaluation of common components establishes the foundation for future investigations into more complex devices to explore the many other aspects of implanted user interfaces.

For example, we disregarded security concerns in our exploration. Wireless implanted devices need to prevent malicious activities and interactions from users other than the host user, such as stealing or altering stored information and manipulating the devices' operating system [7,15].

The processing capabilities of the devices that were implanted during the technical evaluation, as well the *3in3out* device, require only simple processing on the microchip. More work is necessary to investigate if and how implanted devices can perform more computationally intensive operations (e.g., classification tasks using machine learning [17,37]) and how this affects the needs for power supply.

Social perception of implanted interfaces, both by host users as well as public perception requires more studying. Although this has been studied with implanted *medical* devices [6], social perception of invisible and implanted *user interfaces* and devices remain to be examined.

We conducted our qualitative evaluation with participants in the summer, which is why all participants wore short-sleeve shirts. In the winter, cloth will additionally cover implanted input and output components [35] and interfere with interaction, which raises new challenges.

Study Limitations

Our technical evaluation comprised a single specimen. In addition, we carried out the staircase evaluations with a single participant. As such, the metrics we have collected can serve as baselines for future experimentations, but should be generalized with caution. Furthermore, our evaluation captured technical metrics from the devices, and not human factor results. In the future, it may be interesting to have external participants interact with the implanted devices and study task performance levels.

CONCLUSIONS

The technological transition society has made in the past 30 years is astounding. Technology, and the way we use it, continues to evolve and no one can tell what the future holds. Several experts have predicted that cyborgs are coming [32, 42], and devices will become indistinguishable from the very fabric of our lives [47]. If we look at how much has changed, it should not be hard to believe that we will one day interact with electronic devices that are permanent components of our body. Our work takes a first step towards understanding how exactly this might be accomplished, and begins to ask and answer some of the important technical, human factors, and medical questions.

ACKNOWLEDGMENTS

We thank Frank Li, Azam Khan, Justin Matejka, Alex Tessier and Gord Kurtenbach for feedback and discussions.

REFERENCES

1. Anderson, S.D. Practical Light Embalming Technique for Use in the Surgical Fresh Tissue Dissection Laboratory. *Clin Anat.*, 19(1), (2006), 8-11.
2. Ashbrook, D., Clawson, J., Lyons, K., Patel, N., Starner, T., Clara, S. Quickdraw: the impact of mobility and on-body placement on device access time. *Proc. CHI '08*, 219-222.
3. Badshah, A., Gupta, S., Cohn, G., Villar, N., Hodges, S., Patel, S.N. Interactive generator: a self-powered haptic feedback device. *Proc. CHI '11*, 2051-2054.
4. Brumberg, J.S., Nieto-Castanon, A., Kennedy, P.R., Guenther, F.H., Brain-computer interfaces for speech communication, *Speech Communication*, 52(4), Silent Speech Interfaces, April 2010, 367-379.
5. Cornsweet, T.N. The Staircase-Method in Psychophysics. *Amer. J. Psychol.*, 75(3), (1962), 485-491.
6. Denning, T., Borning, A., Friedman, B., Gill, B.T., Kohno, T., Maisel, W.H. Patients, pacemakers, and implantable defibrillators: human values and security for wireless implantable medical devices. *Proc. CHI '10*, 917-926.
7. Denning, T., Matsuoka, Y., Kohno, T. Neurosecurity: security and privacy for neural devices. *Neurosurg. Focus*, 27(1), E7.
8. Drew, T., Gini, M. Implantable medical devices as agents and part of multiagent systems. *Proc. AAMAS '06*, 1534-1541.
9. Fitzpatrick, R.C., Day, B.L. Probing the human vestibular system with galvanic stimulation. *Journal of Applied Physiology*, June 2004, 96(6), 2301-2316.
10. Fornage, B.D., Deshayes, J. Ultrasound of Normal Skin. *J Clin Ultrasound* 14, (1986), 619-622.
11. Gelfand, S.A. Hearing: An introduction to psychological and physiological acoustics. 1990, 2nd edition. New York and Basel: Marcel Dekker, Inc.
12. GivenImaging. http://www.givenimaging.com
13. Gustafson, S., Holz, C., Baudisch, P. Imaginary Phone: Learning Imaginary Interfaces by Transfer of Spatial Memory from a Familiar Screen Device. *Proc. UIST '11*, 283-292.
14. Hakoama, M. Hakoyama, S. The impact of cell phone use on social networking and development among college students. *AABSS Journal*, 15, (2011).
15. Halperin, D., Heydt-Benjamin, T.S., Ransford, B., Clark, S.S. Defend, B. Morgan, W. Fu, K., Kohno, T., Maisel, W. Pacemakers and Implantable Cardiac Defibrillators: Software Radio Attacks and Zero-Power Defenses. *Proc. SP '08*, 129-142.
16. Harrison, C., Benko, H., Wilson, A.D. OmniTouch: Wearable Multitouch Interaction Everywhere. *Proc. UIST '11*, 441-450.
17. Harrison, C., Tan, D. and Morris, D. Skinput: appropriating the body as an input surface. *Proc. CHI '10*, 453-462
18. Hinckley, K., Pierce, J., Sinclair, M., Horvitz, E. Sensing techniques for mobile interaction. *Proc. UIST '00*, 91-100.
19. Ho, H., Saeedi, E., Kim, S.S., Shen, T.T., Parviz, B.A. Contact lens with integrated inorganic semiconductor devices. *Proc. MEMS '08*, 403-406.
20. Holz, C. and Baudisch, P. The Generalized Perceived Input Point Model and How to Double Touch Accuracy by Extracting Fingerprints. *Proc. CHI '10*, 581-590.
21. Huo, X., Wang, J., Ghovanloo, M. 2008. A magneto-inductive sensor based wireless tongue-computer interface. *IEEE Trans on Neural Sys Rehab Eng.* 16(5), 497-504.
22. Jovanov, E., Milenkovic, A., Otto, C., de Groen, P.C. A wireless body area network of intelligent motion sensors for computer assisted physical rehabilitation. *NeuroEng Rehab*, 2(6).
23. Kaiser, M., Proffitt, D. Observers' sensitivity to dynamic anomalies in collisions. *Percept. Psychophysics* 42, 3, 275-280.
24. Karrer, T., Wittenhagen, M., Lichtschlag, L., Heller, F., Borchers, J. Pinstripe: eyes-free continuous input on interactive clothing. *Proc. CHI '11*, 1313-1322.
25. Lambert, M., Chadwick, G., McMahon, A., Scarffe, H. Experience with the portacath. *Hematol Oncol*, 6(1), 57-63.
26. Levitt, H. Transformed up-down methods in psychoacoustics. *J. Acoust. Soc.* Am., 49(2), (1971), 467-477.
27. Li, Z., Wang, Z.L. Air/liquid pressure and heartbeat driven flexible fiber nanogenerators as micro-nano-power source or diagnostic sensors. *Adv. Mater.* 23, (2011), 84-89.
28. Luhrmann, T. What students can teach us about iPhones. Salon May 30, (2010). http://salon.com/a/sT_weAA
29. Masters, A., Michael, K. Humancentric Applications of RFID Implants: The Usability Contexts of Control, Convenience and Care. *Proc. WMCS '05*, 32-41.
30. Moore, M.M., Kennedy, P.R. Human factors issues in the neural signals direct brain-computer interfaces. *Proc. Assets '00*, 114-120.
31. Ni, T. and Baudisch, P. Disappearing mobile devices. *Proc. UIST '09*, 101-110.
32. Norman, D. Cyborgs. *Commun. ACM* 44, 3 (Mar 2001), 36-37.
33. Orth, M., Post, R., Cooper, E. Fabric computing interfaces. *Proc. CHI '98*. 331-332.
34. *Powermat* inductive charging. http://www.powermat.com.
35. Rekimoto, J. GestureWrist and GesturePad: unobtrusive wearable interaction devices. *Proc. ISWC '01*, 21–27.
36. Saponas, T.S., Kelly, D., Parviz, B., Tan, D. Optically sensing tongue gestures for computer input. *Proc. UIST '09*, 177-180.
37. Saponas, T.S., Tan, D.S., Morris, D., Balakrishnan, R., Turner, J., Landay, J.A. Enabling always-available input with muscle-computer interfaces. *Proc. UIST '09*, 167-176.
38. Smith, D.V., Margolskee, R.F. Making sense of taste. *Sci. Am.* 2001 Mar, 284(3), 32-39.
39. Starner, T. Human-powered wearable computing. *IBM Systems Journal*, 35 (3), (1996), 618-629.
40. Starner, T. The Challenges of Wearable Computing: Part 1. *IEEE Micro 21*, 4 (July 2001), 44-52.
41. Starner, T. The Challenges of Wearable Computing: Part 2. *IEEE Micro 21*, 4 (July 2001), 54-67.
42. Starner, T. The cyborgs are coming. *Tech Report* 318, Perceptual Computing, MIT Media Labaratory, November 1995.
43. Stelarc. Official website. http://www.stelarc.org
44. Tamaki, E., Miyaki, T., Rekimoto, J. PossessedHand: a hand gesture manipulation system using electrical stimuli. *Proc. AH '10*, Article 2, 5 pages.
45. Ullah, S, Higgin, H, Siddiqui, M, Kwak, K. A Study of Implanted and Wearable Body Sensor Networks. *Proc. KES-AMSTA '08*, 464-473.
46. Warwick, K. Project Cyborg. Official website. http://www.kevinwarwick.com/
47. Weiser, M. The Computer for the 21st Century. *Scientific American* Special Issue on Communications, Computers, and Networks, 265(3), Sept. 1991, 94-104.
48. Wishnitzer, R., Laiteerapong, T., Hecht, O. Subcutaneous implantation of magnets in fingertips of professional gamblers-Case report. *Plast Reconstr Surg*, 71(3):473-474, 1983.
49. Wolpaw, J.R., Birbaumer, N., McFarland, D.J., Pfurtscheller, G., Vaughan, T.M. Brain-computer interfaces for communication and control. *Clin Neurophysiol.*, 113(6), (2002), 767-791.
50. Yatani, K., Truong, K.N. SemFeel: a user interface with semantic tactile feedback for mobile touch-screen devices. *Proc. UIST '09*, 111-120.

EEG Analysis of Implicit Human Visual Perception

Maryam Mustafa
TU Braunschweig
mustafa@cg.tu-bs.de

Lea Lindemann
TU Braunschweig
lindemann@cg.tu-bs.de

Marcus Magnor
TU Braunschweig
magnor@cg.tu-bs.de

ABSTRACT
Image Based Rendering (IBR) allows interactive scene exploration from images alone. However, despite considerable development in the area, one of the main obstacles to better quality and more realistic visualizations is the occurrence of visually disagreeable artifacts. In this paper we present a methodology to map out the perception of IBR-typical artifacts. This work presents an alternative to traditional image and video quality evaluation methods by using an EEG device to determine the implicit visual processes in the human brain. Our work demonstrates the distinct differences in the perception of different types of visual artifacts and the implications of these differences.

Author Keywords
Perception;artifacts;EEG;visual processing;HVS;

ACM Classification Keywords
H.5.m. Information Interfaces and Presentation (e.g. HCI): Miscellaneous.

INTRODUCTION
The advantage of perceptual based graphics has been apparent for a long time, and while a considerable amount of work has been done in measuring conscious, cognitive processing [13, 2, 1], much less has been done in Computer Graphics to take advantage of covert(brain) measurements and visual processing. In this paper we present a new approach that uses an electroencephalograph (EEG) to interface with the human brain and measure the output of implicit (covert) visual processing in the brain in response to artifacts in image sequences. The way videos are perceived by people is becoming increasingly important in visual media. Image and video based rendering techniques allow for the creation of complicated 3D scenes and videos from a few images. The ubiquitous use of 3D cinema, affordable display technology, and the merging of real world scenes with computer graphics allows for the creation and pervasive use of realistically rendered images and videos for movies such as Avatar. Similarly applications like Google Street View use a sparse set of images to create complex visualizations, and Microsoft photosynthesis uses image based rendering to transition between images

CHI'12, May 5–10, 2012, Austin, Texas, USA.

Figure 1. Left: ghosting. Right: dashed: area for static blurring and popping, solid: moving frame for blurring and popping on person.

[12]. However, one of the main areas that still require a lot of research is the assessment and perception of the rendered output. Rendering systems can now closely approximate a real scene but physical or statistical accuracy does not necessarily amount to visual accuracy. During rendering visually objectionable artifacts can arise which limit the application of most rendering algorithms. The most common artifacts that occur in rendered images are ghosting, blurring and popping [13]. In this paper we perform an experiment to analyze the perception of these artifacts. Traditionally the quality of a video has been judged by either user-studies or the use of quality assessment algorithms. Apart from requiring a large number of participants, user-studies can at best only measure the explicit output of the visual cognitive process [5].Quality ratings obtained by user studies are always filtered by some decision process which, in turn, may be influenced by the task and/or rating scale the participants are given [9]. The subjective judgment of a viewer is often biased by external factors such as mood, expectation or past experience.While current work in computer vision and graphics focuses on the explicit (overt)output of the human visual system(HVS) we propose to use the implicit(covert) processing of the HVS [4] to determine the perception and quality of a video. There is extensive literature dealing with implicit and explicit processing in the human brain [10]. Koch and Tsuchiya [4] discuss the evidence showing that visual processing can occur without conscious perception or attention and that conscious awareness of a stimulus is preceded by complex visual decision making processes. We propose to use this covert processing in the human brain to assess the quality of a video with artifacts. In our study we also specifically chose to look at motion in rendered sequences as motion plays an important role in perception owing to effects such as speed and direction of motion, visual tracking of moving objects and motion saliency. Given the complexity of the HVS in perceiving motion, traditional systems based on it have not been able to effectively model temporal aspects of human vision [9].

There are several advantages to developing methodologies that merge covert human visual processing with traditional computer graphics and vision techniques. First the analysis of visual information processing that occurs in the absence of conscious attention will allow boosting of traditional masking and rendering algorithms and introduce the robustness and flexibility associated with human vision. Secondly, such an analysis of the covert visual processes reveals aspects of how these artifacts are viewed by the HVS that have not yet been accurately modeled by computer vision algorithms. Given that it is more important for rendered images and videos to be perceptually accurate as opposed to physically accurate, rendering times can be shortened by eliminating computations that calculate image features that are not apparent to the human eye [8]. Computer graphics algorithms can take advantage of the limitations of the human eye to compute just enough detail in an image or video to convince the observer without a perceived deterioration in quality. Specifically, our main contribution is a methodology for the analysis of artifacts in videos using an EEG to interface with the human brain and mine the covert visual processing.

In this paper we present the design and results from our experiments with video stimuli containing five different types of artifacts. We present an analysis and comparison of the covert visual decision making about the video quality obtained from the EEG with the conscious video quality judgment obtained via direct user feedback which serve as initial proof of concept for our ideas.

RELATED WORK

There has been recent interest in studying visual processing for image rendering and analysis techniques [2]. However very little work has been done in using implicit visual decision making processes for video assessment. Shenoy et al. [10] present the idea of Human-Aided Computing which uses an EEG to label images implicitly. They use brain processes to show that users can implicitly categorize pictures based on content. Their work however required users to memorize the images and to be attentive to the content viewed. Our work looks to analyze the implicit visual processing behind viewing videos with motion and not static images. Similarly, Vangorp et al. [13] conduct psychophysical experiments to understand the perception of artifacts in synthetic rendering. They looked at the user feedback from rendered sequences that moved over facades of buildings. This work focused on the output of conscious visual cognitive processes.

Recently Lindemann et al. [6, 7] have been using an EEG to assess the quality of compressed images and video artifacts. They reported that when shown different images of decreasing quality the participants EEG results showed corresponding detected changes in image quality. Their work showed that the brain response varied with the image compression value.

EXPERIMENT

This experiment was designed to measure the covert (implicit) visual processing associated with three basic types of artifacts that typically occur in image based rendering. 8 (3 male, 5 female) healthy participants with an average age of 25 and with normal or corrected-to-normal vision took part in the experiment. All participants had average experience with digital footage and no involvement in professional image/video rendering or editing. The basic stimulus for the experiment was a 5.6 second video (resolution: 1440x1024, 30 fps) of a person walking along a park trail from left to right. The occurrence of the artifact was delayed by 4 frames (132ms) to avoid locking the participants attention to a fixed time. Five different kinds of artifacts were incorporated into the scene. These artifacts included both temporal and spatial aspects. The following 6 test cases were shown (Figure 1):

1. Popping on Person: a small rectangular area (marked with solid line in Figure 1) containing the walking person freezes for one frame

2. Popping: A static rectangular area of the image (marked with dashed line in Figure 1) freezes for one frame.

3. Blurring on person: a small rectangular area containing the walking person is blurred with a Gaussian kernel with a size of 15 pixels in 10 successive frames. The blurring area moves along with the motion of the person

4. Blurring: A static rectangular area (Figure 1) in the center of the scene is blurred with a Gaussian kernel with a size of 15 pixels in 10 successive frames.

5. Ghosting on Person: A partly transparent silhouette of the person stays behind for 10 frames, fading to invisibility in the last 5 frames (left part of Figure 1).

6. Ground truth: No artifacts.

One trial consisted of a ready screen followed by the video with artifacts which was instantly followed by the quality assessment screen. Participants were instructed to follow the moving person with their gaze and rate the quality of every test case on an integer 1(worst) to 5(best) mean opinion score (MOS) scale [3]. The participants were not informed about the presence of artifacts in the videos.

They were instructed orally and received a training in which every one of the 6 videos was shown 3 times. This prepared for the procedure and showed the whole range of available video qualities. During the main experiment all videos were shown 30 times resulting in 180 trials per participant. The videos were played in a block-wise randomized order and the same video was not shown twice in a row.

An EEG was recorded with 32 electrodes attached according to the international 10-20 system. Additionally a 4 channel EOG and mastoids were recorded which were used as a reference to remove data with accidental eye movements. The recorded data were referenced to the mastoids and filtered with a high-pass filter with a cutoff frequency of 0.1 Hz to remove DC-offset and drifts. Trials of a length of 1.2 seconds time locked to the appearance of the artifact occurrence were extracted from the continuous data. All trials with blinks, severe eye movements and too many alpha waves were manually removed.

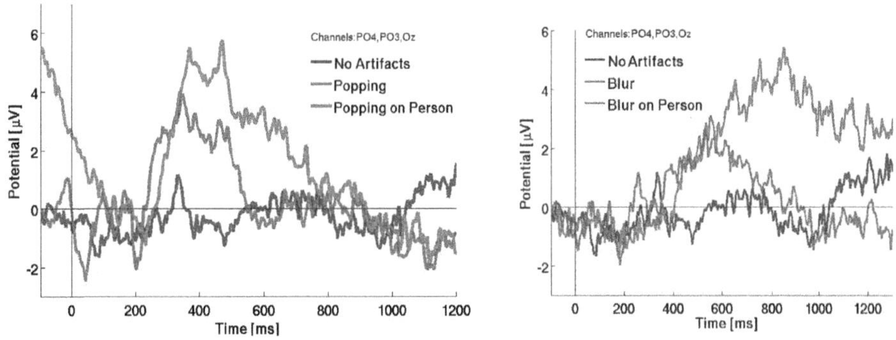

Figure 2. The ERPs for artifacts Popping and Popping on Person , Blurring, Blurring on Person, and no artifact for comparison.

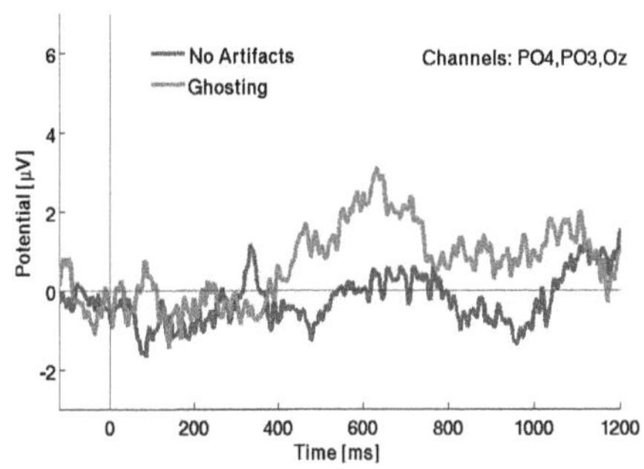

Figure 3. The ERPs for artifacts Ghosting and no artifact for comparison.

The eye movements from watching the video were the same for all trials and all artifacts over all participants. All videos were exactly the same including the reference video (ground truth) and induced identical eye movements. Due to the identical nature of the stimulus the results can be compared.

RESULTS

Figures 2, and 3 show the different ERPs averaged over all participants over all trials and over electrodes PO4, PO3 and Oz and as compared with the no artifact ERP with time 0 corresponding to the appearance of the artifact. Firstly, all artifacts were detected by the brain, albeit with varying strength. The artifact which evoked the greatest response was popping on the moving person which has a latency of 264ms and reaches a maximum amplitude of 5.758μV. This is followed closely by blurring on the moving person. Static popping and blurring evoke a smaller response. Popping is a more obviously perceived artifact and evokes a quicker response. Ghosting however requires the brain to process the perceived distortion before a response occurs. This latency due to processing of the perceived stimuli is also seen with blurring, which is also a less obvious artifact. Table 1 shows the detailed latency and maximum potential responses for all artifacts. From both the ERP figures and Table 1 the second result that becomes clear is the difference in the perception of artifacts related to motion and those independent of motion. Both popping and blurring linked with the motion of the person produce a much larger response potential than popping and blurring not linked with the motion of the person.

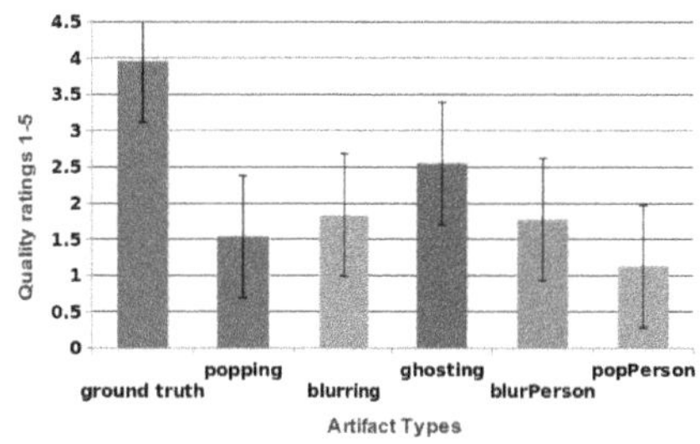

Figure 4. Participants average responses to videos

Figure 4 shows an average of the participant responses for all trials for each video. As can be seen participants rated the quality of the video with the ghosting artifact as the best after ground truth. This is in contradiction with what the ERPs showed where although the latency of both blurring and ghosting was the same the ghosting artifact evoked a response with a maximum potential of 3.082μV as opposed to 2.681μV for blurring. The most obvious difference between the explicit quality rating and the implicit brain reaction can be seen with the Popping on Person and Popping artifact. Participants rated the two with almost the same rating (1-1.5) whereas the ERPs show a marked difference in the response of the brain to either artifact. This same difference is also observed in the two blurring artifacts. The participants rated them both equally whereas the ERPs show a marked difference between the two (5.58μV and 2.68μV) with the same latency.

We also ran a standard two-tailed t-test to confirm the validity of the curves as shown in Figures 2 and 3. For all artifact cases the two tailed t-test was run for the stimuli time pe-

Artifacts	Peak Latency (ms)	Peak Amplitude (μV)
Popping on pers.	264	5.758
Popping	200-250	3.928
Blurring on pers.	400	5.58
Blurring	400	2.681
Ghosting	400	3.082

Table 1. Peak latency and amplitude for all artifacts.

riod against the same ground truth time period. In all cases the null hypothesis was rejected. The p-values were popping p=4.5×10^{-9}, popping on person p=1.1×10^{-36}, ghosting p=5.89×10^{-5}, blurring p=0.0031 and blurring on person p=3.14×10^{-13}. Given the rejection of the null hypothesis in all cases and the fact that the probabilities are all less than 0.05(5%) there is sufficient evidence for the statistical significance of the results. We also ran the two-tailed t-test between popping and popping on person and blurring against blurring on person. Both of these tests also rejected the null hypothesis with p-values of p=6.3×10^{-12} and p=5.03×10^{-5}. Given these values we can safely assume a statistically significant difference between the responses over all artifacts.

To determine the deviation of individual participants from the average we also ran a two-tailed t-test of one randomly selected participant against the averaged results of all the other participants. For all stimuli the null hypothesis was accepted and the p-values were popping p =0.14, popping on person p=0.854, blurring=0.85, blurring on person=0.97 and ghosting p=0.74. Given these p-values and the acceptance of the null hypothesis it is clear that any one participants response is close to the average. There are no statistically significant differences.

The analysis of the ERPs from this experiment also indicate a potential emotional reaction to the artifacts. Previous data from EEG studies and emotion has provided evidence of lateralization of emotion in the frontal cortex [11]. This theory predicts right hemisphere dominance for negative emotions. The results from our experiment show an increased output in the right frontal cortex for test cases with more severe artifacts where the maximum output was for popping on the moving person. This can theoretically be explained by the negative emotions elicited by bad video quality.

CONCLUSION

We showed that the covert (implicit) and overt (explicit) output of the human visual processing does differ and in some cases the difference is striking. We also showed that the brain responds very differently to not only different types of artifacts but also to artifacts specifically linked with motion. Artifacts linked with motion evoke a much larger response in the brain. We also showed that it is possible to categorize artifacts based on how they are perceived. This provides information on the perception of videos which has previously not been modeled. This also creates the possibility of shortening rendering times by eliminating computations that calculate image features which do not evoke a strong reaction in the brain as opposed to those which do. The brains response to artifacts is also essential for the modeling of masking algorithms for rendered image sequences. While the current experimental setup provides new and relevant information it has some limitations. The main issue we see is the absence of eye movement information. Eye tracking would allow us to incorporate information regarding the exact viewing pattern of the participants during stimuli presentation. A more complete picture of participants eye gaze pattern during stimuli presentation is essential for advances in realistic image and video synthesis. Also using sensors to capture physiological data would provide more concrete information regarding the participants emotional state during trials.

ACKNOWLEDGMENTS

This work was funded in part by ERC grant #256941 'Reality CG'.

REFERENCES

1. Anderson, E., Potter, K., Matzen, L., Shepherd, J., Preston, G., and Silva, C. A user study of visualization effectiveness using EEG and cognitive load. *Computer Graphics Forum 30* (2011), 791–800.
2. Ferwerda, A. J., Shiley, P., Pattanaik, N., and Greenberg, P. A model of visual adaptation for realistic image synthesis. In *Proc. ACM SIGGRAPH* (1996), 249–258.
3. International Telecommunication Union. Mean opinion score (MOS) terminology. In *ITU-T Recommendation* (2006), P.800.1.
4. Koch, C., and Tsuchiya, N. Attention and consciousness: two distinct brain processes. *Trends in Cognitive Sciences 11*, 1 (2007), 16–22.
5. Korsar, R., Healey, C. G., Interrante, V., Laidlaw, D. H., and Ware, C. Thoughts on user studies: Why, how, and when. *Computer Graphics and Applications 23*, 4 (2003), 20–25.
6. Lindemann, L., and Magnor., M. Assessing the quality of compressed images using EEG. In *Proc. IEEE International Conference on Image Processing (ICIP)* (2011), 3170–3173.
7. Lindemann, L., S., W., and M., M. Evaluation of video artifact perception using event-related potentials. *ACM Applied Perception in Computer Graphics and Visualization (APGV)* (2011), 1–5.
8. McNamara, A., Mania, K., Banks, M., and Healey, C. Perceptually-motivated graphics, visualization and 3D displays. In *Proc. ACM SIGGRAPH* (2010), 1–159.
9. Ponomarenko, N., Lukin, V., Zelensky, A., Egiazarian, K., Astola, J., Carli, M., and Battisti, F. A database for evaluation of full-reference visual quality assessment metrics. *Advances of Modern Radioelectronics 10*, 10 (2009), 30–45.
10. Shenoy, P., and Tan, D. Human-aided computing: utilizing implicit human processing to classify images (2008). 845–854.
11. Silberman, E., and Weingartner, H. Hemispheric lateralisation of functions related to emotion. *Brain and Cognition 5* (1986), 322–353.
12. Snavely, N., Seitz, M., and Szeliski, R. Photo tourism: exploring photo collections in 3D. *ACM Trans. Graph. 25* (2006), 835–846.
13. Vangorp, P., Chaurasia, G., Laffont, P.-Y., Fleming, R. W., and Drettakis, G. Perception of visual artifacts in image-based rendering of facades. *Computer Graphics Forum 30* (2011), 1241–1250.

Development and Evaluation of Interactive System for Synchronizing Electric Taste and Visual Content

Hiromi Nakamura
Meiji University
1-1-1, Higashimita, Tama-ku,
Kawasaki City Kanagawa 214-8571
hirominakamura.b@gmail.com
+81-44-934-7238

Homei Miyashita
Meiji University
CREST, Japan Science and Technology Agency
1-1-1, Higashimita, Tama-ku,
Kawasaki City Kanagawa 214-8571
homei@isc.meiji.ac.jp
+81-44-934-7238

ABSTRACT
Electric taste is a characteristic taste produced when the tongue is electrically stimulated. We have proposed apparatuses to add electric taste to food and drink. An interactive system could be developed to synchronize video contents using the reversibility and instantaneity of electric taste. However, to do so, the presentation time must be determined based on the different latency for the perception of each sense. We measured the latencies for electric taste and visual stimuli as a basic evaluation for a content presentation system in which electric taste and visual content are synchronized.

Author Keywords
Electric taste, gustatory presentation system, multimodal information system, latency difference of several sensations

ACM Classification Keywords
H.5.1 Multimedia Information Systems

General Terms
Design, Experimentation, Human Factors

INTRODUCTION
Humans perceive external stimuli through five senses: sight, hearing, smell, taste, and touch. Some sensory information can produce actions and feelings as a response. Many studies have proposed applications of multimodal information presentation for producing more realistic sensations and entertainment; some have proposed applications that use one of the five senses for more realistic sensation. However, whereas many applications use vision and audition, few use olfaction and gustation. This is because whereas the former senses require a physical structure, the acceptor reactions of the latter occur in response to chemical signals. Gustation, in particular, is attributed to taste buds located on top of the tongue. Treating gustatory information requires solutions to many complex problems. Chief among these is the fact that most foods and drinks are irreversible, that is, additives, once added, are very difficult to remove. Therefore, foods and drinks must be made anew to undo their taste. Some studies overcame this problem by using pseudo sensations and dietary environments; however, they only changed the feeling of taste, and not the taste itself. Furthermore, the sensing and detecting mechanisms involved were complicated.

In a recent study, we used electric taste to study the problem of irreversible change [6]. Humans perceive electric stimuli as a characteristic electric taste, which is used in gustatory testing. This taste is irreversible and is perceived immediately when the stimulus exceeds a certain threshold. Therefore, the addition of some electric stimulus in foods and drinks would constitute new and additional information, that is, an electric taste, that has not been perceived before and that can present reversibly and instantly. We can control this information using a simple electric circuit. Additionally, by detecting whether an electric circuit is completed, we can not only detect whether we eat or drink but also whether the taste has been changed. We can thus realize an interactive system triggered by our eating and drinking. The reversible change allows us to control our gustatory perception based on human–computer interactions. In addition, it may augment realistic sensations if utilized as an entertainment system in conjunction with other senses such as vision or audition.

In this study, we propose some apparatuses for adding electric stimuli to foods and drinks and introduce a method for using these apparatuses. We conducted an experiment to measure the latency between presentation and perception using visual and electric taste stimuli. We also analyzed the difference in perception and discussed a multimodal system using this method. Finally, we have discussed future possibilities arising from this study.

ELECTRIC TASTE APPARATUSES
We developed apparatuses that create circuits comprising some foods/drinks, metal cutleries, and our body and

tongue in order to add new gustatory information to food and drink based on electric taste. We have already proposed the polar opposite circuit [6], and we newly propose the single-pole circuit. Herein, we introduce these apparatuses.

When we eat and drink using these apparatuses, by presenting electric taste through food and drink, we get a greater impression of metallic, sour, or salty taste. This is consistent with findings of many previous studies that investigated electric taste using electrogustometry (directly touching an electrode on the tongue). Whether the change in taste change is considered positive depends on the food and drink.

Apparatuses for adding electric taste to drink

The apparatus for changing the taste of drink consists of a cup/bottle, electric circuit to present electric stimuli, and 1–2 straws to add stimuli to the drink. Stimuli are presented through a polar opposite or single-pole type circuit.

Polar opposite circuit for drink

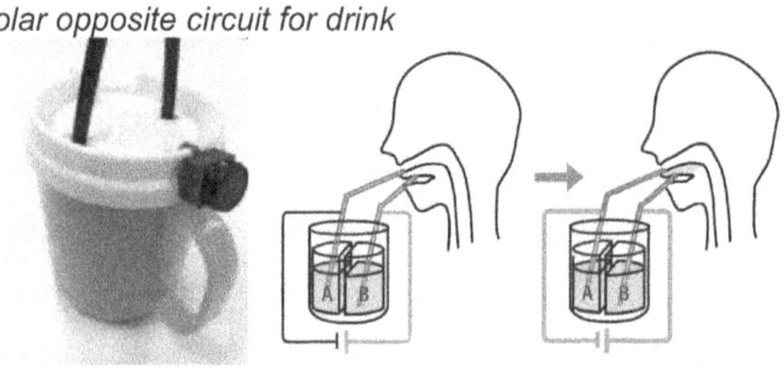

Figure 1. Polar opposite circuit to add electric taste to drink

This circuit consists of cup (separated from each other by smaller cups) and straws and a conducting wire. First, the user pours drinks into cups separately. Next, s/he inserts a negative electrode into one straw and a positive electrode into another (Figure 1). The circuit is switched on and off using the switch on the bottom.

Single-pole circuit for drink

Figure 2. Single-pole circuit to add electric taste to drink

This circuit utilizes the human body as a part of the circuit. Hence, we use a cup/bottle and two electrodes—one in contact with the body and the other with the straw (Figure 2). We can drink the beverage with electric taste using the straw when we touch one electrode. To do so, a wristband can be attached to the skin surface; attaching a copper foil seat on the grip of the cup/bottle is easier. This apparatus includes a miniature potentiometer for voltage adjustment.

Apparatuses for adding electric taste to food

The apparatus for changing the taste of food consists of metal cutlery through which electric stimuli are presented using one of the two circuits mentioned above.

Polar opposite circuit for food

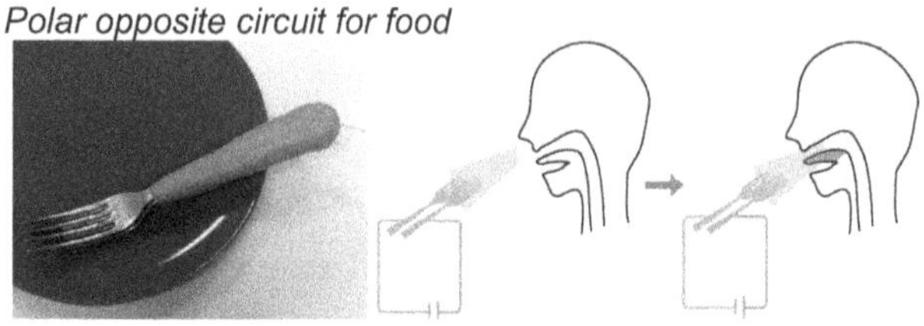

Figure 3. Polar opposite circuit to add electric taste to food

This circuit consists of a conducting wire and two metal cutleries, say, two forks, one of which is connected to the positive electrode and the other to the negative electrode (Figure 3). The right and left tines of the fork are connected to the negative and positive electrodes, respectively. The user has to break the connection between the two tines.

Single-pole circuit for food

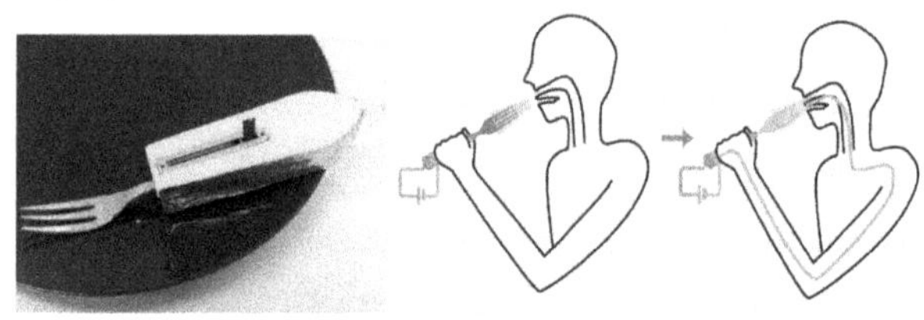

Figure 4. Single-pole circuit to add electric taste to food

This circuit, too, utilizes the human body as a part of the circuit. One electrode is connected to our body using copper foil and the other is connected to metal cutlery (Figure 4). We can eat the food with electric taste using the metal cutlery when we touch one electrode. This apparatus, too, includes a miniature potentiometer.

Method for presenting electric stimulus

These apparatuses use two 9V batteries to present electric taste. However, batteries provide a flat sensation of electric stimulus because they use direct current. Therefore, we tried other electric stimuli such as a pulsating voltage or one with time series variations (such as an auditory signal) to change the taste and we found that it produces greater and noticeable variation in taste. Such voltages are amplified and outputted using an amp. Our preliminary investigation suggested that most subjects could distinguish the difference in frequency with such signals. For example, one subject described coarse and keen feelings at lower and higher registers, respectively. There were individual variations in how subjects felt depending on the type of signal. Nevertheless, saw tooth waves were commonly considered harsh, and noise felt harsher than a saw tooth wave.

EXPERIMENTS

Mutually synchronized multimodal media provide a wholesome feeling, and it would be beneficial for content such as games and visual content to be more realistic and expressive. However, the latency time between presentation and perception depend on the organ and sensation.

We should measure these latencies and adjust them to realize effective multimodal presentation. Some studies have already done so; for example, Kim et al. developed the Aroma-Chip based Olfactory Display and measured the latency between the start (end) of diffusion and the start (end) of perception [3]. Similarly, we measured the latency of visual and electric taste stimuli and analyzed the perceptual traits of electric taste using our apparatuses.

Experimental method

We used the color change of a rectangle to measure visual stimulus latency and the gustatory change with DC and varying voltage to measure electric taste stimulus latency.

For the latter, we used the polar opposite drink apparatus. Subjects could indicate when they perceived a stimulus using a switch. Before starting the experiment, we allowed the nine subjects (excluding the experimenter) to familiarize themselves with our apparatus (the time required depended on the subjects). This method required subjects to keep drinking before we presented the electric taste stimulus, and we informed them about how long they had to drink before we added the stimulus.

The experimental program was developed using Max/MSP. We measured 14 visual stimuli followed by 14 gustatory ones. Subjects were previously informed of which stimulus would be presented first. We repeated each experiment 14 times but excluded the top and bottom two results because subjects occasionally could not perceive the electric taste stimulus. Voltages of 0.3–0.5 V were presented, and all subjects could perceive this electric stimulus as electric taste. When we measured the latency of visual/electric taste stimulus, we verified whether the stimuli were felt by subjects on a separate display monitor. Subjects were asked to report if they did not feel any stimulus.

Results

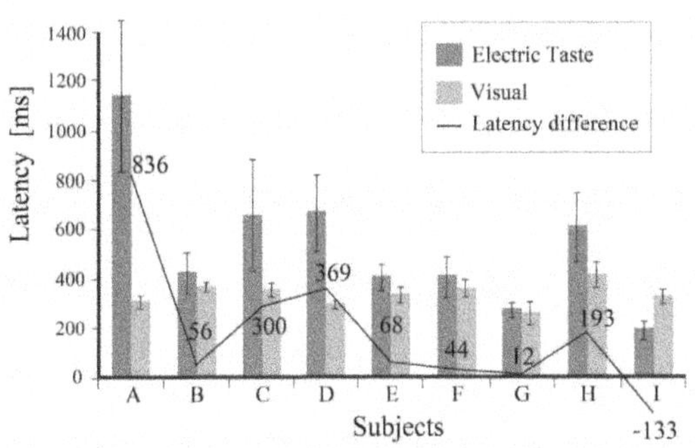

Figure 6. Average latency during perception stimulus change

For most subjects, the latency for electric taste stimulus was greater than that for visual stimulus. The difference between latencies ranged from 13 to 837 ms (Figure 6). Only one subject perceived electric taste stimulus before visual stimulus, with the difference between latencies being 134 ms; this subject's visual perception was not anomalous, with the latency for visual stimulus agreeing with that of other subjects.

DISCUSSION

Our results show that if visual and electric taste stimuli are presented simultaneously, most people perceive the latter last. However, the subjects showed greatly varying electric taste stimulus latencies, and only one perceived the latter first. Therefore, we should adjust the presentation time of each stimulus according to each subject's perception latency. However, for subjects B, E, F, and G, the difference between latencies was small, so we did not adjust the presentation times if the visual and electric taste stimuli were presented realistically. Toward this end, we performed comparative experiments and adjusted the presentation times using examples from our experiments. We used very simple changes in stimuli because we needed to measure the ordinary change in each stimulus. We intend to perform comparative experiments using more complex stimuli in order to utilize our system to enjoy games and visual contents more richly.

In this experiment we required subjects to keep drinking before we presented the electric stimulus. However, such a compulsion might cause users some mental stress and reduce the entertainment derived from content. We considered this method impractical for lengthy content and variable use. Therefore, we proposed a method for detecting whether the electric circuit is complete. We added a circuit and program for measuring the voltage change. In addition, we added a very low voltage that cannot be perceived as taste in order to measure whether the user drinks, based on the voltage change. This method can also be applied to control the presentation time of other senses by checking the latency of each sense and adjusting the time. This enables multi-synchronized presentation using electric taste and other sensations.

A limitation of our work is that the electric taste is currently limited to metallic, sour, and salty tastes. Therefore, we should carefully select the foods used.

In future work, we will conduct experiments on the latency of haptic, olfactory, and auditory senses in conjunction with the gustatory sense. This will enable richer and varied experiences when enjoying entertainment content.

RECENT WORK

Many studies have focused on the structure of taste. The perception of and reaction to taste is generally attributed to taste buds located on top of the tongue. Mouth orifice side cells perceive a chemical agent and depolarize to generate a potential. This potential is delivered from the bottom side cells to the gustatory nerve. Depolarization is attributed to direct ion influx into cells, interface potential difference between sapid substances and the tongue surface, and receptor attachment due to a reaction with sapid and protein substances [10].

Electric taste was discovered by Sulzer in 1754 when he placed two different metals on his tongue. Volta later hypothesized that this taste was attributable to an electric stimulus flowing from one metal to the other metal through taste sensors on the tongue [9]. Many studies analyzed the quality of electric taste and its thresholds. Tomiyama et al. reported that the threshold increased with age, and they reported no significant variation with bilateral differences, sexual differences, smoking history, artificial dentition, and dental metallic crowns. They reported that the most commonly perceived tastes were, in order, metallic and salty and sour tastes, and that humans can perceive AC stimuli [11]. Another study reported that the quality of metallic taste using AC stimuli is stronger than that of copper pennies [5]. One study determined the condition of taste buds using electric taste in a gustatory test [8]. BrainPort, a tongue output system, was proposed to convert visual images to strengthen electric stimuli and provide an output to the tongue [1]. This system enables a visual image to be seen based on the strength of the electric stimulus. It can also be used in evaluation experiments to support surgery [12]. In these studies, an electrode was directly attached to the tongue to present electric taste; in contrast, we add electric taste to food and drink.

Some studies reported that other senses and dietary environment affect gustatory perception. Therefore, Toko et al. presented a chart affected to build daintiness. Olfaction and texture are considered essential to gustation, whereas vision and audition have lesser influence. Therefore, tastes can be changed through pseudo sensations such as a sense of vision or smell. Narumi et al. proposed Meta Cookie, a method to change taste using augmented reality (AR) and scent [7]. This system changes the perceived taste of a cookie based on cross-modal effects evoked by overlaying visual information (texture) and scent onto a real cookie using an AR marker. Food Simulator [2] and ChewingJockey [4] were proposed to add food textures using haptic or auditory information. The former uses a haptic and sound interface to apply pressure to the tongue and produces a biting sound to enhance virtual taste. The latter measures biting using a photo reflector and presents a filtered and designed sound effect through a bone-conduction speaker. Our work presents taste directly, allowing us to use other perceptions for multimodal and unrealistic expressions.

Some studies described how humans visualize feelings of taste and quantity of taste. Flavor visualization is a co-cooking interface system that presents unique tastes through graphical information. Electric taste can be visualized easily because we can manipulate it using electrical circuits and a computer. However, the quality of taste depends on each individual, and therefore, we should design the system to represent a subjective taste.

ACKNOWLEDGEMENTS
This work was funded in part by the Information Technology Promotion Agency, Japan (IPA).

REFERENCES

1. Arnoldussen, A., Nemke, C., Hogle, A.R., and Skinner, K.: BrainPort plasticity, balance and vision applications, *Proc. of the 9th International Conference on Low Vision* (2008).
2. Iwata, H., Yano, H., Uemura, T., and Moriya, T.: Food simulator: A haptic interface for biting, Proc. IEEE Virtual Reality (2004), 51-57.
3. Kim, D.W., Cho, Y.H., Nishimoto, K., Kawakami, Y., Kunifuji, S., and Ando, H.: Development of Aroma-Card Based Soundless Olfactory Display, *Proc. of the 16th IEEE International Conference on Electronics, Circuits, and Systems* (2009).
4. Koizumi, N., Tanaka, H., Uema, Y., and Inami, M.: Chewing Jockey: Augmented food texture by using sound based on the cross-modal effect, *Proceedings of the 8th International Conference on Advances in Computer Entertainment Technology* (2011) 21, 1-4.
5. Lawless, H.T., Stevens, D.A., Chapman, K.W., and Kurtz, A.: Metallic taste from electrical and chemical stimulation. Chem Senses Vol. 30 (2005), 185-194.
6. Nakamura, H., and Miyashita, H.: Communication by change in taste, *Ext. Abstracts CHI 2011*, ACM Press (2011), 1999-2004.
7. Narumi, T., Kajinami, T., Tanikawa, T., and Hirose, M.: Meta Cookie, ACM SIGGRAPH 2010 Emerging Technologies (2010) 18-1.
8. Rion Co., Ltd. Electrogustometer TR-06 http://www.rion.co.jp/asp/product/me/ProB.asp?pos=B1 6
9. Sato, M., and Ogawa, T.: Science of Taste (in Japanese), Asakura Publishing Co., Ltd. (1997), 183.
10. Toko, K.: Taste Sensor, Asakura Publishing Co., Ltd. (1993), 43-49.
11. Tomiyama, H., Tomita, H., and Okuda, Y.: Normal level of electric taste(in Japanese), *Journal of the Oto-Rhino-Laryngological Society of Japan* (Nippon Jibiinkoka Gakkai Kaiho),Vol. 74, No.11 (1971), 1580-1587.
12. Vazquez-BuenosAires, J., Payan, Y., and Demongeot, J.: Electro-stimulation of the tongue as a passive surgical guiding system, ICAR 03, IEEE (2003).

Empathy, Participatory Design and People with Dementia

Stephen Lindsay[1], Daniel Jackson[1], Cas Ladha[1], Karim Ladha[1], Katie Brittain[2], Patrick Olivier[1]

Culture Lab
[1] School of Computing Science
Newcastle University, UK
{stephen.lindsay/p.l.olivier}@ncl.ac.uk

Culture Lab
[2] Institute for Health and Society
Newcastle University, UK
katie.brittain@ncl.ac.uk

ABSTRACT

We describe the development, application and evaluation of a design method tailored for working with people with mild to moderate dementia. Our experiences with the approach highlighted areas where designers and participants held radically different views. The tenet of our approach was that to overcome these differences we needed to create an empathic relationship between participants and designers. To achieve this we modified participatory design techniques to foster respectful engagement with participants in the development of a digital aid to facilitate 'safe walking'. The process begins with broad qualitative scoping and design work then moves to developing personally tailored, individual designs to further exploration of the experiential elements of the domain while reducing the need for the participants to engage in abstract thought. Reflection highlights a number of important areas that demand consideration when undertaking research in this area and, more generally, when performing design work with people with dementia.

Author Keywords

Dementia; participatory design; empathy; experience; prompting; cognitive impairment.

ACM Classification Keywords

H5.m. Information interfaces and presentation (e.g., HCI): Miscellaneous.

INTRODUCTION

The aging population is one of the defining characteristics of the 21st century [26]. Although widely regarded as a positive trend, with the increase in life expectancy comes with an associated increase in the number of age-related health problems. Amongst the most significant of these is dementia [28]. By 2030 it is estimated that more than 65 million people will have some form of dementia [28]. The mental functions of a person with dementia deteriorate over a period of months or years to the point where they require constant care to perform basic activities of daily living. This is provided by either a professional or informal caregiver. The burden on caregivers' time, effort, and resources can be enormous [21] and, for many informal caregivers, leads to considerable distress as they witness firsthand the debilitative affects of dementia on their loved one.

Appropriately designed assistive technologies can help people with dementia to maintain their independence for longer and their caregivers to provide more comprehensive care. However, designing appropriately for this group is challenging [11]. Human-computer interaction research places an increasing emphasis on designing for peoples experiences with technology [30], but when designing for people with dementia there is a tendency to focus on the impairments that characterize dementia at the expense of the experiential consequences of design choices. There is a need to also understand the person with dementia's point of view in order to design technologies they will use [24], as Keith and Whitney say *"people are not just the sum of their acquired impairments"* [12].

However, even if a designer accepts the need to be attentive to the experiential consequences of their designs, there is still an enormous gulf between their life-experiences and those of people with dementia. In designing for the experiences of people with dementia, a designer's intuition can drastically mislead them [11] and there is a clear need to bridge this gulf in experiences. Kitwood [13] was concerned with the neglectful culture in dementia healthcare work in the UK, how one could understand the experiences of a person with dementia and ensure they are afforded the respect they deserve. His process of "person centered care" (PCC) focused on respecting the "personhood" and experiences of the person with dementia and understanding that, while their experiences might arise from irrational perceptions of the world around them, for that person those experiences are just as significant as they are for a cognitively unimpaired individual. PCC requires extensive, respectful dialogue with the person being cared for and aims to foster an understanding of their experiences on the part of healthcare professionals.

This paper aims to be a starting point for understanding how empathic relationships can be used to bridge gulfs in experience. While our goal s not to introduce new *methods*, we give details of our approach to framing participatory design to create empathic relationships between participants and designers. We document our experiences of applying this approach to the design of a 'safe walking aid' and present our insights into working with people with dementia in participatory design process.

DEMENTIA, EMAPTHY AND PARTICIPATION

The values espoused by Kitwood are similar to those proposed in *empathic design* [25]. Wright and McCarthy identified three qualities that are central to developing an empathic relationship with participants in design: (i) a quality relationship between the designer and the user that allows the designer to be attuned to their needs; (ii) a sympathetic disposition towards the user; and, (iii) an attention to the affective and emotional quality of their experiences [29]. These need to be realized through a specific design approach. We used participatory methods because: (i) they democratize the design environment [18] mirroring the respect that Kitwood suggests is needed to understand people with dementia's experiences [13] and; (ii) the close contact that they require between the designers and participants, which has that potential to foster the empathy that Wright and McCarthy propose [29].

However, participatory design methodologies originated in workplace contexts as part of the effort to democratize the introduction of new technologies in Sweden in the 1970s. Due to this, many participatory design techniques make inherent assumptions that are not immediately applicable to the daily lives of people with dementia. For example, participatory design techniques assume that there are specific tasks to be understood and designed for, that there are a range of experts that need to be engaged in the design, that the focus is work and productivity, and that the participants are cognitively able. This means that specific techniques within participatory design do not necessarily translate to being used in social contexts, or where issues of experience dominate those of function. However, participatory approaches have been modified, for example, "Empathy probes" [16] are a participatory design approach that promotes a holistic understanding of day-to-day experiences. In addition, there are several examples of participatory techniques being used with older adults [15] and with younger cognitively impaired people [31].

Beyond insights into the experiences of people with dementia, empowering them through engagement in design has the potential to alter the ways in which we think about the role of technology in their lives. Typically, it is the caregiver who is the source of information in the design process [20] and people with dementia are not engaged directly [27]. Consequently, commercially available assistive technologies for people with dementia generally have a *safety focus*. When people with dementia are empowered through being given a voice in design, this has given rise to designs that address social interaction with others [6], facilitate reminiscing about their past or that help the person with dementia maintain their autonomy through support for activities of daily living [9].

The caregiver is not a suitable *substitute* for talking directly to people with dementia. Previous work has shown there was a gap in the requirements generated by caregivers and people with dementia [20] and found that family caregivers do not accurately represent the needs of their loved ones [5]. However, despite caregiver bias, interactions with them were still informative. We need to talk to both people with dementia and their caregivers; but need to engage with caregivers' responses critically if we are to design appropriately for people with dementia.

Empowering people with dementia through design also has practical benefits. When safety-oriented systems are imposed, people do not recognize their utility and tend to be less patient or willing to use them [20]. Even the design of safety oriented technologies can benefit if they can be framed as "enabling" rather than disempowering or dehumanizing. For example, members of the Alzheimer's Society are optimistic about the role that electronic tracking technology can play in the lives of people with dementia because of its potential to let them reclaim the ability to walk safely [1]. However, further work must include people with dementia and caregivers to avoid the tendency to focus on safety oriented technology. In this way, technology can empower the people with dementia rather than simply addressing their impairments.

THE KITE PROJECT'S APPROACH TO DESIGN

The KITE project's design approach engages people with dementia in participatory design. Specifically, the process (Figure 1) aims to foster an empathic relationship between designers and people with dementia by demanding close, respectful contact. The approach focuses on trying to develop a holistic understanding of people with dementia's day-to-day lives and acknowledges that there is likely to be a wide gulf between designers' and people with dementia's life experiences. To address this, the initial stages of the process elicit participants' accounts of experiences relevant to the domain and allow a shared understanding of the domain to develop which can be built upon in later work. In a final, iterative stage the design approach works with individuals to produce personally tailored prototypes that reduce the need for abstract thinking (which can be challenging for people with dementia) and allow an in-depth exploration of individual's thoughts and experiences with the prototypes.

Bridging Divides in Experience

The main tenet of the approach used in the KITE project is creating an empathic relationship between the designers, people with dementia and caregivers. Fostering a sympathetic, empathic disposition on the part of the designers will develop an environment in which people with dementia can speak openly. The attitude of the designer towards the participants is central to creating this relationship. We propose that, for designers to be able to understand the perspective of people with dementia, they need to uncritically accept and engage with the accounts put forward by the participants with dementia. We suggest, as Kitwood did [13], that the factual accuracy of a person's narrative is secondary to what it reveals about their own experiences. Ultimately, the designer comes to the person

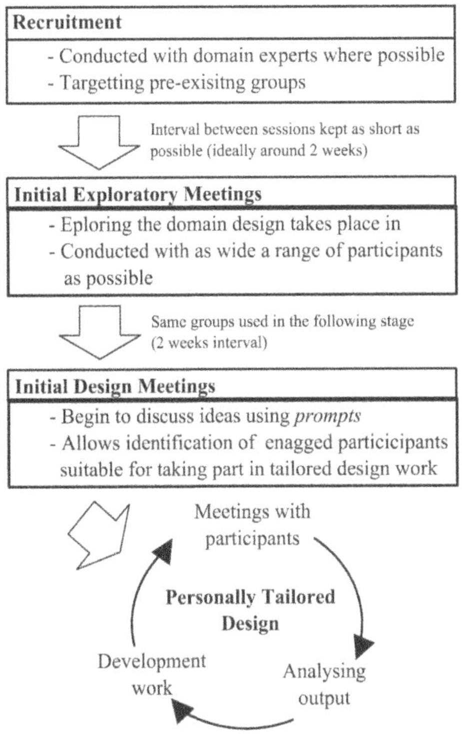

Figure 1. The KITE approach showing early scoping work and the later, iterative personally tailored design cycles

with dementia in the hope of learning from them. This explicit approach lets participants know that they can state what they feel without the need to justify or defend it.

Achieving this requires designers talking to participants in a way that is clear and free of jargon. The act of sharing experiences and analyzing and developing designs should lead to the development of an understanding of the domain shared between all the design session members. Where possible, the terms that are used by participants need to be used by the designer in facilitating these discussions, (i.e. not the language of the designer). We refer to this as creating a *common frame of reference*.

Addressing Issues Arising from Cognitive Impairment

When they were created, many assumptions were made about the environment in which participatory design techniques would be applied in and the people that would involved. There are several strategies we adopt throughout our process to alleviate issues that arise where these assumptions intersect with cognitive impairment when engaging people with dementia in participatory design. Incorporating *review* into the structure of the meetings focuses attention, ensures that the design team's interpretation of what the participant says is accurate and helps the participants remember the discussion later in the process [23]. This requires the creation of extensive documentation throughout the process. The act of cementing user concerns into this documentation – whether in the form of writing down a note, making a point for a recording device or altering a paper prototype – serves to focus participants' attention and ensures that concerns are voiced more readily should a participant feel that a point is being made erroneously. If all the participants are consulted at this point, the act also ensures everyone has a chance to voice their opinion and this allows the discussion to move to a new topic by giving a clear indication of the closing of the previous topic.

In our approach, each group will be involved in at least two meetings so as to reduce confusion the meetings will be facilitated by the same person, a *consistent point of contact*. The consistent contact is the closest member of the design team to the participants and will gain the greatest insight into their experiences. The consistent contact can also introduce other members of the design team into meetings with participants, allowing their voice to be heard by, and directly influence the rest of the design team.

Articulating personal narratives can be challenging for people with dementia. The use of *existing groups* can help the individuals articulate themselves. Many people with dementia regularly attend support groups (typically run by voluntary organizations) to help them learn strategies to cope with problems they may face and to provide a venue to talk with other, sympathetic people who understand the challenges they face. Support groups are an ideal place to recruit existing groups as they are a normal venue for the discussion of personal problems for people with dementia. Talking to established support groups leverages existing dynamics within the group (to provide mutual support) and the trusted environment (in which participants feel safe discussing sensitive issues). This approach builds on the underlying focus group concept: that the interplay between the participants can generate new data [7]. This effect can be enhanced by conducting meetings in *familiar environments* in which participants are more likely to feel at ease [8].

Caregivers can also provide support for the person they care for in conversation, when a person with dementia struggles to articulate themselves their caregiver can often help them. However, caregivers may be able to articulate themselves more easily than the person they care for, and therefore it is important that the designer ensures that the caregivers' voices do not dominate discussions. An important role of the consistent contact within the KITE approach is to balance the voice and concerns of the caregiver with the voice of the person with dementia.

At each of the initial stages, one group that exclusively involves caregivers shall be conducted. Talking with caregivers in this way allows the identification of areas of conflict or inconsistencies between their accounts and those put forward in the other groups by people with dementia. These conflicts highlight areas where design work might be focused and helps designers infer which issues that arise in design sessions may be more relevant to caregivers [5,20].

Previous work has highlighted the benefits of working with people with *milder levels of cognitive impairment* as opposed to working with people with severe cognitive impairment [31]. Although conducting a review of the severity of someone's dementia would be impractical, the venues through which people are recruited, and the participants themselves, can provide an indication of the severity of their dementia. As a general rule, support groups for people still living independently are likely to include people less severely impaired than day care centers for people with dementia, which in turn will include people less severely affected than those in dementia care homes.

Identifying *appropriate stakeholders* is a critical part of any participatory design process. The process needs to engage with caregivers as well as people with dementia, engage with people with milder dementia where possible and work with existing groups. These people can be contacted through charitable organizations, support groups, and day care centers. The involvement of professionals with experience of working with people with dementia is particularly helpful at this stage because they can provide insights into stakeholder identification and the avenues for recruiting participants.

Transcript Analysis

Analysis is not the preserve of traditional participatory design practices as participants would usually be more directly involved in the construction of explicit requirements (for themselves and the designers). However, we transcribe all meetings with participants and use a Thematic Analysis [4] of the transcripts to allow designers to engage with the people with dementia and their caregiver's narratives and provide clarity, through reflection on an accurate account of the meetings in the event that a person with dementia cannot clearly articulate their thoughts or experiences due to cognitive impairment.

The analysis begins with identification of interesting or significant sections of the transcript and highlighting, or 'coding', them. Groups of codes with a common underlying theme are identified is a second reading and are grouped into themes. Themes are then grouped into categories which will include all coded sections related to them. Under the hierarchy of concepts and categories, coded work can be re-examined and theories about the domain constructed. The themes and concepts, which the analysis draws out, need to be validated by the participants before they are accepted by re-presenting the themes to them.

Initial Exploratory Meetings

Exploratory meetings develop a broad understanding of living with dementia and establish a common frame of reference for the consistent point of contact and participants. The aim of these sessions is not to imagine new designs so discussion of technology should be limited to accounts of previous encounters with it. As many people with dementia and caregivers as possible should be engaged at this stage. Each meeting will last between forty-five and ninety minutes and should ideally involve 3-6 people with dementia and their caregivers or 6-8 caregivers [2]. Our experiences showed that in practice numbers cannot be precisely controlled.

The meetings follow a focus group structure, questions are left open in order to stimulate discussion and allow co-questioning to emerge in the process [7]. Co-questioning, when participants ask each other questions rather than the facilitator leading discussion, is particularly valuable at this early stage in the process as it leads to questions that a facilitator who is unfamiliar with the domain might not think to ask. However, meeting facilitators should be prepared to start discussion so research into the design domain should be done to help in the construction of a *topic guide* for the meeting that outlines relevant topics for discussion. The Thematic Analysis of these meetings gives the designers ideas about possible technological interventions. In the next stage of the process the design team will have the chance to feed back their analysis to participants through the *prompts* they select.

Initial Design Work

The aim of the initial design work is to elicit participants' reactions to the designs proposed in response to the Thematic Analysis of the exploratory meetings. Workshops are conducted with the same groups that participated in the exploratory stage. These workshops use the brainstorming technique [23] to generate large amounts of raw ideas. These meetings begin by reviewing the analysis of the previous meetings to focus the attention of participants onto the topics being discussed and to validate it. This also reinforces the common frame of reference for the meetings. The meetings move on to discuss initial design concepts created based on the analysis.

Previous work has noted that many older participants struggle to envision new technologies or discuss intangible issues [15]. To help with this, the consistent point of contact will present a range of physical artifacts to the participants to *prompt* discussion. These devices are chosen to be physical representations of design concepts. The physical devices serve as tangible prompts that remind the participant what is being discussed. A wide range of artifacts should be presented allowing participants to lead the discussion by selecting the ones they want to discuss. Groups with caregivers are presented with the same technologies and asked to envision their own devices. They are also asked about the sorts of devices that their loved ones might carry and their functionality. These sessions are recorded and transcribed and the analysis is used to distil the output of these sessions into problem descriptions and requirements that the design team can respond to.

The most important outcome of these meetings is the identification of participants who are suitable to continue working with. These are participants who are engaged in the process, identify with the problem area and are in some way invested in addressing it. They will be asked to take part in personally tailored design exercises. In addition, designers should also gain ideas about what sorts of designed interventions are appropriate in this domain.

Personally Tailored Design

The personally tailored design work focuses on developing the relationship between participants and designers through the process of creating individually tailored prototypes. We work with individuals as it is not feasible to create tailored prototypes for all the participants. In addition, the personal nature of the work (addressing the participants own lives and individual problems) can reduce the barrier to envisioning new technology that older adults struggle with [e.g. 15] by reducing the need for them to think in abstract terms. For example, they no longer need to think in generalized terms about the ways that a device might be used or try to imagine what it may look like. The quality of the relationship at this stage should improve designers' understanding of the participant's experiences and the design domain, and allow more critical debate in the meetings to help designers further their understanding. The production of such personal designs might be considered by some to limit the generalizability of the final design; however, others argue that , while the devices produced may not be generalizable [3], the personal approach gives more in-depth insights that can inspire ideas that better generalize to a wider group [10]

This stage follows an iterative approach, with the development cycling every 3-4 weeks with a focus on producing new designs or prototypes to be presented to the participants. This allows them to see that they are having an impact on the process and how their input is being interpreted. These sessions involve prompts in the form of new design objects, storyboards and paper prototypes that help the participants envisioning novel technology. The focus on their own very personal experience of living with dementia contributes significantly to their engagement and, when coupled with the frequent meetings, reduces the chances that topics discussed in one session will be forgotten by the next. The information gathered in these sessions is combined with the information taken from the wider selection of people interviewed in the exploratory stage to produce the design artifacts and, eventually, prototype devices for participants to use. There are a variety of techniques that can concrete user issues in these design sessions and gather more information from the participants. Physical objects are central to these techniques as they play to the strengths of older participants [15].

Storyboards promote discussion around participants' routines, a designer creates storyboards showing how they perceive a typical day in the participants' lives. The participants fill in dialogue and thought bubbles to indicate what they would be thinking about in the various scenes to allow designers to introduce a sense of context to the design of future devices as well as to get at the routines of the participants. *Paper Prototyping* design activities allow the user to show their ideas on paper. The sessions require a degree of creative engagement (problematic for individuals with cognitive impairment [31]) but allows participants to express themselves through a new modality which may be easier for them to communicate in. These sessions also focus discussion on the problems that the participants have using specific features in relation to their own personal issues. Both approaches allow notes to be tied to visual cues for individuals' reference and places focus on a physical artifact. *Functional prototypes* allow users to evaluate designs by letting them use it in their everyday life. This removes part of the conceptual element of the design process and gives them something very concrete to critique, playing to their strengths in design work [15].

EXPERIENCES WITH THE KITE METHOD

The KITE project design work examined the potential for designing a digital intervention to promote safe walking for people with dementia [22], i.e. walking outdoors unaccompanied by a caregiver with minimal risk of becoming lost or experiences of anxiety. Being able to walk safely has many benefits including reduced reliance upon caregivers, exercise and helping to promote a sense of personhood. However, safe walking activity is threatened by wandering behavior. Wandering behavior is difficult to define but can generally be characterized as occasions when a person with dementia walks somewhere but is not motivated by a specific goal, or is motivated by one that is not rational. A precise definition of wandering is problematic because it has to take into account a wide variety of causes and resultant behaviors [14] ranging from rational movement in the service of non-rational goals, to non-rational movement in pursuit of rational goals.

Stakeholder Identification and Recruitment

We worked with a Social Gerontologist (SG) and General Practitioner (GP) to identify and recruit appropriate stakeholders. They were able to identify suitable venues to perform recruitment and leverage existing contacts with two charitable groups: the Alzheimer's Society (AS), a UK based charity that performs advocacy work for people with dementia and runs support groups. We also worked with The Dementia Care Partnership (DCP), a not-for-profit group that runs day care centers for people with dementia

Workers in these groups were contacted and, because they were familiar with the SG and GP, were happy to engage with us. They discussed the project to get a thorough sense of its aims before offering to approach support groups for people with dementia and caregivers to gauge their interest in the project. The support groups were pre-existing, close-knit, tending to make their decisions as a group, and discussed our proposal in their meetings. At this stage the project was presented as looking at "getting out and about" when someone had dementia with terms felt to be more intimidating, like "wandering" and "participatory design", being avoided because it was felt the might be intimidating. The team was aware that there would be an issue if some members of the groups wanted to take part and others did not. Given how important these regular support meetings were to the people involved, we felt it was unethical to risk disrupting the groups. Our decision was to only work with groups if all the members agreed to participate. In practice we found that the collective decision making of the groups lead to them reaching their own consensuses on participation.

Initial Exploratory Meetings

The participants from AS1-4 (Table 1) quickly engaged with the idea of "getting out and about" and had many stories about their experiences. Distinct themes emerged around the role of *anxiety and confidence* in getting out and about that related to either the curtailment of walking alone or the need to not allow fears to get in the way, as one female participant said: *"just get on with it"*. This discussion highlighted the *tensions* that emerged between people, one male participant said: *"the family really, they're frightened, you know, but I'm not"*. Many caregivers talked about an *incident* that changed their attitudes towards the person they were caring for *"after that, if I went anywhere, he had to stand beside me you know"*.

When discussing strategies for dealing with the threat of becoming lost some participants *used low fidelity solutions: "I always made sure that in his wallet, he had his name and address, as well as our phone number"* A lot of discussions centered on the use of *technology*. Many participants owned mobile phones and at least one male participant had used one when lost *"right, I'm such and such a place, where are you? You stay there and I'll come and find you"*. However, most experiences and opinions of technology were negative: *"once you reach my age, you are faced with something electronic, you would ignore it"*.

There was a lot of concern over the *stigma* that might be associated with carrying devices to help with becoming lost *"if somebody sees you have a card or something, they think well, I'm stupid you know"*. Some people felt the mobiles needed to be *discreet* so they wouldn't make their carriers targets for criminals *"you'd find they'd be getting mugged for it"*. Our understanding of the domain was that the participants wanted to walk outdoors but didn't because of a fear of wandering (or getting lost as they usually termed it). They needed a system in place to provide reassurance and improve their confidence.

Group	Caregivers	People with Dementia
AS 1	2 Volunteers	2 People with dementia
AS2	2 Caregivers 1 Volunteer	3 People with dementia
AS 3	3 Caregivers	4 People with dementia
AS 4	6 Caregivers	None
DCP 1	1 Caregiver	5 People with dementia
DCP 2	None	2 People with dementia

Table 1. Group profiles engaged in the process.

Initial Design Work

We worked with AS 1, AS 2, DCP 1 and DCP 2 to develop initial design concepts. The AS participants were still living independently but the DCP participants were not and struggled more with the design process. Nevertheless, they still identified with the concept of "getting out and about" and engaged with the ideas from previous sessions and the AS groups were starting to develop a rapport with the consistent point of contact.

The concepts developed in response to the issues raised in the exploratory meetings were presented through a set of *prompts*. An *iPod-nano* was selected to prompt discussion around futuristic aesthetic as we felt participants would feel it was intended for a younger generation. *Digital Jewelry* [19], a custom made piece tailored to an individual, was intended to demonstrate to participants that technology did not have to look like a mobile phone or a computer if they did not want it to. The desire for *discreet* devices also seemed to be important to many participants, and both the *iPod* and *digital jewelry* were relatively small. A *Nokia N95 Smartphone* served the purpose of provoking discussion around using Smartphone's as they would allow self-orientation through their GPS and could call a caregiver if help was needed. The *PDA* was intended to spark discussion around touch screen interaction with devices. Demonstrating how a *TomTom* worked was intended to introduce the concept of location aware technologies. Finally, a *Tracking Bracelet* and *Fall Alarm* were intended to promote discussion of tracking and alarm technologies.

Distinct themes emerge in these meetings, the need for devices to be *specific to individuals* was important because individuals' circumstances were so varied. This can be realized through performing personally tailored design. Integration into *routine* was another important aspect of day-to-day life that was identified as determining if a new device would be accepted. This is of note because it is almost a direct articulation of our underlying motivation for carrying out the process: to tap into participants' day-to-day experiences. The participants felt that they used routine to cope with many issues they faced and that new devices would have their benefit weighed up against the cost in terms of disruption to routine. Finally, people identified the main threat to safe walking as *anxiety* about becoming lost and there was *speculation around device function*. These related to three steps taken when lost: self orientation, asking for help and summoning help. There was a distinct lack of discussion around the ethics of tracking with no one taking issue with the concept of tracking people in these sessions. This suggested we needed to develop our relationship with the participants so they would feel more confident working with us in the personally tailored design stage and be more prepared to criticize the designs we proposed.

Personally Tailored Design

Two members of AS2 were particularly engaged with the ideas being developed: Alice lived on her own, with mild dementia, and John showing signs of early onset dementia and his wife Mary. They were chosen due to the mild nature of their impairments, their very different personal circumstances, and their enthusiasm for the process. John and Alice wanted to maintain their independence; John was a keen runner, and Alice still regularly drove alone to the shops or to visit friends. John had been diagnosed with dementia two years ago but Alice had only been diagnosed recently and both behaved in ways that were consistent with someone with mild dementia. John occasionally displayed some confusion in meetings and both Alice and John struggled to remember past events including discussions from previous meetings. John lived with his wife whilst Alice lived alone, this opened up a field of inquiry that, until this point, had not been drawn out of the work: what the designs could do if no caregiver was available. John did not have any other medical conditions but Alice had arthritis and a problem with her ankle that meant she struggled to manipulate small objects and used a walking stick. Alice and John talked at length about the importance of routine in their lives including its significance when remembering to carry things with them when they went out and remembering to charge mobile phones for later use.

The first personally tailored design meeting presented sketches of designs to participants illustrating a variety of ideas. The second meeting focused on storyboards and eliciting ideas about routine. At this stage, Alice started to express that she would like to be tracked, even if the person informed in the event of a problem could not be established. The debate in the meetings was becoming notably more animated and when the team proposed putting a tracking device on Alice's walking stick (that previous storyboarding revealed as central to routines when leaving the house), she vigorously argued against it. At first Alice could not articulate why, but eventually she revealed it was because she had *"a hatred"* for the stick (*"the blasted thing!"*). Alice had hoped her device could be something she was proud to show off to her friends and placing it on her walking stick, which had the opposite emotional association, was not something she would countenance.

The third meeting focused on trying to paper prototype the interface to the devices and the final meeting presented final prototypes (Figure 2) to the participants. The final prototypes constantly reported their position to a central server that could be interrogated online through a mobile interface. Both devices had a panic button that could be pressed to send a phone call to a pre-determined mobile phone. If the signal was not acknowledged, it could be propagated to other devices. The aesthetic of John's prototype mimicked a runner's arm-band-mp3 holder to

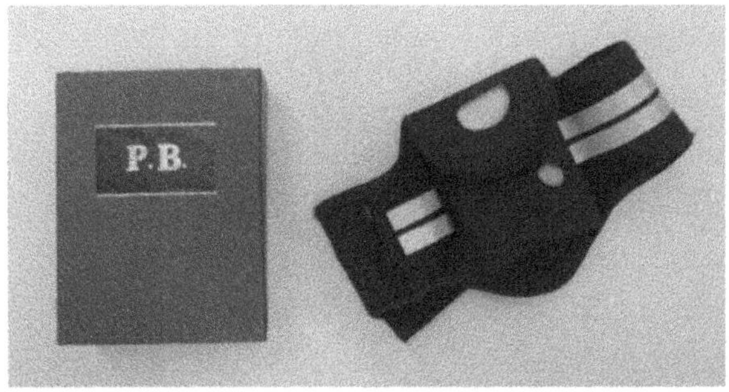

Figure 2. Alice's notebook (left) and John's running band

disguise its tracking functionality. Alice's device was built into a leather bound notebook with her initials embossed on the front. While the size of the device was still an issue for Alice, John liked his device and was happy to carry it on a test run with him after our fourth meeting. He was enthusiastic about the device but still had some small criticism to offer with regards to simple usability issues such as placement of buttons and feedback from the device.

DEMENTIA AND EXPERIENCES WITH TECHNOLOGY

The final designs illustrate key, experiential elements of design in this field. We present our insights in the hopes that others designing aids to promote safe walking, or developing other assistive technologies, might be able to better understand their participants from the outset and so have more meaningful conversations with them.

Safety and design

Both the devices had a GPS tracking system and a GSM unit that could be used to raise an alarm on a caregivers' phone with the carrier's location should they become lost. Despite previous works findings suggesting people with dementia are not concerned about their personal safety [27], this backup needed to be in place before the participants would consider using the devices. The design sessions revealed a desire for a device that went beyond simply tracking its carrier but there was a lack of willingness to engage with less familiar design concepts without this safety net in place. For example, Mary would not consider having a device that gave implicit feedback about John and Alice asked for the device she had to have a tracking unit built into it in the later stages of design process.

The significance of routine in everyday life

The ways that a device interacts with the existing routine of a person with dementia is critical when they are deciding whether or not to use it. The participants used routine as a way to cope with their increasing cognitive impairment, so were sensitive to anything new that interfered with it. They felt integrating into routine, as opposed to being forced to create new ones by new devices, was central to ensuring a device was carried and remembering to charge it. The idea of having a home base for the devices to charge at, some device that looked incongruous without the device plugged into it, arose from aiming to embed our devices into participants routines.

Everyday uses for a device

The participants felt that the designs they created should have some added value beyond just being tracking and locating devices. This stemmed from their desire to not carry a device with them that reminded them they have dementia and that something may go wrong even when performing simple everyday activities. As one participant said, they did not want to have to carry a device that made them *"feel disabled"*.

Concerns about stigma associated with devices

Initially, the participants did not want their devices to identify them as having dementia, they wanted something small enough to hide out of sight or that was disguised as something else, as others have found when working with disabled users [17,24]. However, when the devices were shown to them and were considered aesthetically pleasing this attitude shifted, and the participants became happy to talk about the devices even wanting to show them off to their friends. This sentiment became explicit when Alice was challenged in discussion about having her device built into her walking stick and she resisted the idea, in part because that would mean she would not value it as much.

DISCUSSION

Our experiences showed that working with participants with cognitive impairments poses a variety of challenges for both designers and participants. This discussion highlights three areas we found particularly interesting or challenging in working with our cognitively impaired participants and some of the strategies that we employed to help improve the quality of our relationship with them. We believe that other designers and researchers working with people with dementia (or possibly more generally, with cognitively impaired individuals) might benefit from implementing these strategies.

Working with pre-existing groups was one of the most useful aspects of our work and had an impact in all of the following domains. The environment in these groups lent confidence to the participants and they were able to support each other when articulating their thoughts or in recalling stories they had previously shared in the support group.

Inadvertently Disempowering People with Dementia

Engaging with people with dementia in design is a rarity and our process empowered the participants by giving them a voice in regards to technologies being produced for them. However, the process of analyzing transcripts from the later tailored design sessions with participants with dementia and adding our own layer of interpretation to the needs that they expressed, sometimes had unanticipated adverse effects on this. The analysis could, inadvertently, disempower the participants and undermine our relationship with them if we took action on our analysis too early in the process. For example, when discussing how to feed-back information on the devices location, the designers discounted their desire to get feedback through their TV, instead interpreting it as a desire to have feedback integrated into their day-to-day lives. The participants had actually carefully considered this issue and further exploration of their idea revealed just how central the TV specifically was to their lives. However, the analysis did reveal interesting aspects of the participant's experiences and underlying themes that tied these together (particularly in the initial exploratory meetings). As such, the process of reflecting on the transcripts is still valuable in the initial stages of the KITE approach.

Taking decisions for participants based on needs that they do not directly articulate (which stemmed from our belief that participants would not be able to articulate themselves) in the personally tailored design work ran counter to our goal of respecting their experiences (and their accounts of these experiences). Our assumption that participants could not directly articulate their needs echoes some of the issues that were highlighted in our review of previous work which spoke to caregivers instead of people with dementia [20] on the assumption that the people with dementia would not be capable of contributing meaningfully to the design process. In the future, we would work harder in these sessions to explicitly construct requirements with the participants.

Empathy's Role Bridging the Gulf in Experience

The time spent with participants fostered a quality relationship between them and the team members present. This changed the nature of the relationship between the consistent point of contact and other members of the design and development team. In addition, because of insights into the participants lives gained from active debates with them, the consistent point of contact found that they became an advocate for the participants at design team meetings that were conducted without them, where their opinions might otherwise have been marginalized. The consistent point of contact and designers who had been introduced to the participants frequently argued for the participants with dementia in these meetings. This created an unusual dynamic in the work with the consistent point of contact becoming more aligned with the group of participants with dementia and less aligned with the rest of the design team during the tailored design process. Furthermore, team members often expressed surprise at the opinions of the people with dementia and re-evaluated their opinions on different aspects of the design as a consequence of members meeting with them. Such meetings were easily facilitated by having the consistent point of contact to make introductions at group meetings.

An example of this was that, although ethical issues around privacy and tracking were frequently discussed in the meetings, participants in the tailored design were unconcerned by the threat to privacy posed by caregivers knowing where they were. This highlighted how the world view of people with dementia differed dramatically from those of the designers and echoes the warnings found in previous work about the gulf in experiences, and the resultant gulf in outlook, between younger and older people [11]. This lack of concern seemed to arise because the people with dementia could not envisage reasons that their caregiver, typically a partner or adult daughter, should not know where they were. The participants with dementia suggested they would get a sense of comfort either from their spouse knowing their location or, more interestingly, in knowing that their spouse was not worried about them.

Another example of this was the surprising insight in the personally tailored design meetings that John was not afraid for his own safety but wanted something to reassure his wife that he was "okay". An awareness of the problems caregivers encounter is not unknown amongst people with dementia but the desire to lessen that burden is not something we have seen mentioned in other design work. This highlights the emotional burden a person with dementia can experience if they feel, in some ways, they encumber their loved ones.

An issue that arose from the relationship that we had not anticipated was that sometimes participants were unwilling to critique the designs that we placed in front of them. We speculate this is because they were concerned we would be offended if they were too critical. When the consistent point of contact emphasized that the devices were prototypes and downplayed the effort placed into developing them, the participants were much more willing to criticize. A strategy that emerged during this process was establishing a clear separation between the people that they met in design meetings and the rest of the design team through careful use of language. For example, we would ask if "they" (designers) should keep a switch in its location or if "we" (participants and consistent contact) wanted it moved. This strategy emerged naturally and was symptomatic of the shifting alignment of the consistent point of contact.

Mitigating the Impact of Cognitive Impairment

The strategies that we employed to mitigate the impact that our participants' cognitive impairment had on the design process may be more broadly applied to other design projects that engage with people with a variety of cognitive impairments. Giving participants access to physical artifacts to critique, whether prompts as seen in early exploratory work or design artifacts in the tailored design work, helped elicit feedback on designs and design questions. The rapid development of prototypes was crucial, and frequent meetings were also helpful in achieving this. Ensuring that participants felt that their contributions were being acknowledged also maintained their interest in the project. This meant being able to show them, in each meeting, how their contributions have impacted on the design. However, this process could also lead to participants becoming fixated on specific details or characteristics of a prototype that were never intended to be included in final designs and so needs to be carefully managed. Whilst leading into topics which needed discussion was something that was aspired to, there were concerns over certain design decisions being suggested to the participants by the prompts.

When discussing intangible issues of design, such as the safety issues around tracking or alert propagation, participants were much less vocal. The participants struggled to envision theses issues as we did not have physical prompts for them. However, the rare informative discussions around these issues often started based on the tangible prompts. The problem lay in understanding which of the prompts would provoke discussion around more intangible or conceptual aspects of the design and the direction in which the participants would take discussion based on these prompts. The next design process will consider how to better utilize this phenomenon.

The inclusion of family caregivers, who took part in the meeting alongside the person with dementia they cared for helped in discussion as they could articulate problems their loved ones struggled with. However, they were used to speaking for their loved ones and the consistent contact had to be aware of the correspondence between what a caregiver said, and the views expressed (or not expressed) by the person that they cared for. This was done by listening to the caregiver speak on behalf of their loved one then asking the person with dementia the same question the caregiver had just answered, to see if they agreed or had anything to add. Occasionally this revealed new issues, but most of the time the person with dementia simply expressed agreement. In other cases the consistent point of contact aggregated and contrasted the points made by both the caregivers and people with dementia, both within and across meetings. The caregiver meetings acted as a baseline for this process and allowed us to identify more caregiver issues.

CONCLUSION

This paper presents our attempts to design in a participatory manner with frequently marginalized people with dementia and their caregivers. In adopting a participatory approach to design we were able to engage with the participants and develop an empathic relationship that improved both our understanding of the domain we worked in and the issues we encountered. The approach we followed contributes explicit scaffolding for anyone wishing to engage people with dementia in design and the strategies that emerged in meetings may be applied more broadly in work with numerous groups with cognitive impairment.

However, the scope of the work is limited by our decision to work with more cognitively able participants and, to some extent, by the inclusion of caregivers (who introduce their own agenda) into the sessions. In the future, we hope others will develop the use of empathy in understanding different groups in participatory design. Ultimately, if designers and researchers are motivated enough to engage with people with dementia, they will gain unexpected insights and, while our approach holds many lessons for these researchers, it is secondary to their willingness to learn from this group.

ACKNOWLEDGEMENTS
This research was jointly funded by Centre for Excellence in Life Sciences, and SiDE the RCUK Research Hub in Social Inclusion through the Digital Economy.

REFERENCES
1. Alzheimers Society. *Policy position: Electronic tagging*.
2. Barrett, J. and Kirk, S. Running focus groups with elderly and disabled elderly participants. *Applied Ergonomics 31*, 6 (2000), 621-629.
3. Boehner, K., Sengers, P., and Warner, S. Interfaces with the ineffable. *ACM TOCHI 15*, 3 (2008), 1-29.
4. Braun, V. and Clarke, V. Using thematic analysis in psychology. *Qualitative research in psychology 3*, 2 (2006), 77-101.
5. Cohene, T. and Baecker, R. Designing interactive Life Story Multimedia for a family affected by Alzheimer's disease: A case study. *In Proc. CHI 2005 EA*, ACM Press (2005).
6. Dishman, E., Morris, M., and Lundell, J. Catalyzing social interaction with ubiquitous computing: a needs assessment of elders coping with cognitive decline. *In Proc. CHI' 2004 EA*, (2004).
7. Gibbs, A. Focus groups. *Social Research Update 19*, 8 (1997).
8. Hawkey, K., Inkpen, K.M., Rockwood, K., McAllister, M., and Slonim, J. Requirements gathering with Alzheimer's patients and caregivers. *In Proc. ASSETS 2005*, (2005), 142-149.
9. Hoey, J., Plotz, T., Jackson, D., Monk, A., Pham, C., and Olivier, P. Rapid Specification and Automated Generation of Prompting Systems to Assist People with Dementia. *Pervasive and Mobile Computing 7*, 3 (2010), 299-318.
10. Holmquist, L.E. User-Driven Innovation in the Future Applications Lab. *CHI'2004*, (2004), 1091-1092.
11. Keates, S. and Clarkson, P.J. Countering design exclusion: bridging the gap between usability and accessibility. *Universal Access in the Information Society 2*, 3 (2003), 215-225.
12. Keith, S. and Whitney, G. Bridging the gap between young designers and older users in an inclusive society. *In Proc. The good, the bad and the challenging: the user and the future of ICT*, (1998).
13. Kitwood, T. *Dementia Reconsidered*. Open University Press, 1997.
14. Lai, K.Y. and Arthur, D.G. Wandering behaviour in people with dementia. *Advanced Nursing 44*, 2 (2003).
15. Massimi, M., Baecker, R.M., and Wu, M. Using participatory activities with seniors to critique, build, and evaluate mobile phones. *In Proc. ASSETS 2007*, (2007), 155-162.
16. Mattelmäki, T., C, H., and Helsinki, F.I.N. Empathy Probes. *in Proc. PDC 2002*, (2002).
17. McNaney, R., Lindsay, S., Ladha, K., Ladha, C., Schofield, G., Plötz, T., Hammerla, N., Jackson, D., Walker, R., Miller, N., et al. Cueing Swallowing in Parkinson ' s Disease. *In Proc. CHI 2011*, (2011), 619-622.
18. Muller, M. *PICTIVE: Democratizing the dynamics of the design session*. Lawrence Erbaulm, 1993.
19. Olivier, P. and Wallace, J. Digital Technologies and the Emotional Family. *IJHCS 67*, 2 (2009).
20. Orpwood, R., Chadd, J., Howcroft, D., Sixsmith, A., Torrington, J., Gibson, G., and Chalfont, G. User-led design of technology to improve quality of life for people with dementia. In P. Langdon, J. Clarkson and P. Robinson, eds., *Designing Inclusive Futures*. Cambridge, 2008, 185-195.
21. O'Shea, E. Costs and Consequences for the Carers of People with Dementia in Ireland. *Dementia 2*, (2003), 201-219.
22. Robinson, L., Brittain, K., Lindsay, S., Jackson, D., and Olivier, P. Keeping In Touch Everyday (KITE) project: developing assistive technologies with people with dementia and their carers to promote independence. *21*, 03 (2009), 494-502.
23. Roulston, K. *Reflective Interviewing: A Guide to Theory and Practice*. SAGE Ltd, 2010.
24. Shinohara, K. and Wobbrock, J.O. In the Shadow of Misperception : Assistive Technology Use and Social Interactions. *CHI'11*, (2011), 705-714.
25. Suri, J.F. The next 50 years: future challenges and opportunities for empathy in our science. *Ergonomics 44*, 14 (2001), 1278-1289.
26. United Nations. *World Population Ageing: 1950 - 2050*.
27. Wherton, J.P. and Monk, A.F. Technological opportunities for supporting people with dementia who are living at home. *IJHCS 66*, 8 (2008), 571-586.
28. Wimo, A. and Prince, M. *World Alzheimer's Report 2010*. .
29. Wright, P. and McCarthy, J. Empathy and experience in HCI. *In Proc. CHI 2008*, (2008), 637-646.
30. Wright, P.C. and McCarthy, J. *Technology as Experience*. MIT Press, 2004.
31. Wu, M., Baecker, R., and Richards, B. Participatory design of an orientation aid for amnesics. *In Proc. CHI 2005*, (2005), 511-520.

From Death to Final Disposition: Roles of Technology in the Post-Mortem Interval

Wendy Moncur[1], Jan Bikker[1], Elaine Kasket[2], John Troyer[3]

University of Dundee[1]
Dundee, DD1 4HN, UK
{wmoncur, j.bikker}
@dundee.ac.uk

London Metropolitan
University[2]
London, E1 7NT, UK
e.kasket@londonmet.ac.uk

Centre for Death & Society[3],
University of Bath,
Bath, BA2 7AY, UK.
J.Troyer@bath.ac.uk

ABSTRACT
In this paper, we describe collaborative processes and stakeholders involved in the period from when a person dies until they are laid to rest: the funeral, final disposition of the body, and (in some circumstances) victim identification. The rich mixture of technologies currently deployed during this brief period are categorized and critically analyzed. We then reflect on the implications of our findings, both for the design of technology that takes the end of life into account, and for the wider HCI community.

Author Keywords
End of life, collaboration, coordination, thanatosensitive design, funerals, final disposition, victim identification.

ACM Classification Keywords
H.5.3. [Group and Organization Interfaces]: Computer-supported cooperative work;

INTRODUCTION
The Human Computer Interaction (HCI) community is beginning to consider the design of technology for the end of life (EoL) and for memorialization [25,41]. In this paper, we bring the HCI community's attention to bear on the processes and stakeholders involved in the period immediately after death: the *post-mortem interval (PMI)*. We acknowledge that this is a challenging and sensitive area [31]. It is also an important one, which we should not shy away from if we are truly to design technology to "*meet human needs across the life-span*" [26, p989] and beyond.

Previous research in this domain has taken various approaches – e.g. sociological [31], critical humanist [5], design-oriented [40] – yet a standard methodology is absent [25]. We are still learning how best to 'do' design for EoL. Our research adopted a process-oriented participatory approach, working in a hybrid interdisciplinary space where we could "*combine diverse knowledge with new insights, ...learning reciprocally and creating new ideas*" [30, p1062]. By adopting this approach, we gained a new understanding of a specific brief time period which is densely packed with collaborative activities, and which is increasingly supported and mediated by technologies.

In the first part of this paper, we examine the processes that occur in the immediate PMI, and the stakeholders involved in them. We focus on (1) the organization and conduct of the *funeral* and (2) the *final disposition* (the burial, interment, cremation, or other authorized disposition of a dead body). These processes are routine. The third process, (3) *victim identification*, is necessary if the deceased was the victim of a disaster, accident or suspicious death. Identification is usually essential before the funeral and final disposition can occur. Increasingly, stakeholders are using technology to expedite or augment these three processes.

In the second part of this paper, we identify how technologies are being used, highlighting the remarkable diversity of technology applications in the immediate PMI. The stakeholders involved are diverse, and go beyond the four groups (the living, the dying, the dead and the bereaved) previously identified in work that scopes thanatosensitive design [26]. We highlight the involvement of a fifth group, '*death workers*' [42], comprised of the individuals who conduct specialized work after a death and support the preceding four groups. Death workers include funeral directors, celebrants, bereavement counselors, lawyers, police, coroners, embalmers and Disaster Victim Identification (DVI) workers.

In the final part of this paper, we consider implications for the design of technology that takes the end of life into account, and for the wider HCI community.

Our research focused on processes and stakeholders common to the UK, and is grounded in conformist Christian faiths, unless specifically identified as being otherwise. We acknowledge that processes and stakeholders vary across the dimensions of faith, community and country, and encourage research into how these dimensions impact technology design. However, such a discussion is beyond the scope of this paper.

CHI'12, May 5–10, 2012, Austin, Texas, USA.

METHODOLOGY

In generating a shared understanding of this cross-disciplinary area, we adopted a participatory approach. The lead author framed the initial question of how technology is used in the PMI, and then interviewed three experts (EX) with specialist domain understanding, and invited them to collaborate. The experts were (1) Jan Bikker, a practicing forensic anthropologist, with field experience of victim identification in the aftermath of disasters worldwide, (2) Elaine Kasket, a practicing psychologist, who specializes in death and bereavement, and (3) John Troyer, a Death Studies researcher.

The initial interviews informed the design of subsequent semi-structured interviews conducted with 9 UK-based death workers (DW) (7 male, 2 female), who worked as funeral directors (n=2), funeral celebrants (n=3), social media entrepreneurs specializing in legacies and memorialization (n=2), a crematorium manager (n=1) and an international disaster management company representative (n=1). Acting as key informants, DWs were able to give insights into both their own technology deployment, and that of the many bereaved individuals that they supported – e.g. one of the funeral directors who we interviewed carried out around 500 civilian and military funerals a year.

Participants were recruited at an international conference, *Death and Dying in the Digital Age* (organized by the Centre for Death and Society, University of Bath), and also through emails and phone calls. Research was subject to ethical approval at the University of Dundee. All participants gave informed consent to participation. Interviews were conducted by telephone/ Skype (n=4) or face-to-face at participants' workplaces (n=5). Interviews were structured around set topics which allowed for comparison across participants:

- How participants used technology to support their work.
- Participants' observations of how other death workers involved in funerals and final disposition used technology to support their work.
- How the bereaved used technology in organizing and contributing to the funeral.

Most participants volunteered much extra information. Interviews lasted between ½ - 3 hours, and were recorded and transcribed. Visits to workplaces (crematorium, church, funeral parlor, disaster management facility, home office) furthered contextual understanding and delivered surprising insights. For example, the crematorium manager claimed "*We don't use any technology at all here*" during a tour of his facility, yet demonstrated complex furnace control software. Analysis of the interview data was conducted and verified, and then themes were synthesized. Interpretation was member-checked with available DW participants (n=3).

Following on from the interviews, we conducted extensive systematic internet searches of products currently on the market, based on criteria generated from EX and DW interviews.

PROCESSES AND STAKEHOLDERS IN THE PMI

Despite its brevity, the PMI is densely packed with processes and stakeholders. We provide a description of these as a background to the subsequent description of the role of technology after the end of life, and the analysis of design implications. Table 1 provides a supporting summary of the activities and stakeholders involved in the two routine processes: the funeral and final disposition.

The Funeral

Consistent with other milestone events in people's lives, such as births and weddings, it is customary in the UK to mark a death with a ritualized social event. In the case of death, this event is a funeral. The funeral ritual serves as a point of discontinuity in the mourners' physical connection to the deceased, and hence helps mourners to accept the reality of the loss. At the same time, however, a 'good' funeral facilitates a sense of continuing bond to the deceased. It achieves this by interpreting and conveying an accurate picture of the person to the community through the eulogy/tribute, and by providing an opportunity for mourners to begin or continue the process of (re)constructing the deceased's identity [20]. This helps form a '*durable biography*' with which the living will continue to connect [42]. Failure of these processes may result in a 'bad' funeral that, in the worst case scenario, adversely affects the grieving process on an individual and community level.

Unlike other milestone events, there may be intense time pressures in organizing and conducting a funeral. Even when a death is expected, its specific date is not set in advance. As funerals are usually held within a week of the death, this leaves a short space of time in which to organize an event that brings together people from across an individual's social networks. Efficient event facilitation is essential. Organization and execution of a funeral is a collaborative process, involving a number of stakeholders, who are shown in Table 1. They include the deceased, the chief mourner(s)[1], the funeral director/ undertaker, the funeral celebrant, family and friends. The role of chief mourner may not always be taken by the legal next-of-kin: this depends on legal and social constructions over kinship and marriage, and the availability and willingness of someone to take on this role [39].

The deceased may have left instructions for how they wish their funeral to be carried out, and have paid for the funeral directors' services in advance. Otherwise, the chief mourner

[1] There may be more than one chief mourner; however, we refer to *one* chief mourner for simplicity in the remainder of the text.

Process	Task	Stakeholders								
		De	*CM*	*NK*	*FD*	*Cel*	*FF*	*Med*	*BgC*	*Gov*
Funeral	Appoint funeral director	Y	Y							
	Inform social network of death / funeral	Y	Y		Y		Y			
	Arrange venue, transport, flowers, catering	Y	Y		Y					
	Viewing the body		Y		Y		Y			
	Write eulogy	Y	Y			Y				
	Select music	Y	Y			Y				
	Attend funeral	Y	Y	Y	Y	Y	Y			
	Book of remembrance		Y				Y			
	Memorialization	Y	Y		Y		Y			
	Arrange bereavement counseling		Y		Y	Y	Y	Y		
Final disposition	Lay body out		Y		Y					
	Process death certificate			Y	Y			Y		Y
	Administration			Y						Y
	Purchase of burial plot	Y	Y	Y	Y				Y	
	Reserve crematorium for use		Y		Y				Y	
	Order coffin & headstone	Y	Y		Y				Y	

Table 1: Tasks and Stakeholders for Funeral & Final Disposition

De= Deceased; CM=Chief mourner(s); NK=Next-of-kin; FD=Funeral director; Cel=Celebrant; FF= Friends & Family; Me= Medical staff; BgC = Burial ground/ Crematorium workers; Gov=Govt/Municipal administrators;

will select a funeral director, if they intend to use one. A funeral celebrant[2] (e.g. religious officiant, humanist celebrant) is also selected and instructed, either by the bereaved or the funeral director. A venue for the funeral must be booked, potential attendees notified of the death and invited to the funeral, transport for the deceased and close family members arranged, the eulogy written and music chosen. In the immediate aftermath of the funeral, the chief mourner and attendees at the funeral may write comments about the deceased in a Book of Remembrance, or take other steps to memorialize them. Those experiencing a high level of distress may also seek out bereavement counseling – perhaps through a counselor recommended by the funeral director or celebrant.

While the nature of the event itself is likely to be shaped by faith, culture and community, its format is not static. As one celebrant described, in the past, "*you very rarely …talked about the person …there was never much in the way of real flavor (*of the deceased)". However, "*what has happened over the years, in all sections of society, is that people are now much more intentional and informed about the funeral, and they want it individualized".* Individualization is achieved through use of "*…a bit of music they liked, some readings, some poetry, a few memories …friends saying something about the person*".

[2] In the UK, it is common for the celebrant to read the eulogy and lead the ceremony.

Final disposition

In contrast to the funeral, final disposition of the body is a predominantly physical and administrative process. This process may involve the chief mourner, next-of-kin, funeral director and associated staff, government and municipal departments, medical staff, and employees of a cemetery or crematorium. '*Next-of-kin*' is a legally recognized administrative role, distinct from that of chief mourner. Separate people may fulfill these two roles - although such cases have arisen most frequently in same-sex partnerships where the couple cannot marry *and* the deceased has not designated a non-family member as the official next-of-kin.

Before final disposition can occur, a death certificate must be issued by the Registrar [9]. Issue is contingent on the next-of-kin providing numerous official documents, including a medical certificate signed by a doctor indicating cause of death, a birth certificate, and evidence of the deceased's last address. The next-of-kin is also responsible for informing numerous government and municipal departments of the death – e.g. to cancel the deceased's passport, driving license and government-supplied pension.

The body is prepared ('laid out') for final disposition by the chief mourner, or by the funeral director and their staff. A coffin and perhaps a headstone are chosen by the chief mourner. Once the death certificate is issued, the body is usually buried or cremated. If the body is to be buried, the location of a vacant plot in the cemetery must be identified, and its future occupant recorded by an administrator. The plot must be purchased - usually by the chief mourner or by the deceased when they were alive. If the body is to be cremated, a time slot must be booked at the crematorium.

Victim Identification

The funeral and disposition of the body usually occur only after the body has been identified. Identification may be required in cases of suspicious and non-natural death, medico-legal investigation and cases in which questions arise as to the identity of the deceased (e.g. when a body is washed ashore). In the case of a natural disaster, accident or deliberate attack – e.g. the 2010 earthquake in Haiti - identification may be a "*highly complex and sensitive task*" [21, p98] involving victims, their family and friends, and multiple agencies: governments, non-governmental organizations (NGOs) such as the Red Cross, local and international law enforcement agencies, medical teams, disaster management companies and Disaster Victim Identification (DVI) teams. Especially in a large natural disaster, this process may be conducted against a backdrop of infrastructure breakdown and escalating health risks, as transport and communication links are severed and basic sanitation fails. In extreme conditions (e.g. massive fatalities following a natural disaster), it may be impossible to identify all fatalities.

The agencies engaged in victim identification – notably the DVI team or forensic scientists - will draw upon ante-mortem and post-mortem data to assist them in their task [4]. For each potential missing person, ante-mortem data will be collected and may include medical and dental records, photos, and even criminal records, drawn from multiple sources. Those that knew the missing person also have a role to play in describing them, what they were wearing when last seen, and the personal effects that they commonly carried. Post-mortem data is assembled from the body and from artifacts at the scene such as jewelry and mobile phones. The DVI team will endeavor to find a match between ante-mortem and post-mortem data, and thus identify the missing person and unidentified remains.

TECHNOLOGY DEPLOYMENT DURING THE PMI

In the funeral, final disposition and victim identification, stakeholders are increasingly using technologies to support the processes that they are engaged in, through:

- Facilitation of service provision
- Information seeking
- Mediated communications
- Personalization of artifacts/ events

Some technologies are designed specifically for purpose, others are repurposed. This technology deployment is not without problems, which we reflect upon here.

Funerals

Facilitation of service provision

The chief mourner's quest for a suitable funeral director may be facilitated by online searches. She/ he may even organize the funeral and burial/ cremation through an online funeral director – although this service is currently limited to the US and Canada [13]. Funeral directors can get online training in how to mobilize social media resources to attract potential clients via the internet[3].

Funeral directors may also use technology to expedite routine tasks, to the benefit of their clients:

*"I was with the husband of this lady that died and I've got an iPad. It beeped and up came an email from the local newspaper which confirmed the name of his dead wife and also had a proof of the way it (*death notice*) would look in the paper. I was able to hand him the iPad and he was like 'My God! That's really great!' I was able to get an approval on that literally in seconds."* Funeral director

Information seeking

The chief mourner(s) may seek advice online about how to organize a funeral. It may be difficult for them to identify which sites to trust. In the absence of consistent credentialing for sites, the bereaved are likely to make judgments on what online advice to take based on a professional 'designed' appearance, ease of understanding and ease of use [35], yet these sites may lack impartiality and reliable content. For example, [12] offers a "*free consumer information, education and resource community*", yet the proffered services are provided through "*strategic (*commercial*) alliances*". The same site provides bereavement advice based on Kubler-Ross's outmoded '5 Stages of Grief' model – a model challenged by empirical research [23]. Advice based on this model may be unhelpfully misleading and potentially distressing to bereaved individuals, by making them feel that the course of their grief is not 'normal'.

Mediated communications

Organization of the funeral may involve computer-mediated communications (CMCs). Although the initial meeting between the chief mourner and funeral director is likely to be face-to-face, subsequent communications may be mediated synchronously (e.g. Skype) or asynchronously (e.g. SMS). The funeral director may use email to manage potential conflicts between mourners:

[3] http://www.funeralfuturist.com/social-media-week/

"*... You can ensure that everybody gets exactly the same information at exactly the same time. Not keeping everyone informed is one of the big dangers you see. If you say to one person 'Who do you want to receive the information?' and they go 'You better send it to him, 'cos he's the eldest', you can end up with conflict within the family, because what happens if the eldest decides he doesn't want to show the rest of the family? It's a good way of resolving that problem.*" Funeral director

CMCs may also be used to give news of a death and funeral arrangements to the deceased's wider social network. Whilst those directly affected by the death are likely to be informed by the chief mourner in person or by phone, the burden of communicating to the wider social network may be alleviated through use of CMCs – e.g. use of emails and a posting on the social network site (SNS) previously used by the deceased. CMCs may also be used to avoid interaction, when those giving news do not feel like talking, yet need to convey information in a timely manner [24]. When the deceased has kept contact information for their social networks in a password-protected repository, and not shared their password, it may be difficult or impossible to give those in the wider social network the news, online or offline.

News also travels by word-of-mouth, and through '*death notices*'. Death notices are traditionally placed in a local or national newspaper, but are now frequently transferred online, either as part of the service provided by the newspaper publisher, or by the appointed funeral director. Some online sites for death notices are poorly implemented and display inappropriate advertising. For example, we searched for a death notice relating to a specific, recently deceased individual on one popular site[4], using the person's full name and location. Her husband had placed the death notice in the local newspaper. Unexpectedly, 3,602 results were returned in apparently random order for name and date of death, despite the deceased having an unusual name. The resulting search pages also displayed adverts for *"Over 60s Dating Exclusively for seniors. Join free!"* - overstepping boundaries of appropriateness.

Remote participation in the funeral itself is made possible through technology. This is becoming more common as population mobility, increasing secularity, and the ubiquity of social media erode the convention of attending a funeral in person [17]. The cost of travel and the swift turnaround time from death to disposition also play their part:

"*We recently had a lady, she'd just turned 50. She died of cancer ...but she knows people all over the world. So we broadcast the funeral live. We had something like 60 computers watching it. Some people can't afford to travel, or ...because of the short notice they can't, so you stream it online. Now, we guesstimated that there was 100+, a family of 5, lots of individuals, lots of little groups of friends who knew her, who sat down & watched it together.*" Celebrant

Such remote participation raises questions of privacy, access and performance. It is common for webcast access to be by invitation only, controlled by a password [45]. The process of gaining secure access to the webcast may itself present an obstacle to legitimate viewing, through poor usability - e.g. secure access to one funeral webcast site involves a minimum of eight separate steps after the user has been sent the password [45]. Viewers of the funeral webcast may also experience technology failures, leading them to miss out on some/ all of the funeral [3]. Such failures may cause disappointment to the bereaved. Furthermore, as the funeral may be instrumental in helping the bereaved to accomplish one of the basic tasks of adapting to a death – accepting the reality of the loss [44] – a technology failure has the potential to interfere with progress through this task, which in turn could increase the risk of complicated grief [33].

Bereaved individuals who are significantly affected by a death may seek counseling that is mediated via the Web. It can be difficult for the bereaved to identify a reputable, qualified counselor online. Numerous ethics codes identify critical areas of concern in online counseling with vulnerable individuals: specifically, credentialing, duty to warn and protect, informed consent, and confidentiality [36]. The efficacy and ethics of commercial online counseling services certainly vary. Some offer superficial services – e.g. *"365 days of emails to cheer you up!"*[5] Others offer interactive online videos and virtual meetings where *"family members living in different parts of the world can come together online to share the healing process, under the guidance of a trained grief counselor"*[6]. It is critical to note that bereaved persons may need the help of a professional to assess their needs, and to provide tailored intervention where there is risk – rather than just picking a service online without guidance. While the majority of bereaved individuals negotiate the grieving process effectively and well, grief is idiosyncratic, and a significant minority experience serious ill effects and negative outcomes, including early mortality [14]. The individual nature of grief means that 'one-size-fits-all' counseling services, online or otherwise, risk being ineffective or even harmful.

Personalization of artifacts/ events

Increasingly, technology is playing a role in the personalization of funerals. The deceased may have articulated how they want their funeral to be conducted in advance, perhaps using an end-of-life planning tool [7] to store music and photos for use at the service, and to propose

[4] http://www.iannounce.co.uk/.

[5] http://www.mountcastle.net/grief-and-healing/365-days-of-grief-support

[6] http://www.funeralone.com/aftercare/

what should be said in the eulogy. Such tools are available online (e.g. www.aftersteps.com), and as an iPhone app (www.legacyorganiser.com). In the absence of posthumous instructions, the bereaved may prepare their own materials. They may draw on digital photos to create a personalized Order of Service sheet, or use a digital soundtrack to evoke memories of the deceased:

"He liked birdwatching. They sent him off to a chorus of birdsong they got from a CD." Celebrant

A multimedia backdrop to the funeral service may be created to great effect, repurposing personal images, video and music:

"I did a funeral for a lady in her late forties. She'd done a parachute jump for charity not long before she died. That was projected onto a big screen in the church, the video of her doing the jump, and it was set to music, to 'Viva la Vida'. People sat & watched that for 7-8 minutes and it brought her to life in some ways." Funeral director

Personalization may be achieved through ordinary desktop software such as Microsoft Office, through software designed specifically for the task[7], or through specialist commercial services [12]. Where digital artifacts are available, their repurposing is creating a new role amongst the bereaved. If a chief mourner lacks technology skills, they may seek help in preparing a digital tribute from (often younger) members of the deceased's social network:

"His (the chief mourner's) *teenage step-daughter got the music together. He didn't know how to do it."* Celebrant

Children and younger adults have traditionally been excluded from the organization of a funeral, and friends have often been disenfranchised in mourning [11]; however, friends and young people often have privileged access to a repository of information about deceased individuals via social networks, giving them a valuable part to play in constructing the deceased's identity [42]. However, opportunities for personalization may be significantly reduced if the digital artifacts belonging to the deceased are password protected. No consistent mechanism exists across internet service providers to bequeath digital assets [7,28]. In the short term, this may limit the ability to create a personalized funeral tribute. In the longer term, precious resources which help people to grieve and to maintain a continuing bond with the deceased may be lost.

Final disposition

Information seeking

Those who are preparing the body for final disposition can access online training in how to do it, both through text-based instructions [10] and YouTube videos[8]. Information is available on all aspects of final disposition, including embalming. Videos are not usually flagged as potentially disturbing to watch, despite their challenging content. While moderate/safe filters try to eliminate sites that contain explicit sexual content from video search results, they lack the sophistication to identify other 'difficult' and potentially distressing content – such as laying out or embalming a body.

Facilitation of service provision

The death of an individual involves an administrative final disposition, as well as a physical one. When reporting a death in the UK, next-of-kin can be drawn into a byzantine paperwork process involving up to 22 different government and municipal departments. In some areas, a central government service called *Tell Us Once* [43] enables next-of-kin to report the death just once. This automated service then facilitates the provision of updates to all necessary departments, reducing costs for the departments and effort and distress for the next-of-kin. However, this service is limited to government and municipal departments: it does not notify banks, utility companies, insurers, etc. Next-of-kin still have a vast array of individual companies to update. There is much to be done to streamline the routine administrative processes required once a death certificate is issued.

The routine processes involved in the management and care of cemeteries are gradually evolving, as municipal bodies, private cemetery owners and archaeological groups involved in the management and care of cemeteries adopt commonly-available technologies to facilitate records management, using mapping software to document the location of vacant/ occupied burial plots, where individuals are buried, and their date of burial[9]. Through a process of digital curation, the central database[10] for UK burials and cremations also provides online access to cremation and burial records, digital scans of cremation and burial registers and books of remembrance. Such practices improve accessibility of information for the public.

Crematoria also deploy technology. In their case, it is to facilitate the safe, pollution-free operation of furnaces. Although cremation uses the same physical processes as it did in the 19th Century, the software[11] used to control the operation of crematorium furnaces is entirely contemporary [39]. As well as controlling temperature and operating time, the crematorium furnace software plays a key role in ensuring legal UK and EU emission limits are not breached. It is vital that the user interface for operating the furnace is straightforward: a furnace malfunction can result in an explosion, causing distress to the bereaved whose loved one

[7] E.g. http://www.funeralhymnsheets.co.uk/

[8] E.g. http://www.youtube.com/watch?v=PdRC9SCvHlo

[9] E.g. http://www.trail.ca/mapping/cemetery.php

[10] http://www.deceasedonline.com/

[11] E.g. http://www.facultatieve-technologies.com

was being cremated. Some crematoria also use tracking software, to ensure that the correct cremated remains (ashes) are returned to the bereaved. The tracking software hinges on the use of a ceramic or metal barcode tag (a remembrance code) which can withstand extreme temperatures [39]. The tag is placed in the furnace with the body of the deceased, and stays with the resulting ashes as they are processed and returned to the bereaved[12].

Personalization of artifacts/ events

Traditional methods of personalizing funeral goods (e.g. headstone, casket) are being augmented/ replaced by technology-based personalization. Funeral urns, used to store ashes, can now incorporate a screen that displays digital images of the deceased [16]. Further repurposing of digital images – and indeed of ashes – can be seen in the service offered by memorial artists[13] who incorporate ashes into a painting. The painting is often based on a digital photo of either the deceased or a favorite location that they had. QR codes and RFID tags attached to headstones [1] enable visitors who carry an internet-enabled phone to discover additional information about the deceased. Content is usually provided by the bereaved. The use of technology in these contexts calls for technological longevity. UK graveyards contain headstones that are many centuries old, with durable stone inscriptions which provide vivid insights into the lives of the long-dead. Will QR codes and RFID tags be as durable, as technology storage and access methods evolve with rapidity?

The search for funeral goods may be facilitated through online shopping, where the chief mourner may find a wider range of goods than is offered by the average local funeral director [15]. Internet-based marketplaces can deliver increased personalization and customization of products, and competitive pricing strategies [2]. However, the online provision of funeral goods has encountered opposition from some in the funeral trade, who have traditionally acted as a lucrative 'one-stop shop' in providing goods and services to the bereaved. In many US states, online sales of coffins and memorials are also constrained by regulations [8]. This situation is at odds with competitive practice in other retail spheres, but is on the cusp of change as the US considers legislative changes.

Victim Identification

Facilitation of service provision

Before the attack on the World Trade Center, "*software tools for storing, tracking, comparing, annotating and curating* (DVI) *data had never been considered a priority in North America*"[6]. Since the attack, there has been considerable effort invested into developing such tools, both in North America and worldwide. Although victim identification is ultimately reliant on human expertise, DVI software tools can speed up efforts in disasters involving a large number of deaths. Automated comparison of ante-mortem and post-mortem data can expedite the matching process and provide a shortlist of candidates [4, 22]. Technology deployment may involve multiple systems, and stakeholders from multiple agencies and/or governments. Some systems integrate multiple identification methods - e.g. Plassdata™, used by Interpol, performs matches on dental features, physical and medical characteristics, personal belongings and DNA. Other systems are designed to use a single identification method - e.g. OptoSearch™ calculates the frequency of occurrence for specific or generalized eye or eyeglass prescriptions [4]. However, such custom-designed software is costly. National efforts and laboratory-based solutions using standard PC applications such as Microsoft Excel spreadsheets and Photoshop have also been used in a number of disasters - e.g. [32].

The multiple stakeholders and systems involved in victim identification can create data management and integration challenges, exacerbated by international variation in standards – e.g. in the UK, identification of 7 corresponding fingerprint characteristics between ante- and post-mortem data constitutes a confirmed match, yet in the US, 15 characteristics are required. Further problems can be caused by inconsistent naming conventions: cultural variations on 'family name' and 'first name' may cause confusion, causing investigators to look for the wrong person – e.g. 'Wayne John', rather than 'John Wayne'. These challenges can impact adversely on timely victim identification, unless a central system is put in place to integrate data. As far as we are aware, Kenyon Response™ [19] is the only system to do this.

Information seeking & mediated communication

In addition to specialist DVI software tools, Web 2.0 applications have been used in disasters, circumventing organizational barriers to share information between government and non-governmental organizations (NGOs), family and friends [18]. These applications have assisted in victim identification, reuniting families and friends, and organizing aid – e.g. the Facebook site *Haiti Earthquake Hotel Montana*[14], (also used more recently to maintain a social network amongst those bereaved in the earthquake and to commemorate the anniversary of the event), and Google's *Person Finder* (used in the aftermath of natural disasters, such as the 2011 New Zealand earthquake and the 2011 earthquake in Japan[15]). An international cohort of volunteers and relatives have contributed data to *Person Finder*, by scraping websites and extracting information

[12] E.g. http://www.matthewscremation.com/technology/security.aspx

[13] E.g. http://www.cremationsolutions.com/

[14] http://www.facebook.com/#!/pages/Haiti-Earthquake-Hotel-Montana/245595172631

[15] http://japan.person-finder.appspot.com/?lang=en

from blogs, texts and tweets, then adding relevant information to the site. This surge of benign global activity has had many positive benefits. However there have been some issues with information validity. Instances of malign individuals (trolls) giving fake reports of deaths [29] were met with a swift response by Google.

DVI teams may also use Web 2.0 resources to gather ante-mortem data, to help them to identify victims when routine methods fail. Images available on SNS of a suspected victim can provide vital clues to appearance, showing features that family members are perhaps unaware of. For example, family members may not know that the victim had a distinctive tattoo on their body, yet the victim may have shared a photo of it with friends via an SNS. DVI teams may face difficulties in accessing these materials, depending on the privacy settings in place for the SNS page. Further, if the next-of-kin asks for the victim's SNS account to be closed, this vital resource is lost to the DVI team.

IMPLICATIONS FOR DESIGN

Fresh design insights can be distilled from consideration of the roles played by technology after EoL, and the identified problems.

Funerals

While technology can play a useful role in organizing and carrying out a funeral, problems of *credibility, appropriateness, access* and *usability* emerge. Some of these problems generalize beyond the context of the PMI. Websites containing credible information and services may be hard for users to identify - not only for bereavement counseling [36], but also for health, politics and finance [37]. Recommender systems fail to make wholly appropriate recommendations for users who search online [38], whether the user is the widower viewing their wife's death notice online who we described earlier, or a US lawyer unaccountably receiving recommendations for Korean news broadcasts [46]. Users' desires for ease of access may be confounded as tensions persist between the diametrically opposed needs for security and usability in password-based systems, whether their goal is to access a secure funeral webcast or to legitimately withdraw money at the cashpoint [27].

Final disposition

When conducting an administrative 'final disposition', the absence of a seamless central process to inform all interested commercial, governmental and municipal parties of a person's death leads to increased effort and distress for the next-of-kin. Can technology designers mitigate this process by creating a comprehensive version of the *Tell Us Once* service [43] which reduces or eliminates costly duplication across commercial, government and municipal boundaries, and calls on the next-of-kin to take a single administrative step, rather than many separate ones?

Instructional videos for final disposition highlight the inadequacy of current video 'safe' search facilities. Users vary in what content they find offensive/ distressing – e.g. a funeral director and a university student will almost certainly differ. Final disposition videos highlight the need for personalization of safe search categories that go beyond current ones for merely sexual/ pornographic content.

The question of technology longevity, raised in relation to QR codes and RFID tags, generalizes to the question of how we design for memorialization, and to storing important information in any context. With the rapid evolution of technology, there is a risk that vital data becomes unreadable in the future. How can we ensure that this risk is eliminated?

Victim Identification

Even when data is readable, we have described how it may have different meanings to different stakeholders, and result in unnecessary confusion. The integration problems experienced in DVI, generated through the use of multiple systems by multiple stakeholders, highlight the need for international, cross-cultural consistency in the design of universally common data items such as a person's name.

The use of SNS data as a piece of the puzzle in victim identification creates a new role for SNS accounts – and perhaps a need for a new status category. Some SNS (e.g. Facebook) already allow next-of-kin to memorialize a deceased individual's account. We propose that an additional status should be "*Missing*". Associated with this status, read-only rights of access could be granted to recognized agencies that are assisting in the search for the individual in question. Rather than messages to reconnect being disabled (as they are when an individual's page is memorialized), these messages could be replaced with requests for network members to contact a central point, if they have information that helps to find or identify the missing person. Such a change would assist DVI teams and police.

We have described the remarkable leveraging of human goodwill which has emerged from the global use of Web 2.0, as information about those missing in recent natural disasters and accidents was input and analyzed. The abuse of Web 2.0 by 'trolls' in the wake of these events [29] provokes questions of access and accountability. Enabling continued use of Web 2.0 in this socially benign vein, whilst excluding irresponsible trolling and fake reports, remains a worthwhile challenge to be addressed.

DISCUSSION

In broadening existing discussions of technology design for EoL to include a critical, underexplored time period and its stakeholders, we have two aims. Firstly, to motivate designers to consider ways in which personal data has utility after a user's death, beyond recent HCI work focusing on bereavement and memorialization. Secondly, to inform the design of technologies that help to coordinate processes in the PMI, through provision of new cross-disciplinary understanding of technology deployment.

In this paper, we have focused specifically on three processes involved in the PMI, where technology acts as a servant of the stakeholders by facilitating provision of services and information, mediating communications, and assisting in the personalization of artifacts and events. The adoption of a process-oriented participatory approach allowed us to combine knowledge across the disciplines of HCI, forensic anthropology, psychology and death studies, and to draw on the knowledge of professional death workers. Through this approach, we developed a fresh understanding of the role that technology plays after EoL, and the associated problems.

The brief period from death to final disposition involves a series of remarkably rich collaborative processes, made up of sets of discrete, complex and sensitive tasks, carried out by stakeholders with clear roles. While the specificity of roles and the time pressures involved in PMI task completion are common to many CSCW activities, the sensitivities of the PMI and the extreme 'remote location' of the central actor (the deceased) generate unique demands. Through this uniqueness, we hope to create a lens that can offer fresh design insights for the HCI community, drawing on the concept of "*extra-ordinary users*" and the opportunity for "*radical starting points*" [34, p257] to inspire fresh solutions which generalize beyond the PMI.

ACKNOWLEDGMENTS

We are grateful for the insights provided by death workers who assisted us in our research, and to Dr Rachid Hourizi, for his constructive review of this paper. Wendy Moncur acknowledges the financial support of the EPSRC, grant no. EP/I026304/1.

REFERENCES

1. Anderson, K. The Value-added Tombstone. *The Death Reference Desk*, 2011. http://deathreferencedesk.org/2011/05/22/the-value-added-tombstone/.
2. Bakos, Y. The Emerging Role of Electronic Marketplaces on the Internet. *Communications of the ACM 41*, 8 (1998).
3. Bambuck, M. Online Funerals a Growing Trend? - ABC News. *ABC News*, 2007. http://abcnews.go.com/International/story?id=2947262&page=1.
4. Bikker, J. Experimental studies into modal and joint modal comparison of compromised genetic and dental data in disaster victim identification. Doctoral Thesis. University of Sheffield. 2008.
5. Brubaker, J.R. and Vertesi, J. Death and the Social Network. *Proc. CHI Workshop on Death and the Social Network*, (2010).
6. Budowle, B., Bieber, F.R., and Eisenberg, A.J. Forensic aspects of mass disasters: Strategic considerations for DNA-based human identification. *Legal Medicine 7*, 4 (2005), 230-243.
7. Carroll, E. and Romano, J. *Your Digital Afterlife*. New Riders, Berkeley, CA, 2011.
8. Chevalier, J. and Morton, F.S. State Casket Sales and Restrictions: A Pointless Undertaking? 2006, 1-31. http://www.nber.org/papers/w12012.
9. Citizens Advice Bureau. What to do after a death. 2011. http://www.adviceguide.org.uk/index/your_family/family_index_ew/what_to_do_after_a_death.htm.
10. Cowling, C. The Good Funeral Guide. 2011. http://www.goodfuneralguide.co.uk/.
11. Doka, K.J. *Disenfranchised grief: Recognizing hidden sorrow*. Lexington Books, Lexington, MA, USA, 1998.
12. FuneralResources.com. Funeral Memorial Services,Funeral Plan,Funeral Costs,Grief. 2010. http://www.funeralresources.com/.
13. Gonsalves, A. Basic Funerals Bets Baby Boomers Will Arrange Cremations Online. *Bloomberg News*, 2011. http://www.bloomberg.com/news/2011-04-05/basic-funerals-bets-baby-boomers-will-arrange-cremations-online.html.
14. Haley, W.E., Larson, D.G., Kasl-Godley, J., Neimeyer, R.A., and Kwilosz, D.M. Roles for Psychologists in End-of-Life Care: Emerging Models of Practice. *Professional Psychology: Research and Practice 34*, 6 (2003), 626-633.
15. Harrington, D.E. Breathing Life into the Funeral Market. *Regulation Spring*, 2003, 14-18.
16. Holle, M. Inventing the Future of Death. *Death Reference Desk*, 2010. http://deathreferencedesk.org/2010/05/24/inventing-the-future-of-death/.
17. Holson, L.M. Private Funerals Now Streamed Online. *NYTimes.com*, 2011. http://www.nytimes.com/2011/01/25/fashion/25death.html?_r=1.
18. Hughes, A.L., Palen, L., Sutton, J., Liu, S.B., and Vieweg, S. Site-seeing in disaster: An examination of on-line social convergence. *Proc. 5th International ISCRAM Conference*, (2008).
19. Kenyon International Emergency Services. Kenyon Response is here! 2011. http://www.kenyoninternational.com/forum/showthread.php?t=241.

20. Klass, D., Silverman, P.R., and Nickman, S.L. *Continuing bonds: new understandings of grief.* Taylor & Francis, Washington, DC., USA, 1996.

21. London Assembly. *Report of the 7/7 review committee.* London, UK, 2006.

22. Lorton, L. and Langley, W. Design and use of a computer-assisted postmortem identification system. *J Forensic Sci 3*, (1986), 972-981.

23. Maciejewski, P.K., Zhang, B., Block, S.D., and Prigerson, H.G. An empirical examination of the stage theory of grief. *JAMA 297*, 7 (2007), 716-23.

24. Massimi, M. and Baecker, R.M. Dealing with death in design: Developing systems for the bereaved. *Proc. CHI'11*, ACM (2011), 1001-1010.

25. Massimi, M., Moncur, W., Odom, W., Banks, R., and Kirk, D. Memento Mori: Technology Design for the End of Life. *Proc. CHI'12*, ACM (2012).

26. Massimi, M., Odom, W., Banks, R., and Kirk, D. Matters of life and death: Locating the end of life in lifespan-oriented HCI research. *Proc. CHI'11*, ACM (2011).

27. Moncur, W. and LePlatre, G. Pictures at the ATM□: Exploring the usability of multiple graphical passwords. *Proc. CHI'07*, ACM (2007), 887-894.

28. Moncur, W. and Waller, A. Digital Inheritance. *RCUK Digital Futures 2010*, Horizon Digital Economy Research (2010).

29. Mullany, A. and Jantzen, D. After Japan's earthquake and tsunami, tech tools provide information and help families reconnect. *NYDailyNews.com*, 2011. http://www.nydailynews.com/tech_guide/2011/03/11/2011-03-11_how_technology_is_helping_in_the_aftermath_of_japans_earthquake_and_tsunami.html.

30. Muller, M.J. Participatory design: The third space in HCI. In A. Sears and J.A. Jacko, eds., *The Human-Computer Interaction Handbook.* Lawrence Erlbaum Associates, Oxford, UK, 2008, 10610-1081.

31. Odom, W., Harper, R., Sellen, A., Kirk, D., and Banks, R. Passing on and putting to rest: Understanding bereavement in the context of interactive technologies. *Proc. CHI'10*, ACM (2010), 1831-1840.

32. Piccinini A., Betti F., Capra M., Cattaneo, C. The identification of the victims of the Linate air crash by DNA analysis. *International Congress Series 1 1261*, (2004), 39-41.

33. Prigerson, H.G. and Jacobs, S.C. Traumatic grief as a distinct disorder: A rationale, consensus criteria, and a preliminary empirical test. In M.S. Stroebe, R.O. Hansson, W. Stroebe and H.A.W. Schut, eds., *Handbook of Bereavement Research: Consequences, Coping, and Care.* American Psychological Association, Washington, DC, USA, 2001, 613-647.

34. Pullin, G. and Newell, A. Focussing on extra-ordinary users. *Proceedings of the 4th international conference on Universal access in human computer interaction: coping with diversity*, Springer-Verlag (2007), 253-262.

35. Robins, D. and Holmes, J. Aesthetics and credibility in web site design. *Information Process Management 44*, 1 (2008), 386-399.

36. Ross, W. Ethical issues involved in online counseling. *Journal of Psychological Issues in Organizational Culture 2*, 1 (2011), 54-66.

37. Schwarz, J. and Morris, M. Augmenting web pages and search results to support credibility assessment. *Proc. CHI'11*, ACM Press (2011), 1245-1254.

38. Tintarev, N. and Masthoff, J. Evaluating the effectiveness of explanations for recommender systems: Methodological issues and empirical studies on the impact of personalization. *UMUAI* (Accepted, to appear).

39. Troyer, J. *Technologies of the Human Corpse.* University of North Carolina Press, 2012.

40. Uriu, D. and Okude, N. ThanatoFenestra: photographic family altar supporting a ritual to pray for the deceased. *Proc. DIS'10*, ACM (2010), 422-425.

41. Walter, T., Hourizi, R., Moncur, W., and Pitsillides, S. Does the internet change how we die and mourn? An overview. *Omega: Journal of Death & Dying 64*, 4 (2011-12), 275-302.

42. Walter, T. Mediator Deathwork. *Death Studies 29*, 5 (2005).

43. Wirral Borough Council. Tell Us Once service. 2011. http://www.wirral.gov.uk/my-services/community-and-living/deaths-cemeteries-and-crematoria/registering-death/tell-us-once-service.

44. Worden, J.W. *Grief Counseling and Grief Therapy: A Handbook for the Mental Health Practitioner.* Springer Publishing Company, New York, NY, USA, 1982.

45. Worthing Borough Council. Attend a Service Web-cast. 2008. http://www.worthing.gov.uk/worthings-services/cemeteriesandcrematoriums/crematoriums/attendaserviceweb-cast/.

46. Zaslow, J. If TiVo Thinks You Are Gay, Here's How to Set It Straight. *Wall Street Journal November 2*, (2002).

On Saliency, Affect and Focused Attention

Lori McCay-Peet
Dalhousie University
Halifax, Nova Scotia, Canada
mccay@dal.ca

Mounia Lalmas
Yahoo! Research
Barcelona, Spain
mounia@acm.org

Vidhya Navalpakkam
Yahoo! Research
Santa Clara, California, USA
nvidhya@yahoo-inc.com

ABSTRACT
We study how the visual catchiness (saliency) of relevant information impacts user engagement metrics such as focused attention and emotion (affect). Participants completed tasks in one of two conditions, where the task-relevant information either appeared salient or non-salient. Our analysis provides insights into relationships between saliency, focused attention, and affect. Participants reported more distraction in the non-salient condition, and non-salient information was slower to find than salient. Lack-of-saliency led to a negative impact on affect, while saliency maintained positive affect, suggesting its helpfulness. Participants reported that it was easier to focus in the salient condition, although there was no significant improvement in the focused attention scale rating. Finally, this study suggests user interest in the topic is a good predictor of focused attention, which in turn is a good predictor of positive affect. These results suggest that enhancing saliency of user-interested topics seems a good strategy for boosting user engagement.

Author Keywords
User engagement; saliency; focused attention; positive affect; user interests; news entertainment

ACM Classification Keywords
H5.m. Information interfaces and presentation: Miscellaneous.

General Terms
Human Factors, Experimentation, Measurement

INTRODUCTION
In web applications, *user engagement* refers to the quality of the user experience emphasizing the positive aspects of the interaction, in particular the phenomena associated with being captivated by the application, and wanting to use it frequently. User engagement is a key concept in the design of web applications, motivated by the observation that successful applications are not just used, they are engaged with. In a world full of choices, it is essential that technology providers do not just design systems but that they design engaging experiences [21].

User engagement can be improved by serving not only the most relevant content/functionality to users, but also by displaying it in a *visually catchy way*. The sensory and visual appeal of a web page is an important factor for engagement [18]. In the context of online shopping, web searching, educational webcasting and video games [18], web page style has been related to factors such as screen layout, graphics and the use of design principles such as symmetry and balance. In the context of multimedia design [8], web page style (here with respect to media quality) has been related to *positive affect* and to promote *focused attention*.

Positive affect and focused attention are important characteristics of user engagement [1]. Focused attention refers to the exclusion of other things [18]; while affect relates to the emotions experienced during the interaction. Jennings et al. [8] argue that affective experiences are intrinsically motivating and that, in relation to engagement, an initial affective hook can induce a desire for exploration or active discovery. One important, albeit less studied, aspect, of web page style, is the visual catchiness of items, known as *visual saliency*. The aim of this work is to study the effect of saliency on focused attention and positive affect.

Research in cognitive psychology and neuroscience show that when users see a display or visually search for a target object in a cluttered display, their attention and eye gaze are drawn to salient objects that appear visually different from the rest of the display [24]. For example, big, bolded, italicized and colored text surrounded by plain text appears visually catchy or salient and draws attention, due to the difference in size, orientation and color. More generally, differences in features such as color, brightness, edge orientation, size, motion and flicker are known to draw attention, independently of the user goal or intent [26].

While saliency is known to attract eye gaze in displays, we do not know if it leads to a better user affect and focused attention. To answer this question, we carried out a study within the news entertainment domain, where we measured, both quantitatively and qualitatively, affect and focused attention for a large sample of participants drawn from Amazon Mechanical Turk [13].

We carefully varied the saliency of the headlines in a news page from non-salient to salient, while keeping everything else fixed, and tested whether increasing saliency can help improve user task performance, and whether it impacts focused attention and affect. To help calibrate saliency of the headlines, we turn to a model of saliency [7] that takes in a screenshot of the news page as an input and predicts the salient hotspots that will likely draw user attention in the first few seconds of visiting that page.

CHI'12, May 5–10, 2012, Austin, Texas, USA.

The paper is organized as follows. We start with a description of our methodology. Next, we present our results, which we then discuss and relate to results from the literature. We end with implications and suggestions for future work.

METHODOLOGY

Our goal was to explore the impact of saliency on positive affect and focused attention. We selected the entertainment news domain knowing that the internet is a common way for people to get their entertainment news [20]. To ensure control of the saliency of web pages we were restricted in terms of the tasks to create. However, these restrictions allowed a more focused study at a more granular level, albeit at the expense of a less natural reading experience.

Participants drawn from Amazon Mechanical Turk were asked to complete an online study. There were two conditions for this study, salient and non-salient.

- *Salient:* this group is shown only entertainment web page images in which the task-based information is salient
- *Non-salient:* this group is shown only entertainment web page images in which the task-based information is not salient

The following hypotheses were tested using both quantitative and qualitative measures:

- *H1: Saliency of task-relevant information leads to greater task performance, both actual and perceived*
- *H2: Affect improves when the task-relevant information is salient compared to when it is not salient.*
- *H3: Saliency of task-relevant information leads to higher levels of focused attention.*

We were also interested in the interaction between participants' level of interest in the entertainment web page content with affect and focused attention, but due to its exploratory nature, we did not formulate hypotheses.

Saliency model

We used the saliency model of visual attention developed by Itti and Koch [7], inspired by how the primate visual cortex processes information to drive attention while freely viewing the display, in the absence of user goal. Extensions of this model have shown to predict user attention during visual search for a target object in a display [14], while watching video [4], and playing exploratory video games [22]. While the model is precognitive and agnostic to the semantics and user biases, it is a good predictor of attention in the first few seconds of seeing the display and hence serves as a good starting point to predict what might catch the users' eye as soon as they see the display.

In the first stage, the model extracts a set of biologically inspired features, such as color, brightness intensity, and edge orientation at various spatial scales. Feature difference maps are computed by determining the pair-wise difference in feature response at every image location between spatial scales. This results in 42 feature difference maps. In the second stage, the model mimics competitive interactions between neutrons by applying a difference of Gaussian filter (mimics the narrow self-excitatory connections between nearby neutrons and the broad inhibitory connections between far away neurons). This is followed by rectification to remove negative values.

A few iterations of such nonlinear competitive interactions results in highlighting only the salient hotspots in the display in each feature dimension i.e., those display regions whose features are different from the rest of the display. Finally, in the third stage, the model linearly combines the saliency maps from the various feature dimensions to a single master saliency map. Attention is then guided in decreasing order of saliency in this map, starting with the most salient hotspot, followed by the next most salient hotspot and so on until the entire display is visited.

Tasks

There were eight tasks in total for each participant to perform. Each task involved finding the latest news or headline on a different celebrity or entertainment topic (e.g., "Find the headline on Brad Pitt on the next page"). Task topics included Justin Bieber (singer), Sam Worthington (actor), Brad Pitt (actor), Halle Berry (actress), Disney (media conglomerate), Britney Spears (singer), David Letterman (television host), Brendan Gleesan (actor). Entertainment news web pages were selected from a variety of sources to ensure diversity of topic and presentation format (e.g., OMG Yahoo!, CinemaBlend.com, BBC Entertainments & Arts). Only the screenshots of the web pages were manipulated by condition. For consistency, the following manipulation criteria were applied:

1. All web page screenshots have a width:length ratio of 2:3
2. Location of headline on the pages is the same between conditions, although it may vary within a condition
3. Though pages may be scrolled, all headlines appear on the visible page (screen resolution of 1024 x768)
4. According to the saliency model of visual attention, headlines in the non-salient condition do not register as salient; those in the salient condition register as salient

Manipulations included increases in font size, changes in color of font or background, and addition or removal of image or icon. For example, Figure 1 shows the Justin Bieber task web page screenshot images. The headline (lower center of each image) has been manipulated in the salient condition; the font size has been increased, the subtitle font color has been altered and two large exclamation points added. To ensure these web page images contained a non-salient and a salient Bieber headline for their respective conditions, these visible page screenshots were uploaded to a program which automatically applies the saliency model of visual attention described in the previous section to the images. The

Figure 1. Web page screenshots for the Bieber task (non-salient condition at top, salient at bottom).

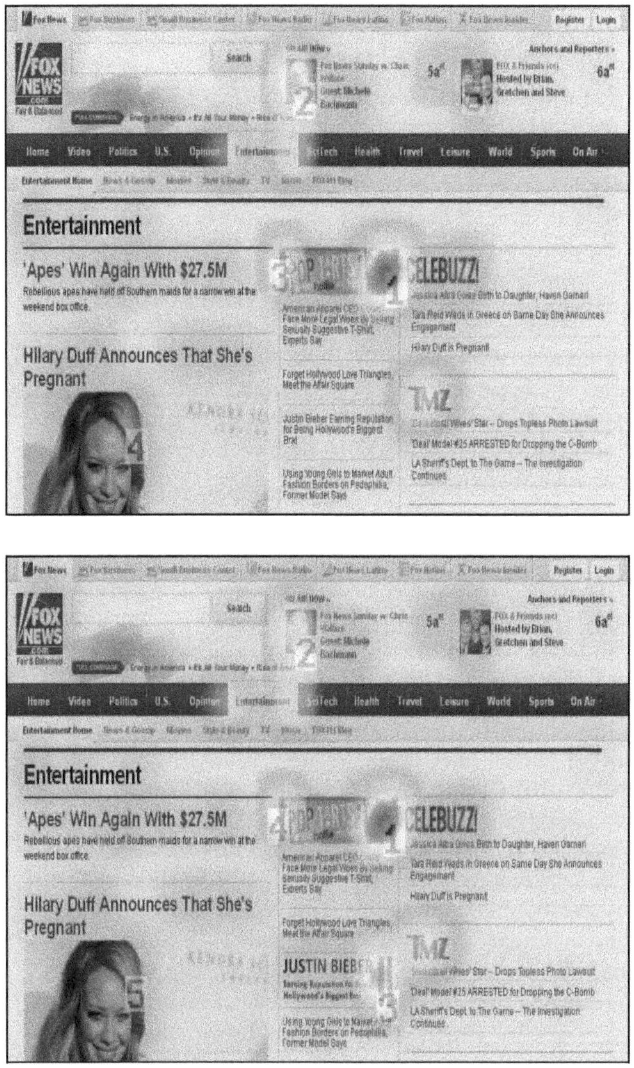

Figure 2. Saliency maps for the Bieber task (non-salient condition at top, salient at bottom)

program outputs a saliency map like those displayed in Figure 2 that identify and number the five most salient spots on the web page images. While the Bieber headline does not register as salient in the non-salient condition, the headline registers as the third most salient item on the page in the salient condition. A score of "1" indicates the feature has the highest level of saliency on the page followed by "2" and so on.

Qualitative and quantitative measures

Affect

Affect was measured pre- and post- task using the Positive and Negative Affect Schedule (PANAS) [25], a 20-item scale that is one of the most commonly used measures of affect. It includes 10 items measuring positive affect (PAS), such as determined, attentive, and enthusiastic and 10 items measuring negative (NAS) including jittery, hostile, and afraid. Participants responded with their agreement on a 5-point scale (very slightly or not at all; a little; moderately; quite a bit; extremely) to the following statement relating to each item: "You feel this way right now, that is, at the present moment."

Affect was also measured by asking users to respond to the question: "Overall, did you feel positive or negative while completing the news headline tasks? [positive, negative, neither positive nor negative]". A follow-up question was designed to understand the reasons behind these feelings (e.g., "Why did you feel positive while completing the news headline tasks?").

Focused attention

Focused attention was measured in a number of ways. First, the 7-item *focused attention* subscale, part of the 31-item user engagement scale [16], was adapted to fit in the context of finding news headlines. It consisted of the following items:

1. I lost myself in this news tasks experience

2. I was so involved in my news tasks that I lost track of time
3. I blocked things out around me when I was completing the news tasks
4. When I was performing these news tasks, I lost track of the world around me
5. The time I spent performing these news tasks just slipped away
6. I was absorbed in my news tasks
7. During the news tasks experience I let myself go

Participants were instructed to respond to each item on a 5-point scale (strong disagree to strong agree): "Based on this experience finding celebrity and entertainment news headlines, please indicate whether you agree or disagree with each statement".

Two questions were included to measure participants' perceptions relating to focus and distraction: "Was it easy to focus on finding the news headlines you were asked to find? [yes, no, somewhat]" and "Did you find anything distracting when you were searching for the headlines? [On the web pages or in your own environment.] [yes, no, somewhat]". These questions were followed with "why" questions to understand reasons for their perceptions.

As perceived time is an integral component of focused attention [16], the actual time spent on the entertainment web page displays looking for headlines was measured as well as perceived time. Perceived time was measured using the question: "Please estimate in minutes the total time you think you spent finding the eight news headlines on the entertainment web pages. [not including time spent reading the questions or selecting multiple choice answers]."

Interest

The participants' level of interest in topics (pre-task) was measured using a 5-point level of interest scale with an option to indicate that they did not know who/what this was. Post-task, interest was measured on a 5-point agreement scale using the following questions: "Though it wasn't possible, I wanted to click on links within the web pages", "I was interested in the content of the web pages" and "I wanted to find out more about the topics that I encountered on the web pages."

Task ease

Perception of task ease was measured based on responses on a 5-point agreement scale to the following two questions: "I am confident I found the headlines I was asked to find" and "It was easy to locate the headlines I was asked to find." Actual time spent finding the headlines was also used as a measure of task ease; the easier the task is to complete, the less time it should take.

Mechanical Turk

The use of Mechanical Turk (MTurk) in research has been explored in detail elsewhere, e.g., [10, 13]. MTurk has been used successfully in the recruitment of participants for external surveys that require longer than your average Mechanical Turk HIT [12], providing a convenient participant pool. To our knowledge, this is the first time that MTurk (or similar platform) was used to study affect and focused attention.

Pilot Studies

We conducted a series of three pilot studies. These pilots enabled us to test the validity of our use of the focused attention subscale, previously applied to the online shopping domain [18]. In the initial pilot study (N=191) confirmatory factor analysis was performed using the Principal component analysis method of extraction and Varimax rotation; a single factor was extracted and Cronbach's alpha (.93) indicated high reliability. The second and third pilot studies further confirmed its reliability; Cronbach's alphas of .90 (N=81) and .88 (N=46) were found. The pilots also allowed us to test the study design and led to a number of significant changes in task, question order and delivery, the types of questions asked, and payment structure.

It was imperative that we control users' view of the web page images as much as possible given that they would be in their own environments rather than in a controlled lab setting. Complaints regarding slow page loading in the first pilot, for example, led us to insert coding to help ensure that web pages pre-loaded. This reduced the chance that participants would see the page slowly appear from top to bottom, thus impacting saliency predictions.

Comments in the original pilot study suggested that some tasks meant to be in the salient condition were considered difficult to spot while some in the non-salient condition stood out. Most of the complaints regarding the non-salient headlines in the salient condition were related to highlighting that impaired readability; new tasks were created with this in mind. The second and third pilots became pared-down versions of the study (e.g., PANAS questionnaire removed) in order to get the tasks "right".

The original pilot study included follow-up questions designed to engage the participants in the content. Comments suggested this was too artificial given the lack of ability to engage with the web pages via links; as well, those with no interest in entertainment news complained vehemently. Given the sensitivity of the PANAS, follow-up questions were removed and replaced with a question that simply asked them to select the correct headline from a list of headlines. The number of tasks was also reduced to eight from ten to reduce emotions not associated with saliency itself. The polarized reactions to entertainment and celebrity news led us to add a few questions relating to interest in the web page content.

Overview of study protocol

The study took place over a period of approximately 12 hours in August, 2011. **Error! Reference source not**

found. outlines the flow of the study from its introduction to Amazon Mechanical Turk Workers and acceptance of the HIT assignment to their return to the Amazon site to submit the HIT after completing the study. Participants were instructed that the study would take approximately 15 minutes to complete, though they would be given 60 minutes between the time they accepted and submitted the HIT. They were informed that they could only participate in this study once and they would not be paid if they had participated in one of the two previous pilot studies that employed the same tasks. Payment for study completion was $1.50. Upon accepting the HIT, participants were randomly assigned to one of 8 surveys by clicking the link to the external survey.

Items in the PANAS and focused attention scale were randomized as were questions in the pre-task interest questionnaire and the interest and task ease questions. Task order was partially randomized; four surveys were created for each condition and the task order in each set manipulated to reduce location bias. Participants were all given the same instructions and tasks. No time constraints for task completion were imposed. Tasks consisted of three parts to ensure the accurate capture of time data relating to time spent on web pages: 1) instructions to find a headline, 2) display of web page screenshot where headline could be found, 3) selection from a list of 4 possible headlines, all drawn from actual news headlines, plus an "I don't know" option. Participants were unable to return to previous pages.

<table>
<tr><td colspan="2">Mechanical Turk: Introduction/Consent, HIT acceptance</td></tr>
<tr><td colspan="2">Link to external survey; entry of MTurk worker ID</td></tr>
<tr><td colspan="2">Pre-task PANAS</td></tr>
<tr><td colspan="2">Pre-task topic interest questions</td></tr>
<tr><td>8 Non-Salient tasks</td><td>8 Salient tasks</td></tr>
<tr><td colspan="2">Self-report of time spent finding headlines</td></tr>
<tr><td colspan="2">Post-task PANAS</td></tr>
<tr><td colspan="2">Self-report of affect</td></tr>
<tr><td colspan="2">Focused attention scale</td></tr>
<tr><td colspan="2">Self-report of focused attention</td></tr>
<tr><td colspan="2">Interest and task ease questions</td></tr>
<tr><td colspan="2">Monitor size and perception of page loading time questions</td></tr>
<tr><td colspan="2">Demographics questionnaire</td></tr>
<tr><td colspan="2">Comments</td></tr>
<tr><td colspan="2">Return to MTurk to submit HIT</td></tr>
</table>

Table 1 Study protocol

Participants

Participants were drawn from the MTurk population and screened based on location (United States) and HIT approval rate (> 95%), as recommended in the literature [13] and communications with crowd-sourcing experts. The 189 participants (female=65.1%, male=34.4%, prefer not to say=0.5%) were mainly under the age of 41 (79.9%) with the largest group between the ages of 24-29 (32.8%). Participants tended to have a bachelor (39.2%) or some college degree (22.8%). They were primarily employed for a company or organization (42.9%), though there were a number of self-employed (14.8%), students (18.5%), and not employed (20.6%).

Most indicated using a monitor that was 18" or less (73.2%) with the most commonly reported monitor size of 15-16" (30.1%). Regarding page loading time, 23 (12.2%) agreed or strongly agreed that it took a long time for the pages to load. Overall, participants expressed the least amount of interest in Gleeson (N=88, M=1.83, SD=1.06) and the most in Disney (N=189, M=3.33, SD=1.29). Many participants indicated not knowing Worthington (41%) or Gleeson (53%). However, no more than 1% indicated not knowing the other headline topics and 47% of participants agreed/strongly agreed that they follow entertainment news. Unlike a 2010 Pew study that indicates that 47% of Americans get their celebrities or entertainment news online [20], 79% of the participants in our study indicated getting their entertainment news via the internet. No significant differences ($p > .05$) were found between the two conditions (salient and non-salient) relating to demographics, monitor size, page loading, or entertainment news behaviors.

Analysis

All quantitative analyses were conducted in SPSS. The open-ended responses relating to overall feelings, ease of focus and distraction were analyzed through a process of inductive, thematic coding. The first author developed a coding manual that included definitions and examples of each of the codes. An independent researcher was asked to code 50 responses from each of the three questions using the coding manual. Based on this initial step, code definitions were clarified to improve coding consistency. Both the researcher and the independent researcher then re-coded all three sets of responses independently using the revised coding manual. Kappa was used to determine the reliability of the coding; Kappas > .75 are considered excellent agreement beyond chance [3]. This criteria was met for all three questions (overall feelings = .85); ease of focus = .78; and distraction = .83). The researchers then reached agreement on those responses where their coding conflicted.

RESULTS

The average time for completion of the study was approximately 13 minutes. Of the 200 participants, 96 (48%) were in the salient condition and 104 (52%) were in the non-salient condition. Of these, two were found to have repeated the study after abandoning the study part-way through therefore these were deleted. Those unable to correctly answer at least 6 of the 8 tasks (N=2) were also eliminated. Given the easy nature of the tasks, these participants were not making a sufficient attempt to find the headlines. To the "confident I found the headlines"

Variable	*M*	*SD*	1	2	3	4	5	6	7	8	9
1. Pre-PAS	28.28	8.94	-								
2. Post-PAS	27.47	9.65	.88**	-							
3. Focused Attention Scale	20.72	6.84	.30**	.44**	-						
4. Time on web pages	3.38	1.92	.13	.16*	.19*	-					
5. Perceived time	5.38	3.36	.14*	.14*	.15*	.53**	-				
6. Easy to locate headlines	4.44	0.81	.22**	.23**	.12*	-.18*	-.11	-			
7. Wanted to click links	3.19	1.40	.24**	.32**	.42**	.22**	.09	.06	-		
8. Interest in webpage content	3.34	1.26	.33**	.42**	.50**	.27**	.10	.05	.79**	-	
9. Wanted to find out more	3.27	1.34	.27**	.35**	.50**	.19**	.05	.12	.78**	.84**	-

Note. $N = 189$. $*p < .05$, $**p < .01$.

Table 2 Summary of Inter-correlations, Means, and Standard Deviations of Study Variables

statement 92.3% responded "agree" or "strongly agree"; no further analysis was performed due to this unanimity.

All missing values were NMAR (not missing at random) and included responses such as "don't know" and "cannot say/not applicable". Six data sets were removed as a result of this NMAR data, leaving N=190. The negative affect scale (NAS) of the PANAS was non-normally distributed, showing extreme signs of skew and kurtosis even after log base-10 transformation. As NAS violated the assumption of linearity required for this study's analyses and as our main focus of this study was the PAS rather than the NAS, no further analysis was done using the NAS.

Univariate outliers were examined; a number were identified but their removal did not change the results therefore these data sets were retained. Using Mahalanobis distance five multivariate outliers were identified (p <.001); however, Cook's distance values for all but one of the cases fell below the generally accepted cutoff of 1 [23]. This case was deleted, leaving N=189 for the analyses reported in this paper. Table 2 contains the descriptive statistics and inter-correlations of the study variables.

There was a relatively even split by condition with 90 (47.6%) in the salient task condition and 99 (52.4%) in the non-salient task condition. Of these, 83.1% (N = 157) answered all 8 news headline tasks, 12.7% (N = 24) answered 7 of the tasks correctly and 4.2% (N = 8) answered 6 of tasks correctly. There were no significant differences by condition relating to task accuracy.

Several themes emerged from the qualitative analysis of the three open-ended questions relating to overall affect, easy to focus, and distractions. Only those themes relating to our hypotheses and exploration of user interests, focused attention, and affect are explored in this paper. Discussion of these themes is interwoven through the discussion of the quantitative results in the following sections. Results are organized according to our hypotheses and exploratory examination of user interests, focused attention and affect. Participants are referred to by condition and number. For example, S130 refers to participant 130 in the *salient* condition; NS21 refers to participant 21 in the *non-salient* condition.

Hypothesis 1: Task performance and saliency

Saliency of task-relevant information leads to greater task performance, both actual and perceived.

Analysis of actual time spent (in minutes) finding the headlines indicates a significant effect for saliency, $t(170.06) = 3.60$, $p < .001$; those in the salient condition (M = 2.77, SD = 1.75) found the headlines faster than those in the non-salient condition (M = 3.94, SD = 2.68). As well, there was a significant effect for saliency, $t(182.43) = -2.49$, p=.01 with those in the salient task condition finding it easier to locate the headlines (M = 4.59, SD = .69) than those in the non-salient condition (M = 4.30, SD = .89). However, does this positive effect on task performance translate to positive feelings and emotions upon task completion?

Hypothesis 2: Affect and saliency

Affect improves when the task-relevant information is salient compared to when it is not salient.

There was no significant effect for saliency between the two groups relating to post positive affect, t (187) = -.35, p = .73. Positive affect, however, significantly decreased from pre- to post-task t (188) = 2.41, p = .02. Pre- and post-PAS scores were examined for each of the two conditions. In the non-salient condition there was a significant difference between positive affect before (M = 28.3, SD = 9.1) and after (M = 27.2, SD = 10.1) the tasks were performed, t (98) = 2.25, p = .03, with a decrease in affect post-task representing a small effect size of r = .23. This same result was not observed in the salient condition, t (89) = 1.09, p = .28, where there was no change in affect between pre- and post-task affect scores.

Analysis of the "Overall, did you feel positive or negative while completing the news headline tasks?" question revealed no differences by condition, χ^2 (2, N = 189) = 2.25, p = .32. Thematic analysis of responses to the why participants felt positive of negative, or somewhat positive or negative revealed similar patterns in both the salient task group and non-salient task group responses. Both groups, for example, tended to associate positive feelings with performance, indicating the tasks were easy or relatively easy to perform. One participant wrote: "I felt like I was able to find the headlines quickly and efficiently" (S121) while another noted "I felt positive because I was able to find the headlines quickly" (NS40). Despite the ease of the tasks, another theme to emerge across both conditions was that the web pages were cluttered or there was too much content. Negative feelings emerged because "There was too much at which to look. The page was too busy" (NS29).

Hypothesis 3: Focused attention and saliency

Saliency of task-relevant information leads to higher levels of focused attention.

There was no significant effect for saliency, t (187) = -.09, p = .93 in the focused attention scale scores. Likewise, there were no significant differences in their likelihood to overestimate or underestimate time spent finding the headlines (χ^2 = 3.43, df = 1, p = .06). Condition also had no significant impact on the extent of overestimation (F = .06, df = 1, 149, p = .81), underestimation (F = .002, df = 1, 36, p = .97), or absolute error in estimation (F = .04, df = 1, 187, p = .83).

Responses to the question, "Did you find anything distracting when you were searching for the headlines?" did not differ by saliency condition, χ^2 (2, N = 189) = 5.78, p = .06. However, the open-ended responses relating to distraction suggests that those in the non-salient condition appeared more apt to be distracted by web page format, layout or image saliency. One participant (NS100) wrote: "Some of the pictures and large graphics were distracting when the headline I was looking for was in small type".

This pattern of responses is reflected in the responses to the question "Was it easy to focus on finding the news headlines you were asked to find?" There were significant differences by saliency condition, χ^2 (2, N = 189) = 7.73, p = .02 (Table 3). Due to some cell counts of less than five, a Fisher exact test was performed which confirmed the significance of this result (p < .01). Those in the non-salient condition were more likely to be "on the fence" in their response to this question with more indicating "somewhat" than their salient condition counterparts.

	Condition		
Easy to focus?	Non-Salient (N=99)	Salient (N=90)	χ^2
Yes	81	85	7.73*
Somewhat	17	4	
No	1	1	

Note. * p < .05

Table 3 Cross Tabulation of Easy to Focus and Condition

Responses to the "why?" portion of the easy-to-focus question indicated that saliency was perceived to play a role in whether or not they found it easy to focus on finding the headlines. Those in the salient condition indicated that the location or (more often) the salience of the task headlines made it easy to focus. S14 noted that it was easy to focus "because they were all close to the top and had a picture or were bolded or highlighted" while S74 wrote "Because most of the headlines that I was looking for stood out from the rest".

Exploration: User interests, focused attention and affect

While saliency impacted focused attention and affect, a prominent theme to emerge from the thematic analysis of the open-ended questions was the impact that web page content had on participants' focus. One participant wrote: "My attention was drawn at first to headlines regarding things that I am particularly interested (i.e., the Grey's Anatomy episode blurb). But once I gave myself an attention check, it was easy to find the headlines" (NS190). Others were able to stay focused due to lack of interest in the celebrity news: "I don't really care about celebrity news, so I didn't get distracted very easily" (NS181).

Multiple regression analysis was used to test whether interest in topics, wanting to click on the links, and wanting to find out more were related to focused attention scores (results summarized in Table 4). The results indicated that the three independent variables explained 27% of the variance. However, while interest in content (β = .30, p < 0.01) and wanting to find out more (β = .27, p = 0.03), each contributed significantly to the prediction of focused attention scores, wanting to click on links was not a significant predictor (β = -.03, p = 0.78).

Model	b	$SE\ b$	β	t	*Sig.*
Constant	11.27	1.23		9.19	.00*
Interest in content	1.64	.67	.30	2.45	.02
Wanted to click on links	-.15	.53	-.03	-.28	.78
Wanted to find out more	1.36	.63	.27	2.17	.03

Note. R^2 = .27, *p < .001.

Table 4 Multiple Regression for Focused Attention Scores

As well as engagement in the web page content, engagement in the task itself appeared to be an integral reason behind open-ended responses. In order to focus, one participant noted that "[...] I made it into a game with myself" (S182). Another who found it easy to focus wrote that "It was kind of like a puzzle trying to find them amid all the other useless information on those pages" (S22). Likewise, the gaming aspect led some to express positive emotions as a result of the experience: "I enjoyed the game of it [...]" (NS98); "It's interesting, like a hide and find" (S87). Others expressed neutral feelings relating to their experience noted "It was just a game of finding the headlines, but not that interesting a game" (S169). This leads to the question: does focused attention, an aspect of user engagement, predict positive affect?

Simple linear regression was used to test whether focused attention scores significantly predicted post-positive affect. Regression results are summarized in Table 5.

Model	*B*	*SE b*	*β*	*T*	*Sig.*
Constant	14.66	2.03		7.24	.00*
Focused Attention	.62	.09	.44	6.66	.00*

Note. $R^2 = .19$, $*p < .001$.

Table 5 Simple Linear Regression for Post Positive Affect

The results of the regression indicated that focused attention scores contributed significantly to the prediction of post-positive affect scores ($\beta = .44$, $p < .001$) and explained 19% of the variance. Pre- positive affect also significantly predicts focused attention ($\beta = .30$, $p < .001$), and explained 10% of the variance.

DISCUSSION

Saliency of task-relevant information leads to better task performance, both actual and perceived (H1)

When the task relevant information is salient, it is found faster, and participants report that it is easier to find the headlines. This hypothesis is thus fully supported.

The connection between task difficulty and time on task has been noted previously [5] and this study confirms that saliency contributes to both subjective measures of task difficulty and actual measures of time. Salient headlines helped participants complete the task more quickly. While the tasks were easy for both groups to complete, those provided with salient headlines perceived the tasks were easier. But does this benefit in task performance translate to a positive affect?

Affect improves when the task-relevant information is salient compared to when it is not salient (H2)

This hypothesis was supported through the results of the pre- and post- positive affect scores, though unsupported through the responses to the overall affect question.

In general, entertainment news web pages are cluttered and have several visual elements; there are a multitude of images and advertisements, headlines and bodies of text on a single page. This is also true of the web pages that our participants were shown; there was a lot of information on the pages. Web pages that are cluttered demand a lot of attention [19] and the stylistic properties of retrieved documents such as presentation of information have been found to arouse both positive and negative emotions [11, 17]. Emotions have also previously been shown to change from positive to negative as task difficulty increases [1]. Saliency of relevant information provided a way to navigate through the page clutter more effectively, making tasks easier for those in the salient condition. This in turn appears to have allowed their emotions to remain positive and stable from pre- to post-task, mitigating a decrease in positive affect. Previous studies [5, 11] examining task type and topic as factors contributing to mood changes before and after online information searching indicated that mood remained stable, however these studies manipulated the tasks rather than the features of the web pages themselves.

Saliency of task-relevant information leads to higher levels of focused attention (H3)

This hypothesis was unsupported through the sum scores of the focused attention scale and estimation of the time spent finding headlines. Focused attention does not increase when the task relevant information is salient nor does a lack of saliency increase distortions of time perception. In contrast, users reported that it was easier to focus when the headlines appeared salient. Why the contradiction?

Recall that responses to the focused attention scale were based on the *experience* of finding news headlines on the web pages. The tasks themselves were easy, short, and involved only a single change in headline saliency between the two groups. The user engagement scale was developed to measure engagement in interactive systems [18]. Perhaps engagement with multiple non-interactive web page screenshots in the entertainment news was not enough to make an impact on perceived focused attention based on saliency alone. Measurement of any potential differences was thwarted possibly in part by our study design. Allowing interaction with web pages, however, would have made it impossible to control saliency to the degree that we did in this study. Due to the lack of interaction with the web page screenshot, the focused attention subscale may have been too abstract. As evidenced in the qualitative analysis, participants reported that it was easier to focus in the salient condition, suggesting that this question helped them think more concretely about what helped them focus.

Like focused attention, distortion of time perception was expected to be greater when the task-based information was salient than when it was not salient. Time distortion or lack of awareness of time occurs when the user is focused on or immersed in an activity [18, 15]. While we expected that saliency would help participants maintain their focus, become engaged with the task and therefore lose track of time, this did not occur. Perhaps it was the case that the task was simply too easy for those looking for salient headlines; a certain amount of challenge is necessary if a user is to become engaged or immersed in their activity and lose themselves, often referred to as the experience of flow [9]. Jennett et al. [9] found that level of immersion in a game was higher than that of immersion in a controlled activity. As both participants in the salient and non-salient conditions were asked to perform tasks that were essentially controlled activities, this level of control may have mitigated against focused attention in both conditions.

Exploration: User interests, focused attention and affect

Our exploratory analysis of the interactions between user interests, focused attention and positive affect suggest a number of relationships between these both within and outside the remit of saliency.

Relationships between user interests and focused attention

Interest in content predicts focused attention. Similar to other findings [6, 19], our study suggests that when engaged in a goal-based task, users often make a concerted effort to stay focused and block out non-relevant web page content despite efforts to draw their attention. As responses to the follow-up questions suggested, some made a game out of the tasks to maintain their focus. By doing so, they tapped into their attention mechanism, allowing them to control which visual stimuli are processed [19]. By making relevant, goal-oriented information salient, this aids the attention mechanism, allowing users to complete the task-at-hand [19].

Despite the focused task we designed, non-relevant content not only captured attention, but also curiosity, and played a significant role in the perception of distraction during the tasks. This reinforces previous findings suggesting that content and web links of interest to or relevant to the user's goal positively influence focusing of attention on the information-seeking activity; likewise, interesting content and links not relevant to the user's goal have a positive influence on the user's *specific* or *diversive* curiosity in a topic [19]. It seems intuitive, but the degree of interest people have in the content they are encountering has an impact on how engaged they become with this content. A recent quasi-experimental study by O'Brien [17] concluded that the user engagement scale which includes the focused subscale should be expanded to include content as a quality of user engagement due to the emergence of a relationship found between content and the way it is presented on web pages.

Relationship between focused attention and positive affect

Immersion in gaming can sometimes lead to positive affect and other times negative affect [9]. Both negative and positive emotions have also been expressed in relation to reading online news [17]. Our results suggest that focused attention, whether influenced by the non-task-based content or by focused attention to the task itself influences how they feel once they have disengaged. While mood prior to entertainment news tasks influences focused attention, there is a strong relationship between focused attention during the tasks and post-task emotions. The relationship between focused attention and affect therefore merits further investigation.

CONCLUSIONS

This paper presented a study of the impact of saliency of task-relevant information on two engagement metrics, focused attention and affect. Participants were recruited via Amazon Mechanical Turk to respond to an online survey that included information seeking tasks; half were provided with web pages where the task-related headlines were salient while the other half were given web pages where the headlines were not salient. This paper makes three novel contributions:

- This paper detailed the first study showing how saliency impacts metrics associated with user engagement (positive affect and focused attention).
- We showed that when the headlines that users seek appear visually non-salient, users are slow at finding them, report more distraction due to web page features, and show a drop in affect. In comparison, when the headlines appear visually catchy or salient, they find them faster, report that it is easy to focus, and maintain positive affect. This shows that saliency is helpful in task performance, focusing/avoiding distraction and in maintaining positive affect.
- By adapting the focused attention subscale from the online shopping domain [16] to the entertainment news domain, we studied how saliency impacts focused attention. Although users reported that it was easier to focus in the salient condition, we found no significant improvement in the focused attention subscale or differences in perceived time spent on tasks. Instead, we find that user interest in web page content is a good predictor of focused attention, which in turn is a good predictor of positive affect.

Our results ultimately suggest that the interaction of saliency, focused attention, and affect, together with user interest, is complex.

Examining saliency and engagement simultaneously in this study was a challenge. Salient features of a web page draw user attention within the first few seconds of visiting a page, but engagement happens after, sometimes long after, that initial exposure. Moreover, the impact that the manipulation of our perceptual environment has on our feelings and emotions is difficult to measure. Nonetheless, the use of multiple measures helped us gain a richer understanding of the complex relationships between saliency, focused attention, affect and user interest.

Performing this study online with no control over screen size, internet connection speed, or other variables we would normally control for in a laboratory setting presented further challenges. However, while the use of Amazon Mechanical Turk as a platform for online recruitment took much of the environmental control away that we could have maintained in a lab setting, it also allowed for more rapid testing and a larger and more diverse participant base than the average user study. In addition, the Mechanical Turk Workers made excellent participants, contributing through their post-study comments suggestions for study improvements. Responses to open-ended questions were equally thoughtful and contributed significantly to the interpretation of our results.

While we were limited in the present study to working with static web pages, future studies should allow participants to engage more naturally with the website content. As well, we were limited in this study to static forms of salience, the manipulation of color, images, and font size. Future studies should explore the impact that common dynamic web page features such as animation or simple flickering may have on affect and focused attention. Findings would be of interest to any website owner, entertainment-oriented or other, interested in not only in catching users' attention, but also maintaining it.

We did not control for interest in this study, but future studies could incorporate this into the design by gathering users' interests on different topics in advance (e.g., sports, finance, entertainment, travel, fashion). A more naturalistic study could subsequently be conducted. Salience of information that the participant is known to enjoy or have an interest in could be manipulated to test how saliency, user interests, affect and focused attention, and perhaps other aspects of user engagement, interact. We speculate that increasing the salience of information of personal interest to users might improve focused attention and create positive affect, though this needs to be tested rigorously in future work. Rather than imposing a goal-oriented, externally-imposed task, facilitating more natural interactions will broaden our understanding of the impact of saliency on users.

ACKNOWLEDGMENTS

We would like to thank Diego Sáez for his support in implementing the online study and Ioannis Arapakis for assistance with the qualitative data analysis. This study was completed while the first author was on an internship at Yahoo! Research in Barcelona, Spain.

REFERENCES

1. I. Arapakis, J.M. Jose & P.D. Gray. Affective feedback: An investigation into the role of emotions in the information seeking process. In *Proc. SIGIR2008,* ACM press (2008), 395-402.
2. S. Attfield, G. Kazai, M. Lalmas & B. Piwowarski. Towards a science of user engagement (Position Paper), WSDM Workshop on User Modelling for Web Applications (2011).
3. M. Banerjee, M. Capozzoli, L. McSweeney, & D. Sinha. Beyond kappa: A review of interrater agreement measures. *Canadian Journal of Statistics, 27,* 1 (1999).
4. R. Carmi & L. Itti. Visual causes versus correlates of attentional selection in dynamic scenes. *Vision Research, 46,* 26 (2006).
5. J. Gwizdka & I. Lopatovska. The role of subjective factors in the information search process. *JASIST, 60,* 12 (2009).
6. M.H. Huang. Designing website attributes to induce experiential encounters. *Computers in Human Behavior, 19,* 4 (2003).
7. L. Itti and C. Koch. A saliency-based search mechanism for overt and covert shifts of visual attention. *Vision Research, 40,* 10-12 (2000), 1489-1506.
8. M. Jennings. Theory and models for creating engaging and immersive e-commerce websites. In *Proc. SIGCPR 2000,* ACM Press (2000).
9. C. Jennett, A.L. Cox, P. Cairns, S. Dhoparee, A. Epps, T. Tijs & A. Walton. Measuring and defining the experience of immersion in games. *International Journal of Human-Computer Studies, 66,* 9 (2008), 641-661.
10. A. Kittur, E.H. Chi & B. Suh. *Crowdsourcing user studies with Mechanical Turk.* In *Proc. SIGCHI* 2008, ACM Press (2008).
11. I. Lopatovska. Searching for good mood: Examining relationships between search task and mood. *American Society for Information Science and Technology, 46,* 1 (2009), 1-13.
12. C.C. Marshall & F.M. Shipman. The ownership and reuse of visual media. In *Proc. JCDL 2011,* ACM Press (2011).
13. W. Mason & S. Suri. Conducting behavioral research on Amazon's Mechanical Turk. *Behavior Research Methods* (2010), 1-23.
14. V. Navalpakkam & L. Itti. Search goal tunes visual features optimally. *Neuron, 53,* 4 (2007), 605-617.
15. T.P. Novak, D.L. Hoffman, & Y. Yiu-Fai. Measuring the Customer Experience in Online Environments: A Structural Modeling Approach. *Marketing Science, 19,* 1 (2000), 22-42.
16. H.L. O'Brien. *Defining and Measuring Engagement in User Experiences with Technology.* PhD Thesis, 2008.
17. H.L. O'Brien. Exploring user engagement in online news interactions. In *Proc. ASIST 2011* (forthcoming).
18. H. O'Brien & E. Toms. The development and evaluation of a survey to measure user engagement. *JASIST 61,* 1 (2010).
19. S. Pace. A grounded theory of the flow experiences of Web users. *International Journal of Human-Computer Studies, 60,* 3 (2004), 327-363.
20. K. Purcell, L. Rainie, A. Mitchell, T. Rosenstiel, & K. Olmstead. *Understanding the Participatory News Consumer.* Pew Internet & American Life Project (2010).
21. K. Overbeeke, T. Djajadiningrat, C. Hummels, S. Wensveen & J. Frens. Let's make things engaging. *Funology.* Kluwer, 2003.
22. R. Peters & L. Itti. Applying computational tools to predict gaze direction in interactive visual environments. *ACM Transactions on Applied Perception (TAP), 5,* 2 (2008).
23. B.G. Tabachnick & L.S. Fidell. *Using Multivariate Statistics* (4th ed.). Boston, MA: Allyn and Bacon, 2001.
24. A. Treisman & G. Gelade. A feature-integration theory of attention. *Cognitive Psychology, 12,* 1 (1980).
25. D. Watson, L.A. Clark & A. Tellegen. Development and validation of brief measures of positive and negative affect: The PANAS Scales. *Journal of Personality and Social Psychology, 47* (1988).
26. J. Wolfe & T. Horowitz. What attributes guide the deployment of visual attention and how do they do it? *Nature Reviews Neuroscience, 5,* 6 (2004), 495-501.

The Way I Talk to You: Sentiment Expression in an Organizational Context

Jiang Yang, Lada A. Adamic, Mark S. Ackerman
University of Michigan
Ann Arbor, MI 48109, USA
{yangjian, ladamic, ackerm}@umich.edu

Zhen Wen, Ching-Yung Lin
IBM T. J. Watson Research Center
Hawthorne, NY 10532, USA
{zhenwen, chingyung}@us.ibm.com

ABSTRACT
Sentiment is a rich and important dimension of social interaction. However, its presence in computer-mediated communication in corporate settings is not well understood. This paper provides a preliminary study of people's expression of sentiment in email conversations in an organizational context. The study reveals that sentiment levels evolve over time during the process of newcomers' socialization, that sentiment varies according to tie-strength with the recipient, and that sentiment patterns can be indicative of one's position in the corporate social network as well as job performance. These findings shed light on the complex and dynamic nature of sentiment patterns, and would inspire further explorations and applications of sentiment analysis in organizations.

Author Keywords
Sentiments; Computer-Mediated-Communication (CMC); organization science; social network; socializing; email.

ACM Classification Keywords
H.5.m [Information interfaces and presentation (e.g., HCI)]: Miscellaneous;

INTRODUCTION
Understanding social interaction in computer-supported collaborative systems is crucial in order to better design tools and systems to support communication and collaboration in groups. A wealth of literature has attempted to do so from a variety of angles: studying, e.g., the intensity of social relationships in social networking sites (SNS) [5], social exchange activities in online communities [10], and new members' socialization in SNS [2], online groups [1], and organizations [3].

Recently, sentiment analysis has added another dimension to the study of online interactions. It has been used to track aggregate trends in social media, from understanding aggregate mood of a nation to predicting product reviews and sales (e.g. [4, 6, 7]). However, the expression of sentiment as a rich and important dimension of social interaction, so far, has rarely been explored in an organizational context. This short paper aims to investigate several basic aspects of sentiment expression patterns to shed light on the complex and dynamic nature of sentiment in computer mediated interactions in an organizational context.

By applying sentiment analysis to communication data within a large global company, we sought to answer the following: whether the level of sentiment expressed evolves over time; whether it depends on the strength of tie with the recipient of the communication; and whether it varies by individuals' status within the organization. Each of these questions will be addressed in the Analysis section.

DATA AND APPROACH
Data Description
Our empirical study resides in a global company devoted to information technologies and consulting, with over 400,000 employees across more than 200 countries. In particular, we use a dataset of 15 million email conversations of 8,592 volunteer employees who agreed to share their outgoing messages when signing up for an Intranet service. They were recruited via snowball sampling, by allowing existing users to invite their contacts to join the service. As a result, users in our pool are scatted throughout the corporation's different divisions and countries. A prior study based on the same dataset compared the network characteristics and job roles of the sampled users to the rest of the firm and found minimal differences between the two distributions [9].

Each log entry of the communication records specifies the sender and receiver(s), a timestamp, the subject, and the content of the body of the message. To preserve privacy, the email addresses of users are hashed and the content is transformed into a vector of term frequencies. In order to focus on social interaction patterns, we eliminated spam and mass email announcements (refer to [4] for more information about the pre-processing of the dataset).

We also collected financial performance data for a subset of employees (more than 10,000), all of whom are dedicated business consultants and thus are comparable to each other in terms of job role and performance metrics. These consultants generate revenue by logging "billable hours" and [9] found the ability to generate revenue is an appropriate measure for productivity. Therefore for each consultant, performance is measured by the revenue he/she generated during a fiscal year.

It is important to note that our data does not capture a myriad of factors affecting sentiment expression: the individuals' personality, conversation topics, or global time-varying factors such as the financial performance of the company. Therefore each of the measured factors: tenure with the company, strength of tie, and organizational status, can be expected to individually account for at most a very small fraction of the observed variance in sentiment expression.

Methods

We employ a commonly used method for evaluating sentiment, based on frequency of occurrence of words in text based on a subjectivity lexicon [8]. The lexicon includes a list of over 8,000 subjectivity clues that have been annotated as strongly positive (++, e.g., "successful"), weakly positive (+, e.g., "suggestion"), weakly negative (-, e.g., "wrong"), or strongly negative (--, e.g., "suffering"). At the aggregate level, we calculate the frequency of all subjectivity terms to quantify the degree of subjectivity of a set of conversations (see Eq. 1, where F is the frequency count). Thus we measure sentiment-level for each user along each of the four dimensions separately, from strongly positive to strongly negative.

$$sentiment\_level = \sum F_{\text{sentiment\_terms}} / \sum F_{\text{all\_terms}} \quad \text{(Eq 1)}$$

Term-frequency is a simplified method for sentiment analysis, and we recognize that it cannot precisely detect the sentiment of an individual conversation. However, by extracting aggregate patterns over many conversations, we can capture the degree to which an individual tends to express each kind of sentiment.

Since our subjectivity lexicon contains only English terms, we confine our analysis to emails written in English. We further limit the analysis to the 50% of employees who are in the US, as well as 2491 additional employees from Canada, the United Kingdom, and India, retaining nearly 80% of our sample. This restriction minimizes language issues, such as switching to another language to communicate different types of information. Finally, we conduct correlation and regression tests to explore patterns in expression of each polarity and intensity of sentiment separately[1].

ANALYSIS AND RESULTS

Sentiments in Newcomers' Socialization

Upon joining a new group and environment, an individual often goes through a period of socializing and adaptation [3]. Sentiment, as an important attribute of communication, might reflect this adjustment process to some degree. We therefore examine whether people change the polarity and amount of sentiment they express as they gain more experience in the company.

[1] While normally the use of multiple tests would be a concern, the large sample size produces statistically significant results even if the p-values are inflated by an appropriate factor using the Bonferroni correction.

We assess the sentiment level expressed by an employee in their email messages for each month since they first appeared in our dataset. Employees are encouraged to keep all emails, which are automatically archived by the corporate email system. These records are included in our dataset upon the agreement of the volunteers. Even if some individual emails have been deleted, we expect this to have limited effect on the measurement of aggregate sentiment level. In addition, we confine our analysis to the most recent three years, to minimize the occurrence of missing data, and to draw from a sample of employees who had been hired relatively recently and exposed to similar developments within the company. The resulting dataset contains email records of 2586 users who joined since 2007 and had been with the company for at least 12 months.

Figure 1 presents how the sentiment levels for new employees evolve in each of the four dimensions. In general, expression of strong sentiment increases slightly within the first year (--: ρ=.029, sig.<10^{-7}; ++: ρ=.026 sig.<10^{-6}), while people use weak sentiments more frequently and consistently (sig. -: .08; +: .49). A possible explanation is that newcomers are more tentative in expression of sentiment, but gradually become somewhat more comfortable in voicing their opinion.

Comfort level may also increase within individual relationships. We therefore examine whether sentiment level changes over time as one continues to communicate with the same contact. We selected user-contact pairs that had exchanged more than 50 messages and computed the sentiment level for each batch of 10 sequential messages. There are small correlations between time-order and sentiment levels (-: ρ =.02, sig.<10^{-3}; --: ρ=.017, sig.<10^{-3}; +: ρ=.014, sig<10^{-2}; ++: ρ=.01, sig.<.05), suggesting that people tend to feel more comfortable expressing sentiment as they continue to communicate with the same individual.

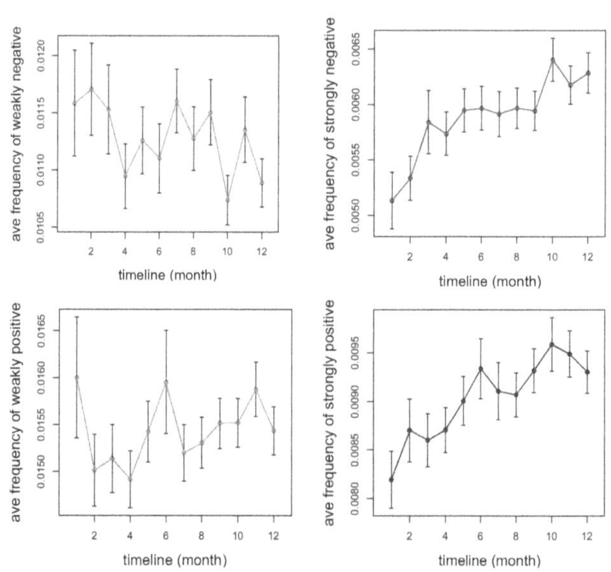

Figure 1. Change of sentiment levels since joining

Sentiments in Social Networks

Prior work (e.g., [5]) found that tie strength is reflected in the type and frequency of interaction in online settings. We thus further analyze whether the strength of a tie relates to the expression of sentiment in this organizational context.

We define tie-strength by the ranked position of a contact in terms of communication frequency. Thus tie-strength is defined relative to communication with one's remaining social contacts. In order to obtain enough observations in terms of both size of the social network and number of conversations, we only include the 3590 users who communicated with more than 100 contacts and sent more than 4000 messages. Please note this is also necessary since our relative tie-strength definition would only make sense when social networks are comparable in size. In particular, we group employee's contacts into three sets: $1\sim10^{th}$, $11\sim40^{th}$, $>40^{th}$, which correspond to weak, moderate, and strong ties in their social networks.

Figure 2 shows how frequently people express different sentiment levels to a tie of a specified strength. Sentiment levels are normalized for each individual's basic sentiment profile. Except for the weak-positive dimension, there are significant differences between different conversation pairs of different tie-strength (sig.$<10^{-7}\sim10^{-16}$). In fact, there are weak correlations between tie-strength rank and sentiment levels on negative (-: $\rho = -.05$, sig.$<10^{-7}$; --: $\rho = -.06$, sig.$<10^{-10}$) and strong-positive dimensions ($\rho = .10$, sig.$<10^{-16}$). In general, people tend to be more negative when conversing along strong ties and more positive when communicating with infrequent contacts.

Sentiments and Social Network Size

The size of one's social network, namely the number of contacts one has communicated with, is an indicator of an employee's level of activity and engagement within the organization. We study whether people with different sizes of social networks exhibit different patterns of sentiment expression. The number of contacts and sentiment levels were computed within a 6-month period, and we confirmed that the results are consistent when the start and duration of the observation period is varied.

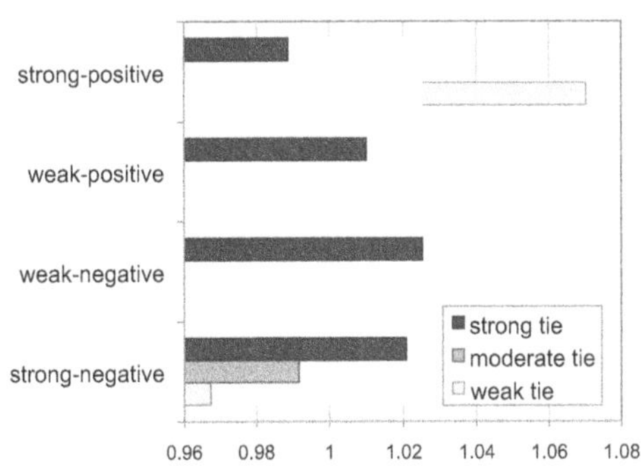

Figure 2. Sentiment levels (normalized) by tie-strength, ranked by communication frequency

For the 4114 users included in our observation period (the one we selected to present here), the mean of the network size is 138 and median is 98.

With the exception of the strong-negative dimension, there are weak correlations between the number of contacts and the level of sentiment expressed. In particular, people with larger social networks tend to express more positive sentiments (+: $\rho=.11$, sig.$<10^{-10}$; ++: $\rho = .07$, sig.$<10^{-5}$), and slightly fewer negative ($\rho= -.04$, sig.$= .005$). Since network size and the length of time with the company are correlated ($\rho=.10$, sig.$<10^{-8}$), we ran regression of sentiment_level over both variables and found that the network size variable shows a consistent relationship with sentiment, even controlling for length of time in the company.

In order to better observe the pattern, we divided employees into three equal-sized groups, according to the size of their social networks: small, medium, and large. As shown in Figure 3, the trend is generally consistent with the correlation pattern: people who maintain larger social networks tend to be more positive and less negative than those with smaller social networks.

Sentiments as Indicator of Performance

Prior work has found that social network size is not significantly correlated with one's performance in an organization, but having strong connections to authorities is positively associated with revenue [9]. We further examine whether sentiment is correlated to job performance within the company. As explained, we confine this analysis to 549 individuals in our sample who reside within the business consultant group, who have the same job role, and who are evaluated using the same metric: the amount of yearly revenue they generate for the company. In particular, this measure naturally combines two dimensions of a business consultant's performance: value of a unit working hour (hourly pay) and productivity (total consulting work one has done).

For simplified illustration, we divided the sample into high, middle, and low performance groups. Figure 4 shows that the high-performance group more frequently expresses weak positive and negative sentiment than the other two groups (sig. +: =.005; -: =.01), but there is no significant difference

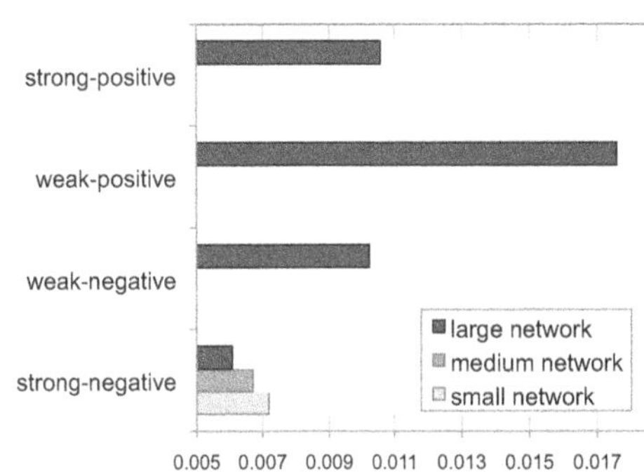

Figure 3. Sentiment levels and social network size

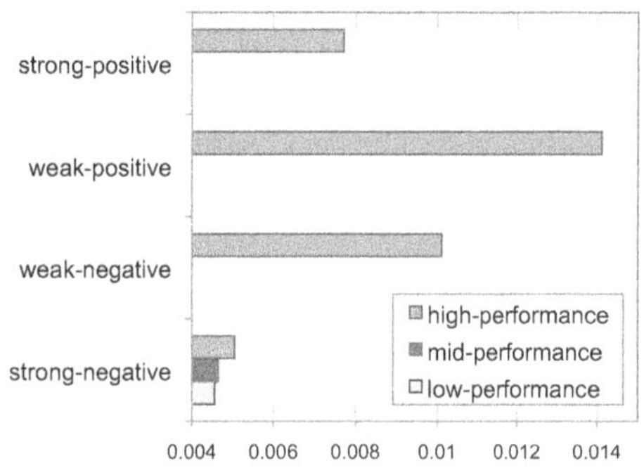

Figure 4. Sentiment levels by performance-groups

between mid and low performance groups. In fact, there is a positive correlation between performance (log-revenue) and expression of weak-positive sentiment (ρ=.09,sig.<.05), which may suggest positive reinforcement between performance and sentiment.

DISCUSSION

In this paper we presented a preliminary exploration of several basic aspects of sentiment expressed in CMC conversations in an organizational context. The results suggest that sentiment expression depends on the individuals' tenure and performance in the company, as well as their relationships with others. These dynamic and multifaceted characteristics of sentiment could have important implications for designing collaborative systems.

First, during the initial socializing process, newcomers adjust their sentiment levels. Through their first year, they increase their use of strong sentiment words, both positive and negative. In addition, between pairs of individuals who continue to communicate, sentiment is also increasingly expressed. This implies that sentiment expression increases as employees become more comfortable with their environment and build stronger social bonds with other people. This dynamic aspect of sentiment might suggest using sentiment as a dimension to assess newcomers' adjustment progress and status. Moreover, some design features to support proper sentiment expression might be helpful to alleviate some newcomers' shyness in communication, for example, indicating others' sentiment levels might encourage newcomers to adapt to the norms within the participants' organizational context.

Within one's social network, people tend to use positive sentiment words when communicating with infrequent contacts and express negative sentiment more frequently to their strong-tie contacts. This might indicate a higher comfort level in expressing negative thoughts in close relationships, while putting up a positive front to those one does not know well. But when email messages are forwarded, the strength of tie context may be lost. Tools that flag strong sentiment in email may allow users to write and forward email more carefully in intercultural contexts.

Finally, sentiment expression differs according to one's social position in the organization. In particular, people with larger social networks tend to be more positive while less negative. Higher-performers tend to express more sentiment in their messages. Although it is difficult to identify the casual relationship between sentiment and these status variables, we tend to believe that they form some mutual reinforcement dynamics. This kind of association should be worth mentioning in employee training. In addition, giving users feedback on how their sentiment expression compares to others' of similar position and tenure with the company should help users be aware of and adjust their sentiment expression.

ACKNOWLEDGMENTS

The University of Michigan authors were partially supported by NSF IIS-0948639 and NSF IIS-0746646.

REFERENCES

1. Arguello, J., Butler, B., Elisabeth, J., Kraut, R., Ling, K.S., Rose, C., and Wang, X. *Talk to Me: Foundations for Successful Individual-Group Interactions in Online Communities*. in *CHI* (2006).
2. Burke, M., Marlow, C., and Lento, T.M. *Feed me: motivating newcomer contribution in social network sites*. in *CHI* (2009), 945-954.
3. Chan, D. and Schmitt, N., Interindividual differences in intraindividual changes in proactivity during organizational entry: A latent growth modeling approach to understanding newcomer adaptation. *Journal of Applied Psychology* **85**, 2 (2000), 190-210.
4. Diakopoulos, N.A. and Shamma, D.A. *Characterizing debate performance via aggregated twitter sentiment*. in *CHI* (2010), 1195-1198.
5. Gilbert, E. and Karahalios, K. *Predicting tie strength with social media*. in *CHI* (2009), 211-220.
6. Mishne, G. and Rijke, M.d., *Predicting movie sales from blogger sentiment*, in *AAAI 2006 Spring Symposium on Computational Approaches to Analysing Weblogs (AAAI-CAAW 2006)*. 2006.
7. Pang, B., Lee, L., and Vaithyanathan, S. *Thumbs up? Sentiment Classification using Machine Learning Techniques*. in *Proc.Empirical methods in natural language processing*, ACL (2002), 79-86.
8. Wilson, T., Wiebe, J., and Hoffmann, P. *Recognizing Contextual Polarity in Phrase-Level Sentiment Analysis*. in *Proc. HLT-EMNLP*, (2005).
9. Wu, L., Lin, C.-Y., Aral, S., and Brynjolfsson, E., *Value of Social Network -- A Large-Scale Analysis on Network Structure Impact to Financial Revenue of Information Technology Consultants*. 2009.
10. Yang, J., Ackerman, M., and Adamic, L. *Virtual Gifts and Guanxi: Supporting Social Exchange in a Chinese Online Community*. in *Proc.CSCW*, ACM (2011), 45-54.

"A Pace Not Dictated by Electrons": An Empirical Study of Work Without Email

Gloria J. Mark[1], **Stephen Voida**[1]
Department of Informatics
University of California, Irvine
Irvine, CA 92697-3440 USA
{gmark, svoida}@uci.edu

Armand V. Cardello
U.S. Army Natick Soldier R, D & E Center
Natick, MA 01760 USA
armand.cardello@us.army.mil

ABSTRACT
We report on an empirical study where we cut off email usage for five workdays for 13 information workers in an organization. We employed both quantitative measures such as computer log data and ethnographic methods to compare a baseline condition (normal email usage) with our experimental manipulation (email cutoff). Our results show that without email, people multitasked less and had a longer task focus, as measured by a lower frequency of shifting between windows and a longer duration of time spent working in each computer window. Further, we directly measured stress using wearable heart rate monitors and found that stress, as measured by heart rate variability, was lower without email. Interview data were consistent with our quantitative measures, as participants reported being able to focus more on their tasks. We discuss the implications for managing email better in organizations.

Author Keywords
Email; multitasking; interruptions; empirical study; sensors

ACM Classification Keywords
H.5.3 [Information Interfaces and Presentation (e.g., HCI)]: Group and Organization Interfaces; K.4.m [Computers and Society]: Miscellaneous.

INTRODUCTION
Less than a year ago, a New York Times article drew an analogy between zombies and emails: you keep killing them (or deleting them), and they never stop coming [20]. This tongue-in-cheek commentary brings to light a broader issue associated with being continually connected to ICTs and email in particular—we just can't seem to keep up. The wide adoption of ICTs in the workplace enables people to stay continually up-to-date and connected with others, but critiques as in the New York Times article raise important questions about how continual connectivity might impact aspects of our psyche and behavior such as creating stress and distraction.

Does being continually connected provide benefits to information workers? Wacjman and Rose [29] claim that being continually connected gives agency to workers; information workers are constantly negotiating how to manage information, when to respond to communications, and how to prioritize tasks and information. Email is currently considered the tool *de rigueur* of the workplace, cf. [3]. However, being continually connected on email has also drawn criticism, expressed by Turkle, who writes "*we don't do email, our email does us*" [28]. Bolstering this view is a result from a study of email use where 45% of participants associated email with a loss of control [2].

Though we might surmise that we are overburdened with a huge volume of email, how much attention does email demand? Wacjman and Rose [29] found that, on average, information workers engage in more mediated communication each day than face-to-face communication, of which email is the most common. The picture that Jackson et al. [19] found is rather dismal: they found that 70% of emails were attended to within six seconds of arriving. Email may not be distracting if workers quickly returned to their interrupted task; however, it took an average of 64 seconds to resume an interrupted task.

Email is a multi-functional tool in the workplace; not only is it used for communication, but it also serves as a to-do list and personal information management tool [3], for archiving information, as a mechanism to foster coordination and collaboration among colleagues, and as a source for assigning and delegating tasks [30]. Barley et al. [2] summarize this multi-functional character of email by claiming it to be a symbol for work.

In this paper, we address the issues of email and distractions. Whereas email use has been studied through *in situ* observation [3, 25] and surveys [10], we approach email usage from an inverted perspective. We investigate how people perform work in the *absence* of email—a world free of the "zombies" that vex so many in information work.

[1] Authors Mark and Voida contributed equally to this work and share primary authorship.

EMAIL AND MULTITASKING

Studies of information workers have consistently revealed that they experience high levels of multitasking and interruptions [8, 12, 21]. Interruptions can be beneficial, for example, in gaining relevant information, addressing the task at-hand [21], or as a way to exert control over work by choosing when to respond to others [29]. However, some argue that interruptions can have a negative impact on work when they cause people to switch contexts or create redundant work [21], if they occur at inappropriate times [8], or if they lead users to forget their main task focus [9]. Evidence suggests that fragmented work patterns negatively impact work productivity [24].

Observation of information workers reveals that they switch tasks on average every three minutes [12]. Much switching concerns email: studies show with consistency that people spend about 23% of their time on email [8, 25], with an estimate that people check email about 36 times an hour [25]. This could be an overestimation, but even if halved, and if true, it would comprise a large component of multitasking. Further, people self-report that a high amount of email is associated with a high level of stress [2, 10].

Different theories have been proposed to explain how email creates overload for people. Managing the sheer volume of email is one factor [29], but the more time spent on email, the more likely it creates a feeling of overload [2]. Poor email management strategies also play a role [10, 29], as does the effort to keep track of separate email threads [3]. Recipients generally need to meet the task demands of the sender, which can exacerbate this sense of overload [25].

Despite the wide attention that email overload has received, it is still unclear to what extent email actually contributes to multitasking. Does email lead people to focus less on the task at-hand? In this paper, we address the following research questions related to email and multitasking:

- How is multitasking affected in the absence of email? Is multitasking fueled by email, or would multitasking occur at the same rate in today's information work climate without email use? Does email lead to the increased fragmentation of work?
- Though stress has been self-reported to correspond to email use, to date no study has ever *directly* measured the effect that email has on stress. Stress associated with email has been based on self-reports through surveys or logging [2, 10, 25]. Yet there may be biases in self-reports of stress—for example, in overestimating it. We therefore ask the question: how much stress does email use actually cause? We measure stress directly during *in situ* work using mobile wearable sensors.

There are several reasons why it is important to take an inverted perspective and investigate how work might change when email is removed. First, it enables us to understand whether it is possible to create an environment in which people can focus more closely on their tasks. Since people self-interrupt to check email often [19, 21, 29], would they be able to spend longer durations on tasks when email is not available and when keeping up-to-date with incoming email is no longer a concern? Ultimately, we are interested in providing support to avoid work fragmentation, given the negative consequences associated with this problem [24]. Second, we are interested in learning whether—and how much—stress might be reduced without email. While it is not realistic for an organization to eliminate email usage, this study can shed light on how email management and organizational email policies might be improved.

Our method to directly address the role of email in multitasking was to design an intervention in which multitasking is observed both *with* and *without* email. It is only by comparing a baseline condition (the status quo, i.e., typical email usage) with an experimental manipulation (the absence of email) that we can directly examine the effects email plays on multitasking and stress in the workplace.

RESEARCH SETTING

The study was conducted in a large scientific research organization located on the east coast of the United States. For the current study, participants were recruited by inviting them to information sessions. A total of 13 participants volunteered for the study (6 females, 7 males, mean age = 46). Additionally, 36 of their colleagues (13 females, 23 males) in their workplace social network volunteered to provide end-of-day surveys during the study. Our study was approved by institutional review boards at our home institutions and at the field site.

All of our participants were information workers whose job titles included chemical engineer, materials scientist, psychologist, biologist, food technologist, and research administrator; four of the 13 worked as managers or mentors with significant supervisory responsibilities. Their self-reported job characteristics revealed, on average (using a 5-point scale, where 5 was high), relatively high levels of creativity ($M = 4.5$, $SD = 0.52$), autonomy ($M = 4.3$, $SD = 0.9$), and day-to-day task variety ($M = 4.4$, $SD = 0.5$). All participants had some level of postsecondary education, and averaged employment in their current job for 8.4 years.

Methodology

Our study was a within-subjects design, with each participant taking part in a three-day baseline data collection phase and a five-day experimental ("No Email") condition. In both of these conditions, we collected data using a combination of ethnographic methods and automatic, computer log and sensor-based data collection.

On the first day of the study, we conducted an initial semi-structured interview with each participant to ask about his or her existing multitasking and email usage strategies. After installing a custom window activity logging application on his or her computer and providing instruction about how to use the heart rate monitor, a researcher spent the rest of the day conducting an in-person ethnographic observation of a typical, "baseline" workday. We also began recording activity in the office using our logging software to capture shifts in document and application windows as a measure of how often people were multitasking in their electronic work, a process that we repeated for two additional days (and sometimes more), to ensure that our system collected several days' worth of baseline data.

On the fourth day of the study, participants experienced the No Email experimental condition—complete email cutoff for a five-day period. During these days, we created a Microsoft Outlook email-processing rule that would automatically file away incoming messages without triggering any pop-up notifications. We also asked the participants to voluntarily refrain from sending work-related email. However, because so many participants used other facets of the Outlook software (e.g., contacts, the calendar, SharePoint shared folders), we allowed participants to use Outlook and access emails that had been received prior to the onset of the experimental condition.

We recorded activity in the office for all five of the No Email days using the window activity logging software. A researcher returned on the final day of the experimental condition to conduct a second day of ethnographic observation. At the conclusion of the study, we conducted a semi-structured interview in which we asked about the participant's activity management strategies and about their experiences of not having email available. Post-study interviews lasted about one hour.

Our use of ethnographic methods was intended to provide a rich corpus of data for understanding the complex actions in the workplace. To understand multitasking behavior *in situ*, we needed to capture details of process and content of our participants' workplace activities. An alternative technique, videotaping our participants, was not permitted by our field site. Thus, we used a "shadowing" observation technique similar to that used in previous time management and multitasking studies [12, 21, 22]. A researcher sat with the participant in his/her workspace and followed the individual, whenever possible, to meetings or other activities. The researcher recorded every action that the participant performed to the second, such as opening a computer application or making a phone call. Details about each event were also noted. All interactions with colleagues were documented, including details about the conversation topic, documents used (if possible) and persons involved. We conducted this in-depth observation for two days of the study—the first day of the Baseline condition and the last day of the No Email condition.

Our custom window activity logging application was designed to collect real-time data about our participants' multitasking behavior. This application was installed on each participant's computer workstation before we began data collection, and it ran for the entire duration of the study. The software recorded the frequency of switches between document or program windows where electronic work is carried out (after [18, 23]). In order to gather more objective measures of stress and arousal, the participants wore an electronic heart rate monitor while working—the Garmin ForeRunner 301, consisting of a chest strap and wristwatch receiver—for the duration of the study, i.e., in both the Baseline and No Email conditions.

We administered survey instruments at the beginning and end of the study, as well as at the end of each day. Pre-study survey questions included a demographic questionnaire and a polychronicity preference instrument (IPV) [6], which measures the extent to which participants prefer to work in a polychronic or monochronic manner. At the end of each workday, we delivered several surveys electronically from our data collection software, including the NASA TLX workload scale [15].

Finally, in order to assess the impact of disconnecting a colleague from email, we asked members of the participants' workplace teams to serve as peripheral participants in the study. We asked these team members to complete short surveys at the end of each day about their own perceived productivity, their ability to get information needed to accomplish work on that particular day, and their success (or failure) in getting information that they needed from the main participants, given the changes in their accessibility via email.

RESULTS

Over the course of the study, we conducted nearly 137 hours of ethnographic observation. Our automated sensors captured over 25,000 window changes and recorded over 1.6 million sensor events over a total of more than 700 hours of data collection. The heart rate monitors provided readings of heart rate every few seconds; we received over 40,000 of these readings during the course of the study.

Sometimes illness, vacations, and technology failures interfered with our study schedule. When these incidents occurred, we rescheduled our informants so that they experienced email cut off for a period of five consecutive days. In some cases, this led to our extending Baseline or No Email data collections beyond the typical 8-day window.

We asked participants at the end of each day of the study if they considered that day to be "normal" in terms of the volume and type of work they did. We found no statistical difference for participants in the number of days judged to be normal between the Baseline and No Email conditions. Approximately 65% of study days were reported as being normal workdays.

Workplace Activity: Shadowing of Participants

We observed and classified a total of 5,643 activities carried out by our 13 participants over the course of our in-person shadowing sessions, comprising 71 hours of data collected in the Baseline condition and nearly 66 hours in the No Email condition.

Activity Type	Baseline		No Email	
	Mean	*SD*	Mean	*SD*
Out of office* (work-related)	412.32	938.14	1195.24	2048.88
Computing tasks	52.47	90.52	50.32	82.81
Physical tasks (e.g., reading, jotting notes)	41.06	75.55	56.55	69.86
Communication in the office (excl. email)	84.82	256.94	60.15	103.68
Email (new/filed)	40.65	60.71	36.94	64.85
Metawork*	21.41	28.04	29.14	41.76
Other tasks	56.12	205.58	31.33	54.50
Overall	**74.81**	**375.37**	**102.85**	**510.81**

Table 1. Means and *SDs* of the observed durations (in seconds) of types of activities, excluding personal breaks. * = sig. difference between Baseline and No Email at $p < .05$.

In general, participants reacted well to being cut off from email. Typically, participants stayed connected with their colleagues during the No Email condition through a combination of face-to-face meetings, telephone calls, and by having team members notify them (mostly face-to-face) of critical emails sent to the entire work group or laboratory. Although participants checked email habitually in the Baseline condition, by the fifth day of email cutoff, we observed that participants rarely tried to check email.

The actions recorded from shadowing were categorized into *categories* of activities, as shown in Table 1. A three-way ANOVA of the *duration* of observed activities with condition, participant, and activity type as factors reveals a significant main effect of condition, $F(1, 12) = 6.881$, $p < .05$, indicating that, overall, participants spent longer in activities on average in the No Email condition than they did in the Baseline condition. We also found a significant main effect of activity type, $F(6, 76) = 14.301$, $p < .001$, and a significant interaction of condition by activity type, $F(6, 69) = 8.753$, $p < .001$, suggesting that our participants allocated their time differently across different kinds of activities when access to email was limited. We also observed significant interactions of condition by participant, $F(11, 95) = 3.432$, $p < .001$, and condition by activity type by participant, $F(60, 5474) = 4.849$, $p < .001$, suggesting that there were individual differences in how participants reacted to changes in email availability and in their strategies for multitasking in each of the conditions.

In order to better understand the effect of cutting off email on activities, we ran a series of paired t-tests on the mean durations that participants spent working in each type of activity. We found significant differences in just two of the activity types. First, participants spent significantly longer on out-of-office activities in the No Email condition compared to the Baseline condition: $t(12) = -3.001$, $p < .05$.

Second, we found that participants spent significantly more time carrying out metawork (i.e., activities not connected with any single project but associated with managing all of them [12]) in the No Email condition than they did in the Baseline condition: $t(12) = -2.558$, $p < .05$. This difference might be explained by the fact that coordination work, often carried out via email, is frequently interleaved with metawork activities; without email, this coordination work may be deferred, leading to larger contiguous blocks of metawork.

Surprisingly, the duration of time spent in each session reading, writing, or reviewing attachments to emails—either newly-arrived or those archived in the participants' stored folders—did not differ significantly between the two conditions. Although this is a counterintuitive finding since email was cut off, a potential explanation can be found in the data we collected about the *frequency* (i.e., the total number of activities observed) in which participants engaged in each category of activity in the different conditions. A three-way ANOVA of the *frequency* of switching observed activities yielded a significant main effect of activity type, $F(7, 73) = 28.526$, $p < .001$, as well as significant interactions of condition by activity type, $F(6, 60) = 2.412$, $p < .05$, and condition by participant, $F(11, 60) = 4.160$, $p < .001$. We also ran paired t-tests on these data to determine whether there were any differences in the frequencies at which participants switched activity types across the two conditions. The only activity type that showed statistically significant differences was the email activity; participants worked in their email client significantly less frequently in the No Email condition compared to the Baseline condition, $t(11) = 3.964$, $p < .01$. Thus, though participants used their email client less often when email was cut off, we found no difference between the amount of time they spent using Outlook in either condition (e.g., in the No Email condition, they read emails received prior to the study).

Multitasking Measures: Window Switches

Next, we looked at the sensor data that were collected from tracking computer window switches over the entire 8-day duration of the study. To measure differences in multitasking between the Baseline and No Email conditions, we looked at the duration and frequency of window switches. Table 2 shows, for each participant, the means and standard deviations of the durations (in seconds) that application and document windows were left open, as well as the frequency of window switches (in switches per hour) during each hour that our sensors collected data. We counted all window switches, including when auxiliary windows were invoked (e.g., reading a PDF attachment from a past email). Seven extreme outliers were removed from our set of over 25,000 data points.

For all but one participant, the mean window duration was longer during the No Email condition compared to Baseline. A paired t-test comparing each participant's

P	Baseline Duration *M*	Baseline Duration *SD*	Baseline Frequency *M*	Baseline Frequency *SD*	No Email Duration *M*	No Email Duration *SD*	No Email Frequency *M*	No Email Frequency *SD*
1	76.4	466.7	36.2	34.3	106.1	621.6	12.7	21.2
2	72.6	329.7	27.2	26.0	214.0	729.9	9.1	14.1
3	79.4	450.1	39.2	33.5	121.9	536.2	25.4	20.8
4	53.2	166.9	53.9	34.5	109.8	322.7	24.6	17.7
5	133.8	554.8	17.5	18.5	216.6	882.3	8.2	13.1
6	55.3	275.9	44.2	32.7	83.4	285.0	24.1	23.3
7	67.4	397.9	45.1	33.1	115.7	596.9	25.8	28.1
8	100.6	402.1	26.7	23.0	156.8	821.5	16.2	41.5
9	78.8	369.9	40.1	26.1	181.6	658.1	9.0	12.2
10	53.8	181.0	47.5	29.5	198.4	828.1	16.2	25.2
11	130.5	421.9	23.4	18.8	180.7	560.5	17.5	17.1
12	99.4	400.7	25.5	24.1	126.8	441.9	24.1	17.2
13	62.3	438.2	42.7	33.3	56.7	156.4	30.6	32.0
M	**75.5**	**394.3**	**37.1**	**31.4**	**131.9**	**568.1**	**18.2**	**23.5**

Table 2. Mean and *SD* of window duration (in seconds) and frequency of window switches (switches/hour in which data were collected) for each participant.

window duration during the Baseline and No Email conditions showed that participants spent highly significantly longer times in a document or program window in the No Email condition: $t(12) = -5.00$, $p < .001$. Combining participants' data, an ANOVA with condition and participant as factors shows a highly significant difference between conditions: $F(1, 14) = 28.01$, $p < .0001$. There was no significant difference between participants: $F(12, 12) = 2.37$, $p > .05$. There was, however, a significant condition by participant interaction: $F(12, 25094) = 3.18$, $p < .0001$. Thus, the data show that there was a significant change in the length of time that participants' windows were active between conditions: in the No Email condition, participants had individual application windows open for a significantly longer duration before switching to another window, compared to those in the Baseline condition.

We also examined the frequency of window switches. Table 2 shows that all participants had a lower mean frequency of window switches in the No Email condition. A paired t-test comparing participants' frequencies in Baseline to No Email showed a highly significant difference: $t(12) = 6.50$, $p < .0001$. Thus, participants in the No Email condition switched their windows significantly less often than in the Baseline condition. Combining participants' data, an ANOVA showed a highly significant difference between Baseline and No Email: $F(1, 13) = 44.23$, $p < .0001$, with a significant difference between participants: $F(12, 12) = 3.14$, $p < .05$. There was also a significant condition by participant interaction: $F(12, 903) = 1.97$, $p < .05$. Thus, overall, the window logging data show that participants in the No Email condition had individual application and document windows active for longer durations and switched between them less often than they did in the Baseline condition, when email was available.

Email and Stress: Heart Rate Monitoring

We also directly measured participants' level of stress when working with and without email through the use of heart rate monitors. Participants wore the heart rate monitors full time while at work. Heart rate variability (HRV) is widely used as an indicator of mental stress (see [1, 4, 5] for reviews). The lower the measure of HRV, the higher the amount of stress that an individual experiences. The correlation between stress and HRV is high; as arousal increases, HRV decreases. The body responds to stressful circumstances by regulating itself: the sympathetic nervous system is very good at responding to stress. Similarly, when people are not experiencing stress, HRV is higher, as the heart rate fluctuates more, i.e., the body is not regulating itself. A lowering of HRV has been associated with other factors related to stress (e.g., depression [14] and anxiety [31]). HRV has been used to measure a variety of phenomena, including stress during computer work [17].

A recommended measure of overall HRV is the standard deviation of heart periods [5]. Our goal was to measure study participants' stress during the Baseline and No Email conditions and we did so by measuring HRV continually as participants went about their normal work. Due to technical difficulties, we were only able to capture data across both the Baseline and No Email conditions from seven of our participants. Table 3 shows the number of days for these participants in which heart rate data were captured. In post-study interviews, no one reported that wearing the heart rate monitor was obtrusive or that it affected their behavior. Nearly all participants reported that once they put the chest strap on, they forgot about it. One participant wore the monitor home once because she forgot that she was wearing it. Another participant reported that he tended to "sit back more" but did not believe it changed his behavior. A third person reported that it was "a bit annoying," but she wore it on all of the study days except one.

We computed the HRV using the standard deviation of the recorded heart rate, which is the standard way to measure HRV [5]. Table 3 shows measures averaged for each participant and for each condition over all the days that data were collected. A paired comparisons t-test between the Baseline and No Email conditions shows a very strong trend that people in Baseline had lower HRV (i.e., higher

Subj.	Baseline # days	Baseline Mean	Baseline *SD*	No email # days	No email Mean	No email *SD*
2	6	76.35	8.43	5	79.29	10.60
3	4	88.99	9.82	3	93.70	9.85
4	3	71.31	7.06	3	76.07	5.36
5	5	74.92	23.72	5	75.61	25.93
6	3	95.88	18.80	8	100.00	23.39
8	2	77.15	8.75	7	78.99	13.03
11	3	62.26	9.40	4	67.22	18.22
Total	**26**	**77.03**	**16.173**	**35**	**80.39**	**18.36**

Table 3. Mean and *SD* of heart rate monitor data and number of days that data were captured for each condition.

stress) than those in No Email (Mean difference = −2.926, $SD = 3.425$, $t(6) = -2.260$, $p = .065$). Levene's test conducted on the comparison of the standard deviations of all Baseline data with all No Email data shows this difference to be highly significant: SD(Baseline) = 16.17, SD(No Email) = 18.36, $F(1, 40409) = 170.86$, $p < .0001$. These results indicate that participants experienced less stress when their email was cut off than in the baseline condition when they had email access.

An ANOVA conducted on the mean heart rate with Condition and Participant as factors shows that the measure was significantly less in Baseline than in the No Email condition: $F(1, 40409) = 33.40$, $p < .001$. There was also a significant difference between participants, $F(6, 40409) = 206.34$, $p < .0001$, and a significant interaction of condition by participant, $F(6, 40409) = 16.30$, $p < .0001$. Thus, mean heart rate was higher in the No Email condition. While there could be a number of explanations for this result, heart rate generally increases with activity. This notion is consistent with our observations, which showed that without email, participants engaged in more "Out of office" activities (see Table 1).

Attitudes of Multitasking and Email: Surveys

Surveys were deployed to help us understand whether immersion in an "email free" work environment might be affected by—or influence—participants' attitudes about multitasking and feelings of productivity, time pressure, and frustration. We asked participants at the beginning of the study questions drawn from the Inventory of Polychronic Values (IPV), an instrument designed to assess

> *the extent to which people in a culture: (1) prefer to be engaged in two or more tasks simultaneously; and (2) believe that their preference is the best way to do things* [6].

Relative to the results reported by Bluedorn et al. [6], four out of 13 participants were categorized as having a high preference for polychronicity and nine participants measured an average preference for polychronicity. There was no significant relationship between polychronicity preference scores and mean window durations in either the Baseline or No Email conditions.

At the end of each day of the study, participants completed the NASA TLX workload assessment [15], which measures mental, physical, and temporal demands, as well as performance, effort, and frustration. An ANOVA conducted on participants' responses between the Baseline and No Email conditions showed no significant differences. These findings suggest that foregoing the use of email at work does not fundamentally change the subjective workload that a person experiences—in either direction.

Colleagues' Perspectives: End-of-Day Self-Reports

A person's availability via email has the potential to impact not only their own multitasking and stress levels, but also to affect the ability of their colleagues to find information they need to collaborate and to delegate tasks. For each of our study participants, we recruited a group of 2–7 of that person's closest team members to answer a short series of survey questions at the end of each day of the study. These questions combined general queries about the success and stress level of the colleagues' day (e.g., "Rate the following statement: I was able to get the information I needed to conduct my work today" and "How productive do you think you were today?") and a question specifically geared to determining the impact of the main participant's availability or unavailability via email ("Rate the following statement: It was easy for me to reach [name] to get information I needed from [him/her]").

An ANOVA showed no significant difference in team members' responses between the Baseline and No Email conditions for these questions. However, a trend approaching statistical significance revealed that team members agreed more strongly with the statement "I was able to get the information I needed to conduct my work today" in the Baseline condition ($M = 4.53$, $SD = 0.28$) than in the No Email condition ($M = 3.71$, $SD = 0.26$), $F(1, 47) = 3.221$, $p < .08$.

QUALITATIVE DATA ANALYSIS

How did our informants feel when their email was cut off for five days? The post-study interview data was open-coded and themes were identified. Not surprisingly, nearly all informants viewed email as "*double-edged*," having pros and cons. Attitudes towards email could be categorized in two ways. To two informants, they viewed email primarily as a communication tool in their work—these people missed email the most when it was cut off. The second category—the rest of the informants—expressed an attitude that email was primarily a burden. A common reason expressed by this latter group was due to the volume, e.g.:

> *My work has become how to manage email.*
>
> *I have so many emails, I don't even read them.*
>
> *With email, it's a train wreck... you can't look away from it.*

One informant's attitude was extreme:

> [Email is] *an annoyance, a giant to-do list. I got to the point where, being overwhelmed, I gave up.... That would be nirvana—to tell everyone I'm wiping out my email.... It's ruining my life, it's interfering with my happiness.*

Only one informant considered herself addicted to email. She explained that she takes her BlackBerry on vacation but then locks it in the hotel safe to keep from checking email. One informant explained she was not addicted but would not want to live without it. Still another admitted that at times he felt addicted to email.

Lack of Agency

Another reason why informants viewed email as a burden was that they felt that it affected their agency to work. About half of the informants described that they felt like they were not in control of their email, and consequently not in control of their work. Attitudes were expressed as:

It ruled my life—that made me feel depressed, and now I feel liberated [without email]...*too much headache trying to keep on top of everything.*

I let the sound of the bell and the pop-ups rule my life.

[When email was cut off]: *Felt it was under my control.*

It prompts me. When you come back, it's waiting.

In contrast, when asked how they felt about working without email, nearly all informants described that their pace was more relaxed. One informant described he felt "*liberated*"; another informant expressed the biggest benefit as "*peace*"; still another described it as "*refreshing.*"

Email, Communication, and Relationships

A theme that emerged was that when email was cut off, face-to-face interactions with other colleagues in the workplace increased. All informants reported that with email cut off, they interacted with people more, both face-to-face and by phone, whereas they would usually send emails instead. They viewed this change as a benefit. Nearly all informants described how they walked around the workplace more to visit their colleagues for face-to-face interactions in the No Email condition; some even walked to other buildings on the campus. Some visits to colleagues were by choice, as opposed to placing a telephone call[2].

The lack of access to email enabled the informants to reflect more deeply on how email affects their relationships with their colleagues. The informants expressed that during the time of email cut off, they became aware that the use of email hindered their work relationships. Some representative comments that express this idea were:

...Email can be a superficial blanket that distances you from real relationships where you're really working together.

I socialize and the social aspect became that much greater.

I was surprised at how much all that human interaction came in to fill the vacuum [i.e., when having no email].

[Working without email] *helps with one-on-one relationships.*

Email is easier, but getting up and walking around, it's a lot easier to talk face-to-face. You can pick up more vibes of the relationship thing that you can't do with email.

Focus

Our quantitative results showed that in the No Email condition, people switched tasks less and spent longer durations on each window screen before switching. The interview data corroborate this result. A common theme that was expressed by nearly all informants was that during the time that email was cut off, they were able to spend longer periods of time on a task and focus more intently on their work. One informant described that during the study, he learned that email was his main source of self-distraction. The word "focus" was found often throughout our interview data. Typical comments included:

It gave me more focus.

It gave me time to think about [work] *more.*

I was able to spend time actually doing tasks that had to be done.... It was nice to be able to sit and work on a manuscript for the whole morning.

When I didn't have email, multitasking, I had three projects done. I was more focused.

[I] *wasn't distracted by checking email. It was nice. I was able to plan more what I was doing for a chunk of time.*

I was writing a report, and I could focus on the report.

Only one person told us that she was surprised that, despite expecting to be able to accomplish a larger number of projects in the No Email condition, she did not.

Feeling Cut Off

The biggest disadvantage expressed by the informants when they did not have email was that they felt "cut off." Two informants did not report feeling cut off (one reported that he did not miss anyone); one informant felt cut off "a little bit" but was "OK" with it. Only one informant mentioned from whom she felt cut off (off-site customers). About half the informants described it as a general sense of isolation:

You have that sense that there's something really important, there's a deadline that you missed... not knowing.

The hardest thing was not being sure what I missed.

I felt disconnected for sure. When email is down, it makes me crazy. I don't feel as productive...it was difficult.

Yes—hands down—it isolates you as the one person who's not "plugged in."

There was a little uneasiness...felt I was missing something.

I didn't like knowing that information was coming or not 'cause there's the expectation that you're on email.

Thus, though most informants reported feeling cut off from others, this feeling seemed to be grounded in a fear that they were potentially missing out on information being exchanged within the organization.

As a result of not using email in the workplace, the informants could describe their actual experiences of how email affects work, as opposed to their perceptions. The interview data revealed that there were various ways that email was reported to be burdensome. First, the social norm that surrounds email use is primarily what causes it to be a burden. The informants commonly expressed that there is a norm or expectation that the email recipient will respond to an email quickly. For example, one informant comes into work two hours later than her colleagues. She described how her colleagues, who arrived at work and sent out emails two hours prior, expect an answer to their emails as soon as she arrives. Second, email is a burden due to the

[2] In our shadowing observation, we could not always follow informants when they left the office; the activity of interacting with others outside the office is characterized as "Out of office" in Table 1.

sheer volume of email that people receive. The informants commonly reported not being able to keep up with their email. They referred to important emails that get lost in the flood of incoming messages. Third, the informants admit that they lack self-control to not check email regularly. In some cases, this lack of self-control translates into a lack of agency in the workplace, as two informants described: a "lack of control" and that it "rules their life." Last, email is a burden when it is used as a channel for delegating work. Aside from the two informants who viewed email primarily as a communication tool, to the other informants, it was a channel for delegating tasks to others. One informant's experience is an illustration—this informant receives "taskers" from his superiors. These refer to tasks that he needs to do immediately. As a lab scientist, this interferes with his ability to set up and run experiments without interruption. When his email was cut off, the taskers suddenly stopped. Though his superiors could have called him on the phone or walked down the hall to delegate the task to him, this did not happen. This experience led him to believe that the taskers he had been receiving by email were either not important or that the senders had taken initiative to find the information themselves when he was off email.

DISCUSSION

We set out to discover whether email was a significant component of multitasking behavior, and whether, by removing email, people would focus more on their tasks and multitask less. Our results show that without email, people did multitask less and had a longer task focus, as measured by a longer duration of time spent working in each application window and a lower frequency of shifting between windows. In other words, our data show that email usage leads to more work fragmentation. Perhaps this is not surprising, as other studies have shown how often people check email [19, 25]. Our study confirms, that without email, multitasking would be reduced. This raises a number of other questions, such as: how much information sent through email is actually necessary or desirable for work?

We also directly measured whether email causes stress. We found a strong trend that stress, as measured by HRV, was lower when email was removed. We expect that this result would achieve significance with more subjects. If workplace stress is detrimental to health, as some research suggests [16], then our results may even suggest that email could contribute to workplace health problems by raising stress levels. This is a topic for further research.

It is possible that the out-of-office activity could have affected HRV. Though HRV is reported higher in athletes [7] and in older adults doing aerobic activity [27], there is little data about the relationship between HRV and physical activity or exercise in the general population. In our study, any activity (e.g., walking to meetings) was a random effect variable—it occurred in both conditions of our study, and is therefore an unlikely contributor to the trend that we observed between conditions.

It is difficult to disentangle the different sources of stress in the workplace, so we can only speculate as to whether it is the volume of email, social expectations and organizational conventions associated with email, or the symbolism of email as a delegator of work [2] that lead to the increase in stress that we observed. It is noteworthy that we found stress levels to change within a period of just five days without email. This suggests that short "vacations" from email may be sufficient to reduce stress in the workplace. At the same time, the higher mean heart rate that we found without email use is consistent with both our observations and our interviews, which show that without email, people take more frequent work breaks, during which they move around the workplace more. This would suggest that not only might reducing email reduce stress, but that reducing use of email may even be good for health. Of course, further research would be needed to examine this hypothesis. Overall, our results suggest that the reduction of email needs to be taken seriously by organizations and they raise a number of potentially interesting issues for future study.

Email and Non-mediated Interaction

One of the interesting findings that emerged from the interview data was that not having email led to more face-to-face interaction. On the whole, the informants reported that they enjoyed their social life at work with their colleagues more when email was cut off. Combined with lower stress levels and the reports of being more relaxed, this leads us to question more broadly how email is affecting workplace relationships.

Interestingly, the colleagues in the participants' work groups did not report detrimental effects when their colleagues were off email. Aside from reporting that it was harder to get information from their colleague (which was expected), their satisfaction, productivity, and stress levels were not affected. As a result, we might hypothesize that when a person upon whom one relies for information becomes unavailable for a period of time, this will increase the self-initiative of the information seeker to find the information or to solve the problem on their own.

The Pace of Work

Our findings suggest that email speeds up the pace of work. Participants switched between windows more often, and the amount of time they spent in any one window before moving on was shorter with email. At the same time, from the interviews, nearly all informants reported that email creates expectations that the receiver will respond quickly. When we combine our quantitative and qualitative results, we see support for the idea that email drives a cycle of working at a faster pace. We cannot say whether this is positive or negative for organizations; our study results do not address whether a faster work pace is associated with higher productivity or efficiency. What we can say from our data is that the study participants overall preferred a slower pace of work based on their reactions to work life without email. Perhaps this is best expressed by the informant who described not having email as allowing him to work at "a pace not dictated by electrons."

Implications for Organizations

Our results suggest several implications for organizations in alleviating the burden of email on employees. First, our results reinforce some existing recommendations that reading email in batches might be efficacious [26]. Our informants were off of email for five days. In the interviews, most of the informants described that they dreaded reading their email when they concluded participation in the study. However, the process of catching up was not as bad as they anticipated. One informant, for example, said that when he returned to email, he read through his inbox quickly and learned a strategy of eliminating emails based on their subject header. He claimed that this took far less time than handling emails by checking them regularly throughout the day. This finding illustrates a contrast to the survey responses reported by Dabbish and Kraut [10]; our informants reported feeling *less* overloaded with restricted email use. These differences might be explained by the evolution of email management strategies over the last several years, the specific culture of email usage in the organization we studied, or the fact that we were examining email usage in the broader context of multitasking and information work. While we do not suggest that reading email should be done in batches of several days, organizations could consider experimenting with establishing practices of exchanging email—at least within particular work groups—at certain intervals, such as first thing in the morning, after lunch, and in the evening. Organizations could also try deferring informational emails to a pull-oriented channel (e.g., an intranet website or RSS feed), rather than sending email "blasts" that necessitate action by every employee.

One of our intriguing results was that without email, our informants consistently reported feeling relaxed and more focused. This suggests that an organization should consider the immaterial benefits for workers in restricting, filtering, or actively managing the delivery of email.

Are we suggesting that organizations cut off email? Absolutely not. We did learn a great deal from this study, as did our participants. For example, informants reported that when someone needed to reach them and email was not available, they often used an alternative means. Perhaps if communication is dispersed within an organization across various media, e.g., IM, telephone, or face-to-face, it would create less email traffic and may lower stress. Of course, dispersed communication channels lead to other problems such as not knowing which means to use to reach someone. This is a topic of ongoing research.

Limitations

Although we studied a relatively small group of 13 participants (and surveyed their immediate colleagues), we do not feel that this factor adversely affected the validity of our findings, for two main reasons. First, this participant size is consistent with previous, observation-only studies of workplace multitasking (cf. [12]). Second, our combination of qualitative and quantitative data collection techniques provided an enormous amount of data from each participant over almost two weeks of authentic, *in situ* work.

One of the main limitations of the study is that we collected data at only a single field site, a decision that we made because of these workers' willingness to commit to a demanding study schedule, including observation and the use of heart rate recording devices, and the support that we received from the field site administrators in allowing us to ask employees to forego use of email for an entire week. Even within this organization, we may have unintentionally encountered some bias due to participant self-selection, since only a portion of those people who voluntarily attended a study information session consented to be in the study. Thus, our participants may have self-selected on the basis of their attitudes toward their email workload, concern with multitasking in the workplace, or for some other reason. From our initial interviews, we know that most participants considered email to be a burden, at least some of the time. We are also aware that some potential participants excluded themselves from the study because their jobs were solely focused on responding to email. We would strongly advocate that similar studies be run in a variety of different work contexts to help validate the findings with information workers that may have different practices and different relationships with the use of email.

We also encountered some technical difficulties with the heart rate monitors that prevented us from capturing data from all participants. However, our findings show a strong trend that would very likely reach significance with additional participants.

CONCLUSIONS

Our study has shown that there are benefits to not being continually connected by email. Without email, our informants focused longer on their tasks, multitasked less, and had lower stress. It is an open question to what extent the effects we found in our study might be sustainable. How the benefits of reduced email usage might outweigh the known benefits of email in reaching larger numbers of people rapidly with information is not clear. What our study suggests is that the tradeoffs among email usage, work pace, stress, and collaboration need to be more closely explored. There will always be new "zombies" lurking with advances in information technology, and we must continue to be vigilant in assessing the human costs that are incurred when these advances are adopted in the workplace.

ACKNOWLEDGMENTS

This work was supported by the National Science Foundation under award CNS-0937060 to the Computing Research Association for the Computing Innovation Fellows Project, as well as by the U.S. Army Natick R, D & E Center. We would like to thank the members of the executive steering committee at our field site for their support of our study and our informants for their time (and patience).

REFERENCES

1. Acharya, U.R., Joseph, K.P., Kannathal, N., Lim, C.M., and Suri, J.S. Heart rate variability: A review. *Medical & Bio Engineering & Comp 44*, 12 (2006), 1031–1051.
2. Barley, S., Myerson, D., and Grodel, S. E-mail as a source and symbol of stress. *Organization Science 22*, 4 (2011), 887–906.
3. Bellotti, V., Ducheneaut, N., Howard, M., Smith, I., and Grinter, R.E. Quality versus quantity: E-mail-centric task management and its relation with overload. *Human-Computer Interaction 20*, 1 (2005), 89–138.
4. Berntson, G.G. and Cacioppo, J.T. Heart rate variability: Stress and psychiatric conditions. In M. Malik and A.J. Camm (Eds.), *Dynamic Electrocardiography*, Blackwell Publishing, Oxford, UK, 2007.
5. Berntson, G., Bigger, J., Eckberg, D., Grossman, P., Kaufmann, P., Malik, M., Nagaraja, H., Porges, S., Saul, J., Stone, P., and van der Molen, M. Heart rate variability: Origins, methods, and interpretive caveats. *Psychophysiology 34*, 6 (1997), 623–648.
6. Bluedorn, A., Kalliath, T., Strube, M., and Martin, G. Polychronicity and the Inventory of Polychronic Values (IPV): The development of an instrument to measure a fundamental dimension of organizational culture. *J of Managerial Psychology 14*, 3/4 (1999), 205–231.
7. Boutcher, S.H., Nugent, F.W., McLaren, P.F., and Weltman, A.L. Heart period variability of trained and untrained men at rest and during mental challenge. *Psychophysiology 35*, 1 (1998), 16–22.
8. Czerwinski, M., Horvitz, E., and Wilhite, S. A diary study of task switching and interruptions. In *Proc. CHI 2004*, ACM Press (2004), 175–182.
9. Cutrell, E., Czerwinski, M., and Horvitz, E. Notification, disruption, and memory: Effects of messaging interruptions on memory and performance. In *Proc. INTERACT 2001*, IOS Press (2001), 263–269.
10. Dabbish, L.A. and Kraut, R.E. Email overload at work: An analysis of factors associated with email strain. In *Proc. CSCW 2006*, ACM Press (2006), 431–440.
11. Fogarty, J., Hudson, S.E., Atkeson, C.G., Avrahami, D., Forlizzi, J., Kiesler, S., Lee, J.C., and Yang, J. Predicting human interruptibility with sensors. *ACM Trans. Computer–Human Interaction 12,* 1 (2005), 119–146.
12. González, V.M. and Mark, G. "Constant, constant, multitasking craziness": Managing multiple working spheres. In *Proc. CHI 2004*, ACM Press (2004), 113–120.
13. González, V.M., Nardi, B., and Mark, G. Ensembles: Understanding the instantiation of activities. *Information Tech & People 22*, 2 (2009), 109–131.
14. Gorman, J.M. and Sloan, R.P. Heart rate variability in depressive and anxiety disorders. *American Heart Journal 140,* 4, Part B (2000), 77–83.
15. Hart, S.G. and Staveland, L.E. Development of NASA-TLX (Task Load Index): Results of empirical and theoretical research. In P.A. Hancock and N. Meshkati (Eds.), *Human Mental Workload*. North-Holland, Amsterdam (1988), 239–250.
16. Hewlett, S.A. and Luce, C.B. Extreme jobs: The dangerous allure of the 70-hour workweek. *Harvard Business Review 84*, 12 (2006), 49–59, 162.
17. Hjortskov, N. Rissén, D., Blangsted, A., Fallentin, N., Lundberg, U., and Søgaard, K. The effect of mental stress on heart rate variability and blood pressure during computer work. *Eur J of Appl Phys 92*, 1-2 (2004), 84–89.
18. Hutchings, D.R., Smith, G., Meyers, B., Czerwinski, M., and Robertson, G. Display space usage and window management operation comparisons between single monitor and multiple monitor users. In *Proc. AVI 2004*, ACM Press (2004), 32–39.
19. Jackson, T., Dawson, R., and Wilson, D. Reducing the effect of email interruptions on employees. *International J of Information Management 23*, 1 (2003), 55–65.
20. Klosterman, C. My zombie, myself: Why modern life feels rather undead. *The New York Times*, Dec. 3, 2010.
21. Mark, G., González, V., and Harris, J. No task left behind? Examining the nature of fragmented work. In *Proc. CHI 2005*, ACM Press (2005), 321–330.
22. Mintzberg, H. Structured observation as a method to study managerial work. *J Mgt Stud 7*, 1 (1970), 87–104.
23. Nair, R., Voida, S., and Mynatt, E.D. Frequency-based detection of task switches. In *Proc. HCI 2005*. Springer (2005), 94–99.
24. Perlow, L.A. The time famine: Towards a sociology of work time. *Admin Sci Quarterly 44*, 1 (1999), 57–81.
25. Renaud, K., Ramsay, J., and Hair, M. "You've got e-mail!" ... shall I deal with it now? Electronic mail from the recipient's perspective. *IJHCI 21*, 3 (2006), 313–332.
26. Robbins, S. Tips for mastering e-mail overload. *Harvard Business School Working Knowledge* (2004, Oct 25). http://hbswk.hbs.edu/archive/4438.html.
27. Stein, P.K., Ehsani, A.A., Domitrovich, P.P., Kleiger, R.E., and Rottman, J.N. Effect of exercise training on heart rate variability in healthy older adults. *American Heart Journal 138*, 3 (1999), 567–576.
28. Turkle, S. *Alone Together*. MIT Press, Cambridge, MA, 2010.
29. Wacjman, J. and Rose, E. Constant connectivity: Rethinking interruptions at work. *Organization Studies 32*, 7 (2011), 941–961.
30. Whittaker, S., and Sidner, C. Email overload: Exploring personal information management of email. In *Proc. CHI 1996*, ACM Press (1996), 276–283.
31. Yeragani, V.K., Sobolewski, E., Igel, G., Johnson, C., Jampala, V.C., Kay, J., Hillman, N., Yeragani, S., and Vempati, S. Decreased heart-period variability in patients with panic disorder: A study of Holter ECG records. *Psychiatry Research 78*, 1–2 (1998), 89–99.

"You've Got Video": Increasing Clickthrough When Sharing Enterprise Video with Email

Mercan Topkara[1] **Shimei Pan**[1] **Jennifer Lai**[1] **Ahmet E. Dirik**[2] **Steve Wood**[1] **Jeff Boston**[1]
[1]IBM T. J. Watson Research Center
19 Skyline Dr, Hawthorne, NY, USA
{mtopkara, shimei, jlai, woodsp, daddyb} @us.ibm.com
[2]Uludag University
Gorukle Campus, 16059, Bursa, TURKEY
edirik@uludag.edu.tr

ABSTRACT

In this Note we summarize our research on increasing the information scent of video recordings that are shared via email in a corporate setting. We compare two types of email messages for sharing recordings: the first containing basic information (e.g. title, speaker, abstract) with a link to the video; the second with the same information plus a set of video thumbnails (hyperlinked to the segments they represent), which are automatically created by video summarization technology. We report on the results of two user studies. The first one compares the quality of the set of thumbnails selected by the technology to sets selected by 31 humans. The second study examines the clickthrough rates for both email formats (with and without hyperlinked thumbnails) as well as gathering subjective feedback via survey. Results indicate that the email messages with the thumbnails drove significantly higher clickthrough rates than the messages without, even though people clicked on the main video link more frequently than the thumbnails. Survey responses show that users found the email with the thumbnail set significantly more appealing and novel.

Author Keywords
Video sharing; thumbnail view; email overload; link sharing

ACM Classification Keywords
H5.m. Information interfaces and presentation (e.g., HCI): Miscellaneous.

General Terms
Human Factors, Design

INTRODUCTION
Increasingly talks, as well as meetings, are recorded and made available after the fact as a video recording. These videos tend to be much longer than the average YouTube video, often lasting up to 60 minutes. Current methods of sharing video as an attachment or a link in an email are sub-optimal since one method has bandwidth and storage costs, and neither provide the recipient with sufficient information to determine if it is worth their time to view the recording. Corporate file-sharing systems notify users that a file has been shared with them by sending an email with a link to the file. These online systems were developed in an attempt to increase knowledge sharing, and reduce reliance on sharing files as attachments [5]. However, given the well documented phenomena of 'email overload' [4], users already feel that they receive and send more email than they can handle, and have developed triage methods for their email to help with the handling of the daily onslaught [3]. Thus receiving an email with a link to a video, which may or may not be of interest to the user, is most frequently ignored, unless the link is sent directly to the recipient by a trusted source [2].

In an attempt to address these issues we experimented with the use of a video processing technology we developed that allows the creator/owner of the video to share a set of automatically selected shot thumbnails via email (see Figure 1). We evaluated whether recipients of these messages would be more or less inclined to view the video, and their subjective reactions to this type of information notification. A within-subjects study showed a higher number of clickthroughs originating from emails that included the visual thumbnail set and responses to a survey indicate that users found the email with the visual thumbnail set more appealing and novel.

In the next section we briefly describe the video summarization technology, and then introduce key related work. We subsequently describe the two studies with their results. Lastly we discuss limitations of this work.

VIDEO SUMMARIZATION TECHNOLOGY
We developed a low complexity unsupervised video summarization technology for use with recordings of talks. The summary consists of salient thumbnails selected from video frames based on a ranking algorithm that takes into consideration several heuristics based on the characteristics of the domain. The thumbnails are presented in 200x150 pixel size due to the limited real estate available in emails. The technique uses the following standard steps: shot detection; shot clustering; slide detection; shot ranking; and selection of top 10 representative frames. We refer to a sequence of successive frames with similar content as a

"shot". Shot detection is the step of segmenting video into shots. Only one representative frame from each shot is used during the clustering and ranking steps. Shot detection uses color histogram to evaluate the similarity of frames, which is standard for this technology.

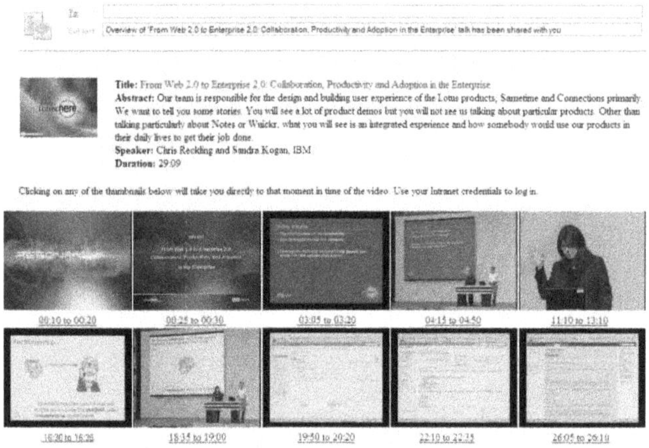

Figure 1. An email with thumbnails

We used several heuristics in ranking the representative frames. A cluster's rank is directly correlated with the total shot duration in that cluster. Also, a cluster with a higher information value (i.e., different from the rest of the clusters) is ranked higher. The first shot in a slide cluster shots is selected as representative for that cluster, which aims to catch the title slide or the first slide of a new discussion point. We perform OCR analytics on all slide shots, and the number of characters extracted from a slide shot is *inversely* correlated with its rank (to provide thumbnails with readable text on them). Slides with greater graphic and visual appeal measures, as computed by intensity histograms, are ranked higher.

Once representative frames from the top ranked non-slide-clusters are added to the summary, slide frames from the top ranked slide-clusters are selected based on their ranking within the cluster. After an initial set of frames is selected, the diversity among these frames is re-evaluated. Low ranking frames are swapped with the next top ranked frame in the cluster until the similarity among the selected frames in the set is below a threshold value.

RELATED WORK

Given the nature of Note, we will contain our references to just the work focused on the effect of previews on content sharing.

Several studies show improvement in user experience when visual context is provided for web page previews (in search results or mobile web previews) [1, 6]. Aula et al. showed that users overestimated the helpfulness of a web page when they were provided only a textual snippet, and they underestimated the helpfulness when given only visual thumbnail of the page. The best judgment was achieved when both were available. Our findings also suggest that users found it more useful when visual thumbnails were added to the general information about the video.

Song et al.'s work focuses directly on the usefulness of audio and visual 'surrogates' for deciding whether to download a video [8]. They used a web interface to provide the users with three different types of surrogates: audio (spoken) description, a visual storyboard and both. Users performed best on the sense-making tasks when both surrogates were available. By contrast, in our work we focused on the effect of an automatically created visual summary together with manually created basic information.

USER STUDY 1: VALIDITY OF SUMMARIZATION TECHNOLOGY

The goal of this study was to verify that the technology used to select the 10 thumbnails sent in the email did a sufficient job to represent the video. To measure this we compared the set of thumbnails selected by the technology with sets selected by 31 humans for the same videos.

Setup

We provided representative shots from four videos of recorded talks (Video 1: 91 shots; Video 2: 147 shots; Video 3: 182 shots: Video 4: 192 shots;) in a web interface and asked participants to select 10 shots that represented the video and would give another person an idea of what the talk was about. The frames were presented as 200 x 150 pixel thumbnails. Participants ranged in age from mid 20s to mid 50s from different ethnic backgrounds, all working in software technology at a large research company.

	Video1	Video2	Video3	Video4
System's Agreement	70%	76.3%	47.1%	44.8%
Average User Agreement	65.9%	76.7%	43.5%	59.2%
STD of User Agreement	0.58	0.62	1.01	1.00

Table 1. System Agreement with Users

Results

We calculated the agreement of each participant with the other study participants as well as the agreement of the system's selection with that of all participants. The agreement value is calculated by performing 1 by N color histogram similarity comparison on each of the thumbnails in the set. As shown in Table 1 there was a high variance in user agreement. For example, for video 1, when comparing sets selected by participants, there was only 65.9% agreement among participants. This result supports other research that reported that human participants do not agree strongly on a common summary [7, 9].

We modeled our evaluation on TRECVID (a video summarization benchmarking effort), which has recently started using a similar process of creating a ground truth with 5 trained annotators analyzing 8 hrs of BBC news videos. This truth is then used in evaluating the video summarization techniques [11].

The variance in participants' agreement increased as the number of total shots increased. Yet in 3 out of 4 videos the technology's agreement with the participants' selections is within the standard deviation, indicating that the system did as well as any single participant. Only in Video 4, the system's selection was outside of the standard deviation, which was due to the nature of this particular talk that included a review of several projects at a fast pace with only screen shots. As a result, for Study 2, we only used videos of talks that included speaker, screen shots (i.e. slides or demo) and audience shots. This was the same nature as videos 1 through 3.

USER STUDY 2: SHARING VIDEO VIA EMAIL

The focus of this research is on increasing the informativeness of the email when sharing a link to a video. Part of the goal is to support knowledge sharing within the enterprise, since if I share a video with you and you never follow the link because you can't invest the time to see if it is truly relevant, there is a potential missed opportunity cost.

Our hypothesis was that when people can view the summary thumbnails they will be more inclined to take the time to view the video, or segments of the video, since the information scent would be higher. This hypothesis is supported by the feature integration theory in human visual attention [10], which indicates that color and intensity are primitive features and are included in the fast and pre-attentive feature search.

Our assumption was that all videos selected for the study have the same relative degree of interest to the target population since they were talks of general interest to the HCI community and the distribution list was made up of 428 people who had registered an interest in this topic.

We performed a within-subject study that involved sending the distribution list four email messages. Recipients were randomly assigned to either Group1 or Group 2. The four videos were all similar including views of the speaker, his/her slides and the audience. The durations ranged from 59 minutes to 71 minutes.

We prepared two different types of emails for each of the four videos. The first type (WoMT – with only main thumbnail) included a main thumbnail from the video (first non-blank keyframe automatically selected by the video processing system), a link to the video, the title of the talk, the name of the speaker, 2-3 sentence abstract of the talk that was manually created by the content owner, and its duration. The second email type (WTS – with thumbnail summary) included exactly the same information as the first type, plus the automatic thumbnail summary. The thumbnails were hyperlinked to the moment in time they represented in the video. In both types of messages, clicking on the link to the video started playing the video in a new window at the start of the video recording. For the messages in WTS format, clicking on any of the thumbnails started playing the video at that moment in time of the recording.

We added the main thumbnail to both types of emails to minimize any bias based solely on the fact that one format was text only and the other was text plus image. In this way, each format had some visual element, but the WTS format had more. We sent out each email at the same time to the two groups. The emails were sent on Tuesdays and Thursdays for 2 weeks. We alternated the type of email each group received in consecutive emails. Group 1 received information about Video A in WoMT format, Video B in WTS format, Video C in WoMT format, and Video D in WTS format. This sequence of email types was reversed with Group 2.

On the third week, we sent out a survey to both groups to solicit subjective opinions in addition to the clickthrough data resulting from the email messages.

Results

In total there were 175 clickthroughs to video playback originating from these emails. 112 of these clicks came from WTS type emails and 63 came from WoMT type emails. We performed a paired t test and the mean difference between the WTS and WoMT conditions (mean WoMT = 28, WTS = 15.75) is statistically significant ($p=0.037$).

Additionally we got 27 responses to the survey. The survey questions include eleven agreement questions on the usability and attractiveness for each of the two types of emails (boring, complicated, confusing, novel, easy to use, appealing, error-prone, frustrating, intuitive, quick and satisfying.). We also asked seven questions on how users interacted with the emails they received (e.g. whether a thumbnail was clicked and what would constitute a useful thumbnail). Lastly we included five general agreement questions on the usability of the thumbnails (e.g. thumbnails are useful, informative, easy to use).

Our click-through data showed that most of the recipients preferred to click on the hyperlinked title to play back the video from the beginning in both types of emails. Several survey respondents mentioned that they needed more context (in addition to the visual thumbnails) about the segments in order to decide if they wanted to start watching from that segment. This feedback is also supported by the work presented in [1], where users judged the 'helpfulness' of a webpage better when the preview included both a textual and a visual snippet as compared to having only one of these types.

Respondents' top choices for the type of thumbnails they would like to see in a summary were: representative of long segments in the video (N=13), 'with readable text' feature (N=10) and with 'graphics and charts' (N=7).

We used a 9-point Likert scale for all the agreement questions. In general, a majority of respondents favored the usefulness and ease-of-use of the emails with the thumbnail set. The mean response to judging the usefulness of email with thumbnail set was 6.08, when compared to neutral with one sample t-test we get t=2.2, p=0.038. When asked whether users preferred to receive just a link and a two-sentence summary, a high number of the respondents (16) gave a score of less than 5 (indicating disagreement).

We also provided two tables with an identical list of adjectives to measure respondents' agreement with the descriptors for each of the email formats. Respondents found the email with thumbnail summary (WTS) significantly less boring, more novel and more appealing than the WoMT format.

Measure	T	df	p
Boring	-3.242	17	0.005*
Complicated	1.531	18	0.143
Confusing	-0.230	18	0.820
Novel	6.364	18	0.000*
Easy-to-use	0.473	18	0.642
Appealing	2.122	18	0.048*
Error-prone	-0.470	18	0.644
Frustrating	-0.087	18	0.932
Intuitive	2.044	18	0.056
Quick	0.829	18	0.418
Satisfying	1.019	18	0.322

Table 2. Survey responses to two e-mail formats (WTS vs WoMT) using paired t-tests.

Several users mentioned that while they did not clickthrough to view the video, they saved these emails in a folder to view at a later time. They mentioned that these thumbnails would also provide a mechanism to recall which talk had the information they were looking for. One of them mentioned that the images helped sell the content of the talk whereas an attached powerpoint requires effort to load and view in order to decide if the talk is interesting.

LIMITATIONS OF THE STUDY

We feel this is preliminary work that indicates a promising direction for increasing the information value of messages when sharing video content. A limitation of the finding is that like many studies, there is a self selecting population that responds to either one of the messages, or the survey. The very busy people (or people with different email triage methods) did neither. Also, a finding that the interface with the thumbnails is significantly more novel should not be surprising, since this email type was compared with a more traditional type containing a link and descriptive text. However, of note is the finding that the email format with thumbnails was significantly more appealing, and that it drove significantly more clickthroughs. With the increased use of video in organizations it is key to understand how to best share the content contained in them.

We would like to gather additional data on the thumbnails (e.g. which types, if any, result in higher clickthrough) as well as test different layouts for the email message. Some respondents indicated that they clicked on the main link rather than the thumbnails since they did not realize the latter were clickable. Even though the message stated this, and each thumbnail had a blue colored link under it, this must have been missed as users quickly scanned the content of the message.

ACKNOWLEDGMENTS

We thank the users for their participation in our studies and the anonymous reviewers for insightful comments.

REFERENCES

1. A. Aula, R. M. Khan, Z. Guan, P. Fontes, and P. Hong. A comparison of visual and textual page previews in judging the helpfulness of web pages. WWW '10.
2. M. S. Bernstein, A. Marcus, D. R. Karger, and R. C. Miller. Enhancing directed content sharing on the web. CHI '10.
3. L. A. Dabbish and R. E. Kraut. Email overload at work: an analysis of factors associated with email strain. CSCW '06.
4. N. Ducheneaut and V. Bellotti. E-mail as habitat: an exploration of embedded personal information management. *Interactions* 8, 5 (September 2001), 30-38.
5. M. Muller, D. R. Millen, and J. Feinberg. Patterns of usage in an enterprise file-sharing service: publicizing, discovering, and telling the news. CHI '10.
6. H. Lam and P. Baudisch. Summary thumbnails: readable overviews for small screen web browsers. CHI '05.
7. A. Nenkova. Summarization evaluation for text and speech: issues and approaches. INTERSPEECH-2006.
8. Y. Song and G. Marchionini. Effects of audio and visual surrogates for making sense of digital video. CHI '07.
9. Y. Song, G. Marchionini, C. Y. Oh. What are the most eye-catching and ear-catching features in the video?: implications for video summarization. WWW '10.
10. A. Treisman, and G. Gelade. A feature integration theory of attention. *Cognitive Psychology, 12, 97-136.*
11. P. Over, A. F. Smeaton, and G. Awad. The trecvid 2008 BBC rushes summarization evaluation. TVS '08

Impression Formation in Corporate People Tagging

Daphne R. Raban and Avinoam Danan
Graduate School of Management
University of Haifa, Israel
draban@univ.haifa.ac.il; noam.da1@gmail.com

Inbal Ronen and Ido Guy
IBM Research Lab
Mt. Carmel, Haifa 31905, Israel
{inbal, ido}@il.ibm.com

ABSTRACT
This research explores the relationship between self-presentation and perception by others as manifested explicitly through the use of tags in a people tagging system. The study provides insights relevant for the organizational context since it is based on a system implemented within IBM. We developed a detailed codebook and used it to categorize 9,506 tags assigned to a sample of taggers. Our analysis examines the use of self tags versus social tags (assigned by others) across different categories and sub-categories. While overlap exists, self tags tend to be more factual describing technology expertise, social tags augment the individual tags by adding a personal dimension.

Author Keywords
Impression management; presentation of self; perception of others; people tagging.

ACM Classification Keywords
H.5.3 Group and Organization Interfaces: Computer-supported cooperative work.

General Terms
Design; Experimentation; Human Factors

INTRODUCTION
Internet technology offers users new tools and multiple opportunities for expressing themselves online. Social information technologies allow users to interact, collaborate, and socialize with each other in new and diverse forms such as blogs, social networks, wikis, content sharing applications and more.

As the web is transforming from a content focus to an increasingly social arena, the importance of self-presentation and the perception by others becomes evident. Even President Obama who is famous for efficiently using the social web in his 2008 election campaign alluded to the importance of self-presentation by his remark to high school students: "*Be careful what you post on Facebook.*" Moreover, impressions are perceived fast and sometimes remain regardless of newer information that is received about people. This has been studied in the marketing literature as the halo effect, in decision making as the confirmation bias and in the usability and visual appeal of web sites [12]

Impressions online can be based on implicit or explicit cues through which people present themselves on the web. An explicit form of describing people is a people tagging system. In this system people describe themselves and their peers by the use of tags. This presents a unique opportunity to study explicit self-presentation and perception by others using real-life data.

Online impressions have been studied to some extent as we describe later, however, we wish to shed new light by examining the following dimensions:

1. Studying self-presentation and concurrently the perception by others.
2. Focusing on the organizational environment.
3. Analyzing a system that offers an explicit form of self-presentation and perception.

This paper will briefly describe the major domains that are related to the research: people tagging, self presentation and perception of others. We then outline a research question, and the research method selected for the current work. Subsequently, we provide results based on a sample of 9,506 tags by a sample of 281 most active taggers, analyze their implications and suggest future research directions.

PEOPLE TAGGING
In online information systems terminology, a tag is a non-hierarchical keyword or term assigned to a piece of information in order to indicate identity, mark ownership, contextualize, etc. Tags enrich the information about an item and can be used for later retrieval. Since tagging is usually done by end-users, the result is the creation of a web of human topical interest.

Tags can be chosen from a controlled vocabulary or they can be free text assigned by the user. When free text is used, the resulting metadata can include homonyms, synonyms, spelling mistakes and errors which can lead to inappropriate connections between items and insufficient outcomes for information searches. On the other hand, with free text the user can use terms he thinks are appropriate to describe or help him recall information without the burden of selecting a category from a known taxonomy. Free text also allows for a dynamic update of the vocabulary, maintaining its relevance.

It is worth noting that tags are often presented in the form of tag clouds which are a graphical presentation of a weighted list of words. Is word frequency the only valuable way to organize tags? This practical design question may benefit from the outcome of the present study.

The special case where the resources to tag are people, is referred to as people tagging. The uniqueness of people tagging in contrast to other tagging applications can be derived from the Social Relations Model (SRM) [11], which argues that perception of people is different from perception of objects in four ways: it is reciprocal, it invokes thoughts about how the other will receive what one has told him (meta-perception), other perception is closely linked to self perception, and finally, perception may change over time. From the individual's perspective, people tagging systems can be described as two-sided, enabling use for acting and reacting, posting or replying [16], therefore, it is an opportunity for a field study of the SRM.

In their study, Ehrlich and Cash claimed that people in an enterprise can provide valuable expertise to solve problems [4]. Knowledge work (e.g expertise, unique knowledge) often involves finding opportunities to contribute to collaborative work, and one way, possibly the simplest way, of finding those opportunities is to "advertise" one's skills to other members of the organization through the use of tags [14].

In fact, the most common use of people tagging systems is for contact management. People use the application to arrange their friends and colleagues in a social network system [6]. Beyond contact management, people tagging enables the formation of an organizational community which collectively maintains each others' interests and expertise. This expanded profile is searchable and available for later recall about employees associated with a project or a needed skill or knowledge.

SELF PRESENTATION

In order to be socially-accepted or cultivate certain reputation or recognition, people tend to try and control the information they present about themselves in one-to-one encounters as well as in group meetings or before large audiences. Goffman distinguished between two kinds of expression of the self: expressions one gives, and expressions one gives off [8]. The first involves relatively easily controlled, presumably intentional expressions, conveyed through traditional verbal communication [15, 23]. The other kind, implicit expression, is considered to be more theatrical and contextual, nonverbal, and presumably unintentional [15].

Any situation of appearance before others involves self presentation and induces people to express themselves explicitly and implicitly. By attempting to control or manage the impression others receive people will calculate behavior so that the audience will believe what they see [8].

Self Presentation Online

Self presentation, also referred to as impression management, implies that every individual performs a certain role while appearing in public [23]. The internet and organizational systems provide several ways for online self presentation such as personal home pages, the profile one accumulates for oneself on a variety of online systems, blogs, email, instant messaging, social networks, dating sites and intranet tools for contact management within organizations.

In each of these tools, the participant chooses how to introduce himself, how to manage his impression, and what is his preferred level of participation. A user can introduce himself by choosing nicknames and perhaps forfeiting age, gender, workplace, or other cues [18]. The web offers opportunities to expose multiple senses of self or personas in different contexts [24] to the point of playfulness or fantasy as forms of misrepresentations. There is a tension between idealizing the self and presenting truthfully, however, individuals usually know how to balance their desire for self-promotion with their need for accurate self-presentation [5][1][13].

Anticipation of a future meeting has been shown to favor truthful self presentation [7]. While online self-presentation is more malleable and subject to self-censorship than face-to-face self-presentation [26], under certain conditions the online medium may enable participants to express themselves more openly and honestly than in face-to-face contexts [9]. An investigation of truthfulness of presentation was done in a dating web site where people used single adjectives, somewhat similar to the notion of tagging, to describe themselves and their desired partners. The results showed that interacting over the Internet led to a more truthful self presentation leading to a better match [27]. Thus the internet serves as a social lubricant by delivering a clear self-presentation which meets the expectations of others.

In a work environment, the tension between the need for self-promotion and truthful representation is expected to be minimal because people participate in the system as part of professional community building. If they describe themselves as having a certain skill they do so out of confidence in their ability in this area. We see no particular motivation to idealize one's skills in an organization.

Overall, we believe that in organizations, self-presentation will tend to be less personal, more professional – less about appearance or age and more about knowledge and skills, and similar to the dating studies cited here, it will be truthful. The purpose of organizational self-presentation is social in a work-related sense – to find like-minded people or locate experts to help in promoting a project [2].

People tagging is uniquely reciprocal, as users can tag themselves, others or both. While people share information as a form of self presentation, other individuals may perceive them differently than what they present and tag them using other terms.

PERCEPTION OF OTHERS

Perception of others online is distinct from face-to-face situations. Rouse and Haas [19] pointed out the main factors that explain the differences between online and face-to-face interactions: 1. Physical appearance has a less meaningful effect. 2. People may behave differently online especially when anonymized. 3. In online communication there may be a heightened level of ambiguity due to the lack of vocal inflection and facial expression.

Online perception can be either synchronous or asynchronous. A person creates an impression by his digital artifacts such as writing, photos, selection of materials for inclusion in a web page or personal profile [21]. Impressions can form through synchronous conversation but also by a visit to a homepage or profile page. As the interaction progresses more information accumulates, verbal and non-verbal cues are taken into consideration and affect the impression [20]. Perception of others online is constructed according to the explicit and implicit cues observed. In order to make a positive impression a person will carefully select the explicit cues to manifest. The online perceiver is aware of that and is likely to notice the implicit cues as well.

An example of such a communication was identified in Q&A websites where both the asker and the answerer tried to make a positive impression on each other; the asker for getting valuable answers and the answerer for being rewarded positive feedback and a monetary tip for his answer [17]. The present study focuses on explicit cues.

Prior research suggests that explicit cues will deliver a reliable representation of a person especially when a future meeting is anticipated [5, 9]. Why, then, is tagging practiced both by the person himself and by his perceiver? Why is there a need to tag a person beyond his own self-description? According to the SOKA model (Self Other Knowledge Asymmetry) differences between self and other-perception derive from informational differences in perspective (i.e., the salience of overt vs. covert aspects of a person) and motivational significance (such as the need for self-enhancement) [25]. Thus, self descriptions are more accurate than others for internal, unobservable, less evaluative traits (e.g. neuroticism), and others are slightly more accurate than the self for external, observable and evaluative traits (e.g. intelligence). Therefore, the perspectives offered by the actors themselves vs. those offered by their peers are expected to differ and complement each other. Corporate people tagging offers a window for examining the degree of similarity or difference in the explicit presentation and perception of employees using the tagging system.

RESEARCH QUESTION

People tagging offers a unique opportunity to study explicit self-presentation and perception by others by analyzing tags. Tags are explicit cues because users describe themselves or others using individual words or short phrases, without implicit effects such as writing style, manners, or use of personal pronouns. We use the tags in order to examine both sides of the coin: self-presentation and perception by others, and to learn whether and how they complement each other.

Using the database of a people tagging application implemented in a large enterprise we explore the following question: What terms do people use to tag themselves (presentation of self) compared to terms used by others (perception by others)? To what degree are the self descriptions similar to or different from the tags assigned by others? Do self tags converge with incoming tags or is a larger number of tags associated with a more diverse description?

METHOD

The data was harvested from an organizational profile application within IBM which included a people tagging system based on free-text tags. It represents a period of three years during which the application was deployed on the organization's intranet. Each employee in the application had a profile page which exposed the tags used by the employee to tag himself (referred to as ***self tags***) and a tag cloud of the tags assigned to him by other employees (referred to as ***social tags***). Additionally, profile information was shown such as the person's name, photo, job title, department and others. The same social tag could be applied several times by different persons. A self tag could be applied only once. Employees used the people tagging application both to tag themselves (self presentation) and to assign tags to others (perception of others). Figure 1 shows an anonymized screenshot of a typical profile in the application. For the present research the preferred methodology is content analysis which allows an understanding of the meaning of the tags.

The people tagging application kept each tag with the id of the tagged person, the tagger and the date of the tagging event in a database. A tag was stored normalized, such that the terms of a multi-term tag were separated by a hyphen. We extracted the tags related to a person by querying this database through SQL.

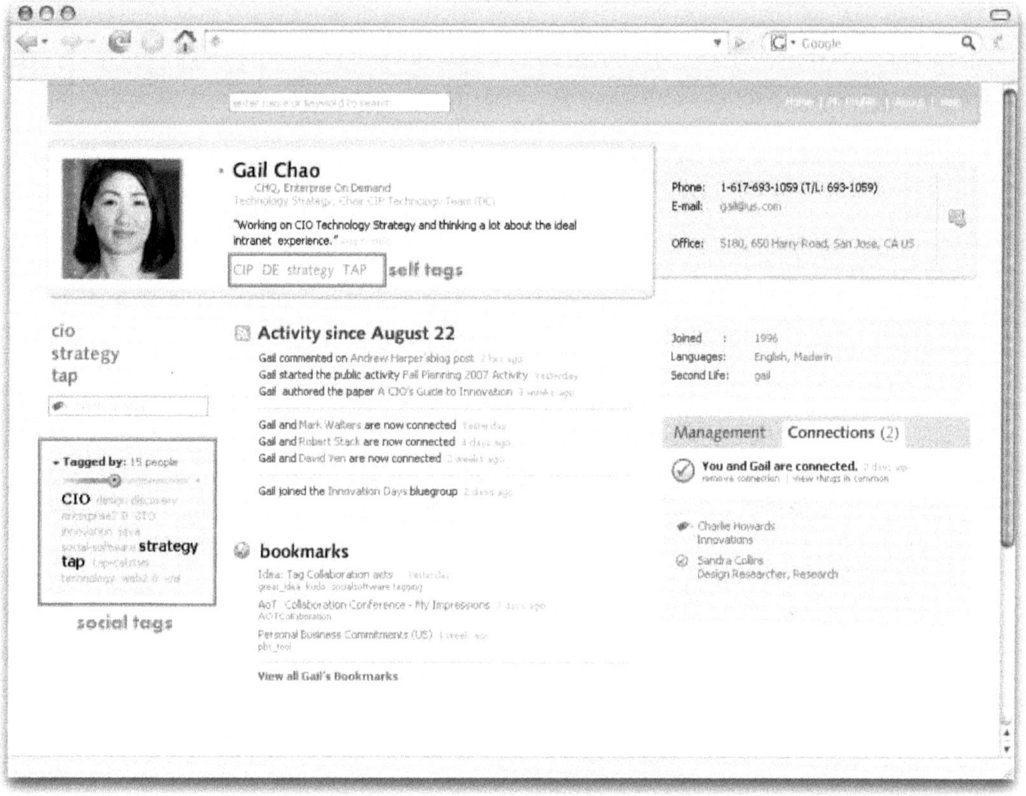

Figure 1. Profile Page in People Tagging application (anonymized)

Variables

Self Tags: tags assigned to a user by himself, representing the presentation of self.

Social Tags: tags assigned to a user by other users, representing the perception by others. Each unique social tag was counted once even if it was used by more than one person to tag the same peer.

Sample

The complete data included the tagging activity by 62,332 system participants. As in many web-based applications the distribution of tags followed a power law function; hence, random sampling would not be representative of the full data. The focus of this study is on the comparison of self tags to social tags; therefore, both types of tags must have significant counts. Based on the frequency of self and social tags we decided that a minimum of 10 in each tag set would be the cutoff for the sample. This resulted in a group of 281 users who had a total of 9,506 tags.

Content Analysis

Kaid and Wadsworth [10] suggest seven steps for implementing content analysis:

1. Formulate the hypotheses or research question.
2. Select the sample to be analyzed.
3. Define the categories to be applied.
4. Outline the coding process and train coders.
5. Implement the coding process.
6. Determine reliability and validity.
7. Analyze the results from the coding process.

Codebook development: The heart of content analysis is the coding process. We prepared a codebook by assigning the tags of 25 random system users (not from the 281 people) to three coders. Each coder described the tags according to his understanding. Then a meeting was held to form an agreement on the coding categories. Having organized the tag descriptions we identified 3 main categories: technology, environment, and individual. Every main category contains 6 sub-categories that represent the fine-tuned aspects of the category (see Table 1).

Inter-coder reliability: This is a measure of whether independent judges make the same coding decisions while characterizing the data. Without reliability of the coding, the analysis cannot be trusted [22]. We conducted inter-coder reliability for the three coders by using a new random sample of 30 participants, not from the 281 most active users. For each participant the self tags and the social tags were coded. For the first 9 people all three coders worked jointly to reach an agreed understanding of the use of the codebook. Then each coder coded independently the self and other tags for the remaining 21 people. A total of 175 self tags and 434 social tags were coded to test inter-coder reliability. Krippendorf's alpha for the three coders was 0.75 for the self tags and 0.73 for the social tags for the sample of 30 participants. Both values are above the threshold of 0.7 needed in order to determine the coding process as reliable.

Main Cat.	Sub-category	Description	Examples
Technology	Information Technologies	Information technologies and systems	linux, android, ooa, eclipse-plugins
	Internet Technologies	Internet programming, technologies and systems	web20, secondlife, atom, javascript, 3dinternet
	Theme	broad topic	collaboration, knowledge-management, legacy-transformation
	IBM Product	products developed and sold by IBM	websphere-commerce lotus-notes lotus-domino websphere-portal sametime, quickr
	External Product	Products not developed or sold by IBM	photoshop, mac, iphone
	Project	Projects (not products) of IBM	project-zero, p-vista oasis, bluepedia
Environment	Group Affiliation	Groups such as conferences and internal or external events	cscw2011, web20forbiz, helsinki-2007, class-of-78, Vienna-team
	Organizatio-nal Group	Departments and organizational groups at IBM	research, sales, services, corporate
	Country	Country names	Norway, Canada
	City	City names	Hamburg, Cambridge
	Customer	Customer and partners of IBM	Philips, Miele, Rails, Citybank
	Organization	Organization names which are not customers or partners of IBM	BMW, Cisco, Apple, Daimler, Teva
Individual	Name	Name, Last Name, Nickname	Bob, Laszlo
	Training	Academic or professional degree, training, institution	MBA, Certified-IT-Specialist, Miami-University
	Job Description	Description of job responsibility	architect, presales, manager, designer
	Special Skill	work related skills	hacker, mentor, demo-guru, speaker, bilingual
	Hobby	Non work related hobby or interest	Skiing, karaoke, photography, rocker, piano, soccer-fan
	Personal Adjective	personality related characteristics	leadership, traveler, creative, funny, supergenious, storyteller, recycler

Table 1. Codebook categories, sub-categories, and examples.

For the sample of 281 highly active participants, we applied the coding retrieved in the previous step and extracted only those tags that had not been coded before. These were distributed among the coders for independent coding. All the coded tags were then aggregated to assign the coded tags to each system participant in the sample.

RESULTS

Tag Volumes and Ratio

We first inspect the volumes of self and social tags across the three main categories. On average, each of the 281 taggers was tagged with 16.26 self tags and 17.57 social tags, leading to an overall of 4569 self tags and 4937 social tags inspected in our study.

	Mean Self Tags	Mean Social Tags	Ratio of Means (self/social)
Technology	9.15	8.02	1.14
Environment	4.0	5.03	0.8
Individual	3.11	4.52	0.69

Table 2. Mean tags per user in the 3 main categories (N=281).

Table 2 shows the mean number of self and social tags. The rightmost column in Table 2 highlights the overall ratio between self and social tags. The most active category is Technology, which is also the only category where the volume of self tags is higher than social tags. While taggers sharply prefer to tag themselves with Technology tags (over 56% of the self tags belong to Technology), this tendency is milder for social tags (less than 46% of the social tags belong to Technology). On the other hand, while only 19.2% of the self tags are Individual, 25.7% of the social tags are Individual.

A correlation analysis shows a statistically significant correlation between tagging in one main category and tagging in other main categories. This relationship is stronger for social tagging ($r=.45$ to $.50$, $p<.01$) than for self tagging ($r=.19$ to $.25$, $p<.01$).

Table 3 lists the means and ratios across the 18 sub-categories with noteworthy observations in boldface. For Technology sub-categories, the most frequent sub-categories are Theme and IBM Product. The ratio of the External Product sub-category is exceptionally high, while the ratio for Project is especially low. It seems that taggers prefer to associate others with internal projects, probably for personal bookmarking purposes [6], than to associate themselves with such projects. Interestingly the ratio difference between IBM Product and External Product suggests that the latter has stronger preference for usage as a self tag.

	Mean Self Tags	Mean Social Tags	Ratio of Means (self/social)
Information Tech	0.85	0.78	1.09
Internet Tech	1.93	1.67	1.16
Theme	**2.54**	**2.16**	1.18
IBM Product	**3.03**	**2.64**	1.15
External Product	0.37	0.17	**2.15**
Project	0.43	0.6	**0.72**
Group Affiliation	**1.57**	**1.93**	0.81
Org Group	**0.89**	**1.5**	**0.59**
Country	0.32	0.36	0.89
City	0.35	0.41	0.84
Customer	0.43	0.32	**1.34**
Organization	0.44	0.5	0.88
Name	0.05	0.13	0.41
Training	0.18	0.13	1.38
Job Description	**1.09**	**1.64**	0.66
Special Skill	**0.74**	**1.06**	0.7
Hobby	0.32	0.32	**1.0**
Personal Adj	**0.72**	**1.23**	0.59

Table 3. Mean tags per user across the 18 sub-categories.

Among the Environment sub-categories, Group Affiliation is the most frequently used, followed by Organizational Group. The latter has the lowest self-to-social ratio within the Environment category. This implies that people are less passionate to tag themselves with their organizational affiliation and aim to tag others with such affiliation more frequently. The difference in the ratio between these two sub-categories may result from the person himself being more knowledgeable than his peers about his own external group affiliations. Customer is the sub-category with highest ratio. We again observe that tags of an external entity or affiliation are more frequently used as self tags than as social tags.

As for the Individual category, Job Description is the most frequently used sub-category, followed by Personal Adjective and Special Skill. Name is used very infrequently, mostly as a social tag, hinting that taggers view it as redundant information. Training is also quite infrequent, used more often as a self tag. The low activity around academic or professional training may imply a greater focus on actual work experience.

The relatively low ratio of Personal Adjective may reflect that some employees feel uncomfortable tagging themselves with such subjective tags. Interestingly, Hobby has exactly the same number of self and social tags. The relatively high ratio implies that people feel more comfortable to testify on themselves with respect to hobbies than with respect to other subjective traits, such as adjectives or special skills.

Overall, the three most frequent sub-categories for self tags are related to Technology. They represent over 46% of the total self tags. The three leading sub-categories for social tags represent only 38% of the total social tags, indicating more diversity across social tags.

Overlap Analysis

We next set to explore the agreement between self and social tags per user across the different categories and sub-categories. We define *overlapping tags* as tags that

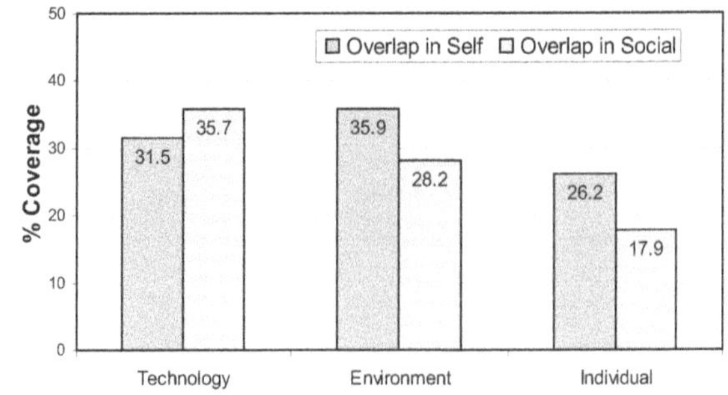

Figure 2. Overlap between self and social tags across the 3 main categories.

appear both as self and social tags for the same user. We examine two measures: (1) *overlap in self tags*, defined as the percentage of overlapping tags out of all self tags, averaged across all 281 taggers, and (2) *overlap in social tags*, defined as the percentage of overlapping tags out of all social tags, averaged across all taggers.

Figure 2 shows these two measures for the three main categories. The left bars represent the overlap in self tags and the right bars represent the overlap in social tags. Inspecting both Table 2 and Figure 2 shows that a lower mean number of tags in one of the main categories is associated with a lower overlap in the same category. The Technology category has the highest number of tags and the highest rate of overlap, while the Individual category has the lowest number of tags and the lowest overlap.

Figure 3 shows the overlap analysis for the sub-categories across the 3 main categories. For the Technology category, the two sub-categories with highest overlap are IBM Product and Internet Technology. The sub-category with least overlap is Non-IBM Product.

For the Environment category, most noticeable is the high overlap in self tags for Organizational Group. The lowest overlap was associated with Group Affiliation.

Overlap in the Individual category is generally lower than in the other main categories. Note that the overlap for Name and Training is based on especially low volume of tags (see Table 2) and should thus be treated with a grain of salt. Special Skill has the highest overlap between self and social tags. The overlap in self tags for Job Description is lower than for Personal Adjective and for Special Skill. This is an interesting finding: people's presentation of self regarding their unique skills agrees with the perception of others more often than for their job description. While hobbies have identical volumes of self and social tags, the overlap of their content is only 18%. It seems that the hobbies people want to be associated with are not the ones others associate them with.

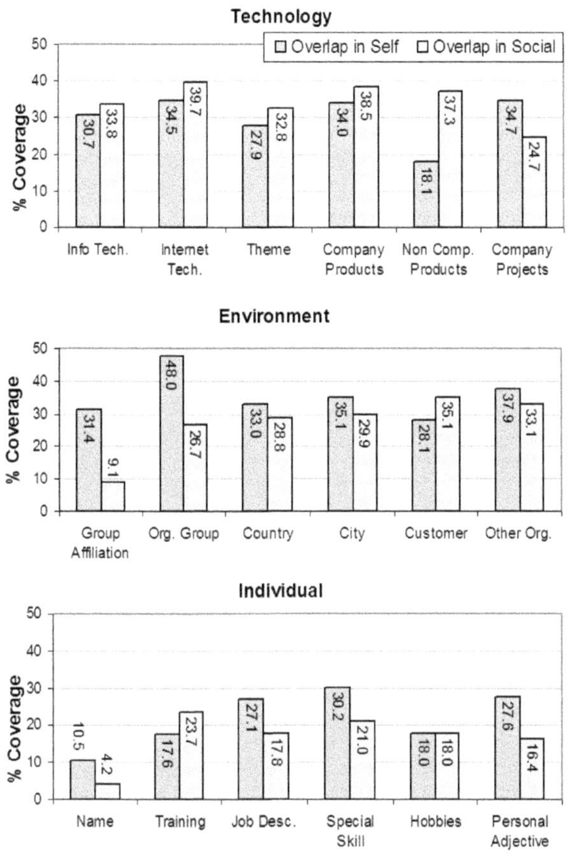

Figure 3. Self and Social Overlap across the 18 sub-categories.

Tag Popularity Analysis

In this part of the analysis we focus on the most popular tags in each category and sub-category. Table 4 shows the three most popular tags in each of the three main categories. The right section of the table indicates the overlap between the k most popular self and social tags, for k=1,5,10. We denote by *ovl@k* the portion of tags that are amongst the k most popular self tags as well as the k most popular social tags. For example, an ovl@5 of 0.6 indicates 3 overlapping tags within the 5 most popular. Note that the binary ovl@1 directly indicates whether the most popular tag is identical for self and social tags.

Table 5 shows the most popular self and social tags, as well as their overlap, for the sub-categories. We excluded the Name and Training sub-categories since they did not have enough tags to generate rich enough popularity lists.

In general, the overlap rates for the sub-categories are high: 12 of the 16 sub-categories have an identical top tag for self and social; the rates for ovl@5 and ovl@10 range mostly from 0.4 to 0.8. Sub-categories with higher volumes of tags have higher overlap, suggesting convergence. The overlap rates also point at sub-categories with more narrow and/or well-defined vocabularies. For example, Organizational Group has very high overlap and so does IBM Product (in spite of disagreement on the top tag).

	Popular Self Tags	Popular Social Tags	ovl @1	ovl @5	ovl @10
Technology	web20 secondlife collaboration	web20 collaboration secondlife	1	0.8	0.7
Environment	lotus web204biz vuccore	lotus web204biz group2	1	0.4	0.7
Individual	blogger architect competitive	blogger architect innovator	1	0.4	0.5

Table 4. Popular tags and their overlap across the 3 main categories.

There is less agreement within the most popular Individual tags, implying that people use somewhat different vocabularies when describing self versus others with tags that tend to be more subjective. For example, consider the Personal Adjective sub-category: 'competitive' is among the top three for self tags, but is not among the top 10 for social tags, as it might be sensed as a negative perception of another person. When testified by self, it can be perceived as a more positive quality in a workplace. On the other hand, 'innovator' is the top social tag, representing a tag that one would mostly want to get from others rather than use for self tagging. There are also common adjectives for self and social, such as 'early adopter' or 'evangelist'.

DISCUSSION

This research set out to explore how people present themselves, compared to how they are perceived by their peers in a corporate setting when they are given a tool for explicit description, the people tagging system. Our analysis goes from broad to focused view. We started by looking at overall and mean tag counts in the three main categories. We, then, zoomed into the sub categories to gain a finer description of the person by himself and by his peers. Next, we employed overlap analysis to assess the degree of similarity between self and social tagging. Lastly, the focus was on the most frequently used overlapping tags.

The Broad View

The sample analyzed is the group of the 281 most active taggers with ten or more self and social tags each. By focusing on this group we ensured a sufficient description for each person in the sample. While this may not be representative of the average user, learning how the most active taggers act can be a point of reference for system designers.

Looking across the rows in the broad view presented in Table 2, the number of self tags is quite similar to the number of social tags per category. Previous work [16] showed that self tagging corresponds with more incoming, social, tags. Table 2 suggests that not only does tagging invoke tagging but also of the same category.

	Popular Self Tags	Popular Social Tags	ovl @1	ovl @5	ovl @10
Info Tech	linux java css	linux java visualization	1	0.6	0.6
Internet Tech	web20 secondlife social-networking	web20 secondlife social-networking	1	0.8	0.7
Theme	collaboration innovation social-computing	collaboration innovation work	1	0.8	0.8
IBM Product	webssphere-portal lotus-connections lotus-notes	lotus-connections sametime websphere-portal	0	0.8	0.9
External Product	twitter eclipse mac	twitter mac moleskine	1	0.6	0.4
Project	dogear bluepedia beehive	beehive bluepoints ets	0	0.6	0.5
Group Affiliation	web20forbiz vuccore blueiq	web20forbiz blueiq vuccore	1	0.8	0.8
Org Group	lotus websphere swg	lotus gbs sales	1	0.8	0.9
Country	Germany Australia Austria	Germany UK Austria	1	0.8	0.7
City	Hamburg Hursley Stuttgart	Hamburg Hursley Berlin	1	0.6	0.4
Customer	ebic goverment itil	ebic deutsche-bank siemens	1	0.2	0.2
Org	Cisco SAP Apple	Cisco Apple Xing	1	0.4	0.7
Job Desc	architect tech-sales manager	architect manager tech-sales	1	0.6	0.5
Special Skill	blogger mentor community-builder	blogger mentor 5live-speaker	1	0.5	0.6
Hobby	photography writer soccer	biker photography writer	0	0.4	0.3
Personal Adj	evangelist early-adopter competitive	innovator evangelist early-adopter	0	0.4	0.7

Table 5. Most popular tags and their overlap across 16 of the sub-categories.

A person who tags himself with Technology or Environment tags, is likely to be similarly tagged by others. Possibly at the Individual category social tagging is more intensive because people may shy away from assigning themselves personal descriptors. The self-to-social ratio supports this direction showing that people are more comfortable tagging themselves with matter-of-fact technology tags. Peers make a greater effort to augment the individual tags, adding a personal dimension to the tag cloud.

Correlation analysis confirmed that tagging in one main category was associated with tagging in other main categories. Moreover, this relationship was stronger for social tagging which suggests diversification. More tags lead to a more diverse description of a person over the three main categories, not "more of the same" tags in a specific category.

The Deeper View

The sub-categories in Table 3 help to understand what specific information is more useful to system users. Here, we see that in the Technology category the most used sub-categories were IBM Product, Theme and Internet Technology, in that order. These sub-categories are an indication of the employee's specific context (Product) as well as his general knowledge or association (Theme, Internet Technology). The self-to-social ratio in all three leading sub-categories is higher than 1, suggesting the importance of these sub-categories for the presentation of self which tends to be factual. On the other hand, perception by others is based more on the sub-categories belonging to the Environment and Individual categories. Specifically, perception is based on the sub-categories Group Affiliation, Organizational Group, Job Description, Special Skill, and Personal Adjective. For all these sub-categories the self-to-social ratio is smaller than 1 – taggers feel they need to augment these socially-oriented sub-categories more than other factual technology descriptions. This is in line with the SOKA model [25] in two ways. First, tagging is complementary by contributing different perspectives, and second, social tags tend to be more about external circumstances or character traits that a person might not think about highlighting for oneself.

Sub-categories used in the Individual category underscore what personal information is useful. It is a mixture of fairly objective information such as Job Description (e.g. programmer, architect, manager) with subjective information: Special Skill (hacker, speaker, mentor) and Personal Adjective (innovator, creative, funny). These unique descriptions add a human dimension to the system and enhance the formal, general, descriptions, with qualities unique to the person. To determine the degree of uniqueness of the descriptions we turn to overlap analysis.

Overlap in Presentation and Perception

The degree of overlap reflects the agreement between self tags and social tags per user, by considering the portion of tags that appeared as both. Overlap is an indication of common knowledge which can be viewed as part of corporate cultural capital. Overlap also indicates where we might obtain new information – categories with the lowest overlap. We should encourage users to populate those categories more.

The Technology category has the highest number of tags and the highest rate of overlap. The more people get tagged, the more overlap develops. This suggests that convergence is occurring: more tags result in more similarity in tagging in line with an earlier study [16]. This is also in line with the SRM model which predicts similarity in presentation and perception [11].

Within the Technology category, we observe high agreement on IBM Product, as opposed to low agreement with regards to Non-IBM Product. In the Environment category, there is a high agreement on Organizational Group and a low agreement on Group Affiliation. Both findings indicate that presentation of self and perception by others more often agree when it comes to organizational association, be it a product or a group, than an external one. Within the Individual category, there is surprisingly more agreement for Special Skill than for the supposedly-more-objective Job Description.

Popular Tags

The results in Table 4 indicate that for all three main categories the most popular tag is identical for self and social tags. In general, the overlap within the popular tags is considerably higher than the overall overlap, as depicted in Figure 2, indicating that both types of tags converge to a similar vocabulary. The Technology category has the highest overlap, presumably due to its higher volumes of tags, which allows for more convergence.

The overlap in the most highly used, popular, tags is very high, indicating that almost a consensus is reached in the overall usage of terms. This can be seen as kind of a 'wisdom of crowds', surfacing the organizational vocabulary or cultural capital. The agreement is reached for quite general terms such as listed in Table 5 (Linux, Web 2.0 etc.). What individuates a user is found further down the path of tags in the less popular areas of the tag list.

Another insight from this very high overlap in the top tags is that tagging is to a large extent reciprocal. For example, if a user tags himself with 'Linux' statistical probability suggests that he will be tagged by a peer with the same term and vice versa.

Study Limitations

The current study is based on a sample of the most active taggers of the people-tagging system; therefore, the results are limited to understanding the practices of this sub-population. On the other hand if we treat this group as a benchmark for the system's potential then we can identify goals for further system development. A similar study based on a representative sample of the entire population of users could help mark the starting point and suggest paths from the lower levels of activity to higher ones.

From a technical standpoint, we did not identify multi-term tags which had no explicit separation between the terms. For example, social-networking and social networking were treated as different tags. No stemming or synonym identification has been done. We estimate that these issues introduce an error rate of 3% at the most so correcting them would not make a significant difference in the results presented here.

CONCLUSIONS

We studied presentation of self and perception by others as reflected through enterprise people tagging. People use tagging in critically different ways, but as a collective enterprise use it well. The most common form of self presentation is through Technology tags, mainly IBM Product, Theme, and Internet Technology. While there is considerable overlap, especially for popular tags, there is also a substantial degree of complementary tagging, bringing new information to the system.

Self presentation often relies on Technology tags and is less personal than one would expect from people describing themselves. People use less individuating tags when managing their own impression. This is filled-in to some extent by the social tags. Possibly, the work context induces this type of presentation vs. perception so it is even more important in this context to cultivate more uniqueness in impression management.

Environmental and Individual tags are generally used more for augmenting the perception of people than for self presentation. Exceptions to this rule include the Customer and Training sub-categories, which are used more for self presentation. Customer probably reflects the greater knowledge one has and wished to expose regarding the customers relevant to his work. This may not be well-known by one's colleagues. Training is typically known by the person and is used for self-advertising and not so much for identification by others.

The broad view we presented suggests diversification of tags while the overlap and popular tags analyses point toward convergence. Both processes are likely to occur – to corroborate this proposition a future study should examine a group of people with a moderate amount of tags.

This study highlights a need for individuation. While the concept of 'folksonomy' heralds the development of cultural capital in the form of commonality of interests, when it comes to describing people, we would recommend the augmentation of uniqueness and areas of specialty. Tagging system designers should consider the deep difference between tagging people and objects. They should not import the same technology used for objects and apply it to people, but they are advised to consider the goals of tagging people, such as impression management, and design the system accordingly.

Finally, tag clouds are designed so that popular tags appear in large and bold font and are more prominent in the tag cloud than less popular tags. Is this a good practice when it comes to people tagging? Do we prefer to identify the maximum number of people based on large, bold, tags or do we want the tagging system to help us to identify the uniqueness of people, be it on a professional or personal basis? We leave these as questions for further thought and discussion indicating the importance of this study for system design.

ACKNOWLEDGEMENT

This work is partially supported by the EC co-funded project SocIoS. SocIoS is an FP 7 STREP project (Project number: 257774. Call Identifier FP7 ICT 2009.1.2: Internet of Services, Software and Virtualisation). For more information see http://www.sociosproject.eu.

The work on this paper was partially supported by an Open Collaborative Research grant from IBM.

REFERENCES

[1] Back, M. D., Stopfer, J. M., Vazire, S., Gaddis, S., Schmukle, S. C., Egloff, B. and Gosling, S. D. Facebook profiles reflect actual personality, not self-idealization. Psychological Science, 21, 3 (2010), 372.

[2] DiMicco, J., Millen, D. R., Geyer, W., Dugan, C., Brownholtz, B. and Muller, M. Motivations for social networking at work. In Anonymous *Proceedings of the 21st ACM conference on Computer supported cooperative work.* ACM, , 2008, 711-720.

[3] Dominick, J. R. Who Do You Think You Are? Personal Home Pages and Self-Presentation on the World Wide Web. Journalism and Mass Communication Quarterly, 76, 4 (1999), 646-658.

[4] Ehrlich, K. and Cash, D. Turning information into knowledge: Information finding as a collaborative activity. In Anonymous *Proceedings of Digital Libraries.* (1994), 119-125.

[5] Ellison, N., Heino, R. and Gibbs, J. Managing Impressions Online: Self-Presentation Processes in the Online Dating Environment. Journal of Computer-Mediated Communication, 11, 2 (2006), 415-441.

[6] Farrell, S., Lau, T., Nusser, S., Wilcox, E. and Muller, M. Socially augmenting employee profiles with people-tagging. In Anonymous *Proceedings of the 20th annual ACM symposium on User interface software and technology.* (2007) , 91-100. ACM New York, NY, USA.

[7] Gibbs, J. L., Ellison, N. B. and Heino, R. D. Self-Presentation in Online Personals: The Role of Anticipated Future Interaction, Self-Disclosure, and Perceived Success in Internet Dating. Communication Research, 33, 2 (2006), 152.

[8] Goffman, E. *The presentation of self in everyday life.* Allen Lane, , 1959.

[9] Joinson, A. N. European Journal of Social Psychology, 31, 2 (2001), 177-192.

[10] Kaid, L. L. and Wadsworth, A. J. Content analysis. Measurement of communication behavior, (1989), 197–217.

[11] Kenny, D. A. *Interpersonal perception: A social relations analysis.* The Guilford Press, , 1994.

[12] Lindgaard, G., Fernandes, G., Dudek, C. and Brown, J. Attention web designers: You have 50 milliseconds to make a good first impression! Behaviour & information technology, 25, 2 (2006), 115-126.

[13] Marcus, B., Machilek, F. and Schütz, A. Personality in cyberspace: Personal web sites as media for personality expressions and impressions. J. Pers. Soc. Psychol., 90, 6 (2006), 1014.

[14] Muller, M. J., Ehrlich, K. and Farrell, S. *Social tagging and self-tagging for impression management.* TR 06-02. IBM Research technical report, 2006.

[15] Papacharissi, Z. and Rubin, A. M. Predictors of Internet use. Journal of Broadcasting & Electronic Media, 44, 2 (2000), 175-196.

[16] Raban, D. R., Ronen, I. and Guy, I. Acting or Reacting? Preferential Attachment in a People Tagging System. Journal of the American Society for Information Science & Technology, 62, 4 (2011), 738-747.

[17] Raban, D. R. Self-Presentation and the Value of Information in Q&A Web Sites. Journal of the American Society for Information Science and Technology, 60, 12 (2009), 2465-2473.

[18] Rafaeli, S., Raban, D. R. and Kalman, Y. Social Cognition Online. In Amichai-Hamburger, Y. ed. *The social net: The social psychology of the internet.* Oxford University Press, Oxford, England, 2005.

[19] Rouse, S. V. and Haas, H. A. Exploring the accuracies and inaccuracies of personality perception following Internet-mediated communication. Journal of research in personality, 37, 5 (2003), 446-467.

[20] Savicki, V., Kelley, M. and Oesterreich, E. Judgments of gender in computer-mediated communication. Comput. Hum. Behav., 15, 2 (1999), 185-194.

[21] Schau, H. J. and Gilly, M. C. We are what we post? Self-presentation in personal web space. Journal of Consumer Research, (2003), 385-404.

[22] Singletary, M. W. *Mass communication research: Contemporary methods and applications.* Longman White Plains, NY, 1994.

[23] Trammell, K. D. and Keshelashvili, A. Examining the new influencers: A self-presentation study of A-list blogs. Journalism & Mass Communication Quarterly, 82, 4 (2005), 968-982.

[24] Turkle, S. *Life on the Screen: Identity in the Age of the Internet.* Simon & Schuster, New York, 1995.

[25] Vazire, S. Who knows what about a person? The self–other knowledge asymmetry (SOKA) model. J. Pers. Soc. Psychol., 98, 2 (2010), 281.

[26] Walther, J. B. Computer-Mediated Communication: Impersonal, Interpersonal, and Hyperpersonal Interaction. Communication Research, 23, 1 (1996), 3.

[27] Whitty, M. T. Revealing the [] real'me, searching for the [] actual'you: Presentations of self on an internet dating site. Comput. Hum. Behav., 24, 4 (2008), 1707-1723.

Too Close for Comfort: A Study of the Effectiveness and Acceptability of Rich-Media Personalized Advertising

Miguel Malheiros, Charlene Jennett, Snehalee Patel, Sacha Brostoff, M. Angela Sasse
University College London
Gower Street
London WC1E 6BT, UK
{m.malheiros, c.jennett, s.brostoff, a.sasse}@cs.ucl.ac.uk, snehalee.patel.10@ucl.ac.uk

ABSTRACT
Online display advertising is predicted to make $29.53 billion this year. Advertisers believe targeted and personalized ads to be more effective, but many users are concerned about their privacy. We conducted a study where 30 participants completed a simulated holiday booking task; each page showing ads with different degrees of personalization. Participants fixated twice as long when ads contained their photo. Participants reported being more likely to notice ads with their photo, holiday destination, and name, but also increasing levels of discomfort with increasing personalization. We conclude that greater personalization in ad content may achieve higher levels of attention, but that the most personalized ads are also the least acceptable. The noticeability benefit in using someone's photo to make them look at an ad may be offset by the privacy cost. As more personal data becomes available to advertisers, it becomes important that these trade-offs are considered.

Author Keywords
Targeted advertising; personalization; privacy.

ACM Classification Keywords
H.1.2 User/Machine Systems: Human Factors.

General Terms
Human Factors

INTRODUCTION
Display advertising (banner ads and pop-ups) accounts for approximately one third of the total online advertising market and is predicted to reach $29.53 billion this year [21]. Many users are desensitized to traditional display advertising and actively avoid looking at online banner ads [10]. Over time, response rates to banner ads have fallen dramatically [15]. Techniques used by advertisers to overcome this problem include targeted advertising and personalization. *Targeted advertising* refers to the practice where ads are matched to the user's interest. The more relevant the ad is to the user, the more attractive it is. *Personalization* refers to the inclusion of information in the ad content that identifies or characterizes the recipient. It is sometimes used alongside targeting to further increase the appeal of an ad. These techniques have been found to achieve higher click-through rates [33] and in turn more sales. However, they also create ads which have the potential to be more invasive to users, intruding on their privacy [31]. Yet there exists scope for even greater personalization of advertisements. Facebook, for example, is planning to allow companies to advertise products on users' profiles [11]. What will happen to internet users' perceptions of privacy should these more powerful techniques for personalization become common? Will increasingly personalized ads lead to increased revenues for advertisers and their clients, or might it lead to a still greater experience of privacy invasion, and rejection of products, services and sites hosting the ads?

We report a study that explored participants' responses to ads with varying degrees of personalization toward the individual recipient, including a newer type that incorporates personally identifying information (PII) about the viewer within each ad (i.e. the participant's name and photograph). We first present background on users' perceptions of targeted advertising and personalization. We then describe the study where participants interacted with web pages with increasingly targeted and personalized ads. Their attention towards the ads was measured using eye-tracking while their perceptions were collected using questionnaires and interviews. The results show that greater personalization in ad content may achieve higher levels of attention, with participants spending almost twice as much time looking at an ad containing a photo of themselves than at a standard picture ad. However, increasing personalization also increased discomfort, with 80% of participants uncomfortable with their photos being used in the ads. We conclude that advertisers should strive to identify high-value data items that can be used to achieve 'sweet spot' personalization that results in noticeable, interesting ads that are also comfortable for the user, and avoid data items that may increase the noticeability of their ads at the expense of users' comfort.

BACKGROUND

Display Advertising

Targeted ads are mainly plain content text ads – such as Google's AdSense, which generates $6 billion in revenue [12]. The two most common forms of targeting are contextual and behavioral. *Contextual advertising (CA)* describes ads delivered based on an automated matching of keywords from the content a user is currently viewing with keywords for an advertisement. CA aims to complement the website content and relies on information collected in real-time. *Behavioral advertising* (BA) describes ads which are delivered based on information collected about a user's web browsing behavior over time, such as websites visited, topics viewed and search engine queries. This data is used to profile users into interest categories (e.g. 'golf enthusiast') and relevant ads are served. Examples of BA ad networks include Google's Double Click, Yahoo! Network, AOL Advertising and Scientific Media.

Past research suggests that BA can improve the click-through rate (CTR) of an ad by as much as 670% [33]; and the action-through rates (ATR; percentage of ads resulting in sale) are more than double those of standard advertising, 6.8% and 2.8% respectively [4]. It is likely that targeted ads are more effective because they are more relevant to users. A strong correlation was found between users liking an ad and its perceived relevance, those who dislike advertising being the least likely to see any relevance in what they see [16].

There is also evidence to suggest that BA is more effective than CA. Studies conducted by advertising agencies found that the same ads received 17% more fixations in unrelated-content sites than related-content sites [20]; and the CTR was more than 100% higher for ads in unrelated-content sites, and the ATR was 19% higher, compared to related-content sites [26]. Such results could be due to the '*surprise effect*': when a user looking for a product finds an ad on an unrelated site, s/he might react to the unexpected event by engaging with the ad [20, 26]. Another explanation is that contextual ads could suffer from the '*clamor effect*': when too many adverts for the same product try and catch the user's attention, the user might avoid looking at any of them and instead choose to stay focused on the editorial content [20, 26].

However, being served more relevant adverts does not necessarily mean that users will perceive targeted advertising positively – as can be seen in Table 1, studies exploring the perceptions of users have had mixed results.

Reasons for disliking targeted advertising include **perceived privacy costs**. Users dislike the idea of being followed, describing BA as '*invasive*' [16, 24]. This has

Researchers	Year	N	Population	Survey Method	Findings
Internet Advertising Bureau and Olswang [15]	2009	1,004	UK	Online	23% found the concept of BA appealing and 20% found it unappealing. When asked whether they would prefer BA as opposed to non-targeted ads, 27% opted for BA while 17% preferred non-targeted ads.
Turow et al. [30]	2009	1,000	US	Phone	66% did not want ads tailored to their interests, compared to 32% yes and 2% maybe.
McDonald and Cranor [23]	2009 2010	14 314	US US	In-depth interviews. Online	Only 21% wanted the benefits of relevant advertising. 40% said that they would be more careful online if they knew that advertisers were collecting data; 15% said that they would stop using sites with BA.
Hastak & Culnan [13]	2010	2,064	US	Online	46% were uncomfortable with BA, 31% were neutral and 22% were comfortable.
Office of Fair Trading [26]	2010	1,320	UK	Not Reported	40% held neutral views about BA, 28% disliked it and 24% welcomed it. 57% said that the practice of BA would make no difference to their internet use, 5% that they would limit their internet use, and 1% that they would stop using the internet altogether.
TrustE [1]	2011	1,004	US	Not Reported	54% did not like BA and 37% had experienced a time when they had felt uncomfortable with a targeted online ad.

Table 1. Surveys investigating targeted advertising

been termed the '*creepiness factor*', a sense that someone has been 'snooping' into a part of your life that should remain private [17]. Other perceived privacy costs identified in the literature include:

- Cookies being installed on the user's computer [27];
- The storage of personal data without the user's knowledge [16];
- PII being attached to the user's Internet browsing [1];
- Being labeled by advertisers in ways the user considers unfair [31];
- Potential embarrassment to the user if using a shared computer [27];
- Other companies having access to the user's data [16];
- Data collected being used for purposes other than advertising [27].

CA raises fewer objections than BA [27]; because no tracking is involved, there are fewer risks associated with data storage or data sharing.

The **benefits** of targeted ads include:

- Free access to ad-funded content [2, 27];
- A reduction in irrelevant ads [27];
- A reduction in the cost of good services [27];
- Decreased search times [27].

The Internet Advertising Bureau suggest that the benefit of ad-funded Internet services to the user outweighs the privacy costs: they found that users were only prepared to pay one-sixth of the total surplus gained to avoid advertising and personal information-usage nuisance [2]. Users might argue, however, that it is not fair for advertisers to expect them to make such a trade-off. McDonald and Cranor [24] found that 69% believe privacy is a right, 61% think it is 'extortion' to pay to keep their data private, and only 11% say they would pay to avoid ads.

Factors that could help alleviate users' privacy concerns include transparency and control. Research findings suggest that users feel more comfortable with BA in situations where they are actively told when targeted ads are being shown [14, 27]. Users are also more comfortable after finding out PII is not stored [1, 16] and that they have the option to opt-out [14, 16, 27].

Rich Media

Rich media - such as images, video and pop-ups – are increasingly being used in display advertising. By making the ad highly visible relative to the website content, the ad is made harder for the user to ignore. Pop-ups have been found to be more memorable than standard banner ads [9]. However, such advertising can also be experienced as *disruptive* because it diverts the user from their online goals. When an ad is considered disruptive, negative attitudes can develop, affecting brand perception and leading to '*ad avoidance*' [23]. The more important the task, the more disruptive the interruption is likely to be perceived.

With the growth of targeted ads, it is possible that advertisers will try to combine targeting with high visibility. Only one study has investigated users' possible response to this approach. Goldfarb and Tucker [12] conducted a large-scale field experiment on 2,892 web advertising campaigns, comparing CA campaigns, rich media campaigns, and campaigns that did both. They conclude that users' purchase intent increased when CA and rich media were used as separate strategies; but when these strategies were combined, users' purchase intent decreased. They suggest that users may tolerate CA more than other ads because they potentially provide useful information; however, when such ads are made highly visible, this has a negative effect because it increases the user's awareness of being targeted and their perceptions of being manipulated by advertisers.

Personalization

Personalization is said to increase the appeal of an ad, because the user is more likely to assume that there is a match between his/her self and the product [3]. However, highly personalized messages can also have negative effects, depending on the degree to which the personal information used in the message uniquely identifies or characterizes the recipient. This is referred to as '*personalization reactance*' - when the user feels constrained in the sense of being too identifiable or observable by the firm. White et al. [32] suggest that three factors influence personalization reactance: the level of personalization, whether or not justification for personalization is present, and the perceived utility of the service. In their study, they used highly personalized email ads that addressed the customer by their name, state of residence and movie preferences. They found that when the perceived utility of the service was low, participants experienced personalization reactance in response to highly personalized messages that were not justified, resulting in lower click-through intentions. By contrast, when the perceived utility of the service was high, the justification of personalization was less important because highly personalized messages were less likely to elicit reactance.

Only one research study has investigated the effects of targeted display advertising and personalization. Tucker et al. [30] conducted a randomized field experiment where they compared the CTRs of two different Facebook ad formats, before and after the introduction of improved privacy controls. In the targeted and personalized ad format, the ad explicitly mentioned the user's undergraduate institution, or the name of a celebrity the user was a 'fan' of, e.g. '*As a [undergraduate institution name] graduate, you know that strong women matter...*' In the targeted and non-personalized format, the message referred to a broader user characteristic, e.g. '*You know that strong women matter...*' They found that after Facebook's introduction of improved privacy controls, users were twice as likely to click the targeted personalized ads. As a result, they suggest that if sites are successful at reassuring consumers that they are in control of their privacy, personalization of online ads can be used to generate higher CTR.

Compared to email personalization, relatively low levels of personalization are currently used in targeted display ads. In particular, PII has not yet been used to personalize targeted display ads. PII has been formally defined as '*information that can be used to distinguish or trace an individual's identity*'; examples include a person's name and photographic images [22]. Research studies suggest that PII can make a message more noticeable. For example, in psychology, the famous 'cocktail party effect' describes how a person can hear his/her own name being said amongst many voices in a crowded room [6, 25]. More recently, it has been suggested that people have prioritized processing for their own name and their own face [29], and that people have difficulty disengaging their attention from self-referential stimuli [7, 8].

The majority of advertisers involved in BA claim not to keep people's real names in their databases and often cite this layer of anonymity as a reason why BA should not be considered intrusive [28]. However, it is reported that some companies, such as Rapleaf, do keep PII [28]. Also there is evidence to suggest that advertisers have access to PII, even if they are not using it: several studies have found that there is 'information leakage' from online social networks to third-party advertisers, which can include PII and sexual-orientation [13, 18, 19].

Another relevant finding is that it is a common belief amongst Internet users that advertisers have access to PII. A recent study found that over 30% of users believed that sites they are registered with (e.g. Facebook, Google, Microsoft Live, Yahoo) share PII with advertisers without their consent; and more than half of users (52%) believe that their PII are attached to tracking activity [1]. Following on from this, we question how would users respond if advertisers were open about having access to PII, and PII was used to personalize advertising content?

Research Aims

The effects of personalization and the use of rich-media in TA have been under-investigated in previous research. In this paper we ask: what will happen to internet users' perceptions of privacy when these powerful advertising techniques become more common? This question gains relevance now that companies like Facebook plan to leverage their users' profiles to advertise products [11].

In particular, we wanted to explore and compare participants' reactions to the following types of ads:

- Untargeted rich media ads;
- Targeted rich media ads;
- Personalized rich media ads, using PII of first name and photo.

User studies investigating people's opinions of targeted ads have tended to be survey-based, asking participants to rate their level of agreement with various statements [15, 23, 13]. We argue however, that how a person feels about the practice of targeting might be different to how they feel when presented with targeted ads in an actual browsing situation. To explore people's responses to our ad types, we designed a study where participants were given the task of booking a holiday. As the participant went through the booking process, they were exposed to ads that became increasingly personal – on the first page they were presented with standard ads, on the second page they were presented with ads that targeted them based on their holiday booking input, and on the final page they were presented with personalized ads that used their name and photo in the ad content. In particular, we wanted to understand the following research questions:

RQ1. Which ads did participants notice most / least?

RQ2. Which ads did participants find the most comfortable / uncomfortable?

RQ3. Which ads were participants most / least likely to take an interest in?

METHOD

Participants

There were 30 participants (15 male, 15 female). Their ages ranged from 19 to 55 years (mean age = 28 years, SD = 10.1). 22 were university students and 8 were university staff, recruited from an opportunity sample.

Stimuli

A travel website ('Flyaway') was created using HTML, CSS and JavaScript. The website was split into three pages, each page containing four banner adverts (top left, top right, bottom left, bottom right). The adverts were all the same size (221 by 336 pixels) and consisted of text and rich media. See Figure 1 for examples of the adverts.

Page 1 allowed the participant to select their journey information (destination, journey type, departure date and time, return date and time) and a series of additional questions to 'qualify for our exclusive offers' (relationship status, do you own a car, do you have travel insurance, age group). The ads on this page were general ads about holidays and flights. See Figure 1, top left ad, for an example.

Figure 1. Examples of 'Flyaway' ads. Top left: a general holiday ad. Top right: a holiday ad based on holiday selection 'Dubai'. Bottom left: an ad based on the age selection '18-34'. Bottom right: an anti-aging cream ad using the participant's first name and modified photo

Page 2 allowed the participant to select the number of tickets and to enter their name, address and payment details. The ads on this page were targeted using the holiday destination the participant chose on Page 1 (e.g. local hotels, restaurants) and their answers to the additional questions on Page 1 (e.g. dating website, car loan, travel insurance). See Figure 1, top right, for an example.

Page 3 confirmed the booking and informed the participants that their booking reference would be emailed to them shortly. The ads on this page were targeted using the age range the participant chose on Page 1 (e.g. clubbing, life cover), addressed the participant by their first name, and used the participant's photo (both modified and unmodified) to show them what they could look like with / without a particular product (e.g. hair salon, anti-wrinkle cream). See Figure 1, bottom left and right ads, for examples. The participant's photo was obtained from the university database when the participant signed up for the study and was modified using Photoshop. The modifications were changing the hair-style in one version, and artificially aging the appearance of the individual by 40 years in another version.

Apparatus

The website was displayed on a Dell desktop computer using Internet Explorer 7. Eye movements were measured with a Tobii X50 eye tracker and Tobii Studio 2.0.4 software. Total fixation duration (TFD) was collected in order to gauge noticing of the stimuli ads (RQ1), with longer durations indicating ads that had been noticed more. The post-task interview was recorded using an audio recorder.

Materials

A post-task questionnaire was created that consisted of 13 statements, which participants had to rate how on a 5-point scale, indicating their level of agreement. Q1 was a general statement, where participants rated their awareness of the website's ads. The 12 questions that followed then focused on four of the targeted ads: holiday destination, age, name and photo. Participants were asked to rate each of the ad types for how likely they were to notice the ad (RQ1), how comfortable they felt with the ad (RQ2) and how likely they were to take an interest in the ad (RQ3).

Procedure

The experimenters applied for permission to conduct the study through the university's ethical review process. Permission was granted to use the participant's university ID photo (from a publicly accessible page) and to display modified versions of it to the participant during the study.

The study took place in a usability lab and took approximately 30 minutes per participant. It was advertised as an experiment to investigate 'Perceptions of a Travel Website.' Participants signed a consent form detailing the procedure of the experiment, what equipment would be used, informed that the data would be held in accordance with local data protection law, and of their right to withdraw from the experiment at any time without consequence. However, participants were not told that the focus of the study would be the website's adverts, and that their photo would be used for a subset of the ads.

Participants were asked to book a flight to a destination of their choice and to 'talk aloud' about their thoughts of the website. While they did the task, eye tracking and video recording were used to record their reactions. Once the task was completed, the researcher reviewed the Tobii screen recording with the participant and this time asked participants to specifically talk about what they thought of the ads on each page.

Next participants were asked to complete a post-study questionnaire, which asked them to rate the ads with regard to how noticeable, comfortable and likely to elicit interest they were. They then took part in an interview exploring their perceptions of targeted and personalized advertising in the context of their prior experience.

At the end of the study participants were fully debriefed and informed that the photos of themselves would not be published, and that all data relating to them from the experiment could be destroyed at their request. All participants were paid £5 for their time.

RESULTS

Attention

Eye tracking data was analyzed using Tobii Studio 2.0.4 Software. The four ads on each page were defined as areas of interest (AOI). Aggregating the data for the four AOIs, descriptive statistics for total fixation duration (TFD) were then calculated for each page. (Note that 5 participants were excluded from the sample due to poor data quality.)

Page	Total Fixation Duration (s)	
	Mean	SD
1	4.6	3.8
2	4.7	5.4
3	9.5	6.3

Table 2. Descriptive statistics for total fixation duration (n=25)

As can be seen in Table 2, the ads on Page 3 received twice as much attention (mean TFD = 9.5 seconds) as the ads on Page 1 and Page 2. A repeated measures one-way ANOVA was revealed that there was a significant effect for TFD, F (2, 48) = 10.16, p<.001. Bonferroni-corrected pairwise comparisons (sig. level = .016) revealed that the TFD for Page 3 was significantly higher than Page 1 (p=.009) and Page 2 (p<.001).

Two ads on Page 3 were compared, to test the effect of displaying an ad with the participant's photo while controlling for potential differences between pages. An ad which used the participant's age and a standard picture (which appeared on the top-left of the webpage) was compared against an anti-ageing cream ad using the participant's photo (which appeared on the top-right). The ad with the participant's photo was looked at for 5.8 seconds longer than the standard picture ad (mean TFDs = 13.0 seconds and 7.2 seconds respectively). A repeated measures t-test revealed that this difference was statistically significant, t (24) = 3.2, p=.003.

Questionnaire Results

The questionnaire responses for all participants (n=30) were analyzed using SPSS. Four questions were negated (Q6, Q7, Q9, Q11), so that for all items 1 = strongly disagree, 2 = disagree, 3 = neutral, 4 = agree and 5 = strongly agree.

Likely to Notice

The majority of participants agreed that they were more likely to notice ads that use their photo (97%), holiday destination (77%) and name (57%); see Table 3. Descriptive statistics revealed that participants rated adverts using their photo highest for being noticeable (M=4.6), followed by adverts using their holiday destination (M=3.8), their name (M=3.5) and age (M=3.0).

I am more likely to notice adverts that use my...	+ ve	0	- ve
Holiday destination (Q2)	23 (77%)	5 (17%)	2 (7%)
Age (Q5)	7 (27%)	13 (43%)	9 (30%)
Name (Q8)	17 (57%)	6 (20%)	7 (23%)
Photo (Q11)	29 (97%)	0 (0%)	1 (3%)

Table 3. Frequencies for Noticing. +ve = Strongly Agree or Agree, 0 = Neutral, - ve = Disagree or Strongly Disagree (n=30)

A repeated-measures one-way ANOVA revealed that there was a significant effect for Noticing, F (3, 87) = 16.0, p<.001. Bonferonni-corrected pairwise comparisons (sig. level =.008) revealed that photo was rated significantly more noticeable than holiday destination (p=.005), age (p<.001) and name (p<.001). Holiday destination was rated significantly more noticeable than age (p<.001).

Feeling Comfortable

87% of participants agreed that they would feel comfortable with their holiday destination being used in ads and more than two-thirds of participants disagreed that they would feel comfortable with their photo (80%) or name (66%) being used in ads; see Table 4.

I feel comfortable with adverts that use my...	+ ve	0	- ve
Holiday destination (Q3)	26 (87%)	3 (10%)	1 (3%)
Age (Q6)	7 (23%)	13 (43%)	10 (33%)
Name (Q9)	7 (23%)	4 (13%)	19 (66%)
Photo (Q12)	3 (10%)	3 (10%)	24 (80%)

Table 4. Frequencies for Comfort. +ve = Strongly Agree or Agree, 0 = Neutral, - ve = Disagree or Strongly Disagree (n=30)

Descriptive statistics revealed that participants rated adverts using their holiday destination (M=4.0) as most comfortable, followed by adverts using their age (M=2.9), their name (M=2.3) and photo (M=1.7). A repeated measures one-way ANOVA was conducted to test for significance. To compensate for violations of the sphericity assumption (Mauchley's W(df=5) = .65, p=.037), the significance levels were adjusted according to the lower-bound procedure. There was a significant effect for Comfort, F (1, 30) = 26.7, p<.001. Bonferonni-corrected pairwise comparisons (sig. level = .008) revealed that holiday was rated significantly more comfortable than age ($p<.001$), name $p<.001$) and photo ($p<.001$). Age was rated as significantly more comfortable than photo ($p=.001$).

Taking An Interest
77% of participants agreed that they would be more likely to take an interest in ads that used their holiday destination and over half of participants disagreed that they would be more likely to take an interest in ads that used their photo (67%) or name (57%); see Table 5.

I'm more likely to take an interest in adverts that use my...	+ ve	0	- ve
Holiday destination (Q4)	23 (77%)	6 (20%)	1 (3%)
Age (Q7)	7 (30%)	16 (53%)	5 (17%)
Name (Q10)	5 (17%)	8 (27%)	17 (57%)
Photo (Q13)	10 (23%)	0 (0%)	20 (67%)

Table 5. Descriptive statistics for Interest. +ve = Strongly Agree or Agree, 0 = Neutral, - ve = Disagree or Strongly Disagree (n=30)

Descriptive statistics revealed that participants rated adverts using their holiday destination (M=3.9) highest for interest followed by adverts using their age (M=3.1), their name (M=2.4) and photo (M=2.4). A repeated-measures one-way ANOVA was conducted to test for significance. To compensate for violations of the sphericity assumption (Mauchley's W(df=5) = .47, $p<.001$), the significance levels were adjusted according to the lower-bound procedure. There was a significant effect for Interest, F (1, 30) = 13.7, $p<.001$. Bonferonni-corrected pairwise comparisons (sig. level = .008) revealed that holiday was rated significantly more comfortable than age ($p<.001$), name ($p<.001$) and photo ($p<.001$).

Interviews

Interview transcripts were analyzed using thematic analysis, a "method for identifying, analyzing and reporting patterns (themes) within data" [5]. This type of analysis involves coding (tagging) interesting sections of the transcript in a consistent way and subsequently grouping those codes into themes. The identification and interpretation of themes help explain what the data means and relate it to the research questions [5]. Five major themes are described in this section: (1) relevance of the ads; (2) perception of own photo; (3) how advertisers obtain personal data; (4) the extent to which advertisers access and use personal data; and (5) other people seeing ads with another person's data.

Relevance
The majority of participants (23) identified 'relevance' of the ads as an important factor in how they perceived targeted and personalized advertising. A relevant ad was described as an ad which was related to the individual's interests, activity on the website, or topic of the website. In the context of our study that meant ads related to holidays were considered by these participants as more relevant. Relevance was associated to a more positive perception of the ads. P5 said *"I mean I think that they are more attractive if they have things that are relevant to me [...]"*.

Own photo
More than half the participants (19) expressed negative reactions to seeing ads with their own photo. When referring to the ads in the study that manipulated their photo into looking older and having different haircuts these participants used adjectives such as: *"disturbing"* (P2, P25), *"strange"* (P4), *"weird"* (P12, P13), *"freaky"* (P13), *"creepy"* (P14), or *"terrible"* (P17).

When asked how they would react to ads that used their own photo these participants said they would feel uncomfortable. P1 said *"[...] the face is a very important thing and identifying yourself is important but umm it's creepy yeah and it might turn me off and it might turn several people off a lot."*

In order to gauge the strength of feeling and judge possible consequences for ad-hosts of using this level of personalization, participants were asked about how they would feel if a site that is frequently used and relied upon, such as Facebook, started using their photo in ads targeted at them. 5 participants said they would quit the site. 6 said they would continue using it even though they would feel uncomfortable about the use of their photo. 7 said they would be comfortable.

17 participants mentioned that ads with their own photo would be more noticeable. P27 said *"[...] well in terms of advertising it might work well if you use someone's picture because you immediately notice that."*

How did they get my data?
For 18 participants, how advertisers had obtained their data and where it had come from influenced how they perceived targeted ads. One specific issue was data from one website or company being used to show ads on another website. P10 said *"I don't understand how they know what you've been looking at on another website."*

Understanding how the ad had been created had a comforting effect. P18 said *"Yeah, I would prefer targeted adverts as long as I knew how they got the fact that they're targeted. As long as, yeah, I was aware of, it was just you know that I could see that I looked at it before and they were just advertising something, and that was it, then I'd be more comfortable and happy with that [...]"*

In our study, the photos of participants were obtained from the university pages. Knowing this made participants more comfortable with its use in ads. P5 said *"Yeah I would be surprised and a bit umm not comfortable with it, I mean the fact that I know that it is a university, that it is my university picture and that I am at university, then it doesn't make me uncomfortable [...]"*. Not realizing where the photo came from made participants uncomfortable. P14 said *"I think that's weird, because I'm like 'Where did they get that picture?'"*

Access to / use of personal data

For 17 participants the extent of personal data that advertisers had access to, and used for creating ads, had an effect on their perceptions. For example, P7 said *"I don't want anything specifically focused on me because then again it presumes that my life is pretty open but for instance if you're digging into my life it's none of your business."*

Consent to use personal data in targeted advertisement was mentioned by 5 participants. Using individual's personal data without consent in order to create ads was perceived negatively. P4 said *"[...] I don't think I would want my image being used for something without my knowledge, I mean if they like approached people and asked to use it then that would be different but I wouldn't want it used without my knowledge."*

Other people seeing ads with my data

9 participants were concerned about the potential for other people to see ads with their data because of errors in the targeting, or people sharing computers. For example, if personalized ads started to make use of personal photos, the wrong photo could be displayed to the wrong person. P19 said *"Well they have to be rather accurate to know which ... I mean there may be ... are so many, many names, have the same name so they may get the wrong picture from a person with the same name."* Computers storing an individual's web browsing behavior could also introduce problems if they are shared. P11 said *"The computer or the website will have the memory of my searching. The next time my friend or somebody else uses my computer they can see what I bought. If I just, I only buy the cream or moisturizer, those kind of things, that's okay. But if it's very private I don't want them to be able to see that."*

DISCUSSION

The goal of the study was to explore participants' perceptions of rich-media targeted and personalized advertising. We investigated how participants perceive targeted and personalized ads that use increasingly personal data with regards to noticeability, interest, and comfort.

Questionnaire results indicate that depending on the data item used to create an ad it can become significantly more or less noticeable. Ads which use the participant's photo, name, or holiday destination are more likely to be noticed. Ads that used their photo were perceived by participants as being significantly more noticeable than ads that used their age, name, or holiday destination. An individual's photo is not commonly displayed without her/his knowledge as part of an ad in commercial websites, so it is possible that they were considered highly noticeable due to a 'surprise effect' [20, 26]. An additional explanation is that individuals are slower to disengage their attention when looking at a photo of themselves [7, 8], so it's possible that they looked at ads with their photo for longer periods of time and more times than the other ads. This possibility is supported by the mean TFD results. Ads on Page 3 were looked at for significantly longer than ads on Pages 1 and 2. Also, when comparing the ads at the top of Page 3, the ad with the participant's photo was looked at for significantly longer than the ad with the standard picture.

The level of interest participants had in the different types of ads was significantly influenced by the type of data item used. Questionnaire results revealed that they were more likely to take an interest in ads that use their holiday destination, and less likely to take an interest in ads that use their name and photo. The use of age had no effect on interest. Ads that used holiday destination were considered significantly more likely to raise interest than ads that used age, name, or photo. This can be attributed to the fact that the task participants were asked to complete was intrinsically related to holidays; thus ads with holiday destination may have been seen as more relevant in the context than the other ads. This explanation is supported by the interviews which show that the majority of participants identified 'relevance' of an ad as having a positive influence in how they perceived it. The link between relevance of an ad and whether people like it has also been suggested in past research [16]. This supports the conclusion that in order to make users interested in their ads advertisers should make an effort to make ads relevant for the context users are engaging with.

The type of data item used in the ads has a significant effect on how comfortable participants were with it. Participants reported being comfortable with ads using their holiday destination, neutral about ads using their age, and uncomfortable with ads using their name or photo. Ads that used holiday destination were rated significantly more comfortable than ads that used the other three types of data. Ads that used photo were rated significantly less comfortable than ads that used age and holiday destination, with the majority of participants saying they felt uncomfortable with the use of their photos in ads. Again, relevance of the ad may be used to explain these results: previous research has shown that individuals are more comfortable with personal data use in ads when it is perceived as relevant [32]. It is likely that participants perceived holiday destination as a relevant data item in that context, but not their own photo. Additionally, the interviews indicated that not knowing how advertisers had obtained the data used to create targeted ads was discomforting. It is possible that, while it was clear for participants that holiday destination had been collected from the form they were filling in, it was more difficult to remember the source of their photo. Advertisers should avoid using personal data that make users feel uncomfortable about ads. The use of personal photos in particular may upset users and lead them to reject services, as indicated by participants' answers to the possibility of Facebook employing this type of advertising. The interviews suggest that asking users for consent before using their data in advertising could alleviate their concerns.

The type of personal data used in creating the targeted ads has, according to the questionnaire results, a highly significant effect on noticeability, interest, and comfort. Items such as holiday destination in our scenario help to create ads which are both considered noticeable, interesting, and comfortable – so should be of great value for advertisers since they will help get the attention of potential customers, convert that attention into purchases, while not creating feelings of privacy invasion on the individual. Identifying these data types in different contexts on the web should be of great interest to advertisers. At the same time advertisers should also be careful with data items that can increase noticeability of ads but which are considered too sensitive to be used in ads by individuals. There could be a short term benefit in using someone's photo to make them look at an ad, but if that ad makes the individuals uncomfortable then the privacy cost may offset the noticeability benefit. As more personal data becomes available to advertisers on the web, it becomes more important that these trade-offs are considered.

CONCLUSIONS

The findings described in this paper suggest that users' perceptions of targeted ads using rich-media vary depending on the type of data used to create the ads, with comfort decreasing as the level of personalization increases. Advertisers should strive to identify high-value data items that can be used to achieve 'sweet spot' personalization that results in noticeable, interesting ads that are also comfortable for the user. At the same time, advertisers should be wary of using data items that can increase the noticeability of their ads at the expense of users' comfort since this could be counterproductive for the advertised brand. Our findings can be used as guidance for future research aimed at understanding how to design more attractive and less intrusive ads.

To our knowledge, this is the first study of how personalized rich media ads are perceived by users and where different types of personalization were compared with regards to their impact on user perceptions. Past studies on targeted advertising have typically been surveys, whereas we gauged participant's live reactions to adverts in the lab. It was also the first study to investigate users' reactions to ads that used their own photo. Targeted advertising seeks to make ads more relevant to the recipient and related to their interests. It is becoming increasingly prevalent and, with advertising companies having access to new sources of personal data such as social networks, we believe the trend toward targeting may become a trend toward personalization (see [11]). Therefore, by using participants' photos in ads for anti-aging cream or makeovers we are anticipating what the future of display advertising can be.

The main limitation of this study was the size and composition of the participant sample. It was also participants' first interaction with ads that used their photo. Further research is needed to determine whether users habituate to these ads over time, if different users perceive these ads more positively than others, or if combination with other types of content changes users' perceptions. A longitudinal between-subjects study with different groups being subject to different types of ads would help answer these questions. Participants being asked to 'talk aloud' may also have artificially increased their sensitivity for the ads.

Although this was a first-step study, we can state confidently that the use of PII in this context is a complex issue that needs to be handled with care and that imprecise targeting or personalization could deter potential customers from engaging with the brand. The effects of data quality errors and imprecise targeting in advertising are currently under-researched topics which we would like to pursue in future research.

REFERENCES

1. 2011 Consumer Research Results: Privacy and Online Behavioral Advertising, TRUSTe, 2011.
2. Consumers driving the digital update: The economic value of online advertising-based services for consumers, IABEurope, London, 2010.
3. Anand, B. and Shachar, R. Targeted advertising as a signal. *Quantitative Marketing and Economics*, *7* 3 (2009), 237-266.
4. Beales, H. The Value of Behavioral Targeting, Network Advertising Initiative, Washington, D.C., 2010.
5. Braun, V. and Clarke, V. Using thematic analysis in psychology. *Qualitative Research in Psychology*, *3* (2006), 77-101.
6. Cherry, E. Some Experiments on the Recognition of Speech, with One and with Two Ears. *J. Acoust. Soc. Am.*, *25* 5 (1953), 975.
7. Devue, C. and Brédart, S. Attention to self-referential stimuli: Can I ignore my own face? *Acta Psychologica*, *128* 2 (2008), 290-297.
8. Devue, C., Van der Stigchel, S., Brédart, S. and Theeuwes, J. You do not find your own face faster; you just look at it longer. *Cognition*, *111* 1 (2009), 114-122.

9. Diao, F. and Sundar, S.S. Orienting Response and Memory for Web Advertisements. *Communication Research, 31* 5 (2004), 537-567.
10. Drèze, X. and Hussherr, F.-X. Internet advertising: Is anybody watching? *Journal of Interactive Marketing, 17* 4 (2003), 8-23.
11. Fiveash, K. Facebook shoves your face into creepy "sponsored stories" in 2012. *The Register*, London, 2011. Available at: http://www.theregister.co.uk/ 2011/12/21/facebook_sponsored_stories/. [Accessed January 9, 2012].
12. Goldfarb, A. and Tucker, C. Online Display Advertising: Targeting and Obtrusiveness. *Marketing Science* (2011).
13. Guha, S., Cheng, B. and Francis, P., Challenges in Measuring Online Advertising Systems. in *IMC '10: Proceedings of the 10th ACM SIGCOMM conference on Internet measurement conference*, ACM, (2010).
14. Hastak, M. and Culnan, M.J. Future of Privacy Forum Online Behavioral Advertising "Icon" Study Summary of Key Results, 2010.
15. Hollis, N. Ten Years of Learning on How Online Advertising Builds Brands. *Journal of Advertising Research, 45* 02 (2005), 255-268.
16. Kean, A. and Dautlich, M. A guide to online behavioural advertising, Internet Advertising Bureau, London, 2009.
17. Knowledge@Wharton. Privacy on the web: Is it a losing battle? *Knowledge@Wharton* Philadelphia, PA, 2008.
18. Korolova, A., Privacy Violations Using Microtargeted Ads: A Case Study. in *Data Mining Workshops (ICDMW), 2010 IEEE International Conference on*, (2010) 474-482.
19. Krishnamurthy, B. and Wills, C., On the leakage of personally identifiable information via online social networks. in *WOSN '09: Proceedings of the 2nd ACM workshop on Online social networks*, ACM, (2009) 7-12.
20. Marcus, N. Behavioral Targeting Has More Visibility *iMEDIA CONNECTION*, 2006.
21. MarketingCharts. Global web ad spend to rise 31% in 2 yrs, Watershed Publishing, 2011.
22. McCallister, E., Grance, T. and Scarfon, K. Guide to Protecting the Confidentiality of Personally Identifiable Information (PII), NIST, Gaithersburg, MD 2010.
23. McCoy, S., Everard, A., Polak, P. and Galletta, D. The effects of online advertising. *Commun. ACM, 50* 3 (2007), 84-88.
24. McDonald, A.M. and Cranor, L.F. Beliefs and behaviors: Internet users' understanding of behavioural advertising *Telecommunications Policy Research Conference*, 2010.
25. Moray, N. Attention in dichotic listening: Affective cues and the influence of instructions. *Quarterly Journal of Experimental Psychology, 11* 1 (1959), 56-60.
26. Newcomb, K. Behavioral ads convert better out of context *Clickz*, New York, 2006.
27. OFT. Online targeting of advertising and prices: A market study, Office of Fair Trading, London, 2010.
28. Steel, E. A web pioneer profiles users by name *Wall Street Journal*, New York, NY, 2010.
29. Tacikowski, P. and Nowicka, A. Allocation of attention to self-name and self-face: An ERP study. *Biological Psychology, 84* 2 (2010), 318-324.
30. Tucker, C. Social Networks, Personalized Advertising, and Privacy Controls, NET Institute, 2010.
31. Turow, J., King, J., Hoofnagle, C.J., Bleakley, A. and Hennessy, M. Americans Reject Tailored Advertising and Three Activities that Enable It. *SSRN* (2009).
32. White, T., Zahay, D., Thorbjørnsen, H. and Shavitt, S. Getting too personal: Reactance to highly personalized email solicitations. *Marketing Letters, 19* 1 (2008), 39-50.
33. Yan, J., Liu, N., Wang, G., Zhang, W., Jiang, Y. and Chen, Z. How much can behavioral targeting help online advertising? *Proceedings of the 18th international conference on World wide web*, ACM, Madrid, Spain, 2009, 261-270.

Why Johnny Can't Opt Out: A Usability Evaluation of Tools to Limit Online Behavioral Advertising

Pedro G. Leon, Blase Ur, Rebecca Balebako, Lorrie Faith Cranor, Richard Shay, and Yang Wang
Carnegie Mellon University, Pittsburgh, PA
{pedrogln,bur,balebako,lorrie,rshay,yangwan1}@cmu.edu

ABSTRACT

We present results of a 45-participant laboratory study investigating the usability of nine tools to limit online behavioral advertising (OBA). We interviewed participants about OBA and recorded their behavior and attitudes as they configured and used a privacy tool, such as a browser plugin that blocks requests to specific URLs, a tool that sets browser cookies indicating a user's preference to opt out of OBA, or the privacy settings built into a web browser. We found serious usability flaws in all tools we tested. Participants found many tools difficult to configure, and tools' default settings were often minimally protective. Ineffective communication, confusing interfaces, and a lack of feedback led many participants to conclude that a tool was blocking OBA when they had not properly configured it to do so. Without being familiar with many advertising companies and tracking technologies, it was difficult for participants to use the tools effectively.

Author Keywords

Usability; Privacy; Online Behavioral Advertising; Cookies

ACM Classification Keywords

H.5.2 Information Interfaces and Presentation: Miscellaneous

General Terms

Human Factors; Experimentation; Security

INTRODUCTION

The United States Federal Trade Commission (FTC) and other groups have voiced privacy concerns about online behavioral advertising (OBA) for over a decade [8]. The FTC defines *online behavioral advertising* as "the practice of tracking an individual's online activities in order to deliver advertising tailored to the individual's interests" [9]. Industry organizations have developed self-regulatory principles that call for companies to empower consumers to control targeted advertising. [1] [2]

[1] http://www.networkadvertising.org/networks/principles_comments.asp
[2] http://www.aboutads.info/principles/

Consumers may control OBA using a number of tools. However, to use these tools successfully, users must be able to install a tool, configure it to match their preferences, and effectively use it. While these tools have the potential to satisfy the concerns of consumers and regulators, there has been little rigorous evaluation of their usability and effectiveness.

In this paper, we present results of an in-depth study investigating the usability of tools that limit OBA. We found serious usability flaws in all nine tools we examined. The online opt-out tools were challenging for users to understand and configure. Users were confused by technical jargon and complicated settings in some tools. Users also struggled to install and configure Tracking Protection Lists (TPLs) and other blacklists to make effective use of blocking tools. They often erroneously concluded the tool was blocking OBA when they had not properly configured it to do so.

In the next section, we present background and related work. We then describe the privacy tools that we tested, present our testing methodology, and discuss our results. We conclude with a discussion and design recommendations.

BACKGROUND AND RELATED WORK

Online advertisers track users as they navigate the Internet to construct profiles for targeting advertisements. They typically use third-party HTTP cookies to track users [13]. Unlike first-party cookies, which are placed by the domain a user is visiting, third-party cookies are placed by another domain, such as an advertising network. Other tracking mechanisms, such as Flash Local Shared Objects (LSOs) and HTML 5 local storage, enable tracking even when the user clears cookies or switches browsers [1].

User concerns about behavioral advertising

According to a 2009 study [19], if given a choice, 68% of Americans "definitely would not" and 19% "probably would not" allow advertisers to track them online even if their activities would remain anonymous. McDonald and Cranor found that only 20% of their respondents prefer targeted ads to random ads, and 64% find the idea of targeted ads invasive [17].

Industry self-regulation and browser-based solutions

The Network Advertising Initiative (NAI) and Digital Advertising Alliance (DAA) self-regulatory principles require that companies allow users to opt out of targeting. Both organizations host websites where users can set opt-out cookies, signaling that they do not wish to receive targeted ads. However, Komanduri et al. found many instances of non-compliance with the NAI and DAA requirements [12]. A 2010 FTC staff report stated that "industry efforts to address privacy through self-regulation have been too slow, and up to now have failed to provide adequate and meaningful protection" [10].

Another example of attempted industry self-regulation is the Platform for Privacy Preferences (P3P), a computer-readable privacy policy standard published by the World Wide Web Consortium (W3C) in 2002. P3P compact policies (CPs) are a set of tokens that summarize a website's privacy policy regarding cookies. Internet Explorer 9 (IE9) uses CPs to evaluate websites' data practices and can reject cookies based on user preferences [4]. Leon et al. found that more than 20 of the 100 most-visited sites have inaccurate CPs and discovered "thousands of sites using identical invalid CPs that had been recommended as workarounds for IE cookie blocking" [15].

Two recent browser-based methods for controlling OBA are Do Not Track (DNT) and Tracking Protection Lists (TPLs). Users can configure their web browser to send a DNT header with HTTP requests, signaling that they do not want to be tracked. However, there is not yet a consensus on how to define tracking or what websites should do upon receiving a DNT header. In IE9, Microsoft introduced TPLs, lists of filter rules that block content and scripts from specified domains.

Usability of privacy tools

Prior studies have examined the usability of privacy tools. Cranor et al. designed and evaluated a privacy agent that fetched P3P policies and indicated whether they were consistent with configured preferences [6]. Ha et al. conducted focus groups to examine users' awareness of cookies and asked participants to evaluate two cookie-management tools, finding cookie management to be confusing to users [11].

A number of authors have offered guidance for the developers of privacy tools. Lederer et al. described five pitfalls in the design of privacy tools. They cautioned against designs that "require excessive configuration to manage privacy" [14]. Brunk offered recommendations for developers of privacy software including giving "the user feedback that preventative features are operational" [2]. Cranor advised privacy software developers to avoid privacy jargon, ease configuration, educate users, and use persistent indicators to convey information about the tool's capabilities and current state [5].

PRIVACY TOOLS TESTED

We tested the usability of nine tools from three broad categories for controlling behavioral advertising. This list includes three *opt-out tools*, two *built-in browser settings*, and four *blocking tools*. The tools we selected are representative of the range of tools currently available. Where we were aware of multiple similar tools, we selected those that we judged most comprehensive or easiest to use. Tests of IE 9 were conducted on Windows 7. All other tools were tested with Firefox 5.0.1 on Windows 7 or Mac OS X Leopard.

Opt-out tools

Opt-out tools allow users to set opt-out cookies for one or more advertising networks. If a user sets an opt-out cookie for a particular advertising network, that network should not show a user advertising based on his or her browsing behavior, but may continue to track and profile that user.[3] A separate opt-out cookie must be set for each network. To simplify this process, some opt-out tools let users opt out of dozens or hundreds of networks all in one place.

DAA Consumer Choice is a web-based opt-out tool hosted by the DAA. Consumers can go to the DAA website's "Consumer Choice" page,[3] select some or all of the participating companies, and click a button to set opt-out cookies. At the time of our testing, there were 79 participating companies.

Evidon Global Opt-Out is an opt-out tool hosted by Evidon, a company that provides technology to help advertisers comply with industry self-regulatory programs.[4] Similar to the DAA opt-out site, Evidon's opt-out page allows consumers to select companies from which to opt out of OBA. In addition, Evidon provides links to other companies from which a consumer may opt out through other means. At the time of testing, Evidon provided direct opt-out for 184 companies and links to opt-out information for 118 others.

PrivacyMark is a JavaScript bookmark tool that sets opt-out cookies. PrivacyMark[5] is offered by Privacy Choice, a company that sells privacy-related services to companies and offers free consumer privacy tools. At the time of our testing, the tool set opt-out cookies for over 160 companies.

Browsers' built-in settings

All major web browsers include privacy options among their built-in settings. We tested the privacy settings on Internet Explorer and Firefox, the browsers that currently have the highest market share.[6] These browsers offer the ability to block cookies selectively based on a variety of factors, including whether they are first-party or third-party cookies.

Internet Explorer 9 (IE9) includes an Internet options panel with a privacy tab that displays a six-level privacy slider. These levels restrict or block cookies based on a website's P3P CP. A user can also choose advanced settings that block all first-party or third-party cookies, setting exceptions on a per-site basis. IE9 offers additional privacy features, which we discuss with the *blocking tools*.

Mozilla Firefox 5 includes a privacy panel with a check box to "Tell web sites I do not want to be tracked" by sending a DNT header to each website a user visits. In addition, the privacy panel allows users to select options to delete browsing history automatically or choose to accept no cookies, accept cookies except from third-parties, or accept all cookies, including the option to set exceptions on a per-site basis.

Blocking tools

We tested four blocking tools, which allow users to choose domains or patterns to block. When using a blocking tool, users rely on the scope of a list of blocking rules rather than

[3]http://www.aboutads.info/choices/
[4]http://www.evidon.com/consumers/profile_manager#tab3
[5]http://www.privacychoice.org/privacymark
[6]http://gs.statcounter.com/

on the good faith of the advertising networks. When a site is blocked, the browser will not communicate with that site, preventing that site from tracking the user.

Adblock Plus 1.3.9 is an open-source tool that relies on subscription lists to determine what to block. When a user installs Adblock Plus,[7] he or she chooses one or more filter subscriptions maintained by third parties.

IE9 Tracking Protection is a mechanism built into IE9 that blocks websites based on TPLs, which are blacklists of domains. Users may subscribe to TPLs curated by third parties.

Ghostery 2.5.3 is a browser plugin available for all major web browsers. When a user visits a website, Ghostery[8] finds and disables cookies, scripts, and pixels that are used for tracking. It notifies users about which companies have been blocked and gives users the option of selectively unblocking these companies. Ghostery is owned by Evidon.

TACO 4.0 by Abine blocks tracking by particular advertising companies, sets opt-out cookies, and deletes LSOs. In addition, TACO[9] offers other privacy features, including disposable email addresses. The version of TACO we tested has since been rebranded as Privacy Suite.

METHODS

We conducted a 45-participant, between-subjects laboratory study in which each participant tested one of nine tools that control OBA. The study took place on Carnegie Mellon University's Pittsburgh campus during August 2011.

Recruitment

We sought nontechnical participants who were not knowledgable about privacy enhancing tools, but who were interested in trying them. Since we were using IE9 on Windows 7 and Firefox 5 on Windows 7 and Mac OS X as our testing platforms, we recruited participants who had experience using one of these operating system and browser combinations. Participants, who received $30 Amazon gift cards, were recruited from the Pittsburgh region using Craigslist, flyers, and a university electronic message board. Recruitment material directed prospective participants to a screening survey. We recruited five participants for each of the nine tools we tested, for a total of 45 participants. Prior research has shown that many usability problems that are likely to occur in a given population can be identified with only five participants [16].

Testing protocol

Each 90-minute individual session was moderated by one of two researchers who had jointly moderated 11 pilot sessions. We used audio recording and screen capture to document each session. Participants were randomly assigned to the tools considering their browser and OS preferences. We began each session with a semi-structured interview to gather perceptions, knowledge, and attitude about online advertising. We then showed the participant an informational *Wall Street Journal* video about OBA.[10] Following the video, we probed the participant's attitudes and perceptions about behavioral advertising. Next, we asked participants to perform three types of tasks using a computer in our laboratory configured with their preferred Internet browser and operating system. We reset the browser settings both between participants and between tasks. We asked participants to think aloud as they performed each task and to work as though they were using their own computer.

Installation and Initial Configuration. We provided a simulated email from a friend recommending the assigned tool. The email linked to a website from the tool provider where the participant could download, use, or learn about the tool. After the participant installed and configured the tool to match his or her personal preferences, we asked an After Scenario Questionnaire (ASQ) [16] and open-ended questions to measure his or her perceptions and understanding of the tool.

Configuration of Specified Settings. We next asked participants to configure the tools to match specifications we provided. Tools in the same category had similar specifications. Evidon and DAA participants were asked to opt out of 13 specific companies. Ghostery and TACO participants were asked to block the same 13 companies, which were selected from the pool of companies common to these tools. Participants also chose specific settings for the tool's notification messages. AdBlock Plus participants were asked to subscribe to a specific filtering list and add a specific filtering rule. IE-TPL participants installed a specific TPL and also blocked a specific domain. IE and Firefox participants blocked third-party cookies, allowed first-party cookies, and added two exceptions. Participants using PrivacyMark did not perform this task since that tool cannot be configured. Participants then answered another ASQ survey and verbal questions.

Fine Tuning Settings to Resolve Problems. We then configured the tool to a fairly protective setting and asked the participant to perform five typical browsing tasks with the tool installed and active. Three of these tasks required third-party content, cookies, or scripts to function properly, and thus could not be completed when some of the tools were set to block tracking. We advised the participant to change the tool's settings if he or she faced difficulty completing these tasks. In one task, we asked participants to watch a video on nytimes.com. Participants testing AdBlock Plus or Ghostery could only see the video after unblocking brightcove.com, disabling the tool on nytimes.com, or completely disabling or uninstalling the tool. Similarly, we asked participants to shop for a laptop on dell.com. When participants testing Ghostery or TACO clicked a button to proceed to the checkout page, nothing happened unless they unblocked omniture.com, disabled the tool on dell.com, or uninstalled the tool. Finally, we asked participants to log into Facebook, using an account we provided, and invite a friend to play Farmville. Participants testing Ghostery and TACO saw whitespace where the game should have been. Participants then answered questions and filled out a System Usability Scale (SUS) questionnaire [7].

[7]http://adblockplus.org/en/
[8]http://www.ghostery.com/
[9]http://abine.com/preview/taco.php
[10]http://online.wsj.com/video/92E525EB-9E4A-4399-817D-8C4E6EF68F93.html

Limitations

Due to the limited recruitment area, our participants are not representative of the general Internet population. We make no effort to draw statistically significant conclusions, but instead focus on understanding the underlying problems faced by each participant. As with any laboratory study, participants were not in their usual working environments. Participants only used their assigned tools for about an hour; an experiment over an extended time period might reveal further insights about how users interact with the tools over time and might reveal changes in behavior as users become more familiar with the tools. However, we note that a user who is dissatisfied with a tool within the first hour may opt not to continue using it. Furthermore, because most of these tools offer few visual indicators of what they are doing and do not require ongoing interaction with the user interface, users may not gain much additional familiarity through continued use.

RESULTS

We first describe our participants' demographics. Then, we present usability results for all three categories of evaluated tools. We summarize our results in Table 1.

Participants

Our participants were fairly well-educated, with some concerns about online privacy. They included 15 males and 30 females between the ages of 19 and 57 (mean age 29); each condition had both males and females. Eight were undergraduate students, 15 were graduate students, two were unemployed, and 20 were employed. None had a background in computer science or web development. The level of initial knowledge about OBA was fairly uniform across conditions. Participants' quotes are attributed to an identifier consisting of an abbreviation for the tool they tested (e.g. "EV" for Evidon) and their subject number (1 to 5) within that tool.

In our initial interview, a number of participants expressed awareness that the ads they see are sometimes tailored to their interests, though they conflated contextual and behavioral advertising. When asked how they think online advertising companies decide which ads may be relevant to users, half of the participants mentioned web browsing history or web searches, while many others mentioned social networks and email. A few participants mentioned that cookies might be involved, though they did not know how. None of the participants demonstrated an understanding of the mechanisms used for tracking. After they viewed the informational video, most participants were able to explain roughly behavioral advertising and third-party cookies. When asked about ways to stop receiving targeted ads, most participants mentioned deleting cookies, while some mentioned antivirus software. Only a few mentioned built-in browser settings.

Opt-out tools

Configuration

Participants had difficulty using the DAA's opt-out website both when attempting to navigate from the site's homepage to the opt-out page and also when choosing the companies from which to opt out. DAA-1 and DAA-4 were unable to find the opt-out page, which is linked from the homepage, until the moderator provided written instructions. Both of these participants accidentally navigated to the page on which advertising companies register to join the DAA, mistakenly believing that this was the opt-out page. DAA-1 remarked, "The application to opt out it is a bit expensive: $5,000 a year."

Once they arrived on the DAA's opt-out page, participants did not always notice that the page had three tabs: *All Participating Companies, Companies Customizing Ads For Your Browser* (the default view), and *Existing Opt-Outs*. In our test, in which each user began with a new Firefox profile, Yahoo! always appeared alone on this list of companies that had already begun tracking them. Both DAA-3 and DAA-5 only opted out of Yahoo! even though both expressed a desire to opt out of all behavioral advertising. They didn't realize that they needed to switch tabs to choose all companies. The other three DAA participants opted out of all participating companies. Since participants had difficulty navigating the DAA site, the opt-out process took a relatively long time. Participants expressed displeasure when the DAA website displayed a message stating that certain opt-outs had failed.

All five participants who tested Evidon successfully located the opt-out mechanism, although EV-2 complained that "the opt-out option is hidden." EV-1 initially had problems finding it, saying, "I am not sure where to go to opt out," and EV-3 requested assistance finding the opt-out tab once he landed on the profile page. EV-1 and EV-3 both chose to "Select All" companies whose opt-out could be completed on Evidon's page, while EV-4 chose to opt out of all companies except Google, 24/7 Real Media, AOL Advertising, and YouTube, which he identified as those he uses and trusts.

Although Evidon provides the most comprehensive list of trackers, including links to manually opt out of sites, users who wish to opt out of all companies linked from Evidon's page may expend a large amount of time doing so. Both EV-2 and EV-5 wanted to opt out of all companies available, including those that required manual opt-out. EV-5 spent 47 minutes completing the opt-out process, including landing on opt-out pages in five different languages. "How am I gonna opt-out of this one?" he remarked when he arrived on a Japanese language opt-out page. He completed these non-English opt-outs by using Google Translate.

The installation process for PrivacyMark requires dragging an icon to a browser's bookmarks toolbar, an unfamiliar process. PM-1 was initially confused about where the bookmarks toolbar was located. PM-4 remarked, "Usually software goes through a different installation process." The instructions provided incorrectly assume that the user has previously enabled the bookmarks toolbar. This toolbar is not enabled by default in recent versions of Firefox.

Understanding

No participants who tested the DAA website understood what opting out means in this context. Four participants incorrectly stated that opting out will stop tracking. Only DAA-5 did not

Tool	Capabilities	Strengths	Weaknesses
Blocking			
AdBlock Plus	Blocks tracking, blocks ads	Facilitates awareness of trackers when users click icon. Users are guided to pick a filtering list.	Configuration interface confusing, includes jargon. Difficult for participants to find specific trackers to unblock. Difficult for participants to understand differences between filtering lists.
Ghostery	Blocks tracking	Facilitates awareness of trackers through on-screen alerts. Alerts helped resolve broken website elements. Easy installation.	Configuration interface includes jargon. Participants unaware that default settings don't block trackers. Multiple steps required to enable blocking.
IE-TPL	Blocks tracking, enables DNT headers	Easy to install TPLs from provider websites.	Configuration interface confusing. Participants unaware that default settings don't block trackers. Participants did not realize they had to choose a TPL in order to be protected. Even when prompted, participants were unable to choose a TPL using the interface. Difficult to unblock specific trackers.
TACO	Blocks tracking, sets permanent opt-out cookies and blocks third-party cookies	Sets opt-out cookies by default and prevents deletion. Facilitates awareness of trackers from icons and alerts. Suggests workarounds for broken website elements. Provides diverse privacy features.	Large number of privacy features overwhelmed participants. Configuration interface confusing, includes jargon. Initial configuration took a long time. Difficult for participants to find specific trackers to unblock. Participants unaware that default settings don't block trackers. Participants didn't notice workaround suggestions.
Opt-out			
DAA	Sets opt-out cookies for 79 advertising companies	Provides links to more information about each tracker. Easy to select specific trackers.	Initial configuration took a long time. Difficult to navigate to actual opt-out page. Not obvious that opting out of all trackers requires switching out of default tab on opt-out page. Participants incorrectly believed that they were opting out of tracking. Participants did not realize that deleting cookies nullifies opt-outs. Opt-outs sometimes fail. Participants unable to confirm opting out was effective.
Evidon	Sets opt-out cookies for 184 advertising companies and provide links to opt out of 118 additional companies	Provides links to more information about each tracker. Easy to select specific trackers. Provides links to non-standard opt-outs. Provides the most comprehensive list of tracker and advertising opt-outs.	Initial configuration took a long time. Participants incorrectly believed that they were opting out of tracking. Difficult to navigate to actual opt-out page. Participants did not realize that deleting cookies nullifies opt-outs. Difficult for users to complete non-standard opt-outs. Opt-outs sometimes fail. Participants confused by "opt-out request sent" messages with no additional information. Participants unable to confirm opting out was effective.
PrivacyMark	Sets opt-out cookies for 160 advertising companies	One-click opt-out.	Participants did not realize that deleting cookies nullifies opt-outs. Participants unable to confirm opting out was effective. Requires dragging icon to bookmarks toolbar, which participants could not find. Tutorial video states incorrectly that tool will stop tracking. Participants thought clicking icon would delete cookies.
Built-in			
IE-Settings	Blocks specified cookie types	Default settings provide some protection.	Configuration interface confusing, includes jargon. Participants couldn't figure out how to block all third-party cookies.
Firefox	Blocks specified cookie types, DNT	Participants could easily block third-party cookies and enable DNT headers.	Participants didn't know what protection DNT provided.

Table 1. Summary of strengths and weaknesses of each tool identified by observing participants during usability testing.

mention tracking, but she thought that opting out "makes it easy to block advertisers from sending you ads."

All participants who used Evidon's opt-out tool similarly misunderstood opt-out to mean that they could not be tracked or would receive fewer ads. However, Evidon's opt-out website explicitly states, "If you opt out, you will still see ads online, and in some cases data may be collected about your browsing activity."[11] After opting out initially, EV-1's expectation was that she would see "probably only 10% of the ads that I used to see." Most participants mistakenly believed they could no longer be tracked. EV-3 thought that Evidon's opt-out configures "who gets your information and whether they can/cannot use it," while EV-4 believed he was "telling ad companies that I do not wish to participate in tracking behaviors." EV-5 thought he could now browse without "worrying about my information being collected."

The mechanism for opting out confused users. None of the participants who tested the DAA's website, and only two of the participants who tested Evidon's website, understood that opting out sets an opt-out cookie on their computer. All other participants who mentioned cookies mistakenly thought that cookies were being blocked. DAA-1 thought he was temporarily stopping cookies, DAA-2 expected that opting out "prevents third-party cookies from being installed on my computer," and DAA-3 said, "it blocks cookie creation and transfer." Evidon participants also thought opt-out blocks access to cookies. For instance, EV-2 said, "Somehow, it will prevent those companies from looking at the cookies that accumulate in my computer." Although they misunderstood the opt-out process, some participants liked the links to learn about the companies that participate in the opt-out program.

None of the PrivacyMark participants initially understood that the purpose of the tool was to set opt-out cookies. Three of the participants watched the video on PrivacyChoice's website, which states incorrectly that this tool stops online tracking. Common misconceptions were that PrivacyMark either prevented cookies from being sent or deleted cookies. In the eyes of PM-2, PrivacyMark "clears cookies, prevents cookies from being sent, or encodes cookies so that advertisers cannot see them." Participants retained their misconceptions of PrivacyMark's purpose even after performing a number of browsing tasks with the tool installed.

[11] http://www.evidon.com/consumers/profile_manager#tab3

Three of the participants who tested either the DAA or Evidon websites drew parallels between opting out and Do Not Call lists. DAA-4 expressed a negative attitude, saying that the DAA opt-out is "almost like Do Not Call lists, not like that works." DAA-5 said, "Everyone gets ads. You have to intentionally remove yourself, like Do Not Call."

Four of the participants who tested Evidon noted disliking the "opt-out request sent" message that sometimes appeared in place of "opted out." EV-1 was representative in saying, "I do not have a way to verify that I successfully opted out. The request was sent, but I am not sure if I actually opted out." Another participant received an "opt-out failed" message, leading him to question the effectiveness of the process.

Users were unhappy that Evidon's "Select All" option selected only companies whose opt-out could be completed on Evidon's page. EV-1 felt that the idea that "if you select all, you will not opt-out of *all* is misleading."

Overall, users were unsure of how successful their opt-outs were, with EV-2 stating, "You just have to hope that it is working." EV-4 similarly wondered, "I do not know if I actually did anything." He was also confused about the meaning of the trade group affiliations listed on Evidon's opt-out page, saying, "It would be nice to know what these [DAA, NAI] affiliations are." EV-5, who was redirected to the NAI website a handful of times during his 47-minute Evidon opt-out process, said that he believed that the NAI is an "ad agency" used by a number of companies.

PrivacyMark's lack of communication with users was its major usability issue; users wanted an indication that PrivacyMark was working. For instance, PM-2 described the feature she wanted to see in PrivacyMark as "a little notification telling you that it is working, blocking something." PM-5 suggested that she "would like to be able to check from which companies I have opted out. I want to choose specific companies I want to block." PM-4 felt that the lack of communication meant that it was not doing anything.

Finally, most participants who used cookie-based opt-out tools mistakenly believed that deleting their cookies would further protect their privacy. However, unless they use a tool designed to prevent opt-out cookie deletion (e.g. TACO, Beef TACO, "Keep my opt-outs" by Google, "Keep more opt-outs" by PrivacyChoice), users who delete their cookies inadvertently delete their opt-out cookies, undoing their opt-out.

Built-in tools

Browsers differ in the ease of changing settings

Most participants were able to find their browser's privacy settings page, although they were confused by the page's interface and jargon. IE users were unsure how IE's P3P-based settings related to third-party cookies. IE-1 spent more than 10 minutes trying to find the Internet Options window. Although she eventually found the window, she never clicked on the 'Privacy' tab. The other four participants were able to find the settings page, but the settings they chose differed from their expectations in all cases. For instance, IE-4 incorrectly expected that the default settings "will block third-party cookies." IE-5, who chose the 'High' privacy setting, was unsure what that setting actually meant. She said, "I hope what I chose, 'high,' will block cookies from dangerous websites, but from safe ones everything will get through." The explanations next to the privacy levels are based on P3P Compact Policies, which are likely unfamiliar to an average user.

In contrast, participants testing Firefox were able both to configure and describe accurately their privacy settings. For example, FF-1 blocked both first- and third-party cookies, but added exceptions for websites she uses, such as Amazon.com. She explained that Firefox "seems to be effective at limiting cookies... I like more stringent privacy setttings, but I have some exceptions, mainly entertainment." FF-4 accepted first-party and blocked third-party cookies, saying that her configuration "clears away all the cookies that you do not want...I wanted less cookies, less tracking, less invasion." The three other Firefox participants kept the default cookie settings, which allow both first- and third-party cookies. However, these participants demonstrated awareness of their settings. For instance, FF-3 explained that she "didn't want it to not track completely since I'm sometimes interested in ads."

We observed a stark difference in the performance of participants testing IE and Firefox. When asked to do so, none of the IE participants were able to allow first-party and block third-party cookies. The option to block third-party cookies is contained in the 'Advanced' menu, which only IE-2 opened. Rather than blocking third-party cookies as they had been instructed, IE-2, IE-3, and IE-5 chose the 'Low' setting on Internet Explorer's privacy slider, falsely believing they had accomplished their goal. In contrast, all five Firefox users were able to configure the specified settings, including blocking third-party cookies, in 1 to 4 minutes.

Users like 'Do Not Track' but are skeptical of its effectiveness

When asked to configure Firefox's privacy settings as they would on their own computer, four of the five Firefox participants enabled DNT. This behavior suggests that participants like the idea of stopping tracking with a single click. Nevertheless, users were skeptical about DNT's effectiveness. For example, FF-5 said, "[DNT] would probably just put a wrench in their program, but they could probably figure something else out." Both FF-1 and FF-3 correctly realized that DNT relies on advertisers' good faith. FF-1 had learned this fact from the Firefox privacy webpage, explaining, "Firefox says that DNT is voluntary. I would like to think websites will actually respect my preferences, but I am not sure."

Participants did not understand the details of the DNT mechanism, though they expressed their desire for it to stop tracking. For example, FF-3 felt that DNT meant, "Don't allow behavioral advertising to happen. Don't share...my browser history or my information," whereas FF-4 thought it meant that "websites will not be allowed to collect cookies on me. They will not be able to remember what I have done."

Fine tuning settings to fix broken elements

Both IE and Firefox users were able to remove Facebook from a blacklist in order to log in. All five IE users and all five Firefox users correctly recognized that they were unable to login to Facebook because Facebook had been blacklisted. Although all participants removed Facebook from the blacklist, IE-1 never refreshed Facebook's page after changing her settings and thus she was not able to login after 10 minutes of trying. It took the other four users between 1 and 5 minutes from when they noticed there was a problem to successfully logging in. Removing Facebook from the list of blacklisted domains was sufficient for IE users to complete the task of inviting a friend to Farmville, but Firefox users needed to perform an extra step that proved difficult for most. Only two Firefox participants were able to invite their friends to Farmville by enabling third-party cookies. Although FF-4 solved the problem, she was confused by why her solution worked, stating, "I think I am getting confused between third-party cookies and others." FF-1 displayed similar confusion during her unsuccessful attempt to load Farmville's 'Invite Friends' feature, commenting, "I do not know why cookies are required to invite friends."

Blocking tools

While participants were able to install all four of the blocking tools, they had trouble configuring them to match their preferences. In many cases, participants erroneously believed they had chosen configurations that would block most or all third-party tracking. When the tools blocked content participants needed to complete browsing tasks, they were often unable to take appropriate corrective action, instead either failing to complete the task or disabling the tool entirely.

Installing blocking tools is easy

Overall, participants experienced few difficulties installing blocking tools. All participants who tested Ghostery, TACO, and IE-TPL were able to install the tool without any assistance, although TACO took participants longer to install. Four of the participants testing AdBlock Plus installed the tool without assistance, while one participant required assistance finding the options menu. Participants found the installation process for Ghostery to be especially simple.

Participants tried and failed to configure strong protections

Although participants were able to install the blocking tools with relative ease, they experienced difficulty configuring these tools appropriately. Participants were confused by jargon in the interface, and in some cases thought erroneously that they had chosen the most protective configuration when the tool was actually doing little.

Ghostery permits users to block tracking cookies and web bugs, but these options are off by default. Users must navigate multiple steps filled with jargon to turn on blocking. Only one participant blocked all available trackers, the highest level of protection. Three participants did not block any trackers, but two of these participants nonetheless believed they had configured the tool to block all trackers. The remaining participant selected a handful of trackers and cookies to block.

All participants who tested TACO selected the default blocking and opt-out features, which set (and prevent the deletion of) opt-out cookies, yet do not block any trackers. This configuration does not exploit the tool's significant privacy-enhancing features. Two TACO participants attempted to use the tool's identity protection features, even though neither configured any options to opt out of or block web tracking. TACO-2 spent 15 minutes installing the tool and setting preferences, attempting yet failing to configure TACO's "safe e-mail" and "safe phone number" features. Although she stated that she hoped to block cookies, she was unable to; although she remembered seeing an option to block cookies, she later forgot where this option was amid TACO's many features. TACO-4 stated that she was very concerned with privacy and was determined to use all of TACO's features. After spending 24 minutes trying to configure the tool and watching its video tutorials, she questioned TACO's trustworthiness. She remarked, "I think this is a false sense of security. Give us your information and we will anonymize it. Yeah, sure!"

Four of the AdBlock Plus participants chose the default filtering subscription list without changes, while ABP-4 chose the default list but unblocked Google AdSense. However, none of our participants understood what they were blocking, and most were unsure how to differentiate between filtering lists.

All participants testing IE Tracking Protection also kept the default setting, which provides minimal protection because it only sends a DNT header without subscribing users to a TPL. However, participants believed they were configuring the tool protectively. For instance, TPL-2 explained the rationale for his configuration as, "I just tried to get like the maximum privacy." Many of the usability problems encountered by participants testing Tracking Protection Lists had been previously identified by Cranor [3].

Changing configurations is difficult

When asked to configure blocking tools according to a specified configuration, participants' initial problem was often finding the tool again in order to change its settings. Although the add-ons toolbar was enabled, participants ABP-2, ABP-3, GH-2, and TACO-4 all required assistance finding their respective tools. Many of these participants mistakenly looked for these tools in the "All Programs" area of the Windows Start Menu. Others clicked on "Add-Ons" to open the add-ons manager, but never realized that they needed to click on "Extensions" to see which add-ons were already installed.

Only two TACO participants were able to configure TACO according to the specification we provided, spending 6 minutes and 16 minutes to do so. The three other TACO participants were unable to block web trackers. TACO-2, who spent 8 minutes before giving up, never realized that she could click on the "Not Blocked" text listed under web trackers to block them. TACO-4, who worked for 12 minutes before giving up, didn't realize that clicking on a category of trackers produced a drop-down menu of the companies whose trackers were blocked. All participants who realized they could click on this drop-down menu complained that companies were presented in a seemingly random, rather than alphabetical, order.

Similarly, only two AdBlock Plus participants configured the tool as we specified. Two others didn't select the specified filter subscription, and one gave up. Participants had trouble navigating AdBlock Plus' interface and understanding the jargon that accompanied filtering rules. However, four of the Ghostery participants correctly configured the tool. The remaining participant required assistance finding the tool's options page and also neglected to enable one specified feature.

When asked to add a specific IE TPL, all five participants were able to do so. However, three participants were unsure how to use the IE interface to add TPLs, instead using a search engine to find the TPL on the web. Participants were also unsure whether they actually downloaded any TPLs. In addition, none of the the IE TPL participants were able to configure custom preferences that unblock specific trackers.

Fine tuning settings to fix broken elements

AdBlock Plus, Ghostery, and TACO participants encountered problems at websites because of the tool. IE TPL participants did not encounter any problems because the TPL that was installed did not block critical content at the visited sites.

In the nytimes.com task, participants noticed that there was a problem when they could not watch the required video. All five AdBlock Plus participants and four of the Ghostery participants realized that the tools were preventing the video from showing up. Every participant who noticed the problem eventually solved it. One AdBlock Plus participant unblocked a single tracking domain, while the other four participants disabled AdBlock Plus on nytimes.com. For instance, ABP-3 realized in less than a minute that something had been blocked, and he spent eight minutes trying unsuccessfully to unblock particular trackers. In the end, he disabled AdBlock Plus on nytimes.com. The Ghostery participants who solved the problem unblocked a single tracking domain.

In the Dell scenario, problems were more opaque. The mouse pointer started blinking and the site never responded after participants clicked the checkout button, leading many to believe that the Internet was temporarily slow. However, two TACO participants did not experience this problem due to changes made to the Dell website during the course of the study.

Three of the Ghostery participants realized that there was a problem, albeit after waiting for over two minutes. The other two participants waited for over four minutes until they were primed by the moderator to consider whether Ghostery might be causing the problem. At this point, GH-4 speculated that it was "maybe because I am about to enter personal information," whereas GH-5 attributed the delay to Dell's website. Four of the Ghostery participants solved the problem by unblocking specific trackers, while the other participant uninstalled Ghostery.

None of the three affected TACO participants realized by themselves that something was wrong. After the moderator waited four minutes and then asked the participant whether TACO might be causing the problem, TACO-1 concluded that TACO was the cause. However, TACO-2 still attributed the delay to the webpage, thinking that because she had successfully navigated past the first page of Dell's website, TACO was not causing problems. She said, "I'm like into the page now, so I'm thinking if anything it's just the webpage itself is slow or something... I don't know why it would have anything to do with TACO." TACO-3 also attributed the delay to network issues, explaining, "It just seems to be taking a few minutes." When asked whether TACO might be causing the problem, she decided that TACO might be protecting her from entering personal information. The only TACO participant who solved the problem, TACO-1, unblocked one web tracker and solved the problem in about two minutes.

The Facebook/Farmville task was easier for many participants than the Dell task, both because they had learned about unblocking trackers in previous tasks and because the failure was more evident. In the Facebook/Farmville task, all Ghostery participants experienced problems inviting friends yet were able to solve the problem in about one minute. Four of these participants unblocked specific trackers, while the other participant simply uninstalled Ghostery.

Four of the TACO participants experienced problems inviting friends. By contrast, TACO-1 did not experience problems since she noticed TACO's message that other participants have recommended different settings for this site, and she chose to accept those changes. None of the other TACO participants noticed this message even though all received it. TACO-3 again thought that TACO might be blocking her actions because she was about to enter personal information, although she was not certain that TACO was causing the problem. Neither of the other two TACO participants ever considered TACO as the culprit. TACO-3 gave up after seven minutes without ever noticing the alert about recommended changes. After it was pointed out by the moderator, TACO-4 noticed the TACO alert at the top of the page, but she decided to reject the changes and gave up. TACO-5, however, found an alternate route through the page that circumvented the blocked objects, never realizing that TACO had caused any problems.

Opinions and understanding of tools' capabilities

Following the testing session, we administered a System Usability Scale (SUS) survey in order to evaluate participants' opinions of the usability of the tool tested. All the tools scored between 40 and 50 out of 100 points. According to previous research [18], SUS scores below 50 points should be assigned a failing grade.

In order to evaluate participants' understanding of the capabilities of the tool they tested, we asked true-false questions after the "Configuration of Specified Settings" task and at the end of the testing session. Though none of the tools were particularly good at communicating its purpose, participants found the feedback provided by Ghostery and TACO useful. All five IE TPL participants misunderstood what IE TPLs do and were unable to differentiate between them. Participants did not trust the third-parties that produce TPLs. For example, TPL-4 erroneously believed that Fanboy, a popular TPL curator, "is probably a top advertising company." Participants testing opt-out tools incorrectly believed that those tools would stop online tracking.

DISCUSSION AND DESIGN IMPLICATIONS

None of the tools we tested empowered study participants to control OBA effectively according to their personal preferences. We identify the usability problems that appear endemic to this space and split them into thematic strands.

Users can't distinguish between trackers

The opt-out websites, as well as the Ghostery and TACO browser add-ons, provide users with lists of companies that they can block or from which they can opt out. However, users don't recognize most of these companies. We observed that users generally chose the same settings for all companies. Only a few users made exceptions for a handful of companies with names they recognized. Users were unable to set opt-out or blocking preferences meaningfully on a per-company basis. In order to align better with user expectations, blocking and opt-out tools should allow users to opt-out easily of all tracking. They should provide more fine-grained choices as an advanced setting and allow users to configure exceptions if they so desire, but not assume that most users are going to exercise such fine-grained control. Filter subscriptions and TPLs allow users to delegate these decisions to trusted experts; however, tools need better interfaces for selecting and installing these lists. In addition, tool providers should develop and test other ways of grouping trackers into meaningful categories that allow users to block or set opt-outs on a per-category basis rather than a per-company basis.

Inappropriate defaults

None of the tools that are not bundled with browsers have default settings that are appropriate for their target audience. If a user proactively downloads a browser add-on like Ghostery or TACO, or proactively visits an opt-out website, this action indicates that he or she likely intends to block tracking. However, Ghostery and TACO do not block any trackers by default, and enabling tracking involves multiple clicks. Similarly, no advertising companies are selected by default on the DAA and Evidon opt-out sites.

The general population of Firefox and IE users may have different expectations. Thus, it might be appropriate for browsers' built-in privacy settings to have less protective defaults. However, once a user enables a browser privacy feature such as TPLs, a protective default for that feature seems reasonable. IE Tracking Protection users must subscribe to a TPL before the feature provides additional protections, yet the interface did not lead participants to do so. While automatically subscribing users to a TPL would require Microsoft to select a default TPL, user interface changes could make users more aware that they need to select a TPL, guiding them to do so.

Communication problems

The tools we tested were ineffective at communicating their purpose and guiding users to configure them properly. The tools tended to present information at a level that is either too simplistic to inform a user's decision or too technical to be understood. For instance, IE9 provides a simplistic privacy slider whose six levels (e.g. "medium") do not describe their functionality. In contrast, participants were unable to understand the jargon-filled technical explanations next to the slider. Ghostery and TACO used the following terms whose distinction was meaningless to participants: Web Tracker, Web Bug, Flash Cookie, Silverlight Cookie, Tracking Cookie, Script, IFrame, and Targeted Ad Network. In addition, participants testing opt-out tools did not understand what the tools would opt them out of, mistakenly believing that they were protected against tracking. Furthermore, opt-out tool users thought deleting cookies would protect their privacy even more, not realizing that deleting their cookies would also delete their opt-out cookies and undo their opt-out.

Need for feedback

Many of the tools we tested provide insufficient feedback to users. Participants were left unaware whether or not most tools were working and oblivious to what they were doing. None of the opt-out tools tested notify users while they are browsing that their preferences are being respected. Furthermore, participants were unsure of what it meant to be opted-out and how they could tell whether opt-out was working. Participants who tested the browser cookie settings also had no mechanism for understanding what was happening behind the scenes unless websites didn't work. DNT mechanisms also provided no feedback; however, there is currently no way for tools to confirm that DNT preferences are being honored.

While AdBlock Plus did not provide explicit feedback, users noticed the absence of all ads on pages they visited and inferred that the tool was effective. Ghostery and TACO users received notifications on every website about what companies were attempting to track them and whether trackers had been blocked. Users appreciated this feedback and gained an understanding of what the tool was doing. However, future work is needed to determine whether these notifications become annoying or users stop noticing them over time.

Users want protections that don't break websites

Participants had difficulty determining when the tool they were using caused parts of websites to stop working. In cases where some content was not displayed or features stopped working, it appeared to participants that the problem was due to their Internet connection.

Some participants suggested that the tools should be able to detect these problems automatically and change their settings accordingly. TACO is able to detect browsing problems and suggest changes based on feedback from other users. However, most participants didn't see TACO's notification about these recommendations. An improved notification might be helpful. An alternative would be to adjust settings automatically. However, there is a risk that companies might game the crowdsourcing system to have their trackers unblocked. TPLs have the potential to address this problem by allowing users to subscribe to a list that has been curated to block most trackers, except those necessary for sites to function. However, participants in our study were unaware of the need to select a TPL and unsure how to decide which TPL to select. In addition, users wanted an easier way to delete all tracking cookies without losing essential site functions. This suggests that built-in browser tools should provide an easy way not only to block third-party cookies but also to delete third-party cookies without deleting first-party cookies.

Confusing interfaces

The tools we tested suffered from major usability flaws. For instance, multiple participants opted out of only one company on the DAA's website despite intending to opt out of all. Participants testing TACO never realized that they were not blocking any trackers and multiple participants never realized they could block tracking or third-party cookies since they were confused by features related to anonymous email. Participants did not understand AdBlock Plus' filtering rules. None of the participants who tested IE Tracking Protection realized that they needed to subscribe to TPLs until prompted in a later task. When we asked them to subscribe to a particular TPL, most participants did not use the IE TPL interface but instead performed a Google search for the name of the specified TPL and subscribed via its website.

Conclusion

We found serious usability flaws in all nine tools evaluated, demonstrating that the status quo is insufficient for empowering users to protect their privacy. While we recognize that the advertising industry, browser vendors, and third parties have contributed an assortment of tools to this ecosystem, we encourage a greater emphasis on usability moving forward.

Our results suggest that the current approach to OBA self-regulation through opt-out tools is fundamentally flawed. It is very difficult for users to distinguish between advertising companies. They also lack sufficient knowledge about tracking technology to use existing privacy tools effectively.

There are significant challenges in providing easy-to-use tools that give users meaningful control without interfering with their use of the web. The list of tracking companies and technologies is changing constantly, making it difficult for tool providers, let alone users, to keep up. It is difficult and time consuming to determine the purpose and privacy practices associated with every tracker on a website. It is also difficult to determine which trackers can be blocked without breaking desired website features. Even with additional education and better user interfaces, it is not clear whether users are capable of making meaningful choices about trackers.

Acknowledgements

This research was funded in part by a grant from The Privacy Projects and by NSF grants DGE0903659, CNS1012763, and CNS0831428.

REFERENCES

1. Ayenson, M., Wambach, D. J., Soltani, A., Good, N., and Hoofnagle, C. J. Flash cookies and privacy II. *http://ssrn.com/abstract=1898390* (2011).
2. Brunk, B. A user-centric privacy space framework. In *Security and Usability*, L. F. Cranor and S. Garfinkel, Eds. O'Reilly, 2005, ch. 20, 401–420.
3. Cranor, L. F. A first look at Internet Explorer 9 privacy features. *http://www.techpolicy.com/Blog/March-2011/A-first-look-at-Internet-Explorer-9-privacy-featur.aspx.*
4. Cranor, L. F. *Web Privacy with P3P*. O'Reilly & Associates, Inc., Sebastopol, CA, USA, 2002.
5. Cranor, L. F. Privacy policies and privacy preferences. In *Security and Usability*, L. F. Cranor and S. Garfinkel, Eds. O'Reilly, 2005, ch. 22, 447–472.
6. Cranor, L. F., Guduru, P., and Arjula, M. User interfaces for privacy agents. *ACM Transactions on Computer-Human Interaction 13* (2006).
7. Dumas, J. S. *The Human-Computer Interaction Handbook*. Lawrence Erlbaum Associates, 2003, 1093–1117.
8. Federal Trade Commission. Online Profiling: a Report to Congress: Part 2 Recommendations, July 2000.
9. Federal Trade Commission. Self-regulatory principles for online behavioral advertising, 2009.
10. Federal Trade Commission. Protecting consumer privacy in an era of rapid change, 2010.
11. Ha, V., Inkpen, K., Al Shaar, F., and Hdeib, L. An examination of user perception and misconception of internet cookies. In *CHI Extended Abstracts* (2006).
12. Komanduri, S., Shay, R., Norcie, G., and Cranor, L. F. AdChoices? compliance with online behavioral advertising notice and choice requirements. CyLab Technical Report CMU-CyLab-11-005, 2011.
13. Krishnamurthy, B., and Wills, C. Privacy diffusion on the web: a longitudinal perspective. In *Proc. WWW* (2009), 541–550.
14. Lederer, S., Hong, J., Dey, A., and Landay, J. Personal privacy through understanding and action: five pitfalls for designers. *Personal and Ubiquitous Computing 8*, 6 (2004), 440–454.
15. Leon, P. G., Cranor, L. F., McDonald, A. M., and McGuire, R. Token attempt: the misrepresentation of website privacy policies through the misuse of P3P compact policy tokens. In *Proc. WPES* (2010), 93–104.
16. Lewis, J. R. *Handbook of Human Factors and Ergonomics*. John Wiley & Sons, Inc., 2006, ch. 49 Usability Testing, 1275–1316.
17. McDonald, A. M., and Cranor, L. F. Beliefs and behaviors: Internet users' understanding of behavioral advertising. In *TPRC* (2010).
18. Sauro, J. *A Practical Guide to the System Usability Scale (SUS): Background, Benchmarks & Best Practices.* Denver, CO: Measuring Usability LLC., 2011.
19. Turow, J., King, J., Hoofnagle, C. J., Bleakley, A., and Hennessy, M. Americans reject tailored advertising and three activities that enable it. *http://ssrn.com/abstract=1478214* (2009).

<Insert Image>: Helping in the Legal Use of Open Images

Herkko Hietanen [a], Antti Salovaara [a], Kumaripaba Athukorala [a], Yefeng Liu [b]

[a] Helsinki Institute for Information Technology HIIT
Aalto University
PO Box 19215, 00076 Aalto, Finland
firstname.lastname@hiit.fi

[b] Department of Computer Science
Waseda University
3-4-1 Ohkubo, Shinjuku-ku, Tokyo, Japan 169-8555
yefeng@dcl.info.waseda.ac.jp

ABSTRACT
Media creation applications cater poorly to one very common usage: Situations in which the users need media that they do not own and for which they are unwilling to pay. Finding and using externally produced media is currently a cumbersome process. Often, users locate the content using a search engine, copy it into their work, cross their fingers, and hope they do not infringe on any copyrights. While the authors have shared hundreds of millions of images with permissive licenses, the license terms are too complicated for other users to follow. In our studies, we found that even the well-intentioned users still fail to respect copyrights in simple image reuse situations. We therefore introduce an *Open Media Retrieval* (OMR) model to remedy this problem and supplement it with prototypes that access various legal image sources directly within the creative work flow and provide automatic credits to the original authors.

Author Keywords
Creative Commons; attribution; open content; open media retrieval; copyright

ACM Classification Keywords
H.3.3 [Information Storage and Retrieval]: Information Search and Retrieval - Retrieval models;

General Terms
Design, economics, human factors, legal aspects, management

INTRODUCTION
In our networked society, users are inserting more visual elements into their everyday communications. People create and share presentations online, post blogs, and upload videos more than ever. Our Information Society has become what Lessig calls a read-write society [13] where culture is no longer consumed only by viewing it, but also as a source for remixed creativity. *Remix culture* can be defined as a "global activity consisting of the creative and efficient exchange of information made possible by digital technologies" and is supported by the practice of cut/copy/paste [17]. The term *remix* refers to "separating and recombining many types of media, including images, video, literary text, and video game assets" [5]. Consequently, *remixers* are those users who use different types of media in creating their works. They need external content to fuel their creative processes and thus the *search* for suitable content is an integral part of their remix creation processes.

With growing demand for free and remixable content, millions of creators have realized that in the *remix culture*, exclusive copyrights can be a serious hindrance. They have helped to create a pool of openly licensed works by making hundreds of millions of works available free of charge using Creative Commons (CC) licenses. CC images are royalty free and available to anyone. However, they all have some restrictions on their use. *Compliance* to the license terms has become another important part of legal remixing. Unfortunately, this is an area where the marriage of remix culture and the CC licensed content faces a problem. For example, every CC license requires the licensee to give proper credit to the original author. Recent studies suggest that users fail to properly attribute CC licensed works [18]. This mismatch of media use motivated us to address a number of research issues including:

- Do people use open content according to the license terms provided with the content? If there are infringements, how prevalent are they?
- Why and how do people fail in using open content appropriately?
- How can we improve this situation?
- Can an improved media management concept be more generally applied to remix applications and different media formats?

This paper describes an *Open Media Retrieval* (OMR) model in which the use of legally available media is automated. This is exemplified with two media creation systems, their pilot studies, and our analysis of the implications. We started our research by studying how users find and use media. This led to many insights into the problems of users' behavior with existing tools and how the needs of users can be facilitated with improved tools. This enabled us to envision improved interaction principles to facilitate the use of open content in a media creation process. To evaluate the model, we developed two search functionalities for open content retrieval.

Open Content Ribbon is a MS PowerPoint add-on that enables users to search and retrieve CC-licensed images in the sidebar of the program's window. The application automatically attributes the authors according to the license terms. *AudioImager* is a video editor that can be used from a web browser. It inserts still images into the audio track based on users' search queries. These studies were focused on CC-licensed image use, but the lessons and the OMR model apply to other copyrighted media as well.

THE COST OF THE MEDIA RETRIEVAL PROCESS

Remixers do not always have the exact media file they need in their collections. This triggers a media retrieval process. At first, the user needs to reach a source where a suitable media can be found. The user's subsequent actions are directed at finding particular piece of media that satisfies the search criteria [1]. This is followed by insertion of the media file from the Internet into user's media creation application. However, media retrieval and usage come with legal costs.

Legal Costs

In principle, legal restrictions are one of the biggest obstacles in using online media. Default search engine results present mostly copyright-protected media. These media files can be copied and used, but without permission from the rights owner, this use can easily infringe on copyright law. However, in practice, some users decide to ignore copyrights and infringe anyway. They purposefully choose to risk the legal repercussion of their infringement.

Lessig has criticized excessive copyrighting for hurting modern creativity, where remixing is the modus operandi [13]. Copyrighting creates an obstacle for the use of media files that were not created by the user. It grants the author an exclusive right to reproduce and publicly display or perform images, videos, and other creative works. Fortunately, authors and service providers have created markets for commercial and free exchanges of works, thereby helping to match supply to demand. These markets carry various direct and indirect costs.

Users can overcome copyright's exclusive nature by getting permission from the rights owner. However, finding the rights owner does not guarantee his/her willingness to license the content. Individual licensing is rarely efficient and several rights owners have a policy of non-cooperation, which means that he/she is not willing to license work to individuals, even for a fee [12]. Luckily the digital content markets are highly competitive and offer several options for obtaining content from content brokers like stock content services. However, rights owners typically set a price to license their otherwise exclusive rights and for many users even the smallest *direct license cost* can limit the use of the work.

Licensing also includes *indirect transaction costs*, for example, the search costs of finding the content, the licensor and negotiation costs to reach an agreement in terms of use, and enforcement costs to make sure that the use complies with the licensing terms [9].

Many commercial stock media services have reduced transaction costs by providing tools that simplify the licensing and retrieval processes. There are several add-ons[1] that plug and integrate the search, payment, and downloading of stock photos and other media for media creation applications. However, many users are either unable or unwilling to pay direct licensing costs for commercial content.

Fortunately, there are several sources for getting remixable media free of charge. In 2007, Wikimedia Commons[2] adopted by far the most popular open licensing scheme—Creative Commons—that is currently used to license millions of media files. The files are crowd-selected, annotated, and structured in a hierarchical ontology. Another source is Flickr[3] with its 200 million CC-licensed images. As a result, during the past few years, we have witnessed an increasing number of users sharing, promoting, and spreading their works and ideas [3, 15, 4] under CC licenses. CC-licensed material provides an attractive means for end-users to overcome the direct and indirect licensing costs because the licensed content is royalty free and getting the license does not involve laborious negotiations with the rights owners. Also, it seems that the quality of even the least restrictive CC-licensed images is comparable to Flickr's "all rights reserved" images [7]. The CC license's attribution requirements, however, lead to a design challenge, which we describe below.

Open Content Transaction Costs

A growing pool of open content is licensed with various public licenses (such as CC) that permit sharing and often remixing of the works. While these licenses reduce legal restrictions and are often gratis, they include a search cost for finding the content, a technical cost for downloading the content, and a compliance cost for making sure that the intended use falls within the license's scope. For a user, a proper licensed use of works involves numerous steps.

Figure 1 describes the required steps for using CC-licensed content. It illustrates the number of effort-related actions that the licenses impose on the users. Most of these steps are aimed at ensuring the correct *attribution* alongside the actual content. The attribution requirement is defined in detail in a long legal document that few licensees have ever read. CC licenses require the proper attribution to include 1) the Uniform Resource Identifier (URI) of the CC license

[1] E.g., iStock Office (www.istockphoto.com/istockphoto-office-ribbon) and Getty Images Photoshop (www. gettyimages.com/creative/frontdoor/adobeplugin) plug-ins.

[2] http://commons.wikimedia.org/.

[3] http://www.flickr.com/creativecommons/.

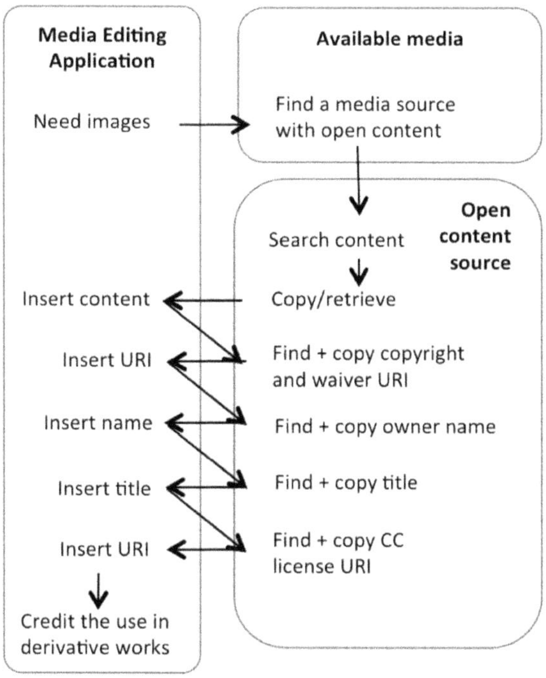

Figure 1. Media retrieval process with CC content.

used, 2) the name of the author, 3) the title of the work, 4) the copyright and the disclaimer of warranties' URIs if provided by the licensor, and 5) a credit identifying the use of the licensed work in the derivative work.

At least a dozen separate tasks are needed to ensure the compliance with the attribution terms. Such a procedure is prone to errors. Unfortunately, none of the major media creation applications are optimized to support a retrieval process in which remixers search and use open content. Therefore, remixers have the responsibility to study the details of the license terms and follow all of them. Failing to do so can lead to a grave situation as a CC license states that any breach of the license terms will terminate the license.[4] As any non-compliant attribution will terminate the license, the licensee can be left defenseless. The licensor could bring an infringement lawsuit against the licensee. Had the licensee followed the license terms to the letter, the licensee would have a legal defense against such claims.

RELATED WORK

Lawrence Lessig [13] has criticized our legal system for criminalizing the new remix generation. The web-savvy generation uses remixing as a self-expression tool involving borrowing and recombining works for which they do not own the copyrights. Studies on content reuse indicate unanimously that consumers' respect for copyrights leaves room for improvement.

Kantar Media's copyright survey [10] revealed that 73% of the respondents were not sure what is legal or illegal under the copyright laws. However, around half of the subjects who shared files illegally had also used legal online services. End users may therefore value convenience and availability over legality in their media use activities.

Similarly, Hietanen et al.'s quantitative survey [8] on illegal file sharers' attitudes toward copyrights showed that illegal file sharers do understand that infringements are both morally and legally wrong. However, they conceive the probability of getting caught as likely as winning a lottery and compare the moral dilemma to jaywalking [8]. It is noteworthy that, while there are hundreds of millions of CC-licensed works available, only few infringement cases have ended up in courts.

Diakopoulos et al. [5] found that users actually had a positive attitude toward the attribution of copyright contents. However, Seneviratne et al. [18] estimated that 70%–90% of Flickr's CC-licensed images have been reused in an improper fashion. They contend that users may be ignorant of the meaning of the licenses; do not read the license terms; use incorrect licenses in their derivative works, which violates the original content creator's intention; or even intentionally ignore the license due to their own interests. Similarly, most websites lack adequate functionality for finding licensed content, remixing, and attributing sources for remixes [19]. As a result, end users lack opportunities for effortless and appropriate media reuse.

Because of this pressing need, applications have been developed for easier attribution management in open content reuse. ThinkFree[5] lets users directly pick images from Flickr and inject license metadata automatically with them into a document. Zemanta[6] is a browser add-on for searching and recommending reusable media while working with the content. AuthorSTREAM[7] enables users to search images and videos from several online sources within PowerPoint and features an automatic attribution. However, it does not limit the search to legally reusable content. OpenOfficeOrg Addin[8] lets presentation creators set sharing and reuse permissions to their work and insert legally reusable images from Flickr, Wikimedia Commons, and OpenClipart.org. Firefox browser plug-ins such as OpenAttribute[9] and Semantic ClipBoard[10] simplify attribution by parsing the webpage contents and displaying

---

[4] Creative Commons Attribution 2.0. Available at http://creativecommons. org/licenses/by/2.0/legalcode.

[5] www.thinkfree.com.

[6] www.zemanta.com.

[7] www.authorstream.com.

[8] wiki.creativecommons.org/OpenOfficeOrg_Addin.

[9] openattribute.com.

[10] dig.csail.mit.edu/2009/Clipboard/.

the license and attribution information separately. Finally, developers have been active in helping CC authors to enforce their rights. Many prototypes and algorithms have been developed to monitor the Web for illegal re-use of open content and to inform the original contributors automatically.[11]

Although the media retrieval process is simplified with such tools, Monroy-Hernández et al. [16] have shown that automatic attribution also has drawbacks. It does not increase the content author's social value as much as a credit provided by a human user. However, our assumption is that automated attributions are a major improvement to the current situation where users fail to properly attribute altogether.

PRE-STUDIES

We carried out two pre-studies to answer our research questions: 1) How prevalent is the inappropriate use of works? 2) Why are users failing to follow the terms of open content reuse? 3) How can we improve the situation by identifying the difficulties?

Image Reuse in SlideShare.net

To get an idea of how image copyrights are currently respected, we analyzed image reuse in presentations. SlideShare[12] is the largest on-line presentation slide hosting and sharing service with 16 million unique visitors a month and about 100 million registered users. Our goal was to examine the image sources that people use when preparing presentations and to study whether they knew how to correctly credit the original authors. We analyzed 51 popular presentations on SlideShare that were randomly selected from the first five pages of results among the most viewed, most downloaded, and featured works. The presentations had an average of 300,000 views. All but one of the presentations were in English.

We reviewed the images in these slides and developed a binary classification tree (see Figure 2) to categorize the presentations into seven copyright treatment categories: No photos, own images, stock images (i.e., purchased content), images under fair use (e.g., screenshots from a website, see [14]), infringing images (either non-CC-licensed photos used without permission or CC-licensed images with improper attribution), and CC-licensed images with proper attribution.

For each image, we started by searching for a URL to the image source. If one was found, we checked whether the image was CC-licensed and continued by checking the status of proper attribution. If the URL was not available,

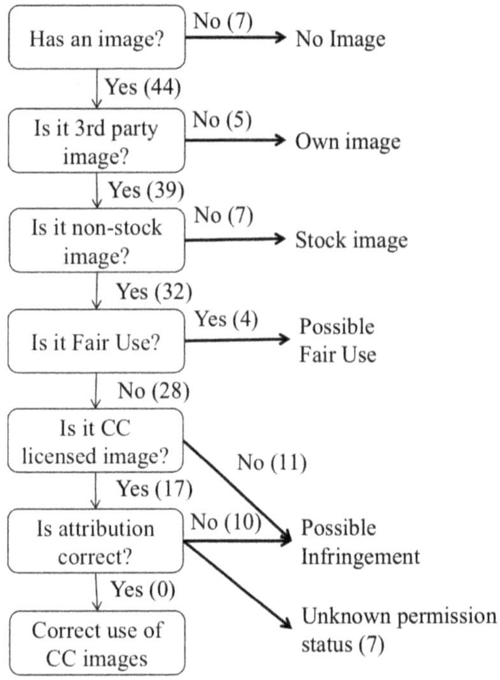

Figure 2. Categorization of images in SlideShare presentations.

we used the image recognition feature in Google Image Search[13] to find the source. If the search led to stock photos, we assumed that the image had been appropriately purchased. However, it was difficult to tell stock photos from non-CC-licensed photos used without permission. We had to mark seven cases as "Unknown permission status."

As a result, we found that, although 10 authors used CC-licensed images and tried to attribute, not one had managed to do so correctly. The most common mistakes included missing the URL for the specific CC license and the lack of an original image title. In particular, one of the infringing presentations was about the appropriate use of CC-licensed images in presentations! Eleven presentations had more obvious infringements by containing non-CC-licensed images without the authors' permissions.

The users we studied had released 16 of the presentations with a CC license, five of which clearly contained stock images or non-CC-licensed images, causing a likely copyright infringement. We believe that most of the creators of these infringing presentations had, in fact, released the presentations under the CC license with good intentions. This shows that while CC licenses are familiar to some users, the details of the licenses can be challenging to understand and internalize even for experienced users.

Image Reuse Processes

To find out in more detail why users find it hard to respect copyrights, we conducted a study on users' image search

[11] Attribution License Violations Validator for Flickr [18]; qSign algorithm [11], License Validation Service by CC organization (validator.creativecommons.org), and Attributor (www.attributor.com).

[12] www.slideshare.net.

[13] images.google.com.

strategies. We were interested in how users initiate their image searches, whether they pay attention to copyrights during their searches, whether they know which images they are allowed to use, and how they credit the author of the image when they include it in a presentation.

The test resembled a traditional usability study. We presented a story of an upcoming academic conference for which the participants were asked to prepare a three-slide presentation. The slides had to be prepared so that they could be uploaded to the Internet without any copyright infringements. The three slides had to contain images suitable for a welcoming speech to our home city and for two social events which were a horseback-riding excursion and a trip on a pirates' ship. For each slide, the participants had to find one image to illustrate their topic. We asked the participants to focus on finding suitable images and ignore all fine-tuning of the slides. We videotaped all the sessions so that only hands, keyboards, mice, and the displays were visible, and we asked the participants to verbalize their processes by thinking aloud. We let each participant find at least one image. If the image was found and included in the presentation in less than five minutes, we let the participant move onto the next slide and interrupted him or her when five minutes had passed.

Twelve lecturers (five males, average age 40) from our home university participated in the study. They came mostly from cartography (3) and computer science departments (5). On average, they gave eight lectures or other presentations per month, always using some kind of presentation software.

Initially, all participants remembered the requirement that the presentation should respect copyrights. As expected, based on the SlideShare study, none of the participants succeeded in creating slides that would respect copyrights. When analyzed using the schematic task sequence of necessary steps presented in Figure 1, our participants failed in performing these steps:

- Use of a media source with open images: 6/12. One participant attempted to find open images but failed because of the choice of keyword ("non-commercial"). Five participants made no attempt to use open media sources and performed normal Google or Flickr searches.
- Insert copyright and waiver URI: 0/12
- Insert author name: 0/12. Three users incorrectly provided the name of the service (e.g., Wikimedia).
- Insert title of the work: 0/12
- Insert CC license URI: 0/12

In short, while seven participants out of 12 tried to respect image authors' copyrights by starting to search for open images, they all failed in the process in multiple ways.

None of the participants stated that they did not care about the copyright-related instructions in our task, and therefore all the observed infringements were unintentional. Inspection of the videotapes showed some salient reasons for this. First, five participants seemed to forget the need to use open images altogether and made no attempt to direct their searches to correct sources. This was possibly because the search for a suitable image caught their attention, making them forget the related requirements.

Second, the participants were unaware of advanced search features. Of the seven participants who attempted to find open images, five used Google or Flickr (among other services), but only two used the advanced search feature that limited the results to CC-licensed images.

Third, the participants did not possess the knowledge of the steps required by the CC license for image use. While six participants finally chose an image that would have not infringed on any copyrights, none of them performed the attribution-related steps successfully. Three of the attempts were erroneous because they only attributed the media source (e.g., Wikimedia), and not the author, and they did not include a link to the specific CC license.

The study therefore showed that those content users who would like to respect the copyrights would need assistance in all of the required steps. The primary reasons for infringements seemed to be related to forgetting the latter steps when a suitable image was finally found and the lack of knowledge about the required steps.

Summary

Throughout the studies, we confirmed that appropriate remixing of digital media is a challenging task. We observed failures in all parts of the image retrieval process presented in Figure 1: in media source selection, in content searching, and in content attribution.

Nowadays, users commonly have the skill to look for images via search engines or other popular on-line image databases. However, it seems that many users copy/paste the images without attention to copyright issues. In some slides analyzed in the SlideShare study, the images even contained watermarks of a copyright notice, suggesting the users' ignorant attitude towards digital copyrights.

One noticeable thing in the studies was the fact that many users were aware of CC licenses and were able to find CC-licensed images. These users had at least basic awareness of copyrights, had an intention to respect them, and tried to show their respect to the original authors. However, even with their respectful attitude, all participants still failed in the attribution task. It appears that the current CC licenses are too difficult and confusing even for fairly advanced users. Moreover, even if they understand the requirements, the transaction costs are high: for every attribution, they have to move between different programs and repeat copy-and-paste actions several times.

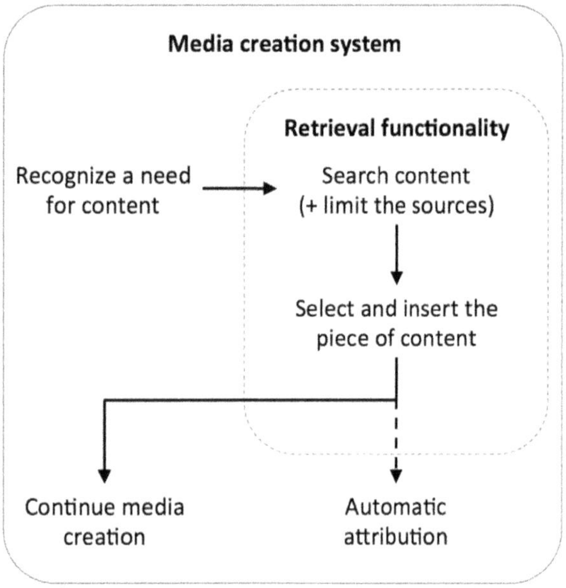

Figure 3. Open media retrieval model.

OPEN MEDIA RETRIEVAL MODEL

To solve the issues in open content remixing, we have developed a solution that we call the *Open Media Retrieval* (OMR) model. The model integrates searches into the user's creative workflow and automates the attribution process. It treats the remix process as a collection of tightly coupled searches. The media creation application's role is to act as a composing platform through which the user controls how the search results are presented to the audience. For example, presentation software is used to control the slide order and timing, and video editing software controls the synchronization of clips and images with audio.

Our goal has been to minimize the tasks a user needs to perform to import CC works into the media creation application. The OMR model reduces the task load from twelve to two tasks: 1) users enter a query and 2) users select a media file to be attached. The second task can be avoided if the system enables the automatic insertion of suggested media from the best-matching search results. Optionally, the user can refine the search to include only certain media sources or search for more media. Figure 3 presents the model.

Developers can integrate this search into their media creation applications and call image repository APIs directly or they can rely on a separate backend service to which the application can delegate the queries. In our tests, we reduced the complexity of the application by creating a backend system that provided the query process as a web service. The majority of the task load is delegated to the backend system, which has a list of suitable CC media repositories. The features of one possible implementation of the OMR model can be listed as follows:

1. Repository contains CC-licensed content.
2. Repository is aware of all the information necessary for proper attribution.
3. Repository has a policy that permits connections to the stored works and their metadata.
4. Repository has an API that provides structured access to all required attribution metadata: title of the work, author and rights owners' names, licensing information and the URL of additional copyright information.

For the end user, the media creation application has to provide integrated retrieval functionality or allow third-party functionality (e.g., a plug-in) to be connected with it for automatic content searches and insertions. This functionality will communicate with the backend service that connects to a repository with the above-listed features. By using the backend's API, the application either gets a URL to the original source of the media or retrieves the content from the backend's database. It then presents the results to the user and takes care of the proper attribution.

The media creation application also needs to be able to read and analyze the author and copyright metadata and translate both into a suitable attribution format that can be embedded in the remixed content. Here the model can take advantage of the CC licensing structure, which was designed to automate the tedious license compliance issues. CC licenses come with three versions that serve different needs. 1) The "lawyer readable" license is a long legal document that includes the terms of the license written in detailed court enforceable language. 2) The "human readable" version is a simple summary of the central concepts of the license and is intended to make the license more approachable. 3) The "machine readable" version uses a rights description language to describe the license terms. Because the CC licenses come in a machine-readable form, the system can automatically help users with correct attributions. The OMR systems can use the machine-readable feature when individual works are imported to the system.

The OMR model is independent of the media format that is remixed. Depending on the media format, the content needs to be embedded differently. In our implementation, we focused on CC-licensed images. While Google and Wikimedia Commons provide ways to search CC-licensed content, Flickr is the only service that provides the means for making the required metadata requests. Because of the speed limitations of the Flickr's API, in our implementation, we downloaded a three-million image subset of Flickr's CC-licensed images along with their metadata to our own server. Next we present applications that we created that implement the OMR model.

Study 1: Open Image Ribbon for PowerPoint

Open Image Ribbon is our implementation of the OMR model for one of the most popular remix platforms: Microsoft PowerPoint. It runs as an add-on, providing a

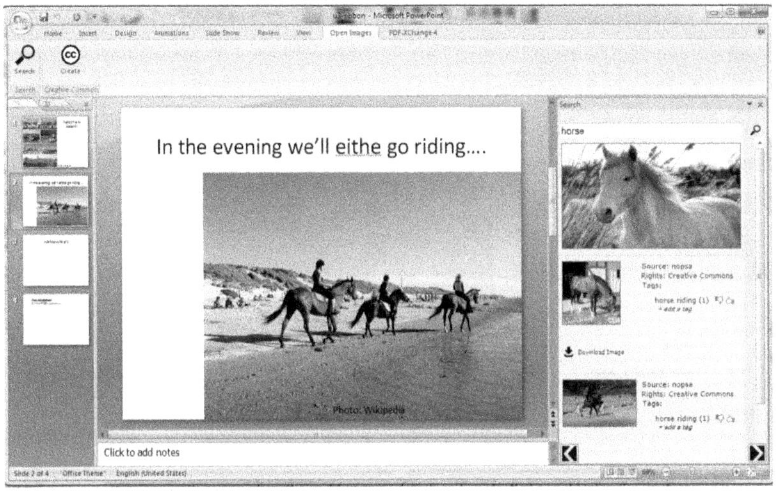

Figure 4. Screenshot from PowerPoint, with Open Image Ribbon's sidebar at right.

sidebar so the user can perform queries for CC-licensed images (see Figure 4). Integrating search and retrieval into PowerPoint saves the user from leaving the program and performing the multiple copy-and-paste tasks presented in Figure 1. Following the OMR model, the Ribbon can do these tasks automatically, letting the user focus on the choice of keywords and browsing the results. Every time the user inserts an image that the plugin has retrieved into the presentation, the Ribbon automatically adds an attribution to a separate attribution slide to the end of the presentation.

We carried out a lightweight comparative evaluation of Open Image Ribbon along with our study of image search processes (presented above). In the same sessions, we asked our participants to create the same presentations using our Ribbon tool. We measured the difference between the Ribbon and the Baseline conditions (i.e., the image search processes study) using the following two measures:

- *Task load:* After each condition, the participants filled in the Raw NASA-TLX questionnaire [2, 6] that measures the participants' subjective task load using six statements on a seven-point semantic differential scale (e.g., "How hard did you have to work to accomplish your level of performance?").

	Ribbon	Baseline	Significance of difference*
N	8	8	
Raw NASA-TLX, mean	2.5 (sd .90)	2.5 (sd .75)	Wilk's λ = .86, $F(1,7)$ = 1.152, p = .32
Slide creation speed, slides / 5 mins	1.8 (sd .88)	1.4 (sd .72)	Wilk's λ = .94, $F(1,7)$ = 0.484, p = .51

* Within-subjects repeated measures ANOVA

Table 1. Summary of results from Study 1.

- *Speed:* How many slides (0–3) did the participants create within the first five minutes of the task?

In the analysis, we had to drop the number of participants to N=8 because of a bug that caused very slow image retrievals for four participants. All the participants carried out the tasks in both conditions. We switched the order of the two tasks every time for the next participant. The results, analyzed using a within-subjects repeated-measures ANOVA, are presented in Table 1, showing that while the averages were slightly in favor of the Ribbon in both measures, these differences were not significant on either of the measures, neither on the task load nor on the slide creation speed.

While these statistical results are tentative, they point to a conclusion that using Ribbon was not more difficult than creating the slides using the familiar method. When participants spent a long time using Ribbon, it was because they were dissatisfied with the retrieved images. This

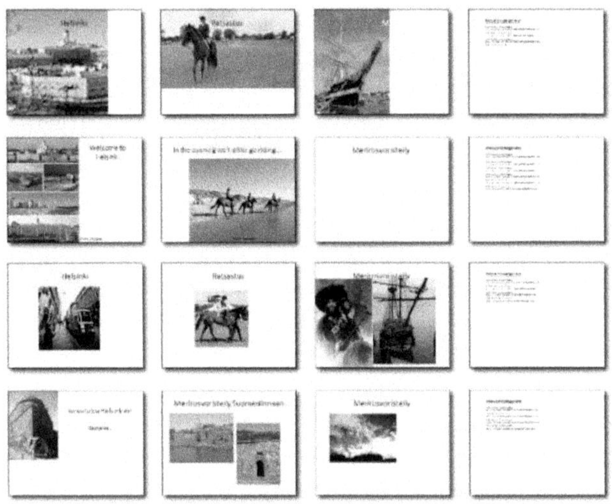

Figure 5. Examples of content created using Open Image Ribbon. Attributions are presented on the last slides.

Figure 6. Screenshot of AudioImager. The search box is always presented at the point where video editing takes place.

happened fairly often and was due to the limited number of images in our database, most of which are snapshots taken by Flickr users without explicit intentions for remixing. Also, our database did not have as sophisticated rating algorithm as Google does. Therefore, the best images are not presented first in a set of retrieved images. The Ribbon was therefore handicapped in terms of image quality. We still find the results promising in this light.

Obviously, all the presentations respected the copyrights, since the Ribbon actively enforced that. Failing in this aspect could only happen if the participants had deleted the presentation's last slide or its information on purpose.

Study 2: AudioImager

Video creation is another application class where the OMR model can be applied. To study this scenario, we created a prototype video creation application called AudioImager. We treated the process of video creation as a chain of image searches synchronized to audio.

AudioImager helps users turn audio files into videos. Users create videos by typing keywords while they listen to the audio file. When a user types a keyword and presses "Enter," the application automatically retrieves CC-licensed image that matches the keyword and inserts it on the timeline.

After the initial round of insertions, the user can change the images as needed from the selections shown on both sides of the video window. Also the exact transition times of the images are adaptable through image border dragging. When the user chooses to publish the video, the system creates the required attribution information as end credits.

In the AudioImager's design, we strove for an integrated image search and subsequently adapted the OMR model to follow a principle of a *within-workspace search*. By this, we mean that the image search task is integrated into the primary work area of the application. Thus, while Open Image Ribbon provided an image search in the sidebar, Figure 6 shows how the users could search for images in AudioImager inside the workspace. In terms of the image retrieval process and the OMR model, the primary difference between AudioImager's within-workspace design and the sidebar-based design featured in the Open Content Ribbon is that the search and the selection tasks are restructured: First, the search queries are entered one after another for all images, and then the user can start selecting the final images.

We conducted a study on AudioImager to analyze whether the within-workspace search model is suitable for the OMR model. We installed the system on workstations at a public library for one evening during an art festival. Our participants (N=16) constituted a self-selected sample of people with ages ranging from five to 70 years. First, the participants watched a one-minute demo video of the use of the AudioImager. Then we let them select a song and start creating videos. We measured the video creation durations (from the start time to the press of a publish button) and the numbers of images that the participants added to the timeline during this process. We asked the participants to work on three CC-licensed song clips, each having one-minute duration.

It took 5.7 minutes on average (sd 2.8 min) from the participants to create a 60-second video. On average, the videos had 11.3 (sd 6.2) images. All participants succeeded in video creation, and the reorganized task sequence, consisting of rapid image searches followed by a more relaxed period of detailed image selection, ensured that the timeline of the video was filled with content that was leisurely improved. We found that the within-workspace design was suitable for this task.

In terms of the evaluation of the OMR model, the within-workspace search feature portrayed an alternative, more compressed way to implement an image retrieval functionality that follows the OMR model. The successful design of two systems—Open Image Ribbon and AudioImager—implemented using two different interaction principles, indicates that the OMR model is more generally applicable to a class of open content retrieval applications.

DISCUSSION

This paper has examined the difficulties that remixers have with the reuse of open content, specifically CC-licensed images. The results have been difficult with regard to the primary intentions of CC licensing: Following the licenses' rules requires a multitude of steps from the users; users lack the necessary knowledge about the requirements that the licenses put on them; they misuse content with good intensions; and they sometimes forget to search content under the CC license because they get carried away in the process of searching suitable images from sources where all content is not CC-licensed.

The paper has presented a series of small studies, following a research approach that prioritized exploration and breadth over depth. This approach helped us examine the scope of the problem in a wide range of different content remixing activities. However, the studies involved only a small number of participants and were based mostly on quantitative measures. For example, we could not prove the superiority of our Open Image Ribbon over the baseline solution in terms of usability. A more finely tuned interaction design, larger user sample, and a wider range of measures could have probably done that, but now that has to be left for future research. However, our results have provided a promising start in that direction.

With the scale of participants used and the research methods applied, the results should not be treated as "proof" that copyright infringements permeate all remix cultures. Likewise, the results do not present direct design solutions that would remedy such infringements. Instead, they should be understood as an indication that legal reuse of digital content involves solvable issues that have social, motivational, and design-oriented dimensions. These dimensions should be studied in more detail using qualitative methods and targeted interaction design studies.

Qualitative studies would be critically needed to understand the social and motivational basis of law-respecting remixing. We believe that these two dimensions are closely interlinked. Our assumption is, pending verification, that users, when they remix others' material, need a feeling that they are doing it in the right way and take *pride* in doing so. They understand that remixing is reusing the material of authors very much like themselves. The motivation would therefore have a social basis, arising from peer loyalty and wishes to be perceived as reputable creators.

Regarding the design dimension, designers of media editing software can make use of this aspect of pride in at least two ways. As the user edits content, the user interface may continuously confirm and indicate points where the program knows that copyrights have been properly managed. This will increase the user's confidence and erase doubts of unintended infringement. Another suggestion is that the program adds a logo or a note to the final output file (e.g., the last slide in the slideset) indicating that a program was used to ensure that copyrights were managed when preparing the content. When other users see creations having that sign, they can then choose to adopt the same procedure in their creations. This increases awareness of copyright issues and points to a location where the work and more information can be found. In this way, the users can learn the correct methods from each other. Currently the opposite is true: Users mimic content reuse practices with good intentions from others and inadvertently sustain the infringing practices. However, eventually, when there are enough works with proper attributions, the users can spot the infringing forms of attribution. Also, with proper attributions, the licensors can use search engines to follow where and how their works are being used. This can form social pressure that starts correcting false practices.

As a general interaction design strategy, we find that users should only have to care about licensing to the level that they need to know that copyrights exist and that they are being respected. The system should hide the functionality as much as possible without forgetting the license requirements that make it mandatory. By correctly attributing the reused works, users know that they are giving the credit in a proper way to those who deserve it.

On the other hand, we do not find it fruitful that systems could force correct attributions. This would irritate users and backfire with intentional infringements. In addition, in many media formats, especially images and text, enforcements can be easily bypassed with copy/pasting and screenshots. We believe that positive encouragement is likely to lead to better results.

The OMR model presented in the paper serves as a guideline for implementing automatic attributions that save users from error-prone manual attribution tasks. The space for design explorations is large. The two sample systems—Open Image Ribbon and AudioImager—addressed the seamlessness of search functionality: While the Ribbon presented a search box and the results on the sidebar, AudioImager featured a search directly within the workspace. Longer-term studies in real use are needed to better understand how users will perceive and understand the OMR model's content retrieval paradigm, which is tightly integrated into the content creation software. Studies should also examine more extensively how such designs compare to the current practices that often involve separate web searches, downloads, and insertion phases.

Wide-scale adoption of copyright-compliant creations could also have positive second-order effects. For example, proper attribution information could be used for improving search engine results. Engines could use the copyright metadata as hints of content that users have found valuable and which is also legally reusable, meaning that it should be ranked high in retrieval results. Also, the content creators would get more credit for their work.

We find that application developers and vendors should start taking into account those users who want to use open content in their creations. Providing powerful open content retrieval tools within media creation applications would increase users' expressive capabilities for content creation. Powerful tools would lead to more attractive-looking contents. These, in turn, would receive attention from other users, and thereby increase the interest toward those applications. Also the Creative Commons organization and the rights owners should consider how to react to the attribution problem. While the license terms can be hard to understand, they serve valid purposes and cannot be changed much. One of the tasks for Creative Commons has been to educate users in copyright issues. Based on this study, the organization could think how to include also application developers into their education efforts.

While the current situation with license compliance looks bleak, we believe that the problem can be addressed with changes to existing software by following the OMR model or its derivatives. The demand for remix features and the growing number of remixers should present an easy business case for software companies. For the open content movement, the correct attribution could also create more visibility for CC-licensed content and in time help to improve the quality of the open content in the long run.

ACKNOWLEDGMENTS

The research was funded by Finnish Funding Agency for Technology and Innovation. The PowerPoint Ribbon coding was done in Google Summer of Code project by Hasanat Kazmi.

REFERENCES

1. Broder, A. Taxonomy of web search. *SIGIR Forum 36*,2 (2002), 3-10.
2. Byers, J. C., Bittner, A. C., and Hill, S. G. Traditional and raw task load index (TLX) correlations: Are paired comparisons necessary? In A. Mital (Ed.) *Advances in Industrial Ergonomics and Safety, Vol 1.* Taylor & Francis (1989), 481-485.
3. Cheliotis, G. and Jude Y. An analysis of the social structure of remixculture. In *Proc. C&T 2009*, ACM Press (2009), 165-174.
4. Cheliotis, G. From open source to open content: Organization, licensing and decision processes in open cultural production. *Decision Support Systems*, *47*, 3 (2009), 229-244.
5. Diakopoulos, N., Luther, K., Medynskiy, Y.E. and Essa, I. The evolution of authorship in a remix society. In *Proc. HT 2007*. ACM Press (2007), 133-136.
6. Hart, S.G. and Staveland, L.E. Development of NASA-TLX (Task Load Index): Results of empirical and theoretical research. Human mental workload, *Advances in psychology, 52*, Oxford, England: North-Holland (1988), 139-183.
7. Hietanen, H., Athukorala, K. and Salovaara, A. What's with the free images? A study of Flickr's creative commons attribution images. *In Proc. MindTrek 2011*, ACM Press (2011).
8. Hietanen, H., Huttunen, A. and Kokkinen, H. Criminal friends of entertainment: Analysing results from recent peer-to-peer surveys, *SCRIPTed—A Journal of Law, Technology & Society*, *5*, 1, (2008).
9. Hietanen. H. *The Pursuit of Efficient Copyright Licensing — How Some Rights Reserved Attempts to Solve the Problems of All Rights Reserved.* PhD dissertation, Acta Universitatis Lappeenrantaensis 325, Lappeenranta, Finland (2008).
10. Kantar Media. *Time to change the tune: Consumer research briefings on copyright.* Technical Report, Consumer Focus. London, UK, 2009.
11. Kim, J.W., Candan, K.S. and Tatemura, J. Efficient overlap and content reuse detection in blogs and online news articles. In *Proc. WWW 2009*, ACM Press (2009), 81-90.
12. Lasica, J.D. *When the studios won't give permission, Darknet: Hollywood's War against the Digital Generation.* A blog post at www.darknet.com/2005/07/when_the_studio.html -blog, July 8, 2005.
13. Lessig, L. Remix: *Making Art and Commerce Thrive in the Hybrid Economy*. Penguin, New York, USA, 2008.
14. Leval, P.N. Toward a fair use standard. *Harvard Law Review, 103*, 5 (1990), 1105–1136.
15. Loren, L.P. Building a reliable semicommons of creative works: Enforcement of creative commons licenses and limited abandonment of copyright. *George Mason Law Review*, *14*, (2007), 271.
16. Monroy-Hernández, A., Hill, B.M., Gonzalez-Rivero, J. and Boyd, D. Computers can't give credit: How automatic attribution falls short in an online remixing community. In *Proc. CHI 2011*. ACM Press (2011), 3421-3430.
17. Navas, E. Regressive and Reflexive Mashups in Sampling Culture. In Sonvilla-Weiss, S. (Ed.), *Mashup Cultures*, Springer (2010), 157-177.
18. Seneviratne, O., Kagal, L., and Berners-Lee, T. Policy-aware content reuse on the web. In *Proc. ISWC 2009, ACM* Press (2009), 553-568.
19. Seneviratne, O., Monroy-Hernández, A. Remix culture on the web: A survey of content reuse on different user-generated content websites. In *Proc. WebSci 2010.*

Fighting for My Space: Coping Mechanisms for SNS Boundary Regulation

Pamela J. Wisniewski, Heather Richter Lipford, and David C. Wilson
University of North Carolina at Charlotte
9201 University City Blvd., Charlotte, NC 28223
{pjkarr, Heather.Lipford, davils} @uncc.edu

ABSTRACT
Sharing information online via social network sites (SNSs) is at an all-time high, yet research shows that users often exhibit a marked dissatisfaction in using such sites. A compelling explanation for this dichotomy is that users are struggling against their SNS environment in an effort to achieve their preferred levels of privacy for regulating social interactions. Our research investigates users' SNS boundary regulation behavior. This paper presents results from a qualitative interview-based study to identify "coping mechanisms" that users devise outside explicit boundary-regulation interface features in order to manage interpersonal boundaries. Our categorization of such mechanisms provides insight into interaction design issues and opportunities for new SNS features.

Author Keywords
Boundary Regulation; Social Networking Sites; Coping

ACM Classification Keywords
H.5.2 [Information Interfaces and Presentation]: User Interfaces – Evaluation/methodology;

INTRODUCTION
Facebook's CEO Mark Zuckerberg has said that sharing is our new social norm and believes that Facebook's role is "to constantly be innovating and be updating what [Facebook's] system is to reflect what the current social norms are" [14]. However, even though sharing personal information online appears to be at an all-time high, there is strong evidence that users are also dissatisfied with their online social interactions [10]. An explanation for this dichotomy may be found in Altman's seminal work, *The Environment and Social Behavior*: "if privacy and its associated mechanisms are ignored or rigidly incorporated into designs ...then people will have to *struggle against the environment* to achieve what they consider to be appropriate degrees of interaction" [3]. Social Networking Sites (SNSs) are more than just websites; they are social environments in which we have to navigate how we interact with each other. Therefore, established theories of social psychology should be leveraged when designing these environments to facilitate optimal and desired levels of social interaction.

Altman's theories of environmental design for regulating social interactions in physical spaces are often referenced in Social Network Site (SNS) privacy literature but are rarely applied as principles of design for SNS interfaces. As a result, SNS users do struggle in their attempts to maintain appropriate levels of social interaction within their online social networks [10]. Therefore, coping behaviors are employed to reduce emotional distress when desired privacy levels have not been achieved [3]. As Ellison et al. note "privacy behaviors on SNSs are not limited to privacy settings" [7]. For instance, some SNS users create multiple Facebook profiles [20] to manage their information disclosure for different groups.

Our research investigates users' SNS boundary regulation behavior, and this paper focuses specifically on how users try to overcome functionality that does not meet their privacy needs. Through a qualitative study, we identify and categorize the myriad of coping mechanisms SNS users have developed to manage their social interactions. We define *coping mechanisms* as the behaviors developed by SNS users outside of the SNS interface or through the unintended use of interface features in an attempt to effectively maintain or regain their interpersonal boundaries. These round-about and often sub-optimal approaches give us insight into interactional design problems SNS users face when trying to socialize online. They also afford design opportunities for SNS developers.

BACKGROUND
Privacy can be conceptualized as "an interpersonal boundary process by which a person or group regulates interaction with others," by altering the degree of openness of self to others [3]. Ineffective boundary regulation can lead to a state of social crowding or isolation, having much more or much less social interaction than one desires [3]. In these states, individuals experience stress and develop coping mechanisms to reduce that stress. Altman (also referencing Milgram) outlined a number of coping mechanisms individuals employ in the physical world in order to achieve acceptable levels of stimulation [3, 15].

They included reducing interaction through filtering, ignoring, and blocking as well as withdrawing from interaction or meeting it with aggression. For instance, crime, juvenile delinquency, homicide, and civil strife have all been related to social crowding and high population density. In some cases, individuals adjust their desired privacy level instead of trying to alter the social environment [3]. These categorizations corresponded closely to Horney's mature theory and coping strategies related to patterns of neurotic needs: compliance, aggression, and detachment [9].Yet, manifestations of these coping mechanisms have not been examined within the context of SNSs.

While a breadth of research has addressed SNS privacy e.g [1, 5, 6, 7, 8, 12, 13, 16, 20, 21, 22, 23], very few researchers have examined coping mechanisms in response to undesirable privacy outcomes. Stutzman examined the creation of multiple profiles on social media websites, primarily Facebook, as an information regulation mechanism. Through grounded-theory, he identified three types of boundary regulation within this context (pseudonymity, practical obscurity, and transparent separations), as well as four over-arching motives for these mechanisms (privacy, identity, utility, and propriety) [20]. Tufekci examined disclosure mechanisms used by college students on MySpace and Facebook to manage the boundary between private and public. Findings suggest that students are more likely to adjust profile visibility rather than limiting their disclosure [21]. Lampinen et al. created a framework of strategies for managing private versus public disclosures. It defined three dimensions by which strategies differed: behavioral vs. mental, individual vs. collaborative, and preventative vs. corrective [12].

The related research in privacy and coping strategies often studies a specific coping mechanism in detail [20], uses students as a sampling frame [12, 21], and defines privacy in terms of private versus public information disclosures [12, 20, 21]. While this past research is closely related, our research differs in several distinct ways. First, we studied a variety of emergent coping mechanisms and applied existing social theory to our findings. Second, we felt that it was important to examine how a diverse set of adults coped in this new social environment, and sought a variety of non-student participants. Third, past research does not make a distinction between strategies readily supported by SNS interface capabilities and those that are not [12, 21]. Both coping and technology-supported strategies are types of boundary mechanisms for regulating different types of interpersonal boundaries. We distinguish between *technology-supported boundary mechanisms* which are behaviors supported through SNS interface controls and *coping mechanisms* which are an individual's response outside of these confines to mitigate potential boundary interpersonal violations. Technology-supported boundary mechanisms are specifically designed to address particular boundary regulation needs through interface controls. For instance, untagging is a technology-supported boundary mechanism for managing photo sharing, while using chat to negotiate with friends which photos should appear online is a form of coping.

Finally, and most importantly, we do not characterize privacy as only a means to regulate private versus public disclosures. This conceptualization comes most readily from Petronio's well known Communication Privacy Management (CPM) theory, an extension of Altman's work specifically dealing with private disclosures [3, 17]. However, not all interpersonal boundaries revolve around disclosure. In a broader sense, interpersonal boundaries help us define who we are, who we interact with, how and when. Our previous work identified the different types of interpersonal boundaries users need to manage within their SNSs [10]. Table 1 summarizes our taxonomy. We found that in addition to *disclosure* boundaries, SNS users can also negotiate *relationship*, *network*, *territorial*, and *interactional* boundaries to regulate their privacy levels. For instance, rejecting a friend request defines a *relationship boundary*. Hiding annoying posts from a friend's game application helps regulate *inward-facing territories* (such as one's News Feed), but has nothing to do with whether or not the information was considered private [10]. Therefore, when we discuss coping mechanisms for interpersonal boundary regulation in this paper, we included coping behaviors from this broader perspective instead of limiting our scope to public and private disclosures.

METHODOLOGY

We conducted semi-structured interviews of SNS users on how they manage their social interactions online. For instance, we asked participants how they managed friending and unfriending, overlapping social circles, personal disclosures, updates from others, and conflicts within their SNS. Participants were asked to base their responses on actual past experience as opposed to speculating what they would do given a particular scenario. We did this because previous research suggests a "privacy paradox," where an individual's stated privacy concerns do not necessarily correspond to their actual behavior [1].

Interview participants were recruited between September 2010 and July 2011 via postings on Facebook and email. Interviews were conducted via Google Voice, Skype, or email. Interviews were transcribed using InqScribe and qualitatively coded using Atlas.ti 5.5. As a foundation, we used Altman's definition of coping along with our conceptual distinction between technology-supported boundary mechanisms and coping mechanisms.

Table 1: Taxonomy of SNS Interpersonal Boundary Types

Boundary Type	Dimensions	Definition
Relationship	Connection	Regulating whom to let into one's social network
	Context	Regulating appropriate interpersonal interactions given the type of relationship
Network	Discovery	Regulating access others have to one's network connections
	Intersection	Regulating social interactions between connections or groups of connections
Territorial	Inward-Facing	Regulating incoming content for personal consumption
	Outward-Facing	Regulating semi-public content available through interactional spaces
Disclosure	Self-Disclosure	Regulating what personal information one discloses within one's network
	Confidant-Disclosure	Regulating how co-owned personal information is disclosed within one's network
Interactional	Disabling	Regulating potential interaction through turning on/off interface features
	Blocking	Regulating overall access of oneself to specific individuals outside of one's network

Next, we applied open coding [19] to uncover different types of coping behaviors exhibited by our participants. These codes were then conceptually grouped based on the coping mechanisms outlined by Altman to determine if similar coping mechanisms were observed in SNS environments. Quotes and anecdotes from participants are presented using a pseudonym first name for anonymity, profession, and age then consistently used throughout this paper.

Participants

We collected interview data from 21 participants, 10 females and 11 males. Participants were recruited through Snowball sampling [4] via email and Facebook. In order to participate, they had to be over 18 years old and have been an active member of a social networking website (such as Facebook, MySpace, LinkedIn, etc.) within the past year. Thirteen interviews were audio recorded, averaging 58 minutes each. Eight interviews were completed via email with follow up questions totaling 50 single-spaced pages (out of over 200 pages of transcripts overall). The average age of our participants was 36 years old, ranging from 21 to 60. Only one of our participants was a student with others ranging from an administrative assistant, minister, dating coach, photographer, restaurant manager, security officer, to a stay-at-home mother. Participants primarily used Facebook, with 16 participants logging in daily and four participants logging in weekly. Six participants reported using MySpace weekly to annually, and three said they used to have MySpace accounts but had deactivated them. Eight participants reported having Twitter accounts, and six participants had LinkedIn accounts. Participants also reported being active on a variety of other SNSs, including Ning, Hi5, LibraryThing, Shelfari, and Xanga. One participant was active through his wife's Facebook account, but chose to refrain from creating any SNS account of his own due to privacy concerns.

RESULTS

The interviews confirmed our priori codes were present within SNS environments; filtering, ignoring, blocking, withdrawal, aggression, and compliance are all coping mechanisms previously identified as ways to reduce emotional stress and anxiety [3, 9, 15]. However, the specific behaviors associated with these mechanisms drastically differ from the physical world. To Altman's coping mechanisms, we added one additional coping strategy – compromise. While we originally sought to match each coping mechanism to the boundary regulation taxonomy we had previously defined (Table 1), we found that many strategies were used across various boundaries. However, for the most common trends we observed, we will relate the coping mechanisms to the boundary types.

Filtering

"Reduction of intensity of inputs by *filtering* devices [3, 15]" was a coping mechanism participants often used specifically when regulating their *relationship boundaries* such as choosing with whom to connect and managing SNS interactions based on relationship context [10]. Filtering as a means for relationship boundary management may be one way participants avoided "overmanning," which occurs when the capacity of a space is exceeded by the number of applicants. In other words, there are more people than the setting can handle. This "results in pressure to reduce applicants, raise the standard for those admitted, or increase the setting capacity" [3]. Even though SNS participants are not confined due to physical space, many of our participants found that social networks that were too large became too cumbersome to manage.

"I pretty much let everybody in, so it is tough to manage. I've got 1600 [Facebook friends] now. . . Within the last week I think I've had 100 new people so I can't manage it. . . it is just too much." –Tyrone, Photographer, 31

Therefore, some individuals coped with this problem by leveraging small social cues as filtering devices for relationship management. For instance, four participants noted that they use a person's profile picture as a way to decide if they would accept or deny a friend request from someone they did not know.

"If it is a picture of somebody and they are half naked in it, then I don't accept it. So if you are showing your boobs in your picture, I am going to say no to that. Those I will turn down if it is obvious, but if it is not obvious, I will accept it." –Kristine, Author, 37

Two participants relied on relationships with mutual friends when determining if they would form a new relationship connection.

"If we have absolutely no friends in common, I will not accept it at all." –Lynn, Photographer, 30

Overall, the reliance on such minor social cues when determining whom to friend reveals that SNS users must sometimes use sub-optimal mechanisms when developing criteria for filtering potential relationship connections. Therefore, in addition to social cues, SNS users have developed other filtering mechanisms. Our previous work showed that group management within one SNS account was rarely used for regulating social interactions [10], instead SNS users segregated friends through separate SNS profiles or even different SNSs. Consistent with past research [20], four of our participants explained the need for two SNS profiles within the same SNS to separate personal interactions from work.

"I chose to keep my work and play profiles separate. I don't need any [co-workers] reading my work rants!... I don't accept any friend requests on my [work] page from real friends, and vice versa." –Tia, Administrative Assistant, 37

Four other participants mentioned accepting different types of friends on different SNSs (i.e. Facebook versus LinkedIn) in order to maintain appropriate network intersection boundaries.

"I, for example, do not have some IRC friends on Facebook since they smoke marijuana. I do not. ... I keep them on MySpace, mainly so they don't make me look bad, as well as harass the attractive friends I have [on Facebook] when they are high." –Allen, Technical Services, 31

The use of separate profiles or different SNSs to manage social interactions by *relationship context* possibly reduced the cognitive filtering process instead of doing so within one SNS account. A disadvantage of using relationship management filtering as one's primary boundary regulation mechanism was the upfront time investment required to properly leverage this technique. Consistent rules for filtering need to be developed from the onset because implementing them after-the-fact is often difficult to do.

"It is so hard to do at this point. If I had started off that way, I think it would have worked. [Some authors] use the fan page just for fan stuff and their regular Facebook page just for people they really know. But I think at this point I have over 1000 friends on Facebook that it would be impossible to separate it out." –Kristine, Author, 37

Ignoring

When individuals are presented with more information than they have the time or cognitive ability to process, they tend to make satisficing decisions versus optimal decisions due to their limited capacity [2, 18]. In addition to experiencing social crowding, more social interaction than one desires [3], participants also struggled with information overload which was exacerbated by the amount of content enabled through SNSs. Often, individuals felt overwhelmed by the amount of interaction they could engage in or information they could consume within their online social networks.

"I don't see how people can maintain if they have 1,000 friends. If I had 1,000 friends and 1/4 them are posting, I mean that is 250 posts a day. I am trying to keep it at a reasonable number." –Gordon, Restaurant Manager, 48

An identified coping mechanism for this is a "disregard of low-priority inputs which results in *ignoring*," giving attention only to interactions that have direct, personal meaning [3, 15]. Within SNSs, ignoring is most strongly associated with *inward-facing territories* such as one's Facebook News Feed. Eight of our participants mentioned reducing the amount of attention they paid to News Feed content. They skimmed or ignored incoming content because they characterized it as "annoying" or "too much," and they did not feel it pertained directly to them.

"It's a really long list that I haven't read yet, and I'll just read the first, whatever comes up on the screen, and I won't use the scroll bar. If it's something that I needed to know, they would have contacted me directly. They would have either sent me a message on Facebook or a text or a phone call or an email. Chances are if they didn't do that

then I really didn't need to know it." –Lorrie, Security Officer, 22

Alternatively, three participants actually expected their friends' to ignore (or hide) them if they did not like what they posted or were annoyed by over postings. That way, they did not have to censor what they wanted to post. However, a negative consequence of ignoring was that SNS users often missed important information that was shared within their networks which, at times, resulted in hurt feelings. For instance, Gordon recounted how he felt when one of his close friends who was also in his Facebook network missed his posts about his daughter's heart surgery:

"She had so many friends that mine was just another post. It had obviously slipped through the cracks. It hurt a little bit thinking that, hey, I am reading your posts but you are not reading mine." –Gordon, Restaurant Manager, 48

Blocking

Individuals who feel filtering and ignoring are not adequate coping mechanisms may escalate to blocking [3, 15] Interestingly, blocking is a feature that is built into most SNS interfaces that we characterized as an *interactional boundary mechanism*; however, individuals rarely take advantage of this technology-supported boundary mechanism [10]. Instead, they develop coping mechanisms for blocking unwanted interactions with others. For instance, Dollie and Alana use pseudonyms on Facebook even though the SNS encourages individuals to use their real names.

"I changed my name because I was hiding. I wanted to be less able to be found. I changed my name, but it didn't work. Because then I realized that people were finding me under other people's names ...My sister was still able to find me." –Dollie, Mother, 34

Another way SNS users block interactions with others is by using someone else's Facebook account and never creating their own. Richard does not have an SNS account but logs into his wife's Facebook account more often than she does; Becky's husband benefits from her SNS interactions in a similar way.

"My husband does not have a Facebook page. He doesn't understand why I check it all the time but does enjoy the 'gossip' when I tell him about recent updates. He sometimes asks me to check his sister's or brother's status to figure out where they are, if he can't get in touch with them ...(I think he just feels left out!)" –Becky, Elementary School Teacher, 29

Blocking through the use of pseudonyms or someone else's account can effectively remove unwanted social interactions while allowing one to still participate as part of an SNS. However, blocking as a coping mechanism often does not derive the same level of benefits enjoyed by others. Both Richard and Becky's husband (according to Becky) feel isolated from others by not having their own SNS accounts where they can be active participants.

Due to the high potential for boundary violations, four participants felt that proactive and retroactive blocking were not enough to protect them from negative consequences. Therefore, they were forced to find ways to constantly monitor their *outward-facing territories* and *confidant disclosures* so that they could block any threats in as close to real-time as possible. Kristine used social aggregators such as TweetDeck to monitor her MySpace comments. Tyrone and Tia frequently checked Facebook from their mobile phones.

"When I do get comments or tagging pictures or something that comes to my phone and says hey, so and so commented. If it is something that I am like 'this is not kosher,' then I can logon and delete that comment." –Tia, Administrative Assistant, 37

Withdrawal

Withdrawal is characterized as an "allocation of less time to each of the many inputs" [3, 15] in which an individual can interact or a general unwillingness to help others [3]. Individuals withdraw to distance themselves from perceived threats in order to avoid harm [9]. Our participants showed evidence of withdrawal through self-censorship, detachment, and retreat. Seventeen, almost all, of our participants felt that they needed to censor what they shared within their SNS. Because most of them do not limit their sharing based on *relationship context* [10] through the creation of friend lists or groups, they used the heuristic of only sharing what was appropriate based on everyone in their network seeing it. Therefore, *self-disclosure* was reduced to the lowest common denominator and stripped of personal intimacy.

"There's certain things you maybe want to post about, but there's people on there that you maybe really don't want to know that, or you don't really want to share that with, so yeah, I've censored myself and/or not put things on there that I would have otherwise." –Nelson, Office Manager, 53

In this case, Nelson was unaware that he could limit the visibility of posts on Facebook to specific friend lists using existing controls. In other cases, individuals censored themselves in the present out of fear that those interactions could persist and harm them in the future.

"You don't want people to get things that they can hold against you. It's difficult because you post something and you are friends with someone, or a company you want to

hire you comes and looks at it and then your relationship with that person or company changes and what was ok before isn't ok now." –Lorrie, Security Officer, 22

Therefore, many participants compensated for this by only accentuating the positive when sharing within their SNS. Eight participants said they suppressed any negative thoughts or feelings and only shared content they felt was positive or humorous. In fact, they frowned upon other people not doing the same.

"Some people use it as a diary. I would not do that. I would not tell how I feel...if I say anything on my wall it is going to be either, one, that I am going to complement something that someone else already said ...or it's going to be something positive. I feel like I will never put anything that has negative energy on my wall." –Tyrone, Photographer, 31

In addition to censoring themselves, six SNS users managed their boundaries by carefully staying out of any conflict they observed between others.

"I don't usually interject myself in those kind of posts. I figure somebody's upset somebody but I really don't need to know about it." –Regina, HIV Awareness Coordinator, 60

In a sense, this was their way of withdrawing by "shifting social transactions to others" [3, 15], by offloading the responsibility of managing conflict to others. However, when avoiding conflict was not a successful mechanism for maintaining their boundaries, some participants resorted to retreat. They created *interactional boundaries* of retreat through dropping off conversation threads, not logging in to their SNS, or even deactivating their account completely. For example, Gordon and Edward abandoned arguments that were started on Facebook for a time or indefinitely.

"What I do is I just back off and try to come back to it later. And just say 'Ok, This conversation about the ethics of termination of unborn children is not a really a conversation I'm happy having right now. ... I probably need to take a step back.'" –Edward, Youth Minister, 30

Kristine explained that she needed a break from her SNSs when she could not maintain a positive persona for her readers.

"I do take Twitter Holidays or Twitter-cations where you don't go on for a while. Same thing with Facebook. Sometimes if I am feeling down or depressed, I don't want to go on Twitter and Facebook. One of the bad things about having all these people who are fans or whatever or that aren't family and friends, who are in a third category is that they expect you to be on and up and they don't expect you to have doubts or things like that." –Kristine, Author, 37

Alana has deactivated and reactivated her Facebook and MySpace accounts on multiple occasions as she is generally ambivalent about online social networking, believing that its main purpose is to violate one's privacy.

"I get on it to start off with, save all my good friends, even post updates to start off ...then my friends and I catch up in real life, have our girlfriend powwows and the pizazz of the site goes away. I don't use it, realize over and over that my most meaningful relationships benefit little from social networking, and I stray away from the site." –Alana, Substance Abuse Counselor, 28

Dollie completely deleted her Facebook account until after her daughter was born. This happened because an acquaintance inadvertently disclosed to Dollie's network that Dollie was pregnant before Dollie herself was comfortable revealing the information. Dollie believes that when Facebook becomes more of a nuisance than a positive social outlet, the best thing to do is to remove herself from it completely.

"If I don't like Facebook, if I don't like being there, I could as easily get out of it. I can just delete the whole thing and leave. Delete is fabulous. I can delete you or delete myself and all my issues go away." –Dollie, Mother, 34

Self-censorship, detachment, and retreat are ways that SNS users withdraw from social interactions within SNSs, often when they feel there are no other ways to engage without being harmed. Withdrawal is an extreme coping mechanism for protecting oneself by limiting one's own behaviors in contrast to blocking which limits the actions of others. In both cases, social interaction is limited because the cost of interacting is perceived to be higher than the benefits.

Aggression

Filtering, ignoring, blocking, and withdrawal are all characterized as defensive coping mechanisms. However, some SNS users resort to offensive measures within their SNSs in order to hurt others. *Aggression* is a coping mechanism where individuals threaten those they perceive as a threat in order to protect themselves [9]. For instance, aggression due to social crowding in physical spaces may manifest as violence or verbal behaviors [3]. However, within SNSs, aggression is a coping mechanism that tends to be used to seek revenge in a covert yet public way, leveraging *outward-facing territories* such as Wall posts. Interestingly, aggression within SNSs was a response to neurotic needs of acceptance and approval [9] instead of social crowding [3]. SNS users leveraged aggression to get attention or enhance the level of social interaction within their networks, even if the interaction was negative. Seven participants explained using or having a friend use a status update to all of their friends as a way to retaliate against one particular person and garner attention or sympathy.

"[My boyfriend's daughter] would make a comment on her Facebook page to look at it would be kind of general but then for us to read it to know what situation she's talking about it is like wait a minute why are you putting our business out on the street? It is more of a connotation, I am not saying your name, but I am talking to you." – Tia, Administrative Assistant, 37

Kurt went as far as to create a separate Facebook page and change his profile visibility to Friends of Friends in order to make his ex-girlfriend jealous and regret breaking up with him.

"I had the bachelor of the year thing which was a good way to get back at her and say look, you gave this shit up. Now all your friends are going to see. They would say it why did you walk away from that he has all these other qualities and he is hot too?" –Kurt, Dating Coach, 32

Aggression also surfaced, at times, when SNS users enjoyed generating discussion and even causing conflict between their friends, possibly even pitting them against one another and intentionally converging one's *network intersection boundaries*. Regina, Larry, and Dollie often found entertainment value in starting political arguments on their Facebook Walls. Edward and Nelson often encouraged religious debates. Kurt, in general, liked provoking his audience as a means of personal promotion and even used them to bolster his own causes.

However, being the target or even just witness of others' aggression certainly has negative consequences. Having experienced some form of aggression in the past, participants tended to have a tainted view of SNSs as environments that breed drama and revert adults back to juvenile tendencies. Six participants emphasized the need to avoid the "drama" present within online social networks.

"The site causes enough drama, as it is, or rather the people on the site using it in nefarious ways. Same thing for Myspace and all the others." –Allen, Technical Services, 31

Compliance

Compliance is a "self-effacing solution" to boundary turbulence and leads to sacrificing one's own needs to accommodate others and avoid harm [9]. Altman explained that individuals do this in response to, "repeated failures to achieve a balance between achieved and desired levels of privacy" [3]. Often, compliance was implemented without any boundary discussion with others; therefore, adjustment towards more mutually acceptable boundaries would not occur in the future. Six participants admitted to adjusting their boundaries and relinquishing their interactional privacy needs to please others. This resulted in changing their disclosures, friending and unfriending preferences, and even their offline behaviors to account for the inevitable sharing within their social networks.

"I am worried what people say or tag of me or whatever, so I do not engage in as many crazy drinking sessions with people who might not execute the best judgment when uploading, or the very least, marking who has access to view the more unsuitable photos. I do not say or do crazy things with my friends in town (usually) and keep some things I might normally share by my nature, to myself, so it doesn't end up on Facebook." –Allen, Technical Services, 31

Being able to properly maintain one's interpersonal boundaries is important for self realization and healthy relationship management [3, 9, 11, 17]. Therefore, over accommodation of others could result in a perceived loss of control over one's social interactions. As Allen admitted above, he feels that he cannot always be himself, even offline, due to the online interactions that may occur as a result.

Compromise

Many SNS behaviors we saw, as illustrated above, fit nicely within the coping mechanisms previously identified by Altman for dealing with stress in social environments[3, 15]. However, Horney identified one "healthy" coping mechanism to meet neurotic needs that Altman did not mention. *Compromise* [9] involves the interpersonal process of communicating, agreeing, disagreeing, compromising, and reaching mutual decisions. In effect, compromise is the primary mechanism for regulating interpersonal boundaries instead of satisficing through compensatory actions. We observed boundary coordination through compromise in our study, but ironically, this coordination almost always happened *external* to the SNS environment. SNS users found ways to use offline or private communication with others in order to coordinate boundaries beforehand (as a preventative strategy [12]), and subsequently (as a corrective strategy [12]). When SNS users were confronted with interpersonal conflict or negative social interactions, they made a point to take the interaction off of *outward-facing territories* to other more private mediums. It was important to our participants to not allow interpersonal conflict to be visible to everyone within their networks. Communication was initiated either through the SNS's private email messaging capabilities or by more direct communication such as calling or face-to-face conversations.

Compromise through boundary coordination was most frequently observed for photo posting or tagging, which were part of *confidant disclosures* in our boundary mechanism taxonomy. Besmer and Lipford examined photo tagging and untagging behaviors in detail on Facebook [5]. In most cases, coordination happened before the photo was posted. Generally, people were very accommodating when it came to posting and tagging photos of others. However, photo tagging was also a point of contention where most SNS users said they had untagged a picture of themselves in the past. (Note: Our interviews were conducted prior to Facebook's recent changes that allow tag review.)

"I texted her and asked her if she wanted me to email her the pictures or did she want me to tag it? I wanted to tag it because I thought it was a hot picture. She said no no no you can't tag it, I am about to graduate . . . The shoot didn't show any nudity or anything. I think it was just really tight clothing, and it was really sexy but she did not want that to get out. She said that no do not ever tag me and that image." –Tyrone, Photographer, 31

We also observed this process when setting *relationship connection boundaries*. Becky and Dollie told co-workers in person that they did not accept friend requests from co-workers so as to manage their expectations.

"I don't want to have coworkers on my page ... I would say it at work, 'oh no, don't send me a friend request because I don't allow coworkers on my page.'" –Dollie, Mother, 34

While the primary response to conflict was to withdraw, an alternative strategy 13 SNS users employed was private confrontation for reconciliation. However, the effort to reach a compromise or truce was reserved for close friends as opposed to acquaintances. A benefit of this approach, however, was that SNS users were often able to resolve misunderstandings instead of ending the relationship or propagating drama within their SNSs.

"If it [conflict occurring] was just in my news feed, I would filter them out, if it was on my wall, I would probably just unfriend them unless they were a close friend, then I would ask them to stop." –Fred, Sales Manager, 33

DISCUSSION

We have created a framework of SNS coping strategies by identifying analogous online behaviors to theoretically based, offline coping mechanisms. Filtering, ignoring, blocking, withdrawal, aggression, compliance, and compromise are all strategies SNS users have developed in an attempt to achieve their desired level of privacy and social interaction outside of the use of traditional SNS privacy controls. Table 2 summarizes the types of coping mechanisms described in this paper, gives a specific example, and relates the example to types of interpersonal boundary management.

Table 2: Coping Mechanisms with Examples

Coping Mechanism	Example (*Boundary Type*)
Filtering	Creating two separate SNS profiles to segregate different circles of friends (*Relationship Context*)
Ignoring	Skimming or ignoring one's News Feed (*Inward-Facing Territorial*)
Blocking	Using a pseudonym so that others cannot find oneself (*Interactional/Relationship Connection*)
Withdrawal	Censoring oneself (*Self-Disclosure*)
Aggression	Intentionally starting arguments between one's friends (*Network Intersection/Outward-Facing Territorial*)
Compliance	Accepting almost all friend requests and rarely unfriending (*Relationship Connection*)
Compromise	Confirming that it is okay to tag someone in a picture (*Confidant-Disclosure*)

Such adaptations suggest, first, that social interactions through SNSs frequently cause emotional distress that users feel the need to mitigate. Second, it suggests that SNS environments are not optimally designed to be responsive and flexible to SNS user privacy needs. Third, such coping mechanisms tend to produce sub-optimal social outcomes such as neurotic tendencies [9] and additional stress. With the exception of compromise, these coping strategies tend to be maladaptive, where short term stress may be decreased but potentially at the cost of increasing long term stress [9]. For instance, feeling like you constantly have to monitor your SNS, participate using a pseudonym, or even change your offline behavior due to potential SNS interactions are generally not beneficial coping behaviors and can be stressful in and of themselves.

As an example, Dollie, who is an extreme filterer when it comes to *relationship connection boundaries* (not allowing family or coworkers into her network) does so because she has been hurt in the past. She only has 62 Facebook friends and unfriends often in order to avoid conflict or compromise. However, this coping behavior reduces her opportunity to forge deeper relationships with these individuals through her SNS at any point in the future. Individuals like Kurt and Tyrone, who use their SNSs for professional marketing, often ignore their News Feed, or *inward-facing territories*, due to the sheer volume of status updates from their extremely large networks, and miss important updates from true friends. Therefore, while they welcome others to interact with them, they rarely engage others in the same level of interaction in return, possibly making others feel ignored or unimportant. Individuals who withdraw emotionally through self-censorship tend to express a dissatisfaction of not being able to present an authentic self to others and feel a reduced sense of intimacy within their SNSs.

In addition to these coping behaviors, all of our participants exhibited the use of *incongruent boundary mechanisms* given a boundary goal. For instance, if someone is not one's friend, a congruent boundary mechanism would be to unfriend them. Thus, an appropriate relationship connection boundary would be established. However, the most common incongruency we observed was when SNS users crossed *relationship connection boundaries* with *inward-facing territorial boundaries*. For example, quite a few participants hid someone from their News Feed who was no longer a friend, while others unfriended a real friend due to an annoyance such as over-posting. In most cases, when a boundary mechanism was incongruent with the boundary goal, it also created potential for negative consequences. For instance, hiding someone still allows that person access to one's network, personal disclosures, and future interactions. Inversely, unfriending someone who is truly a friend removes the possibility of future interactions that could strengthen the relationship, and could even harm the relationship by emotionally hurting the other person.

Understanding SNS coping mechanisms can help pinpoint areas where improved interface design can potentially enhance online social interactions. Our findings can inform design guidelines that can improve SNS interface support for interpersonal boundary regulation. For instance, SNSs could support one's relationship connection filtering process by requiring more information as to the motivation one wants to connect with another. This would have saved Gordon from significant emotional torment when a high school bully friend-requested him on Facebook.

"He used to bully the shit out of me in high school. I am looking at him, and I am thinking, why in the world would he send a friend request to me when he tortured me in high school? I really struggled over it, and I was about to decline him actually. I decided to say yes, to see what's going on ...the next day he sends an email in which he apologizes for the grief that he gave me through high school." –Gordon

SNS interfaces would also benefit from better *inward-facing territorial boundary* support to reduce cognitive overload from updates streaming in from one's friends. For instance, many Facebook users reported frustration that Facebook controls who they see in their News Feed instead of allowing them to do so themselves. Because SNSs often take control of boundary regulation for end users, they have to find ways to regain control. For instance, when Edward wants to see a particular friend show up in his Facebook News Feed, he makes sure to post a comment on their Wall so that the recent interaction bumps them into his Top News. To address this problem, in September 2011, Facebook just rolled out a change to filter one's News Feed by different friend lists.

Overall, the biggest gap our study highlights in SNS interface design for boundary regulation support is a lack of built-in capabilities to compromise by actively negotiating one's boundaries with others. SNS users are forced to use communication mediums outside of the SNS interface to coordinate interpersonal boundaries with others. Therefore, the SNS environment is not responsive to these needs. SNS interfaces, such as Facebook, are designed to encourage sharing and being open, and de-emphasize boundary coordination. For instance, many of our participants expressed anguish over having no closure from being unfriended. SNSs do not notify and certainly do not facilitate communication to explain why the relationship was severed or attempt to reconcile conflict. There also are no tools for explicitly signaling or collaboratively negotiating disclosure for co-owned information such as pictures and tags. SNS users have to resort to external coordination though such means as private messaging or face-to-face conversations. By integrating this negotiation process into SNS interfaces in positive ways, it could facilitate and make online boundary regulation a more socially acceptable process.

CONCLUSION

Now that individuals are interacting online instead of merely sharing information asynchronously, it is important to reapply existing psychology of social interaction and behavior to virtual, social environments. This research applied social theories of interpersonal boundary regulation through boundary and coping mechanisms to the unique social environments of SNSs. We found that filtering, ignoring, blocking, withdrawal, aggression, compliance, and compromise represent coping mechanisms individuals use within SNSs to maintain their interpersonal boundaries. In many cases, coping and incongruent boundary mechanisms created sub-optimal social networking experiences or introduced unnecessary complexity, which in turn reduced end user satisfaction with the SNS and negatively impacted their social interaction with others.

Hence, when SNS users employ coping strategies, this can signify opportunities for improved interactional interface design. Integrating, improving or realigning boundary mechanisms supported by SNS interfaces could actually enhance relationship development. Privacy through effective interpersonal boundary regulation serves as a way to improve how individuals connect and share with others. In contrast to definitions that tend to depict privacy as a means restricting information disclosure and promoting social withdrawal [7, 21, 23], a direct negation of social networking goals, interpersonal boundary regulation can increase one's level and quality of engagement through SNSs. Therefore, improved interface design to better support interpersonal boundary regulation could serve to improve, instead of prevent, higher levels of social interaction. Our future research will continue along this path - to examine interpersonal boundary regulation within online social networks as a means to align interactional privacy needs with social networking goals.

REFERENCES

1. Acquisti, A. and Gross, R. *Imagined Communities: Awareness, Information Sharing, and Privacy on the Facebook*. Springer Berlin / Heidelberg, (2006).
2. Agosto, D. E. Bounded Rationality and Satisficing in Young People's Web-Based Decision Making. *Journal of American Society for Information Science and Technology* 53, 1, (2002), 16-27.
3. Altman, I. *The environment and social behavior*. Brooks/Cole Monterey, CA, (1975).
4. Babbie, E. *The Practice of Social Research*. Wadsworth Publishing Company, Belmont, CA., (2004).
5. Besmer, A. and Lipford, H. R. Moving beyond untagging: photo privacy in a tagged world. *Proceedings of the 28th international conference on Human factors in computing systems*, Atlanta, Georgia, USA, ACM. (2010).
6. Debatin, B., Lovejoy, J. P., Horn, A.-K. and Hughes, B. N. Facebook and Online Privacy: Attitudes, Behaviors, and Unintended Consequences. *Journal of Computer-Mediated Communication* 15, 1, (2009), 83-108.
7. Ellison, N. B., Vitak, J., Steinfield, C., Gray, R. and Lampe, C. (In press). Negotiating Privacy Concerns and Social Capital Needs in a Social Media Environments.
8. Gross, R. and Acquisti, A. Information revelation and privacy in online social networks. *Proceedings of the 2005 ACM workshop on Privacy in the electronic society*, Alexandria, VA, USA, ACM. (2005).
9. Horney, K. *Our Inner Conflicts: A Constructive Theory of Neurosis*. W W Norton & Company Inc, New York, (1945).
10. Karr-Wisniewski, P., Lipford, H. and Wilson, D. (2011). *A New Social Order: Mechanisms for Social Network Site Boundary Regulation.* Americas Conference on Information Systems. Detroit, MI.
11. Katherine, A. *Boundaries: Where You End and I Begin.* MJF Books Hazelden Foundation, (1991).
12. Lampinen, A., Lehtinen, V., A., L. and Tamminen, S. We're in It Together: Interpersonal Management of Disclosure in Social Network Services. *CHI'11 Proceedings of the annual conference on Human factors in computing systems*, Vancouver, BC. (2011).
13. Lipford, H. R., Besmer, A. and Watson, J. Understanding Privacy Settings in Facebook with an Audience View. *Usability, Psychology, and Security 2008 (UPSEC 2008)*, Berkeley, CA. (2008).
14. Matyszczyk, C. (2010). Zuckerberg: I know that people don't want privacy. Retrieved February 21, 2011, from http://news.cnet.com/8301-17852_3-10431741-71.html?tag=digg2.
15. Milgram, S. The experience of living in cities. *Science* 167, (1970), 1461-1468.
16. Palen, L. and Dourish, P. Unpacking "privacy" for a networked world. *Proceedings of the SIGCHI conference on Human factors in computing systems*, Ft. Lauderdale, Florida, USA, ACM. (2003).
17. Petronio, S. *Boundaries of privacy: dialectics of disclosure*. SUNY Press, (2002).
18. Simon, H. A. A Behavioral Model of Rational Choice. *Quarterly Journal of Economics* 69, 1, (1955), 99-118.
19. Strauss, A. L. and Corbin, J. M. *Basics of qualitative research: techniques and procedures for developing grounded theory*. Sage Publications, (1998).
20. Stutzman, F. and Hartzog, W. Boundary Regulation in Social Media. *AOIR 2009*, Milwaukee, WI. (2009).
21. Tufekci, Z. Can You See Me Now? Audience and Disclosure Regulation in Online Social Network Sites. *Bulletin of Science, Technology & Society* 28, 1, (2008), 20-36.
22. Tyma, A. Rules of Interchange: Privacy in Online Social Communities–A Rhetorical Critique of MySpace. Com. *JCSTAND*, (2007), 31-31.
23. Xu, H., Reddy, M. and Zhang, X. L. Collaborative Privacy Practices in Social Media. *The 2011 ACM Conference on Computer Supported Cooperative Work*, Hangzhou, China. (2011).

TeleAdvisor: A Versatile Augmented Reality Tool for Remote Assistance

Pavel Gurevich, Joel Lanir, Benjamin Cohen, Ran Stone
IBM Haifa Research Lab
Mt. Carmel, Haifa, 31905, Israel
{pavelg, yoell, cohen, ranst} @ il.ibm.com

ABSTRACT
TeleAdvisor is a novel solution designed to support remote assistance tasks in many real-world scenarios. It consists of a video camera and a small projector mounted at the end of a tele-operated robotic arm. This enables a remote helper to view and interact with the workers' workspace, while controlling the point of view. It also provides the worker with a hands-free transportable device to be placed anywhere in his or her environment. Active tracking of the projection space is used in order to reliably correlate between the camera's view and the projector space.

Author Keywords
Augmented Reality; Mobile projector; Remote assistance.

ACM Classification Keywords
H.5.3 [Information Interfaces and Presentation]: Group and Organization Interfaces – Computer-supported cooperative work;

INTRODUCTION
A remote assistance task around a physical object is characterized by the presence of one or more objects that a person (the worker) focuses on and interacts with to complete the task. The worker lacks some knowledge pertaining to the object or the operation of the task, and a emote expert (the helper) aids the worker to diagnose the problem and provide instructions on how to perform unfamiliar operations. Often, the worker uses other objects such as tools to interact with the focus object. Examples of such tasks may include a customer calling a call center to help troubleshoot a printer, a novice technician calling an expert for guidance in repairing a complex device (e.g., an aircraft engine), or a medical expert guiding a local doctor through a complex procedure.

Studies have shown that a shared visual representation of the workers' space, including the task object, tools being used, and a view of the workers' actions is highly useful in supporting such tasks [2]. Still, video-mediated dialogs were found less efficient than side-by-side ones [3]. This was explained by the fact that the worker has difficulties establishing what visual information was shared, and more importantly, the helper could not use gestures to refer efficiently to task objects [2].

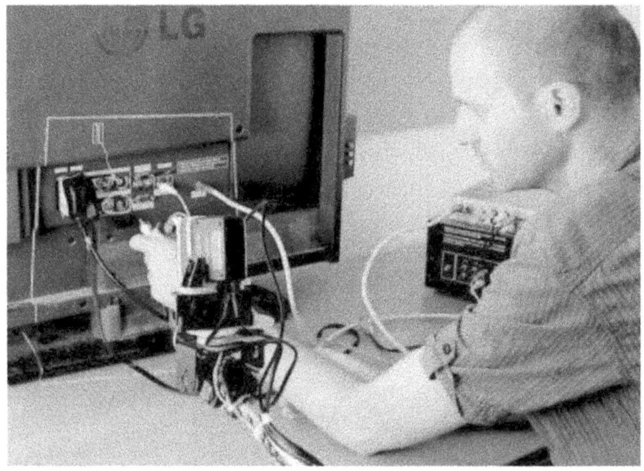

Figure 1. Using TeleAdvisor to remotely assist a person in executing a complex wiring task

A promising method for gesturing combines the gesture representation with the physical objects themselves, mostly using Augmented Reality (AR) tools. Kirk et al. [4, 5] projected the gestures onto the workers' workspace using top-mounted projectors. Top-mounted projectors have a large projection area and can support high-resolution projection, however, they are stationary and are limited to a prearranged work area, on which the projector was mounted prior to the task. Many scenarios require more flexibility, and cannot set the workspace ahead of time. With the advent of pico projectors, it is now possible to create a transportable appliance that the worker would be able to easily situate anywhere in his or her work environment.

We present TeleAdvisor, a remote assistance tool that uses a small video camera alongside a pico projector to capture the worker's environment and project on top of it (Figure 1). TeleAdvisor is designed to be transportable and hands-free, transmitting the captured video and helpers' gestures over the network, so the worker would be able to situate it anywhere needed and use both hands to interact with the object. Furthermore, the camera and projector are mounted on top of a robotic arm to enable the helper fine-level control of the view and projection area. Finally, TeleAdvisor is equipped with an enhanced set of annotation tools which include the ability to project a pointer, freehand sketches, text and images. The combination of transportability, hands-free unobtrusive usage, and zero training of the worker, provides a solid basis for the deployment of a versatile ubiquitous appliance that can be used in all types of scenarios, such as working on the back of a washing machine or under a car. In this paper, we describe the technical challenges that stem from the dynamic field of view of TeleAdvisor and discuss the design decisions we have made. We also describe an initial evaluation that we conducted in order to examine the viability of the system.

RELATED WORK

Many studies have examined different mechanisms to allow a remote helper to assist or guide a worker through various tasks involving the use of physical objects. These studies have shown that it is important to enable the helper to view the remote workspace in order to improve coordination and maintain a shared context of the task [3, 10]. Other studies have suggested to further improve the communication between the worker and helper by communicating helpers' gestures in the form of pointers [6], sketches [2] or full images of the helpers' hands [4] to the worker. Early technologies overlaid these gestures on top of the worker's workspace video feed to be sent back and shown to the worker on a display located in the workspace [2, 6]. However, this may cause a fractured ecology in which the worker needs to split attention between the task and the external display [9].

To address this, several studies have looked on using Augmented Reality (AR) solutions for helping remote users perform various tasks. Bauer et al. [1] used a telepointer for supporting field workers undertake technical activities with the aid of a remote expert. GestureCam [6] implements a solution that comprises of camera and a Head Mounted Display (HMD) that are worn by the worker. The camera's image is sent to the helper, whose gestures in front of a display are captured and sent back to the workers' HMD. In addition, the helper can control an actuator with a second camera mounted to top that provides him or her with a static view of the object. A laser pointer is mounted on the actuator to enable remote pointing. O'Neill et al [9] examined a mixed reality solution in which the object representation is 3D model shared by the helper and worker and connected to the physical object itself.

Finally, other studies have used a camera in conjunction with a mobile projector for other tasks [7, 8]. The Sixth sense [8] combined a mobile projector and camera to create a wearable gestural appliance that augments the physical world with digital information and uses hand gestures to interact with that information.

TELEADVISOR

TeleAdvisor includes two remotely located parts: the TeleAdvisor device and the Controller interface. The

Figure 2. The TeleAdvisor end-point device prototype.

TeleAdvisor device part (Figure 2) is comprised of a robotic arm on which are mounted a camera and pico projector. The camera captures visual data which is transmitted to the Controller. The projector projects information sent from the Controller on top of objects in the worker's environment. The worker can easily situate TeleAdvisor in his or her environment, directing the camera and projector to the point of need, and can carry on a voice conversation with the helper while having both hands free to work on the object.

Controller's interface

The Controller interface (Figure 3) is located remotely and its purpose it to enable the helper to view the worker's workspace via the live stream of the TeleAdvisor's camera, and to gesture onto the worker's workspace. In addition, the helper can use the Controller to move the robotic arm in order to change the point of view and projection area. Gestures are made by annotations and graphics that are overlaid on the video stream using the Controller interface. The annotations are sent back to the projector via the network and projected on top of the objects at the worker's location. In addition to using a pointer or free sketched ink in various colors and sizes, the helper can choose a set image (or icon) to be pinpointed to a specific location. For example, the helper can attach a pre-set "rotate clockwise" icon to a screw in the user's environment. The helper can also add a "bubble" in which it is possible to enter text and attach it to an object. For example, the helper can mark a

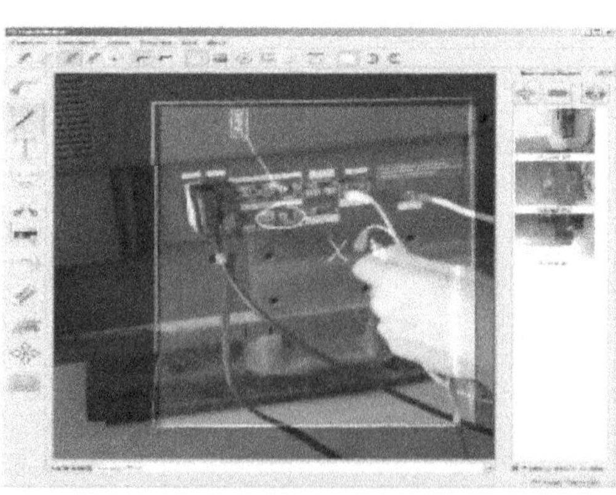

Figure 3. Controller interface (See Figure 1 to view corresponding workspace).

certain object with a bubble with the words "don't touch this".

Stroke annotations that are overlaid on top of the helpers' view are erased after a pen-up event. After that, the real projected annotations are seen by the helper through the video captured view of the worker's workspace. We considered enhancing the helpers' view with the annotation drawings, but after several experimentations decided against it. The main reason was that the annotations did not always align pixel-to-pixel with the real-world projected annotation causing visual clutter and misunderstanding. In addition, we felt it diminished helpers' understanding of what exactly the worker sees and how the annotations are perceived by the worker.

Helper's control of the point of view

A fixed-view camera can provide a good overview image but is fixed and cannot view detail, while a camera mounted on the worker's head constraints the helper's view to what the worker is focused on and can be jittery [6]. Ranjan et al. [10] propose using motion tracking technology to track the workers' hands and move the camera accordingly. Our approach leaves control in the helper's hand by enabling him or her to move the camera's view and to electronically zoom in and out in order to view in more detail.

The TeleAdvisor robotic arm allows for five degrees of freedom (DOF) rotation and azimuth angle. It consists of a base unit, a first arm connected to a second arm with an elbow joint, and a wrist joint at the end of the second arm with a clamp unit that holds the combined video camera and a projector assembly (See Figure 2). Although the robotic arm allows five DOF, its movements are mapped into two dimensions on the Controller interface. We decided to narrow down the movement of the arm to two dimensions in order to match the helper's 2D view, and thus reduce the helpers' cognitive load. From our experimentations, 2 DOF with the addition of electronic zoom were enough to reach a wide area of workspace including views of several planes. Finally, we implemented *positional bookmarks*. The helper at any time can bookmark a view. Later, selecting this bookmark will move the arm back to the exact same position.

Active tracking of the projection space

TeleAdvisor is designed to be transportable. Furthermore, the view position of TeleAdvisor's camera is constantly moving in response to the helper's control. This introduces a challenge to reliably derive the correlation between the camera and the projector space which is needed in order to know where exactly to project the annotation. A parallax is created between the camera and the projector due to the distance between them. This may cause the projected annotation to be inaccurate. While in a stationary solution, this distortion can be calibrated once and fixed accordingly, this is not possible in a mobile solution where the distance between the surface and the camera/projector may be different every time. Moreover, the surface angle compared

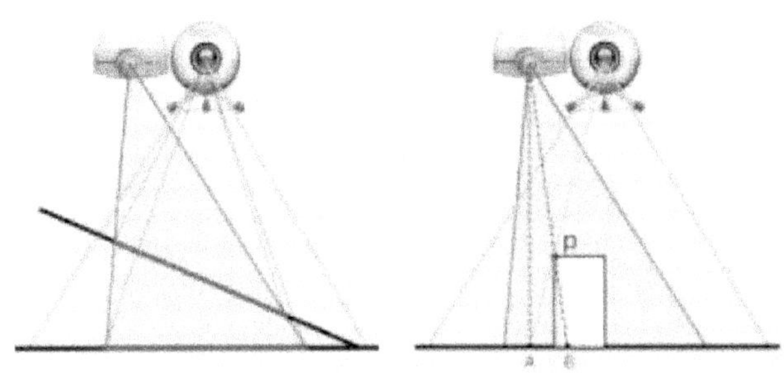

(a) (b)

Figure 4. (a) Because the distance between the surface and the camera/projector varies in distance and angle, the need for active tracking of the projector area arises. (b) Distortion problem caused by height of object

to the device might not be straight causing even more distortions. Figure 4a illustrates this problem showing the differences in parallax between a straight surface (in blue) and a tilted surface (in red).

To address this, we actively track the effective projector area and accommodate the changes accordingly. The projector continuously projects a green rectangle on the boundary of the projection area, and the system tracks it. The green rectangle also provides the worker with knowledge of the annotation and viewing space of the helper, which is important for the reciprocal communication between helper and worker [2]. For the tracking we used OpenCV primitives to build a robust and fault-tolerant detection algorithm. To alleviate laser flicker due to camera-projection scan asynchronization, we average three image frames back. Several filters are applied to remove extra details from the image and improve fault-tolerance. First, the noise edge-like lines are detected and masked out of the green channel. Then, only lines that are at least half of the frame are preserved. Second, space separation criterion is examined - four corner points should be sufficiently separated in space. Third, a median filter is applied to the individual history of each candidate corner point to avoid glitches. After the frame boundaries are detected, the reverse transformation is calculated and is applied to the live view of the helper. The annotations added by the helper are applied to the forward transformation and appear in the correct place when projected to the worker.

Another type of distortion can be caused when projecting on 3D objects because of the height of the object (Figure 4b). The correction described earlier is efficient for planar objects but can introduce distortions when the target object (p) to project on is significantly non planar with respect to the correction plane (black line). The correction procedure will result in highlighting point A instead of P. Currently, we do not have an automatic solution for this problem. However, in our experimentations, we saw that the distortion caused by the height of the objects do not exceed a few millimeters. TeleAdvisor allows the helper to move an existing annotation a few pixels in each direction to correct these kinds of distortions. Future solutions may examine the use of depth perception cameras to include the depth of the object.

INITIAL EVALUATION

We conducted an initial user evaluation of TeleAdvisor to examine the use of the software and its features and assess user acceptance. The purpose of the evaluation was to test TeleAdvisor and get feedback on the usability and usefulness of such a tool. We therefore performed a qualitative study rather than a comparative one.

We recruited three participants to be helpers. Helpers were first fully trained to use the Controller interface, after which they got full training performing the tasks themselves. We recruited 10 participants (7 female) for the role of workers. Each helper worked with 3-4 workers for an experimental session. Workers did not get any initial training. Two tasks were given. The first was a Lego assembly task which is common in similar previous works [2, 4, 5]. The task consisted of connecting small pieces of Lego situated on one plane (the table), where the helper held the manual for the given model while the worker constructed the model using the helpers' instructions. The second task was designed to be more realistic. The task consisted of connecting various cables between a TV set, a DVD and an AV receiver box. The TV and DVD were set perpendicular to each other and to the table (see Figure 1) to create a realistic 3D scenario in 3 planes. The worker and helper sat in the same room enabling regular voice communication. They were separated using partitions to ensure they only had visual access to each other through TeleAdvisor.

Observations indicated that helpers were able to effectively use TeleAdvisor to complete the tasks. Similar to [5], helpers repeatedly used annotations, accompanying them with phrases such as: "put it *here*" and "move it *there*" to establish common ground using deictic references. The active tracking worked well, and almost no glitches or distortions were observed. Helpers mostly used the free sketch tool for annotation. Pointer was used a few times while text or icons were not used at all. Helpers explained that sketches were most useful for deictic gestures, highlighting a specific object or location (usually by circling it), while pointers were useful for more accurate and transient gestures. Helpers heavily relied on the movement of the robotic arm since both tasks required a wider point of view of the workspace than the camera provided. For both tasks, helpers easily managed to view the entire workspace including all three planes of the second task, supporting our approach of providing only 2DOF movements. All three helpers manually moved the viewpoint as well as used the position bookmarks to mark and return to specific areas. They all indicated in post-interviews that bookmarks were extremely useful. All workers reported that TeleAdvisor was intuitive, very useful, and saw much value in having projected annotations in such a setting. Workers easily understood the novel interaction paradigm. This is probably due to the fact that they did not need to operate anything with the device which seamlessly integrated in the environment. Workers also reported that the visible rectangle helped them be aware of the helpers' view. Most workers said that using the system was as effective as having a person giving instructions in the same room and one person even said that it was better, since it was less stressful.

CONCLUSION

Many remote assistance and remote collaboration tasks require flexibility and mobility at the workspace. We showed that it is possible to create a tool that would effectively support remote gesturing while being transportable, and robust. Future work may look at anchoring annotations to specific locations using computer vision techniques allowing the object or the device to move while keeping the annotations in the same relative location.

REFERENCES

1. Bauer, M., Kortuem, G., Segall, Z. Where are you pointing at? A study of remote collaboration in a wearable videoconference system. International Symposium on Wearable computers (1999).
2. Fussell, A. R., Setlock, L. D., Yang J., Ou J., Mauer E., and Kramer, A. D. I. Gestures Over Video Streams to Support Remote Collaboration on Physical Tasks, Human-Computer Interaction, 19: 3, 273 - 309 (2004)
3. Gergle, D., Kraut, R.E., and Fussell, S.R. Action as language in a shared visual space. *In Proceedings of. CSCW'04*, ACM Press (2004), 487-496.
4. Kirk, D., Fraser, D. S., Comparing remote gesture technologies for supporting collaborative physical tasks. *In Proc. CHI '06*, ACM Press (2006), 1191-1200.
5. Kirk, D., Rodden, T., Fraser, D. S. Turn it this way: grounding collaborative action with remote gesture. In *Proc. CHI '07*, ACM Press (2007), 1039-1048.
6. Kuzuoka, H., Kosuge, T., & Tanaka, K. GestureCam: A video communication system for sympathetic remote collaboration, *Proceedings of CSCW'94* (35-43). NY: ACM Press. (1994)
7. Linder, N, Maes, P. LuminAR: portable robotic augmented reality interface design and prototype. *In Adjunct proceedings of UIST '10.* ACM, New York, NY, USA, 395-396 (2010).
8. Mistry, P., Maes, P., Chang, L. WUW – wear Ur World: a wearable gestural interface. *In proceedings of extended abstracts of CHI'09*. ACM Press. (2009)
9. O'Neill J., Castellani S., Roulland F., Hairon N., Juliano C, Dai L. From ethnographic study to mixed reality: a remote collaborative troubleshooting system. *Proceedings of CSCW'11*, ACM Press. 225-234. (2011)
10. Ranjan, A., Birnholtz, J. P., Balakrishnan, R., Dynamic Shared Visual Spaces: Experimenting with Automatic Camera Control in a Remote Repair Task. *In Proceedings of CHI 2007*, ACM Press (2007)

DragLocks: Handling Temporal Ambiguities in Direct Manipulation Video Navigation

Thorsten Karrer Moritz Wittenhagen Jan Borchers
RWTH Aachen University
52074 Aachen, Germany
{karrer, wittenhagen, borchers}@cs.rwth-aachen.de

ABSTRACT

Direct manipulation video navigation (DMVN) systems allow to navigate inside video scenes by spatially manipulating objects in the video. Problems arise when dealing with temporal ambiguities where a time span is projected onto a single point in image space, e.g., when objects stop moving. Existing DMVN systems deal with these cases by either disabling navigation on the paused object or by allowing jumps in the timeline. Both of these workarounds are undesirable as they introduce inconsistency or provoke loss of context. We analyze current practices regarding temporal ambiguities and introduce two new methods to visualize and navigate object pauses. User tests show that the new approaches are better suited for navigation in scenes containing temporal ambiguities and are rated higher in terms of user satisfaction.

Author Keywords

Video navigation; direct manipulation; accessing pauses.

ACM Classification Keywords

H.5.2 Information Interfaces and Presentation: User Interfaces. - Interaction styles.

INTRODUCTION

Navigating in videos, i.e., accessing a certain frame inside a length of video material for viewing, still frame extraction, or editing, has traditionally been performed using indirect controls such as the timeline slider or direct entry of frame numbers and time codes. Recently, several approaches have been proposed that allow navigation by interacting with the content of the video directly. With these direct manipulation video navigation (DMVN) systems, objects in the video can be grabbed and dragged along their motion trajectories, causing the video to advance or reverse accordingly [3, 4, 6, 7].

While DMVN systems have been shown to significantly increase efficiency for certain in-scene navigation tasks [3, 6], the interaction fails in the presence of certain object motion

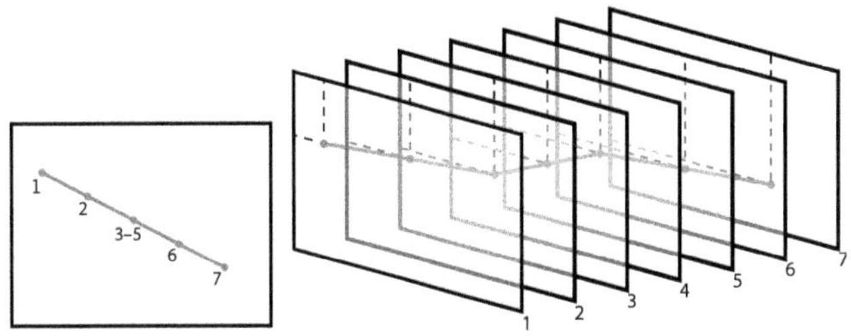

Figure 1. If an object occupies the same position in multiple frames, e.g., while pausing, the trajectory through these positions collapses to a single point. The frames then cannot be accessed using DMVN techniques.

patterns. Figure 1, e.g., shows an object that halts its movement for a couple of frames. When dragging the object across the screen, those frames either have to be skipped—losing the context of what else happens in the scene—or one has to give up on the direct mapping between the positions of the cursor and the object. Clearly, similar problems occur whenever an object occupies the same position in the scene at multiple times; the object's trajectory exhibits *temporal ambiguities*. Three different cases of motion patterns related to this problem can be identified:

Recurring movements, e.g., the rotating hands of a clock or a ball bouncing up and down. Here, problems arise mainly because it is difficult to know in which 'iteration' of the movement the object is at the moment. When the trajectory forms a cusp, it is unclear if the video is to be advanced forward or backward in time when dragging an object away from the cusp; to counter this problem, some DMVN systems enforce directional continuity constraints [3, 7].

Self-intersecting trajectories, e.g., a looping roller coaster or a car heading straight towards the camera. Similar to the case of recurring movements, the mapping problems can be mitigated by employing temporal or arc-length continuity constraints during the navigation [3, 6]. If the object is at a position where the trajectory self-crosses many times it may still be confusing to the user.

Pauses, e.g., a model walking down the catwalk, striking a pose and holding it for a few seconds before moving on. Ideally, when interacting with an object, a DMVN technique should allow access to those parts of the video where the object is pausing: Assume, for example, that we drag the model into the pose and then want to navigate to a frame *inside that pause* where the lighting is perfect or the model assumes a certain facial expression. This is a situation in which most strategies of existing DMVN systems fail. Because the pause only occupies a single pixel on the movement trajectory (cf. Fig.2b) it is skipped entirely. Thus, users either miss everything that is happening in the video while the object stops, possibly failing to notice the existence of a pause at all, or they have to switch to another means of navigation, like the timeline slider (cf. Fig.2a), to access the video frames in the pause. Although pauses structure a scene temporally—which should help with navigation—, DMVN systems cannot leverage this advantage but are hindered by them.

In the remainder of the paper, we analyze existing approaches to deal with temporal ambiguities and propose two different solutions that allow pause navigation without relinquishing control of the dragged object. We then report on a controlled experiment, where we evaluated the effectiveness and usability of our techniques compared to the existing approaches.

TEMPORAL AMBIGUITIES IN CURRENT DMVN SYSTEMS

The existing literature discusses recurring movements and self-intersecting trajectories together with techniques to suppress undesired jumps in the video while navigating. Pauses have been neglected so far. The current approaches rely on modifying the distance measure d that is used to determine the next frame f to be displayed during the interaction:

$$f(p,T) = [\underset{t\in T}{\text{argmin}}(d(p,t))]_f$$

where p is the screen position the user is dragging the object to and $T \subseteq F \times P$ is the object's trajectory consisting of tuples (t_f, t_p) of a frame number and a position.

Two classes of distance measures have been proposed: *purely spatial* distance measures depending only on t_p, and *spatio-temporal* distance measures depending on both t_p and t_f.

The most straightforward implementation of a purely spatial distance measure is found with Goldman et al. [4].

$$d_1(p,t) \cong \|p - t_p\|$$

While dragging an object, the system will always display the frame where the object's position is closest to the mouse cursor. The advantage of this technique is that objects can be very quickly repositioned along their trajectory. However, the playback position may freely jump discontinuously over the length of the video. Time ranges where the object pauses are not accessible so users have to resort to using the timeline slider to navigate inside a pause. In fact, the pauses are skipped completely and can only be detected by sudden changes in the rest of the frame when dragging across the pause position.

Dragicevic et al. [3] propose a spatial distance measure that reduces the frequency of jumps and ensures directional continuity at cusp points:

$$d_2(p,t) \cong \|p - t_p\| + \|\text{arclen}(t_p, o_p)\| + k_D$$

with o_p being the object's current position and $k_D > 0$ being added whenever the arc-length changes signs from the last step. In their paper, they specifically discuss the problems of recurring movements at cusp points and self-intersecting trajectories, and they formulate directional continuity and arc-length continuity as two requirements for DMVN systems. Due to d being a purely spatial metric, however, their system also skips object pauses.

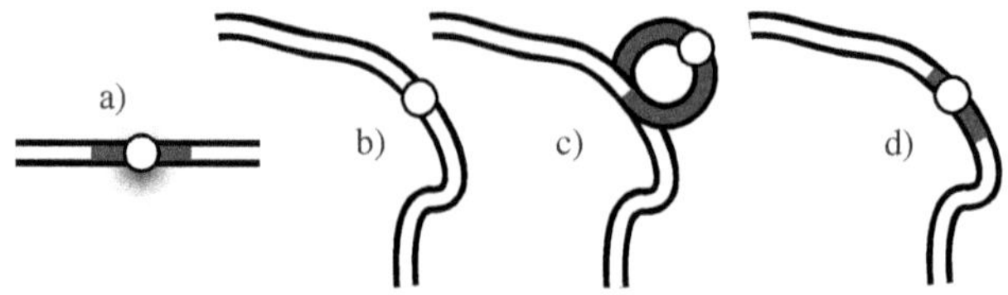

Figure 2. Schematic of the spatial extent of a pause (blue) for a) *timeline slider*: No special handling of pauses, all frames are distributed evenly. b) *DMVN*: Pause has no extent. c) *DMVN with embedded timeline*: Pause is distributed over a part of the trajectory. d) *DMVN with loop*: The trajectory form is altered to contain a loop representing the pause.

Karrer et al. [6] discuss the need to disambiguate situations of recurring movements and to avoid jumps in the video during navigation. They propose a spatio-temporal distance function that includes the current frame number o_f.

$$d_3(p,t) \cong \|(p_x - t_{p_x}, p_y - t_{p_y}, o_f - t_f)^T\|$$

This approach works reasonably well when it comes to self-intersecting or recurring movement trajectories (but not cusps), and it allows to easily spot pauses; the dragged object will 'stick' to the beginning of the pause. Dragging the object further, the spatial distance component outweighs the temporal one and the object will 'snap' to a position some time after the pause. While accessing the frames after the pause is possible by backtracking along the trajectory, navigating the contents of the pause is not possible.

Kimber et al. [7] propose a similar spatio-temporal distance measure that also ensures directional continuity at cusps.

$$d_4(p,t) \cong c_\theta \cdot \|p - t_p\| + \|o_f - t_f\| + k_D$$

with k_D defined as above. Otherwise, this approach behaves like d_3 but includes a time-dependent term c_θ that makes the 'snapping' across pauses happen more easily the longer the dragging takes.

We can see that spatio-temporal distance measures mitigate the problem of jumps during the interaction and at least allow to recognize object pauses. At the same time, they do not help to navigate the pauses, and they introduce a number of additional problems on their own: these compound measures have to be weighted according to the spatial and temporal sampling rates of the video—there is no universal answer to the question "how many pixel worth is one frame?".

PROPOSED SOLUTIONS

Outside the domain of DMVNs, solutions to a similar class of problems have been proposed for some time in the context of the general domain of direct manipulation control elements like sliders and selectors. Accessing elements in a list without mapping each element to its own pixel on a slider has been investigated among others by [1] and [2]. This problem setting is akin to navigating object pauses in DMVN in so far as the time range of a pause is mapped in its entirety to a single pixel, too, and thus cannot be navigated. Our approach thus borrows from these techniques: instead of changing the distance measure to navigate pauses, we locally extend the geometry of the trajectories—a technique inspired by the Popup-Vernier [2]. Alternatively, we dynamically change the mapping along the trajectory depending on the location of the interaction; this idea is akin to the Alphaslider [1].

Loop

Our first technique expands the single spatial point of a pause to a *loop* on the trajectory (Fig. 2c). Thus, the pause can now be navigated in one stroke, without having to re-home to the timeline slider. The distinct shape of a loop is a recognizable pattern that gives users a good hint of its special meaning. The user can navigate to the beginning (or the end respectively) of the pause by dragging the object to the base of the loop. Frames inside the pause are equally distributed on the loop and are now accessible as if on a curved timeline slider.

Navigation inside the loop can be performed at different temporal granularities depending on the radius of the dragging gesture; this is similar to the micrometer interface [1] or the mobile zoom slider [5]. Finally, the loop ensures that the rest of the trajectory is unmodified, guaranteeing direct manipulation of the object on the rest of the trajectory. To avoid the need of traversing the loop when the user intends to navigate to a time after the pause, the loop could be deactivated via a *quasimode* [8], e.g., by holding down the control key.

Embedded Timeline

For our second technique, we change the mapping along a short extent of the trajectory around the pause location, so that this part controls the time of the video instead of the location of the object (Fig. 2d). All time points on this part of the trajectory are redistributed equally. The embedded timeline thus does not change the form of the trajectory but changes its meaning in a local area around the pause. Expanding the pause into the spatial domain guarantees that we can navigate the pause in one stroke without having to leave the object of interest. Conserving the trajectory shape allows navigation to a point after the pause while retaining of what happens during a pause. This comes at the cost of decoupling navigation from the object on that part of the trajectory that is used for the expansion. With this technique there is no way to identify the pause from the shape of the trajectory alone; thus, we set the color of the embedded timeline to be different from that of the rest of the trajectory. For longer pauses, this technique will show the same resolution problems as the timeline slider, making it hard to navigate to a specific frame inside the pause.

Both techniques work best if used with either a spatio-temporal distance measure or a spatial distance measure that ensures arc-length continuity. Although pauses would be accessible even with a metric like d_1, the extended geometry could very easily be skipped involuntarily during the interaction.

NAVIGATION AROUND PAUSES

We identified four different target areas on a trajectory in regard to navigation around pauses: *Before the pause*, at the *edge of the pause*, *in the pause*, and *after the pause*. In the following, we describe these cases for forward navigation. Navigation *before the pause* (cf. Fig 1, frames 1–2) is equivalent to not having a pause at all and thus is already covered by the standard DMVN approaches. The *edge of a pause* (cf. Fig 1, frame 3) is the point were an object stops moving. It is accessible easily when using spatio-temporal distance measures, because of the 'sticking', and when using the loop, because the pause is visually distinguishable. Navigating to the edge is harder when using purely spatial distance measures or the embedded timeline. Loop and embedded timeline both support navigation *in a pause* (cf. Fig 1, frames 3–5). We expect the loop to perform better for longer pauses because the embedded timeline will suffer from resolution issues. Existing DMVN systems—regardless of the choice of distance measure—require the use of the timeline slider to navigate in the pause since the pause has no spatial extent. Navigation to the area *after the pause* (cf. Fig 1, frames 6–7) requires crossing the pause. This is easiest for purely spatial distance measures, only requiring to drag the object to the target position. Spatio-temporal distance measures may require the help of the timeline slider to cross the pause. Both loop and embedded timeline allow crossing the pause easily; if the quasimode mentioned above is not implemented the loop requires the traversal of the extended shape of the path.

EXPERIMENT

We conducted an experiment to investigate navigation performance for *purely spatial* and *spatio-temporal* distance measures (d_1 and d_3) and the *loop* and *embedded timeline* techniques. In our implementation of loop and embedded timeline, we also used d_3 as distance measure. In the loop condition, there was no quasimode and the loops were always visible. We tested these four techniques in six different experiments: navigation to a point on the *edge*, *inside*, and *after* a pause, each in separate versions for long (>25s) and short (<5s) pauses. For each of the six experiments, we used a different section of a longer video showing two people playing a board game. Trajectories were created using optical flow fields as described in [6]. We detected a pause when an object was not moving for more than 0.2s.

Participants used a Wacom Cintiq 12WX and a stylus as an input device. They were introduced to DMVNs before the experiment and had time to familiarize themselves with each of the four techniques on a separate video. For each experiment, subjects were given a simple navigation task ("Navigate to the frame where the right player rolls a six."). After each experiment, people were asked to rank the four techniques in order of their personal preference. To avoid learning effects, participants watched each video scene twice before performing the task. At the end, we performed a short structured interview with the participant.

The study design was within-subjects; subjects performed the task in each experiment using all techniques. The order of techniques was randomized for each participant using a balanced 4x4 latin square. We measured the navigation time in each trial, defined as the time between acquisition of the object to lifting the stylus in a 0.5s range of the target

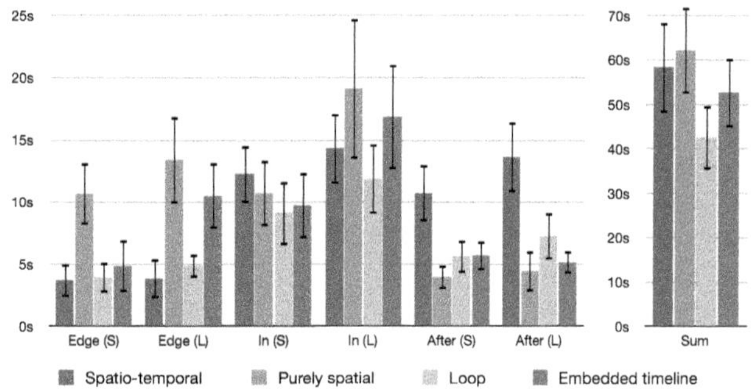

Figure 3. Summary of navigation times. Left: Means of navigation time and 95% confidence intervals for all techniques and experiments. Navigation to the *edge*, *in*, and *after* short (S) and long (L) pauses. Right: Means of the sum of navigation times for each technique.

time. We analyzed the measurements with a repeated measures ANOVA using Greenhouse-Geisser correction and, in case of significance, post-hoc analysis employing paired t-tests with Bonferroni correction. For nonparametric data, we used a Friedman test and Wilcoxon signed-rank tests.

28 users (four female) between 21 and 36 years were recruited from our university's campus. Free snacks and drinks were offered during the study and we raffled an Amazon gift card.

Results

Before analyzing the data, we removed two outliers where a participant misunderstood the task. Figure 3 shows a summary of the recorded navigation times. When looking at the sum of navigation times for each technique, subjects were fastest when using loop ($M = 42.1s$, $SD = 17.2s$), followed by embedded timeline ($M = 50.5s$, $SD = 18.8s$), spatio-temporal ($M = 58.5s$, $SD = 24.9s$) and purely spatial ($M = 62s$, $SD = 23.7s$). Differences were strongly significant between loop and purely spatial ($p < .001$), and significant for loop and spatio-temporal ($p < .05$).

Navigation to the edge of a pause was significantly faster for the spatio-temporal and loop conditions than for the purely spatial condition ($p < .001$). Embedded timeline was only faster than purely spatial for short pauses ($p < .05$).

When navigating to a point after a pause the purely spatial, loop, and embedded timeline conditions were significantly faster than the spatio-temporal condition ($p < .001$). Additionally, purely spatial and embedded timeline performed significantly better than loop for long pauses ($p < .05$).

The data revealed that our participants strongly preferred loop over all other techniques ($p < .001$). Also, the embedded timeline technique was preferred over the spatio-temporal condition ($p < .001$).

During the interview, when asked if they ever felt that they did not know where they were in the video with any of the techniques, one participant named loop, two embedded timeline, four the spatio-temporal and 12 the purely spatial technique, indicating that, indeed, the purely spatial navigation can provoke a loss of context. When being asked if they could keep a good overview over what was happening in the video with any of the techniques, the results were consistent (loop: 17, embedded timeline: 8, spatio-temporal: 4, purely spatial: 4).

CONCLUSION AND FUTURE WORK

The results indicate that both the spatio-temporal and the purely spatial conditions do not perform well overall in regard to pauses. Embedded timeline works well for short pauses but is problematic in long pauses. Loop seems to be a viable alternative for all tested situations and was the preferred technique by our users. For future work we plan looking into techniques that deal with the limitations of the work presented here. Limitations we identified are overlapping loops or embedded timelines on paths containing frequent pauses and the added overhead of having to navigate several pauses even when navigating to a time after all pauses. For the latter, using a quasimode to dynamically disable the loop would be helpful to quickly get across pauses. Further work includes a similar analysis of recurring movements and combining the conclusions with the ones presented here. Also, we plan to further analyse pauses, especially of varying lengths, and variations of the techniques presented here, e.g. different visualizations.

ACKNOWLEDGMENTS

This work was partially funded by the German B-IT Foundation and by the German Government through its UMIC Excellence Cluster for Ultra-High Speed Mobile Information and Communication and its HumTec Human Technology Center at RWTH Aachen University.

REFERENCES

1. Ahlberg, C., and Shneiderman, B. The Alphaslider: A rapid and compact selector. In *Proc. of CHI'94* (1993).

2. Ayatsuka, Y., Rekimoto, J., and Matsuoka, S. Popup vernier: a tool for sub-pixel-pitch dragging with smooth mode transition. In *Proc. of UIST'98* (1998).

3. Dragicevic, P., Ramos, G., Bibliowitcz, J., Nowrouzezahrai, D., Balakrishnan, R., and Singh, K. Video browsing by direct manipulation. In *Proc. of CHI'08* (2008).

4. Goldman, D., Gonterman, C., and Curless, B. Video object annotation, navigation, and composition. In *Proc. of UIST'08* (2008).

5. Hürst, W., and Götz, G. Interface designs for pen-based mobile video browsing. In *Proc. of DIS'08*, ACM Press (2008).

6. Karrer, T., Weiss, M., Lee, E., and Borcers, J. DRAGON: a direct manipulation interface for frame-accurate in-scene video navigation. In *Proc. of CHI'08* (2008).

7. Kimber, D., Dunnigan, T., Girgensohn, A., Shipman, F., Turner, T., and Yang, T. Trailblazing: Video Playback Control by Direct Object Manipulation. In *Proc. of ICME'07, IEEE* (2007).

8. Raskin, J. *The humane interface*. New directions for designing interactive systems. Addison-Wesley, 2000.

CamBlend: An Object Focused Collaboration Tool

James Norris, Holger Schnädelbach
Mixed Reality Laboratory
University of Nottingham,
Nottingham, NG8 1BB
{psxjn, holger.schnadelbach}@nottingham.ac.uk

Guoping Qiu
Intelligent Modeling and Analysis
University of Nottingham,
Nottingham, NG8 1BB
guoping.qiu@nottingham.ac.uk

ABSTRACT
CamBlend is a new focus-in-context panoramic video collaboration system designed to facilitate the interaction with and around objects in a lightweight, flexible package. As well as the ability to view very high resolution local and remote video that covers a full 180° field of view, the system contains a number of tools which facilitate bi-directional pointing between two remote spaces. In the first quasi-naturalistic exploratory study on a focus-in-context video system, we show a number of unique object referencing behaviours, including un-intentional or 'implicit' pointing and a number of scenarios where this was advantageous. Additionally the study highlighted some of the problems inherent in aligning between screen-based and real-world perspectives.

Author Keywords
CSCW; collaboration; interaction analysis; focus+context

ACM Classification Keywords
H.4.3. Communications Applications: Computer conferencing, teleconferencing, and videoconferencing

INTRODUCTION
Video communication technologies are widely used by organisations to support teams in remote collaboration [14], whether this is on the desktop or in the boardroom [22]. Whilst such tools can and are frequently used for purely discursive ends it is quite common to wish to use video-technologies to support a collaborative task at a distance which might entail access to the connected/shared spaces, specific artefacts and resources located in those spaces and of course the team members involved. In the majority of video communication set-ups in use today, this access is impeded by principal technical limitations.

Spatial inconsistencies are introduced because of the anisotropy of video communication (different set-ups at each node create interactionally different views) and the way the pinhole camera model does not preserve lines of sight [8]. Secondly, standard cameras have a much more limited field of view (FOV) compared to human vision. These technical limitations have an impact on interaction, and the interactional issues that emerge around the shared access to distributed resources and the conduct of team members are well documented in the literature [20, 21].

CamBlend is a new focus-in-context panoramic video collaboration system that solves several technical limitations inherent in current systems that increase FOV. The system design is exploited to provide facilities which help with some of the problems generated through the spatial inconsistencies of video communication. There are two contributions, firstly in this technical system, and secondly by the first exploratory study of a focus-in-context video collaboration system.

RELATED WORK
The problems with spatial consistency are usually manifested in the inability to point to, or reference artefacts in either local (in order to show a remote participant something) or remote environments. Collaborative tasks are frequently grounded through referential statements and gestures made in relation to objects of common interest. Direct manipulation of the objects themselves is also a means by which action is coordinated and made accountable to others. This is particularly relevant for expert helper tasks [3, 6, 23] as well as more generally in workplace environments [12, 20]. These problems stem from the fracturing of interaction spaces [20] and the technical limitations in maintaining consistent spatial relationships. In this context, Fussell et al provide a succinct classification of classes of visual information necessary to ground conversations [6]. Views of participants' heads and their faces, of their bodies and actions, of shared task objects and of the work context, support joint attention, the monitoring of comprehension and conversational efficiency to varying degrees, by establishing a shared visual interaction space.

Some high-end (expensive, custom built) systems address those issues by careful architecture of the interaction environment, including HP Halo [19] and t-Room [22], but as well as being costly these systems are inflexible in how and where they're deployed. The remote-controlled GestureMan [18] system is more flexible, allowing remote pointing with the use of a laser pen, but end-users found it difficult to relate the robot to activities in the remote environment. More lightweight is a cursor pointing system [5], which although limited in its expressive capacity,

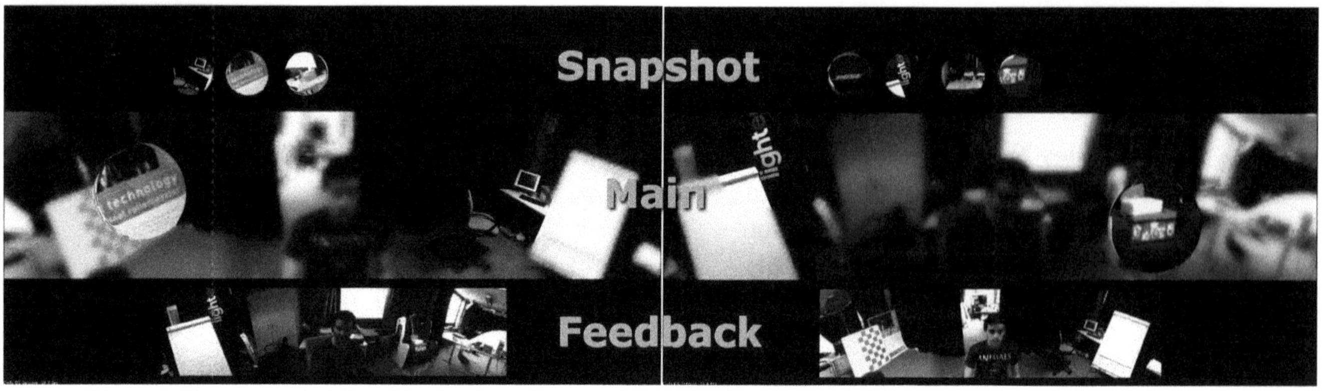

Figure 1. Two connected CamBlend nodes with snapshot mechanism (top), main remote feed and feedback (bottom)

provides a flexible solution, and the study of which showed that with it participants were faster in locating objects.

The inability to reference objects is compounded by the limited FOV of standard cameras, limiting the contextual information that end-users have. They are often unaware of objects that surround the narrow camera FOV and are therefore unable to reference them as they would in a face-to-face scenario, which has been shown in generic collaboration tasks [10, 15], expert helper systems [6] and collaboration over CVEs [13]. There are various methods to increase FOV, including fish-eye lenses, curved mirrors and camera arrays. The relationship between resolution and FOV means that they all require much more bandwidth in order to represent the fidelity of standard video. Simply using very high resolution imagery is unmanageable in three areas: in terms of live communication, as it cannot be streamed in real time; in terms of computational power required, as it cannot be encoded/decoded or otherwise processed in real time; in a display sense, as monitors cannot render the resolutions that would be required. Further, we hypothesise that systems which only increase the FOV of cameras will produce video which contains large areas of redundancy, areas that do not change and are not central to the interaction, as interactions usually occur in narrow, focused areas, unpredictably located.

Previously, this has been addressed by providing multiple but related views into the same space, in order to provide both detailed focused views and wide-angle contextual overviews [3, 9]. This work can most usefully be categorised in terms of the focus plus context literature [2], which looks at efficient ways to find areas of detail within a large dataset. Video systems in this space include for example the Polycom CX5000 (formerly Microsoft Roundtable) [4], which uses a camera array to provide a full 360° FOV for connecting meeting rooms. The system automatically selects regions of interest using directional microphones. Other systems include the Extra-Eyes [24] system, using motorised pan-tilt-zoom cameras for detail together with a wide-angle fish eye camera for overview. This design has more recently been used in a range of expert/helper experiments [3, 23], which concentrate on discovering the most effective visual information configuration and focal point control schema.

As well as problems with scalability, speed and control, a theme that runs through all the above work is that of reconciliation between different camera views. Although most pronounced in the MTV studies [9], the Extra-Eyes [24] work also reported on the performance benefits of linking detailed views and overviews. The focus plus context work by Baudisch et al [2] shows that for dynamically changing information, keeping the focused view in context allows for more effective use of peripheral information. Arguably, the closer and more 'linked' these views are, the less effort might be required in relating them.

CAMBLEND DESIGN

CamBlend is addressing the established challenge of providing flexible, cost-effective access to remote spaces, artefacts and people, by combining wide camera FOV with multiple controllable, in-context views of detail. Camblend is a video collaboration system covering 180° FOV, which represents the area of focus contextually within its background. It also contains a set of tools which provide bi-directional pointing facilities. CamBlend scales to a number of focus areas that can each be manipulated independently, and without observable latency. CamBlend is designed to be a portable video conferencing technology that could be deployed on a desktop or large screen media space, requiring a self-contained camera unit and custom software. The following describes its two main development iterations.

The Core System – ITERATION 1

At its core CamBlend is a focus plus context video system that represents areas of attention in high resolution, contextually inside a wide-angle, low-resolution background. The system is scalable in that multiple users can each own unique views into the same space.

Implemented in C++ and CUDA [1], the system creates a panoramic video stream from 3 high resolution (1024x768) cameras aligned to cover a 180° FOV. A very high resolution panorama is generated (3072x768) using the FlyCam method [7], implemented on the GPU. This high resolution panoramic image forms the base dataset, from which many concurrent focus areas can be extracted and transmitted in real-time. As shown in Figure 1, the background rendered is a very low resolution (256x60) version of the panoramic image. Overlaid onto this, in context, are high resolution (368x368) focus windows. Users may manipulate the position of these focus windows without observable latency by dragging them over the contextual view.

It is also possible to have the focus windows zoom into the remote space, shown in Figure 1. This is performed in-context, so that areas around the focus window are not occluded. A focus plus context technique is used [17], where linear and non-linear magnification is combined in order to preserve straight lines while zoomed, but smoothly blend between the focused and contextual areas. Because the full resolution of the panorama is so large, this zoom functionality becomes a 'real' zoom, revealing extra underlying information.

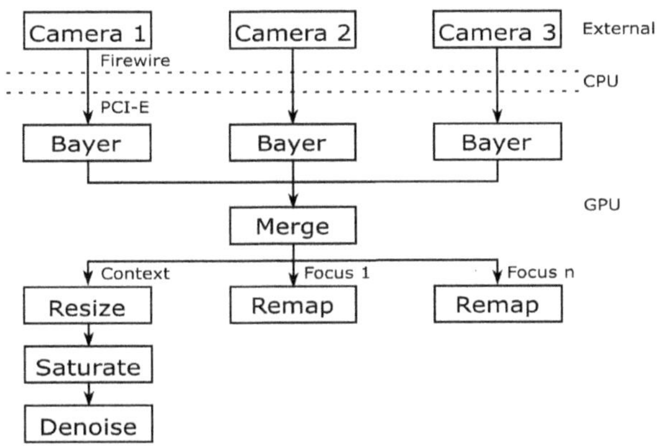

Figure 2. The video pipeline shows the processing of image data from camera hardware (top) to screen (bottom). Further processing for over the air communication (OTA) is missing. The implementation has not been necessary for the study but newer versions of CamBlend include a full OTA stream.

Until recently this design (visualized in figure 2) might only have been possible by building some custom digital signal processing (DSP) hardware. Now with the use of CUDA [1] as a GPGPU programming language, it will run on most desktop PCs. This system design improves on the PTZ camera pair design [24] in three ways; firstly movement is instant without the physical limitations of motorized cameras; secondly the focused and contextual views are seamlessly blended by being generated from the same image; thirdly there is a scalability dimension which allows the same person to have multiple views into a single space (explored in the study) and multiple people unique views into a single space (explored in principle), both of which would require multiple PTZ cameras.

Focus Groups Feedback

Iteration 1 was deployed as a single node demonstration, exposing the interaction paradigm of user-controllable focus windows, visually it matched Figure 1, but did not contain the snapshot and feedback features shown. This version was discussed with two focus groups. The aim was to collect feedback very early on in the development. Participants within both focus groups had no previous knowledge of the system or input into the development. Both sessions were audio recorded and the main points have been drawn out of this recording below.

One focus group was to a group of seven teachers at a technology-focused secondary school in the UK. The teachers were asked about their thoughts on the interaction paradigm, as well as potential use-cases within the school they could imagine. CamBlend was setup and trained to view a doorway area where people were frequently entering and exiting. The teachers were able to list a large number of scenarios where the system could be used. These included observing a remote, inaccessible location, for example an archaeological dig site from the classroom, and a tool to record, annotate and playback dance classes, where children are recorded as they perform and the clip is collectively scrutinised, annotated and saved. There were also ideas around video editing and directing, recording and later filtering to show only relevant clips, as well as suggestions to use CamBlend to connect remote classrooms for creative activities. Focus windows could be used to make groups of pupils aware of attention that they are currently receiving.

Another session was held with five researchers within our department, chosen for their HCI and development experience. As well as feedback on the interaction paradigm, this session was also to get expert advice into the design decisions required to enable the effective interaction with objects. For this session we were able to prepare the study space with some objects to interact with, including some Lego, a laptop, a white-board and some posters with various sized text. Participants were asked questions about the system and encouraged to interact with it over the course of a two-hour session. The feedback again was positive; participants had no trouble grasping the concept or interaction technique. Researchers here identified the potential of the focus windows of representing areas of attention, and suggested a feedback mechanism to allow them to understand what others see of their local space.

The focus groups highlighted the wide range of possible application areas but also drew attention to potential areas for further development. In particular, features for recording, features for making others aware of one's attention and features for view feedback were those that seemed most promising to improve support for interaction. These areas were addressed in the final version. The aim was to both respond to the very initial focus group feedback and to devise a prototype that could be studied in a laboratory setting in a formative way.

Refining Interaction Support – ITERATION 2 (Studied)

The panorama generated with 3 cameras (aspect ratio 4:1) forms the main window showing the remote scene (see Figure 1 showing two symmetrical networked nodes). The panorama is centrally placed on screen. Focus windows are floating over this contextual background and can be dragged to any position using a mouse. There is then space above and below the panorama for additional features described briefly below.

Recording Snapshots

One advantage of segmenting the panorama for the generation of focus areas is that those streams can be easily digitised for further processing. This creates possibilities in saving, sharing or documenting video or image resources. One feature that touches on these affordances is the snapshot window. When a user clicks the right mouse button over a focus window, a screenshot is taken of the focus window area, which displays at the top of the screen in one of several slots (we have allowed for six here because of the task, but it is flexible). This feature allows users to document objects or events, which interest them. Figure 1 shows several recorded snapshots.

Feedback and bi-directional referencing

The feedback window renders at the bottom of the screen as a miniature panorama, showing the user's own space with the other user's focus window positions augmented over the top with a blue cross. The blue crosses can in turn be directly manipulated, allowing users to point in their own space. Taken together, this provides both control and awareness in both directions and provides for a shared visual interaction space, which is widely reported as being beneficial throughout the video collaboration literature [6, 9, 19]. For example, a user has the ability to look into a remote space to explore. Due to the remote users live feedback window they are also implicitly stating, "I am looking at this". This then provides the ability to implicitly point, to direct attention 'without' intention. In addition a user may also manipulate a remote user's focus window by dragging the blue cross, to state "I want you to look at this", while this can also be used to explore one's own space.

This implicit pointing ability depends on the use of the focus windows to view objects in detail. If the background provided enough detail users needn't use the windows. Conversely the background must provide enough detail to be useful as a source of contextual information, i.e. by representing motion and basic image outlines clearly. Through a series of informal iterations, a balance between these two was reached. The final system uses both a k-nearest-neighbour de-noise algorithm, and a colour de-saturation algorithm which results in a near grey-scale background image with a 'glazed' effect. A flexible network layer provides a high level TCP socket interface supporting all other control and synchronization functionality.

STUDY

A lab based formative user study was held with this version of the system. The objective was firstly to evaluate the basic interaction design and identify any interactional problems. We were particularly interested in the ways that the multiple views would be reconciled by users and the way that the focus windows would be used for awareness and pointing. In order to spur the intensive use of the system the study was designed around a lab based collaborative object finding task. Despite the somewhat artificial nature of the task, we feel it remains representative of a workplace scenario that involves the referencing of local and remote objects (and there is a precedent for the use of such tasks in related HCI research e.g., [19, 20, 24]). Initially two participants were recruited for a pilot study, in order to validate and refine the task. After some minor tweaks to object placement and user instructions, 12 participants (6 pairs) were run through the task. Participants were mostly PhD students from other departments within the University, they were recruited on a self-selected basis responding to an advert and participants were offered £10 compensation. Each pair was gender balanced and all participants had normal or corrected-to-normal vision.

Task overview

The objective was to find and record, using the CamBlend snapshot feature, a set of six different objects provided to each participant via an image sheet. Each participant received a different set of six images making a total of twelve objects to find using the system. In order to enforce collaboration the objects were mixed and placed on either side of the screen. As snapshots can only be recorded of the remote space, individually participants could only record some of the images provided to them. As a consequence participants were required to exchange responsibility for recording snapshots. Finally one object from each image sheet did not exist at all, and participants were encouraged to draw that object on a whiteboard provided.

Participant Instructions

Participants were told that they would need to work together to record all twelve images and that this would involve exchanging images to record. It was made clear that there was no competition element and that participants should take their time. They were encouraged to physically explore their side of the screen, because objects would not be immediately visible and that all the objects could be found within a curtained area. Participants were told that one image from each sheet would need drawing on the whiteboard provided and that the only rule was not to take snapshots of the image sheet. Participants were guided through the task as follows; firstly they were given an instruction sheet detailing all system features and asked to spend some time reading it; they were then led into the study area from separate directions and placed at the CamBlend terminal; participants were given some time to familiarise themselves with the system, the moderator worked with them to make sure all system features were understood and demonstrated in practice; participants were then given the image sheets and the task was explained. After the task was completed pairs of participants were interviewed. In some specific cases where participants exhibited particular behaviour or problems, this was also an opportunity to query the participant about that.

Environment setup

The system was setup to simulate a two-person teleconference, with two terminals in a partitioned room viewing the opposing space (as described, the studied system does not contain the video encoding necessary for a remote set-up), see Figure 3.

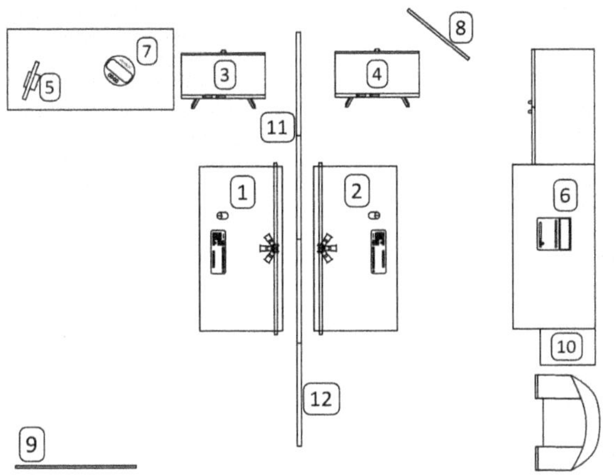

1, 2 CamBlend terminals 7 Battery charger 10 Bose speaker
3, 4 Whiteboards 8 Light poster 11 Map of the world image sheet
5, 6 Image cycling monitors 9 CBI poster 12 Eagle image sheet

Figure 3. The study area for the task, each space is separated by a non-transparent screen shown.

Each terminal was configured with two focus windows, with the intention that they could permanently focus on something static (the remote participants face) while moving the other around. No suggestions were given to participants on how to use them though.

As well as the objects being searched for, each space was relatively cluttered with general office equipment. This included various computing peripherals, some DIY equipment, some office storage including desk draws and a cupboard. The objects participants were asked to locate were designed to emulate physical properties of objects that might be interesting within an office environment, that is they were either fixed in position, occluded by other objects or the participant themselves, out of camera view (and thus required users to move and 'frame' the object), restricted in their movement by a cable, clearly outside of a normal camera FOV, or needed to be created by drawing on a whiteboard provided. Some of the objects were chosen because they do not have a name, requiring participants to in some way negotiate a shared language to describe them, and others were common objects that can easily be recognised. There were also two monitors behind each user on each side of the screen that cycled through a different set of images. Each monitor was directed towards the CamBlend system so snapshots could be recorded of the contents of the screen.

Methods

To record the study session both the CamBlend screens were recorded via screen capture software, and each participant was recorded via an external fixed position camcorder. The video capture configuration resulted in 4 video feeds to analyse for each group. The 4 video streams were aggregated into a single synchronised high-resolution video stream showing all the recordings together. This video consisted of a 2x2 grid of the source video streams, using the audio track of the video camera with the best audio quality. The analysis of this data uses qualitative video analysis [11], which draws on conversation and interaction analysis techniques [16]. Our primary analytic concern was our participants' practical accomplishment of reciprocal object-focused referencing and how issues of view reconciliation interplay with that accomplishment.

RESULTS

All groups of participants completed the task within 20 minutes, with the fastest group taking just 9 minutes. The moderator who remained in close proximity throughout observed no significant problems with task completion.

Interview data

The questions in a semi-structured interview covered task comprehension, system interface, system feature use and potential problems or improvements. The interviews were recorded via audio and the main points are discussed below. All participants stated that the task was straight forward, that the controls were intuitive and no groups could suggest any improvements to the controls or interface. Most groups said that they enjoyed the task, and that it would have been very difficult without the feedback and pointing tools provided. No groups reported problems with view reconciliation, i.e. reconciling the detail with the overview, and one group reported the opposing problem that they sometimes found it difficult to find the focus windows within the background. Some participants stated that the low resolution provided basic awareness without invading the space, maintaining a level of privacy. At the same time, participants reported feeling uncomfortable using the focus windows to zoom in on faces unless it was clearly necessary. However, they did want to see faces, but wanted it automated both for convenience, and so it was known that they weren't intentionally concentrating on the face. The two participants who didn't like the design of CamBlend both separately described how it felt unfamiliar to have a video stream with differing levels of detail.

Most participants said that screen to physical space transitions were fine, despite evidence during the task of short confusion. Groups described two tactics they used to avoid the need to perform a conversion. One was to rely on the physical space by exploring locally and then physically pointing. The other was to rely exclusively on the system, to '*give over to [the system]*' and ignore your physical surroundings. Also some participants would have liked the feedback window to be mirrored. Several application areas were brought up, including cross-campus lab sessions, a collaborative storyboarding or documenting tool and as an exploration game. Additionally, improvements were suggested including enhanced snapshot features, privacy controls, better zoom detail and object tracking technology.

Video data

Beyond the interview data, which has a provided an initial overview of system use, the video material provided a more detailed window into intricacies of interaction through and around CamBlend. From this material, it was evident that participants structured the way they handled the task into a number of activities. These were exchanging information on objects left to find (*informing*), exploring to find an object either locally or remotely (*exploring*), communicating the location of objects (*directing*) and framing to record an object (*recording*). The task parameters dictate that each of these activities was of a collaborative nature. To analyse the video it was split temporally into episodes. Those which demonstrated the activities introduced above were transcribed and analysed in detail, resulting in 60 episodes across the six pairs of participants. All names in the following transcript sections have been anonymised. The transcription orthography is based on [11], except that delays are rounded to the nearest half-second, and some notation is omitted, including raising/falling intonation, emphasis and audible inhalations. The original orthography is for short highly detailed transcriptions of around 30s, these changes accommodate for the longer data here.

Informing

Although not suggested by the moderator, most participants opted to hold their image sheet up to the camera in order to communicate which images are remaining to find, rather than trying to verbally describe the images in turn. In holding the image sheet up participants would demonstrate one of two tactics. Either they would hold the image sheet still, allowing the remote participant to explore the images. Or sometimes if a particular object was already in discussion, they would attempt to place this image directly over the remote participants focus window, circumventing the remote participants need to operate the system at all. In both cases participants who held an image sheet up demonstrated use of the feedback window to understand remote participants attention area. Often this information was used to query specific images, without the need to describe them. Two episodes are detailed below showing examples of both these techniques.

Session 1, Episide 1

This episode was at the very start of the session, participants are showing each other their entire image sheet with no specific image in mind.

```
L. Right I'll show you
J. °That's the CBI° so you've got a bose speakers
(0.5) er °lets have a° (3.5) can you just pull it
back a bit towards you slightly (1) So we've got a
boot (.) light (.) a globe (0.5) what's this one
here? (1.5)
L. Er:: it's a drop of water=
J. =Drop of water (.) ok
```

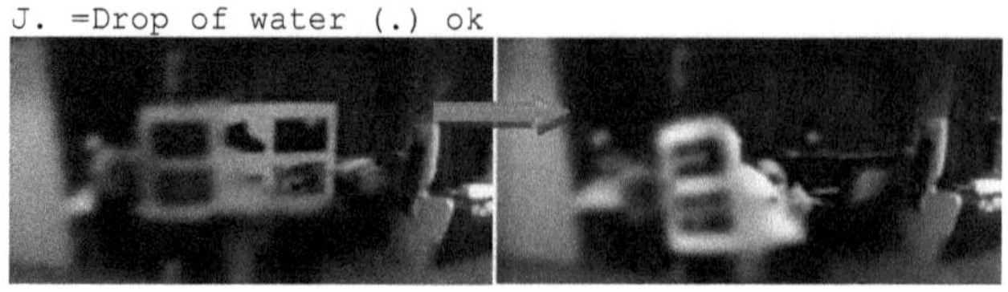

Lucy raises her image sheet up to the camera so that John can explore them using his focus window. Initially Lucy holds the sheet too close and John asks it to be moved back. He then moves his focus window over the images one by one, positioning his focus window onto the centre of each image in turn, he pauses over the drop of water and asks '*what's this one here?*'. Lucy then curls the image sheet back where Johns focus window rests and describes the image. Lucy was able to understand immediately which image John meant without the need for any verbal description of the object. In order to understand which image John was querying, Lucy must have been watching the feedback window on her screen from underneath the image sheet as she holds it. This behaviour of watching the feedback window was consistent through all groups.

Session 3, Episode 6

In the following episode Steve requires Rachel to record an image behind him. Steve first needs Rachel to understand which object he has found for her to take a snapshot.

```
S. Oh the bose, sorry on my umm: (0.5) I'll show
you where that is hang on ee:: its behind me: (.)
there we go
S. Yeah so this: (1) this this bose logo (.) there
R. Ah yeah
S. Yep (.) t- that's that's there
R. Ah ok (.) I'll zoom [ (in on that)
S.                     [ on the speaker
R. Sorted (.) so
```

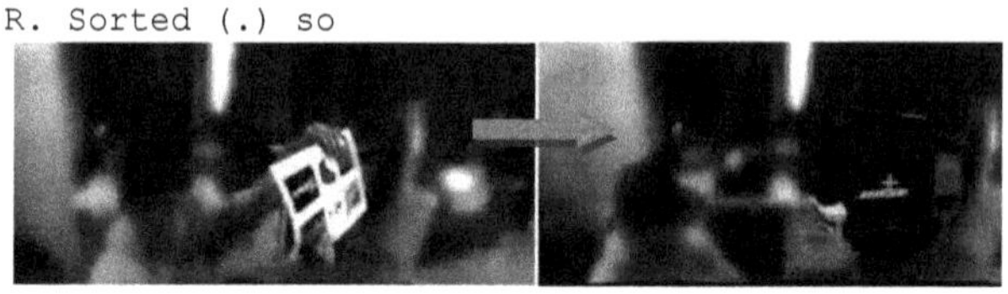

Steve starts by moving Rachel's focus window over to the Bose speaker behind him. Once Rachel's focus window is lined up he shows her which object he requires by holding the image sheet up, he lines it up precisely so the speaker logo is already over Rachel's focus window. Then when he lowers the image sheet Rachel is already looking at the real object. Steve was easily able to convey to Rachel which image he needed, and subsequently where that object was located in the physical environment. Rachel had very little input to the episode, simply confirming her understanding of the situation and then later recording the snapshot.

Exploring

A centre point of the task was actually finding the objects provided to participants via their image sheet. There were three different tactics demonstrated to achieve this. Either participants would look around themselves and explore the space without using the system. They would use the system to explore the opposing space, ignoring the space local to them. Or they would explore their local space using the feedback window, instead of turning around. Participants when appropriate were also combining the tactics. Below are two examples of exploring using the system.

Session 4, Episode 4

Here Emily and James are both exploring the remote space using the system.

```
E. Alright (.) around you is there a shoe?
J. A shoe
E. A black sho- a black boot (.) shoe (10)
J. What behind you (or)
E. Th- there isn't (1) I can't see any shoes near
me (.) I can't see any shoes near you either
J. No
E. So I'm wondering whether my sh- the shoe is the
(.) potential red herring
```

Here participants are moving their focus windows systematically over the remote environment, zooming into some objects to get more detail as they go. Although some objects were deliberately occluded from the system, this tactic of relying on the system correctly brings them to conclude that the shoe is the extra object that they must draw. This is an example of system reliance described later.

Session 2, Episode 4

Here Harry has found some writing off a poster by directing Jenny's focus window towards it.

```
H. I've got a board that says supported by CBI
voice of business
J. °Ah: ok:°
H. Ah (.) I think its right behind me (1) there
(1.5) I think that ones there
J. Ah:: yeah y- y- yeah
H. Is [ that it?
J.    [ Um
J. I- I've got (.) I can see CBI in: the if I
magnify it
H. Right yeah yeah
```

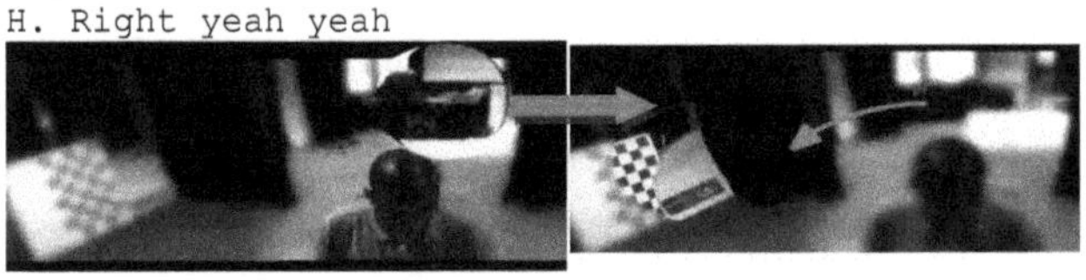

Harry spots the "CBI" writing from the feedback window, without looking behind himself. He then directs Jenny towards the poster by dragging her focus window over to it. When Jenny recognises the object Harry then opts to ask Jenny whether it is the correct image (rather than turning around). It seems here that Harry would rather rely on the system than actually look behind himself at the poster, even to the extent that he asks Jenny to identify the object using the zoom functionality at her disposal.

Directing

The task required two different scenarios for directing attention. Either an object was found locally, so participants would need to direct remote attention towards that object. Or vice-versa if an object was found in the remote space (using the system) participants would need to direct a remote users attention to that object. Although it might be possible to avoid one or the other via carefully exchanging responsibilities, all groups demonstrated using both. Depending on how the object was found, the study revealed a multitude of tactics appropriate to either local or remote directing. For instance if a local object is found that is portable, often attention was drawn by simply picking that object up. Additionally, participants sometimes opted to explore their local space using the system rather than physically, so attention could easily be drawn by moving a remote focus window. Below are some examples.

Session 1, Episode 2

Here Lucy believes she has found a shoe on the desk near John, but it is partially occluded and the system doesn't provide enough fidelity for her to recognise. She wants John to look at the desk to check. This is an example of directing remote attention towards a local object.

```
L. Is that a boot? (3)
J. Where are you looking?
L. On the desk
J. °er::° (1) so that's right left so it's near
the board (3) I can't see one on there, there's a
bag (.) on the desk (2)
L. Yeah
```

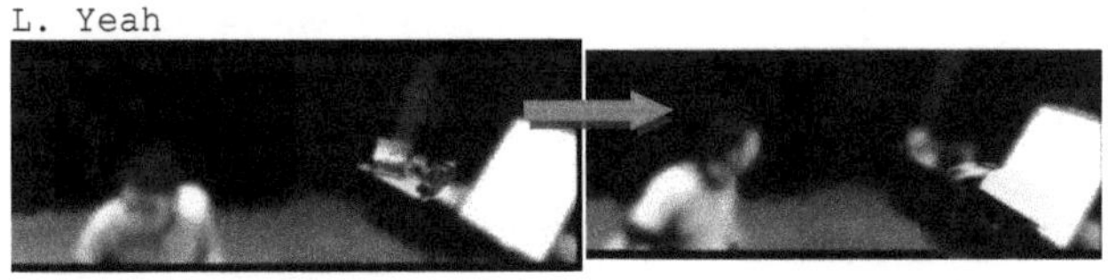

Although John does ask Lucy to describe the location of the shoe "on the desk", he still opts to find it using the feedback window. Here there are clear screen to physical space conversion problems verbalised by John as he calculates the position of the desk. As John states 'so that's right left so' he is turning is head, acting the calculation process. Later he finds the desk and tells Lucy that there is no shoe. This episode also shows that Lucy has implicitly pointed to the desk in the process of attempting to identify the shoe. It's clear that John is using the feedback window in order to identify the shoe location, rather than the verbal description.

Session 5, Episode 2

Sarah has found one of the objects embedded in a poster behind her, so Graham must take a snapshot of it. This is an example of directing remote attention towards local objects.

S. So, I need something from you as well [Graham], so behind me there is this poster, has two green bits, er, I need the bottom one that says CBI (.) the voice of business
S. I think yeah I think you're you're about right no- there yeah (0.5) that should be correct
G. Ok (.) got that
S. Yep (.) ok

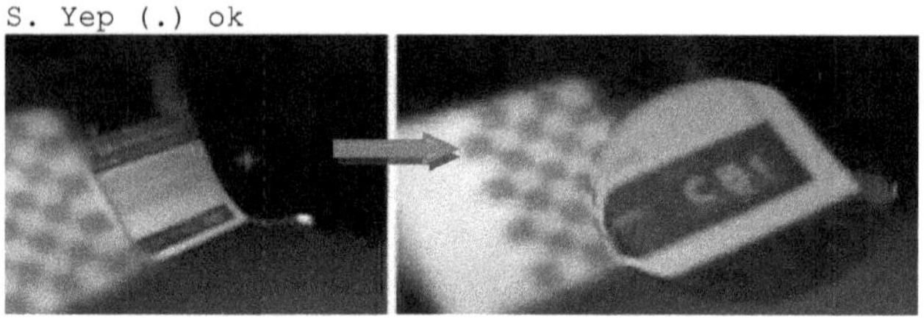

After the initial description Graham understands the general area that Sarah means, so his focus window moves over to the poster and scans around to find the specific writing. Sarah now plays a sort of "hot and cold" game to direct Graham onto the writing, encouraging him when his focus window gets nearer. Graham didn't need to relay information back to Sarah on whether he had located the poster, Sarah was watching the feedback window and thus was aware that Graham was searching the poster area. This is an example of implicitly pointing. Had there been enough resolution for Graham to recognise the poster, he needn't have moved his focus window over to it. Further, recognition via resolution is not sufficient to gain a mutual understanding of which object is correct. Although Graham has received some verbal directions he could only guess exactly which object is in question without confirmation.

Session 4, Episode 2

Emily has spotted one of the objects behind her and directs James over to it in order to take a snapshot. She does so by manipulating James' focus window.

E. E:rm (0.5) so (.) behind me (.) I know where one is ones behind me (.) where I've l- moved my marker where it says light (1.5)
J. Oh yeah
E. Can you take a picture of that?
J. Yep (.) er:: (.) done it yep

Here Emily opts to find the object using the system, even though it might have been easier to turn around and look. After she locates the object, she direct James' attention by manipulating his focus window. James then records a snapshot and verbally confirms that he has done so. As the object was found using the system, it was easy for Emily to manipulate the remote focus window to direct attention, avoiding the need to physically locate the object.

Recording

Recording an object means lining up the focus window over the object and taking a snapshot. If the object was visible and accessible, there were no recorded problems in recording the object. As described, sometimes the object required bringing into the camera view to record, and here participants needed to 'frame' the object to be recorded.

Session 3, Episode 4

Rachel has her focus window already over the monitor behind Steve, she is waiting for a parrot to appear. Meanwhile Steve spots the owl image sheet and brings it into the camera view for Rachel to record.

R. [OK I'll] get that I'll get that when it comes up next
S. [Umm]
S. OK (.) Yeah I've got I've got (1) where's my crosshair (0.5) oh there you go
S. [(like that)] is that in the right place?
R. [°Ah ok°]
R. Yeah, perfect

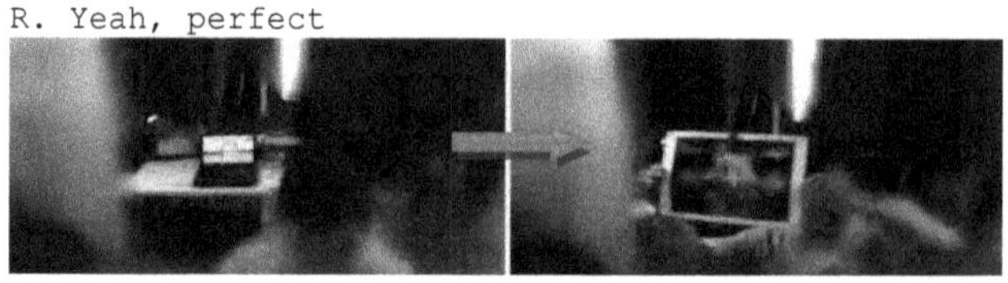

Steve knew that Rachel was waiting for the parrot on the monitor behind him, and so places the image sheet of the owl directly over her focus window. Rachel doesn't need to move her focus window at all to record both images, she takes a snapshot when Steve holds the image and again later to record the parrot. In waiting for the parrot, Rachel doesn't really intend to point at the monitor, but is implicitly doing so. Steve uses this information to position the owl sheet over her view.

DISCUSSION

The implementation of this focus-in-context video system means that it remains scalable in principle, with multi-point access to the connected spaces available, in contrast to PTZ implementations [24]. Sets of focus windows are then controllable in a distributed fashion, with both the consumer and the server of the views able to move their position. Control remains fast, with no observable latency in moving focus windows over the context background, while this has only been tested with two nodes and four focus areas at present. Although relatively expensive mid-range cameras were used for CamBlend at this stage, much lower cost cameras would principally work with the software infrastructure, resulting in a cost-effective but high-quality video collaboration tool, which can be flexibly deployed. The potential bandwidth savings of the focus-in-context video approach are significant, this test setup uses in the order of 15x fewer pixels in comparison to streaming the entire image. Even though available bandwidth is constantly increasing, such bandwidth savings remain attractive. This is especially so when one considers that many more than three cameras might be assembled resulting in ultra-high resolution live imagery, only sub-sections of which ever need to be streamed, while those sub-sections remain in context of the scene.

As interview and video data have highlighted, CamBlend supported the study task well. Across six pairs the overall task was broken down into the four mentioned activities, for which different strategies were found. Analysis of system use showed that participant conversation tended to transcend the tools with participants talking about the objective at hand. The data collected also allows a brief reflection on some key aspects of interaction.

Reconciling focus and context views

CamBlend provides multiple views into the connected remote space, one context overview and multiple lenses visually imbedded in this overview. The analysis of system use of this focus-in-context video system has shown that this strategy does seem to address the previously reported interactional issues with view reconciliation [9]. It also confirms previous work emphasising the importance of providing legible links between overview and detail views [24]. With CamBlend, those links are established by leaving the detailed view within the context itself. The success of this strategy is evident in the fact that no examples of problems with focus and context view reconciliation can be found in interview or video analysis. To the contrary, some participants identified the integration of detail view into context view as a potential problem, as it was difficult to tell them apart, unless the detail view was zoomed. The visual manipulations on the background image (saturation, de-noising) were partly introduced to avoid this confusion.

Object Referencing

In referencing local or remote objects during the study task, there were two principal observations.

Line of sight

It has been noted that during video collaboration, when making reference to remote resources users often attempt to point 'at screen' into the remote space [15]. The spatial inconsistencies of video break line of sight and thus cause interactional problems. CamBlend does not attempt to repair the video to restore line of sight, in fact displaying the whole panorama accentuates these problems via representation of a much more extreme aspect ratio and FOV. A gesture towards the side of the screen refers to an object sharply to the side of the remote participant, but looks like a gesture pointing roughly forwards.

However, it seems that the flexibility and speed of the focus windows allowed physical 'at-screen' pointing to be all but replaced. This seems to be well represented during the study, where participants never attempted to point 'at-screen' to reference remote objects. By looking into the remote space, participants implicitly indicated their focus of attention, as this was visible in the feedback window. Equally where participants pointed to resources locally, the feedback window enabled this to happen in reverse. This allowed participants to point at artefacts in their physical space. The episode shown in Session 3, Episode 6 demonstrates the success of this mechanism, highlighting the system internal line of sight established in CamBlend. The focus window establishes line of sight between participant and remote artefact. This line of sight is legible and can be acted upon by the remote participant via the feedback window.

Conversion Problems

In addition to a view into the connected remote space, CamBlend also provides a perspective on the local space via the feedback window. All groups demonstrated the process of finding an object physically that was referred to on-screen inside this feedback window. In doing so participants sometimes had problems converting between the physical and screen spaces, shown most clearly inside Session 1, Episode 2. These conversion problems are reflected in similar issues surrounding the motivations for shared visual spaces [6], in that separate interaction spaces trigger delays or confusion in reconciling these views.

During the interviews some participants seemed aware of these problems, and gave one of two tactics for coping. Participants would rely exclusively on either the physical or screen spaces, and try to ignore the other. What is interesting is that the task dictated these tactics would be unlikely to work, via a combination of occluded objects forcing physical exploration, and fixed objects forcing system exploration (even if first found physically a participant would still need to take a snapshot). Further, in some interviews participants were pushed to recall examples of a conversion, successful or not, and they struggled to do so. This suggests that although participants were aware of the difficulty (by recalling a mechanism to cope), they weren't aware that it was a problem. What we suggest is that groups naturally converged into shared tactics for referencing objects, tactics more complex than exclusively screen or physical spaces. This seems to be broadly backed up by the video analysis when all episodes for a group are considered together.

Reflection on application areas

Although the analysis categories (informing, exploring, directing, recording) were chosen to reflect the arrangement of participants activities to complete the study task, here it is briefly shown how each of these categories relate to application areas suggested in the focus groups and beyond. *Informing*, or describing an item to a remote participant is common when establishing a mutual understanding of objects local to one participant, useful for example in the connected classroom scenario supporting creative sessions. *Exploring* is especially useful in observation scenarios where remote users may be unable to help, as for example in the example of connecting to an archaeological dig site. *Directing* remote attention has application areas where attention could be focused on either side of the collaboration, for example the teacher directing attention to a particular student group. Finally *recording* finds application when the review of data is critical, as in the example of CamBlend as a tool to record dance classes and to review progress. In addition to those, the current system design has also highlighted other potential application areas, such as CCTV, flexible video broadcasting and expert-helper scenarios. We acknowledge that some of these applications would require a substantially different system design and that our study results would not directly be transferrable to those.

CONCLUSION

CamBlend is a lightweight video collaboration tool, which addresses the aforementioned technical problems of scalability, speed and view reconciliation involved in increasing the FOV of video in a novel way. The study of CamBlend highlighted a number of successful examples of object referencing using the pointing tools provided. These included pointing implicitly, explicitly and referencing objects in either local or remote spaces. The problem of screen to physical space transition is identified and a number of tactics, which participants used to cope with the scenario, are highlighted.

ACKNOWLEDGMENTS

We thank all study participants and gratefully acknowledge support from the EPSRC through grants EP/P504252/1 and EP/J006688/1, the Creativity Greenhouse project.

REFERENCES

1. NVidia CUDA. http://www.nvidia.com/cuda.
2. Baudisch, P., Good, N., Bellotti, V., Schraedley, P., Keeping things in context: a comparative evaluation of focus plus context screens, overviews, and zooming, *Proc. CHI '02*, ACM (2002). 259-266
3. Birnholtz, J., Ranjan, A., Balakrishnan, R., Providing Dynamic Visual Information for Collaborative Tasks: Experiments With Automatic Camera Control, *Human-Computer Interaction 2010*, 261-287
4. Cutler, R., Rui, Y., Gupta, A., Cadiz, J.J., Tashev, I., He, L., Colburn, A., Zhang, Z., Liu, Z. and Silverberg, S. Distributed meetings: A meeting capture and broadcasting system, in *Proc. ACM Multimedia* (2002)
5. Fussell, S. R., Setlock, L.D., Yang, J., Ou, J., Mauer, E. M., & Kramer, A., Gestures over video streams to support remote collaboration on physical tasks. *Human-Computer Interaction 2004,* 273-309
6. Fussell, S.R., Kraut , R.E., and Siegel, J., Coordination of communication: effects of shared visual context on collaborative work, in *Proc. CSCW'00* ACM (2000)
7. Foote, J. and Kimber, D., FlyCam: Practical panoramic video and automatic camera control. in *Multimedia '00* (2000), 487-488.
8. Gaver, W.W., The affordances of media spaces for collaboration, in *Proc. CSCW'92*. ACM (1992), 17-24.
9. Gaver, W.W., Sellen, A., Heath, C and Luff, P., One is not enough: multiple views in a media space, in *Proc. INTERACT '93 and CHI '93.* ACM (1993), 335-341.
10. Heath, C. and Luff, P., Disembodied conduct: communication through video in a multi-media office environment, in *Proc. CHI '91,* ACM (1991), 99-103.
11. Heath, C., Hindmarsh, J., and Luff, P., Video in Qualitative Research, *SAGE.*
12. Heath, C., Knoblauch, H., and Luff, P., Technology and social interaction: the emergence of 'workplace studies'. In *The British Journal of Sociology,* (2000), 299-320.
13. Hindmarsh, J., Fraser, M., Heath, C., Benford, S and Greenhalgh, C, Object-focused interaction in collaborative virtual environments. *TOCHI '00*, ACM (2000), 477-509.
14. Hinds, P.J and Keisler, S. Distributed Work: *MIT Press.*
15. Isaacs, E.A., and Tang, J.C., What video can and cannot do for collaboration: A case study. *Proc. MULTIMEDIA '93* (1993), ACM, 199-206.
16. Jordan, B and Henderson, A., Interaction Analysis: Foundations and Practice. in *Journal of Learning Sciences,* PARC (1994), 39-103
17. Keahey, T.A., and Robertson, E.L., Techniques for non-linear magnification transformations. In *Proc. Inf. Vis. '96*, IEEE (1996), 38-45
18. Kuzuoka, H., Oyama, S., Yamazaki, K., Suzuki, K and Mitsuishi, M., GestureMan: a mobile robot that embodies a remote instructor's actions, in *Proc. CSCW '00.* ACM (2000), 155-162
19. Luff, P., Yamashita, N., Kuzuoka, H and Heath, C, Hands on hitchcock: embodied reference to a moving scene, In *Proc. CHI '11,* ACM (2011), 43-52
20. Luff, P., Heath, C., Kuzuoka, H., Hindmarsh, J., Yamazaki, K and Oyama, S, Fractured Ecologies: Creating Environments for Collaboration. In *Human-Computer Interaction 2003,* 51-84
21. Mantei, M.M., Baecher, R.M., Sellen, A.J., Buxton, W.A.S., Milligan, T and Wellman, B., Experiences in the Use of a Media Space. In *CHI '91.* ACM (1991)
22. O'hara, K., Kjeldskov, J., and Paay, J., Blended interaction spaces for distributed team collaboration. In *TOCHI '11*. ACM (2011)
23. Ranjan, A., Birnholtz, J, P., and Balakrishnan, R., An exploratory analysis of partner action and camera control In a video-mediated collaborative task. *Proc. CSCW '06,* ACM (2006), 403-412.
24. Yamaashi, K., Cooperstock, J, R., Narine, T., Buxton, W., Beating the limitations of camera-monitor mediated telepresence with extra eyes, in *Proc. CHI '06.* ACM (1996), 50-5

Swift: Reducing the Effects of Latency in Online Video Scrubbing

Justin Matejka, Tovi Grossman, George Fitzmaurice
Autodesk Research, Toronto, Ontario, Canada
{*firstname.lastname*}@autodesk.com

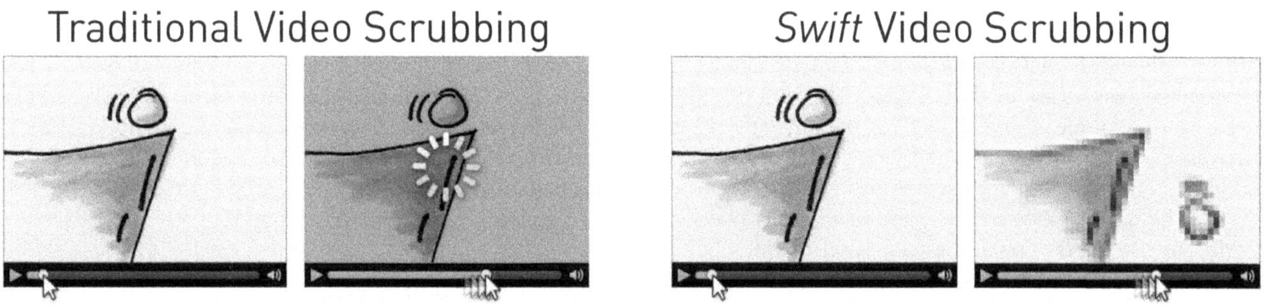

Figure 1. An illustration of the scrubbing behavior of a traditional streaming video player and the *Swift* player. With the *Swift* system a quick-to-download low resolution version of the video is displayed while scrubbing.

ABSTRACT
We first conduct a study using abstracted video content to measure the effects of latency on video scrubbing performance and find that even very small amounts of latency can significantly degrade navigation performance. Based on these results, we present *Swift*, a technique that supports real-time scrubbing of online videos by overlaying a small, low resolution copy of the video during video scrubbing, and snapping back to the high resolution video when the scrubbing is completed or paused. A second study compares the *Swift* technique to traditional online video players on a collection of realistic live motion videos and content-specific search tasks which finds the *Swift* technique reducing completion times by as much as 72% even with a relatively low latency of 500ms. Lastly, we demonstrate that the *Swift* technique can be easily implemented using modern HTML5 web standards.

Author Keywords
Video; Video Navigation; Online Streaming

ACM Classification Keywords
H.5.m [Information interfaces and presentation (e.g., HCI)]: Graphical User Interfaces.

INTRODUCTION
Streaming online video players have given internet users the instant gratification of watching a video play immediately, as opposed to the previous workflow of downloading a video and then viewing it using a local player. With recent advancements in both internet download speeds, and faster CPUs, the quality of streaming videos has improved drastically. High definition videos are now standard, and full length television shows and movies are readily available on sites such as Netflix and Hulu.

Although very popular, streaming videos have limitations when it comes to navigation. In most desktop media players, the user is able to "scrub" the video by moving a slider along the timeline and the current frame of the video updates in real-time. In contrast, streaming video players request new frames from the server to update the view, introducing a significant amount of latency. This latency makes the scrubbing experience very choppy at best, and for many players, the view does not start updating until after the mouse button has been released (Figure 1).

For many usage scenarios, the ability to scrub video timelines is critical to the viewing experience. For example, a user may wish to find a particular scene in a movie, look for when a particular operation was performed in a software tutorial video, or skip past an advertisement while watching a sporting event. While scrubbing is sometimes enabled once a video is cached, fully downloading a video can take a considerable amount of time. Furthermore, it might not be desirable, or even possible, to cache a large video file for reasons such as the bandwidth costs incurred by the server and/or user, or the storage capacity of the playback device.

Many aids for navigating videos have been explored [21]. However, most require additional visual elements such as summary storyboards [25] or video analytics [22], and few enhance the ubiquitous scrubbing behavior. Furthermore, most enhancements are designed for desktop systems and assume random access availability to the video. Despite the ubiquity of online video players, we are unaware of any research to date which has empirically measured the user performance impact of latency during video scrubbing.

In this paper, we first conduct a study to measure the impact of latency in a controlled abstract environment. We find that even extremely short delays (20ms) can cause significant difficulty when navigating videos, and with latencies users typically experience (1000ms or more), seeking tasks can take up to 10 times longer.

To combat these observed effects of latency, we present *Swift*, a technique that supports real-time scrubbing of streaming videos even in high latency conditions. *Swift* works by overlaying a small, low resolution copy of the video during video scrubbing, and snaps back to the high resolution video when the scrubbing is completed or paused. The technique has no impact on the user interface controls or layout. By fixing the resolution and number of video frames to the number of input pixels on the timeline slider, the size of the low-resolution copy can be kept at a fixed size of approximately 1MB, regardless of the duration or size of the original source video.

In a second study, using real video content, we evaluate *Swift*, against video navigation with traditional browsers in 20ms and 500ms latency environments. Swift significantly decreased task completion times, in some cases by 72%. After providing an analysis of the results, we demonstrate a simple HTML5 implementation of *Swift*. Based on these results, we believe the *Swift* technique can be integrated into today's online video players, and significantly improve the user's viewing experience.

RELATED WORK

Video Navigation

There have been many projects exploring improvements to video navigation. A number of approaches have looked at using the traditional timeline slider augmented with different dynamics such as the AV-ZoomSlider [12], which uses the additional dimension of the y-axis to enable more precise control. The PVSlider [20] provides an elastic scrubbing experience for more fluid control.

Several systems have been developed to augment the traditional video timeline with additional graphical elements and information. The Video Explorer [22] uses additional timeline strips to visualize low level video features. Bailer et. al.'s SVAT [2] visualizes scene boundaries and motion events on the timeline. Chronicle [8] uses additional rows on the timeline to display document workflow events based on captured metadata. Joke-o-mat HD [14] and emoPlayer [4] both support navigating videos based on user contributed metadata.

An alternate way to get an overview of an entire video is through a collection of scene thumbnails [11, 25]. Truong and Venkatesh [24] provide a thorough summary and classification of work in both the creation of thumbnails and video skimming. This includes techniques that display thumbnails hierarchically [6], thumbnails lists [3], and fisheye views of thumbnails [5].

While these described techniques all aid video navigation in interesting ways, they typically require a local cache of the video, or its thumbnails, to function, and do not support real-time scrubbing in an online environment.

Existing Deployed Technologies

The internet is full of sites with streaming video players and we tested over 30 unique implementations. The most popular video streaming site, YouTube, currently hosts more than 350 million streaming videos. While scrubbing, the YouTube player does not update the position in an un-cached video until the mouse button is released. This general interaction model is representative of the majority of streaming players we have found.

Several players such as the ones found on Hulu and ESPN.com support enhanced video navigation by providing a thumbnail preview while hovering over the timeline. These thumbnails are not pre-loaded so they suffer from the same latency issues as the full video, but they do present an interesting interaction model.

The PC version of the Netflix streaming video player is the only example we have found to support real-time scrubbing. When the user begins scrubbing, sequential thumbnail images are displayed in the center of the screen, and update in real-time as the user scrubs (Figure 2).

Figure 2. PC version of the Netflix streaming video player.

We are unaware of any archived publication or white paper describing its behavior, and so its technical implementation is unknown. However, the real-time scrubbing seems to only be enabled once a full set of thumbnails has been downloaded. For some movies, the scrubbing is enabled within 10 seconds, however, for others, we found it could take several minutes before the real-time scrubbing begins to work, even with a high-speed broadband connection.

Despite its limitations, the Netflix player should be considered closely related to *Swift*. That said, *Swift* does contribute a scalable technique, where real-time scrubbing only requires 1MB of data, regardless of the source video resolution or duration. Furthermore, we demonstrate a simple implementation using modern web standards consisting of less than 30 lines of javascript and HTML5 code, and provide a public dissemination of its implementation and related technical details to the research community.

DEFINITIONS

Before describing the first experiment, we will outline definitions for the two main factors being tested.

Simulated Network Latency

All computer systems have some amount of inherent input latency. Using the technique from [17] we calculated the average delay between when the mouse is moved to when the cursor actually moves on the screen to be 37ms. For our video navigation tasks we refer to *simulated network latency* (or *sn-latency*) as the time between when a frame is requested by the user and when the frame is displayed on the screen, less the inherent system latency. With an online video player this is the time it takes to request a new play position from the server, and have the server transfer enough frames to buffer the video sufficiently to begin playing again. While the effects of latency on some interaction tasks has been studied [16, 18], its impact on video scrubbing is unknown.

Classification of Video Types for Navigation Tasks

We restrict our evaluation to tasks where the user knows what scene they are looking for, and would recognize when they have successfully navigated to it. Within such a task, a user's knowledge of the target video content and scene organization provides information and orientation which may affect scrubbing behaviors. Thus we found it useful to divide videos into three main *video type* categories:

Sequential

In a *sequential* video, the scenes have a natural order which is known to the user. It is therefore possible for a user to estimate where the target scene is, and to "jump" to the approximate point in the timeline. During the navigation task the user is able to tell if they have gone too far, or not far enough, and also judge how far away from the target they are. An example of a sequential video seeking task is finding a particular time in a televised sporting event: to find "the beginning of the 4th quarter" in a basketball game, the user could jump to about 75% into the video and then looking at the game clock, adjust accordingly.

Ordered

With an *ordered* video it is possible for a user to tell if they are before or after the target scene, but not how far away they are. An example would be navigating through a commercial break to get back to the television show. After navigating, the user would know if they have gone too far, or, if they still see a commercial, had not gone far enough. Without real-time scrubbing, the optimal strategy for this type of task may be a binary search of the timeline, reducing the search space by half in each step.

Random

In a video with a completely *random* ordering, the user does not know where the target scene is likely to be located in the timeline, and has no cues as to where the target sits in relation to their current position. There are no particularly intelligent strategies for this type of task; the user is forced to try and look at each scene. A primary example of this type of task is for a user to find a particular scene in a movie which they have never seen before.

The exact same video could have different navigation characteristics for different users; finding a scene in a movie that one person is unfamiliar with would be a *random* searching task. For a person who is very familiar with the move, it would be more of a *sequential* seeking task. These classifications also do not necessarily have hard boundaries between them. For example a sporting event which only displays the clock some of the time could present a primarily *sequential* seeking task, but the segments without a clock present would represent a *random* seeking sub-task. Even though the distinctions are not always clear, this categorization of video types will be useful when studying navigation techniques over a range of potential scene finding scenarios.

EXPERIMENT ONE

To better understand how latency affects video navigation tasks we conducted a controlled experiment. Specifically, we wanted to test video scrubbing performance while navigating to a target scene with varying levels of latency and for differing video types. To ensure a controlled environment, this experiment was carried out with abstracted video content simulating three types of videos: *sequential*, *ordered* and *random*, and two different scene counts to simulate shorter (*12*) and longer (*24*) videos.

Participants and Apparatus

Twelve paid volunteer participants (8 female) were recruited though an online classified posting. Users had varying levels of computer experience, with daily usage ranging between 2 and 10 hours.

The experiment was conducted in a private office on a 3.16GHz quad-core desktop computer running Windows 7 64-bit Edition. The graphics card was an nVidia Quadro FX 5600 and was driving a 24" Dell LCD monitor with a resolution of 1920 by 1200.

Design

A repeated measures within-participant design was used with the independent variables being *video type* (*sequential, ordered, random*), *number of scenes* (*12, 24*), and *sn-latency* (*1000ms, 500ms, 100ms, 20ms, 0ms, 0ms-lowRes*). The ordering of *sn-latency* and *number of scenes* were counterbalanced and *video type* was randomized. A fully crossed design resulted in 36 combinations of variables.

Each participant performed the experiment in one session lasting approximately one hour. The study was divided into two blocks, with each condition run 4 times per block.

Video Player

A custom video player with a playback resolution of 800 by 600 pixels was used for the study. The player was programmed as a stand-alone application to allow for precise control of the latency, and to support high frequency logging capabilities. The interface was intentionally simple, with just the video playback window and a timeline slider (Figure 3). In the *0ms* condition, dragging the slider along the timeline would update the video frame to the appropriate location immediately (less the 37ms inherent system input latency). In the other conditions, the frame would only update if the slider remained stationary for the condition's associated latency duration. It was not necessary to mouse-up to trigger the update, dwelling in place was sufficient. During the latency period, the screen would display a "Loading" message on top of the previous frame to help the user understand the player's state. Playback was disabled, as we were only testing seeking behaviors.

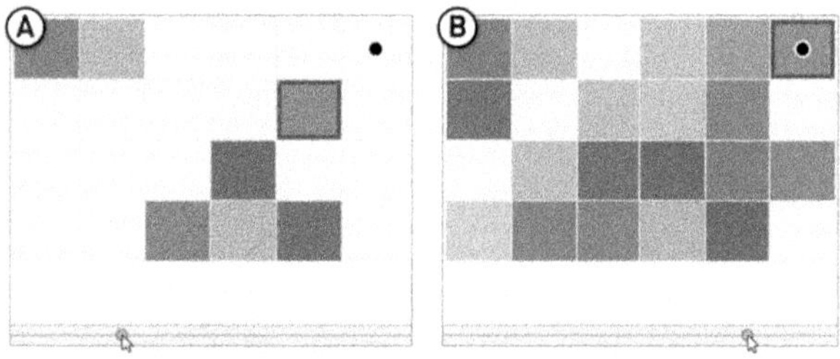

Figure 3. Video player used in the experiment near the beginning of a trial (A) and at the target scene (B). The most recently drawn square, representing the current scene, was outlined with a wide border. The goal scene is marked with a black dot.

Simulated Network Latency

Five different simulated network latency levels were used for the first study ranging from 1000ms down to 0ms. The *1000ms* condition is typical of what we have observed on a fast (~18MB/s) network when viewing a 480p video on YouTube. When viewing 720p content the delay is generally more than 2000ms. We also tested shorter delays of 500ms and 100ms, which are both faster than what we have been able to achieve on any deployed network, but might be conceivably possible. We also tested with 20ms as an approximate "theoretical limit" based on the average *network* latency, or ping times, of 20 to 40ms.

The *0ms* condition was included to simulate the baseline scenario, of watching the video on a desktop player capable of real-time scrubbing, or an online player once the video has been fully cached. To begin to understand the effects of video resolution on navigation tasks, the final condition (*0ms-lowRes*) was the same as the *0ms* condition, except that while scrubbing the timeline, the frame displayed was a 64 by 48 pixel version of the current frame which had been scaled up to 800 by 600 and bilinearly smoothed. In particular, we hoped to see if switching between a crisp view and a blurry view of the same video content would affect navigation performance.

Video Content

The video content for the study was a grid of procedurally generated squares that faded in one at a time. There were an equal number of squares as *number of scenes* (i.e., 12 squares for *12* scenes, and 24 squares for *24* scenes). During each scene a different square would be filled in. To make it easier to determine which was the last square to be drawn (i.e. the current "scene"), the most recently drawn square was outlined with a 10px wide border (Figure 3). The timeline was divided into equally spaced segments so each scene was of the same length. Because playback was disabled, the scenes, and video, did not have an absolute duration. The timeline was 800 pixels wide and each scene occupied 800/12=67 pixels in the *12 scene* conditions, and 800/24=33 pixels in the *24 scene* conditions.

To represent each of the video orderings in a controlled fashion, the order for which the squares appeared differed:

SEQUENTIAL: The squares filled in from left-to-right and top to bottom (Figure 4). This made it possible to tell how far the target scene was into the video so the user could make a large movement and "jump" to the correct area of the timeline if desired.

Figure 4. First three scenes in a *sequential* scene ordering. The order which the squares fill in is fixed.

ORDERED: For the *ordered* condition the squares were filled in a random order, and once a square filled in, it remained colored for the rest of the video (Figure 5). With this configuration the user could tell if they were not far enough (the target square was not filled), or too far (the target square was filled, but not outlined) but could not tell how far forward or back they needed to navigate.

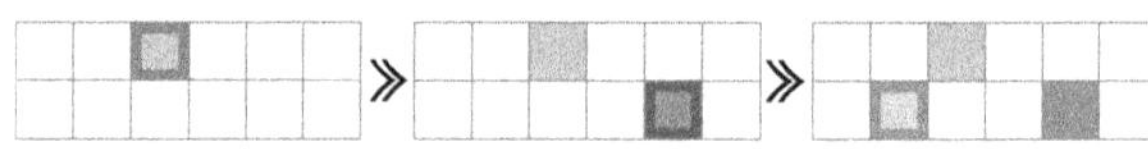

Figure 5. First three scenes in an *ordered* scene ordering. The order which the squares fill in is random.

RANDOM: With the *random* ordering, the squares would become filled in a random order, however they would only remain filled in for one scene (Figure 6). This gave no information to the user in terms of if they were before or past the target scene; they could only know if they were exactly at the target scene.

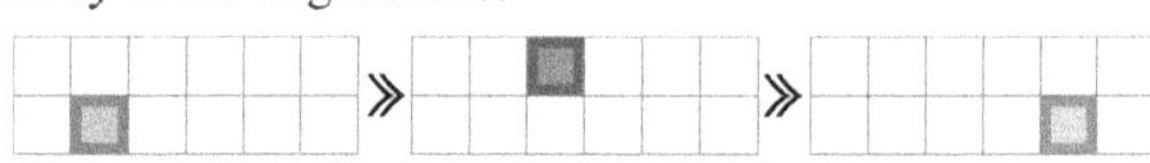

Figure 6. First three scenes in a *random* scene ordering. The order which the squares fill in is random.

Task

In all trials, the user's task was to find a target scene in the video. More specifically, the user had to find the part of the video where a target square was the last to be filled in. The target square was indicated with a black dot overlaid on the video (Figure 3). The first and last scenes were never chosen for a trial, and the same scene was never selected for consecutive trials. Additionally, the timeline was halved, and half of the trials were selected from each section.

Procedure

At the beginning of the study the examiner explained and showed the user examples of each video type. Once the differences between the video types were understood, the participants spent two minutes becoming accustomed to the different latency conditions.

Each trial began when the cursor entered the timeline slider, and at that time the dot would appear over the target square. Participants were instructed to click and hold the mouse button down while searching for the target scene and to release the button once it was found. Errors were not possible as the trial ended only once the target scene was found. Between each block users were given a short break, and the next condition was described on the screen. If the participant was unclear how the next condition would work they had the opportunity to execute several practice trials.

Results

The primary independent variable was *completion time* for each task. Repeated measure analysis of variance showed a main effect for *video type* ($F_{2,22} = 79.2$, $p < .0001$), *number of scenes* ($F_{1,11} = 39.4$, $p < .0001$), and *latency* ($F_{5,55} = 73.5$, $p < .0001$). Additionally, *video type* had a significant interaction with *number of scenes* ($F_{2,22} = 14.6$, $p < .0001$) as well as with *ns-latency* ($F_{10,110} = 22.3$, $p < .0001$).

Looking at the results for each *video type* we can see that overall the completion times increase as the latency increases (Figure 7). Of particular interest is the large jump in completion times between *0ms* and *20ms* conditions with overall mean completion times of 3210ms and 6175ms respectively ($p < .0001$). It is important to recall that the *20ms* latency condition represents a theoretical limit, and is much lower than any existing online video player that we are aware of. This result suggests that even optimal latency levels will not approximate the efficiency of real-time scrubbing capabilities.

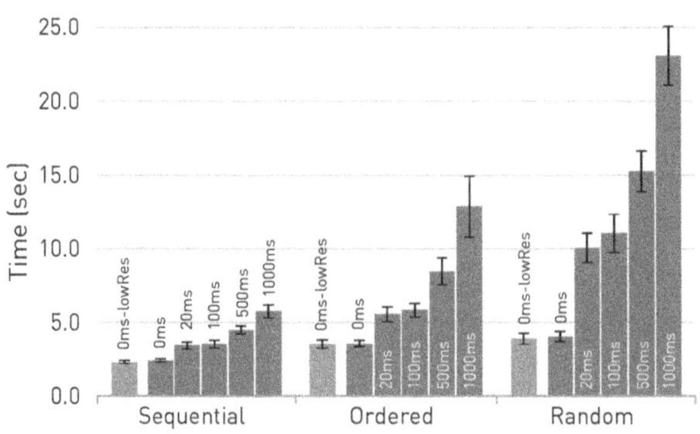

Figure 7. Average median navigation completion times for each combination of *video type* and *ns-latency.* (Note: error bars report standard error).

When we compare the *0ms* and *0ms-lowRes* conditions we see that the average *completion times* were 3.21s and 3.22s respectively. This result indicates that exploring the use of a lower resolution video while scrubbing could be a promising direction.

Figure 8 illustrates the completion times for each individual video type. It can be seen that after the initial jump from 0ms to 20ms, completion times increase in a fairly linear fashion with latency. The exception is the Random video type with 24 scenes, where the *1000ms* latency condition possesses additional difficulty.

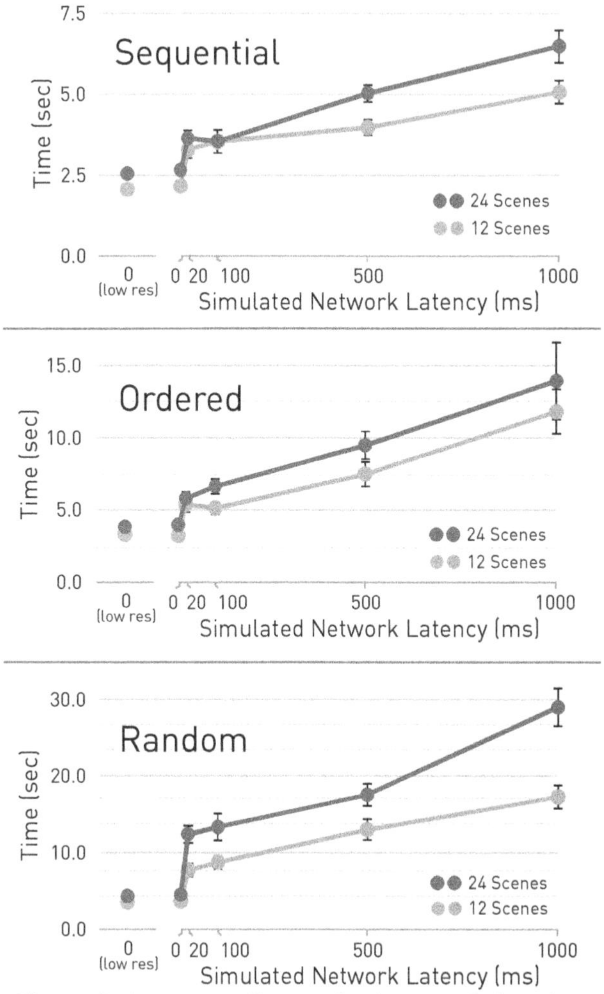

Figure 8. Average median navigation completion time divided into groups based on *video type.* (Note: error bars report standard error).

Frames Seen

In addition to completion time, it is interesting to look at how efficient users are being in their searching behaviors. One way to do this is to look at how many times a new video frame is seen by the user while completing a task. For conditions with no latency we cannot tell when a user has seen a new frame, as they are being displayed constantly. However, for the conditions with latency we can count the number of frames seen during each trial (Figure 9).

Across all *video type* and *number of scene* combinations the trend is for the number of frames seen to go down as the latency increases. This matches with the observed behavior of users being more "careful" with their movements as the penalty for each additional search step became greater. That is, when the penalty for a poor strategy is small, users were more likely to randomly search around in the video than to make a calculated decision of where to look next. So although latency is detrimental to performance times, users can partially make up some of the time in higher latency conditions with improved search strategies.

Figure 9. Average number of frames seen per trial.

Anecdotally, we found that most users were using near optimal strategies of jumping to the approximately correct position with the *sequential* videos, and linearly searching through the *random* videos. With the *ordered* videos however, few participants performed an optimal binary search of the video scenes, however, many participants performed a somewhat "partial binary" search by first seeking to near the middle of the video, and then searching linearly in one direction to find the target scene.

THE *SWIFT* TECHNIQUE

Our controlled evaluation on the effects of latency indicates a significant performance decrease when real-time scrubbing is not available. One possible way to address this limitation is to use a lower resolution version of the video that can be cached immediately and used for scrubbing. The Netflix player comes close to doing so, but its implementation details are unknown, and there is a noticeable delay before scrubbing is enabled. As such, we developed *Swift* to support *immediate* low resolution scrubbing. This technique will allow us to empirically evaluate if low-resolution scrubbing could address the performance limitations identified in our first experiment.

Overview

The idea behind *Swift* is to display a fully cached, low resolution copy of the video during video scrubbing, and snap back to the high resolution video when scrubbing is completed or paused. Since the low resolution version of the video is fully cached ahead of time, it can be scrubbed in real-time and used to find the desired scene in the video. Displaying the low resolution version overlaid onto the entire size of the high resolution version allows for spatial congruence and tracking video content while scrubbing.

User Interface

There is a large base of existing streaming videos on the internet, and a broad demographic spectrum of users who consume them [9]. As such, it is important for the navigation mechanism to be simple and have minimal impact on the existing user interfaces. Introducing advanced controls could impact ease-of-use, and hosting sites may be reluctant to adopt major changes to the interface layout.

To this end, our technique requires no changes to the traditional video player interface, and no changes to the interaction model. It would be relatively straightforward to retrofit an existing player to use our technique, and we believe any user familiar with a traditional timeline slider would be able to use the *Swift* interface on first exposure based on our results and observations from the *0ms-lowRes* condition in the first study.

Low Resolution Videos

The human visual system has an amazing tolerance to degradation in image resolution. For example, as little as 16 × 16 pixel images are suitable for face recognition [1]. Torralba et. al. found that human scene recognition on images with a resolution of 32 × 32 was 93% of the recognition at the full resolution of 256 × 256 source images, despite having only 1.5% the number of pixels as the original [23]. This findings support the idea that low resolution videos might be suitable for recognition tasks.

Increases in internet bandwidth and advances in video compression and streaming technology [10, 15] will continue to drive the movement to higher quality streaming videos. Those same advancements make lower resolution videos extremely efficient to transfer.

Video Size Analysis

The success of *Swift* depends on a low-resolution video small enough that it can be cached almost immediately after a page is loaded, but large enough to give a reasonable depiction of the video. Our hope was to use a video size of approximately 1MB, which would take less than a second to download with most broadband internet connections.

To determine appropriate parameters for the lower-resolution video, we looked at file sizes generated by a modern codec. We used the H.264/MPEG-4 AVC high profile codec, given its high quality, low file sizes, and HTML5 compatibility. Videos were converted to .mp4 files with this codec using the "mp4" option of "Miro Video Converter", a free video conversion tool. A one hour full motion movie was used for the evaluation, at 800 × 600 resolution. For the evaluation, we varied the video resolution, ranging from 320×240 to 32×24.

In addition, we varied the total number of frames encoded. A key insight is that only a subset of the video's frames need to be encoded for real-time scrubbing, equal to the pixel width of the timeline slider. For instance, a slider with a width of 600 pixels can only access one of 600 frames during scrubbing, regardless of the actual length of the video. We varied frame totals from 50 (representing low granularity scrubbing) to 1600 (representing high granularity scrubbing in a full screen playback mode). To convert the videos to a desired frame total, n, the playback speed was modified using a video editor to run exactly n seconds, and the video was then encoded at 1fps.

Figure 10 shows the resulting mp4 file sizes, at different resolutions and frame counts. It can be seen that video sizes drastically decrease as the resolution decreases. It can also be seen that there are a group of candidate parameters that result in video sizes close to 1MB. Based on these results, we choose to use a video size of 134 × 100, with a frame count of 800. This gave us the file size we wanted and the resolution seemed to provide adequate visual cues during navigation tasks. If the aspect ratio of a video was wider than 4:3, the height could be reduced instead of increasing the width, so that the file size would not increase.

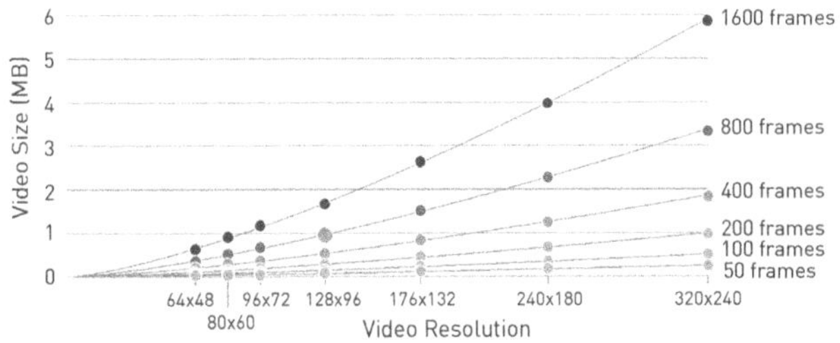

Figure 10. Encoded file sizes using varying resolutions and frame counts.

Because we fix the total frames encoded, and the frame resolution, these parameters should reduce *any* source video into the range of a 1MB file, regardless of its initial resolution, duration, or frame rate. The compressibility of the video content will have some effect on the resulting video size, however, the most complicated videos we tried still had files sizes of approximately 1MB, and for some videos we achieved sizes as small as 0.2MB.

EXPERIMENT TWO

To validate the *Swift* technique we conducted a second controlled experiment using an actual full-motion video and content-specific search tasks.

Participants and Apparatus

Twelve paid volunteer participants (7 female) were selected from the same recruiting pool as used for the first experiment. Participants reported using a computer for an average of between 2 and 14 hours per day (μ = 6.5 hours) and watching between 0 and 200 online videos per month (μ = 47 videos). The experiment was conducted in the same office and on the same machine as the first study.

Design

A repeated measures within-participant design was used with the independent variables being *video type* (*sequential, ordered, random*), target *discernibility* (*low, high*), *sn-latency* (*20ms, 500ms*), and *technique* (*traditional, swift*). The ordering of *video type*, *discernibility*, and *technique* were counterbalanced and the order of *sn-latency* was randomized. A fully crossed design resulted in 24 conditions. Each participant performed the experiment in one session and each condition was run 5 times, with the first trial discarded as practice.

For the *traditional* technique the *sn-latency* value had the same effect as in the first study (the frame would update after *x* ms), and with the *Swift* technique the low resolution version of the video was shown while scrubbing and the full resolution version would appear after the *x* ms delay.

Latency values of *20ms* and *500ms* were selected from the values used in the first study, with again the *20ms* condition serving as an approximate "theoretical limit" assuming infinite download speed and fast network ping responses and the *500ms* representing a level of latency still lower than what we have found on any existing online player.

Video Content

In video seeking tasks, the distinguishing feature of a target scene could have varying degrees of visibility. To examine this dimension, videos representing two levels of *discernibility* were selected for each *video type*; the *high discernibility* condition contained targets which were easier to recognize than the *low discernibility* conditions. We specifically chose videos that the subjects would not have seen prior to the study. Also, as described below, the experimental design tried to minimize learning effects from memorizing the video content.

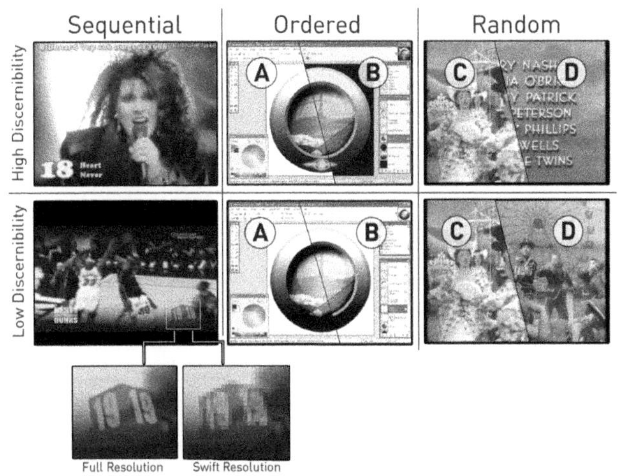

Figure 11. Frames taken from the target scenes for each *video type* and *discernibility* combination used in the study. For the *ordered* examples, (A) is from before the change occurring, and (B) is from after. In the *random* examples, (C) is a typical scene from the movie and (D) is the target scene.

SEQUENTIAL: The *sequential* videos used for the study were both "countdown" videos which presented a number of clips in decreasing numerical ranking. For the *high discernibility* condition, a countdown of the Top 25 Music Videos of 1986 was used (Figure 11). This video displayed the number of the current video prominently in the bottom left corner of the screen. Each video took the same fraction of time to play making the target size on the timeline 800/25 = 32 pixels wide. The *low discernibility* video was a countdown of the Top 50 Basketball Dunks. The decreasing numbers were shown on a slightly transparent rotating cube in the bottom right corner of the frame. The clips in this video were of varying length, but the ones used in the task each occupied 12 pixels on the timeline.

ORDERED: For the *ordered* condition we used a software tutorial video and simulated the situation where a user wants to find out how a particular piece of the design was created. Both the *high* and *low discernibility* videos were taken from a tutorial video of the drawing program Paint.NET. In the *high discernibility* condition the user needed to find when the background of the drawing changed from white to black, while in the *low discernibility* condition the user needed to find the point where the inner bevel was added to the porthole (Figure 11). Participants were not required to find the exact single frame where the change occurred, but were given a 5 pixel buffer on either side making for an 11 pixel range on the timeline.

To enable positioning the target point at different locations on the timeline, each of the *ordered* videos were constructed in three parts: a seamless loop of material before the change, a small section of video where the change occurred, and a seamless loop of material from after the change. From these "master" videos, a portion was trimmed from each end, positioning the change in the desired location; half of the trials occurred at a random location in the first half of the timeline, and the remainder occurred in the second half.

RANDOM: The video used for the *random* conditions was the 1946 movie "Till the Clouds Roll By" (Figure 11). To counter the potential learning bias of users memorizing the movie, participants were required to find one particular scene which was placed at a random location within the video. For the *high discernibility* condition the scene was the easily recognizable opening credits (taking up 32 pixels on the timeline), and for *low discernibility* the scene was a dance number where the actors were wearing red and green costumes (a 3 minute scene, taking 34 pixels).

Procedure

The examiner began by using a sample video to show each of the *technique/latency* combinations to the participant. The examiner demonstrated how each worked, and observed the user interacting with the player to ensure that they understood. The trials were ordered with *video type* at the outermost level, and *discernibility* at the second level. This created 6 occasions when a new video or target type would be introduced. At these times the examiner would verbally explain the video and target to accompany the written description presented on the screen. Four trials with a 0ms latency, full resolution video player were presented for the user to become accustomed to the new video and target content, and then the balance of the trials began.

The trial timing behavior and interaction instructions were the same as in the first study.

Results

As in the first study, the primary independent variable was *completion time* for each task. Repeated measure analysis of variance showed a main effect for *technique* ($F_{1,11}$ = 100.3, $p < .0001$) with means of 7.01s for *swift* and 12.51s for *traditional*. Additionally, significant effects were found for *video type* ($F_{2,22}$ = 91.6, $p < .0001$), *discernibility* ($F_{1,11}$ = 7.15, $p < .05$), and *sn-latency* ($F_{1,11}$ = 32.3, $p < .0001$).

Looking at the *technique* pairs for each of the *video type/discernibility/sn-latency* conditions (Figure 12) we see that in all cases the *Swift* technique performed faster than *traditional*. Post-hoc analysis shows the effect to be significant for all pairs except the *20ms* conditions in the *sequential* videos, and the *20ms/ordered/low* condition.

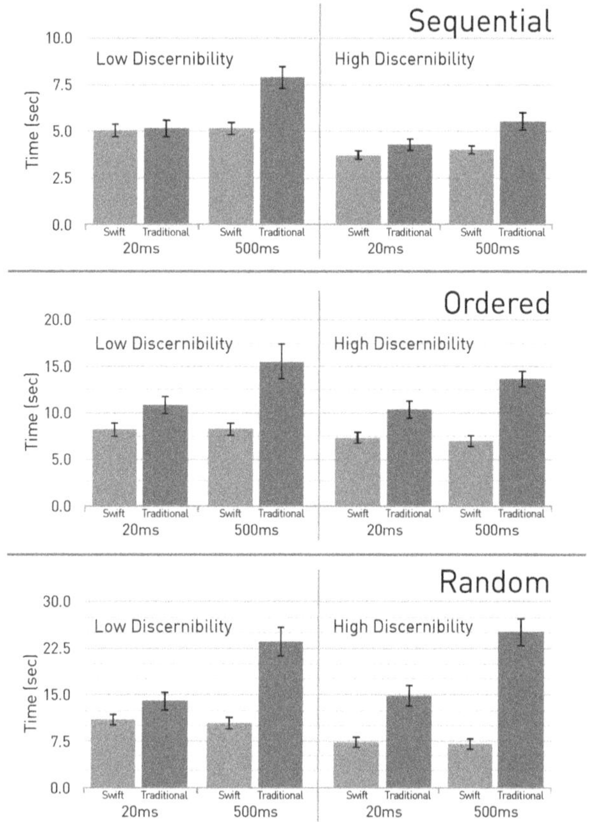

Figure 12. Results for the three video types. (Note: error bars report standard error).

It is interesting to see that for each *video type/discernibility* condition, the performance of the *Swift* technique stayed relatively constant across the two latency values. With the *traditional* player the completion times increased significantly overall from 9.9s in the *20ms* conditions to 15.1s during the *500ms* conditions ($F_{1,11}$ = 40.4, $p < .0001$). Based on the increasing trend of the results from the first study, it is reasonable to project that the gap in performance would continue to increase as the latency increased.

As in the first study, the overall task completion times increased as the tasks moved through the *video types* from *sequential* to *ordered* to *random*. As the tasks became more difficult, the benefit of the *Swift* technique became more pronounced, with *traditional* taking between 2 and 3.5 times as long as *Swift* in the *random/500ms* conditions. So as not to make the study unnecessarily hard, the target scenes were relatively long, and the movie relatively short. As the total length of the movie increases and the length of the target decreases, the benefits of *Swift* would become even more pronounced.

HTML5 IMPLEMENTATION

In this section we describe a simple HTML5 implementation of *Swift*, which demonstrates that the technique can work in today's web browsers. Two videos are rendered with the HTML5 <video> tag, with the small video above the large video, but initially invisible. The *Swift* technique is implemented with less than 20 lines of javascript code (Listing 1). A custom slider is configured to make the small-resolution video visible when sliding begins, and update its position as it slides. The position of the full resolution video is not updated until the sliding completes. The small-resolution video is not hidden until the full resolution video has finished seeking to the desired frame, resulting in a seamless transition between resolutions. Our testing of this code indicated that by default, the small and large video are downloaded in parallel, resulting in a close to instant download of the small video. However, further code could be investigated to force the initial download of the small-resolution video.

```
var small_length = 800;
var large_length = 3999.929;
var large = document.getElementById("lmovie");
var small = document.getElementById("smovie");
document.getElementById("slider").max = small_length;

function startSlide() {
  small.style.visibility = 'visible';
}

function Slide(newValue) {
  small.currentTime = newValue;
}

function endSlide() {
  var t = small.currentTime;
  large.currentTime = ((t) * (largelength)) / small_length;
}

function Seeked() {
  small.style.visibility = 'hidden';
}
```

```
<video STYLE="position:absolute;" id="lmovie" src="large.mp4"
    onseeked="Seeked()" width="800" height="600" preload controls>
</video>

<video STYLE="position:absolute; visibility:hidden" id="smovie"
    src="small.mp4" width="800" height="600" preload>
</video>

<input STYLE="position:absolute; TOP:608px; WIDTH:800px" type="range"
    id="slider" value="0" onchange="Slide(this.value)"
    onmousedown="startSlide()" onmouseup="endSlide()">
```

Listing 1. Javascript and HTML code for basic implementation of Swift technique.

Unfortunately, supported codecs and input elements still vary from one browser to the next. The listed code is fully functional in Google Chrome, and minor adjustments would be required for other HTML5 enabled browsers.

DISCUSSION AND LIMITATIONS

We have presented the empirical results from two novel experiments related to navigating online videos. Our first study demonstrated that even a small amount of network latency (20ms) can significantly hinder performance in video navigation tasks. Our second study demonstrated that real- time, low resolution scrubbing, significantly improves performance, in both high and low latency environments. The new empirical data provided by these studies will help practitioners and researchers better understand the benefits of enabling real-time scrubbing in online video players.

In addition to being beneficial in online environments, our results are applicable to desktop video players as well. Many such players still do not support real-time scrubbing, and only update their frames when a seek operation has completed. While transitioning to a lower resolution version in a desktop environment may not be necessary, this could actually improve the display rate of frames during a scrubbing operation, due to the reduced CPU load.

An important aspect of our implementation, *Swift*, is that it limits the download capacity required to enable real-time scrubbing to approximately 1MB, regardless of the source video's resolution, frame rate, and duration. As such, real-time scrubbing is available almost immediately when viewing videos with a broadband connection. We are unable to verify the Netflix implementation, but we did find it usually takes at least 10 seconds, and often several minutes before real-time scrubbing is enabled. Limiting the download size is also important as many internet providers are employing download caps and pay-per-use models.

Another advantage of *Swift* is its simple HTML5 compatibility. We demonstrated how real-time scrubbing could be enabled with less than 30 lines of HTML5 and javascript code. However, for a video sharing site to implement the technique, a service to create the low-resolution videos would be required. This should not be problematic, since sites, such as YouTube already have services to convert videos into multiple versions at different resolutions.

One potential limitation of low-resolution scrubbing is that it may be impossible to discern low-granularity details while scrubbing. Although prior research indicates very little resolution is required to identify features in images, small text fonts for example would be unreadable. Although we do not believe it is common for users to be searching for such fine grain details while navigating videos, it should be noted that low-resolution scrubbing would not aid such a task. In our future work section, we discuss possible ways for which fine grain details could be represented.

FUTURE WORK AND CONCLUSION

There are a number of other techniques in the literature that aid video navigation, although most do not focus on the scrubbing interaction. Low-resolution scrubbing could potentially be used in combination with these techniques. For example, Pongnumkul et al.'s content-aware dynamic timeline control [19] could be used while scrubbing, so that instead of frames flashing quickly by, salient scenes could be displayed at a more digestible rate. Additionally, direct manipulation video navigation systems such as DRAGON [13] and DimP [7] could utilize a low-resolution overlay.

Our implementation of *Swift* overlaid the low-resolution version of the video across the entire video player canvas. In contrast, the Netflix player displays multiple smaller thumbnails centered on the canvas. We did not become aware of the Netflix player until our studies were completed, but it would be interesting in the future to compare these two approaches. Another alternative design worth exploring is displaying a small thumbnail just above the timeline, offset from the cursor position. Some players, such as Hulu, already do this when hovering over the timeline, but do not pre-cache these thumbnails.

It would also be interesting to look at alternative low-data representations of the content while scrubbing, other than a literal down-sampling of the entire video. For example, the low resolution video could be a zoomed in view of the full resolution video, showing an area that has important details. Alternatively, metadata could be stored alongside the video and rendered instead of frames from the actual video. For example, when scrubbing through a sporting event, the current score or time remaining in the game could be overlaid. When scrubbing a movie or music video, the closed captions or lyrics could be displayed.

While our implementation used a fixed 1MB file size, our analysis of the H.264 codec performance showed that representations could be made as small as 29KB. To support low speed connections, it could be useful to have multiple low-resolution files available, and possibly progressively download and use larger versions.

Our study focused on scrubbing under uniform latency values while in practice, users may experience a range of latencies and this would be interesting to examine further.

Finally, we feel low-resolution scrubbing is particularly suited for mobile devices, as it reduces both bandwidth and CPU load. Our implementation should work with minimal modification on HTML5 supported mobile devices, such as the iPad, and it would be interesting to evaluate such an implementation.

To conclude, we have contributed empirical data demonstrating the impact of latency on online-video navigation tasks, demonstrated that low-resolution real-time scrubbing can significantly improve performance, and provided a simple HTML5 compatible implementation. Given today's prevalence of online streaming video sites, we feel these are important and timely contributions.

REFERENCES

1. Bachmann, T. (1991). Identification of spatially queatized tachistoscopic images of faces: How many pixels does it take to carry identity? *European J. of Cog. Psychology.* 3:85-103.
2. Bailer, W., Schober, C., and Thallinger, G. (2006). Video Content Browsing Based on Iterative Feature Clustering for Rushes Exploration. *TRECVID Workshop*. 230-239.
3. Chang, L., Yang, Y., and Hua, X.S. (2008). Smart Video Player. *IEEE Multimedia and Expo*. 1605-1606.
4. Chen, L., Chen, G.C., Xu, C.Z., March, J., and Benford, S. (2008). EmoPlayer: A Media Player for Video Clips with Affective Annotations. *Int. with Comp.* 20:17-28.
5. Divakaran, A. and Forlines, C. and Lanning, T. and Shipman, S. and Wittenburg, K. (2005). Augmenting Fast-Forward and Rewind for Personal Digital Video Recorders. *ICCE*. 43-44.
6. Doulamis, A.D. and Doulamis, N.D. (2004). Optimal Content-based Video Decomposition for Interactive Video Navigation. *IEEE CSVT.* 757-775.
7. Dragicevic, P., Ramos, G., Bibliowitcz, J., Nowrouzezahrai, D., Balakrishnan, R., and Singh, K. (2008). Video browsing by direct manipulation. *CHI.* 237-246.
8. Grossman, T., Matejka, J., and Fitzmaurice, G. (2010). Chronicle: Capture, Exploration, and Playback of Document Workflow Histories. *UIST.* 143-152.
9. Hanson, G. and Haridakis, P. (2008). YouTube Users Watching and Sharing the News: A Uses and Gratifications Approach. *Journal of Electronic Publishing.* 11:3.
10. Hefeeda, M. and Hsu, C.H. (2008). Rate-Distortion Optimized Streaming of Fine-Grained Scalable Video Sequences. *ACM TOMCCAP.* 1-28.
11. Holthe, O. and Ronningen, L.A. (2006). Video Browsing Techniques for Web Interfaces. *IEEE CCNC.* 1224-1228.
12. Hürst, W. (2006). Interactive Audio-Visual Video Browsing. *ACM MM.* 675-678.
13. Karrer, T., Weiss, M., Lee, E., and Borchers, J. (2008). DRAGON : A Direct Manipulation Interface for Frame-Accurate In-Scene Video Navigation. *CHI.* 247-250.
14. Janin, A., Gottlieb, L., and Friedland, G. (2010). Joke-o-Mat HD: Browsing Sitcoms with Human Derived Transcripts. *ACM MM.* 1591-1594.
15. Krasic, C. and Légaré, J.S. (2008). Interactivity and Scalability Enhancements for Quality-Adaptive Streaming. *MM.* 753-756.
16. MacKenzie, I.S. and Ware, C. (1993). Lag as a Determinant of Human Performance in Interactive Systems. *CHI.* 488-493.
17. Pavlovych, A. and Stuerzlinger, W. (2009). The Tradeoff between Spatial Jitter and Latency in Pointing Tasks. *ACM Symposium on Eng. Interactive Comp. Syst.* 33-44.
18. Pavlovych, A. and Stuerzlinger, W. (2011). Target Following Performance in the Presence of Latency, Jitter, and Signal Dropouts. *GI.* 33-44.
19. Pongnumkul, S., Wang, J., Ramos, G., and Cohen, M. (2010). Content-Aware dynamic timeline for video browsing. *ACM UIST.* 139-142.
20. Ramos, G. and Balakrishnan, R. (2003). Fluid Interaction Techniques for the Control and Annotation of Digital Video. *ACM UIST.* 105-114.
21. Schoeffmann, K., Hopfgartner, F., Marques, O., Boeszoermenyi, L., and Jose, J.M. (2010). Video browsing interfaces and applications: a review. *SPIE Reviews.* 18004:1-35.
22. Schoeffmann, K., Taschwer, M., and Boeszoermenyi, L. (2010). The Video Explorer – A Tool for Navigation and Searching within a Single Video based on Fast Content Analysis. *ACM SIGMM.* 247-258.
23. Torralba, A., Fergus, R., and Freeman, W.T. (2008). 80 million tiny images: A large data set for non-parametric object and scene recognition. *IEEE Pattern Analysis and Machine Intelligence.* 1958-1970.
24. Truong, B.T. and Venkatesh, S. (2007). Video Abstraction: A Systematic Review and Classification. *ACM TOMCCAP.* Appl. 3, 1, Article 3.
25. Uchihashi, S., Foote, J., Girgensohn, A., and Boreczky, J. (1999). Video Manga: Generating Semantically Meaningful Video Summaries. *ACM CHI.* 383-392.

Video Summagator: An Interface for Video Summarization and Navigation

Cuong Nguyen, Yuzhen Niu, and Feng Liu
Portland State University
Portland, OR 97207-0751
{cuong3,yuzhen,fliu}@cs.pdx.edu

ABSTRACT
This paper presents *Video Summagator* (*VS*), a volume-based interface for video summarization and navigation. *VS* models a video as a space-time cube and visualizes the video cube using real-time volume rendering techniques. *VS* empowers a user to interactively manipulate the video cube. We show that *VS* can quickly summarize both the static and dynamic video content by visualizing the space-time information in 3D. We demonstrate that *VS* enables a user to quickly look into the video cube, understand the content, and navigate to the content of interest.

Author Keywords
Video Visualization; Navigation; Summarization

ACM Classification Keywords
H.5.2 Information Interfaces and Presentation: User Interfaces—*Graphical User Interfaces*

INTRODUCTION
Video capturing and displaying devices are ubiquitous now. Capturing, sharing, and watching videos has become a common practice. Meanwhile, the human video interaction tools, mainly video players, remain almost unchanged in user interface design. A typical video player consists of a display window to show a video one frame at a time and a slider to navigate through the video. While such a player prevails, it is often inconvenient for video browsing. It cannot fully and quickly convey important aspects of the video content.

This paper describes *Video Summagator* (*VS*), a 3D volume-based interface for video summarization and navigation. *VS* considers a video as a cube, with time as the third dimension, as shown in Figure 1. It employs real-time volume rendering techniques to quickly visualize the cube in a 3D volume [10]. *VS* seamlessly combines video summarization and navigation. By visualizing and deforming the video cube, *VS* can quickly convey important visual content that otherwise

Figure 1. ***Video Summagator*** **visualizes a video in 3D, allowing a user to look into the video cube, and enables rapid visualization and navigation.**

would be time-consuming to find and easy to miss. *VS* allows a user to look into the video cube, summarize the video, quickly identify the content of interest and navigate to it.

The main idea behind *VS* is to visualize a time sequence in 3D. *VS* is inspired by recent research that summarizes a video clip into a 2D image [1, 5, 12]. *VS* extends the 2D display space of these methods to 3D, which provides more visualization space and better conveys space-time video content. It also extends these methods with interactive video manipulation and visualization, and handles a wider variety of camera and object motion. An important aspect of *VS* is direct manipulation for video browsing inspired by [9, 13]. But *VS* is different from these methods because it visualizes the whole video, enables a user to manipulate the entire video cube, and then navigate to the interesting part by clicking the corresponding region in the cube.

RELATED WORK
A rich literature exists on video summarization that selects a key frame sequence or key segments from an input video as a concise video representation. A good review can be found in [22]. Our work is particularly relevant to video summarization methods that represent a video clip as a still picture like panorama and action synopsis [1, 5, 12, 21]. These methods can create high-quality pictures; however, they are typically time-consuming. Compared to these methods, our work models a video as a cube and uses real-time volume rendering techniques to show the video cube in 3D. Our method supports interactive video cube manipulation and navigation. While our method sometimes cannot create final

images equal in quality to these dedicated video summarization methods, our results are good for quick video browsing.

Our work builds on video cubism research that models a video as a space-time volume and manipulates a cut surface through the volume to display the video content [11]. This method has also been extended for non-photorealistic rendering [16]. Unlike these methods, our method visualizes the whole video volume instead of the cut surface to more concisely summarize the video. Our method also allows interactive volume manipulation to visualize complex motion. Bennett and McMillan extend video cubism for convenient space-time video editing [3]. Their method does not work for visualization. Daniel and Chen visualize a video in a transparent cube or other pre-defined volume [8]. This technique has been extended to visualize human activities [4, 20]. Our work extends it to support interactive video cube manipulation to facilitate video summarization and browsing.

Our work is relevant to research on video player design. Adaptive fast-forwarding is designed for quick video browsing with predefined semantic rules [6]. The video speed and playing speed are decoupled and content analysis is adopted to play interesting shots at an intelligible speed [18]. Besides the player bar, maps have also been used for browsing domain-oriented videos, such as lecture videos [7] and tour videos [17]. Our work is inspired by direct manipulation that allows users to browse videos by directly dragging the video content and frees them from the player bar [9, 13, 14, 15]. Unlike these methods, our method enables a user to manipulate the whole video cube and navigate to the interesting part by clicking the corresponding region in the cube. Our work is also relevant to video collection browsing in 3D that reconstructs the 3D scene and uses video-based rendering to create novel views [2]. Our method is different in that it does not require 3D scene reconstruction although it visualizes the video content in 3D. Our 3D visualization typically does not correspond to the 3D scene structure.

VIDEO SUMMAGATOR

Two common types of user interaction with videos are quickly skimming through a video for overview and slowly navigating in interesting segments for detail [18]. We develop *Video Summagator* (*VS*), a 3D volume-based interface, to support both video summarization and navigation. Below we first describe how we model and render a video as a cube (volume), with time as the third dimension. We then describe how *VS* supports a user to interactively manipulate the video cube to visualize video content. We finally describe exemplary scenarios of using *VS* for summarization and navigation.

Video Cube Modeling and Rendering

We consider a video as a cube V that contains a set of voxels:

$$V = \{v_{x,y,t} | 1 \le x \le w, 1 \le y \le h, 1 \le t \le n\} \quad (1)$$

where voxel $v_{x,y,t}$ corresponds to pixel (x, y) at frame t. w and h are the video frame width and height, and n is the number of video frames. Each voxel is associated with a set of features, including the voxel's 3D coordinates, color, and

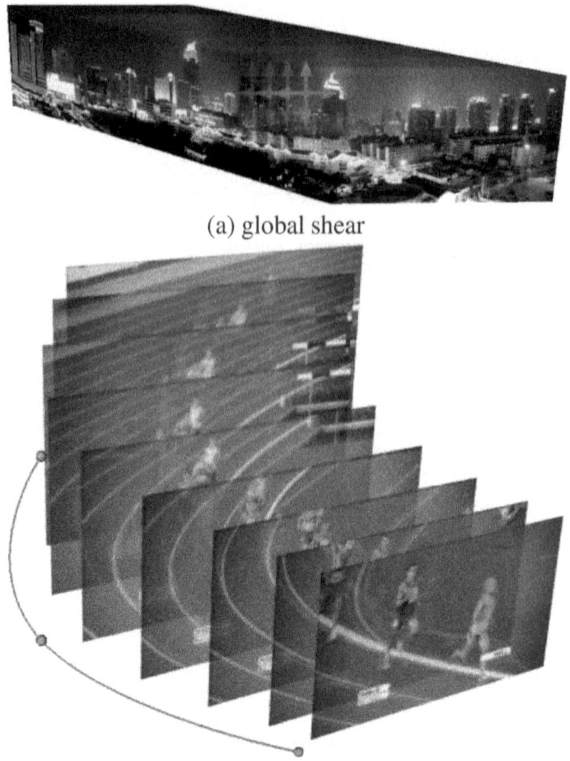

(a) global shear

(b) skeleton-based deformation

Figure 2. Video cube deformation. ***VS*** **supports a user to globally shear the video cube to create a panoramic summarization (a). The user can also use a spline interface to deform the cube to better arrange the video content in the 3D space. For the example in (b), the user define three control points (in green) to define a new spline to deform the cube.**

opacity. A voxel takes its color from the corresponding pixel. Its coordinates and opacity are controlled by a user for video summarization and navigation, as described in the next subsection. With the volume features, *VS* uses the state-of-the-art volume rendering techniques from the Visualization Toolkit [1] to quickly render the video cube.

User Interaction

A user interacts with *VS* by controlling three features of a video cube: opacity, shape, and video frame sampling.

The voxel opacity value ranges from 0 to 1, with 0 being fully transparent and 1 fully opaque. *VS* uses off-the-shelf computer vision algorithms to detect dynamic voxels and assigns higher opacity values to them than the stationary ones to clearly convey the video dynamics. *VS* allows a user to control the opacity values of the dynamic, static, and boundary voxels using a slider interface.

VS supports a user to translate, rotate, scale, and deform a video cube to clearly visualize its content. These user interactions are mapped to the coordinates of the voxels. We use the standard 3D interface for translation, rotation and scaling. We design two interactive deformation modes in *VS* . One is to shear the cube globally, as shown in Figure 2 (a). This is implemented by applying a shearing transformation to the

[1] http://www.vtk.org

(a) front view

(b) side view

Figure 3. Video summarization. Rendering a video cube from the front view often suffers from self-occlusion, as shown in (a). This problem can often be solved by simply rotating the video cube, as shown in (b).

cube. The other is skeleton-based local shearing transformation. We define a video skeleton as a spline that is perpendicular to each video frame. For the original cube, its skeleton is a line parallel to the t axis. We provide a spline-based interface for adjusting the skeleton to deform the video cube and create the output volume. As shown in Figure 2 (b), a user can create control points and move them to define a new skeleton.

VS uses two methods to select key frames, as rendering all the video frames will lead to a cluttered visualization. The first is frame-based uniform sampling (default rate 1/20). A user can control the sampling rate through a slider-based interface. Uniform sampling is used to create all the examples except Figure 5. The second is importance sampling, which is more applicable for a long video. We consider that the probability of a frame being a key frame is proportional to the amount of foreground motion. Then, we select a sequence of key frames according to this distribution [19].

VS allows a user to get a quick overview of a video typically with two steps: adjust the opacity values of the stationary and dynamic pixels to see the activities and rotate the video cube if there exists self-occlusion. Since *VS* renders the cube at an interactive speed, these two steps together take less than 5 seconds, which is typically shorter than the video length. With a preview of the video, the summarization can be further improved by adjusting the cube parameters.

Video Summarization

We now show how *VS* can be used to summarize a range of videos with different camera and scene motion.

(a) scene panorama

(b) action synopsis

Figure 4. Video summarization. A user creates scene panorama or action synopsis by globally shearing the video cube.

Static camera with moving objects. Figure 3 shows a street show video captured by an almost static camera. Dynamic voxels are assigned bigger opacity values than the background ones to reveal the magician's activity. For this video, since the camera is almost static and the magician moves in a small region, looking into the video cube suffers from self-occlusion, as shown in Figure 3 (a). This problem can be simply solved by rotating the cube, as shown in Figure 3 (b). For (b), the opacity values for the left, back, and bottom cube faces are set to a big value to better visualize the background scene.

Panning camera motion. Consider a video with the camera panning horizontally. *VS* enables a user to easily create a panorama by shearing the video cube, as shown in Figure 4 (a). For this application, the opacity values for all the voxels are uniformly set to 1. If the video contains a moving object, *VS* then creates an action synopsis that visually depicts the object activity, as shown in Figure 4 (b). For this example, the moving objects are automatically separated horizontally as the cube is being sheared. The opacity value for the back and right cube face is set to 1 to visualize the background.

Moving camera following actions. Consider a video with the camera following the athletes. *VS* supports a user to first create a mosaic image by shearing the cube globally. Then, the user refines the result with local adjustments using the skeleton-based interface, as shown in Figure 2 (b). Since *VS* provides online visual feedback, this can be done quickly. For this example, the opacity values for the voxels on the key frames are set to 0.9 and the others are set to 0.

Video Navigation

VS also provides an intuitive interface for video navigation. *VS* associates the (possibly curved) time axis with a 3D volume-based summarization. With the overview of the video, a user can quickly navigate to the interesting video segment by clicking and selecting the corresponding area in the summarization. For example, given a surveillance video, a user rotates the whole video cube so that the evolution of video content shows clearly in the display window. Looking into the video cube, the user spots the region in the cube with human activity and selects this region by drawing a line indicating the region of interest, as shown in Figure 5. *VS* maps the selected region to the time axis by projection and automatically navigates to the corresponding video segment.

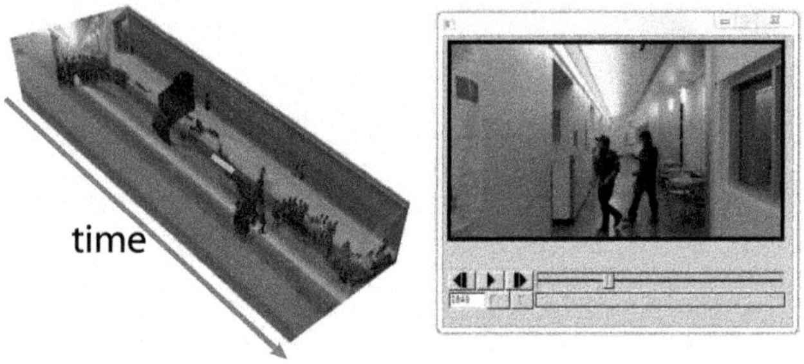

Figure 5. Video navigation. Video Summagator enables a user to look into the video cube and navigate to the interesting part by selecting the corresponding area (marked in green) in the 3D summarization.

To handle a long video, we down-sample the video frame size and adaptively sample the video frames using importance sampling. On a desktop machine with 6G memory and AMD Phenom II X6 2.8 GHz CPU, *VS* currently can allow a user to interactively manipulate a video cube with as many as 3000 key frames with frame size 480×270. Figure 5 shows a video cube that samples 1500 frames from an input video with totally 10000 frames.

CONCLUSION

This paper described Video Summagator, a 3D volume-based interface for interactive video summarization and navigation. We model a video as a space-time cube and visualize the video cube in a 3D volume using volume rendering techniques. We show that Video Summagator supports a user to manipulate the video cube to quickly summarize a video, identify the content of interest, and navigate to it.

Currently, we use off-the-shelf computer vision algorithms for moving object detection, which is sometimes not very reliable and causes visual artifacts, as shown in Figure 1. The advance in computer vision research can benefit our results. In future, we plan to extend *VS* to handle a streaming video such as webcam videos. We also plan to integrate more video analysis to better handle complex videos. Our visualization is not necessarily physically correct, so we plan to design user study to more thoroughly evaluate how people perceive the video content from our summarization.

REFERENCES

1. Assa, J., Caspi, Y., and Cohen-Or, D. Action synopsis: pose selection and illustration. *ACM Trans. Graph. 24* (July 2005), 667–676.
2. Ballan, L., Brostow, G. J., Puwein, J., and Pollefeys, M. Unstructured video-based rendering: interactive exploration of casually captured videos. *ACM Trans. Graph. 29* (2010), 87:1–87:11.
3. Bennett, E. P., and McMillan, L. Proscenium: a framework for spatio-temporal video editing. In *ACM Multimedia* (2003), 177–184.
4. Botchen, R. P., Bachthaler, S., Schick, F., Chen, M., Mori, G., Weiskopf, D., and Ertl, T. Action-based multifield video visualization. *IEEE Trans. Vis. Comput. Graphics 14* (2008), 885–899.
5. Caspi, Y., Axelrod, A., Matsushita, Y., and Gamliel, A. Dynamic stills and clip trailers. *Vis. Comput. 22* (September 2006), 642–652.
6. Cheng, K.-Y., Luo, S.-J., Chen, B.-Y., and Chu, H.-H. Smartplayer: user-centric video fast-forwarding. In *ACM CHI* (2009), 789–798.
7. Corsten, C. Dragonfly: spatial navigation for lecture videos. In *ACM CHI EA* (2010), 4387–4392.
8. Daniel, G., and Chen, M. Video visualization. In *IEEE Visualization* (2003), 409–416.
9. Dragicevic, P., Ramos, G., Bibliowitcz, J., Nowrouzezahrai, D., Balakrishnan, R., and Singh, K. Video browsing by direct manipulation. In *ACM CHI* (2008), 237–246.
10. Engel, K., Hadwiger, M., Kniss, J., Rezk-Salama, C., and Weiskopf, D. *Real-Time Volume Graphics*. 2006.
11. Fels, S., Lee, E., and Mase, K. Techniques for interactive video cubism. In *ACM Multimedia* (2000), 368–370.
12. Goldman, D. B., Curless, B., Salesin, D., and Seitz, S. M. Schematic storyboarding for video visualization and editing. *ACM Trans. Graph. 25* (2006), 862–871.
13. Goldman, D. B., Gonterman, C., Curless, B., Salesin, D., and Seitz, S. M. Video object annotation, navigation, and composition. In *ACM UIST* (2008), 3–12.
14. Karrer, T., Weiss, M., Lee, E., and Borchers, J. Dragon: a direct manipulation interface for frame-accurate in-scene video navigation. In *ACM CHI* (2008), 247–250.
15. Karrer, T., Wittenhagen, M., and Borchers, J. Pocketdragon: a direct manipulation video navigation interface for mobile devices. In *MobileHCI* (2009), 47:1–47:3.
16. Klein, A., Sloan, P.-P. J., Colburn, R. A., Finkelstein, A., and Cohen, M. F. Video cubism. In *Microsoft Research Technical Report* (2001), MSR-TR-2001-45.
17. Pongnumkul, S., Wang, J., and Cohen, M. Creating map-based storyboards for browsing tour videos. In *ACM UIST* (2008), 13–22.
18. Pongnumkul, S., Wang, J., Ramos, G., and Cohen, M. Content-aware dynamic timeline for video browsing. In *ACM UIST* (2010), 139–142.
19. Press, W., Teukolsky, S., Vetterling, W., and Flannery, B. *Numerical Recipes: The Art of ScientiŒ Computing*. 2007.
20. Romero, M., Vialard, A., Peponis, J., Stasko, J., and Abowd, G. Evaluating video visualizations of human behavior. In *ACM CHI* (2011), 1441–1450.
21. Teodosio, L., and Bender, W. Salient stills. *ACM Trans. Multimedia Comput. Commun. Appl. 1*, 1 (2005), 16–36.
22. Truong, B. T., and Venkatesh, S. Video abstraction: A systematic review and classification. *ACM Trans. Multimedia Comput. Commun. Appl. 3*, 1 (2007), 3:1–3:37.

Video as Memorabilia: User Needs for Collaborative Automatic Mobile Video Production

Sami Vihavainen[1], Sujeet Mate[2], Lassi Liikkanen[1], Igor D.D. Curcio[2]

[1]Helsinki Institute for Information Technology HIIT, Aalto University, P.O.Box 19215, 00076 Aalto, Finland
{sami.vihavainen, lassi.liikkanen}@hiit.fi

[2]Nokia Research Center
P.O. Box 1000, 33721 Tampere, Finland
{sujeet.mate, igor.curcio}@nokia.com

ABSTRACT
Digital memorabilia, such as video remixes, can increase the value of attending music events. Remixes can be made using video clips recorded by attendees during the event; however, producing them is a laborious task. In this paper we study the prospects of automatic video remixing and present the results of a study on users' perceptions and attitudes towards collaborative automatic mobile video production. The three findings are as follows: People assess automatic video remix memorabilia as fairly equal to amateur-made manual ones, even if the manually-created video remixes are better in overall quality; as a remixing actor, a computer can be perceived to be more trustworthy than a human remixer; and, the quality of the video remix and the publication forum of the remix outcome plays a significant role when people are deciding whether or not they need public acknowledgement for their contribution. We conclude by discussing the design implications for collaborative automatic mobile video production.

Author Keywords
Mobile video; CSCW; live music; memorabilia; authorship; crowdsourced media

ACM Classification Keywords
H.5.1 [Information Interfaces And Presentation]: Multimedia Information Systems - Evaluation/methodology;

General Terms
Design

INTRODUCTION
Live music events are one of the most important sources of revenue for artists. Many people invest considerable time, effort, and money to attend live performances. Different types of artist memorabilia from concerts provide added value for music consumers. Technology facilitates this process; nowadays it has become common for the audience to capture video clips and photos with smartphones during live music performances. This trend produces a pool of underutilized material that could become part of video remixes that combine material from several points-of-view to create novel memorabilia, thus enhancing the experience. However, producing multi-camera video remixes is laborious due to material handling and the number of people involved. Previous research shows that automating the editing process can ease the burden of remixing [13], but this requires human-produced video material to edit. Users must also be willing to hand over their personally-recorded footage to the automatic system.

This study aims to provide design insights to the CHI community for building collaborative video production tools. We believe the insights can be valuable also to video or photography services for large-scale events in general. Through our earlier study with an automatic video remixer [13], three issues emerged. It was unknown how potential users would perceive automatic video remixing systems in terms of *personal value*, *need for control* and *public acknowledgement*. By *personal value,* we mean how useful people perceive the mobile video remixes as memorabilia. Previous research has shown the importance of visual media for reliving an event [1,7]. Also more broadly, mobile media plays a major role in attendees' active construction of a shared experience at large-scale events like music festivals [6]. By *need for control* we mean the level of control that people desire when contributing personal video content to be remixed by an automatic video remixing system. Previous research has shown that too much automation with too little user control may affect the perceived usefulness of the system [11] and cause withdrawal [12]. By *public acknowledgement,* we mean peoples' attitudes about being publicly acknowledged if their clips were used in the remix. Previous research has shown that in remixing culture, acknowledgement plays a significant role in the negotiation of rights to use material [4, 10, 9].

METHODS
We arranged a two-day field trial at Provinssirock music festival in Finland during summer 2010. We collaborated with two of the performing rock bands and recruited 51 festival attendees to take mobile video clips during two concerts. A real-world trial was conducted to ascertain user attitudes based on experiences in the context for which the system was designed. We recruited 22 users via the bands' Facebook sites and 29 on-site. All recruits were young adults, no minors. The participants were given Nokia smartphones for the task. They formed groups of three to

CHI'12, May 5–10, 2012, Austin, Texas, USA.

five people and were instructed to record video clips during the concerts. They were told that, after the festival, all the video clips would be used as material for video remixes produced by the Nokia's automatic video remixer system (AVRS); their material also would be made available for video remixing using a web-based video editor called Jaycut [5]. After the event, we encouraged the participants over email to create video remixes. All together, four automatic and six user-generated video remixes were made. After receiving the artists' permission, we published eight of them on YouTube (two automatic and six manual) to give them visibility.

We invited the participants to complete a web-based questionnaire, which also included links to five of the YouTube remixes (two automatic and three manual). The questionnaire asked: How do people perceive automatic remixes as memorabilia? How do people perceive the sharing of personal video with an AVRS compared to the music artist or an unknown peer as the editor? What kind of attitudes do people have about receiving public acknowledgment for contributing their videos? We compared the automatic system with the two human actors (Artist and Peer) to ascertain if there were dimensions other than human vs. automation in terms of how people perceive the remixing actors. "Artist" here includes all representatives of the artist (e.g. the record company).

The automatic video remixing system

The AVRS utilizes context data from multiple sensors, including a compass, GPS, and an accelerometer. The availability of these sensors is becoming increasingly common on mobile devices. The multiple modalities of context data, which is obtained from these sensors, is stored as time-stamped data while the video recording is in progress. AVRS is critical to generate memorabilia for events. Since the initial version [13], the AVRS was improved to include interesting happenings and information from the live music event, thus adding to the video remix's value as memorabilia. This information is enabled by analysis of context data jointly with the recorded videos, contributed by the users attending the event [3]. This data is used to determine interesting occurrences, perspectives and high quality media segments; which are then included in the video remix [2, 3]. The higher the number of video clips contributed and the greater the number of users contributing clips, the higher the probability of capturing interesting occurrences from the event. Such capturing has the capacity to fill in the experience gap of an individual's video recordings providing added value to the experience. Such added value signifies the high importance one must assign to designing the AVRS in a way that reassures that users' content and identities will be used properly and respectfully.

Questionnaire

The questionnaire contained open-ended and order-ranking questions on a Likert scale (1='strongly disagree', 5='strongly agree'). In the analysis, the scale was simplified by combining the 'strongly agree' and 'agree', and 'strongly disagree' and 'disagree' into two categories, resulting in a one- to three-point scale (1='disagree', 2='nor agree or disagree', 3='agree'). The questionnaire was pre-tested with eight researchers.

In the first section, the respondents gave their subjective assessments about automatic and manual *remixes as memorabilia*. They were asked to watch the five remixes: Auto1 and Auto2, and Manual1, Manual2, and Manual3. (Man# and Auto# in the paper). They were then asked to respond to the claim: "This remix works very well as memorabilia from the concert". They were also asked for a rationale in an open-ended field and to put the remixes in order based on their overall quality. The labels of Auto1 and Man1 did not indicate whether they were manual or automatic but this information was visible in the other remixes. However, we found that the labeling did not influence the ratings significantly.

In the second section, we concentrated on how much people want to *have control over their video clips*. We presented claims concerning sharing video clips to other actors to be remixed (Actors: the artist, an unknown concert attendee, the AVRS). We presented three claims related to each actor. The claims were as follows: If the [actor] is the one who makes the public remix, I'm willing to share my clips 1) immediately after recording a video clip, 2) after viewing the video clips, and 3) after watching the final video remix.

In the third section, we asked about people's *willingness to receive public acknowledgment* if their clips were used as part of a video remix. We presented two claims and an open-ended question about willingness to get one's name published as part of the video remix. The claims were again presented three times, separately concerning each actor. In the open-ended question, we asked about their reasons for wanting or not wanting acknowledgement.

RESULTS AND DISCUSSION

The questionnaire was sent to 43 participants of the field study via email. 19 responded (ten males and nine females for a response rate of 44%). Since we did not want to force people to respond, N varied for the different survey items.

Automatic remixes as memorabilia

The results of rating automatic and manual remixes show that the best of the manual ones were perceived as better than the automatic ones overall (Table 1). Man2 and Auto2 were significantly different (Mann-Whitney, p=.036). The remixes separated into two groups, Man3 and Man2 being significantly better in overall quality than the rest (unadjusted for multiple comparisons).

However, when the participants were asked to rate the same video remixes based on their value as memorabilia, the remixes were rated much closer to each other (Table 1, the next page). Man1 had a median of 2 and all others were 3

Rank: Please, order the remixes based on overall quality.
Claim: This remix works very well as a memorabilia from the concert.

Remix	Rank	Claim	Rank	Claim	Rank	Claim
	Median		Mode		N	
Man3	5	3	5	3	16	12
Man2	4	3	4	3	16	11
Auto2	3	3	3	3	16	11
Auto1	2	3	2	3	16	11
Man1	1.5	2	1	3	16	11

Table1. Rank: Order based on overall quality. (1=worst, 5=best); Claim: Personal memorabilia value. (1=disagree, 3=agree)

(scale 1= disagree to 3 = agree). A significant difference was found only between Man1 and Man3 (Mann-Whitney, $p=.038$). The results indicate that, although the automatic remixes were not perceived to be as good as the best manual ones, they were still perceived to be good memorabilia.

In the open-ended questions, some of the respondents described the automatic remixes as a bit convoluted and bumpy. However, many also described the automatic remixes as representing the overall atmosphere well. They also noted familiar angles of view:

"I was in the front of the stage. There the atmosphere was different than at the back: jumping, raging...Because the picture was shaky in places and the cuts were fast, this remix was able to capture my concert feeling."

The need for control of clips

We sought to study if users' need for control of their clips depended upon the actor with whom the clips were to be shared. As such, we compared control variable scores of the three actors (Table 3). Significant differences were found between AVRS and Peer (Mann-Whitney, $p=.029$) as well as between Artist and Peer (Mann-Whitney, $p=.038$). Interestingly, this finding implies that respondents preferred to hand over clips to the AVRS over an unknown peer. It might also be that in the case of the artist and the AVRS as the actor, the users did not feel a need for control because they trusted these entities more than an unfamiliar person. Trust itself always involves risk [8], and is crucial in systems of distributed agency like our collaborative video remixing where labor is allocated to external actors. It might be that the participants feel that the risk involved in their clips being used in an unpleasant way is greater with a peer as an actor compared to the AVRS or artist. They might perceive the AVRS as "deterministic" and incapable of "abusing" the material, and trust that AVRS will not violate their impression management goals. Also in a long run, trust on the system may change depending on the type and frequency of possible faults. Fault in this case would occur if a user was associated with a published video remix that is not in line with the public profile she is building.

Claims: If the [actor] is the one who makes the public remix, I'm willing to share my clips 1) immediately after taking a video clip, 2) after checking the video clips, and 3) after watching the final remix.

Actor	Median	Mode	Reliability	N
Artist	5.5	4	α=.823, 1.comp. 74%	18
Peer	7.5	9	α=.718, 1.comp. 66%	18
AVRS	6.0	6	α=.729, 1.comp. 65%	18

Table3. Need for control of clips (3=low, 9=high). Sum variable from three claims: 1), 2) and 3). Cronbach's α and PCA's 1. component as reliability measure for sum variable.

Attitudes for public acknowledgement

Based on medians and modes (Table 4), we can see that most of the participants do not want to get public acknowledgement when the AVRS makes the remix. However, most of them did want to receive authorship if the artist made a video remix. We believe this finding might indicate that the respondents perceive the AVRS as a black box. The artist, on the other hand, represents something that the participants probably want to be associated with. Nonetheless, the differences between the actors were not statistically significant (Mann-Whitney, $p<0.05$). Based on median and mode values, the respondents were less likely to want to see the final video remix before deciding whether to be acknowledged in the case of the AVRS than in the cases of peer and artist as actors. In this case also, the differences were not statistically significant.

The open-ended question on whether and why the participants ($N=16$) would like to be publicly mentioned as the authors of the final mix (regardless of who made the remix) showed that half expected acknowledgement. More importantly, acknowledgement expectations were divided among conditional and definite opinions. Only a few participants expressed an unconditional desire for acknowledgment or desire for publicity ("definitely yes"). The people who expressed a conditional need for acknowledgement would like to provide their consent after their evaluation of their own or the final content. There were several reasons for not wanting an acknowledgement. For example, one participant said that because of professional reasons he does not want his name to appear on the Internet. Many respondents indicated skepticism towards the technical quality of the recording, their own capacity, or the quality of the final video remix. Identification concerns were evident because the

Actor	Median	Mode	N
Claim: If the remix made by [actor] includes my video clips, I want my name to be mentioned in the remix.			
Artist	3	3	18
Peer	2	2	18
AVRS	2	1	18
Claim: If the remix is made by [actor], it is important for me to see the complete remix before I decide if I want my name to be published as part of the remix.			
Artist	2.5	3	18
Peer	3	3	18
AVRS	2	2	18

Table4. Attitudes on acknowledgement (1=disagree, 3=agree)

people did not want to be associated with dubious publications nor with dubious forums. One respondent mentioned consideration of fair use, the need for awareness of commercial or any other type of use that was previously unknown. No one explicitly expressed a need for individual parts of the video remix to be attributed to them.

CONCLUSIONS AND IMPLICATIONS FOR DESIGN

Based on the results about how people perceive collaborative automated mobile video production in live music context, we draw the following conclusions:

For memorabilia, remixes do not have to be perfect

The overall quality of the automatic remixes did not match the quality of the best manual remixes. However, the automatic video remixes were perceived to be as good as memorabilia as the manual ones. This finding indicates that the video remix does not have to be superb in order to trigger memories from the music event. One way to provide that emotional response is to offer varied perspectives of the event through different camera angles. This technique allows people to relate to the video because they see views from places they themselves had occupied during the show.

Proper control helps to hand over the clips

People need significantly less control of their personal clips when sharing them with an AVRS, as compared to other concert attendees with whom they are not familiar. We believe that this result indicates that the automatic remixing system was seen as trustworthy with regards to sharing one's personal video clips to be used in creating a public video remix. With an AVRS, a user veto may not be required before publishing the automatic video remix. However, users should not be hurried into handing over their video clips to the system either; they should have a chance to preview their clips. Only the clips that are explicitly chosen should be included for remixing.

No to automatic acknowledgement

Novice users are uncertain about the outcome and thus unlikely to want to be acknowledged without the chance to review the video remix. The willingness to share is largely dependent on the quality and subjective meaningfulness of the final content as well as the reputation of the venue where the final content will be published. It seems that people want to be aware of how they are presented as part of the outcome and want to control it in such a way that matches their impression management goals. Since many of the participants did not expect acknowledgment and many saw it as very conditional, we do not think people should be acknowledged as a default, unless they separately agreed to do so. Users should be informed from the start about the intended use and licensing. However, they should not necessarily be asked for consent for acknowledgement at an early stage, either before recording or after uploading the material. If after production consent is impractical, the decision should be made thoughtfully.

We hope that our study will be a useful reference for designers of video production tools who need to know peoples' perceptions on collaborative video remixing and how to deal with control and acknowledgement issues.

ACKNOWLEDGMENTS

We thank Provinssirock, Fullsteam Records, Lapko, Disco Ensemble, and Teosto organizations. Anonymous CHI reviewers, and additional researchers Lassi Seppälä, Suvi Silfverberg., Arto Puikkonen, Pirkka Åman, Francesco Crikri, and Vilma Lehtinen for organizing the study. Academy of Finland project MusiQuitous funded work at HIIT.

REFERENCES

1. Chalfen R., Snapshot versions of life. Bowling Green State University, Bowling Green Ohio, 1987.
2. Cricri, F., Curcio, I.D.D., Mate, S., Dabov, K., Gabbouj, M., Sensor-based Analysis of User Generated Video for Multi-Camera Video Remixing. *Proc. MMM 2012*, 255-265.
3. Cricri, F., Dabov, K., Curcio, I., Mate, S., Gabbouj, M. Multimodal Event Detection in User Generated Videos, *Proc. IEEE ISM 2011.*
4. Diakopoulos, N., Luther, K., Medynskiy, Y. E., Essa, I. The evolution of authorship in a remix society. *Proc. HT 2007*, ACM Press (2007).
5. Jaycut. http://jaycut.com/ (accessed 9.1.2012)
6. Jacucci, G., Oulasvirta, A. & Salovaara, A. Active construction of experience through mobile media: A field study with implications for recording and sharing. *Personal and Ubiquitous Computing* 11, 4 (2007), 215-234.
7. Lehmuskallio, A., Sarvas, R., Snapshot Video: Everyday Photographers Taking Short Video-Clips. *Proc.* NordiCHI 2008, ACM Press (2008), 257-265.
8. Luhmann N., *Familiarity, confidence, trust: Problems and alternatives.* Basil Blackwell, Oxford, 1990.
9. Marsh*all, C.C. & Shipman, F.M., The ownership and reuse of visu*al media. *Proc. JCDL*, 11, pp.13-17.
10. Monroy-Hernández, A., Hill, B.M. & Gonzalez-Rivero, J., boyd, d. 2011. Computers can't give credit: how automatic attribution falls short in an online remixing community. *Proc. CHI 2011.* ACM Press, (2011).
11. Sheridan T., *Humans and automation: System design and research issues.* Wiley Inter-Science, 2002
12. Vihavainen, S., Mate, S., Seppälä, L., Cricri, F., Curcio,I.D.D. We Want More: Human-Computer Collaboration in Mobile Social Video Remixing of Music Concerts. *Proc. CHI 2011.* ACM Press (2011), 287-296.
13. Vihavainen, S., Oulasvirta, A., Sarvas, R.: "I Can't Lie Anymore - The Implications of Location Automation for Mobile Social Applications. *Proc.* MobiQuitous 2009, IEEE Press (2009).

Collapse Informatics: Augmenting the Sustainability & ICT4D Discourse in HCI

Bill Tomlinson[1], M. Six Silberman[2], Don Patterson[1], Yue Pan[3], and Eli Blevis[3]

[1]University of California, Irvine, CA, USA, {wmt, djp3}@uci.edu

[2]Bureau of Economic Interpretation, San Francisco, CA, USA, six.silberman@gmail.com

[3]Indiana University, Bloomington, IN, USA, {panyue, eblevis}@indiana.edu

ABSTRACT

Research in many fields argues that contemporary global industrial civilization will not persist indefinitely in its current form, and may, like many past human societies, eventually collapse. Arguments in environmental studies, anthropology, and other fields indicate that this transformation could begin within the next half-century. While imminent collapse is far from certain, it is prudent to consider now how to develop sociotechnical systems for use in these scenarios. We introduce the notion of collapse informatics—the study, design, and development of sociotechnical systems in the abundant present for use in a future of scarcity—as a complement to ICT4D and mitigation-oriented sustainable HCI. We draw on a variety of literatures to offer a set of relevant concepts and articulate the relationships among them to orient and evaluate collapse informatics work. Observing that collapse informatics poses a unique class of cross-cultural design problems, we sketch the design space of collapse informatics and provide a variety of example projects. We explore points of connection and distinction between collapse informatics and sustainable HCI, ICT4D, and crisis informatics. Finally, we discuss next steps and comment on the potential value of collapse informatics work even in the event that collapse never occurs.

Author Keywords

Sustainable HCI; collapse; sustainability; mitigation; adaptation; ICT4D; cross-cultural design.

ACM Classification Keywords

H.5.m [Information interfaces and presentation (e.g., HCI)]: Miscellaneous; K.4.m [Computers and Society]: Miscellaneous.

General Terms

Design; Human Factors; Theory.

CHI'12, May 5–10, 2012, Austin, Texas, USA.

INTRODUCTION[1]

History documents the rise and fall of many complex societies. Large human civilizations form over long periods of expansion, sometimes lasting centuries; however, most civilizations that have ever existed have collapsed [6,31]. The archaeologist Joseph Tainter defines collapse as "a rapid, significant loss of an established level of sociopolitical complexity" ([31], p. 7). In his parlance, "rapid" means "no more than a few decades" ([31], p. 4). Collapse manifests as the loss of the hallmarks of political complexity, namely: *"a lower degree of stratification and social differentiation; less economic and occupational specialization, of individuals, groups, and territories; less centralized control; that is, less regulation and integration of diverse economic and political groups by elites; less behavioral control and regimentation; less investment in the epiphenomena of complexity, those elements that define the concept of 'civilization': monumental architecture, artistic and literary achievements, and the like; less flow of information between individuals, between political and economic groups, and between a center and its periphery; less sharing, trading, and redistribution of resources; less overall coordination and organization of individuals and groups; a smaller territory integrated within a single political unit"* ([31], p. 4).

We live in a world that includes the first global civilization. Despite the relatively continuous growth that this civilization has experienced over the past two centuries (or, perhaps, because of it), it is plausible that this civilization may someday enter a period of decline. Many scholars have suggested that this decline may have already begun, or may begin within the next several decades [6,31].

The collapse of global civilization, whether imminent or not, would carry enormous costs that novel research may be able to reduce. It is time to consider how the CHI community can help civilization react to, and perhaps plan for, global collapse.

In this paper, we propose that there is a need for research in *collapse informatics*—the study, design, and development

[1] Portions of the document adapted from several non-archival publications, specifically: [2,25,29].

of sociotechnical systems in the abundant present for use in a future of scarcity. The term ICT4D—or Information & Communications Technologies for Development—already denotes a well-established area of inquiry, referring to the role and potential effects of ICT in helping the so-called developing world, the 'development' of which is part of our collective global fate. In HCI, under the banners of sustainable interaction design, sustainable HCI, and green IT, there is much literature targeted at mitigating the forces—especially social-behavioral forces—that also threaten standards of living around the globe. This work to date has focused primarily on mitigating the possibility of climate change effects, although some of the sustainability work specifically included in this present paper has stated the need to focus on adaptation as well [2]. Collapse informatics, then, is the third in this trilogy of concerns, focusing on the role and potential effects of ICT in dealing with changes—however induced—that create massive shifts in the way humanity must adapt to survive in its environments—political, social, and ecological. Collapse informatics is broader than notions of adaptation in the general literature on sustainability, since the concern is for preparation and adaptation to change, whether induced by climate change or other forces.

Just as the Americans with Disabilities Act produced innovations that had far-reaching social benefits beyond simply helping those with disabilities, collapse informatics may well produce innovations that are broadly useful, for example, in localized collapse situations, disaster-preparedness and response, or in ICT4D, even in the event that the global community is able to sustain itself indefinitely. Moreover, the study of mechanisms of preparation for and adaptation to collapse has important implications for the discourse on sustainable interaction design/HCI, and ICT4D. Through this research, we envision the possibility of a future characterized by scarcity and shrinking opportunity, and seek to make that future a better place.

COLLAPSE IS NOT APOCALYPSE

If collapse is potentially in our civilization's future, it is relevant to consider how soon and in what styles, collapse may occur. Hollywood movies (e.g., *Carriers*, *28 Days Later*, *The Terminator, 2012*) and survivalist fiction (e.g., [26]), often focus on very rapid collapse, occurring on the scale of days or weeks—an apocalypse.

While rapid and powerful events such as nuclear attacks may cause events to unfold in a way that merits the term "apocalypse", and while various "tipping point" phenomena [6,14] may cause non-linear changes to occur very rapidly (as is common in ecosystems), Tainter [31], geographer Jared Diamond [6], and others note that collapse frequently occurs more gradually. In the popular press recently, there has been discussion of a "double dip recession" [23]; collapse could well take the form of an "N-dip recession."

TIMING OF COLLAPSE

When, exactly, collapse may begin is difficult to predict with precision. Many scholars tie the collapse timeline to our primarily fossil fuel-based energy supply. "Recent history seems to indicate that we have at least reached declining returns for our reliance on fossil fuels, and possibly for some raw materials," writes Tainter ([31], p. 215). He continues: "[a] new energy subsidy is necessary if a declining standard of living and a future global collapse are to be averted." One barrel of oil does an equivalent amount of work to 25,000 hours of human manual labor [18]; it is the subsidy and externalized costs from this vast resource that makes our current ways of living possible. The term "peak oil" has entered popular parlance to describe the point at which global oil production reaches its highest point and then enters a period of decline. There is some debate over the timing of this phenomenon; some researchers say it has already occurred, others that it will occur within the next several decades. If collapse is tied to dwindling supplies of fossil fuels, collapse may well be in the offing.

Diamond also argues that environmental problems that could cause civilization-scale collapse will manifest within the century. "[A]t current rates most or all of the dozen major sets of environmental problems ... will become acute within the life-time of young adults now alive" ([6], p. 513). These kinds of predictions are made as well by Lovelock (e.g., [14]). Lovelock's notion of Gaia Theory, which holds that the Earth is a self-regulating system, has been cited in the HCI literature [6,13] in the context of describing the controversies surrounded his theories. The much less controversial Intergovernmental Panel on Climate Change (IPCC) ([24], p. 7, Figure SPM.5) states that we are very likely to reach a tipping point by 2040 with respect to global warming/climate change unless we are able to reduce our GHG emissions to 1999 levels by the year 2015.

Taken together, these sources suggest that collapse could begin within the next several decades. If it does, it is likely to usher in profound changes.

EFFECTS OF COLLAPSE

In this document we use the term 'civilization' to mean a large, complex society, where a society is a collection of cooperating individuals (or smaller such collections). A civilization including cooperation between globally distributed individuals or collections can be described as a 'global civilization'. With these definitions we can describe a 'collapse of global civilization' as the transition from a state of affairs in which such cooperation exists to one in which it no longer exists. (Note: No moral valuation is intended by our use of the term 'civilization'.)

Diamond and Tainter describe numerous examples of collapse across the history of human civilizations, and point to scarcities of many kinds, including dramatic shortfalls in food, energy, and raw materials. In a scarce, post-collapse future, we may see crumbling infrastructures as well (e.g., power, manufacturing, government regulation). In the "Inside Risks" column in *CACM*, Horning and Neumann note that "[c]ivilization and infrastructure are intimately intertwined. Rising civilizations build and benefit from their infrastructures in a 'virtuous cycle.' As civilizations decline, their infrastructures decay—although unmaintained vestiges, such as roads and aqueducts, may outlive them" ([12], p. 112). In the wake of collapse, the largest level of human organization is likely to be a smaller social unit than the current global civilization [31]. We may see scarcities of energy in the wake of peak oil, and scarcities of other resources as a result of reduced global trade. The lack of infrastructures, energy sources, and trade would likely impact food supplies for a large portion of the world population, who either do not raise their own food, or do so relying on imported water, seed, fertilizers, pesticides, and other supplies. Taken together, these kinds of civilizational repercussions would bring about non-trivial lifestyle changes for many people.

ICT AND COLLAPSE

This paper focuses on the potential contribution that the field of HCI can make in preparation for and adaptation to collapse. Computer-based ICT systems are among the most powerful tools humanity has ever created; understanding how to design ICT and sociotechnical systems to enable social wellbeing in times of collapse could benefit many.

There has been some discussion of collapse in the computing community (e.g., [22]). Within HCI specifically, Blevis and Blevis [6] have written about the need to emphasize adaptation in addition to mitigation. They write: *"We are at a crossroads where the logic that applies is the logic of hoping for the best and preparing for the worst—that is, we need to continue our efforts to develop digital interactivity to induce people and societies to engage in behavioral changes that reduce our greenhouse gas emissions, and we also need to develop digital interactivity that allows us to prepare for and adapt to climate change under the possibility that we will reach a tipping point, or the possibility that we have already done so"* (p. 26).

Wong has discussed the need for a broadening of the scope of research in order to have effects that are sufficiently impactful to address the gravity of the crises facing human civilizations [37]. In Wong's view, researchers "should also consider … the design context to be a world radically altered by environmental damage; solutions that fit into today's lifestyles risk irrelevance" ([37], p. 1).

Silberman and Tomlinson have described a need for "apocalypse-related … approaches to technology design" ([29], p. 1). They consider how HCI research may be relevant to contexts characterized by a "rapid, significant loss of sociopolitical complexity which in itself constitutes an event whose impacts exceed the responsive capacities of [those] affected" ([29], p. 1).

Despite these initial forays by HCI researchers into the space of research relating to collapse and similar phenomena, we as a discipline have largely failed to appreciate the need to design and build technologies that may be of use on the "downward slope" of social complexity. This paper seeks to bring together ideas from these early works with research in other fields to articulate the concerns, goals, assumptions, and concepts of this emerging genre of HCI research. We use the term "genre" following DiSalvo *et al.* [7], who describe genres as "common frameworks that structure how researchers define [a problem] and structure what is an appropriate solution" (p. 1975). While we believe collapse informatics constitutes a substantive departure from the approaches developed thus far in sustainable HCI and ICT4D, we recognize the risks of "carving up" the intellectual terrain, or proliferating subfields unnecessarily.

It is worth noting that ICT may also play a prominent role in *bringing about* collapse. ICT is a force multiplier and has hastened the development of the various environmental issues that surround us [33]. With regard to the recession in the late 2000s, *CACM* editor Moshe Vardi argues that "information technology played a major role in the crisis" ([34], p. 5). Recalling points made by Tainter, Vardi offers: "A common thread to these disasters is that our financial system has reached a level of complexity that makes it opaque even to the 'high priests of finance'" ([34], p. 5). Vardi gives examples showing how ICT is linked to economic complexity. And then he makes the link to collapse explicit: "if a massive electromagnetic pulse wiped out our computing infrastructure, our society would face a catastrophic collapse" ([34], p. 5).

ICT is a powerful form of technology. Because of ICT's great power, and because it is deeply embedded in global industrialized civilization, understanding how it may be of service in a potential collapse is of critical importance.

Many people in the modern world look at the past several hundred years of fairly steady growth, and see growth as eternal and unconditionally desirable. Growth has led to higher standards of living in many areas, and, as an idea, is supported by the bulk of major governments and corporations of the world. However, continuous growth is, by definition, not sustainable indefinitely.

The bulk of ICT innovations in the past half-century reflect an implicit expectation of perpetual growth. Infrastructures will expand, markets will grow, and materials will become more readily available. Recently, "green" technologies have begun to consider that it might be desirable to have civilization plateau, and achieve a sustainable steady state or dynamic equilibrium [4,5].

Civilizational collapse is the condition for which this paper seeks to help civilization prepare. Thoughtful development of computing technologies, and the removal of certain technologies as well, are methods of preparing. The goal is to adapt to potential futures that may involve collapse, rather than preserving the "business as usual" that may, in fact, be hastening collapse.

SCOPE, CONCEPTS, AND CONCERNS

Software engineering researcher Douglas Schuler suggests that "[w]hether or not humankind successfully navigates itself away from the rocky shoals it faces will depend to no small degree on whether the right type of sociotechnological infrastructure is conceptualized, developed and used" ([27], p. 63). Collapse informatics seeks to build this sociotechnological infrastructure.

Adaptation and Mitigation

Adaptation describes changes in a system's structure or behavior in response to changes in its external environment (e.g., [38]). When the systems under study are humans or groups of humans, we can focus on adaptations to practices for fulfilling human needs. The economist Manfred Max-Neef argues that the fundamental human needs are subsistence, protection, affection, understanding, participation, idleness, creation, identity, and freedom [17]. This particular list is not essential to collapse informatics, but a distinction between finite, broadly relevant (if not universal) needs and culturally idiosyncratic, arbitrarily extensible wants must be made in some way to predict the likely goals of users in the face of collapse.

In global climate change discourse, "adaptation"—the mobilization of effective responses to the effects of environmental change (e.g., climate change) is complementary to "mitigation," the *a priori* reduction of the magnitude of change by reducing the causes of change (e.g., greenhouse gas emissions). Mitigation reduces the need for future adaptation, if it occurs soon enough and with sufficient scale to avoid a tipping point. But, if change becomes inevitable and begins to occur (i.e., as opportunities to mitigate are foregone or mitigation efforts fail), prevention is no longer possible and adaptation is required. Further, because adaptation takes time, it is necessary to begin adapting even before changes occur in order to be successful. Climate science predicts that a certain amount of global warming and sea level rise will occur as a result of past emissions [16,21,36]. While mitigation remains important, the need for a certain amount of adaptation is already assured.

Vulnerability and Adaptive Capacity

The work of adapting *a priori* to expected effects of global change can be described in terms of reducing vulnerability and increasing adaptive capacity. Amy Luers *et al.* [15] note that it is hard to discuss with precision the 'general' vulnerability of a system, and instead study vulnerability in terms of variables that relate to the well-being of the system (p. 257). For example, in studying a farming community one might investigate the vulnerability of crop yields to climate change. In studying a city one might investigate the vulnerability of food availability to changes in oil prices.

Luers *et al.* define vulnerability in terms of (a) the sensitivity of the system's well-being (or its proxy) to changes in the value of the environmental variable in question and (b) the proximity of the system to a threshold below which the system is said to be 'damaged.' Specifically, large changes in well-being resulting from small changes in the environment are indicative of high vulnerability, as is proximity to the damage threshold [15] (pp. 257-8).

Luers *et al.* define adaptive capacity as "the extent to which a system can modify its circumstances to move to a less vulnerable condition." Quantitatively, it is the difference between a system's current vulnerability and its vulnerability under some condition to which it could shift. This does not include adaptations already made in response to past disturbances; those adaptations are represented by the system's current vulnerability. Adaptive capacity indicates changes that could be made to reduce vulnerability to future disturbance ([15], p. 259). Vulnerability describes actual conditions; adaptive capacity describes possible conditions.

These concepts describe two categories of work that supports adaptation to collapse: reducing vulnerability and increasing adaptive capacity. We aim to reduce vulnerability of fulfillment of fundamental human needs to the disturbances we expect in association with global change (climate change, sea level rise, degradation of ecosystems and their services, etc.). Once existing adaptive capacity has been exploited, adaptive capacity must be increased to further reduce vulnerability. One component of adaptive capacity is knowledge; we cannot change our ways unless we know how. Thus increasing adaptive capacity entails, among other things, gathering and developing knowledge relevant to fulfilling fundamental human needs in various contexts despite the disturbances of global change. Reducing vulnerability means helping interested parties deploy that knowledge. There are different appropriate times for work in these two categories. To the extent that increasing adaptive capacity has low opportunity costs — and this may hold for much of the 'knowledge work' involved — it can be undertaken even in situations of uncertainty. Reducing vulnerability to changes in one variable, however, may increase vulnerability to changes in others. Thus the appropriate action depends on our degree of certainty about what the future holds. Research on decision making under uncertainty abounds in the policy, business, decision theory, and computer science literatures and is likely to be of value in choosing between possible adaptations.

To increase adaptive capacity is to increase the number of options. To reduce vulnerability to changes in a particular variable is to change our way of life to reduce the costs of anticipated disturbances associated with that variable.

The question of time is central to this work. It takes time to change a way of life, even for an individual. How long might it take for an entire city to develop local food production in anticipation of rising oil prices? At least years; perhaps decades. Thus if we think that severe disturbances are decades, not centuries, away, it makes sense to begin increasing adaptive capacity now.

COLLAPSE INFORMATICS AS A STRATEGIC DESIGN PROBLEM

The core challenge of collapse informatics involves designing sociotechnical systems in our present context, even though the primary usage of these systems will occur in a very different situation. Essentially, collapse informatics is a cross-cultural design problem.

However, whereas most cross-cultural design efforts span two communities that are contemporary but spatially and culturally distinct (e.g., designers from one country attempting to design systems for users in a different country), the cross-cultural design problem in collapse informatics spans two communities that may exist in the same location but are temporally and culturally distinct (e.g., designers in the present attempting to design systems for their future selves and families in a time of scarcity). What makes this effort particularly challenging is that it is impossible for a researcher or designer to engage with the anticipated users and seek to understand their needs and ways of viewing the world in which they live, or engage in action research (cf. [11]). This is not to say that typical cross-cultural design is easy; meeting and interacting with the people for whom we design is different from understanding their needs and desires. But in most cross-cultural design it is at least logically possible to attempt to establish understanding, work with users to evaluate prototypes, and iterate on designs. In collapse informatics the imagined users are not yet in the imagined context of use (collapse). They may not have even been born yet.

Collapse informatics focuses on the difference in availability of resources and infrastructure between when systems are designed and when they may be used. These systems are designed in times of relative abundance in many places around the world, building on the wealth of resources and expanding infrastructures brought about by fossil fuels and globalization. In present times, we have the cognitive surplus [28] to design systems for purposes beyond immediate survival, and the excess materials and energy to bring these systems to fruition.

Not all sociotechnical interventions involve building and deploying systems. Fry's notions of "redirective practice" (e.g., using a push mower instead of a gas powered lawn mower) and "acts of elimination" (e.g., replacing lawns with small scale crop gardens or wildflowers) [10] instead point to the potential need to remove components of complex sociotechnical systems. In Tainter's analysis [31], complexity itself sets the stage for collapse; therefore, reducing complexity in sociotechnical systems while maintaining their viability could be an important means both of avoiding collapse and of creating systems that are viable post-collapse. Understanding how our research may be most effectively brought to bear on this suite of concerns, whether through the introduction of new technologies or the elimination of problematic ones, is an important consideration of the proposed project.

To design these interventions, and begin exploring how they interact with human civilizations, we return to Max-Neef's concept of basic human needs [17]. Understanding how sociotechnical systems may support and provide for these needs in a sustainable way in a time of scarcity is the core of the collapse informatics design problem.

Despite the possibility of widely-shared human needs, we also recognize the existence of many different social, biological, and biogeographic contexts (e.g., [8]). What serves a human need in one culture (even a collapsed one) may be very different than what serves the same need in a different culture. What serves a need across various ecological habitats differs as well, especially as climate changes make ecologies dynamically unstable.

Finally, collapse informatics systems should also operate in future scenarios characterized by minimal, intermittent, and/or alternative infrastructure—or even "anti-infrastructure," such as a local despot who takes most things of value for his or her own use.

RELATION TO OTHER GENRES OF HCI RESEARCH

Collapse informatics is both a separate concern and a part of the discourse for sustainable HCI, ICT4D, crisis informatics, and potentially other genres within and outside HCI. (See Figure 1.) These genres aim to increase human well-being. But their operating contexts and orienting assumptions are different to those of collapse informatics.

Sustainable HCI has been mainly focused on mitigation,

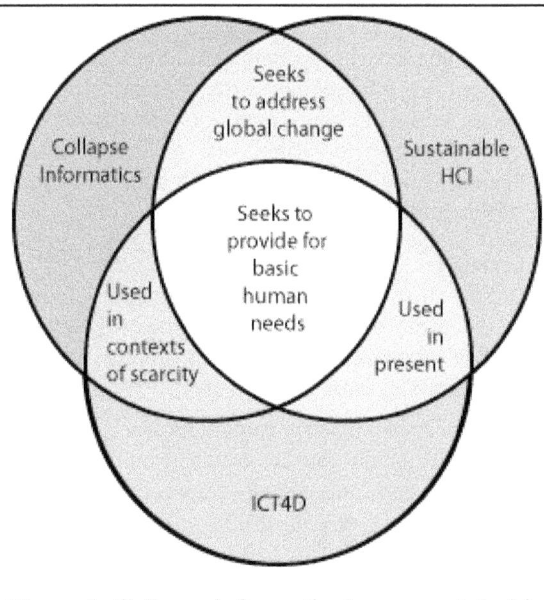

Figure 1: Collapse informatics has a great deal in common with sustainable HCI research and ICT4D.

and tends to assume that the infrastructures relied on by most interactive technologies will persist as the risks incurred by current unsustainable practices become urgent challenges to well-being and survival. Collapse informatics distinguishes itself from this work by its orientation to adaptation rather than mitigation and by imagining those infrastructures as at risk, and subject to design and redesign, rather than as stable elements of the environment [30].

ICT4D has been mainly focused on increasing standards of living in 'developing' countries, often by importing or adapting technologies created and used in 'developed' countries. This work can increase human well-being in the short and medium term and is therefore deeply important. But the use practices and infrastructures surrounding most of these technologies, developed in countries whose economic growth has been made possible by abundant fossil fuels [32], may not be sustainable in the long term (i.e., decades to centuries). Collapse informatics distinguishes itself from ICT4D by considering long term scenarios of global change, in which the infrastructural conditions in current high-consumption countries begin to look more like those currently prevalent in 'developing' countries, and the continued appropriation of non-local resources and associated notions of externalized costs are no longer supported by post-collapse global conditions.

The nascent field of crisis informatics is also concerned with saving life and maintaining well-being in the context of dramatic change. These are urgent, difficult, and important design challenges, especially given the possibility that disasters will increase in frequency and severity as global change unfolds. Thus collapse informatics overlaps with this work, but here again distinguishes itself by taking a longer and broader view. Disasters are bounded in space and time; by designing to support users in disaster contexts we can assume that (a) the disaster will end and (b) users in the disaster context can be supported by users outside it (with access to functioning infrastructure). In collapse informatics work, the new conditions are not necessarily bounded in space or time; in collapse scenarios, infrastructure failures are likely to be spatially extensive and for all practical purposes permanent.

EVALUATION

A critical question when designing systems for a future that has not yet come to pass is "How do you know it will work?" The question of evaluation looms large over collapse informatics work.

Key elements of a proposed approach to collapse informatics evaluation can be drawn from the history of collapse. Two core ingredients frame our approach to evaluation: smaller social group size and unreliable infrastructure. The approach is this: create models and/or conduct real world experiments with willing participants in which certain constraints are placed on a person or group's existence, and explore the viability and usefulness of the proposed design or actual working system in that context. For example, if one model of collapse entails no electricity, then any system that relies on electricity is a failure. If another entails the lack of reliable federal or state governments, the bulk of civil services will no longer be available. Existing measures of quality of life [9] and assessments based on basic human needs [17] may then be used to assess the implications of collapse informatics research projects used in these circumstances.

In addition to evaluating the success or failure of a particular system, these models may be used to generate questions (cf. [1]), principles, heuristics, and indices [30] to help understand the set of relevant issues more fully. Researchers may also consider what kinds of emergent and network effects may be valuable or problematic in a range of collapse contexts.

We acknowledge that evaluation is a difficult and rich topic of critical importance to collapse informatics, and fertile ground for future work in this area.

EXAMPLES

To explore the range of potential collapse informatics projects, first we include a somewhat detailed sketch for an application in progress called "The Climate Change Habitability Index," to serve as an example of the type of interactive technology application we have in mind. Next, we include a series of ideas for applications and contexts targeted to motivate near-future collapse informatics research.

The Climate Change Habitability Index

The Climate Change Habitability Index (CCHI) is a design exercise and catalyst to a program of ongoing research. The idea of the CCHI is to allow ordinary individuals—rather than just climate scientists—to understand the state of the world in terms of habitability at particular places. In the face of climate change, individuals will need to be able to use the CCHI and other measures to answer questions such as: (a) *can I continue to live where I am living,* (b) *where can I move if I can't continue to live where I'm living,* and (c) *how many people can the place where I live sustainably support, if where I live continues to be habitable?* The CCHI needs to be stated in a way that is as easily understood by ordinary people as other summary reporting such as weather forecasting.

Definition

The CCHI is defined abstractly as a metric that can be stated in ordinary language and diagrams which allow people to answer the above three questions related to sustainability and adaptation to climate change about particular places on Earth.

By "*can I continue to live where I am living,*" we mean to ask if a place is habitable enough for people to live in accordance with water and food supplies, health conditions, and the habitability of coastal environments in particular and other environments in general.

By "*where can I move if I can't continue to live where I'm living*," we mean to ask which places are habitable or have better, more sustainable living affordances respective of the five factors identified by the IPCC ([24], p. 16, Figure SPM.2)—namely water, coasts, food, health, and ecosystems. This question relates to a person's ability to understand the habitability of where she or he lives now and to make plans for moving in the future, if necessary.

By "*how many people can the place where I live sustainably support, if where I live continues to be habitable*," we mean to ask how can we inform policies and decisions related to migration and absorption of immigrants in a manner that promotes peaceful and orderly sustainable practice in the face of the potential and realized effects of climate change.

The CCHI aims to provide a metric to enable everyone from individuals to intergovernmental bodies to plan for the dynamic and orderly migration and absorption of populations as climate change alters the suitability of various regions of the planet for sustainable habitation. Finally the notion of making the habitability index as highly accessible as a notion like "temperature" is co-requisite to the social imperative to provide for the safety and security of every person and creature whose life or home may be impacted by climate change events and effects.

Initial Design for the CCHI

We are designing a tool to support the summarization of the suitability of any particular place for habitation as a dynamically changing metric corresponding to historical, current, and predicted states of water systems, ecosystems, food supplies, coastal conditions, and health conditions, as well as the likelihood of hazard events. Interactivity of the habitability index may be presented using cloud-based technologies, such as layers implemented as part of the "Google Earth" or "Google Maps" APIs, or other GIS systems. Figure 2 shows the essential interactivity elements

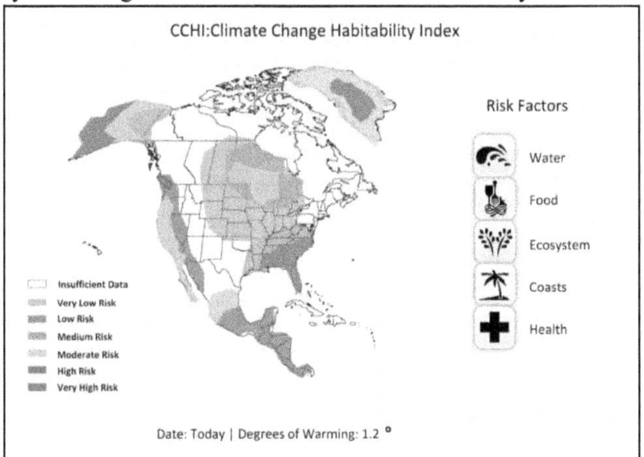

Figure 2: CCHI view on a specific day given a specific amount of warming. (*Not real data—For illustrative purposes only.*)

we imagine are needed to support interactivity with the CCHI representation as a cascading summary of more detailed data. Our design is deliberately minimalist and it is easy to image a gray scale version as a matter of accessibility. The regions defined in the map denote a cumulative summary of the risk factors indicated by the risk factor icons.

Time & Temperature

Another two essential features of CCHI are time and degrees of warming (or cooling). Our purpose is to allow people to see historical trends and future predictions about how climate change affects the Earth over periods of time. People need to be able to see what the Earth may look like when the average temperature increases by a specific amount which in the IPCC summary diagrams ([24]) ranges from 0 to 6 degrees Celsius of warming. Two degrees Celsius of warming is generally considered to be the dangerous tipping point. Based on the assumptions of the IPCC reports, we define year 2000 to be the base point and set the temperature change to be 0 for 2000 ([24]).

The CCHI seeks to provide access to data about the current and possible future habitability of particular regions [6]. Making this information readily available to ordinary people will increase the likelihood that the evacuation and absorption of populations in the face of climate change will be orderly and peaceful.

Application Ideations and Context Scenarios

The following are unimplemented "fictional abstracts" for research projects that serve as ideas we hope others will take up, or which we ourselves will investigate in future work. These ideas/scenarios illustrate the range of what may be possible in terms of collapse informatics.

Predicting and Preparing

Designing ICT Systems for Post-Collapse Deployment: Most current ICT systems are designed for deployment in contexts much like those in which they were developed – industrialized, stable, infrastructure-rich, and communication-enabled. In the case of civilizational collapse, though, the lack of infrastructure and other resources may make deployment of these systems challenging – there may not be access to the most recent version of a system, or critical updates, or server-based license management systems. This project would develop a new class of ICT systems – "collapse-compliant systems" – that are designed for use after the industrialized context has begun to decay. For example, collapse-compliant systems should be 1) always ready (the most recent version must be locally cached with some regularity); 2) critically useful (explicitly serve a physiological or psychological need of humans or some other species); and 3) robust (must contain source code or some other mechanism for repair/adaptation). A Wikipedia dump that locally auto-archives a subset of articles based on user-specified keywords and total file size would be one example of a collapse-compliant system. An online community could emerge around this and other collapse-compliant systems, so that interested individuals and organizations could benefit from each other's preparedness.

Modeling Survivable Whole Life Systems: Many researchers (e.g., Max-Neef [17]) suggest that humans have an assortment of basic needs. In any viable, long-term survival scenario, all basic human needs must be met. This project would simulate an arbitrary-sized population of human-like agents and examining the interdependencies among individuals and their various needs. For example, two agents may reciprocally provide affection for each other, but compete with each other for subsistence in the context of scarce food resources. By modeling basic human needs, this system may allow individuals and institutions to plan more effectively for both emergency and everyday lifestyles.

Visualizing Collapse Via Markers of Social Complexity: This project would create a means of monitoring and visualizing key indicators of the collapse process. The system would track metrics such as unemployment rates, bond ratings, border security, governmental solvency, and incidence of martial law; integrate these factors via a user-customizable algorithm; and present the results via a dynamically-updated interactive visualization. Enabling the citizenry to monitor and predict the process of collapse may enable broader preparedness for the reduction of social complexity.

Peak ICT: Peak oil will usher in profound changes across many facets of society. Since ICT systems rely extensively on fossil fuels for their creation and operation, these systems are likely to be heavily affected by declining fuel availability. Barring a new power source to replace fossil fuels, eventually ICT will reach a point where the maximum information storage, manipulation, and transmission will be reached ("Peak ICT"), and human civilizations will enter a time of declining information availability. While studies suggest that people preferentially expend scarce resources ICT over many other things (even, sometimes, food), and therefore Peak ICT may lag behind Peak Oil by some months or years, an awareness of the likelihood of Peak ICT may be helpful for both individual and institutional planning efforts. This project would explore the characteristics, timing, and implications of Peak ICT.

Surviving and Thriving

Local Smart Grids: A great deal of research has explored the use of smart electrical grids for increasing energy efficiency, and tracking energy usage for a variety of other purposes. However, the bulk of this research focuses on centralized grids used by large-scale institutions such as power companies or universities. Despite this focus, many of these advances may be able to be applied to local power contexts such as off-the-grid communities and self-sufficient survival retreats. These contexts tend to have much more stringent constraints on power; as such, they would benefit greatly from intelligent power tracking and management. This project would explore how sensing, measurement, and control techniques developed for large smart grids may be adapted to help local smart grids address canonical concerns in renewable energy such as the intermittency problem, in which energy sources such as solar or wind power vary dramatically based on cloud cover, time of day, etc.

Tracking Post-Collapse Food Sources: One of the most basic human needs is reliable access to food sources. However, vagaries of climate, seasons, access, and other factors may compromise this access. While researchers have previously explored ways of dynamically mapping the flows of materials through product supply chains outside collapse contexts [3], this project would seek to create an interactive system for monitoring a diverse array of food resources. The system could feature arbitrary ranges for various resources, with user-specified fuzziness of boundaries, and blendable confidence values to manage resource information from multiple sources. By providing a central and shareable way to track food sources, this system could be of significant use both to individuals foraging repeatedly in a given range, and to communities wishing to benefit mutually from shared food-gathering experiences.

Optimizing Arbitrage in Dynamic Barter Markets: In the absence of governmental infrastructure and stable currencies, it may be difficult to establish reliable exchange rates among various barter goods. Prices may vary across vendors in a market context, or across time in a series of interactions with one or more vendors. This project would build a computational system for optimizing trading policies in both concurrent and iterated exchanges. The system could take as input the available exchange rates in as many interactions are available, in whatever commodities are available. It would then seek to create transitive mappings across multiple commodities, as well as to perform predictive modeling of likely values of various commodities. The results of these calculations would be used to suggest optimal trading strategies and exchange rates. By optimizing arbitrage policies, this system could provide users with a competitive advantage in an unregulated and low-information-exchange market setting.

Currency, Infrastructure, and Societal Gatekeeping: Societies require the storage of value using media of exchange such as currencies in order to enable the easy transfer of seasonal and localized work across time and distance. Currencies typically require exchange participants to trust the issuer of the currency as well as the validity of the physical currency itself. The infrastructure of currency, however, enables the central authority to act in other gatekeeping roles as well. For example, flows of money across national borders are restricted, tax structures can be enforced, and a primary crime can be effectively punished on the basis of tax evasion as a secondary crime. When the trust in the centralized authority of the physical currency fails, not only does the currency system fail but so do the gatekeeping roles as well. This project would examine sources of trust in alternative digital currencies and how they span the digital-physical border. The examination would be done in light of how existing gatekeeping roles could be restructured and reimagined.

WHAT IF COLLAPSE NEVER COMES?

As has been evidenced time and time again across history, humans have a remarkable supply of ingenuity. Therefore, we may well avert collapse through a new energy source, geoengineering, the colonization of space, or some other as-yet-unconsidered approach. If collapse is somehow avoided, or delayed to the point where it's not yet relevant to give it much thought, won't the work on collapse informatics have been wasted?

We propose that no, the work will not have been wasted, for two main reasons. First, as was discussed in the previous section, collapse informatics has much in common with other HCI work. The overlap among projects and approaches among these genres makes a large portion of any research findings that may arise from collapse informatics efforts broadly relevant.

To offer a specific example, following publication of the results of the World3 model in the widely-circulated *Limits to Growth* [20], the 'Bariloche Group' of Latin American systems modelers offered the following critique: "The view that global crises will occur in the future reflects a parochial, developed-world perspective. For two-thirds of the world's population, crises of scarce resources, inadequate housing, deplorable conditions of health, and starvation are already at hand" ([19], p. 45). Given these crises, a subset of collapse informatics research efforts may be usefully adapted for use in other cultures and contexts.

Second, one of the key concepts of collapse informatics is designing sociotechnical systems with basic human needs at the heart of the process. Many research projects and commercial undertakings focus instead on perceived needs or manufactured needs, which then leads to a proliferation of complexity in many people's lives. This complexity not only hastens our progress toward collapse [31], but it also potentially compromises our quality of life. Humans evolved to deal with much narrower suites of issues than those that currently confront us [33]; the vast complexity of many people's lives may contribute to a lack of societal wellbeing via cognitive overload [35]. By seeking to foster more direct paths to meeting human needs, collapse informatics may also find new ways to make people happy.

FUTURE WORK

There are several main domains of future work that are relevant to collapse informatics. First, more work is needed to understand the details of how previous studies of collapse and various collapse scenarios may influence the goals and processes of collapse informatics as a genre of research.

Second, there are abundant potential projects in this area, across a wide variety of human needs, contexts, and habitats. The selection of fictional abstracts above provides just a small sampling of the wide range of potential research efforts that could be undertaken, and that could help improve human quality of life in collapse contexts.

Third, the question of how best to evaluate collapse informatics projects is of critical importance. The particular challenges of this class of cross-cultural design problem make evaluation an exciting area for future research.

Finally, there may be ways that collapse informatics can lay the groundwork for research outside of HCI pertaining to collapse, providing new kinds of collapse-compliant infrastructures that support efforts in other domains. To use a term from economics, computers are powerful "general purpose technologies" – their ability to amplify human efforts could have a profound effect on a range of other disciplines.

CONCLUSION

This paper is based on the possibility that global industrial civilization may enter a period of collapse, rather than indefinitely continuing the growth that has been its hallmark for much of the past two centuries. We propose that it is now appropriate for CHI researchers to begin exploring how our discipline may help to address the problems that would be likely to arise in such a scenario.

In this paper, we have defined collapse informatics as encompassing the study, design, and building of ICT and sociotechnical systems in the abundant present for use in a future of scarcity. Work in this area would seek to serve basic human needs, situated in particular contexts and habitats. We have drawn connections between collapse informatics and existing areas, offered initial thoughts on how research in this area may be evaluated, and provided a selection of potential projects that would be relevant to this domain.

While we see collapse as an unfortunate potential future, it is one that humanity's current ways of living make increasingly likely. There are many efforts afoot across many disciplines to enable sustainability; however, these efforts are often diametrically opposed to the culture of growth and consumption that pervades industrialized society. Perhaps by thinking now about life after collapse, we may both prepare ourselves for such an outcome, and also make that outcome less likely.

ACKNOWLEDGMENTS

The authors wish to thank the reviewers for their helpful feedback. We also thank Bonnie Nardi, Shunying Blevis, Sam Kaufman, Chit Meng Cheong, Rebecca Black, the Donald Bren School of Information and Computer Sciences, and the California Institute for Telecommunications and Information Technology. This material is based upon work supported in part by the

National Science Foundation under Grant No. 0644415 and by the Alfred P. Sloan Foundation.

REFERENCES

1. Baumer, E.P.S. and Silberman, M.S. When the implication is not to design (technology). *Proceedings of the 28th international conference on Human factors in computing systems (CHI 2011),* (2011), 2271.
2. Blevis, E. and Blevis, S. Hope for the best and prepare for the worst: interaction design and the tipping point. *interactions 17*, 5 (2010), 26-30.
3. Bonanni, L., Hockenberry, M., Zwarg, D., Csikszentmihalyi, C., and Ishii, H. Small business applications of sourcemap. *Proceedings of the 28th international conference on Human factors in computing systems (CHI 2010)*, (2010), 937.
4. Costanza, R., Cumberland, J.H., Daly, H., Goodland, R., and Norgaard, R.B. *An Introduction to Ecological Economics*. CRC Press, 1997.
5. Daly, H.E. *Toward a Steady-state Economy*. W.H.Freeman & Co Ltd, 1973.
6. Diamond, J. *Collapse: How Societies Choose to Fail or Succeed.* Viking Adult, 2004.
7. DiSalvo, C., Sengers, P., and Brynjarsdóttir, H. Mapping the landscape of sustainable HCI. *Proceedings of the 28th international conference on Human factors in computing systems (CHI 2010)*, (2010), 1975-1984.
8. Dourish, P. What we talk about when we talk about context. *Personal and Ubiquitous Computing 8*, (2004), 19-30.
9. Fayers, P.M. and Machin, D. *Quality of life: the assessment, analysis and interpretation of patient-reported outcomes*. Wiley, 2007.
10. Fry, T. *Design futuring: sustainability, ethics, and new practice*. Berg, 2008.
11. Hayes, G.R. The relationship of action research to human-computer interaction. *ACM Trans. Comput.-Hum. Interact. 18*, 3 (2011), 15:1-15:20.
12. Horning, J. and Neumann, P.G. Risks of neglecting infrastructure. *Comm. ACM 51*, (2008), 112.
13. Laurel, B. Gaian IxD. *interactions 18*, 5 (2011), 38-46.
14. Lovelock, J. *The Vanishing Face of Gaia: A Final Warning*. Basic Books, 2009.
15. Luers, A.L., Lobell, D.B., Sklar, L.S., Addams, C.L., and Matson, P.A. A method for quantifying vulnerability, applied to the agricultural system of the Yaqui Valley, Mexico. *Global Environmental Change 13*, 4 (2003), 255-267.
16. Matthews, H.D. and Weaver, A.J. Committed climate warming. *Nature Geosci 3*, 3 (2010), 142-143.
17. Max-Neef, M. *Human scale development: conception, application and further reflections*. The Apex Press, 1991.
18. McKibben, B. *Eaarth: Making a Life on a Tough New Planet*. Times Books, 2010.
19. Meadows, D. *Groping in the Dark: The First Decade of Global Modelling*. John Wiley & Sons Inc, 1982.
20. Meadows, D.H. *Limits to Growth*. Signet, 1972.
21. Meehl, G.A., Washington, W.M., Collins, W.D., et al. How Much More Global Warming and Sea Level Rise? *Science 307*, 5716 (2005), 1769 -1772.
22. Nelson, T.H. Crush and crash: logic of a terrible tomorrow. *Comm. ACM 40*, (1997), 90-91.
23. Norris, F. Time to Say It: Double Dip May Be Happening. *The New York Times*, 2011. http://www.nytimes.com/2011/08/05/business/economy/double-dip-recession-may-be-returning.html.
24. Pachauri, R.K. *Climate Change 2007: Synthesis Report. Contribution of Working Groups I, II and III to the Fourth Assessment Report of the Intergovernmental Panel on Climate Change*. IPCC, 2007.
25. Pan, Y., Cheong, C.M., and Blevis, E. The climate change habitability index. *interactions 17*, 6 (2010), 29-33.
26. Rawles, J.W. *Patriots: Surviving the Coming Collapse: A Novel of the Turbulent Near Future*. Xlibris Corporation, 2006.
27. Schuler, D. Communities, technology, and civic intelligence. *Proceedings of the fourth international conference on Communities and technologies*, (2009), 61-70.
28. Shirky, C. Gin, Television, and Social Surplus - Here Comes Everybody. 2008. http://www.herecomeseverybody.org/2008/04/looking-for-the-mouse.html.
29. Silberman, M.S. and Tomlinson, B. Precarious infrastructure and postapocalyptic computing. *Examining Appropriation, Re-use, and Maintenance for Sustainability, workshop at CHI 2010*, (2010).
30. Silberman, M.S. and Tomlinson, B. Toward an ecological sensibility: tools for evaluating sustainable HCI. *CHI EA '10 Proceedings of the 28th of the international conference extended abstracts on Human factors in computing systems* (2010), 3469.
31. Tainter, J.A. *The Collapse of Complex Societies*. Cambridge University Press, 1990.
32. Tainter, J.A. Social complexity and sustainability. *ecological complexity 3*, 2 (2006), 91-103.
33. Tomlinson, B. *Greening through IT: Information Technology for Environmental Sustainability*. The MIT Press, 2010.
34. Vardi, M.Y. The financial meltdown and computing. *Communications of the ACM 52*, (2009), 5.
35. Walsh, R. Lifestyle and mental health. *American Psychologist*, (2011).
36. Wigley, T.M.L. The Climate Change Commitment. *Science 307*, 5716 (2005), 1766-1769.
37. Wong, J. Prepare for Descent: Interaction Design in our New Future. *Defining the Role of HCI in the Challenges of Sustainability, workshop at CHI 2009*, (2009).
38. Vulnerability, Resilience and Adaptation. 16:25:48.679192. http://ihdp.unu.edu/article/adaptation.

Beyond Energy Monitors: Interaction, Energy, and Emerging Energy Systems

James Pierce, Eric Paulos
Human-Computer Interaction Institute, Carnegie Mellon
5000 Forbes Avenue, Pittsburgh, PA, USA
{jjpierce, paulos} @ cs.cmu.edu

ABSTRACT
Motivated by a recent surge of research related to energy and sustainability, this paper presents a review of energy-related work within HCI as well as from literature outside of HCI. Our review of energy-related HCI research identifies a central cluster of work focused on electricity consumption feedback (ECF). Our review of literature outside of HCI highlights a number of emerging energy systems trends of strong relevance to HCI and interaction design, including smart grid, demand response, and distributed generation technologies. We conclude by outlining a range of opportunities for HCI to engage with the experiential, behavioral, social, and cultural aspects of these emerging systems, including highlighting new areas for ECF research that move beyond our field's current focus on energy feedback displays to increase awareness and motivate individual conservation behavior.

Author Keywords
Energy; Electricity; Sustainability; Design

ACM Classification Keywords
H.5.m [Information Interfaces and presentation (e.g., HCI)]: Miscellaneous;

General Terms
Theory

INTRODUCTION
Energy has become established as an important topic of concern for HCI, particularly with respect to the area of sustainable HCI [e.g.,6,15]. Given the proliferation of research within HCI related to energy, now is a good time to review and assess current work within our field, as well as trends in literature from outside of HCI. Our review of energy-related work within HCI highlights a range of innovative contributions related to the design of energy feedback systems that aim to motivate sustainable consumption. However our review also reveals that current work is narrowly focused on a specific set of goals and interventions, namely increasing users' cognitive awareness of electricity consumption and promoting electricity conservation behavior by means of consumption feedback, particularly by visualizing energy consumption data. Our review of literature outside of HCI highlights a number of key areas of emerging energy systems that have not—with some notable exceptions [e.g.,48,55,61,70]—been significantly engaged with, including smart grid technologies, demand response appliances and infrastructure, real-time energy pricing, and small to large scale distributed and renewable generation such as wind and solar power.

Our primary goal and contribution in this paper is to help expand the types of energy-related work within HCI, both with respect to energy feedback systems and beyond. We give special attention to emerging energy systems, and outline and concretely illustrate that these types of systems offer a rich space for innovative and important HCI contributions. In line with others [e.g.,13,48,56,61,62], we draw attention to the emergence of new energy infrastructure, policy and areas of consumer applications as key opportunities for designers and researchers to intervene in order to redesign and reconfigure sustainable everyday technologies, practices, lifestyles and behaviors. Similar to the ways in which the introduction of electricity and accompanying technologies transformed everyday life and gave rise to new ways of living, the emergence of new energy systems are poised to have potentially radical effects on how energy is used and experienced in domestic, workplace and public contexts. At the same time, however, the opportunities for radical change afforded by shifts in energy regimes should be tempered with caution and concern for the potentially far-reaching negative consequences that may be introduced unintentionally by design [e.g.,9,57].

In what follows, we first give a review of energy-related HCI research and identify a dominant cluster of this work focused on electricity consumption feedback (ECF). While this paper is not specifically aimed at critiquing this cluster of work, we note that prior work within and outside of HCI has raised a number of criticisms of the types of approaches we have characterized as ECF. For example, Elizabeth Shove has argued that approaches to sustainable consumption aimed at changing individuals' behaviors and attitudes often have difficulty dealing with the dynamics of social change and the ways behavior is constrained by forces outside an individual's control [57]. Related criticisms can be found in the work of Dourish [17], DiSalvo et al. [15], Strengers [61] and others [e.g., 3,47].

Following our discussion of ECF research within HCI, we outline several critical yet largely overlooked areas of emerging energy systems for HCI. Surprisingly, given our field's concern with the topic of energy consumption and more generally with emerging technologies, many of these areas have yet to be explicitly highlighted and significantly engaged with within the HCI literature (and yet are pervasive across the more general body of literature dealing with energy systems research, development, policy, legislation, and design). Next we highlight several interactive projects that variously engage with aspects of the emerging energy systems presented. Some of this work is drawn from the authors' prior and ongoing research.

We conclude by outlining a range of opportunities and challenges for HCI and interaction design research related to energy and sustainability. These include both ways of expanding ECF research, as well as ways that HCI can expand beyond the goal of promoting sustainable behavior change by means of electricity consumption feedback.

ENERGY-RELATED RESEARCH WITHIN HCI

In this section we characterize and give an overview of current HCI research related to energy. This is based on our review of 51 papers related to "energy" [1] from HCI-oriented venues including the ACM CHI, OZCHI, UbiComp, DIS, TEI, NordiCHI, Persuasive and Pervasive conferences. Specifically we identified 2 journal articles, 32 papers published in conference proceedings, and 17 papers in extended abstracts. We did not review workshop papers or other non-peer reviewed papers.

Our review reveals a central cluster of research that we refer to as *electricity consumption feedback research* (ECF). This area represents roughly 70% of the HCI literature we reviewed dealing with electricity consumption, and 100% of the subset of this work that is both self-identified as related to "sustainability" and primarily contributes a novel design artifact. ECF is characterized by the following themes:

1. **Consumption feedback.** ECF research is focused on a specific type of intervention, namely presenting users with feedback based on electricity consumption data (e.g., the amount of electricity a home is consuming), typically displayed to users via a computational visualization.
2. **Energy awareness and conservation behavior**. ECF research is focused on a specific goal, namely promoting individual energy conservation behavior and/or cognitive awareness of energy consumption.

With only a few notable exceptions that contextualize their work within recent energy trends such as smart metering [e.g.,7,39,53,55], ECF can further be characterized by a third theme:

3. **Lack of engagement with emerging energy systems.** ECF research is mostly framed within current paradigms of energy production/consumption, namely centralized systems of production with limited capacity for integration with smart metering infrastructure, demand response, or distributed and renewable generation (areas which we review later in this paper).

Our review reveals three clusters of energy feedback research: (1) ECF displays and interfaces, (2) ECF technical infrastructure, and (3) qualitative studies informing ECF research and design. We give an overview of each in turn.

ECF displays and interfaces

The majority of the papers we reviewed focus on the design, implementation and/or evaluation of technologies that involve "feeding back" electricity consumption data to users via a computational display (27 papers total, roughly half of the literature we reviewed). 23 of these papers present a design artifact [e.g.,5,20,28,31,33,35,43,71]); 3 focus on outlining design recommendations or strategies for energy feedback design [21,27,45]; the remaining paper is a review of eco-feedback, which does not exclusively focus on electricity but does identify electricity consumption as the predominant focus of eco-feedback technology within HCI [22]. The majority of the papers focus on a specific context of electricity consumption, namely the domestic environment. Exceptions include a paper that focus on workplace consumption behavior [33] and a tool that provides feedback to software engineers [2]. We further note that all of the papers we reviewed were focused on electricity consumption in industrialized or "developed" contexts, typically upper-middle class populations (an issue also highlighted by Dillahunt et al. [14]).

Most papers employ a screen-based computational visualization [e.g.,7,31,35,43]. Others employ ambient displays utilizing lighting other than pixel-based displays [e.g.,23,28,33]). Most of these papers focus on energy consumption for the entire home or broken down for specific appliances. Only a few target interactions with a specific appliance or device via a display integrated with that appliance or device. These include feedback integrated with an electrical power cord [23], mobile screen-based devices [26], individual home power outlets [28,59], and home computers [35]. Most focus on providing feedback in order to inform or motivate conscious decision-making. A

[1] This group of 51 papers does not include papers we reviewed that focused on energy resources other the electrical energy. Interestingly, though perhaps not surprisingly, we found relatively few papers that focused on non-electrical energy. Two of these dealt with transportation and two with carbon-tracking more generally. We also found four papers that dealt with water consumption, each of which focused on feedback similar to that which characterizes ECF. Although these papers are relevant to our concern with energy and emerging energy systems, we chose to exclude them for simplicity and given they were relatively few in number.

few focus on unconsciously processed information, including subliminal information [24] and "unconscious", affordance-based persuasion [59]. One of the papers we reviewed is a persuasive game that did not directly measure energy consumption but rather simulated it in order to educate users about efficient consumption behaviors [5].

While we characterize this cluster as focused on the goals of increasing user awareness and/or motivating conservation behavior change via energy feedback, it is important to clarify that many of these papers additionally address some broader goals and concerns, such as curiosity and engagement [7], aesthetic experience [31], and playful competition [58]

ECF technical infrastructure

We identified a much smaller set of HCI-related papers that focus more on the technical challenges of sensing and feedback infrastructure for feedback interfaces, rather than the design of feedback interfaces themselves [42,51,54]. We also note that outside of HCI venues but within the computing literature more broadly (e.g., ACM conferences such as E-Energy and Build-Sys, and journals such as IEEE Pervasive Computing), a great deal of attention has been given to the technical challenges and opportunities presented by emerging energy technologies, such as the smart grid concept we discuss in the next section [e.g., 50,52].

Qualitative studies informing ECF research and design

We identified a number of papers that focus on user studies or other qualitative studies of electricity feedback systems and energy consumption practices [e.g.,10,11,14,53,55]. We characterized these studies as ECF research because they focus on design recommendations for energy feedback systems that encourage energy awareness and conservation behavior. However it should be noted that these papers also discuss some broader concerns such as power imbalances between landlords and tenants [14], limitations of financial incentives [10], and privacy issues related to personal energy consumption information [55].

Non-ECF research

We identified 4 clusters of research related to energy and HCI that we did not characterize as ECF. These were: (1) critical perspectives on energy feedback [46,47,60,61], (2) qualitative studies of energy consumption (without a predominant focus on ECF design recommendations) [8,40,70], (3) energy harvesting and human-powered interaction techniques [e.g.,4,41,66,67], and (4) design-theoretic treatments of energy [3,48,49]. (Here we reference two noteworthy papers [3,41] that deal with interactive technologies but which fall outside of the mainstream HCI venues we reviewed.) Collectively these papers deal with a range of emerging energy technologies, such as smart metering and small-scale power generation technologies. Later in this paper we highlight some of these projects in more detail. Next we discuss emerging energy systems.

EMERGING ENERGY SYSTEMS

We are currently witnessing a surge of technical and social innovation in the energy sector across various areas of academic research, government, and industry. However our review reveals that the HCI community has been slow to fully and explicitly engage with important areas of this work—either to build upon it or critique it. In this section we draw out and summarize several key areas for HCI research and design based on our review of literature related to emerging energy systems. In doing so, we highlight important opportunities for HCI and interaction design to play a role in proposing, exploring and shaping (or un-shaping) new interactive applications based on emerging technologies. We outline four commonly discussed areas of emerging energy systems (with a focus on technical infrastructure rather than social, cultural, economic, and political factors) that have strong relevance for HCI and interaction design. We conclude this section with a brief discussion of some criticisms of emerging energy systems.

Smart grid

Since the introduction of modern electricity generation in the late 1800's, modern electrical power grids have undergone remarkable evolution. Despite Thomas Edison's original vision of a largely distributed generation system [32], the modern power grids in most developed countries are centralized systems comprised primarily of large central-station generation connected by a high voltage network of grid to local electric distribution systems that serve homes, businesses and industry [18]. While this system has served industrial countries well in many regards, a host of concerns have arisen with this system, including climate change, energy security, the need to keep up with aging infrastructure, and risk of nuclear disaster (a concern rekindled by the recent Fukushima Dai-ichi nuclear disaster) [e.g.,30,64].

In response to these concerns, a "smart" electrical power grid, or *smart grid*, is being advocated, developed and in some cases implemented in countries around the world including Europe, the U.S., Australia, and China. While various definitions and visions of the smart grid exist across academic literature and publications from government and industry [30], the central aspect shared by these notions is the use of information technology applied to the electric power system [50]; "At a basic level, the smart grid will serve as the information technology backbone that enables widespread penetration of new technologies that today's electrical grid cannot support." [30, p. 30]. Other sources envision that smart grids of the future will be characterized by a shift "from a centralized, producer-controlled network to one that is less centralized and *more consumer-interactive* [emphasis added]." [64, p. 10].

Advanced metering infrastructure and smart meters

The concept of *advanced metering infrastructure (AMI)* is central to various definitions of the smart grid [30]. AMI refers to a network that allows for two-way communication between an electricity provider and the customer meter [30]. *Smart meters*, built on top of AMI, are utility meters that record real-time electricity consumption and report this data back to utility providers. Smart meters have been installed or are planned to be installed in countries including Italy, Japan, Canada, the U.K., the U.S., and Australia (see, e.g., [60,61,64,68]). In-home displays (IHDs) that report real-time energy consumption data enabled by smart meters are frequently discussed in the smart grid literature [e.g.,30], and have been implemented and studied [e.g.,60,61,70]. Smart meters and IHDs clearly dovetail with the types of home energy monitoring displays characteristic of current ECF research. However, AMI and smart meters are also significant in that they enable time-based electricity rates and demand response programs, which we discuss in the following section.

Demand response

ECF systems within HCI typically focus on motivating conservation behaviors such as turning off lights when not in use. However there is another major approach to improving the overall efficiency of the power grid called demand response. *Demand response (DR)* refers to a variety of programs and actions that involve customer/user response to particular conditions within the electricity system, such as peak period network congestion or high prices [63]. Demand response programs aim to transfer customer loads during periods of high-demand to off-peak periods, a strategy referred to as *load shifting* [12]. Load shifting can improve the overall efficiency of the power grid by flattening load curves and allowing more electricity to be provided by less expensive base load generation [12]. Demand response can also reduce the need for building additional generation capacity [12, 25].

Demand response and load shifting are particularly interesting areas to explore for HCI and interaction design because they can involve behavior and lifestyle changes that may be quite different from those falling in the category of energy conservation.

Distributed generation and renewable energy resources

The centralized power grids of most industrialized countries rely on large central generation facilities, typically fossil fuel or nuclear plants [18], which are tied to a range of concerns including global warming, threat of terrorist attack, and nuclear disaster. In response to these issues associated with centralized power systems a new trend toward developing distributed energy generation is emerging [e.g.,1,68,72]. While there is no clear consensus on the term *distributed generation (DG)* or related terms such as decentralized generation or on-site generation, DG is typically characterized by energy conversion units with smaller generation capacities (~3-10,000 kW) and which are situated physically closer to energy consumers [1,72]. In the most extreme case of distributed generation, buildings are completely self-supported with respect to generation of their electricity, heat and cooling energy [1]. Some common distributed generation systems include combined heat and power (CHP), fuel cells, microturbines, biomass, photovoltaic systems, and small-scale wind power systems. Generation using such sources to meet ones own energy needs is often referred to as *microgeneration*, and localized groupings of electricity generation and storage is typically referred to as a *microgrid*, or a *grid-tied electrical system* when it is linked to a centralized system (see, e.g., [68,72]).

While distributed and renewable generation has been advocated as means of addressing the inefficiencies with and environmental degrading nature of current centralized power systems, a number of challenges are presented by decentralized power systems, including high costs to produce, implement, and maintain them [e.g.,72]. A major issue discussed in the literature is the intermittent and distributed nature of distributed generation that is determined by local environmental conditions such as wind speeds and cloud cover, which can vary significantly even over short periods of hours or minutes [52]. This is often framed as an engineering problem in which strategies such as demand-response will have to be utilized to ensure electricity demand is matched to the available supply [52, 64]. Others have argued that the "problematic" intermittent and local character of distributed generation actually offer new opportunities for social empowerment [65], energy systems that are more compatible with "social diversity and freedom of choice" [38, p. 54], energy awareness and citizen participation in energy issues [13], more active consumer engagement through the co-provision of microgeneration services [68], and positive experiential engagement with one's local environment and community [48,62].

DG and its potentials for both integration with and independence from centralized power systems and the smart grid suggest a broad range of opportunities and challenges for HCI and interaction design. These range from new financial and non-financial incentives to conserve energy (e.g., by designing to amplifying feelings of ownership and responsibility over locally produced energy) to the design of new community sharing norms and practices.

Criticism of emerging energy systems

While proponents of a "smart grid" and related technical innovations argue these technologies can help solve pressing societal problems such as climate change and energy security, others have raised substantial criticisms of these technologies. One area of criticism highlights technical and economic issues. For example, some critics have questioned the cost-effectiveness of installing smart meters. Another area of criticism more deeply challenges the way emerging energy technologies are being positioned socially and politically. For example, Nobel Laureate John Byrne and colleagues argue that proponents of renewable generation hope to achieve technological revolution without addressing the social issue of "energy obesity" [9]. Such

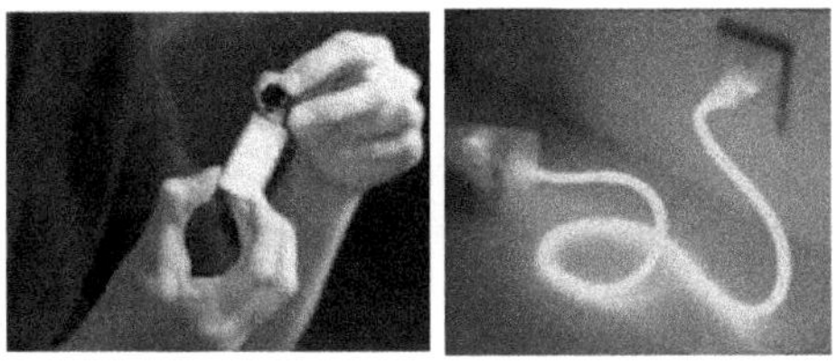

Figure 1. Energy Memento (left) and Power-Aware Cord (right, image courtesy of Interactive Institute).

criticisms are echoed in recent critiques within HCI [e.g.,6,15,17,48,61]. While this paper focuses on highlighting the opportunities presented by emerging energy systems, these types of criticisms should be taken into account. Indeed, they can be productively drawn on and developed by designers and researchers of interactive technologies in order to propose new ways of positioning and shaping emerging energy systems.

DESIGN CASES: INTERACTION FOR EMERGING ENERGY SYSTEMS

In this section we highlight several projects and areas of research involving interactive designs that variously deal with aspects of the emerging energy systems outlined previously. Some of these examples fall within mainstream HCI research while others originate from outside of HCI. We present these examples in order to concretely illustrate interaction-oriented energy research at the periphery of ECF research. Each project departs in some noteworthy way from either the goal of energy conservation/awareness or the design of a display for monitoring and displaying consumption data, or both. We organize these projects into three scales of focus: energy as a material, energy devices, and energy homes/communities.

Energy as a material

Static! and the aesthetics of energy

The Static! research group at the Interactive Institute was focused on a novel approach to interactive design research around energy. Two ideas were central to the group's research: exploring the aesthetics of energy as a design material and promoting critical reflection with respect to the use of energy [3]. The group prototyped an impressive range of artifacts related to these themes. One of the most commonly referenced artifacts is the Power Aware Cord, an electrical cord that visualizes the amount of electricity flowing through it using pulsing LED lighting (Figure 1). Several projects also made use of energy from small-scale renewable sources, including the Energy Tap—a public hand-crank electricity generator (Figure 3). While the presentation of several of these projects such as the Power Aware Cord fit within our characterization of ECF [23], the broader design theoretic approach presented by the Static! group [3] is unique in the way it moves beyond concerns with behavior change by conceptualizing ways that designers can craft electrical energy as a material in aesthetic and provocative ways.

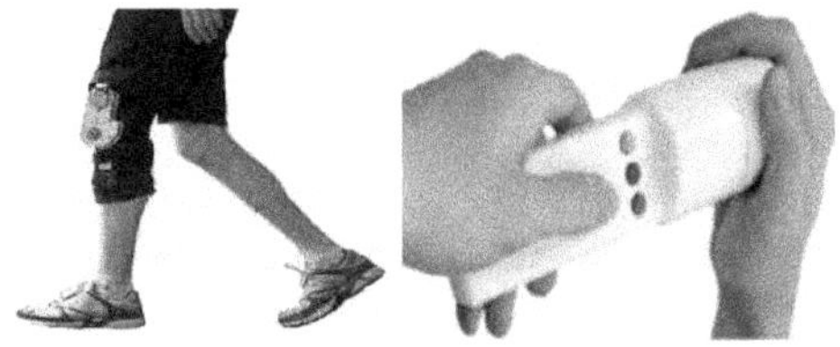

Figure 2. Bionic Energy Harvestor (left, image courtesy of Max Donelan) and Peppermill (right, image courtesy of Nicolas Villar and Steve Hodges).

Energy Mementos and energy metadata

Building on the work of the Static! group, authors Pierce and Paulos have designed a series of "Energy Mementos" with a goal of exploring energy as material that is experienced as a unique and meaningful thing [48]. A central theme this project investigates is the extent to which people can interpret and treat some energy differently than other energy. For example, the Shake-light bottle (Figure 1) allows someone to generate energy by shaking the bottle. The energy is then stored and may be given as a gift. Opening the bottle activates the energy as a stream of lights that directly correspond to the unique magnitudes of power generated by the individual that created the energy. Energy Mementos build on the concept of *energy metadata* that captures attributes of electrical energy [48]. These may include more commonly discussed attributes such as cost or technical characteristics such as voltage or frequency. However the metadata concept emphasizes a much broader range of less conventional attributes of electricity, such as how it was produced (e.g., wind, solar, coal), where it was produced, who produced it, and how far it has traveled.

Energy devices and interactions

Energy harvesting

Energy harvesting (or energy scavenging) is an area of research concerned with capturing and utilizing energy from human activities and other external sources such as ambient heat, often for mobile and wireless applications. A well-known example within the energy scavenging literature is Schenck and Paradiso's shoe-mounted piezoelectronic device (discussed in [41]). A more recent example is the knee-mounted biomechanical energy harvester that captures energy from walking [16] (Figure 2). Other types of energy scavenging devices capture ambient environmental energy from thermal, light and vibrational sources [41].

Human-powered electrical and electronic applications

While energy harvesting applications typically focus on extracting *passively* generated energy from humans or ambient environmental sources, other applications are designed for more *active* human-power generation. Current consumer applications of this variety include hand-powered flashlights, radios, and mobile phone chargers. A recent research exemplar is Villar and Hodges' Peppermill, a device that can power web-applications with human energy

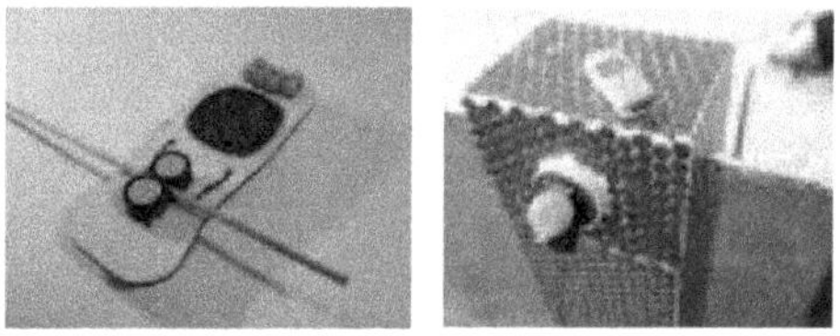

Figure 3. An Exertion Instrument (left, image courtesy of Noah Vawter) and Energy Tap (right, image courtesy of Interactive Institute).

[67] (Figure 2). Another noteworthy example is InGen, a self-powered wireless rotary input device that can generate haptic feedback without external power requirements [4]. Human-power generation and energy harvesting both offer a range of possibilities for new types of interactive applications.

Exertion Instruments

Designed and built by Noah Vawter at the MIT Media Lab, Exertion Instruments are hand-powered musical instruments that use electric or electronic oscillators for sound generation [66]. Exertion instruments are similar to traditional acoustic instruments in that the acoustic energy generated is directly proportional to the player's kinetic energy exerted into the instrument. Vawter has built a range of such instruments using a number of different types of interactive methods of electricity generation (e.g., Figure 3). Exertion instruments exemplify a novel application of human-powered electricity generation in order to explore new ways of engaging with and through electricity.

Energy homes and communities

The GridWise testbed demonstration

The Pacific Northwest GridWise Testbed demonstration was a field demonstration of smart grid technologies and programs that took place from 2006-2007 in the Pacific Northwest region of the U.S [25]. The project was funded by the U.S. Department of Energy and local utility companies. The GridWise project implemented and tested a wide range of smart grid technologies across approximately 100 homes, including the use of two-way communication between the power grid and microturbine distributed generation resources, real-time utility pricing for residential customers, and residential demand response for electric water heating, space heating and clothes dryers. Residents were able to set the "price responsiveness" based on a "comfort setting" for thermostats and water heaters, and clothes dryers were modified to display current pricing conditions. Residents were also able to view detailed historic and aggregated energy information for their homes from a website. Overall the project reports to have demonstrated peak load reduction based on demand response management and real-time price contracts.

Demand response and renewable energy displays

Within and outside of HCI, there have also been a number of qualitative studies of emerging energy technologies that are currently being manufactured, installed, and adopted in homes, such as domestic microgeneration and demand response displays. Woodruff et al. [70] have studied how

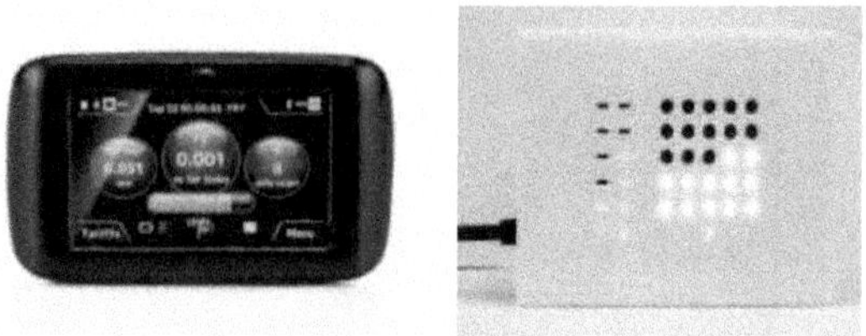

Figure 4. Landis+Gyr ecoMeter (left, image courtesy of Landis+Gyr) and The Local Energy Indicator (right).

eco-conscious consumers adopt and use new energy technologies. Strengers [61] has investigated how Australian eco-communities use the commercially available ecoMeter, which is unique from many other home energy monitors in that it displays periods of high, medium and low energy demand. Authors Pierce and Paulos have explored other ways of displaying information about the source of electricity [48], such as a lamp that communicates the source of energy by changing its color, and a home display showing the amount of available wind and solar energy (Figure 4).

RESEARCH AND DESIGN OPPORTUNITIES

Based on the areas of emerging energy systems and specific projects we have highlighted, we outline a number of opportunity areas for energy-related HCI research. Our goal is to demonstrate and advocate a broadening of research concerns, approaches, and projects within HCI and interaction design.

Designing new data, products, services and systems (Beyond monitoring home energy consumption)

We have characterized current energy-related HCI research as focused on a particular type of technology: energy feedback displays for consumption data. Here we outline a broader range of data, products, environments, services, and systems that ECF and other areas of HCI can engage with, particularly in the context of emerging energy systems.

Displaying new data

Emerging energy systems suggest sets of data (or energy metadata [48]) that can be visualized and displayed in addition to the amount of energy consumed by a person or household. In the context of distributed and renewable generation, energy displays could also visualize the source of energy for homes connected to microgrids and distributed resources (e.g., Figure 4). Another emerging area is the display of dynamic energy pricing information. More generally, the emergence of demand response systems opens up a space for communicating not only energy consumption but also energy *demand*, such as informing dwellers of critical peak periods.

Redesigning everyday product interfaces and interactions

Prior work has tended to focus on displays that report aggregated or disaggregated consumption data for an entire household or building. However, there are also many unexplored opportunities to redesign everyday appliances and devices, ranging from mobile phone chargers to dishwashers to thermostats. One important emerging application area is demand response appliances. An example of DR appliance development is the GridWise study that utilized demand response electric clothes dryers, hot water heaters and thermostats. Projects such as the PowerAware Cord [23] (Figure 1) further suggest ways that different types of energy can be reflected in the interface of a product, possibly based on new types of energy metadata [48].

Bodily energy interaction (without visualization)

We have also reviewed projects that explore new product-level energy interactions that focus on bodily, tactile engagement more than visual or cognitive engagement. These include human-powered and other energy harvesting applications such as the shoe-mounted energy harvester, the Peppermill, and InGen [4,41,67]. There are also opportunities to build on these types of technologies to design new forms of experiential and social engagement, as demonstrated by projects like Exertion Instruments and the Energy Tap. These types of applications highlight the potential for designing new ways of engaging with, experiencing, and understanding energy based on a more direct, visible, and physical connection to the production of energy.

Designing for other types and contexts of energy

The vast majority of the projects we reviewed and highlighted focus on the consumption of electricity in domestic contexts. Only a few papers engaged with other contexts such as the workplace [e.g.,2,33,55]. With a few exceptions [e.g.,3,31], none focused on design for public or communal spaces such as cafes, parks, schools or museums. (However, outside of academic research artists and designers have engaged with such contexts; see, e.g., [45].) Our review also did not reveal any papers that focused on "developing contexts", such as intermittent electricity supply in areas of India. Finally, the overwhelming focus of the works we reviewed was electrical energy, rather than other energy resources like natural gas—a point that has been noted previously by Froelich et al. [22]. While there are good reasons to focus on electricity, the home, and developed contexts, there are also opportunities to expand beyond these focuses.

Using energy differently (beyond "using less")

We have argued that energy-related HCI research is currently narrowly focused on the goal of promoting conservation behavior, i.e., using less energy by, for example, turning lights off when they are not in use. However, new types of interactions, behaviors and practices are already beginning to emerge in the context of new energy systems. We outline several such areas to consider.

Shifting energy consumption

Demand response and load-shifting are noteworthy areas in that they challenge a dominant assumption underlying how energy is currently consumed, namely that energy supply can and should always meet consumer demand. Instead of strictly focusing on conservation behaviors (using less energy), demand response is concerned primarily with *shifting* consumption behaviors to different times or places [46]. For example, while an energy conservation approach may aim to promote individuals to consolidate loads of laundry or use more efficient settings when running the automatic clothes washer and dryer, a demand response approach may aim to shift the practice of laundering from mid-day periods of high demand to nighttime or weekend periods of lower demand. Energy feedback research can play an important role in motivating and facilitating shifting behaviors. There are also opportunities to redesign individual products for integration with demand response systems. Companies are already beginning to develop DR appliances that can, for example, display changing market prices for energy or automatically respond to user defined preferences to stop or delay functions. Distributed and renewable generation also provides a very interesting context for designing shifting practices and behaviors because of its intrinsically intermittent character. Designing for shifting in this context suggests a potential reconfiguration of practices in a way that more directly relates to local weather conditions [e.g.,48,62].

Energy selection

Electricity that flows into the home and is tagged with energy metadata would allow people to know previously unknown or unconsidered characteristics of the energy they consume, such as where it was produced, how it was produced and who produced it [48]. Local distributed and renewable generation, ranging from large-scale distributed generation (such as the GridWise project) to small-scale applications (like the Peppermill and InGen) make it possible for individuals to literally see and even touch the technologies that are generating the energy they are consuming. Such contexts offer a largely unprecedented opportunity for energy consumers: selecting the type of energy or particular energy that one uses.

Sharing energy

In the future individuals and groups may not simply acquire and use energy, but additionally may be actively involved in distributing and sharing energy. For example, grid-tied homes equipped with solar or wind generation often sell power back to the electrical grid when they generate more energy than they require to meet their own energy demands. The emergence of microgrids could allow for more nuanced decisions and policies regarding how energy is shared and distributed within and between communities and households. For example, dwellers may be able to set home preferences for whether to store excess energy on-site or distribute it, and to whom. Sharing energy may also occur at the device-level. For example, microgenerated energy from energy harvesting application could be stored and shared amongst individuals, as suggested by projects like Energy Mementos and the Energy Tap.

Acquisition and adoption of energy technologies
How and why people acquire and adopt new technologies is also an important area of concern. Prior work has highlighted that current eco-feedback approaches tend to focus on curtailing the use of resources, such as curtailing hot water consumption when showering, rather than acquiring efficiency upgrades, such as acquiring a more efficient hot water heater [22]. Such efficiency upgrades have been suggested as more significant than curtailment behaviors in terms of reducing overall energy consumption. In the context of emerging energy systems, the acquisition and adoption of new technologies becomes increasingly important. For example, designers can think about ways of designing home microgeneration systems (e.g., photovoltaic) that people desire because they are fun and engaging or symbolically project important values.

Engaging with other approaches to consumption (Beyond attitude and behavior change)

Much of the energy-related HCI research we reviewed draws predominantly on theories and approaches from the fields of behavioral and social psychology. However there are many other theories of consumption developed in fields such as anthropology, sociology, geography, material culture studies, and philosophy. Several of these approaches have already seen inroads into HCI [e.g.,19,48,60,61,70]. For example, Strengers' studies of energy feedback [60,61] are interpreted through the lens of social practice theory [e.g.,56]. Practice theory offers a different theoretical perspective on how social change happens and draws attention to practices as embedded in social contexts. Consequently, Strengers' work draws attention to ways that current energy feedback technologies conflict with how people actually go about their everyday lives. The value of different theories of consumption is that they offer different ways of understanding energy consumption, and in turn focus on a range of different concerns that design can address (e.g., behavior change, self-identity, the dynamics of social systems) and types or scales of design interventions (e.g., product, service, system, policy).

Another area to consider is developing energy and consumption theory *within* HCI, rather than only applying or being guided by theory originating from outside of our field. For example, sociologists have noted the lack of rigorous theoretical engagement with energy consumption [e.g.,56,57]. Recent sociologically-informed studies of eco-feedback technologies [60,61] suggest ways such research can not only inform HCI/design but also make theoretical contributions that help explain how energy and energy technologies are (and are not) consumed. Recently there have been several works that offer design-theoretic treatments of electricity [3,49].

Engaging with energy infrastructure, service and policy (Beyond the individual consumer)

Most of the work we reviewed is predominantly focused on the individual user (and the design of product-level interventions), rather than engaging more broadly with various social groups (e.g., communities, the state), and the design of infrastructure and "behind the scenes" technologies (e.g., solar panels, water heaters), services (consisting of material and immaterial technologies), and public policy and legislation. The importance, and substantial challenges, of sustainable HCI and HCI in general moving beyond the individual has been raised previously [e.g.,15,17,29,70]. Outside of HCI there have been similar critiques of policy focused on targeting individual behaviors, attitudes and choices [e.g.,57]. These works collectively question and challenge the notion that problems of sustainability are best framed as matters of individual behavior and choice, and addressed by interventions at this level.

Although there are many interventions at the infrastructure and policy level that are largely outside the scope of HCI, there are nonetheless important opportunities to engage with these often overlooked aspects of technology design. Throughout we have suggested and demonstrated one way of engaging with infrastructure, services and policy: building upon and intervening within emerging energy systems with the design of new interactions and applications. For example, while the Energy Tap is in one sense a product for individuals to interact with, it is positioned and deployed so as to engage users and designers in a discussion around how energy is situated within public spaces.

Another important role that HCI can play is prototyping future energy applications *before* the technical infrastructure, service and policy systems to support them are fully in place. Such prototyping can serve a number of goals, including exploring, testing, and evaluating future ways of interacting with energy before they are, or can be, fully actualized. Another role that such prototyping can play is to directly inform the design and development of infrastructure, services and policy, for example, by creating compelling visions of future energy applications, interactions and practices. This type of work can take a much longer-term approach to intervention, aiming to inform technology design broadly and many years out into the future, rather than exclusively focusing on immediate applications. The extent to which HCI as a field has agency to impact policy and infrastructure is unclear, but this is a question worthy of stronger investigation.

CONCLUSION

A primary goal of this paper has been to demonstrate and advocate ways of expanding and refocusing various aspects of energy-related HCI research and design. We identified a central cluster of energy-related HCI research focused electricity consumption feedback (ECF). We further outlined a range of emerging energy technologies and socio-technical systems with strong relevance to HCI research. Based on our reviews, we outlined opportunities and challenges including new areas for ECF research as well as areas that move beyond this focus. It is our hope that this work will both further new and innovative HCI contributions, as well as further discussion within our field about the role and value of energy-related research.

ACKNOWLEDGEMENTS

We thank the anonymous reviewers for their helpful comments on this paper. Financial support was provided in part by National Science Foundation Grant #IIS-1018340.

REFERENCES

1. Allane, K. & Saari, A. 2006. Distributed generation and sustainable development. Renew. & sust. energy rev. 10(6).
2. Amsel, N. & Tomlinson, B. 2010. Green tracker: a tool for estimating the energy consumption of software.CHI EA '10.
3. Backlund, S. et al. 2006. Static! The aesthetics of energy in everyday things. Proc. of DRSIC.
4. Badshah, A., Gupta, S., Cohn, G., Villar, Hodges, S. & Patel, S. 2011. Interactive generator: a self-powered haptic feedback device. CHI '11.
5. Bang, M., Gustafsson, A., Katzeff, C. 2007. Promoting new patterns in household energy consumption with pervasive learning games. Persuasive'07.
6. Blevis, E. 2007. Sustainable interaction design: invention & disposal, renewal & reuse. CHI '07.
7. Broms, L., Katzeff, C., Bång, M, Nyblom, A., Hjelm, S. & Ehrnberger, K. 2010. Coffee maker patterns and the design of energy feedback artefacts. DIS '10.
8. Busse, D. 2011. Who Needs Energy Management? Reducing Energy Consumption in Manufacturing Industries - Early Results of Research into Industrial Energy Management Users. CHI EA '11.
9. Byrne, J. et al. 2009. Relocating energy in the social commons: Ideas for a sustainable energy utility. Bulletin of science, technology and society, 29(2):81-94.
10. Chetty, M., Tran, D. & Grinter, R. 2008. Getting to green: understanding resource consumption in the home. UbiComp '08.
11. Chetty, M., Brush, A.J., Meyers, B. & Johns, P.. 2009. It's not easy being green: understanding home computer power management. Proc. CHI '09. 1033-1042.
12. Davito et al. 2010. McKinsey on Smart Grid: The smart grid and the promise of demand-side management
13. Devine-Wright, P. 2006. Energy citizenship: psychological aspects of evolution in sustainable energy technologies. In J. Murphy (ed.) Governance of Sustainable Technology.
14. Dillahunt, T., Mankoff, J., Paulos, E. 2010. Understanding Conflict Between Landlords and Tenants: Implications for Energy Sensing and Feedback. UbiComp '10.
15. DiSalvo, C., Sengers, P., and Brynjarsdóttir, H. 2010. Mapping the landscape of sustainable HCI. CHI '10.
16. Donelan, J.M et al. 2008. Biomechanical energy harvesting: Generating electricity during walking with minimal user effort. Science, 319:807–810.
17. Dourish, P. 2010. HCI and environmental sustainability: the politics of design and the design of politics. DIS '10.
18. EPRI. 2011. Estimating the Costs and Benefits of the Smart Grid – A Preliminary Estimate of the Investment Requirements for a Fully Functioning Smart Grid.
19. Fallman, D. 2011. The new good: exploring the potential of philosophy of technology to contribute to human-computer interaction. CHI '11.
20. Foster, D., Lawson, S., Blythe, M., & Cairns, P. 2010. Wattsup?: motivating reductions in domestic energy consumption using social networks. NordiCHI '10.
21. Fitzpatrick, G., Smith, G. 2009. Technology-enabled feedback on domestic energy consumption: articulating a set of design concerns. Perv. Computing, 8(1):37-44.
22. Froehlich, J., Findlater, L., & Landay, J. 2010. The design of eco-feedback technology. In Proc. CHI '10.
23. Gustafsson, A. & Gyllenswärd, M. 2005. The power-aware cord: energy awareness through ambient information display. CHI EA '05.
24. Ham, J., Midden, C., and Beute, F. (2009). Can ambient persuasive technology persuade unconsciously? Using subliminal feedback to influence energy consumption ratings of household appliances. Persuasive '09.
25. Hammerstrom, D. et al. 2007. Pacific Northwest GridWise(TM) Testbed Demonstration Projects: Part I. Olympic Peninsula Project. Richland, Washington, Pacific Northwest National Laboratory
26. Harter, T., Vroegindeweij, S., Geelhoed, E., Manahan, M., & Ranganathan, P. 2004. Energy-aware user interfaces: an evaluation of user acceptance. CHI'04.
27. He H., Greenberg, S. & Huang, E. 2010. One size does not fit all: applying the transtheoretical model to energy feedback technology design. CHI '10.
28. Heller, F. & Jan Borchers. 2011. PowerSocket: towards on-outlet power consumption visualization. CHI EA '11.
29. Hirsch, T. & Anderson, K. 2010. Cross currents: water scarcity and sustainable CHI. CHI EA '10.
30. Hledick, R. 2009. How green is the smart grid? Electricity, 22(3).
31. Holmes, T. G. Eco-visualization: combining art and technology to reduce energy consumption. C&C '07.
32. Hughes, T. 1983. Networks of power. John Hopkins.
33. Johnson, L., Broms, L. & Katzeff, C. 2010. Watt-Lite: energy statistics made tangible. DIS '10.

34. Kim, T., Hong, H., & Magerko, B. Coralog: use-aware visualization connecting human micro-activities to environmental change. Proc. CHI EA '09.

35. Kim, T., Hong, H., & Magerko, B. 2010. Design requirements for ambient display that supports sustainable lifestyle. Proc. DIS '10.

36. Kim, Y. Schmid, Charbiwala, & Srivastava. 2009. ViridiScope: design and implementation of a fine grained power monitoring system for homes. UbiComp '09.

37. Lehrer, D. & Vasudev, J. 2011. Evaluating a social media application for sustainability in the workplace. CHI EA '11.

38. Lovins, A. 1977. Soft energy paths. Penguin.

39. Monigatti, P., Apperley, M., & Rogers, B. 2010. Power and energy visualization for the micro-management of household electricity consumption. AVI '10.

40. Nathan, L. 2008. Ecovillages, Values, and Information Technology: Balancing Sustainability with Daily Life in 21st Century America. CHI EA '08.

41. Paradiso, J. & Starner, T. 2005. Energy scavenging for mobile and wireless electronics, IEEE Perv. Comput,

42. Patel, S., Gupta, S. & Reynolds, M. 2010. The design and evaluation of an end-user-deployable, whole house, contactless power consumption sensor. CHI '10.

43. Petersen, D. et al. 2009. WattBot: a residential electricity monitoring and feedback system. CHI EA '09.

44. Petkov, P., Köbler, F., Foth, M., Medland, R. & Krcmar, H. 2011. Engaging energy saving through motivation-specific social comparison. CHI EA '11. 1945-1950.

45. Pierce, J., Odom, W., Blevis, E. 2008. Energy Aware Dwelling: A Critical Survey of Interaction Design for Eco-Visualizations. Proc. OZCHI '08, 2008.

46. Pierce, J., Schiano, D., & Paulos, E. 2010. Home, habits and energy: examining domestic interactions and energy consumption. CHI '11.

47. Pierce et al. 2010. Some consideration on the (in)effectiveness of energy feedback systems. DIS '10.

48. Pierce & Paulos. 2010. Materializing energy. DIS '10.

49. Pierce, J. & Paulos, E. A phenomenology of human-electricity relations. CHI '11.

50. Potter, C et al. 2009. Building a smarter smart grid through better renewable energy information. IEEEPES Power Systems Conference and Exposition.

51. Quintal, F., Nunes, N., Ocneanu, A. & Berges, M. 2010. SINAIS: home consumption package: a low-cost eco-feedback energy-monitoring research platform. DIS '10.

52. Ramchurn, S. et al. 2011. Putting the ``Smarts" into the Smart Grid: A Grand Challenge for Artificial Intelligence. Communications of the ACM . (In Press)

53. Riche, Y., Dodge, J. & Metoyer, R. 2010. Studying always-on electricity feedback in the Home. CHI '10.

54. Rodgers, J. & Bartram, L. 2010. ALIS: an interactive ecosystem for sustainable living. Ubicomp '10.

55. Schwartz, T., Betz, M., Ramirez, L., & Stevens, G. 2010. Sustainable energy practices at work: understanding the role of workers in energy conservation. NordiCHI '10.

56. Shove, E. 2003. Comfort, cleanliness and convenience: the social organisation of normality. Berg.

57. Shove E. 2010. Beyond the ABC: climate change policy and theories of social change, Env. and Planning, 42.

58. Shrubsole, P. et al. 2011. Flo: raising family awareness about electricity use. CHI EA '11.

59. Sohn, M. et al. 2009. Designing with unconscious human behaviors for eco-friendly interaction. CHI EA '09.

60. Strengers, Y. 2008. Smart metering demand management programs: challenging the comfort and cleanliness habitus of households. OZCHI '08.

61. Strengers, Y. 2011. Designing eco-feedback systems for everyday life. CHI '11.

62. Tatum, J. 1994. Technology and value: getting beyond the 'device paradigm' impasse. Science, Tech. and Hum. Values, 19:70-87

63. Torriti, J., Hassan, M., Leach, M. 2009. Demand response experience in Europe: Policies, programmes and implementation. Energy, 35(4): 1575-1583.

64. US DOE (2006). Benefits of demand response in electricity markets and recommendations for achieving them. February 2006.

65. Vaitheeswaran, V. 2003. Power to the People: How the Coming Energy Revolution Will Transform an Industry, Change Our Lives, and Maybe Even Save the Planet.

66. Vawter, N. 2010. Exertion music. Unpublished PhD thesis.

67. Villar, N. & Hodges, S. 2010. The peppermill: a human-powered user interface device. Proc. TEI '10.

68. Watson et al. 2006. Unlocking the power house: policy and system change for domestic microgeneration in the UK.

69. Wilson, C. & Dowlatabadi, H. 2007. Models of Decision Making and Residential Energy Use. Annual Review of Environment and Resources, 32.

70. Woodruff, A., Hasbrouck, J., Augustin, S. 2008. A bright green perspective on sustainable choices. CHI '08.

71. Yun, T. 2009. Investigating the impact of a minimalist in-home energy consumption display. CHI EA'09.

72. Zareipour et al. 2004. Distributed Generation: Current Status and Challenges. IEEE Proc. of NAPS '04.

The Dubuque Water Portal: Evaluation of the Uptake, Use and Impact of Residential Water Consumption Feedback

Thomas Erickson, Mark E. Podlaseck, Sambit Sahu, Jing D. Dai, Tian Chao, Milind Naphade
IBM T. J. Watson Research Center
P.O. Box 704, Yorktown Heights, NY 10598 USA
{snowfall | podlasec | sambits | jddai | tian | naphade}@us.ibm.com

ABSTRACT
The Dubuque Water Portal is a system aimed at supporting voluntary reductions of water consumption that is intended to be deployed city-wide. It provides each household with fine-grained, near real time feedback on their water consumption, as well as using techniques like social comparison, weekly games, and news and chat to encourage water conservation. This study used logs, a survey and interviews to evaluate a 15-week pilot with 303 households. It describes the Portal's design, and discusses its adoption, use and impacts. The system resulted in a 6.6% decrease in water consumption, and the paper employs qualitative methods to look at the ways in which the Portal was (or wasn't) effective in supporting its users and enabling them to reduce their consumption. The paper concludes with a discussion of design implications for residential feedback systems, and possible engagement models.

Author Keywords
Water; smart meters; sustainability; behavior change; water and energy feedback systems; social comparison; games

ACM Classification Keywords
H.5.2 [Information Interfaces And Presentation]: User Interfaces - Graphical user interfaces (GUI);

General Terms
Design, Experimentation, Human Factors.

INTRODUCTION
Lack of fresh water is a worldwide problem: a billion people lack access to clean water, and 3 million die every year due to water-related diseases [18]. Water use is growing twice as fast as the population [19]. Even where plentiful, surface water is being increasingly polluted and aquifers depleted [3]. According to the UN, "*By 2025 1.8 billion people will be living in countries ... with absolute water scarcity, and two-thirds of the world population could be under conditions of water stress.*" [19, p10]

Water is also important in producing energy [10]. It is critical to hydroelectric, geothermal and nuclear power generation. It is used to extract natural gas and oil from shale, to produce 'clean coal' and to grow biofuels. Many of these uses chemically alter the water, or disrupt natural systems that depend on water, requiring further energy to ameliorate. In sum, the increasing scarcity of fresh water is a problem that requires global attention.

Water scarcity is a complex problem, with many ways of addressing it. This study is concerned with a system for promoting water conservation among residential users in a U. S. city. While residential water consumption is far from the heaviest use in the U.S. (power plant cooling uses 50%, and irrigation 35%), it nevertheless costs $33 billion a year, with an equivalent amount required to manage the resulting wastewater [9]. Finally, as per capita U.S. water use is the highest in the world, twice that of Japan and over four times that of most northern European countries, it would appear that there are considerable savings to be had.

This paper evaluates a 15-week pilot deployment of a system aimed at supporting voluntary reductions of water use among 303 households in a mid-sized U.S. city. The system collected data from 'smart' water meters, analyzed it, and used a variety of techniques – usage graphs, alerts, incentives, games and chat – to encourage water conservation among residential users. This paper offers an in-depth, multi-method evaluation of the system.

PREVIOUS WORK
Over the last decade HCI has devoted increasing attention to sustainability (cf., [2]). Much of this has focused on resource conservation, and especially on energy. Space precludes a comprehensive review of this literature, but fortunately there are several excellent review papers. DiSalvo et al. [7] review of sustainability research within HCI, identifying axes along which work differs and highlighting emerging issues. Froehlich et al. [11] do a superb review of eco-feedback technologies that encompasses work in both HCI and environmental psychology, noting that the two literatures rarely refer to each other, and calling out differences between the fields. Pierce et al. [15] classify eco-visualizations, discuss design rationales and identify new challenges and opportunities. Finally, Darby [4] reviews the environmental psychology literature on energy feedback, finding that direct feedback can reduce energy consumption by 5% to 15%.

Eco-feedback also has its critics. Strengers [17] argues that such systems assume that their users will act as rational resource managers, and that this assumption is challenged by the fact that water and energy use is part of daily practices that are shaped by social and cultural norms (e.g., daily showering as a hygenic practice) and often viewed as largely non-negotiable. Similarly, Pierce et al. [15, 16] argue that much everyday energy use is not the result of conscious and motivated action, and that feedback may reinforce norms by reifying a household's "baseline" usage (which users may try to avoid exceeding but don't consider trying to reduce).

This paper addresses two issues that have been noted as deserving further attention. Froehlich, et al. [11] note that environmental psychology has used large, long-term field studies to quantify the effect of feedback, but pays little heed to the design of the feedback mechanisms, "*while HCI has concentrated on the production of the eco-feedback artifact and rarely on conducting fields studies to actually study behavior change*" [11, p. 2,003]. This paper bridges this gap with a 15-week field study of a complex eco-feedback portal. Further, researchers from both HCI and environmental psychology (e.g., [6, 16]) have called for work that, rather than treating the household as a black box, looks at "*how individuals engage or do not engage with feedback*" [16, p 244]. This work addresses this as well.

While energy has gotten the most attention, water has received some notice. Most work on water feedback has focused on point of use feedback at the tap and the showerhead [1, 12, 13]. These studies are limited by the fact that they are short-term, with small numbers of subjects, and have produced mixed results. The most positive result was a reduction in water consumption during showering of about 10% [12]. While feedback at the point of use seems, *a priori*, the most effective approach, a practical limitation is that the costs of purchasing and installing such devices city-wide seem formidable in an era of increasingly-constrained spending on urban infrastructure. Alternatives would be useful.

Work on water consumption feedback at the residential scale is rare. Petersen et al. [14] staged a two-week "energy reduction" contest at Oberlin during which they delivered feedback on water and energy consumption to 18 student dorms. Feedback was either delivered in near real time or once a week, and was delivered via student-accessible web pages and kiosks located in the dorms. The results were mixed: energy use dropped by 32%, but water use only by 3%. Although the students' 32% reduction in energy use considerably exceeded the 5–15% reduction usually achieved by energy feedback systems, the 3% reduction in water consumption is very small. It raises the question of whether residential-scale water feedback would be effective at all under circumstances more ordinary than an inter-dorm competition among college students.

In summary, it is clear that providing energy feedback, particularly in near real-time, can reduce resource consumption; it is less clear whether that is true in the realm of water. This study provides a data point – derived from a longer study of a broader population – that will provide a useful supplement to Petersen et al's [14] work. Finally, and more generally, as called for by other researchers, it would be valuable to have a deeper understanding of how feedback mechanisms are used, understood and experienced so as to be able to more effectively design such systems.

BACKGROUND: SITE, SYSTEM, PILOT AND PORTAL

The Site

The system this study evaluates was deployed in Dubuque Iowa. The choice of Dubuque was opportunistic, due to a convergence of factors including: Dubuque had established a strong sustainability agenda; Dubuque was in the process of switching from traditional water meters to smart water meters; and the researchers' organization had developed a good working relationship with the City. Dubuque does not have water scarcity problems: water is cheap.

The System

The system was designed for the City of Dubuque, and responded to their requirements both in specific features (e.g., showing water consumption in gallons, dollars and pounds of CO_2), and at a general level (e.g., a strong focus on maintaining privacy). In brief, the system worked as follows: Smart meters recorded consumption every 15 minutes. Each home's data was sent to a cloud-based repository every 4 hours where it was analyzed, typically with a 2-3 hour delay. The resulting feedback was provided (in aggregate, anonymized form) to the City's Water Agency, and (privately) to individual homes. Further details of the system architecture, data collection and analyses can be found in [4] and the final project report [8].

The Pilot Project

The portal was deployed to 303 volunteer households located in a few contiguous neighborhoods (due to constraints on proximity to data collection points) in early September. The deployment had two phases. During the first 9 weeks, half the participants were given access to the Portal, and half were not, allowing a controlled comparison of its impact on water consumption. Phase 2 started after a 1-week break, and during its 6 weeks everyone used the Portal. Because the pilot ran into the year-end holiday season, interviews were carried out in early December and the survey ran from late December into January.

The pilot project involved more than just turning on a web portal: sustained efforts were made to publicize the project and engage participants. The Mayor wrote letters to recruit participants and to update them on the pilot's progress. Dubuque 2.0, a non-profit sustainability organization, held various events to encourage participation. Training classes gave participants hands-on experience with the Portal.

Weekly prizes were awarded for participation, and weekly emails announced winners, prizes and tips. Web sites run by the City and by Dubuque 2.0 also provided publicity.

The public nature of the pilot project had consequences. Its stakeholders, particularly elected officials, were aware that problems could reflect back on them. Thus, it was not acceptable to recruit volunteers for the pilot and then tell half that they could not use the Portal at all because they needed to serve as controls. Nor was it acceptable to make water consumption data from the pilot public (even though water usage data is, legally, public, and available to anyone who asks). Strict user ID and password requirements were enforced out of concern that users might expose their usage. In general, concerns of this sort sometimes drove the design of the system and the pilot in ways that were not ideal for research, particularly with respect to the more social features of the system.

The Water Portal User Interface

Each household had a private portal, as shown in Figure 1. Just below the user ID (①), the timeline shows the daily water usage for the last year (②). Moving a 'thumb' along the timeline, shows a graph of the hour-by-hour usage for each day (③). The "Weekly Usage" tab displays a bar graph that shows usage for the week, each day broken into 4 periods. The "Compare" tab displays a bar graph that contrasts usage per day of the week for the last 3 weeks.

The last tab, "This Week's Game," provides two means of socially shaping behavior. The first (④) shows the ongoing results of a weekly game. Each week teams of 4 to 6 households were automatically created by the system. Each team was matched against another team that was expected – based on previous consumption patterns – to use about the same amount of water during the upcoming week. The goal was, of course, to use less water than the opposing team. The results were updated throughout the week (with each household being able to see how it and each of its (anonymous) teammates were performing (via the segments in the bar in the graph). Finally, the farthest bar to the right (⑤) shows the amount of water used by "Neighbors Like You," to which users can compare to their own usage. At the top right are statistics that provide various metrics of how the household is doing such as rank, and a menu bar that provides access to chat and news functionality (⑥).

THE STUDY

The Portal was deployed to 303 households for 15 weeks. Multiple measures – logs, a survey and interviews – were used to evaluate its effects on its users' behavior, beliefs and experience. The study examines the following areas:

- **Degree of usage**. How many households made use of the Water Portal, and what usage patterns did they exhibit?

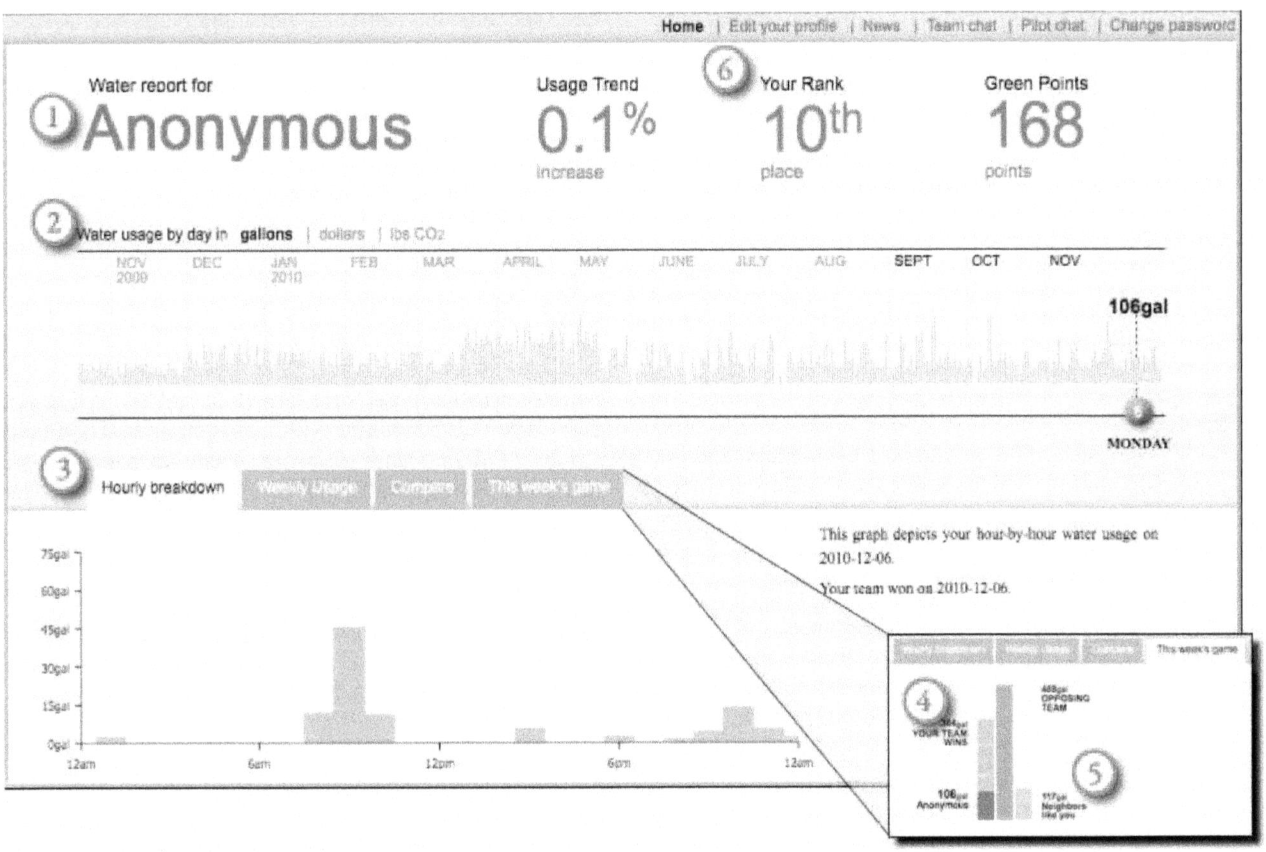

Figure 1. The Water Portal.

- **Manner of usage**. Which features of the Water Portal did participants use, and how and why did they use them?
- **Impacts of use**. What kind of impact did using the Water Portal have? Did users learn things from the information presented? Did they change their behavior, or make changes to their water appliances, to reduce their water consumption? And so on.

Participants
Because of privacy concerns, participants were identified only by anonymized IDs. Because the pilot was restricted to one area of the city, we can infer that participants were mostly middle class and lived in single-family dwellings.

Limitations
Our ability to generalize from this study is limited by two factors. First, as noted above, participants were not a random sample of the city population, but were primarily middle class residents of single-family dwellings. Second, participants were volunteers. On the one hand, it can be argued that as a consequence they are highly motivated and will be more inclined to use the Portal than the general populace. On the other hand, it can be argued that the same attitudes that led them to volunteer may mean that they have already taken actions to conserve water and thus there is little more they can do – i.e., the low hanging fruit is already picked. The study will shed more light on this.

While it is important to keep these factors in mind when generalizing from this research, it should be noted that issues like this are characteristic of most *in situ* studies of this type. Thus readers should draw conclusions, keep the limitations in mind, and over time, as more deployments of this type of technology occur, the field as a whole will develop a more general understanding of this domain.

Usage Logs
Two types of usage information were logged. Throughout the pilot Portal usage was tracked via login records. During phase 2, fine-grained logging was added to track use of individual user interface components.

The Survey
The survey consisted of 36 questions, 1 open-ended and the rest a mix of multiple choice and Likert scale questions, with valences mixed where appropriate. It took about ten minutes to complete. Participants received an email with a link to an online survey; two reminders were sent.

The survey began asking about the frequency of Water Portal usage. Those who rarely or never used it were asked about barriers to their usage; the others were asked which components of the Water Portal they used, how they used (and whether they understood) those components, and what impact they believed using the Water Portal had on them. After that, all participants answered questions about their attitudes and actions with respect to water usage.

The survey received 89 responses (2 other responses in which only 1 question was answered were omitted), which is a 29% response rate. With respect to the focus of this evaluation – the use of the Water Portal – 62 of the respondents reported using the Portal at least once, which, since the logs show that 106 distinct users logged onto the Portal, gives a 58% response rate for Water Portal users. Thus the survey provides a good picture of those who used the Portal; it has much less to say about non-users.

The Interviews
Interviews were conducted near the end of the deployment; their purpose was to provide illustrations and context and to inform the design of the survey. The 10 informants (3 women, 6 men, and 1 couple) were diverse in age, attitudes towards water conservation, and in the degree and ways in which they used the Portal. Semi-structured interviews were conducted in a city office and lasted about 45 minutes. They were digitally recorded, with permission, and later roughly transcribed. Interviews enquired about issues such as motivation, degree and manner of use of the Portal (using screenshots as prompts), and the impacts of using it.

FINDINGS
Of the 303 households in the pilot, 106 (35%) logged onto the Portal at least once. (Note: 28 households lacked internet access and received their results on paper; we do not report on these households). We discuss the results in three sections: the degree to which the Portal was used; the manner in which it was used; and the impacts it had. We also note implications for design, to which we return later.

How Often was the Portal Used?

Those who used the Portal Little or Not at All
The survey asked users who didn't use the Water Portal (at all or very much) the reasons for their lack of use. Significantly, only 4% of the respondents said that they found the Portal too difficult or complex to use; respondents had only minor suggestions for improving the user interface of the Portal. The most frequent reason for non-use was that they "kept forgetting" (49%). While some users reported difficulties with managing user IDs (random strings of digits) and passwords (sent on paper by U.S. mail), we believe that there is a larger issue of how (and whether) tracking water consumption fits into people's daily lives. We will return to this issue later.

Of the 32 respondents who used the Portal infrequently, 41% choose the response "After looking at it a few times I'd learned all I wanted." In the interviews, users spoke of wanting to 'establish a baseline.' One informant said "*I probably used it more frequently at the beginning – more interested in what the baselines were, and once I knew that, my access to it probably dropped off.*" Another said: "*I was looking at it every day just out of curiosity, but it doesn't do anything… <laughs> You know, it gets kind of boring after a while. I decided once a week I'd just check it and see* *what the past week was like.*" Both made it clear that initially they found the Portal quite interesting, and learned some things about their water usage, but after a while they 'figured out' what they did, and that was sufficient. With regard to designing future systems, this raises the question of how to best engage users over longer periods.

Those who Used the Portal More Frequently

About 27% of the survey respondents reported that they were using the Water Portal regularly – about once a week or more frequently. While some of these might still have been in the process of establishing a baseline and would subsequently reduce their frequency of use, it was clear from the interviews that some of participants 'got into' using the Water Portal. One said: "*I would say* [I use it] *maybe 2 or 3 times a week. I mean I don't check it every day cause I kind of know what's going to be there. But it's interesting to see the game and how I stack up against other users and how many green points I got today.*" Another said, "*I check it religiously every day.* [...] *I do look at kind of the team thing. I usually check first thing in the morning – I get up around 6 and the numbers are low. And then when I come home I also look to see what's going on.*"

The existence of this set of more frequent users raises the question of why they kept returning to the Portal and what they did while they were there, which we will turn to next.

What Parts of the Portal were Used, and Why?

This section focuses on the 56 survey respondents who used the Portal multiple times, hereafter referred to as "the Portal Users." This section also draws on the interviews.

Table 1 shows the user interface components that users reported most frequently looking at. This largely corresponds to the fine-grained usage logs that tracked time per component, except that they indicated that more time was spent using news and chat than looking at "Neighbors Like You" and the weekly game. This discrepancy between what people "usually did" and "time spent" is not troubling since both news and chat involve switching to another page and reading text, which might be expected to take more time than looking at bars on a graph for the "Neighbors Like You" and the weekly game results. This ordering is also consistent with our impressions from the interviews.

Table 1: What users reported that they usually looked at

I usually looked at	N	%
The hourly graph of water usage	49	88%
How I compared with Neighbors Like You	37	66%
The weekly game results	27	48%
The news	23	41%
The chat	17	30%

The Hourly Usage Graph

The hourly usage graph is among the most looked at elements of the Water Portal. One question going into the study was to what extent users would be able to connect what they saw in their usage graphs to their actual water use. This was a key question because the Water Portal did not indicate which appliances – showers, sinks, toilets – had used the water, and there was a 2-3 hour delay before usage was reflected in the Portal. Another question was whether this information would be useful. From the two survey questions shown in Table 2, it's evident that almost all respondents found the hourly usage graph understandable, and half reported learning surprising things from it.

Table 2. Questions about the hourly water usage graph

Question	Agree-Neutral-Disagree (NA)	% agreed
When I looked at the graph of my hourly water usage, I could usually understand what the peaks in the graph corresponded to	51- 2- 2 (1)	91%
I was surprised by some of the things I saw in my water usage graph	28-17- 8 (3)	50%

While the Portal did not show which appliances contributed to water consumption, users found this easy to infer by mapping their recent experience to the peaks they saw in the hourly usage graph. One said he could see that one toilet used twice as much as the other, and another that it was nice to see that his new energy star dishwasher really *was* efficient. Other interviewees provided more details: "*I was knock-your-socks-off impressed at the detail that you could see. Wow! Here's the shower I took this morning. Here's the shower [my wife] took this morning. Here's where I came home during the middle of the day and washed my hands and used the toilet. Here's where I filled the dog's dish.*" Another said "*When I look at it you can tell alright this is when we've gotten up and are getting ready, and* [this is] *when I get home and I start doing laundry or baking or cooking and running a dishwasher.*"

A recurrent theme was the power of visualization. It was clear that informants not only found the graph useful but also *enjoyed* looking at it and seeing their activities reflected in it. This suggests that visualizations can a play a dual role: they are powerful communications mechanisms, and they are also effective ways of engaging people. One informant said, "*I know I have a leak in my house ...it's a leaky faucet. ... I just never took the time because I never saw a graphical representation. ... You can really picture – I mean a gallon is a gallon of milk, and you can see fifteen of those going down your drain! That makes a heck of a difference!*" Another said, "*When I wash I can really see the spike!*" and wondered aloud whether a new washer might be a good idea. Informants made similar comments about the year-long timeline, one noting a huge peak on thanksgiving when she had 25 people over and saying that "*it was nice to be able to connect [the peak] with something and see that it was going to be tracked.*" Others commented on the big peaks that signified the start of summer with the watering of new grass and the filling of the swimming pool.

"Neighbors Like You" and "This Week's Game"

"Neighbors Like You" and "This Week's Game" both involved comparisons or competitions with others – but (because of privacy concerns) *anonymous* others. Thus, unlike many gaming situations, users didn't know who was on their team, or against whom they were competing. Would the Portal Users find these 'invisible' competitions and comparisons interesting and engaging?

Interestingly enough, 66% (37) of the Portal Users reported usually looking at the "Neighbors Like You" comparison, and 48% (27) reported usually looking at the weekly game. Given that the team and neighbors comparisons are side by side, it is interesting that some users paid attention to "Neighbors Like You" but not "This Week's Game," and *vice versa* – in fact, a total of 16 users followed one but not the other, with more favoring "Neighbors Like You."

The interviews provide some insight here. Two of the informants were engaged by the game. One said, "*That's the one I concentrate on* [pointing to "This week's game"], *I guess because I'm competitive and trying to see what my team is doing... And um, it would be kind of nice to know who your team was.*" Another explained that he had turned the Portal over to his kids: "*I think the competition was a perfect thing to do. ... I saw it as an opportunity to get my kids excited. Because they can earn points and they can win stuff.*" And this had ramifications: "*I did notice an impact right away. That the kids were – either jokingly or seriously, it's hard to tell – that 'you're going to make our usage go up and we're going to lose again!'*"

Interestingly, three other informants explained that they "followed" the game, even though they didn't actually care about winning and said they didn't change their behavior to try to win the game. One said "*it's interesting to compare myself against neighbors like myself – households with four people of a certain size and a certain makeup.*" Another said "*This down here* [pointing to the "This Week's Game" graph] *...my team always loses! ... I'm like, 'We're doing our part people, come on!'*" These informants liked seeing their household compared against others, perhaps in contrast to "Neighbors Like You" in which they were compared to an average.

Finally, although the sample is too small to draw firm conclusions from, it is telling that of the 15 survey respondents who reported logging on more than once a week, all but one reported that they "looked to see how my team was doing," and/or "made an effort to reduce my water consumption to help my team." While the game only engaged a minority of the Portal Users, playing or following the game is highly correlated with frequent visits.

News and Chat

News and Chat saw the least usual use (41% and 31%). This corresponds with our impressions from the interviews, where informants said little about either function, except that some looked at them and occasionally saw things of interest. With respect to chat, none of the informants reported seeing any content in the team chat; for pilot chat (the chat open to all users), while some reported posting comments or reading, they felt it was not well attended, and no one reported having real back-and-forth conversations.

These impressions are reinforced by an analysis of the system's chat logs. Team chat was very lightly used. Eighteen comments were posted by 11 people, 7 of whom posted only one comment. The most common posts were those intended to encourage or congratulate the team such as "*good job team!*" and "*OK team, are you ready to win!!,*" (further illustration that some users were engaged by the game). No comments directly responded to others.

Pilot chat was used more than team chat. Fifty-seven distinct comments were posted by 18 people, twenty-four of these by the project administrator (e.g., answering questions, thanking users for input, and offering "tips of the day"). Besides the administrator, only 3 people posted three or more comments, 5 posted two, and 7 posted one. Except for the administrator, only 2 users replied to others; most non-administrative posts were general comments about water use (15), questions about water use (11), or questions or suggestions relating to the web site (7).

In summary, although Pilot chat was used more than team chat, it was used for informational purposes. Virtually no conversation, in the sense of users responding to one another, took place in either chat room. One reason may be that users were anonymous, and thus there were few openings for conversation. Another may be that there were few users online at any one time: the Water Pilot may have fallen short of the "critical mass" needed for robust online conversation A third reason is that conversations are most apt to start when there is something to talk about. Several informants commented that they just didn't have much to say about their water use. Regardless of the reason, examining ways of encouraging conversation in systems like this seems like an important area for further work.

Impact of Use

About the Users

Before examining the impact of the Water Portal, we will look more closely at the participants in the pilot. Recall that the pilot participants were all volunteers, and therefore may have been exceptional. And indeed, the survey indicates that the Portal Users were already attuned to water conservation: 73% reported that before the pilot started they had made at least one change to their behavior to conserve water (e.g., shorter showers, running dishwashers only with full loads, etc.), and 57% reported that they had made at least one change to their water infrastructure (e.g., installing low-flow showerheads, efficient toilets, etc). So, for Pilot participants it seems that much of the low hanging fruit was already gone.

That makes the actual finding of a water consumption reduction quite impressive. As reported elsewhere [8], during the first 9 weeks of the deployment, when Group 1 was using the Portal and Group 2 was not, Group 1's water normalized water consumption was reduced 6.6% compared to that of Group 1. This is similar to that achieved by residential energy feedback systems (5 – 15%), and better than that observed for water by Petersen [14].

So what accounts for this reduction?

Increased Understanding

The survey asked a number of questions about the impact using the Water Portal had on users (Table 3). Large majorities of the Portal Users agreed that it increased their understanding of how they use water (77%) and enabled them to see the effects of changes they made (70%). As we've described earlier in this section, the ten informants described ways in which the Portal – especially the hourly water usage graph – did this: from seeing how much water a particular appliance used, to seeing that an appliance that claimed to be water efficient actually was.

Table 3. Questions on the general impact of the Portal

Question	Agree-Neutral-Disagree (NA)	Summary
Using the Water Portal increased my understanding of how I use water	43- 7- 5 (1)	77% agreed
The Water Portal allowed me to see that changes I've made do affect my water usage	39-13- 3 (1)	70% agreed
The Water Portal helped our household conserve water	27-21- 8 (0)	48% agreed
I discussed water usage information from the Water Portal with other members of my household	12 (Never) 6 (Once) 29 (A few times) 9 (Once a week or more)	79% discussed at least once
I discussed water usage information from the Water Portal with people who do NOT live in my household	21 (Never) 6 (Once) 23 (A few times) 6 (Once a week or more)	62% discussed at least once

Water Conservation: Reinforcing Existing Practices

Yet, in the third question, a smaller proportion of the Portal Users (48%) said that the Water Portal actually helped them conserve water. Why is this? A number of the interviewees commented that while they liked the Water Portal and the information it provided, they were, in the words of one couple, "pretty frugal anyway." Another said, "*This, for us, reinforces what we're doing and keeps us doing it, rather than changing the mode of operation in our house.*" Still others reported taking a wait and see approach – "*It's just got us thinking about it. And put it into focus that this is real, we have some control over this, and in the end our faucet controls how much is going down the drain*" – sometimes because they are contemplating major appliance purchases that they don't want to rush in to.

Talking with Others

We were interested in the extent to which the Portal Users discussed their experiences with others. Such talk within the household is crucial to enabling collective discussion and decision-making about household water use. And talk beyond the household can be important in encouraging system adoption and shifting public norms.

A large majority (79%) of the Portal Users discussed their water use with others in their household (note that some members of the pilot group lived by themselves). For instance, one informant recounted how looking at the hourly usage graph led to "*some comedic banter with [my wife] about how come your shower has such a bigger bar than my shower has. And that kind of caught her attention.*" In another instance, the kids in the family, motivated by winning the weekly game, nagged their father: "*My kids said 'Dad, you gotta fix that faucet, it's dripping so much!*'

A majority of The Portal Users (62%) also reported discussing their results with those outside of the household. One informant described giving out his user ID and password to his extended family so they could log in and see his results. Another printed out screenshots to show people. And still others mentioned carrying on discussions with their co-workers. No doubt some of this is due to the novelty of the Water Portal, but nevertheless this can facilitate adoption.

Water Conservation: Changes to Appliances and Behaviors

The survey asked the Portal Users about changes they had made *during the pilot*, or *planned to make in the future*. Although many of the Portal Users had made such changes before the pilot began, many also reported making other changes during the pilot, or planning to in the future.

- 39% of the Portal Users reported making at least one change to their water infrastructure, with the most frequent being fixing a leak (29%). 45% reported plans to make such changes, with the most frequent planned alteration being to purchase a water efficient toilet (18%).
- 45% of the Portal Users reported making at least one change in their water consumption behavior during the pilot. The most popular of these behavioral changes was to avoid unnecessarily running the faucet – e.g., while washing dishes or brushing teeth – and was reported by 33% of the Portal Users. Only 20% of the Portal Users reported plans to make further behavioral changes, perhaps because, unlike making changes to water appliances, advance planning is not so necessary.

Overall, a total of 61% of the Portal Users reported making a change to either a water appliance or the ways in which they used water (or both) during the pilot, and 48% reported plans to do so. These reports are consistent with the observed reductions in water use.

DISCUSSION AND CONCLUSION

A web-based Water Portal was deployed to 303 volunteer households in Dubuque Iowa for 15 weeks. The system, designed to be deployed city-wide, was intended to reduce water consumption by providing near real time feedback, social comparisons, a weekly game, and news and chat. Portal Users reported that feedback, social comparisons and the game had impacts on their behavior (in that order); majorities reported increased understandings of their consumption, seeing that changes they made had an effect, and discussing their consumption with those within and outside their households. Quantitative measures showed a 6.6% reduction in water use during an experimental/control contrast for the first 9 weeks of the pilot study; this is striking, since most participants reported that they'd taken measures to reduce their use long before the pilot began.

Degree of Use

The aggregate usage pattern for the Water Portal is an initial burst of logons followed by a gradual decline to a lower and steadier pattern of use. It is evident from both survey and interview responses that a portion of the users were interested in gaining an understanding of their water usage patterns, but once they'd done that they lost interest in the Portal. In the interviews, those who fit this pattern commented that they were already quite frugal in their use of water. This is in line with other reports [16, 17], and consistent with concerns that eco-feedback systems may, in part, work to reify existing norms. On the other hand, the Portal did result in a reduction in consumption, and some users engaged with the Portal throughout the deployment.

What of the households that rarely or never used the Portal? That is more difficult to say. Of the relatively small proportion of those users who responded to the survey, the most frequently cited reason for their infrequent or non- use was that they "kept forgetting." This is a curious response, and it raises two possibilities, both of which we suspect have some truth to them. First, users had to navigate to a web page that was not part of their usual routine, and that required a special ID and password. This may be too much to expect, and as we discuss later, the engagement model may need to be re-thought. Second, it may be that, in line with criticisms of eco-feedback systems, many users are not interested in acting as "managers" of their consumption, and thus feedback is beside the point. In this view, progress lies in the re-design of point-of-use appliances and services.

User Experience

In an ideal world, this study would have been much larger, and different versions of the Portal could have been deployed to different groups, allowing a crisp assessment of the relative importance of various user interface components. That was not the case, and so the best we can do is rely upon users' reports as uncovered by the survey and interviews.

The hourly usage graph received the most attention. Most importantly, Portal Users reported that it was easy to map their daily experience to the hourly usage graph, and thus make inferences about the impacts of particular appliances and practices on their consumption. Because they were able to draw such inferences, they got value from the hourly usage graph in several ways. It enabled identification of the activities (e.g., showers, watering the lawn as part of a grub control treatment) and appliances (e.g., washing machines, toilets) that were consuming larger than expected quantities of water. It allowed them to compare activities (my shower versus your shower) and appliances (downstairs versus upstairs toilet) *vis a vis* their consumptions. It provided validation that some appliances (e.g., the energy star dishwasher) actually did use small amounts of water. It enabled visualization of the cumulative impact of leaks (e.g., the leaky faucet that accounts for 15 gallons a day).

Of the Portal Users, 66% usually looked at "Neighbors Like Me," and 48% followed the results of the weekly games. Although both these techniques involve social comparison, it is worth noting that they appealed to somewhat different sets of users. The attention devoted to the weekly games is of interest because the 'teams' were composed of anonymous households, and although teammates could in principle chat with one another, no such conversations took place. Apparently, even something that lacks many of the characteristics of online games can still succeed in engaging people. Finally, of the 15 participants who used the system more than once a week, 14 followed the weekly game, suggesting that although not for everyone, games may be of value for encouraging frequent use.

The other social aspects of the Water Portal – News and Chat – saw the least "usual" use according to the survey (41% and 31%), which corresponds to impressions from the interviews. While users appreciated these functions, and gained useful information from them, analysis of the chat logs and comments in the interviews show that the chat function was not used for conversations among ordinary users: it was instead used as a place for posting information, and supporting Q&A between users and the administrator.

Impact

As noted earlier, use of the Water Portal resulted in a reduced consumption of water. This is striking in view of the fact that 70% of the Portal Users noted that they'd tried to conserve water for a long time, and 79% had made some kind of change to their water appliances or the ways they used water before the pilot began.

While this study does not have the data to reveal which aspects of portal use led to a reduction in water consumption, much of what participants reported in the surveys and interviews could have contributed. The 56

Portal Users reported seeing the most benefits. 77% reported that using the Portal increased their understanding of their water use, and interviewees gave examples ranging from understanding the amount of water wasted by a leak to realizing how much water a washer or dishwasher used. And informants reported that these realizations led to changes in behavior …fixing leaks, running dishwashers and washers only with full loads, and contemplating the purchase of more water efficient appliances. More generally, 61% of Portal Users reported making changes either to a water appliance (e.g., 29% reported fixing a leak) or their water use behavior (e.g., 33% reported letting the faucet run less) during the pilot study, and 48% stated they planned to make other changes in the future.

Design Implications and Issues

This examination of how Portal Users used and experienced the Water Portal suggests areas for future work.

The Value of Aggregate Visualizations

There is value in providing near real time graphs of water consumption, even if it does not show what is responsible for the consumption. The finding that participants could make sense of their graphs ..mapping the graphs' peaks and valleys to their practices and appliance use ..is an important finding. This is useful to know because the additional instrumentation needed to tie usage to particular appliances is quite expensive when scaled up to the number of households in a city. Furthermore, the enjoyment that users exhibited when interpreting their water graphs suggests that they might also serve as motivational mechanisms.

Social Comparisons

The "Neighbors Like You" comparison and the weekly games were effective as well, albeit for a smaller set of Portal Users. It was interesting to note that although the comparison and game graphs were shown side by side, some users only paid attention to one or the other. This suggests that it is useful to provide a variety of mechanisms to have the best chance of engaging the broadest array of users. Of particular interest were those who "followed" the game but didn't care about winning …the comments of these users suggest that they liked seeing themselves compared against individual households, even though those households were anonymous. This distinction, between comparisons with an average and comparisons with similar but anonymous households would be interesting to understand more deeply. Regardless, there appears to be considerable opportunity for future development of both comparisons and games.

Chat

While the chat was used for posting information and Q&A, there was almost no conversation among participants. This is disappointing, because such discussion could provide a channel for participants to share practical knowledge and even to question the existing norms that underlie consumption (as suggested by Strengers [17]).

This merits further exploration because there are many examples of online communities that sustain rich and varied conversations, and thereby attract and retain participants. If the difficulty is simply lack of a critical mass of conversants, the problem may solve itself as the technology is deployed city-wide. Conversation might also be encouraged by providing a richer interaction model than the Portal's simple chat-in-a-single-window. One that allowed users to create and monitor separate topics with practical orientations ..e.g., "How to save water in the summer," or "Are front loading washers worth it" …might encourage chat. Finally, encouraging participants to use real identities rather than anonymous ID's might provide more grounds for discussion, particularly among neighbors.

Identity and Anonymity, Privacy and Visibility

Real identities could be usefully surfaced not only in chat but in other parts of the Water Portal. This, of course, raises a number of issues having to do with privacy and visibility. Interestingly enough, individual water usage information is not private in Dubuque: in theory, anyone can call up the city water department and request the water usage data for any address. While this policy was understandable when water usage data consisted of monthly consumption, it clearly needs to be revisited given the detailed and intimate picture of household activity made possible by the per-hour-usage view provided by the Portal.

At the same time, majorities of consumers discussed their water usage with others outside their households. While some of this is no doubt a function of the novelty of the Portal, and of the fact the pilot participants were enthusiastic volunteers, enabling the sharing of some degree of usage information seems crucial to promoting discussion of everything from community norms to city policy. One approach could be to share data aggregated at the neighborhood, parish, or school district level. Another approach could be to make it easy for individual users to publish their water usage on social networking systems.

Engagement Models

Finally, at a more general level, we are interested in the issue of engagement models. It seems unrealistic to envision a world where people wake up every morning and eagerly check their water usage. Perhaps games will engage some users in a persistent way, but engaging the others who most likely constitute the majority remains a challenge.

How might we move beyond the current default, the seek-out-and-use paradigm? Perhaps efforts could be made to periodically re-engage participants. This might be done occasionally, in response to sporadic or seasonal changes that impact water usage. Another approach would be to develop what we refer to as pseudo-ambient displays. While ambient displays at the point of use seem promising, as we've noted they are expensive when scaled to entire urban populations. We might tap some of the advantages of ambient displays by redesigning the Portal so that portions of it could be embedded in or 'on the way to' a frequently visited site: perhaps a social networking site, or an online bill-paying application. One of our informants, in discussing his vision of the future, sketched out a similar idea: "*It's all going to come together and it will probably end up merged in with your television and you'll have a touch screen on your TV and you'll just check everything while you're watching the news at the same time.*"

A final, more speculative idea has to do with enabling different groups to appropriate feedback technology. While working on this project, we've been struck by the number and diversity of community groups that care about resource conservation. At the same time, not all groups identified themselves as "green;" some were wary of being seen as "tree huggers" and/or being drawn into the global warming debate. Framings of resource conservation ranged from it being an intrinsic part of local (rural) values of frugality, to religiously grounded beliefs about stewardship, to good business sense, to civic-minded promotion of the city's image. And, yes, there was a group of ten ladies who met weekly to talk about how to save the earth. It might be useful to explore ways of disseminating information from government to citizens *via* community groups which can reframe ideas in ways that speak to their constituents. As one informant said, "*You just have to find a way to engage folks and then it's fine. So whether that is through newspaper or radio, or by going to their Lions or Kiwanis club, if they hear their friends and their small group of folks say 'this is great and here's how it worked for me.' For folks who may not ordinarily take the plunge that is a better way to get people involved and engaged in the process.*"

ACKNOWLEDGMENTS

This project would not have been possible with the support of the City of Dubuque, the Dubuque 2.0 NGO, and the 303 households who participated in the pilot study.

REFERENCES

1. Arroyo, E., Bonanni, L., Selker, T. Waterbot: exploring feedback and persuasive techniques at the sink. *Proc. CHI 2005*, ACM (2005), 631-639.
2. Blevis, E. Sustainable interaction design: Invention & disposal, renewal & reuse. *Proc. CHI 2007*, ACM (2007), 503-512.
3. Brown, L. *Outgrowing the Earth: The Food Security Challenge in an Age of Falling Water Tables and Rising Temperatures.* Norton, 2005.
4. Chen, F., Dai, J., Wang, B., Sahu, S., Naphade, M. and Lu, C. Activity Analysis Based on Low Sample Rate Smart Meters. *Proc. Intl. Conf. on Knowledge Discovery and Data Mining*. ACM (2011), 240-248.
5. Darby, S. The effectiveness of feedback on energy consumption. 2006. http://www.eci.ox.ac.uk/research/energy/electric-metering.php. Accessed 9-11-11.
6. Darby, S. Social learning and public policy: Lessons from an energy-conscious village. *Energy Policy 34* (2006), 2929–2940.
7. DiSalvo, C., Sengers, P., and Brynjarsdóttir, H. Mapping the landscape of sustainable HCI. *Proc. CHI 2010*, ACM (2010), 1975-1984.
8. IBM Research. *Smart Water Pilot Report*. June 10, 2011. [Public report] http://www.cityofdubuque.org/DocumentView.aspx?DID=3116. Accessed 9-11-11.
9. ICF International. *Water and Energy: Leveraging Voluntary Programs to Save Both Water and Energy*. March 2008. http://water.epa.gov/scitech/wastetech/upload/Final-Report-Mar-2008.pdf. Accessed 9-11-11.
10. IEEE. Water Vs. Energy: Special Report. *IEEE Spectrum, 47*:6, June 2010.
11. Froehlich, J., Findlater, L., and Landay, J. The design of eco-feedback technology. *Proc. CHI 2010*. ACM (2010), 1999-2008.
12. Kappel, K. and Grechenig, T. "show-me": Water consumption at a glance to promote water conservation in the shower. *Proc. Pervasive 2009*. ACM (2009), 1-6.
13. Kuznetsov, S. and Paulos, E. 2010. UpStream: motivating water conservation with low-cost water flow sensing and persuasive displays. *Proc. CHI 2010*, ACM (2010), 1851-1860.
14. Petersen, J.E., V. Shunturov, K. Janda, G. Platt, K. Weinberger. Combining real-time feedback on resource use with incentives stimulates dormitory residents to reduce electricity consumption. *Int. J. of Sustainability in Higher Education, 8,* (2007), 16-33.
15. Pierce, J., Odom, W., and Blevis, E. Energy aware dwelling: A critical survey of interaction design for eco-visualizations. *Proc. OZCHI 2008*, ACM (2008), 1-8.
16. Pierce, J., Fan, C., Lomas, D., Marcu, G. and Paulos, E. Some consideration on the (in)effectiveness of residential energy feedback systems. *Proc. DIS 2010*, ACM (2010), 244-247.
17. Strengers, Y. Designing eco-feedback systems for everyday life. *Proc. CHI 2011*. ACM (2011) 2135-2144.
18. UNICEF. *UNICEF Handbook on Water Quality*. 2008. http://www.unicef.org/wash/files/WQ_Handbook_final_signed_16_April_2008.pdf. Accessed 9-11-11.
19. UN Water. *Coping with Water Scarcity – Challenge of the Twenty-first Century*. UN Water, 2007. http://www.fao.org/nr/water/docs/escarcity.pdf. Accessed 9-11-11.

Embedded interaction in a Water Fountain for Motivating Behavior Change in Public Space

Ernesto Arroyo
Universitat Pompeu Fabra
Barcelona, Spain
ernesto.arroyo@upf.edu

Leonardo Bonanni
MIT Media Lab
Cambridge, MA
amerigo@media.mit.edu

Nina Valkanova
Universitat Pompeu Fabra
Barcelona, Spain
nina.valkanova@gmail.com

ABSTRACT
This paper presents an interactive installation for a public space aimed at motivating new behaviors by augmenting the space with subtle and playful audiovisual interaction aesthetically integrated in a shared environment. Designed to complement an existing water fountain with projected light and sound, the embedded installation encouraged people to take a drink, increasing the proportion of people who used the water fountain by 42% to 57% approximately for nine months. Sensors evaluated the impact of multiple interaction modalities on actual water usage. We found that subtle interaction can improve the experience of a space, in particular for those that use it frequently, and lead to sustained behavior change, especially when its modalities are responsive to the level of activity in the space.

Author Keywords
Embedded Interaction; Design; In-the-wild; Behavior Change; Augmented Public Spaces; Water; Persuasion.

ACM Classification Keywords
H5.m. Information interfaces and presentation: Miscellaneous. H.5.2.i Information Technology and Systems: Interaction styles. C.3.h Computer Systems Organization: Ubiquitous computing.

INTRODUCTION
Many of the spaces we walk through every day go unnoticed. How can we influence the way people perceive, experience, and move through shared spaces while maintaining their appeal? Embedded interaction, if properly designed, can improve the perceived quality of public spaces and attract attention to motivate new behaviors. This paper focuses on the design and evaluation of an installation with minimal and subtle interactions that increase the perceived quality of a space that is passed through by thousands of people every day. The installation seeks to motivate new behaviors by enriching an existing everyday experience in a shared public space. We chose a seldom-used water fountain in a crowded hallway on a university campus, and augmented it with an aesthetic self-monitoring light-and-sound system responsive to use and proximity, called *Gurgle* (see Fig. 1). *Gurgle* also acts as an experimental platform that helps us understand whether and how audiovisual feedback can change behavior and provide long lasting engagement. A long-term field study conducted in a public environment evaluated how people who work and visit the space responded to and used *Gurgle*. Results showed sustained behavior change reflected by an increase in the proportion of people who used the water fountain relative to a baseline of several months. The data revealed an effect of feedback modality and the number of people in the space on user behavior that can be used as a resource for more effective design.

Figure 1. *Gurgle* is an interactive installation in a public corridor that augments an existing water fountain with watery reflections and sound with the aim of encouraging people to pause and take a drink.

BACKGROUND
This work falls within the field of augmented urban environments which aims at developing strategies for articulating public domains that connect physical urban spaces and new media technologies to foster their positive potential. Everyday urban environments can benefit from sensory interfaces to make spaces more enjoyable, informative and persuasive [3]. Previous research suggests that augmenting everyday spaces with simple interfaces has the power to motivate more sustainable behaviors, especially if these interfaces are designed to be unobtrusive and aesthetically pleasing [1,10]. An augmented faucet was able to make people more conscious of their water consumption without being overbearing, by including playful sounds and attractive lights in the stream of water

[1]. Interactive installations have been also successful at motivating healthier behaviors such as taking the stairs instead of the escalator [7,10]. However, research also suggest, that embedded interactive systems can be annoying if they are not perceived as having added value to the space and their effect can fade over time [5,4]. In the real world, this type of interaction can include systems for conducting in-the-wild evaluation and improving upon its impact. Mr. Java, for example, is a communal coffee machine that logs usage data to help anticipate demand [6]. Our overall research objective is to investigate whether and how augmenting shared public spaces with different kinds of audiovisual feedback might lead to engagement and sustained behavior change. In particular, we were interested in the effect of simple interactions of light and sound that change in response to people's movement and activity in the shared space.

DESIGN

The design concept was of an embedded installation that could be experienced while walking through a shared space characterized by an intense flux of people. As a real-world test bed, we chose the crowded central corridor of a large university building. This is a transition space where people rush-by every day without taking the time to be aware of their surroundings or to relax. Our goal was to design a system, which allows for a unique experience and motivates positive behaviors in the shared space. We aimed for a design that attracts attention of passersby and entices them to take a refreshing drink from a water fountain in the corridor. It was considered important that it fitted properly into the environment and so considerable attention was given to designing it to be aesthetically pleasing. To do so, we created an appealing, but discrete and robust interaction and physical design as to complement the space and its activities without being obtrusive.

Interaction Design

We augmented the space by embedding interactive light and sound feedback into one of the seldom-used water fountains in the space. We were inspired by Sensory Rooms that contain interactive sound machines and dynamic lighting that target specific sensory modes, which have been shown to promote relaxation and concentration [2]. The proximity of passersby in the corridor triggers *Gurgle* to briefly illuminate. If they stop to take a drink, the entire nook that contains the fountain is transformed by watery reflections with sound of a gurgling stream. This is inspired by research suggesting that projected colors and simple contextualized animations (i.e. of fire, water and snow) can effectively communicate meaning without being distracting [3], while being aesthetically pleasing. The designed behavior seeks to provide rushed passersby with unexpected moments of meditation and needed hydration.

Physical Design

Gurgle was designed to be both reliable as a permanent art installation and flexible as an experimental platform. The main consideration of the physical design was to make an aesthetically pleasing interactive light and sound installation with hardware that is unobtrusive, robust, easy to maintain and hard to steal. An *Aquasplash* stage light commonly used in aquariums that produces a light similar to the reflection of wavy water was chosen to produce the rippling water illusion because of its robustness, cost and beauty. The light was hidden behind a wall-mounted water fountain. As *Gurgle* is a prototype for improving everyday public spaces, it was designed to cost under $300 - equivalent to the price of an industrial light fixture.

System Description

Based on our desire for flexibility, reliability and low cost, *Gurgle* was built with pre-existing hardware and a modular structure for easy maintenance. The hardware includes a microcontroller board, a light source, an mp3-player, speakers, infrared proximity sensors and control circuitry. The microcontroller controls the feedback and interaction behavior in *Gurgle* and additional EEPROM memory logs usage data. A serial port allows downloading logged data and changing its behavior by reprogramming new firmware. Infrared proximity sensors were mounted to the wall and under the water fountain in the hallway (see Fig. 2). The sensors located at different angles measure how many people are passing in the hallway and how many are in position to use the fountain. A micro-switch inside the fountain trigger measures actual water usage.

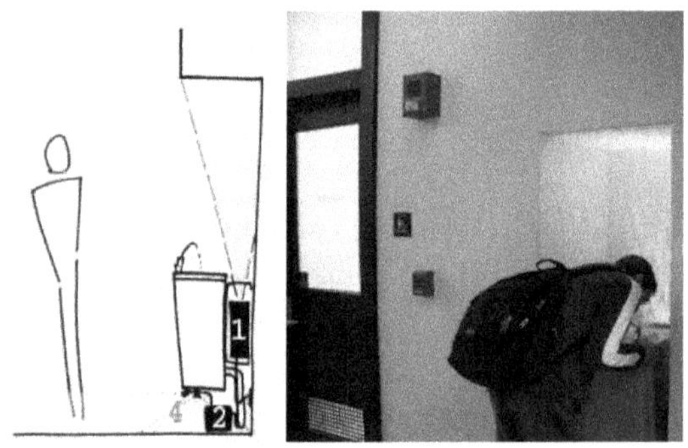

Figure 2. *Gurgle*: physical installation in the hallway includes a light projector, a controller box, a subwoofer and proximity sensors (left). It can be activated while drinking water (right).

EVALUATION

The evaluation goal was two-fold: 1) confirming that public space augmentation with a contextualized interactive installations can lead to changing behavior and 2) investigating how various feedback modalities can change behavior and provide long lasting engagement on a public space. We conducted a long-term in-the-wild study to evaluate *Gurgle*'s impact on water drinking behavior and to compare the effectiveness of audiovisual feedback. A mixed evaluation method included measures of user satisfaction alongside traditional performance measures due to the inherent problems associated with evaluating the effectiveness of aesthetic displays in public spaces characterized by a continuous flow of people and activity.

A one-month pilot installation at an art gallery validated the appeal of the audio-visual feedback and the robustness of the technical system with 3,000 visitors. A second version was installed for nine months (including 2.5 months for baseline and accommodation) on its permanent location in a public corridor. Evaluation of *Gurgle* over the nine months suggests that the installation achieved a sustained (water drinking) behavior change and that the audiovisual feedback should vary based on time of day and the number of people in the space. Qualitative studies suggested an improved experience and perception of the space.

Usage Study

As public environments have many potential external factors that could affect the outcome of an intervention, we chose to periodically cycle through the interaction modalities for the duration of the study in order to equally distribute the possible effects from external factors while also limiting the effects of unexpected conditions. *Gurgle*'s randomly cycled through 4 interaction modes in 4-hour intervals: responsive light, responsive sound, responsive sound and light, and no interaction that served as the baseline for usage. Motion, distance and trigger sensors allowed *Gurgle* to measure its own impact according to three metrics: hallway activity, attracting passersby and activating the water fountain.

Baseline and novelty effect

At first, only usage and motion sensors were installed in the water fountain to measure passersby and general use for establishing baseline data. A consistent activity pattern was identified for weekdays, with activity peaking at noon (see Fig. 3), thus the results presented in this paper are focused on weekday activity.

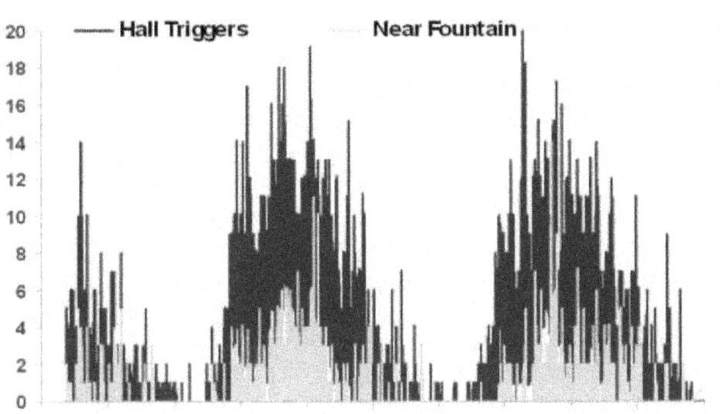

Figure 3. Triggers per minute of the Hall and Fountain proximity sensors show a consistent cyclical pattern with activity peaking at noon during weekdays.

We also found that usage varied according to the number of people in the space: the more people passed through, the proportion of people that used the water fountain decreased (see Fig. 4). This water drinking behavior remained consistent through the duration of the study (summer and fall) and across all hours of day. Based on our observations we attribute this effect to the increased difficulty in crossing over to the fountain with more people in the space, and to passersby rushing to their goal destination (lecture, bus, etc), thus probably possessing less attention capacity to attend the fountain.

We accounted for novelty effects by activating *Gurgle* for three weeks and turning it off for three more. After the initial baseline logging and subsequent novelty control, one month of usage was logged and analyzed, half of which occurred during the summer term and half during the fall term. On average roughly 2,600 walked past the fountain daily during the summer term and 8,900 during the busier fall term. Approximately 2.5% and 4.7% of passersby used the water fountain when *Gurgle* was not active for the summer and fall terms respectively.

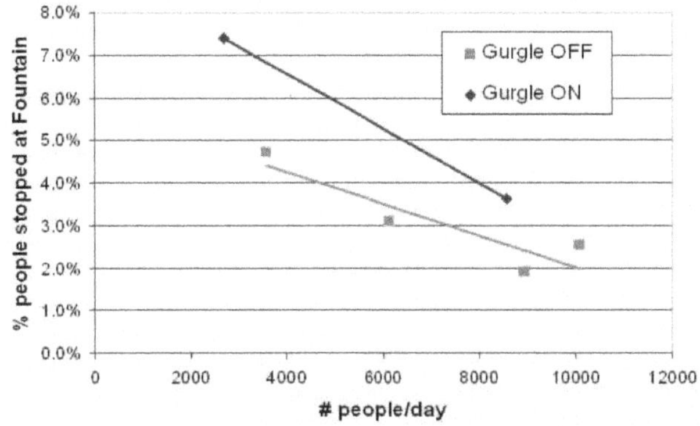

Figure 4. *Gurgle* increases overall water fountain use. However as the number of passersby increases the number of people that pause to drink decreases.

Motivating usage and attracting passersby

The data indicates that *Gurgle* increased the proportion of people who used the water fountain during the time it was active A multivariate ANOVA using the Wilks Lambda criteria showed a statistically significant difference between the interaction modes on people and fountain activity, $F(8, 4096) = 253.7$; $p>0.001$). With *Gurgle* enabled, the ratio of passersby that took a drink from the fountain improved significantly $F(4, 2049)=53.6$, $p<.001$). It increased 3.6%, for the summer ($p<.01$) and 7.4% for the fall period ($p>.001$). This represents a 42% (summer) and 57% (fall) sustained usage increase in water fountain use when *Gurgle* was fully active compared to when it was absent.

Effect of interaction modalities and people in the space

A cycling program compared the effects of light, sound, and audiovisual feedback. Tukey's HSD post-hoc tests suggest differences in the proportion of people who used the water fountain depending on the interaction mode: 3.0% for sound ($p<.001$), 3. 6% for sound and light ($p<.01$, and 4.6% for light only ($p<.001$). This might indicate that the sound is perceived as annoying, however, when these results are compared taking into account the number of people passing by, sound works better than other modes with 0-0.5 people per minute (ppm), while light alone works best for 0.5-1 ppm, and the three modes are comparable with >1ppm (see Fig. 5). This means, that sound may feel more personal and be better perceived with less passersby (and less ambient noise), and light may be better perceived when there are more people in the hall. The data also reflects trend that general usage falls off with many people in the corridor, no matter the feedback type.

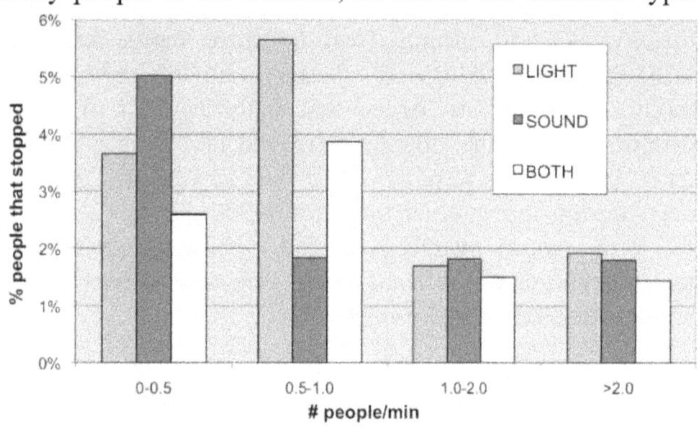

Figure 5. Effectiveness varies according to feedback type and the number of people per minute passing by.

People's perceptions

We observed the way people perceived and approached the installation by direct observation and by inviting students to give feedback through a campus-wide magazine. The responsive shimmering light lured passersby to approach the installation. Lots of them expressed curiosity and amusement using the fountain. Comments from passersby reported that they enjoyed the light and sound feedback, mostly for bringing attention to a neglected part of campus ("*I never actually think of the hallway as I pass by*", "*It's not really a place one expects to be enjoyable*"). People who used the fountain every day approached us wanting to know more about the water fountain and remarked that they were delighted to use it. Some seem to have adopted *Gurgle* as an important and integral part of their environment ("*I would like the other fountains on campus to be like this one*", "*I often go out of my way and tell other people to try it*") and others even showed attachment: "*I wish I could keep it*", "*I don't like it when it doesn't work, I always go to drink without knowing what is going to happen*". Finally, student's feedback indicated that *Gurgle* reached campus-wide impact and awareness as many people heard about it through word-of-mouth and were generally eager to look out for it and see it activate.

DISCUSSION & FUTURE WORK

Our studies suggest that *Gurgle* is effective at motivating more people to take a drink from the water fountain. We have learnt that the design of *Gurgle* could be more effective by taking into account the intensity of the human flow to maximize its impact. Feedback modes could vary based on how many people are passing by and on the time of day. Sound could be effective when few people are present; light when more are around, and when the hallway is busiest, feedback could fade away or a new more noticeable feedback could be designed (i.e.. color animation). An embedded installation like *Gurgle* could one day use sensing and variable feedback to automatically configure itself for greatest impact. When designing an installation for a public space it is also important to understand the proportion of regular users to new visitors. In *Gurgle,* the random cycling of modes acted as variable schedule of reinforcement that intrigued regular users and kept them from predicting its behavior. Varying the interaction modes through the day is one technique that could be used to remain engaging over the long term.

CONCLUSION

Our results show that augmenting the experience of an everyday public shared space with simple and aesthetically pleasing interactions can improve the perception of a space and motivate new behaviors. We presented *Gurgle*, an interactive installation that augments a water fountain in a public hallway with sound and light designed to lure passersby, incite them to take a drink and reward them with an aesthetic experience. Usage sensors in the installation confirmed sustained increased usage and a cycling pattern of feedback modes revealed that embedded interactions can be more effective at engaging the public if they vary feedback and are responsive to the number of people within the space: Sound is preferable with few people whereas light is preferable with many people in the space.

REFERENCES

1. Arroyo, E., et. al. Waterbot: Exploring Feedback and Persuasive Techniques at the Sink. In *Proc. CHI'05*, ACM Press (2002).
2. Backlund, S, Gyllenswärd, M. et al. STATIC! The Aesthetics of Energy in Everyday Things. In *Design Research Society Wonderground Conference* (2006)
3. Baillon et. al., Multi-Sensory Therapy in Psychiatric Care. In *Advances in Psychiatric Treatment* 8, (2002).
4. Bonanni, L., Living with Hyper-Reality. In *Ambient Intelligence in Everyday Life*, Lecture Notes in Artificial Intelligence #3864, Springer, (2006).
5. Cialdini, R. The Science of Persuasion. In *Scientific American*, (2001), 76-81.
6. Fogg, B.J. *Persuasive Technology: Using Computers to Change What We Think and Do*: Morgan K.P (2003).
7. Kaye, J and Matsakis, N. Mr Java in Information Appliances. In *IEEE Computer Graphics and Applications*, 20,3 (2000), 21-31.
8. Intille S.S., et. al. Just-in-Time Technology to Encourage Incremental, Dietary Behavior Change. In *AMIA* 2003 Symposium, (2003).
9. Pousman, Z., Stasko, J. and Mateas, M. Casual Information Visualization: Depictions of Data in Everyday Life. In *IEEE Transactions on Visualization and Computer Graphics*, 13, 6, (2007). 1145-1152.
10. Rogers, Y., Hazlewood H.R., et al. Ambient influence: can twinkly lights lure and abstract representations trigger behavioral change?. In *Proc. Ubicomp'10,* ACM Press, (2010)

A Transformational Product to Improve Self-Control Strength: the *Chocolate Machine*

Flavius Kehr
University of Koblenz-Landau
flavius.kehr@web.de

Marc Hassenzahl
Folkwang University of Arts
marc.hassenzahl @folkwang-uni.de

Matthias Laschke
Folkwang University of Arts
matthias.laschke @folkwang-uni.de

Sarah Diefenbach
Folkwang University of Arts
sarah.diefenbach @folkwang-uni.de

ABSTRACT
Lack of self-control is at the heart of many undesirable behaviors, such as overeating, overspending, and even overworking. While the field of Persuasive Technologies searches for ways to change attitudes and behaviors, it often neglects the science of self-control. We present the *Chocolate Machine*, an exploratory interactive product to train self-control strength based upon *Ego Depletion* theory. A field study showed the machine to increase perceived self-control over time, while providing a sustained positive experience. This makes the machine *transformational*, aiming at facilitating behaviors people find worthwhile, but hard to implement.

Author Keywords
Transformational Product; Persuasive Technology; Self-Control; Willpower; Experience Design;

ACM Classification Keywords
H.5.m [Information Interfaces And Presentation]: Miscellaneous;

General Terms
Design, Experimentation, Human Factors

INTRODUCTION
Chocolate is far too delicious. Although we are all well aware of the fact that it should be consumed moderately, we – at least now and then – indulge ourselves in the vice. If chocolate is not what you prefer (we almost hear your smug denial), it will surely be cake, pretzels, crisps, steaks, French fries, Italian salami, beer, wine, soft drinks, or cigarettes. We too often indulge in too much of everything unhealthy. When confronted with the choice between a *Mars* bar and an apple (given a preference for the *Mars* bar), we must weigh our immediate desire against future costs. While in the long run, staying in shape is certainly preferable to a *Mars* bar, the choice is nevertheless a difficult one. From our vantage point (with the *Mars* bar in full view), staying healthy is a vague and abstract remote future outcome, while the sweet fudge is concrete and now. At the heart of this problem is *temporal discounting* (see [4] for an overview), a psychological principle, responsible for the existence of interest rates and the conviction that "a bird in the hand is worth two in the bush." Discounting describes people's tendency to devalue future outcomes due to their inherent uncertainty. The bird in the hand is certain; the birds in the bush can still fly away. Steep discounting surfaces as impulsivity and impatience. However, people can counteract impulsivity by exerting *self-control*, a highly adaptive cultural technique. Agriculture, for example, is impossible without the farmer's capability to reserve a part of the crop for future sowing – no matter how hungry he is.

Self-control lies at the heart of change. Even after having accepted all arguments in favor of a beneficial behavior, an individual still needs to implement this new behavior – each and every day. Successful persuasion thus turns into an individual self-control problem. Interestingly, while the field of Persuasive Technologies [1] explicitly searches for ways to change attitudes and behaviors, it often neglects the science of self-control (for an exception, see [3]). It rather focuses on monitoring devices and feedback, that is, arguments and information, than addressing change directly. In contrast, focusing on self-control implies focusing on the *transformation* of people according to their own aspirations. Zimmerman [11], for example, argued to *Design for the Self*, to strive for products "that help people move closer to their idealized sense of self" (p. 395). We call those products *transformational*. Their primary objective is not to maximize change *per se* (e.g., reducing energy consumption, buying more chocolate bars), but to support people with realizing the goals, they find worthwhile, but hard to implement [2].

EGO DEPLETION AND THE CHOCOLATE MACHINE
The present paper explores the notion of transformational products aimed at increasing individual self-control through an exploratory object – the *Chocolate Machine* – based on *Ego Depletion* Theory (e.g., [6]). *Ego Depletion*, views self-control strength as analogous to a muscle. The implications are twofold: First, like the muscle, self-control strength will fatigue the more it is used without time for regeneration. Second, self-control strength can be trained. The latter was the starting point for the *Chocolate Machine*

(Figure 1). It consists of a slender container filled with wrapped chocolate balls placed at a study desk. Every 40 to 60 minutes the machine releases a chocolate ball onto the desktop. The user can either eat the chocolate or put it back into the machine, which is registered by a counter. Repeatedly resisting the chocolate trains self-control strength, just like working out trains muscles.

THE COCOLATE MACHINE AT HOME

To explore individual responses to the *Chocolate Machine* and its potential impact on perceived self-control, we conducted a 14-day field study. Twenty-four individuals, predominantly students, participated (15 female; age: M=26, Min=22, Max=28). The study was introduced as self-control training. After a pre-study, participants were assigned to either a treatment or a control group. Both groups were matched according to the participants' preference for chocolate, general self-control capability (measured as a trait by the 13-item version of the *Self-Control-Scale*, [10] , Cronbach's α=.77), general motivation to change, a number of contextual aspects (e.g., participants own a desk), and demographics (age, sex).

Participants in the treatment group (N=10) got a *Chocolate Machine* installed at their desk at home for 14 days. It initially contained 25 chocolate balls of different flavors selected by the participants according to their personal preference. We told people that they were free to eat the chocolate balls when dispensed by the machine. However, to practice self-control, it would be good to resist temptation and to put the ball back into the machine. Participants in the control group (N=14) got 14 daily sets of easy math exercises and the instruction to work through them day by day to practice self-control. Those exercises are perfect control tasks, because they *appear* to the participants as requiring self-control, however without actually depleting self-control strength [8].

Every second day (i.e., seven measurement points), participants got an online questionnaire to fill in (i.e., a logbook). We were interested in two aspects: participants' *perceived required self-control strength* (low, high; in short: *self-control*) and the *valence* (positive, negative) of their experience. *Self-control* was measured with three five-point Likert items (e.g., "The task required a lot of self-discipline" adapted from [8]) ranging from *fully disagree* (0) to *fully agree* (4). The items were averaged to derive a scale value (Cronbach's α: from .51 to .88 for the different measurement points) with high numbers indicating a high requirement of self-control. We expected more required self-control for the *Chocolate Machine* (compared to math exercises), which, however, decreases over time as a consequence of the training. *Valence* of experience was measured with two seven-points semantic differential items (*happy.unhappy*, *satisfied.unsatisfied*) ranging from -3 to 3. The items were averaged to derive a scale value (Cronbach's α: from .67 to .97 for the different measurement points) with positive numbers indicating a positive and negative numbers a negative experience of the task (chocolate machine, math exercise). We expected a more positive experience of the *Chocolate Machine* (compared to math exercises), which is sustained over time.

After the 14 days, the first author visited each participant at home. The first author ran episodic interviews focusing on participants' experiences, self-observed changes in behavior, improvement suggestions and ideas. We obtained 434 statements, which were further grouped and categorized to explore feelings, thoughts and actions related to using the *Chocolate Machine*.

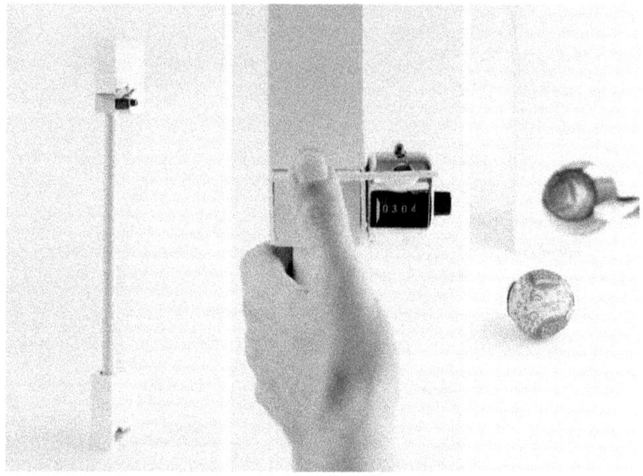

Figure 1: The *Chocolate Machine* (see http://youtu.be/pr-gtnMcFnE?hd=1 for a video figure)

In addition to the qualitative interview and the quantitative logbook data, we were interested in estimating potential generalization instilled by using the *Chocolate Machine*. *Ego Depletion* theory assumes that not only the specific self-control problem (here: resisting chocolate) but also self-control strength in general will benefit from the training. To study this, we measured participants' initial level of self-control strength (as a part of the pre-study) with a widely-used procedure (e.g., [7]): We first depleted participants' self-control strength (by an exhausting but monotonous task) and then asked them to work through and solve a list of eleven anagrams with a length of five to fifteen letters (e.g., GERTI > TIGER). All but two anagrams were solvable. The measure for self-control strength was the minutes spent on the anagrams (i.e., *persistence*). The task was announced as an intelligence test and people were told that only the number of solved anagrams was important, not the time spent on task. The same procedure was repeated at the end of the study (as a part of closing interview) to register changes in self-control strength.

RESULTS AND INTERPRETATION

The presentation of the results starts with the major insights revealed by the qualitative interviews, complemented with the quantitative data from the logbook and the more controlled self-control strength assessment.

Qualitative data

Nine (of 10) *Chocolate Machine* users expressed positive feelings towards the training and the machine. Two participants mentioned the attention needed: "You need to take care, like with a *Tamagotchi*". Another three anthropomorphized … they wanted to make a good impression or do the machine a favor. Eight (of 10) shared their results with family and friends. Negative feelings resulted from technical problems, the noise the machine made and the occasional search for chocolate balls strewn on the floor. The math exercise generated neutral or even negative feelings (6 of 14), such as being irritated, finding it monotonous, or being indifferent.

The participants experienced the temptation represented by the *Chocolate Machine* as significant. Over time, seven (of 10) found it easier to resist. They reported the gradual acquisition of two different strategies to deal with the temptation: *reinterpretation* (e.g., thinking of the chocolate balls as wooden), and *tabooing* (e.g., thinking of the chocolate balls as belonging to somebody else). Such strategies lie at the heart of self-control (e.g., [5]). *Chocolate Machine* users incorporated the machine into daily habits and routines. For example, five (of 10) participants told us that upon returning home, they immediately checked the status of the machine and dealt with the chocolate balls dispensed while being away. When at home, nine (of 10) dealt with a ball the moment it was dispensed. Participants in the control group found the math exercises neither a temptation nor especially hard to carry out. As expected, this task did not tap much into self-control strength.

Participants (8 of 10) were skeptical about potential generalizations from resisting a chocolate ball to other self-control problems. However, some participants (3 of 10) coupled the machine with daily tasks, which afford self-control. Through this, one participant reported about increased work performance with the machine at his desk, the others tidied up more often or decreased smoking. Five (of 10) participant found themselves to be more self-reflective because of the machine. They thought more about themselves and their motives and were more aware of their own behavior. Participants in the control group did not believe in generalization either (10 of 14). The math exercises were predominantly perceived as meaningless, some even started to question their relation to self-control.

Quantitative data

Figure 2 shows the mean *perceived required self-control* for the treatment and the control condition. As expected, the initial mean required self-control (Figure 2, day 2) was higher for the treatment (M=2.63, SD=.78) compared to the control group (M=1.14, SD=.96), t(22)=4.05, p<.01. Resisting chocolate was a much more potent self-control problem than solving math exercises. To estimate change over time, we correlated the self-regulation measure with time point (day) for each participant. This captured each participant's linear change over time. The mean correlation (using Fisher-Z-transformations) over time was a large and significant -.61 for the treatment group, df=8, p<.05, one-tailed, but only a small and insignificant -.22 for the control group, df=12, ns, one-tailed. All in all, while resisting the chocolate initially posed a stronger self-control problem, the required self-control did not stay on this level but constantly decreased (down to the level of the math exercises). Resisting the chocolate became easier each day. Combined with the interviews, this supports the notion of a training effect instilled by the machine.

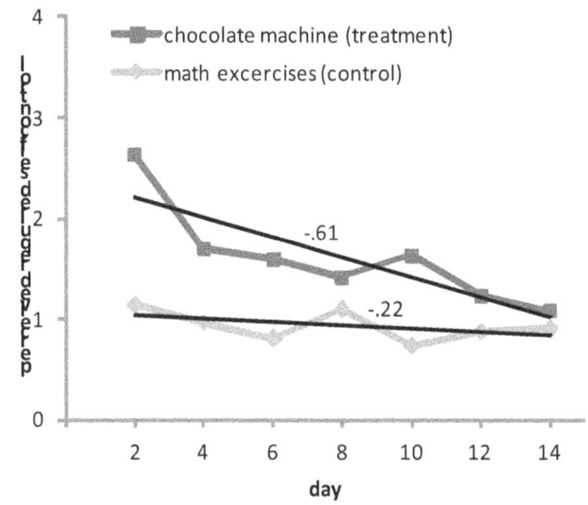

Figure 2: Perceived required self-control strength over time

From an experience point of view, participants experienced the *Chocolate Machine* as more positive (M=1.60, SD=0.63) compared to the math exercises (M=0.63, SD=1.21), t(22)=2.31, p<.05. This did not change much over time. Linear change (estimated analogous to *self-control*) was only -.10 for the treatment group and -.03 for the control group, both p>.05. As already apparent in the interviews, the *Chocolate Machine* was more fun, and this did not change over the course of the 14 days.

We measured general self-control strength as minutes spent on a difficult anagram task (i.e., *persistence*) before and after the training to get an idea of the behavioral and generalizing effects of using the *Chocolate Machine*. We performed a 2x2 mixed analysis of variance with *time* (before vs. after the study) as within-subjects factor, *treatment* (chocolate machine, math exercise) as between-subjects factor and *persistence* as independent variable. To control confounding aspects, we included general motivation to change as a covariate, i.e., we partialled out the effect of general motivation. In addition, we controlled the effect of the *valence* of the experience on *persistence* after the study by a regression. By this, we focused on training effects *not* instilled by general motivation or the attitudinal effects resulting from a positive/negative subjective experience of either the math exercise or the *Chocolate Machine*. The analysis revealed a significant

Time x *Treatment* interaction only, $F(1, 19)=4.94$, $p<.05$, partial $\eta^2=.21$. While persistence was in general poorer after the study (a difference of -12.5 minutes on the absolute values) – an effect well-known from literature (e.g.,[7]) – the *reduction* of persistence in the *Chocolate Machine* group was only 8.5 minutes compared to 16 minutes in the math exercise group. To summarize, other than participants themselves suspected, there was a generalization effect of the *Chocolate Machine*, in the sense that persistence of participants in the treatment group decreased less than persistence of participants in the control group.

SUMMARY AND CONCLUSION

The *Chocolate Machine* is a transformational product not so much targeted at a particular behavior (e.g., saving energy, stopping overeating), but at general self-control strength. Our study showed that people get better in resisting over time, presumably because they acquire strategies to deal with the temptation, such as reinterpretation. Metcalfe and Mischel [5] argued that resisting will get the harder the more consummatory, action-oriented (i.e., "hotter") the outcome representation is. "Cooling it down" through reinterpretation or tabooing is, thus, an effective strategy acquired by using the machine. The acquisition of useful strategies as well as the subjective feelings of being more self-reflective and self-aware may further be the basis for a potential generalization from resisting a chocolate ball to resisting other vices.

Many persuasive technologies rely on monitoring, feedback, and competition alone. They hope to get people to do things by simple recording and rewarding, without voicing much of a position themselves. In contrast, we assume that people can readily see what is potentially good for them (after a little eye-opener, maybe), but have problems with accepting and implementing change. We all know that fast food is bad – and a stroke the worst – but it simply tastes so good. People may pretend not to know, or even deliberately abstain from related information, but they are not stupid. To approach these problems as deficits of information and monitoring seems at best naïve (at worst it is patronizing). What is needed beyond information is an alternative position to rub against or to align with. *Transformational products* deliberately take a position. They are "materialized arguments" (see [9]) provided by us, the designers. Transparency and humor seems crucial to this. A *Chocolate Machine* user was always fully aware of what we intended. Nothing is concealed. Admittedly, the machine slightly mocks people, it is a troublemaker, but it does so in a light way. By that, it draws its users into a playful "dialog loop" about their current Self and potential alternative Selves. And people seem to happily submit to it, as reflected by the positive feelings towards the device. To us, this playful, positive confrontation with own attitudes and behavior seems crucial to a persuasive technology. To create this requires a new approach to the design of according interactive products – away from an aesthetic of convenience to one of playful positive friction.

REFERENCES

1. Fogg, B.J. *Persuasive Technology: Using Computers to Change What We Think and Do.* Morgan Kaufmann, 2003.
2. Laschke, M., Hassenzahl, M., and Diefenbach, S. Things with attitude: Transformational Products. In *Create11 Conference* (2011), 1-2, Retrieved from http://www.create-conference.org/storage/create11papersposters/Things with attitude.pdf
3. Lee, M.K., Kiesler, S., and Forlizzi, J. Mining behavioral economics to design persuasive technology for healthy choices. In *Proceedings of the 2011 annual conference on Human Factors in Computing Systems - CHI '11*, ACM Press (2011), 325.
4. Loewenstein, G. The Fall and Rise of Psychological Explanations in the Economics of Intertemporal Choice. In G.F. Loewenstein and J. Elster, eds., *Choice over time*. Russell Sage, 1992, 3-34.
5. Metcalfe, J. and Mischel, W. A hot/cool-system analysis of delay of gratification: dynamics of willpower. *Psychological Review* 106, 1 (1999), 3-19.
6. Muraven, M. and Baumeister, R.F. Self-regulation and depletion of limited resources: does self-control resemble a muscle? *Psychological Bulletin* 126, 2 (2000), 247-259.
7. Muraven, M., Baumeister, R.F., and Tice, D.M. Longitudinal improvement of self-regulation through practice: building self-control strength through repeated exercise. *Journal of Social Psychology* 139, 4 (1999), 446-457.
8. Muraven, M. Building self-control strength: Practicing self-control leads to improved self-control performance. *Journal of Experimental Social Psychology* 46, 2 (2010), 465-468.
9. Redström, J.H. Persuasive design: Fringes and foundations. In *Proceedings of the first international conference on Persuasive Technology for Human Well-Being (PERSUASIVE'06)*, Springer (2006), 112–122.
10. Tangney, J.P., Baumeister, R.F., and Boone, A.L. High self-control predicts good adjustment, less pathology, better grades, and interpersonal success. *Journal of Personality* 72, 2 (2004), 271-324.
11. Zimmerman, J. Designing for the self: making products that help people become the person they desire to be. In *Proceedings of the 2009 annual conference on Human Factors in Computing Systems - CHI '09*, ACM Press (2009), 395–404.

Ripple Effects of an Embedded Social Agent: A Field Study of a Social Robot in the Workplace

Min Kyung Lee[1], Sara Kiesler[1], Jodi Forlizzi[1], Paul Rybski[2]
Human-Computer Interaction Institute[1], Robotics Institute[2]
Carnegie Mellon University
5000 Forbes Ave, Pittsburgh, PA 15213 USA
{mklee, kiesler, forlizzi, rybski}@cs.cmu.edu

ABSTRACT
Prior research has investigated the effect of interactive social agents presented on computer screens or embodied in robots. Much of this research has been pursued in labs and brief field studies. Comparatively little is known about social agents embedded in the workplace, where employees have repeated interactions with the agent, alone and with others. We designed a social robot snack delivery service for a workplace, and evaluated the service over four months allowing each employee to use it for two months. We report on how employees responded to the robot and the service over repeated encounters. Employees attached different social roles to the robot beyond a delivery person as they incorporated the robot's visit into their workplace routines. Beyond one-on-one interaction, the robot created a ripple effect in the workplace, triggering new behaviors among employees, including politeness, protection of the robot, mimicry, social comparison, and even jealousy. We discuss the implications of these ripple effects for designing services incorporating social agents.

Author Keywords
Social agent, human-robot interaction, service design, workplace, field study, embodiment, organizational technology

ACM Classification Keywords
H5.0. Information interfaces and presentation: General.

General Terms
Design, Experimentation

INTRODUCTION
Increasingly, computational agents assist in real world tasks. Examples include Aethon's hospital delivery robot, the Autom robotic weight coach, a therapeutic robot called Paro, and online social customer agents such as IKEA's Anna. Other service agents are in development as instructor

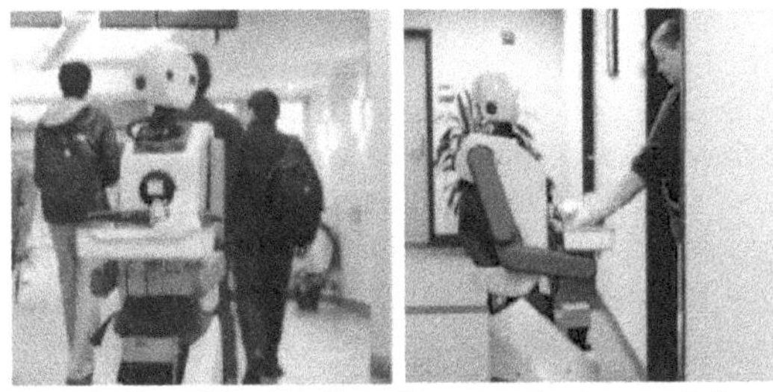

Figure 1. Snackbot delivering snacks to participants

agents for language learning [17], office and hospital work assistants [4, 31], and rehabilitation or assistive robots [10].

Most of the agents mentioned above have social skills and attributes such as speech, humanlike appearance, conversational strategies, or social responses to human input. Research suggests there are benefits of an agent having such social capabilities. For instance, small talk and empathic language have been shown to improve people's liking, engagement and trust for agents [3, 5, 6]. However, most of this work has been conducted in labs or public settings in which repeated encounters with the agent were not tracked over time. We do not know if an agent's social skills become annoying or boring over time, or how socially interactive systems fit into the culture of a real workplace.

This research explores the experiences of employees with a snack delivery service and robot that delivered the snacks in their workplace over a period of four months (Figure 1). We followed participating employees over the two months they each were allotted for the service to understand their responses to the robot and to the service.

This paper makes two contributions to the human computer interaction community beyond prior studies of social agents and robots. First, we describe the adoption of a service employing an embodied social agent in a workplace, showing how acceptance grew and social dynamics matured over time. Second, we describe changes in employees' interactions with one another surrounding the service. We describe the development of protective norms as the robot came to be understood as a workplace member, and how deliveries became occasions for taking breaks and celebrations. We characterize these phenomena as ripple effects, a chain of events in which social interactions affect situations not directly related to the initial interaction. As agents become more embedded in workplaces and other organizations, ripple effects will make for interesting design challenges.

Social Aspects of Agents

Computer-based agents, whether animations, avatars, text-based conversational agents or embodied robots, are considered "social" when they exhibit human-like attributes such as faces or conversational dialogue or respond socially to human input. Researchers have explored the effects of agents' appearance [28, 39], conversational strategies [3, 5, 6], gestures [2, 18, 31], touch [25] and normative behavior [26]. More sophisticated strategies attempt to match the social response of the agent to the personality of the user [35], to the task [14], or to the culture [9]. Much of this work has been performed in labs [2, 3, 6, 9, 14, 25, 28, 35] and demonstration projects in public settings such as museums [26]. The work suggests that a social agent can improve people's engagement and trust of the system, and liking of the agent, even in a utilitarian and task-oriented setting [2]. Studies of entertainment and commercial robots [36] suggest that people can form a relationship with a robot dog [12], or even to a vacuum cleaner [34].

Some researchers have begun to study people's response to social agents that deliver real services in work settings [17, 24, 30, 31]. To our knowledge, no studies have followed the same employees over an extended period. Our development of a sturdy mobile robot platform allowed us to track a snack service and the same set of users and their repeated interactions with the robot. Using this approach, we could observe the integration of the social agent in the workplace beyond its novelty effect. To guide our observations, we drew on research about the introduction of technology in work organizations [1, 27]. Two important concepts in this literature are "organizational routines" [11] and "sensemaking," the social process of making sense of new situations and events [38]. We observed both processes emerge in our study.

ROBOTIC SNACK DELIVERY SERVICE

We designed our robotic snack service, with the robot, Snackbot, to fit the workplace of our university [19]. From a preliminary survey conducted the previous year, we determined that employees would value snack deliveries, especially deliveries of fresh, healthy snacks. We also believed robotic deliveries would have application to other domains (e.g., hospital, warehouse deliveries) and to assisting the mobility impaired [31].

Components

The Snackbot service was comprised of a front stage consisting of services that participants encountered directly, and a back stage consisting of the underlying system that they did not see [32].

Front stage

Participants ordered snacks using a snack ordering website [23]. They specified the snack type, delivery day, and office number. We offered fresh fruits and sweet snacks that were not always available in the workplace.

Snackbot [20], a 4.5-foot tall anthropomorphic robot, made the snack deliveries. The robot has wheels, an articulated head, and an animated LED mouth to smile, frown, or show a neutral expression. The robot was designed following a human-centered design approach. Its form was determined through iterative tests, with the goal of creating a robot that is social and friendly but not misleadingly smart. The robot uses a SICK LIDAR to traverse the office environment autonomously (with obstacle avoidance and path planning). In our study, the website information was not linked to the robot, so an operator specified the office destinations. The robot used the Cepstral text to speech program with a male voice. The robot carried a web camera and a microphone on its chest to record interactions. Speech was controlled remotely with a laptop connected to the robot through a wireless network.

Back stage

A laptop running a custom interface was used to remotely control robot's head and mouth movements, dialog system, and navigation when the robot was not able to navigate autonomously. The interface showed the video feed from the robot, the robot's location on the building map, its head position, and a number of dialogue scripts. The operators could see and hear participants' actions through the video/audio feed on the interface.

The operator translated orders on the website into a delivery schedule, specifying customer names, snack names, and delivery location. Locations were mapped into the navigation system, and snacks were loaded on the robot's tray. The operator initialized and localized the robot at the start of each delivery run, and opened hallway doors so the robot could pass through. The operator loaded an appropriate dialogue script (according to the interaction timeline) and clicked each node based on human responses. Even though we used a Wizard of OZ technique, which is commonly used in HRI, the interaction sets and dialogues were built in a way that they could automatically unfold using basic speech recognition. We used this method since we did not want our participants to wear headsets that would interfere with their natural interaction with the robot.

Interaction Design

The main interactions between participants and the service took place through website orders and interactions with the robot, the latter of which became a main focus of our design efforts. We built the interaction scripts before we launched the service, considering potential events and user behaviors.

Structure of interaction

The interaction design was meant to convey an image of a polite and friendly service provider in the workplace. We started with a prototypical interaction structure, informed by the interactions we observed between a hot dog vendor and his long-time customers. These interactions start with the vendor identifying the customer, greeting and engaging in small talk with the customer, engaging in the snack transaction, and performing social leave-taking. Below is an example script that the operator would have selected on an early day in the trial.

[At the office door] Excuse me. I have an order for David. [Robot looks straight ahead.]
Hello, David. Nice to meet you [Robot looks up to make eye contact with David.]
{...social interaction...}
Please take your apple. [Robot looks down at the tray and then looks up at David.]
Thanks, David. Bye, I'm leaving now. [Robot looks straight]

The robot followed pre-set scripts, to maintain consistency across participant experiences and prohibit improvisations of the operator. The robot's responses were built in a way that made sense regardless of the participants' response (e.g., "I see."), or had two different alternative responses, each for participants' yes or no answers. When there were no appropriate scripts matching a participant's comment, the robot said, "I have no idea," or laughed. In considering the context of the workplace, we were also attentive to the right time to interrupt. For example, the robot promised to return if a meeting or a phone call were taking place.

Categories	Topics	Examples
Temporal and seasonal	Days of the week, holidays (April Fool's Day, Memorial Day), seasons	"You've got something on your face! [pause] April fools!"
Organizational	Festivals, exam time, breaks	"Do you have any plans for Carnival?"
Regional	Local sports teams	"It is baseball season. Do you follow the Pirates?"
Task-talk	Snack-related information	"Bananas are a really good source of potassium and vitamin B6. Excellent choice."
Small-talk	Jokes, local weather	"It is a nice day today. I am glad to see you again and hope you are doing well."

Table 1. Examples of social interaction dialogues

Categories	Topics	Examples
Snack choices	Most ordered snacks; orders of healthy snacks, variety of snacks; group's snack consumption patterns	"It seems as though you really like [snack]. This is the [nth] time you have ordered one. "
Service usage patterns	Whether they were regular weekly users; had they been in their office when the robot was there; times when they did not use the snack service	"I missed you during my snack deliveries [n] times so far. I am glad to finally see you again."
Robot's behaviors	Frequency of breakdowns and apology (no breakdowns to frequent breakdowns)	"I was thinking about my first month here. I realized that I broke down and made mistakes [n] times in front of you. Sorry for that, and thank you for being patient with me."

Table 2. Examples of personalized interaction dialogues

Social interaction

Following the model of the hot dog vendor, we created social as well as instrumental dialogues (Table 1). These responses were designed to be agreeable and honest (i.e., admitting inability to understand many topics), and to emphasize similarity between participants and the robot, following politeness principles [7].

Personalization

For half of the participants, we designed dialogues that built on their prior interactions with the robot and the service (Table 2). These referred to previous snack choice patterns, service usage patterns, and the robot's behaviors and breakdowns [22]. Because these interactions were based on participants' prior history with the robot and snack service, they were introduced after four deliveries had occurred.

Mitigation of service breakdowns

Despite our efforts to create natural interactions, the robot had significant limitations that were evident to participants. It followed pre-set scripts. There were frequent delays in the dialogue. Sometimes the system froze when there were wireless network problems. To mitigate these events, the robot was designed to initiate and guide conversation. For example, the robot led the conversation by asking questions. To address situations where the robot could not process human behaviors, the robot used dialogues to encourage participants or passersby to behave in a manner that could be processed by the robot (e.g., "Can you please stand in front of me?" "I have bad ears, so sometimes I cannot hear very well. Can you repeat, please?").

METHOD

We conducted a field study from February to June, 2011 in the workplace.

Field Site and Participants

Employees solicited for the service and study were distributed across 16 offices located in 10 hallways on one floor of an office building at a US university. We used flyers, postcards, and snowball sampling to recruit participants. The study required participants to have offices in our field site, and generally to be in their offices at least one afternoon a week. We had 21 participants: eight women, ranging in age from 23–49, and 13 men, ranging in age from 22-51. The participants included eleven graduate students, eight staff, one post-doc, and one faculty member. All were members of the computer science school; but half of the participants had no programming knowledge. Only one participant had prior exposure to the robot.

Procedure and Data Sources

The robot delivered snacks from 2:30 – 4 p.m. Mondays, Wednesdays, and Fridays. We provided free snacks to compensate for participation in surveys and interviews. Participants could place an order anytime before noon on the day of snack delivery. If participants were not in their offices, their snack was placed in a paper bag and hung on their office door. Because we could not deliver snacks to all

21 participants in a day, those who joined the service early were retired from the study after two months of usage.

Surveys

The initial background survey included questions about participants' demographic information, their expectation about the service, and their snacking routines. The exit survey included service satisfaction questions in 7-point Likert scales.

Interaction logs

The robot's camera and microphone recorded all interactions between the robot and participants. Except for one day when the robot's recording was turned off accidentally, and a few other cases when the camera was turned away from participants, 175 interactions were audio recorded and 161 interactions were video recorded.

To measure cooperation with the robot, it initiated three new interactions near the end of each participant's trial [21]: (1) a help request when the robot asked the participant for tour locations for visitors, (2) a suggestion to take a break and join the robot doing a "neck stretch," and (3) carrying a mystery snack that participants could choose instead of the snack that they ordered.

Interviews

The first author conducted 30..60 minute semi-structured interviews with the 21 participants at the end of the study. The interview began with questions about participants' experiences with the robot and the service. Then, we asked participants how they felt their experiences with the robot changed over time, whether they saw other participants interacting with the robot, how other people around them behaved, what types of breakdowns they experienced and how they reacted to them, what they liked and disliked about the service, whether they had any concerns about the service. All but one participant consented to audio recording of the interview.

Analyses

We transcribed the interviews and interaction logs and did thematic coding, using the NVivo 8 software. We followed an inductive process that involved reading through the interview and interaction scripts and investigating emerging categories and relationships [33]. We started by open coding a small sample of scripts, adjusted and added categories, and then proceeded to open coding of all the data. In the phase 2, we grouped the lower-level codes into thematic clusters and drew connections among them to tell a story about how participants made sense of the robot, and how the robot changed and evoked social behaviors that created interesting ripple effects. We do not report themes that concern functional and aesthetic qualities of the robot, and ideas for new features; they were practical suggestions unique to our service platform. In this process, we compared what we were learning with existing concepts such as sensemaking and structuration. We also counted how much participants spoke and relational behaviors from the interaction logs.

For analysis of behavior change over time, we defined the first four interactions during delivery as Period 1, and the rest as Period 2. We used a multi-level regression model to analyze the codes from the interaction logs, comparing responses during Period 1 versus Period 2.

FINDINGS

As noted above, the robot was social with all participants (Table 1), but half of the participants also received a more personalized service in Period 2 (Table 2). Personalized interaction was more successful in eliciting cooperation, sustaining engagement, and building stronger rapport; we report a detailed analysis of the effects of personalization in [21]. In this paper, we report findings that were common to all participants. When they were not, we note that fact.

Participants interacted with the robot 9 times on average (SD=3.07) over the two months they could receive service, and made 12 orders (SD=3.96) on average, resulting in 261 orders in total for all participants. Participants were typically in their offices for snack deliveries. Each interaction averaged one minute and six seconds long (SD=37 seconds), including 7 turns (SD=2.28) from the participant and 8 turns (SD=2.27) from the robot. The average number of words in participants' dialogues was 35.13 (SD=23.08) (Participants spoke more words in Period 2 than Period 1, but the difference was not significant if we controlled for the number of turns from the robot.).

On the initial background survey, participants' expected utilitarian benefits such as good quality snacks, and convenience. Participants did not expect to interact with an embodied robot; they thought it would be like a delivery cart that left snacks. With the exception of one participant who did not want to continue the service at the end of the study, participants reported that they liked the service and the robot, talked about the service with their friends and families, and got positive feedback about it.

Change over Time

Over the course of the snack service trial, two notable phenomena emerged. Participants began to attach a workplace role to the robot, and incorporated the service into their daily routine. Further, these interactions had rippling effects on others in the workplace, resulting in new social dynamics within the organization.

Routinization

Participants said their initial excitement wore off after two to three interactions with the robot. They learned how the interactions generally unfolded, and got used to seeing the robot; it became a routine [11]. Some participants looked forward to their interactions with the robot, and made an effort to be in their offices when it arrived:

Participant U: *Yeah, it was definitely something we added to my Monday, Wednesday and Friday routine and I was always sad if I missed it.*

Participant O: *I was having a conversation with a coworker about whatever it was that I was going to do that afternoon, and I realized, I heard myself say, "Well, it doesn't matter, 'cause I'm not missing my Snackbot visit now."*

Participant M: *Oh yeah, [my boss's] office is down the hall from mine, and I was in a meeting with him and then I heard Snackbot coming down the hall towards my office, and so I ran out of the meeting to go to my office and wait for Snackbot...*

Sensemaking

Research shows that new or unfamiliar situations, new technology, or new services trigger a process of sensemaking, whereby people attach particular meaning to events [38]. After our participants experienced deliveries by a robot that talked with them, they began to think of the robot as a member of the workplace:

Participant D: *I like the snack delivery thing. Sometimes I would actually come to campus just because I ordered a Snackbot snack, and I liked to be here when he showed up. Other times, I was kind of cranky and didn't feel like talking to him and sort of wanted to just grab the snack and walk away. But I felt bad, so I didn't do that.*

Participant M: *Snackbot is non-judgmental, yet you can kind of feel like you have some sort of some kind of relationship. I mean, whether it'd be a deep relationship, probably not, but just that constancy.*

Participant O: *[the robot] reminded me of a coworker that I used to have that used to stop by and, like, make sure that you got a break during the day. And so it was, kind of, interesting. Because I was, like, wow. This is just a machine that comes to visit me. But it actually makes me feel better and reminds me of people that aren't around me anymore. Which is, I think, kind of, important to me.*

Those who were exposed to personalized dialogues tended to anthropomorphize the robot:

Participant E: *But the one thing that really shocked me was the day, it was a few weeks ago, when he came to the office and said that he was embarrassed because he broke down the first few times in front of my office. And I was, I felt bad for the robot. And suddenly, I noticed I was suddenly thinking it was a person, or reacting to him like a person.*

Participant E put a flashlight battery in the robot's tray, as a gift during the robot's last visit, in case the robot would run out of battery life as had happened during a prior delivery.

As with any technology used in real world settings, robot breakdowns were not an uncommon event. Breakdowns were occasions for people to change their conceptions of the robot and to reevaluate their connections to it.

For example, Participant E thought that the robot could recognize people until she saw the robot talking to a closed door:

Participant E: *Because he didn't realize the door was closed.*
Interviewer: *Wait, so he was trying to talk to people there?*
Participant E: *Yeah, but he was talking to the door saying, "May I pass?"*

Breakdowns caused further sensemaking and some reality-checking as the robot performed behaviors a person would not do:

Participant J: *Are we having a staring contest? I think you will win.*
Snackbot, after 18 second delay: *Please take your Snickers.*

Participants' emotional responses to breakdowns differed depending on what they expected from the robot. For those who lacked a social connection to the robot, breakdowns were instances that highlighted the robot's incapability. On the other hand, for those who had a connection to the robot, breakdowns shattered the illusion of the robot having social intelligence:

Interviewer: *Any suggestions for the next version of the service?*
Participant M: *Not to talk to a door. . . I thought it was sad. Talking to a door, you know it's undignified. . . you know just in general, don't embarrass yourself, you're supposed to be a human here. You know, don't ruin the illusion.*

For other participants, the robot's breakdowns were entertaining, robot-like qualities that they desired in a delivery robot. For example, Participant J said:

If he had just come and, you know, had a nice little conversation and given me the snack, I actually don't think I would've liked it as much as I did. ... But if it's just, sort of, cutely robotic in a way where it's not able to accomplish what a human could. Then, it's, like, better than if it was just really, really good at what it did, I think. Because ultimately, you know you're interacting with a computer. You're not going to be tricked into thinking it's a person.

Five participants of the 21 made sense of the robot as a failed person. They concluded that social interaction with the robot was meaningless because the robot was not a creature or a person, and that social interaction was not something they desired from a delivery person in any case.

For example, Participant C, who described the robot as "*an ATM that dispenses snacks,*" said:

Yes, I know the robot's not a person that's going to miss me so it's like somebody has programmed it to say "I'm going to miss you," and it's just like funny in a way, it is, but it's not meaningful.

Participant A: *"Do you want a service robot to be very conversational?" ...I'm a little reluctant with these human analogies in general, but in the sense that if you're in a hotel room and somebody knocks and says, "Room service," you don't start chatting with them.*

The robot's inability to carry out natural conversation contributed to these reactions. All participants thought that the robot should know if they were hurried or busy with work before it started social conversation:

Ripple Effects in the Workplace

As the service ran, we observed new social practices among employees.

Formation of norms through interpersonal influence

All robot deliveries happened at employees' office doors, and conversations with the robot could be overheard by officemates or passersby. Both participants and non-participants eavesdropped and observed others' interactions with the robot. Surprising to us, these behaviors continued throughout the service deployment. Recorded interaction logs showed that often one or more people were watching when someone interacted with the robot. When something out of the ordinary happened, for example, if the robot made a funny comment, observers laughed or remarked about the incident. On one occasion, the robot came to a participant's office door while the participant remained at her desk and yelled at the robot. At this point the robot said, "Please stand in front of me." Everyone in the office laughed.

Some participants said they felt self-conscious or awkward when others overheard their interactions:

Participant J: *If people were in the hallway or across in their offices, and you're just, sort of, the spotlight's... on you a little bit when he comes to your door.*

In overhearing and observing other participants' interactions, employees developed a consensus on how a typical interaction should unfold and the types of inputs that the robot could understand:

Participant B: *I think definitely seeing maybe what worked when people interacted with him and what didn't kind of like primed you like how or things you should kind of say or could say to Snackbot in order for him to understand you.*

Participants learned to be polite to the robot. For example, they waited until the robot was finished speaking, took snacks only after the robot invited them to do so, and did not make impolite remarks:

Participant R: *I think I was a little bit meaner to Snackbot before I saw [Participant O] talking to him. I was like, "Oh, she's actually really nice and she says bye properly and "Have a good day," whereas I'm just like, "Bye Snackbot." After I saw her, I was like, "Oh, I should really be nicer to Snackbot.*

The analysis of interaction logs of the participant above shows that, in her earlier interactions, she took a snack before the robot was finished talking, and used more directive language (e.g., "Snackbot, go away."). In her later interactions, she was more conversational and polite.

Robot as member of the workplace

After a few weeks, some participants in the workplace began treating the robot like a member of the workplace, and it became the norm to protect the robot from criticism. For example, the interaction log of Participant N shows when he complained that the robot was slow, his officemate made excuses for it:

Participant J: *Hey, it's Monday.*

Another participant talked about this phenomenon as follows:

Participant F: *Snackbot doesn't have feelings but I wouldn't want to just take the snack and shut the door in its face.*

Or one time I told Snackbot--I think Snackbot asked me if there was maybe a tour of [building] or something, which room should Snackbot take me up to, and I just told Snackbot that probably someone would program it. It's a robot. It's probably not going to make those choices. And then my office mate was like, "Oh. Now you've gone and made Snackbot feel bad." So I think part of it is about how my relationship with Snackbot is not just about Snackbot but about other people who are around and kind of see us.

In the subsequent visit after the incident reported above, Participant F apologized to the robot.

The behavior logs show participants exhibited more relational and in-group member interactions over time. On average, more percentage of participants made meta-relational comments during their interaction (e.g., using "us" or referring to the robot as "friend") in Period 2 ($M = 0.25$, $SE = 0.05$) than Period 1 ($M = 0.13$, $SE = 0.05$), $F(1, 161.3) = 4.56$, $p = .03$. Significantly fewer percentage of participants took snacks before the robot gave permission to do so in Period 2 ($M = 0.18$, $SE = 0.05$) than Period 1($M = 0.05$, $SE = 0.04$), $F(1, 136.1) = 7.73$, $p <.01$. Finally, they smiled more frequently during the interaction in Period 2 ($M = 1.51$, $SE = 0.26$) than in Period 1 ($M = 2.10$, $SE = 0.25$), $F(1, 136.9) = 8.44$, $p < .01$).

One issue was that our interaction design did not allow for an easy way for people to interrupt and end a conversation. Participants may have felt some social pressure to be polite, even when they wanted to end the dialogue because they were busy, or the robot was experiencing a delay:

Participant N: *It's kind of awkward because when [the robot] crashes you don't know what to do because sometimes it turns away and you're trying to take the cookie or something and then people will be like why are you stealing from Snackbot? Snackbot didn't ask you to take the cookie yet.*

In all social groups, people develop feelings around fairness and the distribution of resources [8]. In one hallway where five participant's offices were located, perceptions of the robot as a workplace member developed to the point that participants seemed to think that the robot had personal preferences for some workers and felt slightly envious when the robot seemed to prefer others. For example, a purely mechanical decision, such as the order of office visits, was interpreted as evidence for the robot's preference.

Participant L: *I don't know if it was numeric or just alphabetic or whatever it was and we thought "Oh, why he always goes to her first because he likes her best."*

Participant E: *I think he's flirting with her. I wonder if he likes her. Because he seemed to talk to her longer than anyone else.*

The analysis of the interaction logs showed that the robot spoke the same amount of words to Participant J as to any other participant.

When the robot made the mistake of calling Participant J's name at a different participant's office, participants interpreted the mistake as additional evidence for the robot's "crush" on Participant J.

Participant L: *We were kind of all at our doors here looking this way and [then] he then went over to Participant M's [office] and asked for Participant J again . . .and we all said "I knew it! I knew he has a crush on [Participant J] because he keeps looking for her." I think it was because we thought he was talking to her more than he was talking to the rest of us. That's what made us first think. We said "Oh, gosh. He says so many different things to her."*

Being the first to receive a personalized interaction from the robot also made some participants feel special:

Participant L: *Like when he had the mystery snack for me and he hadn't given it to anybody else.*

Personalization strategies also contributed to social comparison:

Participant J: *Yeah, I think that the robot complimented one girl, [Participant E], one lady, on always being in her office. And how she must be a hard worker. How he would miss her and things like that. And then, I felt a little jealous.*

Deliveries as an occasion to socialize

The initial survey and the exit interview included questions about participants' snacking routines before the study. Participants ate snacks during long afternoons, usually at their desks; many made individual trips to vending machines without socializing. This practice may reflect US workplace culture that values efficiency. Snack consumption increased when the service was used to get snacks regularly (to have healthy snacks or curb hunger), and did not change when the service substituted snacks that participants used to bring from home. Participants' experiences did not differ by these snacking patterns.

In one hallway where many participants' offices were near each other, participants began to routinely socialize when Snackbot visited, calling the days the robot made deliveries "Snackbot days":

Participant N: *I really liked, enjoyed the Snackbot. And it has been like in the hallway of like the [building] [room number], everyone is looking forward to Monday, Wednesday and Friday. They call it Snackbot day. Sometimes I go into the office and people will be yelling today is Snackbot day.*

Participant J: *I'm just finishing up my first year over here. And people, kind of, mostly keep to themselves. And a lot of times, people aren't even in their office. And I think people might've even been showing up more to get the snacks. So it's usually pretty, like, quiet in my hall. You know, even if people are in, they might close their door or something. But I think people are more likely to be around and laughing and feeling sociable when the robot was there.*

Participants' responses suggest that the robot became a common boundary object that participants could easily relate to, creating a topic of conversation and an occasion to socialize, in the way that dogs do in a public park [29].

In another hallway, a few participants who shared a lab space started impersonating each other during the Snackbot visit when the participants who ordered a snack were not in their office. While doing this, they usually mimicked personal characteristics such as tone of voice and accent to entertain themselves and other passersby.

Participant B: *Let's see, who was I? I was Participant S who wasn't in the lab. And my other friend, [Participant U], I think he was [Participant I]. Participant I is Australian, so he tried to do an Australian accent. But Snackbot didn't seem to like that. <laughing>. [...] I guess I tried to impersonate his mannerisms and the way he interacted with Snackbot. I mean, it really wasn't really for entertainment purposes with the robot. It was more for the other people that were in the office.*

When probing further, the participants who impersonated each other could not explain why they started; they said someone started and it seemed fun. It became a pattern to imitate anyone who was not in the office when the robot came to make a delivery.

DISCUSSION

Our findings show employees attached different social roles to the robot beyond a delivery person as they incorporated the robot's visit into their workplace routines. Beyond one-on-one interaction, the robot created a ripple effect in the workplace, triggering new positive and negative behaviors among employees, including politeness, protection of the robot, mimicry, social comparison, and even jealousy.

The ripple effects were quite unanticipated, and they lasted and grew richer over time. This was not our design intention. The initial purpose of this study had been to evaluate the feasibility and usefulness of a social robot to perform delivery services in a workplace, and to examine how the robot's interactions could be designed to support repeated interactions with customers. Yet, we gathered a great deal of evidence to support the fact that social dynamics around the robot and service evolved. In the following sections, we discuss different aspects of the ripple effect, and how the design of the robot and the workplace culture contributed to these effects. We believe that this result is partly due to the interaction and service design of the robot, with its repeated travels and conversations through the workplace.

The robot interacted through conversations that could be overheard, causing people to pay attention and to observe what was going on. The robot's mobile form also made the robot easy to be noticed, as compared, for example, to a screen agent on a kiosk or a computer. Perhaps another influence was the afternoon delivery time, possibly more conducive to socializing than mornings.

To make the robot more sociable and interesting, we designed the dialogues to change over time, using different topics, and (for half of the participants) building on prior events to spark more personalized interactions. We think if the robot had enacted the same dialogues for four months, interest would probably have flagged.

Our results also suggest that the decision of anthropomorphic vs. non-anthropomorphic systems has tradeoffs, and social qualities should be employed adaptively depending on individual preferences and situational contexts (e.g., busyness). The literature suggests that services can be successfully transactional or social depending on the situation (e.g., a postman who delivers mail to a large city apartment vs. a postman who delivers mail to a small community over time, and is treated as a community member) [16]. We explored a social interaction model appropriate for our workplace context ...the same robot visiting people's offices repeatedly, unfolding social interaction over time. To our surprise, 75% of the participants appreciated these interactions over time. However, for 25%, social interactions were a reason to devalue the service as it incurred interruption or did not match their conception of the robot as machine.

Limitations

Conducting the field study provided participants a realistic experience with a novel service and system, but also entailed many limitations. The study was conducted on one floor of a computer science building, where the robot had a floor map and could operate reliably; the location also offered easier access to engineering help if it broke down. This could cause a potential bias in knowledge about the robot's underlying technology. People with programming skills may anthropomorphize robots less than others. However, half of the participants in the study did not have much programming knowledge. None of our participants were part of the Snackbot development team. Furthermore, studying a prototype in the same organization it was developed in, especially when it is novel, is not uncommon (e.g., [31, 37]). The university building lobby houses a reception robot, and most participants interacted with it 1-2 times when it was introduced, so they may be less subject to the novelty effect. However, the robots differ in their roles (receptionist vs. delivery), mobility (kiosk vs. mobile), input method (keyboard vs. speech), and interaction (reactive vs. proactive). Our study used a Wizard of Oz technique to select nodes in the dialog script, and the operator was in the vicinity of the robot for control and security reasons. This could cause a bias in whether people understand the robot to be autonomous or not. When we asked participants about the robot's mechanisms, they wondered how much the robot was autonomous, but no one believed that they were communicating with the operator through the robot. Participants could not see the operators when interacting with the robot but if they participants knew of their presence, operators may have increased participants' positive reactions to the robot. The interviewers could be a source of bias, though they explained to participants that they did not build/implement the robot.

The specifics of our study also limit the external generalizability of the results. The snack service was operated as compensation for participating in the field study, having all interactions recorded, completing surveys and interviews. Free snacks may have contributed to high service satisfaction. We recorded all the interactions with participants' consent, which may have influenced their behavior. Participants had time to interact with and assess the robot beyond their initial excitement, yet different practices may have emerged or disappeared (unpredictably) in a longer study. We tested our interaction and service design strategy in the domain of snack delivery. The robot was anthropomorphic, and the conversation was not fluid as human conversation is. Generalizing the results to different service domains and to different kinds of agents will require further investigation.

IMPLICATIONS FOR DESIGN

Most studies of screen-based and robotic social agents have been conducted in isolated settings. We have shown, however, that interpersonal interactions in the workplace influenced the social dynamics that unfolded around the technology we studied, and future research should take into account this organizational and social context. To support services using agent-based technology in an organization, we propose the following design considerations.

Leveraging the Ripple Effect

Much discussion of social agents has concerned their immediate effect on individuals and tasks [e.g., 5]. We believe positive ripple effects instigated through group interaction can be anticipated and leveraged to help members of an organization to adopt, and adapt [27] new technology in the workplace. Here we present a few factors that are important in promoting positive ripple effects.

Making interaction visible

Our findings show several benefits of having the interaction between social agents and people in a place where other people can overhear or join in. This visibility of interaction helps people learn how to interact with a novel system by providing examples, and developing usage norms based on a group consensus. Increasing visibility of interaction can create a passive form of socialization, for example, as happens often in online communities when newcomers watch how old timers interact. Many online community members derive entertainment and learning benefits from watching other people's conversations online. Watching prepares them to join the interaction and socialize with others later. Features like embodiment, interaction location, and timing can be used to increase the visibility of agent-group interaction.

Harnessing in-group effects

As workers in our study began to think of the robot as a part of the organization, a desire to protect it emerged. Previous research shows that the influence of a person in the group gets stronger as group members like each other [13]. Having social agents perceived as a group member can encourage the development of norms that are more favorable and generous to a social agent. In our study, repeated, consistent exposure to employees, social interaction around organizational topics, and the robot's persona (not pretending to be more capable than it actually was) seemed to contribute to people's acceptance of it as a member of the organization.

Encouraging and discouraging social comparison

A few participants compared the robot's treatment of them with how the robot treated others. They attributed preferences to the robot, even when it was a result of a purely mechanical decision. People's tendency to anthropomorphize an agent could be used to encourage more frequent interaction with the agent. For example, an agent in a rehabilitation center could publicly encourage a patient who followed its orders well to promote social comparisons. In other cases where such attribution is not desirable, designers should make it clear that the social agent does not have such biases or preferences.

Promoting socializing

Our field study suggests social agents can be used to promote social activities and even celebrations among people. In our study, the robot's visit created an occasion to socialize. It offered topics of conversation and an excuse to take a break. Engaging in topics that are of interest to a group will be one way for an agent to facilitate socializing.

Starting and ending interactions

Research has shown that interaction has a natural opening, middle section, and closing [15]. Limitations in our dialogue design meant that these rules were often violated as people waited uneasily for the robot to finish its script. To encourage better adaptation to a busy workplace, a social agent must be able to start and end an interaction fluidly at any moment. Social interaction with an agent may be too demanding at a given time, therefore, agents need to offer a graceful way for people turn down an interaction.

Social context awareness

For social agents to instigate or encourage group interaction, they need to be aware of the possibilities for social interaction to unfold. To improve this capability, they should be aware of who might be near the focal person or persons, and be able to adaptively deliver personalized messages aimed at the group. Additionally, recognizing who is busy and who is free to socialize or interact will be important.

CONCLUSION

Prior research has investigated the effect of interactive social agents presented on computer screens or embodied in robots mostly in labs and brief field studies. We evaluated a snack delivery robot in the workplace, over a period of four months where each participant interacted with the robot for two months. Despite workers' knowledge of the robot as a machine, they developed a variety of social relationships with the robot. In addition, we witnessed ripple effects as new social norms and practices developed in the workplace. We hope that the design implications offered by this work will assist in the development of agents, avatars, and robots that can benefit individuals and organizations.

ACKNOWLEDGEMENTS

This work was supported by NSF grants 0624275 and 709077. We thank John Antanitis, Sarun Savetsila, Alex McCluskey, Leonard Turnier, Katherine Cuti, Ahmad Shamsuddin, and Junior Baboolall for their assistance.

REFERENCES

1. Barley, S. R. (1986). Technology as an occasion for structuring: Evidence from observations of CT scanners and the social order of radiology departments. *Administrative Science Quarterly, 31(1),* 78-108.
2. Bethel, C. L. & Murphy, R. (2006). Affective expression in appearance constrained robots. *Proc. of HRI'06*, 327-328.
3. Bickmore, T. & Cassell, J. (2001). Relational agents: A model and implementation of building user trust. *Proc. of CHI'01*, 396-403.
4. Bickmore, T., Pfeifer, L & Jack, B. (2009). Taking the time to care: Empowering low health literacy hospital patients with virtual nurse agents. *Proc. of CHI'09*, 1265-1274.
5. Bickmore, T. & Picard, R. (2005). Establishing and maintaining long-term human-computer relationships. *Transactions on Compt.-Hum. Interact., 59(1)*, 21-30.
6. Brave, S., Nass, C. & Hutchinson, L. (2005). Computers that care: Investigating the effects of orientation of emotion exhibited by an embodied computer agent. *International Journal of Human-Computer Studies, 62*, 161-178.

7. Brown, P. & Levinson, S. (1987). *Politeness: Some universals in language usage*. Cambridge Univ. Press.

8. Diekmann, K., Samuels, S., Ross, L. & Bazerman, M. (1997). Self-interest and fairness in problems of resource allocation: Allocators vs. recipients. *Journal of Personality and Social Psychology, 72,* 1061-1074.

9. Evers, V., Maldonado, H., Brodecki, T. & Hinds, P. J. (2008). Relational vs. group self-construal: Untangling the role of national culture in HRI. *Proc. of HRI'08*, 255-262.

10. Feil-Seifer, D. & Mataric, M. J. (2005). Defining socially assistive robotics. *Proc. of ICORR'05*, 465-468.

11. Feldman, M., & Pentland, B. (2003). Reconceptualizing organizational routines as a source of flexibility and change. *Administrative Science Quarterly, 48*, 94-118.

12. Friedman, B., Kahn, P. & Hagman, J. (2003). Hardware companions?: What online AIBO discussion forums reveal about the human-robotic relationship. *Proc. of CHI'03*, 273-280

13. Fulk, J. (1993). Social construction of communication technology. *Academy of Management Journal,* 921-950.

14. Goetz, J., Kiesler, S. & Powers, A. (2003). Matching robot appearance and behavior to tasks to improve human-robot cooperation. *Proc. of ROMAN'03*, 55-60.

15. Goffman, E. (1963). *Behavior in public places*. The Free Press.

16. Gwinner, K.P., Gremier, D.D., & Bitner, M.J. (1998). Relational benefits in services industries: The customer's perspective. *Journal of Academy of Marketing Science, 26(2),* 101-114.

17. Kanda, T., Hirano, T., Eaton, D. & Ishiguro, H. (2004). Interactive robots as social partners and peer tutors for children: A field trial. *Hum.-Comput. Interact.,* 61-84.

18. Kuno, Y., Sadazuka, K., Kawashima, M., Yamazaki, K., Yamazaki, A. & Hideaki Kuzuoka. (2007). Museum guide robot based on sociological interaction analysis. *Proc. of CHI'07*. 1191-1194.

19. Lee, M.K. & Forlizzi, J. (2009). Designing adaptive robotic services. *Proc. of IASDR'09*.

20. Lee, M.K., Forlizzi, J., Rybski, P.E., Crabbe, F., Chung, W., Finkle, J., Glaser, E. & Kiesler, S. (2009). The Snackbot: Documenting the design of a robot for long-term human-robot interaction. *Proc. of HRI'09*, 7-14.

21. Lee, M. K., Forlizzi, J., Kiesler, S., Rybski, P., Antanitis, J., & Savetsila, S. (2012). Personalization in HRI: A longitudinal field experiment. To appear in *Proc. of HRI'12*.

22. Lee, M.K., Kiesler, S., Forlizzi, J., Srinivasa, S., & Rybski, P. (2010). Gracefully mitigating breakdowns in robotic services. *Proc. of HRI'10*, 203-210.

23. Lee, M. K., Kiesler, S., & Forlizzi, J. (2011). Mining behavioral economics to design persuasive technology for healthy choices. *Proc. of CHI'11*, 325-334.

24. Mutlu, B. & Forlizzi, J. (2008). Robots in organizations: The role of workflow, social, and environmental factors in human-robot interaction. *Proc. of HRI'08*, 239-248.

25. Nakagawa, K., Shiomi, M., Shinozawa, K., Matsumura, R., Ishiguro, H. & Hagita, N. (2011). Effect of robot's active touch on people's motivation. *Proc. of HRI'11*, 465-472.

26. Nakauchi, Y. & Simmons, R. (2002). A social robot that stands in line. *Autonomous Robots, 12*, 313-324.

27. Orlikowski, W. J. (2000). Using technology and constituting structures: A practice lens for studying technology in organizations. *Org. Science, 11*, 404-428.

28. Powers, A., Kiesler, S., Fussell, S. & Torrey, C. (2007). Comparing a computer agent with a humanoid robot. *Proc. of HRI'07*, 145-152.

29. Robins, D., Sanders, C. & Cahill, S. (1991). Dogs and their people: Pet-facilitated interaction in a public setting. *Journal of Contemporary Ethnography,20*, 3-25.

30. Sabelli, A. M., Kanda, T. & Hagita, N. (2011). A conversational robot in an elderly care center: An ethnographic study. *Proc. of HRI'11*, 37-44.

31. Severinson-Eklundh, K., Green, A. & Hüttenrauch, H. (2003). Social and collaborative aspects of interaction with a service robot. *Robotics and Autonomous Systems, 42(3-4),* 223-234.

32. Shostack, L. (1982). How to design a service. *European Journal of Marketing*, 16, 49-63

33. Strauss, A. L. & Corbin, J. (1998). *Basics of qualitative research: Techniques and procedures for developing grounded theory* (2nd ed.). Thousand Oaks: Sage.

34. Sung, J., Guo, L., Grinter,R. & Christensen, H. (2007). "My Roomba is Rambo": Intimate home appliances. *Proc. of Ubicomp'07*, 145-162.

35. Tapus, A. & Mataric, M. (2008). User personality matching with a hands-off robot for post-stroke rehabilitation therapy. *Experimental Robotics,* 165-175.

36. Turkle, S. (2005). Relational artifacts/children/elders: The complexities of cyber companions. *Proc. of CogSci Workshop on Android Science*, 62-73.

37. Venolia, G., Tang, J., Cervantes, R., Bly, S., Robertson, G. G., Lee, B. & Inkpen, K. (2010). Embodied Social Proxy. *Proc. of CHI'10,* 1049-1058.

38. Weick, K. (1979). *The Social Psychology of Organizing (*2nd ed.). Addison-Wesley.

39. Yee, N., Bailenson, J. & Rickertsen, K. (2007). A meta-analysis of the impact of the inclusion and realism of human-like faces on user experiences in interfaces. *Proc. of CHI'07*, 1-10.

Designing Effective Gaze Mechanisms for Virtual Agents

Sean Andrist, Tomislav Pejsa, Bilge Mutlu, Michael Gleicher
Department of Computer Sciences, University of Wisconsin–Madison
1210 West Dayton Street, Madison, WI 53706, USA
{sandrist, tpejsa, bilge, gleicher}@cs.wisc.edu

ABSTRACT
Virtual agents hold great promise in human-computer interaction with their ability to afford embodied interaction using nonverbal human communicative cues. Gaze cues are particularly important to achieve significant high-level outcomes such as improved learning and feelings of rapport. Our goal is to explore how agents might achieve such outcomes through seemingly subtle changes in gaze behavior and what design variables for gaze might lead to such positive outcomes. Drawing on research in human physiology, we developed a model of gaze behavior to capture these key design variables. In a user study, we investigated how manipulations in these variables might improve affiliation with the agent and learning. The results showed that an agent using affiliative gaze elicited more positive feelings of connection, while an agent using referential gaze improved participants' learning. Our model and findings offer guidelines for the design of effective gaze behaviors for virtual agents.

Author Keywords
Nonverbal behavior; gaze; virtual agents; affiliation; learning

ACM Classification Keywords
H.1.2 Models and Principles: User/Machine Systems—*Human factors*; H.5.2 Information Interfaces and Presentation: User Interfaces—*Evaluation/methodology, User-centered design*

General Terms
Design, Experimentation, Human Factors

INTRODUCTION
Virtual agents hold tremendous potential for computer interfaces with their unique ability to embody humanlike attributes [7]. These attributes form rich communication mechanisms with which people are intimately familiar and afford intuitive interactions. Variations in these attributes activate key social and cognitive processes, in turn eliciting significant positive outcomes such as improved learning and rapport in key application domains such as education [33], collaboration [46], and therapy [49]. A deeper understanding of how humans use these attributes in social interactions might enable designers to create more effective virtual agents in these domains.

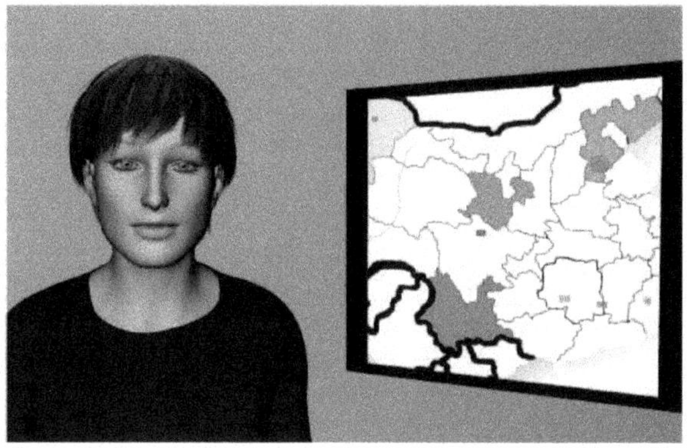

Figure 1. Erin, one of the humanlike virtual agents we used in our study which examined how virtual agents could use their gaze effectively in an educational scenario. Here Erin is giving a lecture on geographical locations of ancient China.

Gaze cues are an important subset of the embodied cues that people employ in social interactions. Using gaze cues, people can control the flow of a conversation, indicate interest in or appraisal of objects and people, improve listeners' comprehension, express complex emotions, and facilitate interpersonal processes [1, 3, 36]. In order to design virtual agents that achieve such significant effects, we must first design mechanisms that capture key variables of gaze and generate appropriate gaze behaviors. However, creating effective gaze cues for virtual characters is an open challenge, as humans have built and finessed subtle but complex patterns in which they use these cues over thousands of years of evolution and developed a sensitivity to observing them in others [42]. Furthermore, how these design variables might be varied to achieve specific high-level social and cognitive outcomes is not well understood. The goal of our research is to explore how agents might achieve these outcomes through subtle variations in gaze behaviors and what design variables might enable such variations. We contextualize the work presented in this paper in an educational scenario, in which virtual agents promise improvements in affiliation with students and in learning.

In this paper, we demonstrate that virtual agents can use subtle variations in gaze to achieve significant high-level outcomes. We present a parametric model that synthesizes appropriate gaze behaviors and allows for systematic variations in these behaviors, which we validated through an online user study with 96 participants. Our design of the gaze model draws on research in human physiology, which precisely describes how humans coordinate various gaze parameters such as the movements of the eyes and the head when executing *gaze shifts*—the intentional redirection of gaze toward a particular piece of information in the context of interaction. Gaze shifts are a fundamental building block of overall gaze behavior. Through subtle variation in timing and movement of the head and eyes, individuals construct a range of high-level behaviors. Our model of gaze was designed and parameterized in such a way as to provide sufficient control over the subtleties of head and eye movements, enabling a virtual agent to naturally display these behaviors.

We also present a user study with 20 participants, in which we investigated how a virtual agent (Figure 1) might manipulate low-level gaze parameters to achieve high-level effects such as improved learning and feelings of rapport in a storytelling context. We manipulated the parameters of our gaze model to create *affiliative gaze*—maintaining a head orientation toward the participant to emphasize the social interaction [12]—and *referential gaze*—maintaining a head orientation toward shared visual space to emphasize the information to which the speaker is referring [30]. In both cases, the agent looks at the same targets; the difference lies in the timing and the degree to which the agent uses its head or eyes to look at these targets. The results showed that these manipulations generated significant social and cognitive effects; the use of affiliative gaze improved the perceptions of the agent and the use of referential gaze increased recall performance.

The remainder of the paper provides related work on gaze from a number of perspectives, describes our model and a validation study, outlines the design and results of our user study, and discusses our findings and their implications for the design of effective gaze mechanisms for virtual agents.

BACKGROUND

Gaze is an important social cue that has been studied under a number of different academic disciplines. First we present work in psychology on how humans use their gaze in social interactions, as well as some of the achievable high-level effects of gaze. Next we discuss related work on embodied conversational agents in the computer graphics and HCI literatures.

Gaze in Human Communication

In general, being gazed at by another person can result in a number of interesting effects. Gaze is predominantly interpreted as being attended to, and depending on the context of interaction, being gazed at can lead to discomfort from feeling observed, or lead to genuine social interaction [1]. A person who makes increased eye contact is associated with greater perceived dynamism, likeability, and believability [4]. These people are also seen as more truthful or credible [1]. One illustrative study specifically showed that people who spend more time gazing at an interviewer receive higher socioemotional evaluations [16]. On the other hand, gaze aversion produces consistently negative effects in impressions of attraction, credibility, and relational communication [5].

An important construct in the study of nonverbal behavior is *immediacy*, defined as the degree of perceived physical or psychological closeness between people [37]. Gaze has been found to be a significant component of immediacy, especially in the context of improving educational outcomes [21]. Students from primary school age through college have been shown to learn better when they are gazed at by the lecturer [41, 47]. Learning in these cases was usually measured by the students' performance on recall tasks. In a similar study, gazing into the camera during a video link conversation was shown to increase the recall of the viewer at the other end [14]. Gaze's positive effect on recall is usually attributed to its role as an arousal stimulus, which increases attentional focus and therefore enhances memory [26].

The above work shows that gaze as a whole can create positive interactions and learning effects. Our goal is to investigate how subtle parameters of gaze might serve to strengthen or weaken these effects. One of these parameters is the alignment of the head, which plays a substantial role in shifting a viewer's visual attention [23]. Gazing at someone with the head fully aligned (affiliative gaze) might be perceived differently than gazing at someone out of the corner of the eyes with the head aligned towards information of interest in the context of interaction (referential gaze). A virtual agent might be able to manipulate this, and other parameters, to achieve specifically desired effects.

Embodied Conversational Agents

Our work builds on previous research in the area of embodied conversational agents. Developing embodied agents that can communicate effectively is a significant area of research. Giving these agents more complex and human-like behaviors has been a longstanding goal, for example to make inhabited interfaces and agents in VR environments more effective [40]. The ability to use non-verbal communicative behavior is very important as it increases positive feelings of copresence and familiarity, and in general makes agents more effective communicators [2].

An agent's gaze behavior is very important to providing rich interactions; well-designed gaze mechanisms–e.g., gazing at turn-taking boundaries during conversation–can result in more efficient task performance and more positive subjective evaluations [22]. However, poor gaze behavior can be worse than no gaze at all. The positive effects of having an embodied agent–as opposed to only audio or text–can be completely lost if the gaze is very poor or random [15]. Gaze behavior of a female virtual agent, when coupled with the agent's appearance, can make the difference between enhancing negative attitudes toward women or breaking gender stereotypes [10]. The high-level effects of gaze discussed above have been shown to also extend to physical embodiments, such as robots. For example, the learning effect of gaze has been observed in human-robot interactions; increased gaze from a storytelling robot facilitates greater recall of the story [39].

Previous work on modeling human gaze to inform the design of agents includes the area of turn management [8, 43], figuring out where agents should be looking and why they should be looking there [25, 31], or how an agent should make random eye saccades in idle situations [6] or face-to-face conversations [32]. Some attempts have been made to model head and eye motions for virtual agent gaze, including data-driven [9]

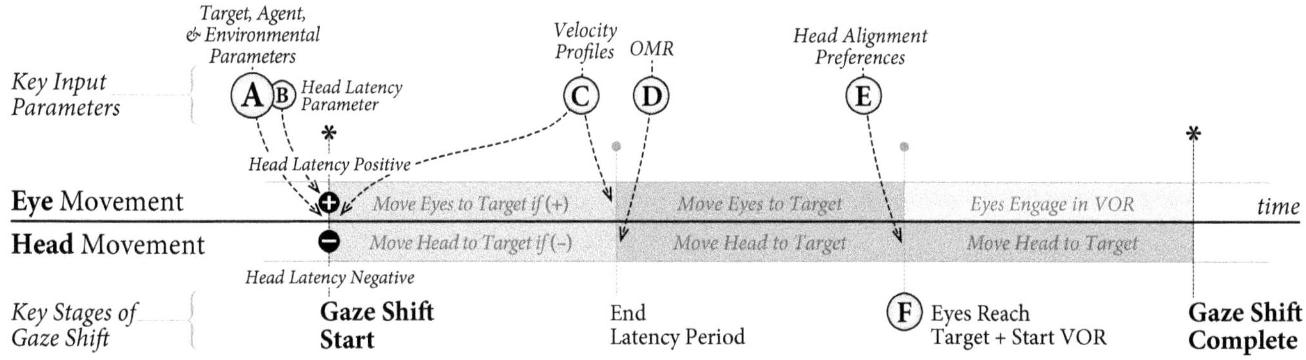

Figure 2. A visual representation of our model of gaze shifts mapped onto time. Key input variables and processes include (A) target, agent, and environmental parameters, (B) head latency, (C) velocity profiles for head and eye motion, (D) oculomotor range (OMR) specifications, (E) head alignment preferences, and (F) the vestibulo-ocular reflex (VOR)[1].

and procedural [45] approaches, as well as a hybrid between the two [29]. In general, existing research has proven that more realistic gaze behavior for humanoid avatars results in considerably improved and fluid communication [15]. At the very least, simply *conveying* gaze direction eases turntaking and is essential to establishing who is talking and listening to whom in multiparty mediated communication [50].

While previous research has explored how gross manipulations in gaze behavior might shape user experience and perceptions of virtual characters, how specific parameters in the control space for gaze might be mapped to specific outcomes in interaction has not been explored. Our work seeks to fill this knowledge gap. Our model of gaze, presented next, provides parameters that work as low-level gaze variables, and allows us to investigate their impact on high-level outcomes in a principled way. Advantages of our model include its procedural simplicity, grounded nature, and proven ability to produce large objective and subjective high-level effects through the manipulation of very subtle parameters.

DESIGNING EFFECTIVE GAZE MECHANISMS

In order to design virtual agents to be effective communicators, we must develop a deeper understanding of how humans use subtle gaze behavior to achieve high-level outcomes. We turn to research in neurophysiology to develop this understanding. Neurophysiologists have studied how humans and other primates coordinate head and eye movements during gaze shifts, in the process revealing potential parameters of gaze that might eventually lead to the positive social outcomes we wish to create with virtual agents. Here we present the most relevant findings from neurophysiology literature which we combine into a model of gaze shifts useful to virtual agents. We also present a validation of our model, taking the form of a user study, which shows that virtual agents using the model can execute gaze shifts that are both communicative and natural. [1]

Given the current configuration of the head and eyes and input parameters indicating movement characteristics and target gaze direction, our model computes a trajectory for the head and eyes. It first computes a few key variables for the movement, and then computes velocities for the head and eye rotations for each frame of the animated movement, keeping the gaze on target until the eyes and head have reached their final target rotations. The model is presented graphically in Figure 2, and includes six main components: (A) target, agent, and environmental parameters, (B) head latency, (C) velocity profiles for head and eye motion, (D) oculomotor range (OMR) specifications, (E) head alignment preferences, and (F) the vestibulo-ocular reflex (VOR).

The first variable to compute when executing a gaze shift is head movement latency in relationship to the eye movement (Figure 2b). This head latency can vary from person to person and task to task. Factors such as target amplitude, the predictability of the target [44], modality of the target (visual or auditory) [17, 18], target saliency, vigilance of the subject, and whether the gaze shift is forced or natural [51] have an effect. These factors serve as the target, agent, and environmental input parameters to our model (Figure 2a). Our model stochastically combines these parameters to determine the head latency based on findings from Zangemeister et al. [51]. A positive latency results in a period of eye motion during which the head remains fixed, while a negative latency result in a period of head motion while the eyes remain fixed.

Once the head latency period is complete, both the eyes and head begin simultaneously moving towards the target. Both during and after the latency period, each eye and the head follow velocity profiles (Figure 2c) that resemble standard ease-in and ease-out functions [27, 32]. These movements prevent unnatural head motions caused by high-frequency signals [35]. The maximum velocity of the eyes and head—the peaks of the velocity profiles—are computed based on positive linear relationships with the amplitude of the intended gaze shift [20]. Once the maximum velocity for the gaze shift is computed, the shift is executed by computing the actual velocity for each frame of the animation. The velocity is determined by a piecewise polynomial function derived to approximate the published experimental data. This polynomial function can be expressed as follows, where g is the proportion of the gaze shift completed, V_{max} is the maximum velocity, and V is the current calculated velocity.

[1]A full specification of the model, including documented pseudocode, full details of the validation, and videos of animated characters using the model for their own gaze behavior, can be found at http://hci.cs.wisc.edu/projects/gaze.

$$V = \begin{cases} 2V_{max} \cdot g & g \in [0, 0.5) \\ 4V_{max} \cdot g^2 - 8V_{max} \cdot g + 4V_{max} & g \in [0.5, 1] \end{cases}$$

An important component of the model is the oculomotor range (OMR) (Figure 2d), which limits rotation of the eyes such that they don't roll back into the head. The human OMR has been estimated to be between 45° and 55°. A virtual character's baseline OMR can be determined based on the size of the eye cavities and the size of its pupils and irises. However, merely encoding these OMR values as static parameters is not sufficient, as the *effective* OMR may fluctuate during the course of a single gaze shift. The fluctuation is a product of the neural (as opposed to mechanical) nature of the limitation imposed on eye motion. The virtual agent's eye rotations are never allowed to surpass the current *effective* OMR.

At the onset of a gaze shift, effective OMR is computed based on the initial eye position and the baseline OMR. Initial eye position is measured in degrees as a rotational offset of the current eye orientation from a central (in-head) orientation. This value is only non-zero when the rotational offset is contralateral (on the opposite side of center) to the target. When the eyes begin the gaze shift at these angles, the effective OMR has a value close to the original baseline value. When the eyes begin the gaze shift closer to a central orientation in the head, the effective OMR diminishes [11]. Effective OMR is also updated throughout the gaze shift at every time step according to the concurrent head velocity. As the head moves faster, the effective OMR diminishes [20]. See the online supplement for details on the effective OMR computations, including equations and empirically derived constants.

The next component of the model is a user-defined parameter specifying the *head alignment* preferences of the agent (Figure 2e). Head alignment—how much individuals use their heads in performing a gaze shift—is highly idiosyncratic, and creates a differential directness of gaze at the target [13]. A parameter value of 0% for head alignment indicates that once the eyes have reached the gaze target, the head stops moving, resulting in gaze at the target out of the corner of the eyes. On the other hand, at a 100% parameter value for head alignment, the head continues rotating until it is completely aligned with the target, with concomitant compensatory eye movement to keep the eyes directed toward the target, resulting in gaze with the eyes and head both fully directed towards the target. Head alignment values between these two extremes can be computed using spherical linear interpolation between the two corresponding rotational values. This parameter can be manipulated to create affiliative gaze–keeping high head alignment with a conversational partner and low head alignment with everything else–or referential gaze–keeping high head alignment with information being referred to in the environment and low head alignment with the conversational partner. Head alignment is the most directly controllable input parameter to the model, and as such is the parameter we focus on in our experimental methodology.

Once the eyes have reached their target, the vestibulo-ocular reflex (VOR) keeps them locked to the target while the head finishes its rotation (Figure 2f). This component of gaze, the final in our model, is handled by rotating the eyes in the opposite direction of head motion as the head completes its portion of the gaze shift, keeping the eyes fixated on the gaze target even as the head keeps rotating.

Ancillary components of our model include a blink controller for generating both random and gaze-evoked blinking as described by Peters [45], and idle gaze behavior. When the agent is not actively engaging in a gaze shift following our model, the eyes are controlled by an implementation of the model presented in Lee et al. [32]. This implementation of subtle random eye movements has been shown to dramatically increase the realism of the character. The virtual character's eyelids also move with vertical shifts of the eyes, rising up as the eyes pitch upwards and dropping down as the eyes pitch downward [48]. Lastly, we implemented ambient facial and bodily cues for our virtual characters to prevent the unnatural rigidity inherent to a static character. When the character is in an idle state, these cues include smiles and slight movements of the arms and the head.

Model Validation

Our model development was followed by an empirical evaluation of the communicative accuracy and perceived naturalness of gaze shifts generated by our model. We compared gaze shifts generated by our model against those generated by a baseline model and those displayed by a human.

Participants – Ninety-six participants (50 males and 46 females) took part in the validation study. The participants were recruited through Amazon.com's Mechanical Turk online marketplace, following crowd-sourcing best practices to minimize the risk of abuse and to achieve a wide range of demographic representation [28, 24]. Participants received $2.50.

Study Design – In the study, participants were shown a series of videos in which either an animated virtual character or a human confederate shifted gaze toward one of sixteen objects arranged on a desk. This simplified scenario allowed us to focus our evaluation on the effectiveness and naturalness of gaze shifts, while minimizing contextual and interactional

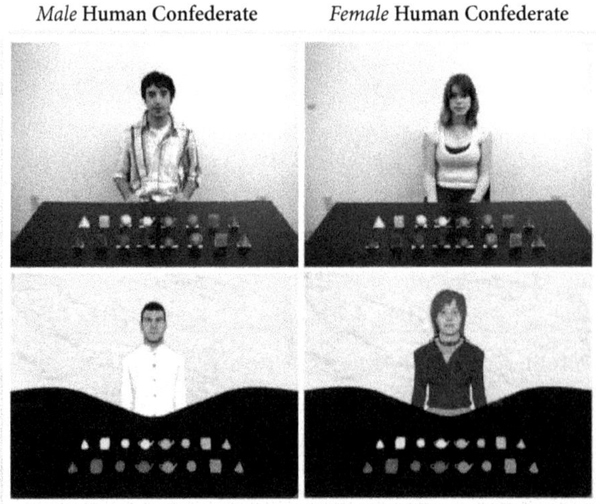

Figure 3. Still images from the videos presented to the participants.

factors and facilitating the matching of animated and real world conditions. Participants observed the agent from the perspective of a collaborator seated across from the agent or the human confederate. The objects on the desk were separated into four groups, distinguished by color and shape. Still images from the videos are shown in Figure 3.

The study followed a two-by-four split-plot design. The factors were gender–participant matched with agent–varying between participants, and model type, varying within participants. The model type independent variable included gaze shifts generated by a baseline gaze model from Peters [45], and those produced by our model. The model type independent variable also included two control conditions. In the first control condition, a virtual agent with a male or female appearance maintained gaze toward the participant (i.e., the camera) without producing any gaze shifts at all. In the second control condition, a male or female human confederate presented gaze shifts toward the object on a desk in front of him/her. The order in which the conditions were presented to each participant was counterbalanced.

Procedure – Each participant was shown 32 videos of a virtual character or human. In the videos, the agents or the confederates gazed toward the participant (i.e., the camera), announced that they are about to look toward an object of a specific color on the table, shifted their gaze toward the object, and moved their gaze back toward the participant. Following each video, the participants answered a set of questions that measured the dependent variables. Participants evaluated each condition four times in a stratified order. Each video was approximately 10 seconds, with the overall study lasting around 20 minutes.

Measures – The validation study used two dependent variables: *communicative accuracy* and *perceived naturalness*. Communicative accuracy was measured by capturing whether participants correctly identified the object toward which the gaze shift of the agent was directed. Perceived naturalness was measured with a four-item scale with high reliability, including *naturalness*, *humanlikeness*, *lifelikeness*, and *realism*, Cronbach's $\alpha = .94$.

Results – We conducted a mixed-model analysis of variance (ANOVA) on the data to determine the effect that different

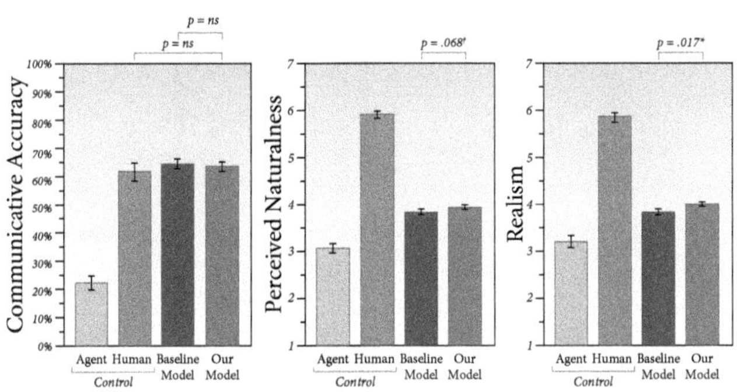

Figure 4. Results from the communicative accuracy, perceived naturalness, and realism measures. Conditions are from left-to-right: agent control (no gaze shifts, only idle gaze), human control (video of a gazing human), agents shifting their gaze using a previously published baseline gaze model [45], and agents shifting their gaze using our model of gaze.

gaze models had on how accurately participants identified the object that the agents or the human confederates looked toward and the perceived naturalness of the gaze shifts. Overall, model type had a significant effect on communicative accuracy, $F(7, 46.67) = 16.77, p < .001$, and perceived naturalness, $F(7, 46.67) = 151.03, p < .001$.

Pairwise comparisons found no significant differences in the *communicative accuracy* of the gaze shifts produced by our model and those produced by human confederates, $F(1, 14.91) = 0.03, p = ns$. Similarly, no differences in accuracy were found between our model and the baseline model, $F(1, 1958) = 0.17, p = ns$. The results suggest that the gaze shifts generated by our model are just as accurate as those performed by human confederates and those generated by the baseline model.

Comparisons across conditions showed that participants rated gaze shifts generated by our model as marginally more *natural* than those generated by the baseline model, $F(1, 1967) = 3.34, p = .068$. Comparisons over *realism* (one of the items included in the perceived naturalness scale) found that gaze shifts produced by our model were rated as significantly more realistic than those generated by the baseline model, $F(1, 1963) = 5.75, p = .017$. Results on the communicative accuracy, perceived naturalness, and realism measures are illustrated in Figure 4.

EXPERIMENTAL EVALUATION

The validated model of gaze shifts provides parameters that allow us to explore how manipulation of these low-level parameters can achieve valuable high-level effects. The main study of this paper explores manipulating the *head alignment* parameter in order to create more affiliative or more referential gaze cues, with the goal of increasing feelings of connection with the agent and increasing learning respectively. The experiment was carried out in the context of an educational scenario, with the virtual agent serving as a lecturer to the human participant. The virtual agent taught the participant about a specific subject from ancient Chinese history. A map of China was used as a reference to facilitate the descriptions of geographical locations. An example of the interface presented to participants is shown in Figure 1.

Hypotheses

We designed an experiment to test three hypotheses. First, we wished to merely confirm that the presence of an agent will elicit better learning than only audio.

Hypothesis 1 – The presence of an embodied agent will result in better recall performance than only hearing audio with no accompanying agent.

The literature strongly supports the first hypothesis, in which it is shown that teachers who gaze at their students lead the students to learn better [41, 47]. We seek to show these same effects can be achieved by virtual agents using our gaze model.

Hypothesis 2 – An agent which employs more affiliative gaze (maintains higher head alignment with the participant) will garner higher subjective evaluations than one which uses more

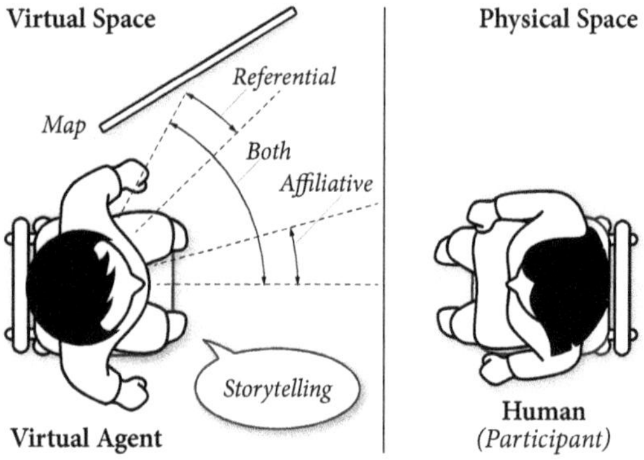

Figure 5. A diagram of the setup of the study showing the range of the agent's head movements for each gaze condition. The agent's eye motions (not depicted) always move the full distance from eye contact with the participant to eye contact with each map location being referred to.

referential gaze (maintains higher head alignment with the information being referred to).

This hypothesis is supported by the fact that people are perceived as being more intelligent, more trustworthy, and more friendly if they make more direct eye contact [1, 14]. We wish to extend this work to show that head alignment makes an impact on the positive subjective effects of mutual gaze, and that our model is capable of achieving these effects.

Hypothesis 3 – Viewing an agent using more referential gaze should result in better recall performance. This will especially be true when the information to be recalled relies on building associations to objects in the environment.

Referential gaze helps build associations between information and objects in the environment. In communication between a human and virtual agent with a shared environment, being able to perceive the agent's eye gaze to different objects in the environment reduces the time and verbal communication needed for grounding references [34]. We believe that head alignment has the ability to strengthen or weaken this effect since it plays a substantial role in shifting a viewer's visual attention [23]. When the agent's head is aligned more fully with the object under consideration, this should serve as a stronger referential gaze cue than if the head is not aligned. We wish to show that our gaze model can achieve this effect.

Participants

We recruited 20 participants for our study (10 males and 10 females), with ages ranging from 19 to 65 ($M = 27.8$, $SD = 14.3$). Fifteen participants were students and five were working members of the community. All were native English speakers. Student participants came from a number of different fields, including psychology, engineering, and business. All participants were recruited using a combination of campus flyers and on-line student job forums.

Study Design

We employed a within-subjects design for this study. Our experiment involved one factor, *type of gaze*, with four levels, each of which is defined as follows:

- **Audio**: The agent is shown briefly during its introduction. Then the lights in the virtual scene are extinguished for the duration of the lecture, except for a spotlight on the map, so only the map can be seen and the agent is in complete darkness. At the end of the lecture, the scene lights turn back on for the agent to give its instructions to the participant on taking the subjective evaluation and quiz for the lecture.
- **Affiliative**: The agent keeps its head aligned with the participant as much as possible during the lecture. When the agent is making direct eye contact with the participant, the head is fully aligned with the participant. When the agent shifts its eye gaze to refer to something on the map, the head aligns as little as possible with the map – as much as the agent's OMR will allow – so as to keep the head aligned towards the participant.
- **Referential**: The agent keeps its head aligned with the map as much as possible during the lecture. When the agent is gazing at the map, the head is fully aligned with the map. When the agent shifts its eye gaze back to the participant, the head aligns as little as possible with the participant – as much as the agent's OMR will allow – so as to keep the head aligned towards the map. The referential condition is "more referential" (borrowing the term "referential" from linguistics) because the head maintains alignment with the information being referred to on the map, both when looking at the participant (out of the corner of the eyes) and when looking at the map (head and eyes fully aligned).
- **Both**: When gazing at the participant, the agent keeps its head fully aligned to the participant. When gazing at the map, the agent aligns its head fully with the map.

Figure 5 and Figure 6 illustrate the difference in head motion between the three conditions *affiliative*, *referential*, and *both*. It should be stressed that in all three of these conditions, the agent's eyes move the full distance from eye contact with the participant to each map location being referred to. The agent's eyes always converged on each map location while it was being referred to.

Each participant viewed four lectures given by four different virtual agents, each utilizing a different gaze condition. Thus, every participant was exposed to all four gaze conditions. All agents, three of which can be seen in Figures 1 and 6, were specifically designed to look and sound androgynous so as to eliminate gender biases as much as possible. Each agent always gave the same lecture, but pairings between agent and gaze condition were stratified across participants for balance.

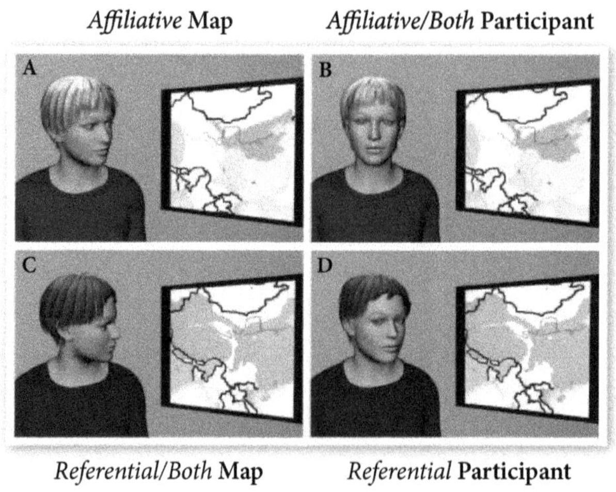

Figure 6. A visual depiction of an agent in different gaze conditions: (A) Affiliative, looking at map, (B) Affiliative (and Both), looking at participant, (C) Referential (and Both), looking at map, (D) Referential, looking at participant.

Figure 7. The physical setup of the experiment.

The order in which the lectures – and accordingly gaze conditions – were presented to the participants was completely randomized to offset any bias due to fatigue. Lectures were also kept informationally distinct in an attempt to decrease learning bias. Each lecture was carefully controlled to be near the same length–approximately three minutes.

During each lecture, the agent makes eleven gaze shifts to the map, each followed shortly by a gaze shift back to the participant. The agent fixates its gaze on different targets on the map as they are mentioned, e.g. while giving facts about a Chinese city visible on the map. Timing of this gaze shift is done according to Griffin [19] and Meyer et al. [38], which indicate that a deictic gaze shift should occur 800 - 1000 ms before the object being gazed at is mentioned in speech.

Implementation – The experiment was implemented using a custom framework built on top of the Unity game engine (www.unity3d.com). The gaze model was implemented as a Unity script. The characters were created using a commercially available parametric base figure. Audio was prerecorded and pitch-shifted to sound androgynous.

Procedure

The experiment was conducted in a closed study room with no outside distraction. Participants entered the experiment room and were asked to sit at a table with a single computer monitor and mouse. The monitor was a 32-inch flat panel display, allowing the virtual agent representation (only head and shoulders) to be near life size. This setup can be seen in Figure 7. The experimenter gave the participant a brief description of what they would be asked to do in the experiment, and then asked them to review and sign a consent form. The experimenter told the participants that they were going to be listening to and quizzed on four short lectures from different virtual lecturers, each on a topic pertaining to ancient China.

After consenting, the experimenter told participants that they could press the start button on the screen after he left the room. Upon pressing the start button, the first lecturer (randomly chosen by the software) began introducing itself and giving its lecture. Upon completion of the lecture the screen went black, and participants filled out on paper a subjective evaluation of the lecturer they had just viewed, followed by a quiz on the material presented in the lecture. During the initial instructions, the experimenter made it clear that the quiz was to be filled out *after* the subjective evaluation had been completed. This allows the subjective evaluation to double as distractor task, strengthening any subsequent recall measures. All participants were monitored via closed-circuit camera by the experimenter to ensure that these instructions were followed, but no participants were observed to neglect the instructions.

After filling out the subjective evaluation and quiz, the participant could go back to the monitor and click the on-screen button to begin the next lecture. This process was repeated until all four lectures had been viewed, rated, and quizzed. At this point, the experimenter re-entered the room with a short questionnaire of demographic information. Following completion of the questionnaire, the experimenter debriefed and payed the participant. The total experiment took approximately 30 minutes, and participants were paid $5.

Measures

Our experiment involved one independent manipulated variable, *type of gaze*, manipulated within participants. The dependent variables included objective measurements for evaluating participants' recall of the lecture material and subjective measurements for evaluating the participants' impressions of the virtual agent.

The objective measurement of recall involved quizzes taken by all participants following each lecture. Each quiz had ten short-answer questions. These questions were split into three categories (not visible to the participant). One category included three questions that asked about information not directly associated with information on the map. Thus, referential gaze should not have had an effect on the recall of this information. An example question in this category would be, "In what year did the Jin dynasty overtake control of China?" The Jin dynasty was not represented on the map during the associated lecture. The second category, consisting of four questions, asked about purely spatial information. For example, one question here was "Which of the *Three Kingdoms* dynasties extended farthest south?" This question is only answerable by having studied the map. The third category, including the remaining three questions of the quiz, relied on building associations between verbal lecture content and spatial map locations. For example, "Give one reason why Emperor Wen declared the city of Luoyang to be his capital city." Referential gaze was expected to make the biggest impact on questions from the latter two categories. Questions from all three categories were randomly permutated to create the final ten-question quiz.

The subjective measurements were split into six broad indicators. Each question within the indicators took the form of a seven-point rating scale. Item reliability (Cronbach's α) was acceptable or better for all except *skilled communicator*.

1. *Likeability*: Four-item measure of how likeable the participant found the agent to be. Includes questions on perceived friendliness and helpfulness. (Cronbach's $\alpha = .78$)

2. *Rapport*: Six-item measure of how much the participant felt feelings of rapport in relation to the agent. Questions asked, e.g., how well the participant felt he or she connected with the agent and how willingly he or she would disclose personal information to the virtual agent following the lecture. (Cronbach's $\alpha = .84$)

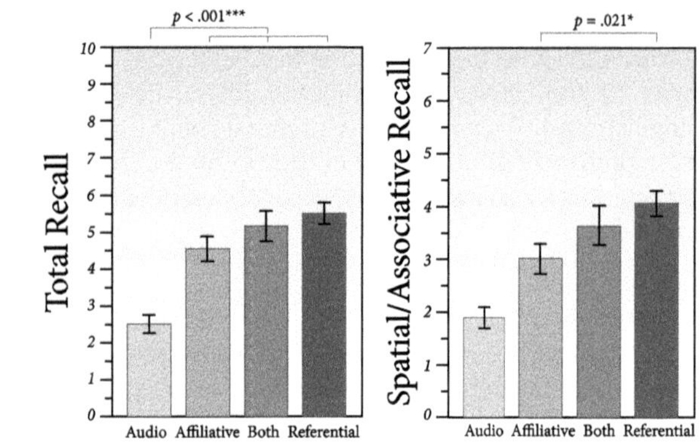

Figure 9. Objective measure (recall measured by post-lecture quiz). On the left is the total quiz performance, on the right is the quiz performance when only considering a subset of the questions: those dealing with spatial information and building associations.

3. *Trust*: Two-item measure of how trustworthy the participant perceived the agent to be. Includes ratings of trustworthiness and honesty. (Cronbach's $\alpha = .72$)
4. *Intelligence*: Three-item measure of how intelligent the participant perceived the agent to be. Includes ratings of competence and expertise. (Cronbach's $\alpha = .84$)
5. *Skilled Communicator*: Three-item measure of how effective at conveying lecture material the participant perceived the agent to be. Item reliability was questionable (Cronbach's $\alpha = .62$)
6. *Engagement*: Six-item measure of how engaged the participant felt during the lecture. Includes personal ratings of focus, attentiveness, and satisfaction. (Cronbach's $\alpha = .89$)

Manipulation Checks

To check that our *gaze type* manipulations were being noticed between the visible agent conditions, we asked the participants to rate from 0% to 100% how much they felt the agent was paying attention to them and to the map. We expected that participants would feel more attended to in the *affiliative* and *both* conditions than in the *referential* condition. Conversely, we expected participants to feel like the agent was attending to the map more in the *referential* and *both* gaze conditions than in the *affiliative* condition.

Results

Analysis of our data was conducted using a repeated measures analysis of variance (ANOVA). We used Tukey-Kramer HSD to control the experiment-wise error rate in all post-hoc tests. Our analysis started with the manipulation check. We found that participants felt more attended to in the *affiliative* gaze condition versus the *referential* condition, $F(1, 69) = 12.53, p < .001$. They also felt more attended to in the *both* condition versus *referential*, $F(1, 69) = 4.37, p = .040$. Finally, participants felt that the agent attended to the map more in the *referential* condition versus *affiliative*, $F(1, 69) = 7.75, p = .007$. This difference was not found to be significant for the *both* condition versus *affiliative*, $F(1, 69) = 0.37, p = .55$, however participants rated the agent as attending more to the map in the *referential* condition over the *both* condition, $F(1, 69) = 4.75, p = .033$.

Next we analyzed the objective results in the form of recall quiz scores (Figure 9). In terms of overall score, the *audio* condition resulted in significantly lower recall than the other three visible agent conditions, including *affiliative* gaze, $F(1, 69) = 19.38, p < .001$, *referential* gaze, $F(1, 69) = 37.78, p < .001$, and *both*, $F = 31.91, p < .001$. When considering only the seven (out of ten total) questions that dealt with purely spatial map information and building associations between verbal lecture content and locations on the map, we found that the *referential* gaze condition resulted in significantly better recall performance than the *affiliative* gaze condition, $F(1, 69) = 5.62, p = .021$. The increase in recall performance from the *both* condition over *affiliative* does not quite reach significance, $F(1, 69) = 2.58, p = .11$. *Referential* and *both* were not significantly different, $F(1, 69) = 0.59, p = .45$.

Finally, we analyzed the subjective measures. Here we observed that on the *likeability* scale, the *referential* condition rated lower than both the *affiliative* condition, $F(1, 69) = 58.86, p < .001$, and *both* condition, $F(1, 69) = 52.65, p < .001$. On the *rapport* scale, the *referential* condition also rated lower than both *affiliative*, $F(1, 69) = 13.25, p < .001$, and *both*, $F(1, 69) = 7.95, p = .006$. The *trust* scale had similar results, with the *referential* condition rated lower than both *affiliative*, $F(1, 69) = 8.63, p = .005$, and *both*, $F(1, 69) = 5.55, p = .021$. The *intelligence* scale again shows the *referential* condition getting rated lower than *affiliative*, $F(1, 69) = 11.38, p = .001$, and *both*, $F(1, 69) = 10.99, p = .002$. The *skilled communicator* scale yielded no significant results be-

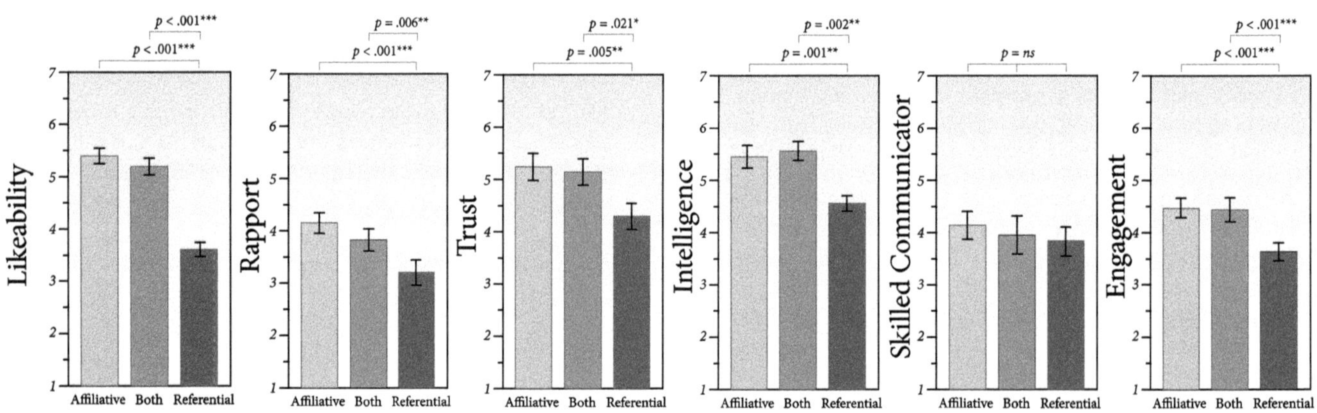

Figure 8. Results for subjective evaluations (likeability, rapport, trust, intelligence, skilled communicator, and engagement) based on gaze condition.

tween conditions, but the *engagement* scale showed the *referential* condition getting rated significantly lower than the *affiliative* condition, $F(1,69) = 14.53, p < .001$, and *both* condition, $F(1,69) = 17.16, p < .001$. These results are summarized in Figure 8.

DISCUSSION

The purpose of the experiment was to demonstrate how subtle changes in gaze behavior can lead to significant high-level effects, with the goal of improving learning and positive feelings of affiliation. To do this, we manipulated the *head alignment* parameter in our model implemented on various virtual lecturing agents. We showed that by manipulating just this parameter for a virtual agent shifting its gaze from the participant to an object in the scene (i.e., the map of China) and back again, the agent could achieve very different subjective and objective effects, including the participant's feelings toward the agent and information recall respectively.

Confirming our first hypothesis, the mere presence of an agent resulted in better recall performance than audio alone, no matter which gaze condition was being used. For five out of six subjective scales, the *affiliative* and *both* gaze conditions achieved better ratings than the *referential* condition. This leads us to accept our second hypothesis, showing that human listeners prefer when the virtual agent speaker aligns its head fully with the participant while speaking, rather than looking out of the corners of its eyes with its head aligned towards something else. The *skilled communicator* scale did not exhibit this effect, which could mean that participants thought the agent was doing a similarly decent job of communicating the lecture content no matter which gaze condition was used. We also have strong support for our third hypothesis, where we showed that *referential* gaze results in better participant recall than *affiliative* gaze. By keeping its head aligned with the map as much as possible, the agent compelled the participant to concentrate more on the map and learn the spatial locations better, while building associations between verbal lecture content and those same locations. As a reminder, the same amount of gaze was used by the agent in both the *affiliative* and *referential* gaze conditions. Hence in both conditions the participant was able to benefit from gaze as an arousal stimulus to learn the lecture material better. The difference lies in the way each gaze shift was performed, proving that not all ways of gazing are equal and subtle changes can create significant outcomes. Overall, this study showed that our model was capable of achieving targeted outcomes.

Design Implications

Embodied agents' potential in computer interfaces is increasing with the ever-growing popularity of interactive games and computer-based tools for learning, motivation, and rehabilitation. However, agent designers need controllable models of interactive behavior and evidence that these models effectively improve outcomes such as learning and rapport. Our work provides one such example in the context of gaze.

We have shown that it is possible to implement in virtual agents the very subtle gaze cues that humans use to great effect in social situations, and that manipulating these cues can achieve significant objective and subjective high-level effects in a human interacting with the agent. Designers of virtual agents can use these subtle gaze behaviors, such as head alignment, to reach different desired outcomes. If the agent designer wants human interlocutors to pay more attention to specific objects in the environment, possibly to learn more about them, the agent could be programmed to use high head alignment when gazing to those objects. Similarly, if the agent designer wants the agent to build a stronger relationship with the human interlocutor, increasing feelings of, e.g., rapport and trust, the agent should be programmed to use high head alignment when gazing towards the human. Our model of gaze behavior offers a simple and effective means to control the low-level gaze parameters found in physiological research. Virtual agent designers can use and build off of this model to create rich, compelling gaze behaviors that accomplish the high-level effects they wish to achieve.

Limitations and Future Work

Our gaze mechanisms are currently focused on the contributions of the head and eyes alone. Future extensions should consider the movement of other body parts, such as employing the neck in performing head movements. While the work presented here explored our gaze shift model on very humanlike characters, we intend to explore its application to different character designs, e.g., stylized cartoons, and embodiments, e.g., storytelling robots [39]. We also intend to run future studies exercising different parameters of the model (e.g., head latency) and measuring the effects of subtle gaze cues in different interaction modalities, such as VR and mobile devices.

CONCLUSIONS

Gaze is a complex and powerful cue. Through subtle changes in gaze, people can achieve a wide range of social and communicative goals, affecting their partner of interaction in a variety of different ways. Gaze cues, as with all embodied communication cues, hold a strong fundamental connection with key social, cognitive, and task outcomes. This connection reveals an opportunity for designing embodied dialog with virtual agents. Designing gaze behaviors for virtual agents that can achieve specifically targeted high-level outcomes has long been a difficult problem. By creating a mechanism for synthesizing gaze shifts in a natural, yet parameterized fashion, we have provided a building block for creating high-level social and communicative behaviors. In this paper we presented a model of gaze shifts validated to achieve humanlike gaze for virtual agents, and a study which shows that it can achieve interesting subjective and objective effects through manipulation of low-level gaze parameters. These subtle gaze cues are effective in the context of our gaze model due to the grounded physiological approach we took in designing it. By manipulating and combining them in different ways, we believe that virtual agents will soon have access to a rich new source of possible gaze behaviors, resulting in human-agent interactions that are more effective and rewarding.

ACKNOWLEDGMENTS

This research was supported by National Science Foundation award 1017952. We would like to thank Allison Terrell, Danielle Albers, and Erin Spannan for their help in creating the videos used in the experiments described in this paper.

REFERENCES

1. Argyle, M., and Cook, M. *Gaze and mutual gaze*. Cambridge University Press Cambridge, 1976.
2. Bailenson, J., Yee, N., Merget, D., and Schroeder, R. The effect of behavioral realism and form realism of real-time avatar faces on verbal disclosure, nonverbal disclosure, emotion recognition, and copresence in dyadic interaction. *Presence: Teleoperators and Virtual Environments 15*, 4 (2006), 359–372.
3. Bayliss, A., Paul, M., Cannon, P., and Tipper, S. Gaze cuing and affective judgments of objects: I like what you look at. *Psychonomic bulletin & review 13*, 6 (2006), 1061–1066.
4. Beebe, S. Effects of eye contact, posture and vocal inflection upon credibility and comprehension.
5. Burgoon, J., Coker, D., and Coker, R. Communicative effects of gaze behavior. *Human Communication Research 12*, 4 (1986), 495–524.
6. Cafaro, A., Gaito, R., and Vilhjálmsson, H. Animating idle gaze in public places. In *Intelligent Virtual Agents*, Springer (2009), 250–256.
7. Cassell, J., Bickmore, T., Billinghurst, M., Campbell, L., Chang, K., Vilhjálmsson, H., and Yan, H. Embodiment in conversational interfaces: Rea. In *Proceedings of the SIGCHI conference on Human factors in computing systems: the CHI is the limit*, ACM (1999), 520–527.
8. Cassell, J., Torres, O., and Prevost, S. Turn taking vs. discourse structure: How best to model multimodal conversation. *Machine conversations* (1999), 143–154.
9. Deng, Z., Lewis, J., and Neumann, U. Automated eye motion using texture synthesis. *IEEE Computer Graphics and Applications* (2005), 24–30.
10. Fox, J., and Bailenson, J. Virtual virgins and vamps: The effects of exposure to female characters sexualized appearance and gaze in an immersive virtual environment. *Sex roles 61*, 3 (2009), 147–157.
11. Freedman, E., and Sparks, D. Activity of cells in the deeper layers of the superior colliculus of the rhesus monkey: evidence for a gaze displacement command. *Journal of neurophysiology 78*, 3 (1997), 1669.
12. Frischen, A., Bayliss, A., and Tipper, S. Gaze cueing of attention: Visual attention, social cognition, and individual differences. *Psychological bulletin 133*, 4 (2007), 694.
13. Fuller, J. Head movement propensity. *Experimental Brain Research 92*, 1 (1992), 152–164.
14. Fullwood, C., and Doherty-Sneddon, G. Effect of gazing at the camera during a video link on recall. *Applied Ergonomics 37*, 2 (2006), 167–175.
15. Garau, M., Slater, M., Bee, S., and Sasse, M. The impact of eye gaze on communication using humanoid avatars. In *Proceedings of the SIGCHI conference on Human factors in computing systems*, ACM (2001), 309–316.
16. Goldberg, G., Kiesler, C., and Collins, B. Visual behavior and face-to-face distance during interaction. *Sociometry* (1969), 43–53.
17. Goldring, J., Dorris, M., Corneil, B., Ballantyne, P., and Munoz, D. Combined eye-head gaze shifts to visual and auditory targets in humans. *Experimental brain research 111*, 1 (1996), 68–78.
18. Goossens, H., and Opstal, A. Human eye-head coordination in two dimensions under different sensorimotor conditions. *Experimental Brain Research 114*, 3 (1997), 542–560.
19. Griffin, Z. Gaze durations during speech reflect word selection and phonological encoding. *Cognition 82*, 1 (2001), B1–B14.
20. Guitton, D., and Volle, M. Gaze control in humans: eye-head coordination during orienting movements to targets within and beyond the oculomotor range. *Journal of neurophysiology 58*, 3 (1987), 427.
21. Harris, M., and Rosenthal, R. No more teachers dirty looks: Effects of teacher nonverbal behavior on student outcomes. *Applications of nonverbal communication* (2005), 157–192.
22. Heylen, D., Van Es, I., Van Dijk, E., NI-JHOLT, A., van Kuppevelt, J., Dybkjaer, L., and Bernsen, N. Experimenting with the gaze of a conversational agent, 2005.
23. Hietanen, J. Does your gaze direction and head orientation shift my visual attention? *Neuroreport 10*, 16 (1999), 3443.
24. Ipeirotis, P. Demographics of Mechanical Turk. Tech. Rep. CeDER-10-01, 2010. Accessed on 10-Mar-2010 at http://hdl.handle.net/2451/29585.
25. Itti, L., Dhavale, N., and Pighin, F. Photorealistic attention-based gaze animation. In *2006 IEEE International Conference on Multimedia and Expo*, IEEE (2006), 521–524.
26. Kelley, D., and Gorham, J. Effects of immediacy on recall of information. *Communication Education* (1988).
27. Kim, K., Brent Gillespie, R., and Martin, B. Head movement control in visually guided tasks: Postural goal and optimality. *Computers in Biology and Medicine 37*, 7 (2007), 1009–1019.
28. Kittur, A., Chi, E., and Suh, B. Crowdsourcing user studies with Mechanical Turk. In *Proceeding of the twenty-sixth annual SIGCHI conference on Human factors in computing systems*, ACM (2008), 453–456.
29. Lance, B., and Marsella, S. The expressive gaze model: Using gaze to express emotion. *Computer Graphics and Applications, IEEE 30*, 4 (2010), 62–73.
30. Langton, S., and Bruce, V. Reflexive visual orienting in response to the social attention of others. *Visual Cognition* (1999).
31. Lee, J., Marsella, S., Traum, D., Gratch, J., and Lance, B. The rickel gaze model: A window on the mind of a virtual human. In *Intelligent Virtual Agents*, Springer (2007), 296–303.
32. Lee, S., Badler, J., and Badler, N. Eyes alive. In *ACM Transactions on Graphics (TOG)*, vol. 21, ACM (2002), 637–644.
33. Lester, J., Towns, S., Callaway, C., Voerman, J., and FitzGerald, P. Deictic and emotive communication in animated pedagogical agents. *Embodied conversational agents* (2000), 123–154.
34. Liu, C., Kay, D., and Chai, J. Awareness of partners eye gaze in situated referential grounding: An empirical study. *2nd Workshop on Eye Gaze in Intelligent Human Machine Interaction* (2011).
35. Ma, X., Le, B., and Deng, Z. Perceptual analysis of talking avatar head movements: A quantitative perspective. *CHI'11* (2011).
36. Mason, M., Tatkow, E., and Macrae, C. The look of love: Gaze shifts and person perception. *Psychological Science* (2005), 236–239.
37. Mehrabian, A. Immediacy: An indicator of attitudes in linguistic communication. *Journal of Personality 34*, 1 (1966), 26–34.
38. Meyer, A., Sleiderink, A., and Levelt, W. Viewing and naming objects: Eye movements during noun phrase production. *Cognition 66*, 2 (1998), B25–B33.
39. Mutlu, B., Forlizzi, J., and Hodgins, J. A storytelling robot: Modeling and evaluation of human-like gaze behavior. In *Humanoid Robots, 2006 6th IEEE-RAS International Conference on*, IEEE (2006), 518–523.
40. Nijholt, A., Heylen, D., and Vertegaal, R. Inhabited interfaces: Attentive conversational agents that help. In *Proceedings 3rd international Conference on Disability, Virtual Reality and Associated Technologies-CDVRAT2000, Alghero, Sardinia* (2000).
41. Otteson, J., and Otteson, C. Effect of teacher's gaze on children's story recall. *Perceptual and Motor Skills* (1980).
42. Parke, F., and Waters, K. *Computer facial animation*. AK Peters Ltd, 2008.
43. Pelachaud, C., and Bilvi, M. Modelling gaze behavior for conversational agents. In *Intelligent Virtual Agents*, Springer (2003), 93–100.
44. Pelz, J., Hayhoe, M., and Loeber, R. The coordination of eye, head, and hand movements in a natural task. *Experimental Brain Research 139*, 3 (2001), 266–277.
45. Peters, C. Animating gaze shifts for virtual characters based on head movement propensity. In *2010 Second International Conference on Games and Virtual Worlds for Serious Applications*, IEEE (2010), 11–18.
46. Rickel, J., and Johnson, W. Task-oriented collaboration with embodied agents in virtual worlds. *Embodied conversational agents* (2000), 95–122.
47. Sherwood, J. Facilitative effects of gaze upon learning. *Perceptual and Motor Skills* (1987).
48. Steptoe, W., and Steed, A. High-fidelity avatar eye-representation. In *Virtual Reality Conference, 2008. VR'08. IEEE*, IEEE (2008), 111–114.
49. Tartaro, A., and Cassell, J. Authorable virtual peers for autism spectrum disorders. In *Proceedings of the Combined workshop on Language-Enabled Educational Technology and Development and Evaluation for Robust Spoken Dialogue Systems at the 17th European Conference on Artificial Intellegence*, Citeseer (2006).
50. Vertegaal, R. The gaze groupware system: mediating joint attention in multiparty communication and collaboration. In *Proceedings of the SIGCHI conference on Human factors in computing systems: the CHI is the limit*, ACM (1999), 294–301.
51. Zangemeister, W., and Stark, L. Types of gaze movement: variable interactions of eye and head movements. *Experimental Neurology 77*, 3 (1982), 563–577.

"Baby It's Cold Outside": The Influence of Ambient Temperature and Humidity on Thermal Feedback

Martin Halvey, Graham Wilson, Stephen A. Brewster
School of Computing Science, University of Glasgow, Glasgow, United Kingdom G12 8QQ
{first.last}@glasgow.ac.uk, gawilson@dcs.gla.ac.uk

Stephen A. Hughes
SAMH Engineering, 1 Leopardstown Drive, Blackrock, Dublin Ireland
stephenahughes@gmail.com

ABSTRACT
Thermal feedback is a new area of research in HCI and, as such, there has been very little investigation of the impact of environmental factors on its use for interaction. To address this shortcoming we conducted an experiment to investigate how ambient temperature and humidity could affect the usability of thermal feedback. If environmental conditions affect perception significantly, then it may not be suitable for mobile interactions. Evaluations were conducted outdoors in varying environmental conditions over a period of 5 months. Results showed that the ambient temperature has a significant impact on people's ability to detect stimuli and also their perception of these stimuli. Humidity has a negligible effect for most humidity values. Despite this, previous thermal feedback design recommendations still hold in varying temperatures and humidities showing that thermal feedback is a useful tool for mobile interaction.

Author Keywords
Thermal feedback; mobile interaction; environment; temperature; humidity, ambient; non-visual feedback

ACM Classification Keywords
H.5.2 [Information Interfaces And Presentation]: User Interfaces - Haptic I/O;

General Terms
Design, Human Factors

INTRODUCTION
Physical interactions such as multitouch and 3D spatial input through gestures are becoming more prominent in modern mobile devices. While the use of haptic feedback is common and has received a lot of attention, this has mostly been through the vibrotactile actuators built into phones. Other aspects of touch can be exploited to enhance interaction with mobile devices. In particular, in this work we focus on thermal feedback which has a number of potential benefits. It can act as a non-visual notification channel for situations that are too bumpy or noisy for vibrotactile or audio feedback. It can enhance both visual and non-visual feedback by adding extra depth to the interaction experience, e.g. thermal feedback could be used to add affect that is not provided by other modalities [11, 18]. Thermal output is also entirely private; audio may be heard by others, vibrotactile may be heard and felt by others and visual may be seen by others. Currently, the basis for designing thermal feedback comes from the wealth of research on temperature perception from the psychology literature, where the goals are very different, e.g. the investigation of the characteristics and limits of perception, pain thresholds etc.

No previous work in HCI investigating thermal feedback has taken environmental factors, such as ambient temperature or humidity, into account. This means it is not clear if the same thermal feedback could be used in Northern Europe during winter and in the Middle East during summer. If the wrong feedback is delivered in the wrong environmental conditions then the thermal feedback may become ineffective, e.g. warm feedback in hot and humid conditions may be uncomfortable and difficult to use. Thus, it is important to investigate these contextual factors to design effective and usable thermal feedback. With the goal of examining the impact of ambient temperature and humidity on an individual's ability to detect and use thermal feedback, we present a study into how well users perceive hot and cold stimuli on the hand and wrist. Evaluations were carried out outdoors in varying environmental conditions over a period of 5 months. In addition, we examine if any impact of environmental conditions can be overcome with training. The results will help us understand how to construct thermal feedback for a user interface that is usable in a wider range of usage contexts.

BACKGROUND
Temperature Perception
The skin rests in a narrow 'neutral' zone, ranging from ~28°C up to ~40°C when in all but the most extreme environmental conditions [13]. The size of this zone is relatively constant across individuals, at around 6-8°C, but the relative position of each individual's neutral zone varies. Within the neutral zone there is no discernible thermal sensation [13]. Outside of this range a constant sensation of warmth (above) or cold (below) is perceived [15]. Thermal *thresholds* (the amount of temperature change required before a stimulus becomes perceivable, measured from a set baseline temperature) are inextricably linked to both the skins current temperature and the rate of stimulus change

(i.e. rate of warming or cooling). There is a roughly U-shaped relationship between rate of change (ROC) and thermal threshold, in ideal laboratory settings using highly trained individuals. Thermal thresholds decrease to as small as 0.5°C as ROC increases from 0.01°C/sec to 3°C/sec. They then increase again under faster changes, due to conduction velocity as well as reaction and cognition time [9]. This would suggest that, as ROC increases, stimuli become more salient, however, above a set speed, even if salience increases, the ROC 'over-takes' reaction time so that further increases in stimulation have occurred by the time the participant could react. As the skin adapts to the warm or cool extreme of the neutral zone, warm and cold thresholds, respectively, decrease and decrease more as the stimulus intensity approaches the heat/cold pain thresholds (~45°C and 11-15°C respectively [12, 20]). Conversely, warm and cold thresholds increase as the skin is cooled and warmed respectively. From this, and other evidence, it is clear that the thermal sense is more sensitive to *changes* in temperature, rather than the temperature itself.

Thermal sensitivity is not uniform; there are marked variations between different body locations and different skin types. Glabrous skin (hairless skin as found on the fingertips, palm and volar/under surface of the arm) is generally less sensitive than non-glabrous/hairy skin with normal and pain thresholds generally larger on glabrous skin [9]. This is due to the thickness of glabrous skin compared to hairy skin [9]. The Thenar eminence (the bulbous region of the palm adjoining the thumb) has higher sensitivity than the rest of the palm [7] but is still not as sensitive as non-glabrous skin on the hand [9]. In general, thermal sensitivity is best on the head and trunk but worse towards the extremities [7].

Influence of Environment and Context

A number of studies outside of computing have investigated the effect of the environment on thermal perception and pain thresholds. Strigo *et al.* [21] investigated the effect of ambient temperature on stimulus intensity, pain intensity and unpleasantness of thermal stimuli applied to the volar forearm. The ambient temperatures they used were 15°C (cool), 25°C (neutral) and 35°C (warm) and their thermal stimuli was in the range 0-50°C. They found that mean skin temperature, heat perception (44-50°C) and cold perception (0-25°C) were affected by ambient temperature. They also found that cold stimuli were rated as being more unpleasant in cold conditions, with warm stimuli being more unpleasant in warm conditions. In related work, Gagge *et al.* [3] investigated the effect of ambient temperature on comfort and thermal sensation for seated unclothed subjects. The ambient temperatures they investigated were in the range 12-48°C. They found neutral temperatures to be in the range of 28-30°C. They also found that discomfort increased more rapidly for cool (<28°C) than warm (>30°C) environments, while thermal sensation increased outside the neutral zone. Discomfort increased for cool stimuli in cold environments and for warm stimuli in hot environments. In general, discomfort was linked to a change in average body temperature from 36.5°C. Hagander *et al.* [7] reported that warm and cool pain thresholds were independent of local skin temperature, when temperatures range between 27-37°C. Hirosawa *et al.* [10] found that warm and cold thresholds at the middle fingertips were affected by room temperature, from a neutral zone of 15-25°C.

With respect to humidity, Givoni *et al.* [4] report the results of 5 comfort studies to investigate the impact of humidity on perceived levels of comfort. The 5 studies cover both indoor and outdoor conditions and were conducted in a number of countries (Thailand, Singapore, Indonesia and Japan). They report the effect of humidity on perceived comfort to be small to negligible. They note that the participants were acclimatised to the environment of the country in which the evaluation was conducted.

Although not investigating ambient temperature and humidity, Halvey *et al.* [8] examined how clothing might affect usability of thermal feedback. They studied how well users perceive hot and cold stimuli on the hand, thigh and waist. Evaluations were carried out with cotton and nylon between the thermal stimulators and the skin. Results showed that the presence of clothing required higher intensity thermal changes for detection but that these changes were more comfortable than direct stimulation on the skin.

Most of the studies mentioned above were conducted in tightly controlled laboratory settings with users who often had many hours of training in making fine judgments on small changes in thermal stimulation. It is important to investigate these phenomenons and their application to HCI in more realistic usage scenarios.

Thermal Feedback in HCI

In their review of thermal perception and the design of thermal feedback, Jones and Berris [13] summarised what they saw as the "desired features" of a thermal display. These were based on both VR research and psychophysical evidence and indicate the range of control a system would need to have to make full use of the thermal sense. They recommend using stimulus temperatures of 22-42°C and employing higher rates of change so as to maximize detection of stimuli. However, they also suggest a thermal interface should be capable of heating and cooling resolutions of 0.001°C and 0.002°C respectively, to mimic the subtle differences in the thermal conductance of different materials (their work was on discrimination of materials in VR environments). These features are extremely exact, and necessarily so for the VR application, however this level of accuracy may not be necessary or even useful for everyday indoor and outdoor mobile thermal feedback needs.

Wettach *et al.* [22] designed a Peltier-based thermal feedback apparatus for mobile devices and tested users' ability to differentiate three stimulus temperatures (32°C, 37°C and 42°C). Initially error rates were around 65%, although this number dropped to 25% after long-term training. None of these temperatures would normally be considered 'cool' and so this study suggests that individuals can identify varying degrees of warmth, not simply a change from one temperature to another. However, if users can only distinguish these three relatively disparate temperatures at 75% accuracy it is unlikely they will be able to differentiate stimuli at the resolutions suggested by Jones and Berris [13]. Wilson *et al.* [23] presented two studies into how well users could detect hot and cold stimuli presented to the fingertips, the palm, the dorsal (upper) surface of the forearm and the dorsal surface of the upper arm. Evaluations were carried out in static and mobile settings. Results showed that the palm was most sensitive, cold was more perceivable and comfortable than warm and that stronger and faster-changing stimuli were more detectable but less comfortable.

Gooch [5] found that adding thermal feedback to remote, PC-mediated interpersonal communication increased feelings of 'social presence'. Nakashige *et al.* [18] accompanied photographs of warm and cold scenes (food such as soup and ice cream, and environmental examples like fire and snow) with either warm or cold feedback. A small informal study indicated that the foods appeared more appealing when accompanied by the corresponding temperature and a small number of users reported an impression of a "loving home" from the warm soup. Both Iwasaki *et al.* [11] and Fujita and Nishimoto [2] have suggested systems that could be used to convey emotional information to another user through either augmentation of an existing mobile phone [11] or through a simple device worn around the neck. Lee and Lim [17] discussed existing preconceptions about the meaning or significance of thermal sensations in general. They found that users did not treat sensations as binary (i.e. warm and cold) but as a continuum; sensations were almost meaningless without context and that it was a very unobtrusive form of feedback. They also found that cold stimuli were generally less preferred than warm.

Recently, Kushiyama and colleagues [16] developed thermal display technology utilising Peltier elements and Narumi *et al.* [19] developed a contextual/ambient thermal display for more mobile scenarios. Neither piece of technology has been evaluated but both hold promise for future use. Thermo-pict [16], in particular, stands out as it has the opportunity to provide patterns of thermal stimulation not possible with more limited hardware, including thermal 'pictures'.

There are large differences in feedback design requirements for VR, abstract uses of thermal output or for highly controlled lab settings. For use in real world applications more robust evaluations of thermal output must be conducted. Many of the studies looking at the impact of temperature and humidity were conducted with different goals to ours, e.g. they focus on pain thresholds or are conducted in highly controlled environments. Therefore, we conducted a long term evaluation to investigate the impact of ambient temperature and humidity on thermal feedback usability.

EVALUATION

The main goal of this evaluation is to investigate the impact of environmental factors on thermal feedback. There are a number of specific research questions that we investigated:

1. Wilson *et al.* [23] put forward a number of design recommendations for use of thermal interfaces for mobile interaction, namely: (1) the Thenar eminence is the optimal location for feedback, but non-glabrous arm locations are also suitable, (2) 1°C/sec and 3°C/sec changes are both usable and (3) Warm and cool stimuli are both suitable for use, although users have a preference for cool. Their recommendations were based on indoor conditions. We wanted to examine if these recommendations still held in different environmental conditions?
2. Does ambient temperature have an impact on people's ability to detect and perceive thermal stimuli?
3. Does ambient humidity have an impact on people's ability to detect and perceive thermal stimuli?
4. Can repeated use of thermal interfaces help users to overcome any influence of temperature and humidity?

Equipment

For our evaluation we used a microcontroller connected to a four-channel Peltier heat pump designed and built by SAMH Engineering [23] (Figure 1). Peltier heat pumps allow for a high level of control over temperature output and also allow for both heating and cooling from the same pump. All four Peltier devices could be independently controlled over USB, with the temperature set anywhere within the range of -20°C to +45°C, accurate to 0.1°C. The Peltiers themselves were bonded to circuit boards and therefore it was necessary to bond heat sinks to an exposed copper strip on the underside of the boards to help dissipate this heat.

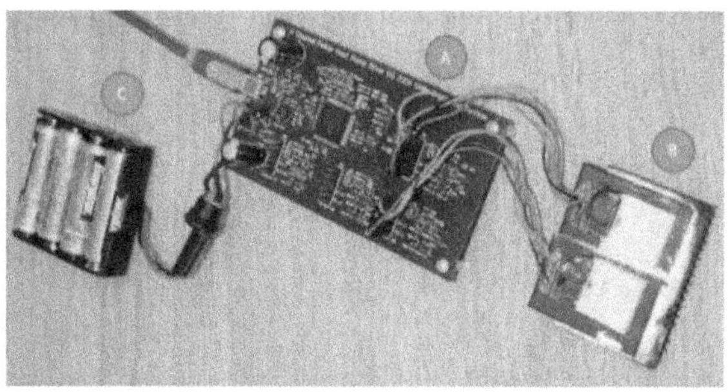

Figure 1: Microcontroller (A), battery pack (C) and Peltier stimulators (B)

Although our device can control four Peltier pumps, only two were used for this study, placed next to each other to stimulate adjoining areas of the skin. The larger the area of stimulation, the greater the thermal sensation, known as spatial summation [20]. Thus using two Peltiers instead of one (i.e. having a larger area of stimulation) meant that we needed lower intensity output to produce threshold sensations, compared to using one. We chose not to employ more than two, even though this could have reduced the intensity requirements further, as this would have required too large an area of skin to fit with the premise of mobile use.

Stimuli

We replicated the design of the study of Wilson *et al.* [23] to get a baseline for indoor performance, so the thermal stimuli used were the same as theirs. Using similar stimuli to previous evaluations allows us to compare our results directly with results of other experiments. A neutral starting temperature of 32°C was chosen as this is within the defined 'neutral zone' of thermal sensation [14, 23]. The skin was adapted to this temperature before each trial session and was returned to it between each stimulus presentation. Two different rates of stimulus change were used: 1°C/sec and 3°C/sec. Three different stimulus intensities were used: 1°C, 3°C and 6°C. Employing each intensity change in both directions from 32°C neutral gave absolute stimulus temperatures of (in increasing order): 26°C (-6°C), 29°C (-3°C), 31°C (-1°C), 33°C (+1°C), 35°C (+3°C) and 38°C (+6°C). Every temperature was away from the cold and heat pain thresholds (approximately 11-15°C and 45°C respectively). Each stimulus in this set was delivered twice, giving a total of 24 stimuli presented at each location (3 intensities x 2 directions x 2 rates x 2 presentations).

As our interest is in mobile interaction, we selected 2 body locations that could be used for thermal feedback: the Thenar eminence and the back of the wrist. An additional reason for choosing these locations is that they are often exposed and not covered by clothing. Thus they are exposed to the environment and our evaluations would not be hindered by participants wearing different clothing in different environmental conditions. The Thenar eminence was chosen specifically over the central palm itself due to its increased sensitivity to thermal stimuli [23]. If a person was to hold a mobile device in his/her hand it would be in direct contact with the Thenar. The wrist/dorsal surface (hairy skin) of the forearm was chosen as it has differing thermal sensitivity to the Thenar eminence [6, 23] but also as it is conceivable that a watch or wristband could be worn which forms part of an interaction paradigm for mobile devices. The volar surface (underside) of the forearm was specifically not chosen as research has shown it has equivalent sensitivity to the Thenar eminence [7].

Variables

For this study we were interested in identifying what stimuli produce threshold sensations from a neutral base temperature, i.e. which stimuli were noticeable and so be best suited for use in thermal feedback design. The independent variables were: (1) rate of change (ROC), (2) stimulus intensity, (3) direction of change (warm or cool), (4) body location and (5) user experience with thermal feedback.

The dependent variables were: (1) threshold perception (if one was perceived), (2) threshold time (how long after the initiation of a stimulus that the threshold was perceived), (3) subjective comfort of stimulus and (4) subjective intensity of stimulus. Threshold size (distance in °C from neutral when the stimulus was felt) was also considered as a dependent variable but was removed as it is correlated with threshold time i.e. given a rate of change and time to detection we can calculate threshold size. We recorded user subjective reports of the intensity of the stimulation (a 7-point Likert scale from "Very Cold" up to "Very Hot") and the comfort level of the stimulus (a 7-point Likert scale from "Very Uncomfortable" up to "Very Comfortable") similar to others used before [1, 3, 21, 23]. For analysis, the intensity scales were mapped to a 0-3 scale, with 0 being neutral and 3 being very hot or very cold for the hot or cold stimuli.

Procedure

The task was split into 2 conditions based on the location of stimulation, with all participants taking part in both conditions in a counterbalanced order. Each participant was seated outdoors at a desk upon which there was a laptop and mouse. The Peltier stimulator lay on the desk in front of the participant, facing up so that he/she could lay a hand or wrist on the stimulator (see Figure 2).

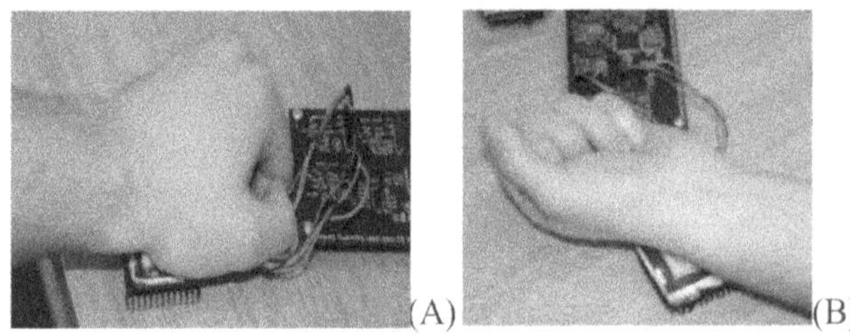

Figure 2: Stimulator locations for Thenar (A) and forearm (B) conditions

Figure 3: Locations for evaluation, (A) garden area and (B) covered entrance way

Two different outdoor locations were used for the experiment to provide a robust and realistic test environment. Both were sheltered to reduce effects of wind. The first was in a small garden area (see Figure 3A), however when it was raining it was not possible to use this location and a covered entrance way was used (see Figure 3B). The garden area was preferred, as the shading in the entrance way meant that we might not get a large range of temperatures.

The stimulator was contacted with the skin of the non-dominant hand/arm (by resting on top) at the beginning of each condition and remained in contact for the duration of that condition. Green [6] found that participants reported higher intensity perceptions when they were in contact with a stimulator between successive stimuli, compared to removing their hand between trials. At the start of each condition the Peltiers were set to the neutral starting temperature of 32°C for two minutes so as to adapt the skin to this temperature. After the two minutes of adaptation all 24 stimuli were presented in random order. A stimulus presentation comprised of 10 seconds of stimulus followed by a return to the neutral temperature and 30 seconds of adaptation. There were no visual or auditory clues as to when stimuli were presented.

Participants were instructed to click the left mouse button as soon as they felt a change in thermal stimulation, in any direction and at any intensity. Once this occurred, the time elapsed since the initiation of the stimulus was taken as an indication of the threshold time. At this point the two Likert scales appeared on screen asking the individual to rate the stimulus in terms of intensity and comfort. They then clicked on a submit button and another stimulus was presented after the 30 seconds of adaptation had completed. If the participant clicked the button before the full 10 seconds of stimulation had passed, the Peltiers were immediately returned to neutral and the following scale ratings corresponded to the preceding stimulus. If a stimulus was not felt, and so ran its 10 second presentation with no click from the participant, the Peltiers were then returned to neutral and the 30 seconds of adaptation began. In this case, the participant may have felt the transition back to neutral and so a click during this period produced exactly the same scales and data as before, however they corresponded to the transition back to neutral and not the initial stimulus.

Participants

Two groups of users participated: single session users and repeated users. Single session users participated in one session of the study only. Repeated users took part in a session once a month for the five months of the study. Each month six single session users took part, resulting in a total of 30 single session users. Six repeated users started the evaluation; however one had to withdraw, leaving a total of five who completed the whole study. One month was chosen as the time between sessions to provide a greater chance of different environmental conditions (see Figure 4 for example environmental conditions over the period of the study).

The single session group consisted of 18 males and 12 females aged 21 to 39 (mean = 28.77, median = 29), the majority of whom were studying or working at the University. 28 were right-handed and paid £6 for participation, which lasted just under an hour. The repeated session group consisted of 5 males aged 24 to 31 (mean = 26.2, median = 24), all studying or working at the University. All were right-handed and paid £6 per session. The majority of participants were of Northern European origin, although there were individuals from Asia, Africa, North America and South America. All were living in Northern Europe and in that respect can be considered acclimatised.

Environmental Conditions

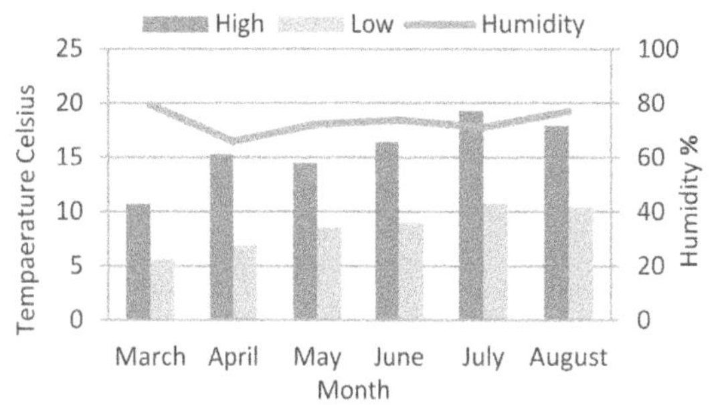

Figure 4: Environmental conditions over 5 months of the study (August is included as some of the July participants finished in the first few days of August)

Participants were tested from March to July (some of the July participants took part in the evaluation in the first few days of August). During each trial, the ambient temperature and humidity were recorded. Temperature and humidity readings were taken 3 times during the evaluation, as over the period of the evaluation these conditions could change, allowing us to calculate the average ambient temperature and humidity. Temperature was measured to an accuracy of 0.1°C and humidity to an accuracy of 0.1%. Figure 4 shows the average daily high and low temperature and average daily humidity per month for the duration of the experiment. These figures were collected daily from local weather reports for the duration of the evaluation. Initially, we had considered beginning the experiment when temperatures were cooler, however, for ethical, safety and comfort reasons we did not want to have participants seated outside in cold temperatures.

Over all of the evaluation sessions, temperature ranged from a minimum of 8.45°C to a maximum of 27.75°C, with humidity from 31.4% of to a maximum of 93.2%. Due to the range of environmental conditions, the data was grouped based on temperature and humidity. Temperature data was grouped in blocks of 5°C. Previous work by Hirosawa *et al.* [10] found that the neutral zone for thresholds is in the range 15-25°C. The grouping chosen maintains this neutral zone, while at the same time allows a finer grained analysis of the data. Had we used the 10°C gap for the 15-25°C neutral zone, we would only have had three groups; the larger number of groups still allows us to conduct the same analysis. This resulted in 5 temperature based groups <10°C, 10-15°C, 15-20°C, 20-25°C and >25°C. Where for example the 10-15°C range includes temperatures starting at 10°C up to 15°C, so there was no overlap between ranges. Humidity data were grouped in blocks of 10%, resulting in 7 blocks: 30%, 40%, 50%, 60%, 70%, 80% and 90%. Givoni *et al.* [4] reported that humidity has a negligible effect on comfort, as such we believed that this grouping would allow us to investigate this phenomenon while still be fine grained enough to show any effects. Figure 5 shows the breakdown of user evaluation sessions by temperature and humidity ranges. While Figure 4 shows the seasonal changes over the course of the experiment, Figure 5 shows the fluctuations for sessions involving experimental participants. As can be seen many of the sessions were conducted in the mid-range temperature and humidities.

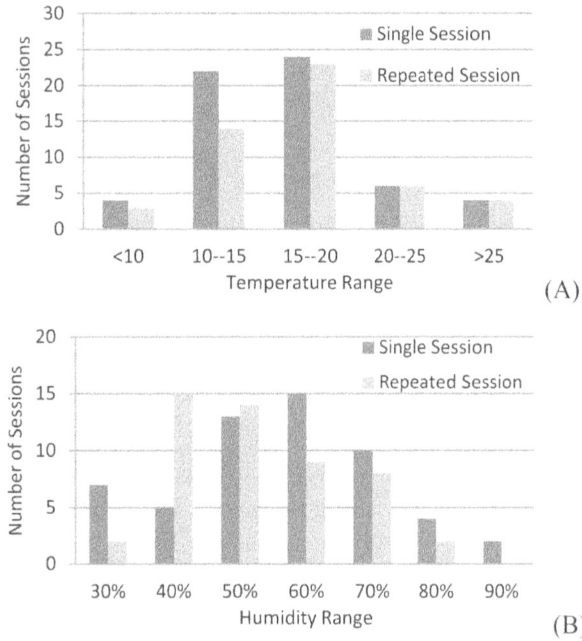

Figure 5: Experimental sessions broken down by temperature (A) and humidity (B) ranges. Session refers to one body location per evaluation participation.

RESULTS

Single Session

In this section we present an analysis of the factors for the single session participants. The independent variables were analysed as follows: a Friedman's analysis of variance by ranks was used to analyse the effect of ambient temperature, humidity and intensity of change. Wilcoxon pair-wise comparisons were also used to determine the effect of location, ROC and direction of change.

Number of Detections

Table 1 shows the performance for the different ambient temperatures and it can be seen clearly that detection rate peaks in the 15-20ºC temperature range. Indeed ambient temperature was found to have a significant effect on the number of thresholds produced (χ^2 (4)=68.325, p<0.001). In addition there are significant differences between a number of the temperature bands (as shown in Table 2). This indicates that effect of ambient temperature might be more fine grained than indicated by previous research [10]. Table 3 shows the figures for the impact of humidity on user performance. Humidity was found to have a significant effect on the numbers of thresholds produced (χ^2 (6)=28.74, p<0.001). It can be seen from viewing the figures in Table 3 that the detection rates are mostly in a similar range with the exception of extreme humidities (i.e. >90% and <30%). *Post hoc* Wilcoxon T comparisons between all humidities showed that the differences between the extreme humidities and more central humidities were significant (figures not shown for reasons of space). While some other differences were found there was no distinct pattern other than differences at the extreme humidity values, in keeping with the findings of Givoni *et al.* [4].

	<10ºC	10-15ºC	15-20ºC	20-25ºC	>25ºC
Detection Rate (Accuracy %)	82.29 σ=38.37	74.7 σ=43.48	84.25 σ=36.44	79.84 σ=40.27	35.56 σ=48.13
Detection Time (Sec.)	3.46 (3.36) σ=1.37	3.23 (2.82) σ=1.70	3.03 (2.68) σ=1.52	4.14 (3.65) σ=2.25	3.7 (3.93) σ=1.92
Comfort (Scale 0-6)	3.11 (3) σ=1.05	2.09 (2) σ=1.53	1.82 (1) σ=1.61	2.71 (2) σ=1.60	2.38 (2) σ=1.45
Intensity (Scale 0-3)	1.24 (1) σ=0.72	1.52 (1) σ=0.73	1.67 (2) σ=0.74	1.72 (2) σ=0.83	1.38 (1) σ=0.71

Table 1: Average performance relative to temperature, median in brackets where appropriate.

With respect to the other variables, intensity of change was found to have a significant effect on the number of thresholds produced (χ^2 (2)=192.412, p <0.001). The number of stimuli detected increased with intensity, with means of 53.55% (σ=49.93), 83.93% (σ=36.77) and 90.26% (σ=29.68) for 1°C, 3°C and 6°C intensities respectively. *Post hoc* Wilcoxon *T* comparisons showed significant differences in the number of detections between all stimulus intensities: 1°C vs. 3°C (z=9.62, T = 16884.0, p<0.001), 1°C vs. 6°C (z=11.84, T=19458.0, p<0.001) and 3°C vs. 6°C (z=3.08, T=2028.0, p<0.002). There was no significant effect of direction of stimulation. ROC had a significant effect (z=2.54, T=13375.0, p=0.011) with the higher ROC having a better detection rate (78.47% σ=41.13) than the lower ROC (73.06% σ=44.39). Location had a significant effect (z=4.16, T=9545.0, p<0.001) with the Thenar (80.41% σ=39.72) having a better detection rate than the wrist (71.14% σ=45.35). All of these findings are consistent with those of previous evaluations of thermal stimuli [23].

Time to Detection

Ambient temperature was found to have a significant effect on time to detection (χ^2 (4)=28.4, p <0.001). Once again performance peaks in the 15-20ºC range, see Table 1. This is further indication that thermal interfaces may be more sensitive to ambient temperature than indicated by prior research. Humidity was found to have a significant effect on the time to detection (χ^2 (6)=13.948, p =0.03). *Post hoc* Wilcoxon T comparisons showed significant effects at a number of values; however there was no pattern in the differences between humidities.

		<10°C v 10-15*°C*	*<10°C* v 15-20*°C*	*<10°C* v 20-25*°C*	*<10°C* v >25*°C*	10-15*°C* v 15-20*°C*	10-15*°C* v 15-20*°C*	10-15*°C* v >25*°C*	15-20*°C* v 15-20*°C*	15-20*°C* v >25*°C*	15-20*°C* v >25*°C*
Number of Detections	Z	1.616	0.928	0.686	5.632	3.533	1.483	5.000	1.859	6.040	5.374
	p	0.106	0.353	0.493	0.000*	0.000*	0.138	0.000*	0.063	0.000*	0.000*
Time to Detection	Z	2.307	5.867	1.706	0.860	3.713	3.400	0.037	6.456	3.291	1.683
	p	0.021*	0.000*	0.088	0.390	0.000*	0.001*	0.970	0.000*	0.001*	0.092
Perceived Comfort	Z	3.542	6.597	2.024	2.097	2.365	1.84	2.583	6.074	2.462	2.495
	p	0.001 *	0.000 *	0.043*	0.036*	0.018*	0.066	0.010*	0.000*	0.014*	0.013*

Table 2: Pairwise comparison of different temperature bands using Wilcoxon Sign Ranked test. Intensity not shown as it had no significant effect.

	30%	*40%*	*50%*	*60%*	*70%*	*80%*	*90%*
Detection Rate (Accuracy %)	57.41, σ=49.60	77.45, σ=41.99	81.44 σ=38.94	81.22 σ=39.11	79.09 σ=40.76	82.11 σ=38.53	34.37 σ=48.26
Detection Time (Sec.)	2.91(2.59), σ=1.50	2.99(2.6) σ=1.53	3.69 (3.31) σ=2.02	3.06(2.61) σ=1.57	3.22(3.02) σ=1.41	3.26(2.69) σ=1.61	4.99(4.85) σ=2.53
Comfort (Scale 0-6)	2.30 (2), σ=1.39	1.82 (2) σ=1.57	2.67 (2) σ=1.55	2.42 (2) σ=1.53	1.74 (1) σ=1.39	1.27 (1) σ=1.59	1.63 (1) σ=1.36
Intensity (Scale 0-3)	1.53 (1), σ=0.72	1.67 (1.5) σ=0.76	1.61 (2) σ=0.81	1.47 (1) σ= 0.72	1.69 (2) σ=0.75	1.71 (2) σ=0.79	1.60 (1.5) σ=0.69

Table 3: Average performance relative to humidity, median in brackets where appropriate.

Intensity of change was found to have a significant effect on time to detection (χ^2 (2)=56.167, p<0.001). The time to detection decreased as the intensity increased with means/medians of 3.98/3.59 (σ=1.97) seconds, 3.04/2.64 (σ=1.59) seconds and 3/2.74 (σ=1.49) seconds for 1°C, 3°C and 6°C respectively. *Post hoc* Wilcoxon *T* comparisons showed significant differences in the time to detection between 1°C and the other intensities: 1°C vs. 3°C (z=6.22, T=22642.0, p<0.001) and 1°C vs. 6°C (z=6.58, T=22873.0, p<0.001). Direction of stimulation had a significant effect on time to detection (z=5.71, T=251982.0, p<0.001) with cool stimuli (mean=3.04, median=2.61, σ=1.69) being detected more quickly than warm stimuli (mean=3.38, median=3.01, σ=1.67). Location had an effect on time to detection (z=5.47, T=76690.5, p<0.001). With stimuli on the Thenar (mean=3.04, median=2.59, σ=1.69) detected significantly more quickly than on the wrist (mean=3.48, median=3.1, σ=1.68). ROC (z=5.37, T=45071.5, p<0.001) also had an effect on time to detection with the higher rate of change resulting in a faster time to detection (mean=3.01, median=2.64, σ=1.59) that the lower rate (mean=3.51, median=3.08, σ=1.78). Once again these results are consistent with the results of previous evaluations [23].

Subjective Stimulus Comfort

Ambient temperature was found to have a significant effect on perceived comfort (χ^2 (4)=34.247, p<0.001). Once again, the best comfort ratings occur in the 15-20°C range indicating the fine grained nature of the impact of ambient temperature (see Table 1 and Table 2). Humidity had a significant effect on perceived intensity (χ^2 (6)=21.338, p=0.002). Once again as with time to detection there is no real pattern in the differences. Intensity of change had a significant effect on perceived comfort (χ^2 (2)=35.154, p<0.001). *Post hoc* Wilcoxon *T* comparisons showed significant differences in the time to detection between 6°C and the other intensities: 1°C vs. 6°C (z=4.28, T=11936.0, p<0.001) and 3°C vs. 6°C (z=5.39, T=28537.0, p<0.001). The perceived comfort decreased as intensity increased with means/medians of 1.73/1 σ=1.37, 1.89/1 σ=1.45 and 2.58/2 σ=1.71 for 1°C, 3°C and 6°C intensities respectively. Direction had a significant effect on perceived comfort (z= 4.21, T=148932.0, p<0.001) with cool stimuli (mean=1.98, median=2, σ=1.47) being more comfortable than warm (mean=2.28, median=3, σ=1.68). Location had an effect on perceived comfort (z=2.16, T=38112.5, p=0.031). With stimuli to the Thenar (mean=2.1, median= 2, σ=1.59) being more comfortable than to the wrist (mean=2.16, median=2, σ=1.56). ROC (z=4.47, T=41652.0, p<0.001) also had an effect on comfort with the higher rate of change (mean=2.37 median =2, σ=1.67) being less comfortable than the lower rate of change (mean=1.86 median = 1, σ=1.43). As with detection rate and time to detect these findings are consistent with the results of evaluations conducted by Wilson et al. [23].

Subjective Stimulus Intensity

Statistical tests showed that ambient temperature did not have an effect on perceived intensity, as can be seen in Table 1 the figures for perceived intensity are in a similar range. Also humidity did not have a significant effect on intensity, as can be seen un Table 3.

As expected, intensity of change had a significant effect on the perceived intensity (χ^2 (2)=174.69, p<0.001). *Post hoc* Wilcoxon *T* comparisons showed significant differences in the perceived intensity of change between all intensities: 1°C vs. 3°C (z=7.53, T=6342.0, p<0.001), 1°C vs. 6°C (z=10.78, T=14406.5, p<0.001) and 3°C vs. 6°C (z=9.51, T=25474.0, p<0.001). The perceived intensity increased as the intensity increased with means/medians of 1.09/1 σ=0.49, 1.43/1 σ= 0.61 and 1.99/2 σ= 0.78 for 1°C, 3°C and 6°C intensities. Direction had a significant effect on perceived intensity (z=3.582, T=113226.5, $p<0.001$) with cool stimuli (mean=1.45, median=1, σ=0.79) perceived as less intense than warm (mean=1.57, median=1, σ=0.81). Location did not have an effect on perceived intensity. ROC also had an effect on intensity (z=7.02, T=33958.5, $p<0.001$) with the higher rate of change (mean=1.74, median =2, σ=0.81) being more intense than the lower rate of change (mean=1.39, median = 1, σ=0.64).

Direction of Change in Relation to Ambient Temperature

To provide a more in depth analysis of the effect of direction of stimulation and ambient temperature, we compared warm and cool stimuli in all temperature bands using Wilcoxon sign ranked tests. There was no effect of direction on detection rate in any band. For detection time there was an effect in the most sensitive temperature bands 10-15°C (z=2.25, T=10456.0, p=0.025) and 15-20°C (z=4.53, T=16293.0, $p<0.001$). For comfort only the 10-15°C (z=3.18, T=2889.5, p=0.001) had an effect with cool being more comfortable than warm. Finally for intensity there was an effect for the most sensitive temperature bands 10-15°C (z=2.58, T=4271.0, p=0.01) and 15-20°C (z=1.98, T=6339.5, p=0.048), where cool was less intense than warm. These results are interesting, warming or cooling changes were not affected by more extreme warm or cool conditions, but rather by the more favourable ambient conditions. In future work we plan to investigate this in more detail with larger temperature ranges.

Repeated Sessions

Between Session Comparison

	Session1	Session2	Session3	Session4	Session5
Detection Rate (Accuracy %)	87.03 σ=33.67	84.65 σ=36.12	81.14 σ=39.21	81.36 σ=39.03	87.61 σ=33.02
Detection Time (Sec.)	2.69 σ=1.54	2.94 σ=1.83	2.61 σ=1.38	2.77 σ=1.51	2.43 σ=1.36
Comfort (Scale 0-6)	2.42 σ=1.47	2.65 σ=1.27	2.59 σ=1.34	2.50 σ=1.35	2.69 σ=1.27
Intensity (Scale 0-3)	1.49 σ=0.69	1.55 σ=0.73	1.41 σ=0.67	1.41 σ=0.72	1.42 σ=0.67
Temperature Avg/Min/Max	11.31/ 9.25/ 14.15	16.01/ 12.40/ 20.5	16.76/ 10.35/ 24.60	16.75/ 14.55/ 18.90	22.02/ 16.50/ 27.75
Humidity Avg/Min/Max	65.68/ 56.2/ 78.95	50.95/ 44.85/ 58.90	68.59/ 51.60/ 79.10	50.86/ 45.60/ 59.50	51.55/ 33.10/ 87.70

Table 4: Average performance relative to temperature, median in brackets where appropriate.

As well as analysing the performance of the single session participants, the performance and responses of the repeated users were analysed relative to each other and relative to the single session participants. All sessions were compared using Friedman's Analysis of Variance by Ranks, with individual sessions compared using Wilcoxon pair-wise comparisons. The different sessions did not have an effect on detection rate (χ^2 (4)=6.5, p=0.165). The time to detection was significantly different between the sessions (χ^2 (4)=12.94, $p<0.012$). Details of the average detection times are available in Table 4, with Session 2 having slowest detection time and Section 5 the fastest detection time. Overall there were significant differences between the following sessions a number of sessions, but there was no pattern in the differences. There was no effect of repeated sessions on comfort (χ^2 (4)=8.665, p=0.07). There was no effect of repeated sessions on intensity (χ^2 (4)=6.452, p=0.168). These results indicate that training did not improve or degrade user performance. However, to ensure larger changes in environmental conditions we used a large time gap between sessions (1 month), perhaps in other conditions with shorter gaps between sessions a training effect could be found.

Comparison to Single Users

To provide a more in depth analysis of any training effects, comparisons were made between the repeated user and single user sessions based on temperature and humidity. Comparisons were made between individual sessions and the performance of the single session users for both the same temperatures and humidities using the Mann Whitney U test. While some differences were found, these did not follow any particular pattern. Table 5 provides an example of a comparison for a repeat user R2 and the general population. As can be seen, R2 has some sessions where he outperformed the general population and some where he was in line. His five sessions were spread across two temperature bands and performance was consistent within those bands. For all repeat users, there was no evidence of performance improving with more training and sessions. A full discussion of the implications of this finding and indeed all of the findings in this section is given in the next section.

	Session1	Session2	Session3	Session4	Session5
Temperature Range	*10-15*	*10-15*	*10-15*	*15-20*	*15-20*
Detection Rate (Accuracy %)	89.58*	83.33	89.58*	83.33	89.36
	74.7	74.7	74.7	84.25	84.25
Detection Time (Sec)	2.35*	3.13	2.5*	2.53*	2.52*
	3.23	3.23	3.23	3.03	3.03
Comfort (Scale 0-6)	0.77*	1.11*	1.53	1.28	1.43
	2.09	2.09	2.09	1.82	1.82
Intensity (Scale 0-3)	1.3	1.27	1.35	1.23*	1.14*
	1.52	1.52	1.52	1.67	1.67

Table 5: Repeat user R2 in comparison to general population. R2 performance is on top and general performance below. Significant differences are marked with an asterisk.

DISCUSSION

RQ1: Comparison with Existing Design Recommendations

Wilson *et al.* [23] made a number of recommendations for the design of thermal feedback for interaction: (1) the Thenar eminence is the optimal location for feedback, but non-glabrous arm locations are also suitable, (2) 1°C/sec and 3°C/sec changes are both suitable and (3) warm and cold stimuli are both suitable for use, although users have a preference for cold stimuli. Despite the different temperatures and humidities encountered by the participants in this experiment, the design recommendations made by Wilson *et al.* still hold. In our experiment, for measures of number of stimuli detected, threshold time and perceived comfort the Thenar eminence outperformed the wrist showing it to be the most sensitive area, and confirming the results of Wilson *et al.* However, while the Thenar was the best location the wrist was still suitable. Similar to the results of Wilson *et al.* [23], our results indicate that both rates of change are suitable for use, each with slightly different characteristics. While 1°C/sec changes are slower and require a longer time to detect, they are more comfortable and less intense than the larger ROC. 3°C/sec changes are more likely to be detected and are much faster to detect, but are less comfortable. Finally, although both warm and cold stimuli are equally detectable and are perceived to have equal intensity, cold stimuli are faster to detect and are more comfortable as they feel less intense. More in depth investigation of direction of change in different ambient temperatures also indicates that cool changes are preferable to warm changes, with both still being usable. Research by Halvey *et al.* [8] indicted that warm stimuli might be more comfortable, however in this evaluation different clothing materials were placed between the Peltiers and the skin. So, for direct contact with the skin cool stimuli are more comfortable based on both the results of this experiment and the results of Wilson *et al.*

RQ2: Effect of Ambient Temperature

Hirosawa *et al.* [10] investigated the relationship between room temperature and warm and cold thresholds on the middle fingertips. They found that the warm and cold thresholds were affected by room temperature changes, with a neutral zone of 15-25°C for thresholds. However, the results of our analysis indicate that the effect of ambient temperature on thermal feedback perception appears to be finer grained than previously reported. Ambient temperature had a significant effect on the number of stimuli detected, threshold time and perceived comfort. Ambient temperature was not found to have an effect on perceived intensity. Our results indicate that the optimal performance in terms of detection rate (84.25%) and time to detection (3.03 seconds) is in the range 15-20°C. With performance degrading in both warm and cool direction around the 15-20°C temperature zone. While the differences are significant, with the exception of detection rate for >25°C, all of the other results are useable and indicate that thermal interfaces could be used. It should be noted that the >25°C is one of the more sparse data points in our data and the low detection rate might be due to individual thermal sensitivity of the users, this point should be investigated further in future work. Interestingly, the 15-20°C range also had the most favourable comfort ratings; again the ratings indicated that stimuli were perceived as being less comfortable in both the warm and cool directions. It should be noted that the average comfort rating (2.13) is not in the uncomfortable range. This indicates, once again, that while ambient temperature affects comfort, the thermal stimuli used in this evaluation were still comfortable and useable.

RQ3: Effect of Ambient Humidity

Givoni *et al.* [4] reported the effect of humidity on perceived comfort to be small. However, the results of our study indicate that humidity had a significant effect on the number of stimuli detected, threshold time and perceived comfort. Pairwise comparisons for detection rate showed that the differences in detection rate were for more extreme humidities, i.e. <30% (57.41% accuracy) and >90% (34.37% accuracy), with all other humidity ranges having detection rates in the range 77%-82%. This result is in keeping with the findings of Givoni *et al.* [4] where there are some effects at extreme humidities but otherwise the differences are negligible. While significant differences were reported for threshold time and perceived comfort, the differences between humidity ranges did not follow any particular pattern. Perhaps these differences could be attributed to some sparsity for particular humidity ranges and as such those ranges were affected more by the thermal sensitivities of the individual users. Further experimentation is needed to explore this.

RQ4: Training Effects

The results from the repeated user sessions indicate that there is very little difference between performance and perception in the different sessions, as can be seen in Table 4. There was no significant difference between the five sessions for the number of stimuli detected, the perceived comfort of the stimuli and the perceived intensity of the stimuli. There was a significant effect for threshold time. However, there was no clear pattern of improvement or degradation as the exposure to the stimuli increased over the sessions, although Session 5 did have the fastest detection time (2.43 sec.) and Session 2 the slowest (2.94 sec.). To gain further insight into any possible learning effect, individual performances were compared to the general population (as represented by the single session users) for the same temperature and humidity ranges. This comparison, while showing some differences, did not reveal any patterns and certainly no increase in performance for the repeated users. These results suggest that users learn the thermal feedback quickly and it would be usable for single or repeated use in an interface.

CONCLUSIONS

This paper has presented a detailed study investigating how well users were able to detect warm and cool stimuli presented to two body locations while outdoors. Our aim was to identify the sensitivity of thermal stimulus presentation to environmental factors in order to inform thermal feedback design for HCI and as such our novel contributions can be summarised as follows 1) Proposed design recommendations for thermal interfaces are based on a very recent study [23]. The confirmation that they hold across environmental conditions is a novel, useful and non-obvious finding. In addition the confirmation that cool stimuli directly on the skin are preferred is important, as other different studies have found that in some cases warm stimuli are preferred [8, 22]. 2) Ambient temperature affects stimuli detection rates and this effect is at a more fine grained level than presented in the psychophysical literature [10]. This knowledge is essential for designing thermal UIs. 3) Humidity does not appear to have the same effect as ambient temperature with the differences being at extreme humidities. While Givoni et al. [4] had a similar finding, they were not concerned with direct stimulation as we are. 4) No training effect was found for this evaluation; however a large gap between sessions was used.

In conclusion this paper has shown that while thermal feedback is sensitive to ambient temperature that previous recommendations are still valid, and as such we can design and use thermal feedback in a wide range of usage settings.

ACKNOWLEDGEMENTS

This research has been funded by the Industrial Members of MobileVCE (www.mobilevce.com), with additional financial support from EPSRC grant EP/G063427/1.

REFERENCES

1. Cherycroze, S., *Painful Sensation Induced by a Thermal Cutaneous Stimulus*. Pain, 1983. **17**(2): p. 109-137.
2. Fujita, H. and K. Nishimoto, *Lovelet: a heartwarming communication tool for intimate people by constantly conveying situation data*. Proc. CHI 2004.
3. Gagge, A., J. Stolwijk, and J. Hardy, *Comfort and Thermal Sensations and Associated Physiological Responses at Various Ambient Temperatures*. Environ Res, 1967. **1**(1): p. 1-20.
4. Givoni, B., J. Khedari, N.H. Wong, H. Feriadi, and M. Noguchi, *Thermal sensation responses in hot, humid climates: effect of humidity*. Building Research & Information, 2006. **34**(5): p. 496-506.
5. Gooch, D., *An Investigation into Communicating Social Presence With Thermal Devices*. MSc Dissertation, University of Bath, 2009: p. 1-390.
6. Green, B.G., *Temperature perception on the hand during static versus dynamic contact with a surface*. Atten Percept Psycho, 2009. **71**(5): p. 1185-1196.
7. Hagander, L., H. Midani, and M. Kuskowski, *Quantitative sensory testing: effect of site and skin temperature on thermal thresholds*. Clinical Neurophysiology, 2000.
8. Halvey, M., Y. Vazquez-Alvarez, G. Wilson, and S. Brewster. *The Effect of Clothing on Thermal Feedback Perception*. Proc ICMI 2011: p. 217-220.
9. Harrison, J. and K. Davis, *Cold-evoked pain varies with skin type and cooling rate: a psychophysical study in humans*. Pain, 1999. **83**(2): p. 123-135.
10. Hirosawa, I., H. Dodo, M. Hosokawa, S. Watanabe, K. Nishiyama, and Y. Fukuichi, *Physiological Variations of Warm and Cool Sense with Shift of Environmental-Temperature*. Int J Neurosci, 1984. **24**(3-4): p. 281-288.
11. Iwasaki, K., T. Miyaki, and J. Rakimoto, *AffectPhone: A Handset Device to Present User's Emotional State with Warmth/Coolness*. BIOSTEC2010, 2010. **2010**(B-Interface Workshop): p. 1-6.
12. Johnson, K., I. Darian-Smith, and C. LaMotte, *Peripheral neural determinants of temperature discrimination in man: a correlative study of responses to cooling skin*. Journal of Neurophysiology, 1973.
13. Jones, L.A. and M. Berris, *The Psychophysics of Temperature Perception and Thermal-Interface Design*. 10th Symposium on Haptic Interfaces for Virtual Environment and Teleoperator Systems, 2002: p. 1-6.
14. Kenshalo, D., C.E. Holmes, and P.B. Wood, *Warm and Cool Thresholds as a Function of Temperature Change*. Perception & Psychophysics, 1968. **3**(2A): p. 4.
15. Kenshalo, D. and H. Scott, *Temporal course of thermal adaptation*. Science, 1966.
16. Kushiyama, K., T. Baba, K. Doi, and S. Sasada, *Thermo-Pict neo*. Proc SIGGRAPH 2010: p. 1-1.
17. Lee, W. and Y.K. Lim, *Thermo-Message: Exploring the Potential of Heat as a Modality of peripheral Expression*. Proc CHI Extended Abstracts 2010: p. 1-6.
18. Nakashige, M., M. Kobayashi, and Y. Suzuki, *"Hiya-Atsu" media: augmenting digital media with temperature*. Proc. CHI 2009: p. 3181-3186.
19. Narumi, T., T. Akagawa, Y.A. Seong, and M. Hirose, *Thermotaxis*. Proc. SIGGRAPH 2009: p. 1-1.
20. Stevens, J.C., *Thermal Sensibility*, in *The Psychology of Touch*, M.A. Heller and W. Schiff, Editors. 1991, Lawrence Erlbaum: New Jersey.
21. Strigo, I., F. Carli, and M. Bushnell, *Effect of ambient temperature on human pain and temperature perception*. Anesthesiology, 2000. **92**(3): p. 699-707.
22. Wettach, R., C. Behrens, A. Danielsson, and T. Ness, *A thermal information display for mobile applications*. Proc. MobileHCI 2007: p 182-185.
23. Wilson, G., M. Halvey, S.A. Brewster, and S. Hughes, A., *Some Like it Hot? Thermal Feedback for Mobile Devices*. Proc. CHI 2011: p 2555-2564.

PINOKY: A Ring That Animates Your Plush Toys

Yuta Sugiura[1&2], Calista Lee[1&2], Masayasu Ogata[1&2], Anusha Withana[1], Yasutoshi Makino[1], Daisuke Sakamoto[2&3], Masahiko Inami[1&2], Takeo Igarashi[2&3]

[1]Graduate School of Media Design, Keio University, 4-1-1 Hiyoshi, Kohoku, Yokohama, 223-8526 Japan

[2]JST ERATO Igarashi Design Interface Project, 1-28-1-7F Koishikawa, Bunkyo, Tokyo, 112-0002 Japan

[3]Department of Computer Science, The University of Tokyo, 7-3-1 Hongo, Bunkyo, Tokyo, 113-0033 Japan

{y-sugiura | calista | anusha | inami}@kmd.keio.ac.jp, makino@sdm.keio.ac.jp
sakamoto@is.s.u-tokyo.ac.jp, takeo@acm.org

ABSTRACT

PINOKY is a wireless ring-like device that can be externally attached to any plush toy as an accessory that animates the toy by moving its limbs. A user is thus able to instantly convert any plush toy into a soft robot. The user can control the toy remotely or input the movement desired by moving the plush toy and having the data recorded and played back. Unlike other methods for animating plush toys, PINOKY is non-intrusive, so alterations to the toy are not required. In a user study, 1) the roles of plush toys in the participants' daily lives were examined, 2) how participants played with plush toys without PINOKY was observed, 3) how they played with plush toys with PINOKY was observed, and their reactions to the device were surveyed. On the basis of the results, potential applications were conceptualized to illustrate the utility of PINOKY.

Author Keywords

Interactive Plush Toy; Tangible User Interface; Robots; Ubiquitous Computing;

ACM Classification Keywords

H5.m. Information interfaces and presentation (e.g., HCI): Miscellaneous.

General Terms

Design

INTRODUCTION

Plush robots have not only served as toys for children [5] but have also contributed significantly in the areas of medical therapy [28] and communication media [22]. During the March 11 disaster in Japan in 2011, Paro (a seal-like robot) was used as a means of stress reduction for victims in the affected areas [21]. Due to its soft body and friendly appearance, it provides an emotionally richer user experience than typical robots [15]. However, its electrical components (microcontroller, actuators, etc.) must be inserted during fabrication. Also, the behaviors have to be hard-coded and are not configurable by the user. Our goal was to design a system that would enable the user to customize the movement of a plush robot.

Figure 1. PINOKY attached to the right arm of plush toy, enabling the arm to be moved.

Another goal was to convert an existing plush toy into an interactive robot by augmenting it with a computer system. In the area of ubiquitous computing, there have been several attempts to insert computing systems into everyday objects to convert them into highly compatible user interfaces in the home [2][12]. We chose to focus on plush toys as they are commonly found in the home. Because plush toys typically have an anthropomorphic embodiment, augmenting them with a computer system would enable them to play significant roles as communication agents (for example, between a person and a home appliance or with another person). Depending on the personal memory associated with the plush toy, there could be a variety of service and entertainment possibilities. For example, a grandson and his family could communicate with their grandfather living in a distant location through a plush toy given to the grandson by the grandfather for his birthday many years ago. However, implementing a computer system with actuators in a non-intrusive manner is problematic as it requires the cutting of the body of the user's favorite plush toy. Therefore, we focused on designing a device that converts an existing plush toy into an interactive robot system in the least intrusive way.

The device we developed is called "PINOKY." It is a wireless ring-like device that can be used to animate any plush toy, such as by moving its limbs, ears, or tail (Figure 1). Since PINOKY is battery-powered and equipped with wireless communication, it can easily be attached to a toy externally, the same way a person puts on an accessory. PINOKY consists of a microcontroller, motors, photoreflectors, a wireless module, and a battery. The motors are used to animate the toy, and the photoreflectors are used to sense and record the direction and amount of user-defined movement.

We conducted a user study to 1) examine the role of plush toys in the participants' daily lives, 2) observe how the participants played with plush toys without PINOKY, 3) observe how they played with plush toys with PINOKY, get their reactions to the device, and to get their thoughts on the concept. The results of our qualitative and quantitative analysis showed that users were able to enjoy using the system much more than we had expected.

Our work to convert an existing plush toy into an interactive soft robot has five significant contributions.

- A method has been developed for externally actuating a plush toy in a non-intrusive manner. Current methods require the cutting of the toy's body.
- A palm-sized, battery-operated, ring-like device equipped with wireless communication has been developed. It can be easily attached to various parts of a plush toy as an accessory.
- Our user study revealed how plush toys are used in daily life.
- Our user study clarified the usability of our device and revealed how the participants reacted to it.
- Several example application scenarios for the device were conceptualized.

RELATED WORK

Our work builds upon five distinct areas of prior research that are covered in turn in this section. The first is the body of work on puppets and their significance; the second is the body of work on plush toy interfaces; the third is the body of work on plush animal robots; the fourth is the body of work on giving movement to everyday objects; and the fifth is the body of work on configurable robots.

Animating Puppets

When talking about animating inanimate objects in play, one of the first things that comes to mind is puppetry. Puppets have been in existence for decades, and are present in a wide number of cultures all over the world. Via the usage of strings, sticks or hand movements to manipulate the puppet's limbs, puppeteers breathe "life" into the puppets by giving them motion. This is similar to PINOKY animating previously inanimate plush toys by manipulating the limb it is attached to. Puppets have important roles to play in many situations, for example in regular play, entertainment, education, therapy, and so on. McDonald's Camp Quality Puppets have been used effectively to bring across messages to children on how it is like to live with cancer [3]. Puppets in Education is an educational puppet troupe that utilizes puppets to educate their audience on difficult social issues such as bullying and autism [19]. Hadari has educated others for years on using puppets for education, as a means of social communication, and for therapy purposes [9].

Plush Toy Interfaces

The transition from infancy to childhood to adolescence is characterized by certain behaviors, such as remaining attached to a plush toy [29]. Even adults often display an instinctive desire to touch a plush toy. This has led to the introduction of interactive plush toys to provide an emotionally richer user experience [15]. Yonezawa et al. made an interactive plush toy by equipping it with seven types of sensors (bend, microphone, etc.) [30]. They also created an application to be used with this toy that composes music on the basis of the intensity and frequency of interaction.

Plush toy interfaces are sometimes used to control a character in the virtual environment. Johnson et al. developed the Sympathetic Interface, a plush doll embedded with a wireless module that is used to manipulate a virtual character in an iconic and intentional manner [11]. In a similar manner, Shimizu et al. developed a plush robotic toy interface with haptic feedback [23].

Plush Animal Robots

Plush robots have long been popular as children toys [5]. In recent years, many researchers have developed more intelligent plush robots and tested their use for various applications such as medical therapy [28], collaborative agents [1], communication media [22], and interior lighting [27]. Wada et al. developed Paro, a life-like robot baby harp seal, which is designed to be used for therapy in hospitals [28]. Microsoft's ActiMates Barney Doll is a plush toy embedded with pressure and light sensors, a wireless data connection, voice output, and a simple arm motor [25]. Barney is designed to be a social robot, commenting using computer media at crucial moments to facilitate learning. Leonardo, developed by Breazeal et al., is an agent that supports the user's work by providing accompanying gestures and social cues [1]. Sekiguchi et al. created RobotPHONE [22], a telecommunications device in the form of a plush toy that the caller manipulates to animate another person's plush toy that functions as a telecommunications device. The concept of PINOKY is similar but takes it to the next level by enabling the user to customize and add similar functionality to any plush toy.

There have been several attempts to actuate plush toys. Many existing plush robotic toys use a servomotor at a joint because it is stable, easily handled, and small but with high power [5]. Stiehl et al. used a voice coil actuator instead of a motor because such actuators have a smooth motion without backlash, resulting in life-like motion [24]. These methods impair the softness of the plush toy, and actuators have to be inserted into the toy beforehand. Ishikawa et al. used strings to pull on the surface of the plush toy [10]. However, this makes it difficult for the user to configure and customize the movements.

For the methods above to animate plush animal robots, a microcontroller and actuators must be embedded into the plush toy during manufacture. Additionally, their behaviors have to be hard-coded and are not configurable by the user. The PINOKY device, on the other hand, can be attached to and removed from any plush toy, and is thus able to convert any existing plush toy into an interactive robot.

Giving Movement to Everyday Objects

Physical computing is becoming more commonplace [8]. In the area of ubiquitous computing, there have been several attempts to insert computers into everyday objects [4]. LilyPad is a wearable microcontroller designed to introduce computing into fabrics [2]. Sugiura et al. developed a sensor module that enables the user to convert a soft household object into a touch input interface [12].

Several techniques have been proposed for giving movement to everyday objects. Osawa et al. developed customizable robot parts that personalize existing home appliances and give them movement [16]. Animated Paper enables the user to give movement to paper [13]. A shape memory alloy is attached to the paper and given movement by heating it from a distance using a laser. Probst et al. developed an intelligent paper clip for easily converting conventional Post-it® notes to physical I/O media [18]. Coelho et al. developed shape-changing paper, foam, and cloth [4]. Both the clip and the shape-changing materials use shape memory alloy for giving physical movement. Furukawa et al. found that an animal's fur can be made to stand up by the usage of simple vibration motors [6].

There have been numerous researches on robotic exoskeletons being used to facilitate motion in inanimate beings. One such example is the Berkeley lower extremity exoskeleton that Ghan et al. developed, which works to enhance the strength and endurance of a pilot [7]. Robot Suit HAL by Taal and Sankai is another wearable robot which aids in human motion [26].

These prior works infuse computing into our daily lives, which is what we aimed to do as well. Thus, with PINOKY, we aim to introduce computing into plush toys.

Configurable Robots

Many researchers have explored different types of configurable robots for several purposes, such as smart machines capable of doing tasks that people cannot do [31], as an educational tool kit that children can use to learn about programming [14] or kinetic movement [20], and simply as toys [17]. These configurable robots can be switch between varying forms and behavior autonomously or by user control.

Lego Mindstorm is a programming environment that creates a robot application by graphical programming. Each hardware component is packaged in one module, and can be connected in a simple manner (without requiring soldering) [14]. The Topobo is an educational tool kit for children to learn about kinetic movement and locomotion [20]. Topobo allows the user to record their desired movement by twisting the motorized pieces.

The PINOKY is also a configurable robot module that allows the user to transform any plush toy into an interactive robot by augmenting it with a computer system. The device can work as a standalone or in a network, and they communicate with each other over a wireless network system. Thus, the number of devices can be changed freely according to the user's requirement.

DESIGN GOAL

PINOKY was designed to convert existing plush toys into soft interactive robots. Because PINOKY is to be attached to a user's personal plush toys, we needed to be careful when coming up with the design. We thus set the following design goals:

Easy to use ...The device must be able to be used by children as well, so its usage should be intuitive.

No damage to plush toy ...Using the device should not damage or require the user to modify the plush toy in any way, because it is the user's personal item.

Easily attachable and removable without requiring special tools ...Children should be able to attach and remove the device easily and quickly without help from adults.

Scalability ...The device should be attachable to any plush toy on almost any location on the toy. More than one device should be attachable.

Aesthetically pleasing ...Aesthetics is essential for plush toys, so the device should look aesthetically pleasing on the toy even when not in use.

Safe and robust ...As the device is attached externally, it should be safe (for example, it should not catch the user's fingers). Moreover, it should not break if dropped.

Adequate movement actuation ...The device should be able to recreate most animations that users use when playing with plush toys.

We will discuss the validity of our design in the Discussion section on the basis of the results obtained from the user study.

THE PINOKY SYSTEM

A major innovation of PINOKY is that it is unobtrusive and easy to attach. It is an external attachment that can animate any part of any plush toy. PINOKY is easy to attach and remove, similar to how one puts on and removes a bracelet, and is crafted to look like an accessory. All electronic parts are packaged in the module, and it is used wirelessly.

Overview

The PINOKY system (Figure 2) consists of a microcontroller (Arduino Pro Mini), a pair of DC servomotors, a pair of photoreflectors (photosensor, IR light), a wireless module (XBee Series 1), and a Li-Po battery. Each servomotor is in contact with the surface of the plush toy through an arm, and causes the area in contact to bend by pushing on the covering. The photoreflectors are used to measure the angle at which the joint is bent. A pair of strong magnets holds PINOKY in position, enabling the user to attach and remove it without using special tools. The user is also able to synchronize the motors of multiple PINOKYs using ZigBee communication. The case is made of laser-cut acrylic and covered with felt to give it a look and feel similar to that of a plush toy (Figure 3).

Actuation

Preliminary design experiments

Before we decided on the current method that we are using to animate plush toys, we developed two prototypes. One was a clip-type device that creates motion by clipping the surface of the plush toy. However, this method does not enable dynamic swinging movement. The other, an implementation more similar to that of the current system, uses a pair of DC motors and gears. However, we abandoned this idea because the gears damage the surface of the plush toy due to friction.

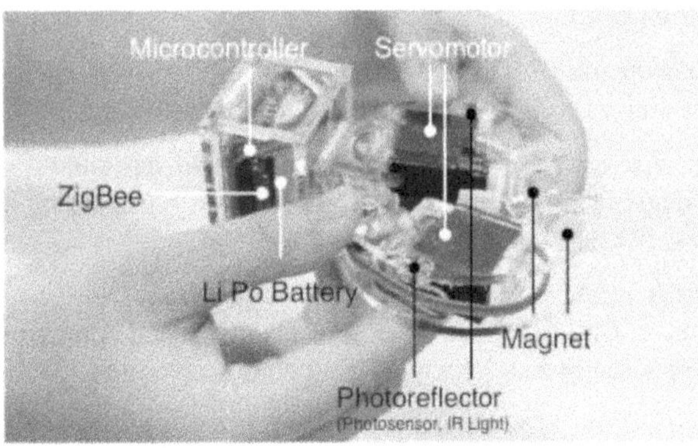

Figure 2. Hardware components.

Figure 3. Design prototypes of PINOKY.

Current implementation

We developed a ring-type actuator that can be attached to and removed from any plush toy. Our prototype actuator creates joint movement using two servomotors (CORONA CS-929MG). Each is fitted with an arm that displaces the surface of the toy. The joint is bent by pushing on the cover (Figure 4). By changing the servomotor speed and rotation angle, we can dynamically control the speed and joint angle of the plush toy. The arms are positioned so that they do not extend beyond the device. We have successfully used PINOKY on plush toys with knit and fleece fabrics. However, it is less effective on cotton stretch fabrics. Filling material like cotton, beans, and sponge can be used without any problems. However, PINOKY is less able to generate identifiable motion on plush toys with high-density filling material (e.g. sand). The diameter of plush toy that can be used depends on device diameter. In our observations, if the PINOKY ring has a diameter d, plush toys within the range of diameter d - 1cm to d + 2cm can be used. The maximal velocity of limb is 0.23sec/60°, and maximal resolution is 0.67° per 1 step. For an 8.5 cm plush toy limb, the joint angle range is $-50° < \theta < 50°$.

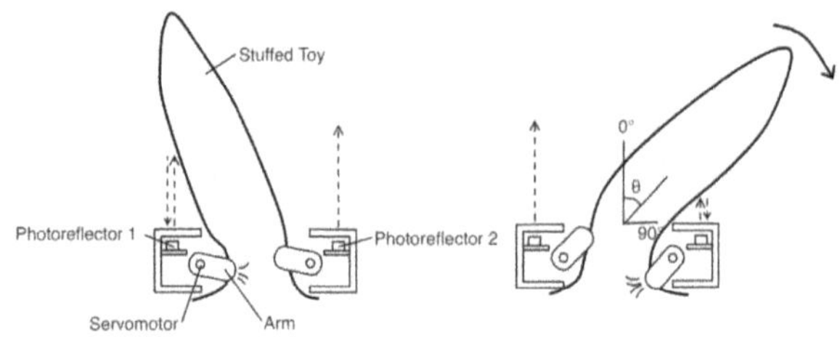

Figure 4. Actuation principle: a pair of DC servomotors push on the toy's cover; two photoreflectors sense joint angle θ by measuring distance between sensor and cover.

Sensing

To measure the joint angle, we use a pair of photoreflectors (photosensor and IR LED), which are generally used to measure the distance to objects. As shown in Figure 4, they are embedded in the device at either end of the ring, and they measure the distance to the surface of the toy. When the joint bends, one of the sensors becomes closer to the surface.

We conducted an experiment to investigate the relationship between the change in the joint angle and the photoreflective properties of the sensors (Figure 5). The limb length was 8.5 cm, and the limb was bent from −50 degrees to 50° by hand at intervals of 2°. The results are shown in Figure 5; the red line shows the photovoltaic voltage when a hand covered the sensor. As shown in the figure, the range of joint angles that the system can measure is $\theta < -31.2°$, $34.2° < \theta$.

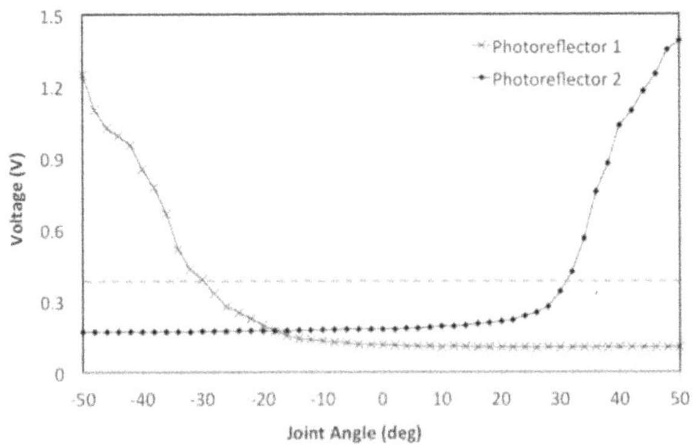

Figure 5. Measurable joint angle range.

Communication

A wireless communication device (ZigBee) is embedded in PINOKY. It is energy efficient and has a self-organization network function. The ZigBee module is able to communicate not only with PCs but also with other ZigBee modules directly without using a server on a PC. In this work, it was used as a standalone module without PC support. However, the device is designed to support other configurations. The use of ZigBee enables the number of devices to be flexibly increased.

Basic Interaction

We created two basic interaction modes for PINOKY on the basis of those of Topobo [20]. The user can switch between them by pushing one of the three colored buttons on the side of the device (see Figure 3).

Record and play mode

In record and play mode, the user can record the behavior desired by directly moving the joint to which the device is attached. The microcontroller memory is sufficient to record behavior for up to 1 minute. The plush toy can then execute the recorded movements.

Synchronize mode

Through the ZigBee network, multiple PINOKYs can be synchronized with each other.

USER STUDY

A user study was conducted to determine the validity of our design direction, evaluate the usability of the PINOKY device, and see how participants react to the concept. Basic interactions between participants and the devices were observed, and feedback was obtained from the participants for the purpose of improving future versions. There was no comparison study performed as there are no existing devices that control plush toys in a similar manner.

Participants

We recruited 51 participants by placing a poster describing PINOKY at the entrance to the study area (in a science museum in Japan) that invited passersby to participate. They were between 2 and 70 years old (average: 23.8 years, standard deviation (SD): 19 years); 24 were male and 27 were female. The number of children from 2 to 9 years old was 18. Participants who were 3 years old and younger were assisted by a parent and the experimenter while using the device. All participants had no prior experience using the device.

Environmental Setup

A closed environment was created by using screen partitions. The participants were seated (individually or in a group) across a table from the experimenter. Each trial was video-recorded.

Experimental Design

Each experimental session consisted of three phases: 1) completion of a questionnaire to survey how plush toys are used in the participant's daily life, 2) observation of how the participants played with plush toys without PINOKY, 3) observation of how they played with plush toys with PINOKY, completion of a questionnaire to survey their reactions to the device, and an interview to solicit their thoughts on the concept.

For the first phase, the participants aged 14 and older (30 participants) completed a pre-experiment questionnaire about the plush toys that they owned. The purpose was to learn about the participants' impressions of plush toys, how many and what types of plush toys they owned, and what kind of memories they associated with them. Occasionally, a casual interview would be carried out as well.

The second phase was a general observation of how the participants interacted with plush toys. They were not told of this observation so that they would not feel self-conscious, thus enabling us to observe their natural interactions with plush toys. During this phase, we did not show the device to the participants. We also carried out a casual interview after the observation.

In the third phase, the PINOKY device was introduced by the experimenter, who explained and demonstrated the two basic functions (record and playback, and synchronization). 5 devices and 12 plush toys (6 humanoid, 3 fish, a teddy bear, an octopus, and a snake) were placed on the table. The participants were then allowed free selection of the number of devices and the type of plush toy to play with, and were allowed a minimum of 10 minutes to freely play with them. Their actions were observed. At the end of this phase, the participants aged 10 and older (32 participants) answered a post-experiment questionnaire about their reactions to PINOKY, and they were interviewed about their thoughts on the concept.

RESULTS

Plush Toy Usage in Daily Life

The 30 participants who answered the pre-experiment questionnaire about the plush toys that they owned ranged in age from 14 to 70 (average: 34.7 years, standard deviation (SD): 13.7 years), 11 male and 19 female. They were encouraged to describe their plush toys: shape and size, location in the house, memories associated with them, and so on. The results showed that about 70% of the participants owned more than one plush toy. The mean number of plush toys owned was 13.6 (SD: 14.5) and was affected by the family configuration.

Participants remembered the circumstances under which they received the plush toys, and had some memory associated with about 76% of the plush toys on the list: about 58% of them were received as a gift on special occasions such as a birthday.

The results also showed that about 73% of the participants' plush toys were placed at easily visible locations, such as around the bed (~34%), on a shelf (~16%), and on the sofa (~9%). However, about 23% had been hidden away in a closet, a toy box, or elsewhere.

How Participants Played with Plush Toys without PINOKY

Our observations of how participants played freely with the plush toys were useful when designing the interactions using PINOKY to convert an existing plush toy into an interactive toy. We focused on how the participants interacted with the plush toy.

Some movements we observed the participants making with the plush toy were dancing and jumping. Most participants pretended that the plush toy was alive and used it to talk to someone else. One participant said, "*I often use a plush toy as spokesperson to help me convey what I want to tell my child.*" Several other participants used plush toys to play house. Another participant said that her child found it interesting when she synchronized the movements of two plush toys. For these activities, the plush toys' gestures were created by bending the arms, legs, neck, and tail, and voice was added accordingly (Figure 6).

How Participants Played with Plush Toys with PINOKY

Usability

All participants, across a wide age range (2 to 70 years old), were able to easily attach and remove the device from almost any part of a plush toy. While a quick demonstration was given to all participants before the experiment began, it was observed that some children were able to attach and remove the device even before the demonstration was given. This shows that our device design makes it generally intuitive to use.

The post-experiment questionnaire consisted of eight ease-of-use statements. The results are shown in Table 1, which

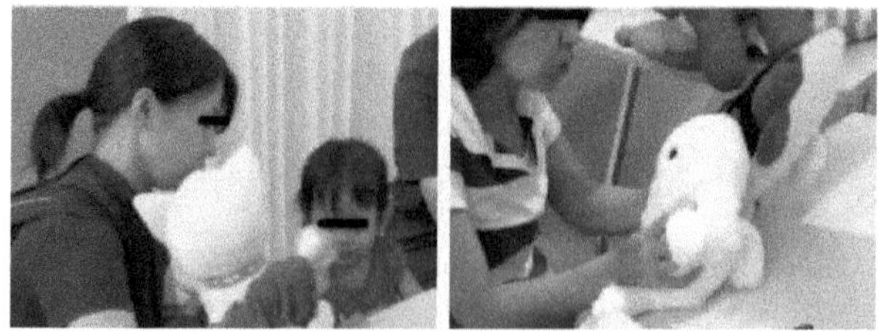

Figure 6. Participants demonstrate how they play with plush toys, bending the limbs (left), synchronizing the movements of similar-shaped plush toys (right).

Table 1. Results of post-experiment questionnaire

No.	Question	Mean	SD	%
1	It was enjoyable to me that the plush toy moved.	5.19	1.07	78.1
2	I was able to use the device easily.	5.16	1.54	71.9
3	I was able to use the device to give movement to the plush toy easily.	5.16	1.44	71.9
4	I was able to use the device with confidence.	4.34	1.57	43.8
5	I think that most people will be able to use the device to animate their plush toys.	4.81	1.42	59.4
6	I think that the device is an adequate one to animate the plush toy.	4.16	1.35	43.8
7	I felt the need to learn many things in order to operate the device.	3.59	1.56	31.3
8	I felt the need to concentrate while using the device.	3.19	1.57	18.8

shows the mean, SD, and percentage of positive responses (>4 on a 7-point Likert scale). 25 users reported that the device was enjoyable to use (Q1: 78.1% positive responses). 23 reported that the device was easy to use (Q2: 71.9%). Many participants (68.7%) reported that they did not feel the need to have to learn how to use it (Q7) and that they could easily use it to give movement to a plush toy (Q3). However, 56.2% of the participants reported that they did not feel confident using the device (Q4).

Number of devices, location of attachment

It was observed that many participants realized that they could attach multiple devices to a plush toy such as an octopus (one to each tentacle) or a snake (multiple devices along the body) and thereby create more complex animations using synchronization mode. It was also observed that different users attached the devices to different parts of a plush toy (Figure 7).

Difference between user expectations and system performance

As this device is still in the early prototype phase, only two sensing points were provided. Initially, some participants were unable to manipulate the plush toy to enable the sensors to detect the user-input movement properly when using the record and playback function. However, once the sensor locations were pointed out to them, they were able to use the function without any problem. Furthermore, there were times when the limb of the plush toy was too short to have its movement detected by the sensors.

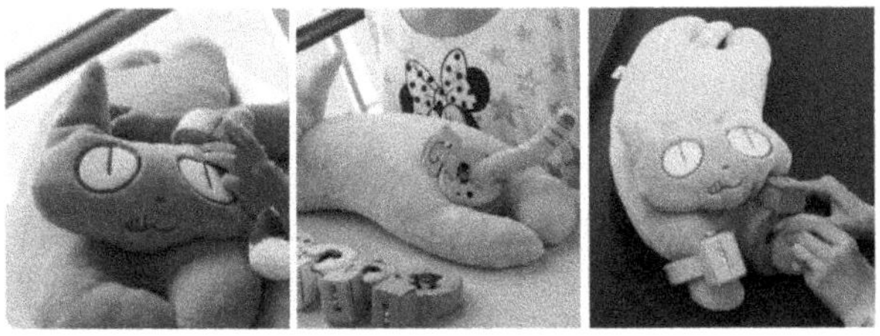

Figure 7. Attachment location: ear (left), tail (center), and arms (right).

Likewise, when told about the record and playback function, many users expected full functionality. Thus, while the device is only able to record a forward/backward motion, there were some users who tried to make the plush toy move in a circular manner.

Finally, some of the participants expressed a desire for a smaller device as they felt that it was too chunky. While a smaller device is also something that we hope to create, it is difficult to do so with current technology.

Different styles of play related to demographics

Since all the participants were allowed to freely play with the device, we could observe the relationship between demographics and device use (Figure 8).

Male participants tended to use the devices on more than one plush toy. They also tended to use more devices than the female participants.

Participants who were 2 years old played with the device under the guidance of an adult (parent or experimenter). A 2-year-old girl found the device scary and vehemently refused to allow her mother to attach the device to the plush toy, immediately removing it if attached. A few 2-year-old participants showed no interest in the device. This might be because they were unable to fully understand the concept or because the movements of the plush toys were not big enough. In general, it was observed that the 2-year-old participants were unable to operate the device on their own. The attachment and removing of the device was mostly left up to the adult, with the child occasionally trying to help.

The 3-year-old participants generally needed the guidance of an adult (although one did not need help). One 3-year-old boy was observed using the record and playback function successfully. However, during the synchronization, he focused on moving the plush toy instead of watching the synchronized animation. Another 3-year-old participant was observed attaching the device to random locations on the plush toy. Instead of deriving fun from seeing the plush toy become animated, she seemed to have more fun opening and closing the device. In general, the participants of this age were able to attach and remove the device without help and were able to grasp how to operate the device on their own.

Participants of elementary and junior high school age were allowed to play with the device without adult guidance. Two participants were observed to enjoy playing with the device but eventually removed all the devices and proceeded to have fun hitting each other with the plush toys. In general, all participants were observed to be able to fully utilize the device without any problem. They tried both functions of the device on several different plush toys. These participants tended to enjoy the playtime more in the presence of another person (participants showed off the movements they created to their family).

Participants in the age range of 20 to 39 years, although to varying degrees, showed surprise and a sense of wonderment when the plush toy moved. These reactions were typically more clearly expressed by female participants, with the younger participants showing bigger reactions. Participants also showed an interest (more so for male participants) in the technology behind the device.

There seemed to be a correlation between the age of the participants and how much emotion they displayed. As compared to the previous age category (20 to 39), participants in the age range of 40 to 59 were observed to generally have less reaction and to have more of an air of understanding after they managed to make the device move as demonstrated. There was, however, one exception to this observation. One 59-year-old participant showed much joy when the plush toy moved. She also enjoyed attaching many devices to the plush toy and synchronizing all of them. This might be a cultural difference as this participant was an Australian, while the rest of our participants were Japanese.

Lastly, participants 60 years old and above did not show much reaction. Most of these participants were able to understand the operation of the device. However, there was one participant (70 years old) who took some time to fully comprehend the idea and operate the device properly.

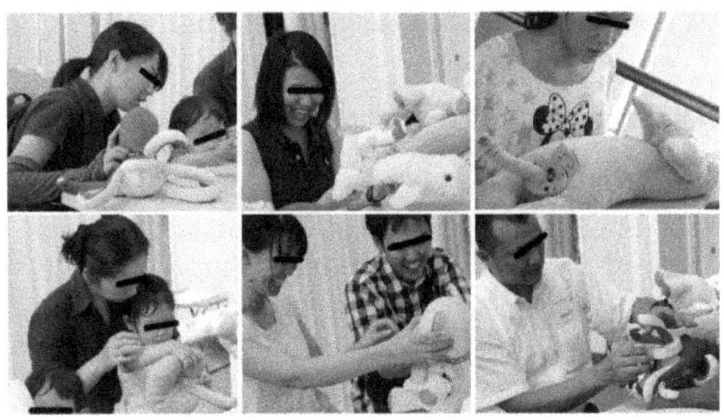

Figure 8. Images of participants using PINOKY.

Difference in impressions between individual experience and group experience

There was a noticeable difference in the amount of satisfaction the participants derived from using PINOKY individually and in a group (two people or more). The results were analyzed with a between-subjects design analysis of variance (ANOVA). The survey responses from the participants who used the device in a group situation were more positive than those from the participants who used the device individually: Q1 ($F(1,30) = 36.8750, p<.01$) and Q3 ($F(1,30) = 66.2188, p<.05$). This may be because the participants in a group were able to share their play experience with each other and take turns controlling in synchronization mode (one participant commented that it was more enjoyable to him that someone else animated his plush toy rather than animating the plush toy himself). Additionally, participants in a group found the device easier to use than participants who used the device individually. This may be because they had someone (who was not a stranger) to turn to for help if they were unable to make the device operate as they intended.

DISCUSSION

Plush Toys in the Home

From the survey results in phase 1, we can conclude that ownership of plush toys is common, that they are easily visible in the home, and that most owners have memories associated with them. Also, from our observations of how the participants naturally played with plush toys, we can conclude that most of the participants played with a plush toy by giving it some form of animation.

Validity of Design

Here we review the appropriateness of our design goals on the basis of the results of the survey and our observations of the participants' interactions with plain plush toys. We also examine whether our implementation satisfies these goals on the basis of our observations of how the participants used PINOKY.

Easy to use ...The child participants started playing with the plush toys immediately upon picking them up. Any enhancement to a plush toy should not interrupt such immediate interaction. All participants were observed to be able to use the device without any practice, showing that the device is easy to use.

No damage to plush toy ..From the survey, we learned that many of the participants had strong attachments to their plush toys, so they would likely not be happy to have their plush toys cut open so that movement actuators can be embedded. Our device does not require any alteration to the plush toy, and no damage to the surface of any of the plush toys used in the experiment was detected after their use.

Easily attachable and removable without requiring special tools ...One participant commented: "*I wash my plush toy whenever it gets dirty.*" This shows the importance of the design goal: easily attachable and removable. The plush toy should be easily washable. Our device is held in place by a pair of magnets, and it was observed that even some of the 2-year-old participants were able to attach and remove the device without help.

Scalability ...We observed that participants move various parts of a plush toy when playing with it. This shows the importance of scalability. Participants were seen to able to attach and use as many devices as they pleased, as the ZigBee module enables multiple simultaneous connections. Some participants encountered the size limitation of PINOKY when they tried to attach it to a part of the toy that was too big to fit within the device.

Aesthetically pleasing ...Many participants indicated that they display their plush toys in their rooms, which shows the importance of aesthetics. Covering the device with felt so that it matched the texture and look of plush toys seems to be effective as there were no complaints from the participants about device appearance. However, from earlier observations of the 2-year-old participants, it was seen that some tore off the device. This may be because they still saw it as an alien object, different from their familiar mental image of a plush toy. This shows that there is still room for improvement, such as by shrinking the size to something more acceptable, and redesigning the appearance to look more similar to that of an accessory or a wearable.

Safe and robust ..Children often played with the plush toys in a rough manner, so safety and robustness are important. None of the participants were injured during the course of the experiment, demonstrating that the device can be safely used even by very young children. Devices were dropped many times during the experiment, and some participants exerted much force on them. After four days of tests, all the devices were examined and found to be still working properly, showing that our design is stable and durable.

Adequate movement actuation ...Our observations of how the participants play with plush toys revealed that plush toys can be animated so as to perform various types of movement: jumping, walking, and so on. The swing motion that PINOKY was designed to create constituted the most often used animation during our observations. We believe that the swing motion is an adequate one for expressing many different types of emotions (for example, many different expressions such as agreement and dislike can be created by manipulating the neck of a plush toy using the swing motion). Therefore, we can say that our design is sufficient to accommodate most motions that users would expect from a plush toy.

From the observations and survey results, we can see that the device design fulfills almost all the requirements we set at the beginning, thus making it a very effective one. In general, the users reacted very positively, and it was observed that they derived enjoyment from seeing the plush toy moves autonomously. They were pleasantly surprised by the movement, and some even commented that it was as if the toy was alive. However, there was a slight problem with regards to scalability, and this will be discussed in the Limitations and Future Work section.

Example Applications

Since users are now able to do things previously impossible, such as controlling multiple plush toys simultaneously, and recording motion data and have it played back. This opens up a variety of new play experiences with plush toys. On the basis of our results, we conceptualized several potential applications of PINOKY.

Telecommunications

Our observation that some participants used a plush toy as an avatar raises the possibility of using PINOKY for a new form of communication, over and above voice and video communication. Plush toys located remotely can be synchronized so that callers communicate not only by voice but also by using the toy's movements to express their thoughts and feelings. A system could be developed for synchronizing PINOKY devices through a TCP/IP network, and other interfaces such as iPhone and Kinect could be used to expand the range of communication.

Story telling

From our user study, we learned that children sometimes create stories using plush toys by giving them voice and movement. Plush toys typically have a humanoid or animal shape, so they are well suited for use as characters in a story. Since PINOKY can be easily programmed, children can easily input the desired movement by simply manipulating the toy. Since the input data is archived, children can program several plush toys and then have them interact.

Watching television programs with PINOKY

Being able to watch television programs with one's favorite plush toy is a unique and enjoyable experience. Although we have created a prototype PINOKY that would cause a plush toy to react during the climax of a horror movie or comedy in order to enhance the emotions of fear or amusement, the behavior currently needs to be hard-coded. In the future, we hope to combine this with an existing video service such as YouTube. By using the annotation function, anyone could control the reaction timing (if they provide the API and if PINOKY can understand the language that the user inputs).

Limitations and Future Work

Our ring device is a "proof-of-concept" implementation, so there are some hardware limitations. We observed that for the plush toys with thinner limbs, the participants had to ensure that the limb was properly inserted between the actuators to be able to obtain the correct movement. We hope to develop a device that is able to adapt its size to the target part of the plush toy. Also, some participants indicated that they would prefer a smaller device. PINOKY is currently implemented using a general-purpose microcontroller (Arduino) and a commercial ZigBee module. In a more customized implementation, we could select components with a smaller footprint and integrate them into a more power-efficient system with a smaller form factor. Moreover, there is a trade-off between servomotor size and torque. While small plush toys can be controlled via other methods such as using smaller actuators with lower torque (such as bio-metal ones), bigger plush toys cannot. The development of smaller actuators with high torque would greatly reduce device size. In the meantime, we are currently working to make the device less noticeable by packaging it into accessories for plush toys, such as the shoulder straps of a backpack.

While it is possible to express many different emotions using the swinging motion that PINOKY can actuate, there are still some emotions that cannot be expressed yet as they require different movements. We are looking at designing a device that can create other types of movement: twisting, expansion and contraction, and so on. We are also working on other attachable devices that can create a jumping and swinging movement for the whole plush toy (for example, a tail-like device that can cause a body-shaking movement). With the new devices, we will conduct another test to see how the new motions affect how participants play with plush toys, and whether it enhances the play experience.

Another limitation of PINOKY is its sensitivity to sunlight. This is because we use photoreflectors, which detect both the infrared light from the emitters and infrared radiation from the sun. This may be solvable using an ultrasonic sensor. Some participants had expressed a wish for alternative input methods, such as using voice instructions. We will thus also look at introducing more input methods, e.g., making a plush toy react by shaking or squeezing it (done by attaching a sensor module consisting of acceleration and pressure sensors to the toy's surface material). Furthermore, by using a motion sensor, we can cause a plush toy react when someone enters the room. Ultimately, we aim to utilize these tangible I/O modules as a programming environment to convert a personal plush toy into an interactive robot.

CONCLUSION

PINOKY is a ring-like device that is able to give movement to a plush toy, such as moving its limbs or tail. As opposed to actuators that have to be embedded into the plush toy, our device operates externally. Thus, the user can convert any plush toy into an interactive robot in a non-intrusive manner without having to make any alterations to the toy. Because the electronic parts (microcontroller, battery, sensor, and actuator) are in one package and do not require external wiring, the user can easily attach the device to any plush toy as an accessory.

We conducted a user study to determine the validity of the design direction of PINOKY, and evaluate the usability of the device. Our surveys of how plush toys are used in daily life showed that ownership of plush toys is common (about 70% of the participants owned more than one plush toy) and that most owners have memories associated with them. Our observations of how the participants used PINOKY showed that all of them were able to fully utilize the device without any serious problems. The results indicate that there are various potential applications of PINOKY.

REFERENCES

1. Breazeal, C., Kidd, C., Thomaz A. L., Hoffman, G. and Berlin, M. Effects of Nonverbal Communication on Efficiency and Robustness in Human-Robot Teamwork. In *Proc. IROS '05*, IEEE (2005), 708..713.
2. Buechley, L., Eisenberg, M., Catchen, J. and Crockett, A. The LilyPad Arduino: using computational textiles to investigate engagement, aesthetics, and diversity in computer science education. In *Proc. CHI '08*, ACM (2008), 423..432.
3. Camp Quality. http://www.campquality.org.au/
4. Coelho, M. and Zigelbaum, J. Shape-changing interfaces. Personal Ubiquitous Comput. 15, 2, 161..173.
5. Furby (1998). Furby, from http://www.furby.com
6. Furukawa, M., Uema, Y., Sugimoto, M. and Inami, M. Fur interface with bristling effect induced by vibration. In *Proc. AH '10*, ACM (2010), Article 17, 6 pages.
7. Ghan, J., Steger, R. and Kazerooni, H. Control and system identification for the Berkeley lower extremity exoskeleton (BLEEX), *Advanced Robotics 20*, 9 (2006), 989..1014.
8. Greenberg, S. and Fitchett, C. Phidgets: Easy development of physical interfaces through physical widgets. In *Proc. UIST '01*, ACM (2001), 209..218.
9. Hadari, F. http://www.speakingpuppetry.com/
10. Ishikawa, T. and Hasegawa, S. The Motion Control of Soft Feeling Stuffed Animal Robot. *Technical Report of Information Processing Society of Japan (2011)*, Vol.2011-EC-19, No.13. (in Japanese)
11. Johnson, M. P., Wilson, A., Blumberg, B., Kline, C. and Bobick, A. Sympathetic interfaces: using a plush toy to direct synthetic characters. In *Proc. CHI '99*, ACM (1999), 152..158.
12. Sugiura, Y., Kakehi, G., Withana, A., Lee, C., Nagaya, N., Sakamoto, D., Sugimoto, M., Inami, M. and Igarashi, T. Detecting shape deformation of soft objects using directional photoreflectivity measurement, In *Proc. UIST '11*, ACM (2011), 509 .516.
13. Koizumi, N., Yasu, K., Liu, A., Sugimoto, M. and Inami, M., Animated paper: A toolkit for building moving toys, *Computers in Entertainment (CIE) 8*, 2 (2011).
14. Lego. Lego Mindstorm. http://mindstorms.lego.com/
15. Marti, S. and Schmandt, C. Physical embodiments for mobile communication agents. In *Proc. UIST '05*, ACM (2005), 231..240.
16. Osawa, H., Ohmura, R. and Imai, M. Using Attachable Humanoid Parts for Realizing Imaginary Intention and Body Image, *International Journal of Social Robotics 1*, 1 (2009), 109..123.
17. Oschuetz, L., Wessolek, D. and Sattler, W. Constructing with movement: kinematics. In *Proc. TEI '10*, ACM (2010), 257-260.
18. Probst, K., Seifried, T., Haller, M., Yasu, K., Sugimoto, M. and Inami, M. Move-it: interactive sticky notes actuated by shape memory alloys. In *Ext. Abst. CHI '11*, ACM (2011), 1393..1398.
19. Puppets in Education. http://www.puppetsineducation.org/
20. Raffle, H., Parkes, A. and Ishii, H. 2004. Topobo: A Constructive Assembly System with Kinetic Memory. In *Proc. CHI '04*, ACM (2004), 869..877.
21. Robot to reduce the stress for victims, Tech-On, Nikkei BP net (June 20, 2011). http://techon.nikkeibp.co.jp/article/NEWS/20110615/192583/. (in Japanese)
22. Sekiguchi, D., Inami, M. and Tachi, S. RobotPHONE: RUI for Interpersonal Communication. In *Ext. Abst. CHI '01*, ACM (2001), 277..278.
23. Shimizu, N., Koizumi, N., Sugimoto, M., Nii, H., Sekiguchi, D., Inami, M. A Teddy-Bear-Based Robotic User Interface, *Computers in Entertainment (CIE) 4*, 3 (2006).
24. Stiehl,W. and Breazeal, C. Design of a Therapeutic Robotic Companion for Relational, Affective Touch. In *Proc. RO-MAN '05*, IEEE (2005), 408..415.
25. Strommen, E. When the interface is a talking dinosaur: learning across media with ActiMates Barney. In *Proc. CHI '98*, ACM (1998). 288..295.
26. Taal, S.R. and Sankai, Y., Exoskeletal Spine and Shoulders for Full Body Exoskeletons in Health Care, *Advances in Applied Science Research 2*, 6 (2011), 270... 286.
27. Ueki, A., Kamata, M. and Inakage, M. Tabby: designing of coexisting entertainment content in everyday life by expanding the design of furniture. In *Proc. ACE '07*, ACM (2007), 72..78.
28. Wada, K. and Shibata, T. Social effects of robot therapy in a care house - change of social network of the residents for two months. In *Proc. ICRA '07*, IEEE (2007), 1250..1255.
29. Winnicott, D. Transitional objects and transitional phenomena - A Study of the First Not -Me Possession, *Int. J. Psychoanal. 34*, (1953), 89-97.
30. Yonezawa, T., Clarkson, B., Yasumura, M. and Mase, K. Context-aware sensor-doll as a music expression device. In *Ext. Abst. CHI '01*, ACM (2001), 307..308.
31. Yoshida, E., Murata, S., Kamimura, A., Tomita, K., Kurokawa, H. and Kokaji, S. A Motion Planning Method for a Self-Reconfigurable Modular Robot, In *Proc. IROS '01*, IEEE (2001), 590..597.

Shape-Changing Interfaces: A Review of the Design Space and Open Research Questions

Majken K. Rasmussen[1], Esben W. Pedersen[2], Marianne G. Petersen[3], Kasper Hornbæk[2]

[1]Aarhus School of Architecture
majken.kirkegaard.rasmussen@aarch.dk

[2]Department of Computer Science
University of Copenhagen
{esbenwp, kash}@diku.dk

[3]Department of Computer Science
Aarhus University
mgraves@cs.au.dk

ABSTRACT
Shape change is increasingly used in physical user interfaces, both as input and output. Yet, the progress made and the key research questions for shape-changing interfaces are rarely analyzed systematically. We review a sample of existing work on shape-changing interfaces to address these shortcomings. We identify eight types of shape that are transformed in various ways to serve both functional and hedonic design purposes. Interaction with shape-changing interfaces is simple and rarely merges input and output. Three questions are discussed based on the review: (a) which design purposes may shape-changing interfaces be used for, (b) which parts of the design space are not well understood, and (c) why studying user experience with shape-changing interfaces is important.

Author Keywords
Shape-changing interfaces; shape displays; organic user interfaces; actuated interfaces; non-visual actuators

ACM Classification Keywords
H5.2. Information interfaces and presentation (e.g., HCI): User Interfaces---Haptic I/O, Input Devices and strategies, Interaction styles.

General Terms
Human Factors

INTRODUCTION
The ability of objects to change shape plays a key role in nature (e.g., the Southern White-faced Owl can enlarge its body to scare enemies or shrink it to appear as a tree branch), in design (e.g., the invention of self-inflating life vests), in architecture (e.g., buildings that automatically reconfigure offices based on occupants' habits), as well as in many other fields. The research area of shape-changing interfaces aims at using some of these qualities to enhance our interaction with digital information.

Examples of shape-changing interfaces include displaying directions on a mobile phone through deformations of its shape [15], a foam surface with embedded shape-memory alloys that may be programmed to change shape [10], a water faucet that uses changing postures to raise awareness about water consumption [48], and buttons capable of modifying their shape [12]. Recent reviews contain many other examples (see [9,37]).

In spite of the inventiveness of these examples, we see a number of limitations of the research on shape-changing interfaces. First, the literature mainly contains point designs. Few papers survey the design space for shape-changing interfaces, so as to put existing work into perspective and identify underexplored directions. Second, research on shape-changing interfaces is mostly a technical enterprise. The psychological and artistic aspects of shape change are rarely discussed. Third, research in shape-changing interfaces rarely focuses on interaction and does not relate shape change to models of interaction (e.g., on reality-based interaction [24] or tangible user interfaces [11,49]).

The aim of this paper is to review existing research on shape-changing interfaces. We analyze the change in shape, the dynamics of change, the interaction, and the design purposes. Based on the review of these parameters of the design space, we discuss open research questions and under-researched areas. For practitioners, the paper aims at providing an overview of the design possibilities in shape-changing interfaces. For researchers, the benefit of the paper is to outline open research questions.

SCOPE AND MOTIVATION
The interfaces relevant to the present paper have been discussed under different headings: Actuated Interfaces [37], Kinetic Interaction [34], Organic User Interfaces [9], Kinetic Organic Interfaces [34], Pro-active Architecture [31] and Computational Composites [50]. The present paper discusses these together under the phrase shape-changing interface. A shape-changing interface uses physical change of shape as input or output. We follow earlier work that has used self-actuated change as a defining characteristic for such interfaces [37]. Additionally, we require that the self-actuation must be controllable so that the object can return to its initial state and repeat the shape change. Interfaces that cannot directly control their shape are thus left out of

this paper. Finally, we are concerned only with non-WIMP types of interfaces and non-desktop hardware.

Previous papers have begun to characterize the potential of interfaces using shape change. In 2008, Communications of the ACM ran a special issue on organic user interfaces [52], the TEI conference has featured several overviews of shape-changing interfaces [37], and Coelho and Zigelbaum [9] recently reviewed the potential of shape-changing materials to HCI, focusing in particular on technology for invoking shape change.

Compared to these earlier reviews, the present paper offers three novelties. First, we base our review on a selection of 44 papers on shape change. We collected these by browsing proceedings of relevant conferences, following references in and citations to well-known papers on shape change, and searching the reference lists of the reviews mentioned above. The list of papers is available from the authors. Second, we discuss four aspects of shape change: the change in shape, the dynamics of change, the interaction, and its purpose. Previous reviews have only focused on a subset of these. Third, we discuss state-of-the-art, as well as open research questions and blind spots. In particular, existing reviews have mostly been about technology; we try to complement this by also focusing on the experience of using shape-changing interfaces.

TYPES OF CHANGE IN SHAPE

This section presents an overview of the types of change in shape that are used in the papers informing this review (see Figure 1). The types are changes in: *orientation, form, volume, texture, viscosity, spatiality, adding/subtracting,* and *permeability*. Changes in viscosity and spatiality do not necessarily deform objects (i.e., change shape in a strong sense), but are included because they may lead to the experience of shape change.

Changes in *orientation* distort the original shape through rotations or changes in direction, while preserving the recognisability of the original form. Orientation is a widely used means to establish shape change [6,33,39,44,48]. The Thrifty Faucet [48] communicates information on water consumption and hygiene to the user through deforming its shape into various postures, using changes in rotation and direction.

Form changes are defined by transformations that preserve the approximate volume of the shape while changing its overall form [10,26,27,32,33,47,56]. Horev's Morphing Harddisk concept [20] changes form by sucking in or blowing up a cube shape, thereby hiding or revealing the cube's skeleton structure. The concept applies the form change to visualize information about harddisk activity, synchronization, and the remaining space on the harddisk. Another example is the Shape-Changing Mobile [17], a mock-up phone that changes its form by using a set of small motors embedded in a flexible chassis.

Changes in *volume* maintain the approximate form and are used in some shape-changing interfaces [16,26,32,59]. The Inflatable Mouse [26] uses change in volume, through inflating and deflating a form, in order to accommodate both fitting into the PC card slot on a computer and having the volume of a comfortable, ergonomic mouse. Although the inflatable mouse changes form to some extent, the most pronounced change is in the change of volume.

Textural changes are small changes on the surface of the shape that add visual and tactile properties without affecting

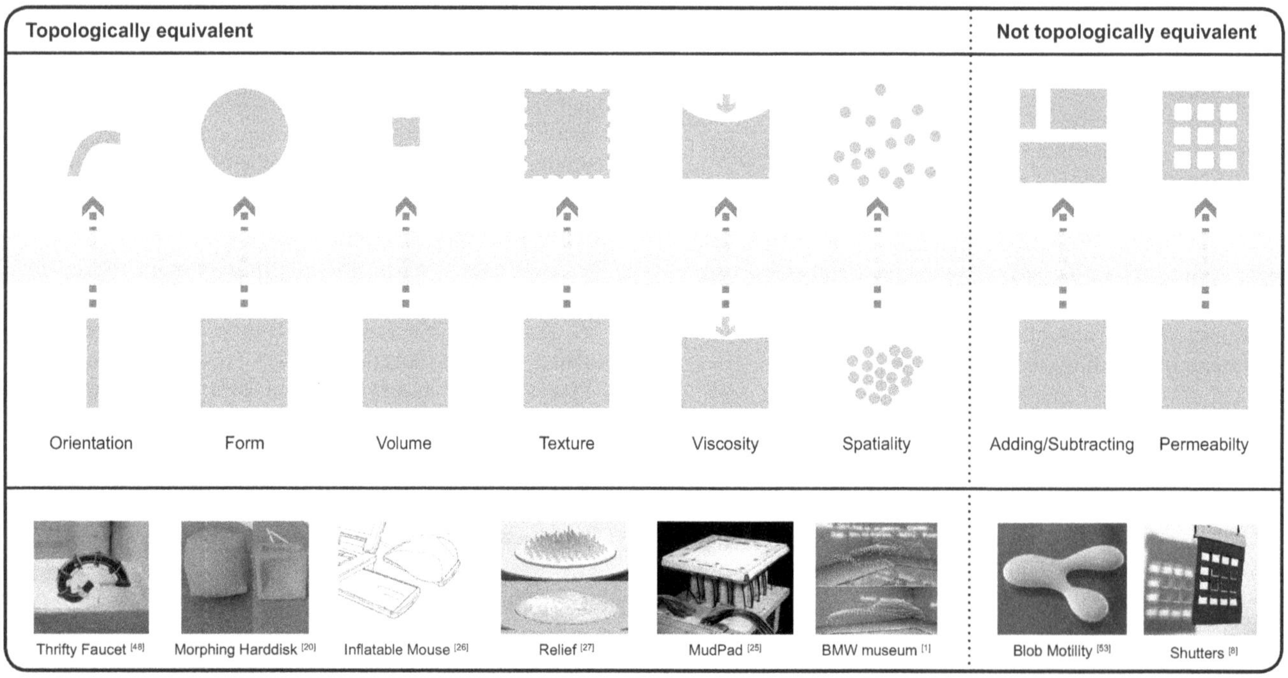

Figure 1. Types of shape change.

the overall form [4,7,12,21,23,38,40,44]. The surface of Leithinger and Ishii's [27] Relief is actuated by an array of 120 motorized pins, which allow users to create and experience digital models of, for instance, a geographical terrain. The pins are covered with lycra, which causes movements of the individual pins to be perceived as textural changes on the surface.

Changes in *viscosity* can result in both physical shape changes and in the illusion of shape change, where the viscosity changes while the original form is maintained. Mudpad [25] uses changes in viscosity as haptic output for a multi-touch surface. The change in viscosity is for instance used for the play button feedback: When the play button is pressed it becomes fluid and the user's finger sinks in. As the music starts playing, a tactile representation of the music's amplitude can be felt on the button. The viscosity change of the surface causes an illusion of the interface changing shape, as users perceive the surface as shifting between hard, soft, and vibrating. In the sample of papers, only Mudpad exploits this means of shape change.

Changes in *spatiality* do not automatically create the illusion of shape change. A change of one element's position in space does not create the illusion of shape change, as the change is typically seen as a repositioning in space. The illusion of shape change through spatial repositioning depends on individual elements being seen as part of a collective structure. When multiple elements are repositioned spatially, they may be perceived as part of the same structure. Like schools of fish group in spherical formations to confuse enemies, changes in the spatial position of individual elements changes the composite form. The only example of shape change through spatial repositioning in the sample of papers is the Kinetic sculpture at the BMW museum in Munich [1] illustrated in Figure 2. The sculpture consists of 714 metal spheres that can be repositioned vertically and thereby lead to perception of a composite form, rather than of individual elements.

All the types of shape change mentioned above are topological equivalent, meaning shapes that can pass from one form to another through continuous deformation, without dividing or joining elements (the left part of Figure 1). Next we describe changes that are not topologically equivalent, for instance because shapes are being split, united, or perforated. However, interfaces rarely use such changes because few materials are capable of producing them.

Shape change through *adding or subtracting* is achieved by transformations that unite or divide elements, while being able to return to the initial shape or shapes. The Blob Motility [53] is an example of an interface that explores the possibilities of creating shape changes that break homeomorphism, through using a magnetic fluid as an interface that is able to split, merged, and moulded into organic shapes through changes in the magnetic field.

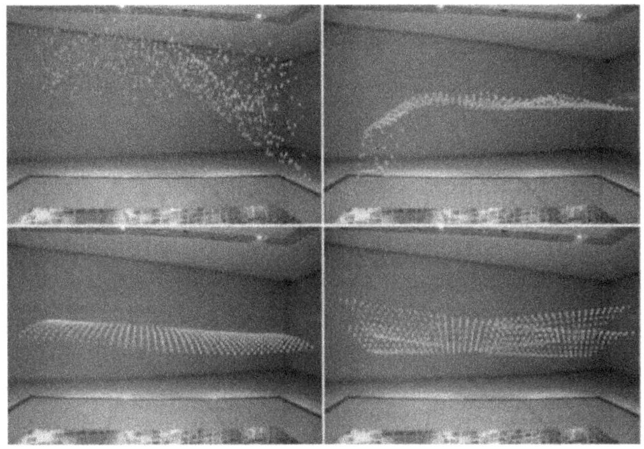

Figure 2. BMW museum kinetic sculpture [1].

Changes in *permeability* are defined by transformations, where the shape is perforated, but able to return to its initial shape. Permeable transformations offer interesting design possibilities, for instance for creating architecture that allow regulation of ventilation flow, daylight intake, or visual privacy. However, current materials are not able to realize this ideal. Shutters [9] imitates a permeable transformation, where parts of a surface can open and close to regulate the flow of air and light. Although the example does not break the homeomorphism of the surface, the imitation exemplifies the potential of permeable transformations.

TYPES OF TRANSFORMATION

In the previous section, we described the endpoints of a change in shape; this section describes the phase between endpoints. We characterize the transformations using the work of Vaughan [51] and its adaptation by Young et al. [55]. Figure 3 shows the kinetic parameters of transformations at the bottom; the top of the figure illustrates how transformations are perceived (expressive parameters).

Kinetic Parameters

Kinetic parameters are physical specifications of the transformation (e.g., speed, tempo, frequency). They include:

Velocity: Describes the speed, acceleration, tempo, vibration, and frequency of an object's movement. The Inflatable Mouse [26] uses changes in tempo and intensity of its up and down movement to express various emotions. Shutters [8] seeks to determine what is the ideal speed for a louver to move. MudPad [25] describes the speed of the changes in viscosity of the interface, being able to switch back and forth within 5 ms.

Path: Describes the movement pattern of a transformation, and thus the line that an object moves along, and whether that movement is smooth/jerky, linear/curved, continuous/intermittent, or pattern/random. Togler and colleagues [48] use a series of images to describe different movement patterns of the Thrifty Facet.

Direction: Describes the directions in which the object moves. The BMW museum kinetic sculpture [1] uses simple up and down movements to create the fluid shape-changing sculpture.

Space: Describes the use of space by the interface, including scale change and form change. In the InSync hard drive [20] the space transformation is described as follows: "Two of the prototype adjacent planes were sliding in parallel to each other, causing the envelope to twist in a way that appeared as if the cube lost its alignment." (p. 27).

A few papers describe these parameters in detail. Shape-changing Mobiles [17] include precise details of how the back plate of the mobile phone change by "...tilting of its back plate by 10° into each direction, extending by up to 15mm in depth" (p. 3077). Several papers mention kinetic changes [5,31,48], but provide few details on how the transformation occurs. It is thus hard to discuss in depth how transformations happen. One reason seems to be that movements often are complex and thus hard to express in text. Videos might provide raw information about the transformation used. For Shade Pixel [21], for example, a video is available that shows the prototype, contextualizes it in relation to related work, and explains its technical construction. Videos are not, however, available for all papers in the sample and often do not focus on illustrating transformations.

Expressive Parameters

Expressive parameters account for how the effect of the kinetic parameters is perceived. A fast, pumping motion might be experienced as agitated; slow, flowing movements might be experienced as similar to grass moved by the wind. The expressive parameters are divided into two types: association and adjectives.

Association

This type of expressivity is about the associations generated by the transformation, in particular whether it is perceived as mechanical or organic. Several of the reviewed papers seek to give "life" to the interfaces through movement. Often papers do not distinguish whether the goal is anthropomorphic or zoomorphic. Togler and colleagues [48] describe The Thrifty Faucet, which "move and behave in life-like manners" (p. 43) and the authors emphasize how continual, small movements "enriched the impression of a living object" (p. 44). In the Inflatable Mouse, life is expressed as a heartbeat, which can alter tempo to create tension [26]. Along the same line, other examples aim to create interfaces that appear to be "living" [6,23,48].

Other researchers seek to use movement to embody the interface with a sense of nature. The movements of Slow Furl [47] are described as a glazier, a frozen river, a landscape, a cloud formation, and an ice wall. In the case of Bamboostic [31], the movement of the individual mechanical "trees" creates the "feel of a rather natural landscape" (p. 76).

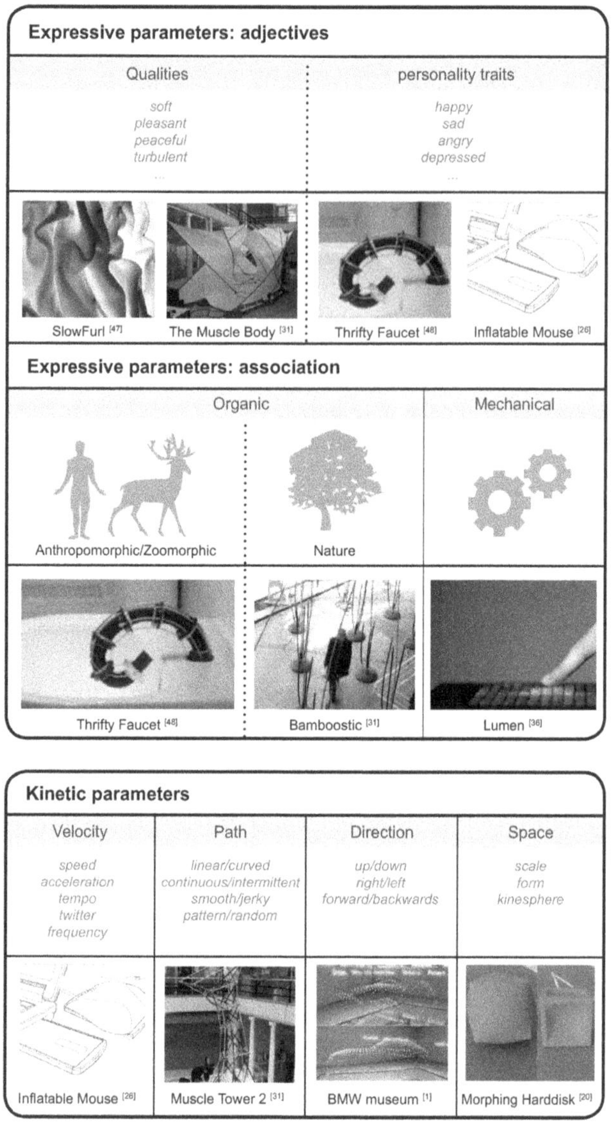

Figure 3. Transformation vocabulary.

Mechanical characteristics are less sought in shape-changing interfaces, possibly because researchers seek to answer the question "what would computers look like if they were more curved, flexible and delicate" [19]. Although a more organic sense is sought, some of the examples might be perceived as mechanical. In Kinematics [32] the two types of kinematic blocks, one shape changing and one rotating, move with repetitive and jerky movements, which give the movement a mechanical feel.

Adjectives

Adjectives describe what type of traits and qualities are ascribed to the movements. The category is divided into *qualities* and *personality traits*. If an interface transforms with a continuous smooth movement, it can be perceived as having pleasant and peaceful *qualities*. Likewise, the movement can be ascribed certain *personality traits*, by associating the movement with the interface being, for instance, relaxed or tired.

The Thrifty Faucet [48] seeks to ascribe personality traits to the faucet through movements. It moves between poses being intended as curious, seeking, or rejecting [48]. Ambient Life [18] aims at giving life to mobile phones and uses, for example, movements of "excitement" to get the user's attention. Oosterhuis and Biloria describe the movements made possible by the muscle wire as soft luxuriant undulations [31], and thus use adjectives to characterize the movement.

The expressive parameters above are often combined, serving both to describe the user experience of transformations and to account for the designer's intentions with the movements. Expressive descriptions that recount the designer's intention with the movements tend to be rather subjective and provide little information about the movements necessary to obtain it. Furthermore, it is rare to see studies of how users actually experience the prototypes. Such studies would allow us to see or validate if the intended experience materializes. Exceptions include The Thrifty Faucet [48] and Topobo [39], both of which report evaluations of how users perceive the movements.

INTERACTION

Next, we survey how shape-changing interfaces use physical transformation as input and output. In the reviewed sample of papers, we see three approaches to interaction (see Figure 4): *No interaction* where shape change is used solely as output, *indirect interaction* where shape change occurs based on implicit input, and *direct interaction* where shape change is used as both input and output.

Shape-changing interfaces have the potential to create a bidirectional relationship between the physical and the digital: The shape can be changed both physically by the user (as a means of input) and digitally by the interface (as a means of output). *Direct interaction* takes advantage of this bidirectional relationship, and in some cases *indirect interaction* also uses digital input to change the physical form. However, the majority of reviewed examples only use shape change as a means of output, focusing on the ability to alter the physical shape.

Shape-changing Output - No Interaction

The category of shape-changing interfaces without interaction uses shape change solely as output and disregards user input [4,5,6,8,21].

Some of these interfaces change shape in order to display digital information in physical form, either visually or haptically. For example, Shutters [8] and Shade Pixel [21] use a limited number of "pixels" to communicate with the user, while BubbleWrap [4] vibrates a set of electromagnetic actuators to provide haptic feedback.

Other interfaces use shape change more randomly without attempting to convey information. SlowFurl [47] changes in its own rhythm, engaging a "geological time of imperceptible flow" (p. 2). Likewise, Skorpions [6] (four different kinetic garments) and Vilkas [5] (a kinetic dress) all change shape autonomously and independently of the users' actions.

Indirect Interaction

The interfaces employing indirect interaction use shape change as output, but base the change in shape on implicit

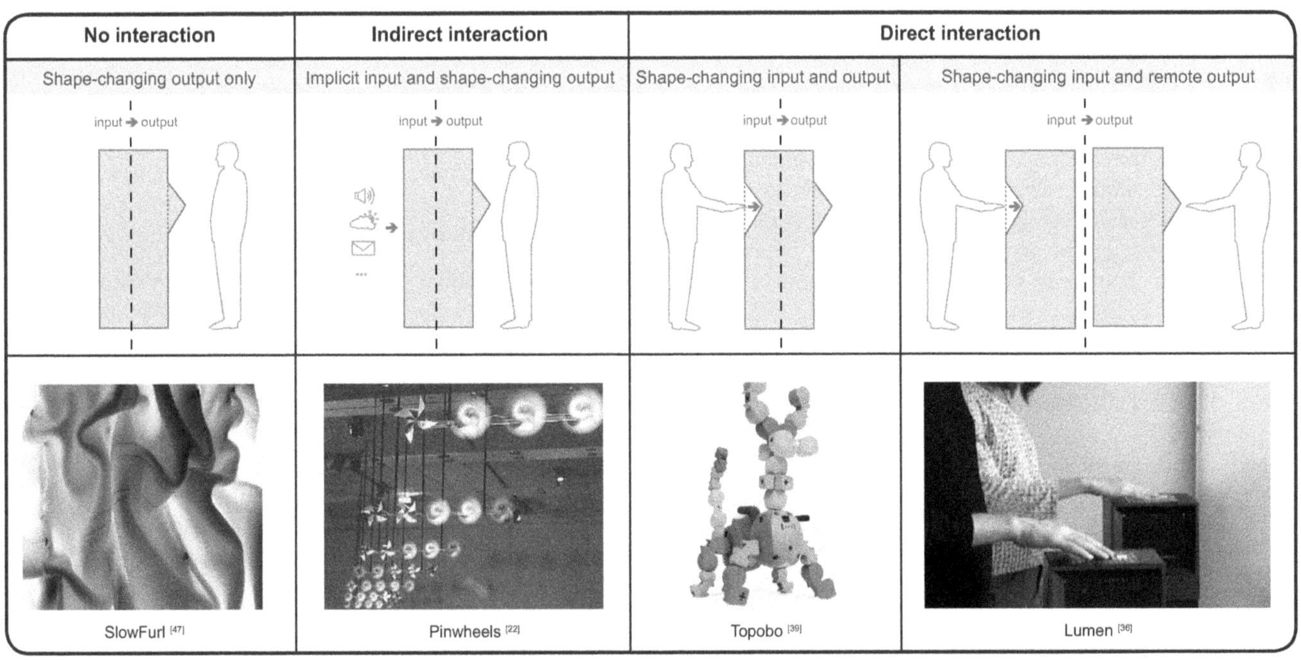

Figure 4. Three approaches to interacting with shape-changing interfaces.

input. We characterize input as implicit, when users may not realize that their actions are being used as input. The Pinwheels installation [22] exemplifies this approach. In Pinwheels, the system monitors human behaviour in its environment and spins its wheels when certain activities occur (e.g., when a person uses the elevator or sends an e-mail). Similarly, Murmur [41], a sonic sculpture, responds to sound input from its surroundings. Oosterhuis and Biloria employ implicit input as the basis for their proactive architectural spaces [31], the muscle projects (Muscle Tower, Muscle Body, Muscle Space and Bamboostic). All of these interfaces respond implicitly to the users' movements in the installation space.

Direct Interaction: Merging Input and Output

This category is defined by interfaces that use shape change both as input and output. The user interacts intentionally with the system through deforming the shape, while changes in shape are simultaneously used as output [20,26,36]. Within the reviewed papers, two approaches to using shape change as input and output exist: *action and reaction* and *input and output.*

With the *action and reaction* approach, the user transforms the shape, which triggers a shape transformation corresponding to the one that the user inputs. For example, the InSync' harddisk [20] must be twisted in order for it to be re-synced. As the synchronization progresses, the twisted cube realigns by slowly twisting back to its initial cubical shape. In Bodyscape [35], a kinetically transformable meshed textile interface, and Topobo [39], a kinetic toy, the user can record an action through transforming the shape and a corresponding movement is played back.

Whereas the *action and reaction* approach employs a turn-taking relationship between the shape-changing input and output, many systems use *input and output* that are not directly related. In the Inflatable Mouse [26], users can input through shape change, either by squeezing the sides or pressing the top of the mouse, thereby manipulating the shape of the mouse. Simultaneously, the mouse may be deformed as means of output by inflating or deflating the shape. This is used for expressing a heartbeat, which could be applied to create tension while playing a game or inform the user of program errors and system warnings. This example uses both shape changing input and output, but in a decoupled manner. Another example is Sprout I/O [7], an array of soft and kinetic textile strands, that uses shape memory alloys both to sense touch and move to display images and animations.

Direct Interaction: Remotely Merging Input and Output

The direct interactions described in the previous category may also be used for linking remotely located interfaces. In this way, the shape changes performed on one interface are transferred to an identical interface, where they are reproduced. One of the applications of the Lumen display [36] uses two separate displays, in order to establish haptic communication between remote participants. The setup allows users to remotely touch and draw simple traces on each other's hand using the Lumen shape display.

PURPOSES OF SHAPE CHANGE

One way to understand shape-changing interfaces is to understand the purpose with which they are designed (i.e., the aims and goals pursued by designers and researchers). In this section we review the purposes as stated by the authors of the papers we review. Typically, the purposes are stated in abstracts, descriptions of prototypes, conclusions, or application scenarios. In the sample of papers, we see four main purposes of using shape change: *functional, hedonic, explorative*, and supplying the field with *toolkits* for designing shape-changing interfaces (Figure 5). Many papers address more than one purpose, but for the sake of mapping the design space of shape-changing interfaces, we discuss each of the four purposes separately in the following sections.

Functional Aims of Shape Change

Within the sample of papers we found a number of specific functional purposes for using shape change, which we present below. In the majority of cases, the purpose reflects the designers' intentions rather than studies of how users experienced the interfaces.

The main functional purpose of applying shape change is to *communicate information* (e.g., [8,17]). Shape change is here used to encode information in a more expressive or efficient manner. Shape-changing Mobiles [17], for instance, uses changes in thickness of the phone to guide users to move in a particular direction, by making the phone slightly thinner in the direction in which to move. In other cases, changes in shape are used as "information displays" [8, p. 13] or to "visualize information" [21, p. 1].

Dynamic affordances are another functional purpose, where shape change is used to communicate possibilities for action. As an example, Harrison and Hudson [12] use pneumatics to add physical shape to buttons, allowing for dynamic affordances depending on digital content. Papers in our review use phrases like "just-in-time affordances" [10, p. 3433] and "dynamic ergonomics" [17, p. 3077].

Another functional purpose of shape change is to use it for providing *haptic feedback* [4,7,12,25,27]. One aim of using shape change as haptic feedback is to provide tactility to touch displays. BubbleWrap [4] uses electromagnetic actuators enclosed in fabric to provide haptic information by making the surface bulge or vibrate or by changing its firmness. Whereas the interfaces mentioned above use haptic feedback to improve usability, systems like Super Cilia Skin [38] and Lumen [36] use haptic feedback for more explorative purposes. Here, haptic feedback is used to create social presence by recording the interactions of one user and play them back either locally or on remotely placed device.

Some research prototypes use the capability to change shape because it is a *practical* solution to a problem. One example of this is the Inflatable Mouse [26] that can be inflated to the size of a regular mouse and deflated in order to fit inside a PC card slot. Another example is Shutters [8], where the permeability of a fabric is changed by opening small louvers in the fabric to change daylight intake and ventilation.

Several papers describe the use of shape-changing interfaces for *construction* [32], where the user can assemble a dynamic form and manipulate it. Both Kinematics [32] and Topobo [39] allow users to construct different shape-changing kinetic structures through assembling parts.

Hedonic Aims of Shape Change

A number of design goals of shape-changing interfaces are hedonic, that is, focus primarily on non-instrumental goals [3,13] such as stimulation, aesthetics, identification, and fun. An illustrative example of such a hedonic aim is found in Pinwheels: "Pinwheels acted as kinetic sculptures that are beautiful and poetic in and of themselves" [22, p. 112]. Below we present the specific hedonic aims.

Several papers use shape change for *aesthetical* aims [5,26,48]. The interfaces in the aesthetics category derive from domains such as fashion [6], art [40], and architecture [47].

Another frequent use of shape change technologies is to engender *emotion* (e.g., [26,48]). A commonly used approach to portray emotions is to use organic and life-like movements. The Inflatable Mouse [21] simulates breathing to "express the motion of taking a nap when it is not in use." [26, p. 213]. The Thrifty Faucet [48] is neither functional nor aesthetic. Rather, by ascribing life-like behaviour to the faucet, Togler and colleagues sought to "step into dialogue with the user" (p. 43) and communicate emotions through motions and postures. In the case of the faucet, emotional responses from users have been studied empirically [48].

Stimulation and provocation are also pursued as design goals [6,31]. One prominent purpose of using shape change is to challenge our understanding of materiality. This use is illustrated by Oosterhuis and Biloria with their Muscle Projects [31]. By incorporating interactivity as a key component, they seek to "suggest and provoke the possibilities of engaging with space" (p. 75) and to "break the stereotype of the façade of a building as a barrier separating the interior from the external environment" (p. 78).

Explorative

Some papers report on conceptual experiments with shape-changing materials and technologies. Their goals are typically technical and aim at increasing our understanding of the materials involved in shape change. Examples of such explorations have concerned soap bubbles [45], shape memory alloys [10], silicone [44], and the use of ferrofluid [25]. Few focus on exploring the design potential of shape change unencumbered by technical limitations. SpeakCup [56], however, explores the design potential of shape change in relation to simplicity.

Toolkits for Programming Shape Change

A few papers discuss shape change in terms of toolkits for programming it. Bosu [33] is an example of this aim. Bosu makes it possible to iteratively experiment with shape actuation by making it possible to use soft materials to record and play back motion in 3-D space.

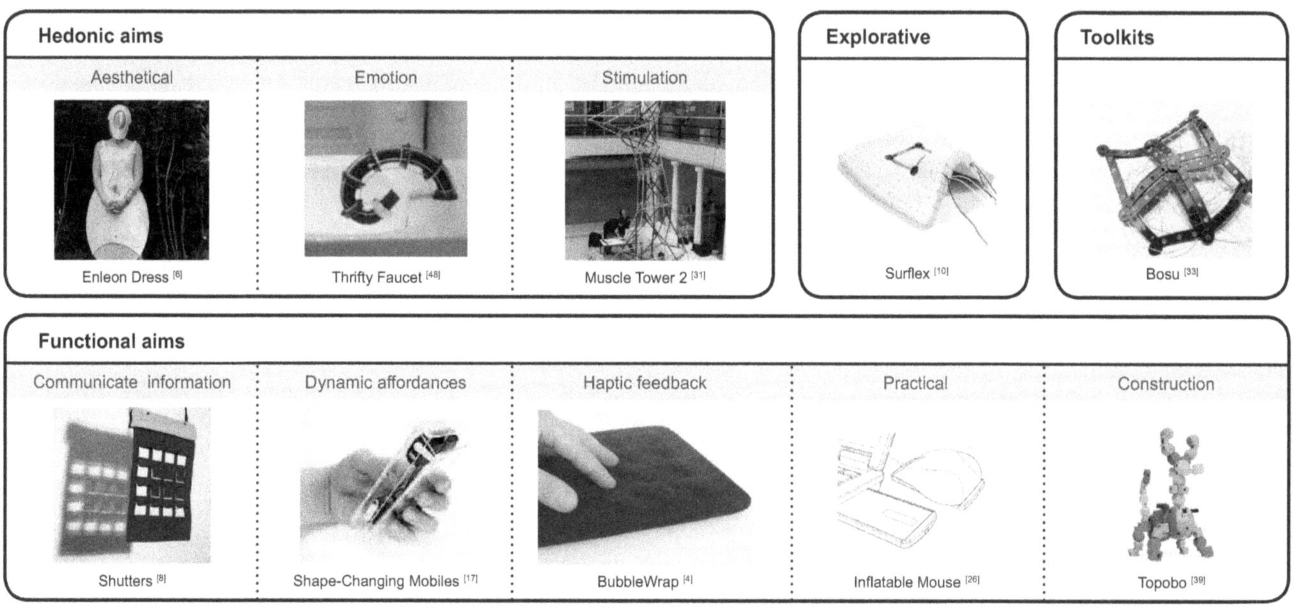

Figure 5. Four purposes of using shape change.

DISCUSSION AND CONCLUSION

We have reviewed 44 papers on shape-changing interfaces in order to outline the design space and provide a basis for discussing open research questions. Papers were analyzed with respect to which aspects of shape they manipulated (e.g., form, volume) and how transformation between shapes was achieved (e.g., animation type). We also discussed the broad types of interaction (e.g., integrated input/output) and the purpose intended with shape-changing interfaces (e.g., communication, artistic expression). Three questions spring from the review, which we discuss next.

The Purpose of Shape Change

The first question concerns the purpose to which designers put shape-changing interfaces. We have shown how many purposes are pursued in the literature, something not brought up in previous reviews of shape-changing interfaces [9,35]. Each purpose raises different questions on the suitability of using shape change and on how to assess whether the purpose was successful.

Many of the interfaces we have discussed aim to communicate information. Surprisingly few of them, however, answer the question whether shape change is a good modality for accurate and precise communication. Shade Pixel [21] for instance, has a resolution of 7×11 pixels; Shutters [8] offers 4×4. As communication devices in a strict sense, are these resolutions interesting? Limited bandwidth communication can be very rich (e.g., the 12Pixel project, [54]), but we would like to see more discussion of the viability of this particular purpose. For instance, what is the inherent communication quality of shape and transformation? What is the potential of ambiguity, subtleness, growth, or related shape notions for designing expressive and engaging interfaces?

As discussed earlier, many shape-changing interfaces use life-like movements (e.g., [48]; see also [42]). But what is the purpose of life-like movements, besides serving as design inspiration? Further, whereas life-like technology is often pursued early in the life cycle of a technology, its later utility is sometimes questioned. We suggest future research to be clearer about the purposes and benefits of imitation of life; the papers in the present sample are not.

Our classification of purpose was cumbersome and proceeded on limited information; few papers succeed in articulating the design aim of using shape change and making plain why that purpose is better accomplished with shape change, rather than another interaction style (say, a tangible user interface or direct manipulation). Recent reviews of tangible user interfaces (e.g., [43]) have begun a careful, data-driven discussion of the purposes and tasks for which tangibility is suitable. We suggest future research to do the same for shape-changing interfaces.

The Design Space of Shape Change

The second question concerns the design space of shape change, as exemplified by the sampled papers.

Undoubtedly, what we have called transformation is a key aspect of making shape-changing interfaces useful and usable, just as transformation is part of the magic of animation [46]. Unfortunately, current descriptions (incl. videos) do not give sufficient detail to discuss this aspect of shape-changing interfaces in depth. Also, we have seen no systematic exploration of how different types of transformation may be used and to what effects.

We have attempted to outline the design space of shape-changing interfaces; others have provided complementary accounts (e.g., [9,35]). Whereas individual papers combine design space parameters, we see no systematic attempt to explore this space and investigate new combinations of purpose, shapes, transformations, and input/output configurations. Future work should do so, possibly using a design research approach [57,58], which seems ideal for exploring design opportunities, yet curiously underused in work on shape-changing interfaces. One benefit of exploring the field through design would be to illustrate how shape-changing interfaces can integrate into and benefit from different use contexts, as well as gaining an understanding of how shape-changing interfaces can enter people's lives in new and unexpected ways.

At the level of modeling interaction, Parkes [33,35] has discussed how shape-changing interfaces advance tangible user interfaces. We would like to see this discussion followed up by further studies on, for instance, hybrid materiality, that is, the combination of structural stable parts of shape and more malleable parts [33]. Thus, at the level of modeling the distinct characteristics of shape-changing interfaces and exploring them through design-based research, we have seen no systematic approaches in our sample. Finally, the relation between input and output in the present sample of shape-changing interfaces is underexplored.

User Experience and Shape Change

The third question we wish to raise is about users' experience with shape change. Overall, about one fourth of the papers in our sample evaluate users' reactions to the interfaces; in our view, many of these offer valuable insights [12,16]. On the one hand, this percentage may be seen as adequate for a technology-driven field in its early stages. On the other hand, many evaluations are sketchy and based on exhibitions or workshops. Few papers in our sample build on recent progress in conceptualizing and studying user experience [13,29]. This is unfortunate for three reasons. First, it is unclear whether the designer's conceptual model (in the terms of Norman [30]) is in agreement with what is being experienced by the user. Thus, we do not know enough about whether the many purposes that designers imagine for shape-changing interfaces will materialize in user studies or in real use. Second, many questions on the utility of particular transformations, shapes, or purposes are empirical. For instance, one potential of shape-changing interfaces is to allow for dynamic affordances, that is, perceived action possibilities that change with changes in shape. To our knowledge, however, how users experience dynamic affordances has not been investigated. Third, shape-changing interfaces are a case in point with respect to Bannon's [2] recent critique of the HCI field as having too little of a human-centred focus. A key objective for future research is to generate more, high-quality data on the user experience with shape-changing interfaces.

Let us suggest two ways of how to generate such data. One way is about understanding the vocabulary of shape-changing interfaces and how this may be used. As an analogy, studies of graphical perception have long investigated the expressivity and accuracy of graphical marks (e.g., [14,28]). Similarly, we would find it highly valuable to see in-depth studies of the expressivity of the eight shape types outlined earlier as well as of how to transform among them. Another way is to study overall reactions to interfaces, in particular to involve users' tasks (or aspirations for experiences) and user context. The current literature rarely discusses suitable tasks for shape-changing interfaces and we found no investigations of how use context may impact the performance of and preference for shape-changing interfaces.

Limitations

We have argued in the introduction that the present review's strengths are to build on a solid base of papers and to discuss shape-changing interfaces in a broader manner than existing reviews. However, it has several limitations. First, we have established the sample of studies in an ad hoc way, based on references in and citations to well-known papers on shape change. A more systematic review could complement this approach. Second, the research on shape change is multidisciplinary, bordering fields and traditions where research papers are rarely the prime documentation of designs and prototypes. A different approach to obtaining descriptions (e.g., video, catalogue entries, exhibitions) of shape-changing interfaces would be complementary and, we believe, valuable. Finally, the reader may object that the discussion ignores that shape-changing interfaces is a primarily technology-driven research area; the discussion above about purpose and user experience is therefore irrelevant. We disagree. One reason is similar to that offered by Bannon [2], another is that we believe that the research suggestions above are likely to improve our understanding of shape-changing interfaces markedly, in turn informing the necessary technical development of such interfaces.

ACKNOWLEDGEMENTS

We are thankful for permission to use images of shape-changing interfaces. Susanne Bødker and Kim Halskov provided thoughtful comments on a draft.

REFERENCES

1. Art+com. BMW museum sculpture. Retrieved from http://www.artcom.de/index.php?lang=en&option=com_acprojects&id=62&page=6.
2. Bannon, L. Reimagining HCI: toward a more human-centered perspective. *interactions 18*, 4 (2011), 50-57.
3. Bargas-Avila, J.A. and Hornbæk, K. Old wine in new bottles or novel challenges. *CHI'11*, (2011), 2689-2698.
4. Bau, O., Petrevski, U., and Mackay, W. BubbleWrap. *CHI EA'09*, (2009), 3607-3612.
5. Berzowska, J. and Coelho, M. Kukkia and Vilkas: Kinetic Electronic Garments. *ISWC'05* (2005), 82-85.
6. Berzowska, J. and Mainstone, D. Skorpions: kinetic electronic garments. *ACM SIGGRAPH'08 art gallery*, (2008), 92-94.
7. Coelho, M. and Maes, P. Sprout I/O: A Texturally Rich Interface. *TEI'08*, (2008), 221-222.
8. Coelho, M. and Maes, P. Shutters: A Permeable Surface for Environmental Control and Communication. *TEI'09*, (2009), 13-18.
9. Coelho, M. and Zigelbaum, J. Shape-changing interfaces. *Personal and Ubiquitous Computing 15*, 2 (2010),161-173.
10. Coelho, M., Ishii, H., and Maes, P. Surflex: a programmable surface for the design of tangible interfaces. *CHI'08*, (2008), 3429-3434.
11. Fishkin, K. A taxonomy for and analysis of tangible interfaces. *Personal and Ubiquitous Computing 8*, 5 (2004), 347-358.
12. Harrison, C. and Hudson, S.E. Providing dynamically changeable physical buttons on a visual display. *CHI'09*, (2009), 299-270.
13. Hassenzahl, M. *Experience Design: Technology for All the Right Reasons*. Morgan and Claypool Publishers, (2010).
14. Heer, J. and Bostock, M. Crowdsourcing graphical perception. *CHI'10*, (2010), 203-212.
16. Hemmert, F., Hamann, S., Löwe, M., Wohlauf, A., Zeipelt, J., and Joost, G. Take me by the hand: haptic compasses in mobile devices through shape change and weight shift. *NordiCHI'10*, (2010), 671-674.
15. Hemmert, F., Hamann, S., Löwe, M., Wohlauf, A., and Joost, G. Shape-changing mobiles: tapering in one-dimensional deformational displays in mobile phones. *TEI'10*, (2010), 249-252.
17. Hemmert, F., Hamann, S., Löwe, M., Zeipelt, J., and Joost, G. Shape-changing mobiles: tapering in two-dimensional deformational displays in mobile phones. *CHI EA'10*, (2010), 3075-2079.
18. Hemmert, F. Ambient Life: Permanent Tactile Life-like Actuation as a Status Display in Mobile Phones. *UIST'08 Adjunct Proceedings* (2008).
19. Holman, D. and Vertegaal, R. Organic user interfaces: Designing computers in any way, shape, or form. *Communications of the ACM 51*, 6 (2008), 48-55.

20. Horev, O. 'TALKING TO THE HAND' An exploration into shape shifting objects and morphing interfaces, Master Thesis, Interaction Design Institute Ivrea, (2006).
21. Hyunjung, K. and Woohun, L. Shade Pixel: Interactive Skin for Ambient Information Displays. *CHI'09*, (2009), 1-4.
22. Ishii, H., Ren, S., and Frei, P. Pinwheels: Visualizing Information Flow in an Architectural Space. *CHI'01* (2001), 111-112.
23. Iwata, H., Yano, H., Nakaizumi, F., and Kawamura, R. Project FEELEX: : adding haptic surface to graphics. *SIGGRAPH'01*, (2001), 469-476.
24. Jacob, R.J.K., Girouard, A., Hirshfield, L.M., et al. Reality-based interaction: a framework for post-WIMP interfaces. *CHI'08*, (2008), 201-210.
25. Jansen, Y. Mudpad: Fluid Haptics for Multitouch Surfaces. *CHI EA'10*, (2010), 4351-4356.
26. Kim, S., Kim, H., Lee, B., Nam, T.-J., and Lee, W. Inflatable mouse: Volume-adjustable Mouse with Air-pressure-sensitive Input and Haptic Feedback. *CHI'08*, (2008), 211-214.
27. Leithinger, D. and Ishii, H. Relief: A Scalable Actuated Shape Display. *TEI'10*, (2010), 221-222.
28. Mackinlay, J. Automating the design of graphical presentations of relational information. *ACM Transactions on Graphics 5*, 2 (1986), 110-141.
29. McCarthy, J. and Wright, P. Technology as experience. *interactions 11*, 5 (2004), 42-43.
30. Norman, D.A. Cognitive Engineering. In *User Centered System Design: New Perspectives on Human-Computer Interaction*, D. A. Norman and S. W. Draper, Eds. Hillsdale, NJ: Lawrence Erlbaum Associates (1986), 31-61.
31. Oosterhuis, K. and Biloria, N. Interactions with proactive architectural spaces. *Communications of the ACM 51*, 6 (2008), 70-78.
32. Oschuetz, L., Wessolek, D., and Sattler, W. Constructing with movement: Kinematics. *TEI'10*, (2010), 257-260.
33. Parkes, A. and Ishii, H. Bosu: A Physical Programmable Design Tool for Transformability with Soft Mechanics. *DIS'10*, (2010), 189-198.
34. Parkes, A., Poupyrev, I., and Ishii, H. Designing kinetic interactions for organic user interfaces. *Communications of the ACM 51*, 6 (2008), 58-65.
35. Parkes, A. Phrases of the Kinetic: Dynamic Physicality as a Construct of Interaction Design, *MIT Doctoral Dissertation*, (2009).
36. Poupyrev, I., Nashida, T., Maruyama, S., Rekimoto, J., and Yamaji, Y. Lumen: Interactive Visual and Shape Display for Calm Computing. *SIGGRAPH'04*, (2004), 17.
37. Poupyrev, I., Nashida, T., and Okabe, M. Actuation and tangible user interfaces: the Vaucanson duck, robots, and shape displays. *TEI'07*, (2007), 206-212.
38. Raffle, H., Joachim, M.W., and Tichenor, J. Super Cilia Skin. *CHI'03*, (2003), 1-19.
39. Raffle, H.S., Parkes, A.J., and Ishii, H. Topobo: A Constructive Assembly System with Kinetic Memory. *CHI'04*, (2004), 647-654.
40. Rozin, D. Peg Mirror. Retrieved from http://www.smoothware.com/danny/pegmirror.html.
41. Rydarowski, A., Samanci, O., and Mazalek, A. Murmur: Kinetic Relief Sculpture, Multi-Sensory Display, Listening Machine. *TEI'08*, (2008), 231-238.
42. Schmitz, M. Concepts for life-like interactive objects. *TEI'11*, (2011), 157-164.
43. Shaer, O. and Hornecker, E. Tangible User Interfaces: Past, Present and Future Directions. *Foundations and Trends in Human-Computer Interaction, 3* 1-2 (2010), 1-137.
44. Slyper, R., Poupyrev, I., and Hodgins, J. Sensing through structure. *TEI'11*, (2011), 213-220.
45. Sylvester, A., Döring, T., and Schmidt, A. Liquids, smoke, and soap bubbles. *TEI'10*, (2010), 269-270.
46. Thomas, F. *Disney animation: The illusion of life*. Abbeville Press, New York, 1981.
47. Thomsen, M.R. Textile Logics in a Moving Architecture. *CHI 09 Workshop on Transitive Materials*, (2009).
48. Togler, J., Hemmert, F., and Wettach, R. Living interfaces: The Thrifty Faucet. *TEI'09*, (2009), 43-44.
49. Ullmer, B. and Ishii, H. Emerging frameworks for tangible user interfaces. *IBM Systems Journal 39*, 3 (2000), 915-931.
50. Vallgårda, A. and Redström, J. Computational composites. *CHI'07*, (2007), 513-522.
51. Vaughan, L.C. Understanding movement. *CHI'97*, (1997), 548-549.
52. Vertegaal, R. and Poupyrev, I. Organic User Interfaces: Introduction. *Communications of the ACM 51*, 6 (2008) 48-55.
53. Wakita, A. Blob Motility. Retrieved from http://metamo.sfc.keio.ac.jp/project/blob/.
54. Willis, K.D.D. and Poupyrev, I. 12Pixels: Exploring Social Drawing on Mobile Phones. *Pervasive'10*. (2010), 391-408.
55. Young, R., Pezzutti, D., Pill, S., and Sharp, R. The language of motion in industrial design. *Design and semantics of form and movement*, (2005), 6-12.
56. Zigelbaum, J., Chang, A., Gouldstone, J., Monzen, J.J., and Ishii, H. SpeakCup: Simplicity, BABL, and Shape Change. *TEI'08*, (2008), 145-146.
57. Zimmerman, J., Forlizzi, J., and Evenson, S. Research through design as a method for interaction design research in HCI. *CHI'07*, (2007), 493-502.
58. Zimmerman, J., Stolterman, E., and Forlizzi, J. An analysis and critique of Research through Design. *CHI'10*, (2010), 310-319.
59. Apple patent. Retrieved from http://www.patentlyapple.com/patently-apple/2010/06/apple-introduces-the-incredible-shape-shifting-device-interface.html.

MimicTile: A Variable Stiffness Deformable User Interface for Mobile Devices

Yusuke Nakagawa
The University of Tokyo
qq106313@iii.u-tokyo.ac.jp

Akiya Kamimura
National Institute of Advanced Industrial Science and Technology, AIST
kamimura.a@aist.go.jp

Yoichiro Kawaguchi
The University of Tokyo
yoichiro@iii.u-tokyo.ac.jp

ABSTRACT
MimicTile is a novel variable stiffness deformable user interface for mobile devices that implements two key features. The first feature is an input interface that accepts a variety of deformation-based gestures, providing a user with several ways of interacting with a small mobile device. The other feature is the ability to provide information to the user through haptic feedback by varying the stiffness of the interface. The features are suitable for enhancing mobile applications. They were implemented using only shape memory alloy (SMA) wires as the actuator. SMA wire is extremely flexible, making it ideal for deformable user interfaces. In MimicTile, SMA wires act as both actuators and external input sensors. The actuator function works by altering stiffness based on user input. This study also discusses ideas for further development of deformable user interfaces.

Author Keywords
Mobile devices; deformable user interfaces; gestures; haptic feedback; shape memory alloy

ACM Classification Keywords
H.5.2 Information Interfaces and Presentation: User Interfaces—*Input devices and strategies*

General Terms
Design, Human Factors

INTRODUCTION
Although mobile devices have become increasingly popular in recent years, there are significant limitations. One limitation is that mobile devices offer very limited input methods, which is an input side problem. In addition, the ability to provide feedback to the user is limited to features such as the display and vibration functions, which overlap with the input area as the small display can only show a limited amount of information; this is an output side problem. Several approaches have been proposed for overcoming these issues. One possible approach for resolving the input side problem is a deformable user interface [12, 6].

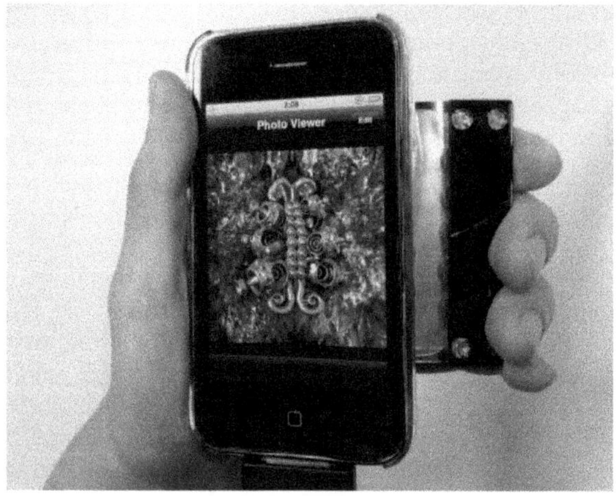

Figure 1. External appearance of MimicTile.

Deformable user interfaces do not require space for buttons. A system incorporating a deformable interface can provide more input methods than conventional devices. These input methods enable flexible and intuitive user interaction by allowing users to interact with the device through actions they are familiar with from their everyday life. For example, lifting the right side upward is an action that is similar to turning the page of a book. This gesture based interaction style forms the basis of an intuitive input method for mobile devices.

Several studies have proposed the use of haptic feedback to resolve the output side problem [9, 4]. Through haptic feedback, additional information can be provided even on a device with a small display. For example, when a smartphone vibrates in response to touchscreen input, haptic feedback can inform the user that the input is invalid. Thus, haptic feedback and deformable interfaces have several potential applications in mobile devices.

However, to the best of our knowledge, no single device has implemented both of these features thus far.

Therefore, we propose a novel mobile device called MimicTile (Fig.1) that recognizes deformation-based gestures and mimics the stiffness of several materials to provide haptic feedback.

RELATED WORKS
Several deformable user interfaces and interaction methods for mobile devices have been developed and studied. GUMMI [12] is a well-known bendable user interface for mobile devices. It is comprised of an LCD display with bend sen-

sors attached to its front and back and a 2D position sensor. Bending the device is registered as a gesture, with its creators describing the use of GUMMI with applications. PaperPhone [6] was the first prototype that integrated an actual flexible display. Earlier deformable user interface designs and interaction methods were previously proposed in the hope that flexible displays will become practical in future. Thus, PaperPhone was the first time such a display was realized and tested. Looser [8] et al. proposed a flexible and tangible magic lens that uses AR maker to present meta information overlaid on the real object. Lee et al. investigated how users may manipulate future deformable devices by making dummy devices from various materials [7]. They attempted to identify the optimal deformable interfaces and interaction styles by using devices made of plastic sheets, paper, and elastic cloth. They found that users had a higher preference for gestures with more flexibility.

Haptic feedback has been the subject of several studies. The Haptic Chameleon [9] was the first example of a shape changing interface implementing haptic feedback. Users can change the shape of the Haptic Chameleon, responding through haptic and tactile feedback. The SqueezeBlock [4] enables eyes-free interaction with a mobile device by altering the stiffness and size of the virtual spring to provide haptic feedback. A proposed application of this approach is to indicate the arrival of new email messages by altering stiffness. Users would be alerted without needing to take the mobile out of their pockets. Interactive Generator [2] also utilizes changes in stiffness. However, unlike the other haptic feedback devices described thus far, it is self-powered. Other haptic feedback devices require large amounts of energy from the mobile battery, and Interactive Generator avoids this issue.

As mentioned earlier, no single device implements both haptic feedback and a deformable interface.

BASIC CONCEPT

The basic design of MimicTile (Fig.2) introduces the following unique features:

- the ability to recognize several deformation-based gestures.
- a flexible, variable stiffness device - stiffness can be varied to provide haptic feedback.
- a thin, lightweight, simple structure.

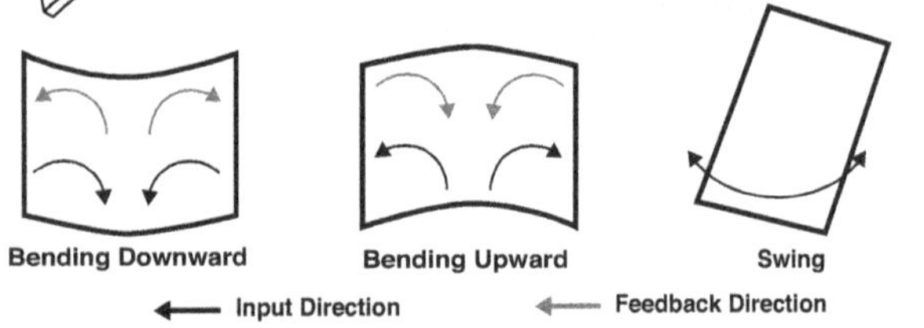

Figure 2. The concept design of MimicTile. The top row demonstrates how it can mimic the stiffness of materials like wood and paper and the bottom row shows the available deformation-based gestures.

Deformation-based gestures

Based on previous studies [7], we selected three gestures that can be performed using a plastic sheet. The gestures were chosen for their high user preference score on a device similar to a plastic sheet i.e. bending upward, bending downward and the swing gesture [7]. Bending upward and downward were also selected as basic gestures in [12, 6]. Lee et al. concluded that materials such as paper and elastic cloth are preferable to a plastic sheet. However, current technology does not allow usable devices to be made from materials similar to paper or elastic cloth. Therefore, we focus on plastic sheet based gestures. We selected three gestures because once our device is able to recognize these gestures, other gestures can be realized by adding more sensors to the device. For instance, the gesture of bending the left or right side upwards may then be realized by adding more sensors to the device. Since flipping the device over in a clockwise or counterclockwise direction are not deformation-based gestures, they were not selected. Such gestures can be detected easily by adding a gyro sensor to the device.

Haptic feedback

MimicTile varies its stiffness between differing levels to provide haptic feedback, as shown in Fig.2. Such feedback can be felt natural as deformation-based gestures encourage the user to enter input by taking advantage of device flexibility. If device flexibility is decreased, such flexibility dependant input is no longer available. In other words, a change in stiffness varies the ability to accept deformation based input. However, providing haptic feedback for the swing gesture is difficult as the swing gesture is fast. Thus, we only provide haptic feedback for the bending upward/downward gestures.

Hardware design and system

The proposed design meets the basic requirements of flexibility and the device is small enough to grasp with one hand. MimicTile is comprised of two SMA wires, heat-resistant pulleys, a polycarbonate plate, acrylic plates, and a silicon rubber sheet. Both SMA wires provide sensor and actuator functions. Most common deformation-based gesture and haptic feedback implementations require many sensors and actuators, which makes their structure extremely complex and compromises system robustness. Using SMA wires that work as both sensors and actuators can resolve this issue. In addition, general actuators such as servo motors are too heavy and rigid to use in mobile devices and deformable user interfaces. However as SMA is thin, flexible, and lightweight, the device will have the same properties.

The SMA wire used is BioMetal Fiber 150[1] ; it is the most powerful SMA wire produced by Toki Corporation. Its diameter is 0.15 mm and the nominal practical force produced is 150 gf. We placed a 24 cm long SMA wire with heat-resistant pulleys on both surfaces of the device (Fig.3(c, d)). Pulleys on one side are placed 1.0 mm higher than the other side to adjust the tension of the SMA wire (Fig.3(c)). A polycarbonate plate is used as SMA wires become hot when they conduct electricity and the plate offers high heat resistance. Acrylic plates limit the bendable area and transmit the force from SMA wires to the user more efficiently. The acrylic plates and silicon rubber sheets protect user's hand not to touch the

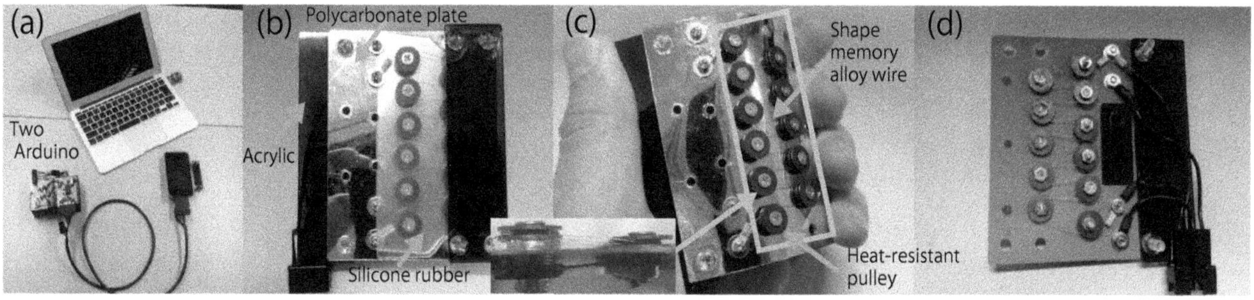

Figure 3. (a) Whole setup. (b) Front. (c) Detail. (d) Back.

SMA wires (Fig.3(b)). We use two Arduino platforms, a PC and an iPhone for testing (Fig.3(a)). Unfortunately, flexible displays are not available currently, and in its place we use the iPhone in the current system. The first Arduino communicates with the PC through XBee and the second Arduino communicates with the iPhone through a Redpark serial cable. Each Arduino communicate through I2C. The first Arduino and PC control the SMAs and classify the input gestures into the three available gestures based on the values of the SMA sensors. The second Arduino retrieves analysis data from the first Arduino and uploads it to the iPhone, which is running some applications. The two Arduinos and the SMA are powered by a Li-po battery(11.1V, 910mAh). Thus, MimicTile can function wirelessly.

METHODOLOGY

For this study, the most important aspects are controlling the SMA wires and gesture recognition.

Control method of shape memory alloy

SMA wires function as both sensors and actuators. The electrical resistance of SMA wires changes with wire length; thus, they are able to function as sensors [5]. Thus, when the device is bent, one SMA wire is stretched while the other contracts, creating a difference in the resistance of the two SMA wires. We map this difference to the bending angle. As the SMA wires function as actuators and are controlled by PWM, the stiffness of the device can be varied.

However, the resistance changes when the SMA is actuated and hysteresis prevents the resistance from stabilizing quickly. When SMA is used for external force sensors and variable stiffness actuators, it is important to detect the change in resistance that is caused by the external input only. Previous studies have used SMA as sensors in the area of human interface design. Sprout I/O [3] uses SMA for electrostatic capacity sensors, although the method used is not suitable for deformation-based gestures. Research in the area of robotics by Ikuta et al. and Toki Corporation led to the development of self-sensing actuators using SMA only [5, 1]. However, these methods do not accept input applied as an external force, making them unsuitable for our requirements. In the proposed device, two identical SMA wires are used for the front and back and the difference between the SMA resistance values is the sensor value. If both SMAs are actuated by the same PWM pulse, the change in resistance and hysteresis will be identical as long as other factors are unchanged. Therefore, even if the SMAs are actuated accidentally, the difference between their resistance values will remain zero in the absence of external force input. On the other hand, when an input is received, the difference is non-zero and can easily be mapped to a bending angle. This technique can be used to extract the change in resistance due to external input force only without needing to consider the effects of hysteresis and the actuation. We measure the resistance using a bridge circuit operating at 21 Hz. To estimate input magnitude, we first create a table of the resistance differences against the PWM and then determine the input by comparing with this table. Thus, the input magnitude can then be estimated by consulting this table.

It is also important to prevent over-heating of the SMA wires and to avoid using them continuously at high power. With these precautions, the response is fast and consistent and the device is able to maintain a temperature acceptable for human hands without requiring a cooling mechanism.

Gesture classification

In this section, we describe how MimicTile classifies input as the three gestures based on the measured SMA resistance. Such deformation-based gestures cannot be classified using thresholds. PaperPhone implements the k-nearest neighbor algorithm for this purpose [6]. The proposed device applies a wavelet transform (WT) and artificial neural network (ANN) based algorithm [10, 11]. The WT extracts the feature space from the sensor data received at that time and the ANN classifies the feature space based on the data learned previously. The sensor data from motion gestures usually contains local features. Unlike the Fourier transform method, WT can detect local features. Thus, this method can detect time varying movement gestures such as the swing gesture easily. In this study, we use the multi-resolution wavelet transformation shown in Fig.4.

The data values and algorithms used for the classification are as follows. The data input for the WT is the measured resistance difference of the SMA wires. The WT used is the Haar wavelet transform and three rules (average, max, min) are used to extract the feature space. The ANN learns teaching data through the back propagation algorithm.

DISCUSSION

Three experiments were performed using MimicTile. The first experiment tests the recognition system. Before the experiment is performed, the device learns approximately 120 sample data values and another 50 sample data values are used in the test. During this experiment, the shape memory

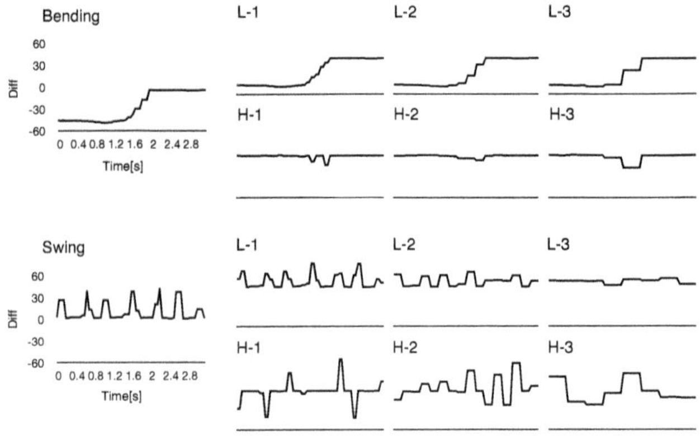

Figure 4. The multi-resolution wavelet transform repeatedly decomposes the original data into low and high frequency waves while reducing the resolution. The six graphs (L-1 : H-3) show multi-resolution analysis performed using the wavelet transform. For example, the L-1 graph is the level 1 low frequency graph generated from the original data and H-2 is the level 2 high frequency graph generated using data from the L-1 graph. Levels 4 and higher graphs are not shown here.

alloy received a random pulse. Our device distinguished approximately 98% of the gestures correctly. This experiment proved that the device could recognize the three deformation-based gestures with high accuracy. Experimental results showed that the maximum bending frequency that is measured accurately by this system is about 5 Hz, which is adequate for normal use.

In the second experiment, three test participants (two males and one female) were asked to report if they could recognize or feel stiffness changes in the device. Each person recorded ten sets of observations with one hand and another ten sets with both hands. Before the experiment, the participants were allowed to feel the three different levels of stiffness. When the device stiffness was set to the maximum level, the participants could not bend the device with one hand easily. For each test set, we randomly activated one of the three stiffness levels and the participants recorded the stiffness level they felt. The test participants correctly identified the stiffness 90% of the time.

In the third experiment, we evaluated the usability of MimicTile by implementing a simple application. The application is a simple photo viewer, where the gestures for bending upward, bending downward, and swing gestures are mapped to zoom out, zoom in, and to 'restart application' functions, respectively. We used a flick gesture to change photos. When the photo was completely zoomed in and could not be zoomed in any further, the device provides feedback by altering its stiffness. The three test participants were asked to use the application as they wished. All participants were able to use the basic functions of the device correctly and said they felt the haptic feedback clearly and that the haptic feedback was useful. In addition, two participant said they found it easier to interact with mobile devices using only one hand.

CONCLUSION

MimicTile, a novel variable stiffness deformable device, was proposed. The device accurately recognizes three deformation-based gestures and provides feedback to the user through haptic feedback. Such an interface is extremely useful for mobile phones and devices, which can only display a limited amount of information. Experimental results showed that the device performed as intended. The structure of the proposed device is extremely simple and easy to extend. In future work, we plan to implement more user-defined interaction methods and haptic feedback in suitable applications.

ACKNOWLEDGMENTS

We thank all the participants for their time. This research is supported by JST CREST.

REFERENCES

1. Toki corporation. http://www.toki.co.jp/.
2. Badshah, A., Gupta, S., Cohn, G., Villar, N., Hodges, S., and Patel, S. N. P. Interactive generator: A self-powered haptic feedback device. *In Proceedings of CHI 2011*, 2051–2054.
3. Coelho, M., and Maes, P. Sprout I/O: A texturally rich interface. *In Proceedings of TEI 2008*, 221–222.
4. Gupta, S., Campbell, T., Hightower, J. R., and Patel, S. N. Squeezeblock: Using virtual springs in mobile devices for eyes-free interaction. *In Proceedings of UIST 2010*, 10–14.
5. Ikuta, K., Tsukamoto, M., and Hirose, S. Shape memory alloy servo actuator system with electric resistance feedback and application for active endoscope. *In Proceedings of ICRA 1988*, 427–430.
6. Lahey, B., Girouard, A., Burleson, W., and Vertegaal, R. Paperphone: Understanding the use of bend gestures in mobile devices with flexible electronic paper displays. *In Proceedings of CHI 2011*, 1303–1312.
7. Lee, S.-S., Kim, S., Jin, B., Choi, E., adn Xu Jia, B. K., Kim, D., and Lee, K.-P. How users manipulate deformable displays as input devices. *In Proceedings of CHI 2010*, 1647–1656.
8. Looser, J., Grasset, R., and Billinghurst, M. A 3D flexible and tangible magic lens in augmented reality. *In Proceedings of ISMAR 2007*, 51–54.
9. Michelitsch, G., Williams, J., Osen, M., Jimenez, B., and Rapp, S. Haptic chameleon: a new concept of shape-changing user interface controls with force feedback. *In Proceedings of CHI 2004 extended abstracts*, 1305–1308.
10. M.W.Jiang, R.C.Wang, J.Z.Wang, and D.W.Jin. A method of recognizing finger motion using wavelet transform of surface emg signal. *International Conference of the Engineering in Medicine and Biology Society* (2005), 2672–2674.
11. Oropesa, E., Cycon, H. L., and Jobert, M. Sleep stage classification using wavelet transform and neural network. *International Computer Science Institute* (1999).
12. Schwesig, C., Poupyrev, I., and Mori, E. Gummi: A bendable computer. *In Proceedings of CHI 2004*, 263–270.

Animating Paper using Shape Memory Alloys

Jie Qi
75 Amherst St. E14-548
Cambridge, MA 02139
jieqi@media.mit.edu

Leah Buechley
75 Amherst St. E14-548
Cambridge, MA 02139
leah@media.mit.edu

ABSTRACT
Our aim is to make shape memory alloys (SMAs) accessible and visible as creative crafting materials by combining them with paper. In this paper, we begin by presenting mechanisms for actuating paper with SMAs along with a set of design guidelines for achieving dramatic movement. We then describe how we tested the usability and educational potential of one of these mechanisms in a workshop where participants, age 9 to 15, made actuated electronic origami cranes. We found that participants were able to successfully build constructions integrating SMAs and paper, that they enjoyed doing so, and were able to learn skills like circuitry design and soldering over the course of the workshop.

Author Keywords
paper craft; paper mechanisms; paper electronics; shape memory alloy; education; origami

ACM Classification Keywords
J.5 [Arts and Humanities]: Arts, fine and performing; B.m [Hardware]: Miscellaneous

General Terms
Design

INTRODUCTION
Paper has long been used as a versatile building material. Soft enough to manipulate by hand yet rigid enough to hold a shape, while also inexpensive and plentiful in diverse forms, paper offers endless creative possibilities. As a result there has been a growing interest in combining the technological and aesthetic promises of paper with the interactive power of electronics. This has inspired novel techniques for fabrication such as embedding circuitry directly into the paper [2] and new technologies like electronically augmented pop-up interfaces [5], and kits for drawing electronic circuits on paper [?]. These examples demonstrate not only the functional aspect of paper electronics, but also its expressive and creative potential.

Recent works also examine how the mechanical nature of paper can be controlled with electronics and thus programmed.

To make these mechanisms move electronically, nontraditional actuators that are lighter than traditional actuators–motors and solenoids–must be used to prevent destroying the paper as well as for direct integration with the material. Shape memory alloys (SMAs), which are metals that change shape in response to heat, are a popular solution precisely for their light weight and flexibility. One example is the programmable matter project, in which an array of custom made SMA hinges actuated a sheet to fold autonomously into various forms [3]. Saul et al. used SMA wires to make paper robots that bobbed and bounced [6]. The Animated Paper toolkit uses scanning and targeted lasers to heat the SMA precisely and wirelessly [4].

While research has been done on the use of shape memory alloys and paper, it is still largely an underused material. For beginner users of SMAs, the material is often prohibitively difficult to use and the effects are frequently not as dramatic as desired.

In this paper we introduce simple methods for incorporating SMAs into paper, including a series of reliable mechanisms for getting different movements. We then present a case study of using SMAs in an educational setting. Finally, we examine how effectively the activity works to inspire interest and teach topics in electronics.

SMA MATERIAL PROPERTIES
Shape memory alloys are metals that change shape with respect to temperature. At deactivated temperatures the metal is malleable and when heated to an activation temperature the metal returns to a "remembered" shape. Since setting SMAs requires specialized equipment, to make our research accessible we focus on a pre-trained form of SMA called muscle wire. This wire is commercially available and comes in the form of wire that contracts approximately ten percent of its original length upon heating. While heat can be applied through various methods including light and body heat [4], we heat the muscle wire by running electric current through so that movement can be controlled electronically and be used in programmable interfaces.

WORKING WITH MUSCLE WIRE ON PAPER
Working with muscle wire is a process of experimenting to find an optimal combination of mechanism, structural force and electrical power. Keeping the wire taut in the mechanism ensures that the full contraction is used to move the structure. Heating the muscle wire for the first time often causes some strain in the wire, so it is important to re-tension the wire after initial heating for maximum movement. The electrical power used to heat the wire must be strong enough to run the desired

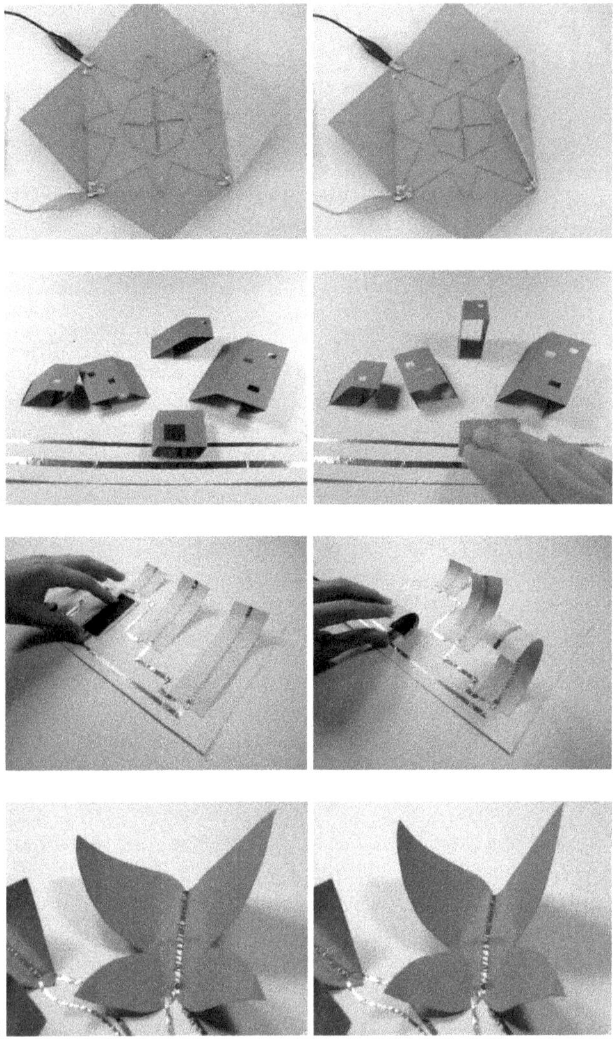

Figure 1. SMA paper mechanisms: folding flap (a), parallelogram (b), curling flap (c) and clam shell (d)

amount of current through, without overheating and straining the wire.

Paper as a medium is easy to manipulate through cutting, folding, drawing, sewing and so forth. Using a basic set of mechanisms, an endless variety of creative works can be made. A flap that curls up and down can be transformed into petals on a flower, the tongue of a snake, or even a skirt blowing in the wind. Paper is particularly appropriate for working with shape memory metals due to its high temperature tolerance as well as light, and pliable nature.

The first step in working with muscle wire is connecting the wire to the circuit. Since it has an oxidized coating, it cannot be easily soldered. One solution is to fold wire tip into a "u" and insert into a crimp bead [1]. Folding prevents the wire from slipping out of the crimp bead while the bead provides a large surface area for soldering. We have found that cylindrical jewelry crimp beads, in silver or copper, work well for this purpose.

Next it is crucial to anchor the wire firmly to the structure and maintain tension in the wire, so that when the wire contracts, it pulls the structure along. We have found that adhesive on copper tape is strong enough to anchor the copper to the paper. Finally, the crimped muscle wire can be soldered directly to the copper tape, which also functions as a circuit element to deliver current to the wire. Since the wire tends to lengthen slightly after the its initial contraction, we found it helpful to retention the wire after this initial activation.

MECHANISMS

The following are several simple muscle wire mechanisms that we designed to have reliably dramatic effects. We used papers that have medium weight, from printer paper to card stock, which provides sufficient structural strength to hold the mechanism together while remaining pliable enough for the wire to overcome. In all of the following mechanisms, we use the natural springiness of paper to act as the restoring force for returning the structure to its deactivated form.

Folding Flap

In this mechanism the muscle wire pulls a flap along a crease, causing the flap to fold (see figure 1.a). The folding flap is built by anchoring two ends of the muscle wire to the base and attaching the middle of the muscle wire to the flap, so that the wire is taught when the flap is flattened. The simplest way for attaching the wire to the flap is to thread the wire through the paper itself. In this configuration, the flap acts as a lever and the muscle wire is the pulling actuator. The closer the wire is attached to the crease, the greater the degree of folding. Using longer wire will result in more dramatic folding only when the straight path of the wire elongates.

Parallelogram

The parallelogram mechanism lifts a plane out and parallel to the base when activated (see figure 1.b). This mechanism uses the same muscle wire attachment as the folding mechanism. However, here the flap to be actuated is one leg of the parallelogram. Lifting the parallelogram is achieved easily with the muscle wire but getting the parallelogram to lay back flat often requires reinforcing the legs of the parallelogram to be flat against the background. Here it is important to avoid strongly pre-creasing the legs of the parallelogram, or the restoring force will not be strong enough to return the structure to its flattened state.

Curling Flap

In the curling flap mechanism, the flap lays flat against the base when deactivated and curls out from the page upon activation (see figure 1.c). This mechanism is constructed by sewing the muscle wire to the paper or by even threading the muscle wire through small slits in the paper itself. It works by holding the muscle wire against the paper as it contracts, forcing the paper to curl to accommodate the shorter length of wire. For this mechanism it is important to use medium weight paper that the does not simply wrinkle when the wire contracts.

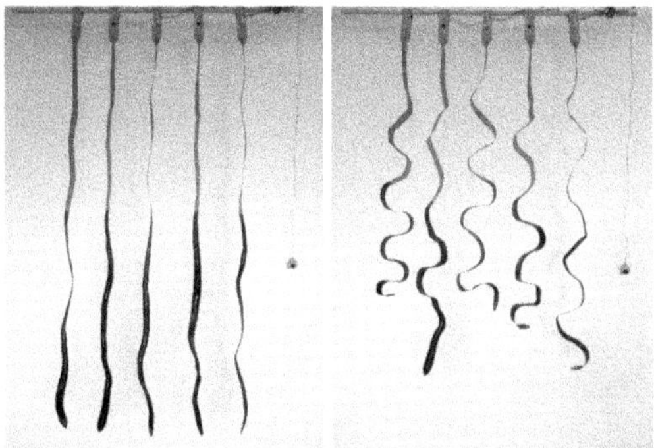

Figure 2. Wall hanging constructed using chained curling mechanisms

Clam shell

In this mechanism, two flaps rise upward symmetrically like two shells of a clam(see figure 1.d). This mechanism is constructed based on the curling mechanism with the addition that each side along the curl is now folded with arced creases. The result is that as the central paper curls down, the side flaps fold upward. This mechanism multiplies the effect of the curling mechanism by links two folding elements, so one actuation point results in three movements result.

DESIGNING FOR MAXIMAL EFFECT

In addition to achieving desired motion, various properties of muscle wire can be exploited to get the most magical effect out of this medium.

With the muscle wire mechanisms presented, it is possible to keep the wires flush with the surface of the paper, which integrates the material nicely into the structure. This also prevents tangling of the wires and thus keeps the circuitry organized and more robust. This can be done easily by sewing the wire directly through the paper structure.

Even though individual movements may be limited, for more startling effects large motions can be made by cascading multiple moving elements. For example, a chain of curling elements can be used to make large snaking motions (see figure 2). Here, the curling and contraction of each unit lifts the following unit, so that the motion adds linearly with each additional unit and the entire chain moves much more dramatically as a whole. Using multiple moving elements in close proximity with contrasting or opposing motions also heightens the effect of the movement.

Finally, the actuation of the wire is silent compared to traditional actuators such as motors or solenoids which produce a whirring or clicking noise. This gives space for emphasizing the sound of motion such as the creaking of materials sliding against one another, the crackling of paper or the collision of one material against another.

EVALUATION

Once several basic mechanisms for muscle wire were determined, we decided to design a simple example project as a case study for testing these techniques and materials in an educational setting. We aimed to teach paper actuation and electronics building an accessible manner that both teaches electronics concepts and draws on participants' arts and crafts background. Through our study, we wanted to see whether participants were capable of using the materials to build functioning, moving circuits and whether the experience inspires interest in pursing these activities further.

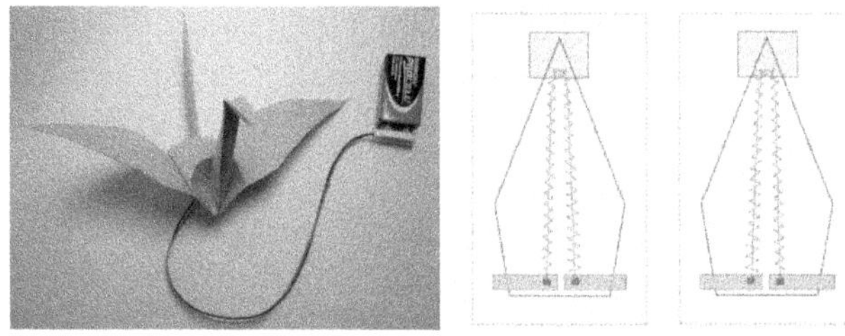

Figure 3. Electronic origami crane (left) and SMA wing template (right)

Electronic Origami Crane

Our goal for the example project and companion activity was to create a project that is simple to make, reliably functions electronically and teaches basic electronics theory and techniques.

We decided to augment the traditional origami crane with wings that curl and created a step by step tutorial for the project [1]. We chose the crane because is a popular model to fold and flapping wings is natural movement that matches both the concept of model and the capabilities of the muscle wire. Pockets in the wings of a traditional origami crane also provides a convenient location for curling wing inserts, so that the electronics portion of the activity is decoupled from the folding portion.

We chose a simple circuit to made up of a 9V battery, 0.006" high-temperature Flexinol muscle wire [1], connecting wires and two pieces of copper tape to make a switch. Touching copper tapes together closes the circuit connecting the battery to the muscle wire, which activates wire and curls the wings down. Separating the copper tapes opens the circuit, allowing the muscle wire to cool down and the wings to rise up. Since the switch is made of two pieces of copper tape, they can be placed anywhere on the model, which gives individuals freedom to design the form of the switch. In the tutorial, we suggest putting the copper tapes on the tail of the crane, so that when the tail is squeezed, the wings curl down.

Preliminary Electronic Origami Workshop

As part of the Cambridge Science Festival, we held a four-hour workshop on making the electronic origami crane. Our workshop was attended by ten participants– five female and five male– ages nine to fifteen. Each student was accompanied by a parent or guardian. All of our participants had some experience with paper craft but only 50% had previous experience with electronics.

We began the workshop with a survey on the participants' previous experience and expectations for the workshop. The

[1] `http://hlt.media.mit.edu/?p=1448`

first half hour of the workshop was a lesson on how to fold origami cranes. Next, we helped students build the curling SMA wing inserts. This session included a demonstration of soldering and a short explanation of the circuit. Finally, we had students assemble the crane by embedding their wings into the origami model. We concluded with a show-and-tell and a discussion of how participants felt about the experience. Before leaving, we gave participants a post-workshop survey designed to gauge how much was learned, what the participants enjoyed and what participants found challenging.

Analysis

All participants successfully completed the tasks–folding the crane, sewing the mechanism, and soldering the electrical connections. Everyone completed the pre-workshop survey and 9 out of 10 completed the post-workshop survey. By the end of the workshop, even though not everyone had cranes that successfully flapped, every respondent said that they had made a project they were happy with and 89% of respondents replied they were interested in learning more about electronics.

It is worth mentioning that, despite the template we provided, 67% of participants who responded on the post survey found that the greatest challenge was getting the desired motion from their wings. Participants were prone to keep the wings activated for extended periods of time in hopes of more dramatic curling. However, this had the effect of overheating the muscle wire, which reduced the contracting abilities of the metal. As a result, half of the participants were faced with the challenge of rebuilding their wing inserts. While upsetting, this provided an interesting lesson (for the participants and the authors) in debugging. Most participants were not terribly discouraged and were able to make dramatically flapping cranes the second time around.

Ultimately, we feel that the workshop successfully introduced participants to the idea and process of crafting electronics. Our pre and post workshop surveys show learning and increased self efficacy. At the beginning of the workshop 40% of students said they they were comfortable working with electronics. This percentages jumped to 78% of respondents at the conclusion of the session. Additionally, 89% of participants who responded on our post survey indicated that they were interested in learning more about electronics. Students felt that they learned valuable lessons in the workshop including, how a circuit functions, and how to solder electronics. One participants parent sent us a message after the workshop explaining that her son was so excited by the workshop that they purchased a soldering iron and electronics kit so that he could continue explorations on his own.

Though these results are preliminary, derived from a single session attended by a small number of students, we believe that they indicate that activities like this one, that blend paper crafting with electronics, are promising activities for engaging diverse youth in building electronics. We believe that the novelty and magic of self-moving paper motivated our participants to build and debug a delicate circuit. Our participants demonstrated that SMAs can be used successfully in introductory electronics workshops. In fact, the sensitive nature of the material arguably supports teaching important concepts like debugging. As one participant remarked on the survey, "you learn from your mistakes." In sum, introducing technical skills like soldering a circuit around familiar activities like cutting and folding paper effectively engaged participants in tasks that they might otherwise not have been exposed to, or thought they were capable of.

CONCLUSION

We presented techniques and approaches for working with SMAs and paper and demonstrated that starting with simple techniques, a wide range of creative works can be made. We also successfully introduced a group of young students to circuits and paper crafting, hopefully inspiring a deeper interest in electronics. We plan to continue to develop SMA mechanisms and activities to help students use SMAs to animate their paper projects.

ACKNOWLEDGEMENTS

We would like to thank Ed Baafi, Emily Lovell, David Mellis and Hannah Perner-Wilson for their advice and support of this work.

This material is based upon work supported by the National Science Foundation under Grant No. 0940484 and an NSF Graduate Research Fellowship under Grant No. 1122374. Any opinions, findings, and conclusions or recommendations expressed in this material are those of the author(s) and do not necessarily reflect the views of the National Science Foundation. This work was also supported by the MIT Media Lab consortium.

REFERENCES

1. Technical Characteristics of Flexinol Actuator Wire. `http://www.dynalloy.com`.
2. Coelho, M., Hall, L., Berzowska, J., and Maes, P. Pulp-based computing: a framework for building computers out of paper. In *Proceedings of the 27th international conference extended abstracts on Human factors in computing systems*, CHI EA '09, ACM (New York, NY, USA, 2009), 3527–3528.
3. Hawkes, E., An, B., Benbernou, N., Tanaka, H., Kim, s., Demaine, E. D., Rus, D., and Wood, R. J. Programmable matter by folding. *Proceedings of the National Academy of Sciences in the United States of America 107*, 28 (2010), 12441–12445.
4. Koizumi, N., Yasu, K., Liu, A., Sugimoto, M., and Inami, M. Animated paper: A toolkit for building moving toys. *Comput. Entertain. 8* (December 2010), 7:1–7:16.
5. Qi, J., and Buechley, L. Electronic popables: exploring paper-based computing through an interactive pop-up book. In *Proceedings of the fourth international conference on Tangible, embedded, and embodied interaction*, TEI '10, ACM (New York, NY, USA, 2010), 121–128.
6. Saul, G., Xu, C., and Gross, M. D. Interactive paper devices: end-user design & fabrication. In *Proceedings of the fourth international conference on Tangible, embedded, and embodied interaction*, TEI '10, ACM (New York, NY, USA, 2010), 205–212.

Intimacy in Long-Distance Relationships over Video Chat

Carman Neustaedter
School of Interactive Arts + Technology
Simon Fraser University
102 – 13450 102nd Avenue, Surrey, BC, Canada
carman_neustaedter@sfu.ca

Saul Greenberg
Department of Computer Science
University of Calgary
2500 University Drive NW, Calgary, AB, Canada
saul.greenberg@ucalgary.ca

ABSTRACT
Many couples live a portion of their lives in a long-distance relationship (LDR). This includes a large number of dating college students as well as couples who are geographically-separated because of situational demands such as work. We conducted interviews with individuals in LDRs to understand how they make use of video chat systems to maintain their relationships. In particular, we have investigated how couples use video to "hang out" together and engage in activities over extended periods of time. Our results show that regardless of the relationship situation, video chat affords a unique opportunity for couples to share presence over distance, which in turn provides intimacy. While beneficial, couples still face challenges in using video chat, including contextual (e.g., location of partners, time zones), technical (e.g., mobility, audio/video quality, networking), and personal (e.g., a lack of physicality needed by most for intimate sexual acts) challenges.

Author Keywords
Long-distance relationships; video chat; intimacy

ACM Classification Keywords
H.5.3 [Information interfaces and presentation]: Group and Organization Interfaces - Computer Supported Cooperative Work;

General Terms: Design, Human Factors

INTRODUCTION
Long-distance relationships (LDRs) are those where partners expect to continue a close relationship but communication opportunities are restricted because of geographic distance [22]. In present culture, LDRs are fairly common [22]. Work may force partners to live apart because of a "two-body problem" where partners cannot find work in the same city [1]. It may be voluntary, such as dual-career and dual-residence couples who choose to live separately due to career demands, desires for autonomy [25], and/or desires to live geographically close to family. Certain jobs require people to live in different places or to travel for long durations, such as in professional athletics, the military, offshore oil workers, people who do extensive work in the field, or mariners who are off at sea. Crisis (such as ailing parents) may force one person to temporarily reside elsewhere. School studies also separate partners. In fact, studies of college students estimate that about 75% of college students have been involved in a LDR [22,24].

The low cost and ubiquity of computer-mediated communication (CMC) tools seemingly lessen the limitations of distance. Email, instant messaging (IM), cell phone calling, texting, video chat, and social networking sites all create easy ways for LDR partners to communicate. Media is now increasingly rich, and multiple channels provide support for a range of communicative activities [9,22], including even intimate activities like cybersex [20]. Studies have shown that CMC can ease loneliness [1] and increase feelings of closeness [1], relationship satisfaction, trust, and commitment, while lowering jealousy [5].

Recent studies have looked at the way video chat systems are used by family members to stay connected over distance [2,10,14]. However, none of these studies look specifically at the way LDR couples use video chat to help maintain their relationship. We also have seen a number of next generation video systems designed for the home [11,12,15, 19,29], however, their focus is not on connecting couples in LDRs. Thus, within this sphere, there has yet to be any focused study of how partners in LDRs make use of video chat systems to help maintain their relationship.

Our paper focuses on understanding and documenting this niche. In particular, we investigate how couples in serious LDRs (as opposed to casual dating) make use of video chat systems to help maintain their relationship. Our emphasis is on documenting the core practices of LDR couples to show how video affords unique opportunities for intimacy, a shared sense of presence, and even intimate (and sometimes sexual) interactions. This presents a detailed foundation for future design work. First, we outline related work on long distance relationships and studies of video chat systems. Second, we describe our interview methodology. Third, we step through our findings to illustrate the benefits and challenges that LDR couples face with video chat systems when used in a (somewhat) "always-on" setting. We conclude with a starting point for discussions about the impact of these routines for design.

RELATED WORK
Relationship maintenance is the cornerstone of all couple

relationships [4,22,24]. Whether people notice it or not, many of their common everyday activities relate to relationship maintenance. This includes positivity (e.g., being polite, avoiding criticism), being open, providing assurances about the relationship, expressing one's love physically, managing conflicts, and sharing tasks or chores [4]. When it comes to LDRs, the same basic relationship maintenance strategies are used [4,7].

Relationships will deteriorate if people do not actively work to maintain them using some or all of the above maintenance activities [4]. In fact, studies have also looked at the factors that relate to relationship satisfaction and they are very similar, if not the same, as the maintenance activities [28]. Such factors include satisfaction with communication, influence in the relationship, sexual activities, one's leisure (the way each partner spends free time), division of household tasks, time together (just the two partners), time with other friends/family, and finances [28]. Of all of these, satisfaction with communication is the strongest predictor of marital satisfaction [28].

A common assumption is that partners in LDRs are not as satisfied with their relationship because of the distance [22]. However, this is most often not the case: People find ways to achieve the previously mentioned relationship behaviors in spite of being separated by distance [22]. Relationship satisfaction in LDRs can also be explained by comparing the communication in LDRs with that of geographically-close relationships. Many relationships (regardless of distance) begin with partners seeing their relationship in an idealized form [28]. This view typically deteriorates over time as partners increase self-disclosure and become more open with each other [4]. But LDR partners often hold off on this degree of disclosure, talk more positively about their relationship, and avoid conflicting topics [23,26]. When together, LDR partners may be on their "best behavior" in order to cherish their time together [5]. Thus, LDR partners are just as satisfied with their relationships as geographically-close couples because they avoid conflict [4,23]. Studies of LDRs that become geographically-close show that once partners are together, they open up, discuss more conflicting topics, and the idealized view of the relationship dissipates [25]. In fact, this is one of the main reasons that a third of LDRs that move to geographic proximity end within three months of reunion [25].

CMC technologies have changed the nature of LDRs by providing an ever-increasing range of ways to be connected. Access to a remote partner is now faster and cheaper than ever [6]. Novel research prototypes are even being designed to specifically target couples and the need to maintain their relationships over distance. For example, couples can now share melodies over their cell phones [21] or click to say, "I love you" [13]. However, such CMC technologies are not without their challenges. Scheduling times for communication over such channels is not always an easy task [1] and is certainly more problematic than 'bumping into' one's partner while at home. Many communication channels are also not very rich when compared to face-to-face situations.

One technology that does show promise, given its similarity to face-to-face settings, is video chat systems. A variety of studies have explored this space and illustrate the ways in which families make use of the technology and the challenges associated with it. First, studies have shown that feelings of "being there" are one of the largest benefits of video chat [2] and such systems make people feel closer to the remote person than other CMC technologies [14]. Second, we know that some people will leave their video link open for an extended period of time [10,14]. This occurs most often for families with children so that they can "share everyday life" with remote family members such as grandparents [10]. Third, studies have shown that it isn't easy to initiate video calls and people commonly use other technologies like the phone or instant messaging clients to first check the remote party's availability and willingness to video call before calling [2,10]. In some cases, people will stay 'offline' until they receive such a request [10]. Once calls are established, people face additional technical challenges in keeping the connection going [2,14].

Our own research builds on this related work. Given that video chat has already been shown to be left open over long periods of time, we wondered if and how this practice might extend to couples in LDRs. That is, how does the richer communication channel afforded by always-on video—or "hanging out" via video—support relationship maintenance over distance? Are there social and technical challenges introduced by this technology that affect its use in LDRs? This is the focus of our inquiry, described next.

METHODOLOGY

We conducted semi-structured interviews with fourteen people in LDRs, focusing on their use of video chat .

Participants

We recruited participants through snowball sampling, word-of-mouth, presentations on related topics, and ads on Facebook, Twitter, and an online forum devoted to LDRs. We selected participants who already used video chat as a primary technology for communicating with their distant partner, preferably where they kept a video link open with their partner for extended periods of time. We did not select for a particular kind of LDR relationship dynamic, which meant our sample included a variety of relationships, e.g., dating, living together, engaged, married. As is standard in qualitative research, we recruited and interviewed participants iteratively. Our interviews ceased once we no longer saw new practices emerge.

Participants ranged in age from 19 to 35 years old and half were female. Two participants were in same-sex relationships (one male, one female). All participants were in serious relationships (albeit to a varying degree). All participants currently resided in either the United States or

Canada, but some were originally from other countries. The geographical distance between partners varied heavily. The closest couple was a two-hour drive apart. The furthest had partners across the world, where they were separated by large time zone differences of 10-12 hours. Due to our recruitment process, about half of our participants were graduate students, post-doctoral fellows, or researchers; yet, their partners' occupations varied broadly.

Interview Method and Analysis

We conducted semi-structured interviews with each participant individually. Only 2 of the 14 were part of the same couple and were interviewed separately. Interviews lasted between 60 and 90 minutes. Five interviews were conducted over Skype and nine were conducted in person in a private office. Questions explored participants' relationships and routines in detail, their use of video chat systems, and their use of other CMC systems in comparison to video chat. We kept handwritten or typed interview notes and audio recorded all interviews. The focal points of our interviews were transcribed and the remainder of the audio was used for reference as needed. We inductively analyzed our interviews using open, axial and selecting coding [27].

What we found remarkable with our participants was that each, regardless of the relationship dynamics, was able to maintain large degrees of intimacy in their LDR because the video channel afforded unique opportunities to connect the partners' physical locations and created a shared sense of presence between the partners. In the following sections, we document this along with the social and technical challenges that participants faced in using video chat. Again, our emphasis is on providing descriptive details on the routines of our participants.

REASONS FOR USING OTHER CMC MEDIA *VS* VIDEO

Participants used a variety of CMC technologies to connect with their distant partner. Each fulfilled a specific need. They commonly used SMS texting for short greetings such as "Good Morning" or "I love you", quick questions during the day, for security where some would check to ensure their partner had made it home safely, and (for some) just to stay in somewhat constant contact. Instant messaging was similar, yet it also afforded asynchronous conversations over a longer time period, such as while one of the partners was at work. They used email (or Facebook private messaging) for sharing stories or funny items, reminiscing about their relationship, coordinating tasks such as paying bills and planning trips, or reviewing documents. They used the telephone for deeper conversations, where partners needed to focus on one another and their discussion. This might include talking about their relationship or other potentially emotional topics. They said it was also useful for short and timely interactions, because it was fast to phone someone. They predominantly used cell phones in situations when one or both partners were mobile.

Participants most often used Skype or Google Chat to video chat with their partners and video chat played a somewhat different role than other technologies. All participants stated they had used video chat as a communication tool for their relationship either before they became separated by distance, or immediately after moving apart. A few began using video chat for pragmatic reasons, such as that it was faster to simply talk rather than type, and that Skype calls were free. In those few cases, video usage began because it was a byproduct of these voice calls, but then became more valued over time. However, for the vast majority of cases, and as one might expect (and similar to families' use of video chat [2,10,14]), people primarily wanted to *see* the other person when apart, and share their day-to-day life by *hanging out* together. Both provided an additional level of emotional connection that other CMC technologies could not provide. We provide details in the following sections.

VIDEO CHAT IS FOR SEEING

First and foremost, they simply wanted to see their partner's face, as it made them feel emotionally closer to each other.

"I could not stand not seeing my husband. I mean, I needed him, I needed to see him, and actually everyday we also talk by our cell phone but it's not enough for us. I need to see his face. And he also has the same feeling"- P12

"The voice is not enough. The relationship is so physical and visual. It's not just about hearing and talking." – P13

They also described video as a way to see their partners' facial expressions and body language. In some cases, this helped avoid miscommunications.

"I always apparently sound pretty harsh when I'm talking ...even when I'm joking it doesn't sound like I'm joking...I would sometimes upset her without even knowing I upset her and, of course, without intending...With video, the problem I had on the phone goes away because she can see that I'm smiling, she can see that I'm being supportive, she can see that I'm not frowning or being angry at her, so you know in that kind of sense it removed those obstacles." – P3

"You don't have to talk. You can see smiles." – P13

"It's just that if you see someone you feel it's real ... you see their reaction instantly. With audio it's harder to get the same information of how someone feels." – P14

They also said that video helped them see the emotional demeanor of others. One participant said that seeing their partner looking tired and worn out helped him understand her state of mind, where he would empathize with her.

Video helped them see their partner's surroundings, whether it was just part of the background or purposely shared by giving the other a video tour around the area.

"It's really nice to see where the other person is situated... she's always at home but it's nice to see she's at home, see cats running around in the background." – P1

Partners commonly "showed off" new things visually over video chat. This ranged from haircuts to modeling clothes and glasses they just purchased.

Some people were very aware of their appearance. Even though they shared intimate relationships and had seen each other "at their worst," three participants would only video chat after they had made themselves "look good."

"We kinda prepare to see each other. One thing we found really bad is seeing each other right after waking up." – P5

"I just feel like I'm on stage when we're on Skype. And I know I look different when I'm on video. It's not like being in person...Having to be confronted with how you look continuously is different than having a face-to-face conversation with someone. You're more aware... I still like put makeup on and do my hair before Skypying..." – P6

Overall, participants said that they used video because it created a unique sense of presence with their partners. In fact, this was one of the fundamental reasons that many couples used video, and only part of this relates to seeing. We return to this in subsequent results.

A MATTER OF ROUTINE: INITIATION AND TIMING

On the downside, video chat was seen as more challenging to initiate a connection with than other technologies. Thus, it was used more commonly in situations when both partners had the time to stay connected for longer durations. People managed this by the way they initiated and timed their video chat sessions.

Like other studies of video chat [2,10], we also found that nearly all of our participants would use other technologies to check if their remote partner was available to video chat prior to video calling them. This varied between using text messages, the phone, or instant messaging to find out if the partner was in a location conducive to video chat (e.g., at home vs. work) and if they were not busy. While some used the IM capabilities by staying online continuously, others did not as they did not want to be available for video-calls by people other than their partner.

However, most video chats were not totally serendipitous or one-person initiated. Instead, partners developed routines of when they would be available to each other. Much like a couple living together, they would try and expect to see each other once they had arrived at home after work or school in the evenings, or early mornings, or at other key times during the day. For example, one couple said they usually contacted each other in the evening, just after dinner, and kept the connection open for an hour or two.

Yet time zone differences—which is a fact of life for LDRs living far apart—strongly influenced how they fashioned their video call routines. Usually this meant juggling their schedules to fit their windows of opportunity, e.g., compensating for mismatches between when they would get up, arrive or leave at work, have dinner, or go to bed. A bigger issue is that the larger the time difference, the fewer the number of hours they would have together. For example, a couple in the same time zone would often have three or four hours to spend together in the evenings. Yet a couple with a partner on (say) each coast of North America might only have one hour to spend together before one had to go to bed.

Extreme time zone differences (e.g., 10-12 hours apart) introduced further challenges. Our four participants in this category worked around this, but it was not always easy. The first participant had a partner who worked from home so they would routinely video call while she was at home during her evening and he was working during his morning. The second couple had work schedules that were aligned so that they both had the same six hours off of work together; for one this was in the evening, and for the other it was in the morning. The third couple did not work so they could alter their sleep schedules to be awake during a larger time overlap. The fourth couple had no such options because both had fairly rigid work times. To compensate, they scheduled their video time together on the weekend.

HANGING OUT: DAY-TO-DAY SHARED LIVING

We purposely tried to recruit participants who used a video chat system for extended durations of time, and, as it turned out, all but one participant did indeed do this. This participant simply did not have enough overlapping "free time" with his partner to allow them to stay connected for more than an hour at a time. On the other hand, all of our other participants "hung out" with their partners over video links for several hours at a time. The video link supported two primary behaviors: partners doing different activities in parallel where the video link provided a view onto each other's activities, and partners doing shared activities together. We describe each in detail.

Parallel Activities

Eleven participants described doing parallel activities with their partners over a video chat system. That is, partners would be connected over a video link but each would be doing his or her "own thing." As in day-to-day domestic life, parallel activities varied, but included house-cleaning, work, cooking, eating, reading, playing games, or watching television, where each partner would be doing a different thing on his or her own. Sometimes activity would occur in front of the camera, and other times it might only be visible over the link part of the time. Partners would periodically look to see what their remote partner was doing.

"Once [video] starts I just kinda sit back in the sofa, put the laptop on the coffee table, eat dinner, watch tv, sometimes do work (on my other laptop)... Most of that time she's off playing her own games on her phone or iPod... she might stream something from NetFlix... and she's just there on the screen." – P3

Conversation routinely would come and go during video sessions containing parallel activities. That is, partners might periodically get the attention of the other person and talk to them. Otherwise, the two were not normally engaged in conversation.

"I would sometimes be reading or something while we'd be on video ...we'd just have [Skype] open, and sometimes

we'd not really say anything for like 15 minutes, 20 minutes you know but I'd be able to talk to her. So it was kinda like being in the same room as her but not necessarily interacting actively." – P2

"Usually he's sitting on the couch and eating some kind of snack or dinner ... if there's something that we need to say to each other we'll chime in every now and then. It's almost like you're sitting and watching TV together...Typically it's we keep it running and live our lives kind of deal. And it's typical evening stuff, making dinner, making sure things are cleaned up, getting things ready, taking care of personal business, stuff like that." – P7

Some participants even said they muted their microphone so that unnecessary sounds from their end were not transmitted, such as a TV, music, or keyboard typing. If they wanted to get their partner's attention, they would just unmute their microphone.

"We use video as a method to simulate shared living. Even if we aren't talking, the video channel is open. In fact, even when open it is on mute most of the time ... We do the things we would normally do if we were together and can see one another doing it." – P10

Regardless of the specific activities that were occurring, participants predominantly told us that the purpose of having the video link open was to simply feel the presence of their remote partner. This made them feel more comfortable and even closer to their partner.

"At home, a lot of times at night, he likes to put on his pjs and turn out all the lights and sit there with a snack and, you know, watch TV. So sometimes it's hard to see him but other than that, as long as you can see the form of somebody that's a nice thing. I think it's just the comfort of knowing that they're there." – P7

Shared Activities

Seven participants talked with us about doing shared activities—beyond talking—with their partners over a video chat system. These activities formed a core part of their relationship maintenance. Routine shared activities usually occurred during weekday evenings *vs.* the weekend, as weekend schedules were less predictable. Several activities are listed below, where all reported the same benefit: they would be doing a routine, everyday activity together.

Watching Television or Videos. Seven participants watched television or videos together. This often involved them placing a laptop or computer near or in front of a couch and then broadcasting their reactions to the show to their remote partner. Sometimes remote partners would watch the same show if they had the same channels. Other times, they might watch their own show. Some participants would even try to synchronize the watching of movies together.

"We video Skyped while we both had this movie and we watched it at the same time ... we were like Skyping at the same time so we could see each other's reaction, like he was small and in the corner so I could see his reaction...it was nice, I actually mentioned it to him the other day that I wanted to do that again, it was nice because there was more of the idea that the person was there... that was a very prime part in our relationship ... I could see him laugh at the funny parts or I could see his reaction to something ridiculous." – P9

Two participants watched music videos together so they could both listen to the same music at the same time. In these cases they would share links to YouTube videos and then both try to synchronize the starting of them. Both participants enjoyed seeing their partners' facial reactions to the songs and videos over their Skype connections.

Three issues arose when partners would try to watch shows or videos together. First, partners who tried to watch the same interactive content (e.g., online streaming of TV shows, YouTube videos) found it difficult to synchronize them. One couple resorted to counting down numbers from 5 to 1 out loud before hitting play. Second, if the show/movie was watched on a TV, then it was easy to see the remote partner on the separate computer. Yet if the show was being watched on the computer, participants would have to toggle between seeing their partner and seeing the show, or strategically place the video window such that both could be seen (if this was even possible with the participants' software). Third, audio was a significant problem; sound from the show or video would broadcast over the video link at the expense of the partners' voices. This created duplicate (and somewhat unsynchronized) sound if the partners were watching the same show.

"What happens is both of us watch TV a lot, so when she streams she mostly streams Netflix...the audio comes through really loud... my volume of her is at 5% so I can [only] hear her if she says 'hey' really loud." – P3

"The reason why we watch together is to see and hear each other's reactions for the shows that we like so much. And that's the crappy part about Skype and watching TV together because you can't talk because the audio is so loud from the show on both ends ... When we were [face-to-face], it was like constant conversation and making jokes and laughing about stupid things people say...it's more like a tool to get to know each other." – P6

Sharing Meals. Two participants were fortunate enough to have similar enough time zones and eating schedules that they could occasionally sit down together and eat dinner over Skype. One described this as being similar to the way a collocated couple might routinely eat together as opposed to a date or special occasion.

"This year we started video chatting and having dinner, which has been nice...it'll be a sushi night and we'll get sushi and ahh, umm, so yah, as much as we can to sort of normalize this ridiculous long distance relationship we try...In a way we both know that it's not a date, it's just we're having dinner together in front of Skype." – P9

Playing Video Games. One participant described how he would play video games on his computer with his distant boyfriend. Being able to see him periodically over the video link added to the gaming experience.

"Most of the time we have the window in front of the video anyhow where we're not just really watching exclusively the video...But you can just click over and see him." – P10

Time with Others. Nearly all shared activities occurred between just the two partners; rarely did they ever have other friends participate in their shared activities. In fact, most participants said that they compromised the time that they spent with other family or friends, and would instead spend the majority of their spare time with their partner.

LOCATION AND ENVIRONMENT

We saw several important instances where the location or environment affected the use of video chat in relation to privacy, mobility, and varying situational contexts.

Private vs. Shared Dwellings. Video chats predominantly occurred from within the participants' own homes or dwellings. For those who lived alone (which included the majority of our participants and their partners), they could easily hang out over video chat without family members or roommates observing. Those who lived in shared dwellings with either family members (e.g., parents, siblings) or roommates had other concerns. Somewhat surprisingly, while our participants did exhibit some privacy worries, they were often more anxious about disturbing their roommates. Consequently, they would try to video chat within a private bedroom as opposed to a communal room.

"Normally I'd just be in my bedroom... we had a living room and dining room but they were a really big open communal space and there'd be other people there. A lot of the times if I was on video people would be bothered by me talking. So typically I'd just be in my bedroom." – P2

To ensure privacy, some participants used other technologies before initiating a video call to check if other people were around. They also reported adjusting their computational and physical environment to safeguard their partner's privacy when others were around. For example, one person (who was in a private dwelling) described how her remote boyfriend would adjust his environment to make her comfortable with his roommates:

"There are sometimes if I am already in bed and I'm like in my pjs and stuff I'm not necessarily the most comfortable with his roommates seeing that...so [my boyfriend] will umm you know like push down his computer screen or just minimize the video because he knows about my comfort levels. Usually if we're talking about something more personal he'll just close the door and his roommates will know not to bother him or they'll knock first." – P9

Of course, the challenge here is that the girlfriend must rely on her remote partner to adjust *his* environment in order to ensure *her* privacy is not compromised.

Fixed vs. Mobile Locations. When spending time together over video, nearly all participants used a laptop to run their video chat system; only two used a desktop computer. However, many participants would leave their video chat system running from a fixed location in their home even if it was on a laptop. They reported that laptops were not really mobile: they were too cumbersome to move given their weight, the auxiliary wiring, or a deteriorating battery. Some considered fixed locations simply as "good enough."

Others found great value in being able to easily move a laptop around the home. They would typically bring the laptop into the room they were in so their partner could still see them and "be present" in the same space. This included moving the laptop between the living room, kitchen, bedroom, and even bathroom. For example, several participants described how they would bring their laptop into the bathroom when showering or putting on make-up. Here the act was not typically sexual in nature.

Regardless of whether the computer was stationary or mobile, many participants periodically rotated their camera or laptop (with embedded camera) to the general direction they were located in so their partner could see them.

"While I'm not in the living room, I basically turn the laptop so she can see me in the kitchen. I turn the laptop when I'm sitting on the sofa." – P3

"Sometimes he'll be playing a video game in which case he'll turn the camera to face him. But most of the time this is his world of me ..." – P10

Connecting at Work. Five people said they connected with their partners either from their own workplace or to their partner's workplace. Participants were conscious of intruding on work activities or being noisy or distracting to other co-workers who might also be present. As a result, most used earphones or microphones to control audio. One participant told us he would only connect with his fiancée over Skype from his work on weekends, as others were not typically around. Another participant only used Skype from work in the early morning before her colleagues arrived.

"I can video chat at work for a few minutes if I need to. And if no one is around I'll do the same kind of thing [hanging out]...I'll turn on my video chat and just do my [work] and that way I can see him." – P7

One participant told us that because of the extreme time zone difference she could *only* see her boyfriend while he worked. On at least one occasion, this created an interesting situation because of the mixed home-work context:

"Last night I was watching something on TV and he had a meeting and uh he just cut my voice... I could see him and of course the person he was meeting with couldn't see me but I was just, you know, doing my own thing and no sound but we could see each other... his office is in his house. I was minimized so the person with him couldn't see what was happening on the computer. I just look at him once in a

while and then he comes back and tells me he is done and I shush him because I am still watching TV." – P4

Several participants did not connect from or to their partner at work, and some were even adamantly opposed to doing so. One participant comments:

"I tried to call her at work once. She was just really embarrassed and was like 'why are you trying to call me at work.' We only ever talk from home...I think maybe just because there are other people around. It's kinda like how you don't want to talk on a cell phone on a bus because you don't want to disturb people and maybe you don't want them listening in on your conversation. And I think that's even more so when there is video involved." – P1

CONVERSATION & (LACK OF) IDEALIZATION

All participants said that they talked with their partners over video chat before, after, or periodically during their time together. Conversations covered nearly any topic, including day-to-day activities, mutual or non-mutual friends, family members, problems at work, finances, trip planning, sports, and hobbies. Video chat supported such conversations for the most part, although some commented that maintaining eye contact was a challenge.

As mentioned, previous work in LDRs reported idealization behavior, e.g., partners tend to talk more positively, avoid conflicting topics, and be on best behaviours [23,26]. This contrasted with what our participants reported. Nearly all talked about discussing negative topics either at the onset of their time apart or within a few weeks of it. This included discussions of relationship issues, religion, or problematic finances. Several people even openly argued over video chat and felt that it aided their ability to argue.

"Even when we fight we prefer to fight online and see each other because we can see the facial expression of the other person...I think in some cases it can make it worse. In some cases, it can soften it, depending on our reactions really. If say I get so upset I'm bursting into tears, he calms down. Or if something is happening and I'm getting really angry and I'm just ignoring him, he gets more angry so really it depends on the reactions of the person. But the good thing about it is you can see the other person's facial expression because it gives you an idea of what the person is feeling at that moment. If we want to hurt each other more we can, if we want to calm down more we can." – P4

A few purposely chose not to argue over video chat, even though they would sometimes talk about negative topics. One participant did not want her partner to see her face when she was upset with him, not wanting to "give him the satisfaction." Two participants felt that video chat would force them to stay in front of the camera and this did not match their preferred style of arguing, which involved moving between rooms to "get away" from their partner.

"I would never want to have an argument on Skype. I'd much rather have an argument over the telephone...when you're on Skype, you are expected to look straight into the camera. A lot of my argument style involves not looking at the other person." – P6

Another participant commented that video chat did not enable her and her husband to resolve an argument the way they might in person. Typically they would leave the same room during an argument and then return to kiss or hug the other person. Such physical touch is not possible in video chat systems. Yet we did see one couple produce a workaround with a similar effect: They would argue over video chat, but then send resolving terms of endearment through a different medium, be it text or instant messaging.

INTIMATE AND SEXUAL ACTS

Participants also told us about shared acts that they would do together over video that were of a more intimate or sexual nature. These fell into several categories.

Hugging and Kissing. All but two participants told us that they would express their love with their partner by virtually kissing or hugging them over the video link. This occurred at the end of conversations, but also periodically if the moment warranted it. In spite of problems caused by the separation of the camera from the screen and/or video window, people found workarounds. They or their partners would blow kisses in the air, kiss the area in front of the laptop screen, or hold their arms out as though they were hugging the person in real. One participant even said his partner would stroke his head and shoulder by cupping her hand around his video image and moving it up and down.

"Every now and then like every night we'll typically sign off by giving each other kisses, which is actually like kissing the webcam so it actually looks like you're kissing. If you kiss the screen you get the other person's forehead. Sometimes we'll pretend to hug the laptop. And... surprisingly... it's not like getting a real hug, but it is kind of rewarding in a way." – P1

"I'm trying to kiss her on the camera... and sometimes she opens her collar and says 'kiss me here'." – P11

For many, kissing and hugging over the link was intimate. Yet a few thought it wasn't serious, where it brought more humor to the relationship and moment.

"I'll make a kiss face at her over video sometimes. I have like hugged my computer and made it look like I was hugging the video but normally this is something I'd just do because it was silly to make her laugh." – P2

Going To Bed / Falling Asleep. Six participants told us that they would sometimes watch their partner fall asleep, or vice versa. These partners would be using video chat during the evening until the point when one of them would be ready to go to bed. That person would then bring their laptop into the bedroom and set it so that it could capture them falling asleep. In one instance, both partners fell asleep together because they shared the same sleep pattern and time zone.

"I will move [the laptop] to my bedroom. The light is on normally because if I don't turn it on he can't see me...and he normally cuts his voice off so I don't wake up from his phone calls or him talking to people. And at a point in time the computer goes to sleep....it's on the bedside table and I normally position it towards my face." – P4

They also reported several issues. Video quality often deteriorated significantly because of the dark room. Some used the lit computer screen to illuminate themselves (and also to see their partner as they fell asleep), but at the cost of a bright light affecting their slumber. Location and equipment stability was problematic. They said they had to carefully place the laptop (and camera) on a stand, chair, pillow, or blanket so that it had the right camera angle to capture themselves, all while ensuring it didn't shift or fall over. Some participants were also cautious because their laptops might overheat on bedding.

"Often she'll have it in her lap... and then she pulls up a chair next to her bed and she places the laptop on that chair...and then she just kinda falls asleep that way." – P3

"When you're on a desk you're alright, but that time I wanted to go on the bed and everything was more soft and would move. This was hard. This was a challenge... because the camera would just fall off... because it was on a soft pillow or on the blanket." – P8

Sexual Activities and Nudity. Only two participants said they regularly engaged in full cybersex activities with their partner, where the participants and their partners would both mutually satisfy themselves through masturbation. One of these participants commented that even though they had cybersex, it highlighted the challenges of the act more than anything. They realized more fully that they couldn't actually touch each other and this caused them to miss each other more. For the other couple, cybersex became so important that it was necessary to see the remote partner to be sexually satisfied. Two other participants had tried cybersex, but stopped because it became "awkward."

The ten remaining participants had not tried cybersex for a variety of reasons (we did not notice any obvious gender differences). Several said either they or their partners were too shy to engage in cybersex. Some simply felt it was not a core need for their relationship. Privacy was a concern: two participants didn't want their partners to get completely naked because they had a fear that the video might somehow be recorded or seen by others.

"I feel it goes back to that culture thing, the shyness... you feel like it's not right. Maybe he feels more distant when he's on the video." - P4

"I felt a little uncomfortable about trying to touch myself on video. I didn't feel very comfortable or in the mood." – P8

"We attempted to have video chat intimate relations and it was very awkward and didn't work out...Maybe it's because I'm insecure but I don't want to look fat or unattractive...I'm a little square in the corner and he sees a lot more of me than i do. I just can't stop thinking about it and so it decreases any other enjoyment that I might get out of it." – P6

Some people reported using nudity to visually tease or emotionally connect to their partner as opposed to a physical sexual act such as masturbation. For example:

"But I did like to just strip tease and have this fun with the video and just showing parts of clothing or parts of skin. Like playing with the frame... I'd step away and just show my bra...or showing my back so not really showing everything but still teasing." – P8

However, others disagreed, as sexual nudity without physical proximity did not have the same intimate connotations. As one participant noted:

"Maybe it's like I'm being watched or something. A lot of times when people ask do you have intimate stuff going on online I always think to myself that they are talking about a porn movie. I don't want to be in a porn movie for my boyfriend... he could just go watch a porn movie, why should I do it.... there's no real intimacy after that." – P4

One participant found it easier to "talk dirty" with her boyfriend over IM because of her shyness. She also had "phone sex" with him on a few occasions and thought this offered more of an exchange than video cybersex because it produced more feelings of equality. Another participant commented that the use of the phone was more intimate because it was like "whispering" in his fiancée's ear.

In addition to intimate sexual acts, three participants also talked about seeing their partner either nude or partly naked at times, either while changing or coming out of the shower. In these cases, the viewing was not sexual in nature.

"There were a few times where if I was changing or whatever if I was putting my pajamas on I'd just pull off my clothes and not bother to turn the camera off. It wasn't in a sexual context... and she does the same thing." – P2

Overall, cybersex was a very personal choice that depended on the couple's values, perceptions of the video media, and the degree they could emotionally connect (or not) over a progression of cybersex activities. For most, the discussion centered around intimacy: the degree of cybersex involved—whether via hugging, kissing, virtual touching, nudity, or masturbation—was more a projection of how that cybersex supported or interfered with feelings of intimacy.

DISCUSSION

We now discuss our findings and highlight a series of core problems that suggest design directions for future systems.

Shared Living. First, our study reveals a pattern of communication that has moved beyond phone call-like usage. Regardless of the relationship situation, couples appropriated video technologies in a new way that made more sense to them. They turned video chat systems into tools that connected two locations in a more permanent fashion. This in turn produced a shared living experience that modeled face-to-face settings more than other CMC technologies. In this joint setting, partners pursued their independent activities, took part in shared activities, and conversed as needed. When conversing, the video added a crucial element of seeing the other person's face and facial expressions. When performing activities, having one's partner 'around' created stronger feelings of connectedness. Together, this shows that intimacy between couples in LDRs is not necessarily about sexual intimacy. It is more importantly about being able to spend time together, whether people are doing the same activity together or not.

These situations certainly create interesting challenges for technology design. Partners would find great value in being able to move throughout their home while using a video chat system and still be on camera. Yet they currently cannot because of power issues, the mobility of devices, audio and camera capture range, etc. Smartphones with Skype or Apple's FaceTime provide one partial solution to mobility, but issues remain and they introduce their own problems (e.g., holding the camera, framing, audio fidelity). Video capture devices also need to be able to be situated in locations that are less conducive to technology placement (e.g., a laptop sitting on a bed). Present technologies are not designed well for these locations.

Partners also need to be able to perform multiple activities on their device at the same time as using a video chat system. For example, many want to video chat while watching television or listening to music. Google+ now provides one way of synchronizing video viewing while using video chat but it is situated more for work meetings and not LDRs. Audio mixing and cancelling is particularly problematic given the various audio channels available (microphones, video, etc).

There also exist challenges with mixed lighting conditions such as poorly lit living rooms or bedrooms when a partner wants to see the other person but not wake them. This suggests research in image enhancement, camera sensitivity, device/screen design, or illumination balancing.

In addition, many social issues exist that are perhaps more difficult to solve through design. People are hesitant to broadcast video for extended periods of time from work or they may not be allowed to; this forces connections into the evening hours. Sometimes people can work around this by working from home. Yet this brings challenges with connecting mixed contexts. This includes connecting not only work and home, but one person's private home with their partner's shared living arrangements.

Sexual Intimacy. Our findings also revealed that, for many, complete sexual intimacy is difficult to gain over a video channel because there is a lack of true physicality between partners. Video chat systems are simply not designed with cybersex in mind, akin to the way that sex toys are now being carefully designed for aesthetics, embodied pleasure, and intimate experiences [3]. Clearly partners need better ways to physically interact over distance as cybersex is extremely limiting. For physical acts such as kissing, hugging and touching, the separation of the camera from the video window is also challenging. Yet beyond these design challenges, what was common to all our couples was that they described sex—no matter how far they took it—entirely as an extension of intimacy. That is, it wasn't so much about the sex, but rather about being together and being intimate together. This further exemplifies the role of presence in supporting and maintaining LDRs.

Idealization. We also found that couples in our study did not idealize about their relationship in the same ways that the existing literature has described LDRs [5,23,28]. Most partners discussed conflicting topics and they had very realistic views (as opposed to idealized ones) of the nature of their relationship. While we cannot draw any causal conclusions, we hypothesize that this reduced idealization was at least partially due to the manner in which our participants used the video link to simulate shared living and promote behaviors more similar to face-to-face relationships. Further study is warranted to fully investigate this aspect though.

CONCLUSION

Our paper has detailed the ways in which couples in long-distance relationships stay connected by using a video chat system. In particular, we have explored situations where partners hang out together by leaving their video chat system running over extended periods of time. Overall, our research suggests an avenue of design that directly supports creating a shared sense of presence between partners in long-distance relationships. Feeling intimately connected to a remote partner is not just about saying 'I love you.' It is about being a part of his or her life, about being day-to-day companions. Video chat is one tool that supports this, despite its limitations and challenges. We suggest that designers, researchers, and practitioners consider other mediums in addition to video to explore how they too can provide a rich experience that allows partners to feel like they are a part of their remote companion's life.

Our findings point the way, but we recognize its limitations. First, our participants may not be representative of the population at large. They were all of younger ages, reasonably savvy about technology, and comfortable enough to talk—quite openly—about how they used video chat. Second, most were (broadly) part of Western culture, although a few were from regions outside of Europe and North America. LDRs in other cultures and other demographics may appropriate and use video chat systems in different ways, and have different views and behaviors when it comes to on intimacy, sexual activities, and relationships. Some may even be opposed to utilizing a video link in the same way as our participants. In spite of these caveats, our participants were uniform in how they viewed video as a way to maintain intimacy and to be present in each other's daily lives. We encourage others to continue this research and explore the cross-cultural variations that may exist in long-distance relationships.

ACKNOWLEDGMENTS

This research was funded by the Natural Sciences and Engineering Research Council and the GRAND NCE as part of the AFEVAL project. We thank our participants for sharing intimate details about their relationships.

REFERENCES

1. Aguila, A.P.N. Living Long Distance Relationships through Computer-Mediated Communication, *Social Science Diliman* 5:1-2, (2009), 83-106.
2. Ames, M., Go, J., Kaye, J., Spasojevic, M., Making Love in the Network Closet: The Benefits and Work of Family Videochat, *Proc. CSCW,* ACM Press (2010).
3. Bardzell, J., and Bardzell, S. Pleasure is Your Birthright: Digitally Enabled Designer Sex Toys as a Case of Third-Wave HCI, *Proc. CHI,* ACM Press (2011).
4. Canary, D., and Stafford, L. Maintaining Relationships through Strategic Routine Interactions, *Communication & Relational Maintenance,* Academic Press, (1994).
5. Dainton, M., and Aylor, B. Patterns of communication channel use in the maintenance of long distance relationships, *Communication Research Reports,* 19, (2002), 118-129.
6. Dimmick, J., Kline, S., and Stafford, L. The gratification niches of personal email and the telephone: Competition, displacement, and complementarity, *Communication Research,* 27, 227-248.
7. Dindia, K., and Emmers-Sommer, T.M. What partners do to maintain their close relationships, In *Close relationships: Functions, forms and processes*, New York: Psychology Press (2006), 305-324.
8. Duck, S. W., Steady s(he) goes: Relational maintenance as a shared meaning system. In D. J. Canary & L. Stafford (Eds.), *Communication and relational maintenance*, San Diego, CA: Academic Press (1994)
9. Johnson, A.J., Haigh, M., Becker, J., Craig, E., and Wigley, S. College Students' Use of Relational Management Strategies in Email in Long-Distance and Geographically Close Relationships, *J. Computer Mediated Communication,* 13, 381-404, (2008).
10. Judge, T.K. and Neustaedter, C., Sharing Conversation and Sharing Life: Video Conferencing in the Home. *Proc. CHI*, ACM Press (2010), 655-658.
11. Judge, T.K., Neustaedter, C. and Kurtz, A., The Family Window: The Design and Evaluation of a Domestic Media Space. *Proc. CHI*, ACM Press (2010).
12. Judge, T. Neustaedter, C., Harrison, S., and Blose, A., The Family Portals: Connecting Families Through a Multifamily Media Space. *Proc. ACM CHI*, (2011).
13. Kaye, J. I just clicked to say I love you, *Extended Abstracts of Proc. CHI,* ACM Press (2006).
14. Kirk, D., Sellen, A., and Cao, X., Home Video Communication, *Proc. CSCW,* ACM Press (2010).
15. Neustaedter, C. and Judge, T. Peek-A-Boo: The Design of a Mobile Family Media Space, Video, *Proc. Ubicomp*, Springer (2010).
16. Pistole, M.C., Roberts, A., Chapman, M.L. Attachment, relationship maintenance, and stress in long distance and geographically close romantic relationships, *J. Social and Personal Relationships*, Vol. 27(4), (2010).
17. Pistole, M.C., Roberts, A., Mosko, J. Commitment Predictors: Long-Distance Versus Geographically Close Relationships, *J. Counseling and Development,* Spring 2010, Volume 88, (2010), 146-153.
18. Raffle, H., Ballagas, R., Revelle, G., Horii, H., Follmer, S., Go, J., Reardon, E., Mori, K., Kaye, J., and Spasojevic, M. (2010) Family story play: reading with children, *Proc. CHI,* ACM Press (2010).
19. Raffle, H., Revelle, G., Mori, K., Ballagas, R., Buza, K., Horii, H., Kaye, J., Cook, K., Freed, N., Go, J., Spasojevic, M. Hello, Is Grandma There? StoryVisit: Family Video Chat and Connected E-Books, *Proc. CHI*, ACM Press (2011).
20. Rumbough, T., The development and maintenance of interpersonal relationships through computer-mediated communication, *J. Communication Research*, 18(3).
21. Shirazi, A., Alt, F., Schmidt, A., Sarjanoja, A., Hynninen, L., Hakkila, J., and Holleis, P. Emotion Sharing via Self-Composed Melodies on Mobile Phones, *Proc. Mobile HCI*, ACM Press, (2009).
22. Stafford, L. Maintaining Long-Distance and Cross-Residential Relationships, Lawrence Erlbaum, (2005).
23. Stafford, L. Geographic Distance and Communication During Courtship, *J. Communication Researc*h, 37(2), (2010), 275-297.
24. Stafford, L., & Canary, D. J., Maintenance strategies and romantic relationship type, gender, and relational characteristics, *J. Social and Personal Relationships,* 8, (1991), 217-242.
25. Stafford, L., Merolla, A., and Castle, J. When long-distance dating partners become geographically close, *J. Social and Personal Relationships*, 23 (6), (2006), 901-919.
26. Stafford, L., and Reske, J. Idealization and Communication in Long Distance Premarital Relationships, *J. Family Relations*, 39 (3), (1990).
27. Strauss, A. and Corbin, J. *Basics of Qualitative Research*, 2nd Edition, Sage Publications (1998).
28. Vangelisti, A., and Huston, T. Maintaining Marital Satisfaction and Love, *Communication and Relational Maintenance*, Academic Press, (1994).
29. Yarosh, S., Cuzzort, S., Mueller, H., and Abowd, G.D., Developing a Media Space for Remote Synchronous Parent-Child Interaction, *Proc IDC*, ACM Press (2009).

How Do Couples Use CheekTouch over Phone Calls?

Young-Woo Park, Seok-Hyung Bae, Tek-Jin Nam
Department of Industrial Design, KAIST
291 Daehak-ro, Yuseong-gu, Daejeon 305-701, Republic of Korea
{pyw, seokhyung.bae, tjnam}@kaist.ac.kr

ABSTRACT
In this paper we introduce CheekTouch, an affective audio-tactile communication technique that transmits multi-finger touch gestures applied on a sender's mobile phone to a receiver's cheek in real time during a call. We made a pair of CheekTouch prototypes each with a multi-touch screen and vibrotactile display to enable bidirectional touch delivery. We observed four romantic couples in their twenties using our prototype system in a lab setting over five consecutive days, and analyzed how CheekTouch affected their non-verbal and emotional communication. The results of the user study showed that CheekTouch could effectively support audio-tactile communication in various ways – persuading, conveying status, delivering information, emphasizing emotion/words, calling for attention, and being playful.

Author Keywords
Affective communication; on-the-cheek interaction; multi-finger touch; vibrotactile feedback; remote touch; mobile phone;

ACM Classification Keywords
H.5.2 [Information Interfaces And Presentation]: User Interfaces - Input devices and strategies;

General Terms
Design;

INTRODUCTION
Mobile phones are now an essential medium of our daily communication. We use mobile phones to share information, ideas, music, photos, feelings and emotions with family members, friends, and colleagues. Because mobile phones help us feel connected with others, their importance as an emotional communication medium is growing as our life style is being more individualized and isolated.

Emotional communication using traditional phones depends on phonetic information such as amplitude variation, pitch inflection, tempo, duration, filtration, tonality and rhythm. For effective emotional communication, however, verbal and non-verbal behaviors such as facial expressions and touches should be in harmony.

A number of past projects have explored touch channels to support emotional communication in distance. However, most of them required additional equipment, such as pads [3], woofers [5], rollers [1], and arm-band type devices [7]; users should put their palm on the desk, or push the device with both hands to use. They make remote emotional communication arguably difficult; users cannot maintain the conventional phone calling posture, which consists of the receiver on the ear and the transmitter on the mouth [4], that is, a device on the cheek. In addition, they have rarely been evaluated in real time [2] and discussed in enough detail to show their practicality in remote emotional communication [3].

In this paper, we suggest a novel audio-tactile communication technique called CheekTouch, which allows sharing touches over phone calls by transmitting multi-finger touch gestures applied on a sender's touch screen of a mobile phone to a receiver's cheek using vibrotactile stimulation, in real time. In addition to applying only components that current smart phones normally use while not requiring additional special devices, it makes possible for users to share their emotions in the conventional phone call posture. To examine its usefulness, we observed four romantic couples using CheekTouch in phone call situations over five consecutive days. Here we illustrate the potential of CheekTouch with findings of the user study about how it can help non-verbal and emotional communication.

CHEEKTOUCH
To make remote emotional communication natural and effective without changing the conventional style to use phones, we identified the following design considerations.

- One-hand interaction: Users should express touch gestures with the fingers of the hand holding the phone.
- On-the-cheek interaction: Users should apply finger gestures and feel tactile feedback without the need of taking the phone away from the cheek.
- Localized tactile rendering: The area to which vibrotactile stimulation applies should be minimized (on the cheek only while not spreading to the hand holding it and other components of the mobile device).
- Real-time touch communication: Touches during a voice call should be delivered immediately.

Touch Input

We used a portable multi-touch mobile device, the iPod touch (Figure 1(f) and (i)), to enable multi-finger touch input while speaking on the phone.

Vibrotactile Output

First, we used an existing mobile phone's vibration motor because they can be easily adapted even if they are used in large numbers compared to other actuators. We placed nine coin-type vibrotactile actuators (10mm diameter, 3mm thickness) in a 3×3 grid (Figure 1(c)) to represent simple finger touch patterns (tapping, sliding back and forth), which might be applied with one or two fingers of the hand holding the phone during a call. The distance between each of the nine actuators was set to 7mm because the two-point discrimination threshold on the cheek is 7mm on average. We inserted (8mm depth) the coin-type actuators (Figure 1(c)) into a high-density sponge (Figure 1(b)) so that each actuator's axis of rotation is perpendicular to the sponge surface's normal vector, in order to stimulate local cheek area more efficiently. Also, we inserted an acrylic panel (8mm thickness, Figure 1(a)) and sponges (5mm thickness, Figure 1(e)) between the actuator part (Figure 1(b) and (c)) and the iPod touch (Figure 1(f)) to prevent undesired vibration from spreading over the entire device. Figure 1(g) and (h) show the actual CheekTouch prototype fully implemented. During our observation, we covered the protruding actuators with thin tissue (Figure 1(d)) in order for them not to directly contact participants' cheeks.

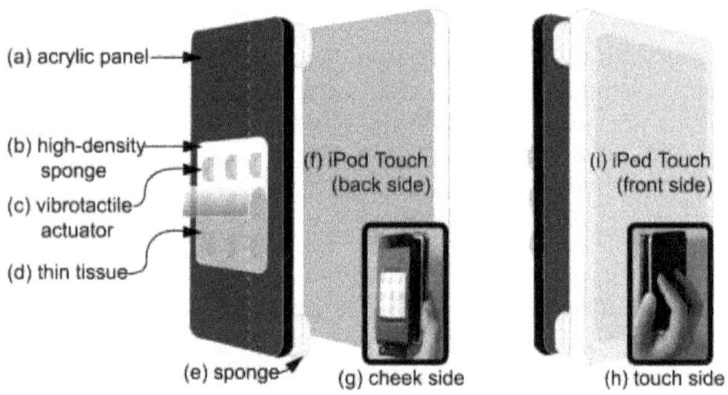

Figure 1. Implemented CheekTouch prototype.

Touch Input to Vibrotactile Output

Figure 2 shows the bidirectional communication diagram of CheekTouch. When one user's finger(s) touches on the touch input area, the touch information is sent to the other user's PC in an OSC (Open Sound Control) message using OSCemote [6] through a Wi-Fi network (- - - ➔).

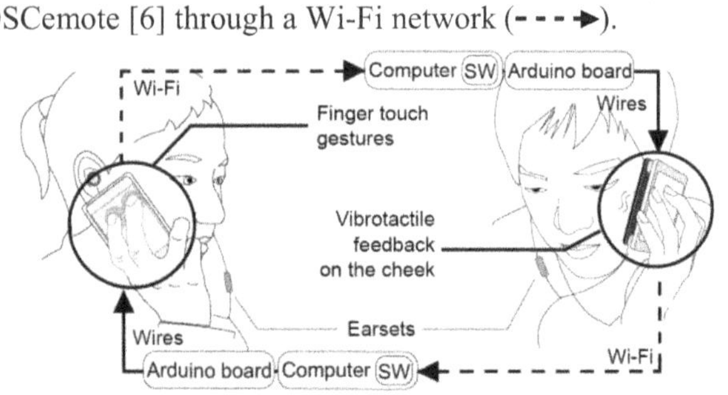

Figure 2. Communication diagram of CheekTouch.

The received information is used to activate the vibrotactile actuator(s) that corresponds to the touch location by using the Arduino board (——➔). In this way, one user's finger motion on the touch screen is rendered on the other user's vibrotactile display in real time.

EXPLORATIVE USER STUDY

We conducted an explorative user study to find the usage patterns of CheekTouch in phone call situations and examine its usefulness. Specifically, what kinds of touch gestures are exchanged in what situations in CheekTouch communication? And do the touch gestures help non-verbal and emotional communication?

Four couples in romantic relationships (aged 25 ~ 30) participated. We expected that real couples would express more feelings and emotions in their communication than people in formal relationships. Each couple was led to two separate rooms for five consecutive days, and asked to have a phone call using CheekTouch for 20 minutes per day. The rooms were well set for natural phone conversations. On Day 1, we taught them the basics of CheekTouch for five to ten minutes, including how to hold the device, how to apply touches, and how to receive tactile feedback. Because we wanted to find as many potential usage patterns using CheekTouch as possible, we ran a minimal instruction session and did not introduce any predefined gestures. A short interview was conducted every day after the call. As our observation was done in a lab setting, we could record the voice communication and videotape the finger gestures; all the touch event signals were logged by our gesture analyzing software. In the daily interview, we gathered each couple' comments on differences between the usual audio-only call and audio-tactile call using CheekTouch based on the day's experience, how well their specific touch gestures were conveyed to each other, and overall usability issues.

FINDINGS: CHEEKTOUCH USAGE PATTERNS

We identified 675 touch gestures from 400 minutes of phone calls made by the four couples (Figure 3). That is, CheekTouch was used every 35 seconds on average. Through a careful examination of the audio and voice records, we found numerous unique patterns which could not be seen in regular voice phone calls.

Persuading

- Comforting: Patting with one or two fingers was used for meaning *"It's okay."* In particular, C1 (Couple 1: Sally and Charlie – we use aliases) used a total of 21 times with voice (6 times) or without voice (15 times). Sally was depressed because the roommate – her best friend – left the dorm after graduation. Charlie patted with two fingers on the CheekTouch device while saying *"It's okay <pat>, you can find a better roommate. I know you have a lot of good friends in the school. Don't worry."* Sally said that Charlie's patting on her cheek was comforting like his tapping on her shoulder in their face-to-face conversation.

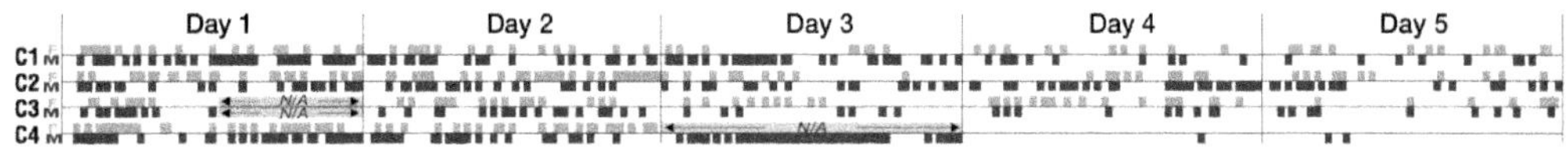

Figure 3. CheekTouch usage log showing all the frequency of CheekTouch uses by male (M) and female (F) participants of the four couples (C1 ~ C4) over five consecutive days (Day 1 ~ Day 5).

- Whining, grumbling, pestering, urging and forcing: We found 59 cases in which touch gestures were used to whine and grumble. These changed the atmosphere of conversation in a positive way, making the other laugh. Single tapping, multi tapping, drawing Z's or squares and long press-and-holding were used.
- Negative opinions: When it was difficult to answer directly through voice, they expressed their opinions using touch gestures in indirect and passive ways. In C1's conversation, Charlie responded with multi tapping (patting) without directly saying *"No"* when Sally made unreasonable demands. Sally said that she could detect his reluctance to accept her requests, and then changed topics not to hurt the conversation mood. Similarly, when the other's talk was boring or hard to listen to, they indirectly expressed their opinions by multi tapping or applying tickling gestures to prevent their conversation from turning sour.

Conveying Status

- I'm hearing: In all four couples' conversations, we found that touch gestures were used to express that they were listening to the other's talk sincerely; they used drawing circles, stroking, and multi tapping using one or two fingers.
- I'm thinking: We observed stroking and double tapping were used to express that they were thinking and considering seriously. For example, *"Well, I don't know ... <double taps>" "Um....<double taps>" and "<multi taps>... That goes for you too!"*
- I'm still here: CheekTouch was used to fill the gaps that happened during the conversation. By horizontally stroking, drawing circles or squares, multi tapping, and tickling, they conveyed their presence to the other even when nobody talked on the phone. *"Charlie (C1): We often scribble on the other's hand when we meet. When I sensed Sally was doing something, even though the feelings of the tactile gesture were not that precise, it seemed to me we were more closely connected."*
- Mimicking: The participating couples often mimicked the other's tactile patterns in turn. Colin (C4) created tactile patterns in the middle of conversations habitually, and Emily (C4) liked to imitate them. They said they could confirm the other's presence in a positive way. Also C3 unconsciously killed time for 2~5 minutes when the verbal conversation died down by mimicking each other's tactile gestures.

Information

- Number: Multi tapping was used to count objects.
- Shape: They used touch gestures to describe the shape of objects or body behaviors, for example, expressing the shape of objects like hair and noodles, or expressing the behaviors like clapping, body twisting, sighing, and crying. In particular, C3 described the structure and shape of the room where they were seated by drawing patterns on the touch input screen. C2 and C4 mentioned that they could actually feel the expression of noodles and clapping in the context of conversation and the following conversation proceeded in a delightful direction. Furthermore, CheekTouch was used with various onomatopoeia (e.g., licking, sobbing, humming, ambulance sounds) while tapping, stroking, and alternating finger gestures. Also there were cases that used CheekTouch in expressing mimetic words; Emily (C4) mentioned that wriggling and simmering have the image of shaking, which was similar to the feeling of the vibration.
- Delimiting: Some touch gestures such as side-to-side, tapping, drawing circles or squares, tickling, and stroking, were used to depict the end of a sentence as if they were a period, question mark, or exclamation mark. Interestingly, single tapping replaced *"Yes"* sometimes.

Emphasis

- Emotion: CheekTouch was often used for highlighting emotions like envy, vexation, surprise, and love. Double tapping, tickling, pinching, and patting were used depending on the situation.
- Word/syllables: Single tapping was used to put an emphasis on a particular word or even each syllable of a word.

Attention

- When they wanted to call for the other's attention, they used to press the input screen with one finger to generate a long vibration. If the person on the line was quiet, sometimes they applied tapping gestures to check whether s/he was there. Some tapped when they started a conversation to notify the other.

Play

- They played with CheekTouch during a call – mimicking touch patterns with complex rhythm, giving a quiz for pattern matching, teasing with tickling or slapping gestures. C4 used CheekTouch to massage the back of the other's neck using the vibration; they mentioned that the vibration delivered by touching the screen with three or four fingers for a long time was like a real massage with hands. In addition, C2 used CheekTouch in a role playing game; Rachel played a dentist treating Brian's cavities by placing the device close to the cheek near his teeth.

DISCUSSIONS

CheekTouch in Negative Atmosphere

CheekTouch was not used much when they were angry, or were expressing negative emotions directly. They mentioned that tactile stimulation on the cheek in a negative situation could make them angrier and more irritated. We found in C4's conversation, *"Keep your hand off"* in this kind of situation. *"Colin (C4): I might not use it when I feel bad. Because I think it would be better not to stimulate her. I try not to touch Emily until the atmosphere becomes better."* C4 only used CheekTouch for three times on the fourth and fifth days of the experiment, during which they fought. Interestingly, we observed that they pressed the touch screen hard for a long time to express angry feelings.

Vibration Control

All four couples mentioned that the vibrotactile feedback didn't disturb their conversation. Some said they could hear weak vibrating sound, however in most cases it was not continuous and did not cause any inconvenience. *"Sally (C1): Vibration noise didn't disturb at all. Even I could not hear the sound.* However, C1 and C2 mentioned the needs of turning on and off, or controlling vibration intensity. *"Brian (C2): When I feel good, it's okay, but when I feel bad, it makes me feel worse, so there should be an on/off function." "Charlie (C1): I don't know if it is vibrating when I am concentrating on something. There should be a function to control the strength of vibration stimulation."*

Gesture Ambiguity

Some participants wanted to confirm if their gestures had been delivered safely and see the other's actual finger motions that resulted in the incoming tactile stimulus. *"Colin (C4): I was concerned that I could not know if my gesture patterns had been delivered. I hoped to have established some patterns that she and I both knew. Sometimes I asked her the meaning of tactile patterns that she had sent." "Brian (C2): I wanted to know what and how Rachel was touching. I wish I could see it from the screen."*

Unintended Touch

Sometimes the fingers unconsciously touched the touch screen during a phone call and a vibration was sent to the other inadvertently. *"Brian (C2): I didn't know that I was touching the screen until she asked me to stop touching it."*

Needs for Free Gestures

Touch gestures used were different depending on the context of the conversation and each individual's character and habits. Especially, a variety of touch gestures were used when asking, answering, whining, forcing, and calling for attention. The participant who usually gave short answers mostly did single or double tapping gestures; positive answers like *"Yeah, it's okay"* were often accompanied with tickling gestures. Answers like *"Um...I don't know exactly"* with scratching gestures on the screen were like they usually scratch their head; questions like *"Does your head or back hurt?"* with patting gestures; playful questions with interesting scratching patterns; questions for short answers with single or double tapping gestures. Active and delightful people like Sally (C1) often used double tapping gestures when whining and pestering, whereas quiet and shy people like Emily (C4) moved fingers side-to-side weakly when asking for something.

CONCLUSIONS

In this study, we developed CheekTouch to enrich emotional mobile communication with touch while preserving the traditional interaction style of phone calls. We observed that CheekTouch could help phone calls in terms of supporting non-verbal communication and delivering tele-presence. CheekTouch can be used effectively to give comfort and lead a conversation in a positive way, which might had flowed in a negative way with voice alone. It allows touches normally seen in face-to-face communication, which emphasize emotion/words, which call for attention, and which describe the shape of objects and body motions, in mobile phone conversations. Also it helps people going through remote communication feel more closely connected by giving ways of revealing their presence with touches, which fill conversation gaps during a call and express *"I'm hearing/thinking/here,"* and which mimic each other's touch patterns. Built on current smart phone technologies, CheekTouch has shown a new possibility of enriching emotions with touch over phone calls in the near future.

ACKNOWLEDGMENTS

This research was supported by the SW Computing R&D Program of KEIT (2011-10041313, UX-oriented Mobile SW Platform) funded by the Ministry of Knowledge Economy, Republic of Korea.

REFERENCES

1. Brave, S., Ishii, H. and Dahley, A. Tangible interfaces for remote collaboration and communication. Proc. CSCW 1998, ACM Press (1998), 169-178.
2. Brown, L., Sellen, A., Krishna, R. and Harper, R. Exploring the potential of audio-tactile messaging for remote interpersonal communication. Proc. CHI 2009, ACM Press (2009), 1527-1530.
3. Chang, A., O'Modhrain, S., Jacob, R., Gunther, E. and Ishii, H. ComTouch: design of a vibrotactile communication device. Proc. DIS 2002, ACM Press (2002), 312-320.
4. Fukumoto, M. and Tonomura, Y. Whisper: a wrist-watch style wearable handset. Proc. CHI 1999, ACM Press (1999), 112-119.
5. Hashimoto, Y. and Kajimoto, H. Emotional touch: a novel interface to display emotional tactile information to a palm. SIGGRAPH 2008 new tech demos, ACM Press (2008), Article 5.
6. OSCemote. www.appstorehq.com/oscemote-iphone/.
7. Wang, R. and Quek, F. Touch & talk: contextualizing remote touch for affective interaction. Proc. TEI 2010, ACM Press (2010), 13-20.

The Spread of Emotion via Facebook

Adam D. I. Kramer
Facebook, Inc.
1601 Willow Rd, Menlo Park, CA
akramer@fb.com

ABSTRACT
In this paper we study large-scale emotional contagion through an examination of Facebook status updates. After a user makes a status update with emotional content, their friends are significantly more likely to make a valence-consistent post. This effect is significant even three days later, and even after controlling for prior emotion expressions by both users and their friends. This indicates not only that emotional contagion is possible via text-only communication and that emotions flow through social networks, but also that emotion spreads via indirect communications media.

Author Keywords
Computer-mediated communication; emotional contagion; emotion; Facebook; social networks

ACM Classification Keywords
H.5.m. Information interfaces and presentation (e.g., HCI): Miscellaneous.

General Terms
Human factors, measurement, languages, verification

INTRODUCTION
Emotional contagion is the process by which people "catch" emotions from each other. This process, which can be as simple as becoming happier in the presence of a smiling friend, is important to psychological and physiological functioning, and vital for healthy relationships [1,12].

Prior research suggests that nonverbal communication is the means by which emotions are contracted. Some research even claims that nonverbal cues are "necessary" for contagion [1,5], but this may not be the whole story: Recent papers indicate that emotion can be contracted through computer-mediated communication (CMC) systems [8,9] in a similar manner to the emotional contagion traditionally observed during in-person interactions [10,11,12]. Overall, emotional contagion has been demonstrated in real life, in laboratory settings, and most recently via CMC.

This is especially important as human social relationships and interactions have been moving into the online world in the form of social networking sites (SNS), and are being increasingly supported via CMC. Facebook, a very popular SNS claiming over 800M users as of publication, is a common means by which people interact with each other both directly (such as via messages, chatting, wall posts, comments), and indirectly (such as via status updates).

In this paper, we examine an important implication of emotional contagion theory: whether and how emotions "spread" via SNSs. The examination of how emotions spread through a textual medium such as an internet SNS is very interesting: If such a process can be shown, this provides evidence for basic psychological processes re-exhibiting themselves in new media, and also contributes to a growing body of evidence suggesting that interaction with "friends" on SNSs mirrors the manner by which people interact with others in offline life [4,10].

Though the current studies are correlational, they address several confounds in prior results by making use of the undirected nature of Facebook "status updates:" Prior research on emotional contagion has usually examined situations in which the expresser and observer of an emotion are communicating directly. In that case, the process by which the emotion is transmitted is ambiguous. For example, in the case of a positive emotion such as joy, the observer is faced with a joyful communicator. If they then become joyful themselves, is it direct transmission of the partner's joyfulness, or simply a peripheral effect of having a joyful interaction? Happier individuals are more expressive, creative, and generous [7], suggesting that interacting with an individual in a good mood would be a pleasant experience—and thus explain increased positive mood. Conversely, would an angry communicator cause anger in a friend through negative, angry interaction, or would the friend become angry merely because of emotional contagion? Further, even if emotion is not actually felt by the conversant, disclosure norms may require that they respond in a similar manner. By examining status updates, which are not specifically "directed" towards a conversation partner (their "friend," in the Facebook case), any observed effects should not be due to effects of proximal communication.

There are still concerns that disclosure norms may affect valenced responses on SNSs, as people strategically present themselves to others in order to achieve certain social goals [18]. However, others have shown both that Facebook profiles seem to reflect actual personality rather than idealized forms ([1], which also reviews the literature on presentation), and "word count" methods of examining natural language production are largely immune to self-presentational concerns [15]. Thus, our strategy to evaluate the downstream emotion expression by the friends of those who express emotion: Examination of status updates. To reduce social demands, we examine emotion expression by users via their undirected updates, and to control for self-presentation, we evaluate emotion expression by those users' friends similarly.

A second confound present in emotional contagion research is the possibility that emotions are not actually being "contracted," but that a single event is causing emotion in both parties. For example, if I am happy because my paper is accepted, and I share this with a friend, the friend may become happy because my paper was accepted (and not simply because I am happy). Similarly, mere exposure to a certain writing or self-expression style in the Facebook feed may lead to conversational mimicry despite the undirected nature of the communication. To address this potential confound, we utilize a multi-day lagged regression design. We predict that when users use positive or negative words (i.e., express positive or negative affect [13]), their friends' emotional states will be affected: Those friends will express more of the corresponding emotion (i.e., use positive or negative words in subsequent updates). In order to address the "same event" confound, we examine their friends' use of positive words on the same day, but also on the two subsequent days, using the days in between as statistical controls. The end analysis, then, examines a three-day lagged effect: If a user posts a positive update today, is the user's friend more likely to post a positive update three days from now? If they are yet more likely to do so than we would expect, given all the words used by both users and friends in the subsequent days, we suggest that the "shared experience" confound is eliminated, as any shared emotional experience would be encoded into the language of both on the same timescale.

Though this research is correlational and thus cannot be argued to represent "contagion" of emotion, showing that emotion spreads through SNSs despite these confounds controlled tests a key corollary of emotional contagion theory and motivates future experimental work.

In sum, we predict that when a user uses an emotion word in a status update, their friends will be more likely to do so subsequently, in a valence-consistent way: If a user uses positive words, their friends will be more likely to use positive words as well (and less likely to use negative words), and vice versa.

METHOD

Participants

Participants were classified into two groups: First, the "users" group was comprised of the set of all active Facebook users who chose to view Facebook in English and who posted at least one status update on three consecutive days (in order to control for subsequent posts when conducting the three-day analysis). From this group of users, one million were chosen at random. The second group of participants was the English-speaking set of these users' friends, consisting of approximately 150m users.

From these users and friends, we then selected a random subsample of users (and all of the friends of those users) that together occupied approximately 5 million rows of data for analysis, in order to produce a set that was appropriately sized for analysis using modern statistical software. This end result constituted a sample of $n = 61,289$ users.

It is important to note that we did not systematically include or exclude friends from analysis based on what those friends saw or commented on. In other words, we examine posts by friends, whether or not they saw the users' initial post, as doing so would not be computationally feasible: A single view of one's newsfeed might produce 5 viewed posts, with many more appearing on each page-down. However, this inability does not confound our results as there is little reason to expect that a friend's expression of emotion would somehow be affected by updates they did not see; rather, it constitutes error that should make it more difficult to find statistically significant results.

Procedure

As in [13], all status updates posted by both users and friends during a three-day window were processed using the list of positive and negative emotion dictionaries from LIWC 2007 [15], using the Hive database system [18], which allowed for parallel computation in order to complete the word-counting task rapidly. Use of the LIWC software package itself was not possible as these status updates constituted far more data that would fit on a single contemporary computer. Because this work was completed in an entirely computational manner, no researchers ever saw any user-generated text in an identified form[1], in compliance with Facebook's Terms of Service [6].

RESULTS AND DISCUSSION

To test our hypotheses, we predicted word usage (positive or negative) by friends from word usage (ibid), by users. This was done using "Hierarchical Logistic Regression," a system similar to the now-common "hierarchical linear modeling" techniques, but adapted to use a logistic regression model. This multi-level technique was necessary because users have different numbers of friends. This analysis was completed using the "glmer" function in the lme4 library for R [3,16].

Same-day analysis

Our analysis was tiered based on the day of prediction: For our first analysis, we predicted whether a friend would use

[1] More specifically, researchers did not see any user-generated text that they would not otherwise have been able to see; procedures were validated via analyses of the researchers' own status updates.

a positive word if the user used a positive word on the same day. This effect was significant and positive[2], $\beta = 0.076$, $z = 24.98$, $p < .001$. We replicated this effect by examining the corresponding effect for users and their friends on all three days of data collection; these effects were all significant and in the same direction.

Single-day lag

Examining only the first day's worth of data, however, is not sufficient to draw strong conclusions. For example, many people may share common interests and be aware of the same goings-on in the world around them. This could lead to a "third variable" problem, in which a single event (say, a college football team winning a game) or a homophily effect (i.e., happier people having happier friends) would make both users and their friends happy. To address this issue, we predicted friends' word usage on Day 2 instead of Day 1, using their own words on Day 1 and the users' words on Day 2 as controls: Thus, the question becomes "does a user's emotion expression on Day 1 predict their friends' emotion expression on Day 2 *above and beyond* their friends' emotion expression on Day 1." For this analysis, we hypothesized that users' words on both Days 1 and 2 would be significant and positive predictors of friends' words on Day 2, but that the coefficient for the same-day effect would be larger than the prior day's.

These hypotheses were supported: Controlling for friends' and users' words on Day 1, users' words on both Days 1 and 2 still predicted friends' words on Day 2, β's = 0.046, 0.050, z's = 16.0, 17.7, p's < .001, respectively, and with the same-day coefficient being larger than the prior day's. In this model the friends' own words on Day 1 were also significant (and much stronger) predictors of word use on Day 2, $\beta = 0.931$. As above, this effect was replicated using data for Days 2 and 3 instead of Days 1 and 2; effects were similar (β's = .051, .053, and .961 respectively; p's < .001).

Two-day lag

Finally, we took this analytic process one step further, predicting friends' word use on Day 3 from users' word use on Days 1, 2, and 3, controlling for their own word use on the two prior days. As predicted, all three coefficients were significant: Friends' word usage was predicted by users' word use on Day 1 ($\beta = 0.031$), Day 2 ($\beta = 0.037$), and Day 3 ($\beta = 0.040$), as well as their own word use on Day 1 ($\beta = 0.743$) and Day 2 ($\beta = 0.824$); all p's < .001.

Negative words

We then took the same approach to the analysis of negative words; all effects across all replications were significant, with even larger effect sizes: β's were all positive and p's < .001; β's around 0.092 for same-day analysis; around 0.053 (users' words on Day 1) and 0.058 (Day 2) for single-day lag; and 0.0384 (Day 1), 0.0379 (Day 2) and 0.0367 (Day 3) for two-day lag.

Emotional suppression

Finally, we examined what we call "emotional suppression," with "suppression" taken as the opposite of "spreading:" Whether using *positive* words would decrease friends' use of *negative* words, effectively *suppressing* the counter-valenced emotion, or whether using negative words would similarly suppress friends' positivity. To examine this effect, we fit two additional two-day lag models as described above: One predicting friends' positive emotion word usage and one predicting friends' negative emotion word usage. In this analysis, however, we used all of the inputs as predictors: Both positive and negative word usage by users on Days 1 through 3, and both positive and negative word usage by friends on Days 1 and 2.

As expected, we observed a cross-valence suppression effect, in which users' use of negative words suppressed use of positive words by friends over the three day time period, β's = -.015, -.013, -.011 for Days 1-3, and users' use of positive words buffered their friends against negativity over the same timeframe, β's = -.022, -.013, -.016, all p's < .05.

GENERAL DISCUSSION

Over the course of several analyses of a very large data set, we show a consistent pattern: When a Facebook user posts, the words they choose influence the words chosen later by their friends. This effect is consistent with prior research on emotional contagion, in that the friends of people who express emotional language end up expressing more same-valenced language as well. We have also shown preliminary evidence for what might be called "emotional suppression," in which the use of positive (or negative) words buffers users' friends against negativity (positivity).

These effects are present despite the fact that we operationalized emotion as the use of an emotion word in a status update, which was not directed from "users" to their friends, who may not have seen the initial update, and whose subsequent updates were not "responses" to the initial updates, and were persistent even three days later.

The implications of this research are highly suggestive: It supports years of research into emotional contagion processes [12], suggesting that certain supposed confounds may not fully explain the effect. Further, these results suggest that posts to Facebook have the ability to affect our friends' subsequent posts. This is *not* to say, however, that they affect our *friends;* further research is necessary to make this claim. Even if they did, however, we would not advise Facebook users to go around expressing disingenuous positivity or to suppress the expression of negative emotions in order to keep one's friends happy: The psychological history of humans likely indicates that these expression strategies probably help us to remain psychologically healthy, by allowing others to share in our joy and helping us recruit social support from our friends

---

[2] β here is a logistic regression "log-odds" coefficient: $\beta = .076$ means that positive posts by users predicts friends' likelihood of doing so to become $e^{0.08} = 1.08$ times larger.

when needed. Sharing negative emotions may also be important for building feelings of closeness [10].

CAVEATS AND FUTURE DIRECTIONS

The current study does not permit the causal conclusion that emotions in friends are caused by emotions in users. This would require an experimental approach, rather than the current correlational design. One could also argue that our effect sizes are quite small (or perhaps even trivial): Our smallest significant effect size was a mere 1.1% decrease in friends' likelihood of using negative words when a user uses a positive word. We note, however, that word usage is a rather noisy measure of emotion: Prior research has shown significant (but small to moderate) correlations between word usage in status updates and overall positivity (e.g., [13] showed only $r = 0.17$ with Satisfaction with Life). Additionally, we were unable to exclude "friends" from analysis when they had not seen the users' posts, further reducing our observed effect size. However, we observed a high frequency of emotionality in updates: 55% of updates contained a positive word, and 34% contained a negative word. These high rates suggest that even low rates of "spread" may indeed be meaningful.

The "bag of words" approach also comes with its own disadvantages: We did not explicitly exclude negations or conduct a revalidation of the LIWC [15] dictionary, which may increase the noisiness of the LIWC analysis. However, we argue that while these effects are small, they are not trivial considering the enormous scale of SNS usage: In a domain as large as Facebook, if expressing positivity on one day causes one out of 100 friends to post positively three days later (when they otherwise would not have), then the tens of millions of people posting each day may be responsible for hundreds of thousands of positive posts that would not have otherwise occurred, and which in turn could cause thousands more; we do not consider this trivial.

ACKNOWLEDGMENTS

I thank James Fowler, Itamar Rosenn, Cameron Marlow, Jeff Hancock, and Jamie Guillory for the several theoretical discussions that led to this paper and analysis, and Carmen Jackson and James Fowler for reading initial drafts. I also thank the Facebook Data Team for their continued support.

REFERENCES

1. Back, M. D., Stopfer, J. M., Vazire, S., Gaddis, S., Schmuckle, S. C., Egloff, B., & Gosling, S. D. (2010). Facebook profiles reflect actual personality, not self-idealization. *Psychological Science, 21*, 372-374.
2. Barsade, S. G. (2002). The ripple effect: Emotional contagion and its influence on group behavior. *Administrative Science Quarterly, 47*(4), 644-677.
3. Bates, D. & Maechler, M. (2010). lme4: Linear mixed-effects models using S4 classes. Retrieved from http://CRAN.R-project.org/package=lme4 .
4. Burke, M., Marlow, C., & Lento, T. (2010). Social network activity and social well-being. In *Proc. CHI 2010*, ACM Press (2010), 1909-1912.
5. Ekman, P. (1992). An argument for basic emotions. *Cognition & Emotion, 6*, 169-200.
6. Facebook Terms of Service (2011). Retrieved 9/19/11 from http://www.facebook.com/terms.php .
7. Fredrickson, B. L. (2001). The role of positive emotions in positive psychology: The broaden-and-build theory of positive emotions. *American Psychologist, 56,* 218-226.
8. Guillory, J., Spiegel, J., Drislane, M., Weiss, B., Donner, W., & Hancock, J. (2011). Upset now?: Emotion contagion in distributed groups. In *Proc. CHI 2011*, ACM Press (2011), 745-748.
9. Hancock, J. T., Gee, K., Ciaccio, K., & Lin, J. M. H. (2008). I'm sad you're sad: Emotional contagion in CMC. In *Proc. CSCW 2008*, ACM Press (2008), 295-298.
10. Hatfield, E., Cacioppo, J. T., & Rapson, R. L. (1992). Primitive emotional contagion. In R. L. Clark, & S. Margaret (Eds.), *Emotion and social behavior, review of personality and social psychology*, Vol. 14 (pp. 151-177). Thousand Oaks, CA: Sage.
11. Hatfield, E., Cacioppo, J. T., & Rapson, R. L. (1993a). Emotional contagion. *Current Directions in Psychological Science, 2*(3), 96-100.
12. Hatfield, E., Cacioppo, J. T., & Rapson, R. L. (1993b). *Emotional contagion*. Cambridge, UK: Cambridge University Press.
13. Kramer, A. D. I. (2010). An unobtrusive model of "Gross National Happiness." In *Proc. CHI 2010*, ACM Press (2010), 287-290.
14. Murray, E. J., Lamnin, A. D., & Carver, C. S. (1989). Emotional expression in written essays and psychotherapy. *Journal of Social and Clinical Psychology, 8*(4), 414-429.
15. Pennebaker, J. W., Chung, C. K., Ireland, M., Gonzales, A., & Booth, R. J. (2007). *The development and psychological properties of LIWC2007.* Retrieved from http://www.liwc.net .
16. R Develompent Core Team (2011). R 2.13.1, http://cran.r-project.org.
17. Rachman, S. (1980). Emotional processing. *Behaviour Research and Therapy, 18*, 51-60.
18. Schlenker, B. R., & Leary, M. R. (1982). Audience's reactions to self-enhancing, self-denigrating, and accurate self presentations. *Journal of Experimental Social Psychology, 18*, 89-104.
19. Thusoo, A., and Facebook Data/Infrastructure (2009). Hive ..A warehousing solution over a map-reduce framework. *Proc. VLDB*.

It's Complicated: How Romantic Partners Use Facebook

Xuan Zhao, Victoria Schwanda Sosik, Dan Cosley
Cornell University
301 College Ave., Ithaca, NY, 14850
{xz298, vls48, drc44}@cornell.edu

ABSTRACT
Romantic partners face issues of relational development including managing information privacy, tension between individual and relational needs, and accountability to existing friends. Prior work suggests that affordances of social media might highlight and shape these tensions; to explore this, we asked 20 people to reflect daily for two weeks on feelings and decisions around their own and others' Facebook use related to their relationships. Most generally, we find that tensions arise when romantic partners must manage multiple relationships simultaneously because Facebook audiences are so present and so varied. People also engage in subtle negotiation around and appropriation of Facebook's features to accomplish both personal and relational goals. By capturing both why people make these decisions and how Facebook's affordances support them, we expect our findings to generalize to many other social media tools and to inform theorizing about how these tools affect relational development.

Author Keywords
Social media, interpersonal communication, romantic relationships, self-presentation

ACM Classification Keywords
H.5.2 [Information interfaces and presentation]: Social and Behavioral Sciences.

General Terms
Design, human factors

INTRODUCTION
Imagine you are selecting photos to upload to Facebook. Since you don't want to disclose too much information about your personal life, especially to your boss and family members, you choose to exclude some intimate photos with your girlfriend. Then you get an angry message: "Why did you exclude pictures of us? Are you ashamed of me?"

Traditional models of information privacy assume that information has a single owner, the originator. However, as social networking sites afford the exchange of social data such as pictures that contain multiple people, issues of co-ownership and mutual decisions arise. An emerging line of work in collaborative privacy management looks at how these issues of privacy and boundary regulation evolve beyond individual decisions, emphasizing the importance of socially negotiated boundaries [2,6] where multiple stakeholders need to make mutually agreeable decisions on whether and how to publish the co-owned content online.

These issues of shared ownership and control become even more pronounced in the case of interpersonal relationships, which previous work in interpersonal communication [5,30] suggests may play an important role in decisions about what to share and what to hide. As shown in the opening example, people often find themselves balancing multiple, sometimes contradictory, relational and identity needs—and that this balancing act is made trickier in "masspersonal" social networking platforms like Facebook where some information is notionally private but actually visible to many people. We believe that approaching the issue of boundary negotiation from multiple theoretical perspectives will be useful for both better explaining the phenomena and informing technology designs that promote relationship well-being and social capital development.

In this paper, we present the results from a two-week study in which we examine how romantic partners present themselves and interpret others' behavior on Facebook. Although it has been well-studied as a way to maintain weak ties and friendships [16], and is not the primary means of communication for many romantic partners, Facebook provides a useful real-world context to examine how multiple relational goals (e.g., romantic relationships and friendships) interact with personal needs in a setting where the relationship activity is literally embedded in a larger social network [27].

We asked participants to keep a two-week diary in which they recorded their reasons and feelings when they made decisions about creating (or not creating) content on Facebook, as well as their reactions to other people's use of Facebook that made them think about their own romantic relationship. We found a wide range of uses and meanings attached to Facebook features, and how they contributed to both outwards tensions around publicizing the relationship and inwards tensions related to managing decisions around autonomous versus shared decision-making. These uses and features, these inwards and outwards tensions, and Facebook norms sometimes combined to create complex situations to negotiate. However, people exhibited a number of subtle strategies for managing both the features and the tensions. Below, we start by laying out theories around privacy management, identity management, and interpersonal communication that can help us understand how these tensions might arise.

RELATED WORK

Much social media research has discussed privacy and online impression management (e.g., [1,15]), focusing on issues of boundary regulation during self-disclosure, primarily as an individual process [10]. Social networking sites afford the exchange of personal information and provide rich opportunities for people to deliberately create digital traces to construct their identities in the online space [14,19]. However, people also need to draw boundaries between their selves and others to avoid exposing too much personal information in front of a mixed public [3,23].

Following Altman's theory on interpersonal boundary regulation [3], we see an emerging line of research on collaborative privacy (e.g. [6,21]) that explores online boundary regulation over co-owned content on social networking sites. The issue of limited control over online content has been highlighted as one important challenge in recent empirical studies around, e.g., controlling identity data revealed through online searches [11,26]. A recent study by Lampinen et al. emphasized the co-ownership issue over content on Facebook and highlights the role of collaborative privacy management [21]. Their work considers disclosure as an interdependent process where people choose what to disclose for each other and develop strategies or rules to manage different expectations.

Other work focuses on the collaborative process of identity management. Similar to how people intentionally manage their ideal self-presentations online [14,19], people also try to present the best of their relationships in public [18]. Bowe's recent study [7] explored relationship rituals on Facebook, such as posting relationship statuses and the public display of affection, and explored why people accept or reject these rituals from a sociological perspective. This study shed light on how people incorporated relationship considerations into their Facebook activities.

However, even though collaborative privacy research has explored how to enhance individual control over joint content [6,21] and informed design for interdependence in managing privacy and regulating publicness of content, the relational subtleties involved in this negotiation process are yet to be explored. The negotiation and reworking of boundary rules does not happen in a vacuum, but in a relational context. A user taking down a wall post by her ex-boyfriend probably does not impact anyone else's privacy, but is driven by her intention to protect her relationship with her current romantic partner. In this vein, Petronio's communication privacy management theory (CPM) [30] views boundary management as a rule-based process and provides a rich framework to think about how people regulate the co-ownership of information, focusing on how people disclose within relationships.

Some earlier work on interpersonal communication also speaks to how boundary management takes place in a relational context. Baxter and Wildenmann [5] explore the topics that people in romantic relationships choose to reveal and conceal to their offline social networks, the strategies they use to manage disclosure of relationship information, and the reasons behind these decisions. This work uncovers a complicated pattern of information management activity that is contingent on a variety of factors including oneself, one's partner, third parties, and factors in the relationship.

We are interested in exploring how these relational dynamics affect people's boundary regulation behaviors on Facebook, a semi-public online environment. Aspects of Facebook such as having multiple audiences and being more visible, searchable, and easily accessible than offline interaction [8,9] may highlight tensions between partners related to disclosing information to others. These tensions also exist offline since interpersonal relationships are inevitably connected to each person's social network [27], but Facebook's gathering of one's personal connections from different spheres of life—"context collapse" [24,33]—complicates decisions about appropriate online disclosure. When romantic partners connect to each other on Facebook, their separate but increasingly overlapping networks [27] can further complicate the issue of context collapse by creating more needs that need to be served.

We are also interested in exploring the role that social networking sites play in people managing their close relationships. Previous work on social networking sites [22,25,28] has shown how Facebook use plays an important role in helping people to understand their intimate relationships. For instance, people sometimes make sense of others' relationships based on aggregated interaction data such as Facebook's "See Friendship" page [32]. Based on this after-the-fact use of interaction data, here we ask questions about the relational and identity goals behind people's decision making to self-disclose, how they negotiate and balance different relational and identity goals, and how features of the sites provide new resources for negotiating these goals.

STUDYING FACEBOOK PRACTICE

Following Child and Petronio's call for work that explores how people adjust SNS privacy management practices around life changes such as romantic relationships [10], here we explore how relational factors interact with boundary management on Facebook. We explore how and why people use Facebook to express their relationships, and when they choose not to. We also look at how people's relationships with others and the masspersonal nature of Facebook shape these decisions, highlighting aspects of privacy management, boundary negotiation, and the need to balance attention between individual needs, the romantic relationship, and relationships with third parties. Finally, we look at the impact these decisions and tensions, and Facebook itself, can have on people's relationships.

Data Collection

We collected data through pre-surveys, diary entries, and post interviews. The pre-survey asked questions about demographic information, the length of a participant's current romantic relationship, and communication tools they frequently used with their partner. After completing the survey, participants started a two-week long diary task. Each day they were reminded via e-mail to fill out an online form prompting them to reflect on how their romantic relationship affected decisions they made about what to do or not to do on Facebook or other social media, how Facebook and other social media made them think about their relationships, and what and why they chose to communicate in private rather than public. We used a diary method to capture the daily decision-making process close to when it happened, instead of asking participants to recall decisions after the fact, as well as to capture decisions of non-use that otherwise would not have been available to reflect on during the interview.

After completing the two-week diary task, we brought participants to the lab, asked them to review their diary, and conducted semi-structured interviews. We asked them to log on to Facebook and allowed them to reference both Facebook and diary content during the interview. We first asked them to reflect on the experience of doing the diary task, followed by questions about how they incorporate their romantic relationships into their Facebook profiles and how their relationship has or has not been affected by decisions around Facebook behaviors. While we focused mainly on Facebook because of its popularity, participants sometimes compared their Facebook use with other tools such as IM, email, phone, and Google+. Interviews were audio recorded and took about an hour.

Participants

We recruited participants from a student subject pool at a large Northeastern U.S. university. To satisfy study goals, participants were required to be active FB users currently in a romantic relationship. We recruited both individuals and couples, in the hope that interviewing couples would provide insights into how romantic partners negotiate their decisions together, while individuals would be more likely to present uncensored opinions about their Facebook behaviors. To recruit couples, we asked participants if they would like to bring their partners to the study as they signed up. Our goal was 20 participants (5 pairs, 10 individuals), so once we reached five couples, we stopped asking people to recruit their partners. All participants completed the pre-survey and diary entries individually, but those participating as couples were interviewed together. Participants were compensated with $15.

We did find 5 pairs and 10 individuals, making a total of 20 participants who completed the study (9 male, 11 female; 9 White/Caucasian, 10 Asian, 1 Hispanic/Latino; average age 21). All participants were in heterosexual relationships, with an average relationship length of 15.6 months, ranging from 1 to 48 months. Nine of the ten Asian participants were raised in the U.S., so our sample is rooted primarily in American culture and practices.

Data Analysis

Diary and interview data was analyzed using the grounded approach [17]. Diary and interview data, and data from both individuals and pairs, were analyzed together to support a holistic understanding of how people make decisions. After interviews were fully transcribed, two researchers together iteratively developed a codebook and coded the data using TAMSAnalyzer. We then used this coded data to identify themes across categories.

We found themes at a number of levels: meanings people attached to specific Facebook features, their role in managing both outwards concerns around relationship presentation and inwards conflict around autonomy and collectiveness, the interplay between these outwards and inwards tensions, and ways in which Facebook both highlights—and sometimes helps people negotiate—this interplay.

USE OF FACEBOOK FEATURES

Here we describe how participants use certain Facebook features in the context of their relationships and the types of relational meaning they attach to these uses. We focus on the most commonly mentioned features: relationship status, friending, photos, and wall posts. Participant numbers are noted after each quote ('I': individual participants; 'P': pair participants, numbered by pair; 'F', female participants; 'M', male participants; 'diary': quote drawn from a diary record instead of interview).

Relationship Status

A fundamental aspect of romantic relationships on Facebook is the relationship status feature, which appears as part of a person's profile. Besides providing a list of different types of relationship statuses such as "in a relationship", "it's complicated", and "married", Facebook provides flexible display options. People can choose whether they want to connect their profile with their partner's via relationship status, and can make this status visible to their whole network or to specific people via Facebook's privacy settings. This feature is an explicit indicator of "state of relationship", the most common topic that romantic partners choose to reveal or to conceal from their offline networks [5].

Further, there is a "Facebook official" norm that states that people in relationships should explicitly indicate this by using the relationship status feature. Over half of our participants recognize the norm and consider listing each other in a relationship on Facebook as *"the standard for knowing when someone is in a relationship."* (I-9-F)

This public display of mutual connection explicitly verifies the identity of being a couple and signals territory to others [12]. People commonly described an affirming effect of listing each other as in a relationship, as well as an opposite effect of doubt and confusion when the status was not displayed.

"Just seeing the fact that we are in a relationship and knowing that the online community can see that makes me feel good about our relationship. It's like he's proud to be with me." (P-2-F)

"Because when we first started dating, his profile said single and I told him that girls tend to Facebook stalk other people's Facebook profiles and if it said single then it sends out like the wrong message like I'm available when I'm not, and because there wasn't really like any sign of me as his girlfriend on his page at all, I was like 'can you just take off the single status?'" (I-25-F)

Even though "Facebook official" has become the norm for most participants, a small number of them acknowledge it also imposes pressures that could lead to the feeling of conformity and loss of identity as a couple.

"Facebook like dulls the uniqueness of our partnership. Because everyone is just...it is Facebook official, we are a Facebook couple...it is an aspect of our relationship that is kind of standardized and gets weighted against a bunch of other couples." (P-6-M)

Friending One's Partner's Friends

Participants reported that being Facebook official often led to an increasing overlap of Facebook friends. The linking feature of relationship status provides one partner's friends easy access to their romantic partner's profile, and the ease of friending someone on Facebook further enables this kind of "cross interaction" between one person and their partner's friends.

As with posting a relationship status, romantic partners' increasingly overlapping networks signal to them the importance of their relationship.

"Thinking about adding my boyfriend's family on social networks made me think about how momentous a relationship step that is. I'm basically saying that I'm committed enough to my relationship with my boyfriend that I'm willing to treat his family as though they were my family, even though if our relationship should go bad I'll likely never see them again..." (I-9-F-diary)

The trend of increasing mutual friends on Facebook could also bring an affirming effect to romantic partners, both as a natural part of relational development and as a strategic move to increase closeness.

"He probably went out of his way to friend them (my friends) as well, at least like my close friends, when we were starting to date, and getting to know them but he probably didn't really reach out to them that much as when we started dating I mean on Facebook, like writing on their profiles and stuff." (I-17-F)

A small number of participants also feel defensive about the increasing number of mutual friends, because of the pressure to maintain relationships with their partners' friends, and the increased cost if the relationship goes bad.

"I would feel much worse if anything went bad in our relationship because these other bonds have been created and that's going to be probably difficult to sever." (I-9-F)

Photos

Friending a partner's friends is one way to express tangible connection in Facebook; another common way to do this is through uploading photos that picture both partners together. Unlike relationship status, posting a photo does not require mutual agreement—but tagging another person's presence in a posted photo does require negotiation, because people can un-tag themselves. Besides their own postings, one's photo collection also contains pictures they are tagged in that are uploaded by their romantic partners and other friends in the network, which raises interesting control and privacy management issues.

Participants attached relational meaning to photos because they depict who people spend time and attend events with; such activities and events around a relationship are another topic that people often revealed to their offline social networks [5].

Facebook users can choose one "profile picture" to represent themselves in Facebook; it is displayed in a prominent place in the profile and alongside the user's other content such as comments and wall posts they make. Because people use profile pictures for explicit self-presentation, choosing profile pictures that contain both romantic partners has important relational meanings. Most participants who don't have their relationship status listed see profile pictures as an alternative to announce the existence of their relationships.

"Well definitely that we're in our profile pictures together, that I'm listed on his profile and he's listed on my profile definitely shows a lot." (I-17-F)

Reciprocity of profile pictures can also be used to signal the quality of relationships, for better and for worse.

"Yeah we were both always in our profile pictures and then when we had our like first fight he took me off of his and then that was kind of like we stopped putting each other in our profile pictures and that was kind of an indication." (P-5-F)

Uploading pictures is commonly used to signal possessiveness, especially among female participants.

"I posted these photos and made them public to friends of friends, because I knew that his ex girlfriend would see them..." (I-17-F-diary)

A less mentioned but interesting point is, because others can contribute to a Facebook user's photo collection, third-party photos can also have important affirming effects for romantic partners.

"My boyfriend's friend putting me in his profile picture made me see our relationship positively." (I-17-F-diary)

Wall Posts

Unlike photos, which are usually visible to the whole network, wall posts are always directed to a specific person. However, they are still visible to those who can see both partners' profiles, including their overlapping mutual friends. Thus, third parties often use wall posts to understand relationships from the outside [32], while couples use them to think about their partner's relationships with third parties. Common tactics that people use to reveal or conceal relationship information, such as affect display [5], often happen in wall posts.

"And we have this thing where we'll always post one more heart than the last person posted." (P-5-F)

Most participants talked using wall posts to communicate with their partners in a playful or indirect way. Such posts could be *"mysterious and subtle"*, as in this description of using the status update *"like...here is to a great two years"* (P-6-M) to quietly celebrate an anniversary.

"I mean if you don't really have any context going in...it could have been about anything. Here is to two great years of college or two great years of whatever..." (P-6-F)

Even though people don't often directly communicate about their relationships in public, both because some topics are private and there are norms around appropriate levels of public display of affection, they do pay attention to how other couples interact via this feature and make judgments about their relationships. For example, people can learn or infer aspects of other relationships from seeing changes in language use and communication frequency in wall posts.

"Because of Facebook I got to know that my friend T and her boyfriend broke up. I guess like from the tone of their messages it started getting less intimate." (I-5-F)

OUTWARDS AND INWARDS TENSIONS

In this section we discuss the overarching themes that cut across people's decision-making for incorporating their romantic relationships into specific Facebook features: managing both outwards and inwards tensions.

Outwards Tension: How Public Should We Be?

The outwards tension comes about from people's need to balance disclosing their romantic relationships in the public context and protecting themselves from exposing too much or being seen in a negative light in public. The mixture of audiences on Facebook, the ease of becoming friends, and the possibility of losing control over content linked to an individual all highlight difficulties in trying to reveal an appropriate amount of relationship information, which for most people falls somewhere between completely public and completely private.

On one hand, going public is important for people in romantic relationships, and participants frequently used a variety of features to signal elements of their relationship to others. This is largely attributed to the need to inform network members about their relationship information. Most people feel this need to maintain a shared image by interacting with third parties.

"I certainly have an image to I guess to keep up... You have got to keep up your appearances on her wall...if I'm never with my girlfriend...people are like why aren't you ever around?" (I-2-M)

Another commonly mentioned reason for going public is to satisfy third parties' curiosity about their relationships or partners.

"I didn't want to [post a relationship status]. I never had a boyfriend before. I was like no I don't know what is going on... But now they (my friends) would make fun of me if it wasn't there." (P-6-F)

Participants had mixed feelings about this interaction with third parties. Positive feedback motivates people to be more open about the relationship, because *"It keeps the high going when people are all just congratulating me and like think it is cute or whatever."* (P-6-M). However, people also worry that going public might bring negative feedback or indifference from the audience.

"If I want to send him something sort of cheesy...like animal pictures that we both love...I won't necessarily put them all on his wall just because his friends...they are just going to make fun of him..." (P-2-F)

"See the reason [not to disclose] is most people tend to ignore us. There is always this other couple that gets more attention than us. And they get more positive feedback." (P-4-F)

People also worry that disclosing relationship information might be inappropriate for a mixture of audiences.

"We just want to let know our close friends and share it with them. But not everybody, all our friends on Facebook." (P-3-M)

"I also tend to keep it private...and also his parents go on his Facebook so I can't really...that is a major influence." (P-4-F)

Over half of participants feel the need to balance the presence of friends and romantic partners. People worry that having too much interaction with their partners via wall posts or uploading too many "couple pictures" will alienate others or be misinterpreted by some audiences.

"Since he and I talk so frequently, posting on his Facebook wall every time I wanted to tell him something would mean that his entire wall would be made up of comments from me, which would decrease the privacy of our relationship and alienate others." (I-17-F-diary)

"Even though there are a lot more pictures of me and her than there are of other people, I make sure to include

certain other people in there…if I see someone else, like a good photo like the kissing is alright really romantic like in Rome or whatever. But if it is constant like picture after picture, they don't put any pictures of their friends but just the two of them I would think that that is just a little strange." (P-2-M)

Inwards Tension: How Autonomous Should We Be?

The inwards tension refers to the control and interpersonal influence a couple has over each other's behaviors. The fact that Facebook affords awareness of others' activities and interactions can lead to tensions within the relationship about how partners expect each other to behave in public. For example, reciprocity is often important—and sometimes required, as when linking profiles together via the relationship status—in decision-making around how to use Facebook. When one partner posts this status, the other often feels obligated to reciprocate. These tensions can lead to compromises or feelings of giving in.

"I want to do that, not like be more lovey dovey… I don't know because I'm a girl or whatever. But he didn't really want to do that. He wants to keep it super private, so I kinda felt that and like, OK, if that's what you want I'll either have to deal with it or break up with him. So I just dealt with it." (I-5-F)

Facebook's affordances can make these tensions more salient. The visibility of Facebook activities allows people to "watch" how their partner interacts with their own personal networks. Participants, especially those in long-distance relationships, sometimes take advantage of this visibility to keep up with each other's personal life.

"I certainly spend the most time on his profile. So like I'm checking his profile all the time [laughs]…and certainly more since it's been long distance…" (P-5-F)

A common theme across most couples is that the visibility can serve more explicit surveillance functions, such as reading wall posts between their partner and third parties as a way to understand their partner's relationships.

"My boyfriend wrote on one of his friend's walls about going to an Asian restaurant. I'm unsure if the restaurant was the one he went to last night with visiting friends from his high school (his ex girlfriend included)." (I-17-F-diary)

A few participants also felt pressure from being in a relationship to change their behaviors toward their friends.

"Due to the fact that I am in a relationship, I tend to not check as many of my male friends' profiles than I might have when I was single." (I-24-F-diary)

"I made a naughty joke or something on our friend's wall, she was like, J! You know, you really embarrassed me…and I just go yeah, I took it down." (I-23-M)

Similarly, the visibility of others' interactions on Facebook also creates expectations for a couple's own relationship.

"Yeah, yeah. So sometimes I would be like oh I wish we can be like more like them. Mainly like when I see couples upload like couple pictures together and it's usually like they do a lot of things together and they're always taking pictures and then I wish I have more of that." (I-25-F)

Differing expectations bring an important question of whether romantic partners should reach an agreement over how to behave, and how much control or influence they have over each other's Facebook behaviors.

"During the summer he is like purging his photos and I actually specifically asked him to remove certain photos of him. It was at a party and he was like…he was drinking. That part always bothered me." (P-4-F)

"I upload a lot more pictures than he does and I haven't actually uploaded a lot of our pictures together just because like I feel like he doesn't really want them on there." (I-25-F)

However, these expectations are balanced with the desire to claim one's own autonomy, such as making one's own decisions on how to manage their online photos, show their relationship status, and interact with third parties. For example, this participant expressed his unwillingness to let his girlfriend "friend" his friends.

"The friends I do have on my own, I try and make it as my escape zone and if she gets in there then I have nowhere to go, I guess I've got to keep that curtained off. She can have her own friends if she wants…if she ever gets sick of me they need to be there…you've got to have something to yourself." (I-2-M)

This kind of negotiation of expectations rarely discussed explicitly. Most of the time it is by using understanding or *"intuition"* (P-3-M) developed in offline interactions, or by observing each other's online behaviors. For example, this participant talked about how she uses the boyfriend's behavior as a reference point for her own behaviors.

"Yeah because I mean I wouldn't like it if he would respond to other people in a way that's somewhat flirtatious or made it seem that he was interested in that person. So I would kind of like to reciprocate that because he hasn't done that so I try not to do that too." (I-24-F)

Two extreme cases of this negotiation of expectation came about where people accessed their partner's account and changed public content—a source of conflict.

"I changed his profile picture to include (me)…then I guess he didn't like it so he took it off." (I-25-F)

Finally, people sometimes use the negotiation of Facebook features such as asking one's partner to post relationship status to explicitly raise or resolve relationship issues.

"There was a point two years ago when he cheated on me, and I was like really upset… He was super private about his relationship with me… I was like, it's on and off, and I

want you to [post our relationship status]. So he just did that... It was such a point of contention for our relationship. He finally just gave in I guess..." (I-5-F)

INTERACTION BETWEEN OUTWARDS AND INWARDS

We see that each individual involved in a romantic relationship is dealing with both the outwards tension which is concerned with their relationship with third parties, and the inwards tension which is concerned with their relationship with their romantic partner.

These observations have been made before in the interpersonal communication literature [5] when they found the couples' boundary regulation strategies depend on a various factors including needs from the self, the partner, and third parties. However, our results suggest this picture may be even more complicated on Facebook because these concerns often arise simultaneously.

At times these different relational goals harmonize nicely. A fairly common theme was that the public nature of Facebook provides opportunities for the couples to have necessary interactions with their social networks, as suggested by Parks [27]. Information such as relationship status could be both affirming for couples and informing for third parties. A few participants also noted that revealing romantic relationships could align with personal needs for third party validation around self-identity.

"*I guess I was always a dork and I always tried to get a girlfriend in high school and it never worked. And I just wanted to gloat a little bit that look at me I'm at the beginning of college and I already have a girlfriend.*" (P-6-M)

However, publicity also creates problems. Facebook's "context collapse" of connections from different spheres of life [24] complicates decisions about appropriate disclosure. Unlike the offline world, where people can manage their communication with romantic partners and with third parties in separate spaces and develop different disclosure management strategies, users often have to balance these needs when they publish content in Facebook. Male participants, in particular, tended to worry that putting up a relationship status might alienate friends.

"*Like being part of a frat is like, when you take your girlfriend...even though there is no intention to, it puts a divide between the guys a little bit... So for me it was a lot bigger than saying well we are in a relationship. We are dating. We are going to spend some time...I'm calling you my girlfriend. It was more than that.*" (P-2-M)

The mixture of audiences created by the increasing overlap of social networks creates another kind of context collapse. Personal networks associated with each partner might have different needs and expectations that need to be satisfied, and somehow couples need to work out strategies to present their relationships appropriately in front of their separate but somewhat overlapping networks.

"*I'd get rid of [relationship status] if she didn't really care.*" (P-6-M)

"*You don't have engineering boys to worry about though.*" (P-6-F)

The need to publicly affirm relationships also sometimes conflicted with norms for public behavior. For instance, almost all interviewees reacted negatively to excessibe public displays of affection, ranging from sending "lovey dovey messages", constantly uploading intimate pictures, hints for sexual activities, and so on.

"*I have one friend who's always like, I love my girlfriend so much, blah-blah...it makes me want to vomit.*" (I-23-M)

Affordances of social media sites, such as visibility, highlight the need to simultaneously manage outwards and inwards tensions. The following two quotes from the same participant shows how individuals both exploit visibility and recognize the problems it can create.

"*I don't think I really trust him as much as I thought I did... I went on his Facebook one day, he set his Facebook to private, I was like, is he doing something he doesn't want me to see, so I checked [his Facebook].*" (I-5-F)

"*I think a lot of things could be misconstrued on Facebook. Like friendships between two people, it can be interpreted as two-way romantic attention; you see you are still friends with your ex...and that causes problems too.*" (I-5-F)

Thus, people weigh the relative importance of romantic relationships and relationships with third parties when they make decisions. In fact, we found people weigh these relationships differently at different relational stages of romantic relationships. For example, evidence suggests in the initial stage of the romantic relationship, more energy is geared towards managing the inwards tension, while as the romantic relationship develops, people might be less likely to sacrifice their concern for third parties to protect their partners' feelings. This finding is partly consistent with studies that suggest the dialectic between openness and closedness is most salient early in relationships [4].

"*I just certainly feel a lot more confident now than I did at that time [the beginning of the relationship] about Eric caring about me and about displaying affection.*" (P-5-F)

STRATEGIES FOR MANAGING TENSIONS

So far we have mostly focused on the ways in which Facebook's affordances such as specific features, privacy controls, and visibility intensify tensions and bring potential problems to relationship management. However, these features also support strategies that can help people manage these tensions.

Mutual rules, mediated by others

In dealing with the tension, one common strategy developed by couples is to develop rules within their own relationships with regard to how they use Facebook.

"It varies from person to person. We have decided that we don't want to put anything related to our relationship on Facebook. So it is our decision." (P-3-M)

The visibility that Facebook affords makes it possible to use other couples' behaviors as a reference point for regulating their own presentations, such as avoiding excess displays of affection.

"I mean, there are couples…we both talked, how we don't want that, like I love you baby, on the wall, it's just so corny to us." (I-23-M)

Shared meanings but separated behaviors

Another common way to negotiate these issues is for one person to "specialize" in a behavior that is more appropriate for their social network than their partner's. For instance, one person might upload a photo and tag both themselves and their partner. This would support relational goals of having a shared image, but are not as salient a self-presentation act as uploading pictures to one's own photo album, allowing people to finesse friends' expectations.

"If someone is just looking at Leslie's page you know they'll see a bunch of photos of us together. Like I'm not asking her to take those out, like I don't want her to take those down. But on my wall personally, I kind of make sure that everything stays that both of us like it a lot." (P-2-M)

Shared meanings but different affordances

Couples also leveraged the variety of Facebook features available to communicate closeness, choosing features that allow partners to manage the inward tension, presenting the relationship while maintaining some autonomy.

"I guess I've asked him before…why he doesn't have a [profile] picture that has me in it but he has never really given me an answer besides that he's not ashamed of me because obviously like his Facebook status says that he's in a relationship with me." (I-25-F)

Selective presentation through privacy features

Another way to resolve outwards versus inwards tensions, though least mentioned by our participants, is to use Facebook's privacy controls to present different inwards and outwards faces. This participant did not want to make the relationship status public, but her boyfriend wanted the affirmation, so she strategically made her relationship status visible only to her boyfriend.

"He actually didn't know that I hid it for a while because I set it so that only he can see it so he just assumes that everyone else can see it too." (I-25-F)

Likewise, people can control the notifications Facebook generates on their behalf, allowing actions such as setting a relationship status to serve relational goals but without as many public side effects, such as appearing "corny".

"Immediately when I found the newsfeed (of my relationship status), I removed that post because I hate that… I don't know, it's corny. Just weird to me." (I-23-M)

FACEBOOK CAN PROVIDE RELATIONAL CONTEXT

Finally, Facebook can also serve a place where people understand their romantic relationship, both in the context of others—as a platform for enacting the embeddedness of interpersonal relationships [27]—and in the historical context of their own relationship.

Third parties as references and support

For instance, Facebook provides a gallery of behaviors for people to reflect on, adopt, or avoid. The visibility of how other couples interact creates reference points not just for choosing appropriate behaviors, as described earlier, but also for people to reflect on the quality and value of their own relationships.

"When I see people fighting on Facebook, it makes me think of how lucky I am to be in a relationship with my boyfriend, in which we don't fight but rather discuss our disagreements." (I-24-F-diary)

Facebook also allows couples to get external affirmation for their relationships. Publicizing the relationship doesn't just satisfy third parties' needs for information, but allows those third parties to provide social support necessary for relationship development [13].

"I think it's a relief to know that my [Facebook] friends are just as open as I am because no one has really like judged me for dating someone who's African American." (I-25-F)

Reviewability as a mirror

The reviewability of prior Facebook activity allows partners to reflect on or reminisce about their relationship, a theme also seen in earlier studies of using social media content for reflection [29, 32].

"It's strange, just going back now that I'm doing this experiment and looking at our wall posts. Normally I wouldn't really read old posts but now I'm going back and looking. It makes me remember what we've talked about, then actually planned and done." (P-2-M)

During our interview, one participant reported that thinking about how they and their partner use Facebook even helps her value the relationship differently.

"I think this experience of doing the activity makes me realize I was not as happy as I thought I am in this relationship. I question a lot of things, I'm leaning towards breaking up with him. I guess." (I-5-F)

CONCLUDING REMARKS

Our study shows the need to better understand interpersonal boundary regulation when people are dealing with tensions emerging from multiple relational contexts on Facebook. It also suggests that affordances of social networking sites such as Facebook highlight the tensions that arise as individuals simultaneously manage the need to interact and maintain relationships with both personal network members and romantic partners.

These findings about inwards and outwards tensions extend previous research on romantic relationships and social media [e.g. 25, 34], which suggests that the use of social media might have negative effects on the relationship, increasing jealousy and relationship dissatisfaction. Our description of the layers of tensions people manage offers a different lens to think about the issue of online disclosure and close relationships and the role social media plays in resolving or intensifying these tensions.

Our findings also have the potential to extend previous theoretical perspectives on relationship maintenance. For example, previous research on relational dialectics mostly examined internal and external relational tensions separately [4]. However, our findings highlight the need to examine internal and external tensions simultaneously, as new technologies blur the boundary between interpersonal communication and communication to a mass audience.

From the design side, our focus on affordances of social media features people used, rather than specific features themselves, and our asking people about not just their behaviors but the reasons behind them, may help designers apply these findings in new contexts. For instance, we explicitly prompted people to reflect on past content and behavior in order to examine the effect of reviewability in media. In the 2011 version of Facebook, such review is somewhat artificial, and prompting it may have affected people's responses. However, with the advent of features such as Facebook's Timeline that make historical content more salient and accessible, we expect this kind review and reflection to become increasingly common in social media. This may in turn change people's interpretations and norms around behavior in social media—but that itself would be interesting to study. Further, it points out the need to go beyond the observation that social media are *in principle* reviewable and consider about how well the interface supports such review and the goals people might serve by reviewing this content [31].

As another example, many participants compared Facebook to Google+, and their comments suggest that its privacy management mechanisms will lead to new strategies. Google+ makes it easier to set different levels of publicness for relationship status, as one of our participants did. This will give partners more flexibility in managing the openness of their relationship, but the level of display might then itself become a point of controversy. Google+ also allows people to create custom audiences through its circles that might reduce context collapse and allow for more nuanced expression of the relationship.

"I do have a circle that's for like really close friends. I think if I were to share my relationship status on Google+ I will only do it for the really close friends and it'll be not showing for any of the others." (I-25-F)

However, this would reduce the visibility of each other's social media activity, which people valued, and could change the ways people think about enacting their relationships and interpreting their partner's behavior.

"I would say I would prefer to see what he's doing like publicly to everyone, I guess I prefer the Facebook way just because I feel like almost if I'm in a circle but I can't see a lot of stuff that he's doing in other circles... It just makes me wonder what is it that is like so like secretive almost that you don't want me to see." (I-28-F)

Our study focused on a tool and participants rooted in American culture, but many other design and cultural contexts exist. For instance, the Lover Space feature of the Chinese social networking site Renren[1] allows couples to construct a shared user profile for presenting "their relationship". Based on our analysis, we might expect that such a profile would help manage the outwards tension but explicitly highlight inwards negotiation over how partners should manage their online presentation in this shared space. But, this would also depend on how Lover Space interacts with other features of RenRen, the values, norms, and practices of RenRen users, and more generally how relationships are perceived and publicized in Chinese culture, which may be quite different from the "WEIRD" (Western, Educated, Industrialized, Rich, and Democratic) [20] context of our study.

There is plenty of other future work beyond culture. Our sample was too small to look deeply at sub-groups, but some of our data suggests that gender (e.g., males being more worried about friends' reactions), relationship stage (e.g., needing more affirmation early on), and relationship types that might lead to social stigma (e.g., worrying about reactions to an interracial relationship) may all impact both design and theory around online disclosure of romantic relationships.

Still, our work casts light on the fundamental observation that the technical affordances and norms of online social networking sites create a number of situations in which couples must—and do—manage both inwards and outwards tensions in their relationships simultaneously. We hope it provides useful examples and ideas for thinking about the design of social network sites and for theorizing about how they affect the ways people manage information privacy, tensions between individual and relational needs, accountability to existing friends' relational dynamics, and other fundamental aspects of relationship development.

ACKNOWLEDGMENTS

We would like to thank Sneha Kanneganti for helping with transcribing interviews, the NSF for support under IIS 0835451 and a Graduate Research Fellowship.

[1] www.renren.com.

REFERENCES

1. Acquisti, A., Gross, R. (2006). Imagined communities: Awareness, information sharing, and privacy on Facebook. In *Proc. PET'06*.
2. Ahern, S., Eckles, D., Good, N., King, S., Naaman, M., Nair, R. (2007). Over-exposed? Privacy patterns and considerations in online and mobile photo sharing. In *Proc. CHI'07*.
3. Altman, I. (1975). *The environment and social behavior*. Monterey, CA: Brooks/Cole.
4. Baxter, L. (1990). Dialectical contradictions in relationship development. *Journal of Social and Personal Relationships*, *7*, 69–88.
5. Baxter, L, Widenmann, S. (1993). Revealing and not revealing the status of romantic relationships to social networks. *J Social & Pers Relationships*, *10*, 321–338.
6. Besmer, A., Richter, L. (2010). Moving beyond untagging: Photo privacy in a tagged world. *Proc. CHI*.
7. Bowe, G. (2010). Reading romance: The impact Facebook rituals can have on a romantic relationship. *J of Comparative Research in Anthro & Soc*, *1*, 61–77.
8. boyd, d. (2008). *Taken out of Context: American Teen Sociality in Networked Publics*. Ph.D. dissertation, University of California at Berkeley, School of Information. URL: http://bit.ly/4AOhPS.
9. boyd, d., Ellison, N. (2008). Social network sites: Definition, history, and scholarship. *JCMC*, *13*, 210–30.
10. Child, J.T., Petronio, S. (2011). Unpacking the paradoxes of privacy in CMC relationships: The challenges of blogging and relational communication on the internet. In *Computer-mediated communication in personal relationships*, 21–40. New York: Peter Lang.
11. Donath, J., et al. (2010). Data portraits. *Leonardo, 43,* 375–383.
12. Donath, J., boyd, d. (2004). Public displays of connection. *BT Technology Journal, 22,* 71–82.
13. Eggert, L., Parks, M.R. (1987). Communication network involvement in adolescents' friendships and romantic relationships. *Comm Yearbook, 10,* 283–322.
14. Ellison, N. (2006). Managing impressions online: Self presentation processes in the online dating environment. *JCMC, 11,* article 2.
15. Ellison, N., Steinfield, C., Lampe, C. (2011). Connection strategies: social capital implications of Facebook-enabled communication practices. *New Media & Society*, *13,* 873–892.
16. Ellison, N.B., Steinfield, C., Lampe, C. (2007). The benefits of Facebook "friends:" Social capital and college students' use of online social network sites. *JCMC, 12*, article 1.
17. Glaser, B., Strauss, A. (1967). *The discovery of grounded theory: Strategies for qualitative research*. Chicago: Aldine Publishing Company.
18. Goffman, E. (1959), *The Presentation of the Self in Everyday Life*. New York: Anchor.
19. Hancock, J.T., Toma, C. (2009). Putting your best face forward: The accuracy of online dating photographs. *Journal of Communication, 59,* 367–386.
20. Henrich, J., Heine, S.J., Norenzayan, A. (2010). Most people are not WEIRD. *Nature, 466*, 29.
21. Lampinen, A., Lehtinen, V., Lehmuskallio, A., Tamminen, S. (2011). We're in it together: Interpersonal management of disclosure in social network services. In *Proc. CHI'11*.
22. Lewis, J., West, A. (2009). 'Friending': London-based undergraduates' experience of Facebook. *New Media & Society, 11,* 1209–1229.
23. Lewis, K., Kaufman, J., Christakis, N. (2008). The taste of privacy: An analysis of college student privacy settings in an online social network. *JCMC, 14,* 79–100.
24. Marwick, A., boyd, d. (2011). I tweet honestly, I tweet passionately: Twitter users, context collapse, and the imagined audience. *New Media & Society, 13,* 114–133.
25. Muise, A. (2009), More information than you ever wanted: Does Facebook bring out the green eyed monster of jealousy. *Cyberpsych Behavior, 12,* 441–444.
26. Palen, L., Dourish, P. (2003). Unpacking "privacy" for a networked world. In *Proc. CHI'03.*
27. Parks, M.R. (2007). *Personal relationships and personal networks.* Lawrence Erlbaum Associates.
28. Pascoe, C.J. (2009), Intimacy in hanging about, messing around and geeking out. In *Kids living and learning with new media,* 117–149. University of California Berkeley.
29. Peesapati, S.T., Schwanda, V., et al. 2010. Pensieve: supporting everyday reminiscence. In *Proc. CHI 2010.*
30. Petronio, S. (2002). *Boundaries of privacy: Dialectics of disclosure.* New York: State U. of New York Press.
31. Sellen, A.J., Whittaker, S. (2010). Beyond total capture: a constructive critique of lifelogging. *Commun ACM, 53*, 70–77.
32. Sosik, V.S., Zhao, X., Cosley, D. (2012). See friendship, sort of: How conversation and digital traces might support reflection on friendships. In *Proc. CSCW*.
33. Stutzman, F., Kramer-Duffield, J. (2010). Friends only: Examining a privacy-enhancing behavior in Facebook. In *Proc. CHI.*
34. Utz, S., Beukeboom, C.J. (2011). The role of social network sites in romantic relationships: Effects on jealousy and relationship happiness. *JCMC, 16*, 511–527.

Lost in Translation: Understanding the Possession of Digital Things in the Cloud

William Odom[1], Abigail Sellen[2], Richard Harper[2], Eno Thereska[2]

Carnegie Mellon University[1]
Human-Computer Interaction Institute
PA 15213 Pittsburgh, USA
wodom@cs.cmu.edu

Microsoft Research Cambridge[2]
Cambridge CB3 0FB, UK
{asellen, r.harper, etheres}@microsoft.com

ABSTRACT

People are amassing larger and more diverse collections of digital things. The emergence of Cloud computing has enabled people to move their personal files to online places, and create new digital things through online services. However, little is known about how this shift might shape people's orientations toward their digital things. To investigate, we conducted in depth interviews with 13 people comparing and contrasting how they think about their possessions, moving from physical ones, to locally kept digital materials, to the online world. Findings are interpreted to detail design and research opportunities in this emerging space.

Author Keywords

Possession; Materiality; Interactive Systems Design; Human-Centered Architectures; Cloud Computing.

ACM Classification Keywords

H.5.m. Information interfaces and presentation (e.g., HCI): Miscellaneous.

INTRODUCTION

"*...the more I talk about it, the idea of owning something digital seems lost in translation.*" (P4)

People are continuing to amass larger, more diverse and deeply valued collections of digital things. In the past few years, the factors shaping people's relationships with their digital materials has become a focus for HCI research [e.g., 6, 16, 21]. This body of work has produced many worthwhile contributions aimed at better supporting people's values, practices and desires surrounding their digital content kept locally on domestic computers and devices. However, the convergence of social and Cloud computing, along with the growing presence of networked devices, are creating new opportunities for people to move personal files to online places, as well as create new digital content through online services. Despite these real and growing changes, relatively little is known about how they might shape people's orientations toward their digital possessions.

The standard view – certainly the one outlined in advertising [e.g., 2] – is that, with 'the Cloud', people will be able to keep their digital assets more securely and, potentially, more cheaply. By moving away from local storage, users can be sure that when their devices crash or get stolen, or when they suffer from the myriad other mishaps of daily life, their data will be safe. There is no doubt that such concerns do motivate people to move the data they care about online. Recently, for example, Odom et al. [15], reported on the fear that drives many teenagers to seek remote back-up: the likelihood that they might lose their devices or get them stolen, combined with their own poor data management practices, make Cloud-like services especially appealing.

But, perhaps this view is overly simplistic. As we shall discuss in this paper, there are many reasons people engage with the Cloud when producing, accessing, sharing and keeping their digital materials. Such activities have many benefits, yet at the same time, as we shall see, the result of these new kinds of interactions can also alter users' orientations to their digital "belongings" in complex and nuanced ways. Indeed, it can lead to complexities, concerns and conundrums in the way people reason about and act upon their online resources. We will argue that part of the complexity here is bound to the design of the devices and services that people use. As we move forward into an ever more networked, multiple device and data-centric world, it seems important to investigate and design around human centered preferences and orientations to data, where storage, and 'safety', is simply one manifestation of that orientation.

It is the purpose of this paper to present research findings based on this premise. We begin the paper with a review of the sociological and anthropological literature on the topic of materiality. We shall see that modern anthropology has become increasingly concerned with possession and materiality, examining in much detail the ways people relate to 'things' as a way of constituting identity and social location. Sociology, meanwhile, has focused on how the orientation that people have to their material possessions needs to be examined as a set of 'reflexive practices' manifest in their daily interactions both with these materials and with others around them.

We will then explore data gathered from qualitative interviews with a diverse sample of 13 people in which we examined how they orient both to their physical and virtual possessions. Specifically, we investigate similarities and differences in how they consider their physical things, their locally kept digital materials, and their things in the online world. Here we shall see that possession is at once a noun for a type of object (physical or virtual) and a verb that labels ways of treating things, again both physical and virtual. This data also illustrates how people are concerned not only with their own possessions, but with others' possessions too. But, beyond this, we shall see that their key concern is that possession be a declarative property of objects, one that can be 'seen' somehow in the type of object—in its location and in the way it is handled by those who have rights to it and concomitantly how it is not handled by those who do not.

With this as a background, the last section of the paper considers how the design of services that allow for the production, gathering, sharing, and storing of digital stuff may proceed in such a fashion that these declarative properties may be embedded in sensible ways. Specifically, we contribute several design considerations to sensitize the design space encompassing Cloud-based interactive systems to better support the possession of personal digital stuff, and the many properties associated with it. To do this, we shall suggest, will not require simple tweaking of current technology, but careful reconfiguration of many aspects of interaction design around digital stuff in all its varieties.

LITERATURE REVIEW

In what immediately follows, we review literature on the topic of materiality in anthropology and sociology. We then describe related works in HCI.

Any investigation of the current literature in anthropology will likely cite Daniel Miller's work. In numerous books he has sought to show how material objects and the study of materiality are fundamental to anthropological research [e.g., 14]. Instead of seeing identity as merely a product of social structure, he shows that identity is partly made in the assemblies of artifacts constitutive of homes in which people live, as well as in their material practices elsewhere (e.g., at work). His study of material displays within homes in South London is a case in point [13]. Here, he argues that 'who you are' is writ large in the things that one possesses and one chooses not to possess; materiality speaks volumes in what it is made up of and what it is does not contain. Miller builds his view through claiming that prior interest in materiality had tended to be at such a high level that it did not account for the richness and diversity of material possessions, a richness that Miller himself tries to convey in the various vignettes presented in his books.

Within sociology, interest in materiality and possession is represented most recently in the work of Shove et al [18]. Shove's work is predicated on a similar presumption to Miller; namely, that the relationship between material objects and identity is to be uncovered through examining the myriad forms that possession can take. She notes that possession is not only something that can apply to a thing but to spaces, practices, and of course, power. From this view, materiality and possession cannot be examined through the limited lens of the persons being studied, through their own subjectivity, but only through theoretical elaboration: key to this is an analysis of the reflexive ways power is manifest in material practices. A somewhat different view within sociology suggests that focus should be placed on people's own orientations and practices which are not to be dismissed as subjective, but as being based on 'lay theorizing'. It is the relationship between this theorizing and material practices that produces the world of everyday life. This perspective has been especially influential in HCI in the work of Suchman [19] and many others.

Turning to work within HCI, there has been a growing interest in how people value or keep digital things, and how this contrasts with physical objects. Much of this research focuses on the concerns of the users, and in this resonates with the ethnomethodological approach. Several researchers explore the practices surrounding valued material archives, for example, and then use these to inform the design of interactive systems. The goal of these systems is to better support personal archiving in 'everyday life' [e.g., 5] and the safekeeping of 'the cherished', digital and otherwise [e.g., 6]. Other researchers have investigated how people's personal archives could be leveraged to better support reflection on the past and meaningful experiences with others [e.g., 16, 21].

Collectively, these works and many others have produced significant contributions to understanding how to better support people's practices and desires surrounding their digital things, most often kept locally on domestic computers and devices.

The convergence of social and Cloud computing, meanwhile, has created new opportunities for people to move increasing amounts of their personal data to online places. Along with these shifts there is now a substantial amount of literature (as well as an active community) within HCI focused on understanding the range of experiences and practices that unfold in online places, such as social networking and media sites. This body of work is too large to cover here, but it suffices to say that researchers have explored issues such as how these sites are used to maintain social relationships [1] and how unwanted self disclosure might be better avoided [17].

However, one topic that has received conspicuously little attention is the question of how the placement of an individual's personal digital stuff in online places might alter their perceptions of these things. Very recently, Odom et al. [15] reported on teenagers' drive to put their "virtual possessions" in Cloud computing services to make them more available and present in their lives. This work also described how teens curated their digital things to exercise a higher level of authorship over their online places compared to their bedrooms. Additionally, Marshall and others [10] have begun to explore implications surrounding the archiving of Internet-based personal information, which revealed people perceived information online to generally be enduring, while also perplexingly susceptible to unanticipated loss. Marshall et al. [9] also investigated peoples' attitudes toward 'owning' social media content on Twitter.com. This study reported that users desired to retain control over the content they produced and to personally archive it, although currently there are no clear ways for this to be achieved. More broadly, there is a history of work in Digital Rights and Digital Identity Management. The former explores how to create technologies used to limit the use of digital content, often to fight copyright infringement [8], while the later aims to verify the identity credentials of a person to decide whether they should be granted access to sensitive content [see 11].

Despite these emerging strands of research, little is collectively known about how the emergence of one's digital stuff in the Cloud might alter people's perceptions of it. In our work, we attempt to address this gap and contribute a more concrete understanding of how people experience the possession of their things in the Cloud, and how this knowledge could better support users' relationships with the digital materials they value.

FIELD STUDY METHOD

The approach we adopted was to recruit a diverse sample of people to elicit a wide range of rich descriptions about how possession of personal digital content is perceived and experienced online. This approach clearly has limitations; for example, it makes the results hard to generalize to any sub-population of users. However, considering the paucity of work in this area and following Edmondson & McManus [3], we wanted to begin with a diverse group to gain a rich, descriptive understanding of the space as a whole to inform what might be salient issues for future research.

With that in mind, a total of 13 participants (7 female and 6 male) were recruited through word of mouth and advertisements; all came from the South Eastern region of the United Kingdom. Participants were screened over the phone to ensure we recruited a range of ages and occupations. Participants' computing practices and expertise varied; however, all owned personal computers, used them relatively frequently (the majority on a daily basis), and had maintained at least one online account at some point (e.g., email, dating website, Facebook). Importantly, in this paper, when we say "online places", we mean any internet-enabled service. This includes but is not limited to Cloud-based storage services (e.g., Dropbox.com), social media/networking sites (e.g. Facebook,), email accounts, and other sites (e.g. location or photo sharing services).

Our resulting sample represented people at many different life stages and in many different occupations. The ages of the participants were as follows: Teenagers [**P1** (aged 16), **P2** (aged 17), **P3** (aged 16)]; Mid-20s [**P4, P5**]; Mid-30s [**P6, P7**]; Mid-40s [**P8, P9, P10**]; Mid-50s [**P11, P12**]; Mid-60s [**P13**]. Occupations included student, architect, bank teller, homemaker, tour guide, and retired dancer.

Semi-structured interviews were conducted in participants' homes, lasting between 70-120 minutes. Interviews aimed to develop an understanding of each participant's orientations toward their (i) material things, (ii) locally stored digital content, and (iii) digital stuff appearing in online places. We began by asking participants to describe the material things they possessed that they considered important. We also asked participants to describe material things that were once valued, but possession had since been relinquished (if any came to mind). Participants then gave us a tour of where these artifacts were kept in the home (in the case of teens, this occurred mostly in their bedroom). This was followed by a tour of participants' digital stuff kept on local devices. We similarly asked participants to describe what they perceived to be valued digital things, with emphasis on probing motivations and strategies for holding onto these things. We then asked participants to give us a tour of their digital stuff kept in online environments. Across these themes, we asked participants to reflect on similarities and differences among their material and digital things; we paid close attention to the language participants used to categorize and describe similarities and differences. We were careful to not offer participants any definitions of 'possession' throughout the interviews; when necessary we prompted them to clarify their orientations toward their various material and digital things.

All interviews were audio-taped, which produced nearly 18 hours of recordings. The first author conducted all of the interviews. All authors met weekly for 1-3 hours to review and analyze the data. Documents for each interview were created and contained transcribed segments relevant to our research questions (as opposed to idle chit chat). Documents were coded by researchers before weekly meetings; overlaps and differences in interpretations of the data were discussed. Data were then organized into themes. Meetings were also held with researchers outside of the project to challenge our assumptions and to corroborate the themes. In what follows, we present several examples taken from field observations with participants, which we feel capture the core themes emerging across our interviews.

FINDINGS

In what immediately follows, we briefly describe the main findings related to participants' material possessions and their perceptions with regard to digital stuff kept locally on devices in the home. We then unpack apparent differences that emerged as participants compared these orientations to their digital things kept in online places or when attempts were made to move them from one to the other.

The Possessing of Things: Material and Virtual

Interviews and observations in participants' homes confirmed the insights that Miller offers in his *The Comfort of Things* [15]. The way our subjects spoke about and presented their possessions revealed a range of deeply held values, values to do with who they were and how they wanted to convey that to those they shared their lives with – at home, at work and even to strangers, like us, the researchers. Material possessions are essential to the repertoire of identity, we learnt. A sample of the materials used in identity production included photographs of family and friends, mementos from trips, and objects symbolic of personal relationships. All the homes we studied contained family heirlooms, for example, tying identity in the here and now with what it was (except P5 and the bedrooms of P1-P3). In some cases these things were on display in the home, and, following Miller, we took this as indicating that the subjects wanted to 'make them present and accessible'. Examples of these included handmade ceramics on a living room mantle. Other artifacts were stored away (in closets or cupboards) but the participants brought them to bear by reporting on how they 'knew' where these things were, and though they might be hidden away in the service of their preservation, their presence remained real, nonetheless. One example of this was a family bible in a bedroom chest. Discussions also revealed material possessions participants had intentionally discarded. The impetus for some of these behaviors simply owed to a loss of utility (e.g., broken mobile phone). But participants also described why some things were discarded because they evoked painful memories or no longer represented their values or desires. What was gone from the material record thus became another resource to account for identity.

Material things were not the only things that our participants had. All owned or had access to a personal computer they were the primary user of. Interviews revealed digital collections of varying sizes kept locally on these machines and other devices (e.g., digital camera, mobile media player). Across all participants, the personal computer functioned as the primary place where their digital content was locally kept. These collections contained such things as: music files, photo collections, personal documents, personal diaries, financial documents, computer game information, and so on. Older participants emphasized the importance of their digital photo collections documenting family members; some of which were expansive. This may be related to the fact that, aside from P10, all of our participants aged 30 and above had children. It was clear that parents perceived these archives to be deeply valued; in fact, several desired to pass them down to their children. In this view, being a parent seemed to imply acting as custodian in this regard, a role that would be 'handed down'.

Some participants raised concerns over their growing size, their importance notwithstanding. For example, P9 compares his archive of nearly 4000 photos (kept on his PC) with physical photo albums, "*....The digital ones, they are my possession, but I don't know exactly what's in there anymore and that sense of not knowing, or not easily knowing, makes possessing them feel somewhat different.*" This quote captures how a lack of awareness of the specificity of a personal archive (the contents in other words) shaped the perception of possessing it. As we will describe, lack of knowledge in this respect emerged as a core factor shaping participants' orientations toward their digital things online, and did so in several ways: the role of curator can become complicated if one does not know what one is curating.

Younger participants (P1-P5) reported keeping less expansive digital archives locally. We observed older participants organized their personal content relatively carefully, often copying it to external hard drives or physical media. By contrast, younger participants generally had less developed practices for organizing files locally, and reported rarely backing their content up. This may be due to the trend among younger participants to put content such as digital photos online [7]. However, as we shall discuss, this transition appeared to cause complications when these participants were asked to discuss their orientations toward these digital things, particularly in terms of issues of control over and awareness of these things once they were online.

Transitioning to Online Places

Several factors shaped participants' motivations to put their personal digital stuff on the internet. These relate to matters which have to do with identity through the management and display of possessions and because of matters that can best be described as practical. All told these can be broadly characterized as the following: (i) to share digital content with others (and potentially acquire new value through the accrual of social metadata), (ii) to make digital things more ubiquitously accessible, opening up the possibility of drawing on these things across different physical places, and (iii) to put in an alternative place of storage for back-up purposes (in case hardware should break down, for example).

While the second and third reasons above treat the online world much like a networked "storage box", the first reason—to share information with others—is perhaps the most compelling. This is because posting information to online sites for sharing fundamentally alters and potentially adds value to these possessions. At the same time, it is clear that the attribution of social metadata, such as comments and tags, seemed to change participants' perceptions of the digital thing itself. In a sense, these digital "things" are transformed into actions and, through this process, transformed into something else.

For example, P8 describes the distinction between digital photos on her hard drive and the 'same' copies uploaded online: "*...they get comments from my friends and family, and those acknowledgments and stories become part of them. ...When I think about the photos as my possessions, I think about the ones on my computer and the ones on my Facebook as different. My* [local] *photos are me saving them for my family, for the future. ...On Facebook, the photos are me and my family and the connections we have with other people through the comments. I want both of them.*"

Discussions with younger and older participants also illustrated how metadata was used as a resource to create a sense of sharing things among friends. For example, consider P2 (our youngest participant): "*I upload photos of when I'm out with friends. ...Like one time is at the mid-summer fair. I posted photos* [on Facebook] *and tagged* [my friends]. *...We write things if something catches our attention or* [we] *remember something happened in that photo. ...I posted them, but I put them up there to share and it's like when we all write on them and tag them, it's those things that make it feel like we all have them together.*"

These reflections help illustrate how the act of sharing online shapes orientations toward this content, possessed in some sense collectively, but still content which participants wanted to keep for themselves. This also shaped participants' orientations toward their own material possessions and digital collections kept locally in the home. Further, while research has described this general phenomenon in the context of teenagers [15], our discussions suggest it was widely applicable to participants from various generations.

Complicating and complicated notions of possession

The case of social metadata as a motivation for posting online highlights how the notion of "possession", in the ways it has traditionally been described, begins to break down in online places. When we talked to participants more closely about whether they possessed this content, and how it compares to digital content they keep locally, or indeed physical possessions, we see that it begins to make people question what this means, and struggle to articulate it.

This is nicely summed up by P8 who describes how placing photos into his Flickr account both created deeply valued digital things she desired to possess, whilst simultaneously prevented him from doing so, "*...When I think of my most important possessions, this is at the top of the list. But at the same time, I have no idea how to get them, not just the photos, but everything together. ...that's where 'possessing' them breaks down. ... I want them, I'm entitled to them, and they're there* [motioning to screen] *but do I have them? ...it feels like there's this illusion that they're mine. ...it's a very strange thing that I do not know how to resolve.*"

So what does it mean to "have", to "own" or to "possess" something? It is clear that the online world brings into question notions that we almost take for granted in the material world. In fact, it may help to appeal to participants' orientations toward what it means to possess something in the physical world to see how those basic concepts are altered, undermined or made more complex once our digital stuff begins to live on the network or in the Cloud.

In what follows, we examine how these basic, implicit assumptions are challenged. In doing so, we will show that two emergent themes run throughout: that posting something online, in today's world, can mean *relinquishing control* over the things that you care about, but also *losing awareness* of what exists, where it is, who has access to it, who is accountable for it, and what is being done with it.

Knowing what you have

In the physical world, one of the characteristics of the things we possess is that we generally have some sense of what we own and where these things are, at least in some approximate way. We organize our possessions in containers, put them in special places, or at least have some loose idea of where something we value resides. At the highest level, our homes, offices and even cars act as a kind of physical boundary around the collection of material things we possess, and within those we may have special places to further contain them, as against other members of the household, for example.

When it comes to online data, there is no equivalent sense of a place where something resides, let alone a clear boundary to understand the limits of what is ours and what is not ours. Participants expressed concerns about not knowing "where" their data lives, what it means for something to reside online, and not really knowing where the entirety of their valued things might actually exist. In this way, notions of *where you have* things are entwined with knowing *what you have*. In other words, it is difficult to take inventory on what you own without knowing where to look.

An excellent illustration of this was given by P12, who had recently experienced a hard drive crash, losing her digital photo collection in the process. As it turns out, many of these photos were also on Facebook, and she had recently taken to copying the online photos onto the local hard drive on her new laptop: "*...I feel like I need to copy them somewhere, have them covered. ...I do that and I've done that and I don't even think about why I do it. I am scared of losing them, but I didn't realize it until I started talking, right here, consciously you know. ...I use the sentence 'I've got some photos', so I've said it, but I don't know really if I possess them, not until they're here* [pointing at laptop], *at least then I know where they are.*"

Despite her recent loss of data on her local hard drive, P12 was driven to move her things from an online place to her local hard drive to have a better understanding of where they are, which appeared in part tied to the experience of possessing them. Being aware of where something resides, and being able to point to that physical place, reinforced her perception of owning those things, despite the fact it might be risky in the long term, as she had learned.

Having access when you want

In the physical world, another benefit of knowing where your things live is that you can have quick access to them. A major concern voiced by participants centered on their perceptions that since they had no discernable control over the services that host the place(s) where their digital stuff "lives", they might temporarily or even permanently lose access to them.

In all, 10 of our 13 participants noted similar concerns. For example, consider P4's discussion of her Facebook content: "*I have this fear that all of a sudden it's going to get shutdown and they're going to wipe* [it] *and I won't be able to get it back. So it doesn't feel like I'm fully possessing it, I mean I feel like it's my information ...but it's like I'm not in charge of it fully. Like it's at the mercy of someone else."*

P6 similarly described a deep attachment to her travel blog, which she now thinks of as a travel memento: "*I put a lot of work into it, but it doesn't feel exactly like mine because, let's face it, that site isn't going to be around forever. I'm thinking to back it up, but how do I do that? If I put it on a CD it's probably going to get lost.*"

The teenagers we interviewed all used social networking sites, uploading digital photos, among other things, frequently. All three teens, along with P6, reported maintaining minimal digital photo collections locally, generally opting to delete photos from their computer, camera, or phone after they had been uploaded. Discussions revealed these participants generally considered their online content would last indefinitely into the future. However, they did raise other concerns, when reflecting on differences between their access to and control over their material possessions compared to their digital things online: "*What if Facebook would block me from coming in or didn't recognize me 'as me.' I might never get those things back. I'd be distraught. ...With Facebook, there are so many things on there that are important to me but they're different than my* [physical] *things because there's this chance I'd never be able to get to them. That fine line can change a lot about how I think of them. It's like possessing them, but not quite.*" (P2).

Alongside fears that services or organizations might block access to one's treasured digital things, the following poignant example shows that this can also happen because others may have rights over content that undermine your access. P5 described how the deletion of his departed friend's Facebook account (by the bereaved parents) also erased the social metadata his friend had created previously: "*Those comments were a big part of what I had left from him. ...his personality really came out in them. ...Now they're gone, just gone and they can't be replaced. Even if I could get them back, it wouldn't be the same. It's not just the text ...it's the time he wrote it, the day he wrote it. It's like this marker of him and it all came together into something special. ...made me realize how fragile things online can be.*"

What we want to highlight across these instances is that while it came naturally to participants to describe their material things, they often struggled to articulate how these orientations mapped to their digital stuff in online places. Specifically, they help illustrate how participants simultaneously had deep convictions that their online content belongs to them, while feeling ambivalent over whether access to them would continue to persist. This in part appeared to be due to a loss of control—participants could control what was stored in and presented through their online places, however higher level concerns over how these places would endure appeared to unsettlingly place their contents, as P4 put it, "at the mercy of someone else."

Being accountable for care and protection

A related issue is that knowing where something is kept is often bound up with a responsibility to care for and protect those objects. In other words, it is not solely a matter of knowing where things are, and being able to access them when you want, but there is accountability implicated in many things that one possesses. This can be, for example, a duty to keep those objects safe for someone else's sake, or to pass on to future generations [6]. What our interviews revealed was that keeping things online in some sense hands that accountability over to some unknown, unseen entity—and further that people may have very little faith in its persistence or reliability.

These issues were highlighted by three participants in possession of digital content that they had acquired from departed friends or family members. In one instance, P9 described how her lack of trust in online services complicated transitioning digital photos and documents from her father's computer to the Cloud: "*I felt like I needed to protect it* ...[put] *it in a special place. ...I did think about putting it online, but it didn't feel right. ...It probably wouldn't* [disappear], *but who knows? ...What if it was accidentally erased? ...Those are chances I can't take.*" When probed further on the very real possibility that the hard drive in her personal computer could crash, she pointed to a higher level moral concern: "*I know my computer could die, but at least it would be* ***on me****. ...it's my responsibility to take care of it. Leaving it up to a website, there's no guarantee it's going to stay around. I can't live with that.*" As another example, P8 described complications after uploading digital photos that had belonged to a departed friend to his DropBox.com account: "*My first thought was to put them on DropBox, like if my computer dies, they'll be somewhere else. Then this whole thing came out* [about] *nothing on DropBox being safe and heaps of people's accounts weren't as private as they thought. ...I had this wretched feeling, like I was being lazy about him. ...I took them down immediately. ...They're backed up on my* [computer] *hard drive and on a CD. I'm more in command of their destiny.*"

What is interesting in both of these examples, (and in P12's earlier reflection on backing up photos onto a new hard disk after the old one died), is that having data in some physical form in one's own possession appears to reinstate a sense of responsibility and control over it. This is despite the fact that such storage devices can and do become corrupted.

As a final example, P5 was in possession of 5 digital photos downloaded from Facebook that a friend had tagged him in on the same day of his accidental death. His reflection further highlights how a lack of awareness and control diminished his sense of guardianship over this content: "*...there's all these contradictions with putting something of that weight online because there's a need to watch over it.* ...[but] *there's this sense that it's more out of my hands. Maybe someone copies it, or it gets deleted, or gets harder to find. ...maybe nothing happens, but it's about the fact* *that when it goes online it is in a situation where all those things become possible.*"

What is interesting about this last example is that it draws attention not just to the issue of personal accountability, but to the issue that the uncertainty about handing over care of one's data to an online entity is potentially exacerbated by the actions of others. It is this issue that we turn to next.

Giving access or rights to others

One aspect of possessing a material thing is that there is some level of implicit control over others' access to it. In other words, if you possess something, you have the right to alter that thing, or to give or loan it to someone else. On the flipside, others have no rights to alter, take, or borrow your possessions without your permission. Again, this is an issue that becomes more complicated in the online world.

Part of this owes to the fact that digital things can be copied. Those copies can easily be controlled by someone other than the original owner. This is illustrated in the following example where P12 describes an undesirable experience she had on an online dating site: "*I used to be on a dating site and I had a photo of myself on it. ...after a disagreement, a man I'd been talking to took it from my page. He sent me a message saying, 'If I can't have you, at least I can have your picture on my computer.' ....He put it on his desktop* [background image]*! ...that was 'my' page, 'mine', he shouldn't have been able to do that! I couldn't get rid of it* [on his computer] *because it's not 'mine' anymore. ...I possess the original copy, but that doesn't feel like mine anymore because of what happened.*"

Similarly, P1, one of our youngest participants, described how lack of awareness of the duplication of photos online could shift perceptions of possessing them: "*...the real way you can keep some possession of a photo online* [is] *knowing who can look at it. ...once someone has viewed it they take some possession of it, but if I am the one letting that happen, then it's still mine. ...but if someone gets the photo without you knowing, then I don't know if you can ever really get it 'back'. Because who knows what's going to happen with it once they get it.*"

In a more drastic example, P5 describes the experience of having his house burgled in comparison to when possession of his Facebook account was temporarily assumed by an ex-lover and his personal content was altered: "*When* [my account] *got hacked, it's more like they came in and dressed me up in a weird way that's not quite me. ...so it is weird, like getting burgled with everyone watching but not realizing that someone else is making me look different.*"

Collectively, these instances highlight how the fact that digital content can be taken, copied, or otherwise appropriated by others profoundly undermined our participants' notions of possession. Clearly part of the complexity bound up in these examples is tied to the 'public' and 'semi-public' online places they unfold in, where digital content is visible to anyone (e.g. travel blog) or select subgroups of people (e.g., social networking sites). Nonetheless, these complications were in part due to the affordances of digital media and its inherent reproducibility. They were also a function of the lack of awareness of the actions of others—not knowing who had access to personal content, who at looked at it, and who had appropriated it—as well as lack of control over all of these aspects of the data. This is summed up nicely by P5's reflection on his photos and social networking content spread across Flickr and Facebook: "*I 'have' them so 'I' should have access to them and be able to decide who else does too. ...but once it goes online it, it's like a void. ...who knows where it will go, or really where it is. ...For me possession is about knowing my things.*"

Being able to relinquish possession

A key property of possessing a thing is the ability to relinquish possession of it. Whether through throwing away love letters or deleting digital photos on their computer, all participants described experiences of relinquishing possession of things they no longer wanted in their lives. In all but two interviews (P1, P3), stark contrasts to these instances emerged as participants described how these processes unfold in online places. For example, P12 describes relinquishing possession of photos on her computer compared to on Facebook and Picasa: "*...online, well I can try to delete something, but who knows? Who deletes the deleted? Where does it go? I don't know, but I don't think it disappears, and that's odd come to think about it. ...You can't very well possess something if you can't 'unpossess' it.*"

P5 describes recurrent complications experienced as he compares relinquishing possession of material things symbolic of a past relationship to similar digital things on Facebook: "*all of a sudden a photo of my Ex comes up that she's tagged me in and I want to be done with it and I'm trying to get rid of those things. ...In the real world, I removed these stimuli from my life. ...*[online] *it can feel impossible.*" P4 similarly described how she fully relinquished material things associated with a past relationship, while similar associations continued to linger on Facebook. She concluded the discussion with this reflection: "*There's this ironic thing about the idea of possessing something online. ...you can feel like you can't really 'have it' but then when you don't want it, it's not always so easy to get away from it.*" P4 provides a salient point capturing the complex nature of possessing digital things online: when possession begins and ends, particularly as we understand it in the material world, can remain highly ambiguous in online places that are neither entirely 'public' nor 'private'.

DISCUSSION AND IMPLICATIONS

It is clear that people's notions about what it means to own something digital can be both complicated and difficult to articulate—difficulties exacerbated by the shift of personal data to the Cloud. A key contribution of our study is to present evidence that helps illustrate just what these are. What should be clear is that, even though people may deploy different strategies, the choices people make reflect a common set of concerns and orientations. It seems too that commonalities in the concerns and strategies we observed can be understood with reference to how people think about and deal with physical things. Either this is because there is something fundamental about the link between materiality and possession, or it is that such notions are so deeply embedded in our dealing with the physical world that people cannot but help use them in their dealings with the digital. Nevertheless, some of the properties of the digital are themselves so new that no analogue for them can be found. This makes the case that people must learn new ways of thinking about digital properties and adjust their notions of ownership accordingly. At the same time, when translating notions of possession from the material to the online world causes difficulties, there may be ways of leveraging concepts of physical ownership to improve the way we deal with digital materials.

One powerful motivation for putting things online is to share them with others. Material things are of course shared too, but the digital allows new forms of sharing. This sometimes alters the thing itself in ways that are more difficult to achieve with material things. For example, the history of some real artifact can be reflected in the markings that give it a patina. But who made the markings or why they were made is often lost–the markings cannot tell that tale. But social metadata may be much richer in that respect: the residue they leave may allow for much deeper interpretations of doings-with-the-object that can change people's perceptions of the digital things in question.

It is not all positive, however. The placement of a digital thing online can have perplexing effects for people, in particular when it challenges ingrained notions about material things. This includes the fact that material things reside in places—places that one can control access to, and keep safe if need be. Possession becomes a difficult concept when the thing possessed has no geographic locale. It seems reasonable then that there are deep concerns and unresolved tensions when valued things have to go online: for this can mean relinquishing control over that thing, and this itself implies something about the 'owners' competence.

The flipside of knowing where something is, is knowing that something is gone. In the physical world, once something is destroyed, it no longer exists. In the online world, the notion of deleting something is undermined when objects can be replicated many times over. The irony here is that the very thing that may drive people to put things online—to share them—leaves those materials susceptible to the actions of others. All of this has implications not just for a person's sense of control of digital objects, but their awareness of them: location is no longer a resource that can be used to judge the safety of a thing. Likewise absence in a location is no guarantee something no longer exists.

There are many other such complications. Some are paradoxical. For example, putting things online is most often done to make them available to oneself or to others. But it can also raise the possibility that access to those things will temporarily or permanently cease. Part of the fragility of online things is not a mirror of the delicate nature of local hardware, such as the PC. It is because of the apparent arbitrariness of the services and service providers, as well as network fragility. At least with a PC, one can own responsibility for damage to it; with the Cloud, there is often little knowing why access is denied.

The point here is that online digital things (or even online places) break "the rules" of how we understand possession of material things. Further, these are issues that seem not to overly concern people in their day to day lives. Not, that is, until something unsettling happens. Just as with a car, ownership of it does not really preoccupy the owner until the day their car is stolen. Likewise, it is when a hard disk fails, a photo is appropriated by someone with mal intent, or when one suddenly loses access to the things they care about that the issues come home to roost. Apart from such events, people's feelings about digital ownership are better described as either uncertainty or uneasiness, revealing themselves very much in the process of asking our participants to reflect on their own experiences and perceptions.

Design Considerations

So how then, might we think about new ways to design Cloud technology? One might approach this through better digital rights or digital identity management solutions, or through more secure storage systems. However, such incremental enhancements in our view may only further burden users' interactions with the Cloud, not to say further complicate notions of ownership. The sensitive and complex issues outlined above suggest that we might instead reexamine how we interact with the Cloud and with the data we keep there in a more fundamental way. In what follows, we outline several design considerations emerging from this study that suggest areas for future research. Some of these have to do enabling users to have better control over their digital things they care about, and others focus on augmenting users' awareness of interaction with their stuff. Still other ideas suggest we may need to propose new properties for files, ones that extend beyond today's file types.

Knowing what you have—What would it take to give people back a sense of "having" a collection of digital objects, of feeling that they own them? One of the main findings was that a lack of awareness of the totality of one's digital assets was a major factor in undermining a sense of possession. This was in part due to the fact that these materials "lived" in many different places—in fact too many to keep track of. A workaround for many was to create local copies of online things to be able to give these materials a sense of place on a hard disk, or on CDs in a shoebox, even if this could be a risky strategy in the long run. For one thing this potentially complicates the situation for people grappling already with too many copies of too many things.

A different approach is to bring together interaction designers and systems developers to create a circumscribed but virtual place where all of the digital assets one cares about are represented. In other words, the suggestion is that there is a place where "my stuff" can be found, even if, in technical terms, it exists on many different servers, or many applications. Such a collection or visual inventory would allow these materials to be browsed through, giving users a sense of what they have. Critical here is that users could also use this as a way to find where the original objects can be located. In other words, objects in the inventory can be interrogated and used as quick ways to navigate to the place where the data resides, offering up access to its original context, metadata and so on. Such an approach could help reinstate that essential sense of awareness that people wish to have, while offering up the control they need to be able to find the objects they care about. This direction also opens up questions about how different forms and presentations of one's virtual inventory could shape interactions with and perceptions of it, and how they could be embodied through applications, devices or appliances.

Retaining guardianship—Another issue that arose was the need for users to have some way of caring for and protecting certain kinds of digital data, without depending on some other entity for guardianship. The findings showed participants had a strong desire to be accountable for safeguarding significant digital materials for future generations.

One approach to this would be to propose a new kind of file property we might call *permanency*, by which we mean the capacity to make a digital thing incapable of being deleted and thus to ensure its safety. There are, of course, Web services that offer this kind of security, but this is to place the trust in some organization "in the ether", something our participants were clearly concerned about, especially for their most sensitive materials. We propose instead that the stuff itself and the architecture of where it is stored should have demonstrable properties that prohibit or make especially difficult the destruction of them. These immutable file types and how they might be constructed will of course be a technical challenge, but the essential value of them would be to place control over guardianship back in the hands of the owners of the data. Additionally, recent work outside of HCI [12] has described new techniques for interfacing cloud computing with personal networks and devices. Those techniques could be used to create 'private clouds', where Cloud services obtain 'leases' from the user for how long their data can be 'used' and when the Cloud-based caches of this stuff expires. These advances could potentially enable people to backup the files they care about simultaneously on multiple devices, and thus deeply safeguard them, while, in a sense, still keeping them 'in the Cloud'—suggesting a body a work that could be productively drawn on in the service of future research in HCI.

Giving rights or access to others—A core motivating factor for putting things online is to share them with others. These actions occurred through various platforms, such as email services, social networking sites, and personal blogs; they offered opportunities to connect with people and in some cases accrue social metadata. The act of sharing online can also transform the thing in question when this metadata comes to extend the meaning of that originating object or stuff. The thing then becomes something that is collectively possessed. Yet we have seen that this can be problematic, leading to confusions over ownership and uncertainty about the actions of others in relation to an object, such as whether it has been copied and so on.

Here it might be valuable to devise a means by which people can retain some sense of the originating file, and of the life history of an object: allowing shared possession but pointing somehow to the original object. In a sense, what we propose is ways to extend representations of data to people without fully relinquishing it to them.

If one can extend such rights to people for joint ownership, it must also be possible to withdraw those rights. People's ability to give up their rights to access digital things are dramatically underdeveloped in online places. Current architectural design in many systems provides little choice other than letting data persist on the network or removing it completely, which, as we saw, can have significant consequences for the people invested in these things. There is a need to more sensitively handle the nuanced social connections among people. In some cases, this might mean removing connections among some people, while retaining others.

Another approach would be more focused on awareness rather than different mechanisms for control. In this approach, people can query any object they own to view other people's actions in relation to that object. In doing so, they can find out who else has made copies, who has modified an object, who has added metadata and so on. This would be a kind of "object lens" allowing people to interrogate their digital things to see what has happened to them, and who has interacted with them. This obviously raises some challenging issues for privacy. But it might be that the owner or creator of the "original" object has certain rights or priorities to view subsequent actions upon that object, as is the case now with many online services.

Being able to relinquish possession—A final aspect of ownership, confounded by the online world, is the right to get rid of something that we own. We might be able to remove material possessions from our lives that evoke memories we wish to forget, however we may be peculiarly unable to free ourselves of these things in our digital world [11]. Collectively, there is a clear need for people to be able to permanently dispossess things online.

Based on these findings, we propose that just as digital objects might have properties that make them permanent, so should it be possible to delete them forever from the context of an online system. In part, this requires that these kinds of objects keep track of actions done to them, and copies taken from them, making sure that this network of relationships is bound up with the action of permanently deleting that object. Moreover, such objects should enable users to see that this is possible, so that if they want to keep copies, one must negotiate the right to do so. We can imagine this applied to not only digital objects (e.g., photos), but other data created as a result of interactions, such as social metadata or machine-produced metadata (e.g., timestamps, frequency of views). Emerging work in the Systems community, such as the Vanish project [4], is beginning to develop new techniques that could help address some of these concerns. More generally, this and the other considerations we have outlined suggest that there is a significant opportunity for HCI and Systems researchers to work together in developing new interventions that could influence the design and implementation of cloud-based systems.

CONCLUSION

Of course many more suggestions probably come to the mind of the astute reader; all the more so if that individual is well versed in the often arcane structures of the systems that allow the PC to connect to the Cloud and for sharing and posting to occur over different social networking services. We aimed to present those suggestions that the qualitative data gathered here suggest; other techniques for data gathering might well suggest alternatives to our proposals. Additionally, there are clear opportunities for future comparative cross-cultural research investigating people's orientations toward their digital content,

Importantly, what we want to emphasize is that our research shows that the 'materiality' of digital artifacts is of prime importance for future HCI research. This turns around the subtle and delicate properties associated with the term possession. We have seen that to possess is not merely a noun nor a verb, but a complex set of actions that transform the relationship between a thing (virtual or physical) and a person. Like physical possessions, virtual ones too play an important role in how people assert their identity, realize their aspirations and interconnect with the lives of others. It is no wonder, then, that as users of contemporary technology increasingly engage with their digital stuff, seeking to place it in secure storage, sharing it with others, and sometimes wanting to know 'who has it' or 'where it has gone', that they end up worrying about rather profound issues. As the online world threatens to complicate our lives further, it is a good time to rein in, reflect on and re-design our interactions with our digital possessions.

ACKNOWLEDGMENTS

We thank the participants for their time and the Computer-Mediated Living group at Microsoft Research Cambridge.

REFERENCES

1. Barkhuss, L., Tashiro, J. 2010. Student socialization in the age of facebook. *Proc. of CHI '10*, 133-142.
2. Crosett, K. 2011. Marketers to Promote Cloud Computing to Consumers. Marketing Forecast. Last accessed: Sept 17, 2011. http://www.marketingforecast.com/archives/11007
3. Edmondson, A., McManus, S. 2007. Methodological Fit in Management Field Research. *Academy of Management Review*, Vol. 32, No. 4, 1155-1179.
4. Geambasu, R., Kohno, T., Levy, A., Levy, H. 2009. Vanish: increasing data privacy with self-destructing data. *Proc. of Usenix Security Symposium'09*, 299-316.
5. Kaye, J. et al. 2006. To have and to hold: Exploring the personal archive. Proc. of CHI'06, 275–284
6. Kirk, D., Sellen, A. 2010. On Human Remains: Values and Practice in the Home Archiving of Cherished Objects. *TOCHI*, 17, 3, 1-43.
7. Lenhart, A. 2010. Social Media and Young Adults. *Pew Internet & American Life Project Report.*
8. Liu, Q., Safavi-Naini, R., Seppard, S. 2003. Digital rights management for content distribution. *Proc. of ACSW '03*, 49-58. ACM press.
9. Marshall, C., Shipman, F. 2011. Social media ownership: using twitter as a window onto current attitudes and beliefs. *Proc. of CHI '11*, 1081-1090.
10. Marshall, C. 2007. McCown, F., Nelson, M. 2007. Evaluating Personal Archiving Strategies for Internet-based Information. *Proc. of IS&T Archiving*, 151-156.
11. Mayer-Schoenberger, V. 2011. *Delete: The Virtue of Forgetting in the Digital Age.* London: Guardian Press.
12. Mazurek, M.L, Thereska, E., Gunawardena, D., Harper, R., Scott, J. 2012. ZZFS: A hybrid device and cloud file system for spontaneous users. *Proc. of FAST' 12.*
13. Miller, D. 2009. *The Comfort of Things.* Polity Press.
14. Miller, D. (ed.). 2005. *Materiality.* Duke University.
15. Odom, W., Zimmerman, J., Forlizzi, J. 2011. Teenagers and Their Virtual Possessions: Design Opportunities and Issues. *Proc. of CHI '11*, 1491-1500.
16. Petrelli, D., Whittaker, S., Brockmeier, J. 2008. AutoTopography: what can physical mementos tell us about digital memories? *Proc. of CHI '08*, 53-62.
17. Stutzman, F., Kramer-Duffield, J. 2010. Friends Only: Examining a Privacy-Enhancing Behavior in Facebook. *Proc. of CHI '10*, 1553-1562.
18. Shove, E., Watson, M., Hand, M., Ingram, J. 2007. *The Design of Everyday Life.* Berg.
19. Suchman, L. 1987. *Plans and Situated Actions.* Cambridge University Press.
20. Van Dyne, L., Pierce, J. 2003. Psychological ownership and feelings of possession. *J. Organiz. Behav.* 25, 439-459.
21. Whittaker, S., Bergman, O., Clough, P. 2010. Easy on that trigger dad: a study of long term family photo retrieval. *Personal Ubiquitous Comput.* 14, 1, 31-43.

Understanding Negotiation in Airtime Sharing in Low-income Microenterprises

Nithya Sambasivan
Department of Informatics
University of California
Irvine, CA 92617
nsambasi@uci.edu

Ed Cutrell
Microsoft Research India
Sadashivanagar
Bangalore, India 560080
cutrell@microsoft.com

ABSTRACT

Shared access to airtime is a prominent mode of connectivity access in the developing world. We seek to understand airtime sharing among low-income microenterprises in India (small, low-capital businesses, such as flower sellers and milkmen), that constitute 90% of the total enterprises in India. We introduce social *negotiation* as the foundation of airtime sharing. We highlight negotiation mechanisms in the microenterprise, showing how shared resources are used towards personal interests amidst tensions and value conflicts, by adapting, modifying, subverting, and repurposing airtime. We then explore the design space of airtime and bandwidth sharing in low-income communities, including designing for negotiation and improving readability of airtime.

Author Keywords

HCI4D; ICT4D; Microenterprises; negotiation; sharing; airtime; bandwidth; India

ACM Classification Keywords

H.5.0 [Information interfaces and presentation]: General

INTRODUCTION

Airtime is the unit of connectivity for mobile phones. Airtime connectivity profoundly impacts its users, especially in the developing world where mobiles are major ICTs, e.g., by leading to livelihood productivity gains [12] and amplifying social networking [11]. In Human Computer Interaction, airtime connectivity is assumed to be readily available to individual subscribers on their personal and private devices. However, in developing countries, the connectivity infrastructure is fraught with high ownership costs [3,18]. For example, in the United States, airtime expenditure is 2% of the average income of lowest income segment; in contrast, despite being the fastest growing mobile market in the world [21], airtime costs in India can be greater than 10% of the average low income[1]. Shared access or multiple users for a single airtime resource is a prominent mode of phone use in these contexts.

Our paper is the first to study airtime sharing in the commercial enterprise in the developing world. We report the results of our fieldwork on airtime sharing practices in a spectrum of 58 microenterprises in two cities in southern India. In India, a country of over 1.2 billion people, microenterprises account for over 90% of the total enterprises [22]. Airtime impacts several functions of the microenterprise, such as procurement and sales of goods; and better price information exchange [5]. Understanding the usage practices and design space of airtime sharing in the microenterprise could impact the livelihoods of millions of people in the developing world. We seek to understand how airtime is shared, apportioned, and controlled among member of an enterprise, supplementing, complementing, or opposing the rules of an enterprise. Sharing airtime bits across a network pipe leads to new tensions, negotiations, and usage practices. Our study points to the foundational phenomenon of *negotiation* in airtime sharing—wherein multiple users repurpose airtime usage towards personal interests—by taking advantage of the opacity of airtime in showing usage of multiple users, and cost and infrastructure constraints.

We present a spectrum of airtime sharing practices across informal enterprises in the wild—sharing airtime, airtime subsidy, and device provision. We show how accountability and subterfuge of employees, airtime economics, and access control are negotiation mechanisms in the enterprise. Airtime sharing is fundamentally *bandwidth* sharing and the design space is relevant for various kinds of bandwidth sharing, beyond just the microenterprise and developing world. We feel our primary contribution is the introduction of negotiation as the foundation of airtime sharing in the microenterprise. We contribute to the HCI for Development (HCI4D) discourse on livelihoods by providing an account of technology access and benefit through airtime sharing in

[1] The average annual income of the lowest quintile in the USA was $22,629[1]. The average cellular package is $40[2]. The average annual Indian income of a microenterprise employee in our study was Rs. 36000 (800 USD) whereas the Arjun Sengupta report[3] estimates that 77% of Indians live on less than Rs. 7300 (162 USD) a year. Average airtime costs were Rs. 300 (6.66 USD) per month in our study.

[1]www.nytimes.com/packages/html/national/20050515_CLASS_GRAPHIC/index_01.html
[2] www.att.com
[3] http://nceuis.nic.in/Condition_of_workers_sep_2007.pdf

the microenterprise. Finally, we discuss design for airtime and bandwidth sharing in low-income communities.

In the remainder of this paper, we report the results of our survey and fieldwork on airtime sharing practices among 58 microenterprises in India. We situate our research amongst other contributions on technology sharing, explaining how non-remunerative sharing takes place in commercial environments. We provide a brief orientation to the airtime landscape in India, followed by a characterization of the types of microenterprises we studied. We then present our findings on the various ways in which negotiation takes place in airtime sharing, such as tracking, seepage between home and work domains, and economics of airtime. We conclude with some thoughts on design, including designing for negotiation and shared usage.

BACKGROUND

Negotiation

Negotiation is the "discussion between two or more parties with the apparent aim of resolving a divergence of interests" [14]. Fisher *et al.*, note that a good negotiation should satisfy three criteria: produce a wise agreement if agreement is possible, be efficient, and not damage the relationship between the parties [9]. In a related strand in HCI, Gaver *et al.*, call for ambiguity in system design, arguing that leaving interpretation open to people allows for greater conceptual grappling and deeper, personal relations with the system [10]. Aoki and Woodruff note that while participants in an interaction observe and account for the actions of others, it is not always desirable for all parties to be able to account accurately and precisely [1]. The ambiguity discourse offers us relevant concepts like openness in interpretation, which we extend in our work.

We define negotiation in airtime sharing as the repurposing of airtime usage towards personal interests, amidst shared interests. Negotiation occurs when there are conflicting technological goals, user interests, or activities. When there is a gap between the expected social norm and the user's action, the subsequent process of achieving the user's expected goal or a compromised version of the goal is negotiation. For example, while the microenterprise expects the employee to use his airtime for professional calls, the employee may also repurpose airtime towards making personal calls. An employee's daughter may also call her boyfriend surreptitiously on her mother's phone. The daughter may account for her usage by claiming to make a call to a client or supplier. It is not just the *process* of achieving the goal, but also the supporting *narratives*, *tensions*, and *re-alignments* in interactions that constitute a negotiation. Negotiations are built upon trust and social understandings. They are ongoing dialogues, with constant back-and-forth between the two parties, be they between employer-employee, family members, or coworkers.

Studies of sharing of technology

Previous studies in HCI have examined technology and content sharing among multiple users. Karlson *et al.*, describe how users are selective about the kind of smart phone function or content they want to share [13]. Brush and Inkpen observed technology sharing in domestic environments, noting that families wish to have a shared device with personal profiles [2]. Voida *et al.*, discuss music sharing in iTunes in a corporate environment, highlighting how impression management was an important part of sharing [19].

Previous ICTD studies have predominantly focused on the household and village communities. In her examination of shared access of mobiles among Ghanian households, Burrell describes multiple roles in mobile phone usage—the user, purchaser, owner, possessor, or operator [3]. Donner *et al.*, in their study of urban middle-class Indian families, argue that mobile sharing is born not merely out of economics, but may also be influenced by cultural factors [6]. Sambasivan *et al.*, describe intermediated usage, a shared usage phenomenon in low-income communities where digitally skilled users enable technology use to those without devices or necessary skills [17]. The Grameen "Village Phone" extends technology sharing to village communities through paid phones [8].

Yet, little is known empirically about sharing in the low-income enterprise, where sharing is neither borne out of tight family structures nor remunerative. It is in this context that we wish to explore how microenterprises share airtime, the ways in which they share, and what the notion of airtime sharing means to them.

Airtime technology

We refer to the credit (measured in minutes) used for services spent on the phone as airtime[1]. In the UK and USA, airtime refers to the minutes spent on a call, whereas in India, airtime is fungible—it is currency for a number of services, such as outgoing calls (incoming calls are free), SMS, MMS, mobile Internet, ringtones, data, and subscription alerts. As of March 2011, airtime was provided by sixteen Cellular Service Providers (CSPs) in India, covering 811.59m subscribers, out of which 381.40m used data on their mobiles [21]. Airtime can be loaded on a phone in two ways: postpaid and prepaid.

Post-paid airtime:

Post-paid connections charge the subscriber on a monthly basis. These are similar to cellular plans common in countries like the USA, except that the subscriber sets a maximum credit limit on the account. Postpaid airtime can only be purchased at dedicated CSP outlets. The postpaid model offers the subscriber an option to view per-call billing history on a monthly basis for a fee.

Pre-paid airtime:

Prepaid subscribers dominate the Indian airtime landscape, comprising 96.81% and 95.30% of the GSM and CDMA

[2] Note that airtime is different from talk-time, which is the maximum expected duration a fully charged battery is expected to last under perfect conditions.

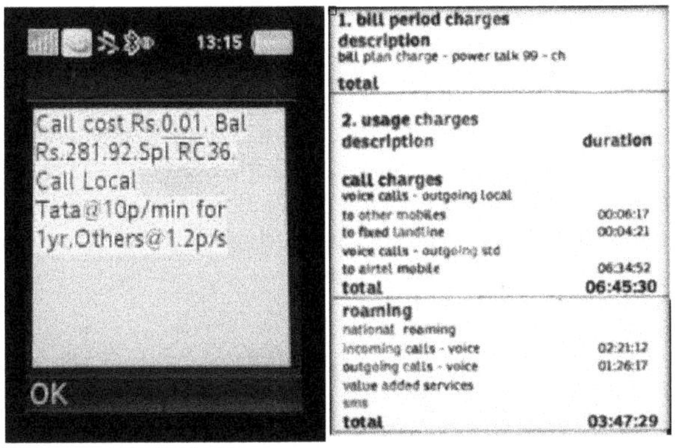

Figure 1. (Left) Prepaid and (right) postpaid notifications

total subscriber base [21]. Pre-paid airtime allows a variety of tailor-made recharge coupons with different denominations, starting at as low as Rs. 10 (0.25 USD). Mobile Internet is available both as integrated with prepaid and in standalone packages, starting at Rs. 9 (0.20 USD) for 10 MB, making access affordable. Usage tracking in pre-paid is fairly limited. The CSP sends out notifications after terminating every call, reflecting the current airtime balance, previous call duration and expense (see figure 1).

Microenterprises

Microenterprises are major employers in both developed and developing countries, spanning both formal and informal economies [23]. They are significant in number in developing countries where the informal economy is significant in employment and GDP. In India, they account for over 90% of the total enterprises and 45% of the manufacturing output [22]. Microenterprises typically have low capital, no legal status, produce goods and services for sale in the marketplace, and do not completely account their activities [23]. The International Labor Union defines microenterprises as enterprises with 25 workers or less [23] whereas the European Union caps the number at less than 10 [24]. In our study, we define a microenterprise as an urban, non-farm enterprise; with 10 or less employees; without a formal payroll; and sometimes tax-paying.

RESEARCH DESIGN

In order to understand the landscape of informal (non-tax paying, low capital) businesses, we decided to study a continuum of microenterprises in Bangalore and Chennai. Using revenue as a defining axis, we approached five income brackets of microenterprises, which we call *tiers*. As we go from tiers one to five, monthly revenues increase in a scalar fashion (Rs. 2,500, Rs. 5,000, Rs. 10,000, Rs. 18,000, and Rs. 40,000). Tier one businesses were highly informal with family members as employees (e.g., street-side vegetable-sellers) whereas tier five businesses were nearing formality with formal employees (e.g., computer businesses). This scheme offers a range of social structures, formality, technology ecologies and usage, employee strength, and organization. All our field studies were carried out in Tamil, Kannada, and Hindi by the first author.

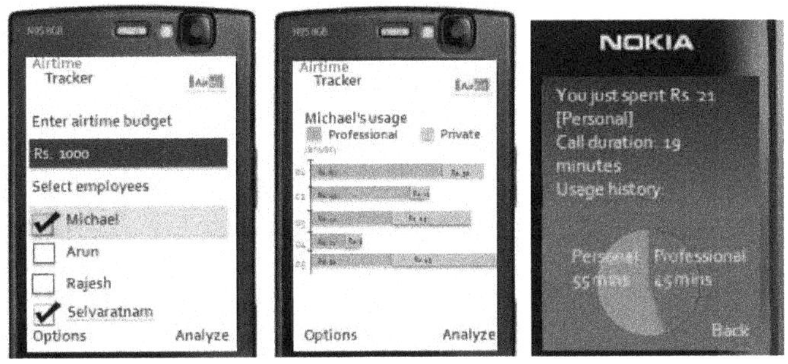

Figure 2. Design concepts for the employer and employee

Survey

We conducted a preliminary survey to understand the socio-economic profiles and technology practices of the microenterprise spectrum. Our goal was to study diverse microenterprises and not limit ourselves to a particular type, commodity, or service. We were interested in eliciting data on socio-economic profiles, household consumption, ICT ownership (appliances, phones, Internet, & PCs), sharing behavior, and communication ecology in the enterprise. To explore this, we surveyed 58 microenterprises. The survey exercise took us two months to complete.

Fieldwork

We conducted a qualitative field study to further understand the social protocol, workflow, technological practices, and airtime sharing. We conducted intensive field observations and open-ended interviews with 10 microenterprises (two in each tier) for three months.

Design provocations

Based on our results from the fieldwork, we were interested in using airtime as a lens to study sharing of technology, social relations, and economics. To this end, we employed two methods, One, we took design concepts to provoke participants and elicit their reactions and broader feelings on airtime sharing (Figure 2). We designed concepts for the employer, to track their employees' usage; and for the employee, to balance their personal-professional usage. Two, we designed paper-based diaries to understand a "day-in-the-life-of" mobile phones among multiple users (Figure 3). Diaries probed into who the user of the mobile was, features used, whether it was a business or family call, location of usage, duration of usage, and airtime balance at the end of the day. Diaries were partitioned into three-hour slots from morning to night, and lasted a weekend and two weekdays. Seven participants out of our initial pool were recruited. We offered airtime recharges as incentives.

MICROENTERPRISE CHARACTERIZATION

We studied a continuum of microenterprises to understand the transition points across each tier and to sketch out the trajectory of microenterprises to small-and-medium enterprises. Based on our survey and interview findings, we characterize each tier as follows (see Table 1 and Figure 4).

Tier one (T1)

T1 businesses are informal street-side businesses such as flower-sellers and vegetable-sellers. They are run by family members who each help out with the various aspects of

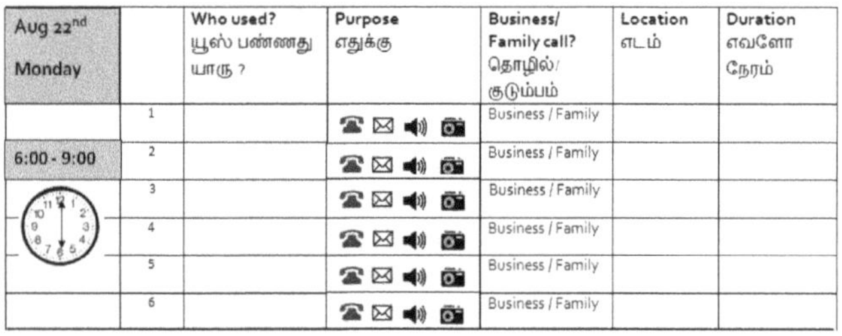

Figure 3. Mobile phone diaries

running a store. T1 businesses do not pay a monthly rent. However, locations are fixed due to social negotiations and understandings. T1 businesses do not maintain financial records. As we see in Figure 4, most of the infrastructure equipment is portable, like baskets and plastic sheets. T1 microenterprises are usually run by middle-aged women who have studied up to the 5th grade.

Mobile phones are the only information technology used by T1. Almost every mobile is a low-end, basic phone, used mainly for phone calls, low-resolution photos, and radio. Although every family member owns their mobile phone, usage is frequently shared among multiple users. T1 businesses form sharing communes of mobile phones and other resources with neighboring enterprises, with a technology expert in every commune (more detail in the next section) [17].

Tier two (T2)

T2 businesses are street-side businesses, but are no longer family-run. They are more formalized than T1 enterprises, with at least one formal employee. Examples include purse and jewellery stores. T2 businesses pay a monthly rent for their spot on the street and the store equipment is portable (wooden supports). Record-keeping is done on pieces of paper. The employer visits the store once in a day or few days, and this necessitates phone calls from employees every night to check-in the day's sales. The employee is responsible for all the activities of running the store, from sales to procurement of goods. Employees are typically young males who have studied up to 8th grade.

In T2, mobile phones are the only information technology used. Mobile Internet (GPRS) connectivity is used for entertainment (multimedia and games downloads). A typical mobile in T2 is a dual-SIM feature (multimedia) phone. One SIM card is used for personal calls and the other for professional calls. Similar to T1, sharing communes with neighboring microenterprises are formed. In addition, these communes are derived from religion (we observed two Muslim communes).

Tier three (T3)

For T3, we were interested in coordination businesses with a major mobility component. We studied milkmen, *iron-wallahs* (steam-iron pushcarts), newspaper stands, and mobile tea shops. In contrast to T2, 2-3 delivery boys are employed at specific times of the day to deliver the goods to the customers, e.g., the milk and newspaper delivery usually deliver in early mornings. The store remains open throughout the day, usually run solely by the employer. A monthly rent is usually paid. Record-keeping is more formal than in T2, and is maintained in ledgers. Employees are typically young males educated up to 10th grade.

Similar to T2, the average mobile is a feature (multimedia) phone with mobile Internet (3G), used primarily for phone calls and entertainment. Unlike T1 and T2, sharing of technology is restricted to coworkers.

Tier four (T4)

T4 microenterprises are regular grocery and wholesale stores such as grocery stores, tailoring stores, and pharmacies. Unlike the previous tiers, T4 stores have concrete storefronts with shutters. A monthly rent is paid. Similar to T3, financial records are maintained in ledgers. Two-three young males are employed in running the store, and the employer is co-present. There is a small delivery component at certain times of the day. Employees are typically young males educated up to the 12th grade.

T4 includes more technologies than the other tiers, such as individual mobile phones, landlines, and personal computers. A typical mobile phone of an employee is a low-end smart phone with mobile Internet (3G), used primarily for Orkut, Facebook, and personal e-mail. Technology sharing with coworkers is frequent.

Figure 4: Sample microenterprises in tiers 1- 5

Tier five (T5)
In contrast to the above tiers, T5 microenterprises are at the cusp of formality, e.g, mobile phone and computer hardware retail and services. Similar to T4, a monthly rent is paid for a permanent concrete store. The workforce is larger than the other tiers, typically constituted by ten employees, including 1-2 family members that hold key positions. Employees are men and women who have graduated from college.

In T5 for the first time, we see heavy use of high-end technologies for work, such as multiplr landlines, mobile phones with mobile Internet (3G and Wi-fi), and PCs with broadband. Unlike the previous tiers, a typical mobile is a high-end smart phone. Employees use two mobile phones each—one for personal use and one for professional use. For the first time, an official e-mail address is used; e-mail is supported by mail clients like Outlook and IM clients like GoogleTalk. T5 record-keeping is done on MS-Excel and Tally. Sharing with coworkers is seen.

SHARING ECOLOGY IN THE MICROENTERPRISE

Airtime sharing practices and the social norms around them extend from and modify the existing ways of sharing non-technological goods in the microenterprise, such as sharing a cup of tea or lunch, looking after each other's shops, borrowing bicycles, as well as other cultural productions such as gossip and humor.

Values in airtime sharing
Airtime sharing is built upon a shared value system and cultural understandings. We encountered a range of values underpinning the airtime sharing ethos including trust, reciprocity, symbolism, and communal shareholding. Depending on who was sharing what with whom, values varied. Motivations to share at work varied from social ties to obligations to colleagues. For example, Raman, a young employer in T2 shared his Nokia C7 with his employees so he could "*make them feel comfortable, make them feel that he is like their elder brother* [...] *unlike older bosses who are not very friendly with employees*." In contrast, Mohammed, an employer in T3 was hesitant about sharing his mobile, stating that, "I already pay my employees, so I offer my phone to them only when they ask me. It's not nice to say "no"." In T1 we observed that sharing in businesses was largely motivated by family ties. Airtime sharing was reciprocated in the form of favors, content, and gifts.

Location, timing, and users:
Shared access to airtime varied with time and location of both the owner and the borrower, as a result of varying relationships, devices, communication needs, and accountabilities across different spaces. For example, 6 am sharing was different from 6 pm sharing; sharing in the street-side shop was different from sharing in one's home. The results of our mobile diary exercise show that all seven participants shared their phones at home with their family and at work, including two participants in T1 whose family members were also coworkers. On average, two family members and one colleague shared the mobile every day.

A total of 302 calls were made by the participants, out of which 176 were professional and 126 were personal calls. Calls were dialed across home, work, supplier stores, delivery locations, temples, and relatives. Professional calls were more frequent during mornings and nights. They tended to be short in length (avg. of 2 minutes) and were largely coordination calls for deliveries. Airtime sharing with coworkers was seen. Personal calls were made during afternoons and nights, and tended to be longer (avg. call length = 4 minutes), but fewer. Airtime was shared heavily with family members at nights. Our findings point to seepages between personal and professional airtime usage.

	Monthly revenue	# Employees	Education	Modal mobile	Year when first mobile was purchased	Mobile Internet penetration and predominant type	Internet penetration and predominant type	Pay for employee airtime	Shared airtime at work
Tier one *(n=19)*	Rs. 2500 (55 USD)	1	5th grade (regional)	Nokia 2600	2008	5.26% (n=1), GPRS	Work = 0, Home = 0	100% (n=19)	100% (n=19)
Tier two *(n=17)*	Rs. 5000 (110 USD)	1	8th grade (regional)	Nokia 5235	2006	41.18% (n=7), GPRS	Work = 0, Home = 23.53% (n=4) Broadband wired	88.23% (n=15)	100% (n=17)
Tier three *(n=7)*	Rs. 10000 (222 USD)	2	10th grade (regional)	Nokia 5530 Express Music	2006	42.86% (n=3), 3G	Work = 0, Home = 28.57% (n=2), Broadband wired	85.71% (n=6)	85.71% (n=6)
Tier four *(n=5)*	Rs. 18000 (400 USD)	2	12th grade (regional)	Samsung Corby	2004	80% (n=4), 3G	Work = 60% (n=3), Home = 80% (n=4) Broadband wired & datacard	80% (n=4)	100% (n=5)
Tier five *(n=10)*	Rs. 40000 (889 USD)	10	College (English-medium)	Nokia C6-01	2003	100% (n=10), 3G and Wi-fi	Work = 100% (n=10), Home = 81.82% (n=9) Broadband Wi-fi	100% (n=10)	100% (n=10)

Table 1: Characteristics of the microenterprises we studied

TYPOLOGY OF SHARING IN MICROENTERPRISES

We limit sharing to instances where shared usage happened more than once or on a recurring basis. We present a range of technology sharing within the microenterprises (Table 2).

Shared airtime

Shared airtime occurs when multiple users share a connection or airtime minutes. Airtime may be shared either by allocating a particular device as the shared instrument or by freely sharing all instruments for calls. Shared airtime is independent of device ownership, i.e., each user may own their device and SIM card yet share airtime on other phones. Shared usage occurs throughout the five tiers, but is pronounced in T1, which consists of family members. In other tiers that are more formal, shared airtime coexists with professional sharing. Rules of access govern shared airtime usage. For example, the mother keeps a watchful eye on the son's usage of the phone.

Airtime subsidy

Airtime subsidy occurs when the employer provides a nominal amount of money every month to the employee towards professional airtime. An allowance of Rs. 200-300 (5-7 USD) is provided each month. Employees own their mobiles and SIM cards. Airtime subsidy comes with an expectation that the employee will make instrumental (professional) use of the subsidy. In T2, employees purchase dual-SIM phones and use one SIM towards personal and the other towards professional calls. In T3 and T4, employees own a mobile each, and the subsidy is used to top-up the existing airtime minutes.

Device provision

In the case of T5, dedicated mobile phones with postpaid connections are handed over to the employee for professional calls. In addition, employees own personal mobile phones. Shared devices allow tighter control for the employer. There is some understanding between employers and employees that a certain percentage of phone calls is towards personal purposes.

Trajectory of microenterprises:

As we move from T1 to T5, we notice a change in devices, technology behavior, and practices (Table 1). Technologies become more sophisticated with each tier, although the big leap from personal to productive use of Internet happens only in T5. We see shifts in airtime technology from prepaid to postpaid; in device models from low-end to high-end smart phones; and in infrastructure from WAP to Wi-fi/3G. Technologies shape the negotiation process: with more capabilities and skills, there are stronger accountabilities, novel responses to accountabilities, and complex accounts of usage.

NEGOTIATION MECHANISMS

Shared access in low-income communities is a site of contestation, where a technological resource is shared among multiple users with various capabilities and interests. The personal and professional coexist in microenterprises, resulting in further conflicts and tensions. Negotiation in the microenterprise entails activities that modify and stretch the properties of technology towards gainful use, amidst checks and balances, rules of access, and cost constraints. In our study, airtime negotiation revealed itself as a set of complex practices. Salient among them were four negotiation mechanisms: accountability of employees, subterfuge of employees, the economics of airtime, and access control.

Accountability

By accountability we refer to the ways in which the employee is obligated to use airtime towards professional purposes and the checks and balances involved in doing so.

Tracking airtime

Enterprises had several ways to maintain airtime expenditure within limits. Since prepaid airtime offers limited means to track airtime, employers checked on their employees through conspicuous and "innocuous" means. Employers in T2 and T3 sometimes checked on dialed numbers in the phone. Anbu, an employer in T2, noted, "*I give Rajesh [his employee] an allowance of Rs. 300.* [...] *Sometimes when I see him, I ask if I can borrow his phone to call, but look up the dialed numbers.*" Airtime tracking was more common in T1. Since members shared a device for work, there was increased surveillance in checking recent calls.

In T5, airtime tracking was better supported by the CSP. Selva, a manager, gave out five post-paid phones to his marketing employees. Monthly bills usually came up to Rs. 5000 (110 USD) per phone. Selva pointed to the Airtel CSP bill and said, "*I could trace individual calls by requesting a detailed call history from Airtel for an additional Rs. 30.*" He went on to add, "*I usually don't do it* [...] *not unless the bill is outrageous. I allow anywhere between Rs. 250 – 750 on personal calls per month.*" He detected personal calls on the list by looking at call lengths and frequencies. He noted, "*Relatives from native villages usually want to talk for a long time and don't hang up. Professional calls don't last longer than 2 minutes. One usually just coordinates when and where to meet.*" In reality, however, he did *not* request detailed call history for phones. Accountability belies the nuances of social understandings and trust, wherein Selva *allowed* personal calls and did not check calls unless the bill skyrocketed.

We created a design provocation to help employers allocate airtime to employees and track individual usage (Figure 2). Our design was deliberately "extreme" in being intrusive and violating privacies of employees. We were interested in understanding the social context and values that airtime sharing is embedded in, not a response to the usability of our designs. While the sentiment of apportioning resources and knowing how airtime was used struck a chord with the employers ["*good to see how productive they are*"], they seemed ambivalent about the idea of tracking minutiae of employee usage ["*not sure if I need to know so much*"].

Limiting calls beforehand

As a preemptive measure, some employers provided airtime by estimating the number of professional calls for the month. In T3 and T4, the frequency and timing of communication were estimated to calculate airtime minutes. Swarna, owner of a vegetable wholesale store, noted, "My delivery boys call up our customers to first decide the *time to deliver. They call me next to notify whether it is done or not. Sometimes I make the calls to customers on my phone. This is cheaper for the boys and makes my life easier. I give them Rs. 200 per month regularly because they cannot possibly exceed the amount even if they make five calls a day.*" In practice, airtime sharing rested in a gray area where Swarna could guess the number of professional calls, but saved her delivery boys a little money by allowing them to borrow her phone.

Reportage

In a few stores in T2, employers required daily and weekly reports of airtime usage from the employee. Shahul Hameed, owner of a street-side jewelry store, sometimes asked his employee how he had spent his day's airtime during the daily sales report. Employers were not interested in accuracy in reportage; rather they made an attenuated enquiry into usage as an accountability check, yet respecting the social relationships. As a repeated social process, this became a less effective means to check usage, as employees learned to invent narratives to account for usage, as we shall see in the next section.

Subterfuge

As an oppositional move to counter the employer's ways of airtime accounting, employees created inventive ways to camouflage their personal usage. It should be noted that in these cases, employees "stole" resources provided by the employer, but this adjusted itself within the social context or the employee provided tales to cover such usage.

Deleting phone numbers

Since prepaid does not provide detailed accounts of usage and the CSP notifications after each call are transient (they disappear after 'OK' is pressed), deleting numbers was a commonly employed strategy. In T2, Sugan was paid for professional airtime but used the minutes to call his village friends and those working on the same street to coordinate lunch or to chit-chat. Sugan regularly deleted his friends' numbers from call history on his phone, leaving behind only family and professional calls. He told us, "*Sometimes owner Sir visits and uses my phone to make calls* [...] *I don't want him to think that I am gossiping here. I want him to know how hardworking I am. Family is OK. It shows that I talk to my mother and father, but friends* [...] *he may think I am wasting time.*" Sugan maintained an impression of being a diligent employee by appropriating the phone content to his advantage. Negotiations in airtime sharing are concerned with what *kind* and how *much* information to reveal.

Exploiting illiteracy

In the lower tiers, where employers were educated in the regional language or were non-literate, employees crafted their usage stories to avoid raising suspicion. Contacts were generally not stored on the phone due to non-literacy or complexity of the phone interface. Phone numbers were either freshly dialed or retrieved from the phone history. Ammulu, daughter of one of the flower-sellers in T1, was a heavy phone user. She attended school and helped out her mother in the evenings. Ammulu had a boyfriend from the neighboring school. "*My mother asks me, "Whose number is this?" My mother does not know how to read English. I tell her it is one of the customers or flower suppliers. Since my mother may eventually recognize the number, I alternate between my boyfriend's mobile and his best friend's number that I have stored as different supplier names. I only call him when I am at work.*" Ammulu created a perfectly logical narrative for her mother, taking into account how her mother may recognize names and numbers through symbolic literacy and numeracy; the credibility in calling professional contacts; and economizing her and her boyfriend's airtime by taking turns—all without raising an eyebrow.

Misnaming contacts

In T5, where employers had college degrees, storing contact names was a common practice. In enterprises where employees were expected to submit weekly reports, employees forged friends' and family names as supply chain contacts like customers, suppliers, or company agents. In the words of Satish, an employee in T5, "*If my boss checks my calls, he will see that I have been calling only my clients and agents.*" When asked if his employer would suspect, he replied, "*No. I store friends and family as frequently dialed clients* [...] *I differentiate like Arun Airtel* [customer] *and Arun Reliance* [*brother*]. *So instead of three calls to Arun, my boss would see four.*" We see how T5 employees and Ammulu leveraged the legitimacy of professional contacts to camouflage and negotiate personal use.

Self-regulation

Employees negotiated, managed and regulated their usage of airtime through self-created personal-professional quotas. These quotas were usually informally fixed per month. In the words of Sugan: "*Each month I use about 30 minutes of airtime to call my family. My boss pays me Rs. 300 per month. But when I exceed 30-35 minutes, I start using my personal SIM. I want to be true to my conscience and job.*" Sugan created a moral threshold above which surreptitious usage of professional airtime for personal calls became "wrong." Within this self-regulated framework, airtime quotas were carried over from one month to another. Sugan added, "*But if I use only 10 minutes this month, I will try to use 50 minutes next month to made up for it.*" Sugan's words were echoed by Akhil, a T2 employee, "*Arre* [Oh], *my boss does not even pay me enough to survive. I have to care of a wife and three kids in Rajasthan. So I try to be make good use of* [justify] *the minutes he gives me, but after that it is for my calls to family.*"

Our designs for employees were created keeping in mind the delicate, inconspicuous balance between personal and professional airtime. Employees responded positively to the idea of differentiating and tracking the two, saying "*warning SMS would help me adjust my usage*" and "*would be useful*". Such responses point to the problematic nature of current airtime technology in supporting different *kinds* of use, that coexist, but are siloed into public and private.

Economics

As we have seen, airtime sharing is negotiated by the push and pull of employers and employees. But how is the valuable resource of airtime managed with multiple users amidst cost and device constraints? Recall that airtime expenditure constitutes over 10% of the employee's salary.

Airtime repurposing (switching SIMS)

Different CSPs charge differently for calls, motivating employees to switch between networks to keep costs minimal. In T2, dual-SIM phones used SIMs from two different CSPs. Vijay, an employee, swapped between two SIMs. His professional SIM (subsidized) had cheaper calling rates, whereas his personal SIM had lower SMS rates. So he tended to send text messages and get incoming calls on the personal SIM and make outgoing, including personal, calls, on the professional SIM. Arul in T5 owned a personal phone and used a postpaid work mobile. He received missed calls on the personal phone and called the person back using the work mobile or landline.

Reading usage

Given the constraints of limited resources, low incomes, and opacity of airtime usage information in prepaid airtime, we found that microenterprises went to extra lengths to make airtime usage more visible and cost-effective. When an airtime pipe was shared, keeping track of individual and total usages became important to keep costs down. One of the commonly employed techniques in T1-T3 was to jot down minutes spent in a notebook. Alongside the name of the person who made the call, the dialed phone number and whether it was a local or STD call were noted.

Our informants had several ways of discerning airtime usage. When the balance notification showed a drastic decrease, Pushpa, an owner in T1, immediately suspected her son of calling his friends when she was not around. She told us, "*Such* thiruttu [sneaky] *usage drives me mad. If I knew how much was spent by whom, I can show them proof and keep the costs low.*" In another case, Shekar, an employee in T5, told us how he figured his son used the phone while he was taking a bath. The phone battery had drained out suddenly and the instrument was warm.

Access control

Airtime sharing, like other forms of communal sharing, is governed by rules of access. Negotiation involves ways of creating adherence to the rules, as well as the transgression and circumvention of them without damaging the social relationships among multiple parties involved.

Physical access

Many informants reported exercising additional control over usage through physical presence. According to Ammulu, her mother made it hard for her to make personal calls, because, "*she is always around me, so I can't call my boyfriend whenever.*" Shanthi, an employer in T4 told us, "*I allow my employees to borrow my phone, but I am present when they make calls [...] sitting at the cash counter* [...] *they cannot exploit the phone when I am there.*" In T5, some employers required phones to be returned at the end of each day. The device boundaries were the data boundaries, since anyone using the device had access to all the data stored on it.

Permissiveness and exclusivity

Some of our informants reflected upon social conventions of permission before sharing. Permission control was largely seen in co-worker relations, and less so in families. Both employees and employers reported asking the other's permission before sharing a device, except when it was marked as a shared technology. In T1 and T2 where sharing communes were formed, airtime sharing outside of the communes was uncommon. Roles and privileges of access were evident—not everyone was allowed commensurate access to technologies. In T5 stores, postpaid phones were not shared with non-marketing employees. As shown elsewhere [16], sharing occurs freely within certain realms whereas tight control is exhibited in others.

THE DESIGN SPACE OF AIRTIME SHARING

Our study reveals how airtime sharing is a set of complex, conflicting, and contested practices. Airtime sharing is an instance of bandwidth sharing in general, where the utility of a volume of data is shared by multiple users. Understanding the design space in airtime sharing may be relevant to other kinds of bandwidth sharing, like shared cable/DSL Internet and TV and radio on-demand in the home. Interfaces for these infrastructures are typically designed for personal and private use, and suffer from scalability for supporting multiple users. Bandwidth is a scarce resource with usage caps in place in several countries [4]; multiple users for bandwidth calls for better representations of usage. Some questions emerge: what does it mean to share a connection? How can we design for multiple users when the subscription or profile is customized to the logged-in user? Moreover, the "user" is not a single person, but an address of a general entity (family, enterprise, or coworkers).

As more users in the developing world subscribe to data services (indeed our study points to the definite entry of mobile Internet (Table 1) and 100% airtime penetration among our informants), understanding the user and usage of these infrastructures is crucial to HCI. In the developing world, airtime sharing is a prominent mode of infrastructure access and coexists with direct ownership and usage. Our study points to problem areas in resource contention among multiple users, the conflict between personal usage and *expected* usage, economics of managing a constrained and valuable resource, and mechanisms to control access to the resource. We see how negotiation is a *fundamental* means to secure a resource for use and to stretch the use within socially accepted limits in a multi-user setting. Using negotiation as a design construct, we offer a few design concerns for both airtime and bandwidth sharing in HCI.

Designing for shared usage

Airtime sharing occurs when a network pipe is shared by multiple users. It occurs in several forms: one device, multiple users; one device, multiple SIMs; and one SIM, multiple airtimes. Unlike using a dedicated device for home Internet sharing or TV viewing, airtime can be shared through multiple devices and multiple users, adding complexity to use. Whereas the owner of the device is typically the consumer in the personal-private model, we find a separation of ownership, authority, and usage in the shared use scenario. Differential access emerges from the negotiated configuration of who owns the device, who has authority, and who has usage.

Our findings point to a problem area in current bandwidth technology for apportionment, brokering, and management among multiple users. Resource management systems with social accountabilities may allow for better apportioning and tracking. Profiles have been suggested as a means to customize individual use on shared devices [15], but studies have shown that users do not always prefer profiles [2]. We suggest airtime quotas as an alternative approach. Allocating multiple users with individual airtime quotas and numeric passwords may help resolve contention and confusion in apportionment. The community may regulate information by deciding the quota limits, accountabilities, and penalties. A snapshot of the various users and their usage can help in understanding resource consumption. Such a system can scale up to other domains where bandwidth is shared, such as Internet and TV on-demand.

Shared usage is a complex socio-technical process. People create several rules of access to help distinguish between different types of relationships—be they professional coworkers, friends, family members, or strangers. Sharing depends upon the user, time of day, and location. As more devices become mobile, such as laptops, mobile phones, and tablets, application designers for bandwidth management should take context into account when designing for multiple users. In addition to the user's identity and their device model, when and where they use the device matters. For example, usage varies tremendously across home and work; usage depends on whether it is their own phone, employer's phone, or a family member's phone. How can we design services for personal use that can be used on professional phones, or vice versa? For example, can we create websites that consume bandwidth according to the facet of the phone used—a Facebook application that consumes less bandwidth if used on an employer's phone? A URL that appears inconspicuous to the employer? A missed call [7] application to communicate with friends on a family phone?

Improving readability of airtime

Current airtime systems are highly opaque in providing usage and expenditure information. As a result, people compensate for airtime tracking through non-technological means, such as notebooks, looking for drops in airtime balance, and checking battery levels. Such compensatory checking may provide imprecise readings. As noted earlier, airtime expenditure is substantial for the microenterprises we studied (roughly 10% of the monthly income). Richer information systems for reading airtime balance are needed to save airtime amidst constraint. Current notifications in the prepaid model provide individual call statistics, whereas postpaid does not allow instantaneous tracking. An aggregate account of usage per day or week may help the user evaluate how airtime was spent and make decisions to spend the valuable resource constructively.

Our study points to certain parameters that may be useful to know in tracking: how much airtime was spent per day or week; dialed calls; call lengths; the breakdown of calls, messages, and data; and the current airtime balance. By visually reifying airtime spending, the user is presented with better tools for decision making on expenditure. The system can reside locally on the device and extract call logs to avoid network overheads. These parameters can be broadly applicable to improving readability of bandwidth in general, especially in emerging infrastructures like mobile Internet that suffer from opacity in showing usage.

Designing for negotiation

Broadband technologies like airtime and Internet are not neutral media; they are entrenched in the value systems of the users and designers. Any airtime design intervention should take into account the politics, ethics, and value conflicts embedded in the infrastructure. As political theorist Langdon Winner argued, "*the process of technological development is critical in determining the politics of an artifact; hence the importance of incorporating all stakeholders in it*" [20], a design solution for the microenterprise should arise from a dialogue with both employers and employees.

We propose negotiation as a design feature. Our findings show how the bulk of the sharing exchange is negotiated socially, by forging contacts, deleting calls, and creating narratives around airtime appropriation. A potentially dangerous solution to information asymmetry between various users (vis-à-vis the owner) is information transparency [1]. Design should be careful to not introduce friction or fear of the enterprise among employees. By showing less yet pertinent information and allowing room for social negotiation, design could prevent misuse of information. For example, while the employers were aware of employees making personal calls using professional airtime, knowing exactly who was called and how long the calls lasted may be incriminating to the employee. A safer approach may be to show aggregate call information instead of individual calls (instead of '*1 call to X for 50 minutes*', show '*5 calls today for a total of 120 minutes*').

A coarse-grained approach is one where the employer can assign upper limits for personal and professional calls and be notified when usage exceeds the quota. The system could support interpretation and dissembling in ways beneficial to the employer and employee. This is in line with the current practice of allowing personal calls within limits. By negotiating how many minutes could be spent on personal calls per month, a mechanism for compromise can be built in, where the employee can negotiate with the employer if the personal quota is underused (carry forward to next month) or overused (ignore or deduct from salary) for the month. For the employees, showing personal/professional airtime usage and action items (*'you just exceeded 20% personal usage. Restrict your personal calls'*) resonated with their current methods of controlling personal quotas. By controlling the quantity and presentation of information and by introducing social negotiation, bandwidth systems can be rendered useful where multiple users, different domains, and cost constraints collide.

Contention arises in any shared technology usage, beyond just the microenterprise or airtime sharing. Whenever a resource is shared among multiple users, the technology is appropriated towards their personal interests. In some cases this involves explicit repurposing, such as using professional airtime towards personal calls, whereas in some others it is a customization of a device. Negotiation is highly relevant to the design of bandwidth sharing systems, where multiple users share an invisible infrastructure and interfaces can foreground selective aspects of usage, users, and analytics of the network.

CONCLUSION

Our paper explored airtime sharing practices in low-income microenterprises in India. Specifically, we examined the phenomenon of negotiation in airtime sharing. Our work shows us how shared resources are used towards personal interests amidst tensions and value conflicts, by adapting, modifying, subverting, and repurposing technology. By being sensitive to social relationships, practices, and values, negotiation in design allows room for diversity and individuality of multiple users by carefully balancing technological encoding with social dialogue. While microenterprises are sites of personal-professional conflicts, there is always a conflict of interest in shared systems. Our findings and design concerns have relevance for the developed world. They point to new ways for the HCI and UbiComp communities to think about shared use by designing social negotiation that goes beyond personal profiles. To HCI4D, we highlight emerging ways of accessing airtime and bandwidth in the microenterprise, where mobiles are the primary ICTs. Our study suggests that building negotiation, improving usage readability, and supporting resource management are important design concerns for bandwidth sharing systems.

ACKNOWLEDGMENTS

We sincerely thank our informants for their time and Jonathan Donner for his helpful advice.

REFERENCES

1. Aoki, P.M. and Woodruff, A. Making space for stories: ambiguity in the design of personal communication systems. *CHI*, (2005), 181–190.
2. Brush, A.J. and Inkpen, K., M. Yours, Mine and Ours? Sharing and Use of Technology in Domestic Environments. In *Proc. Ubicomp*, (2007).
3. Burrell, J. Evaluating Shared Access: social equality and the circulation of mobile phones in rural Uganda. *CMC. 15*, 2 (2010), 230-250.
4. Chetty, M., Banks, R., Brush, A.J., Donner, J., and Grinter, R. While The Meter Is Running: Computing in A Capped World. *Interactions*, 2011.
5. Donner, J. and Escobari, M.X. A review of evidence on mobile use by micro and small enterprises in developing countries. *Journal of International Development 22*, 5 (2010), 641-658.
6. Donner, J., Rangaswamy, N., Steenson, M., and Wei, C. Express yourself" / "Stay together": Tensions surrounding mobile communication in the middle-class Indian family. In *J. Katz (Ed.), Handbook of mobile communication studies*. MIT Press, 325-337.
7. Donner, J. The rules of beeping: Exchanging messages via intentional "missed calls" on mobile phones. *CMC 13*, 1.
8. Donner, J. User-Led Innovations in Mobile Use in Sub-Saharan Africa. Receiver Newsletter. http://www.receiver.vodafone.com/14/articles/pdf/14_02.pdf.
9. Fisher, R., Ury, W., and Patton, B. *Getting to yes:negotiating agreement without giving in*. Houghton Mifflin Harcourt.
10. Gaver, B., Beaver, J., and Benford, S. Ambiguity as a resource for design. 233-240.
11. Horst, H. and Miller, D. *The Cell Phone: An Anthropology of Communication*. Berg publishers, 2006.
12. Jensen, R. The Digital Provide: Information (Technology), Market Performance, and Welfare in the South Indian Fisheries Sector. *The Quarterly Journal of Economics 122*, 3 (2007), 879-924.
13. Karlson, A., Brush, A.J., and Schechter, S. Can I Borrow Your Phone? Understanding Concerns When Sharing Mobile Phones. In *Proc. CHI* (2009), 1647-1650.
14. Pruitt, D.G. and Carnevale, P.J. *Negotiation in social conflict*. 1993.
15. Rangaswamy, N. Personalizing the Shared Mobile Phone. *HCI EA 2009*.
16. Sambasivan, N., Cutrell, E., and Weber, J. Designing a Phone Broadcasting System for Urban Sex Workers in India. In *Proc. CHI 2011*, 267-276.
17. Sambasivan, N., Cutrell, E., Toyama, K., and Nardi, B. Intermediated technology use in developing communities. In *Proc. CHI 2010*, 2583–2592.
18. Sambasivan, N., Rangaswamy, N., Cutrell, E., and Nardi, B. Ubicomp4D: infrastructure and interaction for international development–the case of urban indian slums. In *Proc. UBICOMP 2009*, 155–164.
19. Voida, A., Grinter, R., Ducheneaut, N., Edwards, W.K., and Newman, M. Listening In: Practices Surrounding iTunes Music Sharing. In *Proc. CHI*, (2005), 191-200.
20. Winner, L. Do artifacts have politics? *Daedalus 109*, 1.
21. TRAI. http://www.trai.gov.in/WriteReadData/trai/upload/PressReleases/756/pr7sep.pdf.
22. MSIM Microenterprises. http://msme.gov.in/msme_aboutus.htm.
23. ILO. http://www.ilo.org/wcmsp5/groups/public/---ed_emp/---ifp_skills/documents/publication/wcms_103625.pdf.
24. EU SME Definition. http://ec.europa.eu/enterprise/policies/sme/facts-figures-analysis/sme-definition/index_en.htm.

Author Index

www.ingramcontent.com/pod-product-compliance
Ingram Content Group UK Ltd.
Pitfield, Milton Keynes, MK11 3LW, UK
UKHW051454290926
15471UKWH00008B/1205

9 781450 319386